GROVE'S

DICTIONARY OF MUSIC

AND · MUSICIANS

EDITED

BY

J. A. FULLER MAITLAND, M.A., F.S.A.

IN FIVE VOLUMES

VOL. IV

THEODORE PRESSER COMPANY

PHILADELPHIA, PA.

1926

Norwood Press
J. S. Cushing Co. — Berwick & Smith Co.
Norwood, Mass., U.S.A.

LIST OF ILLUSTRATIONS

LIST OF CONTRIBUTORS

The names of deceased writers are printed in italics

W. A. Aikin, Esq.	W. A. A.
R. Aldrich, Esq., 'New York Times'	R. A.
E. Heron-Allen, Esq.	E. H-A.
Carl Armbruster, Esq.	C. A.
David Baptie, Esq.	D. B.
Mrs. Edith Oldham Best	E. O. B.
J. R. Sterndale-Bennett, Esq.	J. R. S.-B.
D. J. Blaikley, Esq.	D. J. B.
William Chappell, Esq., F.S.A.	W. C.
Alexis Chitty, Esq.	A. C.
M. Gustave Chouquet	G. C.
W. W. Cobbett, Esq.	W. W. C.
Frederick Corder, Esq.	F. C.
Major G. A. Crawford	G. A. C.
William H. Cummings, Esq., Mus.D., F.S.A., Principal of the Guildhall School of Music	W. H. C.
Sir William George Cusins	W. G. C.
Edward Dannreuther, Esq.	E. D.
Herr Paul David	P. D.
J. H. Davie, Esq.	J. H. D.
J. W. Davison, Esq.	J. W. D.
H. C. Deacon, Esq.	H. C. D.
E. J. Dent, Esq.	E. J. D.
L. MᶜC. L. Dix, Esq.	L. MᶜC. L. D.
Thomas Elliston, Esq.	T. E.
Gustave Ferrari, Esq.	G. F.
W. H. Grattan Flood, Esq., Mus.D., M.R.I.A.	W. H. G. F.
Rev. W. H. Frere	W. H. F.
H. Frederick Frost, Esq.	H. F. F.
John T. Fyfe, Esq.	J. T. F.
Rev. F. W. Galpin	F. W. G.
Nicholas Gatty, Esq., Mus.B.	N. G.
Dr. Franz Gehring	F. G.
J. C. Griffith, Esq.	J. C. G.

S. J. Spurling, Esq.	S. J. S.
William Barclay Squire, Esq.	W. B. S.
Miss C. Stainer	C. S.
Sir John Stainer, Mus.D.	J. S.
W. W. Starmer, Esq.	W. W. S.
E. Irenaeus Prime Stevenson, Esq.	E. I. P. S.
T. L. Stillie, Esq.	T. L. S.
William H. Stone, Esq., M.D.	W. H. S.
R. A. Streatfeild, Esq.	R. A. S.
Franklin Taylor, Esq.	F. T.
Alexander W. Thayer, Esq.	A. W. T.
Miss Bertha Thomas	B. T.
Herbert Thompson, Esq.	H. T.
F. Gilbert Webb, Esq.	F. G. W.
C. Welch, Esq.	C. W.
H. A. Whitehead, Esq.	H. A. W.
C. F. Abdy Williams, Esq.	C. F. A. W.
Mrs. Edmond Wodehouse	A. H. W.
J. Muir Wood, Esq.	J. M. W.
The Editor	M.

DICTIONARY

OF

MUSIC AND MUSICIANS

Q

QUADRILLE (German *Contretanz*), a dance executed by an equal number of couples drawn up in a square. The name (which is derived from the Italian *squadra*) was originally not solely applied to dances, but was used to denote a small company or squadron of horsemen, from three to fifteen in number, magnificently mounted and caparisoned to take part in a tournament or carousal. The name was next given to four, six, eight, or twelve dancers, dressed alike, who danced in one or more companies in the elaborate French ballets[1] of the 18th century. The introduction of ' contredanses' into the ballet, which first took place in the fifth act of Rousseau's 'Fêtes de Polymnie' (1745), and the consequent popularity of these dances, are the origin of the dance which, at first known as the ' Quadrille de Contredanses,' was soon abbreviated into 'quadrille.' [The use of the Spanish equivalent, *cuadrilla*, for the party of four *banderilleros* associated with each *torero* in a bull-fight, and the familiar name of a card-game once very popular, may be mentioned.] The quadrille was settled in its present shape at the beginning of the 19th century, and it has undergone but little change, save in the simplification of its steps. It was very popular in Paris during the Consulate and the first Empire, and after the fall of Napoleon was brought to England by Lady Jersey, who in 1815 danced it for the first time at Almack's[2] with Lady Harriet Butler, Lady Susan Ryde, Miss Montgomery, Count St. Aldegonde, Mr. Montgomery, Mr. Montague, and Mr. Standish. The English took it up with the same eagerness which they displayed with regard to the polka in 1845, and the caricatures of the period abound with amusing illustrations of the quadrille mania. It became popular in Berlin in 1821.

The quadrille consists of five distinct parts, which bear the name of the ' contredanses' to which they owe their origin. No. 1 is ' Le Pantalon,' the name of which is derived from a song which began as follows :

Le pantalon
De Madelon
N'a pas de fond,

and was adapted to the dance. The music consists of 32 bars in 6–8 time. No. 2 is ' L'Été,' the name of a very difficult and graceful ' contredanse' popular in the year 1800 ; it consists of 32 bars in 2–4 time. No. 3 is ' La Poule' (32 bars in 6–8 time) which dates from the year 1802. For No. 4 (32 bars in 2–4 time) two figures are danced, ' La Trénise,' named after the celebrated dancer Trenitz, and ' La Pastourelle,' perhaps a survival of the old 'Pastorale.' No. 5—'Finale'—consists of three parts repeated four times. In all these figures (except the Finale, which sometimes ends with a coda) the dance begins at the ninth bar of the music, the first eight bars being repeated at the end by way of conclusion. The music of quadrilles is scarcely ever original ; operatic and popular tunes are strung together, and even the works of the great composers are sometimes made use of.[3] The quadrilles of Musard are almost the only exception ; they may lay claim to some recognition as graceful original musical compositions.   W. B. S.

QUAGLIATI, PAOLO, born about 1560, was a musician living in Rome, who in 1608 is indicated as holding the position of organist at the Liberian Basilica of Santa Maria Maggiore. In 1585 he edited a collection of Spiritual Canzonets for three voices, containing, besides sixteen numbers by himself, some contributions by Marenzio, Nanino, and Giovanelli. His other publications before 1600 consist of two books of Secular Canzonets *a* 3. Two Canzonets *a* 4 with cembalo and lute accompaniment appear in Verovio's collection of 1591, which has been recently republished complete by Alfred Wotquenne. After 1600 he appears to have followed with interest the twofold direction in music emanating from Florence and Venice respectively, the Florentine *Stile rappresentativo* for solo voices, and the Venetian concerted style with

---

[1] The Ballets were divided into five acts, each act into three, six, nine, or twelve 'entrées,' and each ' entrée' was performed by one or more 'quadrilles' of dancers.
[2] See Captain Gronow's *Reminiscences* (1861).

[3] Some readers may recollect the clever 'Bologna Quadrilles' on themes from Rossini's 'Stabat Mater,' which were published shortly after the appearance of that work. The plates of these quadrilles were destroyed on the publishers learning the source from which the author (popularly supposed to be J. W. Davison) had obtained the melodies. [Hans von Bülow wrote a set of quadrilles on airs from Berlioz's ' Benvenuto Cellini.']

basso continuo. In 1606 he composed an opera with libretto by his pupil Pietro della Valle, entitled 'Carro di fedeltà d' amore,' which was performed on a Carnival car in the streets of Rome. It has five solo voices, and was published in 1611, with the addition of several Arie a 1-3. His other works are a book of Concerted Madrigals a 4 for voices and instruments, with a separate book for Basso Continuo, some other books of Spiritual Madrigals a 1-3, and two books of Sacred Motets and Dialogues for two and three choirs in the concerted style with Basso Continuo (Rome, 1612-27). In Diruta's 'Il Transilvano' there appears a toccata by Quagliati for organ or clavier, which has been republished by L. Torchi in *L'Arte Musicale in Italia*, vol. iii.   J. R. M.

QUALITY. See TONE.

QUANTITY. See METRE, vol. iii. p. 186.

QUANTZ, JOHANN JOACHIM, celebrated flute-player and composer, born, according to his autobiography in Marpurg's *Beiträge zur Aufnahme der Musik*, Jan. 30, 1697, at Oberscheden, a village between Göttingen and Münden. His father, a blacksmith, urged him on his death-bed (1707) to follow the same calling, but, in his own words, 'Providence, who disposes all for the best, soon pointed out a different path for my future.' From the age of eight he had been in the habit of playing the double-bass with his elder brother at village fêtes, and judging from this that he had a talent for music, his uncle Justus Quantz, Stadtmusikus of Merseburg, offered to bring him up as a musician. He went to Merseburg in August 1708,[1] but his uncle did not long survive his father, and Quantz passed under the care of the new Stadtmusikus, Fleischhack, who had married his predecessor's daughter. For the next five and a half years he studied various instruments, Kiesewetter being his master for the pianoforte. In Dec. 1713 he was released from his apprenticeship, and soon after became assistant, first to Knoll, Stadtmusikus of Radeberg, and then to Schalle of Pirna near Dresden. Here he studied Vivaldi's violin-concertos, and made the acquaintance of Heine, a musician in Dresden, with whom he went to live in March 1716. He now had opportunities of hearing great artists, such as Pisendel, Veracini, Sylvius Weiss, Richter and Buffardin, the flute-player. In 1717 he went, during his three months' leave, to Vienna, and studied counterpoint with Zelenka, a pupil of Fux. In 1718 he entered the chapel of the King of Poland, which consisted of twelve players, and was stationed alternately in Warsaw and Dresden. His salary was 150 thalers, with free quarters in Warsaw, but finding no opportunity of distinguishing himself either on the oboe, the instrument for which he was engaged, or the violin, he took up the flute, studying it with

[1] Not 1707, as Mendel states.

Buffardin. In 1723 he went with Weiss to Prague, and the two played in Fux's opera 'Costanza e Fortezza,' performed in honour of the coronation of Charles VI. Here also he heard Tartini. In 1724 Quantz accompanied Count Lagnasco to Italy, arriving in Rome on July 11, and going at once for lessons in counterpoint to Gasparini, whom he describes as a 'good-natured and honourable man.' In 1725 he went on to Naples, and there made the acquaintance of Scarlatti, Hasse, Mancini, Leo, Feo, and other musicians of a similar stamp. In May 1726 we find him in Reggio and Parma, whence he travelled by Milan, Turin, Geneva, and Lyons to Paris, arriving on August 15. In Paris—where his name was remembered[2] as 'Quouance'—he remained seven months, and occupied himself with contriving improvements in the flute, the most important being the addition of a second key, as described by himself in his *Versuch einer Anweisung die Flöte . . . zu spielen*, vol. iii. chap. 58 (Berlin, 1752). He was at length recalled to Dresden, but first visited London for three months. He arrived there on March 20, 1727, when Handel was at the very summit of his operatic career, with Faustina, Cuzzoni, Castrucci, Senesino, Attilio, and Tosi in his train. He returned to Dresden on July 23, 1727, and in the following March re-entered the chapel, and again devoted himself to the flute. During a visit to Berlin in 1728 the Crown Prince, afterwards Frederick the Great, was so charmed with his playing, that he determined to learn the flute, and in future Quantz went twice a year to give him instruction. In 1741 his pupil, having succeeded to the throne, made him liberal offers if he would settle in Berlin, which he did, remaining till his death on July 12, 1773. He was Kammermusicus and court-composer, with a salary of 2000 thalers, an additional payment for each composition, and 100 ducats for each flute which he supplied. His chief duties were to conduct the private concerts at the Palace, in which the king played the flute, and to compose pieces for his royal pupil. He left in MS. 300 concertos [but see the *Quellen-Lexikon*, p. 99, on this number] for one and two flutes—of which 277 are preserved in the Neue Palais at Potsdam—and 200 other pieces; flute solos, and dozens of trios and quatuors, of which 51 are to be found at Dresden. His printed works are three—'Sei Sonate' dedicated to Augustus III. of Poland, op. 1, Dresden, 1734; 'Sei duetti,' op. 2, Berlin, 1759; [six sonatas for two flutes, op. 3, of doubtful authenticity, London, Walsh; five sonatas for flutes, also op. 3, Paris, Boivin], a method for the flute—*Versuch einer Anweisung die Flöte traversière zu spielen*—dedicated to Frederick 'Könige *in* Preussen,' Berlin, 1752, 4to, with twenty-four copper-

[2] In Boivin's *Catalogue*.

plates. This passed through three (or four) German editions, and was also published in French and Dutch. He left also a serenata, a few songs, music to twenty-two of Gellert's hymns, 'Neue Kirchenmelodien,' etc. (Berlin, 1760), and an autobiography (in Marpurg's *Beiträge*). Three of the Melodien are given by von Winterfeld, *Evang. Kircheng.* iii. 272. Besides the key which he added to the flute, he invented the sliding top for tuning the instrument. His playing, which was unusually correct for the imperfect instruments of the day, delighted not only Frederick, but Marpurg, a more fastidious critic. He married, not happily, in 1737; and died in easy circumstances and generally respected at Potsdam, July 12, 1773.

All details regarding him may be found in *Leben und Werken*, etc., by his grandson Albert Quantz (Berlin, 1877).   F. G.

QUARENGHI, Guglielmo, violoncellist and composer, born at Casalmaggiore, Oct. 22, 1826, died at Milan, Feb. 4, 1882. He studied at the Milan Conservatoire, 1839-42, occupied the post of first violoncello at the Scala Theatre in 1850; became professor of his instrument at the Milan Conservatoire in 1851, and in 1879 Maestro di Cappella at the Milan Cathedral. As a composer he contributed an opera entitled 'Il dì di Michel'; published in 1863 some church music and transcriptions, as well as an interesting method for the violoncello; a valuable treatise upon the origin of bow instruments precedes this *Metodo di Violoncello* (Milan, 1876), in which he compares the earliest forms with the various barbaric and semi-barbaric instruments previously in use amongst primitive nations. In addition the author gives the 'Personaggi' of Monteverde's 'Orfeo,' and the tuning of the earliest viols. — Riemann, *Lexikon*; Baker, *Biog. Dict. of Music.*   E. H-A.

QUARLES, Charles, Mus. B., graduated at Cambridge in 1698. He was organist of Trinity College, Cambridge, from 1688 to 1709. He was appointed organist of York Minster, June 30, 1722; and died at York early in 1727. 'A Lesson' for the harpsichord by him was printed by Goodison about 1788.   W. H. H.

QUART-GEIGE. See Violin.

QUART-POSAUNE. See Trombone.

QUARTERLY MUSICAL MAGAZINE AND REVIEW, conducted by R. M. Bacon of Norwich. [See vol. i. p. 181; vol. iii. p. 680.]   G.

QUARTET (Fr. *Quatuor*; Ital. *Quartetto*). A composition for four solo instruments or voices.

I. With regard to instrumental quartets the favourite combination has naturally been always that of two violins, viola, and violoncello, the chief representatives since the days of Monteverde of soprano, alto, tenor, and bass, in the orchestra: in fact, when 'quartet' only is spoken of, the 'string quartet' is generally understood;

any other combination being more fully particularised; and it is to the string quartet we will turn our principal attention. The origin of the quartet was the invention of four-part harmony, but it was long before a composition for four instruments came to be regarded as a distinct and worthy means for the expression of musical ideas. Even the prolific J. S. Bach does not appear to have favoured this combination, though he wrote trios in plenty. With the symphony was born the string quartet as we now understand it—the symphony in miniature; and both were born of the same father, Haydn. [See Form.]

The early quartets of Haydn seem to us sadly feeble in the present day; there is not enough flesh to cover the skeleton, and the joints are terribly awkward; but there is the unmistakable infant quartet, and certainly not more clumsy and unpromising than the human infant. In the course of his long life and incessant practice in symphonic composition, Haydn made vast progress, so that the later quartets (op. 71, etc.) begin to show, in the lower parts, some of the boldness which had before been only allowed to the 1st violin. Eighty-three quartets of Haydn are catalogued and printed, while of the ninety-three of his contemporary Boccherini, scarcely one survives.

Mozart, with his splendid genius for polyphony as well as melody, at once opened up a new world. In the set of six dedicated to Haydn we notice, besides the development in form, the development of the idea, which it has only been given to Beethoven fully to carry out—the making each part of equal interest and importance. Theoretically, in a perfect quartet, whether vocal or instrumental, there should be no 'principal part.' The six quartets just spoken of were so far in advance of their time as to be considered on all sides as 'hideous stuff.' In our time we find little that is startling in them, except, perhaps, the famous opening of No. 6, which will always sound harsh from the false relations in the second and fourth bars.

Adagio.   etc.

Mozart's twenty-six quartets all live, the six dedicated to Haydn and the last three composed for the King of Prussia being immortal.

Those writers whose quartets were simply the echo of Mozart's—such as Romberg, Onslow, Ries, and Fesca—made no advance in the treatment of the four instruments.

It is not our province here to speak of the

growth of the symphonic form as exhibited in the string quartet, this subject having been already discussed under FORM, but rather to notice the extraordinary development of the art of part-writing, and the manner in which the most elaborate compositions have been constructed with such apparently inadequate materials. In these points the quartets of Beethoven so far eclipse all others that we might confine our attention exclusively to them. In the very first (op. 18, No. 1) the phrase

of the first movement is delivered so impartially to each of the four players, as though to see what each can make of it, that we feel them to be on an equality never before attained to. If the 1st violin has fine running passages, those of the 2nd violin and viola are not a whit inferior. Does the 1st violin sing a celestial adagio, the violoncello is not put off with mere bass notes to mark the time. All four participate equally in the merriment of the scherzo and the dash of the finale. This much strikes one in the earlier quartets, but later we find that we are no longer listening to four voices disposed so as to sound together harmoniously, but that we are being shown the outline, the faint pencil sketch, of works for whose actual presentation the most perfect earthly orchestra would be too intolerably coarse. The posthumous quartets are hardly to be regarded as pieces written for violins, but we are rather forced to imagine that in despair of finding colours delicate and true enough the artist has preferred to leave his conceptions as charcoal sketches. This fancy is borne out when we note how large a compass the four parts are constantly made to cover, a space of nearly five octaves sometimes being dashed over, with little care for the inevitable poverty of tone produced.

There is a wide contrast between these stupendous works of genius and the polished and thoroughly legitimate workmanship of Schubert's quartets. Here we find everything done which ought to be done and nothing which ought not. They are indeed irreproachable models. One little point deserves notice here as illustrating the comparative strength of two great men : Beethoven gives frequent rests to one or two of the players, allowing the mind to fill in the lacking harmony, and thus producing a clearness, boldness, and contrast which no other composer has attained ; Schubert, on the other hand, makes all four parts work their hardest to hide that thinness of sound which is the drawback of the quartet.

Mention of Spohr's quartets might almost be omitted in spite of their large number and their great beauty. Technically they are no more advanced than those of Haydn, the interest

lying too often in the top part. They also lose much through the peculiar mannerism of the composer's harmony, which so constantly occupies three of the parts in the performance of pedal notes, and portions of the chromatic scale.

Still more than Schubert does Mendelssohn seem to chafe at the insufficiency of four stringed instruments to express his ideas. Not only this, but he fails, through no fault of his own, in one point needful for successful quartet-writing. Beethoven and Schubert have shown us that the theoretically perfect string-quartet should have an almost equal amount of interest in each of the four parts ; care should therefore be taken to make the merest accompaniment-figures in the middle parts of value and character. *Tremolos* and reiterated chords should be shunned, and indeed the very idea of *accompaniment* is barely admissible. The quartet, though differing from the symphony only in the absence of instrumental colouring and limitation of polyphony, is best fitted for the expression of ideas of a certain delicacy, refinement and complexity, anything like boldness being out of place, from the weakness of the body of tone produced. Now the chief characteristic of Mendelssohn's music is its broad and singing character, passage-writing is his weak point. Consequently, however good his quartets, one cannot but feel that they would sound better if scored for full orchestra. Take the opening of op. 44, No. 1, for instance : this is not quartet-writing at all ; there is a melody, a bass, and the rest is mere filling-up ; in the second, we have here as thorough an orchestral theme as could be devised — the ear longs for trumpets and drums in the fourth bar. The name symphony in disguise has often, and not unjustly, been applied to these works. This is curious, because Mendelssohn has shown himself capable of expressing his ideas with small means in other departments. The four-part songs for male voices, for instance, are absolutely perfect models for what such things ought to be. Schumann (op. 41) is the only writer who can be said to have followed in the wake of Beethoven with regard to using the quartet as a species of shorthand. All his three quartets have an intensity, a depth of soul, which, as with Beethoven, shrinks from plainer methods of expression.

Of the earnest band of followers in this school—Bargiel, Rheinberger, and others—all that can be said is that they *are* followers. [Brahms's three quartets, opp. 51, 67, are perfect examples of the art of spreading the interest over all the parts, and the way the return is made to the opening subject of op. 67 at the close of the variations is a touch of unmistakable genius.]

II. Quartets for strings and wind instruments are uncommon, but Mozart has one for oboe, violin, viola, and violoncello. Next to the string quartet ranks the pianoforte quartet, which, however, is built on quite a different principle : here the composition becomes either equivalent to an accompanied trio, or to a symphony in which the piano takes the place of the 'string quartet,' and the other instruments—usually violin, viola, and violoncello —the place of wind instruments. In any case the piano does quite half the work. Mozart has written two such quartets, Beethoven only one, besides three early compositions, Mendelssohn three, Schumann and Goetz one each, while Brahms (opp. 23, 26, 60) and the modern composers have favoured this form of quartet still more.

III. Vocal quartets are so called whether accompanied by instruments or not. The four-part songs of Mendelssohn have been mentioned. For many years no oratorio was considered complete without its unaccompanied quartet, Spohr having set the fashion with ' Blest are the departed ' in the ' Last Judgment.' Modern opera is learning to dispense with concerted music, Richard Wagner having set the fashion. To enumerate the fine operatic quartets from ' Don Giovanni' to ' Faust,' would be useless. [Brahms's first set of ' Liebeslieder ' for piano duet and four voices *ad libitum,* was one of the compositions which began his popularity in England ; in the second set, and in opp. 92, 103, and 112, he has left notable examples. Henschel's ' Serbisches Liederspiel,' op. 32 ; Stanford's quartets from Tennyson's ' Princess '; Walford Davies's ' Pastorals '; and Ernest Walker's songs from *England's Helicon,* may also be mentioned.]

IV. The whole body of stringed instruments in the orchestra is often incorrectly spoken of as ' the Quartet,' from the fact that until the time of Beethoven the strings seldom played in other than four-part harmony. It is now the usual custom to write the parts for violoncello and double bass on separate staves ; in Germany (and in the present day in England) these instruments are grouped apart, a practice which is decidedly unwise, seeing that the double bass requires the support of the violoncello to give the tone firmness, more especially the German four-stringed instrument, the tone of which is so much lacking in body.

V. The term is also applied to the performers of a quartet, as well as to the composition itself.   F. C.

VI. The word is used of a set of stringed instruments, corresponding to the old phrase ' a chest of viols.' Although, accurately speaking, quartets of musical instruments were not employed in chamber music, as we understand the term, until the era of Monteverde (1568-1643), yet the literature and art records of past centuries seem to point to the existence of 'sets' of instruments, analogous in pitch to the soprano,

alto, tenor, and bass voices, from very early times. Some ground for this assumption may be found in the following examples :—The concert of eight flutes (in four sizes) discovered on one of the tombs in the Necropolis of Gizeh, dating—according to Lepsius—from the fifth Dynasty (B.C. 2000) which are reproduced in Carl Engel's *Catalogue* of the Exhibition of Musical Instruments, South Kensington Museum, 1874. Certain Hebrew coins in the British Museum ascribed to Simon Maccabaeus (of the second century of the Christian era) depicting lyres differing in size, shape, and number of strings, and a pertinent passage, quoted from Aristides Quintilianus (about B.C. 110, in Burney's *History of Music,* vol. i. p. 513). Mention may also be made of the string trio portrayed on the splendid Greek Vase in the Munich Museum. The three figures, grouped in the manner of our modern trio performers, appear to be playing ensemble music. Two of the performers have lyres of different sizes and stringing, whilst the third, Polyhymnia, plucks a small harp.

Passing hence to the 11th century, it would appear from Dr. Ruhlmann's *Geschichte der Bogeninstrumente,* that a ' set' of crouths is to be seen in an old MS. prayer-book of that period (vide *Gebetbuch des Erzh. Leopold d'Heil von Osterreich.* Bibl. zu Kloster Neuburg bei Wien, Codex, No. 98, Fol. 110, XI Jahrh.). Four centuries later (April 14, 1401) Charles VI. granted ' Lettres-Patentes,' to the Society of Minstrels who styled themselves ' joueurs d'Instruments tant haut que bas,' and in the following century the ' sets' of viols began to make their appearance. In Martin Agricola's *Musica Instrumentalis deutsch* (1528), woodcuts of a complete quartet of viols may be seen, as also ' Rebecs,' in four different sizes, which he designates, ' Discantus,' ' Altus,' ' Tenor,' ' Bassus.' [In the same year, in the *Cortigiano* of Bald. Castiglione, there is a reference to music played on ' quattro viole da arco.'] In 1566, Andreas Amati (see that name) made the famous set of bow instruments for the French King Charles IX. It consisted of twelve large and twelve small pattern violins, six tenors and eight basses, and in all probability these instruments were the finest examples of this maker's work. On the backs were painted the arms of France and other devices, and the motto ' Pietate et Justitia.' During the French revolution the mob took these instruments out of the chapel at Versailles (on Oct. 6 and 7, 1789), and destroyed all but two violins which were afterwards recovered by Viotti's pupil, J. B. Cartier. One of the small violins is now, or was recently, the property of Mr. George Somes. In the following century numbers of ' Chests of Viols ' (two trebles, two tenors, two basses), for the performance of the elaborate compositions in parts, called ' Fantasies,' were made, and the growing adoption of instrumental music at the Royal Courts of Europe induced Antonio Stradivari (see that name) to turn his attention to the making of 'sets' of instruments, comprising violins, tenors, and basses. The first 'set' of instruments, recorded as by this maker, is that mentioned in the Arisi MSS., a document written by Desiderio Arisi, a Cremonese priest of the order of St. Jerome and belonging to the Church of St. Sigismondo (see *Antonio Stradivari, his Life and Work*, W. E. Hill & Sons). He states that Stradivari received an order, in 1682, from the Venetian banker Michele Morigi, for a complete 'sett' of instruments, destined to be presented to James II. of England. As no trace of these instruments has as yet been found, their existence rests entirely upon the statement made in the MSS. referred to. In 1690 the same maker produced the so-called 'Tuscan Concerto,' or 'set' of instruments, for Cosmo di Medici. This probably consisted of two or three violins, a contralto (small tenor), a tenore (large tenor), and a violoncello. The tenore of this set[1] has been preserved in its original state, and may be seen, together with the violoncello, in the Musical Institute at Florence. In 1696 Stradivari made the inlaid quintet which for some years was owned by Philip IV. of Spain, and at the end of the 17th century and the beginning of the 18th, the 'set' (dated 1696-1709) destined to have been presented to Philip V. of Spain, but not sold until after Stradivari's death, when his son Paolo disposed of it (in 1775) to a priest named Padre Brambrilla for £148, and later it became the property of Don Carlos, afterwards Charles IV. of Spain. This 'set' consisted of two violins, two violas, one tenore, and a violoncello. The large tenore vanished at the dispersal of the royal collection, and the rest of the 'set' were submitted to such barbarous reparations at the hands of Dom Vincenzo Acenzo and his successor Ortega, that, especially in the case of the violoncello now in the Chapel Royal, Madrid, little of their original character remains.

In modern times 'sets' of instruments by one maker have been largely collected by ardent connoisseurs. We are told that the Dumas family, friends of Beethoven, assembled a quartet of Gio. Paolo Maggini's instruments, violin, viola, violoncello, and small bass, and that with the exception of the last, they are some of the finest specimens of this master's work. The Prince J. de Caraman Chimay owned a very interesting quartet of instruments by Stradivari's pupil (?) Ambrose de Comble of Tournay (about 1750) and also an ornamented quartet (copies of Stradivari) made by J. B. Vuillaume in 1865. [These instruments were exhibited in the Albert Hall in 1885.] Quartets of Stradivari's instruments have been collected by

[1] For the history of the violin of this set see article MOSEL.

the following : Count Archinto of Milan, who died in 1860. This quartet passed into the hands of J. B. Vuillaume, and the violoncello (1689) was the instrument used by Mons. Jules Delsart. Nicolo Paganini also owned a quartet by this maker. The Duc de Camposelice, who died in Paris in 1887, possessed about twenty of the great master's instruments, and M. Wilmotte of Antwerp, who died in 1893, left eight violins, two violas, and two violoncellos. M. de St. Senoch's quartet—violin, 1737[*]; second violin, 1704 ; viola, 1728 ; violoncello, 1696—was sold after his death in 1886, at the Hôtel Drouot. At the present time Stradivari quartets are owned by Baron Knoop, Dr. R. E. Brandt, and the Herren Mendelssohn. The late Dr. Charles Oldham's quartet was bequeathed to the British Museum. The quartet of Stradivaris employed by Lady Hallé and her collaborators at the St. James's Hall Popular Concerts were dated as follows :—Lady Hallé's violin, 1709 ; Mr. Ries' violin, 1710 ; Mr. Gibson's viola, 1728 ; and Signor Piatti's violoncello, 1720. It would appear that the only present-day instrumentalists who play upon a complete set of Stradivari's instruments are the Joachim quartet. Dr. Joachim's violin is dated 1715, Prof. Hausmann's violoncello, 1724, Prof. Carl Halir's violin is a long-pattern Stradivarius, and the fine viola played upon by Prof. Wirth is lent to the quartet by the Herren Mendelssohn.—Agricola, *Musica Instrumentalis* ; Burney, *History of Music* ; Hawkins, *History of Music* ; de Laborde, *Essai sur la Musique* ; Hart, *The Violin* ; Hill, *Antonio Stradivari* ; Engel, *Catalogue, South Kensington Exhibition of Instruments*, 1874 ; *Catalogue of Inventions Exhibition*, 1885 ; von Moser, *Joseph Joachim.*   E. H-A.

QUARTET ASSOCIATION, THE. A Society for the performance of chamber music, started in 1852 by Messrs. Sainton, Cooper, Hill, and Piatti, with such eminent artists as Sterndale Bennett, Mlle. Clauss, Mme. Pleyel, Arabella Goddard, Pauer, Hallé, etc., at the pianoforte. They gave six concerts each season at Willis's Rooms, but ended with the third season, the time not having yet arrived for a sufficient support of chamber music by the London public. The programmes were selected with much freedom, embracing English composers—Bennett, Ellerton, Loder, Macfarren, Mellon, etc. ; foreign musicians then but seldom heard— Schumann, Cherubini, Hummel, etc., and Beethoven's Posthumous Quartets. The pieces were analysed by G. A. Macfarren.   G.

QUASI, as if—*i.e.* an approach to. 'Andante quasi allegretto' or 'Allegretto quasi vivace' means a little quicker than the one and not so quick as the other—answering to poco allegretto, or più tosto allegro.   G.

QUATRE FILS AYMON, LES. An opéra-comique ; words by MM. Leuven and Brunswick, music by Balfe. Produced at the Opéra-

Comique, Paris, July 15, 1844, and at the Princess's Theatre, London, as 'The Castle of Aymon, or The Four Brothers,' in three acts, Nov. 20, 1844.　　　　G.

QUAVER (Ger. *Achtelnote*, whence American 'eighth note'; Fr. *Croche*; Ital. *Croma*). A note which is half the length of a crotchet, and therefore the eighth part of a semibreve; hence the German and American names. It is written thus ♪, its Rest being represented by ♪.

The idea of expressing the values of notes by diversity of form has been ascribed by certain writers to De Muris (about 1340), but this is undoubtedly an error, the origin of which is traced by both Hawkins (*Hist. of Music*) and Fétis (art. 'Muris') to a work entitled *L'antica Musica ridotta alla moderna Prattica*, by Vicentino (1555), in which it is explicitly stated that De Muris invented *all* the notes, from the Large to the Semiquaver. It is, however, certain that the longer notes were in use nearly 300 years earlier, in the time of Franco of Cologne [NOTATION, vol. iii. p. 399], and it seems equally clear that the introduction of the shorter kinds is of later date than the time of De Muris. The fact appears to be that the invention of the shorter notes followed the demand created by the general progress of music, a demand which may fairly be supposed to have reached its limit in the quarter-demisemiquaver, or $\frac{1}{16}$ of a quaver, occasionally met with in modern music.

The Quaver, originally called *Chroma* or *Fusa*, sometimes *Unca* (a hook), was probably invented some time during the 15th century, for Morley (1597) says that 'there were within these 200 years' (and therefore in 1400) 'but four [1] (notes) known or used of the musicians, those were the Long, Breve, Semibreve, and Minim'; and Thomas de Walsingham, in a MS. treatise written somewhat later (probably about 1440), and quoted by Hawkins, gives the same notes, and adds that 'of late a New character has been introduced, called a Crotchet, which would be of no use, would musicians remember that beyond the minim no subdivision ought to be made.' Franchinus Gafurius also, in his *Practica Musicae* (1496), quoting from Prosdocimus de Beldemandis, who flourished in the early part of the 15th century, describes the division of the minim into halves and quarters, called respectively the greater and lesser semiminim, and written in two ways, white and black (Ex. 1). The white forms of these notes soon fell into disuse, and the black ones have become the crotchet and quaver of modern music.[2]

[1] There were really five, including the Large, which Morley calls the Double Long.

[2] It is worthy of notice that in the ancient manuscript by English authors known as the Waltham Holy Cross MS., a note is mentioned, called a 'simple,' which has the value of a crotchet, but is written *with a hooked stem* like a modern quaver. That a note half the value of a minim should at any period have been written with a hook may help to account for the modern name crotchet, which, being clearly derived from the French *croc*, or

Greater　　Lesser
Semiminim.　Semiminim.

The subdivision of the quaver into semiquaver and demisemiquaver followed somewhat later. Gafurius, in the work quoted above, mentions a note $\frac{1}{8}$ of a minim in length, called by various names, and written either ♪ or ♪, but the true semiquaver or *semichroma*, the earliest form of which was ♪, does not appear until later, while the demisemiquaver must have been a novelty as late as 1697, at least in this country, judging from the 13th edition of Playford's *Introduction to the Skill of Musick*, in which, after describing it, the author goes on to say 'but the Printer having none of that character by him, I was obliged to omit it.'

When two or more quavers (or shorter notes) occur consecutively, they are usually grouped together by omitting the hooks and drawing a thick stroke across their stems, thus ♫♫.

[This grouping, which had been in use for centuries in MS. music, was one of the great difficulties in the way of printing from music-types; it was not overcome until about 1690, when John Heptinstall brought it into use. See HEPTINSTALL, and MUSIC-PRINTING.]

In vocal music, quavers which have to be sung to separate syllables are written detached, while those which are sung to a single syllable are grouped; for example:—

The peo-ple that walk-ed in dark · · · · ness, that
　　　　　　　　　　　　　　　　　　　　F. T.

One quaver of historical importance deserves mention, that which Handel added in pencil to the quintet in 'Jephtha' in 1758, six years after he is supposed to have lost his sight, and which in Schoelcher's words shows that by 'looking very closely at a thing he was still able to see it a little.'　　　　G.

QUEEN OF SHEBA. (i.) LA REINE DE SABA, in four acts; words by Barbier and Carré, music by Gounod. Produced at the Opéra, Feb. 28, 1862. Adapted as 'Irene' by H. B. Farnie, and produced as a concert at the Crystal Palace, August 12, 1865. The beautiful Airs de ballet contain some of Gounod's best music.　　　　G.

(ii.) See KÖNIGIN VON SABA.

QUEISSER, CARL TRAUGOTT, a great trombone player, was born of poor parents at Döben, near Leipzig, Jan. 11, 1800. His turn for music showed itself early, and he soon mastered all the ordinary orchestral instruments. He ultimately confined himself to the viola, and to the trombone, which he may really be said

crochet, a hook, is somewhat inappropriate to the note in its present form, which has no hook.

to have created, since, for instance, the solo in the *Tuba mirum* of Mozart's Requiem was before his time usually played on a bassoon. In 1817 he was appointed to play the violin and trombone in the town orchestra, and by 1830 had worked his way into the other orchestras of Leipzig, including that of the Gewandhaus. He played the viola in Matthäi's well-known quartet for many years ; was one of the founders of the Leipzig ' Euterpe,' and led its orchestra for a long time ; and in short was one of the most prominent musical figures in Leipzig during its very best period.

As a solo trombone-player he appeared frequently in the Gewandhaus Concerts, with concertos, concertinos, fantasias, and variations, many of them composed expressly for him by C. G. Müller, F. David, Meyer, Kummer, and others ; and the reports of these appearances rarely mention him without some term of pride or endearment. ' For fulness, purity and power of tone, lightness of lip, and extraordinary facility in passages,' says his biographer, ' he surpassed all the trombone-players of Germany.'[1] There was a Leipzig story to the effect that at the first rehearsal of the Lobgesang, Queisser led off the Introduction as follows :—

to Mendelssohn's infinite amusement. *Se non è vero, è ben trovato.*

Queisser was well known throughout Germany, but appears never to have left his native country. He died at Leipzig, June 12, 1846.   G.

QUICK-STEP (Fr. *Pas redoublé* ; Ger. *Geschwind Marsch*) is the English name for the music of the Quick march in the army, a march in which 116 steps of 30 inches go to the minute. (See Boosé's *Journal of Marches, Quicksteps, Dances,* etc.) It may be well to mention that in the Slow march there are 75 steps of 30 inches, and in the ' Double' 165 of 33 inches. [See MARCH, vol. iii. p. 50.]   G.

QUILISMA. An ancient form of Neuma, representing a kind of shake. [See NOTATION, vol. iii. p. 396.]   W. S. R.

QUINIBLE. See QUINTOYER.

QUINT. An organ stop which causes the fifth above a given note to sound as well as the note belonging to the key which is pressed down. From the note and its fifth there arises a differential tone an octave below the note. By this mixture an organ with 16-ft. pipes can be made to sound as if with 32-ft. pipes ; that is the pitch of the lowest note, but of course it sounds with far less energy than if properly produced with a 32-ft. pipe.   T. E.

QUINTA FALSA (False Fifth). The forbidden interval between Mi in the Hexachordon durum, and Fa in the Hexachordon naturale—

[1] *Allg. musikalische Zeitung,* July 8, 1846.

the Diminished Fifth of modern music. [See MI CONTRA FA.]   W. S. R.

QUINTE. The name given in France, during the latter half of the 17th and part of the 18th centuries, to the now obsolete five-stringed tenor viol. Five-stringed viols were amongst the earliest in use. Praetorius (*Organographia,* 1619) says they were employed in ancient times, and Agricola (*Musica Instrumentalis,* 1532) gives the tuning of the five-stringed viols then in vogue. Although composers of vocal music during the 16th century not infrequently called their tenor part ' Quinte' or ' Quintus,' viols of that denomination remained under the title of tenor until a later period ; and probably the first instance where ' Quintus' designates a musical instrument occurs in the overture to Claudio Monteverde's opera, ' Orfeo' (Venice, 1609-1613). *L'État de France,* in 1683, gives the name of ' Fossart,' who played the ' Quinte de Violon' in the Queen's band, and in 1712-13 the Paris opera orchestra included two ' Quintes' amongst the instruments. In 1773 there were four ' Quintes' amongst the musicians of the ' Grande Chapelle,' and ' Quintes' were employed in all the orchestras. Jean Jacques Rousseau (*Dictionnaire de Musique,* Paris, 1708) gives a good deal of information concerning the ' Quinte.' Under ' Viole' he says that in France the ' Quinte' and the ' Taille' (a large six-stringed tenor viol), contrary to the Italian custom, played the same part, and under ' Partie' mentions that the ' Quinte' and ' Taille' were united under the name ' Viole.' The highest and lowest notes of these instruments, according to the same writer, were—

Quinte or Viola.   Taille.

from which it is to be inferred that the tuning was the same as that given by Agricola in 1532, *i.e.*

Alto and Tenor.

In England the two tenor viols which formed a part of the ' Chests of six Viols,' so much in vogue during the 17th and beginning of the 18th centuries, were probably identical with the ' Quinte' and ' Taille' ; but the French title was never adopted in this country. The bulky size of the ' Quinte' rendered it such an awkward instrument to play upon that its dimensions gradually diminished from century to century, and when the violin came into more general use, it melted into the ' Haute Contre' (alto viol). In the second half of the 18th century it developed into a tenor violin with four strings, and adopted the C clef on the third line which was formerly the clef of the 'Haute Contre' or alto viol. (See TENOR VIOL.)—Agricola (Martinus), *Musica Instrumentalis* ; Praetorius, *Organographia* ; Rousseau (J. J.), *Dictionnaire de Musique* ; La Borde, *Essai sur la Musique* ; Grillet (Laurent), *Ancêtres du Violon* ; Hart, *The Violin*.   E. H-A.

QUINTET (Fr. *Quintuor* ; Ital. *Quintetto*). A composition for five instruments or voices with or without accompaniment.

I. Quintets for strings have been far less often written than quartets, owing to the greater complexity demanded in the polyphony. Boccherini, however, published 125, of which twelve only were written for two violins, two violas, and one violoncello, the others having two violoncellos and one viola. The former is the more usual choice of instruments, probably because the lower parts are apt to be too heavy sounding with two violoncellos, owing to the greater body of tone in this instrument. Schubert's noble Quintet in C (op. 163) is for two violoncellos, but the first is used constantly in its upper octave, soaring above the viola. Onslow's—thirty-four in number—are for a double bass and violoncello.

Beethoven's two Quintets, in E♭ and C, belong to his earlier periods, and have therefore none of the extraordinary features of the later quartets. Mendelssohn's Quintet in B♭ (op. 87) is so orchestral as to seem almost a symphony in disguise, but that in A (op. 18) is an exquisite specimen of what a string quintet should be.

Many other combinations of five instruments have found favour with musicians, mostly including a pianoforte. Thus there is Mozart's Quintet in E♭ for oboe, clarinet, horn, bassoon, and piano—which the composer esteemed the best thing he ever wrote,—the beautiful one for clarinet and strings, and another for the piquant combination of flute, oboe, viola, violoncello, and harmonica. Perhaps the most effective association is that of piano, violin, viola, violoncello, and double bass, as in Schubert's well-known 'Trout' Quintet (op. 114). [The splendid quintets of Schumann and Brahms for piano and strings are for the ordinary combination above referred to, as are also those of Dvořák, Dohnányi, and others. The quintet by Brahms for clarinet and strings is one of his most beautiful works.] Beethoven's quintet for piano and wind instruments (op. 16), in E♭ is a noble representative of a very small class. Hummel has also written a well-known one.

II. In vocal music none who have ever heard it can forget the admirable quintet (for two soprani, contralto, tenor, and bass) which forms the finale to Act 1 of Spohr's 'Azor and Zemira.' In modern opera the most striking specimen occurs in Wagner's 'Meistersinger.' Five-part harmony has a peculiarly rich effect, and deserves to be more practised than it is, especially in oratorio chorus. It is, however, by no means easy to write naturally.   F. C.

QUINTON [See VIOL, TREBLE].

QUINTOYER (Old Eng. Quinible). To sing in Fifths—a French verb, in frequent use among extempore Organisers during the Middle Ages. [See ORGANUM, PART-WRITING.]   W. S. R.

QUINTUPLE TIME. The rhythm of five beats in a bar. As a rule quintuple time has two accents, one on the first beat of the bar, and the other on either the third or fourth, the bar being thus divided into two unequal parts. On this account it can scarcely be considered a distinct species of rhythm, but rather a compound of two ordinary kinds, duple and triple, employed alternately. Although of little practical value, quintuple time produces an effect sufficiently characteristic and interesting to have induced various composers to make experiments therein, the earliest attempt of any importance being a symphony in the second act of Handel's 'Orlando' (1732), in which the hero's perturbation is represented by this peculiar time (see Burney, *History*, iv. 364). The same rhythm occurs in an air to the words 'Se la sorte mi condanna' in the opera of 'Ariadne' by Adolfati, written in 1750, and it is also met in some of the national airs of Spain, Greece, Germany, etc. Thus Reicha, in a note to No. 20 of his set of 36 fugues (each of which embodies some curious experiment in either tonality or rhythm), states that in a certain district of the Lower Rhine, named Kochersberg, the airs of most of the dances have a well-marked rhythm of five beats, and he gives as an example the following waltz :—

In the above example the second accent falls on the third beat, the rhythm being that of 2–8 followed by 3–8, and the same order is observed in a charming movement by Hiller, from the Trio, op. 64.

In Reicha's fugue above referred to, the reverse is the case, the fourth beat receiving the accent, as is shown by the composer's own time - signature, as well as by his explicit directions as to performance. The following is the subject :—

Other instances of quintuple rhythm are to be found in a Trio for strings by K. J. Bischoff, for which a prize was awarded by the Deutsche Tonhalle in 1853 ; in Chopin's Sonata in C minor, op. 4 ; in Hiller's 'Rhythmische Studien,' op. 52 ; in 'Viens, gentille Dame' ; in Boieldieu's 'La Dame blanche' ; Löwe's Ballad 'Prinz Eugen' ; a number in Rubinstein's 'Tower of Babel,' etc.   Another characteristic example occurs in the 'Gypsies' Glee,' by W. Reeve (1796). This may fairly be considered an example of genuine quintuple rhythm, for instead of the usual division of the bar into two parts, such as might be expressed by alternate bars of 3–4 and 2–4, or 2–4 and 3–4, there are five distinct beats in every bar, each consisting of an accent and a non-accent. This freedom from the ordinary alternation of two and three is well expressed by the grouping of the accompaniment. [The same true quintuple time, as distinguished from a combination of triple and duple time, distinguishes the best-known example of all, the second movement of Tchaikovsky's 'Pathetic' symphony. The passage in the third act of 'Tristan und Isolde,' occurring at a most exciting moment in the drama, is apt to escape the attention of many hearers who are only conscious of the impatient effect it produces. See RHYTHM.]   F. T.

QUINTUS (the Fifth). The Fifth Part in a composition for five voices ; called also Pars quinta and Quincuplum. In music of the 15th and 16th centuries, the Fifth Part always corresponded exactly in compass with one of the other four ; it would, therefore, have been impossible to describe it as First or Second Cantus, Altus, Tenor, or Bassus.   W. S. R.

QUIRE. Another way of spelling CHOIR.
                                       G.

QUODLIBET (Lat. 'What you please '), also called QUOTLIBET ('As many as you please '), and in Italian MESSANZA or MISTICHANZA ('A mixture '). This was a kind of musical joke in the 16th and early part of the 17th centuries, the fun of which consisted in the extempore juxtaposition of different melodies, whether sacred or secular, which were incongruous either in their musical character, or in the words with which they were associated ; sometimes, however, the words were the same in all parts, but were sung in snatches and scraps, as in the quodlibets of Melchior Franck. (See Praetorius, *Syntagma Musicum*, tom. iii. cap. v.) There were two ways of performing this : one was to string the melodies together simply and without any attempt at connecting them by passages such as those found in modern 'fantasias' ; the other, the more elaborate method, consisted in singing or playing the melodies simultaneously, the only modifications allowed being those of time. The effect of this, unless only very skilful musicians engaged in it, must have been very like what we now call a 'Dutch chorus.' This pastime was a favourite

one with the Bachs, at whose annual family gatherings the singing of quodlibets was a great feature (see Spitta, *J. S. Bach* (Engl. transl.) i. 154, iii. 172-6). Sebastian Bach himself has left us one delightful example of a written-down quodlibet, at the end of the '30 variations ' in G major, for a detailed analysis of which see Spitta. The two tunes used in it are 'Ich bin so lang bei dir nicht gewest,' and 'Kraut und Rüben, Haben mich vertrieben.' One of the best modern examples, although only two themes are used, is in Reinecke's variations for two pianos on a gavotte of Gluck's, where, in the last variation, he brings in simultaneously with the gavotte the well-known musette of Bach which occurs in the third 'English ' suite. A good instance, and one in which the extempore character is retained, is the singing of the three tunes 'Polly Hopkins,' 'Buy a Broom,' and 'The Merry Swiss Boy' together, which was formerly sometimes done for a joke. A very interesting specimen of a 16th-century quodlibet by Johann Göldel, consisting of five chorale-tunes — viz. (1) 'Erhalt uns, Herr bei deinem Wort,' (2) 'Ach Gott, von Himmel,' (3) 'Vater unser im Himmelreich,' (4) 'Wir glauben all,' (5) 'Durch Adam's Fall '— is given as an appendix to Hilgenfeldt's Life of Bach. We quote a few bars as an example of the ingenuity with which the five melodies are brought together :—

M.

R

RAAFF, ANTON, one of the most distinguished tenors of his day; born 1714 in the village of Holzem, near Bonn, and educated for the priesthood at the Jesuit College at Cologne. His fine voice so struck the Elector, Clement Augustus, that he took him to Munich, where Ferrandini brought him forward in an opera. After studying for a short time with Bernacchi at Bologna, Raaff became one of the first tenors of his time. In 1738 he sang at Florence on the betrothal of Maria Theresa, and followed up this successful début at many of the Italian theatres. In 1742 he returned to Bonn, and sang at Vienna in Jommelli's 'Didone' (1749), to Metastasio's great satisfaction. In 1752 he passed through Italy to Lisbon; in 1755 he accepted a summons to Madrid, where he remained under Farinelli's direction, enjoying every favour from the court and public. In 1759 he accompanied Farinelli to Naples. In 1770 he entered the service of the Elector, Karl Theodor, at Mannheim. In 1778 he was in Paris with Mozart, and in 1779 he followed the court to Munich, where Mozart composed the part of Idomeneo for him. He died in Munich, May 27, 1797. Mozart in his letters speaks of him as his ' best and dearest friend,' especially in one from Paris, dated June 12, 1778. He composed for him in Mannheim the air, ' Se al labbro mio non credi ' (Köchel, 295).　　　　　　　　　　　　　C. F. P.

RABAN, EDWARD, was an Englishman, and after having fought in the wars of the Netherlands, from the year 1600, settled at Edinburgh, at the Cowgate Port, as a printer, in 1620. One work with the Edinburgh imprint alone remains, and in the same year he removed to St. Andrews, and finally to Aberdeen in 1622. In this place he was under the patronage of the town dignitaries, and had the friendship of Bishop Forbes. It was, no doubt, these circumstances that enabled him to carry on his craft unmolested, unlike John Forbes of the same city who, at a later date, suffered fine and imprisonment for infringing the monopoly held by the King's printer in Scotland. Raban at once commenced the printing of liturgical works, including a prayer-book, dated 1625, which is stated to have the music to the Psalms. In 1629 he printed two editions of *CL. Psalmes of the princelie prophet David*, a quarto for binding with Bibles and a 16mo edition. Also, in 1633, two editions of *The Psames of David in prose and metre according to the Church of Scotland. . . . In Aberdene, imprinted by Edward Raban for David Melvill*, 1633, 8o. These have the music to the Psalms printed from movable type. Though probably not so well executed as the music of Andro Hart of Edinburgh, these are of great interest in the history of Scottish music-printing. Raban gave up business in 1649, dying in 1658. F. K.

RACCOLTA GENERALE DELLE OPERE CLASSICHE MUSICALI. A collection of pieces of which the full title is as follows : 'Collection générale des ouvrages classiques de musique, ou Choix de chefs d'œuvres, en tout genre, des plus grands compositeurs de toutes les Écoles, recueillis, mis en ordre et enrichis de Notices historiques, par Alex. E. Choron, pour servir de suite aux Principes de Composition des écoles d'Italie.' A notice on the wrapper further says that the price of the work to subscribers is calculated at the rate of 5 sous per page, The numbers were not to be issued periodically, but the annual cost to subscribers was fixed at from 36 to 40 francs. The work was in folio, engraved by Gillé fils, and published by Leduc & Co., Paris, Rue de Richelieu, 78, with agents at Bordeaux, Marseilles, Leipzig, Munich, Vienna, Lyon, Turin, Milan, Rome, and Naples. It was got up with great care and taste, but seems to have ceased after about six numbers.

For ALFIERI'S 'Raccolta di musica sacra' see vol. i. p. 66.　　　　　　　　　　　G.

RACHMANINOV, SERGEÏ VASSILIEVICH, a pianist of repute, and one of the most talented of the younger Moscow school of composers ; born in the Government of Novgorod, April 1 (March 20, O.S.), 1873. At nine years of age he entered the St. Petersburg Conservatoire, where he remained three years, making the pianoforte his chief study. Three years later, in 1885, he was transferred to the Conservatoire at Moscow. Here he studied the pianoforte, first with Tchaikovsky's friend, Zvierev, and afterwards with Siloti. His masters for theory and composition were Taneiev and Arensky. The musical influences of Moscow are clearly evident in the works of Rachmaninov. In 1892 he won the gold medal for composition, and on quitting the Conservatoire, in the same year, he started on a long concert-tour through the chief towns of Russia. In 1899 Rachmaninov appeared in London at one of the concerts of the Philharmonic Society, and made a good impression in the threefold capacity of composer, conductor, and pianist. In 1893 he was appointed professor of pianoforte to the Maryinsky Institute for girls, in Moscow, a post which he still holds. Several of Rachmaninov's songs and pianoforte pieces, especially the famous prelude in C♯ minor, have attained immense popularity. His compositions are as follows :—

A. ORCHESTRAL

'The Rock,' fantasia, op. 7; Gipsy Capriccio, op. 12; Symphony, op. 13 (1895).

B. PIANOFORTE

Two Concertos, opp. 1 and 18; two Suites, opp. 5 and 17; six pieces for four hands, op. 11; five pieces for two hands, op. 3

(including the C♯ minor prelude) ; seven pieces, op. 10 ; six Moments Musicaux, op. 16 ; variations on the theme of Chopin's Prelude in C minor, op. 22.

C. CHAMBER MUSIC

Elegiac trio (in memory of Tchaikovsky) for pianoforte, violin, and violoncello, op. 9 (1893) ; sonata for violoncello and pianoforte, op. 19 ; two pieces for violin and pianoforte, op. 6 ; two pieces for violoncello and pianoforte, op. 2.

D. VOCAL

Six choruses for female voices, op. 15 ; humorous chorus for mixed voices ; Cantata, 'Spring,' for chorus, baritone solo, and orchestra, op. 20 ; six songs, op. 4 ; six ditto, op. 8 ; 12 ditto, op. 14 ; 'Fate' (to Beethoven's Fifth Symphony), op. 17. 'Aleko,' opera in one act, first performed at the Imperial Opera-House, Moscow, 1892.

R. N.

RACKET, RACKETT, or RANKETT (also known as Cervelat). An obsolete instrument of small cylindrical bore, played with a double reed of the bassoon type. It is described both by Praetorius and by Mersenne, and was made both of wood and ivory. The *apparent* length of the instrument was very small, as the bore doubled many times upon itself, the true length being thus disguised. In addition to the holes or ventages closed by the tips of the fingers in the usual way, the doubling of the tube allowed of the piercing of several holes which were closed by other joints of the fingers, or soft parts of the hand. According to Praetorius the rackets were made in families, the compass of a set of four extending from C to *d'*.   D. J. B.

RADICATI, FELICE DA MAURIZIO DI, violinist and composer, born at Turin in 1778 ; died, according to the *Quellen-Lexikon*, at Vienna, April 14, 1823. His parents belonging to the poor nobility of Italy, the child's singular interest in music was encouraged the more, and he began his studies at a very early age. Pugnani taught him the violin. Profiting by the precepts of this great master, Radicati acquired many of Pugnani's finer qualities, and, on reaching manhood, toured with unqualified success in Italy, France, and England. The love of his native land, however, and the additional inducement of a post at the Court of King Victor Emanuel V., drew him back to Italy, whither he returned, accompanied by his accomplished wife Teresa BERTINOTTI. In the year 1815 the town of Bologna announced a competition for the post of leader of the town orchestra—at that time celebrated ; but when it came to be known that Radicati had entered the lists, no one would contend against him ; with the result that he was elected to the post on March 31, 1815, without contest. After this his talents obtained for him the appointments of director of the great orchestra of the Basilica di S. Pietro, and professor of the violin at the famous Liceo Filarmonico of Bologna. His career was calamitously cut short, in the prime of life, by a fatal carriage accident.

The authorities on the subject of Radicati's career give but few dates. According to the *Quellen-Lexikon* he was in London 1806-7, and toured in Lombardy (Fétis, *Biog. des Mus.*) in 1816. His principal biographer, Carlo

Pancaldi—a Bolognese lawyer—wrote an eulogy in his memory, but unfortunately mentions but one date, that of his election at Padua on March 31, 1815. As a violinist his qualities appear to have been those of a musician rather than those of a virtuoso. Pancaldi tells us that his style was dignified and his tone sonorous, that he counted Haydn, Beethoven, and Romberg among his friends, and that he was well educated in other respects than music. As a composer he devoted himself especially to perfecting the Quartet, which at that time— in spite of Boccherini's influence—was less thought of in Italy than in other countries. It would seem that his interest in the cause of chamber music was aroused by a German critic, who, reviewing some of Radicati's quartets performed in Vienna, remarked that 'The Italian mind is not apt to compose works of the highest character ; in this matter the Germans seem to take precedence. Radicati's quartets are nothing more than melodies accompanied by harmonies in secondary parts.' This so incensed Radicati that he gave a number of concerts of Italian music in Vienna, in order that the German critic might be convinced of his error ; and, on his return to Italy, not only devoted himself to the writing of many quartets and quintets, but also endeavoured to induce other Italian composers to do likewise, and thus efface the stigma cast upon Italian music by the Germans. Besides his numerous contributions to chamber music, Radicati wrote six or seven operas, among which are included his 'Ricardo Cuor di Leone,' produced at Bologna ; a couple of farces, 'I due Prigionieri,' 'Il Medico per forza' ; a concerto for violin, and a number of small 'Arias,' 'Cavatinas,' etc. All these were in the possession of his son in 1828. The most complete list of his compositions—published and MS.—is probably that given in the *Quellen-Lexikon*. Radicati's wife and his son Karolus, who became a lawyer, erected a monument to his memory in the Campo Santo at Bologna.—Pancaldi (Carlo), *Cenni intorno Felice Radicati*, Bologna, 1828 ; Eitner, *Quellen-Lexikon* ; Fétis, *Biog. des Mus.* ; Baker, *Biog. Dict. Mus.*   E. H-A.

RADZIWILL, ANTON HEINRICH, Prince of, Royal Prussian 'Statthalter' of the Grand Duchy of Posen, born at Wilna, June 13, 1775, married in 1796 the Princess Luise, sister of that distinguished amateur Prince Louis Ferdinand of Prussia. [See vol. ii. p. 772.] Radziwill was known in Berlin not only as an ardent admirer of good music, but as a fine violoncello player, and 'a singer of such taste and ability as is very rarely met with amongst amateurs.'[1] Beethoven was the great object of his admiration. He played his quartets with devotion, made a long journey to Prince Galitzin's on purpose to hear the Mass in D, was invited by

<hr>

[1] *A.M.Z.* 1831, July 27. See also 1809, June 28 ; 1814, Sept. 28.

JOSEPH JOACHIM RAFF

Beethoven to subscribe to the publication of that work, and indeed was one of the seven who sent in their names in answer to that appeal. To him Beethoven dedicated the Overture in C, op. 115 (known as 'Namensfeier'), which was published as 'Grosses Ouverture in C dur *gedichtet*,' etc., by Steiner of Vienna in 1825.

Radziwill was not only a player, a singer, and a passionate lover of music, he was also a composer of no mean order. Whistling's *Handbuch* (1828) names three Romances for voice and PF. (Peters), and songs with guitar and violoncello (B. & H.), and Mendel mentions duets with PF. accompaniment, a Complaint of Maria Stuart, with PF. and violoncello, and many part-songs (still in MS.) composed for Zelter's Liedertafel, of which he was an enthusiastic supporter.[1] But these were only preparations for his great work, entitled 'Compositions to Goethe's dramatic poem of Faust.' This, which was published in score and arrangement by Trautwein of Berlin in Nov. 1835, contains twenty-five numbers, occupying 589 pages. A portion was sung by the Singakademie as early as May 1, 1810 ; the choruses were performed in May 1816, three new scenes as late as Nov. 21, 1830, and the whole work was brought out by that institution after the death of the composer, which took place April 8, 1833. The work was repeatedly performed during several years in Berlin, Danzig, Hanover, Leipzig, Prague, and many other places, as may be seen from the index to the *A. M. Zeitung*. It made its appearance in a performance at Hyde Park College, London, on May 21, 1880, under the direction of L. Martin-Eiffe. A full analysis of it will be found in the *A. M. Zeitung* for 1836, pp. 601, 617 ; and there is a copy in the British Museum.   G.

RAFF, JOSEPH JOACHIM, born May 27, 1822, at Lachen on the Lake of Zurich. He received his early education at Wiesenstetten in Wurtemberg, in the home of his parents, and then at the Jesuit Lyceum of Schwyz, where he carried off the first prizes in German, Latin, and mathematics. Want of means compelled him to give up his classical studies, and become a schoolmaster, but he stuck to music, and though unable to afford a teacher, made such progress not only with the piano and the violin, but also in composition, that Mendelssohn, to whom he sent some MSS., gave him in 1843 a recommendation to Breitkopf & Härtel. This introduction seems to have led to his appearing before the public, and to the first drops of that flood of compositions of all sorts and dimensions which from 1844 he poured forth in an almost unceasing stream. Of op. 1 we have found no critical record ; but op. 2 is kindly noticed by the *N. Zeitschrift* for August 5, 1844, the

reviewer finding in it 'something which points to a future for the composer.' Encouraging notices of opp. 2 to 6 inclusive are also given in the *A. M. Zeitung* for the 21st of the same month. Amidst privations which would have daunted any one of less determination he worked steadily on, and at length having fallen in with Liszt, was treated by him with the kindness which always marked his intercourse with rising or struggling talent, and was taken by him on a concert-tour. Meeting Mendelssohn for the first time at Cologne in 1846, and being afterwards invited by him to become his pupil at Leipzig, he left Liszt for that purpose. Before he could carry this project into effect, however, Mendelssohn died, and Raff remained at Cologne, occupying himself *inter alia* in writing critiques for Dehn's *Cäcilia*. Later, in 1854, he published *Die Wagnerfrage*, a pamphlet which excited considerable attention. Liszt's endeavours to secure him a patron in Vienna in the person of Mecchetti the publisher, were frustrated by Mecchetti's death while Raff was actually on the way to see him. Undismayed by these repeated obstacles he devoted himself to a severe course of study, partly at home and partly at Stuttgart, with the view to remedy the deficiencies of his early training. At Stuttgart he made the acquaintance of Bülow, who became deeply interested in him, and did him a great service by taking up his new Concertstück, for PF. and orchestra, and playing it (Jan. 1, 1848).

By degrees Raff attached himself more and more closely to the new German school, and in 1850 went to Weimar to be near Liszt, who had at that time abandoned his career as a virtuoso and was settled there. Here he remodelled an opera, 'König Alfred,' which he had composed in Stuttgart three years before, and it was produced at the Court Theatre, where it was often performed. It has also been given elsewhere. Other works followed—a collection of PF. pieces called 'Frühlingsboten' in 1852, the first string quartet in 1855, and the first grand sonata for PF. and violin (E minor) in 1857. In the meantime he had engaged himself to Doris Genast, daughter of the well-known actor and manager, and herself on the stage ; and in 1856 he followed her to Wiesbaden, where he was soon in great request as a pianoforte teacher. In 1858 he composed his second violin sonata, and the incidental music for 'Bernhard von Weimar,' a drama by Wilhelm Genast, the overture to which speedily became a favourite, and was much played throughout Germany. In 1859 he married. In 1863 his first symphony, 'An das Vaterland,' obtained the prize offered by the Gesellschaft der Musikfreunde in Vienna (out of thirty-two competitors), and was followed by the 2nd (in C) and the 3rd (in F, 'Im Walde') in 1869, the 4th (in G minor) in 1871, the 5th ('Lenore') in 1872, the 6th ('Gelebt, gestrebt, gelitten, gestritten, gestorben, umworben') in 1876, and the 7th ('Alpensinfonie') in 1877, the 8th ('Frühlingsklänge') in 1878, and the 9th ('Im Sommerzeit') in 1880. A 10th ('Zur Herbstzeit') was played at Wiesbaden ; and the 11th, left unfinished at his death, was revised by Erdmannsdörfer. In 1870 his comic opera 'Dame Kobold' was produced at Weimar. Other operas for which he himself wrote the libretti have not been performed in public. Two cantatas, 'Wachet auf,' and another written for the Festival in commemoration of the battle of Leipzig, were his first works for men's voices, and are popular with choral societies. His arrangement of Bach's six violin sonatas for PF. is a work of great merit.

Detailed analyses of the first six of these Symphonies will be found in the *Monthly Musical Record* for 1875, and from these a very good idea of the composer's style may be gathered. Remembering his struggles and hard life it is only a matter for wonder that he should have striven so earnestly and so long in a path that was not his natural walk. A glance at the nearly complete list of his works at the foot of this notice will explain our meaning. The enormous mass of 'drawing-room music' tells its own tale. Raff had to live, and having by nature a remarkable gift of melody and perhaps not much artistic refinement, he wrote what would pay. But on looking at his works in the higher branch of music—his symphonies, concertos, and chamber music—one cannot but be struck by the conscientious striving towards a high ideal. In the whole of his published Symphonies the slow movements, without a single exception, are of extreme melodic beauty, although weak from a symphonic point of view ; the first movements are invariably worked out with surprising technical skill, the subjects appearing frequently in double counterpoint and in every kind of canon. And however modern and common his themes may appear, they have often been built up with the greatest care, note by note, to this end ; showing that he does not, as is often said, put down the first thing that comes into his mind. Observe the following treatment of the first subject in his 1st Symphony 'An das Vaterland' :—

a canon in augmentation and double augmentation. Such instances as this are numerous, and the art with which these contrapuntal devices

are made to appear spontaneous is remarkable. In the Pianoforte Concerto in C minor (op. 185), in each movement *all* the subjects are in double counterpoint with one another, yet this is one of Raff's freshest and most melodious works. To return to the Symphonies: the Scherzos are, as a rule, weak, and the Finales without exception boisterous and indeed vulgar. Writing here, as ever, for an uneducated public, Raff has forgotten that for a symphony to descend from a high tone is for it to be unworthy of the name.

A remarkable set of thirty Songs (Sanges-Frühling, op. 98) deserves notice for its wealth of fine melodies, some of which have become national property ('Kein Sorg um den Weg' ; 'Schön' Else,' etc.) ; and among his pianoforte music is a set of twenty Variations on an original theme (op. 179) which displays an astonishing fertility of resource, the theme—of five and seven quavers in the bar—being built up into canons and scherzos of great variety and elegance.

Raff's Pianoforte Concerto was very popular, and his Suite for Violin and Orchestra (op. 180) only little less so. His versatility need not be enlarged upon. In all the forms of musical composition he showed the same brilliant qualities and the same regrettable shortcomings. His gift of melody, his technical skill, his inexhaustible fertility, and above all his power of never repeating himself—all these are beyond praise. But his very fertility was a misfortune, since it rendered him careless in the choice of his subjects ; writing 'pot-boilers' injured the development of a delicate feeling for what is lofty and refined ; in short, the conscientious critic hesitates to allow him a place in the front rank of composers.

Even those who have least sympathy with Raff's views on art must admire the energy and spirit with which he worked his way upwards in spite of every obstacle poverty could throw in his way. He was a member of several societies, and received various orders. In 1877 he was appointed with much éclat director of the Hoch conservatorium at Frankfort, a post he held until his death, in the night of June 24-25, 1882. [Since his death his music has passed, alike in Germany and England, into an oblivion which cannot excite surprise in those who realise the inherent weaknesses of the composer ; and the sudden change on the part of the public, from a widespread admiration to almost complete neglect, is of itself a severe criticism on his work.]

The first of his large works performed in this country was probably the Lenore Symphony at the Crystal Palace, Nov. 14, 1874. [The *Musical World* of August 1890, p. 629, contains a translation of Raff's letters explaining the meaning of the work.] This was followed by the 'Im Walde,' and the PF. Concerto in C minor (Jaell), at the Philharmonic ; the Symphonies in G minor, 'Im Walde,' 'Frühlings-klänge' and 'Im Sommerzeit,' with the Concertos for violoncello and violin, and the Suite for PF. and orchestra, at the Crystal Palace. His Quintet (op. 107), two Trios (opp. 102, 112), Sonata (op. 128), and other pieces, were played at the Monday Popular Concerts.   F. G.

Catalogue of Raff's Works.[1]

Op.

1. Serenade. PF. solo. Andre.
2. Trois pièces caractéristiques. PF. solo. B. & H.[2]
3. Scherzo (C minor). PF. solo. B. & H.
4. Morceau de Salon . . . sur 'Maria de Rudenz.' PF. solo. B. & H.
5. 4 Galops. PF. solo. B. & H.
6. Morceau inst. Fantaisie et Varns. PF. solo. B. & H.
7. Rondeau sur 'Io son ricco.' PF. solo. B. & H.
8. 12 Romances in form d'Études; en 2 Cahiers. PF. solo. B. & H.
9. Impromptu brillant. PF. solo. B. & H.
10. Hommage au Néoromantisme. Grand Caprice. PF. solo. B. & H.
11. Air suisse, transcrit. PF. solo. B. & H.
12. Morceau de Salon. Fant. gracieuse, PF. solo. B. & H.
13. Valse. Rondino sur 'Les Huguenots.' PF. duet. B. & H.
14. Sonata & Fugue (E♭ minor). PF. solo. B. & H.
15. 6 Poèmes. PF. solo. Schott.
16. Impromptus for PF. Unpublished.
17. Album Lyrique. PF. solo. Schuberth (4 books containing 9 pieces).
18. Paraphrases (on Liszt's songs) PF. solo. Eck.
19. Fantaisie dramatique. PF. solo. Litolff.
20. 2 Morceaux de Salon. Sérénade italienne; Air Rhenan. PF. solo. Litolff.
21. Loreley. Dichtung ohne Worte. PF. solo. Spina.
22. 2 Rhapsodies élégiaques. PF. solo. Spina.
23. 3 Pièces caractéristiques. PF. solo. Kistner.
24. Valse mélancolique. PF. solo. Spina.
25. Romance-étude. PF. solo. Spina.
26. Den Manen Scarlattis. Scherzo. PF. solo. Spina.
27. Angelens letzter Tag im Kloster. Ein Cyclus, etc. (12 pieces in 2 books). PF. solo. Kistner.
28. 2 airs from 'Robert le Diable,' transcribed for PF. Unpublished.
29. Liebesfrühling, songs.
30. 2 Mazurkas and Serenade, for PF.
31. Tarantelle, for PF. Cranz.
32. Am Rhein, Romanze. PF. solo. Spina.
33. Albumstück, for PF. Unpublished.
34. 6 Liederübertragungen, for PF. Ebner.
35. Capriccietto (on themes from 'Freischütz'). PF. solo. Schuberth.
36. Fantaisie Militaire (on themes from 'Huguenots'). PF. solo. Schuberth.
37. Mélange (on themes from 'Sonnambula'). PF. solo. Schuberth.
38. Grand Mazourka. PF. solo. Schuberth.
39. Nocturne (on romance by Liszt). PF. solo. Kistner.
40. Capriccietto à la Bohémienne. PF. solo. Kistner.
41. Romance. PF. solo. Kistner.

Op.

42. 'Le Prétendant' . . . de Kücken (3 Nos.). PF. solo. Kistner.
43. Divertissement sur 'La Juive.' PF. solo. Schuberth.
44. Fantasina sur 'Le Barbier de Seville.' PF. solo. Schuberth.
45. Souvenir de 'Don Giovanni.' PF. solo. Schuberth.
46. 'La dernière Rose' — (The last rose of summer). Impromptu. PF. solo. Cranz.
47. 3 Lieder (by J. G. Fischer) for Bar. or Alto and PF. Senff.
48. 2 Lieder for Voice and PF. Senff.
49. 3 Lieder (by J. G. Fischer) for Voice and PF. Heinrichshofen.
50. 2 Italienische Lieder (by Sternau) for Voice and PF. Heinrichshofen.
51. 5 Lieder for Voice and PF. Kistner.
52. 3 Lieder for Voice and PF. Schlesinger.
53. 2 Lieder vom Rhein for Voice and PF. Bahn.
54. Tanz-capricen (4). PF. solo. Bahn.
55. Frühlingsboten — 12 short pieces for PF. solo. Schuberth.
56. 3 Salonstück. PF. solo. Bachmann.
57. 'Aus der Schweiz.' Fantastische Egloge. Bachmann.
58. 2 Nocturnes. PF. and violin. Schuberth.
59. Duo in A. PF. and violoncello. Nagel.
60. Schweizerweisen (9 Nos.). PF. solo. Schuberth.
61. No. 1. Wagner's 'Lohengrin,' 'Lyrische Fragmente.' PF. solo.—No. 2. Do. 'Tannhäuser,' Fantasie. PF. solo.—No. 3. Do. 'Fliegende Holländer,' Reminiscenzen. PF. solo.—No. 4. Schumann's 'Genoveva,' PF. solo. Schuberth.
62. Salon-Etuden from Wagner's operas. PF. solo. Schlesinger. No. 1. Andante from 'Fliegende Holländer.'—No. 2. Sestet from 'Tannhäuser.'—No. 3. Lohengrin's farewell.
63. Duos on motifs from Wagner's operas. PF. and V. Siegel. No. 1. 'Fliegende Holländer.'—No. 2. 'Tannhäuser.'—No. 3. 'Lohengrin.'
64. Capriccio in F minor. PF. solo. Leuckart.
65. No. 1. Fantaisie on motifs from Berlioz's 'Benvenuto Cellini.' PF. solo.—No. 2. Caprice on motifs from Raff's 'Alfred.' PF. solo. Schuberth.
66. 'Traum-König und sein Lieb' (Geibel). Voice and PF. Schuberth.
67. 'La Fée d'Amour.' Morceau caractéristique pour Violon de Concert avec PF. Schott.
68. 5 Transcriptions (Beethoven, Gluck, Mozart, Schumann, Spohr). PF. solo. Peters.
69. Suite. PF. solo. Körner.
70. 2 Paraphrases de Salon (Trovatore, Traviata). PF. solo. Peters.

Op.

71. Suite in C. PF. solo. Kühn.
72. Suite in E minor. PF. solo. Kühn.
73. 1st Grand Sonata. PF. and V. (E minor). Schuberth.
74. 3 PF. solos (Ballade, Scherzo, Metamorphosen). Schuberth.
75. Suite de (12) Morceaux pour les petites mains. PF. solo. Kistner.
76. Ode au Printemps. Morceau de Concert. PF. and Orch. Schott.
77. Quatuor (No. 1) in D minor, for Strings. Schuberth.
78. 2nd Grand Sonata for PF. and V. (in A). Schuberth.
79. Cachoucha, Caprice. PF. solo. Peters.
80. 'Wachet auf' (Geibel). Men's voices, Solo, Chorus, and Orchestra. Schott.
81. No. 1. Sicilienne de l'Opéra des 'Vêpres Siciliennes.'—No. 2. Tarantelle de ditto. PF. solo. Peters.
82. Suite de (12) Morceaux pour les petites mains. PF. duets. Schuberth.
83. Mazourka-Caprice. PF. solo. Schott.
84. 'Chant de l'Ondin,' Grande Étude de l'Arpeggio tremolando. PF. solo. Peters.
85. 6 Morceaux. PF. and V. Kistner.
86. 2 Fantaisiestücke, PF. and V'cello. R. B.[3]
87. Introduction and Allo scherzoso. PF. solo. R. B.
88. 'Am Giessbach,' Étude. PF. solo. R. B.
89. Vilanella. PF. solo. R. B.
90. Quartet. No. 2, in A, for Strings. Schuberth.
91. Suite in D. PF. solo. Peters.
92. Capriccio in D minor. PF. solo. Peters.
93. 'Dans la nacelle,' Rêverie-Barcarolle. PF. solo. Peters.
94. Impromptu Valse. PF. solo. Peters.
95. 'La Polka de la Reine,' Caprice. PF. solo. Peters.
96. 'An das Vaterland.' Prize Symphony (No. 1). Schuberth.
97. 10 Lieder for Male Voices. Kahnt.
98. 'Sanges-Frühling.' 30 Romanzen, Lieder, Balladen, and Gesänge, for Sopr. and PF. Schuberth.
99. 3 Sonatilles (A minor; G; C). PF. solo. Schuberth.
100. 'Deutschlands Auferstehung.' Fest Cantate on the 50th anniversary of the Battle of Leipzig, for Male Voices and Orch. Kahnt.
101. Suite for Orchestra. Schott.
102. 1st Grand Trio, for PF., V., and violoncello. Schuberth.
103. Jubilee Overture, for Orchestra. Kahnt.
104. 'Le Galop,' Caprice. PF. solo. Peters.
105. 5 Eglogues. PF. solo. Peters.
106. Fantaisie-Polonaise. PF. solo. Peters.
107. Grand Quintuor (A minor). PF., 2 VV., viola, and violoncello. Schuberth.
108. Saltarello. PF. solo. R. B.
109. Rêverie-Nocturne. PF. solo. R. B.
110. 'La Gitana,' Danse Espagn. Caprice. PF. solo. R. B.
111. Boleros and Valse, 2 Caprices. PF. solo. Schuberth.
112. 2nd Grand Trio (in G). PF. V., and violoncello. R. B.
113. Ungarische Rhapsodie. PF. solo. Forberg.
114. 12 Songs for 2 voices and PF. Forberg.
115. 2 Morceaux lyriques. PF. solo. Forberg.
116. Valse Caprice. PF. solo. Forberg.
117. Festival Overture (in A), for Orchestra. Kistner.

Op.

118. Valse favorite. PF. solo. Kistner.
119. Fantasie. PF. solo. Kistner.
120. Spanish Rhapsody, for PF. Kistner, 1855.
121. Illustrations de 'L'Africaine' (4 Nos.). PF. solo. B. B.[4]
122. 10 Songs for Men's Voices. Kahnt.
123. Concert-Overture (in F). Siegel.
124. Festival-Overture on 4 favourite Student-songs, for the 50th anniversary of the 'Deutschen-Burschenschaft.' PF. 4 hands. Praeger.
125. Gavotte; Berceuse; Espiègle; Valse. PF. solo. Siegel.
126. 3 Clavierstücke — Menuet, Romance, Capriccietto. PF. solo. Praeger.
127. 'Ein' feste Burg,' overture to a drama on the 30-years' war. Orchestra. Hofmeister.
128. 3rd Grand Sonata. PF. and V. (in D). Schuberth.
129. 4th Grand Sonata. PF. and V. 'Chrom. Sonate in einem Satze.' (G minor). Schuberth.
130. 2 Études mélodiques. PF. solo. Schuberth.
131. Styrienne. PF. solo. Hofmeister.
132. Marche brillante. PF. solo. Hofmeister.
133. Élégie. PF. solo. Hofmeister.
134. 'Vom Rhein,' 6 Fantasiestücke. PF. solo. Kistner.
135. 'Blätter und Blüthen,' 12 pieces for PF. solo. Kahnt.
136. 3rd String quartet (E minor). Schuberth.
137. 4th String quartet (A minor). Schuberth.
138. 5th String quartet (G). Schuberth.
139. Festmarsch, for Orchestra. Schott.
140. 2nd Symphony (in C), for Orchestra. Schott.
141. Psalm 130 ('De Profundis'). 8 voices and Orch. Schuberth.
142. Fantaisie (F♯). PF. solo. Kistner.
143. Barcarolle (E♭). PF. solo. Kistner.
144. Tarantella (C). PF. solo. Kistner.
145. 5th Grand Sonata. PF. and V. (C minor). Schuberth.
146. Capriccio (B♭ minor). PF. solo. R. B.
147. 2 Meditations. PF. solo. R. B.
148. Scherzo in E♭. PF. solo. R. B.
149. 2 Elégies for PF. solo. R. B.
150. Chaconne (A minor). 2 PFs. R. B.
151. Allegro agitato. PF. solo. R. B.
152. 2 Romances. PF. solo. R. B.
153. 3rd Symphony, 'Im Walde' (F). Orchestra. Kistner.
154. 'Dame Kobold,' Comic opera. B. B.
155. 3rd Grand Trio. PF., V., and violoncello. B. B.
156. Valse brillante (E♭). PF. solo. Ries.
157. Cavatine (A♭) and Étude 'La Fileuse.' PF. solo. Seitz.
158. 4th Grand Trio (D). PF., V., and violoncello. Seitz.
159. 1st Humoreske (D) in Waltz form. PF. duet. B. B.
160. Reisebilder (10 Nos.). PF. duet. Siegel.
161. Concerto for Violin & Orch. (B minor). Siegel.
162. Suite in G minor. PF. solo. Challier.
163. Suite in G major. PF. solo. Seitz.
164. Sicilienne, Romanze, Tarantelle. PF. solo. B. B.
165. 'La Cicerenella, Nouveau Carnaval.' PF. solo. Siegel.

---

[1] The Editor desires to express his obligations to Messrs. Augener & Co. for great assistance kindly rendered him in the difficult task of drawing up this list.

[2] B. & H. = Breitkopf & Härtel.

[3] R. B. = Rieter-Biedermann & Co.

[4] B. B. = Bote & Bock.

Op.
166. Idylle : Valse champêtre.
     PF. solo. Seitz.
167. 4th Symphony (G minor).
     Orchestra. Schuberth.
168. Fantaisie-Sonate (D minor),
     PF. solo. Siegel.
169. Romanze ; Valse brillante.
     PF. solo. Siegel.
170. La Polka glissante, Caprice.
     PF. solo. Siegel.
171. 'Im Kahn' and 'Der Tanz.'
     2 songs for Mixed Choir
     and Orchestra. Siegel.
172. 'Maria Stuart, ein Cyclus
     von Gesängen,' for Voice
     and PF. (11 Nos.) Siegel.
173. 8 Gesänge for Voice and PF.
     Seitz.
174. 'Aus dem Tanzsalon, Phan-
     tasie Stücke' (12 Nos.). PF.
     4 hands. Seitz.
175. 'Orientales,' 8 Morceaux.
     PF. solo. Forberg.
176. Octet for strings (C). Seitz.
177. 5th Symphony, 'Lenore.'
     Orch. Seitz.
178. Sestet. 2 VV., 2 violas, 2
     violoncellos. Seitz.
179. Variations on an original
     theme. PF. solo. Seitz.
180. Suite for Solo V. and Orch.
     Siegel.
181. 2nd Humoreske in Waltz
     form, 'Todtentanz (Danse
     macabre).' PF. duet. Siegel.
182. 2 Romances for Horn (or
     violoncello) and PF. Siegel.
183. Sonata for PF. and violon-
     cello. Siegel.
184. 6 Songs for 3 women's voices
     and PF. Siegel.
185. Concerto. PF. and Orch. (C
     minor). Siegel.
186a. Morgenlied for Mixed Choir
     and Orch. Siegel.
186b. Einer entschlafenen. So-
     prano solo, Chor. and Orch.
     Siegel.
187. Erinnerung an Venedig (6
     Nos.). PF. solo. Seitz.
188. Sinfonietta for wind instru-
     ments. Siegel.
189. 6th Symphony (D minor),
     'Gelebt, gestrebt, gelitten,
     gestritten, gestorben, um-
     worben.' Orch. B. B.
190. Feux follets, Caprice-étude.
     PF. solo. Siegel.
191. Blumensprache. Six Songs.
     Ries and Erler.
192. 3 String Quartets. No. 6. (C
     minor) Suite älterer Form.
     —No. 7. (D) Die schöne
     Müllerin.—No. 8. (C) Suite
     in Canon-form. Kahnt.
193. Concerto (D minor). Violon-
     cello and Orch. Siegel.
194. 2nd Suite in Ungarischer
     Weise (F). Orch. Bahn.
195. 10 Gesänge for men's voices.
     Kahnt.
196. Étude 'am Schiff'; Ber-
     ceuse ; Novelette ; Im-
     promptu. PF. solo. Seitz.
197. Capriccio (Db). PF. solo.
     Seitz.

Op.
198. 10 Gesänge for Mixed Choir.
     Seitz.
199. 2 Scenes for Solo Voice and
     Orch. 'Jäger-braut' and
     'Die Hirtin.' Siegel.
200. Suite in Eb for PF. and
     Orch. Siegel.
201. 7th Symphony, 'In the
     Alps' (Bb). Orch. Seitz.
202. 2 Quartets for PF. V. Va.
     and violoncello (G). Siegel.
203. 'Volker,' cyclische Tondich-
     tung (9 Nos.). V. and PF.
     Siegel.
204. Suite (Bb). Orch. Challier.
205. 8th Symphony 'Frühlings-
     klänge' (A). Orch. Siegel.
206. 2nd Concerto for V. and
     Orch. (A minor). Siegel.
207a. Phantasie (G minor). 2
     PFs. Siegel.
207b. The same arranged for PF.
     and strings. Siegel.
208. 9th Symphony (E minor),
     'Im Sommer.' Orch. Sie-
     gel.
209. 'Die Tageszeiten,' for Choir,
     PF., and Orch. B. & H.
210. Suite for Vln. and PF. Siegel.
211. 'Blondel de Nesle,' Cyclus
     von Gesängen. Barit. and
     PF. B. & H.
212. Weltende — Gericht — Neue
     Welt, oratorio. B. & H.
213. 10th Symphony, 'Zur Herbst-
     zeit.' Siegel.
214. 11th Symphony, 'Der Win-
     ter.' Siegel.
215. 'Von der schwäbischen Alb,'
     10 PF. pieces. Siegel.
216. 'Aus der Adventzeit.' 8 PF.
     pieces. Bahn.

WORKS WITHOUT OPUS-NUMBER.

Valse-rondino on motifs from
  Saloman's 'Diamantkreuz.'
  Schuberth.
Reminiscences of the 'Meister-
  singer' (4 Pts.). Schott.
Valse - impromptu à la Tyro-
  lienne. Schott.
Abendlied by Schumann. Con-
  cert-paraphrase. Schuberth.
Berceuse on an Idea of Gounod's.
  Siegel.
Improvisation on Damrosch's
  Lied 'Der Lindenzweig.' Lich-
  tenberg.
Valse de Juliette (Gounod).
  Siegel.
4 Capriccios on Wallachian (2)
  and Servian (2) themes. Siegel.
Introduction and Fugue for Or-
  gan (E minor), R. B.
Raff-Album—containing op. 156 ;
  157, Nos. 1, 2 ; 166, No. 2 ; 196,
  Nos. 1–4 ; 197. Seitz.
Oper im Salon—containing op.
  35—37, 43—45, 61, 65. Schu-
  berth.
Frühlings-Lied. Mez. Sop. and
  PF. Schott.
Ständchen for Voice and PF.
  Cotta.

RAG TIME. A modern term, of American
origin, signifying, in the first instance, broken
rhythm in melody, especially a sort of continuous syncopation. 'Rag time tunes' is a
name given in the States to those airs which
are usually associated with the so-called ' coon '
songs or lyrics, which are supposed to depict
negro life in modern America.   F. K.

RAIF, OSKAR (born July 31, 1847, at
Zwolle, in Holland, died July 29, 1899, in
Berlin), was a pupil of Tausig, and occupied a
post as pianoforte teacher in the Royal Hochschule at Berlin, with the title of Königlicher Professor, from 1875 till the time he died. H. V. H.

RAIMONDI, IGNAZIO, Neapolitan violinist
and composer. The date of his birth is unknown,
but, judging by the fact that he went to
Amsterdam in 1760, and there produced his

first compositions, we may infer that he was
born about 1735 or 1740. He died in London
at his own house, 74 Great Portland Street,
January 14, 1813. During his residence in
Amsterdam he established periodical concerts,
and produced his symphony entitled 'The
Adventures of Telemachus.' From Amsterdam
he went to Paris, where his opera, 'La Muette,'
was performed, and about 1790-91 he came to
London, where he received sufficient encouragement to induce him to make it his permanent
home. His compositions became very popular
in England, particularly a symphony entitled
'The Battle.' On June 1, 1791, he gave a
benefit concert at the Hanover Square Rooms,
at which he figured both as violinist and composer ; he was assisted by Signor Pacchierotti,
Madame Mara, Lord Mornington, and Monsieur
Dahmer (vide *Morning Chronicle*, June 1, 1791).
The following year he gave a series of subscription concerts at Willis's Rooms, and at these
he both played solos and led the orchestra.
Emanuele Barbella is said to have taught
Raimondi the violin, but whether this be fact
or no, we may infer from Dr. Burney's remark
(*History of Music*, vol. iii.), 'The sweet tone
and polished style of a Raimondi,' that this
artist's technique was of the then greatly admired Tartini school. Raimondi's published
compositions include two symphonies—besides
the 'Telemachus' above mentioned, a number
of quartets for two violins, viola, and violoncello, two sets of six trios for two violins and
violoncello, and some sonatas for two violins,
violin and violoncello, and violin and viola.—
Dr. Burney, *History of Music* ; Park (W. T.),
Musical Memoirs ; Fétis, *Biog. des Mus.* ; Eitner,
Quellen - Lexikon ; *The Gentleman's Magazine*,
Jan. 1813 ; *The Times*, May 14, 1800. E. H-A.

RAIMONDI, PIETRO, was born at Rome of
poor parents Dec. 20, 1786. At an early age
he passed six years in the Conservatorio of the
Pietà de' Turchini at Naples, and after many
wanderings, mostly on foot—from Naples to
Rome, from Rome to Florence, from Florence to
Genoa—and many years, he at length found an
opportunity of coming before the public with an
opera entitled 'Le Bizzarrie d'Amore,' which was
performed at Genoa in 1807. After three years
there, each producing its opera, he passed a
twelvemonth at Florence, and brought out two
more. The next twenty-five years were spent
between Rome, Milan, Naples, and Sicily, and
each year had its full complement of operas and
ballets. In 1824 he became director of the
royal theatres at Naples, a position which he
retained till 1832. In that year the brilliant
success of his opera buffa, 'Il Ventaglio' (Naples,
1831), procured him the post of Professor of
Composition in the Conservatorio at Palermo.
Here he was much esteemed, and trained several
promising pupils. In December 1852, he was
called upon to succeed Basili as Maestro di

Cappella at St. Peter's ; a post for which, if knowledge, experience, and ceaseless labour of production in all departments of his art could qualify him, he was amply fitted. Shortly before this, in 1848, he had after four years of toil completed three oratorios, 'Potiphar,' 'Pharaoh,' and 'Jacob,' which were not only designed to be performed in the usual manner, but to be played all three in combination as one work, under the name of 'Joseph.' On August 7, 1852, the new Maestro brought out this stupendous work at the Teatro Argentina. The success of the three single oratorios was moderate, but when they were united on the following day—the three orchestras and the three troupes forming an *ensemble* of nearly 400 musicians—the excitement and applause of the spectators knew no bounds, and so great was his emotion that Raimondi fainted away. He did not long survive this triumph, but died at Rome, Oct. 30, 1853.

The list of his works is astonishing, and embraces 62 operas ; 21 grand ballets, composed for San Carlo between 1812 and 1828 ; 8 oratorios ; 4 masses with full orchestra ; 2 ditto with 2 choirs a cappella ; 2 requiems with full orchestra ; 1 ditto for 8 and 16 voices ; a Credo for 16 voices ; the whole Book of Psalms, for 4, 5, 6, 7, and 8 voices ; many Te Deums, Stabats, Misereres, Tantum ergos, psalms, and litanies ; two books of 90 *partimenti*, each on a separate bass, with three different accompaniments : a collection of figured basses with fugued accompaniments as a school of accompaniment ; 4 fugues for 4 voices, each independent but capable of being united and sung together as a quadruple fugue in 16 parts ; 6 fugues for 4 voices capable of combination into 1 fugue for 24 voices ; a fugue for 16 choirs ; 16 fugues for 4 voices ; 24 fugues for 4, 5, 6, 7, and 8 voices, of which 4 and 5 separate fugues will combine into one. A fugue in 64 parts, for 16 four-part choirs, is said to exist. Besides the above feat with the three oratorios he composed an opera seria and an opera buffa which went equally well separately and in combination. Such stupendous labours are, as Fétis remarked, enough to give the reader the headache : what must they have done to the persevering artist who accomplished them ? But they also give one the heartache at the thought of their utter futility. Raimondi's compositions, with all their ingenuity, belong to a past age, and we may safely say that they will never be revived.   G.

RAINFORTH, ELIZABETH, born Nov. 23, 1814, studied singing under George Perry and T. Cooke, and acting under Mrs. Davison, the eminent comedian. After having gained experience at minor concerts, she appeared upon the stage at the St. James's Theatre, Oct. 27, 1836, as Mandane, in Arne's 'Artaxerxes,' with complete success. She performed there for the remainder of the season, and then removed to the English Opera-House. Subsequently to her public appearance she took lessons from Crivelli. In 1837 she sang in oratorio at the Sacred Harmonic Society, and continued to do so for several years. She made her first appearance at the Philharmonic, March 18, 1839. In 1840 she sang at the Antient Concerts, and in 1843 at the Birmingham Festival. After performing at Covent Garden from 1838 to 1843 she transferred her services to Drury Lane, where she made a great hit by her performance of Arline, in Balfe's 'Bohemian Girl,' on its production, Nov. 27, 1843. In the previous year she had a most successful season in Dublin, and repeated her visits to Ireland in 1844 and 1849. She was engaged as prima donna at the Worcester Festival of 1845. She continued to perform in the metropolis until about 1852, when she removed to Edinburgh, where she remained until about 1856. She then retired, and in 1858 went to live at Old Windsor, and taught music in the neighbourhood until her complete retirement in March 1871, when she removed to her father's at Bristol. Her voice was a high soprano, even and sweet in quality, but deficient in power, and she possessed great judgment and much dramatic feeling. Although her limited power prevented her from becoming a great singer, her attainments were such as enabled her to fill the first place with credit to herself, and satisfaction to her auditors. She died at Redland, Bristol, Sept. 22, 1877.   W. H. H.

RALLENTANDO, RITARDANDO, RITENENTE, RITENUTO—'Becoming slow again,' 'Slackening,' 'Holding back,' 'Held back.' The first two of these words are used quite indifferently to express a gradual diminution of the rate of speed in a composition, and although the last is commonly used in exactly the same way, it seems originally and in a strict sense to have meant a uniform rate of slower time, so that the whole passage marked *ritenuto* would be taken at the same time, while each bar and each phrase in a passage marked *rallentando* would be a little slower than the one before it. That there exists a difference in their uses is conclusively proved by a passage in the Quartet op. 131 of Beethoven, where in the 7th movement (allegro) a phrase of three recurring minims, which is repeated in all five times, has the direction 'Espressivo, poco ritenuto' for its first three appearances, which are separated by two bars *a tempo*, and for the last two times has *ritardando*, which at length leads into the real *a tempo*, of which the former separating fragments were but a presage. This is one of the very rare instances of the use of the word *ritenuto* by Beethoven. The conclusion from it is confirmed by a passage in Chopin's Rondo, op. 16, consisting of the four bars which immediately precede the entry of the second subject. Here the first two bars consist of a fragment of a preceding figure which is repeated, so that both these bars are exactly the same ; the last two bars, however, have a little chromatic cadence leading into the second subject. The direction over the first two bars is 'poco ritenuto,' and over the last two 'rallentando,' by which we may be quite sure that the composer intended the repeated fragment to be played at the same speed in each bar, and the chromatic cadence to be slackened gradually.

Ritenente is used by Beethoven in the PF. Sonata, op. 110, about the middle of the first movement, and again in the Sonata, op. 111, in the first movement, in the seventh and fifteenth bars from the beginning of the *Allegro con brio*. It would seem that the same effect is intended as if ' ritenuto ' were employed ; in each case, the words ' meno mosso ' might have been used. Beethoven prefers *Ritardando* to *Rallentando*, which latter is common only in his earlier works.   M.

RAMANN, LINA, musical writer and educationist, was born at Mainstockheim, near Kitzingen, in Bavaria, June 24, 1833. Her turn for music and her determination to succeed were evident from a very early age. It was not, however, till her seventeenth year that she had any instruction in music. At that time her parents removed to Leipzig, and from 1850 to 1853 she there enjoyed the advantage of pianoforte lessons from the wife of Dr. F. Brendel, herself formerly a scholar of Field's. From this period she adopted the career of a teacher of music, and studied assiduously, though without help, for that end. After a period of activity in America, she opened (in 1858) an institute in Glückstadt (Holstein) for the special training of music-mistresses, and maintained it till 1865, in which year she founded a more important establishment, the Music School at Nuremberg, in conjunction with Frau Ida Volkmann of Tilsit, and assisted by a staff of superior teachers, under Frl. Ramann's own superintendence. The school was transferred to Aug. Göllerich in 1890, when Frl. Ramann moved to Munich. With a view to the special object of her life she has published two works—*Die Musik als Gegenstand der Erziehung* (Leipzig: Merseburger, 1868), and *Allgemeine Erzieh- und Unterrichts-lehre der Jugend* (Leipzig : H. Schmidt, 1869 ; 2nd ed. 1873), which were both received with favour by the German press. From 1860 she was musical correspondent of the Hamburg *Jahreszeiten*. A volume of her essays contributed to that paper has been collected and published, under the title of *Aus der Gegenwart* (Nuremberg : Schmid, 1868). In the early part of 1880 she published a study of Liszt's ' Christus ' (Leipzig, Kahnt), and later in the year the first volume of a *Life of Liszt*, completed in two volumes in 1894 (Leipzig, Breitkopf). The first portion was translated by Mrs. S. H. Eddy, Chicago, and by Miss E. Cowdery, and published in two vols.

in 1882. This is an important work. It suffers somewhat from over-enthusiasm, but it is done with great care, minuteness, and intelligence, and obviously profited largely by direct information from Liszt himself. She also edited Liszt's writings (1880-83, in six volumes). Her cousin,

BRUNO RAMANN, was born April 17, 1832, at Erfurt, and was brought up to commerce, but his desire and talent for music were so strong, that in 1857 or 1858 he succeeded in getting rid of his business and put himself under Dr. F. Brendel and Riedel, for regular instruction. He then for five years studied under Hauptmann at Leipzig, and was a teacher and composer at Dresden from 1867 until his death, March 13, 1897. His works are numerous, but they consist almost entirely of songs for one or more voices, and of small and more or less sentimental pieces for the pianoforte. He also wrote poetry, and some dramatic pieces. G.

RAMEAU, JEAN PHILIPPE, eminent composer, and writer on the theory of music, born at Dijon, Oct. 23, 1683,[1] in the house now No. 5 Rue St. Michel. His father,[2] Jean, was a musician, and organist of Dijon cathedral, in easy circumstances. He intended Jean Philippe, the eldest of his three sons, to be a magistrate, but his strong vocation for music and obstinacy of character frustrated these views. According to his biographers he played the harpsichord at seven, and read at sight any piece of music put before him : music indeed absorbed him to such an extent when at the Jesuit College that he neglected his classical studies, and was altogether so refractory that his parents were requested to remove him. Henceforth he never opened a book, unless it were a musical treatise. He quickly mastered the harpsichord, and studied the organ and violin with success, but there was no master in Dijon capable of teaching him to write music, and he was left to discover for himself the laws of harmony and composition.

At the age of seventeen he fell in love with a young widow in the neighbourhood, who indirectly did him good service, since the shame which he felt at the bad spelling of his letters drove him to write correctly. To break off this acquaintance his father sent him, in 1701, to Italy, where, however, he did not remain long, a mistake which, in after life, he regretted. He liked Milan, and indeed the attractions of so great a centre of music must have been great ; but for some unknown reason he soon left with a theatrical manager whom he accompanied as first violin to Marseilles, Lyons, Nîmes, Montpellier, and other places in the south of France. How long the tour lasted it is impossible to ascertain, as no letters belonging to this period are to be found. From his ' Premier Livre de

1 [The date of birth is taken from the composer's monument at Dijon : the first edition of this Dictionary gives the more usual date, Sept. 25, 1683.]
2 His mother's name was Claudine Demartinécourt.

JEAN PHILIPPE RAMEAU

pièces de clavecin' (Paris, 1706) we learn that he was then living in Paris, at a wig-maker's in the Vieille Rue du Temple, as Haydn did at Keller's, though without the disastrous results which followed that connection. Meantime he was organist of the Jesuit convent in the Rue St. Jacques, and of the chapel of the Pères de la Merci. No particulars, however, of the length of his stay in Paris are known, nor how he occupied the interval between this first visit and his return about 1717. In that year a competition took place for the post of organist of the church of St. Paul, and Rameau was among the candidates. Marchand, then at the head of the organists in Paris, was naturally one of the examiners ; and either from fear of being outshone by one whom he had formerly patronised, or for some other reason, he used his whole influence in favour of Daquin, who obtained the post. Mortified at the unjust preference thus shown to a man in all points his inferior, Rameau again left Paris for Lille, and became for a short time organist of St. Étienne. Thence he went to Clermont in Auvergne, where his brother Claude[1] resigned the post of organist of the cathedral in his favour. In this secluded mountain town, with a harsh climate predisposing to indoor life, he had plenty of time for thought and study. The defects of his education drove him to find out everything for himself. From the works of Descartes, Mersenne, Zarlino, and Kircher he gained some general knowledge of the science of sound, and taking the equal division of the monochord as the starting-point of his system of harmony, soon conceived the possibility of placing the theory of music on a sound basis. Henceforth he devoted all his energies to drawing up his *Treatise on Harmony Reduced to its Natural Principles*, and as soon as that important work was finished he determined to go to Paris and publish it. His engagement with the chapter of Clermont had, however, several years to run, and there was great opposition to his leaving, owing to the popularity of his improvisations on the organ, in which his theoretical studies, far from hampering his ideas, seemed to give them greater freshness and fertility.

Once free he started immediately for Paris, and brought out his *Traité de l'Harmonie* (Ballard, 1722, 4to, 432 pp.).[2] The work did not at first attract much attention among French musicians, and yet, as Fétis observes, it laid the foundation for a philosophical science of harmony. Rameau's style is prolix and obscure, often calculated rather to repel than attract the

reader, and the very boldness and novelty of his theories excited surprise and provoked criticism. His discovery of the law of inversion in chords was a stroke of genius, and led to very important results, although in founding his system of harmony on the sounds of the common chord, with the addition of thirds above or thirds below, he put both himself and others on a wrong track. In the application of his principle to all the chords he found himself compelled to give up all idea of tonality, since, on the principles of tonality he could not make the thirds for the discords fall on the notes that his system required. Fétis justly accuses him of having abandoned the tonal successions and resolutions prescribed in the old treatises on harmony, accompaniment, and composition, and the rules for connecting the chords based on the ear, for a fixed order of generation, attractive from its apparent regularity, but with the serious inconvenience of leaving each chord disconnected from the rest.

Having rejected the received rules for the succession and resolution of chords which were contrary to his system, Rameau perceived the necessity of formulating new ones, and drew up a method for composing a fundamental bass for every species of music. The principles he laid down for forming a bass different from the real bass of the music, and for verifying the right use of the chords, are arbitrary, insufficient in a large number of cases, and, as regards many of the successions, contrary to the judgment of the ear. Finally, he did not perceive that by using the chord of the 6–5–3 both as a fundamental chord and an inversion he destroyed his whole system, as in the former case it is impossible to derive it from the third above or below.[3] After more study, however, particularly on the subject of harmonics, Rameau gave up many of his earlier notions, and corrected some of his most essential mistakes. The development and modification of his ideas may be seen by consulting his works, of which the following is a list :—*Nouveau système de musique théorique . . . pour servir d'Introduction au traité d'Harmonie* (1726, 4to) ; *Génération harmonique*, etc. (1737, 8vo) ; *Démonstration du principe de l'harmonie* (1750, 8vo) ; *Nouvelles réflexions sur la démonstration du principe de l'harmonie* (1752, 8vo) ; *Extrait d'une réponse de M. Rameau à M. Euler sur l'identité des octaves*, etc. (1753, 8vo)—all published in Paris. To these specific works, all dealing with the science of harmony, should be added the *Dissertation sur les différentes méthodes d'accompagnement pour le clavecin ou pour l'orgue* (Paris, Boivin, 1732, 4to), and some articles which appeared in the *Mercure de France*, and in the *Mémoires de Trévoux*.

---

[1] Claude Rameau, a man of indomitable will and capricious temper, and a clever organist, lived successively at Dijon, Lyons, Marseilles, Clermont, Orléans, Strasburg, and Autun. His son Jean François, a gifted musician, but a dissipated man, is admirably portrayed by Diderot in his *Neveu de Rameau*. He published in 1766 a poem in five cantos called *Le Raméide*, followed in the same year by *La nouvelle Raméide*, a parody by his schoolfellow Jacques Cazotte. He is mentioned by Mercier in his *Tableau de Paris*.

[2] The third Part of this was translated into English fifteen years later with the title *A Treatise of Music containing the Principles of Composition*. London, no date, 8vo, 180 pp.

[3] Fétis has explained, detailed, and refuted Rameau's system in his *Esquisse de l'Histoire de l'Harmonie*, which has been used by the writer, and to which he refers his readers.

The mere titles of these works are a proof of the research and invention which Rameau brought to bear on the theory of music; but what was most remarkable in his case is that he succeeded in lines which are generally opposed to each other, and throughout life occupied the first rank not only as a theorist, but as a player and composer. Just when his *Traité de l'Harmonie* was beginning to attract attention he arranged to make music for the little pieces which his fellow-countryman, Alexis Piron, was writing for the Théâtre de la Foire, and accordingly, on Feb. 3, 1723, they produced 'L'Endriague,' in three acts, with dances, divertissements, and grand airs, as stated in the title. In Jan. 1724 he obtained the privilege of publishing his cantatas, and various instrumental compositions, amongst others his ' Pièces de clavecin, avec une Méthode pour la mécanique des doigts,' etc., republished as ' Pièces de Clavecin, avec une table pour les agréments ' [1] (Paris, 1731 and 1736, oblong folio).

As the favourite music-master among ladies of rank, and organist of the church of Ste. Croix de la Bretonnerie, Rameau's position and prospects now warranted his taking a wife, and on Feb. 25, 1726, he was united to Marie Louise Mangot, a good musician, with a pretty voice. The disparity of their ages was considerable, the bride being only eighteen, but her loving and gentle disposition made the marriage a very happy one.

A few days later, on Feb. 29, Rameau produced at the Théâtre de la Foire, a one-act piece called 'L'Enrôlement d'Arlequin,' followed in the autumn by ' Le faux Prodigue,' two acts, both written by Piron. Such small comic pieces as these were obviously composed, by a man of his age and attainments (he was now forty-two), solely with the view of gaining access to a stage of higher rank, but there was no hope of admission to the theatre of the Académie without a good libretto, and this it was as difficult for a beginner to obtain then as it is now. There is a remarkable letter, still extant, from Rameau to Houdar de Lamotte, dated Oct. 1727, asking him for a lyric tragedy, and assuring him that he was no novice, but one who had mastered the 'art of concealing his art.' The blind poet refused his request, but aid came from another quarter. La Popelinière, the *fermier général*, musician, poet, and artist, whose houses in Paris and at Passy were frequented by the most celebrated artists French and foreign, had chosen Rameau as his clavecinist and conductor of the music at his fêtes, and before long placed at his disposal the organ in his chapel, his orchestra, and his theatre. He did more, for through his influence Rameau obtained from Voltaire the lyric tragedy of ' Samson,' which he promptly

[1] Both Fétis and Pougin have fallen into the mistake of considering this a separate work.

set to music, though the performance was prohibited on the eve of its representation at the Académie—an exceptional stroke of ill-fortune. [On the history of this work, see Hugues Imbert's *Symphonie* (1891), and for a résumé of the facts, see *Musical Times*, 1898, p. 379 ff.] At last the Abbé Pellegrin agreed to furnish him with an opera in five acts, 'Hippolyte et Aricie,' founded on Racine's ' Phèdre.' He compelled Rameau to sign a bill for 500 livres as security in case the opera failed, but showed more sagacity and more heart than might have been expected from one

> Qui dînait de l'autel et soupait du théâtre,
> Le matin catholique et le soir idolâtre,

for he was so delighted with the music on its first performance at La Popelinière's, that he tore up the bill at the end of the first act. The world in general was less enthusiastic, and after having overcome the ill-will or stupidity of the performers, Rameau had to encounter the astonishment of the crowd, the prejudices of routine, and the jealousy of his brother artists. Campra alone recognised his genius, and it is to his honour that when questioned by the Prince de Conti on the subject, he replied, ' There is stuff enough in Hippolyte et Aricie for ten operas; this man will eclipse us all.'

The opera was produced at the Académie on Oct. 1, 1733. Rameau was then turned fifty years of age, and the outcry with which his work was greeted suggested to him that he had possibly mistaken his career; for a time he contemplated retiring from the theatre, but was reassured by seeing his hearers gradually accustoming themselves to the novelties which at first shocked them. The success of ' Les Indes galantes' (August 23, 1735), of 'Castor et Pollux,' his masterpiece (Oct. 24, 1737), and of ' Les Fêtes d'Hébé ' (May 21, 1739), however, neither disarmed his critics, nor prevented Rousseau from making himself the mouthpiece of those who cried up Lully at the expense of the new composer. But Rameau was too well aware of the cost of success to be hurt by epigrams, especially when he found that he could count both on the applause of the multitude, and the genuine appreciation of the more enlightened.

His industry was immense, as the following list of his operas and ballets produced at the Académie in twenty years will show:—

Dardanus, five acts and prologue (Oct. 19, 1739).	Platée, three acts and prologue (Feb. 4, 1749).
Les Fêtes de Polymnie, three acts and prologue (Oct. 12, 1745).	Naïs, three acts and prologue (April 22, 1749).
Le Temple de la Gloire, Fête, in three acts and prologue (Nov. 27, 1745).	Zoroastre, five acts (Dec. 5, 1749).
Zaïs, four acts and prologue (Feb. 29, 1748).	La Guirlande, ou les Fleurs enchantées, one act (Sept. 21, 1751).
Pygmalion, one act (Aug. 27, 1748).	Acanthe et Céphise, three acts (Nov. 18, 1751).
Les Fêtes de l'Hymen et de l'Amour, three acts and prologue (March 15, 1747).	Les Surprises de l'Amour, three acts (July 12, 1757).
	Les Paladins, three acts (Feb. 12, 1760).

Besides these, Rameau found time to write divertissements for ' Les Courses de Tempé,' a

Pastoral (Théâtre Français, August 1734), and 'La Rose' (Théâtre de la Foire, March 1744), both by Piron. From 1740 to 1745 the director of the Opéra gave him no employment, and in this interval he published his 'Nouvelles Suites de Pièces de clavecin' and his 'Pièces de clavecin en concerts avec un violon ou une flûte' (1741), remarkable compositions which have been reprinted by Mme. Farrenc ('Le Trésor des Pianistes') and M. Poisot. He also accepted the post of conductor of the Opéra-Comique, of which Monnet [1] was manager, probably in the hope of attracting public attention, and forcing the management of the Académie to alter their treatment of him. Finally he composed for the Court 'Lysis et Délie,' 'Daphnis et Eglé,' 'Les Sybarites' (Oct. and Nov. 1753) ; 'La Naissance d'Osiris,' and 'Anacréon' (Oct. 1754), all given at Fontainebleau. Some years previously, on the occasion of the marriage of the Dauphin with the Infanta, he had composed 'La Princesse de Navarre' to a libretto of Voltaire's (three acts and prologue, performed with great splendour at Versailles, Feb. 23, 1745). This was the most successful of all his *opéras de circonstance*, and the authors adapted from it 'Les Fêtes de Ramire,' a one-act opera-ballet, also performed at Versailles (Dec. 22, 1745).

In estimating Rameau's merits we cannot in justice compare him with the great Italian and German masters of the day, whose names and works were then equally unknown in France ; we must measure him with contemporary French composers for the stage. These writers had no idea of art beyond attempting a servile copy of Lully, with overtures, recitatives, vocal pieces, and ballet airs, all cast in one stereotyped form. Rameau made use of such a variety of means as not only attracted the attention of his hearers, but retained it. For the placid and monotonous harmonies of the day, the trite modulation, insignificant accompaniments, and stereotyped ritornelles, he substituted new forms, varied and piquant rhythms, ingenious harmonies, bold modulations, and a richer and more effective orchestration. He even ventured on enharmonic changes, and instead of the time-honoured accompaniments with the strings in five parts, and flutes and oboes in two, and with *tuttis* in which the wind simply doubled the strings, he gave each instrument a distinct part of its own, and thus imparted life and colour to the whole. Without interrupting the other instruments, he introduced interesting and unexpected passages on the flutes, oboes, and bassoons, and thus opened a path which has been followed up with ever-increasing success. He also gave importance to the orchestral pieces, introducing his operas with a well-constructed overture, instead of the meagre introduction of the period, in which the same phrases were repeated *ad*

[1] See Monnet's *Supplément au Roman comique*, p. 51. This fact seems to have escaped all Rameau's biographers.

nauseam. Nor did he neglect the chorus ; he developed it, added greatly to its musical interest, and introduced the syllabic style with considerable effect. Lastly, his ballet-music was so new in its rhythms, and so fresh and pleasing in melody, that it was at once adopted and copied in the theatres of Italy and Germany.

We have said enough to prove that Rameau was a composer of real invention and originality. His declamation was not always so just as that of Lully ; his airs have not the same grace, and are occasionally marred by eccentricity and harshness, and disfigured by roulades in doubtful taste ; but when inspired by his subject Rameau found appropriate expression for all sentiments, whether simple or pathetic, passionate, dramatic, or heroic. His best operas contain beauties which defy the caprices of fashion, and will command the respect of true artists for all time.

But if his music was so good, how is it that it never attained the same popularity as that of Lully ? In the first place, he took the wrong line on a most important point ; and in the second, he was less favoured by circumstances than his predecessor. It was his doctrine, that for a musician of genius all subjects are equally good, and hence he contented himself with uninteresting fables written in wretched style, instead of taking pains, as Lully did, to secure pieces constructed with skill and well versified. He used to say that he could set the *Gazette de Hollande* to music. Thus he damaged his own fame, for a French audience will not listen even to good music unless it is founded on an interesting drama.

Much as Rameau would have gained by the co-operation of another Quinault, instead of having to employ Cahusac, there was another reason for the greater popularity of Lully. Under Louis XIV. the king's patronage was quite sufficient to ensure the success of an artist ; but after the Regency, under Louis XV., other authorities asserted themselves, especially the 'philosophes.' Rameau had first to encounter the vehement opposition of the Lullists ; this he had succeeded in overcoming, when a company of Italian singers arrived in Paris, and at once obtained the attention of the public, and the support of a powerful party. The partisans of French music rallied round Rameau, and the two factions carried on what is known as the 'Guerre des Bouffons,' but when the struggle was over, Rameau perceived that his victory was only an ephemeral one, and that his works would not maintain their position in the *répertoire* of the Académie beyond a few years. With a frankness very touching in a man of his gifts, he said one evening to the Abbé Arnaud, who had lately arrived in Paris, 'If I were twenty years younger I would go to Italy, and take Pergolesi for my model, abandon something of my harmony, and devote myself to attaining truth of declamation, which should be the sole guide of musicians. But after sixty one cannot change ; experience points plainly enough the best course, but the mind refuses to obey.' No critic could have stated the truth more plainly. Not having heard Italian music in his youth, Rameau never attained to the skill in writing for the voice that he might have done ; and he is in consequence only the first French musician of his time, instead of taking his rank among the great composers of European fame. But for this, he might have effected that revolution in dramatic music which Gluck accomplished some years later.

But even as it was, his life's work is one of which any man might have been proud ; and in old age he enjoyed privileges accorded only to talent of the first rank. The directors of the Opéra decreed him a pension ; his appearance in his box was the signal for a general burst of applause, and at the last performance of 'Dardanus' (Nov. 9, 1760) he received a perfect ovation from the audience. At Dijon the Académie elected him a member in 1761, and the authorities exempted himself and his family for ever from the municipal taxes. The king had named him composer of his chamber music in 1745 ; his patent of nobility was registered, and he was on the point of receiving the order of St. Michel, when, already suffering from the infirmities of age, he took typhoid fever, and died Sept. 12, 1764. All France mourned for him ; Paris gave him a magnificent funeral, and in many other towns funeral services were held in his honour. Such marks of esteem are accorded only to the monarchs of art.

Having spoken of Rameau as a theorist and composer, we will now say a word about him as a man. If we are to believe Grimm and Diderot, he was hard, churlish, and cruel, avaricious to a degree, and the most ferocious of egotists. The evidence of these writers is, however, suspicious ; both disliked French music, and Diderot, as the friend and *collaborateur* of d'Alembert, would naturally be opposed to the man who had had the audacity to declare war against the Encyclopedists.[1] It is right to say that, though he drew a vigorous and scathing portrait of the composer, he did not publish it.[2] As to the charge of avarice, Rameau may have been fond of money, but he supported his sister Catherine[3] during an illness of many years, and assisted more than one of his brother artists—

[1] Rameau was asked to correct the articles on music for the *Encyclopédie*, but the MSS. were not submitted to him. He published in consequence : *Erreurs sur la musique dans l'Encyclopédie* (1755) ; *Suite des Erreurs, etc.* (1756) ; *Réponse de M. Rameau à MM. les éditeurs de l'Encyclopédie sur leur Avertissement* (1757) ; *Lettre de M. d'Alembert à M. Rameau, concernant le corps sonore, avec la réponse de M. Rameau* (undated, but apparently 1759)—all printed in Paris.
[2] We refer to Diderot's violent satire on the morals and philosophic tendencies of the 18th century, entitled *Le Neveu de Rameau*. It is a curious fact that this brilliantly written dialogue was only known in France through a re-translation of Goethe's German version. The first French edition, by Saur, appeared in Paris only in 1821.
[3] A good player on the harpsichord ; she lived in Dijon, and died there, 1762.

such as Dauvergne, and the organist Balbâtre. He was a vehement controversialist, and those whom he had offended would naturally say hard things of him. Tall, and thin almost to emaciation, his sharply marked features indicated great strength of character, while his eyes burned with the fire of genius. There was a decided resemblance between him and Voltaire, and painters have often placed their likenesses side by side. Amongst the best portraits of Rameau may be specified those of Benoist (after Restout), Caffieri, Masquelier, and Carmontelle (full length). In the fine oil-painting by Chardin in the Museum of Dijon, he is represented seated, with his fingers on the strings of his violin, the instrument he generally used in composing. The bust which stood in the *foyer* of the Opéra was destroyed when the theatre was burnt down in 1781 ; that in the library of the Conservatoire is by Destreez (1865). A bronze statue by Guillaume was erected at Dijon in 1880. The fine medal of him given to the winners of the *grand prix de Rome* was engraved by Gatteaux.

There are many biographies of Rameau ; the most valuable are, among the older, Chabanon's *Eloge* (1764) ; Maret's *Eloge historique* (1766) ; and the very curious details contained in De Croix's *L'Ami des Arts* (1776) ; among the more modern, the notices of Adolphe Adam, Fétis, Poisot (1864), Nisard (1867), and Pougin (1876).

Rameau had one son and two daughters, none of them musicians. He left in MS. four cantatas, three motets with chorus, and fragments of an opera 'Roland,' all which are now in the Bibliothèque Nationale. None of his organ pieces have survived ; and some cantatas, mentioned by the earlier biographers, besides two lyric tragedies 'Abaris' and 'Linus,' and a comic opera, 'Le Procureur dupé,' are lost ; but they would have added nothing to his fame.

Some of his harpsichord pieces have been published in the 'Trésor des Pianistes' ; in the 'Alte Klaviermusik' of Pauer (Ser. 2, pt. 5) and of Roitzsch ; also in Pauer's 'Alte Meister,' and in the 'Perles Musicales' (51, 52). A new edition, with a preface by Saint-Saëns, appeared in Paris in 1905.　　　G. C.

RAMONDON, LEWIS, presumably a Frenchman, and at first a singer in the pre-Handelian Italian operas. He appeared in 'Arsinoe,' 1705 ; in 'Camilla,' 1706 ; and 'Pyrrhus and Demetrius,' 1709. He sometimes took Leveridge's parts in these operas, but about 1711 he ceased to be a public singer, and turned his talents to composition. He brought out the series called 'The Lady's Entertainment' in 1709, 1710, 1711, and 1738. He arranged for the harpsichord the song-tunes in 'Camilla,' using, perhaps for the first time in music-notation for this instrument, a five instead of a six-line stave, and giving as the reason—'that the lessons being placed on five lines renders them proper for a violin and a base.' His vocal compositions were in high favour, and half a dozen or so may be seen in Walsh's 'Merry Musician, or a Cure for the Spleen,' vol. i., 1716 ; others are on the single song sheet of the period. A tune of his, 'All you that must take a leap in the dark,' attained some degree of popularity by being sung by Macheath in the 'Beggar's Opera.' It is probable that he died about 1720, as his name does not appear to occur on any fresh work after that date ; but biographical details regarding him are lacking.   F. K.

RAMSEY, ROBERT, was organist of Trinity College, Cambridge, from 1628 to 1644 inclusive, and 'Magister Choristarum' from 1637 to 1644 inclusive ; but whether before or after those dates is not certain in either case. He took the degree of Mus.B. at Cambridge in 1616, and was required to compose a 'Canticum' to be performed at St. Mary's Church. A Morning and Evening Service in F by him is contained in the Tudway Collection (Harl. MS. 7340) and in the Ely Library, where, and at Peterhouse College, Cambridge, there are also two anthems of his. Add. MS. 11,608 in the British Museum contains a setting by him of the dialogue between Saul, the witch, and Samuel—'In guiltie night,' which was afterwards set by Purcell. Tudway miscalls him John. A madrigal by him is in the British Museum, and a 'commencement song' a 8 was sold at Warren's sale in 1881.   G.

RANDALL, JOHN, Mus.D., born 1715, was a chorister of the Chapel Royal under Bernard Gates. He was one of the boys who shared in the representation of Handel's 'Esther' at Gates's house, Feb. 23, 1732, he himself taking the part of Esther. He graduated as Mus.B. at Cambridge in 1744, his exercise being an anthem. In 1743 he was appointed organist of King's College, and on the death of Dr. Greene in 1755 was elected Professor of Music at Cambridge. In 1756 he proceeded Mus.D. He composed the music for Gray's Ode for the Installation of the Duke of Grafton as Chancellor of the University in 1768, and some church music. He was organist of Trinity College in 1777. He died at Cambridge, March 18, 1799. His name is preserved in England by his two Double Chants.   W. H. H.

RANDALL, P., a London music-seller and publisher, who had a shop at the sign of 'Ye Viol and Lute,' at Paul's Grave, without Temple Bar, in 1707, and for some years later. He may have been related, by marriage, to John Walsh, senior, the great music-publisher of this period. Before 1710 he was a partner with Walsh, and had abandoned his own place of business for Walsh's address in Katherine Street, Strand. His name, in conjunction with Walsh's, appears on many imprints of Walsh's

publications. Later issues of these publications have Randall's name erased, and before 1720 his name entirely disappears from them.

RANDALL, WILLIAM, is presumed to be a son of the preceding P. Randall. At the death of John Walsh, junior, Jan. 15, 1766, William Randall succeeded to the extensive business in Catherine Street, and shortly afterwards was for a couple of years or less in partnership with a person named Abell. Randall & Abell issued in large folio in 1768 what is practically the first complete edition of the 'Messiah,' as well as some minor issues. Randall was in business alone in 1771, and besides reprinting the Walsh publications, he published many interesting works. One of these was a reissue in 1771 of Morley's *Plaine and Easie Introduction*. Collections of Vauxhall or other songs came forth, country dances, and the like. William Randall died about 1780, and his widow, Elizabeth, carried on the business until it was taken over, about 1783, by Messrs. Wright & Wilkinson, who made a great business almost solely by reprinting Handel's works from the original plates.   F. K.

RANDEGGER, ALBERTO, composer, conductor, and singing-master, was born at Trieste, April 13, 1832. He began the study of music at the age of thirteen, under Lafont for the PF., and L. Ricci for composition, soon began to write, and by the year 1852 was known as the composer of several masses and smaller pieces of Church music, and of two ballets—'La Fidanzata di Castellamare' and 'La Sposa d' Appenzello,' both produced at the Teatro grande of his native town. In the latter year he joined three other of Ricci's pupils in the composition of a buffo opera to a libretto by Gaetano Rossi, entitled 'Il Lazzarone,' which had much success, first at the Teatro Mauroner at Trieste, and then elsewhere. In the next two years he was occupied as musical director of theatres at Fiume, Zara, Sinigaglia, Brescia, and Venice. In the winter of 1854 he brought out a tragic opera in four acts, called 'Bianca Capello,' at the chief theatre of Brescia. At this time he was induced to come to London. He gradually took a high position there, and has become widely known as a teacher of singing, conductor, and composer, and an enthusiastic lover of good music of whatever school or country. He has resided in England ever since, and is one of the most prominent musical figures in the metropolis. In 1864 he produced at the Theatre Royal, Leeds, 'The Rival Beauties,' a comic operetta in two acts, which has had much success in London and many other places. In 1868 he became Professor of Singing at the Royal Academy of Music, and has since been made an honorary member and director of that institution and a member of the Committee of Management. He is a Professor of Singing at the Royal College of Music, and is on the Board

of Professors. In the autumn of 1857 he conducted a series of Italian operas at St. James's
Theatre, and in 1879-85 the Carl Rosa Company. [He conducted grand opera under Harris's
management at Drury Lane and Covent Garden
in 1887-98. He conducted the Queen's Hall
Choral Society in 1895-97, but his most important position of this kind was the conductorship of the Norwich Festival, which he held
with great success from 1881 to 1905 inclusive.]

Mr. Randegger's published works are numer-
ous and important. They comprise a dramatic
cantata (words by Mme. Rudersdorff), entitled
'Fridolin,' composed for the Birmingham Festival, and produced there with great success,
August 28, 1873 ; two soprano scenas—'Medea,'
sung by Mme. Rudersdorff at the Gewandhaus,
Leipzig, in 1869, and 'Saffo,' sung by Mme.
Lemmens at the British Orchestral Society,
March 31, 1875 ; the 150th Psalm, for soprano
solo, chorus, orchestra, and organ, for the Boston
Festival, 1872 ; Funeral Anthem for the death
of the Prince Consort, twice performed in
London ; a scena, 'The Prayer of Nature,' sung
by Edward Lloyd at a Philharmonic concert in
1887 ; and a large number of songs and concerted vocal music for voice and orchestra or
PF. He is also the author of the *Primer of
Singing* in Novello's series. As a teacher of
singing, Mr. Randegger has a large number of
pupils now before the English public as popular
singers. (See the *Musical Times* for 1899, p.
653 ff.)   G.

RANDHARTINGER, BENEDICT, an Austrian musician, memorable for his connection
with Schubert. He was born at Ruprechtshofen,
in Lower Austria, July 27, 1802 ; at ten years
old came to the Convict school at Vienna, and
was then a pupil of Salieri's. He afterwards
studied for the law, and for ten years was Secretary to Count Széchényi, an official about the
Court. But he forsook this line of life for
music ; in 1832 entered the Court Chapel as a
tenor singer ; in 1844 became Vice-Court-Capell-
meister, and in 1862, after Assmayer's death,
entered on the full enjoyment of that dignity.
His compositions are more than 600 in number,
comprising an opera, 'König Enzio'; 20 masses ;
60 motets ; symphonies ; quartets, etc. ; 400
songs, 76 4-part songs, etc. Of all these,
124, chiefly songs, are published ; also a vol.
of Greek national songs, and a vol. of Greek
liturgies. His acquaintance with Schubert
probably began at the Convict, and at Salieri's ;
though as he was Schubert's junior by five years,
they can have been there together only for a
short time ; but there are many slight traces of
the existence of a close friendship between them.
He was present, for example, at the first trial
of the D minor String Quartet (Jan. 29, 1826),
and he was one of the very few friends who
visited Schubert in the terrible loneliness of his
last illness. But for Randhartinger it is almost

certain that Schubert's 'Schöne Müllerin' would
never have existed. He was called out of his
room while Schubert was paying him a visit,
and on his return found that his friend had
disappeared with a volume of W. Müller's
poems which he had accidentally looked into
while waiting, and had been so much interested
in as to carry off. On his going the next day
to reclaim the book, Schubert presented him
with some of the now well-known songs, which
he had composed during the night. This was
in 1823. It is surely enough to entitle Randhartinger to a perpetual memory.

He had a brother JOSEF, of whom nothing
is known beyond this—that he was probably
one of the immediate *entourage* of Beethoven's
coffin at the funeral. He, Lachner, and
Schubert are said to have gone together as
torch-bearers (Kreissle von Hellborn's *Schubert*,
p. 266).   G.

RANDLES, ELIZABETH, an extraordinary
infant musical prodigy and performer on the
pianoforte. She was born at Wrexham, August
1, 1800, and played in public before she was
fully two years of age. Her father, a blind
harper and organist of Wrexham, of some degree
of local fame (1760-1820), placed her under
John Parry the harper, and afterwards took
her on tour to London, where she attracted
much attention, and was made a pet of by the
Royal family. A second visit to London was
undertaken in 1808, and a concert for her
benefit given in the Hanover Square rooms.
At this Madame Catalani and other singers
and instrumentalists gave their gratuitous services, Sir George Smart conducting. She settled
in Liverpool as a music teacher about 1818,
and died there in 1829.   F. K.

RANELAGH HOUSE AND GARDENS
were situated on the bank of the Thames,
eastward of Chelsea Hospital. They were
erected and laid out about 1690 by Richard
Jones, Viscount (afterwards Earl of) Ranelagh,
who resided there until his death in 1712. In
1733 the property was sold in lots, and eventually the house and part of the gardens came
into the hands of a number of persons who
converted them into a place of public entertainment. In 1741 they commenced the erection
of a spacious Rotunda (185 feet external, and
150 feet internal diameter), with four entrances
through porticos. Surrounding it was an
arcade, and over that a covered gallery, above
which were the windows, sixty in number. In
the centre of the interior and supporting the
roof was a square erection containing the
orchestra, as well as fireplaces of peculiar
construction for warming the building in
winter. Forty-seven boxes, each to contain
eight persons, were placed round the building,
and in these the company partook of tea and
coffee. In the garden was a Chinese building,
and a canal upon which the visitors were

rowed about in boats. Ranelagh was opened with a public breakfast, April 5, 1742. The admission was 2s. including breakfast. On May 24 following it was opened for evening concerts ; Beard was the principal singer, Festing the leader, and the choruses were chiefly from oratorios. Twice a week ridottos were given, the tickets for which were £1:1s. each, including supper. Masquerades were shortly afterwards introduced, and the place soon became the favourite resort of the world of fashion. Ranelagh was afterwards opened about the end of February for breakfasts, and on Easter Monday for the evening entertainments. On April 10, 1746, a new organ by Byfield was opened at a public morning rehearsal of the music for the season, and Parry, the celebrated Welsh harper, appeared. In 1749, in honour of the Peace of Aix-la-Chapelle, an entertainment called 'A Jubilee Masquerade in the Venetian manner,' was given, of which Horace Walpole, in a letter to Sir Horace Mann, dated May 3, 1749, gives a lively description.

This proved so attractive that it was repeated several times in that and succeeding years, until the suppression of such entertainments in 1755. In 1751 morning concerts were given twice a week, Signora Frasi and Beard being the singers. At that date it had lost none of its charm. 'You cannot conceive,' says Mrs. Ellison, in Fielding's *Amelia*, 'what a sweet elegant delicious place it is. Paradise itself can hardly be equal to it.' In 1754 an entertainment of singing, recitation, etc. was given under the name of 'Comus's Court,' which was very successful. In 1755 a pastoral, the words from Shakespeare, the music by Arne, was produced ; Beard and Miss Young were the singers ; Handel's 'L'Allegro ed Il Pensieroso' was introduced on Beard's benefit night, and Stanley was the organist. In 1759 Bonnell Thornton's burlesque Ode on St. Cecilia's Day was performed with great success. In 1762 Tenducci was the principal male singer. In 1764 a new orchestra was erected in one of the porticos of the Rotunda, the original one being found inconvenient from its height. On June 29, 1764, Mozart, then eight years old, performed on the harpsichord and organ several pieces of his own composition for the benefit of a charity. In 1770 Burney was the organist. Fireworks were occasionally exhibited, when the price of admission was raised to 5s. In 1777 the fashionable world played one of its strange, unreasoning freaks at Ranelagh. Walpole wrote on June 18 :—'It is the fashion now to go to Ranelagh two hours after it is over. You may not believe this, but it is literal. The music ends at ten, the company go at twelve.' This practice caused the concert to be commenced at a later hour than before. In 1790 a representation of Mount Etna in eruption, with the

Cyclops at work in the centre of the mountain, and the lava pouring down its side, was exhibited. The mountain was 80 feet high. In 1793 the Chevalier d'Éon fenced in public with a French professor, and about the same time regattas on the Thames in connection with the place were established. In 1802 the Installation Ball of the Knights of the Bath was given at Ranelagh, and also a magnificent entertainment by the Spanish Ambassador. These were the last occurrences of any importance ; the fortunes of the place had long been languishing, and it opened for the last time July 8, 1803. On Sept. 30, 1805, the proprietors gave directions for taking down the house and rotunda ; the furniture was soon after sold by auction, and the buildings removed. The organ was placed in Tetbury Church, Gloucestershire. No traces of Ranelagh remain ; the site now forms part of Chelsea Hospital garden.   w. h. h.

RANK. A rank of organ-pipes is one complete series or set, of the same quality of tone and kind of construction from the largest to the smallest, controlled by one draw-stop, acting on one slider. If the combined movement of draw-stop and slider admits air to two or more such series of pipes, an organ-stop is said to be of two or more ranks, as the case may be. Occasionally the twelfth and fifteenth, or fifteenth and twenty-second, are thus united ; forming a stop of two ranks ; but, as a rule, only those stops whose tones are reinforcements of some of the higher upper-partials of the ground-tone are made to consist of several ranks, such as the Sesquialtera, Mixture, Furniture, etc. These stops have usually from three to five ranks each, reinforcing (according to their special disposition) the ground-tone by the addition of its 17th, 19th, 22nd, 24th, 26th, 29th,—that is, of its 3rd, 5th, and 8th in the third and fourth octave above. [See SESQUIALTERA and MIXTURE.]   j. s.

RANSFORD, EDWIN, baritone vocalist, songwriter, and composer, born March 13, 1805, at Bourton-on-the-Water, Gloucestershire, died in London, July 11, 1876. He first appeared on the stage as an 'extra' in the opera-chorus at the King's Theatre, Haymarket, and was afterwards engaged in that of Covent Garden Theatre. During Charles Kemble's management of that theatre he made his first appearance as Don Caesar in 'The Castle of Andalusia,' on May 27, 1829, and was engaged soon afterwards by Arnold for the English Opera-House (now the Lyceum). In the autumn of 1829, and in 1830, he was at Covent Garden. In 1831 he played leading characters under Elliston at the Surrey Theatre, and became a general favourite. In 1832 he was with Joe Grimaldi at Sadler's Wells, playing Tom Truck, in Campbell's nautical drama 'The Battle of Trafalgar,' in which he made a great

c

hit with Neukomm's song, 'The Sea.' At this theatre he sustained the part of Captain Cannonade in Barnett's opera 'The Pet of the Petticoats.' He afterwards fulfilled important engagements at Drury Lane, the Lyceum, and Covent Garden. At Covent Garden he played the Doge of Venice in 'Othello,' March 25, 1833, when Edmund Kean last appeared on the stage, and Sir Harry in 'The School for Scandal' on Charles Kemble's last appearance as Charles Surface. His final theatrical engagement was with Macready at Covent Garden in 1837-38. He wrote the words of many songs, his best being perhaps 'In the days when we went gipsying.' In later years his entertainments, 'Gipsy Life,' 'Tales of the Sea,' and 'Songs of Dibdin,' etc., became deservedly popular. As a genial *bon camarade* he was universally liked. [He was also a music-seller and publisher, and during the forties and fifties issued a great number of the popular songs of the day. His shop was in Charles Street, Soho, but in 1850 he moved to 461 Oxford Street. In 1869 he went into partnership with his son, William Edwin, at 2 Princes Street, Cavendish Square. The son, who continued the business after his father's death, was a tenor vocalist of ability. He died Sept. 21, 1890.   F. K.]   W. H.

RANTZAU, I. Opera in four acts, text by G. Targioni-Tazzetti and G. Menasci, music by Mascagni. Produced at the Pergola, Florence, Nov. 10, 1892, and at Covent Garden, July 7, 1893.

RANZ DES VACHES (*Kuhreihen, Kuhrei-gen*; Appenzell patois *Chüereiha*), a strain of an irregular description, which in some parts of Switzerland is sung or blown on the Alpine horn in June, to call the cattle from the valleys to the higher pastures. Several derivations have been suggested for the words *ranz* and *reihen* or *reigen*. *Ranz* has been translated by the English 'rant,' and the French 'rondeau,' and has been derived from the Keltic root 'renk' or 'rank,' which may also be the derivation of *reihen*, in which case both words would mean the 'procession or march of the cows.' Stalder (*Schweizerisches Idiotikon*) thinks that *reihen* means 'to reach,' or 'fetch,' while other authorities say that the word is the same as *reigen* (a dance accompanied by singing), and derive *ranz* from the Swiss patois 'ranner,' to rejoice.

The Ranz des Vaches are very numerous, and differ both in music and words in the different cantons. They are extremely irregular in character, full of long cadences and abrupt changes of tempo. It is a curious fact that they are seldom strictly in tune, more particularly when played on the Alpine horn, an instrument in which, like the BAGPIPE, the note represented by F is really an extra note between F and F$\sharp$. This note is very characteristic of the Ranz des Vaches; passages like the following being repeated and varied almost *ad infinitum*.

The most celebrated Ranz des Vaches is that of Appenzell, a copy of which is said to have been sent to our Queen Anne, with whom it was a great favourite. The first work in which it was printed is Georg Rhaw's *Bicinia* (Wittenberg, 1545). It is also to be found in a dissertation on Nostalgia in Zwinger's *Fasciculus Dissertationum Medicarum* (Basle, 1710). Rousseau printed a version in his *Dictionnaire de Musique*, which Laborde arranged for four voices in his *Essai sur la Musique*. It was used by Grétry in his Overture to 'Guillaume Tell,' and by Adam in his *Méthod de Piano du Conservatoire.*[1] It has been also arranged by Webbe, Weigl, Rossini ('Guillaume Tell'), and Meyerbeer.   W. B. S.

RAPPOLDI, EDUARD, born at Vienna, Feb. 21, 1831. He was placed by his father at an early age under Doleschall, and made his first appearance in his seventh year as violinist, pianist, and composer. His talent for the pianoforte was so great as to induce the Countess Banffy to put him under Mittag, Thalberg's teacher. But the violin was the instrument of his choice, and he succeeded in studying it under Jansa, who induced him to go to London in 1850. Here he made no recorded appearance. On his return to Vienna he was so far provided for by the liberality of the same lady, that he became a pupil of the Conservatorium under Hellmesberger from 1851 to 1854. He then put himself under Böhm, and shortly began to travel, and to be spoken of as a promising player. The first real step in his career was conducting a concert of Joachim's at Rotterdam in 1866, where he had been concertmeister since 1861. At the end of that year he went to Lübeck as capellmeister, in 1867 to Stettin in the same capacity, and in 1869 to the Landestheater at Prague. During this time he was working hard at the violin, and also studying composition with Sechter and Hiller. From 1871 to 1877 he was a colleague of Joachim's at the Hochschule at Berlin —where he proved himself a first-rate teacher—and a member of his quartet party. In 1876 he was made Royal

[1] There is a curious analogy between the above and the following strain, which is sung with infinite variations in the agricultural districts near London to frighten away the birds from the seed. In both passages the F is more nearly F$\sharp$.

[2] Other examples and descriptions will be found in the following works:—Cappeller's *Pilati Montis Historia* (1757); Stolberg's *Reise in Deutschland, der Schweiz, etc.* (1794); Ebel's *Schilderung der Gebirgsvölker der Schweiz* (1798); Sigmund von Wagner's *Acht Schweizer Kuhreihen* (1805); the article on Viotti in the *Décade Philosophique* (An 6); Castelnau's *Considérations sur la Nostalgie* (1806); Edward Jones's *Musical Curiosities* (1811); *Recueil de Ranz des Vaches et de Chansons Nationales Suisses*, third edition, Berne, 1818, also Tarenne's *Sammlung von Schweizer Kuhreihen und Volksliedern* (1818); Huber's *Recueil de Ranz des Vaches* (1830); and Tobler's *Appenzellischer Sprachschatz* (1837).

Professor, and soon after received a call to a court concertmeistership at Dresden. This, however, his love for Joachim and for Berlin, where he had advanced sufficiently to lead the Quartets alternately with his chief, induced him for a long time to hesitate to accept, notwithstanding the very high terms offered. At length, however, he did accept it, and became (in 1877) joint concertmeister with Lauterbach at the Dresden opera, and chief teacher in the Conservatorium. He retired in 1898, after which time he only taught a few favoured pupils; he died in Dresden, May 16, 1903. Though a virtuoso of the first rank he followed in the footsteps of Joachim by sacrificing display to the finer interpretation of the music, and succeeded in infusing a new spirit into chamber-music at Dresden. He composed symphonies, quartets, sonatas, and songs, some of which have been printed. They are distinguished for earnestness, and for great beauty of form, and a quartet was performed in Dresden in the winter of 1878 which aroused quite an unusual sensation. In 1874 Rappoldi married a lady nearly as distinguished as himself, LAURA KAHRER, who was born in Vienna, Jan. 14, 1853, and whose acquaintance he made many years before at Prague. Her talent, like his, showed itself very early. On the nomination of the Empress Elisabeth she became a pupil of the Conservatorium at Vienna, under Dachs and Dessoff, from 1866 to 1869. After taking the first prize, she made a *tournée* to the principal towns of Germany, ending at Weimar. There she studied under Liszt, and matured that beauty of touch, precision, fire, and intelligence, which have raised her to the first rank of pianists in Germany, and which induced Herr von Bülow—no lenient critic—to praise her playing of Beethoven's op. 106 in the highest terms. She was the worthy colleague of her husband in the best concerts of Dresden. G.

RASELIUS, ANDREAS, was born at Hahnbach near Amberg in the Upper Palatinate some time between 1562 and 1564. He was the son of a Lutheran preacher, who had studied at Wittenberg under Melanchthon, and whose original name, Rasel, Melanchthon latinised into Raselius. From 1581 to 1584 Andreas attended the then Lutheran University of Heidelberg, taking his degree as Magister Artium in the latter year. In the same year he was appointed cantor and teacher at the Gymnasium of Ratisbon, then conducted under Lutheran auspices. In his capacity as cantor he published in 1589 a Musical Instruction book with the title *Hexachordum seu Quaestiones Musicae Practicae sex capitibus comprehensae*, which was still in use at Ratisbon in 1664. In 1599 appeared his 'Regenspurgischer Kirchen-Contrapunkt,' which contains simple settings *a* 5 of 51 of the older Lutheran Psalm-tunes and chorales. The full title describes them as set

so that the congregation may easily sing the chorale-tune while the trained choir provide the harmonies. The chorale-tune is in the upper part, but the harmonies are not always mere note-for-note counterpoint as in a modern hymn-tune. A few specimens of these settings are given in Schöberlein's *Schatz*. Other published works of Raselius are 'Teutsche Sprüche aus den Sonntäglichen Evangelia . . .,' 53 German Motets *a* 5 (Nuremberg, 1594), and 'Neue Teutsche Sprüche auf die . . . Fest und Aposteltage . . .,' 22 Motets *a* 5-9, described as composed on the 12 Modes of the Dodecachordon (Nuremberg, 1595). Besides these published works there remain in MS. several collections of Latin and German motets and magnificats by Raselius. He is also known as the author of a historical work, a chronicle of Ratisbon, originally written both in Latin and German, of which only the German edition survives. Raselius remained at Ratisbon till 1600, when he received a pressing invitation from the Elector Palatine Frederick IV. to return to Heidelberg as Hofcapellmeister. This higher post of honour he was not permitted to retain long, as death carried him off on Jan. 6, 1602. A monograph on Raselius by J. Auer of Amberg appeared as a Beilage to Eitner's *Monatshefte* of 1892.   J. R. M.

RASOUMOWSKY,[1] ANDREAS KYRILLO-VITSCH, a Russian nobleman to whom Beethoven dedicated three of his greatest works, and whose name will always survive in connection with the 'Rasoumowsky Quartets' (op. 59). He was the son of Kyrill Rasum, a peasant of Lemeschi, a village in the Ukraine, who, with his elder brother, was made a Count (Graf) by the Empress Elisabeth of Russia. Andreas was born Oct. 22, 1752, served in the English and Russian navies, rose to the rank of admiral, and was Russian ambassador at Venice, Naples, Copenhagen, Stockholm, and Vienna. In England his name must have been familiar, or Foote would hardly have introduced it as he has in 'The Liar' (1762). At Vienna he married, in 1788, Elisabeth Countess of Thun, one of the 'three Graces,' elder sister of the Princess Carl Lichnowsky [see vol. ii. p. 723*a*]; and on March 25, 1792, had his audience from the Emperor of Austria as Russian ambassador, a post which he held with short intervals for more than twenty years. He was a thorough musician, an excellent player of Haydn's quartets, in which he took second violin, not improbably studying them under Haydn himself. That, with his connection with Lichnowsky, he must have known Beethoven is obvious; but no direct trace of the acquaintance is found until May 26, 1806 (six weeks after the withdrawal of 'Fidelio'), which Beethoven—in his usual polyglot—has marked on the first page of the

[1] Rasumoffsky and Rasoumoffsky are forms used by Beethoven in various dedications.

Quartet in F of op. 59, as the date on which he began it—'Quartetto angefangen am 26ten May 1806.'

In 1808 the Count formed his famous quartet party—Schuppanzigh, first violin; Weiss, viola; Lincke, violoncello; and he himself second violin—which for many years met in the evenings, and performed, among other compositions, Beethoven's pieces, 'hot from the fire,' under his own immediate instructions.

In April 1809 appeared the C minor and Pastoral Symphonies (Nos. 5 and 6), with a dedication (on the Parts) to Prince Lobkowitz and 'son excellence Monsieur le Comte de Rasumoffsky' (Breitkopf & Härtel). These dedications doubtless imply that Beethoven was largely the recipient of the Count's bounty, but there is no direct evidence of it, and there is a strange absence of reference to the Count in Beethoven's letters. His name is mentioned only once— July 24, 1813—and there is a distant allusion in a letter of a much later date (Nohl, *Briefe B.* 1865, No. 354). In the autumn of 1814 came the Vienna Congress (Nov. 1, 1814– June 9, 1815), and as the Empress of Russia was in Vienna at the time, the Ambassador's Palace was naturally the scene of special festivities. It was not, however, there that Beethoven was presented to the Empress, but at the Archduke Rodolph's.[1] The Count's hospitalities were immense, and, vast as was his palace, a separate wooden annexe had to be constructed capable of dining 700 persons.

On June 3, 1815, six days before the signature of the final Act of the Congress, the Count was made Prince (Fürst), and on the 31st of the following December the dining-hall just mentioned was burnt down. The Emperor of Russia gave 400,000 silver roubles (£40,000) towards the rebuilding, but the misfortune appears to have been too much for the Prince; he soon after sold the property, pensioned his quartet, and disappears from musical history. The quartet kept together for many years after this date, Sina playing second violin. Beethoven mentions them àpropos of the Galitzin Quartets in the letter to his nephew already referred to, about 1825.   A. W. T.

The three quartets to which Rasoumowsky's name is attached come under op. 59, and are in F, E minor, and C respectively. The first of the three, as already mentioned, was begun May 26, 1806, and the whole three were finished and had evidently been played before Feb. 27, 1807, the date of a letter in the *Allg. mus. Zeitung* describing their characteristics.[2] They were published in January 1808 (Vienna Bureau des Arts; Pesth, Schreyvogel), and the dedication (on the Parts) begins 'Trois Quatuors

très humblement dediées à son Excellence Monsieur le Comte,' etc. Beethoven himself mentions them in a letter to Count Brunswick, which he has dated May 11, 1806, but which Thayer (iii. 11) sees reason to date 1807.

The Quartet in F is the one which Bernard Romberg is said to have thrown on the ground and trampled upon as unplayable.—The slow movement is entitled in the Sketchbook 'Einen Trauerweiden oder Akazienbaum aufs Grab meines Bruders'—'A weeping willow or acacia tree over the grave of my brother.' But which brother? August died in 1783, twenty-three years before, Carl not till ten years after, and Johann not till 1848. Carl's marriage-contract had, however, been signed only on May 25, 1806. Is it possible that this inscription is a Beethovenish joke on the occasion? If so, he began in fun and ended in earnest. The finale has a Russian theme in D minor for its principal subject, and the second of the three has a Russian theme in E major as the Trio of its third movement.   G.

[The tunes are given in Köhler's 'Album Russe' as Nos. 188 and 175 respectively; and are also in 'Chants Nationaux Russes,' Nos. 13 and 45.]

RATAPLAN, like Rub-a-dub, is an imitative word for the sound of the drum, as Tan-ta-ra is for that of the trumpet, and Tootle-tootle for the flute.[3] It is hardly necessary to mention its introduction by Donizetti in the 'Fille du Regiment,' or by Meyerbeer in the 'Huguenots'; and every Londoner is familiar with it in Sergeant Bouncer's part in Sullivan's 'Cox and Box.' 'Rataplan, der kleine Tambour' is the title of a Singspiel by Pillwitz, which was produced at Bremen in 1831, and had a considerable run both in North and South Germany between that year and 1836.   G.

RAUZZINI, VENANZIO, born 1747, in Rome, where he made his début in 1765, captivating his audience by his fine voice, clever acting, and prepossessing appearance. In 1766 or 1767 he was at Munich, where Burney heard him in 1772, and where four of his operas were performed. He sang at various places during this period. In London he made his first appearance in 1774, in Corri's 'Alessandro nell' Indie.' [His appearance in a pasticcio of 'Armida' in the same year has resulted in the attribution to him of an opera of that name dated 1778, and the error has been copied into most dictionaries from the first edition of this work.] He also distinguished himself as an excellent teacher of singing, Miss Storace, Braham, Miss Poole (afterwards Mrs. Dickons), and Incledon, being among his pupils. In 1778 and 1779 he gave subscription concerts with the violinist Lamotte, when they were assisted by such eminent artists as Miss Harrop, Signor Rovedino,

---

[1] Schindler, i. 233 (quoted by Thayer, iii. 321).
[2] They are again alluded to in the number for May 5 as more and more successful, and possibly to be soon published; and then, with astonishing *naiveté*, follows 'Eberl's newest compositions, too, are anticipated with great pleasure'!

[3] Other forms are Patapataplan, Palalalalan, Bumberumbumbum. See the *Dictionnaire Encyclopédique* of Sachs & Villatte.

Fischer, Cervetto, Stamitz, Decamp, and Clementi. He also gave brilliant concerts in the new Assembly Rooms (built 1771) at Bath, where he took up his abode on leaving London. Here he invited Haydn and Dr. Burney to visit him, and the three spent several pleasant days together in 1794. On this occasion Haydn wrote a four-part canon (or more strictly a round) to an epitaph on a favourite dog buried in Rauzzini's garden, 'Turk was a faithful dog and not a man.' (See TURK.) Rauzzini's operas performed in London were 'Piramo e Tisbe' (March 16, 1775, and afterwards in Vienna), 'Le Ali d'Amore' (Feb. 27, 1776); 'Creusa in Delfo' (1783); 'La Regina di Golconda' (1784); and 'La Vestale' (1787). 'L' Eroe Cinese,' originally given at Munich in 1771, was performed in London in 1782. (These dates are from the *Public Advertiser*.) He composed string-quartets, sonatas for PF., Italian arias and duets, and English songs; also a Requiem produced at the little Haymarket Theatre in 1801, by Dr. Arnold and Salomon. He died, universally regretted, at Bath, April 8, 1810. His brother

MATTEO, born in Rome 1754, made his first appearance at Munich in 1772, followed his brother to England, and settled in Dublin, where he produced an opera, 'Il Rè pastore,' in 1784. He had written 'Le finte Gemelli' for Munich in 1772, and 'L' opera nuova' for Venice in 1781. He employed himself in teaching singing, and died in 1791.   C. F. P.

RAVENSCROFT, JOHN, one of the Tower Hamlets waits, and violinist at Goodman's Fields Theatre, was noted for his skill in the composition of hornpipes, a collection of which he published. Two of them are printed in Hawkins's *History*, and another in vol. iii. of 'The Dancing Master.' A set of sonatas for two violins and violone or arch-lute, were printed at Rome in 1695. He died about 1745.   W. H. H.

RAVENSCROFT, THOMAS, Mus. B., born in 1593, was a chorister of St. Paul's under Edward Pearce, and graduated at Cambridge in 1607. In 1609 he edited and published 'Pammelia. Musickes Miscellanie: or Mixed Varietie of pleasant Roundelayes and delightful Catches of 3, 4, 5, 6, 7, 8, 9, 10 Parts in one '—the earliest collection of rounds, catches, and canons printed in this country. A second impression appeared in 1618. Later in 1609 he put forth 'Deuteromelia; or the Second Part of Musick's Melodie, or melodius Musicke of Pleasant Roundelaies; K. H. mirth, or Freemen's Songs and such delightfull Catches'; containing the catch, 'Hold thy peace, thou knave,' sung in Shakespeare's 'Twelfth Night.' In 1611 he published 'Melismata. Musicall Phansies, fitting the Court, Citie, and Countrey Humours, to 3, 4 and 5 Voyces.' In 1614 he published 'A Briefe Discourse of the true (but neglected) use of Charact'ring the Degrees by their Perfection,

Imperfection, and Diminution in Mensurable Musicke against the Common Practise and Custome of these Times ; Examples whereof are exprest in the Harmony of 4 Voyces Concerning the Pleasure of 5 vsuall Recreations. 1. Hunting. 2. Hawking. 3. Dancing. 4. Drinking. 5. Enamouring '—a vain attempt to resuscitate an obsolete practice. The musical examples were composed by Edward Pearce, John Bennet, and Ravenscroft himself. [Much of the material is found in a MS. in the Brit. Mus. Add. MS. 19,758 (*Dict. of Nat. Biog.*). In 1618-22 he was music-master at Christ's Hospital (*Mus. Times*, 1905, p. 580.)] In 1621 he published the work by which he is best known, 'The Whole Booke of Psalmes : With the Hymnes Evangelicall and Spirituall. Composed into four parts by Sundry Authors with severall Tunes as have been and are usually sung in England, Scotland, Wales, Germany, Italy, France, and the Netherlands.' Another edition was published in 1633. Four anthems or motets by Ravenscroft are among the MSS. in the library of Christ Church, Oxford. [For other music by him see the *Quellen-Lexikon*.] The date of his death is not known. It is said by some to have been about 1630, and by others about 1635.   W. H. H.

RAVINA, JEAN HENRI, a pianoforte composer, was born May 20, 1818, at Bordeaux, where his mother was a prominent musician. At the instance of Rode and Zimmermann the lad was admitted to the Conservatoire of Paris in 1831. His progress was rapid—second prize for PF. in 1832 ; first prize for the same in 1834 ; first for harmony and accompaniment in 1835, a joint professorship of PF. Nov. 1835. In Feb. 1837 he left the Conservatoire and embarked on the world as a virtuoso and teacher. He resided exclusively at Paris, with the exception of a journey to Russia in 1853, and Spain in 1871. He received the Legion of Honour in 1861. His compositions are almost all salon pieces, many of them very popular in their time, graceful and effective, but with no permanent qualities. He also published a 4-hand arrangement of Beethoven's nine symphonies. Ravina died in Paris, Sept. 30, 1906.—The above sketch is indebted to M. Pougin's supplement to Fétis.   G.

RAWLINGS, or RAWLINS, THOMAS, born about 1703, was a pupil of Dr. Pepusch, and a member of Handel's orchestra at both opera and oratorio performances. On March 14, 1753, he was appointed organist of Chelsea Hospital. He died in 1767. His son, ROBERT, born in 1742, was a pupil of his father, and afterwards of Barsanti. At seventeen he was appointed musical page to the Duke of York, with whom he travelled on the continent until his death in 1767, when he returned to England and became a violinist in the King's band and Queen's private band. He died in 1814, leaving a son, THOMAS A., born in 1775, who studied music under his father and Dittenhofer. He composed some instrumental music performed at the Professional Concerts, became a violinist at the Opera and the best concerts, and a teacher of the pianoforte, violin, and thorough-bass. He composed and arranged many pieces for the pianoforte, and some songs, and died about the middle of the 19th century.   W. H. H.

RAYMOND AND AGNES. A ' grand romantic English Opera in three acts ' ; words by E. Fitzball, music by E. J. Loder. Produced at Manchester in 1855, and at St. James's Theatre, London, June 11, 1859.   G.

RE. The second note of the natural scale in solmisation and in the nomenclature of France and Italy, as Ut (or Do) is the first, Mi the third, and Fa the fourth—

> *Ut* quant laxis *re*sonare fibris
> *Mi*ra gestorum, *fa*muli tuorum.

By the Germans and English it is called D.   G.

RE PASTORE, IL. A dramatic cantata to Metastasio's words (with compressions), composed by Mozart at Salzburg in 1775, in honour of the Archduke Maximilian. First performed April 23, 1775. It contains an overture and fourteen numbers. The autograph is in the Royal Library at Berlin, and the work is published in Breitkopf's complete edition as Series V. No. 10. Aminta's air, ' L' amerò,' with violin obbligato, is the number by which the work is most widely known.   G.

REA, WILLIAM, born in London, March 25, 1827 ; when about ten years old learnt the pianoforte and organ from Josiah Pittman, for whom he acted as deputy for several years. In about 1843 he was appointed organist to Christchurch, Watney Street, St. George's-in-the-East, and at the same time studied the pianoforte, composition, and instrumentation under Sterndale Bennett, appearing as a pianist at the concerts of the Society of British Musicians in 1845. On leaving Christchurch he was appointed organist to St. Andrew Undershaft. In 1849 he went to Leipzig, where his masters were Moscheles and Richter ; he subsequently studied under Dreyschock at Prague. On his return to England, Mr. Rea gave chamber concerts at the Beethoven Rooms, and became (1853) organist to the Harmonic Union. In 1856 he founded the London Polyhymnian Choir, to the training of which he devoted much time, and with excellent results ; at the same time he conducted an amateur orchestral society. In 1858 he was appointed organist at St. Michael's, Stockwell, and in 1860 was chosen by competition organist to the corporation of Newcastle-on-Tyne, where he also successively filled the same post at three churches in succession, and at the Elswick Road Chapel. At Newcastle Mr. Rea worked hard to diffuse a taste for good music, though he met with less encouragement

than his labours and enthusiasm deserved. Besides weekly organ and pianoforte recitals, he formed a choir of eighty voices, which in 1862 was amalgamated with the existing Sacred Harmonic Society of Newcastle. In 1867 he began a series of excellent orchestral concerts which were carried on every season for nine years, when he was compelled to discontinue them, owing to the pecuniary loss which they entailed. In 1876 he gave two performances of 'Antigone' at the Theatre Royal, and devoted much of his time to training his choir (200 voices), the Newcastle Amateur Vocal Society, and other Societies on the Tyne and in Sunderland, besides giving concerts at which the best artists performed. His published works comprise four songs, three organ pieces, and some anthems. At the close of 1880 he was appointed organist of St. Hilda's, S. Shields, in 1888 he resigned the corporation appointment. [He was an honorary Fellow of the Royal College of Organists, and in 1886 received the honorary degree of Mus.D. from the University of Durham. He composed a ' Jubilee Ode ' for the Newcastle Exhibition of 1887, and he died at Newcastle, March 8, 1903. An account of his life and works is in *Musical Times*, April 1903. His wife, Emma Mary (*née* Woolhouse), was an accomplished musician, actively connected with the musical life of Newcastle. She died May 6, 1893.   F. K.]   W. B. S.

READE, CHARLES, English dramatist and novelist—born June 8, 1814, died April 11, 1884—claims a notice in his capacity of expert connoisseur, and one of the earliest collectors of old violins. He devoted much time to the study of violin construction, and—as his sons put it—acquired ' as keen a scent for the habitat of a rare violin, as the truffle dog for fungus beneath the roots of the trees.' He gathered much of this accurate knowledge from one Henri, a player and a maker to boot, resident in Soho, with whom he engaged in experiments in varnish, and in the business of importing fiddles from abroad for the English dealers. Frequent visits to Paris, in the latter connection, resulted sometimes in profit, and at other times in financial catastrophe ; but they succeeded in bringing to England some of the finest specimens of Cremona instruments that are known to-day. They were in Paris, buying a stock of thirty fiddles, when the Revolution of 1848 broke out, and Henri threw aside fiddle-dealing and joined the revolutionists. He was shot before his friend's eyes at the first barricade, and Charles Reade escaped with difficulty, leaving the fiddles behind. These were found stored away in a cellar after the Revolution, and eventually reached Reade, who records that he sold one of them for more than he paid for the whole lot. At the time of the Special Loan Exhibition of Musical Instruments held at the South Kensington Museum in 1872, Reade wrote a series of letters upon Cremona fiddles in the *Pall Mall Gazette*, in which he propounded the theory that the 'Lost Cremona Varnish' was a spirit varnish laid over an oil varnish. Coming as it did from so noted a connoisseur, there were many who accepted the theory as the solution of the question. These letters were privately reprinted by G. H. M. Muntz, under the title *A Lost Art Revived: Cremona Violins and Varnish* (Gloucester, 1873), and again in the volume entitled *Readiana* (Chatto & Windus, 1882). In later life Charles Reade abandoned fiddles and fiddle-trading, but we find traces of his infatuation in his writings. The adventurous career of John Frederick Lott, the violin-maker, is told by him, somewhat romantically, in his novel *Jack of all Trades*; whilst interesting matter concerning the violin comes into *Christie Johnstone*, and his collection of tales entitled *Cream*.—Reade (Charles L., and Rev. Compton), *Charles Reade*; Coleman (John), *Charles Reade*; Sutherland - Edwards, *Personal Recollections*; Hart (G.), *The Violin*; *Dict. of Nat. Biog.*   E. H-A.

READING, JOHN. There were three musicians of these names, all organists. The first was appointed Junior Vicar Choral of Lincoln Cathedral, Oct. 10, 1667, Poor Vicar, Nov. 28, 1667, and Master of the Choristers, June 7, 1670. He succeeded Randolph Jewett as organist of Winchester Cathedral in 1675, and retained the office until 1681, when he was appointed organist of Winchester College. He died in 1692. He was the composer of the Latin Graces sung before and after meat at the annual College election times, and the well-known Winchester School song, 'Dulce Domum'; all printed in Dr. Philip Hayes's 'Harmonia Wiccamica.' The second was organist of Chichester Cathedral from 1674 to 1720. Several songs included in collections published between 1681 and 1688 are probably by one or other of these two Readings. The third, born 1677, was a chorister of the Chapel Royal under Dr. Blow. In 1696-98 he was organist of Dulwich College [information from Dr. W. H. Cummings]. He was appointed Junior Vicar and Poor Clerk of Lincoln Cathedral, Nov. 21, 1702, Master of the Choristers, Oct. 5, 1703, and Instructor of the choristers in vocal music, Sept. 28, 1704. He appears to have resigned these posts in 1707, and to have returned to London, where he became organist of St. John, Hackney (in 1708), St. Dunstan in the West, St. Mary Woolchurchhaw, Lombard Street, and St. Mary Woolnoth. He published 'A Book of New Songs (after the Italian manner) with Symphonies and a Thorough Bass fitted to the Harpsichord, etc.,' and (about 1709) 'A Book of New Anthems.' One of the Readings was also the reputed composer of the tune to 'Adeste fideles.' He died Sept. 2, 1764.

There was another person named Reading,

who was a singer at Drury Lane in the latter part of the 17th century. In June 1695 he and Pate, another singer at the theatre, were removed from their places and fined 20 marks each for being engaged in a riot at the Dog Tavern, Drury Lane, but were soon after reinstated.

A Rev. John Reading, D.D., Prebendary of Canterbury Cathedral, preached there a sermon in defence of church music, and published it in 1663.   W. H. H.

REAL FUGUE. See FUGUE.

REAY, SAMUEL, born at Hexham, March 17, 1822, was noted for his fine voice and careful singing as a chorister at Durham Cathedral; and under Henshaw the organist, and Penson the precentor there, became acquainted with much music outside the regular Cathedral services. After leaving the choir he had organ lessons from Mr. Stimpson of Birmingham, and then became successively organist at St. Andrew's, Newcastle (1845); St. Peter's, Tiverton (1847); St. John's Parish Church, Hampstead (1854); St. Saviour's, Warwick Road (1856); St. Stephen's, Paddington; Radley College (1859, succeeding Dr. E. G. Monk); Bury, Lancashire (1861); and in 1864 was appointed 'Song-schoolmaster and organist' of the parish Church Newark, retiring from the latter post in 1901, but retaining that of Song schoolmaster on the Magnus foundation until his death, which took place at Newark, July 22, 1905. In 1871 Reay graduated at Oxford as Mus.B. In 1879 he distinguished himself by producing at the Bow and Bromley Institute, London, two comic cantatas of J. S. Bach's ('Caffee-cantate' and 'Bauern-cantate'), which were performed there —certainly for the first time in England—on Oct. 27, under his direction, to English words of his own adaptation. Mr. Reay was noted as a fine accompanist and extempore player on the organ. He published a Morning and Evening Service in F, several anthems, and two madrigals (all Novello); but is best known as a writer of part-songs, some of which ('The clouds that wrap,' 'The dawn of day,' written for the Tiverton Vocal Society) are deservedly popular.   G.

REBEC (Ital. *Ribeca, Ribeba*; Span. *Rabé, Rabel*). The French name (said to be of Arabic origin) of that primitive stringed instrument which was in use throughout western Europe in the Middle Ages, and was the parent of the viol and violin, and is identical with the German 'geige' and the English 'fiddle'; in outline something like the mandoline, of which it was probably the parent. It was shaped like the half of a pear, and was everywhere solid except at the two extremities, the upper of which was formed into a peg-box identical with that still in use, and surmounted by a carved human head. The lower half was considerably cut down in level, thus leaving the upper solid part of the instrument to form a natural finger-board. The portion thus cut down was scooped out, and over the cavity thus formed was glued a short pine belly, pierced with two trefoil-shaped sound-holes, and fitted with a bridge and sound-

post. The player either rested the curved end of the instrument lightly against the breast, or else held it like the violin, between the chin and the collar-bone, and bowed it like the violin. It had three stout gut strings, tuned like the lower strings of the violin (A, D, G). Its tone was loud and harsh, emulating the female voice, according to a French poem of the 13th century.

> Quidam rebecam arcuabant,
> Muliebrem vocem confingentes.[1]

An old Spanish poem speaks of ' el rabé gritador,'[2] or the 'squalling rebec.' This powerful tone made it useful in the mediæval orchestra ; and Henry the Eighth employed the rebec in his state band. It was chiefly used, however, to accompany dancing ; and Shakespeare's musicians in *Romeo and Juliet*, Hugh Rebeck, Simon Catling (Catgut), and James Soundpost, were undoubtedly rebec-players. After the invention of instruments of the viol and violin type it was banished to the streets of towns and to rustic festivities, whence the epithet 'jocund' applied to it in Milton's *L'Allegro*. It was usually accompanied by the drum or tambourine. It was in vulgar use in France in the 18th century, as is proved by an ordinance issued by Guignon in his official capacity as ' Roi des Violons' in 1742, in which street-fiddlers are prohibited from using anything else ; ' Il leur sera permis d'y jouer d'une espèce d'instrument à trois cordes seulement, et connu sous le nom de rebec, sans qu'ils puissent se servir d'un violon à quatre cordes sous quelque prétexte que ce soit.' A similar order is extant, dated 1628, in which it is forbidden to play the treble or bass violin ' dans les cabarets et les mauvais lieux,' but only the rebec. The rebec was extinct in England earlier than in France. It is now totally

disused, and no specimen was known until, at the exhibition of Musical Instruments at Milan in 1881, six genuine specimens were shown. Representations of it in sculpture, painting, manuscripts, etc., are abundant. The illustration is from an Italian painting of the 13th century engraved in Vidal's *Instruments à Archet*. [The custom of playing songs in unison with the voice, which came into vogue in the 15th century, resulted in the classification of rebecs into definite 'sets' answering in pitch to the Treble, Alto, Tenor, and Bass voices. Martin Agricola, in his *Musica Instrumentalis*, 1528, gives woodcuts of a 'set' of rebecs which he calls Discant, Altus, Tenor, and Bassus. E. H-A.]   E. J. P.

REBEL, JEAN FÉRY, born in Paris about 1661, [the son of JEAN, a singer in the service of the French court, from 1661 to his death in 1692.] After a precocious childhood he entered the Opéra as a violinist. In 1703 he produced ' Ulysse,' opera in five acts with prologue, containing a *pas seul* for François Prévôt to an air called ' Le Caprice,' for violin solo. The opera failed, but the Caprice remained for years the test-piece of the *ballerine* at the Opéra. After this success, Rebel composed violin solos for various other ballets, such as ' La Boutade,' ' Les Caractères de la Danse' (1715), 'Terpsichore' (1720), ' La Fantaisie' (1727), ' Les Plaisirs Champêtres,' and ' Les Éléments.' Several of these were engraved, as were his sonatas for the violin. In 1713 he was accompanist at the Opéra, and in 1717 was one of the ' 24 violons,' and by 1720 'compositeur de la chambre' to the King. [This latter office he resigned in 1727, in favour of his son François, and later passed on to him the duties of conductor of the Opéra, which he had fulfilled for many years.] He died in Paris, 1746 or 1747, and was buried on Jan. 3, 1747. [His sister, ANNE-RENÉE, born 1662, became one of the best singers of the court, and from the age of eleven years, appeared in the ballet, etc. She was married in 1684 to Michel Richard de LALANDE (see vol. ii. p. 623), and she died in 1722.]

Jean-Féry's son FRANÇOIS, born in Paris, June 19, 1701, at thirteen played the violin in the Opéra orchestra. It seems to have been at Prague, during the festivities at the coronation of Charles VI. in 1723, that he became intimate with François Francœur ; the two composed conjointly, and produced at the Académie, the following operas :— ' Pyrame et Thisbé' (1726) ; ' Tarsis et Zélie' (1728) ; 'Scanderbeg' (1735) ; ' Ballet de la Paix' (1738) ; ' Les Augustales' and ' Le Retour du Roi' (1744) ; ' Zélindor,' ' Le Trophée' (in honour of Fontenoy, 1745) ; ' Ismène' (1750) ; ' Les Génies tutélaires' (1751) ; and ' Le Prince de Noisy' (1760) ; most of which were composed for court fêtes or public rejoicings. [Rebel

[1] D'Aymeric de Peyrat; see Du Cange's *Glossarium*, s.v. ' bandora.'
[2] Don Ant. Rod. de Hita; see Vidal, *Les Instruments à archet*.

seems to have been the sole author of a 'Pastorale héroïque' (1730).]

From 1733 to 1744 Rebel and Francœur were joint leaders of the Académie orchestra, and in 1753 were appointed managers. They soon, however, retired in disgust at the petty vexations they were called upon to endure. Louis XV. made them surintendants of his music, with the Order of St. Michel. In March 1757 these inseparable friends obtained the privilege of the Opéra, and directed it for ten years on their own account, with great administrative ability.

Rebel died in Paris, Nov. 7, 1775. He composed some cantatas, a Te Deum, and a De Profundis, performed at the Concerts Spirituels, but all his music is now forgotten, excepting a lively air in the first finale of 'Pyrame et Thisbé' which was adapted to a much-admired *pas seul* of Mlle. de Camargo, thence became a popular contredanse—the first instance of such adaptation—and in this form is preserved in the 'Clé du Caveau,' under the title of 'La Camargo.' [A very interesting account of the family, with detailed notices of the music of G. F. Rebel, appeared in the *Sammelbände* of the *Int. Mus. Ges.* vol. vii. p. 253, by M. L. de la Laurencie.]   G. C.

REBER, NAPOLÉON-HENRI, born at Mülhausen, Oct. 21, 1807 ; at twenty entered the Paris Conservatoire, studying counterpoint and fugue under Seuriot and Jelensperger, and composition under Lesueur. Circumstances led him to compose chamber-music, after the success of which he attempted opera. His music to the second act of the charming ballet 'Le Diable amoureux' (Sept. 23, 1840) excited considerable attention, and was followed at the Opéra-Comique by 'La Nuit de Noël,' three acts (Feb. 9, 1848), 'Le Père Gaillard,' three acts (Sept. 7, 1852), 'Les Papillotes de M. Benoît,' one act (Dec. 28, 1853), and 'Les Dames Capitaines,' three acts (June 3, 1857). In these works he strove to counteract the tendency towards noise and bombast then so prevalent both in French and Italian opera, and to show how much may be made out of the simple natural materials of the old French opéra-comique by the judicious use of modern orchestration.

In 1851 he was appointed Professor of harmony at the Conservatoire, and in 1853 the well-merited success of 'Le Père Gaillard' procured his election to the Institut as Onslow's successor. Soon after this he renounced the theatre, and returned to chamber-music. He also began to write on music, and his *Traité d'Harmonie* (1862) went through many editions, and is without comparison the best work of its kind in France. The outline is simple and methodical, the classification of the chords easy to follow and well connected, the explanations luminously clear, the exercises practical and well calculated to develop musical taste—in a

word, everything combines to make it one of the safest and most valuable of instruction-books. The second part especially, dealing with 'accidental' notes—or, notes foreign to the constitution of chords—contains novel views, and observations throwing light upon points and rules of harmony which before were obscure and confused.

In 1862 M. Reber succeeded Halévy as Professor of composition at the Conservatoire ; since 1871 he was also Inspector of the *succursales* or branches of the Conservatoire. He died in Paris, after a short illness, Nov. 24, 1880, and was succeeded as Professor by M. Saint-Saëns.

His compositions comprise four symphonies, a quintet and three quartets for strings, one PF. ditto, seven trios, duets for PF. and violin, and PF. pieces for two and four hands. Portions of his ballet 'Le Diable amoureux' have been published for orchestra, and are performed at concerts. In 1875 he produced a cantata called 'Roland,' but 'Le Ménétrier à la cour,' opéra-comique, and 'Naïm,' grand opera in five acts, have never been performed, though the overtures are engraved. His best vocal works are his melodies for a single voice, but he has composed choruses for three and four men's voices, and some sacred pieces.   G. C.

RECITA (Ital.), 'performance.'

RECITAL, a term which has come into use in England to signify a performance of solo music by one performer. It was probably first used by Liszt at his performance at the Hanover Square Rooms, June 9, 1840, though as applying to the separate pieces and not to the whole performance. The advertisement of the concert says that 'M. Liszt will give Recitals on the Pianoforte of the following pieces.' The name was afterwards adopted by Hallé and others, and is in the present day often applied to concerts when two or more soloists take part.

The term Opera Recital is used for a concert in which the music of an opera is sung without costume or action.   G.

RECITATIVE (Ital. *Recitativo* ; Germ. *Recitativ* ; Fr. *Récitatif* ; from the Latin *Recitare*). A species of declamatory music, extensively used in those portions of an Opera, an Oratorio, or a Cantata, in which the action of the drama is too rapid, or the sentiment of the poetry too changeful, to adapt itself to the studied rhythm of a regularly constructed Aria.

The invention of Recitative marks a crisis in the history of music, scarcely less important than that to which we owe the discovery of harmony. Whether the strange conception in which it originated was first clothed in tangible form by Jacopo Peri, Giulio Caccini, or Emilio del Cavalìeri, is a question which has never been decided.

Thus first launched upon the world, for the purpose of giving a new impetus to the progress of art, this particular style of composition has undergone less change, during the last 300 years, than any other. What simple or unaccompanied Recitative (*Recitativo secco*) is to-day, it was, in all essential particulars, in the time of ' Euridice.' Then, as now, it was supported by the lightest possible accompaniment, originally a figured-bass. Then, as now, its periods were moulded with reference to nothing more than the plain rhetorical delivery of the words to which they were set ; melodious or rhythmic phrases being everywhere carefully avoided, as not only unnecessary, but absolutely detrimental to the desired effect—so detrimental that the difficulty of adapting good recitative to poetry written in short rhymed verses is almost insuperable, the jingle of the metre tending to crystallise itself in regular form with a persistency which is rarely overcome except by the greatest masters. Hence it is, that the best poetry for recitative is blank verse ; and hence it is, that the same intervals, progressions, and cadences have been used over and over again by composers who, in other matters, have scarcely a trait in common. We shall best illustrate this by selecting a few examples from the inexhaustible store used by some of the greatest writers of the 17th, 18th, and 19th centuries ; premising that, in phrases ending with two or more reiterated notes, it has been long the custom to sing the first as an appoggiatura, a note higher than the rest. We have shown this in three cases, but the rule applies to many others.

The universal acceptance of these, and similar figures, by composers of all ages, from Peri down to Wagner, sufficiently proves their fitness for the purpose for which they were originally designed. But the staunch conservatism of *Recitativo secco* goes even farther than this. Its accompaniment has never changed. The latest composers who have employed it have trusted for its support to the simple *Basso continuo*, which neither Peri, nor Carissimi, nor Handel, nor Mozart cared to reinforce by the introduction of a fuller accompaniment. The chief modification of the original idea which has found favour in modern times was when the harpsichord and the pianoforte were banished from the opera orchestra, and the accompaniment of Recitativo secco was confided to the principal violoncello and double bass ; the former filling in the harmonies in light arpeggios, while the latter confined itself to the simple notes of the *Basso continuo*. In this way the Recitatives were performed at Her Majesty's Theatre for more than half a century by Lindley and Dragonetti, who always played at the same desk, and accompanied with a perfection attained by no other artists in the world, though Charles Jane Ashley was considered only second to Lindley in expression and judgment. The general style of their accompaniment was exceedingly simple, consisting only of plain chords, played *arpeggiando* ; but occasionally the two old friends would launch out into passages as elaborate as those shown in the following example ; Dragonetti playing the large notes, and Lindley the small ones.

governed by no law whatever beyond that of euphony. Its harmonies exhibit more variety now than they did two centuries ago ; but they are none the less free to wander wherever they please, passing through one key after another, until they land the hearer somewhere in the immediate neighbourhood of the key chosen for the next regularly constructed movement. Hence it is that recitatives of this kind are usually written without the introduction of sharps or flats at the signature ; since it is manifestly more convenient to employ any number of accidentals that may be needed, than to place three or four sharps at the beginning of a piece which is perfectly at liberty to end in seven flats.

But notwithstanding the unchangeable character of *Recitativo secco*, declamatory music has not been relieved from the condition which imposes progress upon every really living branch of art. As the resources of the orchestra increased, it became evident that they might be no less profitably employed in the accompaniment of highly impassioned recitative than in that of the aria or chorus ; and thus arose a new style of rhetorical composition, called accompanied recitative (*Recitativo stromentato*), in which the vocal phrases, themselves unchanged, received a vast accession of power, by means of elaborate orchestral symphonies interpolated between them, or even by instrumental passages designed expressly for their support. [The

In no country has this peculiar style been so successfully cultivated as in England, where the traditions of its best period are scarcely yet forgotten. [On an interesting MS. of Mendelssohn's, showing the kind of treatment he preferred while following the English practice, see *Musical Times*, 1902, p. 727.] A return was made to the old method by the employment of the piano, first by Mr. Otto Goldschmidt at a performance of Handel's 'L'Allegro' in 1863, and more recently by Sir John Stainer, at St. Paul's, in various oratorios.

Again, this simple kind of recitative is as free now as it was in the first year of the 17th century, from the trammels imposed by the laws of modulation. It is the only kind of music which need not begin and end on the same key. As a matter of fact it usually begins upon some chord not far removed from the tonic harmony of the aria or concerted piece which preceded it ; and ends in or near the key of that which is to follow ; but its intermediate course is

first example of it seems to be in Landi's 'San Alessio' (1634)], and its advantages in telling situations were so obvious that it was immediately adopted by other composers, and at once recognised as a legitimate form of art—not, indeed, as a substitute for simple recitative, which has always been retained for the ordinary business of the stage, but as a means of producing powerful effects, in scenes, or portions of scenes, in which the introduction of the measured aria would be out of place.

It will be readily understood that the stability of simple recitative was not communicable to the newer style. The steadily increasing weight of the orchestra, accompanied by a correspondent increase of attention to orchestral effects, exercised an irresistible influence over it. Moreover, time has proved it to be no less sensitive to changes of school and style than the aria itself ; whence it frequently happens that a composer may be as easily recognised by his accompanied recitatives as by his regularly constiucted movements. Scarlatti's accompaniments exhibit a freedom of thought immeasurably in advance of the age in which he lived. Sebastian Bach's recitatives, though priceless as music, are more remarkable for the beauty of their harmonies than for that spontaneity of expression which is rarely attained by composers unfamiliar with the traditions of the stage. Handel's, on the contrary, though generally based upon the simplest possible harmonic foundation, exhibit a rhetorical perfection of which the most accomplished orator might well feel proud ; and we cannot doubt that it is to this high quality, combined with a never-failing truthfulness of feeling, that so many of them owe their deathless reputation—to the unfair exclusion of many others, of equal worth, which still lie hidden among the unclaimed treasures of his long-forgotten operas. Scarcely less successful, in his own peculiar style, was Haydn, whose 'Creation' and 'Seasons' owe half their charm to their pictorial recitatives. Mozart was so uniformly great, in his declamatory passages, that it is almost impossible to decide upon their comparative merits ; though he has certainly never exceeded the perfection of ' Die Weiselehre dieser Knaben,' or ' Non temer.' Beethoven attained his highest flights in ' Abscheulicher ! wo eilst du hin ?' and 'Ah, perfido ! '; Spohr, in 'Faust,' and 'Die letzten Dinge' ; Weber, in ' Der Freischütz.' The works of Cimarosa, Rossini, and Cherubini abound in examples of accompanied recitative, which rival their airs in beauty ; and it would be difficult to point out any really great composer who has failed to appreciate the value of the happy invention.

Yet even this invention failed either to meet the needs of the dramatic composer or to exhaust his ingenuity. It was reserved for Gluck to strike out yet another form of recitative, destined to furnish a more powerful engine for the production of a certain class of effects than any that had preceded it. He it was who first conceived the idea of rendering the orchestra and the singer to all outward appearance entirely independent of each other ; of filling the scene, so to speak, with a finished orchestral groundwork, complete in itself, and needing no vocal melody to enhance its interest, while the singer declaimed his part in tones which, however artfully combined with the instrumental harmony, appeared to have no connection with it whatever ; the resulting effect resembling that which would be produced, if, during the interpretation of a symphony, some accomplished singer were to soliloquise aloud in broken sentences, in such wise as neither to take an ostensible share in the performance nor to disturb it by the introduction of irrelevant discord. An early instance of this may be found in ' Orfeo.' After the disappearance of Euridice, the orchestra plays an excited crescendo, quite complete in itself, during the course of which Orfeo distractedly calls his lost bride by name, in tones which harmonise with the symphony, yet have not the least appearance of belonging to it. In ' Iphigénie en Tauride,' and all the later operas, the same device is constantly adopted ; and modern composers have also used it freely—notably Spohr, who opens his ' Faust' with a scene, in which a band behind the stage plays the most delightful of minuets, while Faust and Mephistopheles sing an ordinary recitative, accompanied by the usual chords played by the regular orchestra in front.

By a process of natural, if not inevitable development, this new style led to another, in which the recitative, though still distinct from the accompaniment, assumed a more measured tone, less melodious than that of the air, yet more so, by far, than that used for ordinary declamation. Gluck has used this peculiar kind of *Mezzo Recitativo* with indescribable power, in the prison scene, in ' Iphigénie en Tauride.' Spohr employs it freely, almost to the exclusion of symmetrical melody, in ' Die letzten Dinge.' Wagner makes it his *cheval de bataille*, introducing it everywhere, and using it as an ever-ready medium for the production of some of his most powerful dramatic effects. His theories on this subject have already been discussed so fully that it is unnecessary to revert to them here. Suffice it to say that his *Melos*, though generally possessing all the more prominent characteristics of pure recitative, sometimes approaches so nearly to the rhythmic symmetry of the song, that—as in the case of ' Nun sei bedankt, mein lieber Schwan ! '— it is difficult to say, positively, to which class it belongs. We may, therefore, fairly accept this as the last link in the chain which fills up the long gap between simple ' Recitativo secco ' and the finished aria. [The free declamation, built on the natural inflexions of the speaking voice, which is employed for the vocal part of Debussy's ' Pelléas et Mélisande,' though not styled ' recitative,' has much in common with it.]   w. s. r.

RECITING-NOTE (Lat. *Repercussio, Nota dominans*). A name sometimes given to that important note, in a Gregorian Tone, on which the greater portion of every verse of a psalm or Canticle is continuously recited ; and it is commonly used of the corresponding note in Anglican chant.

As this particular note invariably corresponds with the Dominant of the Mode in which the Psalm-Tone is written, the terms, Dominant, and Reciting-Note, are frequently treated as interchangeable. [See Modes and Psalmody.]

The Reciting-Note makes its appearance twice in the course of every tone ; first, as the initial member of the Intonation, and afterwards as that of the Ending ; the only exception to the general rule is to be found in the

Tonus Peregrinus (or Irregularis), in which the true Dominant of the Ninth Mode (E) is used for the first Reciting-Note, and D for the second.

The Reciting-Notes of Tones III, V, VII, VIII, and IX, are so high that they cannot be sung, at their true pitch, without severely straining the voice ; in practice, therefore, these tones are almost always transposed. An attempt has been sometimes made so to arrange their respective pitches as to let one note—generally A—serve for all. This plan may, perhaps, be found practically convenient ; but it shows very little concern for the expression of the words, which cannot but suffer, if the jubilant phrases of one Psalm are to be recited on exactly the same note as the almost despairing accents of another.   w. s. r.

RECORDER. A name given in England to a kind of flute, now discarded, but once very popular in Western Europe. The verb 'to record' was formerly in common use in the sense of to warble or sing as a bird, *e.g.*, 'Hark ! hark ! oh, sweet, sweet ! How the birds record too' (Beaumont and Fletcher). A recorder, then, is a warbler, than which a more appropriate appellation for the instrument, looking to its sweetness and facility for trilling, it would be hard to find. When the word sprang up is uncertain. There is reason for believing that it was in use in the 14th century ; it is indisputable that in the 15th it was known from Cornwall to Scotland ; for in a miracle-play in the Cornish language, the manuscript of which is of that date, we have 'recordys ha symphony' (recorders and symphony), and in the Scottish work entitled the *Buke of the Howlate maid be Holland* (*c.* 1450), 'The rote, and the recordour, the ribup, the rist.'

The recorder belonged to the fipple flute family (see FIPPLE FLUTE), of which the flageolet is a familiar example. It was distinguished from the other members of the family by the number and position of its finger-holes. Their number was eight. The highest, which was closed with one of the thumbs, was pierced at the back, the lowest, played with a little finger, at the side, of the tube. The remaining six were placed in the front of the instrument. In early recorders, which were made in one piece, the lowest hole was duplicated for the accommodation of left-handed players ; there were thus two holes for the little finger, but one of them was kept stopped with wax. The duplication of the hole explains a paradox. Although the recorder was an eight-holed instrument, it was called in France (in addition to *la flûte douce* and *la flûte d'Angleterre*) *la flûte à neuf trous*, or the nine-holed flute. The largest contrabass recorders were pierced with three holes below the eight. They were covered with keys, the two lowest of which were closed in some instruments by the otherwise unemployed thumb, in others by the feet, of the

player. An existing contrabass measures 8 feet 8 inches; its lowest note is D below the bass stave.

Instruments of different families were formerly kept apart, each family forming a consort, or band, of its own. The basis of the consort was the quartet—the discant, the alto, the tenor, and the bass. But the consort was not confined to the quartet ; thus Virdung, referring to recorders, writes : 'Generally, one makes four flutes in one case, or six ; this is called a set, two discant, two tenor, and two bass.' The circumstance that each set was kept in a separate case, enables us to say how many recorders were played together. In the time of Henry VIII. the number rose to seven, eight, and nine, as the inventory of that monarch's recorders shows. When Praetorius wrote twenty-one were required to form a full flute consort. Dr. Burney saw a set at Antwerp comprising no less than thirty or forty, the case for which, when filled, was so heavy that eight men were required to raise it from the ground. By the middle of the 18th century the number had dwindled in France to five, and in a very late set, now in the Grosvenor Museum at Chester, it is reduced

Discant.   Alto.   Tenor.   Bass.
THE CHESTER FLUTES.

to four. The date of this set is unknown, but they are marked with the name of Bressan, a maker of whose flutes Sir John Hawkins speaks in a way which shows that they were in common use in his time (1719-89) ; in 1724 Mr. Bressan, by whom presumably the Chester set was made, was carrying on business at the Green Door in Somerset House Yard, in the Strand.

The tone of the recorder was remarkable for two characteristics, solemnity and sweetness.

Bacon twice alludes to its solemnity ; Milton speaks of its 'solemn touches,' and under the name of 'the solemn pipe,' mentions it as one of the instruments played on a great occasion in Heaven. Its sweetness was ineffable. Referring to the effect of recorders used at a theatre to represent a choir of angels, Pepys writes : 'But that which did please me beyond anything in the whole world was the wind-musique when the angel comes down, which is so sweet that it ravished me, and indeed, in a word, did wrap up my soul so that it made me really sick, just as I have formerly been when in love with my wife ; that neither then, nor all the evening going home, and at home, I was able to think of anything, but remained all night transported, so as I could not believe that ever any musick hath that real command over the soul of a man as this did upon me : and makes me resolve to practice wind-musique, and to make my wife do the like.' Some weeks afterwards he buys a recorder, 'which,' he says, 'I do intend to learn to play on, the sound of it being of all sounds in the world, most pleasing to me.'

The 'command' which recorders had 'over the soul of a man,' and their

—power to mitigate and 'swage
With solemn touches troubled thoughts, and chase
Anguish, and doubt, and fear, and sorrow, and pain
From mortal or immortal minds—

may serve to explain why Hamlet, in the frenzied state to which he had been wrought by the spectacle of the murder of his father played before his guilty uncle, should bethink him of the calming influence of a consort of these instruments. 'Come,' he cries, 'some music ; come, the recorders.' If Shakespeare's design were carried out, instead of the two musicians we generally see furnished with little pipes not unlike penny whistles, there would come upon the stage in the recorder scene at least four recorder players carrying instruments varying in length from nearly two to nearly four feet. It is needless to say that even the discant is far too stout to be snapped like a twig, so that the act of violence sometimes seen, the breaking to pieces of the recorder borrowed of the player, would be as impracticable as it is foreign to the true spirit of the scene, and out of keeping with the nature of the gentle Hamlet.

With the advance of the orchestra the consorts of wind instruments broke up and disappeared, only such members of each family being retained as were most suitable for the new combination. The member of the recorder family which survived had a compass of two octaves, from *f'* to *f'''*, fingerings up to *a'''* being sometimes given. About the end of the 17th century the instrument ceased to be called the recorder, retaining only the appellation of flute, and descending after a time to that of the Common flute. In France it came to be styled the *flûte à bec*. The change of name led to a strange chapter in the history of music—a chapter which should be a warning to those who attempt to reconstruct extinct instruments out of preconceived ideas of what they might, or must, have been. For more than a hundred years the recorder was enshrouded in mystery. It was asked, What was a recorder ? Sir John Hawkins put forward the notion that it was a flageolet, and persuaded himself that Lord Bacon had spoken of the recorder as having six holes, the number of those of the flageolet. Burney, writing thirteen years after Sir John, stated authoritatively that a recorder was a flageolet, thereby revealing the secret that he had availed himself of his rival's labours without acknowledging his obligation. Next came Mr. William Chappell, who brought himself to the belief that he had discovered in a book of instructions for the recorder the statement that the instrument was pierced with a hole called the recorder. He fancied that the recorder took its name from the hole, and drawing further on his imagination, supposed the hole to be covered with a piece of thin skin. Finally, Carl Engel acquired a Common flute (it is now in the South Kensington Museum) in which there was a hole covered with membrane. He pronounced this flute to be a recorder of the 17th century, and explained that the hole thus covered was intended to make the sound reedy and tender ; whereas an examination of the instrument would have shown him that his recorder of the 17th century was made in New Bond Street between 1800 and 1812, and that the hole covered with membrane was so placed that it was impossible for it to affect the tone.

The claim of the recorder to be considered the head of instruments of the flute kind was destined to be called in question. Its supremacy was challenged by the transverse flute, an instrument called by the French the German flute, to distinguish it from the recorder, which they termed the English flute. In lip flutes, to which family the German flute belongs, the channel from which the jet of air issues (see FLUTE) is formed by the lips. The control exercised by the lips over the shape of the jet and the size of the opening of the mouth-hole of the flute enables the player to influence the intonation and the quality of the tone, advantages (not to mention greater power) more than sufficient to compensate for inferiority in sweetness and dignity. In Handel's orchestra the German and the Common flute existed side by side, a circumstance which enabled Handel to express niceties of flute *timbre* to which we are strangers. Thus in 'Judas Maccabæus' he was able to avail himself of the martial strains of two German flutes for 'See the Conquering Hero comes,' but to assign the cajolery of 'Wise men flattering may deceive you' to the cooing blandishments of two Common flutes. We can always tell which flute he intends to be used, for he terms the Common flute *Flauto* ; the German flute *Traversa, Traverso, Traversière, Traversiera* ; sometimes, but rarely, *Flauto Traverso.* Scarcely ever does he leave open which flute is to be employed ; there is, however, in ' Parnasso in Festa,' a passage marked *Flauto ou Trav. I., Flauto ou Trav. II.* Handel's orchestra is known to have contained four hautboys and four bassoons ; his flutes, as will be shown, were still more numerous. He once uses *una traversa bassa.* When he wrote *traversieri tutti,* he no doubt expected not short of four treble transverse flutes to respond. It seems certain that he had at his command as many Common flutes ; for the fourth scene of the first act of ' Giustino ' opens with a passage in which not less than four *Flauti* and a *Basso de' Flauti* play together. We are not bound to suppose that Handel had in his pay ten musicians who devoted themselves exclusively to the flute ; performers on other instruments, especially the hautboy, were expected to take the flute when required.

Handel could call for not only five but six fipple flutes, his *ottavino* being a *flauto piccolo,* or octave Common flute, not a transverse instrument. This does not seem to be even suspected, yet the evidence is quite conclusive. Here one proof must suffice. The accompaniment to ' Augelletti che cantate ' (the air in ' Rinaldo,' on the singing of which birds were let loose) is marked in the conducting score *flauto piccolo,* but in the autograph copy in Buckingham Palace Handel has written ' Flageolett.' Now Handel would never have called a transverse piccolo a flageolet. The usual description of this accompaniment, that it is scored for two flutes and a piccolo, gives to the modern reader a false impression, neither the flutes nor the piccolo being the instruments we now call by those names. It is a trio for three fipple flutes, a *flauto piccolo* and two *flauti* ; the *flauto piccolo* playing a brilliant solo which the *flauti* support. The accompaniment has been pronounced by a musician to be the ' loveliest imaginable ' ; the scoffing Addison writes of it, ' The musick proceeded from a concert of flagelets and bird-calls which were planted behind the scenes.' Handel uses the *flauto piccolo* in a Tamburino in ' Alcina,' and in two movements of the Water Music. In the latter two piccolos which play in unison are employed. They are not in the same key as the orchestral piccolo, but, like it, they were fipple flutes. Thrice the *flauto piccolo* furnishes a florid accompaniment to the soprano voice ; in ' Augelletti che cantate,' just mentioned, in a song in ' Riccardo,' and in ' Hush, ye pretty warbling choir,' in ' Acis and Galatea.' The *obbligato* in the last-named work to the bass solo, ' O ruddier than the cherry,' is marked in the score *flauto,* but seems to have been always assigned to the *flauto piccolo.* As late as

the third decade of the 19th century, long after that instrument had been banished from the orchestra, the second hautboy player used to play the part on a so-called flageolet at the Antient Concerts. As the society was established in 1776, only seventeen years after Handel's death, it is reasonable to suppose that the practice was handed down from the time of the great composer.

When the orchestra was remodelled by Haydn only the transverse flute was retained, the Common flute being altogether rejected. The German flute having thus captured its rival's place, proceeded to usurp its title of *Flauto,* and to drop its old name, *Traversa.* Its superiority for orchestral purposes was already so marked as to cause Haydn's choice to fall upon it ; but during Haydn's career as a composer it received an improvement which gave the *coup de grâce* to the old favourite. The improvement consisted in boring new holes in the tube and covering them with keys kept closed by springs. To make clear the importance of this step it is necessary to explain that in the one-keyed flute, which was then in use, there were no holes for four of the notes of the chromatic octave. When the player was in want of either of them, he muffled, and to some extent flattened, the note above the accidental needed by closing one or more holes below the hole from which the note to be flattened issued. Although the spurious notes thus obtained were so impure, feeble, and out of tune as to make the flute and those who played it bywords amongst musicians, the one-keyed flute held its ground for a period of not far short of a century. Remonstrances on the subject of its imperfections were put to silence by the *dictum* that the flute, like the violin, was perfect ; the player, it was asserted, not the instrument, was at fault. At length a stand was made against authority. The rebellion broke out in England, where two professional players named Tacet and Florio had the courage to adopt a flute with no less than six keys. Their example was quickly followed. Between 1770 and 1780 the six-keyed flute came into use in this country, and by degrees, in spite of opposition, the keys were introduced abroad.

The advantages conferred on the transverse flute by the completion of the chromatic octave were so immense that it is inconceivable that the makers of the time should not have thought of applying the system to the Common flute. Why the idea was not carried out is unknown, but it may be conjectured that mechanical difficulties stood in the way. Of the ten digits with which the hands of man are furnished but nine are available for execution, the tenth being required for holding the flute. As the Common flute was pierced with eight holes, only one finger was free when they were all closed. Possibly, then, the makers may have been unable to contrive a method of acting on the five keys required for the chromatic octave, being baffled by the want of fingers for the purpose ; but whatever was the cause, closed keys did not find their way to the Common flute, and so the instrument after a time fell completely into disuse. (See *Proceedings of the Musical Association*, 1897-98, pp. 145-224 ; 1900-1, pp. 110-120 ; and 1901-2, pp. 105-137.) The above is epitomised from the writer's *Lectures on the Recorder*, to be published shortly.   c. w.

RECTE ET RETRO, PER (*Imitatio cancrizans, Imitatio per Motum retrogradum, Imitatio recurrens* ; Ital. *Imitazione al Rovescio, o alla Riversa* ; Eng. *Retrograde Imitation*). A peculiar kind of Imitation, so constructed that the melody may be sung backwards as well as forwards ; as shown in the following two-part canon, which must be sung, by the first voice, from left to right, and by the second, from right to left, both beginning together, but at opposite ends of the music.

The earliest known instances of Retrograde Imitation are to be found among the works of the Flemish composers of the 15th century, who delighted in exercising their ingenuity, not only upon the device itself, but also upon the Inscriptions prefixed to the canons in which it was employed. The Netherlanders were not, however, the only musicians who indulged successfully in this learned species of recreation. Probably the most astonishing example of it on record is the motet,[1] 'Diliges Dominum,' written by William Byrd for four voices— Treble, Alto, Tenor, and Bass—and transmuted into an eight-part composition, by adding a second Treble, Alto, Tenor, and Bass, formed by singing the four first parts backwards. It is scarcely possible to study this complication attentively, without feeling one's brain turn giddy ; yet, strange to say, the effect produced is less curious than beautiful.

There is little doubt that the idea of singing music from right to left was first suggested by those strange Oracular Verses [2] which may be read either backwards or forwards, without injury to words or metre ; such as the well-known Pentameter—

Roma tibi subito motibus ibit amor.

or the cry of the Evil Spirits—

In girum imus noctu ecce ut consumimur igni.

The canons were frequently constructed in exact accordance with the method observed in these curious lines ; and innumerable quaint conceits were invented, for the purpose of giving the singers some intimation of the manner in which they were to be read. 'Canit more Hebraeorum' was a very common motto. 'Misericordia et veritas obviaverunt sibi' indicated that the singers were to begin at opposite ends, and meet in the middle. In the second 'Agnus Dei' of his 'Missa Graecorum,' Hobrecht wrote, 'Aries vertatur in Pisces'—Aries being the first sign of the Zodiac, and Pisces the last. In another part of the same Mass he has given a far more mysterious direction—

Tu tenor cancriza et per antifrasin canta,
Cum furcis in capite antifrasizando repete.

This introduces us to a new complication ; the secret of the motto being, that the tenor is not only to sing backwards, but to invert the intervals (' per antifrasin canta '), until he reaches the 'Horns'—that is to say, the two cusps of the semicircular Time-Signature—after which he is to sing from left to right, though still continuing to invert the intervals. This new device, in which the intervals themselves are reversed, as well as the sequence of the notes, is called 'Retrograde Inverse Imitation' (Lat. *Imitatio cancrizans motu contrario* ; Ital. *Imitazione al contrario riverso*). It might have been thought that this would have contented even Flemish ingenuity. But it did not. The part-books had not yet been turned upside down ! In the subjoined example we have endeavoured to show, in an humble way, the manner in which this most desirable feat may also be accomplished. The two singers, standing face to face, hold the book between them ; one looking at it from the ordinary point of view, the other, upside down, and both reading from left to right—that is to say, beginning at opposite ends. The result, if not strikingly beautiful, is, at least, not inconsistent with the laws of counterpoint. (For other examples see INSCRIPTION.)

Lau-da-te Dominum, om-nes   gen - tes,   om-nes   gen - tes, lau-da-te Do-mi-num.

Retrograde Imitation has survived, even to our own day ; and in more than one very popular form. In the year 1791 Haydn wrote for his Doctor's degree, at the University of Oxford, a 'Canon cancrizans, a tre' ('Thy Voice, O Harmony'), which will be found in vol. ii. p. 357, and he has also used the same device in the minuet of one of his symphonies. Some other modern composers have tried it, with less happy effect. But perhaps it has never yet appeared in a more popular form than

---

[1] Reprinted by Hawkins, *History*, ch. 96.
[2] Versus recurrentes, said to have been first invented by the Greek Poet, Sotades, during the reign of Ptolemy Philadelphus. The examples we have quoted are, however, of much later date ; the oldest of them being certainly not earlier than the 7th century.

that of the well-known Double Chant by Dr. Crotch.

It would be difficult to point to two schools more bitterly opposed to each other than those of the early Netherlanders, and the English Cathedral writers of the 19th century. Yet here we see an artifice, invented by the former, and used by one of the latter, so completely *con amore*, that, backed by the harmonies peculiar to the modern 'free style,' it has attained a position quite unassailable, and will probably last as long as the Anglican Chant itself shall continue in use. [Sir John Stainer wrote a hymn-tune 'Per Recte et Retro' in 1898 for the Church Hymnary (No. 381); it is also No. 81 of Novello's edition of the composer's hymns. It reads backwards in all the parts.] With these things before us, we shall do well to pause, before we consign even the most glaring pedantries of our forefathers to oblivion. w. s. r.

REDEKER, Louise Dorette Auguste, a contralto singer, who made her first appearance in London at the Philharmonic Concert of June 19, 1876, and remained a great favourite until she retired from public life on her marriage with Dr. (now Sir) Felix Semon, Oct. 19, 1879. She was born at Duingen, Hanover, Jan. 19, 1853, and from 1870 to 1873 studied in the Conservatorium at Leipzig, chiefly under Konewka. She sang first in public at Bremen in 1873. In 1874 she made the first of several appearances at the Gewandhaus, and was much in request for concerts and oratorios in Germany and other countries during 1874 and 1875. In England she sang at all the principal concerts, and at the same time maintained her connection with the Continent, where she was always well received. Her voice is rich and sympathetic; she sings without effort and with great taste. g.

REDEMPTION, THE. A Sacred Trilogy, written and composed by Charles Gounod. First performed at the Birmingham Festival, August 30, 1882, under the composer's direction. m.

REDFORD, John, was organist and almoner, and master of the Choristers of St. Paul's Cathedral in the latter part of the reign of Henry VIII. (1491-1547). Tusser, the author of the *Hundred good Points of Husbandrie*, was one of his pupils. An anthem, 'Rejoice in the Lorde alway,' printed in the appendix to Hawkins's *History* and in the Motett Society's first volume, is remarkable for its melody and expression. Some anthems and organ pieces by him are in the MS. volume collected by Thomas Mulliner, master of St. Paul's School, afterwards in the libraries of John Stafford Smith and Dr. Rimbault, and now in the British Museum. A motet, some fancies, and a voluntary by him are in MS. at Christ Church, Oxford. [See also the *Monatshefte* for 1902, for list of other works by him.] His name is included by Morley in the list of those whose works he consulted for his 'Introduction.' w. h. h.

REDHEAD, Richard, born March 1, 1820, at Harrow, was a chorister at Magdalen College, Oxford, 1829-36, having received his musical education there from Walter Vicary, the organist. He was organist at Old Margaret Chapel (now All Saints' Church), Margaret Street, in 1839-1864, and from the latter date at St. Mary Magdalene, Paddington, a post he held till his death at Hellingley, Sussex, April 27, 1901. His works are almost exclusively written or compiled for use in the Church of England service, viz. 'Church Music,' etc., 1840, 'Laudes Diurnae, the Psalter and Canticles in the Morning and Evening Service,' 1843, Music for the Office of the Holy Communion,' 1853; 'O my people,' anthem for Good Friday; 'Church Melodies, a collection of short pieces and Six Sacred Songs,' 1858; 'The Celebrant's Office Book,' 1863; 'Ancient Hymn Melodies, Book of Common Prayer with Ritual music, Canticles at Matins and Evensong, pointed as they are to be sung in churches and adapted to the Ancient Psalm Chants, and Parish Tune Book and Appendix,' 1865; 'The Universal Organist, a Collection of Short Classical and Modern Pieces,' 1866-81; 'Litany with latter part of Commination Service, Music to the Divine Liturgy during the Gradual, Offertorium and Communion, arranged for use throughout the year,' 1874; Festival Hymns for All Saints and St. Mary Magdalene Days, Hymns for Holy Seasons, Anthems, etc. a. c.

REDOUTE. Public assemblies at which the guests appeared with or without masks at pleasure. The word is French, and is explained by Voltaire and Littré as being derived from the Italian *ridotto*—perhaps with some analogy to the word 'resort.' They soon made their way to Germany and England. They are frequently mentioned by Horace Walpole under the name 'Ridotto,' and were one of the attractions at Vauxhall and Ranelagh in the middle of the 18th century. In Germany and France the French version of the name was adopted. The building used for the purpose in Vienna, erected in 1748, and rebuilt in stone in 1754, forms part of the Burg or Imperial Palace, the side of the oblong facing the Josephs-Platz. There was a *grosse* and a *kleine* Redoutensaal. In the latter Beethoven played a concerto of his own at a concert of Haydn's, Dec. 18, 1795. The rooms were used for concerts till about 1870. The masked balls were held there during the Carnival, from Twelfth Night to Shrove Tuesday, and occasionally in the weeks preceding Advent; some being public, *i.e.* open to all on payment of an entrance fee, and others private. Special nights were reserved for the court and the nobility. The 'Redoutentänze'—Minuets, Allemandes, Contredanses, Schottisches, Anglaises, and Ländler—were composed for full orchestra, and published (mostly by Artaria) for pianoforte. Mozart,[1] Haydn, Beethoven,[2] Hummel, Woelfl, Gyrowetz, and others, have left dances written for this purpose.   C. F. P.

REDOWA, a Bohemian dance which was introduced into Paris in 1846 or 1847, and quickly attained for a short time great popularity, both there and in London, although it is now never danced. In Bohemia there are two variations of the dance, the Rejdovák, in 3–4 or 3–8 time, which is more like a waltz, and the Rejdovacka, in 2–4 time, which is something like a polka. The ordinary Redowa is written in 3–4 time (M.M. $\downarrow$=160). The dance is something like a Mazurka, with the rhythm less strongly marked. The following example is part of a Rejdovák which is given in Köhler's 'Volkstänze aller Nationen'—

W. B. S.

REED (Fr. *Anche*; Ital. *Ancia*; Germ. *Blatt*, *Rohr*). The speaking part of many instruments, both ancient and modern; the name being derived from the material of which it has been immemorially constructed. The plant used for it is a tall grass or reed, the *Arundo Donax* or *Sativa*, growing in the South of Europe. The substance in its rough state is commonly called 'cane,' though differing from real cane in many respects. The chief supply is now obtained from Fréjus on the Mediterranean coast. Many other materials, such as lance-wood, ivory, silver, and 'ebonite,' or hardened india-rubber, have been experimentally substituted for the material first named; but hitherto without success. Organ reeds were formerly made of hard wood, more recently of brass, German silver, and steel. The name Reed is, however, applied by organ-builders to the metal tube or channel against which the vibrating tongue beats, rather than to the vibrator itself.

Reeds are divided into the Free and the Beating; the latter again into the Single and the Double forms. The Free reed is used in

the harmonium and concertina, its union with Beating reeds in the organ not having proved successful. [See FREE REED, vol. ii. p. 106.] The vibrator, as its name implies, passes freely through the long slotted brass plate to which it is adapted; the first impulse of the wind tending to push it within the slot and thus close the aperture. In 'percussion' harmoniums the vibrator is set suddenly in motion by a blow from a hammer connected with the keyboard. [See HARMONIUM, vol. ii. p. 303.] [The Beating reed in its single form is that of the organ and the clarinet. In this the edges of the vibrator overlap the slot leading into the resonating pipe or tube, and so close it periodically during vibration. The reed, which is a thin blade or lamina, has roughly the form of a long parallelogram, and it is firmly secured for a portion of its length to the bed or table of the tube or mouthpiece in which the slot is cut. In the organ reed the necessary opening for the entrance of the wind at the free end is obtained by giving a slight curvature to the blade or reed; the pressure of the wind tends to close this opening, and vibration is thus set up. In the clarinet the same result is obtained by giving a slight curvature to the bed of the mouthpiece towards its tip, the under side of the reed itself being left perfectly flat (see CLARINET).

The Double reed, as used in the oboe and the bassoon, is constructed of two segments united in a tubular form at one end, and splayed out and flattened at the other so as to leave a slight opening in shape like the section of a double-convex lens. The bassoon reed is placed directly upon the 'crook' of the instrument, but the oboe reed is built up upon a small tube or 'staple.' The exact appearance of both single and double reeds will be gathered better from the drawings than from a more detailed description.

1.   2.   3.   4.

Single Reed:—1. Clarinet reed, as held to the mouthpiece by a metal ligature.
Double Reeds:—2. Bassoon reed. 3. Bassoon reed, foreshortened to show the opening between the two blades. 4. Oboe reed.

The single reed is used also on the saxophone, and the double reed for the chaunter of the Highland bagpipe, but the drones of the bag-

1 See Köchel's Catalogue, No. 599, etc.
2 See Nottebohm's Thematic Catalogue, Section ii. pages 135-37.

pipe are sounded by single reeds of a most rudimentary character. It is possible to replace the double reed of the oboe and bassoon by a single reed of the clarinet type fitted to a small mouthpiece. The old dolcino or alto-fagotto was so played in the band of the Coldstream Guards by the late Mr. Henry Lazarus when a boy. The idea has been revived of late years as a novelty, but neither the oboe nor the bassoon is capable of improvement in this way, although the saxophone, also a conical tube, is well adapted to the single reed, being an instrument of wider calibre.] w. h. s. ; with additions by d. j. b.

REED, THOMAS GERMAN, born at Bristol, June 27, 1817. His father was a musician, and the son first appeared, at the age of ten, at the Bath Concerts as a PF. player with John Loder and Lindley, and also sang at the Concerts and at the Bath Theatre. Shortly after, he appeared at the Haymarket Theatre, London, where his father was conductor, as PF. player, singer, and actor of juvenile parts. In 1832 the family moved to London, and the father became leader of the band at the Garrick Theatre. His son was his deputy, and also organist to the Catholic Chapel, Sloane Street. German Reed now entered eagerly into the musical life of London, was an early member of the Society of British Musicians, studied hard at harmony, counterpoint, and PF. playing, composed much, gave many lessons, and took part in all the good music he met with. His work at the theatre consisted in great measure of scoring and adapting, and getting up new operas, such as 'Fra Diavolo' in 1837. In 1838 he became Musical Director of the Haymarket Theatre, a post which he retained till 1851. In 1838 he also succeeded Mr. Tom Cooke as Chapelmaster at the Royal Bavarian Chapel, where the music to the Mass was for long noted both for quality and execution. Beethoven's Mass in C was produced there for the first time in England, and the principal Italian singers habitually took part in the Sunday services. At the Haymarket, for the Shakespearean performances of Macready, the Keans, the Cushmans, etc., he made many excellent innovations, by introducing, as overtures and entr'actes, good pieces, original or scored by himself, instead of the rubbish usually played at that date. During the temporary closing of the theatre, Reed did the work of producing Pacini's opera of 'Sappho' at Drury Lane (April 1, 1843—Clara Novello, Sims Reeves, etc.). In 1844 he married Miss Priscilla Horton, and for the next few years pursued the same busy, useful, miscellaneous life as before, directing the production of English opera at the Surrey, managing Sadler's Wells during a season of English opera, with his wife, Miss Louisa Pyne, Harrison, etc., con-

ducting the music at the Olympic under Mr. Wigan's management, and making prolonged provincial tours.

In 1855 he started a new class of performance which, under the name of 'Mr. and Mrs. German Reed's Entertainment,' made his name widely and favourably known in England. Its object was to provide good dramatic amusement for a large class of society who, on various grounds, objected to the theatres. It was opened at St. Martin's Hall, April 2, 1855, as 'Miss P. Horton's Illustrative Gatherings,' with two pieces called 'Holly Lodge' and 'The Enraged Musician' (after Hogarth), written by W. Brough, and presented by Mrs. Reed, with the aid of her husband only, as accompanist and occasional actor. In Feb. 1856 they removed to the Gallery of Illustration, Regent Street, and there produced 'A Month from Home,' and 'My Unfinished Opera' (April 27, 1857); 'The Home Circuit' and 'Seaside Studies' (June 20, 1859)—all by W. Brough; 'After the Ball,' by Edmund Yates; 'Our Card Basket,' by Shirley Brooks; 'An Illustration on Discord' ('The Rival Composers'), by Brough (April 3, 1861); and 'The Family Legend,' by Tom Taylor (March 31, 1862). They then engaged Mr. John Parry, and produced the following series of pieces specially written for this company of three, and including some of Mr. Parry's most popular and admirable songs in the characters of Paterfamilias at the Pantomime, Mrs. Roseleaf, etc. etc. :—

'The Charming Cottage.' April 6, 1863.
'The Pyramid.' Shirley Brooks. Feb. 7, 1864.
'The Bard and his Birthday.' W. Brough. April 20, 1864.
'The Peculiar Family.' Do. March 15, 1865.
'The Yachting Cruise.' F. C. Burnand. April 2, 1866.

'A Dream in Venice.' T. W. Robertson. March 18, 1867.
'Our Quiet Château.' R. Reece. Dec. 26, 1867.
'Inquire within.' F. C. Burnand. July 22, 1868.
'Last of the Paladins.' R. Reece. Dec. 23, 1868.

At this period the company was further increased by the addition of Miss Fanny Holland and Mr. Arthur Cecil, and soon after by Mr. Corney Grain and Mr. Alfred Reed. The following was the repertory during this last period :—

'Lischen and Fritschen.' Offenbach. Feb. 8, 1869.
'No Cards,' W. S. Gilbert, and 'Cox and Box,' Burnand and Sullivan. March 29, 1869. (A. Cecil's first appearance.)
'Ages Ago.' W. S. Gilbert and F. Clay. Nov. 22, 1869.
'Beggar my Neighbour.' F. C. Burnand. March 28, 1870.
'Our Island Home.' W. S. Gilbert. June 20, 1870.
'The Bold Recruit.' F. Clay. July 19, 1870.
'A Sensation Novel.' Do. Jan. 30, 1871.

'Near Relations.' Arthur Sketchley. August 14, 1871.
'King Christmas.' Planché. Dec. 26, 1871.
'Charity begins at Home.' B. Rowe and Cellier. Feb. 7, 1872.
'My Aunt's Secret.' Burnand and Molloy. March 3, 1872.
'Happy Arcadia.' W. S. Gilbert and F. Clay. Oct. 28, 1872.
'Very Catching.' Burnand and Molloy. Nov. 18, 1872.
'Mildred's Well.' Burnand and German Reed. May 5, 1873.

During this period a diversion was made by the introduction of 'Opere di Camera,' for four characters. These comprised :—

'Jessy Lea.' Oxenford and Macfarren.
'Too Many Cooks.' Offenbach.
'The Sleeping Beauty.' Balfe.
'The Soldier's Legacy.' Oxenford and Macfarren.

'Widows bewitched.' Virginia Gabriel.
'A Fair Exchange'; 'A Happy Result'; 'Ching Chow Hi.' All three by Offenbach.

While the entertainment still remained at the Gallery of Illustration, Reed became lessee of St. George's Hall for the production of Comic Opera. He engaged an orchestra of forty and a strong chorus, and 'The Contrabandista' (Burnand and Sullivan), 'L'Ambassadrice' (Auber), and the 'Beggar's Opera' were produced, but without the necessary success. Mr. Reed then gave his sole attention to the Gallery of Illustration, in which he was uniformly successful, owing to the fact that he carried out his entertainments, not only with perfect respectability, but always with great talent, much tact and judgment, and constant variety.

When the lease of the Gallery of Illustration expired, the entertainment was transferred to St. George's Hall, and there the following entertainments were produced :—

'He's Coming.' F. C. Burnand and German Reed.	Gilbert A'Beckett and German Reed.
'Too Many by One.' F. C. Burnand and F. Cowan.	'Matched and Match.' F. C. Burnand and German Reed.
'The Three Tenants'; 'Ancient Britons.' Gilbert A'Beckett and German Reed.	'A Puff of Smoke.' C. J. Rowe and Mme. Goetz.
'A Tale of Old China.' F. C. Burnand and Molloy.	'Our Dolls' House.' C. J. Rowe and Cotsford Dick.
'Eyes and no Eyes.' W. S. Gilbert and German Reed.	'A Night's Surprise.' West Cromer and German Reed.
'A Spanish Bond'; 'An Indian Puzzle'; 'The Wicked Duke.'	'Foster Brothers.' F. C. Burnand and King Hall.
	'Happy Bungalow.' A. Law.

The following were produced under the management of Mr. Corney Grain and Mr. Alfred Reed :—

'No. 204.' F. C. Burnand and German Reed.	'A Water Cure.' A. Law, Arnold Felix, and George Gear.
'Once in a Century.' G. A'Beckett and Vivian Bligh.	'A Moss Rose Rent.' A. Law and A. J. Caldicott.
'Our New Dolls' House.' W. Yardley and Cotsford Dick.	'A Double Event.' A. Law, Alfred Reed, and Corney Grain.
'Answer Paid.' F. C. Burnand and W. Austin.	'Fairly Puzzled.' Oliver Brand and Hamilton Clarke.
'Doubleday's Will.' Burnand and King Hall.	'A Terrible Fright.' A. Law and Corney Grain.
'Artful Automaton.' Arthur Law and King Hall.	'Old Knockles.' A. Law and A. J. Caldicott.
'A Tremendous Mystery.' F. C. Burnand and King Hall.	'A Peculiar Case.' A. Law and G. Grossmith.
'Enchantment.' A. Law and German Reed.	'Hobbies.' Stephens, Yardley, and G. Gear.
'Grimstone Grange.' G. A'Beckett and King Hall.	'A Pretty Bequest.' M. Watson and Hamilton Clarke.
'£100 Reward.' A. Law and Corney Grain.	'A Night in Wales.' H. Gardner and Corney Grain.
'Back from India.' Pottinger Stevens and Cotsford Dick.	'In Cupid's Court.' M. Watson and A. J. Caldicott.
'The Pirate's Home.' G. A'Beckett and Vivian Bligh.	'A United Fair.' Comyns Carr and A. J. Caldicott.
'A Christmas Stocking.' G. A'Beckett and King Hall.	'The Friar.' Do.
'Castle Botheren.' A. Law and Hamilton Clarke.	'The Naturalist.' Comyns Carr and King Hall.
'The Three Hats.' A. A'Beckett and Edouard Marlois.	'Tally-Ho!' M. Watson and A. J. Caldicott.
'A Flying Visit.' A. Law and Corney Grain.	'Wanted an Heir.' Do.
'The Turquoise Ring.' G. W. Godfrey and Lionel Benson.	'The Bo'sun's Mate.' W. Browne and A. J. Caldicott.
'A Merry Christmas.' A. Law and King Hall.	'Brittany Folk.' Walter Frith and A. J. Caldicott.
'Sandford and Merton.' Burnand and A. S. Gatty.	'Tuppins and Co.' Malcolm Watson and Edward Solomon.
'All at Sea.' A. Law and Corney Grain.	'The Verger.' Walter Frith and King Hall.
'Many Happy Returns.' G. A'Beckett and Lionel Benson.	'Carnival Time.' M. Watson and Corney Grain.
'A Bright Idea.' A. Law and Arthur Cecil.	'Possession.' Walter Browne and A. J. Caldicott.
'Cherry Tree Farm.' A. Law and Hamilton Clarke.	'Killiecrumper.' M. Watson and E. Solomon.
'The Head of the Poll.' A. Law and Eaton Faning.	'The Old Bureau.' H. M. Paull and A. J. Caldicott.
'Nobody's Fault.' A. Law and Hamilton Clarke.	'The Barley Mow.' Walter Frith and C. Grain.
'A Strange Host.' A. Law and King Hall.	'Dan'l's Delight.' Archie Armstrong and J. W. Elliott.
'That Dreadful Boy.' G. A'Beckett and Corney Grain.	'An Odd Pair.' M. Watson and A. J. Caldicott.
'A Mountain Heiress.' G. A'Beckett and Lionel Benson.	'Peggy's Plot.' Somerville Gibney and Walter Slaughter.
'Treasure Trove.' A. Law and A. J. Caldicott.	'A Big Bandit.' M. Watson and W. Slaughter.
	'Melodramania.' Do.
	A. C.

The accompaniments to these pieces were played on a pianoforte and harmonium. For many years the 'Musical Sketches' of Mr. Corney Grain were a principal attraction of the entertainment. German Reed died at Upper East Sheen, Surrey, March 21, 1888, and in 1895 the entertainments came to an end, with the deaths of Alfred German Reed, March 10, and Corney Grain, March 16. An attempt was made to revive the enterprise, but without effect.

Mrs. GERMAN REED, née PRISCILLA HORTON, was born at Birmingham, Jan. 1, 1818. From a very early age she showed unmistakable qualifications for a theatrical career, in a fine strong voice, great musical ability, and extraordinary power of mimicry. She made her first appearance at the age of ten, at the Surrey Theatre, under Elliston's management, as the Gipsy Girl in 'Guy Mannering.' After this she was constantly engaged at the principal metropolitan theatres in a very wide range of parts. Her rare combination of great ability as a singer, with conspicuous gifts as an actress, and most attractive appearance, led to a very satisfactory step in her career. On August 16, 1837, she signed an agreement with Macready for his famous performances at Covent Garden and Drury Lane, in which she acted Ariel, Ophelia, the Fool [1] in 'Lear,' the Attendant Spirit in 'Comus,' Philidel in 'King Arthur,' and Acis in 'Acis and Galatea.' After the conclusion of this memorable engagement, Miss Horton became the leading spirit in Planché's graceful burlesques at the Haymarket Theatre. On Jan. 20, 1844, she married Mr. German Reed, and the rest of her career has been related under his name. She died at Bexley Heath, March 18, 1895, a few days after her son and Corney Grain.　　　　　　　　　　G.

REED-STOP. When the pipes of an organ, controlled by a draw-stop, produce their tone by means of a vibrating tongue striking the face of a reed, the stop is called a Reed-stop ; when the pipes contain no such reeds, but their tone is produced merely by the impinging of air against a sharp edge, the stop is called a Flue-stop. Any single pipe of the former kind is called a Reed-pipe, any single pipe of the latter kind, a Flue-pipe. Pipes containing Free reeds are seldom used in English organs, but are occasionally found in foreign instruments under the name of Physharmonika, etc. [See HARMONIUM, REED.] The reed-stops consisting of 'striking-reeds' are voiced in various ways to imitate the sounds of the Oboe, Cor Anglais, Clarinet, Bassoon, Horn, Cornopean, Trumpet, etc., all of which are of 8-ft. pitch (that is, in unison with the diapason). The Clarion 4-ft. is an octave reed-stop. The Double Trumpet 16-ft. is a reed-stop one octave lower in pitch than the diapason ; it is also called a Contra-posaune, or sometimes a Trombone. Reed-stops

[1] See *Macready's Reminiscences*, by Sir F. Pollock, ii. 97.

of the trumpet class are often placed on a very high pressure of wind under such names as Tuba mirabilis, Tromba major, etc. ; such high-pressure reed-stops are generally found on the Solo-manual ; the reed-stops of the Great organ being of moderate loudness ; those on the Choir organ altogether of a softer character. A very much larger proportion of reed-stops is usually assigned to the Swell organ than to any other manual, owing to the brilliant *crescendo* which they produce as the shutters of the swell-box open. Reed-stops are said to be 'harmonic' when the tubes of the pipes are twice their normal length and perforated half-way with a small hole. Their tone is remarkably pure and brilliant. The best modern organ-builders have made great improvements in the voicing of reed-stops, which are now produced in almost infinite variety both as to quality and strength of tone.   J. S.

REEL (Anglo-Saxon *hreol*, connected with the Suio-Gothic *rulla*, 'to whirl'). An ancient dance, the origin of which is enveloped in much obscurity. The fact of its resemblance to the Norwegian *Hallung*, as well as its popularity in Scotland, and its occurrence in Denmark, the north of England, and Ireland, has led most writers to attribute to it a Scandinavian origin, although its rapid movements and lively character are opposed to the oldest Scandinavian dance-rhythms. The probability is that the reel is of Keltic origin, perhaps indigenous to Britain, and from there introduced into Scandinavia. In Scotland the reel is usually danced by two couples ; in England—where it is now almost only found in connection with the Sword Dance, as performed in the North Riding of Yorkshire—it is danced by three couples. The figures of the reel differ slightly according to the locality ; their chief feature is their circular character, the dancers standing face to face and describing a series of figures of eight. The music consists of 8-bar phrases, generally in common time, but occasionally in 6-4. The Irish reel is played much faster than the Scotch ; in Yorkshire an ordinary hornpipe-tune is used. The following example, 'Lady Nelson's Reel,' is from a MS. collection of dances in the possession of the present writer :—

[In *News from Scotland* (1591) it is stated

that 'Giles Duncan did go before them playing a *reill* or dance upon a small trump.' The Irish reel, which is apparently alluded to here, is in 2-4, or common time, and is always danced singly : the first eight bars, danced in steps, are followed by a round for the next eight bars, when the original steps are resumed, but reversed. W. H. G. F.]

An example of the Danish reel will be found in Engel's 'National Music' (London, 1866).

One of the most characteristic Scotch reels is the Reel of Tulloch (Thulichan) :—

Others, equally good, are 'Colonel M'Bean's Reel,' 'Ye're welcome, Charlie Stuart,' 'The Cameronian Rant,' 'Johnnie's friends are ne'er pleased,' and 'Flora Macdonald.'

For the slow Reel see STRATHSPEY.   W. B. S.

REEVE, WILLIAM, born 1757 ; after quitting school, was placed with a law stationer in Chancery Lane, where his fellow-writer was Joseph Munden, afterwards the celebrated comedian. Determined, however, upon making music his profession, he became a pupil of Richardson, organist of St. James's, Westminster. In 1781 he was appointed organist of Totnes, Devonshire, where he remained till about 1783, when he was engaged as composer at Astley's. He was next for some time an actor at the regular theatres. In 1791, being then a chorus singer at Covent Garden, he was applied to to complete the composition of the music for the ballet-pantomime of 'Oscar and Malvina,' left unfinished by Shield, who, upon some differences with the manager, had resigned his appointment. Reeve thereupon produced an overture and some vocal music, which were much admired, and led to his being appointed composer to the theatre. In 1792 he was elected organist of St. Martin, Ludgate. In 1802 he became part proprietor of Sadler's Wells Theatre. His principal dramatic compositions were 'Oscar and Malvina,' and 'Tippoo Saib,' 1791 ; 'Orpheus and Eurydice,' partly adapted from Gluck, 1792 ; 'The Apparition,' 'British Fortitude,' 'Hercules and Omphale,' and 'The Purse,' 1794 ; 'Merry Sherwood' (containing Reeve's best-known song, 'I am a Friar of orders grey'), 1795 ; 'Harlequin and Oberon,' 1796, 'Bantry Bay,' 'The Round Tower,' and 'Harlequin Quixote,' 1797 ; 'Joan of Arc,' and 'Ramah Droog' (with Mazzinghi), 1798 ; 'The Turnpike Gate' (with Mazzinghi), 'The Embarkation,' and 'Thomas and Susan,' 1799 ; 'Paul and Virginia' (with Mazzinghi), and 'Jamie and Anna,' 1800 ; 'Harlequin's Almanack,' 'The Blind Girl' (with Mazzinghi), 1801 ; 'The Cabinet' (with Braham, Davy, and Moorehead), and 'Family Quarrels' (with Braham and Moorehead), 1802 ; 'The Caravan,'

1803 ; 'The Dash,' and 'Thirty Thousand' (with Davy and Braham), 1804 ; 'Out of Place' (with Braham), and 'The Corsair,' 1805 ; 'The White Plume,' 'Rokeby Castle,' and 'An Bratach,' 1806 ; 'Kais' (with Braham), 1808 ; 'Tricks upon Travellers' (part), 1810 ; and 'The Outside Passenger' (with Whitaker and D. Corri), 1811. He wrote music for some pantomimes at Sadler's Wells ; amongst them 'Bang up,' by C. Dibdin, jun., containing the favourite Clown's song, 'Tippitywitchet,' for Grimaldi. He was also author of *The Juvenile Preceptor, or Entertaining Instructor*, etc. He died June 22, 1815.   W. H. H.

REEVES, JOHN SIMS, son of a musician in the Royal Artillery, was born at Woolwich, Sept. 26,[1] 1818 (*Memoirs of the Royal Artillery Band*, by H. G. Farmer (1904), p. 74 ff.). He received his early musical instruction from his father, and at fourteen obtained the post of organist at North Cray Church, Kent. Upon gaining his mature voice he determined on becoming a singer, and [after a year spent in studying for the medical profession] in 1839 made his first appearance at the Newcastle-upon-Tyne Theatre, as the Gipsy Boy in 'Guy Mannering,' and subsequently performed Dandini in 'La Cenerentola,' and other baritone parts. The true quality of his voice, however, having asserted itself, he placed himself under J. W. Hobbs and T. Cooke, and in the seasons of 1841-42 and 1842-43 was a member of Macready's company at Drury Lane, as one of the second tenors, performing such parts as the First Warrior in Purcell's 'King Arthur,' Ottocar in 'Der Freischütz,' and the like. He then went, to prosecute his studies, first to Paris under Bordogni, and subsequently to Milan under Mazzucato ; he appeared at the Scala as Edgardo in Donizetti's 'Lucia di Lammermoor' with marked success. Returning to England he [appeared at various concerts, and] was engaged by Jullien for Drury Lane, where he made his first appearance on Monday, Dec. 6, 1847, as Edgar in 'The Bride of Lammermoor,' and at once took position as an actor and singer of the first rank. 'His voice had become a pure high tenor of delicious quality, the tones vibrating and equal throughout, very skilfully managed, and displaying remarkably good taste. His deportment as an actor was natural and easy, his action manly and to the purpose, and exhibiting both passion and power, without the least exaggeration.' A fortnight later he performed his first original part, Lyonnel in Balfe's 'Maid of Honour.' [Berlioz, who conducted the performance, engaged him for the performance of two parts of *La Damnation de Faust* at Drury Lane, Feb. 7, 1848.] In 1848 he was engaged at Her Majesty's Theatre, and came out as Carlo in

[1] Or possibly Oct 21 (he entered his name in a 'birthday book' as born on that day).

Donizetti's 'Linda di Chamounix,' appearing also as Florestan in 'Fidelio.' [His operatic career was more or less overshadowed by the great place he made for himself in oratorio ; he sang the part of Faust when Gounod's opera was given for the first time in English, at Her Majesty's Theatre, and for a few performances he sang Braham's old part of Sir Huon in 'Oberon.' Captain Macheath, in 'The Beggar's Opera,' was one of the last operatic parts in which he appeared.] In the autumn of 1848 he was engaged at the Norwich Musical Festival, where he showed his ability as an oratorio singer by an extraordinarily fine delivery of 'The enemy said' in 'Israel in Egypt.' On Nov. 24 following he made his first appearance at the Sacred Harmonic Society in Handel's 'Messiah.' The rapid strides which he was then making towards perfection in oratorio were shown—to take a few instances only—by his performances in 'Judas Maccabæus' and 'Samson,' 'Elijah,' 'St. Paul,' and 'Lobgesang,' and 'Eli' and 'Naaman' (both composed expressly for him). [He sang in Bach's 'St. Matthew Passion,' under Sterndale Bennett, when the work was given for the first time in England in 1854.] But his greatest triumph was achieved at the Handel Festival at the Crystal Palace in 1857, when, after singing in 'Messiah' and 'Judas Maccabæus' with increased reputation, he gave 'The enemy said' in 'Israel in Egypt' with such remarkable power, fire, and volume of voice, breadth of style, and evenness of vocalisation, as completely electrified his hearers. He repeated this wonderful performance at several succeeding festivals, and in the Handelian repertory nothing was more striking than his delivery of 'Total Eclipse' from 'Samson.' [He was the first representative of various tenor parts in oratorios and cantatas that are for the most part forgotten in the present day, such as Benedict's 'St. Peter,' Bennett's 'May Queen,' Sullivan's 'Prodigal Son' and 'Light of the World.' His singing of 'Tom Bowling' and 'Come into the garden, Maud' remained unapproachable until the end of his life. It was unfortunate that he was compelled by adverse circumstances to go on singing after his voice had begun to decay. His farewell concert took place at the Albert Hall on May 11, 1891, but he sang afterwards at Covent Garden, and at music halls. Some critics, who only heard him in his last days, were inclined to question whether he had ever been great, but their doubts were without foundation. In the quarter of a century during which his voice was at its best, he sang on the orchestra with Jenny Lind, Clara Novello, Tietjens, Adelina Patti, and Christine Nilsson, and held his own with them all. Assuredly none but a great artist could have done that. Even in his vocal decay there was nothing harsh or ugly. He never sang off the key, and even when he was nearly seventy his legato singing was a model of steadiness and breath management. The expression 'voice colouring' was not much used in Sims Reeves's day, but of the art implied in the words he was a past master. No one could with greater certainty find the exact tone to fit the most varied emotions. It was a comprehensive talent indeed that could range at will from the levity of Captain Macheath's songs to the poignant pathos of Handel's 'Deeper and deeper still,' the emotional warmth of Beethoven's 'Adelaide,' or the cycle 'An die ferne Geliebte.' He died at Worthing, Oct. 25, 1900.] Sims Reeves married, Nov. 2, 1850, Miss EMMA LUCOMBE, soprano singer, who had been a pupil of Mrs. Blane Hunt, and appeared at the Sacred Harmonic Society's concert of June 19, 1839, and sang there and at other concerts until 1845, when she went to Italy. She returned in 1848, and appeared in opera as well as at concerts. She retired from public life and occupied herself as a teacher of singing, for which she had a deservedly high reputation. [She died at Upper Norwood, June 10, 1895 ; and in the same year her husband married his pupil, Miss Maud Rene, with whom he went on a successful concert tour in South Africa in 1896.] His son HERBERT, after a careful education under his father and at Milan, made his successful début at one of Mr. Ganz's concerts (June 12, 1880), and met with considerable favour from the public. w. H. H. ; additions from the *Dict. of Nat. Biog.*, S. H. Pardon, Esq., etc.

REFORMATION SYMPHONY, THE. Mendelssohn's own name for his Symphony in D minor, written with a view to performance at the Tercentenary Festival of the Augsburg Protestant Confession, which was intended to be celebrated throughout Germany on June 25, 1830. The first mention of it appears to be in a letter of his own from North Wales, Sept. 2, 1829. On May 25, 1830, he writes from Weimar that it is finished, and when copied will be sent to Leipzig. It was not, however, then performed ; the political troubles of that year prevented any festive demonstrations. In January and March, 1832, it was in rehearsal in Paris, but it did not come to actual performance till November 1832, when it was played under his own direction at Berlin. It was not repeated during his life, but was revived at the Crystal Palace, Nov. 30, 1867. It was afterwards played at the Gewandhaus, Leipzig, Oct. 29, 1868, and was published in score and parts by Novello & Co., and by Simrock as 'Symphony No. 5'—op. 107, No. 36 of the posthumous works. The first Allegro is said to represent the conflict between the old and new religions, and the Finale is founded on Luther's Hymn, 'Ein' feste Burg ist unser Gott.' One of the most prominent themes of the work is the beautiful ascending phrase

known as the 'Dresden Amen,' which has been used with marvellous effect in Wagner's 'Parsifal.'   G.

REFRAIN (Fr. *Refrain* ; Germ. *Reimkehr*). This word is used in music to denote what in poetry is called a 'burden,' *i.e.* a short sentence or phrase which recurs in every verse or stanza. It was probably first employed in music in order to give roundness and unity to the melody, and was then transferred to the poetry which was written especially for music. Such collections as the 'Échos du temps passé' give an abundance of examples in French music, where songs with refrains are most frequently to be found. 'Lilliburlero' may be cited as one English instance out of many. [See vol. ii. p. 731.] Schubert's four Refrain-Lieder were published as op. 95.   M.

REGAL (Fr. *Régale* ; It. *Régale* or *Ninfale*). [The word may be derived from 'regulus,' the idea of gradation being inherent in a keyboard. The wooden harmonicon, when played with a keyboard, was at one time called 'régale en bois.'] This name describes a variety of organ, which is especially interesting as being in some ways the prototype of the modern harmonium. It consists of a single row of 'beating' reeds, the pipes of which are in some instances so small as hardly to cover the reeds. A fine specimen is in the possession of the Brussels Conservatoire, and was lent to the Inventions Exhibition in 1885. The name 'bible regal' is the title of another variety, the peculiarity of which consists in its being arranged to fold in two, on a similar principle to that on which leather backgammon boards are made. The bellows are covered with leather, so that when the instrument is folded it presents the appearance of a large book. Praetorius in his *Syntagma*, vol. iii. pl. iv., gives a view of one, which in its extended condition, bellows and all, appears to be about 3 ft. 6 in. by 3 ft. He ascribes (ii. p. 73) the invention to a nameless monk ; others give it to Voll, an organ-builder at Nuremberg in 1575. The specimen preserved in the Musée of the Conservatoire at Paris is said to date from the end of the 16th century, and has a compass of four octaves. The instrument has been long since extinct, but the name 'regal' is still applied in Germany to certain reed-stops. [The word is used by Fétis, Rimbault, and Engel to denote the portable organ of the 12th and 13th centuries. Mr. Hipkins possessed a remarkably fine specimen, believed to be unique as far as Great Britain is concerned. It is smaller than the Brussels one, being 2 ft. 5 in. wide, and (with the bellows) 3 ft. 8 in. long. The compass is from E to *c'''*. The sharps are of boxwood stained black, the naturals of bird's-eye maple. The keys are not balanced, but hinged. The instrument is of oak, and is dated 1629, with no maker's name.]

In the inventory of Henry VIII.'s musical

instruments [Harleian MS., 1419, A fol. 200],
we find thirteen pairs of single regalls (the 'pair'
meant only one instrument) and five pairs of
double regalls (that is with two pipes to each
note). The name continued in use at the English Court down to 1773, the date of the death
of Bernard Gates, who was 'tuner of the Regals
in the King's household.' For further particulars the reader is referred to Mr. A. J. Hipkins's *Musical Instruments* (A. & C. Black,
1887), where instruments are figured; also to
the same writer's *History of the Pianoforte*,
1898. G.; with additions from MS. notes left
by Mr. Hipkins.

REGAN, ANNA, soprano singer. [See
SCHIMON.]

REGER, MAX, was born March 19, 1873, at
Brand, a village near Kemnath in Bavaria, and
left his native place when but a year old for
Weiden, whither his father, who was a teacher,
was transferred in 1874. There he received his
first musical training through his father and the
organist, whose name was Lindner. In 1890
he went to study with Riemann at Sondershausen, whom he followed to Wiesbaden on the
latter's appointment to the Conservatorium, and
became himself a teacher there in 1895, till
in 1896 he was called to the service of his
country. After recovering from a severe illness
he returned to his own home in 1898, removed
again in 1901, this time to Munich, where he
married.

Of all the composers of the modern German
school of chamber and church music Herr Reger
occupies a place that is probably the most prominent of any, and the fact that his publishers
attest to an enormous sale of his works in Berlin
and other musical centres must contribute to
that belief. It cannot be denied that he is a
composer gifted, as a celebrated German critic
remarks, with strong individuality, and that he
handles with the utmost facility the art of
counterpoint; but to a large number of persons
at the present day his resources of harmony and
his indulgences in rhythm and in form will
appear so infinite as to fog even a most attentive
and experienced listener with their complexity.
Truly, however, his compositions contain remarkable and original effects. In his songs, to quote
the aforesaid critic, 'hat er sich vielfach von
einer Strömung fortreissen lassen, welche das
Grundwesen des Liedes zerstört.' To which he
adds that Herr Reger's powers of invention are
so rich that only the employment of a conscious
limitation of his artistic means instead of an
intentional eclipse of his forerunners is to be desired of him, and he would then be *the* master to
continue the direct line of the great German composers. For a man of thirty-four years of age
the number of his compositions is enormous, as
will be seen from the catalogue below, which, it
will be noticed, contains only one number for
orchestra (op. 90).

Op.
1. Sonata for violin and piano, in D minor.
2. Trio for piano, violin and viola.
3. Sonata for violin and piano, in D.
4. Six Songs.
5. Sonata for violoncello and piano, in F minor.
6. { Two Sacred Songs with organ.
   { Songs for 4 voices with piano.
7. Three Organ pieces.
8. Five Songs.
9. 'Walzer Kapricen' (piano pieces for 4 hands).
10. 'Deutsche Tänze' (piano pieces for 4 hands).
11. Waltzes for PF., solo.
12. Five Songs.
13. 'Lose Blätter,' PF. solo.
14. Duets for soprano and alto, with piano.
15. Ten Songs.
16. Suite in E minor, for organ.
17. 'Aus der Jugendzeit,' twenty pieces for PF. solo.
18. 'Improvisation,' PF. solo.
19. Two Sacred Songs, with organ.
20. Five Humoresken for PF. solo.
21. Hymn 'An der Gesang' (male chorus, with orchestra).
22. Six Waltzes, for piano (4 hands).
23. Four Songs.
24. Six Pieces for PF. solo.
25. Aquarellen for PF. solo.
26. Seven Fantasiestücke for PF. solo.
27. Fantasie for organ on 'Ein' feste Burg.'
28. Sonata for piano and violoncello, in G minor.
29. Fantasie and Fugue, C minor, for organ.
30. Fantasie for organ on 'Freu' dich sehr, o meine Seele.'
31. Six Songs.
32. Seven Characteristic Pieces for PF. solo.
33. Sonata for Organ, F♯ minor.
34. 'Pièces Pittoresques' for piano (4 hands).
35. Six Songs.
36. Bunte Blätter, nine small pieces for PF. solo.
37. Five Songs.
38. { Two volumes of Folk-songs for male chorus (a 5-9).
   { Two volumes of Folk-songs for mixed chorus (a 6-8).
   { Sacred German Folk-songs (a 7-12).
   { Seven Choruses for male voices.
39. Three Six-part Choruses for mixed voices.
40. { I. Fantasie on 'Wie schön leucht't uns der Morgenstern.'
   { II. Ditto on 'Straf mich nicht in deinem Zorn' (both for organ).
41. Sonata in A for violin and piano.
42. Four Sonatas for violin, in D minor, A, B minor, and G minor.
43. Eight Songs.
44. Piano Solos.
45. Six Intermezzi for piano.
46. Phantasie and Fugue on B A C H for organ.
47. Six Trios for organ.
48. Seven Songs.
49. { Four Sonatas for violin alone (one in the style of Bach).
   { Two Sonatas for clarinet and piano.
50. Two Romances for violin in G and D.
51. Twelve Songs.
52. { Organ Fantasie on 'Alle Menschen müssen sterben.'
   { Ditto. 'Wachet auf, ruft uns die Stimme.'
   { Ditto. 'Halleluja, Gott zu loben.'
53. 'Silhouetten' for piano.
54. Three String Quartetts in G, A, and D minor.
55. Fifteen Songs.
56. Five easy Preludes and Fugues for organ.
57. { Variations on 'Heil unserm König, Heil.' } for organ
   { Symphonic Fantasie and Fugue. }
58. Six Burlesken for PF. (4 hands).
59. Twelve Pieces for organ.
60. Sonata for organ in D minor.
61. { 'Palmsonntagmorgen' (5 voices a cappella).
   { Der evangelische Kirchenchor (for 4 voices), forty Easy Com-
     positions for church performance.
62. Sixteen Songs.
63. Twelve Monologues for organ.
64. String quintet in C Minor (two violins, two violas, and violon-
     cello).
65. Twelve Pieces for organ.
66. Twelve Songs.
67. Fifty-three Easy 'Choral Vorspiele.'
68. Six Songs.
69. Ten Organ Pieces.
70. Seventeen Songs.
71. 'Gesang der Verklärten' (for 5-voiced choir and grand or-
     chestra).
72. Sonata for piano and violin.
73. Variations and Fugue on an original theme for organ.
74. String quartet in D minor.
75. Eighteen Songs.
76. Fifteen 'Schlichte Weisen' for piano and voice.
77. (a) Serenade in D for flute, violin, and viola.
    (b) Trio in A minor for violin, viola, and violoncello.
78. Sonata for violoncello and PF. in F.
79. Fourteen volumes of Pieces for piano, for organ, for piano and
     violin, for piano and violoncello, and songs.
80. Five Easy Preludes and Fugues, Bach's Two-part Inventions
     arranged as organ trios (with K. Straube), and twelve
     pieces for organ.
81. Variations and Fugue on a theme of J. S. Bach, for PF. solo.
82. Twelve small pieces for PF. solo, 'Aus meinem Tagebuche.'
83. Eight Songs for male chorus.
84. Sonatas for PF. and violin in F♯ minor.
85. Four Preludes for the organ.
86. Variations and Fugue on a theme by Beethoven for two PFs
     (4 hands).
87. Two Compositions for violin and PF.
88. Four Songs.
89. Two Sonatas (E minor and D) for PF. solo.
90. Sinfonietta for orchestra.

Without opus numbers are :—
    Two Books of Canons (1895) for PF.
    PF. Transcriptions of Bach, Kuhlau, etc., for PF. solo and
        duets.
    Four 'Heitere Lieder.'
    Four Sacred Songs.
    Four PF. Studies for the left hand alone.
    Five PF. Studies (arrangements of Chopin's works).
    'Wiegenlied.'
    Piano Transcriptions of songs by Hugo Wolf and Richard
        Strauss.
    Der Evangelische Kirchenchor, consisting of—
        Book I. Forty easy sacred songs (S.A.T.B.) for all festivals,
            in four series.
        Book II. Cantata 'O wie selig' for mixed choir and con-
            gregation, with accompaniment of strings and organ.
        Book III. Cantata for Good Friday, 'O Haupt voll Blut
            und Wunden,' for alto and tenor (or sopr.) solos, mixed
            choir, violin solo, oboe solo, and organ.
    For male chorus :—
        Nine volkslieder.
        Five volkslieder.
        Twelve madrigals.
    For mixed choir :—
        Eight volkslieder.
        Six volkslieder.
    Twelve German sacred songs (in three books).
        'Komm, heiliger Geist.'
        'Es fiel ein Thau,' for 5-part choir.
        'Vom Himmel hoch,' for 4-part chorus, two solo violins,
            choir, and congregation, with organ or harmonium.
    For Organ :—Schule des Triospiels (arrangements of Bach's
        2-part inventions, with K. Straube).
        Romanze, also for harmonium.
    Arrangements of fifteen of Bach's clavier works for organ.
        Arrangements of songs for harmonium.
    PF. and violin :—Petite Caprice, Romanze (G major), and
        Wiegenlied.
    For PF. and violoncello :—Caprice.
    For voice and PF. :—Sixteen songs.
    PF. solo :—Perpetuum mobile, Elegie, Humoreske, Romanze,
        Moment musical, Scherzino, Albumblatt, Frühlingslied,
        Mélodie, two Humoresken, Nachtstück.
    Canons in all major and minor keys, Book I. in two parts,
        Book II. in three parts.
    Four special studies for left hand alone :—Scherzo, Humoreske,
        Romance, and Prelude and Fugue.
    Regiments-Marsch der ehemaligen Hannoverschen Armee
        (arrangement).
    A new set of orchestral variations is announced for perform-
        ance in the winter of 1907-8.
    Literary work :—Beiträge zur Modulationslehre (Contribution to
        the Rules of Modulation).   H. V. H.

REGGIO, PIETRO, born at Genoa in the first
quarter of the 17th century, was private musician (lutenist and singer) to Queen Christina
of Sweden after her abdication. After her final
departure from Rome, Reggio came to England
and settled at Oxford, where, in 1677, he published *A Treatise to sing well any Song whatsoever.* In 1680 he issued a book of songs dedicated to the king, and containing the earliest
setting of 'Arise, ye subterranean winds,' from
Shadwell's 'Tempest,' afterwards set by Purcell.
(See *Sammelbände* of the *Int. Mus. Ges.* v. 553.)
Seven Italian songs are in the British Museum
in MS., two duets in the Fitzwilliam Museum
at Cambridge, and a three-part motet in the
Christ Church Library, Oxford. Reggio died
in London, July 23, 1685 (Hawkins), and was
buried in St. Giles's in the Fields.   M.

REGIS, JEAN, a Flemish musician of the
latter part of the 15th century, usually reckoned
along with Busnois, Caron, Obrecht, and Okeghem
as belonging to the transitional school of composers between Dufay and Binchois on the one
hand, and Josquin Després on the other. Tinctoris
mentions him with special distinction. He was
for a time master of the choir-boys in Antwerp
Cathedral, and is also supposed to have been in
personal relation with Dufay. Though he does
not appear, like Dufay, to have ever been a
member of the Papal Choir, two of his masses
were copied into the great choir-books of the

Sistine Chapel, which are so far interesting as
showing the curious custom of the time in
combining different liturgical texts. Thus, in
one of them, while the two upper voices sing the
usual words of the mass the tenor sings the 'Ecce
ancilla Domini,' and the Bass 'Ne timeas Maria,'
which would seem to show that this mass was
specially composed for the festival of the
Annunciation. . In the other, the Alto and
Tenor sing 'Dum sacrum mysterium cerneret
Joannes,' which would imply the work to be
intended for the festival of St. John the
Evangelist. Regis is also the author of a mass
'L'omme arme,' in the Archives of Cambrai,
and of a few other pieces in the collections of
Petrucci. The setting of a popular song 'S'il
vous plaisait' *a* 4, transcribed by Kiesewetter in
his *Schicksale und Beschaffenheit des weltlichen
Gesanges,* serves to show the skill of Regis as a
contrapuntal harmonist of the time in a very
favourable light.   J. R. M.

REGISTER, of an organ. Literally, a set
of pipes as recorded or described by the name
written on the draw-stop ; hence, in general, an
organ-stop. The word 'register' is, however,
not quite synonymous with 'stop,' for we do
not say 'pull out, or put in, a register,' but,
'a stop,' although we can say indifferently 'a
large number of registers' or 'of stops.' The
word is also used as a verb ; for example, the
expression 'skill in registering' or 'registration'
means skill in selecting various combinations
of stops for use. The word 'stop' is, however,
never used as a verb in this sense.   J. S.

REGISTER is now employed to denote a
portion of the scale. The 'soprano register,'
the 'tenor register,' denote that part of the
scale which forms the usual compass of those
voices ; the 'head register' means the notes
which are sung with the head voice ; the 'chest
register' those which are sung from the chest ;
the 'upper register' is the higher portion of
the compass of an instrument or voice, and so
on. How it came to have this meaning, the
writer has not been able to discover.   G.

REGISTRATION (or REGISTERING) is
the art of selecting and combining the stops
or 'registers' of the organ so as to produce the
best effect. See ORGAN-PLAYING, vol. iii. pp.
562-64.

REGNART, surname of a family of Flemish
musicians who flourished towards the end of
the 16th century. There were five brothers,
one of whom, Augustin (not August, as given
by Eitner, which would correspond to Augustus
in Latin but not to Augustinus) was a canon
of the Church of St. Peter's, Lille (not Douai, as
Eitner suggests in the *Quellen-Lexikon,* forgetting the words of the dedication partly quoted
by himself in his *Bibliographie,* p. 216),[1] and
in 1590 edited and published at Douai a

[1] See also Goovaert's *Bibliographie,* p. 268 ; but he contradicts
himself by elsewhere (p. 52) describing Augustin Regnart as Canon
of St. Peter's, Louvain.

Collection of thirty-nine Motets, a 4-6, composed
by his four brothers Francis, Jacob, Paschasius,
and Charles Regnart. The work appropriately
bears on its title-page the motto, 'Ecce quam
bonum et quam jucundum fratres habitare in
unum,' Psal. 132. The full title is 'Novae
Cantiones Sacrae, 4, 5, et 6 vocum tum instrumentorum cuivis generi tum vivae voci
aptissimae, authoribus Francisco, Jacobo, Pas-
casio, Carolo Regnart, fratribus germanis' (another incidental mistake of Eitner is that of
taking the word 'germanis' as indicative of
nationality, and explaining it on the ground
that Flanders was then part of Germany, while
all that the word really implies is that the
brothers were full brothers). Of the four
brothers only two attained any real position or
eminence as composers, Francis and Jacob. The
other two are only represented by three motets
a piece in this Collection, and of their careers
nothing is known with any certainty. Of
Francis, Augustin tells us that he had pursued
his studies at the University of Douai and the
Cathedral of Tournai. Besides the twenty-four
motets in the Collection above mentioned,
Francis Regnart is chiefly known by a book of
fifty Chansons a 4-5, 'Poésies de Ronsard et
autres,' originally published at Douai by Jean
Bogaerd in 1575, and afterwards at Paris by
Le Roy and Ballard in 1579. These Chansons
have now been republished in modern score by
H. Expert in his collection 'Les Maîtres
Musiciens de la renaissance Française.' Fétis
mentions a book of Missae tres a 4-5, by
Francis Regnart, published by Plantin in 1582,
but there is no trace of such a publication in
Goovaert's *Bibliographie*, and Eitner knows
nothing of it.

Of the life and works of Jacob Regnart
we have fuller information. He was early
received as an Alumnus of the Imperial Chapel
at Vienna and Prague. In 1564 he is designated as tenor singer in the chapel ; and as a
member of the chapel accompanied the Emperor
to the Augsburg Diet of 1566. In 1573 he is
mentioned as musical preceptor to the boys of
the choir, and before 1579 became the vice-
capellmeister. In 1580 he was offered by the
Elector of Saxony the post of capellmeister at
Dresden vacant by the death of Scandelli, but
declined. In 1582, however, he left the
imperial service to enter that of the Archduke
Ferdinand at Innsbruck, where he remained as
capellmeister till 1595. He then returned to
Prague, where he died in 1600. Shortly before
his death, in the dedication of a book of Masses
to the Emperor, Rudolf II., which, however,
was not published till afterwards, he recommended to the care of the Emperor his wife
and six children. The widow, a daughter of
Hans Vischer, the famous bass singer in the
Electoral Chapel at Munich under Orlando
Lassus, returned to Munich, where she occupied

herself in preparing for publication in 1602-3
three volumes of her husband's Masses, containing altogether 29 a 4, 5, 6, 8, and 10, also a
book of Sacrae Cantiones, a 4-12, 35 Nos.
The other sacred works of Regnart which appeared during his lifetime were a book of
Sacrae Cantiones, a 5-6, 1575, and one a 4,
1577 ; also one entitled *Mariale*, 1588, Marian
Motets composed by way of thanksgiving for
recovery from severe illness. He was, however,
even more widely known by his secular works,
which consist of (1) two books of Canzone
Italiane, a 5 (1574-81), (2) two books entitled
Threni Amorum, German secular songs, a 5
(1595), and (3) several collections, a 3, 4, 5,
entitled 'Kurtzweilige teutsche Lieder nach Art
der Neapolitanen oder welschen Villanellen'
(1576-91). Of the latter, the collection of
67 a 3 was republished by Eitner in modern
score in 1895. They are written in the simple
melodious Italian canzonet style, without any
artificiality of counterpoint. In some introductory lines of verse the composer apologises
for his frequent intentional employment of
consecutive fifths in the harmony as being in
accordance with the simple popular character he
wished to give these songs. The melody of
one of them, 'Venus du und dein Kind,' has
become, with a slight alteration in the first line,
the chorale tune well-known later, 'Auf meinen
lieben Gott.' Two of Regnart's other songs,
a 5, which have something more of imitative
counterpoint, have been reprinted in Commer's
selection of 'Geistliche und weltliche Lieder
aus der xvi-xvii Jahrh.' None of his Latin
motets have been reprinted, with the exception
of one which found admission into the *Evan-
gelical Gotha Cantional* of 1655, whence it has
been reproduced in Schöberlein's *Schatz*. His
Masses, several of them based on the themes of
German popular songs, must have been popular
in their day, judging from the MS. copies of
them enumerated in Eitner as surviving in
various church archives. A Passion according
to St. Matthew, a 8, by Regnart survives only
in MS., of which some account is given in
Kade, *Die aeltere Passionskompositionen*, pp.
60-62.   J. R. M.

REGONDI, GIULIO, of doubtful parentage,
born at Geneva in 1822. His reputed father
was a teacher in the Gymnasium of Milan. The
child appears to have been an infant phenomenon on the guitar, and to have been sacrificed
by his father, who took him to every court of
Europe, excepting Madrid, before he was nine
years old. They arrived in England in June
1831 ; and Giulio seems never to have left the
United Kingdom again except for two concert
tours in Germany, one with Lidel, the violoncellist, in 1841, the other with Mme. Dulcken
in 1846. On the former of these tours he played
both the guitar and the melophone (whatever
that may have been), and evoked enthusiastic

praises from the correspondents of the *A. M.
Zeitung* in Prague and Vienna for his extraordinary execution on both instruments, the very
artistic and individual character of his performance, and the sweetness of his *cantabile.* The
concertina was patented by Sir Charles Wheat-
stone in 1829 [see Concertina], but did not come
into use till Regondi took it up. He wrote two
concertos for it, and a very large number of
arrangements and original compositions. He also
taught it largely, and at one time his name was
to be seen in almost all concert programmes. He
was a great friend of Molique's, who wrote for
him a Concerto for the Concertina (in G) which
he played with great success at the concert of
the Musical Society of London, April 20, 1864.
When he went abroad for his second tour, his
performance and the effect which he got out of
so unpromising and inartistic an instrument
astonished the German critics. (See the *A. M.
Zeitung* for 1846, p. 853.) Regondi appears to
have been badly treated by his father, and to
have had wretched health, which carried him
off on May 6, 1872.   G.

REHEARSAL (Fr. *Répétition*, Ger. *Probe*).
In the case of concerts, a trial performance preliminary to the public one, at which each piece
included in the programme is played through
at least once, if in MS. to detect the errors inevitable in the parts, and in any case to study
the work and discover how best to bring out
the intentions of the composer, and to ensure
a perfect *ensemble* on the part of the performers.
In England, owing to many reasons, but principally to the over-occupation of the players, sufficient rehearsals are seldom given to orchestral
works. The old rule of the Philharmonic Society
(now happily altered) was to have one rehearsal
on Saturday morning for the performance on
Monday evening, and the Saturday Popular Concerts were originally, in like manner, rehearsals
for the Monday evening concerts. No new works
can be efficiently performed with less than two
rehearsals ; and in the case of large, intricate,
and vocal works, many more are requisite. We
have it on record that Beethoven's Eb Quartet,
op. 127, was rehearsed seventeen times before
its first performance ; the players therefore must
have arrived at that state of familiarity and
certainty which a solo player attains with a
concerto or sonata.

In the case of Operas, every practice of either
chorus, principals, or orchestra, separately or
together, is termed a rehearsal. These will sometimes continue every day for six weeks or two
months, as the whole of the voice-music, dialogue,
and action has to be learnt by heart. Whilst
the chorus is learning the music in one part of
the theatre, the principals are probably at work
with the composer at a piano in the green-room,
and the ballet is being rehearsed on the stage.
It is only when the music and dialogue are known
by heart that the rehearsals on the stage with

action and business begin. The orchestra is
never used until the last two or three rehearsals,
and these are termed Full Band Rehearsals
(Germ. *General-probe*). Last of all, before the
public production of the work, comes the Full
Dress Rehearsal, exactly as it will appear in
performance.   G.

REICHA, Anton Joseph, born at Prague,
Feb. 27, 1770, lost his father before he was a
year old ; his mother not providing properly
for his education, he left home, and took refuge
with his grandfather at Glattow, in Bohemia.
The means of instruction in this small town
being too limited, he went on to his uncle
Joseph Reicha (born in Prague, 1746, died at
Bonn, 1795), a violoncellist, conductor, and
composer, who lived at Wallerstein in Bavaria.
His wife, a native of Lorraine, speaking nothing
but French, had no children, so they adopted
the nephew, who thus learned to speak French
and German besides his native Bohemian. He
now began to study the violin, pianoforte, and
flute in earnest. On his uncle's appointment,
in 1788, as musical director to the Elector of
Cologne, he followed him to Bonn, and entered
the band of Maximilian of Austria as second
flute. The daily intercourse with good music
roused the desire to compose, and to become
something more than an ordinary musician,
but his uncle refused to teach him harmony.
He managed, however, to study the works of
Kirnberger and Marpurg in secret, gained much
practical knowledge by hearing the works of
Handel, Mozart, and Haydn, and must have
learned much from his constant intercourse with
Beethoven, who played the viola in the same
band with himself and was much attached to
him. At length his perseverance and his success
in composition conquered his uncle's dislike. He
composed without restraint, and his symphonies
and other works were played by his uncle's
orchestra.[1]

On the dispersion of the Elector's Court in
1794, Reicha went to Hamburg, where he remained till 1799. There the subject of instruction in composition began to occupy him, and
there he composed his first operas, 'Godefroid
de Montfort,' and 'Oubaldi, ou les Français en
Egypte' (two acts). Though not performed,
some numbers of the latter were well received,
and on the advice of a French émigré, he started
for Paris towards the close of 1799, in the hope
of producing it at the Théâtre Feydeau. In this
he failed, but two of his symphonies, an overture, and some 'Scènes Italiennes,' were played
at concerts. After the successive closing of the
Théâtre Feydeau and the Salle Favart, he went
to Vienna, and passed six years (1802-8), in
renewed intimacy with Beethoven, and making
friends with Haydn, Albrechtsberger, Salieri,
and others. The patronage of the Empress Maria

---

[1] See an interesting notice by Kastner, quoted by Thayer,
Beethoven, i. 188.

Theresa was of great service to him, and at her request he composed an Italian opera, 'Argina, regina di Granata.' During this happy period of his life he published symphonies, oratorios, a requiem, six string quintets, and many solos for PF. and other instruments. He himself attached great importance to his '36 Fugues pour le piano,' dedicated to Haydn, but they are not the innovations which he believed them to be ; in placing the answers on any and every note of the scale he merely reverted to the Ricercari of the 17th century, and the only effect of this abandonment of the classic laws of Real fugue was to banish tonality.

The prospect of another war induced Reicha to leave Vienna, and he settled finally in Paris in 1808. He now realised the dream of his youth, producing first 'Cagliostro' (Nov. 27, 1810), an opéra-comique composed with Dourlen ; and at the Académie, 'Natalie' (three acts, July 30, 1816), and 'Sapho' (Dec. 16, 1822). Each of these works contains music worthy of respect, but they had not sufficient dramatic effect to take with the public.

Reicha's reputation rests on his chamber-music, and on his theoretical works. Of the former the following deserve mention : a diecetto for five strings and five wind instruments ; an octet for four strings and four wind instruments ; twenty-four quintets for flute, oboe, clarinet, horn and bassoon ; six quintets and twenty quartets for strings ; one quintet for clarinet and strings ; one quartet for PF., flute, violoncello, and bassoon ; one do. for four flutes ; six do. for flute, violin, tenor, and violoncello ; six string trios ; one trio for three violoncellos ; twenty-four do. for three horns ; six duets for two violins ; twenty-two do. for two flutes ; twelve sonatas for PF. and violin, and a number of sonatas and pieces for PF. solo. He also composed symphonies and overtures. These works are more remarkable for novelty of combination and striking harmonies, than for abundance and charm of ideas. Reicha's faculty for solving musical problems brought him into notice among musicians when he first settled in Paris, and in 1818 he was offered the professorship of counterpoint and fugue at the Conservatoire. Among his pupils there were Boilly, Jelensperger, Bienaimé, Millaut, Lefebvre, Elwart, Pollet, Lecarpentier, Dancla, and others.

His didactic works, all published in Paris, are : Traité de Mélodie, etc. (4to, 1814) ; Cours de composition musicale, etc. (1816) ; Traité de haute composition musicale (first part 1824, second 1826), a sequel to the other two ; and Art du compositeur dramatique, etc. (4to, 1833).

Fétis has criticised his theories severely, and though highly successful in their day, they are now abandoned, but nothing can surpass the clearness and method of his analysis, and those who use his works will always find much to be grateful for. Czerny published a German translation of the Traité de haute composition (Vienna, 1834, four vols. folio), and in his Art d'improviser obviously made use of Reicha's Art de varier—fifty-seven variations on an original theme.

Reicha married a Parisian, was naturalised in 1829, and received the Legion of Honour in 1831. He presented himself several times for election to the Institut before his nomination as Boieldieu's successor in 1835. He only enjoyed his honours a short time, being carried off by inflammation of the lungs, May 28, 1836. His death was deplored by the many friends whom his trustworthy and honourable character had attached to him. A life-like portrait, somewhat spoiled by excessive laudation, is contained in the Notice sur Reicha (Paris, 1837, 8vo), by his pupil Delaire.   G. C.

REICHARDT, ALEXANDER, a tenor singer, was born at Packs, Hungary, April 17, 1825. He received his early instruction in music from an uncle, and made his first appearance at the age of eighteen at the Lemberg theatre as Rodrigo in Rossini's 'Otello.' His success there led him to Vienna, where he was engaged at the Court Opera, and completed his education under Gentiluomo, Catalani, etc. At this time he was much renowned for his singing of the Lieder of Beethoven and Schubert, and was in request at all the soirées ; Prince Esterhazy made him his Kammersänger. In 1846 he made a tournée through Berlin, Hanover, etc., to Paris, returning to Vienna. In 1851 he made his first appearance in England, singing at the Musical Union, May 6, and at the Philharmonic, May 12, at many other concerts, and before Queen Victoria. In the following season he returned and sang in Berlioz's 'Romeo and Juliet,' at the new Philharmonic Concert of April 14, also in the Choral Symphony, Berlioz's 'Faust,' and the 'Walpurgisnight,' and enjoyed a very great popularity. From this time until 1857 he passed each season in England, singing at concerts, and at the Royal Opera, Drury Lane, and Her Majesty's Theatre, where he filled the parts of the Count in 'The Barber of Seville,' Raoul in 'The Huguenots,' Belmont in the 'Seraglio,' Don Ottavio in 'Don Juan,' and Florestan in 'Fidelio.' The last was a very successful impersonation, and in this part he was said 'to have laid the foundation of the popularity which he has so honourably earned and maintained in London.' He also appeared with much success in oratorio. In 1857 he gave his first concert in Paris, in the Salle Erard, and the following sentence from Berlioz's report of the performance will give an idea of his style and voice. 'M. Reichardt is a tenor of the first water—sweet, tender, sympathetic and charming. Almost all his pieces were re-demanded, and he sang them again without a sign of fatigue.' In 1860 he settled in Boulogne, where he died March 14, 1885. After he retired from the active exercise of his profession he was not idle. He organised a Philharmonic Society at Boulogne ; he was President of the Académie Communale de Musique, and his occasional concerts for the benefit of the hospital — where one ward is entitled 'Fondation Reichardt' — were among the chief musical events of the town. Reichardt was a composer as well as a singer. Several of his songs were very popular in their day. G.

REICHARDT, JOHANN FRIEDRICH, composer and writer on music ; son of a musician ; born Nov. 25, 1752, at Königsberg, Prussia. From childhood he showed a great disposition for music, and such intelligence as to interest influential persons, under whose care he was educated and introduced into good society, and thus formed an ideal both of art and of life which he could scarcely have gained had he been brought up among the petty privations of his original position. Unfortunately, the very gifts which enabled him to adopt these high aims, fostered an amount of conceit which often led him into difficulties. His education was more various than precise, music he learned by practice rather than by any real study. His best instrument was the violin, on which he attained considerable proficiency under Veichtner, a pupil of Benda's ; but he was also a good pianist. Theory he learned from the organist Richter. On leaving the university of Königsberg he started on a long tour, ostensibly to see the world before choosing a profession, though he had virtually resolved on becoming a musician. Between 1771 and 1774 he visited Berlin, Leipzig, Dresden, Vienna, Prague, Brunswick, and Hamburg, made the acquaintance of the chief notabilities—musical, literary, and political—in each place, and became himself in some sort a celebrity, after the publication of his impressions in a series of *Vertraute Briefen eines aufmerksamen Reisenden*, in two parts (1774 and 1776). On his return to Königsberg he went into a government office, but hearing of the death of Agricola of Berlin, he applied in person to Frederick the Great for the vacant post of Capellmeister and Courtcomposer, [sending him his opera ' Le feste galanti,'] and though barely twenty - four obtained it in 1776. He at once began to introduce reforms, both in the Italian opera and the court orchestra, and thus excited much opposition from those who were more conservative than himself. While thus occupied he was indefatigable as a composer, writer, and conductor. In 1783 he founded the ' Concerts Spirituels ' for the performance of unknown works, vocal and instrumental, which speedily gained a high reputation. He published collections of little - known music, with critical observations, edited newspapers, wrote articles and critiques in other periodicals, and produced

independent works. But enemies, who were many, contrived to annoy him so much in the exercise of his duties, that in 1785 he obtained a long leave of absence, during which he visited London and Paris, and heard Handel's oratorios and Gluck's operas, both of which he heartily admired. In both places he met with great success as composer and conductor, and was popular for his social qualities ; but neither of his two French operas 'Tamerlan' and 'Panthée,' composed for the Académie, was performed. On the death of Frederick the Great (1786) his successor confirmed Reichardt in his office, and he produced several new operas, but his position became more and more disagreeable. His vanity was of a peculiarly offensive kind, and his enemies found a weapon ready to their hand in his avowed sympathy with the doctrines of the French Revolution. The attraction of these views for a buoyant, liberal mind like Reichardt's, always in pursuit of high ideals, and eager for novelty, is obvious enough ; but such ideas are dangerous at court, and after further absence (from 1791) which he spent in Italy, Hamburg, Paris, and elsewhere, he received his dismissal from the Capellmeistership in 1794.[1] He retired to his estate, Giebichenstein, near Halle, and occupied himself with literature and composition, and occasional tours. In 1796 he became inspector of the salt works at Halle. After the death of Frederick William II. he produced a few more operas in Berlin, but made a greater mark with his Singspiele, which are of real importance in the history of German opera. In 1808 he accepted the post of Capellmeister at Cassel to Jerome Bonaparte, refused by Beethoven, but did not occupy it long, as in the same year we find him making a long visit to Vienna. On his return to Giebichenstein he gathered round him a pleasant and cultivated society, and there, in the midst of his friends, he died, June 17, 1814.

Reichardt has been, as a rule, harshly judged ; he was not a mere musician, but rather a combination of musician, litterateur, and man of the world. His overweening personality led him into many difficulties, but as a compensation he was endued with great intelligence, and with an ardent and genuine desire for progress in everything— music, literature, and politics. As a composer his works show cultivation, thought, and honesty: but have not lived, because they want the necessary originality. This is specially true of his instrumental music, which is entirely forgotten. His vocal music, however, is more important, and a good deal of it might well be revived, especially his Singspiele and his Lieder. Mendelssohn was no indulgent critic, but on more than one occasion he speaks of Reichardt with a warmth

1 There was apparently some dissatisfaction with Reichardt's efficiency as a musician as well as with his political opinions, for Mozart's remark that ' the King's band contains great virtuosi, but the effect would be better if the gentlemen played together,' certainly implied a reflection on the conductor. Neither does Reichardt seem to have appreciated Mozart (Jahn's *Mozart*, ii. 410).

which he seldom manifests even towards the greatest masters. He never rested until he had arranged for the performance of Reichardt's Morning Hymn, after Milton, at the Düsseldorf Festival of 1835 ; and his enthusiasm for the composer, and his wrath at those who criticised him, are delightful to read.[1] Years afterwards, when his mind had lost the ardour of youth, and much experience had sobered him, he still retained his fondness for this composer, and few things are more charming than the genial appreciation with which he tells Reichardt's daughter of the effect which her father's songs had had, even when placed in such a dangerous position as between works of Haydn and Mozart, at the Historical Concert at the Gewandhaus in Feb. 1847. It is the simplicity, the naïveté, the national feeling of this true German music that he praises, and the applause with which it was received shows that he was not alone in his appreciation. Amongst Reichardt's numerous works are eight operas; eight Singspiele, including four to Goethe's poems, ' Jery und Bätely,' (1789), ' Erwin und Elmire,' 'Claudine von Villabella,' and ' Lilla ' ; five large vocal works, including Milton's ' Morning Hymn,' translated by Herder, his most important work, in 1835 ; a large number of songs, many of which have passed through several editions, and been published in various collections.

Reichardt's writings show critical acumen, observation, and judgment. Besides the letters previously mentioned, he published—*Das Kunstmagazin*, eight numbers in two vols. (Berlin, 1782 and 1791) ; *Studien für Tonkünstler und Musikfreunde*, a critical and historical periodical with thirty-nine examples (1792) ; *Vertraute Briefe aus Paris*, three parts (1804) ; *Vertraute Briefe auf einer Reise nach Wien*, etc. (1810) ; fragments of autobiography in various newspapers ; and innumerable articles, critiques, etc. The *Briefe* are specially interesting from the copious details they give, not only on the music, but on the politics, literature, and society of the various places he visited. A biography, *J. F. Reichardt, sein Leben und seine musikalische Thätigkeit*, by Herr Schletterer, Capellmeister of the cathedral of Augsburg, is unfinished, two volumes only having been published at Augsburg in 1865. [For list of compositions and writings, see the *Quellen-Lexikon*.]   A. M.

REICHER-KINDERMANN, HEDWIG, the daughter of the celebrated baritone, Kindermann (*q.v.*), was born, July 15, 1853, at Munich. She was taught the piano first by her mother, and at the School of Music, but abandoned the same in favour of singing, on the advice of Franz Wüllner. She received her vocal instruction from her father, and made her début at the Munich Opera as one of the boys in the ' Meistersinger,' and next played small parts in the opera, drama, and ballet, besides singing in the chorus, in order to gain experience. She sang the alto part in Franz Lachner's Requiem at Leipzig in 1871 with such success that she became engaged at Carlsruhe. She played ' as guest ' at Berlin as Pamina, June 5, and Agathe, June 9, 1874 ; she then returned to Munich, and sang Daniel in Handel's ' Belshazzar,' April 14, 1875. Soon after she married Emanuel Reicher, an actor at the Gärtnerplatz theatre, and for a time sang there in opéra bouffe, but returned to opera and played Grimgerde in the 1st Cycle, and Erda in the 2nd Cycle, at Bayreuth in 1876. She next played at Hamburg, Vienna (where she appeared as Leah on the production of Rubinstein's ' Maccabees '), and again at Munich. Having received instruction for the purpose from Faure and Jules Cohen at Paris, she sang in French at Monte Carlo in 1880 with such success that she received an offer to sing at La Scala, Milan, but declined it in favour of an engagement under Neumann at Leipzig, where she made her début as Fidelio, May 12, 1880. She became a great favourite, and remained there until 1882. She played in Neumann's company in the Trilogy at Berlin and other German towns, in London, and lastly at Trieste, where she died June 2, 1883. [See Neumann's *Erinnerungen*, etc., 1907.]

She made a great impression at Her Majesty's Theatre as Fricka on the production of ' Rheingold,' May 5, and of ' Walküre,' May 6, 1882, and still more as Brünnhilde in the 2nd Cycle ; ' not only was her magnificent voice equal to all the demands upon it, but her presentation of the character was full of force and of pathos. While no less touching than Frau Vogl in the truthfulness of her expression, she was more heroic and dignified ; the supernatural element was brought into stronger relief . . . in the grand awakening scene her manner was perhaps too coldly dignified and wanting in the impulsiveness which characterises the heroine when she has finally abandoned her supernatural attributes and become a true woman.'[2]   A. C.

REICHMANN, THEODOR, was born at Rostock, March 15, 1849, was taught to sing at first by Mantius, and subsequently by Lamperti in Milan ; he made his début as a baritone at Magdeburg in 1869, and sang at Berlin, Rotterdam, Strasburg (1872), Hamburg (1873), Munich (1875), and was a member of the Court Opera at Vienna in 1882-89. In 1882 he sang the part of Amfortas at Bayreuth for the first time, and was identified with it for some ten years, after which differences with the authorities resulted in his non-appearance there until 1902. In the seasons between 1889 and 1891 he sang in New York, and in the latter year returned to Vienna, becoming once more a member of the Opera Company in 1893. In that year he sang the part of Creon in ' Medea' at an operatic festival at Gotha.

He appeared in London at Covent Garden in 1884, and at Drury Lane and Covent Garden in 1892, singing the parts of Wotan, Hans Sachs, Flying Dutchman, Pizarro, and the Trompeter von Säkkingen. He was far more popular in Germany than in England, where he had to stand comparisons with voices of far more beautiful quality than his. He died at Marbach, on the Lake of Constance, May 22, 1903.   M.

REID, GENERAL JOHN, [born Feb. 13, 1721, was the son of Alexander Robertson of Straloch, Perthshire, was educated at Edinburgh University, and entered Lord Loudoun's regiment of Highlanders in 1745. He subsequently adopted the surname by which he is known. After the quelling of the Jacobite rebellion, he saw active service in Flanders, Martinique, Havanna, and North America. He was in the 42nd Highlanders in 1751-70, was promoted colonel in 1777 and major-general in 1781. In 1794 he became colonel of the 88th foot, and general in 1798, dying in London, Feb. 6, 1807, possessed of a fortune of £50,000.] By his will, made in 1803, he directed his trustees, in the event of his daughter dying without issue, to found a Professorship of Music in the University of Edinburgh, ' for the purpose also, after completing such endowment as hereinafter is mentioned, of making additions to the library of the said University, or otherwise promoting the general interest and advantage of the University in such . . . manner as the Principal and Professors . . . shall . . . think most fit and proper.' In a codicil, dated 1806, he adds —' After the decease of my daughter . . . I have left all my property . . . to the College of Edinburgh where I had my education . . . and as I leave all my music books to the Professor of Music in that College, it is my wish that in every year after his appointment he will cause a concert of music to be performed on the 13th of February, being my birthday.' He also directed that at this annual ' Reid Concert' some pieces of his own composition should be performed ' by a select band.'

When by the death of General Reid's daughter in 1838 some £70,000 became available, it seems to have been handed over to the University authorities without sufficient attention to the italicised portion of the following instruction in the will: ' that . . . my said Trustees . . . shall and do, *by such instrument or instruments as may be required by the law of Scotland* make over the residue of my . . . personal estate to the Principal and Professors of the said University.' And as no particular sum was specified for foundation and maintenance of the Chair of Music, considerable latitude being allowed to the discretion of the University authorities, the secondary object of the bequest received far greater care and attention than the primary one, and for years the Chair was starved. [On the history of the professorship, see vol. iii. p. 816.] In 1851, anticipating Professor Donaldson's intention of petitioning Parliament, the Edinburgh Town Council, as ' Patrons' of the University, raised an action against the Principal and Professors for alleged mismanagement and misappropriation of the Reid Fund. A long litigation followed, and by decree of the Court of Session in 1855 the University authorities were ordered to devote certain sums to the purchase of a site, and the erection of a building for the Class of music. The class-room and its organ were built in 1861, and the Professor's salary—which had been fixed at the very lowest sum suggested by the founder, viz. £300—as well as the grant for the concert, were slightly raised, and a sum set apart, by order of the Court, for expenses of class-room, assistants, instruments, etc. H. S. O.; with additions from *Dict. Nat. Biog.*

REID CONCERTS. These concerts passed through vicissitudes almost as unfortunate as those to which the Reid Professorship was subjected. The earliest concerts under Professors Thomson and Bishop, considering the then musical taste of Scotland, were not unworthy of General Reid's munificent bequest. The £200 allowed out of the Reid Fund was wholly inadequate to the cost of a grand concert 400 miles from London. The Senate therefore decided that, besides this grant, all the tickets should be sold, and that the proceeds should assist Professor Thomson in giving a fine concert; and the following note was printed in the first Reid Concert Book [1] in 1841 :—' The Professors desire it to be understood that the whole of these sums '—*i.e.* the grant and the proceeds— ' is to be expended on the concert ; and that in order to apply as large a fund as possible for the purpose, they have not reserved any right of entry for their families or friends.'

This system was continued by Sir H. R. Bishop, and in 1842 and 1843 the sale of tickets enabled him to give concerts which were at least creditable for the time and place.

Upon Professor Donaldson's accession a plan was initiated by him which proved most unfortunate. He altered the system of admission by payment to that of invitation to the whole audience ; and in consequence the Reid Concerts began to decline, and became an annual source of vexation to the University, public, and Professor. The grant, which under legal pressure afterwards seems to have been raised to £300, was then only £200, and therefore not only was it impossible to give an adequate concert without loss, but the distribution of free tickets naturally caused jealousies and heartburnings to ' town and gown,' and the Reid Concert became a byword and the hall in which it was held a bear-garden. Matters seem to have culminated

[1] Remarkable as the first programme issued in Great Britain with analytical notes.

in 1865, when a large number of students, who thought that they had a right of entry, broke into the concert-hall.

Such was the state of things on Professor Oakeley's appointment in 1865. Finding it impossible, after twenty years, to return to the original system of Thomson and Bishop, he made a compromise, by giving free admissions to the Professors, the University Court, the students in their fourth year at college, and a few leading musicians in the city, and admitting the rest of the audience by payment. From this date a new era dawned on the Reid Concerts; the university and the city were satisfied, and the standard of performance at once rose.

In 1867 the engagement of Manns and of a few of the Crystal Palace orchestra produced very good results.

In 1869 Hallé and his band were engaged, and the demand for tickets soon became so great that the Professor organised two supplementary performances on the same scale as the 'Reid,' and thus, from concerts which on some occasions seem to have been a mere performance of ballads and operatic music by a starring party, the Reid Concert grew into the 'Edinburgh Orchestral,' or 'Reid Festival,' which in turn was converted into the series of historical concerts described in vol. iii. p. 816. The Scottish Universities Commission abolished the 'Reid Concert' itself, about 1893.   G.

REIMANN, IGNAZ (born Dec. 27, 1820, at Albendorf in the district of Glatz, died June 17, 1885), became principal teacher and choirmaster at Rengersdorf in Silesia, having been a pupil of the Breslau Seminary. He was an excessively diligent and fluent composer of church music, and wrote no fewer than 74 masses, of which only 18 were published, 24 Requiems (4 published), 4 Te Deums (3 published), 37 Litanies, 4 Oratorios, 83 Offertories (48 published), 50 Gradualien (40 published), besides many burial-songs, wedding cantatas, Salves, Aves, etc., and 9 overtures, and other instrumental works.

HEINRICH (son of the above) was born March 14, 1850, at Rengersdorf, and received musical instruction from his father. He passed the Gymnasium at Glatz, and studied philology at Breslau from 1870 to 1874, graduated the following year, and taught at the gymnasia of Strehlen, Wohlau, Berlin, Ratibor, and Glatz, for a year in each place successively, till in 1885 he became director of that at Gleiwitz, in Upper Silesia. There he quarrelled with the authorities, threw up his post, embraced the Protestant faith, and thenceforth devoted himself entirely to music. As a schoolboy (Gymnasiast) he had already conducted an orchestral and choral society, and had composed church and chamber music, and as a student had led the academical singing-club (Gesangverein), 'Leopoldina,' studying incidentally with Moritz

Brosig; had founded and directed a musical society at Ratibor, which performed oratorios, etc., under him, and had become known during 1879 and 1880 as musical reporter to the *Schlesicher Zeitung*, and by other literary works (*Nomos*, 1882 ; *Prosodics*, 1885-86). After he definitely took to music, he published some vocal and organ compositions (sonatas, studies, etc.), and a biography of Schumann, which was published by Peters in 1887, and in that year he moved to Berlin to act as musical critic for the *Allgemeine Musikalische Zeitung*. For a time he was occupied at the Royal Library, besides being teacher of organ-playing and theory at the Scharwenka-Klindworth Conservatorium till 1894, and organist of the Philharmonic till 1895, in which year the Kaiser appointed him to the great church in the Augusta-Victoriaplatz, erected to the memory of the Emperor William I., where he enjoyed a great reputation as an organ virtuoso, and directed some of the most magnificent and impressive performances of oratorios, masses, and church music generally, given in any church in Germany. In 1897 he received the title of Professor, and in 1898 founded a Bach Society. He died at Charlottenburg, May 24, 1906.

His compositions include duets for female voices; love scenes in waltz form for four voices; a chorus for four male voices ; an album of children's songs for solo voice; toccata for organ in E minor (op. 23); piano duets ; two wedding songs for bass voice ; arrangements of twenty-five German songs, 'Das deutsche Lied,' of the 14th to the 19th centuries, also for bass voice ; a prelude and triple fugue in D minor for the organ; and ciacona for organ in F minor. His writings are numerous, and include a contribution on the theory and history of Byzantine music (1889) ; two volumes of musical retrospects, *Wagneriana-Lisztiana* ; an opening volume to his own collection of lives of celebrated musicians, being the biography of Schumann already mentioned, to which he added those of Bülow and J. S. Bach.   H. V. H.

REIMANN, MATTHIEU (Matthias Reymannus), (born 1544 at Löwenberg, died Oct. 21, 1597, at Prague), was a Doctor of Law and Imperial Councillor under Rudolf II., and wrote two works for the lute; the one entitled 'Noctes musicae' appeared in 1598, and the other, 'Cithara sacra psalmodiae Davidis ad usum testudinis,' in 1603.   H. V. H.

REINACH, SALOMAN (THÉODORE), born June 3, 1860, at St. Germain-en-Laye, was at first educated at the École Normal in that place. His bent was always for languages, and especially for Archæology. His occupation of the post of Conservator (curator) of the Museum of Antiquities at St. Germain—which was both the reward of, and the ever-fresh incentive to, his taste for original research—afforded

CARL HEINRICH CARSTEN REINECKE

him ample opportunities for carrying out his
natural proclivities to investigation and critical
inquiry into the methods of the past. His
works include a Latin Grammar, a Greek Epi-
graphy, a Manual of Classical Philology (2nd
ed., Paris, 1883-84, 2 vols.) and Archæological
researches in Tunis. His editorship of the
Revue des Études Grecques (1888 and following
years) was marked by valuable researches into
the music of ancient Greece, and his translation
of the hymns discovered at Delphi gave rise
to much discussion.　　　　　D. H.

REINAGLE, JOSEPH, senior, said to have been
born near Vienna, and to have served in the
Hungarian army. In 1762 he was at Portsmouth, where his sons were born. By the
influence of the Earl of Kelly, he was appointed
in 1762 trumpeter to the king, presumably in
Scotland, as he appears to have at that time
removed to Edinburgh. See SCHETKY.

ALEXANDER REINAGLE was probably his
eldest son ; he was born in 1756 at Portsmouth.
He accompanied his younger brother, HUGH,
to Lisbon, and after his death, went to America
about 1786, dying at Baltimore, Md., Sept. 21,
1809. His name is attached to ' A Collection
of the most Favourite Scots tunes with Variations
for the Harpsichord by A. Reinagle, London,
printed for and sold by the author,' folio. This
scarce and rudely printed volume is advertised
in Aird's ' Selection,' vol. ii. 1782, and though
bearing ' London ' as an imprint was most likely
issued from Glasgow.

The second son, JOSEPH REINAGLE, junior,
was born at Portsmouth in 1762, and was first
intended for the navy, and next apprenticed to
a working jeweller in Edinburgh. He took up
music as a profession, and studied the French
horn and the trumpet under his father and
subsequently the violoncello under J. G. C.
Schetky, who had married his sister. He
became a noted player at the Edinburgh
concerts, but abandoned the instrument as a
consequence of his brother's superior skill on it,
resuming it after Hugh's death. He became
violin and viola player and leader of the orchestra
at St. Cecilia's Hall, Edinburgh. He came to
London, and was one of the second violins at
the Handel Commemoration in 1784. In the
following year he became associated with Haydn
and Salomon and played at their concerts. Early
in the 19th century he removed to Oxford, and
died there in 1836. His published works
include ' Twenty-four progressive lessons for the
pianoforte ' 1796. ' Duets for the Violoncello '
quartets for strings, besides an *Introduction to the
Art of Playing the Violoncello*, which ran through
several editions. In Gow's ' Fifth Collection
of Strathspey Reels ' are some airs by Mr.
Joseph Reinagle ; one, ' Dumfries Races,' became
well known.

The third son, HUGH, became a proficient
violoncellist, and went to Lisbon for the benefit

of his health in 1784 ; he died there of consumption, March 19, 1785.

ALEXANDER ROBERT REINAGLE, the son of
the younger Joseph, was born at Brighton,
August 21, 1799, and settled with his father in
Oxford, where he became teacher, organist, and a
well-known figure in musical circles. He was
organist of the church of St. Peter in the East.
He composed a number of sacred pieces, including the well-known ' St. Peter ' psalm-tune.
He also wrote and compiled many books of
instruction for the violin and violoncello. He
died at Kidlington near Oxford, April 6, 1877.

His wife, CAROLINE REINAGLE (*née* ORGER)
was born in London in 1818, and married
Reinagle in 1846. She was associated with
her husband as a teacher, and wrote some
technical works for the pianoforte, besides a
concerto, and several chamber compositions.
She also attained some success as a pianist.
She died March 11, 1892.　F. K. ; with additions from *Musical Times*, 1906, pp. 541, 617,
and 683.

REINE DE SABA, LA. See QUEEN OF
SHEBA.

REINE TOPAZE, LA. Opéra-comique in
three acts ; words by Lockroy and Battes, music
by Victor Massé. Produced at the Théâtre
Lyrique, Dec. 27, 1856. In English, as ' Queen
Topaze,' at Her Majesty's Theatre, Dec. 24,
1860.　　　　　G.

REINECKE, CARL HEINRICH CARSTEN, composer, conductor, and performer, director of the
Gewandhaus concerts at Leipzig, the son of a
musician, born June 23, 1824, at Altona, was
from an early age trained by his father, and at
eleven performed in public. As a youth he was
a first-rate orchestral violin-player. At eighteen
he made a concert tour through Sweden and
Denmark, with especial success at Copenhagen.
In 1843 he settled in Leipzig, where he studied
diligently, and eagerly embraced the opportunities for cultivation afforded by the society
of Mendelssohn and Schumann, with a success
which amply shows itself in his music. In
1844 he made a professional tour with
Wasielewski to Riga, returning by Hanover and
Bremen. He was already in the pay of Christian
VIII. of Denmark, and in 1846 he again visited
Copenhagen, remaining there for two years.
On both occasions he was appointed court-pianist.
In 1851 he went with the violinist Otto von
Königslöw to Italy and Paris ; and on his
return Hiller secured him for the professorship
of the piano and counterpoint in the Conserva-
torium of Cologne. In 1854 he became conductor
of the Concertgesellschaft at Barmen, and in
1859 Musikdirector to the University of Breslau.
On Julius Rietz's departure from Leipzig to
Dresden in 1860 Reinecke succeeded him as
conductor at the Gewandhaus, and became at
the same time professor of composition in the
Conservatorium. Between the years 1867 and

1872 he made extensive tours ; in England
he played at the Musical Union, Crystal Palace,
and Philharmonic, on the 6th, 17th, and 19th
of April, 1869, respectively, and met with great
success both as a virtuoso and a composer. He
reappeared in this country in 1872, and was
equally well received. [In 1895 he resigned
the post of conductor of the Gewandhaus
concerts, but kept his position in the Conservatorium, being appointed in 1897 director of
musical studies until 1902, when he retired
altogether.]

Reinecke's industry in composition is great,
his best works, as might be expected, being those
for piano ; his three PF. sonatas indeed are excellent compositions, carrying out Mendelssohn's
technique without indulging the eccentricities of
modern virtuosi; his pieces for two PFs. are also
good ; his PF. Concerto in F$\sharp$ minor, a well-
established favourite both with musicians and
the public, was followed by two others in E
minor and C respectively. Besides other instrumental music—a wind octet, quintets, four string
quartets, seven trios, concertos for violin and
violoncello, etc.—he has composed an opera in
five acts, 'König Manfred,' and two in one act
each, ' Der vierjährigen Posten ' (after Körner)
and ' Ein Abenteuer Händel's ' ; 'Auf hohen
Befehl' (1886), and 'Der Gouverneur von Tours'
(1891) ; incidental music to Schiller's 'Tell ' ;
an oratorio, ' Belsazar' ; cantatas for men's voices
' Hakon Jarl ' and ' Die Flucht nach Aegypten ' ;
overtures, 'Dame Kobold,' 'Aladdin,' 'Friedensfeier,' an overture, ' Zenobia,' and a funeral march
for the Emperor Frederick (op. 200) ; two
masses, and three symphonies, (op. 79 in A,
op. 134 in C minor, and op. 227 in G minor) ;
and a large number of songs and of pianoforte
pieces in all styles, including valuable studies
and educational works. Of his settings of fairy
tales as cantatas for female voices, ' Schnee-
wittchen,' ' Dornröschen,' ' Aschenbrödel,' and
several others are very popular. His style
is refined, his mastery over counterpoint and
form is absolute, and he writes with peculiar
clearness and correctness. He has also done
much editing for Breitkopf's house. His
position at Leipzig speaks for his ability as a
conductor ; as a pianist (especially in Mozart)
he kept up a high position for many years ; as
an accompanist he is first-rate ; and as an
arranger for the pianoforte he is recognised as
one of the first of the day. Various contributions to musical literature will be found
enumerated in Riemann's *Lexikon*. [See also
E. Segnitz, *Carl Reinecke*.]　　　　　　F. G.

REINER, JACOB, born about 1559 or 1560
at Altdorf in Würtemberg, was brought up at
the Benedictine Monastery of Weingarten, where
he also received his first musical training. We
have it on his own authority that he was afterwards a pupil of Orlando Lassus at Munich,
where his first publication, a volume of

Motets *a* 5-6, appeared in 1579. Incidentally
it may be mentioned that in 1589 Lassus dedicated a book of six masses, the eighth volume
of the *Patrocinium Musices*, to the Abbot of
Weingarten. Reiner himself returned to Weingarten, and from at least 1586 to his death on
August 12, 1606, was engaged as lay singer and
choir-master to the monastery. His publications are fairly numerous, and consist of several
volumes of motets, masses, and magnificats, which
need not here be specified in detail, especially
since part-books are frequently missing, also
two volumes of German songs *a* 3-5. Three
settings *a* 5 of the Passion exist in MS., of a
similar character to those by Lassus. The first
volume of Reiner's Motets was reproduced in
lithograph score by Ottomar Dresel in 1872,
and one of the numbers also appears in the
supplement to Proske's ' Musica Divina,' edited
by F. X. Haberl in 1876.　　　　　J. R. M.

REINHOLD, HUGO, born March 3, 1854, in
Vienna, was a choir-boy of the Hofkapelle of his
native city and a pupil of the Conservatorium
der Musikfreunde till 1874, where he worked
with Bruckner, Dessoff, and Epstein under the
endowment of the Duke of Saxe-Coburg and
Gotha, and obtained a silver medal. He has
presented various compositions, numbering up
to op. 59, to the public, including piano
music and songs, a string quartet (op. 18 in A
major), a suite in five movements for piano and
strings, and a Prelude, Minuet, and Fugue for
stringed orchestra. The two latter were performed at the Vienna Philharmonic Concerts of
Dec. 9, 1877, and Nov. 17, 1878, respectively,
and were praised by the Vienna critic of the
Monthly Musical Record for their delicate character and absence of undue pretension. The
quartet was executed by Hellmesberger. H. V. H.

REINHOLD, THEODOR CHRISTLIEB, born in
1682, died in 1755, was the teacher of Johann
Adolf Hiller (Hüller), the composer of numerous
motets, and cantor of the Kreuzkirche at Dresden
from 1720 till his death.　　　　　H. V. H.

REINHOLD, THOMAS, born at Dresden about
1690, was the reputed nephew, or, as some said,
son, of the Archbishop of that city. He had an
early passion for music, and having met Handel
at the Archbishop's residence conceived so
strong a liking for him that after a time he
quitted his abode and sought out the great composer in London, where he appeared in various
works of Handel's, after making his first appearance in July 1731 at the Haymarket Theatre
as a singer in ' The Grub Street Opera.' He
died in Chapel Street, Soho, in 1751.

His son, CHARLES FREDERICK, born in 1737,
received his musical education first in St. Paul's
and afterwards in the Chapel Royal. On Feb. 3,
1755, he made his first appearance on the stage
at Drury Lane as Oberon in J. C. Smith's opera,
' The Fairies,' being announced as ' Master
Reinhold.' He afterwards became organist of

St. George the Martyr, Bloomsbury. In 1759
he appeared as a bass singer at Marylebone
Gardens, where he continued to sing for many
seasons. He afterwards performed in English
operas, and sang in oratorios, and at provincial
festivals, etc. He was especially famed for
his singing of Handel's song, 'O ruddier than
the cherry.' He was one of the principal
bass singers at the Commemoration of Handel
in 1784. He retired in 1797, and died in
Somers Town, Sept. 29, 1815. See *Musical
Times*, 1877, p. 273.   W. H. H.

REINKEN, JOHANN ADAM, or JAN ADAMS
REINCKEN, eminent organist, born at Wils-
hausen in Lower Alsace, April 27, 1623, a
pupil of Heinrich Scheidemann, became in
1654 organist of the church of St. Catherine at
Hamburg, and retained the post till his death,
Nov. 24, 1722, at the age of ninety-nine. He
was a person of some consideration at Hamburg,
both on account of his fine playing, and of his
beneficial influence on music in general, and
the Hamburg opera in particular, but his vanity
and jealousy of his brother artists are severely
commented on by his contemporaries. So great
and so widespread was his reputation that Sebastian Bach frequently walked to Hamburg from
Lüneburg (1700 to 1703), and Cöthen (1720),
to hear him play. Reinken may be considered
the best representative of the North-German
school of organists of the 17th century, whose
strong points were, not the classic placidity of
the South-German school, but great dexterity
of foot and finger, and ingenious combinations
of the stops. His compositions are loaded with
passages for display, and are defective in form,
both in individual melodies and general construction. His works are very scarce ; ' Hortus
Musicus,' for two violins, viol da gamba and
bass (Hamburg, 1704) is reprinted as No.
XIII. of the publications of the Maatschappij
tot bevordering der Toonkunst (Amsterdam,
1887). No. XIV. of the same publication consists of Reinken's 'Partite Diverse' (variations),
but even in MS. only very few pieces are
known—two on Chorales, one Toccata, and
two sets of Variations (for Clavier).[1] Of the
first of these, one—on the chorale ' An Wasser-
flüssen Babylons' — is specially interesting,
because it was by an extempore performance on
that chorale at Hamburg in 1720 that Bach
extorted from the venerable Reinken the words,
' I thought that this art was dead, but I see
that it still lives in you.' Two organ fugues,
a toccata in G, Variations on chorales and on a
'ballet,' etc. are in MSS. at Dresden, Leipzig, and
Darmstadt. (See the *Tijdschrift* of the Vereeniging voor N.-Nederlands Muziekgeschiedenis, vi.
pp. 151-8, the *Quellen-Lexikon*, etc.) A. M.

REINTHALER, KARL MARTIN, conductor
of the Private Concerts at Bremen, born Oct.
13, 1822, at Erfurt, was early trained in music

[1] Spitta's *Bach*, Engl. transl. i. 197-9.

by G. A. Ritter, then studied theology in
Berlin, but after passing his examination, devoted himself entirely to music, and studied
with A. B. Marx. His first attempts at
composition, some psalms sung by the Cathedral
choir, attracted the attention of King Frederick
William IV., and procured him a travelling
grant. He visited Paris, Milan, Rome, and
Naples, taking lessons in singing from Geraldi
and Bordogni. On his return in 1853 he
obtained a post in the Conservatorium of
Cologne, and in 1858 became organist in the
Cathedral of Bremen, and conductor of the
Singakademie. He had already composed an
oratorio, ' Jephta' (performed in London by
Hullah, April 16, 1856, and published with
English text by Novellos), and in 1875 his
opera ' Edda' was played with success at
Bremen, Hanover, and elsewhere. His
'Bismarck-hymn' obtained the prize at Dort-
mund, and he composed a symphony, and
a large number of part-songs. [He was a
member of the Berlin Academy from 1882,
and had the title of Royal Professor in 1888.
His cantata ' In der Wüste' had a great success,
and his opera 'Käthchen von Heilbronn' received a prize at Frankfort. He retired from
the Singakademie in 1890, and died at Bremen,
Feb. 13, 1896.]   F. G.

REISSIGER, KARL GOTTLIEB, son of Christian Gottlieb Reissiger, who published three
symphonies for full orchestra in 1790. Born
Jan. 31, 1798, at Belzig near Wittenberg,
where his father was Cantor, he became in
1811 a pupil of Schicht at the Thomasschule, Leipzig. In 1818 he removed to the
University with the intention of studying
theology, but some motets composed in 1815
and 1816 had already attracted attention, and
the success of his fine baritone voice made him
determine to devote himself to music. In
1821, he went to Vienna and studied opera
thoroughly. Here also he composed 'Das
Rockenweibchen.' In 1822 he sang an aria of
Handel's, and played a PF. concerto of his own
composition at a concert in the Kärnthnerthor
theatre. Soon after he went to Munich, where
he studied with Peter Winter, and composed
an opera. 'Dido,' which was performed several
times at Dresden under Weber's conductorship.
At the joint expense of the Prussian government
and of his patron von Altenstein, a musician,
he undertook a tour in 1824 through Holland,
France, and Italy, in order to report on the
condition of music in those countries. On his
return he was commissioned to draw up a
scheme for a Prussian national Conservatorium,
but at the same time was offered posts at the
Hague and at Dresden. The latter he accepted,
replacing Marschner at the opera, where he
laboured hard, producing both German and
Italian operas. In 1827 he succeeded C. M.
von Weber as conductor of the German Opera

at Dresden. Among his operas, 'Ahnenschatz' (1824), 'Libella,' 'Turandot,' 'Adèle de Foix,' and 'Der Schiffbruch von Medusa,' had great success in their day, but the term 'Capellmeistermusik' eminently describes them, and they have almost entirely disappeared. The overture to the 'Felsenmühle,' a spirited and not uninteresting piece, was occasionally played. Masses and church music [an oratorio, 'David '], a few Lieder, numerous chamber compositions, particularly some graceful and easy trios for PF. violin and violoncello, made his name very popular for a period. He is generally supposed to have been the composer of the piece known as 'Weber's Last Waltz.' Reissiger died Nov. 7, 1859, and was succeeded at Dresden by Julius Rietz.   F. G.

REISSMANN, August, musician and writer on music, born Nov. 14, 1825, at Frankenstein, Silesia, was grounded in music by Jung, the Cantor of his native town. In 1843 he removed to Breslau, and there had instruction from Mosewius, Baumgart, Ernst Richter, Lüstner, and Kahl, in various branches, including pianoforte, organ, violin, and violoncello. He at first proposed to become a composer, but a residence in 1850-52 at Weimar, where he came in contact with the new school of music, changed his plans and drove him to literature. His first book was *Von Bach bis Wagner* (Berlin, 1861) ; rapidly followed by a historical work on the German song, *Das deutsche Lied*, etc. (1861), rewritten as *Geschichte des Deutschen Liedes* (1874). This again was succeeded by his General History of Music—*Allg. Geschichte der Musik* (3 vols. 1864, Leipzig), with a great number of interesting examples ; *Allg. Musiklehre* (1864) ; and *Lehrbuch der musik. Kompositionen* (3 vols. Berlin, 1866-71). His later works were of a biographical nature, attempts to show the gradual development of the life and genius of the chief musicians—Schumann (1865), Mendelssohn (1867), Schubert (1873), Haydn (1879), Bach (1881), Handel (1882), Gluck (1882), Weber (1883). In 1877 he published a volume of lectures on the history of music, delivered in the Conservatorium of Berlin, where he resided from 1863. His chief employment from 1871 was the completion of the *Musik Conversationslexikon*, in which he succeeded Mendel as editor, after the death of the latter. The 11th volume, completing the work, appeared in 1879, and it will long remain as the most comprehensive lexicon of music. Dr. Reissmann unfortunately thought it necessary to oppose the establishment of the Hochschule in 1875, and to enforce his opposition by a bitter pamphlet, which, however, has long since been forgotten. Many treatises on musical education were written in the later part of his life. As a practical musician Dr. Reissmann was almost as industrious as he was in literature. The operas, 'Gudrun' (Leipzig, 1871), 'Die Bür-

germeisterin von Schorndorf' (Leipzig, 1880), and 'Das Gralspiel' (Düsseldorf, 1895), a ballet, 'Der Blumen Rache' (1887), a work for singing and speaking soloists, with choir and piano, 'König Drosselbart' (1886), dramatic scenas, an oratorio, 'Wittekind' (1888), a concerto and a suite for solo violin and orchestra ; two sonatas for pianoforte and violin ; and a great quantity of miscellaneous pieces for piano solo and for the voice are mentioned. In 1881 he edited an Illustrated History of German music. [He died in Berlin, Dec. 1, 1903.]   G.

RELATION is a general term implying connection between two or more objects of consideration, through points of similarity and contrast. In other words, it is the position which such objects appear to occupy when considered with reference to one another. It is defined by its context.

The relations of individual notes to one another may be described in various ways. For instance, they may be connected by belonging to or being prominent members of the diatonic series of any one key, and contrasted in various degrees by the relative positions they occupy in that series. A further simple relation is established by mere proximity, such as may be observed in the relations of grace-notes, appoggiaturas, turns, and shakes to the essential notes which they adorn ; and this is carried so far that notes alien to the harmony and even to the key are freely introduced, and are perfectly intelligible when in close connection with characteristic diatonic notes. The relations of disjunct notes may be found, among other ways, by their belonging to a chord which is easily called to mind ; whence the successive sounding of the constituents of familiar combinations is easily realised as melody ; while melody which is founded upon less obvious relations is not so readily appreciated.

The relations of chords may be either direct or indirect. Thus they may have several notes in common, as in Ex. 1, or only one, as in Ex. 2,

Ex. 1.   Ex. 2.   Ex. 3.

to make simple direct connection, while the diversity of their derivations, or their respective degrees of consonance and dissonance, afford an immediate sense of contrast. Or they may be indirectly connected through an implied chord or note upon which they might both converge ; as the common chord of D to that of C through G, to which D is Dominant, while G in its turn is Dominant to C (Ex. 3). The relation thus established is sufficiently clear to allow the major chord of the supertonic and its minor seventh and major and minor ninth to be systematically affiliated in the key, though its third and minor ninth are not in the diatonic series.

A further illustration of the relations of chords is afforded by those of the Dominant and Tonic. They are connected by their roots being a fifth apart, which is the simplest interval, except the octave, in music; but their other components are entirely distinct, as is the compound tone of the roots, since none of their lower and more characteristic harmonics are coincident. They thus represent the strongest contrast in the diatonic series of a key, and when taken together define the tonality more clearly than any other pair of chords in its range.

The relations of keys are traced in a similar manner; as, for instance, by the tonic and perfect fifth of one being in the diatonic series of another, or by the number of notes which are common to both. The relations of the keys of the minor third and minor sixth to the major mode (as of E♭ and A♭ with reference to C) are rendered intelligible through the minor mode; but the converse does not hold good, for the relations of keys of the major mediant or submediant to the minor mode (as of E minor and A minor with reference to C minor) are decidedly remote, and direct transition to them is not easy to follow. In fact the modulatory tendency of the minor mode is towards the connections of its relative major rather than to those of its actual major, while the outlook of the major mode is free on both sides. The relation of the key of the Dominant to an original Tonic is explicable on much the same grounds as that of the chords of those notes. The Dominant key is generally held to be a very satisfactory complementary or contrast in the construction of a piece of music of any sort, but it is not of universal cogency. For instance, at the very outset of any movement it is almost inevitable that the Dominant harmony should early and emphatically present itself; hence when a fresh section is reached it is sometimes desirable to find another contrast to avoid tautology. With some such purpose the keys of the mediant or submediant have at times been chosen, both of which afford interesting phases of contrast and connection; the connection being mainly the characteristic major third of the original tonic, and the contrast being emphasised by the sharpening of the Dominant in the first case, and of the Tonic in the second. The key of the subdominant is avoided in such cases because the contrast afforded by it is not sufficiently strong to have force in the total impression of the movement.

The relations of the parts of any artistic work are in a similar manner those of contrast within limits of proportion and tonality. For instance, those of the first and second section in what is called ' first movement ' or ' sonata ' form are based on the contrast of complementary tonalities as part of the musical structure, on the one hand; and on contrast of character and style in the idea on the other; which between them establish the balance of proportion. The relation of the second main division—the ' working-out ' section—to the first part of the movement is that of greater complexity and freedom in contrast to regularity and definiteness of musical structure, and fanciful discussion of characteristic portions of the main subjects in contrast to formal exposition of complete ideas; and the final section completes the cycle by returning to regularity in the recapitulation.

The relations of the various movements of a large work to one another are of similar nature. The earliest masters who wrote Suites and Sonate da Camera or da Chiesa had but a rudimentary and undeveloped sense of the relative contrasts of keys; consequently they contented themselves with connecting the movements by putting them all in the same key, and obtained their contrasts by alternating quick and slow movements or dances, and by varying the degrees of their seriousness or liveliness: but the main outlines of the distribution of contrasts are in these respects curiously similar to the order adopted in the average modern Sonata or Symphony. Thus they placed an allegro of a serious or solid character at or near the beginning of the work, as typified by the Allemande; the slow or solemn movement came in the middle, as typified by the Sarabande; and the conclusion was a light and gay quick movement, as typified by the Gigue. And further, the manner in which a Courante usually followed the Allemande, and a Gavotte or Bourrée or Passepied, or some such dance, preceded the final Gigue, has its counterpart in the Minuet or Scherzo of a modern work, which occupies an analogous position with respect either to the slow or last movement. In modern works the force of additional contrast is obtained by putting central movements in different but allied keys to that of the first and last movements; the slow movement most frequently being in the key of the Subdominant. At the same time additional bonds of connection are sometimes obtained, both by making the movements pass without complete break from one to another, and in some cases (illustrated by Beethoven and Schumann especially) by using the same characteristic features or figures in different movements.

The more subtle relations of proportion, both in the matter of the actual length of the various movements and their several sections, and in the breadth of their style; in the congruity of their forms of expression and of the quality of the emotions they appeal to; in the distribution of the qualities of tone, and even of the groups of harmony and rhythm, are all of equal importance, though less easy either to appreciate or to effect, as they demand higher degrees of artistic power and perception; and the proper adjustment of such relations is as vital to operas, oratorios, cantatas, and all other forms of vocal music, as to the purely instrumental forms.

The same order of relations appears in all parts of the art ; for instance, the alternation of discord and concord is the same relation, implying contrast and connection, analogous to the relation between suspense or expectation and its relief ; and, to speak generally, the art of the composer is in a sense the discovery and exposition of intelligible relations in the multifarious material at his command, and a complete explanation of the word would amount to a complete theory of music.   c. h. h. p.

RELATIVE is the word used to express the connection between a major and a minor key which have the same signature ; A minor is the 'relative' minor of C, C the 'relative' major of A minor. In other words, the relative minor of any key is that which has its keynote on the submediant of the major key. The term is used to distinguish this minor key from the other, which is perhaps as closely allied to the major, that which has the same keynote as the major, and is consequently called the 'tonic' minor. The 'tonic' minor of C is C minor, the 'tonic' major of C minor is C ; in this case, the key-signature is of course changed.   M.

RELLSTAB, Johann Karl Friedrich, was born in Berlin, Feb. 27, 1759. His father, a printer, wished him to succeed to the business, but from boyhood his whole thoughts were devoted to music. He was on the point of starting for Hamburg to complete, with Emmanuel Bach, his musical studies begun with Agricola and Fasch, when the death of his father forced him to take up the business. He added a music-printing and publishing branch ; was the first to establish a musical lending library (1783) ; founded a Concert-Society, on the model of Hiller's at Leipzig, and called it 'Concerts for connoisseurs and amateurs,' an unusually distinctive title for those days. The first concert took place April 16, 1787, at the Englisches Haus, and in course of time the following works were performed ; Salieri's 'Armida,' Schulz's 'Athalia,' Naumann's 'Cora,' Hasse's 'Conversione di San Agostino,' Bach's 'Magnificat,' and Gluck's 'Alceste,' which was thus first introduced to Berlin. The Society at last merged in the Singakademie. He wrote musical critiques for the Berlin paper, signed with his initials ; and had concerts every other Sunday during the winter at his own house, at which such works as Haydn's 'Seasons' were performed ; but these meetings were stopped by the entry of the French in 1806, when he frequently had twenty men and a dozen horses quartered on him ; lost not only his music but all his capital, and had to close his printing-press. In time, he resumed his concerts ; in

1809 gave lectures on harmony ; in 1811 travelled to Italy. Not long after his return he was struck with apoplexy while walking at Charlottenburg, August 19, 1813, and was found dead on the road some hours afterwards. As a composer he left three cantatas, a 'Passion,' a Te Deum, and a Mass. Also an opera ; songs too numerous to specify ; vocal scores of Graun's 'Tod Jesu,' and Gluck's 'Iphigénie' ; and a German libretto of Gluck's 'Orphée' apparently from his own pen. Of instrumental music he published—marches for PF., symphonies and overtures ; a series of pieces with characteristic titles, 'Obstinacy,' 'Sensibility,' etc. ; twenty-four short pieces for PF., violin and bass, etc. Also *Versuch über die Vereinigung der mus. und oratorischen Deklamation* (1785) ; *Ueber die Bemerkungen einer Reisenden* . . . (1789) (see Reichardt) ; and *Anleitung für Clavierspieler* (1790). These works, for the most part bibliographical curiosities, are very instructive.

Rellstab had three daughters, of whom Caroline, born April 18, 1794, died Feb. 17, 1813, was a singer, distinguished for her extraordinary compass. His son,

Heinrich Friedrich Ludwig, born April 13, 1799, in Berlin, though delicate in health, and destined for practical music, was compelled by the times to join the army, where he became ensign and lieutenant. In 1816, after the peace, he took lessons on the piano from Ludwig Berger, and in 1819 and 1820 studied theory with Bernhard Klein. At the same time he taught mathematics and history in the Brigade-schule till 1821, when he retired from the army to devote himself to literature, ultimately settling in Berlin (1823). He also composed much part-music for the 'jüngere Liedertafel,' which he founded in conjunction with G. Reichardt in 1819, wrote a libretto, 'Dido,' for B. Klein, and contributed to Marx's *Musikzeitung*. A pamphlet on Madame Sontag (*Henriette, oder die schöne Sängerin*) procured him three months' imprisonment in 1826, on account of its satirical allusions to a well-known diplomatist. In 1826 he joined the staff of the *Vossische Zeitung*, and in a short time completely led the public opinion on music in Berlin. His first article was a report on a performance of 'Euryanthe,' Oct. 31, 1826. Two years later he wrote a cantata for Humboldt's congress of physicists, which Mendelssohn set to music.

Rellstab was a warm supporter of classical music, and strongly condemned all undue attempts at effect. He quarrelled with Spontini over his 'Agnes von Hohenstauffen' (Berlin *Musikalische Zeitung* for 1827, Nos. 23, 24, 26, and 29), and the controversy was maintained with much bitterness until Spontini left Berlin, when Rellstab, in his pamphlet *Ueber mein Verhältniss als Kritiker zu Herrn Spontini*, (1827) acknowledged that he had gone too far.

Rellstab's novels and essays are to be found for the most part in his *Gesammelte Schriften*, 24 vols. (Leipzig, Brockhaus). A musical periodical, *Iris im Gebiet der Tonkunst*, founded by him in 1830, survived till 1842. His recollections of Berger, Schroeder-Devrient, Mendelssohn, Klein, Dehn, and Beethoven (whom he visited in March 1825) will be found in *Aus meinem Leben* (2 vols. Berlin, 1861). He was thoroughly eclectic in his taste for music, and, though not an unconditional supporter, was no opponent of the modern school of Liszt and Wagner. He died during the night of Nov. 27, 1860.   F. G.

REMBT, JOHANN ERNST, was born in 1749 or 1750 at Suhl, in the Thüringer-Wald, where in 1773 he was also appointed organist, and remained till his death on Feb. 26, 1810. He was distinguished as a performer, and, devoting himself to the study of the works of Sebastian Bach, he worthily upheld the more solid traditions of the Bach school of organ-playing against the prevailing shallowness of his time. Messrs. Breitkopf & Härtel still retain in their catalogue some of his works originally published by them, such as his six Fugued Chorale-preludes, six Organ Trios, and various Chorale-preludes in Trio-form. Various Fughettas for the Organ also appear in Volkmar's 'Orgel-Album.'   J. R. M.

REMÉNYI, EDUARD (real name HOFFMANN), a famous violinist, was born in 1830 at Heves (according to another account at Miskolc) in Hungary, and received his musical education at the Vienna Conservatorium during the years 1842-45, where his master on the violin was Joseph Böhm, the famous teacher of Joachim. In 1848 he took an active part in the insurrection, and became adjutant to the famous general Görgey, under whom he took part in the campaign against Austria. After the revolution had been crushed he had to fly the country, and went to America, where he resumed his career as a virtuoso. [The details of his German tour in 1852-53, which indirectly had so great an influence on the career of Brahms, may be read in Florence May's *Life of Brahms*, vol. i. pp. 92-104.] In 1853 he went to Liszt in Weimar, who at once recognised his genius and became his artistic guide and friend. In the following year he came to London and was appointed solo violinist to Queen Victoria. In 1855 he was in America, and in 1860 he obtained his amnesty and returned to Hungary, where some time afterwards he received from the Emperor of Austria a similar distinction to that granted him in England. After his return home he seems to have retired for a time from public life, living chiefly on an estate he owned in Hungary. In 1865 he appeared for the first time in Paris, where he created a perfect furore. Repeated tours in Germany, Holland, and Belgium further spread his fame. In 1875 he settled temporarily in Paris, and in the summer of 1877 came to London, where also he produced a sensational effect in private circles. The season being far advanced he appeared in public only once, at Mapleson's benefit concert at the Crystal Palace, where he played a fantasia on themes from the 'Huguenots.' In the autumn of 1878 he again visited London, and played at the Promenade Concerts. He was on his way to America, where he gave concerts and took up his residence. In 1887 he undertook a tour of the world, in the course of which he appeared in private in London in 1891 and 1893. As an artist he combined perfect mastery over the technical difficulties of his instrument with a strongly pronounced individuality. His soul was in his playing, and his impulse carried him away as he warmed to his task, the impression produced on the audience being accordingly in an ascending scale. Another important feature in Reményi's playing was the national element. He strongly maintained against Liszt the genuineness of Hungarian music, and showed himself thoroughly imbued with that spirit by writing several 'Hungarian melodies,' which have been mistaken for popular tunes and adopted as such by other composers. The same half-Eastern spirit was observable in the strong rhythmical accentuation of Reményi's style, so rarely attained by artists of Teutonic origin. Reményi's compositions are of no importance, being mostly confined to arrangements for his instrument, and other pieces written for his own immediate use. [His name is known to music-lovers in the present day by the circumstance that Brahms went on a tour with him as his accompanist, and was 'discovered' by Joachim in this capacity. Reményi died during a concert at which he was playing at San Francisco, May 15, 1898.]   E. H-A.

REMOTE is a term used in speaking of modulation from one key to another, or in regard to the succession of keys in a work in several movements. A remote key has little in common with the key which may be called the starting-point. Thus a key with many sharps or flats in the signature will probably be very 'remote' from the key of C. In the early days of the harmonic period, the nearest keys to a major key were considered to be its dominant, subdominant, relative and tonic minors; and the nearest to a minor key were its relative and tonic majors, the dominant major, and the subdominant minor. As the art progressed, it was gradually admitted that keys which stood to each other in the relation of a third, whether major or minor, were not to be considered remote from each other. Beethoven, in the piano sonata in C, op. 2, No. 3, puts his slow movement into the key of E major; in op. 106, in B flat, the slow movement is in F sharp minor; and Schubert, in his sonata in the same key, employs C sharp minor for his slow movement ; the connection, in this last instance, is attained by a kind of unconscious mental process, involving a silent modulation through the key of the tonic minor, B flat minor, and its relative major, C sharp major. This is an unusual succession of keys, even with Schubert ; but other examples, quite as strange, are in Beethoven's 'posthumous' quartets, and elsewhere. Of the eleven semitones apart from the keynote, six were now accepted as within the scope of modulation without a long and complex process ; two others, the whole tone above and below the keynote, involve a double modulation, the tone above being the dominant of the dominant, and the tone below being the subdominant of the subdominant. There remain, therefore, three keys which are very remote, the semitone above and below the keynote, and the augmented fourth of the key. Even these are nowadays brought within fairly easy distance, by the fact that for the semitone above, it is only necessary to regard the keynote as the leading-note of the new key ; and for the semitone below, a 'Phrygian cadence' (such as is figured in the last two examples in vol. i. p. 436, column a) may be imagined. The semitone above the keynote is used for the slow movement of Brahms's sonata for violoncello and piano, op. 99, in F, where F sharp major is the key chosen for the slow movement. As transition to the augmented fourth of the key involves several steps of modulation, this may be considered the most remote part of the octave. (It is not quite obvious why minor keys should almost always be remote from other minor keys, but they certainly are, from almost all excepting the key of their subdominant minor. See RELATION.) In relation to any given major keynote, we may recognise four degrees of proximity, besides its relative and tonic minors. In relation to the key of C, the notes F and G stand nearest of all ; next come E flat, E, A flat and A, as standing in the relation of thirds, major or minor ; next, as requiring a double modulation, D and B flat; and farthest of all, C sharp, B, and F sharp, the last being the extreme of remoteness. Before equal temperament was a part of practical music, the inherent error in the scale was confined by tuners to the 'remote' keys, that term being used simply of the keys which had many sharps or flats, leaving the key of C perfectly in tune, and F and G almost perfect.   M.

RÉMY, W. A., the name by which an eminent musician and teacher in Prague preferred to be known. His real name was Wilhelm Mayer, and he was the son of a lawyer in Prague, where he was born, June 10, 1831. A pupil of C. F. Pietsch, he appeared at the age of seventeen years as the composer of an overture to Sue's 'Fanatiker in den Cevennen '; but in obedience to the parental desires, he studied law, took the degree of Dr.Jur. in 1856, and did not take up music as his profession until 1862, when he

became conductor of the Steiermärkische Musïk-verein, and earned experience as an orchestral director. He kept the post till 1870, composing many orchestral works during the period, among them an overture to 'Sardanapalus,' and a symphonic poem, 'Helena,' as well as his first symphony in F. The three works made their way as far as Leipzig, where they were received with great success. From the date of his resignation he lived as an unofficial teacher, and devoted himself to composition, until his death at Prague, Jan. 22, 1898. His works include two more symphonies (in F and E flat), a 'Phantasiestück' for orchestra, given at the Vienna Philharmonic concerts under Dessoff ; a 'Slawische Liederspiel' for solos and chorus, with accompaniment of two pianos, another work of the same kind, 'Oestliche Rosen,' a concert-opera, 'Waldfräulein,' and many songs, etc. Among his most eminent pupils may be mentioned Busoni, Kienzl, Heuberger, von Rezniczek, and Felix Weingartner. (Neue Musik-Zeitung, 1890, p. 261.)   M.

RENAUD, MAURICE ARNOLD, born 1862, at Bordeaux, studied singing at the Conservatoire, Paris, and subsequently at that of Brussels. From 1883 to 1890 he sang at the Monnaie, Brussels, in a variety of parts, making a great impression ; on Jan. 7, 1884, as the High Priest in Reyer's 'Sigurd,' and on Feb. 10, 1890, as Hamilcar in Reyer's 'Salammbô,' on production of these operas ; he also sang baritone or bass parts in 'Manon,' 'Lakmé,' etc., and as Kothner in 'Meistersinger.' On Oct. 12, 1890, he made his début at the Opéra-Comique, Paris, as Karnac in 'Le Roi d'Ys,' and sang on Dec. 3 as the hero of Diaz's new opera 'Benvenuto.' On July 17, 1891, he made a very successful début at the Opéra as Nelusko, and remained there until 1902. On Feb. 29, 1892, he sang the modest part of Leuthold, in 'Tell,' at the Rossini centenary ; he added to his repertory the parts of Telramund, Wolfram, Iago, Beckmesser, Hilperic in Guiraud's 'Frédégonde,' completed by Saint-Saëns, the Shepherd in Bruneau's 'Messidor,' and, on Nov. 15, 1899, Chorèbe in Berlioz's 'Prise de Troie.' On leave of absence, on June 23, 1897, he made his début at Covent Garden as Wolfram and De Nevers in selections from 'Tannhäuser' and 'Huguenots,' at the State performance in honour of the Diamond Jubilee of Queen Victoria ; and in the same season he sang the above parts, Don Juan, and Juan in D'Erlanger's 'Inez Mendo.' He fully confirmed his Parisian reputation by his fine voice and presence, and excellent singing and acting. From 1898 to 1905 he has re-appeared here frequently at the above theatre, singing the part of Henry VIII. in Saint-Saëns's opera, July 19, 1898, that of Hares in De Lara's 'Messaline,' July 13, 1899 ; and appearing as Hamlet, Rigoletto, Valentine, Escamillo, etc. In 1903 M. Renaud sang at the Gaité, in Paris, as Herod in Massenet's 'Hérodiade,' and both there, and at the Opéra-Comique in 1904 as Don Juan, and the Flying Dutchman, always with great success. He sang at Monte Carlo in 1907 in Bruneau's 'Nais Micoulin.'   A. C.

RENCONTRE IMPRÉVUE. See PILGRIME VON MEKKA.

RENDANO, ALFONSO, born April 5, 1853, at Carolei, near Cosenza, studied first at the Conservatorio at Naples, then with Thalberg, and lastly at the Leipzig Conservatorium. He played at the Gewandhaus with marked success on Feb. 8, 1872. He then visited Paris and London, performed at the Musical Union (April 30, 1872), the Philharmonic (March 9, 1873), the Crystal Palace, and other concerts, and much in society ; and after a lengthened stay returned to Italy. He was a graceful and refined player, with a delicate touch, and a great command over the mechanism of the piano. His playing of Bach was especially good. He published some piano pieces of no importance.   G.

REPEAT, REPETIZIONE, REPLICA (Ger. *Wiederholung*; Fr. *Répétition*, which also means 'rehearsal'). In the so-called sonata form, there are certain sections which are repeated, and are either written out in full twice over, or are written only once, with the sign 𝄇 at the end, which shows that the music is to be repeated either from the beginning or from the previous occurrence of the sign. The sections which, according to the strict rule, are repeated, are—the first section of the first movement, both sections of the minuet or scherzo at their first appearance, and both sections of the trio, after which the minuet or scherzo is gone once straight through without repeats. The latter half of the first movement, and the first, or even both, of the sections in the last movement, may be repeated ; see for instance Beethoven's Sonatas, op. 2, No. 2 ; op. 10, No. 2 ; op. 78 ; Schubert's Symphony No. 9. Also, where there is an air and variations, both sections of the air and of all the variations, should, strictly speaking, be repeated. This undoubtedly arose from the facility with which on a good harpsichord the player could vary the qualities of tone, by using different stops ; and there was a tradition that, on that instrument, a change of 'register' should be made at every repetition. Although it is a regular custom not to play the minuet or scherzo, after the trio, with repeats, Beethoven thinks fit to draw attention to the fact that it is to be played straight through, by putting after the trio the words 'Da Capo senza repetizione,' or 'senza replica,' in one or two instances, as in op. 10, No. 3, where, moreover, the trio is not divided into two sections, and is not repeated ; in op. 27, No. 2, where the Allegretto is marked 'La prima parte senza repetizione' (the first part without repeat). In his Fourth and Seventh Symphonies he has

given the trio twice over each time with full repeats.   M.

RÉPÉTITION. (Fr.) REHEARSAL.

REPETITION (PIANOFORTE). The rapid reiteration of a note is called repetition ; a special touch of the player facilitated by mechanical contrivances in the pianoforte action ; the earliest and most important of these having been the invention of SEBASTIAN ERARD. [See the diagram and description of Erard's action under PIANOFORTE, vol. iii. p. 730.] By such a contrivance the hammer, after the delivery of a blow, remains poised, or slightly rises again, so as to allow the hopper to fall back and be ready to give a second impulse to the hammer before the key has nearly recovered its position of rest. The particular advantages of repetition to grand pianos have been widely acknowledged by pianoforte makers, and much ingenuity has been spent in inventing or perfecting repetition actions for them ; in upright pianos, however, the principle has been rarely employed, although its influence has been felt and shown by care in the position of the 'check' in all check action instruments. The French have named the mechanical power to repeat a note rapidly, 'double échappement'; the drawbacks to double escapement—which the repetition really is—are found in increased complexity of mechanism and liability to derangement. These may be overrated, but there always remains the drawback of loss of tone in repeated notes ; the repetition blow being given from a small depth of touch compared with the normal depth, is not so elastic and cannot be delivered with so full a *forte*, or with a *piano* or *pianissimo* of equally telling vibration. Hence, in spite of the great vogue given to repetition effects by Herz and Thalberg, other eminent players have disregarded them, or have even been opposed to repetition touches, as Chopin and von Bülow were ; see p. 7, § 10 of the latter's commentary on selected studies by Chopin (Aibl, Munich, 1880), where he designates double escapement as a 'deplorable innovation.'

A fine example of the best use of repetition is in Thalberg's A minor Study, op. 45—

where the player, using the first two fingers and thumb in rapid succession on each note, produces by these triplets almost the effect of a sustained melody with a tremolo. Repetition is an old device with stringed instruments, having been, according to Bunting, a practice with the Irish harpers, as we know it was with the common dulcimer, the Italian mandoline, and the Spanish bandurria.

A remarkable instance may be quoted of the

F

effectivé use of repetition in the Fugato (piano solo) from Liszt's 'Todtentanz' (Danse Macabre).

But there need be no difficulty in playing this on a well-regulated and checked single escapement. With a double escapement the nicety of checking is not so much required. A. J. H.

REPORTS (the word seems not to be used in the singular), an old English and Scottish term for points of imitation. From the eight examples in the Scottish Psalter of 1635 (reprinted in the Rev. Neil Livingston's edition, 1864) it would seem that the term was used in a more general sense, of a setting of certain tunes in which the parts moved in a kind of free polyphony, not in strictly imitative style. In Purcell's revision of the treatise which appears in the third part of Playford's *Introduction to the Skill of Musick* (twelfth edition, 1694), the term is mentioned but not explained, further than as being synonymous with 'imitation' : 'The second is *Imitation* or *Reports*, which needs no Example.' (See *Sammelbände* of the *Int. Mus. Ges.* vi. p. 562.) M.

REPRISE, repetition ; a term which is occasionally applied to any repetition in music, but is most conveniently confined to the recurrence of the first subject of a movement after the conclusion of the working out or *Durchführung*. [In Couperin, Rameau, and other French composers, the term is used of a short refrain at the end of a movement, which was probably intended to be played over more than twice, as sometimes it contains the ordinary marks of repetition within the passage covered by the word.] G.

REQUIEM (Lat. *Missa pro Defunctis* ; Ital. *Messa per i Defunti* ; Fr. *Messe des Morts* ; Germ. *Todtenmesse*). A solemn Mass, sung annually, in Commemoration of the Faithful Departed, on All Souls' Day (Nov. 2) ; and, with a less general intention, at funeral services, on the anniversaries of the decease of particular persons, and on such other occasions as may be dictated by feelings of public respect or individual piety.

The Requiem takes its name [1] from the first word of the Introit—'Requiem aeternam dona eis, Domine.' When set to music, it naturally arranges itself in nine principal sections : (1) The Introit— 'Requiem aeternam' ; (2) the 'Kyrie'; (3) the Gradual, and Tract—'Requiem aeternam,' and 'Absolve, Domine' ; (4) The Sequence or Prose—'Dies irae' ; (5) The Offertorium—'Domine Jesu Christi' ; (6) the Sanc-

tus' ; (7) the 'Benedictus'; (8) the 'Agnus Dei' ; and (9) the Communio—'Lux aeterna.' To these are sometimes added (10) the Responsorium, 'Libera me,' which, though not an integral portion of the Mass, immediately follows it, on all solemn occasions ; and (11) the Lectio —'Taedet animam meam,' of which we possess at least one example of great historical interest.

The Plain-song Melodies adapted to the nine divisions of the mass will be found in the Gradual, together with that proper for the Responsorium. The Lectio, which really belongs to a different Service, has no proper Melody, but is sung to the ordinary 'Tonus Lectionis.' [See INFLEXION.] The entire series of Melodies is of rare beauty, and produces so solemn an effect, when sung in unison by a large body of grave equal voices, that most of the great polyphonic composers have employed its phrases more freely than usual, in their Requiem Masses, either as Canti fermi, or in the form of unisonous passages interposed between the harmonised portions of the work. Compositions of this kind are not very numerous ; but most of the examples we possess must be classed among the most perfect productions of their respective authors.

Palestrina's 'Missa pro Defunctis,' for five voices, first printed at Rome in 1591, in the form of a supplement to the Third Edition of his 'First Book of Masses,' was reproduced in 1841 by Alfieri, in the first volume of his 'Raccolta di Musica Sacra' ; again, by Lafage [2] in a valuable 8vo volume, entitled 'Cinq Messes de Palestrina' ; and by the Prince de la Moskowa in the 9th volume of his collection [see vol. iii. p. 271], and has since been included by Messrs. Breitkopf & Härtel, of Leipzig, in their complete edition. This beautiful work is, unhappily, very incomplete, consisting only of the 'Kyrie,' the 'Offertorium,' the 'Sanctus,' the 'Benedictus,' and the 'Agnus Dei.' We must not, however, suppose that the composer left his work unfinished. It was clearly his intention that the remaining movements should be sung, in accordance with a custom still common at Roman funerals, in unisonous plain-song ; and, as a fitting conclusion to the whole, he has left us two settings of the 'Libera me,' in both of which the Gregorian melody is treated with an indescribable intensity of pathos. [3] One of these is preserved in MS. among the archives of the Pontifical Chapel, and the other, among those of the Lateran Basilica. After a careful comparison of the two, Baini arrived at the conclusion that that belonging to the Sistine Chapel must have been composed very nearly at the same time as, and probably as an adjunct to, the five printed movements, which are also founded, more or less closely, upon the original Canti fermi, and so constructed as to bring their

<hr />

[1] That is to say, its name as a special Mass. The Music of the ordinary Polyphonic Mass always bears the name of the Canto fermo on which it is founded.

[2] Paris, Launer et Cie.; London, Schott & Co.
[3] See Alfieri, *Raccolta di Musica Sacra*, tom. vii.

characteristic beauties into the highest possible relief—in no case, perhaps, with more touching effect than in the opening 'Kyrie,' the first few bars of which will be found at vol. ii. p. 613.

Next in importance to Palestrina's Requiem is a very grand one, for six voices, composed by Vittoria for the funeral of the Empress Maria, widow of Maximilian II. This fine work— undoubtedly the greatest triumph of Vittoria's genius—comprises all the chief divisions of the Mass, except the Sequence, together with the Responsorium and Lectio, and brings the plain-song subjects into prominent relief throughout. It was first published at Madrid in 1605—the year of its production. In 1869 the Lectio was reprinted at Ratisbon, by Joseph Schrems, in continuation of Proske's 'Musica Divina.' A later issue of the same valuable collection contains the Mass and Responsorium. The original volume contains one more movement—'Versa est in luctum'—which has never been reproduced in modern notation; but, as this has now no place in the Roman Funeral Service, its omission is not so much to be regretted.

Some other very fine Masses for the Dead, by Francesco Anerio, Orazio Vecchi, and Giov. Matt. Asola, are included in the same collection, together with a somewhat pretentious work by Pitoni, which scarcely deserves the enthusiastic eulogium bestowed upon it by Dr. Proske. A far finer composition, of nearly similar date, is Colonna's massive Requiem for eight voices, first printed at Bologna in 1684— a copy of which is preserved in the Library of the Royal College of Music.

Several modern Requiem Masses have become very celebrated.

(1.) The history of Mozart's last work is surrounded by mysteries which render it scarcely less interesting to the general reader than the music itself is to the student. (See vol. iii. p. 308 ff.)

(2.) For Gossec's 'Messe des Morts' see vol. ii. p. 203.

(3.) Next in importance to Mozart's immortal work are the two great Requiem Masses of Cherubini. The first of these, in C minor, was written for the Anniversary of the death of King Louis XVI. (Jan. 21, 1793), and first sung on that occasion at the Abbey Church of Saint-Denis in 1817; after which it was not again heard until Feb. 14, 1820, when it was repeated in the same church at the funeral of the Duc de Berri. Berlioz regarded this as Cherubini's greatest work. It is undoubtedly full of beauties. Its general tone is one of extreme mournfulness, pervaded throughout by deep religious feeling. Except in the 'Dies irae' and 'Sanctus' this style is never exchanged for a more excited one; and, even then, the treatment can scarcely be called dramatic. The deep pathos of the little movement, inter-

posed after the last 'Osanna,' to fulfil the usual office of the 'Benedictus'—which is here incorporated with the 'Sanctus'—exhibits the composer's power of appealing to the feelings in its most affecting light.

The second Requiem, in D minor, for three male voices is in many respects a greater work than the first; though the dramatic element pervades it so freely that its character as a religious service is sometimes entirely lost. It was completed on Sept. 24, 1836, a few days after the composer had entered his seventy-seventh year; and, with the exception of the sixth quartet and the quintet in E minor, was his last important work. The 'Dies irae' was first sung at the concert of the Conservatoire, March 19, 1837, and repeated on the 24th of the same month. On March 25, 1838, the work was sung throughout. In the January of that year Mendelssohn had already recommended it to the notice of the committee of the Lower Rhine Festival; and in 1872 and 1873 it was sung as a funeral service in the Roman Catholic Chapel, in Farm Street, London. It is doubtful whether Cherubini's genius ever shone to greater advantage than in this gigantic work. Every movement is full of interest; and the 'whirlwind of sound' which ushers in the 'Dies irae' produces an effect which, once heard, can never be forgotten. w. s. r.

[Schumann's Requiem, op. 148, is of comparatively small importance; more beautiful compositions of his with the same title are the 'Requiem for Mignon,' and a song included in op. 90. These two have, of course, nothing to do with the words of the Mass which are here under discussion; nor has the famous 'German Requiem' of Brahms, which has been noticed in its own place (see vol. i. p. 384). Verdi's Requiem, written in memory of Manzoni, startled the purists when it was produced in 1874, but it gradually won the enthusiastic approval even of the most ardent classicists, for it is a masterpiece in its way. Among later Requiem Masses may be mentioned Stanford's work in memory of Lord Leighton, given at the Birmingham Festival of 1897; Henschel's expressive Requiem, written in memory of his wife, in 1902; and Sgambati's in memory of King Humbert, published 1906.]

RESIN. See COLOPHANE, and ROSIN.

RESINARIUS, BALTHASAR, is possibly, but not certainly, identical with Balthasar Harzer or Hartzer. He was born at Jessen early in the 16th century, took clerical orders and became Bishop of Leipa in Bohemia about 1543. He had been a chorister in the service of the Emperor Maximilian I. He is said to have been a pupil of Isaac, and he published at Wittenberg in 1543 'Responsorium numero octoginta de tempore et festis . . . libri duo.'

RESOLUTION is the process of relieving dissonance by succeeding consonance. All dissonance is irritant, and cannot be indefinitely dwelt upon by the mind, but while it is heard the return to consonance is awaited. To conduct this return to consonance in such a manner that the connection between the chords may be intelligible to the hearer is the problem of resolution.

The history of the development of harmonic music shows that the separate idea of resolution in the abstract need not have been present to the earliest composers who introduced discords into their works. They discovered circumstances in which the flow of the parts, moving in consonance with one another, might be diversified by retarding one part while the others moved on a step, and then waited for that which was left behind to catch them up. This process did not invariably produce dissonance, but it did conduce to variety in the independent motion of the parts. The result, in the end, was to establish the class of discords we call suspensions, and their resolutions were inevitably implied by the very principle on which the device is founded. Thus when Josquin diversified a simple succession of chords in what we call their first position, as follows—

Ex. 1.

it seems sufficiently certain that no such idea as resolving a discord was present to his mind. The motion of D to C and of C to B was predetermined, and their being retarded was mainly a happy way of obtaining variety in the flow of the parts, though it must not be ignored that the early masters had a full appreciation of the actual function and effect of the few discords they did employ.

Some time later the device of overlapping the succeeding motions of the parts was discovered, by allowing some or all of those which had gone on in front to move again while the part which had been left behind passed to its destination; as by substituting (b) for (a) in Ex. 2.

Ex. 2.

This complicated matters, and gave scope for fresh progressions and combinations, but it did not necessarily affect the question of resolution, pure and simple, because the destination of the part causing the dissonance was still predetermined. However, the gradually increasing frequency of the use of discords must have habituated hearers to their effect and to the consideration of the characteristics of different groups, and so

by degrees to their classification. The first marked step in this direction was the use of the Dominant seventh without preparation, which showed at least a thorough appreciation of the fact that some discords might have a more independent individuality than others. This appears at first merely in the occasional discarding of the formality of delaying the note out of a preceding chord in order to introduce the dissonance; but it led also towards the consideration of resolution in the abstract, and ultimately to greater latitude in the process of returning to consonance. Both their instinct and the particular manner in which the aspects of discords presented themselves at first led the earlier composers to pass from a discordant note to the nearest available note in the scale, wherever the nature of the retardation did not obviously imply the contrary; and this came by degrees to be accepted as a tolerably general rule. Thus the Dominant seventh is generally found to resolve on the semitone below; and this, combined with the fact that the leading note was already in the chord with the seventh, guided them to the relation of Dominant and Tonic chords; although they early realised the possibility of resolving on other harmony than that of the Tonic, on special occasions, without violating the supposed law of moving the seventh down a semitone or tone, according to the mode, and raising the leading note to what would have been the Tonic on ordinary occasions. However, the ordinary succession became by degrees so familiar that the Tonic chord grew to be regarded as a sort of resolution in a lump of the mass of any of the discords which were built on the top of a Dominant major concord, as the seventh and major or minor ninth, such as are now often called Fundamental discords. Thus we find the following passage in a Haydn Sonata in D—

Ex. 3.

etc.

in which the Dominant seventh is not resolved by its passing to a near degree of the scale, but by the mass of the harmony of the Tonic following the mass of the harmony of the Dominant. Ex. 4 is an example of a similar use by him of a Dominant major ninth.

Ex. 4.

A more common way of dealing with the resolution of such chords was to make the part having the discordant note pass to another position in the same harmony before changing, and allowing another part to supply the contiguous note; as in Ex. 5 from one of Mozart's Fantasias in C minor.

Ex. 5.   Ex. 5a.

Some theorists hold that the passage of the ninth to the third—as D♭ to E in Ex. 5a (where the root C does not appear)—is sufficient to constitute resolution. That such a form of resolution is very common is obvious from theorists having noticed it, but it ought to be understood that the mere change of position of the notes of a discord is not sufficient to constitute resolution unless a real change of harmony is implied by the elimination of the discordant note; or unless the change of position leads to fresh harmony, and thereby satisfies the conditions of intelligible connection with the discord.

A much more unusual and remarkable resolution is such as appears at the end of the first movement of Beethoven's F minor Quartet as follows—

Ex. 6.

where the chord of the Dominant seventh contracts into the mere single note which it represents, and that proceeds to the note only of the Tonic; so that no actual harmony is heard in the movement after the seventh has been sounded. An example of treatment of an inversion of the major ninth of the Dominant, which is as unusual, is the following from Beethoven's last Quartet, in F, op. 135:—

Ex. 7.

etc.

There remain to be noted a few typical devices by which resolutions are either varied or ela-

borated. One which was more common in early stages of harmonic music than at the present day was the use of representative progressions, which were, in fact, the outline of chords which would have supplied the complete succession of parts if they had been filled in. The following is a remarkable example from the Sarabande of J. S. Bach's Partita in B♭:—

Ex. 8.

etc.

which might be interpreted as follows:—

Ex. 9.

Another device which came early into use, and was in great favour with Bach and his sons and their contemporaries, and is yet an ever-fruitful source of variety, is that of interpolating notes in the part which has what is called the discordant note, between its sounding and its final resolution, and either passing direct to the note which relieves the dissonance from the digression, or touching the dissonant note slightly again at the end of it. The simplest form of this device was the leap from a suspended note to another note belonging to the same harmony, and then back to the note which supplies the resolution, as in Ex. 10; and this form was extremely common in quite the early times of polyphonic music.

Ex. 10.

But much more elaborate forms of a similar nature were made use of later. An example from J. S. Bach will be found in vol. i. p. 314b of this Dictionary; the following example, from a Fantasia by Emanuel Bach, illustrates the same point somewhat remarkably, and serves also as an instance of enharmonic resolution:—

Ex. 11.

The minor seventh on C in this case is ultimately resolved as if it had been an augmented sixth composed of the same identical notes according to our system of temperament, but derived from a different source and having consequently a different context. This manner of using the same group of notes in different senses is one of the most familiar devices in modern music for varying the course of resolutions and obtaining fresh aspects of harmonic combinations. [For further examples see MODULATION, CHANGE, ENHARMONIC.]

An inference which follows from the use of some forms of Enharmonic resolution is that the discordant note need not inevitably move to resolution, but may be brought into consonant relations by the motion of other parts, which relieve it of its characteristic dissonant effect ; this is illustrated most familiarly by the freedom which is recognised in the resolution of the chord of the sixth, fifth, and third on the subdominant, called sometimes the added sixth, sometimes an inversion of the supertonic seventh, and sometimes an inversion of the eleventh of the Dominant, or even a double-rooted chord derived from Tonic and Dominant together.

It is necessary to note shortly the use of vicarious resolutions—that is, of resolutions in which one part supplies the discordant note and another the note to which under ordinary circumstances it ought to pass. This has been alluded to above as common in respect of the so-called fundamental discords, but there are instances of its occurring with less independent combinations. The Gigue of Bach's Partita in E minor is full of remarkable experiments in resolution ; the following is an example which illustrates especially the point under consideration :—

Ex. 12.

etc.

The inference to be drawn from the above examples is that the possible resolutions of discords, especially of those which have an individual status, are varied, but that it takes time to discover them, as there can hardly be a severer test of a true musical instinct in relation to harmony than to make sure of such a matter. As a rule, the old easily recognisable resolutions, by motion of a single degree, or at least by interchange of parts of the chord in supplying the subsequent consonant harmony, must preponderate, and the more peculiar resolutions will be reserved for occasions when greater force and intensity are required. But as the paradoxes of one generation are often the truisms of the next, so treatment of discords such as is utterly

incredible to people who do not believe in what they are not accustomed to, is felt to be obvious to all when it becomes familiar ; and hence the peculiarities which are reserved for special occasions at first must often in their turn yield the palm of special interest to more complex instinctive generalisations. Such is the history of the development of musical resources in the past, and such it must be in the future. The laws of art require to be based upon the broadest and most universal generalisations ; and in the detail under consideration it appears at present that the ultimate test is thorough intelligibility in the melodic progressions of the parts which constitute the chords, or in a few cases the response of the harmony representing one root to that representing another, between which, as in Examples 3 and 4, there is a recognised connection sufficient for the mind to follow without the express connection of the flow of the parts. Attempts to catalogue the various discords and their various resolutions must be futile as long as the injunction is added that such formulas only are admissible, for this is to insist upon the repetition of what has been said before ; but they are of value when they are considered with sufficient generality to help us to arrive at the ultimate principles which underlie the largest circle of their multifarious varieties. The imagination can live and move freely within the bounds of comprehensive laws, but it is only choked by the accumulation of precedents.   C. H. H. P.

RESPOND (Lat. *Responsorium*) a form of ecclesiastical chant which grew out of the elaboration of the primitive RESPONSORIAL PSALMODY. Some of the Responds have been frequently treated in the Polyphonic Style, with very great effect, not only by the Great Masters of the 16th century, but even as late as the time of Colonna, whose Responsoria of the Office for the Dead, for eight voices, are written with intense appreciation of the solemn import of the text.

A large collection of very fine examples, including an exquisitely beautiful set for Holy Week, by Vittoria, will be found in vol. iv. of Proske's ' Musica Divina.'   W. S. R.

RESPONSE, in English church music, is, in its widest sense, any musical sentence sung by the choir at the close of something read or chanted by the minister. The term thus includes the ' Amen' after prayers, the ' Kyrie' after each commandment in the Communion Service, the ' Doxology' to the Gospel, and every reply to a Versicle, or to a Petition, or Suffrage. In its more limited sense the first three of the above divisions would be excluded from the term, and the last-named would fall naturally into the following important groups : (1) those which immediately precede the Psalms, called also the Preces ; (2) those following the Apostles' Creed and the Lord's Prayer ; (3) those following the Lord's Prayer in the Litany ; (4) and the Responses of the first portion of the Litany, which, however, are of a special musical form which will be fully explained hereafter. Versicles and Responses are either an ancient formula of prayer or praise, as, 'Lord, have mercy upon us,' etc., 'Glory be to the Father,' etc., or a quotation from Holy Scripture, as,

℣ O Lord, open Thou our lips.
℞ And our mouth shall shew forth Thy praise.

which is verse 15 of Psalm li. ; or a quotation from a church hymn, as,

℣ O Lord, save Thy people.
℞ And bless Thine inheritance.

which is from the *Te Deum* ; or an adaptation of a prayer to the special purpose, as,

℣ Favourably with mercy hear our prayers.
℞ O Son of David, have mercy upon us.

The musical treatment of such Versicles and Responses offers a wide and interesting field of study. There can be little doubt that all the inflections or cadences to which they are set have been the gradual development of an original monotonal treatment, which in time was found to be uninteresting and tedious (whence our term of contempt 'monotonous'), or was designedly varied for use on special occasions and during holy seasons. [See IN-FLEXION.]

The word 'Alleluia' is found as a Response in the Prayer-Book of 1549, for use between Easter and Trinity, immediately before the Psalms ; during the remainder of the year the translation of the word was used. Here is Marbeck's music for it (1550)—

Prayse ye the Lorde.

When this was in later editions converted into a Versicle and Response, as in our present Prayer-Book, the music was, according to some uses, divided between the Versicle and Response, thus—

℣ Praise ye the Lord.   ℞ The Lord's name be praised.

But as a matter of fact these 'Preces' in our Prayer-Book which precede the daily Psalms have never been strictly bound by the laws of 'ecclesiastical chant,' hence, not only are great varieties of plain-song settings to be met with, gathered from Roman and other uses, but also actual settings in service-form (that is, like a motet), containing contrapuntal devices in four or more parts. Nearly all the best cathedral libraries contain old examples of this elaborate treatment of the Preces, and several have been printed by Dr. Jebb in his 'Choral Responses.'

As then the Preces are somewhat exceptional, we will pass to the more regular Versicles and Responses, such as those after the Apostles'

Creed and the Lord's Prayer. And here we at once meet the final 'fall of a minor third,' which is an ancient form of inflec-tion known as the *Accentus Medialis*—

This is one of the most characteristic progres-sions in plain-song versicles, responses, con-fessions, etc. It must have already struck the reader that this is nothing more or less than the 'note' of the cuckoo. This fact was prob-ably in Shakespeare's mind when he wrote,

The finch, the sparrow, and the lark,
The *plain-song* cuckoo gray.

This medial accent is only used in Versicles and Responses when the last word is a poly-syllable ; thus—

Medial Accent.

℞ And grant us Thy salva-tion.

When the last word is a monosyllable or is accented on its last syllable, there is an ad-ditional note, thus—

Moderate Accent.

℞ As we do put our trust in Thee.

This may be said to be the only law of the *Accentus Ecclesiasticus* which the tradition of our Reformed Church enforces. It is strictly observed in most of our cathedrals, and considering its remarkable simplicity, should never be broken. The word 'prayers' was formerly pronounced as a dissyllable ; it therefore took the medial accent thus—

Favourably . . . . our pray-ers.

but as a monosyllable it should of course be treated thus—

Favourably . . . . our prayers.

In comparing our Versicles and Responses with the Latin from which they were trans-lated, it is important to bear this rule as to the 'final word' in mind. Because the Latin and English of the same Versicle or Response will frequently take different 'accents' in the two languages. For example, the following Versicle takes in the Latin the *medial accent* ; but in the translation will require the *moderate accent.*

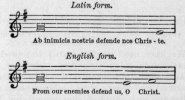

Latin form.

Ab inimicis nostris defende nos Chris - te.

English form.

From our enemies defend us, O   Christ.

It has been just stated that the early part of the Litany does not come under the above laws of 'accent.' The principal melodic progression is, however, closely allied to the above, it having merely an addi-tional note, thus—

This is the old and common Response—

O - ra pro no-bis.

and to this are adapted the Responses, 'Spare us, good Lord'; 'Good Lord, deliver us'; 'We beseech Thee to hear us, good Lord'; 'Grant us Thy peace'; 'Have mercy upon us'; 'O Christ, hear us' (the first note being omitted as redundant); and 'Lord, have mercy upon us; Christ, have mercy upon us.' At this point, the entry of the Lord's Prayer brings in the old law of medial and moderate accents; the above simple melody, therefore, is the true Response for the whole of the first (and principal) portion of the Litany. It is necessary, however, to return now to the preliminary sentences of the Litany, or the 'Invocations,' as they have been called. Here we find each divided by a colon, and, in consequence, the simple melody last given is lengthened by one note, thus—

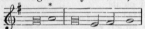

This is used without variation for all the Invocations. The asterisk shows the added note, which is set to the syllable immediately preceding the colon. It happens that each of the sentences of Invocation contains in our English version a monosyllable before the colon; but it is not the case in the Latin, therefore both Versicle and Response differ from our use, thus—

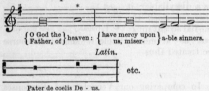

{ O God the } heaven: { have mercy upon } a-ble sinners.
{ Father, of }   { us, miser-   }

Latin.

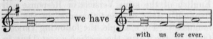

Pater de coelis De - us.

In the petitions of the Litany, the note marked with an asterisk is approached by another addition, for instead of

 we have

with us for ever.

The whole sentence of music therefore stands thus—

(Petition chanted by　　(Response by Choir and
Priest.)　　　　　　　People.)

We have now shortly traced the gradual growth of the plain-song of the whole of our Litany, and it is impossible not to admire the simplicity and beauty of its construction.

But the early English church-musicians frequently composed original musical settings of the whole Litany, a considerable number of which were printed by Dr. Jebb; nearly all, however, are now obsolete except that by Thomas Wanless (organist of York Minster at the close of the 17th century), which is occa-

sionally to be heard in our northern cathedrals. The plain-song was not always entirely ignored by church-musicians, but it was sometimes included in the tenor part in such a mutilated state as to be hardly recognisable. It is generally admitted that the form in which Tallis's responses have come down to us is very impure, if not incorrect. To such an extent is this the case that in an edition of the 'people's part' of Tallis, published not many years since, the editor (a cathedral organist) fairly gave up the task of finding the plain-song of the response, 'We beseech Thee to hear us, good Lord,' and ordered the people to sing the tuneful superstructure—

We be-seech Thee to hear us, good Lord.

It certainly does appear impossible to combine this with

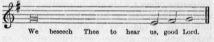

We beseech Thee to hear us, good Lord.

But it appears that this ancient form existed—

Chris-te ex - au - di nos.

This, if used by Tallis, will combine with his harmonies; thus—

We be-seech Thee to hear us, good Lord.

(Plain-song in Tenor.)

Having now described the Preces, Versicles and Responses, and Litany, it only remains to say a few words on (1) Amens, (2) Doxology to Gospel, (3) Responses to the Commandments, all of which we have mentioned as being responses of a less important kind.

(1) Since the Reformation two forms of *Amen* have been chiefly used in our church, the monotone, and the approach by a semitone, generally harmonised thus—

A - men.　　　　　　A - men.

The former of these 'Amens' in early times was used when the choir *responded* to the priest; the latter, when both priest and choir sang together (as after the Confession, Lord's Prayer, Creed, etc.). Tallis, however, *always* uses the monotonic form, varying the harmonies thrice. In more modern uses, however, the ancient system has been actually reversed, and (as at St. Paul's Cathedral) the former is only used when priest and choir join ; the latter when the choir responds. In many cathedrals no guiding principle is adopted ; this is undesirable.

(2) The Doxology to the Gospel is always monotone, the monotone being in the Tenor, thus—

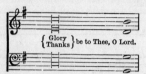

{ Glory Thanks } be to Thee, O Lord.

There are, however, almost innumerable original settings of these words used throughout the country.

(3) The Responses to the Commandments are an expansion of the ancient—

Kyrie eleison,
Christe eleison,
Kyrie eleison,

made to serve as *ten* responses instead of being used as one responsive prayer. The ancient form actually appears in Marbeck (1550), and the so-called Marbeck's ' Kyrie' now used is an editorial manipulation. Being thrown on their own resources for the music to these ten responses, our composers of the reformed church always composed original settings, sometimes containing complete contrapuntal devices. At one period of vicious taste *arrangements* of various sentences of music, sacred or secular, were pressed into the service. The ' Jommelli Kyrie' is a good—or rather, a bad—example. It is said to have been adapted by Attwood from a chaconne by Jommelli, which had already been much used on the stage as a soft and slow accompaniment of weird and ghostly scenes. The adaptation of 'Open the heavens' from ' Elijah' is still very popular, and may be considered a favourable specimen of an unfavourable class. [Both these have happily passed out of general use at present, 1907.]

The re-introduction of choral celebrations of Holy Communion has necessitated the use of various inflexions, versicles, and responses, of which the music or method of chanting has, almost without exception, been obtained from pre-Reformation sources.   J. S.

RESPONSORIAL PSALMODY is the earliest form in which psalms have been sung in the Christian Church. It is a development from inflected monotone (see INFLEXION). In the earliest Christian days the recitation of the psalms was carried out by a single soloist, who monotoned the greater part of the psalm, but inserted various cadences or inflexions at certain points of distinction in the verse. This was very probably but the carrying on of what had long been current in the Synagogue. (See PLAIN-SONG, SYNAGOGUE MUSIC.) It was very advisable not to leave the whole of the performance of the psalm to the soloist ; and it became customary for the congregation to interject some small response

at the close of each verse. Such a response was known among the Greeks as an acrostic (ἀκροστίχιον or ἀκροτελεύτιον), and the technical word in Latin for this performance by the congregation was *Respondere* ; hence this form of psalmody was called 'Responsorial Psalmody.' The refrain was originally very brief,—an Amen or an Alleluia, a short text like the ' For his mercy endureth for ever' of Psalm cxxxvi. or some pregnant sentence drawn from the Psalm which was being sung. In the earliest days the soloist's text was very little removed from monotone, but already by the time of St. Augustine it had become more elaborate, and the ancient simplicity was looked upon as an archaism. The result was a performance somewhat resembling the familiar Litany. The psalmody remained such a short time in this comparatively simple stage that very few actual monuments of it have survived. The Responsorial Psalmody that exists is of the elaborate sort. Partly as a result of the growing artistic feeling, partly also in consequence of the existence of trained singers in the great Song School at Rome, the music, alike of the soloist who sang the verses of the psalm and of the choir who responded, was elaborated to a very high pitch. Then, since it was impossible to sing the whole psalm to a highly ornate chant habitually, certain verses were selected from the psalm for this elaborate treatment ; and there grew up, therefore, the musical form called the Respond, which consisted in its simplest shape of a choral melody (called the Respond proper), alternating with one or more Verses sung by the soloist. This form is found both in the music of the Mass and in that of Divine Service, and mainly as an interlude between the reading of lessons. In the former it is called for distinction's sake *Responsorium Graduale* or the Gradual. In the latter case it is simply called *Responsorium* ; for the lesser Offices, which were sung without musical elaboration, there came to be a few simple forms of Responsorial music, modelled on the elaborate responds of Mattins but differing from them in being simpler in texture. This brief form was then called *Responsorium breve* as distinct from the *Responsorium prolixum.*

The highest development of elaboration was reached in the Gradual ; but even there, in spite of all the embroidery, the primitive monotone around which everything else centres is still traceable ; and careful analysis will show that with all its elaboration the chant is still an inflected monotone. This statement can most easily be proved by the study of a single group of Graduals which are ordinarily ascribed to the second mode, and are decorated with similar melodic themes.

The music falls into eight divisions, each of which consists of (*a*) an intonation, (*b*) the recitation in inflected monotone, (*c*) the cadence or

f

pneuma or *melisma*. There are in all fifteen different texts set to this scheme of music ; the *Justus ut palma* is given here as being the best representative of the group ; but in two of the divisions another text is given as well, in order to reveal the structure the more clearly.

Gloria patri as well, in the early shape in which it consisted of one phrase, not two. Further, it became customary in France to repeat after the Verse not the whole of the respond but only a part of it ; and this custom spread till it was universal.

The same plan holds good with the responds of the Office which are found for the most part in the service of Mattins. It is visible more plainly in the verses of the responds than in the responds themselves. Those of the Office use a set of invariable psalm-melodies, one belonging to each mode ; in these the monotone is very clear, and yet there is much elaboration in the cadences, and the forms are so plastic that they can by certain well-defined rules be readily adapted to the various texts of the verses. (See PSALMODY.) The Graduals in the mass do not utilise these common forms for their Verses ; each Verse is peculiar to the Gradual ; but even so there is much similarity observable amongst them both in general structure and in detail. In exceptional cases even the responds of the Office have their Verses set to a special melody and not to the common one.

As regards liturgical (as distinct from musical) structure the respond of the Office is like the gradual-respond of the Mass, but not identical. In neither case is it common now to find more than one Verse, but the respond in the Office is often accompanied by the

The following respond, then, which belongs to Mattins of the First Sunday in Advent and stands at the head of the series, may be taken as representing this form of composition in an unusually full shape.

Three boys sing the Respond—

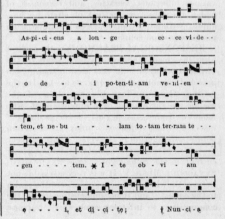

no - bis si tu es ip - se,   ‡ Qui

reg-na-tu - rus   es   ⊗ In po - pu - lo

Is - ra - el.

A boy sings the first Verse to the psalm melody of the Seventh mode (see PSALMODY)—

Quique terrigenae et filii hominum, simul in unum dives et pauper (Ps. xlix. 2).

The choir repeats the Respond from *Ite* onwards. A second boy sings a second Verse as before—

Qui regis Israel intende, qui deducis velut ovem Joseph (Ps. lxxx. 1).

The choir repeats the Respond from *Nuncia*. A third boy sings a third Verse—

Excita domine potentiam tuam, et veni ut salvos facias nos.

The ℞ is repeated from *Qui regnaturus*. The three boys sing the *Gloria patri* (down to *Sancto* only) to the same psalm melody, and the choir repeats the closing section of the Respond—*In populo Israel*.   W. H. F.

RESPONSORIUM. See RESPOND, and RESPONSORIAL PSALMODY.

REST (Fr. *Silence, Pause* ; Ger. *Pause* ; Ital. *Pausa*). The sign of silence in music, the duration of the silence depending upon the form of the character employed to denote it. The employment of the rest dates from the invention of 'measured music,' that is, music composed of notes of definite and proportionate values. [See MUSICA MENSURATA ; NOTATION.] In earlier times the *cantus* was sung without pauses, or with only such slight breaks as were necessary for the due separation of the sentences of the text, but so soon as the relative duration of the notes was established, the employment of rests of like proportionate values became a necessity. Franchinus Gafurius, in his *Practica Musicae* (1496), says that the Rest 'was invented to give a necessary relief to the voice, and a sweetness to the melody ; for as a preacher of the divine word, or an orator in his discourse, finds it necessary oftentimes to relieve his auditors by the recital of some pleasantry, thereby to make them more favourable and attentive, so a singer, intermixing certain pauses with his notes, engages the attention of his hearers to the remaining parts of his song.'

(Hawkins, *Hist. of Music*, chap. 63.) Accordingly we find rests corresponding in value to each of the notes then in use, as shown in the following table.

Maxima.	Longa.		Brevis.	Semibrevis.

Maxima. Longa perfecta. Longa imperfecta. Pausa. Semipausa.

Minima.	Semiminima.	Fusa.	Semifusa.

Suspirium. Semisuspirium. Pausa Fusæ. Pausa Semifusæ.

Of these rests, two, the *semipausa* and *suspirium*, have remained in use until the present day, and appear, slightly increased in size but of unchanged value, as the semibreve and minim rests. Two of the longer rests are also occasionally used in modern music, the *pausa*, or breve rest, to express a silence of two bars' duration, and the *longa imperfecta* a silence of four. These rests are called in French *bâtons*, and are spoken of as ' bâton à deux mesures,' ' à quatre mesures.'

The rests employed in modern music, with their names and values in corresponding notes, are shown in the table below.

By a license the semibreve rest is used to express a silence of a full bar in any rhythm (hence the German name *Taktpause*) ; its value is therefore not invariable, as is the case with all the other rests, for it may be shorter than its corresponding note, as when used to express a bar of 2–4 or 6–8 time, or longer, as when it occurs in 3–2 time. To express a rest of longer duration than one bar, either the *bâtons* of two or four bars are employed (Ex. *a*), or, more commonly, a thick horizontal line is drawn in the stave, and the number of bars which have to be counted in silence is written above it (Ex. *b*).

(a)   (b)   10

Like the notes, the value of a rest can be increased by the addition of a dot, and to the same extent, thus ━• is equal to ━𝄽, 𝄽 • to 𝄾 𝄿, and so on.

In the earlier forms of the ancient ' measured music ' rests were used as a part of the time-signature, and placed immediately after the clef. In this position they did not denote silence, but merely indicated the description of Mood to be counted. [See NOTATION, MOOD, TIME, SIGNATURE.]

(a)   (b)   (c)   (d)   (e)   (f)   (g)

ENGLISH.	FRENCH.	GERMAN.	ITALIAN.
(a) Semibreve rest.	(a) Pause.	(a) Taktpause.	(a) Pausa della Semibreve.
(b) Minim rest.	(b) Demi-pause.	(b) Halbe Pause.	(b) Pausa della Minima.
(c) Crotchet rest.	(c) Soupir.	(c) Viertelpause.	(c) Pausa della Semiminima, or Quarto.
(d) Quaver rest.	(d) Demi-soupir.	(d) Achtelpause.	(d) Pausa della Croma, or Mezzo Quarto.
(e) Semiquaver rest.	(e) Quart-de-soupir.	(e) Sechzehntelpause.	(e) Pausa della Semicroma, or Respiro.
(f) Demisemiquaver rest.	(f) Demi-quart-de-soupir.	(f) Zweiunddreissigstheilpause.	(f) Pausa della Biscroma.
(g) Semidemisemiquaver rest.	(g) Seizième-de-soupir.	(g) Vierundsechszigstheilpause.	(g) Pausa della Semibiscroma. F. T.

RESULTANT TONES (Fr. *Sons résultans*; Ger. *Combinationstöne*) are produced when any two loud and sustained musical sounds are heard at the same time. There are two kinds of resultant tones, the Differential and the Summational. The 'Differential tone' is so called because its number of vibrations is equal to the difference between those of the generating sounds. The 'Summational tone' is so called because its number of vibrations is equal to the sum of those of the generating sounds. The following diagram shows the pitches of the differential tones of the principal consonant intervals when in perfect tune.

Generators.

Differentials.

If the interval be wider than an octave, as in the last two examples, the differential is intermediate between the sounds which produce it. These tones can be easily heard on the ordinary harmonium, and also on the organ. They are not so distinct on the piano, because the sounds of this instrument are not sustained. By practice, however, the resultant tones can be distinguished on the piano also.

Dissonant as well as consonant intervals produce resultant tones. Taking the minor Seventh in its three possible forms the differentials are as follows :—

The first form of minor Seventh is obtained by tuning two Fifths upwards (C–G–D) and then a major Third downwards (D–*/* B♭) : its differential tone is */* A♭, an exact major Third below C. The second form is got by two exact Fourths upwards (C–F–B♭): the differential is then \A♭, which is flatter than the previous */* A♭ by the interval 35 : 36. The third form is the so-called Harmonic Seventh on C, whose differential is G, an exact Fourth below C. The marks \, */*, here used to distinguish notes which are confused in the ordinary notation, will be found fully explained under TEMPERAMENT. We may briefly remark that the acute sign */* refers to notes in an ascending series of Fifths, the grave sign \ to those in a descending series of Fifths.

Hitherto we have spoken only of the differential tones which are produced by the fundamentals or prime partial tones of musical sounds. [See PARTIAL TONES.] But a differential may also arise from the combination of any upper partial of one sound with any partial of the other sound ; or from the combination of a differential with a partial, or with another differential. Thus the major Third C–E may have the following differential tones :—

All these tones are heard simultaneously; but for convenience the differentials of the first, second, third, and fourth orders are written in notes of different length. We see, then, that the number of possible resultant tones is very great ; but only those which arise from the primes of musical sounds are sufficiently strong to be of practical importance.

In enabling the ear to distinguish between consonant and dissonant intervals, the differential tones are only less important than the upper partials. Thus if the chord G–E–C be accurately tuned as 3 : 5 : 8, the differential of G–C coincides with E, and that of E–C with G. But if the intervals be tempered the differentials are thrown out of tune, and give rise to beats. These beats are very loud and harsh on the ordinary harmonium, tuned in equal temperament. Again, in the close triad C–E–G the differentials of C–E and of E–G coincide and give no beats if the intervals be in perfect tune. On a tempered instrument the result is very different. If we take C to have 264 vibrations, the tempered E has about $332\frac{1}{2}$, and the tempered G about $395\frac{1}{2}$ vibrations. The differential of C–E is then $68\frac{1}{2}$, and that of E–G 63. These two tones beat $5\frac{1}{2}$ times each second, and thus render the chord to some extent dissonant.

In the minor triad, even when in just intonation, several of the resultant tones do not fit in with the notes of the chord, although they may

be too far apart to beat. In the major triad, on the contrary, the resultant tones form octaves with the notes of the chord. To this difference Helmholtz attributes the less perfect consonance of the minor triad, and its obscured though not inharmonious effect.

The origin of the differential tones has been the subject of much discussion. Thomas Young held that when beats became too rapid to be distinguished by the ear, they passed into the resultant tone. This view prevailed until the publication in 1856 of Helmholtz's investigations, in which many objections to Young's theory were brought forward. To explain what these objections are, it would be necessary to treat at some length of the nature of beats, and the reader is therefore referred to the article BEATS, for this side of the question. The later mathematical theory given by Helmholtz is too abstruse to admit of popular exposition.

It was also part of Young's theory that the differential tone was produced in the ear alone, and not in the external air. But Helmholtz found that stretched membranes and resonators responded very clearly to differentials produced by the siren or the harmonium. This he considers to prove the existence of vibrations in the external air corresponding to the differential tones. But when the two generating tones were produced by separate instruments, the differential, though powerfully audible, hardly set the resonator in vibration at all. Hence Helmholtz concludes that the differential tone is for the most part generated in the ear itself. He further points out that certain features in the construction of the ear easily permit the action of the law which he has stated. The unsymmetrical form of the drum-skin of the ear, and the loose attachment of the ossicles are, he thinks, peculiarly favourable to the production of resultant tones. [A practical use of resultant tones is shown in the article ORGAN, vol. iii. p. 552a.]

As a consequence of his theory, Helmholtz deduced a different series of resultant tones, which he calls *summational* tones, because their number of vibrations is the *sum* of those of the generators. The existence of the summational tones which Helmholtz believed he verified experimentally, has recently been called in question by Dr. Preyer. He points out that in some intervals, as, for instance, 1 : 2, 1 : 3, 1 : 5, there will be a partial tone present of the same pitch as the presumed summational tone, and these cases therefore prove nothing. Again, if we take 2 : 3, the note 5 is not necessarily a summational tone, but may be the differential of 4 and 9, which are the 2nd partial of 2 and the 3rd of 3 respectively. Dr. Preyer was unable to find any trace of the summational tones when care had been taken to exclude the upper partials. But to do this he could only use sounds of tuning-forks gently bowed, which were far too weak to produce any resultant tones in the air. The question, however, is one of theoretic interest merely.

Not only the origin, but also the discovery of differential tones has been disputed. The earliest publication of the discovery was made by a German organist named Sorge in 1745. Then came Romieu, a French savant, in 1751. Lastly, the great Italian violinist, Tartini, made the phenomenon the basis of his treatise on Harmony in 1754. But Tartini explicitly claims priority in these words :— 'In the year 1714, when about twenty-two years of age, he discovered this phenomenon by chance on the violin at Ancona, where many witnesses who

remember the fact are still living. He communicated it at once, without reserve, to professors of the violin. He made it the fundamental rule of perfect tuning for the pupils in his school at Padua, which was commenced in 1728 and which still exists ; and thus the phenomenon became known throughout Europe.'[1]

Tartini in some cases mistook the pitch of the differential tone ; but there does not appear to be any reason for taking from him the credit of the discovery which has so long been associated with his name.   J. L.

RESZKE, DE, EDOUARD, born at Warsaw, Dec. 23, 1855, was taught singing by his brother Jean, Ciaffei, Steller, and Coletti, and made his début April 22, 1876, as the King in ' Aïda,' on its production at the Italiens, Paris. He sang there with success for two seasons, and afterwards went to Italy, where, in 1880, at Turin, he made a success in two new parts—the King in Catalani's ' Elda,' Jan. 31, and Charles V. in Marchetti's ' Don Giovanni d'Austria,' March 11, and appeared at Milan on the production of Ponchielli's ' Figliuol Prodigo,' Dec. 26. From 1880 to 1884, he was engaged with the Royal Italian Opera, until its collapse. He made his début on April 13, 1880, as Indra ('Roi de Lahore '), but his success as a foremost lyric artist was established by his admirable performances of St. Bris, the Count in ' Sonnambula,' Basilio, and later as Walter (' Tell '), Peter the Great, Prince Gudal (' Demonio '), June 21, 1881 ; Sénon (Lenepveu's ' Velleda '), July 4, 1882 ; Almaviva ; Mephistopheles ; Alvise, on production of ' La Gioconda,' May 31, 1883 ; Hagen, on production of Reyer's ' Sigurd,' July 15, 1884, etc. In 1883-84 he reappeared in Paris at the Italian Opera (Théâtre des Nations), with great success, in ' Simone Boccanegra' ; in Massenet's ' Herodiade,' on its production in Paris; in Dubois' ' Aben Hamet,' Dec. 16, 1884, and in other operas. He was engaged at the French Opéra, where he first appeared April 13, 1885, as Mephistopheles, a part he sang subsequently in the 500th performance of ' Faust.' He appeared as Leporello in the centenary performance of ' Don Juan,' Nov. 4, 1887, and has sung in ' Le Cid ' and ' Patrie.' He played at the Italian Opera at Drury Lane in 1887 the part of Ramfis in ' Aïda,' and sang during the season as Basilio, St. Bris, Mephistopheles, and Henry the Fowler (' Lohengrin '). From 1888 to 1900 he sang every season (except 1899), and added to his repertory the parts of Almaviva, Marcel, the Mefistofele of Boïto, and the Wagnerian parts of Hans Sachs, King Mark, Hunding, and Hagen. From 1890, for many seasons, he sang in America with his brother, with the greatest success. He sang at the Mozart (concert) Festival at the Nouveau Théâtre in Paris in the spring of 1906, under the direction of M. Reynaldo Hahn. In Feb. 1907 he advertised

[1] *De Principii dell' Armonia*, Padova, 1767, p. 34.

his intention of opening a school of singing in London, and appeared there on June 13.

His brother, JEAN (more correctly JAN MECZISLAW) born at Warsaw, Jan. 14, 1850,[1] was the eldest son of the controller of the government railways, was taught singing by his mother, a distinguished amateur, and at the age of twelve sang solos in the Cathedral there. He was taught later by Ciaffei, Cotogni, and Sbriglia. Under the name ' De Reschi ' he made his début at Venice as Alfonso (' Favorita ') in Jan. 1874, according to an eye-witness with success.[2] He made his début at Drury Lane on April 11 of the same year, and in the same part, and played there two seasons as Don Giovanni, Almaviva, De Nevers, and Valentine. A contemporary[3] spoke of him as one of whom the highest expectations might be entertained, having a voice of delicious quality; he phrased artistically and possessed sensibility, but lacked experience such as would enable him to turn his vocal gifts to greater account and to become an effective actor. It is interesting to find that the quality of the organ was even then considered to be more of the robust tenor timbre than a baritone. Under his own name he made his début at the Italiens as Fra Melitone (' Forza del Destino '), Oct. 31, 1876, with some success, and as Severo (Donizetti's ' Poliuto ') Dec. 5, Figaro (' Barbiere ') Dec. 19. He made his tenor début as ' Robert ' at Madrid in 1879 with great success, and was engaged at the Théâtre des Nations in 1884. He played there the part of St. John the Baptist on the production of ' Hérodiade ' so much to the satisfaction of Massenet, that he procured him an engagement at the Académie to create the title-part of ' Le Cid,' in which he made his début on its production, Nov. 30, 1885. He was engaged there for four years, and sang the usual tenor parts, notably Don Ottavio (' Don Juan ' centenary) and Romeo (in 1888, on the production of Gounod's opera at the Grand Opéra). On June 13, 1887, he reappeared at Drury Lane as Radames, and sang as Lohengrin, Faust, and Raoul. He worthily fulfilled his early promise by the marked improvement both in his singing and acting, and by his ease and gentlemanly bearing, the improvements being almost entirely due to his own hard work and exertions. On June 4, 1888, as Vasco de Gama, he made his first appearance at Covent Garden, and from that season dates the revival of opera as a fashionable amusement in London. Till 1900 inclusive, he sang nearly every year here, his parts including John of Leyden, the Duke in ' Un Ballo,' Don José, Phoebus in Goring Thomas's ' Esmeralda,' Lancelot in Bemberg's ' Elaine,' Werther (in Massenet's opera). In the great parts of Wagner, such as Walther, Tristan, and Siegfried, he was unrivalled, throwing new light upon the music by his wonderful power of interpreting the

1 See *Truth*, July 15, 1897.
2 Letter of Mr. Michael Williams in *Musical World*, Jan. 31, 1874.
3 *Athenæum*, April 18, and July 25, 1874.

dramatic side, without losing sight of vocal purity. He sang for several seasons in America with his brother, and at Warsaw and St. Petersburg. On Dec. 11, 1890, he assisted gratuitously in the performance of ' Carmen ' at the Opéra-Comique in Paris, where Mme. Galli-Marié reappeared in her original part, and Melba and Lassalle were in the cast. He reappeared at intervals at the Paris Opéra, singing in 'Siegfried' and ' Pagliacci ' on the Paris production of those operas. He was announced in Reyer's ' Sigurd ' in 1904, but was unable to appear through illness. He is living in Paris, and devotes himself to teaching.

Their sister, JOSEPHINE, educated at the Conservatorium of St. Petersburg, attracted the notice of M. Halanzier at Venice, and was engaged by him at the Académie, where she made her début as Ophelia, June 21, 1875. She sang there with success for some time, where she was the original Sita (' Roi de Lahore '), April 27, 1877. Later she was very successful at Madrid, Lisbon, etc. ; sang at Covent Garden as Aïda, April 18, 1881, and again in Paris at the Th. des Nations as Salome (' Hérodiade '), March 13, 1884. She retired from public on her marriage with M. Leopold de Kronenburg of Warsaw ; she died there Feb. 22, 1891.   A. C.

RETARDATION is a word used by some theorists to distinguish a small group of discords which are similar in nature to suspensions, but resolve upwards, as in Ex. 1.

The ground for making this sub-class is that it appears inaccurate to describe as suspensions notes which are delayed or retarded in ascending. A comparison of Ex. 2, which would be distinguished as a suspension, with Ex. 1, will show the identity of principle which underlies the two discords ; while the fact of their ascending or descending is clearly not an attribute but an accident. So in this case there is no other ostensible reason for breaking up a well-defined class but the fact that the common designation in use is supposed, perhaps erroneously, to be insufficient to denote all that ought to come under it. On the other hand it requires to be noted that as all discords of this class are discords of retardation, and as those which rise are very much less common than those which descend in resolution, the name which might describe the whole class is reserved for the smallest and least conspicuous group in that class.   C. H. H. P.

REUTTER, GEORG, born 1656 at Vienna, became in 1686 organist of St. Stephen's, and in 1700 Hof- and Kammer-organist. He also played the theorbo in the Hofcapelle from

1697 to 1703. In 1712, he succeeded Fux as Capellmeister to the Gnadenbild in St. Stephen's, and in 1715 became Capellmeister of the cathedral itself. He died August 29, 1738. His church music (see list in the *Quellen-Lexikon*), was sound, without being remarkable. On Jan. 8, 1695, he was knighted in Rome by Count Francesco Sforza, on whose family Pope Paul III. had bestowed the privilege of conferring that honour in 1539. His son,

GEORG KARL (generally known by his first name only), according to the cathedral register, was born in Vienna, April 6, 1708, became Court-composer in 1731, and succeeded his father in 1738 as Capellmeister of the cathedral. In 1746 he was appointed second Court-capellmeister, his duty being to conduct the music of the Emperor's church, chamber, and dinner-table. On Predieri's retirement in 1751 Reutter exercised the functions of chief Court-capellmeister, but did not receive the title till the death of the former in 1769. As an economical measure he was allowed the sum of 20,000 gulden (£2000) to maintain the court-capelle (the whole body of musicians, vocal and instrumental), and he enjoys the melancholy distinction of having reduced the establishment to the lowest possible ebb. Reutter composed for the court numerous operas, cantatas *d'occasion*, and Italian oratorios for Lent; also a requiem, and smaller dramatic and sacred works. His grand masses are showy, with rapid and noisy instrumentation, so much so that 'rushing (rauschende) violins *à la Reutter*' became a proverb. Burney heard one of them during his visit to Vienna in 1772, and says 'it was dull, dry stuff; great noise and little meaning characterised the whole performance' (*Present State of Music in Germany*, i. 361). In 1731 Reutter married Therese Holzhauser, a court singer of merit, who died in 1782. His own death took place March 12, 1772. He was much favoured at court owing to his great tact; and Maria Theresa ennobled him in 1740 as 'Edler von Reutter.' His name is inseparably associated with that of Haydn, whom he heard sing as a boy in the little town of Hainburg, and engaged for the choir of St. Stephen's, where he sang from 1740 to 1748. His treatment of the poor chorister, and his heartless behaviour when the boy's fine voice had broken, are mentioned under HAYDN, vol. ii. pp. 349-350. See Stollbrock's biography in the *Vierteljahrsschrift*, 8, p. 165 ff., also the *Quellen-Lexikon*, where a list of his compositions will be found.   C. F. P.

RÊVE, LE. Lyric drama in four acts, text by Louis Gallet after Zola, music by Alfred Bruneau. Produced at the Opéra-Comique, Paris, June 18, 1891, and at Covent Garden, Oct. 29, 1891.

REVEILLÉ. See MILITARY SOUNDS AND SIGNALS, vol. iii. pp. 204-209.

REVERSE. See RECTE ET RETRO, ROVESCIO.

REVUE ET GAZETTE MUSICALE, the oldest and most complete of French musical periodicals. This branch of literature has taken root in France with great difficulty. So far back as Jan. 1770, M. de Breuilly and other amateurs founded the *Journal de Musique* (monthly, 8vo), which after a troubled existence of three years was dropped till 1777, and then resumed for one year more. In 1810 Fayolle started *Les Tablettes de Polymnie* (8vo), but it did not survive beyond 1811. Undeterred by these failures, Fétis brought out the first number of the *Revue musicale* in January 1827. It appeared four times a month, each number containing twenty-four pages 8vo, till Feb. 5, 1831, when it was published weekly, in small 4to, double columns. La *Gazette musicale de Paris*, started Jan. 5, 1834, was similar in size to Fétis's *Revue* and also weekly, but issued on Sunday instead of Saturday. The two were united on Nov. 1, 1835, since which date the *Revue et Gazette musicale* twice enlarged its form, in 1841 and in 1845, at which date it became what it was till its last number, Dec. 31, 1880.

The property of the publishers Schlesinger & Brandus, this periodical was always noted for the reputation and ability of its editors. Amongst its regular contributors have been: Berlioz, P. Bernard, M. Bourges, Chouquet, Comettant, Danjou, Ernest David, F. J. Fétis, O. Fouque, Heller, A. Jullien, Kastner, Lacome, A. de La Fage, Liszt, d'Ortigues, Pougin, Monnais ('Paul Smith'), Richard Wagner, and Johannes Weber. A careful reader of the forty-seven volumes will easily recognise the sentiments of the various editors through whose hands it passed; among those deserving special mention are Fétis, Édouard Monnais, and M. Charles Bannelier, who conducted it from 1872 with equal learning and taste. The indexes given with each volume are a great boon, and constitute one of its advantages over other French periodicals of the same kind.   G. C.

REY, JEAN BAPTISTE (I), born at Lauzerte (Tarn et Garonne), France, Dec. 18, 1724. His musical studies began at an early age at Toulouse, where he became a chorister at the Abbey of Saint Sernin. There he remained until the age of seventeen, when he competed for and obtained the position of Maître de Chapelle at the Cathedral of Auch. Three years later, in 1739, a dispute with the authorities caused him to resign this position and return to Toulouse, where he became *chef d'orchestre* at the opera. Until the age of forty he filled similar posts at Montpellier, Marseilles, Bordeaux, and Nantes. It was at the last-named town that a summons to Paris to assist in the production of Gluck's 'Alceste' reached him in 1776. Three years later Louis XVI. appointed him *Maître de la Musique de Chambre*, with a salary of 2000 frs. In the same year the King decorated him with the Order of Saint Michel, and appointed him *Surintendant de la Chapelle.* According to Fétis and Brenet, Rey conducted the orchestra of the Concert Spirituel between 1782 and 1786, and some of his compositions were performed there. After the French Revolution, he was elected a member of the Committee of Administration for the Affairs of the Opera, and the decree which established the Conservatoire of Music in 1795, named him one of the professors of harmony. It was there that F. J. Fétis became a pupil of Rey, and was instructed by him according to the complicated principles of Rameau. So staunch was his adherence to bygone traditions that he became involved in the turbulent discussions which were roused by Catel's innovations. Finally his championship of his friend Lesueur brought about his dismissal from the Conservatoire in 1802. Napoleon soothed his wounded feelings by nominating him his *Maître de Chapelle* two years later. He held this appointment for five years, but the death of his daughter, who was a talented pianist, plunged him into an abandonment of grief, which caused his death, July 15, 1810. As a conductor, Rey was closely associated with all the great composers of his day and assisted in the productions of the masterpieces of Piccini, Gluck, Paisiello, Grétry, Lemoine, and Méhul. Sacchini, on his deathbed, entrusted the completion of his opera ' Armire et Evelina ' to his friend Rey. This commission was conscientiously executed by him, and the opera was produced April 29, 1788. He is also said to have written all the ballet music in the same composer's opera ' Oedipe à Colone,' and in Salieri's ' Tarare.'

His original compositions comprise some MS. motets with orchestra, several of which were performed in the *Chapelle du Roi,* and some solfège studies which are included in the third part of the ' Solfèges du Conservatoire de Paris.' His two-act opera ' Diana and Endymion' was produced in Paris in 1791, and the opera in one act, entitled ' Apollon et Coronis,' was performed at the Académie Royale de Musique, in 1781. This last was written in conjunction with his brother,

REY, LOUIS CHARLES JOSEPH, who was born at Lauzerte, Oct. 26, 1738, and died May 12, 1811. Also a chorister at the Abbey of St. Sernin, Toulouse, he became a violoncellist in the theatre orchestra at Montpellier, and came to Paris in 1755 to profit by Berteau's teaching. Two years later he occupied the post of violoncellist at the principal theatre in Bordeaux, an appointment which he held for nine years. At the end of the year 1766, he became a member of the Paris opera orchestra, and in 1772 was admitted into the orchestra of the Chapelle du Roi. After forty years' service Rey retired from the orchestra with a

pension in 1806. Fétis says that he cut his throat in delirium caused by a nervous fever. He wrote some trios for two violins and violoncello ; some duos for violin and violoncello, etc., and a *brochure* entitled : *Mémoire justicatif des Artistes de l'Académie Royale de Musique, ou response à la lettre qui leur a été adressée le 4 Sept. 1789.* This last was a reply to Papillon de Laferté's complaints of the behaviour of the members of the opera orchestra.—Brenet, M., *Les Concerts en France* ; Saint Laurent, *Dictionnaire Encyclopédique* ; *Nouvelle Biographie Générale,* Paris, 1843 ; Fétis, *Biog. des Mus. Journal de Paris,* July 19, 1810.   E. H-A.

REY, JEAN BAPTISTE, (II), born at Tarascon about 1760, is said to have taught himself the harpsichord, violin, and violoncello ; occupied the post of *Maître de Musique* at the cathedrals of Verviers and Uzes, and went to Paris in 1785, establishing himself there as a professor of music. A year later he was admitted into the opera orchestra, and held an appointment as violoncellist until his death, at Paris in 1822. A potpourri (op. 1) of his for pianoforte was published by Leduc, in Paris, and Nadermann of Paris brought out his *Cours élémentaire de Musique et de Piano.* In 1807 the same firm published his *Exposition élémentaire de l'harmonie; théorie générale des accords d'après les différents genres de Musique.* Copies of this last work are in the Bibliothèque at Brussels, in the British Museum, London, and also in Glasgow. The *Quellen-Lexikon* mentions twelve sonatas for violoncello, op. 4.—J. B. Wekerlin, *Bibl. du Conservatoire Nat. de Paris* ; Fétis, *Biog. des Mus.*   E. H-A.

REYER, ERNEST, whose real name is Rey, was born at Marseilles, Dec. 1, 1823. As a child he learned solfège at the free school of music founded by Barsotti (born in Florence, 1786 ; died at Marseilles, 1868), and became a good reader, though he did not carry his musical education far. At sixteen he went to Algiers as a government official, but continued his pianoforte practice, and began to compose without having properly learned harmony and counterpoint. He was soon able to write romances which became popular, and composed a mass which was solemnly performed before the Duc and Duchesse d'Aumale. The Revolution of 1848 deprived him of the support of the Governor-General, and he returned to Paris, and placed himself in the hands of his aunt Mme. Louise Farrenc, who completed his musical education, and before long he found an opportunity of coming before the public. From his friend Théophile Gautier he procured the libretto of ' Le Selam,' an oriental ' Symphony' in four parts, on the model of David's ' Le Désert.' It was produced with success, April 5, 1850, and then Méry furnished him with ' Maître Wolfram,' a one-act opera, which was also successful, at the Théâtre Lyrique, May 20,

ERNEST REYER

1854. (Revived at the Opéra-Comique, 1873.) His next work was 'Sacountala' (July 20, 1858), one of the charming ballets of Théophile Gautier; and 'Victoire,' a cantata, was given at the Opéra, June 27, 1859 ; but his full strength was first put forth in 'La Statue,' a three-act opera produced at the Théâtre Lyrique, April 11, 1861, and containing music which is both melodious and full of colour. (It was revived in 1878 at the Opéra-Comique, and in 1903 at the Grand Opéra.) 'Erostrate' (two acts) was performed at Baden in 1862, and reproduced at the Académie, Oct. 16, 1871, for two nights only. Among his earlier works may be mentioned a 'Recueil de 10 Mélodies' for voice and PF.; songs for a single voice ; and some pieces of sacred music.   G. C.

After numerous attempts on Reyer's part to secure an unmutilated performance of 'Sigurd' at the Paris Opéra, he produced it at the Théâtre de la Monnaie, Brussels, Jan. 7, 1884, with great and lasting success.   On July 15 of the same year it was produced at Covent Garden.   The first performance of the work in France was at Lyons, on Jan. 15, 1885, when it was received with marked success.   On June 12, 1885, 'Sigurd' was performed at the Grand Opéra in Paris, but at the general rehearsal the directors thought fit to make curtailments in the score, and the composer retired, protesting against the proceeding, and yet unwilling to withdraw a work on which so much trouble and expense had been bestowed, on the eve of its production.   He threatened never to set foot in the opera-house until his score should have been restored to its original integrity, and he kept his word.   The public, less exacting than the composer, received the opera, which in many passages must have considerably surprised them, with increasing sympathy, and its success was all the more remarkable as it was entirely unassisted either by the composer, who appeared to take no interest in its fate, or by the directors, who would not have been sorry had it failed. It has definitely taken a high place in the repertory.   The qualities which are most prominent in 'Sigurd' are the individual charm of its musical ideas, the exact agreement between the words and the music, vain repetitions and conventional formulas being generally absent ; and lastly, the richness and colouring of the instrumentation, the style of which was greatly influenced by Reyer's favourite masters, Weber and Berlioz, and in places by Wagner. No charge of plagiarism from the last-named composer is intended to be suggested, nor could such a charge be substantiated.   It is true that the subjects of 'Sigurd' and the 'Ring des Nibelungen' are identical, but this is a mere coincidence.   The plot of the libretto, which was written by Du Locle and A. Blau, is taken from the Nibelungen Nôt, the source that

inspired Wagner, who, however, went further back and took his subject direct from the Eddas, moulding it after his own conception. In 1868 the libretto of Wagner's trilogy had been published for fifteen years, but it was completely unknown in France, and when the trilogy was produced in 1876, Reyer's score was nearly finished and ready for production. Reyer was decorated with the Légion d'Honneur in August 1862, and was raised to the rank of an officer in Jan. 1886.   In 1890 his grand opera on Flaubert's 'Salammbô,' was produced in Brussels, and was given at the Grand Opéra in Paris, on May 16, 1892, with great success. It has been frequently revived.

Besides being reckoned among the most poetical of French musicians, M. Reyer is an accomplished *feuilletoniste*.   After writing successively for the *Presse*, the *Revue de Paris*, and the *Courrier de Paris*, he became editor of the musical portion of the *Journal des Débats*, having succeeded d'Ortigue, who followed Berlioz.   He has collected his most important articles and published them under the title of *Notes de Musique* (Paris : Charpentier, 1875).   In both literature and composition he is the disciple and admirer of Berlioz, in whose collected essays, published as *Les Musiciens*, there is an interesting article on 'La Statue' on p. 333.   It is curious that M. Reyer, having succeeded F. David at the Institut (1876), who himself succeeded Berlioz in 1869, should thus occupy the positions, both in music and literature, of the master whose legitimate successor he may well claim to be.   A. J.

REZNICEK, EMIL NICHOLAUS VON, born on May 4, 1861, at Vienna, was at first, like so many other musicians, destined for a legal career, and for that purpose was entered as a law student ; but, rebelling against the irksomeness of that kind of employment, he became a student at the Leipzig Conservatorium. Being drawn towards the dramatic side of music, he presently undertook the duties of theatre conductor at Graz, Zürich, Stettin, Berlin, and at other places; and then, branching out in a different direction, obtained an appointment as military conductor in Prague. [For a short time he was Court Capellmeister at Weimar, and in 1896-99 held a similar post at Mannheim.   In 1902 he moved to Berlin, where he founded the 'Orchester-Kammer-Konzerte' for works requiring a small orchestra. He also directs the monthly concert of the Warsaw Philharmonic Society, and makes frequent journeys to Russia, where he is as highly appreciated as he is in Berlin.   He became teacher of composition at the Klindworth-Scharwenka Conservatorium in 1906.   He conducted two concerts in London in Nov. 1907.]   All his operas are of distinctly Czechish character ; although the libretti, as will be seen below, are founded on stories derived from various nations. The operas, with one exception, were all produced in Prague, where they met with great success. Their titles and dates of production are as follow : ' Die Jungfrau von Orleans,' 1887 ; ' Satanella,' 1888 ; ' Emmerich Fortunat,' 1889 ; ' Donna Diana,' 1894 ; ' Till Eulenspiegel,' 1901. Of these the most celebrated is ' Donna Diana,' a comic opera, of which the scene is laid in the castle of Don Diego at Barcelona, at the period of the independence of Catalonia ; the libretto is by Moreto. ' Till Eulenspiegel ' is a ' folk - opera,' dealing with the jokes of the well - known German comical character ; it was produced at Carlsruhe, on the date given above, and repeated at Berlin in 1903.

[His compositions include a Requiem for Schmeykal, for chorus, orchestra, and organ ; a Mass in F for the Jubilee of the Emperor Francis Joseph II. (1898) ; ' Ruhun und Ewigkeit,' a poem of Fr. Nietzsche set for tenor voice and orchestra ; a Comedy Overture, a Symphonic Suite in E minor, and another in D major ; some songs and piano pieces ; a String Quartet in C minor ; an Idyllic Overture (Berlin : Nikisch, 1903) ; a Tragic Symphony in D minor (Berlin : Weingartner, 1904) ; Three Volkslieder for voice and small orchestra (Kammer-Orchester-Konzerte, 1905) ; Ironic Symphony, B major (do.) ; a String Quartet in C♯ minor (Berlin : Dessau Quartet, 1906) ; Nachtstück for v'cello, with accompaniment for harp, four horns, and string quartet ; a Serenate for strings, and an Introduction and Valse-Caprice for violin and orchestra (Kammer-Orchester-Konzerte, 1906) ; Fugue in C♯ minor, originally for strings, and subsequently for full orchestra.]

D. H. ; additions by H. V. H.

RHAMES, a family of Dublin music-publishers. Benjamin Rhames was established, about the year 1765, at 16 Upper Blind Quay, at the sign of the Sun. Dr. W. H. Grattan Flood informs the writer that the father, Aaron Rhames, was issuing sheet-music in Dublin, circa 1729 to 1732. Benjamin Rhames was in an extensive way of trade, and published great quantities of single sheet songs, mainly of contemporary English music. He was succeeded by his widow, Elizabeth, about 1773 or 1775. In the year 1776 the name Upper Blind Quay was altered into Exchange Street, and the later imprints of Elizabeth Rhames bear the new address with the same number, 16. She remained in business until about the year 1790, when Francis Rhames, her son, took over the concern and greatly increased the output of music sheets. In or near the year 1811 Paul Alday bought the business and remained at the same address until 1823 or 1824, removing then to 10 Dame Street. Elizabeth Rhames and her son published, among other Irish works, pieces by Sir John Stevenson, the copyright of which, after being held by Alday, was transferred to James Power of London.　F. K.

RHAPSODY. The Greek Rhapsodist ('Ραψ-ῳδός) was a professional reciter or chaunter of epic poetry. 'Ραψῳδία is the Greek title of each book of the Homeric poems, the first book of the Iliad being 'Ραψῳδία A, and so forth. The Rhapsody was the song of the Rhapsode ; a sequel of Rhapsodies when sung in succession or written down so as to form a series, constituted an epic poem, and when a long poem was chanted in sections at different times and by different singers it was said to be rhapsodised.

The usual derivation of 'Ραψῳδία is ῥάπτω = I sew, and ᾠδή = song, ode.

Musicians might speak, in Hamlet's phrase, of a ' rhapsody of words,' or of tunes—that is to say, of a string of melodies arranged with a view to effective performance in public, but without regular dependence of one part upon another. Such a description would seem to apply pretty closely to Liszt's fifteen Rhapsodies Hongroises, and to his 'Reminiscences d'Espagne' (a fantasia on two Spanish tunes, ' Les Folies d'Espagne ' and ' La Jota Aragonesa,' 1844-45) which, in 1863, he republished as a 'Rhapsodie Espagnole.' The history of the latter piece is similar to that of the Hungarian rhapsodies—portions of which were originally published under the title of ' Mélodies Hongroises—Ungarische National-melodien '—short transcriptions of Hungarian tunes as they are played by the wandering bands of Gipsies, the national musicians of Hungary. The prototype of these ' melodies ' in all probability was Schubert's ' Divertissement à la Hongroise,' in G minor, op. 54—a piece Liszt was always fond of, and of which he produced several versions—as of the whole for pianoforte solo, and of the march in C minor for orchestra.[1] Liszt's ten sets of ' Mélodies Hongroises ' date from 1839 to 1847 ; the fifteen so-called Rhapsodies Hongroises from 1853 to 1854.

In 1859 Liszt published a book in French Des Bohémiens et de leur Musique en Hongrie— a late and overgrown preface, as he confesses, to the Rhapsodies. In this brilliant, though at intervals somewhat meretricious work,[2] an effort is made to claim for the set of Rhapsodies the dignity of an Hungarian Epic sui generis. Be this as it may, the term ' Rhapsodie ' remains as one of Liszt's many happy hits in the way of musical nomenclature.

Brahms has adopted the term ' Rhapsodie ' both in Liszt's sense and in that of the Greek Rhapsodists ; and, as usual with him, he has added weight to its significance. His original ' Rhapsodien,' op. 79, for pianoforte solo—in B minor and G minor—are abrupt, impassioned aphoristic pieces of simple and obvious structure, yet solidly put together. The ' Rhapsodie ' in C, op. 53, for contralto, male chorus, and orchestra, justifies its title, in the Greek sense, inasmuch as it is a setting—a recitation, a rhapsody—of a portion of Goethe's poem ' Harzreise im Winter ' ; it, also, is a compact and carefully balanced piece. The last pianoforte piece, in op. 119, is a noble Rhapsody, in which there is perhaps rather more of the quality that is usually called 'rhapsodical' than is to be found in Brahms's other rhapsodies.

Among later rhapsodies may be named Mackenzie's Scottish Rhapsodies, Stanford's Irish Rhapsodies, German's Welsh Rhapsody, and ' Rhapsody on March Themes.'

1 He played his version of the march in London, April 1886.
2 Like Liszt's Chopin, this book is on good authority reported to be the joint production of himself and certain female friends.

The last movement of Parry's 'Suite Moderne in A minor for orchestra,' entitled 'Rhapsodie,' consists of a systematised series of melodies on the plan familiar in the Rondo.   E. D.

RHAW, or RHAU, GEORG, born about 1488 at Eisfeld in Franconia, was Cantor at the Thomasschule at Leipzig till 1520, after which he settled at Eisleben as a schoolmaster, and subsequently at Wittenberg, where he became a printer, issuing books both in ordinary typography (including many first editions of Luther's writings) and in musical notes, including his own works, *Enchiridion musices ex variis musicorum libri*, etc., 1518 (often reprinted), *Enchiridion musicae mensuralis*, 1520, etc. He also brought out many collections of musical works (see the *Quellen-Lexikon*); Winterfeld ascribes some chorales to him. He died at Wittenberg, August 6, 1548.

RHEINBERGER, JOSEF GABRIEL, was born March 17, 1839, at Vaduz (Liechtenstein). At an early age he showed extraordinary musical aptitude, and when five years old had attained to considerable local reputation. His father, who was financial agent to Prince Liechtenstein, though unmusical himself, was quick to recognise and encourage the uncommon talent of his son. He accordingly placed him in charge of Sebastian Pöhly, a superannuated schoolmaster in Schlanders, who gratuitously gave him lessons in musical theory, pianoforte, and organ. The organ pedals not being within reach, Pöhly arranged a second pedal board for the convenience of his pupil. In 1846, when only seven years of age, Rheinberger was appointed organist at Vaduz Parish Church, and during the following year his first composition —a three-part mass with organ accompaniment —was publicly performed. Shortly after this event the Bishop of Chur invited Rheinberger senior to bring his son to the cathedral in order that his musical ability might be tested. A 'Salve Regina' for four male voices and organ was placed before the young musician, which he was requested to play whilst the bishop and clergy sang. The performance, however, was brought to an unexpected conclusion by young Rheinberger, who abruptly ceased his accompaniment and exclaimed, 'But, Herr Bishop, you continually sing out of tune!' ('Aber, Herr Bischof, Sie singen ja immer falsch!')

Even at this early stage of his career Rheinberger had very decided opinions upon any music which came under his notice. Disapproving of certain masses composed by one Franz Bühler, an Augsburg musician, the young organist one day during service stuffed them all into a stove. The volume of smoke arising in consequence alarmed the assembled congregation, and the culprit had probably his youth to thank that this *auto da fé* had no unpleasant result.

In November 1848 Rheinberger heard a string quartet for the first time when a few dilettanti came over to Vaduz for the day from the neighbouring town of Feldkirch. The boy was allowed to turn the leaves for the leader, a revenue official named Schrammel. When the tuning began Josef promptly remarked, 'Your A string sounds a semitone higher than my piano at home.' As the boy's statement turned out to be perfectly accurate, the interest of Schrammel was aroused. Realising the possibilities of a musical career for the talented child, the violinist approached Rheinberger's father, who was finally induced to allow his son to reside in Feldkirch under Schrammel's protection, and receive musical instruction from the choir director there, Philipp Schmutzer. A special condition attached to the permission was that the organist's duties at Vaduz should not be abandoned; so for two years the boy walked the ten miles between Vaduz and Feldkirch every Saturday and Monday. In Feldkirch Rheinberger made rapid progress in his musical studies. It was here that he acquired, though under somewhat strict conditions, his intimate knowledge of the music of the great masters. He was allowed to study only one piece at a time, and this he had to play from memory before exchanging for another. Such strict discipline, however, had a beneficial influence. It laid that foundation of thoroughness which was so distinguishing a characteristic in later life.

In 1850 Rheinberger left Feldkirch, and after a year of careful preparation entered the Munich Conservatorium (founded in 1846 by Franz Hauser by command of King Ludwig I.). Here he remained from 1851 to 1854, studying the piano with Julius Emil Leonhard, the organ with Joh. Georg Herzog, and counterpoint with Jul. Jos. Maier, the learned curator of the musical department of the Munich Library. On leaving the Conservatorium Rheinberger obtained the highest honours granted by that institution, and he particularly impressed the ministerial examiner, Professor von Schafhäutl, by an extempore performance on the organ of a complete four-part fugue. To show his appreciation of the youth's talent, Schafhäutl presented him with a copy of Oulibicheff's biography of Mozart, and ever afterwards remained his true friend and adviser.

Rheinberger then became a private pupil of Franz Lachner, and remained in Munich supplementing his small income by giving lessons. A series of 124 youthful compositions bears eloquent testimony to his untiring energy and enthusiasm at this time. On Leonhard's resignation in 1859 Rheinberger was appointed to succeed him as professor of pianoforte at the Conservatorium, and after holding this position about a year he was given the more important office of professor of composition. When the

Munich Conservatorium was dissolved Rheinberger was appointed 'Repetitor' at the Court Theatre, where he at once favourably impressed his colleagues by playing and transposing *a prima vista* Wagner's 'Flying Dutchman.' The environment of the theatre, however, proved uncongenial. He therefore retired from active service in 1867, retaining, however, his interest in the stage.

Much of Rheinberger's earliest success as a composer was due to his Wallenstein and Florentine Symphonies. He at one time thought of setting the complete Wallenstein trilogy to music. The project, however, was discarded in favour of a Symphony, which was published and first performed in Munich in 1866. The Florentine Symphony was commissioned by the Società Orchestrale of Florence. In 1868 Rheinberger revised his opera, 'Die sieben Raben,' and composed the music to Raimund's 'Die unheilbringende Krone.' Both works were successfully produced in Munich the following year. From 1860 to 1866 Rheinberger was organist of the Court Church of St. Michael. He had been since 1854 accompanist to the Munich Choral Society, and in 1864 he became director. When the present (1907) 'Königliche Akademie der Tonkunst' was founded in 1867 by Hans von Bülow, he accepted the position of composition and organ professor and inspector of instrumental and theory classes, a post which he held with ever-increasing fame until the year of his death. The title of Royal Professor was conferred upon him soon after his installation in the Conservatorium, and in the same year he married Frau von Hoffnaass, *née* Fraulein Jägerhüber (born October 1822, died December 31, 1892), a gifted authoress and singer, who wrote the words of many of her husband's most successful choral works. In 1877 he was offered the directorship of the newly-founded Hoch Conservatorium at Frankfort-on-Main, but being unwilling to forsake the congenial artistic surroundings of Munich, he declined the invitation. King Ludwig II., to mark his approval and appreciation, conferred upon him the order of knighthood of St. Michael. In the same year Rheinberger resigned his position as musical director of the Munich Choral Society and succeeded Franz Wüllner as director of the Court Church music (Königliche Hofcapellmeister). This appointment stimulated Rheinberger to compose many ecclesiastical works, one of which —a mass in eight parts, dedicated to Pope Leo XIII.—obtained for him the order of knighthood of Gregory the Great. In 1899, on his sixtieth birthday, Rheinberger was created Doctor *honoris causa* of the University of Munich—*modorum musicorum inventorem fecundissimum artis ad leges sevoriores adstrictae praeceptorem subtilissimum preisend*. He died in Munich, Nov. 25, 1901.

It is comparatively seldom that a highly distinguished composer attains great success as a teacher. Rheinberger, however, was accounted one of the foremost musical theorists and teachers of his day. Students came to his composition classes at the Munich Conservatorium not only from his own country but from many European countries, as well as from America. Three years were required to complete the full course of theoretical instruction in these classes. In the first year students were taught free harmonisation of chorales, including *canto fermo* in alto, tenor, and bass— the same for strings with free florid counterpoint. Second and third year : form, double counterpoint, fugue, vocal and instrumental in two to six parts, instrumentation, scoring of movements from Mozart's and Beethoven's sonatas and quartets, etc.

As an organ teacher Rheinberger's activity in his later years was somewhat restricted. His organ class consisted of four advanced students, generally chosen because of marked ability. The organ works of Bach and Mendelssohn, and Rheinberger's own organ sonatas, received the greatest amount of attention. He insisted upon a clear and noble delivery, his remarks upon the interpretation of his own works being especially valuable.

Rheinberger's compositions embrace almost every branch of musical art. All his works show marked individuality, together with an absolute mastery of musical technique. It is, however, as a choral writer and composer for the organ that he is especially distinguished. His twelve masses, Stabat Mater, De Profundis, and many other examples of church music are marked by earnestness and deep religious feeling. In 'Christophorus' (Legend for soli, chorus, and orchestra, op. 120) Rheinberger combines religious and secular sentiment in a masterly and convincing manner. The Christmas cantata, 'Stern von Bethlehem' (for soli, chorus, and orchestra, op. 164), is also remarkable for its sustained beauty and loftiness of conception. Amongst his finest secular vocal compositions are the 'Seebilder,' 'Das Thal des Espingo,' 'Am Walchensee,' 'Wittekind,' 'Montfort,' 'Toggenburg,' 'Die Rosen von Hildesheim.'

Hans von Bülow and Sir Charles Hallé were the first to introduce Rheinberger's music into England. At a pianoforte recital which Bülow gave in London in 1873, he played the 'Andante and Toccata,' op. 12, one of the finest and most brilliant of Rheinberger's pianoforte compositions. In the same year at the Musical Union, and also in the following year at a popular concert, Bülow gave the Pianoforte Quartet in E flat, op. 38, which achieved a wide popularity. Among his pianoforte compositions which have been received with special favour are the three 'Kleine Concertstücke,' op. 5, and 'Aus Italien,' op. 29.

Rheinberger's twenty organ sonatas are undoubtedly the most valuable addition to organ music since the time of Mendelssohn, and it is probably upon the artistic worth of these works that his position as a composer ultimately depends. They are characterised by a happy blending of the modern romantic spirit with masterly counterpoint and dignified organ style. As perfect examples of organ sonata form they are probably unrivalled. With the object of obtaining external and material relationship between the chief movements, Rheinberger generally introduced as a coda to his finale a brief summary of one or more of the chief subjects of the first movement. Another device with the same object in view—the unifying of the sonata—was the re-introduction, generally with fine artistic effect, of a first-movement subject as an integral part of the last movement. An instance of this procedure is found in Sonata No. 9 in B flat minor (op. 142). Here the principal subject of the first movement is re-introduced in the finale as the second subject and developed in connection with the fugal subject of this last movement. Similar examples of this method are found in Sonatas No. 16 (op. 175) and No. 17 (op. 181). Throughout the whole of the organ sonatas there is a constant flow of beautiful ideas, though a considerable distance separates his best and weakest movements. There is occasionally a tendency to prolong some of the movements, considering the materials upon which they are built. The two concertos for organ and orchestra show real breadth of treatment and a freedom of manipulation that appeal strongly to the musical sense.

Rheinberger was not much in sympathy with modern art. He strongly disapproved of Wagner's methods and theories. In the antechamber of his class-room were lying one day the opened scores of 'Lohengrin' and 'Der Freischütz,' the former on the top of the latter. As Rheinberger passed through, he glanced at the books, and then with a gesture full of meaning, as if to say, 'This is how it ought to be,' pulled out the 'Freischütz' and placed it on the top. In his later years Rheinberger suffered from a chronic lung disease contracted by excessive exposure when making a mountain tour in the Tyrol. His constant ill-health and naturally austere, retiring disposition precluded much personal intercourse with the outside world. Towards his pupils he was invariably exacting and often severe, but his musical genius and commanding personality never failed to compel their respect.

Rheinberger's individuality is faithfully reflected in his compositions. Thoroughness and unpretentiousness are qualities equally characteristic of the artist and of his work. His musical themes are for the most part of great beauty. Much of his work, however, betrays a lack of strong impassioned enthusiasm, and seldom, if ever, attains to that degree of exalted musical inspiration which marks the finest creations of a great genius.

CATALOGUE OF RHEINBERGER'S COMPOSITIONS

Op.
1. 4 Pieces, pf.
2. 5 Part-songs.
3. 7 Songs.
4. 5 Songs.
5. 3 Small pf. pieces.
6. 3 Studies, pf.
7. 3 Characteristic pieces, pf.
8. 'Waldmärchen,' pf.
9. 5 Studies, pf.
10. 'Wallenstein,' symphony.
11. 5 Pieces, pf.
12. Toccata, pf.
13. 'Tarantella,' pf., 4 hands.
14. 24 Preludes, pf.
15. Duo, 2 pfs.
16. 'Stabat Mater,' soli, chorus, and orch.
17. 2 Four-part Ballads.
18. Overture, 'Taming of the Shrew.'
19. Toccatina, pf.
20. 'Die Sieben Raben,' romantic opera in 3 acts.
21. 'Wasserfee,' vocal quartet and pf.
22. 4 Songs.
23. Fantasia, pf.
24. 4 Vocal quartets.
25. 'Lockung,' vocal quartet and pf.
26. 7 Songs.
27. 1st Organ Sonata, in C minor.
28. 4 Humoresken, pf.
29. 'Aus Italien,' 3 pf. pieces.
30. 7 Pf. duets (from the music to 'Der Wunderthätige Magus').
31. 5 Part songs.
*32. 'Daughter of Jairus,' cantata for children.
33. Prelude and fugue, pf.
34. Trio, pf. and strings.
35. Hymn for female choir, organ, and harp.
36. 9 Duets, pf. (from the music to 'Die unheilbringende Krone').
*37. 'Poor Henry,' comic opera for children.
38. Quartet, pf. and strings, in E flat.
39. 6 Pf. pieces, in fugal form.
*40. 5 Motets, choir.
41. 7 Songs.
42. Étude and fugato, pf.
43. Capriccio giocoso, pf.
44. 3 Male choruses.
45. 2 Pf. studies on a theme by Handel.
46. 'Passion Music,' choir and organ.
47. Symphonic sonata, pf.
48. 4 Male choruses.
49. 10 Organ trios.
50. Ballad, 'Das Thal des Espingo,' male chorus and orch.
51. Improvisation on a theme from 'Die Zauberflöte,' pf.
52. 5 Part-songs.
53. 3 Studies, pf.
54. 4 Hymns, mezzo-soprano and organ, or pf.
55. 8 Songs.
56. 4 Vocal quartets, with strings and pf.
57. 7 Songs.
58. 6 Hymns, choir.
59. Pf. study.
60. Requiem, soli, chorus, and orch.
61. Theme and variations, pf.
62. Mass for one voice and organ.
63. 8 Part-songs.
*64. 'May Day,' 5 three-part female choruses, with pf.
65. 2nd Organ sonata in A flat.
66. 3 Studies, pf.
67. 6 Preludes, pf.
68. 6 Pieces, in fugal form.
69. 3 Sacred part-songs.
70. 'Thurmers Töchterlein,' comic opera in 4 acts.
71. Ballad, 'König Erich,' chorus with pf.
72. 'Aus den Ferientagen,' 4 pf. duets.
73. 5 Male choruses.

Op.
74. 5 Male choruses.
*75. 2 Vocal quartets, with pf.
*76. 'Toggenburg,' soli, chorus, and pf.
77. Sonata, vln. and pf., or v'cello and pf.
78. 3 Pf. pieces.
79. Fantasia, orch. or pf., 4 hands.
80. 5 Part-songs.
81. 'Die todte Braut,' romance, mezzo-soprano, choir, and orch., or pf.
82. String quintet, in A minor (or pf. duet).
83. Missa brevis in D minor, choir.
84. Requiem in E flat, choir.
85. 7 Male choruses.
86. 4 Epic songs, male choir.
87. Symphony ('Florentine') in F.
88. 3rd Organ sonata ('Pastoral') in G (or pf. duet).
89. String quartet in C minor.
90. 'Vom Rheine,' 6 male choruses.
91. 'Johannisnacht,' male choir and pf.
92. Sonata, pf. and v'cello, in C (or vln. and pf.).
93. Theme and variations, string quartet in G minor (or pf. duet).
94. Concerto, pf. and orch. in A flat.
95. 2 Choruses with orch. or pf.
96. 3 Latin hymns, three-part female choir and organ.
*97. Ballad, 'Clarice of Eberstein,' soli, chorus, and orch.
98. 4th Organ sonata, 'tonus peregrinus,' in A minor (or pf. duet).
99. Pf. sonata in D flat.
100. 7 Songs, male choir.
101. 3 Studies, pf.
102. Ballad, 'Wittekind,' male chorus and orch., or pf.
103. 3 Vocal duets, sop., bass, and pf.
104. Toccata, pf.
105. Sonata, vln. and pf., in E minor.
106. 2 Romantic songs, choir and orch., or pf.
107. 5 Hymns for choir.
108. 'Am Strom,' 6 part-songs.
109. Mass in E flat for double choir, ded. to Leo XIII.
110. Overture to Schiller's 'Demetrius' (or pf. duet).
111. 5th Organ sonata in F sharp (or pf. duet).
112. 2nd Trio, pf., vln. and v'cello, in A.
113. 6 Studies for pf. (left hand).
114. Quintet, pf. and strings, in C.
115. Toccata, pf. in C minor.
116. 4 Songs, male choir.
117. Missa Sanctissimæ Trinitatis,' choir, in F.
118. 6 Two-part hymns, with organ.
119. 6th Organ sonata, in E flat minor (or pf. duet).
*120. Legend, 'Christophorus,' soli, chorus, and orch., or pf.
121. Trio, pf. and strings, in B flat.
122. Sonata, C minor, pf., 4 hands (or 2 pfs., 8 hands).
123. 24 Fughetten for organ.
124. 8 Part-songs.
125. 7 Male choruses.
126. Mass, three-part female choir, in A.
127. 7th Organ sonata in F minor (or pf. duet).
128. 4 Elegiac songs, with organ.
129. 3 Italian songs.
130. 6 Male choruses.
131. 6 Female choruses.
132. 8th Organ sonata, in E minor (or pf. duet).
133. 4 Motets, six-part choir.
134. Easter hymn, double choir.

Op.
135. Pf. sonata, in E flat.
136. 14 Songs.
137. Organ concerto in F, with orch. (or pf. duet).
138. Stabat Mater, choir, string orch. and organ.
139. Nonet, wind and strings (or pf. duet).
140. 5 Hymns, choir and organ.
141. 6 Male choruses.
142. 9th Organ sonata, in B flat minor (or pf. duet).
143. 'Die Rosen von Hildesheim,' male chorus and wind instruments.
144. 3 Male choruses.
145. 'Montfort,' soli, chorus, and orch.
146. 10th Organ sonata, in B minor (or pf. duet).
147. String quartet in F.
148. 11th Organ sonata in D minor (or pf. duet).
149. Suite, organ, violin, v'cello, and string orch.
150. 6 pieces, violin and organ, or v'cello and organ.
151. Mass in G.
152. 30 Children's songs.
153. 'Das Zauberwort,' singspiel, in 2 acts, for children.
154. 12th Organ sonata, in D flat (or pf. duet).
*155. Mass, three-part female choir and organ.
156. 12 Characteristic pieces for organ.
157. 6 Sacred songs, with organ.
158. 8 Soprano (or baritone) songs.
159. Mass, four-part choir and organ, in F minor.
160. 7 Male choruses.
161. 13th Organ sonata, in E flat (or pf. duet).
162. 'Monologue,' 12 organ pieces.
*163. 5 Motets, five-part choir.
*164. 'Star of Bethlehem,' Christmas cantata, soli, chorus, and orch., or pf.
165. 14th Organ sonata, in C (or pf. duet).
166. Suite, vln. and organ, in C minor.
167. 'Meditations,' 12 organ pieces.
168. 15th Organ sonata, in D (or pf. duet).
169. Mass, soli, choir, and orch., or strings and organ.
170. 8 Four-part songs, 'Sturm und Frieden.'
*171. 'Marianische Hymnen,' voice and organ, or pf.
172. Mass, male choir with organ, or wind insts.
173. 4 Male choruses.
174. 12 Organ pieces.

Op.
175. 16th Organ sonata, in G sharp minor (or pf. duet).
176. 9 Advent-Motetten, choir.
177. 2nd Concerto for organ and orch., in G minor (or pf. duet).
178. Sonata for horn and pf.
179. 'Hymnus an die Tonkunst,' for male chorus and orch.
180. 12 Characteristic pieces for pf.
181. 17th Organ sonata in B.
182. 'Vom goldenen Horn,' Türkisches Liederspiel with pf.
183. 12 Studies, pf.
184. Romantic sonata for pf., in F sharp minor.
185. 7 Male choruses.
186. 8 Four-part songs, 'Jahreszeiten.'
*187. Mass, for female voices and organ, in G minor.
188. 18th Organ sonata, in A.
189. 12 Organ trios.
190. Mass, for male choir and organ, in F.
191. Trio, for pf., vln., and v'cello, in F.
192. Mass, 'Misericordias Domini,' choir and organ, in E.
193. 19th Organ sonata, in G minor.
194. Requiem, for chorus and organ.
195. 'Akademische' overture, fugue with 6 themes for orch.
196. 20th Organ sonata, 'Zur Friedensfeier,' in F.
197. Mass (posthumous), choir and organ (finished by Louis Adolph Coerne of Boston).

Without Opus Numbers.
*'Ave Maria,' soprano and organ, or five-part female choir.
Romance, for soprano and harp.
'Carmina sacra,' songs with organ.
Arrangement of Bach's 30 variations, for 2 pfs.
Three five-part songs.
Idylle for v'cello and pf.
Rhapsodie, for flute and pf., in B.
'Trennung,' for voice, pf., or organ.
'Waldbächlein,' for choir.
Pastorale, for oboe and organ, from op. 98.
Rhapsodie, for oboe and organ, or vln. and organ, from op. 127.
Tarantella from op. 122, for 2 pfs., 8 hands.

* Works possessing English text.   J. W. N.

RHEINGOLD, DAS. The 'Vorabend' of Wagner's trilogy. See RING DES NIBELUNGEN.

RHINE FESTIVALS. See NIEDERRHEINISCHE MUSIKFESTE, vol. iii. p. 377.

RHUBEBA. See REBEC.

RHYTHM. This much-used and many-sided term may be defined as 'the systematic grouping of notes with regard to duration.' It is often inaccurately employed as a synonym for its two subdivisions, ACCENT and TIME, and in its proper signification bears the same relation to these that *metre* bears to *quantity* in poetry.

The confusion which has arisen in the employment of these terms is unfortunate, though so frequent that it would appear to be natural, and therefore almost inevitable. Take a number of notes of equal length, and give an emphasis to every second, third, or fourth, the music will be said to be in 'rhythm' of two, three, or four —meaning in *time*. Now take a number of these groups or bars and emphasise them in the same way as their subdivisions: the same term will still be employed, and rightly so. Again,

instead of notes of equal length, let each group consist of unequal notes, but similarly arranged, as in the following example from Schumann—

etc.

or in the Vivace of Beethoven's No. 7 Symphony: the form of these groups also is spoken of as the 'prevailing rhythm,' though here *accent* is the only correct expression.

Thus we see that the proper distinction of the three terms is as follows :—

Accent arranges a heterogeneous mass of notes into long and short ;

Time divides them into groups of equal duration ;

Rhythm does for these groups what Accent does for notes.

In short, Rhythm is the Metre of Music.

This parallel will help us to understand why the uneducated can only write and fully comprehend music in complete sections of four and eight bars. [Rhythm is an essential part of all primitive music, and every folk-song has a distinct rhythmical character. It was long before this characteristic was introduced into serious music, which had been rhythmless because the notes of plain-chant exist only with reference to the words.] In polyphonic music the termination of one musical phrase (foot, or group of accents) is always coincident with, and hidden by, the commencement of another. And this although the subject may consist of several phrases and be quite rhythmical in itself, as is the case in Bach's Organ Fugues in G minor and A minor. The *Rhythmus* of the ancients was simply the accent prescribed by the long and short syllables of the poetry, or words to which the music was set, and had no other variety than that afforded by their metrical laws. Modern music, on the other hand, would be meaningless and chaotic—a melody would cease to be a melody—could we not plainly perceive a proportion in the length of the phrases.

The bar-line is the most obvious, but by no means a perfect, means of distinguishing and determining the rhythm ; but up to the time of Mozart and Haydn the system of barring, although used more or less accurately from the time of the Elizabethan composers, in Virginal music, etc., was but imperfectly understood. Many even of Handel's slow movements have only half their proper number of bar-lines, and consequently terminate in the middle of a bar instead of at the commencement; as, for instance, 'He shall feed His flock' (which is really in 6–8 time), and 'Surely He hath borne our griefs' (which should be 4–8 instead of C). Where the accent of a piece is strictly *binary* throughout, composers, even to this day, appear to be often in doubt about the rhythm, time, and barring of their music. The simple and unmistakable rule for the latter is this: the last strong accent will occur on the first of a bar, and you have only to reckon backwards. If the piece falls naturally into groups of four accents it is four in a bar, but if there is an odd two anywhere it should all be barred as two in a bar. Ignorance or inattention to this causes us now and then to come upon a sudden change from **C** to 2–4 in modern music.

With regard to the regular sequence of bars with reference to close and cadence—which is the true sense of rhythm—much depends upon the character of the music. The dance-music of modern society must necessarily be in regular periods of 4, 8, or 16 bars. Waltzes, though written in 3–4 time, are almost always really in 6–8, and a dance-music writer will sometimes, from ignorance, omit an unaccented bar (really a half-bar), to the destruction of the rhythm. The dancers, marking the time with their feet, and feeling the rhythm in the movement of their bodies, then complain, without understanding what is wrong, that such a waltz is 'not good to dance to.'

In pure music it is different. Great as are the varieties afforded by the diverse positions and combinations of strong and weak accents, the equal length of bars, and consequently of musical phrases, would cause monotony were it not that we are allowed to combine sets of two, three, and four bars. Not so freely as we may combine the different forms of accent, for the longer divisions are less clearly perceptible; indeed, the modern complexity of rhythm, especially in German music, is one of the chief obstacles to its ready appreciation. Every one, as we have already said, can understand a song or piece where a half-close occurs at each fourth and a whole close at each eighth bar, where it is expected; but when an uneducated ear is continually being disappointed and surprised by unexpected prolongations and alterations of rhythm, it soon grows confused and unable to follow the sense of the music. Quick music naturally allows—indeed demands—more variety of rhythm than slow, and we can scarcely turn to any scherzo or finale of the great composers where such varieties are not made use of. Taking two-bar rhythm as the normal and simplest form—just as two notes form the simplest kind of accent—the first variety we have to notice is where one odd bar is thrust in to break the continuity, as thus in the Andante of Beethoven's C minor Symphony:

This may also be effected by causing a fresh phrase to begin with a strong accent on the weak bar with which the previous subject ended, thus really eliding a bar, as for instance in the minuet in Haydn's 'Reine de France' Symphony:

Here the bar marked (*a*) is the overlapping of two rhythmic periods.

Combinations of two-bar rhythm are the rhythms of four and six bars. The first of these requires no comment, being the most common of existing forms. Beethoven has specially marked in two cases (Scherzo of Ninth Symphony, and Scherzo of C♯ minor Quartet) 'Ritmo di 4 battute,' because, these compositions being in such short bars, the rhythm is not readily perceptible. The six-bar rhythm is a most useful combination, as it may consist of four bars followed by two, two by four, three and three, or two, two and two. The well-known minuet by Lulli (from 'Le Bourgeois Gentilhomme') is in the first of these combinations throughout.

And the opening of the Andante of Beethoven's First Symphony is another good example. Haydn is especially fond of this rhythm, especially in the two forms first named. Of the rhythm of thrice two bars a good specimen is afforded by the Scherzo of Schubert's C major Symphony, where, after the two subjects (both in four-bar rhythm) have been announced, the strings in unison mount and descend the scale in accompaniment to a portion of the first theme, thus:

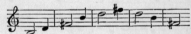

A still better example is the first section of 'God save the King.'

This brings us to triple rhythm, uncombined with double.

Three-bar rhythm, if in a slow time, conveys a very uncomfortable lop-sided sensation to the uncultivated ear. The writer remembers an instance when a band could hardly be brought to play a section of an Andante in 9–8 time and rhythm of three bars. The combination of $3 \times 3 \times 3$ was one which their sense of accent refused to acknowledge. Beethoven has taken the trouble in the Scherzo of his Ninth Symphony to mark 'Ritmo di tre battute,' although in such quick time it is hardly necessary ; the passage,

being understood as though written—

Numerous instances of triple rhythm occur, which he has not troubled to mark ; as in the Trio of the C minor Symphony Scherzo :—

Rhythm of five bars is not, as a rule, productive of good effect, and cannot be used—any more than the other unusual rhythms—for long together. It is best when consisting of four bars followed by one, and is most often found in compound form — that is, as eight bars followed by two.

Minuet, Mozart's Symphony in C (No. 6).

A very quaint effect is produced by the unusual rhythm of seven. An impression is conveyed that the eighth bar—a weak one—has got left out through inaccurate sense of rhythm, as so often happens with street-singers and the like. Wagner has taken advantage of this in his 'Dance of Apprentices' ('Die Meistersinger'), thus :—

It is obvious that all larger symmetrical groups than the above need be taken no heed of, as they are reducible to the smaller periods. One more point remains to be noticed, which, a beauty in older and simpler music, is becoming a source of weakness in modern times. This is the disguising or concealing of the rhythm by strong accents or change of harmony in weak bars. The last movement of Beethoven's Pianoforte Sonata in D minor (op. 31, No. 2) affords a striking instance of this. At the very outset we are led to think that the change of bass at the fourth bar, and again at the eighth, indicates a new rhythmic period, whereas the whole

movement is in four-bar rhythm as unchanging as the semiquaver figure which pervades it. The device has the effect of preventing monotony in a movement constructed almost entirely on one single figure. The same thing occurs in the middle of the first movement of the Sonatina (op. 79, Presto alla Tedesca). Now in both of these cases the accent of the bars is so simple that the ear can afford to hunt for the rhythm and is pleased by the not too subtle artifice ; but in slower and less obviously accented music such a device would be out of place ; there the rhythm requires to be impressed on the hearer rather than concealed from him.

On analysing any piece of music it will be found that whether the *ultimate* distribution of the accents be binary or ternary, the larger divisions nearly always run in twos, the rhythms of three, four, or seven being merely occasionally used to break the monotony. This is only natural, for, as before remarked, the comprehensibility of music is in direct proportion to the simplicity of its rhythm, irregularity in this point giving a disturbed and emotional character to the piece, until, when all attention to rhythm is ignored, the music becomes incoherent and incomprehensible, though not of necessity disagreeable. In 'Tristan und Isolde' Wagner has endeavoured, with varying success, to produce a composition of great extent, from which rhythm in its larger signification shall be wholly absent. One consequence of this is that he has written the most tumultuously emotional opera extant ; but another is that the work is a mere chaos to the hearer until it is closely studied.   F. C.

RIBATTUTA (re-striking), an old contrivance in instrumental music, gradually accelerating the pace of a phrase of two notes, until a trill was arrived at. Beethoven has preserved

it for ever in the Overture 'Leonore No. 3' (bar 75 of *Allegro*).

See too another passage farther on, before the Flute solo. [See TRILL.]   G.

RIBIBLE, an obsolete instrument played by a bow. It is mentioned by Chaucer and other early writers, and appears to have been either the rebec itself, or a particular form of it. Sometimes it is spelled 'rubible.' It has been suggested that both 'rebec' and 'ribible' are derived from the Moorish word 'rebeb' or 'rebab,' which seems to have been the name of a somewhat similar musical instrument. (See REBEC.)   F. K.

RIBS (Fr. *Éclisses*; Germ. *Zarge*). The sides of stringed instruments of the violin type, connecting the back and the belly. They consist of six (sometimes only five) pieces of maple, and should be of the same texture as the back, and if possible cut out of the same piece. After being carefully planed to the right thickness, they are bent to the required shape, and then glued together on the mould by means of the corner and top and bottom blocks, the angles being feather-edged. The back, the linings, and the belly are then added, and the body of the violin is then complete. The ribs ought to be slightly increased in depth at the broader end of the instrument, but many makers have neglected this rule. The flatter the model, the deeper the ribs require to be; hence the viol tribe, having perfectly flat backs and bellies of slight elevation, are very deep in the ribs. The oldest violins were often very deep in the ribs, but many of them have been since cut down. Carlo Bergonzi and his contemporaries had a fashion of making shallow ribs, and often cut down the ribs of older instruments, thereby injuring their tone beyond remedy. Instruments made of ill-chosen and unseasoned wood will crack and decay in the ribs sooner than in any other part; but in the best instruments the ribs will generally outlast both belly and back. Some old makers were in the habit of glueing a strip of linen inside the ribs.   E. J. P.

RICCI, LUIGI, born in Naples, June 8, 1805, in 1814 entered the Royal Conservatorio, then under Zingarelli, of which he became in 1819 one of the sub-professors together with Bellini. His first work, 'L' Impresario in angustie,' was performed by the students of the Conservatorio in 1823, and enthusiastically applauded. In the following four years he wrote 'La Cena frastornata,' 'L' Abate Taccarella,' 'Il Diavolo condannato a prender moglie,' and 'La Lucerna d'Epitteto,' all for the Teatro Nuovo. In 1828 his 'Ulisse,' at the San Carlo, was a failure. In 1829 'Il Colombo' in Parma and 'L'Orfanella di Ginevra' in Naples were both successful. The winter of 1829-30 was disastrous for Ricci, his four new operas ('Il Sonnambulo,' 'L' Eroina del Messico,' 'Annibale in Torino,' and 'La Neve') being all unsuccessful. In the autumn

of 1831 he produced at the Scala, Milan, 'Chiara di Rosemberg,' and this opera, performed by Grisi, Sacchi, Winter, Badioli, etc., was greatly applauded, and soon became successful in all the theatres of Italy. 'Il nuovo Figaro' failed in Parma in 1832. In it sang Rozer, who afterwards married Balfe. The same fate attended 'I due Sergenti' at the Scala in 1833, where the following year he gave 'Un' Avventura di Scaramuccia,' which was a very great success, and was translated into French by Flotow. The same year 'Gli esposti,' better known as 'Eran due ed or son tre,' was applauded in Turin, whilst 'Chi dura vince,' like Rossini's immortal 'Barbiere,' was hissed at Rome. It was afterwards received enthusiastically at Milan and in many other opera-houses of Europe. In 1835 'Chiara di Montalbano' failed at the Scala, while 'La serva e l' ussero' was applauded in Pavia. Ricci had thus composed twenty operas when only thirty years old; and although many of his works had met with a genuine and well-deserved success, he was still very poor and had to accept the post of musical director of the Trieste Cathedral and conductor of the Opera. In 1838 his 'Nozze di Figaro' was a fiasco in Milan, where Rossini told him that its fall was due to the music being *too serious*.

For the next six years Ricci composed nothing. In 1844 he married Lidia Stoltz, by whom he had two children, Adelaide, who in 1867 sang at the Théâtre des Italiens in Paris, but died soon after, and Luigi, who lives in London. 'La Solitaria delle Asturie' was given in Odessa in 1844; 'Il Birraio di Preston' in Florence in 1847; and in 1852 'La Festa di Piedigrotta' was very successful in Naples. His last opera, 'Il Diavolo a quattro,' was performed in Trieste in 1859.

Luigi Ricci composed in collaboration with his brother FEDERICO 'Il Colonnello,' given in Rome, and 'M. de Chalumeaux,' in Venice, in 1835; in 1836 'Il Disertore per amore' for the San Carlo in Naples, and 'L'Amante di richiamo,' given in Turin in 1846. Of these four operas, 'Il Colonnello' alone had a well-deserved reception. But Ricci's masterpiece, the opera which has placed him in a very high rank among Italian composers, is 'Crispino e la Comare,' written in 1850 for Venice, and to which his brother Federico partly contributed. This opera, one of the best comic operas of Italy, enjoyed a long success all the world over.

Shortly after the production of 'Il Diavolo a quattro' in 1859, however, symptoms of insanity showed themselves, and the malady soon became violent. He was taken to an asylum at Prague, his wife's birthplace, and died there Dec. 31, 1859. He was much mourned at Trieste; a funeral ceremony was followed by a performance of selections from his principal works, his bust was placed in the lobby of the Opera-house, and a pension was granted to his widow. He

g

published two volumes of vocal pieces entitled 'Mes Loisirs' and 'Les inspirations du Thé' (Ricordi), and he left in MS. a large number of compositions for the cathedral service. His brother,

FEDERICO, was born in Naples, Oct. 22, 1809, entered the Royal Conservatorio of that town, where his brother was then studying, and received his musical education from Bellini and Zingarelli. In 1837 he gave 'La Prigione d'Edimburgo' in Trieste. The barcarola of this opera, 'Sulla poppa del mio brick,' was for long one of the most popular melodies of Italy. In 1839 his 'Duello sotto Richelieu' was only moderately successful at the Scala, but in 1841 'Michelangelo e Rolla' was applauded in Florence. In it sang Signora Strepponi, who afterwards married Verdi. 'Corrado d'Altamura' was given at the Scala in the same year. At the personal request of Charles Albert he composed in 1842 a cantata for the marriage of Victor Emmanuel, and another for a court festival. In 1843 his 'Vallombra' failed at La Scala. 'Isabella de' Medici' (1844) in Trieste, 'Estella' (1846) in Milan, 'Griselda' (1847) and 'I due ritratti' (1850) in Venice, were all failures. 'Il Marito e l'Amante' was greatly applauded in Vienna in 1852, but his last opera, 'Il paniere d'amore,' given there the following year, did not succeed. He was then named Musical Director of the Imperial Theatres of St. Petersburg, which post he occupied for many years.. Of the operas written in collaboration with his brother we have already spoken.

He brought out at the Fantaisies-Parisiennes, Paris, 'Une Folie à Rome,' Jan. 30, 1869, with great success. Encouraged by this he produced an opéra-comique in three acts, 'Le Docteur rose' (Bouffes Parisiens, Feb. 10, 1872), and 'Une Fête à Venise,' a reproduction of his earlier work, 'Il Marito e l'Amante' (Athénée, Feb. 15, 1872). Shortly after this Federico retired to Conegliano in Italy, where he died Dec. 10, 1877. He was concerned partially or entirely in nineteen operas. Of his cantatas we have spoken. He also left two masses, six albums or collections of vocal pieces (Ricordi), and many detached songs.　　　　L. R.

RICCIO, TEODORO, a native of Brescia, who after holding the post of choirmaster at one of the churches of Brescia was in 1576 invited by George Frederick, Margrave of Brandenberg-Anspach, to be his capellmeister at Anspach. When in 1579 George Frederick became also Duke of Prussia, Riccio accompanied him as capellmeister to his new capital Königsberg, where, like Scandello, also a native of Brescia, in similar circumstances at Dresden, Riccio adopted the Lutheran faith, and seems to have settled for the rest of his life with an occasional visit to Anspach. His adoption of Lutheranism made little difference to the nature of his compositions for use in church, as Latin was still largely used in the services of Lutheran court chapels, and so we find that his publications mainly consist of various volumes of Latin masses, motets, and magnificats, a 4 to 8 or 12. Probably Johann Eccard, who was called to be his coadjutor at Königsberg from 1581, provided the music required for German texts. Besides the Latin works the *Quellen-Lexikon* mentions two incomplete books of madrigals a 5 and 6, and one book of Canzone alla napolitana. Riccio is supposed to have died between 1603 and 1604, since in the latter year Eccard is known to have definitely succeeded him as capellmeister.　　　　J. R. M.

RICERCARE, or RICERCATA (from *ricercare*, 'to search out'), an Italian term of the 17th century, signifying a fugue of the closest and most learned description. Frescobaldi's Ricercari (1615), which are copied out in one of Dr. Burney's note-books (Brit. Mus. Add. MS. 11,588), are full of augmentations, diminutions, inversions, and other contrivances, in fact *recherchés* or full of *research*. J. S. Bach has affixed the name to the 6-part Fugue in his 'Musikalisches Opfer,' and the title of the whole contains the word in its initials—Regis Iussu Cantio Et Reliqua Canonica Arte Resoluta. But the term was also employed for a fantasia on some popular song, street-cry, or such similar theme. Dr. Cummings has a MS. book, dated 1580-1600, containing twenty-two ricercari by Cl. da Coreggio, Gianetto Palestina (*sic*), A. Vuillaert (*sic*), O. Lasso, Clemens non Papa, Cip. Rore, and others—compositions in four and five parts, on 'Ce moy de May,' 'Vestiva i colli,' 'La Rossignol,' 'Susan un jour,' and other apparently popular songs. This use of the word appears to have been earlier than the other, as pieces of the kind by Adriano (1520-67) are quoted.　　　　G.

RICH, JOHN, son of Christopher Rich, patentee of Drury Lane Theatre, was born about 1682. His father, having been compelled to quit Drury Lane, had erected a new theatre in Lincoln's Inn Fields, but died in 1714 when it was upon the eve of being opened. John Rich, together with his brother Christopher, then assumed the management and opened the house about six weeks after his father's death. Finding himself unable to contend against the superior company engaged at Drury Lane, he had recourse to the introduction of a new species of entertainment—pantomime—in which music, scenery, machinery,[1] and appropriate costumes formed the prominent features. In these pieces he himself, under the assumed name of Lun, performed the part of Harlequin with such ability as to extort the admiration of even the most determined opponents of that class of entertainment. [He played Harlequin in 'Cheats, or the Tavern Bilkers,' a pantomime by John

---

[1] Most of Rich's machinery was invented by John Hoole, the translator of Tasso, and his father, Samuel Hoole, an eminent watchmaker.

Weaver (adapted from 'Les Fourberies de Scapin'), with music by Dr. Pepusch, in 1716-17. w. h. g. f.] [See also Beggar's Opera, vol. i. p. 277 ; Lincoln's Inn Fields Theatre, vol. ii. p. 733 ; Pantomime, vol. iii. p. 616.] Encouraged by success he at length decided upon the erection of a larger theatre, the stage of which should afford greater facilities for scenic and mechanical display, and accordingly built the first Covent Garden Theatre, which he opened Dec. 7, 1732. Hogarth produced a caricature on the occasion of the removal to the new house, entitled 'Rich's Glory, or his Triumphal Entry into Covent Garden,' copies of which will be found in Wilkinson's *Londina Illustrata*, and in H. Saxe Wyndham's *Annals of Covent Garden Theatre*, vol. i. He conducted the new theatre with great success until his death, relying much upon the attraction of his pantomimes and musical pieces, but by no means neglecting the regular drama. In his early days he had attempted tragic acting, but failed. He died Nov. 26, 1761, and was buried Dec. 4, in Hillingdon churchyard, Middlesex. (See list of productions, etc., in the *Dict. of Nat. Biog.*)   w. h. h.

RICHAFORT, Jean, a Flemish musician of the earlier part of the 16th century, whom we know on the authority of the poet Ronsard to have been a pupil of Josquin Després. He was one of the more distinguished composers of the period immediately after Josquin, in which with the retention of what was valuable in the older technique of contrapuntal artifice, there was, as Mr. Wooldridge observes, a greater approach made towards purity of sound and beauty of expression. The only known dates of Richafort's career are that between 1543 and 1547 he was choirmaster of the church of St. Gilles, Bruges, but this is supposed to have been towards the end of his life, since as early as 1519 a motet of his composition appears in one of the collections of Petrucci, the Motetti de la Corona, lib. ii. His works appeared only in the collections of the time, and specially in those of Attaignant and Modernus between 1530 and 1550. Two masses are specially mentioned, one 'O genetrix gloriosa' published by Attaignant 1532, and afterwards copied into the Sistine chapel and other choir-books ; the other, ' Veni Sponsa Christi,' 1540, based on one of his own motets, which Ambros describes as the finest of the collection of motets in which it appears. The motet has been reprinted in Maldeghem's 'Trésor.' A Requiem, a 6, would seem from the account which Ambros gives of it to be on the whole more curious than beautiful, though it testifies to the aim after intensity of expression. While the other voices sing the ritual text, the two tenor sing in canon 'Circumdederunt me gemitus mortis,' and also reply to each other as if with exclamations of personal sorrow, 'c'est douleur non pareille.' If some of Richafort's

works retain a character of antique severity, others, as Eitner observes, are remarkable for their wonderful beauty, clearness, and simplicity. Several of his motets Ambros singles out for high praise. Of one which he mentions, ' Quem dicunt homines,' the opening portion is given by Mr. Wooldridge in the *Oxford History of Music*, vol. ii. pp. 269-70. Glarean gives in full Richafort's motet ' Christus resurgens ' as a good example of the polyphonic treatment of the Ionic mode. Of the fifteen chansons of Richafort in various collections, two fine specimens are accessible in modern reprints, ' De mon triste déplaisir' in Commer Collectio xii., and 'Sur tous regrets' in Eitner's republication of Ott's ' Liederbuch,' 1544.   j. r. m.

RICHARD CŒUR DE LION. An opéra-comique in three acts ; words by Sedaine, music by Grétry. Produced at the Opéra-Comique Oct. 21, 1784. The piece has a certain historical value. One of the airs, ' Une fièvre brûlante,' was for long a favourite subject for variations. Beethoven wrote a set of eight upon it (in C major), published in Nov. 1798, having probably heard the air at a concert of Weigl's in the preceding March. Another set of seven (also in C) were for long attributed to Mozart, but are now decided not to be by him. The air 'Ô Richard, ô mon roi, l'univers t'abandonne,' was played on a memorable occasion in the early stage of the French Revolution—at the banquet at Versailles on Oct. 1, 1789. [Two versions were made for the English stage ; General Burgoyne's was acted at Drury Lane in 1786, and Leonard MacNally's at Covent Garden in the same year. Thomas Linley adapted Grétry's music to one of them and the opera remained a standard work for many years.   f. k.]   g.

RICHARDS, Henry Brinley, son of Henry Richards, organist of St. Peter's, Carmarthen, was born there Nov. 13, 1817, and intended for the medical profession, but preferred the study of music, and became a pupil of the Royal Academy of Music, where he obtained the King's scholarship in 1835, and again in 1837. He soon gained a high position in London as a pianist. As a composer he was financially very successful, his song 'God bless the Prince of Wales' (published in 1862) having reached a high pitch of popularity, even out of England, and his sacred songs, part-songs, and pianoforte pieces having been most favourably received. [An overture in F minor was performed in 1840.] He composed additional songs for the English version of Auber's 'Crown Diamonds,' when produced at Drury Lane in 1846. He especially devoted himself to the study of Welsh music (upon which he lectured), and many of his compositions were inspired by his enthusiastic love for his native land. He exerted himself greatly in promoting the interests of the South Wales Choral Union on its visits to London in 1872 and 1873, when they successfully competed at the National Music Meetings at the Crystal Palace. [He died in London, May 1, 1885.] (Additions from *Dict. of Nat. Biog.*)   W. H. H.

RICHARDSON, JOSEPH, an eminent flute-player, born in 1814, and died March 22, 1862. He was engaged in most of the London orchestras, was solo player at Jullien's concerts for many years, and afterwards became principal flute in the Queen's private band. [He played at the Melodists' Club and the Società Armonica in 1836, and was a member of the Liszt concert party in 1841, and visited Dublin in that capacity. W. H. G. F.] His neatness and rapidity of execution were extraordinary, and were the great features of his playing. He composed numerous fantasias for his instrument, usually extremely brilliant.   G.

RICHARDSON, VAUGHAN, born in London in the latter half of the 17th century, was in 1685 a chorister of the Chapel Royal, under Dr. Blow. He was possibly a nephew of Thomas Richardson (alto singer, gentleman of the Chapel Royal from 1664 to his death, July 23, 1712, and lay vicar of Westminster Abbey), and a brother of Thomas Richardson, who was his fellow-chorister. In June 1693 he was appointed organist of Winchester Cathedral. In 1701 he published 'A collection of Songs for one, two, and three voices, accompany'd with instruments.' He was author of some church music : a fine anthem, 'O Lord God of my salvation,' and an Evening Service in C (composed in 1713), are in the Tudway Collection (Harl. MSS. 7341 and 7342), and another anthem, 'O how amiable,' also in Tudway, and printed in Page's 'Harmonia Sacra'; others are in the books of different cathedrals. He was also composer of 'An Entertainment of new Musick, composed on the Peace' [of Ryswick], 1697 ; 'A Song in praise of St. Cecilia,' written for a celebration at Winchester about 1700, and a 'set of vocal and instrumental music,' written for a like occasion in 1703. [An autograph volume of music, containing fourteen anthems, a 'Song for the King' (1697), six sonatas for strings, etc., is in the possession of J. S. Bumpus, Esq.] He died before June 26, 1729, and not, as commonly stated, in 1715.   W. H. H.

RICHAULT, CHARLES SIMON, head of a family of celebrated French music-publishers, born at Chartres, May 10, 1780, came early to Paris, and served his apprenticeship in the music-trade with J. J. Momigny. From him he acquired a taste for the literature of music and chamber compositions ; and when he set up for himself at No. 7 Rue Grange Batelière in 1805, the first works he published were classical. He soon perceived that there was an opening in Paris for editions of the best works of German musicians, and the early efforts of French composers of promise. His calcula-

tion proved correct, and his judgment was so sound that his business increased rapidly, and he was soon obliged to move into larger premises in the Boulevard Poissonnière, first at No. 16, and then at No. 26. Here he published Mozart's Concertos in 8vo score, and other works of the classical composers of Germany, and acquired the bulk of the stock of the firms of Frey, Naderman, Sieber, Pleyel, Petit, Erard, and Delahante. He moved in 1862 to No. 4 in the Boulevard des Italiens. In this house he died, Feb. 20, 1866, well known as a publisher of judgment and ability, a man of keen intellect, and a pleasant social companion. His son, GUILLAUME SIMON, born in Paris, Nov. 2, 1806, had long been his father's partner, and continued in the old line of serious music. At the same time he realised that in so important a business it was well that the Italian school should be represented, and accordingly bought the stock of the publisher Pacini. On his death, Feb. 7, 1877, his son, LÉON, born in Paris, August 6, 1839, resolved to give a fresh impetus to the firm, which already possessed 18,000 publications. Bearing in mind that his grandfather had been the first to publish Beethoven's Symphonies and Mozart's Concertos in score ; to make known in France the oratorios of Bach and Handel, and the works of Schubert, Mendelssohn, and Schumann ; to bring out the first operas of Ambroise Thomas and Victor Massé ; to encourage Berlioz when his 'Damnation de Faust' was received with contempt, and to welcome the orchestral compositions of Reber and Gouvy ; M. Léon Richault above all determined to maintain the editions of the German classical masters which had made the fortune of the firm. His intelligent administration of his old and honourable business procured him a silver medal at the International Exhibition of 1878, the highest recompense open to music-publishers, the jury having refused them the gold medal.   G. C.

RICHTER, ERNST FRIEDRICH EDUARD, son of a schoolmaster, born Oct. 24, 1808, at Grossschönau in Lusatia ; from his eleventh year attended the Gymnasium at Zittau, managed the choir, and arranged independent performances. In 1831 he went to Leipzig to study with Weinlig, the then Cantor, and made such progress that soon after the foundation of the Conservatorium, in 1843, he became one of the professors of harmony and counterpoint. Up to 1847 he conducted the Singakademie ; he was afterwards organist successively of the Peterskirche (1851) and the Neukirche and Nicolaikirche (1862). After Hauptmann's death, Jan. 3, 1868, he succeeded him as Cantor of the Thomasschule. Of his books, the *Lehrbuch der Harmonie* (afterwards called *Praktische Studien zur Theorie*), (12th ed. 1876), has been translated into Dutch, Swedish, Italian, Russian, Polish, and English. The *Lehre von der Fuge*

HANS RICHTER

has passed through three editions, and *Vom Contrapunct* through two. The English translations of all these are by Franklin Taylor, and were published by Cramer & Co. in 1864, 1878, and 1874 respectively. Richter also published a *Catechism of Organ-building*. Of his many compositions *de circonstance* the best known is the Cantata 'Dithyrambe,' for the Schiller Festival in 1859. Other works are—an oratorio, 'Christus der Erlöser' (March 8, 1849), masses, psalms, motets, organ-pieces, string-quartets, and sonatas for PF. He became one of the King's Professors in 1868, died at Leipzig, April 9, 1879, and was succeeded as Cantor by W. Rust.   F. G.

RICHTER, FERDINAND TOBIAS, a native of Würzburg, the date of whose birth is given as 1649, succeeded Alessandro Poglietti as Imperial Court organist at Vienna in 1683. In the *Quellen-Lexikon* he is wrongly said to have been the teacher in composition of the Emperor Leopold I., but he was undoubtedly music teacher to Leopold's children, the future Emperor Joseph I., and the three Archduchesses. Richter enjoyed a high reputation as organ-player and composer. Several even of Pachelbel's pupils at Nuremberg came afterwards to Vienna to perfect themselves in organ-playing by further instructions from Richter, and Pachelbel himself must have held Richter in high esteem, since in 1699 he dedicated to him along with Buxtehude his organ or clavier work entitled 'Hexachordum Apollinis.' It is all the more remarkable that so few organ works of Richter have been preserved. In a recent volume of the Denkmäler der Tonkunst in Oesterreich (Jahrg. xiii. Th. 2) three clavier suites out of a set of five, and an organ toccata with short fugued Versetti out of a set of five on the church tones intended for liturgical use, have been printed for the first time, but hardly suffice to explain his great reputation. The Imperial Library at Vienna preserves in MS. two serenatas by Richter evidently intended for court festivities, 'L' Istro ossequioso,' and 'Le promesse degli Dei ;' also five spiritual dramas composed for performance by the pupils of the Jesuit college at Vienna. There are also some instrumental works, a sonata *a* 7 (described as for two Trombe, one Timpano, two violini, two viole da braccio e cembalo), along with some Balletti *a* 4 and *a* 5, also two Sonatas *a* 8. Richter died at Vienna in 1711.   J. R. M.

RICHTER, FRANZ XAVER, was born at Höllischau in Moravia on Dec. 1 or 31,[1] 1709. His first official post was that of capellmeister to the Abbot of Kempten, which he held from 1740 until 1750, when difficulties appear to have arisen with the authorities as the result of his duplication of posts. He had been a bass-singer at

the court of Mannheim since 1747, and no doubt this was the cause of his dismissal from Kempten. He is stated by F. Walter, *Geschichte des Theaters*, etc. (1898), to have appeared in operatic performances in 1748 and 1749. He was also engaged as leader of the second violins in the orchestra. An oratorio, 'La deposizione della croce,' was performed at Mannheim in 1748. He left Mannheim for Strasburg in 1769, becoming capellmeister at the Minster, and spending the remainder of his life there. He died Sept. 12, 1789, and was succeeded by Ignaz Pleyel, who, according to Fétis, had acted as his assistant for six years. Burney, in his *Present State (Germany)*, ii. 327, speaks of the great reputation Richter enjoyed, and of the want of real individuality in his music. He speaks of his frequent employment of the device called ROSALIA. He left sixty-four symphonies, of which the themes of sixty-two are given in the volume devoted to the Mannheim school of symphonists in the *Denkm. der Tonk. in Bayern*, vol. iii. 1. Three of the symphonies are printed in full, and the preface contains a detailed account of the composer. An enormous mass of church music is ascribed to him in Riemann's *Lexikon*, such as twenty-eight masses, two requiems, sixteen psalms, thirty-eight motets, etc. The *Quellen-Lexikon* gives a more limited list of extant works, and contains many doubtful statements concerning the composer.   M.

RICHTER, HANS, celebrated conductor, born April 4, 1843, at Raab in Hungary, where his father was capellmeister of the cathedral. His mother, *née* Josephine Csazinsky, sang the part of Venus in 'Tannhäuser' at the first performance in Vienna in 1857 ; she was afterwards a very successful teacher of singing in Vienna, and died Oct. 20, 1892. The father died in 1853, and Hans was then placed at the Löwenburg Convict-School in Vienna. Thence he went into the choir of the Court chapel, and remained there for four years. In 1860 he entered the Conservatorium, and studied the horn under Kleinecke, the violin under Heissler, and theory under Sechter. After a lengthened engagement as horn-player in the orchestra of the Kärnthnerthor opera he was recommended by Esser to Wagner, went to him at Lucerne, remained there from Oct. 1866 to Dec. 1867, and made the first fair copy of the score of the 'Meistersinger.' In 1868 he accepted the post of conductor at the Hofund National Theatre, Munich, and remained there for a year. He next visited Paris, and after a short residence there, proceeded to Brussels for the production of 'Lohengrin' (March 22, 1870). He then returned to Wagner at Lucerne, assisted at the first performance of the 'Siegfried Idyll' (Dec. 1870), and made the fair copy of the score of the 'Nibelungen Ring' for the engraver. In April 1871 he went to Pesth as chief conductor of the National Theatre, a post to which he owes

[1] Gerber's *Lexikon*, followed by Riemann, in his *Lexikon*, and in his preface to the Denkm. volume containing works by Richter, gives Dec. 1 as the date of birth ; Eitner's *Quellen-Lexikon* follows Lobstein's *Beiträge*, etc., in giving Dec. 31 as the date.

much of his great practical knowledge of the stage and stage business. In Jan. 1875 he conducted a grand orchestral concert in Vienna, which had the effect of attracting much public attention to him, and accordingly, after the retirement of Dessoff from the Court opera, Richter was invited to take the post, which he entered upon in the autumn of 1875, concurrently with the conductorship of the Philharmonic Concerts. In 1884-90 he acted as conductor of the concerts of the Gesellschaft der Musikfreunde.

He had conducted the rehearsals of the 'Nibelungen Ring' at Bayreuth, and in 1876 he directed the whole of the rehearsals and performances of the Festival there, and, at the close of the third set of performances, received the Order of Maximilian from the King of Bavaria, and that of the Falcon from the Grand Duke of Weimar. In 1877 he produced the 'Walküre' in Vienna, and followed it in 1878 by the other portions of the trilogy. In 1878 he was made court capellmeister, and received the Order of Franz Josef. His first introduction to English audiences was at the famous Wagner Concerts given in the Albert Hall in 1877, when he shared the duties of conductor with Wagner himself. In 1879 (May 5-12), 1880 (May 10-June 14), and 1881 (May 9-June 23) were started what were at first called 'Orchestral Festival Concerts,' but afterwards the 'Richter Concerts,' in London, which excited much attention, chiefly for the conductor's knowledge of the scores of Beethoven's symphonies and other large works, which he conducted without book. [The Richter Concerts went on for many years with great success, but after the great conductor went to live in Manchester in 1897, as director of the Manchester Orchestra, the London concerts were given less regularly. In 1882 and 1884 he conducted important performances of German operas in London, introducing 'Die Meistersinger' and 'Tristan' to the London public. The special performances of German opera which form part of the Covent Garden season have been conducted by Richter since 1904. Since 1885 he has conducted the Birmingham Festival. In that year he received the honorary degree of Mus.D. at Oxford. He has numberless decorations. (See *Musical Times*, 1899, pp. 441-6.) A special concert in celebration of his thirty years' work in England took place at the Queen's Hall, June 3, 1907.]

Herr Richter is certainly one of the very greatest of conductors. He owes this position in great measure to the fact of his intimate practical acquaintance with the technique of the instruments in the orchestra, especially the wind, to a degree in which he stands alone. As a musician he is a self-made man, and enjoys the peculiar advantages which spring from that fact. His devotion to his orchestra is great, and the high standard and position of the band of the Vienna opera-house is due to him. He is a

great master of *crescendo* and *decrescendo*, and of the finer shades of accelerating and retarding the time.   F. G.

RICOCHET. The employment of the bounding staccato—*staccato à ricochet*—is thus indicated in violin music. As the best examples of this bowing are to be found in the works of the French and Belgian composers, it is probable that it owes its invention to the father of virtuosity—Paganini. The same system which governs the flying staccato—so brilliantly applied by Paganini, de Bériot, Wieniawski, Vieuxtemps, and latter-day virtuosi, to the execution of swift chromatic passages—dominates the ricochet, but being thrown upon the strings less rapidly, and with more force, the effect is heavier. To accomplish this style of bowing neatly, the stick should be held so that the full breadth of the hair at the upper part shall fall upon the strings accurately. The wrist must remain flexible, while the fingers grip the bow firmly and relax to allow the bow to rebound. Two graceful examples of the application of the ricochet are to be found in the Bolero of de Bériot's 'Scène de Ballet,' and in the Polonaise of Vieuxtemps's 'Ballade et Polonaise.'   O. R.

RICORDI, GIOVANNI, founder of the well-known music-publishing house in Milan, where he was born in 1785, and died March 15, 1853. He made his first hit with the score of Mosca's 'Pretendenti delusi.' Since that time the firm has published for all the great Italian *maestri*, down to Verdi and Boïto, and has far outstripped all rivals. The *Gazzetta musicale*, edited with great success by Mazzucato, has had much influence on its prosperity. It possesses the whole of the original scores of the operas it has published—a most interesting collection. Giovanni's son and successor TITO (born Oct. 29, 1811, died Sept. 7, 1888) further enlarged the business. The catalogue issued in 1875 contains 738 pages large 8vo. The present head of the firm is his son GIULIO DI TITO, born Dec. 19, 1840, who is a practised writer, a skilled draughtsman, a composer of drawing-room music, under the pseudonym of Burgmein, and in all respects a thoroughly cultivated man.   F. G.

RIDDELL, JOHN (or 'Riddle'), composer of Scottish dance music, born at Ayr, Sept. 2, 1718. It is stated in 'The Ballads and Songs of Ayrshire,' 1846, that Riddell was blind from infancy, also that he was composer of the well-known tune 'Jenny's Bawbee.' This latter statement is not authenticated. Burns mentions him as 'a bard-born genius,' and says he is composer of 'this most beautiful tune' ('Finlayston House').

Riddell published about 1766 his first 'Collection of Scots Reels, or Country Dances, and Minuets,' and a second edition of it, in oblong folio, in 1782. He died April 5, 1795.   F. K.

RIDDELL, ROBERT, a Scottish antiquary,

and friend of Robert Burns. He was an army (or Volunteer) captain, and resided on the family estate Glenriddell, Dumfriesshire. He was an amateur composer of Scottish dance music, and wrote the music to one or two of Burns's songs. His most interesting publication (1794) is ' A Collection of Scotch, Galwegian, and Border Tunes . . . selected by Robert Riddell of Glenriddell, Esq.,' folio. He died at Friars' Carse, April 21, 1794.   F. K.

RIDOTTO. See REDOUTE.

RIEDEL, CARL, born Oct. 6, 1827, at Kronenberg in the Rhine provinces. Though always musically inclined he was educated for trade, and was at Lyons in the silk business until 1848, when he determined to devote himself to music as a profession. He returned home and at once began serious study under the direction of Carl Wilhelm, then an obscure musician at Crefeld, but destined to be widely known as the author of the ' Wacht am Rhein.' Late in 1849 Riedel entered the Leipzig Conservatorium, where he made great progress under Moscheles, Hauptmann, Becker, and Plaidy. He had long had a strong predilection for the vocal works of the older masters of Germany and Italy. He practised and performed in a private society at Leipzig Astorga's ' Stabat,' Palestrina's ' Improperia,' and Leo's ' Miserere,' and this led him to found a singing society of his own, which began on May 17, 1854, with a simple quartet of male voices, and was the foundation of the famous Association which, under the name of the ' Riedelsche Verein,' was so celebrated in Leipzig. Their first public concert was held in November 1855. The reality of the attempt was soon recognised ; members flocked to the society ; and its first great achievement was a performance of Bach's B minor Mass, April 10, 1859. At that time Riedel appears to have practised only ancient music, but this rule was by no means maintained ; and in the list of the works performed by the Verein we find Beethoven's Mass in D, Kiel's ' Christus,' Berlioz's ' Messe des Morts,' and Liszt's ' Graner Messe ' and ' St. Elizabeth.' Riedel's devotion to his choir was extraordinary : he was not only its conductor, but librarian, secretary, treasurer, all in one. His interest in the welfare of music was always ready and always effective, and many of the best vocal associations of North Germany owe their success to his advice and help. He was one of the founders of the ' Beethovenstiftung,' and an earnest supporter of the Wagner performances at Bayreuth in 1876. His own compositions are chiefly part-songs for men's voices, but he edited several important ancient works by Praetorius, Franck, Eccard, and other old German writers, especially a ' Passion ' by Heinrich Schütz, for which he selected the best portions of four Passions by that master—a proceeding certainly deserving all that can be

said against it. Riedel died in Leipzig, June 3, 1888.   G.

RIEM, WILHELM FRIEDRICH, born at Cölleda in Thuringia, Feb. 17, 1779, was one of J. A. Hiller's pupils in the Thomasschule at Leipzig. In 1807 he was made organist of the Reformed church there, and in 1814 of the Thomasschule itself. In 1822 he was called to Bremen to take the cathedral organ and be director of the Singakademie, where he remained till his death, April 20, 1837. He was an industrious writer. His cantata for the anniversary of the Augsburg Confession, 1830 (for which Mendelssohn's Reformation Symphony was intended) is dead ; so are his quintets, quartets, trios, and other large works, but some of his eight sonatas and twelve sonatinas are still used for teaching purposes. He left two books of studies for the PF., which are out of print, and sixteen progressive exercises, besides useful compositions for the organ.   G.

RIEMANN, KARL WILHELM JULIUS HUGO, was born at Grossmehlra near Sondershausen, July 18, 1849, and studied law, etc., at Berlin and Tübingen. He saw active service in the Franco-German war, and afterwards devoted his life to music, studying in the Leipzig Conservatorium. After some years' residence at Bielefeld as a teacher, he was appointed to the post of ' privatdozent ' in the University of Leipzig, which he held from 1878 to 1880, going thence to Bromberg ; in 1881-90 he was teacher of the piano and theory in the Hamburg Conservatorium, and subsequently (after a three-months' stay at the conservatorium of Sondershausen) was given a post at the Conservatorium of Wiesbaden (1890-95). In the latter year he returned to Leipzig, as a lecturer in the University, and in 1901 was appointed professor. He has been amazingly active as a writer on every branch of musical knowledge, but his work is as thorough as if it had been small in extent. On the teaching of harmony, on musical phrasing and the peculiarities of notation required for explaining his system to students, he has strongly supported various innovations, most of them due to his own inventive faculty. The complete list of his works is given in his own *Musiklexikon*, to which the reader must be referred ; *Die Natur der Harmonik* (1882), *Vereinfachte Harmonielehre* (1893), *Lehrbuch des . . . Contrapunkts* (1888), have been translated into English, as well as the various catechisms dealing with every branch of musical study, and the famous *Musiklexikon* (first edition, 1882, sixth, 1905, Engl. translation, 1893, etc.). The useful *Opernhandbuch* (1884-93) and works on musical history must not be forgotten. As a practical illustration of his excellent method of teaching the art of phrasing, his editions of classical and romantic pianoforte music, called 'Phrasierungsausgaben,' may be mentioned. He has edited many masterpieces of ancient music, as, for instance, the works of Abaco and the Mannheim symphonists for the Denkmäler der Tonkunst in Bayern (1900 and 1902 respectively). His original compositions—for he has found time to write music as well as musical literature—are numerous but not very important, being mainly of an educational kind ; but his position in the musical world of Germany is deservedly a very high one.   M.

RIEMSDIJK, J. C. M. van, born 1843, died June 30, 1895, at Utrecht, was a member of an aristocratic family, and thus grew up amid the best and most powerful social influences. An enthusiastic amateur musician, he threw himself into the work of furthering the cause of music. A cultivated scholar, he devoted himself to editing the old songs of the Netherlands with marked success. A practical and business-like citizen, he became Technical Director of the State railway. His house was always open to any artists, and his welcome was always ready for those who followed music as a profession.

He was chairman of the 'Society of Musical history in the North Netherlands,' in which capacity he doubtless had many facilities for collecting old Netherland Folk-Songs, of which he availed himself in the most able manner. His works are as follows :—

1881. *State Music School of Utrecht* 1631-1881 (a complete history of the Art of Music in the Netherlands between those dates).
*1882. Netherland Dances arranged for PF. Duet.
1883. The two first Music books of Tylman Susato (c. 1545), a collection of Netherland Folk Songs of the 16th century.
*1888. Hortus Musicus of J. A. Reinken (1623-1722) for two violins, viola, and bass (translation into Dutch).
*1890. Twenty-four Songs of the 15th and 16th centuries with PF. accompaniment.
1896. Folk Song book of the Netherlands (posthumous).
   The works marked thus * are among the publications of the Vereeniging voor N.-Nederlands Musikgeschiedenis.   D. H.

RIENZI, DER LETZTE DER TRIBUNEN (the last of the Tribunes). An opera in five acts ; words (founded on Bulwer's novel) and music by Wagner. He adopted the idea in Dresden in 1837 ; two acts were finished early in 1839, and the opera was produced at Dresden, Oct. 20, 1842. 'Rienzi' was brought out in French (Nuitter and Guillaume) at the Théâtre Lyrique, April 16, 1869, and in English at Her Majesty's Theatre, London (Carl Rosa), Jan. 27, 1879.   G.

RIES. A distinguished family of musicians.
1. JOHANN RIES, native of Benzheim on the Rhine, born 1723, was appointed Court trumpeter to the Elector of Cologne at Bonn [with a salary of 192 thalers], May 2, 1747, and violinist in the Capelle, March 5, 1754. On April 27, 1764, his daughter Anna Maria was appointed singer. In 1774 she married Ferdinand Drewer, violinist in the band, and remained first soprano till the break-up in 1794. Her father died at Cologne in 1784. Her brother, FRANZ ANTON, was born at Bonn, Nov. 10, 1755, and was an infant phenomenon on the violin ; learned from J. P. Salomon, and was able to take his father's place in the orchestra at the age of eleven. His salary began

when he was nineteen [at 25 thalers a year ; he occupied the post until 1774]. In 1779 he visited Vienna, and made a great success as a solo and quartet player. But he elected to remain, on poor pay, in Bonn, and was rewarded by having Beethoven as his pupil and friend. [On March 2, 1779, he petitioned the Elector Maximilian for a post, and received it on May 2.] During the poverty of the Beethoven family, and through the misery caused by the death of Ludwig's mother in 1787, Franz Ries stood by them like a real friend. In 1794 the French arrived, and the Elector's establishment was broken up. Some of the members of the band dispersed, but Ries remained, and documents are preserved which show that after the passing away of the invasion he was to have been Court-musician.[1] Events, however, were otherwise ordered ; he remained in Bonn, and at Godesberg, where he had a little house, till his death ; held various small offices, culminating in the Bonn city government in 1800, taught the violin, and brought up his children well. He assisted Wegeler in his Notices of Beethoven, was present at the unveiling of Beethoven's statue in 1845, had a Doctor's degree and the Order of the Red Eagle conferred on him, and died, Nov. 1, 1846, aged ninety-one all but nine days.

2. Franz's son FERDINAND, who with the Archduke Rudolph enjoys the distinction of being Beethoven's pupil, was born at Bonn in November (baptized Nov. 28) 1784. He was brought up from his cradle to music. His father taught him the pianoforte and violin, and B. Romberg the violoncello. In his childhood he lost an eye through small-pox. After the break-up of the Elector's band he remained three years at home, working very hard at theoretical and practical music, scoring the quartets of Haydn and Mozart, and arranging the 'Creation,' the 'Seasons,' and the Requiem with such ability that they were all three published by Simrock.

In 1801 he went to Munich to study under Winter, in a larger field than he could command at home. Here he was so badly off as to be driven to copy music at 3d. a sheet. But poor as his income was he lived within it, and when after a few months Winter left Munich for Paris, Ries had saved seven ducats. With this he went to Vienna in October 1801, taking a letter from his father to Beethoven. Beethoven received him well, and when he had read the letter said, 'I can't answer it now ; but write and tell him that I have not forgotten the time when my mother died' ; and knowing how miserably poor the lad was, he on several occasions gave him money unasked, for which he would accept no return. The next three years Ries spent in Vienna. Beethoven took

[1] See the curious and important lists and memorandums, published for the first time in Thayer's *Beethoven*, i. 248.

a great deal of pains with his pianoforte-playing, but would teach him nothing else. He, however, prevailed on Albrechtsberger to take him as a pupil in composition. The lessons cost a ducat each ; Ries had in some way saved up twenty-eight ducats, and therefore had twenty-eight lessons. Beethoven also got him an appointment as pianist to Count Browne, the Russian *chargé d'affaires*, and at another time to Count Lichnowsky. The pay for these services was probably not over-abundant, but it kept him, and the position gave him access to the best musical society. Into Ries's relations with Beethoven we need not enter here. They are touched upon in the sketch of the great master in vol. i. of this work, and they are fully laid open in Ries's own invaluable notices. He had a great deal to bear, and considering the secrecy and imperiousness which Beethoven often threw into his intercourse with every one, there was probably much unpleasantness in the relationship. Meantime of course Ries must have become saturated with the music of his great master ; a thing which could hardly tend to foster any little originality he may ever have possessed.

As a citizen of Bonn he was amenable to the French conscription, and in 1805 was summoned to appear there in person. He left in Sept. 1805, made the journey on foot *via* Prague, Dresden, and Leipzig, reached Coblenz within the prescribed limit of time, and was then dismissed on account of the loss of his eye. He then went on to Paris, and existed in misery for apparently at least two years, at the end of which time he was advised to try Russia. On August 27, 1808, he was again in Vienna, and soon afterwards received from Reichardt an offer of the post of capellmeister to Jerome Bonaparte, King of Westphalia, at Cassel, which Reichardt alleged had been refused by Beethoven. Ries behaved with perfect loyalty and straightforwardness in the matter. Before replying, he endeavoured to find out from Beethoven himself the real state of the case ; but Beethoven having adopted the idea that Ries was trying to get the post over his head, would not see him, and for three weeks behaved to him with an incredible degree of cruelty and insolence. When he could be made to listen to the facts he was sorry enough, but the opportunity was gone.

The occupation of Vienna (May 12, 1809) by the French was not favourable to artistic life. Ries, however, as a French subject, was free to wander. He accordingly went to Cassel, possibly with some lingering hopes, played at Court, and remained till the end of February 1810, very much applauded and fêted, and making money—but had no offer of a post. From Cassel he went by Hamburg and Copenhagen to Stockholm, where we find him in Sept. 1810, making both money and reputation.

He had still his eye on Russia, but between Stockholm and Petersburg the ship was taken by an English man-of-war, and all the passengers were turned out upon an island in the Baltic. In Petersburg he found Bernhard Romberg, and the two made a successful tour, embracing places as wide apart as Kiev, Reval, and Riga. The burning of Moscow (Sept. 1812) put a stop to his progress in that direction, and we next find him again at Stockholm in April 1813, *en route* for England. By the end of the month he was in London.

Here he found his countryman and his father's friend, Salomon, who received him cordially and introduced him to the Philharmonic Concerts. His first appearance there was March 14, 1814, in his own PF. Sextet. His symphonies, overtures, and chamber works frequently occur in the programmes, and he himself appears from time to time as a PF. player, but rarely if ever with works of Beethoven's. Shortly after his arrival he married an English lady of great attractions, and he remained in London till 1824, one of the most conspicuous figures of the musical world. 'Mr. Ries,' says a writer in the *Harmonicon* of March 1824, 'is justly celebrated as one of the finest pianoforte performers of the day ; his hand is powerful and his execution certain, often surprising ; but his playing is most distinguished from that of all others by its romantic wildness.'

His sojourn here was a time of herculean labour. His compositions numbered at their close nearly 180, including 6 fine symphonies ; 4 overtures ; 6 string quintets, and 14 do. quartets ; 9 concertos for PF. and orchestra ; an octet, a septet, 2 sextets, and a quintet, for various instruments ; 3 PF. quartets, and 5 do. trios ; 20 duets for PF. and violin ; 10 sonatas for PF. solo ; besides a vast number of rondos, variations, fantasias, etc., for the PF. solo and duet. Of these 38 are attributable to the time of his residence here, and they embrace 2 symphonies, 4 concertos, a sonata, and many smaller pieces. As a pianist and teacher he was very much in request. He was an active member of the Philharmonic Society. His correspondence with Beethoven during the whole period is highly creditable to him, proving his gratitude towards his master, and the energy with which he laboured to promote Beethoven's interests. That Beethoven profited so little therefrom was no fault of Ries's.

Having accumulated a fortune adequate to the demands of a life of comfort, he gave a farewell concert in London, April 8, 1824, and removed with his wife to Godesberg, near his native town, where he had purchased a property. Though a loser by the failure of a London bank in 1825-26, he was able to live independently. About 1830 he removed to Frankfort. His residence on the Rhine brought him into close contact with the Lower Rhine

Festivals, and he directed the performances of the years 1825, 1829, 1830, 1832, 1834, and 1837, as well as those of 1826 and 1828 in conjunction with Spohr and Klein respectively. In 1834 he was appointed head of the town orchestra and Singakademie at Aix-la-Chapelle. But he was too independent to keep any post, and in 1836 he gave this up and returned to Frankfort. In 1837 he assumed the direction of the Cecilian Society there on the death of Schelble, but this lasted a few months only, for on Jan. 13, 1838, he died after a short illness.

The principal works which he composed after his return to Germany are ' Die Räuberbraut,' which was first performed in Frankfort probably in 1829, then in Leipzig, July 4, and London, July 15, of the same year, and often afterwards in Germany ; another opera, known in Germany as 'Liska,' but produced at the Adelphi, London, in English, as 'The Sorcerer,' by Arnold's company, August 4, 1831, and a third, 'Eine Nacht auf dem Libanon ' ; an oratorio, 'Der Sieg des Glaubens' (The Triumph of the Faith), apparently performed in Dublin for the first time in 1831[1] and then at Berlin, 1835 ; and a second oratorio, 'Die Könige Israels' (The Kings of Israel), Aix-la-Chapelle, 1837. He also wrote much chamber music and six symphonies. All these works, however, are dead. Beethoven once said of his compositions, ' he imitates me too much.' He caught the style and the phrases, but he could not catch the immortality of his master's work. One work of his will live—the admirable *Biographical Notices of Ludwig van Beethoven*, which he published in conjunction with Dr. Wegeler (Coblenz, 1838). The two writers, though publishing together, have fortunately kept their contributions quite distinct ; Ries's occupies from pp. 76 to 163 of a little duodecimo volume, and of these the last thirty-five pages are occupied by Beethoven's letters. The work is translated into French by Le Gentil (Dentu, 1862), and partially into English by Moscheles, as an Appendix to his version of Schindler's *Life of Beethoven*.

3. HUBERT, youngest brother of the preceding, was born at Bonn, April 1, 1802. He made his first studies as a violinist under his father, and afterwards under Spohr. Hauptmann was his teacher in composition. From 1824 he lived at Berlin. In that year he entered the band of the Königstadt Theatre, Berlin, and in the following year became a member of the Royal band. In 1835 he was appointed Director of the Philharmonic Society at Berlin. In 1836 he was nominated Concertmeister, and in 1839 elected a member of the Royal Academy of Arts. [In 1851 he became a teacher at the Kgl. Theater-instrumentalschule, from which he retired with a pension in 1872.] A thorough musician and a solid violinist, he was held in great esteem as

[1] Information from L. M'C. L. Dix, Esq.

a leader, and more especially as a methodical and conscientious teacher. His Violin-School for beginners is a very meritorious work, eminently practical, and widely used. He published two violin-concertos, studies and duets for violins, and some quartets. An English edition of the Violin-School appeared in 1873 (Hofmeister). He died in Berlin, Sept. 14, 1886. Three of his sons gained reputation as musicians :—

LOUIS, violinist, born at Berlin, Jan. 30, 1830, pupil of his father and of Vieuxtemps, has, since 1853, been settled in London, where he enjoys great and deserved reputation as violinist and teacher. He was a member of the Quartet of the Musical Union from 1855 to 1870, and held the second violin at the Monday Popular Concerts from their beginning in 1859, until his retirement in 1897.

ADOLPH, pianist, born at Berlin, Dec. 20, 1837, died in April 1899. He was a pupil of Kullak for the piano, and of Boehmer for composition, and lived in London as a pianoforte teacher. He published a number of compositions for the piano, and some songs. A. W. T. ; with additions in square brackets by E. H.-A.

RIES, FRANZ, violinist and composer, was born on April 7, 1846, in Berlin. His musical gifts were apparent in early youth. The possessor of an alto voice of exceptional beauty, he was admitted at the age of twelve to the *Königl. Domchor* (royal Cathedral choir), which then, under Neithardt's direction, enjoyed considerable reputation in the musical circles of Berlin. He studied the violin in the first instance under his father, and afterwards, in Paris, under Léon Massart and Henri Vieuxtemps. In composition he was a pupil of Friedr. Kiel. Gained in 1868 the first prize at the Paris Conservatoire, and was active in the musical life of the city as soloist and also as viola-player in the Vieuxtemps Quartet. In 1870 he migrated, owing to the Franco-German war, to London, appearing as a soloist at the Crystal Palace. But in 1872 an unfortunate nerve affection of the left hand compelled him to renounce the career of an executive artist. He founded in 1874 a publishing business in Dresden, and ten years later became partner in the firm Ries & Erler in Berlin, where he still resides. As a composer his main successes have been made in four suites for violin and pianoforte, which are in the repertory of almost every famous violinist. He has also written a string quintet, two string quartets, a dramatic overture, piano and violin solos and arrangements, besides a series of songs, one of which, the ' Rheinlied,' has taken rank in the Rhine provinces as a Folk-song.   W. W. C.

RIETER - BIEDERMANN. An eminent German firm of music-publishers. The founder was Jacob Melchior Rieter-Biedermann (born May 14, 1811 ; died Jan. 25, 1876), who in June 1849 opened a retail business and lending-library at Winterthur. Since the first work was published in 1856, the business has continually improved and increased. In 1862, a publishing branch was opened at Leipzig. The stock catalogue of the firm includes music by Berlioz, Brahms (PF. Concerto, PF. Quintet, Requiem, Magelone-Lieder, etc.) ; A. Dietrich ; J. O. Grimm ; Gernsheim ; von Herzogenberg ; F. Hiller ; Holstein ; Kirchner ; Lachner ; F. Marschner ; Mendelssohn (op. 98, Nos. 2, 3 ; opp. 103, 105, 106, 108, 115, 116) ; Raff ; Reinecke ; Schumann (opp. 130, 137, 138, 140, 142) ; etc.   G.

RIETZ (originally RITZ [1]) EDUARD, the elder brother of Julius Rietz, an excellent violinist, was born at Berlin, Oct. 17, 1802. He studied first under his father, a member of the royal band, and afterwards, for some time, under Rode. He died too young to acquire more than a local reputation, but his name will always be remembered in connection with Mendelssohn, who had the highest possible opinion of his powers as an executant,[2] and who counted him amongst his dearest and nearest friends. It was for Rietz that he wrote the Octet which is dedicated to him, as well as the Sonata for PF. and violin, op. 4. For some years Rietz was a member of the royal band, but as his health failed him in 1824 he had to quit his appointment and even to give up playing. He founded and conducted an orchestral society at Berlin, with considerable success ; he died of consumption Jan. 23, 1832. Mendelssohn's earlier letters teem with affectionate reference to him, and the news of his death affected him deeply.[3] The Andante in Mendelssohn's string quintet, op. 18, was composed at Paris ' in memory of E. Ritz,' and is dated on the autograph ' Jan. 23, 1832,' and entitled ' Nachruf.'   P. D.

RIETZ, JULIUS, younger brother of the preceding, violoncellist, composer, and eminent conductor, was born at Berlin, Dec. 28, 1812. Brought up under the influence of his father and brother, and the intimate friend of Mendelssohn, he received his first instruction on the violoncello from Schmidt, a member of the royal band, and afterwards from Bernhard Romberg and Moritz Ganz. Zelter was his teacher in composition. Having gained considerable proficiency on his instrument, he obtained, at the age of sixteen, an appointment in the band of the Königstadt Theatre, where he also achieved his first success as a composer by writing incidental music for Holtei's drama, ' Lorbeerbaum und Bettelstab.' In 1834 he went to Düsseldorf as second conductor of the opera. Mendelssohn, who up to his death showed a warm interest in Rietz, was at that time at the head of the opera, and on his

resignation in the summer of 1835, Rietz became his successor. He did not, however, remain long in that position, for, as early as 1836, he accepted, under the title of ' Städtischer Musik-director,' the post of conductor of the public subscription-concerts, the principal choral society, and the church-music at Düsseldorf. In this position he remained for twelve years, gaining the reputation of an excellent conductor, and also appearing as a solo violoncellist in most of the principal towns of the Rhine-province. During this period he wrote some of his most successful works—incidental music to dramas of Goethe, Calderon, Immermann, and others ; music for Goethe's Liederspiel ' Jery und Bätely,' his first Symphony in G minor ; three overtures —' Hero and Leander,'[4] Concert overture in A major, Lustspiel-overture, the ' Altdeutscher Schlachtgesang' and ' Dithyrambe '—both for men's voices and orchestra. He was six times chief conductor of the Lower Rhine Festivals— in 1845, 1856, and 1869 at Düsseldorf ; in 1864, 1867, and 1873 at Aix.

In 1847, after Mendelssohn's death, he took leave of Düsseldorf, leaving Ferdinand Hiller as his successor, and went to Leipzig as conductor of the opera and the Singakademie. [He gave up the post at the opera in 1854.] From 1848 we find him also at the head of the Gewandhaus orchestra, and teacher of composition at the Conservatorium. In this position he remained for thirteen years. Two operas, ' Der Corsar' and ' Georg Neumark,' were failures, but his Symphony in E♭ had a great and lasting success. At this period he began also to show his eminent critical powers by carefully revised editions of the scores of Mozart's symphonies and operas, of Beethoven's symphonies and overtures for Breitkopf & Härtel's complete edition, and by the work he did for the Bach and (German) Handel Societies. His editions of Handel's scores contrast very favourably with those of some other editors. An edition of Mendelssohn's complete works closed his labours in this respect.

In 1860 the King of Saxony appointed him Conductor of the Royal Opera and of the music at the Hofkirche at Dresden. He also accepted the post of Artistic Director of the Dresden Conservatorium. In 1874 the title of General-Musikdirector was given to him. The University of Leipzig had already in 1859 conferred on him the honorary degree of Doctor of Philosophy.

Rietz was for some time one of the most influential musicians of Germany. He was a good violoncellist, but soon after leaving Düsseldorf he gave up playing entirely. As a composer he showed a rare command of all the resources of the orchestra and a complete mastery of all technicalities of composition. Yet few of Rietz's works have shown any vitality.

---

[1] Uniformly so spelt by Mendelssohn.
[2] ' I long earnestly,' says he, in a letter from Rome, 'for his violin, and his depth of feeling ; they come vividly before my mind when I see his beloved neat handwriting.'
[3] Mendelssohn's *Letters from Italy and Switzerland,* English translation, p. 327.
[4] See Mendelssohn's *Letters,* ii. p. 234 (Eng. ed.).

As a composer he can hardly be said to show distinct individuality ; his ideas are wanting in spontaneity, his themes are generally somewhat dry, and their treatment often rather diffuse and laboured. In fact Rietz was an excellent musician, and a musical intellect of the first rank—but not much of a poet. His great reputation rested, first, on his talent for conducting, and secondly on his rare acquirements as a musical scholar. An unfailing ear, imperturbable presence of mind, and great personal authority, made him one of the best conductors of modern times. The combination of practical musicianship with a natural inclination for critical research and a pre-eminently intellectual tendency of mind, made him a first-rate judge on questions of musical scholarship. After Mendelssohn and Schumann, Rietz probably did more than anybody else to purify the scores of the great masters from the numerous errors of text by which they were disfigured. He was an absolute and uncompromising adherent of the classical school, and had but little sympathy with modern music after Mendelssohn ; and even in the works of Schubert, Schumann, and Brahms he was over-apt to see the weak points. As to the music of the newest German School, he held it in abhorrence, and would show his aversion on every occasion. He was, however, too much of an opera-conductor not to feel a certain interest in Wagner, and in preparing his operas would take a special pride and relish in overcoming the great and peculiar difficulties contained in Wagner's scores.

Rietz had many personal friends, but, as will appear natural with a man of so pronounced a character and opinions, also a number of bitter enemies. He died at Dresden, Sept. 12, 1877, leaving a large and valuable musical library, which was sold by auction in Dec. 1877. Besides the works already mentioned he published a considerable number of compositions for the chamber, songs, concertos for violin and for various wind-instruments. He also wrote a great Mass.   P. D.

RIGADOON (French *Rigadon* or *Rigaudon*), a lively dance, which most probably came from Provence or Languedoc, although its popularity in England has caused some writers to suppose that it is of English origin. It was danced in France in the time of Louis XIII., but does not seem to have become popular in England until the end of the 17th century. According to Rousseau it derived its name from its inventor, one Rigaud, but others connect it with the English 'rig,' *i.e.* wanton or lively.

The Rigadoon was remarkable for a peculiar jumping step (which is described at length in Compan's *Dictionnaire de la Danse*, Paris, 1802) ; this step survived the dance for some time. The music of the Rigadoon is in 2-4 or C time, and consists of three or four parts, of which the third is quite short. The number of bars is unequal, and the music generally begins on the third or fourth beat of the bar. The following example is from the third part of Henry Playford's ' Apollo's Banquet' (sixth edition, 1690). The same tune occurs in ' The Dancing Master,' but in that work the bars are incorrectly divided.

W. B. S.

RIGBY, GEORGE VERNON, born at Birmingham, Jan. 21, 1840, when about nine years old was a chorister of St. Chad's Cathedral, Birmingham, where he remained for about seven years. In 1860, his voice having changed to a tenor, he decided upon becoming a singer, tried his strength at some minor concerts in Birmingham and its neighbourhood, and succeeded so well that in 1861 he removed to London, and on March 4, appeared at the Alhambra, Leicester Square (then a concert room, managed by E. T. Smith), and in August following at Mellon's Promenade Concerts at Covent Garden. In 1865 he sang in the provinces as a member of H. Corri's Opera Company, until November, when he went to Italy and studied under Sangiovanni at Milan, where, in Nov. 1866, he appeared at the Carcano Theatre as the Fisherman in ' Guglielmo Tell.' He next went to Berlin, and in Jan. 1867 appeared at the Victoria Theatre there, in the principal tenor parts in ' Don Pasquale,' ' La Sonnambula,' and ' L'Italiana in Algieri.' He then accepted a three months' engagement in Denmark, and performed Almaviva in the ' Barbiere,' the Duke in ' Rigoletto,' and other parts, in Copenhagen and other towns. He returned to England in Sept. 1867, and sang at various places. In 1868 he was engaged at the Gloucester Festival with Sims Reeves, whose temporary indisposition afforded him the opportunity of singing the part of Samson in Handel's oratorio, in which he acquitted himself so ably that he was immediately engaged by the Sacred Harmonic Society, where he appeared, Nov. 27, 1868, with signal success, and immediately established himself as an oratorio singer, appearing at all the principal festivals. In 1869 he appeared on the stage of the Princess's Theatre as Acis in Handel's ' Acis and Galatea.' His voice was of fine quality, full compass, and considerable power, and he sang with earnestness and care. Since an appearance at Brighton in 1887 in 'Eli,' he has virtually retired.   W. H. H.

RIGHINI, VINCENZO, a well-known conductor of the Italian opera in Berlin, born at Bologna, Jan. 22, 1756. As a boy he was a chorister at San Petronio, and had a fine voice, but owing to injury it developed into a tenor of so rough and muffled a tone, that he turned his attention to theory, which he studied with Padre Martini. In 1776 he sang for a short time in the Opera buffa at Prague, then under Bustelli's direction, but was not well received. He made a success there, however, with three operas of his composition, 'La Vedova scaltra,' 'La Bottega del Caffè,' and 'Don Giovanni,' also performed in Vienna (August 1777), whither Righini went on leaving Prague in 1780. There he became singing-master to Princess Elisabeth of Würtemberg, and conductor of the Italian opera. He next entered the service of the Elector of Mainz, (1788-92) and composed for the Elector of Treves 'Alcide al Bivio' (Coblenz) and a missa solemnis (1790). In April 1793 (owing to the success of his 'Enea nel Lazio') he was invited to succeed Alessandri at the Italian Opera of Berlin, with a salary of 3000 thalers (about £450). Here he produced 'Il Trionfo d'Arianna' (1793), 'Armida' (1799), 'Tigrane' (1800), 'Gerusalemme liberata,' and 'La Selva incantata' (1802). The last two were published after his death with German text (Leipzig, Herklotz).

In 1793 Righini married Henriette Kneisel (born at Stettin in 1767, died of consumption at Berlin, Jan. 25, 1801), a charming blonde, and according to Gerber, a singer of great expression. After the death of Friedrich Wilhelm II. (1797) his post became almost a sinecure, and in 1806 the opera was entirely discontinued. Righini was much beloved. Gerber speaks in high terms of his modesty and courtesy, and adds, 'It is a real enjoyment to hear him sing his own pieces in his soft veiled voice to his own accompaniment.' As a composer he was not of the first rank, and of course was eclipsed by Mozart. His best point was his feeling for *ensemble*, of which the quartet in 'Gerusalemme' is a good example. He was a successful teacher of singing, and counted distinguished artists among his pupils. After the loss of a promising son in 1810, his health gave way, and in 1812 he was ordered to try the effects of his native air at Bologna. When bidding good-bye to his colleague, Anselm Weber, he said, 'It is my belief that I shall never return ; if it should be so, sing a Requiem and a Miserere for me'—touching words, too soon fulfilled by his death at Bologna, August 19, 1812. His own Requiem (score in the Berlin Library) was performed by the Singakademie in his honour.

Besides twenty operas, of which a list is given by Fétis (thirteen are mentioned in the *Quellen-Lexikon* as still extant), Righini composed church music—a Te Deum and a Missa Solennis were published—several cantatas, and innumerable Scenas, Lieder, and songs ; also a short ballet, 'Minerva belebt die Statuen des Dädalus' (1802), and some instrumental pieces, including a serenade for two clarinets, two horns, and two bassoons (1799, Breitkopf & Härtel). One of his operas, 'Il Convitato di pietra, ossia il dissoluto,' will always be interesting as a forerunner of Mozart's 'Don Giovanni.' It was produced at Vienna, August 21, 1777 (ten years before Mozart's), and is described by Jahn (*Mozart*, ii. 333). His best orchestral work is his overture to 'Tigrane,' which was often played in Germany and England. Breitkopf & Härtel's Catalogue shows a tolerably long list of his songs, and his exercises for the voice (1804) are amongst the best that exist. English amateurs will find a duet of his, 'Come opprima,' from 'Enea nel Lazio,' in the 'Musical Library,' vol. i. p. 8, and two airs in Lonsdale's 'Gemme d'Antichità.' He was one of the sixty-three composers who set the words 'In questa tomba oscura,' and his setting was published in 1878 by Ritter of Magdeburg.   F. G.

RIGOLETTO. An opera in three acts ; libretto by Piave (founded on V. Hugo's *Le Roi s'amuse*), music by Verdi. Produced at the Teatro Fenice, Venice, March 11, 1851, and given in Italian at Covent Garden, May 14, 1853, and at the Italiens, Paris, Jan. 19, 1857.   G.

RILLÉ, FRANÇOIS ANATOLE LAURENT DE, the composer of an enormous number of partsongs and other small choral works, born at Orleans in 1828. He was at first intended to be a painter, but altered his purpose and studied music under an Italian named Comoghio, and subsequently under Elwart. His compositions, of which a list of the most important is given in the supplement to Fétis, have enjoyed a lasting popularity with 'orphéoniste' societies, and although they contain few if any characteristics which would recommend them to the attention of earnest musicians, they have that kind of vigorous effectiveness which is exactly suited to their purpose. A large number of operettas of very slight construction have from time to time been produced in Paris, and the composer has made various more or less successful essays in the department of church music.   M.

RIMBAULT, EDWARD FRANCIS, LL.D., son of Stephen Francis Rimbault, organist of St. Giles in the Fields, was born in Soho, June 13, 1816. He received his first instruction in music from his father, but afterwards became a pupil of Samuel Wesley. At sixteen years old he was appointed organist of the Swiss Church, Soho. He early directed his attention to the study of musical history and literature, and in 1838 delivered a series of lectures on the history of music in England. In 1840 he took an active part in the formation of the Musical Antiquarian and Percy Societies, of both which he became secretary, and for both which he edited several works. In 1841 he was editor of the musical publications of the Motet Society. In the course of the next few years he edited a collection of Cathedral Chants ; The Order of Daily Service according to the use of Westminster Abbey ; a reprint of Lowe's *Short Direction for the performance of Cathedral Service* ; Tallis's Responses ; Marbeck's Book of Common Prayer, noted ; a volume of unpublished Cathedral Services ; Arnold's Cathedral Music ; and the oratorios of ' Messiah,' ' Samson,' and ' Saul,' for the Handel Society. In 1842 he was elected a F.S.A. and member of the Academy of Music in Stockholm, and obtained the degree of Doctor in Philosophy. He was offered, but declined, the appointment of Professor of Music in Harvard University, U.S.A. In 1848 he received the honorary degree of LL.D., from the university of Oxford. He lectured on music at the Collegiate Institution, Liverpool ; the Philosophic Institute, Edinburgh ; the Royal Institution of Great Britain, and elsewhere. He published *The Organ, its History and Construction* (1855) (in collaboration with Mr. E. J. Hopkins), *Notices of the Early English Organ Builders* (1865), *History of the Pianoforte* (1860), *Bibliotheca Madrigaliana* (1847), *Musical Illustrations of Percy's Reliques, The Ancient Vocal Music of England, The Rounds, Catches, and Canons of England* (in conjunction with Rev. J. P. Metcalfe), two collections of Christmas Carols. ' A Little Book of Songs and Ballads,' etc. etc. He edited North's *Memoirs of Musick* (1846), Sir Thomas Overbury's Works (1856), the *Old Cheque Book of the Chapel Royal* (1872), and two Sermons by Boy Bishops. He arranged many operas and other works, was author of many elementary books, and an extensive contributor to periodical literature. His compositions were but few, the principal being an operetta, ' The Fair Maid of Islington' (1838), music to ' The Castle Spectre' (1839), and a posthumous cantata, 'Country Life.' His pretty little song, 'Happy Land,' had an extensive popularity. After his resignation of the organistship of the Swiss Church, he was successively organist of several churches and chapels, such as St. Peter's, Vere Street. He died, after a lingering illness, Sept. 26, 1876 (buried at Highgate Cemetery), leaving a fine musical library, which was sold by auction at Sotheby's on July 3, 1877, and following days. See an account of the library in the *Musical World*, 1877, p. 539. An obituary notice appeared in the *Musical Times*, 1877, p. 427, and other papers. The most complete list of his works is in *Brit. Mus. Biog.*   W. H. H.

RIMSKY-KORSAKOV, NICHOLAS ANDREIE-

VICH, was born March 18 (O.S. March 6), 1844, in the little town of Tikhvin, in the Government of Novgorod. The child's earliest musical impressions were derived from a small band, consisting of four Jews employed upon the family estate. These musicians mustered two violins, cymbals, and a tambourine, and were often summoned to the house to enliven the evenings when there was company or dancing. At six years old the boy began to be taught the piano, and at nine he made his first attempts at composition. His talent for music was evident to his parents, but being of aristocratic family he was destined for one of the only two professions then considered suitable for a young man of good birth. In 1856 Rimsky-Korsakov entered the Naval College in St. Petersburg, where he remained until 1862. This period of his life was not very favourable to his musical development, but he managed on Sundays and holidays to receive some instruction in the violoncello from Ulich, and in the pianoforte from an excellent teacher, Fedor Kanillé. His acquaintance with Balakirev, dating from 1861, was the decisive moment in his career. Intercourse with the young but capable leader of the new Russian school of music, and with his disciples, Cui, Moussorgsky, and Borodin, awoke in the young naval cadet an ambition to study the art to more serious purpose. He had only just begun to profit by Balakirev's teaching when he was sent abroad ; but, undaunted by the interruption, during this cruise, which lasted three years (1862-65), he completed a symphony, op. 1. From the letters which he wrote at this time to César Cui it is evident that he composed under great difficulties, but the work was completed in spite of them, and, movement by movement, the manuscript was sent to Balakirev for advice and correction. The work was performed for the first time in December 1865, when Balakirev conducted it at one of the concerts of the Free School of Music, St. Petersburg. It was the first symphony from the pen of a native composer, and the public, who gave it a hearty reception, were surprised when a youth in naval uniform appeared to acknowledge their ovation. Rimsky-Korsakov now remained in St. Petersburg, and was able to renew his musical studies and his close association with the circle of Balakirev.

The compositions which followed the First Symphony—the symphonic poem 'Sadko' (1867), and the opera ' Pskovitianka' ('The Maid of Pskov ')—called the attention of all musical Russia to this promising composer. In 1871 he was appointed professor of composition and instrumentation in the St. Petersburg Conservatoire. He retired from the navy, which can never have been a congenial profession, in 1873, and at the wish of the Grand Duke Constantine Nicholaevich was appointed

NICHOLAS ANDREIEVICH RIMSKY–KORSAKOV

inspector of naval bands, a post which he held until it was abolished in 1884. From 1883 to 1884 he was assistant director to the Court Chapel under Balakirev. Succeeding to Balakirev, he became director and conductor of the Free School Concerts from 1874 to 1881, and conducted the Russian Symphony Concerts, inaugurated in St. Petersburg by Belaiev, from 1886 to 1900. His gifts in this respect, although ignored in England, have been highly appreciated in Paris and Brussels. Rimsky-Korsakov's career has remained closely associated with St. Petersburg, which was the scene of his earliest successes, and on more than one occasion he has declined the directorship of the Moscow Conservatoire. His pupils number some distinguished names : Liadov, Ippolitov-Ivanov, Sacchetti, Grechianinov, and Glazounov have all studied under him for longer or shorter periods. In 1873 Rimsky-Korsakov married Nadejda Nicholaevna Pourgold, a gifted pianist, who proved a helpmeet in the truest sense of the word. This lady and her sister, A. P. Molas, have played important parts in the history of the modern Russian school ; the former by her clever pianoforte arrangements of many of the great orchestral works, while the latter, gifted with a fine voice and dramatic instinct, created most of the leading female rôles in the operatic works of Cui, Moussorgsky, and Borodin, before they obtained a hearing at the Imperial Opera.

Rimsky-Korsakov had already composed his symphonic works 'Sadko' and 'Antar,' and his opera ' Pskovitianka,' and had been appointed professor at the St. Petersburg Conservatoire, when his 'ideal conscientiousness' awoke in him some doubts as to the solidity of his early musical education. Admirably as the system of self-education had worked in his case, he still felt it a duty to undergo a severe course of theoretical study in order to have at his disposal that supreme mastery of technical means in which all the great classical masters excelled. Accordingly he began to work at fugue and counterpoint, thereby calling forth from Tchaikovsky, in 1875, this tribute of admiration : ' I do not know how to express all my respect for your artistic temperament. . . . I am a mere artisan in music, but you will be an artist in the fullest sense of the word.' Most of Rimsky-Korsakov's early works have been revised since this period of artistic discipline. In the earlier phases of his career he was obviously influenced by Glinka and Liszt, and in a lesser degree by Schumann and Berlioz. The imitative period was, however, of short duration, and perhaps no contemporary composer can boast a more individual and distinctive utterance than Rimsky-Korsakov. But its distinctiveness lies in extreme refinement and restraint rather than in violent and sensational expression. He wins but does not force our

attention. A lover of musical beauty rather than musical truth—or, to put it more justly, believing truth to lie in idealistic rather than realistic methods of creation, he was never deeply influenced by the declamatory and naturalistic style of Dargomijsky and Moussorgsky. Like Tchaikovsky, he has divided his career between operatic and symphonic music, but with a steadily increasing tendency towards the former. After his first symphony, written on more or less conventional lines, he showed a distinct preference for the freer forms of programme music, as shown in the symphonic poem 'Sadko,' the Oriental Suite 'Antar,' and the Symphonic Suite 'Scheherezade.' In the Sinfonietta upon Russian themes, and the Third Symphony in C major, he returns to more traditional treatment. Of all his orchestral works the Spanish Capriccio seems to have met with the greatest appreciation in England. Almost without exception Rimsky-Korsakov's symphonic works are distinguished by a poetic and tactful expression of national sentiment. His art is rooted in the Russian soil, and the national element pervades it like a subtle but unmistakable aroma. We may be repelled or fascinated by it, according to individual taste, but we are forced to recognise that this is not mere local colour laid on by a coarse brush to give factitious and sensational interest to music which would be otherwise commonplace in character, but an essential product of the national spirit.

His music invariably carries the charm of expressive orchestration. Taking it up where Glinka left it in his 'Jota Aragonese' and incidental music to 'Prince Kholmsky,' Rimsky-Korsakov has developed this characteristic quality of Russian musicians beyond any of his contemporaries, without, however, overstepping the bounds of what sane minds must still regard as legitimate effect. He is at his best in descriptive orchestration—in the suggestion of landscape and atmospheric conditions. But his clear objective outlook leads him to a luminous and definite tone-painting quite different from the subtle and dreamy impressionism of Debussy. The musical pictures of Rimsky-Korsakov are mostly riant and sunny ; sometimes breezy and boisterous, as in the sea-music of 'Sadko' and 'Scheherezade' ; often full of a quaint pastoral grace, as in the springtide music in his opera 'The Snow Maiden.' His harmony has freshness and individuality. He makes considerable use of the old Church modes and Oriental scales.

All Rimsky-Korsakov's operas, except 'Mozart and Salieri,' are based upon national subjects, historical or legendary. Tales from the Slavonic mythology, which combine poetical allegory with fantastic humour, exercise the greatest attraction for him. In his first opera, 'The Maid of Pskov,' he evidently started under the partial influence of Dargomijsky's 'The Stone Guest,' for the solo parts consist chiefly of mezzo-recitative, the dryness of which is compensated by the orchestral colour freely employed in the accompaniments. In the two operas which followed, 'A Night in May' and 'The Snow Maiden,' the dramatic realism of his first work for the stage gives place to lyrical inspiration and the free flight of fancy. With 'Mozart and Salieri'— a setting of Poushkin's dramatic duologue— and 'The Boyarina Vera Sheloga' Rimsky-Korsakov shows a return to the declamatory style, while 'Sadko,' which appeared in 1896, is a skilful compromise between lyrical and dramatic forms, and may be accepted as the mature expression of his artistic creed. Of all his operatic works, 'The Snow Maiden,' founded upon Ostrovsky's poetical legend of the springtide, has perhaps the most characteristic charm, and seems best calculated to win popular favour outside Russia. 'Sadko,' the thematic material for which is partly drawn from the symphonic poem of the same name, is more epic in character and full of musical interest. It must be surmised that it is only the peculiarly national character of the libretto which has hindered this remarkable work from becoming more widely known. Time, which must inevitably bridge over this intellectual gulf which separates eastern and western Europe, will probably bring these two masterpieces of Russian art to Paris, and perhaps farther afield. Most of Rimsky-Korsakov's operas combine with this strong national element that also of the neighbouring East.

As a song-writer he takes a high place in a school which has shown itself pre-eminent in this branch of art. He has composed about eighty songs, remarkable for an all-round level of excellence, for few are really poor in quality, while the entire collection comprises such lyrical gems as 'Night,' the Hebrew song ('Awake, long since the dawn appeared'), 'A Southern night,' 'Spring,' and 'Come to the kingdom of roses and wine.' In his songs, as in his operas, he inclines more to the lyrical grace of Glinka than to the declamatory force of Dargomijsky. His melodies are not lacking in distinction and charm, especially when they approach in style to the melodies of the folk-songs; but in this respect he is somewhat lacking in impassioned inspiration and copious invention. The richness and picturesqueness of his accompaniments make the characteristic interest of his songs.

A close study of the works of Rimsky-Korsakov reveals a distinguished musical personality; a thinker, a fastidious and exquisite craftsman, an artist of that refined and discriminating type who is chiefly concerned in satisfying the demands of his own conscience rather than the tastes of the general public. Outside Russia he has been censured for his exclusive devotion to national ideals. On the

other hand, some Russian critics have accused him of opening the door to Wagnerism in national opera. This is only true in so far as he has grafted upon the older lyrical forms the use of some modern methods, notably the occasional employment of the *leitmotif*. As regards instrumentation he has a remarkable faculty for the invention of new and brilliant effects, and is a master in the skilful use of onomatopœia. Given a temperament, musically endowed, which *sees* its subject with the direct and observant vision of the painter, instead of *dreaming* it through a mist of subjective exaltation, we get a type of mind that naturally tends to a programme which is clearly defined. Rimsky-Korsakov belongs to this class. We feel in all his music the desire to *depict*, which so often inclines us to the language of the studio in attempting to express the quality of his work. His music is entirely free from that tendency to melancholy unjustly supposed to be the characteristic of all Russian art. The folk-songs of Great Russia—the source from which the national composers have drawn their inspiration—are pretty evenly divided between the light and shade of life; it is the former aspect which makes the strongest appeal to the vigorous, optimistic, but highly poetical temperament of this musician.

Many gifted members of the New Russian School were prevented by illness, by the enforced choice of a second vocation, and by the imperfect conditions of artistic life fifty or sixty years ago, from acquiring a complete musical education. Rimsky-Korsakov, out of the fulness of his own technical equipment, has ever been ready to sacrifice time and labour in the interest of his fellow-workers. Thus, he orchestrated 'The Stone Guest' which Dargomijsky endeavoured to finish on his death-bed; part of Borodin's 'Prince Igor' and Moussorgsky's operas 'Khovantshina' and 'Boris Godounov.'

In 1889, during the Paris Exhibition, he conducted two concerts devoted to Russian music given in the Salle Trocadéro. In 1890 and again in 1900 he conducted concerts of Russian music in the Théâtre de la Monnaie, Brussels.

In March 1905, in consequence of a letter published in the *Russ*, in which he advocated the autonomy of the St. Petersburg Conservatoire, hitherto under the management of the Imperial Russian Musical Society, and complained of the too stringent police supervision to which the students were subjected, Rimsky-Korsakov was dismissed from his professorship. This high-handed action on the part of the authorities was deeply resented by all his colleagues, and Glazounov, Liadov, and Blumenfeld immediately resigned their posts by way of protest. By the autumn of the same year the Conservatoire had actually wrested some powers of self-government from the Musical Society, and having elected Glazounov as director, the new committee lost no time in re-instating Rimsky-Korsakov in the professorship of composition and instrumentation which he had honourably filled since 1871. The following is a list of Rimsky-Korsakov's numerous compositions :—

ORCHESTRAL

Symphony No. 1, E♭ minor, op. 1, afterwards transposed into E minor; Symphony No. 2, 'Antar,' op. 9, afterwards entitled 'Oriental Suite'; Symphony No. 3, C minor, op. 32, 1873, revised 1884; Sinfonietta on Russian themes, A minor, op. 31. Overture on Russian themes, op. 28 ; 'Easter,' overture, op. 36, 1888 ; 'Sadko, musical picture, op. 5, 1867, revised 1891 ; Serbian Fantasia, op. 6 ; 'A Tale,' op. 29, subject from the Prologue of Pouskin's 'Russlan and Lioudmilla'; Capriccio on Spanish themes, op. 34, 1887; Symphonic Suite 'Scheherezade' (from the *Arabian Nights*), op. 35, 1888 ; Suites from the operas 'The Snow Maiden' and 'Tsar Saltana,' and the opera-ballet 'Mlada,' op. 57 ; prelude 'At the Grave,' op. 61 ; Suite from the opera 'Christmas Eve' (chorus *ad lib.*).

CHAMBER MUSIC

String quartet, F major, op. 12 ; string sextet, A major (MS.); first movement of the string quartet on the theme B-la-f, (Belaiev) ; third movement of the quartet 'for a Fête Day'; allegro of the string quartet in the collection 'Fridays' ; Serenade for violoncello and pianoforte, op. 37.

ORCHESTRA AND SOLO INSTRUMENTS

Pianoforte concerto, C♯ minor, op. 30; Fantasia on Russian themes for violin and orchestra.

PIANOFORTE

Six variations on the theme B-a-c-h, op. 10 ; four pieces, op. 11; three pieces, op. 15; six fugues, op. 17; eight variations on a folktune (no op. number); five variations for the 'Paraphrases' (see BORODIN).

CHORAL WITH ORCHESTRA

Folk-song, op. 20 ; 'Slava,' op. 21 ; cantata for soprano, tenor, and mixed chorus, op. 44; 'The Fir and the Palm' (from op. 3) for baritone ; two ariosos for bass, 'Anchar' (The Upas Tree) and 'The Prophet,' op. 49; trio for female voices, op. 53 ; 'The Legend of St. Olga,' cantata for soli and chorus, op. 58 ; 'Fragment from Homer,' cantata for three female voices and chorus, op. 60.

CHORUS ONLY

Two trios for female voices, op. 13 ; four variations and a fughetta for female quartet, op. 14; six choruses a cappella, op. 16 ; two mixed choruses, op. 18 ; fifteen Russian folk-songs, op. 19 ; four trios for male voices, op. 23.

SONGS, ETC.

Four songs, op. 2 ; four songs, op. 3 ; four songs, op. 4 ; four songs, op. 7 ; six songs, op. 8 ; two songs, op. 25 ; four songs, op. 26 ; four songs, op. 27 ; four songs, op. 39 ; four songs, op. 40 ; four songs, op. 41 ; four songs, op. 42 ; four songs, op. 43 ; four songs, op. 45 ; five songs, op. 46 ; two duets, op. 47 ; four duets, op. 50 ; five duets, op. 51 ; two duets, op. 52 ; four duets for tenor, op. 55 ; two duets, op. 56.

SACRED WORKS

The liturgy of St. John Chrysostom (a portion only), op. 22 ; six transpositions, including the psalm 'By the waters of Babylon,' op. 22 *a* ; 'We praise Thee, O God' (MS. 1883).

OPERAS

'The Maid of Pskov' ('Pskovitianka '), libretto from a drama by Mey (1870-72); performed St. Petersburg, 1873, revised in 1894); 'A Night in May,' text from Gogol (1878, St. Petersburg, 1880) ; 'The Snow Maiden,' text from Ostrovosky (1880-81, St. Petersburg, 1882) ; 'Mlada,' fairy opera-ballet (St. Petersburg, 1893) ; 'Christmas Eve,' legendary opera, text from Gogol, 1874 (Maryinsky Theatre, St. Petersburg, 1895) ; 'Sadko,' epic-opera, 1895-96 (Private Opera, Moscow, 1897 ; St. Petersburg, 1901) ; 'Mozart and Salieri,' dramatic scenes, op. 48, 1898 (Private Opera, Moscow, 1898) ; 'Boyarina Vera Sheloga,' musical dramatic prologue to 'The Maid of Pskov,' op. 54 (Private Opera, Moscow, 1899 ; St. Petersburg, 1902) ; 'The Tsar's Bride,' 1898 (Private Opera, Moscow, 1899 ; St. Petersburg, Maryinsky Theatre, 1902) ; 'The Tale of Tsar Saltana, etc.,' 1899-1900 (Private Opera, Moscow, 1900) ; 'Servilia' (Maryinsky Theatre, St. Petersburg, 1902) ; 'Kostchei the Immortal,' an autumn legend (Private Opera, Moscow, 1902) ; 'Pan Voyevoda,' 'The Tale of the Invisible City of Kitezh and the Maiden Fevronia.'

One hundred Russian folk-songs, op. 24 (1877) ; forty Russian folk-songs (1882) ; *A Practical Guide to the Study of Harmony* (1888).

R. N.

RINALDO. (i.) Handel's first opera in England ; composed in a fortnight, and produced at the King's Theatre in the Haymarket, Feb. 24, 1711. The libretto was founded on the episode of Rinaldo and Armida in Tasso's *Gerusalemme liberata* (the same on which Gluck based his 'Armida '). Rossi wrote it in Italian, and it was translated into English by Aaron Hill. The opera was mounted with extraordinary magnificence, and had an unin-

terrupted run of fifteen nights—at that time unusually long. The march, and the air 'Il tricerbero,' were long popular as 'Let us take the road' ('Beggar's Opera '), and 'Let the waiter bring clean glasses.' 'Lascia ch'io pianga '—made out of a saraband in Handel's earlier opera 'Almira' (1704)—is still a favourite with singers and hearers. [John Walsh published the songs in folio with the title 'Arie del' opera di Rinaldo composta dal Signor Hendel, Maestro di Capella di sua Altezza Elettorale d'Hannover. London, printed for J. Walsh, Servant in ordinary to her Britannick Majesty.' It is said that Walsh made £1500 by the publication, and that the composer addressed to him a satirical letter :— ' My dear Sir, as it is only right that we should be on an equal footing, you shall compose the next opera, and I will sell it.' F. K.]   G.

(ii.) Cantata for male voices, set to Goethe's words, by Johannes Brahms (op. 50). First performed by the Akademisches Gesangverein, Vienna, Feb. 28, 1869.

RINALDO DI CAPUA, an Italian composer of the 18th century, of whose life very little is known. Burney made his acquaintance in Rome in 1770, and since he describes him as an old man we may suppose him to have been born about 1700-10. Fétis gives 1715 as the year of his birth, and Rudhardt 1706, but neither writer states his authority for the date. According to Burney he was 'the natural son of a person of very high rank in that country [*i.e.* the kingdom of Naples], and at first studied music only as an accomplishment ; but being left by his father with only a small fortune, which was soon dissipated, he was forced to make it his profession.' It has been assumed that he was born at Capua, and took his name from that place ; but it may be noted that whether Rinaldo had a legitimate claim to it or not, Di Capua was a fairly common surname in the neighbourhood of Naples at that time. He composed his first opera at the age of seventeen, at Vienna, according to Burney ; Spitta showed that no opera by Rinaldo was ever produced at Vienna, but thought it probable that he had some connection with that city, since Metastasio's 'Ciro Riconosciuto,' which formed the libretto of an opera by Rinaldo produced at Rome in 1737, was set to music for the first time by Caldara for performance at Vienna on August 28, 1736. A further connection with the imperial court is shown by the fact that he composed a special work to celebrate the election of Francis I. in 1745. It seems, therefore, not unreasonable to take Burney's words literally, and to understand that the opera 'Ciro Riconosciuto,' though performed in Rome, was composed in Vienna. If this was his first opera, it would settle 1720 as the year of Rinaldo's birth. Spitta was, however, not aware of the existence of a few airs from a comic opera, the title of which has not been

h

preserved, produced at the Teatro Valle in Rome in the autumn of 1737. Of the subsequent history of Rinaldo's life nothing is known. Burney informs us that 'in the course of a long life he has experienced various vicissitudes of fortune ; sometimes in vogue, sometimes neglected.' Most of his operas were given at Rome, a few being produced at Florence and Venice ; although described in some libretti as a Neapolitan, no opera of his is known to have been performed in Naples. The Bouffons Italiens performed an intermezzo of his, 'La Zingara' (La Bohémienne), at Paris in 1753, in a version which included songs by other composers ; among these was the well-known 'Tre giorni son che Nina,' generally ascribed to Pergolesi, and on this account attributed to Rinaldo by Spitta. The song has, however, been recently proved to be by another composer [TRE GIORNI SON CHE NINA]. When Burney knew him he was in somewhat impoverished circumstances, owing to the indifference of the public which had once applauded him. He had collected his works with a view to making provision for his old age, but at the moment when they were required, discovered that his son had sold them for waste paper. The date of his death is not known. Burney mentions an intermezzo composed for the Capranica theatre in 1770 ('I finti pazzi'), when he was already an old man. Another opera, 'La donna vendicativa' (ascribed by Clément and Larousse to 1740, though on no apparent authority), was performed in Rome in 1771, and this was probably his last work. After this date we know only of 'La Giocondina' (Rome, 1778), which was probably a revival of an earlier work. Burney, with characteristic kindliness, recommended him as a teacher to William Parsons, who had studied at a Neapolitan conservatorio, where according to his own account he learnt nothing. Parsons became Master of the King's Musick in 1786, to the great disappointment of Burney, to whom the post had been promised. Another pupil of Rinaldo's was Antonio Aurisicchio.

Rinaldo was supposed to have been the inventor of accompanied recitative ; Burney pointed out that this invention belonged to Alessandro Scarlatti. Rinaldo himself only claimed 'to have been among the first who introduced long *ritornellos* or symphonies into the recitatives of strong passion and distress, which express or imitate what it would be ridiculous for the voice to attempt.' An example from 'Vologeso' is in the Fitzwilliam Museum. His musical education having been that of an amateur, his technique of composition was sometimes defective ; but apart from this slight weakness of harmony, he was one of the best composers of his period for dramatic power and melodic beauty. He was especially successful in brilliant coloratura, but was also

capable of producing most attractive light operas. To judge from the few fragments of his work that remain, 'Ciro Riconosciuto' and 'Vologeso' seem to have been his most important dramatic works.

CATALOGUE OF EXTANT WORKS OF RINALDO DI CAPUA

OPERAS

A comic opera, name unknown (Rome, T. Valle, 1737). Fragments: Palermo R.C.M.
Ciro Riconosciuto (Rome, T. Tordinona, 1737 ; revived Rome, 1739). Fragments: formerly in possession of Spitta ; Brit. Mus.; Münster.
La Commedia in Commedia (Rome, T. Valle, 1738). Libretto: Brussels Conservatoire. Fragments: Palermo R.C.M. Revived at Venice (T. San Cassiano, 1749). Libretto: Venice, Bibl. Marc. The opera was also performed in London ; Walsh printed five airs as 'The favourite Songs in the Opera call'd La Comedia in Comedia.' Rinaldo's name is not mentioned, and the work was probably a pasticcio ; one song, however, 'Non so la prole mia,' is in the Palermo collection, which bears Rinaldo's name.
Farnace (Venice, T. S. Giovanni Grisostomo, 1739). Libretto: Venice, Bibl. Marc.
Vologeso Re de' Parti (Rome, T. Argentina, 1739). Libretto: Bologna, Lic. Mus. Fragments: Brit. Mus. ; Brussels Cons. ; Cambridge, Fitz. Mus. ; Dresden ; Münster ; New York, in possession of H. E. Krehbiel, Esq.
La Libertà Nociva (Rome, T. Valle, 1740). Libretto: Bologna, Brussels Cons. Fragments: Brit. Mus. ; Cambridge, Fitz. Mus. Revived in Florence (T. Cocomero, 1742), Bologna (T. Formagliari, 1743). Libretti: Bologna. Also at Venice (T. San Cassiano, 1744). Libretto: Bologna, Venice.
Turno Herdonio Aricino (Rome, T. Capranica, 1743). Libretto: Bologna, Brussels Cons.
Le Nozze di Don Trifone (Rome, T. Argentina, 1743). Libretto: Bologna.
L' Ambizione delusa (Venice, T. S. Cassiano, 1744). Libretto: Bologna, Venice. Revived at Milan (T. Ducale, 1745). Libretto: Bologna.
La Forza del Sangue (intermezzo), (Florence, T. Pallacorda, 1746). Libretto: Brussels Cons.
Il bravo è il bello (intermezzo), (Rome, T. Granari, 1748). Libretto: Brussels Cons.
Mario in Numidia (Rome, T. Dame, 1749). Libretto: Bologna. Fragments: Brit. Mus., Dresden, Munich.
Il Bravo Burlato (intermezzo), (Florence, T. Pallacorda, 1749). Libretto: Brussels Cons.
A comic opera (Rome ? 1750). Fragments: Dresden.
Il Ripiego in Amore (Rome, T. Valle, 1751). Libretto: Bologna.
Il Cavalier Mignatta } (intermezzi), (Rome, T. Capranica, 1751). Il Galloppino   } Libretto: Brussels Cons.
La Donna superba (intermezzo), (Paris, Opéra, 1752). Libretto: Brussels Cons. Fragments (with French words) : Brussels Cons.
La Forza della Pace (Rome, T. Pace, 1752). Libretto: Bologna.
La Zingara (intermezzo), (Paris, Opéra, 1753). Libretto: Brussels Cons. Score, printed in Paris, Brussels Cons. Revived at Pesaro, 1755, as 'Il Vecchio Amante e la Zingara.' Libretto: Bologna.
La Serva Sposa (Rome, T. Valle, 1753). Libretto: Bologna.
La Chiavarina (Rome, T. Valle, 1754). Libretto: Bologna.
Attalo (Rome, T. Capranica, 1754). Libretto: Brussels Cons. Rinaldo di Capua appears here under the pseudonym of Cleofante Doriano.
Adriano in Siria (Rome, Argentina, 1758). Libretto: Brussels Cons. Fragments: Brit. Mus.
La Smorfiosa (Florence, T. Cocomero, 1758). Libretto: Bologna.
Le Donne Ridicole (intermezzo), (Rome, T. Capranica, 1759). Libretto: Brussels Cons.
Il Caffè di Campagna (farsetta), (Rome, T. Pace, 1764). Libretto: Bologna, Brussels Cons.
I Finti Pazzi per Amore (farsetta), (Rome, T. Pace, 1770). Libretto: Bologna, Brussels Cons.
La Donna Vendicativa (farsetta), (Rome, T. Pace, 1771). Libretto: Bologna. Score: Brit. Mus.
La Giocondina (farsetta), (Rome, T. Pace, 1778). Libretto: Brussels Cons.
[La Statua per Puntiglio, ascribed to R. di Capua by Eitner, is by Marcello di Capua.]

SACRED MUSIC

Cantata per la Natività della Beata Vergine (Rome, Collegio Nazareno, 1747). Score: Münster. Paris, Bibl. Nat. ? (Eitner).

A few other works are mentioned by Eitner: symphonies, probably opera overtures, and cantatas (Venice) ascribed to Cavaliere Rinaldi, who may have been a different composer.
Airs from operas not yet unidentified are at Cambridge, Fitz. Mus., Münster, and Montecassino.
The writer is indebted to Mr. H. E. Krehbiel for notice of the airs in his possession ; the MS. from which they are taken formerly belonged to Thomas Gray, the poet, and is described in Mr. Krehbiel's *Music and Manners in the Classical Period.* Other authorities consulted: Burney's *Present State of Music in France and Italy* (1771) ; an article by Spitta in the *Vierteljahrsschrift für Musikwiss.,* vol. iii. (1887), and A. Wotquenne's *Catalogue* of the library of the Brussels Conservatoire, vol. i. (1898). The two latter works give fuller bibliographical details than we have space for here.

E. J. D.

RINCK, or RINK, JOHANN CHRISTIAN HEINRICH, celebrated organist and composer for his instrument, was born at Elgersburg in Saxe-Gotha, Feb. 18, 1770, and died at Darmstadt, August 7, 1846. His talent developed itself at an early period, and, like JOHANN SCHNEIDER, he had the advantage of a direct traditional reading of the works of Sebastian Bach, having studied at Erfurt (in 1786-89) under Kittel, one of the great composer's best pupils. Rinck having sat at the feet of Forkel at the University of Göttingen, obtained in 1790 the organistship of Giessen, where he held several other musical appointments. In 1805 he became organist at Darmstadt, and 'professor' at its college ; in 1813 was appointed Court organist, and in 1817 chamber musician to the Grand Duke (Ludwig I.). Rinck made several artistic tours in Germany, his playing always eliciting much admiration. At Trèves, in 1827, he was greeted with special honour. He received various decorations,—in 1831 membership of the Dutch Society for Encouragement of Music ; in 1838 the cross of the first class from his Grand Duke ; in 1840 ' Doctor of Philosophy and Arts ' from the University of Giessen. Out of his 125 works a few are for chamber, including sonatas for PF., violin, and violoncello, and PF. duets. But his reputation is based on his organ music, or rather on his 'Practical Organ School,' a standard work. Rinck's compositions for his instrument show no trace of such sublime influence as might have been looked for from a pupil, in the second generation, of Bach ; indeed, throughout them fugue-writing is conspicuous by its absence. But without attaining the high standard which has been reached by living composers for the instrument in Germany, his organ-pieces contain much that is interesting to an organ student.

Rinck's name will always live as that of an executant, and of a safe guide towards the formation of a sound and practical organ-player ; and his works comprise many artistic studies. Amongst these the more important are the 'Practical Organ School,' in six divisions (op. 55, re-edited by Otto Dienel, 1881), and numerous ' Preludes for Chorales,' issued at various periods. He also composed for the church a ' Pater Noster' for four voices with organ (op. 59) ; motets, ' Praise the Lord ' (op. 88) and 'God be merciful' (op. 109) ; twelve chorales for men's voices, etc.   H. S. O.

RINFORZANDO, ' reinforcing ' or increasing in power. This word, or its abbreviations, *rinf.* or *rfz*, is used to denote a sudden and brief *crescendo*. It is applied generally to a whole phrase, however short, and has the same meaning as *sforzando*, which is only applied to single notes. It is sometimes used in concerted music to give a momentary prominence to a subordinate part, as for instance in the Beethoven Quartet, op. 95, in the Allegretto, where the violoncello part is marked *rinforzando*, when it has the second section of the principal subject of the movement.   M.

RING DES NIBELUNGEN, DER, 'The Ring of the Niblung,' a tetralogy or sequence of four music-dramas (more correctly a 'trilogy' with a preludial drama), words and music by Richard Wagner, was first performed in its entirety at Bayreuth, August 13, 14, 16, and 17, 1876, and repeated during the two following weeks. The book, which is written in an alliterative style modelled on that of the ' Stabreim,' is founded on the Icelandic Sagas, and has little in common with the Nibelungenlied, or more correctly ' Der Nibelunge Nôt,' a mediæval German poem of the beginning of the 13th century, in which the mythical types of the old Norse sagas appear in humanised modifications. The poem was completed in 1852. The whole was given at Her Majesty's Theatre, under the management of Angelo Neumann and the conductorship of Anton Seidl, on May 5-9, 1882 ; four performances of the complete cycle took place. The dates of first performances of the separate parts are appended :—

DAS RHEINGOLD. The 'Vorabend,' or Preludial Evening, was first performed at Munich, Sept. 22, 1869.

DIE WALKÜRE was completed in 1856, and the first performance took place at Munich June 25, 1870. It was given in English at Covent Garden, Oct. 16, 1895.

SIEGFRIED was completed early in 1869, and first performed in its place in the cycle, at Bayreuth, August 16, 1876. It was given in French at Brussels, June 12, 1891, and subsequently at the Opéra in Paris ; and in English, by the Carl Rosa Company, in 1898.

GOTTERDÄMMERUNG, completed in 1874, was first heard at Bayreuth, August 17, 1876. The whole trilogy was announced for production in English at Covent Garden in the winter season of 1907-8.   M.

RIOTTE, PHILIPP JACOB, born at St. Mendel, Trèves, August 16, 1776. André of Offenbach was his teacher in music, and he made his first appearance at Frankfort in Feb. 1804. In 1806 he was music-director at Gotha. In 1808 he conducted the French operas at the Congress of Erfurt. In April 1809 his operetta ' Das Grenzstädtchen' was produced at the Kärnthnerthor Theatre, and thenceforward Vienna was his residence. In 1818 he became conductor at the Theatre an-der-Wien, beyond which he does not seem to have advanced up to his death, August 20, 1856. The list of his theatrical works is immense. His biography in Wurzbach's *Lexicon* enumerates, between 1809 and 1848, no less than forty-eight pieces, operas, operettas, ballets, pantomimes, music to plays, etc., written mostly by himself, and sometimes in conjunction with others. In 1852 he wound up his long labours by a cantata 'The Crusade,' which was performed in the great Redoutensaal, Vienna, with much applause. He wrote an opera called ' Mozart's Zauberflöte' at Prague about 1820. He left also a symphony (op. 25), nine solo-sonatas, six do. for PF. and violin, three concertos for clarinet and orchestra, but these are defunct. He became very popular by a piece called 'The Battle of Leipzig,' for PF. solo, which was republished over half Germany, and had a prodigious sale.　　　　　　　　　　　　G.

RIPIENO, 'supplementary.' The name given in the orchestral concertos of the 17th and 18th centuries, to the accompanying instruments which were only employed to fill in the harmonies and to support the solo or 'concertante' parts. [See CONCERTANTE, and CONCERTINO, vol. i. pp. 576-7.]　　　　　　　　　M.

RIPPON, JOHN, born at Tiverton, April 29, 1751. Died in London, Dec. 17, 1836 (*Brit. Mus. Biog.*). He was a doctor of divinity, and had a meeting-house for a number of years in Carter Lane, Tooley Street. His 'Selection of Psalm and Hymn Tunes,' from the best authors in three and five parts (1795) was a tune-book in much request for congregational singing, and ran through a large number of editions. In its compilation and arrangement he was assisted by T. Walker. Rippon was composer of an oratorio 'The Crucifixion,' published in 1837.　　　　　　　　　　　　F. K.

RISELEY, GEORGE, born at Bristol, August 28, 1845, was elected chorister of Bristol Cathedral in 1852, and in Jan. 1862 articled to Mr. John Davis Corfe, the Cathedral organist, for instruction in the organ, pianoforte, harmony, and counterpoint. During the next ten years he was organist at various churches in Bristol and Clifton, at the same time acting as deputy at the Cathedral. In 1870 he was appointed organist to the Colston Hall, Bristol, where he started weekly recitals of classical and popular music, and in 1876 succeeded Corfe as organist to the Cathedral. In 1877 he started his orchestral concerts, which have won for him a well-deserved reputation. Notwithstanding considerable opposition, and no small pecuniary risk, he has continued, during each season, to give fortnightly concerts, at which the principal works of the classical masters have been well performed, and a large number of interesting novelties by modern writers, both English and foreign, produced. [In 1878 he was appointed conductor of the Bristol Orpheus Society, and has enlarged its scope and greatly increased its reputation. He is conductor of the Bristol Society of Instrumentalists, and was the founder of the Bristol Choral Society in 1889. He retired with a pension from the cathedral appointment in 1898, and was appointed conductor of the Alexandra Palace, and of the Queen's Hall Choral Society. In 1896 he conducted his first Bristol Festival, with great success. His compositions include a Jubilee Ode (1887), part-songs, etc. See an interesting article on him in *Musical Times*, 1899, p. 81 ff.]　　　　　　　　　　　W. B. S.

RISLER, JOSEPH EDOUARD, born at Baden, Feb. 23, 1873, studied at the Paris Conservatoire, where he gained, among other distinctions,

first medals in solfège and elementary piano in 1887, a first piano prize (in Diémer's class) in 1889, a second harmony prize in 1892, and the first prize for accompaniment in 1897. On leaving the Conservatoire, Risler made further studies with Dimmler, Stavenhagen, D'Albert, and Klindworth. In 1896 and 1897 he was one of the 'Assistenten auf der Bühne' at Bayreuth, and took part as 'répétiteur,' in preparing the 'Meistersinger' for the Paris Opéra. In 1906 he was appointed a member of the Conseil supérieur of the Paris Conservatoire. Risler has given many pianoforte recitals in France, Germany, Holland, Russia, Spain, etc. His first appearance in England took place at Prince's Hall, May 17, 1894, when he played two sonatas of Beethoven, a master for whom he has a special predilection. His playing was then found to be singularly free from affectation, although in his later years he has yielded to certain mannerisms which detract from the artistic beauty of his earlier performances. His technique is very remarkable. He played the thirty-two 'sonatas of Beethoven in London in 1906. He has written a concert-transcription of Strauss's 'Till Eulenspiegel,' etc.　G. F.

RISPOSTA (Lat. *Comes*; Eng. 'Answer'). The Answer to the subject of a Fugue, or point of imitation. [See PROPOSTA.]

In Real Fugue, the answer imitates the subject, interval for interval. In Tonal Fugue, the Tonic is always answered by the Dominant, and *vice versa*. In both, the imitation is usually conducted, either in the fifth above the Proposta, or the fourth below it, when the subject begins upon the Tonic ; and, in the fourth above, or the fifth below, when it begins upon the Dominant. [See FUGUE, SUBJECT.]　　　　　　　　　　　W. S. R.

RITARDANDO ; RITENENTE ; RITENUTO. [See RALLENTANDO.]

RITORNELLO (Abbrev. *Ritornel., Ritor.* ; Fr. *Ritournelle*). I. An Italian word, literally signifying a little return or repetition ; but more frequently applied, in a conventional sense, (1) to a short instrumental melody played between the scenes of an opera, or even during the action, either for the purpose of enforcing some particular dramatic effect or of amusing the audience during the time occupied in the preparation of some elaborate 'set-scene' ; or, (2) to the symphonies introduced between the vocal phrases of a song or anthem.

1. The earliest known use of the term, in its first sense, is to be found in Peri's 'Euridice,' in connection with a melody for three flutes, which, though called a 'Zinfonia' on its first appearance, is afterwards repeated under the title of 'Ritornello.' 'Euridice' was first printed at Florence in 1600, and at Venice in 1608.

A similar use of the term occurs soon afterwards in Monteverde's 'Orfeo,' printed at Venice in 1609, and republished in 1615. In this work, the Overture—there called Toccata—is followed by a 'Ritornello' in five parts, the rhythmic form of which is immeasurably in advance of the age in which it was produced. [Both toccata and ritornello are printed in the *Musical Times* for 1880, in an essay on Monteverde ; and the toccata is given in Parry's *Seventeenth Century* (*Oxford Hist. of Music*, vol. iii.), p. 51.]

2. When vocal music with instrumental accompaniment became more extensively cultivated, the word was brought into common use, in its second sense, as applied to the instrumental symphonies of a song, or other composition for a solo voice. Ritornelli of this kind were freely used by Cavalli, Cesti, Carissimi, and many other composers of the early Venetian dramatic school, who imitated their manner. An example from Cavalli's 'Il Giasone' will be found at vol. iii. p. 440. Towards the close of the 17th century such instrumental interpolations became very common, in all styles and countries. For instance, in early editions of the Verse Anthems, of Croft, Greene, and other English composers, of the 17th and 18th centuries, we constantly find the words 'Ritornel.,' 'Ritor.,' or 'Rit.,' printed over little interludes, which, unknown in the more severe kind of ecclesiastical music, formed a marked feature in works of this particular school, frequently embodying some of its choicest scraps of melody, as in Dr. Boyce's Anthem, 'The Heavens declare the glory of God.'

In later editions the term disappears, its place being supplied, in the same passages, by the words 'Organ,' or 'Sym.' ; which last abbreviation is almost invariably found in old copies of Handel's songs, and other similar music, in which the symphonies are interpolated, as often as opportunity permits, upon the line allotted to the voice.

II. An ancient form of Italian verse, in which each Strophe consists of three lines, the first and third of which rhyme with each other, after the manner of the *Terza rima* of Dante. Little Folk-Songs of this character are still popular, under the name of 'Ritornelli' or 'Stornelli,' among the peasants of the Abruzzi and other mountain regions of Italy.   w. s. r.

RITTER, Frédéric Louis, born at Strasburg, June 22, 1834. His paternal ancestors were Spanish, and the family name was originally Caballero. His musical studies were begun at an early age under Hauser and Schletterer, and continued at Paris (whither he was sent when sixteen years of age) under the supervision of his cousin, Georges Kastner. Possessed with the idea that beyond the Rhine he would find better opportunities for the study of composition, he ran away to Germany, where he remained for two years, assiduously pursuing his studies with eminent musicians, and attending concerts whenever good music could be heard. Returning to Lorraine, aged eighteen, he was nominated professor of music in the Protestant seminary of Fénéstrange, and invited to conduct a Société de Concerts at Bordeaux. The representations made by some of his family who had settled in America induced him to visit the New World. He spent a few years in Cincinnati, where his enthusiasm worked wonders in the development of taste. The Cecilia (choral)and Philharmonic (orchestral) Societies were established by him, and a large number of important works presented at their concerts for the first time in the United States. In 1861 Ritter went to New York, becoming conductor of the Sacred Harmonic Society for seven years, and of the Arion Choral Society (male voices), and instituting (1867) the first musical festival held in that city.   In 1867 he was appointed director of the musical department of Vassar College, Poughkeepsie, whither he removed in 1874 on resigning his conductorships. The University of New York conferred on him the degree of Doctor of Music in 1878. He died at Antwerp, July 22, 1891. Ritter's literary labours have included articles on musical topics printed in French, German, and American periodicals. His most important work is *A History of Music, in the Form of Lectures*—vol. i. 1870 ; vol. ii. 1874, Boston ; both republished by W. Reeves, London, 1876. *Music in England* appeared in New York in 1883, and *Music in America* in the same year.

The following works have appeared in the catalogues of Hamburg, Leipzig, Mainz, and New York publishers :—

Op. 1. 'Hafis,' cyclus of Persian songs.	Op. 10. Five songs. Ten Irish Melodies with new PF. acct.
2. Preambule Scherzo, PF.	11. Organ fantasia and fugue.
3. Ten children's songs.	12. Voices of the Night, PF.
4. Fairy Love.	'O Salutaris,' baritone, organ.
5. Eight PF. pieces.	'Ave Maria,' mezzo-sopr., organ.
6. Six songs.	'Parting,' song, mezzo-soprano.
7. Five choruses, male voices.	A practical Method for the Instruction of Chorus-classes.
8. Psalm xxiii. female voices.	

The following are his most important unpublished compositions :—

3 Symphonies—A, E minor, Eb.	One string quartet; three PF.
'Stella,' Poème - symphonique, d'après V. Hugo.	Do.
Overture, 'Othello.'	Psalm iv. baritone solo, chorus, and orchestra.
Concerto, PF. and orch.	Psalm xlvi., solo, chor. and orch.
Do. violoncello and orch.	Psalm xcv. female voices with organ.
Fantasia, bass clarinet and orch.	

Dr. Ritter's wife, *née* Raymond, is known under the name of Fanny Raymond Ritter (born at Philadelphia in 1840), as an author and translator of works on musical subjects. She brought out translations of Ehlert's *Letters on Music, to a Lady*; and of Schumann's Essays and Criticisms—in two series, as *Music and Musicans* ; and a pamphlet entitled *Woman as a Musician* — all published by Reeves, London.   f. h. j.

RITTER, Hermann, son of a German government official, was born at Wismar, Mecklenburg, Sept. 26, 1849. A gifted writer and able violinist and musician, he attracted considerable public interest in Germany during the latter half of the 19th century by his performances on the 'Viola Alta,' an instrument which he claimed to be his own invention. While studying history and art at the Heidelberg University, Herr Ritter became deeply interested in the history of musical instruments, and the desire to improve the muffled tone of the ordinary viola induced him to attempt the construction of a similar instrument which should possess the acute resonant qualities of the violin. According to his own account, this consummation was effected by the aid of the rules laid down by Antonio Bagatella in his pamphlet entitled *Regole per la costruzione di Violini, Viole, Violoncelli, e Violoni,* etc. etc., Padua, 1786, of which a second edition appeared in Padua in 1883, and German translations at Padua in 1786 and Leipzig in 1806. In point of fact Hermann Ritter's 'Viola Alta' was in reality a revival of the large 'Tenor Viol,' that direct descendant of those *instruments de remplissage* the *Quinte* and *Haute Contre,* which he methodised into a tenor of extra large proportions constructed on the scientific acoustical basis appertaining to the violin. His public appearances with the instrument began in 1876. They attracted the consideration of many eminent composers, and Wagner, who was at that time occupied with his 'Nibelungen,' invited his aid for the production of that opera in the same year. After completing this engagement Herr Ritter travelled for several years, touring in Germany, Austria, Switzerland, Holland, Russia, England, and Scotland, and in 1879 he was appointed professor of musical history and æsthetics, as well as of the viola, at the Royal School of music at Würzburg. There his talents and personal influence were the means of attracting a vast number of students, who assisted in spreading the fame of his invention, and in 1889 five of his pupils were playing in the orchestra of the Bayreuth festival. In 1889 he was learnedly advocating the use of a three-footed binder in a pamphlet entitled *Der Dreifüssige oder Normal-Geigensteg* (Würzburg, G. Hartz).

The Grand Duke of Mecklenburg appointed Herr Ritter his 'Court Chamber Virtuoso,' and the Emperor Ludwig II. of Bavaria gave him the title of 'Court Professor.' He married the singer Justine Haecker in 1884. He wrote and arranged an immense amount of music for his 'Viola Alta' and traced its history in his book entitled *Die Geschichte des Viola Alta* (Leipzig, Merseburg). (See VIOLA.) G. Adema, *Hermann Ritter und seine Viola alta* (Würzburg, 1881, 2nd edition, 1890); Hermann Ritter, *Die Viola alta oder Altgeige* (Leipzig, 1885), 1st edition, Heidelberg, 1876, 2nd edition, Leipzig, 1877. (Riemann, *Dict. of Music.*) E. H-A.

RITTER (properly BENNET), THEODORE, born near Paris, April 5, 1841, was a pupil of Liszt and wrote a number of successful drawing-room pieces ('Chant du braconnier,' 'Sylphes,' etc.). He produced two operas ('Marianne,' at

Paris in 1861, and 'La dea risorta,' at Florence, 1865); he died in Paris, April 6, 1886.

RIVARDE, SERGE ACHILLE, violinist, was born on Oct. 31, 1865, in New York of an American mother, his father being a Spaniard. He lived in America till the age of eleven, receiving lessons successively from Felix Simon, Henri Wieniawski and Joseph White (a man of colour). Coming to Europe he entered the Paris Conservatoire, to become a pupil of Charles Dancla. He won a first prize in July 1879, sharing the same with Franz Ondricek. In 1881 he returned to America, where he stayed three years, and then gave up violin-playing entirely for a time. In 1885 he came back to Paris and entered Lamoureux's orchestra, in which he remained for five years as principal violin, and occasional soloist. He gave up the appointment in 1891 and made his début in London in 1894. In 1899 he took the post of violin professor at the Royal College of Music. He is occasionally heard as soloist in London and abroad, being the possessor of an exceptionally pure style, but spends most of his time in teaching. Until recently he played almost exclusively upon violins made by a modern maker, Szepessy Bela, but recently has taken to a Nicolas Lupot. w. w. c.

RIVISTA MUSICALE ITALIANA, an important quarterly review on music, published by the firm of Bocca in Turin, and edited by L. Torchi. Each quarterly 'fascicolo' contains about 200 pages in Italian or French, the articles headed 'Memorie' dealing frequently with points of musical archæology, while 'Arte contemporanea' is the heading of those which treat of current events or the criticism of new music. Operas and other works of importance are discussed in detail, there are illustrations, musical and otherwise, and shorter reviews of musical books appear under the title of 'Recensioni.' A useful feature is a list of articles on music which appear in other periodicals. Among the Italian contributors to the first volume may be mentioned Signori Chilesotti, Giani, de Piccolellis, Tacchinardi, Tebaldini, and Valdrighi; while the names of some of the most eminent writers of other countries, such as Guido Adler, F. Draeseke, F. A. Gevaert, Adolphe Jullien, Arthur Pougin, Saint-Saëns, Philipp Spitta, and J. Weckerlin, appear in the list of contributors. The publication began in 1894, and has maintained a high standard of excellence ever since. M.

RIZZIO, DAVID (RIZZI, or RICCI), the son of a professional musician and dancing-master, born at Turin, in Italy, in the early years of the 16th century. He obtained a post at the court of the Duke of Savoy, and came over to Scotland in the train of the ambassador in 1561. With his brother Joseph he remained in the service of Queen Mary, in the first instance as a bass singer, receiving £80 per year.

He so won his way into her favour (no doubt primarily by his ability in connection with court masques, of which she was so fond), that he became, in 1564, her foreign secretary. By this he aroused political and other feelings, and he was stabbed to death, almost in the Queen's presence, in Holyrood Palace, on the evening of March 9, 1566.

There is no doubt that Rizzio exercised some influence on the music then fashionable in Scotland (or at least in Edinburgh), and there appears to have been a very strong tradition that he was the composer of several of the well-known Scots tunes. In 1725 William Thomson in the 'Orpheus Caledonius' puts this tradition into definite form by affixing a mark to seven of the airs there engraved, stating them to be the composition of Rizzio (see ORPHEUS CALEDONIUS). James Oswald and others have in one or two instances also assigned other airs to Rizzio with probably less of tradition to justify them.   F. K.

ROAST BEEF OF OLD ENGLAND, THE. An English national song whose tune has become associated with the serving of dinner at public functions, and occasionally used as a signal for the same in the army.

The air is a fine marked specimen of English melody, and is probably the composition of Richard Leveridge, who doubtless sang the song in public. The first two verses were inserted in Henry Fielding's ballad opera, 'Don Quixote in England,' produced in 1733. They are considered to be by Fielding himself, and are marked as to be sung to the air 'The Queen's old Courtier.' Another claim, however, arises. In Walsh's *British Musical Miscellany* or *The Delightful Grove*, vol. iii., is 'A Song in praise of Old English Roast Beef : the words and Musick by Mr. Leveridge.' This is a version of seven verses, including the two, with slight verbal differences, already placed in Fielding's 'Don Quixote.' The tune is, however, the now well-known melody as under—

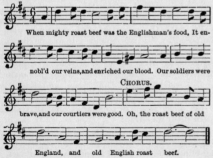

When mighty roast beef was the Englishman's food, It en-

nobl'd our veins, and enriched our blood. Our soldiers were

CHORUS.

brave, and our courtiers were good. Oh, the roast beef of old

England, and old English roast beef.

The melody has been used for many songs, one, formerly well known in the north, being 'The Kail Brose of auld Scotland.' 'The Roast Beef Cantata' was a well-known piece originally published about 1760-70. Headed by a copy of Hogarth's picture the 'Gate of Calais,' the

subject of which is the carrying of a huge piece of beef before a starved French sentry, the praises of roast beef are set to several popular airs, concluding with the 'Roast Beef of Old England.'   F. K.

ROBARTT, of Crewkerne, was an 'orgyn maker' who let out organs to churches by the year. The Mayor of Lyme Regis, in 1551, paid him ten shillings for his year's rent.   V. DE P.

ROBERT BRUCE. A pasticcio adapted by Niedermeyer from four of Rossini's operas— 'Zelmira,' the 'Donna del Lago,' 'Torvaldo e Dorliska,' and 'Bianca e Faliero.' Produced without success at the Académie Royale, Dec. 30, 1846. It is published in Italian as 'Roberto Bruce' by Ricordi.   G.

ROBERT LE DIABLE. Opera in five acts ; words by Scribe, music by Meyerbeer. Produced at the Académie, Paris, Nov. 21, 1831. In London, and in English, imperfectly, as 'The Demon, or the Mystic Branch,' at Drury Lane, Feb. 20, 1832, and as 'The Fiend Father, or Robert of Normandy,' at Covent Garden the day following ; as 'Robert the Devil' at Drury Lane (Bunn), March 1, 1845. In French, at Her Majesty's, June 11, 1832, with Nourrit, Levasseur, Damoreau. In Italian, at Her Majesty's, May 4, 1847 (first appearance of Jenny Lind and Staudigl).   G.

ROBERTO DEVEREUX, CONTE D'ESSEX. (1) Opera in three acts, text by Romani (from Corneille), music by Mercadante. Produced at Milan, March 10, 1833. (2) An opera in three acts ; libretto by Camerano from Corneille's 'Comte d'Essex,' music by Donizetti. Produced in Naples in 1837 ; at the Italiens, Paris, Dec. 27, 1838 ; at Her Majesty's Theatre, London, June 24, 1841. The overture contains the air of 'God save the King.'   G.

ROBERTS, HENRY, a music and an ornamental engraver, who issued several notable books of songs with music, now much sought after, mainly on account of their decorative character. In these works the pieces are headed with pictorial embellishments. The earliest of Roberts's publications is 'Calliope, or English Harmony,' in two volumes octavo. It was issued by and for the engraver in periodical numbers of 8 pp. and commenced late in the year 1737. Twenty-five numbers formed the first volume, which was completed in 1739. The second volume began in this year, but from some cause now unknown, the publication came to a standstill when half through, and was not resumed until 1746, when it came out with the imprint of John Simpson (*q.v.*). This volume contains 'God save the King,' which, from the date 1739 appearing on some of the plates, has been hastily assumed to be prior to the copy in the *Gentleman's Magazine* of 1745 ; this, however, is not the case, for ample proof exists that this portion of the volume was not issued before the spring of 1746. The plates of 'Calliope,' thirty or forty years afterwards, came into possession of Longman & Broderip, who reprinted from them. Roberts's other famous work is 'Clio and Euterpe,' precisely similar in style, which, issued in two volumes, bears the dates 1758 and 1759. A later edition has a third volume added, and is dated 1762. A fourth was again added when re-issued by John Welcker. Henry Roberts kept a music and a print-shop in Holborn 'near Hand Alley almost opposite Great Turnstile.' His name is attached as engraver to several pieces of decorative engraving on music-sheets.   F. K.

ROBERTS, JOHN, composer of sacred music, born in Wales, Dec. 22, 1822. Before 1839 he had adopted the name 'Ieum Gwyllt.' He removed to Liverpool and became editor of a Welsh newspaper, besides writing upon musical matters. In 1858 he again returned to Wales, and at Aberdare set up as a music teacher. On Jan. 10, 1859, he founded there the first of a long series of Welsh musical festivals, and in the same year published a tune-book, 'Llyfr Tonau,' which was much used throughout Wales, and passed through many editions. Roberts was a strong advocate of temperance, and preached as a Calvinistic Methodist. He died May 6, 1877. [Information principally from *Dict. Nat. Biog.*]   F. K.

ROBERTS, J. VARLEY, Mus.D., native of Stanningley, near Leeds, born Sept. 25, 1841. He early exhibited much ability for music, and at twelve was appointed organist of S. John's, Farsley, near Leeds. In 1862 he became organist of S. Bartholomew's, Armley, and in 1868 organist and choirmaster of the parish church, Halifax. In 1871 he graduated Mus.B., and in 1876 Mus.D., at Christ Church, Oxford. During his organistship at Halifax, upwards of £3000 was raised to enlarge the organ, originally built by Snetzler—the instrument upon which Sir William Herschel, the renowned astronomer, formerly played—and it is now one of the finest and largest in the North of England. In 1876 Dr. Roberts became a Fellow of the Royal College of Organists, London. In 1882 he was elected organist at Magdalen College, Oxford, succeeding Mr. (now Sir Walter) Parratt. In 1884 the University Glee and Madrigal Society was founded under his conductorship. In 1885-93 he was organist of St. Giles's, Oxford, and in the former year was appointed examiner in music to the Oxford Local Examinations, and also became conductor of the Oxford Choral Society. In 1883 he was appointed one of the University examiners for musical degrees. In 1907 he presented a new organ to his native village of Stanningley. His compositions include sacred cantatas, 'Jonah,' for voices and orchestra; 'Advent,' 'The Story of the Incarnation,' 'The Passion,' for church choirs; Psalm ciii. for voices and orchestra; six services, one an evening service in C written for

the London Church Choir Association Festival in 1894; about fifty anthems, besides part-songs, and organ pieces. His *Practical Method of Training Choristers*, 1898, 1900, and 1905, is very useful.   W. B. S.

ROBIN ADAIR. [See EILEEN AROON, vol. i. p. 770.]

ROBIN DES BOIS. The title of the French version of 'Der Freischütz' at its first appearance in Paris (Odéon, Dec. 7, 1824; Opéra-Comique, Jan. 15, 1835; Lyrique, Jan. 24, 1855). The libretto was made by Sauvage; the names of the characters were changed, the action and the story were altered, portions of 'Preciosa' and 'Oberon' were introduced, and the piece was made to end happily. The alterations were due to Castil Blaze, who, to save expense, scored the music himself from a PF. copy. Nevertheless, with all these drawbacks, so great was the popularity of the music that Castil Blaze made a large sum of money by it. For the translation by Pacini and Berlioz see FREISCHÜTZ, vol. ii. p. 107.   G.

ROBIN HOOD. An opera in three acts; words by John Oxenford, music by G. A. Macfarren. Produced at Her Majesty's Theatre, London, Oct. 11, 1860, and had a very great run.   G.

Other operas on the same subject have been produced, besides many masques of the 16th and 17th centuries, more or less associated with the May Day games and observances; of these early pieces little record as to detail has survived.

A ballad opera of the name was acted at Lee & Harper's great booth, at St. Bartholomew's Fair, in 1730; the music and libretto of this was published by John Watts in the year of production. A different 'Robin Hood,' by Moses Mendez, was performed at Drury Lane in 1750, the music being supplied by Charles (afterwards Dr.) Burney. Another English ballad opera in three acts, which attained some degree of fame, was entitled 'Robin Hood, or Sherwood Forest.' This was written by Leonard Mac-Nally, with the music selected, arranged, and composed by William Shield. It was produced at Covent Garden Theatre in 1784, the principals being Mrs. Kennedy, Mrs. Martyr, Mrs. Banister, and Miss Kemble, while the male singers were Banister, Johnstone, and Edwin. The piece had a considerable run, and several of the songs lasted in popularity long after the opera itself was dead.   F. K.

ROBINSON, ANASTASIA, born about 1698, was daughter of a portrait painter, who, becoming blind, was compelled to qualify his children to gain their own livelihood. Anastasia received instruction from Dr. Croft, Pier Giuseppe Sandoni, and the singer called The Baroness, successively. She appeared in 'Creso,' in 1714; as Ariana in Handel's 'Amadigi,' May 25, 1715; and in 1720 at the King's Theatre as

Echo in Domenico Scarlatti's opera, 'Narciso.' She afterwards sang in the pasticcio of 'Muzio Scevola,' in Handel's 'Ottone,' 'Floridante,' 'Flavio,' and 'Giulio Cesare'; in Buononcini's 'Crispo' and 'Griselda,' and other operas. Her salary was £1000 for the season, besides a benefit-night. She possessed a fine voice of extensive compass, but her intonation was uncertain. She quitted the stage in 1724, having two years previously been privately married to the Earl of Peterborough, who did not avow the marriage until shortly before his death in 1735, although, according to one account, she resided with him as mistress of the house, and was received as such by the Earl's friends. According to another account, she resided with her mother in a house at Parson's Green, which the Earl took for them, and never lived under the same roof with him, until she attended him in a journey in search of health, a short time before his death. She died at Bevis Mount, Southampton, in April 1755, and was buried at Bath Abbey. There is a fine portrait of her by Faber after Bank, 1727.

Her younger sister, ELIZABETH, intended for a miniature painter, preferred being a singer. She studied under Buononcini, and afterwards at Paris under Rameau; but though an excellent singer, was said to have been prevented by timidity from ever appearing in public.[1] A fortunate marriage, however, relieved her from the necessity of obtaining her own subsistence. w. h. h.; with additions from the *Dict. of Nat. Biog.*

ROBINSON, JOHN, born 1682, was a chorister of the Chapel Royal under Dr. Blow. He became organist of St. Lawrence, Jewry, in 1710 and St. Magnus, London Bridge, in 1713. Hawkins, in his History, describes him as 'a very florid and elegant performer on the organ, inasmuch that crowds resorted to hear him'; and elsewhere says: 'In parish churches the voluntary between the Psalms and the first Lesson was anciently a slow, solemn movement, tending to compose the minds and excite sentiments of piety and devotion. Mr. Robinson introduced a different practice, calculated to display the agility of his fingers in *allegro* movements on the cornet, trumpet, sesquialtera, and other noisy stops, degrading the instrument, and instead of the full and noble harmony with which it was designed to gratify the ear, tickling it with mere airs in two parts, in fact solos for a flute and a bass.' On Sept. 30, 1727, Robinson was appointed to succeed Dr. Croft as organist of Westminster Abbey. He had an extensive practice as a teacher of the harpsichord, and will be long remembered by his double chant in Eb. He died April 30, 1762, and was buried, May 13, in the north aisle of Westminster Abbey. He married, Sept. 6, 1716, Ann,

[1] A 'Miss Robinson, jun.,' appeared at Drury Lane, Jan. 2, 1729, as Ariel in 'The Tempest.' It is possible that this was Margaret Robinson.

youngest daughter of William Turner, Mus.D. She was a singer, and appeared at the King's Theatre in 1720 in Domenico Scarlatti's opera 'Narciso,' being described as 'Mrs. Turner-Robinson' to distinguish her from Anastasia Robinson, who sang in the same opera. She died Jan. 5, and was buried Jan. 8, 1741, in the west cloister of Westminster Abbey. Robinson had a daughter, who was a contralto singer and the original representative of Daniel in Handel's oratorio 'Belshazzar,' 1745, and also sang in others of his oratorios. w. h. h.

ROBINSON, JOSEPH, was the youngest of four brothers, born and resident in Dublin. Their father Francis was an eminent professor of music, and in 1810 was mainly instrumental in founding 'the Sons of Handel,' probably the earliest society established there for the execution of large works. His eldest son Francis, Mus.D., born about 1799, had a tenor voice of great beauty and sympathetic quality; was a vicar-choral of the two Dublin Cathedrals; and, at the Musical Festival in Westminster Abbey, in June 1834, sang a principal part. He died Oct. 31, 1872. Another son, William, had a deep bass of exceptional volume; while John, born about 1812, died in 1844, the organist of both Cathedrals and of Trinity College, had a tenor ranging to the high D. The four brothers formed an admirable vocal quartet, and were the first to make known the German Part-songs then rarely heard either in England or Ireland.

JOSEPH ROBINSON, born August 20, 1815, was a chorister of St. Patrick's at the early age of eight, and afterwards a member of all the choirs, where his fine delivery of recitative was always a striking feature. He also played in the orchestra of the Dublin Philharmonic. But it is as a conductor that his reputation is best established. In 1834 he founded the 'Antient Concert Society,' of which he was conductor for twenty-nine years, and which ceased to exist soon after his resignation. It commenced its meetings in a private house, then took a large room, now the Royal Irish Academy of Antiquities, and in 1843 had made such progress that it purchased and remodelled the building since known as the 'Antient Concert Rooms.' Amongst the last things written by Mendelssohn was the instrumentation of his 'Hear my Prayer' (originally composed for voices and organ only), expressly for Mr. Robinson to produce at the 'Antients.' It did not reach him till after the composer's death. [See MENDELSSOHN, vol. iii. p. 145a, note 2.] In 1837 he became conductor of the 'University Choral Society,' founded by the students. At one of its concerts the music of 'Antigone' was given for the first time out of Germany. He continued to conduct the Society for ten years. [In 1849 he married Miss Fanny Arthur (see below).] In 1852, at the opening of the Cork Exhibition, Mr. Robinson conducted the music, which was on a large scale, and included a new cantata by Sir Robert Stewart. In 1853, an International Exhibition was opened in Dublin ; there he assembled 1000 performers, the largest band and chorus yet brought together in Ireland.

In 1856 efforts were made to revive the 'Irish Academy of Music,' founded in 1848, but languishing for want of funds and pupils. (See ROYAL IRISH ACADEMY.) Mr. and Mrs. Robinson joined as Professors, and nearly all the Irish artists, both vocal and instrumental, who appeared during their time, owed both training and success to their teaching ; and when, after twenty years, Mr. Robinson resigned, the institution was one of importance and stability. In 1859, for the Handel Centenary, he gave the 'Messiah,' with Jenny Lind and Belletti among the principals. The net receipts amounted to £900, an unprecedented sum in Dublin. In 1865 the large Exhibition Palace was opened by the Prince of Wales, and Robinson conducted the performance with a band and chorus of 700.

After the cessation of the 'Antients,' there was no Society to attempt systematically the worthy production of great works. To remedy this a chorus was trained by Robinson, and established in 1876 as the 'Dublin Musical Society.' The last concert conducted by Robinson was on Dec. 6, 1888, previous to which the members presented him with an address and a purse of 100 sovereigns. The purse was returned by him with warm expressions of gratitude, but with the characteristic words, 'While I think a professional man should expect his fair remuneration, yet his chief object may be something higher and nobler—the advancement of art in his native city.' The Society was revived in 1889, under the conductorship of Dr. Joseph Smith, but collapsed after some years. He wrote a variety of songs, concerted pieces and anthems, besides arranging a number of standard songs and Irish melodies. In 1881 he married for the second time ; he died August 23, 1898.

In 1849 a young pianist, Miss FANNY ARTHUR (born Sept. 1831), arrived in Dublin from Southampton, and made her first successful appearance there—Feb. 19, 1849. She had studied under Sterndale Bennett and Thalberg. Mr. Robinson and she were married July 17 following, and she continued for thirty years to be an extraordinary favourite. Her first appearance in London was at the Musical Union, June 26, 1855, when she played Beethoven's Sonata in F (op. 24), with Ernst, and received the praises of Meyerbeer ; also at the New Philharmonic in 1856, where she played Mendelssohn's Concerto in D.

Mrs. Robinson also passed a very active musical life, though it was often interrupted by nervous illness. In teaching she had a peculiar power of infusing her own ideas into others. She played from time to time at concerts of a high class, and herself gave a very successful

concert in Paris, at the Salle Erard (Feb. 4, 1864). Her pianoforte compositions are numerous and graceful. Her sacred cantata, 'God is Love,' was repeatedly performed throughout the kingdom. On Oct. 31, 1879, she met a sudden and tragic end, which caused profound regret. H. M'C. D. ; with additions from *Brit. Mus. Biog.*, *Musical Times*, Sept. 1898, p. 609, and from W. H. Grattan Flood, Esq. [See also an article by Sir C. V. Stanford in *Cornhill Magazine*, June 1899.]

ROBINSON, THOMAS, was author of a curious work published at London in folio in 1603, bearing the following title—*The Schoole of Musicke : wherein is taught the perfect method of the true fingering of the Lute, Pandora, Orpharion and Viol de Gamba.* In 1609 he published 'New Citharen Lessons.' Nothing is known of his biography.   W. H. H.

ROBSON, JOSEPH, organ - builder. See APOLLONICON, vol. i. p. 95, and FLIGHT, vol. ii. p. 61.

ROCHE, EDMOND, born at Calais, Feb. 20, 1828, died at Paris, Dec. 16, 1861, began life as a violin-player, first as Habeneck's pupil at the Conservatoire, but quickly relinquished music for literature. Roche undertook the translation of the libretto of 'Tannhäuser' for its representation at the Opéra, March 13, 1861, and in a preface to his *Poésies posthumes* (Paris, Lévy, 1863) M. Sardou has described the terrible persistence with which Wagner kept his translator to his task. (See Pougin's supplement to Fétis.) In Jullien's *Richard Wagner*, 1887, the facts of the case were made public ; it seems that Roche, not knowing German, had recourse to the services of a friend named Lindau, and the translation, when sent to the director of the Opera, was rejected, as it was in blank verse ; the necessary alteration into rhyme was made by Roche, Nuitter, and Wagner in collaboration. On this Lindau brought an action against Wagner, to enforce the mention of his name as one of the translators ; the case was heard on March 6, 1861, a week before the first representation of the opera, and it was decided that no name but that of Wagner should appear in the books. So that Roche had not even the satisfaction of seeing his name in print, in connection with the work, for even Lajarte (*Bibl. Mus. de l'Opera*, ii. 230) gives Nuitter as the author of the French words. Besides the poems contained in the volume cited, Roche contributed critical articles to several small periodicals.   M.

ROCHLITZ, JOHANN FRIEDRICH, critic, and founder of the *Allgemeine musikalische Zeitung*, born of poor parents at Leipzig, Feb. 12, 1769. His fine voice procured his admission at thirteen to the Thomasschule, under the Cantorship of Doles, where he spent six years and a half. He began to study theology in the University, but want of means compelled him to leave and take a tutorship, which he supplemented by writing. [For the titles of his non-musical works see Riemann's *Lexikon*.] He also attempted composition, and produced a mass, a Te Deum, some part-songs for male voices, a setting of Ps. xxiii., and a cantata, 'Die Vollendung des Erlösers.' In 1798 he founded the *Allgemeine musikalische Zeitung* (Breitkopf & Härtel), and edited it till 1818, during which period his articles largely contributed to the improved general apprecia-tion of the works of the three great Austrian composers, Haydn, Mozart, and Beethoven, in North Germany. The best of these were after-wards re-published by himself under the title of *Für Freunde der Tonkunst*, in four vols. (1824 to 1832, reprinted later by Dörffel, third edition, 1868). It contains, amongst other matter, an interesting account of a visit to Beethoven at Vienna in 1822. Another im-portant work was a collection in three vols. (Schott, 1838 to 1840) of vocal music, from Dufay to Haydn, in chronological order, of which the contents are given below. The first two volumes of the *A.M.Z.* contain a series of anecdotes on Mozart, whose acquaintance he made during Mozart's visit to Leipzig ; but Jahn, in the preface to his *Mozart*, has com-pletely destroyed the value of these as truthful records. Rochlitz was a good connoisseur of paintings and engravings. In 1830 he was one of the committee appointed by the Council of Leipzig to draw up a new hymn-book, and some of the hymns are from his own pen. He also wrote the libretto for Schicht's 'Ende des Gerechten,' Spohr's 'Last Judgment' and 'Calvary,' and for Bierey's opera 'Das Blumen-mädchen.' He was a Hofrath of Saxony, and died Dec. 16, 1842. F. G.

The following are the contents of the collec-tion mentioned above—'Sammlung vorzüglicher Gesangstücke vom Ursprung gesetzmässiger Harmonie bis auf die neue Zeit' :—

First Period (1380-1550)

1. Dufay. Kyrie, a 4. Se la face ay pale.
2. Do. Kyrie, a 4. 'L'omme armé.'
3. Okeghem. Kyrie and Christe, a 4.
4. Josquin de Près. Hymnus, a 4 Tu pauperum refugium.
5. Do. Zwischengesang einer der grössten Messen des Meisters, et incarnatus, a 4.
6. Do. Motet, Misericordias Do-mini, a 4.
7. O. Lasso. Regina Coeli, a 4.
8. Do. Salve Regina, a 4.
9. O. Lasso. Angelus pastores, a 5.
10. Do. Miserere, Amplius, Cor mundum, Ne proficeas, Redde mihi, etc., a 5.
11. C. Goudimel. Domine quid multiplicati, a 4.
12. Ch. de Morales. Kyrie et Christe, a 4.
13. Do. Gloria.
14. T. Tallis. Verba mea, a 4.
15. L. Senfl. Motet on a Choral. 'Mag ich unglück,' a 4.
16. Do. Deus propitius esto, a 5.
17. Do. Nunc dimittis, a 4.

Second Period (1550-1630)

1. Palestrina. Adoramus, a 4.
2. Do. Gloria, two choirs, a 4.
3. Do. Pleni sunt, a 3.
4. Do. O bone Jesu, a 4.
5. Do. Popule meus, two choirs, a 4.
6. Do. Madrigal, 'Cedro gentil,' a 5.
7. Do. Lauda anima mea, a 4.
8. G. M. Nanini. Stabat mater, a 4.
9. Do. Exaudi nos, a 4.
10. Do. Haec dies, a 5.
11. Vittoria. Jesu dulcis, a 4.
12. Do. O quam gloriosum, a 4.
13. F. Anerio. Adoramus, a 4.
14. Do. Christus factus est, a 4.
15. Allegri. Miserere, two choirs, a 5.
16. Gabrieli. In excelsis. Soprano solo. Tenor solo and chorus, a 4, with three horns, two trombones and violins.
17. Do. Benedictus, three choirs, a 4.
18. Böhm. Brüder. Two Lieder, a 4: Der Tag vertreibt; Die Nacht ist kommen.
19. Do. Two Lieder, a 4: Ver-leih' uns Frieden; Nimm' von uns.
20. Walther. Æterno gratias, a 4.
21. Gesänge Martin Luthers, a 4: Mit Fried und Freud: Es woll' uns Gott: Nun komm der Heiden Heiland. Christ lag; Jesus Christus.

22. Gallus. Ecce quomodo mori-tur justus, a 4.
23. Do. Adoramus, a 6.
24. Do. Media vitae, two choirs, a 4.
25. Vulpius. Exultate justi, a 4.
26. Do. Surrexit Christus, two choirs, a 4.
27. Walliser. Gaudent in coelis, two choirs, a 4.
28. Praetorius. Ecce Dominus, a 8.

Appendix

Palestrina. Et incarnatus, etc. (from mass 'Assumpta est'), a 6.
Praetorius. O vos omnes.

Third Period (1600-1700)

1. Caccini. Solo and chorus, Funeste piaggie.
2. Do. Chorus, Biondo arcier.
3. Carissimi. Recitative and chorus, Turbabuntur (from Cantata 'Plaintes des ré-prouvés ').
4. Do. Ardens est cor, four solos and chorus.
5. Do. O sacrum convivium, three solo voices.
6. Do. Cantemus omnes, chorus and scena (Jefta). Plorate, a 6.
7. Benevoli. Sanctus, four choirs, a 4.
8. Do. Christe, a 4.
9. Bernabei. Alleluja, a 4.
10. Do. Salve regina, a 4.
11. A. Scarlatti. Kyrie, a 4.
12. Do. Gloria, a 5.
13. Do. Vacuum est, Canto solo and chorus, with violins.
14. Do. Sanctus, a 4, and Agnus, a 7.
15. Caldara. Salve regina, a 3.
16. Do. Agnus, alto and tenor.
17. Do. Qui tollis, a 4.
18. Astorga. Stabat.
19. Do. Fac me.
20. Do. O quam.
21. Durante. Kyrie.
22. Do. Regina angelorum.
23. Do. Requiem aeternam.
24. Do. Domine Jesu.
25. Lotti. Crucifixus, a 6.
26. Do. Qui tollis, a 4.
27. Do. Crucifixus, a 8.
28. Marcello. Udir' le orecchie, Ps. xliv. a 4.
29. Do. Et incarnatus, a 4.
30. Hasler. Pater noster, a 7.
31. H. Schütz. Selig sind die Todten, a 4.
32. Do. Chorus, Christus ist hier, a 4.
33. Do. Psalm, Was betrübst du?
34. Do. Vater unser.
35. V. Leisring. Trotz sey dem Teufel, two choirs, a 4.
36. Grimm. Gloria, a 5.
37. J. J. Fux. Domine Jesu, a 4.
38. Do. Trema la terra. Coro from oratorio 'La Deposi-zione.'

Fourth Period (1700-1760)

1. Handel. Te Deum, in D, Gloriae tuae.
2. Do. He sent a thick dark-ness.
3. Do. He rebuked the Red Sea.
4. Do. And Israel saw.
5. Do. Behold the Lamb of God.
6. Do. He was despised.
7. Do. Thy rebuke.
8. Do. Lift up your heads.
9. Do. Hear, Jacob's God.
10. Do. Zadok the Priest.
11. Christoph Bach. Ich lasse dich nicht.
12. J. S. Bach. Nimm' von uns Herr.
13. Do. Mache dich mein Geist.
14. Do. Wir setzen uns mit Thränen nieder.
15. Do. Wie sich ein Vater. Lobet den Herrn.
16. Zelenka. Credo.
17. Telemann. Amen. Lob und Ehre, a 8.
18. Stölzel. Gloria.
19. Homilius. Vater unser, a 4.
20. Pasterwitz. Requiem.
21. Hasse. Duet and Chorus, Le porte a noi.
22. Hasse. Alto solo, Ad te clama-mus.
23. Do. Miserere, and Benigni.
24. Do. Te Deum, a 4.
25. Graun. Machet die Thür weit.
26. Do. Tu rex gloriae, a 4.
27. Do. Freuet euch (Tod Jesu).
28. Do. Wir hier liegen. Do.
29. Rolle. Der Herr ist König.
30. Do. Welt-Richter (Tod Abel).
31. Wolf. Laus et perennis gloria, a 4.
32. Do. Des Lebens Fürsten.
33. C. P. E. Bach. Et miseri-cordia, a 6, from Magnificat.
34. Do. Heilig, two choirs, a 4.
35. M. Haydn. Salvos fac nos.
36. Do. Tenebrae factae.
37. Do. Miserere.
38. Leo. Coro, Di quanta pena (S. Elena).
39. Do. Et incarnatus.
40. Do. Miserere ; Ecce enim, a 8.
41. Jommelli. Confirma hoc Deus, five solos and chorus.
42. Do. Miserere.
43. Pergolesi. Eja ergo (Salve Regina).
44. Do. Qui tollis, a 4.
45. Do. Stabat Mater.

           G.

ROCK, MICHAEL, was appointed organist of St. Margaret's, Westminster, June 4, 1802, in succession to William Rock, junr., who had filled the office from May 24, 1774. He com-posed some popular glees—'Let the sparkling wine go round' (which gained a prize at the Catch Club in 1794), 'Beneath a churchyard yew,' etc. He died in March 1809. W. H. H.

ROCKSTRO (originally RACKSTRAW), WILLIAM SMITH, born at North Cheam, Surrey, on Jan. 5, 1823, and baptized at Morden church. The form of his surname by which he was known was an older style resumed after 1846. He was successively pupil of John Purkis, the blind organist, of Sterndale Bennett, and at the Leipzig Conservatorium, where he studied from 1845 till 1846. He enjoyed the special friendship and tuition of Mendelssohn, and was with Hauptmann for theory and with Plaidy for pianoforte. For some years after his return to England, he was active as a teacher and performer in London, being regular accompanist at the 'Wednesday concerts,' where Braham and other eminent singers were to be heard. At this period he wrote his most popular and beautiful song, 'Queen and huntress'; and his pianoforte editions of classical and other operas led the way in popularising that class of music in an available form for the use of those who could not read full scores; and in his indications of the orchestral instruments above the music-staves he did much to point the way towards a general appreciation of orchestral colour. In the early sixties he left London for Torquay on account of his mother's health and his own, and on her death in 1876, he openly became a member of the Roman communion. He had been organist and honorary precentor at All Saints' Church, Babbacombe, from 1867, and won a high position as a teacher. He published, with T. F. Ravenshaw, a 'Festival Psalter, adapted to the Gregorian Tones,' in 1863, and 'Accompanying Harmonies to the Ferial Psalter,' in 1869. These were the first-fruits of his assiduous study of ancient music, on which he became the first authority of his time in England. A couple of valuable text-books, on harmony (1881) and counterpoint (1882) respectively, had a great success, and in the latter part of the first edition of this Dictionary he wrote a large number of articles on musical archæology generally. In the present day, musical research has been sedulously carried on in other countries, and it is inevitable that some of his conclusions should have been controverted, if not disproved; but, considering the state of musical education at the time he wrote, the value of his contributions to such subjects as the music of the period which closed in 1600, can hardly be exaggerated. He was too ardent a partisan to be an ideal historian, but his *History of Music for Young Students* (1879) and his larger work *A General History of Music* (1886) contain much that is of permanent value. His *Life of Handel* (1883) and *Mendelssohn* (1884) are fine examples of eulogistic biography, though they are hardly to be recommended as embodying a calmly critical estimate of either composer. In his larger *History* he showed that he was, nevertheless, not above owning himself in the wrong, and his recantation of certain excessive opinions expressed by him in the Dictionary against Wagner's later works was due to true moral courage. He conducted a concert of sacred music of the 16th and 17th centuries at the Inventions Exhibition of 1885, and in 1891 gave up Torquay for London, giving lectures at the Royal Academy and Royal College of Music, and holding a class for counterpoint and plain-song at the latter institution. Here he imparted the true principles of the ancient music with great success to many worthy pupils; and as a singing-master and teacher of the pianoforte his method of imparting instruction was remarkably successful. As a composer, he never quite freed himself from the powerful influences engendered by his studies; the lovely madrigal, 'O too cruel fair,' was judged unworthy of a prize by the Madrigal Society on the ground that it was modelled too closely on Palestrina; and his oratorio, 'The Good Shepherd,' produced at the Gloucester Festival of 1886 under his own direction, was found to bear too many traces of Mendelssohnian influence to deserve success. In 1891, he collaborated with Canon Scott Holland in writing the life of his old friend, Jenny Lind-Goldschmidt; an abbreviated edition came out in 1893, and with Mr. Otto Goldschmidt he wrote a still shorter book, *Jenny Lind, her Vocal Art and Culture* (partly reprinted from the biography). For many years his health had been bad, and he had many adverse circumstances to contend with. He fought bravely for all that he held best in art, and boundless enthusiasm carried him through. He died in London, July 2, 1895. (*Dict. of Nat. Biog.* etc.)   M.

RODE, JACQUES PIERRE JOSEPH, a great violinist, was born at Bordeaux, Feb. 16, 1774. When eight years of age he came under the tuition of Fauvel aîné, a well-known violinist of his native town, and studied under him for six years. In 1788 he was sent to Paris. Here Punto (or Stich), the famous horn-player, heard him, and being struck with the boy's exceptional talent, gave him an introduction to Viotti, who at once accepted him as his pupil. With this great master he studied for two years, and in 1790 made his first public appearance, when he played Viotti's 13th Concerto at the Théâtre de Monsieur with complete success. Although then but sixteen years of age, he was appointed leader of the second violins in the excellent band of the Théâtre Feydeau. In this position, appearing at the same time frequently as soloist, he remained till 1794, and then started for his first tour to Holland and the north of Germany. His success, especially at Berlin and Hamburg, was great. From the latter place he sailed for his native town, but the vessel was compelled by adverse winds to make for the English coast. So Rode came to London; but he only once appeared in public, at a concert for a charitable purpose, and left England again for Holland and Germany. Finally he returned to France and obtained a professorship of the violin at the newly established Conservatoire at Paris. He was solo violin at the Opéra until November 1799. In 1799 he went to Spain, and at Madrid met Boccherini, who is said to have written the orchestration for Rode's earlier concertos, especially for that in B minor. On his return to Paris in 1800 he was appointed solo-violinist to the First Consul, and it was at that period that he achieved his greatest success in the French capital. In 1803 he went with Boieldieu to St. Petersburg. Spohr heard him on his passage through Brunswick, and was so impressed that for a considerable time he made it his one aim to imitate his style and manner as closely as possible. Arrived at the Russian capital, Rode met with a most enthusiastic reception, and was at once attached to the private music of the Emperor with a salary of 5000 roubles (about £750). But the fatigues of life in Russia were so excessive that from this period a decline of his powers appears to have set in. On his return to Paris in 1808 his reception was less enthusiastic than in former times, and even his warmest friends and admirers could not but feel that he had lost considerably in certainty and vigour. From 1811 we find him again travelling in Germany. Spohr, who heard him in 1813 at Vienna, tells in his Autobiography (i. 178) of the disappointment he felt at Rode's playing, which he now found mannered, and deficient in execution and style.

In Vienna Rode came into contact with Beethoven, who finished the great Sonata in G, op. 96, expressly for him. It was played by Rode and the Archduke Rudolph, Beethoven's pupil, at a private concert, but as far as the violin part was concerned, not much to the composer's satisfaction. Soon afterwards, at any rate, Beethoven requested the Archduke to send the violin part to Rode that he might play it over before a second performance, and he adds: 'He will not take it amiss; certainly not! would to God there were reason to beg his pardon for doing so.'[1] Fétis's statement that Beethoven wrote a Romance for Rode, probably rests on a confusion of the G major Sonata with the Romanza in the same key.

In 1814 Rode went to Berlin, married, and remained for some time. He then retired to his native place. At a later date he made an ill-advised attempt to resume a public career. But his appearance at Paris proved a complete failure, and Mendelssohn, writing from thence in April 1825, says that he was fixed in his resolution never again to take a fiddle in hand.[2] This failure he took so much to heart that his health began to give way, and he died at Bordeaux, Nov. 25, 1830.

Rode was one of the greatest of all violinists. During the earlier part of his career he displayed all the best qualities of a grand, noble, pure, and thoroughly musical style. His intonation was perfect; his tone large and pure; boldness and vigour, deep and tender feeling, characterised his performances. In fact he was no mere virtuoso, but a true artist. His truly musical nature shows itself equally in his compositions. Although his general

[1] Thayer, *Life of Beethoven*, iii. p. 223.
[2] *Die Familie Mendelssohn*, i. p. 149.

musical education appears to have been, like that of most French violinists, deficient (we have already mentioned that Boccherini added the simple orchestration to his earlier concertos), yet his works, especially his concertos, have a noble dignified character and considerable charm of melody, while, it need hardly be added, they are thoroughly suited to the nature of the violin. On the other hand, they hardly show high creative power; of thematic treatment there is very little, the form, though not unsymmetrical, is somewhat loose, and the instrumentation poor.

He published ten concertos (three more were issued after his death); five sets of quartets; seven sets of variations; three books of duos for two violins, and the well-known twenty-four caprices.

Of his concertos, the 7th in A minor is still in the repertory of some eminent violinists. The variations in G major—the same which the famous singer Catalani and other celebrated vocalists after her have made their *cheval de bataille*—are occasionally heard. But above all, his '24 caprices or études' will always, along with Kreutzer's famous forty caprices, hold their place as indispensable for a sound study of the violin.

Although, owing to his life of travel, he had but few direct pupils, his influence through his example and compositions on the violinists of France, and more especially of Germany, was very great indeed. Böhm, the master of Joachim, and Eduard Rietz, the friend of Mendelssohn, both studied under him for some time.   P. D.

RODWELL, GEORGE HERBERT BONAPARTE, born Nov. 15, 1800, brother of J. T. G. Rodwell, part proprietor and manager of the Adelphi Theatre, London, and author of several dramatic pieces, was for many years music-director of the Adelphi. On the death of his brother, in March 1825, he succeeded to his share in the theatre. He was a pupil of Vincent Novello and Henry Bishop, and became in 1828 professor of harmony and composition at the Royal Academy of Music. He was the composer of very many operettas and other dramatic pieces, of which the following are the principal: 'The Flying Dutchman' (Adelphi, 1826); 'The Cornish Miners' (English Opera-House, 1827); 'The Bottle Imp' and 'The Mason of Buda' (partly adapted from Auber's 'Le Maçon'), 1828; 'The Spring Lock,' 'The Earthquake,' and 'The Devil's Elixir,' 1829; 'The Black Vulture,' 1830; 'My Own Lover,' and 'The Evil Eye,' 1832; 'The Lord of the Isles,' 1834; 'Paul Clifford' (with Blewitt), 1835; 'The Spirit of the Bell' (Lyceum, 1835); 'The Sexton of Cologne,' 1836; 'Jack Sheppard,' 1839; and 'The Seven Sisters of Munich,' 1847. In 1836 he was director of the music at Covent Garden, where he brought out many adaptations of operas, etc., 'anticipating the

repertory of Drury Lane' (*Dict. of Nat. Biog.*).
He was author of several farces and other
dramatic pieces, amongst which were 'Teddy
the Tiler' (written in 1830 for Tyrone Power,
and eminently successful), 'The Chimney-Piece,'
'The Pride of Birth,' 'The Student of Lyons,'
and 'My Wife's Out'; of three novels, 'Old
London Bridge,' 'Memoirs of an Umbrella,' and
'Woman's Love'; and of 'The First Rudiments
of Harmony,' 1831. He composed also two
collections of songs: 'Songs of the Sabbath
Eve,' and 'Songs of the Birds' (1827). He
for many years persistently advocated the
establishment of a National Opera. He married
the daughter of Liston, the comedian; died in
Upper Ebury Street, Pimlico, Jan. 22, 1852, and
was buried at Brompton Cemetery.   w. h. h.

ROECKEL, PROFESSOR JOSEPH AUGUST, was
born August 28, 1783, at Neumburg vorm
Wald, in the Upper Palatinate.   He was
originally intended for the church, but in 1803
entered the diplomatic service of the Elector
of Bavaria as Private Secretary to the Bavarian
Chargé d'Affaires at Salzburg.   On the recall
of the Salzburg Legation in 1804, he accepted
an engagement to sing at the Theatre an-der-
Wien, where, March 29, 1806, he appeared as
Florestan in the revival of 'Fidelio.'[1]   In 1823
Roeckel was appointed Professor of Singing at
the Imperial Opera ; in 1828 he undertook the
direction of the opera at Aix-la-Chapelle, and
in the following year made the bold experiment
of producing German operas in Paris with a
complete German company.   Encouraged by
the success of this venture, Professor Roeckel
remained in Paris until 1832, when he brought
his company to London, and produced 'Fidelio,'
'Der Freischütz,' and other masterpieces of the
German school, at the King's Theatre ; the
principal artists being Schröder-Devrient and
Haitzinger, with Hummel (Roeckel's brother-in-
law) as conductor.   In 1835 he retired from
operatic life, and in 1853 finally returned to
Germany, where he died, at Anhalt-Cöthen, in
September 1870.

AUGUST, his eldest son, was born Dec. 1,
1814, at Graz.   He was Musikdirector at Bamberg, at Weimar (1838-43), and lastly was
Musikdirector at the Dresden Opera in 1843-49,
and so a colleague of Richard Wagner ; being,
like the latter, involved in the Revolution of
1848 (he had also witnessed the Paris revolution
of 1830), he abandoned music and devoted
himself entirely to politics.   He spent thirteen
years in prison (1849-62), and on his release
became editor of various newspapers, at Coburg,
Frankfort, Munich, and Vienna, successively.
He published an account of his imprisonment
(*Sachsen's Erhebung*, etc.).   Wagner's letters to
him were published in 1894, and translated
into English by Miss E. C. Sellar shortly after-

wards.   From admiration of Wagner's genius,
Roeckel withdrew an opera of his own, 'Farinelli,'
which had been accepted for performance at
Dresden.   See also Praeger's *Wagner as I knew
him*, p. 119 ff.   He died at Buda-Pesth on
June 18, 1876.

EDWARD, the second son of Professor Roeckel,
was born at Trèves on Nov. 20, 1816, and
received his musical education from his uncle
J. N. Hummel.   He came to London in 1835,
and gave his first concert in 1836 at the King's
Theatre.   He subsequently went on a concert-
tour in Germany, and performed with great
success at the courts of Prussia, Saxony, Saxe-
Weimar, Anhalt-Dessau, etc.   In 1848 Roeckel
settled in England, and resided at Bath, where
he succeeded the late Henry Field.   He died there
Nov. 2, 1899.   He published a considerable
quantity of pianoforte music.

JOSEPH LEOPOLD, the youngest son of Professor
Roeckel, was born in London, April 11, 1838.
He studied composition at Würzburg under
Eisenhofer, and orchestration under Götze at
Weimar.   Like his brother, Mr. J. L. Roeckel
settled in England, and lives at Clifton ; he is
well known as a teacher and a voluminous
composer of songs.   His orchestral and instru-
mental compositions are less well known, but
his cantatas 'Fair Rosamond,' 'Ruth,' 'The
Sea Maidens,' 'Westward Ho,' and 'Mary
Stuart,' 'The Victorian Age' (1887), and many
others, have been received with much favour.
The first of these was performed at the Crystal
Palace in 1871, and a baritone scena with
orchestra, 'Siddartha,' was produced at the
Bristol Festival of 1896.   A song-cycle was
brought forward at the same festival in 1902.
In 1864 Roeckel married Miss Jane Jackson,
a successful pianist, who did much good work as
a teacher at Clifton, and wrote pianoforte pieces,
etc., under the name of Jules de Sivrai.   She died
at Clifton on Aug. 26, 1907, aged 73.   w. b. s.

RÖNTGEN, ENGELBERT, born Sept. 30, 1829,
at Deventer in Holland, entered the Conservatorium at Leipzig in 1848, as a pupil of David
for violin and of Hauptmann for theory.   Upon
graduating at the Conservatorium, Röntgen was
engaged as a first violin both in the Opera
orchestra and in the famous Gewandhaus orchestra.   In 1869 he became professor of the
violin at the Conservatorium ; second Concertmeister of the Gewandhaus orchestra, and, on
the death of his illustrious master, David, in
1873, he was made first Concertmeister in his
place.   Röntgen was a fine violinist although he
never adopted the career of a virtuoso, and his
careful editing of Beethoven's Quartets proves
him to have been a scholarly musician.   He
married a daughter of Moritz Klengel, himself
Concertmeister at the Gewandhaus.   He died in
Leipzig, Dec. 12, 1897.—A. Ehrlich's *Celebrated
Violinists* ; Bachmann, *Le Violon* ; Lahee's
Famous Violinists.   E. H-A.

---

[1] For Roeckel's own account of his intercourse with Beethoven
see Thayer, vol. ii. p. 294, and vol. iii. p. 269.

His son, JULIUS, was born at Leipzig, May 9, 1855, and soon displayed a great gift for music. His parents were his first teachers, and he afterwards learned from Hauptmann, Richter, Plaidy, and Reinecke. In 1872 he went to Munich, and remained there for some time studying counterpoint and composition under Franz Lachner. A tour with Stockhausen in 1873-74, during which he played chiefly his own compositions, launched him favourably before the world. [He now lives in Amsterdam, where he was teacher in the Conservatorium for some years before succeeding Verhulst as director of the Maatschappij tot Bevordering der Tonkunst in 1886. He was also conductor of the Felix Meritis society for the last two years of its existence. Since 1898 Röntgen has devoted himself entirely to teaching and composition.] His published works amount to eighteen, almost all of a serious character. They are, for the PF.—a duet for four hands, in four movements (op. 16); two sonatas (opp. 2, 10), a phantasie (op. 8); a suite (op. 7); a ballade (op. 5), a cyclus of pieces (op. 6), and a theme with variations (op. 17), etc. etc.; a sonata for PF. and violin (op. 1) and for PF. and violoncello (op. 3); a concerto for PF. and orchestra (op. 18); a serenade for seven wind instruments (op. 14); 'Toskanische Rispetti,' a Liederspiel (op. 9); nine songs (op. 15) etc. etc. The violoncello sonata was played at the Monday Popular Concert of Feb. 14, 1881, and was well received.   G.

ROGEL, JOSÉ, Spanish conductor and composer, born at Orihuela, Alicante, Dec. 24, 1829; began music under Cascales and Gil, organist and conductor of the cathedral, and made great progress, till sent to Valencia by his father to study law. The six years which he spent there were, however, devoted much more to music than to law, under the guidance of Pascual Perez, a musician of ability, from whom he learned composition and other branches of practical music. After completing his legal course and taking his degree at Madrid, Rogel was able to indulge his taste, plunged into music without restraint, and became, or at any rate acted as, conductor and composer to several theatres. The notice of him in Pougin's supplement to Fétis, from which this notice is taken, enumerates no fewer than sixty-one zarzuelas or dramatic pieces of his composition, fourteen of them in three acts, eight in two acts, and the remainder in one act, besides a dozen not yet brought out. The titles of the pieces are of all characters, ranging from 'Revista de un muerto' and 'Un Viage de mil demonios' to 'El General Bumbum.' No criticism is given on the merits of the music, but it must at least be popular.   G.

ROGER, ESTIENNE, an Amsterdam music-publisher, who was in a very extensive way of business from 1696 to 1722. His work is of the highest class of music-printing and engraving,

and is from copper plates. It is said that he was one of the first to introduce the practice of punching the notes on the copper as a substitute for engraving. Walsh and Hare are stated to have taken this idea from him and to have used pewter, a cheaper and a more ductile metal. He translated the Traité de la composition of de Nivers into Flemish (1697).

Among other works Roger issued, circa 1720, a fine edition of Corelli's four sets of Sonatas, and also of the same composer's Concertos. Several collections of miscellaneous works are mentioned in the Quellen-Lexikon.

Roger either died or gave up business about 1725 (his last dated publication is 1722), leaving as his successor Michel Charles Le Céne, who reissued many of his predecessor's publications.   F. K.

ROGER, GUSTAVE HIPPOLITE, eminent French singer, born Dec. 17, 1815, at La Chapelle-Saint-Denis, Paris. He was brought up by an uncle, and educated at the Lycée Charlemagne for the legal profession, but his studies were so neglected for an amateur theatre of which he was the leading tenor and self-constituted manager, that he was at length allowed to follow his real vocation. He entered the Conservatoire in 1836, and after studying for a year under Martin carried off the first prizes both for singing and opéra-comique. He obtained an immediate engagement, and made his début at the Opéra-Comique, Feb. 16, 1838, as Georges in 'L'Éclair.' To a charming voice and distinguished appearance he added great intelligence and stage tact, qualities which soon made him the favourite tenor of the Parisian world, and one of the best comedians of the day. Ambroise Thomas composed for him 'Le Perruquier de la Régence' and 'Mina,' Halévy gave him capital parts in 'Les Mousquetaires de la Reine' and 'Le Guitarrero,' and Auber secured him for 'Le Domino Noir,' 'La Part du Diable,' 'La Sirène,' and 'Haydée.' Meyerbeer declared him to be the only French artist capable of creating the part of John of Leyden. In consequence, after ten years of uninterrupted success, Roger left the Opéra-Comique for the Académie, where on April 16, 1849, he created an immense sensation with Mme. Viardot, in 'Le Prophète.' His acting was quite as good in tragedy as it had been in comedy, but his voice could not stand the wear and tear of the fatiguing répertoire he had now to undertake. During the next ten years, however, he was invaluable at the Opéra, creating new parts in the 'Enfant prodigue,' the 'Juif errant,' and many more. His best creation after John of Leyden, and his last part at the Opéra, was Hélios in David's 'Herculanum' (March 4, 1859). In the following autumn he lost his right arm while shooting, by the bursting of a gun; he reappeared with a false one, but with all his skill and bravery he could not conceal his misfortune, and found

himself compelled to bid farewell to the Académie and to Paris.

He went once more to Germany, which he
had been in the habit of visiting since 1850,
and where he was invariably successful, partly
owing to his unusual command of the language.
After this he sang in the principal provincial
theatres of France, and in 1861 reappeared at
the Opéra-Comique in his best parts, especially
that of Georges Brown in 'La Dame Blanche,'
but it was evident that the time for his retirement had arrived. He then took pupils for
singing, and in 1868 accepted a professorship
at the Conservatoire, which he held till his
death, Sept. 12, 1879.

Roger was of an amiable and benevolent disposition. He talked well, wrote with ease, and
was the author of the French translation of
Haydn's 'Seasons,' and of the words of several
romances and German Lieder. His book, *Le
Carnet d'un ténor* (Paris, Ollendorff, 1880), is a
portion of his autobiography. It contains an
account of his visits to England in 1847 (June),
and 1848 (June–Nov.), when he sang at the
Royal Italian Opera, and made an artistic tour
in the provinces with Mlle. Jenny Lind, and
other artists.   G. C.

ROGERS, BENJAMIN, Mus.D., son of Peter
Rogers, lay-clerk of St. George's Chapel, Windsor, was born at Windsor in 1614. He was
a chorister of St. George's under Dr. Giles,
and afterwards a lay-clerk there. He succeeded Jewett in 1639 as organist of Christ
Church, Dublin, where he continued until the
rebellion in 1641, when he returned to Windsor
and obtained a lay-clerk's place there; but
on the breaking up of the choir in 1644 he
taught music in Windsor and its neighbourhood,
and obtained some compensation for the loss of
his appointment. In 1653 he composed some
airs in four parts for violins and organ, which
were presented to the Archduke Leopold, afterwards Emperor of Germany, and favourably
received by him. In 1658 he was admitted
Mus.B. at Cambridge. (See Carlyle's *Oliver
Cromwell*, v. 243, 244 (People's edition).) In
1660 he composed a 'Hymnus Eucharisticus'
in four parts, to words by Dr. Nathaniel Ingelo,
which was performed at Guildhall when Charles
II. dined there on July 5.[1] About the same
time he became organist of Eton College. On
Oct. 21, 1662, he was reappointed a lay-clerk
at St. George's, Windsor, his stipend being
augmented by half the customary amount; and
he also received out of the organist's salary £1
per month as deputy organist. On July 22,
1664, he was appointed Informator Choristarum
and organist of Magdalen College, Oxford. On
July 8, 1669, he proceeded Mus.D. at Oxford.
In Jan. 1685 he was removed from his place at
Magdalen College on account of irregularities

---

[1] The hymn was different from that, bearing the same title, which
Rogers afterwards set for Magdalen College, Oxford.

(see West's *Cath. Org.*, p. 120), the College, however, assuring to him an annuity of £30 for life.
He survived until June 1698, on the 21st of
which month he was buried at St. Peter-le-Bailey.
His widow, whom the College had pensioned
with two-thirds of his annuity, survived him
only seven months, and was laid by his side
Jan. 5, 1699.—Rogers composed much church
music; four services are printed in the collections
of Boyce, Rimbault, and Sir F. Ouseley; another,
an Evening Verse Service in G, is at Ely in MS.
Some anthems were printed in 'Cantica Sacra,'
1674, and by Boyce and Page; and many others
are in MS. in the books of various cathedrals
and college chapels. Four glees are contained
in Playford's 'Musical Companion,' 1673, and
many instrumental compositions in 'Courtly
Masquing Ayres,' 1662. [Some MS. organ
compositions are in the library of the Royal
College of Music, and Mr. J. S. Bumpus possesses
a volume in the handwriting of Dr. Philip Hayes,
containing the whole of Rogers's compositions
for the church.] His 'Hymnus Eucharisticus'
(the first stanza of which, commencing 'Te Deum
Patrem colimus,' is daily sung in Magdalen
College Hall by way of grace after dinner, and
is printed in the Appendix to Hawkins's *History*)
is sung annually on the top of Magdalen tower
at five in the morning of May 1 in lieu of a
requiem which, before the Reformation, was
performed in the same place for the soul of
Henry VII. His service in D and some of his
anthems, which are pleasing and melodious in
character, are still sung in cathedrals. W. H. H.

ROGERS, JOHN, a famous lutenist, born in
London, was attached to the household of
Charles II. in 1661-63. He lived near Alders-
gate, and died there about 1663.   W. H. H.

ROGERS, SIR JOHN LEMAN, Bart., born April
18, 1780, succeeded his father in the baronetcy
in 1797. He became a member of the Madrigal
Society in 1819, and in 1820 was elected its
permanent President (being the first so appointed), and held the office until 1841, when
he resigned on account of ill-health. He composed a cathedral service, chants, anthems,
madrigals, glees, and other vocal music. [See
Hullah's PART MUSIC, Class A, and VOCAL
SCORES.] He was an ardent admirer of the
compositions of Tallis, and by his exertions an
annual service was held for several years in
Westminster Abbey, the music being wholly
that of Tallis. He died Dec. 10, 1847. W. H. H.

ROGERS, ROLAND, Mus.D., born at West
Bromwich, Staffordshire, Nov. 17, 1847, where
he was appointed organist of St. Peter's Church
in 1858. He studied under Mr. S. Grosvenor,
and in 1862 obtained by competition the post
of organist at St. John's, Wolverhampton. In
1867 he similarly obtained the organistship
of Tettenhall parish church, and in 1871 was
appointed organist and choirmaster of Bangor
Cathedral, a post which he resigned at the end

of 1891. He took the Oxford degree of Mus. B. in 1870, and that of Mus. D. in 1875. Dr. Rogers's published works are 'Prayer and Praise,' a cantata, a prize cantata, 'The Garden' (Llandudno, 1896), Evening Services in B♭ and D, Anthems, Part-songs, Organ Solos, and Songs; a Symphony in A, a Psalm 'De Profundis,' and several Anthems and Services are still in MS.   W. B. S.

ROGUES' MARCH, THE. Originally a military quickstep, which from some cause has become appropriate to use when offenders are drummed out of the army. When, from theft, or other crime, it is decided to expel a man from the regiment, the buttons bearing the regimental number, and other special decorations, are cut from his coat, and he is then marched, to the music of drums and fifes playing 'The Rogues' March,' to the barrack gates, and kicked or thrust out into the street. The ceremony still continues at the present day. The writer, though he has made diligent search, cannot find traces of the tune before the middle of the 18th century, although there can be but little doubt that the air, with its association, had been in use long before that time. About 1790, and later, a certain more vocal setting of the air was used for many popular humorous songs. 'Robinson Crusoe,' 'Abraham Newland,' and the better-known 'Tight little Island,' are among these. The latter song, as 'The Island,' was written by Thomas Dibdin about 1798, and sung by a singer named Davies at Sadler's Wells in that year.

The original 'Rogues' March' stands thus—

It is found in many 18th-century collections of fife and flute music; the above copy is from 'The Compleat Tutor for the Fife,' London, printed for and sold by Thompson & Son, 8vo, *circa* 1759-60.   F. K.

ROHR FLUTE (Rohrflöte). See FLUTE-WORK, vol. ii. pp. 68-9.

ROI DE LAHORE, LE. Opera in five acts, libretto by Louis Gallet, music by Jules Massenet. Produced at the Grand Opéra, Paris, April 27, 1877, and at Covent Garden, Royal Italian Opera, June 28, 1879.

ROI DES VIOLONS—'King of the violins' —a title of great interest as illustrating the struggle between Art and Authority. On Sept.

14, 1321, the *ménestriers* or fiddlers of France formed themselves into a regular corporation, with a code of laws in eleven sections, which was presented to the Prevôt of Paris, and by him registered at the Châtelet. The Confraternity, founded by thirty-seven *jongleurs* and *jongleresses*, whose names have been preserved, prospered so far as in 1330 to purchase a site and erect on it a hospital for poor musicians. The building was begun in 1331, finished in 1335, and dedicated to St. Julien and St. Genest. The superior of this 'Confrérie of St. Julien des ménétriers' was styled 'king,' and the following were 'Rois des ménétriers' in the 14th century:—Robert Caveron, 1338; Copin du Brequin, 1349; Jean Caumez, 1387; and Jehan Portevin, 1392.

In 1407 the musicians, vocal and instrumental, separated themselves from the mountebanks and tumblers who had been associated with them by the statutes of 1321. The new constitution received the sanction of Charles VI., April 24, 1407, and it was enacted that no musician might teach, or exercise his profession, without having passed an examination, and been declared *suffisant* by the 'Roi des ménestrels' or his deputies. These statutes continued in force down to the middle of the 17th century. History, however, tells but little about the new corporation. The only 'rois' whose names have been preserved in the charters are—Jehan Boissard, called Verdelet, 1420; Jehan Facien, the elder, and Claude de Bouchardon, oboes in the band of Henri III., 1575; Claude Nyon, 1590; Claude Nyon, called Lafont, 1600; François Rishomme, 1615; and Louis Constantin, 'roi' from 1624 to 1655. Constantin, who died in Paris 1657, was a distinguished artist, violinist to Louis XIII., and composer of pieces for strings in five and six parts, several of which are preserved in the valuable collection already named under PHILIDOR, vol. iii. p. 703.

In 1514 the title was changed to 'roi des ménestrels du royaume.' All provincial musicians were compelled to acknowledge the authority of the corporation in Paris, and in the 16th century branches were established in the principal towns of France under the title of 'Confrérie de St. Julien des ménétriers.' In Oct. 1658, Louis XIV. confirmed Constantin's successor, Guillaume Dumanoir I., in the post of 'Roi des violons, maîtres à danser, et joueurs d'instruments tant haut que bas,' ordaining at the same time that the 'Roi des violons' should have the sole privilege of conferring the mastership of the art throughout the kingdom; that no one should be admitted thereto without serving an apprenticeship of four years, and paying sixty livres to the 'roi,' and ten livres to the masters of the Confrérie; the masters themselves paying an annual sum of thirty sous to the corporation, with a further commission to the 'roi' for each pupil. The masters alone were privileged to play in taverns and other public places, and in case this rule were infringed, the 'roi' could send the offender to prison and destroy his instruments. This formidable monopoly extended even to the King's band, the famous 'twenty-four violons,' who were admitted to office by the 'roi' alone on payment of his fee. [See VINGT-QUATRE VIOLONS.]

So jealously did Guillaume Dumanoir I. guard his rights, that in 1662 he commenced an action against thirteen dancing-masters, who, with the view of throwing off the yoke of the corporation, had obtained from Louis XIV. permission to found an 'Académie de danse.' The struggle gave rise to various pamphlets,[1] and Dumanoir was beaten at all points. He bequeathed a difficult task to his son Michel Guillaume Dumanoir II., who succeeded him as 'roi' in 1668, and endeavoured to enforce his supremacy on the instrumentalists of the Académie de Musique, but, as might have been expected, was overmatched by Lully. After his difficulties with the director of the Opéra, Dumanoir II., like his father, came into collision with the dancing-masters. In 1691 a royal proclamation was issued by which the elective committee was abolished, and its place filled by hereditary officials, aided by four others appointed by purchase. Against this decree the corporation and the thirteen members of the Académie de danse protested, but the Treasury was in want of funds, and declined to refund the purchase money. Finding himself unequal to such assaults Dumanoir resigned in 1693, and died in Paris in 1697. He delegated his powers to the privileged committee of 1691, and thus threw on them the onus of supporting the claims of the Confrérie over the clavecinists and organists of the kingdom ; a parliamentary decree of 1695, however, set free the composers and professors of music from all dependence on the corporation of the ménétriers. This struggle was several times renewed. When Pierre Guignon (born 1702, died 1775), a good violinist, and a member of the King's chamber-music, and of the Chapel Royal, attempted to reconstitute the Confrérie on a better footing, it became evident that the musicians as a body were determined to throw off the yoke of the association. Guignon was appointed 'Roi des violons' by letters patent, June 15, 1741, was installed in 1742, and in 1747 endeavoured to enforce certain new enactments, but a parliamentary decree of May 30, 1750, put an end to his pretended authority over clavecinists, organists, and other serious musicians. The corporation was maintained, but its head was

[1] Of these the principal are *Etablissement de l'Académie royale de dance* [sic] *en la ville de Paris, avec un discours Académique pour prouver que la dance, dans sa plus noble partie, n'a pas besoin des instruments de musique, et qu'elle est en tout absolument indépendante du violon* (Paris, 1663, 4to), and *Le mariage de la musique et de la dance, contenant la réponce* [sic] *au livre des treize prétendus académiciens touchants ces deux arts* (Paris, 1664, 12mo).

obliged to be content with the title of 'Roi et maître des ménétriers, joueurs d'instruments tant haut que bas, et hautbois, et communauté des maîtres à danser.' Roi Guignon still preserved the right of conferring on provincial musicians the title of 'lieutenants généraux et particuliers' to the 'roi des violons,' but even this was abrogated by a decree of the Conseil d'État, Feb. 13, 1773. The last 'roi des violons' at once resigned, and in the following month his office was abolished by an edict of the King dated from Versailles.

This hasty sketch of a difficult subject may be supplemented by consulting the following works : *Abrégé historique de la Ménestrandie* (Versailles, 1774, 12mo) ; *Statuts et réglements des maîtres de danse et joueurs d'instruments . . . registrés au Parlement le 22 Août 1659* (Paris, 1753) ; *Recueil d'édits, arrêts du Conseil du roi, lettres patentes, . . . en faveur des musiciens du Royaume* (Ballard, 1774, 8vo) ; and *Les Instruments à archet*, by A. Vidal (i. and ii. Paris, 1876, 1877, 4to), which last contains nearly all the necessary information. G. C.

ROI D'YS, LE. Opera in three acts, text by Édouard Blau, music by Édouard Lalo, produced at the Opéra-Comique, Paris, May 7, 1888, and at Covent Garden, July 17, 1901.

ROI L'A DIT, LE. Opéra-comique in three acts, text by Edm. Gondinet, music by Léo Delibes ; produced at the Opéra-Comique, Paris, May 24, 1873, in English at Prince of Wales's Theatre, by the Royal College of Music, Dec. 13, 1894.

ROI MALGRÉ LUI, LE. Opéra-comique in three acts, text by Emile de Najac and Paul Burani, music by Emmanuel Chabrier ; produced at the Opéra-Comique, Paris, May 18, 1887.

ROITZSCH, F. AUGUST, born Dec. 10, 1805, at Gruna, near Görlitz, won a high reputation as a careful editor of old music, and more especially of Bach's instrumental compositions, in the valuable cheap editions of the firm of Peters. He died at Leipzig, Feb. 4, 1889. M.

ROKITANSKY, HANS, FREIHERR VON, born March 8, 1835, at Vienna, eldest son of Carl Freiherr von Rokitansky (1804-78), an eminent medical professor. He studied singing chiefly at Bologna and Milan, and first appeared in England at concerts in 1856. In 1862 he made his début at Prague in 'La Juive,' and fulfilled a very successful engagement there of two years. In 1863 he sang the same part at Vienna, in 1864 obtained an engagement there, and was a member of the opera company for many years, retiring in 1892. His voice was a basso-profondo of great compass and volume, very equal in all its range ; he had a commanding presence, and was an excellent actor. His operas include 'La Juive,' 'Robert le Diable,' 'Les Huguenots,' 'Don Juan,' 'Zauberflöte,' 'Guillaume Tell,' 'Le Prophète,'

'Aïda,' 'Faust,' 'Vestale,' 'Medea,' and Wagner's operas. On June 17, 1865, he reappeared in London at Her Majesty's as Marcel with very great success, and then sang there and at Drury Lane for four consecutive seasons, and was greatly esteemed. He played with success as Rocco, Sarastro, Leporello, Il Commendatore, Oroveso, Falstaff, Osmin (June 30, 1866, on production in Italian of Mozart's 'Entführung'), and Padre Guardiano in 'La Forza del Destino,' June 22, 1867. He returned for the seasons of 1876 and 1877 in some of his old parts, and played for the first time the King in 'Lohengrin,' and Giorgio in 'I Puritani.' He retired from public life at the end of 1894, and is now a professor in the Vienna Conservatorium.   A. C.

ROKITANSKY, VICTOR. A younger brother of the above, and a fashionable singing-master at Vienna. Born July 9, 1836. From 1871 to 1880 he filled the post of Professor of Singing at the Conservatorium of Vienna ; he published *Ueber Sänger und Singen* in 1894, and died in Vienna, July 17, 1896.   A. C.

ROLFE & CO., pianoforte makers. William Rolfe was at 112 Cheapside in 1796 as a music-seller and publisher of minor musical works, also as maker of musical instruments. Before this date he was partner in a small music-publishing firm, Culliford, Rolfe, & Barrow, at the same address, about 1790. With Samuel Davis, Rolfe took out a patent for improvements in pianofortes on Jan. 31, 1797, and his pianofortes had some degree of reputation. His business continued until 1806, when the firm was William Rolfe & Sons, and in 1813 they had additional premises at 28 London Wall. Rolfe & Sons (or Co.) remained in Cheapside for many years. In 1850 the number had been changed to 61, and the London Wall premises to 31 and 32. They removed to 12 Great Marlborough Street (1869), and then (1878) to 11 Orchard Street. During the eighties their place of business was at 6 Lower Seymour Street, but after 1890 the writer can find no traces of them.   F. K.

ROLL, in drumming, is a tremolo effect on the side-drum, produced by a certain varied method of playing according to the kind of roll desired. The first practice of this is called 'daddy mammy,' which, commencing deliberately, with a long stroke for each syllable, gradually increases in speed until the beats are merged into one continuous roll. The 'long roll' is an alternate beat of two with the left stick, followed by two with the right. The 'five stroke roll' is two with the left, two with the right, one with the left, two with the right, two with the left, and one with the right ; or more briefly—L L R R . L ; R R L L . R. The 'seven stroke roll' is—L L R R L L . R. The 'nine stroke roll' is—L L R R L L R R . L followed by a short rest, and R R L L R R L L . . R. Rolls

on the timpani are made by the simple alternation of strokes with the two sticks. See DRUM.   F. K.

ROLL-CALL. See MILITARY SOUNDS AND SIGNALS.

ROLLA, ALESSANDRO, violinist and composer, born at Pavia, April 22, 1757. He first studied the pianoforte, but soon exchanged it for the violin, which he learned under Renzi and Conti. He had also a great predilection for the viola, and wrote and performed in public concertos for that instrument. In 1782-1802 he was leader of the band at Parma, and it was there that Paganini was for some months his pupil. [See PAGANINI.] In 1802 he went to Milan as leader and conductor of the opera at La Scala, in which position he gained a great reputation. He became in 1805 a professor at the Conservatorio of Milan, and died in that town, Sept. 15, 1841, aged eighty-four. His compositions, now entirely forgotten, had considerable success in their time ; they consist of a large number of violin duets, some serenades, trios, quartets, and quintets for stringed instruments, and concertos for the violin and for the viola, as well as songs. (See the *Quellen-Lexikon*.) His son and pupil, Antonio, violinist, was born at Parma, April 18, 1798 ; from 1823 till 1835 was leader of the Italian Opera band at Dresden, and died there, May 19, 1837. He published concertos and other solo pieces for the violin. P. D.

ROLLE. A German musical family. The father, CHRISTIAN FRIEDRICH, was town musician of Quedlinburg and of Magdeburg in 1721, and died there in 1751. Of his three sons, CHRISTIAN CARL, born at Quedlinburg in 1714, was Cantor of the Jerusalem Church, Berlin, about 1760, but was apparently of no account. He had sons, of whom FRIEDRICH HEINRICH left a biography of his father ; while CHRISTIAN CARL (the younger) succeeded him as Cantor. 2. A second son is mentioned, but without name. 3. The third, JOHANN HEINRICH, was born at Quedlinburg, Dec. 23, 1718, and at an early age began to play and to write. He held the post of organist at St. Peter's, Magdeburg, in 1732 when only fourteen years old (*Quellen-Lexikon*). He was at the Leipzig University in 1736, and migrated to Berlin in hopes of some legal post ; but this failing he adopted music as his career, and about 1740 entered the Court chapel of Frederick the Great as a chamber musician (viola player). There he remained till 1746, and then took the organist's place at the Johanniskirche, Magdeburg, as town musician, worked there with uncommon zeal and efficiency, and died at the age of sixty-seven, Dec. 29, 1785. His industry seems almost to have rivalled that of Bach himself. He left several complete annual series of church music for all the Sundays and Festivals ; cantatas for Easter, Whitsuntide, and Christmas,

of which many are in the Royal Library at
Berlin ; five Passions, and at least sixty other
large church compositions. Besides these there
exist twenty-one large works of his, of a nature
between oratorio and drama, such as ' Saul, or
the power of Music,' ' Samson,' ' David and
Jonathan,' ' The Labours of Hercules,' ' Orestes
and Pylades,' ' Abraham on Moriah,' ' The
Death of Abel,' etc. The last two were for
many years performed annually at Berlin, and
were so popular that the editions had to be
renewed repeatedly. In addition to these he
left many songs and compositions for organ,
orchestra, and separate instruments. (See the
Quellen-Lexikon for list.) All have now as
good as perished ; but those who wish to know
what kind of music they were, will find a
specimen in Hullah's ' Vocal scores,' ' The Lord
is King.' It has a good deal of vigour, but
no originality or character. Others are given
in the collections of Sander and Rochlitz, and
a set of twenty motets for four voices was published at Magdeburg by Rebling (1851-66.)   G.

ROLLI, PAOLO ANTONIO, an Italian poet, a
Florentine, who was employed by the managers
of the Italian opera to supply the libretti for
several of the operas put before the English public
in the early years of the 18th century. It is
said that he was originally a pastry-cook, but
coming to England about 1718, his productions
pleased the public, and he became much noticed.
In 1727 he issued a small book of canzonets
and cantatas, with the music, dedicated to the
Countess of Pembroke. At a later date he set
up as teacher of the Italian language, and left
England for Italy in 1744. Two stanzas of
his poem, ' Se tu m' ami,' were set by Pergolesi,
and three by J. J. Rousseau ; and his whole
book of canzonets and cantatas was adapted
to new music by William De Fesch about
1745-46, and published with a fresh dedication
to Lady Frances Erskine.   F. K.

ROMANCE (Germ. *Romanze*). A term of
very vague signification, answering in music to
the same term in poetry, where the characteristics are rather those of personal sentiment and
expression than of precise form. The Romanze
in Mozart's D minor PF. Concerto differs (if it
differs) from the slow movements of his other
Concertos in the extremely tender and delicate
character of its expression ; in its form there is
nothing at all unusual : and the same may be
said of Beethoven's two Romances for the violin
and orchestra in G and F (opp. 40 and 50), and
of Schumann's ' Drei Romanzen ' (op. 28).
Schumann has also affixed the title to three
movements for oboe and PF. (op. 94), and to a
well-known piece in D minor (op. 32, No. 3),
just as he has used the similar title, ' in Legen-
denton.' The Romance which forms the second
movement of his symphony in D minor, is a
little poem full of sentimental expression.

In vocal music the term is obviously derived
from the character or title of the words. In
English poetry we have few ' romances,' though
such of Moore's melodies as ' She is far from the
land where her young hero sleeps ' might well
bear the title. But in France they abound, and
some composers (such as Puget and Panseron)
have derived nine-tenths of their reputation
from them. ' Partant pour la Syrie ' may be
named as a good example, well known on this
side the water. Mendelssohn's ' Songs without
Words ' are called in France ' Romances sans
Paroles.'   G.

ROMANI, FELICE, a famous Italian littérateur, born at Genoa, Jan. 31, 1788. He was
educated for the law, but soon forsook it for
more congenial pursuits, and was in early life
appointed to the post of poet to the royal
theatres, with a salary of 6000 lire. The fall
of the French government in Italy drove him
to his own resources. He began with a comedy,
' L' Amante e l' Impostore,' which was very successful, and the forerunner of many dramatic
pieces. But his claim to notice in a dictionary
of music rests on his opera-librettos, in which
he was for long the favourite of the Italian composers. For Simone Mayr he wrote ' Medea '
(1812), ' La Rosa bianca e la Rosa rossa,' and
others ; for Rossini, ' Aureliano in Palmira,'
and ' Il Turco in Italia ' ; for Bellini, ' Bianca
e Faliero,' ' La Straniera,' ' La Sonnambula,'
' Il Pirata,' ' Norma,' ' I Capuletti,' and ' Beatrice
di Tenda ' ; for Donizetti, ' Lucrezia,' ' Anna
Bolena,' ' L' Elisir d' amore,' and ' Parisina ' ;
for Mercadante, ' Il Conte d' Essex ' ; for Ricci,
' Un Avventura di Scaramuccia ' ; and many
others, in all fully a hundred. As editor for
many years of the *Gazzetta Piemontese*, he was
a voluminous writer.

In the latter part of his life he became blind,
and was pensioned by government, and spent
his last years in his family circle at Moneglia,
on the Riviera, where he died full of years and
honours, Jan. 28, 1865.   G.

ROMANO, one of the names (derived from
his birthplace) of a certain ALESSANDRO, who
was also known under the name of ALESSANDRO
DELLA VIOLA from his favourite instrument—
a composer and performer on the viola, was born
at Rome about the year 1530. His published
works include a set of madrigals, Venice, 1554
(Royal College of Music, etc.); five-part madrigals,
Ib. 1565 ; two books of Canzoni Napolitane for
five voices (Venice, 1572 and 1575) ; a set of
motets in five parts (Venice, 1579). A five-
part madrigal by him, 'Non pur d' almi splendori,'
is published in the ' Libro terzo delle Muse '
(Venice, Gardano, 1561). [See the *Quellen-
Lexikon, s.v.* Alessandro.]   P. D.

ROMANTIC is a term which, with its antithesis CLASSICAL, has been borrowed by music
from literature. But so delicate and incorporeal
are the qualities of composition which both
words describe in their application to music, and

so arbitrary has been their use by different writers, that neither word is susceptible of very precise definition. The best guide, however, to the meaning of 'romantic' is supplied by its etymology. The poetic tales of the Middle Ages, written in the old Romance dialects, were called Romances. In them mythological fables and Christian legends, stories of fairyland, and adventures of Crusaders and other heroes of chivalry, were indiscriminately blended, and the fantastic figures thus brought together moved in a dim atmosphere of mystic gloom and religious ecstasy. These mediæval productions had long been neglected and forgotten even by scholars, when, about the close of the 18th century, they were again brought into notice by a group of poets, of whom the most notable were the brothers August Wilhelm and Friedrich von Schlegel, Ludwig Tieck, and Friedrich Novalis. They set themselves to rescue the old romances from oblivion, and to revive the spirit of mediæval poetry in modern literature by the example of their own works. Hence they came to be called the Romantic School, and were thus distinguished from writers whose fidelity to rules and models of classic antiquity gave them a claim to the title of Classical.

It was not long before the term Romantic was introduced into musical literature ; and it was understood to characterise both the subjects of certain musical works and the spirit in which they were treated. Its antithetical significance to the term Classical still clung to it ; and regard to perfection of form being often subordinated by so-called romantic composers to the object of giving free play to the imaginative and emotional parts of our nature, there grew up around the epithet Romantic the notion of a tendency to depart more or less from the severity of purely classical compositions. But, in truth, no clear line divides the romantic from the classical. As we shall endeavour to show, the greatest names of the Classical school display the quality of romanticism in the spirit or expression of some of their works,[1] while, on the other hand, the compositions of the Romantic school are frequently marked by scrupulous adherence to the forms of traditional excellence. Again, as the associations of the word Classical convey the highest meed of praise, works at first pronounced to be romantic establish, by general recognition of their merit, a claim to be considered classical. What is 'romantic' to-day may thus grow, although itself unchanged, to be 'classical' to-morrow. The reader will thus understand why, in Reichardt's opinion, Bach, Handel, and Gluck were classical, but Haydn and Mozart romantic ; why later critics, in

presence of the fuller romanticism of Beethoven, placed Haydn and Mozart among the classical composers ; and why Beethoven himself, in his turn, was declared to be classical.

The propriety of applying the term Romantic to operas whose subjects are taken from romantic literature, or to songs where music is set to romantic words, will not be questioned. And from such works it is easy to select passages which present romantic pictures to the mind, as, for instance, the Trumpet passage on the long B♭ in the bass in the great Leonore overture, the three horn notes in the overture to 'Oberon,' or the three drum notes in the overture to 'Der Freischütz.' But in pure instrumental music the marks of romanticism are so fine, and the recognition of them depends so much on sympathy and mental predisposition, that the question whether this or that work is romantic may be a subject of interminable dispute among critics. Sometimes the only mark of romanticism would seem to be a subtle effect of instrumentation, or a sudden change of key, as in the following passage from the Leonore Overture :—

Another example from Beethoven is supplied by the opening bars of the PF. Concerto in G major, where after the solo has ended on the dominant the orchestra enters *pp* with the chord of B major. The whole of the slow movement of this Concerto is thoroughly romantic, but perhaps that quality is most powerfully felt in the following passage :—

Yet so subtle is the spell of its presence here that it would be difficult to define where its intense romanticism lies, unless it be in the abrupt change both in key (A minor to F major), and in the character of the phrase, almost forcing a scene, or recollection, or image, upon the hearer.[2] Indeed, romantic music possesses in the highest degree the power of evoking in the mind some vivid thought or conception—as for instance, in a passage from the Adagio of the Ninth Symphony, where a sudden transition into D♭ seems to say, 'Vanitas vanitatum, omnia vanitas' ; and again in the 'Eroica,' where at the end of the Trio, the long holding notes and peculiar harmony in the horns seem to suggest the idea of Eternity :—

---

[1] Premonitions of musical romanticism existed in fact long before the word came into use. To our modern ears, now conscious of this special quality, traces are clearly discernible. As examples we may take J. S. Bach's preludes Nos. 14 and 18 in the second book of the 'Wohltemperirtes Clavier,' or the Arioso 'Am Abend da es kühle war' from the Matthew Passion. Also many passages from Gluck's and Mozart's operas.

[2] Pater's definition may well be applied to this example: 'The essence of romanticism is the blending of strangeness with the beautiful.'

That there are times when music has a fuller and wider range of meaning than language, and defies expression in words, might be illustrated by many passages in Beethoven's B flat trio or the last five sonatas. But with regard to the choice of examples we must remind the reader that, where the standpoint of criticism is almost wholly subjective, great diversities of judgment are inevitable.

It was not until after the appearance of the works of Carl Maria von Weber, who lived in close relation with the romantic school of literature, and who drew his inspirations from their writings, that critics began to speak of a 'romantic school of music.' Beethoven had by this time been accepted as classical, but in addition to Weber himself, Schubert and afterwards Mendelssohn, Schumann, and Chopin were all held to be representatives of the romantic school. Widely as the composers of this new school differed in other respects, they were alike in their susceptibility to the tone of thought and feeling which so deeply coloured the romantic literature of their time. None of them were strangers to that weariness of the actual world around them, and those yearnings to escape from it, which pursued so many of the finest minds of the generations to which they belonged. To men thus predisposed, it was a relief and delight to live in an ideal world as remote as possible from the real one. Some took refuge in mediæval legends, where no border divided the natural from the supernatural, and where nothing could be incongruous or improbable ; some in the charms and solitudes of nature ; and others in the contemplation of peace and beatitude beyond the grave. But in all there was the same impatience of the material and mundane conditions of their existence, the same longing to dwell in the midst of scenes and images which mortals could but dimly see through the glass of religious or poetic imagination. As might have been expected of works produced under such influences, indistinctness of outline was a common attribute of compositions of the romantic school. The hard, clear lines of reality were seldom met with in them, and the cold analysis of pure reason was perpetually eluded. It was equally natural that the creations of minds withdrawn from contact with the actual world and wrapt in their own fancies, should vividly reflect the moods and phases of feeling out of which they sprang—that they should be, in short, intensely subjective. Nor was it surprising that when impatience of reality, indistinctness of outline, and excessive

subjectivity co-existed, the pleasures of imagination sometimes took a morbid hue. Such conditions of origin as we have been describing could not fail to affect the forms of composition. It was not that the romanticists deliberately rejected or even undervalued classic models, but that, borne onward by the impulse to give free expression to their own individuality, they did not suffer themselves to be bound by forms, however excellent, which they felt to be inadequate for their purpose. Had the leaders of the romantic school been men of less genius, this tendency might have degenerated into disregard of form ; but happily in them liberty did not beget license, and the art of music was enriched by the addition of new forms. 'The extremes,' says Goethe, speaking of the romantic school of literature, 'will disappear, and at length the great advantage will remain that a wider and more varied subject-matter, together with a freer form, will be attained.' Goethe's anticipations were equally applicable to music.

Among masters of the romantic school, Weber stands second to none. In youth he surrendered himself to the fascination of literary romanticism, and this early bias of his mind was confirmed in later years by constant intercourse at Dresden with Holtei, Tieck, E. T. A. Hoffmann, and other men of the same cast of thought. The subjects of Weber's operas were selected exclusively from romantic literature, and the 'Romantic Opera,' of which Germany has so much reason to be proud, owed to him its origin and highest development, although the names of Spohr,[1] Marschner, Lindpaintner, Kreutzer, Lortzing, and others are justly associated with it. The romantic effects which Weber could produce in his instrumentation are indisputable, and never, even in the least of his pianoforte works, did he cease to be romantic.

Though Weber holds the first place in the opera of the romantic school, he was surpassed in other branches of composition by his contemporary, Franz Schubert. Pure and classic as is the form of Schubert's symphonies and sonatas, the very essence of romanticism is disclosed in them. His unrivalled wealth of melody was the gift of romanticism. It gave him also a certain indefiniteness and, as it were, indivisibility of ideas, which some critics have judged to be a failing, but which were in fact the secret of this strength, because they enabled him to repeat and develop, to change and then again resume his beautiful themes and figures in long and rich progression, without pause and without satiety. None have known, as he knew, how to elicit almost human sounds from a single instrument—as for instance, in the well-known passage for the horn in the second movement of the C major Symphony, of which Schumann said that ' it seems to have come

[1] These points, and Spohr's claim to priority of invention of the Romantic opera, are discussed in OPERA, vol. iii. p. 456, etc.

to us from another world.' Many glorious passages might be pointed out in this Symphony, the romanticism of which it would be difficult to surpass ; for instance, the second subject in the first movement, the beginning of the working out in the Finale, etc. etc. In Song Schubert stands alone. Even from boyhood he had steeped his soul in romantic poetry ; anᴋ so expressive is the music of his songs that they require no words to reveal their deeply romantic character. Few were the thoughts or feelings which Schubert's genius was unable to express in music. 'He was' (to quote Schumann again) 'the deadly enemy of all Philistinism, and after Beethoven the greatest master who made music his vocation in the noblest sense of the word.'

Schumann's own enmity to Philistinism was not less deadly than that of Schubert, and romanticism was its root in both men. So strongly did Schumann resent the popularity of Herz, Hünten, and other Philistines, whose works were in vogue about the year 1830, that he founded the Davidsbund to expose the hollowness of their pretensions. And equally dissatisfied with the shallow and contracted views of the musical critics of that day, he started his *Neue Zeitschrift für Musik* to vindicate the claims of music to freedom from every limitation, except the laws of reason and of beauty. Even in childhood Schumann was an eager reader of romantic literature, and the writings of Hoffmann and Jean Paul never lost their charm for him. He told a correspondent that if she would rightly understand his 'Papillons,' op. 2, she must read the last chapter of Jean Paul's *Flegeljahre* ; and from Hoffmann he borrowed the title of 'Kreisleriana.' It was not, however, the imaginary sufferings of Dr. Kreissler, but the real deep melancholy of Schumann's own soul, which expressed itself in these noble fantasias. Though perfect in form, they are thoroughly romantic in thought and spirit. Not less romantic were the names he gave to his pianoforte pieces. These names, he said, were scarcely necessary—'for is not music self-sufficing ? does it not speak for itself?'—but he admitted that they were faithful indexes to the character of the pieces. The clearest tokens of the same source of inspiration may be found in his Fantasie, op. 17, which bears as its motto a verse from Schlegel. In the last part a deeply moving effect is produced by the abrupt change of key in the arpeggios from the chords of C to A and then to F. But changes of key were not his only resource for the production of romantic effects. Excepting Beethoven, none have illustrated the power of rhythm so well as Schumann. He often imparts a strange and entirely novel significance to commonplace or familiar phrases by syncopated notes, by putting the emphasis on the weak part of the bar, or by accents so marked as to give the impression of a simultaneous combination of triple and common time. These strong and eccentric rhythms appear in all his works ; and the frequent directions *Marcato assai* or *Molto marcato* show what stress he laid upon emphasis. The influence of Jean Paul may be traced also in Schumann's sometimes grave and sometimes playful humour. Many of his pianoforte pieces are marked *mit Humor* or *mit vielem Humor*. And in this respect he is inferior only to Beethoven, of whose 'romantic humour' he so often speaks in his *Gesammelte Schriften*. The romantic bias of Schumann's mind was not less evident in his treatment of Oriental subjects. The colouring of his 'Paradise and the Peri,' and of his 'Bilder aus Osten,' is vividly local. And of his songs we may cite the 'Waldesgespräch' (op. 39, No. 3) as an example of the purest essence of romance. Full as the poem is in itself of romantic feeling and expression, the music interprets the words, rather than the words the music.

The romantic spirit found a less congenial abode in the happy, equable disposition, and carefully disciplined imagination of Mendelssohn ; but his genius was too sensitive and delicate to remain unaffected by the main currents of his age.[1] Take, for example, the first four chords in the overture to 'A Midsummer Night's Dream.' And could it indeed be possible to illustrate Shakespeare's romantic play in music with fuller success than Mendelssohn has done ? The overtures 'The Hebrides,' 'Melusine,' and 'Calm Sea and Prosperous Voyage,' are likewise full of the brightest qualities of romanticism.

Not unlike Mendelssohn was William Sterndale Bennett ; and the points of resemblance between them were strict regard to form, clearness of poetic thought, and cultivated refinement of taste. Romantic, too, Bennett certainly was ; as may at once be seen in his overtures, 'The Naiads' and 'The Wood Nymphs.' So tranquil, clear and perfect in detail are most of Bennett's compositions, so delicate was the touch which fashioned them, that they have been likened to the landscapes of Claude Lorraine. Yet there were rare moments when Bennett's habitual reserve relaxed, and to the inspiration of such moments we may ascribe the romantic passages which occur in his beautiful 'Paradise and the Peri' and 'Parisina' overtures.

Notice of the modern German composers on whom the stamp of Schumann is so unmistakable, would lead us too far, but the names of Robert Franz and Adolf Jensen cannot be omitted. Some of the tenderest and most delicate attributes of romanticism are to be found in their songs, as for instance in the 'Dolorosa' cycle of the latter composer. Peter Cornelius's spirit moves in a different atmosphere ; a poet himself, he casts a peculiar and magic

[1] In describing to Reichardt's daughter the success of her father's 'Morgengesang' at the Rhine Festival, Mendelssohn adds, 'At the words *Und schlich in dieser Nacht* the music becomes so romantic and poetical that every time I hear it, I am more touched and charmed.'

spell of romance over his music. Wagner we pass by, because he cannot be counted among the followers of the romantic school, and, within the limits of this article, it would be impossible to show the points wherein he differs from all former romanticists. We may, however, designate one of the greatest of modern composers as one of the greatest romanticists ; and it is no disparagement to the individuality of Johannes Brahms to say that he is in many respects the disciple of Schubert and Schumann. The romanticism of such productions as the beautiful romances from Tieck's 'Magelone' (op. 33) or the cantata 'Rinaldo' (op. 50) is of course visible at a glance, and there are many other songs in which the presence of romantic sensibility is felt throughout. For instance in one of his most exquisite songs 'Immer leiser wird mein Schlummer,' the phrase 'Eh' die Drossel singt im Wald' reaches a point of romantic emotion difficult to describe. In Brahms's greater works the romanticism seems sometimes veiled, but there are passages in his chamber-music and symphonies where this quality in its deepest sense resides. As examples, the romanticism of which could hardly be surpassed, we may cite the slow movement of the A major pianoforte quartet and the opening of the last movement of the C minor symphony ; or the last part of the first movement of the D major symphony (seventy-three bars before the end, where the horns enter and the strings are kept in the low register) ; or the andante of the third symphony in F, where the different instruments softly call to each other, as if from another world after the passionate working-up twenty-seven bars before the close.

Chopin holds a solitary position in romantic art. No school can claim him wholly for its own, and the best poetic gifts of the French, German, and Sclavonic nationalities were united in him. 'Chopin,' says Liszt, 'refused to be bound by deference to rules which fettered the play of his imagination, simply because they had been accepted as classical.' But the classic training and solid studies of his youth, combined with his exquisite taste and innate refinement, preserved him from abuse of the liberty which he was determined to enjoy. The mental atmosphere of his life in Paris may be felt in his works. In hatred of whatever was common-place and ordinary, he was one with the French romantic school ; but unlike them he would not allow originality alone to stand in his compositions. Beauty there must always be to satisfy him ; and he would have recoiled from the crudities and extravagances which disfigure some works of the French romantic period. So uniformly romantic was Chopin in every stage of his career, that it would be impossible to illustrate this quality of his music by extracts. Among the Sclavonic and Scandinavian races the romantic element is especially marked ; a study of the poetic creations of Tchaikovsky and Grieg will illustrate this.

The French romantic school of literature was of later date than the German, and was considerably affected by it. The general features of the two schools were very similar, but the French authors wrote even more than the German in the mediæval and mystic vein, and were more prone to unhealthy exaggeration. In France, moreover, the antagonism between the romantic and classical schools was carried to a pitch that had no parallel in Germany. The completeness and universality of the empire which classic example and tradition had gained over the educated public of France intensified the revolt against them, when at last it arrived. The revolt was as widespread as it was uncompromising : there was not a field of art or literature in which the rebel flag of the new school was not unfurled, and a revolutionary temper, inflamed perhaps by the political storms of that time, was manifest in all that they did. In the false simplicity and sickly sentimentality, in the stilted diction and threadbare forms of expression affected by the reigning school, the insurgent authors had indeed much to provoke them. But in the vehemence of their reaction against such faults they were apt to fall into an opposite extreme ; and thus, finish of form, clearness of outline, and coherent sequence of thought are too often absent from their works.

With respect to music, Berlioz is the typical name of the renaissance of 1830 ; but Liszt, on whom the French school exercised so strong an influence, may be associated with him. So far were these composers and their countless followers borne by the revolutionary impulse, that they did not shrink at times from a total rejection of the old traditional forms in their instrumental music ; but it cannot be said that very valuable results were obtained by their hardihood. They chose indeed romantic subjects for musical representation, as Weber and Schumann had done, but there the resemblance ceased. They aimed not, as the earlier masters did, to reproduce the feelings stirred in them by external objects, but rather to present the objects themselves to the minds of an audience.

To this kind of music, the term programme-music has been applied, and we may here perhaps fitly show wherein it differs from romantic music, with which there is a tendency in the present day to confound it. In reality a distinct line divides the two. Romantic music implies an emotional and imaginative atmosphere, combined with an idealistic, as distinct from an imitative presentment of whatever theme may be associated with the music. Programme-music avowedly endeavours to depict and imitate the actual scenes and sounds so literally that no doubt is left in the mind of the hearer as to what the composer desired to represent or reproduce. Neither emotional nor imaginative qualities are essential to it. Romantic music does not necessarily desire to call up a given picture, but to induce a mental attitude. Unconsciously the romantic composer may have written passages which evoke as clearly, but not in so limited a degree, some mental image in the mind of the hearer. The composer has stimulated the imagination of his hearer, and left it free to conjure up what it wills. Herein lies the difference between the two schools. Individualism or subjectivity, the characteristic mark of the romantic movement in philosophy and literature, asserts itself as distinctively in music. Programme or pictorial music stands on a lower plane. It is purely imitative work on the composer's part; it gives no scope for, and makes no demands upon the imagination of the hearer. An undoubted loss of romantic effect was the consequence of this method. It produced in the younger French romanticists an excessive realism, which too readily sacrificed artistic beauty to originality and vivid representation. Nor can we deny the frequent obscurity and incoherence of their compositions, though we are unable to acquiesce in the imputation so often fastened upon them that their romanticism was merely the veil of ignorance, and that they violated rules because they knew no better. As a matter of fact, even those among them who pushed extravagances to the farthest point were thorough masters of the strictest rules and severest forms of musical composition.

To sum up, in conclusion, our obligations to the masters of the romantic school, we must acknowledge that they saved music from the danger with which it was at one time threatened, of being treated as an exact but dry and cold science; that they gave it a freer and more elastic form; that they developed the capabilities and technique of various instruments; that being themselves always filled with a deep reverence for their art they have added, by their own genius and labour, many a noble masterpiece to the treasures of music.[1]   A. H. W.

ROMBERG. One of those musical families of whom, from the Bachs downwards, so many are encountered in Germany. The founders were ANTON and HEINRICH, a pair of inseparable brothers, who dressed alike, and lived together in Bonn. They were still alive in 1792. Another ANTON, a bassoon-player, born in Westphalia, March 6, 1742, lived at Dinklage (Duchy of Oldenburg), gave concerts

at Hamburg, and died in Dec. 14, 1814, living long enough to play a concerto for two bassoons with his youngest son ANTON, born 1777. His eldest son, BERNHARD, born Nov. 12, 1767, at Dinklage, is justly regarded as head of the school of German violoncellists. When only fourteen he attracted considerable attention in Paris during a visit there with his father; from 1790 to 1793 he was in the band of the Elector of Cologne at Bonn, at the same time with Ferdinand Ries, Reicha, and the two Beethovens. During the French invasion he occupied himself in a professional tour in Italy, Spain, and Portugal, and was well received, especially in Madrid, where Ferdinand VII. accompanied him on the violin. His cousin Andreas went with him, and on their return through Vienna late in 1796, they gave a concert at which Beethoven played (Thayer, ii. 16). After his return Bernhard married Catherine Ramcke at Hamburg. From 1801 to 1803 he was a professor in the Paris Conservatoire, and we next find him in the King's band at Berlin. Spohr (*Autob.* i. 78) met him there at the end of 1804, and played quartets with him. Perhaps the most remarkable fact he mentions is that after one of Beethoven's early quartets (op. 18) Romberg asked how Spohr could play 'such absurd stuff' (*barockes Zeug*). It is of a piece with the well-known anecdote of his tearing the copy of the first Rasoumowsky quartet from the stand and trampling on it.

The approach of the French forces in 1806 again drove Romberg on the world, and in 1807 he was travelling in South Russia, but returned to Berlin, and was Court-Capellmeister, 1815-19, when he retired into private life at Hamburg. [In 1814 he visited England, giving a concert under the patronage of Prince Blucher and the Hetman of the Cossacks, at Willis's Rooms, June 27. A. F. H.] In 1822 he went to Vienna, in 1825 to St. Petersburg and Moscow, to Frankfort in 1836, and in 1839 to London [2] and Paris, where his *Method for the Violoncello* (Berlin, Trautwein, 1840) was adopted by the Conservatoire. He died at Hamburg, August 13, 1841.

The great importance of B. Romberg both as composer and executant arises from the fact that he materially extended the capabilities of the violoncello. His celebrated concertos may be said to contain implicitly a complete theory of violoncello playing, and there are few passages known to modern players the type of which may not be found there. Probably no better knowledge of the finger-board could be gained than by studying these concertos. Although they are now seldom played in public, being somewhat too old-fashioned

[1] For the foregoing article the following works have been consulted:—Schumann, *Gesammelte Schriften*; Liszt, *Chopin*; Hostinsky, *Die Lehre der formalen Aesthetik*; Küster, *Populäre Vorträge*; La Mara, *Musikalische Studien-köpfe*; Wasielewski, *Schumann*; Weber, Max v., *C. M. v. Weber*; Hoffmann, *Kreisleriana*; Gautier, *Histoire du Romantisme*; *N. Zeitschrift f. Musik*, 1834-39; Riehl, *Charakterköpfe*; Brockhaus, *Conversationslexicon*; Eckermann, *Gespräche mit Goethe*; Mendel, *Lexikon*; Brendel, *Geschichte der Musik*; Marx, *Musik des Neunzehnten Jahrhunderts*; Köstlin, *Geschichte der Musik*; Weitzmann, *Geschichte des Clavierspiels*; Reissmann, *Von Bach bis Wagner*; Letters from Dr. Zopff and Dr. Ludwig. See also Prof. F. Niecks's article on Romanticism, in *Musical Times*, December 1899; vol. vi. of the *Oxford History of Music* (*The Romantic Period*), by E. Dannreuther; *The Quarterly Review* for October 1906, pp. 357-74; and Daniel Gregory Mason's *From Grieg to Brahms*, and *The Romantic Composers*.

[2] He does not seem to have played on this occasion; but a slight trace of his presence is perhaps discoverable in an overture of his nephew's, which closes the Philharmonic programme of June 17, 1839.

to hit the taste of modern artists and audiences, they are yet of considerable merit as compositions, and contain passages of distinct grace and charm. It may be gathered from the character of his compositions, that his tone was not so full and powerful as that of artists who confine themselves more to the lower register of the instrument, and to passages of less complication. As an indication that this view agrees with that which prevailed during his lifetime, we find him for instance spoken of as follows by a correspondent of the *Allgemeine Musikalische Zeitung* for 1817, who had heard him play at Amsterdam:—'The visit of B. Romberg had long been eagerly looked for. The immense reputation which preceded him caused his first concert to be crowded to excess. He played a concerto ('die Reise auf den Bernhardsberg') and a capriccio on Swedish national airs. In regard to the perfection and taste of his performance, to the complete ease and lightness of his playing, our great expectations were far exceeded—but not so in respect of tone—this, especially in difficult passages, we found much weaker than the powerful tone of our own Rauppe, and indeed scarcely to compare with it.' At a second concert Romberg played his well-known Military Concerto, and the same view was reiterated.

Bernhard Romberg composed violoncello solos of various kinds ; string quartets ; PF. quartets ; a funeral symphony for Queen Louise of Prussia ; a concerto for two violoncellos (Breitkopf & Härtel), his last work ; and operas —'Die wiedergefundene Statue,' words by Gozzi von Schwick (1790), and 'Der Schiffbruch' (1791, Bonn), 'Don Mendoce,' with his cousin Andreas (Paris), 'Alma,' 'Ulysses und Circe' (July 27, 1807), and 'Rittertreue,' three acts (Jan. 31, 1817, Berlin). His son KARL, also a violoncellist, born at St. Petersburg, Jan. 17, 1811, played in the court band there from 1832 to 1842, and afterwards lived at Vienna.

Anton Romberg, the father of Bernhard, had a brother GERHARD HEINRICH, born August 8, 1745, a clarinet-player, and Musikdirector at Münster, who lived with him for some time at Bonn, and had several children, of whom the most celebrated was ANDREAS JAKOB, a violinist, born April 27, 1767, at Vechta, near Münster. When only seven he played in public with his cousin Bernhard, with whom he remained throughout life on terms of the closest friendship. At seventeen he excited great enthusiasm in Paris, and was engaged for the Concerts Spirituels (1784). In 1790 he joined his cousin at Bonn, played the violin in the Elector's band, and accompanied him to Italy in 1793. In Rome they gave a concert at the Capitol (Feb. 17, 1796) under the patronage of Cardinal Rezzonico. Andreas then made some stay in Vienna, where Haydn showed great interest in his first quartet. In 1797 he

went to Hamburg, and in 1798 made a tour alone. In 1800 he followed Bernhard to Paris, and composed with him 'Don Mendoce, ou le Tuteur portugais.' The opera failed, and the success of their concerts was but partial, so Andreas left for Hamburg, where he married, and remained for fifteen years. He next became Court-Capellmeister at Gotha, where he died, in very great destitution, Nov. 10, 1821. Concerts were given in various towns for the benefit of his widow and children. The university of Kiel gave him a degree of Doctor of Music. He composed six symphonies, quartets, quintets, and church music ; a Te Deum, Psalms, a Dixit, Magnificat, and Hallelujah, in four, five, eight, and sixteen parts ; several operas—' Das graue Ungeheuer' (1790, Bonn), 'Die Macht der Musik' (1791), 'Der Rabe,' operetta (1792). 'Die Grossmuth des Scipio,' and 'Die Ruinen zu Paluzzi,'—the two last not performed. His best-known work is the music for Schiller's 'Lay of the Bell,' which kept its place in concert programmes for many years. His music is solid, but not original, being too closely modelled on Mozart. His larger works are well known in England. 'The Transient and the Eternal,' 'The Harmony of the Spheres,' 'The Power of Song,' and a Te Deum (in D), as well as 'The Lay of the Bell,' are all published with English words by Novello. His Toy-symphony is now and then played as an alternative to Haydn's, and was chosen for performance by an extraordinary company, embracing most of the great artists of London, May 14, 1880. Two sons, CYPRIAN and HEINRICH are mentioned in the *Allg. musikalische Zeitung.* [The former, a violoncellist, pupil of his uncle, was born at Hamburg, Oct. 28, 1807, and died there Oct. 14, 1865 ; he made concert-tours, became a member of the court orchestra of St. Petersburg, and published compositions for his instrument. Riemann's *Lexikon.*] Andreas's brother BALTHASAR, born 1775, and educated for a violoncellist, died aged seventeen. His sister THERESE, born 1781, had a considerable reputation as a pianist.   F. G.

ROME. The early music schools of Rome, from the time of St. Sylvester to that of Palestrina, were so closely connected with the papacy that their history, as far as it is known, may be read in the article SISTINE CHOIR.

Whether or not Guido d'Arezzo founded a school of singing at Rome in the first half of the 11th century is only a matter of conjecture ; the probabilities are in favour of the theory, as it is known that Guido spent a short time, at least, at the capital about the year 1032, and that the then Pope John XIX. was so delighted with his method of teaching singing that he urged him to take up his residence in Rome, an invitation which only ill-health prevented Guido from accepting. (See vol. ii. p. 256.) In any case there can be no reasonable doubt that the papal choir received many valuable hints from him.

The Sistine Chapel was not the only one which had a school or college of music attached to it, though it was by far the earliest. In 1480 Sixtus IV. proposed the formation of a 'cappella musicale' in connection with the Vatican, distinct from the Sistine; his idea was not, however, realised till the time of Julius II., when the 'Cappella Giulia' was founded (in 1513) for twelve singers, twelve scholars, and two masters for music and grammar. Arcadelt was the first 'Maestro de' Putti' (in 1539), Palestrina the first 'Maestro della cappella della basilica Vaticana' (1551-54); among celebrated 'maestri' in later days were Tommaso Bai (1713-1715), and Domenico Scarlatti (1715-19). The 'Cappella musicale nella protobasilica di S. Giovanni in Laterano' was founded in 1535 by Cardinal de Cupis; one of the earliest 'Maestri de' Putti' was Lasso (1541); Palestrina held the office of 'Maestro di cappella' here after his exclusion from the Vatican chapel (1555-61). The 'Cappella di Musica nella basilica Liberiana' (or Sta. Maria Maggiore) was founded about the same time as the Lateran chapel, and numbers among its maestri Palestrina (1561-71), Giov. Maria Nanini (1571-1575), and Alessandro Scarlatti (1703-9).

Besides these exclusively ecclesiastical schools, others were established by private individuals. The first man who is known to have kept a public music school at Rome was a certain Gaudio Mell, whose school is supposed to have been founded about the year 1539; and among his earliest pupils were Palestrina, Giovanni Animuccia, and Giovanni Maria Nanini. In 1549, Nicola Vicentino, the would-be restorer of the ancient Greek Modes, opened a small private school at Rome, into which a few select pupils were admitted, whom he endeavoured to indoctrinate with his musical views. But it was not till a quarter of a century later that a public music school was opened by an Italian. Whether it was that Nanini was inspired by his master's example, or, which is still more likely, was stirred by the musical agitation of the day, is of little importance; but it is certain that the year to which the opening of his school is attributed was the same which saw the foundation of the order of Oratorians, who in the person of their leader, St. Filippo Neri, were then doing so much for the promotion of music. Nanini soon induced his former fellow-pupil, Palestrina, to assist him in teaching, and he appears to have given finishing lessons. Among their best pupils were Felice Anerio and Gregorio Allegri. After Palestrina's death, Nanini associated his younger brother Bernardino with him in the work of instruction, and it was probably for their scholars that they wrote jointly their treatise on counterpoint. Giovanni Maria dying in 1607 was succeeded by

Bernardino, who was in his turn succeeded by his pupil and son-in-law Paolo Agostini. It must have been this school that produced the singers in the earliest operas and oratorios of Peri, Caccini, Monteverde, Cavaliere, Gagliano, etc. In the second quarter of the 17th century a rival school was set up by a pupil of B. Nanini, Domenico Mazzocchi, who, with his younger brother Virgilio, opened a music school, which was soon in a very flourishing condition; this was due in a great measure to the fact that the masters were themselves both singers and composers. Their curriculum differed but slightly from that of the Palestrina-Nanini school. In the morning one hour was given daily to practising difficult passages, a second to the shake, a third to the study of literature, and another hour to singing with the master before a mirror; in the afternoon an hour was occupied in the study of the theory of music, another in writing exercises in counterpoint, and another in literature; the remainder of the day (indoors) was employed in practising the harpsichord and in composition. Outside the school the pupils used sometimes to give their vocal services at neighbouring churches, or else they went to hear some well-known singer; at other times they were taken to a spot beyond the Porta Angelica to practise singing against the echo for which that neighbourhood was famous. In 1662 Pompeo Natale kept a music school, at which Giuseppe Ottavio Pitoni, the reputed master of Durante and Leo, learnt singing and counterpoint. G. A. Angelini-Buontempi, a pupil of the Mazzocchis, writing in 1695, says that Fedi, a celebrated singer, had opened the first school exclusively for singing at Rome. His example was soon followed by Giuseppe Amadori, with equal success; the latter was a pupil of P. Agostini and no doubt had not entirely forgotten the teachings of the old school; but by the end of the 17th century its traditions were gradually dying out, to be replaced by the virtuosity of the 18th century.

We must now retrace our steps and give some account of the most important musical institution at Rome of past or present time—the 'Congregazione dei Musici di Roma sotto l' invocazione di Sta. Cecilia.' It was founded by Pius V. in 1566, but its existence is usually dated from 1584, when its charter was confirmed by Gregory XIII.; almost all the masters and pupils of the Palestrina-Nanini school enrolled their names on its books, and their example has been since followed by over 4000 others, including every Italian of note, and in the 19th century many illustrious foreigners, such as John Field, Wagner, Liszt, Gounod, etc. etc.

The officers originally appointed were a Cardinal Protector, a 'Primicerio' or president, usually a person of high position, a 'Consiglio dirigente' of four members (representing the four sections—composition, the organ, singing, and instrumental music), a Secretary, a Chancellor, twelve Counsellors, two Prefects, etc. ; there were also professors for almost every branch of music ; Corelli was head of the instrumental section in 1700. Those qualified for admission into the institution were chapel-masters, organists, public singers, and well-known instrumentalists. By a papal decree of 1689 all musicians were bound to observe the statutes of the Academy ; and by a later decree (1709) it was ordained that its licence was necessary for exercising the profession. Soon after this the Congregation began to suffer from an opposition which, though covert, was none the less keenly felt ; and in 1716 a papal decree unfavourable to the institution was passed. In 1762 it was flourishing again, for in that year we find that a faculty was granted to the cardinal protector, to have the general direction of all ecclesiastical music at Rome. By another decree of 1764, it was enacted that none but those *skilled* in music should be in future admitted as members. The entrance-fee was, as it has continued to be, a very small one. The demands made upon members were also very slight. At first they were only expected to assist, by their compositions or performances, in the grand annual festival in honour of the patron saint. Towards the close of the 17th century were added one or two annual services in memory of benefactors ; in 1700 a festival in honour of St. Anna, and in 1771 a '*piccola* festa di Sta. Cecilia.'

The Congregation originally took up its quarters at the College of Barnabites (afterwards Palazzo Chigi) in the Piazza Colonna, where they remained for nearly a century ; thence they moved to the Convent of Sta. Maria Maddalena, and again to another college of Barnabites dedicated to San Carlo a Catinari. Here they resided for the greater part of two centuries, and, after the temporary occupation of premises in the Via Ripetta, finally, in 1876, settled at their present quarters, formerly a convent of Ursuline nuns, in the Via dei Greci. Besides the hostility which the Congregation had to undergo, as we have seen, from outsiders, at the beginning of the 18th century—which was repeated in another form as late as 1836—it has had its financial vicissitudes. Indeed at the end of the 18th, and beginning of the 19th century, the funds were at a very low ebb, from which they have been gradually recovering. The institution was dignified with the title of Academy of Gregory XVI. in 1839. Two years later Rossini's 'Stabat Mater' was performed for the first time in Italy in its entirety by the members of the Academy. Pius IX., who became Pope in 1846, though he founded several other schools for singing, such as that of 'S. Salvatore in Lauro,' did little more for the Academy than to bestow upon it the epithet 'Pontificia.' [During the early years of his reign two attempts were made to found a Liceo musicale or music-school in connection with the Academy. The first, in 1847, received encouragement and sympathy from the pontiff, but efforts to obtain a government subsidy for the purpose failed owing to the political disturbances of 1848-49. Another endeavour by Professor Filippo Bornia in 1857 had no better result. It was not until 1869, when two young associates of the institute, Giovanni Sgambati and Ettore Penelli, opened gratuitous classes for pianoforte and violin on the premises of the Accademia that a practical start was made in this direction. In the following year the two professors sought and obtained from Cardinal Di Pietro, Protector of the Accademia, official sanction for their venture. This was given in a decree, dated May 23, 1870, establishing the classes on a recognised footing as belonging to and dependent upon the institution. The fresh departure received further impetus later in the same year. Soon after the fall of the pontifical government in September, the associates of the Accademia, now a 'Royal' institution, expressed in general assembly unanimous approval of the classes, and entrusted a provisional committee with Professor Bornia at its head with the task of formally constituting a Liceo Musicale.

From this period the energies of the Accademia, which until now had been little more than a body of examiners and licentiates, became centred in the new development, and its history identified with that of the daughter-institute of which the classes formed by Sgambati and Penelli were the nucleus, and of which, therefore, they are rightly considered the founders. The provisional committee remained in office until 1875, when its duties were taken over by the Accademia's newly constituted Council of Direction, of which Comm. Emilio Broglio was president. Meanwhile the music-school had been rapidly growing. Sgambati had engaged three assistants for pianoforte teaching, Alessandro Orsini with a sub-professor had opened classes for singing, and violoncello and brass instruments were being taught by Ferdinando Forino and Vedasto Vecchietti. At length after seven years of careful preparation the Liceo Musicale was formally constituted under the direction of a 'Commissione disciplinare' and a 'Comitato tecnico,' with a staff of twenty-nine professors. The new institute was launched on March 3, 1877, in the presence of the Crown Prince and Princess (Umberto and Margherita) of Italy.

The Accademia now occupied itself with the compilation of a Statute for the Liceo, and in accordance with the wishes of the Government the 'Commissione disciplinare' was substituted, in 1886, by an administrative council. On this the Government, the Province of Rome, and the Municipality, as contributors to the maintenance of the Liceo, were represented, while its Director was nominated by the Accademia itself. The first to occupy the newly created post was Comm. Filippo Marchetti, who vacated the presidential chair of the Accademia to undertake it.

In 1907 the Liceo had 225 students and a professorial staff of about forty. In the first twenty-five years of its existence instruction was given to 1387 pupils, of whom 415 received diplomas. Every branch of practice and theory is taught, besides Italian literature and the history of music. The charge for instruction is so low (five francs a month) that tuition is, to all intents and purposes, free. The Liceo receives yearly subsidies from the Government (£1600), from the Province of Rome (£320), and from the Municipality (£1200). Arrangements are now pending to place it directly under the Government, and its professors will then enjoy the distinction, highly prized in Italy, of State officials. Professors Sgambati and Penelli, after thirty-eight years, still take an active part in examining and teaching. The director is Comm. Stanislao Falchi, who succeeded Comm. Marchetti in 1901.

To its premises in the Via dei Greci the Accademia, assisted by contributions from the Government and Queen Margherita, has added a spacious concert-hall with an organ, opened in 1895. Here, during winter and spring, public orchestral and chamber concerts are given. The library also constitutes an increasingly important branch of its influence. Originally small, the collection of books and MSS. was increased by the musical library of Gregory XVI. bequeathed in 1846. It was still further enriched in 1875 by the Orsini collection, and later by the musical works which had formerly belonged to the dissolved monasteries. In 1882 were added all obtainable modern musical publications since 1500, so that the Accademia now possesses one of the largest and most important musical libraries in Italy (see vol. ii. p. 714a). The books having been removed to the ground floor, the library and reading-room are the more easily accessible to the public. The Accademia still enjoys royal patronage, and the King of Italy is its honorary president, while the Conte di San Martino is at the head of its Council of Direction.

Quite apart from the Accademia, which with its Liceo is the musical centre of Rome, much has been done for the improvement of the popular taste in music. For this the municipal orchestra, under Signor Alessandro Vessella, has been chiefly responsible. Concerts are given weekly during the greater part of the year at the Argentina theatre. Formerly, popular audiences in Rome were for the most part intolerant of music which was not Italian. Thanks to the courage and perseverance of Signor Vessella this is the case no longer. His pro-

grammes, open to composers of all nationalities, have familiarised the Roman public with classical and modern works—Bach, Haydn, Beethoven, Mozart, Mendelssohn, Berlioz, Liszt, Wagner, Tchaikovsky, and Elgar being often associated with Rossini, Verdi, Puccini, and Mascagni. As an operatic centre, however, Rome lacks the prestige of Milan and Naples.

Ecclesiastical music in the Italian capital still leaves much to be desired, the excellent ideals of Pius X. being as yet far from any wide realisation. Divine service is sometimes accompanied by devout and careful singing, as at the church of Santa Maria dell' Anima and at St. John Lateran under Maestro Filippo Capocci; but artistic performances are unhappily rare, and organ-playing is, too generally, careless and vulgar.] A. H-H.; with additions in square brackets by H. A. W.

ROMEO AND JULIET. A subject often set by opera composers ; e.g.—

1. Roméo et Juliette ; three acts ; words by de Ségur, music by Steibelt. Théâtre Feydeau, Paris, Sept. 10, 1793.

2. 'Giulietta e Romeo.' Opera seria in three acts, words by Giuseppe Foppa, music by Zingarelli. Produced at the Scala, Milan, Jan. 30, 1796.

3. 'Giulietta e Romeo,' three acts, words by Romani, music by Vaccaj. Produced at the Teatro della Canobbiana, Milan, Oct. 31, 1825 ; King's Theatre, London, April 10, 1832.

4. 'I Capuletti ed i Montecchi,' in three acts ; libretto by Romani, music by Bellini. Produced at Venice, March 11, 1830. It was written for the two Grisis and Rubini. King's Theatre, London, July 20, 1833.

5. 'Les Amants de Vérone,' five acts, text and music by the Marquis d'Ivry (under the pseudonym of Richard Yrvid), written in 1864, performed privately in 1867, and publicly at the Salle Ventadour, Oct. 12, 1878. At Covent Garden, May 24, 1879.

6. 'Roméo et Juliette,' in five acts ; words by Barbier and Carré, music by Gounod. Produced at the Théâtre Lyrique, April 27, 1867. In London, at Covent Garden, in Italian, July 11, 1867.

7. In addition to these it has been made the subject of a work by Berlioz, his Fifth Symphony —'Roméo et Juliette. Symphonie dramatique avec chœurs, solos de chant, et prologue en récitatif choral, op. 17.' Dedicated to Paganini. The words are Berlioz's own, versified by Emil Deschamps. It was composed in 1839, and performed three times consecutively at the Conservatoire, first on Nov. 24, 1839. In England the First Part (four numbers) was executed under Berlioz's direction at the New Philharmonic Concerts of March 24, and April 28, 1852, and the entire work by the Philharmonic Society (Cusins), March 10, 1881.

8. A symphonic poem by Tchaikovsky was first

performed at the Musical Society in Moscow, March 4, 1870. It was published by Bote & Boch in the following year, and was afterwards, (in 1881) issued in a curtailed and revised form. G.

ROMER, EMMA, soprano singer, pupil of Sir George Smart, born in 1814, made her first appearance at Covent Garden, Oct. 16, 1830, as Clara in 'The Duenna.' She met with a favourable reception, and for several years filled the position of prima donna at Covent Garden, the English Opera-House, and Drury Lane, with great credit. In 1852 she took the management of the Surrey Theatre, with a company containing Miss Poole and other good singers, and brought out a series of operas in English. Miss Romer was rarely heard in the concert-room, but appeared at the Westminster Abbey Festival in 1834. She was the original singer of the title-parts in Barnett's 'Mountain Sylph' and 'Fair Rosamond.' Her performance of Amina in the English version of Bellini's 'Sonnambula' was much admired. She married a Mr. Almond, and died at Margate, April 14, 1868. W. H. H.

RONALD, LANDON. See RUSSELL, HENRY.

RONCONI, DOMENICO, was born July 11, 1772, at Lendinara-di-Polesine in Venetia. He first appeared on the stage in 1797 at La Fenice, Venice, and obtained great renown both as a singer and actor, there and in other Italian cities, sang in Italian opera at St. Petersburg (1801-5), was director of the Italian opera in Vienna in 1809, sang in Paris in 1810, and was engaged at Munich in 1819-29, becoming a teacher of singing there. He founded a vocal school in 1829 at Milan. He died at St. Petersburg, April 13, 1836. Of his three sons,

FELICE, born in 1811, at Venice, under the direction of his father devoted himself to instruction in singing, and became a professor in 1837 at Würzburg, at Frankfort, and, in 1844-48, at Milan. He was similarly engaged for some years in London, and finally at St. Petersburg, where he died Sept. 10, 1875. He was the author of a method of teaching singing, and of several songs. His elder brother,

GIORGIO, the celebrated baritone, was born at Milan, August 6, 1810. He received instruction in singing from his father, and began his dramatic career in 1831, at Pavia, as Arturo in 'La Straniera.' He played in some of the small Italian cities, then at Rome, where Donizetti wrote for him 'Il Furioso,' 'Torquato Tasso,' and 'Maria di Rohan,' in which last, as the Duc de Chevreuse, he obtained one of his greatest triumphs—also at Turin, Florence, and Naples, where he on Oct. 8, 1837, married Signorina Elguerra Giannoni, who, according to some accounts, had recently sung with success at the Lyceum and King's Theatres, London. He began his career in England at Her Majesty's, April 9, 1842, as Enrico in 'Lucia,' and was

well received during the season in that character and in those of Filippo ('Beatrice di Tenda'), Belcore('L' Elisir'), Basilio,Riccardo('Puritani'), Tasso, etc. In the last opera his wife played with him, but neither then, nor five years later as Maria di Rohan, did she make the least impression on the English public. He then made a provincial tour with her, Thalberg, and John Parry. In the winter he played at the Italiens, Paris, with such success that he was engaged there for several subsequent seasons, and at one time was manager of the theatre, and was also engaged at Vienna, Pesth, Madrid (where he was manager), Barcelona, and Naples. He re-appeared in England, April 13, 1847, at Covent Garden, as Enrico, and also played Figaro ('Barbiere'), May 8, De Chevreuse on the production in England of 'Maria di Rohan,' and the Doge on the production of Verdi's 'I due Foscari,' June 19, in which 'by his dignity and force he saved the opera . . . from utter condemnation' (Chorley). 'There are few instances of a voice so limited in compass(hardly exceeding an octave), so inferior in quality, so weak, so habitually out of tune. . . . The low stature, the features, unmarked and commonplace when silent, promising nothing to an audience, yet which could express a dignity of bearing, a tragic passion not to be exceeded, or an exuberance of the wildest, quaintest, most whimsical, most spontaneous comedy. . . . These things we have seen, and have forgotten personal insignificance, vocal power beyond mediocrity, every disqualification, in the spell of strong real sensibility'(Ib.). There have been few such examples of terrible courtly tragedy as 'Signor Ronconi's Chevreuse—the polished demeanour of his earlier scenes giving a fearful force of contrast to the latter ones. . . .' (Ib.) He sang at the Italian Opera every season until 1866 inclusive, excepting in 1855 and 1862. His parts included Don Juan, Papageno, Leporello, Masetto, Iago, Podestà ('La Gazza Ladra'), Isidoro ('Matilda di Shabran'), Nabucco, Faust (Spohr), Rigoletto, Lord Allcash ('Fra Diavolo'), Dandolo('Zampa'), Barberino ('Stradella'), and Crispino ('Crispino e la Comare'), etc. His Rigoletto was unrivalled, but his Don Juan was a disappointment. He sang in America (1866-74) with great success, and on his return to Europe he became a teacher of singing at the Conservatorio at Madrid. In 1863 he founded a school of singing at Granada. He died at Madrid, Jan. 8, 1890. A warm appreciation of his powers appears in Santley's *Student and Singer*.

SEBASTIANO, the other son, also a baritone, born May 1814, at Venice, received instruction from his father and the elder Romani, and made his first appearance in 1836, at the Teatro Pantera, Lucca, as Torquato Tasso, in which part throughout his career he made one of his greatest successes. He enjoyed considerable popularity in his own country, at Vienna, and in Spain, Portugal, and America, as an able artist in the same line of parts as his brother —unlike him in personal appearance, being a tall thin man, but like him in the capability of his face for great variety of expression. He appeared in England on Dec. 17, 1836, at the Lyceum, as Cardenio in Donizetti's 'Furioso,' and also sang for a few nights at the King's Theatre, as well as at the Philharmonic, Feb. 27, 1837. He reappeared in 1860 at Her Majesty's, as Rigoletto, Masetto, and Griletto ('Prova d' un Opera Seria'). He retired from public life after a career of thirty-five years, and settled in Milan as a teacher of singing.[1]   A. C.

RONDEAU. A French name for a short poem of six or eight lines, containing but two rhymes, and so contrived that the opening and closing lines were identical, thus forming as it were a circle or *round*. The name has come to be used in music for a movement constructed on a somewhat corresponding plan. [See RONDO.] G.

RONDO (Fr. *Rondeau*). A piece of music having one principal subject, to which a return is always made after the introduction of other matter, so as to give a symmetrical or *rounded* form to the whole.

From the simplicity and obviousness of this idea it will be readily understood that the Rondo-form was the earliest and most frequent definite mould for musical construction. For a full tracing of this point see FORM, vol. ii. p. 74, etc. In fact the First Movement and the Rondo are the two principal types of Form, modifications of the Rondo serving as the skeleton for nearly every piece or song now written. Marx (*Allgemeine Musiklehre*) distinguishes five forms of Rondo, but his description is involved, and, in the absence of any acknowledged authority for these distinctions, scarcely justifiable.

Starting with a principal subject of definite form and length, the first idea naturally was to preserve this unchanged in key or form through the piece. Hence a decided melody of eight or sixteen bars was chosen, ending with a full close in the tonic. After a rambling excursion through several keys and with no particular object, the principal subject was regained and an agreeable sense of contrast attained. Later on there grew out of the free section a second subject in a related key, and still later a third, which allowed the second to be repeated in the tonic. This variety closely resembles the first-movement form, the third subject taking the place of the development of subjects, which is rare in a Rondo. The chief difference lies in the return to the first subject immediately after the second, which is the invariable characteristic of the Rondo. The first of these classes is the Rondo from Couperin to Haydn, the second

1 We are indebted to him and Mr. J. C. Griffith of Sydney for much of the above information with regard to his family.

and third that of Mozart and Beethoven. The fully developed Rondo-form of Beethoven and the modern composers may be thus tabulated :—

1st sub.	(domi-nant).	1st sub.	3rd sub.	1st sub.	2nd sub. (tonic).	Coda.
	2nd sub.					

In the case of a Rondo in a minor key, the second subject would naturally be in the relative major instead of in the dominant.

One example—perhaps the clearest as well as one of the best known in all music—will suffice to make this plan understood by the untechnical reader. Taking the Rondo of Beethoven's 'Sonate Pathétique' (op. 13) we find the first subject in C minor :—

this is of 17½ bars in length, and ends with a full close in the key. Six bars follow, modulating into E♭, where we find the second subject, which is of unusual proportions compared with the first, consisting as it does of three separate themes :—

After this we return to the first subject, which ends just as before. A new start is then made with a third subject (or pair of subjects) in A♭ :—

this material is worked out for twenty-four bars and leads to a prolonged passage on a chord of the dominant seventh on G, which heightens the expectation of the return of the first subject by delaying it. On its third appearance it is not played quite to the end, but we are skilfully led away, the bass taking the theme, till, in the short space of four bars, we find the whole of the second subject reappearing in C major, Then, as this is somewhat long, the first subject comes in again for the *fourth* time and a *Coda* formed from the second section of the second subject concludes the Rondo with still another 'positively last appearance' of No. 1.

Beethoven's Rondos will all be found to present but slight modifications of the above form. Sometimes a 'working-out' or development of the second subject will take the place of the third subject, as in the Sonata in E minor (op. 90), but in every case the principal subject will be presented in its entirety at least three times. But as this was apt to lead to monotony—especially in the case of a long subject like that in the Sonata just quoted—Beethoven introduced the plan of varying the theme slightly on each repetition, or of breaking off in the middle. It is in such delicate and artistic modifications and improvements as these that the true genius shows itself, and not in the complete abandonment of old rules. In the earliest example we can take—the Rondo of the Sonata in A (op. 2, No. 2)—the form of the opening *arpeggio* is altered on every recurrence, while the simple phrase of the third and fourth bars

is thus varied :—

In the Rondo of the Sonata in E♭ (op. 7) again, we find the main subject cut short on its second appearance, while on its final repetition all sorts of liberties are taken with it ; it is played an octave higher than its normal place, a free variation is made on it, and at last we are startled by its being thrust into a distant key —E♮. This last effect has been adopted by many a composer since—Chopin in the Rondo of his E minor Pianoforte Concerto, for instance. It is needless to multiply examples : Beethoven shows in each successive work how this apparently stiff and rigid form can be invested with infinite variety and interest ; he always contradicted the idea (in which too few have followed him) that a Rondo was bound in duty to be an eight-bar subject in 2-4 time, of one unvarying, jaunty, and exasperatingly jocose character. The Rondo of the E♭ Sonata is most touchingly melancholy, so is that to the Sonata in E minor (op. 90), not to mention many others. There will always remain a certain stiffness in this form, owing to the usual separation of the subject from its surroundings by a full close. When this is dispensed with, the piece is said to be

in Rondo-form, but is not called a Rondo (*e.g.* the last movement of Beethoven's Sonata op. 2, No. 3).

Modern composers, like Chopin, with whom construction was not a strong point, often omit the central section, or third subject, together with the repetition of the first subject which accompanies it, and thus what they call a Rondo is merely a piece on the plan of a French overture ; that is to say, having produced all his material in the first half of the piece, the composer repeats the whole unchanged, save that such portions as were in the Dominant are, in the repetition, given in the Tonic. Chopin's ' Rondeau brillant ' in E♭, the ' Adieu à Varsovie '—indeed all his Rondos—show this construction.   F. C.

RONZI. [See BEGNIS, DE, vol. i. p. 278.]

ROOKE, WILLIAM MICHAEL, son of John Rourke, or O'Rourke, a Dublin tradesman, was born in South Great George's Street, Dublin, Sept. 29, 1794. His bent for music, which displayed itself at an early age, was sternly discouraged by his father, who wished him to follow his own avocation, but before he was sixteen, he was, by his father's death, left free to follow his own inclination. He studied, almost unaided, so assiduously, that in 1813 he took to music as a profession (having altered the form of his name), learned counterpoint under Dr. Cogan, a Dublin professor, and became a teacher of the violin and pianoforte. Among his pupils on the former instrument was Balfe, then a boy. In 1817 he was appointed chorus-master and deputy leader at the theatre in Crow Street, Dublin, and soon afterwards composed a polacca, ' Oh Glory, in thy brightest hour,' which was sung by Braham, and met with great approbation. [In 1818 he composed his first opera, ' Amilie ' (see below), and in 1822 he removed to England, where he became chorus-master at Drury Lane Theatre, under Tom Cooke, and, in 1830-33, leader at Vauxhall, under Sir Henry Bishop. W. H. G. F.] A few years later he removed to England. In 1826 he was leading oratorios at Birmingham, and in the same year came to London, and sought the appointment of chorus-master at Drury Lane, and established himself as a teacher of singing. His opera, ' Amilie, or The Love Test,' after he had waited many years for an opportunity of producing it, was brought out at Covent Garden, Dec. 2, 1837, with decided success, and at once established his reputation as a composer of marked ability. He immediately commenced the composition of a second opera, and on May 2, 1839, produced at Covent Garden 'Henrique, or, The Love Pilgrim,' which, although most favourably received, was withdrawn after five performances on account of a misunderstanding with the manager. He composed two more entitled ' Cagliostro,' and ' The Valkyrie,' which have never been performed.

He died Oct. 14, 1847, and was buried in Brompton Cemetery.   w. h. h.

ROOT. The classification of the chords which form the structural material of modern harmonic music is attained by referring them to what are called their roots; and it is mainly by their use that these harmonic elements are brought into intelligible order.

As long as the purely polyphonic system was in full force, the chordal combinations were merely classified according to recognised degrees of consonance and dissonance, without any clear idea of relationship: but as that system merged by degrees into the harmonic system, it was found that fresh principles of classification were indispensable; and that many combinations which at first might appear to have quite a distinct character must somehow be recognised as having a common centre. This centre was found in an ultimate bass note, namely, the bass note of the complete chord in what would be considered its natural or first position; and this was called the Root, and served as the common indicator of all the various portions of the complete chord which could be detached, and their test of closest possible relationship. Further, these roots were themselves classified according to their status in any given key; and by this means a group of chords which were related to one another most closely by having the same root, might be shown to be related severally and collectively to the group which belonged to another root; and the degree of relationship could be easily and clearly ascertained according to the known nearness or remoteness of the roots in question. By this means the whole harmonic basis of a piece of music can be tested; and it must be further noted that it is only by such means that the structural principles of that kind of music which has been called 'absolute' because of its dissociation from words, is rendered abstractedly intelligible.

The principle upon which modern Instrumental Music has been developed is that a succession of distinct tunes or recognisable sections of melody or figures can be associated by the orderly distribution of harmonies and keys in such a manner that the mind can realise the concatenation as a complete and distinct work of art. It is obvious that fine melodic material is a vital point; but it is not so obvious that where the dimensions of the work are such that a continuous flow of melody of a uniform character is impossible, the orderly arrangement of the materials in successions of keys and harmonies is no less vital. The harmonic structure requires to be clearly ascertainable in works of art which are felt to be masterpieces of form, and to be perfectly understood and felt by those who attempt to follow such models: hence, in discussing the structure of works of this kind, the frequent use of such terms as Tonic, or Domi-

nant or Subdominant harmony, which is only a short way of describing harmony of which these respective notes are the roots.

The simplest and most stable of complete combinations in music are the chords consisting of a bass note with its third and perfect fifth; and of these the bass note is considered the root. In most cases such a root is held to be the fundamental sound of the series of harmonics which an essential chord may be taken to represent. For instance, the chord of the major third and perfect fifth on any note is supposed to represent the ground tone or generator with two of its most distinct and characteristic lower harmonics; and whatever be the positions of the individual notes in respect of one another, they are still referred to this ground-tone as a root. Thus the chord GBD

(a) would be taken to be the representative of the ground-tone G with its second and fourth harmonics (b); and every transposition or 'inversion' of the same notes, such as BDG, or DGB in close or open order (as in c), or even lesser portions to which the implication of a context would afford a clue, would be referred alike to this same root. If F be added (d) to the above chord it may be taken to represent the sixth harmonic (b), and similar 'inversions' of the component portions of the chord will similarly be referred to the note G. If A be added further above the F of the preceding chord, producing GBDFA (as in e), that is commonly taken as a yet more complete representation of the group of harmonics generated by the sounding of G, of which it is the eighth; and, as before, all the different portions which could be intelligibly isolated, and all the transpositions of its component notes, would be still referable to the one root G. If A♭ had been taken instead of A♮, the same general explanation would hold good, though the special question might remain open whether it was a representative of the 16th harmonic, which is four octaves from the fundamental sound, or an artificial softening of the clear and strong major ninth, A♮. Some theorists carry the same principles yet further, and include the C above A, and even the E and E♭ above that in the group which represents the harmonic series of G, calling them respectively the

k

eleventh and major and minor thirteenths of that note.

The discords contained in the above series are frequently styled fundamental from this supposed representation of the group of harmonics generated by their fundamental or root note ; they are characterised among discords by the peculiar freedom of the notes of which they are composed, on both sides. It will be observed that they are all members of the Diatonic series of the key of C, major or minor ; and as G, their root note, is the Dominant of that key, they represent the scope of what is called the Dominant harmony of C, which of course has its counterpart in every other key. No other note than the Dominant serves to this extent as the root of chords of this class which are Diatonic. The Tonic, for instance, can only supply the third and fifth, and even the minor seventh is a chromatic note. Nevertheless this chromatic chord and the ninths which are built upon it are commonly used as if they belonged to the key of C ; and the same remark applies to the similar discords founded on the Supertonic root (as D in the key of C) ; and these are most readily intelligible through their close connection as Dominant harmony to the Dominant of C.

The roots of the various combinations which are arrived at by modifying the intervals of such distinct and essential harmonies as the above, are of course the same as those of the unmodified harmonies. Thus the roots of suspensions are the same as those of the harmonies upon which they are said to resolve, because they are modifications of that which follows in its complete state, and not of that which precedes ; and the same applies to the combinations produced by adventitious notes, such as appoggiaturas and the like.

The combinations which arise from the simultaneous occurrence of ordinary passing notes must find their root in the chord which precedes, as that has possession of the field till new harmony presents itself.

From these considerations it will be obvious that a very considerable variety of apparently different combinations are referable to a single root. In fact a great portion of music is built upon very few roots ; many examples of good popular music especially do not exceed the limits of Tonic and Dominant harmony with an occasional move as far as the Subdominant, and next to no modulation. Even in works which belong to the domain sometimes distinguished as high art, a great deal is often done within very narrow limits. For instance, the whole of the first section of a violin and pianoforte sonata of Mozart's in A is based on six successive alternations of Tonic and Dominant harmony, and modulation to the new key for the second section is effected merely by the Dominant and Tonic harmony of that key.

Notwithstanding the importance which attaches to a clear understanding of the classification of chords according to their roots, there are some combinations upon whose derivation doctors disagree ; and it must be confessed that the theory of music is yet far from that complete and settled stage which would admit any hope of a decisive verdict in the matter at present. In such circumstances variety of opinion is not only inevitable but desirable ; and though the multitude of counsellors is a little bewildering there are consolations ; for it happens fortunately that these differences of opinion are not vital. Such chords, for instance, as augmented sixths have so marked and immediate a connection with the most prominent harmonies in the key, that the ascertainment of their roots becomes of secondary importance ; and even with the chord which stands as $\left.\begin{array}{l}D \\ C \\ A \\ F\end{array}\right\}$ in the key of C for instance (f), it is not so indispensable to decide whether G or F or D is the root, or whether indeed it is even a double-rooted chord, because, among other reasons, the very attention which has been called to it and the very characteristics which have made it difficult to classify have given it a prominence and a unique individuality which relieves it of the need of being assigned to any category ; and even when it is an important factor in the harmonic structure, the process of analysis need not be rendered doubtful, because its actual position in the key is so thoroughly realised. Other disputed points there are having reference to roots, which are even of less importance. For instance, whether what is called an augmented fifth is really an augmented fifth or a minor thirteenth ; or whether the augmented octave which Mozart uses with such marked emphasis in the third bar of the Allegro in the overture to 'Don Giovanni' is properly a minor ninth, as some maintain—since happily the roots would be the same in both cases.   C. H. H. P.

ROOT, GEORGE FREDERICK, an American popular composer, born at Sheffield, Mass., U.S.A., August 30, 1820. He studied under Webb of Boston, and afterwards in Paris in 1850. He was a music-publisher in Chicago in 1859-71. He was associated with Lowell Mason in popularising music in American schools, etc., and had a musical doctor's degree conferred on him at the Chicago University. He died at Barley's Island, August 6, 1895. He wrote various cantatas, such as 'The Flower Queen,' 'Daniel,' and others, but is best known as composer of certain songs much sung during the American Civil War, as, 'The Battle-Cry of Freedom,' 'Just before the Battle, Mother,' but his composition of the spirited 'Tramp, tramp, tramp, the boys are marching,' now almost better known as 'God save Ireland,' should entitle him to rank among the makers of living national music. His son, FREDERICK WOOD-MAN ROOT, born at Boston, June 13, 1846, has done useful work as a teacher of singing, both individually and in large classes.   F. K.

ROPARTZ, J. GUY, born at Quingamp (Côtes du Nord), June 15, 1864, was a pupil of Dubois and Massenet in the Paris Conservatoire, and afterwards studied with César Franck. Though his life has been chiefly devoted to composition he has, since 1894, directed the Conservatoire of Nancy with great success, and has given a strong impulse to the symphony concerts in that town. His dramatic works include two pieces in one act, ' Le Diable couturier ' and ' Marguerite d'Écosse ' ; he has written incidental music for 'Pêcheur d'Islande' (Loti and Tiercelin), played in Paris, 1893 ; ' Paysages de Bretagne ' (written for a ' théâtre d'ombres chinoises '), ' Les Landes,' ' Marie endormie,' and five short pieces, a ' Marche de fête,' three ' Airs de ballet,' a suite in four movements called 'Dimanche breton,' a symphony on a Breton chorale, a ' Serenade,' etc., and among his smaller published works which have been brought to a hearing are a string quartet and a ' fantaisie ' for strings, some church music (Psalm xxxvi. for choir, organ, and orchestra), songs, and pieces for organ and for piano. G. F.

RORE, CIPRIANO DE, composer of the Venetian school, born at Mechlin (or possibly Antwerp) about 1516. He studied under Willaert,[1] chapel-master of St. Mark's, Venice, and was probably in early life a singer in that cathedral. In 1542 he brought out his first book of madrigals a 5, and in 1550 his first book a 4 appeared, a work long held in favour,[2] and for the next seven or eight years published continually.[3] About 1550[4] he appears to have left Venice for the court of Hercules II., Duke of Ferrara, and for some years we hear nothing of him.[5] [In 1558 he was given leave of absence to visit his parents

[1] See title-page ' Fantesie e Recerchari, etc., composti da lo Eccell. A. Vuegliart e *Cipriano suo Discepolo*, etc., Venetiis, 1549 ' (Brit. Mus. A. 287).
[2] The Fétis library at Brussels contains imperfect copies of three editions, 1552, 1569, and 1582. The edition in the British Museum is 1575.
[3] The following list of books of motets and madrigals is taken from Fétis's *Biographie*, Eitner's *Bibliographie*, the *Quellen-Lexikon*, and the catalogues of the British Museum and Fétis libraries. Some contain work by other composers, but in all cases they bear Cipriano's name, and he is the chief contributor. The date given is that of the supposed first edition :—
 Motets. Bk. i. a 5, Venice, 1544 (Brit. Mus.); bk. ii. a 4 and 5, Venice, 1547 (Fétis, Biogr.); bk. iii. a 5, Venice, 1549 (Eitner).
 Madrigals. Bk. i. a 5, Venice, 1542; bk. ii. a 5, Venice, 1544 (Brit. Mus., the *Quellen-Lexikon* gives 1552 as the first edition); bk. iii. a 5, Venice, 1544. The 1562 edition in Brit. Mus. ; bks. iv. and v. (1557 and 1566). (The fifth book contains an ode to the Duke of Parma, and from the events of the composer's life we may assume this volume to be one of his latest publications.) For the first book of madrigals a 4, see above; the second was printed in 1557, and in 1565 came out a selection of the four- and five-part madrigals, as ' Le vive fiamme,' etc. A large number of the four-part madrigals were brought out in score in 1577.
 Chromatic madrigals. Bk. i. a 5, 1544 (Brit. Mus.; the word 'ri-stampato' on title-page shows that this is not the first edition). The first book was reprinted as late as 1593 (Fétis library). Burney has inserted one number in his *History*.
[4] In this year a reprint of his first book of madrigals was brought out at Ferrara.
[5] Except the publication of two Passions (Paris 1557) with the following curious titles: ' Passio D. N. J. Christi in qua solus Johannes canens introducitur cum quatuor vocibus' and ' Passio . . . in qua introducuntur Jesus et Judaei canentes, cum duabus et sex vocibus.'

at Antwerp, and soon afterwards visited the court of Margaret of Austria, Governess of the Netherlands, whose husband, Duke Ottavio Farnese, engaged him as his maestro di cappella at Parma.] On the death of Willaert he was appointed his successor, Oct. 18, 1563. He resigned this position almost immediately, and returned to the court of Parma in July 1564, where he died, in the autumn of 1565, at the age of forty-nine. He was buried in the cathedral of that city, and the following epitaph gives an authentic sketch of his life :—

> Cypriano Roro, Flandro
> Artis Musicae
> Viro omnium peritissimo,
> Cujus nomen famaque
> Nec vetustate obrui
> Nec oblivione deleri poterit,
> Hercules Ferrariens. Ducis II.
> Deinde Venetorum,
> Postremo
> Octavi Farnesi Parmae et Placentiae
> Ducis II Chori Praefecto.
> Ludovicus frater, fil. et haeredes
> Moestissimi posuerunt.
> Obiit anno MDLXV. aetatis vero suae XLIX.

The position to which Rore attained at St. Mark's, and the rank as a musician which contemporary writers assigned him, point to his having been something of an innovator, and a really original composer. His sacred and secular compositions were frequently reprinted, and were included in many collections of the time.[6] (See the *Quellen-Lexikon* for these and for MS. copies.) We know that they were held in high esteem in the court chapel at Munich, and were constantly performed there under Lassus's direction.[7] Duke Albert of Bavaria caused a superb copy of Rore's motets to be made for his library, where it remains to this day, with a portrait of the composer on the last page, by the court painter Mielich.   J. R. S.-B.

ROSA (ROSE), CARL AUGUST NICOLAS, born at Hamburg, March 22, 1842, was educated as a violin-player and made such progress as to be sent to the Leipzig Conservatorium, which he entered in 1859. [He afterwards studied at the Paris Conservatoire, and obtained the post of concertmeister at Hamburg in 1863.] In 1866 he came to England and appeared as a solo player at the Crystal Palace on March 10. After a short stay in London he joined Mr. Bateman in a concert-tour in the United States, and there met Madame Parepa, whom he married at New York, in Feb. 1867. His wife's success on the stage led to the formation of a company under the management and conductorship of Mr. Rose, which, during its early campaigns could boast such names as Parepa, Wachtel, Santley, Ronconi, and Formes among its artists. Early in 1871 Mr. Rose—who by this time had changed his name to Rosa to avoid mistakes

[6] Fetis mentions a book of Cipriano's masses, a 4, 5, 6 (Venice, 1566) on the authority of Draudius's *Bibliotheca Classica*. This is probably ' Liber Missarum' a 4, 5, 6 (Venice, 1566) to which Cipriano only contributes the first mass ' Doulce memoyre.'
[7] *Discorsi delli triomphi*, etc. nelle nozze dell' illustr. duca Gugl. etc. da Massimo Trojano (Monaco, Berg. 1508).

in pronunciation—returned to England with his wife, and then made a lengthened visit to Egypt for health. After this they again returned to London, but only for the lamented death of Madame Parepa-Rosa, which took place Jan. 21, 1874. Mr. Rosa, however, was resolved, notwithstanding this serious blow, to test the fortunes of English opera in London, and on Sept. 11, 1875, he opened the Princess's Theatre with a company including Miss Rose Hersee as prima donna, Mr. Santley, and other good singers. He closed on Oct. 30, having produced 'Figaro,' 'Faust,' *'The Porter of Havre'[1] (Cagnoni), 'Fra Diavolo,' 'Bohemian Girl,' 'Trovatore,' *'The Water-Carrier' (Cherubini), and 'Siege of Rochelle.'

The season of 1876 was undertaken at the Lyceum (Sept. 11–Dec. 2). It included 'The Water-Carrier'; 'The Lily of Killarney' (with additions; 'Sonnambula'; 'Faust'; *'Giralda' (Adam); 'Bohemian Girl'; *'Flying Dutchman'; 'Zampa'; 'Trovatore'; 'Montana'; *'Joconde' (Nicolò); 'Fidelio'; 'Fra Diavolo'; *'Pauline' (Cowen): 'Porter of Havre.' The next season was at the Adelphi Theatre (Feb. 11–April 6, 1878). It included *'The Golden Cross,' by Brüll; 'The Merry Wives'; 'The Flying Dutchman'; 'The Lily of Killarney,' and others of those already named. For the fourth season Mr. Rosa took Her Majesty's Theatre, Jan. 27–March 22, 1879), brought out *'Rienzi,' *'Piccolino' (by Guiraud), and *'Carmen,' and played 'The Golden Cross,' 'Huguenots,' 'Lily of Killarney,' etc. etc. His fifth season was at the same theatre (Jan. 10– March 6, 1880); *'Mignon' (Thomas), *'Lohengrin,' and *'Aida' were all produced for the first time in English; and 'The Taming of the Shrew' (Goetz), 'Carmen,' 'Rienzi,' etc., were performed. In 1882 a season was given at Her Majesty's Theatre, from Jan. 14 to March 11. 'Tannhäuser' and Balfe's *'Painter of Antwerp' ('Moro') were produced, and Mme. Valleria joined the company. For the season of 1883 (March 26–April 21) the company moved to Drury Lane, which was its London centre until 1887. Thomas's *'Esmeralda' and Mackenzie's *'Colomba' were produced, and Mme. Marie Roze appeared as 'Carmen,' etc. In 1884 (April 14–May 10) Stanford's *'Canterbury Pilgrims' was the only new work produced. In 1885 (April 6–May 30) Thomas's *'Nadeshda' and Massenet's 'Manon' were given. In 1886 (May 23–June 26) Mackenzie's *'Troubadour,' and in 1887 (April 7–June 11) Corder's *'Nordisa' were the novelties. In 1888 'Robert the Devil,' 'The Puritan's Daughter,' 'The Star of the North,' and 'The Jewess' were produced; and on Jan. 12, 1889, Planquette's 'Paul Jones' at the Prince of Wales's Theatre, London.　　　G.

[1] The asterisk prefixed to these names signifies that the works had not been before produced in England, at least in English.

After the death of Carl Rosa, which took place in Paris, April 30, 1889, the company began to lose a little of the prestige it had formerly enjoyed. An amalgamation with Harris, which had just been entered into at the time of Rosa's death, had no very artistic results, although a few works of importance were given from time to time. It must of course be remembered that the chief influence of such a company is in the provinces rather than in London, and as a rule, from this time, the first performances of the Carl Rosa productions took place away from London. Cowen's *'Thorgrim' was the main attraction of a Drury Lane season in 1890; and the production of MacCunn's *'Jeanie Deans' in Edinburgh took place in November 1894. In December 1894, the company again laid London musicians under a great obligation, by producing *'Hänsel and Gretel' with Mozart's early *'Bastien et Bastienne' at Daly's Theatre. In 1896 the same theatre was occupied for a short series of miscellaneous performances. 1897 was an eventful year in the life of the company, and in its course permission was granted to prefix the word 'Royal' to the name. In January 'Die Meistersinger' was given at the Garrick Theatre; in April, Puccini's *'La Bohème' was introduced to England at Manchester, and in October they gave a season at Covent Garden (opening with the work just named), in the course of which MacCunn's *'Diarmid' was produced. After *'Siegfried' (1898) the energy of the company failed for some time. A series of performances of 'popular' operas at the Lyceum in 1899 was attended by no remarkable success; but in November 1900, at the Coronet Theatre, Notting Hill, they introduced Gounod's *'Cinq Mars,' and in the following week, at the Brixton Theatre, gave Goldmark's *'Heimchen am Herd' to the English public. In the following October they gave 'Siegfried,' and in April 1902, Giordano's *'André Chenier' was given for the first time in England. The company's record is an honourable one, and its influence on English music cannot be denied; with rather higher aims, its prestige might have been kept up at the same level that was attained during the founder's lifetime, but the usual temptation to beat successful rivals on their own ground, and to present the 'popular' operas in ultra-'popular' style, was too strong to be quite resisted, and the result has been that the most artistic productions have perhaps been suspected by the cultivated amateurs who were the company's best patrons in former times.　　　M.

ROSA, SALVATOR, was born at Arenella, near Naples, July 21, 1615. His father Vito Antonio de Rosa sent him to be educated at the college of the padri Somaschi. He soon began to study music, and became an expert player of the lute, improvising accompaniments and interludes to his own verses. His ambition to go to Rome and devote himself seriously to painting seemed on the point of being fulfilled in 1635, when he visited Rome for the first time. But becoming ill, he returned to Naples at the end of six months, and there became a pupil of the painter, Aniello Falcone, until 1637. Then again he went to Rome, and accompanied a friend, Mercurio, in the service of the Cardinal Brancaccio, to Viterbo, where he received a commission to paint an altar-piece.

After a visit to Naples, he was again in Rome in 1638 until September 1640, when he went to Florence to take an appointment as painter to the court of the Medici, a post he held for nearly nine years. During this time he met Filippo Lippi, poet and painter, and Cesti, the musician, and wrote *La Strega*, to which Cesti composed the music, and *Il Lamento*, later on set to music by Bandini. It was probably towards the end of 1640 that he wrote the satire *La musica*, a violent attack on the depraved taste shown in Italian church music. It was not published till some years after Rosa's death, and evidently caused much agitation. It was answered with a bitterness almost equal to its own by Mattheson in his *Mithridat wider den Gift einer welschen Satyre, genannt la Musica*, Hamburg, 1749 ; in which a German translation of the satire is given, with pages of comments and annotations. The six satires, *La Musica, La Poesia, La Pittura, La Guerra, La Babilonia*, and *L' Invidia*, written by Rosa between 1640 and 1669, were probably first published in Rome in 1695 ; the title-page, without date, and with Amsterdam falsely indicated as the printing place, is as follows : *Satire di Salvator Rosa dedicate a settano. In Amsterdam presso Severo Prothomastix*, 12mo, p. 161. It was followed by numberless unauthorised editions. The first dated edition of 186 pages was printed in Amsterdam by J. F. Bernard in 1719, the second edition is dated 1781, and the third 1790. In 1770 there was an edition *Con note di A. M. Salvini*, printed at Florence, but with Amsterdam on the title-page ; this was reprinted in 1781, 1784, and 1787.

Rosa on leaving Florence was in Volterra for a time, and then returned to Rome in February 1649. The year 1647 was certainly passed peaceably in Tuscany, in spite of the legend which has it that Rosa was at Naples during the insurrection in July 1647, and was one of the 'compagnia della morte' under the leadership of the painter Falcone. To begin with, no such company existed, and secondly, there are letters preserved, written by Rosa to his friend Maffei, one from Pisa, on Jan. 9, 1647, and another from Florence, on Sept. 26, 1647, in which the tumults at Naples are not even alluded to (Cesareo, *Poesie e lettere*, 1892, p. 55). In 1650 Rosa again visited Florence, Pisa, and Siena, returning to Rome in December,

where he worked at his painting, finding relaxation in writing songs to which either he or his friend Cavalli, then in Rome, composed the airs.

Rosa died in Rome on March 15, 1673, at the age of fifty-eight, and was buried in the church of Santa Maria degli Angioli alle Terme di Diocleziano.

Little of Rosa's music is known, with the exception of the songs published in the 'Gemme d'antichità' and other modern collections. His position, however, was one of some musical interest. A personal friend of some of the leading composers of the time—Cavalli, Cesti, Bandini and others—he was so far in touch with the new ideas just germinating, as to adopt the method of writing for a single voice with *basso continuo* accompaniment.

In 1770 Dr. Burney acquired from a great-grand-daughter of Rosa, occupying the same house on the Monte Santa Trinità in Rome in which he had lived and died, a musical manuscript in Rosa's handwriting, containing, besides airs and cantatas by Cesti, Rossi, etc., eight cantatas written and composed by Rosa himself. The airs are melodious and vivacious, and have a good deal of charm. Burney (*Hist. of Music*, iv. pp. 165-8) gives the music of a certain number of them ; they were also included by N. d' Arienzo in his paper on Rosa in the *Rivista Mus. Ital.* 1894, i. 389.

The better-known airs are 'Vado ben spesso,' printed by Dr. Crotch in *Specimens of Various Styles*, 1808. Edited by H. Bishop in 'Gemme d'antichità,' No. 26, and in *La scuola antica*, No. 24, also in Marx's *Gluck und die Oper*, 1863. Beilage, No. 2. 'Star vicino,' edited by W. H. Callcott, 'Gemme,' No. 27. And 'Selve voi che,' edited by J. Pittmann, London, 1878. A manuscript copy of the latter is in the Vienna Imperial Library, No. 19,242 in Mantuani's catalogue. C. S.

ROSALIA (Germ. *Vetter Michel, Schusterfleck*). A form of melody, vocal or instrumental, in which a figure is repeated several times in succession, transposed a note higher at each reiteration.

The name is derived from an old Italian Canto popolare, 'Rosalia, mia cara,' the Melody of which is constructed upon this principle.

The well-known German Volkslied, 'Gestern Abend war Vetter Michel da,' begins with a similar repetition, and hence the figure is frequently called in Germany, 'Vetter Michel.' These titles, as well as that of 'Schusterfleck' —a cobble—are of course given to it in derision —for writers on composition regard its frequent introduction as indicative of poverty of inventive power. Nevertheless, it is frequently employed by the great masters, with charming effect, as may be seen in the Minuet in Handel's 'Ariadne,' in which it will be observed that the figure is suffered to appear three [1] times only in succession. Almost all great writers have imposed this limit upon its employment, experience having proved that a fourfold repetition generally tends to render the passage wearisome. Strikingly effective instances of threefold repetition will be found, in Mozart's Requiem, at the words 'Ingemisco tamquam reus'; in Spohr's 'Last Judgment,' at 'The grave gives up its dead'; and in a remarkably forcible passage in the 'Rigaudon' from Rameau's 'Dardanus.' Still, this restriction is frequently disregarded. Vallerano has left a Canon,[2] which ascends a Tone higher at each repetition, *ad infinitum*; and the resulting effect is far from inharmonious, though the work must be regarded rather as a musical curiosity than a serious composition.

Closely allied to this figure is another, in which the leading phrase is transposed one or more notes lower at each repetition; as in 'Habbiam vinto' from Handel's 'Scipio,' in which the transposition proceeds by thirds.

Here, again, the figure breaks off after a threefold reiteration; and, in two cases in which Mozart has employed the same device, in his Requiem—at the words 'Qui Mariam absolvisti,' and 'Oro supplex et acclinis'—it is relinquished after the second enunciation. [For a fivefold repetition see the Branle given under FORM, vol. ii. p. 75a.] This kind of imitation is, indeed, subject to exactly the same form of treatment as the true Rosalia; though it would be inexact to call it by that name, and equally so to apply the term to the regular ascents or descents of a sequence—as constantly exhibited in the fugues of Seb. Bach; or to those of vocal divisions—as in 'Every Valley,' or Rossini's 'Quis est homo'; or to the scene, in 'Tannhäuser,' in which the stanzas of 'Dir töne Lob' are sung a note higher at each repetition.

Schumann was accused of writing Rosalie *usque ad nauseam.* He does employ them very frequently: but often—as in the opening of his 'Arabeske' (op. 18)—with an effect which true genius alone could have dictated. This is not the place for a detailed criticism of Schumann's principles of composition: but when—as in a bitter article, by Joseph Rubinstein, which appeared in *Bayreuther Blätter*—his masterly use of this particular device is made

[1] Sometimes called 'Les trois Révérences.'
[2] Reprinted in vol. i. of Clementi's *Practical Harmony.*

to serve as an excuse for its unqualified condemnation, as a 'vicious monotony-producing repetition of musical phrases on related degrees, which the student of composition loves to introduce in his first exercises,' we naturally revolt from a conclusion so illogical. That a form which neither Handel, nor Mozart, nor Beethoven, nor any other great writer has disdained to employ, can possibly be, in its own nature, 'vicious,' we cannot believe. With equal reason might we condemn the 'monotony-producing' effect of a regular figure. It is, indeed, quite possible to make such a figure monotonous to the last degree; yet nearly the whole of Beethoven's 'Andante in F' (op. 34), is founded on the rhythmic form of the first four notes of the opening subject. The truth is, that, in the hands of a great master, all such devices are made productive of pure and beautiful effects; while all are 'vicious' when viciously misused.   w. s. r.

ROSAMOND. An opera by Joseph Addison, music by Thomas Clayton; produced at Drury Lane Theatre on March 4, 1707, but only ran three nights.

Thomas Augustine Arne, many years later, took the libretto for one of his early musical efforts; and produced a work that bore considerable promise of his future excellence. His setting of the opera was given at the Little Theatre in the Haymarket, on March 7, 1733.   F. K.

ROSAMUNDE FÜRSTIN VON CYPERN (Rosamond, Princess of Cyprus). A romantic play in four acts; written by Wilhelmine Christine von Chezy, the overture and incidental music by Franz Schubert (op. 26). Produced at the Theatre an-der-Wien, Vienna, Dec. 20, 1823, and only performed twice. The music as then played is as follows:—

* 1. Overture (D minor).
† 2. Entr'acte between Acts 1 and 2 (B minor).
† 3. Ballo (B minor), and Andante un poco assai (G).
  4. Entr'acte between Acts 2 and 3 (D).
* 5. Romance for soprano, 'Der Vollmond strahlt' (F minor).
* 6. Chorus of Spirits.
* 7. Entr'acte between Acts 3 and 4 (B♭).
  8. Shepherds' Melody.
* 9. Shepherds' Chorus.
*10. Huntsmen's Chorus.
†11. Air de Ballet (G).

The overture played at the performances was published in 1827, for PF. four hands, by Schubert himself, as op. 52, under the title of 'Alfonso und Estrella' (now op. 69). The overture (in C), known as the 'Overture to Rosamunde' (op. 26) was composed for the melodrama of the 'Zauberharfe,' or Magic Harp (produced August 19, 1820), and was published by Schubert with its present name and opus-number for PF. four hands, in 1828. The pieces marked have been published — those marked with * by Schubert himself, as op. 29; those marked with † more recently. For particulars see Nottebohm's Thematic Catalogue, pp. 46, 84. The Entr'acte in B minor is one of the finest of all Schubert's works ; the Romance, the Entr'acte No. 7, the Shepherds' Melody, and the Air de Ballet (in G), are all admirable, the Shepherds' Melody for two clarinets especially characteristic. The second Trio to the Entr'acte No. 7 was previously composed, in May 1819, as a song, 'Der Leidende.' G.[1]

ROSE or KNOT (Fr. *Rosace* ; Fr. and Germ. *Rosette* ; Ital. *Rosa*). The ornamental device or scutcheon inserted in the sound-hole of the belly of stringed instruments, such as the lute, guitar, mandoline, dulcimer, or harpsichord, serving not only a decorative purpose, but—in the Netherlands especially—as the maker's 'trade mark.' In the harpsichord and spinet there was usually but one sound-hole with its rose ; but owing to the origin of these keyboard instruments from the psaltery, their analogy with the lute, and the fact of the Roman lutes having three, several sound-holes were sometimes perforated. In fact, a harpsichord dated 1531 was seen in Italy by the eminent art critic, Mr. T. J. Gullick, which possessed no less than five, each with a rose inserted. From the analogy above referred to, the old Italian harpsichord makers named the bottom of the instrument ' cassa armonica ' (sound-chest) ; as if its office were like that of the back of the lute or viol, while the belly was the ' piano armonico ' (sound-flat).[2] The Flemings, retaining the sound-hole, doubtless adhered more or less to this erroneous notion of a sound-chest. The Hitchcocks in England (1620 and later) appear to have been the first to abandon it ; no roses are seen in their instruments. Kirkman in the next century still adhered to the rose and trade scutcheon, but Shudi did not. In the *Giornale de' Litterati d' Italia* (Venice, 1711, tom. v.), Scipione Maffei, referring to Cristofori, who had recently invented the pianoforte, approves of his retention of the principle of the rose in his ordinary harpsichords, although contemporary makers for the most part had abandoned it. But Cristofori, instead of a large rose, to further, as he thought, the resonance, used two small apertures in the front. Under the head RUCKERS will be found illustrations of the rose or *rosace*, as used by those great makers. A. J. H.

ROSE OF CASTILE. An opera in three acts ; compiled by Messrs. Harris & Falconer (from 'Le Muletier de Tolède'), music by M. W. Balfe. Produced at the Lyceum Theatre (Pyne and Harrison), London, Oct. 29, 1857. G.

ROSE OF PERSIA, THE. Comic opera in two acts, libretto by Basil Hood, music by Arthur Sullivan, produced at Savoy Theatre, Nov. 29, 1899.

---

[1] [Sir George Grove, with characteristic modesty, here omits all reference to the fact that he himself discovered the missing portions of the music. See vol. ii. p. 247b, and *infra*, p. 301a.]
[2] In modern Italian we more frequently meet with 'tompagno,' 'tavola armonica,' and 'fondo,' meaning 'belly,' or ' sound-board.'

ROSEINGRAVE or ROSINGRAVE, DANIEL, Church musician and organist. The exact date of his birth is not known. He received his early musical education as one of the children of the Chapel Royal ; though whether before 1660, under Captain Cook, or after that date, under Pelham Humfrey, is uncertain. He is stated subsequently to have studied under Dr. John Blow and Henry Purcell. He was organist of Gloucester Cathedral from 1679 to 1681, of Winchester Cathedral from 1682 to 1692, of Salisbury Cathedral from 1692 to 1698, was appointed organist and Vicar-choral of St. Patrick's Cathedral, Dublin, in the year 1698, and organist and stipendiary of Christ Church Cathedral, Dublin, in the same year. He retired from the organistship of St. Patrick's in 1719 in favour of his son Ralph, but remained organist of Christ Church until his death in 1727. He married Ann, daughter of the Rev. Thomas Washbourne, D.D., who survived him, and by whom he had several children, including his sons Thomas and Ralph, who were also distinguished musicians. There appear to have been Roseingraves in Ireland before Daniel Roseingrave's time, as mention is made in the Chapter Acts of Christ Church of a lease from the Dean and Chapter to one Ralph Roseingrave in 1661.

Daniel Roseingrave succeeded Robert Hodge as organist of St. Patrick's. Hodge, who resigned the post of organist, was thereupon appointed ' Master of the song to the Quire,' apparently as a *solatium* for losing the post of organist. The arrangement does not appear to have been a happy one, for in 1699 we find a Chapter Act in the following words : ' The said Dean and Chapter having received information that Mr. Hodge and Mr. Rosingrave, two of the Vicars-choral, gave each other very scurrilous language in Christ Church, Dublin, and after went together to the taverne and there fought, upon which the said Hodge and Roseingrave were ordered to appear before the said Dean and Chapter to answer in their places touching such their misdemeanours. And upon hearing what they could severally say for themselves touching the matter. And it thereupon appearing to the said Dean and Chapter that Mr. Roseingrave was ye first and chief aggressor, and that also the said Mr. Hodge was to blame. It was thereupon ordered by the aforesaid Dean and Chapter that the said Mr. Daniell Roseingrave should forthwith pay into the hands of ye steward of the said Vicars choralls the sume of three pounds and the said Mr. Hodge the sume of 20s. sterling for a penall mulct for such their offences, the same to be disposed of as the said Dean shall think fitt, and that the said Mr. Roseingrave should then and there beg publick pardon of the said Mr. Hodge for the scurillous language hee gave him as aforesaid, which was accordingly done in the presence of the said Dean and

Chapter.' Robert Hodge, it may be mentioned, had previously, when organist of Wells Cathedral (1688), been corrected and admonished for breaking windows.

At Christ Church Cathedral Roseingrave appears to have been equally combative. By a Chapter Act in 1700 the Dean and Chapter, on hearing the Petition of Daniel Roseingrave complaining of assault by Mr. Thomas Finell, 'ordered on hearing the Petition of Daniel Roseingrave and examination of several witnesses that the said Daniel Roseingrave and Thomas Finell be and are hereby suspended *ab officio et beneficio*'; and further ordered 'that from henceforth no Vicar or Stipendiary of this Church do wear a sword under the penalty of expulsion.' This suspension was subsequently removed on payment of 'mulcts' by the offending parties.

By his will, dated Oct. 21, 1724, Daniel Roseingrave left the house in Peter Street, Dublin, in which he then dwelt, to his 'second son Ralph,'[1] to whom he also left the residue of his property, subject to his providing an annuity of £20 for his (Daniel's) wife, the said Ann Roseingrave. To his 'eldest son Thomas' he only left five shillings. Daniel Roseingrave died in 1727, at Golden Lane (the same street where, fifty-five years later, John Field was born), and was buried in the churchyard of St. Bride's Church. His widow died in 1732-3, and was buried in the old churchyard in St. Patrick's Cathedral.

Although Daniel Roseingrave seems to have written a great deal of church music, and is highly spoken of as a composer by Burney and Hawkins, very little of his music is now extant. One of his anthems, 'Lord, Thou art become gracious,' is preserved in manuscript in the library of Christ Church, Oxford, and another, 'Haste Thee, O Lord,' in the Bodleian library. Mr. J. S. Bumpus has autograph scores of four other anthems of his.

By a Chapter Act of Christ Church, Dublin, dated Dec. 15, 1699, it is ordered 'that the Proctor do pay unto Mr. Daniel Roseingrave three pounds as a gratuity for his writing three services and two Creeds for the use of the Church.' Unfortunately all traces of these compositions have long since disappeared.   L. M'C. L. D.

ROSEINGRAVE, THOMAS (1690 to 1766), the second son of Daniel Roseingrave, was born at Winchester in 1690. At the age of seven he came with his father to Dublin, and from him received his early education in music. Thomas Roseingrave entered Trinity College, Dublin, in 1707, and his then age is given in

[1] Although in his will Daniel describes Ralph as his 'second son,' his eldest son was DANIEL ROSEINGRAVE, JUNIOR, who was born at Winchester in 1685, entered Trinity College, Dublin, in 1702, obtained a scholarship in 1705, and took out his B.A. degree in 1707. He was, doubtless, the 'young Roseingrave' who appears by the College Register to have been appointed organist of Trinity College Chapel in 1705, as in that year Thomas was only fourteen, and Ralph still younger. In 1707 he was given leave of absence for one year, 'in order to improve himself in music.' He had probably died some years before 1724, the date of his father's will.

the College Register as sixteen. He did not, however, proceed to his degree in Arts.

In a Chapter Act of St. Patrick's Cathedral, dated 14th December 1709, it is ordered by the Dean and Chapter 'that whenever Thomas Rosseingrave sonn of Daniell Rossingrave, the present organist of the said Cathedrall, being minded to travell beyond seas to improve himself in the art of music, and that hereafter he may be useful and serviceable to the said Cathedrall, yt tenne guineas be by the Proctor of the said Canonry given him as a guift from the said Canonry towards bearing his charges.' He went to Italy in 1710, and at Venice made the acquaintance of the Scarlattis, Alessandro and Domenico. For the latter he appears to have formed a great admiration. Burney (*History of Music*, iv. p. 263) says, that he 'followed him to Rome and Naples, and hardly ever quitted him while he remained in Italy, which was not till after the Peace of Utrecht, [1713], as appears by an anthem which he composed at Venice in 1713, "Arise, shine, for thy light is come."' The manuscript of this anthem, which he wrote with orchestral accompaniment, is preserved in the Tudway collection (Harl. MS. 7342). Burney says of it, 'There is much fire in the introductory symphony, which is of a very modern cast.' How long he continued abroad is not exactly known, but in 1720 we find him in London, where he produced, at the Haymarket Theatre, Domenico Scarlatti's opera, 'Narciso,' with two additional songs and two duets of Roseingrave's own composition.

As a composer and organist he appears to have been held in high estimation, his powers of reading at sight and of improvising being especially dwelt on by his contemporaries. Burney says: 'In his younger days, when he enjoyed the *mens sana in corpore sano*, he was regarded as having a power of seizing the parts and spirit of a score, and executing the most difficult music at sight, beyond any musician in Europe.'

In 1725 he was appointed the first organist of St. George's, Hanover Square. There were seven other competitors, all of whom had to give a performance on the organ before Dr. Greene, Dr. Pepusch, and Mr. Galliard, who acted as judges. Burney says that Roseingrave's performance of the set pieces was by no means good, but that when he was asked to improvise on given themes, he 'treated the subjects with such science and dexterity, inverting the order of notes, augmenting and diminishing their value, introducing counter subjects, and treating the themes to so many ingenious purposes, that the judges were unanimous in declaring him the victorious candidate.'

Archdeacon Coxe, in his *Anecdotes of George Frederick Handel and John Christopher Smith*, speaking of Roseingrave at this time, says:—

' His reputation was at this period so high that on commencing teaching he might have gained one thousand pounds a year, but an unfortunate event reduced him to extreme distress. Among Roseingrave's scholars was a young lady to whom he was greatly attached, and whose affections he had gained, but her father, who intended to give her a large fortune, did not approve of her marrying a musician, and forbade Roseingrave his house. This disappointment affected his brain, and he never entirely recovered the shock. He neglected his scholars and lost his business. He lived upon fifty pounds per annum, which his place produced, and was often in indigence. He was perfectly rational upon every subject but the one nearest his heart ; whenever that was mentioned he was quite insane.'

About the year 1737 he was compelled to give up the organistship, and lived for some time at Hampstead. Thence in about the beginning of 1753 he removed to Dublin, where he probably lived with his nephew, William Roseingrave, a son of Ralph's, who was born in 1725 and at this time (1753) held the Office of Chief Chamberlain of the Exchequer Court.

Mrs. Delany, in her memoirs, under date Jan. 12, 1753, writes :—' Mr. Roseingrave, who was sent away from St. George's Church on account of his mad fits, is now in Ireland, and at times can play very well on the harpsichord ' (*Correspondence*, iii. 194). Faulkner's *Dublin Journal* of Feb. 3, 1753, contains an announcement that ' the celebrated Opera of " Phaedra and Hippolitus," composed by Mr. Roseingrave lately arrived from London, will be performed at the Great Music Hall in Fishamble Street, and conducted by himself on Tuesday the 6th of March. Between the acts Mr. Roseingrave will perform Scarlatti's "Lessons on the Harpsichord," with his own additions, and will conclude with his celebrated "Almand."' And in the same Journal of Feb. 27, we read :—' Yesterday there was a public rehearsal of Mr. Roseingrave's Opera of " Phaedra and Hippolytus" at the great Music Hall in Fishamble Street, to a numerous audience, which met the highest applause, the connoisseurs allowing it to exceed any musical performance ever exhibited here, in variety, taste, and number of good songs.' One wonders if the writer of this notice had been at the production of the ' Messiah' in the same hall eleven years earlier.

Two anthems of Thomas Roseingrave (' Great is the Lord' and ' One Generation ') are included in the manuscript collection of Anthems in the Library of the Royal College of Music. He was an enthusiastic admirer of Palestrina, and is said to have adorned the walls of his bedroom with scraps of paper containing extracts from the works of that master.

He died on June 26, 1766, and is buried in the churchyard of St. Patrick's Cathedral, in the same grave with his brother Ralph. The inscription on the tombstone adds that he died in the 78th year of his age, ' a most celebrated musician and accomplished man.' Although an inscription added to this tombstone at a later date (1802) states that his wife, Mrs. Jane Roseingrave, is also buried there, this is incorrect, as the Jane Roseingrave in question was the wife of the before-mentioned William Roseingrave, who died in 1780, and is buried in an adjoining grave. Thomas Roseingrave does not appear to have been married.

The most important of his published compositions are :—Fifteen Voluntaries and Fugues for the organ or harpsichord ; six double Fugues for the organ or harpsichord ; the Opera ' Phaedra and Hippolytus' ; eight suits of lessons for the harpsichord or spinet ; six cantatas (Italian words) ; the additional songs and duets sung with Scarlatti's Opera 'Narciso' ; and twelve solos for the German flute with thoroughbass for the harpsichord. He edited the ' Forty-Two Suits of Lessons for the Harpsichord by Domenico Scarlatti,' prefixing an introductory movement in G minor.   L. M'C. L. D.

ROSEINGRAVE, RALPH (about 1695 to 1747), the youngest son of Daniel Roseingrave, was born at Salisbury, and received his musical education from his father. In 1718-19 Daniel Roseingrave petitioned the Dean and Chapter of St. Patrick's Cathedral, Dublin, to allow him to resign the post of organist in favour of his son Ralph, who appears to have been forthwith appointed Vicar-Choral, but did not formally succeed his father as organist until 1726. On his father's death in 1727 he also succeeded him as organist of Christ Church Cathedral, Dublin, at a salary of fifty pounds per annum. He appears to have written a good deal of church music. Eight of his Anthems and two Services in C and F are preserved at Christ Church, and some of them are still sung there. Another anthem of his, ' O God of Truth,' is published in Hullah's Part Music, and an old organ book in the possession of Mr. J. S. Bumpus contains a Service of his in F with a setting of the Benedicite. He died in 1747, and is buried in the churchyard of St. Patrick's Cathedral. The headstone mentions that his wife Sarah, who died in 1746, and four of their children, are buried with him, as are also his mother Ann Roseingrave, and his brother Thomas. Ralph Roseingrave is sometimes mentioned as having taken part as a soloist in the production of the ' Messiah' on April 13, 1742, but Dr. J. C. Culwick, in his pamphlet on the original *Word Book of Handel's 'Messiah'* (1891), points out the improbability of his having done so. L. M'C. L. D.

ROSELLEN, HENRI, son of a PF. maker, born in Paris, Oct. 13, 1811 ; took second PF. prize at the Conservatoire, 1827, and first harmony do. 1828. Was a pupil and imitator of Herz. He published nearly 200 works for PF., including a 'Méthode de Piano' (Heugel), a collection of progressive exercises entitled 'Manuel des Pianistes' (*Ibid.*), a trio for piano and strings, and many separate pieces of drawing-room character, one of which, a Rêverie (op. 32, No. 1), enjoyed an extraordinary popularity for many years over the whole of Europe. He died in Paris, March 18, 1876.   G.

ROSENHAIN, JACOB, eldest son of a banker, was born at Mannheim, Dec. 2, 1813. His teachers were Jacob Schmitt, Kalliwoda, and Schnyder von Wartensee. His first appearance as a pianoforte-player was in 1823 at Frankfort, where his success induced him to take up his residence. A one-act piece of his, 'Der Besuch im Irrenhause,' was produced at Frankfort, Dec. 29, 1834, with great success; his second, 'Liswenna,' three acts, was never performed in its original form. In 1837 he came to London, played at the Philharmonic, April 17, and was much heard in the concerts of the day. After this he took up his abode in Paris, where he became very prominent, giving chamber concerts in combination with Alard, Ernst, and other eminent players, and carrying on a school of pianoforte-playing in conjunction with J. B. Cramer. His early opera, 'Liswenna,' was provided with a new libretto (by Bayard and Arago), and brought out at the Grand Opéra as 'Le Démon de la Nuit,' March 17, 1851. It had, however, but a moderate success, and was withdrawn after four representations, though it was afterwards occasionally played in Germany. Another one-act piece, 'Volage et Jaloux,' produced at Baden-Baden, August 3, 1863, completes the list of his works for the stage. In instrumental music he was much more prolific. He composed three symphonies—in G minor (op. 42), played at the Gewandhaus, Leipzig, under Mendelssohn's direction, Jan. 31, 1846; in F minor (op. 43), played at Brussels, and at the Philharmonic, London, April 24, 1854; 'Im Frühling,' in F major (op. 61), rehearsed at the Conservatoire, and played at a Concert Populaire. Four trios for PF. and strings; one PF. concerto; three string quartets; two violoncello sonatas; twelve characteristic studies (op. 17) and twenty-four Études mélodiques (op. 20), both for PF. solo; a PF. concerto, op. 73; Sonata, op. 74; do. PF. and violoncello, op. 98; 'Am Abend' for quartet, op. 99. Also various pieces for piano entitled, 'Poémes,' 'Rêveries,' etc.; a biblical cantata, and various songs, etc. [He died at Baden-Baden, March 21, 1894.] Schumann criticised several of his pieces with kindness and liberality.   G.

ROSENMÜLLER, JOHANN, was born of poor parents about 1619 at Pelsnitz in the Vogtland of Saxony. In spite of the poverty of his parents the arrangements of the time enabled him to obtain a good general education, and in 1640 his name appears inscribed in the Matriculation-book of the University of Leipzig. In 1642 he became Collaborator or Assistant-Master at the Thomasschule. In musical matters he would appear to have been mainly a pupil of Tobias Michael, who then held the important office of Cantor at the school. In 1645 Rosenmüller published his first work, a work for instruments entitled, 'Paduanen, Alemanden, Couranten, Balletten, Sarabanden mit 3 Stimmen und ihrem Basso pro Organo.' A more important work was his 'Kernsprüche,' published in two parts, 1648 and 1652-53, each part consisting of twenty Latin and German Motets on Scripture and other Church Texts for three to seven voices, mostly with accompaniment of two violins, and also occasionally trombones and other instruments with Basso Continuo. When Tobias Michael became too infirm to discharge adequately his duties as Cantor, Rosenmüller acted as his deputy, and in this position gave such satisfaction to the city council as to obtain the promise of succession to the Cantorship. In 1651 he also held the post of organist at the Nikolaikirche. But in May 1655 his prospects of further promotion were blighted by an accusation made against him of some grave moral offence, for which he was temporarily imprisoned. He succeeded in effecting his escape, and betook himself for a time to Hamburg. From Hamburg he is said to have addressed a 'Supplication' to the Elector of Saxony, Johann Georg I., along with a setting of the Hymn of Albinus, 'Straf mich nicht in deinem Zorn.' This would almost seem to be an admission of his guilt, although Winterfeld in his *Evangelischer Kirchengesang* endeavours to prove him innocent of the charge made against him. However the case may be, Rosenmüller did not feel himself safe in Hamburg, but fled to Italy, and settled in Venice as a teacher of music for a considerable number of years. Of his stay in Venice little would have been known if Johann Philipp Krieger, who was afterwards Capellmeister at Weissenfels, had not sought him out and become his pupil in composition. A large number of works existing only in MSS., consisting of Latin Motets, Vesper Psalms, Lamentations, and various parts of the Mass, must be referred to this Venetian stay. The only work published in Venice was one for instruments, entitled 'Sonate da Camera cioe Sinfonie, Alemande, Correnti, Balletti, Sarabande da suonare con 5 strom. da arco et altri' . . . 1670. This work was dedicated to Duke Johann Friedrich of Brunswick, who became acquainted with the composer on the occasion of one of his visits to Venice. It has recently been republished as *Bd. xviii.* of the *Denkmäler deutscher Tonkunst, Erste Folge,* where also in his introduction the editor Karl Nef traces the influence of the Venetian opera-symphonies upon Rosenmüller's style of instrumental composition. The acquaintance with Duke Johann Friedrich had important consequences for Rosenmüller. It led to his recall to Germany. Duke Johann Friedrich recommended him to his brother the reigning Duke Anton Ulrich, who was an enlightened patron of literature and music, and himself a hymn-writer of some reputation. In 1674 Duke Anton Ulrich appointed Rosenmüller Capellmeister at Wolfenbüttel, where he remained for the rest of his life, dying there on 10th or 11th of September 1684. Only one other work was published in this later period of his life, 'Sonate a 2, 3, 4, e 5 Stromenti da Arco et altri . . . Nuremberg, 1682,' dedicated to his patron Duke Anton Ulrich. A large number of German Motets and Cantatas belonging to this time remained unpublished. None of Rosenmüller's vocal works have yet been republished in modern editions, with the exception of two Chorale-tunes and settings—' Straf mich nicht in deinem Zorn ' and ' Welt ade, ich bin dein müde.' The former of these tunes indeed seems far less suitable to its original German words than to those of the Easter hymns to which it has been so successfully adapted in our English hymn-books, 'Christ the Lord is risen again.' Of Rosenmüller's 5-voice setting of ' Welt ade ' it would appear that Sebastian Bach thought so highly that he took it over bodily from Vopelius' ' Leipziger Gesangbuch,' 1682, to incorporate it into his own church-cantata of 1731, ' Wer weiss, wie nahe mir mein Ende.' This led to both tune and setting being afterwards ascribed to Bach in earlier editions of his 'Choral-gesänge.'   J. R. M.

ROSENTHAL, MORIZ, born Dec. 18, 1862, at Lemberg, where his father was a professor in the chief Academy. From him Rosenthal obtained the solid foundation of the philosophical turn of mind which early in his career became very fully developed. At eight years of age the boy began the study of the pianoforte under a certain Galoth, whose method was curious in that he permitted his pupil absolute freedom in sight-reading, transposing, and modulating, without paying over-much attention to the systematic development of his technique. All who have heard the pianist in later life will agree that this system did no harm, for it is probable that there has never lived a player possessing a more perfect technique. Beethoven, Weber, and others were one and all boldly attacked by the youth, who as yet knew not a syllable of the conventional methods of fingering either chords or scales. In 1872 Carl Mikuli, the editor of Chopin, who was then director of the Lemberg Conservatorium, took charge of Rosenthal's education, and within the same year played in public with him Chopin's Rondo in C for two pianos. All this time, however, nothing had been determined as to Rosenthal's ultimate career, and it was only on the urgent advice of Rafael Joseffy that the parents consented to Rosenthal's adoption of a career as pianist. When, in 1875, the family moved to Vienna, Rosenthal became a pupil of Joseffy, who set to work systematically to ground the boy on Tausig's method. The results were astonishing enough, since in 1876 Rosenthal played at his first public recital Beethoven's thirty-two Variations, Chopin's F minor concerto, and some Liszt and Mendelssohn. Promptly a tour followed through Roumania, where at Bucharest the king created the fourteen-year-old lad court-pianist. In the next year Liszt came into Rosenthal's life, and henceforth played a great part therein, and in 1878 and subsequently they were together in Weimar and Rome. As Liszt's pupil Rosenthal then appeared in Paris, St. Petersburg, and elsewhere.

Meanwhile the philosophical studies were by no means neglected, for in 1880 Rosenthal qualified at the Staatsgymnasium in Vienna to take the philosophical course at the University, where he studied with Zimmermann, Brentano, and Hanslick (musical æsthetics). Six years elapsed before he resumed public pianoforte-playing. Then there followed in quick succession, after a triumph in the Liszt Verein at Leipzig, a long series of concert-tours, in America and elsewhere, which brought him ultimately to England in 1895 and to America again later, where in the spring of the present year (1907) he was making a remarkably successful tour. As a master of technique Rosenthal is not surpassed by any pianist of his time, while as an interpreter, especially of music of the modern composers and of Schubert, he has earned a prodigious reputation. To his great technical accomplishment he adds a beautiful touch, and to those who know him personally he is a musician of unquestionable distinction.   R. H. L.

ROSES, JOSE, priest and musician, born at Barcelona, Feb. 9, 1791, learned music from Sampere, chapelmaster at Barcelona ; was first organist of the monastery of San Pablo and then succeeded his master at Santa Maria del Pino, a post which he held for thirty years. During this time he composed a large quantity of music —masses, requiems, motets, graduals, etc., which are preserved in MS. in the church. Among his pupils may be mentioned Calvo, Puig, Rius, Casanovas, etc. He died at his native city, Jan. 2, 1856.   G.

ROSIN, RESIN (Fr. Colophane), a preparation applied to the hair of the violin bow to give it the necessary 'bite' upon the strings. Without some such agent, the horsehair would slip noiselessly over the catgut. Rosin is the residuary gum of turpentine after distillation. The ordinary rosin of commerce is a coarse, hard substance, quite useless to the fiddler, for whom the rough material undergoes a process of refinement. The ancient English recipe was to boil rough rosin down in vinegar, a process no longer in vogue, as excellent French rosin is now to be had at a very trifling cost. It is prepared by dissolving the rough article in a glazed earthen vessel over a slow charcoal fire. As it melts, it is strained through coarse canvas into a second vessel also kept at a moderate heat, from which it is poured into pasteboard or metal moulds. The process requires some delicacy of eye and hand, and the greatest care in handling so inflammable a material, and is usually entrusted to women. Some players affect to prefer the rosin of Gand, others that of Vuillaume, but both are made of the same material and at the same factory. Rosin should be transparent, of a darkish yellow colour in the mass, and quite white when pulverised : it ought to fall from the bow, when first applied to the strings, in a very fine white dust : when crushed between the fingers it ought not to feel sticky. The best rosin is made from Venetian turpentine. The same sort of rosin serves for the violin, viola, and violoncello. The double-bass bow requires a stiffer preparation than pure rosin, and accordingly double-bass rosin is made of ordinary rosin and white pitch in equal proportions. Emery powder and other matters are sometimes added in the composition of rosin, but are quite unnecessary, and even injurious to the tone. A liquid rosin, applied to the bow with a camel's-hair brush, has its advocates. [See COLOPHANE, vol. i. p. 565.]　　　　　　　E. J. P.

ROSINA. An English ballad opera, of the 18th century, which attained an extraordinary degree of popularity, holding the boards, as a stock piece, for nearly half a century. The libretto, written by Mrs. Brooke, is founded on the Scriptural story of Ruth and Boaz ; or of Palemon and Lavinia, in Thomson's 'Seasons,' a subject which has inspired numbers of theatrical pieces.

The opera was first produced at Covent Garden in 1783, and its music was written, selected, and arranged by William Shield. Miss Harper took the title-rôle ; Mrs. Martyr, Phœbe, and Mrs. Kennedy the hero, William, while the rest of the male characters were taken by Messrs. Banister, Brett, and Davies.

A passage in the overture has long been a bone of contention. It is arranged for the oboe, with a bass for ' bassoons, etc. to imitate the bagpipe.' This fragment of melody is exceedingly like that of 'Auld Lang Syne,' and it has, therefore, been contended that Shield was the author of the air for the celebrated Scotch song. This is, however, scarcely proven, for there exist in prior publications other strathspeys, as 'The Miller's Daughter,' and 'The Miller's Wedding,' which also resemble the well-known air, and these, together with a song, are also prototypes of the Scotch national melody.　　　　　　　　　　　F. K.

ROSS, JOHN, born at Newcastle-upon-Tyne,

Oct. 12, 1763, was placed in his eleventh year under Hawdon, organist of St. Nicholas Church, a disciple of Charles Avison, with whom he studied for seven years. In 1783 he was appointed organist of St. Paul's Chapel, Aberdeen, where he remained until his death, July 28, 1837. He composed 'An Ode to Charity,' pianoforte concertos and sonatas, songs, canzonets, hymns, waltzes, etc.　w. h. h. ; additions from Brit. Mus. Biog.

ROSSETER, PHILIP, a lutenist, born about 1575, in 1601 issued ' A Booke of Ayres, set foorth to be song to the Lute, Orpherian, and Base Violl,' containing forty-two songs, the poetry and music of the first twenty-one by Campion, and the rest by Rosseter himself. [A selection of eight of the forty-two songs was reprinted in 1907, as vol. iv. of the Oriana Madrigal Society's publication, 'Euterpe' (Breitkopf & Härtel)]. In 1609 he published ' Lessons for Consort : Made by sundry excellent Authors, and set to sixe severall instruments ; Namely, the Treble Lute, Treble Violl, Base Violl, Bandora, Citterne, and the Flute.' On Jan. 4, 1610, a patent was granted to him and others appointing them Masters of the Children of the Queen's Revels, under which they carried on dramatic performances at the theatre in Whitefriars. In March 1612, Rosseter's company was joined by 'The Lady Elizabeth's Servants,' but the union lasted for a year only. In May 1615 a privy seal for a patent for the erection of a theatre in Blackfriars was granted to Rosseter, Philip Kingman, Robert Jones, and Ralph Reeve, but the Lord Mayor and Aldermen compelled them to surrender it, when the building was nearly finished. [See JONES, ROBERT, vol. ii. p. 544, where the date of the patent is to be corrected.] Rosseter died on May 5, 1623. (Corrections, etc. from Dict. of Nat. Biog.)　　　　　　　　　　w. h. h.

ROSSI. No fewer than twenty-eight musicians of this name are enumerated in the Quellen-Lexikon, and as there are motets and other works in various libraries attributed to ' Rossi ' without further identification, there is still a large field open for careful research before the facts can be absolutely ascertained. Of these older bearers of the name there are seven who may be distinguished as important : (1) SALOMONE, a Jewish musician, was at the court of Mantua from 1587 to 1628, when he appears to have died. He enjoyed such high favour with two successive dukes that he was privileged to dispense with the yellow badge that all Jews were ordered to wear. He issued madrigals and canzonets in 1589, 1600, 1602, 1603, 1610, 1614, and 1628, but his most important works were instrumental, being contained in four books, called 'Sinfonie e Gagliarde' and 'Sonate' (1607, 1608, 1623, and 1636). He wrote twenty-eight compositions (a 4-8) to Hebrew psalms, published in two editions, in

Hebrew and Italian, in 1623. The authority for his life is Birnbaum's *Jüdische Musiker am Hofe zu Mantua.* A selection from his vocal music was published in 1877 by S. Naumburg and Vincent d'Indy, and examples of his instrumental music are included in Riemann's 'Alte Kammermusik.' (2) GIOVANNI BATTISTA, a monk, born at Genoa, who published in 1618 at Venice a book on mensural notation, *Organo de cantori per intendere da se stesso ogni passo difficile,* etc., containing cantilene *a* 2-5, and a book of four-part masses in the same year. M.

(3) MICHAEL ANGELO, a Roman musician of the earlier part of the 17th century, was a pupil of Frescobaldi for organ-playing. He is known as the composer of an opera entitled 'Erminia sul Giordano,' which in 1635 or 1637 (Fétis and Clément, *Dictionnaire Lyrique,* erroneously give the date 1625) was performed with all stage accessories in the Palace of Taddeo Barberini, Prefect of Rome and Prince of Palestrina. It was published in 1637, and dedicated to the Signora Anna Colonna Barberina, the Princess of Palestrina. A full account of the opera, the libretto of which is based on an episode in Tasso's *Gerusalemme Liberata,* is given in H. Goldschmidt's *Studien zur Geschichte der Italienischen Oper,* with some specimens of the music. Like most of the Roman Operas of the period, the music would appear to be utterly wanting in any dramatic power ; the form of the drama is merely an excuse for scenic decorations, and occasional graceful pastoral music. Rossi is better known as a composer for clavier. He published a collection of Toccate e Correnti for organ or cembalo (second edition, Rome, 1657, first edition without date). These are now generally accessible in Torchi's 'L'Arte Musicale in Italia,' vol. iii. They are modelled on the style of the pieces of the same name by Frescobaldi, but show no advance either in technique or treatment, though the Correnti are melodious enough. Previous to this republication by Torchi, there used to appear in various modern collections of older music, such as L. Köhler's 'Maîtres du Claveçin,' Pauer's 'Alte Meister,' and others, an Andantino and Allegro ascribed to Rossi, which have now been proved to be spurious, their whole style showing them to belong to the following century. Ernst von Werra was the first to prove by examination of the genuine works of Rossi previously unknown, the anachronism of this attribution (*Monatshefte für Musikgeschichte,* xxviii. pp. 123 ff.). It would be interesting to know how these two pieces came to be ascribed to M. A. Rossi. J. R. M.

(4) LUIGI, born about the end of the 16th century in Naples, was about 1620 in the service of Cardinal Barberini in Rome as a singer. Through Mazarin's influence he was invited to Paris, where on March 2, 1647, his

opera, 'Le Mariage d'Orphée et Euridice,' was given, being the first Italian opera performed in Paris. Five years before he had composed a dramatic work, 'Il palagio d'Atlante,' to words by G. Ruspiglosi (a copy in the Royal College of Music has the title 'Il Pallazzo incantato'). Gevaert edited a selection of thirteen cantatas by him. (5) FRANCESCO, an Abbate, a native of Apulia (Fétis gives Bari as his birthplace), who brought out several operas in Venice between 1686 and 1689, viz. 'Il Sejano moderno' (1686), 'La Clorilda' and 'La pena degl' occhi' in 1688, and 'Mitrane' in 1689. The last work contains the beautiful air, 'Ah ! rendimi quel core,' by which alone Rossi's name is known in the present day. An oratorio, 'La Caduta dei Giganti,' is in MS. (6) GIUSEPPE, was successively maestro di cappella at the Castle of St. Angelo, Rome, Pistoia, and San Loreto, Rome. He died in Rome about 1719. A mass in twelve parts, divided into three choirs, and two settings of Dixit Dominus for twelve and sixteen voices respectively, are preserved at Bologna, where the latter are ascribed to the later Giuseppe Rossi. (7) Another GIUSEPPE was maestro in the cathedral of Terni, and was the composer of an opera, 'La sposa in Livorno,' given in Rome in 1807. He published a treatise, *Alli intendenti di contrappunto,* in 1809, and several of his motets are at Bologna. M.

There are, furthermore, three modern operacomposers of the name : (8) LAURO, born at Macerata, Feb. 19, 1810, was a pupil of Crescentini, Furno, and Zingarelli at Naples. He began to write at once, and at eighteen had his first two operas—'Le Contesse Villane' and 'La Villana Contessa'—performed at the Fenice and Nuovo Theatres of Naples respectively. Other pieces followed : one of them, 'Costanza ed Oringaldo,' being written expressly for the San Carlo at the request of Barbaja. On the recommendation of Donizetti, Rossi was engaged for the Teatro Valle at Rome, and there he remained for 1832 and 1833, and composed four operas and an oratorio. In 1834 he moved to Milan, and brought out 'La Casa disabitata' (or 'I falsi Monetari'), which, though but moderately successful at the Scala, was afterwards considered his *chef-d'œuvre,* and spoken of as 'Rossi's Barbiere di Siviglia.' It pleased Malibran so much that she induced Barbaja to bespeak another opera from Rossi for the San Carlo, in which she should appear. The opera was composed, and was named 'Amelia' (produced at Naples, Dec. 4, 1834) ; but owing to her caprice was a failure. She insisted on having a *pas de deux* inserted for her and Mathis. The theatre was crowded to the ceiling to see the great singer dance ; but her dancing did not please the public, and the piece was damned. This disappointment, though somewhat alleviated by the success of his

'Leocadia' (1834) seems to have disgusted Rossi with Italy ; he accepted an engagement from Mexico, left Europe, Oct. 15, 1835, and arrived at Vera Cruz the 6th of the following January. From Mexico he went to the Havannah, New Orleans, and Madras ; married in 1841, and returned to Europe, landing at Cadiz, Feb. 3, 1843. He began again at once to compose—'Cellini a Parigi' (Turin, 1845), etc., but with very varying success. In 1846 he reappeared at the Scala at Milan with 'Azema di Granata,' 'Il Borgomastro di Schiedam,' and three or four other operas in following years. His great success, however, appears to have been made with 'Il Domino nero,' at the Teatro Canobbiana, Sept. 1849. In 1850 he was called to be director of the Conservatorio at Milan. For this institution he published a *Guida di armonia pratica orale* (Ricordi, 1858), and between 1850 and 1859 composed a great many operas, and detached pieces for voices and for instruments. After the death of Mercadante in 1870, Rossi succeeded him as head of the Conservatorio at Naples. This office he resigned in 1878, and he went to Cremona in 1880, dying there on May 5, 1885. Lists of his works are given by Florimo (*Cenni Storici*, pp. 948-962), Riemann (*Lexikon*), and Pougin. They comprise twenty-nine operas, a grand mass, and a dozen miscellaneous compositions, including six fugues for strings, two sets of vocal exercises, and the *Guide to Harmony* already mentioned. His best works are 'Cellini a Parigi,' 'I falsi Monetari,' 'La Contessa di Mons,' and 'Il Domino nero.' One of his operas, 'La Figlia di Figaro,' is said to have been produced at the Kärnthnerthor Theatre, Vienna, April 17, 1846 ; and another, 'Biorn,' was announced for performance at the Queen's Theatre, London, Jan. 17, 1877—English libretto by Frank Marshall ; but no notice of either performance can be found. [An oratorio, 'Saul,' elegies on Bellini and Mercadante, a mass, and other works, are mentioned by Riemann.] G.

(9) GIOVANNI GAETANO, born at Borgo San Donnino, Parma, August 5, 1828, studied at the Milan Conservatorio, was leader of the orchestra in the theatre at Parma, and organist of the court chapel there, from 1852 to 1873, and director of the Parma Conservatorio in 1864-1873. In 1873 he became conductor at the Teatro Carlo Felice, Genoa, until 1879 ; he died at Parma, March 30, 1886. His operas were : 'Elena di Taranto' (Parma, 1852), 'Giovanni Giscala' (Parma, 1855), 'Nicolò de' Lapi' (Ancona, 1865), 'La contessa d'Altemberg' (Borgo San Donnino, 1872), and 'Maria Sanz' (Bergamo, 1895). A symphony, 'Saul,' won a prize in Paris in 1878, and Rossi wrote besides three masses, an oratorio, and a requiem.

(10) CESARE, born at Mantua in 1864, has won success as a composer in many branches of art, his opera 'Nadeja' having been received with much favour at Prague in 1903 (Riemann's *Lexikon*, etc.) M.

ROSSINI, GIOACCHINO ANTONIO, was born Feb. 29, 1792, at Pesaro, and was the only child of Giuseppe Rossini of Lugo. The position of his parents was of the humblest ; his father was town-trumpeter (*trombadore*) and inspector of slaughter-houses, and his mother a baker's daughter, but their life was a happy one, and the irrepressible good-humour of the town-trumpeter was celebrated among his friends. In the political struggles of 1796 the elder Rossini declared himself for the French, and for republican government, and was naturally sent to gaol. His wife, thus deprived of her means of subsistence, was driven to turn her voice to account. She went with her little Gioacchino to Bologna, and there made her début as 'prima donna buffa' with such success as to procure her engagements in various theatres of the Romagna during the Carnival. Meantime the *trombadore* had regained his liberty and was engaged as horn-player in the bands of the theatres in which his wife sang ; the child remaining at Bologna, in the charge of an honest pork butcher. In such surroundings it is not wonderful that Gioacchino's learning was confined to reading, writing, and arithmetic. Music he acquired from a certain Prinetti of Novara, who gave him harpsichord lessons for three years ; but the lessons must have been peculiar, for Prinetti was accustomed to play the scale with two fingers only, combined his music-teaching with the sale of liquors, and had the convenient habit of sleeping as he stood. Such a character was a ready butt for the son of a joker like Giuseppe Rossini ; and so incorrigible was Gioacchino's love of mimicking his master that at length he was taken from Prinetti, and apprenticed to a smith.

Ashamed of this result he resolved to amend and apply. In Angelo Tesei he fortunately found a clever master, able to make singing and practical harmony interesting to his pupil ; in a few months he learned to read, to accompany, and to sing well enough to take solos in church at the modest price of three pauls per service. He was thus able, at the age of ten, to assist his parents, who, owing to a sudden change in his mother's voice, were again in misfortune. In his desire to help them he seized every opportunity of singing in public, and eagerly accepted an offer to appear at the theatre of the Commune as Adolfo in Paër's 'Camilla.' This was his first and only step in the career of a dramatic singer, but it must have been often difficult to resist taking it up again, when he saw singers receiving a thousand ducats for appearing in operas which he both composed and conducted for fifty.

Thus at the age of thirteen Rossini was a sufficiently good singer to be well received at the theatre ; he also played the horn by his father's

GIOACCHINO ANTONIO ROSSINI

side, and had a fair reputation as accompanist. At this time he acquired a valuable friend in the Chevalier Giusti, commanding engineer at Bologna, who took a great affection for the lad, read and explained the Italian poets to him, and opened his fresh and intelligent mind to the comprehension of the ideal ; and it was to the efforts of this distinguished man that he owed the start of his genius, and such general knowledge as he afterwards possessed. After three years with Tesei he put himself under a veteran tenor named Babbini to improve his singing. Shortly after this his voice broke, at the end of the autumn of 1806, during a tournée in which he accompanied his father as chorus-master and *maestro al cembalo*, an engagement in which the daily income of the two amounted to 11 pauls, about equal to 4 shillings. The loss of his voice cost him his engagements in church ; but it gave him the opportunity of entering the Conservatorio, or Liceo communale, of Bologna. On March 20, 1807, he was admitted to the counterpoint class of Padre Mattei, and soon after to that of Cavedagni for the violoncello. He little anticipated when he took his first lesson that his name would one day be inscribed over the entrance to the Liceo.

His progress was rapid, and he was soon able to take his part in Haydn's quartets ; but his counterpoint lessons were a trouble to him from the first. Before he entered Mattei's class he had composed a variety of things—little pieces for two horns, songs for Zambini, and even an opera, called 'Demetrio,' for his friends the Mombellis. Unfortunately Mattei was a pedant, who could see no reason for modifying his usual slow mechanical system to suit the convenience of a scholar, however able or advanced. His one answer to his pupil's inquiry as to the reason of a change or a progression was, 'It is the rule.' The result was that after a few months of discouraging labour Gioacchino began to look to instinct and practice for the philosophy, or at least the rhetoric of this art. The actual parting is the subject of an anecdote which is not improbably true. Mattei was explaining that the amount of counterpoint which his pupil had already acquired was sufficient for a composer in the 'free style' ; but that for church-music much severer studies were required. 'What,' cried the boy, 'do you mean that I know enough to write operas ?' 'Certainly,' was the reply. 'Then I want nothing more, for operas are all that I desire to write.' There was in this something of the practical wisdom which distinguished the Rossini of later life. Meantime it was necessary that he and his parents should live, and he therefore dropped counterpoint and returned to his old trade of accompanist, gave lessons, and conducted performances of chamber-music. He was even bold enough to lead an orchestra, and took the direction of the 'Accademia dei Concordi' of Bologna. There is no reason to doubt that it was more by scoring the quartets and symphonies of Haydn and Mozart than by any lessons of Padre Mattei's that Rossini learned the secrets and the magic of the orchestra. His fame at the Liceo increased day by day, and at the end of his first year his cantata 'Il Pianto d'armonia per la morte d'Orfeo' was not only rewarded with the prize, but was performed in public, August 8, 1808. He was then in his seventeenth year. The cantata was followed, not by a symphony, as is sometimes said, but by an overture in the fugued style, in imitation of that to 'Die Zauberflöte,' but so weak, that after hearing it played he lost no time in destroying it. The same fate probably attended some pieces for double bass and strings, and a mass, both written at the instance of an amateur of the double bass. Rossini had hitherto been known at Bologna as 'il Tedeschino'—'the little German'—for his devotion to Mozart ; but such serious efforts as composing a mass, and conducting a work like Haydn's 'Seasons' were probably intended as hints that he wished to be looked upon no longer as a scholar, but as a master waiting his opportunity for the stage.

It may be easier to enter on a career in Italy than elsewhere, but even there it is not without its difficulties. Rossini by his wit and gaiety had, in one of his tours, made a friend of the Marquis Cavalli, who had promised him his interest whenever it should be wanted. The time was now come to claim the fulfilment of the promise, and Rossini's delight may be imagined when he received an invitation to compose an opera, from the manager of the San Mosè theatre at Venice. He hastened to prepare the piece, and 'La Cambiale di Matrimonio' or the 'Matrimonial Market' was produced there in the autumn of 1810. The piece was an opera buffa in one act ; it was supported by Morandi, Ricci, De Grecis, and Raffanelli, and had a most encouraging reception. After this feat he returned to Bologna, and there composed for Esther Mombelli's benefit a cantata called 'Didone abbandonata.' In 1811 he wrote for the Teatro del Corso of Bologna an opera buffa in two acts, 'L' Equivoco stravagante,' which closed the season with success, and in which both he and Marcolini the contralto were highly applauded.

'Demetrio e Polibio' was brought out at the Teatro Valle, by his old friends the Mombellis, in 1811. Early in 1812 he produced, at the San Mosé theatre, Venice, two buffa operas — 'L' Inganno felice,' and 'L' Occasione fa il Ladro, ossia il Cambio della valigia.' The first of these, a *Farsa*, a trifle in one act, was well sung and much applauded, especially an air of Galli's, 'Una voce,' a duet for the two basses, and a trio full of force and original melody. After the Carnival he went to Ferrara, and there composed an oratorio, 'Ciro in Babilonia,' which was brought out during Lent, and proved a fiasco. [It was performed as ' Cyrus in Babylon' at Drury Lane Theatre (Lent Oratorios), Jan. 30, 1823, under Sir George Smart.] Another failure was ' La Scala di Seta,' an opera buffa in one act, produced at Venice in the course of the spring. While the Mombellis were engaged on his serious opera, he flew off to Milan to fulfil an engagement which Marcolini had procured for him, by writing, for her, Galli, Bonoldi, and Parlamagni, a comic piece in two acts called ' La Pietra del Paragone,' which was produced at the Scala during the autumn of 1812, with immense success. It was his first appearance at this renowned house, and the piece is under-lined in the list as ' musica nuova di Gioacchino Rossini, di Pesaro.' The numbers most ap-plauded were a cavatina, ' Ecco pietosa,' a quartet in the second act, the duel-trio, and a finale in which the word ' Sigillara' recurs continually with very comic effect. This finale is memorable as the first occasion of his employ-ing the crescendo, which he was ultimately to use and abuse so copiously. Mosca has accused Rossini of having borrowed this famous effect from his ' Pretendenti delusi,' produced at the Scala the preceding autumn, forgetting that Mosca himself had learned it from Generali and other composers. Such accusations, however, were of little or no importance to Rossini, who had already made up his mind to adopt what-ever pleased him, wheresoever he might find it. In the meantime he took advantage of his success to pass a few days at Bologna with his parents, en route for Venice ; and thus ended the year 1812, in which he had produced no less than six pieces for the theatre.

Nor was 1813 less prolific. It began with a terrible mystification. He had accepted a com-mission of 500 francs for a serious opera for the Grand Theatre at Venice, but the manager of San Mosè, furious at his desertion, in pursuance of some former agreement, forced on him a libretto for that theatre, ' I due Bruschini, o il figlio per azzardo,' which, if treated as intended, would inevitably have been the death of the music. From this dilemma Rossini ingeniously extricated himself by reversing the situations, and introducing all kinds of tricks. The second violins mark each bar in the overture by a stroke of the bow on the lamp shade ; the bass sings at the top of his register and the soprano at the bottom of hers ; a funeral march intrudes itself into one of the most comical scenes ; and in the finale the words ' son pentito' are so arranged that nothing is heard but ' tito, tito, tito.' Those of the audience who had been taken into the secret were in roars of laughter, but the strangers who had paid for their places in good faith, were naturally annoyed, and hissed loudly. But no complaints were of any avail with Rossini, he only laughed at the success of his joke. ' I due Bruschini' dis-

appeared after the first night, and the remem-brance of it was very shortly wiped out by the appearance of ' Tancredi' at the Fenice during the Carnival. The characters were taken by Manfredini, Malanotte, Todran, and Bianchi. A work so important and so full of spirit, effect, and melody, was naturally received with enthusiasm, and nobody had time to notice various plagiarisms from Paisiello and Paër. It was in fact the first step in the revolution which Rossini was destined to effect in Italian opera. All Venice, and very soon all Italy, was singing or humming ' Mi rivedrai, ti rivedrò.' Hardly any one now remembers that it is only to the happy accident that Malanotte was dissatisfied with her air, and insisted on its being rewritten, that we owe the ' Di tanti palpiti,' which was nicknamed the ' aria de' rizzi,' because it was said to have been dashed off while waiting for a dish of rice. One must read the accounts of the day to understand the madness—for it was nothing else—which ' Tancredi' excited among the Venetians. ' I fancied,' said Rossini, with his usual gaiety, ' that after hearing my opera they would put me into a mad-house—on the contrary, they were madder than I.'

Henceforward he was as much fêted for his social qualities as for his music. But he did not give way to such dissipations for long. His next work was ' L' Italiana in Algeri,' an opera buffa produced at the San Benedetto theatre, Venice, in the summer of 1813. Its greatest novelty was the famous trio 'Papataci,' a charm-ing union of melody and genuine comedy ; while the patriotic air, ' Pensa alla Patria,' which closes the work, spoke not less powerfully to the hearts of his countrymen.

' Aureliano in Palmira' and ' Il Turco in Italia' were both brought out at the Scala, Milan, the first in Dec. 1813, the second in August 1814, before an audience somewhat more critical than that at Venice. ' Aureliano,' though it contains some fine things, which were afterwards utilised in ' Elisabetta' and the ' Barbiere,' was a fiasco. The ' Turco,' too, was not received with the applause which it afterwards commanded. Rossini, however, was greatly fêted during his stay in Milan, and among his ' amiable protec-tresses'—to use the expression of Stendhal—was the Princess Belgiojoso, for whom he com-posed a cantata entitled ' Egle ed Irene.' His next opera, 'Sigismondo,' written for the Fenice at Venice, in the Carnival of 1815, was unsuc-cessful, and the failure so far affected him as to make him give up work for a time, and retire to his home at Bologna. There he encountered Barbaja, who from being a waiter at a coffee-house had become the farmer of the public gaming-tables and impresario of the Naples theatre. Barbaja, though rich, was still bent on making money ; he had heard of the success of the young composer, and of his brilliant talents, and was resolved to get hold of him ;

and Rossini, with the support of his parents on his hands, was ready enough to listen to any good proposal. He accordingly engaged with Barbaja to take the musical direction of the San Carlo and Del Fondo theatres at Naples, and to compose annually an opera for each. For this he was to receive 200 ducats (about £35) per month, with a small share in the gaming-tables, amounting in addition to some 1000 ducats per annum, for which, however, he obtained no compensation after the tables were abolished in 1820.

During Murat's visit to Bologna in April 1815 Rossini composed a cantata in favour of Italian independence ; but politics were not his line, and he arrived in Naples fully conscious of this, and resolved that nothing should induce him to repeat the experiment. The arrival of a young composer with so great a reputation for originality was not altogether pleasing to Zingarelli, the chief of the Conservatorio, or to the aged Paisiello. But no intrigues could prevent the brilliant success of 'Elisabetta, regina d' Inghilterra,' which was produced before the Court for the opening of the autumn season, 1815, and in which Mlle. Colbran, Dardanelli, Manuel Garcia, and Nozzari took the principal parts. The libretto of this opera was by a certain Schmidt, and it is a curious fact that some of its incidents anticipate those of 'Kenilworth,' which was not published till January 1821. Two historical facts should be noted in regard to 'Elisabetta.' It is the first opera in which Rossini so far distrusted his singers as to write in the ornaments of the airs ; and it is also the first in which he replaced the *recitativo secco* by a recitative accompanied by the string quartet. The overture and the finale to the first act of 'Elisabetta' are taken from 'Aureliano.'

Shortly before Christmas Rossini left Naples for Rome to write and bring out two works for which he was under engagement. The first of these, 'Torvaldo e Dorliska,' produced at the Teatro Valle, Dec. 26, 1815, was coldly received, but the second, 'Almaviva, ossia l' inutile precauzione,' founded on Beaumarchais' 'Barbier de Séville,' by Sterbini, which made its first appearance at the Argentina, Feb. 5, 1816, was unmistakably damned. The cause of this was the predilection of the Romans for Paisiello, and their determination to make an example of an innovator who had dared to reset a libretto already treated by their old favourite. Rossini, with excellent taste and feeling, had inquired of Paisiello, before adopting the subject, whether doing so would annoy the veteran, whose 'Barbiere' had been for a quarter of a century the favourite of Europe, and not unnaturally believed that after this step he was secure from the ill-will of Paisiello's friends and admirers.[1] But

[1] We have Rossini's own authority for this, and for the opera having been written in thirteen days, in his letter to M. Scitivaux. See *Musical World*, Nov. 6, 1875, p. 751.

the verdict of a theatre crammed with partisans is seldom just. It is also as changeable as the winds, or as Fortune herself. Though hissed on the first night, 'Almaviva' was listened to with patience on the second, advanced in favour night by night, and ended by becoming, under the title of 'Il Barbiere di Siviglia,' one of the most popular comic operas ever composed, and actually eclipsing in spirit and wit the comedy on which it is founded. It was acted by Giorgi-Righetti (Rosina), Rossi (Berta), Zamboni (Figaro), Garcia (Almaviva), Botticelli (Bartolo) and Vitarelli (Basilio). The original overture was lost, and the present one belongs to 'Elisabetta' ; the opening of the cavatina 'Ecco ridente' is borrowed from the opening of the first chorus in 'Aureliano.' The air of Berta, 'Il vecchietto cerca moglie,' was suggested by a Russian tune, and the eight opening bars of the trio 'Zitti, zitti' are notoriously taken note for note from Simon's air in Haydn's 'Seasons.' Indeed it is astonishing that, with his extraordinary memory, his carelessness, and his habitual hurry, Rossini should not have borrowed oftener than he did. He received 400 scudi (£80) for the 'Barbiere,' and it was composed and mounted in a month. When some one told Donizetti that it had been written in thirteen days, 'Very possible,' was his answer, '*he is so lazy.*'

Lazy as he was, Rossini was destined to write twenty operas in eight years, 1815-23. On his return to Naples after the Carnival of 1816, and the gradual success of the 'Barbiere,' he found the San Carlo theatre in ashes. Barbaja undertook to rebuild it more magnificently than before in nine months. He kept his word, and thus acquired not only the protection but the favour of the king. Rossini obtained the same boon by composing a grand cantata entitled 'Teti e Peleo' for the marriage of the Duchesse de Berry. No sooner had he completed this than he dashed off a two-act comic opera entitled 'La Gazzetta' to a libretto by Tottola, which was produced at the Teatro dei Fiorentini, Naples, and which, although in the hands of a clever and charming actress like Chambrand, and of two such public favourites as Pellegrini and Casaccia, was but moderately successful. Rossini completed his reform of serious opera by his 'Otello,' which was brought out at the Teatro del Fondo, Naples, Dec. 4, 1816, with Isabella Colbran, Nozzari, Davide, Cicimarra, and Benedetti as its interpreters. Some of the most remarkable features of this work, such as the finale of the first act, the duet 'Non m'inganno,' and the passionate trio of defiance, were not at first appreciated : the touching air of Desdemona, 'Se il padre,' and the romance of the Willow, with harp accompaniment, were better received ; but the tragic termination of the whole was very distasteful to the public, and when the opera was taken to Rome, it was found necessary to invent a happy conclusion, a fact which throws a curious light on the dramatic taste of the period.

The machinery, and power of rapidly changing the scenes, were at that time so very imperfect in smaller Italian theatres, that Rossini would only accept the subject of Cinderella when proposed to him by the manager of the Teatro Valle at Rome, on condition that the supernatural element was entirely omitted. A new comic piece was therefore written by Ferretti under the title of 'Cenerentola, ossia la bontà in trionfo'; Rossini undertook it, and it was produced at the Carnival of 1817. Its success was unmistakable, though the cast was by no means extraordinary—Giorgi, Catarina, Rossi, Guglielmi, De Begnis, Verni, and Vitarelli.

In the profusion and charm of its ideas this delicious work is probably equal to the 'Barbiere,' but it is inferior in unity of style. No doubt this is partly owing to the fact that many of the pieces were originally composed to other words than those to which they are now sung. The duet 'Un soave non sò chè,' the drinking-chorus, and the mock proclamation of the Baron, are all borrowed from 'La Pietra del Paragone'; the air 'Miei rampolli' is from 'La Gazzetta,' where it was inspired by the words 'Una prima ballerina'; the air of Ramiro recalls that to 'Ah! vieni' in the trio in 'Otello'; the delightful stretto of the finale, the duet 'Zitto, zitto,' the sestet 'Quest' è un nodo avvilupato,' and various other incidental passages originally belonged to the 'Turco in Italia'; and the humorous duet 'Un segreto' is evidently modelled on that in Cimarosa's 'Matrimonio.' Such repetitions answered their purpose at the moment, but while thus extemporising his operas Rossini forgot that a day would arrive when they would all be published, and when such discoveries as those we have mentioned, and as the existence of the principal motif of the duet of the letter in 'Otello' in the agitato of an air from 'Torvaldo e Dorliska,' would inevitably be made. As he himself confessed in a letter about this time, he thought he had a perfect right to rescue any of his earlier airs from operas which had either failed at the time or become forgotten since. Whatever force there may be in this defence, the fact remains that 'Cenerentola' and the 'Barbiere' share between them the glory of being Rossini's chefs d'œuvre in comic opera.

From Rome he went to Milan, to enjoy the triumph of the 'Gazza ladra'—libretto by Gherardini,—which was brought out on May 31, 1817, at the Scala. The Milanese found no difference between the really fine parts of the opera and those which are mere padding—of which the 'Gazza ladra' has several. Nor would any one have noticed, even had they had the necessary knowledge, that in the first duet and the finale—as was the case also in the

finale to the 'Cenerentola'—Rossini had borrowed an effect from the Poco adagio of Mozart's Symphony in C (Köchel, p. 425) by maintaining a sustained accompaniment in the wind while the strings and the voices carry on the ideas and the ornaments.

From Milan he returned to Naples, and produced 'Armida' during the autumn season, a grand opera in three acts, with ballet, which was mounted with great splendour, and enjoyed the advantage of very good singers. The duet 'Amor, possente Nume!'—which was soon to be sung through the length and breadth of Italy, the air 'Non soffiro l' offensa,' the incantation scene, the chorus of demons, and the airs de ballet, would alone have been sufficient to excite the Neapolitans; but these were not the only pieces applauded, and the remarkable trio 'In quale aspetto imbelle,' written for three tenors with extraordinary ease, a pretty chorus of women 'Qui tutto è calma,' and a scena with chorus 'Germano a te richiede'—afterwards employed in the French version of 'Moïse'—all deserve mention.

This fine work had hardly made its appearance before Rossini had to dash off two more— 'Adelaide di Borgogna,' sometimes known as 'Ottone Rè d' Italia,' and an oratorio—'Mosè in Egitto.' 'Adelaide' was produced at the Argentina at Rome, in the Carnival of 1818, was well sung and warmly received. 'Mosè' was written for the San Carlo at Naples, and brought out there in Lent with an excellent cast—Isabella Colbran, Benedetti, Porto, and Nozzari. Here for the first time Rossini was so much pressed as to be compelled to call in assistance, and employed his old and tried friend Carafa in the recitatives and in Pharaoh's air 'Aspettar mi.'[1] The scene of the darkness was another step onwards, and the whole work was much applauded, with the exception of the passage of the Red Sea, the representation of which was always laughed at, owing to the imperfection of the theatrical appliances already spoken of. At the resumption of the piece, therefore, in the following Lent, Rossini added a chorus to divert attention from the wretched attempt to represent the dividing waves, and it is to the sins of the Neapolitan stage machinists that we owe the popular prayer 'Dal tuo stellato soglio.'

As some relaxation after this serious effort he undertook, in the summer of 1818, a one-act piece 'Adina, o il Califfo di Bagdad,' for the San Carlos Theatre, Lisbon; and immediately after, 'Ricciardo e Zoraide' for San Carlo, Naples, which was sung to perfection at the autumn season there by Isabella Colbran, Pisaroni (whose excessive plainness was no bar to her splendid singing), Nozzari, Davide, and Cicimarra.

'Ricciardo' was extraordinarily full of orna-

[1] Omitted in the Italian score published in Paris.

ment, but 'Ermione,' which was produced at San Carlo in the Lent of 1819, went quite in the opposite direction, and affected an unusual plainness and severity. Though splendidly sung, 'Ermione' did not please, and the single number applauded was the one air in which there was any ornamentation. So much for the taste of Naples in 1819 ! An equally poor reception was given to a cantata written for the re-establishment of the health of the King of Naples, and sung at the San Carlo, Feb. 20, 1819. It consisted of a cavatina for Isabella Colbran, and an air with variations, which was afterwards utilised in the ballet of the 'Viaggio a Reims.' The piece was hastily thrown off, and was probably of no more value in the eyes of its author than was an opera called 'Edoardo e Cristina' which was brought out at the San Benedetto, Venice, this same spring, and was in reality a mere pasticcio of pieces from 'Ermione,' 'Ricciardo,' and other operas, hitherto unheard in Venice, attached to a libretto imitated from Scribe. Fortunately the opera pleased the audience, and sent Rossini back to Naples in good spirits, ready to compose a new cantata for the visit of the Emperor of Austria. The new work was performed on May 9, 1819, at the San Carlo, and was sung by Colbran, Davide, and Rubini, to the accompaniment of a military band. This Rossini probably accepted as a useful experience for his next new opera, the 'Donna del Lago,' in the march of which we hear the results of his experiments in writing for a wind band. Even at the present day the first act of the opera is well worthy of admiration, and yet the evening of Oct. 4, 1819, when it was first given, with the magnificent cast of Colbran, Pisaroni, Nozzari, Davide, and Benedetti, was simply one long torture of disappointment to the composer. who was possibly not aware that the storm of disapprobation was directed not against him so much as against Barbaja the manager, and Colbran his favourite.

On the following evening the hisses became *bravos*, but of this Rossini knew nothing, as by that time he was on his road to Milan. The Scala opened on Dec. 26, 1819, for the Carnival season with 'Bianca e Faliero,' libretto by Romani, which was admirably sung by Camporese and others. No trace of it, however, now remains except a duet and quartet, which were afterwards introduced in the 'Donna del Lago,' and became very popular at concerts.

His engagement at Milan over, he hurried back to Naples, to produce the opera of 'Maometto secondo,' before the close of the Carnival. It had been composed in great haste, but was admirably interpreted by Colbran, Chaumel (afterwards Madame Rubini), Nozzari, Cicimarra, Benedetti, and F. Galli, whose Maometto was a splendid success. It was the last opera that Rossini was destined to give at

Naples before the revolt of July 20, 1820, of the Carbonari, under Pepe, which obliged the King to abandon his capital, ruined Barbaja by depriving him at once of a powerful patron and of the monopoly of the gambling-houses, and drove Rossini to make important changes in his life. Having for the moment no engagement for the Scala, he undertook to write 'Matilda di Ciabrano' ('Mathilde di Shabran') for Rome. Torlonia the banker had bought the Teatro Tordinone, and was converting it into the Apollo ; and it was for the inauguration of this splendid new house that Rossini's opera was intended. The opening took place on the first night of the Carnival of 1821. The company, though large, contained no first-rate artists, and Rossini was therefore especially careful of the *ensemble* pieces. The first night was stormy, but Rossini's friends were in the ascendancy, Paganini conducted in splendid style, and the result was a distinct success.

On his return to Naples, Rossini learned from Barbaja his intention of visiting Austria, and taking his company of singers to Vienna. Rossini's next opera, 'Zelmira,' was therefore to be submitted to a more critical audience than those of Italy, and with this in view he applied himself to make the recitatives interesting, the harmonies full and varied, and the accompaniments expressive and full of colour, and to throw as much variety as possible into the form of the movements. He produced the opera at the San Carlo before leaving, in the middle of December 1821. It was sung by Colbran, Cecconi, Davide, Nozzari, Ambrosi, and Benedetti, and was enthusiastically received. On the 27th of the same month, he took his benefit, for which he had composed a special cantata entitled 'La Riconoscenza' ; and the day after left for the North. He was accompanied by Isabella Colbran, with whom he had been in love for years, whose influence over him had been so great as to make him forsake comedy for tragedy, and to whom he was married on his arrival at Bologna. The wedding took place in the chapel of the Archbishop's palace, and was celebrated by Cardinal Opizzoni. Rossini has been accused of marrying for money, and it is certain that Colbran had a villa and £500 a year of her own, that she was seven years older than her husband, and that her reputation as a singer was on the decline.

After a month's holiday, the couple started for Vienna, where they arrived about the end of February 1822. He seems to have made his début before the Vienna public on March 30, as the conductor of his 'Cenerentola,' in the German version, as 'Aschenbrödel,' and his *tempi* were found somewhat too fast for the 'heavy German language.' 'Zelmira' was given at the Kärnthnerthor opera-house on April 13, with a success equal to that which it obtained at Naples. Rossini was not without violent opponents in Vienna, but they gave him no anxiety, friends and enemies alike were received with a smile, and his only retort was a good-humoured joke. He is said to have visited Beethoven, and to have been much distressed by the condition in which he found the great master. The impression which he made on the Viennese may be gathered from a paragraph in the Leipzig *Allgemeine musik. Zeitung*[1] of the day, in which he is described as 'highly accomplished, of agreeable manners and pleasant appearance, full of wit and fun, cheerful, obliging, courteous, and most accessible. He is much in society, and charms every one by his simple, unassuming style.' After the close of the Vienna season, the Rossinis returned to Bologna, where his parents had resided since 1798. There, at the end of September, he received a flattering invitation from Prince Metternich, entreating him to come to Verona, and he accordingly arrived at the Congress in time for its opening, Oct. 20, 1822. Rossini's contribution to the Congress was a series of cantatas, which he poured forth without stint or difficulty. The best known of these is 'Il vero Omaggio'; others are 'L' Augurio felice,' 'La sacra Alleanza,' and 'Il Bardo.'

The Congress at an end, he began to work at 'Semiramide,' which was brought out at the Fenice, Venice, Feb. 3, 1823, with Madame Rossini, the two Marianis, Galli, and Sinclair the English tenor, for whom there were two airs. The opera was probably written with more care than any of those which had preceded it; and possibly for this very reason was somewhat coldly received. The subject no doubt would seem sombre to the gay Venetians, and they even omitted to applaud the fine quartet (which Verdi must surely have had in his mind when writing the Miserere in the 'Trovatore'), the finale, and the appearance of Ninus, the final trio, at once so short and so dramatic, the cavatina with chorus, and all the other new, bold, bright passages of that remarkable work. Rossini was not unnaturally much disappointed at the result of his labour and genius, and resolved to write no more for the theatres of his native country. The resolution was hardly formed when he received a visit from the manager of the King's Theatre, London (Sigr. Benelli), and a proposal to write an opera for that house, to be called 'La Figlia dell' aria,' for the sum of £240—£40 more than he had received for 'Semiramide,' a sum at the time considered enormous. The offer was promptly accepted, and the Rossinis started for England without delay, naturally taking Paris in their road, and reaching it Nov. 9, 1823. Paris, like Vienna, was then divided into two hostile camps on the subject of the great composer. Berton always spoke of him as 'M. Crescendo,' and he was caricatured on the stage as 'M. Vacar-

mini'; but the author of the 'Barbiere' could afford to laugh at such satire, and his respectful behaviour to Cherubini, Lesueur, and Reicha, as the heads of the Conservatoire, his graceful reception of the leaders of the French School, his imperturbable good temper and good spirits, soon conciliated every one. A serenade, a public banquet, triumphant receptions at the opera-house, a special vaudeville ('Rossini à Paris, ou le Grand Dîner')—everything in short that could soothe the pride of a stranger was lavished upon him from the first. He in his turn was always kind and amiable, consenting, for instance, at the request of Panseron—an old colleague at Rome—to act as accompanist at a concert with the object of saving Panseron's brother from the conscription. Under the hands of Rossini the piano became as effective as an orchestra; and it is on record that the first time that Auber heard him accompany himself in a song he walked up to the instrument and bent down over the keys to see if they were not smoking. Paris, however, was not at present his ultimate goal, and on Dec. 13, 1823, Rossini and his wife arrived in London. They were visited immediately by the Russian ambassador, M. de Lieven, who gave the composer barely time to recover from the fatigues of the journey before he carried him off to Brighton and presented him to the King. George IV. believed himself to be fond of music, and received the author of the 'Barbiere' in the most flattering manner. 'Zelmira' was brought out at the Opera on Jan. 24, 1824; and the royal favour naturally brought with it that of the aristocracy, and a solid result in the shape of two grand concerts at Almack's, at two guineas admission. The singers on these occasions were Mme. Rossini, Mme. Catalani, Mme. Pasta, and other first-rate artists, but the novelty, *the* attraction, was to hear Rossini himself sing the solos[2] in a cantata (or 'ottavino') which he had composed for the occasion, under the title of 'Il Pianto delle Muse in Morte di Lord Byron.' He also took part with Catalani in a duet from Cimarosa's 'Matrimonio' which was so successful as to be encored three times. He appeared at the so-called 'Cambridge Festival' again with Catalani, in July 1824. The opera manager was unable to finish the season, and became bankrupt before discharging his engagements with Rossini. Nor was this all. Not only did he not produce the 'Figlia dell' aria,' but the music of the first act unaccountably vanished, and has never since been found. It was in vain for Rossini to sue the manager; he failed to obtain either his MS. or a single penny of the advantages guaranteed to him by the contract. True, he enjoyed a considerable set-off to the loss just mentioned in the profits of the countless soirées at which he acted as accompanist at a fee of £50. At

[1] May 8, 1822, reporting the early part of March.

[2] This recalls the visit of a great composer in 1746, when Gluck gave a concert at the King's Theatre, at which the great attraction was his solo on the musical glasses! [See vol. ii. p. 1835.]

the end of five months he found himself in possession of £7000 ; and just before his departure was honoured by receiving the marked compliments of the king at a concert at the Duke of Wellington's, for which His Majesty had expressly come up from Brighton. [See *Musical Times*, 1900, pp. 18 ff.]

In leaving England on July 26, after so hearty and profitable a reception, Rossini was not taking a leap in the dark ; for through the Prince de Polignac, French ambassador in England, he had already concluded an agreement for the musical direction of the Théâtre Italien, Paris, for eighteen months at a salary of £800 per annum. In order to be near his work he took a lodging at No. 28 Rue Taitbout, and at once set about getting younger singers in his company. Knowing that Paër was his enemy, and would take any opportunity of injuring him, he was careful to retain him in his old post of *maestro al cembalo* ; but at the same time he engaged Hérold (then a young man of twenty-five) as chorus-master, and as a check on the pretensions of Madame Pasta he brought to Paris Esther Mombelli, Schiassetti, Donzelli, and Rubini, successively. To those who sneered at his music he replied by playing it as it was written, and by bringing out some of his operas which had not yet made their appearance in Paris, such as ' La Donna del Lago ' (Sept. 7, 1824), 'Semiramide' (Dec. 8, 1825), and ' Zelmira ' (March 14, 1826). And he gave much éclat to his direction by introducing Meyerbeer's ' Crociato '—the first work of Meyerbeer's heard in Paris—and by composing a new opera, ' Il Viaggio a Reims, ossia l' Albergo del giglio d' oro,' which he produced on June 19, 1825, during the fêtes at the coronation of Charles X. The new work is in one act, and three parts ; it is written for fourteen voices, which are treated with marvellous art. It was sung by Mmes. Pasta, Schiassetti, Mombelli, Cinti, Amigo, Dotti, and Rossi ; and by MM. Levasseur, Zucchelli, Pellegrini, Graziani, Auletta, Donzelli, Bordogni, and Scudo—a truly magnificent assemblage. In the ballet he introduced an air with variations for two clarinets, borrowed from his Naples cantata of 1819, and played by Gambaro (a passionate admirer of his) and by F. Berr. In the hunting scene he brought in a delicious fanfare of horns, and the piece winds up with ' God save the King,' ' Vive Henri Quatre,' and other national airs, all newly harmonised and accompanied. After the Revolution of 1848 the words were suitably modified by H. Dupin, and the piece appeared in two acts at the Théâtre Italien as ' Andremo noi a Parigi,' on Oct. 26 of that year.[1]

After the expiration of Rossini's agreement

as director of the Théâtre Italien, it was a happy idea of the Intendant of the Civil List to confer upon him the sinecure posts of ' Premier Compositeur du Roi ' and ' Inspecteur Général du Chant en France,' with an annual income of 20,000 francs, possibly in the hope that he might settle permanently at Paris, and in time write operas expressly for the French stage. This was also an act of justice, since in the then absence of any law of international [2] copyright his pieces were public property, and at the disposal not only of a translator like Castil-Blaze, but of any manager or publisher in the length and breadth of France who chose to avail himself of them. Fortunately the step was justified by the event. The opera of ' Maometto '—originally written by the Duke of Ventagnano, and produced at Naples in 1820 —had never been heard in France. Rossini employed MM. Soumet and Balocchi to give the libretto a French dress ; he revised the music, and considerably extended it ; and on Oct. 9, 1826, the opera was produced at the Académie as ' Le Siége de Corinthe,' with a cast which included Nourrit and Mlle. Cinti, and with great success. For the new opera Rossini received 6000 francs from Troupenas.

After this feat Rossini turned to another of his earlier works, as not only sure of success but eminently suited to the vast space and splendid *mise en scène* of the Grand Opéra. This was ' Mosè.' He put the revision of the libretto into the hands of Etienne Jouy and Balocchi, and arranged for Cinti, Nourrit, and Levasseur to be in the cast. ' Moïse ' was produced March 25, 1827, and created a profound impression. True, it had been heard in its original form at the Italiens five years before, but the recollection of this only served to bring out more strongly the many improvements and additions in the new version—such as the Introduction to the first act ; the quartet and chorus ; the chorus ' La douce Aurore ' ; the march and chorus, etc. The airs de ballet were largely borrowed from ' Armida' (1817) and ' Ciro in Babilonia' (1812). This magnificent work gave Rossini a sort of imperial position in Paris. But it was necessary to justify this, and he therefore resolved to try a work of a different character, and according to the axiom of Boileau, to pass

From grave to gay, from lively to severe—

not in the direction of comic but of lyric opera. With this view he employed Scribe and Poirson to develop a vaudeville which they had written in 1816 to the old legend of ' Le Comte Ory,' adapting to that lively piece some of his favourite music in the ' Viaggio a Reims,'—the introduction and finale of the first act, the duet of the Count and Countess, and the famous narrative of Raimbaut when he brings up the

---

[1] The score of ' Andremo noi a Parigi ' is in the Library of the Conservatoire, but the finale of the ' Viaggio,' which we have mentioned as containing national airs, is not there, and all trace of this curious feat seems to have vanished.

[2] The custom in Italy in those days was to sell an opera to a manager for two years, with exclusive right of representation ; after that it became public property. The only person who derived no profit from this arrangement was the unfortunate composer.

wine from the cellar, which it is difficult to believe was in its first form applied to the taking of the Trocadéro! Adolphe Nourrit, who was not only a great artist, but a poet of very considerable dramatic power, was privately of much assistance to Rossini in the adaptation of his old music to the new words, and in the actual mounting of the piece in which he was to take so important a share. 'Le Comte Ory' was produced at the Académie, August 20, 1828, and the principal characters were taken by Mme. Damoreau-Cinti, Mlles. Jawurek and Mori, Adolphe Nourrit, Levasseur, and Dabadie. The Introduction is based on the old song which gives its name to the piece. The best thing in the second act is borrowed from the *Allegretto scherzando* of Beethoven's Eighth Symphony. Rossini was at that time actually engaged with Habeneck, the founder of the Concerts of the Conservatoire, and his intimate friend, in studying the Symphonies of Beethoven; and it is easy to understand how impossible it must have been to forget the fresh and graceful movement referred to.

The study of Beethoven was at any rate not a bad preparation for the very serious piece of work which was next to engage him, and for a great portion of which he retired to the château of his friend Aguado the banker at Petit-Bourg. Schiller had recently been brought into notice in France by the translation of M. de Barante; and Rossini, partly attracted by the grandeur of the subject, partly inspired by the liberal ideas at that moment floating through Europe, was induced to choose the Liberator of the Swiss Cantons as his next subject. He accepted a libretto offered him by Etienne Jouy, Spontini's old librettist, who in this case was associated with Hippolyte Bis. Their words, however, were so unmusical and unrhythmical, that Rossini had recourse to Armand Marrast, at that time Aguado's secretary, and the whole scene of the meeting of the conspirators—one of the best in operatic literature, and the only thoroughly satisfactory part of the book of 'Guillaume Tell'—was rewritten by him, a fact which we are glad to make public in these pages.

This grand opera, undoubtedly Rossini's masterpiece, was produced at the Académie on August 3, 1829, with the following cast:— Arnold, Nourrit; Walter Fürst, Levasseur; Tell, Dabadie; Ruodi, A. Dupont; Rodolphe, Massol; Gessler, Prévost; Leutold, Prévôt; Mathilde, Damoreau-Cinti; Jemmy, Dabadie; Hedwige, Mori.

'Tell' has now become a study for the musician, from the first bar of the overture to the storm scene and the final hymn of freedom. The overture is no longer, like Rossini's former ones, a piece of work on a familiar, well-worn pattern, but a true instrumental prelude, which would be simply perfect if the opening and the

fiery peroration were only as appropriate to the subject as they are tempting to the executant. We find no absurdities like those in 'Moïse'— no song of thanksgiving accompanied by a brilliant polonaise, no more cabalettas, no more commonplace phrases or worn-out modulations— in short, no more padding of any kind. True, it would not be difficult to criticise the length of the duet in the second act, which recalls the duet in 'Semiramide,' and breathes rather the concert-room than the stage—or the style of the finale of the third act, which is not appropriate to the situation.

The spectacle of a great master at the zenith of his glory and in the very prime of life thus breaking with all the traditions of his genius and appearing as in a second avatar is indeed a rare and noble one. The sacrifice of all the means of effect by which his early popularity had been obtained is one which Rossini shares with Gluck and Weber, but for which our former experience of his character would hardly have prepared us. He seems at length to have discovered how antagonistic such effects were to the simplicity which was really at the base of the great musical revolution effected by him; but to discover, and to act on a discovery, are two different things, and he ought to have full credit for the courage and sincerity with which, at his age, he forsook the flowery plains in which his genius had formerly revelled, for loftier and less accessible heights.

But the career thus splendidly inaugurated was not destined to be pursued; circumstances, political and domestic, stopped him on the threshold. He was anxious to visit once more the city in which his beloved mother died in 1827, and where his father, who had soon tired of Paris, was awaiting him. With this view he resigned his office as inspector of singing in France, and made an arrangement with the Government of Charles X., dating from the beginning of 1829, by which he bound himself for ten years to compose for no other stage but that of France, and to write and bring out an opera every two years, receiving for each such opera the sum of 15,000 francs. In the event of the Government failing to carry out the arrangement he was to receive a retiring pension of 6000 francs. 'Guillaume Tell' was thus to be the first of a series of five operas.

After a serenade from the opera orchestra, Rossini, therefore, left Paris for Bologna. Here he was engaged in considering the subject of 'Faust,' with a view to his next work, when he received the sudden news of the abdication of Charles X., and the revolution of July 1830. The blow shattered his plans and dissipated his fondest hopes. He flattered himself that he had regenerated the art of singing in France. What would become of it again under a king who could tolerate no operas but those of Grétry? Anxious to know if his friend Lubbert was still at the head of the Académie de Musique, and if the new Intendant of the Civil List would acknowledge the engagements of his predecessor, he returned to Paris in Nov. 1830 ; and intending only to make a short stay, took up his quarters in the upper storey of the Théâtre des Italiens, of which his friend Severini was then director. Here, however, he was destined to remain till Nov. 1836. The new Government repudiated the agreement of its predecessor, and Rossini had to carry his claim into the law-courts. Had his law-suit alone occupied him, it would not have been necessary to stay quite so long, for it was decided in his favour in Dec. 1835. But there was another reason for his remaining in Paris, and that was his desire to hear 'The Huguenots' and ascertain how far Meyerbeer's star was likely to eclipse his own. It is impossible to believe that a mere money question could have detained him so long at a time when almost every day must have brought fresh annoyances. After reducing 'Guillaume Tell' from five acts to three, they carried their love of compression so far as to give only one act at a time, as a *lever de rideau*, or accompaniment to the ballet. This was indeed adding insult to injury. ' I hope you won't be annoyed,' said the Director of the Opera to him one day on the boulevard, ' but to-night we play the second act of "Tell."' 'The whole of it?' was the reply. How much bitter disappointment must have been hidden under that reply ! During the whole of this unhappy interval he only once resumed his pen, namely in 1832 for the ' Stabat Mater,' at the request of his friend Aguado, who was anxious to serve the Spanish minister Señor Valera. He composed at that time only the first six numbers, and the other four were supplied by Tadolini. The work was dedicated to Valera, with an express stipulation that it should never leave his hands. In 1834 he allowed Troupenas to publish the ' Soirées musicales,' twelve lovely vocal pieces of very original form and harmony, several of which have still retained their charm.

The rehearsals of 'The Huguenots' lingered on, and it was not till Feb. 29, 1836, that Rossini could hear the work of his new rival. He returned to Bologna shortly after, taking Frankfort in his way, and meeting Mendelssohn.[1] He had not been long in Bologna before he heard of the prodigious success of Duprez in the revival of ' Guillaume Tell ' (April 17). Such a triumph might well have nerved him to fresh exertions. But it came a year too late ; he had already taken an unfortunate and irrevocable resolution never again to break silence. It would be very wrong to conclude from this that he had lost his interest in music. The care which he bestowed on the Liceo of Bologna, of which he was honorary director, shows that the art still exercised all its claims on him. He was especially anxious to improve the singing of the pupils,

and among those who are indebted to his care, Marietta Alboni held the first rank.

Rossini's father died April 29, 1839, and he soon afterwards learned to his disgust that the MS. of the ' Stabat ' had been sold by the heirs of Señor Valera, and acquired by a Paris publisher for 2000 francs. He at once gave Troupenas full power to stop both publication and performance, and at the same time completed the work by composing the last four movements, which, as we have already said, were originally added by Tadolini. The first six movements were produced at the Salle Herz, Paris, Oct. 31, 1841, amidst very great applause. Troupenas[2] bought the entire score for 6000 francs. He sold the right of performance in Paris during three months to the Escudiers for 8000, which they again disposed of to the director of the Théâtre Italien for 20,000. Thus three persons were enriched by this single work. It was performed complete for the first time at the Salle Ventadour, Jan. 7, 1842, by Grisi, Albertazzi, Mario, and Tamburini.

Notwithstanding its brilliant success, some critics were found to accuse the composer of importing the strains of the theatre into the church ; but it must not be forgotten that religion in the South is a very different thing from what it is in the North. Mysticism could have no place in the mind of such a man as Rossini, who would naturally utter his prayers aloud, in the sunshine of noon, rather than breathe them to himself in the gloom and mystery of night. The prayer and the scene of the darkness in ' Moïse,' as well as the first movement and the unaccompanied quartet in the ' Stabat,' will always hold their place as religious music ; and are of themselves sufficient to show that Rossini, sceptic as he was, was not without religious feeling.

But at the very moment that the ' Stabat ' was making its triumphant progress round the world, Rossini began to suffer tortures from the stone, which increased to such an extent as to force him, in May 1843, to Paris, where he underwent an operation which proved perfectly satisfactory. We next find him writing a chorus to words by Marchetti for the anniversary festival of Tasso at Turin, on March 13, 1844. On the 2nd of the following September ' Othello ' was produced in French at the Académie with Duprez, Barroilhet, Levasseur, and Mme. Stoltz. Rossini, however, had nothing to do with this adaptation, and the divertissement was arranged entirely by Benoist from airs in ' Mathilde de Sabran' and 'Armida.' While ' Othello ' was thus on the boards of the opera, Troupenas brought out ' La Foi, l'Espérance et la Charité' (Faith, Hope, and Charity), three choruses for women's voices, the first two composed many years previously for an opera on the subject of

---

[1] See Hiller's *Mendelssohn*, and M.'s own letter, July 14, 1836.

[2] We have mentioned that he paid 6000 francs for the 'Siége de Corinthe.' For 'Moïse' he gave only 2400 ; but, on the other hand, the ' Comte Ory' cost him 12,000, and 'Guillaume Tell' 24,000.

Œdipus. These choruses are hardly worthy of Rossini. They justify Berlioz's sarcasm—'his Hope has deceived ours ; his Faith will never remove mountains ; his Charity will never ruin him.' It is fair to say that Louis Engel, in his book *From Mozart to Mario,* states that Rossini repudiated them. Troupenas also brought out a few songs hitherto unpublished, and these reattracted the attention of the public in some degree to the great composer. His statue was executed in marble[1] by Etex, and was inaugurated at the Académie de Musique, June 9, 1846. A few months later (Dec. 30), by his permission, a pasticcio adapted by Niedermeyer to portions of the 'Donna del Lago,' 'Zelmira,' and 'Armida,' and entitled 'Robert Bruce,' was put on the stage of the Opéra, but it was not successful, and Mme. Stoltz was even hissed. From his seclusion at Bologna Rossini kept a watchful eye upon the movements of the musical world. It would be interesting to know if he regretted having authorised the manufacture of this pasticcio. If we may judge from the very great difficulty with which, some time later, Méry obtained his permission to translate and produce 'Semiramide,' he did. It is certain that during his long residence at Bologna he only broke his vow of silence for the 'Inno popolare a Pio IX.' The commencement of this was adapted to an air from 'La Donna del Lago,' and its peroration was borrowed from 'Robert Bruce,' which gives ground for supposing that he himself was concerned in the arrangement of that opera, and explains his annoyance at its failure.

The political disturbances which agitated the Romagna at the end of 1847 compelled Rossini to leave Bologna. He quitted the town in much irritation. After the death of his wife (Oct. 7, 1845), he married (in 1847) Olympe Pélissier, with whom he had become connected in Paris at a time when she was greatly in public favour, and when she sat to Vernet for his picture of 'Judith and Holofernes.' In fact at this time the great musician had to a great extent disappeared in the voluptuary. From Bologna he removed to Florence, and there it was that this writer visited him in 1852. He lived in the Via Larga, in a house which bore upon its front the words *Ad votum.* In the course of a long conversation he spoke of his works with no pretended indifference, but as being well aware of their worth, and knowing the force and scope of his genius better than any one else. He made no secret of his dislike to the violent antivocal element in modern music, or of the pleasure he would feel when 'the Jews had finished their Sabbath.' It was also evident that he had no affection for the capital of Tuscany, the climate of which did not suit him. At length, in 1855, he crossed the Alps and returned to Paris, never again to leave it. His

[1] It represented him seated in an easy attitude. It was destroyed when the opera-house was burnt down in 1873.

reception there went far to calm the nervous irritability that had tormented him at Florence, and with the homage which he received from Auber and the rest of the French artists his health returned. His house, No. 2 in the Rue Chaussée d'Antin, and, at a later date, his villa at Passy, were crowded by the most illustrious representatives of literature and art, to such an extent that even during his lifetime he seemed to assist at his own apotheosis. Was it then mere idleness which made him thus bury himself in the Capua of his past successes ? No one who, like the present writer, observed him coolly, could be taken in by the comedy of indifference and modesty that it pleased him to keep up. We have already said that, after Meyerbeer's great success, Rossini had taken the resolution of writing no more for the Académie de Musique and keeping silence.

The latter part of this resolution he did not, however, fully maintain. Thus he authorised the production of 'Bruschino' at the Bouffes Parisiens on Dec. 28, 1857, though he would not be present at the first representation. 'I have given my permission,' said he, 'but do not ask me to be an accomplice.' The discovery of the piece—which is nothing else but his early farce of 'Il figlio per azzardo' (Venice, 1813)—was due to Prince Poniatowski, and some clever librettist was found to adapt it to the French taste. A year or two later Méry with difficulty obtained his permission to transform 'Semiramide' into 'Sémiramis,' and the opera in its new garb was produced at the Académie, July 9, 1860, with Carlotta Marchisio as Semiramis, her sister Barbara as Arsace, and Obin as Assur. In this transformation Rossini took no ostensible part. Carafa at his request arranged the recitatives, and wrote the ballet music. These were mere revivals. Not so the sacred work which he brought out at the house of M. Pillet-Will the banker on March 14, 1864, and at the rehearsals of which he presided in person. We allude to the 'Petite messe solennelle,' which though so called with a touch of Rossinian pleasantry is a mass of full dimensions, lasting nearly two hours in performance. Rossini had always been on good terms with the bankers of Paris, and after Rothschild and Aguado he became very intimate with the Count Pillet-Will (1781-1860), a rich amateur, passionately fond of music, who had learned the violin from Baillot, and amused himself with composing little pieces for that instrument. His son, more retiring but not less enthusiastic than his father, had always been one of Rossini's most devoted admirers, and on the occasion of the inauguration of his magnificent house in the Rue Moncey, it was a happy thought of the composer to allow his 'Petite messe solennelle' to be heard there for the first time. This important composition, comprising solos and choruses, was written with the accompaniment of a harmonium and two

pianos. On this occasion it was sung by the two
Marchisios, Gardoni, and Agnesi, and was much
applauded. Rossini afterwards scored it with
slight alterations for the full orchestra—perhaps
a little heavily—and in this shape it was performed for the first time in public at the Théâtre
Italien, on the evening of Sunday Feb. 28, 1869,
on the seventy-eighth anniversary of the composer's birth as nearly as that could be, seeing
that he was born in a leap year, on Feb. 29.

In the last years of his life Rossini affected
the piano, spoke of himself as a fourth-rate
pianist, and composed little else but pianoforte
pieces. Most of these were in some sense or
other *jeux d'esprit* ; some were inscribed to his
parrot, or had the most fanciful titles—' Valse
anti-dansante,' ' Fausse couche de Polka-ma-
zurka,' ' Étude asthmatique,' ' Échantillon de
blague,' etc. The whole were arranged in cases
with such quaint names as 'Album olla podrida,'
' Les quatre mendiants,' ' Quatre hors-d'œuvre,'
' Album de Château,' ' Album de Chaumière,'
etc. For the Exposition universelle of 1867,
however, he wrote a Cantata, which was performed for the first time at the ceremony of
awarding the prizes on July 1, and was also
executed at the Opéra at the free performances
on August 15, 1867 and 1868. It opens with a
hymn in a broad style, in which the author of
' Sémiramis ' and ' Moïse ' is quite recognisable,
but winds up with a vulgar quick-step on a
motif not unlike the country dance known as
' L' Ostendaise.' The title, which we give from
the autograph, seems to show that the son of the
jolly ' trombadore ' of Pesaro was quite aware of
the character of the finale of his last work.

À Napoléon III.
et
à son vaillant Peuple.

Hymne
avec accompagnement d'orchestre et musique militaire
pour baryton (solo), un Pontife,
chœur de Grands Prêtres
chœur de Vivandières, de Soldats, et de Peuple.
A la fin
Danse, Cloches, Tambours et Canons.
Excusez du peu ! !

The final touch is quite enough to show that
Rossini to the last had more gaiety than propriety, more wit than dignity, more love of
independence than good taste. He preferred the
society of artists to any other, and was never so
happy as when giving free scope to his caustic
wit or his Rabelaisian humour. His *bons mots*
were abundant, and it is surprising that no one
has yet attempted to collect them. One or two
may find place here. One day, in a fit of the
spleen, he cried out, ' I am miserable ; my nerves
are wrong, and every one offers me string instead.' D'Ortigue, the author of the *Dictionnaire
liturgique*, had been very severe on him in
an article in the *Correspondant* on ' Musical

royalties,' and an enthusiastic admirer of the
Italian School having replied somewhat angrily,
Rossini wrote to him, ' I am much obliged to
you for your vigorous treatment (*lavement*) of
the tonsure of my friend the Curé d'Ortigue.'
A number of friends were disputing as to which
was his best opera, and appealed to him. ' You
want to know which of my works I like best?
"Don Giovanni" ! ' He took extreme delight
in his summer villa at Passy, which stood in the
Avenue Ingres, and had a fine garden of about
three acres attached to it. In that house he
died on Friday Nov. 13, 1868, at 9 P.M., after
a long day of agony. His funeral was magnificent. As Foreign Associate of the Institute
(1833) ; Grand Officer of the Legion of Honour
(1864), and the orders of St. Maurice and St.
Lazare ; commander of many foreign orders,
and honorary member of a great number of
Academies and musical institutions—Rossini
had a right to every posthumous honour
possible. The funeral took place at the church
of the Trinité on Saturday Nov. 21, it was
gorgeous, and was attended by several deputa-
tions from Italy. Tamburini, Duprez, Gardoni,
Bonnehée, Faure, Capoul, Belval, Obin, Delle
Sedie, Jules Lefort, Agnesi, Alboni, Adelina
Patti, Nilsson, Krauss, Carvalho, Bloch, and
Grossi, with the pupils of the Conservatoire,
sang the Prayer from ' Moïse.' Nilsson gave
a fine movement from the ' Stabat ' of Pergolesi,
but the most impressive part of the ceremony
was the singing of the ' Quis est homo ' from
Rossini's own ' Stabat mater ' by Patti and
Alboni. To hear that beautiful music rendered
by two such voices, and in the presence of such
artists, over the grave of the composer, was to
feel in the truest sense the genius of Rossini,
and the part which he played in the music of
the 19th century.

At the opening of his career Rossini had two
courses before him, either, like Simone Mayr
and Paër, to follow the footsteps of the old
Neapolitan masters, or to endeavour to revolu-
tionise the Italian opera, as Gluck and Mozart
had revolutionised those of France and Germany.
He chose the latter. We have described the
eagerness with which he threw himself into the
path of innovation, and the audacity with which,
while borrowing a trait of harmony or of piquant
modulation from Majo (1740-71) or the
skeleton of an effect from Generali (1783-1832),
he extinguished those from whom he stole,
according to the well-known maxim of Voltaire.
We have already mentioned his innovations in
the accompaniment of the recitatives, first, in
' Elisabetta,' the full quartet of strings, and
next in ' Otello ' the occasional addition of the
wind instruments. This was a great relief to
the monotony of the old *secco* recitative. But
his innovations did not stop there ; he introduced into the orchestra generally a great deal

more movement, variety, colour, combination, and (it must be allowed) noise, than any of his predecessors had done, though never so as to drown the voices. In Germany the orchestra was well understood before the end of the 18th century ; and we must not forget that—not to speak of Mozart's operas of 'Fidelio' or of Cherubini's masterpieces—before the production of the 'Barbiere' (1816), eight of Beethoven's Symphonies were before the world. But in Italy instrumentation was half a century behind, and certainly none of Rossini's predecessors in that country ever attempted what he did in his best operas, as for instance in the *finale* to 'Semiramide' (1823), where the employment of the four horns and the clarinets, and the astonishingly clever way in which the orchestra is handled generally, are quite strokes of genius. The horns are always favourites of his, and are most happily used throughout 'Guillaume Tell,' where we may point to the mixture of pizzicato and bowed notes in the Chorus of the first act, the harp and bell in the Chorus of the second act, and other traits in the Conspiracy scene as marks of real genius, for the happy and picturesque effects produced by very simple means. Rossini had further, like all the great masters, a strong feeling for rhythm, as the most powerful of all aids to interest and success, and was fond of quick movements and of triple time.[1] But an excessive love of jewels is apt to lead to the use of sham diamonds, and his incessant pursuit of effect led him to excessive ornamentation, to noise, and to a passion for attractive forms rather than for the feeling which should lie at the root of them. Much of this, however, was atoned for in his early operas by the masterly way of writing for the voices, by the strength of his melody, the copious flow of his ideas, and the irresistible contagion of his good spirits, especially in comic opera. Having thus secured his position in public favour, his next step—a very legitimate one—was to satisfy the demands of his own taste and conscience. During this second period the subjects of his operas increase in interest. In 'Mosè' he deals with the religious sentiment. In the 'Donna del Lago' he rivals Walter Scott on his own field ; and in 'Semiramide' he has recourse to oriental history in his endeavour to give an independent value to his drama. During this period his melodies drop some of their former voluptuous character, but in return are more pathetic and more full of colour, though still wanting in tenderness and depth.

Lastly, in his Paris operas, and especially in 'Guillaume Tell,' the influence of French taste makes itself strongly felt, and we find a clearness, a charm, a delicacy in the small details, a sense of proportion and of unity, a breadth of style, an attention to the necessities of the

stage, and a dignity, which raise this epoch of his career far higher than either of the others.

Rossini's music, as we have already said, has been very differently estimated. Ingres, in whose view honesty in art held almost as high a place as genius or originality, has called it 'the music of a dishonest (*malhonnête*) man.' Berlioz would gladly have burnt it all, and Rossini's followers with it.[2] On the other hand, Schubert, though fully alive to his weaknesses, as his caricatures of Rossini's overtures show, and with every reason to dislike him from the fact that the Rossini *furore* kept Schubert's own works off the stage—contrasts his operas most favourably with the 'rubbish' which filled the Vienna theatres at that time, and calls him emphatically 'a rare genius.' 'His instrumentation,' he continues, 'is often extremely original, and so is the voice-writing, nor can I find any fault with the music (of "Otello"), if I except the usual Italian gallopades and a few reminiscences of "Tancredi."'[3] Mendelssohn, too, as is well known, would allow no one to depreciate Rossini. Even Schumann, so intolerant of the Italian School, is enthusiastic over one of his operas, and calls it 'real, exhilarating, clever music.' Such exaggerations as those of Ingres and Berlioz are as bad as intentional injustice ; it is better to recollect the very difficult circumstances which surrounded an Italian composer eighty years ago, and to endeavour to discover why music which was once so widely worshipped has now gone out of fashion. Is it the fault of his librettos ? No doubt he would have been wiser to stick to comic subjects, like that of the 'Barbiere,' and to have confined himself for his librettos to the poets of his own family. Is it the elaborate ornamentation of much of his music ? No doubt ornamented music decays sooner than that of a plainer style, and it is always dangerous, though tempting, to adopt the fashionable forms. But one main reason is to be found in the deterioration of the art of singing ; the Paris opera can now boast neither 'ténor de force' nor 'ténor de grace' ; and the revival of the 'Comte Ory' (on Oct. 29, 1880) showed conclusively the mediocrity of the singers at the Académie. In fact Rossini is now expiating his fault in having demanded too much from his singers.[4] Some feeling of remorse on this head seems to have prompted his efforts to improve the art of singing both in Paris and Bologna. Indeed so keenly alive was he to the tendencies which

---

[1] The English reader will find these points happily touched on in Sutherland Edwards's *History of the Opera*, chap. xvi.

[2] Berlioz, *Memoires*, chap. xiv. The abuse of the 'brutale grosse caisse de Rossini' sounds oddly from Berlioz's pen.

[3] Letter in Kreissle's *Life of Schubert*, chap. vii.

[4] It is amusing to find Rossini accused in his own time, as were both Beethoven and Wagner, of being a destroyer of the voice. The correspondent of the *Allg. Musik. Zeitung*, writing from Venice in April 1819, mentions a certain Countess Dieterichstein at Rome, who pronounced that his passages were so straining and ruinous for both throat and chest that if he wrote operas for ten years longer there would be no more singers left in Italy. 'Giorgi,' continues the correspondent, 'for whom he wrote the "Cenerentola," is already completely ruined.' [It is perhaps only fair to remind the reader that since the above article was written there have been many singers at the Paris Opéra and elsewhere fully capable of performing Rossini's operas if the public wanted them.]

have degraded the stage since 1830, and so anxious to further the love of fresh melody and the prosecution of sound musical study, that he bequeathed to the Institute an annual sum of 6000 francs (£240) for a competition both in dramatic poetry and composition, specifying particularly that the object of the prize should be to encourage composers with a turn for melody. The greater part of his property Rossini devoted to the foundation and endowment of a Conservatorio of Music at his native town Pesaro, of which A. Bazzini and Mascagni were successively directors.

In order to complete this sketch it is necessary to give as complete a list as possible of his works. N.B.—In the column after the names, (1) signifies that the score has been engraved ; (2) that it is published for voices and piano ; (3) that it is still in manuscript.

I. OPERAS

Title.	1=Full Score. 2 = PF. do. 3=MS.	First representation.	First performance in London at King's Theatre.
Adelaide di Borgogna, or Ottone Rè d'Italia	— 2, 3	Rome, Car. 1818	
Adina (farsa)	— 2, 3	Lisbon, 1818	
Armida	— 2, 3	Naples, Aut. 1817	
Assedio di Corinto, L'	— 2, 3	Milan, Dec. 26, 1828	June 5, 1834
Aureliano in Palmira	— 2, 3	Milan, Dec. 26, 1813	June 22, 1826
Barbiere di Siviglia, Il	— 2, 3	Rome, Feb. 5, 1816	Jan. 27, 1818
Barbier de Séville, Le	1, 2, —	Paris, May 6, 1824	
Bianca e Faliero	— 2, 3	Milan, Dec. 26, 1819	
Bruschini, I due (farsa)	——	Venice, 1819	
Bruschino	— 2, —	Paris, Dec. 28, 1857	
Cambiale di matrimonio, La (farsa)	— 2, 3	Venice, Aut. 1810	
Cambio della valigia, Il, or L'occasione, etc. (farsa)	— 2, 3	Venice, 1812	
Cenerentola, La	— 2, 3	Rome, Car. 1817	Jan. 8, 1820
Comte Ory, Le	1, 2, —	Paris, Aug. 20, 1828	Feb. 28, 1829
Dame du Lac, La	1, —	Paris, Oct. 21, 1825	
Demetrio e Polibio	— 2, 3	Rome, 1812	
Donna del Lago, La	— 2, 3	Naples, Oct. 4, 1819	Feb. 18, 1823
Edoardo e Cristina	— 2, 3	Venice, Car. 1819	
Elisabetta	— 2, 3	Naples, Aut. 1815	Apr. 20, 1818
Equivoco stravagante	— 2, 3	Bologna, Aut. 1811	
Ermione	— 2, 3	Naples, Lent, 1819	
Figlio per Azzardo, Il. See Bruschini			
Gazza ladra, La	— 2, 3	Milan, May 31, 1817	Mar. 10, 1821
Gazzetta, La	— 2, 3	Naples, 1816	
Guillaume Tell	1, 2 —	Paris, Aug. 3, 1829	July 11, 1839
Inganno felice, L' (farsa)	— 2, 3	Venice, Car. 1812	July 1, 1819
Isabelle, adapted from do.	— 2, —		
Italiana in Algeri, L'	— 2, 3	Venice, 1813	Jan. 27, 1819
Maometto Secondo	— 2, 3	Naples, Car. 1820	
Matilda di Shabran	— 2, 3	Rome, Car. 1821	July 3, 1823
Mathilde de Sabran	— 2, —	Paris, 1857	
Moïse	1, 2, —	Paris, Mar. 25, 1827	
Mosè in Egitto (2 or 4 acts)	— 2, 3	Naples, Lent, 1818	(Pietro l'Eremita) Apr. 23, 1822
Do. 2nd Italian libretto		Paris, 1827	
Occasione fa il ladro, L', or Il cambio, etc. (farsa)		Venice, 1812	
Otello	— 2, 3	Naples, Dec. 4, 1816	May 16, 1822
Otello, ou le More de Venise (Castil-Blaze)		Lyons, Dec. 1, 1823	
Othello (Royer & Waez)	— 2, —	Paris, Sept. 2, 1844	
Ottone Rè d' Italia. See Adelaide			
Pietra del Paragone, La	— 2, 3	Milan, Sept. 26, 1812	
Pie voleuse, La	1 —	Paris, 1822	
Ricciardo e Zoraide	— 2, 3	Naples, Aut. 1818	June 5, 1823
Robert Bruce		Paris, Dec. 30, 1846	
Scala di seta, La (farsa)	— 2, 3	Venice, Car. 1812	
Semiramide	— 2, 3	Venice, Feb. 3, 1823	July 15, 1824
Sémiramis	— 2, 3	Paris, July 9, 1860	
Siége de Corinthe, Le	1, 2, —	Paris, Oct. 9, 1826	
Sigismondo	— 2, 3	Venice, Car. 1815	
Tancredi	— 2, 3	Venice, Feb. 6, 1813	May 4, 1820
Torvaldo e Dorliska	— 2, 3	Rome, Dec. 26, 1815	
Turco in Italia, Il	— 2, 3	Milan, Aug. 14, 1814	May 19, 1821
Viaggio a Reims, Il		Paris, June 19, 1825	
Zelmira	— 2, 3	Naples, Dec. 1821	Jan. 24, 1824

II. CANTATAS

Il pianto d' armonia, Bologna, 1808.	L' Augurio felice, Verona, 1822.
Didone abbandonata, Bologna, 1811.	La sacra alleanza, Verona, 1823.
Egle ed Irene, 1814.	Il Bardo, Verona, 1822.
Teti e Peleo, 1816.	Il ritorno, 1823.
Igea, 1819.	Il pianto delle Muse, London, 1823.
Partenope, 1819.	I Pastori, Naples, 1825.
La riconoscenza, 1821.	Il serto votivo, Bologna, 1829.
Il vero omaggio, Verona, 1823.	

III. SACRED MUSIC

Oratorio, 'Ciro in Babilonia,' Ferrara, Lent, 1812.
Stabat Mater, 1832-41. 1, 2, 3.
Petite Messe Solennelle, 1864. 2, 3.
Tantum ergo, for 2 tenors and bass, with orchestra. 1, 2, 3. Composed at Bologna, and performed Nov. 28, 1847, for the re-establishment of the service in the church of S. Francesco dei Minori conventuali.
Quoniam, bass solo and orchestra. 1, 2, 3.
O Salutaris, 4 solo voices. Published at Paris in La Maîtrise and reproduced in facsimile by Azevedo in his Rossini.

IV. MISCELLANEOUS VOCAL MUSIC

Gorgheggi e Solfeggi. A collection of exercises for the voice.
Non posso, o Dio, resistere. Cantata.
Oh quanto son grate. Duettino.
Ridiamo, cantiamo, à 4.
Alle voci della gloria. Scena ed Aria.
Les Soirées musicales. 8 ariettas and 4 duets.
Inno populare, on the accession of Pius IX. Chorus.
Dall' Oriente l' astro del giorno, a 4.
Cara Patria. Cantata.
Chant des Titans. Chorus.
Se il vuol la Molinara.—Rossini's first composition.
La Separazione. Dramatic song.

Various other airs and pieces, thirty or forty in number, will be found in the catalogues of Ricordi, Lucca, Brandus (Troupenas), and Escudier, which it is hardly necessary to enumerate here. Probably no composer ever wrote so much in albums as did Rossini. The number of these pieces which he threw off while in London alone is prodigious. They are usually composed to some lines of Metastasio's, beginning ' Mi lagnerà tacendo della sorte amara,' which he is said to have set more than a hundred times. [The famous aria, ' Pietà, Signore,' which credulous amateurs still regard as Stradella's, was, according to Signor Alfredo Piatti, written as a joke by Rossini.]

We have stated that during the latter years of his life Rossini composed a great quantity of music for the PF. solo, both serious and comic. These pieces were sold by his widow *en masse* to Baron Grant for the sum of £4000. After a time the whole was put up to auction in London and purchased by Ricordi of Milan, M. Paul Dalloz, proprietor of a periodical entitled *La Musique*, at Paris, and other persons.

V. INSTRUMENTAL MUSIC

Le rendezvous de chasse. A fanfare for 4 trumpets, composed at Compiègne in 1828 for M. Schikler, and dedicated to him.
3 Marches for the marriage of H.R.H. the Duke of Orleans. Arranged for PF. à 4 mains.
March (Pas redoublé) composed for H.I.M. the Sultan Abdul Medjid. Arranged for PF. solo (Benedict) and à 4 mains.
5 String Quartets, arranged as Sonatines for the PF. by Mockwitz (Breitkopf & Härtel).

To enumerate and elucidate all the biographical and critical notices of Rossini would require a volume ; we shall therefore confine ourselves to mentioning these of importance either from their authority, their ability, or the special nature of their contents ; and for greater convenience of reference we have arranged them according to country and date.

I. ITALIAN

G. Carpani. *Lettera all' anonimo autore dell' articolo sul ' Tancredi' di Rossini.* Milan, 1818, 8vo.

G. Carpani. *Le Rossiniane, ossia Lettere musico-teatrali.* Padua, 1824, 130 pages, 8vo. Portrait.

Nic. Bettoni. *Rossini e la sua musica.* Milan, 1824, 8vo.

P. Brighenti. *Della musica rossiniana e del suo autore.* Bologna, 1830, 8vo.

Lib. Musumeci. *Parallelo tra i maestri Rossini e Bellini.* Palermo, 1832, 8vo.

Anon. *Osservazioni sul merito musicale dei maestri Bellini e Rossini, in riposta ad un Parallelo tra i medesimi.* Bologna, 1834, 8vo. This pamphlet was translated into French by M. de Ferrer, and published as *Rossini et Bellini.* Paris, 1835, 8vo.

Anon. *Rossini e la sua musica ; una Passeggiata con Rossini.* Florence, 1841, 16mo.

Anon. *Dello Stabat Mater di Gioachino Rossini, Lettere Storico-critiche di un Lombardo.* Bologna, 1842, 8vo.

Giov. Raffaelli. *Rossini, canto.* Modena, 1844, 8vo.

Fr. Regli. *Elogio di Gioacchino Rossini.* We have not been able to discover how far Regli (1804-66) has used this work in his *Dizionario biografico* (1860).

E. Montazio. *Gioacchino Rossini.* Turin, 1862, 18mo. Portrait.

Giul. Vanzolini. *Della vera Patria di G. Rossini.* Pesaro, 1873, 8vo.

Ferrucci. *Giudizio perentorio sulla verità della Patria di G. Rossini impugnata dal Prof. Giul. Vanzolini.* Florence, 1874 ; an 8vo pamphlet of 20 pages.

Sett Silvestri. *Della vita e delle opere di G. Rossini.* Milan, 1874, 8vo ; with portrait and facsimiles.

Ant. Zanolini. *Biografia di Gioacchino Rossini.* Bologna, 1875, 8vo ; with portrait and facsimiles.

[R. Gandolfi. *Onoranze fiorentine a Gioacchino Rossini.* 1902.]

II. French

Papillon. *Lettre critique sur Rossini.* Paris, 1823, 8vo.

Stendhal. *Vie de Rossini.* Paris, 1823, 8vo. Stendhal, whose real name was Henri Beyle, compiled this work from Carpani. In many passages in fact it is nothing but a translation, and Beyle's own anecdotes are not always trustworthy. It was translated into English (London, 12mo, 1826) and German (Leipzig, 1824), in the latter case by Wendt, who has added notes and corrections.

Berton. *De la musique mécanique et de la musique philosophique.* Paris, 1824, 8vo ; 24 pages.

Ditto, followed by an *Épitre à un célèbre compositeur français* (Boieldieu). Paris, 1826, 8vo ; 48 pages.

Imbert de Laphaléque. *De la Musique en France : Rossini, 'Guillaume Tell.'* (*Revue de Paris,* 1829.)

J. d'Ortigue. *De la guerre des dilettanti ou de la révolution opérée par M. Rossini dans l'opéra français.* Paris, 1829, 8vo.

N. Bettoni. *Rossini et sa musique.* Paris, Bettoni, 1836, 8vo.

Anon. *Vie de Rossini,* etc. Antwerp, 1839, 12mo ; 215 pages. (By M. Van Damme, who in his turn has borrowed much from Stendhal.)

L. de Loménie. *M. Rossini, par un homme de rien.* Paris, 1842, 8vo.

Aulagnier. *Quelques observations sur la publication du 'Stabat mater' de Rossini.* Paris, 1842, 4to.

Anon. *Observations d'un amateur non dilettante au sujet du 'Stabat' de M. Rossini.* Paris, 1842, 8vo.

E. Troupenas. *Résumé des opinions de la Presse sur le 'Stabat' de Rossini.* Paris, 1842, 8vo ; 75 pages.

Escudier frères. *Rossini, sa vie et ses œuvres.* Paris, 1854, 12mo ; 338 pages.

Eug. de Mirecourt. *Rossini.* Paris, 1855, 32mo.

A. Azevedo. *G. Rossini, sa vie et ses œuvres.* Paris, 1865, large 8vo ; 310 pages, with portraits and facsimiles. This is the most complete and eulogistic work on Rossini. It appeared originally in the *Ménestrel,* but was discontinued there, the editor not approving of a violent attack on Meyerbeer, which Azevedo included in it.

Virmaître et Elie Frébault. *Les maisons comiques de Paris,* 1868, 12mo. One chapter is devoted to the house of Rossini.

N. Roqueplan. *Rossini.* Paris, 1869, 12mo ; 16 pages.

E. Beulé. *Eloge de Rossini.* Paris, 1869.

A. Pougin. *Rossini : Notes, impressions, souvenirs, commentaires.* Paris, 1870, 8vo ; 91 pages. The detailed and annotated chronological list mentioned on p. 8 has not yet been published.

O. Moutoz. *Rossini et son 'Guillaume Tell.'* Bourg, 1872, 8vo.

Vander Straeten. *La mélodie populaire dans l'opéra 'Guillaume Tell'* de Rossini. Paris, 1879, 8vo.

[J. Sittard. *Rossini,* 1882.]

III. German

Oettinger. *Rossini, Komischer Roman.* Leipzig, 1847. A satirical work translated into Danish by Marlow (Copenhagen, 1849, 2 vols. 8vo.) ; into Swedish by Landberg (Stockholm, 1850, 2 vols. 8vo) ; and into French by Royer, *Rossini, l'homme et l'artiste* (Brussels, 1858, 3 vols. 16mo).

Otto Gumprecht. *Musikalische Charakterbilder.* Leipzig, 1869, 8vo.

Fd. Hiller. *Plaudereien mit Rossini.* Inserted (with date 1856) in Hiller's *Aus dem Tonleben unserer Zeit* (Leipzig, 1868) ; translated into French by Ch. Schwartz in *La France musicale,* 1855 ; and into English by Miss M. E. von Glehn in *Once a Week,* 1870.

A. Struth. *Rossini, sein Leben, seine Werke und Charakterzüge.* Leipzig.

La Mara. *Musikalische Studienköpfe,* vo¹. ii. Leipzig, 1874-1876, 2 vols. 12mo.

IV. English

Hogarth. *Memoirs of the Musical Drama.* London, 1838, 2 vols. 8vo.

H. S. Edwards. *Rossini's Life.* London, 1869, 8vo ; portrait.—*History of the Opera,* Ib. 1862, 2 vols. 8vo.—*Rossini and his School,* 1881.

Portraits of Rossini are frequent at all periods of his life. Marochetti's statue, in which he is represented sitting, was erected in his native town in 1864. There is a good bust by Bartolini of Florence. In the 'foyer' of the Opera in the Rue Le Peletier, Paris (now destroyed), there was a medallion of Rossini by Chevalier ; a duplicate of this is in the possession of the editor of the *Ménestrel.* The front of the new opera-house has a bronze-gilt bust by M. Evrard. A good early engraving of him is that from an oil-painting by Mayer of Vienna (1820). Of later ones may be mentioned that by Thévenin after Ary Scheffer (1843) : still later, a full-length drawn and engraved by Masson, and a photograph by Erwig, engraved as frontispiece to the PF. score of Sémiramis (Heugel). Among the lithographs the best is that of Grévedon ; and of caricatures the only one deserving mention is that by Dantan. G.C.

ROTA, or **ROTTA** (Fr. *rote* ; Ger. *rotte,* or *rotta*). (i.) A stringed instrument of the psaltery class, the three (or seven) strings of which were plucked either with the fingers or with a plectrum. It is mentioned as early as A.D. 868 by Otfried. It seems to be allied to the ancient lyre. The derivation of the word from the Irish *crott* or *cruit,* or the Welsh *crwth* (called *chrotta* by Venantius Fortunatus), seems hardly likely without more definite evidence than is before us. The instruments of the crwth kind were generally played with a bow.

(ii.) The name *rota* is applied to the famous round, 'Sumer is icumen in' (see that article), and may have been a generic name for what we now call rounds, the derivation being in that case quite obvious. M.

ROTA, ANDREA, was born in Bologna about 1553, and in 1583 was appointed choir-master to the church of San Petronio in that city. He died in 1597. His publications consist of three books of madrigals, two *a* 5 (Venice, 1579-1589), one *a* 4 (1592) ; two books of motets *a* 5-10 (1584, 1595) ; and one book of masses *a* 4-6 (1595). A very pleasing madrigal *a* 5 is republished in Torchi's 'L'Arte Musicale in Italia,' vol. i., also an Agnus Dei *a* 7 with double canon, and a Dixit Dominus *a* 8. Padre Martini's *Esemplare* contains a Da Pacem by Rota, and Paolucci's 'L'Arte Prattica,' a motet *a* 10.   J. R. M.

ROUGET DE LISLE, CLAUDE JOSEPH, author of the 'Marseillaise,' born at Montaigu, Lons-le-Saulnier, May 10, 1760. He entered the School of Royal Engineers ('École royale du génie') at Mezières in 1782, and left it two years later with the rank of 'aspirant-lieutenant.' Early in 1789 he was made second lieutenant, and in 1790 he rose to be first lieutenant, and was moved to Strasburg, where he soon became very popular in the triple capacity of poet, violin-player, and singer. His hymn, 'à la Liberté,' composed by Ignace Pleyel, was sung at Strasburg, at the fête of Sept. 25, 1791. While there he wrote three pieces for the theatre, one of which, 'Bayard en Bresse,' was produced at Paris, Feb. 21, 1791, but without success. In April 1792 he wrote the 'Marseillaise,' of which an account has been given elsewhere. [See vol. iii. p. 62 ff.] As the son of royalist parents, and himself belonging to the constitutional party, Rouget de Lisle refused to take the oath to the constitution abolishing the crown ; he was therefore stripped of his military rank, denounced, and imprisoned, only to escape after the fall of Robespierre in 1794, [an event he celebrated in a 'Hymne dithyrambique,' etc. A 'Chant des vengeances' (1798) and 'Chant du combat' (1800) are mentioned in Riemann's *Lexikon*.] He re-entered the army, and made the campaign of La Vendée under General Hoche ; was wounded, and at length, under the Consulate, returned to private life at Montaigu, where he remained in the depth of solitude and of poverty till the second Restoration. His brother then sold the little family property, and Rouget was driven to Paris ; and there would have starved but for a small pension granted by Louis XVIII. and continued by Louis Philippe, and for the care of his friends Béranger, David d'Angers, and especially M. and Mme. Voïart, in whose house, at Choisy-le-Roi, he died, June 27, 1836.

Besides the works already mentioned, he published in 1797 a volume of *Essais en vers et en prose* (Paris, F. Didot, an V de la République), dedicated to Méhul, and now extremely rare ; so also is his 'Cinquante chants Français' (1825, 4to), with PF. accompaniment. One of these songs, 'Roland à Roncevaux,' was written in 1792, and its refrain—

Mourir pour la patrie,
C'est le sort le plus beau, le plus digne d'envie—

was borrowed by the authors of the 'Chant des Girondins,' which was set to music by Varney, and played a distinguished part in the Revolution of 1848. [He wrote another set of twenty-five romances with violin obbligato, and two opera-librettos, 'Jacquot, ou l'école des mères' for Della Maria, and 'Macbeth' for Chelard, produced in 1827.] His 'Relation du désastre de Quiberon,' is in vol. ii. of the *Mémoires de tous*. There exists a fine medallion of Rouget by David d'Angers, which is engraved in a pamphlet by his nephew, entitled *La vérité sur la paternité de la Marseillaise* (Paris, 1865). See the volume of M. Le Roy de Ste. Croix (Strasburg, 1880).   G. C.

ROUND. I. 'A species of canon in the unison, so called because the performers begin the melody at regular rhythmical periods, and return from its conclusion to its commencement, so that it continually passes round and round from one to another of them.'[1] Rounds and Catches, the most characteristic forms of English music, differ from canons in only being sung at the unison or octave, and also in being rhythmical in form. Originating at a period of which we have but few musical records, these compositions have been written and sung in England with unvarying popularity until the present day. The earliest extant example of a round is the well-known 'Sumer is icumen in,' as to the date of which there has been much discussion, although it is certainly not later than the middle of the 13th century. [See SUMER IS ICUMEN IN.] Amongst early writers on music, the terms 'round' and 'catch' were synonymous, but at the present day the latter is generally understood to be what Hawkins (vol. ii.) defines as that species of round 'wherein, to humour some conceit in the words, the melody is broken, and the sense interrupted in one part, and caught again or supplied by another,' a form of humour which easily adapted itself to the coarse tastes of the Restoration, at which period rounds and catches reached their highest popularity. That catches were immensely popular with the lower classes is proved by the numerous allusions to 'alehouse catches' and the like in the dramas of the 16th and 17th centuries. According to Drayton (*Legend of Thomas Cromwell*, Stanza 29) they were introduced into Italy by the Earl of Essex in 1510.

The first printed collection of rounds was that edited by Thomas Ravenscroft, and published in 1609 under the title of 'Pammelia. Musickes Miscellanie : or Mixed Varietie of pleasant Roundelayes and delightfull Catches of 3. 4. 5. 6. 7. 8. 9. 10. Parts in one.' This interesting collection contains many English, French, and Latin rounds, etc., some of which are still

[1] 'The Rounds, Catches, and Canons of England ; a Collection of Specimens of the sixteenth, seventeenth, and eighteenth centuries adapted to Modern Use. The Words revised, adapted, or re-written by the Rev. J. Powell Metcalfe. The Music selected and revised, and An Introductory Essay on the Rise and Progress of the Round, Catch, and Canon ; also Biographical Notices of the Composers, written by Edward F. Rimbault, LL.D.,' from which work much of the information contained in the above article has been derived.

popular. Amongst them there is also a curious 'Round of three Country Dances in one' for four voices, which is in reality a Quodlibet on the country-dance tunes 'Robin Hood,' 'Now foot it,' and 'The Crampe is in my purse.' 'Pammelia' was followed by two other collections brought out by Ravenscroft, 'Deuteromelia' in 1609, and 'Melismata' in 1611, and the numerous publications of the Playfords, the most celebrated of which is 'Catch that catch can, or the Musical Companion' (1667), which passed through many editions. The most complete collection of rounds and catches is that published by Warren in thirty-two monthly and yearly numbers, from 1763 to 1794, which contains over 800 compositions, including many admirable specimens by Purcell, Blow, and other masters of the English school. It is to be regretted that they are too often disfigured by an obscenity of so gross a nature as to make them now utterly unfit for performance. A good specimen of the round proper is Hayes's 'Wind, gentle evergreen.' The Round has never been much cultivated by foreign composers. One or two examples are, however, well known, amongst them may be mentioned Cherubini's 'Perfida Clori.'

II. Any dance in which the dancers stood in a circle was formerly called a round or roundel.[1] The first edition of the 'Dancing Master' (1651) has thirteen rounds, for six, eight, or 'as many as will.' Subsequent editions of the same book have also a dance called 'Cheshire Rounds,' and Part II. of Walsh's 'Compleat Country Dancing Master' (1719) has Irish and Shropshire rounds. These latter dances are, however, not danced in a ring, but 'longways,' i.e. like 'Sir Roger de Coverley.' In Jeremiah Clarke's 'Choice Lessons for the Harpsichord or Spinett' (1711), and similar contemporary publications, the word rondo is curiously corrupted into 'Round O.'   w. b. s.

ROUND, CATCH, AND CANON CLUB. A society founded in London in 1843, by Enoch Hawkins, for the purpose of singing the new compositions of the professional members and others, written in the form of Round, Catch, and Canon; hence the title of the Club. Among the original members were Messrs. Enoch Hawkins, Hobbs, Bradbury, Handel Gear, Henry Phillips, Addison, D'Almaine, and F. W. Collard. The meetings were originally held at the Crown and Anchor Tavern whence the Club removed to the Freemasons' Tavern, thence to the Thatched House, again to Freemasons' Tavern, and to St. James's Hall, where, until the demolition of the building, it assembled every fortnight from the first Saturday in November until the end of March, ten meetings being held in each season. [Its meetings are now held in the Criterion Restaurant, and take place on Mon-

day evenings instead of Saturdays.] In the earlier years of its existence the number both of professional and non-professional members at each dinner rarely exceeded eighteen, but now from sixty to seventy dine together. The management of the Club is in the hands of the officers, who are the proprietors, and each of whom in turn takes the chair, and is alone responsible for the entertainment. The musical programmes now consist mainly of glees, although an occasional catch is introduced. [The professional members at present (1907) are Messrs. W. Coward, G. May, E. Dalzell, F. Norcup, G. and H. Stubbs, assisted by a boy treble. The officers are Messrs. J. A. Brown, Fred. Walker, and Robt. Hilton.] For non-professional members there is an entrance fee of three guineas, and an annual subscription for the ten meetings and dinner of five guineas.   c. m.

ROUSSEAU, JEAN JACQUES, born at Geneva, June 28, 1712, died at Ermenonville, near Paris, July 3, 1778, five weeks after Voltaire. The details of his life are given in his *Confessions*; we shall here confine ourselves to his compositions, and his writings on music. Although, like all who learn music late in life and in a desultory manner without a master, Rousseau remained to the end a poor reader and an indifferent harmonist, he exercised a great influence on French music. Immediately after his arrival in Paris he read a paper before the Académie des Sciences (August 22, 1742) on a new system of musical notation, which he afterwards extended and published under the title of *Dissertation sur la musique moderne* (Paris, 1743, 8vo). His method of representing the notes of the scale by figures—1, 2, 3, 4, 5, 6, 7—had been already proposed by Souhaitty, but Rousseau's combinations, and especially his signs of duration, are so totally different as entirely to redeem them from the charge of plagiarism. A detailed analysis and refutation of the system may be found in Raymond's *Des principaux systèmes de notation musicale* (Turin, 1824, 8vo), to which the reader is referred ; but it is evident that, however convenient notation by means of figures may be for writing a simple melody, it becomes as complicated as the old system when modulation or polyphony are attempted. Its very uniformity also deprives the reader of all assistance from the eye ; the sounds must be spelt out one by one, and the difficulty of deciphering orchestral combinations or complicated harmonies becomes almost insuperable.

Copying music had been Rousseau's means of livelihood, and this led him to believe that the best way to learn an art is to practise it ; at any rate he composed an opera, 'Les Muses galantes' (1747), which was produced at the house of La Popelinière, when Rameau, who was present, declared that some pieces showed the hand of a master, and others the ignorance of a schoolboy. Not being able to obtain access to any of the

---

[1] 'Come now a roundel and a fairy song.'
    Midsummer Night's Dream, act ii. sc. 2.

theatres, Rousseau undertook to write the articles on music for the *Encyclopédie*, a task which he accomplished in three months, and afterwards acknowledged to have been done hastily and unsatisfactorily. We have mentioned in the article RAMEAU (*ante*, p. 22) the exposé by that great musician of the errors in the musical articles of the *Encyclopédie*; Rousseau's reply was not published till after his death, but it is included in his complete works.

Three months after the arrival in Paris of the Italian company who popularised the 'Serva padrona'[1] in France, Rousseau produced 'Le Devin du village' before the King at Fountaine-bleau, on Oct. 18 and 24, 1752. The piece, of which both words and music were his own, pleased the court, and was quickly reproduced in Paris. The first representation at the Académie took place March 1, 1753, and the last in 1828, when some wag[2] threw an immense powdered perruque on the stage and gave it its deathblow. [DEVIN DU VILLAGE, vol. i. p. 692a.] It is curious that the representations of this simple pastoral should have coincided so exactly with the vehement discussions to which the performances of Italian opera gave rise. We cannot enter here upon the literary quarrel known as the 'Guerre des Bouffons,' or enumerate the host of pamphlets to which it gave rise,[3] but it is a strange fact, only to be accounted for on the principle that man is a mass of contradictions, that Rousseau, the author of the 'Devin du Village,' pronounced at once in favour of Italian music.

His *Lettre sur la musique Française* (1753) raised a storm of indignation, and not unnaturally, since it pronounces French music to have neither rhythm nor melody, the language not being susceptible of either; French singing to be but a prolonged barking, absolutely insupportable to an unprejudiced ear ; French harmony to be crude, devoid of expression, and full of mere padding ; French airs not airs, and French recitative not recitative. 'From which I conclude,' he continues, 'that the French have no music, and never will have any ; or that if they ever should, it will be so much the worse for them.' To this pamphlet the actors and musicians of the Opéra replied by hanging and burning its author in effigy. His revenge for this absurdity, and for many other attacks, was the witty *Lettre d'un symphoniste de l'Académie royale de musique à ses camarades de l'orchestre* (1753), which may still be read with pleasure. The æsthetic part of the *Dictionnaire de musique* which he finished in 1764 at Motiers-Travers, is admirable both for matter and style. He obtained the privilege of printing it in Paris,

April 15, 1765, but did not make use of the privilege till 1768 ; the Geneva edition, also in one vol. 4to, came out in 1767. In spite of mistakes in the didactic, and serious omissions in the technical portions, the work became very popular, and was translated into several languages; the English edition (London, 1770, 8vo) being by William Waring.

Rousseau's other writings on music are : *Lettre à M. Grimm, au sujet des remarques ajoutées à sa Lettre sur Omphale* (1752), belonging to the early stage of the 'Guerre des Bouffons' ; *Essai sur l'origine des langues*, etc. (1753), containing chapters on harmony, on the supposed analogy between sound and colour, and on the music of the Greeks ; *Lettre à M. l'Abbé Raynal au sujet d'un nouveau mode de musique inventé par M. Blainville*, dated May 30, 1754, and first printed in the *Mercure de France* ; *Lettre à M. Burney sur la Musique, avec des fragments d'Observations sur l'Alceste italien de M. le chevalier Gluck*, an analysis of 'Alceste' written at the request of Gluck himself ; and *Extrait d'une réponse du Petit Faiseur à son Prête-Nom, sur un morceau de l'Orphée de M. le chevalier Gluck*, dealing principally with a particular modulation in 'Orphée.' From the last two it is clear that Rousseau heartily admired Gluck, and that he had by this time abandoned the exaggerated opinions advanced in the *Lettre sur la musique Française*. The first of the above was issued in 1752, the rest not till after his death ; they are now only to be found in his complete works.

On Oct. 30, 1775, Rousseau produced his 'Pygmalion' at the Comédie Française ; it is a lyric piece in one act, and caused some sensation owing to its novelty. Singing there was none, and the only music consisted of orchestral pieces in the intervals of the declamation. He also left fragments of an opera 'Daphnis et Chloé' (published in score, Paris, 1780, folio), and a collection of about a hundred romances and detached pieces, to which he gave the title 'Consolations des Misères de ma vie' (Paris, 1781, 8vo) ; in the latter collection are the graceful 'Rosier,' often reprinted, and a charming setting of Rolli's 'Se tu m'ami.' Rousseau was accused of having stolen the 'Devin du Village' from a musician of Lyons named Granet, and the greater part of 'Pygmalion' from another Lyonnais named Coigniet. Among his most persistent detractors is Castil-Blaze (see *Molière musicien*, ii. 409), but he says not a word of the 'Consolations.' Now any one honestly comparing these romances with the 'Devin du Village,' will inevitably arrive at the conviction that airs at once so simple, natural, and full of expression, and so incorrect as regards harmony, not only may, but must have proceeded from the same author. There is no doubt, however, that the instrumentation of the 'Devin' was touched up, or perhaps

---

[1] It has been generally supposed that the 'Serva padrona' was not heard in Paris before 1752: this, however, is a mistake ; it had been played so far back as Oct. 4, 1746, but the Italian company who performed it was not satisfactory, and it passed almost unnoticed.

[2] Supposed to have been Berlioz, but he exculpates himself in his *Memoirs*, chap. xv.

[3] See Chouquet's *Histoire de la musique dramatique*, pp. 134 and 434.

wholly re-written, by Francœur, on whose advice, as well as on that of Jelyotte the tenor singer, Rousseau was much in the habit of relying. An air (' de trois notes ') and a duettino, melodious and pretty but of the simplest style, are given in the *Musical Library*, vol. iii.   G. C.

ROUSSEAU'S DREAM. A very favourite air in England in the early part of the 19th century. Its first appearance under that name is presumably as 'an Air with Variations for the Pianoforte, composed and dedicated to the Rt. Hon. the Countess of Delaware, by J. B. Cramer. London, Chappell' [1812].

But it is found (with very slight changes) a quarter of a century earlier, under the title of 'Melissa. The words by Charles James, Esq., adapted to the Pianoforte, Harp, or Guitar. London, J. Dale, 1788.' The melody occurs in the 'Pantomime' in Scene 8 of the 'Devin du Village,' where its form is as follows:—

[The tune, no doubt, made its way in England through the adaptation of the opera by Dr. Burney, as 'The Cunning Man,' in 1766. It seems to have been first adapted to a hymn in Thomas Walker's 'Companion to Dr. Rippon's Tunes' (1825), and after its appearance in 'Sacred Melodies' (1843), with the name 'Rousseau' attached to it, became widely popular as a hymn-tune. W. H. G. F.] The origin of the title 'Dream' is not forthcoming. G.

ROUSSEAU, SAMUEL ALEXANDRE, was born at Neuve-Maison (Aisne), June 11, 1853, and studied at the Paris Conservatoire, where he gained successively the first organ prize in 1877, in César Franck's class, and the Grand Prix de Rome in 1878 with 'La Fille de Jephté.' In the latter year the Prix Cressent was awarded to his opéra-comique, 'Dinorah,' which was produced at the Opéra-Comique in December 1879. Works sent from Rome, and executed at the Conservatoire, were 'Labinies' (1880), 'Raddir' (1881), 'La Florentina' (1882). He was for many years maître de chapelle in Sainte-Clotilde, and chorus-master of the Société des

Concerts du Conservatoire. He wrote a great quantity of admirable church music, two masses, motets, organ pieces, etc.; secular choral works, pieces for piano, harmonium, violin, small orchestra, etc. and songs. He was president of the Société des Compositeurs, and vice-president of the Association de la critique musicale et dramatique. His most famous work was the opera, 'La Cloche du Rhin,' in three acts, brought out at the Paris Opéra, June 8, 1898; another three-act opera, 'Mérowig,' gained the prize of the City of Paris, and produced at Nancy, Jan. 12, 1899. Rousseau died of a tumour on the brain, in Paris, Oct. 1, 1904. G. F.

ROVELLI. A family of eminent Italian musicians. GIOVANNI BATTISTA was first violin in the orchestra of the church of S. Maria Maggiore of Bergamo, at the beginning of the 19th century. GIUSEPPE, his son, was a violoncellist, born at Bergamo in 1753, and died at Parma, Nov. 12, 1806. Of ALESSANDRO we only know that he was at one time director of the orchestra at Weimar, and that he was the father of PIETRO, who was born at Bergamo, Feb. 6, 1793, and received his first lessons, both in violin-playing and the general science of music, from his grandfather. By an influential patron he was sent to Paris to study under R. Kreutzer, and his playing attracted much attention there. On his father's appointment to Weimar he joined him for a time. At the end of 1814 we find him at Munich, playing with great applause. He remained there for some years, and was made 'Royal Bavarian chamber-musician,' and 'first concerto-player.' In Feb. 1817 he was playing at Vienna; there he married Micheline, daughter of E. A. Förster, and a fine PF.-player, and in 1819 went on to Bergamo, took the place once occupied by his grandfather, and seems to have remained there, suffering much from bad health, till his death, Sept. 8, 1838. The writer in the *Allg. mus. Zeitung* for Dec. 26, 1838, from whom the above facts have been mainly taken, characterises his playing as 'simple, expressive, graceful, noble; in a word, classical—a style which takes instant possession of the heart of the hearer.' In other notices in the same periodical, he is said to have inherited the pure, singing, expressive style of Viotti, and practised it to perfection. Molique was his pupil at Munich. G.

ROVESCIO, AL. A term used, in instrumental music, to express two different things. (1) An imitation by contrary motion, in which every descending interval in the leading part is imitated by an ascending one, and *vice versa*; see Moscheles's Étude 'La Forza,' op. 51. (2) A phrase or piece which may be played backwards throughout. It is then synonymous with CANCRIZANS. An interesting example occurs in the minuet of a Sonata for PF. and violin by Haydn, in which, on the repetition after the Trio, the minuet is played backwards, so as to end on the first note, Haydn's indication being *Menuetto D.C. wird zurückgespielt.* [SEE RECTE ET RETRO.]

and 'Griselda.' The fourth season lasted from Nov. 7, 1722, to June 15, 1723, and was remarkable for the first appearance in England

Menuetto al Rovescio.

[The Repeat, as played after the Trio.]

F. T.

ROW OF KEYS. A single CLAVIER or MANUAL. The term is not applied, in the organ, to a pedal-clavier from the simple fact that one row of keys is all that is required by the feet; two rows of pedal-keys have sometimes been constructed, but they have proved always unnecessary and generally unmanageable. Harpsichords had often two rows of keys acting on different sets of jacks, and thus allowing of changes of force and quality of tone.　　J. S.

ROYAL ACADEMY OF MUSIC, 1720-1728. From 1717 to 1720 there was no Italian Opera in London, but in the latter year a sum of £50,000 was raised by subscription, and an establishment was founded for the performance of Italian operas. This was the first Royal Academy of Music. It consisted of a Governor, a Deputy-Governor, and twenty Directors. The first governor was the Duke of Newcastle, the deputy-governor was Lord Bingley, and the directors included the leaders of society at the Court of George I. Buononcini was invited to England from Rome, Ariosti from Berlin, and Handel left Cannons and went to Dresden to engage singers. Under these brilliant auspices the Academy opened at the King's Theatre in the Haymarket, on April 2, 1720, with Giovanni Porta's 'Numitor,' and the following strong cast:—Senesino, Durastanti, Boschi, and Berenstadt. The season ended on June 25. It was remarkable for the production of Handel's 'Radamisto' and D. Scarlatti's 'Narciso,' the latter conducted by Roseingrave, and including Mrs. Anastasia Robinson in the cast. The second season lasted from Nov. 19, 1720, to July 5, 1721. The new works performed were 'Astarto' (Buononcini), 'Arsace' (a pasticcio), 'Muzio Scaevola' (Ariosti, Buononcini, and Handel), and 'Ciro' (Ariosti). During the first year of the undertaking £15,000 of the subscription had been spent. The third season began Nov. 1, 1721, and ended June 16, 1722. The new operas were Handel's 'Floridante,' Buononcini's 'Crispo'

of Cuzzoni, who sang in Handel's 'Ottone' on Jan. 12. The other new works (besides 'Ottone') were Ariosti's 'Coriolano,' Buononcini's 'Erminia,' and Handel's 'Flavio.' In the fifth season (Nov. 27, 1723, to June 13, 1724) Buononcini's 'Farnace,' Ariosti's 'Vespasiano,' and a pasticcio called 'Aquilio,' were produced. At the end of the season Mrs. Robinson retired from the stage. The sixth season (Oct. 31, 1724, to May 19, 1725) opened with Handel's 'Tamerlano.' Ariosti's 'Artaserse' and 'Dario' (partly by Vivaldi), Handel's 'Rodelinda,' Buononcini's 'Calfurnia,' and Vinci's 'Elpidia' were the other new works produced. The seventh season (November 1725 to June 1726) ended abruptly, owing to the illness of Senesino, but it was remarkable for the first appearance of the celebrated Faustina Hasse, who sang in Handel's 'Alessandro' on May 5. Handel's 'Scipione' was also produced in March. Owing to Senesino's absence, the operas were suspended till Christmas, and the next season ended on June 6, 1727. Ariosti's 'Lucio Vero,' Handel's 'Admeto,' and Buononcini's 'Astyanax' (the last of his operas performed at the Academy) were the chief works; but the season, although short, was enlivened by the continual disturbances caused by the rivalry between Cuzzoni and Faustina. The ninth season lasted from Oct. 3, 1727, to June 1, 1728. The operas were entirely under Handel's direction: his 'Siroe,' 'Tolomeo,' and 'Riccardo I' were produced, but the success of the 'Beggar's Opera' at Lincoln's Inn Fields Theatre, as well as the continual disputes and dissensions amongst the singers, caused the season to be more than usually disastrous. At the end of it, the whole sum subscribed, as well as the receipts, was found to have been entirely spent. The company was dispersed, and although a few meetings of the court were held during the year, the establishment was allowed to die gradually, and was never revived.[1]　　W. B. S.

[1] Further information as to the Royal Academy of Music will be

ROYAL ACADEMY OF MUSIC. The original plan for this institution was proposed by Lord Westmorland (then Lord Burghersh) at a meeting of noblemen and gentlemen held at the Thatched House Tavern, London, on July 5, 1822. The proposal meeting with approval, at a second meeting, July 12, rules and regulations were drawn up, and a committee was appointed to carry out the undertaking. According to the rules adopted, the constitution of the new Academy was to be modelled upon the British Institution. The king was announced as the principal Patron, the government was to consist of a committee of twenty-five Directors and a sub-committee of nine subscribers, and the school was to be supported by subscriptions and donations. There was also to be a Board, consisting of the Principal and four professors, and the number of pupils was not to exceed forty boys and forty girls, to be admitted between the ages of ten and fifteen, and all to be boarded in the establishment. A sub-committee, the members of which were Lord Burghersh, Sir Gore Ouseley, Count St. Antonio, Sir Andrew Barnard, Sir John Murray, and the Hon. A. Macdonald, was empowered to form the Institution. Dr. Crotch was appointed the first Principal, and by September 1, the sum of £4312 : 10s. had been collected, including an annual subscription of 100 guineas from George IV., which was continued by his successors, William IV. and Queen Victoria. In November the house, No. 4 Tenterden Street, Hanover Square, was taken for the new school, but the opening was deferred until March 1823, on the 24th of which month the first lesson was given by Mr. Cipriani Potter to Mr. Kellow Pye.

The Academy began its labours with the following staff: Head Master—Rev. John Miles. Governess—Mrs. Wade. Principal—Dr. Crotch. Board of Professors—Messrs. Attwood, Greatorex, Shield, and Sir George Smart. Supplementary members of the Board—Messrs. Horsley and J. B. Cramer. Professors—Messrs. Anfossi, Andrew, Bishop, Bochsa, Crivelli, F. Cramer, Clementi, Coccia, Cerruti, Dragonetti, Dizi, Griesbach, Hawes, Ireland, C. Kramer, Liverati, Lindley, Loder, Mori, Macintosh, Nicholson, Cipriani Potter, Puzzi, Ries, H. Smart, Spagnoletti, Watts, Willmann, and Caravita.[1]

The Foundation students who were first elected were the following : Girls—M. E. Lawson, C. Smith, M. Chancellor, S. Collier, E. Jenkyns, M. A. Jay, C. Bromley, H. Little, J. Palmer, C. Porter. Boys—W. H. Holmes, H. A. M. Cooke,[2] A. Greatorex, T. M. Mudie, H. G. Blagrove, Kellow J. Pye, W. H. Phipps, A.

found in Burney's *History of Music*, vol. iv., from which the above is compiled.

[1] Although the above was published in the *Morning Post* as the list of professors, instruction seems only to have been given by the following:—Dr. Crotch, Messrs. Lord, Potter, Haydon, Crivelli, F. Cramer, Spagnoletti, Lindley, Bochsa, Cooke, Caravita, Cicchetti, Goodwin, J B. Cramer, Beale, and Finart; and by Mmes. Biagioli, Reguandin, and Miss Adams. (See First Report of the Committee, June 2, 1823.)

[2] Known as 'Grattan Cooke.

Devaux, C. Seymour, E. J. Neilson, and C. S. Packer. The pupils were divided into two classes, those on the foundation paying ten guineas per annum, while extra students paid twenty guineas, or if they lodged and boarded in the establishment, thirty - eight guineas. Although the first report of the Committee (June 2, 1823) was satisfactory, yet financial difficulties soon made themselves felt. In March 1824, the Committee reported a deficiency for the current year of £1600, if the institution were conducted on the same plan as before. To meet this, the difference between the students' payments was abolished, and the fees were fixed for all at £40, the professors at the same time giving their instruction gratis for three months. Lord Burghersh also applied to the Government for a grant, but without effect. In 1825 further alterations were made as to the admission of students, by which the numbers amounted in four months' time to a hundred, and Lord Burghersh made another appeal for a Government grant. In spite of this, the year's accounts still showed an unsatisfactory financial condition. During the latter part of the year Moscheles was included among the staff of professors. Early in 1826 the increased number of students compelled the Academy to enlarge its premises, the lease[3] of No. 5 Tenterden Street was bought, and the two houses were thrown into one. In February the Government were petitioned for a charter. In reply it was stated that though unwilling to give a grant, they were ready to defray the cost of a charter. In 1827 the financial condition of the Academy was so disastrous that it was proposed to close the institution ; but a final appeal to the public procured a loan of £1469, beside further donations, enabling the Directors to carry on the undertaking on a reduced scale and with increased fees. Henceforward the state of things began to mend. The charter was granted on June 23, 1830. By this document the members of the Academy and their successors were incorporated and declared to be, and for ever hereafter to continue to be by the name of the 'Royal Academy of Music,' under the government of a Board of Directors, consisting of thirty members, with power to make rules and regulations ; a Committee of Management, with full power over the funds and both students and professors ; and a Treasurer.

In 1832 Dr. Crotch resigned his post of Principal, and was succeeded by Cipriani Potter, who retained office until his resignation in 1859. The financial position of the Academy, although not prosperous, remained on a tolerably secure footing. In 1834, William IV. directed that a quarter of the proceeds of the Musical Festival held in Westminster Abbey should be handed over to the institution. This sum, amounting

[3] Relinquished in or before 1853.

to £2250, was devoted by the Committee to the foundation of four King's Scholarships, to be competed for by two male and two female students. Instead, however, of being invested separately, the fund was merged in the general property of the Academy, a mistake which eventually led to the discontinuance of the scholarships. For the next ten years the financial condition of the Academy continued to fluctuate. In July 1853 the Committee of Management (which was totally unprofessional in its constitution) summoned the professors, revealed to them the decline of the funded property, and asked their counsel as to the remedies to be adopted. The professors advised that the management should be made entirely professional. This course was so far adopted that a Board of Professors was appointed to advise the Committee.

The first act of this Board (Sept. 1853) was to recommend the discontinuance of the practice of students lodging and boarding on the premises. This recommendation was adopted, and since that time the Academy only receives day students. The Board formed in 1853 was disbanded by Lord Westmorland in 1856, but after his death in 1859, a new Board was formed ; this, however, found itself obliged to resign in 1864. Before its resignation it drew up a memorial to Government, praying for an annual grant. After a conference with a deputation of Professors, Mr. Gladstone, then Chancellor of the Exchequer, inserted in the estimates for the year a sum of £500 ' to defray the charge which will come in course of payment during the year ending March 31, 1865, for enabling the Directors of the Royal Academy of Music to provide accommodation for the Institution.' In 1866, upon the change of Administration, suggestions were made to the Committee on the part of the Government, and were renewed personally in 1867 by the then Chancellor of the Exchequer, in consequence of which the Committee was induced to expend the whole of its funds, in order to accommodate the institution to the designs in which it was invited to participate. In 1867, Lord Beaconsfield (then Mr. Disraeli), in reply to a question as to the grant, announced in the House of Commons that ' the Government were of opinion that they would not be authorised in recommending any enlargement of the grant, the results of the institution not being in fact of a satisfactory character.' This was followed by the total withdrawal of the grant, in order (to quote from an official letter addressed to Sir W. Sterndale Bennett) ' simply to give effect to the opinion that it was not so expedient to subsidise a central and quasi-independent association, as to establish a system of musical instruction under the direct control of some Department of Government.' In this emergency the Committee decided to close the establishment. The funds

(including the sum devoted to the King's Scholarships) were totally exhausted. The Professors met in 1868 to consider what could be done, and generously offered to accept a payment *pro ratâ*. It was then, however, announced that the Committee had resigned the Charter into the hands of the Queen. Upon this the Professors obtained a legal opinion, to the effect that the Charter could not be resigned without the consent of every member of the Academy. As many of the members protested at the time against the resignation of the Charter, it was returned, and by great exertions on the part of the Professors, a new Board of Directors was formed under the Presidency of the Earl of Dudley, who appointed a new Committee of Management, in which the professional element formed an important ingredient. From the time of this change the institution has continued to prosper. In 1868, on the return to office of the Liberal Ministry, Mr. Gladstone restored the annual grant of £500. In 1876 the number of pupils had so increased that the lease of the house adjoining the premises in Tenterden Street had to be repurchased out of the savings of the institution. This house was joined on to the original premises, and a concert-room was formed out of part of the two houses, which though small has proved a great boon not only to the students for their regular concerts, but to many concert-givers for whose purposes the more extensive rooms of St. James's Hall, Exeter Hall, etc., were too large. [For some time the room was not licensed as a public concert room, and at the present time it is not available for outside performances.] In July 1880 Mr. William Shakespeare was appointed conductor of the Students' Concerts, *vice* Mr. Walter Macfarren. He was succeeded in 1886 by Sir Joseph Barnby, but since the election of Sir A. C. Mackenzie the Principal has conducted the students' concerts. [It is since that appointment of Sir Alexander Campbell Mackenzie as Principal in Feb. 1888 that the real tide of prosperity for the institution set in, since which date it has never slackened. The neighbouring houses, 11 and 12 Dering Street, 6 Tenterden Street, and the upper part of 3 Tenterden Street have been successively added to the premises, and still the accommodation is insufficient. The number of students, which was 300 in 1876, rose to 500 in 1896, and remains at that number, the full capacity of the school.

The following have been the Principals of the Academy from its foundation to the present time : Dr. Crotch (1823-32), Cipriani Potter (1832-59), Charles Lucas (1859-66), William Sterndale Bennett (1866-75), George Alexander Macfarren (1875-87), Alexander Campbell Mackenzie (1888).

The Academy is supported by the Government grant, subscriptions, donations, and fees from students. It is under the direction of a President (H.R.H. the Duke of Connaught and

Strathearn, K.G.), four Vice-Presidents (the Earl of Kilmorey, Lord Strathcona, Lord Glenesk, and Lord Alverstone), about twenty Directors, amongst whom are Earls De Grey and Shaftesbury, Sir Benjamin Baker and other distinguished gentlemen, and a Committee of Management, consisting partly of Professors of the Institution and partly of well-known business men who are so good as to place their powers at the service of the Institution. It was the Principal's wish that his office and that of Chairman of this Committee should be separate functions, and accordingly since 1890 this has been the case. Mr. Thomas Threlfall was elected to the latter post in 1890, and filled it with zeal and distinguished success till his death in February 1907. The Committee therefore consists, at the present date, of Messrs. P. L. Agnew, Oscar Beringer, E. E. Cooper (Treasurer), F. Corder (Curator), C. T. D. Crews, Sir Geo. Donaldson, H. C. Gooch, Sir A. C. Mackenzie (Principal), A. Randegger, C. Rube, John Thomas, F. P. Tosti, Fred Walker, and Hans Wessely. The secretary is Mr. F. W. Renaut, and the Lady Superintendent Miss Marion White. A staff of one hundred and two Professors and about twenty sub-professors (students) gives instruction in every branch of music, besides which there are classes for Languages, Diction, Elocution, Opera, Dancing, Drama, Fencing, and Deportment. Students cannot enter for less than a year, nor for a single subject ; the normal course is three years, and all pupils receive an all-round musical training. The library of the institution has been noticed in vol. ii. pp. 705-6.

The list of scholarships and prizes open to competition is too large for enumeration, being fifty-nine of the former and thirty-three of the latter (not all awarded annually) ; but mention should be made of the noble foundation, by the late Mrs. Ada Lewis Hill, of the fifteen scholarships bearing her name, five of which are awarded each year and tenable for three years. Deserving but indigent musical ability is also assisted by the Students' Aid Fund, of which the interest is appropriated, at the Committee's discretion, towards the reduction of the fees of talented pupils.]

Public performances have been given by the pupils of the Royal Academy at various intervals from the date of its foundation. Their locality was sometimes in the Hanover Square Rooms and sometimes at Tenterden Street. [The present custom is to have Fortnightly Concerts of chamber and organ music at the Academy, and one chamber concert and one Orchestral ditto at the Queen's Hall every term. Public operatic and dramatic performances are also given from time to time, these being sometimes of works by the students themselves. At the orchestral practices on Tuesday and Friday afternoons the pupils have the opportunity of hearing their own instrumental or vocal com-

positions, and of performing concertos and songs with orchestral accompaniments.

An account of the Royal Academy would be incomplete without some reference to the part it has taken in the holding of public examinations —so prominent a factor in modern musical life. For many years the Royal Academy of Music held Local Examinations throughout the kingdom, which were popular and lucrative. In order, however, to raise the standard of these examinations and assist the public towards the elimination of defective instruction in music, the Royal Academy of Music entered into negotiations with the Royal College of Music for combined action in the matter. These negotiations happily resulted in a union of the forces of the two Institutions for the purposes of Local Examinations in Music, and the formation, in the year 1889, of the 'Associated Board,' under the Presidency of H.R.H. the Prince of Wales. The work of the 'Associated Board' of the two great Chartered Schools of Music has already produced excellent results. The scheme includes the Local Examination of Schools, as well as Local Centre Examinations, and has recently been extended to the Colonies.

The Academy continues its own separate Examination in London (independent of Academy Teaching) of music teachers and performers. This is known as the 'Metropolitan Examination.' Successful candidates at this Examination, which increases annually in popular estimation, receive Diplomas certifying to their proficiency, and are created by the Directors, Licentiates of the Royal Academy of Music.] w. b. s. ; with additions by f. c.

ROYAL AMATEUR ORCHESTRAL SOCIETY, THE, was established in 1872 by H.R.H. the Duke of Edinburgh (late Duke of Coburg), who was the first president, and leader of the orchestra for many years. Mr. J. R. Gow was honorary secretary, and Mr. George Mount acted as conductor for the first twenty-six years of the Society's existence, retiring in 1897, when Mr. Ernest Ford, the present conductor, was appointed. Sir Arthur Sullivan conducted the first concert in 1873, and took a lifelong interest in the institution, which has done much to raise the standard of amateur proficiency in London. The subscription is two guineas, and the present honorary secretary is Hermann Schmettau, Esq.   M.

ROYAL CHORAL SOCIETY. On the opening of the Albert Hall, Knightsbridge, in 1871, a choral society was formed by Charles Gounod, and was amalgamated in 1872 with a successful institution called 'Barnby's Choir,' and conducted by that musician, the name being from that time 'The Royal Albert Hall Choral Society.' The change to the present title was made in 1888, by command of Queen Victoria. The conductor was Sir Joseph Barnby until his death in 1896, when he was succeeded by Sir Frederick Bridge, who still fills the post with distinction. The great number of voices required to produce a tone adequate to the size of the building makes it unwise to attempt any very complicated choral music or delicate effects of vocal writing ; this cause, added to the indifference of the musical amateurs in London to new choral works, is responsible for the lack of interest which is sometimes complained of in the Society's repertory. But, although the institution has relied for its chief successes upon the hackneyed oratorios, the list of its achievements is a long and honourable one. Fourteen performances took place, in the earlier years, of Bach's St. Matthew Passion ; three have been given of Beethoven's Choral Symphony, while his Mass in D has been attempted. Gounod's 'Redemption' was for many years a regular attraction, and other choral works of the composer's were frequently given. In addition to the more hackneyed oratorios of Handel, 'Judas Maccabæus,' 'Belshazzar,' 'Theodora,' 'Samson,' 'Jephtha,' 'L' Allegro,' and 'Alexander's Feast' have been performed ; and certain notable foreign compositions have been introduced to England by the Society, such as Verdi's famous 'Requiem,' Wagner's 'Parsifal' (in concert form), and Benoit's 'Lucifer.' The English works given by the Society have been, for the most part, repetitions of oratorios, etc. written for the provincial festivals, and therefore only new as regards London. Parry's 'War and Peace' (1903), and the third part of Coleridge-Taylor's 'Hiawatha,' completing the work, were given by the Society for the first time, as well as Bridge's 'Flag of England' (1897) and 'Ballad of the Clampherdown' (1899). M.

ROYAL COLLEGE OF MUSIC. For information as to the commencement of this institution see NATIONAL TRAINING SCHOOL, vol. iii. p. 354. The new institution was founded by the Prince of Wales at a meeting held at St. James's Palace, Feb. 28, 1882, and was opened by H.R.H. on May 7 of the following year. Negotiations took place with the ROYAL ACADEMY OF MUSIC with the object of a union with the two bodies ; but these unfortunately came to nothing. Like its predecessor, the College rests on the basis of endowed scholarships lasting not less than three years ; but the funds for these are in this case provided by the interest of money subscribed throughout the country and permanently invested. The College opened with fifty Scholars elected by competition, of whom fifteen received maintenance in addition, and forty-two paying students. It was incorporated by Royal Charter on May 23, 1883, and is governed by a Council, presided over by the Prince of Wales (the present King), and divided into a Finance Committee, and an Executive Committee. The staff was as follows:—Director, Sir George Grove, D.C.L. ; Principal Teachers,

forming the board of Professors, J. F. Bridge, Mus.D. ; H. C. Deacon ; Henry Holmes ; Mme. Lind-Goldschmidt ; Walter Parratt ; C. Hubert H. Parry, Mus.D. ; Ernst Pauer ; C. V. Stanford, Mus.D. ; Franklin Taylor ; A. Visetti. Other principal teachers were Mme. A. Goddard ; John F. Barnett ; G. C. Martin, Mus.D. ; R. Gompertz ; C. H. Howell ; F. E. Gladstone, Mus.D. ; J. Higgs, Mus.B. ; G. Garcia, etc. Registrar, G. Watson, jun. At the dissolution of the Sacred Harmonic Society (1882) the valuable library was acquired for the College through the exertions of Sir P. Cunliffe Owen, and the library of the Concerts of Antient Music was given by Queen Victoria. In 1887 the Alexandra House was opened, containing a beautiful concert hall, where the students' concerts were regularly held, as well as accommodation for 100 ladies, some of whom are pupils of the College.

When the accommodation in the old building was found insufficient for the needs of the College, a new site was granted in Prince Consort Road, and the first stone of the new building was laid on July 8, 1890. The structure, erected by the generosity of the late Mr. Samson Fox, M.I.C.E., was formally opened on May 2, 1894, and the fine concert-room connected with it was opened on June 13, 1901. In 1894, on the resignation of Sir George Grove, Sir Hubert Parry was appointed director of the institution, and has filled the post with great distinction till the present time. The Council consists (1907) of the following:—H.R.H. The Prince of Wales, H.R.H. Prince Christian, the Archbishop of Canterbury, the Marquis of Northampton, the Earls of Cawdor, Pembroke, Plymouth, Shaftesbury ; Lords Revelstoke, Althorp, Farquhar, The Lord Mayor ; Messrs. C. B. Stuart Wortley, Herbert J. Gladstone, G. W. Spencer Lyttelton, Robert H. Lyttelton, Robert T. O'Neill, Sir J. Whittaker Ellis, Sir Edward W. Hamilton ; Messrs. Lionel Benson, Jacques Blumenthal, Eaton Faning, A. W. Fox, Rev. Canon F. A. J. Hervey ; Messrs. William H. Leslie, Alfred H. Littleton, C. Harford Lloyd, R. F. M'Ewen, George A. Macmillan, Charles Morley, Howard Morley, S. Ernest Palmer, Edward H. Pember ; and J. W. Sidebotham, Esq.

The Board of Professors includes the following names : for singing, Messrs. Randegger and Visetti ; piano, Mr. Franklin Taylor ; organ, Sir Walter Parratt ; violin, Señor Arbos and Mr. Rivarde ; composition, Sir C. V. Stanford ; harmony, etc., Sir J. F. Bridge. A large number of professors in addition to these are on the staff. At the present time, the number of scholars is 67, and of paying students 352.

In 1889 the College of Music and the Royal Academy joined in forming the 'Associated Board,' intended to bring the local examinations of the two schools into line with each other. Both institutions have benefited by the new undertaking, and the standard of musical education in all parts of the Empire has been importantly raised. In 1894 Sir George Donaldson presented a large collection of musical instruments. (See vol. iii. p. 337.) The 'Patron's Fund' was instituted in 1903 by Mr. S. Ernest Palmer, who handed to the College sums amounting in all to £27,000 for the encouragement of composition by the younger British musicians, etc.   M.

ROYAL COLLEGE OF ORGANISTS. See ORGANISTS, ROYAL COLLEGE OF, vol. iii. p. 564.

ROYAL IRISH ACADEMY OF MUSIC, THE, founded in 1848, was re-organised in 1856, the necessary funds being obtained by private subscription, and by the proceeds of operatic performances given by amateur musicians resident in the country. It was not until 1870 that the English Government, of which Mr. Gladstone was then head, voted it an annual grant of £150, subsequently increased to £300, on condition that £100 should be contributed annually by private subscribers. The title 'Royal' was granted in 1872.

Various capital sums have been acquired by the Academy at different times, chiefly through the agency of Sir Francis Brady, Bart., whose efforts on behalf of the Academy cannot be forgotten. These are: The Begley Fund, £125, the Albert Fund, £940, the Vandeleur Bequest, £4000, and the Coulson Bequest, £13,000. The last named was left by Miss Elizabeth Coulson in 1883, to found a School in which 'the children of respectable Irish parents' could be taught instrumental music. The money was handed over to the Academy for administration in 1887 by the Commissioners of Charitable Donations and Bequests, the Academy having been first reconstituted and incorporated under the Educational Endowments (Ireland) Act of 1885.

The Government of the Academy consists at present of: a Patron, His Majesty the King; a vice-patron, H.R.H. the Duke of Connaught; a President, the Lord Lieutenant of Ireland; nine vice-presidents; a Board of twenty-four Governors, of whom twelve are nominated by subscribers, eight by the Municipal Corporation, three by the Coulson Endowment trustees, and one by the Board of Studies, which consists of the Professors. There is no Director, orders being carried out by a Secretary under direction of the Board of Governors.

From small beginnings the Academy has come to hold a very important position in the musical life of the country. While almost every resident musician of distinction has been among its professors—among others Sir Robert Stewart, Mr. Joseph Robinson, Mrs. Fanny Robinson, Mr. R. M. Levey, Herr Elsner,—it has also been the means of bringing to Ireland many foreign artists of talent who have spent their lives in the country and rendered incalculable service in its musical development.

Notable among these must be mentioned the late Herr Bast the violoncellist, and also Signor Michele Esposito, who has created in Dublin a fine school of pianoforte playing, and founded an Orchestral Society of which he is at present conductor. The teaching staff of the Academy in 1906 numbered forty-one, and the students almost 500.

After 1856, the premises of the Academy were the upper portion of a house No. 18 St. Stephen's Green, the classes having previously been held in the rooms of the Antient Concert Society. In 1871 the Council purchased the present building, No. 36 Westland Row, which was the town residence of Sir FitzGerald Aylmer, a fine old house, but now quite inadequate to the needs of the Academy.   E. O. B.

ROYAL SOCIETY OF MUSICIANS OF GREAT BRITAIN, THE, was founded by the exertions of Festing the violinist, and Wiedemann the flautist, who were struck by the appearance of two little boys driving milch asses, who proved to be orphans of a deceased oboe-player named Kytch. [See FESTING, vol. ii. p. 27.] They immediately raised subscriptions to relieve the family, and feeling that some permanent establishment was required to meet similar cases, induced the most eminent music-professors of the day to associate themselves together as a Society for that purpose. This excellent work was formally accomplished on April 19, 1738, and amongst its first members were Handel, Boyce, Arne, Christopher Smith, Carey, Cooke, Edward Purcell, Leveridge, Greene, Reading, Hayes, Pepusch, and Travers. In 1739 the members of the Society executed a 'deed of trust,' which was duly enrolled in the Court of Chancery; the signatures of the members, 226 in number, include the most eminent professors of music of the time. The deed recites the rules and regulations for membership and for the distribution of the funds, and provides for regular monthly meetings at the sign of Saint Martin, in St. Martin's Lane. Handel took an especial and active interest in the welfare of the Society, composing concertos and giving concerts for the benefit of its funds, and at his death bequeathing to it a legacy of £1000. The Handel Commemoration held in Westminster Abbey in 1784 brought a further addition of £6000. In 1789 George III. granted the Society a charter, by virtue of which its management is vested in the hands of the 'Governors' and 'Court of Assistants.' In 1804 the funds of the Society not being in a flourishing condition, the king gave a donation of 500 guineas. Considerable sums have been given or bequeathed to the Society by members of the music profession, especially Signora Storace £1000, Crosdill £1000, Begrez £1000, Schulz £1000; the latest amount of 1000 guineas being that of Mr. Thomas Molineux (Feb. 10, 1881), for many years an eminent performer on the bassoon and double-bass at Manchester, who died in 1891.

The Society pays away annually to relieve distress over £3000, which amount is provided by donations from the public, subscriptions and donations of members of the Society, and interest (about £2500 per annum) on the Society's funded property.

Members of the Society must be professional musicians, and are of both sexes. The Royal Society of Female Musicians was established in 1839 by several ladies of distinction in the musical profession, amongst others Mrs. Anderson, Miss Birch, Miss Dolby, and Miss Mounsey (Mrs. Bartholomew), in consequence of the Royal Society of Musicians having made no provision in their laws for the admission of female members. Practically it soon became evident that the co-existence of two separate societies with the same aim was resulting in considerable loss of sympathy and support ; and that one expenditure would suffice for the management of both institutions, if they could be amalgamated. With the consent of the trustees and members this happy union was effected in 1866, and the two societies have now become one.

There is, says Dr. Burney, 'no lucrative employment belonging to this Society, except-ing small salaries to the secretary and collector, so that the whole produce of benefits and sub-scriptions is nett, and clear of all deductions or drawbacks.' The large staff of physicians, surgeons, counsel, solicitors, give their gratui-tous services to the Society. The present secretary is Mr. Charles Lucas, and the honorary treasurer Dr. W. H. Cummings. The Society's rooms are at No. 12 Lisle Street, Leicester Square, and contain some interesting memorials of music, as well as a collection of portraits, including Handel, by Hudson ; Haydn ; Corelli, by Howard ; Geminiani, by Hudson ; Purcell, by Closterman ; C. E. Horn, by Pocock ; John Parry, the elder ; Sir W. Parsons ; J. Sinclair, by Harlowe ; Gaetano Crivelli, by Partridge ; Domenico Francesco Maria Crivelli ; J. S. Bach, by Clark of Eton ; Beethoven, with autograph presenting it to C. Neate ; W. Dance by his brother ; and a life-size painting of George III. by Gainsborough.　　　　　　w. h. c.

ROZE, MARIE HIPPOLYTE, née PONSIN, born March 2, 1846, at Paris ; received instruction in singing from Mocker at the Conservatoire, and in 1865 gained first prizes in singing and comic opera. She made her début August 16 of that year at the Opéra-Comique as Marie, in Hérold's opera of that name, and at once concluded an engagement for the next three years there. She created the part of Djelma in 'Le Premier jour de Bonheur' of Auber, at his request, on Feb. 15, 1868. After further instruction from Wartel she appeared at the Opéra as Marguerite in 'Faust' (Jan. 2, 1870),

returned to the Opéra-Comique to create the part of Jeanne in Flotow's 'L'Ombre,' July 7, 1870. At the outbreak of the war she left the opera for the army, and served with zeal in the ambulance. After the war she sang for a season at Brussels and elsewhere, and on April 30, 1872, first appeared in England at the Italian Opera, Drury Lane, as Marguerite, and as Marcelline in 'Les Deux Journées,' on its production (for one night only), June 20, 1872. The ensuing seasons, until 1881 (except 1878 and 1880) she sang at that theatre or at Her Majesty's, becoming a great favourite, both on account of her charm of person and manner, and by her readiness to undertake any part, from the small one of Berengaria in Balfe's 'Talismano' (Drury Lane, June 11, 1874), to Donna Anna, Ortrud, Aïda, etc. She also appeared in the provinces, singing both in Italian and English in opera or the concert-room. In 1874 she married an American bass singer, Julius Edson Perkins, who died in the following year at Manchester. She after-wards married Mr. Henry Mapleson. In the winter of 1877 she made a highly successful visit to America, returning in 1879 to Her Majesty's Theatre, where her parts included Donna Anna, Donna Elvira, Pamina, Susanna, Alice, Leonora (Verdi), Agatha, Mignon, Carmen. Aïda, Ortrud, etc. After singing at the Birmingham Festival of 1882 with great success, she joined the Carl Rosa Company from 1883 to 1889 ; in that time she added to her repertory Fidelio, and Elsa, and was the first representative in England of Manon Lescaut in Massenet's opera of that name. Margaret and Helen in Boito's 'Mefistofele,' Fadette in Maillart's 'Dragons de Villars,' Donna Maria in Marchetti's 'Ruy Blas,' are among the parts which she has sung on the first production of these works in English. Her impersonation of Carmen was her greatest success, as it was full of delicate detail, and presented Bizet's music in an ideal way. Many Carmens before and since have emphasised the wild, lawless nature of the gipsy more realistically than she chose to do ; but none have brought out the in-dividuality and charm of the musical conception so finely. She sang the part first in Italian in 1879 in America and afterwards in London, next in English in 1880 at Boston (U.S.A.), in 1883 at Manchester, and on April 15, 1884, appeared in it at Drury Lane, where it was a constant attraction of the Carl Rosa season. She sang it in 1889 in Italian at Covent Garden. Scarcely less effective was her Manon in Massenet's opera, first sung by her in English at Liverpool, Jan. 17, 1885, and at Drury Lane on May 7. In 1890 she settled in Paris as a teacher of singing, reappearing at long intervals in London and the English provinces in con-certs. She made a farewell tour in 1894 ; her last appearance in London was as late as 1903, when she sang at a concert given by one of her pupils.   A. C.

RUBATO, lit. 'robbed' or 'stolen,' referring to the values of the notes, which are diminished in one place and increased in another. The word is used, chiefly in instrumental music, to indicate a particular kind of licence allowed in order to emphasise the expression. This consists of a slight *ad libitum* slackening or quickening of the time in any passage, in accordance with the unchangeable rule that in all such passages any bar in which this licence is taken must be of exactly the same length as the other bars in the movement, so that if the first part of the bar be played slowly, the other part must be taken quicker than the ordinary time of the movement to make up for it ; and *vice versa*, if the bar be hurried at the beginning, there must be a *rallentando* at the end. In a general way this most important and effective means of expression is left entirely to the discretion of the performer, who, it need scarcely be said, should take great care to keep it within due limits, or else the whole feeling of time will be destroyed, and the emphasis so desirable in one or two places will fail of its effect if scattered over the whole composition. Sometimes, however, it is indicated by the composer, as in the first Mazurka in Chopin's op. 6 (bar 9), etc. This licence is allowable in the works of all the modern 'romantic' masters, from Weber downwards, with the single exception of Mendelssohn, who had the greatest dislike to any modification of the time that he had not specially marked. In the case of the older masters, it is entirely and unconditionally inadmissible, and it may be doubted whether it should be introduced in Beethoven, although many great interpreters of his music do not hesitate to use it. [See TEMPO.]   M.

RUBINELLI, GIOVANNI BATTISTA, celebrated singer, born at Brescia in 1753, made his first appearance on the stage at the age of eighteen, at Stuttgart, in Sacchini's 'Calliroe.' For some years he was attached to the Duke of Würtemberg's chapel, but in 1774 he sang at Modena in Paisiello's 'Alessandro nelle Indie' and Anfossi's 'Demofoonte.' His success was very great ; and during the next few years he performed at all the principal theatres in Italy, In 1786 he came to London, after a journey from Rome by no means propitious. The weather was unusually severe, and, in going through France, his travelling chaise was overturned at Macon ; besides which, when approaching Dover, the boat that landed him was upset, and the unlucky singer remained for a time up to his chin in the water. In spite of these perils he made a successful début in a pasticcio called 'Virginia,' his own part in which was chiefly composed by Tarchi. He next sang with Mara, in 'Armida,' and in Handel's 'Giulio Cesare,' revived for him, with several interpolations from Handel's other works. These are said to have been most admirably sung by Rubinelli.

After his season in London he returned to Italy, where he had enormous success at Vicenza and Verona, in 1791 and 1792, in 'La Morte di Cleopatra' of Nasolini, and 'Agesilao' of Andreozzi. In 1800 he left the stage, and settled at Brescia, where he died in 1829.   F. A. M.

RUBINI, GIOVANNI BATTISTA, one of the most celebrated tenor singers, was born at Romano, near Bergamo, on April 7, 1795. The son of a professor of music, he learned the rudiments of his art from his father, and at eight years old could sing in church choirs and play the violin in an orchestra. He was then placed as a pupil with one Don Santo, a priest, organist at Adro, who, however, soon sent him home again, saying that he had no talent for singing. In spite of this, the father persisted in teaching his unpromising son, and allowed him, at the age of twelve, to appear in public at the Romano theatre in a woman's part. The boy was next engaged at Bergamo as chorus-singer, and to play violin solos in the entr'actes. It happened while he was here that in a new drama that was brought out, an air by Lamberti, of considerable difficulty, had to be introduced, for which it was not easy to find a singer. The song was finally entrusted to young Rubini, who acquitted himself with much applause, and was rewarded by the manager with a present of five francs. His elation at the time must have been sadly damped just afterwards by the refusal of a Milan manager to engage him as chorus-singer, because of his insufficient voice.

After belonging for a time to a strolling company, and making an unsuccessful attempt at a concert tour with a violinist called Madi, he got a small engagement at Pavia, then another at Brescia for the Carnival ; he next appeared at the San Moisè theatre at Venice, and lastly at Naples, where the director, Barbaja (according to Escudier), engaged him to sing with Pellegrini and Nozzari, in two operas written for him by Fioravanti. (The name of one of these operas 'Adelson e Salvina,' is identical with that of an early work of Bellini's, produced about this time.) With the public Rubini was successful, but so little does Barbaja appear to have foreseen his future greatness that he wished to part with him at the end of the first year's engagement, and only consented to retain his services at a reduced salary. Rubini preferred making some sacrifice to leaving Naples, where he was taking lessons of Nozzari, and he acceded to Barbaja's conditions, which very soon, however, had to be rescinded, owing to Rubini's brilliant successes at Rome (in 'La Gazza ladra') and at Palermo. Some time in 1819 he married Mlle. Chomel, known at Naples as La Comelli, a singer of some contemporary

GIOVANNI BATTISTA RUBINI

celebrity, a Frenchwoman by birth, and pupil of the Paris Conservatoire.

His first appearance at Paris was on Oct. 6, 1825, in the 'Cenerentola,' and was followed by others in 'Otello' and 'La Donna del Lago.' He was hailed unanimously as 'King of Tenors,' and began here the series of triumphs which lasted as long as his stage career. He was still bound by his engagement with Barbaja, who by this time had become aware of his worth, and only yielded him for six months to the Théâtre Italien, claiming him back at the end of that time to sing at Naples, then at Milan, and at Vienna.

Up to this time his laurels had been won in Rossini's music, on which his style was first formed, and it was not till now that he found his real element, the vehicle most congenial to his special individuality, and thanks to which he was to reach the summit of his fame. Rubini was the foundation and *raison d'être* of the whole phase of Italian opera that succeeded the Rossinian period. He and Bellini were said to have been born for one another, and in all probability Rubini was not more captivated by the tender, pathetic strains of Bellini, than the sensitive Bellini was influenced by Rubini's wonderful powers of expression. Such a singer is an actual source of inspiration to a composer, who hears his own ideas not only realised, but, it may be, glorified. During the whole composition of 'Il Pirata,' Rubini stayed with Bellini, singing each song as it was finished. To this fortunate companionship it cannot be doubted that we owe 'La Sonnambula' and 'I Puritani.' Donizetti, again, achieved no great success until the production of 'Anna Bolena,' his *thirty-second* opera, in which the tenor part was written expressly for Rubini, who achieved in it some of his greatest triumphs. It was followed by 'Lucia,' 'Lucrezia,' 'Marino Faliero,' and others, in which a like inspiration was followed by the same result.

Rubini first came to England in 1831, when freed from his engagement with Barbaja, and from that time till 1843 he divided each year between Paris and this country, singing much at concerts and provincial festivals, as well as at the Opera, and creating a *furore* wherever he went.

His voice extended from E of the bass clef to B of the treble, in chest notes, besides commanding a falsetto register as far as F or even G above that. A master of every kind of florid execution, and delighting at times in its display, no one seems ever to have equalled him when he turned these powers into the channel of emotional vocal expression, nor to have produced so magical an effect by the singing of a simple, pathetic melody, without ornament of any kind. He indulged too much in the use of head-voice, but 'so perfect is his art,' says Escudier, writing at the time, 'that the transition from one register to the other is imperceptible to the hearer. . . . Gifted with immense lungs, he can so control his breath as never to expend more of it than is absolutely necessary for producing the exact degree of sound he wishes. So adroitly does he conceal the artifice of respiration that it is impossible to discover *when* his breath renews itself, inspiration and expiration being apparently simultaneous, as if one were to fill a cup with one hand while emptying it with the other. In this manner he can deliver the longest and most drawn-out phrases without any solution of continuity.' His stage appearance was not imposing, for his figure was short and awkward, his features plain and marked with small-pox. He was no actor, and seems rarely to have even tried to act. His declamation of recitative left something to be desired. 'In concerted pieces he does not give himself the trouble of singing at all, and if he goes as far as to open his mouth, it is only to preserve the most absolute silence' (Escudier). 'He would walk through a good third of an opera languidly, giving the notes correctly and little more,—in a duet blending his voice intimately with that of his partner (in this he was unsurpassed); but when his own moment arrived there was no longer coldness or hesitation, but a passion, a fervour, a putting forth to the utmost of every resource of consummate vocal art and emotion, which converted the most incredulous, and satisfied those till then inclined to treat him as one whose reputation had been overrated' (Chorley). Some of his greatest effects were produced by an excessive use of strong contrasts between *piano* and *forte*, 'which in the last years of his reign degenerated into the alternation of a scarcely-audible whisper and a shout.' He was the earliest to use that thrill of the voice known as the *vibrato* (with the subsequent abuse of which we are all of us too familiar), at first as a means of emotional effect, afterwards to conceal the deterioration of the organ. To him, too, was originally due that species of musical sob produced by the repercussion of a prolonged note before the final cadence, which, electrifying at first as a new effect, has become one of the commonest of vocal vulgarisms. But such was his perfection of finish, such the beauty of his expression, such his thorough identification of himself, not with his dramatic impersonations but with his songs, that his hold on the public remained unweakened to the last, even when his voice was a wreck and his peculiarities had become mannerisms. He has had numberless imitators, but no rival in the art of gathering up and expressing in one song the varied emotions of a whole opera, and to this may be due the fact that he was as much worshipped and as affectionately remembered by numbers who never set foot in a theatre, as by the most constant of opera-goers.

In 1843 he started with Liszt on a tour

through Holland and Germany, but the two separated at Berlin, and Rubini went on alone to St. Petersburg, where he created an enthusiasm verging on frenzy. By his first concert alone he realised 54,000 francs. The Emperor Nicholas made him ' Director of Singing ' in the Russian dominions, and a colonel into the bargain.

In the summer of this year Rubini went to Italy, giving some representations at Vienna by the way. He returned to Russia in the winter of 1844, but finding his voice permanently affected by the climate resolved to retire from public life. He bought a property near Romano, where he passed his last years, and died, on March 2, 1854, leaving behind him one of the largest fortunes ever amassed on the operatic stage, which, unlike too many of his brother artists, he had not squandered. He seems to have been a simple, kindly-natured man, and letters of his, still extant, show that he was ready and willing to assist needy compatriots.   F. A. M.

RUBINSTEIN, ANTON GREGOR, an eminent composer and one of the greatest pianists the world has ever seen, was born Nov. 28, 1830,[1] of Jewish parents, at Wechwotynetz, in Volhynia, near the Austrian frontier of Russia. He received his first musical instruction from his mother, and afterwards from a pianoforte-teacher in Moscow named Villoing. So early as 1839 he made his first public appearance in Moscow, and in the following year undertook a concert-tour with his teacher, journeying to Paris, where he made the acquaintance of Liszt, who was then teaching in that city, and under whose advice he there pursued his studies. A year later he made a more extended tour, going to England (1842), and thence to Holland, Germany, and Sweden. In 1845 he went to study composition with Professor Dehn in Berlin. From 1846 to 1848 he passed in Vienna and Pressburg, teaching on his own account. In 1848 he returned to Russia, where the Grand Duchess Helen nominated him Kammervirtuos. After studying diligently in St. Petersburg for eight years he appeared as a fully-fledged artist with piles of original compositions, first in Hamburg and then all over Germany, where he found enthusiastic audiences and willing publishers. His early operas, to Russian words, were performed as follows :— 'Dimitri Donskoi,' 1852 ; 'Die Sibirischen Jäger,' 1852 ; 'Toms der Narr,' 1853, and 'Hadji-Abrek,' were not performed. From this time his fame as a pianist and composer spread rapidly over Europe and America. He again visited England in 1857, and made his first appearance at the Philharmonic on May 18. In 1858 he returned home again, gave

[1] Nov. 30 is given in most books of reference, as the equivalent of Nov. 18 (O.S.). In his autobiography (see below) he declares Nov. 16 (O.S.) to be the actual day, but that the 18th had been so long regarded as his birthday that he had no intention of changing it. Nov. 16 (O.S.) is the equivalent of Nov. 28.

brilliant concerts in St. Petersburg, Moscow, etc., and settled in the former city. At this period he was appointed Imperial Concert-director, with a life-pension. Thenceforward he worked in conjunction with his friend Carl Schuberth for the advancement of music in Russia, and had the merit of being the founder of the St. Petersburg Conservatorium in 1862, remaining its Principal until 1867. The Russian Musical Society, founded in 1859, was also his. On leaving Russia he made another triumphant tour through the greater part of Europe, which lasted till the spring of 1870. When in his native country, in 1869, the Emperor decorated him with the Vladimir Order, which raised him to noble rank. In 1870 he rested awhile, and expressed the intention of retiring from public life ; but it was not likely that this desire could be fulfilled. He held the Directorship of the Philharmonic Concerts and Choral Society in Vienna for the next year or two, and this was followed by fresh concert tours. In 1872-73 he toured in America. Every year the same threat of retirement was made, but the entreaties of the public, and, probably, the desire of providing for his wife and family, brought the gifted genius before us again and again. He gave a set of farewell recitals all over Europe in 1885-87, and in 1887-1890 he again undertook the direction of the St. Petersburg Conservatorium, and from the latter year lived for a time in Dresden. In 1889 he celebrated his artistic jubilee and published an Autobiography. He died at Peterhof, Nov. 20, 1894.

Rubinstein's playing was not only remarkable for the absolute perfection of *technique*, in which he was the only rival Liszt ever had, but there was the fire and soul which only a true and genial composer can possess. He could play a simple piece of Haydn or Mozart so as positively to bring tears into the eyes of his hearers, but on the other hand, he would sometimes fall a prey to a strange excitement which caused him to play in the wildest fashion. An example (though hardly a commendable one) of his perfect mastery over tone is to be found in his performance of the Funeral March of Chopin's Sonata in B♭ minor. Regardless of the composer's intentions, he began it *ppp*, proceeding *crescendo*, with perfect gradation, up to the Trio, after which he recommenced *ff* and with an equally long and subtle *diminuendo* ends as softly as he began. As an effect—the idea of a band passing—this is stale and unworthy of an artist, but as a *tour de force* it can only be justly appreciated by those who have heard it done and then sought to imitate it.

The compositions of Rubinstein may be considered as the legitimate outcome of Mendelssohn ; there is a fine broad vein of melody which is supported by true and natural harmony, and a thorough technical skill. But

ANTON GREGOR RUBINSTEIN

there is also the fatal gift of fluency, and the consequent lack of that self-criticism and self-restraint which alone make a composer great. Rubinstein has written in every department of music, but as yet his songs and chamber-music are all that can be called really popular, excepting always his 'Ocean Symphony,' which is known all over the world.[1] This is undoubtedly one of his very best works, the ideas throughout being vivid and interesting, while the workmanship shows unusual care. From the composer's having added an extra Adagio and Scherzo after the first appearance of this Symphony we may presume he had a particular regard for it, though to risk wearying an audience by inordinate length is scarcely the way to recommend a work to their favour. The 'Dramatic' Symphony (op. 95) has been admired, while of the other three symphonies the first and fifth have each only been performed once in England. His Pianoforte Concertos are very brilliant and effective, especially that in G (op. 45); they will perhaps in time take a permanent position. His Violin Concerto (op. 46) is a very fine work, though but little known. The Persian Songs (op. 34) are perhaps the most popular of his vocal works, but there are many very striking and successful specimens among his other songs—'Es blinkt der Thau' and 'Die Waldhexe' for instance—and the duets are full of beauty and passion. The numerous drawing-room pieces which he has written for the piano are far superior to most of their class, his writing for the instrument being invariably most brilliant, as is but natural in so great a pianist. His chamber-music is not much known in England, and he is apt to give the piano an undue prominence in it; the Quintet in F (op. 55) is almost a Pianoforte Concerto in disguise. His operas and oratorios have as yet met with but qualified success, seeming to lack dramatic force. This is in some measure due to his antagonism to the theories and practice of Wagner and the modern German school. He had a preference for sacred subjects, which are but ill fitted for the stage.

List of dramatic works (including the oratorios, or sacred operas, which were all intended for stage-performance):—

Dimitri Donskoi. St. Petersburg, 1852.
Sibirskije Ochotnikie. St. Petersburg, 1852. ('Die Sibirischen Jäger.')
Foma Duratchok ('Toms, der Narr'). St. Petersburg, 1853.
Mest ('Die Rache'). St. Petersburg, 1858.
Hadji-Abrek (apparently not performed).
Die Kinder der Haide, five acts. Vienna, 1861.
Feramors (Lalla Rookh). three acts. Dresden, 1863.
Der Thurm zu Babel ('The Tower of Babel'). Königsberg, 1870 (see op. 80).
Der Dämon, three acts. St. Petersburg, 1875. As 'Il Demonio,' Covent Garden, 1881.
Die Makkabäer, three acts. Berlin, 1875.
Das Verlorene Paradies (Düsseldorf, 1875). A preliminary performance had taken place in 1855 under Liszt at Weimar (see op. 54).
Nero, four acts. Hamburg, 1879.
Kalashnikov Moskovski Kupets ('Der Kaufmann von Moskau'). St. Petersburg, 1880.
Die Rebe ('La Vigne'), 1882.

Sulamith. Hamburg, 1883.
Unter Räubern, one act (Hamburg, 1883, played before 'Sulamith'). Der Papngei, one act. Hamburg, 1884.
Moses (1887), see op. 112.
Gorjushka ('Die Kummervolle'). St. Petersburg, 1889.
Christus. Berlin, 1888, Bremen, 1895, on the stage (see op. 117).

The complete list of Rubinstein's numbered works is as follows:—

Op.		Op.	
1.	6 little Songs in Low German dialect. Voice and PF. Schreiber.	44.	'Soirées de St. Petersbourg.' for PF. solo (6 pieces). Kahnt.
2.	2 Fantasias on Russian themes. PF. solo. Schreiber.	45.	3rd PF. Concerto (G). B. B.
3.	2 Melodies for PF. solo (F, B). Schreiber.	46.	Concerto, Violin and Orch. (G). Peters.
4.	Mazourka-Fantaisie. PF. solo (G). Schreiber.	47.	3 String Quartets (Nos. 4, 5, 6, E min., Bb, D min.). B. & H.
5.	Polonaise, Cracovienne and Mazurka. PF. solo. Schreiber.	48.	12 Two-part Songs (from the Russian) with PF. Senff.
6.	Tarantelle, PF. solo (B). Schreiber.	49.	Sonata for PF. and Viola (F min.). B. & H.
7.	Impromptu - Caprice, 'Hommage à Jenny Lind.' PF. solo (A minor). Schreiber.	50.	6 'Charakter - Bilder.' PF. duet. Kahnt.
8.	6 Songs (words from the Russian). Voice and PF. Senff.	51.	6 Morceaux for PF. Senff.
		52.	3rd Trio. PF. and Strings (Bb). Senff.
9.	Octet in D for PF. V., Viola, Vcello, Bass, Fl., Clar., and Horn. Peters.	53.	6 Preludes and Fugues in free style. PF. solo. Peters.
10.	Kamennoi - Ostrow. 24 Portraits for PF. Schott.	54.	'Paradise Lost.' Sacred Opera after Milton, in 3 parts. Senff.
11.	3 Pieces for PF. and V.; 3 do. for PF. and Vcello; 3 do. for PF. and Viola. Schuberth.	55.	Quintet for PF. and Wind (F). Schuberth.
12.	1st Sonata for PF. solo (E). Peters.	56.	3rd Symphony (A). Schuberth.
13.	1st Sonata for PF. and V. (G). Peters.	57.	6 Songs. Voice and PF. Senff.
		58.	Scena ed Aria, 'E dunque vero?' Sop. and Orch. Schott.
14.	'The Ball,' Fantasia in 10 Nos. for PF. solo. B.[2]	59.	String Quintet (F). Senff.
15.	2 Trios. PF., V., and Vcello (F, G min.). Hofmeister.	60.	Concert Overture in Bb. Senff.
16.	Impromptu, Berceuse and Serenade. PF. solo. Hofmeister.	61.	3 Part-songs for Male Voices. Schreiber.
		62.	6 Part-songs for Mixed Voices. Schreiber.
17.	3 String Quartets (G, C min., F). B. & H.[3]	63.	'Die Nixe.' Alto Solo, Female Chorus, and Orch. Senff.
18.	1st Sonata for PF. and Vcello (D). B. & H.	64.	5 Fables by Kriloff. Voice and PF. Senff.
19.	2nd Sonata for PF. and V. (A min.). B. & H.	65.	1st Concerto for Vcello and Orch. (A min.). Senff.
20.	2nd Sonata for PF. solo (C min.). B. & H.	66.	Quartet. PF. and Strings (C). Senff.
21.	3 Caprices for PF. solo (F#, D, Eb). B. & H.	67.	6 Two-part Songs with PF. Senff.
22.	3 Serenades. for PF. solo (F, G min., Eb). B. & H.	68.	'Faust.' Musical portrait, for Orch. Siegel.
23.	6 Études for PF. solo. Peters.	69.	5 Morceaux for PF. solo. Siegel.
24.	6 Preludes for PF. solo. Peters.	70.	4th PF. Concerto (D min.). Senff.
25.	1st PF. Concerto (E min.). Peters.	71.	3 Morceaux. PF. solo. Siegel.
26.	Romance and Impromptu, PF. solo (F, A minor). Schreiber.	72.	6 Songs for a Low Voice and PF. Senff.
27.	9 Songs (words from Russian). Voice and PF. Schreiber.	73.	Fantaisie for 2 Pianos (F). Senff.
28.	Nocturne (Gb) and Caprice (Eb) for PF. solo. Kistner.	74.	'Der Morgen.' Cantata for Male Voices and Orch. (from the Russian). Senff.
29.	2 Funeral Marches. PF. solo. —1. For an Artist (F min.); 2. For a Hero (C min.). Kistner.	75.	'Album de Peterhof.' 12 Pieces. PF. solo. Senff.
		76.	6 Songs for Voice and PF. Senff.
30.	Barcarolle (F. min.); Allo Appass. (D min.) for PF. solo. Kistner.	77.	Fantaisie for PF. (E min.). Senff.
		78.	12 Songs from the Russian. Voice and PF. Senff.
31.	6 4-part Songs for Male Voices. Kistner.	79.	'Ivan the Terrible.' Musical portrait for Orch. B. B.
32.	6 Songs from Heine. Voice and PF. Kistner.	80.	'The Tower of Babel.' Sacred opera in one act. Senff. Chapell.
33.	6 Songs. Voice and PF. Kistner.	81.	6 Études for PF. solo. B. B.
34.	12 Persian Songs. V. and PF. Kistner.	82.	Album of National Dances (6) for PF. solo. B. B.
35.	2nd PF. Concerto (F). Schreiber.	83.	10 Songs. Voice and PF. B. B.
36.	12 Songs from the Russian. Voice and PF. Schreiber.	84.	Fantasia for PF. and Orch. (C). Senff.
37.	Akrostichon (Laura) for PF. solo. Schreiber.	85.	4th Trio. PF. and Strings (A). Lewy.
38.	Suite (10 Nos.) for PF. solo. Senff.	86.	Romance and Caprice for Violin and Orch. Senff.
39.	2nd Sonata for PF. and Vcello (G). B. & H.	87.	'Don Quixote.' Musical portrait. Humoreske for Orch Senff.
40.	1st Symphony for Orchestra (F). Kahnt.	88.	Theme and Variations for PF. solo (G). Senff.
41.	3rd Sonata for PF. solo (F). B. & H.	89.	Sonata for PF. duet (D). Senff.
42.	2nd Symphony, 'Ocean' (C). Senff.	90.	2 String Quartets (Nos. 7, 8, G min., E min.). Senff.
43.	Triumphal Overture for Orchestra. Schott.		

---

[1] First performed in London by Musical Art Union (Klindworth) May 31, 1861; with extra movements, Crystal Palace, April 12, 1877. Philharmonic, June 11, 1879

[2] B. B.=Bote & Bock.   [3] B. & H.=Breitkopf & Härtel

Op.
91. Songs and Requiem for Mignon (from Goethe's 'Wilhelm Meister') for Solos, Chorus, and PF. Senff.
92. 2 Scenas for Contralto and Orchestra. No. 1. 'Hecuba'; No. 2. Hagar in the desert.' Senff.
93. 9 Books of Miscellaneous Pieces (12) for PF. solo. Senff.
94. 5th PF. Concerto (Eb). Senff.
95. 4th Symphony, 'Dramatic' (D min.). Senff.
96. 2nd Concerto. Vcello and Orch. Senff.
97. Sextuor for Strings(D). Senff.
98. 3rd Sonata. PF. and V. (B min.). Senff.
99. Quintet. PF. and Strings (G min.). Senff.
100. 4th Sonata for PF. solo (A min.). Senff.
101. 12 Songs. Voice and PF. Senff.
102. Caprice Russe. PF. and Orch. Senff.
103. Bal costumé. Set of characteristic pieces (20) for PF. 4 hands. B. B.
104. Élégie; Variations; Étude. PF. solo. B. B.

Op.
105. A series of Russian songs. Voice and PF. B. B.
106. 2 String Quartets (Nos. 9, 10, Ab, F min.).
107. 5th Symphony (G min.). In memory of the Grandduchess Hélène Paulowna. Senff.
108. 5th Trio for PF. and Strings in C minor.
109. Soirées Musicales. 9 PF. pieces.
110. Eroica, Fantasia for PF. and Orchestra.
111. 6th Symphony (A minor).
112. 'Moses,' a Biblical opera in 8 tableaux. Part I. containing four tableaux (Bilder), was published by Senff, 1888.
113. Concertstück for PF. and Orch.
114. Akrostichon, for PF. solo.
115. Songs.
116. Concert- overture, 'Antony and Cleopatra.'
117. Christus, Biblical Opera.
118. Six PF. solos.
119. Suite in Eb for orchestra, in six movements.

Without opus numbers appeared the following :—
Symphonic poem, 'Russj.' Moscow, 1882.
Fantasia eroica for orchestra.
Ouverture solennelle, for orchestra, with organ and chorus (posth.). Three barcarolles (A minor, G, and C minor).
Pianoforte pieces : — 'Valse caprice,' E flat, and 'Ungarische Phantasie,' 'Russische Serenade,' 'Phantasie,' 3 Morceaux charactéristiques,' 6 preludes, cadenzas to Beethoven's pianoforte concertos, and to Mozart's concerto in D minor, arrangement of the march in Beethoven's 'Ruins of Athens.'

Rubinstein's appearance was remarkable. His head was of a very Russian type, without beard or moustache, but with a thick shock of dark-brown hair.

We have said that Rubinstein's first visit to London was in 1842. He was then only just twelve. Mendelssohn and Thalberg were both here, and the Philharmonic was thus naturally already occupied. Mention of him is to be found in Moscheles's Diary for 1842 (*Leben*, ii. 90), where he is spoken of by that genial master as 'a rival to Thalberg . . . a Russian boy whose fingers are as light as feathers, and yet as strong as a man's.' In the *Musical and Dramatic Review* of May 28, 1842, he is mentioned. He did not return to this country till 1857, when he appeared at the Philharmonic on May 18, playing his own Concerto in G. He came back in the following year, played again at the Philharmonic on June 7, and at the Musical Union, May 11. In 1869 he came a fourth time, and played at the Musical Union only (May 18, June 1). In 1876 he made his fifth visit, played at the Philharmonic, May 1, and gave four Recitals in St. James's Hall. In 1877 he again gave recitals, and conducted his 'Ocean' Symphony (six movements) at the Crystal Palace, April 21 ; he conducted his 'Dramatic' symphony, and played Beethoven's Concerto in G, at the Crystal Palace on June 4. In 1881 he gave another series of Recitals at St. James's Hall, his opera 'The Demon' was brought out in Italian at Covent Garden on June 21, and his 'Tower of Babel,' with other music, at the Crystal Palace on June 11. In May and June 1887, he gave a final set of seven historical recitals in St. James's Hall.

Rubinstein made sundry attempts as a writer on musical subjects. The 'Autobiography' spoken of above appeared in German to celebrate his artistic jubilee in 1889, and was translated into English by Aline Delano in 1890. (See *Musical Times*, 1891, p. 105.) 'Die Kunst und ihre Meister' appeared in 1892, as well as 'Erinnerungen aus 50 Jahren.' (German transl. in 1895.) A posthumous supplement to 'Die Kunst,' etc., called 'Gedankenkorb,' was published posthumously in 1897. Among various biographies of Rubinstein may be mentioned those of W. Baskin (1886), N. Lissowski (1889), A. MacArthur (1889), and Sandra Droucker (1904).

NICHOLAS, his younger brother, born at Moscow, June 2, 1835, was also a fine pianist and no mean composer, though overshadowed by the fame of his great brother. He studied under Kullak and Dehn in Berlin during 1844-46. In 1859 he founded at Moscow the Russian Musical Society, which gives twenty concerts each year ; and in 1864 the Conservatorium, and was head of both till his death. In 1861 he visited England, and played twice at the Musical Union (June 4, 18). In 1878 he gave four orchestral concerts of Russian music in the Trocadéro at Paris with great success. He died of consumption in Paris, Mar. 23, 1881, on his way to Nice for his health, widely and deeply lamented. His latest published work is op. 17—'Scène du Bal, Polonaise.' His best-known pupils are Taneiev, Siloti, and Sauer. The Musical Society gives annual concerts in his memory, on the anniversaries of his birth and death.

RUBINSTEIN, JOSEPH—no relation to the foregoing—was born at Staro Konstantinov, in Russia, Feb. 8, 1847, and acquired some fame as a pianist and composer of drawing-room music. He also obtained an unenviable notoriety through certain newspaper articles in the *Bayreuther Blätter* signed with his name, and attacking Schumann and Brahms in a most offensive and vindictive manner. He made some good pianoforte transcriptions of the works of Wagner, of whom he was an ardent if not very judicious propagandist. He committed suicide at Lucerne, Sept. 15, 1884.   F. C.

RUCKERS, harpsichord makers of Antwerp, who were working as masters between 1579 and 1667 or later, the first of whom, Hans Ruckers, is always credited with great improvements in keyboard instruments. It is certain that the tone of the Ruckers harpsichords has never been surpassed for purity and beauty of tone-colour, and from this quality they remained in use in England, as well as in France and the Netherlands, until harpsichords and spinets were superseded, at the end of the 18th century, by the pianoforte. The art of harpsichord making, as exemplified in London by Kirkman and Shudi, was directly derived from Antwerp and the

Ruckers. Time seemed to have no effect with the Ruckers instruments. They were decorated with costly paintings in this country and France, when a hundred years old and more. New keys and new jacks replaced the old ones ; so long as the sound-board stood lasted the ' silvery sweet' tone. It has done so in some instances until now, but modern conditions of life seem to be inimical to the old wood ; it will be difficult, if not impossible, to preserve any of these old instruments much longer. As a work of piety we have catalogued all that we have seen or can hear of, appending the list to this notice.

In John Broadwood's books, 1772-73, are several entries concerning the hiring of Ruker, Rooker, and Rouker harpsichords to his customers ; to the Duchess of Richmond, Lady Pembroke, Lady Catherine Murray, etc. etc. In 1790 Lord Camden bought a 'double Ruker' : in 1792 Mr. Williams bought another, the price charged for each being twenty-five guineas. These entries corroborate the statement of James Broadwood (*Some Notes*, 1838, printed privately 1862) that many Ruckers harpsichords were extant and in excellent condition fifty years before he wrote. He specially refers to one that was twenty years before in possession of Mr. Preston, the publisher, reputed to have been Queen Elizabeth's, and sold when Nonsuch Palace was demolished. To have been hers Hans Ruckers the elder must be credited with having made it.

If the tone caused, as we have said, the long preservation of the Ruckers clavecins, on the other hand the paintings which adorned them not unfrequently caused their destruction. A case in point is the instrument of the Parisian organist, Balbastre, whom Burney visited when on his famous tour. Burney says it was painted inside and out with as much delicacy as the finest coach or snuff-box he had ever seen. Inside the cover was the story of Rameau's ' Castor and Pollux,' the composer, whom Burney had seen some years before, being depicted crowned with a wreath. He describes the tone as delicate rather than powerful (he would be accustomed in London to the sonorous pompous Kirkmans, which he so much admired), and the touch, in accordance with the French practice of quilling, as very light. This instrument was then more than a hundred years old, perhaps more than a hundred and fifty. On the front board above the keys is inscribed a complete piece of clavecin music, ' Pastorale par Mr. Balbastre, le 6 Aoust, 1767,' beginning—

etc.

The stand for this instrument is rococo, and gilt. We learn more of its fate from Rimbault (*The Pianoforte*, 1860, p. 76), who tells us that it became the property of Mr. Goding of London, who sacrificed Ruckers' work, to display the paintings by Boucher and Le Prince that had adorned it, on a new grand piano made for the purpose by Zeitter. This maker showed respect for his predecessor by preserving the sound-board, which he converted into a music-box, the inscription ' Joannes Ruckers me fecit Antverpiae' being transferred to the back. This box ultimately became Rimbault's ; the piano was sold at Goding's sale by Christie & Manson in 1857. In the same house (Carlton House Terrace), and sold by auction at the same time for £290, was an Andries Ruckers harpsichord that had also been made into a pianoforte by Zeitter. In this instrument the original belly, dated 1628, was preserved. The sound-hole contained the rose (No. 6) of this maker. The present compass of the piano is five octaves F—F. Inside the top is a landscape with figures, and outside, figures with musical instruments on a gold ground. Round the case on gold are dogs and birds, a serpent and birds, etc. All this decoration is 18th-century work. The instrument is on a Louis Quinze gilt stand.

It was this intimate combination of the decorative arts with music that led to the clavecin and clavichord makers of Antwerp becoming members of the artists' guild of St. Luke in that city. They were enrolled in the first instance as painters or sculptors. We must, however, go farther back than Hans Ruckers and his sons to estimate truly their position and services as clavecin makers. For this retrospect the pamphlet of the Chevalier Léon de Burbure — *Recherches sur les Facteurs de Clavecins et les Luthiers d'Anvers* (Brussels, 1863), supplies valuable information. We learn that at the end of the 15th and beginning of the 16th centuries, precisely as in England and Scotland at the same period, the clavichord was in greater vogue than the clavecin ; possibly because clavecins were then always long and sometimes trapeze-shaped. It must be remembered that the names Clavicordio in Spain, Clavicordo in Italy, and Clavicorde in France, have been always applied to the quilled instruments. We are not, therefore, sure whether old references to the clavichord are to be taken as describing a plectrum or a tangent keyboard instrument. About the year 1500 the clavecin had been made in the clavichord shape in Venice, and called Spinet. [See SPINET.] This new form must have soon travelled to the Low Countries, and have superseded the Clavichord as it did in England and France about the same epoch.

A clavecin maker named Josse Carest was admitted in 1523 to the St. Luke's guild as a sculptor and painter of clavichords (literally ' Joos Kerrest, clavecordmaker, snyten scildert').[1] Another Carest had been accepted in 1519 as an apprentice painter of clavecins ('Goosen

[1] See *De Liggeren en andere Historische Archieven der Antwerpsche Sint Lucasgilde*. Rombouts en Van Lerius. 2 vols. Baggerman, Antwerp ; Nijhoff, The Hague.

Kareest, schilder en Klavecimbelmaker, gheleert by Peeter Mathys '). This is an earlier instance of the name Clavecin than that quoted by M. de Burbure as the oldest he had found in Belgium, viz. a house in the parish of Notre Dame, Antwerp, which, in 1532, bore the sign of ' de Clavizimbele.' No doubt at that time both clavecins and clavichords were in use in Antwerp, but in a few years we hear of the latter no more ; and the clavecin soon became so important that, in 1557, Josse Carest headed a petition of the clavecin-makers to be admitted to the privileges of the guild as such, and not, in a side way, merely as painters and sculptors of their instruments. Their prayer was granted and the ten petitioners were exempted from the production of ' masterworks,' but their pupils and all who were to come after them [1] were bound to exhibit masterworks, being clavecins, oblong or with bent sides (' viercante oft gehoecte clavisimbale,' square or grand as we should say), of five feet long or more ; made in the workshops of master experts, of whom two were annually elected ; and to have the mark, design, or scutcheon, proper to each maker (syn eygen marck, teecken, oft wapene), that is, a recognised trade-mark on each instrument. We will give these trade-marks of the members of the Ruckers family from sketches kindly supplied by [the late] M. Abel Régibo, of Renaix in Belgium ; three, belonging to Hans and his two sons, having been already published by M. Edmond Vander Straeten in his monumental work La Musique aux Pays-Bas, vol. iii. (Brussels, 1875).[2] It is at once evident that such regulations tended to sound work. The trade-marks we have more particularly described under ROSE. They were usually made of lead, gilt, and were conspicuous in the sound-holes of the instruments.

Some of the contemporary Italian keyboard-instruments might be taken to give a general idea of what the Antwerp ones were like prior to the improvements of Hans Ruckers the elder. In the preparation of the sound-boards the notion of the sound-chest of LUTE and PSALTERY prevailed. Ruckers adhered to this principle, but being a tuner and perhaps a builder of organs, he turned to the organ as a type for an improved clavecin, and while holding fast to timbre as the chief excellence and end of musical instrument making, introduced different tone colours, and combined them after organ analogies and by organ contrivances of added keyboards and registers. It is doubtful what changes of construction Hans Ruckers made in the harpsichord—perhaps the octave strings only. Yet a clavicembalo by Domenico di Pesaro, dated 1590, in the Victoria and Albert Museum, has the octave strings with two stops. Ruckers's great service may after all have only

been to improve what others had previously introduced. It is nearly certain that harpsichords with double keyboards and stops for different registers existed before his time, and their introduction may be attributed to the great favour the Claviorganum, or combined spinet and organ, was held in during the 16th century. The researches of M. Edmond Vander Straeten (La Musique aux Pays-Bas, vol. viii. Brussels, 1885) have done much to bring into prominence the great use of the Claviorganum at an early time ; see Rabelais, who, before 1552, described Carêmeprenant as having toes like an ' épinette organisée.' The merit of Hans Ruckers, traditionally attributed to him, and never gainsaid, was his placing the octave as a fixture in the long clavecin, boldly attaching the strings to hitch-pins on the sound-board (strengthened beneath for the purpose), and by the addition of another keyboard, also a fixture, thus establishing a model which remained dominant for large instruments until the end of the clavecin manufacture.[3] [On the inventions of H. Ruckers the elder, see Hipkins's Pianoforte Primer, p. 81.]

An interesting chapter is devoted to the Ruckers family by M. Edmond Vander Straeten in the work already referred to (vol. iii. p. 325, etc.). He has gathered up the few documentary notices of the members of it discovered by MM. Rombouts and Van Lerius, by M. Génard and by M. Léon de Burbure, with some other facts that complete all that is known about them.

The name Ruckers, variously spelt Rukers, Rueckers, Ruyckers, Ruckaers, Rieckers, and Rikaert, is really a contraction or corruption of the Flemish Ruckaerts or Ryckaertszoon, equivalent to the English Richardson. Hans the elder was certainly of Flemish origin, being the son of Francis Ruckers of Mechlin. He can hardly have been born later than 1555. Married at Notre Dame (the cathedral), Antwerp, June 25, 1575, as Hans Ruckaerts, to Naenken Cnaeps, he was admitted as Hans Ruyckers, ' clavisinbalmakerre,' to the Lucas guild in 1575. It appears strange that he was not enrolled a citizen until 1594, but this may have been, as M. de Burbure suggests, a readmission, to repair the loss of a record burnt when the Spaniards sacked the Hôtel de Ville in 1576. In those troubled times there could have been but little to do in clavecin-making. May we see in this a reason for his acquiring that knowledge of the organ which was to lead ultimately to his remodelling the long clavecin ?

He had four sons, Francis, Hans, Andries, and Anthony. It is only with Hans (baptized Jan. 13, 1578) and Andries (baptized August 30, 1579) that we are concerned, since they

---

[1] Later on, tuners also became members of the guild. For instance Michel Colyns, Claversingelatelder, in 1631-32 ; who was, however, the son of a member.

[2] Burney refers to these marks when writing about the Ruckers.

[3] The end of the manufacture for Antwerp is chronicled by M. de Burbure in one seen by him—he does not say whether single or double—made by a blind man, and inscribed ' Joannes Heineman me fecit A° 1795, Antwerpiae.' The latest harpsichord made (apart from modern revivals) seems to be an instrument by Clementi, dated 1802, and shown at the Bologna Exhibition of 1888.

became clavecin-makers of equal reputation with their father. We learn that in 1591 Hans Ruckers the elder became tuner of the organ in the Virgin's chapel of the Cathedral, and that in 1593 he added fourteen or fifteen stops to the large organ in the same church. In 1598 and 1599 either he or his son Hans (the records do not specify which) had charge of the organs of St. Bavon, and from 1617 to 1623 of St. Jacques. The like doubt exists as to the Hans who died in 1642. We believe that this date refers to the son, as the latest clavecin we have met with of his make is the Countess of Dudley's beautiful instrument dated that year (list, No. 41); the latest certain date of the father's clavecins at present found being 1614. The earliest is 1590, with which date three existing instruments are marked.

JAHS

The trade-mark of Hans the elder is here represented.

Of the instruments catalogued below, it will be observed that twenty are probably by Hans the elder. The long ones are provided with the octave stop and, with a few exceptions, have the two keyboards identified with him as the inventor. But it is interesting to observe the expedients agreeing with the statement of Praetorius, that octave instruments [1] were employed with and in the oblong clavecins. These expedients doubtless originated before Hans Ruckers; indeed in the Museum at Nuremberg, there is an oblong clavecin of Antwerp make, signed 'Martinus Vander Biest,' and dated 1580, that has an octave spinet in it.[2] 'Merten' Vander Biest entered the Guild in Antwerp, as one of the ten clavecin makers, in 1558. Now Messrs. Chappell of London had such an instrument, No. 16 in appended catalogue, made by Hans Ruckers, certainly the elder. No keys remain, but the scale of both the fixed and movable

keyboards is the same, four octaves marked near the wrest-pins *si—si* (B—B). In this clavecin it is the left-hand keyboard which is removable and is tuned an octave higher. In the Museum of the Conservatoire, Brussels, there is an oblong clavecin by Hans the elder (No. 8), wherein the octave spinet is above and not by the side of the fixed one—according to M. Victor Mahillon a later addition, though the work of the maker himself. This curious instrument formerly belonged to Fétis (who sold the paintings that adorned it), and is dated 1610. While on the subject of these removable octave spinets we will refer to one with keyboards side by side, made by Hans the younger (No. 23), and dated 1619, the property of M. Régibo, and another, a long clavecin, also by Hans the younger (No. 44), not dated, now in the Hochschule, Berlin, that has the octave spinet fixed in the angle side, precisely as in a more modern one, made by Coenen of Ruremonde, which may be seen in the Plantin museum, Antwerp. The same construction is found in a harpsichord by Hans the elder (No. 5).

Hans Ruckers the younger—known to the Belgian musicologists as Jean, because he used the initials J. R. in his rose, while the father, as far as we know, used H. R.—was, as we

have said, the second son. M. Régibo has supplied us with three of his roses.

We have given the date of his baptism in the cathedral in 1578, but have no further details to record beyond the ascertained facts that he was married to Marie Waelrant, of the family of the musician Hubert Waelrant,[3] in the cathedral, Nov. 14, 1604; that either he or his brother Andries was admitted as a master in the Guild in 1611; and that he was employed to tune the organ of St. Jacques from 1631 until 1642.

---

[1] We hesitate to accept Praetorius's statement literally as to such spinets being tuned a fifth as well as an octave higher. This more likely originates in the fact that the F and C instruments had before his time been made at one and the same pitch, starting from the lowest key, although the disposition of the keyboards and names of the notes were different; as in organs, where pipes of the same measurement had been actually used for the note F or the note C. See SHORT OCTAVE; Arnold Schlick's *Spiegel der Orgelmacher*, 1511.

[2] A woodcut of this rare instrument is given in Part ix. of Dr. A. Reissmann's *Illustrirte Geschichte der deutschen Musik*, Leipzig, 1881. Both keyboards, side by side, are apparently original, with white naturals and compass of four octaves C—C. It is the right-hand keyboard that is tuned the octave higher, and is removable like a drawer. A full description of this double instrument is reproduced in Reissmann's work, copied from the *Anzeiger für Kunde der deutschen Vorzeit* (Nuremberg, 1879, No. 9).

[3] Dr. John Bull succeeded Rumold Waelrent as organist of the cathedral in 1617, and retained the post until his death in 1628. He must have known Hans Ruckers and his two sons well, and been well acquainted with their instruments.

There is also evidence as to his having died in that year, and not the father, who would seem to have died before.

Mr. Vander Straeten has, however, brought us nearer Hans the younger, by reference to Sainsbury's collection of *Original unpublished papers illustrative of the life of Sir Peter Paul Rubens* (London, 1859, p. 208, etc.), wherein are several letters which passed in 1638 between the painter, Balthazar Gerbier, at that time at Brussels, and the private secretary of Charles I., Sir F. Windebank. They relate to the purchase of a good virginal from Antwerp for the King of England. Be it remembered that up to this time, and even as late as the Restoration, all clavecins in England, long or square, were called Virginals. [See VIRGINAL.] Gerbier saw one that had been made by Hans Ruckers, the younger (' Johannes Rickarts '), for the Infanta. He describes it as having a double keyboard placed at one end, and four stops ; exactly what we should now call a double harpsichord. There were two paintings inside the cover, the one nearest the player by Rubens; the subject Cupid and Psyche. The dealer asked £30 for it, such instruments without paintings being priced at £15. After some correspondence it was bought and sent over. Arrived in London it was found to be wanting six or seven keys, and to be insufficient for the music,[1] and Gerbier was requested to get it exchanged for one with larger compass. Referring to the maker, Gerbier was informed that he had not another on sale, and that the instrument could not be altered. So after this straightforward but rather gruff answer Gerbier was written to not to trouble himself further about it. Mr. Vander Straeten inquires what has become of this jewel ? We agree with him that the preservation of the pictures has probably long since caused the destruction of the instrument. With such decoration it would hardly remain in a lumber-room. Mr. Vander Straeten himself possessed a Jean Ruckers single harpsichord (now in the Berlin Hochschule), restored by M. Ch. Meerens, of which he has given a heliotype illustration in his work. It is a splendid specimen of Hans the younger. (See No. 27 below).

Andries Ruckers (the elder, to distinguish him from his son Andries), the third son of Hans, was, as we have said, baptized in 1579, and was a master in 1610. As a member of the confraternity of the Holy Virgin in the cathedral he tuned the chapel organ gratuitously in 1644. His work, spite of Burney's impression about the relative excellence of his larger instruments, was held in as great esteem as that of his father and brother. In 1671, Jean Cox, choirmaster of the cathedral, left by will, as a precious object, an André Ruckers clavecin. Handel, many years after, did the same. Within the writer's

recollection there have been three honoured witnesses in London to this maker's fame, viz. Handel's (No. 77), dated 1651, given by Messrs. Broadwood to the Victoria and Albert Museum ; Mr. Howard Head's (No. 55), dated 1614; and one belonging to the late Miss Twining, a single keyboard one (No. 74), dated 1640.[2] A tradition exists that Handel had also played upon both the last-named instruments. We do not know when Andries Ruckers the elder died. He was certainly living in 1651, since that date is on

his harpsichord (Handel's) at South Kensington. His roses are here given.

Of Andries Ruckers the younger, the information is most meagre. Born in 1607, he probably became a master in 1636. The Christian name is wanting to the entry in the ledger, but as the son of a master, the son of Andries the elder is apparently indicated. The researches of M. Génard have proved the birth of a daughter to Hans the younger, but not that of a son. It might be Christopher, could we attribute to him a master for a father. Regarding him, however, as living earlier, we are content to believe that Andries the younger then became free of the Guild ; but as his known instruments are of late date, it is possible that he worked much with his father. We know from a baptism in 1665 that the younger Andries had married Catherina de Vriese, perhaps of the family of Dirck or Thierri de Vries, a clavecin-maker whose death is recorded in 1628. Fétis (*Biog. Univ.*, 2nd edit. vii. 346b) says he had seen a fine clavecin made by Andries the younger, dated 1667. M. Régibo possesses undoubted instruments by him, and has supplied a copy of his rose (7). He has done the same for

[1] The Hitchcocks were active in the latter half of the 17th century, and early in the 18th, making spinets in London with five octaves, C—G.

[2] This instrument formerly belonged to the Rev. Thomas Twining, Rector of St. Mary, Colchester, who died in 1804. A learned scholar (he translated Aristotle's *Poetics*) and clever musician, he enjoyed the friendship of Burney and valued highly his favourite harpsichord, on which the great Handel had played. Charles Salaman used both this instrument and Messrs. Broadwood's in his admirable lectures given in 1855-56 in London and the provinces.

Christopher Ruckers (8), of whose make he owns a specimen. M. Vander Straeten refers to another in the Museum at Namur. We cannot determine Christopher's relationship to the other Ruckers, but he might have been the Her Christofel Ruckers, organist and clockmaker of Termonde, where he set up a carillon in 1549 —possibly a priest, at least the title 'Her' would indicate a person regarded with veneration. The same writer, in the 5th vol. p. 393 of *La Musique aux Pays-Bas*, continues, 'who knows if this Christopher did not own a work-shop for clavecin making? The priest was everything at that epoch, and a scholar, an organ or spinet-builder seems to us quite natural and normal.'

We will now give the list of the existing Ruckers instruments as complete as we have been able to make it. The kind and never-tiring help of MM. Mahillon, Meerens, and Vander Straeten of Brussels, and of MM. Snoeck and Régibo of Renaix, as well as of other friends, in compiling it, is gratefully acknowledged.

Catalogue of Ruckers Clavecins, still existing (1907), *as far as possible according to date. Extreme measurements of length and width.*[1]

In all the sound-boards are painted with devices, generally of fruit, birds, and flowers.

I. Hans Ruckers de Oude (the Elder).

No.	Form.	Date.	Dimensions.	General Description.	Present Owner.	Source of Information.
			ft. in.　ft. in.			
1	Bent side.	1590	7　4 by 2　9	2 keyboards, not original; black naturals; 4¾ octaves, G—E; finely painted. Rose No. 1.	Collection of the late M. Régibo, Renaix.	A. Régibo.
2	Bent side.	1590	7　9 by 2 10½	2 keyboards, not original; black naturals; 5 oct.; extended by Blanchet.[2] Inscribed Hans Ruckers me fecit Antverpiae; Rose No. 1.	Musée du Conservatoire, Paris.	G. Chouquet.
3	Bent side.	1590	....	2 keyboards; case 'en laque de Chine'; 5 stops 'à genouillère.'	Château de Pau, France.	Spire Blondel, *La Revue Britannique*, Oct. 1880.[3]
4	Trapeze.	1591	5　7 by 1 11	1 keyboard; compass 3¾ octaves, E—C. White naturals. Rose No. 1. Red and black ornamentation on yellow ground. Inscribed 'Scientia non habet inimicum nisi ignorantem.' Date on cover, 1591.	T. J. Canneel, Director of the Académie Royale, Ghent.	T. J. Canneel.
5	Bent side harpsichord with octave spinet in one.	1594	5 11 by 2　6	2 keyboards; the front one 4 oct., C—C; the side one 3½ oct., E—A, without the highest G♯; 3 stops in original position at the right-hand side; white naturals. Rose No. 1; and Rose to octave spinet an arabesque. Painting inside top showing a similar combined instrument. Mr. Lionel Cust considers the painting to be by Hieronymus Janssens. Inscribed Hans Ruckers me fecit Antwerpia.	Gewerbe Museum, Berlin.	A. J. Hipkins.
6	Oblong.	1598	....	1 keyboard, 4½ oct., G—C (short octave in bass, not original); white naturals. Inscribed Joannes Rvckers Fecit Antwerpiae 1598, and 'Dulcissimum reficit tristia corda melos.'	Mlle. Jeanne Lyon, Paris.	Paris Exhibition, 1889.
7	....	1604	1 mètre. 45 (width)	3½ oct. Rose H.R. Original decoration simple, subsequently painted in grisaille. Inscribed Joannes et Andreas Rvckers Fecervnt 1604.	The late M. Régibo, Renaix.	Vander Straeten.
8	Oblong.	1610	5　7 by 1　7	2 keyboards one above the other; white naturals; 4½ oct., C—F each. The upper and octave instrument a later addition by the maker. Inscribed Hans Ruckers me fecit Antverpiae, 1610.	Musée du Conservatoire, Brussels.	V. Mahillon.
9	Oblong.	1610	....	1 keyboard, 3 octaves, short octave in bass. Inscribed Hans Rvckers me fecit, Antwerp, 1610, and 'Laudabo nomen Dei cum cantico et magnificabo eum in laude.' The case is of ebony inlaid with engraved ivory. A small octave instrument.	Musée du Conservatoire, Paris.	Rev. F. W. Galpin.
10	Oblong.	1611	5　6 by 1　7½	1 keyboard; 3¾ oct., E—C; case patterned paper. Inscribed Joannes Ruckers fecit Antverpiae, 1611; H. R. rose.	Musée du Steen, Antwerp.	E. Vander Straeten and V. Mahillon.
11	Bent side.	1612	7　6 by 2 11	2 keyboards (put in by Messrs. Broadwood, 1885). Rose No. 1. Case and compass as No. 77. New keys, jacks, and stops. Inscribed Joannes Rvckers me fecit Antverpiae, 1612. Found at Windsor Castle, 1883. This may have been the large Harpsichord left by Handel to Smith, and given by the latter to King George III.	H.M. The King.	A. J. Hipkins.

[1] The present ownership of the instruments has not been possible to trace in all cases, owing to the frequent dispersal of private collections.

[2] It was believed by MM. Snoeck, Vander Straeten, Régibo, and V. Mahillon, that few of the Ruckers clavecins were of the original compass of keys. The statements of compass in this list and also in Keyboard should be qualified by this remark. The increase was, however, made long ago, and in some instances possibly by the maker himself. M. Vander Straeten, p. 348, has a passage quoted from Van Blankenburg: 'This was at the time when clavecins had still a narrow keyboard. In the present day (1739?) it would be difficult to meet with one of this kind; all the keyboards having been lengthened.' Again, white naturals are believed to be original

in these instruments. Upon very old alterations it is not easy to decide. We are of opinion that black naturals and ivory sharps were occasionally substituted when the paintings were done. In dealing with these questions, however, it is best to refrain from generalising; many errors having arisen from too hasty conclusions.

[3] M. Spire Blondel (*Histoire Anecdotique du Piano*) mentions a Ruckers clavecin, painted by Gravelot, as finding a buyer at the sale of Blondel d'Azincourt. M. du Sommerard in a private letter refers to one found in a village, probably a Hans Ruckers. There are more in France, as M. Chouquet has heard of three, but has no particulars of them to communicate. Inquiry has failed to discover one in Holland or the Rhenish provinces.

No.	Form.	Date.	Dimensions.	General Description.	Present Owner.	Source of Information.
			ft. in. ft. in.			
12	Bent side.	1612	7 6 by 3 0	2 keyboards; black naturals. Rose No. 1. No name of original maker, but inscribed 'Mis en ravalement par Pascal Taskin, 1774,' meaning that the compass of keys was extended. This beautiful instrument, painted inside and out with Louis XIV. subjects by Vander Meulen, is said to have belonged to Marie Antoinette. It will be remembered as having adorned the Louis Seize Room of the Historic Collection, Inventions Exhibition, London, 1885.	Sir Edgar Speyer.	A. J. Hipkins.
13	Oblong.	1614	5 5½ by 1 7½	1 keyboard; 3¾ oct., E—C; white naturals.	The late M. Snoeck, Renaix.	C. Meerens.
14	Bent side.	1614	7 4½ by 3 3	2 keyboards; not original; 5 oct., etc., F—G; white naturals; curved bent side and round narrow end; 2 genouillères and a sourdine of the 18th century. Rose No. 1.	Museum of the Hochschule für Musik, Berlin.	C. Meerens.
15	Bent side.	1628	7 7¼ by 3 6½	Rose No. 6 in sound-board, which is painted with the usual decoration. The width has been increased to admit of a greater compass.	Walter H. Burns, Esq., and Captain Hall.	A. J. Hipkins.
16	Oblong.	Undated	5 7 by 1 5½	2 keyboards side by side, the left-hand one removable, having its own belly and rose, but to be tuned an 8ve higher than the fixed instrument; no keys left; 4 oct., B—B. Both stretchers inscribed JOANNES RUCKERS ME FECIT. 2 roses No. 1. (See No. 23.) Good paintings. Stand, an arcade with 6 balusters.	Royal College of Music, London.	A. J. Hipkins.
17	Bent side.	..	7 4 by 2 7	2 original keyboards; 4½ oct., C—F (5 keys added); white naturals; 3 stops.	M. Régibo, Renaix.	A. Régibo.
18	Bent side.	..	Not original.	Described on p. 181*a*, *b*.	Panmure Gordon, Esq.	A. J. Hipkins.
19	Oblong.	Undated	....	Double virginal, inscribed JOHANNES RVQVERS ME FECIT. Compass, 4 octaves, C—C. White naturals; not original. Keyboard of the larger instrument to the right, the smaller (octave) instrument enclosed in the larger case to the left.	Morris Steinert Collection, New Haven, Connecticut, U.S.A.	Rev. F. W. Galpin.
20	Oblong.	Undated	....	Virginal, keyboard to right.	Musée du Steen, Antwerp.	Rev. F. W. Galpin.

II. HANS RUCKERS DE JONGE (the Younger).

No.	Form.	Date.	Dimensions.	General Description.	Present Owner.	Source of Information.
21	Bent side.	1617	6 8 by 3 7	2 keyboards; white naturals. Paintings in Vernis Martin, lately removed.	M. Pilette, Brussels, 1878, since sold, Hôtel Drouot.	Victor Mahillon.
22	Oblong.	1618	2 8½ by 1 3	1 original keyboard; 3¾ oct., E—C; white naturals. Inscribed JOANNES RUCKERS FECIT. Rose No. 2.	Musée du Conservatoire, Paris.	G. Chouquet.
23	Oblong.	1619	7 4 by 2 7	2 original keyboards, side by side, 4 stops to the fixed one, the other tuned 8ve higher; 4½ oct., C—F; white naturals. Roses No. 4. (See No. 16.)	M. Régibo, Renaix.	A. Régibo.
24	Oblong.	1619	3 5 by 1 8½	1 original keyboard; 3¾ oct., E—C; white naturals. Rose No. 2.	M. Régibo, Renaix.	A. Régibo.
25	Oblong.	1622	5 7 by 1 7½	1 keyboard; 4½ oct., C—F; white naturals. Inscribed JOANNES RUCKERS FECIT ANTVERPIAE, 1622, and OMNIS SPIRITUS LAUDET DOMINUM.	M. Victor Mahillon, Brussels.	V. Mahillon.
26	Oblong.	1626	4 3 by 1 7	1 keyboard. Inscribed JOANNES RUCKERS FECIT ANTWERPIAE, 1626.	Pley Collection, Brussels (dispersed Nov. 1906).	Rev. F. W. Galpin.
27	Bent side.	1627	6 0 by 2 7½	1 original keyboard; 4⅓ oct., C—E; white naturals; 2 stops; Rose No. 4; painting inside top, drawn in *La Musique aux Pays-Bas*, tome 3. Inscribed as No. 25, and MUSICA DONUM DEI.	Museum of the Hochschule, Berlin.	E. Vander Straeten.
28	Oblong.	1628	5 9 by 1 7½	1 keyboard; 4½ oct., C—F, without lowest C♯; appears to have been extended by the maker from 3¾ oct., E—C. A sourdine 'à genouillère.'	M. Léon Jouret, Brussels.	V. Mahillon.
29	Bent side.	1628	....	1 keyboard; sound-board painted with musical subjects.	Mme. Snoeck, Ghent.	Rev. F. W. Galpin.
30	Bent side.	1629	7 4 by 3 0	2 keyboards; 58 keys, G—F; black naturals. Rose No. 4.	M. Gerard de Prins, Louvain.	F. P. de Prins, Limerick.
31	Bent side.	1630	4 10½ by 2 10	2 keyboards; 4¾ oct., G—E; black naturals; painting inside top said to be by Lancret. Inscribed JOANNES RUCKERS ME FECIT ANTVERPIAE. Case and top black and gold lacquer, Chinese. Drawn in *L'Illustration*, March 13, 1858, and as frontispiece to Chevalier de Burbure's pamphlet.	Baroness James de Rothschild, Paris.	Georges Pfeiffer.
32	Bent side.	1632	8 2 by 3 3	2 keyboards; 5 oct. and 1 note, F—G; white naturals; 4 stops 'à genouillère.' Rose No. 3.	M. Snoeck, Renaix.	C. Meerens.
33	..	1632	....	Top painted. (The date inclines us to attribute this one to Hans the Younger); the rose is not described.	M. De Breyne, Ypres.	E. Vander Straeten.
34	Bent side.	1634	7 3 by 3 2	1 keyboard; compass 4¾ octaves, G—E. White naturals. Name-board, JOHANNES RVCKERS ME FECIT, ANTVERPIAE. On flap, 'Soli Deo gloria.' Inside top, 'Acta virum probant.'	Earl of Dysart.	A. J. Hipkins.
35	Oblong.	1636	5 9 by 1 8	1 keyboard. Inscribed JOANNES RVCKERS, FECIT ANTWERPIAE, 1636. The stand also original.	Pley Collection, Brussels (dispersed).	Rev. F. W. Galpin.
36	Oblong.	1637	....	1 keyboard to right, 4 oct., C—C (short oct. in bass); white naturals. On sound-board the date 1637, and on the cover the inscription— 'Audi Vide et Tace Si vis vivere in Pace.'	Museum of the Hochschule für Musik, Berlin.	Rev. F. W. Galpin.
37	Bent side.	1637	6 1 by 2 9½	1 keyboard; 4⅝ oct., A—F; white naturals. Inscribed as No. 31, with date.	The late John Callcott Horsley, Esq., R.A., London.	J. C. Horsley.
38	Oblong.	1638	5 9 by 1 7	1 keyboard; 4 oct., etc., C—D; white naturals. Inscribed as No. 25, with date, and MUSICA MAGNORUM EST SOLAMEN DULCE LABORUM. Rose No. 2.	Mme. Snoeck, Ghent.	C. Meerens.

No.	Form.	Date.	Dimensions.	General Description.	Present Owner.	Source of Information.
39	Bent side.	1638	ft. in. ft. in. 7 4½ by 2 6	2 original keyboards, the lower, 4 oct. and a note, E—F; the upper, 45 keys, E—C. The upper have prolongations on the lowest F♯ and G♯ keys at an angle to touch the fourths below, in order to preserve the semitonal succession after the short octave of the lower keyboard, while securing the short octave of the upper. Below E of the upper is a wooden block described by Quirin van Blankenburg. This is the only Ruckers known to Mr. Hipkins left unaltered in the instrument and keyboards. A restorer has taken away two rows of jacks and the stops, as may be still seen; making the instrument two independent spinets, an eleventh apart in pitch, so as to set the keyboards with untransposed notes. Painted belly with date; over keys JOANNES RVCKERS FECIT ANTVERPIAE. Paintings inside top, black and gold case and old stand. Formerly in the possession of the late Mr. Spence of Florence. See *Pianoforte Primer*, p. 88.	The late Right Hon. Sir Bernhard Samuelson (1896).	A. J. Hipkins.
40	Bent side.	1639	5 9 by 2 7½	1 keyboard; no keys; 4 stops; Rose No. 4; black and gold case.	South Kensington Museum (gift of Messrs. Kirkman).	A. J. Hipkins.
41	Bent side.	1642	7 4½ by 2 8	2 keyboards; 4½ oct., B—D; 4 stops at the side as originally placed; Rose No. 4; paintings.	Countess of Dudley.	A. J. Hipkins.
42	Bent side.	Undated	7 11 by 3 0	2 keyboards; 5 oct., F—F; painted outside by Teniers or Brouwer, inside by Breughel and Paul Bril. Rose No. 3.	Musée du Conservatoire, Paris (Clapisson Collection).	G. Chouquet.
43	Bent side.	..	7 1 by 2 7	1 keyboard; 4½ oct., G—D; black naturals; Rose No. 4; blackwood case with incrusted ivory, according to M. du Sommerard, Italian work.	Musée de l'Hôtel de Cluny, Paris. Cat. 1875, No. 2825.	A. J. Hipkins.
44	Bent side, with oblong clavecin attached.	..	5 11 by 2 5½	2 keyboards; each 3¾ oct., E—C; black naturals; 2 stops to the bent side instrument and Rose No. 4; to the oblong one, Rose No. 2; superbly painted. The two instruments together form an oblong square.	Museum of the Hochschule, Berlin.	C. Meerens.
45	Bent side.	..	5 11 by 2 7½	4½ oct., C—E; white naturals; superb paintings.	M. Snoeck, Renaix.	C. Meerens.
46		..	6 0 by 2 7	1 original keyboard, 4½ oct., C—F; 5 keys added in treble; white naturals; 3 stops; Rose No. 2; painting of Orpheus playing a bass viol.	M. Régibo, Renaix.	A. Régibo.
47	Bent side.	..	....	1 original keyboard, 4½ oct., C—F; 4 keys added in treble; Rose No. 3, cut in hardwood.	M. Régibo, Renaix.	A. Régibo.
48	Oblong.		....	1 keyboard; 5 oct. and a note, F—G; not original. An exceptional form, allied to the older Italian pentagonal spinets, enclosed in an oblong case.	Museum of the Hochschule, Berlin.	Rev. F. W. Galpin.
49 and 50	} Oblong.	..	....	{ Two specimens in the Flemish collection of the late C. Snoeck.	Mme. Snoeck, Ghent.	Rev. F. W. Galpin.
51	Bent side.	..	....	1 keyboard with two registers, unison and octave.	Musée du Steen, Antwerp.	Rev. F. W. Galpin.

III. ANDRIES RUCKERS DE OUDE (the Elder).

No.	Form.	Date.	Dimensions.	General Description.	Present Owner.	Source of Information.
52	Oblong.	1610	4 4 by 1 6	1 keyboard to the right; 4 oct., C—C; (short oct. in bass); white naturals. Inscribed ANDREAS RVCKERS ME FECIT ANTWERPIAE, and 'Omnis spiritus laudet Dominum.' On the sound-board is the date 1610. A 'sourdine' added in the 18th century.	Rev. F. W. Galpin, Hatfield, Essex.	Rev. F. W. Galpin.
53	Oblong.	1613	3 8½ by 1 4½	1 keyboard; 4 oct., C—C; white naturals. Inscribed ANDREAS RUCKERS ME FECIT ANTVERPIAE, 1613. Belonged to the clavecinist and carillonneur, Matthias Vanden Gheyn, who put his mark upon it in 1740.	Musée du Conservatoire, Brussels.	V. Mahillon.
54	Oblong.	1613	....	1 keyboard to the left; 4 oct., C—C; (short oct. in bass). A small instrument.	Mme. Snoeck, Ghent.	
55	Bent side.	1614	7 6 by 2 8	2 keyboards, not original; 4½ oct., A—E; white naturals; buff leather, lute and octave stops; pedal, not original; case veneered 18th century. Inscribed as No. 53. Rose No. 6. Painting inside top attributed to Van der Meulen.	Howard Head, Esq., London.	A. J. Hipkins.
56	Bent side.	1615	4 0 by ..	Inscribed CONCORDIA RES . PARVAE . CRESCUNT . DISCORDIA . MAXIMAE . DILABUNTUR; was in the Collegiate Church of St. Jacques, Antwerp.	....	Léon de Burbure, p. 26.
57	Bent side.	1618	7 4 by 2 10	4½ oct., C—F; white naturals. Inscribed SOLI DEO GLORIA.	Museum of the Hochschule, Berlin.	C. Meerens.
58	Bent side.	1619	8 10½ by 2 10	2 keyboards; 5 oct., C—C; the lowest note 8ve below cello C; belly gilt and diapered in Moorish style; painting of Orpheus outside. Inscribed as No. 53, with date. Rose No. 5.	M. Régibo, Renaix.	A. Régibo.
59	Bent side.	1620	5 10 by 2 8	2 keyboards; 4½ oct., G—F; (short oct. in bass); 4 stops. Workmanship very similar to No. 14, but has the initials A. R.	Museum of the Hochschule, Berlin.	C. Meerens.
60	Oblong.	1620	....	1 keyboard; 4 oct., C—C; (short oct. in bass); white naturals. Inscribed ANDREAS RUCKERS ME FECIT ANTVERPIAE and SIC TRANSIT GLORIA MUNDI. Perhaps identical with No. 62.	Morris Steinert Collection, New Haven, Connecticut.	Rev. F. W. Galpin.
61	Oblong.	1620	5 8 by 1 7½	1 keyboard to the right; 4 oct., C—C; white naturals; chromatic compass, the short octave having been completed by a later hand. Inscribed ANDREAS RVCKERS ME FECIT ANTWERPIAE, and 'Omnis spiritus laudet Dominum.' On the sound-board the date 1620.	Musée du Conservatoire, Brussels.	Rev. F. W. Galpin.
62	Oblong.	1620	4 1 by 1 3½	1 keyboard; 3¾ oct., E—C; white naturals. Inscribed as No. 53, and inside the top SIC TRANSIT GLORIA MUNDI. See No. 60.	M. Alfred Campo, Brussels.	V. Mahillon.

No.	Form.	Date.	Dimensions.	General Description.	Present Owner.	Source of Information.
			ft. in. ft. in.			
63	Oblong.	1623	5 7½ by 1 7½	1 keyboard; 4 oct., C—C; white naturals. Inscribed as No. 53, with date.	MM. Victor and Joseph Mahillon, Brussels.	V. Mahillon.
64	Bent side.	1623	7 9 by 3 1	2 keyboards; 5 oct., F—F; white naturals; 3 stops; pedal not original; case veneered 18th century. Rose No. 6.	The late John Hullah, London.	H. Holiday.
65	Bent side.	1624	8 0 by 2 10	5 oct., F—F; 3 stops. Inscribed Musica Laetitiae Comes, Medicina Dolorum.	Musée Archéologique, Bruges.	V. Mahillon.
66	Oblong.	1626	4 0 by 3 1½	1 keyboard; 3½ oct. and 2 notes; at least an 8ve added in the 18th century. Inscribed as No. 53, and inside top as No. 62. The stand a row of five balusters.	....	E. Vander Straeten.
67	Oblong.	1632	5 8 by 1 7½	1 original keyboard to right hand of front; 4½ oct., C—F; white naturals. Inscribed inside top Musica . Magnorum . Solamen . Dulce . Laborum. Rose No. 6.	M. Régibo, Renaix.	A. Régibo.
68	Oblong.	1633	2 1½ by 1 6	1 original keyboard to left hand of front; 4½ oct. C—F; white naturals. Inscribed Andreas Ruckers fecit Antverpiae. Hardwood jacks of double thickness; painting inside top. Rose No. 6.	M. Régibo, Renaix.	A. Régibo.
69	Bent side.	1633	7 0 by 2 8	1 keyboard. Inscribed Andreas Ruckers in Antwerpen Anno 1633. Formerly in the collection of Paul de Wit, Leipzig.	Heyer Collection, Cologne.	Rev. F. W. Galpin.
70	....	1634	....	Inscribed Andreas Ruckers Antverpiae.	In a village in Flanders.	E. Vander Straeten.
71	Bent side.	1636	....	2 keyboards not original; 5 oct.; black naturals stops and legs like Taskin's; beautifully painted. Inscribed as No. 53, with date.	.... Dijon, France.	E. Vander Straeten.
72	Bent side.	1636	7 8 by 3 1	2 keyboards. Rose No. 6. Buff stop. Painted on name-board André Ruckers Année 1636. 'Mis en ravalement par Pascal Taskin, 1782.' Case and top Lacquer with Japanese figures. Exhibited, London, 1885.	Museo Civico, Turin.	A. J. Hipkins.
73	Bent side.	1639	6 4 by 2 9 at keyboard.	2 keyboards, compass 4½ octaves G — D, white naturals. Two unisons and octave. Case dark green, powdered with gold. Sound-board painted, and usual A. Ruckers rose.	Morley, London.	Mr. C. Cramp, and E. J. Hipkins.
74	Bent side,	1640	6 0 by 2 5	1 original keyboard; 4 oct., etc., C—D; white naturals. Inscribed Andreas Rukers, 1640; and inside top Musica Laetitiae Comes Medicina Dolorum; inside flap Concordia Musis Amica. 2 stops; Rose No. 6; case patterned paper.	The late Miss Twining, Dial House, Twickenham.	A. J. Hipkins.
75	Oblong.	1644	5 8 by 1 8	1 keyboard; 4 oct., C—C. Inscribed Andreas Ruckers, Anno 1644.	M. Victor Mahillon, Brussels.	V. Mahillon.
76	Bent side.	1646	7 5 by 3 0	2 keyboards, each 5 oct.; black naturals. Rose No. 6. Inscribed Andrea Ruckers me fecit Antverpiae.	M. Paul Endel, Paris.	P. Endel.
77	Bent side.	1651	6 8 by 3 0	2 keyboards not original; nearly 5 oct., G—F, lowest G♯ wanting; white naturals. Inscribed as No. 53, with date, and Sic Transit Gloria Mundi, Musica Donum Dei, and formerly Acta Virum Probant. Concert of monkeys on the belly, one conducting. Rose No. 6.	South Kensington Museum (gift, as having been Handel's, of Messrs. Broadwood).	A. J. Hipkins.
78	Oblong.	Undated	2 7 by 1 3½	1 original keyboard placed in the middle; 4 oct., C—C; white naturals. Rose No. 6.	M. Régibo, Renaix.	A. Régibo.
79	Bent side.	..	7 6 by 2 7	2 keyboards; the lower 4 oct., etc., B—C, the upper 3¾ oct., E—C; only one key, a white natural, left; 3 stops; no name or rose, but style of work of A. R. Inscribed Omnis Spiritus Laudet Dominum Concordia Res Parvae Crescunt Discordia Maximae Dilabuntur.	Musée du Steen, Antwerp.	V. Mahillon.
80	Bent side.	..	7 3 by 2 11	2 keyboards, not original; 5 oct., F—F; black naturals; inscribed as No. 53; date of renovation, 1758, marked on a jack; fine paintings.	Le Baron de Göer, Château de Velu, Pas de Calais, France.	V. Mahillon.
81	Oblong.	..	3 8 by 1 5	1 keyboard; 4½ oct., C—F; white naturals; inscribed as No. 53.	Musée du Conservatoire, Brussels.	V. Mahillon.
82	Bent side.	..	6 6 by 2 8	2 keyboards; 4½ oct., B—F; white naturals; name and rose wanting; attributed to A. R. by the work.	M. Snoeck, Renaix.	C. Meerens.
83	Oblong.	..	3 8 by 1 4	1 keyboard 3¾ oct., E—C. Rose No. 6.	M. Snoeck, Renaix.	C. Snoeck.
84	Bent side.	..	6 1 by 2 10⅝	1 keyboard; 4 oct., C—C; without lowest C♯; white naturals. Rose No. 6; painting of a hunt.	M. G. de Prins.	F. P. de Prins.
85	Four cornered	..	32 in. long, 12½ in. wide, 6 in. deep: keyboard projects 4 in.	White natural keys, E to D, nearly 4 octaves. Inscribed Andreas Ruckers me fecit Antverpiae (Rose No. 6?). Inside surfaces painted in black curved design on a white ground. Red line round the inside. Georgian mahogany case.	The late W. H. Hammond Jones, Esq., Witley, Godalming.	W. H. H. Jones.
86 and 87	Bent side.	..	....	2 specimens each with one keyboard, on one the inscription, 'Sic transit gloria mundi.' The Ruckers rose with the initials A. R.	Musée du Steen, Antwerp.	Rev. F. W. Galpin.
88	Bent side.	..	....	2 keyboards; five oct., G—G, white naturals; 3 stops. Inscribed Andreas Rvckers me Fecit Antwerpiae. Formerly in the Bodlington Collection; sold 1901.	....	Rev. F. W. Galpin.

IV. Andries Ruckers de Jonge (the Younger).

No.	Form.	Date.	Dimensions.	General Description.	Present Owner.	Source of Information.
89	Bent side.	1655	....	Case painted in blue camaieu in rococo style; attribution to the younger A. R. from the late date.	M. Lavignée (from the Château de Perceau, près Cosne).	S. Blondel.
90	Bent side.	1656	5 4½ by 2 2½	1 original keyboard; 4 oct., C—C; white naturals; painting inside top. Rose No. 7.	M. Régibo, Renaix.	A. Régibo.
91	Bent side.	1659	5 10 by 2 4	1 original keyboard; 4 oct., C—C; white naturals. Rose No. 7.	M. Régibo, Renaix.	A. Régibo.
92	Oblong.	..	4 9 by 1 5½	1 original keyboard to the left; 4 oct., etc., D—E; white naturals. Rose No. 7.	M. Régibo, Renaix.	A. Régibo.

V. CHRISTOFEL RUCKERS.

No.	Form.	Date.	Dimensions.	General Description.	Present Owner.	Source of Information.
93	Oblong.	Un-dated	ft. in. ft. in. 3 7 by 1 5½	1 original keyboard to the right ; 4 oct., E—E, without the highest D♯ ; white naturals ; Rose No. 8, with initials C. R. Sound-board and top renewed. Inscribed 'Acta virum probant.'	In the Crosby-Brown Collection, Metro-politan Museum, New York.	A. Régibo.
94	..	..	....	An instrument by Christofel Ruckers was stated by Vander Straeten to be in the museum at Namur.	Museum, Namur.	

A. J. H. ; with additions by Rev. F. W. Galpin and Miss E. J. Hipkins.

RUDDYGORE: OR, THE WITCH'S CURSE (Title afterwards spelt RUDDIGORE). Comic opera in two acts ; the words by W. S. Gilbert, music by Sir Arthur Sullivan. Produced at the Savoy Theatre, Jan. 22, 1887.

RUDERSDORFF, HERMINE, born Dec. 12, 1822, at Ivanowsky in the Ukraine, where her father, Joseph Rudersdorff, a distinguished violinist (afterwards of Hamburg), was then engaged. She learned singing at Paris from Bordogni, and at Milan from de Micherout, also master of Clara Novello, Catherine Hayes, etc. She first appeared in Germany in concerts, and sang the principal soprano music at the production of Mendelssohn's 'Lobgesang' at Leipzig, June 25, 1840. The next year she appeared on the stage at Carlsruhe with great success, and then at Frankfort—where in 1844 she married Dr. Küchenmeister, a professor of mathematics,—and at Breslau, Berlin, etc. Her repertory was large, and included both dramatic and coloratura parts. On May 23, 1854, she first appeared in England in German opera at Drury Lane, as Donna Anna, and was fairly well received in that and her subsequent parts of Constance in Mozart's 'Entführung,' Agatha, Fidelio, and Margaret of Valois, and in English as Elvira in 'Masaniello.' She took up her residence in England for several years, only occasionally visiting Germany for concerts and festivals. She sang at the Royal Italian Opera in 1855, also from 1861 to 1865, as Donnas Anna and Elvira, Jemmy, Bertha, Natalia ('L'Étoile du Nord'), etc. ; and in English at St. James's Theatre for a few nights in Loder's opera, 'Raymond and Agnes.' But it was as a concert-singer that she was best appreciated, her very powerful voice (not always pleasing), combined with admirable powers of declamation, certainty of execution, and thorough musicianship, having enabled her to take high rank as a singer of oratorio. Especially fine was her singing of the opening soprano recitatives in the 'Messiah' with the air, 'Rejoice greatly,' and of the final air and chorus in the 'Israel,' especially at the Handel Festivals, when her voice would tell out with wonderful effect against the powerful band and choir. In concerts, whatever she undertook she always showed herself a thorough artist, being devoted to her art, in which she worked with untiring industry. This she proved by her revival of Mozart's fine scenas 'Ahi lo previdi' and 'Misera dove son,' and of Handel's air from 'Semele,' 'O Sleep,' or by the introduction in their own tongue of Danish melodies and the Spanish songs of Yradier. She was engaged at the Boston festivals of 1871 and 1872, and finally settled in that city, becoming a teacher of singing there. Her best pupils were Misses Emma Thursby and Isabel Fassett. Her son was the well-known actor, Richard Mansfield, for whose revival of *Richard III.* at the Globe Theatre in 1889, Mr. Edward German wrote the incidental music. Mme. Rudersdorff died at Boston, Feb. 26, 1882. For the Birmingham Festival of 1873 she wrote the libretto of Signor Randegger's cantata 'Fridolin,' founded on Schiller's 'Gang nach dem Eisenhammer.' She had previously introduced, in 1869, at the Gewandhaus concerts, Leipzig, the same composer's scena 'Medea,' which she sang also at the Crystal Palace and in 1872 at Boston.   A. C.

RUDHALL. A family of bell-founders of this name carried on business in Bell Lane, Gloucester, from 1648 until late in the 18th century. Its successive members were Abraham, sen., Abraham, jun., Abel, Thomas, and John. From catalogues published by them it appears that from 1648 to Lady Day, 1751, they had cast 2972 bells 'for sixteen cities' and other places 'in forty-four several counties,' and at Lady Day 1774 the number had increased to 3594. The principal metropolitan peals cast by them were those of St. Bride, St. Dunstan in the East, and St. Martin in the Fields. The most eminent member of the family was Abraham junior, who brought the art of bell-casting to great perfection. He was born 1657, and died Jan. 25, 1736, 'famed for his great skill, beloved and esteemed for his singular good nature and integrity,' and was buried in Gloucester Cathedral. His daughter, Alicia, married William HINE, the cathedral organist. W. H. H.

RUDOLPH JOHANN JOSEPH RAINER, ARCHDUKE of Austria, born at Florence, Jan. 8, 1788, died suddenly at Baden, Vienna, July 24, 1831, was the youngest child of Leopold of Tuscany and Maria Louisa of Spain. Music was hereditary in his family. His great-grandfather, Carl VI., so accompanied an opera by Fux, that the composer exclaimed : 'Bravo ! your Majesty might serve anywhere as chief Capellmeister !'

'Not so fast, my dear chief Capellmeister,' replied the Emperor ; 'we are better off as we are !' His grandmother, the great Maria Theresa, was a fine singer ; her children, from very early age, sang and performed cantatas and little dramas, to words by Metastasio, on birthdays and fêtes. His uncle, Max Franz, was Elector of Cologne, viola-player, and organiser of the splendid orchestra at Bonn, to which the Rombergs, Rieses, Reichas, and Beethovens belonged. It was his father, Leopold, who, after the first performance of Cimarosa's 'Matrimonio segreto,' gave all those who took part in the production a supper, and then ordered the performance to be repeated ; and it was his aunt, Marie Antoinette, who supported Gluck against Piccinni at Paris.

Like the other children of the Imperial family, Rudolph was instructed in music by Anton Teyber, and tradition says that as early as twelve or fourteen he gave ample proof of more than ordinary musical talent and taste ; as soon as he had liberty of choice he exchanged Teyber for Beethoven. The precise date and circumstances attending this change have eluded investigation ; but it seems probable that the connection between Rudolph, a youth of sixteen, and Beethoven, a man of thirty-four, began in the winter of 1803-4.

Ries relates that Beethoven's breaches of court etiquette were a constant source of trouble to his pupil's chamberlains, who strove in vain to enforce its rules on him. He at last lost all patience, pushed his way into the young Archduke's presence, and, excessively angry, assured him that he had all due respect for his person, but that the punctilious observance of all the rules in which he was daily tutored was not his business. Rudolph laughed good-humouredly and gave orders that for the future he should be allowed to go his own way.

Beethoven's triple concerto, op. 56 (1804), though dedicated to Prince Lobkowitz, was written, says Schindler, for the Archduke, Seidler, and Kraft. The work does not require great execution in the piano part, but a youth of sixteen able to play it must be a very respectable performer.

The weakness of the Archduke's constitution is said to have been the cause of his entering the Church. The coadjutorship of Olmütz secured to him the succession ; and the income of the position was probably not a bad one ; for, though his allowance as Archduke in a family so very numerous was of necessity comparatively small, yet, in the spring of 1809, just after completing his 21st year, he subscribed 1500 florins to Beethoven's annuity. [See vol. i. pp. 244, 246.] In 1818 Beethoven determined to compose a solemn Mass for the installation service of his pupil, a year or two later. On Sept. 28, 1819, the Cardinal's insignia arrived from the Pope, and the installa-

tion was at length fixed for March 9,[1] 1820. But the Mass had assumed such gigantic proportions that the ceremony had passed nearly two years before it was completed.[2] [See vol. i. p. 253.] Instead of it, the music performed was a Mass in B♭, by Hummel ; a 'Te Deum' in C, by Preindl ; 'Ecce Sacerdos magnus,' by a 'Herr P. v. R.' ; and Haydn's Offertorium in D minor.

Apart from the annuity, Rudolph's purse was probably often opened to his master ; but the strongest proofs of his respect and affection are to be found in his careful preservation of Beethoven's most insignificant letters ; in the zeal with which he collected for his library everything published by him ; in his purchase of the caligraphic copy of his works made by Haslinger ;[3] and in his patience with him, often in trying circumstances. For Beethoven, notwithstanding all his obligations to his patron, chafed under the interference with his perfect liberty, which duty to the Archduke-Cardinal occasionally imposed. There are passages in his letters to Ries and others (suppressed in publication), as well as in the conversation-books), which show how galling even this light yoke was to Beethoven ; and one feels in perusing those addressed to the Archduke how frivolous are some of the excuses for not attending him at the proper hour, and how hollow and insincere are the occasional compliments, as Rudolph must have felt. That Beethoven was pleased to find the Forty Variations dedicated to him by 'his pupil, R. E. H.' (Rudolph Erz-Herzog), was probably the fact ; but it is doubtful whether his satisfaction warranted the superlatives in which his letter of thanks is couched. Other letters again breathe throughout nothing but a true and warm affection for his pupil. Köchel sensibly remarks that the trouble lay in Beethoven's 'aversion to the enforced performance of regular duties, especially to giving lessons, and teaching the theory of music, in which it is well known his strength did not lie, and for which he had to prepare himself.' When the untamed nature of Beethoven, and his deafness, are considered, together with his lack of worldly wisdom and his absolute need of a Maecenas, one feels deeply how fortunate he was to have attracted and retained the sympathy and affection of a man of such sweet and tender qualities as Archduke Rudolph.

We can hardly expect an Archduke-Cardinal to be a voluminous composer, but the Forty Variations already mentioned, and a sonata for PF. and clarinet, composed for Count Ferdinand Troyer, both published by Haslinger, are good specimens of his musical talents and acquire-

---

[1] This date is from the report of the event in the *Wiener musical-ische Zeitung* of March 25, 1820.
[2] Beethoven announces its completion in a letter to the Archduke Feb. 27, 1822.
[3] These, a splendid series of red folio volumes, beautifully copied, are conspicuous in the Library of the Gesellschaft der Musikfreunde at Vienna.

ments. There is also a set of Variations on a theme of Rossini's, corrected by Beethoven in MS. He was for many years the 'protector' of the great Gesellschaft der Musikfreunde at Vienna, and bequeathed to it his very valuable musical library. An oil portrait in the possession of his son, shows a rather intellectual .ace, of the Hapsburg type, but its peculiarities so softened as to be more than ordinarily pleasing, and even handsome.[1]

The Archduke's published works are the two alluded to above : Theme by L. van Beethoven, with Forty Variations—for PF. solo (Haslinger) ; Sonata for PF. and clarinet, op. 2, in A (Haslinger). A. W. T.

RUDORFF, ERNEST, was born in Berlin, Jan. 18, 1840 ; his family was of Hanoverian extraction. At the age of five he received his first musical instruction from a god-daughter of C. M. von Weber, an excellent pianist and of a thoroughly poetical nature. From his twelfth to his seventeenth year he was a pupil of Bargiel in PF. playing and composition. A song and a PF. piece composed at this period he afterwards thought worthy of publication (op. 2, No. 1 ; op. 10, No. 4). For a short time in 1858 he had the advantage of PF. lessons from Mme. Schumann, and from his twelfth to his fourteenth year learned the violin under Louis Ries. In 1857 he entered the Friedrichs Gymnasium, whence in 1859 he passed to the Berlin university. During the whole of this time his thoughts were bent on the musical profession. When Joachim visited Berlin in 1852 Rudorff had played before him, and had made such a favourable impression that Joachim advised his being allowed to follow the profession of music. His father at length consented that he should go at Michaelmas, 1859, and attend the Conservatorium and the University at Leipzig. After two terms of theology and history he devoted himself exclusively to music, and on leaving the Conservatorium in 1861, continued his musical studies for a year under Hauptmann and Reinecke. Rudorff went to Stockhausen early in 1864, conducted those of the Choral Society's concerts in which Stockhausen himself sang, and finally made concert tours with him. In 1865 he became professor at the Cologne Conservatorium, and there in 1867 he founded the Bach Society, whose performance at their first concert in 1869 gave such satisfaction to Rudorff that he at first refused an appointment as professor in the new Hochschule at Berlin under Joachim's direction. He afterwards changed his mind, and since October 1869 has been first professor of PF.-playing and director of the piano classes in that institution, besides conducting part of the orchestral practices, and in Joachim's absence directing the public performances. In the summer of 1880, on Max Bruch's appointment as director of the Liverpool Philharmonic Society,

[1] For a more detailed notice see the *Musical World*, April 2, 1881.

Rudorff succeeded him as conductor of the Stern Singing-Society in Berlin, but without resigning his post at the Hochschule. [He retained the direction of this Society till 1890.]

He has much talent for piano-playing, though an unfortunate nervousness prevents him from exercising it much in public. His tone is beautiful, his conception poetical, and he possesses considerable power of execution, never degenerating into mere display. He is an excellent teacher ; but his greatest gifts are shown in composition. His musical style is founded throughout upon the romantic school of Chopin, Mendelssohn, and Schumann, and especially of Weber. His part-songs interest by their elegance and thoughtfulness, but few, if any, leave a pleasant impression on the mind. This is true also of his solo songs. He has an almost feminine horror of anything rough or common, and often carries this to such a pitch as seriously to interfere with simplicity and naturalness. He has deeply imbibed the romantic charm of Weber's music, but the bold easy mirth which at times does not shrink from trivialities is unfortunately utterly strange to him. His early songs opp. 1 and 2 follow, it is true, closely in Schumann's steps, but they are among the most beautiful that have been written in his style.

Rudorff's works are for the most part of great technical difficulty, and many of them are over-elaborated, a fact which has kept his works from being as well known as they deserve. The following is a list of his published works :—

Op.	Op.
1. Variations for two PFs.	18. 'Der Aufzug der Romanze,' from Tieck, for solos, chorus, and orchestra.
2. Six songs.	
3. Six songs from Eichendorff.	
4. Six duets for PF.	20. Serenade for orchestra.
5. Sextet for strings (played at the Popular Concerts in April 1900 and January 1903).	22. Six three-part songs for female voices.
6. Four part-songs for mixed voices.	24. Variations on an original theme for orchestra.
7. Romance for violoncello and orchestra.	25. Four six-part songs.
	26. 'Gesang an die Sterne,' by Rückert, for six-part chorus and orchestra.
8. Overture to 'Der blonde Ekbert' for orchestra.	27. Six four-part songs.
9. Six part-songs for female voices.	28. Three songs.
	29. Two études for PF.
10. Eight Fantasiestücke for PF.	30. Four part-songs for mixed choir.
11. Four part-songs for mixed voices.	31. Symphony in B flat.
12. Overture to 'Otto der Schütz' for orchestra.	38. Kinderwalzer for PF. duet.
13. Four part-songs for mixed voices.	A second symphony in G minor (1891).
14. Fantasie for PF.	Symphonic variations for orchestra.
15. Ballade for full orchestra.	Scherzo capriccioso for orchestra.
16. Four songs.	
17. Four songs.	

He has also arranged Schubert's 4-hand fantasia in F minor (op. 103) for orchestra. P. S.

RÜBEZAHL. An opera in two acts ; words by J. G. Rhode, music composed by C. M. von Weber, at Breslau, between October 1804 and May 1806. Weber's autograph list shows that the first act contained fifteen scenes, the second twelve. Of these pieces of music, however, only three have survived (in MS.)—a Chorus of Spirits, a Recitative and Arietta, and a Quintet. Of the overture (in D minor) only the last eleven bars of the first violin part exist ; it was recast into the overture called 'The Ruler of the Spirits.'

(See Jähn's List, Nos. 44, 45, 46, 122 ; Anhang 2, No. 27.)   G.

RÜCKAUF, ANTON, was born March 13, 1855, at Prague, and died Sept. 19, 1903, at Schloss Alt-Erlaa. He was a pupil of Proksch, and studied at the same time at the Prague Organ School, taught for a time at Proksch's Institute till he went, at the expense of the state, to further his studies in Vienna, where, advised by Brahms, he learnt counterpoint with Nottebohm and with Nawratil when Nottebohm died. His connection with Gustav Walter, whose permanent accompanist he was, had a great influence over his development as a composer of songs, and having been an excellent pianist himself, he belongs unquestionably to the comparatively small number of modern song-writers, who give equal expression and effect to the formation of the voice-part and accompaniment. His compositions are of various sorts, including songs, 'Balladen,' settings to five Minnelieder of Walter von der Vogelweide, gipsy songs, duets, choral songs with PF. accompaniment and also a cappella, besides a violin sonata (op. 7), a PF. quintet (op. 13), some piano solos and duets, and an opera, 'Die Rosenthalerin,' which was produced at Dresden in 1897, and attracted a considerable amount of attention.   H. V. H.

RUFFO, VINCENZO, a member of a noble Veronese family, who flourished as a composer in the 16th century. His name is included by Baini in his list of the 'good musicians' of his fourth epoch. Unless a five-part magnificat, stated to have been published at Venice in 1539, and to exist at Lüneburg, be a genuine work, his first publication would seem to be a book of motets dated 1542, where he is described as 'musico' (*i.e.* castrato) in the service of the Marchese Alfonso d'Avalli. In 1554 he became maestro di cappella at the cathedral of Verona, and in 1563 was appointed to a similar post at the cathedral of Milan. In 1574-79 he was at Pistoia in the same capacity, and in 1580 we find him again at Milan. His last publication, a book of masses, dated 1592, contains no mention of any official post, and it is argued that he therefore held none in his latest years. The other masses appeared in 1557, 1574, and 1580 ; motets in 1542, 1555, and 1583, settings of the magnificat in 1578, and psalms *a* 5 in 1574. His madrigals were published in 1545, 1554, 1555, 1556, and 1560. The psalms and a mass were written for his patron Saint Carlo Borromeo in accordance with the decrees of the Council of Trent. An Adoramus is printed by Lück, and a madrigal, 'See from his ocean bed,' edited by Oliphant, is in Hullah's Part Music. Torchi, in his 'Arte Musicale in Italia,' vol. i., gives two movements from masses, a motet, and two madrigals. The libraries of Christ Church, Oxford, and the Royal College of Music, contain specimens of his works in

MS., and for others the article in the *Quellen-Lexikon* and an interesting monograph by Luigi Torri in the *Riv. Mus. Ital.* iii. 635, and iv. 233, should be consulted.   M.

RUGGIERI, the name of a celebrated family of violin-makers, who flourished at Cremona and Brescia. The eldest was FRANCESCO, commonly known as 'Ruggieri il Per' (the father), whose instruments date from 1668 to 1720 or thereabouts. JOHN BAPTIST (1700-1725) and PETER (1700-20), who form the second generation of the family, were probably his sons ; and John Baptist (called 'il buono'), who was indisputably the best maker in the family, claims to have been a pupil of Nicholas Amati. Besides these, we hear of GUIDO and VINCENZO Ruggieri, both of Cremona, early in the 18th century. The instruments of the Ruggieri, though differing widely among themselves, bear a general resemblance to those of the Amati family. They rank high among the works of the second-rate makers, and are often passed off as Amatis.   E. J. P.

RUINS OF ATHENS, THE. A dramatic piece (Nachspiel) written by Kotzebue, and composed by Beethoven (op. 113), for the opening of a new theatre at Pesth, Feb. 9, 1812, when it was preceded in the ceremony by 'King Stephen' (op. 117). It contains an overture and eight numbers, and was probably composed late in 1811. The 'Marcia alla turca,' No. 4, is founded on the theme of the Variations in D, op. 76, which was composed two years earlier. The March and Chorus, No. 6, were used in 1822, with the Overture, op. 124, for the opening of the Josephstadt Theatre, Vienna. The Overture to 'The Ruins of Athens' and the Turkish March were published in 1823, but the rest of the music remained in MS. till 1846.   G.

RULE, BRITANNIA! The music of this 'ode in honour of Great Britain,' which, according to Southey, 'will be the political hymn of this country as long as she maintains her political power,' was composed by Arne for his masque of 'Alfred' (the words by Thomson and Mallet), and first performed at Cliefden House, Maidenhead, August 1, 1740. Cliefden was then the residence of Frederick, Prince of Wales, and the occasion was to commemorate the accession of George I., and the birthday of Princess Augusta. The masque was repeated on the following night, and published by Millar, August 19, 1740.

Dr. Arne afterwards altered the masque into an opera [and it was so performed at the Smock Alley Theatre, Dublin, on March 10, 1744. In the advertisement it is announced that 'Alfred' will conclude with a 'favourable Ode in honour of Great Britain, beginning "When Britain first at Heaven's command."' It was not heard in London till March 20, 1745, when it was given at Drury Lane for the benefit of Mrs. Arne. w. h. g. f.]. In the advertisements of that performance, and of another in April, Dr. Arne entitles 'Rule, Britannia!' 'a celebrated ode,' from which it may be inferred that it had been especially successful at Cliefden, and Dublin.

The year 1745, in which the opera was produced, is memorable for the Jacobite rising in the North, and in 1746 Handel produced his 'Occasional Oratorio,' in which he refers to its suppression, 'War shall cease, welcome Peace,' adapting those words to the opening bars of 'Rule, Britannia!'—in itself a great proof of the popularity of the air.

War shall cease,   wel - come Peace.

By a singular anachronism, Schoelcher, in his *Life of Handel* (p. 299), accuses Arne of copying these and other bars in the song from Handel, instead of Handel's quoting them from Arne. He says also: 'Dr. Arne's *Alfred*, which was an utter failure, appears to have belonged to 1751.' It was not Arne's 'Alfred' that failed in 1751, but Mallet's alteration of the original poem, which he made shortly after the death of Thomson. Mallet endeavoured to appropriate the credit of the masque, as he had before appropriated the ballad of 'William and Margaret,' and thereby brought himself into notice.[1] Mallet's version of 'Alfred' was produced in 1751, and, in spite of Garrick's acting, failed, as it deserved to fail.[2]

The score of 'Rule, Britannia!' was printed by Arne at the end of 'The Judgment of Paris,' which had also been produced at Cliefden in 1740. The air was adopted by Jacobites as well as Hanoverians, but the former parodied, or changed, the words.

A doubt was raised as to the authorship of the words of 'Rule, Britannia!' by Dr. Dinsdale, editor of the re-edition of Mallet's *Poems* in 1851. Dinsdale claims for Mallet the ballad of 'William and Margaret,' and 'Rule, Britannia!' As to the first claim, the most convincing evidence against Mallet—unknown when Dinsdale wrote —is now to be found in the Library of the British Museum. In 1878 I first saw a copy of the original ballad in an auction room, and, guided by it, I traced a second copy in the British Museum, where it is open to all inquirers. It reproduces the tune, which had been utterly lost in England, as in Scotland, because it was not fitted for dancing, but only for recitation. Until Dinsdale put in a claim for Mallet, 'Rule, Britannia!' had been universally ascribed to Thomson, from the advertisements of the time down to the 'Scotch Songs' of Ritson—a most careful and trustworthy authority for facts.

[1] For 'William and Margaret,' with and without Mallet's alterations, see Appendix to vol. iii. of *Roxburghe Ballads*, reprinted for the Ballad Society; also an article in No. 1 of the periodical entitled *The Antiquary*.
[2] See Chappell's *Popular Music of the Olden Time*.

Mallet left the question in doubt. Thomson was but recently dead, and consequently many of his surviving friends knew the facts. 'According to the present arrangement of the fable,' says Mallet, 'I was obliged to reject a great deal of what I had written in the other ; neither could I retain of my friend's part more than three or four single speeches, and a part of one song.' He does not say that it was the one song of the whole that had stood out of the piece, and had become naturalised, lest his 'friend' should have too much credit, but 'Rule, Britannia!' comes under this description, because he allowed Lord Bolingbroke to mutilate the poem, by substituting three stanzas of his own for the fourth, fifth, and sixth of the original. Would Mallet have allowed this mutilation of the poem had it been his own ? [During Mallet's lifetime, the words were printed in the second edition of a well-known song-book, 'The Charmer,' in Edinburgh, with the initials of James Thomson.] On the whole, internal evidence is strongly in favour of Thomson. See his poems of 'Britannia,' and 'Liberty.' As an antidote to Dinsdale's character of David Mallet, the reader should compare that in Chalmers's *General Biographical Dictionary*.   w. c.

[See an article by J. Cuthbert Hadden in the *Nineteenth Century* for Dec. 1896 ; and another by Churton Collins in the *Saturday Review* of Feb. 20, 1897.]

'Rule, Britannia!' was first published by Henry Waylett as an appendix (with another song) to Arne's 'Music in the Judgment of Paris.' The copyright privilege is dated Jan. 29, 1740-41. An extraordinary perversion or religious parody was sung as a hymn in the Rev. Rowland Hill's Chapel, and was included in his Surrey Chapel Hymns at the beginning of the 19th century. Since the above account was written no fresh clue has come to light regarding the authorship of the words.   f. k.

Beethoven wrote five variations for the piano upon the air, and besides numberless references to it in occasional compositions of all sorts, mention may be made of Wagner's overture upon it, which was written at Königsberg in 1836, sent to the Philharmonic Society of London in 1840, and apparently lost for many years. A set of parts, no doubt made for some performance which never took place, was acquired by the late Hon. Mrs. Burrell from a German dealer in old music ; and another set came to light in 1904, corresponding exactly with these, from which the score was reconstructed and the work played at the Queen's Hall in Jan. 1905. It is a composition of no intrinsic value, though historically it is of some interest.   m.

RUMMEL. A German musical family. (1) Christian Franz Ludwig Friedrich Alexander was born at Brichsenstadt, Bavaria, Nov. 27, 1787. He was educated at Mannheim, and seems to have had instruction from the Abbé

Vogler. In 1806 he took the post of bandmaster to the 2nd Nassau infantry, made the Peninsular Campaign, married in Spain, was taken prisoner, released, and served with his regiment at Waterloo. He was then employed by the Duke of Nassau to form and lead his Court orchestra, which he did with great credit to himself till 1841, when it was dissolved. Christian Rummel died at Wiesbaden, Feb. 13, 1849. He was not only an able conductor and a composer of much ability and industry, but a fine clarinettist and a good pianist. His works are numerous, and embrace pieces for military band, concertos, quintets and other pieces for clarinet, many pianoforte compositions, especially a sonata for four hands (op. 20), waltzes, variations, etc., and a Method for the PF. (2) His daughter JOSEPHINE was born at Manzanares in Spain during the Peninsular War, May 12, 1812. She was pianist at the Court at Wiesbaden, and died Dec. 19, 1877. (3) His son JOSEPH, born at Wiesbaden, Oct. 6, 1818, was educated by his father in music generally, and in the clarinet and PF. in particular, on both of which he was a good player. He was for many years Capellmeister to the Prince of Oldenburg, then residing at Wiesbaden—a post in which he was succeeded by Adolph Henselt. Up to 1842 he lived in Paris, and then removed to London for five years. In 1847 he returned to Paris, and remained there till driven back to London by the war in 1870 ; and in London he resided till his death, March 25, 1880. Joseph Rummel wrote no original music, but he was one of the most prolific arrangers of operas and operatic selections for the PF. that ever existed. For nearly forty years he worked incessantly for the houses of Schott and Escudier, publishing about 400 pieces with each house under his own name, besides a much larger number under *noms de plume*. His arrangements and transcriptions amount in all to fully 2000. He wrote also a series of exercises for Augener & Co., and for Escudier. (4) Joseph's sister FRANZISKA, born at Wiesbaden, Feb. 4, 1821, was educated by her father until she went to Paris to study singing under Bordogni, and afterwards to Lamperti at Milan. She became principal singer at the Court of Wiesbaden, and at length married Peter Schott, the well-known music publisher at Brussels, who died in 1873. (5) Another son, AUGUST, a capable pianist, born at Wiesbaden, Jan. 14, 1824, became a merchant in London, where he died, Dec. 14, 1886, and where (6) his son FRANZ was born, Jan. 11, 1853. At the age of fourteen he went to Brussels to study the PF. under Brassin, first as a private pupil and afterwards in the Conservatoire. He took the first prize for PF.-playing there in 1872, and afterwards became one of the staff of teachers. He made his first public appearance at Antwerp, Dec. 22,

1872, in Henselt's PF. Concerto ; in July 1873 played Schumann's Concerto at the Albert Hall Concerts, London ; and again at Brussels, before the King and Queen of the Belgians, with great distinction. He remained at the Conservatoire as professor till 1876, when on the advice of Rubinstein he threw up his post and began to travel, playing in the Rhine Provinces, Holland, and France. Early in 1877 he came to London, and played at the Crystal Palace on April 7. Next year he went to America, where he met with great success, though interrupted by a serious accident. He returned in 1881, and played again at the Crystal Palace on April 30. [He was for a long time a teacher in the Stern Conservatorium at Berlin. He afterwards lived at Dessau, and died at Berlin, May 2, 1901.]   G.

RUNGENHAGEN, CARL FRIEDRICH, born at Berlin, Sept. 27, 1778, became in 1815 second director of the Singakademie, and in 1833 succeeded Zelter as first director. In 1843 he received the title of professor : he wrote four operas, three oratorios, a mass, a Stabat Mater for female voices, a great deal of church music, many songs, and orchestral and chamber music, all of which is now forgotten. He died in Berlin, Dec. 21, 1851. (Riemann's *Lexikon*.) M.

RUSSELL, HENRY, was born at Sheerness on Dec. 24, 1812 ; went to Bologna, in 1825, to study music [was for a time a pupil of Rossini in Naples, appeared as a singer at the Surrey Theatre in 1828, and went to Canada about 1833. He was organist of the Presbyterian Church, Rochester (N.Y.), and travelled in America till 1841, when he returned to England and gave entertainments by himself and in company with Charles Mackay. The first took place at the Hanover Square Rooms, March 8, 1842]. In his particular style he had no rival. His songs 'I'm afloat,' 'A life on the ocean wave' (which in 1889 was authorised as the march of the royal marines), 'Cheer, boys, cheer' (the only air played by the regimental drum and fife band when a regiment goes abroad), 'Woodman, spare that tree,' etc., are still familiar, and some of his dramatic songs, as 'The Dream of the Reveller,' 'The Maniac,' 'The Gambler's Wife,' etc., were immensely popular in their day. It may certainly be said that over 800 songs were either written or composed by him. At a time when Australia, Tasmania, and New Zealand were almost unknown, Henry Russell was instrumental, through the Canadian government, in sending over thousands of poor people who are now wealthy. A memoir was published in 1846, and a book of reminiscences, *Cheer, boys, cheer*, in 1895. [He retired from public life in 1865, was fêted at a special concert given in his honour by Sir A. Harris in Covent Garden Theatre, Oct. 12, 1891, and died in London Dec. 8, 1900.] *L' amico dei cantanti* is a treatise on the art of singing. [Two of his sons have attained distinction in music, Henry Russell as a singing master and operatic impresario, and Landon Ronald (born June 7, 1873) as a pianist and composer. The last-named studied at the Royal College of Music, went on tour with 'L'Enfant Prodigue' in 1891 as pianist, conducted opera at Drury Lane in 1896, and has composed many songs of high artistic aims, besides gaining wide popularity as an accompanist and conductor.] J. H. D. ; with additions from *Dict. of Nat. Biog.* (suppl.), *Musical Times* for Jan. 1901, etc.

RUSSELL, WILLIAM, Mus.B., son of an organ builder and organist, was born in London, Oct. 6, 1777. He was successively a pupil of Cope, organist of St. Saviour's, Southwark, Shrubsole, of Spa Fields Chapel, and Groombridge, Hackney and St. Stephen's, Coleman Street. In 1789 he was appointed deputy to his father as organist of St. Mary, Aldermanbury, and continued so until 1793, when he obtained the post of organist at the chapel in Great Queen Street, Lincoln's Inn Fields, which he held until 1798, when the chapel was disposed of to the Wesleyan body. In 1797 he became a pupil of Dr. Arnold, with whom he studied for about three years. In 1798 he was chosen organist of St. Ann's, Limehouse. In 1800 he was engaged as pianist and composer at Sadler's Wells, where he continued about four years. In 1801 he was engaged as pianist at Covent Garden and appointed organist of the Foundling Hospital Chapel. He took his Mus.B. degree at Oxford in 1808. He composed three oratorios, 'The Deliverance of Israel,' 'The Redemption,' and 'Job' (1826) ; a mass in C minor, an 'Ode to Music,' an 'Ode to the Genius of Handel,' Christopher Smart's 'Ode on St. Cecilia's Day,' and an 'Ode to Harmony,' several glees, songs, and organ voluntaries, and about twenty dramatic pieces, chiefly spectacles and pantomimes. He edited in 1809 'Psalms, Hymns and Anthems for the Foundling Chapel.' He was much esteemed both as pianist and organist. He died Nov. 21, 1813.   W. H. H.

RUSSLAN I LIOUDMILLA. A Russian romantic opera, in five acts, based on a poem by Pushkin, the music by Glinka. Produced at St. Petersburg, Nov. 27, 1842. The scene is laid in the Caucasus, in fabulous times, and the music partakes strongly of the oriental character. The overture was played at the Crystal Palace, Sydenham, London, July 4, 1874.   G.

RUST. A distinguished German musical family. FRIEDRICH WILHELM was born at Wörlitz, Dessau, July 6, 1739 ; his father was a person of eminence, and he received a first-rate education. He was taught music by his elder brother, Johann Ludwig Anton, who, as an amateur, had played the violin in J. S. Bach's orchestra at Leipzig ; and at thirteen he played the whole of the 'Wohltemperirtes

Clavier' without book. Composition, organ, and clavier he learned from Friedemann and Emmanuel Bach, and the violin from Höckh and F. Benda ; and in 1765, during a journey to Italy, from G. Benda, Tartini, and Pugnani. In 1766 he returned to Dessau, and became the life and soul of the music there. On Sept. 24, 1774, a new theatre was opened through his exertions, to which he was soon after appointed music-director. He married his pupil, Henriette Niedhart, a fine singer, and thenceforward, with a few visits to Berlin, Dresden, etc., his life was confined to Dessau, where he died March 28, 1796. His compositions include a Psalm for solo, chorus, and orchestra ; several large Church Cantatas ; Duodramas and Monodramas ; Operas ; music to Plays ; Prologues and Occasional pieces, etc. ; Odes and Songs (2 collections) ; Sonatas and Variations for the PF. solo—'4 dozen' of the former and many of the latter—Concertos, Fugues, etc. etc. ; and three Sonatas for violin solo, which have been republished by his grandson (Peters), and are now the only music by which Rust is known ; that in D minor was often played at the Monday Popular Concerts. The sonatas are analysed in Shedlock's *Pianoforte Sonata*, pp. 152 ff. His last composition was a violin sonata for the E string, thus anticipating Paganini. A list of his works, with every detail of his life, extending to $6\frac{1}{2}$ large pages, is given in Mendel. A monograph on him, with list of works, etc., was published in 1882 by W. Hofäus, and Dr. E. Prieger published a pamphlet, *F. W. Rust, ein Vorgänger Beethovens.* His eldest son was drowned ; the youngest, WILHELM KARL, born at Dessau, April 29, 1787, began music very early ; and besides the teaching he naturally got at home, learned thorough-bass with Türk while at Halle University. In Dec. 1807 he went to Vienna, and in time became intimate with Beethoven, who praised his playing of Bach, and recommended him strongly as a teacher. Amongst other pupils he had Baroness Ertmann and Maximilian Brentano. His letters to his sister on Beethoven are given by Thayer, iii. 35–6. He remained in Vienna till 1827, when he returned to his native place, and lived there till his death, April 18, 1855.

WILHELM RUST, the nephew of the foregoing, himself an advocate, and a fine amateur player on both violin and PF., was born August 15, 1822, at Dessau ; he learned music from his uncle and F. Schneider. After a few years' wandering he settled in Berlin, where he soon joined the Singakademie. He played at the Philharmonic Society of Berlin, Dec. 5, 1849, and was soon much in request as a teacher. In Jan. 1861 he became organist of St. Luke's church, and twelve months afterwards director of Vierling's Bach Society, which he conducted till 1874, performing a large number of fine works by Bach and other great composers, many of them for the first time. The list of occasional concerts conducted by him is also very large. In 1870 he undertook the department of counterpoint and composition in the Stern Conservatorium at Berlin, and in 1878 was appointed organist of the Thomaskirche, Leipzig, and in 1880 succeeded E. F. E. Richter as Cantor of the Thomasschule. He was connected with the Leipzig Bachgesellschaft from 1850, and edited vols. v., vii., ix.-xxiii. and xxv. His original works have reached op. 33, of which eight are for the PF. and the rest for voices. [He died at Leipzig, May 2, 1892. A biography appeared in the *Musikal. Wochenblatt* for 1890.]　　　　　　　　　G.

RUTHERFORD, DAVID, a Scotch music publisher in London, who worked in St. Martin's Court, near Leicester Fields, 'at the sign of the Violin and German Flute,' about 1745. His publications consist principally of minor works for the violin, or flute, such as country dances, minuets, and books of airs. He republished in octavo William M'Gibbon's 'Scotch Airs,' and issued song-sheets, etc. He was publisher, and probably author, of several quaint instruction books, as *The Fiddle new model'd, or a useful introduction for the violin, exemplified with familiar dialogues,* circa 1750, 8vo, and *The art of playing on the violin, showing how to stop every note exactly.*

He was succeeded at the same address by John Rutherford, who issued a similar class of works, and who remained in business until 1783, or later.　　　　　　　　　F. K.

RUY BLAS. A play by Victor Hugo, to which Mendelssohn composed an Overture and a Chorus for soprano voices and orchestra. The Overture (op. 95) is in C minor, and the Chorus (op. 77, No. 3) in A. Both pieces were conceived, written, copied, rehearsed, and executed in less than a week (see Letter, March 18, 1839). The first performance was Monday, March 11, 1839. Mendelssohn brought it to London in MS. in 1844, and it was tried at a Philharmonic Rehearsal, but for some reason was not performed till a concert of Mrs. Anderson's, May 25, 1849 ; it is now in the library at Buckingham Palace. The MS. differs in a few passages from the published score, which was not printed till after Mendelssohn's death (No. 5 of the posth. works).　　　　　G.

RYAN, MICHAEL DESMOND, dramatic and musical critic, was born at Kilkenny, March 3, 1816, son of Dr. Michael Ryan. On the completion of his academical education at an early age he entered the University of Edinburgh, early in the year 1832, for the purpose of studying medicine. He remained in Edinburgh steadily pursuing his studies for some three years, after which, being fairly well read, a dabbler in literature, an enthusiastic admirer of art, a good amateur musician, and a keen follower of the stage, Ryan determined to quit Edinburgh and try his fortune in London. Here he arrived in 1836, by chance met with J. W. Davison, and commenced an intimate and lifelong friendship. Ryan now entered upon his literary career in earnest, writing articles and poems for *Harrison's Miscellany,* etc., and producing verses for songs. A set of twelve sacred songs, versified from the Old Testament and set to music by Edward Loder (D'Almaine), may also be mentioned. The 'Songs of Ireland' (D'Almaine), in which, in conjunction with F. N. Crouch, new verses were fitted to old melodies, is another example of effective workmanship. In 1844 Ryan became a contributor to *The Musical World,* and two years later sub-editor, a post which he filled as long as he lived. For years he was a contributor to the *Morning Post, Court Journal, Morning Chronicle,* and other periodicals, writing criticisms on the drama and music, which had the merit of being trenchant, sound, and erudite. In 1849 he wrote the opera libretto of 'Charles II.' for G. A. Macfarren. The subject was taken from a well-known comedy by Howard Payne, rendered popular at Covent Garden by Charles Kemble's acting some quarter of a century before. A short time afterwards Ryan was commissioned by M. Jullien to provide the libretto of a grand spectacular opera, on the subject of Peter the Great—brought out at the Royal Italian Opera on August 17, 1852, under the title of 'Pietro il Grande.' With the late Frank Mori, Ryan collaborated in an opera called 'Lambert Simnel,' originally intended for Sims Reeves, but never performed. In 1857 he formed his first association with the *Morning Herald,* and its satellite the *Standard,* and became permanently connected with those journals in 1862 as musical and dramatic critic. Few temperaments, however, can sustain the excitement and toil demanded in these days of newspaper activity, and after a painful and prolonged illness Ryan quitted this life on Dec. 8, 1868, followed to the grave by the regretful memories of those who had known and esteemed his character.　　　　D. L. R.

S

SABBATINI, GALEAZZO, of Pesaro, was probably maestro di cappella there for some years before 1626 ; this is indicated at any rate in the preface to the 'Sacrae Laudes,' Venice, 1626 (Parisini, *Catalogo*, ii. 492). On the title-pages of his works he is called maestro di cappella di camera to the Duke of Mirandola in 1630 and again in 1636. The dates of his publications range from 1625 to 1640. In G. B. Doni's *Annotazioni*, published in 1640, the 'Discorso primo dell' inutile osservanza de tuoni' (p. 234), is dedicated to 'Signor Galeazzo Sabbatini a Bergamo.' Sabbatini is highly commended by Kircher, *Musurgia universalis*, Rome, 1650, tom. i. p. 460, for his scientific knowledge of music, a 'rarus musicus, qui tria genera novo ausu ad arithmeticas leges revocans, multo plura sanè invenit, quorum diversis in locis huius operis mentio fiet, et inter coetera abacum novum ordinavit exactissimè quicquid in musica desiderari potest referentem, omnibus harmoniis exibendis perfectissimum,' etc. Sabbatini published one theoretical work, on the thorough-bass or basso continuo, which Burney (*Hist. of Music*, iii. p. 538) criticises as inadequate because it only treats of common chords given to every note of the scale. The title is : *Regola facile e breve per sonare sopra il basso continuo, nell' organo, manacordo, ò altro simile stromento.* Composta da Galeazzo Sabbatini. Dalla quale in questa prima parte ciascuno da se stesso potrà imparare da i primi principii quello che sarà necessario per simil' effetto. Venetia per il Salvatori, 1628, 4to. The second edition, dated 1644, is in the British Museum, and a third edition was published in Rome in 1669. No 'seconda parte' of the work is known. Sabbatini's published compositions were as follows :—

1. Il primo libro de' madrigali di Galeazzo de Sabbatini da Pesaro. Concertati a due, tre, e quattro voci. Opera prima. Nouamente composta, e data in luce. Venetia, Aless. Vincenti, 1625, 4to. A second edition was issued in 1627, and a third in 1639.

2. Il secondo libro de' madrigali di G. S., concertati a 2, 3, et 4 voci. Con la risposta a quattro voci e due violini ad alcuni versi che incominciano quando la Donna si dimostra altiera, posti nel terzo de' madrigali a 6 del Sig. Steffano Bernardi, etc. Opera seconda. Nouamente composta et data in luce. Venetia, Aless. Vincenti, 1626, 4to. Second edition in 1636.

3. Sacrae Laudes musicis concentibus a G. S. contextae, 2, 3, 4, et 5 vocibus concinendae. Una cum bassus continuus pro organo, etc. Opus tertium, liber primus. Venetiis, A. Vincentium, 1626, 4to. Second edition, 1637 ; another edition, Antwerp, 1642.

4. Madrigali concertati a cinque voci con alcune canzoni concertate ane' esse diuersamente con sinfonie, e ritornelli, e nel fine una canzonetta con voci, e instromenti, che si concerta in tempo imperfetto, ò in proportione minor perfetta, cioè ò in numero binario, ò in numero ternario. Di G. S. Opera quarta, de' madrigali libro terzo. Nouamente composti e dati in luce. Venetia, Aless. Vincenti, 1627, 4to. Second edition in 1634.

5. Madrigali concertati a 2, 3, 4, e 5 voci. Con alcune canzoni concertate, e tramezzate diuersamente con sinfonie e ritornelli. Di G. S. maestro di cappella di camera dell' eccell. sig. duca della Mirandola. Opera quinta, de' madrigali libro quarto. Nouamente composti e dati in luce. Venetia, A. Vincenti, 1630, 4to. Second edition, 1637.

6. Madrigali concertati a 2, 3, e 4 voci, con alcune canzonette concertate con instromenti, di G. S. mastro di capella di camera dell' eccell. sig. duca della Mirandola, etc. Opera sesta, de' madrigali libro quinto. Nouamente composti e dati in luce, et a sua eccellenza illustrissima dedicati. Veneti, A. Vincenti, 1636, 4to.

7. Sacrarum laudum musicis conceptibus a Galeatio Sabbatino contextarum 2, 3, 4, et 5 vocibus ad organum concinendarum. Liber secundus. Opus septimum, etc. Venetiis, A. Vincentium, 1637, 4to. Another edition was published at Antwerp in 1641.

8. Deiparae Virginis Laudes a G. S. musicis conceptibus cum 3, 4, 5, et 6 vocibus contextae, etc. Opus octavum. Venetiis, A. Vincentium, 1638. 4to.

9. Sacre lodi concerto a voce sola, C.A.T.B. Con la parte continua da sonare di G. S. Opera nona. Venetia, A. Vincenti, 1640, 4to. These are the 'Motetti a voce sola di G. S. Lib. primo.'

10. Libro de' madrigali di G. S. concertati a 2, 3, e 4 voci, con la risposta a quattro voci, e due violini ad alcuni versi che incominciano quando la donna si dimostra altiera. Posti nel terzo de' madrigali a 6 del sig. Steffano Bernardi. Con il basso continuo. Nouamente ristampati. In Anversa presso i heredi di Pietro Phalesio al Re David, 1640, obl. 4to. A reprint of the second volume of madrigals published in 1626.

Compositions in other publications:—

A motet and a mass 'dal sig. Galeazzo Sabbatini, maestro dell' autore,' in Raniero Scarselli's Sacrarum modulationum, Venice, 1637.

'Laudate pueri' for three voices, in Marcello Minozzi's Salmi, Venice, 1638. Minozzi in the preface mentions that Sabbatini was his teacher; 'buono di quel grido che particolarmente è noto a gli intendenti dell' arte.' (Parisini, ii. 275.)

'O nomen Jesu' for three voices, in Ambr. Profius's Ander Theil geistlicher Concerten, Leipzig, 1641 ; 'Jesu Domine' for two voices, in the Dritter Theil, 1642 ; 'Laudate pueri,' 'Omnes sancti,' and a Missa, all for four voices, in the Vierdter und letzter Theil, 1646. One motet in Profius's Cunis solennib. Jesuli recens-nati, 1646.

'Nos autem gloriari' for three voices, in Benedetto Pace's Motetti d' autori eccellentissimi, Loreto, 1646.

'Hò perso il mio core,' in Florido concento di madrigali, Rome, 1653.

MSS. In the Berlin Königl. Bibliothek : MS. 1100, 'Amare desidero.' In the Upsala Univ.-Bibliothek : 'Io amo,' one of the Madrigali concertati a cinque voci, published 1627. In the Westminster Abbey Library : 'Amor porta' for voice with basso continuo, in a 17th-century folio music manuscript. C. S.

SABBATINI, LUIGI ANTONIO, was born in 1732 at Albano Laziale, near Rome. He was educated at Bologna in the Franciscan monastery of minori conventuali, where he studied music under padre G. B. Martini. There is a manuscript in Sabbatini's handwriting in the Bologna Liceo Musicale, which contains the 'Regole per accompagnare del pre. G. B. Martini, min. conle. maestro di cappella di San Francesco in Bologna, 1761. Per suo di Fra Luigi Ant. Sabbatini, min. conle.' (Parisini, *Catalogo*, i. 282). He remained there eight years according to a long and interesting letter which he wrote to Martini from Albano on Nov. 2, 1766, now preserved in the library of the Accademia filarmonica, Bologna (Succi, *Mostra internazionale*, Bologna, 1888). He was afterwards in the Franciscan monastery at Padua, where Vallotti gave him lessons in composition. Eventually he was appointed maestro di cappella at the church of the SS. Apostoli in Rome, a letter in the Bologna collection, written to Martini from Rome, is dated July 17, 1776 (Masseangeli, *Catalogo della collezione de' autografi*, Bologna, 1881).

Before Vallotti, maestro di cappella of S. Antonio, Padua, died in January 1780, he expressed a wish that Sabbatini should be his successor. Sabbatini was offered the post, but, unwilling to leave Rome, he suggested that Agostino Ricci would be a suitable candidate. Ricci was therefore appointed on April 26, 1780, and remained in Padua for six years, but when he left for Assisi, Sabbatini was persuaded to reconsider his decision and was finally appointed to the post on April 22, 1786, which he held until his death on January 29, 1809, in Padua. During these twenty-three years of his life, he enriched the archives of S. Antonio with many compositions, writes Gonzati

(*La Basilica di S. Antonio di Padova*, 1853, ii. p. 453), among which may be especially mentioned his Salmi di Terza, four masses, a vespero, and a Compieta breve, all composed for four voices.

Sabbatini was elected one of the eight members of the music section of the Accademia italiana in May 1807. In 1887 a bust of Sabbatini was placed in the Piazza Feoli, Albano ; this tribute to his memory was due to Signor Cesare de Sanctis, also an Albano musician.

The larger part of Sabbatini's church music remains in manuscript in the archives of S. Antonio, but Tebaldini, who gives a list of eighty-six compositions (*L'Archivio mus. della cappella Antoniana*, 1895, p. 81), has published some examples for four voices with orchestra, which he considers show that Sabbatini instinctively tried for new combinations, new effects, and that he sometimes lent his music quite an individual character by giving the canto fermo to the alto or soprano part instead of the tenor. Sabbatini was generally recognised as a sound and erudite theorist ; Gervasoni (*Nuova teoria di musica*, Parma, 1812, p. 258) testifies to his profound knowledge no less than to his great personal charm.

Some other manuscript compositions are in the Bologna Liceo Musicale ; autograph scores of twelve pieces of sacred music for two and four voices with orchestral accompaniment, in one volume, and three Kyrie, two Gloria, two Credo, and 'Qui habitat,' all for four voices with orchestral accompaniment, in another volume (Parisini, *Catalogo*, ii. pp. 136, 306) ; as well as twenty-one pieces of sacred music for four voices with figured bass ; and ' Atto di contrizione ' for two voices with basso continuo. The nineteenth volume of the Martini correspondence in the same library consists entirely of letters from Sabbatini.

In the Vienna Hofbibliothek in MS. 16,217 there is a mass for four voices with organ accompaniment ; and in MS. 19,103 a treatise on music 'trascritto ad litteram nell' anno 1791. Dal p. L. A. Sabbatini, min. con. maestro di cappella nella sacra Basilica del Santo in Padova ' (Mantuani's *Catalogue*).

The following theoretical works were published :—

Elementi teorici della musica colla pratica de' medesimi, in duetti e terzetti a canone, ecc. di fra L. A. Sabbatini, min. con. già maestro di cappella nella Basilica Costantiniana de' SS. XII. Apostoli in Roma ed al presente in quella del Santo in Padova. In Roma, 1789-90, obl. folio. In three books. A second edition was published at Rome in 1795.
La vera idea delle musicali numeriche segnature ecc. dal fra L. A. S. m.c. maestro di cappella nella Basilica di S. Antonio di Padova. Venezia, 1799, presso Seb. Valle, 4to, pp. 179. A manuscript of Sabbatini's inscribed *Trattato di contrappunto*, which is in the Padua library, would appear to be the first sketch for this more elaborate work.
Trattato sopra le fughe musicali di Fra L. A. S. m.c. corredato da copiosi saggi del suo antecessore P. Franc. Ant. Vallotti. Venezia, 1802, presso Seb. Valle, 4to. In two books. An analysis of Vallotti's fugues with examples taken from his church music.
Solféges ou leçons élémentaires de musique, etc. en canon avec basse continue. Par le R. P. Luigi A. Sabbatini, etc. Publié par M. Alex. Choron, Paris, circa 1810, 8vo, pp. 120. Consists of music taken from *Elementi teorici*, 1789. Another edition was published in 1836.

Besides these works Sabbatini also published a life of Vallotti : *Notizie sopra la vita e le opere del R. P. Fr. Ant. Vallotti* (Padua, 1780) ; and edited a collection of Marcello's psalms which was published at Venice in 1801. (Fétis, *Biogr. univ.*)   C. S.

SABBATINI, PIETRO PAOLO, was a native of Rome. The dates of his published works range from 1628 to 1657, and from their title-pages it is to be gathered that in 1628 he was maestro di cappella dell' Archiconfraternità della morte et oratione di Roma ; 1630-31 maestro di cappella di S. Luigi de' francesi, Rome ; and in 1650 professore di musica. Catalisano alludes to him in his *Grammatica armonica*, 1781, p. xii. ' Per esprimere quanto mai sia tenuto a questi celebri maestri di cappella . . . P. P. Sabbatini,' etc. His published works were :—

1. Il sesto di Pietro Paolo Sabbatini maestro di cappella del l' archiconfraternità della morte et oratione di Roma. Opera VIII. In Bracciano, per And. Fei, stampatore ducale, 1628, folio, pp. 23. Contains songs for one, two, and three voices, some with guitar accompaniment.
2. Intermedii spirituali di P.P.S., etc. as above. Libro I. Opera IX. In Roma appresso Paolo Masotti, 1628, folio, pp. 27. Contains three Intermedii.
3. Psalmi magnificat cum quatuor antiphonis ad Vespera, cum Lettaniis B.V. octonis vocibus, uno cum Basso ad organum decantandi. Auctore P.P.S. romano in Ecclesia S. Aloysii Gallicae nationis musices moderatore, Liber I. Opus XII. Romae, P. Masottum, 1630. 4to.
4. Il terzo di P.P.S. maestro di cappella di S. Luigi de' francesi in Roma. In Roma, appresso P. Masotti, 1631, folio, pp. 19. Contains Villanelle for one, two, and three voices.
5. Il quarto de Villanelle a una, due e tre voci. Del Sig. P.P.S. etc. as above. Roma, G. B. Robletti, 1631, folio, pp. 19. The dedication is written by Pietro Simi, a pupil of Sabbatini, from Rome, May 1, 1631, he states that he rescues from oblivion these Villanelle by P. P. Sabbatini.
6. Canzoni spirituali ad una, a due, et a tre voci da cantarsi, e sonarsi sopra qualsivoglia istromento, Libro II. Opera XIII. de P.P.S. In Roma, appresso Lod. Grignani, 1640, folio, pp. 32.
7. Varii capricci, e canzonette a una e tre voci da cantarsi sopra qualsivoglia istromento con l' alfabeto della chitarra spagnuola, di P.P.S. Romano, Libro VII. Opera XIV. Roma, Vinc. Bianchi, 1641, folio, pp. 32.
8 Prima scelta di villanelle a due voci composte da P.P.S. da sonarsi in qualsivoglia instromento con le lettere accomodate alla chitarra spagnola in quelle più a proposito. In Roma, Vitale Mascardi, 1652, folio, pp. 19.
9. Ariette spirituali a una, doi e tre voci di P.P.S. in diversi stili da cantarsi in qualsivoglia instromento, Libro V. Opera XXI. Roma, Jacomo Fei del q. Andrea, 1657, folio, pp. 24.
The following treatise was also published :—
Toni ecclesiastici colle sue intonazioni, all' uso romano. Modo per sonare il basso continuo, chiavi corrispondenti all' altre chiavi generali, et ordinarie, etc., da P.P.S. Professore della musica. Libro I., Opera XVIII. Roma, Lod. Grignani, 1650, 4to.   C. S.

SACCHINI, ANTONIO MARIA GASPARE, born at Pozzuoli, near Naples, on July 23, 1734. This 'graceful, elegant, and judicious composer,' as Burney calls him, who enjoyed great contemporary fame, and was very popular in this country, was the son of poor fisher-people who had no idea of bringing him up to any life but their own. It chanced, however, that Durante heard the boy sing some popular airs, and was so much struck with his voice and talent that he got him admitted into the Conservatorio of San Onofrio, at Naples. Here he learned the violin from Niccolo Forenza, and acquired a considerable mastery over the instrument, which he subsequently turned to good account in his orchestral writing. He studied singing with Gennaro Manna ; harmony and counterpoint with Durante himself, who esteemed him highly, holding him up to his other pupils, among whom were Jommelli, Piccinni, and Guglielmi, as their most formidable rival. Durante died in 1755, and in the following year Sacchini left the Conservatorio, but not until he had produced an intermezzo, in two parts, 'Fra Donato,' very successfully performed by the pupils of the institution. For some years he supported himself by teaching singing, and writing little pieces for minor theatres, till, in 1762, he wrote a serious opera, 'Semiramide,' for the Argentina theatre at Rome. This was so well received that he remained for seven years attached to the theatre as composer, writing operas not only for Rome but many other towns. Among these, 'Alessandro nelle Indie,' played at Venice in 1768, was especially successful, and obtained for its composer, in 1769, the directorship of the 'Ospedaletto' school of music there. He seems to have held this office for little more than a year, but during that time formed some excellent pupils, among whom may be mentioned Gabrieli, Canti, and Pasquali.

Before 1770 he left Venice, and proceeded by way of Munich, Stuttgart, and other German towns, to England, arriving in London in April 1772. [For Munich he wrote 'Scipione in Cartagena' and 'L'Eroe cinese' in 1770, and for Stuttgart 'Calliroë.'] His continental fame had preceded him to this country, and a beautiful air of his, 'Care luci,' introduced by Guarducci into the pasticcio of 'Tigrane' as early as 1767, had, by its popularity, paved the way for his music. True, a strong clique existed against the new composer, but he soon got the better of it.

In addition to the 'Cid' and 'Tamerlano,' mentioned by Burney, he produced here 'Lucio Vero' and 'Nitetti e Perseo' (1773-74). His perfect comprehension of the art of writing for the voice, and the skill with which he adapted his songs to their respective exponents, contributed an important element to the success of his music, even indifferent singers being made to appear to advantage. His popularity, however, was undermined, after a time, from a variety of causes. Jealousy led to cabals against him. He would probably have lived down calumny, prompted by personal spite, but his idle and dissolute habits estranged his friends, impaired his health, and got him deeply into debt, the consequence of which was that he left this country and settled in Paris—Burney says in 1784; Fétis in 1782. It seems probable that this last date is correct, as several of his operas were produced in the French capital during 1783-84. He had been there on a visit in 1781, when his 'Isola d' Amore,' translated by Framéry and adapted to the French stage, was played there successfully, having been played under the name of 'La Colonie' in 1775. His 'Olimpiade' had been given in 1777. Burney says that in Paris Sacchini was almost adored. He started with an apparent advantage in the patronage of Joseph II. of Austria, who was in Paris at the time, and recommended the composer to the protection of his sister, Marie Antoinette. Thanks to this, he obtained a

hearing for his 'Rinaldo' (rearranged and partly rewritten for the French stage as 'Renaud'), and for 'Il gran Cid,' which, under the name of 'Chimène,' was performed before the Court at Fontainebleau. Both of these works contained great beauties, but neither had more than a limited success. 'Dardanus,' a French opera, was not more fortunate in 1784. 'Œdipe à Colone' was finished early in 1785, and performed at Versailles, April 4, 1786. This, his masterpiece, brought him his bitterest disappointment. The Queen had promised that 'Œdipe' should be the first opera at the royal theatre during the Court's next residence at Fontainebleau. The time was approaching, but nothing was said about it, and Sacchini remarked with anxiety that the Queen avoided him and seemed uneasy in his presence. Suspense became intolerable, and he sought an audience, when the Queen unwillingly and hesitatingly confessed the truth. 'My dear Sacchini, I am accused of showing too much favour to foreigners. I have been so much pressed to command a performance of M. Lemoine's "Phèdre" instead of your "Œdipe" that I cannot refuse. You see the situation; forgive me.' Poor Sacchini controlled himself at the moment, but on arriving at home gave way to despair. The Queen's favour lost, he believed his only chance gone. He took to his bed then and there, and died three months afterwards, on Oct. 7, 1786.

It is very difficult to form a just estimate of this composer, whose merits were great, yet whose importance to the history of Art seems now so small. The dramatic music of the end of the 18th century is summed up to us in the operas of Gluck and Mozart, exclusive of many others, akin to these in style and tendency, deficient only in the vital element which makes one work live while others die out. At the time of their production the line may have seemed more difficult to draw. One drop of essence may be distilled from a large quantity of material, yet without the proportion of material that drop would not be obtained. Among the second-rate writers of this transition period, Sacchini must rank first. A little more force, perhaps a little less facility, and he might have been a great, instead of a clever or a 'graceful, elegant, and judicious' composer. He, better than most Italians, seems to have understood the dawning idea of the 'poetical basis of music'; unfortunately the musical ideas, of which the superstructure must, after all, consist, while good and appropriate as far as they went, were limited. His dramatic sense was keen and just, but was not backed by sufficient creative power to make a lasting mark. Fear, remorse, love, hatred, revenge, — these things repeat themselves in the world's drama from Time's beginning to its end, but their expressions are infinite in variety. They repeat themselves, too, in Sacchini's operas, but always in very much the same way. In his later works, the influence of Gluck's spirit is unmistakable. There is a wide gulf between such early Italian operas as 'L' Isola d' Amore,' consisting of the usual detached series of songs, duets, and concerted pieces, and the 'Œdipe à Colone,' where each number leads into the next, and where vigorous accompanied recitative and well-contrasted dialogued choruses carry on and illustrate the action of the drama, while keeping alive the interest of the hearer. Burney remarks that Sacchini, 'observing how fond the English were of Handel's oratorio choruses, introduced solemn and elaborate choruses into some of his operas ; but, though excellent in their kind, they never had a good effect ; the mixture of English singers with the Italian, as well as the awkward figure they cut as actors, joined to the difficulty of getting their parts by heart, rendered those compositions ridiculous which in still life would have been admirable.' In Paris they managed these things better, for in all the operas of Sacchini's which were composed or arranged for the French stage, choruses are used largely and with admirable effect, while in 'Œdipe' they are the principal feature. A somewhat similar transition to this is apparent in comparing Piccinni's earlier and later works ; but his French operas are only Italian ones modified and enlarged. Sacchini had far more dramatic spirit, and took more kindly to the change. He bears the kind of relation to Gluck that Piccinni does to Mozart, but he approached his model more nearly, for he handled Gluck's theory almost as well as Gluck himself ; had he possessed the one thing lacking—force of originality—there might have been more in his works for criticism to censure, but they might not now have been forgotten. As it was, they made a hard struggle for life. The 'Œdipe' was continuously on the boards of the Académie for fifty-seven years (from 1787 to 1844), which can be said of no other opera. During this time it had 583 representations. It was revived in July 1843, and was performed six times in that year and once in May 1844.

Sacchini understood orchestral as well as choral effect. His scores are small, oboes, horns, and sometimes trumpets and bassoons, being the only additions to the string quartet, but the treatment is as effective as it is simple. His part-writing is pure and good, while the care and finish evident in his scores are hard to reconcile with the accounts of his idle and irregular ways. The same technical qualities are shown in his compositions for the church, which in other ways are less distinguished than his operas from contemporary works of a similar kind.

Much of Sacchini's music is lost. Four oratorios, a mass, and various motets, etc., are mentioned in the Quellen-Lexikon, Fétis gives a list of twenty-one sacred compositions, and the names of forty-one operas, the chief of which **have** been mentioned here, but Burney puts the number of these much higher [twenty-seven are given as still extant in the Quellen-Lexikon]. The last of them, 'Arvire et Evelina,' was left unfinished. It was completed by J. B. Rey, and performed with success after the composer's death (April 29, 1788). He also left two symphonies in D, six trios for two violins and bass ; six quartets for two violins, tenor and bass ; and two sets, each of six harpsichord sonatas, with violin, as well as twelve sonatas (opp. 3 and 4) for clavier solo. These were all published in London. One of the sonatas, in F, is included in Pauer's 'Alte Meister.' [See the list, vol. iii. p. 103.] A couple of cavatinas are given by Gevaert in his 'Gloires d'Italie,' and an antiphon for two voices by Choron in his 'Journal de Chant.'   F. A. M.

SACKBUT, an early name for the trombone, probably derived from the Spanish sacabuche ('draw-tube') i.e. sacar 'to draw,' and bucha 'a pipe,' originally of boxwood (cf. Portuguese saca-buxa), the name being also given to a form of pump. Other derivations, however, are from O.F. saquier-boter ('to pull and to push') or Sp. sacar del buche ('to exhaust the chest'). The form first appears in Spanish literature of the 14th century, the trombone having been evolved from the trumpet about the year 1300. At the beginning of the next century the French form saqueboute is found, and at the close of the same century, when the instrument was introduced into England, it was known as the shakbusshe and subsequently as the saykebud, sackbut, or sagbut. One of the earliest uses of the word in English literature occurs in Hawes's Passetyme of Pleasure (1506). English players were held in high esteem both in this country and on the continent, the popularity of the sackbut continuing till the 18th century, when it gave place to the horn and serpent. Burney (Musical Performances in Westminster Abbey, 1784) relates the difficulty experienced in obtaining players on the sackbut or double trumpet, the only performers to be found in England being the six German musicians of the Royal Band. About the year 1800 the use of the instrument was revived in connection with the Opera, but the old English name was supplanted by the Italian trombone. Notwithstanding Shakespeare's allusion (Coriolanus, Act V. Sc. iv.), there is at present no authority for believing that the sackbut was known to the Romans, the specimen said to have been discovered in the 18th century at Pompeii or Herculaneum having proved a myth. The so-called representation of a 9th-century sackbut in the Boulogne Psalter (MS. No. 20) is also an error, the instrument depicted being a fanciful delineation of the sambuke, an ancient four-stringed lyre. The phrase 'tuba ductilis' applied in later times to the sackbut, originally meant a trumpet of metal beaten or drawn out by the hammer, i.e. not cast. For details of the instrument see art. TROMBONE ; also Mahillon, *Le Trombone*, Brussels, 1906, and Galpin, *The Sackbut, its Evolution and History*, *Mus. Assoc. Proceedings*, 1907.   F. W. G.

SACRED HARMONIC SOCIETY. This Society was originated by Thomas Brewer, Joseph Hart, W. Jeffreys, Joseph Surman, and — Cockerell, who first met, with a view to its establishment, on August 21, 1832. Its practical operations did not, however, commence until Nov. 20 following. Its first meetings were held in the chapel in Gate Street, Lincoln's Inn Fields, where the first concert was given on Tuesday evening, Jan. 15, 1833. The programme comprised selections from Handel's ' Messiah ' and ' Funeral Anthem,' and from Perry's ' Fall of Jerusalem ' and ' Death of Abel,' with Attwood's Coronation Anthem, ' O Lord, grant the king a long life,' and the hymn ' Adeste fideles.' The names of the principal singers were not published ; Thomas Harper was engaged as solo trumpeter. The then officers of the Society were John Newman Harrison, president ; Thomas Brewer, secretary ; J. G. Moginie, treasurer ; Joseph Surman, conductor ; George Perry, leader of the band ; and F. C. Walker, organist. In Nov. 1833, the permission to meet in the chapel being suddenly withdrawn, the Society removed to a chapel in Henrietta Street, Brunswick Square, and shortly afterwards to a room belonging to the Scottish Hospital in Fleur de Lys Court, Fleet Street ; but at Midsummer, 1834, it migrated to Exeter Hall, which was its home until Michaelmas, 1880. The concerts were for the first two years given in the Minor Hall, and consisted principally of selections, in which a few short complete works were occasionally introduced, such as Handel's ' Dettingen Te Deum,' Haydn's ' Mass,' No. 1, Bishop's ' Seventh Day,' and Romberg's ' The Transient and the Eternal.' The Society having on June 28, 1836, given a concert in the Large Hall in aid of a charity with very great success, was shortly afterwards induced to give its own concerts there. At the same time an important change in its policy was effected, viz. the abandonment of miscellaneous selections for complete oratorios, a change which was received by the public with great favour. Up to that period, even at the provincial festivals, it was very rarely that any complete oratorio, except Handel's ' Messiah,' was performed, whilst the programmes of the so-called ' Oratorios ' at the two patent theatres on the Wednesdays and Fridays in Lent were a mongrel mixture of oratorio songs and choruses, secular songs of all kinds, and instrumental solos. The first concert given in the Large Hall on the Society's own account was Handel's ' Messiah,' on Dec. 20, 1836, the orchestra consisting of about 300 performers. In 1837 the works performed included Mendelssohn's ' St. Paul ' (March 7), for the first time in

London and second in England, Handel's ' Messiah,' ' Israel in Egypt,' and ' Dettingen Te Deum,' Haydn's ' Creation,' and the Mass known as Mozart's 12th. On Sept. 12 another performance of ' St. Paul ' was given, in the composer's presence [see MENDELSSOHN, vol. iii. p. 134*a*]. During the year the number of performers was increased to 500. In the same year the formation of a musical library was commenced, and Robert Kanzow Bowley appointed honorary librarian. In 1838 Handel's ' Judas Maccabæus,' ' Samson,' and ' Solomon ' were revived, and Beethoven's ' Mass in C,' Spohr's ' Last Judgment,' and Perry's ' Fall of Jerusalem ' introduced. 1839 witnessed the revival and repetition of Handel's ' Joshua.' A new organ was built for the Society by Walker, and opened Jan. 23, 1840, with a performance by Thomas Adams. Handel's ' Saul ' was revived, and Elvey's ' Resurrection and Ascension,' and Perry's ' Thanksgiving Anthem on the birth of the Princess Royal ' introduced. 1841 was distinguished by a revival of Handel's ' Jephtha,' and by two performances of a selection of anthems. The latter was received with great interest, public attention having been then lately drawn to our cathedral music. The programme was chronologically arranged, and exhibited the various changes in the style of English church music from Tallis to Samuel Wesley, a period of two centuries and a half. It is true that a performance of a so-called ' Selection of Anthems ' had been given in the preceding year, but the programme being injudiciously arranged — a few anthems being interspersed with songs and other pieces in no wise connected with church-music,—had produced but little effect : the distinguishing feature of it was two admirable performances upon the organ by Mendelssohn. Perry's ' Death of Abel ' was brought forward on March 19, 1841. In 1842 Handel's ' Jubilate Deo,' and Beethoven's ' Mount of Olives ' (the ' Engedi ' version), were introduced. In 1843 Spohr's ' Fall of Babylon ' was produced, conducted by the composer, who was then on a visit to England ; Dr. Crotch's anthem, ' The Lord is King,' was performed for the first time ; Mendelssohn's 'Hymn of Praise' was introduced, and also Handel's ' Deborah.' The new introductions in 1844 were a Coronation Anthem and an organ concerto by Handel, Mendelssohn's 42nd Psalm, and Haydn's Mass, No. 16 ; but the season was chiefly distinguished by two performances of Mendelssohn's ' St. Paul,' conducted by the composer. Handel's ' Athaliah,' Purcell's ' Jubilate in D,' and cantata ' Saul and the Witch of Endor,' Neukomm's ' David,' and a new selection of anthems, were brought forward for the first time in 1845. In 1846 the new introductions comprised Perry's ' Belshazzar's Feast,' Mendelssohn's 114th Psalm, Haydn's Mass, No. 2, and some minor pieces.

1847 was an important epoch in the Society's annals; Handel's 'Belshazzar' was revived, and a new selection of Anthems given, but the greatest event was the production for the first time in its improved form of Mendelssohn's 'Elijah,' under his own personal direction. Four performances of it were given, and it at once took that firm position which it has ever since maintained. Subsequently Spohr visited this country at the invitation of the Society and conducted two performances of his 'Fall of Babylon' and one of his 'Christian's Prayer' and 'Last Judgment' (the last for the only time in England under his direction), and produced his '84th Psalm, Milton's version,' composed expressly for the occasion. An incident of this year eventually led to changes which had an important influence on the fortunes of the Society. A committee, appointed to investigate the conduct of Joseph Surman, both in respect of his dealings with the Society and his execution of the office of conductor, having unanimously reported adversely to him, he was removed from his office Feb. 15, 1848. Pending a regular appointment the remaining concerts of the season were conducted by the leader of the band, George Perry. Mr. (afterwards Sir Michael) Costa was elected conductor, Sept. 22, 1848. Very beneficial results followed this appointment: both band and chorus were strengthened and improved, and the number of performers was augmented to nearly 700. The performances of the season consisted principally of more effective renderings of the stock pieces, but Mendelssohn's music for 'Athalie' was introduced with great success. In 1850 nothing new was given but Mendelssohn's 'Lauda Sion' in an English dress. 1851 was chiefly remarkable for the number of concerts given—thirty-one; 'Messiah,' 'Elijah,' and the 'Creation' having been performed alternately, one in each week, from May to September for the gratification of visitors to the Great Exhibition in Hyde Park. Later in the year Haydn's 'Seasons' was introduced for the first time. In 1852 Spohr's 'Calvary' and the fragments of Mendelssohn's 'Christus' were introduced. In 1853 some changes took place in the officers of the Society; R. K. Bowley became treasurer, and W. H. Husk succeeded him as librarian: Mozart's 'Requiem' was first brought forward this year. 1854 was distinguished by two performances of Beethoven's Mass in D. Griesbach's 'Daniel' was also brought forward, and the Society undertook the performance of the music at the opening of the Crystal Palace on May 10. In 1856 Costa's 'Eli' was performed for the first time in London with marked success. In 1857 Rossini's 'Stabat Mater' was introduced, and the Society undertook the musical arrangements for the first Handel Festival at the Crystal Palace. [See HANDEL FESTIVAL.] In 1862 Beethoven's 'Mount of Olives' was given with

its proper libretto. Costa's 'Naaman' was introduced to a London audience in 1865. In 1867 Benedict's 'Legend of St. Cecilia' was given for the first time in London. In 1870 Beethoven's Mass in D was again performed. The Society sustained the loss, by death, of three of its principal officers, J. N. Harrison, president; R. K. Bowley, treasurer; and T. Brewer, secretary and, for a few weeks, president. They were replaced by D. Hill, president; W. H. Withall, treasurer; and J. F. Puttick, secretary. In 1873 the last named died, and E. H. Mannering was appointed in his stead. Bach's 'St. Matthew Passion' was given for the first time. In 1874 Dr. Crotch's 'Palestine' was introduced, and Macfarren's 'St. John the Baptist' given for the first time in London. Mozart's Litany in B♭, in an English dress, was introduced in 1877. In 1878 Rossini's 'Moses in Egypt' was restored to its original position as an oratorio. Nothing new was brought forward in the season of 1879-80, which ended on April 30, 1880, with 'Israel in Egypt.' Owing to a change in the proprietorship of Exeter Hall the Society had to quit that building, and the concerts of the season 1880-81 were given in St. James's Hall, the number of performers being reduced, on account of the limited space of the orchestra, to about 300. The first concert was on Dec. 3. Sullivan's 'Martyr of Antioch' (first time in London) and Cherubini's Requiem in C minor were brought out during the season.

The Society's library was the largest collection of music and musical literature ever gathered together by a musical body in England. Space does not allow here of even a brief list of its principal contents, and the reader is therefore referred to the last edition of its printed catalogue, issued in 1872. It was acquired for the Royal College of Music at the dissolution of the original Society. [See also LIBRARIES, vol. ii. p. 706.] The Society also possessed some interesting original portraits, statuary, and autograph letters. It was in constitution an essentially amateur body, none but amateurs being eligible for membership, and the governing committee being chosen by and from the members. Every member was required to take some part in the orchestra, and a strict examination as to his qualification for so doing was made prior to his admission. The most eminent professors were engaged as principal vocalists and instrumentalists, the rest of the band and the whole of the chorus being amateurs. The members were comparatively few in number, the majority of the amateurs being assistants, who gave their gratuitous services, but paid no subscription. The subscription of members, originally £1, was afterwards £2 : 2s. per annum. The original Society was dissolved in 1882, its last concert being a performance of 'Solomon' on April 28 of that year. Some members of the committee determined to resuscitate the Society, and the new institution was incorporated in 1882. Charles Hallé was appointed conductor, and in 1885 was succeeded by W. H. Cummings, who had, up to that time, acted as assistant conductor. In the autumn of 1888 the new Society ceased to exist.

The Benevolent Fund of the Society was instituted March 14, 1855, for the aid of necessitous persons who had at any time been connected with the Sacred Harmonic Society. The management of the Fund was entrusted to an independent committee, chosen by the Governors of the Fund from the members of the Sacred Harmonic Society.   W. H. H.

SADLER'S WELLS, a place of entertainment near the New River Head, Pentonville, much associated with music from the end of the 17th century. In a garden belonging to a person named Sadler an ancient well was discovered in 1683. The water of the well was chalybeate and ferruginous, and Sadler, who owned a sort of tavern, having attached a wooden 'Music House,' exploited the medicinal qualities in rivalry of the waters at Tunbridge and at Epsom. He laid out the grounds and engaged tumblers and musicians, and the place was much frequented for its open-air concerts. In 1699 James Miles and a Francis Forcer, the latter a musician, were proprietors, and the place became known also as 'Miles's Music House.' Miles having died in 1724, Francis Forcer, junior, increased the attractions, and Forcer dying in 1743, the gardens passed into the hands of one Rosoman, who made many alterations, rebuilding the Music House in brick. This brick structure, erected in 1765, formed part of Sadler's Wells theatre until quite recent years. Mrs. Lampe, Thomas Lowe, and other vocalists of repute sang at Sadler's Wells, and at a later date Miss Romanzini (Mrs. Bland), and Braham were among the performers engaged there. Mrs. Mountain, the singer, whose parents were engaged at Sadler's Wells, was named after Rosoman the proprietor. Charles Dibdin the elder, and his sons Thomas and Charles were all more or less closely connected with Sadler's Wells, writing plays and musical pantomimes for production there. The younger Dibdins were proprietors and managers. Grimaldi's connection with this theatre and that of other pantomimists, tumblers, rope-dancers, and actors, do not concern the musical records of it. The theatre has seen many changes, and it is now a music-hall. Much information regarding details can be gathered from a collection of scraps relating to Sadler's Wells, bound in fourteen volumes, formed by Mr. Percival in the British Museum. *London Pleasure Gardens* by W. and A. E. Wroth, *Old and New London*, and similar works may be also consulted.   F. K.

SAFFO. See SAPPHO.

SAGGIO DI CONTRAPPUNTO (Sample of Counterpoint). A very important work, published at Bologna, in 1774-75, by the Padre Giambattista Martini, in two large 4to volumes, dedicated to Cardinal Vincenzo Malvezzi, and now very scarce. The full title, *Esemplare, o sia saggio fondamentale pratico di contrappunto sopra il canto fermo*, etc., sufficiently explains the design of the work, in which the author endeavours to teach the art of counterpoint rather by reference to the most perfect obtainable models than by any code of written laws. The method adopted for this purpose is above all praise. The bulk of the volume consists of a series of examples, in the form of Motets, Madrigals, Movements from Masses, and other similar compositions, selected from the works of the greatest masters of the 16th and 17th centuries, beautifully printed, from movable types, in lozenge-headed notes, resembling those found in Italian Part-Books of the best period, but without the Ligatures which render those books so puzzling to the modern musician. The masters selected are, Agostini, Animuccia, Barbieri, Baroni, Benevoli, Bernabei, Caresana, Cifra, Clari, Corvo, Falconio, Foggia, Gabussi, Gesualdo, Lotti, Marcello, Marenzio, Minarti, Monteverde, Morales, Navarro di Siviglia, Nitrami, Olstani, Ortiz, Pacchioni, Palestrina, P. Pontio Parmigiano, Pasquale, Perti, Piocchi, Porta, Predieri, Riccieri, Rota, A. Scarlatti, Stradella, Turini, Vittoria, Willaert, Zarlino, and several Anonymi. The works are arranged in accordance with the characteristics of their respective schools ; and each movement is illustrated by a copious series of annotations, explaining its general design, pointing out the various devices employed in its construction, and calling particular attention to its merits, and the lessons to be learned from it. The amount of sound scholarship and able criticism displayed in these annotations renders the work extremely valuable for purposes of study ; while the rarity of the original edition suggests that a careful reprint would be useful.   W. S. R.

SAINT ANNE'S TUNE. This well-known tune, in accordance with a practice of which there are several examples,[1] was constructed by the addition of a new continuation to a fragment of an older melody. A seven-part motet of Palestrina's, published in May 1569, leads off in the first treble with this phrase

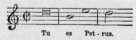

Tu   es   Pet - rus.

identical with the first phrase of St. Anne's ; after which the resemblance ceases. The entire first strain of the tune is said to be traceable to a French chanson of the 16th century. It was adopted by J. S. Bach as the subject of an organ fugue, known in England as 'St. Anne's fugue'—

[1] The 'Old Hundredth' psalm tune is another instance. Its first strain is the commencement of several distinct tunes.

a misleading title, as, except in the identity of its subject with the first strain of St. Anne's, the fugue has no connection with the hymn-tune. As early as 1638 the same strain was employed by Henry Lawes as the commencement of the tunes set by him to the 9th and 136th Psalms in Sandys's 'Paraphrase upon the Psalmes of David.'

St. Anne's tune, under that name, is first found in 'A Supplement to the New Version of the Psalms,' sixth edition, much enlarged, 1708. Dr. Croft's name is not mentioned in the work, but he is believed to have been the musical editor of this edition of the Supplement ; the name of the tune is probably derived from that of the parish, St. Anne's, Westminster, of which church he was then organist, and the tune itself is directly ascribed to him by his contemporaries, viz., Philip Hart in 'Melodies proper to be sung to any of ye Versions of ye Psalms of David,' cir. 1719, and John Church in his 'Introduction to Psalmody,' 1723. The tune appears in the 'Supplement' in the following form :—

Psalm xlii.   *St. Anne's Tune.*

A 2 voc.

See *Musical Times* for 1900, p. 585, where the tune is given in facsimile and Croft's authorship discussed.

Of late years some doubt has been thrown on the authorship of the tune from its having been found in Abraham Barber's 'Book of Psalm Tunes,' a Yorkshire collection, of which the license bears date Feb. 14, 1687, when Croft was but ten years of age. Here the tune appears under the name of 'Leeds,' and is ascribed to 'Mr. Denby,' whose name some editors of hymnals have too hastily substituted for that of Croft. The edition, however, of Barber's Psalms which contains the tune is the seventh, dated 1715, or seven years after the publication of the 'Supplement' already mentioned. This edition contains, besides tunes for Canticles, Psalms, etc., twenty-eight hymn-tunes arranged in four parts, with the melody in the tenor. Of these tunes three only have a composer's name prefixed, and these three, which bear the names of northern towns ('Leverpool,' 'Hallifax,' and 'Leeds'), are all ascribed to 'Mr. Denby.' It may be observed that while the melody of 'Leeds' is identical with that of St. Anne's in the 'Supplement,' the modulation at the end of the third strain is different.

Leeds Tune.   Mr. DENBY.

[Tune.]

The supposition, however, that 'Leeds' was originally in Barber's Psalm-book has been disproved by the recent discovery of a copy of an early edition of the collection, which from the evidence of the preface appears to be either the third or fourth, and to have been published about 1696.[1] The title-page is unfortunately missing. This volume, a smaller book than the edition of 1715, contains but twelve hymn-tunes arranged in two parts, and neither the tune in question nor Denby's name occurs in it. Until, therefore, an edition of Barber's Psalms is found, containing 'Leeds,' and of earlier date than 1708, Denby must be regarded as merely the author of a rearrangement of Croft's tune.

That some confusion existed respecting the authorship may perhaps be inferred from the fact that Dr. Miller, organist of Doncaster Parish Church, in his 'Psalms of David,' 1790, gives 'St. Ann's, Dr. Croft' on one page, and opposite to it 'Leeds, Denby,' in triple time and as a different tune. On the other hand, it may be noticed that in another Yorkshire collection, John and James Green's 'Collection of choice Psalm Tunes' (Sheffield, 3rd ed., 1715), St. Anne's tune is quoted under that name.   G. A. C.

SAINT-AUBIN, JEANNE CHARLOTTE SCHRŒDER, a very remarkable opera-singer, born in Paris, Dec. 9, 1764. She was daughter of a theatrical manager, began to act as a mere child, and, when only nine, charmed Louis XV. by her precocious talent. In 1782 she married Saint-Aubin, an actor in Mlle. Montansier's company, and in 1786 made her first appearance at the Académie, in 'Colinette à la Cour,' but perceiving that she was not qualified for so large a stage, had the good sense to transfer herself to the Comédie Italienne. There her expressive face, graceful acting, and good singing, could

[1] The preface speaks of 'former editions,' and adds—'since the Psalms in metre are this last year much refin'd as to the English by some good grave Divine Persons who hath only left out all the old words and made the meter good English.' The preface to the seventh edition is a different one.

be properly appreciated, and she speedily became a favourite. No actress ever created a greater number of parts, in a variety of styles. She sang romances with great charm, and became the acknowledged star of the company and its most profitable member. She was, however, badly treated by the management, for though admitted as *sociétaire* to the fourth of a share in 1788, she was not advanced to a full share till 1798, after her success in 'Le Prisonnier.'

At her farewell benefit (April 2, 1808) she took the part of Mme. Belmont in this work, leaving Rosine, her own creation, to her second daughter, Alexandrine. Her modest pension of 1900 francs was increased by Louis XVIII. to 3000. She took her final farewell, assisted by her elder daughter, Mme. Duret, on Nov. 7, 1818, in 'Une heure de mariage,' and was as much applauded as ever. Mme. Saint-Aubin lived to a great age, and died in Paris, Sept. 11, 1850. Three of her children distinguished themselves; the son, JEAN DENIS, born at Lyons in 1783, a violinist and composer of great promise, died at Paris in 1810.

The elder daughter, CÉCILE, born at Lyons in 1785, a pupil of Garat, made her début in 1805 at the Opéra-Comique in 'Le Concert interrompu,' but went back to the Conservatoire to study, and did not reappear till 1808. In the interval she gained both style and taste in singing, but remained an indifferent actress. Under the name of Mme. Duret she rose for a short time to distinction as the favourite singer of Nicolo Isouard, who composed several important and difficult parts for her. Her best creations were in 'Le Billet de Loterie,' and 'Jeannot et Colin.' She retired in 1820. Her sister ALEXANDRINE, born at Paris, 1793, made a brilliant début at the Théâtre Feydeau in 1809, and in the following year excited great enthusiasm in Isouard's 'Cendrillon.' This was, however, the only original part in which she distinguished herself, and on her marriage with an actor at the Vaudeville in 1812, she retired from the stage. G. C.

SAINT CECILIA. See vol. i. p. 489 ff.

SAINT CECILIA'S HALL, a famous Edinburgh concert-room, associated, during the last half of the 18th century, with the chief musical events of the northern capital. It was at the foot of Niddry Wynd (now Niddry Street), and almost adjoining the Cowgate. Robert Mylne, the well-known Scottish architect, designed the building, taking the opera-house at Parma for his model. The main hall was a long-shaped oval, and its acoustic properties were admirable. It was opened in 1762, and remained in possession of the Musical Society of Edinburgh from that date to June 1801. It then became successively a Baptist Chapel, a Freemasons' Hall, a school, and, in 1899, a book-binder's works.

Though at the foot of a steep and dirty wynd, in a quarter that had ceased to be fashionable even at the time of its first building, it was frequented by the highest society of Edinburgh. All the important concerts were held here. Previous to its erection the chief concerts were held in St. Mary's Chapel, in the same wynd, as early as 1728. The Taylors' Hall in the Cowgate, the Assembly Rooms, Assembly Close, and the Concert Hall, in Playhouse Close.

At a later date Corri's Rooms and other places, as the New Town began to grow, superseded the Hall. Some interesting reminiscences of the Concerts at St. Cecilia's Hall were contributed in 1847 by George Thomson to Robert Chambers's *Traditions of Edinburgh*. Wilson's *Memorials of Edinburgh*, Grant's *Old and New Edinburgh*, and other works deal with the famous Concert-room. See Mr. Fraser Harris's *Saint Cecilia's Hall in the Niddry Wynd*, 1899. F. K.

SAINT-GEORGES, JULES HENRI VERNOY, MARQUIS DE,—not to be confounded with the notorious Chevalier de Saint-Georges (1745-99 or 1801)—born in Paris, 1801, died there, Dec. 23, 1875, writer of novels, and author of numerous librettos for operas and opéras-comiques, was the favourite collaborator of Halévy. Among his 120 librettos we need only specify those for Donizetti's 'Fille du Régiment'; Adolphe Adam's 'La Marquise,' 'Cagliostro,' 'Le Bijou perdu,' operas: and 'Giselle,' 'La jolie Fille de Gand,' and 'Le Corsaire,' ballets; Auber's 'L'Ambassadrice,' 'Zanetta,' and 'Les Diamants de la Couronne,' with Scribe; Grisar's 'Lady Melvil,' 'Le Carillonneur de Bruges,' and 'Les Amours du Diable'; Clapisson's 'La Fanchonnette'; and Halévy's 'L'Eclair,' 'Les Mousquetaires de la Reine,' 'Le Val d'Andorre,' 'La Fée aux Roses,' 'Le Juif errant,' 'Le Nabab,' and 'Jaguarita l'Indienne.'

From this list it will appear that Saint-Georges was the most prolific, as he was the ablest, of all French contemporary librettists after Scribe. G. C.

SAINT HUBERTY,[1] ANTOINETTE CÉCILE, an eminent French operatic actress, whose real surname was Clavel, was born at Toul, about 1756. Her father, who had previously served in the army, became stage manager to a French opera company at Mannheim, and afterwards at Warsaw, where she studied for four years with Lemoyne, conductor of the orchestra. Her first public appearance was in an opera of his, 'Le Bouquet de Colette.' She then went to Berlin, and is said to have been married there to a certain Chevalier de Croisy, of whom, however, nothing is heard in her subsequent history. For three years she sang at Strasburg, as Mlle. Clavel, and thence went to Paris, and made her début at the Académie as 'un

[1] How she obtained this name is not known.

démon, un plaisir' in the first performance of Gluck's 'Armide' (Sept. 23, 1777). For a considerable time she only played in subordinate parts. Her appearance was not striking; she was fair, thin, and below middle height, with a face expressive, but not beautiful. Her voice was produced badly and with effort, her stage action was spasmodic and exaggerated, and she had a strong German accent. But Gluck found in this ill-trained actress some qualities he may have vainly sought for in more finished singers. She appeared one morning at rehearsal in an old black gown in the last stage of patched decrepitude. 'Here comes Madame la Ressource,' remarked some gay rival (alluding to the character of that name in 'Le Joueur'). 'Well said,' answered Gluck; 'that woman will some day be the *resource* of the opera.' Perhaps she heard the words—we may be sure she heard of them. She laboured to improve herself, and on the retirement of two leading singers succeeded to their parts. Her first great success was as Angélique in Piccinni's 'Roland,' and was followed by others in Floquet's 'Le Seigneur Bienfaisant,' Gossec's 'Thésée' (March 1, 1782), and Edelmann's 'Ariane' (Sept. 24, 1782), all tragic parts; while as Rosette in Grétry's 'L'Embarras des Richesses' (Nov. 26, 1782), she showed all the versatility and vivacity necessary for comedy. As Armide (in Sacchini's 'Renaud'), in 'Didon,' 'Chimène,' 'Les Danaïdes,' 'Alceste,' and 'Phèdre,' she had a succession of triumphs. 'Didon,' Piccinni's masterpiece, made no impression till she undertook the title-rôle, and the composer declared that, without her, his opera was 'without Dido.' On her first appearance in that part (Jan. 16, 1784) she was crowned upon the stage.

In 1785 she made a journey to Marseilles, which resembled a royal progress. The excitement she created amounted to frenzy, and when she left Provence she carried away more than a hundred crowns, many of them of great value. But on her return to Paris she found new rivals to dispute her sway. She failed, too, as Clytemnestra, a part altogether unsuited to her. It ended four years later by her marrying the Comte d'Entraigues, of strong royalist sympathies, in which she participated warmly. In 1790 he had emigrated to Lausanne, and there their marriage took place, at the end of that year. It was only acknowledged, however, in 1797, after the Count, imprisoned at Milan by Bonaparte, had been released by his wife, who found means of enabling him to escape, and of preserving his portfolio, full of political papers. For this service she was rewarded by Louis XVIII. with the Order of St. Michel and, it seems, by her husband with the recognition of their marriage.

The Count afterwards entered the Russian diplomatic service, and was employed on secret missions. The peace of Tilsit changed his tactics. He possessed himself in some manner of a copy of the secret articles of the Treaty, and hastened with them to England to communicate them to the government. For this he is said to have received a pension. He established himself, with his wife, at Barnes, near Richmond, where, July 22, 1812, they were assassinated by their servant, who stabbed them as they were getting into their carriage, and blew out his own brains afterwards. This man had been bribed by emissaries of Fouché's, sent to watch the proceedings of the Comte d'Entraigues, and had allowed them to take copies of correspondence with the Foreign Office, entrusted to his care by his master. He had reason to think that his treachery was being discovered, and fear of the consequences probably prompted him to the dreadful deed. F. A. M.

SAINT JAMES'S HALL CONCERT ROOMS were erected, at the cost of a company with limited liability, from designs by Owen Jones. Messrs. Lucas were the builders.

The project was taken up by two of the music-publishing firms, Messrs. Beale & Chappell of Regent Street, and Chappell & Co. of New Bond Street; and the company was formed mainly by them, and among their friends. Messrs. T. F. Beale and W. Chappell became the tenants of the Crown for the land, holding it in trust for the Company. The capital was fixed at £40,000, because the original estimate for the new building was £23,000 and the remainder was supposed to be an ample sum for compensations, working expenses, etc. It was then unknown that between Regent Street and Piccadilly, was the ancient boundary of Thorney Island with its quicksand, but this was encountered in the course of the building, and had to be saturated with concrete at great cost, in order to make a sure foundation. Other demands raised the cost of the building to beyond £70,000. The Great Hall was opened to the public on March 25, 1858, with a concert for the benefit of Middlesex Hospital, given in presence of the Prince Consort.

The principal entrance to the Great Hall was originally from Regent Street, and that to the Minor Hall from Piccadilly. The dimensions of the Great Hall were 139 feet in length, 60 in height, and 60 in breadth. It seated on the ground floor 1100; in the balcony 517; in the gallery 210; in the orchestra 300; total 2127. Under the platform end of the Great Hall was the Minor Hall 60 feet by 57, having also a gallery, an orchestra, and a small room. This was occupied for many years by the Christy (Moore & Burgess) Minstrels. Under the Regent Street end of the Great Hall was one of the dining rooms, 60 feet by 60, and on the Regent Street level was another dining-room 40 feet by 40, with a large banqueting-room on the floor above, etc.

CHARLES CAMILLE SAINT-SAËNS

In 1860 alterations and additions were made to the restaurant attached to the concert rooms, at a further outlay of £5000. The Company was eventually enabled to pay these charges, through the uncovenanted liberality of some of the directors, in accepting personal responsibility to mortagees and bankers, while they diminished the debt annually through the receipts of the Hall. Many concerts were given for the express purpose of engaging the Hall on off-nights, especially the Monday Popular Concerts, which became a national institution, but were originally started by Chappell & Co. to bring together a new public to fill the Hall on Monday nights. In 1874 three more houses in Piccadilly were purchased to add to the restaurant. The rebuilding of these entailed a further expenditure of £45,000, so that the total cost exceeded £120,000. w. c. [In much later days important alterations were made in the approaches to the hall, a fine marble staircase leading direct from the Piccadilly entrance. In spite of these, there was an element of danger from the presence of kitchens and the Christy Minstrels' hall below, and in spite of the beautiful acoustics of the great hall and its wonderful artistic associations, it was not wholly a misfortune when it was determined to pull it down and use the site for a hotel. The last concert took place on Feb. 11, 1905.]

ST. PATRICK'S DAY. This rousing Irish melody has been regarded for over a century as the unofficial anthem of Ireland. It can be definitely traced back to the first decade of the 18th century, and was very popular, so much so that we find it as one of the two tunes played by the Irish war-pipers at the famous battle of Fontenoy, on May 11, 1745. Between the years 1746 and 1766 it was in vogue in England, and was printed by Rutherford in his 'Country Dances,' in 1749. In 1759 Oswald published a fairly good setting of it in his *Caledonian Pocket Companion* (Bk. xi.), and the Irish dramatist, Isaac Bickerstaffe, set one of his songs in 'Love in a Village' to it, in 1762. Numerous Anglo-Irish songs were adapted to the tune, and at length, in 1810, Moore wrote his lyric 'Tho' dark are our sorrows,' which duly appeared in the fourth number of the 'Irish Melodies' (1811). Oswald's setting is as follows :—

St. Patrick's Day.

Oswald's Setting, 1759.

W. H. G. F.

SAINT-SAËNS, CHARLES CAMILLE, born Oct. 9, 1835, in the Rue du Jardinet (now No. 3), Paris. Having lost his father, he was brought up by his mother and a great-aunt, who taught him the elements of music, and to this day the composer keeps the little old-fashioned instrument on which this dearly-loved relative gave him his first lessons. At seven he began to study the piano with Stamaty, and afterwards had lessons in harmony from Maleden. Gifted with an excellent ear and a prodigious memory, he showed from childhood a marvellous aptitude for music, and an unusual thirst for knowledge. He played at a concert of his own in 1846, and in 1847 he entered Benoist's class at the Conservatoire, and was with Halévy for composition; he obtained the second organ-prize in 1849, and the first in 1851. He left in the following year, but competed for the Prix de Rome, which was, however, won by Léonce Cohen, his senior by six years. He was not more fortunate at a second trial in 1864, although by that time he had made a name in more than one branch of composition. These academic failures are therefore of no real importance, and we merely mention them because it is remarkable that the most learned of French contemporary musicians should have gained every possible distinction except the Grand Prix de Rome.

Saint-Saëns was only sixteen when he composed his first symphony, which was performed with success by the Société de Sainte Cécile. In 1853 he became organist of the church of St. Merri, and shortly after accepted the post of pianoforte professor at Niedermeyer's École religieuse. Though overwhelmed with work he found time for composing symphonies, chamber-music, and vocal and instrumental pieces—and for playing at concerts, where he became known as an interpreter of classical music. In 1858 he became organist of the Madeleine, and distinguished himself as much by his talent for improvisation as by his execution. He resigned this coveted post in 1877, when he was much gratified by the appointment of Théodore Dubois, a solid musician, worthy in every respect to be his successor.

The stage being the sole road to fame and fortune in Paris, all French musicians naturally aim at dramatic composition. Saint-Saëns was no exception to this rule. He was in the first rank of pianists and organists, and his cantata 'Les Noces de Prométhée' had been awarded the prize at the International Exhibition of 1867, and performed with great éclat, but these successes could not content him, and he produced 'La Princesse jaune,' one act, at the Opéra-Comique, June 12, 1872, and 'Le Timbre d'argent,' a fantastic opera in four acts, at the Théâtre Lyrique, Feb. 23, 1877. Both operas were comparative failures ; and, doubtless discouraged by so harsh a judgment from the Parisian public, he produced his next work, 'Samson et Dalila,' a sacred drama (Dec. 2, 1877), at Weimar, and 'Étienne Marcel,' opera in four acts (Feb. 8, 1879), at Lyons. ['Henri VIII.' was produced at the Opéra, March 5, 1883, and not given in England until 1898 ; 'Proserpine' was given at the Opéra-Comique, March 16, 1887, 'Ascanio' at the Opéra, March 21, 1890, 'Phryné' in May 1893, 'Frédégonde' (completion of Guiraud's unfinished opera) in 1895, 'Les Barbares' in 1901, 'Parysatis' in 1902 in the ancient theatre of Béziers, 'Andromaque' in 1903, 'Hélène' (one-act, Monte Carlo, Feb. 18, 1904, and Covent Garden, June 20 of the same year); 'L'Ancêtre,' produced Feb. 24, 1906, at Monte Carlo, is the master's last opera. His 'Javotte,' a two-act ballet, was given at Lyons and Brussels in 1896, music to 'Antigone' (Th. Français, 1893), and 'Déjanire,' incidental music to Gallet's play, at the Odéon, Nov. 11, 1898. He also wrote music to 'Le Malade Imaginaire.']

Saint-Saëns has been an extensive traveller. He has been in Russia, Spain, Portugal, Africa, etc., besides paying repeated visits to Germany, Austria, and England, so that he may be truly said to have acquired a European reputation. His fame mainly rests on his instrumental music, and on his masterly and effective manner of dealing with the orchestra. He is an excellent contrapuntist, shines in the construction of his orchestral pieces, has a quick ear for picturesqueness of detail, and has written enough fine music to procure him an unique position among French composers. He has very great power of combination, and of seizing instantaneously all the latent capacities of a given theme, both in the way of melody and harmony.

[Saint-Saëns is a consummate master of composition, and no one possesses a more profound knowledge than he does of the secrets and resources of the art ; but the creative faculty does not keep pace with the technical skill of the workman. His incomparable talent for orchestration enables him to give relief to ideas which would otherwise be crude and mediocre in themselves ; and it is this talent which makes him the one French musician most fitted to compete with the classic masters of the Symphony. His weakness consists not only in the inequality of his inspiration, but also in the indecision of his artistic principles ; this is shown in all his compositions, and it is this

which leads him to place excellent and objectionable passages in juxtaposition. For the same reason his works are on the one hand not frivolous enough to become popular in the widest sense, nor on the other do they take hold of the public by that sincerity and warmth of feeling which is so convincing. Saint-Saëns, who was made a knight of the Légion d'honneur in 1867, and an officer of the same in July 1884, is always the same incomparable pianist. It would even seem that during the last twenty years his talent in this direction had increased, and such receptions as he has received at the Conservatoire, where he played Beethoven's Choral Fantasia, in Russia, on the occasion of his tour in 1887 with Taffanel, Turban, and Gillet, and in London, on many occasions, as in 1871, 1874, 1879, prove him to be one of the most remarkable and earnest pianoforte players of the day. On June 13, 1892, he received the honorary degree of Mus.D. from the University of Cambridge, where he played his 'Africa' at a concert of the Cambridge University Musical Society on the previous day. On June 2, 1896, the fiftieth anniversary of his first appearance in public was celebrated in Paris.

In addition to his other claims to distinction, Saint-Saëns is a first-rate musical critic, and has contributed articles to La Renaissance, L'Estafette, and Le Voltaire, the best of which were published in 1885, under the title of Harmonie et Mélodie (Paris: Calmann Lévy, 1885), with an introduction and appendix explaining the change which his views have undergone in relation to Richard Wagner. An 'Essai sur les lyres et cithare antique' appeared in 1902, and 'Portraits et Souvenirs' in 1903.] He was elected member of the Institute, vice Henri Reber, Feb. 19, 1881.

LIST OF SAINT-SAËNS'S COMPOSITIONS

Op.
1. Three pieces for harmonium.
2. First Symphony, Eb (published 1855).
3. PF. solos, Bagatelles.
4. Mass for soli, choir, organ, and orchestra.
5. Tantum ergo for 8-part choir with organ.
6. Tarantelle for flute, clarinet, and orch.
7. Rhapsodies on Breton themes for organ.
8. Six duets for harmonium and pf.
9. Scena from Horace.
10. Bénédiction nuptiale, for organ.
11. Duettino in G, for pf.
12. Oratorio de Noël.
13. Élévation for harmonium.
14. Quintet, A minor, for pf. and strings.
15. Serenade for pf., organ, vln., and viola or vcello.
16. Suite for pf. and vcello.
17. First pf. concerto in D.
18. Trio, pf. and strings in F.
19. Les Noces de Prométhée, cantata.
20. First violin concerto, A minor.
21. First Mazurka for pf.
22. Second pf. concerto, G minor.
23. Gavotte for pf.
24. Second Mazurka for pf.
25. March for pf., 'Orient et Occident,' 4 hands.
26. Mélodies Persanes for voice.
27. Romance for pf., organ, and violin.
28. Introduction and Rondo capriccioso for violin and orch.
29. Third pf. concerto, Bb.
30. La Princesse Jaune, opera.
31. Le Rouet d'Omphale, symphonic poem.
32. Sonata in C minor, pf. and vcello.
33. Violoncello concerto, A minor.
34. Marche héroïque for orchestra.
35. Variations for two pfs. on a theme of Beethoven.]
36. Romance, horn or vcello and orch. in F.
37. Romance for flute or vln. in D flat.
38. Berceuse in B flat, pf. and vln.
39. Phaëton, symphonic poem.

Op.
40. Danse macabre, symphonic poem.
41. Quartet for pf. and str. in B flat.
42. Ps. xix. (vulg. xviii.), 'Coeli enarrant,' for soli, choir, and orch.
43. Allegro Appassionato for pf. and vcello.
44. Pf. concerto in C minor.
45. Le Déluge, biblical opera.
46. Les Soldats de Gédéon, for double male chorus, unaccomp.
47. Samson et Dalila, opera.
48. Romance, vln. and orch.
49. Suite for orchestra.
50. La Jeunesse d'Hercule, symphonic poem.
51. Romance in D, pf. and vcello.
52. Six Études for pf.
53. Chanson de grand-père for two female voices, and Chanson d'ancêtre, male choir, baritone solo; accompt. orch. or pf.
54. Requiem for soli, choir, and orchestra.
55. Second symphony, A minor.
56. Minuet and Valse for pf.
57. La Lyre et la Harpe, soli, choir, and orchestra.
58. Second violin concerto in C.
59. Ballade for pf., 4 hands.
60. Suite Algérienne for orchestra.
61. Third violin concerto, B minor.
62. Morceau de Concert, vln. and orch.
63. Une nuit à Lisbonne, Barcarolle for orchestra.
64. Jota Aragonese for orchestra.
65. Septet for pf., 5 stringed instruments, and trumpet.
66. Third Mazurka, B minor, for pf.
67. Romance for horn (from op. 16).
68. Two choruses with ad lib. pf. accompaniment.
69. Hymne à Victor Hugo for orchestra and chorus ad lib.
70. Allegro Appassionato for pf. and orch.
71. Two choruses for male voices.
72. Pf. album.
73. Rhapsodie d'Auvergne, for pf. and orchestra.
74. Saltarelle, for male choir, unaccompanied.
75. Sonata for pf. and vln., D minor.
76. Wedding Cake, caprice-valse for pf. and strings.
77. Polonaise for two pfs.
78. Third Symphony in C minor, orch. organ, pf., 4 hands.
79. Caprice for pf. and three wind instruments, on Danish and Russian airs.
80. Souvenir d'Italie, for pf.
81. Albumblatt for pf., 4 hands.
82. La Fiancée du Timbalier (Victor Hugo's ballade), voice and orch.
83. Havanaise for pf. and vln.
84. Les Guerriers, for male chorus, unaccompanied.
85. Les Cloches du Soir, pf.
86. Pas redoublé for pf., 4 hands.
87. Scherzo for two pfs., 4 hands.
88. Valse canariote for pf.
89. Africa, fantaisie, pf. and orch.
90. Suite, pf.
91. Chant saphique, vcello and pf.
92. Second trio, E minor, pf. and strings.
93. Sarabande and Rigaudon for orchestra.
94. Concertstück for horn.
95. Fantaisie for harp.
96. Caprice Arabe for two pfs., 4 hands.
97. Thème varié, for pf.
98. Pallas Athene, hymn for sop. and orchestra.
99. Three preludes and fugues for organ.
100. Souvenir d'Ismailia, pf.
101. Fantaisie for organ.
102. Second sonata, pf. and violin, E♭.
103. Fifth pf. concerto in F.
104. Valse Mignonne for pf.
105. Berceuse for pf., 4 hands.

    Works without opus numbers—
      Fantaisie for violin and harp (1907).
      Twenty-five motets; songs, part-songs, etc.
      Transcriptions of his own and other music.

G. C.; with additions by MM. Adolphe Jullien and Gustave Ferrari; from the monograph by O. Neitzel in *Berühmte Musiker*; Reimann's and Baker's Dictionaries, etc.

SAINTON, PROSPER PHILIPPE CATHERINE, an eminent violin-player, born June 5, 1813, at Toulouse, where his father was a merchant. He received his education at the College of Toulouse, and was destined to the law, but his great talent for music, combined with other reasons, fortunately altered this, and in Dec. 1831 he entered the Conservatoire at Paris, and studied the violin under Habeneck, taking the first prize in 1834. For two years after this he was a member of the orchestra of the Société des Concerts, and the Grand Opéra; and then made an extended tour through Italy, Germany, Russia, Finland, Sweden, Denmark, and Spain, with great success. In 1840 he was appointed Professor of the violin in the Conservatoire of

his native city. In 1844 he made his first visit to England, and played at the Philharmonic on June 10, and July 8, of that memorable season, under the baton of Mendelssohn. The following year he returned, was appointed Professor at the Royal Academy of Music, and settled in London. He took the first and second violin alternately with Sivori, Ernst, Molique, and Vieuxtemps, at the performances of Beethoven's quartets, at the house of Mr. Alsager in 1845 and 1846, which resulted in the 'Beethoven Quartet Society.' He was also a constant leader at the performances of the Musical Union, the Quartet Association, the Monday Popular Concerts, etc. etc. On the establishment of the Royal Italian Opera at Covent Garden, April 6, 1847, Mr. Sainton became leader of the orchestra, a post which he held until 1871, when he accompanied Sir Michael Costa to the rival house, and remained there till 1880. He was leader of the Philharmonic band from 1846 to 1854 inclusive, and of the Sacred Harmonic Society from 1848, conducting the performances of the latter Society in the absence of his chief, as he did those of the Opera. He was also for many years leader of the Birmingham Festivals, and other provincial musical performances. From 1848 to 1855 he was conductor of the State Band and violin solo to the Queen, resigning the post of his own accord. At the opening of the International Exhibition of 1862 Sainton conducted the performance of Sterndale Bennett's Ode (to Tennyson's words) and was presented by the composer with the autograph of the work as a token of his gratitude and consideration. Among the many pupils whom he formed during his long career as Professor of the Violin at the Royal Academy may be mentioned H. Weist Hill, F. Amor, A. C. Mackenzie, A. Burnett, Gabrielle Vaillant, W. Sutton, and many more good players. His works comprise two Concertos for the violin with orchestra; a Solo de Concert; a Rondo mazurka; three Romances; several airs with variations; and numerous Fantasias on operas. In 1860 Mr. Sainton married Miss Dolby, the well-known English contralto singer. [See below.] His farewell concert took place at the Albert Hall, on June 25, 1883, and he died on Oct. 17, 1890.   G.

SAINTON-DOLBY, CHARLOTTE HELEN, was born in London, May 17, 1821, and gave signs of possessing decided musical talent when still young. Her earliest instructress was a Mrs. Montague, from whom she received pianoforte lessons. On the death of her father Miss Dolby determined to adopt the musical profession, and in Jan. 1834 entered the Royal Academy of Music, where she first studied under Mr. J. Bennett and Mr. Elliott, and then under Signor Crivelli. In 1837 so great was her promise that she was elected a King's Scholar, although her voice was still weak and not fully developed. She remained at the Academy for three years, and after leaving was elected an honorary member of the institution. Almost from the date of her first appearance in public, until her retirement in 1870, she remained unrivalled as a singer of oratorio and English ballads. The admirable skill with which she controlled a powerful contralto voice, the exquisite intonation, perfect enunciation, and noble declamation which distinguished her singing, caused her to take a very high place, not only among English, but among European artists of the 19th century. She made her first appearance at the Philharmonic in a quartet, June 14, 1841, and in a solo, April 14, 1842. In the winter of 1845-1846, Mendelssohn, who had been delighted by her singing in 'St. Paul,' obtained for her an engagement at the Gewandhaus Concerts at Leipzig, where her first appearance took place Oct. 25, 1845, and on Dec. 6 she sang in a duet with Jenny Lind. About this time Mendelssohn dedicated to her his Six Songs [1] (op. 57), besides writing the contralto music in 'Elijah' with the special view to her singing it. Her success in Leipzig was followed by several concert tours in France and Holland, in both of which countries Miss Dolby established her reputation as a singer of the first rank. In 1860 she married M. Prosper Sainton, (see above), and ten years later she retired from public life. In 1872 Mme. Sainton opened her Vocal Academy, at which she successfully trained many excellent artists in the admirable school of pure vocalisation, of which she was herself so distinguished an example. Mme. Fanny Moody is her most eminent pupil. Besides her labours in connection with this Academy, Mme. Sainton appeared before the world as a composer. Her cantatas 'The Legend of St. Dorothea,' and 'The Story of the Faithful Soul,' produced respectively at St. James's Hall on June 14, 1876, and Steinway Hall on June 19, 1879, have been performed in the provinces and the colonies with unvaried success. A fairy cantata for female voices, 'Florimel,' was published after her death, which took place at 71 Gloucester Place, Hyde Park, Feb. 18, 1885; she was buried at Highgate Cemetery, the great concourse of persons assembled testifying to the estimation in which the singer was held. The Royal Academy of Music founded, shortly after her death, a scholarship in memory of the eminent singer, once a student within its walls.   W. B. S.

SAITEN, SAITENINSTRUMENTE (Germ.) Strings, Stringed Instruments.

SALA, NICOLA, born at a little village near Benevento, Naples, in 1701, and brought up in the Conservatorio della Pietà de' Turchini under Fago, Abos, and Leo. He died in 1800, and devoted the whole of a long life to his Conservatorio, in which he succeeded Fago as second master about 1764, and Cafaro in 1787, as first

master. The great work to which all his energies were devoted was his *Regole del contrappunto prattico* in three large volumes, containing methodical instruction in the composition of fugues, canons, etc., which was published in 1794. During the disturbances in Italy the engraved plates vanished for a time and were supposed to be lost. Choron then reprinted the work (Paris, 1808), but the plates were afterwards discovered. Both editions are in the Library of the Royal College of Music. Sala wrote little besides this work. Three operas, 'Vologeso,' 1737; 'Zenobia,' 1761; and 'Merope,' 1769; an oratorio, 'Giuditta,' 1780; three 'Prologues' on the births of kings of Naples; a Mass, a Litany, and a few smaller pieces, are mentioned by Florimo (*Cenno storico*, p. 562).   G.

SALAMAN, CHARLES KENSINGTON, [2] born in London, March 3, 1814; began music early—violin, PF., and composition. In 1824 he became a student of the Royal Academy of Music, but soon left it and studied under Charles Neate, the friend of Beethoven. He made his first public appearance at Blackheath, in 1828, as a PF. player; then went to Paris and took lessons of Herz, and in the following summer returned to London and began teaching, playing, and writing.

In 1830 he played a rondeau brillant of his own in London, and composed an ode for the Shakespeare commemoration, which was performed at Stratford-on-Avon, April 23, and was repeated in London. From 1833 to 1837 he gave annual orchestral concerts in London, at one of which he played Mendelssohn's G minor Concerto for the third time in England—the former two performances having been by the composer himself. [In 1835 he instituted, with Henry Blagrove and others, the Concerti da Camera. He was an associate of the Philharmonic Society from 1837 to 1855.] In 1846, 1847, and 1848 he resided at Rome, and while conducting Beethoven's Symphony No. 2 (for the first time in Rome), the concert was interrupted by the news of Louis Philippe's flight from Paris. [He was made a member of the Academy of St. Cecilia in 1847. He founded an amateur choral society in London in 1849.] On March 18, 1850, he played at the Philharmonic. In 1855 he began a series of lectures on the History of the Pianoforte, and other musical subjects, which he continued both in London and the country for several years. In 1858 he was one of the founders of the MUSICAL SOCIETY OF LONDON, and acted as its honorary secretary until 1865. [He was one of the founders of the Musical Association, and its secretary until 1877.] Mr. Salaman was for many years a well-known professor and teacher of music in London. Besides the ever-popular 'I arise

---

[1] Also dedicated to Mme. Livia Frege.

[2] He assumed this name in 1867 at the desire of his father, who had been born in Kensington in 1789.

ANTONIO SALIERI

from dreams of thee,' he composed many songs, some to Hebrew, Greek, and Latin words; Psalms (the 84th, 29th); anthems, choral works, in Hebrew for the service of the Synagogue, and various PF. pieces. He contributed to various musical journals. [He died in London, June 23, 1901. An interesting obituary notice appeared in the *Musical Times*, 1901, p. 530. Additions from that article and from *Brit. Mus. Biog.*] G.

SALAMMBÔ. Opera in three acts; text by Du Locle, music by E. Reyer. Produced at Brussels, Feb. 9, 1890.

SALCIONAL. See SALICIONAL.

SALE, JOHN, born at Gainsborough, March 19, 1734, was admitted in 1766 a lay clerk of St. George's Chapel, Windsor, and held that post until his death, Oct. 2, 1802.

His son JOHN, born in London in 1758, was in 1767 admitted a chorister of St. George's Chapel, Windsor, and Eton College under William Webb, and so continued until 1775. In 1777 he obtained a lay clerk's place in both choirs. On July 12, 1788, he was admitted a gentleman of the Chapel Royal in the room of Nicholas Lade or Ladd; in 1794 he succeeded John Soaper as vicar choral of St. Paul's; and in 1796 John Hindle as lay-vicar of Westminster Abbey. At Christmas 1796 he resigned his appointments at Windsor and Eton. In 1800 he succeeded Richard Bellamy as almoner and master of the choristers of St. Paul's. On Jan. 14, 1812, he was appointed successor to Samuel Webbe as secretary to the Catch Club, and soon afterwards resigned his places of almoner and master of the choristers of St. Paul's. He was also conductor of the Glee Club. He possessed a rich, full, and mellow-toned bass voice, and sang with distinct articulation and energetic expression. He was for thirty years a principal singer at the Concert of Antient Music and other leading concerts in London, and at various provincial festivals. He composed several glees (published in 1800) and some which were included, with glees by Lord Mornington and other composers, in collections published by him. He died at Westminster, Nov. 11, 1827. He left two sons, viz.—

JOHN BERNARD, born at Windsor, June 24, 1779, and admitted a chorister of St. George's Chapel, Windsor, and Eton College in 1785. [He was in the chorus of the Antient Concerts in 1792, and in 1794 was principal soprano at the Three Choir Festival at Hereford.] In 1800 he succeeded Richard Bellamy as lay-vicar of Westminster Abbey; on Jan. 19, 1803, was admitted a gentleman of the Chapel Royal, in the place of Samuel Champness, and in 1806, on the death of Richard Guise, obtained a second lay-vicar's place at Westminster Abbey.[1] On March 30, 1809, he succeeded Michael Rock as organist of St. Margaret's, Westminster. About

---

[1] In order to understand how one person could perform the duties of two in the same choir it is necessary to explain that by long-standing custom each lay vicar attends during six months of the year only, *i.e.* in each alternate month.

1826 he was appointed musical instructor to the Princess Victoria. In 1838 he was admitted organist of the Chapel Royal on the death of Attwood. His voice was a powerful bass, and his style of singing chaste and refined; he excelled in anthems, glees, and other part-music. He was for many years principal second bass at the Concerts of Antient Music. He long enjoyed a high reputation as a teacher of singing and the pianoforte. His compositions were few, consisting only of some chants, psalm-tunes, Kyries, glees, songs, and duets. One of his duets, 'The Butterfly,' was long in favour. In 1837 he published a collection of psalm and hymn tunes, chants, etc., with a concise system of chanting. He died at Westminster, Sept. 16, 1856. Of his three daughters, two, MARY ANNE and SOPHIA, were organists and teachers of music; Sophia died May 3, 1869. The youngest, LAURA, was the wife of William John Thoms, the antiquary, and originator of *Notes and Queries*.

The other son, GEORGE CHARLES, born at Windsor in 1796, was admitted a chorister of St. Paul's under his father in 1803. He afterwards became a skilful organist; in 1817 succeeded Dr. Busby as organist of St. Mary, Newington, and in 1826 was appointed organist of St. George's, Hanover Square. He died Jan. 23, 1869. W.H.H.

SALICIONAL, or SALICET, a soft-toned organ-stop of a reedy quality. The pipes are of a very small scale, the tenor C being of about the same diameter as the middle C of an ordinary open diapason. The mouth is also much more 'cut up' than that of a diapason pipe. The origin of the word Salicet is plain; to this day country boys make toy wind-instruments out of 'withy'; but withy is also called 'sally,' and 'sally' is *salix*, a willow. In some counties a willow is called (by combining both names) a 'sally-withy.' A Salicet is therefore a stop made to imitate a rustic 'willow-pipe.' The introduction of the Salicional or Salicet was later than that of the Dulciana (said to have been invented by Snetzler), and it must be considered merely as a variety of that stop. It is of 8 ft. or unison pitch.   J. S.

SALIERI, ANTONIO, Court-capellmeister at Vienna, son of a wealthy merchant, born August 19, 1750, at Legnago in the Veronese territory, learnt music early from his brother Franz, a pupil of Tartini. After the death of his parents a member of the Mocenigo family took him to Venice, where he continued his studies, and made the acquaintance of Gassmann, composer and late Capellmeister to the Emperor, who became much interested in him, and took him to Vienna in June 1766. Here Gassmann continued his fatherly care, provided his protégé with teachers, and himself instructed him in composition, made him acquainted with Metastasio, and introduced him to the Emperor Joseph, whose chamber-concerts he henceforth attended, and often took an active part in.

While Gassmann was in Rome, composing an opera for the Carnival of 1770, Salieri conducted the rehearsals for him, and composed his own first comic opera, 'Le Donne letterate,' which received the approval of Gluck and Calzabigi, and was performed with success at the Burg-theater.   On Gassmann's death in 1774 Salieri returned his paternal kindness by doing all in his power for the family, and educating the two daughters as opera-singers.   In the same year the Emperor appointed him court composer, and on Bonno's death in 1788 he became Court-capellmeister.   He was also a director of the opera for twenty-four years, till 1790, when he resigned, and out of compliment to him the post was given to his pupil Weigl.   In 1778 Salieri was in Italy, and composed five operas for Venice, Milan, and Rome.   For the Emperor's newly-founded National Singspiel he wrote 'Der Rauchfangkehrer' (1781), and for a fête at Schönbrunn 'Prima la musica, poi le parole' (1786).[1]   When the Académie de Musique in Paris requested Gluck to suggest a composer who could supply them with a French opera in which his own principles should be carried out, he proposed Salieri, who accordingly received the libretto of 'Les Danaïdes' from Moline, worked at it under Gluck's supervision, and personally superintended its production in Paris (April 26, 1784).[2]   He was entrusted with librettos for two more operas, and returned with a great increase of fame to Vienna, where he composed an opera buffa, 'La Grotto di Trofonio' (Oct. 12, 1785), the best of its kind and one of his finest works, which had an extraordinary success, and was engraved by Artaria.   In 1787 he again visited Paris, where the first of his operas, 'Les Horaces,' had failed (Dec. 7, 1786), owing to a variety of untoward circumstances, a failure amply retrieved, however, by the brilliant success of 'Axur, Re d'Ormus' (June 8, 1787) or 'Tarare,' as it was first called.   This, which has remained his most important work, was first performed in Vienna, Jan. 8, 1788.   Another work composed in Vienna for Paris was a cantata, 'Le Dernier Jugement'[3] (libretto by Chevalier Roger), ordered by the Société d'Apollon, and per-formed there and at the Concerts Spirituels with great applause from the connoisseurs.   In 1801 Salieri went to Trieste to conduct an opera composed for the opening of a new opera-house. This was his last Italian opera, and 'Die Neger' (Vienna, 1804) his last German one, for owing to his dislike to the change of taste in dramatic

music, he devoted himself chiefly to church music, composing also a few instrumental pieces, choruses, and canons in various parts, published as 'Scherzi armonici.'   On June 16, 1816, he celebrated the fiftieth anniversary of the com-mencement of his career in Vienna, when he was decorated with the gold 'Civil-Ehren-medaille' and chain, and honoured by a fête, at which were performed special compositions by each of his pupils, including Schubert.[4] Salieri was also vice-president of the Tonkünstler Societät, and till 1818 conducted nearly all the concerts.   For the twenty-fifth anniversary of its foundation (1796) he composed a cantata 'La Riconoscenza,' and for the fiftieth (1821) a part-song, 'Zu Ehren Joseph Haydn,' to whom the society was largely indebted.   Salieri was also a generous contributor to the funds.   He took great interest in the foundation of the Conservatorium (1817), and wrote a singing-method for the pupils.   He lost his only son in 1805, and his wife in 1807, and never recovered his spirits afterwards.   On June 14, 1824, after fifty years of service at court, he was allowed to retire on his full salary, and died May 7, 1825.

His biographer, Edler von Mosel (*Ueber das Leben und die Werke des Anton Salieri*, Vienna, 1827), describes him as a methodical, active, religious-minded, benevolent, and peculiarly grateful man, easily irritated, but as quickly pacified.   We have seen how he discharged his obligations to Gassmann.   He gave gratuitous instruction and substantial aid of various kinds to many poor musicians, and to the library of the Tonkünstler Societät he bequeathed forty-one scores in his own handwriting (thirty-four operas, and seven cantatas) now in the Hof-bibliothek.   In accordance with his own wish his Requiem was performed after his death at the Italian church.   He remained throughout on cordial terms with Haydn, whose two great oratorios he often conducted, and Beethoven dedicated to him in 1799 three sonatas for PF. and violin, op. 12.   In the first volume of his *Beethoven's Studien* (Rieter-Biedermann, 1873), Nottebohm has printed ten Italian vocal pieces, submitted by Beethoven to Salieri, with the corrections of the latter.   These chiefly concern the arrangement of the notes to the words, so as to conform to the rules of Italian prosody, and produce the best effect.   The pieces are undated, but internal evidence fixes them to the period between 1793 and 1802.   It appears that as late as 1809 the great composer con-sulted his old adviser as to the arrangement of his Italian, probably in the 'Four Ariettas and Duet' of op. 82 ; and that even then, when Beethoven was so fiercely independent of all other musicians, their relations were such that he voluntarily styled himself 'Salieri's

[1] Mozart's 'Schauspieldirector' was given the same evening.
[2] The play-bill of the first twelve performances described it as an opera by Gluck and Salieri, in accordance with a stipulation of the publisher Deslauriers, but before the thirteenth representation Gluck publicly stated in the *Journal de Paris* that Salieri was the sole author.
[3] The following anecdote is connected with this cantata.   Salieri was talking over the difficulties of the work with Gluck, especially as to the voice to be assigned to the part of Christ, for which he finally proposed a high tenor.   Gluck assented, adding, half in joke, half in earnest, 'Before long I will send you word from the other world in what key our Saviour speaks.'   Four days later, Nov. 15, 1787, he was dead. .

[4] The autograph of Schubert's Cantata—both words and music by him—was sold by auction in Paris, May 14, 1881.

pupil.'[1] As regards Mozart, Salieri cannot escape censure, for though the accusation of having been the cause of his death has been long ago disproved, it is more than possible that he was not displeased at the removal of so formidable a rival. At any rate though he had it in his power to influence the Emperor in Mozart's favour, he not only neglected to do so, but even intrigued against him, as Mozart himself relates in a letter to his friend Puchberg.[2] After his death, however, Salieri befriended his son, and gave him a testimonial, which secured him his first appointment.

His works were too much in accordance with the taste, albeit the best taste, of the day to survive. He drew up a catalogue of them in 1818. They comprise five Masses, a Requiem, three Te Deums, and several smaller church works ; four oratorios (including ' La Passione di Gesù Cristo,' performed by the Tonkünstler Societät in 1777) ; one French, three Italian, and two German cantatas, and five patriotic part-songs ; several instrumental pieces ; two operas to French, and thirty-seven to Italian words ; one German Singspiel, three German operas, and numerous vocal pieces for one or more voices, choruses, canons, fragments of operas, etc. [See the *Quellen-Lexikon* for detailed list.]   C. F. P.

SALIMBENE, FRA, a Minorite friar, of Parma, who began his life early in the 13th century, and seems to have lived through the greater part of the same century (achieving a good deal of distinction in his order) and whose extremely curious *Cronaca* or Diary, throws considerable interesting side-light on musical affairs in his time. He was a skilled and passionate music-lover. He gives us our accounts of two or three distinguished monkish composers and singers of his day, including the once-famous Fra Enrico da Pisa, and Fra Vita da Lucca, who were in great demand during their careers. The *Cronaca* was found in the Vatican Library in the middle of the 19th century. It has been printed (though never completely) in the original Latin, and in a translation into Italian made by Cantarelli, and published by Battei, at Parma in 1882. The Latin version is now extremely rare ; and even the Italian text long out of print. But the book deserves the attention of musicians, *passim*, in much the way that Pepys's *Diary* does, on account of its intelligent references to the art of music at a period so early, and not too clearly depicted by contemporaries. A new and complete edition is about to be published (1907).   E. I. P. S.

SALMON, MRS., whose maiden name was Eliza Munday, was born at Oxford in 1787. Her mother's family had produced several good musicians ; her uncle, William Mahon (born 1753, died at Salisbury, May 2, 1816), was

: .[1] See Moscheles's *Life*, i. 10.   [2] Nottebohm's *Mozartiana*, p. 64.

the best clarinettist of his day ; her aunts, Mrs. Warton, Mrs. Ambrose, and Mrs. Second, were excellent singers of the second rank. She was a pupil of John Ashley, and made her first appearance at Covent Garden in the Lenten concerts given by him under the name of ' oratorios,' March 4, 1803. On Feb. 11, 1806, she married James Salmon, and went to reside at Liverpool, where she became distinguished as a concert singer, occasionally appearing in London, and rapidly attaining the highest popularity. In 1812 she sang at the Gloucester Festival, and in 1815 at the Antient Concerts. From that time to the close of her career her services were in constant request at nearly all the concerts, oratorios, and festivals in town and country. Her voice was a pure soprano of the most beautiful quality, of extensive compass, very brilliant tone, and extraordinary flexibility. She excelled in songs of agility, and was unsurpassed for the rapidity, neatness, and certainty of her execution, and the purity of her taste in the choice of ornament. In the higher and more intellectual qualities of singing, expression and feeling, she was wanting. But she extorted admiration, even from those most sensible of her deficiencies, by the loveliness of her voice and the ease with which she executed the most difficult passages. She unfortunately gave way to intemperance, which eventually occasioned derangement of the nervous system, and in 1825 she suddenly lost her voice. She endeavoured to gain a livelihood by teaching singing, but, although she was well qualified for it, the ignorant public concluded that, as she herself had lost the power of singing, she was incapable of instructing others. She remarried a Rev. Mr. Hinde, who died leaving her totally destitute. A concert was given for her relief, June 24, 1840, which proved a complete failure. She gradually sank into a state of the greatest poverty ; in 1845 an effort was made to raise a fund to purchase an annuity for her, but it was only partially successful. She died at No. 33 King's Road East, Chelsea, June 5, 1849. Her death was registered in the names of Eliza Salmon Hinde.

Her husband, JAMES SALMON, son of James Salmon (gentleman of the Chapel Royal, Nov. 30, 1789, vicar choral of St. Paul's, and lay clerk of St. George's Chapel, Windsor, died 1827), received his early musical education as a chorister of St. George's, Windsor. In 1805 he was appointed organist of St. Peter's, Liverpool, and was in much esteem as a performer. In 1813, having fallen into embarrassed circumstances (by some attributed to his wife's extravagance, and by others to his own irregularities), he enlisted, and went with his regiment to the West Indies, where he died.

WILLIAM, another son of James Salmon, sen., born 1789, was also a chorister of St. George's. He was admitted a gentleman of the Chapel

Royal, May 28, 1817, and was also lay vicar of Westminster Abbey and lay clerk of St. George's, Windsor. With an ungrateful voice he sang with much taste and expression, and was an excellent singing-master. He died at Windsor, Jan. 26, 1858.   w. h. h.

SALMON, THOMAS, born at Hackney, Middlesex, June 24, 1648, was on April 8, 1664, admitted a commoner of Trinity College, Oxford. He took the degree of M.A. and became rector of Mepsal or Meppershall, Bedfordshire. In 1672 he published *An Essay to the Advancement of Musick, by casting away the perplexity of different Cliffs, and uniting all sorts of Musick in one universal character.* His plan was that the notes should always occupy the same position on the stave, without regard as to which octave might be used ; and he chose such position from that on the bass stave—*i.e.* G was to be always on the lowest line. Removing the bass clef, he substituted for it the capital letter B, signifying Bass. In like manner he placed at the beginning of the next stave the letter M (for Mean), to indicate that the notes were to be sung or played an octave higher than the bass; and to the second stave above prefixed the letter T (for Treble), to denote that the notes were to be sounded two octaves above the bass. Matthew Locke criticised the scheme with great asperity, and the author published a *Vindication* of it, to which Locke and others replied. [See LOCKE, MATTHEW.] [In 1688 he wrote a book on Temperament, *A Proposal to perform Music in Perfect and Mathematical Proportions*; he lectured before the Royal Society on Just Intonation, in July 1705 ; and in the following December approached Sir Hans Sloane with a view of making researches into the Greek enharmonic music. He died at Mepsal, and was buried there August 1, 1706. For his nonmusical works, see *Dict. of Nat. Biog.*] w. h. h.

SALO, GASPARO DA, a celebrated violinmaker of Brescia. [The career of this maker rested entirely upon conjecture, until the keeper of the Brescian State Archives, Cavaliere Livi, undertook to investigate da Salo's life, and published the result of his researches in the *Nuova Antologia*, on August 16, 1891. The documentary evidence there quoted has proved Gasparo da Salo to have been a member of an artistic family ; that his legitimate name was Gasparo di Bertolotti ; that his grandfather was a lute-maker of Polepenazze, named Santino di Bertolotti ; and that his father was a painter, Francesco di Bertolotti, who was apparently called ' Violino' by his intimate friends. Owing to the loss of certain requisite pages of the parish registers of Salo, the exact date of this violin-maker's birth is still unknown, but calculating by the income-tax returns of Brescia, which declare him to be twenty-six in 1568, and forty-five in 1588, his birth locates itself with some degree of accuracy in the year 1542.

It is supposed that da Salo learnt his art partly from his grandfather and partly from a Brescian viol-maker who stood sponsor to his son Francesco, named Girolamo Virchi. Whether Virchi was da Salo's master or not is merely surmise, but what is certain is that the great Brescian master's earliest efforts met with such small encouragement that he contemplated removing to France, but was turned from his purpose by a loan of 60 lire from a certain brother Gabriel of St. Pietro. This advance was apparently the turning-point in da Salo's career ; it was the moment when hazardous venture gave place to definite aim. In 1568 da Salo was renting a house and shop in the Contrada del Palazzo Vecchio, Brescia, at £20 per annum. He then possessed the title of ' Magistro di Violino,' and owned a stock of musical instruments which he valued at £60. In 1579 there is an added title of ' Magistro a Cittari,' and in 1583 'Artifice d' Instrumenti di Musica.' Five years later, 1588, and twenty after his first establishment in the Contrada del Palazzo Vecchio, he changed his residence to the Contrada Cocere, where he valued his stock of finished and unfinished violins at £200, and styled himself ' Magister instrumentorum musica.' In 1599 he bought a house in Brescia, in a street called St. Peter the Martyr ; and between 1581 and 1607 owned some small properties about Calvagese, near Salo. He died in Brescia on April 14, 1609, and although all trace of the place of his interment is lost, it is known that he was buried at Santo Joseffo in Brescia. His wife's Christian name was Isabella; she was born in the year 1546. G. da Salo's son, Francesco, was born in Brescia, 1565, and died there in 1614 (?). He was married to Signorina Fior of Calvegese, near Salo, in his twenty-third year. He followed the fiddle-making profession during his father's lifetime, but ceased to do so after his death. It is probable that he sold his business to his father's pupil Paolo Maggini, and retired. In any case he apparently left Brescia in 1614, and nothing further is known of him after that date.] Gasparo da Salo was one of the earliest makers of stringed instruments who employed the pattern of the violin as distinguished from that of the viol. His works are of a primitive pattern, more advanced than that of Zanetto and other old Brescian makers, but totally different from that of the contemporary Amati family. The model varies, being sometimes high, sometimes flat ; the middle curves are shallow, and the sound-holes straight and angular. The wood is generally well chosen, and the thicknesses are correct ; and the tone of the instrument, when of the flat model and in good preservation, peculiarly deep and penetrating. [He made many instruments, especially basses, of pear wood as well as sycamore wood. His selection of timber was most careful ; indeed, the remarkable regularity of the grain in the bellies of his instruments bears evidence to this particular trait of the Brescian master. His varnish is principally deep yellow, and rich in tone, though some of his instruments are much darker in colour ; in fact some are almost black, an effect doubtless due to age. The sound-holes are long, parallel, and pointed in form, and in the gambas and viols still retain the more simple C shape ; yet in spite of their length they are in perfect harmony with the form of the instrument. The purfling is usually single, and the general appearance of his work is bold, but not highly finished. His tickets run as follows : ' Gasparo da Salo : In Brescia,' and are undated.]

The pattern of Gasparo da Salo was partially revived in the 18th century, owing no doubt to its great tone-producing capacity, by the celebrated Joseph Guarnerius (see that article), and to a less extent by some of the French makers. As a maker of tenors and double-basses Gasparo da Salo has never had an equal, and his instruments of these classes are eagerly sought after. The objection to his tenors is their great size, but their effect in a quartet is unrivalled. Two remarkably fine specimens, formerly in the possession successively of Dr. Stewart of Wolverhampton, and of Mr. John Adam of Blackheath, are now in the possession of Mr. J. A. Torrens Johnson. [The most perfect specimen of a da Salo viola ever seen by the writer was the one which belonged to Mr. Edward Withers in 1884. This was a fine primitive instrument, and another perfect speci-men was the property of Mr. Tyssen Amherst, an English amateur of celebrity. At the Special Loan Exhibition of Musical Instruments at the Fishmongers' Hall in 1904 there were three of da Salo's masterpieces. One was a viola of 1570, the property of Mr. E. A. Sandermann ; another a viola da gamba of the same date, lent by Messrs. W. E. Hill & Sons ; and a third was a viol of 1565, belonging to F. Pengrie, Esq. (The dates quoted are according to the catalogue.) At the Victoria and Albert Museum there are two Gasparo da Salo Viole da Gamba. One is mounted with seven strings, an innovation attributed to Marais in the 17th century. The sound-holes are in the C form, the ribs curve into the neck in the true viol fashion, the wood of the belly is even in grain, and the varnish is brownish yellow. Its complete length is 4 feet, and it was bought at the sale of the Engel col-lection for £8. The other gamba by this maker is mounted for six strings. The neck terminates in a well-carved grotesque head of an old woman ; the wood of the belly is even in grain ; the sound-holes are in the C form ; the varnish is slightly darker than the instrument mentioned above. The finger-board is ornamented with ivory and tortoise-shell, and bound with catgut frets. The purfling is in one single broad line. It is labelled within ' Gasparo da Salo : In

Brescia.' The length measures 3 feet 9 inches, and it was bought at the sale of the Engel col-lection for £10. The well-known violin-maker, August Reichers of Berlin, possessed a small-sized violoncello by this maker in 1894 (probably a cut-down bass), and Dragonetti possessed three or four double-basses by da Salo. The most celebrated of these instruments was presented to him by the monks of the monastery of St. Marco, Venice, about the year 1776, and was returned to the donors after his death. It would appear that this bass has disappeared. Another of Dragonetti's basses was bequeathed by him to the Duke of Leinster, and a third was in the possession of the Rev. G. Leigh Blake in 1875. In the same year Mr. John Hart owned a Gasparo da Salo bass (small size) in an exceptional state of preservation. The most renowned instrument of this maker is the violin which was made by him to the order of the Cardinal Aldobrandini, a noble patron of the fine arts in Rome, who paid da Salo 3000 Neapolitan ducats for his work, and presented it to the treasury of Innspruck, where it was preserved as a curiosity. The head of this curious violin is said to have been carved by Benvenuto Cellini ; it represents an angel's face carved and coloured, surrounded by flowing locks of hair. Behind this there leans a little mermaid, the human form of which terminates in scales of green and gold. The tail-piece is another mermaid, in bronze colour, and the finger-board is ornamented with ara-besques in blue and gold ; while the bridge is delicately carved in the form of two intertwin-ing fish, similar to the zodiacal sign of the month of February. The belly is made of an exceedingly rare species of Swiss pine, which grows on the Italian side of the Swiss Alps, and is even-grained. When Innspruck was taken by the French in 1809, this violin was carried to Vienna and sold to a wealthy Bohemian amateur named Rahaczek, who was a well-known collector. Ole Bull saw it at Rahaczek's house during a visit to Vienna in 1839, and tried to persuade his host to part with it, but this he refused to do. However, after his death Raha-czek's sons offered it to the great Norwegian virtuoso at a price, and he purchased it from them in the year 1841. At the death of Ole Bull this violin became the property of an American amateur resident in the United States.] Gasparo's violins, which are mostly of small size, are not in request for practical purposes.

M. Fétis, in A. Stradivari (1864), mentions a very remarkable violin of da Salo which was sold at Milan in 1807 ; and that Baron de Bagge also possessed one in the year 1788, of which Rudolph Kreutzer spoke with admiration. An-other violin he states to be in the possession of Mr. T. Forster, an English amateur, and the owner of a numerous collection of violins, which bore the inscription 'Gasparo da Salo: In Brescia, 1613,' but either the ticket or instrument was doubtless counterfeit. On April 21, 1907, commemorative tablets in honour of Gasparo da Salo and G. P. Maggini were placed in the façade of the church of San Giuseppe, and of a house near the Palazzo Vecchio, at Brescia.

Von Lutgendorff, *Die Lautern und Geigenmacher*; Fleming, J. M., *The Fiddle Fancier's Guide*; Schebek, Edmund, *Der Geigenbau in Italien und sein deutscher Ursprung*; Weustenberg, H., *Die alten italienischen Geigenmacher*; Hart, G., 'The Violin,' *Harper's Magazine*, No. 368, Jan. 1881 (No. 2, vol. i., English edition); Bull, Sara, *Ole Bull: A Memoir*.   E. H-A.

SALOMÉ. 'Drama' in one act, founded on the French play by Oscar Wilde, the German version by Frau Hedwig Lachmann, music by Richard Strauss. Produced at Dresden, Dec. 9, 1905. Performed frequently at various German music centres, and in New York, 1907, the representation being forbidden after the first night. Six special representations took place at the Théâtre du Châtelet, Paris, in German, beginning May 8, 1907. The work had previously been performed in Brussels, in French.   M.

SALOMÉ, THÉODORE CÉSAR, born in Paris, Jan. 20, 1834; received his education at the Conservatoire, where he obtained various prizes for harmony, counterpoint, and organ, and gained the second Prix de Rome in 1861. For many years he was organist of the small organ in the church of the Trinité, in 1872-73 taught solfège in the Conservatoire, and was maître de chapelle at the Lycée Saint-Louis, etc. He wrote various excellent organ pieces, and several interesting orchestral works, performed by the Société Nationale in 1877. He died at Saint Germain-en-Laye in July 1896.   G. F.

SALOMON, JOHANN PETER, a name inseparably connected with that of Haydn, born at Bonn,[1] 1745 (christened Feb. 2), early became an expert violinist, and in 1758 was admitted into the orchestra of the Elector Clement August. In 1765 he made a concert-tour to Frankfort and Berlin; and Prince Henry of Prussia, who had an orchestra and a small French opera-company at Rheinsberg, made him his Concert-meister, and composer of operettas. He had already showed his appreciation for Haydn by introducing his symphonies whenever he could. On the prince's sudden dismissal of his band, Salomon went to Paris, where he was well received, but being so near London he determined to go on there, and on March 23, 1781, made his first appearance at Covent Garden Theatre. The pieces on this occasion were Mason's 'Elfrida,' set to music by Dr. Arne, and Collins's 'Ode on the Passions,' with solos and choruses by Dr. Arnold, both of which he led, besides playing a solo in the middle. The *Morning Herald* says of him, 'He does not play in the most graceful style, it must be confessed, but his

tone and execution are such as cannot fail to secure him a number of admirers in the musical world.' From this time he frequently appeared at concerts as soloist, quartet-player (violin and viola), and conductor. He quarrelled with the directors of the Professional Concerts, soon after their foundation, and thenceforward took an independent line. During Mara's first season in London, in 1784, he conducted and played solos at all her concerts. The *Morning Chronicle* says, in 1785, 'Salomon's solo, though perhaps not excelling in tone, was in the greatest point, in pathetic impression, excelled by none! Whose violin-playing approaches nearer the human voice? On the whole Salomon is a mannerist, but he has much originality—he is very susceptible—he is a genius.' In 1786 he gave a series of subscription concerts at the Hanover Square Rooms, and produced symphonies by Haydn and Mozart. From that time he contented himself with an annual benefit concert, but acted as leader at others, both in London, as at the Academy of Ancient Music in 1789, and elsewhere, as at the Oxford Commemoration, Winchester, and Dublin. A grand chorus composed by him in honour of the King's recovery, performed by the New Musical Fund in 1789, and repeated at his own concert, was his one successful vocal piece. He removed in 1790 to No. 18 Great Pulteney Street, in which house Haydn stayed with him in the following year. The two had long been in correspondence, Salomon endeavouring in vain to secure the great composer for a series of concerts; but as he was at Cologne on his way from Italy, where he had been to engage singers for the Italian Opera, he saw in the papers the death of Prince Esterhazy, hurried to Vienna, and carried Haydn back in triumph with him to London. Haydn's two visits to England in 1791 and 1794 were the most brilliant part of Salomon's career as an artist, and after the return of the former to Vienna the two continued the best of friends. [It was at Salomon's suggestion that Haydn undertook to write 'The Creation.' Salomon's most important composition was an opera, 'Windsor Castle,' composed for the Prince of Wales's wedding, April 8, 1795.] In 1796 Salomon resumed his concerts, at which he was assisted by Mara, the young tenor Braham, and his own promising pupil Pinto. On April 21, 1800, he produced Haydn's 'Creation' at the King's Theatre, though not for the first time in England, as he had been forestalled by John Ashley (Covent Garden, March 28). Salomon's active career closes with the foundation of the Philharmonic Society, in which he took a great interest, playing in a quintet of Boccherini's, and leading the orchestra, at the first concert in the Argyll Rooms, March 8, 1813. Up to the last he was busy planning an Academy of Music with his friend Ayrton. A fall from his

---

[1] The Salomons' house was 515 Bonngasse, the same in which Beethoven was born.

horse caused a long illness, from which he died Nov. 25, 1815, at his house No. 70 Newman Street. He was buried Dec. 2 in the south cloister of Westminster Abbey. He bequeathed his house to the Munchs of Bonn, his next of kin ; £200 to F. Ries, for the benefit of his brother Hubert ; and his Stradivarius violin (said to have belonged to Corelli, and to have his name upon it) to Sir Patrick Blake, Bart., of Bury St. Edmunds.[1]

Salomon was, on the whole, a first-rate solo-player, but his special field was the quartet, in which he showed himself a solid and intelligent musician. Haydn's last quartets were composed especially to suit his style of playing.

He was a man of much cultivation, and moved in distinguished society. Bland published an engraving of him by Facius from Hardy's picture. Another portrait by Lansdale was sent by Salomon himself to the Museum at Bonn. [A pencil drawing by Dance is in the Royal College of Music.] His best epitaph is contained in a letter from Beethoven to his pupil Ries in London (Feb. 28, 1816) : 'Salomon's death grieves me much, for he was a noble man, and I remember him ever since I was a child.'[2] C. F. P. ; with additions from the *Dict. of Nat. Biog.*, etc.

SALTANDO. See SAUTILLÉ.

SALTARELLO or SALTARELLA (Latin *saltare*, to jump).

I. In 16th-century collections of dance tunes the melodies usually consist of two distinct divisions, the first of which is written in common time, the second in 3 time. The former was probably danced like our English country-dances (*i.e.* the dancers standing in two lines facing each other) and bore the distinguishing name of the dance, while the latter was like the modern round dance and was variously entitled Nachtanz, Proportio, Hoppeltanz, or Saltarello, the first three being the German and the last the Italian names for the same movement. Thus in Bernhard Schmidt's *Tabulaturbuch* (Strasburg, 1577) are found the following dances : 'Possomezzo Comun' with 'Il suo Saltarello'; 'Ein guter Hofdantz' with 'Nach-dantz' ; 'Alemando novello : Ein guter neuer Dantz' with 'Proportz darauf' and 'Ein guter neuer Dantz' with 'Hoppeldantz darauf.' Similarly in the Fitzwilliam Virginal Book (i. 306) there is an elaborate 'Galiarda Passamezzo' by Peter Philips (dated 1592) which consists of ten 8-bar 'divisions,' the ninth of which is entitled 'Saltarella.' The Saltarello, or Proportio, was always founded on the air of the first part of the dance, played in triple time with a strong accent on the first beat of the bar. The manner in which this was done

will be seen by examining the following example, from the second book of Caroso da Sermoneta's 'Nobiltà di Dame' (Venice, 1600). It is part of a Balletto, 'Laura Soave,' the second part of which (a Gagliarda) and the last forty bars of the Saltarello are not printed here for want of space.

Si torna à far un altra volta.

Gagliarda.   *Saltarella.*

etc.

II. A popular Roman dance, in 3–4 or 6–8 time, danced by one or two persons, generally a man and a woman, the latter of whom holds up her apron throughout the dance. The step is quick and hopping, and the dance gradually increases in rapidity as the dancers move round in a semicircle, incessantly changing their position, and moving their arms as violently as their legs. The music is generally in the minor, and is played on a guitar or mandoline, with tambourine accompaniment. The finale to Mendelssohn's Italian Symphony contains two Saltarello themes, in each of which the jumping or hopping step is very apparent. In contrast to these is a Tarantella, used as a third subject, a continuous flow of even triplets. W. B. S.

SALVAYRE, GERVAIS BERNARD, called GASTON, born at Toulouse, Haute-Garonne, June 24, 1847, began his musical education at the maîtrise of the cathedral, and afterwards studied at the conservatoire of the town, before he was brought by Ambroise Thomas to the Paris Conservatoire, where he studied the organ with Benoist, and composition and fugue with Thomas and Bazin. He gained the first prize for organ in 1868, and competed for the Prix de Rome every year from 1867 to 1872, gaining it at last by sheer force of perseverance. During his stay at Rome, Salvayre worked very hard, and many of his compositions date from this time, notably his opera of 'Le Bravo,' and his sacred symphony in four movements, 'Le Jugement dernier,' of which the first two movements were performed at the Concerts du Châtelet, March 19, 1876. It was given in its entirety at the same concerts on Dec. 3, 1876, under the title of 'La Résurrection,' and again, under a third title, 'La Vallée de Josaphat,' at Lamoureux's concert on April 7, 1882. The remaining works written by Salvayre for the concert-room are an 'Ouverture Symphonique,'

---

[1] See the *Westminster Abbey Registers*, by J. L. Chester, D.C.L. Sir P. Blake's property was sold after his death, and nothing is now known by the family about the violin.
[2] Pohl's *Haydn in London*, pp. 73 to 85. *Beethoven's Sämmtliche Briefe*, No. 411.

performed on his return from Rome at the Concerts Populaires, March 22, 1874 ; a Stabat Mater, given under the care of the Administration des Beaux-Arts (performed in London, April 23, 1879, at one of Mme. Viard-Louis's concerts) ; a setting of Ps. cxiii. for soli, chorus, and orchestra ; and an air and variations for strings, performed in 1877, all the last given as the fruits of his residence in Italy. On his return to Paris, he was appointed chorus master at the Opéra Populaire which it had been attempted to establish at the Théâtre du Châtelet, and he then wrote ballet music for Grisar's 'Amours du Diable,' revived at this theatre Nov. 18, 1874. Three years later he made his real début with his grand opera, 'Le Bravo' (Théâtre Lyrique, April 18, 1877), a noisy and empty composition revealing the true nature of the composer, who loves effect, but is wanting in inspiration, style, and form, and is wholly destitute of any fixed ideal. His little ballet 'Fandango' (Opéra, Nov. 26, 1877), in which he made use of some highly characteristic Spanish melodies, was a decided advance in point of instrumentation ; but his grand opera, 'Richard III.,' performed at St. Petersburg, Dec. 21, 1883, was a dead failure, and in 'Egmont,' produced at the Opéra Comique, Dec. 6, 1886, his chief faults, noisiness, and an amalgamation of different styles, from that of Meyerbeer to that of Verdi, were so predominant that the work was only performed a few times. Salvayre was commissioned to set to music Dumas' drama 'La Dame de Monsoreau,' a subject little fitted for musical treatment. It was produced at the Opéra, Jan. 30, 1888, and was wholly unsuccessful. Salvayre, who has the qualities of a good musician, in spite of his repeated failures, was decorated with the Légion d'honneur in July 1880.   A. J.

SALVE REGINA, one of the most celebrated Latin antiphons. It does not belong to the classical Gregorian plain-song, but both words and music were written in the 10th century. They have been ascribed to various authors, but are with greatest probability assigned to Hermann Contractus (1013-1054), the crippled monk of St. Gall and Reichenau, composer and writer on musical theory and practice. Originally an independent antiphon, this was afterwards assigned a special place of its own and became one of the antiphons of the B.V.M. sung after Compline. The music opens thus—

Sal - ve Re - gi - na mi - se - ri - cor - di - æ, etc.

and continues in pure Dorian classical style. In this respect it is unlike the companion antiphon *Alma Redemptoris mater*, also attributed to Hermann, which shows signs of modern or popular tonality from the very start,

Al - - - - ma Re-demp-to - ris ma - ter, etc.

The *Salve Regina*, text and music, became speedily popular. The words were the subject of sets of sermons by the end of the century, and soon St. Bernard and others still more widely established their popularity. In some rites the antiphon was admitted into the Office itself on one of the festivals of the Blessed Virgin ; it was then naturally associated with the First Tone. In the present Roman Breviary the text has been altered, and many incorrect forms of the music prevail. Apart from the plain-song setting the words have frequently been set in the motet style by Palestrina and others. These antiphons of the B.V.M. were among the earliest texts to be set in 'prick-song,' partly because elaboration was especially connected with such services, and partly because the antiphon at the close of Compline, being extra-liturgical, gave scope for polyphonic treatment, and in fact was among the first to develop into an 'anthem' in the modern sense of the word. Their popularity has survived down to the present time, and many composers great and small have set the *Salve Regina*, the *Alma Redemptoris*, the *Regina coeli*, etc. W. H. F.

SAMARA, SPIRO, the son of a Greek father and an English mother, was born at Corfu, Nov. 29, 1861. He began his musical education at Athens under Enrico Stancampiano, a former pupil of Mercadante, and afterwards studied at the Paris Conservatoire, where his principal master was Léo Delibes. An introduction to the publisher Sonzogno led to the production of his first opera, 'Flora Mirabilis,' which was given at the Teatro Carcano, Milan, May 16, 1886. 'Flora Mirabilis,' which was written to a fantastic libretto by Ferdinando Fontana on a subject possibly suggested by the scene of the flower-maidens in the recently produced 'Parsifal,' was a kind of compromise between opera, ballet, and spectacle. The legendary atmosphere of the tale appealed strongly to the young composer's imagination, and his music, though unequal, showed remarkable promise. Unfortunately that promise has never been redeemed. 'Flora Mirabilis,' after a brief period of popularity, dropped into oblivion, and none of Samara's subsequent operas has won anything like permanent success. 'Medgé' (Rome, 1888), a revised edition of an opera written before the production of 'Flora Mirabilis,' was followed by 'Lionella' (Milan, 1891). In neither work were the hopes founded upon 'Flora Mirabilis' fulfilled. 'La Martire' (Naples, 1894) may best be regarded as a concession to the prevailing taste for squalid melodrama which was engendered by the success of Mascagni's 'Cavalleria Rusticana.' The libretto deals with the painful story of the sorrows and suicide of a woman whose husband has deserted her for a music-hall singer. The opera won a certain measure of success owing to the clever if somewhat brutal treatment of certain realistic scenes, notably that of a *café-concert*, and still more from the remarkably powerful performance of Mme. Bellincioni in the part of the heroine, but the sheer musical value of 'La Martire' was very small. Samara's next two works, 'La Furia Domata' (Milan, 1895), an operatic version of Shakespeare's *Taming of the Shrew*, and 'Storia d' Amore' (Milan, 1903) were completely unsuccessful, but 'Mademoiselle de Belle Isle' (Genoa, 1905) was more favourably received.   R. A. S.

SAMMARTINI. See SAN MARTINI.

SAMSON. Oratorio by Handel, words compiled by Newburgh Hamilton from Milton's 'Samson Agonistes,' 'Hymn on the Nativity,' and 'Lines on a Solemn Musick.' The autograph of the work is in the Buckingham Palace Library, and contains the following dates :—End of first part, 'Sept. 29, 1741' (N.B. 'Messiah' was finished 14th of same month) ; end of second part '⊙ (*i.e.* Sunday) Oct. 11, 1741' ; end of chorus 'Glorious hero,' 'Fine dell' Oratorio,' S.D.G., London, G. F. Handel, ♃ (*i.e.* Thursday) Oct. 29, 1741' ; then the words 'Fine dell' Oratorio' have been struck out, and 'Come, come,' 'Let the bright,' and 'Let their celestial' added, with a note at end, 'S.D.G.— G. F. Handel, Oct. 12, 1742.' It was produced at Covent Garden, Lent 1743—the first after Handel's return from Ireland.

Handel esteemed it as much as the 'Messiah,' and after his blindness wept when he heard the air 'Total eclipse.' It was revived by the Sacred Harmonic Society, Nov. 14, 1838, and has often been performed since. The score was published by Wright ; by Arnold in his edition ; by the Handel Society (edited by Rimbault, 1852) ; and by Breitkopf & Härtel (Chrysander, 1861).   G.

SAMSON ET DALILA. Opera in three acts, text by Ferdinand Lemaire, music by Camille Saint-Saëns ; produced at Weimar under Liszt, Dec. 2, 1877, and in France at Rouen, 1890. Performed at Covent Garden in concert form, Sept. 25, 1893.

SAN CARLO, the largest and most beautiful theatre of Naples, has almost the same proportions as La Scala of Milan, with which it contends for the theatrical primacy in Italy. It was built in 1737 by the architect Carasale, on plans by Medrano, a General of the R. E., and was completed in nine months. Some alterations and improvements were made in it by Fuga and Niccolini towards the end of the 18th century. It was completely burnt down in 1816, and rebuilt even more elegantly and quickly than before, in six months, by the said Antonio Niccolini. In 1844 the San Carlo underwent a thorough restoration and considerable improvement.

The best days of the San Carlo were those in which it was under the management of the great impresario Domenico Barbaja from 1810 to 1839. During that period the greatest singers appeared on its stage, amongst whom we need only name Colbran, Sontag, Grisi, Tamburini, Rubini, and Lablache.   L. R.

SANCTUS. I. The angelic hymn based on Isaiah vi. 3 and St. Matt. xxi. 9, sung in all Liturgies at the beginning of the *Anaphora* or central section of the service. In the Latin rite it is introduced by the Preface (see vol. iii. p. 809), sung by the celebrant, while the hymn itself is sung by the clergy and congregation, or by the choir, according to later usage (see vol. ii. p. 235). The original setting was in the simplest style of recitative like that of the Preface. Later plain-song settings were more elaborate ; see an example given in vol. iii. p. 766.

Various specimens survive of the setting of the Sanctus in prick-song. The first stage here, as elsewhere, was the setting of an *Organum* or free voice part against the plain-song, as in the following instance from the latter part of the Sanctus :—

The original may be seen in facsimile in *Early English Harmony* (Plain-song Soc.), pl. xl. It belongs to the 14th century. This was but a step on the way to developed polyphony. Another Sanctus in three parts written by John Benet in the first half of the 15th century is given at pp. 51, 52 of the same volume, and this may be cited as marking an intermediate stage on the way to the great masters of the 16th century.   W. H. F.

II. These great masters have almost always treated it in Real Fugue, of a peculiarly reverent character, not unlike that of the 'Kyrie,' but developed at greater length, with frequent repetitions of the text, and three distinct subjects, adapted to the words, 'Sanctus,' 'Dominus Deus Sabaoth,' and 'Pleni sunt coeli et terra.' Sometimes—as in Palestrina's Masses, 'Veni, sponsa Christi,' and 'Dum complerentur'—the 'Pleni sunt coeli' forms a separate movement, assigned to three or four solo voices; sometimes the nature of the subject indicates an accelerated tempo, without an actual solution of continuity, as in the same composer's 'Aeterna Christi munera.' The 'Osanna,' with which the whole concludes, is either treated as a supplementary movement, quite distinct from the 'Sanctus' itself; or, less frequently, aids in the development of the fugue, by the addition of a fourth subject, without disturbing the homogeneity of the whole. In the former case, the same 'Osanna' usually serves both for the 'Sanctus' and the 'Benedictus,'[1] as in the 'Missa Papae Marcelli,' and Vittoria's 'Simile est regnum coelorum'; in the latter, the treatment is usually of a very subdued character, as in Palestrina's 'Tu es Petrus,' 'Assumpta est Maria,' 'Aeterna Christi munera,' and 'Missa brevis.' These instances are particularly fine ones; and, indeed, it may be doubted whether even Palestrina's genius ever rose to greater sublimity of conception than in this part of the 'Missa brevis,' which, when interpreted by a large body of voices, singing in the most delicate attainable *pianissimo*, presents us with the highest ideal of the song of the Heavenly Host that has yet been reached.

The treatment of the 'Sanctus,' by modern composers, exhibits an infinite variety of styles; yet the movement is, nearly always, the most solemn one in the Mass. In Bach's great work in B minor, an indescribably massive effect is produced by the passages of sustained chords, beginning at the seventeenth and thirty-fifth bars. [As the Lutheran service enjoined the singing of the 'Sanctus' on certain occasions apart from the rest of the mass, Bach left four compositions besides the glorious chorus already mentioned. They are contained in the B.-G. edition, vol. xi. (i.). The keys are C, D, D minor, and G, the second work being of peculiarly impressive beauty.] Very different is the idea developed in the corresponding division of Beethoven's Mass in D. The awestruck character of the opening 'Adagio. Mit Andacht,' however closely it may border upon the dramatic, can scarcely impress the hearer with any other feeling than that of the most profound reverence; while the 'Allegro pesante' of the 'Pleni sunt coeli' is conceived in strict accordance with the literal meaning of the words, though nothing could possibly be more unsuited to their position in the service. This deplorable incongruity is, however, more or less observable in all masses

with instrumental accompaniment. The same objection may be urged, with equal propriety, against the combined 'Sanctus' and 'Benedictus,' in Cherubini's Requiem in C minor; a comparatively unpretending movement, the persistent *fortissimo* of which can scarcely fail to distract the mind far more seriously than even the sensuous beauty of a movement like that in Rossini's 'Messe Solennelle.'

To particularise the varied readings of the 'Sanctus,' to be found in the masses of even the greatest composers of modern times, would be impossible. The examples to which we have called attention will serve as types of many others; and will, moreover, be valuable, as illustrations of the one practical point of divergence which, more than any other, distinguishes the reading prevalent in the 16th century from that most common in the 19th—the devotional *piano* from the pompous *forte*. So long as drums and trumpets are permitted to take part in the accompaniments of the 'Sanctus,' so long will it fail to attain that æsthetic consistency which alone can ensure its ultimate perfection as a work of art.[2]

III. In Anglican 'Services' the Sanctus is usually a very unpretending movement, written, for the most part, in simple harmony, without any attempt at fugal treatment, or even imitation; though, in the works of such masters as Tallis, Byrd, Farrant, Gibbons, and their contemporaries, it is always noted for a quiet dignity well worthy of the solemnity of the text. [In former days when there was only ante-communion service, the Sanctus was often sung at the conclusion of morning prayer as a sort of Introit leading to the 'second service' at the altar.]   W. S. R.

SANDERSON, JAMES, born in 1769 at Workington, Durham, had from early childhood a passion for music, and, without the assistance of masters, so qualified himself that in 1783 he was engaged as violinist at the Sunderland Theatre. In 1784 he went to Shields as a teacher of the violin and pianoforte, and met with much success. In 1787 he was engaged as leader at the Newcastle-upon-Tyne Theatre, and in 1788 at Astley's Amphitheatre. In 1789 he made his first attempt at dramatic composition by writing instrumental interludes to illustrate the several parts of Collins's 'Ode on the Passions,' which the eminent tragedian, George Frederick Cooke, was to recite on his benefit night at Chester. His next work was 'Harlequin in Ireland' at Astley's in 1792. In 1793 he was engaged at the Royal Circus, afterwards the Surrey Theatre, as composer and music director, a post which he retained for many years. His principal productions during that period were 'Blackbeard,' 1798; 'Cora,'

---

[1] In order to explain the intimate connection between these movements, it is necessary to remind the reader that the first 'Osanna' is immediately followed by the Consecration of the Host, which takes place in silence. This completed, the 'Benedictus,' and second 'Osanna,' are sung, in continuation of the same train of ideas, and not with the intention of introducing a new subject of contemplation.

[2] [It may interest the reader to notice how closely the writer's views on the inappropriateness of certain music to the service of the church foreshadow the famous *motu proprio* of the present Pope, issued in 1903.]

1799 ; 'Sir Francis Drake,' 1800 (in which was the song, 'Bound 'prentice to a waterman,' which became so great a favourite with stage representatives of British sailors that it was constantly introduced into pieces in which a seaman formed one of the characters for fully half a century), and 'Hallowe'en.' His 'Angling Duet,' originally composed for 'The Magic Pipe,' a pantomime produced at the Adelphi, also enjoyed a long popularity. He composed many pieces for the violin. He died in or about 1841.   W. H. H.

In these pantomimes and operas he was associated with J. C. Cross, who wrote most of the words, and contrived the scenic effects. The song 'Gin a body meet a body' is claimed by Chappell as originally appearing in one of these productions, 'Harlequin Mariner,' 1795-96, but the air is found in print in Scottish collections long before this, and there is sufficient evidence to show that Cross and Sanderson had merely adapted the song to London requirements. F. K.

SANDONI. See CUZZONI.

SANDYS, WILLIAM, F.S.A., born 1792, educated at Westminster School, and afterwards called to the bar, is entitled to mention here as editor of 'Christmas Carols, Ancient and Modern, including the most popular in the West of England, with the tunes to which they are sung. Also specimens of French Provincial Carols,' 1833 ; author of *Christmastide, its History, Festivities, and Carols*, with twelve carol tunes, 1852 ; and joint author with Simon Andrew Forster of *The History of the Violin and other Instruments played on with the Bow. . . . Also an Account of the Principal Makers, English and Foreign*, 1864. He died Feb. 18, 1874.   W. H. H.

SANG SCHOOLS. See SONG SCHOOLS.

SAN MARTINI, or SAMMARTINI. Two brothers born at Milan, both musicians, whose works were in great vogue in England during the first half of the 18th century.

GIUSEPPE or GIOSEFFE SAN MARTINI, born about 1693, came to England, according to Burney, in 1723, and according to Hawkins in 1729. This latter date is most probably correct, as Quantz heard him in Milan in 1726. He was well received by Buononcini, Dr. Greene, and others, and was by the influence of the first-named appointed as hautboy player at the Opera. His performance on the instrument surpassed all that had been before heard, and raised it to a great importance. It was thought that much of the fine quality he obtained was by a secret method of manipulating the reed before its insertion. San Martini, having left the Opera, was patronised by Frederick Prince of Wales and his wife, holding in their household the position of musical director of the Chamber Concerts. Hawkins states that he died about 1740, but this date is probably a few years too early. Martini composed many sets of sonatas for flutes and for violins.

To distinguish him from his brother he is frequently named in contemporary references 'St. Martini of London,' his brother being 'of Milan.' His first publication was a set of sonatas for two flutes, issued in 1738. The sale of these being slow he destroyed the plates and the unsold copies, though they were afterwards reissued by Johnson of Cheapside. In the same year six concerti grossi were published. His next work, dedicated to the Princess of Wales, was twelve sonatas for the violin (Walsh, *circa* 1740). Others issued by Simpson are :— 'Six Concertos for violins, etc., in 7 parts,' eight overtures, six more concerti grossi, harpsichord concertos, 'Six Solos for a German flute,' and 'Six Sonatas for two German flutes or violins.' Scattered pieces by him are often found in collections of airs ('Martini's Minuet' being long a favourite), but it is difficult to distinguish them from work by his brother or from that of many other musicians who bore the same surname. (See the *Quellen-Lexikon*.)

GIOVANNI BATTISTA SAN MARTINI of Milan, his younger brother, remained in Italy, and became a prolific composer both for instruments and voices. About 1746 J. Simpson of London published of his works 'Six Sonatas for two violins and a bass,' and Burney says that between 1740 and 1770, in which latter year he saw him in Milan, he produced for the violin 'an incredible number of spirited and agreeable compositions,' and in 1770 'he was *maestro di capella* to more than half the churches in the city, for which he furnished masses upon all the great festivals.' [Many motets, etc., and a great number of concertos, symphonies, overtures, trios, sonatas, etc., are mentioned in the *Quellen-Lexikon*.]   F. K.

SANTA CHIARA. Opera in three acts ; words by Mme. Birch Pfeiffer, music by H.R.H. Ernest, Duke of Saxe-Coburg-Gotha. Produced at Coburg, Oct. 15, 1854 ; at the Opéra, Paris (French translation by Oppelt), Sept. 27, 1855, and, in Italian, at Covent Garden, June 30, 1877.   G.

SANTINI, FORTUNATO, the Abbé, a learned musician, born in Rome, Jan. 5, 1778, early lost his parents, and was brought up in an orphanage, but showed such talent for music that he was put to study with Jannaconi, and received into the Collegio Salviati. During his stay there (until 1798) he occupied himself in copying and scoring the church-music of the great masters, and after his ordination in 1801 devoted his whole life to music, copying, collating, and compiling with unwearied industry. As an ecclesiastic he had the *entrée* to many libraries and collections generally inaccessible, and set himself to the task of scoring all important works then existing only in parts. In 1820 he issued a catalogue (46 pp., 1000 Nos.) of his music, the MS. of which, containing more than the printed one, is in the collection of the writer.[1] A MS. copy of a *Catalogo della musica antica, sacra, e madrigalesca, che si trova in Roma via dell' anima no. 50 presso Fortunato Santini*, is in the Fétis collection at Brussels, No. 5166. His learning, and practical knowledge of church-music, made his assistance invaluable to all engaged in musical research. He did much to make German music known in Italy, translating Rammler's 'Tod Jesu' into Italian, and helping the introduction of Graun's music. Mendelssohn writes (*Letters*, Rome, Nov. 2, 1830): 'The Abbé has long been on the look-out for me, hoping I should bring the score of Bach's "Passion."' And again (Nov. 8): 'Santini is a delightful acquaintance ; his library of old Italian music is most complete, and he gives or lends me anything and everything.' Then he tells how Santini is trying to get Bach's compositions performed at Naples, and goes on (Nov. 16): ' Old Santini continues to be courtesy personified ; if some evening in company I praise anything, or say I do not know such and such a piece, the very next morning he comes knocking gently at my door with the identical piece folded up in his blue handkerchief. Then I go to him in the evenings, and we are really fond of each other.' Santini composed pieces in five, six, and eight real parts. [A Requiem *a* 8 is at Bologna, where are numerous other church compositions. See the *Quellen-Lexikon*.] The Singakademie of Berlin elected him an honorary member. On the death of his sister he sold his valuable collection, stipulating, however, for the use of it for life. He died in 1862. His library is in the episcopal palace at Münster in Westphalia. A pamphlet, *L'Abbé Santini et sa collection musicale à Rome* (Florence, 1854), giving a useful résumé of its contents, was published by the Russian Vladimir Stassov.   F. G.

SANTLEY, SIR CHARLES, son of William Santley, a teacher of music, was born at Liverpool, Feb. 28, 1834. He was a chorister in early life, and, after various appearances as an amateur, he went to Italy to have his beautiful baritone voice trained. Here, at Milan, he was under Gaetano Nava from Oct. 1855. He made a début before very long, as the Doctor in 'La Traviata,' at Pavia, and after singing some other small parts, returned to England in Oct. 1857, and pursued his studies under Manuel Garcia. His first appearance before an English audience was at St. Martin's Hall on Nov. 16, 1857, when he sang the part of Adam in 'The Creation' ; he next sang three times at the Crystal Palace, and again in 'The Creation' (taking the parts of Raphael and Adam), at the Sacred Harmonic Society, Jan. 8, 1858. In March of the same year he undertook, at the same society's concert, the part of Elijah, with which he was afterwards so closely iden-

[1] His address is there given Roma, Via Vittoria, No. 49, while in the Fétis collection it is Via dell' anima, No. 50.

tified. In the following autumn he sang at the first Leeds Festival, taking the bass part of Rossini's 'Stabat Mater,' and other works. His first appearance on the English stage was at Covent Garden, with the Pyne and Harrison Company, as Hoel in ' Dinorah,' in Sept. 1859 ; he sang with the same company in 'Trovatore,' 'Lurline,' and other operas. He took part in a concert performance of 'Iphigénie en Tauride,' under Hallé, about this time. In the winter of 1860-61 he sang in English opera at Her Majesty's Theatre, in 'Robin Hood,' 'La Reine Topaze,' 'Fra Diavolo,' etc. In 1861 he sang for the first time at the Birmingham Festival, and in the winter again at Covent Garden, in 'The Lily of Killarney,' and other things. He first appeared in the Italian opera in England at Covent Garden in 1862 in 'Il Trovatore,' and later in the same season he joined the company of Her Majesty's Theatre under Mapleson, appearing as the Count in 'Figaro,' and Nevers in ' Les Huguenots.' In 1863 he sang the part of Valentine on the production of 'Faust' in England with such success that Gounod wrote the song 'Even bravest heart' ('Dio possente') especially for him, and for the English performance of the work in 1864. He sang at Barcelona in the winter of 1864-65, adding Rigoletto to the number of his characters. At Manchester in Sept. 1865 he sang the part of Don Giovanni for the first time, and later on appeared in London as Caspar in 'Der Freischütz.' In 1870, after singing the part of the Dutchman for the first time in England (as 'L' Olandese dannato'), he gave up Italian opera, and sang at the Gaiety Theatre under Hollingshead, as Zampa, Peter the Shipwright, and Fra Diavolo. In 1871 he made a very successful tour in America in opera and concerts. In 1876 he joined the Carl Rosa Company at the Lyceum Theatre, repeating his memorable performance of the Flying Dutchman in English. After his first festival performance at Birmingham in 1861, he was, of course, in request at all the autumnal festivals, singing, for the first time at the Three Choir Meetings, at Worcester in 1863. He had previously sung at the Handel Festival in 1862, and until 1906 he appeared regularly at these triennial meetings. From about this time his position in oratorio and concert work was ever more and more important. On April 9, 1859, he had married Gertrude Kemble, daughter of John Mitchell Kemble, the eminent Anglo-Saxon scholar, and grand-daughter of Charles Kemble. She appeared as a soprano singer at St. Martin's Hall in the 'Messiah,' but retired from public life on her marriage. Their daughter, EDITH, had a short but brilliant career as a concert-singer (soprano), before her marriage in 1884 with the Hon. R. H. Lyttelton.

Though the versatility of his genius allows him to express any emotion to the full, yet

Santley's singing is identified with certain characteristics in the minds of those who know it best. The quality of the voice was less remarkable for richness or sonority than for its eloquence of expression, and had a *timbre* which in love-music more easily represented fiery passion than soft languor. This *re was never more perfectly in its place than in 'Elijah,' where it was prominent from the opening recitative until the end. His distinct enunciation, and power of varying the tone-colour, were among his technical merits; but, beyond and above these, was the informing spirit of energy finely held in control. This made his singing of songs as dramatic as if they were scenes on the stage, although he never fell into the error of making lyrics sound operatic. His performance of the 'Erl King' (which he always sang in English) can never be forgotten in this respect, and in a kindred mood Hatton's 'To Anthea' became exclusively his own. His interpretation of Handel's 'O ruddier than the cherry' was masterly in delineation and humour. Among the oratorios in which he made the greatest impression, apart from 'Elijah,' must be mentioned 'The Redemption' (Birmingham, 1882), and 'The Spectre's Bride' (Birmingham, 1885). He has found time in the intervals of a wonderfully successful and busy career to compose several works for the service of the Roman Church (which he joined about 1880), such as a mass in A flat, an Ave Maria, and other things. A berceuse for orchestra was performed at Sydney in 1890, when Santley was on a tour in Australia. In 1887 he was created a Knight Commander of St. Gregory the Great by Pope Leo XIII. In 1892 he published an amusing and valuable volume of reminiscences, *Student and Singer.* On May 1, 1907, the 'jubilee' of his artistic career was celebrated at a concert at the Albert Hall, when he appeared with many eminent artists. A money presentation, referred to on that occasion, was made some time afterwards. He was knighted later in the year.   M.

SAPPHO. 1. Saffo. Opera in three acts; text by Cammarano, music by Giov. Pacini. Produced at Naples, Nov. 27, 1840; in London at Drury Lane, in an English version by Serle, April 1, 1843 (Clara Novello as Sappho).

2. Sapho. Opera in three acts; words by Emile Augier, music by Charles Gounod. Produced at the Opéra, April 16, 1851. It was reduced to two acts, and reproduced July 26, 1858. In Italian, as 'Saffo,' at Covent Garden, August 9, 1851. The opera was afterwards remodelled by its composer, extended to four acts, and produced at the Grand Opéra, April 2, 1884, with moderate success.

3. Sapho. Opera in five acts; text by Henri Cain and Arthur Bernède, music by Jules Massenet. Produced at the Opéra-Comique, Paris, Nov. 27, 1897.   G.

SARABAND, a stately dance, once very popular in Spain, France, and England. Its origin and derivation have given rise to many surmises. Fuertes (*Historia de la Musica Española*, Madrid, 1859) says that the dance was invented in the middle of the 16th century by a dancer called Zarabanda, who, according to other authorities, was a native of either Seville or Guayaquil, and after whom it was named. Others connect it with the Spanish Sarao (an entertainment of dancing), and Sir William Ouseley (*Oriental Collections*, 1728, vol. ii. p. 197, misquoted by Mendel, under 'Saraband'), in a note to a Turkish air called 'Ser-i-Kháneh,' or 'the top of the house,' has the following:—'Some tunes are divided into three parts and are marked *Kháne-i sání* "the second part," and *Kháne-i sáliš* "the third part"; near the conclusion of several we also find the Persian words *ser-band*, from which, without doubt, our *sara-band* has been derived.'[1]

Whatever its origin may have been, it is found in Europe at the beginning of the 16th century, performed in such a manner as to render its oriental source highly probable. This may be gathered from the following extract from Chapter xii., 'Del baile y cantar llamado Zarabanda,' of the *Tratado contra los Juegos Publicos* (*Treatise against Public Amusements*) of Mariana (1536-1623): 'Entre las otras invenciones ha salido estos años un baile y cantar tan lacivo en las palabras, tan feo en las meneos, que basta para pegar fuego aun á las personas muy honestas' ('amongst other inventions there has appeared during late years a dance and song, so lascivious in its words, so ugly in its movements, that it is enough to inflame even very modest people'). This reputation was not confined to Spain, for Marini in his poem *L'Adone* (1623) says:

Chiama questo suo gioco empio e profano
Saravanda, e Ciaccona, il nuovo Ispano.[2]

Padre Mariana, who believed in its Spanish origin, says that its invention was one of the disgraces of the nation, and other authors attribute its invention directly to the devil. The dance was attacked by Cervantes and Guevara, and defended by Lope de Vega, but it seems to have been so bad that at the end of the reign of Philip II. it was for a time suppressed. It was soon, however, revived in a purer form, and was introduced at the French court in 1588, where later on Richelieu, wearing green velvet knee-breeches, with bells on his feet, and castanets in his hands, danced it in a ballet before Anne of Austria.

In England the Saraband was soon transformed into an ordinary country-dance. The first edition of Playford's *Dancing Master* (1651) has two examples, one to be danced 'longwayes for as many as will' *i.e.* as 'Sir Roger de

[1] In a MS. collection of dances in the Music School at Oxford is a Saraband by Coleman, entitled 'Seribran.'
[2] 'New Spain' is Castile.

Coverley' is now danced), and the other, 'Adson's Saraband,' to be danced 'longwayes for six.' It was at about this time that the Saraband, together with other dances, found its way into the Suite, of which it formed the slow movement, placed before the concluding Gigue. In this form it is remarkable for its strongly accentuated and majestic rhythm, generally as follows :—

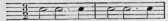

It is written either in the major or the minor key, in 3-2 or 3-4 time, although Walther (*Lexikon*, 1732) says that it may be also written in 2-4 time. It usually consists of two 8- or 12-bar divisions, begins on the down-beat, and ends on the second or third beat. Bach, in the 'Clavierübung,' Pt. I. (B.-G. iii. 76) has a Saraband beginning on the up-beat, and Handel (Suite XI.) has one with variations. Those by Corelli do not conform to the established rules, but are little more than Sicilianas played slowly.

The following Saraband for the guitar is printed in Fuertes' *Historia de la Musica Española*.

Handel's noble air 'Lascia ch' io pianga,' in 'Rinaldo,' is taken with no material alteration from a Saraband in his earlier opera of 'Almira,' in which the majestic rhythm mentioned reigns in all its dignity. See Chrysander's *Händel*, i. 121.   W. B. S.

SARASATE. PABLO MARTIN MELITON DE SARASATE Y NAVASCUES, born at Pampeluna, March 10, 1844, came to France as a child, and entered the Paris Conservatoire, Jan. 1, 1856. The following year he became the favourite pupil of Alard, and gained the first prizes for solfège and violin. He then entered Reber's harmony class, and secured a *premier accessit* in 1859, but shortly after relinquished the study of composition for the more tempting career of a concert player. His beautiful tone, retentive

memory, immense execution, and certainty of finger, added to the singularity of his manners and appearance, ensured his success in Paris, the French provinces, and the Peninsula. The Spaniards naturally honoured an artist whom they looked upon as their own countryman, but Sarasate aspired to make his name known wherever music was appreciated, as well as in the two countries especially his own by birth and adoption. No violinist has travelled more than he ; besides making his way through Europe, from the remotest corner of Portugal to Norway, and from London to Moscow, he has visited America, North and South. In all his wanderings he has contrived to carry on his cultivation, and develop his great natural gifts. To London his first visit was in 1861, when he played at St. James's Hall on May 22 ; he came again in 1874, when he played at the Philharmonic Concert, May 18, and at the Musical Union, June 9, etc. He returned in 1877 (Crystal Palace, Oct. 13), and 1878 (Philharmonic, March 28), and has been a frequent visitor since. In 1885 and 1886 he gave sets of orchestral concerts conducted by Cusins, and at the Birmingham Festival of 1885 played a concerto written for him by Mackenzie.

Sarasate's distinguishing characteristics are not so much fire, force, and passion, though of these he has an ample store, as purity of style, charm, brightness of tone, flexibility, and extraordinary facility. He *sings* on his instrument with taste and expression, and without that exaggeration or affectation of sentiment which disfigures the playing of many violinists. His répertoire is varied, comprising the concertos of German masters—Beethoven, Mendelssohn, and Bruch,—Raff's various works for violin, and the works of the modern French and Belgian schools. Among the former his favourites are the concertos of Saint-Saëns and Lalo, and the Symphonie Espagnole of the last-named composer. [He has avoided the music of Paganini and his followers, partly for want of taste for it, and partly because of the long stretches required, his hand being very small. Although Bach, on the whole, is unsuited to his style for obvious reasons, he gives certain movements with great charm, notably the prelude and gavotte from the E major solo sonata. But he will always be remembered for his rendering of the solos he has written for himself, and plays so exquisitely, giving the spirit of Spanish dance translated into terms of the violin virtuoso. He possesses two fine Stradivari violins, one of which, dated 1724, was presented to him when a boy by Queen Isabella of Spain. This instrument was one of those brought from the chapelle royale at Naples by Charles III. (for whom Boccherini composed his quintets), and upon it he has mainly played throughout his career. A successful copy of it was made by Vuillaume, and is sometimes used by him at rehearsals. Later

PABLO MARTIN MELITON DE SARASATE Y NAVASCUES SARASATE

in life he acquired from the Boissier collection, and occasionally plays on, an exceptionally beautiful instrument, bearing date 1713.] Sarasate has composed for his instrument romances, fantaisies, and especially transcriptions of Spanish airs and dances, all calculated to display his skill as a virtuoso. His 'Zigeunerweisen,' 'Jota Aragonesa,' and the four books of Spanish dances are among the most popular violin solos in existence. [He pays an annual visit to his native town of Pampeluna, where fêtes are held in his honour.] G. C. ; additions, in square brackets, by w. w. c.

SARRUSOPHONE. A brass instrument of conical bore, played with a double reed, designed in 1863 by M. Sarrus, a bandmaster in the French army. The scheme of the inventor comprised a whole family of instruments ranging in pitch from soprano to contra-bass, and his expectation was that they might well take the place of oboes and bassoons in military bands. As regards the contra-bass models, Sarrus was to some extent anticipated by Stehle of Vienna in 1835, who brought out a contra-bassoon in brass, of simple fingering, and whose model has been further developed by Cerveny of Königgratz, and Mahillon of Brussels ; but to Sarrus belongs the credit of designing a whole family of double-reed instruments as possible substitutes for the oboe and bassoon groups. The objection that has been raised to them is that they fail to produce the delicate and distinctive qualities of the wooden double-reed instruments.

The complete family of sarrusophones comprises the sopranino in $e'\flat$, soprano in $b\flat$, alto in $e\flat$, tenor in $B\flat$, baritone in $E\flat$, bass in $B_{,}\flat$, contra-bass in $E_{,}\flat$, and the contra-bassoon in $C_{,}$ or $B_{,,}\flat$. All these have a compass from one tone below the pitch note, to a fifth above its double octave, $b\flat$ to f''', agreeing in this respect with the oboe, and the general scheme of fingering is much like that of the oboe. The tube of all but the small instruments is bent back upon itself, so as to reduce the length to a convenient compass.

The actual use of the sarrusophone in the orchestra has been very limited, but M. Saint-Saëns appears to have thought highly of the contra-bass instrument as an alternative to the double-bassoon, and used it on several occasions. Jules Massenet introduced it in his 'Esclarmonde' with great effect, and other composers have followed his example. It is possible that the bass and contra-bass members of the family may be kept alive, as they have distinctive qualities, but the treble and alto instruments can be regarded only as interesting experiments.   D. J. B.

SARTI, GIUSEPPE, born at Faenza, Dec. 1, 1729, a date differing from that given by most of his biographers, but furnished by Sarti's own grandson to the writer, who has taken great pains to verify it. The son of a jeweller who played the violin in the cathedral, he early learned music, and had lessons in composition —from Vallotti according to his own family, from Padre Martini according to his biographers. Whether at Padua or at Bologna (the respective homes of the two masters), he completed his studies at an early age, for we learn from the chapter archives, still preserved in the library of Faenza, that he was organist of the cathedral from 1748 to April 1750, and director of the theatre from 1752. In 1751 he composed his first opera, 'Pompeo in Armenia,' which was enthusiastically received by his fellow-townsmen, and followed by several more serious works, and 'Il Rè pastore' (Venice, 1753), which had an immense success. So quickly did his fame spread that when he was only twenty-four the King of Denmark (Frederick V.) invited him to Copenhagen as Capellmeister to the Prince Royal, and director of the Italian opera ; and, on the closing of the latter in two years, made him Court-capellmeister. In the summer of 1765 the king determined to reopen the opera, and Sarti went back to Italy after an absence of twelve years to engage singers ; but his plans were upset by the deaths first of the king in 1766, and then of his own mother in 1767, so that it was not till 1768 that he returned to Copenhagen. These three years of trouble were not unfruitful, as he composed five operas, of which two, 'I Contratempi' (1767) and 'Didone abbandonata,' were given in Venice, where he seems chiefly to have resided.

Overskou's carefully compiled *History of the Danish Stage*[1] informs us that Sarti directed the Danish court-theatre from 1770 to May 20, 1775, when he was summarily dismissed. A favourite with Christian VII., and the protégé of Struensee and Queen Caroline Matilda, he was too artless and straightforward to curry favour with the queen dowager and the ambitious Ove Gulberg ; so after the catastrophe of 1772 he found his position gradually becoming worse and worse, and when the oligarchical party had secured the upper hand, imprisoning the queen, and reducing the king to a mere cipher, he had, with other court favourites, to endure much ill treatment, and was finally banished. During this second stay at Copenhagen he married Camilla Pasi, by whom he had two daughters.

Returning to Italy in the summer of 1775, he went first to Venice, became at once director of the Ospedaletto Conservatorio, and administered it with great success for four years. In 1779 the post of maestro di cappella of the cathedral of Milan fell vacant through the death of Fioroni, and Sarti was pronounced successful at a competition held before the

---

[1] Thomas Overskou, *Den danske Skueplads in dens Historie*, 8vo. Copenhagen, 1854, etc.

Conservatorio of Naples. This victory over Paisiello and other eminent musicians greatly increased his reputation, and procured him many distinguished pupils, Cherubini among the number, who indeed was not only his pupil, but for some years his assistant.[1] In 1784 he received an invitation from Russia too advantageous to be refused, but the nine years spent in Milan were the most brilliant of his whole career, and the most prolific, including as they did his most successful operas, ' Le Gelosie villane '[2] and ' Farnace ' (Venice, 1776); ' Achille in Sciro' (Florence, Oct. 1779); ' Giulio Sabino' (Venice, 1781), and ' Fra i due Litiganti' (Milan, 1782). To complete the list, at least ten more operas and several cantatas on a large scale should be added, works for the cathedral choir, including several masses, a Miserere *a* 4, and some important motets.

On his way to St. Petersburg, Sarti made some stay at Vienna, where Joseph II. received him graciously, and granted him the proceeds of a performance of ' I due litiganti,' which had long maintained its place at the Burgtheater, and had helped to fill its coffers, as the monarch politely told the composer. He there made the acquaintance of Mozart, then in the very prime of life, who speaks of him as an ' honest, good man,' and who not only played to him a good deal, but adopted an air from his ' Due Litiganti' as the theme of a set of Variations (Köchel, 460), and as a subject in the second finale of ' Don Juan.' His pleasure in Mozart's playing did not, however, place him on Mozart's level ; and when the famous six quartets were published, Sarti was one of the loudest to complain of their ' barbarisms.' His examination remains mostly in MS., but some extracts are given in the *A.M.Z.* for 1832 (p. 373), including nineteen serious errors in thirty-six bars, and showing how difficult it is even for a very clever composer to apprehend the ideas of one greater than himself.

Catherine II. received him with even greater marks of favour than Joseph, which he repaid by composing several important works for her own choir, and by bringing the Italian opera into a state of efficiency it had never attained before. Among his sacred compositions of this period may be mentioned an oratorio for two choirs ; full orchestra, and band of Russian horns ; a Te Deum for the taking of Otchakow by Potemkin ; and a Requiem in honour of Louis XVI. It was in the Te Deum that Sarti employed fireworks and the discharge of cannon to heighten the martial effect of the music. Among his operas produced at St. Petersburg were ' Armida' (1786), which had an immense success, and was sung to perfection by the celebrated Todi ; and ' Olega,' the libretto of

which was by the Empress herself. In this opera Sarti endeavoured to imitate the music of the ancient Greeks, and made use of some of their modes. A skilled mathematician and physicist, he was fond of explaining to the Empress his theories of acoustics, which he illustrated by many ingenious experiments. He invented a machine for counting the vibrations of sounds, and fixed 436 vibrations[3] for the A, as the normal pitch for his orchestra. For this invention he was elected an honorary member of the Academy of Science in St. Petersburg. Many other honours were conferred upon him, including those of councillor of the University, chief maître de chapelle to the court, and nobility of the first class. Todi's intrigues caused him temporary inconvenience, but he consoled himself for a short period of disgrace by going to a village in the Ukraine, given him by Prince Potemkin, and founding there a school of singing which turned out some remarkable singers. In 1793 the Empress restored him completely to favour, and placed him at the head of a Conservatoire planned after the model of those in Italy. After her death and that of her son Paul I., Sarti determined to revisit his native land, and in the spring of 1802 left Russia, where he had lived for eighteen years without a break. At Berlin he formed an intimacy with the Court-capellmeister, Noël Mussini (born at Bergamo, 1765 ; died at Florence, 1837), who fell in love with his daughter Giuliana, and became his son-in-law.[4] Immediately after the marriage the kind and gentle Sarti fell seriously ill of gout, and died July 28, 1802, aged seventy-three. He was buried in the Catholic church of St. Edwige, where his ashes still remain.

From some unexplained cause very few of Sarti's compositions have been engraved. His Te Deum was printed with Russian words at St. Petersburg, and Breitkopf & Härtel have published two of his sacred pieces, one in eight, the other in six real parts. A French translation of the ' Nozze di Dorina' (identical with ' Fra i due Litiganti '), apparently the only opera of his that has been engraved, appeared in Paris ; but Ricordi of Milan has copies of ' Armida e Rinaldo '; ' I finti Eredi '; ' Le Gelosie villane '; ' Nitteti,' and ' Vologeso.' These scores, as well as those of ' Adriano in Sciro,' ' Alessandro,' ' Gli Amanti consolati,' ' Castore e Polluce,' ' I Contratempi,' ' Didone abbandonata,' ' Erifile,' ' Fra i due Litiganti,' ' Giulio Sabino,' ' Idalide,' ' Ifigenia,' ' Il Medonte,' ' Il Militare bizzarro,' ' Mitridate,' and ' Scipione,' and also of nearly all his sacred works, are in the library of the Paris Conservatoire, from which circumstance the writer is

---

[1] See Cherubini's preface to the Catalogue of his works.
[2] Mozart, in 1791, wrote a final chorus for this, of which, however, nothing has survived but the five bars in his autograph catalogue. (See Köchel, 615.)

[3] The ' diapason normale' fixes 435 vibrations for the same note.
[4] The articles on Sarti and Mussini in Fétis are full of errors and omissions. We have corrected the most glaring mistakes from family papers kindly furnished by the distinguished painter L. Mussini, director of the Museo at Siena, and grandson of the composer.

able to pronounce upon his style. The part-writing is eminently vocal, and the most difficult combinations are mastered with ease, but the scientific element is never unduly forced into notice, owing to Sarti's gift of fresh and spontaneous melody. Most of his operas contain numbers well constructed with a view to stage effect, and full of expression and charm ; indeed so much of his music might still be heard with pleasure that it seems strange that no great artist has attempted to revive it.

His masses alone retain their hold on public favour, and one was performed on Easter Day 1880 in Milan Cathedral, which still has all the MSS.

Sarti left six sonatas for Clavier solo (London, 1762). An Allegro from these is included in Pauer's 'Alte Meister.' Cherubini quotes a 'Cum Sancto' a 8 of his in his *Counterpoint* ; and Fétis a Kyrie from the same mass in his treatise. Breitkopf has published a Fugue for eight voices, a Hymn and a Miserere, and the overture to 'Ciro riconosciuto.' A Rondo for mezzo soprano will be found in Gevaert's 'Gloires d' Italie,' and a Cavatina, from 'Giulio Sabino' in the 'Gemme d'Antichità.'

The Mussini family possess a fine oil-painting of the composer, taken in 1786 by Tonci, an Italian painter settled in St. Petersburg. *Le Chevalier Sarti*, a novel by P. Scudo, appeared first in the *Revue des Deux Mondes*, and has since been published separately (Paris, Hachette, 1857). G. C.

SARTORIS, MRS. See KEMBLE, ADELAIDE.

SATANELLA, OR THE POWER OF LOVE. A 'New Original Romantic Opera,' in four acts ; words by Harris and Falconer, music by Balfe. Produced at the National English Opera, Covent Garden (Pyne and Harrison), Dec. 20, 1858. The story is a version of 'Le Diable boiteux.' G.

SATURDAY POPULAR CONCERTS. See POPULAR CONCERTS.

SATZ. The German term for MOVEMENT, which see.

SAUER, EMIL, born at Hamburg, Oct. 8, 1862, was a pupil of Nicolas Rubinstein at the Moscow Conservatorium in 1876-81, and subsequently studied under Liszt and Deppe. From 1882 he made frequent and successful concert-tours as a virtuoso-pianist. He first appeared in England at eight recitals of his own, in November 1894, and rapidly attained great success in this country. In 1901 he was appointed head of one department of the pianoforte branch of the Vienna Conservatorium, which he gave up in April 1907, going to live at Dresden. His technique is wonderfully neat and accurate, and his playing, though occasionally rather wanting in breadth, is always agreeable. He has written a 'suite moderne' and many slighter pieces for the pianoforte, as well as a Concerto in E minor. He has also pub-

lished a volume of reminiscences, *Meine Welt* (1901). M.

SAUL. 1. An oratorio ; words attributed both to Jennens and Morell, music by Handel. The composition was begun July 23, 1738. The second act was completed August 28, and the whole on Sept. 27, of the same year. First performance at the King's Theatre, Tuesday, Jan. 16, 1739 ; at Dublin, May 25, 1742. Revived by the Sacred Harmonic Society, March 20, 1840. The autograph is in the library at Buckingham Palace. The overture ('Sinfonia') is Handel's longest ; it is in four movements, and the organ is largely employed in it as a solo instrument. The 'Dead March in Saul' has been perhaps more widely played, and is more universally known, than any other piece of music.

2. 'King Saul.' An oratorio ; composed by Sir C. Hubert H. Parry, produced at the Birmingham Festival of 1894. G.

SAURET, ÉMILE, violinist, born at Dun-le-Roi, Cher, France, May 22, 1852, soon attracted the notice of De Bériot, and became his pupil, the last he ever had. He began to travel at an early age, playing in the chief towns of France and Italy, in Vienna and in London, where he played at the International Exhibition of 1862 and also at the Alhambra. More important was his appearance at Alfred Mellon's Concerts, Covent Garden, August 27, 1866. He played often at the French court in the last days of the Second Empire. In 1872 he made his first visit with Strakosch to the United States, and his second in 1874, remaining there till Jan. 1876. In New York he made the acquaintance of von Bülow and Rubinstein, and on his return to Leipzig was welcomed by the latter, then engaged in the rehearsals of his 'Paradise Lost.' Sauret made his début in the Gewandhaus in May 1876 in Mendelssohn's Concerto, and was most warmly received. He took lessons in composition from Jadassohn. He, however, returned immediately to America, and it was not till he came back again in 1877, and went through Germany and Austria in two long and most successful tournées, that his reputation was established in his native country. In England he reappeared in 1880, and played at the Crystal Palace, April 24, and Philharmonic (Bruch's Concerto, No. 1) on the 28th.

Liszt showed him much kindness, and they often played together. In 1872 he married Mme. Teresa Carreño, the marriage being dissolved a few years later. In 1879 he married Miss Emma Hotter of Düsseldorf [and being appointed professor of the violin at Kullak's Academy in Berlin, he settled in that city, remaining there nearly ten years. He relinquished this post, however, in 1890, when the Royal Academy of Music, London, invited him to fill the vacancy caused by the death of the principal violin professor, Prosper Sainton. In 1903 Sauret again gave up this second professorship for a similar position at the Chicago Musical College, where he remained until July 1906. At present he is residing in Geneva, giving private lessons to a small *coterie* of pupils, many of whom have followed him from America. As a virtuoso Mons. Sauret has obtained a greater degree of popularity in America than here. His playing is distinguished by the grace and elegance of the French school, to which is added a conscientious handling of the classics. He is also a thorough musician, and has written a large amount of music, including an excellent method for the violin.]

His published works embrace a Concerto in G minor ; a Ballade, a Légende ; and a Serenade in G—all for solo violin and orchestra ; Caprice de Concert in D ; Scherzo fantastique ; Valse-caprice ; Barcarolle-mazurka, and many other drawing-room pieces, as well as transcriptions from Mendelssohn, Rubinstein, Wagner, etc. G.

[He has also written a Concerto in E major for violin and orchestra, a *Gradus ad Parnassum du Violiniste* (Leipzig, 1894), and a number of Études, small pieces and transcriptions for the violin, with and without orchestra.—Lahee, *Famous Violinists* ; Mason Clarke, *Dictionary of Fiddlers* ; Baker *Dict. of Music* ; *Musical Times*, 1900, p. 9. E. H-A.]

SAUTILLÉ, or SALTANDO. A technical term in violin and violoncello music whereby the executant understands that a certain skipping motion of the bow is to be employed. To the school of classical composers from Corelli to Spohr, *sautillé* was either unknown, or by them ignored ; but with the advent of Paganini this brilliant embellishment came into vogue, and at the present time it is one of the most effective and frequently used *coups d'archet*. Like all the different species of bowing, the manner of playing *sautillé* varies with the tempo of the composition, and the amount of tone required. In slow movements it assumes the form of gentle even taps given with an up-and-down movement in the middle of the bow. To accomplish this accurately, perfect unity of action between the fingers of the left hand and the bow is necessary. The hair of the bow should be slightly turned towards the face, the bow itself being held lightly but firmly ; the forearm must move slightly with each upward and downward stroke of the bow ; the thumb must be almost straight ; the wrist loose, but controlled. Although in a slow movement the bow requires to be raised and lowered by the player, in an allegro or presto movement the bow rebounds of its own accord with such rapidity that the executant has only to keep the forearm quiet ; to have a perfectly loose wrist, and to control the action of the bow by a slight pressure of the first finger upon the stick when required. Excellent studies and examples of this bowing

are to be found in such compositions as Paganini's 'Moto Perpetuo,' Sarasate's 'Ziguenerweisen,' Bohm's two 'Moto Perpetuo,' Arensky's 'Caprice,' Ries's 'Moto Perpetuo,' and in Ernst's, Vieuxtemps's, De Bériot's, Leonard's, Wieniawski's, Nachez's, and Hubay's compositions. The use of the *sautillé* in concerted music, particularly in the quartets of Haydn, Mozart, Beethoven, as well as in the sonatas of the two last-named composers, is universally understood, and enhances the beauties of the old masters with happy effect (see BOWING). O. R.

SAUZAY, CHARLES EUGÈNE, an eminent French violinist, was born at Paris, July 14, 1809. In 1823 he entered the Conservatoire, and in his second year became the pupil of Baillot and of Reicha. He obtained the second violin prize in 1825, the first do., and the second for fugue, in 1827. A few years later he joined Baillot's quartet, first as second violin and then as tenor, *vice* Urhan, married Mlle. Baillot, and continued one of her father's party till its dissolution in 1840. He soon rose rapidly both in society and as a professor. In 1840 he was made first violin to Louis Philippe, and afterwards leader of the second violins to the Emperor Napoleon III. In 1860 he succeeded Girard as professor at the Conservatoire. His own quartet party started after the termination of Baillot's, embracing his wife and Boely as pianists, Norblin and Franchomme ; gave its concerts, sometimes with and sometimes without orchestra, in the Salle Pleyel. Sauzay is mentioned by Hiller as one of Mendelssohn's acquaintances during his stay in Paris in 1830. He was greatly sought after both as a player and a teacher. His publications are not important, and consist of incidental music to 'Georges Dandin' and 'Le Sicilien,' cleverly written in the style of Lully to suit the date of the pieces ; fantasias and romances ; a PF. trio ; a string trio ; songs ; *Haydn, Mozart, Beethoven ; Étude sur le quatuor* (Paris, 1861), a disappointing work from the pen of a musician of so much eminence and experience ; *L'école de l'accompagnement* (Paris, 1869), a sequel to the foregoing. He also composed a series of 'Études harmoniques' for the violin. [He died in Paris, Jan. 24, 1901.] G.

SAVAGE, WILLIAM, born about 1720, was a pupil of Pepusch, and became a gentleman of the Chapel Royal in 1744. He was almoner, vicar-choral, and master of the choristers at St. Paul's Cathedral in 1748, and was the master of Battishill and Stevens. He wrote some chants and church music of little importance, and died in London, July 27, 1789. (*Brit. Mus. Biog.*)

SAVART, FÉLIX. [A French doctor of medicine who abandoned his profession and devoted himself to investigating the theory of the vibration of surfaces and strings. He was the son of Gérard Savart, a mathematical instrument maker of repute, director of the *ateliers* of the École d'Artillerie, and the author of several useful innovations, including an ingenious contrivance for dividing circles. He was born at Mézières, June 30, 1791. Originally established at Metz, he left Paris in 1819, where he was made Conservateur de Physique at the Collège de France, and in 1827 was elected a member of the Académie des Sciences.] Following in the steps of Chladni, whose labours had particularly attracted his attention, he made many investigations in acoustics, which are recorded in the several publications bearing his name. He appears particularly to have thrown light on the nature of that complicated relation between a vibrating body which is the source of sound, and other bodies brought into connection with it, by virtue of which the original sound is magnified in intensity and modified in quality ; well-known examples of such an arrangement being furnished by the *sound-boards* of the violin tribe and the pianoforte.

[In his *Mémoire sur la construction des Instruments à cordes et à archet*, published in Paris in 1819, he explains the series of experiments which led him to construct his 'Trapezoid Violin,' familiarly known in England as Savart's 'Box Fiddle.' The exhaustive tests therein described are the most renowned and convincing that have ever been undertaken. Clearly and distinctly he proved that wood arched in the form ordinarily employed for stringed instruments of the violin tribe does not vibrate in every part of its length and breadth equally ; that there are points where the vibrations decrease, and points—*i.e.* the bouts, corner-blocks and sound-holes—where the vibrations cease ; finally, that a flat piece of wood vibrates more readily and evenly than an arched one. Taking these facts for his basis, he constructed a violin in the form of a box, narrower at the upper than at the lower end. The two tables were flat, planed on the inner side and slightly raised on the outer so as to support the increased pressure of the strings caused by the bridge, which was necessarily higher than usual, so as to allow the bow a free passage across the strings, which would otherwise be hindered by the straight sides of the instrument. In contrast with the customary curved sound-holes of the ordinary violin, Savart cut his straight ; and their position in the belly, and distance apart, he determined by a series of practical experiments which are minutely described in his book. He tried two bass-bars, one placed down the centre joint of the violin, the other crescent-shaped, only touching the belly at a point just below the bridge. Curiously enough both these forms produced apparently identical effects. The sides of the instrument were $\frac{1}{12}$ in. in thickness, and no side linings were employed. The sound-post was placed behind the bridge, but a little more to the right than is customary. To prevent the excessive pull of the strings on the tender part of the belly (inseparable from a tail-piece attached in the ordinary way), Savart carried his strings over a hardwood or ivory nut at the end of the violin and attached them to the tail-pin, which was set slightly below the centre. A jury of the Académie des Sciences, composed of MM. Biot, Charles, Haüy, and De Prony, together with four members of the Académie des Arts, MM. Berton, Catel, Le Sueur, and Cherubini, were appointed to consider the merits of this violin. The eminent violinist M. Lefebvre played alternately on a fine Cremona and M. Savart's violin before this jury, and eventually the latter was pronounced to be equal, if not superior, to the Italian masterpiece.]

Savart's name is also connected with an ingenious little device for measuring, in a manner easily appreciable by a lecture-audience, the number of vibrations corresponding to a given musical note. A wheel, caused to rotate quickly by ordinary mechanical contrivances, is furnished on its circumference with teeth or ratchets, against which a tongue of pasteboard or some other elastic substance is brought into contact. The passage of each tooth gives a vibration to the tongue, and if the wheel revolve fast enough, the repetition of these vibrations will produce a musical sound. Hence, as the number of rotations of the wheel in a given time can be easily counted, the number of vibrations corresponding to the note produced can be experimentally ascertained with tolerable precision. This mode of determining vibration numbers has been since superseded by the more elegant instrument, the SYREN, and by other modes known to modern acoustic physicists, but from the simplicity of its demonstrations it is still often used. Savart also investigated with some attention and success the acoustical laws bearing on wind instruments and on the production of the voice.

[He also wrote *Mémoire sur la Voix Humaine*, published in 1825, and also *Sur la Voix des Oiseaux*, 1826. His complete works were published in the *Annales de Chimie et de Musique*, beginning with the year 1819. He died March 16, 1841.—(P. Davidson, *The Violin* ; Heron-Allen, *Violin-making* ; J. Gallay, *Luthiers Italiens* ; Leon Mordret, *La Luthérie Artistique* ; J. A. Otto, *Über den Bau und die Erhaltung der Geige* ; F. Savart, *Mémoire sur la construction des Instruments, etc.* (a condensed German translation of this work was published in Leipzig in 1844) ; F. J. Fétis, 'Biographical Notice of Nicolo Paganini,' *The Repository of Arts, Literature, and Fashion, etc.*, vol. xi., 2nd Series, Jan. 1, 1821, No. 6, pp. 21 and 80 ; *Nouvelle Biographie Générale publiée par Firmin Didot* ; *Nouveau Larousse Illustré* ; Fétis, *Biog. des. Mus.*)]. W. P. ; additions by E. H-A.

SAVILE, JEREMY, a composer of the middle of the 17th century, some of whose songs are included in 'Select Musicall Ayres and Dialogues,' 1653, is now only known by 'Here's a health unto his Majesty,' and his four-part song, 'The Waits,' printed in Playford's 'Musical Companion,' which, by long-standing custom, is the last piece sung at the meetings of the Madrigal Society and similar bodies.   w. h. h.

SAVONAROLA. Grand opera in a prologue and three acts; words by Gilbert à Beckett, music by C. Villiers Stanford. Produced at the Stadt-Theater, Hamburg (words translated by Ernst Frank), April 18, 1884, and at Covent Garden (German Opera, under Richter), July 9 of the same year.   m.

SAVOY. [See OLD HUNDREDTH, THE.]

SAVOY CHAPEL ROYAL, THE, has a constitution differing widely from the chapel of St. James. While that is maintained out of the Civil List, the Savoy Chapel derives its sustenance from the sovereign's privy purse, and thus in one respect has even greater claim to the appellation of Royal. The salient points in the history of the Savoy may be given in few words, which may tend to remove much prevailing misconception on the subject. In 1246 Henry III. made a grant of land on the banks of the Thames to his wife's uncle, Count Peter of Savoy, and a palatial residence was erected on the site. After Peter's death the estate came into the possession of Queen Eleanor, who bestowed it upon her son Edmund of Lancaster, and it remained in the possession of the Lancastrian branch of the royal family until 1381, when, owing to the unpopularity of John of Gaunt, the palace was wrecked by the insurgents under Wat Tyler. Under the provisions of the will of Henry VII., a hospital was founded there, but though richly endowed, it did not flourish, and the foulest abuses prevailed until 1702, when the institution was dissolved. The Chapel had been used from 1564 until 1717 by the parishioners of St. Mary's, but in 1773 George III. issued a patent constituting it a Chapel Royal, and its title is therefore beyond dispute. From time to time the reigning sovereigns contributed towards its maintenance, but the place attracted little general notice until 1864, when it was partially destroyed by fire. Restored from designs by Sir Sidney Smirke, at a cost to Queen Victoria of about £7000, the Chapel was reopened for Divine Service on Dec. 3, 1865. The appointment is in the gift of the Duchy of Lancaster.   h. f. f.

In the middle of the 18th century the Chapel acquired a dubious celebrity for 'easy marriages.' The inducements are set forth in the following advertisement which appeared in the *Public Advertiser* for June 2, 1754 :—' By authority, marriages performed with the utmost privacy, decency, and regularity, at the Ancient Royal Chapel of St. John the Baptist in the Savoy, where regular and authentic registers have been kept from the time of the Reformation (being two hundred years and upwards) to this day. The expense not more than one guinea, the five shilling stamp included. There are five private ways by land to this chapel, and two by water.' A quaint old custom connected with the Chapel survives in the Court Leet of the Manor Liberty of the Savoy. The Court is held annually at Easter in the vestry hall of St. Clement Danes, to which 'sixteen good men and true' are summoned to appear and 'do their Suit and Service to His Majesty the King,' under penalty of £2. The Court consists of the High Steward, High Bailiff, four burgesses, four assistant burgesses and their beadle. The duty of this company is to report to the Court that the old boundary marks have not been removed and are in good order. In consequence of various improvements some of these boundary marks are now in unexpected places ; one is in a sewer on the Embankment, and others are on the stage of the Lyceum Theatre, at the rear of Child's Bank in Fleet Street, and beneath a stone on the lawn in the Temple. There is evidence to show that the Court has been held since the accession of Henry IV. There is no special endowment fund for the choir, but boys who have the good fortune to be elected receive a free education at the school in connection with the Chapel, of which Mr. H. Kingston is the present master. The services are choral, but almost entirely sung in unison. The chants and tunes are collected from various sources, and comprise a remarkable collection of old and new melodies. A peculiarity of the building is its sensitiveness to the note F, reverberations being felt, even in the vestry, when the low F is sounded on the pedal organ. In consequence of this the responses are sung in F. The two-manual organ, built by Messrs. Willis, has recently been completed.

The names of the chaplains of the Savoy from 1773 are—William Willmot ; Samuel Ayscough, 1778 ; James Hodgsons, 1795 ; Dr. John Banks Jenkinson, 1805, afterwards Bishop of St. David's ; Andrew Brandram, 1825 ; John Foster, 1838, afterwards Rector of Stambourne ; Henry White, 1859, Chaplain-in-Ordinary to H.M. Queen Victoria, Chaplain to the Speaker of the House of Commons ; George Herbert Curteis, 1890, Canon Residentiary of Lichfield ; Paul William Wyatt, 1894, Assistant Chaplain of the Savoy 1885–94, Chaplain of the Order of St. John of Jerusalem in England. Further information will be found in *The Story of the Savoy*, by the Rev. William John Loftie, B.A., F.S.A., and in *The History of the Savoy Chapel*, by John E. Locking.   f. g. w.

SAX, CHARLES JOSEPH, a Belgian musical-instrument maker of the first rank, born at Dinant in Belgium, Feb. 1, 1791 ; died in Paris, April 26, 1865. He was first a cabinet-maker, then a mechanic in a spinning-machine factory, and then set up in Brussels as a maker of wind-instruments. He had served no apprenticeship to the trade, and his only qualification was that he could play the serpent ; he was there-fore obliged to investigate for himself the laws concerning the bore of instruments ; but as he had great manual dexterity, and a turn for invention, he was soon able to produce serpents and flutes of fair quality. He quickly attracted notice by his clarinets and bassoons, which gained him a medal at the Industrial Exhibi-tion of 1820, and the title of musical-instrument maker to the court of the Netherlands, which also encouraged him by advancing him capital. In 1822 he began to make all kinds of wind-instruments, brass and wood, and in 1824 invented an 'omnitonic horn,' which he con-tinued to perfect till 1846. This instrument can be adjusted to any key by means of a piston sliding backwards or forwards on a gra-duated scale of about half an inch long, which sets the body of the instrument in communica-tion with tubes of different lengths corresponding to all the major keys. On a separate elbow is a movable register which the player fixes opposite the number of the key he wishes to use, and the tube of that key being at once brought into position, the instrument is played exactly like an ordinary horn. Sax also invented brass instruments producing every note in the scale, without crooks, pistons, or cylinders. He took out patents for a keyed harp, and a piano and a guitar on a new system, but his efforts were mainly directed to perfecting the clarinet, especially the bass clarinet, and discovering new methods of boring brass and wood wind instruments with a view to make them more exactly in tune. His exertions were crowned with success, and he obtained gratifying dis-tinctions at the Brussels Industrial Exhibition of 1835.

Charles Sax was the father of eleven children, of whom two sons were distinguished in the same line. The eldest of these,

ANTOINE JOSEPH, known as ADOLPHE SAX, born at Dinant, Nov. 6, 1814, was brought up in his father's workshop, and as a child was remarkable for manual skill, and love of music. He entered the Brussels Conservatoire and studied the flute and clarinet,—the latter with Bender, who considered him one of his best pupils. Like his father his efforts were directed mainly to the improvement of that instrument, especially the bass clarinet, and he even designed a double-bass clarinet in B♭. In the course of his endeavours to improve the tune of his favourite instrument he invented an entire family of brass instruments with a new quality of tone, which he called Saxophones (see below). The hope of making both fame and money led him to Paris ; he arrived in 1842, and estab-lished himself in the Rue St. Georges, in small premises which he was afterwards forced to

enlarge. He had no capital beyond his brains and fingers, which he used both as a manu-facturer and an artist ; but he had the active support of Berlioz, Halévy, and G. Kastner, and this soon procured him money, tools, and workmen. He exhibited in the French Exhibi-tion of 1844, and obtained a silver medal for his brass and wood wind instruments, a great stimulus to a man who looked down upon all his rivals, and aimed not only at eclipsing them, but at securing the monopoly of furnishing musical instruments to the French army. In 1845 he took out a patent for the Saxhorn, a new kind of bugle, and for a family of cylinder instruments called Saxotrombas, intermediate between the Saxhorn and the cylinder trumpet. On June 22, 1846, he registered the Saxophone, which has remained his most important dis-covery. A man of such inventive power natu-rally excited much jealousy and ill-feeling among those whose business suffered from his discoveries, but his tact and wisdom made numerous and powerful friends, among others Général de Rumigny, Aide-de-camp to Louis Philippe, and a host of newspaper writers who were perpetually trumpeting his praises. He lost no opportunity of vaunting the superiority of his instruments over those in use in the French military bands, at a special competition held between the two ; and the superiority, whether deserved or not, soon resulted in a monopoly, the first effect of which was to banish from the military bands all horns, oboes, and bassoons.

The Paris Industrial Exhibition of 1849, at which Sax obtained a gold medal, brought his three families of instruments still more into notice ; and he received the Council Medal at the Great Exhibition of 1851. In spite of these merited honours, he became bankrupt in 1852. He soon, however, made an arrangement with his creditors, and on recommencing busi-ness entered for the Paris Exhibition of 1855, and gained another gold medal. When the pitch was reformed in 1859 every orchestra and military band in France had to procure new wind-instruments—an enormous advantage, by which any one else in Sax's place would have made a fortune ; but with all his ability and shrewdness he was not a man of business, and his affairs became more and more hopelessly involved. There was full scope for his inventive faculties under the Second Empire, and he introduced various improvements into the differ-ent piston instruments, only one of which need be specified, viz. the substitution of a single ascending piston for the group of descending ones. This principle he adapted to both conical and cylindrical instruments. He also invented instruments with seven bells and six separate pistons ; instruments with rotatory bells for altering the direction of the sound, and a host of smaller improvements and experiments, all detailed in Fétis's *Rapports de l'Exposition* and *Biographie Universelle.*

At the London International Exhibition of 1862, Sax exhibited cornets, saxhorns, and saxotrombas, with 3 pistons, and with 2, 3, 4, and 5 keys ; and at Paris in 1867 he took the Grand Prix for specimens of all the instruments invented or improved by him.   He afterwards lost his powerful patrons and declined in prosperity year after year.   He was obliged to give up his vast establishment in the Rue St. Georges and to sell (Dec. 1877) his collection of musical instruments.   The printed catalogue contains 467 items, and though not absolutely correct is interesting, especially for the view it gives of the numerous infringements of his patents. The typical instruments of the collection were bought by the Museum of the Paris Conservatoire, the Musée Instrumental of Brussels, and the late M. César Snoeck of Renaix, a wealthy Belgian collector.   Sax died in Paris, Feb. 4, 1894.

Among the numerous works written to advertise the merits of Adolphe Sax's instruments we need only mention two—Comettant's *Histoire d'un inventeur au XIXme Siècle* (Paris, 1860, 552 pp. 8vo, with a fair likeness of Sax) ; and Pontécoulant's *Organographie* (Paris, 1861, 2 vols. 8vo).

ALPHONSE SAX, jun., worked with his brother for some years, and seems to have devoted his attention especially to ascending pistons.   He set up for himself in the Rue d'Abbeville (No. 5 *bis*), but did not succeed.   He published a pamphlet, *Gymnastique des poumons* ; *la Musique instrumentale au point de vue de l'hygiène et la création des orchestres féminins* (Paris, 1865), which is merely a disguised puff.   G. C.

SAXHORN (*Saxtuba, Saxotromba*).   The name given to a family of brass instruments with valves, invented by Adolphe Sax.

' No one can be ignorant,' say the editors of the Method for Saxhorn and Saxo-tromba, ' of the deplorable state in which brass instruments were when M. Sax's method made its appearance. No coherence, no unity between the individual members of the group ; in one case keys, in another valves ; a small compass, an imperfect scale, lack of accurate intonation throughout, bad quality of tone, variations of fingering requiring fresh study in passing from one instrument to another.   The keyed bugle, built on false proportions, offered no prospect of improvement ; the mechanism of the valves themselves, by their abrupt angles, deteriorated the quality of tone ; and the absence of intermediate instruments caused gaps in the general scale, and at times false combinations.'

Sax's first advice to players exhibits the power of his new instruments—that namely of playing in every key without using ' crooks,' as in the French-horn and Trumpet.   [See HORN.]   He also attacked the problem of true intonation in valve instruments, by means of what he terms a compensator.   Besides these improvements he planned all the tubes and mechanism on a far sounder acoustical basis than had been attempted in the fortuitous and disconnected contrivances of former periods. The valve or piston was indeed known, but was open to the objection stated above, and was at best but a clumsy machine.   He unquestionably simplified it by causing fewer turns and corners to interfere with the free course of the vibrating column of air.   It is to be noted, however, that all the instruments of the Sax family, like the ordinary cornet-à-pistons, utilise the harmonic octave below that in which the trumpet and French horn speak, and thus obtain power and facility somewhat at the expense of quality.

[Sax did not aim at designing or improving instruments of the trumpet and horn qualities only, but rather at adapting improved valves systematically to brass instruments of the bugle type ranging in pitch from soprano to contrabass, the lower pitched members of the family being substitutes for the imperfect serpents, ophicleides, and other bass horns then in use. The power and facility of tone production of the instruments known as Saxhorns, whether made by Sax, or by other makers who have followed up his ideas, should therefore be compared with that obtainable on these keyed instruments, rather than with the quality of French horns and trumpets.   The cornet is an instrument standing by itself, as a hybrid between the trumpet and the flügel horn, and its analogy with Saxhorns, as now understood, cannot be pushed beyond the fact that the free use of the second octave in the harmonic series is common to it and to them.

The valve system of the Saxhorn is arranged in such manner that the depression of the second valve flattens the pitch a semitone, the depression of the first valve flattens it a tone, and the third valve a tone and a half.   Whatever the normal pitch of the instrument, the second note of the harmonic series is written as middle *c'* when the treble clef is used, but when the bass clef is employed the notes are written as sounded.   The harmonic scale obtained from the unaltered length of the instrument is supplemented when three valves are used singly and in combination, by six other similar scales, and by this means a complete chromatic scale can be produced.

It will be observed, on comparing the notes on the first and last groups of the scheme, that there is a gap between the open pedal C (No. 1) and the G♭ above it, produced by the combined use of the 1st, 2nd, and 3rd valves, but this is of no practical consequence on the alto, tenor, and baritone instruments, as the quality of the extreme low notes is poor.   With the basses (euphoniums and tubas), however, the case is

SCHEME OF FINGERING FOR THE SAXHORN

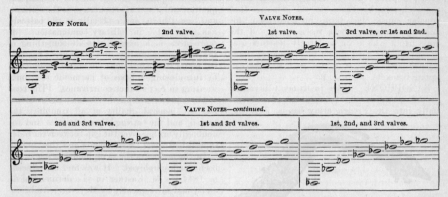

different, as the notes of the pedal octave are required, and to obtain them, a fourth valve, altering the pitch two and half tones, is usually employed. (For explanation of certain inac-

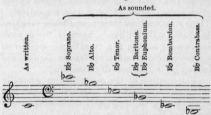

The B♭ Baritone Saxhorn or Althorn.

curacies due to the use of valves in combination see VALVE.)

The range of compass of the Saxhorn family is fully five octaves, the upper limit being approximately that of the soprano voice, and the lower descending an octave lower than the bass voice. Sir Edward Elgar in his 'Cockaigne' Overture has a descending passage for the tuba going to D♭. Although the basses can take three octaves without difficulty, the average *easy* compass of the other instruments is about two octaves or a little less.

The saxhorns chiefly used are the following :—

> E♭ Soprano Flügel Horn.
> B♭ Alto Flügel Horn.
> E♭ Tenor or Althorn.
> B♭ Baritone or Althorn.
> B♭ Bass or Euphonium.
> E♭ Bass Tuba or Bombardon.
> B♭ Contrabass.

but the instruments are sometimes pitched in F instead of E♭ and in C instead of B♭ when required for use in the orchestra. As stated above, the second note in the harmonic series is written as middle C when the treble clef is used, the actual pitch of the note for each of the instruments named being as here shown :—

In every case, however, the note written as middle C is known as the 'low C' of the instrument, the octave below is the 'pedal C,' and the octave above, or No. 4 in the harmonic series, is known as 'middle C.' 'Top C' or No. 8 in the harmonic series is rarely passed.]

There can be no doubt that the inventor of the Saxhorn added greatly to the compass, richness, and flexibility of the military brass and reed bands. But it is a question whether the tone of these powerful auxiliaries blends so well with the stringed instruments as that of the trumpet, French horn, and trombone—and hence their comparative neglect.

[It is to open-air music that we must look to understand the change that has been brought about by the introduction of the saxhorns. Granting that with the exception of the bass tubas, nothing distinctive has been added to the orchestra by them, it yet remains that popular music has been revolutionised, for military bands have been reorganised, and the brass bands which are so largely instrumental in introducing good music 'to the masses, have become possible.]   w. h. s. ; with additions in square brackets, by d. j. b.

SAXOPHONE.   [An instrument invented by Adolphe Sax about 1840, introduced officially into the French army bands, July 31,

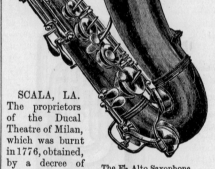

1845, and registered by Sax, June 22, 1846.]   It consists essentially of a conical brass tube furnished with about twenty lateral orifices covered by keys, and with six studs or finger-plates for the first three fingers of either hand, and is played by means of a mouthpiece and single reed of the clarinet kind.   [In addition to lateral holes giving the scale, two small holes opened by keys, and known as 'pipes' or 'speakers,' are also provided, and are used for the production of the octaves.   The saxophones generally in use are the soprano in $b\flat$, the alto in $e\flat$, the tenor in $B\flat$, the baritone in $E\flat$, and the bass in $B,\flat$.   A sopranino in $e'\flat$ is sometimes made, and c and f are occasionally used for the pitch notes instead of $b\flat$ and $e\flat$ respectively.] Those most used are the alto and tenor varieties. In French military bands, however, five or more are in use ; having to a great degree superseded the more difficult but more flexible clarinet, and having quite replaced the bassoon.

[The compass of the saxophone as generally recognised is from b to f''', but all the members of the family are frequently made with an extension of the bell giving $b\flat$, which note is obtained by the closing of an extra open-standing key. The two highest keys, giving e''' and f'''', are, however, seldom fitted to any but the alto and tenor instruments.   The key-system for the right hand is similar to that of the Boehm flute, but for the left hand approaches more nearly to that of the ordinary oboe.   The fundamental sounds from $b\flat$ or $b\natural$ to $c'\sharp$ are obtained by the successive opening of the lateral holes, and by means of the two octave or 'pipe' keys the compass is carried up from d' to $c'''\sharp$.   The four highest notes, d''', $e'''\flat$, e''', and f''', are produced by four keys on the upper part of the instrument, used exclusively for these notes. Since its introduction, many improved or alternative fingerings have been designed for and adopted on the saxophone, but a description of these would unduly extend this article.]

The saxophone, though inferior in compass, quality, and power of articulation to the clarinet, and basset-horn, and especially to the bassoon, has great value in military combinations.   It reproduces on a magnified scale something of the violoncello quality, and gives great sustaining power to the full chorus of brass instruments, by introducing a mass of harmonic overtones wanting in Sax's other contrivance.   [The tone of the soprano saxophone is somewhat strident, but the general quality of all combines the 'vocal' and the 'string' characteristics, and undoubtedly bridges over the gap between the older established 'reed' instruments and the 'brass.'

In the orchestra the saxophone has not as yet been much employed.   It was first introduced, in 1844, by M. Kastner in 'Le dernier Roi de Juda,' and subsequently by Meyerbeer, Ambroise Thomas, and others.   Among recent examples of its use may be mentioned Cowen's 'Thorgrim,' Strauss's 'Domestic Symphony,' and a quartet for saxophones in 'Les Hommages,' by Mr. Joseph Holbrooke.] w. h. s. ; additions by d. j. b.

SCALA, LA. The proprietors of the Ducal Theatre of Milan, which was burnt in 1776, obtained, by a decree of July 15, 1776,

The E♭ Alto Saxophone.

from the Empress Maria Theresa of Austria, leave to build a new opera-house on the site of the church of S. Maria della Scala.   The celebrated architect, Piermarini of Foligno, made the designs, and it was inaugurated August 3, 1778. The building was not only the grandest theatre then existing in Europe, but the most artistically beautiful and complete.   Levati and Reina painted the ceiling, the boxes, and the great hall, or ridotto ; and the curtain, representing Parnassus, was the work of Riccardi.   The cost of the whole amounted to one million lire (£40,000), an enormous sum for that time. Until 1857 the principal entrance of La Scala was from a by-street, but since that date it opens on to a large and beautiful piazza.

The interior of the house is in the horseshoe form, with five tiers of boxes and a gallery above them, all in white, relieved by gilded ornaments. The lowest three tiers have each thirty-six boxes, and a royal box above the entrance to the stalls. The fourth and fifth tiers have each thirty-nine boxes, and there are four on each side of the proscenium, making a total of 194 boxes, besides the large royal box and the gallery, each box having a private room at its back for the convenience of its occupants.

The length of the whole building is 330 ft., and its width 122 ft. The height from the floor to the ceiling is 65 ft. The stage, with the proscenium, is 145 ft. long and 54 wide between the columns of the proscenium, but is 98 ft. wide farther behind. The ridotto, a large hall for promenading between the acts, is 82 ft. long and 30 ft. wide. The total capacity of the house is 3600. This immense institution permanently employs 922 persons on its staff, distributed in the following way:—Artist-singers, 20 ; orchestra, 100 ; band, 28 ; choristers, 110 ; 'comparse,' 120 ; ballet, 140 ; dressmakers and tailors, 150; doctors, 6 ; servants, 36, etc.

The gentlemen who provided the funds for the building of La Scala enjoy the use of its boxes at a nominal rental whenever the theatre is open, each box having its owner. In all other respects the theatre has been the property of the town of Milan since 1872. The municipality grants to its lessee an annual sum of £9800, and the owners of the boxes pay £2920 ; and thus La Scala enjoys an endowment of £12,720 a year. The theatre is controlled by a Commission elected by the Common Council of Milan and the owners of its boxes.

Annexed to the theatre is a celebrated dancing school, with sixty pupils, where the most famous ballet-dancers have been trained, and a singing school for about fifty choristers. Two charitable institutions—*I Filarmonici*, founded by Marchesi in 1783, and the *Teatrale*, by Modrone in 1829—are also dependent for their income upon the greatest theatre of Italy.

The latest restoration of the theatre took place in 1878. Its archives have been most carefully preserved. Further information may be obtained from the *Teatro alla Scala 1778-1862*, by Luigi Romani (Milan, 1862) ; the *Reali Teatri di Milano*, by Cambiasi (Ricordi, Milan, 1881); and *La Scala de Milan*, by Henri de Curzon (*Le Guide Musical*, 1906, pp. 538-40).   L. R.

SCALCHI, SOFIA, was born Nov. 29, 1850, at Turin ; received instruction in singing from Augusta Boccabadati, and made her début at Mantua in 1866 as Ulrica in 'Un Ballo in Maschera.' She afterwards sang at Verona, Bologna, Faenza, Nice, etc., and in England for the first time Sept. 16, 1868, at the Promenade Concerts, Agricultural Hall, with very great success. At the Royal Italian Opera, Covent Garden, she first appeared Nov. 5, of the same year, as Azucena, and after that as Pier-

rotto('Linda'), Urbano, Un Caprajo ('Dinorah'), etc. She sang there every year till 1890 inclusive. Her voice was of fine quality in compass, two octaves and a half from low F to B in alt, enabling her to take both the mezzo-soprano and contralto parts in a great number of operas. In Sept. 1875 she married Signor Lolli, a gentleman of Ferrara. Among her répertoire may be named Leonora ('Favorita'), which she played July 19, 1871, at Mario's farewell appearance ; Estelle in Campana's 'Esmeralda,' June 14, 1870 ; Leonora in Cimarosa's 'Le Astuzie femminili,' July 15, 1871 ; Meala in Massé's 'Paul et Virginie,' June 1, 1878 ; Mrs. Page, July 14, 1877, and Fidès, June 24, 1878, on the respective revivals of Nicolai's 'Lustige Weiber,' and of 'Le Prophète' ; also Arsace, Amneris, Maffeo Orsini, Siebel, etc. One of her most successful impersonations was Wania in Glinka's ' Vie pour le Czar.' She has had frequent engagements in Italy, St. Petersburg, Moscow, Vienna, North and South America, etc.   A. C.

SCALE (from the Latin *Scala*, a staircase or ladder ; Fr. *Gamme* ; Ger. *Tonleiter*, *i.e.* sound-ladder ; Ital. *Scala*), a term denoting the series of sounds used in musical compositions.

The number of musical sounds producible, all differing in pitch, is theoretically infinite, and is practically very large ; so that in a single octave a sensitive ear may distinguish 50 to 100 different notes. But if we were to take a number of these at random, or if we were to slide by a continuous transition from one sound to another considerably distant from it, we should not make what we call music. In order to do this we must use only a certain small number of sounds, forming a determinate series, and differing from each other by well-defined steps or degrees. Such a series or succession of sounds is called a *scale*, from its analogy with the steps of a ladder.

It is unnecessary here to enter into the æsthetical reason for this ; [1] it must suffice to state that all nations, at all times, who have made music, have agreed in adopting such a selection, although they have not always selected the same series of sounds. As a first step towards the selection all musical peoples appear to have appreciated the intimate natural relation between sounds which lie at that distance apart called an *octave* ; and hence replicates of notes in octaves are found to form parts of all musical scales. The differences lie in the intermediate steps, or the various ways in which the main interval of the octave has been substituted.

For modern European music, in ascending from any note to its octave above, we employ, normally, a series of seven steps of unequal height, called the *diatonic* scale, with the power of interposing, accidentally, certain intermediate

---

[1] More complete information on the subject generally may be found in Helmholtz's *Tonempfindungen*, or in *The Philosophy of Music*, by W. Pole (London, 1879).

chromatic steps in addition. The diatonic scale is of Greek origin, having been introduced about the middle of the 6th century B.C. The main divisions of the octave were at the intervals called the fifth and the fourth, and the subdivisions were formed by means of two smaller divisions called a *tone* and a *hemitone* respectively. The tone was equal to the distance between the fourth and the fifth, and the hemitone was equal to a fourth *minus* two tones. The octave was made up of five tones and two hemitones, and the entire Greek diatonic scale of two octaves, as settled by Pythagoras, may be accurately represented in modern notation as follows :—

The Greek Diatonic Scale.

Thus the essence of the diatonic scale was that it consisted of *tones*, in groups of two and three alternately, each group being separated by a *hemitone* from the adjoining one ; and, combining consecutive intervals, any two tones with a hemitone would form a *fourth*, any three tones with a hemitone would form a *fifth*, and any complete cycle of five tones with two hemitones, would form a perfect *octave.*

Now it is obvious that in this series of notes, proved to be in use above two thousand years ago, we have essentially our diatonic scale ; the series corresponding in fact with the natural or white keys of our modern organ or pianoforte. And as this series formed the basis of the melodies of the Greeks, so it forms the basis of the tunes of the present day.

Although, however, the general aspect of the diatonic series of musical sounds remains unaltered, it has been considerably affected in its mode of application by two modern elements —namely, *Tonality* and *Harmony.*

First, a glance at the Greek scale will show that there are seven different diatonic ways in which an octave may be divided ; thus, from A to the A above will exhibit one way, from B to B another, from C to C a third, and so on —keeping to the white keys alone in each case ; and all these various 'forms of the octave' as they were called, were understood and used in the Greek music, and formed different 'modes.' In modern times we adopt only two—one corresponding with C to C, which we call the *Major* mode, the other corresponding with A to A, which we call the *Minor* mode. And in each case we attach great importance to the notes forming the extremities of the octave series, either of which we call the *Tonic* or *Keynote.* We have, therefore, in modern music, the two following 'forms of the octave' in common use. And we may substitute for the Greek word 'hemitone' the modern term 'semitone,' which means the same thing.

Intervals of the Diatonic Scale for the Major Mode.

Intervals of the Diatonic Scale for the Minor Mode.

Although these differ materially from each other, it will be seen that the original Greek diatonic form of the series is in each perfectly preserved. It must be explained that the minor scale is given, under particular circumstances, certain accidental variations [see below], but these are of a chromatic nature ; the normal minor diatonic form is as here shown. The choice of particular forms of the octave, and the more prominent character given to their limiting notes, constitute the important feature of modern music called Tonality.

Secondly, a certain influence has been exercised on the diatonic scale by modern Harmony. When it became the practice to sound several notes of the scale simultaneously, it was found that some of the intervals of the Greek series did not adapt themselves well to the combination. This was particularly the case with the interval of the major third, C to E : according to the Greek system this consisted of two tones, but the perfect harmonious relation required it to be a little flatter. The correction was effected in a very simple manner by making a slight variation in the value of one of the tones, which necessitated also a slight alteration in the value of the semitone. Other small errors have been corrected in a similar way, so as to make the whole conform to the principle, *that every note of the scale must have,* as far as possible, *concordant harmonious relations to other notes ;* and in determining these, the relations to the tonic or keynote are the more important.

The diatonic series, as thus corrected, is as follows :—

Major Diatonic Scale as corrected for Modern Harmony.

The several intervals, reckoned upwards from the lower keynote, are—

C to D, Major tone,
,, E, Major third,
,, F, Perfect Fourth,

C to G, Perfect Fifth,
,, A, Major sixth,
,, B, Major seventh,
,, C, Octave.

In has been stated, however, that for modern European music we have the power of adding, to the seven sounds of the diatonic scale, certain other intermediate *chromatic* notes. Thus between C and D we may add two notes called C♯ and D♭. Between G and A we may add G♯ and A♭, and so on. In order to determine what the exact pitch of these notes should be, it is necessary to consider that they may be used for two quite distinct purposes, *i.e.* either to embellish melody without change of key, or to introduce new diatonic scales by modulation. In the former case the pitch of the chromatic notes is indeterminate, and depends on the taste of the performer ; but for the second use it is obvious that the new note must be given its correct harmonic position according to the scale it belongs to: in fact it loses its chromatic character, and becomes strictly diatonic. For example, if an F♯ be introduced, determining the new diatonic scale of G, it must be a true major third above D, in the same way that in the scale of C, B is a major third above G. In this manner any other chromatic notes may be located, always adhering to the same general principle that they must bear concordant harmonic relations to other notes in the diatonic scale of which they form part.

Proceeding in this way we should obtain a number of chromatic notes forming a considerable addition to the diatonic scale. For example, in order to provide for eleven keys, all in common use, we should get ten chromatic notes in addition to the seven diatonic ones, making seventeen in all, within the compass of a single octave. This multiplication of notes would produce such a troublesome complication in practical music, that in order to get rid of it there has been adopted an ingenious process of *compromising*, which simplifies enormously the construction of the scale, particularly in its chromatic parts. In the first place it is found that the distance between the diatonic notes E and F, and between B and C is *nearly* half that between C and D, or G and A ; and secondly, it is known that the adjacent chromatic notes C♯ and D♭, G♯ and A♭, etc., are not very different from each other. Putting all these things together, it follows that if the octave be divided into *twelve equal parts*, a set of notes will be produced not much differing in pitch from the true ones, and with the property of being *applicable to all keys alike*. Hence has arisen the modern chromatic scale, according to what is called *equal temperament*, and as represented on the key-board of the ordinary pianoforte. According to this, the musical scale consists of twelve *semi-*

tones, each equal to a twelfth part of an octave ; two of these are taken for the *tone* of the diatonic scale, being a very little less in value than the original major tone of the Greek divisions.

This duodecimal division of the octave was known to the Greeks, but its modern revival, which dates about the 16th century, has been one of the happiest and most ingenious simplifications ever known in the history of music, and has had the effect of advancing the art to an incalculable extent. Its defect is that certain harmonic combinations produced by its notes are slightly imperfect, and lose the satisfactory effect produced by harmonies perfectly in tune. The nature and extent of this defect, and the means adopted to remedy it, will be more properly explained under the article TEMPERAMENT, which see.

Minor Scale.—It is a peculiarity of the minor scale adopted in modern music, that its form is frequently varied by accidental chromatic alterations, to satisfy what are assumed to be the requirements of the ear ; and as these alterations most commonly take place in ascending passages, it is usual, in elementary works, to give different forms of the minor scale, for ascending and descending.

For example, the normal form of the scale of A minor is

and in descending, as here shown, the progressions seem natural and proper.

But if the motion take place in the reverse direction, thus :—

No. 1.

it is said that the succession of the upper notes in approaching the key note A, do not give the idea which ought to correspond to our modern tonality. It is argued that the penultimate note, or seventh, being the *leading* or *sensible* note of the key, ought to be only a semitone distant from it, as is customary in all well-defined keys ; and that, in fact, unless this is done, the tonality is not properly determined. This reason has led to the accidental sharpening of the seventh in ascending, thus :—

No. 2.

But here there is another thing objected to ; namely, the wide interval of three semitones (an augmented second) between the sixth and the seventh, F♮ and G♯, which it is said is abrupt and unnatural, and this has led to the sharpening of the sixth also, thus—

No. 3.

to make the progression more smooth and
regular. This is the succession of notes usually
given as the *ascending minor scale*, which with
the descending scale without accidentals is
usually called the *melodic form* of the minor
scale.

The first alteration—namely, the sharpening
of the leading note—is no doubt required if the
perfect modern tonality is to be preserved, for
no doubt an ascending passage, thus—

would give rather the impression of the key of
C or of F than that of A.

But the necessity for sharpening the *sixth* is
by no means so obvious ; it may no doubt be
smoother, but the interval of the augmented
second is one so familiar in modern music, as
to form no imperative reason for the change.
Hence the form marked No. 2 is very commonly
used, both for ascending and descending. It
is called the *harmonic form* of the minor
scale.   W. P.

SCANDELLO, SCANDELLIUS, or SCAN-
DELLI, ANTONIO, was born at Brescia in
1517. In 1553 he was already resident in
Dresden and a member of the Hofcapelle,
but he often returned to visit his native place ;
in 1567, on account of the plague, he and his
family left Dresden and spent four months
there. In 1555 six Italians are mentioned
as being members of the Dresden Hofcapelle :
' welsche Instrumentisten in der Musica,'
among them Anthonius Scandellus, his brother
Angelus Scandellus, and Benedict Tola, the
painter, whose daughter Agnes became Scandello's second wife in June 1568 (*Monatshefte*,
1877, p. 255). The Italians, receiving higher
pay than the Germans, were even then arousing feelings of jealousy, which later, as their
numbers increased, and German music was
pushed more and more into the background,
resulted in open quarrels and opposition.
Their influence was to prove powerful enough
to oust a German capellmeister from his post,
although as is pathetically stated of Mathias
Weckmann, the organist in question, he had
learnt Italian ' mit Fleiss,' and was at first on
a friendly footing with the foreign musicians
(Fürstenau, *Zur Geschichte*, i. 26). In 1555
Scandello, with 250 fl. 16 grs. 9 pf. a year,
was receiving a larger salary than the capellmeister, Matthias Le Maistre, who had only
204 fl. 7 grs. 9 pf. It is also curious to note
that the Italian players were paid on a higher
scale than singers from the Netherlands, the
highest salary to the latter only amounting to
120 fl. (Fürstenau, *Archiv für die sächs. Ge-*

schichte, iv. 1866). It is true that the player
was expected to show facility on a large variety
of instruments ; Scandello himself was a noted
zinke or cornetto player, besides being already
a composer of some repute.

In 1566 Scandello became assistant capellmeister to the ageing Le Maistre, and on his
retirement was appointed capellmeister, Feb.
12, 1568, when his salary altogether amounted
to 400 fl. a year, a large sum for those days.
A letter addressed to the capellmeister on
Jan. 13, 1579, gives leave to his brother Angelo
to go to Venice for three months, to collect
some debts. He retained his post until his
death in Dresden on Jan. 18, 1580, at the age
of sixty-three. One of his sons, August, was
also a member of the Dresden Hofcapelle.

Three motets for six voices, dated 1551, in
a manuscript in the Dresden Library, are probably Scandello's earliest compositions. Next
comes the mass for six voices, in commemoration of the death of the Elector Moritz of
Saxony, July 9, 1553, at the battle of Sievers-
hausen. In the 'Inventarium' of the capelle
music drawn up by the Dresden capellmeister,
Johann Walther, Oct. 16, 1554, for the use
of his successor, Matthias Le Maistre, this mass
is mentioned as being in six little printed part-
books : 'VI kleine gedruckt Partes in pergament,
darinnen das Epitaphium Electoris Mauricii
Antonii Scandelli' (W. Schäfer, *Sachsen-Chronik*,
1853, p. 320). At the present time only a
manuscript copy of it is known, made in Torgau,
in 1562, by one Moritz Bauerbach of Pirna,
tenorist in the Dresden capelle ; very possibly
it was owing to the suggestion of Johann
Walther, then living in retirement at Torgau,
that Bauerbach wrote it. The manuscript was
formerly in the Pirna Stadt-Bibliothek, but is
now in the Dresden Royal Library. A large
part of the mass was scored by Otto Kade and
published in Ambros's *Geschichte der Musik*,
1889, vol. v.

Especial mention must be made of the Passion-
music and the story of the Resurrection, which
were in all probability composed before 1561
(see O. Kade, *Die ältere Passionskomposition*,
1893, p. 191, a reprint of the Passion-music, pp.
306-44). Scandello some years later refers to
them in a document dated July 15, 1573, they
were therefore in existence some fifty years
before Heinrich Schütz's great works were published, his 'Auferstehung' in 1623, and his
'Passionen nach Johannis' not until 1664.
A manuscript copy of Scandello's work, dated
1593, formerly at Grimma, now in the Dresden
Royal Library, is entitled, 'Passio et Resur-
rectio Domini nostri Jesu Christi ab Antonio
Scandello compositae,' the scribe was Johann
Gengenbach of Colditz. It only gives the
tenor part of the choruses ; the music is otherwise complete. The manuscript of the tenor
part-book now in the same library, but formerly

at Löbau, contains the 'Johannispassion' and the 'Auferstehungsgeschichte,' without mention of the composer's name. Another Löbau manuscript contains a complete copy of the 'Auferstehung'; this part of the composition was the first to appear in print. It was published by Samuel Besler at Breslau, 1612, with the title, 'Gaudii paschalis Jesu Christi redivivi in Gloriosissimae Resurrectionis ejus laetam celebrationem. Relatio historia à quatuor Evangelistis consignata, etc., durch Samuelem Beslerum, etc.'

Besler alludes in the preface to the composer, Antonius Scandellus, 'der berhümbte musicus.' It was again published in an adapted form by O. S. Harnisch in 1621. In the same year Besler published the Passion-music; 'Ant. Scandelli . . . Passio, Das Leyden unsers Herrn Jesu Christi nach dem H. Evangelisten Johanne. Durch S. B. mit der Chorstimme vermehrt,' Breslau, 1621. It is from this edition that the chorus parts, missing in the manuscripts, have been filled in. The Passion opens with the words in four-part writing, 'Das Leyden unsers Herrn Jesu Christi wie das der heilige Evangelist Johannes beschreibet.' Throughout, each individual character is represented by a duo, trio, or quartet, with the exception of the Evangelist, who is given the traditional recitative. The words of Christ are invariably set as a solo quartet, those of Peter as a trio, and so on. The concluding chorus and the short, quick outcries of the people are all in five-part writing; possibly the opening chorus should be the same. There is no accompaniment. Schütz also followed this method of dividing the voices, with the addition of a four-part string accompaniment to the recitative, but here all similarity between the two works ceases, for whereas Schütz's music shows an emotional impulse which eventually affected profoundly the devotional rendering of church music, Scandello's retains the clear, fresh simplicity of the olden time with an added wealth of sound which marks a great distinction between it and Joh. Walther's Passion-music; it should be studied as a link in the chain of historical development of the Passion-music. An interesting comparison of the Schütz and Scandello works will be found in Monatshefte für Musikgeschichte, 1882, p. 37, where also the identity of the anonymous 'Auferstehung' published by Vopelius in the Neu Leipziger Gesangbuch, 1682, pp. 311-65 (reprinted by Riegel and Schöberlein, Kirchliche Chorgesänge, 1868, ii. pp. 619-47) with that of Scandello's is pointed out. Scandello was the first composer to set the story of the Resurrection to music, and he followed very closely the lines laid down in his Passion-music.

As to his other compositions, it may be noted that although his Italian madrigals, published 1566 and 1577, are purely vocal works with no accompaniment, the German Lieder, both sacred and secular, published 1568, 1570, and 1575, may be sung to an instrumental accompaniment. Examples are given in Ambros's Geschichte der Musik. v., 'Bonzorno, madonna,' for four voices; 'Der Wein der schmeckt mir' for six voices; and 'Nu komm der Heiden Heiland' for five voices.

List of published works :—

Missa sex vocum super Epitaphium Mauricii Ducis et Electoris Saxoniae ab Anthonio Scandello, Italo, composita, 1553. Walther (1732) states that it was published at Nuremberg, by Georg Fabricius, in 1558.

El primo libro de le canzoni napoletane a IIII voci, composti per Messer Antonio Scandello musico del illus. et eccel. sig. Duca Augusto Elettor di Sassonia. Novamente datti in luce. Noribergae excudebant Ulricus Neuberus et Th. Gerlatzen, 1566, obl. 4to. Four part-books. The dedication to the Elector August is dated from Augsburg. Contains twenty-four canzoni. Later editions were issued at Nuremberg in 1572 and 1583.

Melodia Epithalami in honorem . . . Martini Henrici et filiae Barbarae viri Joh. Schildbergii . . . sex vocum. Witebergae, 1568.

Epithalamia, in honorem . . . Nicolai Leopardi, symphoniacorum puerorum illustrissimi ac serenis. principis Georgii Friderici, marchionis Brandeburgensis . . . praeceptoris, et pudicissimae virginis ac sponsae Kunigundae . . . composita per Ant. Scandellum, Matthaeum Le Maistre, etc. Noribergae apud Th. Gerlatzenum, 1568. Text: Beati omnes qui timent; in two movements, for six voices.

Newe Teutsche Liedlein mit vier und fünff Stimmen, welche gantz lieblich zu singen, und auff allerley Instrumenten zugebrauchen. Durch Anthonium Scandellum, Churfürstlicher G. zu Sachsen Cappelmeister verfertigt. Gedruckt zu Nürnberg, durch Dietrich Gerlatz, inn Johann von Bergs seligen Druckerey, 1568, obl. 4to. Four part-books, containing twelve sacred songs. Includes the well-known chorale 'Lobet den Herrn,' which took a permanent place in church-song, and was reprinted in Joachim Magdeburg's 'Christliche u. tröstliche Tischgesänge,' Erfurt, 1571; the Dresdener Gesangbuch, 1593; J. C. Kühnau's 'Vierstimmige alte u. neue Choralgesänge,' 1790, ii. p. 140; Lützel's Kirchliche Chorgesänge, 1861, No. 11; and with the song 'Allein zu dir' for six voices, in Winterfeld's Evangelische Kirchengesang, 1843, Nos. 38 and 39.

Nawe und lustige weltliche Deudsche Liedlein, mit vier, fünff, und sechs Stimmen, auf allerley Instrumenten zugebrauchen, und lieblich zu singen. Durch Ant. Scandellum, etc. von ihme selbst corrigiret, und in Druck vorfertiget. Gedruckt zu Dresden durch Matthes Stöckel und Gimel Bergen, 1570, obl. 4to. Five part-books, containing twenty songs. A later edition of 1578 had the title-page as above with the exception of the tenor part-book, dated a year later, as follows: Schöne, weltliche und geistliche, nawe, deudsche Liedlein mit vier, fünff und sechs Stimmen, 1579.

Epithalamium in honorem . . . Christophori Waltheri, illustris. Electoris Saxoniae . . . organistae insignis: prudentiss. viri Joannis Waltheri, consulis Dresdensis, ac fautoris musicae singularis . . . filii, et honestissimae foeminae Catherinae Tolae, sponsae ipsius, Benedicti Tolae, musici et pictoris . . . relictae filiae. Compositum sex vocibus ab illus. Electoris Saxoniae . . . musici chori magistro, Antonio Scandello, 1574, 4to. Six part-books.

Nawe ausserlesene Geistliche Deudsche Lieder, mit fünff und sechs Stimmen, gantz lieblich zu singen, und auff allerley Instrumenten zugebrauchen, sampt einem Dialogo mit acht Stimmen. Durch Ant. Scandellum, etc. componirt, auch von ihme selbst corrigirt, und in Druck vorfertiget. Dresden, Gimel Bergen, 1575, obl. 4to. Contains twenty-three compositions, 'meist über ältere Kirchenmelodien.'

Missae sex, quarum priores tres quinque, posteriores vero sex vocum sunt, compositum super has cantionumseil. 1, super: avec que vous; 2. Io mi son giovenetta; 3. Ad aequales; 4. Maria Magdelena; 5. Au premier jour; 6. O passi sparsi. Authore Ant. Scandello Electoris Saxoniae musices praefecto. Monachi, 1576.

Il secondo libro de le canzoni napolitane, a quatro et a cinque voci. Composte per Ant. Scandello, maestro de la capella del illus. et eccel. sig. Elettore di Sassonia, etc. Novamente date in luce. Stampate in Monacho per Adam Berg, 1577, obl. 4to. Five part-books, containing twenty-four canzoni.

COMPOSITIONS IN OTHER PUBLICATIONS

Thesaurus musicus. Noribergae, 1564.
'Imperium Augusti sit foelix,' 'Magnificat,' 'Noe, noe, exultemus,' all for eight voices, in the first volume; 'Alleluia noli flere Maria' for seven voices, in the second.

Beati omnes, Psalmus 128 Davidis. . . . Per Cl. Stephani Buchaviensem. Noribergae, 1569. Includes Scandello's setting of the psalm for six voices (see his Epithalamia, 1568). A manuscript copy is in the Vienna Hofbibliothek, No. 15,591.

Das erste Buch . . . schöner Lautenstück . . . mit vier und fünff Stimmen. Getruckt durch Bernhard Jobin, bürger zu Strassburg, 1572. Includes 'Ich weis mir ein fest gebautes hauss' for five voices, in lute tablature.

Ein new kunstlich Tabulaturbuch . . . durch Eliam Nicolaum Ammorbach, bürger und Organist in Leipzig zu Sanct Thomas, Leipzig, 1575. 'Ich weis mir,' 'Den liebsten Buhlen,' 'Gros lieb hat,' 'Kein lieb ohn leid,' 'Von deinetwegen,' all for five voices, in lute tablature.

Selectae Cantiones octo et septem vocum, etc. Argentorati, 1578. 'Noe, noe exultemus,' for eight voices.

Schöne ausserlesene . . . Teutsche Lieder XX. Durch J. Pühlerum Schvuandorffensem. München, 1585.
'Mancher der spricht,' for four voices.

Corollarium Cantionum sacrarum . . . F. Lindneri, Noribergae, 1590. No. 22. Antonius Scandellus; 'Christus vere languores' in two movements, for five voices. On a manuscript copy in the Zwickau Library is written, 'Ultima cantio Anthonii Scandelli qui 18 Januarii die vesperi hora 7, anno 80, aetatis suae 63 obiit' (Kade, Le Maistre, p. 3). MSS. are also in the Basle, Dresden, and Liegnitz libraries.

Musikalischer Zeitvertreiber, das ist Allerley seltzame lecherliche Vapores und Humores, etc., Nürnberg, 1609. Contains songs for 4, 5, 6, 7 and 8 voices, two compositions are by Scandello.

Triumphi di Dorothea . . . das ist geistliches musicalisches Triumph Cräntzlein . . . durch M. Rinckhardum. Leipzig, 1619. Contains 'Ich weis mir' for five voices.

Engelmann's Quodlibetum novum latinum quinque vocum. Leipzig, 1620. Compositions by Scandello in Part I.

Cantionale sacrum, das ist, Geistliche Lieder mit 3, 4, 5 oder mehr Stimmen unterschiedlicher Autorum. Gotha, 1646-48, 3 volumes. One composition by Scandello, also in the edition of 1651-55-57.

Joh. G. Ebeling's edition of P. Gerhardi geistliche Andachten, 1667. With Scandello's melody to 'Lobet den Herrn.'

A. Neithardt, Sammlung religiöser Gesänge, vii. No. 11. 'Lasset die Kindelein' for five voices.

Franz Commer, Geistliche u. weltliche Lieder. 1870, Nos. 11, 12. 'Ich ruf zu dir' and 'Gelobet seist du,' both for five voices; other motets in Musica Sacra, vols. 15, 19, and 20.

Franz Wüllner, Chorübungen der Münchener Musikschule, 1893, Nos. 63, 99. 'Auf dich trau ich' and 'Mit Lieb bin ich,' both for four voices.

MSS. In Augsburg Library, No. 21, Lib. I. Sacrarum missarum sex vocum variorum authorum haud vulgarium, 1595. Missa super, Maria Magdalena. (Schletterer's *Catalogue.*) Basle Universitäts-Bibliothek, No. 33, Magnificat VIII. toni, in tablature, date about 1585. (Richter's *Catalogue.*) Berlin. Königl. Bibliothek, many sacred songs in score (Eitner).

Breslau Stadtbibliothek, No. 2 (date 1573) in score, and No. 5 in separate part-books, 'Alleluia noli fiere' for seven voices. No. 6 (date 1567) and No. 11 (date 1583) 'Noe, noe exultemus' for eight voices. Both in Thes. mus. 1564. No. 11 and No. 14 (date about 1600). 'Ein Kindelein so löbelich' for six voices, and 'Gelobet seist du' for five voices, both from 'Nawe sch. auss. geistl.' 1575. No. 10, five part-books, nine Italian madrigals from Scandello's second book, 1577. No. 94, six folio part-books, late 16th century, Missae super : Auecque vous ; Io mi son giovenetta ; Ad aequales ; all for five voices, and Missae super : Maria Magdalena ; Au premier jour ; O passi sparsi, all for six voices. The six masses published at Munich in 1576, see above. A MS. copy of the mass 'O passi sparsi' is also in the Vienna Hofbibliothek, date about 1560. (Bohn's *Catalogue.*)

Brieg Gymnasial-Bibliothek. No. 36, six part-books, date 1592, 'Lobet den Herrn' for four voices (see 1568 publication). In Nos. 40, 51, 52, imperfect sets of part-books, 'Ach edler Wein' for five voices ; 'Schöns lied' ; 'S'io canto,' and 'Se per sentir' (from Lib. i. of Canzoni, 1572), all for four voices. (Kuhn's *Catalogue.*)

Dresden Royal Library, No. 1270. Three motets for six voices : 'Christus dicit ad Thomam' dated 1551. 'Hodie Christus natus est,' 1551, and 'Illuminare Jerusalem.' (Kade's *Catalogue.*)

Munich Royal Library, No. 34 (Mus. MS. 509) date 1602, Missa super : O passi sparsi, and Missa super : Au premier jour, both for six voices. No. 207 (Mus. MS. 1501) 'Ich weis mir' for five voices, and 'Ach Gott wem soll ich's' for four voices. No. 132 (Mus. MS. 1536) date 1583, an incomplete set of part-books ; two magnificats, and two motets for eight voices ; one motet for seven, and one for six voices. (Maier's *Catalogue.*) Grimma Library MS. motets written between 1593 and 1595, some for four and five voices by Scandello.

Liegnitz Ritterakademie Bibl. MS. 19, many motets by Scandello.

Pirna Stadtkirche 16th-century MS. 'Auf dich trau ich' for four voices (from 1568 work). Another MS. with 'Dies sanctificatus' for six voices.

Zwickau Ratsschulbibliothek. No. 39, date about 1600, in tablature, 'Mit Lieb bin ich' for four voices (from 'Nawe und lustige Liedlein,' 1578). No. 678, date before 1580, five folio part-books 'Nun kommt der Heiden Heiland' for five voices. No. 679, incomplete set of part-books, Missa super : Germania plange, for six voices. No. 680, incomplete set of part-books, 'Magnus Dominus' in two movements (which was included in Walther's *Inventarium* in 1554), and 'Allein zu dir,' both for six voices. (Vollhardt's *Catalogue.*)

                                            C. S.

SCARIA, EMIL, born Sept. 18, 1840, at Graz, Styria, studied at the Conservatorium, Vienna, under Gentiluomo, made his début at Pesth as St. Bris in the 'Huguenots,' and afterwards sang at Brunn and Frankfort. In 1862 he came to London for the purpose of further study under Garcia, and sang at the Crystal Palace, on April 5, and at a concert given later by Franz Abt, who procured him an engagement at Dessau. He next played at Leipzig (1863-65) and from 1865 to 1872 at Dresden. Among his best parts were Hercules ('Alceste'), Sarastro, Leporello, Caspar, Rocco, Landgrave ('Tannhäuser'), Pogner ('Meister-singer') Burgomaster ('Czaar und Zimmer-mann'), Dulcamara, Geronimo ('Il Matrimonio segreto'), and Falstaff (Nicolai), in which last a critic remarks that he made one of his greatest successes . . . when he was at Dresden, and made it in great measure by his really excellent acting of the character. From 1872 to 1886 he

was engaged at Vienna, where he established his reputation as a versatile singer and actor in both baritone and bass parts, but best in the latter, as his 'carefully deadened high notes form so great a contrast to the vigorous notes of his lower and middle register' (Hanslick). On leave of absence he sang in the principal German cities, in Italian opera in Russia, etc. He sang the part of Escamillo to the Carmen of Bertha Ehnn, Oct. 23, 1875, when Bizet's opera was first given outside France. Among his later parts were Hans Sachs ('Meistersinger') Wotan ('Nibelungen')—for which character he was originally selected by Wagner for Bayreuth, and which he sang at Her Majesty's Theatre in 1882, Micheli ('Wasserträger'), Marcel, Bertram, and (1879) Seneschal ('Jean de Paris'). Finest of all was his Gurnemanz in 'Parsifal,' which he created at Bayreuth in 1882 ; he sang it at the concert-performance of the work in the Albert Hall, London, in 1884. He became insane in 1886, and died on July 22 of that year at Blasewitz near Dresden. A. Neumann's *Erinnerungen an Richard Wagner*, 1907, gives many amusing stories of him.   A. C.

SCARLATTI, ALESSANDRO, was born in Sicily in 1659 or possibly in 1658, as may be deduced from the statement of his age engraved on his tombstone. It has generally been assumed that his birthplace was Trapani, on the strength of an alleged autograph score of his opera 'Pompeo,' which both Fétis and Florimo professed to have seen while in the possession of Gaspare Selvaggi of Naples. Selvaggi's library was bought by the Marquis of Northampton, and presented by him in 1843 to the British Museum ; but no score of 'Pompeo' is to be found there now, nor is it included in the MS. catalogue of the collection drawn up for the donor at the time. The only known score of 'Pompeo' is in the Royal Library at Brussels, and formerly belonged to Fétis ; but it is not autograph, and does not bear the inscription mentioned. This inscription, by the way, is given by Fétis as 'Musica del Signor Alessandro Scarlatti da Trapani,' and by Florimo as 'Pompeo del Cav. Alessandro Scarlatti di Trapani.' Florimo's version can hardly be accepted as genuine, since 'Pompeo' appeared in 1683, while the composer did not receive the title of Cavaliere until many years later. In the records of the Arcadian Academy at Rome, Scarlatti is described as a native of Palermo, but in view of other known errors to be found in these records the evidence of this entry cannot be regarded as infallible. The official record of his birth or baptism has hitherto eluded the most careful research. The fact, however, that he was born in Sicily is proved conclusively by statements in the printed libretti of his early operas, and in MS. chronicles which record their performance, and speak of the composer as a Sicilian. Of his parentage nothing is known, and it seems not improb-

ALESSANDRO SCARLATTI

able that he came of a Tuscan stock, the name Scarlatti being Tuscan and not Sicilian. He must in any case have left the island at an early age ; he is traditionally supposed to have been a pupil of Carissimi in Rome, although that master died when Scarlatti was fifteen years old. His early compositions show the influence of Legrenzi, and more especially of Stradella, whose best work has recently been shown to have been done in Rome ; and his early chamber-cantatas, of which some are probably earlier in date than even his first operas, are generally to be found in MS. alongside of similar music by composers who worked in Rome and northern Italy.

His first known opera was 'L'Errore Innocente ovvero Gli Equivoci nel Sembiante,' produced Feb. 8, 1679, in Rome at the Collegio Clementino. This work won him the interest of Christina Queen of Sweden, who even asserted her protection of him in defiance of the Papal representatives, Scarlatti being in bad odour at the Vatican on account of the misconduct of his sister with an ecclesiastic. In the libretto of his second opera, 'L'Honestà negli Amori' (1680), he is described as Maestro di Cappella to Queen Christina. Both these operas are on a small scale ; 'Pompeo' (Rome, 1683) was probably his first attempt at *opera seria* in the grand manner. In February 1684 'Pompeo' was given at Naples, where 'Gli Equivoci' had also been heard, and on the 17th of the same month he was appointed Maestro di Cappella to the Viceroy, his brother Francesco receiving a post as violinist in the same chapel royal. The two brothers owed their appointments to the influence of their sister, Anna Maria, an opera-singer, who was the mistress of a court official ; and the affair seems to have caused some indignation at Naples, not so much on grounds of morality as from motives of chauvinism. That Scarlatti was regarded as a stranger in Naples seems a sufficient proof that he did not receive his musical education there, as Neapolitan historians of music have tried to maintain. About this time Scarlatti married one Antonia Anzalone, by whom he had three and possibly more children, of whom the eldest, born Oct. 26, 1685, was Giuseppe Domenico, later famous as a composer for the harpsichord. From this time to 1702 he remained at Naples, occupied principally in the composition of operas for production at the royal palace or at the royal theatre of San Bartolomeo. He was also much in demand as a composer of music for aristocratic entertainments, and soon fell into a popular and hasty style of work. His chamber music, however, shows that even at this time his artistic ideals were much higher, and by 1702 Naples had become so irksome to him, both for musical and financial reasons, that he determined to try his fortunes elsewhere. His salary was in arrear, and the political disturbances consequent on the war of the Spanish Succession rendered his position still more insecure. On June 14 he went with Domenico to Florence, where they enjoyed the patronage of Ferdinand III., son of the Grand Duke of Tuscany, a prince who was enthusiastically devoted to music. For his private theatre at Pratolino Scarlatti composed several operas, and the Archivio Mediceo at Florence contains a very interesting correspondence between the prince and the musician on the subject of these works. Ferdinand, however, was not disposed to offer him any permanent post, and Scarlatti being resolved not to return to Naples accepted the humble position of assistant Maestro di Cappella at the church of S. Maria Maggiore in Rome. This was obtained for him by Cardinal Pietro Ottoboni, who had taken an interest in him for some twelve years or more, and who also made him his private Maestro di Cappella. Nevertheless, Scarlatti seems to have been no happier in Rome than in Naples, judging from the contempt for both places which he expresses in his letters to Ferdinand. He had been forced to write down to the level of a Spanish viceroy's taste for the opera-house at Naples ; at Rome the Popes had done their best to suppress opera altogether on grounds of public morality. This must, no doubt, have been a severe blow to Scarlatti, whose real genius sought expression in dramatic music, although it found vent in chamber-music when its natural outlet was obstructed.

On April 26, 1706, Scarlatti was admitted a member of the Arcadian Academy, under the name of *Terpandro Politeio*, Corelli and Pasquini being elected at the same time. Crescimbeni (*Arcadia*, Lib. vii. Prosa v.) gives a charming account of their musical performances at these pastoral assemblies. To this period of Scarlatti's activity belong many of his beautiful chamber-cantatas, and a certain amount of church music. In May 1707, Antonio Foggia died, and Scarlatti succeeded him as principal Maestro at the church of S. Maria Maggiore. He continued to compose operas for Ferdinand de' Medici while living in Rome, but although his voluminous correspondence about these works has been preserved, the scores of them have unfortunately disappeared. In spite of all his efforts to write pleasing music, he seems to have been too severe for the prince's taste, and in 1707 he was dropped in favour of Perti.

In this year he produced two operas, 'Mitridate Eupatore' and 'Il Trionfo della Libertà' at Venice (Teatro S. Giovanni Crisostomo), going there in person to direct them. These works are on a larger scale than any of his previous operas, and the first is one of the best that he ever wrote ; the second has come down to us in so fragmentary a condition that it is hardly possible to form a fair judgment upon it. In all probability Scarlatti remained at Venice to the end of the Carnival, and thence made his way to Urbino, travelling, there is reason to believe, by way of Ferrara.   The reigning pope (Clement XI.) was a native of Urbino, and the Albani family, to which he belonged, were nobles of great importance in that country.   The resident representative of the family, Cardinal Orazio Albani, was interested in music, and although no trace of Alessandro Scarlatti is now to be found there, the Albani library possesses several libretti of Domenico's operas, as well as a few musical treasures of an earlier date.   Scarlatti remained at Urbino until September, but probably returned to Rome for Christmas, since he wrote a mass with orchestral accompaniment for this festival.

Although Scarlatti had left Naples in June 1702, his post at the royal chapel was not filled up until October 1704, when a certain Gaetano Veneziano was appointed.   In December 1707 he was succeeded by Francesco Mancini ; but towards the end of 1708 Cardinal Grimani, the Austrian Viceroy, made an attempt to persuade Scarlatti to return.   It seems that Scarlatti, as might have been expected, declined to accept the post of deputy first organist, which was offered him, having been at the head of the chapel for nearly twenty years, and did not return until he had been restored to the office of Maestro di Cappella, with an increased stipend. Mancini was compensated with the title of Vice-maestro, and the right of succeeding eventually to the post held by Scarlatti.   It is doubtful, however, whether he re-established himself definitely at Naples until 1713.   Although described in the libretti of ' L' Amor Volubile e Tiranno' (1709) and 'La Principessa Fedele' (1710) as *Maestro della Real Cappella*, he does not appear to have written anything more for Naples during the next three years, and on May 27, 1713, the new Viceroy, Count Daun, made a special confirmation of the appointment given him by Cardinal Grimani.   This action secured him for Naples for the next few years.

During this second period of work in Naples Scarlatti was at the height of his fame.   He produced operas on a magnificent scale at the court theatre ; 'Tigrane' (1715) and its contemporaries, though less interesting than his later operas, are brilliant and effective—the leisured work of a man mellowed by success, not the hurried output of one struggling to retain the favour of his patrons at any sacrifice of artistic ideals.   To this period also belong some oratorios, notably 'San Filippo Neri' (1713), and several serenatas for state occasions. The honour of knighthood, which is first vouched for by the appearance of his name with the title Cavaliere in the libretto of 'Carlo Rè d' Alemagna' (1716), was probably conferred upon him in recognition of the serenata and opera which he composed to celebrate the birth of the Archduke Leopold.   It has been suggested that he received the order of the Golden Spur from the Pope, at the request of Cardinal

Ottoboni ; but if this were the case it is only natural to suppose that it would have been conferred upon him while in the Cardinal's service, or even under the pontificate of the Cardinal's uncle, Alexander VIII.   It may, however, be pointed out that in this year, 1716, he composed a mass (known as 'Missa Clementina II.') for Clement XI.   In 1718 he made his one attempt at pure comic opera, 'Il Trionfo dell' Onore,' performed at the Teatro dei Fiorentini.

The interest of the Neapolitans in Scarlatti's music seems to have waned about this time. After 'Cambise' (1719) no more of his operas were heard there, and it is probable that he established himself in Rome, since his stipend as Maestro di Cappella at Naples was not paid to him any more, although he retained the title. At Rome he had a number of admirers sufficient to undertake the production of a series of operas which exhibit the composer in a still more advanced phase of artistic development.   The first of these was 'Telemaco' (1718), which was followed by 'Marco Attilio Regolo' (1719), 'Tito Sempronio Gracco' and 'Turno Aricino' (1720), apparently not so much revivals as entire recompositions of two earlier operas, and finally his 114th and last opera, 'Griselda' (1721).   Since the autograph score of this last informs us that it was composed for Prince Ruspoli, we may suppose that that nobleman (who had interested himself in Scarlatti's work when he was living in Rome before) was the principal organiser of the performances, which took place at the 'Sala degli illustrissimi Signori Capranica.'   In 1721 Clement XI. was succeeded by Innocent XIII., and in November of that year Scarlatti was commissioned by the Portuguese Ambassador to compose a pastorale for the Pope's formal entrance into the Vatican. This appears to have been his last work for Rome, where he had distinguished himself in sacred music as well as in opera, producing a fine mass with orchestra and other works for St. Cecilia's day at the request of Cardinal Acquaviva, who had a special interest in the church of St. Cecilia in Trastevere.   In 1722 he seems to have visited Loreto, where he is supposed to have composed a setting of the Psalm 'Memento Domine David' and an 'Ave Maria.'   The following year probably saw him back at Naples.   He set to work on a serenata for the marriage of the Prince of Stigliano, but appears to have left it unfinished, as the first part only has come down to us.   There is every reason to suppose that he was now living in complete retirement, forgotten by his own generation, and regarded as a crabbed and eccentric harmonist by even so learned a musician as the German theorist Heinichen. In 1724 J. A. Hasse, having quarrelled with Porpora, came to Scarlatti as a pupil ; the old man was attracted by the boy's amiable disposition, and during the few remaining months of Scarlatti's life the two musicians regarded each other with the affection of father and son. Quantz visited Naples in 1725, and stayed with Hasse, whom he begged to introduce him to Scarlatti; Scarlatti, however, merely replied to Hasse's request, 'My son, you know that I cannot endure players of wind instruments, for they all blow out of tune.' Hasse succeeded eventually in inducing him to receive Quantz, who heard him play the harpsichord 'in a learned manner'; Scarlatti even accompanied him in a solo and composed a couple of flute-pieces for him. He died on Oct. 24 of the same year, and was buried in the church of Monte-santo. His epitaph is said to have been written by Cardinal Ottoboni, and runs as follows :—

HEIC · SITVS · EST
EQVES · ALEXANDER · SCARLACTVS
VIR · MODERATIONE · BENEFICIENTIA
PIETATE · INSIGNIS
MVSICES · INSTAVRATOR · MAXIMVS
QVI · SOLIDIS · VETERVM · NVMERIS
NOVA ,· AC · MIRA · SVAVITATE
MOLLITIS
ANTIQVITATI · GLORIAM · POSTERITATI
IMITANDI · SPEM · ADEMIT
OPTIMATIBVS · REGIBVSQ
APPRIME · CARVS
TANDEM · ANNOS · NATVM · LXVI · EXTINXIT
SVMMO · CVM · ITALIAE · DOLORE
IX · KAL^{AS} · NOVEMB^{RIS} · CIƆIƆCCXXV
MORS · MODIS · FLECTI · NESCIA

Scarlatti is one of the most important figures, not only in the history of opera, but in the entire history of music. He is the most import-ant of that group of composers who succeeded the first pioneers of the monodic style, based upon the modern tonal system, and who moulded and developed a musical idiom which served as the language of musical expression down to the days of Beethoven. In his early work he is naturally under the influence of older composers—Carissimi, Luigi Rossi, Stradella, and Legrenzi; indeed, the vague tradition of his having studied in Parma might associate him with the last-named composer as a pupil. His first operas and his early cantatas and church music have, moreover, a certain harshness and crudity which reveals the beginner; Stradella's operas and Rossi's cantatas, though old-fash-ioned in their phraseology, are much more mature and finished in their execution. It is interesting to compare Scarlatti with Purcell, who was his exact contemporary; Purcell was also under Italian influence, and we find in the young Scarlatti many points of resemblance to him, notably in the treatment of harmony,—both composers showing a tendency to think polyphonically, though melodiously, and being either indifferent to, or more probably taking a positive pleasure in, the painful dissonances resulting from their unbending logic. But with his appointment as Maestro di Cappella at Naples, Scarlatti modified his style. Here he

was forced to work with the utmost rapidity, and to work for popular success. The fine detail of his earlier work is swept aside; the curious forms, derived in part from the ground-bass, in which he had once delighted, are abandoned; and he poured forth a long series of operas in which the grace and vigour of his best moments eventually degenerated into insipidity and vulgarity. Three important features charac-terise this somewhat unfortunate period of his career. The da capo aria in ternary form (ABA), though of course not an invention of Scarlatti, is now definitely established as the only type of operatic aria, to the entire exclusion of all other forms. The form of overture known as the 'Italian' overture was introduced in 1696 for the revival of an earlier opera, 'Dal Male il Bene,' and, though subject to much develop-ment, remains constant in its main outlines to the end of the Metastasio period of Italian opera; and lastly, the opera 'Olimpia Vendi-cata' (1686) presents us with the earliest-known example of accompanied recitative. From about 1686 to 1696 Scarlatti's operas have a facile grace that is often far removed from triviality; the operas 'La Statira' (1690), 'La Rosaura' (1690), and 'Pirro e Demetrio' (1694), which was performed in London in an English adapta-tion in 1708, were deservedly popular in their day, and contain music which has even survived down to our own. About 1697 a change comes over Scarlatti's style, due in all probability to the influence of Giovanni Bononcini, whose 'Trionfo di Camilla' was performed at Naples in that year. Bononcini had a certain genius for airs of a spirited martial type—'L' esperto nocchiero' from 'Astarto' is a good specimen—and no doubt they pleased the court, since they were easy to understand, and even a viceroy could beat time to them. Scarlatti, either on his own initiative, or more probably in obedience to orders from above, set to work on the same lines, and from 1697 to 1702 turned out a number of inferior operas, full of airs that are either sugary and cloying, or pompous and stilted. Their only redeeming features, as a rule, are the comic scenes, which are trivial but certainly humorous. Of this phase 'Eraclea' (1700) and 'Laodicea e Berenice' (1701) are the best examples.

There can be little doubt that Scarlatti's most serious work was being put into the operas which he composed for Ferdinand de' Medici. His let-ters give a detailed account of the composition of 'Turno Aricino' (1704), 'Lucio Manlio' (1705), and 'Il Gran Tamerlano' (1706). He speaks with enthusiasm of Stampiglia's libretto to the second of these, and appears to have considered the opera the best that he had hitherto com-posed, although each act was written in a fort-night. The scores of these operas, however, have entirely disappeared, and not even scat-tered fragments of them can be traced. To

what great height he was capable of rising at
this stage may be seen in the opera 'Mitridate
Eupatore,' composed for Venice in 1707. Although the interest is not equally sustained all
through, the work is a very remarkable example
of the classical manner at its grandest. The
libretto is also remarkable, as depending entirely
upon its political interest. There are no love-
scenes at all ; but the devotion of the heroine
for her lost brother is expressed with a passionate sincerity that far transcends anything that
Scarlatti had written before. J. S. Bach at his
best has hardly surpassed the dignified recitative 'O Mitridate mio,' followed by the magnificent aria 'Cara tomba' in Act IV.

With his return to Naples in 1709 Scarlatti
entered upon yet another stage of development.
The deep poetic intention of 'Mitridate' is indeed seldom apparent ; but the experience of
former years had given the composer command
of every resource, and the honour in which he
was held at the Austrian court enabled him to
write in a style more worthy of himself. We
may regret the loss of that tender charm so
characteristic of his early work, but we must
admit the wonderful vigour and brilliance of
such operas as 'La Principessa Fedele' (1710),
'Il Ciro' (Rome, 1712), 'Scipione nelle Spagne'
(Naples, 1714), and above all 'Tigrane' (1715).
In these operas we may notice not only the
more extended development of the ternary aria-
forms, but also an advance towards a more
modern treatment of the orchestra. Scarlatti's
early operas are generally scored for a band of
strings, supported, of course, by the harpsichord
and other harmonic instruments, such as the
lute, playing from the *basso continuo*, which in
this case we can hardly call the *figured* bass,
since Italian accompanists were so fluent in improvisation that the composer could generally
spare himself the trouble of indicating the harmony in the conventional shorthand. To this
band are added occasionally trumpets, flutes,
oboes, and bassoons, not as regular constituents
of the orchestra, but treated more as *obbligato*
instruments, with a view to special colour effects.
The burden of the accompaniment rested on
the harpsichord. Violin-playing was at the
close of the 17th century still so primitive
that the strings of an opera band could seldom
be trusted with the delicate task of supporting
a singer. In most cases they enter only to play
the final noisy *ritornello* at the close of an air ;
sometimes they are given a share in the accompaniment, but treated as a group antiphonal
to the harpsichord. Scarlatti, however, was
evidently interested in the development of
violin-playing, and as time went on he allotted
to the strings a more important share of the
work, stimulated, no doubt, by the influence of
Corelli, who was thought by his contemporaries
to be distinguished more as a conductor than as
a composer. As early as 'Mitridate Eupatore'

(1707) we may observe the tendency to reverse
the principle of the earlier work ; it is the
strings (generally without double-basses) that
accompany the voice, and the harpsichord that
is reserved to add power and brilliance to the
ritornelli. Moreover, Scarlatti's whole outlook
becomes gradually less and less aggressively contrapuntal, the harsh dissonances of his boyhood
are soon smoothed away, and the general scheme
of his musical thought tends more to melody
supported by harmony, although he showed to
the end of his life that he regarded free counterpoint as the most intellectual style of expression. This point of view naturally influences
his instrumentation, and causes his later scores
to have much more affinity to the modern style
of treating the orchestra.

A fifth and final period is exemplified in the
series of operas written for Rome that began
with 'Telemaco' and ended with 'Griselda.'
Twenty years earlier Scarlatti had bitterly
lamented the impossibility of producing operas
in the city that had witnessed his first triumphs.
But the passion for opera, which had attacked
Rome, no less than other Italian cities, during
the baroque period, was too serious to be stifled
by the protests of clerical prudery, and Rome
now showed him that here at last was an audience which could appreciate the full maturity
of the genius which she had been the first to
encourage. In these latest operas we see not
only the furthest development of technical resource, but also the ripened fruits of emotional
experience. Here at last is the whole Scarlatti,
here at last he was able to place upon the stage
something of that passionate tenderness and
serious musical reasoning that he had for so
many years brought to utterance only in the
intimacy of his chamber-cantatas, and exhibit
the whole in all the glory of variegated orchestration, lighted up by the blaze of vocal *coloratura*.

Scarlatti has been remembered in modern
times chiefly on account of his operas ; but we
cannot understand his complete development
without a study of his chamber-music. The
chamber-cantata was to the age of Rossi and
Scarlatti what the pianoforte-sonata or violin-
sonata was to the age of Beethoven and Brahms
—the most intimate and the most intellectual
form of music that could be produced. The
degraded age of vocal virtuosity had not yet
arrived ; the singers were not merely the most
agile performers upon the most perfect of instruments, but the most intellectual exponents
of the art of music. Scarlatti, the greatest
and almost the last of the great writers of
chamber-cantatas, practised in this form, as
Beethoven did in the pianoforte-sonata, from
his earliest years to that of his death. Over
five hundred of his cantatas have come down
to us, representing every period of his life, and
we may often see that for any given period, as

with Beethoven's pianoforte-sonatas, they represent the highest intellectual achievement of the moment. It is unfair to judge them by the standard of Schumann's 'Lieder'; they are not lyrical outbursts, sacrificing formality to the personal emotion of the poet, much less scenes taken out of operas, as has been suggested, but carefully designed studies in composition, often depending for their main interest on the working out of some interesting problem of modulation or of thematic development. Thus in 1712 he sent Gasparini two settings of the cantata 'Andate o miei sospiri' which had been set by Gasparini and sent to him by the composer. The first of these two settings is a beautiful specimen of Scarlatti's work at this period; the second was designed with a view to puzzling his correspondent with the most difficult modulations, both in the recitatives and in the airs. The work is difficult even to the modern reader, but only on account of the terseness of its thought. 'Awkward' and 'experimental' are epithets that could hardly ever be applied to Scarlatti, and his music often fails to interest the modern romantic reader because of the absolute mastery with which he solves his problems.

His instrumental chamber music is of less value. It was apparently traditional to treat this branch of art in a more archaic style; the four 'Sonate a quattro' (string quartets), and even the twelve Symphonies for small orchestra (1715), are more primitive in their methods than the Sonatas of Corelli. He composed a certain amount of music for the harpsichord and organ, but it is for the most part straggling and ineffective, interesting only as showing a certain influence on the early work of his son. His best work for the harpsichord is a set of variations on the theme of Corelli's 'Follia,' recently edited by Aless. Longo, and published by Messrs. Ricordi.

As a church composer Scarlatti is not at his best. The story of his having set the mass two hundred times may be dismissed as a fable. Considering the vast quantity of other music of his that has survived, it can hardly be believed that as many as 190 masses should have been lost. Quantz is the only authority for this statement, and as he never mentions a single composition of Scarlatti's by name, his information deserves little credit. Of the ten surviving masses, the majority are in the strict style kept up to the end of the 18th century and called 'alla Palestrina,' though breaking gradually away from the manner of its illustrious model. Scarlatti treats discords with more freedom, and occasionally shows a more modern feeling for fugue; but his strict masses are on the whole uninteresting. Two masses with orchestra are important in the history of modern church music. The first (1707) is somewhat crude and ineffective, but the second (1720) is a worthy ancestor of the

great masses of Bach and Beethoven. The miscellaneous church music calls for little comment. Roger of Amsterdam printed a collection of 'Concerti Sacri' (about 1710), characterised by a Jesuitical brilliance which is meretricious, but certainly attractive; three motets for double choir 'Tu es Petrus,' 'O magnum mysterium,' and 'Volo, Pater' (about 1707), are broad and dignified; the little 'Laetatus sum' for four voices (printed by Proske) is a model of counterpoint in Leo's manner. The oratorios and secular serenatas are of very varying value, and show the same sort of tendencies as the operas. (See ORATORIO.)

Mention must also be made of Scarlatti as a teacher. The *Regole per principianti*, a MS. treatise on accompaniment, is of interest, as showing that its author was always liberal in his views on the theory of his art. He allows various harmonies (*e.g.* the use of a second inversion of a dominant seventh) which his contemporaries did not, admitting that not everybody would agree with him, but defending himself on the principle that such progressions sound well. To what extent he taught at Naples is not clear. The tendency of modern research is to indicate that the younger generation of composers at Naples were trained for the most part by Nicola Fago and Gaetano Greco; Hasse seems to have been almost the only one who came into intimate relations with him. His frequent absence from Naples must have been a serious interruption to teaching work, and in his latter years he was evidently quite forgotten by the Neapolitan public.

Nevertheless, Alessandro Scarlatti must certainly be regarded as the founder of the Neapolitan school of the 18th century. He was, of course, not the first teacher nor the first opera-composer that appeared in Naples; but Provenzale, a man far inferior to his Venetian and Roman contemporaries, was much too insignificant to be the leader of a new movement. The real celebrity of Naples as an operatic centre dated from Scarlatti's appointment in 1683, and the long series of his operas performed there from 1683 to 1702, and from 1709 to 1719, during which periods he almost monopolised the stage of S. Bartolomeo, caused his artistic influence to be paramount there. But the unfortunate, though natural, consequence was that the younger generation of composers imitated him not at his ripest but at his most successful phase, so that, in spite of the earnest effort of Leo, the later Italian opera proceeded rapidly to that state of decadence against which Gluck finally led the reaction. For this reason Scarlatti has too often been represented as the first composer who took the downward step towards empty formalism and the prostitution of opera to the vanity of singers. This is gross injustice. We may regret that adverse circumstances compelled him to produce much that was unworthy of his best ideals ; but the mass of chamber-cantatas and the later operas show him to have been a thoroughly intellectual musician, a complete master of form in its minutest details, who made as severe demands upon the brains of his interpreters as upon their technical powers.

Scarlatti indeed is the founder of that musical language which has served the classical composers for the expression of their thoughts down to the close of the Viennese period. Thematic development, balance of melodic phrase, chromatic harmony—all the devices which the 17th century had tentatively introduced, are by him woven into a smooth and supple texture, which reached its perfection in one who, although he never knew his true master, was yet his best pupil—Mozart. [For complete list of works, see the writer's Alessandro Scarlatti, 1905, and the Quellen-Lexikon.]   E. J. D.

SCARLATTI, GIUSEPPE DOMENICO, son of Alessandro, born in Naples, Oct. 26, 1685, first learned from his father, and later from Gasparini. [He has been called a pupil of Bernardo Pasquini, but that seems most improbable, seeing that Pasquini was of the school of Palestrina, and wrote entirely in the contrapuntal style, whereas Domenico Scarlatti's chief interest is that he was the first composer who studied the peculiar characteristics of the free style of the harpsichord. Mr. Shedlock's suggestion that he was taught, or at least largely influenced, by Gaetano Greco is far more likely.] His bold style was by no means appreciated in Italy, for Burney remarks (State of Music in France and Italy) that the harpsichord was so little played that it had not affected the organ, which was still played in the grand old traditional style. The first work on which Domenico is known to have been engaged was that of remodelling for Naples, in 1704, Polaroli's opera 'Irene' (Venice, 1695). At Naples 'his talent found scope indeed,' wrote Alessandro to Ferdinand de' Medici on May 30, 1705, ' but it was not the sort of talent for that place. I send him away from Rome also, since Rome has no roof to shelter music, that lives here in beggary. This son of mine is an eagle whose wings are grown ; he ought not to stay idle in the nest, and I ought not to hinder his flight. Since the virtuoso Nicolino, of Naples, is passing through Rome on his way to Venice, I have thought fit to send Domenico with him ; and under the sole escort of his own artistic ability (which has made great progress since he was able to be with me and enjoy the honour of obeying Your Royal Highness's commands in person, three years ago), he sets forth to meet whatever opportunities may present themselves for making himself known—opportunities for which it is hopeless to wait in Rome nowadays.' Domenico duly presented himself to the Prince with this letter, which is now in the Medici

archives at Florence, and presumably continued his journey with Nicolino, at any rate as far as Venice. In 1708 he was in Venice [studying with Gasparini, and making the acquaintance of Handel and later of Roseingrave.] Domenico seems to have accompanied Handel to Rome, for Cardinal Ottoboni held a kind of competition between the two, at which the victory was undecided on the harpsichord, but when it came to the organ, Scarlatti was the first to acknowledge his rival's superiority, declaring that he had no idea such playing as Handel's existed. The two became fast friends from that day ; they remained together till Handel left Italy, and met again in London in 1720. In 1709 he entered the service of Marie Casimire, Queen of Poland, and composed for her private theatre in Rome several operas : a dramma pastorale ' Sylvia ' (libretto in the Paris Bibliothèque Nationale), which was followed by ' Orlando '(1711), ' Fatide in Sciro' (1712), ' Ifigenia in Aulide ' and 'in Tauride' (1713), 'Amor d'un ombra,' and ' Narciso' (1714), and 'Amleto' (1715, Teatro Capranica), interesting as the first musical setting of that subject. Even in extreme old age Handel spoke with pleasure of D. Scarlatti, and Mainwaring (Memoirs, p. 61) relates that when Scarlatti was in Spain, if his own playing was admired, he would turn the conversation on Handel's, crossing himself at the same time as a sign of his extreme reverence. In January 1715 he succeeded Baj as maestro di capella of St. Peter's in Rome, where he composed Masses, Salve Reginas, etc. In 1719 he went to London, where his 'Narciso' was performed (May 30, 1720), and in 1721 to Lisbon, where he became a court favourite. The longing for home and kindred, however, drove him back to Naples, where Hasse heard him play the harpsichord in 1725.

In 1729 he was invited to the Spanish court, and appointed music-master to the Princess of the Asturias, whom he had formerly taught in Lisbon. According to the Gazetta musicale of Naples (Sept. 15, 1838) he returned to Naples in 1754, and died there in 1757. Being an inveterate gambler he left his family in great destitution, but Farinelli came to their assistance. (Sacchi's Vita di Don Carlo Broschi.)

As we have said, Scarlatti was in some sense the founder of modern execution, and his influence may be traced in Mendelssohn, Liszt, and many other masters of the modern school. He made great use of the crossing of the hands, and produced entirely new effects by this means. His pieces, unlike the suites of Handel and his predecessors, were all short. Santini possessed 349 of them. Of these Scarlatti himself only published one book of thirty pieces, entitled ' Esercizii per gravicembalo,' etc., printed according to Burney in Venice, but at any rate before August 1746, when the Prince of the

Asturias, whose name is on the title-page, ascended the throne. In the Fétis collection is a Paris edition, 'Pièces pour le clavecin,' two vols., published by Mme. Boivin (who died Sept. 1733) and Le Clerc.[1] '42 Suits[2] of Lessons' were printed by John Johnson (at the Harp and Crown, Cheapside), London, under the supervision of Scarlatti's friend Roseingrave (between 1730 and 1737, when Roseingrave went out of his mind). In 1752 John Worgan obtained the sole licence to print certain new works by Domenico Scarlatti, and published them (at J. Johnson's, facing Bow Church, Cheapside). These were twelve sonatas, most of them new to England. Czerny's edition (Haslinger, Vienna, 1839), containing 200 pieces, was re-edited (Paris, Sauer, Girod) and revised by Mme. Farrenc from Roseingrave's edition, and MSS. then in possession of Rimbault. There are also 130 pieces in Farrenc's 'Trésor des Pianistes' (1864); sixty Sonatas are published by Breitkopf; and eighteen pieces, grouped as Suites by von Bülow, by Peters. [Tausig arranged several of the sonatas to suit the requirements of modern pianists, but the greatest boon to lovers of Domenico Scarlatti is the publication of a complete edition of his sonatas by Ricordi & Co. under the editorship of Signor Alessandro Longo. Six volumes, containing 300 pieces in all, appeared in 1906, and are to be continued by a further series. The above article has been corrected by reference to a review of this edition written by Mr. E. J. Dent, and published in the *Monthly Musical Record*, Sept. 1906.] Besides these famous works and the operas, among which last are to be included contributions to various pasticcios, Domenico Scarlatti wrote a Stabat Mater for ten voices and organ, and a 'Salve. Regina' for a single voice, stated to be his last composition.   F. G.

SCARLATTI, FRANCESCO, a brother of Alessandro. A mass and Dixit Dominus by him, a 16, are in the Bodleian Library, Oxford, dated 1702 and 1703 respectively. He was for twenty-six years maestro di cappella at Palermo (1689-1715), and in 1719 came to London with his nephew Domenico, giving a concert of his own compositions, Sept. 1, 1720. A Miserere a 5 is in the Court library at Vienna, and some opera airs and cantatas in the Fitzwilliam Museum, Cambridge, and elsewhere. (See the *Quellen-Lexikon*.)   M.

SCARLATTI, GIUSEPPE, son of Domenico, was born at Naples, according to Paloschi in 1712, according to Florimo in 1718. At one time he seems to have been maestro at Pavia, and in the text-book of 'I portentosi effetti,' revived at Berlin, in 1763, he is styled maestro di cappella in Naples. He settled in Vienna in 1757, before which date he had produced the

following operas:—'Merope,' Rome 1740 (repeated at Naples 1755); 'Dario,' Turin, 1741; 'Pompeo in Armenio,' Rome, 1747; 'Adriano in Siria,' Naples, 1752; 'Ezio,' Naples, 1754; 'I portentosi effetti della natura,' Venice, 1754; 'Antigone,' Milan, 1756; 'Chi tutto abbraccia nulla stringe,' Venice, 1756. In Vienna he brought out at the court theatre : 'Il mercato di malmantile' and 'L' isola disabitata,' 1757; 'La serva scaltra,' 1759; 'Issipile' and 'La Clemenza di Tito,' 1760; 'Artaserse,' 1763; 'Li stravaganti,' 1765; 'La moglie padrona,' 1768. He died at Vienna, August 17, 1777. C. F. P.; with additions from the *Quellen-Lexikon*.

SCARLATTI, PIETRO, was probably a nephew of Domenico and was, according to Florimo, maestro di cappella in Naples. In 1728 his opera 'Clitarco' was given at the theatre of San Bartolomeo (a MS. of the work is at Monto Cassino, in which there are intermezzi by Hasse.)   M.

SCENA (Gr. Σκηνή; Lat. *Scena*; Ital. *Scena*. *Teatro, Palco*; Ger. *Bühne, Auftritt*; Fr. *Scène*, *Théâtre*; Eng. *Scene, Stage*). A term, which, in its oldest and fullest significance, applies equally to the stage, to the scenery it represents, and to the dramatic action which takes place upon it. Hence, the long array of synonyms placed at the beginning of this article.

I. Classical authors most frequently use the word in its first sense, as applying to that part of a Greek or Roman Theatre which most nearly answers to what we should now call the stage; and the classical tendencies of the Renaissance movement led to its similar use in the 16th century.

II. In its second sense, the word is commonly applied, in England, to those divisions of a drama which are marked by an actual change of scenery; a method of arrangement which is even extended to English translations of foreign works.

III. In the Italian, German, and French theatres, the word is more frequently used, in its third sense, to designate those subordinate divisions of an act[3] which are marked by the entrance or exit of one or more members of the Dramatis Personae'; a new scene being always added to the list when a new character appears upon or quits the stage, though it be only a messenger, with half-a-dozen words to say or sing.

IV. In a more limited sense, the term Scena is applied by operatic composers to an accompanied recitative, either interspersed with passages of rhythmic melody, or followed by a regular Aria. In the former case, the word is generally used alone—and always in its Italian form : in the latter the composition is sometimes called 'Scena ed Aria.' Less frequently, the

[1] No. 10 in vol. ii. is an organ fugue by Alessandro Scarlatti.
[2] Which are not 'Suites,' but single movements.
[3] Ital. *Atto*; Fr. *Acte*; Ger. *Aufzug*—in allusion to the raising of the curtain.

place of pure recitative is supplied by the introduction of short strains of melody, with strongly-marked variations of tempo. But, in all cases, it is *de rigueur* that the character of the composition should be essentially and unmistakably dramatic throughout. The Scena, thus defined, is as old as the opera itself ; for the name might very well be given to the scene from ' Euridice,' already alluded to ; or to the ' Lamento' in Monteverde's ' Ariana.' A very fine example, much in advance of its age, will be found in 'Ah rendimi quel core,' from Francesco Rossi's ' Mitrane,' 1689. Mozart's peculiar aptitude for this kind of composition is well exemplified in his wonderful scena for two voices, ' Die Weiselehre dieser Knaben,' in ' Die Zauberflöte' ; in innumerable delightful instances in his other operas ; and in a large collection of detached pieces, such as ' Ch'io mi scordi,' ' Bella mia fiamma,' ' Ahi, lo previdi,' ' Misera, dove son ? ' and others, too numerous to mention, most of them written for the stage, though some are clearly intended for the concert-room, notwithstanding their powerful dramatic expression. To this latter class of Scenas must be referred Beethoven's magnificent ' Ah, perfido !' which ranks, with the Scenas for Leonore and Florestan, in 'Fidelio,' among his most passionate compositions for voice and orchestra. The Scena was unquestionably Weber's strongest point—witness his three magnificent examples, ' Durch die Wälder,' ' Wie nahte mir die Schlummer,' and ' Ocean, du Ungeheuer,' and his six ' Concert Arien.' The grand Scena, in B♭, for Kunegunde in ' Faust,' is one of Spohr's most notable masterpieces ; and the same composer's impassioned instrumental ' Scena Cantante ' for violin and orchestra stands quite alone, as an inspiration of the highest order. He also wrote a very fine Scena for the concert-room—' Tu m'abbandoni' (op. 71) ; and Mendelssohn has left us a priceless treasure of this class in his ' Infelice,' which embodies an amount of scenic power no less remarkable than that thrown into the numerous similar movements in his oratorios. The secret of success, in all these cases, lies in the intensity of dramatic expression embodied in the work.   W. S. R.

SCENARIO. An Italian term, meaning a sketch of the scenes and main points of an opera libretto, drawn up and settled preliminary to filling in the detail.   G.

SCHABLONE. The German term for a stencil or pattern, and thence in musical criticism often applied to music written with too much adherence to mechanical form or manner, whether the composer's own or some one else's —made on a cut-and-dried pattern. The term *capellmeister - musik* is used by the German critics for a similar thing. With a slightly different metaphor we should say, ' cast in the same mould.'   G.

SCHACK (properly CZIAK), BENEDICT, the first Tamino, and one of the party [1] who stood round Mozart's bed the night before his death, and at his request sang the completed portions of the ' Requiem ' as far as the first bars of the ' Lacrimosa,' when he broke into violent weeping at the thought that he should never finish it. Schack, who was born at Mirowitz, in Bohemia, in 1758, was a man of general cultivation, a thorough musician, and a good flute-player. He composed several operas for Schikaneder's theatre. Mozart was on intimate terms with him, and would often come and fetch him for a walk, and, while waiting for Schack to dress, would sit down at his desk and touch up his scores. Schack's voice was a fine tenor, flexible and sonorous, and his execution thoroughly artistic, but he was a poor actor.[2] In 1787 he was taking second parts only ; in 1792 he sang Tamino, Count Almaviva, and Don Ottavio (Don Gonsalvo in the German translation), after which we hear no more of him as a singer. [In 1780 he was Capellmeister to a nobleman, and in 1805 retired on a pension. A mass by him was finished by Mozart. (See the *Harmonicon*, vol. ix. p. 298.)] His operas or Singspiele came between 1789 and 1793 ; some were written with Gerl.[3]   C. F. P.

SCHALE (German). A cymbal, used of the halves of a pair, which together are called Becken. ' Beide Schalen' is a direction found after one of the cymbals has been directed to be struck with a drum-stick.

SCHALMEI. See SHAWM.

SCHARWENKA, LUDWIG PHILIPP, born Feb. 16, 1847, at Samter, near Posen, in East Prussia, where his father was an architect. His taste for music showed itself early, but he was unable to cultivate it seriously till the removal of his family to Berlin in 1865, when he entered Kullak's ' New Academy,' studying under Würst and Heinrich Dorn, having previously completed his studies at the Gymnasium in Posen, where his parents settled in 1859. On completing his course at the Academy he remained on the staff as a teacher of theory till 1881, when he became teacher of composition at his brother's newly opened Conservatorium, the direction of which he undertook with Hugo Goldschmidt on his brother's emigration to America in 1891. In 1880 he married the well-known violinist Marianne Stresow, who is at present a violin teacher in the Klindworth-Scharwenka Conservatorium. Besides having made a good name for himself with a long list of interesting compositions, Professor Scharwenka is an accomplished caricaturist.

The compositions of Philipp Scharwenka in-

---

[1] The others were Mozart's brother-in-law, Hofer, the violinist, and Franz Xaver Gerl, a bass-singer, and the first Sarastro. Mozart himself sang the alto.
[2] Jahn's *Mozart*, ii. p. 510.
[3] Gerl sang ' Osmin' in 1797 at the same theatre in the Freihaus, where was produced in 1797 his comic opera in three acts, ' Die Maskerade,' by ' a former member of this theatre.'

clude **a** vast number of piano pieces—Ländler, waltzes, minuets, mazurkas, etc.—of which 'Album Polonais' (op. 33) is best known, many songs, three concert pieces for violin and PF. (op. 17), studies for violin, studies for violoncello, three sonatas for pianoforte (op. 61) ; two choral works with soli and orchestra, 'Herbstfeier' (op. 44) and 'Sakuntala'; a choral work with pianoforte accompaniment *ad lib.*, 'Dörpertanzweise' ; a PF. trio in C♯ minor (op. 100) ; and some orchestral works, two symphonies, a Serenade (op. 19), a Fantasiestück 'Liebesnacht,' a Festival Overture (op. 43), an 'Arcadian Suite' (op. 76), and a Symphonic Poem, 'Frühlingswogen' (op. 87).   H. V. H.

His brother, FRANZ XAVER, was also born at Samter, Jan. 6, 1850 ; and like his brother was at Kullak's Academy in Berlin, where he was well known, while still a pupil, for his PF. playing and composition, which he studied under Kullak and Wüerst respectively. He made his first appearance in public in Berlin at the Singakademie in 1869, and remained for some time at Kullak's as a teacher, until compelled to leave it for his military duties in 1873. After this he began to travel, and was soon renowned as a fine and brilliant player, and a 'young composer of remarkable endowments.' In 1877 he produced his first Concerto for the PF. (in B♭ minor, op. 32), playing it to the meeting of German musicians at Hanover in May ; it was played in England for the first time by Mr. Edward Dannreuther at the Crystal Palace, Oct. 27, 1877. In 1878, Feb. 14, Scharwenka himself played it at the Gewandhaus, Leipzig. In 1879 he made his first appearance in England, playing the same work at the Crystal Palace, March 1, and played at the Musical Union, April 29. In 1880 he returned and played his B♭ minor Concerto at the Philharmonic, Feb.19, and the Beethoven E♭ Concerto on June 9. In 1881 he made a third visit, and played his second Concerto (in C minor, op. 56) which he had produced at the Gesellschaftsconcert at Vienna, Feb. 24 ; but his stay was shortened by his recall to Germany for his military duties, though he found time to appear several times, and deepened the favourable impression he had previously made. In 1899 he made another visit to England and played his Third Concerto (C♯ minor, op. 80).

On Oct. 1, 1881, Scharwenka opened his own Conservatorium in Berlin (staff including his brother Philipp's wife, *née* Marianne Stresow, Albert Becker, Philipp Rüfer, J. Kotek, O. Lessmann, W. Langhans, M. Röder, W. Jähns, A. Hennes, and Philipp Scharwenka), which became amalgamated with that of Klindworth in 1893, is now known as the Klindworth-Scharwenka Conservatorium (and School for Opera and Drama), and run under the artistic direction of the brothers Scharwenka and Capellmeister Robitschek and the administra-

tion of the latter, of which Xaver Scharwenka is the principal.

On Dec. 18 and 19, 1906, the twenty-fifth anniversary of the foundation of the Conservatorium was celebrated.

In 1891, answering a call to found and direct a branch of his Conservatorium in New York, Xaver Scharwenka, his wife and family, with all their belongings, emigrated to the States, where they remained seven years ; he, however, crossing to Europe and back no less than seven times during that period. In the New World he made numerous tours, and to his astonishment discovered that in the West he had already earned a reputation as a pianist through a former pupil of his brother's who had adopted his name and given concerts for two years without his identity being discovered. At present the Scharwenka family live in Berlin, where the Professor is busy morning, noon, and night as composer and teacher.

As a pianist Xaver Scharwenka is renowned above all his other qualifications for the beautiful quality of his tone, which is rich, round, soft, yet great, and singing, for which it would be difficult to name another living pianist as his equal. His power is enormous, yet he never bangs, and has no mannerisms, his arms and body at the piano appearing to be almost entirely without movement. If he is a specialist as interpreter of one composer rather than another it is of Chopin, whose nationality he partly shares, but of the other great masters his readings are always grand and musicianly, while to hear him play a waltz of Strauss is as dance-inspiring as the magic bells of Papageno. His compositions, which possess energy, harmonic interest, strong rhythm, many beautiful melodies, and much Polish national character, include a symphony in C minor (op. 60) ; three PF. concertos in B♭ minor, C minor, and C♯ minor (opp. 32, 56, and 80) ; two PF. trios in F♯ minor and A minor (opp. 1 and 42) ; two v'cello sonatas in D minor and E minor (opp. 2 and 46) ; a PF. quartet in F (op. 37) ; two PF. sonatas in C♯ minor and E♭ (opp. 6 and 36) ; very many piano pieces, mostly Polish dances, but also a scherzo in G, a ballade (op. 8), a concert menuet in B (op. 18), a theme and variations, studies and some songs, besides some books of technical exercises of great value to the modern pianist. A grand opera, without opus number, in four acts, to a libretto by Dr. Ernst Koppel, 'Mataswintha' (from the novel of Felix Dahn, *Ein Kampf um Rom*), was produced at Weimar, Oct. 4, 1896, and at the Metropolitan Opera-House, New York, April 1, 1897. In New York Scharwenka himself conducted ; at Weimar, Stavenhagen.

Xaver Scharwenka is Royal Professor, Imperial and Royal 'Kammervirtuos,' Ordinary Member and Senator of the Royal Prussian Academy of Arts, President of the 'Musik pädagogische' Association, Doctor of Music (America), and bears the title of Ritter hoher Orden. H. V. H.

SCHAUSPIELDIRECTOR, DER, 'Comödie mit Musik in 1 Act' (The Manager, a Comedy with Music in one Act) ; containing an overture and four numbers ; words by Stephanie, jun., music by Mozart. Produced at a Court festival at Schönbrunn, Feb. 7, 1786. Over the terzet (No. 3) is the date, Jan. 18, 1786. It was adapted to a French libretto under the name of 'L' Impresario,' and produced in Paris in 1856. [See vol. ii. p. 462.] A careful version of the entire piece from the German original, by W. Grist, was brought out at the Crystal Palace, London, on Sept. 14, 1877, as 'The Manager,' and repeated several times there and elsewhere.

An interesting little work, full of details on this opera and Mozart in general, is *Mozart's Schauspieldirector* by Dr. R. Hirsch (Leipzig, 1859). G.

SCHEBEK, EDMUND, a distinguished and influential Austrian amateur, Doctor of Law, Imperial councillor, and secretary to the Chamber of Commerce at Prague, was born Oct. 22, 1819, at Petersdorf in Moravia. He began his musical career as head of a Society at Olmütz, and continued it at Prague, where in conjunction with Weiss, the superior of the Capuchins, and Krejci, he revived much of the best old Italian church music. He devoted his attention specially to the construction of the violin, in relation to which he published very interesting treatises—*On the Orchestral Instruments in the Paris Exhibition of 1855*[1] ; *On the Cremonese instruments, àpropos of the Vienna Exhibition of 1873*, and *The Italian Violin manufacture and its German origin*.[2] He also published a valuable little pamphlet on Froberger (1874). Dr. Schebek possessed a fine collection of ancient stringed instruments, Beethoven autographs, etc. G.

SCHEBEST, AGNES, born at Vienna, Feb. 15, 1813, became attached at a very early age to the Court Theatre at Dresden, first in the chorus, and then as singer of small solo parts. Here she had the inestimable advantage of frequently hearing and seeing the great Schroeder-Devrient. In 1833 she left Dresden for Pesth, and from 1836 to 1841 starred throughout Germany with very great applause. Her voice was a fine mezzo-soprano, her style and method were good, her best parts heroic, with much energy and passion. In 1841 she married the great theologian Dr. David Strauss (himself a keen amateur, and author of an interesting paper on the Ninth Symphony), and died Dec. 22, 1869, at Stuttgart. She left an account of her career—*Aus dem Leben einer Künstlerin* (1857), and *Rede und Gebärde* (1862). G.

[1] *Die Orchester-Instrumente auf der Pariser Weltausstellung im Jahre 1855* (Vienna, Staatsdrückerei, 1858).
[2] *Der Geigenbau in Italien und sein deutscher Ursprung* (Vienna, 1872 and 1874).

SCHECHNER-WAAGEN, NANETTE, dramatic singer, born at Munich in 1806. She was employed in the chorus-scenes of the opera, and, on the occasion of Madame Grassini's visit, was chosen to second her in some selections from Cimarosa's 'Gli Orazii e Curiazii.' Schechner's beautiful voice made a great impression, and won for her a patroness in the Queen of Bavaria. After some study in singing and in Italian, she appeared in Italian opera in Munich, until 1827, after which she devoted herself to German opera. In 1826 she was in Vienna, if a curious story, related by Schindler, of a scene in the theatre there, àpropos of an air written for her by Schubert, may be believed. [See SCHUBERT.] It is related by Fétis that, when she first appeared in Berlin in Weigl's 'Schweizerfamilie,' the first act was played to an almost empty house ; but such enthusiasm did her Emmeline arouse in the few listeners, that the report of it spread to the neighbouring cafés during the entr'acte, a large audience was drawn to the theatre for the rest of the performance, and the singer's success was complete. Her Donna Anna, Euryanthe, Fidelio, Reiza, Vestalin and Iphigenie in Tauris excited great admiration in Berlin and Munich. In 1832 she married Waagen, a lithographer and painter. Her voice was powerful, even massive in its tones, and her acting earnest and natural. She took a place in the first rank of German singers, but her brilliant career lasted no longer than ten years. A severe illness injured her voice ; she retired from the stage in 1835, and died April 30, 1860.

Mendelssohn heard her at Munich in 1830, and while he found her voice much gone off and her intonation false, says that her expression was still so touching as to make him weep.[3] L. M. M.

SCHEIBE, JOHANN ADOLPH, born at Leipzig in May 1708, the son of an organ-builder, was educated for the law at the Nicolaischule, and at the University, where Gottsched was at the time professor. In 1735 he set out to try his fortunes as a musician, visiting Prague, Gotha, Sondershausen, and settling in 1736 at Hamburg as a teacher. He composed incidental music to various plays, and wrote a grand opera which only reached the stage of being twice rehearsed. In 1737 he began the publication by which he is famous in the history of German opera. *Der Critische Musikus*, as it was called, came out as a weekly periodical, and carried further the war against Italian operatic conventions which Gottsched had declared in his *Vernünftigen Tadlerinnen*. In 1740 he was appointed Capellmeister to the Margrave of Brandenburg-Culmbach, and also visited Copenhagen, where he settled two years later, and in 1742 became director of the court opera, retaining this post till 1749, when he

[3] Letter, June 6, 1836.

was succeeded by the Italian Sarti. He next devoted himself to literature and composition, becoming for a time head of a music-school at Sonderburg in Holstein. In 1745 he published a second edition of the *Critische Musikus*, (see below), and in 1754 wrote an *Abhandlung vom Ursprung und Alter der Musik.* He contributed a treatise on Recitative, in the composition of which he was a proficient, to the *Bibliothek der schönen Wissenschaften und freien Künste* (vols. xi. and xii.), 1764-65. In 1773 appeared the first of four projected volumes on composition, *Ueber die musikalische Composition*, but no more was finished, as the author died at Copenhagen, April 22, 1776. Apart from his championship of German opera, he obtained an unenviable notoriety by an attack on Sebastian Bach, published in the sixth number of his periodical, under date May 14, 1737. He had competed for the post of organist to the Nikolaikirche in 1729 ; and Bach, one of the judges, had not approved his playing ; furthermore, it seems probable that Bach, in his cantata ' Der Streit zwischen Phöbus und Pan,' had intended the character of Midas as a reference to Scheibe. It is only fair to say that Scheibe recanted his errors in the second edition of the *Critischer Musikus*, issued in 1745. Scheibe wrote an opera, ' Thusnelda,' which was published (with an introductory article on vocal music) at Copenhagen in 1749 ; two oratorios, ' Die Auferstehung' and ' Der wundervolle Tod des Welterlösers ' ; masses, secular cantatas, church compositions to the number of 200 ; 150 flute concertos ; 70 quartets or symphonies, trios, sonatas, existed, for the most part in MS. (*Quellen-Lexikon* ; Riemann's *Lexikon* ; *Sammelbände* of the *Int. Mus. Ges.* ii. 654 ff. ; Spitta, *J. S. Bach* (Engl. transl.) ii. 645-47, iii. 252-55.)   M.

SCHEIBLER, JOHANN HEINRICH, born at Montjoie, near Aix-la-Chapelle, Nov. 11, 1777, died Nov. 20, 1838, silk manufacturer, after many travels settled down at Crefeld, where he was first-assistant-Bürgermeister. In 1812-1813, after some interesting experiments with Jew's-harps, he turned his attention to the imperfections of existing means of tuning. He first tried a monochord, but finding that he could not always get the same note from the same division of his monochord, he endeavoured to help himself by beats, and discovered that each beat corresponded to a difference of two simple vibrations or one double vibration in a second. His plan was to fix the monochord by finding the stopped length which would give a note beating four times in a second with his own fork. Then, after endless trials and calculations, he found similar places for all the divisions of the scale, and finally from the monochord made forks for each note of the perfectly equally tempered scale. By repeated comparisons with his forks he found that it was

impossible to make a mathematically accurate monochord, or to protect it from the effects of temperature. He then hit upon the plan of inserting forks between the forks of his scale, from the lowest A of the violin to the open A, and counting the beats between them. It was this counting that was the trouble, but by highly ingenious mechanical contrivances he was enabled to complete the count of his fifty-two forks within from ·0067 to ·00083 beats or double vibrations in a second, and hence to tune a set of twelve forks so as to form a perfectly equal scale for any given pitch of A. The particulars of his forks and the mode of counting them are contained in his little pamphlet *Der physikalische und musikalische Tonmesser*, (Essen, Bädeker, 1834, p. 80, with lithographic plates),[1] from which the preceding history has been gathered. During his lifetime he issued four smaller tracts, showing how to tune organs by beats, which were collected after his death as *H. Scheibler's Schriften*, etc. (Crefeld, Schmüller, 1838). This is quite out of print, but copies of the former book are still to be bought. [These pamphlets form part of the interesting bequest left to the late A. J. Hipkins, by Dr. A. J. Ellis, and will, it is hoped, complete Mr. Hipkins's gift to the Royal Institution in memory of his friend Dr. Ellis.] His wonderful tonometer of fifty-two forks has completely disappeared. But another one, of fifty-six instead of fifty-two forks, which belonged to Scheibler, still exists, and was inherited by his daughter and grandson, who lent it to Herr Amels, formerly of Crefeld, who again lent it to the late Dr. Alexander J. Ellis, who counted it, and having checked his results by means of M'Leod's and Mayer's machines for measuring pitch, gave the value of each fork in the *Journal of the Society of Arts* for March 5, 1880, p. 300, correct to less than one-tenth of a double vibration. The two extreme forks of this fifty-six fork tonometer agree in pitch precisely with those of the fifty-two fork tonometer, but no other forks are alike, nor could the forks of the fifty-two fork tonometer have been easily converted into those of the other one. In 1834, at a congress of physicists at Stuttgart, Scheibler proposed with approval the pitch A 440 at 69° F. (= A 440.2 at 59° F.) for general purposes, and this has been consequently called the Stuttgart pitch.[2]   A. J. H.

SCHEIDEMANN. The name of a family of organists in Hamburg in the 16th and 17th centuries. Gerber, in his *Lexicon*, mentions Heinrich Scheidemann, born about 1600, died 1654, but appears to confuse him with an older

---

[1] *The physical and musical Tonometer, which proves visibly by means of the pendulum, the absolute numbers of vibrations of musical tones, the principal kinds of combinational tones, and the most rigid exactness of equally tempered and mathematical just chords.*

[2] He selected it as the mean of the variation of pitch in pianos as then tuned at Vienna, and not from the fact that it enables the scale of C major, in just intonation, to be expressed in whole numbers, as has been sometimes stated.

and more important member of the family, David Scheidemann, probably an uncle of Heinrich. The date of David Scheidemann's birth is not ascertained, but in 1585 he was organist of St. Michael's Church, Hamburg. He is chiefly noteworthy as associated with three other Hamburg organists of repute, Jacob and Hieronymus Praetorius, and Joachim Decker, in the compilation of what we should now call a Choralbuch, though this name was not in general use then,[1] a book of the usual hymn-tunes or chorales of the Lutheran Church, simply harmonised in four parts for congregational singing. This book appeared in 1604. Its original title is 'Melodeyen-Gesangbuch, darein Dr. Luthers und ander Christen gebräuchlichste Gesänge, ihren gewöhnlichen Melodien nach . . . in vier stimmen übergesetzt.' The example first set by Lucas Osiander in 1586, of uniformly giving the melody to the soprano part, and not to the tenor, as the older practice was, is here followed, and in the preface attention is called to the greater convenience of this for congregational singing. Of the eighty-eight tunes in the book, David Scheidemann harmonised thirteen or fourteen ; among them there appears for the first time harmonised 'Wie schön leuchtet der Morgenstern.' Gerber, confusing David with Heinrich, attributes both the melody and the setting of this Chorale to Heinrich. But Winterfeld shows (*Ev. Kirch.* i. p. 90) that the melody belongs to neither, but seems to be taken from an old secular song, beginning with similar words ('Wie schön leuchten die Aeugelein'), to the metre of which Philip Nicolai in 1599 wrote the words of his hymn, 'Wie schön leuchtet der Morgenstern.' It should be mentioned, however, that Wackernagel (*Das Deutsche Kirchenlied*, Bd. I. pp. 618-19), after giving the words of the secular song in full, adduces reasons for believing that in this case the secular song is a later parody of Nicolai's hymn, not *vice versa.* Winterfeld praises Scheidemann's settings of the chorales for their fresh animated character, and for the happy way in which the rhythmical peculiarities of the old melodies are brought out. Chorales were not then sung as now, all in slow uniform rhythm, but many of the older melodies had curious changes of rhythm, as from common to triple time, in successive lines. See the

specimens of Scheidemann in Winterfeld, Part I. Nos. 70, 71.

HEINRICH SCHEIDEMANN, mentioned above, was the son of Hans Scheidemann, organist of St. Catherine's Church, Hamburg. In 1616 he and Jacob Praetorius, the younger, were sent at the public expense to Amsterdam, to be initiated into a higher style of organ-playing, under the tuition of the then most famous organ-player of Europe, Peter Sweelinck. In 1625 Heinrich succeeded his father as organist of St. Catherine's. Mattheson says of Scheidemann that his organ-playing and compositions were like himself, popular and agreeable, easy and cheerful, with no pretence or desire for mere show. Some of his organ pieces have been discovered in MS. tablature at Lüneburg, for an estimate of which see Seiffert's *Geschichte der Klaviermusik*, vol. i. pp. 117-19. Heinrich Scheidemann was again associated with Jacob Praetorius in contributing melodies to Rist's 'Himmlische Lieder,' which were published in 1641-42. Praetorius composed ten to the 4th part of Rist's Book, Scheidemann ten to the 5th part, entitled 'Höllenlieder.' One of Scheidemann's melodies in this collection, 'Frisch auf und lasst uns singen,' continued for a while in church use, as it appears again in Vopelius's 'Leipziger Gesangbuch' of 1682. Among Scheidemann's pupils were Werner Fabricius, Matthias Weckmann, and Joh. Adam Reinken, the last of whom became his successor as organist of St. Catherine's, Hamburg, in 1654. Max Seiffert, in the *Sammelbände* of the *Int. Mus. Ges.* ii. p. 117, gives the date of Scheidemann's death as 1663, but Eitner, in the *Quellen-Lexikon*, gives reasons for adhering to the previously accepted date, 1654, as there is no doubt that Reinken succeeded him in that year.   J. R. M.

SCHEIDEMANTEL, CARL, born Jan. 21, 1859, at Weimar, was taught singing by Bodo Borchers, and on Sept. 15, 1878, made his début there as Wolfram. He remained there until 1886, having in the meantime received further instruction from Stockhausen at Frankfort. In 1884, on leave from Weimar, he sang in German at Covent Garden, June 4, as Kothner, as the Minister ('Fidelio'), Herald ('Lohengrin'), Kurwenal, Wolfram, and, July 9, Rucello, on the production of Stanford's 'Savonarola.' He made a very favourable impression, both on account of his fine baritone voice and his excellent singing and acting. In 1886 he sang at Bayreuth as Klingsor, Amfortas, a remarkable performance, and Kurwenal ; after which he made his débuts at Dresden as the Dutchman, and the Templar and Hans Heiling of Marschner, as a permanent member of the company there, as successor to Degele, the result of a successful 'gastspiel' the previous year. Here he has remained ever since (1907), and has gained great popularity in a

---

[1] It is worth while noting that the word Choral (in English usually spelt Chorale), as now restricted to the melodies of German metrical hymns, really originated in a misunderstanding of what Walther meant when he spoke of Luther as having called the 'deutscher Choralgesang' into life. What both Luther and Walther meant by 'Choralgesang' was the old Cantus Choralis or Plain-song of the Latin Church, which Luther himself wished to retain ; and his merit consisted in the adaptation of the chief parts of the Latin Choral to German words, his work in this respect corresponding to Marbeck's 'Book of Common Prayer Noted' with us in England. All the older Lutheran Church-musicians, such as Lucas Lossius and Michael Praetorius, used the words Choral and Choralgesänge in this sense of the old Plain-song melodies to the graduals, sequences, and antiphons, whether sung to Latin or adapted to German words. It was only when German metrical hymns gradually superseded in common use the other choral parts of the service, that the name Choral in course of time became restricted to the melodies of these hymns. See Winterfeld, *Ev. Kirch.* i. pp. 151, 152.

large number of parts. On Dec. 12, 1896, he sang with great success as the hero in Bungert's 'Odysseus' Heimkehr,' on Jan. 29, 1898, in 'Kirke,' and on March 21, 1901, in 'Nansikaa' (the second and third parts respectively of the Homeric tetralogy), on May 21, 1901, in Paderewski's 'Manru,' on the production of that opera. On leave of absence, in 1888, he sang as Hans Sachs at Bayreuth; in 1893, at the Gotha Opera Festival, as Rodolph in the revival of Boieldieu's 'Petit Chaperon Rouge.' On May 27, 1899, he sang again at Covent Garden, as Hans Sachs, a performance remarkable both on account of his fine acting and for the refinement of his singing and declamation. In addition he has sung in the principal cities of Germany and Austria, both in opera and concerts. In 1906 he took the part of Scherasmin in a successful revival of 'Oberon' at Dresden.   A. C.

SCHEIDT, SAMUEL, one of the celebrated three S's (the other two being Heinrich Schütz and Hermann Schein, his contemporaries), the best German organist of his time, was born at Halle in 1587. His father, Conrad Scheidt, was master or overseer of salt-works at Halle. The family must have been musical, as some works are still preserved of Gottfried, Samuel's brother, which A. G. Ritter (*Geschichte der Orgelmusik*) says show considerable musical ability. Samuel owed his training as an organist to the then famous 'Organisten-macher' Peter Sweelinck of Amsterdam. About 1605 he betook himself to Amsterdam, and became a pupil of Sweelinck. In 1608 or 1609 he became organist in the Moritzkirche in Halle, and in 1620 at least, if not earlier, he had received the appointment of organist and capellmeister to Christian Wilhelm, Markgraf of Brandenburg, and then Protestant Administrator of the Archbishopric of Magdeburg. In this capacity Scheidt officiated not at Magdeburg, but in the Hofkirche at Halle. The troubles of the Thirty Years' War and the misfortunes of his patron, the siege and sack of Magdeburg in 1631, and the abdication of Christian Wilhelm in 1638, seem to have made no difference to Scheidt's official position at Halle, though his income and means of living must have suffered; the service in the Hofkirche ceased after 1625, and the Moritzkirche was destroyed by fire in 1637. We have no record as to his personal relations with Christian's successors in the administration of the Magdeburg archbishopric, but Chrysander in the *Jahrbücher für musikalische Wissenschaft*, i. p. 158, prints a letter from Scheidt to Duke Augustus of Brunswick in 1642, which seems to imply that he was then looking for some patronage or assistance from that art-loving prince. Scheidt never left Halle, however, and his circumstances may have improved, as in his will he bequeathed some money for the

sake of the organ in the St. Moritzkirche at Halle. He died at the age of sixty-seven on March 24, 1654.

Scheidt's first published work appeared at Hamburg in 1620 ('Cantiones Sacrae octo vocum'), and consists of thirty-nine vocal compositions, fifteen of which are settings of Lutheran chorales. In 1621-22 appeared the first part of his sacred concertos, in 2-12 vocal parts with instrumental accompaniment. This was followed by successive books of similar pieces, published in 1631, 1634, 1635, and 1640. His fame, however, rests not on his vocal compositions, but on his works for the organ. His next work, also published at Hamburg in 1624, is considered epoch-making in the history of organ music. It consists of three parts, but the whole work bears the general title 'Tabulatura Nova'; the same title, indeed, as many earlier works of the same kind in Germany (*e.g.* Ammerbach, 1571; B. Schmid, 1577; Paix, 1583; Woltz, 1617), from all of which, however, it differs widely both in aim and style, and indeed marks the beginning of a new and better treatment of the organ both with regard to playing and to composition. From 1570 to about 1620, organ playing in Germany almost entirely consisted in what was known as the art of 'coloriren,' the art of 'colouring' melodies sacred or secular by the inserting of meaningless passages, all framed on one and the same pattern, between each note or chord of the melody. These earlier Tablature-books were all compiled simply to teach this purely mechanical art of 'colouring' melodies for the organ. The music was written in the so-called German Tablature, *i.e.* with letters instead of notes.[1] (For a full account of these German 'Coloristen'[2] of the 16th and 17th centuries, see A. G. Ritter's *Geschichte der Orgelmusik*, pp. 111-39.) Scheidt's 'Tabulatura Nova' put an end to this miserable style of playing and composing for the organ, as well as to the old German Tablature. The music in his book is noted in score of four staves, with five lines to the stave, so far differing from the notation both of Frescobaldi and Sweelinck, the former using two staves of six and eight lines respectively, the latter two staves both of six lines. To give an idea of the contents of Scheidt's work, we transcribe in full the separate titles of the three parts :—

I. Tabulatura Nova, continens variationes aliquot Psalmorum, Fantasiarum, Cantilenarum, Passamezo et Canones aliquot, in gratiam Organistarum adornata a Samuele Scheidt Hallense, Reverendiss. Illustrissimique Principis ac Domini, Christiani Guilielmi Archiepiscopi Magdeburgensis, Primatis Germaniae Organista et Capellae Magistro. Hamburgi . . . MDCXXIV.

II. Pars Secunda . . . continens Fugarum, Psalmorum, Cantionum et Echus Tocatae variationes varias et omnimodas. Pro quorumvis Organistarum captu et modulo. . . .

---

[1] For an example of German Organ Tablature, see Schlecht, *Geschichte der Kirchenmusik*, p. 377 ff.

[2] 'Geschmacklose Barbaren' (tasteless barbarians), as Ambros calls them.

III. Tertia et ultima pars, continens Kyrie Dominicale, Credo in unum Deum, Psalmum de Coena Domini sub Communione, Hymnos praecipuorum Festorum totius anni, Magnificat 1–9 toni, modum ludendi pleno Organo et Benedicamus . . . In gratiam Organistarum, praecipue eorum qui musice pure et absque celerrimis coloraturis Organo ludere gaudent . . .

The last words mark an important difference between the third part and the two preceding. In the first two parts the composer appears to wish to show how he could beat the ' Colourists' on their own ground, his figures and passages, however, not being like theirs, absolutely meaningless and void of invention, but new and varied, and having an organic connection with the whole composition to which they belong. He shows himself still as virtuoso, desirous to extend the technique of organ-playing, while at the same time displaying his contrapuntal mastery. So far as technique is concerned, there is to be noticed in Scheidt the extended use of the pedal, so different from Frescobaldi's occasional use of it for single notes merely, also the imitation of orchestral effects, such as what he himself terms ' imitatio violistica,' the imitation of the effects of the different ways of bowing on the violin, and the imitation of an organ tremulant itself by the rapid interchange of the fingers of the two hands on one and the same key ('Bicinium imitatione tremula organi duobus digitis in una tantum clave manu tum dextra, tum sinistra'). The first two parts contain a mixture of sacred and secular pieces, the secular pieces, however, being marked off as for domestic rather than for church use by the absence of a pedal part. The sacred pieces consist of ten fantasias or sets of variations on chorale melodies, with a few fugues or fantasias on another motive, among which is a ' fantasia fuga quadruplici,' on a madrigal of Palestrina's, which Ritter describes as a masterpiece of contrapuntal art, four subjects from the madrigal being treated first singly and then together, and with contrary motion and other devices. The secular pieces consist chiefly of variations on secular melodies, among which appears one entitled an English song ' de fortuna' (i.e. the famous ' Fortune, my foe'). The third part of the ' Tabulatura Nova' stands, however, on a higher level than the first two. The composer expressly renounces the virtuoso; he writes, as the title-page says, for those who delight to play the organ purely musically, and without mere ornamental and passage work. In this third part he gives very full directions with regard to registering both for manuals and pedal. It is intended entirely for church use, and both by the choice of pieces, and the manner in which they are arranged, it gives us an insight into the way in which the organ was very frequently employed in the church services of those days. It was not then generally used to accompany or sustain the voices of the choir or congregation, but rather to alternate with them. Thus,

for instance, between each verse of the ' Magnificat' sung by the choir without accompaniment, the organ would come in independently with some variation or changing harmonies on the plain-song melody. A further use of the organ was even to take the place of the choir in making the responses to the ecclesiastical intonations of the officiating clergy when there was no proper choir to do this. Frescobaldi's works (especially ' Fiori Musicali,' 1635) furnish instances of this use of the organ in the Roman Church. Thus when the priest had intoned the Kyrie of the Mass, in the absence of a proper choir, the organist would answer, as Ambros expresses it, when speaking of Frescobaldi's works of the kind, ' with a kind of artistically-ennobling and enriching echo ' ('mit einer Art von künstlerisch-veredelnden und bereichernden Echo '), that is to say, the organist, taking up the plain-song theme, would not just harmonise it note by note, but treat it in the form of a short polyphonic composition for the organ. (See the quotations from Frescobaldi in Ambros's Geschichte der Musik, iv. pp. 444-50.) The third part of Scheidt's ' Tabulatura' shows that this usage was not confined to the Roman Church, but was also retained for a considerable time in the Lutheran. It opens with twelve short movements based on the plain-song of the different sections of the Kyrie and Gloria of the Mass, and the remark, or rubric, as we might call it, ' Gloria canit Pastor,' shows that they were expressly intended as responses made by the organ to the intonation of officiating clergy. The ' Magnificat' follows, in all the church tones, one verse sung by the ecclesiastic and every alternate verse arranged to be played by the organ in lieu of a choir. This way of treating the ' Magnificat' prevailed in Lutheran Churches, even up to Pachelbel's time (1706), though the plain-song was more and more put into the background, and the practice became simply an excuse for interludes on any motive. After the Magnificat came a series of hymns common to both Roman and Lutheran churches, with their plain-song melodies treated in a similar fashion. The book further contains Luther's version of the Creed ('Wir glauben All' an einen Gott') with its Doric melody, John Huss's Communion Hymn, arranged to be played instead of being sung during Communion. The two last pieces in the book are 6-part movements for the full organ, meant to be played at the end of Vespers. Interwoven with the last is the liturgical melody of the Benedicamus. In all these compositions Scheidt has faithfully adhered to the original plain-song melodies when they appear as Cantus Firmus, but in the further working out has not been content simply to harmonise them according to the laws of the Church modes, but has so far altered them in accordance with the new ideas of harmony then beginning to make way. But

there is still wanting in him a consistent system
of modulation. The chromatic semitones are
still employed by him rather in a haphazard
sort of way.

Twenty-six years later, viz. in 1650, Scheidt
published another work for the organ, hi. second
and last, which shows a different conception as
to the use of the organ in the services of the
Church, and probably marks a change which
was then going on gradually in the practice of
the Lutheran Church. The congregational singing of metrical hymns was gradually superseding
the older liturgical music, and the organ had
more and more to surrender its independence to
accommodate itself to the simple accompaniment
in 4-part harmony of the melodies of these
hymns, which now began to assume exclusively
the name of Choral-musik. This, which was at
first a loss, became in time a gain, as it deepened
the sense of the value of harmony for its own
sake ; and besides, out of this originated the new
art-form of the Choral-Vorspiel of later days.
Scheidt's last organ work was intended to meet
the new requirements.   Its title sufficiently
explains its object : ' Tabulatur-buch 100 geistlicher Lieder u. Psalmen D. Martini Lutheri
und anderer gottseliger Männer für die Herren
Organisten mit der Christlichen Kirchen u.
Gemeine auf der Orgel, desgleichen auch zu Hause
zu spielen u. zu singen, auf alle Fest- u. Sonn- tage
durchs ganze Jahr mit 4 Stimmen componirt
. . . Gedruckt zu Görlitz . . . im 1650 Jahr.'
This work is dedicated to the Magistrates and
Town Council of Görlitz, and the composer
seems to imply that it had been undertaken at
their special desire.   In this, as in his previous
work, there is noticeable, as Ritter points out,
the same undecided struggle in the composer's
mind between attachment to the old and inclination to the new.   Thus, while he strictly
adheres to the original rhythms of the old melodies, he harmonises according to the rules of
modern musical accent, and thus the rhythm of
the melody is not in agreement with the rhythm
implied by the harmony.   See for illustration
his setting of ' Ein' feste Burg ' in Ritter,
Geschichte der Orgel-Musik, p. 19, the first two
bars of which may here be given :—

One chorale appears in this book for the first
time, viz. ' O Jesulein süss, O Jesulein mild,'
which has been adapted in later chorale books
to the words ' O heiliger Geist, O heiliger
Gott.'   As harmonised by Scheidt it is given
in Winterfeld *Ev. K. G.* ii. No. 218, and
Schöberlein, *Schatz des Chorgesangs*, ii. No.
457.

If it is his organ works that now entitle
Scheidt to honourable remembrance, and give
him a distinct position of his own amongst
composers, it was not his organ works, but his
vocal compositions, that procured him the
esteem of his contemporaries, and caused him to
be ranked as one of the celebrated three S's.
Of his vocal works, besides the ' Sacrae Cantiones' of 1620, mentioned above, there are
mentioned ' Liebliche Krafft-Blümlein conzert-
weise mit 2 Stimmen sampt dem General-Basse,'
Halle, 1625. Another work should also be
recorded, consisting of ' Paduana, Galliarda,'
etc. for four and five voices, 1621, the second
part of which was called ' Ludorum musicorum
prima et secunda pars,' and published in 1622.

It is natural to draw comparisons, as Ritter
does in his history above quoted, between
Scheidt and Frescobaldi, whose lives covered
nearly the same period of time, and who may
both be regarded as the true founders of modern
organ music, or rather, the Italian of clavier
music generally, the German of specifically
organ music. Of the two, Frescobaldi is the
greater genius, showing greater force of imagination in the invention of new forms and the
solution of difficult problems ; Scheidt is more
laborious and painstaking, showing greater
study of the capabilities of his instrument, as,
for instance, in the use of the pedal, and in
registering generally, with neither of which
did Frescobaldi concern himself. As Ritter
points out, while Scheidt has thus greater
command of all the resources of expression,
Frescobaldi has more of real poetic expression in
his music itself.   For more detailed comparison
of the two masters it will be sufficient to refer
to Ritter's work. [See Max Seiffert's preface
to the first vol. of the *Denkmäler deutscher
Tonkunst*, containing Scheidt's ' Tabulatura
Nova ' ; the *Vierteljahrsschrift für Musikwiss.*
vii. p. 188 ff.; and the *Sammelbände* of the *Int.
Mus. Ges.* i. p. 401, where a detailed study of
Samuel and Gottfried Scheidt is to be found,
the work of Arno Werner.   Also titles of works
in the *Quellen-Lexikon*.]   J. R. M.

SCHEIN, JOHANN HERMAN, was born Jan.
20, 1586, at Grunhain in Saxony, where his
father was the Lutheran pastor. Having lost
his father at an early age, he was taken to
Dresden and became a chorister in the Court
Chapel there in 1599. His further education
was received at the Gymnasium of Schulpforta
in 1603 and the University of Leipzig (1607).
Of his musical training further than what he
received in the Court Chapel at Dresden we
have no details. In 1615 he was invited to
be capellmeister at Weimar, but held this
post for only two years. On the death of Seth
Calvisius in November 1615 he obtained the
appointment of Cantor to the Thomasschule in
Leipzig, which post he held till his death Nov.
19, 1630.

Schein is chiefly known to later times by his 'Cantional,' first published in 1627. Its original title is 'Cantional oder Gesangbuch Augspurgischer Confession, in welchem des Herrn D. Martini Lutheri vnd anderer frommen Christen, auch des Autoris eigne Lieder vnd Psalmen. . . . So im Chur- vnd Fürstenthümern Sachsen, insonderheit aber in beiden Kirchen und Gemeinen allhier zu Leipzig gebräuchlich, verfertiget und mit 4, 5, 6 Stimmen componirt.' A second (enlarged) edition appeared in 1645 after Schein's death. As the title shows, it consists of Choral-melodies, both old and new, harmonised for ordinary church use, mostly note against note. Schein himself appears in this book in three capacities, viz. as poet, melodist, and harmonist. Of the 200 and odd Choral-melodies in the book about 80 are Schein's own, a few of which have still held their ground in modern chorale books, though some appear to be attributed to him by mistake. Schein's book differs from Crüger's similar book of later date (1648) in retaining the old irregular rhythm of Choral-melodies, while Crüger has transformed their rhythms according to more modern ideas. But if Schein still retains the old rhythm in the melodies, in his harmonies he has almost entirely lost, as Winterfeld points out, the feeling for the peculiarities of the old church modes in which those melodies are written, though otherwise his harmonies are serious and dignified. With Michael Praetorius and Heinrich Schütz, and probably through their influence, Schein was one of the pioneers in Germany of the new movement in music proceeding from Italy at the beginning of the 17th century. Naturally his other works show this more plainly than the 'Cantional,' as many of them are avowedly written in imitation of Italian models. These other works are as follows :—

1. Venus-Kränzlein mit allerley lieblichen und schönen Blumen gezieret und gewunden, oder Neue Weltliche Lieder mit 5 Stimmen, neben etlichen Intraden, Gagliarden, und Canzonen . . . Leipzig, 1609. This work consists of sixteen secular strophic songs a 5 and one a 8, in the simplest Italian canzonetta style, homophonic throughout, besides eight instrumental pieces a 5 and 6.

2. Cymbalum Sionium sive Cantiones Sacrae 5, 6, 8, 10 et 12 vocum. Leipzig, 1615. This work contains thirty sacred motets, some to Latin texts, some to German, besides an instrumental canzone a 5 as Corollarium.

3. Banchetto Musicale, neuer anmuthiger Padouanen, Gagliarden, Courenten und Allemanden a 5 auf allerley Instrumenten, bevorans auf Violen nicht ohne sonderbare gratia lieblich und lustig zu gebrauchen . . . Leipzig, 1617. This work was dedicated to Duke Johann Ernst of Weimar, and contains twenty instrumental suites consisting of Paduanas, Gagliardas, Courentes a 5 and Allemande and Tripla a 4, with two separate pieces at the end.

4. Opella Nova, erster Theil Geistlicher Concerten mit 3, 4 und 5 Stimmen zusampt dem General-Bass auf jetzo gebräuchliche Italienische Invention componirt, Leipzig, 1618. This work contains thirty sacred compositions on German texts in the new Italian style, with instrumental basso continuo, which, however, seems to be purely ad libitum.

5. Musica Boscareccia, Waldliederlein auf Italian-Villanellische Invention, Beides für sich allein mit lebendiger Stim, oder in ein Clavicembel, Spinet, Tiorba, Lauten, etc. This work appeared in three parts published in 1621, 1626, 1628 respectively, and contains altogether fifty secular compositions a 3 on poems by Schein himself written in the artificial pastoral style of the time. These pieces are more polyphonic in their character than those of the 'Venus-Kränzlein,' and, as the title indicates, they may be sung by voices alone or with the substitution of instruments for one or other of the vocal parts or instrumental accompaniment generally. A new edition of the work appeared in 1644, with the substitution of sacred texts for the original secular.

6. Fontana d' Israel, Israels Brünlein auserlesener Kraft-sprüch-lein altes und neuen Testaments von 5 und 6 Stimmen sambt dem General Bass auf eine sonderbare anmutige Italian-Madrigalische Manier sowol für sich allein mit lebendiger Stim und Instrumenten als auch in die Orgel Clavicembel bequemlich zugebrauchen. Leipzig, 1623. This work consists of twenty-six sacred pieces a 5 and 6, on German texts, composed in the later freer Madrigal style of Monteverde and others, allowing greater boldness of harmonic progression.

7. Diletti pastorali, Hirten Lust von 5 Stim. zusampt dem General-Bass auf Madrigal Manier. Leipzig, 1624. 15 Nos.

8. Studenten-Schmaus a 5. Leipzig, 1626. 5 Nos.

9. Opella Nova, Ander Theil Geistlicher Concerten. Leipzig, 1626. Contains thirty-two sacred pieces, twenty-seven with German texts, five with Latin.

Besides these works, and the Cantional of 1627, the *Quellen-Lexikon* enumerates a large number of occasional compositions for weddings and funerals, many of which, however, Schein himself incorporated into the publications above specified.

In 1895 Herr Arthur Prüfer published a monograph on Schein's Life and Works, by way of preparation for a complete edition of his works, two volumes of which have since appeared, containing the 'Venus-Kränzlein,' 'Banchetto Musicale,' and 'Musica Boscareccia.'   J. R. M.

SCHELBLE, JOHANN NEPOMUK, a thoroughly excellent and representative German musician, born May 16, 1789, at Hüfingen, in the Black Forest, where his father was superintendent of the House of Correction. His strict musical education was begun in a Monastery at March-thal 1800-3 ; and continued at Donaueschingen, under Weisse. He then spent some time, first with Vogler at Darmstadt, and then with Krebs, a distinguished singer at Stuttgart, and there, in 1812, he filled the post of elementary teacher in the Royal Musical Institution, a very famous and complete school of those times.[1] In 1813 he went to Vienna, lived in intimate acquaintance with Beethoven, Moscheles, Weigl, Spohr, etc., composed an opera and many smaller works, and went on the stage, where, however, his singing, though remarkable, was neutralised by his want of power to act. From Austria in 1816 he went to Frankfort, which became his home. Here the beauty of his voice, the excellence of his method, and the justness of his expression, were at once recognised. He became the favourite teacher, and in 1817 was made director of the Musical Academy. This, however, proved too desultory for his views, and on July 24, 1818, he formed a Society of his own, which developed into the famous 'Caecilian Society' of Frankfort, and at the head of which he remained till his death. The first work chosen by the infant institution was the 'Zauberflöte' ; then Mozart's Requiem ; then one of his Masses ; and then works by Handel, Cherubini, Bach, etc. In 1821 the Society assumed the name of the 'Cäcilienverein' ; the répertoire was increased by works of Palestrina, Scarlatti, and other Italian masters, and at length, on March 10, 1828, Mozart's 'Davidde penitente' and the Credo of Bach's Mass in B minor were given ; then, May 2, 1829 (stimulated by the example of Mendelssohn in Berlin), the Matthew Pas-

[1] See the *A.M.Z.* 1812, p. 334.

sion ; and after that we hear of ' Samson ' and other oratorios of Handel, Bach's motets, and choruses of Mendelssohn, whose genius Schelble was one of the first to recognise, and whose ' St. Paul ' was suggested to him by the Caecilian Association, doubtless on the motion of its conductor. Whether the Society ever attempted Beethoven's mass does not appear, but Schelble was one of the two private individuals who answered Beethoven's invitation to subscribe for its publication. [See vol. i. p. 255, note 6 ; vol. iii. p. 131a.]

His health gradually declined, and at length, in the winter of 1835, it was found necessary to make some new arrangement for the direction of the Society. Mendelssohn was asked (*Letters*, Feb. 18, 1836), and undertook it for six weeks during the summer of 1836. Mendelssohn's fondness and esteem for the man whose place he was thus temporarily filling is evident in every sentence referring to him in his letters of this date. Schelble died August 7, 1837. His great qualities as a practical musician, a conductor, and a man, are well summed up by Hiller [1] in his book on Mendelssohn, to which we refer the reader. His compositions have not survived him. His biography was published shortly after his death—*J. N. Schelble*, von Weissmann (Frankfort, 1838). G.

SCHELLER, JAKOB, born at Schettal, Rakonitz, Bohemia, May 16, 1759, a very clever violinist. He was thrown on his own resources from a very early age, and we hear of him at Prague, Vienna, and Mannheim, where he remained for two years playing in the court band, and learning composition from Vogler. After more wandering he made a stay of three years in Paris, studying the school of Viotti. He then, in 1785, took a position as *Concertmeister*, or leading violin, in the Duke of Würtemberg's band at Montbéliard, which he held until the establishment was broken up by the arrival of the French in 1792. This forced him to resume his wandering life, and that again drove him to intemperance, till after seven or eight years more he ended miserably, being even obliged to borrow a fiddle at each town he came to.[2] He was more celebrated for his tricks and *tours de force* than for his legitimate playing. Spohr (*Selbstbiog.* i. 280) speaks of his flageolet-tones, of variations on one string, of pizzicato with the nails of the left hand, of imitations of a bassoon, an old woman, etc. ; and Fétis mentions a trick in which by loosening the bow he played on all four strings at once. By these, and probably also by really fine playing, he excited so much enthusiasm, that it used to be said of him ' one God ; one Scheller.' G.

SCHEMELLI, GEORG CHRISTIAN, born at Herzberg about 1678, was a pupil of the Thomasschule at Leipzig from 1695, and was cantor of

the castle at Zeitz. In 1736 he published a ' Musicalisches Gesang-Buch, Darinnen 954 geistreiche, sowohl alte als neue Lieder und Arien, mit wohlgesetzten Melodien, in Discant und Bass, befindlich sind . . . ' In the preface the compiler states that the tunes in his book were partly newly composed, partly improved, by J. S. Bach. Various authorities on the life of Bach have spent much labour in investigating which were the tunes newly composed by him, and which were merely revised and corrected by him. While Spitta attributes twenty-nine out of the sixty-nine tunes to Bach, Herr F. Wüllner, the editor of the volume of the Bach-Gesellschaft (xxxix.) in which the hymns appear, considers that only twenty-four are Bach's ; while Eitner, in the *Quellen-Lexikon*, assigns only twenty-two to the master. His name, curiously enough, is appended to only one of the sacred songs of which the collection mainly consists (the beautiful ' Vergiss mein nicht,' above which is written, ' di J. S. Bach, D. M. Lips.' See S. Spitta, *J. S. Bach*, Eng. trans. i. 367-70 ; iii. 109-114.) M.

SCHENK, JOHANN, (I) was a viol-da-gamba player in the service of the Elector Palatine at Düsseldorf in the latter part of the 17th century. He was afterwards at Amsterdam, where he published numerous works for his instrument, and other compositions. The following are known to have existed, but only a few of them are still extant, according to the *Quellen-Lexikon* :—

Op.
1. Airs from an opera, ' Ceres en Bachus.'
2. Konstoeffeningen (sonatas or suites).
3. Il giardino armonico, sonate da camera *a* 4 (two vlns., gamba, and continuo).
4. Koninklyke Harpliederen, 150 airs for one or two voices, with a prelude and postlude.
6. Scherzi musicali, for viol da gamba and bass.
7. Eighteen sonatas for violin and bass.
8. La ninfa del Reno, twelve sonatas or suites.
9. L'écho du Danube, sonatas.
10. Les Fantaisies bisarres de la goutte, twelve sonatas for viol da gamba.

(*Quellen-Lexikon* ; Riemann's *Lexikon*.) M.

SCHENK, JOHANN, (II) is mainly interesting from his connection with Beethoven ; he was born of poor parents, Nov. 30, 1753,[3] at Wiener Neustadt in Lower Austria, and at an early age was admitted into the Archbishop's choir at Vienna. [In 1774 he was a pupil of Wagenseil.] In 1778 he produced his first mass, which he followed by other sacred pieces, and by many Singspiele and Operas [beginning with ' Die Weinlese,' 1785, and ' Die Weihnacht auf dem Lande,' 1786, and ending with ' Der Fassbinder,' 1802], which gained him a considerable name, and rank with those of Dittersdorf and Wenzel Müller. In addition he wrote symphonies, concertos, quartets, lieder, etc. The autographs of many of these are in the Gesellschaft der Musikfreunde at Vienna, with that of a theoretical work, *Grundsätze des Generalbasses*. [In 1794 he was appointed music-

---

[1] *Mendelssohn*, translated by Miss M. E. von Glehn, p. 8.
[2] Rochlitz, *Für Freunde der Tonkunst*, ii.

[3] So in Riemann's *Lexikon*; Eitner (*Quellen-Lexikon*) gives the date as 1761.

director to Prince Carl von Auersperg; in
1795 his 'Achmet und Almanzine' was brought
out at Vienna, and finally 'Der Dorfbarbier' was
produced at the Kärnthnerthor Theatre, Nov. 7,
1796, a work that was always popular, and
kept its position in the repertory for many
years. Between this, his masterpiece, and
the 'Fassbinder,' already mentioned, came 'Der
Bettelstudent' (1796) and 'Die Jagd' (1797).]
The anecdote of his kissing Mozart's hand during
the overture on the first night of the 'Zauberflöte'
has been already related. [See MOZART, vol. iii.
p. 300a, note 1.] His first meeting with Beethoven
is told in Bauernfeld's biographical sketch of
Schenk in the *Wiener Zeitschrift für Kunst* for
1837 (Nos. 5, 6, and 7). Gelinek mentioned to
Schenk that he had found a young man whose
playing excelled anything ever heard before,
excepting Mozart's, and who had been studying
counterpoint for six months with Haydn, but
to so little purpose that it would be a great
kindness if Schenk would give him some help.
A meeting was arranged at Gelinek's house,
when Beethoven improvised for over half an
hour in so remarkable and unusual a manner
that forty years afterwards Schenk could not
speak of it without emotion. Schenk next went
to see the young artist. Himself a model of
neatness, he was rather taken aback by the
disorderliness of the room, but Beethoven's
reception was cordial and animated. On the
desk lay some short exercises in counterpoint,
in which on the first glance Schenk detected a
few errors. Beethoven's troubles soon came
out. He had come to Vienna aware of his own
ability, but anxious to learn; had at once put
himself in the hands of the first master to be
got, and yet was making no progress. Schenk
at once agreed to help him, and took him
through Fux's 'Gradus ad Parnassum,' with
which indeed Haydn was familiar enough. As
it was essential that Haydn should not be entirely thrown over, Beethoven copied exercises
partly corrected by Schenk,[1] and Haydn was
then able to congratulate himself on the progress
of his hot-headed pupil. The affair was of course
kept strictly secret, but Beethoven having fallen
out with Gelinek the latter gossiped, and
Schenk was deeply annoyed. Beethoven, however, when on the point of following Haydn to
Eisenstadt, wrote very gratefully to Schenk,[2]
and the two remained on pleasant terms. It is
interesting to know that besides Mozart and
Beethoven, Schenk was acquainted with Schubert.
Bauernfeld introduced them, and so congenial
were they that after an hour's talk they parted
like old friends.

Very unassuming in his ways, Schenk was

[1] This surely says a great deal for Beethoven's patience, and for his desire not to offend Haydn.
[2] 'I wish I were not starting to-day for Eisenstadt. I should like to have had more talk with you. In the meantime you may count upon my gratitude for the kindness you have shown me. I shall do all in my power to return it. I hope to see you and enjoy your society again soon. Farewell, and do not forget your BEET-MOVEN.'

respected as a thorough though somewhat
pedantic teacher of the piano and composition.
His portrait, in the Museum of the Gesellschaft
der Musikfreunde in Vienna, shows a pleasing
countenance. [Two cantatas, 'Die Huldigung'
and 'Die Mai,' his last complete compositions,
date from 1819] and at an advanced age he set
about remodelling his 'Jagd,' for which he got
Bauernfeld to write him a new libretto. He
had finished the first act when he died, Dec.
29, 1836.   C. F. P.

SCHERZANDO, SCHERZOSO, playful,
lively; a direction of frequent occurrence, indicating a passage of a light and cheerful
character. It is occasionally used, in combination with some other direction, to indicate the
style of a whole movement, as *Allegro scherzando*,
Allegretto scherzando (Beethoven, Symphony
No. 8), etc., but its more usual and characteristic application is to a phrase which is to be
played in a lively manner, in contrast to the
rest of the movement or to some other phrase.
In such passages, as a rule, the time is intended
to be taken more freely than usual, while any
marks of phrasing which occur should be strictly
adhered to. In fact the phrasing of a *scherzando*
passage is of paramount importance, for by it
alone can the proper character be given.—The
word is found, where one would little expect it,
in the old editions of Beethoven's Mass in D,
near the beginning of the 'Et vitam venturi';
but on reference to Breitkopf & Härtel's complete
edition it turns out to have been read in error
for *sforzando*!   M.

SCHERZO. An Italian word signifying 'jest'
or 'joke.' Its application in music is extensive,
and—as is the case with many other musical
titles—often incorrect. Most of the movements, from the time of Mendelssohn onwards,
would be better designated as 'Caprices' or
'Capriccios.' Obviously the word signifies that
the piece to which it applies is not merely of a
light and gay character, but is of the nature of
a joke, in that it possesses that rare quality in
music, humour. But, exclusive of Haydn and
Beethoven, what musician shows humour, real
unaffected drollery, in his music?

The term seems to have been first employed
(Scherzando) merely as a direction for performance, but there are early instances of its use as
a distinctive title. The light Italian canzonets
popular in Germany in the 17th century were
called *Scherzi musicali*. Late in the 17th
century Johann Schenk published some 'Scherzi
musicali per la viola di gamba.' Later, when
each movement of an instrumental composition
had to receive a distinctive character, the directions *Allegretto scherzando* and *Presto scherzando*
became common, several examples occurring in
the Sonatas of Ph. Em. Bach. But even in
the 'Partitas' of his great father, we find a
Scherzo preceded by a Burlesca and a Fantaisie,
though some modern ears can discover little of

humour or fancy in either of these. Many of the Gigues are far more frolicsome than these.

Coming to the period of the Symphony it may be as well to remind the reader of a fact which will be more enlarged upon under that heading, namely, that the presence of the Minuet or Scherzo in works of the symphonic class, is a matter of natural selection, or survival of the fittest. In the old Suites the Minuet, being of rather shorter rhythm than the other dances, was seized upon, perhaps unconsciously, by the great masters who tied themselves down to the old form, and was exaggerated out of all recognition for the sake of contrast. The actual Minuet, as danced from the 16th century up to the present day (if any one still learns it), is in the time of that famous specimen in Mozart's 'Don Juan,' or say M.M. ♩= 80. Yet even in the Suites of Bach one finds quick and slow Minuets, neither having any regard to the requirements of the dance. [The slow tempo was obligatory only where dancing was concerned ; quicker Minuets were recognised in quite early days.] When we come to Haydn the term Minuet ceases to have any meaning ; the stateliness and character of the dance are quite gone, and what we should call a Waltz appears. But with the true instinct of an artist, Haydn felt that in a work containing such heavy subtleties (for even Haydn was deemed heavy and subtle once) as the ordinary first movement and slow movement, a piece of far lighter character was imperatively demanded. So lighter and quicker and more sportive grew the Minuets, till Beethoven crowned the incongruous fashion with the 'Minuet' of this First Symphony. It should be mentioned, however, that Mozart never departed nearly so far from the true Minuet as Haydn, whose gaiety of musical thought drove him into really inventing the Scherzo, though he did not use the name. The Minuets of many of the String Quartets of Haydn exhibit indeed those quaint and fanciful devices of unexpected reiteration, surprises of rhythm, and abrupt terminations, which are the leading characteristics of the Scherzo, and are completely opposed to the spirit of the true Minuet. One which begins and ends each part with these bars

8ve basso.

is a strong instance in point.

Beethoven quickly gave the Scherzo the permanent position in the Symphony which it now occupies. He also settled its form and character. It is a good answer to those who consider the classical forms worn out and irksome to the flow of inspiration to point out that in the Scherzo, where full rein is given to the individual

caprice of the musician, there is as much attention given to construction as anywhere. In fact, either the bold and masculine First-movement form, or its sister, the weaker and more feminine Rondo form, *must* be the backbone of every piece of music with any pretensions to the name. But, lest the light and airy character of the Scherzo should be spoilt by the obtrusion of the machinery, the greater composers have sought to obscure the form artistically by several devices, the most frequent and obvious being the humorous persistent dwelling on some one phrase—generally the leading feature of the first subject—and introducing it in and out of season, mixed up with any or all of the other subjects. Witness the Scherzo of Beethoven's Ninth Symphony, where the opening phrase for the drums is used as an accompaniment to the second subject—indeed as a persistent 'motto' throughout. Apart from this there is not the slightest departure from rigid First-movement form in this great movement.

The Trio, which is a relic of the Minuet and takes the position of third subject or middle section in a Rondo, survives because of the naturally felt want of a contrast to the rapid rhythm of the Scherzo. Many modern composers affect to dispense with it, but there is usually a central section answering to it, even though it be not divided off from the rest by a double bar. Mendelssohn has been the most successful in writing Scherzos without Trios. The main idea was to have a movement in extremely short and marked rhythm, for which purpose triple time is of course the best. In the Pianoforte Sonatas the Scherzo to that in E♭ (op. 31, No. 3) is the only instance where Beethoven has employed 2–4. The Trios to the Scherzos of the Pastoral and Choral Symphonies are 2–4 and C for special reasons of effect and contrast. It may be worth noticing that Beethoven invariably writes 3–4 even where 6–8 or 3–8 could equally well have been employed. This is no doubt in order that the written notes should appeal to the eye as much as the sounded notes to the ear. In fact three crotchets, with their separate stems, impress far more vividly on the mind of the player the composer's idea of tripping lightness and quick rhythm than three quavers with united tails. Having once ousted the Minuet, Beethoven seldom re-introduced it, the instances in which he has done so being all very striking, and showing that a particularly fine idea drove him to use a worn-out means of expression. In several cases (PF. Sonatas in E♭, op. 7 ; in F, op. 10, etc.) where there is no element of humour, he has abstained from the idle mockery of calling the movement a Minuet, because it is not a Scherzo, as others have done ; yet, on the other hand, the third movements of both the First Fourth, and Eighth Symphonies are called Minuets while having little or nothing in common with even the Symphony Minuets of Haydn and Mozart. Amongst Beethoven's endless devices for novelty should be noticed the famous treatment of the Scherzo in the C minor Symphony ; its conversion into a weird and mysterious terror, and its sudden reappearance, all alive and well again, in the midst of the tremendous jubilation of the Finale. Symphony No. 8, too, presents some singular features. The second movement is positively a cross between a slow movement and a Scherzo, partaking equally of the sentimental and the humorous. But the Finale is nothing else than a rollicking Scherzo, teeming with eccentricities and practical jokes from beginning to end, the opening jest (and *secret* of the movement) being the sudden unexpected entry of the basses with a tremendous C sharp, afterwards turned into D flat, and the final one, the repetition of the chord of F at great length as if for a conclusion, and then, when the hearer naturally thinks that the end is reached, a start off in another direction with a new coda and wind-up.

As a specimen of true Scherzo—that is, a movement in strict form and with quaint and whimsical humorous devices springing up unexpectedly, but naturally, throughout, — the Scherzo of the Ninth Symphony must ever stand without a rival. The tiny phrase which is the nucleus of the whole is eccentrically introduced, and prepares us at the outset for all manner of starts and surprises. The idea of using the drums for this phrase seems to have tickled Beethoven's fancy, as he repeats it again and again.

Humour is more unexpected in Schubert than in Beethoven, and perhaps because of its unexpectedness we appreciate it the more. The Scherzo of the C major Symphony is full of happy thoughts and surprises, as fine as any of Beethoven's, and yet distinct from them. The varied changes of rhythm in two, three, and four bars, the piquant use of the wood wind, and above all the sudden and lovely gleam of sunshine

Flute.

Oboe.

combine to place this movement among the things imperishable. The Scherzos of the Octet, the Quintet in C, and above all, the PF. Duet in C, which Joachim has restored to its rightful dignity of Symphony, are all worthy of honour. The last named, with its imitations by inversion of the leading phrase, and its grotesque bass

is truly comical.

It is much to be regretted that the more modern composers have lost sight of the true bearing of the Scherzo so completely. Mendelssohn indeed has given it an elfish fairy character, but though this is admirable in the ' Midsummer Night's Dream,' it is perhaps a little out of place elsewhere. Lightness and airy grace his Scherzos possess to admiration, in common with his Capriccios, which they closely resemble ; but the musical humour which vents itself in unexpected rhythms and impudent upstartings of themes in strange places, neither he nor any later composer seems to have had an idea of. Mendelssohn has not used the title 'Scherzo' to either of his five symphonies, though the 'Vivace non troppo' of the *Scotch*, the ' Allegretto ' of the *Lobgesang*, and the ' Allegro Vivace ' of the *Reformation* are usually called ' Scherzos.' It is sufficient to name the String Octet, the two PF. Trios and the two Quintets for Strings, as a few of his works which contain the most striking specimens in this line. As before mentioned, his Capriccios for Piano are pieces of the same order, and No. 4 of the ' Sieben Charakter-stücke' (op. 7) may be classed with them.

With Schumann we find ourselves again in a new field. Humour, his music seldom, if ever, presents, and he is really often far less gay in his Scherzos than elsewhere. He introduced the innovation of two Trios in his B♭ and C Symphonies, PF. Quintet, and other works, but although this practice allows more scope to the fancy of the composer in setting forth strongly contrasted movements in related rhythm, it is to be deprecated as tending to give undue length and consequent heaviness to what should be the lightest and most epigrammatic of music. Beethoven has repeated the Trios of his Fourth and Seventh Symphonies, but that is quite another thing. Still, though Schumann's Scherzos are wanting in lightness, their originality is more than compensation. The Scherzos of his orchestral works suffer also from heavy and sometimes unskilful instrumentation, but in idea and treatment are full of charm. Several of his Kreisleriana and other small PF. pieces are to all intents and purposes Scherzos.

Though the modern composers have not produced many remarkable Scherzos, it is not for want of trying. Rubinstein has a very pretty idea in 6-4 time in his Pianoforte Octet, and a very odd one in his A major Trio. The ' Ocean ' Symphony has two Scherzos, in excellent contrast, the first being in 2-4 time, and slightly Schumannish, and the second in 3-4 time, with quite a Beethoven flavour. The first of these is not, however, entitled Scherzo by the composer any more than is the second movement of his 'Dramatic' Symphony.

Unlike Schubert and Beethoven, Brahms seldom wrote a really bright Scherzo, but he published one for PF. solo (op. 4) which is very odd and striking. [It was the work which undoubtedly persuaded Liszt to include Brahms among the partisans of the 'advanced school,' a mistake which had many curious consequences. The PF. sonata (op. 5) has a Scherzo of wonderful vigour.] The Second Symphony has a movement which is a combination of Minuet and Scherzo, and certainly one of his most charming ideas. On somewhat the same principle is the Scherzo of the second String Sextet (op. 36) which begins in 2-4 as a kind of Gavotte, while the Trio is 3-4 Presto, thus reversing the ordinary practice of making the Trio broader and slower than the rest of the piece.

Quite on a pedestal of their own stand the four Scherzos for piano by Chopin. They are indeed no joke in any sense ; the first has been entitled 'Le Banquet infernal,' and all four are characterised by a wild power and grandeur to which their composer seldom attained.

Among other productions may be noticed the Scherzo for orchestra by Goldmark, the so-called Intermezzo of Goetz's Symphony, the Scherzos in Dvořák's Sextet, and other chamber works. We have omitted mention of the strangely instrumented 'Queen Mab' Scherzo of Berlioz—more of a joke in orchestration than anything.

The position of the Scherzo in the Symphony—whether second or third of the four movements—is clearly a matter of individual taste, the sole object being contrast. Beethoven, in the large majority of cases, places it third, as affording relief from his mighty slow movements, whereas most modern composers incline to place it as a contrast between the first and slow movements. The matter is purely arbitrary.   F. C.

SCHETKY, JOHANN GEORG CHRISTOFF, a composer, and an excellent performer on the violoncello. He was born at Hesse-Darmstadt in 1740, and was the son of Louis Schetky, secretary and musician to the Landgrave there. J. G. C. Schetky was intended for the law, but developed musical abilities and became locally famous. He travelled to Italy and France, and obtained recognition and patronage at various courts. He returned to Hesse-Darmstadt, but after the death of the Landgrave set out for London. Robert Bremner, the music-publisher, having been commissioned by the gentlemen directors of St. Cecilia's Hall, Edinburgh, to engage a first violoncellist for the concerts held there, met Schetky at Lille, and brought him to Edinburgh, where he arrived in Feb. 1772, and there spent the remainder of a long life. He played at the Edinburgh concerts, and became associated with the musical life there. He was a friend of Robert Burns, and

at the latter's request set to music his song, 'Clarinda, mistress of my soul,' printed with the music in the second volume of Johnson's *Scots Museum*, 1788. In 1774 Schetky married the daughter of Joseph Reinagle, senior, the Austrian musician, who was then settled in Edinburgh. He had several children by this marriage, one of whom, John Christian Schetky, was marine painter to George IV. and to Queen Victoria. Schetky, the musician, died in Edinburgh on Nov. 29, 1824, aged eighty-four, and was buried in the Canongate burial-ground. His published works consist of concertos, duets, trios, etc., for strings, and some harpsichord sonatas. They were principally, if not all, published by Robert Bremner. A MS. oratorio, 'Die verschmachtende Verspottung des zum Tode verurtheilten Heylandes,' is at Darmstadt. For some details of his life see *Life of John C. Schetky, late Marine Painter*, by his daughter, and *St. Cecilia's Hall*, by David Fraser Harris, Edinburgh, 1899.   F. K.

SCHICHT, JOHANN GOTTFRIED, born at Reichenau, Zittau, Sept. 29, 1753, owed his education to an uncle ; went to Leipzig University in 1776, intending to study law, but gradually adopted music, and was soon chosen by Adam Hiller as solo clavier player at his concerts. On Hiller's retirement he succeeded him in 1785, and at length in 1810 rose to the head of his profession as Cantor of the Thomasschule. He died Feb. 16, 1823, leaving many large works (three oratorios, much church and chamber music), as well as a translation of the PF. Schools of Pleyel and Clementi, and of Pellegrini-Celoni's Singing Method, etc., but only one which will live, his edition of J. S. Bach's motets (Breitkopf & Härtel, 1802-3).   G.

SCHICKHARD, or SCHICKARD, JOHANN CHRISTIAN, a composer resident at Hamburg about 1730. His works were chiefly published at Amsterdam, but were republished by the elder John Walsh in England. They comprise instrumental pieces, including : solos for a flute and bass, op. 17 ; concertos for flutes, op. 19 ; solos for German flute, hautboy, or violin, op. 20 ; sonatas for two violins and a bass, op. 5 ; sonatas for two German flutes and a bass, op. 10 ; and some others. These were all published by Walsh, and reissued by Randall.   F. K.

SCHICKSALSLIED ('Song of Destiny'), a short cantata or ode for chorus and orchestra, words by Friedrich Hölderlin, music by Brahms, op. 54. It was first performed from manuscript by the Carlsruhe Philharmonic Society, under the composer's direction, Oct. 18, 1871. It was published by Simrock in the following December, and was performed early in 1872 at Leipzig, Bremen, Breslau, Frankfort, and Vienna. First performed in England by the Cambridge University Musical Society, March 8, 1877.   M.

SCHIEDMAYER. There are now two firms

of this name in Stuttgart, both enjoying wide reputation as pianoforte-makers, viz. 'Schiedmayer & Sons,' and 'Schiedmayer Pianofortefabrik ; vormals, J. & P. Schiedmayer.' The heads of these firms are the grandsons and great-grandsons of Johann David Schiedmayer, who towards the close of the 18th century was a musical instrument maker at Erlangen, and afterwards at Nuremberg, where he died in 1806. His son Johann Lorenz (born 1786) went after this for two years to Vienna as a workman, and in 1809 established a business at Stuttgart in partnership with C. F. Dieudonné (who died in 1825). Before that time pianoforte-making was virtually unknown in Stuttgart, those who required satisfactory instruments obtaining them from Vienna. Lorenz Schiedmayer's intelligence and aptness for business gained a position for his firm, and it soon became one of the first in Germany. In 1845 Lorenz united his two eldest sons, Adolf and Hermann, to himself, and 'Schiedmayer & Sons' soon became as well known in foreign countries as in Würtemberg. Lorenz died in 1860 and his son Hermann in 1861. The sons of the brothers Adolf (1820-1890) and Hermann, bearing the same Christian names, have been for many years the directors of this firm, which has made both concert and ordinary instruments, and has competed with success in London and Paris and other exhibitions. The two younger sons, Julius (1822-78) and Paul (died June 18, 1890) at first devoted themselves to harmonium-making, then of recent introduction, a practical knowledge of which had been gained by Paul in Paris. They started together in 1854, but after the death of the father, in 1860, turned to pianoforte-making in competition with the elder firm, and the younger firm is now known as 'Schiedmayer, Pianoforte-fabrik.'

Special mention must be made of Julius Schiedmayer's prominence as an expert in the Juries of the great Exhibitions of London, 1862 ; Paris, 1867 ; Vienna, 1873 ; and Philadelphia, 1876.   A. J. H.

SCHIEVER, ERNST, violinist, was born at Hanover on March 23, 1844. Studied under Joachim, 1860-64. In 1868 joined the Müller Quartet, with which he travelled as leader until its dissolution in 1869, and became in the same year a teacher at the Hochschule and a member of the Joachim Quartet. Remained in Berlin two years, organising with Hermann Franke (second violin), Leonhard Wolff (viola), and Robert Hausmann (violoncello) another quartet party, which was engaged subsequently by Count Hochberg, and became known as the 'Gräflich Hochberg Quartet' of Schloss Rohnstock near Striegau in Silesia. Came to England in 1878, making Liverpool his headquarters, and undertaking the leadership of the Richter orchestra, with which he has been connected for nearly thirty years. His sympathy with chamber music remains constant, the 'Schiever Quartet,' in which he is associated with A. Ross (second violin), Carl Courvoisier (viola), and Walter Hatton (violoncello), being an institution favourably known in the north of England.   w. w. c.

SCHIKANEDER, EMMANUEL, theatrical manager, playwright, actor, and singer, born 1751 at Ratisbon, began life as a poor wandering musician, joined some strolling players at Augsburg in 1773, married the adopted daughter of the manager, and at length undertook the direction himself. In 1780 his wanderings brought him to Salzburg, where he fell in with the Mozarts, and at once began to make a profit out of Wolfgang's talents. In 1784 we find him in Vienna, giving with Kumpf a series of excellent performances of German opera, comedy, etc., at the Kärnthnerthor theatre. He appeared on the boards both here and at the Burgtheater, where, however, he did not succeed. He next took the management of the theatre at Ratisbon, but was recalled to Vienna by his wife, who had undertaken the little theatre lately built in the grounds of Prince Starhemberg's house in the suburb of Wieden, for which Schikaneder received a *privilegium* or licence.[1] He had no scruples as to the means to be adopted to make a hit, but in spite of large receipts was continually in difficulty. On one such occasion (March 1791) he had recourse to Mozart, whom he implored to set to music a libretto adapted by himself from a piece by Giesecke, a member of his company. Mozart, always good-natured, especially to a brothermason, consented, and from that moment till its completion Schikaneder stuck closely to him, and did all he could to keep him amused over his work. The history of the 'Zauberflöte' is well known ; Schikaneder made various suggestions in the composition, took the part of Papageno, and found himself saved from ruin by the success of the opera ; but he showed little gratitude to Mozart, and after his death, instead of helping the widow of the man by whom he had benefited so materially, contented himself with loud and vain lamentations. In 1800 he entered into partnership with a merchant named Zitterbarth, who at a short distance from the small theatre just mentioned, built the present 'Theater an-der-Wien,' opened June 13, 1801. Zitterbarth then bought the *privilegium* from Schikaneder, who managed it for him till 1806. His next project was to build, with the assistance of some wealthy friends, a new theatre in the Josephstadt suburb, but this he did not carry out. On his way to Pesth, whither he had been invited to undertake a theatre, he went mad, was brought back to Vienna, and died in great misery Sept. 21, 1812.

Schikaneder wrote the librettos for many

[1] It was popularly called Schikaneder's theatre.

popular operas, Singspiele, and fairy-pieces, the list of which, with year of performance, is here published for the first time :—

'Anton der dumme Gärtner' (Schack and Gerl), 1789 ; 'Die beiden Antons' (with 4 sequels), 'Jakob und Nannerl,' and 'Der Stein der Weisen,' or 'Die Zauberinsel' (Schack and others), 1790 ; 'Die Zauberflöte' (Mozart), 1791 ; 'Der wohlthätige Derwisch,' or 'Die Schellenkappe' (Schack, Gerl, and others), 1792 ; 'Die Eisenkönigin,' 'Die Waldmänner,' and 'Der Zauberpfeil' (Lickl), 1793 ; 'Der Spiegel von Arkadien' (Süssmayer), and 'Die Hirten am Rhein,' 1794 ; 'Der Scheerenschleifer' (Henneberg), 'Der Königssohn aus Ithaka' (A. F. Hoffmeister), and 'Der Höllenberg' (Wölfl), 1795 ; 'Der Tyroler Wastel' (Haibel), and a second part 'Oesterreich's treue Brüder,' 1796 ; 'Das medizinische Consilium' (Haibel), 'Der Löwenbrunnen' (Seyfried), and 'Babylons Pyramiden' (Act i. Gallus, Act ii. Peter Winter), 1797 ; 'Das Labyrinth,' or 'Kampf mit den Elementen' (second part of 'Zauberflöte,' Winter), 1798 ; 'Die Ostindier vom Spittelberg' (Seyfried, Stegmayer, etc.). 'Conrad Langbarth,' or 'Der Burggeist' (Henneberg), 'Minna und Peru,' or 'Königspflicht' (Act i. Henneberg, Act ii. Seyfried), and 'Der Wundermann am Wasserfall' (Seyfried), 1799 ; 'Amors Schiffchen' (Seyfried), 1800. At the Theater an-der-Wien—opening night— 'Alexander' (Teyber), 'Thespis Traum,' and 'Proteus und Arabiens Söhne' (Stegmayer), 1801 ; 'Tsching! Tsching!' (Haibel), 1802 ; 'Die Entlarvten,' a continuation of the 'Waldmänner' (Anton Fischer), and 'Pfändung und Personalarrest' (Teyber), 1803 ; 'Der Stein der Weisen' (Schack and others), 1804 ; 'Swetarda Zauberthal' (Fischer), 1805 ; 'Die Eisenkönigin' (Henneberg), and 'Die Kurgäste am Sauerbrunnen' (Anton Diabelli), Schikaneder's last piece, given for his benefit, 1806.   C. F. P.

SCHILLING, DR. GUSTAV, author of a book much esteemed in Germany, though little known in England—*Encyclopädie der gesammten musikalischen Wissenschaften oder Universal Lexikon der Tonkunst* (7 vols. 8vo, Stuttgart, 1835-40). He was born Nov. 3, 1803, at Schwiegershausen, Hanover, where his father was clergyman. He was brought up at Göttingen and Halle, and in 1830 settled in Stuttgart as director of Stöpel's Music School. In 1857 he went to America, and died at Nebraska in March 1881. He published several other works bearing on music, but none of the importance of that already mentioned.   G.

SCHILLINGS, MAX, was born at Düren in Rheinland, on April 19, 1868. He studied under K. Joseph Brambach and O. F. von Königslow, at Bonn. From the former he derived the traditions of both Hummel and Beethoven, as shown through the medium of the teaching of Hiller, whose pupil Brambach was ; while from the latter he inherited, musically, the methods of David the violinist, and Moritz Hauptmann the distinguished theorist. On leaving Bonn, Schillings continued his studies at Munich, where, after three years spent in perfecting himself in all branches of his art, he decided to settle. He was appointed chorusmaster at Bayreuth in 1902, having acted as one of the assistant stage conductors there in 1892. His compositions, fairly numerous, show a high order of talent ; but the composer is decidedly dominated by the influence of Wagner. Among his published works may be mentioned two Symphonic Fantasias, 'Meergruss' and 'Seemorgen' ; 'Zwiegespräch' for small orchestra, solo violin, and solo violoncello ; 'Abenddämmerung' for baritone, violin, and piano ; 'Improvisation' for violin and piano ; the orchestral accompaniments to Wildenbruch's 'Hexenlied' ; music to 'Oedipus Rex' ; and several books of songs. The operas 'Ingwelde,' three acts, produced at Carlsruhe in 1894,

'Der Pfeifertag,' first performed at Schwerin in 1901, and 'Moloch' (Dresden, 1906) are at present in MS.   D. H.

SCHIMON, ADOLF, son of an Austrian artist, well known for his portraits of Beethoven, Weber, Spohr, etc., was born on Feb. 29, 1820, at Vienna. At sixteen he went to Paris and entered the Conservatoire as a pupil of Berton and Halévy. In 1844 he brought out an opera called 'Stradella,' at the Pergola in Florence. In 1850 he was in London, and took a provincial tour with Balfe, Reeves, and Clara Novello. From 1854 to 1859 he was attached to the Italian opera in Paris, and in 1858 produced a comic opera 'List um List,' which was successful in North Germany. In 1872 we find him again at Florence, where he married Anna Regan. (See below). From 1874 to 1877 he was teacher of singing in the Conservatorium at Leipzig, and from thence was called to Munich, where he was professor of singing in the Royal Music School. His original compositions embrace quartets, trios, and solos for the PF., and songs in various languages, and he edited many vocal pieces by Scarlatti, Porpora, Paradies, and other old Italian masters. He died at Leipzig, June 21, 1887. His wife, ANNA REGAN-SCHIMON, was born at Aich, near Carlsbad, Sept. 18, 1841, and was brought up in the house of Dr. Anger in Carlsbad, till 1859, when she was placed as a pupil with Mme. Schubert (née Maschinka-Schneider) in Dresden. In the following year she accompanied Mme. Sabatier-UNGHER, the great contralto, to Florence, where she remained under the care of that eminent artist till Feb. 1864. During this time she made her first attempts on the stage at Siena, her success in which encouraged her in further study. From 1864 to 1867 she was engaged at the Court theatre at Hanover. Then as Kammersängerin to the Grand Duchess Helena in St. Petersburg, where she sang at three of the seven concerts given by Berlioz. In 1869 she visited London in company with her old friend and teacher, Mme. Sabatier, sang twice at the Philharmonic, and three times at the Crystal Palace, and at Hallé's Recitals, etc. From this time till 1875 she was frequently in England, widely known and much liked for her exquisite delivery of Schubert's and other songs. In 1870 and 1871 she visited Vienna with great success, and in 1872 married Dr. Schimon. She took two brilliant tournées with Mombelli, Sivori, Trebelli, etc., in the winters of 1872 and 1873, and from that time till her death only appeared occasionally at the Gewandhaus Concerts at Leipzig. [After her husband's death she accepted a post in the Royal Music School at Munich, where she died April 18, 1902.]   G.

SCHINDELMEISSER, LOUIS, was born at Königsberg, Dec. 8, 1811, and educated at the Gymnasium at Berlin. Music he learned from a French musician named Hostié, and from Gährich. He first adopted the clarinet, but afterwards took a wider range. From 1832 to 1837 he filled capellmeisters' posts at Salzburg, Innsbruck, Graz, then at Berlin (Königstadt theatre), and at Pesth, where he remained for nine years. He at length came to an anchor as Court-capellmeister at Darmstadt, where he died March 30, 1864. His works embrace six operas—'Mathilde,' 'Ten happy days,' 'Peter von Szapary' (Pesth, 1839), 'Malvina' (Pesth, 1851), 'The Avenger,' 'Melusine' (1861); an oratorio, 'S. Boniface'; an overture to 'Uriel Acosta,' and incidental music to various plays; concerto for clarinet and orchestra; and a concertante for four clarinets and orchestra; songs, PF. pieces, etc.   G.

SCHINDLER, ANTON, the devoted friend and biographer of Beethoven, was born in 1796 at Medl, Neustadt, Moravia, where his father was cantor and schoolmaster. He began the study of music and the violin early in life. While quite young he entered the Vienna University to study law, and assiduously kept up his music by practice in an amateur orchestra. His introduction to Beethoven took place accidentally in 1814, when he was asked to take a note from Schuppanzigh to the great composer. Later in the year he played in Beethoven's two concerts of Nov. 29 and Dec. 2. He and the master met often, and the intimacy increased until, early in 1819, on the recommendation of Dr. Bach, he became a kind of secretary to Beethoven and at length, in 1822, took up his residence in the master's house. He then became conductor at the Josephstadt Theatre, where he studied several of Beethoven's great works under his own direction. Beethoven, however, at last began to tire of his young friend, and after much unpleasantness, in 1824, after the failure of the concert of May 23, the breach came. Beethoven behaved with great violence and injustice, and Schindler was driven from him till Dec. 1826, when he arrived in Vienna from Gneixendorf, to die. Schindler at once resumed his position, attended him with devotion till his death, wrote several letters [1] to Moscheles on the details of the event, and in company with Breuning took charge of Beethoven's papers. Breuning died, and then the whole came into Schindler's hands.

In 1831 he wrote some interesting articles on Beethoven and Schubert in Bäuerle's *Theaterzeitung*. In December he left Vienna, and became capellmeister to the cathedral at Münster, a post which he exchanged four years later for that of music-director at Aix-la-Chapelle. After some years he relinquished this, became first a private teacher and then went entirely into private life. He lived in various towns of Germany, and at length in Bockenheim, near Frankfort, where he died Jan. 16, 1864.

[1] Printed in Moscheles's *Life*, i. 145-79.

His book on Beethoven is entitled *Biographie von Ludwig van Beethoven. Mit dem Porträt Beethoven's und zwei Facsimilen* (Münster, 1840, 1 vol. 8vo).[2] This was followed by *Beethoven in Paris . . . ein Nachtrag zur Biographie Beethoven's*, etc. (Münster, 1842; 1 thin vol. 8vo), and that by a second edition of the *Biographie* with additions (Münster, 1845, 1 vol. 8vo). The third and last edition appeared in 1860. Being so long about Beethoven he accumulated many autographs and other papers and articles of interest, and these he disposed of to the library at Berlin for an annuity. His sister was a singer, who in the year 1830 was engaged at the Königstadt Theatre, Berlin.

Schindler has been the object of much obloquy and mistrust, but it is satisfactory to know, on the authority of A. W. Thayer, that this is unfounded, and that his honesty and intelligence are both to be trusted.   G.

SCHIRA, FRANCESCO, was born at Malta, Sept. 19, 1815, received his early education at Milan, and was placed, at the age of nine (1824), in the Conservatorio, where he learned counterpoint under Basily, principal of that institution. At seventeen, having completed his studies, Francisco was commissioned to write an opera for the Scala, which was produced Nov. 17, 1832. That 'Elena e Malvina' won favourable recognition may be inferred from the fact that a Lisbon *impresario*, being at Milan with the object of forming a company for the Santo Carlos, contracted an engagement with Schira for the forthcoming season as 'Maestro Direttore, Compositore e Conduttore della Musica.' He remained eight years at Lisbon, where he was also appointed Professor of Harmony and Counterpoint at the Conservatorio, composing 'I Cavalieri di Valenza' and 'Il Fanatico per la Musica,' for the Santo Carlos, besides ballets, cantatas, etc.

In January 1842 Schira quitted Lisbon for Paris, with the idea of obtaining some book in the French language which he might set to music. In Paris he made the acquaintance of Mr. Maddox, then in quest of artists for the Princess's Theatre. This led to an offer from the London manager, and Schira was appointed director of music and orchestral chief at that establishment. On Monday, Dec. 26, 1842, the Princess's opened as a lyric theatre, and Schira's appearance at the conductor's desk was his first introduction to the English public. The opera chosen was an English version of 'La Sonnambula,' the leading characters sustained by Mme. Eugenie Garcia, Mme. Feron, Messrs. Templeton, Walton, and Weiss; Mr. Loder (father of Edward Loder) being principal violin. Among notable incidents during Schira's term of conductorship may be specified the production of two operas by Balfe, originally com-

[2] This is the book which was translated or adapted by Moscheles (London, Colburn, 1841), strange to say with no mention of Schindler on the title-page.

posed for the Paris Opéra-Comique—'Le Puits d'Amour,' called 'Geraldine' (Nov. 1843), and 'Les Quatre Fils d'Aymon,' called 'The Castle of Aymon' (Nov. 1844). At the end of 1844 Schira accepted an engagement from Alfred Bunn, then lessee of Drury Lane, to fill the place left vacant by Benedict, who resigned immediately after Balfe's 'Daughter of St. Mark' was brought out. At Drury Lane he remained until the spring of 1847, when Bunn seceded from the management, the committee having entertained the proposal of Jullien to become future lessee ; and here several adaptations of foreign operas, besides a good number of works by English composers, were produced. From the latter it will suffice to name Wallace's 'Maritana' and 'Matilda of Hungary,' Macfarren's 'Don Quixote,' Benedict's 'Crusaders,' Lavenu's 'Loretta' (composed for Mme. Anna Bishop), Balfe's 'Enchantress,' etc. ; among the former, Flotow's 'Stradella' and 'Martha.' In Sept. 1848 Bunn took Covent Garden Theatre, and Schira was again appointed conductor. The season only lasted two months, but comprised the first theatrical engagement after his brilliant success, the year before, at Drury Lane, of Sims Reeves, for whom an adaptation of Auber's 'Haydée' was produced, the great English tenor assuming the part of Loredano ; another English adaptation of Rossini's 'Donna del Lago' ; and an entirely new opera, called 'Quentin Durward,' the composition of Henri Laurent. The success of the enterprise was not in proportion to the expectations of the manager ; 'Quentin Durward' was by no means a hit, and though Bunn had lowered his prices the house was prematurely closed. Thus an opera, entitled 'Kenilworth,' from Schira's own pen, which had already been put into rehearsal, with Sims Reeves in the part of Leicester, was lost to the public, and no more English opera was heard at Covent Garden until Miss Pyne and Mr. Harrison migrated from the Lyceum, to carry on their undertaking in a more spacious arena. Although he had severed his connection with the Princess's as musical director, in which position his worthy successor was Edward Loder, Schira wrote two original works for the theatre in Oxford Street—'Mina,' produced in 1845, and 'Theresa, or the Orphan of Geneva,' in 1850, both, the latter especially, received with marked favour. Schira was once more engaged as conductor at Drury Lane, and the theatre opened on Jan. 23, 1852, with an English version of 'Robert le Diable,' succeeded by 'Fra Diavolo,' with Sims Reeves in the titlepart. The principal incident that marked the season was the production of 'The Sicilian Bride,' by Balfe, in no respect one of his most successful efforts. From this time Schira devoted himself specially to giving instructions in the vocal art. He nevertheless did not

neglect composition, as testified in a number of charming songs, duets, trios, etc., some of which have attained wide popularity. He also was busily employed in the composition of a grand opera called 'Niccolò de' Lapi,' performed with marked applause at Her Majesty's Theatre in May 1863. For the Carnival at Naples, two years later, he wrote another grand opera, entitled 'Selvaggia,' which was given with brilliant success, and represented at Milan, Barcelona, and elsewhere. The reception accorded to 'Selvaggia' led to his being asked to write another opera, 'Lia,' for Venice. This, also brought out during the Carnival, was hardly so much to the taste of the Venetians as its precursor. Nevertheless, there are amateurs who regard 'Lia' as Schira's best work.

The managers of the Birmingham Festival commissioned Schira to write a cantata for the meeting of 1873, and he wrote a piece entitled 'The Lord of Burleigh,' the libretto, by Desmond Lumley Ryan, being founded upon Tennyson's well-known poem, though not a line was appropriated, save the motto which heads the title-page of the printed edition. An operetta entitled 'The Ear-ring' was performed at the St. George's Hall Theatre. His music, while revealing the hand of one who has thoroughly mastered the principles of his art, was free from all pretence, relying upon its unaffected simplicity and grace for its impression. As an instructor in singing Schira always maintained a high position, many a public vocalist of note having profited by his counsels. In his own country and elsewhere abroad, he held the insignia of several orders of merit, the most prized of which was that of 'Commendatore della Corona d' Italia'—prized the more because conferred by King Humbert, motu proprio. Schira died in London, Oct. 16, 1883.   J. W. D.

SCHIRMER, G., is the corporate name under which is carried on the music-publishing and trading business established in New York by Gustav Schirmer, and which has attained to a place among the largest and most important of its kind in the world. Gustav Schirmer, born in Saxony in 1829, went to New York in 1837, and entered the music-shop of Scharfenberg and Luis. In 1854 he became the manager of Breusing's music business, which had been founded in 1848 by Kerksieg and Breusing. In 1861, with B. Beer, he took over this business, which was then carried on under the name of Beer & Schirmer, when Schirmer obtained complete control. Under his management it steadily increased in standing and influence. Gustav Schirmer died in 1893 in Eisenach, while journeying in Germany in the hope of restoring his health. In the same year the business was incorporated by his heirs, and its management undertaken by his two sons Rudolph E. and Gustave Schirmer (the latter died July 15, 1907), who extended it still further in importance, especially the department of publication. The firm has a large engraving and printing plant of its own, being one of the few maintained by American publishing-houses. The catalogue of G. Schirmer numbered about 18,000 active titles in 1906. Among the most important of its publications are the Library of Musical Classics, comprising about 850 numbers and a series of modern operas in vocal score with analytical and historical prefaces written by the foremost musical writers of the United States. G. Schirmer has published the works of many American composers, including DUDLEY BUCK, GEORGE W. CHADWICK, Arthur Whiting, Henry Holden HUSS, HORATIO W. PARKER, ETHELBERT NEVIN, and especially CHARLES MARTIN LOEFFLER. The literary publications of the house include theoretical works by Dr. Percy Goetschius, Dr. Theodore Baker, and others. It established and maintained for many years the principal circulating music library in the United States ; but this was transferred in 1906 to the Institute of Musical Art. R. A.

SCHLAGINSTRUMENTEN. Instruments of percussion, such as drums, cymbals, tambourine, etc.

SCHLEIFER. See SLIDE.

SCHLEPPEN. To drag. A frequent direction in modern scores is 'Nicht schleppend '— Don't drag !

SCHLESINGER. A well-known musical-publishing house in Berlin. It was founded in 1795 by ADOLF MARTIN SCHLESINGER, a man of original character and great ability. Among the principal works issued by him was the edition of Bach's 'Matthew Passion,' one of the fruits of Mendelssohn's revival of it,[1] and an astonishingly bold undertaking for those days —which Schlesinger brought out, according to his favourite expression, 'for the honour of the house.' It was announced in Sept. 1829, and published soon afterwards both in Full and PF. score. He also founded the *Berliner Allg. mus. Zeitung*, which under the editorship of A. B. Marx had for seven years (1824-30) much influence for good in Germany. [See vol. iii. p. 685a.] He died in 1839.

His second son, HEINRICH (born 1807), carried on the business till his death, Dec. 14, 1879. He founded the *Echo* in 1851, a periodical which remained in his hands till 1864, when it was sold to R. Lienau.

The eldest son, MORITZ ADOLF, left Berlin, and in 1819 entered the bookselling house of Bossange père at Paris. In 1823 he endeavoured to found a similar business for himself. Police difficulties prevented him from carrying out his intention, and he founded, in 1834, a music business instead, which for many years has had the lead among French publishers, and is now nearly as famous as Paris itself. He brought his German tastes with him, and an unusual

[1] March 11, 1829. See Marx's *Erinnerungen*, ii. pp. 50, 87.

degree of enterprise. His first serious effort was an edition of Mozart's operas in PF. score, for which Horace Vernet designed the title-page. This was followed by editions of the complete works of Beethoven, Weber, Hummel, etc., and a 'Collection de chefs d'œuvre' in twenty-four vols. He published also the full scores of Meyerbeer's 'Robert,' and 'Les Huguenots'; Halévy's 'L'Éclair,' 'La Juive,' 'Les Mousquetaires,' 'La Reine de Chypre,' 'Guido et Ginevra,' 'Charles VI'; Donizetti's 'La Favorite'; Berlioz's 'Symphonie fantastique,' and overture to the 'Carnaval Romain'; the arrangements of Wagner ; the chamber-music of Onslow, Reissiger, and a host of other pieces of all descriptions, for which the reader must be referred to the catalogue of the firm. Amongst the educational works the 'Méthode des Méthodes' is conspicuous. On Jan. 5, 1834, he issued the first number of the *Gazette Musicale*, which in a few months was united to the *Revue Musicale* and ran a useful and successful course till its expiry in 1880. [See *ante*, p. 79.] In 1846 M. Schlesinger sold the business to MM. Brandus and Dufour, and retired to Baden-Baden, where he died in Feb. 1871. G.

SCHLICK, ARNOLT, the elder, was born in Bohemia about 1460. Like Paumann of Nuremberg he was blind, a fine organist, and a lute-player. He was a member of the Hofkapelle at Heidelberg before 1511, holding the post of organist to the Count Palatine. In the fourth book of the Micrologus, 1517, dedicated to Schlick, 'musico consumatissimo, ac Palatini Principis organiste probatissimo,' Ornithoparcus thus apostrophises him : 'From your sentence no man will enter appeale ; because there is no man either learneder, or subtiler in this art, than your selfe, who besides the practise, hast wisdome, eloquence, gentlenesse, quicknesse of wit, and in all kinds of musicke a divine industry, and further the knowledge of many other sciences. Thou wantest the bodily lamp, but in thy mind shineth that golden light ; . . wherefore not only by thy princes, who are to thee most gracious, but even of all men (like Orpheus and Amphion) art thou loved' (Dowland's translation, 1609). Schlick himself states in the preface to his 'Tabulaturen' that he made tours through Germany and Holland, winning much renown as an organist, and that he was in Worms in 1495, at the time that the Reichstag was held there. Two of Schlick's works are still in existence, the first on organs and organists, the second, a volume of organ and lute pieces in tablature. The former was called : 'Spiegel der Orgelmacher vnd Organisten, allen Stifften vnd Kirchen so Orgel halten oder machen lassen hochnützlich, durch den hochberümpten vnd kunstreichen meyster Arnolt Schlicken Pfalzgrauischen Organisten artlich verfasst,' etc. (1511), small 4to, 30 pages ('Mirror of organ-builders and organists, very useful to all foundations and churches which possess or order organs, excellently composed by the celebrated and gifted master, A. S. organist to the Palatinate '). The only copy known lacks the page at the end which would have given the name of the publisher, but there is little doubt that it was printed by Peter Schöffer, at Mainz. Eitner reprinted the whole work in the *Monatshefte für Musikgeschichte,* 1869, giving a facsimile of the engraved title-page. It deals with the materials to be used for the construction of an organ, its erection, the tuning of the pipes, and other technical and theoretical matters, to which is added a description of the organs then in existence, and some allusions to the music of the period. Mr. A. E. Ellis, in his paper on the history of musical pitch, read before the Society of Arts, March 3, 1880, referred to this book as being of great use in showing the relation between very high and very low church-pitch, and the method of tuning before the invention of the mean-tone temperament. He notes also the curious fact that Schlick recommended both the very sharp and the very flat pitch, and for the same reason, consideration of the convenience of both singer and organist using the old ecclesiastical tones, that is, consideration of the compass of the voice and of ease in fingering. This appears to account for the high and low pitches in the earlier period of church-pitch.

Schlick's work is mentioned in Virdung's *Musica getutscht,* 1511 (see Eitner's reprint, page E. IV. v.) ' Dann ich neulich ein tractetlin han gelesen, das ist der spiegel aller organisten vnn orgelmacher intituliert oder genannt, darin find ich in dem andern capitel, das er spricht der organist well dann per fictam musicam spilen, weste der selb von den dreyen geschlechten zu sagen er wurd sye, nit fictam musicam nennen, dann das er maynt fictam musicam syn, das ist cromaticum genus . . . man soll ihn aber verzeihen dann er hat es übersehen, ists augen schuld, oder der spiegel ist dunckel worden,' etc. These remarks on his use of the term ' musica ficta ' did not at all please Schlick, and in return he made a long attack on Virdung in his preface to the 'Tabulaturen,' published the year after ; there are only two copies known of this important work, one in the Leipzig Stadtbibliothek, the other, without title-page, is in the Berlin Königl. Bibliothek. The full title is :—

Tabulaturen etlicher lobgesang vnd lidlein vff die orgeln vn lauten, ein theil mit zweien stimen zu zwicken vn die drit dartzu singen, etlich on gesangk mit dreien, von Arnolt Schlicken Pfalzgrauischen Churfürstlichen Organisten tabulirt, vn in den truck in d'vrsprungklichen stadt der truckerei zu Meintz wie hie nach volgt verordnet. (On last page) Getruckt zu Mentz durch Peter Schöffern. Vff Sant Mattheis Abent. Anno 1512, small obl. 4to, 83 pages unnumbered.

It contains fourteen organ pieces, twelve songs with lute accompaniment, and three pieces for lute. Eitner reprinted (*Monatshefte,* 1869) all the organ and two lute compositions. They are preceded by a letter from Schlick's son

Arnolt, asking his father to make him a collection of organ and lute music ; it is dated St. Catherine's Day, 1511, and an answer from his father promising to do so, although he has become blind, is dated St. Andrew's Day, 1511. Some satirical verses about Virdung follow. Schlick's method of arranging songs, some with one-voice part and two lutes accompanying, others for three lutes only, is noted by Ambros (*Geschichte der Musik,* iii. 440) as being rather remarkable at that early date. Two examples were transcribed and published by Wilhelm Tappert (*Sang u. Klang aus alter Zeit,* Berlin, 1906). Schlick's volume is also the earliest appearance in print of organ pieces in the German tablature, for Ammerbach's ' Tabulaturbuch ' was not published until 1571, and Bernh. Jobin's work in 1572. The organ pieces are all taken from sacred vocal compositions, but are arranged with intelligence and artistic feeling, and with a musicianly touch that shows a genuine sense of instrumental composition ; the next step in advance was to be taken later on by Buus, Willaert, and others, in their ' Ricercari ' for the organ (Wasielewski, *Geschichte der Instrumentalmusik im XVI. Jahrhundert,* 1878). No. 10 from ' Tabulaturen,' an organ arrangement in three-part writing of ' Maria zart,' was published in A. G. Ritter's *Zur Geschichte des Orgelspiels,* 1884, ii. 96. In the Heilbronn Gymnasialbibliothek is a MS. part-book with the Bass only of a three-part song 'Mi, mi,' by Arnolt Schlick. A manuscript, *Mus. Theoret.* 40, 57, written between 1533 and 1540, in the Berlin Königl. Bibliothek, contains a treatise *De musica poetica,* which has been ascribed to Arnolt Schlick the younger, because of the initials A. S. attached to it. It is described by H. Bellermann (*Der Contrapunct,* 1862, p. 28) who gives a facsimile of one of the musical examples in it, a four-part setting by Heinrich Isaac ; it is interesting because of the different parts being distinguished by different colours, the soprano and bass being written in red, the alto in green, and the tenor in black ink.   c. s.

SCHLICK, RUDOLF, a doctor of medicine who lived in Meissen, published the following work : ' Rodholffi Schlickii R Exercitatio, qua musices origo prima, cultus antiquissimus, dignitas maxima, et emolumenta, quae tam animo quam corpori humano confert summa, breviter ac dilucidè exponuntur. Spirae, typis Bernardi Albini, 1588, 8vo, pp. 48.' A copy is in the Bodleian Library, with ' Robertus Burton, 1600,' on the fly-leaf, probably the author of the *Anatomy of Melancholy.*   c. s.

SCHLOESSER, LOUIS, born at Darmstadt in 1800, learnt music there from Rinck, and in Vienna from Seyfried, Salieri, and Mayseder. In due time he entered the Conservatoire at Paris, and attended the violin class of Kreutzer and the composition class of Lesueur. He then went to Darmstadt and became first leader and then conductor of the Court band. His works comprise five operas, among them ' Das Leben ein Traum ' (1839), and ' Die Braut des Herzogs ' (1847), a melodrama, music to ' Faust,' a mass, a ballet, and a quantity of instrumental music of all descriptions. He died at Darmstadt, Nov. 17, 1886. His son, CARL WILHELM ADOLPH, was born at Darmstadt, Feb. 1, 1830. He was educated by his father, and in 1847 established himself at Frankfort. In 1854 he went to England, where he has been ever since settled in London as an esteemed teacher. He was a professor at the Royal Academy of Music until his retirement in 1903. He has published both in England and Germany a great number of PF. works, both solos and duets ; including a suite dedicated to Cipriani Potter, and a set of twenty-four studies ; many songs and vocal pieces, and has many larger works in MS. His 'Schumann Evenings' in 1868 were well known, and did much to advance the knowledge of Schumann in England.   G.

SCHMELTZL, or SCHMELTZEL, WOLFGANG, a native of Kemnat in the Upper Palatinate, was at first a Protestant cantor at Amberg, where he married, but eventually forsook his wife and children, and became a Roman priest. About 1540 he was a schoolmaster in Vienna, and in 1544 issued the book by which he is known, a collection of 'Quodlibets' for four and five voices, as well as folk-songs of the time. The title is ' Guter seltzamer vnd kunstreicher teutscher Gesang, sonderlich etliche künstliche Quodlibet, Schlacht (bei Pavia), vnd dergleichen mit 4 oder 5 stimmen. . . .' It was printed at Nuremberg in four part-books. Copies are at Berlin, in the British Museum, and elsewhere. (See the Quellen - Lexikon, Eitner's Deutsches Lied, vol. i. and Monatshefte f. Musikgesch. iii. 201. A long account of the book is given in the Sammelbände of the Int. Mus. Ges. vi. 80, by Elsa Bienenfeld.)   M.

SCHMID, ANTON, Custos of the Hofbibliothek in Vienna, born at Pihl, near Leipa in Bohemia, Jan. 30, 1787, entered the Imperial Library at Vienna in 1818, became Scriptor in 1819, Custos in 1844, and died at Salzburg, July 3, 1857. His department as a writer was the history and literature of music and hymns. He contributed to the following works :—Dr. Ferdinand Wolf's Ueber die Lais, Sequenzen, und Leiche (Heidelberg, 1841); Becker's Darstellung der musikalischen Literatur (supplement, Leipzig, 1839); A. Schmidt's Allg. Wiener musik. Zeitung (from 1842 to 1848) ; Dehn's Cäcilia (from 1841 to 1848 ; Mayence, Schott) ; and the Oesterreich Blätter für Lit. und Kunst (1844, 1845). His independent works are Ottaviano dei Petrucci of Fossombrone, the inventor of movable metal types for printing music, and his successors (Vienna, Rohrmann, 1845) ; Joseph Haydn und Nicolo Zingarelli, proving that Haydn was the author

of the Austrian national hymn (Vienna, Rohrmann, 1847) ; Christoph Willibald Ritter vo.. Gluck (Leipzig, Fleischer, 1854) ; also a work on chess, Tschaturanga-vidjâ (Vienna, Gerold, 1847).

To Schmid in the first instance is due the orderly and systematic arrangement of the musical archives of the Hofbibliothek. In recognition of his unwearied industry and research he was made a member of many learned societies in different parts of Europe.   C. F. P.

SCHMIDT, BERNHARD. See SMITH, BERNARD (' FATHER SMITH ').

SCHMIDT, JOHANN CHRISTOPH. See SMITH, JOHN CHRISTOPHER.

SCHMITT, a German musical family founded by a Cantor at Obernburg in Bavaria. His son ALOYS was born at Erlenbach on the Main, August 26, 1788, and taught to play by his father ; he then learned composition from André of Offenbach, and in 1816 established himself in Frankfort as a PF. teacher. After a few successful years there—during which, among others, he had taught Ferdinand Hiller —and much travelling, he migrated to Berlin, then to Hanover, where he held the post of Court Organist (1825-29), and lastly back to Frankfort, where he died July 25, 1866. His reputation as a teacher was great, though he had a passion for journeys, and his pupils complained of his frequent absences. He composed more than 100 works, of all descriptions, including masses, four operas, two oratorios, and string quartets, besides some useful PF. studies.

His brother JAKOB, born at Obernburg, Nov. 2, 1803, was a pupil of Aloys. He settled in Hamburg, where he brought out an opera (' Alfred der Grosse ') and a prodigious amount of music, including many sonatas for the piano, solo and with violin, variations, three books of studies, etc., in all more than 300 works ; and died June 1853.

The son of Aloys, GEORG ALOYS, was born Feb. 2, 1827, during his father's residence at Hanover. Music came naturally to him, but it was not till after some time that he decided to follow it. He was then at Heidelberg university, and put himself under Vollweiler to serious study of counterpoint. His first attempt was an operetta called 'Trilby,' which was performed at Frankfort in 1850, with great success. He then passed some years in various towns of Germany, and at length, in 1856, was called by Flotow to Schwerin as Court-cappellmeister ; [he retired on a pension in 1892, and in the following year became head of the Mozartverein in Dresden]. In 1860 he visited London, and played with éclat before Queen Victoria. He wrote operas, music to plays, and orchestral and other works. [He edited and completed Mozart's great mass in C minor (1901) ; he died at Dresden, Oct. 15, 1902.] Emma BRANDES, now Mme. Engelmann, the eminent pianist, was his pupil.   G.

SCHNEIDER, GEORG ABRAHAM, born April 9, 1770, at Darmstadt, became a proficient on the horn, studied theory with Portmann, whose daughter he afterwards married. He was successively oboist in a Hessian regiment, horn-player in the court bands of Darmstadt, Schwerin, Rheinsberg, and Berlin. In 1812 or 1814 he undertook the duties of theatrical conductor at Reval, but went back to Berlin in 1816, and in 1820 was made capellmeister of the court opera, and director of military bands. He had a rare knowledge of musical instruments of all kinds, and wrote a large number of operettas, masses, cantatas, an oratorio, 'Die Pilgrime auf Golgotha,' symphonies, concertos, and chamber music of all kinds. (*Quellen-Lexikon*; Riemann's *Lexikon*.)   M.

SCHNEIDER, JOHANN CHRISTIAN FRIEDRICH, composer, teacher, and conductor, born Jan. 3, 1786, at Alt-Waltersdorf, near Zittau, composed a symphony at the age of ten. In 1798 entered the Gymnasium of Zittau, and studied music with Schönfelder and Unger. In 1804 he published three PF. sonatas, and having entered the University of Leipzig in 1805 carried on his musical studies to such purpose that in 1807 he became organist of St. Paul's, in 1810 director of the Seconda opera, in 1812 organist of the Thomaskirche, and in 1817 director at the Stadt Theater. There he remained till 1821, when he became capellmeister to the Duke of Dessau, whose music he much improved, and founded in the town a Singakademie, a school-master's choral society, and a Liedertafel. In 1829 he founded a musical Institute, which succeeded well, and educated several excellent musicians, Robert Franz among the number. Schneider was also an industrious composer, his works comprising oratorios—'Die Höllenfahrt des Messias' (1810), 'Das Weltgericht' (1819), 'Totenfeier' (1821), 'Die Sündfluth' (1823), 'Verlorne Paradies' (1824), 'Jesu Geburt' (1825), 'Christus das Kind,' 'Pharao,' and 'Gideon' (1829), 'Absalom' (1830), 'Das befreite Jerusalem' (1835), 'Salomonis Tempelbau' (1836), 'Bonifazius' (1837), 'Christus der Erlöser' (1838), 'Gethsemane und Golgotha' (1838); 14 masses; Glorias and Te Deums; 25 cantatas; 5 hymns; 13 psalms, 7 operas; 23 symphonies; 60 sonatas; 6 concertos; 400 Lieder for men's voices, and 200 ditto for a single voice—all now forgotten except the men's part-songs. Schneider directed the musical festivals of Magdeburg (1825), Nuremberg (1828), Strasburg (1830), Halle (1830 and 1835), Halberstadt (1830), Dessau (1834), Wittenberg (1835), Coethen (1838 and 1846), Coblenz and Hamburg (1840), Meissen (1841), Zerbst (1844), and Lübeck (1847). He also published didactic works—*Elementarbuch der Harmonie und Tonsetzkunst* (1820), translated into English (London,

1828); *Vorschule der Musik* (1827); and *Handbuch des Organisten* (1829-30). The oratorio of the 'Sündfluth' was translated into English as 'The Deluge' by Professor E. Taylor, published in London, and performed at the Norwich Festival of 1833.

Schneider was a doctor of philosophy, and a member of the Berlin and other Academies. He died Nov. 23, 1853. Some traits of his curious jealous temper will be found in Schubring's Reminiscences of Mendelssohn, in *Daheim* for 1866, No. 26. He was vexed with Mendelssohn for his revival of Bach's Passion—but the feeling passed away; and in the *Signale* for 1866, Nos. 46, 47, 48, there are eight letters (1829-1845 (translated in the *Musical World*, Dec. 29, 1866, and Jan. 5, 1867) from Mendelssohn to him showing that they were on very good terms. When Mendelssohn's body passed through Dessau, on its way to Berlin, Schneider met it at the station, with his choir, and a lament was sung, which he had purposely composed, and which will be found in the *A.M.Z.* for 1847, No. 48.   F. G.

SCHNEIDER, JOHANN GOTTLOB, the celebrated Dresden organist, brother of the preceding, was born at Alt-Gersdorf, Oct. 28, 1789. He is said to have begun to learn organ, piano-forte, and violin, when only five. At twenty-two he was organist of the Leipzig University church, and by 1820 was recognised as one of the first organists living. To his fine playing at a Magdeburg Festival in 1825 he owed his Dresden appointment of Court organist, which he held till his death, April 13, 1864. From the organ-loft of the Hofkirche he made his influence felt; how widely, may be gathered from the mere names of his pupils, amongst whom were Mendelssohn, Schumann, Liszt, Merkel, Töpfer, Van Eycken. The last four were amongst the thirty old pupils who composed and presented to him that graceful offering, the 'Jubel Album für die Orgel,' in 1861, the fiftieth year of his artistic career. Schumann's studies with him permanently influenced the composer, and directly inspired or helped to inspire the Pedal Pianoforte Studies, and Fugues on the name of Bach; and Mendelssohn confessed a like obligation and admiration. Schneider's reading of Bach—derived straight from him by direct descent in only three removes—was the best weapon in his equipment as a teacher. He always ended a lesson by playing one of the great fugues, or, especially, 'organ chorales.' Sir Herbert Oakeley (Schneider's last pupil) used to talk much of his playing of these compositions. He liked playing some of 'the 48' on his deep-toned Silbermann organ. Mendelssohn records in one of his letters his surprise at hearing him play the D major. He himself used to tell with pride how he 'tried' upon Mendelssohn and another Professor of Music the B flat minor of the second book. The Professor stood by his side unmoved, but the composer of 'Elijah' disappeared into a remote gallery, to hide his emotion.

Schneider's few published works include an 'answer of thanks' to the 'Jubel Album,' a masterly Fantasia and Fugue in D minor (op. 3), etc.   E. M. O.

SCHNELLER. The German name for the short trill or inverted mordent—

Written.   Played.

SCHNETZLER, JOHANN. See SNETZLER, JOHN.

SCHNORR VON CAROLSFELD, LUDWIG, born July 2, 1836, at Munich, the son of the painter Julius Schnorr von Carolsfeld, first received instruction in music from Julius Otto at Dresden, where, in 1846, his father became director of the Kunst Akademie. In 1854 he was for a short time at the Leipzig Conservatorium, and later in the year studied for the stage under Eduard Devrient at Carlsruhe, where he became engaged. He made his début in the modest part of Napthali in Méhul's 'Joseph,' and later made a great success as Robert (Meyerbeer). About this period he married the singer, Malwina Garrigues (born Dec. 7, 1825). On leave of absence, he sang in opera at Wiesbaden and Frankfort, and at festivals at Mainz and Düsseldorf. From 1860 to 1865 he was engaged at Dresden, where he increased his popularity. In 1862 Wagner heard him when singing at Carlsruhe as Lohengrin, and was so struck with his performance that he determined to confide to him the part of Tristan whenever the opera was produced. Schnorr had been warmly recommended to the composer earlier, both by Tichatschek the singer, and Devrient, but for a time Wagner was not prepossessed in Schnorr's favour, on account of his unromantic figure, in spite of his talent and his enthusiasm for Wagner and his music. (Vide 'Meine Erinnerungen an L. S. v. C.,' Neue Zeitschrift für Musik, Nos. 24 and 25, 1868.) On June 10, 1865, Schnorr and his wife created the parts of Tristan and Isolde, when the opera was produced at Munich, at the express instance of the composer. Their leave of absence being limited, they returned to Dresden, July 15, and the tenor died six days after, of a chill and rheumatism, caught at the first performance of the opera. He was a clever, all-round musician, an excellent pianist and extempore player, a composer, and arranger of songs of Bach, Gluck, and the old Italian school. He was also a painter and a writer of poetry. In 1867 his widow published a volume of poems by herself and her husband. After his death she was engaged at Hamburg, and finally at Carlsruhe, where, on her retirement, she became

a teacher of singing. She died at the Vincentius Hospital there on Feb. 8, 1904.   A. C.

SCHOBERLECHNER, FRANZ, born at Vienna, July 21, 1797. Hummel composed for him his second pianoforte Concerto, in C, which he performed in public with success when only ten years old. The precocious child was taken under the patronage of Prince Esterhazy, and sent to Vienna, to study under Förster. From 1814 he travelled in Austria and Italy. While at Florence he composed a requiem, and a buffa opera, 'I Virtuosi teatrali.' In the next year, having been appointed chapel-master to the Duchess of Lucca, he wrote 'Gli Arabi nelle Gallie,' and subsequently, at Vienna, in 1820, 'Der junge Onkel.' In 1823 he went to Russia. He seems to have written to Beethoven, before starting, for letters of introduction, which the composer refused.[1] At St. Petersburg he recommended himself to dall' Occa, a professor of singing, whose daughter he married in 1824. After travelling in Germany and Italy, the pair returned to St. Petersburg in 1827, where Mme. Schoberlechner was engaged for three years at the Italian Opera at a salary of 20,000 roubles. Her husband composed for her an opera, 'Il Barone di Dolzheim,' which had some success. In 1831 Schoberlechner retired to a country house near Florence. His last opera was 'Rossane,' produced at Milan, Feb. 9, 1839. He died at Berlin on Jan. 7, 1843.

His published works are chiefly for the pianoforte ; a list of them is to be found in Fétis's Biog. d. Mus. His wife,

Madame SOPHIE SCHOBERLECHNER, daughter of Signor dall' Occa, was born at St. Petersburg in 1807. Up to 1827 she appeared only in concerts, but was then engaged at the Italian Opera of St. Petersburg, as we have also already mentioned. She had a very beautiful voice, and for twelve or thirteen years sang with unvarying success in almost all the principal towns of Germany and Italy. In 1840 she left the stage, retired to her husband's property in Tuscany, and died at Florence in 1863. F. A. M.

SCHOBERT, or CHOBERT in Mozart's orthography,[2] a player on the harpsichord, whose sonatas were the delight of our great-grandmothers. His Christian name does not appear, and little is known of his biography. He is said to have been born in 1720, and brought up at Strasburg. He was at one time organist at Versailles, but was dismissed for negligence. He settled in Paris in 1760, in which year his first works were published there, where he was in the service of the Prince de Conti. On the occasion of his death, August 1767, Grimm, no mean judge of music, inserts in his Correspondence a very high eulogium on his merits as a player. He praises him for 'his great ability, his

[1] See Note to Beethoven's Letters, translated by Lady Wallace, vol. ii. p. 118.
[2] See Letter, Oct. 17, 1777.

brilliant and enchanting execution, and an unequalled facility and clearness. He had not the genius of our Eckard, who is undoubtedly the first master in Paris; but Schobert was more universally liked than Eckard, because he was always agreeable, and because it is not every one who can feel the power of genius.' This is the description of a pleasant brilliant player who never soared above the heads of his audience. He left seventeen sonatas for PF. and violin; eleven for PF., violin, and violoncello; three quartets for PF., two violins, and violoncello; six 'sinfonies' for PF., violin, and two horns; six PF. concertos, and four books of sonatas for PF. solo.[1] These seem to have been originally published in Paris, but editions of many of them appeared in London between 1770 and 1780. The particulars of his death are given by Grimm. It was occasioned by eating some fungi which he gathered near Paris, and which killed his wife, his children, a friend, the servant, and himself.[2] Schobert and Eckard are alike forgotten by modern musicians. A Minuetto and Allegro molto in E♭ have been reprinted in Pauer's 'Alte Meister' (the former has been 'freely arranged' in L. Godowsky's 'Renaissance'), other movements in the 'Maîtres du Clavecin,' and a Sonata, so-called, in the Musical Library. These pieces are tuneful and graceful, but very slight in construction, the harmonies consisting chiefly of alternations of tonic and dominant, seldom in more than three parts, often only in two. Burney (*Hist.* iv. 591, 597) remarks that his music is essentially harpsichord music, and that he was one of the few composers who were not influenced by Emanuel Bach.   G.

SCHŒLCHER, VICTOR, French writer and politician, son of a manufacturer of china, was born in Paris, July 21, 1804, educated at the Collège Louis le Grand, and well known as an ultra - republican. On the accession of the Emperor Napoleon III. he was expelled both from France and Belgium, but took refuge in London, where he brought out his *Histoire des crimes du 2 Décembre* (1853), and an English pamphlet entitled *Dangers to England of the Alliance with the men of the Coup d'État* (1854).

Schœlcher remained in England till August 1870, returning to Paris immediately before the Revolution of Sept. 4. As staff-colonel of the Garde Nationale he commanded the Legion of Artillery throughout the siege of Paris. After Jan. 31, 1871, he was elected to the Assemblée Nationale by the Department of the Seine, Martinique, and Cayenne, and sat for Martinique till elected a life-senator (Dec. 16, 1875).

His claim to a place in this work, however, is as a distinguished amateur. His devotion to art of all kinds was proved by his articles in *L'Artiste* (1832), and *La Revue de Paris* (1833),

and he made during his travels a most interesting collection of foreign musical instruments. His long stay in England had a still more remarkable result in his enthusiasm for Handel. Up to 1850 only the 'Messiah' and a few other works of Handel had been given in Paris, but very spasmodically; M. Schœlcher resolved to do something to remove this reproach from France. He accordingly made a collection of Handel's works, and of books and pamphlets bearing on his life and music, a list of which he gives in the beginning of his book. To the autographs in Buckingham Palace and the Fitzwilliam Museum at Cambridge, and to the copies by Smith formerly in possession of Mr. H. B. Lennard, he obtained access, and thus provided, published *The Life of Handel, by Victor Schœlcher*, London, Trübner, 8vo, 1857. The author was materially assisted by Mr. Rophino Lacy,[3] whose labours are amply acknowledged in the preface (p. xxii). The work was written by M. Schœlcher in French, and translated by James Lowe. It contains much information beyond what is indicated in the title, especially with regard to Italian opera and music in general in England during the 18th century. The French MS., *Handel et son temps*, was handed over to La France Musicale, which (August 19, 1860) published the first four chapters, and the beginning of the fifth (Nov. 2, 1862), but there broke off, doubtless for political reasons. The MS. was supposed to have been destroyed, till May 25, 1881, when it was offered for sale by M. Charavay, and at once bought for the library of the Conservatoire, thus completing M. Schœlcher's magnificent gift (Nov. 1872) of all the works, in print or MS., used by him in preparing the book, and his collection of foreign instruments. He later added a quantity of music and rare books bearing on the history of Italian opera in London and on singing and pianoforte-playing, in the United Kingdom. The *Fonds Schœlcher*, as it is called, contains in all 500 volumes uniformly bound with the initials of the donor, and has already been of immense service to French artists and musicologists, whose knowledge of the madrigal writers and pianists of the English school, and indeed of Handel himself, is as a rule but imperfect. [Schœlcher died at the house of a friend at Horville (Seine-et-Oise), Dec. 24, 1893.]   G. C.

M. Schœlcher's work is very inadequate to its purpose. The author was no musician, and was therefore compelled to depend on the labours and judgment of another. His verdicts are deformed by violent and often ludicrous partisanship; and his style, which is extremely French, has had but small assistance from his translator.[4] No man can write a serious book on a

---

[1] Weitzmann, *Geschichte des Clavierspiels.*
[2] Grimm (new ed.), vii. 422.

[3] M. Schœlcher's statement as to Mr. Lacy's assistance should materially modify our inferences from his account of his own part in the examination of Handel's MSS., p. xxi.
[4] Who did not do his work well. Instead of modifying the

great subject without its being of some value, and Schœlcher's dates and lists are alone enough to make the student grateful to him ; it is a great pity that M. Schœlcher's original French work is not published.   G.

SCHÖNBERGER, Benno, born at Vienna, Sept. 12, 1863, was a pupil of Anton Door for piano, Bruckner for counterpoint, and Volkmann for composition, at the Vienna Conservatorium, until 1874, when he played at recitals, and with the Hellmesberger Quartet. He went for a time to study with Liszt, and in 1878 undertook an extended tour in Russia, Germany, Austria, and Belgium. From 1880 to 1885 he taught in Vienna, and after a journey to Sweden in 1886 settled in London, making his first appearance at a recital of his own, in January 1887. Since then he has held an honourable place among the pianists who appear regularly in London, and his interpretations of the classics are always sound and interesting, while his tone and technique are of remarkable excellence. He went to America on tour in 1894. Of late years he has appeared but rarely, owing to ill-health ; but he is a diligent and successful teacher of his instrument. He has published numerous piano pieces and songs. (Baker's *Dictionary*, etc.)   M.

SCHÖNE MINKA. The name by which a certain very popular Ruthenian or Little Russian song is generally known. (The music and original words are given by Prach, *Sobranie russkikh narodnuikh pyesen*, end of vol. i., and the literal German version in Fink, *Musikalischer Hausschatz*, No. 157.)

It is marked by perfect regularity of rhythm and absence of certain eccentricities noted in the article, Song, as common in the Cossack and Little Russian songs ; and the words are a dialogue in rhymed verse. It is an interesting instance of a Volkslied of one country becoming natural over-exuberance of the author he has rather exaggerated it, and has allowed a number of sentences to pass which no literary man of any pretension should have written.

domesticated in the same capacity in another, and also of the extraordinary transformation which the song may undergo in the process. A very loose imitation of the words of this song, beginning ' Schöne Minka ich muss scheiden,' was published by the German poet Ch. A. Tiedge in 1808, and this, with the melody much altered, is now to be found in most collections of German Volkslieder without notice of the Slavonic source. J. N. Hummel has made this air (rather in its original than in the German form) the subject of ' Adagio, Variazionen und Rondo über ein russisches Thema,' for PF., violin, and violoncello, op. 78, and Weber wrote a set of brilliant variations for pianoforte on the same theme. R. M.

SCHOLA CANTORUM, THE, an important institution founded in 1896 in Paris by Charles Bordes, the famous director of the ' Chanteurs de Saint-Gervais,' Alexandre Guilmant, and Vincent d'Indy. Its first object was the execution of plain-song after the Gregorian tradition, and the revival of music of the period of Palestrina. The beginnings were very modest, only twenty-one pupils attending the first course ; but in 1900 its growth had been so rapid that it was found necessary to transfer it from the original premises in the Rue Stanislas, to the large building it now occupies in the Rue Saint Jacques, formerly the Hôtel des Bénédictins Anglais, where the remains of the exiled James II. of England were deposited.

It is now a superior high-class music-school, with more than 300 pupils of both sexes, who receive a thorough musical education, founded (whatever may be the ultimate direction of their studies) upon a knowledge of plain-song, liturgical melodies, and of the religious music of the polyphonic period. The course of training is wisely divided into two sections, one concerned solely with technique and the other with style and the application of technique to art. At the monthly concerts, directed and prepared by M. Vincent d'Indy, the head of the institution, the pupils have opportunities for becoming intimately acquainted with the music of the centuries preceding the 19th. Complete performances are given of works rarely to be heard elsewhere in Paris ; Bach has been represented by more than 20 of the church cantatas, the Christmas Oratorio, all his concertos, the Passion according to St. John, and the B minor Mass ; Gluck, by ' Alceste,' ' Armide,' ' Iphigénie en Aulide ' ; Monteverde by ' Orfeo,' and ' L' Incoronazione di Poppea.' Numberless works by such old French masters as Clérambault, Charpentier, Dumont, Leclair, Lalande, etc., have been revived, as well as Rameau's ' Dardanus,' ' Hippolyte et Aricie,' ' Zoroastre,' ' Castor et Pollux.' There are a certain number of bursaries or scholarships connected with the institution, and by an ingenious system the fees due from the pupils are in many cases balanced by the fees they earn in taking part in the concerts. There is a ' section de propagande' confided to M. Bordes, who has founded affiliated societies at Avignon, Lyons, Marseilles, Bordeaux, Poitiers, Nancy, etc. The 'bureau d'édition' connected with the school has done very useful work in bringing out an 'Anthologie des Maîtres primitifs,' 'Les Archives des Maîtres de l'Orgue,' 'Les Concerts Spirituels,' a collection of modern vocal and organ music, and 'Le Chant Populaire.' An 'Édition mutuelle' of the compositions of the younger men is intended to assure to the composers the profit on the sale and performance of their works. The school also publishes a monthly organ *Les Tablettes de la Schola*, which chronicles the various doings of the institution.   G. F.

SCHOLZ, BERNHARD E., born March 30, 1835, at Mainz, studied the piano with Ernst Pauer (at that time Director of the Liedertafel in that city) and theory with S. W. Dehn, became teacher of theory in the Royal School of Music at Munich in 1856, was Capellmeister at the Hanover Court Theatre from 1859 till 1865, when he went to live in Berlin, until he was summoned to Breslau in 1871 as Director of the Orchesterverein. On April 1, 1883, he became Raff's successor as Director of Dr. Hoch's Conservatorium at Frankfort. There he met with much opposition, and in spite of endless intrigue succeeded in ensuring a prosperous future for the Conservatorium. Since 1884 he has also directed the Gesangverein founded in Mainz by Fried. Wilhelm Rühl.

Many compositions have been written by Bernhard Scholz, including songs, string quartets (opp. 46 and 48), and a quintet (op. 47), a piano concerto, a symphony in B♭ (op. 60) entitled 'Malinconia,' some pieces for orchestra, solos, and chorus, 'Das Siegesfest,' 'Das Lied von der Glocke,' overtures to Goethe's 'Iphigenie' and 'Im Freien,' a requiem, and the operas 'Carlo Rosa' (Munich, 1858); 'Zietensche Husaren' (Breslau, 1869); 'Morgiane' (Munich, 1870); 'Genoveva' (Nuremberg, 1875); 'Der Trompeter von Säkkingen' (Wiesbaden, 1877); 'Die vornehmen Wirte' (Leipzig, 1883); 'Ingo' (Frankfort-a.-M., 1898); and 'Anno 1757' (Berlin, 1903).   H. V. H.

SCHOP, or SCHOPP, JOHANN, a skilful player on the lute, violin, and trombone, who entered the court band at Wolfenbüttel in 1615, was a violinist at the Danish court in 1618-19 (according to one account he went to Denmark in 1615, so that his stay at Wolfenbüttel must have been very short), and in 1621 became director of the Ratsmusik at Hamburg, being appointed later on organist to the town and to the church of St. James. He died about 1664 or 1665. Although he was chiefly renowned as an instrumentalist (Mattheson speaks of him as incomparable in his way), he is at present known mainly as a composer of chorale-tunes, in virtue of his contributions to Rist's hymn-book, published in

1641 as 'Himmlische Lieder.' No copy seems to exist of his 'Neue Paduanen, Galliarden, Allemanden,' published in six parts at Hamburg in 1633-40 ; his 'Geistliche Concerten' appeared in 1643, and many occasional compositions, such as congratulatory odes on weddings, are extant. Besides Rist's book, already alluded to, the following contain tunes by Schop: Rist's 'Frommer und gottseliger Christen alltägliche Hausmusik' (1654), Philip von Zesen's 'Jugend-und Liebes-Flammen,' 1651, and 1653, and from these books the melodies were copied into later collections. (*Quellen-Lexikon*, etc.)   M.

SCHOTT, ANTON, born June 25, 1846, at Castle Staufeneck in the Swabian Alps, was educated at the military academy at Ludwigsburg, Würtemberg, and served as an artillery officer through the war of 1866. Some time after, his voice attracted the attention of Pischek, and of Frau SCHEBEST, from the latter of whom he had much instruction preparatory to his appearance on the stage. On May 8, 1870, Herr Schott made his début at Frankfort, as Max in 'Der Freischütz,' with such success that he determined to abandon the army in favour of music, though prevented for a time by the outbreak of the war of 1870, through which he served and obtained his captaincy. At the end of 1871 he was engaged at Munich, and subsequently at Berlin, Schwerin, and Hanover. At the last place he created the part of Benvenuto Cellini on the revival of Berlioz's opera there under Bülow. He sang in England, June 16, 1879, at piano recitals given by Dr. von Bülow at St. James's Hall, and at a New Philharmonic concert, in all which he was well received. He appeared Jan. 10, 1880, at Her Majesty's Theatre (Carl Rosa), as Rienzi, and afterwards as Lohengrin, with only moderate success, owing to his faulty intonation. He had a fine presence and a good voice. He received further instruction from Blume, and created the part of Azim in Stanford's 'Veiled Prophet' on Feb. 8, 1881, at Hanover. In 1882 he sang with Neumann in Wagner's company in Italy, and in 1884 in Leopold Damrosch's company in America. He afterwards devoted himself exclusively to concert-singing. In his day he was considered one of the best 'heroic tenors' in Germany.   A. C.

SCHOTT (B. SCHOTT'S SÖHNE), the well-known firm of music-publishers at Mainz. This business, the largest of the kind except Breitkopf & Härtel's, was founded in 1773 by BERNHARD SCHOTT, and carried on after his death in 1817 by his sons ANDREAS (born 1781, died 1840), and JOHANN JOSEPH (born 1782, died 1855), who in the early part of the 19th century set up a house of their own at Antwerp (afterwards removed to Brussels) which gave them an advantage both in suppressing pirated editions, and in dealing with the French and Italian composers then in vogue. In 1838 they founded a branch in London, superintended by a third brother, ADAM (who afterwards was a band-master in Canada and India, dying in the latter country), and conducted with great success since 1849 by J. B. Wolf (born 1815, died 1881), and, since his death, by Mr. Carl Volkert. Another branch in Paris soon followed. PETER, a younger brother of FRANZ PHILIPP, and grand-son of Bernhard, lived in Brussels and managed the business of the branches there and in Paris, forwarding at the same time the circulation of the Mainz publications. He died Sept. 20, 1894, in Paris. Besides these four independent houses the firm has depôts in Leipzig, Rotterdam, and New York. FRANZ PHILIPP (born 1811), grandson of Bernhard, took part in the business from 1825, and managed it after the death of his father Andreas, first in partnership with his uncle Johann Joseph, and after his death by himself. Since his death in Milan in 1874 the business has been carried on with the old traditions by PETER SCHOTT (a son of the Brussels Peter), FRANZ VON LANDWEHR (a nephew of the family), and DR. L. STRECKER. The Schotts have been music-publishers to the Court since 1824.

At a time when the book and music trade was regulated by no fixed laws, the correct and elegant editions of Mainz found a ready entrance into foreign countries, and the firm was thus stimulated to keep ahead of rivals by making constant improvements in music-print-ing and engraving. They were the first to use lithography for this purpose, an important turning-point in the printing of music. Their copyright publications now amount to over 23,000, including Beethoven's latest quartets, Ninth Symphony, and Mass in D, nearly all the operas of Donizetti, Rossini, Adam, and Auber, most of Rink's organ-music, 'der Choral-freund,' in nine volumes ; ' École pratique de la modulation,' op. 99 ; 'Gesangstudien' (vocalises, méthode de chant, etc.) by Bordèse, Bordogni, Concone, Fétis, Gavaudé, Garcia, Lablache, Abbé Mainzer, Rossini, Rubini, Vaccaj, etc. To come to later times, Wagner's 'Meistersinger,' 'Ring des Nibelungen,' and 'Parsifal.' The establish-ment has been enlarged by the addition of a printing-office (where have been printed, among others, Gottfried Weber's theoretical works, the periodical *Cäcilia*, 1824-48, etc.), and in 1829 of a piano factory, which, however, was given up in 1860 on account of the extension of the main business.

The Schotts, besides innumerable services to art and artists, have done good work in a smaller circle by fostering music in Mainz itself. Franz and his wife Betty (*née* von Braunrasch, born 1820, died 1875) left a considerable sum for the maintenance of a permanent orchestra and conductor of eminence, in order that Mainz might hold its own in music with the richer cities of the Rhine provinces.   C. F. P.

SCHOTTISCHE ('The Scotch dance'), a round dance very similar to the polka. It must not be confounded with the Écossaise, which was a country dance of Scotch origin introduced into France towards the end of the 18th century. The Schottische was first danced in England in 1848, when it was also known as the German Polka. It does not seem to have been danced in Paris, as Cellarius (*La Danse des Salons*, Paris, 1847) does not include it amongst the dances he describes. The music is almost the same as that of the polka, but should be played rather slower. The following is the tune to which it was originally danced in England.

W. B. S.

SCHRADIECK, HENRY, violinist, was born at Hamburg, on April 29, 1846. He received his first lesson from his father on his fourth birth-day, and already made public appearances in his sixth year. In 1854 Teresa Milanollo heard, and took considerable interest in him, putting him into the hands of Léonard at the Conservatoire in Brussels, where he stayed for four years, and gained the first prize. Afterwards he studied under David at Leipzig (1859-61), obtaining his first important engagement in 1863 as soloist in the so-called 'Private Concerts,' conducted by Reinthaler at Bremen. The following year he was appointed professor of the violin at the Moscow Conservatorium, but in 1868 returned to Hamburg to take the post vacated by Auer as Concertmeister of the Phil-harmonic Society. After six years he moved (in 1874) to Leipzig, becoming Concertmeister at the Gewandhaus concerts, professor at the Conservatorium, and leader of the theatre or-chestra. His pupils became very numerous, and at length he found himself overburdened with so many duties, and accepted an appointment as conductor and teacher of the violin at the College of Music at Cincinnati. Here he worked until 1889, and then returned to his native town, taking his old position as Concertmeister of the Philharmonic Society, besides teaching at the Hamburg Conservatorium. Subsequently he went to New York as principal violin professor at the National Conservatoire, moving in 1899 to Philadelphia, where he teaches at the S. Broad Street Conservatoire.

As a writer of Studies for the violin he stands very high. Amongst them are twenty-five

Grosse Studien for violin alone, three volumes of Technical Studies, Scale Studies, Guide to the Study of Chords, Finger Exercises, and 'The First Position.' He has also interested himself in questions connected with the making of violins.   w. w. c.

SCHRIDER, SCHREIDER, or SCHRÖDER, CHRISTOPHER, was one of Father Smith's workmen, and previous to 1708 had become his son-in-law. After Smith's death he succeeded to his business, and in 1710 was organ-builder to the Royal Chapels. His organs do not appear to be very numerous, that of Westminster being his *chef-d'œuvre*. It was built for the coronation of George II. in 1727, and was presented to the Abbey by the King (Chrysander's *Händel*, ii. 174, note). He put up another organ in Henry the Seventh's Chapel for the funeral of Queen Caroline, Dec. 17, 1737, when Handel's noble anthem, 'The ways of Zion,' was first sung to its accompaniment(*Ibid*. p.437, note; Stanley's *Westminster Abbey*, p. 166). An amusing epitaph is quoted in Scott's *Gleanings from Westminster Abbey*, 2nd ed. p. 279.   V. DE P.

SCHRÖDER-DEVRIENT, WILHELMINE, a highly-gifted dramatic singer, was born at Hamburg, Dec. 6, 1804.[1] Her father, Friedrich Schröder—who died in 1818—had been an excellent baritone singer, a favourite in many operas, especially in Mozart's 'Don Juan,' which he was the first to act in German. Her mother was Antoinette Sophie Bürger, a celebrated actress, sometimes called 'the German Siddons.'

Wilhelmine was the eldest of four children. She enjoyed great advantages of training; dancing lessons, and public appearances in ballets in early childhood, helped her to mastery of attitude and elasticity of movement; afterwards, when her parents' wanderings led them to Vienna, she took such parts as Ophelia, and Aricia (Schiller's 'Phädra'), at the Hofburgtheater, receiving careful instruction in gesture and delivery from her mother, who afterwards superintended her study of operatic parts.

Thus there was no trace of the débutante, when, in 1821, Wilhelmine made a brilliant first appearance at the Vienna opera-house as Pamina in 'Die Zauberflöte.' The freshness of her well-developed soprano, her purity of intonation and certainty of attack, astonished the public. Other early triumphs were Emmeline (Weigl's 'Schweizerfamilie'), Marie (Grétry's 'Barbe bleu'[2]), where she showed herself worthy of all praise 'as well in singing as in acting, especially in parts demanding passionate expression.' As Agathe ('Der Freischütz') her glorious voice and charming appearance won great approval, not only from the public 'who already loved her,' but from

Weber, who presided over the performance at Vienna, March 7, 1822. But her great achievement was the creation of the part of Leonore, on the revival of 'Fidelio' at Vienna later in the year. Hitherto connoisseurs had failed to discover the merits of Beethoven's opera. Mlle. Schröder's impersonation of the heroine, besides laying the foundation of her own fame, redeemed the music from the imputation of coldness, won for the work the praise so long withheld, and achieved its ultimate popularity by repeated performances in Germany, London, and Paris. The story of her first appearance in the part has often been quoted from Glümer's *Erinnerungen an Wilhelmine Schröder Devrient*. Beethoven was present at the performance. 'He sat behind the conductor, and had wrapped himself so closely in the folds of his cloak that only his eyes could be seen flashing from it.' Schröder's natural anxiety only heightened the effect of her acting. A breathless stillness filled the house until Leonore fell into the arms of her husband, when a storm of applause broke out which seemed unceasing. To Beethoven also had his Leonore been revealed in the glowing life of Schröder's representation. He smilingly patted her cheek, thanked her, and promised to write an opera for her. Would that he had!

In 1823 she went to Dresden to fulfil a contract to sing at the Court Theatre for two years, at a salary of 2000 thalers. (At a later period she received 4000 thalers at the same house, for her connection with Dresden never entirely ceased as long as she was on the stage.) She married Karl Devrient, an excellent actor whom she met in Berlin during an engagement there that year. Four children were born, but the marriage was not a happy one, and was dissolved in 1828. During the next eight years she delighted her audiences by her appearance in the great classical characters which ever remained her most successful parts. In Weber's operas, as Preciosa, Euryanthe, and Reiza, she is said to have thrown a new light over both story and music, gradually heightening the interest of the work until a torrent of inspiration carried all before it. In Spontini's 'Vestale' she was the very personification of the spirit of the antique. Yet no less did she succeed, in Paër's comic opera, 'Sargino,' in singing with so much finish, and acting with so much humour, that it became a matter of dispute whether tragedy or comedy was her forte.

In 1830 she passed through Weimar and sang to Goethe on her way to Paris to join Röckel's German company. With an exalted sense of the importance of her mission, she wrote: 'I had to think not only of my own reputation, but to establish German music. *My* failure would have been injurious to the music of Beethoven, Mozart, and Weber.'

---

[1] According to her own account, as quoted in Glümer's *Erinnerungen*, and not in October 1805, as stated by Fétis.
[2] 'Raoul Barbe bleu' (1789), Germanised into 'Raoul der Blaubart.'

This date was an epoch in the history of music in Paris. Bouquets—then an extraordinary manifestation of approval—were showered upon the triumphant singer. In her subsequent visits to Paris, 1831 and 1832, she sang in Italian opera.

In 1832 Schröder-Devrient was heard at the King's Theatre in London, engaging with Mr. Monck Mason to sing ten times monthly during May, June, and July, for £800 and a benefit. Chelard was conductor. 'Fidelio,' 'Don Juan,' and Chelard's 'Macbeth' were repeatedly given, but Chorley (*Musical Recollections*) says, 'Fidelio was the solitary success of a disastrous enterprise. . . . The sensation is not to be forgotten. The Italians (not very strong that year) were beaten out of the field by the Germans. The intense musical vigour of Beethoven's opera was felt to be a startling variety, wrought out as it was in its principal part, by a vocalist of a class entirely new to England. This was Madame Schröder-Devrient. Within the conditions of her own school she was a remarkable artist. . . . She was a pale woman ; her face, a thoroughly German one though plain, was pleasing, from the intensity of expression which her large features and deep tender eyes conveyed. She had profuse fair hair, the value of which she thoroughly understood, delighting, in moments of great emotion, to fling it loose with the wild vehemence of a Mænad. Her figure was superb though full, and she rejoiced in its display. Her voice was a strong soprano, not comparable in quality to some other German voices of its class . . . but with an inherent expressiveness of tone which made it more attractive on the stage than many a more faultless organ. . . . Her tones were delivered without any care, save to give them due force. Her execution was bad and heavy. There was an air of strain and spasm throughout her performance.'

The 'Queen of Tears' (so she was styled) was heard next season in 'Der Freischütz,' 'Die Zauberflöte,' 'Euryanthe,' and 'Otello.' The engagement was to sing for Mr. Bunn at Covent Garden twenty-four times at £40 a night, and once for the benefit of the speculators. However all London was under the spell of Taglioni and of Fanny Elsler. Malibran in the English opera ; Pasta, Cinti-Damoreau, Rubini, and Tamburini, in the Italian opera, sang to empty houses. Again in 1837, after Malibran's death, Mr. Bunn engaged Schröder-Devrient at a double salary. 'Fidelio,' 'Le Sonnambula,' and 'Norma' were performed in English. She broke down in health before the season was over. After a rest, too short to be beneficial, she resumed her work, and was carried home insensible from the theatre. She was able, however, to give a farewell performance of 'Fidelio,' with the last act of the 'Montecchi e Capuletti,' and then discovered that Bunn had declared himself bankrupt and

could pay her nothing. In his book, *The Stage both before and behind the Curtain*, Bunn complains of the singer's attempts at extortion ; says that she demanded the fourth part of the proceeds of each night, but on this sum proving to fall short of the fixed salary, asked for £100.

From 1837 a gradual decline in power was observed in Mme. Schröder-Devrient, though she continued to delight her audiences all over Germany in the parts she had identified herself with. Of Wagner's operas she only appeared in 'Rienzi' as Adriano Colonna, in 'Der fliegende Holländer' as Senta, and in 'Tannhäuser' as Venus. Gluck's masterpieces were among her latest studies. Her last appearance in Dresden was in his 'Iphigenie in Aulis,' in 1847 ; her last appearance on any stage took place at Riga, where she played Romeo. Her concert-singing was greatly admired, and one of the liveliest passages in Mendelssohn's letters [1] describes the *furore* caused by her impromptu execution of 'Adelaide' in her ordinary travelling dress at the Gewandhaus Concert of Feb. 11, 1841.

She had made a second marriage with Herr von Döring, a worthless person, who immediately seized upon his wife's earnings and pension, and left her almost destitute, to recover what she could in a long lawsuit. The marriage was dissolved at her wish. In 1850 she again married Herr von Bock, a man of culture, who took her to his property in Livonia. Passing through Dresden she was arrested on account of the sympathy she had shown with the revolution of 1848. An examination in Berlin resulted in her being forbidden to return to Saxony ; in the meantime she was exiled from Russia. Her husband's exertions and sacrifices secured a reversal of this sentence. In 1856 she visited some German towns, singing Lieder in public concerts. Her interpretations of Beethoven's 'Adelaide' and of Schubert's and Schumann's songs were immensely admired, though by some thought too dramatic. When at Leipzig her strength succumbed to a painful illness. She was devotedly nursed by a sister and a friend at Coburg, and died Jan. 21, 1860.

Even in her best days her voice was of no extraordinary compass, but, to the last, the tones of the middle notes were of exceptionally fine quality. Mazatti's teaching, with further instruction from Radichi and from Miksch (the Dresden Chorus-master), had not been sufficient training for the young girl, who had besides been disinclined to the drudgery of scale-singing. The neglect of system and of careful vocal exercise resulted in faulty execution and too early loss of the high notes. This might have been less observable had she kept to such simple rôles as Pamina and Agathe. But there seemed a discrepancy between the delicate

[1] Letter, Feb. 14, 1841.

WILHELMINE SCHRÖDER–DEVRIENT

organisation of her voice and the passionate energy of her temperament. By force of will she accomplished more than was warranted by her natural powers. 'A portion of her life was exhausted in every song.' As a musical instrument the voice was not under her command ; as a vehicle of expression it was completely so. It was the dramatic genius of this artist which won for her an European reputation. She infused a terrible earnestness into the more pathetic impersonations, while an almost unerring instinct of artistic fitness, combined with a conscientious study of the parts, secured a perfection of performance which reached every detail of by-play. It could be said of her that she never ceased learning, for she toiled at her art to the end. She once wrote as follows : ' Art is an eternal race, and the artist is destroyed for art as soon as he entertains the delusion that he is at the goal. It were certainly comfortable to lay down the task with the costume, and let it rest until its turn comes round again in the répertoire. I have never been able to do this. How often, when the public have shouted approval and showered bouquets on me, have I retired in confusion, asking myself : "Wilhelmine, what have you been about again ?"—then there would be no peace for me, but brooding the livelong days and nights, until I had hit upon something better.'

Her good faith and earnestness led her to condemn a fellow-actress for disrespect to her art when she carelessly threw down behind the scenes a handkerchief which had served on the stage as a Signal of Love. Schröder-Devrient's art generally inspired others with her own spirit. On one occasion it moved a Bluebeard to forget the ordinary artifice used in dragging his Marie off the stage, and to take her literally by the hair. 'Almost unconscious with pain and covered with blood, the artist endured this torture rather than spoil the effect of the tableau.' It was easier for her to forgive an injury arising thus from excess of feeling, than to tolerate the inadequate support of a first tenor, ' half sponge, half wood ' ; or to allow the sleepy acting of a prima donna to go unpunished : as when, in Romeo, she was guilty of tickling the feet of a too unemotional Giulietta, during the caresses of the last scene of Bellini's opera. (See also Moscheles' Life, i. 270.) An audience of ' lederne Seelen ' was her abhorrence, and the ignorance of fashionable London in the forties tried her sorely (Ib. p. 263).

In his Modern German Music (i. 341) Chorley enters upon an analysis of some of Madame Schröder-Devrient's parts. He and Berlioz (the latter in letters to the Journal des Débats, 1843) concur in condemning the mannerisms which grew upon her as time went on. Rellstab has devoted an article to her (Ges. Schriften, ix.). A. von Wolzogen's Wilh. Schröder-

Devrient (Leipzig, 1863) is the best life, and gives a circumstantial, impartial, and interesting account ; while Wagner's Ueber Schauspieler und Sänger eulogises her depth of feeling and power of interpretation.　　　　L. M. M.

SCHROETER, CHRISTOPH GOTTLIEB, born at Hohenstein, Saxony, August 10, 1699, long enjoyed in Germany the honour of having invented the pianoforte. His claims, first published by himself in Mizler's Musikalische Bibliothek (Leipzig, 1738) and repeated in Marpurg's Kritische Briefe (Berlin, 1764) have been examined and set aside in favour of Cristofori. [See PIANOFORTE, vol. iii. pp. 718, 719.] We learn from Schroeter's autobiography that at seven years of age he was placed as a chorister at Dresden, under Capellmeister Schmidt, and that Graun was his companion. The clavichord early became his greatest pleasure. When he lost his voice he entered the Kreuzschule to study thorough-bass, that is, accompaniment as then practised, and learned to quill and tune harpsichords, which led him to the monochord and systems of temperament. On the wish of his mother that he should study theology, he went to Leipzig for that purpose in 1717, but after her death resumed music, returned to Dresden, and was accepted by Lotti to copy for him, and write his middle parts. It was at this time that he endeavoured to combine the characteristics of the harpsichord and clavichord, by inventing two hammer actions, the models of which he deposited at the Saxon Court in 1721 ; but immediately afterwards he left Dresden, taking service with a Baron whom he does not name, to travel in Germany, Holland, and England. In 1724 he went to the University of Jena and began writing upon musical subjects ; in 1726 he took the organist's place at Minden, removing in 1732 to Nordhausen, where he remained until his death in 1782. [He published a treatise, Deutliche Anweisung zum General-Bass, in 1772 at Halberstadt, and his Letzte Beschäftigung mit musikalischen Dingen appeared posthumously in 1782. A list of his polemical pamphlets is given in the Quellen-Lexikon and elsewhere.]　A. J. H.

SCHRÖTER, CORONA ELISABETH WILHELMINE, a celebrated singer of the Weimar court in its most brilliant days, was the daughter of a musician, Johann Friedrich Schröter. According to her latest biographer, Keil (Vor hundert Jahren, Leipzig, 1875), Corona was born Jan. 14, 1751, at Guben, whence the family shortly afterwards migrated to Warsaw, and finally to Leipzig. Corona's voice was trained by her father, and she sang when she was but fourteen at a Leipzig Grosses Concert (1765). From the following year until 1771 she was engaged at these concerts, Schmehling (La Mara) being retained as principal vocalist. Goethe had become acquainted with Schröter in 1766 ; ten years later he conveyed to her the offer of the post of Kammersängerin to the Dowager Duchess of Weimar. Here she made her first appearance Nov. 23, 1776, and soon became the idol of the place. Associated with Goethe himself in the production of his dramas, she created amongst others the part of Iphigenia, completely realising the poet's ideal (see *Auf Mieding's Tod*). Her co-operation in 'Die Fischerin' included the composition of all the music. It was on July 22, 1782, that she was heard as Dortchen, and that 'Der Erlkönig,' with which the play opens, was sung for the first time. [In 1782-84 she sang at the Gewandhaus in Leipzig.] After 1786 Schröter sang little in public, but devoted herself to composition, painting, and a few dramatic pupils. Schiller heard her read Goethe's 'Iphigenie' in 1787, and Charlotte von Schiller, a year or two later, found much to praise in the musical settings of 'Der Taucher' and 'Würde der Frauen,' and their expressive rendering by the famous artist. In the meantime Schröter's health had broken down, and her death, when aged fifty-one, at Ilmenau, August 23, 1802, was not unexpected.

Her songs were published in two books. They are melodious and simple settings of poems by Herder, Matthison, Klopstock, etc. Book I. (25 Lieder, Weimar, 1786) contains Goethe's 'Der neue Amadis' and 'Der Erlkönig.' The second collection of songs was published at Weimar, 1794.

Corona's brothers, Johann Samuel (see below) and Johann Heinrich Schröter (violinist) visited England; the latter published some duos for two violins and for violin and violoncello, in 1782. Besides the life by Keil, Düntzer's *Charlotte von Stein und Corona Schröter* may be consulted for details of her social and artistic successes. In 1778 Schröter handed to Goethe her MS. autobiography, which has never been made public, perhaps has not yet been discovered among his papers, although Goethe noted the receipt of it in his diary.   L. M. M.

SCHRÖTER, JOHANN SAMUEL, an esteemed pianoforte-player and composer for that instrument, was born about 1750 of German parents at Warsaw, where his father, Johann Friedrich, was oboist in the royal orchestra. About 1763 he accompanied his father and sister to Leipzig, and sang there in the Gewandhaus Concerts. On the breaking of his voice he devoted himself entirely to the piano, and travelled with his father, brother, and sister, performing as they went, through Holland to London. There they made their début in the concerts of Bach and Abel at the Thatched House, St. James's Street, May 2, 1772, Schröter playing a concerto on the 'Forte Piano,' which J. Christian Bach had first performed in 1767, the brother Johann Heinrich on the violin, and the sister, Corona, singing. [In 1773 we find evidence of his performance on the harpsichord, as Broadwood's

books show that a harpsichord was sent to Haberdashers' Hall on March 4, for J. S. Schröter (A. J. H.).] After J. C. Bach's death in 1782, he succeeded him as music-master to the Queen. 'Six Sonatas for the harpsichord or piano forte' are announced by W. Napier in the *Public Advertiser* in 1776 as his op. 1. This was followed in 1778 by op. 3, 'Six Concertos with an accompaniment for two violins and a bass'; and this again by three concertos with string accompaniments, op. 4; three, op. 5 (Berlin); op. 6 (Paris); op. 2, six trios (Amsterdam); op. 9, two ditto (Do.). [Many other compositions—quintets, trios, sonatas with and without accompaniment—are enumerated in the *Quellen-Lexikon*.] The *A B C Dario* (p. 144) says of him, 'He has composed the harpsichord parts of some concertos; the accompaniments are by Bach; they are neither new nor very striking. He plays in an elegant and masterly style; his cadences are well imagined, and if his *penchant* was not rather to play rapidly than *al core*, he would excel on the pianoforte.' Burney, on the other hand (in Rees), says, 'He became one of the neatest and most expressive players of his time, and his style of composition, highly polished, resembles that of Abel more than any other. It was graceful and in good taste, but so chaste as sometimes to seem deficient in fire and invention.' He did not remain long before the public in consequence of his marriage with one of his pupils, a young lady of birth and fortune, after which he played only at the concerts of the Prince of Wales and a few others of the nobility. He died on Sunday, Nov. 2, 1788, in his own house at Pimlico, having lost his voice some years before by a severe cold. His marriage was a clandestine one, and brought him into collision with his wife's family, the result of which was his surrendering all his rights for an annuity of £500. She is the lady who took lessons from Haydn during his residence in London, and fell violently in love with him. Haydn spoke of her many years after as a very attractive woman, and still handsome, though over sixty; 'had I been free,' said the patriarch, 'I should certainly have married her'—she was then a widow. He dedicated to her three clavier trios (B. & H., Nos. 1, 2, 6). [See vol. ii. p. 358.]   C. F. P.

SCHROETER, LEONARD, born at Torgau towards the middle of the 16th century, became Cantor of the Cathedral of Magdeburg about 1564, in succession to Gallus Dressler, also a composer of some importance. [His successor was appointed in 1600, so this may be assumed as the year of his death.] Schroeter's chief work is 'Hymni Sacri,' Erfurt, 1587, and consists of 4- and 5-part settings of those Latin Church Hymns which had also been received into the worship of the Lutheran Church.

Winterfeld says of these hymns that they belong to the best musical works of the time ; the harmony is rich, clear, and dignified, and shows an unmistakable advance on the path of the older masters. They are in the same style as the Hymns of Palestrina and Vittoria, only the choral melody is mostly given to the upper voice. Some of these hymns, as well as some of the German psalms of Gallus Dressler, Schroeter's predecessor, are re-published in Schöberlein and Riegel's *Schatz des liturgischen Chorgesangs*, Göttingen, 1868-72. [Earlier publications of hymn-tunes by Schroeter were published in 1562, 1576, 1584, etc. See the *Quellen-Lexikon* for list.] Four Weihnachts-Liedlein of Schroeter's are received into the repertoire of the Berlin Dom-Chor, and are published in Schlesinger's 'Musica Sacra,' No. 11. A German Te Deum for double choir by Schroeter, originally published in 1576, has been printed by Otto Kade in the Notenbeilagen to Ambros's *Gesch. der Musik*, No. 28.   J. R. M.

SCHUBART, CHRISTIAN FRIEDRICH DANIEL, born at Obersontheim in Suabia, in 1739,[1] and brought up, not as a musician, at Nördlingen, Nuremberg, and Erlangen. In 1768 we find him as organist at Ludwigsburg. His life seems to have been a very wild and irregular one, but he must have been a man of great talent and energy to justify the eulogies on him so frequent in the early volumes of the *Allg. musikalische Zeitung*, of Leipzig (see vol. ii. pp. 78, 98, etc.), and the constant references of Otto Jahn in his *Life of Mozart*. He lived in Mannheim, Munich, Augsburg, and Ulm ; founded a *Deutsche Chronik* in 1744 ; was more than once in confinement for his misdeeds, and at length was imprisoned from 1777 to 1787 at Hohenasperg. [On his release he was appointed director of the court theatre ; his paper changed its title to *Vaterlands-Chronik*, and appeared from 1787 until the year of his death.] He died Oct. 10, 1791. An autobiography, written in prison, appeared in 1791-93. His compositions are few and unimportant. [They include a set of 'Musicalische Rhapsodien,' a 'Salve Regina,' variations, and other clavier pieces.] A work of his on musical æsthetics, *Ideen zu einer Aesthetik der Tonkunst*, was published after his death by his son Ludwig (Vienna, 1806). From the notices of it in the *A.M.Z.* (viii. 801, xiii. 53, etc.) and Jahn's citations, it appears to be partly a dissertation on the styles, abilities, and characteristics of great musicians and artists. It also contains some fanciful descriptions of the various keys, which Schumann notices (*Ges. Schriften*, i. 180) only to condemn. But Schubart will always be known as the author of the words of one of F. Schubert's most favourite songs—'Die Forelle' (op. 32). The words of 'An den Tod' and 'Grablied auf einen Soldaten' are also his. His

son further published two vols. of his *Vermischte Schriften* (Zürich, 1812).   G.

SCHUBERT, FERDINAND, one of the elder brothers of FRANZ SCHUBERT, second son of his father (see p. 280), born at Vienna, Oct. 19, 1794. After passing the two-years' course at the Normal School of St. Anna in 1807-8, he became his father's assistant at the school in the Lichtenthal. In Nov. 1810 he was installed as assistant (Gehilfe), and in 1816 teacher, at the Imperial Orphan House (Waisenhaus) in Vienna, where he continued till March 1820, devoting himself specially to the Bell-Lancastrian method. He was then appointed principal teacher and choirmaster to the school at Altlerchenfeld, Vienna, till 1824, when he was nominated to be head teacher of the Normal School of St. Anna, which he held from Jan. 22, 1824, till his appointment as director of the same establishment on March 15, 1854. This position he retained till his death on Feb. 28, 1859. His merits were recognised by the bestowal of the Gold Cross of Merit (Verdienstkreuze), with the Crown. During this long period of useful and efficient service he was twice married, and had in all seventeen children, of whom Ferdinand, Rudolf, and Hermann were living in Vienna in 1882. His daughter Elise married Linus Geisler, and their daughter, Caroline Geisler-Schubert, had a successful career in Vienna as a player and teacher. She is now living in England. Between 1819 and 1853 Ferdinand published twelve school-books on various branches of learning, which came into general use. Music he learnt from his father and from Holzer, and left more than forty works, of which the following were published :— Regina Cœli, *a* 4 and orch. (op. 1) ; German Requiem, *a* 4 with organ (op. 2) ; 4 Waisenlieder (op. 3) ; Cadenzas for PF. in all keys (op. 4) ; Requiem *a* 4 and orch. (op. 9) ; Mass in F, *a* 4 and orch. (op. 10) ; Salve Regina in F, *a* 4 and orch. (op. 11) ; Salve Regina *a* 4 and wind (op. 12) ; original March and Trio. The MS. works contain various other pieces of church music. Of the two Requiems the first is mentioned in his brother's letter of August 24, 1818 (see p. 291) ; the second was performed a few days before Franz's death, and was possibly the last music he heard. The library of the Musikverein at Vienna contains the autograph of Franz Schubert's Mass in G, with oboes (or clarinets) and bassoons, added by Ferdinand, July 23, 1847.

Ferdinand's love for his brother and care of his memory have been often referred to in the following article (pp. 317, 319, 320). An interesting evidence of their attachment is afforded by a letter[2] of his to Franz, dated Vienna, July 3, 1824, and containing the following passage in regard to a clock at the Ungarische Krone in Vienna, which played his brother's music :—

[1] The day is given in the *Quellen-Lexikon* as March 26, and in Riemann's *Lexikon* as April 13.

[2] I owe this letter to Miss Geisler-Schubert.

'This clock delighted me not a little, when one day at dinner for the first time I heard it play some of your waltzes. I felt so strange at the moment that I really did not know where I was ; it was not only that it pleased me, it went regularly through my heart and soul with a fearful pang and longing, which at last turned into settled melancholy.' This may be fanciful, but it is the language of passionate affection, which evidently animated Ferdinand's whole intercourse with his great brother. Franz's reply (July 16-18, 1824) is quite in the same strain. (The above article is indebted to Wurzbach's *Biographisches Lexicon.*)   G.

SCHUBERT,[1] FRANZ PETER, the one great composer native to Vienna, was born Jan. 31, 1797, in the district called Lichtenthal, at the house which is now numbered 54 of the Nussdorfer Strasse,[2] on the right, going out from Vienna. There is now a grey marble tablet over the door, with the words ' Franz Schuberts Geburtshaus' in the centre ; on the left side a lyre crowned with a star, and on the right a chaplet of leaves containing the words, ' 31 Jänner 1797.' He came of a country stock, originally belonging to Zukmantel in Austrian Silesia. His father, Franz, the son of a peasant at Neudorf in Moravia, was born about 1764, studied in Vienna, and in 1784 became assistant to his brother, who kept a school in the Leopoldstadt. His ability and integrity raised him in 1786 to be parish schoolmaster in the parish of the 'Twelve holy helpers' in the Lichtenthal, a post which he kept till 1817 or 1818, when he was appointed to the parish school in the adjoining district of the Rossau, and there he remained till his death, July 9, 1830. He married early, while still helping his brother, probably in 1783, Elisabeth Vitz, or Fitz, a Silesian, who was in service in Vienna, and was, like Beethoven's mother, a cook. Their first child, Ignaz, was born in 1784. Then came a long gap, possibly filled by children who died in infancy—of whom they lost nine in all ; then, Oct. 19, 1794, another boy, Ferdinand ; then in 1796, Karl, then Franz, and lastly, a daughter, Theresia, Sept. 17, 1801, who died August 7, 1878. The hardworked mother of these fourteen children lived till 1812. Soon after her death her husband was married again, to Anna Klayenbök, a

Viennese, and had a second family of five children, of whom three grew up, viz. Josefa (+ 1861), Andreas, an accountant in one of the public offices, and Anton, a Benedictine priest, ' Father Hermann'[3]—the last two living in 1881.

Ignaz and Ferdinand followed their father's calling, and inherited with it the integrity, frugality, and modesty, which had gained him such respect. Of the former we do not hear much ; the one letter by him that is preserved (Oct. 12, 1818), shows him very free-thinking, very tired of schoolmastering, very much attached to his home and his brother.[4] He remained at the Rossau school till his death in 1844. Ferdinand, on the other hand, rose to be director of the chief normal school of St. Anna in Vienna, and played a considerable part in the life of his celebrated brother, by whom he was fondly loved, to whom he was deeply attached, and whose eyes it was given to him to close in death.

Little Franz was no doubt well grounded by his father, and to that early training probably owed the methodical habit which stuck to him more or less closely through life, of dating his pieces, a practice which makes the investigation of them doubly interesting.[5] As schoolmasters the father and his two eldest sons were all more or less musical. Ignaz and Ferdinand had learned the violin with other rudiments from the father, and Franz was also taught it by him in his turn, and the ' clavier' (*i.e.* probably the pianoforte—for Beethoven's op. 31 was published before Schubert had passed his sixth year) by Ignaz, who was twelve years his senior. But his high vocation quickly revealed itself ; he soon outstripped these simple teachers, and was put under Michael Holzer, the choirmaster of the parish, for both violin and piano, as well as for singing, the organ, and thorough-bass. On this good man, who long outlived him, he made a deep impression. ' When I wished to teach him anything fresh,' he would say, ' he always knew it already. I have often listened to him in astonishment.'[6] Holzer would give him subjects to extemporise upon, and then his joy would know no bounds, and he would cry ' The lad has got harmony at his fingers' ends.'[7] Such astonishment was natural enough, but it would have been far better if he had taught him counterpoint. Ignaz too—and an elder brother is not always a lenient judge of his

---

[1] The following abbreviations are used in the notes to this article :—

K.H.=Kreissle von Hellborn's biography. The first reference to the German edition ; the second, in brackets, to Coleridge's translation.

Ferd.=Ferdinand Schubert, in his biographical sketch in Schumann's *Neue Zeitschrift für Musik*, x. p. 129, etc.

A.M.Z.=*Allgemeine Musikalische Zeitung.*

N.Z.M.=*Neue Zeitschrift für Musik.*

W.Z.K.=*Wiener Zeitschrift für Kunst, etc.*

[2] The Nussdorfer Strasse runs north and south. At the time of Schubert's birth it was called 'Auf dem Himmelpfortgrund,' and the house was No. 72. The Himmelpfortgasse (' the street of the gate of heaven') was a short street running out of it westwards towards the fortifications—the same which is now the 'Säulengasse.' The present Schubertgasse did not then exist beyond the opening into the main street. I find all this on a large map of the date in the British Museum.

[3] Author of a sermon on the 1400th anniversary of the birth of St. Benedict (Vienna, 1880), in which he is styled 'Capitularpriester des Stiftes Schotten ; Curat und Prediger an der Stiftspfarre ; Besitzer des gold. Verdienstkreuzes m. d. Krone.'

[4] *K.H.* p. 146 (i. 149).

[5] His usual practice was to write the title of the piece, the date, and his name, ' *Frz Schubert Mpia' (manu propriâ*), at the head of the 'first page, on beginning to compose. In his earlier years he added the full date of completion at the end, even when it was the same day. See Nos. 1, 2, and 5 of the '6 Lieder' (Müller)—all three belonging to 1813, as given in Nottebohm's *Catalogue*, p. 243. Sometimes he has dated each movement, as in the String Quartet in Bb (op. 168), described under 1814. With 1815, however, this minute dating in great measure ceases, and as a rule we find the year or at most the month stated.

[6] *N.Z.M.*   [7] *K.H.* p. 5 (i. 5).

junior—bears similar testimony. 'I was much astonished,' says he, 'when after a few months he told me that he had no more need of any help from me, but would go on by himself ; and indeed I soon had to acknowledge that he had far surpassed me, beyond hope of competition.'

Before he became eleven he was first soprano in the Lichtenthal choir, noted for the beauty of his voice and the appropriateness of his expression. He played the violin solos when they occurred in the service, and at home composed little songs, and pieces for strings or for PF. For a child so gifted, of people in the position of the Schuberts, the next step was naturally the Imperial *Convict*, or school[1] for educating the choristers for the Court-chapel ; and to the *Convict* accordingly Franz was sent in Oct. 1808, when eleven years and eight months old. He went up with a batch of other boys, who, while waiting, made themselves merry over his grey suit, calling him a miller, and otherwise cracking jokes. But the laugh soon ceased when the 'miller' came under the examiners, the Court-capellmeisters Salieri and Eybler, and Korner the singing-master. He sang the trial-pieces in such a style that he was at once received, and henceforth the grey frock was exchanged for the gold-laced uniform of the imperial choristers. The music in the *Convict* had been a good deal dropt in consequence of the war, but after the signing of the treaty of peace, Oct. 14, 1809, it regained its old footing, and then Franz soon took his right place in the music-school. There was an orchestra formed from the boys, which practised daily symphonies and overtures of Haydn, Mozart, Krommer, Kozeluch, Méhul, Cherubini, etc., and occasionally Beethoven. Here his home practice put him on a level with older boys than himself. The leader of the band, behind whom he sat, several years his senior, turned round the first day to see who it was that was playing so cleverly, and found it to be ' a small boy in spectacles named Franz Schubert.'[2] The big fellow's name was Spaun, and he soon became intimate with his little neighbour. Franz was extremely sensitive, and one day admitted to his friend, very confused and blushing deeply, that he had already composed much ; that indeed he could not help it, and should do it every day if he could afford to get music-paper. Spaun saw the state of matters, and took care that music-paper should be forthcoming ; for which and other kindnesses his name will be long remembered. Franz in time became first violin, and when Ruzicka, the regular conductor, was absent, he took his place. The orchestral music must have been a great delight to him, but we only hear that he preferred Kozeluch to Krommer, and that

his particular favourites were some adagios of Haydn's, Mozart's G minor Symphony, in which he said ' You could hear the angels singing,' and the overtures to ' Figaro ' and the ' Zauberflöte.' It is also evident from his earliest symphonies that the overture to ' Prometheus ' had made its mark on his mind. On Sundays and holidays he went home, and then the great delight of the family was to play quartets, his own or those of other writers, in which the father took the violoncello, Ferdinand and Ignaz the first and second violins, and Franz the viola, as Mozart did before him, and Mendelssohn after him. The father would now and then make a mistake ; on the first occasion Franz took no notice, but if it recurred he would say with a smile, in a timid way, ' Herr Vater, something must be wrong there.'

The instruction in the *Convict* was by no means only musical. There was a Curator, a Director (Rev. Innocenz Lang), a Sub-director, an Inspector, a staff of preachers and catechists ; and there were teachers of mathematics, history, and geography, poetry, writing, drawing, French, and Italian.[3] In fact it was a school, apart from its music department. Franz of course took his part in all this instruction, and for the first year is said to have acquitted himself with credit, but his reputation in the school fell off as it increased in the musical department. The extraordinary thirst for composition, which is so remarkable throughout his life, began to assert itself at this time, and appears to have been limited only by his power of obtaining paper ; and it not unnaturally interfered with his general lessons. His first pianoforte piece of any dimensions, and apparently his earliest existing composition, was a four-hand fantasia, containing more than a dozen movements, all of different characters, and occupying thirty-two pages of very small writing. It is dated April 8–May 1, 1810, and was followed by two smaller ones.[4] His brother remarks that not one of the three ends in the key in which it began. The next is a long vocal piece for voice and PF., called ' Hagars Klage ' — Hagar's lament over her dying son—dated March 30, 1811, also containing twelve movements, with curious unconnected changes of key ; and another, of even grimmer character, attributed to the same year, is called ' Leichenfantasie,' or Corpse-fantasia, to the words of Schiller's gruesome juvenile poem of the same name. This has seventeen movements, and is quite as erratic in its changes of key and disregard of the compass of the voice as the preceding.[5] The reminiscences of Haydn's ' Creation,' Mozart's opera airs, and Beethoven's Andantes, are frequent in both. A fourth is ' Der Vatermörder '—the Parricide—

---

[1] In the Piaristengasse in the Josephstadt. See a very full and interesting account of this school in Hanslick's excellent book, *Geschichte des Concertwesens in Wien* (Vienna, 1869), p. 141.
[2] From a sketch by von Köchel, entitled *Nachruf an Joseph von Spaun*, Vienna (privately printed), 1866. I owe the sight of this to my excellent friend Mr. Pohl.

[3] See the list of names in *K.H.* p. 13 (i. 13).
[4] *Ferd.* p. 133. Reissmann (p. 7) gives the inscriptions—'Den 8. Aprill angefangen. Den 1. May vollbracht, 1810.'
[5] The autographs of both are in possession of Herr Nicholas Dumba of Vienna.

for voice and PF., ‘26 Dec. 1811,’ a pleasant Christmas piece ! a decided advance on the two previous songs in individuality of style, and connection.   1811 also saw the composition of a quintet-overture, a string quartet, a second fantasia for four hands, and many songs.[1]   For 1812 the list is more instrumental.   It contains an overture for orchestra in D ; a quartet over-ture in Bb ; string quartets in C, Bb, and D[2] ; a sonata for PF., violin, and violoncello ; varia-tions in Eb, and an andante, both for PF. ; a Salve Regina and a Kyrie.   In 1813 an octet[3] for wind ; three string quartets in C, Bb, Eb, and D ; minuets and trios for orchestra and for PF. ; a third fantasia for the PF., four hands ; several songs, terzets, and canons ; a cantata in two movements, for three male voices and guitar, for his father's birthday, Sept. 27—both words and music his own ; and his first symphony in D,[4] intended to celebrate the birthday of Dr. Lang, and finished on Oct. 28.   With this very important work his time at the *Convict* ended. He might have remained longer ; for it is said that the Emperor, who took an interest in the lads of his chapel, had specially watched the progress of this gifted boy with the lovely voice and fine expression, and that a special decision had been registered in his favour on Oct. 21, assuring him a foundation scholarship in the school, provided that during the vacation he should study sufficiently to pass an examination.[5] To this condition, however, he refused to submit ; and at some time between Oct. 26 and Nov. 6 he left the *Convict* and returned home.[6]   His mother died in 1812, but we hear nothing of the event, unless the octet just named refers to it.   The father married again in about a year, and the new wife, as we shall see, did her duty to her stepson Franz fully, and apparently with affection.

Franz was now just completing his seven-teenth year, and what has been rightly called the first period of his life.   The *Convict* has much to answer for in regard to Schubert.   It was entrusted with the most poetical genius of modern times, and it appears to have allowed him to take his own course in the matter of composition almost unrestrained.   Had but a portion of the pains been spent on the musical education of Schubert that was lavished on that of Mozart or of Mendelssohn, we can hardly doubt that even his transcendent ability would

have been enhanced by it, that he would have gained that control over the prodigious spon-taneity of his genius which is his only want, and have risen to the very highest level in all departments of composition, as he did in song-writing.   But though Eybler and Salieri were the conductors of the choir in chapel, it does not appear that they had any duties in the school, and Ruzicka, the thorough-bass master, like Holzer, was so prostrated by Schubert's facility as to content himself with exclaiming that his pupil already knew all he could teach him, and must have ‘learned direct from heaven.’   If all masters adopted this attitude towards their pupils, what would have become of some of the greatest geniuses ?   The dis-comforts of the school appear to have been great even for that day of roughness.   One of the pupils speaks of the cold of the practice-room as ‘dreadful’ (*schauerlich*) ; and Schubert's own earliest letter, dated Nov. 24, 1812, to his brother Ferdinand, shows that these young growing lads were allowed to go without food for 8½ hours, between ‘a poor dinner and a wretched supper.’   There was not even sufficient music paper provided for the scholars, and Schubert was, as we have seen, dependent on the bounty of the richer pupils.

On the other hand, the motets and masses in the service, the rehearsals in the school, such teaching as there was, and the daily practisings, must have been both stimulating and improving, and with all its roughness a good deal of know-ledge could not but have been obtainable.   One advantage Schubert reaped from the *Convict*— the friends which he made there, many of them for life, Spaun, Senn, Holzapfel, Stadler, and others, all afterwards more or less eminent, who attached themselves to him as every one did who came into contact with him ; a band of young adorers, eager to play, or sing, or copy anything that he composed ; the earnest of the devoted friends who surrounded him in later years, and helped to force his music on an ignorant and preoccupied public.   Nor did the enthusiasm cease with his departure ; for some years afterwards the orchestral pieces which he had written while at the school were still played by the boys from his own MS. copies.   Outside the school he had sometimes opportunities of going to the opera.   The first opera which he is said to have heard was Weigl's ‘Waisenhaus,’ played Dec. 12, 1810 ; but this was eclipsed by the ‘Schweizerfamilie’ of the same com-poser, July 8, 1811 ; that again by Spontini's ‘Vestalin,’ with Milder, Oct. 1, 1812 ; and all of them by Gluck's ‘Iphigenie auf Tauris,’ which he probably heard first April 5, 1815, with Milder and Vogl in the two principal parts, and which made a deep and ineffaceable im-pression upon him, and drove him to the study of Gluck's scores.[7]   During the same years there

1 *Ferd.* p. 138.
2 Kreissle expressly states this (p. 550) and gives the date—‘Nov. 19, 1812.’
3 This octet, dated Sept. 19, is said to be mentioned by Ferdinand Schubert as ‘Franz Schubert's Leichenbegängniss’ (funeral cere-mony).   It is supposed by Kreissle (p. 31) to have been composed for the funeral of his mother ; but it is difficult to believe that the words which he wrote for his father's birthday ode, eight days later, would have had no reference to the mother's death—which they certainly have not—if it had occurred at that date.
4 Adagio and Allegro vivace (D) ; Andante (G) ; Minuet and Trio (D) ; Finale, Allegro vivace (D).   The work was played from MS. at the Crystal Palace, Feb. 5, 1881.   The autograph is in possession of Herr Dumba, Vienna.   5 *K.H.* p. 33 (i. 33).
6 It is stated on Spaun's authority that Schubert was led to this decision by the advice of the poet Theodor Körner.   But Körner, in whose correspondence there is no mention of Schubert, left Vienna at the beginning of this year and died at Gadebusch in August.
7 From Bauernfeld, in *W.Z.K.*

were also many concerts, including those at which Beethoven produced his 5th, 6th, and 7th, Symphonies, the Choral Fantasia, portions of the Mass in C, the Overture to 'Coriolan,' and others of his greatest compositions. Schubert probably heard all these works, but it is very doubtful whether he heard them with the same predilection as the operas just mentioned. We might infer with certainty from the three earliest of his symphonies, that Beethoven's style had as yet taken but little hold on him, notwithstanding the personal fascination which he seems to have felt for the great master from first to last. But, indeed, we have his own express declaration to that effect. Coming home after a performance of an oratorio of Salieri's, June 16, 1816, he speaks of the music in terms which can only refer to Beethoven, as 'of simple natural expression, free from all that *bizarrerie* which prevails in most of the composers of our time, and for which we have almost solely to thank one of our greatest German artists ; that *bizarrerie* which unites the tragic and the comic, the agreeable and the repulsive, the heroic and the petty, the Holiest and a harlequin ; infuriates those who hear it instead of dissolving them in love, and makes them laugh instead of raising them heavenwards.' Mozart was at the time his ideal composer ; this, too, is plain from the symphonies, but here also he leaves us in no doubt. Three days earlier we find in the same diary,[1] apropos of one of the quintets of that great master :—'Gently, as if out of the distance, did the magic tones of Mozart's music strike my ears. With what inconceivable alternate force and tenderness did Schlesinger's masterly playing impress it deep, deep, into my heart ! Such lovely impressions remain on the soul, there to work for good, past all power of time or circumstances. In the darkness of this life they reveal a clear, bright, beautiful prospect, inspiring confidence and hope. O Mozart, immortal Mozart ! what countless consolatory images of a bright better world hast thou stamped on our souls.' There is no doubt to which of these two great masters he was most attached at the time he wrote this. [At the same time it is fair to add that even now his allegiance was divided. In the instrumental compositions of this period, though the style is modelled on Mozart, the subjects are occasionally reminiscent of Beethoven's ideas ; and there is a significant story that when a friend praised some of his settings of Klopstock, and hailed him already as one of the great masters of composition, he answered diffidently, ' Perhaps, I sometimes have dreams of that sort, but who can do anything after Beethoven ?']

We have seen what a scourge the conscription proved in the case of Ries (see *ante*, p. 97), and the uneasiness of Mendelssohn's family till the risk of it was over in his case (vol. iii. p. 121*a*).

To avoid a similar danger [2] Schubert elected to enter his father's school, and after the necessary study for a few months at the Normal School of St. Anna, did so, and actually remained there for three years as teacher of the lowest class. The duties were odious, but he discharged them with strict regularity, and not with greater severity than might reasonably be expected from the irritable temperament of a musician condemned to such drudgery. The picture of Pegasus thus in vile harness, and the absence of any remark on the anomaly, throws a curious light on the beginnings of a great composer. Out of school hours, however, he had his relaxations. There was a family in the Lichtenthal named Grob—a mother, son, and daughter —whose relations to him were somewhat like those of the Breunings to Beethoven (vol. i. p. 218*b*). The house was higher in the scale than his father's, and he was quite at home there. Therese, the daughter, had a fine high soprano voice, and Heinrich Grob played both PF. and violoncello ; the mother was a woman of taste, and a great deal of music was made. It is not impossible that Therese inspired him with a softer feeling.[3] The choir of the Lichtenthal church, where his old friend Holzer was still choirmaster, was his resort on Sundays and feast days, and for it he wrote his first mass, in F—begun May 17, finished July 22, 1814—a fitting pendant to the symphony of the previous October. He was not yet eighteen, and the mass is pronounced by a trustworthy critic[4] to be the most remarkable first mass ever produced, excepting Beethoven's in C, and as striking an instance of the precocity of genius as Mendelssohn's Overture to the ' Midsummer Night's Dream.' It seems to have been first performed on Oct. 16, the first Sunday after St. Theresa's day, 1814—Mayseder, then twenty-five and an acknowledged virtuoso, leading the first violins ; and was repeated at the Augustine Church ten days after. This second performance was quite an event. Franz conducted, Holzer led the choir, Ferdinand took the organ, Therese Grob sang, the enthusiasm of the family and friends was great, and the proud father presented his happy son with a five-octave piano.[5] Salieri was present and loud in his praises, and claimed Schubert as his pupil. He had indeed begun to take some interest in the lad before[6] he left the *Convict*, and continued it by daily lessons ' for a long time.'[7] That interest was probably much the same that he had shown to Beethoven fifteen years before, making him write to Metastasio's words, and correcting the prosody of his music. But there must have been some curious attraction about the old man, to attach two such original geniuses as Beethoven

[1] Quoted by *K.H.* pp. 103, 101 (i. 105, 103).

[2] He was three times summoned to enlist. See *Ferd.* p. 133.
[3] See *K.H.* pp. 141 (i. 144).
[4] Prout, in *Monthly Musical Record*, Jan. and Feb. 1871.
[5] *Ferd.* p. 133*b*.　　[6] *K.H.* i. 27 *note*.
[7] Bauernfeld, in *W.Z.K.* June 9, 1829.

and Schubert to him, and make them willing to style themselves 'scholars of Salieri.' [1] His permanent influence on Schubert may be measured by the fact that he warned him against Goethe and Schiller, a warning which Schubert attended to so far as to compose sixty-seven songs of the one poet, and fifty-four of the other !

Franz's next effort was an opera—a light and absurd supernatural ' opéra - comique ' in three acts, 'Des Teufels Lustschloss,' words by Kotzebue. He probably began it while at the *Convict*, the first act having been completed Jan. 11, 1814 ; the second, March 16 ; and the third, May 15. Two days afterwards he began the mass. That over, he had leisure to look again at the earlier work. The experience gained in writing the mass probably revealed many an imperfection in the opera. He at once rewrote it, and finished the revision of it on Oct. 22. The work was never performed. With all these and other labours he found time to visit the *Convict* [2] in the evenings, take part in the practices, and try over his new compositions. Besides the pieces already mentioned, the productions of 1814 embrace a Salve Regina for tenor and orchestra. Also two string quartets in D and C minor respectively, and a third in B♭, published as op. 168, and remarkable for the circumstances of its composition. It was begun as a string trio, and ten lines were written in that form. It was then begun again and finished as a quartet. The movements are more fully dated than usual. [3] Also five minuets and six Deutsche (or waltzes) for strings and horns ; and seventeen songs, among them 'Gretchen am Spinnrade' (Oct. 19), and Schiller's 'Der Taucher,' a composition of enormous length, begun Sept. 1813, and finished in the following August. On Dec. 10 he began his second symphony, in B♭. [4] The autograph shows that the short Introduction and Allegro vivace were finished by the twenty-sixth of the same month, but its completion falls in 1815. Before the year closed he made the acquaintance of Mayrhofer, a man of eccentric, almost hypochondriac character, and a poet of grand and gloomy cast, who became his firm friend, and fifty-four of whose poems [5] (besides the operas of 'Adrast' and 'Die beiden Freunde von Salamanka'), fortunately for Mayrhofer's immortality, he set to music—some of them

among his very finest songs. The acquaintance began by Schubert's setting Mayrhofer's 'Am See.' He composed it on Dec. 7, and a few days afterwards visited the poet at his lodgings in the Wipplinger Strasse 420 (since destroyed), a small dark room rendered illustrious by being the residence of Theodor Körner, and afterwards of Schubert, who lived there in 1819 and 1820. The visit was the beginning of a friendship which ended only with Schubert's death.

1815 is literally crowded with compositions. Two orchestral symphonies of full dimensions, Nos. 2 and 3 (that in B♭ ended March 24, that in D, [6] May 24–July 19); a string quartet in G minor (March 25–April 1) ; PF. sonatas in C, F, E (Feb. 11) and E (Feb. 18); an adagio in G (April 8), twelve Wiener Deutsche, eight Écossaises (Oct. 3), and ten variations for PF. solo ; two masses, in G [7] (March 2–7) and B♭ (Nov. 11–) ; a new 'Dona' [8] for the mass in F ; a Stabat Mater in G minor (April 4) ; a Salve Regina (July 5) ; five large dramatic pieces —' Der vierjährige Posten,' one-act operetta (ended May 16) ; 'Fernando,' one-act Singspiel (July 3–9) ; 'Claudine von Villabella,' three-act Singspiel (Act 1, July 26–August 5), originally composed complete, but Acts 2 and 3 were used by an officious maid-servant for lighting fires ; 'Die beiden Freunde von Salamanka,' a two-act Singspiel by Mayrhofer (Nov. 18–Dec. 31) ; 'Der Spiegelritter,' three-act opera, of which eight numbers are with the Gesellschaft des Musikfreunde at Vienna ; perhaps also a Singspiel called 'Die Minnesänger,' and 'Adrast,' an opera by Mayrhofer, of which but seven numbers exist. [9] In addition to all these there are no less than 146 songs. In August alone there are over thirty, and in October over twenty, of which eight are dated the 15th and seven the 19th ! And of these 146 songs some are of such enormous length as would seem to have prevented their publication. 'Minona' (MS. Feb. 8), the first one of the year, contains sixteen, and 'Adelwold and Emma' (MS., June 5) no less than fifty-five closely written sides. Of those published, 'Die Bürgschaft' ('Aug. 1815 ') fills twenty-two pages of Litolff's edition, 'Elysium' thirteen, and 'Loda's Gespenst' fifteen of the same. It was the length of such compositions as these — 'pas une histoire, mais des histoires'—that caused Beethoven's exclama-

---

[1] For Beethoven see vol. i. p. 222b. Schubert so styles himself on the title-pages of his 'Fernando' and 'Claudine von Villabella.'

[2] *K.H.* p. 18 (i. 19).

[3] The Allegro has at beginning, '5 Sept. 1814,' at end, 'den 6 Sept. in 4½ Stunden angefertigt,' apparently implying that it was dashed off before and after twelve o'clock at night. Andante, at beginning, 'den 6 Sept. 1814,' at end, 'den 10 Sept. 1814.' Minuet, at end, '11 Sept. 1814.' Finale, at end 'den 13 Sept. 1814.' Autograph with Spina.

[4] At beginning, '10 Dec. 1814'; at end of Allegro, '26 Dec. 1814'; at beginning of Finale, '25 Feb. 1815,' and at end, '24 March 1815.' The movements are Largo and Allegro vivace (B♭) ; Andante (E♭) ; Minuet and Trio (C minor) ; Finale, Presto vivace (B♭). Played from MS. at the Crystal Palace, Oct. 20, 1877. Autograph with Herr Dumba.

[5] Forty-eight published, and six in MS.

[6] It is in the usual number of movements : Adagio maestoso and Allegro con brio (D) ; Allegretto (G) ; Minuet and Trio (D) ; Finale, Presto vivace (D). Dates :—Allegro, at beginning, '24 May 1815 '; end, 'July 12, 1815.' Allegretto, at beginning, 'July 15, 1815.' End of Finale, 'July 19, 1815.' Autograph with Herr Dumba.

[7] Published by M. Berra, of Prague, in 1846, as the composition of R. Führer. [See vol. ii. p. 113b]. The fraud was not exposed till 1847, when it was announced by Ferd. Schubert in the *Allg. Wiener Musikzeitung* of Dec. 14. Ferdinand mentions this mass in his list under 1815. A copy, evidently copied closely from the autograph, but with the addition of oboes (or clarinets) and bassoons by Ferd. Schubert (July 23, 1847), is in the Library of the Gesellschaft der Musikfreunde.

[8] Mentioned by Ferdinand, p. 139a.

[9] Autographs of Fernando, Teufels Lustschloss, and Adrast, are with Herr Dumba.

tion on his deathbed : 'Such long poems, many of them containing ten others,' by which he meant as long as ten. [See p. 309 *b*.] And this mass of music was produced in the mere intervals of his school drudgery ! Well might his brother say that the rapidity of his writing was marvellous.

Amidst all this work and, one might be tempted to believe, all this hurry, it is astonishing to find that some of the songs of these boyish years are amongst the most permanent of his productions. 'Gretchen am Spinnrade,' a song full of the passion and experience of a lifetime, was written (as we have said) in Oct. 1814, when he was seventeen. The 'Erl King' itself in its original form (with a few slight differences)[1] belongs to the winter of 1815, and the immortal songs of the 'Haidenröslein,' 'Rastlose Liebe,' 'Schäfers Klagelied,' the grand Ossian songs, and others of his better-known works, fall within this year. The Mass in G, too, though composed for a very limited orchestra, and not without tokens of hurry, is a masterpiece. The dramatic works contain many beautiful movements, and are full of striking things, but the librettos are so bad, that in their present condition they can never be put on the stage. The symphonies, though not original, are not without original points ; and are so sustained throughout, so full of fresh melody and interesting harmony, and so extraordinarily scored considering their date, that in these respects a man of double Schubert's age might be proud to claim them.

The habit of writing to whatever words came in his way was one of Schubert's characteristics, especially in the earlier part of his career. With his incessant desire to sing ; with an abundant fountain of melody and harmony always welling up in him and endeavouring to escape, no wonder that he grasped at any words and tried any forms that came in his way and seemed to afford a channel for his thoughts. If good, well ; if bad, well too. The reason why he wrote eight operas in one year was no doubt in great measure because he happened to meet with eight librettos ; had it been four or twelve instead of eight the result would have been the same. The variety in the productions even of this early year is truly extraordinary. A glance at the list is sufficient to show that he tried nearly every form of composition, whilst the songs which he set range from gems like Goethe's 'Meeresstille' and 'Freudvoll und leidvoll,' to the noisy ballads of Bertrand ; from Mayrhofer's stern classicality and the gloomy romance of Ossian, to the mild sentiment of Klopstock. No doubt, as Schumann says, he could have set a placard to music.[2] The

spectacle of so insatiable a desire to produce has never before been seen ; of a genius thrown naked into the world and compelled to explore for himself all paths and channels in order to discover by exhaustion which was the best— and then to die.

During this year he taught diligently and punctually in his father's school, and attended Salieri's lessons. His relations to the Lichtenthal remained as before. The Mass in G, like that in F, was written for the parish church, and according to the testimony of one[3] of his old friends was especially intended for those of his companions who had been pupils of Holzer's with him. A pleasant relic of his home life exists in a piece of music written for his father's birthday, Sept. 27, 1815, for four voices and orchestra —'Erhabner, verehrter Freund der Jugend.'[4] He kept up his intercourse also with the *Convict*, and when he had written anything special it was one of the first places to which he would take it. There possibly his Symphonies were tried, though it is doubtful if a juvenile orchestra would contain clarinets, bassoons, trumpets, and horns, all which are present in the scores of the first four Symphonies. There, thanks to the memorandum of another old 'Convicter,' we can assist at the first hearing of the 'Erl King.' Spaun happened to call one afternoon, in this very winter, at the elder Schubert's house in the Himmelpfortgrund, and found Franz in his room, in a state of inspiration over Goethe's ballad, which he had just seen for the first time. A few times' reading had been sufficient to evoke the music, which in the rage of inspiration he was whelming down[5] on to the paper at the moment of Spaun's arrival ; indeed it was already perfect except the mere filling in of the accompaniment. This was quickly done ; and it was finished in the form in which we can now see it in the Berlin Library.[6] In the evening Schubert brought it to the *Convict*, and there first he and then Holzapfel sang it through. It was not altogether well received. No wonder ; the form was too new, the dramatic spirit too strong, even for that circle of young Schubert-admirers. At the words 'Mein Vater, mein Vater, jetzt fasst er mich an !' where G♭, F♮, and E♭ all come together, there was some dissent, and Ruzicka, as teacher of harmony, had to explain to his pupils, as best he might, a combination which now seems perfectly natural and appropriate.

1816 was passed much as 1815 had been, in

---

[1] The Berlin Library possesses an autograph of the earlier form. All the versions are in the complete edition.

[2] 'Qu'on me donne la Gazette de Hollande,' says Rameau. But Schubert could have thrown poetry into an advertisement ! 'Give me the words,' said Mozart, 'and I'll put the poetry to them.'

[3] Herr Doppler. I cannot refrain from mentioning this gentleman, who in 1867 was shopman at Spina's (formerly Diabelli's). I shall never forget the droll shock I received when on asking him if he knew Schubert, he replied, 'Know him ? I was at his christening !' Kreissle's *Life* is indebted to him for many a trait which would otherwise have been lost.

[4] Now in the Imperial Library, Berlin. No doubt there was one every year, though that of 1814 has been lost.

[5] *Hinzuwühlend* is Kreissle's word, doubtless from Spaun's lips.

[6] If indeed this be the actually first original. The omission of bar 8, and its subsequent insertion, however, as well as the clean regular look of the whole, seem to point to its being a transcript. [The various versions of this song, and the stages of its growth, can be seen in the complete edition of Breitkopf & Härtel.]

a marvellous round of incessant work. The drudgery of the school, however, had become so insupportable that Schubert seized the opportunity of the opening of a government school of music, at Laibach, near Trieste, to apply for the post of director, with a salary of 500 Vienna florins—£21 a year. The testimonials which he sent in in April from Salieri, and from Joseph Spendou, Chief Superintendent of Schools, were so cold in tone as to imply that however much they valued Schubert, they believed his qualifications not to be those of the head of a large establishment.[1] At any rate he failed, and the post was given, on the recommendation of Salieri, to a certain Jacob Schaufl. Schubert found compensation, however, in the friendship of Franz von Schober, a young man of good birth and some small means, who had met with his songs at the house of the Spauns at Linz, and had ever since longed to make his personal acquaintance. Coming to Vienna to enter the University, apparently soon after the Laibach rebuff, he called on Schubert, found him in his father's house, overwhelmed with his school duties, and with apparently no time for music. There, however, were the piles of manuscript—operas, masses, symphonies, songs, heaped up around the young schoolmaster-composer, and Schober saw at once that some step must be taken to put an end to this cruel anomaly, and give Schubert time to devote himself wholly to the Art of which he was so full. Schober proposed that his new friend should live with him ; Franz's father — possibly not over-satisfied with his son's performances as a teacher of the alphabet to infants [2] — consented to the plan, and the two young men (Schober was some four months Franz's junior) went off to keep house together at Schober's lodgings in the Landkrongasse. A trace of this change is found on two MS. songs in the Musik Verein at Vienna, 'Leiden der Trennung' and 'Lebenslied,' inscribed 'In Herr v. Schober's lodging,' and dated Nov. 1816. Schubert began to give a few lessons, but soon threw them up,[3] and the household must have been maintained at Schober's expense, since there was obviously as yet no sale for Schubert's compositions. He had good friends, as Beethoven had had at the same age, though not so high in rank—Hofrath von Kiesewetter, Matthäus von Collin, Graf Moritz Dietrichstein, Hofrath Hammer von Purgstall, Pyrker, afterwards Patriarch of Venice and Archbishop of Erlau, Frau Caroline Pichler—all ready and anxious to help him had they had the opportunity. But Schubert never gave them the opportunity. He was a true Viennese, born in the lowest ranks, without either the art or the taste for 'imposing' on the aristocracy (Beethoven's [4] favourite phrase) that Beethoven had ; loving the society of his own class, shrinking from praise or notice of any kind, and with an absolute detestation of teaching or any other stated duties.

But to know him was to love and value him. Three little events, which slightly diversify the course of this year, are of moment as showing the position which Schubert took amongst his acquaintances. The first was the 50th anniversary of Salieri's arrival in Vienna, which he had entered as a boy on June 16, 1766. [See SALIERI, p. 212.] On Sunday, June 16, 1816, the old Italian was invested with the Imperial gold medal and chain of honour, in the presence of the whole body of Court-musicians ; and in the evening a concert took place at his own house, in which, surrounded by his pupils, Weigl, Assmayer, Anna Fröhlich, Schubert, and many others,[5] both male and female, he snuffed up the incense of his worshippers, and listened to compositions in his honour by his scholars past and present. Among these were pieces sent by Hummel and Moscheles, and a short cantata, both words and music by Schubert.[6]

Eight days afterwards, on July 24, there was another festivity in honour of the birthday of a certain Herr Heinrich Watteroth,[7] a distinguished official person, for which Schubert had been employed to write a cantata on the subject of Prometheus, words by Philipp Dräxler, another official person. The cantata has disappeared ; but from a description of it by Leopold Sonnleithner, communicated to ' Zellner's Blätter für Theater,' etc. (No. 19), and reprinted [8] separately, it seems to have been written for two solo voices, soprano (Gäa), and bass (Prometheus), chorus, and orchestra, and to have contained a duet in recitative, two choruses for mixed and one for male voices (the disciples of Prometheus). This last is described as having been in the form of a slow march, with original and interesting treatment. The performance took place in the garden of Watteroth's house in the Erdberg suburb of Vienna. As all the persons concerned in the festivity were people of some consideration, and as the music was very well received, it may have been an important introduction for the young composer. A congratulatory poem by von Schlechta, addressed to Schubert, appeared a day or two later in the *Theaterzeitung*. Schubert had already, in the previous year, set a song of Schlechta's—' Auf einem Kirchhof '—and he promptly acknowledged the compliment by adopting one of more moment from Schlechta's

1 *K.H.* p. 107 (i. 109).   2 There is ground for this supposition.
3 Bauernfeld, *W.Z.K.*   4 *Imponiren.* Thayer, ii. 313.

5 There was a Liszt among Salieri's pupils at this time, but hardly the future Abbé, who was then but five years old. Franz Liszt and Schubert met once—in the curious collection of variations on Diabelli's waltz, to which fifty Austrian composers contributed. Beethoven's contribution being the thirty-three variations, op. 120. Liszt's variations is No. 24, and Schubert's No. 38. Liszt was throughout an indefatigable champion for Schubert.
6 The autograph of this little curiosity was sold in Paris, by auction, May 14, 1881. The words are given by Kreissle, p. 82 (i. 83), but are not worth quoting. They do not possess the individuality of thought which makes Schubert's later verses so interesting, in spite of the crudity of their expression.
7 His birthday was July 12, but the performance was put off on account of the weather.
8 I am indebted for this reprint to my ever-kind friend Mr. C. F. Pohl, of the Gesellschaft der Musikfreunde, Vienna.

'Diego Manzanares,' 'Wo irrst du durch einsame Schatten ?' his setting of which is dated July 30, 1816.[1] Schubert evidently was fond of his cantata. It was performed at Innsbruck by Gänsbacher, and at Vienna by Sonnleithner in 1819. Schubert wished to give it at the Augarten in 1820, and had sent it somewhere for performance at the time of his death. He was paid 100 florins, Vienna currency (or £4) for it, and he notes in his journal that it was the first time he had composed for money.

The third event was the composition of a cantata on a larger scale than either of the others. It was addressed to Dr. Joseph Spendou, in his character of Founder and Principal of the Schoolmasters' Widows' Fund, and contained eight numbers, with solos for two sopranos and bass, a quartet and choruses, all with orchestral accompaniment. Whether it was performed or not is uncertain,[2] but it was published in 1830 in PF. score by Diabelli, as op. 128. The other compositions of the year 1816 are as numerous as usual. There is a fine trio for S.S.A. and PF. to the words of Klopstock's 'grosses Halleluja' (Lf. 41, No. 2); a Salve Regina in F, to German words, for four voices and organ [3] (Feb. 21, 1816) [another, to Latin words, for unaccompanied chorus (Feb. 1816), and a Stabat Mater in F minor (Feb. 28, 1816) to Klopstock's translation of the Latin hymn.] The last of these is written for soprano, tenor, and bass solo, and chorus, and for an orchestra of the usual strings, two flutes, two oboes, two bassoons, one contra-bassoon, two horns, three trombones, two trumpets and drums. These, however, are not uniformly employed ; the trumpets and drums only appear for a few chords in Nos. 9 and 12 ; No. 5, an eight-part chorus, is accompanied by the wind alone, and No. 6, a tenor air, by the strings, with oboe solo. This work was performed in 1841 by the Musik-Verein of Vienna, and in 1863 at the Altlerchenfelder church, but was not published until the appearance of Breitkopf & Härtel's edition. [Among other works of this year are a setting of the Angels' Chorus from *Faust*, ' Christ ist erstanden' (June 1816), a fragment of a Requiem in E♭ [4] (July 1816), which ends with the second bar of the second Kyrie, a Tantum ergo in C (Aug.), a Magnificat in C (Sept.), and a duet, 'Auguste jam coelestium' (Oct.), strongly tinctured by Mozart.[5]]

Of operas we find only one in 1816, probably because only one libretto came in his way. It is called ' Die Bürgschaft,' and is in three acts. The author of the words is not known ; and the quotations in Kreissle show that they are in great part absolute rubbish. Schubert continued his

task to the third act, fifteen numbers, and there stopped. The autograph, in Herr Dumba's possession, is dated May 1816.

The Symphonies of 1816 are two—the fourth, in C minor, entitled ' Tragic Symphony,' and dated April 1816 ;[6] and the fifth, in B♭, for small orchestra, dated Sept. 1816–Oct. 3, 1816.[7] The first of these is a great advance on its predecessors ; the Andante is individual and very beautiful, and the Finale wonderfully spirited. The other, though full of Mozart, is as gay and untrammelled as all Schubert's orchestral music of that day. It is sometimes entitled ' Without Trumpets or Drums,' and is said to have been composed for the orchestra at the Gundelhof, which grew out of the Schubert Sunday afternoon quartets.[8] Both were often played at the Crystal Palace, under Manns's direction, and were among the favourite works in the *répertoire* of that establishment. A string quartet in F ; a string trio in B♭, apparently very good ; a rondo in A for violin solo and quartet (June 1816) ; a violin concerto in C ; three sonatinas for PF. and violin (op. 137) ; a PF. sonata in F, two movements of another in E ; various marches for PF. ; twelve Deutsche (waltzes) ; six Écossaises, with the inscriptions ' Composed while a prisoner in my room at Erdberg' and 'Thank God'—probably the relic of some practical joke—are still existing.

Very little of the above, however interesting, can be said to be of real, first-rate, permanent value. But when we approach the songs of 1816 the case is altered. There are not quite so many with this date as there were with that of 1815, but there are over a hundred in all, and among them are some of his finest settings of Goethe, the three songs of the Harper, in ' Wilhelm Meister' (op. 12, Sept. 6), Mignon's 'Sehnsucht' song (op. 62, No. 4) ; 'Der Fischer' ; 'Der König in Thule' (op. 5, No. 5), 'Jägers Abendlied,' and 'Schäfers Klagelied' (op. 3), 'Wanderer's Nachtlied' (op. 4), ' Schwager Kronos' (op. 19). Of Schiller there are the beautiful ' Ritter Toggenburg,' Thekla's song (op. 58), etc., and to name only one other, the far-famed ' Wanderer,' by Schmidt of Lubeck.

These magnificent pieces are well known to every lover of Schubert, but they are not more valued than such exquisitely simple and touching little effusions as ' An eine Quelle' of Claudius (op. 109, No. 3), ' Der Abend' of Kosegarten (op. 118, No. 2), or ' Der Leidende' of Hölty (Lief. 50, No. 2), all equally bearing his stamp.

The lists of the songs of these two years throw a curious light on Schubert's musical activity and mode of proceeding. Dr. Johnson was said when he got hold of a book to ' tear the heart out of it,' and with Schubert it was very much

---

[1] He returned to this poet in 1820, 1825, 1826, 1828.
[2] Kreissle, i. 88, says that it was.
[3] Nottebohm's *Catalogue*, p. 226.
[4] First printed by Schumann as Appendix to his newspaper, the *N.Z.M.*, for June 18, 1839.
[5] In Brahms's possession. The date is quoted from the *Catalogue* of the accurate Nottebohm. I am bound to say that I saw no date, and Brahms judged it to be later than 1816.

[6] April 1816.—Adagio molto and Allegretto vivace in C minor ; Andante in A♭ ; Menuet and Trio in E♭ ; Finale in C.—The autograph has vanished.
[7] Sept, 1816.—Fine den 3. Oct. 1816. Allegro, B♭ ; Andante con moto, E♭ ; Menuet and Trio, G minor and G major ; Finale, Allegretto vivace, B♭. Autograph with Peters & Co.
[8] Hanslick, *Concertwesen*, p. 142.

the same. To read a poem, and at once to fasten upon it and transcribe it in music seems to have been his natural course ; and having done one he went at once to the next. A volume of Hölty, or Claudius, or Kosegarten came into his hands ; he tore from it in a moment what struck him, and was not content with one song, but must have three, four, or five. Thus, in the summer of 1815, he evidently meets with Kosegarten's poems, and, in July, sets twenty of them. In March 1816 he sets five songs by Salis ; in May, six by Hölty ; in Nov. four by Claudius, three by Mayrhofer, and so on. To read these lists gives one a kind of visible image of the almost fierce eagerness with which he attacked his poetry, and of the inspiration with which the music rushed from his heart and through his pen — 'everything that he touched,' says Schumann, 'turning into music.' Thus, at a later date, calling accidentally on Randhartinger, and his friend being summoned from the room, Schubert, to amuse himself in the interval, took up a little volume which lay on the table. It interested him ; and as his friend did not return he carried it off with him. Anxious for his book, Randhartinger called next morning at Schubert's lodgings, and found that he had already set several pieces in it to music. The volume was Wilhelm Müller's poems ; the songs were part of the 'Schöne Müllerin.' A year or two after this, in July 1826—it is his old friend Doppler who tells the story—returning from a Sunday stroll with some friends through the village of Währing, he saw a friend sitting at a table in the beer-garden of one of the taverns. The friend, when they joined him, had a volume of Shakespeare on the table. Schubert seized it, and began to read ; but before he had turned over many pages pointed to ' Hark, hark, the lark,' and exclaimed, ' Such a lovely melody has come into my head, if I had but some music paper.' Some one drew a few staves on the back of a bill of fare, and there, amid the hubbub of the beer-garden, that beautiful song, so perfectly fitting the words, so skilful and so happy in its accompaniment, came into perfect existence. Two others from the same poet not improbably followed in the evening.[1]

It seems that the Quartet afternoons at the house of Schubert the elder had gradually extended themselves into performances of Haydn's Symphonies, arranged as quartets and played with doubled parts, players of ability and name joined, and a few hearers were admitted. After a time, the modest room became inconveniently crowded, and then the little society migrated to the house of a tradesman named Frischling (Dorotheengasse 1105), wind instruments were added, and the smaller works of Pleyel, Haydn, and Mozart were attacked. In the winter of 1815 another move became

[1] The drinking-song from ' Antony and Cleopatra' (marked ' Währing, July 26 '), and the lovely ' Sylvia' (' July 1826 '). The anecdote is in Kreissle.

necessary, to the house of Otto Hatwig, one of the violins of the Burgtheater, at the Schottenthor, and in the spring of 1818, to his new residence in the Gundelhof, and later still at Pettenkofer's house in the Bauernmarkt. The band now contained some good professional players, and could venture even on Beethoven's first two symphonies, and the overtures of Cherubini, Spontini, Boieldieu, Weigl, etc. Schubert belonged to it all through, playing the viola, and it was probably with the view to their performance by the society that he wrote the two symphonies of 1816 (Nos. 4 and 5), two overtures in the winter of 1817, and his sixth Symphony in the spring of 1818.

Schober and Mayrhofer were Schubert's first friends outside the immediate circle of his youthful associates. He was now to acquire a third, destined to be of more active service than either of the others. This was Vogl. He was twenty years Franz's senior, and at the time of their meeting was a famous singer at the Vienna Opera, admired more for his intellectual gifts than for the technical perfection of his singing, and really great in such parts as Orestes in ' Iphigenie,' Almaviva in ' Figaro,' Creon in ' Medea,' and Telasko in the ' Vestalin.' About the year 1816—the date is not precisely given —Vogl was induced by Schober to come to their lodgings, and see the young fellow of whom Schober was always raving, but who had no access to any of the circles which Vogl adorned and beautified by his presence. The room as usual was strewed with music. Schubert was confused and awkward ; Vogl, the great actor and man of the world, gay, and at his ease. The first song he took up—probably the first music of Schubert's he had ever seen—was Schubart's 'Augenlied.' He hummed it through, and thought it melodious, but slight—which it is. ' Ganymed ' and the ' Schäfers Klage' made a deeper impression ; others followed and he left with the somewhat patronising but true remark, ' There is stuff in you ; but you squander your fine thoughts instead of making the most of them.' But the impression remained, he talked of Schubert with astonishment, soon returned, and the acquaintance grew and ripened till they became almost inseparable, and until in their performances of Schubert's songs, ' the two seemed,' in Schubert's own words, ' for the moment to be one.' In those days songs were rarely if ever sung in concert-rooms ; but Vogl had the *entrée* to all the great musical houses of Vienna, and before long his performances of the ' Erl King,' the 'Wanderer,' 'Ganymed,' 'Der Kampf,' etc., with the composer's accompaniment, were well known. What Vogl's opinion of him ultimately became, may be learnt from a passage in his diary : — ' Nothing shows so plainly the want of a good school of singing as Schubert's songs. Otherwise, what an enormous and universal effect must have been produced throughout the world, wherever the German language is understood, by these truly divine inspirations, these utterances of a musical *clairvoyance* ! How many would have comprehended, probably for the first time, the meaning of such expressions as "speech and poetry in music," "words in harmony," "ideas clothed in music," etc., and would have learnt that the finest poems of our greatest poets may be enhanced and even transcended when translated into musical language ? Numberless examples may be named, but I will only mention " The Erl King," "Gretchen," "Schwager Kronos," the Mignon and Harper's songs, Schiller's "Sehnsucht," " Der Pilgrim," and "Die Bürgschaft." '

This extract shows how justly Vogl estimated Schubert, and how, at that early date, his discernment enabled him to pass a judgment which even now it would be difficult to excel. The word *clairvoyance*, too, shows that he thoroughly entered into Schubert's great characteristic. In hearing Schubert's compositions it is often as if one were brought more immediately and closely into contact with music itself than is the case in the works of others ; as if in his pieces the stream from the great heavenly reservoir were dashing over us, or flowing through us, more directly, with less admixture of any medium or channel, than it does in those of any other writer—even of Beethoven himself. And this immediate communication with the origin of music really seems to have happened to him. No sketches, no delay, no anxious period of preparation, no revision, appear to have been necessary. He had but to read the poem, to surrender himself to the torrent, and to put down what was given him to say, as it rushed through his mind. This was the true 'inspiration of dictation,' as much so as in the utterance of any Hebrew prophet or seer. We have seen one instance in the case of the 'Erl King.' The poem of the Wanderer attracted him in the same way, and the song was completed in one evening. In a third case, that of Goethe's 'Rastlose Liebe,' the paroxysm of inspiration was so fierce that Schubert never forgot it, but reticent as he often was, talked of it years afterwards.[1] It would seem that the results did not always fix themselves in the composer's memory as permanently as if they had been the effect of longer and more painful elaboration. Vogl tells an anecdote about this which is very much to the point.[2] On one occasion he received from Schubert some new songs, but being otherwise occupied could not try them over at the moment. When he was able to do so he was particularly pleased with one of them, but as it was too high for his voice, he had it copied in a lower key. About a fortnight afterwards they were again making music together, and Vogl placed the transposed song before Schubert on the desk of the piano. Schubert tried it through, liked it,

and said, in his Vienna dialect, 'I say ! the song's not so bad ; *whose is it ?*' so completely, in a fortnight, had it vanished from his mind ! Sir Walter Scott attributed a song of his own to Byron ; but this was in 1828, after his mind had begun to fail.[3]

1817 was comparatively an idle year. Its great musical event was the arrival of Rossini's music in Vienna. ' L' Inganno felice ' was produced at the Hoftheater, Nov. 26, 1816, and 'Tancredi,' Dec. 17 ; ' L' Italiana in Algeri,' Feb. 1, 1817, and 'Ciro in Babilonia,' June 18 ; and the enthusiasm of the Viennese—like that of all to whom these fresh and animated strains were brought—knew no bounds. Schubert admired Rossini's melody and spirit, but rather made fun of his orchestral music, and a story is told—not impossibly apocryphal[4]—of his having written an overture in imitation of Rossini, before supper, after returning from 'Tancredi.' At any rate he has left two ' Overtures in the Italian style' in D and C, dated Sept.[5] and Nov. 1817 respectively, which were much played at the time. Schubert made four-hand PF. arrangements of both, and that in C has been since published in score and parts as op. 170, and has been played at the Crystal Palace (Dec. 1, 1866, etc.) and elsewhere. Its caricature of Rossini's salient points, including of course the inevitable *crescendo*, is obvious enough ; but nothing could transform Schubert into an Italian, and the overture has individual and characteristic beauties which are immediately recognisable. The influence of Rossini was no mere passing fancy, but may be traced in the Sixth Symphony, mentioned below, and in music of his later life—in the two Marches (op. 121), the Finale to the Quartet in G (op. 161), and elsewhere.

A third Overture in D belongs to 1817, and, though still in MS., has also been played at the Crystal Palace (Feb. 6, 1869, etc.). It is in two movements Adagio, and Allo. giusto, and the former is almost a draft of the analogous movement in the overture known as 'Rosamunde' (op. 26), though really the 'Zauberharfe.' There the resemblance ceases. What led Schubert to the pianoforte this year in so marked a manner is not known, but his devotion to it is obvious, for no fewer than six sonatas belong to this period, viz. three with opus numbers—op. 122, in E♭ ; op. 147,[6] in B (August); op. 164, in A minor,[7] and three others, in F, A♭, and E minor (June).

Schubert's Sixth Symphony, in C,[8] completed in February 1818, appears to have been begun in the preceding October. It is the first one

[1] Bauernfeld, *W.S.K.*   [2] In *Kreissle*, p. 119 (i. 123).

[3] Lockhart's *Life of Scott*, vii. 129.
[4] *K.H.* 129 (i. 133).
[5] Kreissle says May. September is Nottebohm's date : but there is another Overture in D, and it seems doubtful which of the two is dated May, and which September.
[6] Autograph in possession of Brahms.
[7] Published, by Spina as '7th Sonata.'
[8] Adagio and Allegro in C ; Andante in F ; Scherzo in C, and Trio in E major ; Finale in C.

which he has marked as 'Grand'—'Grosse Sinfonie'—though hardly with reason, as both in form and orchestra it is the same as the early ones. It is an advance on the others, and the Scherzo shows the first decided signs of Beethoven's influence. Passages may also be traced to Rossini and the Italian opera.

The catalogue of the instrumental compositions of this year closes with a string Trio [1] and a Polonaise for the violin. In the number of the vocal compositions of 1817 there is an equal falling off. Rossini's popularity for the time shut the door against all other composers, and even Schubert's appetite for bad librettos was compelled to wait. Not only, however, are there no operas this year, there is no church music, and but forty-seven songs. In quality, however, there is no deterioration in the songs. The astonishing 'Gruppe aus dem Tartarus,' and the 'Pilgrim' of Schiller; the 'Ganymed' of Goethe; the 'Fahrt zum Hades,' 'Memnon,' and 'Erlafsee' of Mayrhofer; and 'An die Musik' of Schober, are equal to any that come before them. Among the MS. songs is one showing the straits to which Schubert was sometimes put, either by the want of materials or by the sudden call of his inspiration. It is the beginning of a setting of Schiller's 'Entzückung an Laura,' and is written on the front page of the second violin part of a duet-fugue by Fux, the words, 'Fuga. Duetto. Violino: Secundo. Del: Sing:[2] Fux.' appearing in the copyist's formal handwriting through Schubert's hasty notes. It is superscribed 'Entzückung an Laura Abschied August 1817. Schubert Mpia'—interesting as showing that in 'Abschied' he has added his own comment to Schiller's words; that he dated his pieces at the moment of beginning them; and that he sometimes signed his name without the 'Franz.'

His circle of intimate friends was increased about this date by Anselm and Joseph Hüttenbrenner and Joseph Gahy. Anselm, four years his senior, was a pupil of Salieri's, and there they had met in 1815. With the younger brother, Joseph, he became acquainted in the summer of 1817.[3] Both were men of independent means, and Anselm was a musician by profession. Gahy was in the government employment, an excellent pianoforte-player, of whom Schubert was for long very fond. The younger Hüttenbrenner was bewitched by Schubert, much as Krumpholz and Schindler were by Beethoven; and was ever ready to fetch and carry for his idol, and to praise whatever he did, till the idol would turn on his worshipper, and be so cruel

as to get the nickname of 'The Tyrant' from the rest of the set.

How Schubert existed since he threw up his place at the school and left his father's house is a point on which we are in entire ignorance, His wants were few, but how even those few were supplied is a mystery. We have seen that he lived rent-free with Schober for a few months in 1816, but the return of Schober's brother put an end to the arrangement,[4] and from that date he must have been indebted to Spaun, or some friend better off than himself, for lodgings, for existence, and for his visits to the theatre, for there is no trace of his earning anything by teaching in 1817, and the few pounds paid him for the Watteroth cantata is the only sum which he seems to have earned up to this date.

In the summer of 1818, however, on the recommendation of Unger, the father of Mme. Unger-Sabatier, the great singer, Schubert accepted an engagement as teacher of music in the family of Count Johann Esterhazy, to pass the summer at his country seat at Zselész, in Hungary, on the Waag, some distance east of Vienna, and the winter in town. He was to be a member of the establishment and to receive two gulden for every lesson. The family consisted of the Count and Countess, two daughters, Marie, thirteen, and Caroline, eleven, and a boy of five. All were musical. The Count sang bass, the Countess and Caroline contralto, Marie had a fine soprano, and both daughters played the piano. Baron von Schönstein, their intimate friend, slightly older than Schubert, a singer of the highest qualities, with a noble baritone voice, made up the party, which certainly promised all the elements of enjoyment. It was a pang to Schubert to part from the circle of his companions, to whom he was devoted, but it is not difficult to imagine how pleasant he must have found the comfort and generous living of the Esterhazy house, while at the same time there would be opportunities of retirement, and abundant means of diversion in a beautiful country, a new people, and the Hungarian and gipsy melodies.

When they left town does not appear.[5] Schubert's Mass in C,[6] his fourth, written like the others, for Holzer, is dated 'July 1818'; but there is nothing to show whether it was finished in Vienna or in the country. A set of MS. Solfeggi for the Countess Marie, also dated July, is perhaps evidence that by that time they were settled at Zselész. Two letters to Schober are printed by Bauernfeld,[7] and

---

[1] In B♭, in one movement.
[2] For 'Sign.' A facsimile is given by Reissmann.
[3] So *Kreissle*, i. 128. But does not the dedication of the song, 'Die Erwartung,' composed Feb. 27, 1815,—'to his friend,' J. H.— show that the acquaintance was of much earlier date? True, it was not published till the April after Schubert's death; and the song may have been prepared by him for publication shortly before, and the dedication added then.

[4] *K.H.* 109 (i. 112).
[5] There is an interesting autograph copy of the 'Forelle' song dated at A. Hüttenbrenner's Lodgings (in Vienna) midnight, Feb. 21, 1818, and besprinkled with ink instead of sand. It has been published in photography. But the 'Forelle' really dates from 1817. (Nottebohm, in the *Them. Catalogue*.)
[6] Published in 1826 as op. 48. Schubert wrote a new and most beautiful Benedictus to it in 1828, only a few months before his death.
[7] In *Die Presse*, Vienna, April 17, 1869. Reprinted in the *Signale*, Nov. 15, 1869.

are dated August 3, and Sept. 18, 1818. The first is addressed to his home circle, his 'dearest fondest friends . . Spaun, Schober, Mayrhofer, and Senn . . . you who are everything to me.' There are messages also to Vogl, and to Schober's mother and sister, and to 'all possible acquaintances,' and an urgent entreaty to write soon—'every syllable of yours is dear to me.' He is thoroughly well and happy, and 'composing like a god. . . Mayrhofer's Einsamkeit is ready, and I believe it to be the best thing I have yet done, for I was *without anxiety*' (*ohne Sorge*—the italics are his own). 'Einsamkeit' is a long ballad, filling nineteen close pages of print, with a dozen changes of tempo and as many of signature ; perhaps not quite coming up to his own estimate of it, though both words and music are often very striking. The length of this and other ballads will probably always hinder their wealth of melody, dramatic effects, and other striking beauties, from being known by the world at large.

The other letter, seven weeks later, throws more light on his position at Zselész 'as composer, manager, audience, everything, in one.' 'No one here cares for true Art, unless it be now and then the Countess ; so I am left alone with my beloved, and have to hide her in my room, or my piano, or my own breast. If this often makes me sad, on the other hand it often elevates me all the more. Several songs have lately come into existence, and I hope very successful ones.' He is evidently more at home in the servants' hall than the drawing-room. 'The cook is a pleasant fellow; the ladies'-maid is thirty ; the housemaid very pretty, and often pays me a visit; the nurse is somewhat ancient ; the butler is my rival ; the two grooms get on better with the horses than with us. The Count is a little rough ; the Countess proud, but not without heart ; the young ladies good children. I need not tell you, who know me so well, that with my natural frankness I am good friends with everybody.' The letter ends with an affectionate message to his parents.

The only songs which can be fixed to this autumn, and which are therefore doubtless those just referred to, besides the great 'Einsamkeit,' are the 'Blumenbrief,' 'Blondel und Maria,' 'Das Marienbild' and 'Litaney,' 'Das Abendroth'—for a contralto, evidently composed for the Countess ; 'Vom Mitleiden Mariä,' and three Sonnets from Petrarch. The Hungarian national songs left their mark in the '36 original dances,' or 'First Waltzes' (op. 9), some of which were written down in the course of the next year. The 'Divertissement à la hongroise,' and the Quartet in A minor (op. 29), in which the Hungarian influence is so strong, belong—the first apparently, the second certainly—to a much later period.

A third letter of this date, hitherto unprinted, with which the writer has been honoured by the grand-daughter[1] of Ferdinand Schubert, to whom it was addressed, is not without interest, and is here printed entire. The Requiem referred to was by Ferdinand, and had evidently been sent to his brother for revision. The letter throws a pleasant light on the strong link existing between Franz and his old home, and suggests that assistance more solid than 'linen' may often have reached him from his fond step-mother in his poverty in Vienna. In considering the pecuniary result of the engagement, it must be remembered that the florin was at that time only worth a franc, instead of two shillings. The month's pay therefore, instead of being £20, was really only about £8. Still, for Schubert that was a fortune.

24 Aug. 1818.

DEAR BROTHER FERDINAND,

It is half-past 11 at night, and your Requiem is ready. It has made me sorrowful, as you may believe, for I sang it with all my heart. What is wanting you can fill in, and put the words under the music and the signs above. And if you want much rehearsal you must do it yourself, without asking me in Zelész. Things are not going well with you ; I wish you could change with me, so that for once you might be happy. You should find all your heavy burdens gone, dear brother ; I heartily wish it could be so.—My foot is asleep, and I am mad with it. If the fool could only write it wouldn't go to sleep !

Good morning, my boy, I have been asleep with my foot, and now go on with my letter at 8 o'clock on the 25th. I have one request to make in answer to yours. Give my love to my dear parents, brothers, sisters, friends, and acquaintances, especially not forgetting Carl. Didn't he mention me in his letter ! As for my friends in the town, bully them, or get some one to bully them well, till they write to me. Tell my mother that my linen is well looked after, and that I am well off, thanks to her motherly care. If I could have some more linen I should very much like her to send me a second batch of pocket-handkerchiefs, cravats, and stockings. Also I am much in want of two pair of kerseymere trousers. Hart can get the measure wherever he likes. I would send the money very soon. For July, with the journey-money, I got 200 florins.

It is beginning already to be cold, and yet we shall not start for Vienna before the middle of October. Next month I hope to have a few weeks at Freystadt, which belongs to Count Erdödy, the uncle of my count. The country there is said to be extraordinarily beautiful. Also I hope to get to Pesth while we are at the vintage at Boszczmedj, which is not far off. It would be delightful if I should happen to meet Herr Administrator Taigele there. I am delighted at the thought of the vintage, for I have heard so much that is pleasant about it. The harvest also is beautiful here. They don't stow the corn into barns as they do in Austria, but make immense heaps out in the fields, which they call *Tristen* They are often 80 to 100 yards long, and 30 to 40 high. and are laid together so cleverly that the rain all runs off without doing any harm. Oats and so on they bury in the ground.

Though I am so well and happy, and every one so good to me, yet I shall be immensely glad when the moment arrives for going to Vienna. Beloved Vienna, all that is dear and valuable to me is there, and nothing but the actual sight of it will stop my longing ! Again entreating you to attend to all my requests, I remain, with much love to all, your true and sincere,

FRANZ Mpia.

A thousand greetings to your good wife and dear Resi, and a very hearty one to aunt Schubert and her daughter.

The inscription 'Zelész, Nov. 1818' on the song 'Das Abendroth' shows that the return to Vienna was not till nearly the end of the year.

[1] Fräulein Caroline Geisler, daughter of Linus Geisler and Ferdinand's second daughter, Elise.

He found the theatre more than ever in possession of Rossini. To the former operas, 'Elisabetta' was added in the autumn, and 'Otello' early in Jan. 1819. But one of the good traits in Schubert's character was his freedom from jealousy, and his determination to enjoy what was good, from whatever quarter it came, or however much it was against his own interest. A letter of his to Hüttenbrenner, written just after the production of 'Otello,' puts this in very good light. '"Otello" is far better and more characteristic than "Tancredi." Extraordinary genius it is impossible to deny him. His orchestration is often most original, and so is his melody; and except the usual Italian gallopades, and a few reminiscences of "Tancredi," there is nothing to object to.' But he was not content to be excluded from the theatre by every one, and the letter goes on to abuse the 'canaille of Weigls and Treitschkes,' and 'other rubbish, enough to make your hair stand on end,' all which were keeping his operettas off the boards. Still, it is very good-natured abuse, and so little is he really disheartened, that he ends by begging Hüttenbrenner for a libretto; nay, he had actually just completed a little piece called 'Die Zwillingsbrüder' ('The Twins'), translated by Hofmann from the French—a Singspiel in one act, containing an overture and ten numbers. He finished it on Jan. 19, 1819, and it came to performance before many months were over.

Of his daily life at this time we know nothing. We must suppose that he had regular duties with his pupils at the Esterhazys' town house, but there is nothing to say so. We gather that he joined Mayrhofer in his lodgings, 420 in the Wipplingerstrasse, early in the year.[1] It was not a prepossessing apartment. 'The lane was gloomy; both room and furniture were the worse for wear; the ceiling drooped; the light was shut out by a big building opposite—a worn-out piano, and a shabby bookcase.' The only relief is the name of the landlady—Sanssouci, a Frenchwoman. No wonder that Mayrhofer's poems—he was ten years Schubert's senior—were of a gloomy cast.

The two friends were on the most intimate terms, and addressed each other by nicknames. What Mayrhofer's appellation may have been we do not know, but Schubert, now and later, was called 'the Tyrant,' for his treatment of Hüttenbrenner; also 'Bertl,' 'Schwammerl,' and, best of all, 'Kanevas'—because when a stranger came into their circle his first question always was, 'Kann er was?' ('Can he do anything?') Their humour took all sorts of shapes, and odd stories are told of their sham fights, their howls, their rough jokes and repartees.[2] Mayrhofer was a Government employé

and went to his office early, leaving his fellow-lodger behind. Schubert began work directly he awoke, and even slept in his spectacles to save trouble; he got at once to his writing, sometimes in bed, but usually at his desk. It was so still, when Hiller called on him eight years later.[3] 'Do you write much?' said the boy, looking at the manuscript on the standing desk—they evidently knew little in North Germany of Schubert's fertility. 'I compose every morning,' was the reply; 'and when one piece is done, I begin another.' And yet this was the *musicien le plus poète que jamais*—it might have been the answer of a mere Czerny! Add to this a trait, communicated to the writer by Schubert's friend, Franz Lachner, of Munich, that when he had completed a piece, and heard it sung or played, he locked it up in a drawer, and often never thought about it again.

This close work went on till dinner-time—two o'clock—after which, as a rule, he was free for the day, and spent the remainder either in a country walk with friends, or in visits—as to Sofie Müller and Mme. Lacsny Buchwieser, whom we shall encounter farther on; or at Schober's rooms, or some coffee-house—in his later days it was Bogner's Café in the Singerstrasse, where the droll cry of a waiter was a never-ending pleasure to him. But no hour or place was proof against the sudden attack of inspiration when anything happened to excite it. An instance occurs at this very time, Nov. 1819, in an overture for four hands in F (op. 34), which he has inscribed as 'written in Joseph Hüttenbrenner's room at the City Hospital in the inside of three hours; and dinner missed in consequence.'[4] If the weather was fine he would stay in the country till late, regardless of any engagement that he might have made in town.

The only compositions that can be fixed to the spring of 1819 are five songs dated February, and one dated March; a very fine quintet for equal voices, to the 'Sehnsucht' song in 'Wilhelm Meister'—a song which he had already set for a single voice in 1816, and was to set twice more in the course of his life (thus rivalling Beethoven, who also set the same words four times); an equally fine quartet for men's voices, 'Ruhe, schönstes Glück der Erde,' dated April; four sacred songs by Novalis, dated May; and a striking overture in E minor, in Ser. II. of the complete edition.

The earnings of the previous summer allowed him to make an expedition this year on his own account. Mayrhofer remained in Vienna, and Vogl and Schubert appear to have gone together to Upper Austria. Steyr was the first point in the journey, a town beautifully situated on the Enns, not far south of Linz. They reached it early in July; it was Vogl's native place, and he had the pleasure of introducing

---

[1] In a letter to Mayrhofer from Linz, dated August 19, 1819, he says, 'Let the bearer have my bed while he stays with you.' *K.H.* p. 159 (i. 160). The bed must have been his before he left town.
[2] *K.H.* p. 51 (i. 51).
[3] In Hiller's *Künstlerleben*, p. 49.   [4] *K.H.* p. 160 (i. 162).

his friend to the chief amateurs of the town, Paumgartner, Koller, Dornfeld, Schellmann— substantial citizens of the town, with wives and daughters, ' Pepi Koller,' ' Frizi Dornfeld,' ' the eight Schellmann girls,' etc., who all welcomed the musician with real Austrian hospitality, heard his songs with enthusiasm, and themselves helped to make music with him. His friend Albert Stadler was there also with his sister Kathi. How thoroughly Schubert enjoyed himself in this congenial *bourgeois* society, and in such lovely country—he mentions its beauties each time he writes—we have ample proof in two letters.[1] Among other drolleries the ' Erl King' was sung with the parts distributed amongst Vogl, Schubert, and Pepi Koller. Perhaps, too, Schubert gave them his favourite version of it on a comb. Vogl's birthday (August 10) was celebrated by a cantata in C, containing a terzet, two soprano and two tenor solos, and a finale in canon, pointed by allusions to his various operatic triumphs, words by Stadler, and music by Schubert.[2] After this the two friends strolled on to Linz, the home of the Spauns, and of Kenner and Ottenwald, whose verses Franz had set in his earlier days ; and thence perhaps to Salzburg, returning to Steyr about the end of the month. Nor did the joviality of these good Austrians interfere with composition. Besides the impromptu cantata just mentioned, the well-known PF. quintet (op. 114), in which the air of ' Die Forelle' is used as the theme of the Andantino, was written at Steyr, possibly as a commission from the good Paumgartner, and was performed by the Paumgartner party. Schubert achieved in it the same feat which is somewhere ascribed to Mozart, of writing out the separate parts without first making a score, and no doubt played the pianoforte part by heart. The date of their departure, Sept. 14, is marked by an entry in the album of Miss Stadler, when Schubert, delivered himself of the following highly correct sentiment :—' Enjoy the present so wisely, that the past may be pleasant to recollect, and the future not alarming to contemplate.' This may pair off with a sentence written by Mozart, in English, in the Album of an English Freemason, which has not yet been printed :—' Patience and tranquillity of mind contribute more to cure our distempers as the whole art of medicine. Wien, den 30te März 1787.'[3]

A few days more saw them again settled in Vienna. Each of the two letters preserved from the journey contains an obvious allusion to some love affair ; but nothing is known of it. He could hardly have adopted a more effectual diversion from such sorrows than the composition of a mass, on an extended scale ; that namely in A♭—his fifth—which he began this

[1] *K.H.* pp. 158-159 (i. 159-160).
[2] Published to other words, ' Herrlich prangt,' as op. 158.
[3] I owe this to my good friend Mr. Pohl, of Vienna.

month under the serious title of ' Missa Solemnis' ; but he seems to have dawdled over it more than over any other of his works ; as it was not finished till Sept. 1822, and contains many marks of indecision.

The most pregnant musical event of this year is the fact that on Feb. 28, 1819, a song of Schubert's was sung in public—the ' Schäfers Klagelied,' sung by Jäger at Jäll's concert, at 5 P.M. at the ' Römische Kaiser,' Vienna. It was Schubert's first appearance before the public as a song-writer [one of the ' Italian' overtures had been given on March 1, 1818, at one of Jäll's concerts], and is noticed by the Leipzig *A.M.Z.* in these terms :— ' Goethe's Schäfers Klagelied set to music by Herr Franz Schubert —the touching and feeling composition of this talented young man was sung by Herr Jäger in a similar spirit.' Such is the first utterance of the press on one who has since evoked so much enthusiasm ! In the course of this year Schubert appears to have forwarded the three songs, ' Schwager Kronos,' ' Ueber Thal ' (Mignon), and ' Ganymed,'—afterwards published as op. 19),—to Goethe ; but no notice was taken by the poet of one who was to give some of his songs a wider popularity than they could otherwise have enjoyed, a popularity independent of country or language ; nor does Schubert's name once occur in all the six vols. of Goethe's correspondence with Zelter.[4]

1820 was again a year of great activity. Owing to Vogl's influence, Schubert was gradually attracting the attention of the managers. The ' Zwillingsbrüder ' had been written for the Kärnthnerthor theatre (see p. 292*a*), and it was not long before the *régisseur* of the rival opera-house, the Theatre an-der-Wien, suggested to him a libretto called the ' Zauberharfe,' or ' Magic harp,' a melodrama in three acts, by the same Hofmann who had translated the former piece. To receive such a proposal and to act upon it was a matter of course with Schubert, and the ' Zauberharfe ' is said to have been completed in a fortnight.[5] But before this, early in the year, he had met with the works of A. H. Niemeyer, Professor of Theology at Halle, and had adopted the poem of ' Lazarus, or the Feast of the Resurrection,' for an Easter Cantata. Easter fell that year on April 2, and his work is dated ' February,' so that he was in ample time. The poem—or drama, for there are seven distinct characters—is in three parts. 1. The sickness and death. 2. The burial and elegy. 3. The resurrection. Of these the first and a large portion of the second were completed by Schubert, apparently without the knowledge of any of his friends. Ferdinand mentions the first part in his list,[6] but the existence of the second was unknown, till, through the instru-

[4] Search should be made in the *Goethe Archiv* at Weimar for the autograph of these songs, and the letter which doubtless accompanied them.
[5] Autograph in Herr Dumba's collection.   [6] *N.Z.M.* p. 139*a*.

mentality of Mr. Thayer, it was unearthed in 1861. These have been published,[1] but no trace of the third act has yet been found, and the work was not performed till long after the composer's death—viz. in 1863.

On June 14 the 'Zwillingsbrüder' or 'Zwillinge' was produced at the Kärnthnerthor theatre. It is a comic operetta ('Posse'), with spoken dialogue, in one act, containing an overture and ten numbers, and turns on the plot that has done duty many times before, the confusion between two twin-brothers, who were both acted by Vogl. The overture was encored on the first night, and Vogl's two songs were much applauded, but the piece was virtually a *fiasco*, and was withdrawn after six representations. Schubert took so little interest in its production that, like Mendelssohn at the 'Wedding of Camacho,' he did not even stay in the house, and Vogl had to appear instead of him in front of the curtain. The libretto, though overburdened with characters, is sadly deficient in proportion, and contains very little action. Schubert's music, on the other hand, is light, fresh, and melodious, pointed, unusually compact, and interesting throughout. In the concerted numbers there is evidence of great dramatic power. To condemn it, as the critics of the day do, as wanting in melody, and constantly striving after originality, is to contradict Schubert's most marked characteristics, and is contrary to the facts. There is possibly more justice in the complaint that the accompaniments were too loud, though that is certainly not the fault in his masses, his only other published works with orchestral accompaniments anterior to this date. The work has been published in vocal score by Peters (1872).

On August 19 the 'Zauberharfe' was produced at the Theatre an-der-Wien. It consists chiefly of chorus and melodrama, with only a few solo passages. There is a fine overture (in C), original, characteristic, and full of beauty, which was published before 1828 as op. 26, under the name of 'Rosamunde,' to which it seems to have no claim.[2] The piece was occasionally brought forward till the winter, and was then dropped. These three vocal works appear so far to have whetted Schubert's appetite that in the autumn he attacked the more important libretto of 'Sakontala,' a regular opera in three acts, by P. H. Neumann, founded on the Indian drama of that name. He sketched two acts, and there it remains; the MS. is in Herr Dumba's possession. Another important and very beautiful piece is the 23rd Psalm,[3] set for two sopranos and two altos with PF. accompaniment, at the instigation of the

sisters Fröhlich, and dated at the beginning '23 Dec. 1820'—perhaps with a view to some private concerts given, now or later, at the old hall of the Musikverein. Another is the 'Gesang der Geister über den Wassern' of Goethe (op. 167). This fine and mystical poem had a strong attraction for Schubert. He set it for four equal voices in 1817; then he reset it for four tenors and four basses with two violas, two violoncellos, and bass, in Dec. 1820; and lastly revised this in Feb. 1821. It was first produced on March 7, 1821, and found no favour, to Schubert's disgust. It was again performed on March 30, before a more receptive audience, with a far better result. It was revived at Vienna in 1858 by Herbeck, and in England was performed with success on March 22, 1881, under the direction of Mr. Prout. It is enormously difficult, and, though perfectly in character with the poem, will probably never be attractive to a mixed audience. Another work of 1820 were some antiphons (op. 113) for Palm Sunday (March 26), composed for Ferdinand, who had been recently appointed Choirmaster at the Altlerchenfelder Church, and found the duties rather too much for him. They are written with black chalk, on coarse grey wrapping paper; and the tradition is that they and two motets were written in great haste, just in time for the service. On Easter Sunday Franz attended and conducted the mass for his brother.

The Fantasia in C for PF. solo (op. 15), containing Variations on Schubert's own 'Wanderer,' is probably a work of this year. It was written for von Liebenberg, a PF. player, to whom Schubert dedicated it. This fine piece was brought into vogue by Liszt's arrangement of it for PF. and orchestra as a concerto; but it is doubtful if it is improved by the process. Schubert never could play it; he always stuck fast in the last movement; and on one occasion jumped up and cried 'Let the devil himself play it!'. Another piece is an Allegro for strings in C minor, dated Dec. 1820, the first movement of a quartet, of which there exist besides forty-one bars of the Andante, in A♭. The Allegro is of first-rate quality, and Schubert in every bar. It was published in 1868 by Senff. The MS. was in Johannes Brahms's fine collection of autographs.

The songs of 1820, seventeen in all, though not so numerous as those of previous years, are very fine. They contain 'Der Jüngling auf dem Hügel' (op. 8, No. 1), 'Der Schiffer,' 'Liebeslauschen,' three grand songs to Mayrhofer's words, 'Orest auf Tauris,' 'Der entsühnte Orest,' and 'Freiwilliges Versinken,' and four Italian Canti, written for Frl. von Romer, who afterwards married Schubert's friend Spaun, and since published with one which was probably written under Salieri's eye as early as 1813. The most remarkable of all is 'Im Walde' or

1 In 1866, by Spina.
2 The overture played to the 'Rosamunde' music is in D minor, and was afterwards published as 'Alfonso & Estrella.' There is, perhaps, another in existence. See the letter to von Mosel quoted farther on.
3 To Moses Mendelssohn's translation.

'Waldesnacht,' a very long song of extraordinary beauty, variety, force, and imagination.

With February 1821 Schubert entered his twenty-fifth year, and it was a good omen to receive such a birthday present as the three testimonials of this date which Kreissle has [1] preserved. The first is from von Mosel, then Court Secretary; the second from Weigl, Director of the Court Opera, Salieri, and von Eichthal; the third from Moritz Count Dietrichstein, whom Beethoven addresses as 'Hofmusikgraf,' and who appears to have been a sort of Jupiter-Apollo with general sway over all Court music. These influential personages warmly recognise his eminent ability, industry, knowledge, feeling, and taste, and profess the best intentions towards him. The three documents were enclosed by the Count in a letter to Vogl, full of good wishes for the future of his friend. Still more gratifying was the prospect, which now at last opened, of the publication of his songs. It was the first good epoch in Schubert's hitherto struggling life. He had now been writing for more than seven years, with an industry and disregard of consequences which are really fearful to contemplate; and yet, as far as fame or profit were concerned, might almost as well have remained absolutely idle. Here at length was a break in the cloud. It was not less welcome because it was mainly due to his faithful friends, the Sonnleithners, who had made his acquaintance through the accident of Leopold Sonnleithner's being at school with him, and ever since cherished it in the most faithful and practical way, Ignaz, the father, having, since 1815, had large periodical music-meetings of artists and amateurs in his house at the Gundelhof, which were nothing less than Schubert propaganda. Here, before large audiences of thoroughly musical people, Schubert's pieces were repeatedly performed, and at length, on Dec. 1, 1820, the 'Erl King' was sung by Gymnich, a well-known amateur, with a spirit which fired every one of the audience with the desire to possess the song, and appears to have suggested to Leopold and Gymnich the possibility of finding a publisher for the inspirations which had for so long been their delight and astonishment. They applied to Diabelli and Haslinger, the leading houses of Vienna, but without success; the main objections being the insignificance of the composer, and the difficulty of his PF. accompaniments. On this they resolved to take the matter into their own hands; and, probably not without misgivings, had the 'Erl King' engraved. The fact was announced at the next Concert at the Gundelhof, and a hundred copies were at once subscribed for in the room—sufficient to defray the cost of the engraving and printing, and of engraving a second song as well. Meantime the 'Erl King' had been sung in public (for

the concerts at the Gundelhof were, strictly speaking, private, limited to the friends of the host) by Gymnich, at an evening concert of the Musikverein, in one of the public rooms of the city, on Jan. 25, 1821, Schubert himself appearing on the platform, and playing the accompaniment. Everything was done by the young enthusiasts to foster the Schubert *furore*, even to the publication of a set of 'Erl King waltzes' by A. Hüttenbrenner, which at any rate must have made the name familiar, though they provoked Schubert, and drew from Kanne some satirical hexameters and pentameters which may be read in Kreissle.[2] On Feb. 8 the programme of the Musikverein Concert included three songs of his, the 'Sehnsucht' by Schiller, 'Gretchen am Spinnrade,' and 'Der Jüngling auf dem Hügel'; and on March 8 the 'Gruppe aus dem Tartarus.' On March 7 the 'Erl King' was again sung, this time by Vogl himself, at an unmistakable public concert, at the Kärnthnerthor theatre, a concert supported by all the most distinguished ladies of the Court, who received the song with loud applause. Think what the first appearance of these godlike pieces must have been! It was the rising of the Sun! He is now an everyday sight to us; but how was it the first time that he burst in all his brightness on the eyes of mortals? In the midst of all this enthusiasm the 'Erl King' was published on the 1st of April 1821, by Cappi and Diabelli, on commission. It was dedicated to Count Moritz Dietrichstein, whose kindness well deserved that recognition. On April 30, 'Gretchen am Spinnrade' appeared as op. 2. The succeeding publications—each made to depend on the success of the last— were as follows :—

May 29.	Op. 3.	Schäfers Klagelied ; Meeres-Stille ; Heidenröslein ; Jägers Abendlied.
Do.	Op. 4.	Der Wanderer ; Morgenlied ; Wanderers Nachtlied.
July 9.	Op. 5.	Rastlose Liebe ; Nähe des Geliebten ; Der Fischer ; Erster Verlust ; Der König in Thule.
Aug. 23.	Op. 6.	Memnon ; Antigone und Oedip ; Am Grabe Anselmos.
Nov. 27.	Op. 7.	Die abgeblühte Linde ; Der Flug der Zeit ; Der Tod und das Mädchen.

Here the publication by commission stopped, the Diabellis being evidently convinced that the risk might be profitably assumed; and accordingly op. 8 appears on May 9, 1822, as 'the property of the publishers.' The dedications of the first seven numbers no doubt furnish the names of Schubert's most influential supporters: 1. Graf von Dietrichstein; 2. Reichsgraf Moritz von Fries; 3. Ignaz von Mosel; 4. Johann Ladislaus Pyrker, Patriarch of Venice; 5. Salieri; 6. Michael Vogl; 7. Graf Ludwig Széchényi. It must be admitted that the above are very good lists, and that if Schubert had waited long for the publication of his works, the issue of twenty songs in eight months, under the patronage of seven such eminent personages, was a substantial compensation. We do not hear, however, that much money came into his hands from the publication. The favourable impression made by the publication may be gathered from the long, intelligent, and sympathetic criticism, 'Blick auf Schuberts Lieder,' by F. von Hentl, which appeared in the *Wiener Zeitschrift für Kunst*, etc.—a periodical belonging to Diabelli's rivals, Steiner & Co.—for March 23, 1822.

Schubert was now a good deal about the theatre, and when it was determined to produce a German version of Hérold's 'Clochette,' as 'Das Zauberglöckchen,' at the Court-opera, he was not unnaturally called upon to insert a couple of pieces to suit the Vienna audience. It was what Mozart often did for the Italian operas of his day—what indeed we know Shakespeare to have done in more than one case. The opera was produced on June 20. The interpolated pieces were a long air for tenor,[1] in three movements—Maestoso, Andante, and Allegro—full of passion and imagination, and a comic duet between the princes B flat and C natural (Bedur and Cedur). They were more applauded than anything else in the work, but Schubert's name was not divulged ; the opera as a whole did not please, and was soon withdrawn.

The little Variation which he contributed, as No. 38, to Diabelli's collection of fifty Variations—the same for which Beethoven wrote his thirty-three (op. 120)—should not be overlooked. Though not published till 1823, the autograph, now in the Hofbibliothek at Vienna, is dated 'March 1821.' The variation is fresh and pretty, in the minor of the theme, but is more noticeable from its situation than from its own qualities. A few dances for PF. solo are dated '8th March' and 'July' in this year, and a collection of thirty-six, containing those alluded to and others of 1816 and 1819, was published by Cappi and Diabelli on Nov. 29, as op. 18. Some of these are inscribed on the autograph 'Atzenbrucker Deutsche, July 1821,' indicating a visit to Atzenbruck, the seat of an uncle of Schober's, near Abstetten, between Vienna and St. Pölten, where a three days' annual festivity was held, to which artists of all kinds were invited, and where Schubert's presence and music were regarded as indispensable.

Whether after this he and Schober returned to Vienna we know not, no letters remain ; but the next event of which any record remains is the composition of a symphony, his seventh, in E, which is marked, without note of place, as begun in August. He did not complete the writing of it, and indeed it is probable that it did not occupy him more than a few hours ; but the autograph, which is in the writer's posses-

sion,[2] is a very curious manuscript, probably quite unique, even among Schubert's feats of composition. It occupies 167 pages of 42 sheets (10 quires of 4, and 1 of 2), and is in the usual movements—Adagio in E minor, and Allegro in E major ; Andante in A ; Scherzo in C, and Trio in A ;[3] and Allegro giusto in E major. The Introduction and a portion of the Allegro are fully scored and marked ; but at the 110th bar —the end of a page—Schubert appears to have grown impatient of this regular proceeding, and from that point to the end of the work has made merely memoranda. But these memoranda are, in their way, perfectly complete and orderly to the end of the Finale. Every bar is drawn in ; the *tempi* and names of the instruments are fully written at the beginning of each movement ; the *nuances* are all marked ; the very double bars and flourishes are gravely added at the end of the sections, and 'Fine' at the conclusion of the whole ; and Schubert evidently regarded the work as no less complete on the paper than it was in his mind. And complete it virtually is ; for each subject is given at full length, with a bit of bass or accompaniment-figure, or *fugato* passage. There is not a bar from beginning to end that does not contain the part of one or more instruments ; at all crucial places the scoring is much fuller ; and it would no doubt be possible to complete it as Schubert himself intended. [It is said that the sketch was submitted to Mendelssohn, who refused to complete it. In later days, at the suggestion of Sir George Grove, Mr. J. F. Barnett undertook the task, and the symphony, scored by him from Schubert's indications, was produced at the Crystal Palace on May 5, 1883. See Barnett's *Musical Reminiscences and Impressions*, pp. 312-22.]

We next find the two friends at the castle of Ochsenburg, a few miles south of St. Pölten, the seat of the Bishop, who was a relative of Schober's ; and there and in St. Pölten itself they passed a thoroughly happy and healthy holiday of some weeks in September and October. The Bishop and Baron Mink, a local magnate, were congenial hosts, and the visit of the two clever young men was the signal for various festivities, in which all the aristocracy of the country-side— 'a princess, two countesses, and three baronesses,' in Schober's enumeration—took part, and in which the music and drollery of Schubert and his friend delighted every one. The great result of the visit, however, was the composition of an opera to Schober's words, on a romantic subject of battles, love, conspiracy, hunting, peasant life, and everything else, so natural in opera librettos,

---

[1] Introduced into 'Alfonso und Estrella' in 1881 by Joh. Fuchs.

[2] I received it in 1868 from the late Paul Mendelssohn, Felix's brother, into whose hands it came after his brother's death. Felix Mendelssohn had it from Ferdinand Schubert direct.

[3] The change in this symphony from the Scherzo in C to the Trio in A, by an E in octaves in the oboes lasting four bars, is an anticipation of the similar change in the same place in the great C major Symphony of 1828, and a curious instance of the singular way in which many of Schubert's earlier symphonies lead up to his crowning effort.

so impossible in real life. It was called 'Alfonso und Estrella,' and two acts were completed before their return to town. The first act is dated at the end of the autograph Sept. 20, and the second Oct. 20. A week later they were back again in Vienna.

The songs composed in 1821 are very important, and comprise some of his very finest, and in the most various styles. It is sufficient to name among the published ones 'Grenzen der Menschheit' (February); 'Geheimes' (March); Suleika's two songs (opp. 14, 31); 'Sei mir gegrüsst' (op. 20, No. 1); and 'Die Nachtigall,' for four men's voices (op. 11, No. 2)—all of the very highest excellence, of astonishing variety, and enough of themselves to make the fame of any ordinary composer. A fine setting of 'Mahomet's song,' by Goethe, for bass (possibly for Lablache), was begun in March.

The third act of 'Alfonso und Estrella' was finished in Feb. 27, 1822. The fact that a thoroughly worldly, mercenary, money-making manager like Barbaja, who was at the same time a firm believer in Rossini, had become lessee of the two principal theatres of Vienna, augured badly for Schubert's chance of success in that direction. But indeed the new piece seems to have been calculated to baffle any manager, not only in Vienna, but everywhere else. It caused, as we shall see, a violent dispute, eighteen months later, between Schubert and Weber, which but for Schubert's good temper would have led to a permanent quarrel. Anna Milder, to whom Schubert sent a copy of the work in 1825, tells him, in a letter full of kindness and enthusiasm, that the libretto will not suit the taste of the Berliners, 'who are accustomed to the grand tragic opera, or the French opéra-comique.' Nor was the libretto the only drawback. Schubert, like Beethoven in 'Fidelio,' was in advance of the modest execution of those days. At Graz, the abode of the Hüttenbrenners, where there was a *foyer* of Schubert-enthusiasts, the opera got as far as rehearsal, and would probably have reached the stage, if the accompaniments had not proved impossible for the band.[1] No performance took place until twenty-six years after poor Schubert's death, namely at Weimar, on June 24, 1854, under the direction of Liszt, who, with all his devotion to the master, had to reduce it much for performance. It was very carefully studied, and yet the success, even in that classical town, and with all Liszt's enthusiasm and influence, seems to have been practically *nil*. At last, however, its time came. Twenty-five years later, in 1879, it was again taken in hand by Capellmeister Johann Fuchs of the Court opera, Vienna, who entirely rewrote the libretto, and greatly curtailed the work; and in this form it was brought to performance at Carlsruhe in March 1881, with great success.

[1] *K.H.* p. 249 (i. 252).

But to return to Schubert and 1822. Early in the year he made the acquaintance[2] of Weber, who spent a few weeks of February and March in Vienna to arrange for the production of his 'Euryanthe.' No particulars of their intercourse on this occasion survive. With Beethoven Schubert had as yet hardly exchanged words. And this is hardly to be wondered at, because, though Vienna was not a large city, yet the paths of the two men were quite separate. Apart from the great difference in their ages, and from Beethoven's peculiar position in the town, his habits were fixed, his deafness was a great obstacle to intercourse, and, for the last five or six years, what with the lawsuits into which his nephew dragged him, and the severe labour entailed by the composition of the Mass in D, and of the Sonatas opp. 106, 109, 110, and 111—works which by no means flowed from him with the ease that masses and sonatas did from Schubert—he was very inaccessible. Any stranger arriving from abroad, with a letter of introduction, was seen and treated civilly. But Schubert was a born Viennese, and at the time of which we speak, Beethoven was as much a part of Vienna as St. Stephen's tower, and to visit him required some special reason, and more than special resolution.

A remark of Rochlitz's[3] in the July of this year shows that Schubert was in the habit of going to the same restaurant with Beethoven, and worshipping at a distance; but the first direct evidence of their coming into contact occurs at this date. On April 19, 1822, he published a set of Variations on a French air as op. 10, and dedicated them to Beethoven as 'his admirer and worshipper' (*sein Verehrer und Bewunderer*). The Variations were written in the winter of 1820-21, and Schubert presented them in person to the great master. There are two versions of the interview,[4] Schindler's and J. Hüttenbrenner's. Schindler was constantly about Beethoven. He was devoted to Schubert, and is very unlikely to have given a depreciating account of him. There is therefore no reason for doubting his statement, especially as his own interest or vanity were not concerned. It is the first time we meet Schubert face to face. He was accompanied by Diabelli, who was just beginning to find out his commercial value, and would naturally be anxious for his success. Beethoven was at home, and we know the somewhat overwhelming courtesy with which he welcomed a stranger. Schubert was more bashful and retiring than ever; and when the great man handed him the sheaf of paper and the carpenter's pencil provided for the replies

[2] For their meeting we have the authority of Weber's son in his biography. ii. 420. But his statement that Schubert was alienated from Weber by Weber's criticism on 'Rosamunde' is more than doubtful, because 'Rosamunde' was probably not composed till some nineteen months later, and because it was not Schubert's habit to take offence at criticism.
[3] *Für Freunde der Tonkunst*, iv. 352. See the lifelike and touching picture by Braun von Braun given in Nohl's *Beethoven*, iii. 682.
[4] Schindler's *Beethoven*, ii. 176.

of his visitors, could not collect himself sufficiently to write a word. Then the Variations were produced, with their enthusiastic dedication, which probably added to Beethoven's good humour. He opened them and looked through them, and seeing something that startled him, naturally pointed it out. At this Schubert's last remnant of self-control seems to have deserted him, and he rushed from the room. When he got into the street, and was out of the magic of Beethoven's personality, his presence of mind returned, and all that he might have said flashed upon him, but it was too late. The story is perfectly natural, and we ought to thank Beethoven's Boswell for it. Which of us would not have done the same ? Beethoven kept the Variations and liked them ; and it must have been some consolation to the bashful Franz to hear that he often played them with his nephew. Hüttenbrenner's[1] story is that Schubert called, but found Beethoven out ; which may have been an invention of Diabelli's to shield his young client.

This autumn Schubert again took up the Mass in A♭, which was begun in 1819 ; finished it, and inscribed it '*im 7ᵇ* $\overline{822}$ *beendet.*'[2] Not that that was the final redaction ; for, contrary to his usual practice—in fact it is almost a solitary instance—he took it up again before his death, and made material improvements[3] both in the position of the voice-parts and in the instrumentation, as may be seen from the autograph score now in the Library of the Gesellschaft der Musikfreunde.

This year seems to have been passed entirely in Vienna, at least there are no traces of any journey ; and the imprisonment in the broiling city, away from the nature he so dearly loved, was not likely to improve his spirits. What events or circumstances are alluded to in the interesting piece called ' My Dream,'[4] dated ' July 1822,' it is hard to guess. It may not improbably have been occasioned by some dispute on religious subjects of the nature of those hinted at in his brother Ignaz's letter of Oct. 12, 1818.[5] At any rate it is deeply pathetic and poetical.

During this summer Joseph Hüttenbrenner was active in the cause of his friend. He made no less than four endeavours to bring out the ' Teufels Lustschloss '—at the Josefstadt

and Court theatres of Vienna, at Munich, and at Prague. At Prague alone was there a gleam of hope. Hollbein, the manager there, requests to have the score and parts sent to him, at the same time regretting that during a month which he had passed in Vienna, Schubert had not once come near him. Hüttenbrenner also urged Schubert on Peters, the publisher, of Leipzig, who in a tedious egotistical letter, dated Nov. 14, 1822, gives the usual sound reasons of a cautious publisher against taking up with an unknown composer—for in North Germany Schubert was still all but unknown. One is sorry to hear of a little rebuff which he sustained at this time from the Gesellschaft der Musikfreunde of Vienna, to whom he applied to be admitted as a practising member (on the viola), but who refused him on the ground of his being a professional, and therefore outside their rules.[6] A somewhat similar repulse was experienced by Haydn from the Tonkünstler Societät. [See vol. ii. p. 354.] On the other hand, the musical societies both of Linz and Graz elected him an honorary member. To the latter of these distinctions we owe the two beautiful movements of the symphony No. 8, in B minor, which was begun at Vienna on Oct. 30, 1822, and intended as a return for the compliment. The Allegro and Andante alone are finished, but these are of singular beauty and the greatest originality. In them, for the first time in orchestral composition, Schubert exhibits a style absolutely his own, untinged by any predecessor, and full of that strangely direct appeal to the hearer of which we have already spoken. It is certain that he never heard the music played, and that the new and delicate effects and orchestral combinations with which it is crowded, were the result of his imagination alone. The first movement is sadly full of agitation and distress. It lay hidden at Graz for many years, until obtained from Anselm Hüttenbrenner by Herbeck, who first produced it in Vienna at one of the Gesellschaft concerts in 1865.[7] It was published by Spina early in 1867 ; was played at the Crystal Palace, April 6, 1867, and elsewhere in England, and always with increasing success. In fact no one can hear it without being captivated by it.

The Songs composed in 1822—fourteen printed and two in MS.—comprise ' Epistel von Collin ' (Jan.) ; ' Heliopolis ' (April) ; ' Todesmusik,' with a magnificent opening (op. 108, No. 2 ; Sept.) ; ' Schatzgräbers Begehr ' (op. 23, No. 4 ; Nov.) with its stately bass ; ' Willkommen und Abschied ' (op. 56, No. 1 ; Dec.) ; ' Die Rose ' (op. 73) and ' Der Musensohn ' (op. 92). The concerted pieces, ' Constitutionslied ' (op. 157 ; Jan.), ' Geist der Liebe ' (op. 11, No. 3), ' Gott in der Natur ' (op. 133), and ' Des Tages Weihe ' (op. 146), all belong to this year.

Publication went on in 1822, though not so

---

[1] *K.H.* p. 261 (i. 264).   [2] 7ᵇ stands for September.
[3] This was kindly pointed out to the writer by Johannes Brahms, who had an early copy of the score, made by Ferdinand Schubert from the autograph in its original condition. In this shape Brahms rehearsed the mass, but found many portions unsatisfactory, and was interested to discover subsequently from the autograph that Schubert had altered the very passages alluded to, and made them practicable.—He made three attempts at the ' Cum Sancto ' before succeeding, each time in fugue, and always with a different subject. Of the first there are four bars ; of the second 199 ; the third is that printed in Schreiber's edition. This edition is unfortunately very incorrect. Not only does it swarm with misprints, but whole passages, and those most important ones (as in the Horns and Trombones of the Dona), are clean omitted. The *nuances* also are shamefully treated.
[4] First printed by R. Schumann in the *Neue Zeitschrift für Musik* for Feb. 5, 1839. See also *K.H.* p. 333 (ii. 16).
[5] *K.H.* p. 146 (i. 148).
[6] *K.H.* p. 280 (i. 283).   [7] See Hanslick. *Concertsaal.* p. 350.

briskly as before. The Variations dedicated to Beethoven (op. 10) were first to appear, on April 19. They were followed by op. 8 (four songs) on May 9, and op. 11 (three part-songs) on June 12. Then came a long gap till Dec. 13, on which day opp. 12, 13, and 14, all songs, appeared at once. We have not space to name them. But with such accumulated treasures to draw upon, it is unnecessary to say that they are all of the first class. The pecuniary result of the publications of 1821 had been good ; 2000 gulden were realised, and of the 'Erl King' alone more than 800 copies had been sold ; and if Schubert had been provident enough to keep his works in his own possession he would soon have been out of the reach of want. This, however, he did not do. Pressed by the want of money, in an incautious moment he sold the first twelve of his works [1] to Diabelli for 800 silver gulden (£80), and entered into some injudicious arrangement with the same firm for future publications. His old and kind friend Count Dietrichstein about this time offered him a post as organist to the Court Chapel,[2] but he refused it, and he was probably right, though in so doing he greatly distressed his methodical old father. His habits, like Beethoven's, made it absurd for him to undertake any duties requiring strict attendance.

The Vienna Theatre being closed to 'Alfonso and Estrella,' Schubert turned his thoughts in the direction of Dresden, where his admirer Anna Milder was living, and where Weber was Director of the Opera ; and we find him in a letter of Feb. 28, 1823 (published in 1881 for the first time)[3] asking his old patron Herr von Mosel for a letter of recommendation to Weber. He is confined to the house by illness, and apologises for not being able to call. There are no traces of reply to this application, but it probably led to nothing, for, as we shall see, the score of the opera was still in his hands in October. He was evidently now set upon opera. In the letter just mentioned he implores von Mosel to entrust him with a libretto 'suitable for his littleness' ; and though he seems never to have obtained this, he went on with the best he could get, and 1823 saw the birth of no less than three dramatic pieces. The first was a one-act play with dialogue, adapted from the French by Castelli, and called 'Die Verschworenen,' or 'The Conspirators.' The play was published in the *Dramatic Garland*—an annual collection of dramas—for 1823. Schubert must have seen it soon after publication, and by April had finished the composition of it. The autograph, in the British Museum, has at

the end the words 'Aprill 1823. F. Schubert, Ende der Oper.' It contains an overture and eleven numbers, and appears from Bauernfeld's testimony to have been composed with a view to representation at the Court theatre. The libretto is a very poor one, with but few dramatic points, and confines the composer mainly to the Chorus. The licensers changed its title to the less suspicious one of 'Der häusliche Krieg' or 'The Domestic Struggle,' and it was duly sent in to the management, but it returned in twelve months without examination. It did not come to performance at all during Schubert's lifetime, nor till 1861. In that year it was given, under Herbeck's direction, by the Musikverein, Vienna, on March 1 and 22 ; and on the stage at Frankfort on August 29 ; since then at the Court theatre, Vienna, at Munich, Salzburg, and other German towns ; in Paris, Feb. 3, 1868, as 'La Croisade des Dames,' and at the Crystal Palace, Sydenham, March 2, 1872, as 'The Conspirators.' In less than two months after throwing off this lively Singspiel, Schubert had embarked in something far more serious, a regular three-act opera of the 'heroico-romantic' pattern—also with spoken dialogue —the scene laid in Spain, with Moors, knights, a king, a king's daughter, and all the usual furniture of these dreary compilations. The libretto of 'Fierrabras,' by Josef Kupelwieser— enough of itself to justify all Wagner's charges [4] against the opera books of the old school—was commissioned by Barbaja for the Court theatre. The book was passed by the Censure on July 21 ; but Schubert had by that time advanced far in his labours, and had in fact completed more than half of the piece. He began it, as his own date tells us, on May 25. Act 1, filling 304 pages of large oblong paper,[5] was completely scored by the 31st of the month ; Act 2, in five days more, by June 5 ; and the whole three acts, fully 1000 pages, and containing an overture and twenty-three numbers, were entirely out of hand by Oct. 2. And all for nothing ! Schubert was not even kept long in suspense, for early in the following year he learnt that the work had been dismissed. The ground for its rejection was the badness of the libretto ; but knowing Barbaja's character, and seeing that Kupelwieser was secretary to a rival house (the Josefstadt), it is difficult not to suspect that the commission had been given by the wily Italian, merely to facilitate the progress of some piece of business between the two establishments.

It is, as Liszt has remarked, extraordinary that Schubert, who was brought up from his youth on the finest poetry, should have unhesitatingly accepted the absurd and impracticable librettos which he did, and which have kept in oblivion so much of his splendid music. His devotion to his friends, and his irrepressible

---

[1] So say the books ; but the works published on commission were opp. 1-7, containing twenty songs.
[2] [The evidence for this transaction is very obscure, and the story may have become confused with a proposed application in 1825. See below, p. 305a.]
[3] In the *Neue Freie Presse* of Vienna, Nov. 19, 1881. The letter, though formal in style, is curiously free in some of its expressions. It mentions the overture to the 1st Act of 'Alfonso und Estrella. What can this be? The overture known under that name (op. 69) is dated 'Dec. 1823,' and is said to have been written for 'Rosamunde.'

[4] Hanslick, *Concertsaal*, p. 150.
[5] The autograph was shown to Sullivan and the writer by the energetic Schubert apostle, Herr Johann Herbeck, in 1868.

desire to utter what was in him, no doubt help to explain the anomaly, but an anomaly it will always remain. It is absolutely distressing to think of such extraordinary ability, and such still more extraordinary powers of work, being so cruelly thrown away, and of the sickening disappointment which these repeated failures must have entailed on so simple and sensitive a heart as his. Fortunately for us the strains in which he vents his griefs are as beautiful and endearing as those in which he celebrates his joys.

His work this summer was not, however, to be all disappointment. If the theatre turned a deaf ear to his strains there were always his beloved songs to confide in, and they never deceived him. Of the Song in Schubert's hands we may say what Wordsworth so well says of the Sonnet :—

> With this key
> Shakespeare unlocked his heart ; the melody
> Of this small lute gave ease to Petrarch's wound.
> .   .   .   .
> .   .   . and when a damp
> Fell round the path of Milton, in his hand
> The thing became a trumpet, whence he blew
> Soul-animating strains, alas too few !

—with the notable difference that it was given to Schubert to gather up and express, in his one person and his one art, all the various moods and passions which Wordsworth has divided amongst so many mighty poets.

And now, in the midst of the overwhelming tumult and absorption which inevitably accompany the production of so large a work of imagination as a three-act opera, brought into being at so extraordinarily rapid a pace, he was to stop, and to indite a set of songs, which though not of greater worth than many others of his, are yet so intelligible, so expressive, address themselves to such universal feelings, and form so attractive a whole, that they have certainly become more popular, and are more widely and permanently beloved, than any similar production by any other composer. We have already described the incident through which Schubert made acquaintance with the Müllerlieder [1] of Wilhelm Müller, twenty of which he selected for the beautiful series so widely known as the 'Schöne Müllerin.' We have seen the enduring impatience with which he attacked a book when it took his fancy, and the eagerness with which he began upon this particular one. We know that the Müllerlieder were all composed this year ; that some of them were written in hospital ; that No. 15 is dated 'October' ; that a considerable interval elapsed between the second and third Act of 'Fierrabras'—probably the best part of July and August. Putting these facts together it seems to follow that the call on Rand-

hartinger (see ante, p. 24) and the composition of the first numbers of the 'Schöne Müllerin' took place in May, before he became immersed in 'Fierrabras.' Then came the first two Acts of that opera ; then his illness, and his sojourn in the hospital, and more songs ; then the third Act of the opera ; and lastly the completion of the Lieder.

Be this as it may, there was no lack of occupation for Schubert after he had put 'Fierrabras' out of hand. Weber arrived in Vienna late in September 1823, and on Oct. 3 began the rehearsals of 'Euryanthe'; and for a month the musical world of Austria was in a ferment. After the first performance, on Oct. 25, Weber and Schubert came somewhat into collision. Schubert, with characteristic frankness, asserted that the new work wanted the geniality and grace of 'Der Freischütz,' that its merit lay mainly in its harmony,[2] and that he was prepared to prove that the score did not contain a single original melody. Weber had been much tried by the rehearsals, by the growing conviction that his work was too long, and by the imperfect success of the performance ; and with a combination of ignorance and insolence which does him no credit replied, 'Let the fool learn something himself before he criticises me.' Schubert's answer to this was to go off to Weber with the score of 'Alfonso and Estrella.' When they had looked through this, Weber returned to Schubert's criticisms on 'Euryanthe,' and finding that the honest Franz stuck to his point, was absurd enough to lose his temper, and say, in the obvious belief that the score before him was Schubert's first attempt, 'I tell you the first puppies and the first operas are always drowned.' Franz, it is unnecessary to say, bore no malice, even for so galling a speech, and it is due to Weber to state that he took some pains later to have the work adopted at the Dresden theatre.[3]

Schubert did not yet know the fate which awaited 'Fierrabras'; all was at present couleur de rose ; and the fascination of the theatre, the desire innate in all musicians, even one so self-contained as Schubert, to address a large public, sharpened not improbably by the chance recently enjoyed by the stranger, was too strong to be resisted, and he again, for the third time in ten months, turned towards the stage. This time the temptation came in the shape of 'Rosamunde, Princess of Cyprus,' a play of ultraromantic character, by Madame von Chezy, authoress of 'Euryanthe,' a librettist whose lot seems to have been to drag down the musicians connected with her. The book of 'Rosamunde' must have been at least as inefficient as that with which Weber had been struggling, to cause the failure of such magnificent and interesting music as Schubert made for it. The drama has disappeared, but Kreissle gives the plot,[4] and

[1] The Müllerlieder, twenty-three in number, with Prologue and Epilogue in addition, are contained in the 1st vol. of the Gedichte aus den hinterlassenen Papieren eines reisenden Waldhornisten (Poems found among the papers of a travelling French-horn-player), which were first published at Dessau, 1821. Schubert has omitted the Prologue and Epilogue, and three poems—'Das Mühlenleben' after 'Der Neugierige'; 'Erster Schmerz, letzter Scherz,' after 'Eifersucht und Stolz'; and 'Blümlein Vergissmein' after 'Die böse Farbe.'

[2] See Mendelssohn's opinion in The Mendelssohn Family, i. 237.
[3] K.H. p. 246 (i. 249) note.   [4] Ibid. p. 285 (i. 282), etc.

it is both tedious and improbable. It had moreover the disadvantage of competition with a sensational spectacular piece, written expressly to suit the taste of the suburban house, the Theatre an-der-Wien, at which 'Rosamunde' was produced, and which, since the time when Schikaneder induced Mozart to join him in the 'Magic Flute,'[1] had a reputation for such extravaganzas. Schubert completed the music in five days.[2] It consists of an Overture in D,[3] since published as 'Alfonso und Estrella,' op. 69 ; three Entr'actes ; two numbers of ballet music ; a little piece for clarinets, horns, and bassoons, called a 'Shepherds' Melody,' of bewitching beauty ; a Romance for soprano solo, and three choruses. The Romance (op. 26), the Shepherds' chorus, the Entr'acte in Bb, and the Air de Ballet in G, are not only very beautiful but very attractive ; and the Entr'acte in B minor, of a grand, gloomy, and highly imaginative cast, is one of the finest pieces of music existing. The play was brought out on Dec. 20, 1823 ; the overture, though the entire orchestral part of the music had only one rehearsal of two hours, was twice redemanded, other numbers were loudly applauded, and Schubert himself was called for at the close ; but it only survived one more representation, and then the parts were tied up and forgotten till the year 1867, when they were discovered by two English travellers in Vienna.[4]

Besides the Müllerlieder several independent songs of remarkable beauty belong to 1823. Conspicuous among these are 'Viola' (Schneeglöcklein ; op. 123), a long composition full of the most romantic tenderness and delicacy, with all the finish of Meissonnier's pictures, and all his breadth and dignity. Also the 'Zwerg' (op. 22, No. 1), by Matthias von Collin, in which Schubert has immortalised the one brother, as Beethoven, in his overture to 'Coriolan,' did the other. This long, dramatic, and most pathetic ballad, which but few can hear unmoved, was written absolutely à l'improviste, without note or sketch, at the top of his speed, talking all the while to Randhartinger, who was waiting to take him out for a walk.[5] Equal, if not superior, to these in merit, though of smaller dimensions, are 'Dass sie hier gewesen' (op. 59, No. 2) ; 'Du bist die Ruh' (do. No. 3) ; the Barcarolle, 'Auf dem Wasser zu singen' (op. 72), to which no nearer date than '1823' can be given. Below these again, though still fine songs, are 'Der zürnende Barde' (Feb.) ; 'Drang in die Ferne' (op. 71 ; March 25) ; 'Pilgerweise' (April) ; 'Vergissmeinnicht' (May). The fine Sonata in A minor for PF. solo, published as op. 143, is

dated Feb. 1823, and the sketch of a scena for tenor solo and chorus of men's voices with orchestra, dated May 1823. The latter was completed by Herbeck, and published in 1868 by Spina as 'Rüdiger's Heimkehr.'

Ten works (opp. 15-24) were published in 1823. The earliest was a collection of dances, viz., twelve Waltzes, nine Écossaises, and seventeen Ländler, op. 18, published Feb. 5 ; the PF. Fantasia, op. 15, followed on Feb. 24. The rest are songs, either solo—op. 20, April 10 ; op. 22, May 27 ; op. 23, August 4 ; op. 24, Oct. 7 ; op. 16, Oct. 9 ; op. 19, twenty-one (no dates)—or part-songs, op. 17, Oct. 9. With op. 20, the names of Sauer & Leidesdorf first occur as publishers.

The year 1824 began almost exclusively with instrumental compositions. An Introduction and Variations for PF. and flute (op. 160), on the 'Trockne Blumen' of the 'Schöne Müllerin,' are dated 'January,' and were followed by the famous Octet (op. 166), for clarinet, horn, bassoon, two violins, viola, violoncello, and contrabass, which is marked as begun in February, and finished on March 1. It was written—not, let us hope, without adequate remuneration, though that was probably the last thing of which its author thought—for Count F. von Troyer, chief officer of the household to the Archduke Rudolph, Beethoven's patron. In this beautiful composition Schubert indulges his love of extension. It contains, like Beethoven's Septet, eight movements ; but, unlike the Septet, it occupies more than an hour in performance. But though long, no one can call it tedious.[6] The Count played the clarinet, and must have been delighted with the expressive melody allotted to him in the Andante. The work was performed immediately after its composition, with Schuppanzigh, Weiss, and Linke, three of the famous Rasoumowsky quartet, amongst the players. His association with the members of this celebrated party may well have led Schubert to write string quartets ; at any rate he himself tells us that he had written two before the 31st March,[7] and these are doubtless those in Eb and E (op. 125), since the only other quartet bearing the date of 1824—that in A minor—has so strong a Hungarian flavour as to point to his visit to Zselész later in the year. How powerfully his thoughts were running at present on orchestral music is evident from the fact that he mentions both octet and quartets as studies for 'the Grand Symphony,'[8] which was then his goal, though he did not reach it till eighteen months later.

A bitter disappointment, however, was awaiting him in the rejection of 'Fierrabras,' which,

[1] Produced at the Theatre an-der-Wien, Sept. 30, 1791.
[2] So says Wilhelm von Chezy, the son of the librettist, who was on terms with Schubert. See his Journal, *Erinnerungen*, etc., 1863.
[3] The autograph is dated 'Dec. 1823.'
[4] [It is hardly necessary to remind the reader that the two travellers were Sir George Grove and Sir Arthur Sullivan.]
[5] Kreissle, *Sketch*, p. 154 note.

[6] Published by Spina in 1854.
[7] In his letter to Leopold Kupelwieser of March 31, *K.H.* p. 321 (ii. 5).
[8] 'In this manner I shall prepare the way to the Grand Symphony (zur grossen Sinfonie).' *Ibid.*

as already mentioned, was returned by Barbaja, ostensibly on account of the badness of its libretto. Two full-sized operas—this and 'Alfonso und Estrella'—to be laid on the shelf without even a rehearsal! Whatever the cause, the blow must have been equally severe to our simple, genuine, composer, who had no doubt been expecting, not without reason, day by day for the last four months, to hear of the acceptance of his work. His picture of himself under this temporary eclipse of hope is mournful in the extreme, though natural enough to the easily depressed temperament of a man of genius. After speaking of himself as 'the most unfortunate, most miserable being on earth,' he goes on to say, 'think of a man whose health can never be restored, and who from sheer despair makes matters worse instead of better. Think, I say, of a man whose brightest hopes have come to nothing, to whom love and friendship are but torture, and whose enthusiasm for the beautiful is fast vanishing; and ask yourself if such a man is not truly unhappy.

My peace is gone, my heart is sore,
Gone for ever and evermore.

This is my daily cry; for every night I go to sleep hoping never again to wake, and every morning only brings back the torment of the day before. Thus joylessly and friendlessly would pass my days, if Schwind did not often look in, and give me a glimpse of the old happy times. . . . Your brother's opera'— this is a letter to Kupelwieser the painter, and the allusion is to ' Fierrabras '—' turns out to be impracticable, and my music is therefore wasted. Castelli's " Verschworenen " has been set in Berlin by a composer there, and produced with success. Thus I have composed two operas for nothing.' This sad mood, real enough at the moment, was only natural after such repulses. It was assisted, as Schubert's depression always was, by the absence of many of his friends, and also, as he himself confesses, by his acquaintance with Leidesdorf the publisher (in Beethoven's banter ' Dorf des Leides,' a very ' village of sorrow '), whom he describes as a thoroughly good, trustworthy fellow, ' but so very melancholy that I begin to fear I may have learnt too much from him in that direction.' It must surely have been after an evening with this worthy that he made the touching entries in his journal which have been preserved ; e.g. ' Grief sharpens the understanding and strengthens the soul : Joy on the other hand seldom troubles itself about the one, and makes the other effeminate or frivolous.' ' My musical works are the product of my genius and my misery, and what the public most relish is that which has given me the greatest distress.' Fortunately, in men of the genuine composer-temperament, the various moods of mind follow one another rapidly. As soon as they begin to compose the demon flies and heaven opens.

That gloomy document called ' Beethoven's Will,' to which even Schubert's most wretched letters must yield the palm, was written at the very time that he was pouring out the gay and healthy strains of his Second Symphony. Schubert left town with the Esterhazys in a few weeks after these distressing utterances, and for a time forgot his troubles in the distractions of country life in Hungary. At Zselész he remained for six months, but his life there is almost entirely a blank to us. We can only estimate it by the compositions which are attributable to the period, and by the scanty information conveyed by his letters, which, though fuller of complaint than those of 1818, are even less communicative of facts and occurrences. To this visit is to be ascribed that noble composition known as the ' Grand Duo ' (op. 140), though designated by himself as ' Sonata for the PF. for four hands. Zselés, June 1824 ' ; a piece which, though recalling in one movement Beethoven's Second, and in another his Seventh Symphony, is yet full of the individuality of its author ; a symphonic work in every sense of the word, which, through Joachim's instrumentation, has now become an orchestral symphony, and a very fine one. To Zselész also are due the Sonata in B♭ (op. 30, May or June), the Variations in A♭ (op. 35, ' middle of 1824 '), two Waltzes (in op. 33, ' 1824, July '), and four Ländler (' July, 1824,' Nott. p. 215)—all for PF. four hands ; other Waltzes and Ländler in the same collections for two hands ; and the ' Gebet ' of Lamotte Fouqué (op. 139a), signed ' Sept. 1824, at Zelész in Hungary '—all evidently arising from the necessity of providing music for the Count's family circle. The young Countesses were now nineteen and seventeen, and doubtless good performers, as is implied in the duet-form of the pianoforte works. We are probably right in also attributing the lovely String Quartet in A minor (op. 29), and the four-hand ' Divertissement à la hongroise ' (op. 54), to this visit, at any rate to its immediate influence. Both are steeped in the Hungarian spirit, and the Divertissement contains a succession of real national tunes, one of which he heard from the lips of a maidservant as he passed the kitchen with Baron Schönstein in returning from a walk. For the Baron was at Zselész on this as on the last occasion, and frequent and exquisite must have been the performances of the many fine songs which Schubert had written in the interval since his former visit.

The circumstances attending the composition of the vocal quartet (' Gebet,' op. 139) just mentioned are told by Kreissle, probably on the authority of Schönstein, and they give a good instance of Schubert's extraordinary facility. At breakfast one morning, in Sept. 1824, the Countess produced Lamotte Fouqué's poem, and proposed to Schubert to set it for the family party. He withdrew after breakfast, taking the book with him, and in the evening, less than ten hours afterwards, it was tried through from the score at the piano. The next evening it was sung again, this time from separate parts, which Schubert had written out during the day. The piece is composed for quartet, with solos for Mme. Esterhazy, Marie, Schonstein, and the Count, and contains 209 bars. A MS. letter of Ferdinand's,[1] dated July 3, full of that strong half-reverential affection which was Ferdinand's habitual attitude towards his gifted brother, and of curious details, mentions having sent him Bach's fugues (never-cloying food of great composers), and an opera-book, 'Der kurze Mantel.' Strange fascination of the stage, which thus, in despite of so many failures, could keep him still enthralled !

The country air of the Hungarian mountains, and no doubt the sound and healthy living and early hours of the château, restored Schubert's health completely, and in a letter of Sept. 21 to Schober he says that for five months he had been well. But he felt his isolation and the want of congenial Vienna society keenly; speaks with regret of having been 'enticed' into a second visit to Hungary, and complains of not having a single person near to whom he could say a sensible word. How different from the exuberant happiness of the visits to Steyr and St. Pölten, when every one he met was a demonstrative admirer, and every evening brought a fresh triumph !

Now, if ever, was the date of his tender feeling for his pupil Caroline Esterhazy, which his biographers have probably much exaggerated. She was seventeen at the time, and Bauernfeld represents her as the object of an ideal devotion, which soothed, comforted, and inspirited Schubert to the end of his life. Ideal it can only have been, considering the etiquette of the time, and the wide distance between the stations of the two ; and the only occasion on which Schubert is ever alleged to have approached anything like a revelation of his feelings, is that told by Kreissle—on what authority he does not say, and it is hard to conceive—when on her jokingly reproaching him for not having dedicated anything to her, he replied, 'Why should I ? everything I ever did is dedicated to you.' True, the fine Fantasia in F minor, published in the March following his death as op. 103, is dedicated to her ' by Franz Schubert,' a step which the publishers would hardly have ventured upon unless the MS.—probably handed to them before his death—had been so inscribed by himself. But it is difficult to reconcile the complaints of isolation and neglect already quoted from his letter to Schober with the existence of a passion which must have been fed every time he met his pupil or sat down to the

piano with her. We must be content to leave each reader to decide the question for himself.

Vocal composition he laid aside almost entirely in 1824. The only songs which we can ascertain to belong to it are four—the fine though gloomy ones called ' Auflösung,' and ' Abendstern,' both by Mayrhofer ; another evening song ' Im Abendroth ' by Lappe, all three in March ; and the bass song, ' Lied eines Kriegers,' with which he closed the last day of the year.[2] Of part-songs there are two, both for men's voices ; one a ' Salve regina,' written in April, before leaving town ; and the other, the ' Gondelfahrer,' or Gondolier, a very fine and picturesque composition, of which Lablache is said to have been so fond that he encored it on first hearing, and himself sang in the encore (Spaun).—A Sonata for PF. and Arpeggione, in A minor, dated Nov. 1824, was probably one of his first compositions after returning to town.[3]

The publications of 1824 embrace opp. 25 to 28 inclusive, all issued by Sauer & Leidesdorf. Op. 25 is the ' Schöne Müllerin,' 20 songs in five numbers, published March 25 ; op. 26 is the vocal music in ' Rosamunde,'[4] the romance and three choruses; op. 27, three fine ' heroic marches,' for PF. four hands ; op. 28, ' Der Gondelfahrer,' for four men's voices and PF., August 12.

1825 was a happy year to our hero—happy and productive. He was back again in his dear Vienna, and exchanged the isolation of Zselész for the old familiar life, with his congenial friends Vogl, Schwind, Jenger, Mayrhofer, etc. (Schober was in Prussia, and Kupelwieser still at Rome), in whose applause and sympathy and genial conviviality he rapidly forgot the disappointments and depression that had troubled him in the autumn. Sofie Müller, one of the great actresses of that day, evidently a very accomplished, cultivated woman, was then in Vienna, and during February and March her house was the resort of Schubert, Jenger, and Vogl, who sang or listened to her singing of his best and newest Lieder,—she herself sang the ' Junge Nonne' at sight on March 3—and lived a pleasant and thoroughly artistic life.[5] Others, which she mentions as new, and which indeed had their birth at this time are ' Der Einsame,' and ' Ihr Grab.' The 'new songs from the Pirate,' which she heard on March 1, may have been some from the ' Lady of the Lake,' or 'Norna's song,' or even 'Anna Lyle,' usually placed two years later. Schubert published some important works early in this year—the Overture in F for four hands (op. 34) ; also the Sonata in B♭ (op. 30), and the Variations in A♭ (op. 35), both for four hands ; and the

1 For which I again gladly acknowledge the kindness of Frl. Caroline Geisler-Schubert, Schubert's grandniece.

2 The autograph, so dated, belongs to Mr. C. J. Hargitt, London.
3 Gotthard, 1871. Autograph in Musikverein.
4 Besides the vocal music, the overture was published about 1828, and the Entr'actes and Ballet music in 1866.
5 See her interesting Journal, in her Leben und nachgelassene Papiere herausg. von Johann Grafen Majláth (Vienna, 1832).

String Quartet in A minor (op. 29)—fruits of
his sojourn in Hungary. The last of these,
the only quartet he was destined to publish
during his life, is dedicated 'to his friend I.
Schuppanzigh,' a pleasant memorial of the
acquaintance cemented by the performance of
the octet, a twelvemonth before. And as on
such publications some amount of money passes
from the publisher to the composer, this fact of
itself would contribute to enliven and inspirit
him. In addition to these instrumental works
some noble songs were issued in the early part
of 1825 — 'Die zürnende Diana,' and the
'Nachtstück,' of Mayrhofer ; ' Der Pilgrim ' and
'Der Alpenjäger,' of Schiller ; and Zuleika's
second song. The two beautiful solo sonatas in
A minor and in C—the latter of which he never
succeeded in completely writing out, but the
fragment of which is of first-rate quality—also
date from this time.

As if to revenge himself for his sufferings at
the Esterhazys', he planned an extensive tour
for this summer, in his favourite district, and
in the company of his favourite friend. Vogl,
on March 31, started for his home at Steyr.
Schubert[1] soon followed him, and the next five
months, to the end of October, were passed in a
delightful mixture of music, friends, fine scenery,
lovely weather, and absolute ease and comfort,
in Upper Austria and the Salzkammergut,
partly amongst the good people who had welcomed him so warmly in 1819, partly among
new friends and new enthusiasm. Taking Steyr
as their *point d'appui* they made excursions to
Linz, Steyreck, Gmunden, Salzburg, and even
as far as Gastein, etc., heartily enjoying the
glorious scenery by day, received everywhere on
arrival with open arms, and making the best
possible impression with their joint performances. The songs from 'The Lady of the
Lake' were either composed before starting or
on the road. At any rate they formed the chief
programme during the excursion. If the whole
seven were sung or not is uncertain ;[2] but
Schubert particularly mentions the 'Ave Maria,'
àpropos of which he makes an interesting
revelation. 'My new songs,' says he, 'from
Walter Scott's "Lady of the Lake," have been
very successful. People were greatly astonished
at the devotion which I have thrown into the
Hymn to the Blessed Virgin, and it seems to
have seized and impressed everybody. I think
that the reason of this is that I never force
myself into devotion, or compose hymns or
prayers unless I am really overpowered by the
feeling ; that alone is real, true devotion.' It
is during this journey, at Salzburg, that he
makes the remark, already noticed, as to the
performance of Vogl and himself. At Salzburg
too, it was the 'Ave Maria' that so riveted
his hearers. 'We produced our seven pieces

before a select circle, and all were much im
pressed, especially by the Ave Maria, which I
mentioned in my former letter. The way in
which Vogl sings and I accompany, so that for
the moment we seem to be one, is something
quite new and unexpected to these good people.'
Schubert sometimes performed alone. He had
brought some variations and marches for four
hands with him, and finding a good player at
the convents of Florian and Kremsmünster, had
made a great effect with them. But he was
especially successful with the lovely variations
from the solo Sonata in A minor (op. 42) ; and
here again he lets us into his secret. 'There I
played alone, and not without success, for I was
assured that the keys under my hands sang like
voices, which if true makes me very glad,
because I cannot abide that accursed thumping,
which even eminent players adopt, but which
delights neither my ears nor my judgment.'
He found his compositions well known throughout Upper Austria. The gentry fought for the
honour of receiving him, and long after old
people were wont to talk with equal enthusiasm
of his lovely music, and of the unaffected gaiety
and simplicity of his ways and manners.

The main feature of the tour was the excursion
to Gastein in the mountains of East Tyrol. To
Schubert this was new ground, and the delight
in the scenery which animates his description
is obvious. They reached it about August 18,
and appear to have remained three or four
weeks, returning to Gmunden about Sept. 10.
At Gastein, among other good people, he found
his old ally Ladislaus Pyrker, Patriarch of
Venice, and composed two songs to his poetry,
'Heimweh ' and 'Allmacht' (op. 79). But the
great work of this date was the 'Grand Symphony' which had been before him for so long.
We found him eighteen months ago writing
quartets and the octet as preparation for it,
and an allusion in a letter[3] of Schwind's shows
that at the beginning of August he spoke of
the thing as virtually done. That it was
actually put on to paper at Gastein at this date
we know from the testimony of Bauernfeld,[4]
who also informs us that it was a special
favourite with its composer. Seven songs in
all are dated in this autumn, amongst them two
fine scenes from a play by W. von Schütz called
'Lacrimas' (op. 124), not so well known as
they deserve.

The letters of this tour, though not all preserved, are unusually numerous for one who so
much disliked writing. One long one to his
father and mother ; another, much longer, to
Ferdinand ; a third to Spaun, and a fourth to
Bauernfeld, are printed by Kreissle, and contain
passages of real interest, showing how keenly
he observed and how thoroughly he enjoyed
nature, and displaying throughout a vein of

[1] For the dates of the early part of the tour, see *K.* ii. 21.
[2] Schubert speaks of them as 'unsere sieben Sachen' (Letter to
Ferdinand, *Kreissle*, p. 363) ; but Nos. 3 and 4 are for chorus.
[3] *K. H.* p. 358 (ii. 43). 'To your Symphony we are looking forward
eagerly,' implying that Schubert had mentioned it in a former
letter.   [4] *W.Z.K.*, June 9-13, 1829.

good sense and even practical sagacity,[1] and a facility of expression, which are rare in him.

At length the summer and the money came to an end, Vogl went off to Italy for his gout, and Schubert, meeting Gahy at Linz, returned with him and the MS. Symphony to Vienna in an *Einspänner*, to find Schober and Kupelwieser both once more settled there. The first thing to be done was to replenish his purse, and this he soon did by the sale of the seven songs from 'The Lady of the Lake,' which he disposed of on Oct. 29 to Artaria, for 200 silver gulden—just £20 ! Twenty pounds, however, were a mine of wealth to Schubert ; and even after repaying the money which had been advanced by his father, and by Bauernfeld for the rent of the lodgings during his absence, he would still have a few pounds in hand.

During Schubert's absence in the country his old friend Salieri died, and was succeeded by Eybler. The Court organist also fell ill, and Schwind wrote urging him to look after the post ; but Schubert made no sign, and evidently did nothing in the matter, though the organist died on Nov. 19. He obviously knew much better than his friends that he was absolutely unfit for any post requiring punctuality or restraint. In the course of this year he was made 'Ersatzmann,' or substitute—whatever that may mean—by the Musikverein, or Gesellschaft der Musikfreunde. Of what happened from this time till the close of 1825 we have no certain information. He set two songs by Schulze in December ; and it is probable that the Piano Sonata in D (op. 53), and the noble funeral march for the Emperor of Russia (op. 55), whose death was known in Vienna on Dec. 14, both belong to that month. What gave him his interest in the death of Alexander is not known, but the march is an extraordinarily fine specimen. A piece for the Piano in F, serving as accompaniment to a recitation from a poem by Pratobevera, a series of graceful modulations in arpeggio form, also dates from this year.[2]

The compositions of 1825 may be here summed up :—Sonata for PF. solo in A minor (op. 42) ; ditto in D (op. 53) ; ditto in A (op. 120) ; unfinished ditto in C ('Reliquie,' Nott. p. 211) ; a funeral march, four hands, for the Emperor Alexander of Russia (op. 55). Songs —'Des Sängers Habe,' by Schlechta, and ' Im Walde,' by E. Schulze ; seven from 'The Lady of the Lake' (op. 52) ; another from Scott's ' Pirate' ;[3] ' Auf der Bruck,' by Schulze ; ' Fülle der Liebe,' by Schlegel ; ' Allmacht' and 'Heimweh,' by Pyrker ; two scenes from ' Lacrimas,' by W. von Schütz ; and ' Abendlied für die Entfernte,' by A. W. Schlegel ; ' Die junge

Nonne,' 'Todtengräbers Heimweh,' and ' Der blinde Knabe,' all by Craigher ; ' Der Einsame,' by Lappe ; and, in December, ' An mein Herz' and 'Der liebliche Stern,' both by Ernst Schulze. It is also more than probable that the string quartet in D minor was at least begun before the end of the year.

The publications of 1825 are :—In January, opp. 32, 30, 34 ; Feb. 11, opp. 36 and 37 ; May 9, op. 38 ; July 25, op. 43 ; August 12, op. 31 ; and, without note of date, opp. 29 and 33. Op. 29 is the lovely A minor Quartet ; and it is worthy of note that it is published as the first of ' Trois quatuors.' This was never carried out. The two others were written, as we have already seen (p. 301*b*), but they remained unpublished till after the death of their author.

1826 was hardly eventful in any sense of the word, though by no means unimportant in Schubert's history. It seems to have been passed entirely in Vienna. He contemplated a trip to Linz with Spaun and Schwind, but it did not come off. The weather of this spring was extraordinarily bad, and during April and May he composed nothing.[4] The music attributable to 1826 is, however, of first-rate quality. The String Quartet in D minor, by common consent placed at the head of Schubert's music of this class, was first played on Jan. 29, and was therefore doubtless only just completed.[5] That in G (op. 161), Schubert himself has dated as being written in ten days (June 20 to June 30), a work teeming with fresh vigour after the inaction of the preceding two months as full of melody, spirit, romance, variety, and individuality, as anything he ever penned, and only prevented from taking the same high position as the preceding, by its great length—due to the diffuseness which Schubert would no doubt have remedied had he given himself time to do so. One little point may be mentioned *en passant* in both these noble works—the evidence they afford of his lingering fondness for the past. In the D minor Quartet he goes back for the subject and feeling of the *Andante* to a song of his own of 1816, and the Finale of the G major is curiously tinged with reminiscences of the Rossini-fever of 1819.

The ' Rondeau brillant' in B minor for PF. and violin (op. 70), now such a favourite in the concert-room, also belongs to this year, though it cannot be precisely dated ; and so does a piece of still higher quality, which is pronounced by Schumann to be its author's 'most perfect work both in form and conception,' the Sonata in G major for PF. solo, op. 78, usually called the ' Fantasia,' owing to a freak of the publisher's. The autograph is inscribed, in the hand of its

---

[1] See his shrewd reasons for not at once accepting Bauernfeld's proposition that he, Schwind and Schubert, should all live together. *K.H.* p. 370 (ii. 57). Also the whole letter to Spaun.
[2] Printed by Reissmann in his book.
[3] So says Sofie Müller (under date of March 1) ; but perhaps it was her mistake for Norman's song in 'The Lady of the Lake.'

[4] See his letter to Bauernfeld and Mayrhofer, in *Die Presse*, April 21, 1869.
[5] *K.H.* p. 391 (ii. 77). The finale was voted too long, to which Schubert, after a few minutes' consideration, agreed, and 'at once cut out a good part.' (Hauer's information.) The autograph has disappeared.

author, 'IV. Sonate für Pianoforte allein. Oct. 1826, Franz Schubert'; above which, in the writing of Tobias Haslinger, stands the title 'Fantasie, Andante, Menuetto und Allegretto.'[1] We may well say with Beethoven, 'O Tobias!'

By the side of these undying productions the 'Marche héroïque,' written to celebrate the accession of Nicholas I. of Russia, and the Andantino and Rondo on French *motifs*—both for PF. four hands, are not of great significance.

An attack of song-writing seems to have come upon him in March, which date we find attached to six songs; or, if the rest of those to Seidl's words forming opp. 105 and 80, and marked merely '1826,' were written at the same time (as, from Schubert's habit of eviscerating his books, they not improbably were)—twelve. Three Shakespeare songs are due to this July— 'Hark! hark! the lark,'[2] from 'Cymbeline'; 'Who is Sylvia?' from the 'Two Gentlemen of Verona'; and the Drinking-song in 'Antony and Cleopatra'—the first two perhaps as popular as any single songs of Schubert's. The circumstances of the composition, or rather creation, of the first of these has already been mentioned (p. 288*a*). The fact of three songs from the same volume belonging to one month (not improbably to one day, if we only knew) is quite *à la Schubert*.—A beautiful and most characteristic piece of this year is the 'Nachthelle' or 'Lovely night'), written to words of Seidl's— not improbably for the Musikverein, through Anna Fröhlich—for tenor solo, with accompaniment of four men's voices and pianoforte, which would be a treasure to singing societies, for its truly romantic loveliness, but for the inordinate height to which the voices are taken, and the great difficulty of executing it with sufficient delicacy. A song called 'Echo' (op. 130), probably written in 1826, was intended to be the first of six 'humorous songs' for Weigl's firm.[3]

We hear nothing of the new symphony during the early part of this year. No doubt it was often played from the MS. score at the meetings of the Schubert set, but they say no more about it than they do of the Octet, or Quartets, or Sonatas, which were all equally in existence; and for aught we know it might have been 'locked in a drawer,' which was often Schubert's custom after completing a work—'locked in a drawer and never thought about again.'[4] It was, however, destined to a different fate. On Sept. 9, 1826, at one of the first meetings of the Board of the Musikverein after the summer recess, Hofrath Kiesewetter reports that Schubert desires to dedicate a symphony to the Society; upon which the sum of 100 silver

[1] See an interesting letter from Ernst Perabo, the owner of the MS. with an extract from the Andante, in the *Monthly Musical Record* for April 1888.
[2] Entitled 'Serenade,' but more accurately an 'Aubade.'
[3] See Nottebohm's *Catalogue* under op. 130.
[4] Lachner's expression to my friend Mr. C. A. Barry in 1881.

florins (£10) is voted to him, not in payment for the work, but as a token of sympathy, and as an encouragement. The letter conveying the money is dated the 12th, and on or even before its receipt Schubert brought the manuscript and deposited it with the Society. His letter accompanying it may here be quoted :—

To the Committee of the Austrian Musical Society.— Convinced of the noble desire of the Society to give its best support to every effort in the cause of art, I venture, as a native artist, to dedicate this my Symphony to the Society, and most respectfully to recommend myself to its protection. With the highest esteem. Your obedt.
FRANZ SCHUBERT.

In accordance with this, the MS. probably bears his formal dedication to the Verein, and we may expect to find that though so long talked of, it bears marks of having been written down as rapidly as most of his other productions.[5] At present, however, all trace of it is gone; not even its key is known. There is no entry of it in the catalogue of the Society's Library, and except for the minute and letter given above, and the positive statements of Bauernfeld quoted below,[6] it might as well be non-existent. That it is an entirely distinct work from that in C, written two and a half years later, can hardly admit of a doubt.

Of the publications of 1826, the most remarkable are the seven songs from 'The Lady of the Lake,' for which Artaria had paid him 200 florins in the preceding October, and which appeared on the 5th of this April, in two parts, as op. 52. They were succeeded immediately, on April 8, by the PF. Sonata in D (op. 53), and the 'Divertissement à la hongroise' (op. 54), both issued by the same firm. For these two splendid works Schubert received from the penurious Artaria only 300 Vienna florins, equal to £12. Songs issued fast from the press at

[5] The documents on which these statements are based are given by Herr C. F. Pohl in his *History of the Gesellschaft der Musikfreunde*—or Musikverein—Vienna, 1871, p. 16; and by Ferdinand Schubert in the *Neue Zeitschrift für Musik*, for April 30, 1839, p. 140.
[6] Bauernfeld, in an article *Ueber Franz Schubert* in the *Wiener Zeitschrift für Kunst, Literatur, Theater, und Mode,* for 9, 11, 13 June, 1829 (Nos. 69, 70, 71), says as follows :—'To the larger works of his latter years also belongs a Symphony written in 1825 at Gastein, for which its author had an especial predilection. . . . At a great concert given by the Musik Verein shortly after his death a Symphony in C was performed, which was composed as early as 1817 [1818], and which he considered as one of his less successful works. . . . Perhaps the Society intends at some future time to make us acquainted with one of the later symphonies, possibly the Gastein one already mentioned.' [N.B. The two movements of the B minor Symphony (1822) were not at this time known, so that by 'later Symphonies' Bauernfeld must surely intend the two of 1825 and 1828.] At the end of the article he gives a 'chronological list of Schubert's principal works not yet generally known.' Amongst these are '1825, Grand Symphony.' . . . '1828, Last Symphony'— 'Grand' (*grosse*) being the word used by Schubert himself in his letter to Kupelwieser referred to above (p. 301*a*). It is plain, therefore, that at this time, seven months after Schubert's death, the Gastein Symphony of 1825, and that in C major of 1828, were known as distinct works. The present writer has collected the evidence for the existence of the Symphony in a letter to the London *Athenæum* of Nov. 19, 1881.
[This note is left as Sir George Grove wrote it. But the existence of the Gastein Symphony rests at present on very imperfect evidence. There is no mention of it in Ferdinand Schubert's catalogue, or in Kreissle von Hellborn's biography, or in the testimony of any one who claims to have seen the score. The symphony accepted by the Gesellschaft der Musikfreunde and performed by them in the year of Schubert's death is the C major, written in 1818 and incorrectly dated, in a Gesellschaft programme, 1825. No copy of the work in question has revealed itself to the most careful research. It is probable that the so-called Gastein Symphony is Schubert's 'No. 6,' possibly retouched during the holiday of 1825, and offered to the Gesellschaft in the following year.]

this date; for on the 6th of April we find op. 56 (three songs) announced by Pennauer, and opp. 57 and 58 (each three songs) by Weigl; on June 10, op. 60 ('Greisengesang' and 'Dithyrambe') by Cappi and Czerny; in Sept. op. 59 (four songs, including 'Dass sie hier gewesen,' 'Du bist die Ruh,' and 'Lachen und Weinen') by Leidesdorf; and op. 64 (three part-songs for men's voices) by Pennauer; and on Nov. 24, op. 65 (three songs) by Cappi and Czerny. Some of these were composed as early as 1814, 1815, 1816; others again in 1820, 1822, and 1823. The Mass in C (op. 48), and three early pieces of church music, 'Tantum ergo' (op. 45), 'Totus in corde' (op. 46), and 'Salve Regina' (op. 47), were all issued in this year by Diabelli. Of dances and marches for piano there are eight numbers:—a Galop and eight Écossaises (op. 49); thirty-four Valses sentimentales (op. 50); 'Hommage aux belles Viennoises' (sixteen Ländler and two Écossaises, op. 67); three Marches (four hands, op. 51)— all published by Diabelli; the two Russian Marches (opp. 55, 56), by Pennauer; six Polonaises (op. 61), Cappi and Czerny; and a Divertissement, or 'Marche brillante et raisonnée,' on French *motifs* (op. 63), Weigl. In all, twenty-two publications, divided among six publishers, and containing 106 works.

We have been thus particular to name the numbers and publishers of these works, because they show conclusively how much Schubert's music was coming into demand. Pennauer and Leidesdorf were his personal friends, and may possibly have printed his pieces from chivalrous motives; but no one can suspect hard and experienced men of business like Diabelli and Artaria of publishing the music of any one at their own risk unless they believed that there was a demand for it. The list is a remarkable one, and will compare for extent and variety with that of most years of Beethoven's life. And even at the incredibly low prices [1] which his publishers gave for the exclusive copyright of his works, there is enough in the above to produce an income sufficient for Schubert's wants. But the fact is that he was mixed up with a set of young fellows who regarded him as a Crœsus,[2] and who virtually lived upon his carelessness and good-nature, under the guise of keeping house in common. Bauernfeld, in an article in the Vienna *Presse* of April 17, 1869, has given us the account with some *naïveté*. A league or partnership was made between himself, Schwind the painter, and Schubert. They had nominally

their own lodgings, but often slept all together in the room of one. The affection between them was extraordinary. Schubert used to call Schwind 'seine Geliebte'—his *innamorata*! A kind of common property was established in clothes and money; hats, coats, boots, and cravats were worn in common, and the one who was in cash paid the score of the others. As Schwind and Bauernfeld were considerably younger than Schubert, that duty naturally fell on him. When he had sold a piece of music he seemed to this happy trio to 'swim in money,' which was then spent 'right and left' in the most reckless manner, till it was all gone, and the period of reverse came. Under these circumstances life was a series of fluctuations, in which the party were never rich, and often very poor. On one occasion Bauernfeld and Schubert met in a coffee-house near the Kärnthnerthor theatre, and each detected the other in ordering a *mélange* (*café au lait*) and biscuits, because neither had the money to pay for dinner. And this in Schubert's twenty-ninth year, when he had already written immortal works quite sufficient to make a good livelihood! Outside the circle of this trio were a number of other young people, artists and literary men, Schober, Jenger, Kupelwieser, etc., attracted by Schubert's genius, good-nature, and love of fun, and all more or less profiting by the generosity of one who never knew what it was to deny a friend. The evenings of this jolly company were usually passed in the Gasthaus, and then they would wander about, till daybreak drove them to their several quarters, or to the room of one of the party. It would be absurd to judge Vienna manners from an English point of view. The Gasthaus took the place of a modern club, and the drink consumed probably did not much exceed that which some distinguished Vienna artists now imbibe night after night, and does not imply the excess that it would infallibly lead to in a Northern climate; but it must be obvious that few constitutions could stand such racket, and that the exertion of thus trying his strength by night and his brain by day, must have been more than any frame could stand. In fact his health did not stand the wear and tear. We have seen that in February 1823, he could not leave the house; that in the summer of the same year he was confined to the hospital; that in March 1824, he speaks of his health as irrecoverably gone; and the dedication of the six four-hand Marches op. 40, to his friend Bernhardt, doctor of medicine, 'as a token of gratitude,' is strong evidence that in 1826, the year of their publication, he had had another severe attack.

It was probably a sense of the precarious nature of such a life that led some of his friends in the autumn of 1826 to urge Schubert to stand for the post of Vice-capellmeister in the Imperial Court, vacant by the promotion of Eybler to that

---

[1] It is said by Schindler that the prices agreed on with him were ten Vienna gulden per Heft of songs, and twelve per pianoforte piece. (The Vienna gulden was then worth just one franc. 'Heft' meant then a single song, not a 'Part' of two or three. This is conclusively proved by Ferdinand Schubert's letter of 1824.) These prices were not adhered to. Thus for the seven 'Lady of the Lake' songs he had 500 paper gulden = £20, or nearly £3 per song. Even that is low enough. On the other hand F. Lachner told Mr. Barry that in the last year of Schubert's life, he took half-a-dozen of the 'Winterreise' songs to Haslinger at Schubert's request, and brought back one gulden a piece (= 10d.) for them!

[2] The expression is Bauernfeld's,

of principal capellmeister ; but the application, like every other of the same kind made by him, was a failure, and the place was given to Joseph Weigl by the Imperial decree of Jan. 27, 1827.

Another opportunity of acquiring a fixed income was opened to him during the same autumn, by the removal of Karl August Krebs from the conductorship of the Court theatre to Hamburg. Vogl interested Duport, the administrator of the theatre, in his friend, and the appointment was made to depend on Schubert's success in composing some scenes for the stage. Madame Schechner, for whom the principal part was intended, a young débutante who was making her first appearance in Vienna, objected at the pianoforte rehearsals to some passages in her air, but could not induce the composer to alter them. The same thing happened at the first orchestral rehearsal, when it also became evident that the accompaniments were too noisy for the voice. Still Schubert was immovable. At the full-band rehearsal Schechner fairly broke down, and refused to sing any more. Duport then stepped forward, and formally requested Schubert to alter the music before the next meeting. This he refused to do ; but taking the same course as Beethoven had done on a similar occasion, said loudly, ' I will alter nothing,' took up his score and left the house. After this the question of the conductorship was at an end. Schubert's behaviour in this matter has been strongly censured, but we do not see much in it. Such questions will always depend on the temperament of the composer. Had it been either Mozart or Mendelssohn we cannot doubt that all would have gone smoothly ; the prima donna would not only not have been ruffled, but would have felt herself complimented, and the music would have been so altered as to meet every one's wish, and yet sound as well as before. On the other hand, had it been Beethoven or Schumann we may be equally sure that not a note would have been changed, and that everything would have ended in confusion. With all Schubert's good-nature, when his music was concerned he was of the same mind as Beethoven and Schumann. There are other instances of the same stubbornness, which will be noticed later.

Some set-off to these disappointments was afforded by the ready way in which his Gastein Symphony was received by the Musikverein, and the sympathetic resolution and prompt donation which accompanied its acceptance, although no attempt to perform or even rehearse it can now be traced. The beautiful ' Nacht-helle,' already referred to, which he composed in September, was rehearsed during the early winter months, and performed by the Society on Jan. 25, 1827.

Some little gratification also he not improbably derived from the letters which during this year he began to receive from publishers in the north. Probst of Leipzig — one of Beethoven's publishers,

predecessor of the present firm of Senff—was the first to write. His letter is dated August 26, and is followed by one from Breitkopf & Härtel of Sept. 7. True, neither are very encouraging. Probst speaks of his music as too often ' peculiar and odd,' and ' not intelligible or satisfactory to the public ' ; and begs him to write so as to be easily understood ; while Breitkopf stipulates that the only remuneration at first shall be some copies of the works. Still, even with this poor present result, the fact was obvious that he had begun to attract attention outside of Austria.

As to Schubert's life in the early part of 1827 we have little to guide us beyond the scanty inferences to be drawn from the dated compositions. The first of these of any moment are eight Variations (the eighth very much extended) on a theme in Hérold's opera ' Marie,' for PF. four hands (op. 82). ' Marie ' was produced on the Vienna boards Jan. 18, 1827 ; and Schubert's Variations are dated ' February,' and are dedicated to one of his friends in Upper Austria, Prof. Cajetan Neuhaus of Linz. The next and still more important work is the first half of the ' Winterreise,' twelve songs (' Gute Nacht' to ' Einsamkeit'), marked as begun in Feb. 1827. Franz Lachner remembers that ' half a dozen' of them were written in one morning, and that Haslinger gave a gulden (that is a franc) apiece for them. The poems which form the basis of this work are by Wilhelm Müller, the poet of the 'Schöne Müllerin,' which the Winterreise closely approaches in popularity, and which it would probably equal if the maiden of the Winter-walk were as definite a creation as the miller's daughter is. They are twenty-four in all, and appear under their now immortal name in the second volume of the work of which vol. i. contained the ' Schöne Müllerin,' and which has the quaint title already quoted (p. 300a).[1] The second volume was published at Dessau in 1824, and did not at once attract Schubert's notice. When it did, he made short work of it. Another important composition of this month (dated Feb. 28) is the Schlachtlied (battle-song) of Klopstock, set for two choirs of male voices, sometimes answering, sometimes in eight real parts, of immense force and vigour, and marked by that dogged adherence to rhythmical monotony so characteristic of Schubert.

He can scarcely have finished with this before the news that Beethoven was in danger spread through Vienna. The great musician got back to his rooms in the Schwarzspanierhaus from his fatal expedition to Gneixendorf in the first week of December, became very ill, and during January was tapped for the dropsy three times. Then Malfatti was called in, and there was a slight improvement. During this he was allowed to read, and it was then that Schindler, a zealous

[1] The order of the songs is much changed in the music.

Schubert-propagandist, took the opportunity to put some of Schubert's songs into his hands.[1] He made a selection of about sixty, in print and MS., including 'Iphigenie,' 'Grenzen der Menschheit,' 'Allmacht,' 'Die junge Nonne,'[2] 'Viola,' the 'Müllerlieder,' etc. Beethoven up to this time probably did not know half-a-dozen of Schubert's compositions, and his astonishment was extreme, especially when he heard that there existed at least 500 of the same kind. 'How can he find time,' said he, 'to set such long poems, many of them containing ten others?' *i.e.* as long as ten separate ones; and said over and over again, 'If I had had this poem I would have set it myself'; 'Truly Schubert has the divine fire in him.' He pored over them for days, and asked to see Schubert's operas and PF. pieces, but the illness returned and it was too late. But from this time till his death he spoke often of Schubert, regretting that he had not sooner known his worth, and prophesying that he would make much stir in the world.[3] Schubert was sure to hear of these gratifying utterances, and they would naturally increase his desire to come into close contact with the master whom he had long worshipped at a distance. It is possible that this emboldened him to visit the dying man. He seems to have gone twice; first with Anselm Hüttenbrenner and Schindler. Schindler told Beethoven that they were there, and asked whom he would see first. 'Schubert may come in first' was the answer. At this visit perhaps, if ever, it was that he said, in his affectionate way, 'You, Anselm, have my mind *(Geist)*, but Franz has my soul *(Seele)*.'[4] The second time he went with Josef Hüttenbrenner and Teltscher the painter. They stood round the bed. Beethoven was aware of their presence, and fixing his eyes on them, made some signs with his hand. No one, however, could explain what was meant, and no words passed on either side. Schubert left the room overcome with emotion. In about three weeks came the end, and then the funeral. Schubert was one of the torch-bearers. Franz Lachner and Randhartinger walked with him to and from the Cemetery. The way back lay by the Himmelpfortgrund, and close by the humble house in which he had drawn his first breath. They walked on into the town, and stopped at the 'Mehlgrube,' a tavern in the Kärnthnerthorstrasse, now the Hotel Munsch. There they called for wine, and Schubert drank off two glasses, one to the memory of Beethoven, the other to the first of the three friends who should follow him. It was destined to be himself.

[1] Schindler, *Beethoven*, ii. 136.
[2] Schindler's list of the songs perused by Beethoven differs in his two accounts. Compare his *Beethoven*, ii. 136, with *K.H.* p. 264 (i. 266).
[3] Schindler, in Bäuerle's *Theaterzeitung* (Vienna), May 3, 1831.
[4] See von Leitner, *Anselm Hüttenbrenner*, Graz, 1868, p. 5. The story has an apocryphal air, but Hüttenbrenner was so thoroughly trustworthy, that it is difficult to reject it. At any rate, Beethoven is not likely to have thus expressed himself before he had made acquaintance with Schubert's music.

Lablache was also one of the torch-bearers at the funeral. This and the part which he took in the Requiem for Beethoven [vol. i. p. 260 *b*] may have induced Schubert to write for him the 'three Italian Songs for a Bass voice,' which form op. 83, and are dedicated to the great Italian basso.

Hummel and Hiller were in Vienna during March 1827, and Hiller describes meeting Schubert and Vogl at Madame Lacsny-Buchwieser's, and his astonishment at their joint performance. 'Schubert,' says Hiller,[5] 'had little technique, and Vogl but little voice; but they had both so much life and feeling, and went so thoroughly into the thing, that it would be impossible to render these wonderful compositions more clearly and more splendidly. Voice and piano became as nothing; the music seemed to want no material help, but the melodies appealed to the ear as a vision does to the eye.' Not only did the boy think it the deepest musical impression he had ever received, but the tears coursed down the cheeks even of the veteran Hummel. Either then or a few evenings afterwards, Hummel showed his appreciation by extemporising on Schubert's 'Blinde Knabe,' which Vogl had just sung—to Franz's delight.

In April Schubert wrote the beautiful 'Nachtgesang im Walde' (op. 139*b*) for four men's voices and four horns; and a 'Spring Song,' also for men's voices. In July we have the very fine and characteristic serenade 'Zögernd leise' (op. 135) for alto solo and female voices, a worthy pendant to the 'Nachthelle,' and written almost *à l'improviste*.[6] A fête was to be held for the birthday of a young lady of Döbling. Grillparzer had written some verses for the occasion, and Schubert, who was constantly in and out of the Fröhlichs' house, was asked by Anna to set them for her sister Josephine and her pupils. He took the lines, went aside into the window, pushed up his spectacles on to his brow, and then, with the paper close to his face, read them carefully twice through. It was enough: 'I have it,' said he, 'it's done, and will go famously.' A day or two afterwards he brought the score, but he had employed a male chorus instead of a female one, and had to take it away and transpose it. It was sung in the garden by moonlight, to the delight of every one, the villagers thronging round the gate. He alone was absent.

1827 witnessed another attempt at an opera—the 'Graf von Gleichen,' written by Bauernfeld, apparently in concurrence[7] with Mayrhofer. Schubert had the libretto in August 1826, submitted it to the management of the Royal Opera-house, and arranged with Grillparzer, in case the Censure should cause its rejection, to

[5] *Künstlerleben* (1880), p. 49.   [6] *K.H.* p. 474 (ii. 160).
[7] See Schubert's letter [May 1826] with Bauernfeld's statements in the *Presse* of April 21, 1869, and *Signale*, Nov. 1869.

have it accepted by the Königstadt Theatre. Owing possibly to the delay of the Censure it was nearly a year before he could begin the composition. The MS. sketch, now in Herr Dumba's collection, is dated at the beginning '17 Juni 1827.' The opera is sketched throughout, and he played portions of it to Bauernfeld. Forty years later the sketch came into the hands of Herbeck, and he began to score it after Schubert's indications—of which there are plenty—but was prevented by death.

A correspondence had been going on for long between the Schubert circle at Vienna and the Pachler family in Graz, the capital of Styria, as to an expedition thither by Schubert, and at length it was arranged for the autumn of this year. Carl Pachler was one of those cultivated men of business who are such an honour to Germany ; an advocate, and at the head of his profession, yet not ashamed to be an enthusiastic lover of music and musicians, and proud to have them at his house and to admit them to his intimate friendship. Amongst his circle was Anselm Hüttenbrenner, the brother of Schubert's friend Josef, himself an earnest admirer of Franz, whose last visit to Vienna had been to close the eyes of his old friend Beethoven. The house was open to painters, singers, actors, and poets, 'the scene of constant hospitalities, the headquarters of every remarkable person visiting Graz.' Such was the family whose one desire was to receive Schubert and Jenger. The journey, now accomplished in 5½ hours, was an affair of two days and a night, even in the fast coach. They left on Sunday morning, Sept. 2, and reached Graz on Monday night. The next three weeks were spent in the way which Schubert most enjoyed, excursions and picnics by day through a beautiful country, and at night incessant music ; good eating and drinking, clever men and pretty women, no fuss, a little romping, a good piano, a sympathetic audience, and no notice taken of him—such were the elements of his enjoyment. The music was made mostly by themselves, Schubert singing, accompanying, and playing duets with Jenger, and extemporising endless dance tunes. He does not appear to have composed anything of great moment during the visit. A galop and twelve waltzes, published under the titles of the 'Grätzer Waltzer' (op. 91) and the 'Grätzer Galoppe' ; [1] three songs (op. 106, 1, 2, 3—the last a particularly fine one) to words by local poets— and the 'Old Scottish Ballad' by Herder (op. 165, No. 5), were probably all that he penned during this festive fortnight ; unless perhaps some of those exquisite little pieces published in 1828 and 1838 as 'Impromptus' and 'Momens musicals' are the result of this time. Two songs, written a couple of years before, 'Im

Walde,' and 'Auf der Bruck,' of the purest Schubert, proved, and justly proved, such favourites that he had them lithographed and published in the place.[2] The visit is further perpetuated by the titles of the dances just mentioned, and by the dedication to Mme. Pachler of op. 106, a collection of four songs, the three already named, and the lovely 'Sylvia.' Schubert seems to have had this set of songs lithographed without name of place or publisher, shortly after his return, on purpose for his hostess.[3]

The journey home was a triumphal progress, and by the 27th they were back in Vienna. Schubert then wrote the second part of the 'Winterreise' (Nos. 13-24), completing that immortal work. The shadows lie much darker on the second than on the first part, and the 'Wegweiser,' 'Das Wirthshaus,' 'Die Krähe,' 'Die Nebensonnen,' and 'Der Leiermann,' are unsurpassed for melancholy among all the songs. Even in the extraordinary and picturesque energy of 'Die Post' there is a deep vein of sadness. Schubert here only followed faithfully, as he always does, the character of the words.

On Oct. 12 he wrote a little four-hand march as a souvenir for Faust Pachler, the son of his host, a trifle interesting only from the circumstances of its composition. In the same month he composed his first PF. trio, in B♭ (op. 99), and in November the second, in E♭ (op. 100). They were both written for Bocklet, Schuppanzigh, and Lincke, and were first heard in public, the one early in January, the other on March 26, 1828. The year was closed with an Italian cantata, dated Dec. 26, 'alla bella Irene,' in honour of Frl. Kiesewetter (afterwards Mme. Prokesch v. Osten), the daughter of his friend the Hofrath, sponsor to the Gastein Symphony (p. 306a). It is probably more interesting for its accompaniment for two pianos than for anything else.

The communications with Probst of Leipzig went on. There is a letter from him dated Jan. 15, and he himself paid a visit to Vienna later in the season, and made Schubert's [4] personal acquaintance, but the negotiations were not destined to bear fruit till next year. But a proof that Schubert was making his mark in North Germany is afforded by a letter from Rochlitz, the sometime editor of the Leipzig *Allgemeine Musikalische Zeitung*, and a great personage in the musical world of Saxony—dated Nov. 7, 1827, proposing that Schubert should compose a poem by him, called 'Der erste Ton,' or 'The first Sound,' a poem which Weber had already set without success, and which Beethoven had refused. Rochlitz's letter was probably inspired by the receipt of three of his songs set by

[1] Published by Haslinger, as No. 10 of the 'Favorite Galops,' 1828.

[2] They stood originally in B♭ minor and A♭, but on republication by Diabelli after his death, as op. 93, the keys were changed to G minor and G major.

[3] Compare Jenger's letter in *K.H.* (ii. 103), note, with Nottebohm's notice under op. 106.

[4] *K.H.* p. 421 (ii. 107).

Schubert as op. 81, and published on May 27. The proposition, however, came to nothing.

Coincident with these communications from abroad came a gratifying proof of the improvement in his position at home, in his election as a member of the representative body of the Musical Society of Vienna. The date of election is not mentioned : but Schubert's reply, as given by Herr Pohl,[1] is dated Vienna, June 12, 1827, and runs as follows :—

The Managing Committee of the Society of Friends of Music of the Austrian Empire having thought me worthy of election as a Member of the Representative Body of that excellent Society, I beg herewith to state that I feel myself greatly honoured by their choice, and that I undertake the duties of the position with much satisfaction.

FRANZ SCHUBERT, Compositeur.

We have mentioned the more important compositions of 1827. There remain to be named two songs by Schober (op. 96, No. 2) ; and one by Reil (op. 115, No. 1) ; a comic trio, 'Die Hochzeitsbraten' (op. 104), also by Schober ; and an Allegretto in C minor for PF. solo, written for his friend Walcher, 'in remembrance of April 26, 1827,' and not published till 1870.

The publications of 1827 are as follows :— the Overture to 'Alfonso und Estrella' (op. 69) ; Rondeau brillant, for PF., and violin (op. 70) ; songs—'Der Wachtelschlag' (op. 68, March 2), 'Drang in die Ferne' (op. 71, Feb.), 'Auf dem Wasser zu singen' (op. 72, Feb.), 'Die Rose' (op. 73, May 10)—all four songs previously published in the Vienna Zeitschrift für Kunst ; four Polonaises, for PF. four hands (op. 75) ; Overture to 'Fierrabras,' for PF. four hands, arranged by Czerny (op. 76) ; twelve 'Valses Nobles,' for PF. solo (op. 77, Jan.) ; Fantasie, etc. for PF. in G (op. 78) ; two songs, 'Das Heimweh,' 'Die Allmacht' (op. 79, 'May 16') ; three songs (op. 80, May 25) ; three ditto (op. 81, May 28) ; Variations on theme of Hérold's (op. 82, Dec.) ; three Italian songs (op. 83, Sept. 12) ; four songs (op. 88, Dec. 12).

We have now arrived at Schubert's last year, 1828. It would be wrong to suppose that he had any presentiment of his end ; though, if a passion for work, an eager use of the 'day,' were any sign that the 'night' was coming 'in which no man could work,' we might almost be justified in doing so. We hear of his suffering from blood to the head, but it was not yet enough to frighten any one. He returned to the extraordinary exertions, or rather to the superabundant productions of his earlier years, as the following full list of the compositions of 1828, in order, as far as the dates permit, will show.

Jan. Songs, 'Die Sterne' (op. 96, No. 1) ; 'Der Winterabend.'
March. Symphony in C, No. 9.
    Oratorio, Miriam's Siegesgesang.
    Song, 'Auf dem Strom,' Voice and Horn (op. 119).
May. Lebensstürme, PF. duet (op. 144).
    Hymn to the Holy Ghost (op. 154), for two Choirs and Wind.
    2 Clavierstücke.
    Song, 'Widerschein.'

[1] Die Gesellschaft der Musikfreunde, etc., p. 16.

June. Mass in E♭ (begun).
    Fugue in E minor, PF. duet, op. 152 ('Baden, Juny, 1828 ').
    Grand Rondeau, PF. duet (op. 107).
July. Psalm 92, in Hebrew, for Baritone and Chorus
August. Songs, 'Schwanengesang,' Nos. 1-13.
Sept. PF. Sonata in C minor.
    Ditto in A.
    Ditto in B♭ ('Sept. 26 ').
Between August and October. Tantum ergo in E flat, and Offertorium in B flat, for tenor solo, chorus, and orchestra. Published 1890 by Peters.
October. Song, 'Schwanengesang,' No. 14.
    New Benedictus to Mass in C.
    'Der Hirt auf den Felsen,' Voice and Clarinet (op. 129)
'1828' only. String Quintet in C (op. 163).

This truly extraordinary list includes his greatest known symphony, his greatest and longest mass, his first oratorio, his finest piece of chamber music, three noble PF. sonatas, and some astonishingly fine songs. The autograph of the symphony, 218 pages in oblong quarto, is now one of the treasures of the Library of the Musikverein at Vienna. It has no title or dedication, nothing beyond the customary heading to the first page of the score 'Symfonie März 1828, Frz. Schubert Mpia,' marking the date at which it was begun. If it may be taken as a specimen, he took more pains this year than he did formerly. In the first three movements of this great work there are more afterthoughts than usual. The subject of the Introduction and the first subject of the Allegro have both been altered. In several passages an extra bar has been stuck in—between the Scherzo and the Trio, two bars ; in the development of the Scherzo itself sixteen bars of an exquisite episode—first sketched in the Octet—have been substituted. The Finale alone remains virtually untouched.[2] But such alterations, always rare in Schubert, are essentially different from the painful writing, and erasing, and rewriting, which we are familiar with in the case of Beethoven's finest and most spontaneous music. This, though the first draft, is no rough copy ; there are no traces of sketches or preparation ; the music has evidently gone straight on to the paper without any intervention, and the alterations are merely a few improvements en passant.[3] It is impossible to look at the writing of the autograph, after Schubert has warmed to his work, especially that of the Finale, and not see that it was put down as an absolute impromptu, written as fast as the pen could travel on the paper.

It seems that Schubert's friends used to lecture him a good deal on the diffuseness and want of consideration which they discovered in his works, and were continually forcing Beethoven's laborious processes of composition down his throat. This often made him angry, and when repeated, evening after evening, he would say, 'So you're going to set upon me again to-day ! Go it, I beg you !' But, for all his annoyance, the remonstrances appear to have had some effect ; and after Beethoven's death he asked

[2] See details by the present writer in Appendix to the Life of Schubert, translated by A. D. Coleridge, Esq., vol. ii. p. 320.
[3] The original MS. orchestral parts show at any rate that the alterations in the score were made before they were copied from it. C. V. Stanford kindly examined them for me with that view.

Schindler to show him the MS. of 'Fidelio.'[1] He took it to the piano, and pored over it a long time, making out the passages as they had been, and comparing them with what they were ; but it would not do ; and at last he broke out, and exclaimed that for such drudgery he could see no reason under any circumstances ; that he thought the music at first just as good as at last ; and that for his part he had really no time for such corrections. Whether the amendments to the Great Symphony were a remorseful attempt on Schubert's part to imitate Beethoven and satisfy the demands of his friends we cannot tell ; but if so they are very unlike the pattern.

The autograph of the E♭ Mass, in the Bibliothek at Berlin, does not show at all the same amount of corrections as that in A♭ (see p. 298a), nor do the fugal movements appear to have given any special trouble. True, the 'Cum Sancto' was recommenced after the erasure of seven bars,[2] but apparently merely for the sake of changing the tempo from C to ₵, and the larger part of the movement was evidently written with great rapidity. In the 'Et vitam' there are barely a dozen corrections, and the 'Osanna' has every mark of extreme haste. Some of the erasures in this work are made with the penknife—surely an almost unique thing with Schubert ! The four-hand PF. fugue in E minor (op. 152, dated 'Baden, June 1828') is not improbably a trial of counterpoint with reference to this Mass.

The Songs of 1828 are splendid. It does not appear that the fourteen which were published after his death with the publisher's title of 'Schwanengesang—'the Swan's song'—were intended by him to form a series of the same kind as the 'Schöne Müllerin' and 'Winterreise' ; but no lover of Schubert can dissociate them, and in the 'Liebesbotschaft,' ' Aufenthalt,' ' Ständchen,' etc., we have some of the most beautiful, and in the 'Atlas,' 'Am Meer,' ' Doppelgänger,' etc., some of the most impressive, of his many songs. The words of some are by Rellstab, and the origin of these is thus told by Schindler.[3] Schubert had been much touched by Schindler's efforts to make Beethoven acquainted with his music, and after the great master's death the two gradually became intimate. Schindler had possession of many of Beethoven's papers, and Schubert used to visit him in familiar style, to look over them. Those which specially attracted him were the poems and dramas sent in at various times for consideration ; amongst others a bundle of some twenty anonymous lyrics which Beethoven had intended to set, and which therefore attracted Schubert's particular

notice.[4] He took them away with him, and in two days brought back the 'Liebesbotschaft,' ' Kriegers Ahnung,' and ' Aufenthalt,' set to music. This account, which is perfectly natural and consistent, and which Mr. Thayer allows me to say he sees no reason to question, has been exaggerated [5] into a desire expressed by Beethoven himself that Schubert should set these particular songs ; but for this there is no warrant. Ten more quickly followed the three just mentioned ; and these thirteen—seven to Rellstab's and six to Heine's words (from the ' Buch der Lieder'[6]), were, on Nottebohm's authority, written in August. The last is by Seidl ; it is dated ' Oct. 1828,' and is probably Schubert's last song.

But it is time to return to the chronicle of his life during its last ten months. Of his doings in January we know little more than can be gathered from the following letter to Anselm Hüttenbrenner, the original of which is in the British Museum (Add. MS. 29,804, f, 24).

VIENNA, Jan. 18, 1828.

MY DEAR OLD HÜTTENBRENNER—You will wonder at my writing now? So do I. But if I write it is because I am to get something by it. Now just listen ; a drawing-master's place near you at Graz is vacant, and competition is invited. My brother Karl, whom you probably know, wishes to get the place. He is very clever, both as a landscape-painter and a draughtsman. If you could do anything for him in the matter I should be eternally obliged to you. You are a great man in Graz, and probably know some one in authority, or some one else who has a vote. My brother is married, and has a family, and would therefore be very glad to obtain a permanent appointment. I hope that things are all right with you, as well as with your dear family, and your brothers. A Trio of mine, for Pianoforte, Violin, and Violoncello, has been lately performed by Schuppanzigh, and was much liked. It was splendidly executed by Boklet, Schuppanzigh, and Link. Have you done nothing new? A propos, why doesn't Greiner,[7] or whatever his name is, publish the two songs? What's the reason? Sapperment !

I repeat my request ; recollect, what you do for my brother, you do for me. Hoping for a favorable answer, I remain your true friend, till death,

FRANZ SCHUBERT Mpia.
of Vienna.

The expression 'till death,' which appears here for the first time in his letters, and the words ' of Vienna,' added to his name, are both singular.

On the 24th, at an evening concert at the Musikverein, the serenade for contralto solo and female chorus just mentioned was performed, and is spoken of by the correspondent of the Leipzig *A.M.Z.* as 'one of the most charming works of this favourite writer.' In February we find three letters from North Germany, one from Probst of Leipzig, and two from Schott. They show how deep an impression Schubert was making outside Austria. Both firms express

1 Schindler, *Erinnerungen*, in *Niederrheinische Musikzeitung*, 1857, pp. 73-78, 81-85.
2 The omission of the words 'Jesu Christe' at the end of the 'Quoniam,' and other omissions, show that he had not conquered the carelessness so frequent in his early Masses as to the treatment of the words.
3 Schindler, *Erinnerungen*, etc., as before.

4 They proved afterwards to be by Rellstab.
5 See Rellstab's *Aus m. Leben*, ii. 245.
6 Baron Schönstein relates—*K.H.* p. 447 (ii. 135)—that he found Heine's ' Buch der Lieder' on Schubert's table some years before this date, and that Schubert lent them to him with the remark ' that he should not want them again.' But such reminiscences are often wrong in point of date : the fact remains ineffaceable in the mind, the date easily gets altered. In fact Heine's ' Buch der Lieder' was first published in 1827. The six songs which Schubert took from it are all from the section entitled ' Die Heimkehr.'
7 A publisher in Graz. His name was Kienreich, and the two songs, 'Im Walde' and 'Auf der Bruck' (op. 93), appeared in May.

warm appreciation of his music, both leave the terms to be named by him, and Schott orders a list of nine important pieces.

On March 26 Schubert gave what we wonder

he never gave before, an evening concert on his own account in the Hall of the Musikverein. The following is the programme exactly reprinted from the original :—

Einladung
zu dem Privat Concerte, welches Franz Schubert am
26. März, Abends 7 Uhr im Locale des oesterreichischen Musikvereins
unter den Tuchlauben No. 558 zu geben die Ehre haben wird.

Vorkommende Stücke.

1. Erster Satz eines neuen Streich Quartetts vorgetragen von
den Herren Böhm, Holz, Weiss, und Linke.

2. a. Der Kreutzzug, von Leitner ⎫ Gesänge mit Begleitung des
   b. Die Sterne, von demselben ⎪ Piano Forte, vorgetragen von
   c. Fischerweise, von Bar. Schlechta ⎬ Herrn Vogl, k. k. pensionirten
   d. Fragment aus dem Aeschylus ⎭ Hofopernsänger.

3. Ständchen von Grillparzer, Sopran-Solo und Chor, vorgetragen von
Fräulein Josephine Fröhlich und den Schülerinnen des Conservatoriums.

4. Neues Trio für des Piano Forte, Violin und Violoncelle,
vorgetragen von den Herren Carl Maria von Boklet, Böhm und Linke.

5. Auf dem Strome von Rellstab. Gesang mit Begleitung
des Horns und Piano Forte, vorgetragen von den Herren
Tietze, und Lewy dem Jüngeren.

6. Die Allmacht, von Ladislaus Pyrker, Gesang mit Begleitung
des Piano Forte, vorgetragen von Herren Vogl.

7. Schlachtgesang von Klopfstock, Doppelchor für Männerstimmen.

Sämmtliche Musikstücke sind von der Composition des Concertgebers.
Eintrittskarten zu fl. 3. W. W. sind in den Kunsthandlungen
der Herren Haslinger, Diabelli und Leidesdorf zu haben.

This programme attracted 'more people than the hall had ever before been known to hold,' and the applause was very great. The net result to Schubert was 800 gulden, Vienna currency, equal to about £32. This put him in funds for the moment, and the money flowed freely. Thus, when, three days later, Paganini gave his first concert in Vienna, Schubert was there, undeterred, in his wealth, by a charge of five gulden. Nay, he went a second time, not that he cared to go again, but that he wished to treat Bauernfeld, who had not five farthings, while with him 'money was as plenty as blackberries.' [1]

This month he wrote, or began to write, his last and greatest Symphony, in C. He is said to have offered it to the society for performance, and in so doing to have expressed himself to the effect that henceforth he wished to have nothing more to do with songs, as he was now planted firmly in Opera and Symphony. This rests on the authority of Kreissle ; [2] the silence of Herr Pohl in his history of the society shows that its minute-books contain no express mention of the reception of the work, as they do that of the symphony in October 1826. There is no doubt, however, that it was adopted by the society, and is entered in the Catalogue, under the year 1828, as xiii. 8024. [3] But this prodigious work was far beyond the then powers of the chief musical institution of Vienna. The parts were copied and some rehearsals held ; but both length and difficulty were against it, and it was

soon withdrawn, on Schubert's own advice, in favour of his earlier Symphony, No. 6, also in C. Neither the one nor the other was performed till after his death.

March also saw the birth of the interesting Oratorio 'Miriam's Song of Victory,' to Grillparzer's words. [4] It is written, as so many of Schubert's choral pieces are, for a simple pianoforte accompaniment ; but this was merely to suit the means at his disposal, and is an instance of his practical sagacity. It is unfortunate, however, since the oratorio has become a favourite, that we have no other orchestral accompaniment than that afterwards adapted by Lachner, which is greatly wanting in character, and in the picturesque elements so native to Schubert. [5] A song to Rellstab's words, 'Auf dem Strom' (op. 119), for soprano, with obbligato horn and PF. accompaniment, written for Lewy, a Dresden horn-player, belongs to this month, and was indeed first heard at Schubert's own concert, on the 26th, and afterwards repeated at a concert of Lewy's, on April 20, Schubert himself playing the accompaniment each time.

To April no compositions can be ascribed unless it be the Quintet in C for strings (op. 163), which bears only the date '1828.' This is now universally accepted not only as Schubert's finest piece of chamber music, but as one of the very finest of its class. The two violoncellos in

---

[1] See Bauernfeld's Letter in the *Presse*, April 17, 1869. *Häckerling*, 'chaff,' is Schubert's word.   [2] *K.H.* p. 445 (ii. 132).
[3] See Herr Pohl's letter to the *Times*, of Oct. 17, 1881.

[4] Kreissle, p. 609 (ii. 285), says that it was produced in the Schubert Concert, March 1828. But this is contradicted by the Programme which is printed above. It was first performed Jan. 30, 1829, at a concert for erecting Schubert's headstone.
[5] It has been performed (with Lachner's orchestration) at the Crystal Palace several times, at the Leeds Festival 1880, and elsewhere in England.

themselves give it distinction ; it has all the poetry and romance of the G major Quartet, without the extravagant length which will always stand in the way of that noble production ; while the Adagio is so solemn and yet so beautiful in its tone, so entrancing in its melodies, and so incessant in its interest, and the Trio of the Scherzo, both from itself and its place in the movement, is so eminently dramatic, that it is difficult to speak of either too highly.

In May we have a grand battle-piece, the 'Hymn to the Holy Ghost,' for eight male voices, written for the Concert Spirituel of Vienna, at first with PF., in October scored by the composer for a wind band, and in 1847 published as op. 154. Also a 'Characteristic Allegro' for the PF. four hands, virtually the first movement of a Sonata—issued some years later with the title 'Lebensstürme' (op. 144) ; an Allegro vivace and Allegretto, in E♭ minor and major, for PF. solo, published in 1868 as first and second of '3 Clavierstücke'; and a song 'Widerschein.'

In June, probably at the request of the publisher, he wrote a four-hand Rondo for PF. in A, since issued as 'Grand Rondeau, op. 107 '; and began his sixth Mass, that in E♭. In this month he paid a visit to Baden—Beethoven's Baden ; since a fugue for four hands in E minor is marked as written there in 'June 1828.' In the midst of all this work a letter[1] from Mosewius of Breslau, a prominent Prussian musician, full of sympathy and admiration, must have been doubly gratifying as coming from North Germany.

In July he wrote the 92nd Psalm in Hebrew for the synagogue at Vienna, of which Sulzer was precentor. In August, notwithstanding his declaration on completing his last Symphony, we find him (under circumstances already described) composing seven songs of Rellstab's, and six of Heine's, afterwards issued as 'Schwanengesang.'

He opened September with a trifle in the shape of a short chorus,[2] with accompaniment of wind band, for the consecration of a bell in the church of the Alservorstadt. A few days after, the memory of Hummel's visit in the spring of 1827 seems to have come upon him like a lion, and he wrote off three fine PF. solo sonatas, with the view of dedicating them to that master. These pieces, though very unequal and in parts extraordinarily diffuse, are yet highly characteristic of Schubert. They contain some of his finest and most original music, and also his most affecting (e.g. Andantino, Scherzo and Trio of the A minor Sonata) ; and if full of disappointment and wrath, and the gathering gloom of these last few weeks of his life, they are also saturated with that nameless personal charm that is at once so strong and so indescribable. The third of the three, that in B♭, dated Sept. 26, has perhaps more of grace and finish than the other two. The sonatas were not published till a year after Hummel's death, and were then dedicated by Diabelli-Spina to Robert Schumann, who acknowledges the dedication by a genial though hardly adequate article in his Ges. Schriften, ii. 239. The second part of the 'Winterreise' was put into Haslinger's hands for engraving before the end of this month.[3]

In October, prompted by some occasion which has eluded record, he wrote a new 'Benedictus' to his early Mass in C, a chorus of great beauty and originality in A minor, of which a competent critic[4] has said that 'its only fault consists in its immeasurable superiority to the rest of the Mass.' To the same period may be assigned a fine offertorium, 'Intende voci orationis meae,' and an extremely beautiful 'Tantum ergo' in E♭, for chorus and orchestra. For some other occasion, which has also vanished, he wrote accompaniments for thirteen wind instruments to his grand 'Hymn to the Holy Ghost'; a long scena or song for soprano—probably his old admirer, Anna Milder—with pianoforte and obbligato clarinet (op. 129) ; and a song called 'Die Taubenpost' ('The carrier pigeon ') to Seidl's words. The succession of these pieces is not known. It is always assumed that the Taubenpost, which now closes the Schwanengesang, was the last. Whichever of them was the last, was the last piece he ever wrote.

The negotiations with Probst and Schott, and also with Brüggemann of Halberstadt, a publisher anxious for some easy PF. pieces for a series called 'Mühling's Museum,' by no means fulfilled the promise of their commencement. The magnificent style in which the Schotts desired Schubert to name his own terms[5] contrasts badly with their ultimate refusal (Oct. 30) to pay more than 30 florins (or about 25s.) for the PF. Quintet (op. 114) instead of the modest sixty demanded by him. In fact the sole result was an arrangement with Probst to publish the long and splendid E♭ Trio, which he did, according to Nottebohm,[6] in September, and for which the composer received the incredibly small sum of 21 Vienna florins, or just 17s. 6d. ! Schubert's answer to Probst's inquiry as to the 'Dedication' is so characteristic as to deserve reprinting :—

VIENNA, Aug. 1.

Euer Wohlgeboren, the opus of the Trio is 100. I entreat you to make the edition correct ; I am extremely anxious about it. The work will be dedicated to no one but those who like it. That is the most profitable dedication. With all esteem,

FRANZ SCHUBERT.

---

[1] K.H. p. 428 (ii. 114).
[2] K.H. p. 443 (ii. 131). This piece, 'Glaube, Hoffnung, und Liebe,' is not to be confounded with one of similar title for a solo voice, published, Oct. 6, 1828, as op. 97.

[3] Schubert's letter to Jenger, Sept. 25. K.H. p. 437 (ii. 124).
[4] Mr. E. Prout in the Monthly Musical Record for 1871, p. 56.
[5] K.H. p. 424 (ii. 109).
[6] Probst announces two long lists of new music in the A.M.Z. for Oct., but makes no mention of the Trio. It is reviewed most favourably in the A.M.Z. for Dec. 10, 1828. Alas ! he was then beyond the reach of praise or blame.

The home publications of 1828 are not so important as those of former years. The first part of the 'Winterreise' (op. 89) was issued in January by Haslinger ; March 14, three songs by Sir W. Scott (opp. 85, 86) by Diabelli ; at Easter (April 6) six songs (opp. 92 and 108), and one set of 'Momens musicals,' by Leidesdorf ; in May, two songs (op. 93) by Kienreich[1] of Graz ; in June or July ('Sommer'), four songs (op. 96) by Diabelli ; Aug. 13, four Refrain-Lieder (op. 95), Weigl. Also the following, to which no month can be fixed :—'Andantino varié and Rondeau brillant' (op. 84), PF. four hands, on French *motifs*, forming a continuation of op. 63, Weigl ; three songs (op. 87), Pennauer ; four impromptus (op. 90), and twelve Grätzer Waltzer (op. 91) for PF. solo, Diabelli ; Grätzer Galoppe, do. Haslinger ; four songs (op. 106) lithographed without publisher's name.

There is nothing in the events already catalogued to have prevented Schubert's taking an excursion this summer. In either Styria or Upper Austria he would have been welcomed with open arms, and the journey might have given him a stock of health sufficient to carry him on for years. And he appears to have entertained the idea of both.[2] But the real obstacle, as he constantly repeats, was his poverty.[3] 'It's all over with Graz for the present,' he says, with a touch of his old fun, 'for money and weather are both against me.' Herr Franz Lachner, at that time his constant companion, told the writer that he had taken half-a-dozen of the 'Winterreise' songs to Haslinger and brought back half-a-dozen gulden —each gulden being then worth a franc. Let the lover of Schubert pause a moment, and think of the 'Post' or the 'Wirthshaus' being sold for tenpence ! of that unrivalled imagination and genius producing those deathless strains and being thus rewarded ! When this was the case, when even a great work like the E♭ Trio, after months and months of negotiation and heavy postage, realises the truly microscopic amount of '20 florins 60 kreutzers' (as with true Prussian businesslike minuteness Herr Probst specifies it), of 17s. 6d. as our modern currency has it—not even Schubert's fluency and rapidity could do more than keep body and soul together. It must have been hard not to apply the words of Müller's 'Leyermann' to his own case—

> Barfuss auf dem Eise
> Wankt er hin und her,
> *Und sein kleiner Teller*
> *Bleibt ihm immer leer.*

In fact so empty was his little tray that he could not even afford the diligence-fare to Pesth, where Lachner's 'Bürgschaft' was to be brought out, and where, as Schindler reminds him, he would be safe to have a lucrative concert of his own music, as profitable as that of March 26. Escape from Vienna by *that* road was impossible for him this year.

Schubert had for some time past been living with Schober at the 'Blaue Igel' (or Blue Hedgehog), still a well-known tavern and resort of musicians in the Tuchlauben ; but at the end of August he left, and took up his quarters with Ferdinand in a new house in the Neue Wieden suburb, then known as No. 694 Firmian, or Lumpert,[4] or Neugebauten, Gasse, now (1881) No. 6 Kettenbrücken Gasse ; a long house with three rows of nine windows in front ; a brown sloping tiled roof ; an entry in the middle to a quadrangle behind ; a quiet, clean, inoffensive place. Here, on the second floor, to the right hand, lived Schubert for the last five weeks of his life, and his death is commemorated by a stone tablet over the entry, placed there by the Männergesang Verein in Nov. 1869, and containing these words :—'In diesem Hause starb am 19 November 1828 der Tondichter Franz Schubert'—(In this house died on Nov. 19, 1828, the composer Franz Schubert). Ferdinand had removed there, and Franz went thare too. He made the move with the concurrence of his doctor, von Rinna, in the hope that as it was nearer the country—it was just over the river in the direction of the Belvedere—Schubert would be able to reach fresh air and exercise more easily than he could from the heart of the city. The old attacks of giddiness and blood to the head had of late been frequent, and soon after taking up his new quarters he became seriously unwell. However, this was so far relieved that at the beginning of October he made a short walking tour with Ferdinand and two other friends to Ueber-Waltersdorf, and thence to Haydn's old residence and grave at Eisenstadt, some 25 miles from Vienna. It took them three days, and during that time he was very careful as to eating and drinking, regained his old cheerfulness, and was often very gay. Still he was far from well, and after his return the bad symptoms revived, to the great alarm of his friends. At length, on the evening of Oct. 31, while at supper at the Rothen Kreuz in the Himmelpfortgrund, an eating-house much frequented by himself and his friends, he took some fish on his plate, but at the first mouthful threw down the knife and fork, and exclaimed that it tasted like poison. From that moment hardly anything but medicine passed his lips ; but he still walked a good deal. About this time Lachner returned from Pesth in all the glory of the success of his opera ; and though only in Vienna for a few days, he called on his friend, and they had two hours' conversation. Schubert was full of plans for the future, especially for the completion of 'Graf von Gleichen,' which, as already mentioned, he had sketched in the summer of 1827.

---

[1] Whom Schubert parodies as 'Greiner' *i.e.* grumbler. Jenger's and Traweger's letters, *K.H.* pp. 416, 427, 431, etc.
[3] Letters, *K.H.* p. 437 (ii. 124), etc.

[4] *K.H.* p. 453 *note.*

He discussed it also with Bauernfeld during the next few days, and spoke of the brilliant style in which he intended to score it. About this time Carl Holz, Beethoven's old friend, at Schubert's urgent request, took him to hear the great master's C♯ minor Quartet, still a novelty in Vienna. It agitated him extremely. 'He got (says Holz) into such a state of excitement and enthusiasm that we were all afraid for him.'[1] On Nov. 3, the morrow of All Souls' day, he walked early in the morning to Hernals—then a village, now a thickly built suburb outside the Gürtelstrasse—to hear his brother's Latin Requiem in the church there. He thought it simple, and at the same time effective, and on the whole was much pleased with it. After the service he walked for three hours, and on reaching home complained of great weariness.

Shortly before this time the scores of Handel's oratorios had come into his hands—not impossibly some of the set of Arnold's edition given to Beethoven before his death, and sold in his sale for 102 florins; and the study of them had brought home to him his deficiencies in the department of counterpoint. 'I see now,' said he[2] to the Fröhlichs, 'how much I have still to learn; but I am going to work hard with Sechter, and make up for lost time'—Sechter being the recognised authority of the day on counterpoint. So much was he bent on this, that on the day after his walk to Hernals, i.e. on Nov. 4, notwithstanding his weakness, he went into Vienna and, with another musician named Lanz, called on Sechter, to consult him on the matter, and they actually decided on Marpurg as the textbook, and on the number and dates of the lessons.[3] But he never began the course. During the next few days he grew weaker and weaker; and when the doctor was called in, it was too late. About the 11th he wrote a note[4] to Schober—doubtless his last letter.

DEAR SCHOBER,
I am ill. I have eaten and drunk nothing for eleven days, and am so tired and shaky that I can only get from the bed to the chair, and back. Rinna is attending me. If I taste anything, I bring it up again directly. In this distressing condition, be so kind as to help me to some reading. Of Cooper's I have read the Last of the Mohicans, the Spy, the Pilot, and the Pioneers. If you have anything else of his, I entreat you to leave it with Frau von Bogner at the Coffee house. My brother, who is conscientiousness itself, will bring it to me in the most conscientious way. Or anything else. Your friend,
SCHUBERT.

What answer Schober made to this appeal is not known. He is said to have had a daily report of Schubert's condition from the doctor, but there is no mention of his having called. Spaun, Randhartinger,[5] Bauernfeld, and Josef Hütten-

brenner, are all said to have visited him; but in those days there was great dread of infection, his new residence was out of the way, and dangerous illness was such a novelty with Schubert that his friends may be excused for not thinking the case so grave as it was. After a few days Rinna himself fell ill, and his place was filled by a staff-surgeon named Behring.

On the 14th Schubert took to his bed.[6] He was able to sit up a little for a few days longer, and thus to correct the proofs of the second part of the 'Winterreise,' probably the last occupation of those inspired and busy fingers. He appears to have had no pain, only increasing weakness, want of sleep, and great depression. Poor fellow! no wonder he was depressed! everything was against him, his weakness, his poverty, the dreary house, the long lonely hours, the cheerless future—all concentrated and embodied in the hopeless images of Müller's poems, and the sad gloomy strains in which he has clothed them for ever and ever—the 'Letzte Hoffnung,' the 'Krähe,' the 'Wegweiser,' the 'Wirthshaus,' the 'Nebensonnen,' the 'Leiermann'—all breathing of solitude, broken hopes, illusions, strange omens, poverty, death, the grave! As he went through the pages, they must have seemed like pictures of his own life; and such passages as the following, from the 'Wegweiser' (or Signpost), can hardly have failed to strike the dying man as aimed at himself:—

Einen Weiser seh' ich stehen,
Unverrückt vor meinem Blick,
Eine Strasse muss ich gehen,
Die noch keiner ging zurück.

Alas! he was indeed going the road which no one e'er retraces! On Sunday the 16th the doctors had a consultation; they predicted a nervous fever, but had still hopes of their patient. On the afternoon of Monday, Bauernfeld saw him for the last time. He was in very bad spirits, and complained of great weakness, and of heat in his head, but his mind was still clear, and there was no sign of wandering; he spoke of his earnest wish for a good opera-book. Later in the day, however, when the doctor arrived, he was quite delirious, and typhus had unmistakably broken out. The next day, Tuesday, he was very restless throughout, trying continually to get out of bed, and constantly fancying himself in a strange room. That evening he called Ferdinand on to the bed, made him put his ear close to his mouth, and whispered mysteriously, 'What are they doing with me?' 'Dear Franz,' was the reply, 'they are doing all they can to get you well again, and the doctor assures us you will soon be right, only you must do your best to stay in bed.' He returned to the idea in his wandering—'I implore you to put me in my own room, and not to leave me in this corner under the earth; don't I

1 Quoted by Nohl, *Beethoven*, iii. 964. Holz says it was the last music that poor Schubert heard. Ferdinand claims the same for his Requiem. At any rate both were very near the end.
2 Kreissle's *Sketch*, p. 152.
3 *K.H.* p. 451 (ii. 138), expressly on Sechter's authority.
4 Given by Bauernfeld, in *Die Presse*, April 21, 1869.
5 Fräulein Geisler-Schubert informs me that Ferdinand's wife (still living, 1882) maintains that Randhartinger was the only one who visited him during his illness; but it is difficult to resist the

statements of Bauernfeld (*Presse*, April 21, 1869) and of Kreissle's informants, p. 452 (ii. 140).
6 Ferdinand, in the *N.Z.M.* p. 143.

deserve a place above ground ?' 'Dear Franz,' said the agonised brother, 'be calm; trust your brother Ferdinand, whom you have always trusted, and who loves you so dearly. You are in the room which you always had, and lying on your own bed.' 'No,' said the dying man, 'that's not true; Beethoven is not here.' So strongly had the great composer taken possession of him! An hour or two later the doctor came, and spoke to him in the same style. Schubert looked him full in the face and made no answer: but turning round clutched at the wall with his poor tired hands, and said in a slow earnest voice, 'Here, here, is my end.' At three in the afternoon of Wednesday the 19th Nov. 1828 he breathed his last, and his simple earnest soul took its flight from the world. He was thirty-one years, nine months, and nineteen days old. There never has been one like him, and there never will be another.

His death, and the letters of the elder Franz and of Ferdinand, bring out the family relations in a very pleasant light. The poor pious bereaved father, still at his drudgery as 'school teacher in the Rossau,' 'afflicted, yet strengthened by faith in God and the Blessed Sacraments,' writing to announce the loss of his 'beloved son, Franz Schubert, musician and composer'; the good innocent Ferdinand, evidently recognised as Franz's peculiar property, clinging to his brother as the one great man he had ever known; thinking only of him, and of fulfilling his last wish to lie near Beethoven,—these form a pair of interesting figures. Neither Ignaz nor Carl appear at all in connection with the event, the father and Ferdinand alone are visible.

The funeral took place on Friday Nov. 21. It was bad weather, but a number of friends and sympathisers assembled. He lay in his coffin, dressed, as the custom then was, like a hermit, with a crown of laurel round his brows. The face was calm, and looked more like sleep than death. By desire of the family Schober was chief mourner. The coffin left the house at half-past two, and was borne by a group of young men, students and others, in red cloaks and flowers, to the little church of S. Joseph in Margarethen, where the funeral service was said, and a motet by Gänsbacher, and a hymn of Schober's, 'Der Friede sey mit dir, du engelreine Seele'—written that morning in substitution for his own earlier words, to the music of Schubert's 'Pax vobiscum'—were sung over the coffin. It was then taken to the Ortsfriedhof in the village of Währing, and committed to the ground, three places higher up than the grave of Beethoven.[1] In ordinary course he would have been buried in the cemetery at Matzleinsdorf, but the appeal which he made almost with his dying breath was naturally a law to the tender heart of Ferdinand, and through his piety and self-

denial his dear brother rested if not next, yet near to the great musician, whom he so deeply reverenced and admired. Late in the afternoon Wilhelm von Chezy, son of the authoress of 'Euryanthe' and 'Rosamunde,' who though not in Schubert's intimate circle was yet one of his acquaintances, by some accident remembered that he had not seen him for many months, and he walked down to Bogner's coffee-house, where the composer was usually to be found between five and seven, smoking his pipe and joking with his friends, and where the Cooper's novels mentioned in his note to Schober were not improbably still waiting for him. He found the little room almost empty, and the familiar round table deserted. On entering he was accosted by the waiter—'Your honour is soon back from the funeral!' 'Whose funeral?' said Chezy in astonishment. 'Franz Schubert's,' replied the waiter, 'he died two days ago, and is buried this afternoon.'[2]

He left no will. The official inventory[3] of his possessions at the time of his death, in which he is described as 'Tonkünstler und Compositeur'—musician and composer—is as follows:— '3 dress coats, 3 walking coats, 10 pairs of trousers, 9 waistcoats—together worth 37 florins; 1 hat, 5 pairs of shoes and 2 of boots—valued at 2 florins; 4 shirts, 9 cravats and pocket handkerchiefs, 13 pairs of socks, 1 towel, 1 sheet, 2 bedcases—8 florins; 1 mattress, 1 bolster, 1 quilt—6 florins; a quantity of old music valued at 10 florins—63 florins (say £2 : 10s.) in all. Beyond the above there were no effects.' Is it possible then, that in the 'old music, valued at 8s. 6d.,' are included the whole of his unpublished manuscripts? Where else could they be but in the house he was inhabiting?

The expenses of the illness and funeral amounted in all to 269 silver florins, 19 kr. (say £27). Of this the preliminary service cost 84 fl. 35 kr.; the burial 44 fl. 45 kr.; and the ground 70 fl.; leaving the rest for the doctor's fees and incidental disbursements. Illness and death were truly expensive luxuries in those days.

On Nov. 27, the Kirchenmusikverein performed Mozart's Requiem in his honour; and on Dec. 23 a requiem by Anselm Hüttenbrenner was given in the Augustine church. On Dec. 14, his early Symphony in C, No. 6, was played at the Gesellschaftsconcert, and again on March 12, 1829. At Linz on Christmas Day there was a funeral ceremony with speeches and music. Articles in his honour appeared in the *Wiener Zeitschrift* of Dec. 25 (by von Zedlitz), in the *Theaterzeitung* of Vienna of the 20th and 27th (by Blahetka); in the Vienna *Zeitschrift für Kunst* of June 9, 11, 13, 1829 (by Bauernfeld); in the Vienna *Archiv für Geschichte* by Mayrhofer); and memorial poems were published by

---

[1] Next to Beethoven came 'Freiherr von Wssehrd'; then 'Joh. Graf Odonel and Gräfin O'Donnell,' and then Schubert.

[2] Wilhelm von Chezy, *Erinnerungen aus meinen Leben* (1863), pp. 182, 183.
[3] Given at length by Kreissle (p. 457)—but entirely omitted in the translation—and materially misquoted by Gumprecht (p. 15).

Seidl, Schober, and others. On Jan. 30, 1829, a concert was given by the arrangement of Anna Fröhlich in the hall of the Musikverein; the programme included 'Miriam,' and consisted entirely of Schubert's music, excepting a set of flute variations by Gabrielsky, and the first Finale in 'Don Juan'; and the crowd was so great that the performance had to be repeated shortly afterwards. The proceeds of these concerts and the subscriptions of a few friends sufficed to erect the monument which now stands at the back of the grave. It was carried out by Anna Fröhlich, Grillparzer, and Jenger. The bust was by Franz Dialler, and the cost of the whole was 360 silver florins, 46 kr. The inscription [1] is from the pen of Grillparzer:—

DIE TONKUNST BEGRUB HIER EINEN REICHEN BESITZ
ABER NOCH VIEL SCHOENERE HOFFNUNGEN.
FRANZ SCHUBERT LIEGT HIER.
GEBOREN AM XXXI. JÆNNER MDCCXCVII.
GESTORBEN AM XIX. NOV. MDCCCXXVIII.
XXXI JAHRE ALT.

MUSIC HAS HERE ENTOMBED A RICH TREASURE,
BUT MUCH FAIRER HOPES.
FRANZ SCHUBERT LIES HERE.
BORN JAN. 31, 1797;
DIED NOV. 19, 1828,
31 YEARS OLD.

The allusion to fairer hopes has been much criticised, but surely without reason. When we remember in how many departments of music Schubert's latest productions were his best, we are undoubtedly warranted in believing that he would have gone on progressing for many years, had it been the will of God to spare him.

In 1863, owing to the state of dilapidation at which the graves of both Beethoven and Schubert had arrived, the repair of the tombs, and the exhumation and reburial of both, were undertaken by the Gesellschaft der Musikfreunde. The operation was begun on the 12th of October and completed on the 13th. The opportunity was embraced of taking a cast and a photograph of Schubert's skull, and of measuring the principal bones of both skeletons. The lengths in Schubert's case were to those in Beethoven's as 27 to 29,[2] which implies that as Beethoven was 5 ft. 5 in. high, he was only 5 ft. and ½ an inch. Schubert was reburied in the central cemetery of Vienna on Sept. 23, 1888. Various memorials have been set up to him in Vienna. The tablets on the houses in which he was born and died have been noticed. They were both carried out by the Männergesang Verein, and completed, the former Oct. 7, 1858, the latter in Nov. 1869. The same Society erected by subscription a monument to him in the Stadt-Park, a sitting figure in Carrara

[1] We have given the inscription exactly as it stands on the monument. Kreissle's version (p. 463), followed by Gumprecht and others, is incorrect in almost every line.
[2] See *Actenmässige Darstellung der Ausgrabung und Wiederbeisetzung der irdischen Reste von Beethoven und Schubert*, Vienna, Gerold, 1863.

marble by Carl Kuntmann, with the inscription 'Franz Schubert, seinem Andenken der Wiener Männergesangverein, 1872.' It cost 42,000 florins, and was unveiled May 15, 1872.

Outside of Austria his death created at first but little sensation. Robert Schumann, then eighteen, is said to have been deeply affected, and to have burst into tears when the news reached him at Leipzig; Mendelssohn too, though unlike Schubert in temperament, circumstances, and education, doubtless fully estimated his loss; and Rellstab, Anna Milder, and others in Berlin who knew him, must have mourned him deeply; but the world at large did not yet know enough of his works to understand either what it possessed or what it had lost in that modest reserved young musician of thirty-one. But Death always brings a man, especially a young man, into notoriety, and increases public curiosity about his works: and so it was now; the stream of publication at once began and is even yet flowing, neither the supply of works nor the eagerness to obtain them having ceased. The world has not yet recovered from its astonishment as, one after another, the stores accumulated in those dusky heaps of music paper (valued at 8s. 6d.) were made public, each so astonishingly fresh, copious, and different from the last. As songs, masses, part-songs, operas, chamber-music of all sorts and all dimensions—pianoforte-sonatas, impromptus and fantasias, duets, trios, quartets, quintet, octet, issued from the press or were heard in manuscript; as each season brought its new symphony, overture, entr'acte, or ballet-music, people began to be staggered by the amount. 'A deep shade of suspicion,' said *The Musical World* of Jan. 24, 1839, p. 150, 'is beginning to be cast over the authenticity of posthumous compositions. All Paris has been in a state of amazement at the posthumous diligence of the song-writer, F. Schubert, who, while one would think that his ashes repose in peace in Vienna, is still making eternal new songs.' We know better now, but it must be confessed that the doubt was not so unnatural then.

Of the MS. music—an incredible quantity, of which no one then knew the amount or the particulars, partly because there was so much of it, partly because Schubert concealed, or rather forgot, a great deal of his work—a certain number of songs and pianoforte pieces were probably in the hands of publishers at the time of his death, but the great bulk was in the possession of Ferdinand, as his heir. A set of four songs (op. 105) was issued on the day of his funeral. Other songs—opp. 101, 104, 106, 110-112, 116-118; and two PF. Duets, the Fantasia in F minor (op. 103) and the 'Grand Rondeau' (op. 107)—followed up to April 1829. But the first important publication was the well-known 'Schwanengesang,' so entitled by Haslinger—a collection of fourteen songs, seven by Rellstab, six by Heine, and one by Seidl—unquestionably Schubert's last. They were issued in May 1829, and, to judge by the lists of arrangements and editions given by Nottebohm, have been as much appreciated as the 'Schöne Müllerin' or the 'Winterreise.' A stream of songs followed—for which we must refer the student to Nottebohm's catalogue. The early part of 1830[1] saw the execution of a bargain between Diabelli and Ferdinand, by which that Firm was guaranteed the property of the following works ; opp. 1-32, 35, 39-59, 62, 63, 64, 66-69, 71-77, 84-88, 92-99, 101-104, 106, 108, 109, 113, 115, 116, 119, 121-124, 127, 128, 130, 132-140, 142-153 ; also 154 songs ; 14 vocal quartets ; the canons of 1813 ; a cantata in C for three voices ; the Hymn to the Holy Ghost ; Klopstock's Stabat Mater in F minor, and Grosse Halleluja ; Magnificat in C ; the String Quintet in C ; four string quartets in C, B♭, G, B♭ ; a string trio in B♭ ; two sonatas in A and A minor, variations in F, an Adagio in D♭, and Allegretto in C♯—all for PF. solo ; Sonata for PF. and Arpeggione ; Sonata in A, and Fantasie in C—both for PF. and violin ; Rondo in A for violin and quartet ; Adagio and Rondo in F, for PF. and quartet ; a Concert-piece in D for violin and orchestra ; Overture in D for orchestra ; Overture to third Act of the 'Zauberharfe' ; 'Lazarus' ; a Tantum ergo in E♭ for four voices and orchestra ; an Offertorium in B♭ for tenor solo, chorus and orchestra.

Another large portion of Ferdinand's possessions came, sooner or later, into the hands of Dr. Eduard Schneider, son of Franz's sister Theresia. They comprised the autographs of Symphonies 1, 2, 3, and 6, and copies of 4 and 5 ; Autographs of operas :—The 'Teufels Lustschloss,' 'Fernando,' 'Der Vierjährige Posten,' 'Die Freunde von Salamanka,' 'Die Bürgschaft,' 'Fierrabras,' and 'Sakontala' ; the Mass in F ; and the original orchestral parts of the whole of the music to 'Rosamunde.' The greater part of these are now (1882) safe in the possession of Herr Nicholas Dumba of Vienna.

On July 10, 1830, Diabelli began the issue of what was entitled 'Franz Schuberts nachgelassene musikalische Dichtungen' ; and continued it at intervals till 1850, by which time 50 Parts (Lieferungen), containing 137 songs, had appeared. In 1830 he also issued the two astonishing 4-hand marches (op. 121) ; and a set of 20 waltzes (op. 127) ; whilst other houses published the PF. Sonatas in A and E♭ (opp. 120, 122) ; the two string quartets of the year 1824 (op. 125) ; the D minor Quartet, etc. For the

progress of the publication after this date we must again refer the reader to Nottebohm's invaluable Thematic Catalogue (Vienna, Schreiber, 1874), which contains every detail, and may be implicitly relied on ; merely mentioning the principal works, and the year of publication :—'Miriam,' Mass in B♭, three last Sonatas and the Grand Duo, 1838 ; Symphony in C, 1840 ; Phantasie in C, PF. and violin, 1850 ; Quartet in G, 1852 ; Quintet in C, and Octet, 1854 ; 'Gesang der Geister,' 1858 ; 'Verschworenen,' 1862 ; Mass in E♭, 1865 ; 'Lazarus,' 1866 ; Symphony in B minor, 1867 ; Mass in A♭, 1875.

Before the complete critical edition of Schubert's works issued by Breitkopf & Härtel was finished, there were many publications of songs, pianoforte pieces, etc., for which the reader is referred to Nottebohm's Thematic Catalogue. Of the Songs two collections may be signalised as founded on the order of opus numbers :—that of Senff of Leipzig, edited by Julius Reitz, 361 songs in 20 vols. and that of Litolff of Brunswick—songs in 10 vols. But neither of these, though styled 'complete' are so. For instance, each omits opp. 83, 110, 129, 165, 172, 173 ; the six songs published by Müller, the forty by Gotthard ; and Litolff also omits opp. 21, 60.

Schumann's visit to Vienna in the late autumn of 1838 formed an epoch in the history of the Schubert music. He saw the immense heap of MSS. which remained in Ferdinand's hands even after the mass bought by Diabelli had been taken away, and amongst them several symphonies. Such sympathy and enthusiasm as his must have been a rare delight to the poor desponding brother. His eagle eye soon discovered the worth of these treasures. He picked out several works to be recommended to publishers, but meantime one beyond all the rest riveted his attention—the great symphony of March 1828 (was it the autograph, not yet deposited in the safe keeping of the Gesellschaft der Musikfreunde, or a copy ?) and he arranged with Ferdinand to send a transcript of it to Leipzig to Mendelssohn for the Gewandhaus Concerts, where it was produced March 21, 1839,[2] and repeated no less than three times during the following season. His chamber-music was becoming gradually known in the North, and as early as 1833 is occasionally met with in the Berlin and Leipzig programmes. David, who led the taste in chamber music at the latter place, was devoted to Schubert. He gradually introduced his works, until there were few seasons in which the Quartets in A minor, D minor (the score of which he edited for Senff), and G, the String Quintet in C (a special favourite), the Octet, both Trios, the PF. Quintet, and the Rondeau brillant, were not performed amid great applause, at his concerts. Schumann had long been a zealous Schubert propagandist. From an early date his *Zeitschrift* contains articles of more or less length, always inspired by an ardent admiration ; Schubert's letters and poems and his brother's excellent short sketch of his life, printed in vol. x. (April 23 to May 3, 1839) —obvious fruits of Schumann's Vienna visit —are indispensable materials for Schubert's biography ; when the Symphony was performed he dedicated to it one of his longest and most genial effusions,[1] and each fresh piece was greeted with a hearty welcome as it fell from the press. One of Schumann's especial favourites was the E♭ Trio ; he liked it even better than that in B♭, and has left a memorandum of his fondness in the opening of the Adagio of his Symphony in C, which is identical, in key and intervals, with that of Schubert's Andante. The enthusiasm of these prominent musicians, the repeated performances of the Symphony, and its publication by Breitkopfs (in Jan. 1840), naturally gave Schubert a strong hold on Leipzig, at that time the most active musical centre of Europe ; and after the foundation of the Conservatorium in 1843 many English and American students must have carried back the love of his romantic and tuneful music to their own countries.

Several performances of large works had taken place in Vienna since Schubert's death, chiefly through the exertions of Ferdinand, and of a certain Leitermayer, one of Franz's early friends ; such as the E♭ Mass at the parish church of Maria Trost on Nov. 15, 1829 ; 'Miriam,' with Lachner's orchestration, at a Gesellschaft Concert in 1830 ; two new overtures in 1833 ; an overture in E, the Chorus of Spirits from 'Rosamunde,' the Grosses Halleluja, etc., early in 1835, and four large concerted pieces from 'Fierrabras' later in the year ; an overture in D ; the finale of the last Symphony ; a march and chorus, and an air and chorus, from 'Fierrabras,' in April 1836 ; another new overture, and several new compositions from the 'Remains,' in the winter of 1837-38. As far as can be judged by the silence of the Vienna newspapers, these passed almost unnoticed. Even the competition with North Germany failed to produce the effect which might have been expected. It did indeed excite the Viennese to one effort. On the 15th of the December following the production of the Symphony at Leipzig its performance was attempted at Vienna, but though the whole work was announced,[2] such had been the difficulties at rehearsal that the first two movements alone were given, and they were only carried off by the interpolation of an air from 'Lucia' between them.

But symphonies and symphonic works can hardly be expected to float rapidly ; songs are more buoyant, and Schubert's songs soon began to make their way outside, as they had long since done in his native place. Wherever they once penetrated their success was certain. In Paris, where spirit, melody, and romance are the certain criterions of success, and where nothing dull or obscure is tolerated, they were introduced by Nourrit, and were so much liked as actually to find a transient place in the programmes of the Concerts of the Conservatoire, the stronghold of musical Toryism.[3] The first French collection was published in 1834, by Richault, with translation by Bélanger. It contained six songs— 'Die Post,' 'Ständchen,' 'Am Meer,' 'Das Fischermädchen,' 'Der Tod und das Mädchen,' and 'Schlummerlied.' The 'Erl King' and others followed. A larger collection, with translation by Emil Deschamps, was issued by Brandus in 1838 or 1839. It is entitled 'Collection des Lieder de Franz Schubert,' and contains sixteen —'La jeune religieuse,' 'Marguérite,' 'Le roi des aulnes,' 'La rose,' 'La sérénade,' 'La poste,' 'Ave Maria,' 'La cloche des agonisants,' 'La jeune fille et la morte,' 'Rosemonde,' 'Les plaintes de la jeune fille,' 'Adieu,' 'Les astres,' 'La jeune mère,' 'La Berceuse,' 'Éloge des larmes.'[4] Except that one—'Adieu'[5]—is spurious, the selection does great credit to Parisian taste. This led the way to the 'Quarante mélodies de Schubert' of Richault, Launer, etc., a thin 8vo volume, to which many an English amateur is indebted for his first acquaintance with these treasures of life. By 1845 Richault had published as many as 150 with French words.

Some of the chamber music also soon obtained a certain popularity in Paris, through the playing of Tilmant, Urhan, and Alkan, and later of Alard and Franchomme. The Trio in B♭, issued by Richault in 1838, was the first instrumental work of Schubert's published in France. There is a 'Collection complète' of the solo PF. works published by Richault in 8vo, containing the Fantaisie (op. 15), ten sonatas, the two Russian marches, Impromptus, Momens musicals, five single pieces, and nine sets of dances. Liszt and Heller kept the flame alive by their transcriptions of the songs and waltzes. But beyond this the French hardly know more of Schubert now than they did then ; none of his large works have become popular with them. Habeneck attempted to rehearse the Symphony in C (No. 10) in 1842, but the band refused to go beyond the first movement, and Schubert's name up to this date (1881) appears in the

[1] *Ges. Schriften,* iii. 195. Schumann's expressions leave no doubt that the Symphony in C was in Ferdinand's possession at the time of his visit. This and many others of his articles on Schubert have been translated into English by Miss M. E. von Glehn, and Mrs. Ritter.
[2] The MS. parts in the possession of the Musikverein show the most cruel cuts, possibly with a view to this performance. In the Finale, one of the most essential and effective sections of the movement is clean expunged.

[3] 'La jeune religieuse' and 'Le roi des aulnes' were sung by Nourrit, at the Concerts of Jan. 18, and April 26, 1835, respectively —the latter with orchestral accompaniment. On March 20, 1836, Marguérite was sung by Mlle. Falcon, and there the list stops.
[4] This list is copied from the Paris correspondence of the *A.M.Z.* 1839, p. 394.
[5] This song is made up of phrases from Schubert's songs and will probably always be attributed to him. It stands even in Pauer's edition. But it is by A. H. von Weyrauch, who published it himself in 1824. See Nottebohm's *Catalogue,* p. 254.

programmes of the Concerts of the Conservatoire attached to three songs only. M. Pasdeloup introduced the Symphony in C and the fragments of that in B minor, but they took no hold on the Parisian amateurs.

Liszt's devotion to Schubert was great and unceasing. We have already mentioned his production of 'Alfonso und Estrella' at Weimar in 1854, but it is right to give a list of his transcriptions, which have done a very great deal to introduce Schubert into many quarters where his compositions would otherwise have been a sealed book. His first transcription— 'Die Rose,' op. 73—was made in 1834, and appeared in Paris the same year.[1] It was followed in 1838 by the 'Ständchen,' 'Post,' and 'Lob der Thränen,' and in 1839 by the 'Erl King' and by twelve Lieder. These again by six Lieder; four Geistliche Lieder; six of the Müllerlieder; the 'Schwanengesang,' and the 'Winterreise.' Liszt also transcribed the Divertissement à la hongroise, three Marches and nine 'Valses-caprices,' or 'Soirées de Vienne,' after Schubert's op. 67. All the above are for PF. solo. He also scored the accompaniment to the 'Junge Nonne,' 'Gretchen am Spinnrade,' 'So lasst mich scheinen,' and the 'Erl King,' for a small orchestra; has adapted the Allmacht for tenor solo, male chorus, and orchestra, and has converted the Fantasie in C (op. 15) into a Concerto for PF. and orchestra. Some will think these changes indefensible, but there is no doubt that they are done in a masterly manner, and that many of them have become very popular.—Heller's arrangements are confined to six favourite songs.

England made an appearance in the field with the 'Moment musical' in F minor in 1831, followed in 1832 by the 'Erl King' and the 'Wanderer.' In 1836 Mr. Ayrton printed 'The Letter of Flowers' and 'The Secret,' in the Musical Library, to Oxenford's translation. Mr. Wessel (Ashdown & Parry) had begun his 'Series of German Songs' earlier than this, and by 1840, out of a total of 197, the list included 38 of Schubert's, remarkably well chosen, and including several of the finest though less known ones, e.g. 'Ganymed,' 'An den Tod,' 'Sei mir gegrüsst,' 'Die Rose,' etc. etc. Ewer's 'Gems of German Song,' containing many of Schubert's, were begun in Sept. 1837. Schubert's music took a long time before it obtained any public footing in this country. The first time it appears in the Philharmonic programmes—then so ready to welcome novelties—is on May 20, 1839, when Ivanoff sang the Serenade in the 'Schwanengesang' to Italian words, 'Quando avvolta.' Staudigl gave the 'Wanderer,' May 8, 1843. On June 10, 1844, the Overture to 'Fierrabras' was played under Mendelssohn's direction, and on June 17 the 'Junge Nonne' was sung to French words by M. de Revial,

Mendelssohn playing the magnificent accompaniment. We blush to say, however, that neither piece met with approval. *The Musical World* (1844, p. 197) says that 'the overture is literally beneath criticism: perhaps a more overrated man never existed than this same Schubert.' Its dictum on the song is even more unfortunate. It tells us that 'it is a very good exemplification of much ado about nothing—as unmeaningly mysterious as could be desired by the most devoted lover of bombast.' Mendelssohn conducted the last five Philharmonic concerts of that season (1844); and amongst other orchestral music new to England had brought with him Schubert's Symphony in C, and his own overture to 'Ruy Blas.' At the rehearsal on June 10, however, the behaviour of the band towards the symphony—excited, it is said, by the continual triplets in the Finale—was so insulting that he refused either to go on with it or to allow his own overture to be tried.[2] But the misbehaviour of our leading orchestra did not produce the effect which it had done in Paris; others were found to take up the treasures thus rudely rejected, and Schubert has had an ample revenge. The centres for his music in England have been—for the orchestral and choral works, the Crystal Palace, Sydenham, and Hallé's Concerts, Manchester; and for the chamber music, the Popular Concerts and Hallé's Recitals. At the Crystal Palace the Symphony in C (No. 10) was in the répertoire of the Saturday Concerts from April 5, 1856; the two movements of the B minor Symphony were first played April 6, 1867, and have been constantly repeated. The six other MS. Symphonies were obtained from Dr. Schneider in 1867 and since, and have been played at various dates, a performance of the whole eight in chronological order forming a feature in the series of 1880-81. The 'Rosamunde' music was first played Nov. 10, 1866, and the 'air de ballet' in G, March 16, 1867. Joachim's orchestration of the Grand Duo (op. 140) was given March 4, 1876. The overtures to 'Alfonso und Estrella,' 'Fierrabras,' 'Freunde von Salamanka,' 'Teufels Lustschloss,' and that 'in the Italian style' have been frequently heard. 'Miriam's Song' was first given Nov. 14, 1868 (and three times since); the 'Conspirators,' March 2, 1872; the 23rd Psalm, Feb. 21, 1874; the E♭ Mass, March 29, 1879. At the Popular Concerts a beginning was made May 16, 1859, with the A minor Quartet, the D major Sonata, and the Rondeau brillant. Afterwards the D minor and G major Quartets, many sonatas and other

[1] These particulars are taken partly from Miss Ramann's *Life of Liszt*, and partly from Liszt's *Thematic Catalogue*. The third No. of the 'Apparitions' is founded on a Waltz melody of Schubert's.

[2] Even fifteen years later, when played at the Musical Society of London, the same periodical that we have already quoted says of it:—'The ideas throughout it are all of a minute character, and the instrumentation is of a piece with the ideas. There is no breadth, there is no grandeur, there is no dignity in either; clearness, and contrast, and beautiful finish are always apparent, but the orchestra, though loud, is never massive and sonorous, and the music, though always correct, is never serious or imposing.' (*Musical World*, April 2, 1859). Is it possible for criticism to be more hopelessly wrong?

PF. pieces were added, and the Octet, the Quintet in C, and the two Trios were repeated season by season, and enthusiastically received. The Quartet in B♭, the trio in the same key, the Sonata for PF. and Arpeggione, etc. were brought to a hearing. A large number of songs were made familiar to the subscribers to these concerts through the fine interpretation of Stockhausen, Mme. Joachim, Miss Sophie Löwe, Mr. Santley, Mr. Henschel, and other singers. At Hallé's admirable recitals at St. James's Hall, from their commencement in 1861 all the published Sonatas were repeatedly played; not only the popular ones, but of those less known none have been given less than twice; the Fantasia in C, op. 15, three times; the PF. Quintet, the Fantasia for PF. and Violin, the Impromptus and Momens musicals, the '5 pieces,' the '3 pieces,' the Adagio and Rondo, the Valses nobles, and other numbers of this fascinating music have been heard again and again.

The other principal publications in England are the vocal scores of the six Masses, the PF. accompaniment arranged from the full score by Ebenezer Prout, published by Augener & Co.—the 1st, 2nd, 3rd, 4th in 1871, the 6th (E♭) in 1872, and the 5th (A♭) in 1875.[1] The Masses have been also published by Novellos, both with Latin and English words ('Communion Service'); and the same firm has published 'Miriam,' in two forms, and the 'Rosamunde' music, both vocal score and orchestral parts. Messrs. Augener have also published editions of the PF. works, and of a large number of songs, by Pauer.

Schubert was not sufficiently important during his lifetime to attract the attention of painters, and although he had more than one artist in his circle, there are but three portraits of him known. 1. A poor stiff head by Leopold Kupelwieser, full face, taken July 10, 1821, photographed by Mietke and Wawra of Vienna, and wretchedly engraved as the frontispiece to Kreissle's biography. 2. A very characteristic half-length, three-quarter-face, in water-colours, by W. A. Rieder, taken in 1825, and now in possession of Dr. Granitsch of Vienna.[2] A *replica* by the artist, dated 1840, is now in the Musikverein. It has been engraved by Passini, and we here give the head, from a photograph expressly taken from the original. 3. The bust on the tomb, which gives a very prosaic version of his features.

His exterior by no means answered to his genius. His general appearance was insignificant. As we have already said, he was probably not more than 5 feet and 1 inch high, his figure was stout and clumsy, with a round back and shoulders (perhaps due to incessant writing), fleshy arms, and thick short fingers. His complexion was pasty, nay even tallowy; his cheeks were full, his eyebrows bushy, and his nose insignificant. But there were two things that to a great extent redeemed these insignificant traits—his hair, which was black, and remarkably thick and vigorous,[3] as if rooted in the brain within; and his eyes, which were truly 'the windows of his soul,' and even through the spectacles he constantly wore were so bright as at once to attract attention.[4] If Rieder's portrait may be trusted—and it is said to be very faithful, though perhaps a little too *fine*—

they had a peculiarly steadfast penetrating look, which irresistibly reminds one of the firm rhythm of his music. His glasses are inseparable from his face. One of our earliest glimpses of him is 'a little boy in spectacles' at the *Convict*; he habitually slept in them; and within eighteen months of his death we see him standing in the window at Döbling, his glasses pushed up over his forehead, and Grillparzer's verses held close to his searching eyes. He had the broad strong jaw of all great men, and a marked assertive prominence of the lips. He had a beautiful set of teeth (Benedict). When at rest the expression of his face was uninteresting, but it brightened up at the mention of music, especially that of Beethoven. His voice was something between a soft tenor and a baritone. He sang 'like a composer,' without the least affectation or attempt.[5]

His general disposition was in accordance with his countenance. His sensibility, though his music shows it was extreme, was not roused

[1] Reviewed by Mr. E. Prout in *Concordia* for 1875, pp. 8, 29, 109, etc.

[2] He bought it in Feb. 1881 for 1205 florins, or about £120. It is about 8 inches high, by 6 wide. It was taken, or begun, while Schubert took refuge in the artist's house from a storm (Pohl).

[3] All three portraits agree in this. An eminent surgeon of our own day is accustomed to say, 'Never trust a man with a great head of black hair, he is sure to be an enthusiast.'

[4] W. v. Chezy, *Erinnerungen*—'with eyes so brilliant as at the first glance to betray the fire within.'　　　[5] Bauernfeld.

by the small things of life. He had little of that jealous susceptibility which too often distinguishes musicians, more irritable even than the 'irritable race of poets.' His attitude towards Rossini and Weber proves this. When a post which he much coveted was given to another,[1] he expressed his satisfaction at its being bestowed on so competent a man. Transparent truthfulness, good-humour, a cheerful contented evenness, fondness for a joke, and a desire to remain in the background—such were his prominent characteristics in ordinary life. But we have seen how this apparently impassive man could be moved by a poem which appealed to him, or by such music as Beethoven's C♯ minor Quartet.[2] This unfailing good-nature, this sweet lovableness, doubtless enhanced by his reserve, was what attached Schubert to his friends. They admired him ; but they loved him still more. Ferdinand perfectly adored him, and even the derisive Ignaz melts when he takes leave.[3] Hardly a letter from Schwind, Schober, or Bauernfeld, that does not amply testify to this. Their only complaint is that he will not return their passion, that 'the affection of years is not enough to overcome his distrust and fear of seeing himself appreciated and beloved.'[4] Even strangers who met him in this *entourage* were as much captivated as his friends. J. A. Berg of Stockholm, who was in Vienna in 1827, as a young man of twenty-four, and met him at the Bogners', speaks of him[5] with the clinging affection which such personal charm inspires.

He was never really at his ease except among his chosen associates. When with them he was genial and compliant. At the dances of his friends he would extemporise the most lovely waltzes for hours together, or accompany song after song. He was even boisterous—playing the 'Erl King' on a comb, fencing, howling, and making many practical jokes. But in good society he was shy and silent, his face grave ; a word of praise distressed him, he would repel the admiration when it came, and escape into the next room, or out of the house, at the first possible moment. In consequence he was overlooked, and of his important friends few knew, or showed that they knew, what a treasure they had within their reach. A great player like Bocklet, after performing the B♭ Trio, could kneel to kiss the composer's hand in rapture, and with broken voice stammer forth his homage, but there is no trace of such tribute from the upper classes. What a contrast to Beethoven's position among his aristocratic friends—their devotion and patience, his contemptuous behaviour, the amount of pressing necessary to make him play, his scorn of emotion, and love of applause after he had finished ! [See vol. i. p. 223b.] The same contrast is visible in the

dedications of the music of the two—Beethoven's chiefly to crowned heads and nobility, Schubert's in large proportion to his friends. It is also evident in the music itself, as we shall endeavour presently to bring out.

He played, as he sang, 'like a composer,' that is, with less of *technique* than of knowledge and expression. Of the virtuoso he had absolutely nothing. He improvised in the intervals of throwing on his clothes, or at other times when the music within was too strong to be resisted, but as an exhibition or performance never, and there is no record of his playing any music but his own. He occasionally accompanied his songs at concerts (always keeping very strict time), but we never hear of his having extemporised or played a piece in public in Vienna. Notwithstanding the shortness of his fingers, which sometimes got tired,[6] he could play most of his own pieces, and with such force and beauty as to compel a musician[7] who was listening to one of his latest Sonatas to exclaim, 'I admire your playing more than your music,' an exclamation susceptible of two interpretations, of which Schubert is said to have taken the unfavourable one. But accompaniment was his *forte*, and of this we have already spoken [see pp. 304b, 309b, etc.]. Duet-playing was a favourite recreation with him. Schober, Gahy, and others, were his companions in this, and Gahy has left on record his admiration of the clean rapid playing, the bold conception and perfect grasp of expression, and the clever droll remarks that would drop from him during the piece.

His life as a rule was regular, even monotonous. He composed or studied habitually for six or seven hours every morning. This was one of the methodical habits which he had learned from his good old father ; others were the old-fashioned punctilious style of addressing strangers which struck Hiller[8] with such consternation, and the dating of his music. He was ready to write directly he tumbled out of bed, and remained steadily at work till two. 'When I have done one piece I begin the next' was his explanation to a visitor in 1827 ; and one of these mornings produced six of the songs in the ' Winterreise ' ! At two he dined—when there was money enough for dinner—either at the Gasthaus, where in those days it cost a ' Zwanziger ' (8½d.), or with a friend or patron ; and the afternoon was spent in making music, as at Mme. Lacsny Buchwieser's [p. 309b], or in walking in the environs of Vienna. If the weather was fine the walk was often prolonged till late, regardless of engagements in town ; but if this was not the case, he was at the coffee-house by five, smoking his pipe and ready to joke with any of his set ; then came an hour's music, as at Sofie Müller's [p. 303b] ;

[1] Weigl. [2] See pages 285, 316. [3] K.H. p. 149 (i. 151). [4] Schwind, in K.H. p. 345 (ii. 28). [5] In a letter to the writer.

[6] Bauernfeld. [7] Horzalka. K.H. p. 128 (i. 132). [8] *Künstlerleben*, p. 49. 'Schubert I find mentioned in my journal as a *quiet man*—possibly not always so, though it was only amongst his intimates that he broke out. When I visited him in his modest lodging he received me kindly, but so respectfully, as quite to frighten me.'

then the theatre, and supper at the Gasthaus again, and the coffee-house, sometimes till far into the morning. In those days no Viennese, certainly no young bachelor, dined at home ; so that the repeated visits to the Gasthaus need not shock the sensibilities of any English lover of Schubert. [See p. 307b.] Nor let any one be led away with the notion that he was a sot, as some seem prone to believe. How could a sot—how could any one who even lived freely, and woke with a heavy head or a disordered stomach—have worked as he worked, and have composed nearly 1000 such works as his in eighteen years, or have performed the feats of rapidity that Schubert did in the way of opera, symphony, quartet, song, which we have enumerated ? No sot could write six of the ' Winterreise' songs—perfect, enduring works of art— in one morning, and that no singular feat ! Your Morlands and Poes are obliged to wait their time, and produce a few works as their brain and their digestion will allow them, instead of being always ready for their greatest efforts, as Mozart and Schubert were. Schubert—like Mozart— loved society and its accompaniments ; he would have been no Viennese if he had not ; and he may have been occasionally led away ; but such escapades were rare. He does not appear to have cared for the other sex, or to have been attractive to them as Beethoven was, notwithstanding his ugliness. This simplicity curiously characterises his whole life ; no feats of memory are recorded of him as they so often are of other great musicians ; the records of his life contain nothing to quote. His letters, some forty in all, are evidently forced from him. ' Heavens and Earth,' says he, ' it's frightful having to describe one's travels ; I cannot write any more.' ' Dearest friend '—on another occasion —' you will be astonished at my writing : I am so myself.' [1] Strange contrast to the many interesting epistles of Mozart and Mendelssohn, and the numberless notes of Beethoven ! Beethoven was well read, a politician, thought much, and talked eagerly on many subjects. Mozart and Mendelssohn both drew ; travelling was a part of their lives ; they were men of the world, and Mendelssohn was master of many accomplishments. Schumann too, though a Saxon of Saxons, had travelled much, and while a most prolific composer, was a practised literary man. But Schubert has nothing of the kind to show. He not only never travelled out of Austria, but he never proposed it, and it is difficult to conceive of his doing so. To picture or work of art he very rarely refers. He expressed himself with such difficulty that it was all but impossible to argue with him.[2] Besides the letters just mentioned, a few pages of diary and four or five poems are all that he produced except his music. In literature his range was wide indeed,

but it all went into his music ; and he was strangely uncritical. He seems to have been hardly able—at any rate he did not care—to discriminate between the magnificent songs of Goethe, Schiller, and Mayrhofer, the feeble domesticities of Kosegarten and Hölty, and the turgid couplets of the authors of his librettos. All came alike to his omnivorous appetite. But the fact is that, apart from his music, Schubert's life was little or nothing, and that is its most peculiar and most interesting fact. Music and music alone was to him all in all. It was not his *principal* mode of expression, it was his *only* one ; it swallowed up every other. His afternoon walks, his evening amusements, were all so many preparations for the creations of the following morning. No doubt he enjoyed the country, but the effect of the walk is to be found in his music and his music only. He left, as we have said, no letters to speak of, no journal ; there is no record of his ever having poured out his soul in confidence, as Beethoven did in the ' Will,' in the three mysterious letters to some unknown Beloved, or in his conversations with Bettina. He made no impression even on his closest friends beyond that of natural kindness, goodness, truth, and reserve. His life is all summed up in his music. No memoir of Schubert can ever be satisfactory, because no relation can be established between his life and his music ; or rather, properly speaking, because there is no life to establish a relation with. The one scale of the balance is absolutely empty, the other is full to overflowing. In his music we have fluency, depth, acuteness, and variety of expression, unbounded imagination, the happiest thoughts, nevertiring energy, and a sympathetic tenderness beyond belief. And these were the result of natural gifts and of the incessant practice to which they forced him ; for it seems certain that of education in music—meaning by education the severe course of training in the mechanical portions of their art to which Mozart and Mendelssohn were subjected—he had little or nothing. As we have already mentioned, the two musicians who professed to instruct him, Holzer and Ruzicka, were so astonished at his ability that they contented themselves with wondering, and allowing him to go his own way. And they are responsible for that want of counterpoint which was an embarrassment to him all his life, and drove him, during his last illness, to seek lessons. [See p. 316a.] What he learned, he learned mostly for himself, from playing in the *Convict* orchestra, from incessant writing, and from reading the best scores he could obtain ; and, to use the expressive term of his friend Mayrhofer, remained a ' Naturalist' to the end of his life. From the operas of the Italian masters, which were recommended to him by Salieri, he advanced to those of Mozart, and of Mozart abundant

[1] *K.H.* p. 368 (ii. 55) ; p. 417 (ii. 104).
[2] Seyfried, in Schilling's *Lexicon.*

traces appear in his earlier instrumental works. In 1814 Beethoven was probably still tabooed in the *Convict*; and beyond the 'Prometheus' music, and the first two Symphonies, a pupil there would not be likely to encounter anything of his.

To speak first of the orchestral works.

The first Symphony dates from 1814 (his 18th year), and between that and 1818 we have five more. These are all much tinctured by what he was hearing and reading—Haydn, Mozart, Rossini, Beethoven (the last but slightly, for reasons just hinted at). Now and then—as in the second subjects of the first and last Allegros of Symphony 1, the first subject of the opening Allegro of Symphony 2, and the Andante of Symphony 5, the themes are virtually reproduced—no doubt unconsciously. The treatment is more his own, especially in regard to the use of the wind instruments, and to the 'working out' of the movements, where his want of education drives him to the repetition of the subject in various keys, and similar artifices, in place of contrapuntal treatment. In the slow movement and Finale of the Tragic Symphony, No. 4, we have exceedingly happy examples, in which, without absolutely breaking away from the old world, Schubert has revealed an amount of original feeling and an extraordinary beauty of treatment which already stamp him as a great orchestral composer. But whether always original or not in their subjects, no one can listen to these first six Symphonies without being impressed with their *individuality*. Single phrases may remind us of other composers, the treatment may often be traditional, but there is a fluency and continuity, a happy cheerfulness, an earnestness and want of triviality and an absence of labour, which proclaim a new composer. The writer is evidently writing because what he has to say must come out, even though he may occasionally couch it in the phrases of his predecessors. Beauty and profusion of melody reign throughout. The tone is often plaintive but never obscure, and there is always the irrepressible gaiety of youth and of Schubert's own Viennese nature, ready and willing to burst forth. His treatment of particular instruments, especially the wind, is already quite his own—a happy *conversational* way which at a later period becomes highly characteristic. At length, in the B minor Symphony (Oct. 30, 1822), we meet with something which never existed in the world before in orchestral music—a new class of thoughts and a new mode of expression which distinguish him entirely from his predecessors, characteristics which are fully maintained in the 'Rosamunde' music (Christmas, 1823), and culminate in the great C major Symphony (March 1828).

The same general remarks apply to the other instrumental compositions—the quartets and PF. sonatas. These often show a close adherence to the style of the old school, but are always effective and individual, and occasionally, like the symphonies, varied by original and charming movements, as the Trio in the E♭ Quartet, or the Minuet and Trio in the E major one (op. 125, 1 and 2), the Sonata in A minor (1817), etc. The visit to Zselész in 1824, with its Hungarian experiences, and the pianoforte proclivities of the Esterhazys, seem to have given him a new impetus in the direction of chamber music. It was the immediate or proximate cause of the 'Grand Duo'—that splendid work in which, with Beethoven in his eye, Schubert was never more himself—and the Divertissement à la hongroise; as well as the beautiful and intensely personal String Quartet in A minor, which has been not wrongly said to be the most characteristic work of any composer; ultimately also of the D minor and G major Quartets, the String Quintet in C, and the last three Sonatas, in all of which the Hungarian element is strongly perceptible—all the more strongly because we hardly detect it at all in the songs and vocal works.

Here then, at 1822 in the orchestral works, and 1824 in the chamber music, we may perhaps draw the line between Schubert's mature and immature compositions. The step from the Symphony in C of 1818 to the Unfinished Symphony in B minor, or to the 'Rosamunde' Entr'acte in the same key, is quite as great as Beethoven's was from No. 2 to the Eroica, or Mendelssohn's from the C minor to the Italian Symphony. All trace of his predecessors is gone, and he stands alone in his own undisguised and pervading personality. All trace of his youth has gone too. Life has become serious, nay cruel; and a deep earnestness and pathos animate all his utterances. Similarly in the chamber music, the Octet stands on the line, and all the works which have made their position and are acknowledged as great are on this side of it—the Grand Duo, the Divertissement Hongroise, the PF. Sonatas in A minor, D, and B♭, the Fantasie-Sonata in G; the Impromptus and Momens musicals; the String Quartets in A minor, D minor, and G; the String Quintet in C; the Rondo brillant,—in short, all the works which the world thinks of when it mentions 'Schubert' (we are speaking now of instrumental music only) are on this side of 1822. On the other side of the line, in both cases, orchestra and chamber, are a vast number of works full of beauty, interest, and life; breathing youth in every bar, absolute Schubert in many movements or passages, but not completely saturated with him, not of sufficiently independent power to assert their rank with the others, or to compensate for the diffuseness and repetition which remained characteristics of their author to the last, but which in the later works are hidden or atoned for by the astonishing force, beauty, romance, and personality inherent in the contents of the music. These early works will always be more than interesting ; and no lover of Schubert but must regard them with the strong affection and fascination which his followers feel for every bar he wrote. But the judgment of the world at large will probably always remain what it now is.

He was, as Liszt so finely said, ' *le musicien le plus poète que jamais* ' [1]—the most poetical musician that ever was ; and the main characteristics of his music will always be its vivid personality, fulness, and poetry. In the case of other great composers, the mechanical skill and ingenuity, the very ease and absence of effort with which many of their effects are produced, or their pieces constructed, is a great element in the pleasure produced by their music. Not so with Schubert. In listening to him one is never betrayed into exclaiming ' How clever !' but very often 'How poetical, how beautiful, how intensely Schubert !' The impression produced by his great works is that the means are nothing and the effect everything. Not that he had no technical skill. Counterpoint he was deficient in, but the power of writing whatever he wanted he had absolutely at his fingers' end. No one had ever written more, and the notation of his ideas must have been done without an effort. In the words of Macfarren,[2] 'the committing his works to paper was a process that accompanied their composition like the writing of an ordinary letter that is indited at the very paper.' In fact we know, if we had not the manuscripts to prove it, that he wrote with the greatest ease and rapidity, and could keep up a conversation, not only while writing down but while inventing his best works ; that he never hesitated ; very rarely revised—it would often have been better if he had ; and never seems to have aimed at making innovations or doing things for effect. For instance, in the number and arrangement of the movements, his symphonies and sonatas never depart from the regular Haydn pattern. They rarely show æsthetic artifices, such as quoting the theme of one movement in another movement,[3] or running them into each other ; changing their order, or introducing extra ones ; mixing various times simultaneously—or similar mechanical means of producing unity or making novel effects, which often surprise and please us in Beethoven, Schumann, Mendelssohn, and Spohr. Nor did he ever indicate a programme, or prefix a motto to any of his works. His matter is so abundant and so full of variety and interest that he never seems to think of enhancing it by any devices. He did nothing to extend the formal limits of Symphony or Sonata, but he endowed them with

a magic, a romance, a sweet naturalness, which no one has yet approached. And as in the general structure so in the single movements. A simple canon, as in the E♭ Trio, the Andante of the B minor or the Scherzo of the C major Symphonies ; an occasional round, as in the Masses and Part-songs ;—such is pretty nearly all the science that he affords. His vocal fugues are notoriously weak, and the symphonies rarely show those piquant *fugatos* which are so delightful in Beethoven and Mendelssohn. On the other hand, in all that is necessary to express his thoughts and feelings, and to convey them to the hearer, he is inferior to none. Such passages as the return to the subject in the Andante of the B minor Symphony, or in the ballet air in G of 'Rosamunde' ; as the famous horn passage in the Andante of the C major Symphony (No. 10)—which Schumann happily compares to a being from the other world gliding about the orchestra—or the equally beautiful violoncello solo farther on in the same movement, are unsurpassed in orchestral music for felicity and beauty, and have an emotional effect which no learning could give. There is a place in the working-out of the Rosamunde Entr'acte in B minor (change into G♯) in which the combination of modulation and scoring produces a weird and overpowering feeling quite exceptional, and the change to the major near the end of the same great work will always astonish. One of the most prominent beauties in these orchestral works is the exquisite and entirely fresh manner in which the wind instruments are combined. Even in his earliest Symphonies he begins that method of dialogue by interchange of phrases, which rises at last to the well-known and lovely passages in the Overture to 'Rosamunde' (2nd subject), the Trios of the B♭ Entr'acte, and the *Air de Ballet* in the same music, and in the Andantes of the eighth and tenth Symphonies. No one has ever combined wind instruments as these are combined. To quote Schumann once more—they talk and intertalk like human beings. It is no artful concealment of art. The artist vanishes altogether, and the loving, simple, human friend remains. It were well to be dumb in articulate speech with such a power of utterance at command ! If anything were wanting to convince us of the absolute *inspiration* of such music as this it would be the fact that Schubert never can have heard either of the two Symphonies which we have just been citing.—But to return to the orchestra. The trombones were favourite instruments with Schubert in his later life. In the fugal movements of his two last Masses he makes them accompany the voices in unison, with a persistence which is sometimes almost unbearable for its monotony. In portions of the C major Symphony also (No. 10) some may possibly find them too much used.[4] But in

---

[1] Liszt's worst enemies will pardon him much for this sentence.
[2] Philharmonic programme, May 22, 1871.
[3] Instances may be quoted from the Rondo brillant, op. 70, where part of the introduction is repeated in the Rondo, and from the pf. trio in E flat, op. 100, where the principal theme of the slow movement is repeated in the Finale.

[4] There is a tradition that he doubted this himself, and referred the score to Lachner for his opinion.

other parts of the Masses they are beautifully employed, and in the Introduction and Allegro of the Symphony they are used with a noble effect, which not improbably suggested to Schumann the equally impressive use of them in his Bb Symphony. The accompaniments to his subjects are always of great ingenuity and originality, and full of life and character. The triplets in the Finale to the tenth Symphony, which excited the *mal à propos* merriment of the Philharmonic orchestra (see p. 321*b*), are a very striking instance. Another is the incessant run of semiquavers in the second violins and violas which accompany the second theme in the Finale of the Tragic Symphony. Another, of which he is very fond, is the employment of a recurring monotonous figure in the inner parts :—

often running to great length, as in the Andantes of the Tragic and B minor Symphonies ; the Moderato of the Bb Sonata ; the fine song ' Viola' (op. 123, at the return to Ab in the middle of the song), etc. etc. In his best PF. music, the accompaniments are most happily fitted to the leading part, so as never to clash or produce discord. Rapidly as he wrote he did these things as if they were calculated. But they never obtrude themselves or become prominent. They are all merged and absorbed in the gaiety, pathos, and personal interest of the music itself, and of the man who is uttering through it his griefs and joys, his hopes and fears, in so direct and touching a manner as no composer ever did before or since, and with no thought of an audience, of fame, or success, or any other external thing. No one who listens to it can doubt that Schubert wrote for himself alone. His music is the simple utterance of the feelings with which his mind is full. If he had thought of his audience, or the effect he would produce, or the capabilities of the means he was employing, he would have taken more pains in the revision of his works. Indeed the most affectionate disciple of Schubert must admit that the want of revision is often but too apparent.

In his instrumental music he is often very diffuse. When a passage pleases him he generally repeats it at once, almost note for note. He will reiterate a passage over and over in different keys, as if he could never have done. In the songs this does not offend ; and even here, if we knew what he was thinking of, as we do in the songs, we might possibly find the repetitions just. In the Eb Trio he repeats in the Finale a characteristic accompaniment which

is very prominent in the first movement and which originally belongs perhaps to the Ab Impromptu (op. 90, No. 4)—and a dozen other instances of the same kind might be quoted.[1] This arose in great part from his imperfect education, but in great part also from the furious pace at which he dashed down his thoughts and feelings, apparently without previous sketch, note, or preparation ; and from his habit of never correcting a piece after it was once on paper. Had he done so he would doubtless have taken out many a repetition, and some trivialities which seem terribly out of place amid the usual nobility and taste of his thoughts. It was doubtless this diffuseness and apparent want of aim, as well as the jolly, untutored *naïveté* of some of his subjects (Rondo of D major Sonata, etc.), and the incalculable amount of modulation, that made Mendelssohn shrink from some of Schubert's instrumental works, and even go so far as to call the D minor quartet *schlechte Musik*—*i.e.* ' nasty music.' But unless to musicians whose fastidiousness is somewhat abnormal—as Mendelssohn's was—such criticisms only occur afterwards, on reflection ; for during the progress of the work all is absorbed in the intense life and personality of the music. And what beauties there are to put against these redundances ! Take such movements as the first Allegro of the A minor Sonata or the Bb Sonata ; the G major Fantasia-Sonata ; the two Characteristic Marches ; the Impromptus and Momens musicals ; the Minuet of the A minor Quartet ; the Variations of the D minor Quartet ; the Finale of the Bb Trio ; the first two movements, or the Trio, of the String Quintet ; the two movements of the B minor Symphony, and the wonderful Entr'acte in the same key in ' Rosamunde' ; the Finale of the tenth Symphony—think of the abundance of the thoughts, the sudden surprises, the wonderful transitions, the extraordinary pathos of the turns of melody and modulation, the absolute manner (to repeat once more) in which they bring you into contact with the affectionate, tender, suffering personality of the composer,— and who in the whole realm of music has ever approached them ? For the magical expression of such a piece as the Andantino in Ab (op. 94, No. 2), any redundance may be pardoned.

In Schumann's words, ' he has strains for the most subtle thoughts and feelings, nay even for the events and conditions of life ; and innumerable as are the shades of human thought and action, so various is his music.'[2] Another equally true saying of Schumann's is that, compared with Beethoven, Schubert is as a woman to a man. For it must be confessed that one's attitude towards him is almost always that of sympathy, attraction, and love, rarely that of embarrassment or fear. Here and there

[1] For a comparison of his Sonatas with those of other masters see SONATA.
[2] *Ges. Schriften*, i. 206.

only, as in the Rosamunde B minor Entr'acte, or the Finale of the tenth Symphony, does he compel his hearers with an irresistible power ; and yet how different is this compulsion from the strong, fierce, merciless coercion, with which Beethoven forces you along, and bows and bends you to his will, in the Finale of the eighth or still more that of the seventh Symphony.

We have mentioned the gradual manner in which Schubert reached his own style in instrumental music (see p. 325). In this, except perhaps as to quantity, there is nothing singular, or radically different from the early career of other composers. Beethoven began on the lines of Mozart, and Mendelssohn on those of Weber, and gradually found their own independent style. But the thing in which Schubert stands alone is that while he was thus arriving by degrees at individuality in Sonatas, Quartets, and Symphonies, he was pouring forth songs by the dozen, many of which were of the greatest possible novelty, originality, and mastery, while all of them have that peculiar *cachet* which is immediately recognisable as his. The chronological list of his works shows that such masterpieces as the 'Gretchen am Spinnrade,' the 'Erl King,' the Ossian Songs, 'Gretchen im Dom,' ' Der Taucher,' 'Die Bürgschaft,' were written before he was nineteen, and were contemporary with his very early efforts in the orchestra and chamber music ; and that by 1822—in the October of which he wrote the two movements of his eighth Symphony, which we have named as his first absolutely original instrumental music—he had produced in addition such ballads as 'Ritter Toggenburg' (1816), and 'Einsamkeit' (1818) ; such classical songs as 'Memnon' (1817), 'Antigone und Œdip' (1817), 'Iphigenia' (1817), 'Ganymed' (1817), 'Fahrt zum Hades' (1817), 'Prometheus' (1819), 'Gruppe aus dem Tartarus' (1817) ; Goethe's 'Wilhelm Meister' songs, 'An Schwager Kronos' (1816), 'Grenzen der Menschheit' (1821), Suleika's two songs (1821), 'Geheimes' (1821) ; as well as the 'Wanderer' (1816), 'Sei mir gegrüsst' (1821), 'Waldesnacht' (1820), 'Greisengesang' (1822), and many more of his very greatest and most immortal songs.

And this is very confirmatory of the view already taken in this article (p. 289a) of Schubert's relation to music. The reservoir of music was within him from his earliest years, and songs being so much more direct a channel than the more complicated and artificial courses and conditions of the symphony or the sonata, music came to the surface in them so much the more quickly. Had the orchestra or the piano been as direct a mode of utterance as the voice, and the forms of symphony or sonata as simple as that of the song, there seems no reason why he should not have written instrumental music as characteristic as his eighth Symphony, his

Sonata in A minor, and his Quartet in the same key, eight years earlier than he did ; for the songs of that early date prove that he had then all the original power, imagination, and feeling, that he ever had. That it should have been given to a comparative boy to produce strains which seem to breathe the emotion and experience of a long life is only part of the wonder which will also surround Schubert's songs. After 1822, when his youth was gone, and health had begun to fail, and life had become a terrible reality, his thoughts turned inwards, and he wrote the two great cycles of the 'Müllerlieder' (1823) and the 'Winterreise' (1827) ; the Walter Scott and Shakespeare songs ; the splendid single songs of 'Im Walde' and 'Auf der Bruck,' 'Todtengräbers Heimweh,' 'Der Zwerg' 'Die junge Nonne'; the Barcarolle, ' Du bist die Ruh,' and the lovely 'Dass sie hier gewesen' ; the 'Schiffers Scheidelied,' those which were collected into the so-called 'Schwanengesang,' and many more.

It is very difficult to draw a comparison between the songs of this later period and those of the earlier one, but the difference must strike every one, and it resides mainly perhaps in the subjects themselves. Subjects of romance—of ancient times and remote scenes, and strange adventures, and desperate emotion—are natural to the imagination of youth. But in maturer life the mind is calmer, and dwells more strongly on personal subjects. And this is the case with Schubert. After 1822 the classical songs and ballads are rare, and the themes which he chooses belong chiefly to modern life and individual feeling, such as the 'Müllerlieder' and the 'Winterreise,' and others in the list just given. Walter Scott's and Shakespeare's form an exception, but it is an exception which explains itself. We no longer have the exuberant dramatic force of the 'Erl King,' 'Ganymed,' the 'Gruppe aus dem Tartarus,' 'Cronnan,' or 'Kolma's Klage'; but we have instead the condensation and personal point of 'Pause,' 'Die Post,' 'Das Wirthshaus,' 'Die Nebensonnen,' the 'Doppelgänger,' and the 'Junge Nonne.' And there is more maturity in the treatment. His modulations are fewer. His accompaniments are always interesting and suggestive, but they gain in force and variety and quality of ideas in the later songs.

In considering the songs themselves somewhat more closely, their most obvious characteristics are :—Their number ; their length ; the variety of the words ; their expression, and their other musical and poetical peculiarities.

1. Their number. The published songs, that is to say the compositions for one and two voices, excluding Offertories and songs in operas, amount to 603.

2. Their length. This varies very much. The shortest, like 'Klage um Aly Bey,' 'Der Goldschmiedsgesell,' and 'Die Spinnerin' (op.

the alteration in the principal subject of the first movement.

Fac-simile page of the manuscript of Schubert's great Symphony in C,

From the original autograph in the possession o

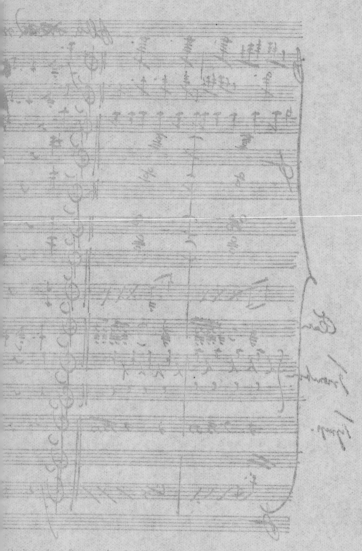

Fac-simile page of the manuscript of Schubert's great Symphony in C.

From the original autograph in the possession o...

118, 6), are strophic songs (that is, with the same melody and harmony unchanged verse after verse), in each of which the voice part is only eight bars long, with a bar or two of introduction or ritornel. The longest is Bertrand's 'Adelwold und Emma' (June 5, 1815), a ballad the autograph of which contains fifty-five pages. Others of almost equal length and of about the same date are :— 'Minona,' 'Die Nonne,' 'Amphiaraos,' etc. Another is Schiller's 'Der Taucher,' which fills thirty-six pages of close print. Schiller's 'Bürgschaft' and the Ossian-songs are all long, though not of the same extent as 'Der Taucher.' These vast ballads are extremely dramatic ; they contain many changes of tempo and of signature, dialogues, recitatives, and airs. The 'Ritter Toggenburg' ends with a strophic song in five stanzas. 'Der Taucher' contains a long pianoforte passage of sixty bars, during the suspense after the diver's last descent. 'Der Liedler' contains a march. The Ballads mostly belong to the early years, 1815, 1816. The last is Mayrhofer's 'Einsamkeit,' the date of which Schubert has fixed in his letter of August 3, 1818. There are long songs of later years, such as Collin's 'Der Zwerg' of 1823 ; Schober's 'Viola' and 'Vergissmeinnicht' of 1823, and 'Schiffers Scheidelied' of 1827, and Leitner's 'Der Winterabend' of 1828 ; but these are essentially different from the ballads ; they are lyrical, and evince comparatively few mechanical changes.

It stands to reason that in 603 songs collected from all the great German poets, from Klopstock to Heine, there must be an infinite variety of material, form, sentiment, and expression. And one of the most obvious characteristics in Schubert's setting of this immense collection is the close way in which he adheres to the words.[1] Setting a song was no casual operation with him, rapidly as it was often done ; but he identified himself with the poem, and the poet's mood for the time was his. Indeed he complains of the influence which the gloom of the 'Winterreise' had had upon his spirits. He does not, as is the manner of some song-composers, set the poet at naught by repeating his words over and over again. This he rarely does ; but he goes through his poem and confines himself to enforcing the expression as music alone can do to poetry. The music changes with the words as a landscape does when sun and cloud pass over it. And in this Schubert has anticipated Wagner, since the words to which he writes are as much the absolute basis of his songs, as Wagner's librettos are of his operas. What this has brought him to in such cases as the 'Erl King,' the 'Wanderer,' 'Schwager

[1] It is strange to find his practice in the Masses so different. There—a critic has pointed out—in every one of the six, words are either omitted or incorrectly jumbled together (Mr. Prout, in *Concordia*, 1875, p. 110a). Was this because he understood the Latin words imperfectly ?

Kronos,' the 'Gruppe aus dem Tartarus,' the Shakespeare songs of 'Sylvia' and 'Hark, hark, the lark !' those of Ellen and the Huntsman in 'The Lady of the Lake,' even Englishmen can judge ; but what he did in the German literature generally may be gathered from the striking passage already quoted from Vogl (pp. 288-9), and from Mayrhofer's confession— doubly remarkable when coming from a man of such strong individuality—who somewhere says that he did not understand the full force even of his own poems until he had heard Schubert's setting of them.

One of his great means of expression is modulation. What magic this alone can work may be seen in the Trio of the Sonata in D. As in his PF. works, so in the songs, he sometimes carries it to an exaggerated degree. Thus in the short song 'Liedesend' of Mayrhofer (Sept. 1816), he begins in C minor, and then goes quickly through E♭ into C♭ major. The signature then changes, and we are at once in D major ; then C major. Then the signature again changes to that of A♭, in which we remain for fifteen bars. From A♭ it is an easy transition to F minor, but a very sudden one from that again to A minor. Then for the breaking of the harp we are forced into D♭, and immediately, with a further change of signature, into F♯. Then for the King's song, with a fifth change of signature, into B major ; and lastly, for the concluding words,

> Und immer näher schreitet
> Vergänglichkeit und Grab—

a sixth change, with eight bars in E minor, thus ending the song a third higher than it began.

In Schiller's 'Der Pilgrim' (1825), after two strophes (four stanzas) of a chorale-like melody in D major, we come, with the description of the difficulties of the pilgrim's road—mountains, torrents, ravines—to a change into D minor, followed by much extraneous modulation, reaching A♭ minor, and ending in F, in which key the first melody is repeated. At the words 'näher bin ich nicht zum Ziel'—we have a similar phrase and similar harmony (though in a different key) to the well-known complaint in the 'Wanderer,' 'Und immer fragt der Seufzer, Wo ?' The signature then changes, and the song ends very impressively in B minor.

These two are quoted, the first as an instance rather of exaggeration, the second of the mechanical use of modulations to convey the natural difficulties depicted in the poem. But if we want examples of the extraordinary power with which Schubert wields this great engine of emotion, we would mention another song which contains one of the best instances to be found of propriety of modulation. I allude to Schubart's short poem to Death, 'An den Tod,' where the gloomy subjects and images of the poet have tempted the composer to a series of successive changes so grand, so sudden, and yet so easy, and so thoroughly in keeping with the subject, that it is impossible to hear them unmoved.

But modulation, though an all-pervading means of expression in Schubert's hands, is only one out of many. Scarcely inferior to the wealth of his modulation is the wealth of his melodies. The beauty of these is not more astonishing than their variety and their fitness to the words. Such tunes as those of 'Ave Maria,' or the Serenade in the 'Schwanengesang,' or 'Ungeduld,' or the 'Grünen Lautenband,' or 'Anna Lyle,' or the 'Dithyrambe,' or 'Geheimes,' or 'Sylvia,' or the 'Lindenbaum,' or 'Du bist die Ruh,' or the 'Barcarolle,' are not more lovely and more appropriate to the text than they are entirely different from one another. One quality only, spontaneity, they have in common. With Beethoven, spontaneity was the result of labour, and the more he polished the more natural were his tunes. But Schubert read the poem, and the appropriate tune, married to immortal verse (a marriage, in his case, truly made in heaven), rushed into his mind, and to the end of his pen. It must be confessed that he did not always think of the compass of his voices. In his latest songs, as in his earliest (see p. 281), we find him taking the singer from the low B♭ to F, and even higher.

The tune, however, in a Schubert song is by no means an exclusive feature. The accompaniments are as varied and as different as the voice-parts, and as important for the general effect. They are often extremely elaborate, and the publishers' letters contain many complaints of their difficulty.[1] They are often most extraordinarily suitable to the words, as in the 'Erl King,' or the beautiful 'Dass sie hier gewesen,' the 'Gruppe aus dem Tartarus,' the 'Waldesnacht' (and many others); where it is almost impossible to imagine any atmosphere more exactly suitable to make the words grow in one's mind, than is supplied by the accompaniment. Their unerring certainty is astonishing. Often, as in 'Heliopolis,' or 'Auflösung,' he seizes at once on a characteristic impetuous figure, which is then carried on without intermission to the end. In 'Anna Lyle,' how exactly does the sweet monotony of the repeated figure fall in with the dreamy sadness of Scott's touching little lament! Another very charming example of the same thing, though in a different direction, is found in 'Der Einsame,' a fireside piece, where the frequently-recurring group of four semiquavers imparts an indescribable air of domesticity to the picture.[2] In the 'Winterabend'—the picture of a calm moonlit evening—the accompaniment, aided by a somewhat similar little figure, conveys inimitably the very breath of the scene. Such atmospheric

effects as these are very characteristic of Schubert.

The voice-part and the accompaniment sometimes form so perfect a whole, that it is impossible to disentangle the two; as in 'Sylvia,' where the persistent dotted quaver in the bass, and the rare but delicious ritornel of two notes in the treble of the piano-part (bars 7, 14, etc.), are essential to the grace and sweetness of the portrait, and help to place the lovely English figure before us. This is the case also in 'Anna Lyle' just mentioned, where the ritornel in the piano-part (bar 20, etc.) is inexpressibly soothing and tender in its effect, and sounds like the echo of the girl's sorrow. The beautiful Serenade in the 'Schwanengesang,' again, combines an incessant rhythmical accompaniment with ritornels (longer than those in the last case), both uniting with the lovely melody in a song of surpassing beauty. In the 'Liebesbotschaft,' the rhythm is not so strongly marked, but the ritornels are longer and more frequent, and form a charming feature in that exquisite love-poem. Schubert's passion for rhythm comes out as strongly in many of the songs as it does in his marches and scherzos. In the two just named, though persistent throughout, the rhythm is subordinated to the general effect. But in others, as 'Suleika,' 'Die Sterne,' the 'Nachtgesang im Walde,' 'Erstarrung,' or 'Frühlingssehnsucht,' it forces itself more on the attention.

Schubert's basses are always splendid, and are so used as not only to be the basis of the harmony but to add essentially to the variety and effect of the songs. Sometimes, as in 'Die Krähe,' they are in unison with the voice-part. Often they share with the voice-part itself in the melody and structure of the whole. The wealth of ideas which they display is often astonishing. Thus in 'Waldesnacht,' a very long song of 1820, to a fine imaginative poem by F. Schlegel, describing the impressions produced by a night in the forest, we have a splendid example of the *organic life* which Schubert can infuse into a song. The pace is rapid throughout; the accompaniment for the right hand is in arpeggios of semiquavers throughout, never once leaving off; the left hand, where not in semiquavers also, has a succession of noble and varied rhythmical melodies, independent of the voice, and the whole is so blended with the voice part—itself extraordinarily broad and dignified throughout; the spirit and variety, and the poetry of the whole are so remarkable, and the mystery of the situation is so perfectly conveyed, as to make the song one of the finest of that class in the whole Schubert collection. The same qualities will be found in 'Auf der Bruck' (1825).

We do not say that this is the highest class of his songs. The highest class of poetry, and of music illustrating and enforcing poetry, must always deal with human joys and sorrows, in

---

[1] Op. 57, containing three songs by no means difficult, was published with a notice on the title-page that care had been taken (we trust with Schubert's consent) to omit everything that was too hard.
[2] A similar mood is evoked in the Andante of the Grand Duo (op. 140).

their most individual form, with the soul loving
or longing, in contact with another soul, or
with its Maker ; and the greatest of Schubert's
songs will lie amongst those which are occupied
with those topics, such as 'Gretchen am Spinnrade,' the 'Mignon' songs, the 'Wanderer,' the
'Müllerlieder,' and 'Winterreise,' and perhaps
highest of all, owing to the strong religious
element which it contains, the 'Junge Nonne.'[1]
In that wonderful song, which fortunately is so
well known that no attempt at describing it
is necessary, the personal feelings and the
surroundings are so blended—the fear, the
faith, the rapture, the storm, the swaying of
the house, are so given, that for the time the
hearer becomes the Young Nun herself. Even
the convent bell, which in other hands might
be a burlesque, is an instrument of the greatest
beauty.

We have spoken of the mental atmosphere
which Schubert throws round his poems ; but
he does not neglect the representation of
physical objects. He seems to confine himself
to the imitation of natural noises, and not to
attempt things which have no sound. The
triplets in the Lindenbaum may be intended to
convey the fluttering leaves of the lime-tree,
and the accompaniment-figure in 'Die Forelle'
may represent the leaps of the trout ; but there
are other objects about which no mistake can be
made. One imitation of the bell we have just
referred to. Another is in the 'Abendbilder,'
where an F♯ sounds through sixteen bars to
represent the 'evening bell' ; in the 'Zügen-
glöcklein' the upper E is heard through the whole
piece ; and the bell of St. Mark's is a well-
known feature in the part-song of the 'Gondelfahrer.' The post-horn forms a natural feature
in 'Die Post,' and the hurdy-gurdy in 'Der
Leiermann.' Of birds he gives several instances ;
the Nightingale in 'Ganymed' and 'Die
gefangene Sänger'; the Raven in 'Abendbilder,'
and perhaps in 'Frühlingstraum' ; the Cuckoo
in 'Einsamkeit,' the Quail in 'Der Wachtelschlag' ; and the Cock in 'Frühlingstraum.'

That hesitation between major and minor
which is so marked in Beethoven is characteristic also of Schubert, and may be found in
nearly every piece of his. A beautiful instance
may be mentioned en passant in the trio of the
G major Fantasia Sonata (op. 78), where the
two bars in E minor which precede the E major
have a peculiarly charming effect. Another is
supplied by the four bars in A minor, for the
question which begins and ends the beautiful
fragment from Schiller's 'Gods of ancient
Greece.' He also has an especially happy way
—surely peculiarly his own—of bringing a
minor piece to a conclusion in the major. Two
instances of it, which all will remember, are in
the Romance from 'Rosamunde' :—

[1] The poems of Craigher, *Poetische Betrachtungen in freyen
Stunden, von Nicolaus, mit einer Vorrede . . . von Friedrich von
Schlegel*, were printed by Gerold of Vienna in 1828.

Du süsses Herz, es ist so schön, wenn treu die Treu-e küsst.

and in the 'Moment musical,' No. 3, in F
minor. This and the ritornels already spoken
of strike one like personal features or traits of
the composer. But apart from these idiosyncrasies, the changes from minor to major in the
songs are often superb. That in the 'Schwager
Kronos' (astonishing[2] production for a lad under
twenty), where the key changes into D major,
and farther on into F major, to welcome the
girl on the threshold, with the sudden return
to D minor for the onward journey, and the
sinking sun—can be forgotten by no one who
hears it, nor can that almost more beautiful
change to D major in the 'Gute Nacht' on the
mention of the dream. This latter, and the
noble transition to F major in the 'Junge Nonne'
are too familiar to need more than a passing
reference, or that to G major in the 'Rückblick,'
for the lark and nightingale and the girl's eyes,
or to D major in the Serenade. 'Irdisches
Glück' is in alternate stanzas of major and
minor. In Schiller's 'Rose' (op. 73) every
shade in the fate of the flower is thus indicated ;
and this is no solitary instance, but in almost
every song some example of such faithful painting may be found. A word will often do it.
With Schubert the minor mode seems to be
synonymous with trouble, and the major with
relief ; and the mere mention of the sun, or a
smile, or any other emblem of gladness, is sure
to make him modulate. Some such image was
floating before his mind when he made the
beautiful change to A major near the beginning
of the A minor Quartet (bar 23).

The foregoing remarks, which only attempt to
deal with a few of the external characteristics of
these astonishing songs, will be of use if they
only encourage the knowledge and study of them.
The chronological list of Schubert's productions
[which appeared in the first edition of the Dictionary, and has now been superseded by the
list in the complete edition of Breitkopf & Härtel]
will throw much light on the progress of his
genius, by facilitating the search where alone
it can be made with profit, namely in the works
themselves. All are worth knowing, though
all are by no means of equal excellence.

I end my imperfect sketch of the life and
works of this wonderful musician, by recalling
the fact that Schubert's songs, regarded as a
department of music, are absolutely and entirely
his own. Songs there were before him, those of
Schulz for instance, and of Zumsteeg, which he
so greatly admired, and of Haydn and Mozart—
touching, beautiful expressions of simple thought
and feeling. But the Song, as we know it in his
hands ; full of dramatic fire, poetry, and pathos ;

[2] Why is this wonderful song never sung in public in England ?

set to no simple Volkslieder, but to long complex poems, the best poetry of the greatest poets, and an absolute reflection of every change and breath of sentiment in that poetry ; with an accompaniment of the utmost force, fitness, and variety— such songs were his and his alone. With one exception. Beethoven left but one song of importance, his ' Liederkreis ' (op. 98), but that is of superlative excellence. The 'Liederkreis,' however, was not published till Dec. 1816, and even if Schubert made its acquaintance immediately, yet a reference to the Chronological List will show that by that time his style was formed, and many of his finest songs written. He may have gained the idea of a connected series of songs from Beethoven, though neither the ' Schöne Müllerin ' nor the ' Winterreise ' have the same intimate internal connection as the 'Liederkreis'; but the character and merits of the single songs remain his own. When he wrote ' Loda's Gespenst ' and ' Kolma's Klage ' in 1815, he wrote what no one had ever attempted before. There is nothing to detract from his just claim to be the creator of German Song, as we know it, and the direct progenitor of those priceless treasures in which Schumann, Mendelssohn, and Brahms have followed his example.

Of Schubert's religion it is still more difficult to say anything than it was of Beethoven's, because he is so much more reticent. A little poem of Sept. 1820, one of two preserved by Robert Schumann (*Neue Zeitschrift für Musik*, Feb. 5, 1839), is as vague a confession of faith as can well be imagined.

THE SPIRIT OF THE WORLD.

Leave them, leave them, to their dream,
    I hear the Spirit say :—
It and only it can keep them
    Near me on their darkling way.

Leave them racing, hurrying on
    To some distant goal,
Building creeds and proofs upon
    Half-seen flashes in the soul.

Not a word of it is true.
    Yet what loss is theirs or mine?
In the maze of human systems
    I can trace the thought divine.

The other, three years later, May 8, 1823, is somewhat more definite. It calls upon a ' mighty father' to look upon His son lying in the dust ; and implores Him to pour upon him the everlasting beams of His love ; and, even though He kill him, to preserve him for a purer and more vigorous existence. It expresses—very imperfectly, it is true, but still unmistakably—the same faith that has been put into undying words in the prologue to *In Memoriam*.

Franz may not have gone the length of his brother Ignaz [1] in vulgar scoffing at religious forms and persons, which no doubt were very empty in Vienna at that date ; but still of formal or dogmatic religion we can find no traces, and we must content ourselves with the practical

[1] See his letter in *Kreissle*, p. 147 (l. 149).

piety displayed in his love for his father and Ferdinand, and testified to by them in their touching words and acts at the time of his death (pp. 316-17) ; and with the certainty that, though irregular after the irregularity of his time, Schubert was neither selfish, sensual, nor immoral. What he was in his inner man we have the abundant evidence of his music to assure us. Whatever the music of other composers may do, no one ever rose from hearing a piece by Schubert without being benefited by it. Of his good-nature to those who took the bread out of his mouth we have already spoken. Of his modesty we may be allowed to say that he was one of the very few musicians who ever lived who did not behave as if he thought himself the greatest man in the world.[2] And these things are all intrinsic parts of his character and genius.

That he died at an earlier age [3] even than Mozart or Mendelssohn, or our own Purcell, must be accounted for on the ground partly of his extraordinary exertions, but still more of the privations to which he was subjected from his very earliest years. His productions are enormous, even when measured by those of the two great German composers just named, or even of Beethoven, who lived to nearly double his years. At an age when Beethoven had produced one Symphony he had written ten, besides a mass of works great and small. ' Fairer hopes' ? Had he lived, who can doubt that he would have thrown into the shade all his former achievements ? But as we have endeavoured to explain, his music came so easily and rapidly that it was probably not exhausting. It was his privations, his absolute poverty, and the distress which he naturally felt at finding that no exertions could improve his circumstances, or raise him in the scale of existence, that in the end dragged him down. Nearly the first distinct glimpse we catch of him is in the winter of 1812, supplicating his brother for a roll, some apples, or a few halfpence, to keep off the hunger of the long fast in the freezing rooms of the *Convict*. Within a year of his death we catch sight of him again, putting up with coffee and biscuits because he has not 8½d. to buy his dinner with ; selling his great Trio for 17s. 6d., and his songs at 10d. each, and dying the possessor of effects which were valued at little more than two pounds. Beside this the poverty of Mozart—the first of the two great musicians whom Vienna has allowed to starve—was wealth.

[2] This modesty comes out in a letter to Ferdinand of July 16-18, 1824, where Schubert says, 'It would be better to play some other quartets than mine' (probably referring to those in E and E♭), 'since there is nothing in them except perhaps the fact that they please you, as everything of mine pleases you. True,' he goes on, ' you do not appear to have liked them so much as the waltzes at the Ungarische Krone,' alluding to a clock at that eating-house of which Ferdinand had told him, which was set to play Franz's waltzes. The clock shows how popular Schubert was amongst his own set, and I regret having overlooked the fact in its proper place.
[3] The following are among the musicians, poets, and painters who have died in the fourth decade of their lives. Shelley, 30 ; Sir Philip Sidney, 32 ; Bellini, 33 ; Mozart, 35 ; Byron, 36 ; Raffaelle, 37 ; Burns, 37 ; Purcell, 37 ; Mendelssohn, 38 ; Weber, 39 ; Chopin, 40.

Such facts as these reduce the so-called friendship of his associates to its right level. With his astonishing power of production the commonest care would have ensured him a good living ; and that no one of his set was found devoted enough to take this care for him, and exercise that watch over ways and means which Nature had denied to his own genius, is a discredit to them all. They prate of their devotion to their friend, when not one of them had the will or the wit to prevent him from starving ; for such want as he often endured must inevitably have injured him, and we cannot doubt that his death was hastened by the absence of those comforts, not to say necessaries, which should have nursed and restored the prodigal expenditure of his brain and nerves.

We are accustomed to think of Beethoven's end as solitary and his death as miserable, but what was his last illness compared to Schubert's? Officious friends, like Pasqualati, sending him wine and delicacies; worshipping musicians, like Hummel and Hiller, coming to his death-bed as if to a shrine; his faithful attendants, Schindler, Hüttenbrenner, and Breuning, waiting on his every wish ; the sense of a long life of honour and renown ; of great works appreciated and beloved ; the homage of distant countries, expressed in the most substantial forms—what a contrast to the early death-bed, and the apparent wreck of such an end as Schubert's ! Time has so altered the public sense of his merits that it is all but impossible to place oneself in the forlorn condition in which he must have resigned himself to his departure, and to realise the darkness of the valley of the shadow of death through which his simple, sincere, guileless soul passed to its last rest, and to the joyful resurrection and glorious renown which have since attended it. *Then* an intelligent and well-informed foreign musician could visit the Austrian capital and live in its musical circles, without so much as hearing Schubert's name.[1] *Now* memorials are erected to him in the most public places of Vienna, institutions are proud to bear his name, his works go through countless editions, and publishers grow rich upon the proceeds even of single songs, while faces brighten and soften, and hands are clasped, as we drink in the gay and pathetic accents of his music.

For even his privations and his obscurity have now been forgotten in the justice since done to him, and in the universal affection with which he was regarded as soon as his works reached the outside world—an affection which, as we have conclusively shown, has gone on increasing ever since his death. In the whole range of composers it may be truly said that no one is now so dearly loved as he, no one has the happy power so completely of attracting both the admiration and the affection of his hearers. To each one he is not only a great musician, not only a great enchanter, but a dear personal friend. If in his 'second state sublime' he can know this, we may feel sure that it is a full compensation to his affectionate spirit for the many wrongs and disappointments that he endured while on earth.

The very wide field over which Schubert ranged in poetry has been more than once alluded to in the foregoing. It would be both interesting and profitable to give a list of the poems which he has set. Such a list, not without inaccuracies, will be found in Wurzbach's *Biographisches Lexicon*, vol. xxxii. p. 94. Here we can only say that it includes over 600 poems by 100 authors of whom the principal are :—

Goethe, 72 ; Schiller, 54 ; Mayrhofer, 48 ; W. Müller, 44 ; Hölty, 25 ; Matthisson, 27 ; Kosegarten, 20 ; F. Schlegel, 19 ; Klopstock, 19 ; Körner, 16 ; Schober, 15 ; Seidl, 15 ; Salis, 14 ; Claudius, 13 ; Walter Scott, 10 ; Rellstab, 9 ; Uz, 8 ; Ossian, 7 ; Heine, 6 ; Shakespeare, 3 ; Pope, 1 ; Colley Cibber, 1 ; etc. etc.

Compared with the literature on other composers that on Schubert is not extensive.

Biographical.—The original sources are scattered in German periodicals and elsewhere.

1. The first place must be given to Ferdinand Schubert's sketch, entitled 'Aus Franz Schuberts Leben,' four short papers which appeared in Schumann's periodical, the *Neue Zeitschrift für Musik*, in Nos. 33 to 36 (April 23-May 3), 1839. These are written with great simplicity, and apparently great exactness ; but might have been extended to double the length with great advantage. 2. Mayrhofer contributed a short article of recollections, *Erinnerungen*, to the *Neues Archiv für Geschichte . . . Literatur und Kunst* (Vienna), Feb. 23, 1829 ; and Bauernfeld a longer paper, *Ueber Franz Schubert*, to Nos. 69, 70, 71, of the *Wiener Zeitschrift für Kunst, Literatur, Theater, und Mode*, for June 9, 11, 13, 1829. These papers, written so shortly after Schubert's death by men extremely intimate with him, are very valuable. 3. Bauernfeld also made two interesting communications to the *Freie Presse* of Vienna, for April 17, and 21, 1869, containing six letters and parts of letters by Schubert, and many anecdotes. These latter articles were reprinted in the Leipzig *Signale* for Nov. 15, 22, 26, 28, 1869 ; translated in the *Musical World*, Jan. 8, 15, Feb. 5, 19, 1870, and in Bauernfeld's *Gesammelte Schriften*, vol. xii. (Vienna, 1873). But recollections written so long after the event must always be taken *cum grano*. 4. Schindler wrote an article in *Bäuerle's Wiener Theaterzeitung*, for May 3, 1831, describing Beethoven's making acquaintance with Schubert's songs on his death-bed ; and other articles in the *Niederrheinische Musikzeitung*, for 1857. He also mentions Schubert in his *Life of Beethoven*, 3rd ed., ii. 136. 5. Schumann printed four letters (incomplete), two poems, and a Dream, by Schubert, as 'Reliquien' in his *Neue Zeitschrift für Musik*, for Feb. 1 and 5, 1839. 6. One of the same letters was printed complete in the *Signale*, No. 2, for 1878. 7. The *Diary* of Sofie Müller (Vienna, 1832), the *Unvergessenes* of Frau von Chezy (Leipzig, 1858), and the *Erinnerungen* of her son W. von Chezy (Schaffhausen, 1863), all afford original facts about Schubert by those who knew him ; and 8. Ferd. Hiller's *Künstlerleben* (Cologne, 1880), contains a paper — 'Vienna 52 years since' — embodying a few interesting and lifelike notices of the year 1827. Of all these, use has been made in the foregoing pages.

9. The first attempt to write a life of Schubert was

---

[1] The allusion is to E. Holmes, the biographer of Mozart, who passed some time in Vienna in the spring of 1827, evidently with the view of finding out all that was best worth knowing in music, and yet does not mention Schubert's name. (See his *Ramble among the Musicians of Germany*.)

made by von Kreissle, who, in 1861 published a small 8vo pamphlet of 165 pages, entitled *Franz Schubert, eine biografische Skizze* ; von Dr. Heinrich von Kreissle. This is a very interesting little book, and though not nearly so long as the second edition, it contains some facts which have dropt out of that. 10. The second edition, *Franz Schubert, von Dr. Heinrich Kreissle von Hellborn* (Vienna, Gerold, 1865), is a large 8vo of 619 pages, with portrait after Kupelwieser. This is a thoroughly honest, affectionate book ; but it is deformed, like many German biographies, by a very diffuse style, and a mass of unnecessary matter in the shape of detailed notices of every one who came into contact with Schubert ; and some of the letters appear to be garbled ; but the analyses of the operas and the lists of works are valuable, and there are some interesting facts gathered from the Fröhlichs, Ferdinand Schubert, Spaun, Hüttenbrenner, and others. It has been translated into English by Mr. A. D. Coleridge (two vols, 8vo, Longman, 1869), with an Appendix by the present writer, containing the themes and particulars of the MS. Symphonies and other MS. music of Schubert, as seen by Arthur Sullivan and him in Vienna in 1867. A résumé of the work is given in English by Wilberforce. *Franz Schubert*, etc. (London, 1866). 11. Both Kreissle's works have been largely utilised by H. Barbedette, in *F. Schubert, sa vie*, etc. (Paris, 1866). This contains an atrocious version of Rieder's portrait, and one new fact —a facsimile of Schober's song ' An die Musik,' valuable because, being dated April 24, 1827 (while the song was composed in 1817), it shows that Schubert did not confine his dates to the original autographs (compare 'The Trout,' p. 329, note 4).
12. The chief value of Reissmann's book, *Franz Schubert, sein Leben u. seine Werke* (Berlin, 1873), consists in the extracts from the juvenile MS. songs, Quintet overture (pp. 12-30), the comparisons of early songs with later revisions of the same (pp. 24, 154, etc.), five pieces printed for the first time, and facsimile of a MS. page.
13. Gumprecht, La Mara, and others have included sketches of Schubert in their works.
14. The article on Schubert in Wurzbach's *Biographisches Lexicon* (Part 32, pp. 30-110 ; Vienna, 1876) is a good mixture of unwearied research, enthusiasm for his hero, and contempt for those who misjudge him (see for example, p. 95*b*). The copious lists are extremely interesting and useful. Unfortunately they cannot always be trusted, and the quotations are sometimes curiously incorrect. Thus Mr. Arthur Duke Coleridge is raised to the peerage as ' Herzog Arthur von Coleridge,' etc. etc. Still all students of Schubert should be grateful for the article.
15. The facsimile of the ' Erl King' in its first form has been mentioned in the body of the article (p. 285*b*). Further consideration convinces me that the original of this cannot be the first autograph, but must be a copy made afterwards by Schubert.
Two documents must be mentioned. 16. *Actenmässige Darstellung der Ausgrabung und Wiederbeeinsetzung der irdischen Reste von Beethoven und Schubert* (Vienna, 1863), and 17. *Vom Wiener Männergesangverein. Festschrift zur Enthüllung des Schubert Denkmales am 15 Mai, 1872*, an account of the unveiling of the statue in the Stadt Park, containing a capital sketch of Schubert's Life, Lists, and many other welcome facts. Herr Dumba's speech on the occasion, and poems by Bauernfeld and Weilen were printed separately. Good photographs of the statue are published by Löwy of Vienna.
18. Since writing the foregoing I have seen the *Life and Works of Schubert*, by A. Niggli, which forms No. 15 of Breitkopf & Härtel's *Musikalische Vorträge* (1880). It appears to be an excellent and generally an accurate compilation,[1] with a great deal of information in small compass, but wants a list of works to make it complete. Also 19, a Life by H. F. Frost in *The Great Musicians*, edited by Francis Hueffer (London, 1881), is readable and intelligent, and has a list of works year by year.
[*Schubert*, by Edmondstoune Duncan, contains a good deal of useful information, and a catalogue of Schubert's works based on the complete edition of Messrs. Breitkopf & Härtel.]
The articles on Schubert's masses by Professor Prout, in the *Monthly Musical Record* for 1871, and the *Concordia* for 1875, are too important and interesting to be omitted. [Among other articles on Schubert, may be especially mentioned those in the *Monthly Musical Record* for Feb.

1897 ; those in the *Musical Times* for August 1893, Jan. and Feb. 1897, Sept. and Oct. 1901, and an interesting critical study by Antonin Dvořák and Mr. H. T. Finck in *The Century* for July 1894. *The Romantic Composers*, by Daniel Gregory Mason (1907), contains a very interesting article on Schubert.]

Thematic Catalogues.

Of these there are two :—

1. *Thematisches Verzeichniss im Druck erschienenen Compositionen von Franz Schubert* (Vienna, Diabelli) [1852], contains the works from Opus 1 to 160 ; Schwanengesang ; Lieferungen 1 to 50 ; and thirty songs (included in the foregoing) of a series entitled ' Immortellen.'
2. *Thematisches Verzeichniss der im Druck erschienenen Werke von Franz Schubert*, herausgegeben von G. Nottebohm. Vienna, F. Schreiber, 1874, pages 1 to 288. This admirable work is as comprehensive and accurate as the previous publications of its author would imply its being. Under the head of printed works it comprises :—(1) works with opus numbers 1 to 173. (2) Nachgelassene Mus. Dichtungen, Lieferungen 1 to 50. (3) Works without opus numbers for orchestra, chamber music, etc. (4) Doubtful and spurious compositions ; works still in MS. ; books, portraits, etc. (5) Index, list of songs, etc.
The information under each piece is not confined to the name and date of publication, but gives in most cases the date of composition, and frequently also such facts as the first time of performance, etc. It is in fact, like all the author's publications, a model of what such a catalogue should be.

Schubert's Letters, etc.

Date	Place.	Addressed to	Where Printed.
1812. Nov. 24	Vienna	Ferd. Schubert	*N.Z.M.* Feb. 1, 1839.[2]
1813. Sept. 27		Poem for his father's birthday	*K.H.* p. 30 *note* (i. 30).[3]
1815. Sept. 27		Poem for his father's birthday	*K.H.* p. 30 *note* (i. 31).
1816. June 16		Poem for Salieri's Jubilee	*K.H.* p. 82 *note* (i. 83).
June 13-16		Diary	*K.H.* pp. 103-105 (i. 103).
1817. Aug. 24		Lied. 'Abschied v. e. Freunde'	*Lief.* xxix. 4.
1818. Feb. 2 (?)		J. Hüttenbrenner	*K.H.* p. 125 (i. 129).
Aug. 3	Zselész	Schober	Bauernfeld, in *Die Presse*, April 17, 1869 ; *Signale*, 1869, p. 978.
Aug. 24	Zselész	Ferd. Schubert	*ante*, p. 291*b*.
1819. (?)	..	J. Hüttenbrenner	*K.H.* p. 126 *note* (i. 132).
May 19	..	A. Hüttenbrenner	*K.H.* p. 152 (i. 154).
July 15	Steyr	Ferd. Schubert	*K.H.* p. 158 (i. 159).
Aug. 19	Linz	Mayrhofer	*K.H.* p. 159 (i. 160).
Sept. 14	Steyr	K. Stadler's album	*K.H.* p. 160 *note* (i. 161).
1820. Sept.	..	Poem, 'Lasst sie nur'	*K.H.* Feb. 5, 1839.
1821. Nov. 2	Vienna	Spaun	*K.H.* p. 231 (i. 234), PS. to Schober's letter.
1822. (?)	⟩ (?)	Hüttenbrenner (?)	*K.H.* p. 236 *note* (i. 239).
July 3		' My dream '	*N.Z.M.* Feb. 5, 1839.
Oct. 31	Vienna	Hüttenbrenner	MS. (in my possession).
1823. Feb. 28	,,	von Mosel	*Neue Freie Presse*, Nov. 19, 1881.
May 8	(?)	'My prayer,' Poem	*N.Z.M.* Feb. 5, 1839.
Nov. 30	Vienna	Schober	Bauernfeld, in *Die Presse*, April 17, 1869 ; *Signale*, 1869, p. 979.
1824. Mar. 27-29	,,	Diary	*K.H.* p. 322 (ii. 5, 6).
Mar. 31	,,	Kupelwieser	*K.H.* p. 319 (ii. 2).
July 16-18	Zselész	Ferd. Schubert	*Signale*, 1878, p. 17.
Sept. 21	..	Schober, with Poem ' Klage an das Volk '	Bauernfeld, in *Die Presse*, April 17, 1869 ; *Signale*, 1869, p. 980.
1825. July 21	Linz	Spaun	*K.H.* p. 341 (ii. 25).
July 25	Steyr	Father and Mother	*N.Z.M.* Feb. 1839.
(?)	Gmunden	Steiger	*K.H.* p. 372 *note* (ii. 58).
Sept. 12-21	,,	Ferd. Schubert	*N.Z.M.*, Feb. 5, 1839.
Sept. 18-19	Steyr	Bauernfeld	*K.H.* p. 370 (ii. 56).
Oct. 10	Vienna	Committee of Musikverein	*Pohl*, p. 16.

---

[1] I am sorry to find the inscription on the tomb very incorrectly given.

[2] *N.Z.M.* = *Neue Zeitschrift für Musik.*

[3] *K.H.* = Kreissle von Hellborn, *Life of Schubert*. The references in parentheses are to Coleridge's translation.

Date.	Place.	Addressed to	Where Printed.
1826. May	Vienna. (?)	Bauernfeld and Mayrhofer	Bauernfeld, *Die Presse*, April 21, 1869; *Signale*, 1869, p. 1011.
1827. June 12	Vienna. (?)	Mme. Pachler	*K.H.* p. 398 (ii. 84).
June 13	Vienna	Committee of Mu-sikverein	*Pohl*, p. 17.
Sept. 27	,,	Herr Pachler	*K.H.* p. 402 (ii. 89).
Oct. 12	,,	Mme. Pachler, with march	*K.H.* p. 404 (ii. 91).
1828. Jan. 18	Vienna	Hüttenbrenner	*K.H.* p. 417 (ii. 104).
April 10	,,	H. A. Probst	MS. in the writer's possession.
Aug. 1	,, (?)	Probst	*K.H.* p. 435 (ii. 122).
Sept. 25	,,	Jenger	*K.H.* p. 437 (ii. 124).
(?)	,, (?)	Sonnleithner	*K.H.* p. 515 (ii. 199).
Nov. 11	,,	Schober	Bauernfeld, *Presse*, 1869; *Signale*, 1869, p. 1028.

It only remains for me to return my sincere thanks to those friends who have helped me with facts and suggestions and with much labour in the execution of the preceding pages ; such as Fräulein Caroline Geisler-Schubert, Father Hermann (Anton) Schubert, and other members of the composer's family ; to Herr Eugen Heilpern and the eminent photographers who act under the name of 'Adéle' in Vienna ; my ever-kind friend Herr C. F. Pohl, Librarian of the Musikverein there ; Dr. Kopfermann, Librarian of the k. k. Bibliothek, Berlin ; Sir C. V. Stanford ; Mr. C. A. Barry ; Sir A. Manns ; Herr A. Dörffel ; Mr. Paul David ; Messrs. Breitkopf & Härtel ; Baron Tauchnitz, jun. ; Mr. L. Engel ; Mr. W. B. Squire ; and many more. To each and to all, I express my hearty acknowledgments.   G. ; revised by w. H. Hᵂ·

SCHUBERT, FRANZ, a violinist, born of a musical family at Dresden, July 22, 1808, was a pupil of Lafont, and rose through various grades to succeed Lipinski in 1861 as first Concertmeister (or leader) in his native city. He retired in 1873, on the fiftieth anniversary of his entrance into the orchestra. He died at Dresden, April 12, 1878. His published works include Studies, a Duo for violin and piano, and two Concertante for violin and violoncello (with Kummer). His little piece, 'L'Abeille' is often to be found on violinists' programmes. Schubert's wife, MASCHINKA, a distinguished bravura singer, was born August 25, 1815, and appeared at the German opera in London in 1832. She died at Dresden, Sept. 20, 1882.   G.

SCHUBERT, LOUIS, violinist and singing-master, born Jan. 27, 1828, at Dessau, went in his eighteenth year to St. Petersburg, and then as Concertmeister to Königsberg, where he remained till 1862. He then returned to Dresden, where he enjoyed a great reputation as a teacher of singing. He published a method of singing in the form of songs, and four of his operettas have become favourites. He died at Dresden, Sept. 17, 1884.   G.

SCHUBERTH, GOTTLOB, born at Carsdorf, August 11, 1778, received his musical education at Jena, and learnt the violin from Stamitz.

In 1804 he went to Magdeburg, resided there for some years, and was distinguished as an excellent clarinet and oboe player. In 1833 he moved to Hamburg, where he died, Feb. 18, 1846. His eldest son

JULIUS FERDINAND GEORG, born at Magdeburg, July 14, 1804, was the founder of the well-known firm of J. Schuberth & Co. in Leipzig and New York. After learning the business of a music-publisher in Magdeburg, he started in 1826 on his own account at Hamburg, whence he was enabled to found branch establishments at Leipzig (1832), and New York (1850). In 1854 he gave up the Hamburg business to his brother Frederick (see below) and devoted himself entirely to Leipzig and New York. Besides his publishing business, Julius Schuberth was an indefatigable student of language, literature, and music. He was publisher, editor, and proprietor of a *Musikalisches Conversations Lexicon* (which has gone through ten editions, and from which the details of the present article have been obtained), the *Kleine Hamburger Musik Zeitung* (1840-50), the New York *Musik Zeitung* (1867), and *Schuberth's kleiner Musik Zeitung* (1871-72). In 1840 he founded the Norddeutscher Musikverein and Preis Institut at Hamburg. He received many decorations from the crowned heads of Germany in recognition of his services to music. In 1874 he settled at Leipzig, where he died, June 9, 1875. His business, which in 1877 comprised over 6000 publications, was carried on with increasing success by his widow and nephew until 1891, when it was bought by F. Siegel.

LUDWIG, the second son of Gottlob, was born April 18, 1806, at Magdeburg. He studied under his father and C. M. von Weber, and when only sixteen was music-director at the Stadt Theater of his native town. He was subsequently Court Capellmeister at Oldenburg, and after living at Riga and Königsberg (1835), became (1845) conductor of the German Opera at St. Petersburg, where he died in 1850. His compositions include some published chamber music, besides operas and symphonies which remain in MS. His younger brother,

CARL, was born at Magdeburg, Feb. 25, 1811. He learnt the piano from his father, and the violoncello from L. Hesse. In 1825 he was placed under Dotzauer at Dresden, and in 1828 made his first concert tour to Ludwigslust and Hamburg. In 1829 he played at Copenhagen and Gothenburg, but a series of misfortunes drove him back to Magdeburg, where he occupied the post of first violoncello in the theatre orchestra. In 1833 he again played in Hamburg with success, and during the next few years gave concerts in all the principal towns of North Germany, Belgium, and Holland, besides visiting Paris and London (1835). In the autumn of the latter year he was appointed solo violoncellist to the Czar. He remained for twenty years at St. Petersburg, occupying the posts of musical director at the University, conductor of the Imperial Court Orchestra, and inspector of the Imperial Dramatic College. He died at Zurich, July 22, 1863. His compositions include chamber music and concertos for the violoncello, etc.

FRIEDRICH WILHELM AUGUST, fifth son of Gottlob Schuberth, was born at Magdeburg, Oct. 27, 1817, and from 1853 was the head of the firm of 'Fritz Schuberth' at Hamburg.   w. b. s.

SCHUCH, ERNST VON, born at Graz, Nov. 23, 1847, was at first intended for the legal profession, but music was too strong (he had appeared as a violinist at the age of seven, and at nine years old played solos on the piano and violin in public), and he received instruction from Eduard Stoltz at Graz, and afterwards from Dessoff in Vienna. In 1867 he was appointed conductor of Lobe's theatre at Breslau, and after short engagements at Würzburg, Graz, and Basle he was engaged by Pollini to conduct a series of Italian operas in different parts of Germany. In March 1872 he conducted his first opera in Dresden, and in August following was appointed capellmeister there. In 1873 he was made court capellmeister, and very soon his great gifts began to make the Dresden opera famous throughout the world for the catholicity of its repertory, the broad views of its conductor, and the excellence of individual performances. Schuch has always given due regard to the art of the *bel canto*, and as an operatic conductor he has few rivals. In 1897 he was ennobled by the Emperor of Austria, and in 1899 he was given the title of privy-councillor. In 1875 he married the singer CLEMENTINE SCHUCH-PROSKA (her maiden name was accurately Procházka), who was born at Vienna, Feb. 12, 1853, was a pupil of Mme. Mathilde Marchesi at the Vienna Conservatoire, and a member of the opera company at Dresden from 1873. Her voice is a light soprano, and she sings florid music with great skill. She appeared in London at some of the early Richter Concerts, and at the Crystal Palace ; she sang the part of Aennchen in 'Der Freischutz' at the German Opera under Richter in 1884, with much success, and also appeared as Eva in 'Die Meistersinger.' She retired from the stage in 1895. (Dr. Sakolowski's monograph on Schuch ; Riemann's *Lexikon*, etc.)   M.

SCHÜRMANN, GEORG CASPAR, one of the early composers of German opera, was the son of a Lutheran pastor in Hanover. He early showed a decided talent for music, first as singer and afterwards as composer. From 1693 to 1697 he was engaged as falsetto singer at the Hamburg Opera, and also for Church service. In 1697 the Duke of Brunswick invited him

to Wolfenbüttel, and shortly afterwards, at the Duke's expense, he visited Italy for the further cultivation of his musical talent. From 1702 to 1707, with the Duke of Brunswick's permission, he entered the service of the Duke of Meiningen, but in the latter year he was recalled to Wolfenbüttel, where he remained till his death, some time after 1741, busily engaged in the composition and production of German operas, in which he himself took a leading part as alto singer, and also from time to time acted as capellmeister. Many of these operas were also produced at Hamburg, but none of them were ever printed during his lifetime, and most of them are only known from their librettos. Of a few only has the music survived. One of them, entitled 'Ludovicus Pius,' or 'Ludewig der fromme,' first produced in 1726, has now been reprinted, though not complete, by Dr. Hans Sommer, from a MS. in his possession, and appears as Band xvii. in Eitner's *Publikation aelterer Musikwerke*. As a Beilage to the *Monatshefte* of 1885, Eitner has also printed an aria from another opera of Schürmann's, entitled 'Henricus Anceps,' or 'Heinrich der Vogler,' besides a complete Church Cantata for the New Year, both of which are calculated to give a very favourable idea of Schürmann's powers as a composer. Eitner is disposed to assign him a very high place even in association with Handel and Bach, both for genuine feeling and contrapuntal skill.   J. R. M.

SCHÜTT, EDUARD, born Oct. 22, 1856, at St. Petersburg, was intended for a mercantile career, but relinquished it for music, which he learned from Petersen and Stein sufficiently to pass the examination at the St. Petersburg Conservatoire, with honour, in 1876. He then entered the Conservatorium at Leipzig, passed the final examination there in 1878, and went to Vienna, where he was elected conductor of the Akademische Wagner-Verein. In January 1882 he played his Concerto (op. 7) in G minor, before the Russian Musical Society at St. Petersburg. It was performed at the Crystal Palace, Sydenham, April 15, 1882, by Mme. Frickenhaus. His published works include—Serenade for strings, op. 6 ; Variations for 2 Pianos, op. 9 ; Songs opp. 18, 19, 22, 23 ; piano pieces, opp. 13, 15, 16, 17, 20, 21, 41, transcription of songs by Brahms, Strauss's Fledermaus waltz, etc.   G.

SCHÜTZ, HEINRICH (name sometimes Latinised SAGITTARIUS), 'the father of German music,' as he has been styled, was born at Köstritz, Saxony, Oct. 8, 1585. His father and grandfather occupied a good social position at Weissenfels, whither his father removed with his family on the death of the grandfather in 1591. Admitted in 1599 as a chorister into the chapel of the Landgraf Maurice of Hesse-Cassel, Schütz had, besides a thorough musical training, the advantage of a good general education in the arts and sciences of the time, which enabled him in 1607 to proceed to the University of Marburg, where he pursued with some distinction the study of law. The Landgraf, when on a visit to Marburg, observing in his *protégé* a special inclination and talent for music, generously offered to defray the expense of his further musical cultivation at Venice under the tuition of Giovanni Gabrieli, the most distinguished musician of the age. Schütz accordingly proceeded to Venice in 1609, and already in 1611 published the first-fruits of his studies under Gabrieli, a book of five-part madrigals dedicated to his patron. On the death of Gabrieli in 1612, Schütz returned to Cassel, and was appointed organist to the Landgraf, but either uncertain himself as to his real vocation for music or induced by his friends, he had still some thoughts of taking up again the profession of law. Perhaps the Landgraf's chapel was too narrow a sphere for him to work in; it was fortunate therefore that in 1614 he received the invitation to undertake the entire direction of the capelle of the Elector Johann Georg of Saxony at Dresden, at a salary of 400 gulden. The Landgraf was unwilling to part with him, and would at first only allow him to accept this position temporarily. He recalled Schütz in 1616, but on the earnest petition of the Elector finally consented to his remaining permanently at Dresden. Schütz's first endeavour at Dresden was to reorganise the electoral music, and indeed, as he had been engaged to do, on the Italian model, for the purpose of introducing the new concerted style of music vocal and instrumental. He procured good Italian instruments and players, and sent qualified members of the capelle to Italy for a time, to perfect themselves in the new style of singing and playing.

His first work of importance appeared in 1619, 'Psalmen David's sammt etlichen Motetten und Concerten mit 8 und mehr Stimmen,' a work which shows the influence of the new Monodic or Declamatory style which Schütz had learned in Italy.

For his purpose Schütz uses the means of expression afforded by contrast of different choirs, or contrast of solo voices with full choir, or contrast of voices with instruments, either the simple Basso Continuo, *i.e.* for organ, lute, or theorbo, or strings with occasional trumpets, etc. His next work, in 1623, was an oratorio on the subject of the Resurrection entitled 'Historia der fröhlichen und siegreichen Auferstehung unsers einigen Erlösers und Seligmachers Jesu Christi.' The occasion for the composition of this work would seem to have been the practice, still kept up at Dresden, Leipzig, and other churches in Saxony, of singing the story of the Resurrection at Easter as that of the Passion in Holy Week. A 'Geistliches Gesangbuch' of 1612 informs us that 'Every year on Easter-day

at Vespers, before the sermon, there is sung in our Christian congregations the Resurrection, so splendidly set by Antonius Scandellus.' This Antonius Scandellus, Scandello, or Scandelli, had been one of Schütz's own predecessors at Dresden from 1568 to 1580, and had written both a Passion and a Resurrection. (See p. 238.) His 'Resurrection' must have continued in use even beyond Schütz's time, since it even appears in Vopelius's 'Leipziger Gesangbuch,' of 1682. It may be seen in Schöberlein and Riegel's 'Schatz des liturgischen Chorgesang,' ii. 619-647. (With regard to the authorship, compare O. Kade's remarks in the Vorwort to the Notenbeilagen to Ambros's *Geschichte*, xlvi.) Schütz's 'Resurrection' follows the line of Scandello's, only whereas Scandello's composition is purely vocal, that of Schütz is adapted to instrumental accompaniment. Both works begin with a setting (in Scandello 5-part, in Schütz 6-part) of the words 'Die Auferstehung unsers Herrn Jesu Christi, wie uns die von den Evangelisten beschrieben wird,' and conclude with a setting (Scandello 5-part, Schütz 8-part) of the words 'Gott sei Dank, der uns den Sieg gegeben hat,' etc. In Scandello, the part of the Evangelist is altogether liturgical, but in Schütz, while it is mostly based on the liturgical melody, the more important passages have given to them a more characteristic and expressive form of declamation, which sometimes rises up to actual melody in the more modern sense of the term, and the Evangelist's part is accompanied throughout either by the organ or preferably by four Viole da Gamba, which are called upon at certain pauses in the narrative to execute appropriate runs or passages ('Zierliche und appropriirte Läufe oder Passaggi machen'). The words of other personages are set for two or more voices, according to their number, as for instance, the words of the three Maries as a trio, of the two angels as a duet, of the eleven disciples as a 6-part chorus, only that usually for single personages two parts are employed (as in Scandelli), though Schütz permits one of these parts to be taken, as he expresses it, *instrumentaliter*. This work of Schütz's is altogether remarkable, as being a highly successful endeavour to unite dramatic expressiveness with reverence for ecclesiastical tradition. The same spirit is shown in another form in his next work of importance, 'Cantiones Sacrae,' for four voices with bass accompaniment for organ. The endeavour here is to unite the older form of the Motet with the newer form of the Concerto, and the Diatonic Church Modes with the use of Chromatic harmonies. In 1627 Johann Georg I. of Saxony wished to signalise the occasion of the marriage of his daughter to the Landgraf of Hesse-Darmstadt by giving the first performance of opera in Germany. The opera had just sprung into life in connection with the new musical movement in Italy, as a supposed revival of the antique music-drama. Schütz was commissioned to procure from Italy Peri's opera 'Dafne.' The poet Opitz was set to the task of translating the Italian text by Rinuccini into German, and as it was found that Peri's music would not quite fit the new German words, Schütz had to adapt them to new music of his own. The opera 'Dafne,' as thus set by Schütz, was performed at Torgau on the 13th of April 1627. Unfortunately the music of this first German opera has not been preserved, and no further account of it has been given. It is probable, however, that Schütz did little else on this occasion than rearrange Peri's music and add something in exactly the same style. In any case the result was not such as to induce Schütz to make any further attempts in music for the theatre, if we except another occasional piece, a Ballet, 'Orpheus und Euridice,' written in 1638, the music of which appears also to be lost. In 1625 appeared his 'Geistliche Gesänge,' and in 1628 Schütz, having lost his wife, found some comfort in his sorrow, as he tells us, by occupying himself with the task of composing melodies with simple 4-part harmony to a rhymed version of the Psalms by Dr. Cornelius Becker. This version by Becker was meant to be a Lutheran rival to an earlier Calvinistic version by Lobwasser, based on the French Psalter of Marot and Beza, and adapted to the same melodies. Later on, Johann Georg II., with a view to the introduction of the Becker Psalter in place of Lobwasser's in the schools and churches of Saxony, urged Schütz to complete his composition of melodies for the work. The task was hardly congenial to our composer, as he himself confesses in the preface to the complete work when it appeared in 1661. Two further editions, however, of this Psalter, with Schütz's melodies, appeared in 1676 and 1712. Some of these melodies passed into later Cantionals, though none have ever taken the same place in general use or esteem that similar work by less eminent composers has done.

Partly to distract himself from his great sorrow, partly to familiarise himself with the still newer development of music in Italy, with which the name of Claudio Monteverde is chiefly associated, Schütz set out on a second visit to Italy in 1629. He found musical taste in Venice greatly changed since the time of his first visit (1612), 'modern ears were being regaled with a new kind of sensation' ('recenti titillatione'). The new style consisted in the greater prominence given to solo singing, and to intensity of expression in solo singing, the freer use of dissonances, and greater richness and variety in instrumental accompaniment. In a series of works entitled 'Symphoniae Sacrae,' Schütz endeavoured to turn to account the new experiences he had gained, without, however, like his new Italian models, turning his back upon his earlier polyphonic training. He never altogether forgot to unite the solidity of the old school with the piquancy of expression of the new. The first part of 'Symphoniae Sacrae' appeared at Venice in 1629, and consists of twenty settings of Latin texts, chiefly from the Psalms and the Song of Songs. A second part of 'Symphoniae Sacrae,' with the sub-title 'Deutsche Concerten,' appeared at Dresden in 1657; a third part also at Dresden in 1650. The two later parts are settings of German Bible texts. They may be described as brief dramatic cantatas for various combinations of voices and instruments, and in virtue of them Schütz may be considered joint-founder with Carissimi of the Dramatic Oratorio. Winterfeld (*Gabrieli*, vol. iii. pp. 82, etc., also *Evang. Kir. Gesang.* vol. ii. p. 315) singles out for special notice from the first part, 'Fili, fili mi, Absalom' (David's lament over Absalom), written for bass solo with accompaniment of four trombones, and from the third part, 'Saul, Saul, was verfolgst du mich?' (a cantata for the festival of the Conversion of St. Paul), and 'Mein Sohn, warum hast du uns das gethan?' (for the first Sunday after Epiphany).

In 1631 and following years Saxony became the scene of war, and one result was the complete disorganisation of the Elector's capelle, means failing for the payment of musicians, and the attention of the Elector and his court being occupied with more serious matters than music. Schütz obtained leave in 1633 to accept an invitation to Copenhagen from King Christian IV. of Denmark. The years 1635-41 were spent in wanderings to and fro between different courts with occasional returns to Dresden, Schütz being still nominally in the service of the Elector. The chief works worthy of notice published during these years are two sets of Geistliche Concerte for one to five voices, with Basso Continuo (1636, 1639), the second set being especially remarkable by the composer's frequent directions for the securing of proper expression in his music. (It is to be remembered that marks and terms of expression were not then in common use.) In 1641 Schütz returned to Dresden to make an effort to reorganise the music, but from want of means his efforts were not crowned with anything like success till 1645 or 1647. A work of importance was written and produced about 1645, though strangely enough it was never printed or published in Schütz's lifetime, and only appeared in print for the first time in 1873, edited by Carl Riedel of Leipzig. It is a small Passion Oratorio on the Seven Words from the Cross. This work is of importance as contributing some new elements to the development of the later Passion Music. First, the part of the Evangelist is no longer based on the liturgical intonation, as in the 'Resurrection' oratorio of 1623, but takes the form of the new 'Arioso Recitative.' For the sake of variety Schütz divides this part among different solo voices, and sets it twice in the form of a quartet. Next, the work is opened and concluded with a chorus (5-part with basso continuo) expressive of the feelings of Christians at the contemplation of our Lord upon the Cross. After the opening, and again before the concluding chorus, there occurs a short 5-part instrumental symphony, which has been aptly described as an ideal raising and dropping of the curtain before and after the action. The instruments to be used are not specified, but strings are probably more intended than anything else. The part of our Lord differs from the other parts in having a 3-part instrumental accompaniment. This probably originated out of the custom in previous 'Passions' (as followed in Scandello's 'Resurrection,' for instance), of setting the words of our Lord in four vocal parts. Schütz here improved upon the idea, first timidly suggested by himself in his 'Resurrection,' of giving the words of a single character to a single voice, for the sake of dramatic consistency, and assigning the accompanying parts to the instruments. The way in which this accompaniment is carried out deserves to be noticed. It is neither in the old style nor in the new, but a curious combination of both ; the lower part is identical with the basso continuo for sustaining the harmony throughout : the other two parts are written in the polyphonic style with the voice, consisting of imitations either preceding or following the vocal phrase. It is well known how Bach in his 'Matthew-Passion' developed this idea of a special accompaniment to the words of our Lord, surrounding Him as it were with a halo. Naturally there are no arias in the modern sense in Schütz's work, all is in the form of expressive recitative. A touching simplicity and tenderness distinguish the whole work. In 1648 appeared his 'Musicalia ad Chorum Sacrum,' a work in quite a different style from those last mentioned, and showing a reaction in Schütz's mind against the exclusive claims of the modern 'Manier.' It consists of twenty-nine pieces to German words, for five, six, and seven voices, in the old motet or strictly polyphonic style, in which the bassus generalis or continuus may be dispensed with (as the title says, 'Wobei der Bassus Generalis auf Gutachten und Begehren, nicht aber aus Nothwendigkeit zugleich auch zu befinden ist'). In the preface he expresses the opinion that no one will become a capable musician who has not first acquired skill in strict contrapuntal work without the use of the basso continuo. Personal reasons to some extent combined with artistic reasons to produce the reaction in favour of the older school of music as against the new, to which we have referred. From 1647 onwards, in spite of the many personal sacrifices he had made on behalf of the Elector's capelle, as for instance by paying or increasing out of his own salary the salaries of others of

the musicians, he appears to have suffered so many annoyances in connection with it as caused him to have almost a disgust for the further cultivation of music at Dresden, and induced him to solicit over and over again in 1651-55 dismissal from the Elector's service. The new Italian element in the chapel was very different from the old ; Schütz was getting involved in continual differences and squabbles with a new Italian colleague Bontempi. Italian art was losing its earlier seriousness of purpose, turning its back upon its older traditions, and aiming simply at the amusement of princes and their courts, and thus acquiring a popularity dangerous to higher ventures of art. The Elector, however, refused to accept the resignation of his Capellmeister, and after 1655 affairs improved somewhat, so far as Schütz was personally concerned, so that he continued quietly at his post for the remaining sixteen years of his life. In 1657 he published 'Zwölf geistliche Gesänge' a 4 for small choirs, a work which we might call a German Communion and Evening Service, consisting, as it does, mainly of settings of the chief portions of the Liturgy in order, viz. the Kyrie, Gloria, Nicene Creed, Words of Institution (usually appointed to be sung in early Lutheran liturgies), a Communion Psalm, Post-Communion Thanksgiving, then a Magnificat and Litany, etc. From 1657 to 1661 our composer would seem to have been occupied with the task enjoined on him by the new Elector, that of composing additional melodies for Becker's Psalter, already mentioned ; work which apparently gave him more trouble than it was worth, and hindered him from devoting himself to other more congenial work. In the preface to this Psalter, 1661, he says that 'to confess the truth, he would rather have spent the few remaining years of his life in revising and completing other works which he had begun, requiring more skill and invention' ('mehr sinnreichen Inventionen'). It is greatly to be regretted that the next work with which Schütz occupied himself has been preserved to us in so incomplete a form. It was a setting of the story of the Birth of our Lord, and as a Christmas oratorio would have been a fitting companion-work to his earlier 'Easter' oratorio and his later 'Passions-Musik.' Only the part of the Evangelist, in recitative with bass accompaniment, has been preserved to us ; but the preface to this (1664) contains a specification of ten so-called 'Concerte' for various voices and instruments which were to come in at different points of the narrative. The introduction, for instance, consisted of the title ('Die Geburt, etc.') set for four vocal and five instrumental parts ; the message of the Angel was set for soprano solo with accompaniment of two violettas and one violone ; the Chorus of Angels for six voices with violins and violas ; the words of the Shepherds for three alto voices with two flutes and bassoon; of the Wise Men for three tenor voices with two violins and bassoon; of the High Priests for four bass voices and two trombones; and so on with the rest of the work. The loss of these concerted movements is the more to be regretted, as they would doubtless have shown Schütz's maturer views on instrumentation and the combination of voices and instruments. The last work of Schütz preserved to us, and perhaps his most famous work, is his setting of the story of the Passions, four settings in all, after the four Evangelists, 'Historia des Leidens und Sterbens unserer Herrn und Heylandes Jesu Christi' (1665-66). This work was never published in his own lifetime, and the only original copy extant is that of the St. John Passion, presented by the composer himself to the Duke of Wolfenbüttel, and now in the library at Wolfenbüttel. The only copy of the other settings is that made by a later hand in 1690, regarding which see below in list of Schütz's works. As we now have the work, it is for voices alone without instruments. It is, therefore, as if the composer here wished to renounce the mere external advantages of the newer concerted and dramatic style for the sake of showing how the spirit of it could be retained and applied to the purely vocal and older polyphonic style. For what specially distinguishes this Passion Music, is the series of brief choruses of surprising dramatic energy and truth of expression, yet never overstepping the bounds of devout reverence inspired by the subject. Otherwise the work is more purely liturgical than later Passions, not having arias and chorales to interrupt the narrative and give that variety of interest so needed for modern concert performance. Each Passion is opened according to old custom with a setting of the title ('the Passion, etc.') and closed with a devotional chorus in motet style, the text taken from some familiar Church hymn. The rest of the work is written in unaccompanied recitative, though parts of it may have been meant to be accompanied in the manner suggested by Schütz himself in his 'Resurrection.' In the 'St. Matthew' the recitative has more of melodic expressiveness than in the other Passions. The 'St. Mark' is peculiar in combining the greatest monotony of recitative with the richest dramatic character in the choruses. Dr. Spitta, the editor of the new complete edition of Schütz's works, is inclined, on this and other grounds, to doubt the authenticity of the 'St. Mark Passion' (see his preface, pp. xx, xxi). But the fact of its being joined with the other undoubtedly authentic Passions without anything to indicate its being by a different author, is sufficient to outweigh mere suspicions. These 'Passions,' compressed by Carl Riedel and so far adapted to the requirements of modern performance, have been repeatedly produced with considerable success by the Riedelsche Verein of Leipzig.

In his later years Schütz's powers began to fail, especially his sense of hearing; and we are told, when he could no longer go out, he spent the most of his time in the reading of Holy Scripture and spiritual books. His last attempts at composition were settings of portions of the 119th Psalm; and no verse indeed of that psalm could have been more fittingly chosen as the motto of both his personal life and his art-work than that on which he was last engaged, but left unfinished: 'Thy statutes have been my songs in the house of my pilgrimage.' He is the true predecessor of Handel and Bach, not so much in the mere form of his work, as the spirit. If in the dramatised Biblical scenes of his 'Symphoniae Sacrae,' he is more especially Handel's predecessor, in his Passion Music he is Bach's. Both Handel and Bach simply brought to perfection what lay in germ in Heinrich Schütz. His great merit consists in this, that at a time when the new dramatic style was threatening the complete overthrow of the older polyphonic style, he saw how to retain the advantages of both, and laboured to engraft the one upon the other. It was thus he prepared the way for the greater work of Handel and Bach after him. Schütz died at Dresden, Nov. 6, 1672. The rather singular coincidence of Schütz's birth-year being exactly a hundred years earlier than the birth-year of Handel and Bach, brought about, on the occasion of the keeping of the bicentenary of the two latter, in 1885, a great revival of interest in the work of their forerunner, which has had this practical result at least, the publication of a monumental edition of his works by Messrs. Breitkopf & Härtel of Leipzig.

The following is a list of Schütz's works, based on Eitner, *Monatshefte für Musikgeschichte*, xviii. pp. 47 ff., and the *Quellen-Lexikon*.

I. WORKS PUBLISHED IN LIFETIME.

1. Il primo libro de Madrigali de Henrico Sagitario Alemanno. Venice, 1611. Dedicated to Landgraf Moritz of Hesse-Cassel. Contains 18 Madrigals *a* 5, and 1 Dialogo *a* 8.
2. 3 Pièces d'occasion, entitled 'Concerte,' published separately. Dresden, 1618.
3. Die Worte Jesus Syrach; Wol dem der ein tugends. Weib, 1618.
4. Concerto in two parts. 1618.
5. Psalmen Davids sampt etlichen Moteten und Concerten mit acht und mehr Stimmen, nebenst andern zweien Capellen dass dero etliche auf drei und vier Chor nach Beliebung gebraucht werden können, wie auch mit beigefügten Basso Continuo vor die Orgel, Lauten, Chitaron, etc. Dresden, 1619. Contains 26 Psalms.
6. Psalm cxxxiii., for 8 voices with Basso Continuo, composed for his brother's wedding. Leipzig, 1619.
7. Syncharma Musicum tribus Choris adornatum, etc. A pièce d'occasion for the restoration of peace in Silesia. Breslau, 1621.
8. Historia der fröhlichen und siegreichen Auferstehung unsers einigen Erlösers und Seligmachers Jesu Christi. In fürstlichen Capellen oder Zimmern um die Osterliche zeit zu geistlicher Recreation füglichen zu gebrauchen. Dresden, 1623. An Oratorio on the Resurrection of Christ. The title shows that it was intended as well for Chamber performance as for Church.
9. Elegy on the Death of 'Fürstin Frau Sophia, Herzogin zu Sachsen.' Melody with Basso Cont. Text by Schütz himself. Freiberg, 1623.
10. Cantiones Sacrae quatuor vocum, cum Basso ad Organum. Freiberg, 1625. Contains 41 pieces *a* 4 with Latin words.
11. De Vitae fugacitate, Aria, unique vocum supra Bassum Continuum. Freiberg, 1625. A pièce d'occasion.
12. Psalmen Davids, in Teutsche Reimen gebrachte durch D. Cornelium Beckern . . . nach gemeiner Contrapunctsart in *4*

Stimmen gestellt . . . Freiberg, 1628. Contains 92 new melodies by Schütz himself and 11 others harmonised by him. An edition, Güstrow, 1640, was published for use in Mecklenburg-Schwerin. A later enlarged edition, with melodies for all the Psalms, appeared, Dresden, 1661.

13. Symphoniae Sacrae . . . variis vocibus ac Instrumentis accomodatae a 3, 4, 5, 6. Opus ecclesiasticum secundum. Venice, 1629. Dedicated to the Elector of Saxony. Contains 20 settings of Latin texts.

14. ' Das ist je gewisslich wahr.' A motet for 6 voices in memory of Johann Hermann Schein, died 1631. Dedicated to Schein's widow and children. Dresden, 1631.

15. Erster Theil Kleiner geistlichen Concerten, mit 1, 2, 3, 4, und 5 Stimmen sammt beigefügten Basso Cont. Leipzig, 1636. Contains 17 pieces to German words.

16. Musicalische Exequien . . . mit 6, 8, und mehr Stimmen zu gebrauchen. Dresden, 1636. Contains 3 funeral pieces.

17. Anderer Theil Kleiner geistlichen Concerten, mit 1, 2, 3, 4, und 5 Stimmen, sammt beigefügten Basso Continuo vor die Orgel. Dresden, 1639. Contains 31 pieces, texts German and Latin.

18. Symphoniarum Sacrarum Secunda Pars . . . Deutsche Concerte mit 3, 4, 5 nämlich einer, zwo, dreien Vocal- und zweien Instrumental-Stimmen. . . . Opus Decimum. Dresden, 1647. Dedicated to Christian V. of Denmark. Contains 27 pieces. German words.

19. Danck-Lied für die hocherwiesene fürstliche Gnade in Weymar, 1647.

20. Musicalia ad Chorum sacrum. Geistliche Chor-Musik mit 5, 6, 7 Stimmen, beides Vocaliter und Instrumentaliter zu gebrauchen . . . Opus Undecimum. Dresden, 1648. Dedicated to the Bürgermeister, etc., of Leipzig, out of respect for the Choir of the Thomas-Schule. Contains 29 Motets to German words.

21. Symphoniarum Sacrarum Tertia Pars. Deutsche Concerte mit 5, 6, 7, 8, nämlich 3, 4, 5, 6. Vocal- und zweien Instrumental-Stimmen. . . . Opus Duodecimum. Dresden, 1650.

22. Canticum B. Simeonis. German text of Nunc Dimittis, 2 settings for 6 voices. (Not perfectly preserved.)

23. Zwölf Geistliche Gesänge a 4. Für Kleine Cantoreien. Opus Decimum Tertium. Dresden, 1657.

24. Historia der Freuden- und Gnaden-reichen Geburt Gottes und Marien Sohnes, Jesu Christi . . . Vocaliter und Instrumentaliter in die Musik versetzt. Dresden, 1664. A Christmas Oratorio, but only imperfectly preserved.

II. WORKS UNPUBLISHED IN LIFETIME.

1. Die Sieben Worte unsers lieben Erlösers und Seligmachers Jesu Christi, so Er am Stamm des heiligen Kreuzes gesprochen, ganz beweglich gesetzt. . . . Parts in manuscript preserved in the Library at Cassel, discovered in 1855 by O. Kade, and first published in Score and adapted for modern performance by Carl Riedel, Leipzig, 1873.

2. Historia des Leidens und Sterbens unsers Herrens Jesu Christi. a. Nach dem Evangelisten St. Matthaeus. b. Nach St. Marcus. c. Nach St. Lucas. d. Nach St. Johannes. An older form of the Johannes Passion exists in MS. 1665. Of the four Passions together there exists only a copy made by J. Z. Grundig in 1690, now in the Leipzig Stadt Bibliothek.

3. Various single motets and concerted pieces, enumerated by Eitner, M.f.M.G., xviii. pp. 62, 67-70, and in the Quellen-Lexikon.

III. WORKS LOST.

1. ' Dafne.' Opera, performed 1627. German text by Opitz, after the original by Rinuccini.

2. A Ballet with Dialogue and Recitative, composed for the marriage of Johann Georg II. of Saxony, 1638. (Another Ballet, ' Von Zusammenkunft und Wirkung der VII. Planeten,' existing in MS., is conjecturally ascribed to Schütz in Eitner's List, M.f.M.G. xviii. p. 69.)

All Schütz's MS. remains at Dresden were destroyed by fire, 1760. The same fate befell in 1794 what he may have left at Copenhagen.

IV. DOUBTFUL WORKS.

Ballet, ' Von Zusammenkunft und Wirkung der VII Planeten,' found in MS. at Dresden. (See above.)

V. NEW EDITION IN SCORE.

Begun on the Tercentenary of the composer's Birthday, 1885. Heinrich Schütz, Sämmtliche Werke, edited by Friedrich Chrysander and Philipp Spitta, and published by Messrs. Breitkopf & Härtel, Leipzig (1885-94).

Vol. 1 contains the ' Resurrection' Oratorio, the Passions-Musik after the four Evangelists, the Seven Words from the Cross, and in an Appendix the imperfect Christmas Oratorio, and the older form of the Johannes-Passion.

Vols. 2 and 3 contain the Psalms and Motets of 1619.
Vol. 4, Cantiones Sacrae, 1625.
Vol. 5, Symphoniae Sacrae, Part I. 1629.
Vol. 6, Geistliche Concerte of 1636 and 1639.
Vol. 7, Symphoniae Sacrae, Part II. 1647.
Vol. 8, Musicalia ad Chorum sacrum, 1648.
Vol. 9, Italian Madrigals, 1611.
Vols. 10 and 11, Symphoniae Sacrae, Part III. 1630.
Vol. 12, Gesammelte Motetten, Concerte, Madrigals, and Arien, i. (containing Nos. 14, 16, and 22, besides other things).
Vol. 13, Ditto. ii. Pss. 24, 8, 7, 85, 127, 15, and motets.
Vol. 14, Ditto. iii. 14 Compositions, including No. 6.
Vol. 15, Ditto. iv. 12 Compositions, including No. 7.
Vol. 16, Psalms for Becker's hymn-book.   J. R. M.

SCHULHOFF, JULIUS—dear to player and dancer for his Galop di Bravura, Impromptu Polka, and many more brilliant and clever PF. pieces—was born at Prague, August 2, 1825. He learned the piano from Kisch, and counter-

point from Tomaschek, and before he was fourteen made a successful appearance as a player. Notwithstanding his success, the boy's ambition was too great to allow him to remain in Prague, and in 1842 he went to Paris, then a hotbed of pianoforte virtuosity. Here a fortunate interview with Chopin gave him his opportunity. He played in public (Nov. 2, 1845), and published his first two works, of which op. 1, an Allegro Brillant, was dedicated to Chopin. After a lengthened residence in Paris he took a very extended tour through France, Austria (1849-50), England, Spain (1851), and even South Russia and the Crimea (1853). He lived in Dresden from 1870, and in Berlin from about 1897; he died in the latter city March 13, 1898. A sonata in F minor, and twelve études, are among his more earnest compositions.   G.

SCHULTHEISS, BENEDICT, was the younger son of HIERONYMUS SCHULTHEISS (1600-69), and his second wife, whom he married in 1648. Benedict became organist at S. Egidius, Nuremberg, but he died at a comparatively early age on March 1, 1693. He published first a set of Clavier pieces: Muth und Geist ermunternder Clavier-Lust. Erster Theil, Nürnberg, 1679; Ander Theil, 1680. Later he seems to have devoted himself entirely to Church music, and composed many Chorales which are still included in the Lutheran Church-song; they will be found in the following works, all published in his lifetime :—

Heiliger Sonntags-Handel und Kirch-Wandel . . . durch Sigmund von Birken. Nürnberg, 1681. Contains two melodies with figured bass by ' Ben. Schulth.'

Der geistlichen Erquick-Stunden des . . . Heinr. Müllers . . . Poetischer Andacht-Klang von denen Blumgenossen verfasset, anjetzo mit 60 Liedern vermehret, und von unterschiedlichen Ton-Künstlern in Arien gesetzt. Nürnberg, 1691. Contains thirteen melodies with figured bass by Schultheiss.

Gott-geheiligter Christen nützlich-ergetzende Seelen-Lust . . . mit lieblich in Noten gesetzten neuen Arien . . . vorgestellet von W. C. D. (W. C. Dessler). Nürnberg, 1692.

It contains twenty-five melodies with figured bass ; Zahn included nine of them in his great work Die Melodien der deutschen evangelischen Kirchenlieder, 1893, and thinks Schultheiss composed all twenty-five, although only the first eleven are initialled B. S.   C. S.

SCHULTHESIUS, JOHANN PAUL, was born at Fechheim, Saxe-Coburg, on Sept. 14, 1748. He received his first lessons in music from his father, a schoolmaster there ; in 1764 he entered the local college to follow a course of theology, became a member of the choir, and remained there six years, acquiring a thorough knowledge of music. From 1770 to 1773 he was at the University of Erlangen, where he completed his theological studies, while he was able to obtain organ lessons from Kehl, an excellent organist. He was then offered a post at Leghorn, as Protestant minister to the colony of Germans and Dutch settled there ; he accepted and went to Italy, where he remained for the rest of his life. Checchi was organist at that time, and gave him lessons in counterpoint and composition. Schulthesius was an excellent performer on the clavier, and in 1782 he was called upon to play some of his own compositions before the Grand Duke of Tuscany, and was very favourably received. He became one of the most erudite musicians of his time, and in 1807 was nominated secretary of the fourth class of the Accademia di scienze, lettere ed arti di Livorno. He died on April 18, 1816, at Leghorn. His treatise on the quality and character of church music: *Sulla musica da chiesa.* Memoria di Gio. Paolo Schulthesius. Livorno, presso Tommaso Masi. 1810, 4to, was also published in the first volume of the *Proceedings* of his Accademia. Letters of his to Marco Santucci are in existence; in one of them he mentions this work, and expresses his desire to hear Santucci's opinion of it. The following compositions were also published :—

Tre sonate per il Cimbalo o piano-forte con l' accompagnamento d'un violino obbligato. Composte da Gio. Paolo Schulthesius. Opera 1. Livorno, 1780, obl. folio. A copy of the second edition is in the British Museum.
Sonate a solo per il cembalo o pianoforte. Op. 2. Livorno, obl. fol.
Deux quatuors pour piano, violon, viola et violoncello. Op. 3. London, 1785.
Otto variazioni facili sopra un Andantino per il cimbalo o pianoforte, violino, viola e violoncello obbligato. Op. 4. Livorno. Four oblong folio part-books.
Allegretto avec 12 variations pour le Clavecin ou pianoforte, violon, viola et violoncello obbligato. Op. 6. Augsburg (Gombart).
Andante grazioso de Pleyel varié pour le clavecin ou pianoforte, violon et violoncello obbligato. Op. 7. Augsburg (Gombart).
Andantino original, avec huit variations pour le piano. Op. 8. Augsburg (Gombart).
Sept variations pour le forte-piano. Op. 9. Augsburg (Gombart). 1797. Dedicated to Joh. Nic. Forkel.
Huit variations sur un air russe pour piano. Op. 10. Livorno.
Douze variations sur l'air de *Malbrouk* pour piano, violon, viola et violoncello. Op. 11. Florence (Nicola Pagni).
La reconciliazione di due amici, tema con variazioni. Op. 12. Augsburg (Gombart). It was dedicated to Haydn.
Otto variazioni sentimentali sopra un tema originale intitolato L' Amicizia per pianoforte, dedicate al signore Carlo Mozart, figlio maggiore del Gran Mozart. Op. 14. Leipzig. Breitkopf.　　C. S.

SCHULTZ. See PRAETORIUS, vol. iii. p. 805.

SCHULZ, JOHANN ABRAHAM PETER, son of a baker, born at Lüneburg, March 30, 1747. His master was Schmugel, a local organist of ability, whose descriptions of Berlin and of Kirnberger's labours so excited him that at the age of fifteen, without money and against the wish of his family, he went thither and put himself under the protection of Kirnberger, who was very good to him, under whom he studied and to whom he became greatly attached. In 1768 he was fortunate enough to travel in France, Italy, and Germany under good auspices. In 1773 he returned to Berlin, and found his old master and Sulzer at work on their *Allgem. Theorie der Schönen Künste,* and undertook the musical portion of it from S to the end. In 1776-78 he was also Capellmeister to the French theatre at Berlin, and afterwards to the private theatre of the Crown Princess at Berlin and that of Prince Henry at Reinsberg, where he stayed for seven years from April 1, 1780. His choruses to 'Athalia,' produced while there, were translated and brought out at Copenhagen, and the result was an offer from the King of Denmark to be his Capellmeister at a salary of 2000 thalers. This he accepted and held for eight years, from

1787, with great credit and advantage to the place. His health at length obliged him to leave, and he departed, Sept. 29, 1795, for Hamburg, Lüneburg, and Berlin. He lost his wife, and at length, on June 10, 1800, died at Schwedt deeply and widely lamented. Schulz was a prolific composer ; his operas are 'Clarisse' (1775), 'La fée Urgèle' (1782), 'Minona,' and ' Le Barbier de Séville' (1786), ' Aline' (1789) ; besides he wrote music to plays, and sacred music such as 'Christi Tod,' 'Maria und Johannes,' etc. The *Quellen-Lexikon* gives the names of many church and chamber works, as well as of his important song-collections. His literary works include a treatise on a new mode of writing music. He also edited Kirnberger's *Wahre Grundsätze zum Gebrauch der Harmonie* (1783). But his true claim to notice rests on his songs. He was the first to give the Volkslied an artistic turn. He was very careful to get good words, and as a considerable move was taking place among the poets at that date (1770-80), and Bürger, Claudius, Hölty, and others were writing, he had good opportunities, and many of his settings were published in the Göttingen *Musenalmanach* and Voss's *Almanach.* He published also 'Lieder in Volkston bey dem Klavier zu singen' (1782), containing forty-eight songs, 2nd ed. (1785) in two parts, and a third part in 1790. (See Reissmann, *Gesch. d. Deutschen Liedes,* p. 149.)　　G.

SCHULZE, J. F. & SONS, a firm of organ-builders, whose founder, J. F. Schulze, was born at Milbitz- bei - Paulinzella, Thuringia, in 1794, and began his manufactory there in 1825. His first organs were for Horba (with ten stops) and Milbitz (twenty-one stops). In 1825 he moved to Paulinzella, where his business largely increased. At this period his principal organs were those for Bremen cathedral and Solingen. In 1851, the firm sent an organ to the International Exhibition in Hyde Park, which obtained a prize medal and was the beginning of much work done for England. This is now in the Town Hall, Northampton. In 1854 they built the great organ in the Marienkirche at Lübeck. J. F. Schulze died in 1858, but was succeeded by his three sons, the most distinguished of whom was Heinrich Edmund, who introduced many improvements. On the rebuilding of the parish church of Doncaster, England, after the fire in 1853, the organ was rebuilt by the Schulze firm, with great success. Besides this fine instrument, their most important organs are in Bremen, Düsseldorf, Söst, and Aplerbeck. H. E. Schulze died in 1878 at the age of fifty-four, and shortly after, on the death of the surviving brother, the firm ceased to exist.

The Schulzes' organs are most celebrated for their flute-pipes, which are constructed so as to admit as much wind as possible. In order to do this the feet are opened very wide, and the pipes are in consequence cut up unusually high.

By this means, with a comparatively low pressure of wind an extraordinarily rich quantity of tone is produced. The Schulzes carried the same principles into their wooden flute pipes. Their organs are also celebrated for their string-toned stops, but the drawback in all of these is a certain slowness in their speech. Besides the organs at Doncaster and Northampton, the Schulzes have instruments in England at churches at Armley ; Leeds (in conjunction with Hill) ; Hindley, Wigan ; Tyne Dock, South Shields ; Harrogate; also at Northampton Town Hall ; Charter-house School, Godalming ; Seaton Carew (Thos. Walker, Esq.). w. b. s.

SCHUMANN, CLARA JOSEPHINE, wife of Robert Schumann, one of the greatest pianoforte players that the world has ever heard, was the daughter of FRIEDRICH WIECK, and was born at Leipzig, Sept. 13, 1819. She began the PF. at a very early age under her father's guidance ; and on Oct. 20, 1828, when she had just completed her ninth year, made her début in public at a concert of Frl. Perthaler's, where she played with Emilie Reinhold in Kalkbrenner's 4-hand variations on the March from 'Moïse.' The notices in the Leipzig *Tageblatt* and *A.M.Z.* show that she was already an object of much interest in the town. At this time she was accustomed to play the concertos of Mozart and Hummel with orchestra by heart, and thus early did she lay the foundation of that sympathy with the orchestra which so distinguished her. On Nov. 8, 1830, when just over eleven, she gave her first concert at the Gewandhaus under the good old name of 'Musikalische Akademie' ; and her performance is cited by the *A.M.Z.* as a proof how far application and good teaching can bring great natural gifts at so early an age. Her solo pieces were Rondo brillant (op. 101), Kalkbrenner ; Variations brillantes (op. 23), Herz ; and variations of her own on an original theme ; and she is praised by the critic just referred to for already possessing the brilliant style of the greatest players of the day. Her next appearance was on May 9, 1831, in pieces by Pixis and Herz —still bravura music. In the same year a set of four polonaises by her was published by Hofmeister. About this time she was taken to Weimar, Cassel, and Frankfort, and in the spring of 1832 to Paris, where she gave a concert on April 9 at which she extemporised for the first time in public. Mendelssohn was there at the time, but was suffering from an attack of cholera, and thus the meeting of these two great artists—destined to become such great friends—was postponed. On July 9, and July 31, 1832, she gives two other 'Musikalische Akademien' in Leipzig, at which, besides Pixis and Herz, we find Chopin's variations on 'La ci darem' (op. 2), a piece which, only a few months before, Robert Schumann had welcomed with his first and one of his most

spirited reviews. At the former of these two concerts Frl. Livia Gerhardt (Mme. Frege) sang in public for the first time.

On Sept. 30, 1832, Clara Wieck seems to have made her début at the Gewandhaus Concerts in Moscheles's G minor Concerto, and from that time forward her name is regularly found in the programmes of those famous Subscription Concerts, as well as of others held in the same hall. Hitherto, it will be observed, her music has been almost exclusively bravura ; but on Oct. 6, 1835, she played with Mendelssohn and Rakemann in Bach's triple Concerto in D minor, and about the same time Moscheles mentions her performance of one of Schubert's Trios, and Beethoven's Trio in B♭. On Dec. 15 she played Beethoven's Choral Fantasia. In the winter of 1837 she made her first visit to Vienna, and remained during the winter playing with great success, and receiving the appointment of 'Kk. Kammer-virtuosin.'

Schumann had been on a very intimate footing in the Wiecks' house for some years, but it was not till the end of 1835 that his attachment to Clara was openly avowed, and it was not till Sept. 12, 1840 (the eve of her birthday), after a series of delays and difficulties which are sufficiently touched upon in the article on Robert Schumann, that they were married. For eighteen months after this event Mme. Schumann remained in Leipzig. We find her name in the Gewandhaus programmes attached to the great masterpieces, but occasionally playing more modern music, as on Dec. 6, 1841, when she twice played with Liszt in a piece of his for two pianos. In the early part of 1842 she and her husband made a tour to Hamburg, which she continued alone as far as Copenhagen. Early in 1844 they went together to St. Petersburg, and at the end of the year Schumann's health made it necessary to leave Leipzig, and remove to Dresden, where they resided till 1850. During all this time Mme. Schumann's life was bound up with her husband's, and they were separated only by the exigencies of her profession. She devoted herself not only to his society, but to the bringing out of his music, much of which—such as the PF. Concerto, the Quintet, Quartet, and Trios, etc.— owed its first reputation to her. In 1846 she met Jenny Lind for the first time at Leipzig, and in the winter of the same year they met again at Vienna, when the two great artists appeared together at a concert in December. England, though at one time in view, was reserved to a later day. At Paris she never played after the early visit already spoken of. The trials which this faithful wife must have undergone during the latter part of her husband's life, from his first attempt at self-destruction to his death, July 29, 1856, need only be alluded to here. It was but shortly before the fatal crisis that she made her first visit to

England, playing at the Philharmonic on April 14 and 28, at the Musical Union on four separate occasions, and elsewhere, her last appearance being on June 24. On June 17 she gave an afternoon 'Recital' at the Hanover Square rooms, the programme of which is worth preserving. 1. Beethoven, Variations in E♭ on Theme from the Eroica ; 2. Sterndale Bennett, Two Diversions (op. 17), Suite de pièces (op. 24, No. 1) ; 3. Clara Schumann, Variations on theme from Schumann's 'Bunte Blätter' ; 4. Brahms, Sarabande and Gavotte in the style of Bach ; 5. Scarlatti, Piece in A major ; 6. R. Schumann's Carnaval (omitting Eusebius, Florestan, Coquette, Replique, Estrella, and Aveu). She returned from London to Bonn just in time to receive her husband's last breath (July 29, 1856).

After this event she and her family resided for some years in Berlin with her mother, who had separated from Wieck and had married a musician named Bargiel ; and in 1863 she settled at Baden-Baden, in the Lichtenthal, which then became her usual headquarters till 1874.

Her reception in this conservative country was hardly such as to encourage her to repeat her visit ; she appeared again at the Philharmonic on June 29, 1857, and on June 27, 1859. In a few years the appreciation of Schumann's music had greatly increased on this side the Channel ; and the anxiety of amateurs to hear an artist whose fame on the continent was so great, became so loudly expressed, that Mme. Schumann was induced to make another visit. She played at the Philharmonic, May 29, 1865, Musical Union, April 18, 25, and June 6, etc. etc. In 1867 she returned again, and after this her visit became an annual one up to 1882, interrupted only in 1878, 1879, 1880, when health and other circumstances did not permit her to travel. She came again in 1885, 1886, 1887, and 1888. In 1866 she again visited Austria, and gave six concerts at Vienna ; and any coldness that the Viennese may have previously shown towards her husband's compositions was then amply atoned for.

In 1878 she accepted the post of principal teacher of the pianoforte in the Conservatoire founded by Dr. Hoch at Frankfort, where she lived and worked with great success until the end of her life. She died there, May 20, 1896.

This is not the place or the time to speak of the charm of Madame Schumann's personality, of the atmosphere of noble and earnest simplicity which surrounded her in private life no less than in her public performance. Those who had the privilege of her acquaintance do not need such description, and for those who had not it is unnecessary to make the attempt. She was deeply and widely beloved, and at a time when there appeared to be a prospect of her being compelled by ill health to abandon her public appearances, the esteem and affection of her numerous friends took the practical form of a subscription, and a considerable sum of money was raised in Germany and England for her use.

———

I am indebted to Mr. Franklin Taylor for the following characterisation of Mme. Schumann's style and works.

As an artist, Mme. Schumann's place was indubitably in the very first rank, indeed she may perhaps be considered to stand higher than any of her contemporaries, if not as regards the possession of natural or acquired gifts, yet in the use she made of them. Her playing was characterised by an entire absence of personal display, a keen perception of the composer's meaning, and an unfailing power of setting it forth in perfectly intelligible form. These qualities would lead one to pronounce her one of the most intellectual of players, were it not that that term has come to imply a certain coldness or want of feeling, which was never perceived in her playing. But just such a use of the intellectual powers as serves the purposes of true art, ensuring perfect accuracy in all respects, no liberties being taken with the text, even when playing from memory, and above all securing an interpretation of the composer's work which is at once intelligible to the listener—this certainly formed an essential element of her playing, and it is worth while insisting on this, since the absence of that strict accuracy and perspicuity is too often mistaken for evidence of deep emotional intention. With all this, however, Mme. Schumann's playing evinced great warmth of feeling, and a true poet's appreciation of absolute beauty, so that nothing ever sounded harsh or ugly in her hands ; indeed it may fairly be said that after hearing her play a fine work (she never played what is not good), one always became aware that it contained beauties undiscovered before. This was, no doubt, partly due to the peculiarly beautiful quality of the tone she produced, which was rich and vigorous without the slightest harshness, and was obtained, even in the loudest passages, by pressure with the fingers rather than by percussion. Indeed, her playing was particularly free from violent movement of any kind ; in passages, the fingers were kept close to the keys and squeezed instead of striking them, while chords were grasped from the wrist rather than struck from the elbow. She founded her *technique* upon the principle laid down by her father, F. Wieck, who was also her instructor, that 'the touch (*i.e.* the blow of the finger upon the key) should never be audible, but only the musical sound,' an axiom the truth of which there is some danger of overlooking, in the endeavour to compass the extreme difficulties of certain kinds of modern pianoforte music.

Mme. Schumann's *répertoire* was very large

CLARA JOSEPHINE SCHUMANN

extending from Scarlatti and Bach to Mendelssohn, Chopin, and Brahms, and it would be difficult to say that she excelled in her rendering of any one composer's works rather than another's, unless it be in her interpretation of her husband's music. And even here, if she was pronounced by general opinion to be greatest in her playing of Schumann, it is probably because it was to her inimitable performances that we owe, in this country at least, the appreciation and love of his music now happily become universal, and thus the player shared in the acknowledgment she won for the composer.

Mme. Schumann's compositions, though not very numerous, evince that earnestness of purpose which distinguished her work in general. Even her earliest essays, which are short pianoforte-pieces written for the most part in dance-form, are redeemed from any approach to triviality by their interesting rhythms, and in particular by the freshness of their modulations, the latter being indeed in some cases original even to abruptness. Their general characteristic is that of delicacy rather than force, their frequent *staccato* passages and the many skipping grace-notes which are constantly met with requiring for their performance a touch of the daintiest lightness; although qualities of an opposite kind are occasionally shown, as in the 'Souvenir de Vienne,' op. 9, which is a set of variations in *bravura* style on Haydn's Austrian Hymn. Among her more serious compositions of later date are a Trio in G minor for pianoforte, violin and violoncello, op. 17, which is thoroughly musicianlike and interesting, three charming Cadenzas to Beethoven's Concertos, opp. 37 and 58, and a set of three Preludes and Fugues, op. 16, which deserve mention not only on account of their excellent construction, but as forming a most valuable study in *legato* part-playing. There is also a Piano Concerto, op. 7, dedicated to Spohr, of which the passages (though not the modulations) remind one of Hummel; but it is a short work and not well balanced, the first movement being reduced to a single solo, which ends on the dominant, and leads at once to the Andante.

In the later works, as might naturally be expected, there are many movements which bear traces of the influence of Schumann's music both in harmony and rhythm, but this influence, which first seems perceptible in the 'Soirées Musicales,' opp. 5, 6, is afterwards less noticeable in the pianoforte works than in the songs, many of which are of great beauty, and some of which (see op. 12) were incorporated into collections by Schumann. Her 'Liebst du um Schönheit' is one of the most expressive songs in existence. Schumann himself has made use of themes by Mme. Schumann in several instances, namely in his Impromptus, op. 5 (on the theme of her Variations op. 3, which

are dedicated to him), in the Andantino of his Sonata in F minor op. 14, and (as a 'motto') in the 'Davidsbündlertänze,' op. 6.

The following is a list of Mme. Schumann's compositions :—

Op.	
1. Quatre Polonaises.	15. Four pièces fugitives.
2. Caprices en forme de Valse.	16. Three preludes and fugues.
3. Romance variée.	17. Trio, PF. and Strings, G minor.
4. Valses Romantiques.	
5, 6. Soirées Musicales, 10 Pièces caractéristiques.	18. (?)
	19. (?)
7. Concerto for pianoforte in A minor.	20. Variations on a theme by Robert Schumann.[1]
8. Variations de Concert, in C, on the Cavatina in 'Il Pirata.'	21. Three romances.
	22. Three romances for PF. and violin.
9. Souvenir de Vienne in E♭, impromptu.	23. 6 Lieder from Rollet's 'Jucunde.'
10. Scherzo, D minor.	'Liebeszauber,' Lied by Geibel.
11. 3 Romances (Mechetti).	Andante and Allegro, PF. solo.
12. 3 Songs in R. Schumann's op. 37 (Nos. 2, 4, 11).	Cadenzas to Beethoven's Concertos in C minor and G, and to Mozart's in G minor.
13. 6 Lieder.	
14. 2nd Scherzo, in C minor.	

[A detailed biography was issued by Prof. Berthold Litzmann of Bonn in 1902-08. (Eng. trans. by G. E. Hadow, 2 vols., 1913.)] G.

SCHUMANN, GEORG ALFRED, born at Königstein on the Elbe, Oct. 25, 1866, was taught the violin by his father, the town musical director there, and the organ by his grandfather, with such good results that at nine years old he played in the orchestra, and at twelve did the organist's duty. At fifteen he played the piano in public, and after learning from some Dresden masters, he went to the Leipzig Conservatorium, remaining there from 1881 to 1888. In 1891-96 he was conductor of a choral society at Danzig, and from 1896 to 1899 director of the Philharmonic orchestra and choir in Bremen. In 1900 he was appointed royal Professor, and made head of the Berlin Singakademie. His compositions, though not very numerous as yet, are in all the larger forms excepting opera. His opus 3 is a choral work, 'Amor und Psyche'; a symphony in B minor won a prize, but has apparently not been published; his first published work for orchestra is a suite 'Zur Karnevalszeit,' op. 22. Op. 24 is a set of Symphonic Variations on 'Wer nur den lieben Gott lässt walten,' for organ and orchestra, and op. 30, 'Variationen und Doppelfuge über ein lustiges Thema für grosses Orchester,' shows much humour and technical skill; a serenade, op. 34, and an overture, 'Liebesfrühling,' are among the orchestral works which have reached their climax in a symphony in F minor, op. 42. Two choral works, the 'Totenklage,' op. 33, and 'Sehnsucht,' op. 40, deserve mention, and his chamber music includes variations and fugue on a theme of Beethoven for two pianos, a quintet for piano and strings in E minor, op. 18, a violoncello sonata, op. 19, two trios, in F and G, two violin sonatas in E minor and C sharp minor, and a pianoforte quartet for piano and strings in F minor, op. 29. Schumann belongs to the more conservative of the two great parties in

[1] From 'Bunte Blätter,' op. 99, No. 4; also varied by Brahms, op. 9.

modern German music, and his sound musicianship the originality of his ideas, and the skill of their treatment, mark him as a worthy member of the party which most strenuously resists the attacks of the ultra-modern writers. (Paul Hielscher, in *Monographen moderner Musiker* ; Riemann's *Lexikon*.)   M.

SCHUMANN, ROBERT ALEXANDER, born June 8, 1810, at Zwickau in Saxony, was the youngest son of Friedrich August Gottlob Schumann (born 1773), a bookseller, whose father was a clergyman in Saxony ; the composer's mother, Johanna Christiana (born 1771), was the daughter of Herr Schnabel, Rathschirurgus (surgeon to the town council) at Zeitz. Schumann cannot have received any incitement towards music from his parents ; his father, however, took a lively interest in the *belles lettres*, and was himself known as an author. He promoted his son's leanings towards art in every possible way, with which however his mother seems to have had no sympathy. In the small provincial town where Schumann spent the first eighteen years of his life there was no musician capable of helping him beyond the mere rudiments of the art. There was a talented town-musician, who for several decades was the best trumpeter in the district,[1] but, as was commonly the case, he practised his art simply as a trade. The organist of the Marienkirche, J. G. Kuntzsch, Schumann's first pianoforte teacher, after a few years declared that his pupil was able to progress alone, and that his instruction might cease. He was so impressed with the boy's talent, that when Schumann subsequently resolved to devote himself wholly to art, Kuntzsch prophesied that he would attain to fame and immortality, and that in him the world would possess one of its greatest musicians. Some twenty years later, in 1845, Schumann dedicated to him his Studies for the Pedal-Piano, op. 56. [See vol. ii. p. 612.]

His gift for music showed itself early. He began to compose, as he tells us himself, before he was seven. According to this he must have begun to play the piano, at latest, in his sixth year. When he was about eleven, he accompanied at a performance of Friedrich Schneider's ' Weltgericht,' conducted by Kuntzsch, standing up at the piano to do it. At home, with the aid of some young musical companions, he got up performances of vocal and instrumental music which he arranged to suit their humble powers. In more extended circles, too, he appeared as a pianoforte-player, and is said to have had a wonderful gift for extempore playing. His father took steps to procure for him the tuition of C. M. von Weber, who had shortly before (1817) been appointed Capellmeister in Dresden. Weber declared himself ready to undertake the guidance of the young genius, but the scheme fell through for reasons

[1] Schumann's *Gesammelte Schriften*, ii. 126 (1st ed.).

unknown. From that time Schumann remained at Zwickau, where circumstances were not favourable to musical progress ; he was left to his own instruction, and every inducement to further progress must have come from himself alone. Under these circumstances, a journey made when he was nine years old to Carlsbad, where he first heard a great pianoforte-player — Ignaz Moscheles—must have been an event never to be forgotten ; and indeed during his whole life he retained a predilection for certain of Moscheles's works, and a reverence for his person. The influence of the pianoforte technique of Moscheles on him appears very distinctly in the variations published as op. 1.

At the age of ten he entered the fourth class at the Gymnasium (or Academy) at Zwickau, and remained there till Easter, 1828. He had then risen to the first class, and left with a certificate of qualification for the University. During this period his devotion to music seems to have been for a time rather less eager, in consequence of the interference of his school-work and of other tastes. Now, at the close of his boyhood, a strong interest in poetry, which had been previously observed in him, but which had meanwhile been merged in his taste for music, revived with increased strength ; he rummaged through his father's book-shop, which favoured this tendency, in search of works on the art of poetry ; poetical attempts of his own were more frequent, and at the age of fourteen Robert had already contributed some literary efforts to a work brought out by his father and called *Bildergallerie der berühmtesten Menschen aller Völker und Zeiten*. That he had a gift for poetry is evident from two Epithalamia given by Wasielewski (*Biographie*, 3rd ed., Bonn, 1880, p. 305). In 1827 he set a number of his own poems to music, and it is worthy of note that it was not by the classical works of Goethe and Schiller that Schumann was most strongly attracted. His favourite writers were Schulze, author of ' Die bezauberte Rose ' ; the unhappy Franz von Sonnenberg ; Byron, and, above all, Jean Paul, with whose works he made acquaintance in his seventeenth year (at the same time as with the compositions of Franz Schubert). These poets represent the cycle of views, sentiments, and feelings, under whose spell Schumann's poetical taste, strictly speaking, remained throughout his life. And in no musician has the influence of his poetical tastes on his music been deeper than in him.

On March 29, 1828, Schumann matriculated at the University of Leipzig as *Studiosus Juris*. It would have been more in accordance with his inclinations to have devoted himself at once wholly to art, and his father would no doubt have consented to his so doing ; but he had lost his father in 1826, and his mother would not hear of an artist's career. Her son dutifully submitted, although he was decidedly averse to the study of jurisprudence. Before actually joining the university he took a short pleasure trip into South Germany, in April 1828. He had made acquaintance in Leipzig with a fellow-student named Gisbert Rosen; and a common enthusiasm for Jean Paul soon led to a devoted and sympathetic friendship. Rosen went to study at Heidelberg, and the first object of Schumann's journey was to accompany him on his way. In Munich he made the acquaintance of Heine, in whose house he spent several hours. On his return journey he stopped at Bayreuth to visit Jean Paul's widow, and received from her a portrait of her husband.

During the first few months of his university life, Schumann was in a gloomy frame of mind. A students' club to which he belonged for a time, struck him as coarse and shallow, and he could not make up his mind to begin the course of study he had selected. A large part of the first half-year had passed by and still—as he writes to his friend—he had been to no college, but 'had worked exclusively in private, that is to say, had played the piano and written a few letters and Jean Pauliads.'

In this voluntary inactivity and solitude the study of Jean Paul must certainly have had a special charm for him. That writer, unsurpassed in depicting the tender emotions, with his dazzling and even extravagant play of digressive fancy, his excess of feeling over dramatic power, his incessant alternations between tears and laughter, has always been the idol of sentimental women and ecstatic youths. 'If everybody read Jean Paul,' Schumann writes to Rosen, 'they would be better-natured, but they would be unhappier; he has often brought me to the verge of desperation, still the rainbow of peace bends serenely above all the tears, and the soul is wonderfully lifted up and tenderly glorified.' Even in his latest years Schumann would become violently angry if any one ventured to doubt or criticise Jean Paul's greatness as an imaginative writer, and the close affinity of their natures is unmistakable. Schumann himself tell us how once, as a child, at midnight, when all the household were asleep, he had in a dream and with his eyes closed, stolen down to the old piano, and played a series of chords, weeping bitterly the while. So early did he betray that tendency to overstrung emotion which found its most powerful nourishment in Jean Paul's writings.

Music, however, is a social art, and it soon brought him back again to human life. In the house of Professor Carus[1] he made several interesting acquaintances, especially that of Marschner, who was then living in Leipzig, and had brought out his 'Vampyr' there in the spring of 1828. His first meeting with Wieck,

the father of his future wife, took place in the same year; and Schumann took several pianoforte lessons from him. Several music-loving students met together there, and all kinds of chamber-music were practised. They devoted themselves with especial ardour to the works of Schubert, whose death, on Nov. 19, 1828, was deeply felt by Schumann. Impelled by Schubert's example, he wrote at this time eight Polonaises for four hands; also a Quartet for piano and strings, and a number of songs to Byron's words; all of which remain unpublished. Besides these occupations, he made a more intimate acquaintance with the clavier works of Sebastian Bach. It is almost self-evident that what chiefly fascinated Schumann in Bach's compositions was the mysterious depth of sentiment revealed in them. Were it not so, it would be impossible to conceive of Bach in connection with the chaotic Jean Paul; and yet Schumann himself says that in early life Bach and Jean Paul had exercised the most powerful influence upon him. Considering the way in which his musical education had been left to itself, the fact of his so thoroughly appreciating the wealth and fulness of life in Bach's compositions at a time when Bach was looked upon only as a great contrapuntist, is clear evidence of the greatness of his own genius, which indeed had some affinity to that of Bach. The ingenuity of outward form in Bach's works was neither strange nor unintelligible to him. For although Schumann had hitherto had no instructor in composition, it need scarcely be said that he had long ago made himself familiar with the most essential parts of the composer's art, and that constant practice in composition must have given him much knowledge and skill in this branch of his art.

At Easter, 1829, Schumann followed his friend Rosen to the university of Heidelberg. The young jurists were perhaps tempted thither by the lectures of the famous teacher, A. F. J. Thibaut; but it is evident that other things contributed to form Schumann's resolution: the situation of the town,—a perfect Paradise,—the gaiety of the people, and the nearness of Switzerland, Italy, and France. A delightful prospect promised to open to him there: 'That will be life indeed!' he writes to his friend; 'at Michaelmas we will go to Switzerland, and from thence who knows where?' On his journey to Heidelberg chance threw him into the society of Willibald Alexis. Alexis had trodden the path which Schumann was destined to follow, and had reached art by way of the law. No doubt this added to Schumann's interest in the acquaintance. It cannot be denied that even in Heidelberg Schumann carried on his legal studies in a very desultory manner, though Thibaut himself was a living proof that that branch of learning could co-exist with a true love and comprehension of music. Only a few years before (in 1825) Thibaut had published

[1] 'Patientibus Carus, sed clarus inter doctos.' (Berlioz, Voyage Musical, Letter IV.)

his little book, *Ueber Reinheit der Tonkunst*, a work which at that time essentially contributed to alter the direction of musical taste in Germany. Just as in his volume Thibaut attacks the degenerate state of church music, Schumann, at a later date, was destined to take up arms in word and deed, against the flat insipidity of concert and chamber music. Nevertheless the two men never became really intimate ; in one, no doubt, the *doctor* too greatly preponderated, and in the other the artist. Thibaut himself subsequently advised Schumann to abandon the law, and devote himself entirely to music.

Indeed, if Schumann was industrious in anything at Heidelberg it was in pianoforte-playing. After practising for seven hours in the day, he would invite a friend to come in the evening and play with him, adding that he felt in a particularly happy vein that day ; and even during an excursion with friends he would take a dumb keyboard with him in the carriage. By diligent use of the instruction he had received from Wieck in Leipzig, he brought himself to high perfection as an executant ; and at the same time increased his skill in improvisation. One of his musical associates at this time used afterwards to say that from the playing of no other artist, however great, had he ever experienced such ineffaceable musical impressions ; the ideas seem to pour into the player's mind in an inexhaustible flow, and their profound originality and poetic charm already clearly foreshadowed the main features of his musical individuality. Schumann appeared only once in public, at a concert given by a musical society at Heidelberg, where he played Moscheles's variations on the ' Alexandermarsch ' with great success. He received many requests to play again, but refused them all, probably, as a student, finding it not expedient.

It will no doubt be a matter of surprise that Schumann could have justified himself in thus spending year after year in a merely nominal study of the law, while in fact wholly given up to his favourite pursuit. A certain lack of determination, a certain shrinking from anything disagreeable, betray themselves during these years as his general characteristics, and were perhaps an integral part of his nature. At the same time his conduct is to a certain extent explicable, by the general conditions of German student-life. Out of the strict discipline of the Gymnasium the student steps at once into the unlimited freedom of the University. It was the intoxicating poetry of the student life which Schumann drank in deep draughts. Its coarseness was repellent to his refined nature, and his innate purity and nobility guarded him against moral degradation ; but he lived like a rover rejoicing in this bright world as it lies open to him, worked little, spent much, got into debt, and was as happy as a fish in the water. Besides its tender and rapturous side,

his nature had a vein of native sharpness and humour. With all these peculiarities he could live his student's life to the full, though in his own apparently quiet and unassertive way. The letters in which he discusses money-matters with his guardian, Herr Rudel, a merchant of Zwickau, show how he indulged his humorous mood even in these : ' Dismal things I have to tell you, respected Herr Rudel,' he writes on June 21, 1830 ; 'in the first place, that I have a *repetitorium* which costs eighty gulden every half-year, and secondly, that within a week I have been under arrest by the town (don't be shocked) for not paying thirty gulden of other college dues.' And on another occasion, when the money he had asked for to make a journey home for the holidays did not arrive : ' I am the only student here, and wander alone about the streets and woods, forlorn and poor, like a beggar, and with debts into the bargain. Be kind, most respected Herr Rudel, and only this once send me some money—only money— and do not drive me to seek means of setting out which might not be pleasant to you.' The reasons he employs to prove to his guardian that he ought not to be deprived of means for a journey into Italy are most amusing : ' At any rate I shall have made the journey : and as I *must* make it once, it is all the same whether I use the money for it now or later.' His compositions, too, plainly show how deeply the poetical aspect of student life had affected him, and had left its permanent mark on him. I need only remind the reader of Kerner's ' Wanderlied ' (op. 35, No. 3), dedicated to an old fellow-student at Heidelberg, and of Eichendorff's 'Frühlingsfahrt' (op. 45, No. 2). Among German songs of the highest class, there is not one in which the effervescent buoyancy of youth craving for distant flights has found such full expression, at once so thoroughly German and so purely ideal, as in this ' Wanderlied,' which indeed, with a different tune, is actually one of the most favourite of student songs. ' Frühlingsfahrt' tells of two young comrades who quit home for the first time, one of whom soon finds a regular subsistence and a comfortable home, while the other pursues glittering visions, yields to the thousand temptations of the world, and finally perishes ; it is a portrait of a German student drawn from the life, and the way in which Schumann has treated it shows that he was drawing on the stores of his own experience.

Several journeys also served to infuse into Schumann's student life the delight of free and unrestrained movement. In August 1829 he went for a pleasure trip to North Italy, quite alone, for two friends who had intended to go failed him. But perhaps the contemplative and dreamy youth enjoyed the loveliness of the country and the sympathetic Italian nature only the more thoroughly for being alone. Nor were little adventures of gallantry wanting. Fragments of a diary kept at this time, which are preserved (Wasielewski, p. 325), reveal to us the pleasant sociableness of the life which Schumann now delighted in. The Italian music which he then heard could indeed do little towards his improvement, except that it gave him, for the first time, the opportunity of hearing Paganini. The deep impression made by that remarkable player is shown by Schumann's visit to Frankfort (Easter, 1830) with several friends to hear him again, and by his arrangement of his 'Caprices' for the pianoforte (opp. 3 and 10). Shortly after this he seems to have heard Ernst also in Frankfort. In the summer of 1830 he made a tour to Strasburg, and on the way back to Saxony visited his friend Rosen at Detmold.

When Schumann entered upon his third year of study, he made a serious effort to devote himself to jurisprudence; he took what was called a *Repetitorium*, that is, he began going over again with considerable difficulty, and under the care and guidance of an old lawyer, what he had neglected during two years. He also endeavoured to reconcile himself to the idea of practical work in public life or the government service. His spirit soared up to the highest goal, and at times he may have flattered his fancy with dreams of having attained it; but he must have been convinced of the improbability of such dreams ever coming true; and indeed he never got rid of his antipathy to the law as a profession, even in the whole course of his *Repetitorium*. On the other hand, it must be said, that if he was ever to be a musician, it was becoming high time for it, since he was now twenty years old. Thus every consideration urged him to the point. Schumann induced his mother, who was still extremely averse to the calling of a musician, to put the decision in the hands of Friedrich Wieck. Wieck did not conceal from him that such a step ought only to be taken after the most thorough self-examination, but if he had already examined himself, then Wieck could only advise him to take the step. Upon this his mother yielded, and Robert Schumann became a musician. The delight and freedom which he inwardly felt when the die was cast, must have shown him that he had done right. At first his intention was only to make himself a great pianoforte-player, and he reckoned that in six years he would be able to compete with any pianist. But he still felt very uncertain as to his gift as a composer; the words which he wrote to his mother on July 30, 1830—'Now and then I discover that I have imagination, and perhaps a turn for creating things myself' —sound curiously wanting in confidence, when we remember how almost exclusively Schumann's artistic greatness was to find expression in his compositions.

He quitted Heidelberg late in the summer of 1830, in order to resume his studies with Wieck in Leipzig. He was resolved, after having wasted two years and a half, to devote himself to his new calling with energetic purpose and manly vigour. And faithfully did he keep to his resolution. The plan of becoming a great pianist had, however, to be given up after a year. Actuated by the passionate desire to achieve a perfect *technique* as speedily as possible, Schumann devised a contrivance by which the greatest possible dexterity of finger was to be attained in the shortest time. By means of this ingenious appliance the third finger was drawn back and kept still, while the other fingers had to practise exercises. But the result was that the tendons of the third finger were overstrained, the finger was crippled, and for some time the whole right hand was injured. This most serious condition was alleviated by medical treatment. Schumann recovered the use of his hand, and could, when needful, even play the piano; but the third finger remained useless, so that he was for ever precluded from the career of a virtuoso. Although express evidence is wanting, we may assume with certainty that this unexpected misfortune made a deep impression upon him; he saw himself once more confronted with the question whether it was advisable for him to continue in the calling he had chosen. That he answered it in the affirmative shows that during this time his confidence in his own creative genius had wonderfully increased. He soon reconciled himself to the inevitable, learned to appreciate mechanical dexterity at its true value, and turned his undivided attention to composition. He continued henceforth in the most friendly relations with his pianoforte-master, Wieck; indeed until the autumn of 1832 he lived in the same house with him (Grimmaische Strasse, No. 36), and was almost one of the family. For his instructor in composition, however, he chose Heinrich Dorn, at that time conductor of the opera in Leipzig, subsequently Capellmeister at Riga, Cologne, and Berlin, who lived till 1892. Dorn was a clever and sterling composer; he recognised the greatness of Schumann's genius, and devoted himself with much interest to his improvement.[1] It was impossible as yet to confine Schumann to a regular course of composition: he worked very diligently, but would take up now one point of the art of composition and now another. In 1836 he writes to Dorn at Riga that he often regrets having learnt in too irregular a manner at this time; but when he adds directly afterwards that, notwithstanding this, he had learnt more from Dorn's teaching than Dorn would believe, we may take this last statement as true. Schumann was no longer a tyro in composition, but had true musical genius, and his spirit was already matured. Under such

[1] Schumann's gratitude to him is thus expressed:—'The man who first gave a hand to me as I climbed upwards, and, when I began to doubt myself, drew me aloft so that I should see less of the common herd of mankind, and more of the pure air of art.'

circumstances he was justified in learning in his own way.

In the winter of 1832-33, he lived at Zwickau, and for a time also with his brothers at Schneeberg. Besides a pianoforte-concerto, which still remains a fragment, he was working at a symphony in G minor, of which the first movement was publicly performed in the course of the winter both at Schneeberg and Zwickau. If we may trust the evidence of the *Musikalisches Wochenblatt*, Leipzig, 1875, p. 180, the whole symphony was performed at Zwickau in 1835, under Schumann's own direction, and the last movement was almost a failure.

At all events the symphony was finished, and Schumann expected it to be a great success ; in this he must have been disappointed, for it has never been published. The first performance of the first movement at Zwickau took place at a concert given there on Nov. 18, 1832, by Wieck's daughter Clara, who was then thirteen years of age. Even then the performances of this gifted girl, who was so soon to take her place as the greatest female pianist of Germany, were astonishing, and by them, as Schumann puts it, 'Zwickau was fired with enthusiasm for the first time in its life.' It is easily conceivable that Schumann himself was enthusiastically delighted with Clara, adorned as she was with the twofold charm of childlike sweetness and artistic genius. 'Think of perfection,' he writes to a friend about her on April 5, 1833, 'and I will agree to it.' And many expressions in his letters seem even to betray a deeper feeling, of which he himself did not become fully aware until several years later.

Schumann's circumstances allowed him to revisit Leipzig in March 1833, and even to live there for a time without any definite occupation. He was not exactly well off, but he had enough to enable him to live as a single man of moderate means. The poverty from which so many of the greatest musicians have suffered, never formed part of Schumann's experience. He occupied himself with studies in composition chiefly in the contrapuntal style, in which he had taken the liveliest interest since making the acquaintance of Bach's works ; besides this his imagination, asserting itself more and more strongly, impelled him to the creation of free compositions. From this year date the impromptus for piano on a romance by Clara Wieck, which Schumann dedicated to her father, and published in August 1833, as op. 5. In June he wrote the first and third movements of the G minor Sonata (op. 22), and at the same time began the F♯ minor Sonata (op. 11) and completed the Toccata (op. 7), which had been begun in 1829. He also arranged a second set of Paganini's violin caprices for the piano (op. 10), having made a first attempt of the same kind (op. 3) in the previous year. Meanwhile he lived a quiet and almost monotonous life. Of family acquaintances he had few, nor did he seek them. He found a faithful friend in Frau Henriette Voigt, who was as excellent a pianist as she was noble and sympathetic in soul. She was a pupil of Ludwig Berger, of Berlin, and died young in the year 1839. Schumann was wont as a rule to spend his evenings with a small number of intimate friends in a restaurant. These gatherings generally took place at the ' Kaffeebaum ' (Kleine Fleischergasse, No. 3). He himself, however, generally remained silent by preference, even in this confidential circle of friends. Readily as he could express himself with his pen, he had but little power of speech. Even in affairs of no importance, which could have been transacted most readily and simply by word of mouth, he usually preferred to write. It was, moreover, a kind of enjoyment to him to muse in dreamy silence. Henriette Voigt told W. Taubert that one lovely summer evening, after making music with Schumann, they both felt inclined to go on the water. They sat side by side in the boat for an hour in silence. At parting Schumann pressed her hand and said, ' To-day we have perfectly understood one another.'

It was at these evening gatherings at the restaurant in the winter of 1833-34 that the plan of starting a new musical paper was matured. It was the protest of youth, feeling itself impelled to new things in art, against the existing state of music. Although Weber, Beethoven, and Schubert had only been dead a few years, though Spohr and Marschner were still in their prime, and Mendelssohn was beginning to be celebrated, the general characteristic of the music of about the year 1830 was either superficiality or else vulgar mediocrity. ' On the stage Rossini still reigned supreme, and on the pianoforte scarcely anything was heard but Herz and Hünten.' Under these conditions the war might have been more suitably carried on by means of important works of art than by a periodical *about* music. Musical criticism, however, was itself in a bad way at this time. The periodical called *Cæcilia*, published by Schott, which had been in existence since 1824, was unfitted for the general reader, both by its contents and by the fact of its publication in parts. The *Berliner allgemeine musikalische Zeitung*, conducted by Marx, had come to an end in 1830. The only periodical of influence and importance in 1833 was the *Allgemeine musikalische Zeitung*, published by Breitkopf & Härtel of Leipzig, and at that time edited by G. W. Fink. But the narrow view taken of criticism in that periodical, its inane mildness of judgment—Schumann used to call it ' Honigpinselei ' or ' Honey-daubing ' —its lenity towards the reigning insipidity and superficiality, could not but provoke contradiction from young people of high aims. And the idea of first bringing the lever to bear on the domain of critical authorship, in order to try their strength, must have been all the more attractive to these hot-headed youths, since most of them had had the advantage of a sound scholarly education and knew how to handle their pens. On the other hand, they felt that they were not yet strong enough to guide tl public taste into new paths by their own musical productions ; and of all the set Schumann was the most sensible of this fact.

Such were the grounds on which, on April 3, 1834, the first number of the *Neue Zeitschrift für Musik* saw the light. Schumann himself called it the organ of youth and movement. As its motto he even chose this passage from the prologue to Shakespeare's *Henry VIII.* :—

> Only they
> Who come to hear a merry bawdy play,
> A noise of targets, or to see a fellow
> In a long motley coat guarded with yellow,
> Will be deceived—

a passage which sufficiently expresses his intention of contending against an empty flattering style of criticism, and upholding the dignity of art. ' The day of reciprocal compliments,' says the preliminary notice, ' is gradually dying out, and we must confess that we shall do nothing towards reviving it. The critic who dares not attack what is bad, is but a half-hearted supporter of what is good.' The doings of ' the three arch-foes of art—those who have no talent, those who have vulgar talent, and those who, having real talent, write too much,' are not to be left in peace ; ' their latest phase, the result of a mere cultivation of executive *technique*,' it is to be opposed as inartistic. ' The older time,' on the other hand, ' and the works it produced, are to be recalled with insistence, since it is only at these pure sources that new beauties in art can be found.' Moreover, the *Zeitschrift* is to assist in bringing in a new ' poetic ' period by its benevolent encouragement of the higher efforts of young artists, and to accelerate its advent. The editing was in the hands of Robert Schumann, Friedrich Wieck, Ludwig Schunke, and Julius Knorr.

Of all these Schunke alone was exclusively a musician. That gifted pianist, who belonged to a widely dispersed family of esteemed musicians, came to Leipzig in 1833, and became a great friend of Schumann's, but died at the end of the following year at the early age of twenty-four. The three other editors were by education half musicians and half *littérateurs*, even Julius Knorr (born 1807) having studied philology in Leipzig. Schumann co-operated largely in Schunke's contributions (signed with the figure 3), for handling the pen was not easy to him. Hartmann of Leipzig was at first the publisher and proprietor of the *Zeitschrift*, but at the beginning of 1835 it passed into the hands of J. A. Barth of Leipzig, Schumann becoming at the same time proprietor and sole editor. He continued the undertaking under

these conditions till the end of June 1844 ; so that his management of the paper extended over a period of above ten years. On Jan. 1, 1845, Franz Brendel became the editor, and after the summer of 1844 Schumann never again wrote for it, with the exception of a short article [1] on Johannes Brahms to be mentioned hereafter.

Schumann's own articles are sometimes signed with a number—either 2 or some combination with 2, such as 12, 22, etc. He also concealed his identity under a variety of names—Florestan, Eusebius, Raro, Jeanquirit. In his articles we meet with frequent mention of the Davidsbündler, a league or society of artists or friends of art who had views in common. This was purely imaginary, a half-humorous, half-poetical fiction of Schumann's, existing only in the brain of its founder, who thought it well fitted to give weight to the expression of various views of art, which were occasionally put forth as its utterances. The characters which most usually appear are Florestan and Eusebius, two personages in whom Schumann endeavoured to embody the dual sides of his nature. The vehement, stormy, rough element is represented by Florestan ; the gentler and more poetic by Eusebius. These two figures are obviously imitated from Vult and Walt in Jean Paul's *Flegeljahre* ; indeed Schumann's literary work throughout is strongly coloured with the manner of Jean Paul, and frequent reference is made to his writings. Now and then, as moderator between these antagonistic characters, who of course take opposite views in criticism, ' Master Raro ' comes in. In him Schumann has conceived a character such as at one time he had himself dreamed of becoming. The explanation of the name 'Davidsbündler' is given at the beginning of a 'Shrove Tuesday discourse' by Florestan in the year 1835. ' The hosts of David are youths and men destined to slay all the Philistines, musical or other.' In the college-slang of Germany the ' Philistine' is the non-student who is satisfied to live on in the ordinary routine of every-day life, or—which comes to the same thing in the student's mind—the man of narrow, sober, prosaic views, as contrasted with the high-flown poetry and enthusiasm of the social life of a German university. Thus, in the name of Idealism, the 'Davidsbündler' wage war against boorish mediocrity, and when Schumann regarded it as the function of his paper to aid in bringing in a new ' poetical phase ' in music he meant just this. Though Schumann was himself the sole reality in the 'Davidsbündlerschaft,' he indulged his fancy by introducing personages of his acquaintance whose agreement with his views he was sure of. He quietly included all the principal co-operators in the *Zeitschrift*, and even artists such as Berlioz, whom he did not know, but in whom he felt an interest, and was thus justified in writing to A. von Zuccalmaglio in

[1] *Neue Bahnen,* Oct. 28, 1853.

1836 : 'By the Davidsbund is figured an intellectual brotherhood which ramifies widely, and I hope may bear golden fruit.' He brings in the brethren, who are not actually himself, from time to time in the critical discussions : and the way in which he contrives to make this motley troop of romantic forms live and move before the eyes of the reader is really quite magical. He could say with justice : 'We are now living a romance the like of which has perhaps never been written in any book.' We meet with a Jonathan, who may perhaps stand for Schunke (on another occasion, however, Schumann designates himself by this name) ; a Fritz Friedrich probably meant for Lyser[1] the painter, a lover of music ; Serpentin is Carl Banck, a clever composer of songs, who at the outset was one of his most zealous and meritorious fellow-workers ; Gottschalk Wedel is Anton von Zuccalmaglio, then living in Warsaw, who had made a name by his collection of German and foreign Volkslieder ; Chiara is of course Clara Wieck, and Zilia (apparently shortened from Cecilia) is probably the same. Felix Mendelssohn appears under the name of Felix Meritis, and the name Walt occurs once (in 1836, *Aus den Büchern der Davidsbündler*, ii. Tanzlitteratur). It cannot be asserted that any particular person was meant, still his direct reference to Jean Paul's *Flegeljahre* is interesting. There is also a certain Julius among the 'Davidsbündler,' probably Julius Knorr. The name occurs in Schumann's first essay on music, 'Ein opus ii.' This is not included in the *Neue Zeitschrift*, but appears in No. 49 of the *Allgemeine Musikalische Zeitung* for 1831 (then edited by Fink). The editor has prefixed a note to the effect that 'it is by a young man, a pupil of the latest school, who has given his name,' and contrasts it with the anonymous work of a reviewer of the old school discussing the same piece of music. The contrast is indeed striking, and the imaginative flights of enthusiastic young genius look strange enough among the old-world surroundings of the rest of the paper.

Schumann placed this critique—which deals with Chopin's variations on 'La ci darem'—at the beginning of his collected writings, which he published towards the close of his life (*Gesammelte Schriften*, 4 vols. Georg Wigand, Leipzig, 1854). It is a good example of the tone which he adopted in the *Neue Zeitschrift*. His fellow-workers fell more or less into the same key, not from servility, but because they were all young men, and because the reaction against the Philistine style of criticism was just then in the air. This may be plainly detected, for instance, in a critique written by Wieck for the periodical called *Cæcilia*, on Chopin's airs with variations. It is easy to

understand that the total novelty of the style of writing of the *Neue Zeitschrift* should have attracted attention to music ; the paper soon obtained a comparatively large circulation ; and as, besides the charm of novelty and style, it offered a variety of instructive and entertaining matter, and discussed important subjects earnestly and cleverly, the interest of the public was kept up, and indeed constantly increased, from year to year. The influence exerted by Schumann on musical art in Germany through the medium of this paper, cannot but be regarded as very important.

It has been sometimes said that Schumann's literary labours must have done him mischief, by taking up time and energy which might have been better employed in composition. But this view seems to me untenable. Up to the period at which we have now arrived, Schumann, on his own statement, had merely dreamed away his life at the piano. His tendency to self-concentration, his shyness, and his independent circumstances, placed him in danger of never achieving that perfect development of his powers which is possible only by vigorous exercise. Now the editing of a journal is an effectual remedy for dreaming ; and when, at the beginning of 1835, he became sole editor, however much he may have felt the inexorable necessity of satisfying his readers week after week, and of keeping his aim constantly in view, it was no doubt a most beneficial exercise for his will and energies. He was conscious of this, or he certainly would not have clung to the paper with such affection and persistency ; and it is a matter of fact that the period of his happiest and most vigorous creativeness coincides pretty nearly with that during which he was engaged on the *Zeitschrift*. Hence, to suppose that his literary work was any drawback to his artistic career is an error, though it is true that as he gradually discovered the inexhaustible fertility of his creative genius, he sometimes complained that the details of an editor's work were a burthen to him. Besides, the paper was the medium by which Schumann was first brought into contact and intercourse with the most illustrious artists of his time ; and living as he did apart from all the practically musical circles of Leipzig, it was almost the only link between himself and the contemporary world.

Nor must we overlook the fact that certain peculiar gifts of Schumann's found expression in his writings on musical subjects, gifts which would otherwise scarcely have found room for display. His poetic talent was probably neither rich enough nor strong enough for the production of large independent poems ; but, on the other hand, it was far too considerable to be condemned to perpetual silence. In his essays and critiques, which must be regarded rather as poetic flights and sympathetic inter-

---

[1] Author of the sketch of Beethoven engraved at p. 225 of vol. i. of this Dictionary.

pretations than as examples of incisive analysis, his poetical gift found a natural outlet, and literature is by so much the richer for them. Nay, it is a not unreasonable speculation whether, if his imaginative powers had not found this vent they might not have formed a disturbing and marring element in his musical creations. Even as it is, poetical imagery plays an important part in Schumann's music, though without seriously overstepping the permissible limits. This, too, we may safely say, that in spite of his silent and self-contained nature, there was in Schumann a vein of the genuine *agitator*, in the best and noblest sense of the word ; he was possessed by the conviction that the development of German art, then in progress, had not yet come to its final term, and that a new phase of its existence was at hand. Throughout his writings we find this view beautifully and poetically expressed, as for instance, ' Consciously or unconsciously a new and as yet undeveloped school is being founded on the basis of the Beethoven-Schubert romanticism, a school which we may venture to expect will mark a special epoch in the history of art. Its destiny seems to be to usher in a period which will nevertheless have many links to connect it with the past century.' Or again : ' A rosy light is dawning in the sky ; whence it cometh I know not ; but in any case, O youth, make for the light.'

To rouse fresh interest and make use of that already existing for the advancement of this new movement was one of his deepest instincts, and this he largely accomplished by means of his paper. From his pen we have articles on almost all the most illustrious composers of his generation — Mendelssohn, Taubert, Chopin, Hiller, Heller, Henselt, Sterndale Bennett, Gade, Kirchner, and Franz, as well as Johannes Brahms, undoubtedly the most remarkable composer of the generation after Schumann. On some he first threw the light of intelligent and enthusiastic literary sympathy ; others he was actually the first to introduce to the musical world ; and even Berlioz, a Frenchman, he eulogised boldly and successfully, recognising in him a champion of the new idea. By degrees he would naturally discern that he had thus prepared the soil for the reception of his own works. He felt himself in close affinity with all these artists, and was more and more confirmed in his conviction that he too had something to say to the world that it had not heard before. In the *Zeitschrift* he must have been aware that he controlled a power which would serve to open a shorter route for his own musical productions. ' If the publisher were not afraid of the editor, the world would hear nothing of me—perhaps to the world's advantage. And yet the black heads of the printed notes are very pleasant to behold.' ' To give up the paper would involve the loss of all the reserve

force which every artist ought to have if he is to produce easily and freely.'

So he wrote in 1836 and 1837. But at the same time we must emphatically contradict the suggestion that Schumann used his paper for selfish ends. His soul was too entirely noble and his ideal aims too high to have any purpose in view but the advancement of art ; and it was only in so far as his own interests were inseparable from those of his whole generation, that he would ever have been capable of forwarding the fortunes of his own works. The question even whether, and in what manner, his own works should be discussed in the *Neue Zeitschrift* he always treated with the utmost tact. In one of his letters he clearly expresses his principles on the subject as follows : ' I am, to speak frankly, too proud to attempt to influence Härtel through Fink (editor of the *Allgemeine mus. Zeitung*) ; and I hate, at all times, any mode of instigating public opinion by the artist himself. What is strong enough works its own way.'

His efforts for the good cause indeed went beyond essay-writing and composing. Extracts from a note-book published by Wasielewski prove that he busied himself with a variety of plans for musical undertakings of general utility. Thus he wished to compile lives of Beethoven and of Bach, with a critique of all their works, and a biographical dictionary of living musicians, on the same plan. He desired that the relations of operatic composers and managers should be regulated by law. He wished to establish an agency for the publication of musical works, so that composers might derive greater benefit from their publications, and gave his mind to a plan for founding a Musical Union in Saxony, with Leipzig as its headquarters, to be the counterpart of Schilling's Deutscher National Verein für Musik.

In the first period of his editorship, before he had got into the way of easily mastering his day's labour, and when the regular round of work had still the charm of novelty, it was of course only now and then that he had leisure, or felt in the mood, for composing. Two great pianoforte works date from 1834 (the 'Carnaval,' op. 9, and the 'Études Symphoniques,' op. 13), but in 1835 nothing was completed. After this, however, Schumann's genius began again to assert itself, and in the years 1836 to 1839 he composed that splendid set of pianoforte works of the highest excellence, on which a considerable part of his fame rests ; viz. the great Fantasia (op. 17), the F minor Sonata (op. 14), Fantasiestücke (op. 12), Davidsbündlertänze, Novelletten, Kinderscenen, Kreisleriana, Humoreske, Faschingsschwank, Romanzen, and others. The fount of his creative genius flowed forth ever clearer and more abundantly. ' I used to rack my brains for a long time,' writes he on March 15, 1839, ' but now I scarcely ever scratch out a note. It all comes from within, and I often feel as if I could go playing straight on without ever coming to an end.' The influence of Schumann the author on Schumann the composer may often be detected. Thus the 'Davidsbündler' come into his music, and the composition which bears their name was originally entitled 'Davidsbündler, dances for the Pianoforte, dedicated to Walther von Goethe by Florestan and Eusebius.' The title of the F♯ minor Sonata, op. 11, which was completed in 1835, runs thus : 'Pianoforte Sonata. Dedicated to Clara by Florestan and Eusebius.' In the 'Carnaval,' a set of separate and shorter pieces with a title to each, the names of Florestan and Eusebius occur again, as do those of Chiarina (the diminutive of Clara), and Chopin ; the whole concluding with a march of the Davidsbündler against the Philistines.

The reception of Schumann's works by the critics was most favourable and encouraging, but the public was repelled by their eccentricity and originality ; and it was not till after the appearance of the 'Kinderscenen' (1839) that they began to be appreciated. Opp. 1 and 2 actually had the honour of a notice in the Vienna *Musikalische Zeitung* of 1832, by no less a person than Grillparzer the poet. Fink designedly took hardly any notice of Schumann in the *Allgemeine musikalische Zeitung*. But Liszt wrote a long, discriminating, and very favourable article in the *Gazette Musicale* of 1837 upon the Impromptus (op. 5), and the Sonatas in F♯ minor and F minor. Moscheles wrote very sympathetically on the two sonatas in the *Neue Zeitschrift für Musik* itself (vols. 5 and 6), and some kind words of recognition of Schumann's genius were published subsequently from his diary (*Moscheles' Leben*, Leipzig, 1873, vol. ii. p. 15 ; English translation by A. D. Coleridge, vol. ii. pp. 19, 20). Other musicians, though not expressing their sentiments publicly, continued to hold aloof from him. Hauptmann at that time calls Schumann's pianoforte compositions 'pretty and curious little things, all wanting in proper solidity, but otherwise interesting.' (See Hauptmann's *Letters to Hauser*, Leipzig, 1871, vol. i. p. 255.)

In October 1835 the musical world of Leipzig was enriched by the arrival of Mendelssohn. It was already in a flourishing state : operas, concerts, and sacred performances alike were of great excellence, and well supported by the public. But although the soil was well prepared before Mendelssohn's arrival, it was he who raised Leipzig to the position of the most musical town of Germany. The extraordinarily vigorous life that at once grew up there under the influence of his genius, drawing to itself from far and near the most important musical talent of the country, has shown itself to be of so enduring a character that even at the present day its influences are felt. Schumann too, who

had long felt great respect for Mendelssohn, was drawn into his circle. On Oct. 4, 1835, Mendelssohn conducted his first concert in the Gewandhaus ; the day before this there was a musical gathering at the Wiecks', at which both Mendelssohn and Schumann were present, and it seems to have been on this occasion that the two greatest musicians of their time first came into close personal intercourse. (*Moscheles' Leben*, vol. i. p. 301 ; English translation, vol. i. p. 322.) On Oct. 5, Mendelssohn, Schumann, Moscheles, Banck, and a few others, dined together. In the afternoon of the 6th there was again music at Wieck's house ; Moscheles, Clara Wieck, and L. Rakemann from Bremen, played Bach's D minor Concerto for three claviers, Mendelssohn putting in the orchestral accompaniments on a fourth piano. Moscheles had come over from Hamburg, where he was staying on a visit, to give a concert in Leipzig. Schumann had already been in correspondence with him, but this was the first opportunity he had enjoyed of making the personal acquaintance of the man whose playing had so delighted him in Carlsbad when a boy of nine. Moscheles describes him as 'a retiring but interesting young man,' and the F♯ minor Sonata, played to him by Clara Wieck, as 'very laboured, difficult, and somewhat intricate, although interesting.'

A livelier intimacy, so far as Schumann was concerned, soon sprang up between him and Mendelssohn. When Mendelssohn had to go to Düsseldorf in May 1836, to the first performance of 'St. Paul' at the Niederrheinische Musikfest, Schumann even intended to go with him, and was ready months beforehand, though when the time arrived he was prevented from going. They used to like to dine together, and gradually an interesting little circle was formed around them, including among others Ferdinand David, whom Mendelssohn had brought to Leipzig as leader of his orchestra. In the early part of January 1837 Mendelssohn and Schumann used in this way to meet every day and interchange ideas, so far as Schumann's silent temperament would allow. Subsequently when Mendelssohn was kept more at home by his marriage, this intercourse became rarer. Schumann was by nature unsociable, and at this time there were outward circumstances which rendered solitude doubly attractive to him. Ferdinand Hiller, who spent the winter of 1839-40 in Leipzig with Mendelssohn, relates that Schumann was at that time living the life of a recluse and scarcely ever came out of his room. Mendelssohn and Schumann felt themselves drawn together by mutual appreciation. The artistic relations between the two great men were not as yet, however, thoroughly reciprocal. Schumann admired Mendelssohn to the point of enthusiasm. He declared him to be the best musician then living, said that he looked up to him as to a high mountain-peak, and that even in his daily talk about art some thought at least would be uttered worthy of being graven in gold. And when he mentions him in his writings, it is in a tone of enthusiastic admiration, which shows in the best light Schumann's fine ideal character, so remarkable for its freedom from envy. And his opinion remained unaltered : in 1842 he dedicated his three string quartets to Mendelssohn, and in the 'Album für die Jugend' there is a little piano piece called 'Erinnerung,' dated Nov. 4, 1847, which shows with eloquent simplicity how deeply he felt the early death of his friend. It is well known how he would be moved out of his quiet stillness if he heard any disparaging expression used of Mendelssohn. Mendelssohn, on the contrary, at first only saw in Schumann the man of letters and the art-critic. Like most productive musicians, he had a dislike to such men as a class, however much he might love and value single representatives, as was really the case with regard to Schumann. From this point of view must be regarded the expressions which he makes use of now and then in letters concerning Schumann as an author. (See Mendelssohn's *Briefe*, ii. 116 ; Lady Wallace's translation, ii. 97 ;[1] and Hiller's *Felix Mendelssohn Bartholdy*, Cologne, 1878, p. 64.) If they sound somewhat disparaging, we must remember that it is not the personal Mendelssohn speaking against the personal Schumann, but rather the creative artist speaking against the critic, always in natural opposition to him. Indeed it is obviously impossible to take such remarks in a disadvantageous sense, as Schumann quite agreed with Mendelssohn on the subject of criticism. One passage in his writings is especially remarkable in this respect. He is speaking of Chopin's pianoforte concerto, and Florestan exclaims, ' What is a whole year of a musical paper compared to a concerto by Chopin ? What is a magister's rage compared to the poetic frenzy ? What are ten complimentary addresses to the editor compared to the Adagio in the second Concerto ? And believe me, Davidites, I should not think you worth the trouble of talking to, did I not believe you capable of composing such works as those you write about, with the exception of a few like this concerto. Away with your musical journals ! It should be the highest endeavour of a just critic to render himself wholly unnecessary ; the best discourse on music is silence. Why write about Chopin ? Why not create at first hand—play, write, and compose ?' (*Gesammelte Schriften*, i. 276 ; Engl. trans. in *Music and Musicians*, series i. p. 205.) True, this impassioned outburst has to be moderated by Eusebius. But consider the significance of Schumann's writing thus in

his own journal about the critic's vocation ! It plainly shows that he only took it up as an artist, and occasionally despised it. But with regard to Schumann's place in art, Mendelssohn did not, at that time at all events, consider it a very high one, and he was not alone in this opinion. It was shared, for example, by Spohr and Hauptmann. In Mendelssohn's published letters there is no verdict whatever on Schumann's music. The fact, however, remains that in Schumann's earlier pianoforte works he felt that the power or the desire for expression in the greater forms was wanting, and this he said in conversation. He soon had reason to change his opinion, and afterwards expressed warm interest in his friend's compositions. Whether he ever quite entered into the individualities of Schumann's music may well be doubted ; their natures were too dissimilar. To a certain extent the German nation has recovered from one mistake in judgment ; the tendency to elevate Schumann above Mendelssohn was for a very long time unmistakable. Latterly their verdict has become more just, and the two are now recognised as composers of equal greatness.

Schumann's constant intimacy in Wieck's house had resulted in a tender attachment to his daughter Clara, now grown up. It was in the latter part of 1835 that this first found any definite expression. His regard was reciprocated, and in September 1837 he preferred his suit formally to her father.[2] Wieck, however, did not favour it ; possibly he entertained loftier hopes for his gifted daughter. At any rate he was of opinion that Schumann's means and prospects were too vague and uncertain to warrant his setting up a home of his own. Schumann seems to have acknowledged the justice of this hesitation, for in 1838 he made strenuous efforts to find a new and wider sphere of work. With the full consent of Clara Wieck he decided on settling in Vienna, and bringing out his musical periodical in that city. The glory of a great epoch still cast a light over the musical life of the Austrian capital—the epoch when Gluck, Haydn, Mozart, Beethoven, and Schubert were living and working there. In point of fact, all genuine music had vanished even during Beethoven's lifetime, and had given way to a trivial and superficial taste. Rossini and his followers were paramount in opera ; in orchestral music there were the waltzes of Strauss and Lanner ; and in vocal music the feeble sentimentalities of Proch and his fellow-composers. So far as solo-playing was concerned, the fourth decade of the century saw it at its highest pitch of executive brilliancy, and its lowest of purpose and feeling—indeed it may be comprehensively designated as the epoch of Thalberg. Thus Schumann would have found in Vienna ample opportunity for doing good

---

[1] Hardly recognisable, owing to *Die musikalische Zeitung* (Schumann's paper) being rendered ' The musical papers.'

[2] [These dates are now finally settled by Litzmann's *Clara Schumann*, vol. i. p. 123, etc.]

work, for the Viennese public was still as ever the most responsive in the world, and one to justify sanguine hopes. Schumann effected his move with the assistance of Professor Joseph Fischhof, his colleague in the paper ; settling himself in October 1838 in the Schönlaterngasse, No. 679. Oswald Lorenz edited the *Zeitschrift* as Schumann's deputy, and for a time it was still to be issued in Leipzig. Schumann hoped to be able to bring it out in Vienna by January 1839, and made every effort to obtain the prompt permission of the authorities, as well as the support of influential persons for himself and his journal. But the consent of the censor's office and the police were long withheld ; and he was required to secure the co-operation of an Austrian publisher, in itself a great difficulty. It is hard to believe that in the great city of Vienna no strictly musical newspaper then existed, and that a small catalogue, the *Allgemeine musikalische Anzeiger*, published weekly by Tobias Haslinger, and almost exclusively devoted to the business interests of his firm, was the only publication which could pretend to the name. But the publishers were either too indolent or too timid to attempt any new enterprise, and sought to throw impediments in Schumann's way.

His courage and hopefulness were soon much reduced. The superficially kind welcome he met everywhere could not conceal the petty strife of coteries, the party spirit and gossip of a society which might have been provincial. The public, though keenly alive to music, was devoid of all critical taste. ' He could not get on with these people,' he writes to Zuccalmaglio as early as Oct. 19, 1838 ; their utter insipidity was at times too much for him, and while he had hoped that on its appearance in Vienna the *Zeitschrift* would have received a fresh impulse, and become a medium of intercourse between North and South, he was forced as early as December to say : ' The paper is evidently falling off, though it must be published here ; this vexes me much.' Sterndale Bennett, who was residing in Leipzig during 1837-38, and who, Schumann hoped, would settle with him in Vienna, was obliged to relinquish his intention ; and in Vienna itself he sought in vain for an artist after his own heart, ' one who should not merely play tolerably well on one or two instruments, but who should be a *whole man*,' and understand Shakespeare and Jean Paul.' At the same time he did not abandon the scheme of making a wide and influential circle of activity for himself ; he was unwilling to return to Leipzig, and when in March 1839 he made up his mind to do so, after trying in vain to carry on the journal in Vienna, it was with the intention of remaining there but a short time. He indulged in a dream of going to England never to return ! What the anticipations could have been that

led him to cherish such an idea we know not ; perhaps his friendship for Bennett may have led to it ; but, in point of fact, he never set foot on English ground.

As far, therefore, as making a home for himself went, his half-year's stay in Vienna was without result. But without doubt Schumann received impulses and incitements towards further progress as a musician through his acquaintance with Vienna life. A work which is to be referred directly to this influence is the ' Faschingsschwank aus Wien ' (op. 26, published by Spina in 1841). In the first movement, which seems to depict various scenes of a masquerade, there springs up quite unnoticed the melody of the ' Marseillaise ' (p. 7, bar 40, etc. ; Pauer's edition, vol. iii. p. 596, l. 1), at that time strictly forbidden in Vienna. Schumann, who had been much worried by the government officials on account of his newspaper, took this opportunity of playing off a good-tempered joke upon them.

It was very natural that, with his enthusiastic admiration for Schubert, he should take pains to follow out the traces of that master, who had now been dead just ten years. He visited the Währing cemetery, where Schubert is buried, divided by a few intervening graves from Beethoven. On the tomb of the latter a steel pen was lying ; this Schumann took possession of, and being always fond of symbolical associations and mystic connections, used on very special occasions. With it he wrote his Symphony in B♭ (op. 38), and the notice of Schubert's C major Symphony, which is found in the *Zeitschrift* for 1840.[1] And here we encounter one of the chief benefits which Schumann received from his stay in Vienna. He visited Franz Schubert's brother Ferdinand, who showed him the artistic remains of his too early lost brother, and among them the score of the C major Symphony. This he had composed in March 1828, but never lived to hear it performed entire, and no one had since cared to take any trouble about it. Schumann arranged for the score to be sent to Leipzig, and there on March 21, 1839, it was performed for the first time under Mendelssohn's direction. Its success was very striking, and was of great influence on the more thorough and widespread appreciation of Schubert's genius. Schumann retained pleasant memories of Vienna throughout his life, in spite of the little notice he attracted on this occasion, and the meagre success of a concert consisting of his own works, which he gave with his wife on a subsequent visit in the winter of 1846. In the summer of 1847 he even wished to apply for a vacant post on the board of direction at the Conservatorium, but when the year 1848 came, he was extremely glad that the plan had come to nothing.

[1] See also the *Gesammelte Schriften*, iii. 195.

At the beginning of April 1839 Schumann returned to his old life in Leipzig. He devoted himself with new zest to the interests of the journal, and delighted in once more being associated with prominent and sympathetic musicians. In the summer he paid a short visit to Berlin, which pleased and interested him from its contrast to Vienna.

Unfortunately Wieck's opinion as to the match between Schumann and his daughter remained unchanged, and his opposition to it became even stronger and more firmly rooted. Since persuasion was unavailing, Schumann was forced to call in the assistance of the law, and Wieck had to account for his refusal in court. The case dragged on for a whole year, but the final result was that Wieck's objections to the marriage were pronounced to be trivial and without foundation. A sensitive nature such as Schumann's must have been deeply pained by these difficulties, and the long-delayed decision must have kept him in disastrous suspense. His letters show signs of this. For the rest, his outward circumstances had so much improved, that he could easily afford to make a home without the necessity of such a round of work as he had attempted in Vienna. 'We are young,' he writes on Feb. 19, 1840, 'and have hands, strength, and reputation; and I have a little property that brings in 500 thalers a year. The profits of the paper amount to as much again, and I shall get well paid for my compositions. Tell me now if there can be real cause for fear.' One thing alone made him pause for a time. His bride-elect was decorated with different titles of honour from the courts at which she had played in her concert-tours. He himself had, it is true, been latterly made a member of several musical societies, but that was not enough. In the beginning of 1840 he executed a scheme which he had cherished since 1838, and applied to the university of Jena for the title of Doctor of Philosophy. Several cases in which the German universities had granted the doctor's diploma to musicians had lately come under Schumann's notice; for instance the university of Leipzig had given the honorary degree to Marschner in 1835, and to Mendelssohn in 1836, and these may have suggested the idea to him. Schumann received the desired diploma on February 24, 1840. As he had wished, the reason assigned for its bestowal is his well-known activity not only as a critical and æsthetic writer, but as a creative musician. At last, after a year of suspense, doubts, and disagreements, the marriage of Robert Schumann with Clara Wieck took place on Sept. 12, 1840, in the church of Schönefeld, near Leipzig.

The 'Davidsbündlertänze,' previously mentioned, bore on the title-page of the first edition an old verse—

In all und jeder Zeit
Verknüpft sich Lust und Leid:
Bleibt fromm in Lust, und seyd
Beim Leid mit Muth bereit;

And when we observe that the two first bars of the first piece are borrowed from a composition by Clara Wieck (op. 6, No. 5), we understand the allusion. Schumann himself admits that his compositions for the piano written during the period of his courtship reveal much of his personal experience and feelings, and his creative work in 1840 is of a very striking character. Up to this time, with the exception of the Symphony in G minor, which has remained unknown, he had written only for the piano; now he suddenly threw himself into vocal composition, and the stream of his invention rushed at once into this new channel with such force that in that single year he wrote above one hundred songs. Nor was it in number alone, but in intrinsic value also, that in this department the work of this year was the most remarkable of all Schumann's life. It is not improbable that his stay in Vienna had some share in this sudden rush into song, and in opening Schumann's mind to the charms of pure melody. But still, when we look through the words of his songs, it is clear that here more than anywhere, love was the prompter —love that had endured so long a struggle, and at last attained the goal of its desires. This is confirmed by the 'Myrthen' (op. 25), which he dedicated to the lady of his choice, and the twelve songs from Rückert's *Liebesfrühling* (op. 37), which were written conjointly by the two lovers. 'I am now writing nothing but songs great and small,' he says to a friend on Feb. 19, 1840; 'I can hardly tell you how delightful it is to write for the voice as compared with instrumental composition, and what a stir and tumult I feel within me when I sit down to it. I have brought forth quite new things in this line.' With the close of 1840 he felt that he had worked out the vein of expression in the form of song with pianoforte accompaniment, almost to perfection. Some one expressed a hope that after such a beginning a promising future lay before him as a song-writer, but Schumann answered, 'I cannot venture to promise that I shall produce anything further in the way of songs, and I am satisfied with what I have done.' And he was right in his firm opinion as to the peculiar character of this form of music. 'In your essay on song-writing,' he says to a colleague in the *Zeitschrift*, 'it has somewhat distressed me that you should have placed me in the second rank. I do not ask to stand in the first, but I think I have some pretensions to a place *of my own.*'

As far as anything human can be, the marriage was perfectly happy. Besides their genius, both husband and wife had simple domestic tastes, and were strong enough to bear the admiration of the world without becoming egotistical. They lived for one another, and for their children. He created and wrote for his wife, and in accordance with her temperament ; while she looked upon it as her highest privilege to give to the world the most perfect interpretation of his works, or at least to stand as mediatrix between him and his audience, and to ward off all disturbing or injurious impressions from his sensitive soul, which day by day became more and more irritable. Now that he found perfect contentment in his domestic relations, he withdrew more than ever from intercourse with others, and devoted himself exclusively to his family and his work. The deep joy of his married life produced the direct result of a mighty advance in his artistic progress. Schumann's most beautiful works in the larger forms date almost exclusively from the years 1841 to 1845.

In 1841 he turned his attention to the Symphony, as he had done in the previous year to the Song, and composed, in this year alone, no fewer than three symphonic works. The B♭ Symphony (op. 38) was performed as early as March 31, 1841, at a concert given by Clara Schumann in the Gewandhaus at Leipzig. Mendelssohn conducted it, and performed the task with so much zeal and care as truly to delight his friend. The other two orchestral works were given at a concert on Dec. 6 of the same year, but did not meet with so much success as the former one. Schumann thought that the two together were too much at once ; and they had not the advantage of Mendelssohn's able and careful direction, for he was spending that winter in Berlin. Schumann put these two works away for a time, and published the B♭ Symphony alone. The proper title of one of these was 'Symphonistische Phantasie,' but it was performed under the title of 'Second Symphony,' and, in 1851, the instrumentation having been revised and completed, was published as the 4th Symphony (D minor, op. 120). The other was brought out under an altered arrangement, which he made in 1845, with the title 'Ouverture, Scherzo, et Finale' (op. 52) ; and it is said that Schumann originally intended to call it 'Sinfonietta.' Besides these orchestral works the first movement of the Pianoforte Concerto in A minor was written in 1841. It was at first intended to form an independent piece with the title of ' Fantasie.' As appears from a letter of Schumann's to David, it was once rehearsed by the Gewandhaus orchestra in the winter of 1841-42. Schumann did not write the last two movements which complete the concerto until 1845.

The year 1842 was devoted to chamber music. The three string quartets deserve to be first mentioned, since the date of their composition can be fixed with the greatest certainty. Although Schumann was unused to this style of writing, he composed the quartets in about

a month—a certain sign that his faculties were as clear as his imagination was rich. In the autograph,[1] after most of the movements is written the date of their completion. The Adagio of the first quartet bears the date June 21, 1842 ; the finale was 'finished on St. John's day, June 24, 1842, in Leipzig.' In the second quartet the second movement is dated July 2, 1842, and the last July 5, 1842, Leipzig. The third is dated as follows : first movement, July 18, second July 20, third July 21, and the fourth Leipzig, July 22, all of the same year. Thus the two last movements took the composer only one day each. These quartets, which are dedicated to Mendelssohn, were at once taken up by the Leipzig musicians with great interest. The praise bestowed upon them by Ferdinand David called forth a letter from Schumann, addressed to him, which merits quotation, as showing how modest and how ideal as an artist Schumann was : — 'Härtel told me how very kindly you had spoken to him about my quartets, and, coming from you, it gratified me exceedingly. But I shall have to do better yet, and I feel, with each new work, as if I ought to begin all over again from the beginning.' In the beginning of October of this year the quartets were played at David's house ; Hauptmann was present, and expressed his surprise at Schumann's talent, which, judging only from the earlier pianoforte works, he had fancied not nearly so great. With each new work Schumann now made more triumphant way—at all events in Leipzig. The same year witnessed the production of that work to which he chiefly owes his fame throughout Europe— the Quintet for Pianoforte and Strings (op. 44). The first public performance took place in the Gewandhaus on Jan. 8, 1843, his wife, to whom it is dedicated, taking the pianoforte part. Berlioz, who came to Leipzig in 1843, and there made Schumann's personal acquaintance, heard the quintet performed, and carried the fame of it to Paris. Besides the quintet, Schumann wrote, in 1842, the Pianoforte Quartet (op. 47) and a Pianoforte Trio. The trio, however, remained unpublished for eight years, and then appeared as op. 88, under the title of ' Phantasiestücke for Pianoforte, Violin, and Violoncello.' The quartet too was laid aside for a time ; it was first publicly performed on Dec. 8, 1844, by Madame Schumann, in the Gewandhaus, David of course taking the violin part, and Niels W. Gade, who was directing the Gewandhaus concerts that winter, playing the viola.

With the year 1843 came a total change of style. The first work to appear was op. 46, the Variations for two pianos, which are now so popular, and to which Mendelssohn may have done some service by introducing them to the public, in company with Mme. Schumann, on August 19, 1843. The principal work

[1] Now in the possession of Herr Raymund Härtel, of Leipzig.

of the year, however, was 'Paradise and the Peri,' a grand composition for solo-voices, chorus, and orchestra, to a text adapted from Moore's 'Lalla Rookh.' The enthusiasm created by this work at its first performance (Dec. 4, 1843), conducted by the composer himself, was so great that it had to be repeated a week afterwards, on Dec. 11, and on the 23rd of the same month it was performed in the Opera House at Dresden. It will be easily believed that from this time Schumann's fame was firmly established in Germany, although it took twenty years more to make his work widely and actually popular. Having been so fortunate in his first attempt in a branch of art hitherto untried by him, he felt induced to undertake another work of the same kind, and in 1844 began writing the second of his two most important choral works, namely, the music to Goethe's 'Faust.' For some time, however, the work consisted only of four numbers. His uninterrupted labours had so affected his health, that in this year he was obliged for a time to forego all exertion of the kind.

The first four years of his married life were passed in profound retirement, but very rarely interrupted. In the beginning of 1842 he accompanied his wife on a concert-tour to Hamburg, where the B♭ Symphony was performed. Madame Schumann then proceeded alone to Copenhagen, while her husband returned to his quiet retreat at Leipzig. In the summer of the same year the two artists made an excursion into Bohemia, and at Königswart were presented to Prince Metternich, who invited them to Vienna. Schumann at first took some pleasure in these tours, but soon forgot it in the peace and comfort of domestic life, and it cost his wife great trouble to induce him to make a longer journey to Russia in the beginning of 1844. Indeed she only succeeded by declaring that she would make the tour alone if he would not leave home. 'How unwilling I am to move out of my quiet round,' he wrote to a friend, 'you must not expect me to tell you. I cannot think of it without the greatest annoyance.' However, he made up his mind to it, and they started on Jan. 26. His wife gave concerts in Mitau, Riga, Petersburg, and Moscow; and the enthusiasm with which she was everywhere received attracted fresh attention to Schumann's works, the constant aim of her noble endeavours. Schumann himself, when once he had parted from home, found much to enjoy in a journey which was so decidedly and even brilliantly successful. At St. Petersburg he was received with undiminished cordiality by his old friend Henselt, who had made himself a new home there. At a soirée at Prince Oldenburg's Henselt played with Mme. Schumann her husband's Variations for two pianos. The B♭ Symphony was also performed under Schumann's direction at a soirée given by the Counts Joseph and Michael Wielhorsky, highly esteemed musical connoisseurs; and it is evident that the dedication of Schumann's PF. Quartet (op. 47) to a Count Wielhorsky was directly connected with this visit.

In June they were once more in Leipzig, and so agreeable were the reminiscences of the journey that Schumann was ready at once with a fresh plan of the same kind—this time for a visit to England with his wife in the following year; not, indeed, as he had once intended, with a view to permanent residence, but merely that she might win fresh laurels as a player, and he make himself known as a composer. He proposed to conduct parts of 'Paradise and the Peri' in London, and anticipated a particular success for it because the work 'had, as it were, sprung from English soil, and was one of the sweetest flowers of English verse.' On June 27, 1844, he writes to Moscheles concerning the project, which had the full support of Mendelssohn; but the scheme ultimately came to nothing, chiefly because of the refusal of Buxton, the proprietor of the publishing firm of Ewer & Co., to bring out 'Paradise and the Peri' with English words. Still Schumann, even long after, kept his eye steadily fixed on England. He was delighted at being told that Queen Victoria often listened to his music, and had had the B♭ Symphony [1] played by the private band at Windsor, and he contemplated dedicating his Manfred music (op. 115) to Her Majesty, but the idea was given up.

Instead of going to England, they at length paid a visit to Vienna in the winter of 1846. Here again Schumann conducted his B♭ Symphony, and his wife played his Pianoforte Concerto. This was on Jan. 1, 1847. But the public were perfectly unsympathetic, and justified an earlier utterance of Schumann's that 'The Viennese are an ignorant people, and know little of what goes on outside their own city.' Nor were matters much more satisfactory in Berlin, whither they went from Vienna to conduct 'Paradise and the Peri'; while in Prague, where they performed on their way, they met with the warmest reception.

The year 1844 was the last of Schumann's residence in Leipzig; for in October he left the town where he had lived and worked with short intervals for fourteen years, and moved to Dresden. He had given up the editorship of the *Neue Zeitschrift* in July, and from April 3, 1843, had held a Professor's chair in the Conservatorium, founded at Leipzig by Mendelssohn's exertions, and opened on that date. [See vol. ii. p. 668; vol. iii. pp. 142, 143.] He was professor of pianoforte-playing and composition; but his reserved nature was little suited to the duties of a teacher, though his name and the example afforded by

---

[1] The first performance of the B♭ Symphony in England was at the Philharmonic Concert, June 5, 1854.

his work were no doubt highly advantageous to the infant institution. Schumann had no disciples, properly speaking, either in the Conservatorium or as private pupils. In a letter to David from Dresden he incidentally mentions Carl Ritter as having instruction from him, and as having previously been a pupil of Hiller's; and he writes to Hiller that he has brought young Ritter on a little. But what the style of Schumann's teaching may have been cannot be told; and a single exception only proves the rule.

The move to Dresden seems to have been chiefly on account of Schumann's suffering condition. His nervous affection rendered change of scene absolutely necessary to divert his thoughts. He had overworked himself into a kind of surfeit of music, so much so that his medical attendant forbade his continually hearing it. In the musical world of Leipzig such a prohibition could not be strictly obeyed, but at Dresden it was quite different. 'Here,' he writes to David on Nov. 25, 1844, 'one can get back the old lost longing for music, there is so little to hear! It just suits my condition, for I still suffer very much from my nerves, and everything affects and exhausts me directly.' Accordingly he at first lived in Dresden in the strictest seclusion. A friend sought him out there and found him so changed that he entertained grave fears for his life. On several occasions he tried sea-bathing, but it was long before his health can be said to have radically improved. In February 1846, after a slight improvement, he again became very unwell, as he did also in the summer of the following year. He observed that he was unable to remember the melodies that occurred to him, when composing; the effort of invention fatiguing his mind to such a degree as to impair his memory. As soon as a lasting improvement took place in his health, he again devoted himself wholly to composition. He was now attracted more powerfully than before to complicated contrapuntal forms. The 'Studies' and 'Sketches' for the pedal-piano (opp. 56 and 58), the six fugues on the name of 'Bach' (op. 60) and the four piano fugues (op. 72), owe their existence to this attraction. The greatest work of the years 1845-46, however, was the C major Symphony (op. 61), which Mendelssohn produced at the Gewandhaus in Leipzig, Nov. 5, 1846. Slight intercourse with a few congenial spirits was now gradually resumed. Among those whom he saw was the widow of C. M. v. Weber, whose fine musical f ⌐⌐ng was highly valued by Schumann. The first year in Dresden was spent with Ferdinand Hiller, who had been living there since the winter of 1844. Their intercourse gradually grew into a lively and lasting intimacy. When Hiller was getting up subscription concerts in the autumn of 1845, Schumann took an active share in the undertaking. With Richard Wagner, too, then Capellmeister at

Dresden, he was on friendly terms. He was much interested in the opera of 'Tannhäuser' and heard it often, expressing his opinion of it in terms of great though not unqualified praise. But the natures of the two musicians differed too widely to allow of any real sympathy between them. Wagner was always lively, versatile, and talkative, while Schumann's former silence and reserve had increased since his illness, and even intimate friends, like Moscheles and Lipinski, had to lament that conversation with him was now scarcely possible.

At the end of Schumann's collected works we find a *Theaterbüchlein* (1847-50), in which are given short notes of the impressions made upon him by certain operas. From this we learn that in 1847 he went comparatively often to the theatre; the reason being that at that time he himself was composing an opera. He had long cherished the idea. So early as Sept. 1, 1842, he writes, 'Do you know what is my morning and evening prayer as an artist? *German Opera.* There is a field for work.' He concludes a critique of an opera by Heinrich Esser in the number of the *Zeitschrift* for September 1842 with these significant words —'It is high time that German composers should give the lie to the reproach that has long lain on them of having been so craven as to leave the field in possession of the Italians and French. But under this head there is a word to be said to the German poets also.' In 1844 he composed a chorus and an aria for an opera on Byron's *Corsair.* The work, however, went no farther, and the two pieces still remain unpublished. He also corresponded with his friend Zuccalmaglio as to the subject for an opera, which he wished to find ready on his return from Russia; and made notes on more than twenty different subjects of all kinds, periods, and nationalities; but none of these were found suitable, and circumstances led to the abandonment of the project. At length, in 1847, he decided on the legend of St. Geneviève. The two versions of the story contained in the tragedies of Tieck and Hebbel (principally that of Hebbel) were to serve as the basis of the text. The treatment of the words he persuaded Robert Reinick, the poet, who had been living in Dresden since 1844, to undertake. Reinick, however, failed to satisfy him, and Hebbel, who came to Dresden at the end of July 1847, could not say that he thought it a satisfactory text, though he declined to assist in remedying the deficiencies and bringing it into the desired form. This, however, was from no lack of interest in Schumann himself. On the contrary Hebbel always preserved the highest esteem for him, and subsequently dedicated to him his drama of *Michel Angelo,* accepting in return from Schumann the dedication of his 'Nachtlied' (op. 108). But it was repugnant to him to see his work mutilated in the way which Schumann considered necessary for an opera. The composer was at last obliged to trust to his own poetic powers, and construct a text himself from those already mentioned.

By August 1848 the music for the opera was so far complete that Schumann thought he might take steps for its performance. His first thought was of the theatre at Leipzig, where he knew that he was most warmly remembered. Wirsing was at that time the director, Julius Rietz the conductor, and the opera was to have been brought out in the spring of 1849, but it came to nothing. In June, when the preparations were to have begun, Schumann was detained by domestic circumstances, and the rest of the year slipped away with constant evasions and promises on the part of the director of the theatre. Even the promise, 'on his honour,' that the opera should be performed at the end of February 1850, at latest, was not kept. And so in this, his very first attempt at dramatic work, Schumann made acquaintance with the shady side of theatrical management in a way which must have disgusted his upright and honourable spirit. In his indignation, he would have made the director's breach of faith public, by invoking the aid of the law; but his Leipzig friends were happily able to dissuade him from this course. At last, on June 25, 1850, the first representation of 'Genoveva' actually took place under Schumann's own direction. But the time was unfavourable. 'Who,' he writes to Dr. Hermann Härtel, 'goes to the theatre in May or June, and not rather into the woods?' However, the number of his admirers in Leipzig was great, and the first opera by so famous a master excited great expectations; the house was full, and the reception by the public, though not enthusiastic, was honourable to the composer. Still, artists and connoisseurs were tolerably unanimous in thinking that Schumann lacked the special genius for writing opera. His almost entire exclusion of recitative was very widely disapproved of. No one but the venerable Spohr, who had attended many of the rehearsals, gave a really favourable verdict upon the work. In his last opera, 'The Crusaders,' Spohr himself had adopted similar methods of making the music follow the plot closely without ever coming to a standstill, and he was naturally delighted to find the same in Schumann's work. After three representations (June 25, 28, 30) 'Genoveva' was laid aside for the time. Schumann, already vexed by the tedious postponements of the first performance, and disappointed by the cold reception of the work, was greatly annoyed by the discussions in the public prints, especially by a critique from Dr. E. Krüger, one of the collaborateurs in the *Neue Zeitschrift*. A letter from Schumann to Krüger, in stronger terms

than might have been expected from him, put an end for ever to their acquaintance.

Schumann derived far more gratification from the reception of his music to 'Faust.' In 1848 he completed the portion he had originally intended to write first, viz. the salvation of Faust, which forms the end of the second part of Goethe's poem, and the music of which is called the 'third part.' On June 25, 1848, the first performance took place among a limited circle of friends, upon whom it made a deep impression. The most cultivated portion of the audience was of opinion that the music made the meaning of the words clear for the first time, so deeply imbued was the composer with the poet's inmost spirit. As the 100th anniversary of Goethe's birthday was approaching (August 28, 1849) it was decided to give a festival concert in Dresden, at which this 'Faust' music and Mendelssohn's 'Walpurgisnacht' should form the programme. When the Leipzig people heard of this intention, they would not be behind Dresden, and also got up a performance of the same works on August 29. In Weimar too the 'Faust' music was performed for the same festivity. Schumann was exceedingly delighted that his work had been employed for so special an occasion. He writes to Dr. Härtel: 'I should like to have Faust's cloak, and be able to be everywhere at once, that I might hear it.' In Dresden the success of the work was very considerable, but it made less impression at its first performance in Leipzig. Schumann took this quite calmly. 'I hear different accounts,' says he in a letter, 'of the impression produced by my scenes from "Faust"; some seem to have been affected, while upon others it made no definite impression. This is what I expected. Perhaps an opportunity may occur in the winter for a repetition of the work, when it is possible that I may add some other scenes.' This repetition, however, did not take place in Schumann's lifetime. He fulfilled his scheme of adding several scenes; and in 1853 prefixed an overture to the whole work, which was divided into three parts. It was not published complete until two years after his death.

In the meantime, Schumann's health had again improved, as was evident from his augmented creative activity. Indeed his eager desire for work increased in a way which gave rise to great apprehensions. In the year 1849 alone he produced thirty works, most of them of considerable extent. It had never seemed so easy to him to create ideas and bring them into shape. He composed as he walked or stood, and could not be distracted, even by the most disturbing circumstances. Thus he wrote Mignon's song 'Kennst du das Land' at Kreischa, near Dresden, in the midst of a group of his noisy children. And in a restaurant near the post-office, much frequented by the artistic

2 a

society of Dresden, where he used to drink his beer in the evening, he would usually sit alone, with his back to the company and his face to the wall, whistling softly to himself, and developing his musical ideas all the time. No preference for any particular form of art can be traced in Schumann's work at this time. Pianoforte works and chamber trios, songs and vocal duets, choruses, choral works with orchestra, concertos with orchestra, compositions for horn, clarinet, oboe, violoncello, or violin, with pianoforte accompaniment, even melodramatic music —all these thronged as it were out of his imagination in wild and strange succession. Among all the beautiful and important works produced at this time, the music to Byron's *Manfred* deserves especial mention. The first stage performance of it was given by Franz Liszt in Weimar on June 13, 1852. For that occasion the drama was adapted for the stage by Schumann himself, in an arrangement which is printed as a preface to the score of the work. The first performance of the music at a concert took place at Leipzig on March 24, 1859.

Dresden was Schumann's place of residence until 1850. In the latter years of his stay there his outward life was more active than before. No journeys of note were made, it is true, with the exception of those to Vienna and Berlin already mentioned, and a longer expedition undertaken in 1850 to Bremen and Hamburg, where many concerts were given. He avoided the passing disturbance occasioned by the Dresden insurrection of 1849, by leaving the town with his family. Though no revolutionary, like Richard Wagner, scarcely even a politician, Schumann loved individual liberty and wished others to enjoy it also. But what gave a different aspect to his life as a musician in the last years of his stay in Dresden, was his occupation as a conductor. Ferdinand Hiller had conducted a choral society for men's voices ; and when he left Dresden to go to Düsseldorf as municipal director of music, Schumann succeeded him in his post. He conducted the society for some time with great interest, and was glad to find that his capacity for conducting was not so small as he had generally fancied it to be. He was even induced to write a few works for male chorus. Three songs of War and Liberty (Kriegs- und Freiheitslieder, op. 62) and seven songs in canon-form, to words by Rückert (op. 65), were written in 1847, and a grand motet for double chorus of men's voices (op. 93) in 1849. But a nature like Schumann's could not thrive in the atmosphere of a German singing-club. He was in all respects too refined for the tone of vulgar comfort, and often even of low sentimentality, which pervades these assemblies, and they could not but be irksome to him. 'I felt myself,' he says, in a letter to Hiller written on April 10, 1849, after his withdrawal, ' out of my element ;

they were such nice (*hübsch*) people.' This is even noticeable in his compositions for male chorus ; they are not of the right kind, and have in consequence never been much sung. Of greater artistic importance was a society of mixed voices which was constituted in January 1848, and of which Schumann was asked to take the lead. It was not very large—in 1849 it numbered only sixty or seventy members— but these were efficient, and Schumann was able ' to perform correctly any music he liked with pleasure and delight.' It was this society that gave the first performance of the third part of ' Faust' in June 1848, at a private party ; Schumann was induced to write many new compositions for them, and they did much service in promoting a knowledge of his music in Dresden by two performances of ' Paradise and the Peri' on Jan. 5 and 12, 1850. They even succeeded in drawing him into social amusements. In August 1848 a general excursion was arranged, in which Schumann took what was, for him, a lively interest.

That Schumann, after so successful a beginning in the art of conducting, considered himself fitted to undertake the direction of performances on a larger scale, is evident from the following circumstance. After Mendelssohn's death the Gewandhaus concerts were conducted by Julius Rietz, who until 1847 had been at work in Düsseldorf. In the summer of 1849 a report reached Dresden that Rietz was going to succeed O. Nicolai as royal Capellmeister at Berlin. Schumann thereupon applied for the post of concert director at the Gewandhaus. Dr. Hermann Härtel was to be the medium of communication, and Schumann, with a well-founded expectation that the choice would fall upon him, gave himself up for a time with great pleasure to the idea of becoming the successor of the honoured Mendelssohn. ' It would give me great pleasure,' he wrote, ' if the thing came to pass. I long for regular duty, and though I can never forget the last few years, during which I have lived exclusively as a composer, and know that so productive and happy a time may perhaps never be mine again, yet I feel impelled towards a life of active work, and my highest endeavour would be to keep up the renown which the institution has so long enjoyed.' This wish was not realised, for Rietz remained in Leipzig. But Schumann's desire for a more extended field of work as a conductor was to be satisfied in another way in the following year.

In 1850 Hiller gave up his post in Düsseldorf to obey a call to Cologne as Capellmeister to that city. He suggested that Schumann should be his successor, and opened negotiations with him. Some efforts were made to keep him in Dresden and to obtain his appointment as Capellmeister to the King of Saxony ; but the attempt was unsuccessful, and Schumann accepted the directorship at Düsseldorf that summer, though he left his native place with deep regret, and not without some suspicions as to the condition of music in Düsseldorf, of which he had heard much that was unfavourable from Mendelssohn and Rietz. In his new post he had the direction of a vocal union and of an orchestra, and a number of concerts to conduct in the course of the winter. He arrived at Düsseldorf, Sept. 2, 1850, and the first winter concert was in some sort a formal reception of him, since it consisted of the overture to 'Genoveva,' some of his songs, and Part I. of 'Paradise and the Peri.' It was under the direction of Julius Tausch, Schumann himself appearing as conductor for the first time on Oct. 24.

He was very well satisfied with his new sphere of work. The vocal resources, as is the case with all the choirs of the Rhine towns, were admirable ; Hiller had cultivated them with special zeal, and he and Rietz had left the orchestra so well drilled that Schumann, for the first time in his life, enjoyed the inestimable advantage of being able to hear everything that he wrote for the orchestra performed immediately. The concerts took up no more of his time than he was willing to give, and left him ample leisure for his own work. Chamber music was also attainable, for in J. von Wasielewski there was a good solo violinist on the spot. Schumann and his wife were at once welcomed in Düsseldorf with the greatest respect, and every attention and consideration was shown to them both. It might be said that their position here was one of special ease, and they soon formed a delightful circle of intimate acquaintances. Little as his music was then known in the Rhine-cities, Schumann's advent in person seems to have given a strong impulse to the public feeling for music in Düsseldorf. The interest in the subscription concerts during the winter of 1850 was greater than it had ever been before ; and the board of directors was able, at the close of the usual series of six concerts, to undertake a second series of three or four. At Schumann's instance one of the winter concerts was entirely devoted to the works of living composers, an idea then perfectly novel, and showing that he had remained faithful to his desire—manifested long before through the *Zeitschrift*—of facilitating the advancement of young and gifted composers. At first Schumann's direction gave entire satisfaction. If some performances were not perfectly successful, they were compensated for by others of special excellence ; and the execution of Beethoven's A major Symphony at the third concert even seemed to show that he was a born conductor. But it was not so in reality ; indeed he was wholly wanting in the real talent for conducting ; all who ever saw him conduct or who played under his direction are agreed on this point.

Irrespective of the fact that conducting for any length of time tired him out, he had neither the collectedness and prompt presence of mind, nor the sympathetic faculty, nor the enterprising dash, without each of which *conducting* in the true sense is impossible. He even found a difficulty in starting at a given *tempo* ; nay, he sometimes shrank from giving any initial beat ; so that some energetic pioneer would begin without waiting for the signal, and without incurring Schumann's wrath. Besides this, any thorough practice bit by bit with his orchestra, with instructive remarks by the way as to the mode of execution, was impossible to this great artist, who in this respect was a striking contrast to Mendelssohn. He would have a piece played through, and if it did not answer to his wishes, had it repeated. If it went no better the second, or perhaps even a third time, he would be extremely angry at what he considered the clumsiness or even the ill-will of the players ; but detailed remarks he never made. Any one knowing his silent nature and his instinctive dislike to contact with the outer world, might certainly have feared from the first that he would find great difficulty in asserting himself as a director of large masses. And as years went on his incapacity for conducting constantly increased, as the issue showed, with the growth of an illness, which, after seeming to have been completely overcome in Dresden, returned in Düsseldorf with increasing gravity. His genius seemed constantly to shrink from the outside world into the depths of his soul. His silence became a universally accepted fact, and to those who saw him for the first time he seemed apathetic. But in fact he was anything rather than that ; he would let a visitor talk for a long time on all kinds of subjects without saying a word, and then when the caller rose to leave, 'not to disturb the master longer,' he would discover that Schumann had followed the one-sided 'conversation' with unfailing interest. When sitting for an hour, as he was accustomed of an evening, with friends or acquaintances at the restaurant, if anything was said that touched or pleased him he would give the speaker a radiant, expressive glance, but without a word ; and the incessant creative labours, to which he gave himself up so long as he was able, are the best proof of the rich vitality which constantly flowed from the deepest sources of his soul. In the family circle he was a different man ; there he could be gay and talkative to a degree that would have surprised a stranger. He loved his children tenderly, and was fond of occupying himself with them. The three piano sonatas (op. 118) composed for his daughters Julie, Elise, and Marie, the Album for beginners (op. 68) ; the Children's Ball (op. 130), and other pieces, are touching evidence of the way in which he expressed this feeling in music.

The first great work of the Düsseldorf period

was the E♭ Symphony (op. 97), marked by the composer as No. 3, although it is really the fourth of the published ones, the D minor Symphony preceding it in order of composition. If we call the Overture, Scherzo, and Finale (op. 52) a symphony too, then the E♭ Symphony must rank as the fifth. It would seem that Schumann had begun to work at it before his change of residence. As soon as he conceived the project of leaving Saxony for the Rhine, he bethought himself of the great musical festival which ever since 1818 had been held in the lower Rhine[1] districts, and was inspired by the idea of assisting at one of these in the capacity of a composer. He wrote down this great work with its five movements between Nov. 2 and Dec. 9, 1850. He has told us that it was intended to convey the impressions which he received during a visit to Cologne ; so that its ordinary name of the 'Rhenish Symphony' may be accepted as correct. It was first performed at Düsseldorf on Feb. 6, 1851, and then at Cologne on Feb. 25, both times under the direction of the composer, but was coldly received on both occasions.[2]

Although Schumann had had no pleasant experiences in connection with the opera 'Genoveva,' he was not to be deterred from making another essay in dramatic composition. In Oct. 1850 he received from Richard Pohl, at that time a student in the Leipzig university, Schiller's 'Bride of Messina,' arranged as an opera libretto. Schumann could not make up his mind to set it to music ; but in Dec. 1850 and Jan. 1851 he wrote an Overture to the ' Braut von Messina ' (op. 100), which showed how much the material of the play had interested him, in spite of his refusal to set it. He inclined to a more cheerful, or even a comic subject, and Goethe's 'Hermann und Dorothea' seemed to him appropriate for an operetta. He consulted several poets concerning the arrangement, and having made out a scheme of treatment, wrote the Overture at Christmas 1851 (op. 136). The work, however, progressed no farther. He subsequently turned his attention to Auerbach's ' Dorfgeschichten,' but without finding any good material, and no second opera from his pen ever saw the light.

He completed, however, a number of vocal compositions for the concert-room, in which his taste for dramatic music had free play. A young poet from Chemnitz, Moritz Horn, had sent him a faery poem, which greatly interested him. After many abbreviations and alterations made by Horn himself at Schumann's suggestion, 'The Pilgrimage of the Rose' (Der Rose Pilgerfahrt, op. 112) was really set to music between April and July 1851. The work, which both in form and substance resembles 'Paradise and the Peri,' except that it is treated in a manner at once more detailed and more idyllic, had at first a simple pianoforte accompaniment, but in

[1] See this Dictionary, vol. iii. pp. 377, 378.
[2] Its first performance in England was at a Concert of Signor Arditi's, Dec. 4, 1865.

November Schumann arranged it for orchestra. June 1851 is also the date of the composition of Uhland's ballad ' Der Königssohn ' (op. 116), in a semi-dramatic form, to which indeed he was almost driven by the poem itself. Schumann was much pleased with his treatment of this ballad, which he set for soli, chorus, and orchestra. In the course of the next two years he wrote three more works of the same kind : ' Des Sängers Fluch ' (op. 139), a ballad of Uhland's ; ' Vom Pagen und der Königstochter ' (op. 140), a ballad by Geibel ; and ' Das Glück von Edenhall ' (op. 143), a ballad by Uhland.

In the last two poems he made alterations of more or less importance, to bring them into shape for musical setting, but the ' Sängers Fluch ' had to be entirely remodelled—a difficult and ungrateful task, which Richard Pohl carried out after Schumann's own suggestions.

At that time this young man, a thorough art-enthusiast, kept up a lively intercourse with Schumann, both personally and by letter. They devised together the plan of a grand oratorio. Schumann wavered between a biblical and an historical subject, thinking at one time of the Virgin Mary, at another of Ziska or Luther. His final choice fell upon Luther. He pondered deeply upon the treatment of his materials. It was to be an oratorio suitable both for the church and the concert room, and in its poetical form as dramatic as possible. In point of musical treatment he intended the chorus to predominate, as in Handel's 'Israel in Egypt,' of which he had given a performance in the winter of 1850. Moreover, it was not to be complicated and contrapuntal in style, but simple and popular, so that ' peasant and citizen alike should understand it.' The more he pondered it the more was he inspired with the grandeur of the subject, although by no means blind to its difficulties. ' It inspires courage,' he says, ' and also humility.' He could not, however, coincide with his poet's opinion as to the extent of the work, the latter having formed the idea of a sort of trilogy, in oratorio form, while Schumann wished the work to be within the limit of one evening's performance, lasting about two hours and a half. In this way the few years of creative activity that were still granted to him slipped away, and the oratorio remained unwritten. The impossibility of satisfying, by the oratorio on Luther, the inclination for grave and religious music which became ever stronger with increasing years, is partly the reason of his writing in 1852 a Mass (op. 147), and a Requiem (op. 148). But to these he was also incited by outward circumstances. The inhabitants of Düsseldorf are mostly Catholics, the organ-lofts in the principal churches are too small to hold a large choir and orchestra, and the regular church-music was in a bad condition. The choral society which Schumann conducted was accustomed, as a reward for its labours, to have several concerts of church music, or at least sacred compositions, every year ; and Schumann was probably thinking of this custom in his Mass and his Requiem, but he was not destined ever to hear them performed.

In the summer of 1851 he and his family made a tour in Switzerland, which he had not visited since the time of his student-life in Heidelberg ; on his return he went to Antwerp, for a competitive performance by the Belgian ' Männergesangverein,' on August 17, at which he had been asked to aid in adjudging the prizes. Two years later, towards the end of 1853, he and his wife once more visited the Netherlands, and made a concert-tour through Holland, meeting with such an enthusiastic reception that he could not help saying that his music seemed to have struck deeper root there than in Germany. In March 1852 they revisited Leipzig, where, between the 14th and the 21st, a quantity of his music was performed ; the Manfred overture and the ' Pilgerfahrt der Rose ' at a public matinée on the 14th ; the D minor Sonata for pianoforte and violin (op. 121) in a private circle, on the 15th ; the E♭ Symphony at a concert at the Gewandhaus on the 18th ; the Pianoforte Trio in G minor (op. 110) at a chamber concert on the 21st. On Nov. 6, 1851, the overture to the ' Braut von Messina ' was also performed at the Gewandhaus. The public had thus, during this season, ample opportunity of becoming acquainted with the latest works of this inexhaustible composer. But although he had lived in Leipzig for fourteen years, and had brought out most of his compositions there, besides having a circle of sincerely devoted friends in that city, he could not on this occasion boast of any great success ; the public received him with respect and esteem, but with no enthusiasm. But in this respect Schumann had lived through a variety of experience ; ' I am accustomed,' he writes to Pohl, Dec. 7, 1851, when speaking of the reception of the overture to the ' Braut von Messina,' ' to find that my compositions, particularly the best and deepest, are not understood by the public at a first hearing.' Artists, however, had come to Leipzig from some distance for the ' Schumann-week ' ; among them Liszt and Joachim.

In August 1852 there was held in Düsseldorf a festival of music for men's voices, in which Schumann assisted as conductor, though, owing to his health, only to a very limited extent. He took a more important part at Whitsuntide 1853, when the 31st of the Lower Rhine Festivals was celebrated in Düsseldorf on May 15, 16, and 17. He conducted the music of the first day, consisting of Handel's ' Messiah ' and of his own Symphony in D minor, which was exceedingly well received. In the concerts of the two following days, which were conducted chiefly by Hiller, two more of Schumann's larger compositions were performed ; the Pianoforte Concerto in A minor, and a newly composed Festival Overture with soli and chorus on the ' Rheinweinlied ' (op. 123). But although Schumann appeared in so brilliant a way as a composer, and as such was honoured and appreciated in Düsseldorf, yet there was no concealing the fact that as a conductor he was inefficient. The little talent for conducting that he showed on his arrival in Düsseldorf, had disappeared with his departing health. It was in fact necessary to procure some one to take his place. An attempt was made after the first winter concert of the year (Oct. 27, 1853) to induce him to retire for a time from the post of his own accord. But this proposal was badly received. The fact, however, remains, that from the date just mentioned all the practices and performances were conducted by Julius Tausch, who thus became Schumann's real successor. No doubt the directors of the society were really in the right ; though perhaps the form in which Schumann's relation to the society was expressed might have been better chosen. The master was now taken up with the idea of leaving Düsseldorf as soon as possible, and of adopting Vienna, for which he had preserved a great affection, as his permanent residence. But fate had decided otherwise.

The dissatisfaction induced in his mind by the events of the autumn of 1853 was, however, mitigated partly by the tour in Holland already mentioned, and partly by another incident. It happened that in October a young and wholly unknown musician arrived, with a letter of introduction from Joachim. Johannes Brahms—for he it was—immediately excited Schumann's warmest interest by the genius of his playing and the originality of his compositions. In his early days he had always been the champion of the young and aspiring, and now as a matured artist he took pleasure in smoothing the path of this gifted youth. Schumann's literary pen had lain at rest for nine years ; he now once more took it up, for the last time, in order to say a powerful word for Brahms to the wide world of art. An article entitled *Neue Bahnen* (New Paths) appeared on Oct. 28, 1853, in No. 18 of that year's *Zeitschrift*. In this he pointed to Brahms as the artist whose vocation it would be ' to utter the highest ideal expression of our time.' He does not speak of him as a youth or beginner, but welcomes him into the circle of Masters as a fully equipped combatant. When before or since did an artist find such words of praise for one of his fellows ? It is as though, having already given so many noble proofs of sympathetic appreciation, he could not leave the world without once more, after his long silence, indelibly stamping the image of his pure, lofty, and unenvious artist-nature on the hearts of his fellow-men.

So far as Brahms was concerned, it is true that this brilliant *envoi* laid him under a heavy debt of duty, in the necessity of measuring his productions by the very highest standard ; and at the time Schumann was supposed to have attributed to Brahms, as he did to the poetess Elisabeth Kulmann, gifts which he did not actually possess. Twenty-eight years have now [1881] passed and we know that Schumann's keen insight did not deceive him, and that Brahms verified all the expectations formed of him. His intercourse with the young composer (then twenty years old), in whom he took the widest and most affectionate interest, was a great pleasure to Schumann.

At that time, too, Albert Dietrich (afterwards Hofcapellmeister at Oldenburg) was staying in Düsseldorf, and Schumann proved to the utmost the truth of what he had written only a few months previously of Kirchner, that he loved to follow the progress of young men. A sonata for pianoforte and violin exists in MS. which Schumann composed during this month (October 1853), in conjunction with Brahms and Dietrich. Dietrich begins with an allegro in A minor ; Schumann follows with an intermezzo in F major; Brahms—who signs himself *Johannes Kreissler junior*—adds an allegro (scherzo) in C minor ; and Schumann winds up the work with a finale in A minor, ending in A major. The title of the sonata is worth noting. Joachim was coming to Düsseldorf to play at the concert of Oct. 27, so Schumann wrote on the title-page 'In anticipation of the arrival of our beloved and honoured friend Joseph Joachim, this sonata was written by Robert Schumann, Albert Dietrich, and Johannes Brahms.'[1]

This interesting intimacy cannot have continued long, since in November Schumann went to Holland with his wife, and did not return till Dec. 22. But he met Brahms again in Hanover in January 1854 at a performance of 'Paradise and the Peri,' where he found also Joachim and Julius Otto Grimm. A circle of gifted and devoted young artists gathered round the master and rejoiced in having him among them, little imagining that within a few months he would be suddenly snatched from them for ever.

Schumann's appearance was that of a man with a good constitution ; his figure was above the middle height, full and well-built ; but his nervous system had always shown extreme excitability, and even so early as his twenty-fourth year he suffered from a nervous disorder which increased to serious disease. At a still earlier date he had shown a certain morbid hypertension of feeling, in connection with his passionate study of Jean Paul, of whom he wrote, even in his eighteenth year, that he often drove him to the verge of madness. Violent shocks of emotion,

as for instance the sudden announcement of a death, or the struggle for the hand of Clara Wieck, would bring him into a condition of mortal anguish, and the most terrible state of bewilderment and helplessness, followed by days of overwhelming melancholy. A predisposition to worry himself, an 'ingenuity in clinging to unhappy ideas,' often embittered the fairest moments of his life. Gloomy anticipations darkened his soul ; 'I often feel as if I should not live much longer,' he says in a letter to Zuccalmaglio of May 18, 1837, 'and I should like to do a little more work' ; and later, to Hiller—'man must work while it is yet day.' The vigour of youth for a time conquered these melancholy aberrations, and after his marriage the calm and equable happiness which he found in his wife for a long time expelled the evil spirit. It was not till 1844 that he again fell a prey to serious nervous tension. This was evidently the result of undue mental strain, and for a time he was forced to give up all work, and even the hearing of music, and to withdraw into perfect solitude at Dresden. His improvement was slow and not without relapses ; but in 1849 he felt quite re-established, as we gather from his letters and from the work he accomplished ; and his condition seems to have remained satisfactory till about the end of 1851. Then the symptoms of disease reappeared ; he had, as usual, been again working without pause or respite, and even with increased severity ; and was himself so much alarmed as to seek a remedy. Various eccentricities of conduct betrayed even to strangers the state of nervous excitability in which he was. By degrees delusions grew upon him, and he fancied that he incessantly heard one particular note, or certain harmonies, or voices whispering words of reproof or encouragement. Once in the night he fancied that the spirits of Schubert and Mendelssohn brought him a musical theme, and he got up and noted it down. He was again attacked by that 'mortal anguish of mind' of which he had had former experience, and which left him perfectly distracted. Still, all these symptoms were but temporary, and between the attacks Schumann was in full possession of his senses and self-control. He himself expressed a wish to be placed in an asylum, but meanwhile worked on in his old way. He wrote some variations for the piano on the theme revealed to him by Schubert and Mendelssohn, but they were his last work, and remained unfinished. On Feb. 27, 1854, in the afternoon, in one of his fits of agony of mind, he left the house unobserved and threw himself from the bridge into the Rhine. Some boatmen were on the watch and rescued him, and he was recognised and carried home. Unmistakable symptoms of insanity now declared themselves, but after a few days a peculiar clearness and calmness of mind returned, and with it his irrepressible love of

---

[1] The MS. was in Joachim's possession, and he permitted the publication of the movement by Brahms, which appeared in 1907.

work. He completed the variation on which he had been at work before the great catastrophe. These last efforts of his wearied genius remain unpublished, but Brahms has used the theme for a set of 4-hand variations which form one of his most beautiful and touching works (op. 23), and which he has dedicated to Schumann's daughter Julie.

The last two years of Schumann's life were spent in the private asylum of Dr. Richarz at Endenich near Bonn. His mental disorder developed into deep melancholy ; at times—as in the spring of 1855—when for a while he seemed better, his outward demeanour was almost the same as before. He corresponded with his friends and received visits, but gradually the pinions of his soul drooped and fell, and he died in the arms of his wife, July 29, 1856, only forty-six years of age.

Soon after Schumann's death his music achieved a popularity in Germany which will bear comparison with that of the most favourite of the older masters. When once the peculiarities of his style grew familiar, it was realised that these very peculiarities had their origin in the deepest feelings of the nation. The desire of giving outward expression to the love which was felt towards him, soon asserted itself more and more strongly. Schumann was buried at Bonn, in the churchyard opposite the Sternenthor, and it was resolved to erect a monument to him there. On August 17, 18, and 19, 1873, a Schumann festival took place at Bonn, consisting entirely of the master's compositions. The conducting was undertaken by Joachim and Wasielewski, and among the performers were Madame Schumann, who played her husband's Pianoforte Concerto, and Stockhausen. The festival was one of overwhelming interest, owing to the sympathy taken in it, and the manner in which that sympathy was displayed. The proceeds of the concerts were devoted to a monument to Schumann's memory, which was executed by A. Donndorf of Stuttgart, erected over the grave, and unveiled on May 2, 1880. On this occasion also a concert took place, consisting of compositions by Schumann, and Brahms's Violin Concerto (op. 77), conducted by himself, and played by Joachim.

Schumann, with his activity both as an author and as a composer, was a new phenomenon in German music. It is true that he had had a predecessor in this respect in C. M. von Weber, who also had a distinct gift and vocation for authorship, and whose collected writings form a literary monument possessing far more than a merely personal interest. Still Weber was prevented by circumstances and by his own natural restlessness from fully developing his literary talent, while Schumann benefited by the restraint and discipline of his ten years of editorship. In 1854 he had his *Gesammelte*

Schriften über Musik und Musiker published in four volumes by Wigand in Leipzig, and it was not long in reaching its second edition, which appeared in two volumes in 1871. This collection, however, is not nearly complete, and the essays it includes have been much altered. A full and correct edition of his writings is still a desideratum.

It must not, however, be imagined that Schumann's aim as an author was to lay down the principles on which he worked as a composer ; it is indeed hardly possible to contrast the critical and the productive elements in his works. His authorship and his musical compositions were two distinct phases of a creative nature, and if it was by composition that he satisfied his purely musical craving it was by writing that he gave utterance to his poetical instincts. His essays are for the most part rather rhapsodies on musical works or poetical imagery lavished on musical subjects than criticisms properly speaking ; and the cases where he writes in the negative vein are very rare exceptions. A high ideal floats before his mind, and supported by the example of the greatest masters of the art, his one aim is to introduce a new and pregnant period of music in contrast to the shallowness of his own time. Again and again he speaks of this as the ' poetic phase '— and here we must guard against a misunderstanding. The term *poetic music* is often used in antithesis to *pure music*, to indicate a work based on a combination of poetry and music ; as, for instance, a song, which may be conceived of either as a purely musical composition founded on the union of definite feelings and ideas, or as intended to express the preconceived emotions and ideas of the poet. But it was not anything of this kind that Schumann meant to convey ; he simply regarded poetry as the antithesis to prose, just as enthusiasm is the antithesis to sober dulness, the youthful rhapsodist to the Philistine, the artist with his lofty ideal to the mechanical artisan or the superficial dilettante. His aim is to bring to birth a living art, full of purpose and feeling, and he cannot endure a mere skeleton of forms and phrases. In this key he pitches his writings on music, and their purport is always the same. He once speaks of reviewers and critics under a quaint simile—' Music excites the nightingale to love-songs, the lap-dog to bark.' Nothing could more accurately represent his own attitude in writing on music than the first of these images. From his point of view a piece of music ought to rouse in the true critic sympathetic feeling, he ought to absorb and assimilate its contents, and then echo them in words—Schumann was in fact the singing nightingale. Though we may not feel inclined to apply his other comparison to every critic who does not follow in his steps, we may at least say that the difference between Schumann's style and that of the musical periodicals of his day was as great as that between a nightingale and a lap-dog. And how strange and new were the tones uttered by this poet-critic! A considerable resemblance to Jean Paul must be admitted, particularly in his earlier critiques: the ecstatic youthful sentiment, the humorous suggestions, the highly wrought and dazzling phraseology, are common to both; but the style is quite different. Schumann commonly writes in short and vivid sentences, going straight at his subject without digressions, and indulging in bold abbreviations. There is a certain indolence of genius about him, and yet a sure artistic instinct throughout. Nor has he a trace of Jean Paul's sentimental 'luxury of woe,' but we everywhere find, side by side with emotional rhapsody, the refreshing breeziness of youth and health.

It has already been said that Schumann connects certain definite characteristics with different feigned names (Florestan, Eusebius, Raro, etc.), a device which none but a poet could have hit on. Indeed, it would be a hindrance to the writing of calm criticism, which must have a fixed and clearly defined position as its basis. But it often introduces a varied and even dramatic liveliness into the discussion, which is very attractive, and leads to a deeper consideration of the subject. Schumann, however, could use still more artificial forms in his critiques. Thus he discusses the first concert conducted by Mendelssohn at the Gewandhaus, October 1835, in letters addressed by Eusebius to Chiara in Italy; and within this frame the details of the concert are gracefully entwined with ingenious reflections and fanciful ideas which add brilliance to the picture. On another occasion, when he was to write about a mass of dance music, Schumann has recourse to the following fiction:—the editor of a certain musical paper gives a historical fancy ball. Composers are invited, young lady amateurs and their mothers, music publishers, diplomatists, a few rich Jewesses, and—of course—the Davidsbündler; the dance-programme includes the music to be criticised, to which the couples whirl about during the whole evening. Hence arise all sorts of humorous incidents—satirical, whimsical, and sentimental outpourings, in which a criticism of the compositions is brought in unperceived. On another occasion, the Davidsbündler have met, and the new compositions are played in turns; during the playing the rest carry on a variety of amusements which culminate in a magic lantern, throwing the figures of a masked ball on the wall, which Florestan, standing on the table, explains, while 'Zilia' plays Franz Schubert's 'Deutsche Tänze.' Anything more vivid, charming, and poetical than this essay, has never been written on music (it is in the *Gesam. Schriften*, vol. ii. p. 9; and is partly translated in *Music and Musicians*, vol. i. p. 102); a little work of art in itself!

Once, in reviewing a concert given by Clara Wieck, he gives us a real poem ('Traumbild, am 9 September, 1838, Abends,' vol. ii. p. 233). In this he combines his own tender sentiments with a skilful characterisation of all that was peculiar in the performance. For sketching character-portraits Schumann shows a conspicuous talent; the articles in which he has characterised Sterndale Bennett, Gade, and Henselt are unsurpassed by anything since written concerning these artists. He seems to have penetrated with the insight of a seer to the core of their natures, and has set forth his conclusions in a delicate and picturesque manner that no one has succeeded in imitating.

The foundation of Schumann's critiques lay in kindness; his fastidious character would simply have nothing to do with anything bad enough to demand energetic reproof. The most cutting and bitter article he ever wrote was the famous one on Meyerbeer's 'Huguenots' (vol. ii. p. 220; translated in *Music and Musicians*. vol. i. p. 302). In its violence it has no doubt somewhat overshot the mark; but nowhere perhaps do the purity and nobleness of Schumann's artistic views shine forth more clearly than in this critique and in the one immediately following on Mendelssohn's 'St. Paul.' It was the great success of the 'Huguenots' which infused the acid into Schumann's antagonism; for when dealing with inoffensive writers he could wield the weapons of irony and ridicule both lightly and effectively. But he is most at his ease when giving praise and encouragement; then words flow so directly from his heart that his turns of expression have often quite a magical charm. As an example we may mention the article on Field's Seventh Concerto (*Ibid.* vol. i. p. 268; *Music and Musicians*, vol. i. p. 267). Anything more tender and full of feeling was never written under the semblance of a critique than the remarks on a sonata in C minor by Delphine Hill-Handley —formerly Delphine Schauroth (*Ibid.* i. 92). Schumann has here given us a really poetical masterpiece in its kind, full of intelligent appreciation of the purport of the work, and giving covert expression to its maidenly feeling, even in the style of his discussion; it must delight the reader even if he does not know a note of the composition. Schumann had fresh imagery always at command, and if in a generally meritorious work he found something to blame, he contrived to do it in the most delicate manner. His amiable temper, his tender heart and his conspicuous talents for literary work combined, never left him at a loss in such cases for some ingenious or whimsical turn. Sometimes, though rarely, in his eager sympathy for youthful genius in difficulty he went too far; Hermann Hirschbach, for instance, never fulfilled the hopes that Schumann formed of him; and even in his remarks on Berlioz, he at first probably said

ROBERT ALEXANDER SCHUMANN
From a daguerrotype

more than he would afterwards have maintained.

In later years Schumann's flowery and poetic vein gave way to a calm and contemplative style. His opinions and principles remained as sound as ever, but they are less keenly and brilliantly expressed than at the earlier period when he took peculiar pleasure in turning a flashing phrase (see *Ges. Schriften*, vol. i. pp. 27, 208). Still, the practical musician always predominates, and Schumann himself confesses that 'the curse of a mere musician often hits higher than all your æsthetics' (*Ibid.* ii. 246). Here and there, however, we come upon a profound æsthetic axiom, the value of which is in no degree diminished by our perception that it is the result rather of intuition than of any systematic reflection. It is universally acknowledged that by his essay 'on certain corrupt passages in classical works' (*Ibid.* iv. 59 ; *Music and Musicians*, i. 26), Schumann gave a real impetus to the textual criticism of music ; historical clues and comparisons are frequently suggested, and though these indications are not founded on any comprehensive historical knowledge, on all important subjects they show a happy instinct for the right conclusion, and are always worthy of attention.

It may be said of Schumann's literary work in general that it was not calculated to attract attention merely for the moment, though it did in fact open up new paths, but that it took the form of writings which have a high and permanent value. They will always hold a foremost place in the literature of music, and may indeed take high rank in the literature of art. For analytical acumen they are less remarkable. Schumann cannot be called the Lessing of music, nor is it by the display of learning that he produces his effects. It is the union of poetic talent with musical genius, wide intelligence, and high culture, that stamps Schumann's writings with originality, and gives them their independent value.

Schumann's literary work was connected with another phase of the musical world of Germany, as new in its way as the twofold development of his genius—the rise of party feeling. No doubt Schumann gave the first impetus to this movement, both by his imaginary 'Davidsbündlerschaft,' and by that Radical instinct which was part of his nature. Schumann's principles as an artist were the same which have been professed and followed by all the greatest German masters ; what was new in him was the active attempt to propagate them as principles. So long as he conducted the *Zeitschrift* he could not of course lend himself to party feeling ; the standard he had assumed was so high that all who took a serious view of art were forced to gather round him. But the spirit of *agitation* was inflamed, and when he retired from the paper other principles of less general application were put forward. It

was self-evident that Schumann was the only contemporary German composer who could stand side by side with Mendelssohn, and they were of course compared. It was asserted that in Mendelssohn form took the precedence of meaning, while in Schumann meaning predominated, striving after a new form of utterance. Thus they were put forward as the representatives of two antagonistic principles of art, and a Mendelssohn party and a Schumann party were formed. In point of fact there was scarcely any trace of such an antagonism of principle between the two composers ; the difference was really one of idiosyncrasy ; and so, being grounded more or less on personal feeling, the parties assumed something of the character of cliques. The literary Schumannites, having the command of an organ of their own, had an advantage over the partisans of Mendelssohn, who like Mendelssohn himself, would have nothing to do with the press. Leipzig was for a time the headquarters of the two parties. There, where Mendelssohn had worked for the delight and improvement of the musical world, it was the fate of his art to be first exposed to attack and detraction, which, to the discredit of the German nation, rapidly spread through wider and wider circles, and was fated too to proceed first from the blind admirers of the very master for whom Mendelssohn ever felt the deepest attachment and respect. That Schumann himself must have been painfully affected by this spirit is as clear as that it could only result in hindering the unprejudiced reception of his works ; and the process thus begun with Schumann has been carried on, in a greater degree, in the case of Wagner.

As a composer Schumann started with the pianoforte, and until the year 1840 wrote scarcely anything but pianoforte music. For some time he used to compose sitting at the instrument, and continued to do so even until 1839, though he afterwards condemned the practice (in his *Musikalische Haus- und Lebensregeln*). At all events it had the advantage of making him write from the first in true pianoforte style. If ever pianoforte works took their origin from the innermost nature of the pianoforte, Schumann's did so most thoroughly. His mode of treating the instrument is entirely new. He develops upon it a kind of orchestral polyphony, and by means of the pedal, of extended intervals, of peculiar positions of chords, of contractions of the hands, and so forth, he succeeds in bringing out of it an undreamt-of wealth of effects of tone. How deeply and thoroughly Schumann had studied the character of the instrument may be seen from the detailed preface to his arrangement of Paganini's caprices (op. 3). Even in his earliest PF. works he nowhere shows any inclination to the method of any of the older masters, except in the variations, op. 1, which betray the influence of the school of Hummel and Moscheles. But it is evident that he knew all that others had done, and the time and attention devoted in his writings to works of technical pianoforte study were no doubt deliberately given. Notwithstanding this his compositions are scarcely ever written in the *bravura* style ; for he seldom cared to clothe his ideas in mere outward brilliancy. Sometimes one is constrained to wonder at his reluctance to use the higher and lower registers of the pianoforte.

As is the case with the technical treatment of the piano, so it is from the beginning with the substance and form of his compositions. Few among the great German masters show such striking originality from their very first compositions. In the whole range of Schumann's works there is scarcely a trace of any other musician. At the outset of his course as a composer he preferred to use the concise dance or song-form, making up his longer pieces from a number of these smaller forms set together as in a mosaic, instead of at once casting his thoughts in a larger mould. But the versatility with which the small forms are treated is a testimony to the magnitude of his creative faculty. The predominance of the small forms is explained by his earlier method of composing. Diligent and constant though he was in later years, in early life his way of working was fitful and inconstant. The compositions of this period seem as if forced out of him by sudden impulses of genius. As he subsequently says of his early works, 'the man and the musician in me were always trying to speak at the same time.' This must indeed be true of every artist ; if the whole personality be not put into a work of art, it will be utterly worthless. But by those words Schumann means to say that as a youth he attempted to bring to light in musical form his inmost feelings with regard to his personal life-experiences. Under such circumstances it is but natural that they should contain much that was purely accidental, and inexplicable by the laws of art alone ; but it is to this kind of source that they owe the magic freshness and originality with which they strike the hearer. The Variations, op. 1, are an instance of this. The theme is formed of the notes A, B(♭), E, G, G. Meta Abegg was the name of a beautiful young lady in Mannheim, whose acquaintance Schumann, when a student, had made at a ball. Playful symbolism of this kind is not unfrequent in him. To a certain extent it may be traced back to Sebastian Bach, who expressed his own name in a musical phrase ; as Schumann afterwards did Gade's. (See 'Album für die Jugend,' op. 68, No. 41.) In the same way (*Ges. Schriften*, ii. 115) he expresses the woman's name 'Beda' in musical notes, and also in the 'Carnaval' made those letters in his own name which stand as notes—*s* (*es*), *c*, *h*, *a*—into a musical phrase. But the idea really came from

Jean Paul, who is very fond of tracing out such mystic connections. Schumann's op. 2 consists of a set of small pianoforte pieces in dance-form under the name of 'Papillons.' They were written partly at Heidelberg, partly in the first years of the Leipzig period which followed. No inner musical connection subsists between them. But Schumann felt the necessity of giving them a poetical connection, to satisfy his own feelings, if for nothing else, and for this purpose he adopted the last chapter but one [1] of Jean Paul's *Flegeljahre*, where a masked ball is described at which the lovers Wina and Walt are guests, as a poetic background for the series. The several pieces of music may thus be intended to represent partly the different characters in the crowd of maskers, and partly the conversation of the lovers. The finale is written designedly with reference to this scene in Jean Paul, as is plain from the indication written above the notes found near the end—' The noise of the Carnival-night dies away. The church clock strikes six.' The strokes of the bell are actually audible, being represented by the A six times repeated. Then all is hushed, and the piece seems to vanish into thin air like a vision. In the finale there are several touches of humour. It begins with an old Volkslied, familiar to every household in Germany as the Grossvatertanz. [2]

In contrast to these two old-fashioned love-tunes is placed the soft and graceful melody of No. 1 of the 'Papillons,' which is afterwards worked contrapuntally with the 'Grossvatertanz.' The name 'Papillons' is not meant to indicate a light, fluttering character in the pieces, but rather refers to musical phases which, proceeding from various experiences of life, have attained the highest musical import, as the butterfly soars upwards out of the chrysalis. The design of the title-page in the first edition points towards some such meaning as this ; and the explanation we have given corresponds with his usual method of composing at that time. There exists, however, no decisive account of it by the composer himself.

In a kind of connection with the 'Papillons' is the 'Carnaval,' op. 9. Here again Schumann has depicted the merriment of a masquerade in musical pictures, and a third and somewhat similar essay of the same kind is his 'Faschingsschwank [3] aus Wien,' op. 26. The 'Carnaval' is a collection of small pieces, written one by one without any special purpose, and not provided either with collective or individual titles until later, when he arranged them in their present order. The musical connection between the pieces is, that with few exceptions they all contain some reference to the succession of notes

---

[1] In a letter to his friend Henriette Voigt, Schumann calls it the *last chapter*. This, although obviously a slip of the pen, has led several writers to wonder what grand or fanciful idea lurks behind the 'Papillons.'
[2] See GROSSVATERTANZ, vol. ii. p. 246.
[3] *Fasching* is a German word for the Carnival

a, es, c, h (A, E♭, C, B) or *as, c, h* (A♭, C, B). Now Asch is the name of a small town in Bohemia, the home of a Fräulein Ernestine von Fricken, with whom Schumann was very intimate at the time of his writing this music. The same notes in another order, *s* (or *es*), *c, h, a*, are also the only letters in Schumann's own name which represent notes. This explains the title 'Sphinxes,' which is affixed to the ninth number on p. 13 of the original edition. The pieces are named, some from characters in the masked ball—Pierrot, Arlequin, Pantalon, and Colombine,—and some from real persons. In this last category we meet with the members of the Davidsbund—Florestan, Eusebius, and Chiarina ; Ernestine von Fricken, under the name Estrella, Chopin, and Paganini ; there is also a 'Coquette,' but it is not known for whom this is intended. Besides these, some of the pieces are named from situations and occurrences at the ball ; a recognition, an avowal of love, a promenade, a pause in the dance (Reconnaissance, Aveu, Promenade, Pause) ; between these are heard the sounds of waltzes, and in one of the pieces the letters A·S·C·H, and S·C·H·A, 'Lettres dansantes,' themselves dance boisterously and noisily, and then vanish like airy phantoms. A piece called 'Papillons' rushes by like a hasty reminiscence, and in the numbers entitled 'Florestan'—an actual passage from No. 1 of the 'Papillons' (op. 2) is inserted. The finale is called 'March of the Davidsbündler against the Philistines.' The symbol of the Philistines is the 'Grossvatertanz,' here called by Schumann a tune of the 17th century. The fact of the march being in 3–4 time has perhaps a humorous and symbolic meaning.

The 'Davidsbündlertänze' (op. 6), the 'Fantasiestücke' (op. 12), 'Kinderscenen' (op. 15), 'Kreisleriana' (op. 16), 'Novelletten' (op. 21), 'Bunte Blätter' (op. 99), and 'Albumblätter' (op. 124), the contents of which all belong to Schumann's early period, and, of the later works, such pieces as the 'Waldscenen' (op. 82) —all bear the impress of having originated like the 'Papillons' and the 'Carnaval,' in the personal experiences of Schumann's life. They are *poésies d'occasion* (Gelegenheitsdichtungen), a term which, in Goethe's sense, designates the highest form that a work of art can take. As to the 'Davidsbündlertänze,' the 'Kreisleriana,' and the 'Novelletten,' Schumann himself tells us that they reflect the varying moods wrought in him by the contentions about Clara Wieck. In the 'Davidsbündlertänze' the general arrangement is that Florestan and Eusebius appear usually by turns, though sometimes also together. The expression 'dance' does not, however, mean, as is sometimes supposed, the dances that the Davidsbündler led the Philistines, but merely indicates the form of the pieces, which is, truth to say, used with scarcely less freedom than that of the march in the finale to the 'Carnaval.'

The 'Kreisleriana' have their origin in a fantastic story with the same title by E. T. A. Hoffmann, contained in his *Fantasiestücke in Callots Manier* (Bamberg, 1814, p. 47). Hoffmann was a follower of Jean Paul, who indeed wrote a preface to *Fantasiestücke*. Half musician, half poet, Schumann must have looked on him as a kindred spirit ; and in the figure of the wild and eccentric yet gifted 'Kapellmeister Kreisler,' drawn by Hoffmann from incidents in his own life, there were many traits in which Schumann might easily see a reflection of himself. Of the 'Novelletten' Schumann says that they are 'long and connected romantic stories.' There are no titles to explain them, although much may be conjectured from the indications of time and expression. But the rest of the works we have just mentioned nearly always have their separate component parts, headed by names which lead the imagination of the player or hearer, in a clear and often deeply poetic manner, in a particular and definite direction. This form of piano piece was altogether a very favourite one with Schumann. He is careful to guard against the supposition that he imagined a definite object in his mind, such as a 'pleading child' (in op. 15) or a 'haunted spot in a wood' (in op. 82), and then tried to describe it in notes. His method was rather to invent the piece quite independently, and afterwards to give it a particular meaning by a superscription. His chief object was always to give the piece a value of its own, and to make it intelligible of itself. This principle is undoubtedly the right one, and, by adopting it, Schumann proved himself a genuine musician, with faith in the independent value of his art. Nevertheless, had he considered the poetical titles utterly unimportant, he would hardly have employed them as he has in so large a majority of his smaller pianoforte pieces. His doing so seems to evince a feeling that in the composition of the piece alone, he had not said everything that struggled within him for expression. Until a particular mood or feeling had been aroused in the hearer or the player, by means of the title, Schumann could not be sure that the piece would have the effect which he desired it to have. Strictly speaking, poetry and music can only be really united by means of the human voice. But in these pianoforte pieces with poetical titles, Schumann found a means of expression which hovered as it were between pure instrumental music on the one hand, and vocal music on the other, and thus received a certain indefinite and mysterious character of its own, which may most justly be called Romantic, but which is entirely apart from any connection with what is now called Programme Music.

Among the compositions consisting of small forms we must count the variations. Schumann treated the variation-form freely and fancifully, but with a profuse wealth of genius and depth of feeling. For the Impromptus on a theme by Clara Wieck (op. 5), Beethoven's so-called 'Eroica Variations' (op. 35), apparently served as a model ; they remind us of them both in general arrangement and in the employment of the bass as a theme, without being in any way wanting in originality. In the Andante and Variations for two pianofortes (op. 46), one of the most charming and popular of Schumann's pianoforte works, he treated the form with such freedom that they are not so much variations as fantasias in the style of variations. [They were at first intended to be accompanied by two violoncellos and horn, and this version is in the supplementary volume of the Breitkopf edition.] His most splendid work in this form is his op. 13 (the 'Études symphoniques'), a work of the grandest calibre, which alone would be sufficient to secure him a place in the first rank of composers for the pianoforte, so overpowering is the display of his own individual treatment of the pianoforte—frequently rising to the highest limits of the bravura style of execution—of his overflowing profusion of ideas, and his boldness in turning the variation form to his own account. In the finale the first two bars only of the theme are employed, and these only occasionally in the 'working-out section.' In other respects the proud edifice of this elaborately worked number has nothing in common with a variation. It contains, however, a delicate reference to the person to whom the whole work is dedicated, William Sterndale Bennett. The beginning of the chief subject is a fragment of the celebrated romance in Marschner's 'Templer und Jüdin' ('Du stolzes England, freue dich,' etc.). It is an ingenious way of paying a compliment to his beloved English composer.[1]

Schumann had made early attempts at works of larger structure, but it cannot be denied that they were not at first successful. The F♯ minor Sonata (op. 11) teems with beautiful ideas, but is wanting in unity to a remarkable degree, at least in the *Allegro* movements. The F minor Sonata (op. 14) shows a decided improvement in this respect, and the Sonata in G minor (op. 22) is still better, although not entirely free from a certain clumsiness. Schumann afterwards showed himself quite aware of the faults of these sonatas in regard to form. They offer the most striking example of his irregular and rhapsodical method of working at that period. The second movement of the G minor Sonata was written in June 1830, the first and third in June 1833, the fourth in its original form in October 1835, and in its ultimate form in 1838, the whole sonata being published in 1839. The F♯ minor Sonata was begun in 1833, and not completed till 1835. The F minor Sonata, finished on June 5, 1836, consisted at first of

five movements, an Allegro, two Scherzos, one after the other, an Andantino with variations, and a Prestissimo. When the work was first published, under the title of 'Concerto sans Orchestre,' Schumann cut out the two scherzos, apparently intending to use them for a second sonata in F minor. This, however, was not carried out, and in the second edition of the work he restored the second of the scherzos to its place.[2] When we observe how he took up one sonata after another, we see how impossible it is that any close connection can subsist between the several parts, or that there should be any real unity in them as a whole.

The Allegro for pianoforte (op. 8) is somewhat disjointed in form, while the Toccata (op. 7), a bravura piece of the greatest brilliance and difficulty in perfect sonata-form, exhibits a great degree of connection and consequence. In the great Fantasia (op. 17) we are led by the title to expect no conciseness of form. The classical masters generally gave to their fantasias a very clearly defined outline, but Schumann in this case breaks through every restriction that limits the form, especially in the first movement, where he almost seems to lose himself in limitless freedom. In order to give unity to the fantastic and somewhat loosely connected movements of this work of genius, he again had recourse to poetry, and prefaced the piece with some lines of F. Schlegel's as a motto :—

Durch alle Töne tönet	Through all the tones that vibrate
Im bunten Erdentraum,	About earth's mingled dream,
Ein leiser Ton gezogen	One whispered note is sounding
Für den der heimlich lauschet.	For ears attent to hear.

The 'earth's mingled dream' is in a manner portrayed in the substance of the composition. Schumann means that 'the ear attent to hear' will perceive the uniting-tones that run through all the pictures which the imagination of the composer unrolls to his view. Schlegel's motto seems almost like an excuse offered by Schumann. The original purpose of this Fantasia was not, however, to illustrate these lines. About Dec. 17, 1835, an appeal having been made from Bonn for contributions to a Beethoven memorial, Schumann proposed to contribute a composition ; and this was the origin of the work now called 'Fantasia,' the three movements of which were originally intended to bear the respective inscriptions of 'Ruins,' 'Triumphal Arch,' and 'The Starry Crown.' By these names the character both of the separate parts and of the whole becomes more intelligible. In order to get into the right disposition for the work Schumann's four articles on Beethoven's monument should be read (*Gesammelte Schriften*, vol. i. p. 215).

Although few of Schumann's pianoforte works of the first period are without defects of form, yet their beauties are so many that we easily forget those defects. In certain ways the com-

---

[1] The five variations left out in the published edition are included in the supplementary volume of Breitkopf's edition.

[2] The first appeared in 1866 as No. 12 of the Posthumous Works published by Rieter-Biedermann, together with the discarded Finale of the Sonata in G minor as No. 13. Both are in the supplementary volume of the Breitkopf & Härtel edition (1893).

positions of the first ten years present the most characteristic picture of Schumann's genius. In after life he proposed and attained loftier ideals in works worthy of the perfect master. But the freshness and charm of his earlier pianoforte works was never surpassed, and in his later years was but rarely reached. A dreamy imaginative nature was united in Schumann's character with a native solidity that never descended to the commonplace. From the first his music had in it a character which appealed to the people —nay, which was in a way national ; and quickly as he reached his present immense popularity in Germany, it will probably be long before he has the same influence in other nations, especially in France and Italy. After Beethoven, Schumann is the only master who possesses the power of giving full and free expression to the humorous element in instrumental music. Both in his writings and compositions he allows it to have full play, and it is in his earlier PF. works that it is most prominent. One of his freshest and fullest works is the Humoreske (op. 20), the most wonderful portrayal of a humorous disposition that it is possible to imagine in music. Schumann's thorough individuality is prominent, alike in harmonies, rhythm, and colouring, and in the forms of the melodies. It is, however, characteristic of his early PF. works that broad bold melodies rarely occur in them, though there is a superabundance of melodic fragments—germs of melody, as they might be called, full of a deep expression of their own. This music is pervaded by a spring-like animation and force, a germ of future promise, which gives it a peculiar romantic character ; a character strengthened by the admixture of poetic moods and feelings. Schumann was both musician and poet, and he who would thoroughly understand his music must be first imbued with the spirit of the German poets who were most prominent in Schumann's youth ; above all others Jean Paul and the whole romantic school, particularly Eichendorff, Heine, and Rückert. And just as these poets were specially great in short lyrics, revealing endless depths of feeling in a few lines, so did Schumann succeed, as no one has done before or since, in saying great things and leaving unutterable things to be felt, in the small form of a short pianoforte piece.

Schumann's enthusiastic admiration and thorough appreciation of Bach have been already described. He shared this with Mendelssohn, but it is certain that he entered more thoroughly than Mendelssohn did into the old master's mysterious depth of feeling. It would therefore have been wonderful if he had not attempted to express himself in the musical forms used by Bach. His strong natural inclination towards polyphonic writing is perceptible even in his earliest pianoforte works, but it was not until 1840 that it comes prominently forward. His six fugues on the name 'Bach' (op. 60), the

four fugues (op. 72), the seven pianoforte pieces in fughetta form (op. 126), the studies in canon form for the pedal-piano (op. 56), and the other separate canons and fugues scattered up and down his pianoforte works—all form a class in modern pianoforte music just as new as do his pianoforte works in the free style. The treatment of the parts in the fugues is by no means always strictly according to rule, even when viewed from the standpoint of Bach, who allowed himself considerable freedom. In employing an accompaniment of chords in one part, he also goes far beyond what had hitherto been considered allowable. But yet, taken as a whole, these works are masterpieces; no other composer of modern times could have succeeded as he has done in welding together so completely the modern style of feeling with the old strict form, or in giving that form a new life and vigour by means of the modern spirit. In these pieces we hear the same Schumann whom we know in his other works ; his ideas adapt themselves as if spontaneously to the strict requirements of the polyphonic style, and these requirements again draw from his imagination new and characteristic ideas. In short, though a great contrapuntist he was not a pedantic one, and he may be numbered among the few musicians of the last hundred years to whom polyphonic forms have been a perfectly natural means of expressing their ideas.

As a composer of Songs Schumann stands by the side of Schubert and Mendelssohn, the youngest of the trio of great writers in this class of music. Schubert shows the greatest wealth of melody, Mendelssohn the most perfect roundness of form; but Schumann is by far the most profoundly and intellectually suggestive. He displays a more finely cultivated poetic taste than Schubert, with a many-sided feeling for lyric expression far greater than Mendelssohn's. Many of his melodies are projected in bold and soaring lines such as we meet with in no other composer but Schubert ; for instance, in the well-known songs ' Widmung ' (op. 25, No. 1), ' Lied der Braut ' (op. 25, No. 12), ' Liebesbotschaft ' (op. 36, No. 6), ' Stille Thränen ' (op. 35, No. 10), and others. Still more frequently he throws himself into the spirit of the German Volkslied, and avails himself of its simpler and narrower forms of melody. Indeed his songs owe their extraordinary popularity chiefly to this conspicuously national element. The reader need only be reminded of the song ' O Sonnenschein ' (op. 36, No. 4), of Heine's ' Liederkreis ' (op. 24), and of the Heine songs ' Hör' ich das Liedchen klingen,' ' Allnächtlich im Traume,' ' Aus alten Marchen ' (op. 48, Nos. 10, 14, 15), of most of the songs and ballads (op. 45, 49, 53), and above all of the 'Wanderlied' (op. 35, No. 3), which sparkles with youthful life and healthy vigour. Besides these there are many songs in which the melody is hardly worked out, and which are—as is also frequently the case with his pianoforte works—as it were, mere sketches, or germs, of melodies. This style of treatment, which is quite peculiar to Schumann, he was fond of using when he wished to give the impression of a vague, dreamy, veiled sentiment ; and by this means he penetrated more deeply into the vital essence and sources of feeling than any other song-writer. Such songs as ' Der Nussbaum' (op. 25, No. 3), or ' Im Walde' (op. 39, No. 11) are masterpieces in this kind. Besides this, Schumann always brought a true poet's instinct to bear on the subtlest touches and most covert suggestions in the poems which he chose for setting, and selected the musical expression best fitted to their purport. Schubert and Mendelssohn set verses to tunes, Schumann wrote poems to them in music. He was the first who ventured to close on the dominant seventh when his text ended with a query (as in op. 49, No. 3). With him also the vocal part often does not end on the common chord, but the true close is left to the accompaniment, so as to give an effect of vague and undefined feeling. The part filled by the pianoforte in Schumann's songs is a very important one. With Schubert and Mendelssohn we may very properly speak of the pianoforte part as an ' accompaniment,' however rich and independent it occasionally appears. But with Schumann the word is no longer appropriate, the pianoforte asserts its dignity and equality with the voice ; to perform his songs satisfactorily the player must enter fully into the singer's part and the singer into the player's, and they must constantly supplement and fulfil each other. It was evidently of moment in the history of his art that Schumann should have come to the work of writing songs after ten years' experience as a composer for the pianoforte, and after instituting an entirely new style of pianoforte music. This style supplied him with an immense variety of delicate and poetic modes and shades of expression, and it is owing to this that he displays such constant novelty in his treatment of the pianoforte part. The forms of phrase which he adopts in his ' accompaniments' are infinitely various, and always correspond with perfect fitness and ingenuity to the character of the verses. In some cases the pianoforte part is an entirely independent composition, which the voice merely follows with a few declamatory phrases (op. 48, No. 9, ' Das ist ein Flöten und Geigen') ; while in others, in contrast to this, the voice stands almost alone, and the pianoforte begins by throwing in a few soft chords which nevertheless have their due characteristic effect (op. 48, No. 13, ' Ich hab' im Traum'). In Schumann's songs the proper function of the pianoforte is to reveal some deep and secret meaning which it is beyond the power of words, even of sung words, to express ; and he always disliked and avoided those repetitions of the words of which other composers have availed themselves in order to fill out in the music the feeling to which the words give rise. When he does repeat he always seems to have a special *dramatic* end in view rather than a musical one, and often makes the piano supplement the sentiment aroused by the text, while the voice is silent. He is particularly strong in his final symphonies, to which he gave a value and importance, as an integral portion of the song, which no one before him had ventured to do, often assigning to it a new and independent musical thought of its own. Sometimes he allows the general feeling of the song to reappear in it under quite a new light ; sometimes the musical phrase suggests some final outcome of the words, opening to the fancy a remote perspective in which sight is lost (a beautiful example is op. 48, No. 16, ' Die alten bösen Lieder'). Or he continues the poem in music ; of which a striking instance is the close of the ' Frauenliebe und Leben' (op. 42), where by repeating the music of the first song he revives in the fancy of the lonely widow the memory of her early happiness. The realm of feeling revealed to us in Schumann's songs is thoroughly youthful, an unfailing mark of the true lyric ; the sentiment he principally deals with is that of love, which in his hands is especially tender and pure, almost maidenly. The set of songs called ' Frauenliebe und Leben' gives us a deep insight into the most subtle and secret emotions of a pure woman's soul, deeper indeed than could have been expected from any man, and in fact no composer but Schumann would have been capable of it.

Schumann also found musical equivalents and shades of colour for Eichendorff's mystical views of nature ; his settings of Eichendorff's poems may be called absolutely classical, and he is equally at home in dealing with the bubbling freshness or the chivalrous sentiment of the poet. Many of Schumann's fresh and sparkling songs have a touch of the student's joviality, but without descending from their high distinction ; never under any circumstances was he trivial. Indeed he had no sympathy with the farcical, though his talent for the humorous is amply proved by his songs. A masterpiece of the kind is the setting of Heine's poem ' Ein Jüngling liebt ein Mädchen' (op. 48, No. 11), with its strange undercurrent of tragedy. It was principally in dealing with Heine's words that he betrays this sense of humour ; ' Wir sassen am Fischerhause' (op. 45, No. 3), is an example, and still more ' Es leuchtet meine Liebe' (op. 127, No. 3), where a resemblance to the scherzo of the A minor String Quartet is very obvious. A thing which may well excite astonishment as apparently quite beside the nature of Schumann's character, is that he could even find characteristic music for Heine's bitterest irony (op. 24, No. 6)

'Warte, warte, wilder Schiffsmann,' and many of the 'Dichterliebe.'

Schumann's Symphonies may, without any injustice, be considered as the most important in their time since Beethoven. Though Mendelssohn excels him in regularity of form, and though Schubert's C major Symphony is quite unique in its wealth of beautiful musical ideas, yet Schumann surpasses both in greatness and force. He is the man, they the youths; he has the greatest amount of what is demanded by that greatest, most mature, and most important of all forms of instrumental music. He comes near to Beethoven, who it is quite evident was almost the only composer that he ever took as a model. No trace whatever of Haydn or Mozart is to be found in his symphonies, and of Mendelssohn just as little. A certain approximation to Schubert is indeed perceptible in the 'working out' (*Durchführung*) of his Allegro movements. But the symphonies, like the pianoforte works, the songs, and indeed all that Schumann produced, bear the strong impress of a marvellous originality, and a creative power all his own. Even the first published Symphony (in B♭, op. 38) shows a very distinct talent for this branch of composition. We do not know that Schumann had ever previously attempted orchestral compositions, except in the case of the symphony written in the beginning of 1830, which still remains in MS. In 1839 he writes to Dorn: 'At present it is true that I have not had much practice in orchestral writing, but I hope to master it some day.' And in his next attempt he attained his object. In a few passages in the B♭ Symphony, the effects of the instruments are indeed not rightly calculated. One great error in the first movement he remedied after the first hearing. This was in the two opening bars, from which the theme of the Allegro is afterwards generated, and which were given to the horns and trumpets. It ran originally thus, in agreement with the beginning of the Allegro movement:

which, on account of the G and A being stopped notes, had an unexpected and very comic effect. Schumann himself was much amused at the mistake; when he was at Hanover in January 1854 he told the story to his friends, and it was very amusing to hear this man, usually so grave and silent, regardless of the presence of strangers (for the incident took place at a public restaurant), sing out the first five notes of the subject quite loud, the two next in a muffled voice, and the last again loud. He placed the phrase a third higher, as it stands in the printed score:

Another, but less important passage for the horns has remained unaltered. In bar 17 of the first Allegro, Schumann thought that this phrase ought to be made more prominent than it usually was on the horns, and requested both Taubert and David, when it was in rehearsal at Berlin and Leipzig in the winter of 1842, to have it played on the trombones.

But in general we cannot but wonder at the certain mastery over his means that he shows even in the first Symphony. His orchestration is less smooth and clear than that of either Mendelssohn or Gade, and in its sterner style reminds us rather of Schubert. But this stern power is suited to the substance of his ideas, and there is no lack of captivating beauty of sound. We even meet in his orchestral works with a number of new effects of sound such as only true genius can discover or invent. Instances of these are the treatment of the three trumpets in the 'Manfred' overture, the use made of the horns in the second movement of the E♭ Symphony, the violin solo introduced into the Romanza of the D minor Symphony, etc. etc. It is hard to decide which of Schumann's four symphonies (or five, counting op. 52) is the finest. Each has individual beauties of its own. In life and freshness and the feeling of inward happiness, the B♭ Symphony stands at the head. Schumann originally intended to call it the 'Spring Symphony'; and indeed he wrote it, as we learn from a letter to Taubert, in Feb. 1841, when the first breath of spring was in the air. The first movement was to have been called 'Spring's Awakening,' and the Finale (which he always wished not to be taken too fast) 'Spring's Farewell.' Many parts of the symphony have an especial charm when we thus know the object with which they were written. The beginning of the introduction evidently represents a trumpet-summons sent pealing down from on high; then gentle zephyrs blow softly to and fro, and everywhere the dormant forces awake and make their way to the light (we are quoting from the composer's own programme). In the Allegro the Spring comes laughing in, in the full beauty of youth.[1] This explains and justifies the novel use of the triangle in the first movement—an instrument not then considered admissible in a symphony. An enchanting effect is produced by the Spring song at the close of the first movement, played as though sung with a full heart; and it is an entirely new form of coda (see p. 67 of the score). In publishing the Symphony, Schumann omitted the explanatory titles, because he believed that the attention of the public is

[1] Schumann intended the *Più vivace* of the Introduction to be taken distinctly faster at once, so that the time might glide imperceptibly into the *Allegro*.

distracted from the main purpose of a work by things of that kind. We may well believe, moreover, that a good part of the spring-like feeling in this symphony comes from the deep and heart-felt joy which Schumann felt at being at last united to his hard-won bride. The same influence is seen in the D minor Symphony (op. 120), written in the same year with that just described, and immediately after it. It is entirely similar to its predecessor in its fundamental feeling, but has more passion. The form too is new and very successful ; the four sections follow each other consecutively without any pauses, so that the work seems to consist of only one great movement. The subjects of the Introduction re-appear in the Romanze, with different treatment, and the chief subject of the first Allegro is the foundation of that of the last. The second part of the first Allegro is in quite an unusual form, and before the last Allegro we find a slow introduction—imaginative, majestic, and most original. As has been already mentioned, Schumann intended to call the work 'Symphonic Fantasia.' Here, too, poetic pictures seem to be hovering round him on every side.

His third symphonic work of the year 1841 is also irregular, but only in form, and has as good a right as the second to the name of 'Symphony.' It appeared, however, under the name 'Overture, Scherzo, and Finale' as op. 52. Of this work, which is charming throughout, the first movement offers us the only example to be found in Schumann of the influence of Cherubini, a master for whom he had a great reverence. perhaps the most lovely movement is the highly poetic Scherzo in gigue-rhythm, which might constitute a type by itself among symphony-scherzos. His other scherzos approximate in style to those of Beethoven, whose invention and speciality this form was, and who had no successor in it but Schumann. The characteristic of the C major Symphony (op. 61) is a graver and more mature depth of feeling ; its bold decisiveness of form and overpowering wealth of expression reveal distinctly the relationship in art between Schumann and Beethoven. The form, too, as far as regards the number and character of the movements, is quite that of the classical masters, while in the last Symphony (Eb, op. 97) Schumann once more appears as one of the modern school. This is divided into five separate movements, including a slow movement in sustained style, and of a devotional character, between the Andante and the Finale. Schumann originally inscribed it with the words ' In the style of an accompaniment to a solemn ceremony' (im Charakter der Begleitung einer feierlichen Ceremonie), and we know that it was suggested to him by the sight of Cologne Cathedral, and the festivities on the occasion of Archbishop von Geissel's elevation to the Cardinalate.

The other movements are powerful, and full of variety and charm, and the whole symphony is full of vivid pictures of Rhineland life. Perhaps the gem of the whole is the second movement (Scherzo), in which power and beauty are mingled with the romance which in every German heart hovers round the Rhine and its multitude of songs and legends. Although written in 1850, when Schumann's imagination was becoming exhausted, the work bears no trace of any diminution of power.

The poetical concert-overture, a form invented by Mendelssohn, and practised by Bennett and Gade, was one never cultivated by Schumann. His overtures are really 'opening pieces,' whether to opera, play, or some festivity or other. In this again he follows Beethoven. His overtures, like those of Beethoven, are most effective in the concert-room, when the drama or occasion for which they were composed is kept in mind. It is so even with the wonderful ' Genoveva' overture, which contains something of Weber's power and swing ; but more than all is it true of the overture to Byron's ' Manfred,' so full of tremendous passion. None of the overtures subsequently written by Schumann reached this degree of perfection, least of all his ' Faust' overture, though that to the ' Braut von Messina' (op. 100) is not much inferior to 'Manfred.' In the last year of his productive activity Schumann was much occupied with this form, but the exhausted condition of his creative powers cannot be disguised, either in the 'Faust' overture or in those to Shakespeare's 'Julius Caesar' (op. 128) and Goethe's 'Hermann und Dorothea' (op. 136), which last he had intended to set as an opera. The festival overture on the ' Rheinweinlied ' (op. 123) is cleverly worked, and a very effective pièce d'occasion.

It was in the spring of 1838 that Schumann made his first attempt, so far as we know, at a String Quartet. It was scarcely successful, for he was too much immersed in pianoforte music ; at any rate the world has hitherto seen nothing of it. In June and July 1842 he was much more successful. The three string quartets (op. 41), written at this time, are the only ones that have become known. They cannot be said to be in the purest quartet style ; but as Schumann never played any stringed instrument, this is not surprising. They still retain much of the pianoforte style ; but by this very means Schumann attains many new and beautiful effects. At the time of writing the A minor quartet Schumann had become acquainted with Marschner's G minor Trio (op. 112), and speaks of it in the Zeitschrift. The fine scherzo of that work struck him very much, and in his own scherzo it reappears, in a modified form certainly, but yet recognisable enough. In spite of this plagiarism, however, we must allow the quartet to be in the highest degree original, and full of richness and poetry.

It contains much enchanting beauty, never surpassed even by Schumann. He seems here to have resumed his practice of mixing up poetic mysticism with his music. What other reason could there be for proposing to use the four bars of modulation from the first quartet (bars 30-34), exactly as they stand, for an introduction to the second quartet? He afterwards struck them out, as may be seen in the autograph. The other quartets also arrived at their present form only after manifold alterations. The slow introduction to the A minor Quartet was at first intended to be played *con sordini*. The third quartet began with a chord of the 6-5 on D, held out for a whole bar. The greatest alterations were made in the first Allegro of the A minor and in the variations in A♭ of the F major Quartets. Whole sections were re-written and modified in various ways. But Wasielewski is mistaken in saying (3rd ed. p. 178, note) that the *più lento* over the coda in these variations is a misprint for *più mosso*. Schumann wrote *più lento* quite plainly, and evidently meant what he wrote. He may possibly have changed his mind afterwards, for in regard to *tempo* he was often moved by the opinions of others.

Of the works for strings and pianoforte, the Quintet (op. 44) is of course the finest; it will always keep its place in the first rank of musical masterpieces. It claims the highest admiration, not only because of its brilliant originality, and its innate power—which seems to grow with every movement, and at the end of the whole leaves the hearer with a feeling of the possibility of never-ending increase—but also because of its gorgeous beauty of sound, and the beautiful and well-balanced relations between the pianoforte and the strings. Musicians are still living, like Carl Reinecke of Leipzig, who at the time of its appearance were in the most susceptible period of youth, and who tell of the indescribable impression the work made upon them. It must have seemed like a new paradise of beauty revealed to their view. The Pianoforte Quartet (op. 47) only wants animation, and a more *popular* character in the best sense of the word, to make it of equal merit with the Quintet. There is much in it of the spirit of Bach, as is perhaps most evident in the wonderful melody of the Andante. A high rank is taken by the Trios in D minor (op. 63) and F major (op. 80), both, as well as the quintet and quartet, written in one and the same year. In the first a passionate and sometimes gloomy character predominates, while the second is more cheerful and full of warmth in the middle movements. The canonic style is employed in the Adagios of both trios with new and powerful effect. The treatment of the strings with respect to the pianoforte may here and there be considered too orchestral in style; but it must not be forgotten that it was adopted to suit the piano

style, which in Schumann is very different from that of the classical masters and of Mendelssohn. The two trios, however, are wanting in that expression of perfect health which is so prominent in both the quintet and the quartet. They show traces of the hurry and breathless haste which in his later years increases the complication of his rhythms. The third and last Trio (G minor, op. 110) is far inferior to the others. There is still the same artistic design, and in isolated passages the noble genius of the master still shines clearly out; but as a whole this trio tells of exhaustion. The same may be said of most of the other chamber works of Schumann's latest years. Among them are two sonatas for piano and violin, gloomy, impassioned compositions, which can hardly be listened to without a feeling of oppression. There are also a number of shorter pieces for different instruments, among which the 'Märchenbilder für Pianoforte und Viola' (op. 113) are prominent. No one who bears in mind Schumann's ultimate fate can hear without emotion the last of these 'Märchenbilder,' which bears the direction 'Langsam, mit melancholischem Ausdruck.'

In the sphere of the concerto Schumann has left an imperishable trace of his genius in the Pianoforte Concerto in A minor (op. 54). It is one of his most beautiful and mature works. In addition to all his peculiar originality it has also the qualities, which no concerto should lack, of external brilliancy, and striking, powerful, well-rounded subjects. The first movement is written in a free form with happy effect; the cause being that Schumann had at first intended it to stand as an independent piece, with the title 'Fantasia.' He did not add the other two movements until two years afterwards.—The 'Introduction und Allegro appassionato,' for pianoforte and orchestra (op. 92), is a rich addition to concerto literature. In Schumann there is a deeper connection between the pianoforte and orchestra than had before been customary, though not carried to such a point as to interfere with the contrast between the two independent powers. He was far from writing symphonies with the pianoforte *obbligato*. His other works in concerto-form, written in the last years of his life, do not attain to the height of the Concerto. Among them is an unpublished violin concerto written between Sept. 21 and Oct. 3, 1853, and consisting of the following movements: (1) D minor alla breve, 'Im kräftigen, nicht zu schnellen Tempo'; (2) B♭ major, common time, 'Langsam'; (3) D major, 3-4, 'Lebhaft, doch nicht zu schnell.' The autograph was in the possession of Joachim. A Fantasia for violin and orchestra, dedicated to the same great artist, is published as op. 131. The Violoncello Concerto (op. 129) is remarkable for a very beautiful slow middle movement. There is also a Concerto for four horns and orchestra (op. 86). Schumann himself thought

2 *b*

very highly of this piece, partly because, as he wrote to Dr. Härtel, 'it was quite curious.' It is indeed the first attempt made in modern times to revive the form of the old *Concerto grosso* which Sebastian Bach had brought to perfection in his six so-called 'Brandenburg' concertos. As these concertos of Bach were not printed until 1850, and Schumann can scarcely have known them in manuscript, it is a remarkable and interesting coincidence that he should thus have followed Bach's lead without knowing it. The piece is particularly hard for the first horn, because of the high notes. When well rendered it has a peculiarly sonorous, often very romantic effect, to which, however, the ear soon becomes insensible from the tone of the four horns.

In his account of Marschner's 'Klänge aus Osten,' a work performed in Leipzig on Oct. 22, 1840, Schumann expresses great admiration for the form, in which it was possible to make use for concert performances of romantic stories, which had hitherto been only used on the stage. He was the first to follow this example in his 'Paradise and the Peri.' The text was taken from Moore's poem, of which Schumann shortened some parts to suit his purpose, while he lengthened others by his own insertions. It was his first work for voices and orchestra, and is one of his greatest and most important. The subject was happily chosen. The longing felt by one of those ideal beings created by the imagination from the forces of nature, to attain or regain a higher and happier existence, and using every means for the fulfilment of this longing, is of frequent occurrence in the German popular legends, and is still a favourite and sympathetic idea in Germany. It is the root of the legends of the Fair Melusina, of the Water Nixie, and of Hans Heiling. Schumann's fancy must have been stimulated by the magic of the East, no less than by Moore's poem, with its poetic pictures displayed on a background of high moral sentiment. The fact of Schumann's having retained so much of Moore's narrative is worthy of all praise ; it is the descriptive portions of the poem that have the greatest charm, and the music conforms to this. True, there will always be a certain disadvantage in using a complete self-contained poem as a text for music, a great deal of which will inevitably have been written without regard to the composer. Much that we pass over lightly in reading has, when set to music, a more definite and insistent effect than was intended. In other places again, the poem, from the musician's point of view, will be deficient in opportunities for the strong contrasts so necessary for effect in music. This is very obvious in Schumann's composition. The third portion of the work, although he took much trouble to give it greater variety by additions to the poetry, suffers from a certain monotony. Not that the

separate numbers are weaker than those of the former parts, but they are wanting in strong shadows. But there is something else that prevents the work from producing a really striking effect upon large audiences, and that is, if we may say so, that there is too much music in it. Schumann brought it forth from the fulness of his heart, and threw, even into its smallest interludes, all the depth of expression of which he was capable. The beauties are crowded together, and stand in each other's light. If they had been fewer in number they would have had more effect. But, with all these allowances, 'Paradise and the Peri' is one of the most enchanting musical poems in existence. And we can now confirm his own words in a letter to a friend after the completion of the work : 'A soft voice within me kept saying while I wrote, It is not in vain that thou art writing' : for this composition will go far to make him immortal. All the choruses in 'Paradise and the Peri,' perhaps with the exception of the last, are fine, original, and effective. But it must be admitted that choral composition was not really Schumann's strong point. In this respect he is far inferior to Mendelssohn. In many of his choruses he might even seem to lack the requisite mastery over the technical requirements of choral composition, so instrumental in style, so impracticable and unnecessarily difficult do they seem. But if we consider Schumann's skill in polyphonic writing, and recall pieces of such grand conception and masterly treatment as the beginning of the last chorus of the 'Faust' music, we feel convinced that the true reason of the defect lies deeper. The essential parts of a chorus are large and simple subjects, broad and flowing development, and divisions clearly marked and intelligible to all. In a good chorus there must be something to speak to the heart of the masses. Schumann took exactly the opposite view. The chorus was usually an instrument unfitted for the expression of his ideas. His genius could have mastered the technical part of choral composition as quickly and surely as that of orchestral composition. But since the case was otherwise, the chief importance of 'Paradise and the Peri' is seen to be in the solos and their accompaniments, especially in the latter, for here the orchestra stands in the same relation to the voice as the pianoforte does in Schumann's songs. A good orchestral rendering of 'Paradise and the Peri' is a task of the greatest difficulty, but one rewarded by perfect enjoyment.

In the fairy-tale of 'The Pilgrimage of the Rose' (op. 112) Schumann intended to produce a companion picture to 'Paradise and the Peri,' but in less definite outline and vaguer colours. The idea of the poem is similar to that of the former work, but Horn's execution of the idea is entirely without taste. Schumann was possibly attracted by its smooth versification and a few really good musical situations. The music contains much that is airy and fresh, as well as a beautiful dirge. On the other hand, it is full of a feeble sentimentality utterly foreign to Schumann's general character, and ascribable only to the decay of his imagination. The insignificant and wholly idyllic subject was quite inadequate to give employment to the whole apparatus of solo, chorus, and orchestra, and Schumann's first idea of providing a pianoforte accompaniment only was the right one. With a small section of Schumann's admirers the work will always keep its place, and produce a pleasing though not very deep effect. His other works in this form consist of four ballads : —'Der Königssohn' (op. 116), 'Des Sängers Fluch' (op. 139), 'Das Glück von Edenhall' (op. 143), all by Uhland ; and 'Vom Pagen und der Königstochter' (op. 140), by Geibel. It is painfully evident that these poems were not really written for music. The way the principal events of the story are described, and the whole outward form of the verses, imply that they were intended to be recited by a single person, and that not a singer but a speaker. If necessary to be sung, the form of a strophic song should have been chosen, as is the case with 'Das Glück von Edenhall,' but this would confine the varieties of expression within too narrow a range. It is as though Schumann's pent-up desire for the dramatic form were seeking an outlet in these ballads ; especially as we know that in the last years of his creative activity he was anxious to meet with a new opera-libretto. The faults of texts and subjects might, however, be overlooked, if the music made itself felt as the product of a rich and unwearied imagination. Unfortunately, however, this is seldom the case. It is just in the more dramatic parts that we detect an obvious dulness in the music, a lameness in rhythm, and a want of fresh and happy contrasts. It must be remarked, however, that isolated beauties of no mean order are to be met with ; such as the whole of the third part and the beginning and end of the second, in the ballad 'Vom Pagen und der Königstochter.' These works, however, taken as a whole, will hardly live.

On the other hand, there are some works of striking beauty for voices and orchestra in a purely lyrical vein. Among these should be mentioned the 'Requiem for Mignon' from 'Wilhelm Meister' (op. 98b), and Hebbel's 'Nachtlied' (op. 108). The former of these was especially written for music, and contains the loveliest thoughts and words embodied in an unconstrained and agreeable form. Few composers were so well fitted for such a work as Schumann, with his sensitive emotional faculty and his delicate sense of poetry ; and it is no wonder that he succeeded in producing this beautiful little composition. But it should never be heard in a large concert room, for which its delicate proportions and tender colouring are utterly unfitted. The 'Nachtlied' is a long choral movement. The peculiar and fantastic feeling of the poem receives adequate treatment by a particular style in which the chorus is sometimes used only to give colour, and sometimes is combined with the orchestra in a polyphonic structure, in which all human individuality seems to be merged, and only the universal powers of nature and of life reign supreme.

Schumann's music to 'Faust' is not intended to be performed on the stage as the musical complement of Goethe's drama. It is a piece for concert performance, or rather a set of pieces, for he did not stipulate or intend that all three parts should be given together. What he did was to take out a number of scenes from both parts of Goethe's poem, and set music to them. It follows that the work is not self-contained, but requires for its full understanding an accurate knowledge of the poem. From the First Part he took the following :—(1) Part of the first scene in the garden between Gretchen and Faust ; (2) Gretchen before the shrine of the *Mater dolorosa* ; (3) The scene in the Cathedral. These three form the first division of his Faust music. From the Second Part of the play he adopted : (1) The first scene of the first act (the song of the spirits at dawn, the sunrise, and Faust's soliloquy) ; (2) The scene with the four aged women from the fifth act ; (3) Faust's death in the same act (as far as the words, 'Der Zeiger fällt—Er fällt, es ist vollbracht'). These form the second division of the music. Schumann's third division consists of the last scene of the fifth act (Faust's glorification) divided into seven numbers. The experiment of constructing a work of art, without central point or connection in itself, but entirely dependent for these on another work of art, could only be successful in the case of a poem like 'Faust'; and even then, perhaps, only with the German people, with whom Faust is almost as familiar as the Bible. But it really was successful, more particularly in the third division, which consists of only one great scene, and is the most important from a musical point of view. In this scene Goethe himself desired the co-operation of music. Its mystic import and splendid expression could find no composer so well fitted as Schumann, who seemed, as it were, predestined for it. He threw himself into the spirit of the poem with such deep sympathy and understanding, that from beginning to end his music gives the impression of being a commentary on it. To Schumann is due the chief meed of praise for having popularised the second part of 'Faust.' In musical importance no other choral work of his approaches the third division of his work. In freshness, originality, and sustained power of invention it is in no way inferior to 'Paradise and the Peri.' Up to about the latter half of the last chorus it is a chain of musical gems, a perfectly unique contribution to concert literature, in the first rank of those works of art of which the German nation may well be proud. The second division of the 'Faust' music, consisting of three other scenes from the Second Part of the poem, is also of considerable merit. It is, however, evident in many passages that Schumann has set words which Goethe never intended to be sung. This is felt still more in the scenes from the First Part, which are, moreover, very inferior in respect of the music. The overture is the least important of all ; in fact the merit of the work decreases gradually as we survey it backwards from the end to the beginning ; a circumstance corresponding to the method pursued in its composition, which began in Schumann's freshest, happiest, and most masterly time of creativeness, and ended close upon the time when his noble spirit was plunged in the dark gloom of insanity.

There exist only two dramatic works of Schumann's intended for the theatre : the opera of 'Genoveva' and the music to Byron's 'Manfred.' The text of the opera may justly be objected to, for it scarcely treats of the proper legend of Genoveva at all ; almost all that made the story characteristic and touching being discarded, a fact which Schumann thought an advantage. This may perhaps be explained by remembering his opinion that in an opera the greatest stress should be laid on the representation of the emotions, and that this object might most easily be attained by treating the external conditions of an operatic story as simply and broadly as possible. He also probably felt that a great part of the Genoveva legend is epic rather than dramatic. He was mistaken, however, in thinking that after the reductions which he made in the plot, it would remain sufficiently interesting to the general public. He himself, as we have said, arranged his own libretto. His chief model was Hebbel's 'Genoveva,' a tragedy which had affected him in a wonderful way ; though he also made use of Tieck's 'Genoveva.' Besides these he took Weber's 'Euryanthe' as a pattern. The mixture of three poems, so widely differing from one another, resulted in a confusion of motives and an uncertainty of delineation which add to the uninteresting impression produced by the libretto. The character of Golo, particularly, is very indistinctly drawn, and yet on him falls almost the chief responsibility of the drama. The details cannot but suffer by such a method of compilation as this. A great deal is taken word for word from Hebbel and Tieck, and their two utterly different styles appear side by side without any compromise whatever. Hebbel, however, predominates. Tieck's work appears in the finale of the first act, and in the duet (No. 9) in the second act, e.g. the line 'Du liebst mich, holde Braut, da ist der Tag begonnen.' Genoveva's

taunt on Golo's birth is also taken from Tieck, although he makes the reproach come first from Wolf and afterwards from Genoveva herself, but without making it a prominent motive in the drama. Beside this several Volkslieder are interspersed. This confusion of styles is surprising in a man of such fine discrimination and delicate taste as Schumann displays elsewhere. The chief defect of the opera, however, lies in the music. In the opera of 'Genoveva,' the characters all sing more or less the same kind of music ; that which Schumann puts to the words is absolute music, not relative, i.e. such as would be accordant with the character of each individual. Neither in outline nor detail is his music sufficiently generated by the situations of the drama. Lastly, he lacks appreciation for that liveliness of contrast which appears forced and out of place in the concert-room, but is absolutely indispensable on the stage. 'Genoveva' has no strict recitatives, but neither is there spoken dialogue ; even the ordinary quiet parts of the dialogue are sung in strict time, and usually accompanied with the full orchestra. Schumann considered the recitative a superannuated form of art, and in his other works also makes scarcely any use of it. This point is of course open to dispute ; but it is not open to dispute that in an opera, some kind of calm, even neutral form of expression is wanted, which, while allowing the action to proceed quickly, may serve as a foil to the chief parts in which highly-wrought emotions are to be delineated. The want of such a foil in 'Genoveva' weakens the effect of the climaxes, and with them, that of the whole. As in the formation of the libretto Schumann took 'Euryanthe' as his model, so as a musician he intended to carry out Weber's intentions still farther, and to write, not an opera in the old-fashioned ordinary sense, but a music-drama, which should be purely national. At the time when 'Genoveva' was written, he was utterly opposed to Italian music, not in the way we should have expected him to be, but exactly as Weber was opposed to it in his time. 'Let me alone with your canary-bird music and your tunes out of the waste-paper basket,' he once said angrily to Weber's son, who was speaking to him of Cimarosa's 'Matrimonio Segreto.' But although he may not have succeeded in producing a masterpiece of German opera, we may appreciate with gratitude the many beauties of the music, the noble sentiment pervading the whole, and the constant artistic feeling, directed only to what is true and genuine. The finest part of the work is the overture, a masterpiece in its kind, and worthy to rank with the classical models.

The music to Byron's 'Manfred' (op. 115) consists of an overture, an entr'acte, melodramas, and several solos and choruses. Byron expressly desired the assistance of music for his work, though not so much of it as Schumann has given.

Schumann inserted all the instrumental pieces in the work, with the exception of the tunes on the shepherd's pipe in the first act; also the requiem heard at Manfred's death, sounding from the convent church. On the other hand, it is remarkable that he left the song of 'The captive usurper' in Act ii. Scene iv. without music. The whole work consists of sixteen numbers, including the overture; this Schumann composed first of all, and probably without intending to write music for the drama itself. Even here he does not evince any special gift for dramatic writing. In the present day Byron's drama is frequently performed upon the stage with Schumann's music, and its effectiveness can thus be tested. The music hardly ever serves to intensify the dramatic effects, and yet this is all that is necessary in a drama. It appears rather to be the outcome of the impression produced on Schumann by Byron's poem. There is one peculiarity about the 'Manfred' music. On the stage it loses a great part of its effect, just as, in my opinion, the poem loses half its fantastic and weird magic by being dressed in the clumsy and palpable illusions of a scenic representation. The overture is a piece of music of the most serious character, and much more fitted for concert performance than for assembling an audience in a theatre. This is still more true of all the other pieces, so delicate in construction and subtle in feeling, the closing requiem by no means excluded. And yet in the concert-room the music does not make its due effect; partly because the hearer is withdrawn from the influence of the action, which is indispensable to the full understanding of the whole work; and also because in the melodramas the spoken words and the music which accompanies them disturb one another more than when performed on the stage. From these remarks it might be imagined that the 'Manfred' music is an inferior work; but strange to say such is by no means the case. It is a splendid creation, and one of Schumann's most inspired productions. It hovers between the stage and the concert-room; and, paradoxical as it may seem, the deepest impression is produced by reading the score, picturing in one's mind the action and the spoken dialogue, and allowing the music to sink deep into the ears of one's mind. Perhaps the most striking parts of it all are the melodramas, and among them the deeply touching speech of Manfred to Astarte; and these all stand out with a peculiar purity and unity, when read as just described. They are in a manner improvements upon those highly poetic piano pieces of Schumann's with superscriptions; and we ought to think of the words when hearing the piece. In this music, if nowhere else, is revealed Schumann's characteristic struggle after the inward, to the disregard of the outward; and we see how diametrically opposed to his nature was the realisation of

dramatic effects where all is put into visible and tangible form. But he devoted himself to the composition of the 'Manfred' music just as if he had been fitted for it by nature. The poet and the composer seem to have been destined for one another as truly as in the case of the Faust music, but in a different way. Byron had no idea of stage representation in writing 'Manfred'; he only wished his poem to be read. Its romantic sublimity of thought, spurning all firm foothold or support on the earth, could only find its due completion in music such as this, which satisfies the requirements of neither stage nor concert-room. That a work of art, mighty and instinct with life, can be produced with a sublime disdain of all limits set by circumstance, provided only genius is at work upon it, is amply proved by Byron and Schumann in this their joint production. It has been already remarked more than once that the gloomy, melancholy, and passionate intensity of strife in Byron's 'Manfred,' heightened by contrast with the splendid descriptions of nature, corresponded to the conditions of Schumann's spirit at the time when the music was written. And indeed a deep sympathy speaks in every bar. But there was in Schumann a longing for peace and reconciliation, which is wanting in Byron. This comes out very plainly in different passages in the music, of which the most striking is the 'Requiem' at the close, which sheds over the whole work a gentle gleam of glory. If we were to go into details, we should neither know where to begin nor to end.

In January 1851 Schumann wrote to a friend, 'It must always be the artist's highest aim to apply his powers to sacred music. But in youth we are firmly rooted to the earth by all our joys and sorrows; it is only with advancing age that the branches stretch higher, and so I hope that the period of my higher efforts is no longer distant.' He is here speaking emphatically of 'sacred,' not of church music. Church music he never wrote, his Mass and his Requiem notwithstanding. It should be adapted to the church-services, and calculated to produce its effect in combination with the customary ceremonial; but sacred or religious music is intended to turn the mind of the hearers, by its own unaided effect, to edifying thoughts of the eternal and divine. Of compositions of this class we possess several by Schumann; nor was it in 1851 that he first began writing them. There is an Advent hymn for solo, chorus, and orchestra (op. 71), written in 1848; a motet for men's voices with organ, subsequently arranged for orchestra (op. 93), of 1849, and a New Year's hymn for chorus and orchestra (op. 144) of the winter of the same year; all three settings of poems by Friedrich Rückert. The Mass (op. 147) and the Requiem (op. 148), on the other hand, were composed in 1852, and Schumann may have been thinking mainly of works of this kind when he wrote the letter quoted above. As a Protestant his relations to the Mass and Requiem were perfectly unfettered ; and in the composition of these works he can have had no thought of their adaptation to divine service, since even in form they exhibit peculiarities opposed to the established order of the Mass. It may, however, be assumed that it was the Catholic feeling of Düsseldorf which suggested them, and that he intended the works to be performed on certain occasions at church concerts. The words of the Mass will always have a great power of elevating and inspiring an earnest artist ; but irrespective of this, the composition of a mass must have had a peculiar attraction for Schumann on other grounds. A poetical interest in the Catholic Church of the Middle Ages was at that time widely prevalent in Germany, particularly in circles which were most influenced by romantic poetry, and found in the Middle Ages the realisation of their most cherished ideals. Schumann shared in this tendency ; a vein of mystical religionism, which otherwise might have lain dormant, often shows itself in his later compositions. For instance, under the name Requiem we find the setting of a hymn, ascribed to Héloïse, the beloved of Abélard (op. 90, No. 7),

Requiescat a labore
Doloroso, et amore, etc.

Other instances are the poems of Mary Stuart (op. 135), and the Requiem for Mignon. In the Mass he has, contrary to custom, introduced an offertorium, Tota pulchra es, Maria, et macula non est in te.

In judging of Schumann's sacred music, it is necessary to repeat that, though the chorus is not, strictly speaking, the musical means by which he was best able to express himself, yet both custom and the character and importance of the subject urged him to make considerable use of it in these works. Thus they contain a contradiction in themselves ; they are all nobly and gravely conceived, but as choral music are only very rarely satisfactory. The Mass, no doubt, ranks highest, and contains much that is very beautiful ; the ' Kyrie,' the ' Agnus,' the beginning and end of the ' Sanctus,' and part of the ' Credo,' being among Schumann's very best choral works. Unfortunately there is less to be said for the Requiem ; we should have expected the mere idea of a mass for the dead to have inspired such a genius as Schumann's, even without recollecting the wonderful tones which he has found for the final requiem in ' Manfred.' But this work was undoubtedly written under great exhaustion ; and the first romantic chorus alone makes a uniformly harmonious impression. It closes the list of Schumann's works, but it is not with this that we should wish to complete the picture of so great and noble a master. He once said with reference to the Requiem, ' It is a thing that one writes for oneself.' But the abundant treasure of

individual, pure, and profound art which he has bequeathed to us in his other works is a more lasting monument to his name, stupendous and imperishable.

Among the published works that treat of Schumann's life and labours, that by Wasielewski deserves the first mention (Robert Schumann, eine Biographie, von Josef W. von Wasielewski ; Dresden, R. Kunze, 1858 ; ed. 3, Bonn, E. Strauss, 1880). Though in time it may yet receive additions and revision, it has still the enduring merit of giving from accurate acquaintance the broad outlines of Schumann's life. [August Reissmann's Robert Schumann, sein Leben und seine Werke (1865, 1871, and 1879) contains analysis of many works.] Other valuable contributions to his biography have been written by Franz Hueffer, Die Poesie in der Musik (Leipzig, Leuckart, 1874) ; by Richard Pohl, Erinnerungen an R. Schumann, in the Deutsche Revue, vol. iv., Berlin, 1878 (pp. 169 to 181, and 306 to 317) ; by Max Kalbeck, R. Schumann in Wien, forming the feuilletons of the Wiener Allgemeine Zeitung of Sept. 24, 29, and Oct. 5, 1880. An accurate and sympathetic essay on Schumann, Robert Schumann's Tage und Werke, was contributed by A. W. Ambros to the Culturhistorische Bilder aus dem Musikleben der Gegenwart (Leipzig, Matthes, 1860 ; pp. 51-96). Schumann's literary work was reviewed by H. Deiters in the Allg. musik. Zeitung (Leipzig, Breitkopf & Härtel, 1865, Nos. 47-49). [The Gesammelte Schriften reached their third edition in 1883 ; and were translated by Fanny Raymond Ritter ; Die Davidsbündler by F. G. Jensen (1883) is full of interest. A collection of the master's Jugendbriefe edited by Clara Schumann, appeared in 1885, and was translated in 1888 ; F. G. Jensen's Neue Folge of letters (1886) appeared as The Life of Robert Schumann told in his Letters, translated by May Herbert (1890). Litzmann's biography of Clara Schumann contains much new information. A large selection from all the letters was published by Dr. Karl Storck in 1907, and translated by Hannah Bryant.]

Schuberth & Co. published in 1860-61 a Thematic Catalogue of Schumann's printed works, extending to op. 143 only. A complete index to all the published compositions of Schumann, with careful evidence as to the year in which each was written, published, and first performed, and their different editions and arrangements, was compiled by Alfred Dörffel as a supplement to the Musikalisches Wochenblatt (Leipzig, Fritzsch, 1875). It is impossible to indicate all the shorter notices of Schumann in books and periodicals. The author of this article has had the advantage of seeing a considerable number of his unpublished letters, and of obtaining much information at first hand from persons who were in intimate relations with him.

CATALOGUE OF SCHUMANN'S PUBLISHED WORKS.

[The complete edition of Breitkopf & Härtel in thirty-four volumes, edited by Clara Schumann and others, was completed in 1893 by a supplementary volume edited by Brahms.]

(All works down to op. 23, inclusive, are for pianoforte solo.)

Op.
1. Variations on the name 'Abegg.'
2. Papillons, twelve pieces.
3. Six Studies after Paganini's Caprices.
4. Intermezzi, six pieces.
5. Impromptus (Variations) on a theme of Clara Wieck.
6. Davidsbündlertänze, eighteen pieces.
7. Toccata.
8. Allegro.
9. Carnaval, twenty-one pieces.
10. Six Studies after Paganini's caprices.
11. Sonata in F sharp minor.
12. Fantasiestücke, eight pieces.
13. Études en forme de variations (Études symphoniques).
14. Sonata in F minor.
15. Kinderscenen, thirteen pieces.
16. Kreisleriana, eight pieces.
17. Fantasia in C.
18. Arabeske.
19. Blumenstück.
20. Humoreske.
21. Novelletten, eight pieces.
22. Sonata in G minor.
23. Nachtstücke, four pieces.
24. Liederkreis (nine songs).
25. Myrthen, twenty-six songs.
26. Faschingsschwank aus Wien, pf. solo.
27. Lieder und Gesänge (5).
28. Three Romances for pf. solo.
29. Three Poems by Geibel (the first for two Sopranos, the second for three sopranos, and the third [Zigeunerleben—'Gipsy Life'] for small Chorus, Triangle, and Tambourines ad lib.).
30. Three songs to Geibel's words.
31. Three songs to Chamisso's words.
32. Scherzo, Gigue, Romanza, and Fughetta, for pf. solo.
33. Six Four-part songs for men's voices.
34. Four Duets for sopr. and tenor.
35. Twelve songs to words by Kerner.
36. Six songs to words by Reinick.
37. Twelve songs from Rückert's 'Liebesfrühling.' (Three Nos. 2, 4, and 11 are by Clara Schumann.)
38. Symphony in B flat.
39. Liederkreis, twelve poems by Eichendorff.
40. Five songs.
41. Three string quartets in A minor, F, and A.
42. Frauenliebe und -Leben, songs by Chamisso.
43. Three two-part songs.
44. Quintet for pf. and strings in E flat.
45. Three Romanzen und Balladen, voice and pf.
46. Andante and variations for two pianos.
47. Quartet for pf. and strings in E flat.
48. Dichterliebe, sixteen songs by Heine.
49. Three Romanzen und Balladen, voice and pf.
50. Paradise and the Peri, cantata for solo voices, chorus, and orch.
51. Five songs.
52. Overture, Scherzo, and Finale, for orch.
53. Three Romanzen und Balladen, voice and pf.
54. Concerto for pf. and orch.
55. Five songs by Burns for mixed chorus.
56. Studies for the pedal piano, six pieces in canon.
57. Belsatzar, ballad by Heine.
58. Four sketches for pedal piano.
59. Four songs for mixed chorus.
60. Six fugues on the name Bach, for piano or organ.
61. Symphony in C, for orch.
62. Three songs for male chorus.
63. Trio for piano and strings in D minor.
64. Three Romanzen und Balladen, voice and pf.
65. Ritornellen, canons for male chorus.
66. Bilder aus Osten, for piano, four hands.
67. Five Romanzen und Balladen, for chorus.
68. Album for the young (forty pieces).
69. Six romances, for female chorus.
70. Adagio and Allegro, for piano and horn (or violoncello or violin).
71. Adventlied, for chorus and orchestra.
72. Four fugues for piano.
73. Three Fantasiestücke for pf. and clarinet (violin or violoncello).
74. Spanisches Liederspiel, for vocal quartet, with pf. acct.
75. Five Romanzen und Balladen, for chorus.
76. Four marches for pf.
77. Five songs.
78. Four duets for sopr. and tenor.
79. Lieder-Album, twenty-eight songs for the young.
80. Trio for pf. and strings in F.
81. Genoveva, opera in four acts.
82. Waldscenen, nine pieces for pf.
83. Three songs.
84. A Parting Song ('Es ist bestimmt'), chorus and orch.
85. Twelve piano duets, 'für kleine und grosse Kinder.'
86. Concertstück, for four horns and orch.
87. Der Handschuh, ballad for voice and pf.
88. Four Phantasiestücke for pf. and violin and violoncello.
89. Six songs.
90. Seven songs.
91. Six romances for female chorus.
92. Introduction and Allegro appassionato, pf. and orch.
93. Motet, 'Verzweifle nicht,' double male chorus with organ acct.
94. Three romances for oboe and pf. (or violin or violoncello).
95. Three songs from Byron's Hebrew Melodies, with acct. of harp or pf.
96. Five songs.
97. Symphony in E flat.
98a. Nine songs from 'Wilhelm Meister.'

Op.
98b. Requiem für Mignon, from the same, for chorus and orchestra.
99. Bunte Blätter for pf. (fourteen pieces).
100. Overture to 'Die Braut von Messina.'
101. Minnespiel for solo voices and pf.
102. Five Stücke im Volkston for violoncello (or violin) and pf.
103. Mädchenlieder, vocal duets.
104. Seven Songs.
105. Sonata for pf. and violin, A minor.
106. Schön Hedwig, ballad for declamation with pf. acct.
107. Six Songs.
108. Nachtlied, for chorus and orch.
109. Ballscenen, nine pieces for pf. duet.
110. Trio for pf. and strings in G minor.
111. Three Fantasiestücke for pf.
112. Der Rose Pilgerfahrt (Pilgrimage of the Rose) for soli, chorus, and orch.
113. Märchenbilder, for pf. and viola (or violin).
114. Three songs for female chorus.
115. Music to Byron's 'Manfred.'
116. Der Königssohn, ballad for soli, chorus, and orch.
117. Four Husarenlieder, for voice and pf.
118. Three pf. sonatas for the young.
119. Three songs.
120. Symphony in D minor.
121. Sonata for pf. and violin, D minor.
122. Two ballads for declamation with pf. acct.
123. Festival Overture on the Rheinweinlied, for orch.
124. Albumblätter, twenty pf. pieces.
125. Five Songs.
126. Seven pieces in fughetta form for pf.
127. Five Songs.
128. Overture to 'Julius Caesar.'
129. Concerto for violoncello and orch.
130. Kinderball, six pieces for pf. duet.
131. Phantasie for violin and orch.
132. Märchenerzählungen, four pieces for pf., clarinet (or violin) and viola.
133. Gesänge der Frühe, five pf. pieces.
134. Concert-allegro with introduction, for pf. and orch.
135. Five Gedichte der Maria Stuart, for voice and pf.
136. Overture to 'Hermann und Dorothea.'
137. Five hunting-songs for male chorus, with acct. of four horns.
138. Spanische Liebeslieder, for soli, solos, with acct. of pf. duet.
139. Des Sängers Fluch, for soli, chorus, and orch.
140. Vom Pagen und der Königstochter, four ballads for soli, chorus, and orch.
141. Four songs for double chorus.
142. Four songs.
143. Der Glück von Edenhall, for soli, chorus, and orch.
144. Neujahrslied, for chorus and orch.
145. Five Romanzen und Balladen, for chorus.
146. Five Romanzen und Balladen, for chorus.
147. Mass, for chorus and orch.
148. Requiem, for chorus and orch.

WITHOUT OPUS NUMBERS

Scenes from Goethe's 'Faust' for soli, chorus, and orch.
Der deutsche Rhein, song with chorus.
Pf. accompaniments to Bach's suites for violin alone.

The following are in the supplementary volume of the complete edition :—
1. Andante and variations for two pianofortes, two violoncellos and horn.
2. An Anna, song.
3. Im Herbste, song.
4. Hirtenknabe, song.
5. Sommerruh', duet with pf. acct.
6. Five extra variations for op. 13.
7. Scherzo for pf. (suppl. to op. 14).
8. Presto for pf. (suppl. to op. 22).
9. Thema in E flat for pf.

P. S.

SCHUMANN-HEINK, ERNESTINE, *née* Roessler, was born, June 15, 1861, at Lieben, near Prague. She was taught singing by Marietta Leclair at Graz, and on Oct. 13, 1878, made her début at Dresden as Azucena, remaining there four years. In 1883 she was engaged at Hamburg, where she remained many years. In 1892, as Frl. Heink, she sang with the Hamburg Company both at Covent Garden and Drury Lane, making her début June 8 (Covent Garden) as Erda in 'Siegfried.' Later she sang as Fricka, Waltraute, and, July 8, as the Countess on the production in England at Drury Lane of Nessler's 'Trompeter von Säkkingen.' She made a great impression, on account of her fine voice, combining mezzo and contralto, and of her excellent singing and acting. From 1897 to 1900 inclusive she sang again at Covent Garden, principally in Wagner parts; July 11, 1898, the music of the Prologue, on the production of Mancinelli's

'Ero e Leandro.' From 1896 to 1906 she has been in continued request at Bayreuth, having in the meantime sung with great success in America, at Berlin as Carmen, etc., and elsewhere. In 1903 she gave a vocal recital in London, and on Dec. 12 sang Mozart's 'Non più di fiori' at the Queen's Hall. She has been twice married; first in 1883 to Herr Heink, secondly, in 1893, to Herr Paul Schumann.   A. C.

SCHUNKE, LOUIS (LUDWIG), pianoforte player and composer, born of a musical family at Cassel, Dec. 21, 1810. His progress was so rapid that at ten he could play the Concertos of Mozart and Hummel with ease. In 1824 he visited Munich and Vienna, and then Paris, where he put himself under Kalkbrenner and Reicha. After some wandering to Stuttgart, Vienna (1832), Prague, and Dresden he came to Leipzig, where he made the acquaintance of Schumann, and an intimate friendship was the result. Schunke was carried off on Dec. 7, 1834, at the early age of not quite twenty-four, to the great grief of Schumann, who indulged his affection in several interesting papers (*Ges. Schrift*. i. 9 2, 325; ii. 56, 277) full of memorials of his friend's characteristics. Schunke was one of the four who edited the *Neue Zeitschrift für Musik* on its first appearance. His articles are signed with the figure 3. His published compositions are for the piano, and show considerable ability.   G.

SCHUPPANZIGH, IGNAZ, celebrated violinist, born 1776, in Vienna, where his father was a professor at the Realschule. He adopted music as a profession about the end of 1792, and that he early became known as a teacher we gather from an entry in Beethoven's diary for 1794, 'Schuppanzigh three times a week, Albrechtsberger three times a week.' Beethoven was studying the viola, which was at that time Schuppanzigh's instrument, but he soon after abandoned it for the violin. Before he was twenty-one he had made some name as a conductor, and in 1798 and 1799 directed the Augarten concerts. The *Allg. mus. Zeitung* of May 1799, after describing the concerts, remarks that 'the zeal shown by Herr Schuppanzigh in interpreting the compositions produced, makes these concerts models worth following by all amateur associations of the kind, and by many conductors.' Beethoven, who had also appeared at the Augarten concerts, kept up a singular kind of friendship with Schuppanzigh. They were so useful to each other that, as Thayer says, they had a great mutual liking, if it did not actually amount to affection. Schuppanzigh was goodlooking, though later in life he grew very fat, and had to put up with many a joke on the subject from Beethoven. 'Mylord Falstaff' was one of his nicknames (letter to Archduke in Nohl, *Neue Briefe*, p. 75). The following piece of rough drollery, scrawled by Beethoven on a

blank page at the end of his Sonata op. 28, is here printed for the first time :—

Lob auf den Dicken.

Schup - pan - zigh ist ein Lump, Lump, Lump, Wer kennt ihn, wer kennt ihn nicht? Den dicken Sau - ma-gen, den auf-ge-blas-nen E - selskopf, O Lump Schup-pan-zigh, O E - sel Schuppanzigh, Wir stim-men al - le ein, Du bist der grosste E - - sel! O Lump! O E - sel! Hi - hi - - ha! O E - sel!

Schuppanzigh was a great quartet-player, and belonged to the party which met every Friday during 1794 and 1795 at Prince Carl Lichnowsky's, where he took the first violin, the Prince himself, or a Silesian named Sina, the second, Weiss the viola, and Kraft, a thorough artist, the violoncello—occasionally changing with Beethoven's friend, Zmeskall. Towards the close of 1808 Schuppanzigh founded the Rasoumowsky quartet, to which he, Mayseder and Linke, remained attached for life. Weiss again took the viola. Beethoven's quartets were the staple of their performances. In the meantime Schuppanzigh had married a Fräulein Kilitzky, the sister of a well-known singer, who sang with little success 'Ah perfido!' at a concert of Beethoven's in 1808, instead of Anna Milder. On this occasion the great joker writes to Graf Brunswick, 'Schuppanzigh is married—they say his wife is as fat as himself—what a family ??' (Nohl, *Neue Briefe*, p. 11.) When the Rasoumowsky palace was burnt down in 1815 Schuppanzigh started on a tour through Germany, Poland, and Russia, and did not return till early in 1824, when the quartets were resumed with the same band of friends (see Beethoven's letters to his nephew, 1825). One of the first events after his return was the performance of Schubert's Octet, which is marked as finished on March 1, and was doubtless played very shortly after. [See *ante*, p. 301.] The acquaintance thus begun was cemented by Schubert's dedication of his lovely Quartet in A 'to his friend I. Schuppanzigh,' a year later. Schuppanzigh was a member of the court-chapel, and for some time director of the court-opera. He died of paralysis, March 2, 1830. Of his compositions the following were printed :—'Solo pour le violon avec quatuor' (Diabelli), 'Variationen über ein russisches Lied' (Cappi), and 'Variationen über ein Thema aus Alcina' (Mollo).　　　　　　　　　　　　　　　F. G.

SCHWARBROOK, THOMAS, a German, was in the employ of Renatus Harris, the organ-builder. Early in the 18th century he left London to live at Warwick, and built many noble instruments. His masterpiece was the organ of St. Michael's, Coventry, built in 1733, which cost £1400. The latest mention of him is in 1752, when he improved the organ of Worcester Cathedral. See vol. iii. p. 537a.　　　　　　　　　　　　　　V. DE P.

SCHWARTZENDORF, J. P. A. See MARTINI IL TEDESCO, vol. iii. p. 68.

SCHWEIZERFAMILIE, DIE. Opera in three acts, words by Castelli, music by Joseph Weigl. Produced at Vienna, March 14, 1809.

SCHWEMMER, HEINRICH, was born March 28, 1621, at Gumbertshausen near Hallburg in Lower Franconia, a place which the Thirty Years' War is said to have wiped out of existence. In his younger years war and the pestilence obliged his family to seek refuge first at Weimar, then at Coburg. According to Gerber he first visited Nuremberg in 1641 as a pupil of the St. Sebald School, and received his musical instruction from the organist Johann Erasmus Kindermann. But the first documentary evidence we have of his presence at Nuremberg is in connection with a great musical festival and banquet held there in 1649, in honour of the Swedish Field-Marshal, after the Peace of Westphalia. Schwemmer appears among the singers on that occasion, though not yet holding any appointment. 1650 is the date of his first appointment at Nuremberg as one of the Assistant Masters at the St. Laurence School. In 1656 he is described as *Director Chori musici* at the Frauen-kirche ; but with this post, which he seems to have retained till his death, May 26, 1696, he was obliged, in accordance with the custom of the time, to combine certain duties of ordinary school instruction at the St. Sebald School. Like greater musicians after him Schwemmer appears to have found his ordinary school duties somewhat irksome, and for an occasional negligence in them came under the censure of the town authorities. In spite of this he was recognised as the best musical teacher in Nuremberg, and the most distinguished of later

Nuremberg musicians, such as Pachelbel, Johann Krieger, and Baltazar Schmidt, were his pupils. He was also the musician most sought after for such occasional compositions as wedding and funeral anthems. The *Quellen-Lexikon* enumerates twenty of such works for voices and instruments. He was also the composer of a large number of melodies for the various Nuremberg hymn-books of the time. In the Denkmäler der Tonkunst in Bayern, Jahrgang VI. there is printed for the first time an Easter Motet by him for voices and instruments, which is characterised by much of the Handelian simplicity and directness of choral effect. Only a few other Church works by him remain in MS.　　J. R. M.

SCHWENKE, or SCHWENCKE, a German musical family, whose founder, JOHANN GOTTLIEB (born August 11, 1744, at Breitenau in Saxony, died at Hamburg, Dec. 7, 1823), was a famous bassoonist and a 'Rathsmusikus.' His son, CHRISTIAN FRIEDRICH GOTTLIEB, was born at Wachenhausen in the Harz, August 30, 1767, was a proficient clavier-player, and appeared in public at Hamburg in a concerto of his father's in 1779, when eleven and a half years old. Emanuel Bach interested himself in the boy's career, and was instrumental in getting him sent to Berlin (1782), where he studied under Kirnberger. He tried for an organist's post at Hamburg in 1783, but was unsuccessful, although Emanuel Bach was a judge. In 1787 and 1788 he studied at the university of Leipzig and Halle, and after the dispute which followed on Emanuel Bach's death in 1789, Schwenke was appointed to succeed him as town-cantor, but the new conditions attached to the post were so irksome that he devoted himself mainly to mathematical problems. As a composer his main importance was in the stress he laid on good accentuation. He set Klopstock's 'Vaterunser' and 'Der Frohsinn' to music, and was a friend of the poet's. Various cantatas for solo and chorus with orchestra, six organ fugues, a concerto for oboe, and clavier sonatas are mentioned in the *Quellen-Lexikon*, from which most of the above information is derived. He was bold enough to re-score the 'Messiah' and Bach's B minor Mass. He died at Hamburg, Oct. 28, 1822. Two of his sons were musicians ; the elder, JOHANN FRIEDRICH, born at Hamburg, April 30, 1792, was a player on the organ, violoncello, and clarinet, was appointed to the Nikolaikirche in Hamburg in 1829, and composed cantatas with organ accompaniment, arrangement, etc., of chorales, a septet for five violoncellos, double bass and drums, and orchestrated Beethoven's 'Adelaide' and 'Wachtelschlag,' among other things. The younger, KARL, born at Hamburg, March 7, 1797, was a clever pianist and an industrious composer ; three sonatas for piano duet, and one for violin, appeared, as well as a symphony performed at the Paris Conservatoire in 1843, and at Hamburg. From 1870,

when he lived near Vienna, all trace of him
is lost.   Johann Friedrich's son and pupil,
FRIEDRICH GOTTLIEB, born Dec. 15, 1823, at
Hamburg, was his successor in the Nikolaikirche,
had success as a pianist and organist in Paris
(1855) and elsewhere.   Two fantasias for organ,
trumpet, trombones, and drums, are his most
important compositions.   He re - edited his
father's collection of chorales, and wrote preludes to them.   He died June 11, 1896, at
Hamburg.   (Riemann's *Lexikon, Quellen-Lexikon*.)   M.

SCHWINDL, or SCHWINDEL, FRIEDRICH,
was a skilful player on the violin, flute, and
clavier, in the 18th century.   He was at the
Hague about 1770, where Burney met him,
and in Geneva and Mülhausen, where he brought
out some operettas, and finally he settled at
Carlsruhe, where he died August 10, 1786,
holding the position of Markgräflich badischer
Concertmeister.   He was one of the followers
of the Mannheim school ; his numerous symphonies, quartets, trios, etc. appeared at Amsterdam, Paris, and London (where his music enjoyed great popularity), from 1765 onwards.   A
Mass in E minor for four voices and orchestra
is in MS. at Milan.   (Riemann's *Lexikon,
Quellen-Lexikon*, etc.)   M.

SCHYTTE, LUDWIG THEODOR, born at
Aarhus, Jutland, Denmark, April 28, 1850,
was originally a chemist, and gave up that
business for music in 1870, when he studied the
pianoforte under Anton Rée and Edmund
Neupert, and composition with Gebauer and
Gade, finally going to Taubert in Berlin, and
Liszt at Weimar.   He had one of the advanced
piano classes in Horák's Academy in Vienna
in 1887-88, and has since resided there, being
distinguished as a player, composer, and teacher.
A very large number of graceful and effective
compositions for pianoforte testifies to his industry, and many have become widely popular,
such as op. 22, ' Naturstimmungen ' ; op. 30,
' Pantomimen ' for PF. duet ; op. 53, sonata.
A pianoforte concerto is op. 28, and among his
many songs, a cycle, ' Die Verlassene,' deserves
mention.   A comic opera, ' Fahrendes Volk,'
was not performed ; but ' Hero,' a one-act opera,
was given at Copenhagen in 1898, and an
operetta ' Der Mameluk ' at Vienna in 1903.
(Riemann's *Lexikon* ; Baker's *Biog. Dict. of
Mus*.)   M.

SCIOLTO, CON SCIOLTEZZA, ' freely ' ; an
expression used in nearly the same sense as *ad
libitum*, but generally applied to longer passages,
or even to whole movements.   It is also applied
to a fugue in a free style.   Thus what Beethoven, in the last movement of the Sonata in
B♭, op. 106, calls ' Fuga con alcune licenze,'
might otherwise be called ' Fuga sciolta.'   M.

SCONTRINO, ANTONIO, born at Trapani in
Sicily, May 17, 1850.   His father, a carpenter
by trade, was an ardent lover of music, play-

ing the violin and guitar as well as singing,
and constructing violins, guitars, violoncellos,
double-basses, and even pianofortes.   With his
children and brothers this keen amateur formed
an orchestra in which, at the age of seven years,
Antonio was persuaded to take part as double-
bass, playing on a violoncello adapted for the
purpose, and provided with three strings only.
In 1861 he took up music in earnest, and entered
the Palermo Conservatorio to study the instrument which chance, rather than choice, had
made his own.   For harmony he was a pupil
of Luigi Alfano, and for counterpoint and composition of Platania, the director of the institution.   In 1870 he left the Conservatorio and
toured as a virtuoso on the double-bass throughout southern Italy ; in the following year he
obtained the libretto of an opera from Leopoldo
Marenco, but the work, ' Matelda,' was not
produced until 1876.   Aided by a grant from
the municipality and province of Trapani,
Scontrino went in 1872 to Munich, where
for two years he studied German music, classical
and modern.   In 1874 he came to England as a
member of Mapleson's orchestra, and afterwards
settled in Milan as a teacher of instrumental,
vocal, and theoretical music.   In 1891 he was
appointed professor of counterpoint and composition in the Palermo Conservatorio, and in
1892 a similar professorship was gained by him
in competition, at the Reale Istituto Musicale
at Florence, where he still resides.   His works
include five operas :—' Matelda,' 4 acts (Milan,
Teatro Dal Verme, 1876) ; ' Il Progettista,' 1
act (Rome, 1882) ; ' Sortilegio,' 3 acts (Turin,
1882) ; ' Gringoire,' 1 act (Milan, 1890) ; and
' Cortigiana,' 4 acts (Milan, 1895-6).   Among
his more important orchestral compositions are
an overture to Marenco's ' Celeste,' incidental
music to D'Annunzio's ' Francesca da Rimini,'
a ' Sinfonia Marinesca ' and ' Sinfonia Romantica.'
Three string quartets and a prelude and fugue
for the same instruments ; various pieces for
violin, violoncello, and double-bass with piano
accompaniment, and several sets of pianoforte
solos are among his instrumental works ; and
his songs, which number about fifty, include
two cycles, ' La Vie Intérieure ' to words by
Sully Prud'homme, and ' Intima Vita ' to
words by E. Panzacchi.   An ' O Salutaris ' and
' Salve Regina ' for two voices with organ
accompaniment, a motet, ' Tota Pulcra,' for
vocal quartet, and a ' Gloria,' an eight-part
fugue for solo voices, are his sacred compositions.   M.

SCORDATURA (mis-tuning).   A term used
to designate some abnormal tunings of the
violin which are occasionally employed to
produce particular effects.   The scordatura
originated in the lute and viol, which were
tuned in various ways to suit the key of the
music.   Their six strings being commonly
tuned by fourths, with one third in the middle,

the third was shifted as occasion required, and an additional third or a fifth was introduced elsewhere, so as to yield on the open strings as many harmonies as possible ; in old lute music the proper tuning is indicated at the beginning of the piece. This practice survives in the guitar. The normal tuning being as at (*a*), very striking effects in the key of E major, for instance, may be produced by tuning the instrument as at (*b*). The scordatura was formerly

often employed on the violin. (1) the tuning (*c*) is extremely favourable to simplicity of fingering in the key of A. It is employed by Tartini in one of his solos, and by Castrucci in a well-known fugue : its effect is noisy and monotonous. It is frequently employed by Scotch reel-players, and in their hands has a singularly rousing effect. The following strain from 'Kilrack's Reel' is to be read by the player as if tuned in the ordinary way, so that the first phrase sounds in the key of A :—

The reel called 'Appin House' and the lively Strathspey called 'Anthony Murray's Reel' are played in the same tuning. (2) The tuning (*d*) employed by Biber (see vol. i. p. 324) is a modification of (*c*), a fourth being substituted for a fifth on the first string ; and (3) the tuning (*e*), also employed by Biber, is a similar modification of the normal tuning by fifths. In these tunings the viol fingering must be used on the first strings. On Biber's use of the scordatura in the eleventh sonata of his second book (reprinted in the Denkm. der Tonk. in Oesterreich, xii. 2) see the *Zeitschr.* of the *Int. Mus. Ges.* viii. p. 471, and ix. p. 29 (both 1907). (4) The tuning (*f*), employed by Nardini in his Enigmatic Sonata, is the reverse of the last, being a combination of the common tuning for the first two strings with the viol tuning in the lower ones. (5) The tuning (*g*) is employed by Barbella in his 'Serenade' and by Campagnoli in his 'Notturno,' to imitate the Viola d'amore, from the four middle strings of which it is copied. Thick first and second strings should be used, and the mute put on. The effect is singularly pleasing : but the G and A on the second string are flat and dull. (6) The tuning (*h*) employed by Lolli, is the normal tuning except the fourth string, which is tuned an octave below the third. If a very

stout fourth string is used, a good bass accompaniment is thus obtainable.

Such are a few of the abnormal tunings employed by the old violinists. The scordatura is seldom used by modern players except on the fourth string, which is often tuned a tone higher, as at (*i*). (De Bériot, Mazas, Prume, etc.) This device may always be employed where the composition does not descend below A ; the tone is much increased, and in some keys, especially D and A, execution is greatly facilitated. Paganini tuned his fourth string higher still, as at (*j*) and (*k*), with surprising effect ; the B♭ tuning was a favourite one with De Bériot. Paganini's tuning in flats (*l*) cannot

be called scordatura, as it consists in elevating the violin generally by half a tone for the sake of brilliancy. The same device was employed by Spohr in his duets for harp and violin, the harp part being written in flats a semitone higher. The fourth string is rarely lowered : but Baillot sometimes tuned it a semitone lower, as at (*m*), to facilitate arpeggios in the sharp keys.

The scordatura (*n*) is employed by Bach in his fifth sonata for the violoncello. It corresponds to the violin tuning (*e*). This depression of the first string, if a thick string be used, is not unfavourable to sonority. When the scordatura is used, suitable strings should be obtained. Thicker ones are necessary where the pitch is depressed, and thinner ones where it is elevated : and the player will find it best to keep a special instrument for any tuning which he frequently employs.   E. J. P.

In engraved music of Scottish reels, etc. the scordatura was marked at the commencement of the piece by the word 'Scordatura' and the tuning in notes. In manuscript music, however, it was frequently more carelessly indicated, or even left without indication. It must be remembered that although all notes on the mistuned strings are affected, yet the notation throughout the piece always stood as if the tuning were normal, and consequently allowance for this must be made in playing on the piano, etc., and in transcripts. In scordatura of the lowest string the sound A is represented by the note G, the sound B by the note A, and so on. For a curious instance of the Scottish scordatura see SIR ROGER DE COVERLY.   F. K.

SCORE (Lat. *Partitio, Partitura, Partitura cancellata* ; Ital. *Partitura, Partizione, Partitino, Sparta, Spartita* ; Fr. *Partition* ; Germ. *Partitur*). A series of staves on which the different parts of a piece of music are written one above another, so that the whole may be read at a glance. The English name is derived from the practice of dividing the music by bass or lines *scored* through the entire series of staves. The Latin term, *Partitura cancellata* owes its origin to the compartments or *Cancelli*, into which the page is divided by the vertical scorings. The word Score, though often misapplied in the present day to what is more correctly called a ' short ' score, a ' vocal ' score, or a ' piano ' score, should properly be reserved for the system which presents on separate staves all the parts that are to be performed simultaneously. The oldest known form of score would seem to be that in the pseudo-Hucbald *Musica Enchiriadis*, a treatise of the 11th century. A specimen will be found in vol. iii. p. 397*a*.)

An interesting early score is in the Brit. Mus. Harl. MS. 978,—the volume which contains the famous Reading *rota* ' Sumer is icumen in.' Below the three voice-parts here shown there is a supplementary *quadruplum*, written on a separate stave, which has no concern with our present purpose. This composition shows that within about ten years of 1226 the essential feature of a score was realised in England.

In Arundel MS. No. 248, fol. 153*a*, 154*b*, 155*a*, and 201*a*, there are two-part compositions regularly scored on staves of eight and nine lines. In the last of these, now nearly illegible, two staves, each consisting of four black lines, are separated by a red line. In the other case the staves consist of eight uniform and equidistant black lines. The following is from fol. 155*a* of the MS., and the lower part of the same facsimile is another hymn ' Salue uirgo uirginū,' for three voices, on a stave of twelve equidistant black lines. The MS. dates

from about the middle of the 13th century. A score of the same kind, about the same date, is referred to by Ambros as being in the Bibliothèque Nationale, Paris.　　　　w. s. r.

It will be observed that in these examples care is taken that the notes which synchronise in time are in the same vertical line. In the *rota* (see the facsimile in the article SUMER IS ICUMEN IN) in the facsimile given in vol. iii. p. 324, and in the 15th century carols edited by J. A. Fuller Maitland and W. S. Rockstro, although the parts are superimposed, yet there is no attempt to make the page really a score.

One of the first printed scores, properly socalled, is that of Cipriano de Rore's madrigals of 1577 ; and one of the first printed orchestral scores, if not the very first, was that of the ' Ballèt comique de la Royne' (Paris, 1582). From the system then adopted to the complicated scores now in use, the process is one of natural development. Down to the days of Bach and Handel, and for some time after them, the orchestral instruments were used rather as an accretion of obbligato parts than as a complex whole ; but from the time that music became a scientific art, some system of grouping instruments of the same class near each other has been followed. The basso continuo or thorough-bass, whether figured or not, has always occupied the lowest stave, and its inseparable companion, the violoncello part, has been placed immediately above it. In purely orchestral music the viola comes next and the two violin parts ; but in vocal music, whether for solos or choruses, the voice-parts, with or without an organ part below them, occupy the position immediately above the violoncello. Sometimes in a concerto the solo instrument has this place, as in the first organ concerto of Handel ; but more often, and in modern music almost universally, the solo instrument in such a composition is placed above the strings. Having arrived at the line for the first violin or violin solo part, it will be most convenient to describe the constitution of the score from the top downwards. In certain instances, such as Beethoven's C minor Symphony, Mozart's 'Jupiter' Symphony, Schumann's in E flat, etc., the drums occupy the top line ; but in far the greater number of cases the piccolos or flutes head the score as the top of the group of 'wood-wind' instruments. Next come the oboes, then the clarinet, with cor anglais immediately above or below them ; the bassoons generally end the group of 'wood,' unless a double-bassoon is used. Some composers write their horn-parts between the clarinet and bassoons, but a more reasonable plan seems to be to let them head the division of 'brass,' and below them to place trumpets, trombones, and tuba. Upon the staves between the last of the brass instruments and the first violin lines are placed the instruments of percussion, generally beginning with the ordinary drums, and including such things as triangles, tambourines, big drum, side drum, cymbals, etc. The staves for the harp or harps are generally placed in this division, often below the big drum line. As a rule, in carefully printed scores, assistance is given to the reader's or conductor's eye by not carrying the bar-lines through all the staves, but leaving spaces in the vertical lines between the various groups of instruments. In a well-edited score, while the whole is joined together at the beginning of each page and the groups are indicated by thicker vertical lines, the bar-divisions will be continuous from the piccolo line to that of the contrafagotto, and from the first horn line to that of the bass tuba ; each instrument of percussion will have its own bar-lines to itself, and the three upper 'strings' will be joined in their bar-lines. If solo parts and a double chorus are employed, each solo part will have its separate bar-lines,

and each choir will have joined bar-lines. Lastly, the violoncello and double-bass part will be barred together. With every kind of difference in detail, this arrangement has continued in use from the classical days to our own, the change of place in the drum-line being the most important alteration. Specimens of various scores may be seen at vol. ii. pp. 474-483. In modern times, the great advance in musical education in England has had the excellent result of increasing the number of full scores published at small cost for the edification of those who listen to orchestral music. It may be presumed that a certain proportion of the many who holds these books in their hands during a performance, are able to read them, or at least to gain from them some kind of information ; but there are so many who confess themselves unable to cope with the difficulties of score-reading that it may not be out of place to consider what their difficulties are. It is even whispered that in England more than one conductor has risen to eminence who has not been able to read a complicated score with the requisite fluency. The art of reading, and still more that of playing from, a full score is one of the most precious a musician can possess ; those who can read the two staves of piano music should find only slight difficulty in reading simple quartets in which the viola part with its alto clef, and the occasional excursions of the violoncello into the tenor clef, are all the problems presented. Vocal music, in which the soprano, alto, and tenor clefs are persistently employed, should be attacked next, and as soon as unaccustomed clefs have lost their terror, the student may gradually attempt the parts for the transposing instruments. The clarinet notation may be conveniently studied in works for clarinet with piano or other instruments ; the principles on which the horn and trumpet transpose are not hard to grasp, but it is undoubtedly difficult to become quite sure what sound is indicated by what note, especially where a horn is directed to change its crook during a few silent bars. Various suggestions have been made at different times for avoiding the difficulty of reading scores by making the players of transposing instruments read the notes that they are to sound, not those they have to play. In practice this would but remove the responsibility of correct transposition from the conductor's shoulders to those of each individual player ; and although the average English orchestral player is accustomed to perform marvels of sight-reading, such a change can hardly be contemplated except by those whose interest it is to increase the number of preliminary rehearsals in the case of any new work.   M.

SCORING. The art of INSTRUMENTATION. See vol. ii. p. 473 ff.

SCOTCH SNAP or CATCH is the name given to the reverse of the ordinary dotted note which has a short note after it—in the snap the short note comes first and is followed by the long one. Inasmuch as it is a national peculiarity of Scottish music, it is characteristic of the slow Strathspey reel, rather than of vocal music, though as Burns and others wrote songs to some of these dance-tunes, it is not infrequently found in connection with words. 'Green grow the rashes,' 'Roy's wife,' and 'Whistle o'er the lave o't,' contain examples of the snap. It was in great favour with many of the Italian composers of the 18th century, for Burney—who seems to have invented the name—says in his account of the Italian Opera in London, in 1748, that there was at this time too much of the 'Scots catch or cutting short of the first of two notes in a melody.' He blames Cocchi, Perez, and Jommelli 'all three masters concerned in the opera "Vologeso"' for being lavish of the snap. [In the hands of Hook and the other purveyors of the pseudo-Scottish music, which was in vogue at Vauxhall and elsewhere in the 18th century, it became a senseless vulgarism, and with the exception of a few songs, such as those mentioned above, and the Strathspey reel in which it is an essential feature, its presence may generally be accepted as proof that the music in which it occurs is not genuine.] An example of it will be found in the Musette of Handel's Organ Concerto in G minor (1739); he also uses it occasionally in his vocal music.

J. M. W.

SCOTCH SYMPHONY, THE. Mendelssohn's own name for his A minor Symphony (op. 56), one of the works in which he recorded the impressions of his Scotch tour in 1829. Other results of that expedition are the 'Hebrides' overture, the PF. Fantasia in F♯ minor (op. 28), originally entitled by its author 'Sonate écossaise,' the PF. Fantasia in A minor, op. 16, No. 1, and the two-part song 'O wert thou in the cauld blast.'

The subject of the opening Andante of the Symphony dates from his visit to Holyrood in the evening of July 30, 1829, when it was written down. The Symphony was planned and begun during his residence in Italy in 1831, but was not finally finished till Jan. 20, 1842, the date on the finished score. It was first performed at a Gewandhaus Concert on March 3 of the same year, again at the Gewandhaus Concert next following. He then brought it to England, conducted it at the Philharmonic Concert, June 13, 1842, and obtained permission to dedicate it to Queen Victoria.

The passage for flutes, bassoons, and horns,

connecting the end of the first movement with the scherzo, was, on the authority of G. A. Macfarren, put in after the rehearsal (under Sterndale Bennett) at the Philharmonic, and added by Goodwin, the copyist, to the Leipzig MS. parts. The score and parts were published (as Symphony No. 3) by Breitkopf & Härtel in March 1843.

The work is peculiar among Mendelssohn's symphonies from the fact that it is not separated by the usual pauses. This is especially enjoined in a preface by the author prefixed to the score, in which the titles and tempi are given differently from what they are at the head of the movements themselves.   G.

SCOTT, CYRIL MEIR, born at Oxton, Cheshire, Sept. 27, 1879, studied the pianoforte until he was seventeen years old, when he went to the Hoch Conservatorium at Frankfort, and studied composition, etc. under Prof. Iwan Knorr. Finding himself hampered by the limitations of musical conventions, he threw himself into the ultra-modern school of composition, and all his works show a remarkable homogeneity of style. He shares (with a good many other people in the present day) the conviction that melody should be continuous, rather than cut up into separate strains, that tonality is an unnecessary limitation, and that the chromatic scale is as satisfactory a basis for composition as the diatonic. His works aim at the portrayal of 'atmosphere,' rather than definite beauty; and they occasionally reach their object. Mr. Scott may best be described as the English counterpart to Debussy, whose vagueness of melody and far-fetched harmonies are reproduced in the works of the younger man. An 'aubade' for small orchestra, a symphony, two rhapsodies, an 'arabesque,' a 'Christmas overture'; overtures to 'Aglavaine et Selysette,' 'Princesse Maleine,' and 'Pelléas et Mélisande,' are among his orchestral works; a setting of 'La Belle Dame Sans Merci' is for soprano, baritone, and orchestra, and 'Helen of Kirkconnel' is for baritone and orchestra. A sextet for piano and strings, op. 26, and a string quartet, op. 28, are among his earlier pieces of chamber music, and op. 57, one of his latest, is a quintet for piano and strings. It is beyond question that the later works show more consideration for the hearer's pleasure than do some of the earlier. His setting of the old English lyrics, 'Lovely kind and kindly loving' and 'Why so pale and wan,' making up his op. 55, are among the most pleasing and original of his songs, though 'My Captain,' to Whitman's words, and 'A Reflection' are very striking. 'Afterday,' and the three songs which make up op. 52, are interesting, and in some ways effective. There are a good many pianoforte pieces, which in name and style fulfil the Debussy ideal of landscape-painting in music.   M.

SCOTT, JOHN, nephew of John Sale, jun., was born about 1776. He was a chorister of St. George's Chapel, Windsor, and Eton College; afterwards studied the organ under William Sexton, organist of St. George's, Windsor, and became deputy for Dr. Arnold at Westminster Abbey. He was also chorus-master and pianist at Sadler's Wells. On the erection of the first organ in Spanish Town, Jamaica, he went out as organist, and died there in 1815. He was composer of a well-known anthem, 'Praise the Lord, O Jerusalem,' as well as of a famous comic song, 'Abraham Newland,'[1] the words of which were also sung to the 'Rogue's March'; [the composition here referred to was more commonly ascribed to Tipton, a Vauxhall writer, and was written about the end of the 18th century. F. K.].   W. H. H.

SCOTT, LADY JOHN DOUGLAS, an amateur composer of Scottish songs. Born Alicia Ann Spottiswoode, in 1810, she was the eldest daughter of Mr. John Spottiswoode, of Spottiswoode in Berwickshire. On March 16, 1836, she married Lord John Montague-Douglas Scott (son of the fourth Duke of Buccleuch), who died in 1860. In 1870, under the will of her father, she resumed her maiden name.

Her best claim to remembrance, musically, is her composition of the song 'Annie Laurie,' which was first published without composer's name in the third volume of Paterson and Roy's 'Vocal Melodies of Scotland' in 1838. So popular was the song during the Crimean war, that a letter from the composer herself, in her last years, by mistake refers to it as being composed about that period. It may be added that the words are altered from a song first published in A Ballad Book collected by Charles Kirkpatrick Sharpe, and privately issued in 1824. A few other of her songs gained but scant favour, although she is sometimes credited with being the composer or adapter of 'The Banks of Loch Lomond,' a Scottish song still much sung.

Throughout her life she upheld the ancient Scottish customs in a manner verging on eccentricity. She died on her estate at Spottiswoode, March 12, 1900, aged ninety.   F. K.

SCOTTISH MUSIC. As national music, that of Scotland has long been held in high esteem. Early notices of it may be meagre, but are always laudatory. Unfortunately, there are no means of proving what it was in remote times, for the art of conveying a knowledge of sounds by comprehensible written signs was a late invention, and music handed down by mere tradition was most untrustworthy. Even after the invention of musical writing, the learned men who possessed the art employed it almost entirely in the perpetuation of scholastic music, having apparently an equal contempt for melody

in general, and for the tunes prized by the uneducated vulgar. The earliest Scottish music was probably constructed on the Pentatonic Scale, which is not, however, peculiar to Scotland, for airs of a similar cast have been found in countries as wide apart as China and the West Coast of Africa. Many conjectures have been made as to the sources of British music in general, but in the absence of any real evidence they must be held to be more or less fruitless.

[In 1780, William Tytler of Woodhouselee contributed A Dissertation on the Scottish Music to Arnot's History of Edinburgh. He attempted to date various well-known Scottish airs, and though not very trustworthy or scientific has been taken as authoritative by many later writers. F. K.]

It is a remarkable fact that the first to write a history of Scottish music based on research was an Englishman, Joseph Ritson, a celebrated antiquary and critic, who wrote towards the end of the 18th century. He seems to have been a man of irascible temperament, but love of truth lay at the root of his onslaughts upon Johnson, Warton, Percy, Pinkerton, and others. Any assertion made without sufficient evidence he treated as falsehood, and attacked in the most uncompromising manner. His Historical Essay on Scottish Song has so smoothed the way for all later writers on the subject that it would be ungenerous not to acknowledge the storehouse from which his successors have drawn their information—in many cases without citing their authority. The early portion of the Essay treats of the poetry of the songs, beginning with mere rhymes on the subject of the death of Alexander III. (1285), the siege of Berwick (1296), Bannockburn (1314), and so on to the times of James I. (1393-1437), whose thorough English education led to his being both a poet and a musician. His 'truly excellent composition At Beltayne or Peblis to the play is still held in high esteem,' but of his music there are no remains. This is the more to be regretted as a well-worn quotation from Tassoni states that James 'not only wrote sacred compositions for the voice, but found out of himself a new style of music, plaintive and mournful, differing from every other.' That James improved Scottish music need not be doubted, but it is altogether absurd to suppose that he invented a style that must have been in existence long before his era. The quotation, however, serves to show that in Italy James and not Rizzio— most gratuitously supposed to have aided the development of Scottish music—was believed to have originated or amended this style. As Tassoni flourished soon after Rizzio's time, he had an opportunity of knowing somewhat more of the question than writers who came a century and a half later. George Farquhar Graham has at some length controverted the Rizzio myth. Graham was a very competent judge of such

---

[1] Abraham Newland was the Chief Cashier of the Bank of England.

matters, and believed that some of our airs might be of the 15th century ; though the earliest to which a date can now be affixed is the 'Lament for Flodden,' 1513, of which further mention will be made.

As so little is known of the popular music of the 15th century, a few extracts from the accounts of the Lords High Treasurers of Scotland may be found interesting. They show the value placed on the services of musicians who at various times visited the Courts of James III. and James IV. Scottish money being usually reckoned as worth only one-twelfth of English money, the payments seem very small ; but are not so in reality. For on consulting a table of prices of provisions supplied for a banquet given by James IV. to the French ambassador, it is found that a gratuity such as that to John Broun would buy seven oxen ; and that the 'twa fithelaris' (fiddlers) who sang 'Graysteil' to the King received the value of three sheep. The sums seem odd, but an examination of the items will show that the payments were made in gold. The unicorn (a Scottish coin that weighed from 57 to 60 grains of gold) is valued in the accounts at eighteen shillings ; and another coin, the equivalent of the French crown, at fourteen shillings—

1474. Item, gevin at the kingis command iijᵒ Septembris, to John Broun, lutare, at his passage our sey to leue (? lere, *i.e.* learn) his craft . v. li.
1489. July 1.—Item, to Wilzeam, sangster of Lithgow for a sang bwke he brocht to the king be a precept, x. li.
1490. April 19.—To Martin Clareschaw and ye toder ersche clareschaw at ye kingis command, xviij. s.
May.—Till ane ersche harper, at ye kingis command, xviij. s.

Mr. Gunn, in his *Enquiry on the Harp in the Highlands*, quotes thus from a work of 1597— 'The strings of their *Clairschoes* (small Gaelic harp) are made of brasse wyar, and the strings of the Harp of sinews, which strings they stryke either with their nayles growing long or else with an instrument appointed for that use.' The correct word is *Clàrsach* ; and the harper *Clarsair*.

1491. Aug. 21.—Item to iiij Inglis pyparis viij unicorns, vij. li. iiij. s.
1497. April 10.—Item to John Hert for bering a pare of monicordis of the kingis fra Abirdene to Strivelin (Stirling) . . . . ix. s.
April 16.—Item, to the tua fithelaris that sang Graysteil to ze king . . . . ix. s.
1500. March 1.—Item, to Jacob lutar, to lowse his lute that lay in wed . . . . xxxij. s.

(Which means that the thriftless Jacob received the value of eleven sheep to redeem his lute that lay in pawn.)

1503. Aug. 13.—Item, to viij Inglish menstrales be the kingis command xl frenche crownis, xxviij. li.
Sept. 10.—Item to the four Italien menstrales to fe thaim hors to Linlithqw and to red thaim of the town, lvj. s.

(Riotous fellows, no doubt, who got a French crown each to clear their 'score' in Edinburgh and hire horses to Linlithgow.)

Information regarding the state of popular music during the 16th century is almost equally meagre. James V. is believed to have written two songs on the subject of certain adventures which befell him while wandering through the country in disguise ; these are 'The gaberlunzie man' and 'The beggar's mealpokes' (mealbags). The airs are said to be of the same date, but of this there is really no certainty ; though Ritson, with all his scepticism, admits them into his list of early tunes ; the second is much too modern in style to have been of James V.'s date. Of Mary's time there are two curious works in which musical matters are mentioned. *The Complaynte of Scotland* (1549), and *The Gude and Godly Ballates* (1578), both of which furnish the names of a number of tunes almost all now unknown. Mr. J. A. H. Murray, in his excellent reprint of the former of these, says 'The Complaynte of Scotland consists of two principal parts, viz. the author's *Discourse* concerning the affliction and misery of his country, and his *Dream of Dame Scotia* and her complaint against her three sons. These are, with other obvious art, connected together by what the author terms his *Monologue Recreative.*'

This Monologue—which, from its being printed on unpaged leaves, Mr. Murray has discovered to be an afterthought—is now the most interesting part of the work. In it the author introduces a number of shepherds and their wives. After 'disjune' (*déjeûner*) the chief shepherd delivers a most learned address, and then they proceed to relate stories from ancient mythology, and also from the Middle Ages. Short extracts to give an idea of the style may not be objected to.

Quhen the scheipherd hed endit his prolixt orison to the laif of the scheiphirdis, i meruellit nocht litil quhen i herd ane rustic pastour of bestialite, distitut of vrbanite, and of speculatione of natural philosophe, indoctryne his nychtbours as he hed studeit ptholome, auerois, aristotel, galien, ypocrites or Cicero, quhilk var expert practiciaris in methamatic art. . . . Quhen thir scheiphyrdis hed tald al thyr pleysand storeis, than thay and ther vyuis began to sing sueit melodius sangis of natural music of the antiquite. the foure marmadyns that sang quhen thetis vas mareit on month pillion, thai sang nocht sa sueit as did thir scheiphyrdis. . . .

Then follows a list of songs, including—

Pastance vitht gude companye, Stil vndir the leyuis grene, Cou thou me the raschis grene, . . . brume brume on hil, . . . bille vil thou cum by a lute and belt the in Sanct Francis cord, The frog cam to the myl dur, rycht soirly musing in my mynde, god sen the duc hed byddin in France, and delaubaute hed neuyr cum hame, . . . o lusty maye vitht flora quene, . . . the battel of the hayrlau, the hunttis of cheuet, . . . My lufe is lyand seik, send hym ioy, send hym ioy, . . . The perssee and the mongumrye met, That day, that day, that gentil day.

With the exception of the ballads, these seem to be chiefly part-songs, some of them English.

Than eftir this sueit celest armonye, tha began to dance in ane ring. euyrie ald scheiphyrd led his vyfe be the hand, and euyrie ȝong scheiphird led hyr quhome he luffit best. Ther vas viij scheiphyrdis, and ilk ane of them hed ane syndry instrament to play to the laif. th fyrst hed ane drone bag pipe, the nyxt hed ane pipe maid of ane bleddir and of ane reid, the third playit on ane trump, the feyrd on ane corne pipe, the fyft playit on ane pipe maid of ane gait horne, the sext playt on ane recordar, the seuint plait on ane fiddil, and the last plait on ane quhissil.

The second instrument seems to have been a bagpipe without the drone ; the third, a jew's-harp, and the last a shepherd's-pipe or *flûte à bec*. Sir J. Graham Dalyell says: 'Neither the form nor the use of the whistle (quhissil) is explicit. It is nowhere specially defined. In 1498 xiiij s. is paid for a whussel to the King. . . . Corn-pipe, Lilt-pipe, and others are alike obscure.'

In the other little book already mentioned, known as the *Gude and Godly Ballates* (1578) there are a number of songs 'converted from profane into religious poetry.' Dr. David Laing, who published a reprint of it in 1868, informs us that the authorship of the work is usually assigned to two brothers, John and Robert Wedderburn of Dundee, who flourished about the year 1540. It is divided into three portions ; the first is doctrinal ; the second contains metrical versions of Psalms, with some hymns chiefly from the German ; the third, which gives its peculiar character to the collection, may be described as sacred parodies of secular songs. They were to be sung to well-known melodies of the time, which were indicated usually by the first line or the chorus ; but as Dr. Laing points out that not one of the secular songs of which these parodies were imitations has come down to us, a few only of the tunes can be ascertained. Three of them are certainly English, 'John cum kiss me now,' 'Under the greenwood tree,' and 'The huntis up.' A fourth is 'Hey now the day dawes,' which Sibbald and Stenhouse have attempted to identify with 'Hey tuti taiti'

The day dawis.

(From the Straloch MS. A.D. 1627.)

(Scots wha hae). This is not only improbable, but is disproved by a tune of the same name being found in the Straloch MS. (1627). It has no Scottish characteristics, and may have been picked up from some of the English or foreign musicians who were frequent visitors at the Scottish Court. It is an excellent lively tune, and may have been that played by the town pipers of Edinburgh in the time of James IV.; if so, the note marked with an asterisk must have been altered to C to suit the scale of the instrument. Dunbar thought it so hackneyed that he complains

> Your common menstrallis has no tone
> But 'Now the day dawis' and 'Into Joun'
> Think ye nocht shame.

Of the other songs, 'Ah my love, leif me not' may be 'I'll never leave thee,' and 'Ane sang on the birth of Christ, to be sung with the tune of Bawlulalu,' may probably be 'Baloo my boy lie still and sleep,' for in both songs the measure and also the subject—sacred for secular—are the same. The words, being in Bishop Percy's ancient MS., are thought to be English, but Dr. Rimbault considered the tune to be Scottish. Sibbald's identifications of a few other tunes are altogether fanciful : 'The wind blaws cauld, furious and bauld,' with 'Up in the morning early' ; 'My luve murnis for me,' with 'He's low down in the broom,' and so on. Altogether not more than a third of the whole can now be even guessed at.

The religious troubles of this and the following reigns would no doubt completely unsettle whatever musical tuition might be carried on by the Romish Church, but the introduction of 'sang schuils' and of Genevan Psalmody would probably soon compensate for any loss thence arising. [SONG SCHOOLS.] It does not come within the scope of this paper to consider such changes ; but the allegation already alluded to, that Rizzio composed some of the finest Scottish melodies, is deserving of a more careful inquiry.

Goldsmith, at the instigation apparently of Geminiani, chose to write an essay on a subject of which he evidently knew very little. He asserts that Rizzio was brought over from Italy by James V., lived twenty years in Scotland, and thus had sufficient time to get a knowledge of the style, and ample opportunities for improving it. It is well known, on the contrary, that Rizzio came over in the suite of the Piedmontese Ambassador in 1561, nineteen years after the death of James V., and was little more than five years in Scotland. That he ever composed anything in any style has yet to be shown. Tassoni, who was born in 1565, and who speaks of Scottish music—as has already been noticed—entirely ignores him. In truth the myth seems to have been got up in London early in the 18th century, probably among his own countrymen. It is first heard of in the 'Orpheus Caledonius' of 1725, where the editor ascribes seven tunes to him. Two at least of these are shown by their style to be very recent compositions ; but the absurdity of the statement must have been quite apparent, as all mention of Rizzio's name was withdrawn in the next edition of the work, 1733.

Oswald helped to keep up the falsehood. Notwithstanding the disclaimers of most of those who have made any research into the question, the belief still exists, and is from time to time propounded (see *ante*, p. 111*a*). For 160 years

2 c

after his death Rizzio is not mentioned as having composed music of any kind. Had he done so, it would have been in the style of France or of Italy, and it may be doubted whether Queen Mary herself would have appreciated any other. It must not be forgotten that she quitted Scotland when little more than five years of age, and returned Queen-Dowager of France, a widow of nineteen, with all her tastes formed and every association and recollection connected with a more civilised country than her own.

Mr. Dauney, in his *Dissertation* prefixed to the Skene MS. gives some interesting information regarding the Chapel Royal in Stirling. It was founded by James III., of whom Lindsay of Pitscottie says that 'he delighted more in musick and in policies of Bigging (building) than he did in the governance of his realm. . . . He delighted more in singing and playing on instruments, than he did in the Defence of the Borders. . . . He took great pleasour to dwell thair (in Stirling) and foundet ane collige within the said Castle callit the Chappell Royal ; also he bigget the great hall of Stirling ; also he maid in the said Chappell Royal all kynd of office men, to wit, the bishop of Galloway archdean, the treasurer and sub-dean, the chantor and sub-chantor, with all other officieris pertaining to a College ; and also he doubled thaim, to that effect, that, they schould ever be readie ; the one half to pass with him wherever he pleased, that they might sing and play to him and hold him merrie ; and the other half should remain at home to sing and pray for him and his successioun' (ed. 1728). All this was afterwards abolished ; but in 1612 its restoration was ordered by James VI., its place of residence to be at 'Halyrudhous'—'the palace of the samyn, and the Chappell not to be called the Chappell royall of Striveling as heretofore but his majesties Chappell Royall of Scotland, and the members to attend his majesty in whatever part of Scotland he may happen to be.' In 1629 Charles I. granted an annual pension of £2000 to the musicians of the Chapel, and preparations were made for the celebration of religious service according to the forms of the Church of England. The nature of these arrangements is very fully given in an *Information to the King by E. Kellie* (1631) ; among other things he was appointed 'to see that none but properly qualified persons should have a place there, and that they should all be kept at daily practise, and for that effect your Majestie appointed mee ane chambre within your pallace of Halyrudhous wherein I have provided and sett up, ane organe, two flutes, two pandores, with violls and other instruments, with all sorts of English, French, Dutch, Spaynish, Latine, Italian, and OLD SCOTCH music, vocall and instrumentall.' The capitals are Mr. Dauney's, who says, 'There can be no doubt that this last expression referred to the popular

national music of Scotland. That sacred musie was here not meant is sufficiently obvious ; the metrical psalmody of the Reformed Church was not old, and the music of the Church in Scotland before the Reformation was identical with that of Rome, and therefore not Scottish.' Here Mr. Dauney surely applies to the music what can only be said of the words of the service ; the latter were the same throughout all Roman Catholic countries, while the music, on the contrary, varied in every locality, being frequently the composition of the chapel-master or of the organist of the church where it was performed. Without insisting on the fact already stated, that James I. of Scotland wrote sacred music—'cose sacre compose in canto '—reference may be made to the Scottish composers mentioned by Dr. David Laing as having written music for the church before the Reformation. Among these are Andrew Blackhall, a canon of Holyrood ; David Peblis, one of the canons of St. Andrews, who in 1530 set the canticle 'Si quis diliget me' in five parts ; and Sir John Futhy (the 'Sir' denotes he was a priest), who wrote a moral song, 'O God abufe,' in four parts, 'baith letter and not,' that is, both words and music—as well as others whose names it is unnecessary to mention. Besides, there need not be a doubt that their predecessors were occasional composers from the time when James I. in 1424 set up organs in churches. That this is the music called Old Scottish in Kellie's *Information* seems to be the only reasonable explanation of these words. For though the members of Kellie's choir in fitting time and place might sing to the king 'to hold him merrie,' this would not be the music which they were called upon to practise twice a week in preparation for the next service.

It is to the reign of Charles I. that we owe the first certain glimpse of early Scottish folk-music. All that was known of it had come down by tradition, till the discovery—only in the 19th century—of two MSS. of this date, which establish the existence of a number of tunes whose age and form were previously entirely conjectural. These are the Straloch and Skene MSS. The first was written by Robert Gordon of Straloch, Aberdeenshire, in 1627-29. (See STRALOCH MS.)

The second is a much more important MS. It was formed by or for John Skene of Hallyards, Midlothian, and has no date ; but its seven parts, now bound together, seem from internal evidence to have been written at various times up to about 1635. In general it is much more correct than the last, its versions are occasionally excellent ; its Scottish airs, after rejecting dances and everything else not of home growth, are not fewer than forty. Above all, it contains the ancient original melody of 'The Flowers of the Forest'; whose simple pathos forbids our believing it to be the expression of any but a true sorrow, the wail of a mourner for those who would never return — and which no doubt is nearly coeval with Flodden. The MS. was published in 1838 by Mr. Wm. Dauney, with a *Dissertation*, excellent in many respects, on the subject of Scottish music. He was greatly assisted by G. Farquhar Graham, who not only translated the MS. from Lute Tablature, but contributed much musical and other information. (See SKENE MANUSCRIPT.)

From some anecdotes told of Charles II. he seems to have had a great liking for Scottish music, and certainly from the Restoration it became popular in England. This is shown by the almost innumerable imitations of the style that are to be found in the various publications of John Playford. They are usually simply called 'Scotch tunes,' but sometimes the name of the composer is given, showing that no idea of strict nationality attached to them. In general they are worthless ; but occasionally excellent melodies appear among them, such as 'She rose and let me in,' 'Over the hills and far away,' 'De'il take the wars,' 'Sawney was tall' (Corn rigs), 'In January last' (Jock of Hazeldean), all of which, with many others of less note, have been incorporated in Scottish Collections, at first from ignorance, afterwards from custom, and without further inquiry. There are however many tunes, not to be confounded with these, which two or even three centuries ago were common to the northern counties of England and the adjoining counties of Scotland, the exact birthplace of which will never be satisfactorily determined ; for of course the first record in print does not necessarily decide the parentage of a tune.

Among these—though rather on account of the words than the music—may be classed the famous song 'Tak your auld cloak about ye,' which having been found in Bishop Percy's ancient MS. has been claimed as entirely English. The Rev. J. W. Ebsworth, a very high authority, believes it to be the common property of the Border counties of both nations. Probably it is so ; yet it seems strange that so excellent a ballad, if ever popularly known in England, should have so utterly disappeared from that country as not to be even mentioned in any English work, or by any English author with the exception of Shakespeare, who has quoted one stanza of it in *Othello*. Not a line of it is to be found in the numerous 'Drolleries' of the Restoration, in the publications of Playford and D'Urfey, or in the 'Merry Musicians' and other song-books of the reign of Queen Anne. Even the printers whose presses sent forth the thousands of blackletter ballads that fill the Roxburgh, Pepys, Bagford and other collections, ignore it entirely. Allan Ramsay, in 1728, was the first to print it, nearly forty years before Bishop Percy gave his version to the world, confessing to have corrected his own

by copies received from Scotland. The question naturally arises, where did Allan Ramsay get his copy of the ballad, if not from the singing of the people ? Certainly not from England, for there it was then unknown.

The half century after the Revolution was a busy one both with Jacobite poetry and music ; in regard to the music, little, if any of it, was new, for the writers of the words had the wisdom to adapt their verses to melodies that every one knew and could sing. Thus many old favourite tunes got new names, while others equally old have perhaps been saved to us by their Jacobite words, their early names being entirely lost. The story of the battle of Killiecrankie (1689) is one of the earliest of these songs, and enjoys the distinction of having a Latin translation, beginning

> Grahamius notabilis coegerat Montanos
> Qui clypeis et gladiis fugarunt Anglicanos,
> Fugerant Vallicolae atque Puritani
> Cacavere Batavi et Cameroniani.

It is sung to a Gaelic tune of its own name, so quickly and so widely spread as to be found in a Northumbrian MS. of 1694, as the *Irish* Gillicranky. It is a stirring bagpipe tune, no doubt older than the words.

A still more celebrated air, now known as 'Scots wha hae,' received its name of 'Hey tuti taiti' from a stanza of a song of 1716 (?), 'Here's to the king, sir ; Ye ken wha I mean, sir.' The stanza is worth quoting, and would be yet more so could it tell us the still earlier name of the tune, a subject which has caused much discussion.

> When you hear the trumpet soun'
> Tuti taiti to the drum,
> Up sword, and down gun,
> And to the loons again.

The words 'Tuti taiti' are evidently only an attempted imitation of the trumpet notes, and not the name of the air. To suppose that the tune itself was played on the trumpet as a battle-call is too absurd for consideration. As the air has a good deal in common with 'My dearie, an thou dee,' there seems considerable probability that it was another version of the same, or that the one gave rise to the other, a thing likely enough to happen in days when there being no books to refer to, one singer took his tune as he best could from his neighbour.

'When the king comes owre the water'— otherwise 'Boyne water'—is a good example of change of name ; the air was discovered in a MS. of 1694, where it is called 'Playing amang the rashes,' a line of an old Scottish song recovered by Allan Ramsay, and printed in his *Tea-Table Miscellany*, 1724—a fact which seems somewhat to invalidate the Irish claim to the tune. The Jacobite words are said to have been written by Lady Keith Marischall, mother of the celebrated Marshal Keith, a favourite general of Frederick the Great.

When the king comes owre the water.
(Playing amang the rashes.)
From W. GRAHAM's Flute Book (MS. 1694).

The old air, already mentioned, 'My dearie, an thou dee,' may be pointed out as the tune of an excellent Jacobite song 'Awa, Whigs, awa,' and of another—the name of which is all that has come down to us—' We're a' Mar's men,' evidently alluding to the Earl of Mar, generalissimo of James's forces in Scotland in 1715.

Another of the songs of 1715, 'The piper o' Dundee,' gives the names of a number of tunes supposed to be played by the piper—Carnegie of Finhaven—to stir up the chiefs and their clans to join the Earl of Mar.

He play'd the ' Welcome o'er the main,'
And ' Ye'se be fou and I'se be fain,'
And ' Auld Stuarts back again,'
    Wi' meikle mirth and glee.
He play'd ' The Kirk,' he play'd ' The Quier,' [choir]
' The Mullin dhu' and ' Chevalier,'
And ' Lang away but welcome here,'
    Sae sweet, sae bonnilie.

Notwithstanding the diligence of collectors and annotators some of these songs and tunes have eluded recognition, chiefly because of a habit of those times to name a tune by any line of a song—not necessarily the first—or by some casual phrase or allusion that occurred in it.

Other noted songs of this date are 'Carle an the King come'; 'To daunton me'; 'Little wat ye wha's comin,' the muster-roll of the clans; 'Will ye go to Sheriffmuir'; and 'Kenmure's on and awa.'

A striking phase of Jacobite song was unsparing abuse of the House of Hanover; good specimens of it are 'The wee wee German lairdie,' 'The sow's tail to Geordie,' and, above all, 'Cumberland's descent into hell,' which is so ludicrous and yet so horrible that the rising laugh is checked by a shudder. This, however, belongs to the '45, the second rising of the clans. Of the same date is 'Johnie Cope,' perhaps the best known of all the songs on the subject. It is said to have been written immediately after the battle of Prestonpans, by Adam Skirving, the father of a Scottish artist of some reputation. No song perhaps has so many versions; Hogg says it was the boast of some rustic singer that he knew and could sing all its nineteen variations. Whether it was really Skirving's or not, he certainly did write a rhyming account of the battle, in fifteen double stanzas relating the incidents of the fight—who fled and who stayed—winding up with his own experiences.

That afternoon when a' was done
    I gaed to see the fray, man,
But had I wist what after past,
    I'd better staid away, man;
On Seton sands, wi' nimble hands,
    They pick'd my pockets bare, man;
But I wish ne'er to drie sic fear,
    For a' the sum and mair, man.

Few of these old songs are now generally known; the so-called Jacobite songs, the favourites of our time, being almost entirely modern. Lady Nairne, James Hogg, Allan Cunningham, Sir Walter Scott, may be named as the authors of the greater portion of them. In most cases the tunes also are modern. 'Bonnie Prince Charlie' and 'The lament of Flora Macdonald' are both compositions of Niel Gow, the grandson of old Niel the famous reel-player—' He's owre the hills that I loe weel,' 'Come o'er the stream, Charlie,' 'The bonnets of bonnie Dundee' (Claverhouse), are all of recent origin; even 'Charlie is my darling'—words and music—is a modern *rifacimento* of the old song. One exception to this ought to be noted; the tune now known as 'Wae's me for Prince Charlie' is really ancient. In the Skene MS. (1635) it is called 'Lady Cassilis' Lilt' (see article LOCHABER NO MORE); it is also known as 'Johnny Faa' and 'The Gypsy Laddie,' all three names connected with what is believed to be a malicious ballad written against an exemplary wife in order to

Charlie is my darling.   The Old Air.

The Modern Air.

annoy her Covenanting husband, the Earl of Cassillis, who was unpopular. [It is especially interesting to trace the course of the story of Lady Cassillis' flight with a gipsy as it appears in the English ballad, 'The Wraggle-Taggle Gipsies oh!' and elsewhere. The story may have suggested Browning's *Flight of the Duchess.*]

Those who wish to know more of these relics of an enthusiastic time will find in the volumes of James Hogg and Dr. Charles Mackay all that is worthy of being remembered of this episode of Scottish song.

OF THE SCOTTISH SCALES.

The existence of Scottish airs constructed on the series 1, 2, 3, 5, 6 of a major diatonic scale is well known and has been already alluded to. Whether this pentatonic series was acquired through the use of a defective instrument, or from the melodic taste of singer or player, must remain mere matter of conjecture. The style itself may be accepted as undoubtedly ancient, whatever uncertainty there may be as to the exact age of the airs constructed on it. These are not by any means numerous, though their characteristic leap between the third and fifth, and sixth and eighth of the scale, is so common in Scottish melody, that many persons not only believe the greater part of our airs to be pentatonic, but do not admit any others to be Scottish. However, the taste for this style may have arisen, the series of notes was a very convenient one; for an instrument possessing the major diatonic scale in one key only, could play these airs correctly in the three positions of the scale where major thirds are found, that is, on the first, fourth, and fifth degrees. In the key of C, these are as shown below, adding the octave to the lowest note of the series in each case.

Pentatonic scale in three positions, without change of signature.

If, reversing the order of the notes given above, we begin with the sixth, and passing downwards add the octave below, the feeling of a minor key is established, and keys of A, D, and E minor seem to be produced. Besides tunes in these six keys, a few others will be found, which begin and end in G minor (signature two flats), though also played with natural notes; for B and E being avoided in the melody neither of the flats is required.

A curious peculiarity of tunes written in this series is, that from the proximity of the second and third positions phrases move up and down from one into the other, thus appearing to be alternately in the adjoining keys a full tone apart, moving for example from G into F and *vice versa.* The following are good examples of the style :—

(1) *Gala Water.*

(2) *Were na my heart licht I wad die.*

(3) *The bridegroom grat.*

When the sheep are in the fauld & the kye at hame, And

a' the warld to sleep are gane, The waes o' my heart fa' in

show'rs frae my e'e, While my gudeman lies sound by me.

The first, 'Gala Water,' is one of the most beautiful of our melodies. The modern version of it contains the seventh of the scale more than once, but Oswald has preserved the old pentatonic version in his *Caledonian Pocket Companion* (1759-65). That version is here given in the large type, the small type showing the modern alterations. The air may be played correctly beginning on E, on A, or on B, representing the third of the keys of C, F, and G; but neither flat nor sharp is required in any of the positions, the notes being all natural throughout.

The second is the melody to which Lady Grizel Baillie wrote (1692) her beautiful ballad, 'Were na my heart licht, I wad die.' It is a very simple, unpretending tune, and is given chiefly on account of its close; indeed, both of these tunes are peculiar, and worth more detailed discussion than can be given them here.

The third is the old tune which was so great a favourite with Lady Anne Lyndsay that she wrote for it her celebrated ballad ' Auld Robin Gray.' Although it has been superseded by a very beautiful modern English air, it ought not to be entirely forgotten.

Another exceedingly beautiful pentatonic melody is that to which Burns wrote 'O meikle thinks my love o' my beauty.' It will be found in E minor in the 'Select Songs of Scotland,' by Sir G. A. Macfarren; but it may also be played in D minor and A minor, in each case without either flat or sharp being required in the melody.

The use of the imperfect pentatonic scale in our early music must gradually have ceased, through acquaintance with the music of the church service, which had its singularly complete diatonic system of modes. The complete diatonic scale, which we find in the simple Shepherd's Pipe or Recorder, is really that on which our older melodies are formed. The pitch note might be D or G, or any other, but the scale would be the ordinary major diatonic with the semitones between the 3rd and 4th and 7th and 8th degrees. The key of C is that adopted in the following remarks. With scarcely an exception the old tunes keep steadily to this scale without the use of any accidental. It will also be seen that the pathos produced by means of the 4th of the key, is a clever adaptation of a necessity of the scale. 'The Flowers of the Forest'—fortunately preserved in the Skene MS. —is a fine example of the skill with which the unskilled composer used the meagre means at his disposal. The first strain of the air is in G major, as will be seen if it be harmonised, though no F sharp was possible on the instrument; in the second strain, no more affecting wail for the disaster of Flodden could have been produced than that effected by the use of the F♮, the 4th of the scale of the instrument, the minor 7th of the original key. With his simple pipe the composer has thus given the effect of two keys.

The Flowers of the Forest.   Ancient Version.

It may be objected that the voice was not tied down to the notes of an imperfect instrument, and could take semitones wherever it felt them to be wanted; [but in the process of transmission the untutored singers, happily ignorant of musical science, adhere rigidly to the original forms of the scales in which they sing.]

The same effect of playing in two keys occurs in 'O waly waly! love is bonnie, a little while when it is new,' but in most modern versions of the melody both the F♮ and F♯ are found; this was not possible on the primitive instrument, though easy on the lute or violin.

O waly waly.

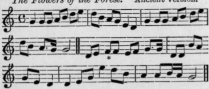

Any air which has the natural as well as the altered note may be set down as either modern, or as having been tampered with in modern times. The major seventh in a minor key is also a fairly good sign of modern writing or modern meddling. In a tune written otherwise in the old tonality, the occurrence of the major seventh sounds weak and effeminate when compared with the robust grandeur of the full tone below.

A few more examples may be given to show the mingling of the pentatonic with the completed scale. 'Adieu Dundee'—also found in the Skene MS.—is an example of a tune written as if in the natural key, and yet really in the Dorian mode.

Adew Dundee.

Another example is 'The wauking of the fauld,' which, played in the same key, has the same peculiarity in the 13th bar; this, however, is the case only in modern versions of the air, for that given by Allan Ramsay in the *Gentle Shepherd* (1736) is without the E.

OF THE GAELIC MUSIC.

If the difficulty of estimating the age of the music of the Lowlands is great, it is as nothing compared to what is met with in considering that of the Highlands.

The Celts certainly had music even in the most remote ages, but as their airs had been handed down for so many generations solely by tradition, it may be doubted whether this music bore any striking resemblance to the airs collected between 1760 and 1780 by the Rev. Patrick Macdonald and his brother. The specimens given of the most ancient music are interesting mainly in so far as they show the kind of recitative to which ancient poems were chanted, for they have little claim to notice as melodies. The example here given is said to be 'Ossian's soliloquy on the death of all his contemporary heroes.'

Slow.

There are, however, many beautiful airs in the collection; they are simple, wild, and irregular ; but their beauty has not a very wide appeal on a first hearing. Of the style of performance the editor says :—

These airs are sung by the natives in a wild, artless and irregular manner. Chiefly occupied with the sentiment and expression of the music, they dwell upon the long and pathetic notes, while they hurry over the inferior and connecting notes, in such a manner as to render it exceedingly difficult for a hearer to trace the measure of them. They themselves while singing them seem to have little or no impression of measure.

This is more particularly the case with the very old melodies, which wander about without any attempt at rhythm, or making one part answer to another. The following air is an excellent example of the style :—

Wet is the night and cold.

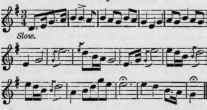

In contrast to these are the LUINIG and JORRAM (see these articles), the former sung by the women at their work, the latter boat-songs.

Patrick Macdonald says 'the very simplicity of the music is a pledge of its originality and antiquity.' Judged by this criticism his versions of the airs seem much more authentic than those of his successors. Captain Fraser of Knockie, who published a very large and important collection of Highland airs in 1816, took much pains, in conjunction with a musical friend, to form what he terms a 'standard.' As he had no taste for the old tonality, he introduces the major seventh in minor keys, and his versions generally abound in semitones. He professed a liking for simplicity, and is not sparing of his abuse of MacGibbon and Oswald for their departures from it ; yet his own turns and shakes and florid passages prove that he did not carry his theory into practice. As, however, a large portion of his volume is occupied with tunes composed during the latter part of the 18th century and the beginning of the 19th century, in these it would be affectation to expect any other than the modern tonality. A specimen of what he calls an ancient Ossianic air is given as a contrast to that selected from Patrick Macdonald. In style it evidently belongs to a date nearer to the times of MacPherson than to those of Ossian. (Compare last example, p. 398*b*, with the first on next column.)

It cannot be denied that though by his alterations of the forms of Gaelic melody Fraser may have rendered them more acceptable to modern ears, he has undoubtedly shorn the received versions of much of their claim to antiquity. The volume published by the Gaelic Society of

An air to which Ossian is recited.

London in 1876, though not faultless in regard to modern changes, has restored some of the old readings ; one example ought to be quoted, for the air 'Mairi bhan og' is very beautiful, and the F♮ in the fourth bar gives us back the simplicity and force of ancient times.

Mairi bhan og.   (Mary fair and young.)

Captain Fraser stigmatises the previous collections of Patrick Macdonald and Alexander Campbell (*Albyn's Anthology*) as very incorrect. But Fraser's own versions have in many cases been much altered in the second edition (1876), while more recent works differ most remarkably from earlier copies. The airs are evidently still in a plastic state, every glen, almost every family seems to have its own version.

There has been a good deal of controversy in former times about Highland and Lowland, Irish and Gaelic claims to certain melodies : most of the former seem pretty well settled, but both Irish and Scot still hold to LOCHABER, and to EILEEN AROON or ROBIN ADAIR (see those articles).

It is evident from the examples given by Patrick Macdonald that in the most ancient times Gaelic music was devoid of rhythm. The Ossianic chants are short and wild. They are succeeded by longer musical phrases, well suited it may be to heighten the effect of the Gaelic verse, but, apart from that, formless to a modern ear. From these emerge airs still wild and irregular, but with a certain sublimity arising from their very vagueness. Even when they become more rhythmic, the airs do not at once settle down into phrases of twos and fours, but retain an easy indifference to regularity ; two alternating with three, four with five bars, and this in so charming a way that the ease and singularity are alone apparent. The air 'Morag' may be quoted ; other examples may be found in *Albyn's Anthology*, 1816-18, and in 'Orain na h-Albain,' an excellent collection of Gaelic airs made by Miss Bell and edited by Finlay Dun.   J. M. W.

George Thomson employed Pleyel, Kozeluch, Haydn, Beethoven, Weber, and Hummel to harmonise and supply symphonies to the Scottish songs which comprised his published collections. The choice in all these instances was not very good. Beethoven appears to have been under the impression that the 'Scotch snap' was characteristic of all Scottish music, whereas, really, it only naturally belongs to the strathspey, the reel, and the Highland fling. Haydn, who seems truly to have had a liking for, and some knowledge of, Scottish vocal music, was certainly better fitted for the task ; he also arranged the two volumes of Scottish songs issued by Whyte in 1806-7.

Sir G. A. Macfarren's collection has already been spoken of, and an excellent set of twelve Scottish songs arranged by Max Bruch was published by Leuckart of Breslau. 'Songs of the North,' with the music arranged by Malcolm Lawson, had a great popularity, but many of the airs suffered a good deal in transmission, and several of them are to be found in a purer form in Macleod's 'Songs of a Highland Home.'

The virulent attack made by the late Mr. William Chappell on the claims advanced for the Scottish origin of certain airs cannot in every case be considered justifiable. There is much truth in what he advances, *i.e.* that a number of Anglo-Scottish Songs of the 17th and 18th centuries have been too readily claimed as Scottish folk-songs, in spite of the fact that they have been sufficiently well ascertained to be the composition of well-known English musicians. See Chappell's *Popular Music*, old edition, pp. 609-616, etc.

It is, however, quite evident that Chappell's irritation has, on some points, led him astray ; for some of his statements can be proved to be wrong ; those for instance regarding 'Jenny's Bawbee,' 'Gin a body,' and 'Ye Banks and Braes' (*q.v.*), and some others. That STEN-HOUSE, up to Chappell's time the chief writer on the history of Scottish Song, makes many lamentably incorrect assertions in his commentary on Johnson's *Scots Musical Museum*, cannot be denied, but that he did so wilfully is quite un-likely. It must be remembered that Stenhouse was handicapped by being four hundred miles from the British Museum Library, a storehouse which supplied Chappell so well, and besides, Stenhouse's work was a pioneer, for his notes were begun in 1817. The late Mr. John Glen in his *Early Scottish Melodies* has much to say regarding Chappell's attack.

The question as to the antiquity of much of Scotland's national music is still undecided.

The dates of manuscripts and of printed books, wherein such music first appears, are not a very trustworthy guide, for it is quite obvious that tradition has carried much of it over a consider-able stretch of time, and also that music was built upon the modes, which remained in popular use for a long period after their abandonment in cultivated music. The existing manuscripts, none of which are prior to the 17th century, show that music-lovers of the day were well acquainted with English and Continental work ; and although there cannot be the slightest doubt that the common people played and sang purely national music, yet this was never written down until late times. Of the country songs mentioned in 'The Complaint of Scotland' and other early works only few are to be recognised and identified with existing copies.

Another class of music which now constitutes part of the national music of Scotland was the compositions of professional or semi-professional musicians. As the fiddle is the national instru-ment of Scotland, so the reel and the strathspey reel are the national dances. A great number of country musicians, particularly in the northern part of Scotland, composed and played these dance tunes for local requirements. These they named either after some patron or gave them a fanciful title. In many instances, by the aid of subscription, the musician was enabled to publish one, or a series of his compositions, and so favourite dance tunes from these works were frequently reprinted and rearranged by other musicians.

Isaac Cooper of Banff, Daniel Dow, William Marshall, and many other lesser-known com-posers, along with the Gow family, have thus enriched Scottish music. We must also remember that where one of this type of musicians has succeeded in getting his compositions into print, there may be many whose tunes have passed into local tradition namelessly, so far as composer is concerned. While there are a great many beautiful and purely vocal airs, yet these instru-mental melodies have largely been used by song-writers in spite of their great compass ; this is one of the factors which makes Scottish song so difficult of execution to the average singer. 'Miss Admiral Gordon's Strathspey,' 'Miss Forbes' Farewell to Banff,' 'Earl Moira's welcome to Scotland,' with others, are well-known examples, and have been selected by Burns and other song-writers for their verses. Another notable one is 'Caller Herring,' which, composed by Nathaniel Gow as a harpsichord piece (one of a series) intended to illustrate a popular Edinburgh Cry, had its words fitted twenty years afterwards by Lady Nairne.

In the 'twenties' and the 'thirties' many now well-known songs in the Scottish vernacular had their birth, possibly owing to the Waverley Novels. Allan Ramsay was the first to collect the Scots Songs into book form from tradition, and from printed ballad sheets and garlands. His first volume of *The Tea-Table Miscellany* was issued in 1724, three others following later. It is rather unfortunate, from an antiquarian point of view, that Ramsay and his friends were not content to leave them as collected, but imparted to many a then fashionable artificial flavour, while boasting in his dedication of the charming simplicity of the Scotch ditties.

In 1769 and 1776 David Herd rendered a more trustworthy account of traditional Scots Song in the two volumes he published ; while Johnson's *Scots Musical Museum* of six hundred songs with the music, was the principal collection of the 18th century.

The following list comprises all the important collections of Scotch National music, including some early manuscripts which contain Scottish airs.

BIBLIOGRAPHY

MANUSCRIPTS

c. 1612-28. The Rowallan MS. In lute tablature on a six-line stave, 50 pp. It belonged to, and was probably written by, Sir William Mure of Rowallan, between the dates 1612 and 1628. It contains several Scottish airs, and is in the library of the Edinburgh University.

c. 1627-29. The Straloch MS. In lute tablature on a six-line stave. Contained Scottish and other airs. The original manuscript is now lost, but a copy of a portion of it was made by G. F. Graham, and is in the Advocates' Library, Edinburgh (see STRALOCH MS.).

16——? The Skene MS. In tablature on a four-line stave. In the Advocates' Library (see SKENE MS.).

c. 1675-80. The Guthrie MS. In tablature, contains a number of Scottish airs or rather, as the late Mr. Glen pointed out, accompaniments for them. In the Edinburgh University.

1683-92. The Blaikie MSS. These two, in tablature for the viol da gamba, belonged to Andrew Blaikie of Paisley, a music-engraver, early in the 19th century. They bore dates as in the margin, but both manuscripts are now lost. Transcripts of portions of them are in the Wighton Library, Dundee.

16——? The Leyden MS. In tablature for the Lyra Viol. It belonged to Dr. John Leyden and is now lost. A transcript made by G. F. Graham is in the Advocates' Library. The contents are much the same as one of the Blaikie MSS. and is apparently of the same date. Another Leyden MS. is in the Advocates' Library, dated 1639, but this does not appear to contain Scottish airs.

1704. Agnes Hume's MS. dated 1704. In the Advocates' Library, ordinary notation.

1709. Mrs. Crockat's MS. Referred to by Stenhouse who once possessed it ; it is said to have been dated 1709, but it is now lost.

1710. Margaret Sinkler's MS. An oblong quarto volume of about a hundred airs, which formerly belonged to the late Mr. John Glen. It bears the date 1710, and is in ordinary notation.

1723-24. Cumming MS. A small volume of airs for the violin, dated 1723 on first leaf, and 1724 on last, with the name of its original compiler, 'Patrick Cumming, Edinburgh.' It contains a number of Scotch airs, up to its date unpublished. In the possession of the present writer.

PRINTED AND ENGRAVED COLLECTIONS

Many Scots and Anglo-Scottish airs appear in Playford's 'Dancing Master' 1650-1728, and other of Playford's publications, also in D'Urfey's 'Pills to purge Melancholy,' 1698-1720. At later dates a great number are also to be found in the London country-dance books of various publishers.

1662, 1666, 1682. Forbes. 'Cantus : Songs and Fancies to three, foure, or five parts, both apt for voices and viols.' John Forbes, Aberdeen, 1662 ; 2nd ed. 1666 ; 3rd, 1682. The first book of secular music printed in Scotland. Contains several Scottish Songs. A reprint of the 1682 ed. was issued by Gardner of Paisley in 1879.

1700-1. H. Playford. 'A Collection of Original Scotch Tunes (full of the Highland Humours) for the Violin.' London, H. Playford, 1700. Ob. 4to.

(A second edition with four more tunes issued with date of 1701. This is the first collection of Scottish airs named as such. There appears to be only one copy of each in existence. Mr. Inglis of Edinburgh holds the 1700 edition, and the British Museum Library the second edition. The work is printed from movable type.)

c. 1700-5. 'A Collection of Original Scotch Tunes for the Violin, the whole pleasant and comical, being full of the Highland Humour.' London, John Young.

(This, and another, with the same title published by John Hare, London, are obviously imitations of Playford's work. The one published by Young is in the library of an Edinburgh gentleman, and the other by Hare is men-

tioned and its contents noted in *Notes and Queries*, 5th series, vol. v. p. 503.)

1725. 'Orpheus Caledonius or a Collection of the best Scotch Songs set to musick by W. Thomson.' London, for the author. Folio, n.d.

(Entered at Stationers' Hall, Jan. 5, 1725. The first collection of Scotch Songs with their airs. The book contains fifty Songs. See separate article, vol. iii. p. 569.)

c. 1726. 'Musick for Allan Ramsay's Collections of Scots Songs set by Alexander Stuart.' Edinburgh. Sm. ob. n.d.

(This was intended to provide the airs for the songs in the *Tea-Table Miscellany*. It is questionable whether a complete copy exists.)

1730. Craig. 'A Collection of the choicest Scots Tunes adapted for the Harpsichord or Spinnet . . . by Adam Craig.' Edinburgh, 1730. Ob. folio.

1733. 'Orpheus Caledonius.' Second edition, Edinburgh, 1733. 2 vols. 8vo. [100 songs.]

(The first volume is practically identical with the first edition. The second volume is additional matter, being fifty more songs with the music.)

1740, etc. Oswald, James. 'A Curious Collection of Scots Tunes for a Violin, Bass viol, or German flute . . . by James Oswald, musician in Edinbr.' Ob. folio. *c.* 1740.

(This is, in all probability, the first of the many volumes of Scots music issued by Oswald. When he arrived in London this work was re-engraved, and with another volume published by John Simpson.)

c. 1742. 'A Collection of Curious Scots Tunes for a Violin, German flute, or Harpsichord.' By Mr. James Oswald. London, J. Simpson.

'A Second Collection of Curious Scots Tunes for a Violin, etc.' (see above ; both were advertised in 1742).

c. 1742-60. Oswald, James. 'The Caledonian Pocket Companion.' London. 12 books, 8vo.

(This important publication of Scottish airs was commenced about 1742-43, and ultimately reached to twelve books about 1760. The first numbers were published by J. Simpson, others by the author, and the whole was reprinted by Straight and Skillern.)

17——? Oswald. 'A Collection of 43 Scots Tunes with Variations . . . by James Oswald.' London, Bland and Weller.

(Originally issued at a much earlier date than these publishers.)

c. 1761-62. Oswald. 'A Collection of the best old Scotch and English Songs set for the voice . . . by James Oswald, chamber composer to His Majesty.' London, n.d.

[1742.] Barsanti. 'A Collection of old Scots Tunes, with a bass for Violoncello or Harpsichord . . . by Francis Barsanti.' Edinburgh, n.d. 4to.

1742, 1746, 1755. M'Gibbon. 'A Collection of Scots Tunes. Some with variations for a Violin, Hautboy, or German Flute . . . by Wm. M'Gibbon.' Edinburgh. Ob. folio, 1742. Second collection, 1746. Third, 1755.

(Afterwards reprinted by N. Stewart, Bremner, and Rutherford.)

c. 1745. 'Twelve Scotch and Twelve Irish Airs with variations . . . by Mr. Bark Thumoth.' London, J. Simpson. 8vo.

[1757.] Bremner, Robert. 'Thirty Scots Songs for a voice and harpsichord . . . the words by Allan Ramsay.' Edinburgh, R. Bremner. Folio, n.d.

'A Second set of Scots Songs.' Bremner. *c.* 1759.

(These two, originally published at Edinburgh, were afterwards reprinted with Bremner's London imprint, and again reprinted by Stewart of Edinburgh with a 3rd vol. added.)

[1759.] Bremner, R. 'A Collection of Scots Reels and Country Dances.' Ob. 4to, n.d.

(Issued in numbers 1759 to 1761.)

[1759.] Bremner, R. 'A Curious Collection of Scots Tunes.' Edinburgh, R. Bremner. Ob. folio, n.d.

(Afterwards reprinted by Ding of Edinburgh.)

[1762.] Peacock. 'Fifty favourite Scotch Airs for a Violin . . . with a Thoroughbass for the Harpsichord.' Francis Peacock Aberdeen. Folio, n.d.

[1761-62.] Stewart, Neil. 'A Collection of the newest and best Reels and Country Dances.' Edinburgh, Neil Stewart. Ob. 4to, n.d.

c. 1762. 'A New Collection of Scots and English Tunes, adapted to the Guittar.' Edinburgh, N. Stewart. Ob. 4to.

'A Collection of Scots Songs adapted for a Voice and Harpsichord.' Edinburgh, N. Stewart. Folio.

1772. M'Lean. 'A Collection of favourite Scots Tunes with Variations for the Violin . . . by Chs. M'Lean and other eminent masters.' Edinburgh, Stewart. Ob. folio.

c. 1775. 'A Collection of Ancient Scots Music for the Violin, Harpsichord, or German Flute, never before printed.' Daniel Dow, Edinburgh. Ob. folio.

(Dow published about this time two other collections of his own compositions, 'Thirty-Seven Reels' and 'Twenty Minuets.')

1780. Cumming, Angus. 'A Collection of Strathspey or Old Highland Reels by Angus Cumming.' Edinburgh. Ob. folio, 1780.

(A later edition is dated 1782.)

[1780.] M'Glashan. 'A Collection of Strathspey Reels,' by Alexander M'Glashan. Ob. folio.

[1781.] —— 'A Collection of Scots Measures.' Alexander M'Glashan. Ob. folio.

[1786.] —— 'A Collection of Reels.' Alex. M'Glashan. Ob. folio.

[1782.] Aird, James. 'A Selection of Scotch English, Irish, and Foreign airs adapted to the fife, violin, or German flute.' Glasgow, Jas. Aird. 6 books, small oblong.

(This series of books are important in the matter of Scottish and Irish music. The first two were issued in 1782, the 3rd 1788, 4th 1794, 5th 1797, and the 6th early in the 19th century.)

1787-1803. Johnson, James. 'The Scots Musical Museum.' Edinburgh, James Johnson. 6 vols. 8vo.

(This important work consists mainly of Scots Songs collected by Johnson and his friends from printed and other sources. Burns interested himself in the publication, and some of his songs were here first issued with music. The first vol. was published in 1787, 2nd 1788, 3rd 1790, 4th 1792, 5th 1797, 6th 1803.)

Gow. (The publications of the Gow family have a strong bearing on the subject of Scottish music. Niel Gow the father and Nathaniel the son, composed, arranged, and adapted a great deal of what now constitutes Scottish National music. Their sheet publications are innumerable, and their collections of Strathspey reels and vocal melodies are named in vol. ii. at p. 2125 of the present work.)

Later collections of Scottish Songs with music were those issued by Wm. Napier, 3 vols., 1790-92 ; Corri, 2 vols. c. 1790 ; Urbani, 6 vols. c. 1792, 1794, 1799, 1800, 1805 ; Dale, 'Sixty Favourite Scottish Songs,' 3 vols. (180 songs), c. 1794-95 ; George Thomson's collections, 1793, etc. (see separate articles) ; Whyte, 2 vols. 1806-7 ; J. Elouis, 2 vols. 1806-7 ; R. A. Smith, 'Scottish Minstrel,' 6 vols. 1820-4, 8vo ; Paterson and Roy, 'Vocal Melodies of Scotland,' 4 vols. 1837-38. Among annotated collections of Scottish music, the following are noteworthy : 'Scotish Songs in two Volumes' [Joseph Ritson], 1794, 8vo (reprinted in 1869) ; Wood's 'Songs of Scotland,' edited by G. F. Graham, 3 vols. 1848, etc., 8vo ; 'The Lyric Gems of Scotland,' Cameron, Glasgow, 2 vols. sm. 4to, 1856 ; 'The Select Songs of Scotland,' Hamilton, Glasgow, folio, 1857 ; 'The Songs of Scotland, prior to Burns,' Chambers, 1862, 8vo ; 'The Minstrelsy of Scotland,' Alfred Moffat, Augener, 1895 ; 'Early Scottish Melodies,' John Glen, 1900, 8vo ; 'The Glen Collection of Scottish dance music,' 1891-95 ; John Glen, 2 vols. folio. Jacobite Songs are best represented in Hogg's 'Jacobite Relics,' 1819-21, 2 vols. 8vo (reprinted in 1874) ; Gaelic music is found scattered through Gow's publications, and other collections of Scottish dance music, and elsewhere, but the best known gatherings into volume form are—Rev. Peter M'Donald's '4Highland Airs,' folio [1783] ; Simon Fraser's 'Airs and Melodies, peculiar to the Highlands and Islands of Scotland,' 1816, folio (reprinted 1876) ; Alexander Campbell's 'Albyn's Anthology,' 1816-18, 2 vols. folio ; 'Orain na h-Albain, collected by Miss G. A. Bell, Edinburgh, c. 1840 ; 'A Treatise on the Language, Poetry, and Music of the Highland Clans,' Donald Campbell, Edinburgh, 1867, 8vo ; 'Ancient Orkney Melodies, collected by Col. Balfour,' 1885 ; 'The Minstrelsy of the Scottish Highlands,' Alfred Moffat, Bayley and Ferguson, Glasgow, 1907, and other works.

The above bibliography represents but a tithe of what might justly be included in it. Although there is much traditional Scottish music found among the quantity of dance collections issued by individual Scottish musicians it is difficult to classify it. Besides the Scottish publications enumerated above, the London country-dance books, from the early part of the 18th century onward, contain much interesting matter in connection with both Scottish and Irish music. Walsh and others issued collections of Scottish Songs and Airs, but they were taken mainly from Thomson's 'Orpheus Caledonius.' His 'Caledonian country dances,' and those published by John Johnson are, however, of much antiquarian interest.

The attention recently paid to folk-song has brought forth enough evidence to show that the published Scottish national music is but a small proportion of what, even now, exists in a traditionary form. Mr. Gavin Greig, Miss Lucy Broadwood, and other workers, have, without much search, brought to light a wealth of Gaelic music of a purely traditional kind. In the Lowlands of Scotland folk-song exists as it does in England, and much of this lowland Scottish folk-song is either almost identical with that found in different parts of England, or consists of variants of it. There is, of course, a certain proportion which may be classed as purely confined to Scotland. One of the first of the modern attempts to tap this stream of traditional music was made by Dean Christie, who published his two volumes of *Traditional Ballad Airs* in 1876 and 1881. This collection of between three and four hundred tunes, noted down with the words in the north of

Scotland, would have been much more valuable if the Dean had been content to present them exactly as noted. Another valuable contribution to the publication of Scottish folk-song is Robert Ford's *Vagabond Songs of Scotland*, first and second series, 1899 and 1900. In both these works folk-song as known in England is largely present. The New Spalding Club of Aberdeen in 1903 made an initial movement towards the rescue of traditional Scottish song. Mr. Gavin Greig (who is also a grantee under the Carnegie Trust given to the Universities of Scotland for research work) was commissioned to collect systematically in the north-east of Scotland. Mr. Greig's able paper, *Folk-Song in Buchan*, being part of the *Transactions of the Buchan Field Club*, gives some of the results of his labours. The Scottish National Song Society, recently founded, is also turning its attention to folk-song research.   F. K.

SCOTTISH ORCHESTRA, THE. The Scottish Orchestra Company, Limited, was formed in 1891 with the object of fostering the study and love of orchestral music in Scotland, and for the purpose of organising and maintaining an efficient orchestra available for concerts throughout Scotland. To this end a fully equipped band of eighty performers, named 'The Scottish Orchestra,' was recruited in 1893 under the leadership of Mr. Maurice Sons, and conducted by Mr. George Henschel. Its headquarters are in Glasgow ; and during the autumn and winter season concerts are given not only in Glasgow, but also in Edinburgh (in the latter city at the series of concerts under the management of Messrs. Paterson & Sons), and less frequently at Aberdeen, Dundee, Dunfermline, Paisley, Greenock, and in many other towns, by this fine combination of players.

Apart from the presentation of purely orchestral compositions the Scottish orchestra has frequently been associated with the principal Scottish choral societies in the production of important choral works. In 1895 Mr. Henschel resigned the post of conductor, and was succeeded first by Herr Wilhelm Kes (1895 to 1898), and later by Herr Wilhelm Bruch (1898 to 1900). Since 1900 the band has been conducted by Dr. Frederic Cowen. In 1903 Mr. Henri Verbrugghen replaced Mr. Sons as leader.

In the absence of the regular conductor, the Scottish Orchestra has played under the direction of many famous conductors, including Richard Strauss, Fritz Steinbach, Edouard Colonne, Hans Richter, Henry J. Wood, and others, and though, in accordance with the purpose for which it was founded, the appearances of this band are appropriately confined mainly to the country north of the Tweed, it has played in London, Leeds, Newcastle, Huddersfield, and elsewhere.   R. F. M^cE.

SCRIABIN, ALEXANDER NICHOLAEVICH. composer and pianist, born in Moscow, Jan. 10,

1872 (Dec. 29, 1871 O.S). He received his early education in the Cadet Corps, but afterwards, abandoning the military career for music, he entered the Moscow Conservatorium, where he studied the piano under Safonov and gained a gold medal in 1892. Having completed his course at the Conservatorium he went abroad, and won considerable reputation both as pianist and composer in Paris, Brussels, Amsterdam, and other cities. From 1898 to 1903 he was professor of pianoforte at the Moscow Conservatorium, but since that time he has devoted himself almost exclusively to composition. Scriabin is regarded as one of the most gifted of the younger Russian composers. He has a distinctive style and seems, like Chopin, by whom he has evidently been influenced, to be attracted to the smaller musical forms. His pianoforte works are delicate and poetical; in his larger compositions it is the orchestration of Wagner rather than of Glinka that he follows with considerable effect. Scriabin's output is not large, but his orchestral works include : two symphonies, E major, op. 26 (with choral finale), and C minor, op. 29 ; ' Rêverie,' op. 24 ; Pianoforte Concerto in F sharp minor, op. 20. For pianoforte : three sonatas (opp. 6, 19, 23) ; Allegro appassionato, op. 4 ; Concert allegro, op. 18 ; Fantasia, op. 28 ; Studies, op. 8 ; Impromptus, opp. 7, 10, 12, 14 ; Mazurkas, opp. 3, 25 ; Preludes, opp. 11, 13, 15, 16, 17, 22, 27 ; besides nocturnes, a valse, and other small pieces.   R. N.

SCRIBE, EUGÈNE, the most prolific of French dramatists, and the best librettist of his day, born in Paris, Dec. 25, 1791. He lost his parents early, and the well-known advocate Bonnet urged him to take to the Bar ; but he was irresistibly drawn to the stage, and from his début at twenty at the Théâtre du Vaudeville till his death, he produced for the different theatres of Paris a rapid succession of pieces which have served as models to a host of imitators. He originated the *comédie-vaudeville*, and attained to high comedy in ' Une Chaîne ' ; but it is in opéra-comique and lyric tragedy that he has given the most striking proofs of his imagination and knowledge of the stage. For half a century he produced on an average ten pieces a year, many, it is true, written conjointly with various authors, but in these ' mariages d'esprit ' Scribe was always the head of the firm.

Meyerbeer's ' Huguenots,' ' Robert,' ' Prophète,' ' L'Étoile du Nord,' and ' L'Africaine ' ; Auber's ' Fra Diavolo,' ' Gustave III.,' ' Cheval de Bronze,' ' Domino Noir,' ' Diamans de la Couronne,' and Verdi's ' Vêpres Siciliennes ' are the most famous of his librettos.

Scribe died suddenly in Paris, Feb. 21, 1861. He had been a member of the French Academy since 1836, and had acquired a large fortune. His complete works have not been published, but there are several editions of his stage-pieces.

That of 1855 comprises 2 vols. of operas, and 3 of opéras-comiques ; and that of Calmann Lévy (1874 to 1881), 6 vols. 12mo of ballets and operas, and 20 of opéras-comiques. A perusal of these gives a high idea of his fertility and resource.   G. C.

SCRIPTORES. There are several great collections of ancient writers on musical theory, both Greek and Latin. In 1652 Meibomius printed a valuable collection of Greek writers which long held the field. It is now, however, superseded by the following :—

Musici Scriptores Graeci, ed. C. Janus (Teubner, 1895), contains, with elaborate prolegomena, the following authors :

1. Aristotle. ' Loci de Musica.'
2. Pseudo-Aristotle. ' De rebus musicis problemata.'
3. Euclides. ' Sectio Canonis.'
4. Cleonides. Εἰσαγωγὴ ἁρμονική.
5. Nicomachus Gerasenus. Ἁρμονικὸν ἐγχειρίδιον & Excerpta.
6. Bacchius. Εἰσαγωγὴ τέχνης μουσικῆς.
7. Gaudentius. Ἁρμονικὴ εἰσαγωγή.
8. Alypius. Εἰσαγωγὴ μουσική.
9. ' Excerpta Neapolitana.'
10. ' Carminum Graecorum Reliquiae.'

The *De Musica* of Aristides Quintilian is not included above, because it had been edited separately by A. Jahn (Berlin, 1882). The *Harmonic Elements* of Aristoxenus are best studied in Macran's edition (Oxford, 1902).

The later Greek writers are to be found as published by Wallis, either separately or in his *Opera Mathematica* (Oxford, 1699), of which vol. iii. contains Ptolemy, *Harmonica*; Porphyry, *Commentary on Ptolemy* ; and Bryennius, *Harmonica*. To these may be added a less important anonymous work, *De Musica*, ed. Bellermann (Berlin, 1841).

For Latin authors reference must first be made to the great collection of Martin Gerbert, *Scriptores Ecclesiastici de Musica*, 3 vols., 1784 (and reproduced in facsimile 1905). It contains the following :—

VOL. I.

1. S. Pambo. ' Geronticon' (in Greek and Latin).
2. ' Monacho qua mente sit Psallendum.'
3. ' Instituta Patrum de modo Psallendi' (? Cistercian).
4. S. Nicetius of Treves. ' De bono Psalmodiae.'
5. Cassiodorus. ' Institutiones musicae.'
6. S. Isidore. ' Sententiae de Musica.'
7. Alcuin. ' Musica.'
8. Aurelian. ' Musica disciplina.'
9. Remigius. ' Musica.'
10. Notker. ' De Musica.'
11. Hucbald. ' De Musica.'
    (Pseudo-Hucbald.) ' Musica Enchiriadis, Commemoratio Brevis de tonis et psalmis modulandis.'
12. Regino. ' De harmonica institutione.'
13. Odo. ' Tonarius,' ' Dialogus de Musica.'
14. Adelbold. ' Musica.'
15. Bernelin. ' Divisio monochordi.'
16. Various anonymous pieces.

VOL. II.

1. Guido of Arezzo. ' De disciplina artis musicae,' ' Regulae musicae rhythmicae,' ' De ignoto cantu,' ' Tractatus correctorius multorum errorum,' ' De tropis sive tonis.'
2. Berno of Reichenau. ' De varia Psalmorum atque cantuum modulatione,' ' De consona tonorum diversitate,' ' Tonarius.'
3. Hermann Contractus. ' Musica,' ' Explicatio signorum,' ' Versus ad discernendum cantum.'
4. William of Hirschau. ' Musica.'
5. Theoger of Metz. ' Musica.'
6. Aribo Scholasticus. ' Musica.'
7. John Cotton. ' De musica.'
8. S. Bernard. ' Tonal.'
9. Gerlandus. ' De musica.'
10. Eberhard of Freisingen. ' De mensura fistularum.'
11. Anonymous. ' De mensura fistularum.'
12. Engelbert of Admont. ' De musica.'
13. Joh. Ægidius. ' Ars musica.'

VOL. III.

1. Franco. 'Ars cantus mensurabilis.'
2. Elias Salmon. 'Scientia artis musicae.'
3. Marchetti of Padua. 'Lucidarium musicae planae,' 'Pomerium musicae mensuratae.'
4. Jean de Muris. 'Summa musicae,' 'Musica speculativa,' 'De numeris,' 'Musica practica,' 'Questiones super partes musicae,' 'De discantu,' 'De tonis,' 'De proportionibus.'
5. Arnulph. 'De differentiis cantorum.'
6. John Keck. 'Introductorium musicae.'
7. Adam of Fulda. 'Musica.'
8 'Constitutiones capellae Pontificiae' (1545).
9. Τεκνή ψαλτική seu Ars Psallendi aut cantandi Graecorum.

A continuation of Gerbert was gathered by Coussemaker under the title *Scriptores de Musica medii aevi* (1864-76). It contains the following works :—

VOL. I.

1. Fra Jerome of Moravia. 'De musica.' With extracts from 'Positio vulgaris.' John de Garlandia, 'De musica mensurabili'; Franco of Cologne, 'Ars cantus mensurabilis'; Peter Picard, 'Musica mensurabilis.'
2. Franco. 'Compendium discantus.'
3. John de Garlandia. 'Introductio musicae.'
4.   ,,   ,,   'De musica mensurabili.'
5. Walter de Odington. 'De speculatione musice.'
6. Aristotle. 'De musica' (12th or 13th century).
7. Petrus de Cruce. 'De tonis.'
8. John Balloc. 'Abbreviatio Franconis.'
9. Anonymus. 'De consonantiis musicalibus.'
10.   ,,   'De discantu.'
11.   ,,   'Cantu mensurabili.'
12.   ,,   'De mensuris et discantu.'
13.   ,,   'De discantu.'
14.   ,,   'De figuris sive de notis.'
15.   ,,   'De musica.'
16. Robert Handlo. 'Regulae.'
17. John Hanboys. 'Summa super musicam.'

VOL. II.

1. Regino of Prüm. 'Tonarius.'
2. Hucbald. 'Musica encheiriadis' (a bit unpublished by Gerbert).
3. Guido of Arezzo, 'De modorum formulis.'
                    'De sex motibus vocum.'
4. Odo. 'Intonarium.'
5. Guido in Caroli-loco Abbas. 'Opusculum.'
6. Jean de Muris. 'Speculum musicae' (books vi. and vii.).
7. A Carthusian. 'De musica plana.'
8. Anonymus. 'De musica.'

VOL. III.

1. 'Marchetti of Padua. 'Brevis compilatio' (see Gerbert).
2. John de Garlandia. 'Introductio de contrapuncto.'
3. Philip of Vitry. 'Ars nova.'
4.   ,,   ,,   'Ars contrapuncti.'
5.   ,,   ,,   'Ars perfecta.'
6.   ,,   ,,   'Liber musicalium.'
7. Jean de Muris. 'Libellus cantus mensurabilis.'
8.   ,,   ,,   'Ars contrapuncti.'
9.   ,,   ,,   'Ars discantus.'
10. Henry of Zeland. 'De cantu perfecto et imperfecto.'
11. Philoppotus Andreas. 'De contrapuncto.'
12. Philip de Caserta. 'De diverais figuris.'
13. Giles de Murino. 'Cantus mensurabilis.'
14. Johannes Verulus de Anagnia. 'De musica.'
15. Theodore de Campo. 'Musica mensurabilis.'
16. Prosdocimus de Beldemandis. 'De contrapuncto.'
17.   ,,   ,,   ,,   'Tractatus practice cantus mensurabilis.'
18.   ,,   ,,   ,,   'Do. ad modum Italicum.'
19.   ,,   ,,   ,,   'Libellus monochordi.'
20.   ,,   ,,   ,,   'Summula proportionum.'
21. Nicasius Weyts, Carmelite. 'Regulae musicae.'
22. Christian Saze of Flanders. 'Tractatus.'
23. Gulielmus Monachus. 'De praeceptis artis musicae.'
24. Antonius de Leno. 'Regule de contraponto.'
25. John de Hothby. 'Regulae super proportionem.'
26.   ,,   ,,   'De cantu figurato.'
27.   ,,   ,,   'Regulae supra contrapunctum.'
Anonymous works, 28-40 (pp. 334-498).

VOL. IV.

1. John Tinctoris. (1) 'Expositio manus'; (2) 'De natura et proprietate tonorum'; (3) 'De notis et pausis'; (4) 'De regulari valore notarum'; (5) 'Liber imperfectionum'; (6) 'Tractatus alterationum'; (7) 'Super punctis musicalibus'; (8) 'De arte contrapuncti'; (9) 'Proportionale musices'; (10) 'Diffinitorium musices.'
2. Simon Tunstede. 'Quatuor principalia musices.'
3. Johannes Gallicus. 'Ritus canendi'; 'Introductio.'
4. Antonius de Luca. 'Ars cantus figurati.'
5. Anonymus. 'De musica figurata.'

For Boethius's *De Institutione musica* recourse may be had to his works in Migne's *Patrologia Latina* or in Teubner's *Bibliotheca* (ed. Friedlein). Note also *Ein anonymer Musiktractat* (ed. J. Wolf), Leipzig, 1893, and a valuable little early tract printed by Wagner in *Rassegna Gregoriana*, iv. 482 (1904).   W. H. F.

SCUDO, PIETRO, born June 6, 1806, at Venice, was brought up in Germany. Some circumstance led him to Paris, and in 1816 he entered Choron's school, and studied singing there at the same time with Duprez. He never became a good singer, and after taking a secondary part in Rossini's 'Il Viaggio a Reims' left the boards, returned to Choron's school, and there picked up a slender knowledge of music. After the revolution of 1830 he played second clarinet in a military band. Returning to Paris he made his way into society, set up as a teacher of singing, and a composer of romances. His knowledge of harmony and the elementary laws of musical accent was but slight, as he himself admits in spite of his vanity. Continuing his career as a professor of singing, he took to writing, and published *Physiologie du rire* and *Les Partis politiques en province* (1838). He gradually restricted himself to musical criticism, but as long as he wrote only for the *Revue de Paris*, the *Réforme*, and the *Revue indépendante*, he was unknown outside certain cliques in Paris. As musical critic to the *Revue des Deux Mondes*, he became a man of mark, though he was never more than a laborious writer, who made good use of German and Italian books, and managed by means of certain dogmatic formulæ and fine writing to conceal his want of knowledge and ideas. Scudo's articles are worth reading as specimens of French musical criticism before Berlioz was known, and while Fétis occupied a field without a rival. They have been mostly republished under the following titles :—*Critique et littérature musicale* (1850, 8vo ; 1852, 12mo), 2nd series (1859, 12mo) ; *La Musique ancienne et moderne* (1854, 12mo) ; *L'Année musicale*, 3 vols. (Hachette, 1860, 1861, and 1862) ; *La Musique en 1862* (Hetzel, 1863) ; and *Le Chevalier Sarti* (1857, 12mo), a musical novel taken from Italian and German sources, of which a continuation, *Frédérique*, appeared in the *Revue des Deux Mondes*, but was not republished. All his works were printed in Paris. Scudo finally became insane, and died Oct. 14, 1864, in an asylum at Blois.   G. C.

SEASONS, THE — Die Jahreszeiten — Haydn's last oratorio. The book was compiled in German from Thomson's 'Seasons' by Van Swieten, who induced Haydn to undertake its composition immediately after the success of the 'Creation'; and the music was written between April 1798 and April 24, 1801, on which day the first performance took place at the Schwarzenberg palace, Vienna. Haydn always averred that the strain of writing it had hastened his death. [See vol. ii. p. 362a.]

It is in four parts. The score was published in 1802-3 (without date) at Vienna; a barbarous English version accompanied the German text.

In 1813 Clementi published a vocal score with a better version. The Rev. John Webb followed with a further improvement, and more recently, in 1840 or 1841, Professor E. Taylor made a fourth. It was in the repertory of the Cecilian Society; and the Sacred Harmonic Society performed it on Dec. 5, 1851, and four times more down to 1877.   G.

SEBASTIANI, JOHANN, was born at Weimar, Sept. 30, 1622. The known facts of his life are few. He is said to have studied music in Italy, but no hint is given as to who his teachers were. He is next heard of as settled at Königsberg in Prussia about 1650, where also in 1661 he was appointed Cantor to the Domkirche in the Kneiphof quarter of the town, and in 1663 became Capellmeister to the Electoral Schlosskirche. He retired on a pension in 1679, and died 1683. He is chiefly known as the composer of a Passion music, which occupies an important place in the development of the form. The full title of the work is 'Das Leyden und Sterben unsers Herrn und Heylandes J. Chr. nach dem heiligen Matthaeo. In eine recitirende Harmoni von 5 singenden und 6 spielenden Stimmen nebst dem Basso continuo gesetzet. Worinnen zu erweckung mehrer Devotion unterschiedliche Verse aus denen gewöhnlichen Kirchenliedern mit einge-führet. . . . Königsberg, 1672.' The work is dedicated to Frederick William, Elector of Brandenburg. As the title indicates, it is a Passion with instrumental accompaniment a 6, and Chorus a 5. The instrumental parts are for first and second violins, three for Viola da Gamba or da Braccio, and one for Viola Bassa. But the full accompaniment is only reserved for the dramatic choruses in the work. Else-where the distinction is made that while the violas alone accompany the words of the Evangelist and other single characters sung by solo voices, the first and second violins alone with basso continuo accompany the utterances of our Lord. There are also short symphonic interludes for violas alone, and the chorale verses are intended to be sung by a solo voice with the accompaniment of violas. The conclu-sion consists of a hymn of thanksgiving, the first four verses of which are sung solo, and only the last verse tutti. The whole interesting work has now been reprinted in Bd. xvii. of the 'Denkmäler Deutscher Tonkunst,' Erste Folge. Other works of Sebastiani, enumerated in the Quellen-Lexikon, are two collections of geistliche und weltliche Lieder bearing the title Parnass-blumen, published at Hamburg 1672 and 1675, also a large number of occasional compositions for weddings and funerals. A few sacred compositions in the concerted style for voices and instruments remain in MS. J. R. M.

SECHTER, SIMON. One of the most import-ant of modern contrapuntists. Born at Fried-berg, in Bohemia, on Oct. 11, 1788. In 1804,

after a moderate musical education, he went to Vienna, where he applied himself with ardour to theoretical studies. In 1809, while Vienna was in the hands of the French, he made the acquaint-ance of Dragonetti—then living in concealment under the curious apprehension that Napoleon would oblige him to go to Paris—for whom he wrote the pianoforte accompaniments to his concertos for the double bass. In 1810 Sechter became teacher of the piano and singing to the Blind Institute, for which he wrote many songs and two masses. During the whole of this time he pushed forward his studies, working more especi-ally at Bach and Mozart. He found a good friend in Abbé Stadler, through whose means three of Sechter's masses were performed at the court chapel. A requiem of his and a chorus from Schiller's 'Bride of Messina' were also executed at the Concert Spirituel with success. In 1824 he became court-organist, first as sub-ordinate, and in 1825, on the death of Worzi-scheck, as chief, an office which he retained till his death. His fame as a theoretical teacher attracted numerous scholars, amongst others the great Schubert, who was on the point of taking lessons from him when attacked by his last illness. (See SCHUBERT, ante, p. 316a.) The Emperor Ferdinand conferred upon him the large gold medal for a grand mass dedicated to his Majesty, which was shortly followed by the order of St. Louis from the Duke of Lucca. In 1850 he became Professor of Composition in the Conservatorium at Vienna. His Aphorisms, etc., which he communicated to the Vienna Allg. musik. Zeitung, show him to have been a profound thinker, and give many instructive hints both to teachers and scholars. His most intimate friends were Staudigl, Lutz, and Hölzel, for whom he wrote a quantity of humorous Volkslieder in contrapuntal style, as well as many comic oper-ettas, ballads, etc. His diligence in study was astonishing. No day passed in which he did not write a fugue. A few years before his death he had the misfortune, through his own good nature, to lose almost everything, and died on Sept. 12, 1867, nearly eighty years old, in poverty and privation. Sechter was much esteemed and beloved for his simplicity and goodness, and it may be truly said that he had no enemies. His system, though severe, was simple, clear, and logical. His scholars were almost innumerable: amongst them may be mentioned, Preyer, Nottebohm, the Prin-cess Czartorijska, Sucher, Bibl, Rosa Kastner (Escudier), Rufinatscha, Bruckner, Otto Bach, Döhler, Schachner, Filtsch, S. Bagge, Benoni, Vieuxtemps, Pauer, C. F. Pohl, and Thalberg. Notwithstanding the multitude of his lessons he found time to compose a great deal of music. His unpublished works in the Imperial Library and the Musikverein at Vienna contain four oratorios, operas and large cantatas, music for voice, organ, and pianoforte, including 104

variations on an original theme of 104 bars ;
also a complete theoretical treatise ready for
publication, in two portions, first on acoustics,
second on canon.   Among his published works
are an edition of Marpurg *On Fugue*, with many
additions ; *Grundsätze der musik. Composition*
(3 vols. B. & H.) ; twelve masses ; *Practical Examples of Accompaniment from Figured Bass*, op.
59 ; *Practical School of Thorough Bass*, opp.49,98 ;
preludes for the organ, in four books ; fugues,
hymns, choral preludes ; four fugues for PF., op.
5, dedicated to Beethoven ; fugue in C minor, to
the memory of Schubert, op. 43 ; etc.   Sechter
completed the grand fugue for orchestra in D
major, left unfinished by Mozart.   C. F. P.

SECOND.   The smallest interval in the scale
used for musical purposes.   It is described by notes
which are next to each other on the stave or by
letters which lie next each other in the alphabet,
as A B, B C, C D♯, E♭ F♯.

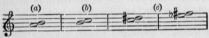

Three kinds can be practically distinguished. The
minor second, which is equal to a semitone, as
at (*b*) in the example ; the major second, which
is equal to a tone (but of which there are two
kinds, grave and acute—see below), as at (*a*) ;
and the augmented second, which is equal
to three semitones, as at (*c*).   They are all
discords, but are characterised by different
degrees of roughness.   The minor second is
extremely harsh, the major decidedly so,
though not so extremely, and the augmented
second but slightly.   In ordinary musical usage
the last is actually the same interval as a
minor third, which is not looked upon as a
dissonance at all ; nevertheless the ear, distinguishing relations instinctively, classifies the
combinations according to their context as
having a dissonant or consonant significance,
Thus when the context suggests the interval A♭
B♮, the mind will not accept it as final, but as
a dissonance requiring resolution ; whereas if
the same interval could be expressed as A♭ C♭,
it might be recognised as a characteristic portion of the minor chord of A♭, and could be
accepted as final without desire for further
motion.—The numerical ratios of the several intervals in just intonation are given as follows :
—the minor second, 16 : 15 ; the grave major
second, 10 : 9 ; the acute major second, 9 : 8 ;
and the augmented second, 75 : 64.   [See SEMI-
TONE.]   C. H. H. P.

SECONDO.   The second player in a duet.
[See PRIMO.]

SEDIE, DELLE, ENRICO, baritone singer,
son of a merchant of Leghorn, was born June
17, 1824.   In the year 1848 he volunteered in
the army of Charles Albert of Piedmont, and
fought against the Austrians in the war for
Italian independence.   He was taken prisoner

at the battle of Curtatone but afterwards released, and at the close of the campaign of
the following year retired from the army with
the rank of lieutenant.   Under the direction of
his fellow-citizen, Orazio Galeffi, he then devoted himself to the study of singing, and in
1851 made his début at Pistoia in Nabucco.

From 1854, when he made a great success as
Rigoletto in Florence, his position was secure.
He appeared with unvarying success at Rome,
Milan, Vienna, Paris, and London, and though
possessed of so little voice as to gain the sobriquet of *Il baritono senza voce*, he made up by
dramatic accent and purity of style for the
shortcomings of nature.   In 1867, at the
earnest request of Auber, he accepted a professorship at the Conservatoire of Paris on the most
advantageous terms hitherto offered.   Under
him a commission was appointed for the entire
remodelling of that institution, but the death
of Auber and the outbreak of the Franco-
Prussian War compelled the government to
abandon their intention.   In 1874 he published a large work upon the art of singing and
musical declamation, under the title of *L'Art
Lyrique*.   Translations of this and other vocal
treatises are published in New York as *A Complete Method of Singing*.

Signor Delle Sedie was Cavaliere of the Order
of the Crown of Italy, for his military services
in the campaigns of 1848, 1849 ; Cavaliere of
the Order of SS. Maurizio and Lazzaro ; and
member of many societies and academies both
of Italy and France.   For some time he lived
in Paris, and devoted himself entirely to the
teaching of his art.   He died there Nov. 28,
1907.   J. C. G.

SEEGR (SEEGER, SEGER, SAGER, SEGERT,
ZECKERT), JOSEPH FERDINAND NORBERT, eminent organist and composer, born at Repin near
Melnik, Bohemia, March 21, 1716.   Educated
at Prague, where he graduated Master of Philosophy.   He was alto singer at St. James's
Church in that city, and, later, organist at St.
Martin's.   In 1735 he was first violinist at the
Tein Church, but was appointed organist in 1741,
which position he retained until his death on
April 22, 1782.   In addition he held the
appointment of organist at the Kreuzherren-
kirche in the Old Town for thirty-seven years
(1745 to 1782).   In this church Joseph II. heard
Seegr play, and was so delighted with the
masterly performance that he at once determined
to give him a Court appointment at Vienna ; but,
sad to say, when the official document containing this preferment arrived, Seegr was no more.
Amongst his pupils were the principal Bohemian
musicians of that time, viz. : Kozeluch, Maschek,
Mysliwecek, Gelinek, Brixi, Kucharz, etc.   That
Seegr was well known to Bach is testified by
the fact that the latter advised Count Millesimo
to place Mathias Sofka under Master Seegr,
remarking that he could not entrust him to a

better teacher. Burney (*Present State of Music*, Germany, vol. ii. pp. 13-14) mentions him as being a fine organ-player, a good linguist, and an excellent musician. The unanimous testimony of his contemporaries proclaims Seegr as one of the finest organists of his time. At his death his compositions were acquired by Ernst, concert-master of Gotha. Daniel Gottlob Turk, music director of Halle, was employed to edit the first posthumous instalment of these compositions—'Eight Toccatas and Fugues' for the organ (published by Breitkopf in 1793), which are up to the present his best known works. The toccatas are in reality preludes—with the exception of No. 5, the style of which is more in accordance with its title. His other compositions consisted of many masses, psalms, litanies, etc., printed copies of which do not exist. After the lapse of nearly a century and a quarter, Messrs. Novello are about to reissue the 'Eight Toccatas and Fugues,' edited by Dom Samuel Gregory Ould, and adapted to the requirements of the modern organ. w. w. s.

SEELING, HANS, was born at Prague in 1828, and towards the end of his life returned to his native city, where he died on May 26, 1862. Failing health obliged him to go to Italy in 1852, and in 1856 he toured in the East, returning to Italy in 1857. After settling in Paris, 1859, he made his home in Germany. An excellent pianist, he met with unfailing success on his tours. Seeling composed a number of brilliant pieces and studies for the piano, of which the best known are the 'Barcarolle,' the 'Lorelei' (op. 2), the 'Concert Studies' (op. 10), and the 'Memories of an Artist' (op. 13). These compositions are highly effective, and their character partakes of Henselt on the one hand and Bendel on the other. D. H.

SEGNO, *i.e.* the sign 𝄋. [See DAL SEGNO.]

SEGUE, 'follows'—as *Segue l' aria*, 'the aria follows'; a direction frequently found at the end of recitatives. It is thus equivalent to the more modern word *attacca*. It is also found occasionally at the foot of a page where a space is left after one movement in order that the next may begin at the top, to avoid turning over in the middle. It then indicates that no stop is to be made between the two movements. M.

SEGUIDILLA (sometimes written SIGUI-DILLA), a popular national dance of Spain. The origin of both name and dance are uncertain; it existed in La Mancha in the time of Cervantes (see *Don Quixote*, part ii. chap. 38), but there is no evidence to show whether it is indigenous, or introduced into Spain by the Moors. It is, however, certain that from La Mancha it spread all over Spain, and it is still danced in both town and country. Seguidillas are divided into three kinds—Seguidillas Manchegas, the original form of the dance, in which it assumes a gay and lively character; Seguidillas

Boleras,[1] more measured and stately ; and Seguidillas Gitanas, danced very slowly and sentimentally. To these some writers add a fourth kind, the Seguidillas Taleadas, said to be a combination of the original Seguidilla with the Cachucha. The music is written in 3-4 or 3-8 time, usually in a minor key, and is performed on the guitar with occasionally a flute, violin, or castanet accompaniment. The *coplas*, or words sung by the musicians, are written in couplets of four short lines followed by an *estrevillo* or refrain of three lines, but some coplas want this latter feature. Both music and words often partake of the character of an improvisation, the former remarkable for strange and sudden modulations, and the latter treating of both serious and comic subjects. A collection of coplas was published at the end of the 18th century by N. Zamacola, writing under the pseudonym of Don Preciso. From the introduction to this book the following quaint description of the Seguidilla is translated : 'So soon as two young people of the opposite sexes present themselves standing face to face at a distance of about two varas[2] in the middle of the room, the "ritornelo" or prelude of the music begins ; then the seguidilla is insinuated by the voice—if it be a manchega, by singing the first line of the copla ; if it be a bolera, by singing two lines, which must only take up four bars. The guitar follows, playing a pasacalle ;[3] and at the fourth bar the seguidilla begins to be sung. Then the dance breaks out with castanets or crotolas,[4] running on for a space of nine bars, with which the first part concludes. The guitar continues playing the pasacalle, during which the dancers change to opposite positions by means of a very deliberate and simple promenade ("paseo"). While singing again, at the beginning of the fourth bar, each goes on for nine bars more, making the variations and differences of their respective schools, which forms the second part. Again they change places, and upon each dancer returning to the spot where they began to dance, the third part goes on in the same way as the second, and on arriving at the ninth bar, the voice, the instrument, and the castanets cease all at once, and as if impromptu, the room remaining in silence, and the dancers standing immovable in various beautiful attitudes, which is what we call "well stopped" (Bien parado).' Space will not allow us to give an example of the music which accompanies this beautiful dance. In Book IV. of Luigi Borghi's 'Opera Dances' (London, 1783) is a seguidilla modified for theatrical representation, and in the first act of 'Carmen' there is a Spanish air which Bizet has entitled 'Seguidille.' Better examples than these will be found in Mendel's *Lexikon* (sub voce Seguidilla),

---

[1] Not to be confounded with the Bolero, said to have been invented in 1780 by Don Sebastian Zerezo.
[2] 1 vara=34 inches.
[3] Literally 'street-pass'; any popular street-song. [See PASSA-CAGLIA, vol. iii. p. 643.]
[4] A kind of castanet.

and in the Appendix to Part I. of Marino Soriano Fuertes's *Historia de la Musica Española* (Madrid, 1855-59), in which specimens are given of the varieties of the dance. With regard to the words, the following copla (from Don Preciso's *Colleccion de Coplas*, Madrid, 1799) may serve as an example :

> El Lunes me enamoro,
> Mártes lo digo,
> Miércoles me declaro,
> Júeves consigo :
> Viérnes doy zelos
> Y Sabado y Domingo
> Busco Amor nuevo. [1]

W. B. S.

SEGUIN, ARTHUR EDWARD SHELDEN, commonly known as EDWARD, was born in London (of Irish descent), April 7, 1809. He received his musical education at the Royal Academy of Music, and first appeared in public in 1828 at concerts and performances of Italian operas given by its pupils. His voice was a deep bass, of very extensive compass, and he met with a very favourable reception. In 1829 he sang at the Exeter Festival. In 1831 he appeared at the theatre in Tottenham Street as Polyphemus in 'Acis and Galatea.' In 1832 he sang at the Concert of Antient Music. In 1833 and 1834 he was engaged at Covent Garden, and in the latter year appeared at the King's Theatre as Il Conte Robinson in Cimarosa's 'Matrimonio Segreto,' and also sang at the Festival in Westminster Abbey. From 1835 to 1837 he was engaged at Drury Lane. In August 1838 he appeared at the English Opera House in Macfarren's 'Devil's Opera,' and soon afterwards quitted England for America, made his first appearance at the National Theatre, New York, as the Count in Rooke's 'Amilie' on Oct. 15, 1838, and was extremely well received. He afterwards formed an opera company named 'The Seguin Troupe,' who performed at various places in the United States and Canada. Amongst other distinctions he was elected a chief by one of the Indian tribes, and received an Indian name, signifying 'The man with the deep mellow voice'; an honour which had never before been conferred on any Englishman, except Edmund Kean, the tragedian. He died at New York, Dec. 9, 1852.

His wife, ANN CHILDE, born in London 1814, was also a pupil of the Royal Academy of Music, and appeared in public as a soprano singer in 1828 in the same performances as her future husband, and with equal success. In 1832 she sang at the Concert of Antient Music, and in 1834 at the Westminster Abbey Festival. After performing for two or three seasons at the King's Theatre as 'seconda donna,' she appeared on the English stage at Drury Lane, Nov. 3, 1837, as Donna Anna in the English

version of Mozart's 'Don Giovanni.' She accompanied her husband to America and performed in opera until his death, when she retired from the stage and taught music in New York, where she died in August 1888.

Seguin's younger brother, WILLIAM HENRY SEGUIN, born in London 1814, also a pupil of the Royal Academy of Music, possessed a light bass voice and was a concert singer and member of the choir of the Temple Church. He died Dec. 28, 1850. He married Miss GOOCH, soprano singer, a fellow pupil at the Academy, who survived him a few years only. His sister ELIZABETH, born in London 1815, was also a singer, and was the mother of Mme. Parepa-Rosa ; she died in London, 1870.   W. H. H.

SEIDL, ANTON, born May 7, 1850, at Pesth, was entered as a pupil at the Leipzig Conservatorium in October 1870. Early in 1872 he went to Bayreuth, and was there employed by Wagner to make the first copy of the score of the Nibelungen trilogy. He also assisted at the festival in August 1876. In 1879, through Wagner's recommendation, he obtained the post of conductor at the Leipzig Opera-House, and remained there until 1882, when he went upon a long tour through Germany, Holland, England, Italy, etc., in the capacity of conductor of Angelo Neumann's 'Nibelungen' opera troupe. The performances were not altogether faultless : it is true that the vocalists were good, but the great music drama was reproduced in a sadly mutilated condition. Yet Seidl proved himself to be an energetic conductor, and was personally successful. In 1883 he became conductor at the Bremen Opera-House. Early in 1885 he married the well-known soprano singer Frl. Kraus, and in September of that year accepted the post of conductor at the New York Metro. Opera-House, which post he filled with great distinction until the temporary eclipse of German opera in favour of Italian. In 1895-97 he again conducted German opera in New York, and in 1897 he conducted at Covent Garden. On Nov. 28, 1898, he died in New York.   C. A.

SEIFFERT, MAX, born at Beeskow on the Spree, Feb. 9, 1868, was educated at his native place and at the Joachimsthal Gymnasium at Berlin, studied musical science and literature under Philipp Spitta, wrote a treatise on Sweelinck for the doctor's degree in 1891 (printed in the *Vierteljahrsschrift* of that year). Besides many contributions to that periodical, to the *Allg. Deutsche Biographie*, the *Tijdschrift* of the Dutch Vereeniging, etc., he wrote a *Geschichte der Klaviermusik* in 1899, and was editor of the complete works of Sweelinck issued in twelve volumes, and of several volumes of the various series of 'Denkmäler der Tonkunst.' Since April 1904 he has been editor-in-chief of the Internationale Musikgesellschaft. (Riemann's *Lexikon*, etc.)   M.

[1] Translation :—'On Monday I fall in love, on Tuesday I say so, Wednesday I declare myself, Thursday I succeed : Friday I cause jealousy, and Saturday and Sunday I seek a fresh love.'

ANTON SEIDL

SEISS, ISIDOR WILHELM, born at Dresden, Dec. 23, 1840, was at first a pupil of F. Wieck for piano and of Julius Otto for theory. In 1858-1860 he studied at Leipzig under Hauptmann. He had a success as a pianist in the following year, and issued several compositions. In 1871 he was appointed a piano-teacher at the Cologne Conservatorium, and in 1878 received the title of professor. He has had a long and successful career there, where he devotes much time to conducting the Musikalische Gesellschaft. His compositions, chiefly educational works for the piano, are tasteful and of high aim; his clever arrangement of Beethoven's 'Contre-danses' and 'Danses allemandes' are among his most famous productions, as well as a revised version of Weber's E flat concerto. A 'Feierliche Szene und Marsch' are for orchestra. (Riemann's *Lexikon.*)   M.

SELBY, BERTRAM LUARD-, born at Ightham, Kent, Feb. 12, 1853, received his musical education at the Leipzig Conservatorium under Reinecke and Jadassohn. Became organist of St. Barnabas, Marylebone, and Highgate School in 1876, and gave chamber concerts in London before his appointment to the post of organist of Salisbury Cathedral in 1881, a post he retained for two years. He was next organist at St. John's, Torquay, in 1884, and of St. Barnabas, Pimlico, in 1886. He was appointed organist of Rochester Cathedral in succession to Dr. John Hopkins, in 1900. His most important works are incidental music to 'Helena in Troas,' performed in London, May 1886, and 'Weather or No,' a musical duologue, produced at the Savoy Theatre in August 1896. An orchestral 'Idyll' was played at one of Henschel's London Symphony Concerts on March 11, 1897. This, two quintets for piano and strings, a suite for violin and piano, many piano pieces, and an opera 'The Ring' (1886), remain unpublished. The list of printed works includes 'The Waits of Bremen,' 'The Dying Swan,' 'Summer by the Sea,' short cantatas, part-songs, 'The Hag,' 'It was a Lover and his Lass,' trios, etc., for female voices, a violin sonata in B minor, some sixteen anthems, ten services, and very numerous organ pieces and some songs, all of which show great taste and refinement of treatment.   M.

SELLINGER'S ROUND, a 16th-century tune and round dance, of unknown authorship, which had immense popularity during the 16th and 17th centuries. The original form of the title was doubtless 'St. Leger's Round.' The delightful vigour and unusual character of the air are felt to-day, when played before a modern audience, as fully as in its own period. It is frequently referred to in 16th- and 17th-century literature, including *Bacchus Bountie*, 1593; Morley's *Plaine and Easie Introduction*, 1597, and elsewhere. In some cases the sub-title 'or the Beginning of the World' is found added to it, and this is partly explained in a comedy

named 'Lingua,' 1607. An excellent version of the tune, arranged with variations by William Byrd, is found in 'The Fitzwilliam Virginal Book,' and other copies of the air are in Lady Neville's Virginal Book and William Ballet's Lute-book.

Printed copies, which differ considerably, and are not so good as those referred to, appear in some of the Playford publications, including early editions of 'The Dancing Master,' 'Musick's Handmaid,' and 'Musick's delight on the Cithren.' The original dance has probably been a May-pole one, and this is borne out by a rude wood-cut on the title-page of a 17th-century 'Garland,' where figures are depicted dancing round a may-pole, and 'Hey for Sellinger's Round' inscribed above them.

The following is the air, without the variations and harmony, in the Fitzwilliam Book.

Sellenger's Round.

From *The Fitzwilliam Virginal Book.*

                      F. K.

SELNECCER, or SELENECCER, NIKOLAUS, born Dec. 6, 1528, at Hersbruck near Nuremberg, was organist of the Burgkapelle in that city, at the age of twelve, and studied at Wittenberg from 1549. From 1557 to 1561 he was court preacher and tutor in Dresden, and subsequently held professional posts in Jena (1561-68), Leipzig (1568-70), Wolfenbüttel (1570-74), Leipzig again (1574-88). In the latter year he was deprived of his offices and became Superintendent at Hildesheim, until at the death of the Elector Christian of Saxony he was reinstated. He was an eminent theologian, and wrote the words and music of many hymns; his great work in this direction was published at Leipzig in 1587, under the title 'Christliche Psalmen, Lieder, vnd Kirchengesenge,' set for four voices, Selneccer's own compositions being marked with his initials. Specimens of his music are given in several of the hymn-books of the 17th century. (*Quellen-Lexikon.*)   M.

SEMBRICH, MARZELLA (original name Praxede Marcelline Kochanska), born Feb. 15, 1858, at Wisniewczyk, Galicia, the daughter of a musician, Kasimir Kochanski, Sembrich being her mother's maiden name. She was taught music by her father, and played in public both piano and violin at the age of

2 d

twelve ; she afterwards received further instruction on these instruments from Stengel (to whom she was afterwards married), and Brustermann, both professors at Lemberg. She then went to Vienna, for completion of her studies under Liszt, but discovering herself to be the possessor of a fine voice, determined to attempt a vocal career, and for that purpose studied singing at Vienna, under Rokitansky, and later at Milan under Lamperti the younger. On June 3, 1877, she made her début at Athens as Elvira in 'I Puritani,' and was highly successful there for two months in that, and as Lucia and Dinorah. She returned to Vienna, studied the German répertoire under Professor Richard Lewy the horn-player, and in October 1878 made a highly successful début at Dresden as Lucia. She remained there until the spring of 1880, becoming famous in coloratura parts. After singing at the Lower Rhine Musical Festival of 1880 she made her first appearance in England on June 12 of the same year at the Royal Italian Opera as Lucia, and was greatly successful in that, Amina, and Margaret of Valois. She returned there for the seasons 1881-84, playing Dinorah, and Constance in the revival of Mozart's 'Entführung.' Dinorah and Astrifiammante were among her best parts. At Benedict's 'Jubilee' Concert at the Albert Hall, June 7, 1884, she sang and played the violin with great success. After singing with much success in Paris, Russia, Spain, the United States, etc., she appeared at L. E. Bach's concert at St. James's Hall, June 25, 1889, and was to have sung in opera at Her Majesty's Theatre, but for the premature closing of the season there. She reappeared as Susanna at Covent Garden in 1895. Of late her career, both in opera and concerts, has been divided between Austria and the United States. Madame Sembrich's voice is about two and a half octaves in compass, viz. from the lower C to F in alt, and is very brilliant in the upper register ; she also possesses great powers of execution. She retired in 1908.   A. C.

SEMELE, a secular oratorio by Handel, was composed in 1743, between June 3 and July 4. The libretto is slightly altered from an opera-book of Congreve's, written in 1707. 'Semele' is termed by Arnold 'A Dramatic Performance,' by Mainwaring 'An English opera but called an Oratorio,' while it was announced at different times in the General Advertiser as 'Semele, after the manner of an Opera,' and 'Semele, after the manner of an Oratorio.' The first performance took place on Feb. 10, 1744, at Covent Garden Theatre, where it was repeated three times in the same year. In the following December it was performed twice, with additions and alterations, at the King's Theatre, Haymarket, and was revived by Smith and Stanley in 1762. The Cambridge University Musical Society revived it on Nov. 27, 1878.

The original MS. is in Buckingham Palace, and there are some interesting sketches (principally of Act iii.) in the Fitzwilliam Museum at Cambridge.   W. B. S.

SEMET, Théophile, born at Lille, Sept. 6, 1824. The prizes he gained at the local Conservatoire procured him a grant from the municipality to study in Paris, and he entered Halévy's class for composition. His first work was merely a few songs and some charming orchestral music for 'La petite Fadette,' vaudeville in two acts (Variétés, Dec. 28, 1850), but he at length procured a better opportunity, and his 'Nuits d'Espagne,' two acts (May 26), and 'La Demoiselle d'honneur,' three acts (Dec. 30), were both produced in 1857 with success at the Théâtre Lyrique ; 'Gil Blas' (March 26, 1860), an opéra-comique in five acts, and 'Ondine,' three acts (Jan. 7, 1863), followed at the same theatre, and his next work, 'La petite Fadette' (Sept. 11, 1869), was produced at the Opéra-Comique.

Besides his operas he composed songs for a piece called 'Constantinople' (1854) ; songs ; a cantata (performed at the Opéra, August 15, 1862) ; airs de ballet for 'Les Pirates de la Savane' (1867), and many part-songs, some of which, especially 'La Danse des Sylphes,' are remarkable. He was drummer at the Opéra for many years ; he died at Corbeil, near Paris, April 15, 1888.   G. C.

SEMIBREVE (Lat. Semibrevis ; Ital. Semibreve ; Fr. Ronde ; Germ. Taktnote, Ganze Note, whence the American term 'whole note'). Franco of Cologne, the earliest-known writer on measured music (Cantus mensurabilis) who furnishes the types from which the forms of our modern notation are evidently derived, describes the semibreve as the shortest note in use, though no very long time elapsed before the minim was added to the list. The forms of these notes are generally supposed to have been suggested by those of the Neumes of an earlier period, the Breve and Semibreve being derived from the Punctum. Don Nicola Vicentino, however, in his L' antica Musica ridotta alla moderna Prattica, printed at Rome in 1555, refers the forms of all these notes to a different origin ; deriving the Large, the Long, and the Breve from the B quadratum, or square B (♮) ; and the Semibreve from the B rotundum (♭) ; the transformation being effected, in each case, by depriving the figure of one or both of its tails. But Vicentino has fallen into so many palpable errors that we cannot trust him ; and, in the present instance, his theory certainly does not accord with that early form of the Semibreve which is produced by cutting the Breve (■) in half, diagonally, thus, (◢). This form soon gave way to the Lozenge (♦ or ◊), which was retained in use until late in the 17th century, when it was replaced in measured music by the round note of our present system (○), though

MARZELLA SEMBRICH

in the Gregorian system of notation the lozenge remains in use to the present day.

Until the beginning of the 17th century, the Semibreve represented one-third of a Perfect Breve, and the half of an Imperfect one. In the Greater Prolation it was equal to three Minims; in the Lesser to two. In either case it was accepted as the norm of all other notes, and was held to constitute a complete measure or stroke. In the Greater Prolation—or, as we should now call it, triple time—this stroke was indicated by a single down-beat of the hand, representing what we write as a dotted Semibreve. In the Lesser Prolation—the common time of the modern system—it was indicated by a down and an up beat, called respectively the *Thesis* and the *Arsis* of the measure. It will be understood that these two beats represented two minims; and, happily for us, we are not left altogether in doubt as to the average pace at which these two Minims were sung, in the great polyphonic compositions of the 15th and 16th centuries: for, apart from the traditions of the Sistine Chapel, early writers have left a very definite rule for our guidance. The Thesis and Arsis of the Lesser Prolation, they say, represent the beats of the human pulse. Now, the rapidity of the human pulse, taking into calculation the variations exhibited at all ages, and in both sexes, ranges between 66·7 and 140 per minute: allowing, therefore, for roughness of calculation, we may say that the compositions of Josquin des Prés, and Palestrina, may be safely interpreted between $\downuparrow$ = 60, and $\downuparrow$ = 140—a sufficiently extended range for any conductor.

In modern music the Semibreve retains more than one of the characteristics that distinguished it in the 15th and 16th centuries. It is now, indeed, the longest instead of the shortest note in common use, for the employment of the Breve is altogether exceptional: but it is none the less the norm from which all other notes are derived. We may say that, of all the notes now in use, the Semibreve is the one which unites us most closely to the system of those who invented the germ of the method we ourselves follow; and it furnishes the safest guide we know of to the right understanding of their works.   W. S. R.

SEMICHORUS, *i.e.* Half-chorus; a word used to denote a kind of antiphonal effect produced by employing half the number of voices at certain points, and contrasting this smaller body of sound with the full chorus.   M.

SEMICROMA (Lat. *Semichroma*; Eng. *Quaver*, or *Semiquaver*). The Italian name for the Semiquaver. Old writers, however, sometimes apply the term Croma to the crotchet, and Semicroma to the quaver; and, so vague was once the distinction between the two, that even Baretti, writing as late as 1824, makes

the word 'Croma' signify 'a crotchet or quaver.' The etymology of the word Chroma is derived from the very early custom of using red notes intermixed with black ones. The red notes being sung more quickly than the black ones, the duration of a red minim was a little longer than that of a black Semiminim (or crotchet); and the note was called *Chroma* on account of its colour. [See NOTATION, QUAVER.]   W. S. R.

SEMIFUSA. The Latin name for the Semiquaver; but sometimes applied to the Quaver also. The etymology of the term is not very clear. The most probable theory is that which traces it to a fancied resemblance between the early form of the Quaver, and that of a spindle (*fusus*). [See NOTATION, QUAVER.]   W. S. R.

SEMIMINIMA MAJOR and MINOR (Eng. *Greater*, and *Lesser Half-Minim* = Crotchet, and Quaver; Ital. *Croma e Semicroma*; Germ. *Viertel und Achtel*; French *Noire et Croche*). Though the Minim was so called, because, at the time of its invention, it was the smallest (*i.e.* the shortest) of all notes, composers soon found it convenient to divide it in half, and even into four parts. Franchinus Gafurius, quoting from Prosdocimus de Beldemandis, describes and figures these divisions in his *Practica Musicae*, printed in 1496. The Greater Semiminima, the equivalent of the modern crotchet, was a black lozenge-headed note, with a tail, $\downarrow$; the Lesser Semiminima, now called the quaver, was a similar note, with a single hook, $\eighthnote$. Sometimes the head of the greater Semiminim was 'void'—that is to say, open or white—in which case, this note also had a hook, to distinguish it from the minim, $\eighthnote$; and, when this hooked form was used, the figure which we have described above as proper to the Greater Semiminim was used for the Lesser one. When black and red notes were used together the red minim served as the diminutive of the black one; and the Semiminim was called *Chroma*, on account of its colour. This name was afterwards applied both to the Greater and the Lesser Semiminim; and hence it came to pass that, in later times, the term Chroma was applied indiscriminately to the crotchet and the quaver. [See NOTATION.]   W. S. R.

SEMIQUAVER (Lat. *Semifusa*; Ital. *Semicroma, Biscroma, Semifusa*; Germ. *Sechzehntel*, whence the American term, *Sixteenth Note*; Fr. *Double croche*). The sixteenth part of a semibreve.

The earliest mention of the Semiquaver occurs in the *Practica Musicae* of Franchinus Gafurius, printed at Milan in 1496. It may be found—though very rarely—in the printed polyphonic music of the 16th century, in the form of a black lozenge-headed note, with a double hook, β or β; and it is manifestly from this early type that our present figure is derived. In the 16th century both Semi-quavers and Quavers were always printed with separate hooks. The custom of joining Quavers together by a single line, and Semiquavers by a double one, dates from the 17th century; and the credit of the invention is generally accorded to John Heptinstall, about 1690. [See NOTATION.]   W. S. R.

SEMIRAMIDE (*i.e.* Semiramis, Empress of Nineveh). A favourite subject with Italian writers of operas. Librettos upon it were written by Moniglia, Apostolo Zeno, and Silvani; and Clément's *Dictionnaire Lyrique* contains a list of twenty-one operas composed to one or other of these by the masters of the 18th century. Voltaire's play on the same subject was adapted to music and set by Graun (Berlin, 1754), and Catel (1802). Rossini's well-known *chef-d'œuvre* was written to a libretto by Rossi, and produced at Venice, Feb. 3, 1823; and in London, at the King's Theatre, July 15, 1824. In French, as 'Semiramis,' it appeared in Paris, July 9, 1860. —SEMIRAMIDE RICONOSCIUTA, words by Meta-stasio, was set by Vinci, Porpora, Cocchi, Sarti, Traetta, Meyerbeer, and Gluck—the last of these at Vienna in 1748.   G.

SEMITONE (from the Greek ἡμιτόνιον). Half a tone; the smallest interval in the ordinary musical scales. The semitone may be of different kinds, each of which has a different theoretical magnitude.

Since the invention of the diatonic scale the natural interval of the fourth has been subdivided artificially into two tones and a semitone. In the ancient Greek time the two tones were both what are now called *major* tones, and the hemitone had a magnitude determined by the difference between their sum and the fourth; but when harmony began to prevail, one of the tones was diminished to a *minor* tone, and this gave the modern semitone a little greater value. The semitone, so formed, as belonging to the diatonic scale (from B to C, or from E to F for example) is called a *diatonic* semitone.

The introduction of chromatic notes gave rise to a third kind of semitone, as from C to C♯ or from G to G♭; this is called a *chromatic* semi-tone and has a less magnitude than the diatonic one.

Finally came the great simplification of music by dividing the octave into twelve equal intervals, each of which was called a *mean* semitone; thus abolishing practically the difference between the diatonic and the chromatic values. A semitone may now be considered, in practical use, as simply the interval between the sounds given by any two adjoining keys on a well-tuned piano.

The relations between the theoretical magni-tudes of the different kinds of semitones are about as follows: If we represent the magnitude of a mean semitone by 25, the true magnitude of a diatonic semitone will be about 28; of a chro-matic semitone about 18; and of the ancient Greek hemitone about 23.   W. P.

SEMPLICE, 'simple'; a direction denoting that the passage so marked is to be performed without any adornment or deviation from the time, used particularly in passages of which the character might possibly be misunderstood. The Arietta which forms the subject of the variations in Beethoven's last PF. Sonata, op. 111, is marked 'Adagio molto semplice cantabile.'   M.

SEMPRE, 'always,' a word used in conjunc-tion with some other mark of time or expression to signify that such mark is to remain in force until a new direction appears. Its purpose is to remind the performer of the directions which might otherwise be forgotten—as in the scherzo of the Eroica Symphony, where the direction *Sempre pp. e staccato* is repeated again and again throughout the movement.   M.

SENAILLÉ, JEAN BAPTISTE, a violinist of eminence, at one time member of the band of Louis XV., born in Paris in the parish of Saint Germain l'Auxerrois on Nov. 23, 1687. He inherited his musical gifts from his father, who played the *hautbois* at the Opéra. He received his earliest violin instruction from Queversin, a member of the famous 'Vingt-quatre violons,' and during his period of study with this master assisted a *maître à danser* named Bonnefons. His next teacher was Corelli's excellent pupil Jean Baptiste Anet, generally known as Baptiste, whose teaching imbued him with such a longing to visit Italy that he travelled to Modena, where he became a pupil of Antonio Vitali. According to the account of Senaillé given by Jacques Lacombe in his *Dictionnaire Portatif des Beaux-arts* (Paris, 1752), Auet's teaching enabled his pupil to surpass the Italian violinist; for on his arrival at Modena, during the time of the annual fair held in the month of May, the composer of the opera then being performed, begged him to play in his orchestra, and on gaining his consent installed him with ceremony in a place prepared for him above the other members of the band. After the performance, he was presented to the Duke and Duchess of Modena: played several of his own sonatas before them and their guests with unqualified success, eventually receiving an appointment in the music of the court. In 1719 he seems to have returned to Paris, where the special recom-mendation of the Duchess of Modena, daughter of the Duke d'Orléans—at that time Regent of France—procured him a position in the Court band. A similar appointment was accorded him in the private band of Louis XV., and he held this until his death, when he was succeeded by Joseph Francœur.

Senaillé ranked as one of the best performers of his time in France. His importation of the Italian methods of playing influenced the French school—at that time in its first state of development—almost as much as did

Leclair. Through his two best pupils Guignon and Guillemain, his traditions were transmitted and preserved. His compositions show the influence of Corelli ; they comprised five books of Sonatas for violin alone, and were published in books of ten sonatas in the following years : 1710, 1712, 1716, 1721, 1727. An Aria of his for Pf. and V. is included in G. Jensen's 'Classische Violin Musik,' Heft iii. A Sarabande and Allemanda (Sonate à violon seul) is arranged by Alfred Moffat. A Sonata in G edited by Alfred Moffat is in Simrock's ' Meister-Schule für Violine mit Begleitung des Pianoforte.' Alard includes Senaillé's Ninth Sonata in his 'Maîtres Classiques de Violon' (1862), and G. Jensen has arranged the same Sonata for piano and violin which is published in 'Classische Violin Musik,' 1890. A composition of Senaillé's is also to be found in E. M. E. Deldevez's ' Pièces diverses choisies' (Paris, Richault, 1858).—A. Vidal, *Les Instruments à Archet* ; G. Hart, *The Violin and its Music* ; Choron et Fayolle, *Dict. Hist. des Mus.* ; Félix Huét, *Études sur les différentes Écoles de Violon* ; Fétis, *Biog. des Mus.* ; J. Lacombe, *Dictionnaire des Beaux-Arts* ; Clarke, *Dict. of Fiddlers.*   E. H-A.

SENESINO, FRANCESCO BERNARDI DETTO, one of the most famous of the sopranists who flourished in the 18th century. He was born about 1680, at Siena (whence he derived his name), and received his musical education from Bernacchi, at Bologna. In 1719 he was singing at the Court theatre of Saxony, and when Handel came to Dresden in quest of singers, was engaged by him for London. His first appearance in this country (Nov. 1720) was in Buononcini's opera ' Astarto,' which at once established him in public favour. He sang next in a revival of Handel's ' Floridante,' and in the celebrated ' Muzio Scævola '; afterwards in Handel's ' Ottone,' ' Flavio,' and ' Giulio Cesare' (1723), 'Tamerlano' (1724), 'Rodelinda' (1725), 'Scipio' and ' Alessandro' (1726), and in various operas and pasticcios by other composers. In ' Giulio Cesare' his declamation of the famous accompanied recitative ' Alma del gran Pompeo' created a special sensation. A writer in the *London Magazine* (Feb. 1733) relates an amusing anecdote of Senesino in this opera: 'When I was last at the opera of "Julius Cæsar," a piece of the machinery tumbled down from the roof of the theatre upon the stage, just as Senesino had chanted forth these words "Cesare non seppe mai che sia timore" (Cæsar never knew fear). The poor hero was so frightened that he trembled, lost his voice, and fell crying. Every tyrant or tyrannical minister is just such a Cæsar as Senesino.' ' Alessandro' had a run of two months, and its last performance, advertised for June 7, was prevented by the sudden illness of Senesino, who, as soon as he was able to travel, set off

for Italy, for the recovery of his health, promising to return the next winter. This promise, however, was not kept in time to enable the Opera-house to open till after Christmas.

Senesino reappeared in Handel's ' Admeto,' early in 1727. This was followed in the same year by ' Riccardo Imo,' and in 1728 by ' Siroe ' and ' Tolomeo,' in which a great effect was made by the echo song, ' Dite che fa,' sung by Cuzzoni, with many of the passages repeated behind the scenes by Senesino. But now, after several unprosperous seasons, the society called the Royal Academy was dissolved. Hawkins attributes to this time the quarrel which ended in a final rupture between Senesino and the great composer. But this is disproved by the fact that Senesino returned to sing for Handel in 1730. That there was, however, much discord in the company before it separated is true enough.

He rejoined the Haymarket company, under Handel's management, at a salary of 1400 guineas, and appeared on Feb. 2, 1731, in ' Poro,' then considered a great success. In the same year were revived ' Rodelinda ' and ' Rinaldo.' ' Ezio ' and ' Sosarme ' were produced in 1732. Besides singing in all these, Senesino took part (May 2, 1732) in ' Esther,' Handel's first oratorio, described as ' a new species of exhibition at the Opera-house,' and on June 10, in a curious performance, under the composer's own direction, of ' Acis and Galatea.' Several airs and three choruses were interpolated on this occasion, from Handel's early Neapolitan Serenata on the same subject, and the piece was sung partly in English and partly in Italian.

The last of Handel's operas in which Senesino appeared, was ' Orlando ' (Jan. 1733), but he took part later in the same season in ' Deborah,' described then as an opera, and performed (as was ' Esther ') on opera nights. The long impending quarrel now came to a crisis. ' All these wealthy adversaries of Handel naturally espoused the cause of Senesino from the outset . . . and ended by demanding that Senesino should be retained . . . Handel replied that Senesino should never reappear in his theatre.' (Schoelcher.) Accordingly, says Burney, ' the nobility and gentry opened a subscription for Italian operas at Lincoln's Inn Fields, inviting Porpora thither to compose and conduct, and engaging Senesino, Cuzzoni, Montagnana, Segatti, Bertolli, and afterwards Farinelli, to perform there.' There Senesino remained till 1735, when he returned to Siena, with a fortune of £15,000, and built himself a house.

Senesino's voice was a mezzo-soprano, or, according to some, a contralto. Although limited in compass it was considered by many good judges to be superior in quality even to that of Farinelli. It was clear, penetrating, and flexible, his intonation faultless, his shake perfect. Purity, simplicity, and expressiveness were the characteristics of his style, while for the delivery of recitative 'he had not his fellow in Europe.'

In 1739 Senesino was living at Florence, and sang a duet with the Archduchess Maria Theresa there. He died about 1750. F. A. M.

SENFF, BARTHOLF, an eminent German music-publisher, was born at Friedrichshall, Coburg, Sept. 2, 1815. He founded the house which bears his name, in Leipzig, in 1850, and his catalogue contains original editions of Mendelssohn, Schumann, Brahms (opp. 5, 6, Gavotte by Gluck, 5 Studien für PF.), Gade, Hiller, Reinecke, Reitz, Rubinstein, and other masters, as well as the excellent educational works of Louis Köhler.

Senff was founder, editor, and proprietor of the well-known musical periodical *Signale für die musikalische Welt.* [See PERIODICALS, MUSICAL, vol. iii. p. 686*a*.] He died at Baden-weiler, June 25, 1900. G.

SENFL, or SENFEL, LUDWIG, born at Zurich towards the end of the 15th century. A volume of MS. songs in the Vienna library contains some verses, written and set to music by Senfl himself, describing his early enthusiasm for music, his education under Heinrich Isaac, and his gratitude to that master. At an early age he entered the Court chapel of Maximilian I., ultimately succeeded Isaac as chapel-master, and held that office till the emperor's death (Jan. 1519), on which occasion he wrote music to the words 'Quis dabit oculis nostris fontem lacrimarum.' In 1520 he was at Augsburg, received a present of fifty gulden from Charles V. on Feb. 19, and in the following November personally edited the 'Liber selectarum Cantionum,' one of the first music books printed in Germany. Thence he went to Munich, though in what capacity is uncertain. On one title-page (1526) he is called 'Musicus intonator,' on another (1534) 'Musicus primarius,' of the Duke of Bavaria, while in his own letters he subscribes himself simply 'Componist zu München.' The date of his death is unknown. In Forster's collection of Liedlein (preface dated Jan. 31, 1556) he is spoken of as 'L. S. seliger' (*i.e.* dead) ; and if the title 'musicus primarius' stands for 'chapel-master' he must have died or retired some years before, since Ludwig Daser had held that office for some years when Lassus went to Munich in 1557.

The well-known letter from Luther to Senfl[1] is no evidence that the composer had worked specially for the Lutheran Church, though the existence of the correspondence has given rise to that idea. Indeed his connection with the strictly Catholic court of Munich would, as Fétis points out, render it most improbable.[2] Four letters written by Senfl to the Margrave

[1] Dated Coburg, Oct. 4, 1530. The letter is printed in *Dr. M. Luther's Gedanken über die Musik,* F. A. Beck (Berlin, 1828), p. 58.
[2] *Biographie des Musiciens,* vi. 44.

Albrecht of Brandenburg and to Georg Schultheis are printed in the *Allgemeine Musik. Zeitung,* for August 12, 1863.

A portrait engraved on a medal by Hagenauer of Augsburg, with the inscription 'Ludovvicus Senfel,' and on the reverse 'Psallam deo meo quamdiu fuero 1529,' is in the collection of coins and medals at Vienna.

The royal library at Munich contains the manuscript church service books begun by Isaac and completed by Senfl, as well as manuscript masses by the latter. His most important published works are (1) 'Quinque salutationes D. N. Hiesu Christi,' etc. (Norimbergae, 1526) ; (2) 'Varia carminum genera, quibus tum Horatius, tum alii egregii poetae . . . harmoniis composita' (*Id.* 1534) ; (3) '121 newe Lieder' (*Id.* 1534), with 81 nos. by L. S. ; (4) 'Magnificat octo tonorum,' *a* 4, 5 (*Id.* 1537) ; (5) '115 guter newer Liedlein' (*Id.* 1544), with 64 nos. by L. S. Besides these Eitner[3] names above 100 separate pieces printed in various collections of the 16th century. (See the *Quellen-Lexikon.*) In modern notation nine sacred pieces (*a* 4) are given by Winterfeld in *Der evangelische Kirchengesang* (Leipzig, 1843), and five Lieder by Liliencron in *Die historischen Volkslieder der Deutschen* (Leipzig, 1865-69). J. R. S.-B.

SENNET—also written SENET, SENNATE, SYNNET, CYNET, SIGNET or SIGNATE—a word which occurs in stage-directions in the plays of the Elizabethan dramatists, and is used to denote that a particular fanfare is to be played. The name is probably derived from Seven, and may indicate a flourish of seven notes, as suggested in Stainer and Barrett's *Dictionary of Musical Terms.* It is a technical term, and what particular notes were played is now unknown. A Sennet was distinguished from a Flourish, as is proved by a stage-direction in Dekker's *Satiromastix,* 'Trumpets sound a florish, and then a sennate.' (Nares's *Glossary.*) W. B. S.

SENZA, 'without'—as *Senza organo,* 'without organ' ; a direction of frequent occurrence throughout Handel's organ concertos ; *Senza repetizione,* 'without repeat' [see REPEAT] ; *Senza tempo,* 'without time,' which occurs in Schumann's Humoreske, op. 20, in the movement marked Precipitoso. The right hand is marked *Come senza tempo* ('Wie ausser tempo,' in German), while the left remains *in tempo.* The same direction is employed at the end of Chopin's Nocturne, op. 9, No. 3. In the 'Sanctus' of Verdi's Requiem both the terms *senza misura* and *senza tempo* occur. M.

SEPTAVE. The compass of seven diatonic notes reckoned upward from the tonic or key-note. The term is occasionally employed by organ-builders. T. E.

SEPTET (Fr. *Septuor* ; Ital. *Septetto*). A composition for seven instruments or voices, with or without accompaniment.

[3] *Bibliographie* (Berlin, 1877).

Beethoven's famous Septet for strings and wind naturally heads the list, and Hummel's for piano, strings, and wind is the next best known, though it is far inferior to Spohr's difficult and brilliant work for a similar combination (op. 147). A striking, though too seldom heard composition, is Saint-Saëns's Septet for piano, strings, and trumpet, op. 65.

Operatic situations have seldom given rise to, or opportunity for, vocal septets, but the magnificent specimen in the last act of Goetz's 'Taming of the Shrew' deserves foremost mention.   F. C.

SEQUENCE is generally taken to mean the repetition of a definite group of notes or chords in different positions of the scale, like regular steps ascending or descending, as in the following outlines :—

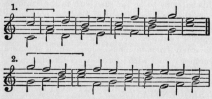

The device has been a favourite one with composers, from Corelli, Bach, and Handel, to Schumann, Brahms, and Wagner. The reason is partly that it is so thoroughly intelligible without being commonplace. The mind is easily led from point to point by recognising each successive step after the first group of chords has been given, and is sufficiently interested by the slight amount of diversity which prevails at each repetition. It thus supplies a vital element of form in a manner which in some cases has certain advantages over simple exact repetition, especially when short phrases are repeated in juxtaposition. It was consequently made much use of by early composers of sonatas, and instrumental works of like nature, such as Corelli and his immediate successors ; and in many cases examples make their appearance at analogous points in different movements, indicating the recognition of formal principles in their introduction. This occurs, for instance, near the beginning of the second half in the following movements from Corelli's Opera Quarta : Corrente and Allemanda of Sonata 1, Allemanda and Corrente of Sonata 2, Corrente of Sonata 3, Corrente and Giga of Sonata 4, Gavotte of Sonata 5, Allemanda and Giga of Sonata 6, and so forth. A large proportion of both ancient and modern sequences are diatonic ; that is, the groups are repeated analogously in the same key series, without consideration of the real difference of quality in the intervals ; so that major sevenths occasionally answer minor sevenths, and diminished fifths perfect fifths, and so forth ; and it has long been considered allowable to in-

troduce intervals and combinations, in those circumstances, which would otherwise have been held inadmissible. Thus a triad on the leading note would in ordinary circumstances be considered as a discord, and would be limited in progression accordingly ; but if it occurred in a sequence, its limitations were freely obviated by the preponderant influence of the established form of motion. Such diatonic sequences, called also sometimes diatonic successions, are extremely familiar in Handel's works. A typical instance is a Capriccio in G major, published in Pauer's 'Alte Meister,' which contains at least fifteen sequences, some of them unusually long ones, in four pages of Allegro. The subject itself is a characteristic example of a sequence in a single part ; it is as follows :—

A kind of sequence which was early developed but which is more characteristic of later music, is the modulatory sequence, sometimes also called chromatic. In this form accidentals are introduced, sometimes by following exactly the quality of the intervals where the diatonic series would not admit of them, and sometimes by purposely altering them to gain the step of modulation. This will be easily intelligible from the following example :—

The usefulness of the device in such circumstances is, if anything, even more marked than it is in a single key, because of the greater breadth of range which it allows, and the closeness and cogency of the successive transitions which it renders possible. A compact and significant example to the point is the following from a fugue by Cherubini in C major :—

Beethoven made very remarkable use of this device, especially in the great Sonata in B♭, op. 106, from which an example is quoted in the article MODULATION [vol. iii. p. 239]. The 'working out' portion of the first movement of the same sonata is an almost unbroken series of sequences of both orders ; and the introduction to the final fugue is even more remarkable, both for the length of the sequence, and the originality of its treatment. The first-mentioned, which is from the slow movement, is further remarkable as an example of a peculiar manipulation of the device by which modern composers have obtained very impressive results. This is the change of emphasis in the successive steps of which it is composed. For instance, if the characteristic group consists of three chords of equal length, and the time in which it occurs is a square one, it is clear that the chord which is emphatic in the first step will be weakest in the next, and *vice versa*. This form will be most easily understood from an outline example :—

A passage at the beginning of the Presto at the end of Beethoven's Leonora Overture, No. 3, is a good example of a sequence of this kind in a single part. It begins in the following quotation at *

The extension of the characteristic group of a sequence is almost unlimited, but it will be obvious at once that in harmonic sequences the shorter and simpler they are the more immediately they will be understood. In long-limbed sequences the hearer may soon perceive that there is a principle of order underlying what he hears, though its exact nature may always elude his apprehension, and in respect of the larger branches of form this is a decided advantage. Among short-limbed emphatic sequences in modern music, the one of eight steps which occurs towards the end of the first full portion of the overture to 'Die Meistersinger' is conspicuous, and it has the advantage of being slightly irregular. The long-limbed sequences are sometimes elaborately concealed, so that the underlying source of order in the progression can only with difficulty be unravelled. A remarkable example of a very complicated sequence of this kind is a passage in Schumann's Fantasia in C major (op. 17), in the movement in E♭, marked 'Moderato con energia,' beginning at the 58th bar. The passage is too long to quote, but the clue to the mystery may be extracted somewhat after this manner :—

In order to see how this has been manipulated reference must be made to the original.

A species of sequence which is familiar in modern music is that in which a figure or melody is repeated a tone higher; this has been termed a Rosalia. [See *ante*, p. 141.] Another, which is equally characteristic, is a repetition of a figure or passage a semitone higher; an example from the Eroica Symphony is quoted in vol. iii. p. 235 of this Dictionary.

The device has never been bound to rigid exactness, because it is easy to follow, and slight deviations seasonably introduced are often happy in effect. In fact its virtue does not consist so much in the exactness of transposition as in the intelligibility of analogous repetitions. If the musical idea is sufficiently interesting to carry the attention with it, the sequence will perform its function adequately even if it be slightly irregular both in its harmonic steps and in its melodic features; and this happens to be the case both in the example from the slow movement of Beethoven's Sonata in B♭, and in the passage quoted from Schumann's Fantasia. It is not so, however, with the crude harmonic successions which are more commonly met with; for they are like diagrams, and if they are not exact they are good for nothing.   C. H. H. P.

SEQUENTIA (*Prosa*; Eng. *Sequence*, or *Prose*). A hymn of peculiar structure, which owes its name to its position in the Mass; it appears there as the continuation or sequence of the Gradual and Alleluia. It originally was a long jubilus or melody without words, attached to the *a* of the Alleluia. (See TROPE.) In the 9th century in France words were adapted to the notes, and these were called a 'Prose,' because they followed the lines of the music and not any scheme of metre. When these compositions had thus won a place for themselves, fresh ones came to be written in regular metre, and the old name Prose being unsuitable gave way to the new name Sequence. From the 12th century to the 15th century such compositions were most popular; and many of the most beautiful specimens we possess were written by the great Hymnologists who flourished during these productive periods. Mediæval Office-Books contain innumerable sequences of striking originality; but at the last revision of the Roman liturgy, by direction of the Council of Trent, the greater number of these were expunged. Five, however, have been retained in the current missal; and these five occupy a very prominent position in the services in which they are incorporated, as well as in the history of ecclesiastical music.

1. The sequence appointed for Easter Sunday is 'Victimae paschali,' the oldest now in use, and in reality a Prose, written by Wipo in the first half of the 11th century.

2. The sequence for Whitsunday, 'Veni Sancte Spiritus,' in rhymed triplets of Trochaic Dimeter Catalectic, was written probably by Innocent III. at the end of the 12th century;

it is called by mediæval writers, 'The Golden Sequence.'

3. For the festival of Corpus Christi, S. Thomas Aquinas wrote the celebrated sequence, 'Lauda Sion,' which is generally believed to date from about the year 1261.

4. To Innocent III. is also attributed the 'Stabat Mater,' sung since 1727 on the 'Feasts of the Seven Dolours of Our Lady' (the Friday in Passion Week, and the third Sunday in September). The authorship, however, has not been certainly ascertained ; and many are inclined to attribute it to Jacobus de Benedictis (Jacopone). (See STABAT MATER.)

5. Even more celebrated than any of these is the 'Dies irae' written, during the latter half of the 12th century or beginning of the 13th century, by Thomas of Celano, and sung in the 'Requiem,' or Mass for the Dead. In the triple stanzas of this wonderful poem the rhymed Latin of the Middle Ages attained its highest perfection ; and, though the 'Stabat Mater' is frequently said to be second only to it in beauty, the distance between the two is very great.

The plain-chant melodies of sequences differ from hymn melodies in their structure. The ancient jubilus was divided into sections, each of which was sung twice, and consequently a sequence melody properly consists of a series of phrases each of which is repeated. Similarly a sequence is a series of verses each dual in structure and consisting of strophe and antistrophe. They may be represented by the formula aa' : bb' : cc', etc. In the early rhythmical proses a, b, c, etc., are usually unlike one another ; in the later metrical proses for the most part the same scheme runs throughout the words though the music varies. The 'Dies irae' is irregular and does not conform to the usual type, because it was not originally a sequence at all. All of these, and other sequences besides, are found in use in whole or in part in Anglican services. For 'Dies irae' see *Hymns Ancient and Modern* (new edition), 302, *English Hymnal*, 351 ; 'Lauda Sion,' *E. H.* 317 ; 'Stabat Mater,' *H. A. and M.*, 132, *E. H.* 115, in part ; 'Veni sancti Spiritus,' *H. A. and M.* 184, *E. H.* 155 ; 'Victimae paschali,' *E. H.* 130. Compare an early French rhythmical prose 'Salus Aeterna,' *E. H.* 10, and contrast it with a late metrical sequence such as 'Sponsa Christi,' *H. A. and M.* 245, *E. H.* 253, both as regards text and melody.

In addition to these plain-song melodies, we possess innumerable settings of all the sequences now in use, by the great masters of the Polyphonic School ; and many by the classical composers of the 18th and 19th centuries. For these see DIES IRAE ; LAUDA SION ; STABAT MATER ; VENI SANCTE SPIRITUS ; AND VICTIMAE PASCHALI.   w. s. r. ; revised by W. H. F.

SERAGLIO, THE.   (i.) The English title of an adaptation (produced 1827) of Mozart's ENTFÜHRUNG AUS DEM SERAIL. See vol. i. p. 784.

(ii.) An opera by Charles Dibdin under this title was produced at Covent Garden, Nov. 14, 1776. Dibdin being then in France, Dr. Arnold, composer to the theatre, had some share in the musical part of it, but it contains Dibdin's fine song 'Blow high, blow low' sung in the opera by Reinhold, and afterwards introduced by Bannister into Arne's opera 'Thomas and Sally.' The opera had very little success, but both libretto and the music were published. Harris the Covent Garden manager had altered the piece considerably for acting purposes.   F. K.

SERAPHIN, SANCTUS (or SANTO SERAFIN) and GIORGIO (uncle and nephew), two celebrated violin-makers of Venice. The uncle, as his label informs us ('Sanctus Seraphin Utinensis fecit Venetiis '), was originally of Udine, a town in the Venetian territory towards the mountains of Carinthia, and probably of Jewish extraction. His violins date from about 1710 to 1740. The nephew, if we may judge from the style of his instruments, worked with the uncle many years, and appears to have succeeded him in the business. The instruments of Sanctus Seraphin occupy a middle place between the Italian and the Tyrolese school. As far as external appearance goes, the maker seems to vacillate between the model of Stainer and that of Nicholas Amati. But in the essential particulars of the art, in the selection of wood of the finest and most sonorous quality, in the proper calculation of the proportions, and the solidity and finish of the parts, he worked on the principles of the Cremona makers. Few equalled him as a workman. Those who wish to see how far mechanical perfection can be carried should examine Seraphin's purfling with a magnifying glass. In Seraphin's earlier years the Stainer character predominates in his instruments ; in his later years he leaned to the Amati model. His instruments are famous for their perfect finish (reminding forcibly of the style of Stradivarius), their remarkably lustrous deep red varnish, and fine mellow tone.

[The period of Sanctus Seraphin's activity extends from about 1678 to 1735. He worked in Udine for nearly twenty years, and during that time he employed an engraved label of large dimensions which runs : 'Sanctus Seraphinus Nicolai Amati Cremonensis Allumnus faciebat : Udine A. 16   ' : It is worthy of note that the dates on Seraphin's labels are in accordance with the rest of his work, neatly written in, and not bungled, as is frequently the case with his contemporaries. The Venetian label quoted at the beginning of this article is larger than any label to be found in a Cremona instrument. The legend on Seraphin's ticket is framed by a design composed on three sides of graceful curving strokes, while the upper side is formed of two fern leaves and elegant curves. On either side there are respectively some rolls of music and a violin. Representations of this ticket are given by M. Laurent Grillet in his *Ancêtres du Violon* and also in Herr von Lutgendorff's *Die Geigen und Lautenmacher*. One of the finest known examples of this maker's work was a violoncello lent to the South Kensington Special Loan Exhibition by its owner Mr. H. B. Heath in 1872.]

George Seraphin followed his uncle's later model with such precision that it is difficult to find any point of difference. Like his uncle, he finished his instruments to a degree of perfection which amounts to a fault, depriving them, as it does, of character and individuality. Like his uncle, he used a large copper-plate label (nearly all the Italian makers used letterpress labels) bearing the inscription 'Georgius Seraphin Sancti nepos fecit Venetiis (1743).' Both makers branded their instruments at the tailpin. Their works are not common in England, and specimens in good preservation realise from £50 upwards.

[A superb violin of Sanctus Seraphin which belonged to Messrs Barré and Bayly's collection realised £280, at a sale by auction in 1894, while a violoncello by the same maker, the property of James Goding, Esq., was sold in a like manner for £56:14s. in 1857. According to Von Lutgendorff, George Seraphin was not Sanctus Seraphin's nephew but his grandson.— Von Lutgendorff, *Die Geigen und Lautenmacher*; Charles Reade, *A Lost Art Revived*; Alberto Bachmann, *Le Violon*; J. M. Fleming, *Old Violins*; Laurent Grillet, *Les Ancêtres du Violon*; G. Hart, *The Violin*; A. Vidal, *Les Instruments à Archet*.] E. J. P.; with additions in square brackets, by E. H-A.

SERAPHINE. In vol. ii. p. 303*a* reference is made to the seraphine as a precursor of Debain's HARMONIUM. It was an English free-reed instrument resembling the German Physharmonica, which latter was brought to England by the Schulz family in 1826. In 1828 a similar instrument, but named Aeol-harmonica, was played by young Schulz at a Philharmonic Concert (Concertante for Aeol-harmonica and two guitars, April 28). In 1833, John Green, who had been Clementi's traveller, and had a shop in Soho Square, brought out the Seraphine. Green engaged Samuel Wesley to give weekly performances upon the seraphine at his shop, and managed for some time to dispose of his instruments at 40 guineas each. But the seraphine was harsh and raspy in tone, and never found favour with sensitive musicians. The wind apparatus, similar to the organ, was a dead-weighted bellows giving a uniform pressure, and a swell was produced by opening a shutter of a box placed over the reeds.

In the year 1841, Mr. W. E. Evans invented the 'Organo Harmonica,' the improvements on the seraphine consisting of thin steel reeds artistically voiced, and coiled springs in the reservoir to enable the player to produce a rapid articulation with a small wind pressure, and to increase the power of tone as the reservoir filled. Eminent musicians publicly pronounced Mr. Evans's instrument more valuable than the seraphine as a substitute for the organ, but neither the one nor the other was capable of what is now known as 'dead expression.'

Patents for various improvements of the seraphine were taken out by Myers and Storer in 1839, by Storer alone in 1846, and by Mott in the same year. There is further reference to it in patents of Pape 1850, and Blackwell 1852. About the last-named date it was entirely superseded by the harmonium.   A. J. H.

SERENADE (Ital. *Serenata*; Fr. *Sérénade*; Germ. *Ständchen*). Evening song, from the Italian *sera*. Hence the word has been applied, indiscriminately, to many different kinds of music intended to be sung or played at night in the open air; and so generally has this connection of ideas been accepted that, by common consent, the term 'Serenade' has identified itself in many languages with the song sung by a lover standing beneath his mistress's window, or the concert of instrumental music substituted for it by an admirer with 'no voice for singing.'

To be true to nature, a serenade of this kind should be simple, melodious, sensuous in expression, and accompanied by some kind of instrument which the lover might carry in his hand. All these conditions are fulfilled in the most perfect example of the style that ever has been, or is ever likely to be written—'Deh vieni alla finestra,' in 'Don Giovanni.' The melody of this is as artless as a folk-song, yet capable of breathing the very soul of voluptuous passion.

[If Mozart created the perfect type of vocal serenade in the song just mentioned, such things as his 'Hafner Serenade' have served as the model of the instrumental serenade, which, like the *divertimento*, is generally in a large number of short movements. The two Serenade trios of Beethoven (opp. 8 and 25) are illustrious specimens of the forms in which each section is of the most concise structure and built upon melodic themes that are easily recognisable by the untutored ear. Two serenades by Brahms are among his earlier works; the first, op. 11, is for full orchestra, in D; and the second, op. 16 in A, has no violins. It does not appear that the German equivalent, *Ständchen*, has found much favour with the composer of instrumental Serenades.]   w. s. r.

SERENATA (Ital. *Serenata*; Fr. *Sérénade*; Germ. *Serenade*). Though the terms Serenata and Serenade are generally regarded as interchangeable—so nearly synonymous, that we have no choice but to give the one as the translated equivalent of the other—they mean, in musical language, two very different things.

The vocal Serenata may be considered as a form of Cantata, which may be either dramatic or imaginative, or even a simple Ode on any subject not actually sacred. Handel applied the term to his Italian Pastoral, 'Aci, Galatea, e Polifemo,' written at Naples in 1709 ; to the Ode composed for the Birthday of Anne of Denmark in 1712 ; and to the English Pastoral 'Acis and Galatea,'[1] written at Cannons in 1720.

We must not omit mention of a Serenata by Stradella in which two lovers, each with his orchestra *in a coach*, serenade a lady, a work which is famous because Handel appropriated a great deal of it in 'Israel.' It was republished as No. 3 of Chrysander's *Supplemente* to the edition of Handel. [See vol. i. p. 535, vol. ii. p. 514.]

The form of the Instrumental Serenata is much more clearly defined, and comprised within much narrower limits. It was very popular during the latter half of the 18th century ; and, for some considerable time, occupied a position midway between those of the Orchestral Suite which preceded, and the Symphony which followed it. From the former it borrowed the multiplicity, and from the latter the colouring, of the long series of lightly developed movements of which it usually consisted. Neither the sequence nor the structure of these movements was subject to any very rigid law. Two forms, however, were considered so necessary that they may almost be described as indispensable—the March and the Minuet. With the former almost every Serenata of any consequence began or ended. The latter was almost always interposed between two Allegros, or an Allegro and an Andante, or, indeed, between any two movements of any other kind ; and used so freely that it frequently made its appearance several times in the course of a composition of importance. The Gavotte and Bourrée so freely used in the older Suite were completely banished from the Serenata. When wind instruments alone were employed, the composition was often called 'Harmoniemusik' ; and this term was so generally received that music for wind instruments is popularly called 'Harmonie' in Germany to the present day. The term Cassation was also frequently applied to works of this kind, whether written for the full orchestra or for wind instruments alone ; and many pieces, not differing very much from these, were called Divertimenti. Sometimes the number of Instruments employed was very small, for the Serenata was almost always intended for private performance, and it was a matter of necessity that it should accommodate itself to the resources of the particular establishment for which it was intended.   w. s. r.

SERES, WILLIAM, an early music-printer

[1] Called also, in early copies, 'Opera,' 'Mask,' and 'Pastoral.'

associated with John Day and others, had a privilege for printing psalters, etc. He was working in 1548, and was one of the early members of the Stationers' Company, filling the offices of Warden and Master. His shop was 'at the signe of the Hedge Hogg.' One of his noteworthy works is Francis Seagar's 'Certayne Psalms select out of the Psalter of David, drawn into English metre with notes to every Psalm in iiij parts to Synge,' 1553.   f. k.

SERGEANT TRUMPETER. See TRUMPETER.

SERMISY, CLAUDE DE, one of the group of French musicians connected with the Chapelle du Roy early in the 16th century, was born about 1490. The following information is based on the researches of the learned M. Michel Brenet (*Sammelbände* of the Int. Mus. Gesell. 1904). Sermisy is first heard of in 1508, when he was appointed 'clerc musicien' in the Sainte-Chapelle du Palais at Paris, his name appears in the Sainte-Chapelle registers as Claude de Cermisy. He was there for a short period, as before 1515 he became a 'chanteur' in the Chapelle de musique du Roy, at that time Louis XII. This post was equivalent to the English 'Gentleman of the Chapel Royal,' and as a chanteur his name occurs in a list of the musicians who were present at the funeral of Louis XII. He eventually succeeded Antoine de Longueval as sous-maître of the Chapelle. In the accounts of payments to the various members of the chapelle in 1533, recently published by M. Brenet, there are some entries concerning Claude de Sermisy. As sous-maître he received the sum of 400 livres tournois (=2400 francs), his wages for the said year, and a sum of 1080 livres tournois (=6480 francs) for the feeding and maintenance of the Children of the Chapelle royale for the year, and another sum of 240 l.t. (=1440 francs) for care of the books belonging to the Chapelle and for the procuring of singing boys, 'pour envoyer quérir des chantres.' This shows his position as sous-maître to have been similar to that of the English 'master of the Children of the Chapel Royal,' who also received like payments, and fees for journeys made to 'press' children for the service of the Chapel.

On Sept. 20, 1533, Sermisy was made a Canon of La Sainte-Chapelle, which gave him a residence and a large salary, and only imposed the obligation of officiating at certain ceremonies ; he retained therefore his post of sous-maître, although he and Louis Hérault are mentioned as joint possessors of the office in 1547, when François I. died. They continued to hold it under Henri II. As a member of the Chapelle du Roi, Sermisy was present on three historical occasions, first at the meeting of François I. with Pope Leo X. at Bologna in 1515, when the French singers vied with the Papal Choir ; then in 1520 when François I. and Henry VIII. met at the Field of the Cloth of Gold, and again

in 1532 when they met at Boulogne ; on both
occasions the English and the French musicians
delighted their hearers with their performances.

A work published in 1554, the *Rudiments
de Musicque* by Maximilien Guilliaud, was dedicated to the 'excellent musicien Monsieur
Maistre Claude de Sermisy, maistre de la Chapelle
du Roy, et chanoine de la Sainte-Chapelle du Palais
Royal à Paris ; 15 Septembre, 1552.' Sermisy
probably resigned the post of sous-maître soon
after this date, but retained his connection with
La Sainte-Chapelle until August 16, 1561, his
name then appearing for the last time on the
rolls of the Chapter meetings. He died in
1562.

Four part-books containing twenty-eight
motets composed by Sermisy were published in
1542 : 'Nova et prima motectorum editio 6, 5,
4, 3, et 2 vocum, Lib. 1, 2, 3, Paris.' Pierre
Attaingnant.

Claude de Sermisy, or Claudin as he is almost
invariably called in music-books, shows an
extraordinarily wide range as a composer ;
love songs, masses, motets were published in
rapid succession, and retained their popularity
for many years after his death, if one may judge
by the number of reprints of his works.

Upwards of 200 of his chansons were included
in the various collections of the period.

The set of song-books published by Pierre
Attaingnant in Paris, commencing in January
1529, with the 'Trente et huyt chansons
musicales à quatre parties,' which were continued until 1535, contained ninety-two chansons
by Claudin. The same publishers commenced
a new series in 1538, 'Premier livre contenant
xxv chansons nouvelles à quatre parties' ; in this
set, up to the 'vingtseptiesme livre' in 1548,
there were thirty-five chansons by Claudin.
About the same time Jacques Moderne in Lyons
was publishing the various volumes of 'Le
Parangon des Chansons,' and in the 2nd, 3rd,
4th, 7th, 9th, and 10th volumes (1538-43),
which were often reprinted, Claudin was represented by about twelve different songs. In
Venice the 'Primo libro de le Canzoni francese,'
published by Scotto in 1535, included 'Faict
ou failly,' for four voices, by Claudin. While
at Anvers, Tylman Susato printed, in 1544,
Claudin's 'O combien est malheureux,' in the
'Quatriesme livre des chansons à quatre parties.'
In Paris, Attaingnant's song-books were being
replaced by Nicolas Du Chemin's publications,
the Premier, Second, and the 'Quart livre du
recueil contenant . . . chansons à quatre parties'
in 1551, contained altogether fifteen of Claudin's
chansons. Shortly before his death, Adrian Le
Roy and Robert Ballard of Paris, the widely
known 'imprimeurs du roy,' who published
much of the music of the 16th century, produced the 'Livre de meslanges, contenant six
vingtz chansons des plus rares . . . soit des
autheurs antiques, soit des plus memorables de

notre temps,' 1560, which contained Claudin's
'Peine et travail me faut' for six voices.

Claudin's claim to be a pupil of the great
Josquin rests on a phrase in the preface to this
volume : 'Josquin des Prez, hennuyer de nation,
et ses disciples, Mouton, Claudin, Jaquet,' etc.
The same publishers also issued in 1571 the
'Second recueil . . . de chansons à quatre parties,'
in which were eight chansons by Claudin.
There is one song in Granjon's 'Trophée, livre 2.'
there are four in 'Il primo libro di madrigali
d'Archadelt a tre voci' (Venetia, Gardano, 1559) ;
another, 'On en dire ce qu'on,' in the 'Troisième
livre delle muse a tre voci' (Venice, Scotto,
1562), and three more in the 'Primo libro de
canzoni francese a due voci' (Venice, Antonio
Gardano, 1564).

In 1532 Attaingnant issued seven volumes
of Masses by various composers, these included
the following by Claudin for four voices :

Liber I. Secunda est 'Philomena praevia.'
  „   II. Secunda est 'Missa IX lectionum.'
  „ III. Prima est 'Missa plurium motetarum.'
  „   IV. Secunda est 'Missa pro defunctis.'
  „ VII. Prima est 'Domini est terra.'

In 1534 Attaingnant published :

Missarum musicalium ad quatuor voces, pares. Liber II. 'Tota
pulchra,' Claudin ; 'Missa ad placitum,' Claudin ; etc.
Liber III.   'Missa Dominus quis habitabit,' Claudin. Paris, 1540.

In 1556 Nicolas Du Chemin published in
Paris a great collection of Masses, among
them :—

Missa cum quatuor vocibus. Ad imitationem moduli : 'Ab initio'
condita . . . auctore D. Claudio de Sermisy Regio Symphoniacorum ordini praefecto et in regali parisiensis palatii sacello
canonico.
Missa cum quatuor vocibus. Ad imitationem cantionis : 'Voulant
l'honneur' condita, etc.
Missa cum quatuor vocibus paribus. Ad imitationem moduli :
'Tota pulchra es' condita, etc.
Missa cum quinque vocibus. Ad imitationem moduli : 'Quare
fremuerunt gentes' condita, etc.

Three of the masses printed in 1532 were
reissued :—

Missae tres Claudio de Sermisy Regii Sacelli magistro, praestantis-
simo musico auctore . . . cum quatuor vocibus . . . 'Novem lectionum' fol. 2; 'Philomena praevia' fol. 13; 'Domini est terra'
fol. 23.
Lutetiae 1558 apud Adrianum Le Roy et Robt. Ballard, folio.

There was another edition in 1583. The
same publishers in the 'Missae tres a Claudio de
Sermisy, Joannes Maillard, Claudio Goudimel,
cum quatuor vocibus conditae,' 1558, included
Claudin's 'Missa plurium modulorum.' His
motets were published in such collections as
the 'Fior de motetti' (? 1526), the 'Motetti
del fiore' (1532). Rhaw's 'Tricinia' (1542),
and Ochsenkuhn's 'Tabulatur Buch' (1558).

MS. copies of Claudin's music are to be found
in different foreign libraries, in Rome, Berlin,
Cambrai, Bologna, in the Dresden Royal Library, MS. 1270, No. 5, a 'Laudate Dominum'
for six voices by Claudin ; in the Munich
Royal Library, MSS. 69, 92, and 132 contain
motets and MSS. 202, 204, 205, and 207
various chansons, all were published in the
16th century.

Of modern reprints, M. Henri Expert's publication 'Les maîtres musiciens' includes Attaingnant's 'Trente et un chansons' (1529), of which

eleven were composed by Claudin. Three chansons are in vol. 23, of the 'Publikation älterer prakt. und theoret. Musikwerke,' Leipzig, 1899. Commer ('Coll. op. mus.' vol. xii.) reprints three, the melodies of which were used for Psalms lxxii., ciii., and cxxviii., in the 'Souter Liedekens,' Antwerp, 1540. Otto Kade in his book *Die ältere Passionskomposition*, Gütersloh, 1893, treats very fully of Claudin's Passion music, published by Attaingnant in 1534. C. S.

SEROV, ALEXANDER NICHOLAEVICH, composer and critic, born Jan. 23, 1820, in St. Petersburg, died in the same city, Feb. 1, (Jan. 20, O.S.), 1871. The son of a government official, he was educated at the School of Jurisprudence, where he only made one intimate friend, Vladimir Stassov, destined afterwards to be his stoutest opponent in matters of art. In his *Reminiscences of the School of Jurisprudence* Stassov has given an interesting account of Serov's student days. He left the institution with a decided hankering after an artistic career, but accepted a clerkship in a government office in obedience to his father's wish. He found, however, some leisure for musical pursuits, studied the violoncello and was busy with the project of composing an opera. From his correspondence with Stassov we gather that he cherished vague, ambitious plans which were hindered by lack of technical training, and by the unsympathetic attitude of his father. In 1848 he was transferred from the capital to the dull provincial town of Simferopol, which proved fatal to his musical schemes. Nevertheless his determination to acquire further technical knowledge was unshaken. Through Stassov he obtained an introduction to the famous theorist Hunke, then living in Petersburg, who undertook to instruct him in counterpoint by correspondence. The method was not very successful, and Serov's progress was slow. It is evident that he was often tempted to throw up his official position for art's sake, but his father sternly discountenanced such a proceeding. Nevertheless, his feeling for music continued to assert itself, and as his ideas assumed more definite shape, he turned to criticism, which at that time was at a low ebb in Russia. His first articles in the Russian *Contemporary* in 1851 created something like a sensation, because he brought to bear upon his æsthetic criticism a highly cultivated intelligence, a distinctive style, and an effective, if ponderous, irony. His early articles dealt with Mozart, Beethoven, Donizetti, Rossini, Meyerbeer, and Spontini, and in discussing the last-named he explained and defended the historical ideal of the music-drama. Considering that at this time Serov was practically ignorant of Wagner's works, the conclusions which he draws do credit to his reflection and foresight. His writings have now lost much of their value because of their polemical character. With

one hand Serov pointed to the great musical movement in Western Europe ; with the other he sought to blind the eyes of Russian society to the awakening which was taking place within. It was not until after his visit to Germany in 1858, from which—in his own words—he returned 'Wagner mad,' that he took up a distinctly hostile attitude to the New Russian School which was striving to express in music the spirit of the race. Then followed that long polemic between Serov and Stassov which was only a side episode in that greater conflict between Western and Slavophil, the echo of which has hardly yet died away. In spite of great popular authority, Serov's position in 1860 was in many respects an isolated and unenviable one. There was neither place nor need for an ardent Wagnerian propaganda in Russia. Between his ungenerous depreciation of the new school and his lukewarm attitude towards Rubinstein, Serov's influence began to wane. Serov had passed his fortieth year before he set to work upon his first opera 'Judith.' With extraordinary energy and determination he surmounted all technical difficulties, and completed the opera in the spring of 1862. In March 1863 Wagner visited St. Petersburg, and Serov submitted to him the score of 'Judith.' Wagner more particularly praised the orchestration, in which he cannot have failed to see the reflection of his own influence. 'Judith' was produced in the course of the season 1863-64, on a scale of magnificence hitherto unknown in the production of national opera, and immediately took the public by storm. The subject was well adapted to Serov's opulent and sensational manner. In general style the work recalls the early Wagnerian operas with some curious reminiscences of Meyerbeer. As regards picturesque effect, 'Judith' is admirable, although the dramatic colour is occasionally coarse and flashy. The many technical defects were easily overlooked by the public in an opera which made so direct an appeal to their sensuous enjoyment. Serov's long apprenticeship to musical criticism taught him what was attractive and practicable for the stage, just as he had acquired from the study of Wagner a considerable power of effective orchestration. 'Judith' fascinated not only the uncritical public, but many of the young musical generation, including Tchaikovsky, who refers to it as one of his 'first loves' in music. It still holds its own in the repertory of Russian opera.

Serov lost no time in following up his first success, and 'Rogneda' was completed and performed in the autumn of 1865. Its success was unprecedented. In 'Rogneda' Serov almost discards the Wagnerian influence for that of Meyerbeer. We look in vain in this work for the higher purpose, the effort at psychological delineation and comparative solidity of execution which are occasional features of 'Judith.' 'Serov knew how to catch the crowd,' writes Tchaikovsky, 'and if this opera suffers from poverty of melodic inspiration, want of organic sequence, weak recitative and declamation, and from harmony and instrumentation that are purely decorative —yet what sensational effects the composer succeeds in piling up ! . . . The whole thing literally crackles with them. Serov had only a mediocre gift, united to great experience, remarkable intellect, and extensive erudition ; therefore it is not astonishing to find in "Rogneda" numbers—rare oases in a desert—in which the music is excellent.' Tchaikovsky stood somewhat apart from the heated conflict with national tendencies in which Serov was constantly involved, therefore his judgment may be accepted as less biassed than that of the majority of his contemporaries. After the triumph of 'Rogneda' Serov rested awhile upon his laurels. The balm of success seems to have done something to soften his hostility to the national school, for the lectures on Glinka and Dargomijsky which he delivered before the Russian Musical Society in 1866 are valuable not only for clearness of exposition, but for fairness of judgment.

For the subject of his third opera Serov turned to contemporary national life as depicted in Ostrovsky's strong, but somewhat sordid, play 'The Power of Evil.' His correspondence reveals his intentions with regard to this work. 'Ten years ago,' he says, ' I wrote much about Wagner. Now it is time to act. To embody the Wagnerian theories in a music-drama written in Russian on a Russian subject. . . . In this work, besides observing as far as possible the principles of dramatic truth, I aim at keeping more closely than has yet been done to the forms of Russian popular music as preserved in our folk-songs.' He is seeking in fact to fuse the methods of Glinka with those of Wagner, and produce a Russian music-drama. Serov was a connoisseur of Russian folk-songs, but he had not the genius of Glinka ; moreover, with all his knowledge of the popular music he was never penetrated by the national spirit as was his great predecessor. In creating this Russo-Wagnerian work Serov created something purely artificial : a hybrid which could bring forth nothing in its turn. The subject of 'The Power of Evil' is exceedingly gloomy and not particularly well adapted to musical treatment, and the work never attained the popularity of 'Judith' and 'Rogneda.'

Serov died of heart disease in January 1871. The orchestration of 'The Power of Evil' was completed by one of his most talented pupils, Soloviev. At the time of his death he was busy with a fourth opera based upon Gogol's 'Christmas Eve Revels,' but this work did not progress beyond a first sketch, from which his widow afterwards arranged an orchestral suite,

published in 1877. Other compositions, all belonging to his later years, are : 'Stabat Mater,' 'Ave Maria,' incidental music to 'Nero' (1869), 'A Christmas Song' and two or three orchestral works, including a 'Gopak' and 'Dance of the Zaporogne Cossacks.' Serov married Valentina Semenovna Bergman, a talented pupil of the St. Petersburg Conservatoire, and the composer of several operas, one of which, 'Uriel Acosta' (Moscow, 1885), brought her some success. She was also a constant contributor to the reviews, and in recent years has devoted her energies to the popularising of music among the masses.   R. N.

SERPENT (Eng. and Fr. ; Germ. *Schlangenrohr* ; Ital. *Serpentone*). A now obsolete instrument forming the natural bass of the ancient cornet family, played with a cupped mouthpiece  similar to that of the bass trombone. It consists of a wooden tube about 8 feet long, increasing conically from ⅝ of an inch in diameter at the mouthpiece to 4 inches at the open end. The name is obviously derived from the curved form into which the tube is contorted, presenting three U-shaped turns followed by a large circular convolution. The bell end is, moreover, turned forward from the player, and the mouthpiece makes a right-angled backward turn to reach his lips. There are six holes on the front of the instrument, to be stopped by the three middle fingers of either hand ; those for the left hand on the third descending branch ; those for the right on the fourth ascending branch towards the bell. The holes are set in groups of three, within reach of the outstretched fingers. The hands are passed through the convolutions to the front of the tube, away from the performer ; the weight of the whole is supported on the upper edges of the two forefingers, and grasped by the two thumbs, which are kept at the back of the instrument.

The serpent is considered to consist of three parts, (1) the mouthpiece, (2) the crook, or curved brass tube leading into (3) the wooden body, which is built up of several pieces held together by a leathern covering. [The whole of the instrument was, however, sometimes made of brass or copper.] It is usually said to have been invented by a canon of Auxerre, named Edmé Guillaume, in 1590. The story bears a somewhat suspicious resemblance to that of the discovery of the bassoon by a canon of Ferrara in the first half of the same century. But there can be no doubt that about this period clerical musicians employed bass reed and brass instruments for the accompaniment of ecclesiastical plain-song. Indeed Mersenne, who gives a remarkably good and complete account of the Serpent, notices that 'even when played by a boy it is sufficient to support the voices of twenty robust monks.' The *Serpent d'Église* is still a recognised functionary in French churches, [and for many years was an indispensable member of the primitive orchestras which accompanied the singing in rural churches in England.]

The scale of the Serpent is in the highest degree capricious, and indeed fortuitous. In this respect it resembles the bassoon. Mersenne gives it a compass of seventeen diatonic notes from 8-foot D upwards, and intimates that the intervening chromatics can be obtained by half-stopping. He does not name the device of cross-fingering so largely employed on the bassoon. Berlioz, who speaks slightingly of it, states that it is in Bb, and that parts for it 'must be written a whole tone above the real sound.' The old parts, however, from which the writer played [in the 'sixties'] at the Sacred Harmonic Society were all, without exception, in C.

It is obvious that the Serpent, like every other instrument with a cupped mouthpiece, can produce the usual harmonic series of notes. These in Mersenne's work seem limited to the fundamental, its octave, and twelfth. There would be no difficulty in obtaining a far larger compass. Lichtenthal[1] who, as an Italian, highly values the Serpent, gives its compass as no less than four full octaves from the *Do bassissimo*, which 'does not exist on the pianoforte (1826), but on the pedal of the organ of 16 feet,' up to the *Do* of the violin on the third space. He states, moreover, that the lowest sound of *Do* can only be used from time to time, 'avendo bisogno di una particolare buona imboccatura'—requiring a specially good lip. [As the fundamental note, pedal, or lowest proper tone of the Serpent was the 8-feet C, just as it is on the trombone, euphonium, or ophicleide in C, the statement of Lichtenthal can only be explained by admitting that certain players, by a peculiarly loose embouchure, could produce notes of a forced or constrained pitch one octave lower than due to the length of tube. The compass given in the scales and tutors is three octaves from C to *c"*, with a possible extension downwards, by slackening the lips, to B, and Bb.]

It will be seen from the woodcut that one hand being applied to an ascending, and the other to a descending branch, the usual sequence of fingering is inverted in the two hands; the scale proceeding downwards in the left and

1 *Dizionario della Musica*, tom. i. p. 193.

upwards in the right. The Serpent is probably the only instrument in existence exhibiting so quaint and unscientific a device. This fact, and the different lengths of sounding-tube intervening between the holes—the distance between the mouthpiece and the first finger-hole being 44 inches; between the next three only about 4 inches in all; between these and the next three for the right hand, 13 inches; and from the last hole to the bell, 31 inches; making 96 inches, or 8 feet—indicate the great imperfection of the instrument mechanically considered, and point to the conclusion that a good player must have relied more on his dexterity and on the strength of his embouchure, as mentioned above, than on the resources of the instrument itself. Later makers, however, added a multiplicity of keys, both above and below, which only complicated without facilitating performance. It is well known that the notes D, A, and some others, the holes for which were the most approximately correct in position, had far greater force and correctness than others less accurately planted on the resonant tube. On the other hand, owing to the material of the Serpent and to its bore, its tone was certainly more tender and less obtrusive than that of the blatant brass valve-instruments which have replaced it in the modern orchestra. It is practically disused except in some few foreign churches, and forgotten by all but musical antiquaries. A part for it is however found in the score of Mendelssohn's overtures 'The Calm Sea and Prosperous Voyage' and 'St. Paul,' in the overtures to 'Masaniello,' 'The Siege of Corinth' (between the second and third trombones), and 'Rienzi.' It is also found in the score of 'I Vespri Siciliani.' It is usually replaced in performance by the ophicleide. A Yorkshireman of Richmond, named Hurworth, who played in the private band of George III., could execute elaborate flute variations with perfect accuracy on this unwieldy instrument.

There is a *Method for the Serpent*, containing studies and duets, published by Cocks. The only concerted music set down to it seems to have been originally intended for the bassoon.

A 'Contra Serpent' was shown in the Exhibition of 1851, made by Jordan of Liverpool. It was in Eb of the 16-foot octave. It was however too unwieldy to be carried by the player, and required independent support. Another modification of this instrument was invented by Beacham and played on by Prospère in Jullien's orchestra. It was named the Serpentcleide, and was essentially an ophicleide with a body of wood instead of brass. [w. h. s.; with additions in square brackets by D. J. B.]

SERPETTE, HENRI CHARLES ANTOINE GASTON, French composer, born at Nantes Nov. 4, 1846, began life as an advocate, but gave up the bar for music. He was a pupil of

Ambroise Thomas at the Conservatoire, and took the 'Grand prix' in 1871 for a cantata ('Jeanne d'Arc') of great promise. On his return from Italy, despairing of acceptance at the Opéra-Comique, he closed with the Bouffes Parisiens, and produced 'La Branche cassée' (three acts, Jan. 23, 1874), with a success which induced him to go on composing works of the same slight character. 'Le Manoir du Pic Tordu' (May 28, 1875), 'Le Moulin du Vert galant' (April 12, 1876), and 'La Petite Muette' (Oct. 3, 1877), all in three acts, followed in Paris, and 'La Nuit de St. Germain' (March 1880) in Brussels. ['Cendrillonette' came out in 1890, 'La dot de Brigitte' in 1895, and 'Le Carillon' in 1896. He died in Paris, Nov. 3, 1904.]   G. C.

SERRANO, EMILIO, born 1850 at Vitoria (Spain), court pianist to the Infanta Isabel (Countess of Girgenti), is Director of the Royal Opera and Professor of the Conservatoire of Madrid. Has composed much music, including grand operas, of which 'Irene de Otranto' (1891) and 'Gonzalo de Córdoba' (1898) were produced with great success in Madrid.   H. V. H.

SERVA PADRONA, LA—the maid turned mistress. An Italian intermezzo, or piece in two acts, containing three characters, one of whom is a mute. Words by Nelli, music by Pergolesi. Written and produced at Naples August 23, 1733, and in Paris first on Oct. 4, 1746, at the Hôtel de Bourgogne, and was revived by the 'Bouffons Italiens' on August 1, 1752. This was followed by an obstinate contest between the reformers, headed by Rousseau, and the conservative musicians—'Guerre des Lullistes et des Bouffonistes.' In 1754 a translation, 'La servante maîtresse,' was brought out, and had a run of 150 consecutive nights. It was revived, August 13, 1862, at the Opéra-Comique, for the début of Mme. Galli-Marié, and was given in London, at the Royalty, March 7, 1873.—An imitation of Nelli's libretto, with the same title, was composed by Paisiello during his stay at St. Petersburg.   G.

SERVAIS, ADRIEN FRANÇOIS, a great violoncellist, was born at Hal, near Brussels, June 6, 1807. His study of music began early, but it was not till he heard a solo by Platel on the violoncello, that he fixed on the instrument on which he became so famous. He became a pupil of Platel's in the Brussels Conservatoire, where he rapidly rose to the first rank. On the advice of Fétis he went to Paris, where his success was great. In 1835 he visited England, and on May 25 played a concerto of his own at the Philharmonic Concert, where he was announced as 'principal violoncello to the King of the Belgians.' He then returned home, and wisely resolved to study for a year, and it was during this period that he formed the style by which he was afterwards known. In 1836 he reappeared in Paris, and the next

dozen years were occupied in a series of long tours through Germany, Holland, Austria, Norway, Russia, and even Siberia. In 1842 he married in St. Petersburg. In 1848 he settled at Brussels as Professor in the Conservatoire, and formed many distinguished pupils. He died at his native village Nov. 26, 1866, of an illness contracted during his third visit to St. Petersburg. His works comprise three Concertos, and sixteen Fantasies, for violoncello and orchestra ; six Études for violoncello and PF.—with Grégoir ; fourteen Duos for ditto ; three Duets for violin and violoncello—with Léonard ; one Duet for ditto—with Vieuxtemps. Servais' tastes were very simple, and his great delight was to slip on a blouse and (like Mozart) play skittles. At the close of his life he became very stout, and the peg now used to support the violoncello is said to have been invented by him as a relief. A biography of Servais was published at Hal by Vanderbroeck Desmeth, 1866. [Interesting reminiscences of him are published in the *Guide Musical* of June 2, 1907, àpropos of the centenary of his birth.] His eldest son JOSEPH, born at Hal, Nov. 28, 1850, succeeded his father in June 1872 as professor of the violoncello at the Brussels Conservatoire. He appeared first at Warsaw with his father, and the pair excited the greatest enthusiasm. In 1868 he was appointed solo violoncellist at Weimar and remained two years. In 1875 he played for the first time in Paris at one of Pasdeloup's Popular Concerts, when some of the journals spoke in terms of extravagant praise of his performance. The instrument used by both father and son is a fine Stradivarius presented by the Princess Yousoupoff. [Joseph Servais died at Hal, August 29, 1885.] A second son, FRANTZ, a successful pianist and composer, was a pupil in the same Conservatoire.   T. P. P.

SERVICE. In matters relating to the Church this word is used in two totally different senses ; first, as a rough translation of *Officium, Ordo, Ritus*, as when we say Communion-service, Ordination-service, and so on : next as a purely musical term, as when we say 'Wesley's Service in E,' etc. It is with this latter application of the word only that we have here to deal.

A Service may be defined as a collection of musical settings of the canticles and other portions of the liturgy which are by usage allowed to be set to free composition. The term, therefore, excludes all versicles or responses, or other portions founded on plain-song ; all chants, whether Gregorian or Anglican ; and all anthems, as their words are not necessarily embodied in the liturgy, but selected at will. On the other hand, it includes the Nicene Creed, *Gloria in excelsis*, and other portions of the liturgy which have from the most ancient times received a more or less free musical treatment.

The origin of the acceptance of the term in this limited musical sense is somewhat obscure. The gradual disuse of distinctive names of offices—such, for instance, as Matins, Vespers, Mass, etc.—after the Reformation, helped to bring the generic word 'service' into very general use ; and it has therefore been supposed that musicians called their compositions 'services' because they were set to certain unvarying portions of the church 'services.' But this explanation is far from satisfactory, for obvious reasons ; it gives too much latitude to the term, and offers no reason why it should ever have become limited to its present meaning.

The fullest form of a set or service would include free musical compositions for (1) The Venite, (2) Te Deum, (3) Benedicite, (4) Benedictus, (5) Jubilate, (6) Kyrie eleison, (7) Nicene Creed, (8) Sanctus, (9) Gloria in excelsis ; (10) Magnificat, (11) Cantate Domino, (12) Nunc Dimittis, (13) Deus Misereatur.

It will be necessary to say a few words about some of these movements separately before making any remarks on our services generally. The *Venite* has long since disappeared from the list of free compositions, and is now universally treated as one of the psalms, and sung to a chant instead of being rendered as a motet. In the form in which the Venite was printed in the Breviary may perhaps be traced the reason why many of our earliest church-composers after the Reformation, such as Tallis, Bevin, Byrd, Gibbons, and others, left settings of the Venite in motet-form. But this treatment of the psalm was probably found to lengthen unduly the time occupied by Matins ; and it may also have been felt that an elaborate choral setting of these particular words seriously injured their force as an invitation to join in public worship. On the whole it is not a matter for regret that the Venite now takes its place merely as an introductory psalm.

The free setting of the *Benedicite omnia opera* did not long maintain its ground, owing probably to its excessive length. Purcell set this canticle, and it is even now occasionally sung to his music ; Blow also wrote an elaborate Benedicite in his Service in E minor. But the canticle itself fell for a long time into neglect, and when revived, it was sung either to a chant in triple measure, or to a 'single' chant, or to a Gregorian tone having a 'short ending.' Hayes contributed one of the earliest triple-measure chants [and there are numerous modern specimens in which waltz-themes, more or less ingeniously disguised, are in use.]

The *Gloria in excelsis*, though set to music by Tallis, fell almost entirely out of the 'service' owing to the loss of choral celebrations of the Holy Communion. On their resumption the *Gloria* was once more included in the set, after a long period of virtual disuse. The *Kyrie eleison* and *Sanctus* maintained their place in the set ;

the former because it was always sung at the so-called 'table prayers' (that is, a Communion-office brought to a conclusion at the end of the Creed, Sermon, or Prayer for the Church Militant) ; the latter lived on as an introit, a duty it fulfilled at one time universally in our cathedrals.

The *Jubilate* completely ousted the *Benedictus* for a long period. The earliest writers of our Reformed Church—Tallis, Byrd, Gibbons, Bevin, Farrant, and others—set the *Benedictus* to music, but it was afterwards practically lost, until, within recent times, a better feeling has restored it to the place which it should hold according to the spirit of the rubric, if not according to its letter.

The *Cantate Domino* and *Deus misereatur* may be said to have been in fashion from time to time. Both Blow and Purcell set these alternative canticles, and later Aldrich also ; but they reached their highest popularity at the end of the 18th and the early part of the 19th century. At the present time they have again fallen somewhat into the background.

To the contents of a service as above enumerated, the most modern composers add musical settings of the Offertory sentences, also of the Doxologies before and after the Gospel, and sometimes also of the *Sursum Corda*, *Agnus Dei*, and *Benedictus*. The Offertory sentences may perhaps be looked upon as a legitimate addition to the set, but the Gospel-doxologies and *Sursum Corda* have both their own ancient plain-song, and the *Agnus Dei* and *Benedictus* are not ordered by our rubric to be sung in the office of Holy Communion.

Having made these few remarks about the contents of a service, we must now discuss the musical character of our English services, assuming that a *Te Deum*, *Benedictus* (or *Jubilate*), *Magnificat*, and *Nunc Dimittis* may be taken as the main framework of an ordinary service. It can hardly be doubted that Tallis, the chief of the early post-Reformation composers, was influenced, when setting his celebrated Te Deum in D minor, by the character of the then well-known Ambrosian Te Deum which Marbeck published in the 1550 Prayer-book. There can be traced an evident wish to form a melody, if not actually in a Church mode, in a tonality closely resembling one of them. Tallis also avoided contrapuntal devices (in which he was a distinguished expert), and limited within strict bounds the *ambitus* of his melody and the number of his harmonic combinations. Anybody who will take the trouble to compare his graceful and melodious anthems 'Hear the voice and prayer' and 'If ye love Me' with his Service, must perceive that he wrote his setting of the canticles under an evident self-imposed restraint. The whole of the Service was made to follow absolutely the style of the Te Deum, and the result is, that music of a dignified and ecclesiastical type has

2 e

been produced—pure, perhaps, but certainly uninteresting. Led in this direction by so great and famous a composer as Tallis, many of his contemporaries and immediate successors followed in his footsteps, and English cathedrals possess a considerable store of plain contrapuntal services in minor keys.

Closely following the class of services just described comes the strict contrapuntal school, of which 'Gibbons in F' forms such a noble example. It must not be thought that Gibbons was the first to write the 'pure contrapuntal' service ; a *Magnificat* and *Nunc Dimittis* by Dr. Tye (who was organist to Edward VI.) show that he transferred his motet-style without any change to his settings of these canticles, which consist almost entirely of short 'points' or phrases of four-part imitation. This is just what Gibbons did, but he threw more melodic freedom and greater breadth into his work, and therefore it has lived, while Tye's *Magnificat* is only known to antiquaries.

Half a century after the death of Gibbons the settings of the canticles had become merely meaningless collections of short 'points' ; and, instead of running on with dignified continuity, the music came to be broken up into a number of small sections, for voices *soli*, alternately with, or in frequent contrast to, short choruses. The influence of the French school, which had the most disastrous effects on English anthems, affected the services also, though to a lesser degree. The services of Purcell and Blow may be considered typical of both the virtues and vices of this school,—melodious, but restless and purposeless.

Seven years before the death of Blow a man was born, who, without possessing any special musical gifts, was destined to bring about a vast change in the character of services ; that man was the very second-rate Charles King. The only possible way of accounting for the enormous popularity of his services is to view them as a protest against contrapuntal devices, and as a restoration of simplicity, even if the simplicity is closely allied to weakness. To the influence of King we probably owe two short but beautiful settings from the pen of Dr. Boyce (who died about thirty years after him) ; one is in the key of C, the other in A.

The next development of the form and character of services was the forerunner of the 'dramatic' school. Attwood deserves an important place in any sketch of the history of services for his bold attempt to attach to the words music which should vary as their character. This had of course been done to some extent before his time, but nearly always with a polite leaning to the conventionalities of the past ; Attwood struck out a fresh path. This fact should be borne in mind by those who are disposed to criticise severely the weak points in his services. Attwood died in 1838, and we soon find ourselves

face to face with S. S. Wesley, whose Service in E has been, and is, a model for many living writers ; and he has been followed by a large group of living composers, all of whom are striving to produce services in which the natural emotions called up by the character of the words shall be reflected in unartificial music.

Those who desire to study the literature of services will find ample materials in Barnard's Collection ; Boyce's Collection of Cathedral Music, 3 vols. ; Arnold's Collection, 3 vols. ; Rimbault's Collection of Services, 1 vol. ; Ouseley's Collection of Services, 1 vol. ; various manuscripts in our cathedrals. Full information as to Barnard's Collection will be found under the head BARNARD. [Of late years efforts have been made to restore the fine old Cathedral Services to general use, from which they were for many years kept by the crowd of 'easy' services purveyed by the least skilful organists and writers of the day. The Church Music Society has already done much good in this direction.]   J. S.

SESQUI. A Latin word signifying, literally, the whole *plus* its half.

In musical terminology, the prefix Sesqui is used in combination with certain numeral adjectives, to express the proportion, either of harmonic intervals or of rhythmic combinations. [See PROPORTION.] Thus, Sesquialtera expresses the proportion of two to three, and therefore represents the perfect fifth, which is produced by sounding two-thirds of a given string. Sesquitertia, indicating (not very correctly) the proportion of three to four, represents the perfect fourth, sounded by three-fourths of the string. Sesquiquarta, or four-fifths, represents the major third. Sesquiquinta represents the minor third, given by five-sixths of the resonant string. Sesquisexta, six-sevenths, and Sesquiseptima, seven-eighths, correspond with no intervals in the accepted canon of the scale : but, Sesquioctava, or eight-ninths, represents the peculiar form of the major second known to theorists as the Greater Tone ; and Sesquinona, nine-tenths, gives the Lesser Tone—an interval, which, though conventionally called a major second, and treated, in practice, as identical with that just described, is less, by one Comma, than the Tone represented by Sesquioctava.[1]

In rhythmic combinations, Sesquialtera is used as the general symbol of triple time. The term Sesquialtera is also applied to passages of three notes sung against two ; Sesquitertia, to three notes sung against four ; and Sesquiquarta, to four notes sung or played against five. [See HEMIOLIA.]   W. S. R.

SESQUIALTERA. A compound organ stop consisting of several ranks of pipes, sometimes as many as five. Various combinations of intervals are used, but they only represent different

---

[1] The Greater and Lesser Tones are, by some theorists, called the Acute and the Grave major second.

positions of the third, fifth, and eighth of the ground-tone in the third or fourth octave above. The sesquialtera thus gives brilliance to the tone by reinforcing these upper partials.

The origin of the term Sesquialtera, as applied to an organ stop, is rather obscure. In the list of ratios given by Boethius, at the close of the 5th or beginning of the 6th century, which were exactly reproduced by almost every writer on music up to the 16th century, the term *proportio sesquialtera* signifies numbers having the ratio 2 : 3 ; the term therefore is really applicable to all stops having pipes at an interval of a fifth (or its octaves) from the groundtone, such as the Quint, Twelfth, Larigot (nineteenth), etc. As stated above, the Sesquialtera organ stop does actually contain pipes having this relation, only, and also contains pipes having the ratio 5 : 4—the tierce—which Boethius called a *proportio sesquiquarta*. On the whole it may be safely said that the word Sesquialtera was originally used for the purpose of showing that the stop contained pipes having ratios other than 2 : 1, or other than an octave-series.　　　　　　　　　　　　　　　J. S.

SESTET, or **SEXTET** (Fr. *Sextuor* ; Ital. *Sestetto*). A composition for six instruments, or six voices, with or without accompaniment.

Instrumental sestets are of two kinds : those for strings only, which belong to the same class as string quartets and quintets, being monochromes in six real parts, and those for various combinations of strings, wind and pianoforte, which belong to the class of pianoforte quartets, etc., and may be regarded as miniature symphonies. The first of these two classes is, naturally, but rarely met with, six-part harmony not being easy to write ; but the few examples we have are striking ones. We may pass over Haydn's solitary specimen, called an 'Echo,' for four violins and two violoncellos, and mention only that of Spohr, in C (op. 140), a charming work ; the two immortal compositions of Brahms (B♭, op. 18 ; G, op. 36), which stand at the head of modern chamber-music ; the Sextet of Raff, op. 178, in G minor ; and that of Dvořák, op. 48.

All the above are for two violins, two violas, and two violoncellos. Turning now to the second and more comprehensive class, we find a few more in point of number but none of much artistic value. The prolific Boccherini wrote sixteen, Haydn one, Mozart only the 'Musical Joke.' Beethoven's Sestet for Strings and two obbligato Horns (op. 81*b*) is interesting, but unfortunately impracticable for modern players.[1] His Sestet for Wind Instruments, op. 71 (for two clarinets, two horns, and two bassoons, in E♭) is an early work and little known. Beethoven himself mentions it in a letter of August

[1] A 1st Horn part is in existence, on which Beethoven has written '6tet of mine. God knows where the other parts are.' The slow movement has been adapted to voices as 'The Vesper Hymn,' and had a wide popularity in 'Orpheus.'

8, 1809, as 'one of my earlier things, and not only that, but written in a single night ; perhaps the only thing in its favour is that it is the work of an author who has at least brought forward better works—though for many such works are the best.' (Nohl's *Neue Briefe*, No. 53.) Sterndale Bennett's Sestet for piano and strings, a very early work (op. 8), is an elegant pianoforte piece with an unimportant though often picturesque accompaniment for strings, in which the piano has an undue share of work. Onslow left two sestets—opp. 30 and 77 *bis*.

It should be noticed that the sestets and quintets of Reicha and other composers, when written for wind instruments only, are practically quartets, one or more of the instruments taking a rest in turn. [Vocal sestets occur in operas whenever the dramatic exigencies of the piece require them ; there are two in 'Don Giovanni,' of which only one, 'Sola, sola,' is performed on the ordinary stage, as the splendid finale is usually left out in the present day. The sestet in 'Lucia' was long famous, and there is a very fine specimen in Berlioz's 'Troyens à Carthage.']　　　　　　　　　　　　　　　F. C.

ŠEVČÍK, OTTAKAR, violinist and pedagogue, was born on March 22, 1852, at Horazdowitz in Bohemia, and is of Czech nationality. His father, a teacher of the violin, after giving him elementary lessons, sent him in 1866 to the Conservatorium in Prague, where he studied under Anton Bennewitz until 1870, and then accepted an appointment as Concertmeister of the Mozarteum in Salzburg. This engagement, varied by the organising of self-supporting concerts at Prague, lasted until 1873, in which year he made his début as a soloist at Vienna, becoming eventually Concertmeister of the Komische Oper in that city. At the closing of the opera-house he gave concerts in Moscow, and in 1875 was appointed Professor at the Imperial Music School in Kiev, remaining there till 1892, when he accepted an invitation from Anton Bennewitz, then director of the Prague Conservatorium, to return to Bohemia and fill the post of principal professor of the violin at that institution. From that day to this, although he has occasionally played in public (for the last time in 1898), he has mainly devoted himself to teaching. His appointment happened to synchronise with the entry, as a pupil, of Jan Kubelik, then twelve years of age, and possessed of a marvellous gift for technique. Ševčík taught him for six years, moulding him in accordance with his own special theories of teaching, to which Kubelik's phenomenal success first drew the world's attention. This success was thought, however, to be very largely due to the young violinist's own natural ability, and it was not until, first, Kocian, and then, in a still greater degree, Marie Hall, confirmed, by the brilliance of their performances, the effectiveness of his system of training, that his reputation became established abroad. Pupils offered themselves in such great numbers, mainly from England and America, that only a small proportion of them could be accepted. Among them were the sons of Wilhelmj and Hugo Heermann, the daughter of Wieniawski, Zacharewitsch, Michel de Sicard, Walter Schulze, Vivien Chartres, Leon Sametini, and many others more locally known, who, after studying under Ševčík, received teaching appointments at various music schools. The number of students working under him varies from 75 to 100 during the winter months, some taking two or three lessons monthly, and others, who also learn from his assistants, one lesson only a month ; whilst during the summer recess many follow him to his country residence at Graz, and continue to get the benefit of his advice in holiday time. Thanks to him, Prague adds to its distinctions that of being a sort of university town of the violin, where students learn and draw inspiration from each other as well as from the Professor. But the latter's personal magnetism is the chief factor in his success in bringing forward so many technically accomplished pupils. He prides himself on 'teaching them how to learn,' and has the gift of stimulating them to an almost superhuman exercise of patience. For as many hours daily as their strength will allow, they play small sections of passages backwards and forwards hundreds, even thousands of times, in every possible fingering and variety of bowing. No other teacher of the violin has the knowledge which Ševčík possesses of the anatomical structure of the hand and arm. The position of the hand holding the violin he regulates according to the physique of the pupil, whose muscles (those controlling the fingers) are systematically trained by his exercises to respond quickly, so that in the end remarkable facility in shifting position is gained. The fingers of the left hand are kept down more rigidly than in the Joachim school, and the management of the bow is taught with extraordinary minuteness of detail. He divides it not only into the usual three sections, but also into subdivisions, and of course the pupil has to apportion each accurately in accordance with the nature of the phrase, thus acquiring great command of tone and accent. In short, under the Ševčík system, nothing is left undone that methodical training of ear or muscles can accomplish. In regard to interpretation, the professor (seated at the pianoforte) teaches all the great concertos on sound technical lines, but the development of the psychical side of the student's nature, the bringing to bear upon him of subtle influences which tend to make him a great interpretative artist, must come from without. In the case of some of his pupils, these influences appear to have been absent, but that is no fault of Ševčík, whose life-

work lies in the domain of pure technique, which he teaches not only to his pupils, but to the world, with a passion which is akin to genius ; to the world by means of his *Method*, which is a monument of patient toil that will secure him fame after his pupils are forgotten. It consists of four books. Book I. is a Violin Method for Beginners (in seven parts, op. 6). In this he has adopted for the early stages of practice what he calls his 'Semitone System.' Whereas in the ordinary diatonic scale the stoppings are unequal, the semitones which occur being produced on almost every string with the aid of different fingers, in this book scales are placed before the beginner, in which all the stoppings are the same on each string. This helps him to acquire quickly pure intonation, and enables him to devote his entire attention to the holding of the violin and the handling of the bow. Book II. contains Studies preparatory to the shake and for developing the touch (in two parts, op. 7). Changes of position and preparatory scale studies, op. 8. and Preparatory Studies in double stopping, op. 9. Book III. is a School of Violin Technique (in four parts, op. 1), for more advanced pupils, and is Ševčík's magnum opus. Book IV. is a School of Bowing Technique (in six parts, op. 2), in which appear some 4000 varieties of bowing in progressive order, with metronome marks, and exhaustive directions tending to the development of the bow arm.

Such is the Ševčík method, for the creating of which he has drawn from the technical storehouse of the past, taken from all schools their characteristics and traditions, arranged them in order, blended them, filtered them through his own originality, and by adding many new features carried them a step farther. His publications include a series of 'Bohemian dances' for violin solo. In 1886 the Czar Alexander II. conferred upon him the Order of St. Stanislaus for pedagogic services. w. w. c.

SEVEN LAST WORDS, THE—*i.e.* the seven last utterances of the crucified Saviour. A composition of Haydn's dating about 1785. It was then the custom in the principal church of Cadiz to have a kind of oratorio during Passion week. The church was hung with black, and a single lamp only was lighted. At noon the doors were shut. An orchestral prelude was played ; then the Bishop mounted the pulpit, read one of our Lord's last 'words,' and made an exhortation upon it. He then came down, and threw himself on his knees before the altar. During this there was again orchestral music. He then mounted the pulpit a second time, and pronounced the second 'word,' and a second discourse, and so on till the last. In 1785 Haydn received a request from Cadiz to compose orchestral pieces for this purpose, each piece to be an adagio of about ten minutes long. This he did, sub-

stituting however (as the original parts show)
for the Bishop's voice a long recitative for a
bass in the case of each of the seven 'words.'
In this form the work was performed at Vienna,
March 26, 1787, and was published in parts
by Artaria in the same year—as '7 sonate, con
un Introduzione, ed al fine un terremoto'—for
orchestra, op. 47; for strings, op. 48; for
piano solo, op. 49.   It quickly spread to other
countries, was sold to Forster of London in the
summer of the same year for five guineas,
Haydn protesting, and endeavouring to obtain
another five, but with doubtful success ;[1] and
was announced by Longman & Broderip in
the *Times* of Jan. 1, 1788, as 'A set of
Quartetts . . . expressive of the Passion of
Our Saviour, op. 48, 8*s*.'   Haydn himself
conducted them (whether with the recitatives
or not does not appear) as the middle part of
a concert at the King's Theatre, Haymarket,
May 30, 1791, and repeated the performance
at the benefit of little Clement the violin-player.
   The work is now known as a cantata, with
words to each movement.   When or by whom
the words were added is not quite clear ; for
the various statements the reader must be
referred to Pohl's *Joseph Haydn* (ii. 217,
218).[2]   Pohl's conclusion appears to be that
Haydn adapted to his music—perhaps with
Van Swieten's assistance—words which he met
with at Passau on his way to England in 1794,
except those to the Earthquake, which are from
Rammler's 'Tod Jesu.'   At the same time he
arranged each of the 'words' in plain harmony,
and added a movement for wind instruments
only between movements 4 and 5.   The 'Seven
Words' were for long a favourite in Vienna
both in church and concert-room.   One of the
last performances was at the Alt-Lerchenfeld church, when Franz Schubert's brother
Anton ('Father Hermann') delivered the discourses.[3]   G.

   SEVENTH.   The intervals which contain
seven notes comprise some of the most important chords in music, and such as have been
peculiarly conspicuous in musical history.   They
are divided mainly into three classes—major
sevenths, minor sevenths, and diminished
sevenths ; as

1. The major sevenths, as CB, FE, GF♯, are
very harsh—in fact the harshest combination
used in modern music except the minor second,
such as BC.   They are only endurable either
when prepared and duly resolved, or when
they result from the use of an appoggiatura or
grace-note, or passing note.   They occur most
commonly as suspensions, resolving either up

<hr />

[1] Pohl, *Haydn in London*, p. 92.
[2] The *Biographie Universelle* states categorically that the adaptation was by Michael Haydn.
[3] See Pohl's *Joseph Haydn*, ii. 214, 341, etc.

or down, while the rest of the chord is stationary, as at (*a*) or (*b*),

or with the condensed forms of resolution, when
the rest of the chord moves simultaneously with
the motion of the discordant note, as at (*c*).
   Of these major sevenths there are several
forms, but as they all have the same general
principles of formation and treatment they do
not require detailed consideration.
   2.   The minor sevenths are more individually
characteristic.   Of these the most important is
the Dominant seventh, as at (*c*), for the key of
C.   The discordance of this combination is very
slight.   By itself it is but little more harsh than

some combinations which are universally accepted as concords, such as the minor sixth ;
but its harshness is increased by the addition
of the other notes which fill up the harmony,
as at (*d*), since the indispensable major third in
the chord makes a diminished fifth with the
seventh.   Nevertheless its mildness has long
been recognised, and it was used as early as
the beginning of the 17th century with greater
freedom than any other discord, by being relieved of the condition of being prepared.   [See
HARMONY, vol. ii. p. 310.]   But the laws of
its resolution continued, and still continue,
more or less restricted.   It naturally resolves
into the tonic chord ; because its third is the
leading note of the key and tends to the tonic ;
its seventh naturally tends to the third of the
tonic chord, which is in the major divided from
it only by the small interval of a semitone ;
and its root or bass note already supplies the
fifth of that chord, which naturally acts as the
connecting link between the two harmonies of
dominant and tonic ; so that all the vital notes
of the tonic chord are, as it were, predicted by
its sounding, and consequently it is the most
natural and forcible penultimate in cadences,
in which it occurs with extreme frequency.
[See CADENCE II. ; HARMONY.]   It is hardly
necessary to point out that it can be resolved
otherwise, since it so often plays a part in
interrupted cadences ; as for instance where the
tonic chord is supplanted by the chord of the
submediant (*e*) ; but it is in consequence of the
very predisposition which it creates to expect
the tonic chord that interrupted cadences have
such marked effect.   [See CADENCE III.]   There
is no other minor seventh in the key which
can be accompanied by a diatonic major third ;
but there are two at least that can be obtained
with one chromatic note in them, and these
are so frequently used as if they belonged to

the key that some theorists have agreed to affiliate them. These are the minor seventh on the supertonic with a chromatic major third, and the minor seventh on the tonic, in which the seventh itself is chromatic, as (*f*) and (*g*), in relation to the key of C. These are respectively the dominant sevenths of the Dominant and Subdominant keys, so that in any sense they lie very close to the principal key, and can resolve into it with the greatest ease ; and they are often taken without preparation as distinct ingredients of its harmonic material without other reference to the keys to which they diatonically belong.

The minor seventh on the supertonic, with a diatonic minor third, is a chord which has much exercised theorists. It comprises the same notes as the chord which has been generally known formerly and even partially now as the Added sixth ; and it is more often met with in the form from which that name was derived. But in whatever position, it has long been peculiar among discords for the variability of its resolution, since the note which would be the seventh if the supertonic were at the bottom of the chord, stands still in resolution almost as often as it moves downwards to the conveniently contiguous leading note of the key. For the various views entertained concerning this chord, see HARMONY and ROOT.

3. The chord of the Diminished seventh is a familiar combination both to theorists and musicians. It is in its complete form composed of a set of minor thirds, and this as much as anything gives it its notoriously ambiguous character, since any of its elements can be treated as the discordant note, with the result of leading to a different key in each several case. It is now commonly held to be the inversion of a minor ninth with the root note omitted. [See DIMINISHED INTERVALS, vol. i. p. 702.]   C. H. H. P.

SEVERN, THOMAS HENRY—brother of Joseph Severn the painter, the intimate friend of Keats, Leigh Hunt, etc.—was born in London, Nov. 5, 1801, and after many difficulties became manager of Farn's music-business at 72 Lombard Street. He was the first conductor of the City of London Classical Harmonists, started in 1831. [See vol. i. p. 526.] He was virtually self-taught, and his knowledge of music was derived from study of the scores of the great masters, and from practice. He died at Wandsworth, April 15, 1881. Severn was the author of an opera, and of various songs which were very popular in their time ; a Cantata, 'The Spirit of the Shell' ; two Te Deums (Novello & Co.), etc., etc.   G.

SEXT (Lat. *Officium* (*vel Oratio*) *ad Horam Sextam* ; *Ad Sextam*). The last but one of the 'Lesser Hours' in the Roman Breviary.

The Office begins, as usual, with the Versicle and Response, 'Deus in adjutorium.' These are followed by a Hymn—'Rector potens, verax Deux'—which never changes ; Verses 81-129 of the Psalm, 'Beati immaculati,' sung in three divisions, but under a single antiphon ; the 'Capitulum' and 'Responsorium breve' for the Season ; and the Prayer (or Collect) for the day.

In Collegiate Churches the Offices of Terce and Sext are usually sung immediately before and after High Mass. The Plain-song Music for Sext will be found in the Antiphonal. W. S. R.

SEXTET. See SESTET.

SEXTOLET (Fr. *Sextolet* ; Ger. *Sextole* ; Ital. *Sestina*). A group of six notes of equal length, played in the time of four ordinary notes of the same species. To distinguish them from regular notes of like form the number 6 is placed above or below the group. The true sextolet is formed from a triplet, by dividing each note into two, thus giving six notes, the first of which alone is accented ; but there is also a similar group of six notes, far more frequently used than the real sextolet, in which a slight accent is given to the fourth note as well as the first. This group, which really consists of two triplets, is properly known as the Double Triplet, and should be marked with the figure 3 over the second and fifth notes, though it is frequently marked with 6, and called a sextolet. The difference is well shown in the following two extracts from the Largo of Beethoven's Concerto in C, op. 15. [See also TRIPLET.]

Double Triplets.

1.

Sextolets.

2.

F. T.

SEXTUS (*Pars sexta, Sextuplum* ; Eng. *The Sixth Voice*, or *Part*). In the Part-books of the 15th and 16th centuries four voices only were, as a general rule, mentioned by name, the Cantus, Altus, Tenore, and Bassus. When a fifth voice was needed, it was called Quintus, or Pars Quinta, and corresponded exactly in compass with one of the first four. When yet another voice was added, it was called Sextus, or Pars Sexta, and corresponded in compass with another original voice-part. The extra part, therefore, represented sometimes an additional treble, sometimes an alto, sometimes a tenor, and sometimes a bass ; and always corresponded in compass with some other part of equal importance with itself. W. S. R.

SEYFRIED, IGNAZ XAVER, RITTER VON, born August 15, 1776, in Vienna, was originally intended for the law, but his talent for music was so decided, that, encouraged by Peter

Winter, he determined to become a professional musician. In this, his intimacy with Mozart and subsequent acquaintance with Beethoven were of much use. His teachers were Kozeluch for the PF. and organ, and Haydn for theory. In 1797 he became joint conductor of Schikaneder's theatre with Henneberg, a post he retained in the new Theatre 'an der Wien' from its opening in 1801 till 1826. The first work he produced there was a setting of Schikaneder's comic opera 'Der Löwenbrunnen' (1797), and the second, a grand opera 'Der Wundermann am Rheinfall' (1799), on which Haydn wrote him a very complimentary letter. These were succeeded by innumerable operas great and small, operettas, singspiele, music for melodramas, plays (including some by Schiller and Grillparzer), ballets, and pantomimes. Specially successful were his biblical dramas, 'Saul, König von Israel' (1810), 'Abraham' (1817), 'Die Maccabäer,' and 'Die Israeliten in der Wüste.' The music to 'Ahasverus' (1823) he arranged from piano pieces of Mozart's, and the favourite singspiel, 'Die Ochsenmenuette' (1823) (an adaptation of Hofmann's vaudeville 'Le menuet du bœuf') was similarly a pasticcio from Haydn's works. His church music, widely known and partly printed, included many masses and requiems, motets, offertoires, graduales, a 'Libera' for men's voices composed for Beethoven's funeral, etc. [See *Quellen-Lexikon*.] Seyfried also contributed articles to Schilling's *Universal Lexikon der Tonkunst*, Schumann's *Neue Zeitschrift für Musik*, the *Leipziger Allg. Zeitung*, and *Cäcilia*, besides editing Albrechtsberger's complete works — the *Generalbass-Schule*, *Compositionslehre*, and a Supplement in three vols. on playing from score (Haslinger) — and Beethoven's *Studies in Counterpoint* (1832). Nottebohm's critical investigations reduced this last work to its proper value. [See vol. i. p. 230, and iii. p. 408.]

Seyfried was elected an honorary or a corresponding member of innumerable musical societies, at home and abroad. His pupils included Louis Schlösser, Karl Krebs, Heinrich Ernst, Skiwa, Baron Joseph Pasqualati, Carl Lewy, Heissler, Kessler, J. Fischhof, Sulzer, Carl Haslinger, Parish-Alvars, R. Mulder, S. Kuhe, Walther von Goethe, Baron Hermann Löwenskiold, F. von Suppé, Köhler, and Basadona. His closing years were saddened by misfortune, and his death took place August 26, 1841. He rests in the Währinger cemetery (Ortsfriedhof), near Beethoven and Schubert.   C. F. P.

SFOGATO (open, airy), a word used in rare instances by Chopin (as in the 'Barcarole') in certain of those little cadenzas and ornaments that he is so fond of using, to indicate what may be called his own peculiar touch, a delicate and, as it were, ethereal tone, which can only be produced upon the pianoforte, and then only by skilful performers. 'Exhalation' is the only word that conveys an idea of this tone when it is produced. A 'Soprano sfogato' is a thin, acute, voice.   M.

SFORZANDO, SFORZATO, 'forced'; a direction usually found in its abbreviated form *sf.* or *sfz.* referring to single notes or groups of notes which are to be especially emphasised. It is nearly equivalent to the accent >, but is less apt to be overlooked in performance, and is therefore used in all important passages. Good instances occur in Beethoven's Sonata for violin and piano in C minor, op. 30, No. 2, in the trio of the Scherzo; in Schumann's Études Symphoniques, Variation 3, etc.   M.

SGAMBATI, Giovanni, a remarkable pianist and composer, born in Rome, May 28, 1843. His mother, an Englishwoman, was the daughter of Joseph Gott the sculptor, a native of London, who had for many years practised his art in Rome. Giovanni was intended for his father's profession, that of an advocate, and he would have been educated with that view but for his strong turn for music. [He took his first lessons in pianoforte-playing at the age of five from Amerigo Barberi, author of a treatise on harmony, who used to pride himself on the fact that his own teacher had been a pupil of Clementi.] After the death of his father in 1849 young Sgambati's mother migrated with her two children to Trevi in Umbria, where she married again. Here Giovanni's lessons, supplemented by a course of harmony, were continued under Natalucci, a former pupil of Zingarelli, at the Conservatorio of Naples. From the age of six the boy often played in public, sang contralto in church, conducted small orchestras, and was known as the author of several sacred pieces. In 1860 he settled in Rome and soon became famous for his playing, and for the classical character of his programmes. His favourite composers were Beethoven, Chopin, and Schumann, and he was an excellent interpreter of the fugues of Bach and Handel. Shortly after this he was on the point of going to Germany to study when the arrival of Liszt in Rome saved him from that necessity. With him Sgambati studied long and diligently. [He soon began to give orchestral concerts in the 'Galleria Dantesca,' which, as the 'Sala Dante,' was for many years the only concert-hall in Rome. Here, under Sgambati's direction, the symphonies and concerts of the German masters, until then unknown in the papal city, at length found a hearing. Beethoven's 'Eroica' was introduced to the Roman public and the 'Emperor' concerto was played to them by Sgambati for the first time, just as later they learned at his hands to know and appreciate Brahms, Saint-Saëns, and later writers.]

At the same time Sgambati was busy with his compositions. In 1864 he wrote a string quartet; in 1866, a pianoforte quintet (F minor, op. 4), an overture for full orchestra to Cossa's 'Cola di Rienzi,' together with other works, and in the same year he conducted Liszt's 'Dante' symphony (Feb. 26) with great success and credit to himself.

In company with Liszt, he visited Germany in 1869, and at Munich heard Wagner's music for the first time. Sgambati's talent naturally attracted the notice of Herr von Keudell, the well-known amateur and German ambassador in Rome. At the orchestral concerts which he conducted at the embassy many of his works were first heard. Here also, in 1876, he made the acquaintance of Wagner [in whose honour the ambassador one evening gave a concert consisting entirely of Sgambati's compositions, including two pianoforte quintets and several songs. Wagner, much surprised to find in Rome a composer who made music of this kind, expressed a wish to hear it again, and on the following evening the programme was privately repeated for the delectation of the master, who immediately wrote to the publishing-house of Schott, advising them to purchase and print Sgambati's works without delay. The firm then published the two quintets, as well as a prelude and fugue for pianoforte.]

Encouraged by this well-merited recognition Sgambati wrote a Festival-overture and a concerto for pianoforte and orchestra. His Symphony in D, produced at a concert in the 'Sala Dante' early in 1881 and repeated on March 28 of that year at the Quirinal, being the first work of the kind ever given at the Italian Court, in the presence of King Humbert and his Consort, Queen Margherita, to whom it was dedicated. In 1882 Sgambati paid his first visit to England and played his pianoforte concerto at the Philharmonic concert of May 11. His symphony was given at the Crystal Palace on June 10 under the composer's direction. Both works were well received, but the symphony made much the greater impression of the two. Though original in its ideas and character it adheres to established forms ; it is at once thoughtfully worked out and gracefully expressed, with a great deal of effect, and no lack of counterpoint.

His quartet for strings in D flat, printed about this time, is one of the works by which Sgambati is best known. First played in London by the Kneisel quartet of Boston, it was afterwards included by Joachim and Piatti, along with his second pianoforte quintet, in the repertory of the famous Popular Concerts, and eventually attained wide popularity throughout Europe. Two years later (1884) Sgambati conducted the symphony in Paris, where he had been invited as representative of Italy at the International Concerts given in the Trocadéro. In 1886 he was named one of the five corresponding members of the French Institute to fill the place vacated by Liszt. In 1887 he

was invited to conduct his second symphony, in E flat (written in 1883 and still unpublished), and to execute his first quintet at the great musical festival of the Tonkünstler-Versammlung in Cologne.

[In the same year he wrote, in honour of the wedding of the Duke of Aosta, an 'Epitalamio Sinfonico,' which takes the form of a suite, though considerably more developed than is usually the case in compositions so described. After its production at Turin the author conducted performances of the work in Milan and Rome, and brought it to London on the occasion of his second visit in 1891, when it was given at a Philharmonic concert. During the same season he gave a concert of his own compositions at Princes' Hall, and was commanded to Windsor where he played before Queen Victoria. One of the most memorable journeys made by Sgambati to foreign countries included a visit to Russia in the autumn of 1903. Received with enthusiasm, he gave concerts, consisting chiefly of his own works, at St. Petersburg, Moscow, and other places in Northern Europe, with such conspicuous success that they would have welcomed him gladly another year.

To commemorate the death of King Humbert he wrote a 'Messa da Requiem' for chorus, baritone solo, and orchestra, which was produced at the Pantheon, Jan. 17, 1896, and several times repeated. It was also given in Germany, at Cologne in November 1906, in the composer's presence, and at Mayence in March 1907. Its reception on both occasions bore testimony to German appreciation of Sgambati, whose work was highly praised. The Requiem is a fine piece of religious writing, in strict conformity with the spirit of the sacred text, modern without extravagance of any kind, and its themes well developed, though not so diffusely as to render it unsuitable for performance on liturgical occasions. It is, perhaps, Sgambati's most ambitious work, and the author's success as a choral writer occasions regret that more of his time had not been given to compositions of the kind.

He preferred, instead, to devote the energies of his best years to teaching ; and, as a result, must be considered the founder, with his colleague Penelli, of the Liceo Musicale in connection with the Accademia di S. Cecilia in Rome (see ROME). Beginning with a free class for the pianoforte in 1869 he has persevered to the present day (1907) in giving instruction of the soundest description. Under him the study of the instrument in Rome has reached an exceptional degree of development, and it cannot be doubted that had Sgambati chosen, as the field of his labours, a city of central Europe, he would have attained a far wider celebrity as a master.

His success as a writer for the pianoforte is due to his rare knowledge of its resources, to his facility in producing required effects with the simplest means, to his complete command of harmonic combinations of the subtlest kind, and to the exquisite finish given to even the least of his inspirations. With Sgambati device is rarely evident. His figures of accompaniment are as spontaneous as the melodies they sustain. Certain of his minor compositions, such as the beautiful intermezzo in op. 21 and certain numbers in his 'Pièces Lyriques' (op. 23) and in his 'Mélodies poétiques' (op. 36) may be cited as exemplifying a level of artistic perfection which in little descriptive pieces of the kind has never, perhaps, been surpassed. His more important pianoforte pieces, his chamber-music, and his orchestral writings, taken together, place him at the head of those Italian musicians of the latter part of the 19th century, who, not writing for the stage, have moulded their work on classic models. Sgambati, in appropriating received forms, has invested them with southern feeling, deep but restrained, rich and even glowing, but utterly free from the meretricious sentiment which served to win immediate popularity for Italian composers of lesser claims. His writings, in a word, possess the qualities which endure.

His native city owes him a lasting debt as its apostle of classical music, as teacher, performer, and director. His efforts have not gone unrecognised in high places. His influence has been felt and appreciated at the Italian court, where he was appointed pianist and director of Queen Margherita's quintet, and named, by *motu proprio* of King Victor Emmanuel III. in 1903, Commendatore of the Order of SS. Maurice and Lazarus. But by his countrymen at large it cannot be said that Sgambati's talent has as yet been estimated at its proper value. This, in a nation so quick to recognise and even exaggerate any indication of artistic eminence, is little short of astounding. The omission may be explained in part by a certain indifference in the musician himself, though not sufficiently to account for the slow awakening of Rome and Italy to the merits of a man who was honoured as a *confrère* by Liszt and Wagner. Yet it is certain, as M. Eugène d'Harcourt wrote in 1906, after he had been commissioned by the French government to report on the state of music in Italy, that 'quand la musique symphonique italienne aura une histoire et qu'on l'écrira, il faudra lui reconnaître, pour véritable fondateur, le Romain Giovanni Sgambati.']

Some of the works mentioned above are still unprinted; his published works include the following:—

Op.
1. Album of five songs.
2. Album of ten songs.
3. Notturno for pf.
4. Quintet, pf. and strings, F minor.
5. Quintet, pf. and strings, B flat.
6. Prelude and fugue for pf. in E flat minor.
10. Two Études for pf., D flat and F sharp minor, written for the Method of Lebert and Stark, Stuttgart.

Op.
12. Fogli volanti for pf., 8 pieces.
14. Gavotte for pf. Easy edition arranged by author.
15. Concerto, pf. and orchestra, in G minor.
16. Symphony in D.
17. Quartet in D flat for strings.
18. Quattro pezzi for pf. Preludio, Vecchio minuetto, Nenia, Toccata.
19. Four Italian songs.
20. Tre Notturni for pf.
21. Suite for pf. (Prelude, Valse, Air, Intermezzo, Étude mélodique).
22. Passiflore, voice and pf.
23. Pièces Lyriques (6) for pf.
24. Due Pezzi for violin and piano.
28. Te Deum laudamus, andante solenne, for strings and organ. The same for full orchestra.
29. Gondoliera for violin and piano.
30. Benedizione nuziale for organ.
31. Fifth Nocturne for pf.
32. Melodie Liriche, four songs.
33. Sixth Nocturne for pf.
34. 'Versa est in luctum cythara mea.' Motet for baritone, organ, and strings (included in opus 38).
35. Quattro melodie per una voce e pf.
36. Mélodies poétiques (12) for pf.
37. 'Tout bas,' Melodia per canto.
38. Messa da Requiem per coro, baritono solo, orchestra ed organo (*ad lib.*).

[The following are without opus number.]
Serenata, per canto e pianoforte.
Ballata, per tenore.
Stornello toscano, per una voce e pianoforte.
Romanza senza parole, pf.
'Il faut aimer,' Gavotte chantée.
La mia stella, Melodia.
Melodie Liriche (five, and a duet).
Two songs—
  1. Fior di siepe.
  2. Fuori di porta.

TRANSCRIPTIONS.
Liszt. Die Ideale, pf. four hands.
Chopin. Canzone lituana, pf. solo.
Gluck. Melodia dell' Orfeo, pf. solo.
'Separazione,' old Italian folk-song (edited and provided with accompaniment by G. Sgambati).

G. ; with additions in square brackets, by H. A. W.

SHAKE or **TRILL** (Fr. *Trille*, formerly *Tremblement*, *Cadence*; Ger. *Triller*; Ital. *Trillo*). The shake, one of the earliest in use among the ancient graces, is also the chief and most frequent ornament of modern music, both vocal and instrumental. It consists of the regular and rapid alternation of a given note with the note above, such alternation continuing for the full duration of the written note. [On other instruments and on the voice, this definition of the shake holds good; text-books and methods will give examples of how the shake should be performed, but it is originally one of the ornaments designed for the keyboard, and most effective there.]

The shake is the head of a family of ornaments, all founded on the alternation of a principal note with a subsidiary note one degree either above or below it, and comprising the MORDENT and PRALLTRILLER still in use, and the RIBATTUTA (Ger. *Zurückschlag*) and *Battement*[1] (Ex. 1), both of which are now obsolete. (See AGRÉMENS.)

1. *Battement.*

Ribattuta.

etc.

[1] Rousseau (*Dict. de Musique*) describes the *Battement* as a trill which differed from the ordinary trill or *cadence* only in beginning with the principal instead of the subsidiary note. In this he is certainly mistaken, since the *battement* is described by all other writers as an alternation of the principal note with the note *below*.

The sign of the shake is in modern music *tr.* (generally followed by a waved line ~~~~~ if over a long note), and in older music *tr.* ⅃⅃⅃, ⅃⅃⅃, and occasionally +, placed over or under the note ; and it is rendered in two different ways, beginning with either the principal or the upper note, as in example 2 :—

2. *Written.*   *Performed.*   *Or thus.*

These two modes of performance differ considerably in effect, because the accent, which is always perceptible, however slight it may be, is given in the one case to the principal and in the other to the subsidiary note, and it is therefore important to ascertain which of the two methods should be adopted in any given case. The question has been discussed with much fervour by various writers, and the conclusions arrived at have usually taken the form of a fixed adherence to one or other of the two modes, even in apparently unsuitable cases. Most of the earlier masters, including Emanuel Bach, Marpurg, Türk, etc., held that all trills should begin with the upper note, while Hummel, Czerny, Moscheles, and modern teachers generally (with some exceptions) have preferred to begin on the principal note. This diversity of opinion indicates two different views of the very nature and meaning of the shake ; according to the latter, it is a trembling or pulsation—the reiteration of the principal note, though subject to continual momentary interruptions from the subsidiary note, gives a certain undulating effect not unlike that of the tremulant of the organ ; according to the former, the shake is derived from the still older *appoggiatura*, and consists of a series of appoggiaturas with their resolutions—is in fact a kind of elaborated appoggiatura,—and as such requires the accent to fall upon the upper or subsidiary note. This view is enforced by most of the earlier authorities ; thus Marpurg says, ' the trill derives its origin from an appoggiatura (*Vorschlag von oben*) and is in fact a series of descending appoggiaturas executed with the greatest rapidity.' And Emanuel Bach, speaking of the employment of the shake in ancient (German) music, says ' formerly the trill was usually only introduced after an appoggiatura,' and he gives the following example :—

3.   *tr.*

Nevertheless, the theory which derives the shake from a trembling or pulsation, and therefore places the accent on the principal note, in which manner most shakes in modern music are executed, has the advantage of considerable, if not the highest antiquity.[1] For Caccini, in

[1] The exact date of the introduction of the trill is not known, but

his Singing School (published 1601), describes the *trillo* as taught by him to his pupils, and says that it consists of the rapid repetition of a *single* note, and that in learning to execute it the singer must begin with a crotchet and strike each note afresh upon the vowel *a* (*ribattere ciascuna nota con la gola, sopra la vocale a*). Curiously enough he also mentions another grace which he calls *Gruppo*, which closely resembles the modern shake.

4. *Trillo.*

Gruppo.

And Playford, in his *Introduction to the Skill of Musick* (1655) quotes an anonymous treatise on ' the Italian manner of singing,' in which precisely the same two graces are described.[2] Commenting on the shake Playford says, ' I have heard of some that have attained it after this manner, in singing a plain-song of six notes up and six down, they have in the midst of every note beat or shaked with their finger upon their throat, which by often practice came to do the same notes exactly without.' It seems then clear that the original intention of a shake was to produce a trembling effect, and so the modern custom of beginning with the principal note may be held justified.

In performing the works of the great masters from the time of Bach to Beethoven then, it should be understood that, according to the rule laid down by contemporary teachers, the shake begins with the upper or subsidiary note, but it would not be safe to conclude that this rule is to be invariably followed. In some cases we find the opposite effect definitely indicated by a small note placed before the principal note of the shake, and on the same line or space, thus—

5. MOZART (ascribed to), ' Une fièvre,' Var. 3.
   tr.   *tr.*

and even when there is no small note it is no doubt correct to perform all shakes which are situated like those of the above example in the same manner, that is, beginning with the principal note. So therefore a shake at the commencement of a phrase or after a rest (Ex. 6), or after a downward leap (Ex. 7), or when preceded by a note one degree below it (Ex. 8) should begin on the principal note.

It is also customary to begin with the principal

Consorti, a celebrated singer (1590), is said to have been the first who could sing a trill (Schilling, *Lexikon der Tonkunst*).

[2] The author of this treatise is said by Playford to have been a pupil of the celebrated Scipione della Palla, who was also Caccini's master.

6.   BACH, Prelude No. 16, Book I.

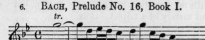

MOZART, Concerto in B♭.

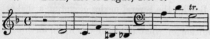

7.   BACH, Art of Fugue, No. 8.

8.   BACH, Sonata for PF. and Flute, No. 6.

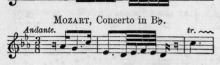

note when the note bearing the shake is preceded by a note one degree above it (Ex. 9), especially if the tempo be quick (Ex. 10), in which case the trill resembles the *Pralltriller* or inverted mordent, the only difference being that the three notes of which it is composed are of equal length, instead of the last being the longest (see vol. iii. p. 808).

9.   BACH, Organ Fugue in F.

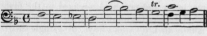

10.   MOZART, Sonata in F.

If, however, the note preceding the shake is slurred to it (Ex. 11a), or if the trill note is preceded by an appoggiatura (Ex. 11b), the trill begins with the upper note ; and this upper note is *tied* to the preceding note, thus delaying the entrance of the shake in a manner precisely similar to the 'bound Pralltriller' (see vol. iii. p. 260, Ex. 13). A trill so situated is called in German *der gebundene Triller* (the bound trill).

11. (a) BACH, Concerto for two Pianos.

(b) HAYDN, Trio in E minor.

When the note carrying a shake is preceded by a short note of the same name (Ex. 12), the upper note always begins, unless the anticipating note is marked staccato (Ex. 13), in which case the shake begins with the principal note.

12.   BACH, Chromatic Fantasia.

Played.

13.   MOZART, Sonata in C minor.

In modern music, when a trill beginning with the subsidiary note is required, it is usually indicated by a small grace-note, written immediately before the trill-note (Ex. 14). This grace-note is occasionally met with in older music (see Clementi, Sonata in B minor), but its employment is objected to by Türk, Marpurg, and others, as liable to be confused with the real appoggiatura of the bound trill, as in Ex. 11. This objection does not hold in modern music, since the bound trill is no longer used.

14. BEETHOVEN, Sonata, Op. 53, Finale.

Immediately before the final note of a shake a new subsidiary note is generally introduced, situated one degree *below* the principal note. This and the concluding principal note together form what is called the *turn* of the shake, though the name is not strictly appropriate, since it properly belongs to a separate species of ornament of which the turn of a shake forms in fact the second half only.[1] [See TURN.] The turn is variously indicated, sometimes by two small grace-notes (Ex. 15), sometimes by notes of ordinary size (Ex. 16), and in old music by the signs ʌʍ, ʍɉ, or ʌʍ.

15.   CLEMENTI,   16. HANDEL, Gigue
     Sonata in C.   (Suite 14).

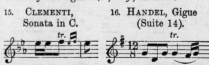

Sometimes the turn is not indicated at all, but it has nevertheless to be introduced if the shake is followed by an accented note (Ex. 17). If, however, the next following note is unaccented, no turn is required, but an extra

---

[1] The turn of a trill is better described by its German name *Nachschlag*, or after-beat.

principal note is added to the last couple of notes, that the trill may end as well as begin with the principal note (Ex. 18). When the trill is followed by a rest, a turn is generally made, though it is perhaps not necessary unless specially indicated (Ex. 19).

17. MOZART, ' Lison dormait,' Var. 8.

18.   CLEMENTI, Sonata in G.

19.   BEETHOVEN, Trio, Op. 97.

When a note ornamented by a shake is followed by another note of the same pitch, the lower subsidiary note only is added to the end of the shake, and the succeeding written note serves to complete the turn. Even when the trill-note is tied to the next following, this extra lower note is required, provided the second written note is short, and occurs on an accented beat (Ex. 20). If the second note is long, the two tied notes are considered as forming one long note, and the shake is therefore continued throughout the whole value.

20.   BACH, Fugue No. 15, Vol. II.

Very similar is the rendering of a shake on a dotted note :—the turn ends on the dot, which thus takes the place of the second of the two notes of the same pitch. Thus the effect of the two modes of writing shown in Ex. 21 *a* and *b*, would be the same. If, however, the dotted note is followed by a note a degree lower, no turn is required (Ex. 22).

21. HANDEL, Suite 10.   Allemande.

Rendering of both.

22.   HANDEL, Suite 10.   Allegro.

Trills on very short notes require no turn, but consist merely of a triplet—thus,

23.   MOZART, ' Ein Weib,' Var. 6.

Played.

Besides the several modes of ending a shake, the commencement can also be varied by the addition of what is called the upper or lower prefix. The upper prefix is not met with in modern music, but occurs frequently in the works of Bach and Handel. Its sign is a tail turned upwards from the beginning of the ordinary trill mark, and its rendering is as follows—

24.   BACH, Partita No. 1, Sarabande.

Played.

The lower prefix consists of a single lower subsidiary note prefixed to the first note of a shake which begins with the principal note, or of two notes, lower and principal, prefixed to the first note of a shake beginning with the upper note. It is indicated in various ways, by a single small grace-note (Ex. 25), by two (Ex. 26), or three grace-notes (Ex. 27), and in old music by a tail turned downwards from the commencement of the trill mark (Ex. 28), the rendering in all cases being that shown in Ex. 29.

25.   26.   27.   28.

29.

From a composer's habit of writing the lower prefix with one, two, or three notes, his intentions respecting the commencement of the ordinary shake *without* prefix, as to whether it should begin with the principal or the subsidiary note, may generally be inferred. For since it would be incorrect to render Ex. 26 or 27 in the manner shown in Ex. 30, which involves the repetition of a note, and a consequent break of legato—it follows that a composer who chooses the form Ex. 26 to express the prefix intends the shake to begin with the upper note, while the use of Ex. 27 shows that a shake beginning with the principal note is generally intended.

That the form Ex. 25 always implies the shake beginning with the principal note is not so clear (although there is no doubt that it usually does so), for a prefix is possible which

30.

leaps from the lower to the upper subsidiary note. This exceptional form is frequently employed by Mozart, and is marked as in Ex. 31. It bears a close resemblance to the Double Appoggiatura. [See that word, vol. i. p. 99.]

31.   Mozart, Sonata in F. Adagio.

Among modern composers, Chopin and Weber almost invariably write the prefix with two notes (Ex. 26) ; Beethoven uses two notes in his earlier works (see op. 2, No. 2, Largo, bar 10), but afterwards generally one (see op. 57).

The upper note of a shake is always the next degree of the scale above the principal note, and may therefore be either a tone or a semitone distant from it, according to its position in the scale. In the case of modulation, the shake must be made to agree with the new key, independently of the signature. Thus in the second bar of Ex. 32, the shake must be made with B♮ instead of B♭, the key having changed from C minor to C major. Sometimes such modulations are indicated by a small accidental placed close to, or above the sign of the trill (Ex. 33).

32.   Chopin, Ballade, Op. 52.

33.   Beethoven, Choral Fantasia.

The lower subsidiary note, whether employed in the turn or as prefix, is usually a semitone distant from the principal note (Ex. 34), unless the next following written note is a whole tone below the principal note of the shake (Ex. 35). In this respect the shake follows the rules which govern the ordinary turn. [See Turn.]

34. Beethoven, Sonata, Op. 10, No. 2.

35.   Mozart, Rondo in D.

A series of shakes ascending or descending either diatonically or chromatically is called a Chain of Shakes (Ital. *Catena di Trille* ; Ger. *Trillerkette*). Unless specially indicated, the last shake of the series is the only one which requires a turn. Where the chain ascends diatonically, as in the first bar of Ex. 36, each shake must be completed by an additional principal note at the end, but when it ascends by the chromatic alteration of a note, as from G♮ to G♯, or from A to A♯, in bar 2 of the example, the same subsidiary note serves for both principal notes, and the first of such a pair of shakes requires no extra principal note to complete it.

36.   Beethoven, Concerto in E♭.

In pianoforte music, a shake is frequently made to serve as accompaniment to a melody played by the same hand. When the melody lies near to the trill-note there need be no interruption to the trill, and either the principal or the subsidiary note (Hummel prescribes the former, Czerny the latter) is struck together with each note of the melody (Ex. 37). But when the melody lies out of reach, as is often the case, a single note of the shake is omitted each time a melody-note is struck (Ex. 38). In this case the accent of the shake must be upon the upper note, that the note omitted may be a subsidiary and not a principal note.

37.   Cramer, Study, No. 11.[1]

38.   Beethoven, Sonata, Op. 109.

[1] Von Bülow, in his edition of Cramer's studies, interprets this passage in a precisely opposite sense to that given above, directing the shake to be performed as in Example 38.

The above arrangement constitutes what is called a false trill, the effect of a complete trill being produced in spite of the occasional omission of one of the notes. There are also other kinds of false trills, intended to produce the effect of real ones, when the latter would be too difficult. Thus Ex. 39 represents a shake in thirds, Ex. 40 a shake in octaves, and Ex. 41 a three-part shake in sixths.

39. MENDELSSOHN, Concerto in D minor.

40. LISZT, Transcription of Mendelssohn's 'Wedding March.'

41. MÜLLER, Caprice, Op. 29, No. 2.

The above method of producing a shake in three parts is generally resorted to when great force is required, otherwise the ordinary method is quite practicable, and both double and triple shakes are frequently met with in modern brilliant music (Ex. 42, 43).

42.   CHOPIN, Polonaise, Op. 26.

43.   BEETHOVEN, Polonaise, Op. 89.

The speed of a shake cannot be exactly defined in notes, since it is usually better, except in the case of very short trills (as in Ex. 23), that the notes of the shake should bear no definite proportion to the value of the written note. Generally, the shake should be as rapid as is consistent with distinctness. When a proportional shake is required it is usually written out in full, as at the end of the Adagio of Beethoven's Sonata in Eb, op. 27, No. 1.   F. T.

SHAKESPEARE, WILLIAM, composer, vocalist, pianist, born at Croydon, June 16, 1849. At the age of thirteen he was appointed organist at the church where formerly he had attracted attention in the choir. In 1862 he commenced a three years' course of study of harmony and counterpoint under Molique ; but after that master's death, having in 1866 gained the King's Scholarship at the Royal Academy of Music, continued his studies there for five years under Sir W. Sterndale Bennett. Whilst at the Royal Academy he produced and performed at the students' concerts a pianoforte sonata, a pianoforte trio, a capriccio for pianoforte and orchestra, and a pianoforte concerto ; and attracted some notice as a solo-player.

He was elected Mendelssohn Scholar in 1871, for composition and pianoforte - playing, and in accordance with the wish of the Committee entered the Conservatorium at Leipzig. There, whilst under the instruction of the director, Carl Reinecke, he produced and conducted in the Gewandhaus a symphony in C minor. Having discovered himself to be the possessor of a tenor voice he was sent by the Mendelssohn Scholarship Committee to study singing with Lamperti at Milan, and there remained for two and a half years. But though singing was his chief pursuit he did not neglect composition, and while in Italy wrote two overtures, two string quartets, and other works.

In 1875 he returned to England, and entered upon the career of a concert and oratorio singer. He was appointed in 1878 Professor of Singing, and in 1880 conductor of the concerts, at the Royal Academy of Music. [This latter office he resigned in 1886. Shakespeare was conductor of the Strolling Players' Orchestral Society in 1901-5.]

His voice, though both sweet and sympathetic in quality, is somewhat deficient in power ; and his success as a singer must therefore be attributed to the purity of his vocal production and to his complete mastery of all styles of music.

His compositions, which are marked by considerable charm and elegance, show the influence of Schumann and Bennett ; and in his overture, performed at the Crystal Palace in 1874, and his Pianoforte Concerto, at the Brighton Festival of 1879, he proves himself an adept at musical form.   J. C. G.

SHALIAPIN, FEDOR IVANOVICH, celebrated opera-singer, born Feb. 11, 1873, at Kazan. His father was a peasant, and unable to give his son any educational advantages, musical or otherwise. At seventeen the young man joined a provincial opera-company, and was soon entrusted with leading parts. In 1892, after a tour in the region of the Caspian Sea and the Caucasus, he found himself in Tiflis, where he studied for a year with Oussatov. Two years later he began to sing in St. Petersburg, at the Summer Theatre, the Aquarium and the Maryinsky Theatre, but it was not until 1896, when he was engaged at the Private Opera in Moscow, that Shaliapin's name became famous. This enterprise, supported by a rich lawyer of the name of Mamontov, made a special feature of national opera, and gave the young singer an opportunity of displaying his exceptional powers. Shaliapin has impersonated, with striking power and originality, most of the chief bass parts in Russian opera : Ivan the Terrible in Rimsky-Korsakov's ' Maid of Pskov,' the title-rôle in Moussorgsky's ' Boris Godounov,' Melnik in Dargomijsky's ' Roussalka,' Yeremka in Serov's ' Power of Evil,' etc. He is an admirable Mephistopheles in ' Faust,' but his predilection for national opera is perhaps the reason for his being so little known out of Russia. He sang in Milan in 1901 (ten performances of Boito's ' Mefistofele '), and again in 1904.   R. N.

SHAMUS O'BRIEN. Romantic comic opera in two acts ; text by G. H. Jessop (after J. Sheridan Le Fanu), music by C. V. Stanford, op. 61. Produced at the Opera-Comique Theatre, London, March 2, 1896.

SHARP (*Diesis*, from Lat. *Divisio*; Fr. *Dièse*). The term which expresses the raising of a note by a less quantity than a whole tone. F sharp is half a tone higher than F natural : a singer ' sang sharp '—that is, sang slightly higher than the accompaniment ; ' the pitch was sharpened ' —that is, was slightly raised.

The sign for a sharp in practical music is ♯, and is derived from the same source as the natural, viz., the *b quadratum* of the ancients, written as ♮ and contrasted with the *b mollis* or ♭, the origin of our flat sign. In French the same signs are used, but the raised note is entitled dièse — Fa dièse, Re dièse, etc. ; in German Fis, Dis, etc., just as E♭, G♭, are designated Es, Ges, and so on.

In the printed music of the 17th century, however, the sign is usually ⤬, and the single cross × was also used to indicate the sharp sign, though now it is the sign for the double-sharp.

In Germany the sign was used to express the major mode, C♯ meaning C major, A♯, A major, and so forth. Thus Beethoven has inscribed the overture to ' Leonora ' known as ' No. 1 ' (which is in the key of C) with the words ' Ouvertura in C♯, Characteristische Ouverture.' The Eroica Symphony, in E♭, was even announced in the programme of Clement's Concert, April 7, 1805, as ' Eine neue grosse Sinfonie in Dis ' (*i.e.* D♯). Instances of the practice are frequent in the Index to the *Allgemeine musikalische Zeitung*.   G.

SHARP (or ACUTE) MIXTURE. An organ stop consisting chiefly of pipes representing the higher partial tones, overtones, or harmonics.

According to Dr. E. J. Hopkins, a sharp mixture is one of four Ranks giving a sharp clear tone, consisting of the following intervals

in relation to the unison : 19th, 22nd, 26th, 29th, or g', c'', g'', c''', in relation to CC or 8 ft. C.   T. E.

SHARPE, ETHEL, born in Dublin, Nov. 28, 1872, was a pupil of the Royal Irish Academy of Music, and subsequently of the Royal College of Music, where, under the tuition of Mr. Franklin Taylor, she became a pianist of remarkable accomplishment. She gave her first concert in Princes Hall, in Nov. 1891, and received the silver medal of the Musicians' Company in the same year. Her début at the Crystal Palace took place on March 26, 1892, and for the next two years she gained experience and pursued her studies on the continent, making a great success at a recital in Vienna in 1894. During her stay at Vienna she enjoyed the friendship of Brahms and other notable musicians. She reappeared in London in 1895, playing again at the Crystal Palace. In that year she married Mr. Alfred Hobday, a distinguished viola-player (*Brit. Mus. Biog.* etc.).   M.

SHARPE, HERBERT FRANCIS, born at Halifax, March 1, 1861, won a pianoforte scholarship at the opening of the National Training School, where he afterwards succeeded Eugène d'Albert as Queen's Scholar. He appeared as a finished pianist in 1882, and gave many concerts in the provinces as well as in London, where he organised several series of very interesting trio concerts in 1899-1902. He was appointed a professor at the Royal College of Music in 1884, and in 1890 became an examiner for the Associated Board. He has written a comic opera in three acts (still in MS.), a concert overture for orchestra, pieces for one and two pianos, for flute or piano, for violin and piano, etc., besides part-songs, vocal trios, and songs. An excellent ' Pianoforte School ' is his op. 60 (*Brit. Mus. Biog.*)   M.

SHAW, MARY (MRS. ALFRED SHAW), daughter of John Postans, messman at the Guard Room, St. James's Palace, was born in 1814. She was a student at the Royal Academy of Music from Sept. 1828 to June 1831, and afterwards a pupil of Sir George Smart. Miss Postans appeared in public as a contralto singer in 1834, and at the Amateur Musical Festival in Exeter Hall in November of that year attracted great attention by the beauty of her voice and the excellence of her style. In 1835 she was engaged at the Concert of Ancient Music and the York Festival, and about the end of the year became the wife of Alfred Shaw, an artist of some repute. In 1836 she appeared at the Norwich and Liverpool Festivals, at the latter of which she sang the contralto part in ' St. Paul,' on its first performance in England. In 1837 she was engaged at the Philharmonic and Sacred Harmonic Societies and Birmingham Festival. In 1838, after fulfilling an engagement at the Gloucester Festival, she left England

and appeared at the Gewandhaus concerts, under Mendelssohn. A letter from him to the Directors of the Philharmonic Society, dated Jan. 19, 1839, speaks of Clara Novello and Mrs. Shaw as 'the best concert-singers we have had in this country for a long time.' From Germany she proceeded to Italy, and appeared at La Scala, Milan, Nov. 17, 1839, in Verdi's 'Oberto.' She returned to England in 1842, and appeared at Covent Garden with Adelaide Kemble; in 1843 at the Sacred Harmonic Society with Clara Novello; and afterwards at the Birmingham Festival. Her brilliant career was suddenly arrested by a heavy visitation. Her husband became deranged, and the calamity so seriously shocked her whole system that the vocal organs became affected, and she was unable to sing in tune. She resorted to teaching, for three or four years appearing in public at an annual benefit concert. After her husband's death in 1847 she married J. F. Robinson, a country solicitor, and retired from the profession. She died at Hadleigh Hall, Suffolk, Sept. 9, 1876.   W. H. H.

SHAWM, a wind instrument of the oboe type, with a double reed but a larger conical bore and a wide bell. The name is generally said to be a corruption of the French *Chalumeau*, but it would be more correct to say that both words have been derived from the same source, the Lat. *Calamus*, 'a reed,' through the diminutive *Calamellus*. In mediæval times the word appears as *Calamel*, *Chalamelle*, or *Chalemie* in France; *Caramillo* and *Charamella* in Spain and Italy; *Schalmei* or *Schalmey* in Germany; and *Shalmele*, *Shalm*, or *Shawm* in England. It is not until the 16th century that the form *Chalumeau* occurs, and in the next century it was used to denote a distinct instrument with cylindrical bore and single reed, the precursor of the modern clarinet. As shown by an ancient fresco in the British Museum, an instrument similar to the Shawm was known to the Romans, but its popularity in Europe is traceable to the Arabic and Saracenic influences of the 12th and 13th centuries (see PIPES, EVOLUTION OF). In the 16th century Shawms were made of various sizes from high treble to contra-bass, the larger forms being generally known on the Continent under the names Pommer and Bombardt. In England the title Shawm included all sizes; hence Drayton (*Polyolbion*, vol. iv.) speaks of the 'shrillest Shawm,' and an old proverb of the time of Henry VII. formerly inscribed on the walls of Leckingfield Manor House, Yorkshire states that :—

A shawme makethe a swete sounde for he tunythe [the] basse :
It mountithe not to hy but kepithe rule and space :
Yet yf it be blowne withe to a vehement wynde,
It makithe it mysgoverne oute of his kynde.
         (MS. copy Brit. Mus. Bib. Reg. 18 D. ii.)

In the Privy Purse Expenses of Henry VIII. is the following entry :—

1530. For ij sagbuttes ij *Tenor* Shalmes and two trebull Shalmesse x li. x s.

Illustrations of the various kinds of Shawms are given by Virdung (*Musica Getutscht*, 1511), Praetorius (*Sciagraphia*, 1620), and Mersenne (*Harmonie universelle*, 1635); also of existing instruments in Day's *Musical Instruments in the Military Exhibition* (1891), Kappey's *Military Music*, and in *Musical Times*, August 1906.

The high treble Shawm is still used on the continent with the bagpipe (cornemuse) by itinerant musicians; in Brittany it is called Bombardt and in Italy Cionnamella or Cennamella (see PIFFERO). The word Shawm disappeared from general use in England during the early part of the 17th century, in favour of the title Hoboy, though this name appears as early as 1561 in the opera 'Ferrex and Porrex.' In 1607 the Edinburgh town musicians consisted of players on 'chalmis and howboyis,' from which it may be inferred that by that time the two instruments had become distinct.

For the term 'wayghte' as applied to the Shawm see WAITS, and for the subsequent history of the instrument see OBOE.   F. W. G.

SHE STOOPS TO CONQUER. A English opera, in three acts; adapted by E. Fitzball from Goldsmith's comedy; music by G. A. Macfarren. Produced at Drury Lane Theatre (Pyne & Harrison), Feb. 11, 1864.   G.

SHEDLOCK, JOHN SOUTH, born at Reading, Sept. 29, 1843, was a pupil of Lübeck for the piano and of Edouard Lalo for composition. Before going to Paris for his musical studies he had taken the degree of B.A. at the London University in 1864. From the time of his return to England he was active as a teacher, and occasionally played in public. In 1879 he was appointed critic of *The Academy*, in succession to Professor Prout, and has since been engaged almost exclusively in musical literature. He was appointed critic of *The Athenæum* in 1901. Besides journalistic work, he has done much of an archæological kind. A series of articles on Beethoven's sketch-books, in the *Musical Times*, 1892, led to his discovery of a copy of Cramer's studies annotated by Beethoven, at Berlin. This was published as 'The Beethoven-Cramer Studies' in 1893. In 1895 he edited two of Kuhnau's 'Biblischen Sonaten,' and a selection of harpsichord pieces by Pasquini and others. In the same year appeared his most important work, a treatise on *The Pianoforte Sonata*, which was translated two years afterwards into German by Olga Stieglitz. His chief composition is a quartet for pianoforte and strings, written in 1886.   M.

SHEFFIELD FESTIVAL. See FESTIVALS, vol. ii. p. 29.

SHEPHERD, SHEPHEARD, SHEPPARD, or SHEPPERD, JOHN, born in the early part of the 16th century, was a chorister of St. Paul's under Thomas Mulliner. In 1542 he was appointed Instructor of the choristers and organist of Magdalen College, Oxford, which office he resigned in 1543, was reappointed to it in 1545, and held it until 1547. He was a Fellow of the College from 1549 to 1551. On April 21, 1554, having then been a student in music for 20 years, he supplicated for the degree of Mus. D., but it does not appear whether he actually took the degree. John Day's 'Morning and Evening Prayer,' etc., 1560, contains two Anthems, a 4, by him—'I give you a new commandment,' and 'Submit yourselves.' The former is reprinted in the 'Parish Choir.' Another book of Day's, the 'Whole Psalms in foure parts,' 1563, has a 'Prayer' by him, 'O Lord of hostes.' Barnard prints a four-part anthem, 'Haste thee.' Hawkins prints a motet in three parts by him, 'Steven first after Christ for Gods worde his blood spent,' and a melodious little 'Poynte'—a fugal piece for four voices of seven bars length. Burney (ii. 565) complains that the motet is not a good specimen, and prints another, 'Esurientes,' for five voices from the Christ Church MSS., on which he pronounces Shepherd to have been superior to any composer of the reign of Henry VIII. [In the Durham part-books, the anthem 'O Lord the maker of all thing' usually assigned to Henry VIII., is accredited to Shepherd. It is more probably by William Mundy.] Much of his church music is preserved in the Music School, Oxford ; the MSS. at Christ Church contain five complete portions of the 'Magnificat' and some motets, also complete. The great majority of Shepherd's motets in the library are incomplete, as the tenor part-book is wanting. [A 'Deus misereatur' and 'Gloria' in short score, written on two six-lines staves and barred with twelve minims to the bar, is in a MS. organ-book, (6).] In the British Museum (Add. MSS. 15,166, 29,289, 30,480) are treble parts of many of his English compositions, amongst them 2 M. and E. Services with Creed ; 2 Te Deums and Magnificats, 2 Creeds, and 7 Anthems. Add. MSS. 4900, 29,246, contain four pieces with lute accompaniment, and Add. MSS. 17,802-5 has no fewer than four Masses— 'The western wynde,' 'The French Masse,' 'Be not afraide,' and 'Playn song Mass for a Mene'; four Alleluias, and ten Latin Motets, all for four voices complete. The library of the Royal College of Music possesses four Latin motets, and a 'First Service' by him. Morley in his *Introduction* includes him amongst 'famous Englishmen.' The date of his death is unknown.

Another John Shepherd, possibly a son of the above, was sworn a Gentleman of the Chapel Royal, Dec. 1, 1606. (Rimbault's *Old Cheque-book*, p. 43.) Perhaps it was he who added a Kyrie to Johnson's service in G, in the Cathedral Library, Ely. (See Dickson's *Catalogue*, 32, 37.) Perhaps, also, he is the 'Thos. Shepherd' of Tudway (iv. 72).   w. h. h.

SHEPHERD, WILLIAM, an Edinburgh composer, violinist, and music-publisher. About 1793 he issued a 'Collection of Strathspey Reels' dedicated to Miss Abercromby, and a similar one about 1802-3. In 1796 he entered into partnership with Nathaniel Gow, in a music-publishing business, at 41 North Bridge, Edinburgh, removing before 1804 to 16 Princes Street.

Gow and Shepherd were unfortunate in their speculations, and Shepherd appears to have been deeply involved at his death, which occurred on Jan. 19, 1812.   F. K.

SHEPHERD'S PIPE. A name given to the pastoral oboe or musette. It was an instrument with a double reed like that of the bagpipe chaunter ; and seems occasionally to have been combined with a windbag as in the latter instrument. It was made in several sizes, constituting a family or 'consort' similar to the viols, recorders, and other instruments. Its origin in the simple reed is well given in Chappell's *History of Music*, vol. i. p. 259.

An excellent drawing of its various forms, with the method of holding it, is to be found in a *Traité de la Musette*, by Jean Girin of Lyons, 1572, where it is distinguished from the 'Cromorne' and 'Hautbois.' The bagpipe form with drones and windbag is also engraved, and interesting details are given as to celebrated makers ; many of whom, like the 'luthiers' of Cremona, seem to have handed down their reputation to their descendants. It appears to have had six holes, and the rudimentary scale and compass of the oboe ; though, of course when played from a bag, and not with the lips, the upper harmonic register must have been deficient.   w. h. s.

SHEREMETIEV, ALEXANDER DMITRIEVICH, Count, born 1859. His ancestor, Peter Borisov, had been one of the first noblemen to establish a private choir in the 17th century, while his father's church choral choir had become widely famous under the bâton of Lomakin. Count Alexander Sheremetiev started his choir in 1884, under the conductorship of Archangelsky. In 1882 he had already organised a symphony orchestra. In 1898 he began to give national concerts in St. Petersburg, which have gradually acquired the character of symphony concerts at popular prices, and are now very highly rated from the artistic point of view. In 1902 Count Sheremetiev became Intendant of the Imperial Court Chapels.   R. N.

SHERRINGTON, MME. LEMMENS. (See vol. ii. p. 674.)

SHERWOOD, PERCY, born at Dresden, May 23, 1866, was a pupil of the Conservatorium of his native place, studying the pianoforte and composition under Draeseke, W. Roth, etc. in 1885-88. In 1889 he won the Mendelssohn prize with a requiem for voices and orchestra. He was appointed a professor in the Dresden Conservatorium in 1893. He has won con-

2 *f*

siderable success both as a pianist and composer in Germany. His works include a piano concerto, a symphony, an overture, a sonata for violoncello, music for piano, organ, etc. as well as songs. In February 1907 he gave a concert of unpublished compositions of his own, in the Palmengarten, Dresden, the programme of which consisted of a sonata for two pianos, a suite for clarinet and piano, and a quintet for piano and strings. (*Brit. Mus. Biog.*; Riemann's *Lexikon*, etc.)   M.

SHIELD, WILLIAM, son of a singing-master, was born March 5, 1748, at Whickham, Durham. He received his first musical instruction when six years old, from his father, but losing his parent three years later, he was apprenticed to a boat-builder at North Shields. His master, however, permitted him to pursue his musical studies, and he obtained some lessons in thorough-bass from Charles Avison, and occasionally played the violin at music meetings in the neighbourhood. On the expiration of his apprenticeship, having acquired sufficient knowledge to lead the subscription concerts at Newcastle, he determined upon making music his profession, and removed to Scarborough, where he became leader at the theatre and concerts. Whilst there he produced his first composition, an anthem for the opening of a new church at Sunderland. Having been heard by Fischer and Borghi, they recommended him to Giardini, by whom he was engaged in 1772 as a second violin in the Opera band. In 1773 he was promoted to the post of principal viola—the favourite instrument of composers—which he held for eighteen years, and which he also filled at all the principal concerts. In 1778 he produced, at the Haymarket, his first dramatic piece, the comic opera 'The Flitch of Bacon.' This led to his being engaged as composer to Covent Garden Theatre, a post which he occupied until his resignation, 1791. During his engagement he composed many operas and other pieces. In 1791 he made the acquaintance of Haydn, and was wont to say that in four days, during which he accompanied Haydn from London to Taplow and back, he gained more knowledge than he had done by study in any four years of his life. In the same year he visited France and Italy. In 1792 he was re-engaged as composer at Covent Garden, in which capacity he acted until 1797. In 1807 he gave up all connection with the theatre. He was appointed Master of the King's Musick in 1817.

He published at various times, 'A Collection of Favourite Songs, To which is added a Duet for two Violins'; 'A Collection of Canzonets and an Elegy'; and 'A Cento, consisting of Ballads, Rounds, Glees, etc.'; likewise 'Six Trios for two Violins and Bass,' and 'Six Duos for two Violins.' He was also author of *An Introduction to Harmony*, 1800; and *Rudi-*

ments of Thorough Bass, about 1815. His dramatic compositions, consisting of operas, musical farces, and pantomimes, were as follow :

'The Flitch of Bacon,' 1778; 'Lord Mayor's Day,' 1782; 'The Poor Soldier,' 'Rosina,' 'Harlequin Friar Bacon,' 1783; 'Robin Hood,' 'The Noble Peasant,' 'Fontainebleau,' 'The Magic Cavern,' 1784; 'Love in a Camp,' 'The Nunnery,' 'The Choleric Fathers,' 'Omai,' 1785; 'Richard Cœur de Lion,' 'The Enchanted Castle,' 1786; 'The Highland Reel,' 'Marian,' 'The Prophet,' 'Aladdin,' 1788; 'The Crusade,' 'The Picture of Paris,' 1790; 'The Woodman,' 'Oscar and Malvina' (with Reeve), 1791; 'Hartford Bridge,' 1792; 'Harlequin's Museum,' 'The Deaf Lover,' 'The Midnight Wanderers,' 'Sprigs of Laurel,' 1793; 'Arrived at Portsmouth,' 'The Travellers in Switzerland,' 'Netley Abbey,' 1794; 'The Mysteries of the Castle,' 1795; 'Abroad and at Home,' 'Lock and Key,' 1796; 'The Italian Villagers,' 'The Village Fête,' 'Wicklow Gold Mines,' 1797 'The Farmer,' 1798; 'Two Faces under a Hood,' 1807.

In many of his pieces he introduced songs, etc., selected from the works of other composers, English and foreign ; and was thereby the means of making the general public acquainted with many beautiful melodies, of which they would otherwise have remained ignorant.

Shield's melodies charm by their simple, natural beauty ; at once vigorous, chaste, and refined, they appeal directly to the hearts of Englishmen. But he also wrote songs of agility, to display the powers of Mrs. Billington and others. Among his most popular songs are 'The Thorn,' 'The Wolf,' 'The heaving of the lead,' 'Old Towler,' 'The Ploughboy,' and 'The Post Captain'; but these are but some of the most prominent. Shield died at his residence in Berners Street, Jan. 25, 1829, and was buried on Feb. 4 in the south cloister of Westminster Abbey. With the exception of his fine tenor, reputed a Stainer, which he bequeathed to George IV. (who accepted the gift, but directed that its utmost value should be paid to the testator's presumed widow), he left his whole estate to his 'beloved partner, Ann [Stokes], Mrs. Shield upwards of forty years.' His valuable musical library was sold in July 1829. [On Oct. 19, 1891, a memorial cross was erected to his memory in Whickham Churchyard, Durham.]   W. H. H.

SHIFT. In playing the violin, or any of the instruments belonging to that family, an executant effects a 'shift' when the left hand passes from one established position to another. Thus, when the hand moves up or down the finger-board the player was said to be 'on the shift.' The term was also used to denote the positions themselves, the second position being known as the 'half-shift,' the third position as the 'whole-shift,' and the fourth position as the 'double-shift.' This technical acquirement, which is now an exact and indispensable means of reaching every note within the compass of the violin, evidently originated in Italy. There is a certain amount of ambiguity surrounding its use by viol-players previous to its introduction among violinists; but it is quite certain that before the 17th century there are no indications of any such custom. During the 17th century, however, there is little doubt that it was employed by the best viol-players of the day. Christopher Simpson clearly demonstrates its use in *The Division Viol* (second edition, London, 1667), wherein he states, under '*The ordering of the fingers in gradual notes*,' that 'In any point of Division which reaches to the lower Frets or *beyond them*; the highest note thereof is always stopt either with the third or fourth finger.' The first tentative advances towards the adoption of the 'shift' took the form of an extension of the little finger in the first position, and the feat of touching the first C on the *chanterelle* of the violin by this means was looked upon as a daring undertaking. As a natural consequence, the executant's ability rested almost entirely upon his manner of playing *l'ut*, and so sensational was the effect of its advent upon the listeners that an involuntary murmur of 'Gare l'ut,' was wont, it is said, to escape from the lips of his listeners. Beyond a doubt, many professional violinists could shift in the first three positions by the year 1655, for Mersenne (*Harmonie Universelle*) speaks with admiration of those players who could mount up to the octave of each string. Then in 1658 Anthony Wood in his *Life* describes the wonderful playing of Thomas Baltzar—the Paganini of his day—whom he saw 'run up his fingers to the end of the finger-board of the violin and run them back insensibly and all with alacrity and in very good tune, which I am sure,' says he, 'any in England never saw the like before.' To Signor Mattaei—who came to England in 1672—is accorded the invention of that *bête noire* of violinists, the 'half shift,' or second position. But although the 'shift' was favoured by professional players of exceptional ability at this period, its adoption was far from general, owing to the confused methods of holding the violin which continued well into the next century. Lully, who was himself a wonderful violinist, gives an idea of the capacity of the ordinary orchestral technique, by choosing a test piece for those desiring to gain the 'dignus est intrare' of his band, in which no C on the *chanterelle* occurred. For thirty years the entr'acte from his opera of 'Atys' served this purpose. Even in Leopold Mozart's time the question of holding the violin was far from settled, for, in his *Violin School* (1756), he mentions that there are two ways of holding the violin, the first being 'against the breast'—which position he regards as an obstacle to 'shifting,'—and the second is to place the violin under the chin and rest it on the shoulder. The best professional players adopted the latter method, and their example finding favour with lesser artists was the means of abolishing the 'breast position' and bringing the 'shift' into general use.

The 'shift' on the violoncello was doubtless derived from the violin, and is governed by the same rules. The 'thumb movement,' or 'shifting of the thumb' which was the means of facilitating the use of the high positions on the violoncello, was first employed—and it is said invented—by the French artist Berteau in the first half of the 18th century.

Huet, Felix, *Étude sur les différentes Écoles de Violon*, Châlons-sur-Marne, 1880 ; Mengy, A., *Quelques Observations sur l'art du Violon*, Paris, 1888 ; Koeckert, G., *Les Principes Rationnels de la Technique du Violon*, Leipzig, 1904 ; Anon., *The Violin, How to master it*, Edinburgh, 1889 ; Courvoisier, Carl, *Technics of Violin-Playing*, London, 1899.   O. R.

SHIFT, in trombone playing, signifies an alteration in position of the movable slide, by means of which the fundamental length of the instrument is increased. The home position of the slide is known as the No. 1 'position,' and the successive shifts, lowering the pitch by successive semitones, give respectively the second, third, fourth, fifth, sixth, and seventh 'positions,' the number of the 'position' being thus always one higher than the number of semitones by which the pitch is lowered (see TROMBONE).   D. J. B.

SHINNER, EMILY, born at Cheltenham, July 7, 1862, began the study of the violin at the age of seven. In 1874 she went to Berlin, and for two years studied under H. Jacobsen, a pupil of Joachim's, female violinists not being at that time admissible to the Hochschule. In 1876 this restriction was taken away, and Miss Shinner was among the first admitted. In October 1877 she became a pupil of Joachim's, and remained with him for three years. In Feb. 1881, she came to London, and after being heard at several private concerts (among others at one given by the Bach Choir), made her début at a concert given by Mr. H. R. Bird in the Kensington Town Hall, in Brahms's Sonata in G, etc. At the London Musical Society's concert of June 29, 1882, she played David's concerto in E minor with great success, and from that time held a high position among English artists, her style being pure and refined, and her power of interpreting works of a high intellectual order being very remarkable. She appeared at the Popular Concert on Feb. 9, and at the Crystal Palace on March 8, 1884 ; in 1887 she organised a successful quartet-party of ladies. In January 1889 she married Capt. A. F. Liddell. She died July 17, 1901.   M.

SHIRREFF, JANE, born 1811, soprano singer, pupil of Thomas Welsh, appeared at Covent Garden, Dec. 1, 1831, as Mandane in Arne's 'Artaxerxes,' with great success. In 1832 she sang at the Concert of Ancient Music, the Philharmonic Concert, and Gloucester Festival, and in 1834 at the Westminster Abbey Festival. Her engagement at Covent Garden continued from 1831 to 1834-35. In 1835 she commenced an engagement at Drury Lane, but in 1837 returned to Covent Garden. In 1838 she went to America, in company with Wilson, E. Seguin, and Mrs. E. Seguin, where she became a universal favourite. On her return to England she married Mr. J. Walcott, and retired into private life. Her voice was full-toned, and powerful in the higher, but somewhat weak in the lower notes ; her intonation was perfect, and she was a much better actress than the generality of singers. She died at Kensington, Dec. 23, 1883. w. h. h.

SHIRREFFS, ANDREW, an Aberdeen musician and poet of the 18th century, born 1762. He wrote a once popular pastoral musical comedy 'Jamie and Bess, or the Laird in disguise' in five acts, modelled upon Allan Ramsay's *Gentle Shepherd*. This was published in 1787 ; and the musical part of it advertised as for sale in 1788. He was composer of 'Forty Pieces of Original Music,' published by Stewart & Co., Edinburgh. Shirreffs was a M.A. of Marischal College, Aberdeen (1783), and edited the *Aberdeen Chronicle* and the *Caledonian Magazine*. He came to London in 1798, and died about 1807. He was originally a bookbinder, was lame, and his portrait is prefixed to his volume of poems, 1790. Burns mentions having met him, and refers to him as 'a little decreped body, with some abilities.'　　　　　　　F. K.

SHOPHAR, or SHOFAR. The Jewish ram's-horn trumpet, used in the synagogue worship. The natural horn is flattened in section, and a cup mouthpiece is formed at the small end. The instrument, or an imitation of its effect, is introduced into the scores of Macfarren's 'John the Baptist' and Elgar's 'Apostles.'　D. J. B.

SHORE, MATHIAS, who in 1665 was one of the trumpeters in ordinary to James II. was, a few years afterwards, promoted to the post of Sergeant Trumpeter, in which he distinguished himself by the rigorous exaction of his fees of office. [See TRUMPETER.] He died in 1700, leaving three children :—

1. WILLIAM, also one of the King's trumpeters in ordinary, succeeded his father as Sergeant Trumpeter, died in December 1707, and was buried at St. Martin's-in-the-Fields. He followed his father's example in the severe exaction of fees.

2. CATHERINE, born about 1668, who was a pupil of Henry Purcell for singing and the harpsichord. In 1693 she became the wife of Colley Cibber, without consent of her father, whose resentment was not, however, of very long duration, as when he made his will, March 5, 1695-96, he bequeathed to her one-third of the residue of his property. Shortly after her marriage Mrs. Cibber appeared on the stage as a singer, and, among other songs, sang the second part of Purcell's air 'Genius of England' ('Don Quixote,' Part II.), to her brother John's trumpet accompaniment. She is said to have died about 1730.

3. JOHN, the most celebrated trumpeter of his time, in 1707 succeeded his brother William as Sergeant Trumpeter. Purcell composed for him obbligato parts to many songs, which may be seen in the 'Orpheus Britannicus,' and

which fully attest his skill. His playing is highly commended in the *Gentleman's Journal* for January 1691-92, where in an account of the celebration on St. Cecilia's day in the preceding November, we read 'Whilst the company is at table the hautboys and trumpets play successively. Mr. Showers hath taught the latter of late years to sound with all the softness imaginable ; they plaid us some flat tunes made by Mr. Finger with a general applause, it being a thing formerly thought impossible upon an instrument designed for a sharp key.' His name appears in 1711 as one of the twenty-four musicians to Queen Anne, and also as lutenist to the Chapel Royal.[1] He is said to have been the inventor of the tuning-fork, and also to have split his lip in sounding the trumpet, thereby incapacitating himself for performing. He died Nov. 20, 1752, at the alleged age of ninety, but it is very probable that his age was over-stated, and did not exceed eighty.　w. h. h.

SHORT, PETER, an early London music-printer and publisher, who printed a number of madrigal books and some early musical treatises. He worked 'at the signe of the Starre' on Bread Street Hill, from about 1584, and his issues include Morley's *Plaine and Easie Introduction to practical Musick*, 1597 ; Holborne's *Cittharn Schoole*, 1597 ; 'Seuen Sobs of a Sorrowfull Soule for Sin,' 1597 ; Dowland's 'First Booke of Songes,' 1597 ; Morley's 'Canzonets,' 1597 ; Farnaby's 'Canzonets,' 1598 ; Cavendish's 'Ayres,' 1599, and some other works. He was succeeded in business, at the same address, between 1603 and 1608, by Humfrey Lowndes, who reissued Morley's *Introduction*.　F. K.

SHORT OCTAVE. In the early days of harmony, and indeed until the whole circle of keys was made available in practical music, the chromatic notes in the lowest octave of the keyboard were not wanted, since they were not required as basses. The evidence of pictorial representations shows that as early as the 14th century the expedient was adopted of omitting some of the strings or organ pipes belonging to such keys, and letting their places be taken by strings and pipes tuned to notes below the apparent notes. Various systems of these effecting a saving of space in the organ will be found explained under ORGAN, vol. iii. p. 528b. For similar expedients in the SPINET see below, pp. 634-36. The Fitzwilliam Virginal Book contains indirect evidence that 'short octaves' were in general use early in the 17th century ; in one piece, the player's left hand is required to strike this chord , which is of course impossible on a full keyboard ; on one with a short octave in which the low G sharp key is attached to the string tuned to the low E, the chord does

---

[1] In the *Cheque Book of the Chapel Royal* he is said to have been appointed lutenist in 1715, but the entry was evidently not made until some time later, and probably from memory only.

not exceed the limit of the ordinary player's hand.   M.

SHRUBSOLE, WILLIAM, organist and hymn composer. He was born at Canterbury in January 1760, and was for seven years chorister at the Cathedral there. He studied the organ during this time, and was in 1782 appointed organist to Bangor Cathedral. While here he gave great offence to the Dean and Chapter by his association with dissenters, and by 'frequenting conventicles'; this led to his dismissal in 1783. He came to London, and immediately got a post as organist at Lady Huntingdon's Chapel, Spafields, Clerkenwell, which he held to his death. This occurred Jan. 18, 1806. He was buried in Bunhill Fields, and his monument was restored in 1892, mainly by the exertions of Mr. F. G. Edwards.

Shrubsole is best remembered by the composition of the fine hymn tune 'Miles Lane,' which appeared in the *Gospel Magazine* as early as 1779.   F. K.

SHUDI, famous harpsichord - maker, and founder of the house of Broadwood. Burkat Shudi, as he inscribed his name upon his instruments, was properly BURKHARDT TSCHUDI, and was a cadet of a noble family belonging to Glarus in Switzerland.[1] He was born March 13, 1702, and came to England in 1718, as a simple journeyman joiner.[2] When he turned to harpsichord-making is not known, but we are told by Burney, who knew Shudi and old Kirkman well, that they were both employed in London by Tabel,[3] a Fleming, and Burney calls them Tabel's foremen, perhaps meaning his principal workmen. The anecdote given by Burney, in Rees's *Cyclopædia*, of Kirkman's hasty wedding with his master's widow, and acquisition with her of Tabel's stock-in-trade, gives no information about Shudi, who, according to the *Daily Advertiser*, Oct. 5, 1742, 'removed from Meard's Street in Dean Street, Soho, to Great Pulteney Street, Golden Square' (the house occupied by his descendants, the Broadwoods, until 1904). Shudi was then styled 'Harpsichord Maker to H.R.H. the Prince of Wales.' [See BROADWOOD; KIRKMAN.]

Kirkman had the King's Arms for the sign of his business in Broad Street, Carnaby Market; Shudi, the Plume of Feathers at the house now 33 Great Pulteney Street. We may trace the choice of signs of these old colleagues and now rival makers to the divided patronage of the King (George II.) and Prince of Wales, who were notoriously unfriendly. No doubt Handel's friendship was of great value to Shudi; few harpsichords were then made, as owing to the

relatively high price, and the great expense and trouble of keeping them in order, they were only for the rich. But the tuning and repairing alone would keep a business going; harpsichords lasted long, and were submitted to restoration and alteration that would surprise the amateur of the present day.[4]

The Shudi harpsichord, formerly Queen Charlotte's, now in Windsor Castle, is dated 1740. It has a 'Lute' stop, a pleasing variation of *timbre*, and, like the pedal, of English invention in the previous century.

James Shudi Broadwood (MS. Notes, 1838) accredits his grandfather Shudi with the gift of a harpsichord to Frederick the Great, Shudi being a staunch Protestant, and regarding Frederick as the leader and champion of the Protestant cause. Mr. Broadwood, moreover, believed that a portrait of Shudi, which remained until a few years since in one of the rooms in Great Pulteney Street, represented him as engaged in tuning the identical harpsichord thus bestowed. Shudi's wife and two sons are also in the picture, a reproduction of which serves as the frontispiece to Rimbault's *History of the Pianoforte*. The elder boy, apparently nine years old, was born in 1736. This synchronises the picture with Frederick's victory and the peace concluded the following year (1745). But the writer could not find this instrument either in Potsdam or Berlin in 1881. The tradition about it is, however, strengthened by the fact that in 1766 Frederick obtained from Shudi two special double harpsichords for his New Palace at Potsdam, where they still remain. Instead of the anglicised 'Shudi,' they are accurately inscribed 'Tschudi.' One has silver legs, etc.; the other rests upon a partially gilded stand. Following Burney, who however only describes the first one, they appear to have been placed in the apartments of the Princess Amelia, and the Prince of Prussia. These instruments, like all Shudi's which still exist, are of the soundest possible workmanship, discrediting Burney's assertion of the want of durability of his harpsichords,[5] a reproach, however, which Burney goes on to say could not be alleged against Shudi's son-in-law and successor Broadwood. He however praises Shudi's tone as refined and delicate. The Potsdam harpsichords were made with Shudi's Venetian Swell, for which the pedals still exist, but it was probably not to the German taste of the time, and was therefore removed. Hopkins, in his comprehensive work upon the Organ, says the original organ swell was the 'nagshead,' a mere shutter, invented by Abraham Jordan in 1712. But to imitate its effect in the harpsichord we know

---

[1] Of the Schwanden branch. Heinrich, born 1074, died 1149, made Feodary of Glarus by the Lady Gutta, Abbess of Seckingen, was the first to adopt the surname Schudi (*sic*). The family tree goes back to Johann, Mayor of Glarus, born about 870.

[2] See *Schweizerische Lexicon*, Zurich, 1795, art. 'Tschudi.'

[3] Messrs. Broadwood's books of 1777 mention a secondhand harpsichord by Tabel (written Table). A harpsichord by Tabel with two manuals, and very like a Kirkman, is in the possession of Helena, Countess of Radnor.

[4] While pianofortes are now kept in tune by yearly contracts, the researches of Mr. William Dale. in Messrs. Broadwood's old books, show that harpsichords in the 18th century were tuned by *quarterly* contracts!

[5] Burney gives as his authority Snetzler the organ-builder, who attached organs to some of Shudi's harpsichords, and was, moreover, Shudi's intimate friend and executor. Shudi left him his ring, containing a portrait of Frederick the Great.

that Plenius about 1750, and also in London, by a pedal movement, gradually raised and lowered a portion of the top or cover. This coming into general use, Shudi improved upon it by his important invention of the 'Venetian Swell' on the principle of a Venetian blind, which he patented Dec. 18, 1769. He probably delayed taking out the patent until it became necessary by his partnership with John Broadwood, who had also become his son-in law,[1] earlier in the same year. This invention was subsequently transferred to the organ. [See vol. ii. p. 331, and the article SWELL.]

A harpsichord exists inscribed with the joint names of Shudi and Broadwood, dated 1770, although Shudi made harpsichords for himself after that date and independent of the partnership, as we know by existing instruments and by his will. About 1772 he retired to a house

in Charlotte Street, leaving the business premises to his son-in-law, John Broadwood, and died August 19, 1773. The next day a harpsichord was shipped to 'the Empress,' ordered by Joseph II. for Maria Theresa. The harpsichord that was Haydn's, acquired for the Museum at Vienna, at a cost of £110 sterling, was also a 'Shudi and Broadwood,' but this was the younger Burkat Shudi, who was in partnership with John Broadwood from 1773 to about 1782, and died in 1803.

A list of the existing harpsichords by Shudi and Shudi & Broadwood, as far as is known (1907),[2] is here appended : all but one are Double harpsichords. The price of a Single harpsichord, about 1770, was 35 guineas ; with Octava (i.e. Octave string), 40 guineas ; with Octava and Swell, 50 guineas. A Double harpsichord with Swell, was 80 guineas.[3]

No.	Date.	Signature.	Present Owner.	Remarks.
94	1740	Burkat Shudi.	H.M. the King, Windsor Castle.	Removed from Kew Palace in 1875.
229	1749	,,	Mr. Warre.	Is a wreck. Double. 5½ C-F, 5 stops, no machine or pedals.
260	1751	,,	F. Fairley, Esq., Newcastle-on-Tyne.	A single keyboard. 5 oct., F-F, with lowest F sharp omitted. 2 stops.
407	1760	,,	W. Dale, Esq.	Double. 5 oct. with F♯ usual stops, added swell on a chest of drawers.
511	1766	Burkat Tschudi.	Emperor of Germany, Potsdam.	Made for Frederick the Great, and described by Burney.
512	1766	,,	,,	Made for Frederick the Great. (Both of 5½ oct., C-F.)
625	1770	Burkat Shudi et Johannes Broadwood.	W. Dale, Esq. ,,	Was in David Hartley's family. 6 stops, 2 pedals, as have nearly all these instruments.
639	1771	Burkat Shudi.	John Broadwood & Sons.	Played upon by Moscheles and by Ernst Pauer in their historical performances.
686	1773	Burkat Shudi et Johannes Broadwood.	Ditto. Lent to the Rev. Sir F. A. G. Ouseley, Bart., Tenbury.	Bought of Mr. T. W. Taphouse, 1861.
691	1773	,,	M. Victor Mahillon, Brussels.	Sent to 'the Empress' (Maria Theresa) Aug. 20, 1773. Obtained by M. Victor Mahillon from Vienna.
750	1775	,,	Messrs. Price & Sons, Yeovil.	Made for Lady Stoverdale, Redlinch, Bruton.
762	1775	,,	Musikverein, Vienna.	Was Joseph Haydn's, and subsequently Herbeck's.
899	1781	,,	The late T. W. Taphouse, Oxford.	5 oct., F-F, 7 stops, 2 pedals. Came from Mrs. Anson's, Sudbury Rectory, Derby.
902	1781	,,	C. Harford Lloyd, Esq., Gloucester.	5 oct., F-F. Restored by Mr. Taphouse.
919	1782	,,	Stephen Stratton, Esq., Birmingham.	Belonged to the Wrottesley family.
1137	1790	,,	..	Instrument mentioned in Mr. Hipkins's notes in the appendix to the first edition of the Dictionary.

A. J. H.

SHUDI, JOSHUA, harpsichord maker and pupil of Burkat Shudi, appears from his advertisement in the Gazetteer of Jan. 12, 1767, to have set up for himself about that time at the Golden Guitar, Silver Street, Golden Square, London. An advertisement of his widow, Mary Shudi, then of Berwick Street, St. James's, in the Public Advertiser of Jan. 16, 1775, announces his death and her continuance of the business, and as there is a fine harpsichord still existing, said to have a romantic history, and bearing the name and date of Joshua Shudi, 1779, it is evident that she continued to use her late husband's name, or dated instruments of his make when she sold them. A. J. H.

SHUTTLEWORTH, OBADIAH, son of Thos. Shuttleworth of Spitalfields, who had acquired some money by vending MS. copies of Corelli's works before they were published in England. He was an excellent violinist, and was principal violin at the Swan Tavern concerts, Cornhill, from their commencement in 1728 until his

[1] By his marriage with Barbara Shudi, baptized March 12, 1748; married to John Broadwood, Jan. 2, 1769; died July 8, 1776. The first wife of John Broadwood, she was the mother of James Shudi Broadwood who was born Dec. 20, 1772, died Aug. 8, 1851; and grandmother of Henry Fowler Broadwood and Walter Stewart Broadwood.

death. He was also a skilful organist, and in 1724 succeeded Philip Hart as organist of St. Michael's, Cornhill, and a few years afterwards was appointed one of the organists of the Temple Church. He composed twelve concertos and some sonatas for the violin, which he kept in MS., his only printed compositions being two concertos adapted from the first and eleventh concertos of Corelli. [These were published by Joseph Hare, at the Viol and Flute in Cornhill, and were engraved by T. Cross : the date is about 1726. F. K.] He died about 1735. W. H. H.

SI. The syllable used, in the musical terminology of Italy and France, to designate the note B, and adapted, in systems of Solmisation which advocate the employment of a movable starting-point, to the seventh degree of the scale.

The method invented by Guido d'Arezzo, in the earlier half of the 11th century, recognised the use of six syllables only—ut, re, mi, fa, sol, la—suggested by the initial and post-cæsural

[2] Additions to the original list are here made from the MS. notes left by Mr. Hipkins.
[3] The altered value of money should be borne in mind in comparing these prices with those of modern pianofortes.

syllables of the hymn, 'Ut queant laxis'; the completion of the octave being provided for by the introduction of certain changes in the position of the root-syllable, *ut*.[1] Until the mediæval theory of the scale was revolutionised by the discovery of the functions of the leading-note this method answered its purpose perfectly; but when the ecclesiastical modes were abandoned in favour of our modern form of tonality, it became absolutely necessary to add another syllable to the series. This syllable is said to have been first used, about 1590, by Erycius Puteanus, of Dordrecht, the author of a treatise on music, entitled *Musathena*; and tradition asserts that it was formed from the initial syllable of the fourth verse—'Sancte Joannes'—of the hymn already alluded to, by the substitution of *i* for *a*. This account, however, has not been universally received. Mersennus[2] attributes the invention to a French musician, named Le Maire, who laboured for thirty years to bring it into practice, but in vain, though it was generally adopted after his death. Brossard[3] gives substantially the same account. Bourdelot[4] attributes the discovery to a certain nameless Cordelier, of the Convent of Ave Maria, in France, about the year 1675; but tells us that the Abbé de la Louette, Maître de Chapelle at Notre Dame de Paris, accorded the honour to a singing-master, named Metru, who flourished in Paris about the year 1676. In confirmation of these traditions Bourdelot assures us that he once knew a lutenist, named Le Moine, who remembered both Metru and the Cordelier, as having practised the new system towards the close of the 17th century—whence it has been conjectured that one of these bold innovators may possibly have invented, and the other adopted it, if indeed both did not avail themselves of an earlier discovery.

Mersennus tells us that some French professors of his time used the syllable *za* to express B♭, reserving *si* for B♮. Loulié, writing some sixty years later, rejected *za*, but retained the use of *si*.[5] The Spanish musician, Andrea Lorente, of Alcala, used *bi* to denote B♮;[6] while in the latter half of the 17th century, our own countryman, Dr. Wallis, thought it extraordinary that the verse, 'Sancte Johannes,' did not suggest to Guido himself the use of the syllable *sa*—and this, notwithstanding the patent fact that the addition of a seventh syllable would have struck at the very root of the Guidonian system.   W. S. R.

SI CONTRA FA. [See MI CONTRA FA.]

SIBELIUS, JEAN, born on Dec. 8, 1865, at Tavastehus in Finland. Like so many other musicians he was at first made a law student,

but, happily for the honour of the music of Finland, he presently found that his real talent lay in the direction of Art, and his real power of speech could only display itself in the language of music. Accordingly, he placed himself under Wegelius at the Helsingfors Conservatorium; and afterwards studied under Becker at Berlin and Goldmark at Vienna. After his return to Finland he accepted the post of Principal of the Conservatorium (which he still holds), and was the fortunate recipient of a handsome annuity from the Senate, which enables him to give the greater part of his time to composition. For so young a man he has written much, his latest opus number being 53. In all his compositions he displays marked ability, a strong individuality, and a decided bias in favour of the Folk-music of his country. Sibelius is a composer who must be taken on his own merits; it would be difficult to compare him to any one else, the whole atmosphere of his work is so strange, and so permeated with lights and shadows that are unfamiliar, and colours that are almost from another world. To understand him it is necessary to understand both the racial descent of the Finns, and their strange, deeply influencing mythology; their racial character is derived partly from the East, and partly from the West, as they are a mixture of Mongolian and Western stock; deriving from the West, vigour and self-reliance, and from the East, languor and mysticism. Even more important is the influence of their mythology. It is hardly too much to say that Sibelius's music seldom gets away from the atmosphere of legend and rune. In idea, rhythm, turn of melody (diction), colour of thought and of orchestration, he keeps within touch of the magic halo which surrounds the 'Kalevala,' which is the great collection of Runes and Folklore made by Dr. Lönnrot in 1835 (the year in which the university of Helsingfors was founded). The 'Kalevala' is a poem which sets forth the mythical history of the Finnish people, just as the 'Nibelungenlied' sets forth the mythical history of the Teutonic nations.

The Finnish music, like the Finnish character, is the outcome of a fearful struggle against unfavourable environment,—a struggle which has literally been for life or death, but which has resulted in a triumphant life. Without some understanding of the Finnish history, religion, and temperament, Sibelius's music is more or less unintelligible; for it does not belong to any family or nation except the Finnish. He has nothing in common with the Russian or German; and even the Swede and the Dane are foreign to him. The Finnish Folk-Song is also a thing by itself; the chief features being the prevalence of 5-4 rhythms, and the repetition of the same note many times (see SONG). Sibelius makes free use of the latter characteristic in most of his compositions, although he

1 See SOLMISATION.   2 *Harmonie Universelle* (Paris, 1636), p. 183.
3 *Dictionnaire de Musique* (Amsterdam, 1703).
4 *Histoire de la Musique*, compiled from the MSS. of the Abbé Bourdelot, and those of his nephew, Bonnet Bourdelot, and subsequently published by Bonnet, Paymaster to the Lords of the Parliament of Paris (Paris, 1705 and 1715; Amsterdam, 1725, 1743).
5 *Éléments ou Principes de Musique* (Amsterdam, 1698).
6 *Porque de la Musica* (1672).

himself says that he does not use Folk-Song. Still, it is obvious that he does not altogether break away from the people's song, and that his mind is in unison with his national trend of thought.   His chief works are the two Symphonies in E and D, 'The Swan of Tuonela,' the Overture and Suite 'Karelia,' 'En Saga,' 'Finlandia,' 'Lemminkâinen,' Incidental music to 'Kuolema,' and the Violin Concerto.   With the exception of the two first named, and the last, the works are entirely founded on the National Legends of Suomi (Finland), in which Tuonela (Hades) and Kuolema (Death) play a large and gloomy part ; so that there is naturally a considerable preponderance of the weird in the music—for example in 'The Swan' it is the strange wild song of the bird swimming on the black still waters which separate man from Hades that inspires awe and almost terror. There is nothing human, but a kind of dark dream of mysticism.   Again, in the music to Yärnfeldt's drama 'Kuolema,' the ideas are those of tragedy, darkness, and horror.   The mother is dying, and in her delirium thinks she is in the ball-room.   Her son cannot detain her, and she rises and dances with imaginary men.   At the height of her frenzy some one knocks ; the vision dies ; the music is silent ; the mother shrieks, for the visitor is Death. It must not be thought that Sibelius is morbid or unmanly from these examples,—on the contrary his main characteristic is enormous power.   He seems at times to be almost beating himself to pieces in the struggle to lash out with his emotions, and gain expression for the feelings that are bursting within him, while every now and then he gives touches of indescribably sad and sweet yearning.   He is the lawful successor of Kollan, Schartz, Faltin, and Kajanus ; but to his inheritance he brings a character, colour, and style, which are entirely his own.   Whether composing for the orchestra, the chorus, or solo voices, Sibelius has much to say ; much that is new, and much that no one else could either imagine or express.   No notice of his work would be complete without an express mention of his songs, which are truly remarkable in every way, and, like all his work, completely foreign to conventional Western thought and manner.   The following is a complete list of Sibelius's compositions ; many of the opus numbers omitted refer to arrangements of works, and are therefore not given here.

Op.
5. 6 Impromptus, PF.
9. En Saga.   Tone-poem for orchestra.
10. Overture Karelia.
11. Suite Karelia.
12. Sonata, PF. Solo.
13. 7 Songs.
15. Skogsräet.
16. Frühlingslied, for Orchestra.
17. 7 Songs.
18. Part-songs for Male voices.
21. Hymn for Male voices, 'Natus in curas.'
22. Legends from the epic 'Kalevala' (Der Schwann von Tuonela and Lemminkäinen zieht heimwärts).
23. Songs for the 'Promotions performances,' 1897 (mixed voices).
24. Piano pieces.
26. Fiulandia (No. 7).   Tone-poem for orchestra.

Op.
27. Incidental Music to King Christian II.
31. Athenian Songs, for boys' voice, solo.   Male chorus.   Horn septet, triangle, cymbals, and large drum.
33. Der Fährmanns Bräute.   Scena for Baritone.
36. 6 Songs.
37. 5 Songs.
38. 5 Songs.
39. Symphony No. 1 in E minor.
41. Kylliki (Lyrical pieces).
43. Symphony No. 2 in D major.
44. Valse triste from Kuolema.
45. Tanz Intermezzo, for orchestra, and for PF. solo.
46. Pelleas and Melisande.   Orch. Suite.
47. Violin Concerto in D minor.
49. Pohgolas Daughter.   Symphonic Fantasia.
51. Balsazars Gastmal.   Symphonic Fantasia.
53. Pan and Echo.

D. H.

SIBONI, GIUSEPPE, born at Forli,[1] Jan. 27, 1780, made his début as a tenor singer at Florence in 1797, and after singing in Genoa, Milan, and Prague, appeared at the King's Theatre, London, in 1806, and sang for the following three seasons.   In 1810, 1811, 1812, 1813, and 1814, he was in Vienna, where he sang at the first performances of Beethoven's 'Wellington's Sieg' and 'Tremate empi.'   In 1813 he sang at Prague, and after engagements at Naples and St. Petersburg (1818) settled at Copenhagen in October 1819, where he lived for the rest of his life, occupying the post of director of the Royal Opera and of the Conservatorium.   He was married three times, his second wife being a sister of Schubert's friend, von Schober, and died at Copenhagen, March 29, 1839.   Many of Paër's tenor parts were written for him.   His son,

ERIK ANTON WALDEMAR, born at Copenhagen, August 26, 1828, learnt the pianoforte from Courländer and Goetze, composition from F. Vogel, and harmony from Prof. J. P. E. Hartmann.   In Sept. 1847 he went to Leipzig, and studied under Moscheles and Hauptmann, but on the outbreak of the Schleswig Holstein insurrection he enlisted as a volunteer in the Danish army, and took part in the campaign of 1848.   In 1851 he went to Vienna, and studied counterpoint under Sechter until 1853, when he returned to Copenhagen, visiting Paris on his way.   Among his pupils at this time were our own Queen Alexandra, her sister, the Empress of Russia, and the Landgrave Frederick William of Hesse Cassel.   In 1864 Herr Siboni was appointed organist and professor of music at the Royal Academy of Music of Sorö, in Seeland, a post he resigned on account of health in 1883 ; he returned to Copenhagen and died there Feb. 22, 1892.   The following are his chief compositions :—

1. PUBLISHED.

Three Impromptus for PF. for 4 hands (op. 1); Organ Preludes; Quartet for PF. and Strings (op. 10); Tragic Overture in C minor (op. 14) ; Songs and PF. pieces.

2. UNPUBLISHED.

Two Danish operas—'Loreley,' in 1 act ; 'Carl den Andens Flugt,' in 3 acts (Libretto on subject from English History by Professor Thomas Overskou), successfully performed at the Royal Theatre of Copenhagen in 1861 ; Psalm cxi. for Bass Solo, Chorus, and Orchestra ; 'Stabat Mater,' for Soli, Chorus, Orchestra, and Organ ; Cantata, 'The Battle of Murten,' for Soli, Male Chorus, and Orchestra ; 'The Assault of Copenhagen,' Cantata for Soli, Chorus, and Orchestra ; two Symphonies ; Concert Overture ; PF. Concerto ; String Quartets ; PF. Trio ; Duet for 2 PFs., Sonatas for PF. and Violin, and PF. and Violoncello, etc., many of them performed at concerts in Copenhagen.

[1] Fétis gives his birthplace as Bologna, and the date as 1782, but the above details are from autobiographical notes supplied by his son.

SICILIANA, SICILIANO, SICILIENNE, a dance rhythm closely allied to the Pastorale. The name is derived from a dance-song popular in Sicily, analogous to the Tuscan Rispetti.[1] Walther (*Lexicon*, 1732) classes these compositions as canzonettas, dividing them into Neapolitan and Sicilian, the latter being like jigs, written in rondo form, in 12–8 or 6–8 time. The Siciliana was sometimes used for the slow movement of Suites and Sonatas (as in Bach's Violin Sonata in G minor), but is of more frequent occurrence in vocal music, in which Handel, following the great Italian masters, made great use of it. Amongst later composers, Meyerbeer has applied the name to the movement 'O fortune, à ton caprice' in the finale to Act I. of 'Robert le Diable,' although it has little in common with the older examples. The Siciliana is generally written in 6–8, but sometimes in 12–8 time, and is usually in a minor key. In the bar of six quavers, the first note is usually a dotted quaver, and the fourth a crotchet, followed by two semiquavers. The Siciliana is sometimes in one movement, but usually ends with a repetition of the first part. It should be played rather quickly, but not so fast as the Pastorale, care being taken not to drag the time and to avoid all strong accentuation, smoothness being an important characteristic of this species of composition.   W. B. S.

SICILIAN BRIDE, THE. A grand opera in four acts ; words translated by Bunn from St. Georges, music by Balfe. Produced at Drury Lane Theatre, March 6, 1852.   G.

SICILIAN MARINER'S HYMN. A hymn-tune at one time very much in vogue, chiefly in Nonconformist chapels. It appears to have been first published in England about 1794. Mr. James T. Lightwood, in *Hymn Tunes and their Stories*, mentions that it occurs in Rev. W. Tattersall's edition of Merrick's 'Psalms,' published in that year. Another copy of it, as 'The Prayer of the Sicilian Mariner,' is found in the fourth volume of Corri's 'Select Collection of the most admired Songs, Duetts, etc.,' *circa* 1794-95. Later ones are printed in Hyde's 'Collection,' 1798, and in Dr. Miller's 'Dr. Watt's Psalms and Hymns,' 1800. Most of the early copies are in three parts, set to a verse beginning—

O Sanctissima, O Purissima.

It appears to have at once become much in fashion in England and to have been soon seized upon for publication in hymnals, having words specially written to it to replace the original ones.   F. K.

SIDE-DRUM (*Caisse roulante*). See DRUM 3 ; MILITARY SOUNDS AND SIGNALS ; ROLL.

SIÉGE DE CORINTHE, LE. Lyric tragedy in three acts ; words by Soumet and Balocchi, music by Rossini. Produced at the Académie,

Oct. 9, 1826. It was an adaptation and extension of 'Maometto Secondo,' produced in 1820. The Andante of the overture, entitled 'Marche lugubre grecque,' is framed on a motif of eight bars, taken note for note from Marcello's 21st Psalm, but with a treatment by the side-drum (*Caisse roulante*), and other instruments, of which Marcello can never have dreamt.   G.

SIEGE OF ROCHELLE, THE. A grand original opera, in three acts ; words by Fitzball, music by Balfe. Produced at Drury Lane Theatre, Oct. 29, 1835.   G.

SIEGFRIED. The third drama of Wagner's Nibelungen tetralogy. See RING DES NIBELUNGEN.

SIFACE, GIOVANNI FRANCESCO GROSSI, DETTO. Too few details are known about the life of this artist, though all the accounts of him agree in representing him as one of the very greatest singers of his time. He was born at Pescia in Tuscany, about the middle of the 17th century, and is said to have been a pupil of Redi. If so, this must have been Tommaso Redi, who became chapel-master at Loretto towards the end of the 17th century, although, as he was Siface's contemporary, it seems improbable that he should have been his instructor. Siface was admitted into the Pope's chapel in April 1675. This disproves the date (1666) given by Fétis and others for his birth, as no boys sang then in the Sistine choir. He would seem at that time to have been already known by the *sobriquet* which has always distinguished him, and which he owed to his famous impersonation of Siface or Syphax in some opera, commonly said to be the 'Mitridate' of Scarlatti ; an unlikely supposition, for besides that Scarlatti's two operas of that name were not written till some forty years later, it is not easy to see what Syphax can have to do in a work on the subject of Mithridates. (See Dent's *Scarlatti*, p. 37.)

Siface's voice, an artificial soprano, was full and beautiful ; his style of singing broad, noble, and very expressive. Mancini extols his choir-singing as being remarkable for its excellence. In 1679 he was at Venice for the Carnival, acting with great success in the performances of Pallavicini's 'Nerone,' of which a description may be found in the *Mercure galant* of the same year. After this he came to England, and Hawkins mentions him as pre-eminent among all the foreign singers of that period. He was for a time attached to James II.'s chapel,[2] but soon returned to Italy. In the second part of Playford's collection, 'Musick's Handmaid' (1689), there is an air by Purcell, entitled 'Sefauchi's farewell,' which refers to Siface's departure from this country.

This great singer was robbed and murdered by his postilion, while travelling, some say from Genoa to Turin, others, from Bologna to Ferrara.

---

[1] For an account of these Sicilian songs see G. Pitrè, *Sui Canti Popolari Siciliani*, Palermo, 1868.

[2] Evelyn heard him there, Jan. 30, 1687, and on April 19 following at Pepys's house. He speaks of him in highly commendatory terms.

According to Hawkins this happened about the year 1699. He is referred to in Durfey's 'Fool's Preferment' (1688), Act I. Sc. i.   F. A. M.

SIGNA. Opera in two acts, libretto (founded on Ouida's story) by G. à Beckett, H. Rudall, and F. E. Weatherley ; Italian version by G. Mazzucato. Music by Frederic H. Cowen. Produced in the Italian version at the Teatro dal Verme, Milan, Nov. 12, 1893, in four acts, reduced to three, and ultimately to two. At Covent Garden, June 30, 1894.   M.

SIGNALS. The drum and bugle calls or 'sounds' of the army. [See vol. iii. p. 204 ff.]   G.

SIGNATURE. I. KEY - SIGNATURE (Fr. *Signes accidentales* ; Ger. *Vorzeichnung*, properly *reguläre Vorzeichnung*). The signs of chromatic alteration, sharps or flats, which are placed at the commencement of a composition, immediately after the clef, and which affect all notes of the same names as the degrees upon which they stand, unless their influence is in any case counteracted by a contrary sign.

The necessity for a signature arises from the fact that in modern music every major scale is an exact copy of the scale of C, and every minor scale a copy of A minor, so far as regards the intervals—tones and semitones—by which the degrees of the scale are separated. This uniformity can only be obtained, in the case of a major scale beginning on any other note than C, by the use of certain sharps or flats ; and instead of marking these sharps or flats, which are constantly required, on each recurrence of the notes which require them, after the manner of ACCIDENTALS, they are indicated once for all at the beginning of the composition (or, as is customary, at the beginning of every line), for greater convenience of reading. The signature thus shows the key in which the piece is written, for since all those notes which have no sign in the signature are understood to be naturals (naturals not being used in the signature), the whole scale may readily be inferred from the sharps or flats which are present, while if there is no signature the scale is that of C, which consists of naturals only. [See KEY.] The following is a table of the signatures of major scales.

Key of   G   D   A   E   B   F sharp   C sharp.

Flat Signatures.

Key of   F   B flat   E flat   A flat   D flat   G flat   C flat.

The order in which the signs are placed in the signature is always that in which they have been successively introduced in the regular formation of scales with more sharps or flats out of those with fewer or none. This will be seen

in the above table, where F♯, which was the only sharp required to form the scale of G, remains the first sharp in all the signatures, C♯ being the second throughout, and so on, and the same rule is followed with the flats. The last sharp or flat of any signature is therefore the one which distinguishes it from all scales with fewer signs, and on this account it is known as the *essential note* of the scale. If a sharp, it is on the seventh degree of the scale ; if a flat, on the fourth. In the present day the place of the signature is marked only once on the stave ; but in the 18th century it was usual to mark it as often as it appeared, so that the keys of B flat and E flat were written thus :—

The signature of the minor scale is the same as that of its relative major, but the sharp seventh—which, though sometimes subject to alteration for reasons due to the construction of melody, is an essential note of the scale—is not included in the signature, but is marked as an accidental when required. The reason of this is that if it were placed there it would interfere with the regular order of sharps or flats, and the appearance of the signature would become so anomalous as to give rise to possible misunderstanding, as will be seen from the following example, where the signature of A minor (*a*) might easily be mistaken for that of G major misprinted, and that of F minor (*b*) for E♭ major. [E. J. Loder tried the odd-looking experiment of indicating the flat sixth and the sharp seventh in the key signature, as at (*c*) in his 'Moonlight on the Lake.']

In former times many composers were accustomed to dispense with the last sharp or flat of the signature, both in major and minor keys, and to mark it as an accidental (like the sharp seventh of the minor scale) wherever required, possibly in order to call attention to its importance as an essential note of the scale, or more probably on account of the influence of the ecclesiastical modes. Thus Handel rarely wrote F minor with more than three flats, the D♭ being marked as an accidental as well as the E♭ (see 'And with His stripes' from 'Messiah') ; and a duet 'Joys in gentle train appearing' ('Athalia'), which is in reality in E major, has but three sharps. Similar instances may be found in the works of Corelli, Geminiani, and others.

When in the course of a composition the key changes for any considerable period of time, it is frequently convenient to change the signature, in order to avoid the use of many accidentals. In affecting this change, such sharps or flats as are no longer required are cancelled by naturals, and this is the only case in which naturals are employed in the signature. (See AUFLÖSUNGS-ZEICHEN.)

In such a case the modulation must be into a sufficiently distant key; modulations into nearly related keys, as, for instance, into the dominant, in the case of the second subject of a sonata, never require a change of signature, however long the new key may continue. Otherwise, there is no limit to the frequency or extent of such changes, provided the reading is facilitated thereby.   **F. T.**

II. TIME-SIGNATURE (Lat. *Signum Modi, vel Temporis, vel Prolationis*; Germ. *Taktzeichen*). A sign placed after the clef and the sharps or flats which determine the signature of the key, in order to give notice of the rhythm in which a composition is written.

Our present Time-Signatures are directly descended from forms invented in the Middle Ages. Mediæval composers used the Circle to denote Perfect (or, as we should now say, Triple) Rhythm; and the Semicircle for Imperfect or Duple forms. The signatures used to distinguish the Greater and Lesser Moods[1] Perfect or Imperfect—*Signa Modi*, Modal Signs—were usually *preceded* by a group of rests,[2] showing the number of Longs to which a Large was equal in the Greater Mood, and the number of Breves which equalled the Long in the Lesser one—that is to say, three for the Perfect forms, and two for the Imperfect. Sometimes these rests were figured once only; sometimes they were twice repeated. The following forms were most commonly used :—

Greater Mood Perfect.

Greater Mood Imperfect.

Lesser Mood Perfect.

Lesser Mood Imperfect.

Combinations of the Greater and Lesser Moods, when both were Perfect, were indicated by a Point of Perfection, placed in the centre of the Circle, as at (*a*) in the following example. When the Greater Mood was Perfect, and the Lesser Imperfect, the Point was omitted, as at (*b*). When both Moods were Imperfect, or the Greater Imperfect, and the Lesser Perfect, the difference was indicated by the groups of Rests, as at (*c*) and (*d*).

(*a*) Both Moods Perfect.   (*b*) Greater Mood Perfect, and Lesser Imperfect.

(*c*) Both Moods Imperfect.   (*d*) Greater Mood Imperfect, and Lesser Perfect.

The Circle and the Semicircle were also used either alone or in combination with the figures 3 or 2, as signatures of time, in the limited sense in which that term was used in the Middle Ages; *i.e.* as applied to the proportions existing between the Breve and the Semibreve only—three to one Imperfect, and two to one in Imperfect forms.

Perfect Time.

Imperfect Time.

The same signs were used to indicate the proportion between the Semibreve and the Minim, in the Greater and Lesser Prolation;[3] but generally with a bar drawn perpendicularly through the Circle or Semicircle, to indicate that the beats were to be represented by minims; and sometimes, in the case of the Greater Prolation, with the addition of a Point of Perfection.

The Greater Prolation.

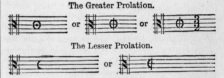

The Lesser Prolation.

Combinations of Mood, Time, and Prolation sometimes give rise to very complicated forms, which varied so much at different epochs, that even Ornithoparcus, writing in 1517, complains of the difficulty of understanding them.[4] Some writers used two Circles or Semicircles, one within the other, with or without a Point of Perfection in the centre of the smaller one. The inversion of the Semicircle (Ɔ) always denoted a diminution in the value of the beats, to the extent of one-half; but it was only at a comparatively late period that the doubled figure (CƆ) indicated an analogous change in the opposite direction. Again, the barred Circle or Semicircle always indicated minim beats; but the unbarred forms, while indicating semibreves in Mood and Time, were used by the Madrigal writers to indicate crotchet beats in Prolation.

The application of these principles to modern time-signatures is exceedingly simple, and may be explained in a very few words. At present we use the unbarred Semicircle to indicate four crotchet beats in a bar; the barred Semicircle to indicate four minim beats, in the Time called *Alla breve*, and two minim beats in *Alla Cappella*. Some German writers once used the doubled Semicircle, barred ($\bigcirc\!\!\!|$) for *Alla breve*—which they called the *Grosse Allabrevetakt*, and the ordinary single form, barred, for Alla Cappella—*Kleine Allabrevetakt* ; but this distinction has long since fallen into disuse.

The Circle is no longer used ; all other forms of rhythm than those already mentioned being distinguished by fractions, the denominators of which refer to the aliquot parts of a semibreve, and the numerators, to the number of them contained in a bar, as $\frac{2}{4}$ ($=\!\diamond$), $\frac{3}{2}$ ($=\!\diamond$), etc. And even in this we only follow the mediæval custom, which used the fraction $\frac{3}{2}$ to denote Triple Time, with three minims in a bar, exactly as we denote it at the present day.

A complete list of all the fractions now used as time-signatures will be found in the article TIME, together with a detailed explanation of the peculiarities of each.   · W. S. R.

SIGURD. Opera in five acts ; text by Dulocle and A. Blau, music by Ernest Reyer. Produced at Brussels, Jan. 7, 1884 ; at Covent Garden, July 15 of the same year, and at the Grand Opéra, Paris, June 12, 1885.

SILAS, ÉDOUARD, pianist and composer, was born at Amsterdam, August 22, 1827. His first teacher was Neher, one of the Court orchestra at Mannheim. He first appeared in public at Amsterdam in 1837 ; he studied the piano in 1839 with Lacombe, and in 1842 he was placed under Kalkbrenner at Paris, and soon afterwards entered the Conservatoire under Benoist for the organ and Halévy for composition, and in 1849 obtained the first prize for the former. In 1850 he came to England ; played first at Liverpool, and made his first appearance in London at the Musical Union, May 21. From that date Mr. Silas was established in London as teacher, and as organist of the Catholic Chapel at Kingston-on-Thames. His oratorio 'Joash' (words compiled by G. Linley) was produced at the Norwich Festival of 1863. A Symphony in A (op. 19) was produced by the Musical Society of London, April 22, 1863 ; repeated at the Crystal Palace, Feb. 20, 1864 ; and afterwards published. A Concerto for PF. and orchestra in D minor is also published. A Fantasia and an Élégie, both for PF. and orchestra, were given at the Crystal Palace in 1865 and 1873. Three Mythological Pieces for orchestra were played at a Philharmonic Concert in 1888. In 1866 he received the prize of the Belgian competition for sacred music for his Mass for four voices and organ.

Mr. Silas is the author of a Treatise on Musical Notation, and an Essay on a new method of Harmony—both unpublished. He has still

in MS. an English opera, 'Nitocris' ; overture and incidental music to 'Fanchette' ; a musical comedietta, 'Love's Dilemma' ; a Cantata ; an 'Ave Verum' ; two 'O Salutaris'; a Symphony in C major ; and other compositions. The list of his published instrumental works is very large, and includes many PF. pieces, among which the best known are Gavotte in E minor, Bourrée in G minor, 'Malvina' (romance), Suite in A minor, op. 103, Six Duets, etc. etc.

Mr. Silas was for many years a teacher of harmony at the Guildhall School of Music and the London Academy of Music.   G.

SILBERMANN. A family of organ-builders, clavichord and pianoforte makers, of Saxon origin, of whom the most renowned were Andreas, who built the Strasburg Cathedral organ, and Gottfried, who built the organs of Freiberg and Dresden, and was the first to construct the pianoforte in Germany. Authorities differ as to whether Andreas and Gottfried were brothers, or uncle and nephew. Following Gerber's *Lexicon* they were sons of Michael Silbermann, a carpenter at Kleinbobritzsch, near Frauenstein in Saxony, where ANDREAS was born May 16, 1678. He was brought up to his father's craft, and travelled, according to the custom of the country, in 1700. He learnt organ-building, and in 1703 we find him settled in that vocation at Strasburg. According to Hopkins and Rimbault [1] he built the Strasburg organ—his greatest work of 29 recorded by them—in 1714-16. He had nine sons, of whom three were organ-builders, and after the father's death, March 16, 1734, carried on the business in common. Of the three, Johann Andreas, the eldest (born June 26, 1712, died Feb. 11, 1783), built the Predigerkirche organ at Strasburg and that of the Abbey of St. Blaise in the Black Forest. In all he built fifty-four organs, in addition to writing a history of the city of Strasburg, published 1775. His son, Johann Josias (died June 3, 1786), was a musical instrument maker. The next son of Andreas, Johann Daniel, born March 31, 1717, died May 6, 1766, in Leipzig, was employed by his uncle Gottfried, and was intrusted after his uncle's death with the completion of the famous organ (in the Hofkirche) in Dresden. Mooser,[2] however, who claims to follow good authorities, attributes the completion of this instrument to Zacharias Hildebrand. Be this as it may, Johann Daniel remained at Dresden, a keyed-instrument maker, and constructor of ingenious barrel-organs. A composition of his is preserved in Marpurg's 'Raccolta' (1757). Johann Heinrich, the youngest son of Andreas, born Sept. 24, 1727, died at Strasburg, Jan. 15, 1799. His pianofortes were well known in Paris ; he made them with organ pedals, and constructed a harpsichord of which the longest strings were of

---

[1] *The Organ, its History and Construction,* London, 1870.
[2] *Gottfried Silbermann.* Langensalza, 1857.

what may be called the natural length, 16 feet!
[The above dates are from Riemann's *Lexikon*.]
But the greatest of the Silbermann family
was GOTTFRIED, who was born in the little
village of Kleinbobritzsch, near Frauenstein, in
1683 (according to Mooser on Jan. 14). He
was at first placed with a bookbinder, but soon
quitted him and went to Andreas at Strasburg.
Having got into trouble by the attempted
abduction of a nun, he had to quit that city in
1707 and go back to Frauenstein, where he built
his first organ (afterwards destroyed by fire, the
fate of several of his instruments). He appears
to have settled at Freiberg in 1709, and
remained there for some years. [He built the
cathedral organ there in 1714.] He built, in
all, forty-seven organs in Saxony.[1] He never
married, and was overtaken by death August 4,
1753, while engaged upon his finest work, the
Dresden Court organ. Although receiving what
we should call very low prices for his organs,
by living a frugal life he became comparatively
rich, and his talent and exceptional force of
character enabled him to achieve an eminent
position. His clavichords were as celebrated as
his organs. Emanuel Bach had one of them for
nearly half a century, and the instrument, many
years after it was made, when heard under the
hands of that gifted and sympathetic player,
excited the admiration of Burney. It cannot be
doubted that he was the first German who made
a pianoforte. He was already settled in Dresden
in 1725, when König translated into German
Scipione Maffei's account of the invention of the
pianoforte at Florence by Cristofori. This fact
has been already mentioned [PIANOFORTE, vol.
iii. pp. 719-20,] and we now add some further
particulars gained by personal search and in-
spection at Potsdam in 1881. We know from
Agricola, one of J. S. Bach's pupils, that in
1736 Gottfried Silbermann submitted two pianofortes of his make to that great master. Bach
finding much fault with them, Gottfried was
annoyed, and for some time desisted from further
experiments in that direction. It is possible
that the intercourse between Dresden and
Northern Italy enabled him, either then or
later, to see a Florentine pianoforte. It is
certain that three grand pianofortes made by
him and acquired by Frederick the Great[2] for
Potsdam—where they still remain in the music-
rooms of the Stadtschloss, Sans Souci, and Neues
Palais,[3] inhabited by that monarch—are, with
unimportant differences, repetitions of the
Cristofori pianofortes existing at Florence.

[1] Five of 3 manuals, Freiberg, Zittau, and Frauenstein; the Frauenkirche and Katholische Hofkirche at Dresden; twenty-four of 2 manuals; fifteen of 1 manual with pedals, and three of 1 manual without pedals. (Mooser, p. 125.)
[2] Probably in 1746. The peace of Dresden was signed by Frederick, Christmas Day, 1745; he would have time after that event to inspect Silbermann's pianofortes.
[3] The Silbermann piano Burney mentions was that of the Neues Palais. He must have heard the one at Sans Souci, although he does not say so. In all probability the piano J. S. Bach played upon specially, on the occasion of his visit to Frederick the Great, was the one still in the Stadtschloss, the town palace of Potsdam.

Frederick is said to have acquired more than
three, but no others are now to be found. Burney's
depreciation of the work of Germans in their
own country finds no support in the admirable
work of Gottfried Silbermann in these pianofortes. If its durability needed other testimony,
we might refer to one of his pianofortes which
Zelter met with at Weimar in 1804, and praised
to Goethe; and to another spoken of by Mooser
in 1857 as having been up to a then recent date
used at the meetings of the Freemasons' Lodge
at Freiberg. Gottfried Silbermann invented the
CEMBAL D' AMORE, a kind of double clavichord. [It is described in Mr. Hipkins's
History of the Piano, p. 65.]   A. J. H.

SILCHER, FRIEDRICH, well-known composer
of Lieder, born June 27, 1789, at Schnaith,
near Schorndorf in Würtemberg, was taught
music by his father, and by Auberlen, organist
at Fellbach near Stuttgart. He was educated
for a schoolmaster, and his first post was at
Ludwigsburg, where he began to compose. In
1815 he took a conductorship at Stuttgart, and
composed a cantata, which procured him, in
1817, the post of conductor to the University
of Tübingen. This he held till 1860, when he
retired, and died shortly after (August 26) at
Tübingen. The honorary degree of Doctor had
been conferred upon him by the University in
1852. His most important publications are—
'Sechs vierstimmige Hymnen' (Laupp), 'Drei-
stimmiges würtemb. Choralbuch' (*Ibid.*), and
'Swabian, Thuringian, and Franconian Volkslieder' (12 parts), many of which are his own
compositions. Several of Silcher's melodies published in his 'Sammlung deutscher Volkslieder,'
etc., have become true songs of the people, such
as 'Aennchen von Tharau,' 'Morgen muss ich
fort von hier,' 'Ich weiss nicht was soll es
bedeuten,' 'Zu Strassburg auf der Schanz,' etc.
The Lieder were published simultaneously for
one and two voices, with PF. and for four men's
voices. He edited a method for harmony and
composition in 1851. A biographical sketch of
Silcher by Köstlin appeared in 1877.   F. G.

SILOTI, ALEXANDER, born Oct. 10, 1863, on
his father's estate near Charkow in Southern
Russia, a remarkable pianist, and one of the most
eminent of Liszt's pupils. He studied at the
Moscow Conservatorium from 1875 to 1881 under
Swerew, Nicolas Rubinstein, Tchaikovsky, and
Hubert, and from 1883 to 1886 with Liszt. Since
1883, when he appeared at Leipzig at a Concert
of the Tonkünstlerversammlung, he has been
regarded as one of the leading Russian pianists,
but he had already appeared with success in
Moscow in 1880. From that year till 1890 he
was Professor at the Moscow Conservatorium;
then he sojourned for several years out of his
own country in such places as Frankfort-on-the-
Main, Antwerp, and Leipzig, conducted the
Moscow Philharmonic concerts in 1901-2, and
since 1903 has figured largely as a conductor

in St. Petersburg, and other great Russian
cities.   H. V. H.

SILVA, ANDREAS DE, was a singer in the
Papal Chapel, 1519, and the first to be described
as Papal composer (Haberl, *Bausteine*, iii. p.
69). In 1522 he appears to have been in the
chapel of the Duke of Mantua. It is natural
to identify him with Andreas Sylvanus, from
whom Glarean quotes the Kyrie and Osanna of
a very peculiar mass for three voices, 'Malheur
me bat,' also with the Andreas Silvanus, to whom
Sebastian Virdung refers as the intimate friend
for whom he wrote his *Musica Getutscht*, 1511.
But Eitner, in the *Quellen-Lexikon* and *Monatshefte*, xxvi. p. 47, refuses to accept this identification, because he thinks Virdung's friend must
have been a German ; and if de Silva had been
a German it is unlikely that his works would
have found their way into French collections
like those of Attaingnant, or Italian collections
like those of Gardane and Petrucci. This
reasoning, however, is not very convincing, all
the less that Eitner himself assumes that the
Sylvanus who is the author of the mass 'Malheur
me bat' is identical with the Silvanus the
friend of Virdung. In any case the Sylvanus
of the mass 'Malheur me bat' is more likely to
have been a Netherlander than a German, and
to be identical with de Silva than with the
Silvanus of Virdung. That de Silva was known
in Germany appears from the reception of an
Italian madrigal by him, 'Che sentisti Madonna,'
in Ott's 'Liederbuch,' 1544, attributed to him
in all the four part-books. This madrigal has
a surprising degree of expressiveness for the
time at which it must be supposed to have been
written. Besides the works of Silva in the
collections of the time, there are two masses
and seven motets by him in the Archives of the
Papal Chapel. One of the motets, 'Illumina
oculos meos, *a* 6,' deserves notice, as being that
on which Palestrina based one of his more important masses *a* 6, bearing the same title.
Among other MS. motets of Silva enumerated
in the *Quellen-Lexikon*, there are two mentioned
together, 'Virtute magna' and 'O Regem
coeli,' both *a* 4. Possibly the theme of the two
four-part masses of Palestrina in his first book,
1554, may be taken from these motets.   J. R. M.

SILVANA : also called 'Silvana das Waldmädchen,' or 'das stumme Waldmädchen'—the
dumb Wood-maiden. A romantic opera in three
acts ; words by F. K. Hiemer, music by Weber ;
his sixth dramatic work, completed Feb. 23,
1810 ; produced at Frankfort, Sept. 16, 1810.
It is probably founded to some extent on his
early opera 'Das Waldmädchen' (1800), which
was afterwards burnt ; and was to a small extent
employed in 'Abu Hassan' and 'Freischütz.'
The overture was used by Weber as the prelude
to his music for the wedding of Prince John of
Saxony ; and he wrote seven variations for
clarinet and PF., for H. Bärmann, on an air

from it, 'Warum musst' ich.' It was produced
in English (as 'Sylvana ') at the Surrey Theatre,
under Elliston's management, Sept. 2, 1828. It
was again revived, with a revised libretto by Herr
Pasqué, and with 'musical amplifications,' at
Hamburg and Lübeck in the spring of 1885.   G.

SILVANI, GROSEFFO ANTONIO, born at
Bologna late in the 17th century, was maestro
di cappella at S. Stefano from 1702 to 1725.
He inherited the publishing business of Marino
Silvani, who may have been his father, and who
issued several important collections of motets,
etc. Gioseffo died before 1727. His published
works are as follows :—

Op.
1. Litanie concertate a 4 voci. 1702.
2. Inni Sacri per tutto l'anno a voce sola. 1702.
3. Sacri Responsorii per . . . la settimana santa, a 4 voci. 1704.
4. Inni sacri per tutto l'anno a 4 voci. 1705.
5. Cantate morali e spirituali a 1, 2, 3 voci. 1707.
6. Stabat mater, Benedictus, Miserere, etc., a 8 voci. 1708.
7. Messe brevi concertate, a 4 voci. 1711.
8. Motetti a 8 voci. 1711.
9. Motetti con le quatro Antifone a voce sola. 1713.
10. Motetti a 2 e 3 voci. 1716.
11. Messe brevi a 4 voci. 1720.
12. Versi della turba, etc., a 4 voci. 1724.
13. Sacre Lamentazioni a voce sola. 1725.
14. Litanie della B.V. a 4 voci concertate. 1725.

All these have accompaniments (some *ad
libitum*) for strings or organ. (*Quellen - Lexikon*.)   M.

SIMAO. [See PORTUGAL, vol. iii. p. 797*a*.]

SIMILI, 'like'; a word commonly used in a
series of passages or figures of similar form, to
be performed in exactly the same way. After
the first few bars of such passages or figures the
word *simili* is used to save trouble of copying
the marks of expression and force at every
recurrence of the figure. 'Simili marks' occur

generally in MS. or old printed music, and
signify that the contents of the previous bar
are to be repeated in every consecutive succeeding
bar in which the marks occur.   M.

SIMON, ANTON YULIEVICH, composer, born
in France in 1851, received his musical education at the Paris Conservatoire and migrated
to Moscow in 1871, where he became conductor
to the Théâtre Bouffe. He was appointed professor of the pianoforte to the school of the
Philharmonic Society, in 1891, and a year or
two later was made superintendent of the
orchestras of the Imperial Theatres in Moscow,
and musical director of the Alexandrovsky
Institute. Simon is a voluminous composer,
the list of his works being as follows.

A. OPERATIC.

'Rolla ' (op. 40, Moscow, 1892) ; 'The Song of Love Triumphant'
(op. 46, libretto from Tourgeniev by N. Wilde, Moscow, 1899) ; 'The
Fishers ' (op. 51, libretto from VictorHugo by N. Wilde, Moscow, 1900) ;
'The Stars' (ballet in 5 acts, Moscow, 1902) ; 'Living Flowers' (op.
58, ballet in 1 act) ; 'Esmeralda' (mimo-drama in 4 acts, Moscow,
1902).

B. ORCHESTRAL.

Overture (op. 13) : Suite (op. 29) ; 'Danse Bayadère' (op. 34) ;
Overture—Fantasia on Malo-Russian themes (op. 35) ; Symphonic
poems: 'The Midnight Review' and 'La Pécheresse' (opp. 36 and
44) ; Triumphal Overture on 3 Russian themes, composed for the
unveiling of the monument to Alexander II., Moscow (op. 54).

C. INSTRUMENTAL AND CHAMBER MUSIC.

Pianoforte concerto (op. 19); clarinet concerto (op. 30); fantasia for violoncello (op. 42); two pianoforte trios (opp. 16 and 25); string quartet (op. 24); quartet for 2 cornets-à-piston and alto and tenor trombones (op. 23); 22 ensemble pieces for wind instruments (op. 26); 4 septets; 4 sextets, 6 quintets; 8 quartets.
A considerable number of pieces for one and two pianos; pieces for violin and pianoforte, including the popular 'Berceuse' (op. 28); a Mass (op. 22); three female choruses (op. 33) and upwards of 80 songs.   R. N.

SIMONE BOCCANEGRA. An opera in three acts, with prologue; libretto by Piave, music by Verdi. Produced at the Fenice Theatre, Venice, March 12, 1857; remodelled and rescored, with a fresh libretto by Boito, and reproduced at La Scala, Milan, March 24, 1881.   G.

SIMONETTI, ACHILLE, violinist and composer, was born at Turin, June 12, 1859. In early youth he studied the violin under Signor Gamba, and composition under Maestro Pedrotti, late Principal of Rossini's Conservatorio in Pesaro. Later, proceeding to Genoa, he placed himself into the hands of Camillo Sivori, who took great interest in him, and whose clear-cut style and Italian temperament are reflected in his playing. After some successful appearances in Marseilles and Lyons he went to Paris to receive further tuition from Charles Dancla (violin), and Massenet (counterpoint), passed four winters at Nice, and then visited England to fulfil an engagement to tour with the Marie Roze Company and B. Schönberger the pianist. His present headquarters are in London, where he is frequently heard as soloist and member of the so-called 'London Trio' (Simonetti, Amina Goodwin, and W. E. Whitehouse), whilst he occasionally visits Vienna and other continental cities. Besides a series of graceful solos for the violin, which have achieved considerable popularity, he has written two sonatas for violin and pianoforte and two string quartets. He plays on a Carlo Bergonzi violin.   w. w. c.

SIMOUTRE, NICOLAS EUGÈNE, a French violin-maker, the patentee of certain inventions by which he claims to improve the tone of violins and instruments of that class—either of defective or feeble *timbre*. The son of a *luthier*, he was born at Mirecourt, April 19, 1839, and was first the pupil of his father, then of Darche in Paris, and lastly of Roth in Strasburg. He began work as an independent maker at Basle in 1859, and there published in 1883 his *brochure* entitled *Aux Amateurs du Violon*. In 1886 a second *brochure—Un Progrès en Lutherie* appeared, a German edition being published at the same time entitled *Ein Fortschritt in der Geigenbaukunst* (Rixheim, 1886, 2nd edition, 1887). In 1889 he brought out a small 'Supplément' to the above pamphlets. The two last-named works deal mainly with his inventions. The principal of these, called 'Le Support Harmonique,' was based upon Savart's scientific discovery that the belly of a violin vibrates unequally. Testing the nodal lines formed by sand distributed upon the belly of

a violin when in vibration, Mons. Simoutre observed that the fibres of the wood vibrated in alternate sections, *i.e.* one and three vibrated in unison, likewise two and four, and that the vibrations of one and two were as much in opposition to one another, as were three and four. Starting from this point, he applied himself to the discovery of a system which should stop the vibrations of alternate fibre sections so as to allow the rest to vibrate in unison, and this he claims to do with his patent 'Support Harmonique.' Briefly, this invention consists in glueing two small sections of wood—variable in form and dimensions according to the effect required—upon the centre of the belly and back of the violin transversely. This method, he considered, concentrated the vibrations near the sound-post—where they are most numerous—and by so doing, increased the sonority of the instrument so furnished, and at the same time prevented the belly from sinking under the pressure of the bridge. Various experiments for ascertaining the best thickness and forms of the 'Support Harmonique' resulted in the discovery that an innovation in the form of the bass bar was necessary where the new system was employed. A semi-detached bar slightly scooped out at the centre, and glued only at each end to the belly of the violin, was patented by Mons. Simoutre, that form proving most efficacious where the violin was free from cracks, etc. A third patent applies to the setting of the sound-post in one of the two small circular grooves made for it in the lower 'Support Harmonique.' In 1890 this maker settled in Paris at 38 Rue de l'Echicquier, where he worked for many years in partnership with his son. — Von Lutgendorff, *Die Geigen und Lautenmacher*, and Mons. Simoutre's works already mentioned.   E. H-A.

SIMPLIFICATION SYSTEM (Organ). This refers to a method formerly in use of planting all the pipes of an organ in semitonal or chromatic order, to simplify the mechanism, but now discontinued for various reasons. (See VOGLER.)   T. E.

SIMPSON, CHRISTOPHER, a distinguished 17th century viola-da-gamba player, famous in his day both as an executant and a theoretic musician. Very little is known of his life, and the exact date of his birth remains problematical, but the few facts that have come to light reveal him to have been the son of a Yorkshire yeoman—a descendant of some Nottinghamshire Simpsons, who spelt their name with a *y* (*vide* Harl. MS. 5800)—a man commended by his fellows for his upright habits, and a staunch upholder of the Cavalier Party against the Parliament. He joined the Royalist army under the command of William Cavendish, Duke of Newcastle, in 1643. He alludes in a passing phrase to the hardships and poverty he endured at this period in his

'Introduction' to the second edition of his *Division Viol*, 1667, when he thanks his patron —Sir Robert Bolles—for the 'Cheerful Maintenance' he had afforded him. This Sir Robert Bolles and his family were all fervent Royalists and ardent patrons of music, and at the end of the civil war Christopher Simpson enjoyed their hospitality at their residence, Scampton, Lincolnshire. To him was assigned the musical tuition of Sir Robert's son and heir, John Bolles and a certain Sir John Barber, and in this congenial musical atmosphere Simpson began to write his valuable book of instructions for the gamba, which he called *The Division Viol*. The excellence of this work is confirmed by Sir Roger L'Estrange, himself a distinguished gamba-player, who remarks in the preface to the second Edition that 'it is not only the *Best* but the *only Treatise* I find extant upon this argument.' Simpson's pupil, John Bolles, attained a high degree of perfection as a viol-da-gamba player, and a laudatory 'Ode' addressed to him while in Rome is inserted by Simpson, with pardonable pride, in the second edition of his *Division Viol*. On assuming the title at the death of his father John Bolles showed his regard for his old master by continuing the patronage which had previously been extended him by Sir Robert. This was fortunate; as was also the fact that Simpson's publications brought him in a good income, for Sir R. Bolles, whose will he witnessed, left him only the sum of £5. Before that event came to pass the eminent gambist had purchased a house and farm—'Hunt-house'—near Pickering, in Yorkshire, and settled this property, by deed, upon his nephew Christopher, the son of Stephen Simpson. According to evidence gained from Simpson's will, he died in the year 1669, between the 5th May and the 29th July. Apparently his demise took place at one of Sir John Bolles's residences, for although Hawkins (*Hist. Mus.*) states that he died at Turnstile, Holborn, where he had lived for many years, his contemporary Anthony à Wood records 'Anno 1669, Mr. Christopher Sympson, a famous musitian, died at Sir John Bolles house, whether in Lyncolnshire or London I know not.' Although nothing is definitely known as to whether Simpson married or not, it may be assumed, from his leaving all his property to his nephew, and all his 'musick-books or whatsoever is of that concernment,' to Sir John Bolles, that he was not.

Simpson's skill was greatly respected by his contemporaries, and musicians such as Lock, Salmon, Mace, and Sir Roger L'Estrange have shown their esteem by their various complimentary allusions to him. He lived in an age when the gamba was much cultivated, both by professionals and amateurs; but besides being the best authority on that instrument he was a composer of talent, and Mace (*Musick's Monu-*

ment, 1676) ranks him with William Lawes and John Jenkins as a composer of 'Fancies.' The Oxford Music School possesses a portrait of Simpson.

LIST OF PUBLISHED WORKS.

1. Annotations on Dr. Campion's *Art of Discant*, 1655. These remarks were introduced into the second edition of Playford's *Brief Introduction*, 1660, and in the other editions until 1684.

2. The Division Violist or an Introduction to the playing upon a ground: Divided into two parts. The first Directing the Hand with other Preparative Instructions. The second, Laying open the Manner and Method of playing Ex-tempore, or Composing division to a ground. To which are Added some Divisions made upon Grounds for the Practice of Learners, London, 1659. W. Godbid, for J. Playford. Fol. (with portrait). Dedicated to Sir Robert Bolles.

Second Edition with title and text in Latin and English thus:—Chelys minuritionum artificio exornata: sive Minuritiones ad Basin, etiam Extempore Modulandi Ratio. In tres partes distributa. The Division Viol or the Art of Playing Extempore upon a Ground. Divided into Three Parts. London, 1665. Fol. with portrait. A further supply of this second Edition was published by W. Godbid for Henry Brome at the Gun in Ivy Lane in 1667. Fol. with portrait by Faithorne engraved from a painting by G. Carwarden. Dedicated to Sir John Bolles.

Third edition published by Pearson, with portrait of Simpson engraved by Faithorne, appeared in 1712. With two Sonatas for the gamba.

3. The Principles of Practicle Musick. . . . either in singing or playing upon an instrument, London, 1665. Dedicated to Sir John Bache—A compendium of Practicall Musick in five parts teaching by a new and easie method. 1. The rudiments of Song. 2. The principles of composition. 3. The use of discords. 4. The form of Figurate Discant. 5. The contrivance of Canon. W. Godbid for H. Brome, 1667. Dedicated to William Cavendish, Duke of Newcastle. The first part of this, the *Rudiments of Song*, was reprinted in a revised form.

Third Edition. London, W. Godbid for Henry Brome, 1678.
Fourth Edition. London. W. Pearson for T. Cullen, 1706.
Fifth Edition. London, 1714.
Sixth Edition. London, 1722.
Seventh Edition. 1727.
Eighth Edition. 1732, W. Pearson.
Ninth Edition, with portrait.

In Playford's 'Catch that Catch can,' 1672-73, there is a composition of Simpson's, and Hawkins (*Hist. of Music*) mentions a 'Division on the Ground' for viola da gamba by Simpson of the year 1665.

In Thomas Campion's *Art of Setting or Composing of Music* there is a composition by Simpson for the viola da gamba.

MS. COMPOSITIONS.

A Series of Suites in Three parts (British Museum Add. MSS. 18,940, 18,944).

Months and Seasons, namely Fancies, Airs, Galliards for two Basses and a Treble (*Ib.* 31,436).

Consorts of Parts for two Basses and two Trebles with figured Bass. (Heidelberg, MS. 3193.)

Rules of Theory (British Museum, MS. 142).
Fancies for a viola da gamba (Christ Church, Oxford).
Fancies and Divisions (British Museum MS. 31,436 and Bodleian Library, Oxford).

Musgrave, in his *Obituary*, mentions a MS. (music) under the date 1666, by Christopher Simpson.

Hawkins, *Hist. Music* ; Burney, *Hist. Music* ; Mace, *Musick's Monument* ; Lock, *Observations* ; Hart, *The Violin and its Music* ; Wasielewski, *Die Violoncell* ; *Quellen-Lexikon* ; Fétis, *Biog. des Mus.* ; Simpson, *The Division Viol* ; Anthony à Wood, *Life*.   E. H-A.

SIMPSON, JOHN, a London music-publisher and instrument-seller of some note. As may be gathered from one of his early engraved labels, he had been employed by Mrs. Hare of Cornhill, the widow of Joseph Hare (see vol. ii. p. 295), but about 1734 he began business on his own account at the 'Viol and Flute' in Sweeting's Alley, a street running out of Cornhill, at the back part of the Royal Exchange. In Simpson's early business career this was named 'Swithen's Alley,' but in 1741 references to Simpson give this address, indifferently, with 'Sweeting's Alley.' He first published sheet songs, which he afterwards gathered into the two volumes as *Thesaurus Musicus* (*circa* 1745-47), and had probably bought the stock and plates of both Mrs. Hare and B. Cooke. He was in business connection with the proprietors of the 'Printing-house in Bow Church yard,' who were successors to Cluer (q.v.).

So far as can be ascertained he died about 1747.

Simpson's most notable publications are : 'Thesaurus Musicus,' in which 'God Save the King' probably first appeared ; Carey's 'Musical Century,' 1740 ; 'Calliope,' 1746 ; and much other music now of considerable antiquarian interest. He was succeeded by John Cox, who reissued from Simpson's plates.

At Cox's death, or retirement, Robert Bremner, Thorowgood, and the Thompson family became possessed of many of Simpson's plates, and republished some of his works. In 1770, and thirty years later, Simpson's premises were occupied by John and James Simpsin, apparently descendants, who were flute-makers, and, in a small way, music-publishers. Later than this (circa 1825) a John Simpson was manufacturer and teacher of the flute and flageolet at 266 Regent Street.   F. K.

SIMPSON, THOMAS, an English musician, who settled in Germany, and in 1610 was viola-player in the Elector Palatine's band ; in 1617-21 he was in the band of the Prince of Holstein Schaumburg. He was subsequently in the royal band at Copenhagen. He published the following works: 'Opusculum neuer Pauanen, Galliarden, Couranten vnd Volten,' Frankfort, 1610 ; 'Pauanen, Volten und Galliarden,' Frankfort, 1611 ; 'Opus Newer Paduanen, Galliarden, Intraden, . . . mit 5 Stim.,' Hamburg, 1617, and 'Taffel Consort allerhand lustige Lieder von 4 Instrumenten und General-bass,' Hamburg, 1621, containing, besides pieces by Simpson himself, some by Peter Phillips, John Dowland, Robert and Edward Johnson, and others.   W. H. H.

SIMROCK. A very famous German music-publishing house, founded in 1790 at Bonn by Nikolaus Simrock (1752-1834), second waldhorn player in the Elector's band, to which Beethoven and his father belonged. The first of Beethoven's works on which Simrock's name appears as original publisher is the Kreutzer Sonata, op. 47, issued in 1805. But he published for Beethoven an 'Edition très correcte' of the two Sonatas in G and D minor (op. 31, Nos. 1 and 2), which Nägeli had printed so shamefully ; and there is evidence in the letters that Simrock was concerned in others of Beethoven's early works. The next was the Sextet for strings and two horns, op. 81b (1810) ; then the two Sonatas for PF. and violoncello, op. 102 (1817) ; the ten themes with variations for PF. and violin or flute, op. 107 (1820). He was succeeded in 1834 by PETER JOSEPH SIMROCK, who died in 1868, and about 1870 his successor, FRIEDRICH SIMROCK, founded the Berlin house, and there published the principal works of Brahms. (Quellen-Lexikon.)   G.

SINCLAIR, GEORGE ROBERTSON, Mus. D., son of Robert Sharpe Sinclair, LL.D., Director of Public Instruction in India, was born at Croydon, Oct. 28, 1863, and was educated at St. Michael's College, Tenbury, and at the Royal Irish Academy of Music. He studied successively under Sir Frederick Gore Ouseley, Sir Robert Stewart, and Dr. C. H. Lloyd. In 1879 he became assistant organist of Gloucester Cathedral, and organist and choirmaster of St. Mary de Crypt, Gloucester ; in 1880, at the age of seventeen, he was appointed organist and choirmaster of Truro Cathedral. Since 1889 he has filled the post of organist of Hereford Cathedral with distinction, and his conducting of the Hereford (Three Choirs) Festivals from 1891 to 1906 brought him into contact with the most eminent English musicians of the time, and ripened his experience as a conductor, a capacity in which he has exhibited very remarkable powers, being in sympathy with every school of excellence, and being able to impress his own reading of the classical and other works upon all under his command. He is conductor of various Hereford and Herefordshire societies, both choral and orchestral, and as an organist he played at six successive Gloucester Festivals. In 1895 he was made an honorary member of the Royal Academy, having been L.R.A.M. since 1887 ; in 1899 he was appointed conductor of the Birmingham Festival Choral Society, and received the degree of Mus. D. from the Archbishop of Canterbury. In 1904 he was made an honorary fellow of the Royal College of Organists. (See Musical Times, 1906, pp. 168, ff.) He is also an ardent Freemason, a Past Grand Organist of England, a Past Master of the Palladian Lodge, No. 120, and Master of the 'Vaga' Lodge, No. 3146. His impetuous character, his skilful pedal-playing, the barking of his dog, and other things, are immortalised in the eleventh variation of Elgar's 'Enigma' set for orchestra.   M.

SINCLAIR, JOHN, born near Edinburgh, Dec. 9, 1791, was instructed in music from childhood, and while still young joined the band of a Scotch regiment as a clarinet player. He also taught singing in Aberdeen, and acquired sufficient means to purchase his discharge from the regiment. Possessed of a fine tenor voice, he was desirous of trying his fortune upon the stage, came to London and appeared anonymously as Capt. Cheerly in Shield's 'Lock and Key' at the Haymarket, Sept. 7, 1810. His success led to his becoming a pupil of Thomas Welsh. He was engaged at Covent Garden, where he appeared Sept. 30, 1811, as Don Carlos in Sheridan and Linley's 'Duenna.' He remained there for seven seasons, during which he had many original parts. He was the first singer of the long popular recitative and air 'The Pilgrim of Love' in Bishop's 'Noble Outlaw,' produced April 7, 1815. He also sang originally in Bishop's 'Guy Mannering' and 'The Slave,' and Davy's 'Rob Roy,' and acquired

2 g

great popularity by his performance of Apollo in 'Midas.' In April 1819 he visited Paris and studied under Pellegrini, and thence proceeded to Milan and placed himself under Banderali. In May 1821 he went to Naples, where he received advice and instruction from Rossini. In 1822 he sang, mostly in Rossini's operas, at Pisa and Bologna. In 1823 he was engaged at Venice, where Rossini wrote for him the part of Idreno in 'Semiramide.' After singing at Genoa he returned to England, and reappeared at Covent Garden, Nov. 19, 1823, as Prince Orlando in 'The Cabinet,' his voice and style having greatly improved. He continued at the theatre for a season or two ; in 1828 and 1829 was engaged at the Adelphi, and in 1829-30 at Drury Lane. He then visited America ; on his return retired from public life, and died at Margate, Sept. 23, 1857.   w. h. h.

SINDING, CHRISTIAN, born Jan. 11, 1856, at Kongberg in Norway ; became a student at Leipzig, and at Munich, and at Berlin. A very talented pianist, he has written much for his own instrument as well as for stringed instruments. His highest opus number is now (1907) 51. His principal works are the Rondo infinito for Orchestra, op. 42 ; Violin Concerto in A, op. 45 ; Piano Concerto in D flat, op. 6 ; Quintet in E minor, op. 5 ; Trio in D major, op. 23 ; Variations for two pianos, op. 2 ; Suite, op. 3 ; Studies, op. 7 ; Sonatas for Violin and Piano ; Suite for Violin and Piano, op. 14 ; Caprices, op. 44 ; Burlesques, op. 48 ; Six pieces, op. 49 ; besides many songs, and many arrangements of Folk-songs. Sinding's music is characterised by great facility in construction, tunefulness, variety, and elegance. He is always intelligent, and even if not deep is a very pleasing writer, who secures the interest of his auditor.   d. h.

SINFONIA. See SYMPHONY.

SINFONIA SACRA (SACRED SYMPHONY). A term used to describe certain short cantatas, in which an unusual closeness of musical connection is to be suggested, such as Parry's 'The love that casteth out fear,' and 'The Soul's Ransom,' Walford Davies's 'Lift up your Hearts,' and Stanford's 'Stabat Mater.'   m.

SINFONIE-CANTATE. The title of Mendelssohn's Lobgesang or Hymn of Praise (op. 52). The term—properly 'Symphonie-Cantate'—is due to Klingemann, according to Mendelssohn's own statement in his published letter of Nov. 18, 1840. Mendelssohn was so much in love with it as to propose to bestow it also on the 'Walpurgisnight' (see the same letter and that to his mother of Nov. 28, 1842). That intention was not, however, carried out.   G.

SINGAKADEMIE, THE, BERLIN, one of the most important art-institutions in Germany. Its founder was Carl Friedrich Christian Fasch, born 1736 and appointed in 1756 cembalist to Frederick the Great of Prussia, after whose death

he led a quiet and retired life in Berlin as music-teacher and composer. The Singakademie originated with some attempts made by Fasch and a few of his pupils and musical friends to perform his own sacred compositions for mixed voices. The actual Akademie was founded on Thursday, May 24, 1791, and up to the present time the weekly practices are still held on a Thursday. The original members were twenty-seven, thus distributed :—seven soprani, five alti, seven tenors, and eight basses. The Society was at first entirely private, the meetings taking place at the house of Frau Voitus (Unter den Linden, No. 59, afterwards Charlottenstrasse No. 61). This character it retained after the practices were held in a room at the Royal Academy of Arts, whence the name of the Society was suggested, and the use of which was granted to the Singakademie, Nov. 5, 1793. The first of the regular public performances took place at Easter, 1801. The proceeds were at first devoted to charitable objects, but after the Akademie had, in 1827, erected its own buildings, where the meetings are still held, and which contain a fine concert-room, it became necessary to have performances for the benefit of the institution, and these are still carried on. The object of the founder was to promote the practice of sacred music both accompanied and unaccompanied, but especially the latter. The Society at first confined itself to Fasch's compositions, singing, amongst others, his 16-part Mass a cappella, but in a short time pieces by Durante, Graun, Leo, Lotti, etc., were added. The first oratorio of Handel's put in rehearsal was 'Judas Maccabæus' (1795). The first performance of Bach's Matthew-Passion in 1829 is well known, and indeed marks an epoch, but the chief credit is due, not to the Singakademie, but to the conductor of the performance, Mendelssohn.

The Berlin Singakademie has served as a model for most of the vocal unions of Germany. Its structure is exceedingly simple, the governing body consisting of a director, who has charge of all musical matters, and a committee of members (ladies as well as gentlemen) who manage the business. All of these are elected at general meetings. Since 1815 the director has had a fixed salary out of the funds of the Society. New members are admitted by the director and the committee. There is a special practice on Wednesdays for less advanced members, who must attain a certain amount of proficiency at this, before being allowed to join the main body. The numbers rose in 1788 to 114, in 1813 to 301, in 1827 to 436, and in 1841 to 618.

Fasch died in 1800, and was succeeded in the directorship by his pupil Carl Friedrich Zelter. An attempt to bring in Mendelssohn having failed, Zelter was succeeded by Carl Friedrich Rungenhagen (1832 to 1851) and he by Eduard

August Grell, who relinquished the directorship in 1876, on account of his advanced age, but retained a seat and vote in the committee, with the title of honorary director. Martin Blumner, the next conductor, was born in 1827, and appointed in 1876 ; [he wrote a history of the Society, which was published in 1891, and shortly before his death in 1901 the present conductor, Georg Schumann, was appointed.]   P. S.

SINGING is the musical expression of the voice. It is part of our natural condition to possess organs for the production of sound, and perceptions to make them musical, and being thus equipped, it is but natural that the art of music should be intimately associated with human life.

Like many of the other animals, we express our pain, sorrow, joy, pleasure, hunger, rage, satisfaction, and love, in sounds which have their vital and instinctive meaning like any of the actions or gestures associated with the elemental functions of human nature. We have no more necessity than they have, however imitative we may be, to look to external phenomena for the origin of this wonderful possession. It is natural to the infant to cry when it is cold or hungry, and crow when it is pleased. So, with the growth of sensibility and perception, a little child knows how to plead with its voice, in tones quite different from those of mere asking, without any vocal training whatever. The same instinct which has enabled the child to appeal to its parents and fellow-creatures, has taught man to approach his God with praise and supplication. But the most remarkable indication of the instinctiveness of song is the characteristic growth of the voice organs at the outset of manhood and womanhood. It is as if the full development of the body were crowned with the completion of the instruments of sound, which express with such particular eloquence the passions and emotions attendant upon the great mystery of sex.

Through the growth and refinement of our perceptions, the art of singing becomes the musical expression of every emotion suggested by thought and imagination.

It not infrequently happens that individuals are born to attain by the light of nature to a high degree of perfection in this art ; and even when this is not so, the inherent sincerity of imperfect singing can sometimes appeal more powerfully to our feelings than the most efficient training could make it do. While the whole of humanity is probably in some measure acquainted with the feeling of a desire to sing, and the form and condition of the vocal instruments appear to be as a rule normally fitted for the production of musical sound, the wonder is that everybody cannot do it. But there is no doubt that the fault lies more often in defective musical perception than in the condition of the organs of voice.

Music demands a high development of a particular sense, the foundation of which is inborn, though its perfection requires cultivation ; and therefore there are individuals who have all the materials for singing, but are still without the faculty of using them for that purpose. Another important obstacle to the acquirement of the power of singing is that, with the intellectual development of the race has arisen a demand for perfection in speech and diction, which often interferes with the process of vocal training.

It should be remembered that language is a purely artificial acquisition of mankind. We all have to spend years in acquiring habits of speech so that we may understand and explain the ordinary circumstances of life. So local is this, that we grow up speaking the language which prevails around us, by the simple process of imitation, without thinking whether its sounds are musical or not, and this introduces a series of common difficulties which are more linguistic than vocal, and which will be considered more fully later on.

It thus becomes apparent that the art of singing has within it a great deal that is quite outside the province of music. For although the musical expression of the voice is of prime importance, the whole foundations of the instruments involved belong strictly to the province of Physiology, like any of the other natural functions of the body, and by far the greater share of its educational side belongs to the study of the speech organs.

The science of Phonology (i.e. the science of vocal sound) has been specialised from its parent science of Physiology, so that it may occupy itself solely with the study of all the problems involved in this important subject, and, by an obligatory knowledge of music and languages, carry out its conclusions in the service of the art.

The first step towards understanding singing is to acquire a knowledge of the forces and instruments which it employs, and their phonological outline should, therefore, be made clear before the fuller details are filled in.

The voice is built upon the same physical principles as a reed-pipe of a church organ. There is (1) a wind-chest in which the air is compressed ; (2) a 'reed' which vibrates and produces the sound ; and (3) a resonator, which gives it certain qualities.

(1) By the act of breathing out, we compress the air which has been taken into the chest. This force in being liberated causes (2) the Vocal 'reed' to vibrate when we bring it into position and the sound thus produced is then modified by (3) the Resonator, formed by the hollows in the neck, mouth, and nose, which give quality to the sound, and impress upon it the characteristics of language.

Under these headings the components of the

voice can be studied separately, and their more complex combined performances are then more easily understood.

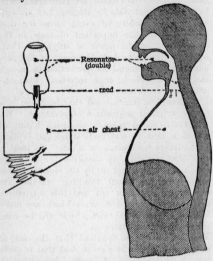

Resonator (double)

reed

air chest

The Breath.—The ordinary breathing of every-day life brings oxygen into contact with the blood in the lungs and carries carbonic acid away from it. Elevation of the ribs expands the chest and increases its circumference, and the contraction of the diaphragm lowers its floor and enlarges its capacity in a downward direction. The two actions go on together and draw a sufficient volume of fresh air (30 cubic inches) into the lungs with a slow, easy movement. The used air is more quickly emitted, principally by the elastic recoil of the lungs and chest, and after that there is a slight pause. This occurs about fifteen times a minute.

Breathing for singing is very different. Its whole object is to maintain a long and well-regulated air-pressure for the production of sound. A full breath must often be taken very rapidly, and then kept in a state of controlled compression for as much as 20 seconds. Thus the number of respirations possible in a minute may be reduced to a minimum. This necessitates a much larger volume of breath than is ordinarily needed, not only for the length of time the sound may have to continue, but also for the supply of oxygen to the blood. The first point is, therefore, to secure the power of taking in a large volume of air as quickly as possible. The second point is to give it out with carefully regulated force, for upon this the controlled production of sound entirely depends.

Breathing in.—The largest amount of air can be inhaled by the properly combined action of raising the ribs (costal breathing) and of contracting the diaphragm (diaphragmatic breathing). The latter has also been called " abdominal " breathing, from the fact that the

diaphragm is hidden and the evidence of its contraction is the protrusion of the abdominal wall caused by lowering the roof of that cavity. Men make more use of the diaphragm than women, whose upper ribs are more movable, but singers of both sexes have to make good use of both diaphragm and ribs.

There are reasons, especially in women, against the extreme use of the diaphragm on account of the pressure it exerts upon the abdominal organs, besides the difficulty of controlling the breath when so taken. This has caused a great deal of misunderstanding between doctors and singing-masters, and has produced extreme views on either side, neither of which can be supported by phonology.

When the ribs are fully raised, and especially the lower ones (6th-10th) which are the most elastic and movable, and correspond to the thickest part of the lungs, not only is the circumference of the chest increased and its floor widened, but the roof and upper part of the abdomen is also enlarged. Under these circumstances a considerable contraction of the diaphragm will cause no more than a protrusion of the upper part of the abdomen, that is, above the waist and between the margins of the ribs in front, without causing any harmful pressure upon the abdominal organs. The more the lower ribs expand, the more the diaphragm may descend with impunity, and a large in-take of breath can be obtained without danger. It has been called ' Central ' breathing, because the principal expansion takes place in the centre at the level of the space between the 6th and 7th ribs, and is designed to promote a good proportion of both actions, and to avoid the disproportionate or exclusive use of either the too high costal and clavicular breathing, or the too low purely abdominal breathing, both of which are sometimes advocated by extremists.

Breathing out.—In order to secure an even and continuous air-pressure three forces have to be considered :—

1. The elastic recoil of the inflated lungs and expanded chest ;

2. The contraction of abdominal muscles that assist the relaxed diaphragm to return to its place ; and

3. The contraction of muscles that pull down the ribs.

The elastic recoil does most of the work in ordinary breathing out, and is most useful in producing sound, only it is a force that begins with a maximum and rapidly diminishes.

To make the force continuous, it must be augmented by one of the others. These may act together or separately. If they act together they must maintain their proper proportion throughout. If they act separately the diaphragm must be replaced by abdominal contraction first, that is, before the ribs are allowed to descend, for, as has already been stated, the subsidence of the expanded chest while the diaphragm is contracted, causes too much abdominal distension.

Those who have developed a good expansion of the lower ribs will be able to maintain that expansion while the diaphragm is supported by the abdominal muscles, and the upper part of the abdomen becomes concave before the ribs are allowed to descend. In this manner very great delicacy in breath-control can be exercised. When the capacity is large enough the ribs can be kept expanded while the diaphragm moves to and fro, opposed by the abdominal muscles, and thus the breathing both in and out becomes entirely diaphragmatic or abdominal. This is the only form in which this is permissible, namely, when the ribs are fully expanded all the time and the movement of the abdominal wall is confined to the region above the waist.

Towards the end of a very long phrase, however, the ribs will have to come down. It is better then, that only the lower ribs should be relaxed while the upper ribs remain raised as part of a permanent position.

The permanent expansion of the ribs is partly secured by straightening the upper part of the spine in standing or sitting up straight, and the larger amount of residual air retained in the lungs is of great value in maintaining continuity of air-pressure and tone.

It will be noted that the form of breathing here explained and advocated is practically invisible. It is also designed to add to volume, the continuity and control of air-pressure necessary to good phrasing. The permanent expansion of the ribs also assists resonation in the neck, an advantage which will be dealt with later.

The vocal reed is formed by two elastic membranes or cords which can be drawn together from their position of rest, so that they meet like curtains, and completely close the air-passage at the upper end of the windpipe, where the larynx begins. Their front ends are fixed close together to the shield cartilage, and behind they are attached to two small triangular cartilages which move very freely upon the thick ring-shaped cartilage supporting them. During breathing in they are wide apart, and during breathing out they approach one another. In the act of whispering, they are definitely drawn, so as to reduce the opening between their edges considerably.

As soon as air-pressure acts upon the elas-

ticity of the edges of the membranes they vibrate, in accordance with the physical laws which govern the action of 'reeds' in general. This may happen before the whole passage is occluded, and a soft 'breathy' note is produced, but the reed acts most strongly and perfectly when the two cartilages are brought into close contact, so that the whole air-pressure acts upon the vibrating edges of the membranes, and is converted into sound.

Singing is practically confined to the last position. The tremor of the elastic membranes rapidly opens and closes the fine slit between their edges and releases the air-pressure in a quick succession of minute puffs. One group of muscles regulates the movements of the small triangular cartilages, by the action of which the membranes are brought together and drawn aside. Another group is concerned with tightening and loosening the membranes, and thereby regulates the tension upon which the rapidity of their vibration depends.

Every vocal reed may be expected to have a compass of two octaves which can be controlled by this function of tension and relaxation, and it must not be forgotten that this tension is an unconscious act guided solely by sound perception or 'ear,' and cannot be appreciated by any muscular sense as in the case of a voluntary movement.

The general pitch of every voice is determined by the size of the membranes. In men they are both wider and thicker than in women, and their length is generally estimated at about $\frac{7}{12}$ths of an inch and $\frac{5}{12}$ths of an inch in women.

Roughly speaking, the male voice is about an octave lower than the female, but in either sex all degrees of general pitch exist between certain limits. For convenience three types are usually considered—high, low, and middle. The majority of voices are near the middle type in both sexes, while exceptional instances of abnormally high or low are sometimes met with.

The male Alto voice has an intermediate position between the two groups, but being an unnatural product it cannot be considered with the others.

Thus every voice has its middle note whence it may be expected to range to the extent of an octave upwards and downwards by performing the same muscular action. In the figure the middle note of each voice is indicated by a double vertical line.

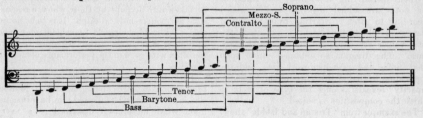

Besides the tension of the membranes there is another physical condition which undergoes variation with every change of pitch, and that is the air-pressure exerted by the breath.

From experiments (M'Kendrick, *Schäfer's Physiology*) it is found that the air-pressure varies in about the same ratio as the tension.

Therefore, in a general plan of the vocal compass the middle note may be regarded as the product of both mean tension and mean air-pressure. The tension is well known to vary in the ratio of the square of the vibrations, and thus both the tension and air-pressure may be represented by the numbers 1, 4, 9, 16, 25, while the vibrations are as 1, 2, 3, 4, 5, in the diagram appended.

Pressure and Tension.	Vibra-tions.	Com-pass.	Working Capacity.
Extreme = 25	5	3rd + 8ve	
High = 16	4		
= 9	3		
Mean = 4	2	Centre	
Low = 1	1	8ve + 3rd	
Extreme			

The working capacity of the voice is here represented by a triangle whose apex is opposite the centre of the compass, which signifies that the middle can do the most work when the whole compass is evenly balanced throughout. Then by a common control of tension and pressure the vibrations are varied so that the notes of a two-octave compass can be used at will. With training an extension upwards and downwards of a third more may still be possible, but it is always desirable that the extremes of the voice should be kept for exceptional use only. Composers are accustomed to fix the voices for which they write by the extreme limits only, which is not phonological. It is more important to adapt the principal share of the work to the centre of the voice.

A more or less exact method of estimating the amount of work demanded by a vocal composition has been made use of in the 'song diagram,' of which two examples are here given. Without considering accidentals, the values of the notes are added together and arranged according to pitch. Starting from a vertical line upon which the pitch is indicated, the total values are expressed in horizontal black lines. The diagram so obtained shows upon what notes the principal work lies, and the application to that of the centre of the 'working capacity' reveals at once the type of voice to which the composition is suited.

The example from 'Tristan and Isolde' shows

that Wagner demands for the part of Isolde a high soprano voice of exceptional development, with its centre on *b'*, and a full compass of over two octaves. Mozart's 'Il mio tesoro' only

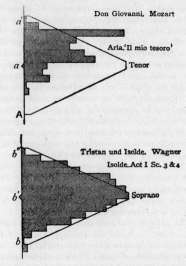

once touches the upper limit of the ordinary tenor compass, and yet it lies so much in the upper part of the voice that it is best suited to a high tenor with a centre above *a*.

The examination of a great number of these diagrams, which are easily made upon paper ruled in squares, will explain a great deal that is interesting to the practical musician, but they do not supply more than a part of what is called the 'tessitura' of vocal music, which includes the length and distribution of phrases and pauses, as well as the declamatory consideration of the question of vocality.

Many voices have been ruined by composers' neglect of vocal considerations, and it is not uncommon to find soprano singers who have lost the middle of the voice entirely. It is not difficult to calculate the great relief to the forces of tension and breath-pressure which even slight transposition will give ; and, conversely, the amount of strain which has to be borne by the voice, if the work is pitched too high, cannot fail to wear out and distort the instrument prematurely.

These considerations might with advantage be taken into account by those who are responsible for modern musical pitch. It is to be hoped that a wider phonological knowledge may tend to remove some of the bitter struggles that are too often witnessed in the performance of modern music.

The question of the attack of a note has been much debated among masters. Manuel Garcia, and others who followed him, have insisted upon what he himself described as a 'very slight cough' before a note in order to secure a distinct attack upon it.

Above the vocal membranes and parallel with them are two muscular folds called the false vocal cords, or ventricular bands. In conjunction with the muscles that bring the membranes together, they form a strong constrictor of the air-passage, to close it firmly when required. This occurs always in swallowing, when the chest has to be held inflated to support a strong muscular action, and also in coughing. The elastic vocal membranes are themselves unable to restrain any air-pressure in the chest, so it was thought necessary to accumulate a little force by constriction with these ventricular bands, and by suddenly relaxing them to allow the force to impinge upon the membranes which were supposed to be held in readiness for the sudden shock. There is no doubt that a crisp attack can be effected in this way, but the sound of the note is always preceded by an explosive noise however lightly it may be done.

The first phonological objection to this 'shock of the glottis' (*coup de glotte*) is that it is quite unnecessary. When the breath is under control and intimately associated as it ought to be with the production of sound, the simultaneous onset of breath force and the proper approximation of the membranes produces a perfectly clear and clean attack, straight upon the note by the ordinary natural action performed with decision.

The introduction of any constriction above the reed cannot be regarded as a natural part of the action of attack. Moreover, the quasi-spasmodic act of constriction produces often an unduly hard attack which is not good for the vocal reed, and its constant repetition produces congestion of the parts around the cartilages, and a troublesome desire to clear the throat.

Phonology insists that the production of sound is always the result of an expiratory act, and that every sound effect, whether it be strong or soft, quick or gradual, must be the outcome of a similar intention in the breath control. Such control leaves the throat free to its unconscious action, which would be destroyed by any muscular constriction in the larynx.

The 'shock of the glottis' is part of a time-worn tradition in the teaching of singing, and is often heard in voices that are beautiful as well as in those that are hard and throaty; it is sometimes regarded as essential to the proper pronunciation of German and some other languages of a guttural nature, but artificial fashions of speech cannot be tolerated if they are opposed to the natural uses of the voice organs.

The cessation of a note is brought about by the withdrawal of the membranes. As a rule the membranes spring back elastically to their open position, and some breath pressure escapes in a puff after the note. The amount of this escape, and consequently the sound it makes,

is a matter of breath-control. A high note is naturally followed by a strong burst, because the pressure is higher than that of a low note. The free release, as this is called, is not objected to in operatic singing, and there is nothing to say against it on phonological grounds. Moreover, it is useful in getting rid of carbonic acid, and in facilitating the quick taking of another breath. It may, therefore, be left to discretion, to make the sound of the release inaudible by breath-control.

Under no circumstances should the note be stopped by constriction of any part of the throat, which is frequently associated with the equally detrimental attack by 'shock' just referred to. Many singers deceive themselves in the belief that their throats remain open when their notes cease.

One of the difficulties in showing the natural behaviour of the vocal membranes with the laryngoscope is that the power of tolerating a mirror in the back of the throat itself requires a long course of training without which the organs under observation cannot act naturally.

The second vocal instrument, the *Resonator*, belongs, as such, to a later date in the evolution of the voice as we now hear it. The particular function of the Resonator, which warrants its being treated as a separate instrument, is its power of modifying sound by assuming different shapes, which is made use of in the formation of language.

Every hollow space enclosed within walls but communicating with the outer air, is capable of allowing only certain sound vibrations or waves to continue within it. This is called its Resonant note, and its pitch corresponds with the size, and its character with the shape, of the resonant cavity or Resonator. The pitch is also affected by the size of its opening. Partly closing it not only changes the character of the note, but also lowers its pitch.

In the case of the voice, in which the reed is strong and the Resonator comparatively weak, much of the fulness of the sound must depend upon keeping the openings free. At the same time the cavities should be made as large as possible in order to keep their resonant pitches low, and thereby impart a richer tone to the voice.

The size of the Resonator varies a little among men; in women it is about 20 per cent smaller, and in children, smaller still. But all, by the same physiological action, can bring it into similar positions, and thus it is the shape of the Resonator that gives characteristic qualities to speech, and language is as intelligible in the mouth of a child as in that of a giant.

The sounds of language are divided into two groups.

1. Vowel sounds, due to open and expanded positions of the Resonator suitable for continuous sounds of the best possible quality.

2. Consonants, due to more or less closed positions, and movements of the Resonator which give certain characters to the approach to and departure from the vowel positions.

The position of the Resonator in forming the vowel sounds is a most important question in the art of singing.

So much latitude is permitted in ordinary speaking that pronunciation in singing has been looked upon as something quite different from it. But when the sound of the voice is at its best, the Resonator is in the position most favourable to sound. This principle applies as strongly to speaking as it does to singing, and when singers do not sing as they would speak, it is either because they do not speak properly, or they do not use the Resonator naturally.

It cannot be too strongly insisted upon that if the principles of good resonation are carefully adhered to from the first, speech, being solely a matter of education, can always be made beautiful.

This is generally neglected in our schools, where children learn their habits of speech, but it is absolutely essential to singing, and not infrequently it happens that a great part of vocal training is spent upon teaching a singer to use the Resonator properly, for the first time.

Vowel Sounds.—In studying the sounds belonging to the five signs U, O, A, E, I, the Italian pronunciation is here adopted—

	U	O	A	E	I
English Equivalent	(oo)	(or)	(ah)	(eh)	(ee)

The position A is that in which the whole passage is open and expanded to the fullest extent convenient (natural habits never go to extremes), and from it the others are differentiated by two principal actions.

1. Closure of the opening by the lips, and
2. Raising and advancing the body of the tongue.

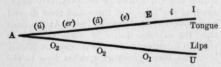

Since A is taken as the basis of our Resonation, its position must be closely defined.

The jaw is open at least an inch between the front teeth.

The lips are at rest upon the teeth, and not retracted at the sides.

The tongue lies flat upon the floor of the mouth with its tip and margins touching the backs of the lower teeth.

The base of the tongue is flat enough to make the back of the throat visible from the front.

The palate is held up just enough to prevent breath passing into the nose, but without any conscious effort.

The neck is fully expanded by the combined actions of holding the head erect, the ribs raised, and drawing down the larynx, more by the action of the sterno-thyroid muscles which act upon the larynx from below, than by the sterno-hyoid muscles which bring down the base of the tongue. This position has the form of a double Resonator, with two principal resonance chambers uniting in the middle at right angles, where they are joined by a third accessory chamber, the nose.

The back chamber in the neck is shaped like a bag, wide below, where the vocal reed is placed, and narrow above, where it opens into the back of the mouth by an oval opening. The front chamber, in the mouth, is shaped like an irregular hemisphere, with a flat floor and an arched roof and a large round opening in front.

Although the whole Resonator acts as one, the back chamber may be said to have most to do with the full resonation of vocal sound ; while to the more variable cavity of the mouth is given the office of forming all the characteristics of language. The accessory cavity of the nose adds to the sound the nasal resonance when required, through the opening controlled by the soft palate. The resonant properties of cavities are demonstrated by blowing a stream of air through or across them, so that their resonant notes can be heard by themselves. This occurs in the whispering voice. The partly closed glottis allows the breath to rush through it without producing any vocal note, and the rushing sound awakens the resonant notes of the air-chambers so distinctly that not only are all the qualities of language distinguishable, but with a little practice the pitch of the resonant notes of the various vowel sounds can be detected. These notes are most distinct, and deeply pitched in the whispering here employed, which requires a fully expanded and open Resonator and a reef out-breath with no constriction of the throat whatever.

Following these rules the pitch of the vowel A is commonly found to be c'' or $c''\sharp$ among men—and about a minor third higher $e''\flat$ or e'' among women.

The double nature of the Resonator can be shown by introducing a tuning-fork of the right pitch, into the throat. A strong reinforcement occurs in that position indicating a 'node' at the junction of the two chambers, as would be expected. The resonant note may, therefore, be said to belong to both the mouth and the neck cavity acting in unison. This is an important acoustical point, which receives further confirmation in the formation of the other vowels.

The first group of vowels derived from A, by closing the opening with the lips, are three varieties of O, and U which is the most closed.

By various degrees of this action, but keeping the jaw still open to the extent of an inch between the front teeth, the positions are obtained for :—

A	O³	O²	O¹	U
English Equivalent ah	not	or	oh	oo.

By every successive degree of closing, the pitch of the resonant note is lowered, and thus are indicated the several positions which produce the notes of a scale as a simple way of fixing them.

By rounding the lips enough to lower the pitch of A a whole fifth, a good resonant position is found for U (oo), and the deep, middle, and shallow forms of O find their proper places upon the three notes intervening.

It will be noticed in practice, as well as in physiological works, that with the closure of the lips there is at the same time a lowering of the larynx and a slight raising of the base of the tongue. Both these actions tend to enlarge and close in the chamber in the neck, and by thus lowering its pitch, they maintain the unison of the two chambers, as may be further shown by tapping the cheek and the neck, when both are found to possess the same note.

Whispered Resonances.

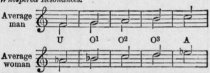

The second group of vowel sounds owe their character to the position of the tongue. The jaw remains open about an inch as before, then the tongue, with its tip against the back of the front teeth, advances and rises. The lips remain still, the larynx is drawn upwards by the movement of the tongue, but this is restrained to some extent by maintaining the expansion of the neck as in the position of A. This action raises the resonant pitch of the mouth because it becomes gradually encroached upon by the body of the tongue, but while it makes the mouth cavity smaller, it makes the neck cavity larger. When the tongue is so far forward as to touch with its margin the upper molar teeth, the pitch of the mouth resonance may be raised a sixth and the neck resonance lowered a third.

This is the position allotted to the vowel E (eh). A still further advance of the tongue to its extreme position, when it has raised the mouth resonance an octave, and lowered the

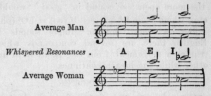

neck resonance a fifth, will give a suitable resonance to the vowel I (ee).

The perfect concords of an octave (1 to 2) and a twelfth (1 to 3) established for the relation of the chambers in these two vowel sounds is not a mere accident. It is more probable that the selection of these sounds as pure vowel sounds in all languages, has been due to their particular resonant advantages, for the resonance of a double resonator can only go on perfectly when the component chambers are either in unison or simply related. A further point in the formation of the vowel sounds E and I, is that the orifice between the two chambers is made smaller by the approach of the tongue to the hard palate. This lowers the pitch of both, so that the division of the chambers does not take place in linear measurement as upon a monochord.

Intermediate between A and E there are several positions which belong to some of the English vowel sounds in common use. The first movement of the tongue is principally forward, and enlarges the opening of the throat, raising the resonant pitch of both chambers while they remain in unison. This position belongs to the sounds of the unaccented *a* in 'álone,' the *u* in 'up,' and the *o* in 'love.' But after this the unison can no longer be maintained owing to the disparity of the chambers, and we find their pitches a third apart, which is not very good for the resonation of the sound *er* as in 'earth.' The shallow *ā* as in 'hat' has resonance chambers a fifth apart, and in the short *ĕ* as in 'get' they differ by a sixth. Hence all these indefinitely resonated sounds are those which are more frequently varied in pronunciation than any others, and are the most difficult to fix in singing. Between E and I is the short *ĭ* as in 'hit,' in which the chambers are a tenth apart.

The full *Resonator Scale* is therefore constructed as follows. The several positions are marked by Roman numbers to indicate them for all voices in relation to the pitch of A, which governs that of the others in each individual case. To these must be added in English

Resonator Scale of Whispered Vowel Sounds.

	I.	II.	III.	IV.	V.	VI.	VII.	VIII.	IX.	X.	XI.	XII.
A Average Man	U	O¹	O²	O³	A	.	.	.	ĕ	E	ĭ	I
	U	oh	or	ŏn	ah	up	her	hăt	get	gate	hit	heat

the more open ' oo ' sound in ' good,' ' would,' etc., which is on I △ between U (oo) and O¹ (oh).

Besides these thirteen simple sounds in English there are several compounds which require a movement from one position to another while the breath continues.

Whispered Resonances.

XI.-I.	VI.-XI.	XI.-VI.	VIII.-VI.	III.-XI.
i — oo	ă — ĭ	ĭ — ă	â — ă	or—i
English: duke	high	hear	hair	boy

The use of the resonator scale is of similar service in fixing the vowel pronunciation of other languages, and French and German sounds have all their places in relation to the sound of A, slight differences only having to be made to suit national peculiarities.

The same relations will be found to exist, whatever the resonant pitch of A may be. The pitch of U, a fifth lower, and of I (ee) an octave higher, will always be the limits of the scale of twelve notes, although in languages with fewer vowels some of the notes will not be occupied.

It must be remembered that all these sounds have to do solely with *whispered* speech, and are in no way connected with the notes of the vocal reed.

With a little practice the notes of the Resonator Scale can be heard without difficulty. By tapping with the finger upon the neck, the resonant notes of the back chamber will be heard to rise with the others, up to No. VI., and then fall again as shown in the scale. They can also be heard by the subject himself when the ears are completely stopped.

The consonants are important to the art of speaking and therefore also to singing, for they all represent different methods of opening and closing the vowel positions. They are conveniently classified as follows :—

It will be noticed that the jaw is only closed when the teeth are obliged to be together to form S.SH, and their sounding companions Z.J (soft), otherwise it must always be kept as wide open as the consonant will allow, in order to have less to do in reaching the vowel positions, which are all open.

What is generally known as ' forward diction ' depends upon this condition, and the free use of the tip of the tongue, the lips, and the teeth.

The base of the tongue in K and G is brought forward to the hard palate, and not allowed to close up the throat at the back.

This action is easier before A, O, and U, when the tongue is either flat or its base somewhat raised ; but before E and I, in which the front of the tongue is high and forward in the

	Larynx.	Base of tongue.	Tip of tongue.	Lips.	Lower lip and upper teeth.	Teeth and tip of tongue.	Teeth.
EXPLOSIVES :							
Plain.	..	K	T	P	..	..	..
With Voice.	..	G	D	B	..	..	..
CONTINUANTS WITH VOICE :							
Nasal.	..	ŃG	N	M	..	..	..
Non-nasal.	...	...	L	..	V	Th (soft)	Z.J (soft)
Roll.	...	..	R	..	..	..	..
ASPIRATES WITHOUT VOICE.	H	..	..	..	F	Th (hard)	S.Sh
	Jaw—open	,, ,,	Very slight closing	Closing lips, not teeth	Lower lip between teeth	Tongue tip ,, ,,	Teeth meet

mouth, the consonants K and G have been softened by all races who have come under Latin influence (French, Spanish, Italian, and part of English) into an aspirated or partly explosive sound better suited to the position of the tongue.

The importation of language into the art of song has thus involved the careful cultivation of those positions and movements of the Resonator which are best calculated to liberate the sound of the vocal reed, and at the same time express with particular distinctness all the various qualities of speech. But the sound of the voice includes yet another quality, namely that of ' tone ' or ' tone colour,' which depends upon whether the maximum of Resonation is used or not. This is the especial function of the chamber in the neck.

The formative actions of the front of the mouth may or may not be accompanied by the full expansion of the back chamber of the Resonator, and thus the total sound will be full and rich or shallow and light, as the singer thinks fit.

After these considerations it is not difficult to perceive that the question of Registers has been confused by the assumption that the different tones of voice were produced by different actions of the vocal reed. The terms 'head register' and 'chest register' have, no doubt, been intended to mean conditions in which the singer has felt the sound in the head and in the chest. The former signifies the absence, and the latter the presence, of expansion in the neck.

The chest itself is occupied with the air-pressure and cannot be regarded as a resonator, since it is practically closed, except for the minute slit through which the pressure issues. The 'head register' has been further confounded with the compression of the membranes which also occurs in the upper notes of many voices.

Certain descriptions of the vocal membranes in explanation of the different 'registers' have been given, and named 'lower thick,' 'upper thick,' 'middle,' 'lower thin,' 'upper thin,' etc. (Lennox Browne), but they have not been confirmed by further observation.

As at present known the membranes behave in the same way throughout the entire compass, and their compression in the high notes must be regarded as a departure from the natural process.

The true high note requires a development of breath power and control, and it would be better for their instrument if singers would refrain from singing by compression, and be satisfied with the compass that their breath power can give them. High notes might become rarer, but their sound would be of better quality.

Other forms of 'register' due to alternative resonation are used as the singer wishes to express different tone-colour. But by insisting upon the maintenance of the double character of the Resonator with all articulation in the front of the mouth, and resonant control in the neck, there are no sudden changes which could produce an obligatory 'register.'

Variety of colour due to control of the resonation of the neck may occur in all parts of the voice. When, however, the base of the tongue is pressed down so as to produce a heavy resonation in the mouth, at the expense of that in the neck, as well as to the detriment of good diction which requires the tongue to be free, it may readily occur that a sudden change has to be made near the middle of the voice, on passing from one note to the next.

Phonology is as much opposed to fictitious tone as to fictitious notes, and prefers to sacrifice the heavy tone of a voice if it is not natural to it, that is, if it is not obtained by the natural actions which are known to govern the sounds of the voice, in this case by expansion of the neck. Therefore the so-called 'Registers' cannot be accepted as natural. That they are often acquired is beyond doubt, but it is astonishing how they disappear when singers are relieved of the necessity of thinking about them.

Phonology does not acknowledge some of the common methods of singing teachers, but it is able to support, on rational grounds, some of the best traditions of the great masters, which are the foundation of the following picture of the use of the singing voice.

The singer stands erect with a broadly expanded chest. He takes a deep breath by expanding both chest and abdomen at the level of the 6th-7th rib. He opens his mouth and throat to the position suitable for the pronunciation of A (ah), and at the same time he thinks of the note he is about to sing. Without allowing the ribs to yield he strikes the note by breathing out with decision, by a contraction at the upper part of the abdomen and a simultaneous approximation of the vocal membranes. If the note is in the middle of his compass, he will sing a succession of notes up to an octave higher and down to an octave lower, and back again, without any movement of his mouth or ribs ; being conscious only of the breath force, which produces the notes he hears in his mind. The notes are lifted up and let down upon the breath pressure, controlled by the muscular action felt in the region of the lower ribs.

By changing the position of the Resonator other vowel qualities can be given to the whole process, but under all circumstances the production of the notes remains the same. By movements of the resonator before and after the open vowel positions the effects of consonants can be introduced for the formation of words. By expanding the neck from below, a full resonant tone can be given, or withheld according to the 'colour' required. The throat is always free, that is, relaxed, open, and unconscious.

This is a brief picture of what singing is in the individual, illustrating the action of the two instruments which combine to produce the sound of the voice. The one instrument expresses in music the emotions of the soul, while the other expresses in words the poetic thoughts of the mind. It is the office of the musical composer to bring these two together into the form of song.

Just as it is essential to the writer of vocal music to understand thoroughly the 'technique' of the living instrument for which he writes, so is it also a necessary part of singing to be acquainted with the manner in which the dual expression is conceived in the song. Phonology has supplied the singer with an absolutely material estimate of work to be done by the voice, in the 'song diagrams' already referred to, but in order to show how the vocal instruments are to be used in the service of Art its analysis of song must be carried farther.

As presented upon the page, a song consists of a line of music written upon a stave, and a line of words below it, in ordinary character. It is evident therefore from the first that the vocal reed or instrument of music has to perform a musical composition ; while the resonator or instrument of speech has to perform a composition in verse. All that can be said about the performance of music by an instrument, or about the recitation of verse, is applicable to the vocal reed and the resonator, each by itself. The vocal reed, however, has two offices to perform. It is either behaving as a true instrument of music, giving utterance to feelings in the direct manner belonging to its nature, or it is lending itself as an instrument of sound to assist, by emphasis and inflexion, the sense of words. In the former case its action is melodic, in the latter, declamatory.

The line of music may be intended by the composer to be interpreted in either of these senses, or it may happen that the feeling suggested by the words is so perfectly treated in the application to it of a form of melody, that both are satisfied, and the song is both melodic and declamatory. Examples of this are rare, and it more often happens that either one or the other element predominates. Not infrequently, however, it occurs that they clash, so that neither is satisfactory.

The rhythm of music, with its division into time measures, and the rhythm of words, with their arrangement into metrical verse, only indicate motion, and when these are applied to one another only the rhythm in which they may move together is emphasised, and nothing more. This cannot be regarded as song composition.

It is the sense of words and not the sound that stimulates the musical sense. The music thus evolved may have no melodic form of its own, in which case it is declamatory, or it may add to the words the power of its own form of expression and become melodic.

Periodicity in poetic expression is as necessary to verse as it is to music, and the study of the works of Heine gives a striking illustration of its force. The period of two lines, in which he usually expressed his thoughts, presented to the musician the simplest foundation for melodic form, and how that appealed to the melodic genius of Schubert is seen distinctly in such a masterpiece as 'Am Meer.' If other poets could speak with such measured simplicity and directness, the art of song would be richer than it is.

The suiting of music to words may appear to be a subject belonging to the art of composition, but it is necessary to consider it from the point of view of singing, since it forms the foundation of the singer's attitude of mind. The singer must know how to direct his technical ability, and must have some distinct mental intention in singing, or the performance will be nothing more than the mechanical recitation of words and notes.

The sense of the words is always to be considered first, since that is generally the most obvious. With a little analysis the poet's scheme of conveying a succession of ideas may next be detected. It will not then be difficult to see at once whether the composer has adapted these ideas to a corresponding scheme of melodic form, or whether he has been content to use his music as a means of supporting the words only ; and the value of the music as depicting the poetic intention can be readily estimated.

It is not within the scope of this article to carry such analysis into the extensive field of existing examples of song-writing. Modern music is full of examples of declamatory song distorted and exaggerated by the musical exigencies of the pianoforte and orchestral accompaniment.

The melodic form is regarded as a survival of the past which does not really belong to present methods of musical expression. In fact, the sound as well as the sense of the voice has been almost swamped by the wealth of instrumentation which is considered necessary for modern ears. How far this can be carried it is impossible to say, but it is quite possible that singing will soon be regarded as a separate form of art, and composers will either write for the voice, or for the orchestra, but not for both together.

In estimating the general character of modern and ancient music the singer can thus realise what part it is that his voice has to take. Throughout the works of the old Italian, English, and German masters, up to the end of the 18th century, he will find abundant opportunity for the full exercise of the natural instrument of song. A more highly cultured and intellectually restrained form was the outcome of the literary period which we owe to the German lyric poets, and perfection of diction, with a refined use of musical expression, characterises the 'Lied,' and those songs of other nations which are conceived upon that model.

Of the vocal necessities of modern music no more need be said than that the singer must be able to realise the situation. The voice is a living thing, and can be ruined by the strain of singing too loud and too high, as only too many modern singers have discovered, but its powers of endurance, if properly treated, are remarkable, and every singer who understands his work ought to know where to stop.

Besides an excellent technique and an intelligent sense for music and poetry, the singer only requires the sincerity which brings to his art the charm of his own personality. If any technique could possibly be learned in order to obtain that inestimable quality, phonology would certainly point to the exercise of the most truly vital of all human functions, and recommend the free and unhindered service of the breath.   W. A. A.

SINGSPIEL. This term has been in use in Germany for the last 300 years to denote a dramatic representation with music; not any one particular kind—singing being capable of being employed in such various ways—but any entertainment in which spoken dialogue and singing alternate. In time speech gave way at intervals not only to singing, but to singing by several voices at once. Later, when the spoken dialogue had been brought into entire subjection to music, as was the case in Italy after the revolution effected in the whole nature of dramatic representation by the rise of opera, not only concerted vocal pieces were introduced into the German Singspiel, but instrumental music and its protégé monody as well. We find the earliest traces of the Singspiel in the German miracle-plays, which were gradually developed outside the churches from the Passions given inside them. The Passions were sung throughout, while in the miracle-plays spoken words in German were introduced, the singing still being in Latin, as for example in the 'Ludus paschalis de passione Domini' MS. of the 13th century. In course of time the Latin text and consequently the music were thrust into the background. In a 14th-century MS. called 'Marienklage,' preserved in the convent of Lichtenthal near Baden, Mary sings in German. Indeed we already find the typical German miracle-play in the 'Spiel von den zehn Jungfrauen' performed at Eisenach in 1322, in which all the words sung are German. These plays were generally performed on the eves of the great festivals, such as Whitsunday, Epiphany, etc. Gradually the ecclesiastical element disappeared, leaving only the secular, and thus originated the Shrove Tuesday plays, in which the characteristics of whole classes of society, priests, doctors, travelling scholars, etc., were held up to ridicule. Nuremberg and Augsburg were specially celebrated for these plays, written for the most part by Hans Rosenblut (about 1405), Hans Folz of Worms (about 1480), both living in Nuremberg, and Nicolaus Mercator. They gradually, however, degenerated into obscene pieces, until in the 16th century Hans Sachs and Jakob Ayrer (both of whom introduced music into their plays) started the movement which ended in the reformation of the German stage. By Ayrer we still have a 'Schöns neus singets Spiel,' 'Der Münch im Kesskorb,' sung in 1618 by five persons 'entirely on the melody of the English Roland.' This melody is repeated fifty-four times, and one cannot help suspecting that the English stage was to some extent Ayrer's model. A reaction from these 'people's plays' (as they might be called) was caused by the 'school plays' in Latin, annually performed by the pupils of the Jesuits. Between the acts German interludes with music were introduced, and these were virtually Singspiele in the modern sense. The first Singspiel in imitation of the Italian opera without any spoken dialogue was the lost 'Dafne,' written by Martin Opitz and composed

by Heinrich Schütz in 1627. The earliest instance of an independent German Singspiel with singing and spoken dialogue was 'Seelewig,' a sacred Waldgedicht or Freudenspiel. In a spoken play of Harsdörffer's (1644) were introduced Arias after the Italian manner, composed (see the *Monatshefte für Musikgeschichte*, 1881, Nos. 4, 5, 6) by Siegmund Gottlieb STADEN. The piece is intended for private performance, and written for three trebles, two altos, two tenors, one bass, three violins, three flutes, three reeds, and one large horn, the bass being taken throughout by a theorbo. No two voices ever sing at the same time, and the instruments have short symphonies to themselves. The only regular stage at that time was the Italian opera-house of each capital (that of Vienna being built in 1651, and that of Dresden in 1667) and of Nuremberg and other Imperial cities. The German Singspiel found a home in Hamburg in the theatre built in 1678, but soon encountered a formidable rival in German opera, founded by Reinhard Keiser. After this, half a century went by before the Singspiel was heard of again. In 1743 the Döbbelin company in Berlin produced without success a German Liederspiel, 'Der Teufel ist los,' founded on the English piece 'The Devil to pay,' followed by Schürer's 'Doris' (1747) and Scheibe's 'Thusnelda' (1749), both very successful. Thus encouraged, Koch's company began to play Singspiele in Leipzig, Weimar, and Berlin, their first piece being 'Die verwandelten Weiber,' another version of 'The Devil to pay,' written by C. F. Weisse, composed by J. A. Hiller, and produced at Leipzig in 1764 with great success. The same authors produced a succession of similar pieces, 'Der lustige Schuster' (1765), 'Lottchen am Hofe,' and 'Die Liebe auf dem Lande' (1767), 'Die Jagd' (1771), 'Aerndtekranz' and 'Der Dorfbarbier' (1772). Neefe, Reichardt, Stegemann, Schweitzer, and others, brought to perfection this new species, now called Operetta. Independently of all this going on in North Germany, the German Singspiel had sprung up in Vienna, starting, curiously enough, with 'Die doppelte Verwandlung' (1767), an adaptation from the French 'Le Diable à quatre,' Sedaine's version of 'The Devil to pay.' Werner, Haydn's predecessor at Eisenstadt, had already produced at the Court German theatre a Tafelstück (*i.e.* piece intended for private performance) called 'Der Wienerische Tändelmarkt' (1760). The marionette plays, of which Haydn was so fond, were Singspicle, and he supplied the court of Esterház with 'Philemon und Baucis' (1773), 'Genoveva' (1777), 'Dido,' a parody on a grand opera (1778), and 'Die erfüllte Rache' (1780). 'Der krumme Teufel,' to words by Kurz, was a real Singspiel. Dittersdorf's 'Doctor und Apotheker,' 'Liebe im Narrenhause,' 'Hieronymus Knicker,' 'Rothe Käppchen,' etc., produced at the Imperial

Nationaltheater, were brilliant successes. Kauer (1751-1831) composed no fewer than 200 Singspiele, and Schenk was almost equally prolific. The classic Singspiel was founded by Mozart with his 'Entführung' (July 12, 1782), which, according to Goethe, threw everything else of the kind into the shade. The 'Zauberflöte' (1791), too, was styled a Singspiel on the title-page of the PF. score. From this point the Singspiel proper becomes continually rarer, though Wenzel Müller's 'Schwester von Prag,' 'Das neue Sonntagskind,' and a few more deserve mention. Lortzing's works are a mixture of opera and Singspiel, certain numbers in the 'Czaar und Zimmermann,' 'Waffenschmied,' and 'Undine' being quite in the Lied-style, and the music consequently of secondary importance, while in others the music undoubtedly assists in developing the characters, and raises these portions to the dignity of opera. We are here brought face to face with the main distinction between Opera and Singspiel ; the latter by no means excludes occasional recitative in place of the spoken dialogue, but the moment the music helps to develop the dramatic dénoûment we have to do with Opera and not with Singspiel. F. G.

SINIGAGLIA, Leone, born at Turin, August 14, 1868, was a pupil of the Conservatorio of his native city, and subsequently studied with Mandyczewski in Vienna, where he enjoyed the friendship and advice of Dvořák, Goldmark, and other musicians. His early works include a number of violin and violoncello pieces, songs, female choruses, etc., and one of these, op. 5, a 'concert étude' for string quartet, was often played by the Bohemian Quartet. His op. 19 is a set of variations on Schubert's 'Haidenröslein' for oboe and piano ; op. 20 is a brilliant and very successful violin concerto in A ; op. 22 is a set of variations on a theme by Brahms, for quartet ; op. 26 is a 'Rapsodia piemontese' for violin and orchestra ; and op. 27 is a string quartet in D, which has won great favour from many of the continental organisations. Two pieces for horn and piano, op. 28, and a romance in A for violin and orchestra, are among his more recent works ; and two 'Danze piemontese' for orchestra, op. 31, are arrangements of genuine popular themes. These have been arranged in a variety of ways, and are very successful. M.

SINK-A-PACE—also written Cinque-pace, Cinqua-pace, Cinque Pass, Cinque Pas, Sinqua-pace, Sinque-pace, Zinck-pass and Sincopas—a name by which the original Galliard was known. Praetorius (Syntagma Mus. vol. iii. chap. ii. p. 24) says that a Galliard has five steps and is therefore called a Cinque Pas. These five steps, or rather combinations of steps, are well described in Arbeau's Orchésographie (Langres, 1588). In later times the Galliard became so altered by the addition of

new steps, that the original form of the dance seems to have been distinguished by the name Cinq Pas. It is frequently mentioned by the Elizabethan writers, well-known examples being the allusions in Shakespeare's 'Much Ado about Nothing' (Act ii. Sc. 1), 'Twelfth Night' (Act i. Sc. 3), Marston's 'Satiromastix' (Act i.), and Sir John Davies's 'Orchestra' (stanza 67). The following less-known quotation is from the 'Histriomastix' (Part 1) of Prynne (who was especially bitter against this dance) : 'Alas there are but few who finde that narrow way . . . and those few what are they? Not dancers, but mourners : not laughers, but weepers ; whose tune is Lachrymæ, whose musicke, sighes for sinne ; who know no other Cinqua-pace but this to Heaven, to goe mourning all the day long for their iniquities ; to mourne in secret like Doves, to chatter like Cranes for their owne and others sinnes.' The following example of a Cinque-pace is given by Wolfgang Caspar Printz, in his Phrynis Mitilenaeus, oder Satyrischer Componist (Dresden, 1696), as a specimen of 'Trichonum Iambicum.' A longer example will be found in Dauney's edition of the 17th-century Skene MS. (Edinburgh, 1838).

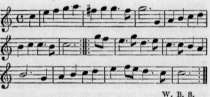

W. B. S.

SIR ROGER DE COVERLY,[1] the only one of the numerous old English dances which has retained its popularity until the present day, is probably a tune of north-country origin. Mr. Chappell (Popular Music, vol. ii.) says that he possesses a MS. version of it called 'Old Roger of Coverlay for evermore, a Lancashire Hornpipe,' and in 'The First and Second Division Violin' (in the British Museum Catalogue attributed to John Eccles, and dated 1705) another version of it is entitled 'Roger of Coverly the true Cheisere way.' Moreover, the Calverley family, from one of whose ancestors the tune is said to derive its name,[2] have been from time immemorial inhabitants of the Yorkshire village which bears their name. The editor of the Skene MS., on the strength of a MS. version dated 1706, claims the tune as Scotch, and says that it is well known north of the Tweed as 'The Maltman comes on Monday.' According to Dr. Rimbault (Notes and Queries, i. No. 8), the earliest printed version of it occurs in Playford's 'Division Violin' (1685). In 'The Dancing Master' it is first found at page 167

---

1 Or more correctly 'Roger of Coverly.' The prefix 'Sir' is not found until after Steele and Addison had used the name in the Spectator.
2 See Notes and Queries, vol. i. No. 23, p. 368.

of the 9th edition, published in 1695, where the tune and directions for the dance are given exactly as follows :—

Roger of Coverly.
Longways for as many as will.

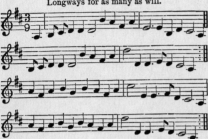

The 1. man go below the 2. wo. then round, and so below the 2. man into his own place ; then the 1. wo. go below the 2. man, then round him, and so below the 2. wo. into her own place. The 1. cu. [first couple] cross over below the 2. cu. and take hands and turn round twice, then lead up through and cast off into the 2. cu. place.   W. B. S.

The Scots song, 'The Maltman comes on Monday,' is not, as erroneously asserted by Chappell, by Allan Ramsay, although it is inserted in the first volume of his *Tea-Table Miscellany*, 1724. The English title is not so easily disposed of.

The *Spectator*, 2nd number, 1711, speaks of Sir Roger de Coverley as a gentleman of Worcestershire, and that 'His great grandfather was the inventor of the famous country dance which is called after him.'

Fanciful as this is, it shows that the dance, at that time, was considered an old one. Another origin for the name of the tune is based on a MS. in the writer's possession, inscribed 'For the violin, Patrick Cumming, his Book : Edinburgh, 1723.' At the end the name is repeated, and the date 1724 given. The

Scor-datura (not given in the MS.). *The Maltman, or Roger the Cavalier.*

tune stands as follows, although the Scottish *scordatura* is likely to puzzle the casual reader, since the first notes which appear as G, A, B, C sound A, B, C, D. (See SCORDATURA.)

It is well known that the name 'Roger' was bestowed upon the Royalists during the Civil War, and it is suggested that 'Coverly' is really a corruption of 'Cavalier.'

As the dance, later, was almost invariably used at the conclusion of a ball, it was frequently called 'The Finishing Dance.' See Wilson's *Companion to the Ball-Room*, circa 1816, and Chappell's *Popular Music* for the modern figure. According to an early correspondent of *Notes and Queries*, the tune was known in Virginia, U.S.A., as 'My Aunt Margery.' F. K.

SIREN. This, though not strictly a musical instrument, has rendered such good service to acoustical science that it deserves brief notice ; for fuller details the works referred to below must be consulted. Lord Rayleigh [1] describes it as 'a stiff disc, capable of revolving about its centre, and pierced with one or more sets of holes arranged at equal intervals round the circumference of circles concentric with the disc. A windpipe in connection with bellows is presented perpendicularly to the disc, its open end being opposite to one of the circles, which contains a set of holes. When the bellows are worked, the stream of air escapes freely if a hole is opposite to the end of the pipe ; but otherwise it is obstructed. As the disc turns, puffs of air in succession escape through it, until when the velocity is sufficient, these blend into a note the pitch of which rises continually with the rapid sequence of the puffs. One of the most important facts in the whole science of Acoustics is exemplified by the siren—namely that the pitch of a note depends upon the period of its vibration. The size and shape of the holes, the force of the wind, and other elements of the problem may be varied ; but if the number of puffs in a given time, such as one second, remains unchanged, so does the pitch. We may even dispense with wind altogether, and produce a note by allowing a card to tap against the edges of the holes as they revolve ; the pitch will still be the same.'

The Siren may be defined as a wind instrument, in which the successive air-waves are produced not at random or by consonance, but by circular rotatory motion, which is susceptible of accurate adjustment as well as measurement. It was originally invented by Cagniard de la Tour, who made it needlessly complicated by using the force of the wind to drive the rotating disc as well as to produce the required note. For this purpose the speaking holes in the top of the small wind-chest were pierced in an oblique direction ; those in the disc sloping in an opposite diagonal. There was also a counting apparatus attached to the upper part of the

[1] *Theory of Sound*, vol. i. p. 5.

main axis, with two dials for registering the number of rotations in a given time. This form has been faithfully reproduced in every manual of Physics up to now.[1] The name is said to have been somewhat fancifully, and indeed incorrectly, given it from Homer's Sirens, on account of its property of singing under water. It is true that if water be forced through it after the fashion of the Turbine, a buzzing or humming sound is produced. Seebeck and others effected material improvements, but the only two which need special notice are the instruments constructed by Helmholtz and Rudolph Kœnig respectively. The former is figured and described in that author's *Tonemp-findungen*,[2] and consists essentially of two sirens united on a single axis, each disc of which possesses four rows of holes susceptible of being separately opened, thus giving means for producing a large variety of intervals.

The upper wind-chest, which looks downwards, can be rotated on its feeding-tube so as to bring about varying changes of phase between the two discs. With this instrument Helmholtz succeeded in producing excellent results, using a small electromotor for driving it at a uniform rate.

The Siren of M. Rudolph Kœnig of Paris is a far more imposing instrument. It was made for W. Spottiswoode, Esq., P.R.S., was exhibited by the writer at the British Association meeting at York in 1881, and is now in the physical laboratory of the College of Science at Bristol. It is furnished with more than a dozen rotating discs of different kinds, which fit on to a vertical spindle, above a wind-chest of large size fitted with a keyboard of eight notes. A strong clockwork actuated by heavy weights forms the motive power, and an ingenious counting apparatus is made not only to record the number of rotations, but also to set going automatically a watch movement, and thus obtain by one motion of the observer's hand the speed of the disc, and the time of the observation. By properly computing the rings of perforations, the harmonic series is given by one disc, and the enharmonic scale by another. Indeed there is hardly any law of musical acoustics which it cannot be made to illustrate.[3] For purposes of demonstration the siren is excellent, and also for the illustration of perfect musical intervals; but for the accurate determination of absolute pitch it is far inferior to Lissajous's optical method; and still more so to the tuning-fork method, described under SCHEIBLER, and to Prof. M'Leod's Cycloscope.   W. H. S.

SIRÈNE, LA.   Opéra-comique in three acts; words by Scribe, music by Auber. Produced at the Opéra-Comique, March 26, 1844. In

English as 'The Syren,' at Princess's Theatre, Oct. 14, 1844.   G.

SIRMEN, or SYRMEN, MADDALENA LOM-BARDINI, a distinguished 18th-century violinist and composer for her instrument, who later, for some unknown reason, discarded her first profession for that of singer. The date of her birth, which it is believed took place at Venice in 1735, is uncertain, and the date of death is unknown. According to Dr. Burney, Maddalena Lombardini received her musical education at the Venetian 'Conservatorio dei Mendicanti,' and ten or more years before Tartini's death in 1770, she was profiting by his tuition. At this time she probably lived in Padua, so as to be near her master, but in 1760 she had apparently returned to Venice, where she received several letters from him, testifying to the keen interest he took in her career. The carefully written instructions as to bowing and fingering which he sent her in a letter dated Padua, March 5, 1760, constitute a valuable treatise on the art of violin-playing. This letter—the autograph of which is preserved at Venice—has been translated into German by J. A. Hiller, and inserted in his *Lebensbeschrei-bungen berühmter Musik-gelehrten.* Dr. Burney's excellent English version appeared in 1779, with the original text and the translation on opposite pages. It was printed in London 'for R. Bremner, opposite Somerset House in the Strand; by George Bigg, successor to Mr. Dryden Leach.' Although a copy of this work is rarely met with now, the substance of the pamphlet has been frequently quoted and reprinted in full in modern works on the violin. Between 1760 and 1768 Maddalena Lombardini toured in Italy, where she is said to have proved a worthy rival of Tartini's greatest pupil,—Nardini. During her travels the young *virtuosa* met Ludovico Sirmen, violinist and conductor at St. Maria Maddalena in Bergamo. The acquaintance eventually ended in marriage, and a visit to Paris, where the couple were heard at a Concert Spirituel on Monday August 15, 1768. The *Mercure de France* speaks in glowing terms of M. and Madame Sirmen's execution of a double violin concerto of their own composition. In 1771, Signora Sirmen came to London, where her début took place at the King's Theatre, on Thursday, Jan. 9. Bach's oratorio, 'Gioas Rè di Giuda' was the *pièce de résistance* of the evening. Duport (cadet) played a violoncello solo after the first Act, and in the Second Act, after the Duettino, there was a 'Concerto on the Violin by the celebrated Mrs. Lombardini Sirmen.' Her success in the Metropolis was apparently instantaneous, and was repeated on the 10th, 16th, 17th, 23rd, and 24th of the same month. During the following February she played frequently at the highest class concerts in London. On Feb. 15 she performed a violin concerto between the first and second parts of Handel's

---

[1] Deschanel, *Nat. Philos.* iv. p. 822; Everitt's translation. Ganot's *Physics*, p. 189; Atkinson's transl.
[2] Helmholtz, *Sensations of Tone*, Ellis's transl. p. 243 *et seqq.*
[3] A description of this instrument is to be found in Poggendorf's *Annalen*, and in the *Philosophical Magazine* for 1876.

'Judas Maccabæus' at Covent Garden, and on the 20th between the first and second parts of the 'Messiah.' Her 'Benefit Concert,' under the direction of Messrs. Bach and Abel, took place at Almack's on April 15, Guadagni, Wendling, Fischer, and other celebrated artists of the day assisted her ; but Madame Sirmen, either for a whim, or by request, abandoned for this occasion the instrument on which she excelled, and, according to the advertisement in the *Public Advertiser* of that date, played 'A Concerto on the Harpsichord.' In the month of May her services as violinist were in constant requisition. She repeated her triumphs at the King's Theatre, and, besides playing her violin concertos, contributed some violin *obbligati* to the songs of the principal vocalists. The *Public Advertiser* of May 28, 1771, announces 'The celebrated Signora Sirmen on the violin, being her last performance this Season.' The following year the gifted lady returned to London, and took up her abode in Half Moon Street, Piccadilly. The high reputation she had established for herself ensured her a welcome on her second arrival, and her services were more than ever sought after. She appeared at nearly all the Lenten Oratorio Concerts at Covent Garden, playing violin concertos between the parts. On March 26, 1772, she had another benefit concert, and on April 1 she introduced a new violin concerto by the eminent violoncellist Signor Cirri, after the second part of Handel's 'Messiah' at Covent Garden. Her final appearance in England is so announced in the *Public Advertiser* of April 10, at the newly organised 'Concert Spirituel' held in the same building. Apparently this was not only Signora Sirmen's last performance in England, but it was the end of her brilliant career as a violinist. Whether she was unable to sustain the high reputation she had achieved, or whether she was drawn away from her original bent by the dazzling example of Miss Schmeling (afterwards Madame Mara), can only be surmised. In any case she came to London again in 1774, and according to Dr. Burney [1] her last visit to the metropolis was in the capacity of a singer, in which her success was questionable. 'In "Sofonisba" and "The Cid"'—runs the note—'Madame Syrmen, the scholar of Tartini who was justly admired for her polished and expressive manner of playing the violin, appeared as a singer in the second woman, but having been first woman so long upon her instrument, she degraded herself by assuming a character in which, though not destitute of voice and taste, she laid no claim to superiority.' After this unfortunate attempt the erstwhile distinguished violinist drifted to the Continent again, and in 1782 she was singing secondary parts at the Court Theatre in Dresden. In May 1785 she made her last recorded appearance as a violinist at a Concert Spirituel in

[1] *Hist. Mus.* vol. iii. p. 500.

Paris, but without success, by reason, according to the *Mercure de France*, of the old-fashioned and worn-out music that she played. The fulfilment of the brilliant promise of Signora Sirmen's early career appears to have been arrested after her two brief seasons in London, and for this reason she is chiefly remembered, not so much as a violinist, but as the recipient of Tartini's notable letter.

Her compositions comprise :—

1. Six trios à deux Violons et Violoncelle obligé. Œuvre Premier (Welcker and Genaud, Soho). 2. Six Quartettes à deux Violons, Alto et Basse (written in conjunction with her husband). Berault, Paris (1769), also Longman & Broderip, London. 3. Six duets for two violins (dedicated to the Duke of Gloucester). William Napier, London. 4. Six concertos for violin with an accompaniment for two violins, Alto, Bass, Hautboy, and two horns. Hummel, Amsterdam. 5. Six Sonates à deux Violons. Hummel, Amsterdam. In the Berlin Bibliothek a copy of these Sonatas is embellished with a picture of Maddalena Sirmen. 6. Six Concertos adapted for the Harpsichord by Signor Giordani. London, 1789, Longman & Broderip, Cheapside, and No. 3 Haymarket. J. A. Hiller mentions a Concerto which was published in Venice.

Burney, *History of Music, The Present State of Music in Italy* ; Castil-Blaze, *L'Opéra Italien* ; Choron and Fayolle, *Dictionnaire Historique des Musiciens* ; *Mercure de France*, Sept. 1768 ; *Public Advertiser*, 1771, 1772 ; Fétis, *Biog. des Mus., Quellen-Lexikon.*   O. R. and E. H-A.

SISTINE CHOIR (Ital. *Il Collegio dei Cappellani Cantori della Cappella Pontificia*). A Collegiate Body, consisting of thirty-two Choral Chaplains, domiciled—though not in any special buildings of their own—at Rome, where, for many centuries, they have enjoyed the exclusive privilege of singing at all those solemn services and ecclesiastical functions in which the Pope officiates in person.

The genealogy of the Papal Choir may be traced back to a period of very remote antiquity. It is said—and the tradition is worthy of credit —that a school for the education of choristers was founded in Rome early in the 4th century by S. Sylvester, whose Pontificate lasted from the year 314 to 335. That S. Hilarius (461-468) established one, not much more than a century later, is certain. These institutions, after the lapse of another hundred years, were supplemented by new ones on a larger scale. On the destruction of the monastery of Monte Cassino, by the Lombards, in the year 580, the Benedictine Fathers fled to Rome ; and, under the protection of Pope Pelagius II. (577-590), established themselves in a new home, near the Lateran Basilica, where they opened schools for the preparation of candidates for holy orders. S. Gregory the Great (590-604) took advantage of this circumstance while working out his system of reform, and turned the seminaries to account as schools of singing. Under his care they prospered exceedingly, and in process of time attained proportions which enabled them to supply the various Basilicas with singers, who assembled on the greater festivals, and attended the Pope wherever he officiated. And thus arose the practice to which the Church was eventually indebted for the magnificent services of the Sistine Chapel.

2 h

These early Scholae Cantorum—sometimes called Orphanotropia, in allusion to the number of fatherless children which they sheltered—were governed by an ecclesiastic, of high rank, called the Primicerius, who, assisted by a Secundicerius destined afterwards to succeed him in his office, exercised absolute control over the youths and children committed to his care. Boys were admitted into the preparatory school (*Parvisium*) at a very early age; and, if of gentle birth, became, at the same time, members of the papal household, holding a status like that of the pages at a secular court. After passing through the necessary preparation, the choristers were permitted to take part in the most solemn services of the Church : and when their voices changed, were either prepared for the priesthood or provided for as Cubicularii. The older members of the Scholae were called Subdeacons; but the title was only an honorary one. By their help Rome was so liberally supplied with singers that, on more than one occasion, the Pope was able to send out skilled instructors for the purpose of encouraging the purest style of ecclesiastical singing in other countries ;[1] and, as we hear of no important modification of the system before the beginning of the 14th century, we are justified in believing that it fulfilled its purpose perfectly.

A great change, however, took place during the Pontificate of Clement V. (1305-14), who in the year 1305 transferred the Chair of S. Peter to Avignon, leaving his Primicerius and Schola Cantorum behind him in Rome. Too much oppressed by political and ecclesiastical troubles to devote his time to the regulation of details, Pope Clement naturally left the management of his chapel to underlings, who suffered the music to degenerate to a very unsatisfactory level. His successor, John XXII. (1316-34), issued in 1323 the well-known Bull, 'Docta sanctorum,' for the purpose of restraining his singers from corrupting the simplicity of plain-song, either by subjecting it to the laws of measured music, or by overloading it with ornamentation. It is doubtful whether the provisions of this Bull were fully carried out after the decease of its author, whose immediate successor, Benedict XII. (1334-42), was too fond of splendid ceremonial to raise any strong objection to the music sung by the twelve Choral Chaplains who officiated in his private chapel, on the score of its elaborateness. Indeed, the management of the choir employed by Benedict and his successors at Avignon differed altogether from that of the Roman Schola, which was still carried on under the Primicerius. In Rome, the choristers were

[1] For this purpose, John the Præcentor was sent to England, during the Primacy of Theodore, Archbishop of Canterbury (669-690). At the request of King Pepin (750-768), Simeon, the Secundicerius of the Roman Schola, was sent, in like manner, to France, but recalled by Pope Paul I. in 763, that he might succeed to the office of the then lately deceased Primicerius, Georgius ; while towards the close of the same century, two celebrated singers, Theodorus and Benedictus, were sent by Hadrian I. (772-795) to Charlemagne

taught on the old traditional system, almost from their infancy. At Avignon, the most welcome recruits were French and Flemish singers, who had already earned a brilliant reputation. Now, in those days the best singers were, for the most part, the best composers also ; and in the Low Countries the art of composition was rapidly advancing towards a state of perfection elsewhere unknown. It followed, therefore, that the choir at Avignon contained some of the greatest musicians in Europe, and was indebted to them for Faux-Bourdons and other polyphonic music, scarcely ever heard at that period except in the Netherlands.

In 1377 Pope Gregory XI. (1370-78) returned to Rome, and carried his choir with him. The contrast between the rival schools now became more apparent than ever ; yet by some means they amalgamated completely. The probability is that Gregory himself united them, forming the two choirs into one body, which was no longer called the Schola Cantorum, nor governed by a Primicerius, but was henceforth known as the Collegio dei Cappellani Cantori, and placed under the command of an ecclesiastic who held the appointment for life, and bore the title of Maestro della Cappella Pontificia. The precise year in which this change took place cannot be ascertained ; though it is certain that the new title was borne by Angelo, Abbot of S. Maria de Rivaldis, in 1397—twenty years after the return from Avignon. After this, we hear of no other Maestro till 1464, when the appointment was conferred upon Niccola Fabri, Governor of Rome, who held it for two years. From 1469 onwards the list includes the names of fourteen ecclesiastics, of whom all, except the last, were Bishops. The most celebrated of them was Elziario GENET, of Carpentras, 'Vescovo in partibus' (1515-26 ?), and the last of the series was Monsignor Antonio Boccapadule (1574-86), whose relations with the reigning Pope, Sixtus V. (1585-90), were disturbed by a misunderstanding, particulars of which will be found in vol. iii. p. 605. That the Pope was highly incensed at the spirit of insubordination shown by his Cantori Cappellani on this occasion is well known ; and it was probably on this account that, instead of appointing a successor to Monsignore Boccapadule, whom he somewhat unceremoniously deposed, he issued, Sept. 1, 1586, a Bull ('In suprema'), by virtue of which he conferred upon the college the right of electing, from among their own body, an officer, to whom was committed the duty of governing the choir, for three, six, or twelve months, or in perpetuity, according to the pleasure of the Electors.[2] It was clear that the Maestri so elected must necessarily be deprived of many of the privileges enjoyed by the ecclesiastical dignitaries who had preceded them ; but, by

[2] Baini, i. p. 272, Note 375.

way of compensation, they were invested with all which were not inseparable from the status of a Bishop ; and these were still further increased, by Pope Clement XIII., in the Bull 'Cum retinendi,' August 31, 1762. It was ultimately arranged that the election should take place annually, and this custom has ever since been strictly observed. The first Maestro so chosen was Giovanni Antonio Merlo, who served during the year 1587. Since his time, the election has always been fixed for Dec. 28 ; and for very many years it has been the invariable custom to elect the principal bass.

The Flemish singers, having once obtained a recognised position in the choir, soon began to exercise an irresistible influence over it, and, through it, over every other choir in Christendom. Among the first of whom we have any certain account, was Guglielmo Dufay, the founder of the older Flemish school, whose name is mentioned in the archives of the Chapel as early as 1380, three years only after the formal settlement of the college in Rome ; whence it has been conjectured that he first sang at Avignon, and afterwards accompanied Pope Gregory XI. to Italy. Dufay died in 1474, leaving many talented pupils.

The number of singers, which at Avignon had been limited to twelve, was in the 16th century increased to twenty-four, and not very long afterwards raised to thirty-two, which figure still represents the normal strength of the Choir, though the assistance of additional *ripieni* is sometimes permitted on extraordinary occasions. After the formal admission of the Netherlanders the compositions sung in the Papal Chapel were almost entirely supplied by the Cappellani Cantori themselves. The custom was, when any member of the college had produced a mass or other great work, to have it roughly written out, and rehearsed by the entire body of singers, who afterwards decided whether or not it was worthy of their acceptance. If the votes were in its favour, the original autograph was placed in the hands of the *Scrittori* —of whom four were usually kept in full employment—and by them copied, in stencilled notes large enough to be read by the entire choir at once, into huge part-books,[1] formed of entire sheets of parchment, of which a large collection, richly illuminated and magnificently bound, is still preserved among the Archives of the Sistine Chapel, though a vast number were destroyed in the conflagration which ensued on the invasion of Rome by Charles V. in 1527.

In the year 1565 Pope Pius IV. conferred upon Palestrina the title of Composer to the Pontifical Chapel, with an honorarium of three scudi and thirty baiocchi per month. The office was renewed, after Palestrina's death, in favour of Felice Anerio, but was never conferred on

any other member of the college. The most famous musicians who sang in the choir, after the expulsion of Palestrina in 1555, were Giov. Maria Nanini, admitted in 1577, Luca Marenzio (1594), Ruggiero Giovanelli (1599), and Gregorio Allegri (1629-52). Adami also mentions Vittoria, whose name, however, is not to be found in any official register. Among more modern Maestri the three most notable were, Tommaso Bai, who held the office of Maestro in 1714 ; the Cavaliere Giuseppe Santarelli— Dr. Burney's friend—who entered the choir as an artificial soprano singer in 1749, and died in 1790 ; and the Abbate Baini, who was received into the college in 1795, became Maestro in 1817, and died in 1844. By special favour of Pope Gregory XVI., Baini retained his office for life—an honour to which, as the greatest ecclesiastical musician of the 19th century, he was most justly entitled ; but no later Maestro has enjoyed the same privilege.

The two settings of the 'Miserere' by Bai and Baini, which for many years past have been used alternately with that of Allegri, are the only works added to the repertory of the chapel since the death of the last-named Maestro. Indeed, neither the constitution nor the habits of the college have, since Palestrina, undergone any important change—except, perhaps, in one particular, to be mentioned presently ; and hence it is that its performances are so infinitely valuable, as traditional indices of the style of singing cultivated at the period which produced the 'Missa Papae Marcelli,' the 'Improperia,' and the 'Lamentations.' Except for these traditions, the works of Palestrina would be to us a dead letter ; under their safe guidance we feel no more doubt as to the tempi of the 'Missa brevis' than we do concerning those of the 'Sinfonia Eroica.'

The one point in which a change has taken place is, the selection of voices ; and it is necessary to remark, that, as the change did not take place until seven years after Palestrina's death, the idea that we cannot sing his music, in England, as he intended it to be sung, for lack of the necessary voices, is altogether untenable. In early times, as we have already seen, the chapel was supplied with Soprani, and in all probability with Contralti also, by means of the Orphanotropia or Scholae Cantorum, exactly as English cathedrals are now supplied by means of the Choristers' Schools. That this plan was continued until quite late in the 16th century is sufficiently proved by the fact that, between 1561 and 1571, Palestrina held the joint offices of Maestro di Cappella and Maestro dei Fanciulli di Coro at the Church of St. Maria Maggiore, while, between 1539 and 1553 the post of Maestro de' Putti, at the Cappella Giulia, was successively filled by Arcadelt, Rubino, Basso, Ferrabosco, and Roselli. During the latter half of the 16th century, however, these youthful

[1] Mendelssohn, in one of his letters, gives an amusing description of one of these enormous books, which he saw carried in front of Baini, as he walked, in procession, up the nave of S. Peter's.

treble voices were gradually supplanted by a new kind of adult male Soprano, called the Soprano falsetto, imported, in the first instance, from Spain, in which country it was extensively cultivated by means of some peculiar system of training, the secret of which has never publicly transpired.[1] At the close of the 16th century, Spanish Soprani were in very great request ; and were, indeed, preferred to all others, until the year 1601, when a far more momentous change was introduced.

During nearly the whole of the 17th and the greater part of the 18th centuries the theatres of Europe were supplied with adult male Soprano and Contralto voices, preserved by a process so barbarous, that at one time it was forbidden in Italy on pain of death.   Yet, notwithstanding this penalty the system prospered, and enriched the stage with many of its most accomplished ornaments, such as Nicolini Grimaldi, Senesino, Carestini, Pacchierotti, Farinelli, and others. It has been said that Farinelli's wonderful voice was accidentally preserved, and the story is probably true ; for it is certain that very fine voices are sometimes preserved by accident, and quite reasonable to suppose that such accidents may very frequently happen, though should the sufferers possess no musical talent one is not likely to hear of them.   In these purely accidental cases no singer, with a good voice, has ever been refused admission into the Pontifical Choir ; but the transgression of the law, which was formerly punishable with death, now renders the offender de facto excommunicate, and therefore effectually prevents his reception into the Collegio.   One of the most learned and accomplished musicians in Rome, in command of one of its most celebrated choirs, remembered the admission of three artificial voices, accidentally produced, while he was studying under Baini.   Two of them proved too weak to be used, except as ripieni ; but the third developed into a magnificent Soprano.   The trained Soprano falsetto, which needs no accident to produce it, is not yet extinct.[2]

Italian choirmasters draw a careful distinction between the different voices they employ. The Voce bianca or naturale is by no means uncommon, but produces only Contralto singers. The true adult Soprano, arte fatta (made by method[3]), is an excessively rare voice, produced 'rather in the head than in the chest or throat,' and lasting, generally, to extreme old age, to the astonishment of the uninitiated hearer, who cannot understand its co-existence with a long white beard.[4] The occurrence of such phenomena

[1] Nevertheless, this secret does not seem to be altogether lost. A lady traveller in Spain and Portugal, amusingly expressed her surprise, on discovering that certain high flute-like notes, which she believed to have been produced by some beautiful young girl, really emanated from the throat of a burly individual *with a huge black beard and whiskers*!
[2] These statements are founded on information supplied to us by gentlemen resident in Rome, whose high position and long experience render their evidence more than ordinarily trustworthy.
[3] i.e. not by operation.
[4] In Adami da Bolsena's *Osservazioni* (Roma, 1711) will be found

is, however, so exceptional, that Pope Pius IX. founded the Scuola di S. Salvatore, near St. Peter's, for the express purpose of supplying the choirs of Rome with boys, subject, as in England, to be discharged on the breaking of their voices.

It remains only to say a few words concerning the style of singing practised by this matchless choir, and the lessons to be learned from it.

For the last three centuries at least there have been preserved certain traditional ornaments and forms of expression which are profound mysteries to the uninitiated.   For instance, the Second and Third Lamentations, on the three last days in Holy Week, are sung, as is generally supposed, by a high voice ; but, when that voice is too weak for the task, it is assisted by another, which, even in the most difficult *Abbellimenti* keeps so exactly with it, that the two voices are invariably mistaken for one. Again, there has long been a traditional way of making crescendi and diminuendi, which has astonished even the most experienced choirmasters.   The secret of this wonderful effect is, that, not only the amount of tone produced by each individual voice, but the actual number of voices employed, is gradually increased in the one case and diminished in the other.   The marvellous effects produced by the 'Miserere' have already been described at vol. iii. p. 216 ; and those associated with the 'Improperia,' at vol. ii. p. 462.   Such effects would no doubt be condemned by English choirmasters as 'tricks' —but they are not tricks.   No means can be so condemned, with justice, provided the effect they produce be artistic and legitimate.   [A catalogue of the singers of the Cappella Pontificia is given in the *Riv. Mus. Ital.* for 1907.] w. s. r.

SIVORI, ERNESTO CAMILLO, a great violinist, born at Genoa, Oct. 25, 1815.   He began the violin at five, under Restano, and continued it under Costa, until about the year 1823, when Paganini met with him, and was so much struck with his talent, as not only to give him lessons, but to compose six sonatas and a concertino for violin, guitar, tenor, and violoncello, which they were accustomed to play together, Paganini taking the guitar.   This was sufficient to launch the lad into Paganini's style.   [After a stay of six months in his native city, Paganini left for a tour in Germany in 1824, but before his departure he demonstrated the interest he took in young Sivori by desiring that he should accompany him on his travels.   Owing to the child's tender years, however, his parents refused to abandon him to the care of the great violinist. This being the case, Paganini recommended the elder Sivori to place his son with his own former master, Giacomo Costa, and for three years this teacher guided the child's studies so adroitly that when Paganini returned to Genoa in 1827, he found him well equipped as a

numerous portraits of Soprani and Contralti, with long beards—many of them priests.

classical player. Though perfectly satisfied with the progress of his *protégé*, he at the same time considered him lacking in virtuosity, and therefore suggested a change from Costa's scholastic method, to the more volatile system of his intimate friend Dellepiane. Again the boy's progress was astonishing, and at length his father, conquering his objections to a musical career for his son, became desirous that he should make some public appearances outside his own country. Accordingly, accompanied by his master Dellepiane, Camillo Sivori travelled first to Turin, where he played at a concert on May 3, 1827. He next appeared at Susa on the 5th, Saint Michel 6th, Chambéry 7th, Lyons 16th, Paris 18th, and made his début in London on the 25th. Two days later he was again in Paris, where the Duchesse de Noailles, the Duc de Berri and most of the *dilettanti* of the town interested themselves in him, as did likewise Rossini, Cherubini, Baillot, and other eminent musicians of the day. He gave a very successful concert in Paris on Dec. 4. In 1828, Sivori repeated his first triumphs in Paris and London. The autumn of the same year was spent by him in touring in the French provinces. After an absence of eighteen months he at length returned to Genoa in January 1829, and devoted himself earnestly to studying composition with Giovanni Serra, a profound theorist of the classical school, then occupying the post of musical director at the Teatro Carlo Felice in Genoa. During the year 1829 Sivori did little else but study, only acting at intervals as Dellepiane's substitute at the Teatro Carlo Felice, and also at the Conservatorio when the latter was taken ill. He generously gave the entire benefit of these services to his old master, and after Dellepiane's death extended the same charity to his impoverished widow and child for the space of a year. February 1834 found Sivori again in England making his début as a quartet-player in the Queen's Square 'Select Society' meetings at Mr. Alsager's house, and on March 28 he played in the first performance of Cherubini's Requiem.] He next traversed Italy, beginning with Florence, in 1839 ; then in 1841 and 1842 visited Prague, Vienna, Leipzig, Berlin, Frankfort, Brussels, St. Petersburg, and Moscow. On Jan. 29, 1843, he made his *rentrée* to Paris with a movement from a concerto of his own, his performance of which carried away his audience and procured him a special medal. He also made a vast impression in chamber-music. [The brilliantly successful appearance of Jan. 29,—when he played his own Concerto in E flat, Paganini's Concerto in B minor, and the same composer's 'Moïse,' for the G string —took place at the Conservatoire, and that institution presented him with its gold medal of honour.] From Paris he went to London, where he made his first appearance at the Phil-

harmonic in May, playing his Concerto in A at the same concerts on June 5, 1843, and repeating it on the 19th (Spohr was in London at the same time) ; returned in 1844, when Mendelssohn, Joachim, Hallé, Piatti, and Ernst were here also, and in 1845, when he assisted in the famous performances of Beethoven's Quartets at Mr. Alsager's house (see vol. i. p. 72), played at the Musical Union on June 24, etc. etc. [Tours in Great Britain and Ireland, and in Holland followed, and in the ensuing year he gave a concert at Brussels (on March 12), returning from thence to Paris and playing *en route* at Liège, Antwerp, Ghent, etc. The season of 1844 was again successfully occupied in London with his own concert at Her Majesty's Theatre, an appearance at a Philharmonic concert under Mendelssohn : a farewell concert at Hanover Square Rooms, where he played the 'Kreutzer Sonata' with Julius Benedict—a performance which was repeated at the Melodists' Club—and numerous private engagements. In August, Sivori in company with Dohler, Piatti, Henry Russell, and Lablache, jun., made a tour of Great Britain. After playing at Hamburg, he came to London again during the season of 1845.] In 1846 he was again here ; on June 27, played Mendelssohn's Concerto at a Philharmonic Concert, and was solo violin at Jullien's 'Concerts d'Été.' He then left for America, in which he remained till 1850, travelling from the Northern States, by Mexico and Panama, to Valparaiso, Rio, Buenos Ayres, and Montevideo, and narrowly escaping death by yellow fever. In 1850 he returned to Genoa, and shortly after lost nearly all the money he had made in the new world by an imprudent speculation. In 1851 he was again in Great Britain, touring throughout the whole country. [In London he played at Professor Ella's Musical Union concert with Golinelli (pianist) and Piatti. In 1852 he played in Beethoven's Triple concerto in C—with Piatti as violoncellist—at the New Philharmonic Society at Exeter Hall under Berlioz's bâton. A tour in Scotland in 1853 was followed by a tour in Switzerland, where he broke his wrist in an unfortunate carriage accident at Geneva. On Dec. 15, Sivori played at the Pergola, Florence, returning to Genoa in time for the opening of the Teatro Apollonio. 1854 brought a tour in France, and the following year, his marriage to the actress Ortensia Damain, after which he toured in Spain, where the Queen made him Knight of the Order of Carlos III. From Spain he went to Portugal, where the King made him Knight of the Order of Christ the King, and in the spring of 1856 he made appearances in Belgium, Holland, and Germany. In 1857 Sivori toured in England with Piatti, and the fourteen-year-old pianist, Arthur Napoleon.] In 1862 he scored one more success in Paris in the B minor Concerto of Paganini. In 1864 he revisited

London, and appeared at the Musical Union and elsewhere. [In 1869 Sivori appeared at some of the Monday Popular Concerts in London, and in 1870 toured in France, after which he returned to Genoa and there led a quiet life until he passed away at his house in the Via Giulia, on Feb. 19, 1894.]

As a man he was always liked—'little, good-tempered, warm-hearted, intelligent Camillo Sivori' is the description of him by an English journalist. He was the only direct pupil of Paganini, and his playing was that of a virtuoso of the Paganini school, with a prodigious command of difficulties, especially of double-stopping, second only to his master. His tone was silvery and clear, but rather thin. His style—judged by a classical standard—was cold and affected, and had little real feeling.

[His compositions include two Concertos for Violin in E flat and A; Cappriccio, La Génoise; op. 12, Tarantelle Napolitaine, Violin and orchestra, or piano; Deux duos concertants for Pianoforte and Violin; Duet for Violin and Double Bass, written with Bottesini; Fantaisie Caprice in E; Fantaisie Étude, op. 10; Fantaisie, Fleurs de Naples; Souvenir de Norma; Carnaval de Chili; Carnaval de Cuba; Carnaval Américain; Tempest Music (Milan, 1860); Folies Espagnoles; Variations on 'Nel cor non piu mi sento' and 'Le Pirate'; Three Fantasias upon airs from 'La Sonnambula,' 'I Puritani,' 'Zapateado'; Fantasia on airs from 'Un Ballo in Maschera,' 'Il Trovatore,' 'Lucia di Lammermoor'; Andante Spianato; 'Trois Romances sans paroles,' with pianoforte accompaniment.]

[Heron-Allen, Camillo Sivori, The Violin Times, March 15, 1894, No. 5, vol. i.; James, E. (Ph. and Lit. D.), Camillo Sivori, a Sketch of his Life, etc.; Benedit, G., C. Sivori (reprinted from the Sémaphore, Marseilles, March 7, 1854); Pierrottet, Adèle, Camillo Sivori (with pictures); Fino, G. da, C. Sivori and F. Romani; Phipson, T. L., Sketches and Anecdotes of Celebrated Violinists; Lahee, H. C., Famous Violinists, Musical Standard, Feb. 24, 1894; Figaro, Paris, April 1, 1894; Journal des Débats, Feb. 28, 1828; Siècle, Paris, Feb. 6, 1843; Moniteur Universel, Paris, Feb. 13, 1843; British Minstrel, vol. ii. pp. 165-6; Fétis, Biog. des Mus.] G.; with additions in square brackets by E. H-A.

SIXTH. The interval which embraces six degrees of the scale. There are three forms—the major, the minor, and the augmented. (1) The major sixth, as CA, contains 9 mean semitones, and the ratio of its limiting sounds in the true scale is 5 : 3. It is a concord, and in harmony is regarded as the first inversion of the minor common chord. (2) The minor sixth, as CA♭ or E C, contains 8 semitones, and the ratio of its limiting sounds is 8 : 5. It is also a concord, and in harmony regarded as the first inversion of the major common chord. (3) The augmented sixth, which is arrived at by flattening the lower or sharpening the upper extreme sound of a major sixth, as D♭ B, or A♭ F♯, contains 10 semitones, and the ratio of the limiting sounds is 125 : 72. The augmented sixth is a discord, and is usually resolved by moving each note a semitone outwards to the octave, the sharpening or flattening of one of the extreme sounds already implying a straining in that

direction. [See HARMONY.] Three forms of the augmented sixth are distinguished by special names : when it is accompanied by the major third it is called 'Italian' (see a); when to this is added the augmented fourth, it is called 'French' (see b); and when the major third and fifth are present (c) it is called 'German.'

The Neapolitan Sixth is the name by which a chord consisting of a minor sixth and minor third on the subdominant has long been known ; as (d) in the key of C minor.

Theorists, starting from different radical assumptions, suggest different derivations for this chord. Some, taking the major and minor scales to comprise all the notes which can be used for essential harmonies, except in the cases where important root notes in those scales bear fundamental harmonies on such principles as they accept, derive the chord from a combination of two roots ; so that the dominant is the root of the two lower notes which are respectively its seventh and minor ninth, and the tonic of the upper, which is its minor ninth. Others, accepting the unquestionably frequent use of some chromatic harmonies in relation to an established Tonic, by many great masters, indicate the major concord on the minor or flat supertonic (as the major common chord of D♭ in relation to the Tonic C) as one of them, and hold the 'Neapolitan sixth' to be its first inversion. Others, again, hold this sixth to be found in the minor scale of the subdominant ; and others, yet further, that it is merely produced by the artificial lowering of the sixth for artistic purposes, similar to the artificial sharpening of the fifth which is commonly met with ; and that its object may either be to bring the supertonic melodically nearer the Tonic in downward progression, or to soften the harshness which results from the augmented fourth in the chord of the sixth and minor third on the subdominant of the usual minor scale. In the theory which explains some chromatic combinations as reflections of the old ecclesiastical modes, this chord would spring from the use of the ecclesiastical Phrygian, which was the same as the Greek Doric mode.   C. H. H. P.

[Concerning one chord of the sixth, that on the supertonic of the key, a good deal of doubtfully authoritative teaching has been made public, in regard to its use mainly in contrapuntal work. There is no doubt that the motion of all three parts is unimpeded ; though the B may usually proceed to C, the keynote, the F moves quite as often up to G as down to E. Yet a certain school of theorists still maintain that the chord is the second inversion of the dominant seventh with the root left out. (See Prout, Harmony,

20th impression, 1903, p. 106.) No explanation is offered concerning the freedom of motion which is admittedly allowed. The fact is that the chord was used commonly by the polyphonic masters long before the dominant seventh was considered as an essential part of the key. The circumstance that each of the upper parts makes a concord with the lowest was held to excuse the discord between the two upper parts, and the same liberty of movement was given as in the case of an undoubted concord. Its occurrence, with this obvious freedom of motion, in compositions of the madrigalian era, is too common to need citation.]

SJÖGREN, EMIL, born June 6, 1853, at Stockholm; studied first at the Conservatoire there, and afterwards at Berlin under Kiel for composition and Haupt for the organ. In 1884-85 he made tours through Europe, visiting Vienna, Munich, Venice, and Paris. During a stay at Meran, he was for six months under the influence of Lange Müller, which affected his work very deeply. Since 1891 Sjögren has been organist at the Yohannes-kyrka at Stockholm, where he has been employed in teaching, and in composition of all kinds; chiefly for piano solo, violin and piano, and songs. He is a composer whose works do not display the almost exclusively Scandinavian character of Grieg; but who shows an infusion of German ideas. Among his best-known works are 'Der Contrabandista,' op. 9, for bass voice; 'Erotikon,' op. 10, for piano; Novelettes, op. 14, for piano; the three Sonatas, op. 19, op. 24, op. 32, in G minor, E minor, and G minor, for violin and piano; the two sonatas, op. 35 and op. 44, in E minor and A major for piano. Besides these Sjögren has written a great number of melodies, and detached pieces for the piano, but up to the present time (1907) he has not produced any compositions in the symphonic style. He has also written much for the voice, as well as many pieces for the organ. His music shows a certain amount of Scandinavian style, coupled with a warm emotionalism which is derived from more southern countries. D. H.

SKENE MANUSCRIPT. A collection of airs, chiefly Scottish, though with a considerable admixture of foreign dance tunes and English vocal melodies, supposed to have been written at various dates between 1615 and 1635. In 1818 the MS. came into the possession of the Faculty of Advocates, Edinburgh, along with a charter chest of documents, by bequest from Miss Elizabeth Skene of Curriehill and Hallyards in Midlothian. She was the last representative in line of the family, and great-great-granddaughter of John Skene of Hallyards, who died in 1644, and was the original possessor and probably also the writer of some parts of the MS. It consisted originally of seven distinct parts, but these have since been bound together, and now form one tiny oblong volume 6½ inches by 4½. It is written in tablature

for a lute with five strings. As amateur scribes however were rarely correct, either in their barring or in marking the lengths of the notes, a translator into modern notation requires much patience, as well as knowledge and ingenuity, to decipher and correct the uncertainties of these MSS. In the present instance the work of translation was undertaken by George Farquhar Graham, whose fitness for the task is sufficiently shown by the article 'Music' which he wrote for the 7th edition of the Encyclopædia Britannica. In 1838 Mr. William Dauney, F.S.A.Scot., urged by his friends and encouraged by the members of the Bannatyne and Maitland Clubs, published the translation in 4to with a very learned preliminary dissertation on the music of Scotland, and an appendix by Finlay Dun containing an analysis of the structure of Scottish music. [See DAUNEY, vol. i. p. 664b.]

The MS. contains 115 airs; of these 85 were published, 11 were found to be duplicates, and the rest were rejected as being either unintelligible or uninteresting. The airs of Scottish origin appear to be about 45, of which 25 were previously unknown. Many of the latter are no doubt sufficiently commonplace in style, but a few are really fine melodies, worthy of a place in our present collections, and worthy of the attention of rising poets. In some instances the airs are in a simple unadorned vocal state, a few being even pentatonic; of which 'Lady Rothiemay's Lilt,' 'Lady Laudian's Lilt,' and the first part of 'Kilt your coat, Maggie,' may be named as examples. In most cases the first half strain of the air is simple, the repetition more florid; this is frequently followed by variations—or divisions as they were then called—consisting of scale and other passages well fitted to show the dexterity of the player. Like many other Scots tunes, a considerable number of the airs are either pentatonic or modal as regards their scale.

The fact of so many duplicates being found in the MS. has caused the remark to be made that the seven parts must have belonged to different individuals. Nothing can be inferred as to the date of either part. Part III., however, differs from the others in certain respects, and not improbably belonged to some other member of the family. It is written for a lute tuned CFADG, all the others being for a lute tuned ADADA. The only air that is said to bring the MS. down to a later date than has been claimed for it (1635) occurs in Part VI. and is named 'Peggie is ouer the sie with the souldier.' This is the tune of an English ballad included in the catalogue issued by Thackeray in 1689. There is a copy of the ballad, printed about 1655, in the Euing collection of Glasgow University, and a still earlier copy in the Roxburghe Ballads; and we learn from Chappell's list of the publishers of black-letter ballads that its date is from 1620 to 1629, both prior to the date claimed for the MS. The simple Skene versions of some of our old melodies, two of which have already been given in this work [see SCOTTISH MUSIC], show how little we really know of the early forms of our airs. The discovery in this MS. of these and of some other tunes, otherwise unknown until the middle of the following century, proves that first appearance in print is no guide whatever to actual age. The appearance also in it of so many as 25 previously unknown airs leads to the belief that the loss of ancient melodies may have been as great even as that of songs, in regard to which Ritson, in a letter to George Paton, after enumerating about 120, adds that he believes he has the names of as many more, none of which he had ever been able to recover. Several of the parts of the Skene MS. contain airs which date themselves ; such as Ostend (taken 1604) ; Prince Henry's masque (1610) ; Lady Elizabeth's masque (1613).

List of the 115 tunes contained in the seven parts of the Skene MS.

The first row of figures shows the order in which they appear in the original ; the second is that of Mr. Dauney's volume. The asterisks point out the duplicates, and the figures after the names show their place in the MS. The omitted tunes are marked by daggers. The double dagger in the first line of figures between 29 and 30 shows the place of a tune omitted in Mr. Dauney's list.

PART I. (24 leaves.)

1. 38. Male Simme.
2. 40. Doun in yon banke.
3. 76. O Sillie soule alace.
4. 10. Long ere onie old man.
5. 63. The Spanishe Ladie.
6. 8. My dearest sueate is fardest fra me.
7. 41. I long for your verginitie. *48.
8. † Hutcheson's Galziard.
9. 59. Pitt in an inche and mair of it
10. † A French volt.
11. 69. Lady Elizabeth's Maske.
12. 47. Kette Bairdie.
13. 85. Trumpeters Currand. * 50.
14. 60. Joy to the persone.
15. 68. Comedians maske.
16. 42. Aderneis Lilt.
17. 78. Sommersetts Maske.
18. 36. John Devesonnes pint of wine.
19. † Horreis Galziard. * 45.
20. 64. Froggis Galziard.
21. 22. I cannot liue and want thee.
22. 20. I mett her in the medowe.
23. 9. Prettie weil begunn man.
24. 67. Prince Henreis Maske. Finis quod Skine.

PART II. (8 leaves.)

25. † Lady wilt thou love me. (Fragment.)
26. 37. The lass o Glasgowe.
27. 25. Shoe looks as shoe wold lett me.
28. 1. Alace yat I came owr the moor and left my love behind me. * 42.
29. 34. Bone Jeane makis meikill of me.
‡ 27. Let never crueltie dishonour bewtie.
30. 17. My love she winns not her away.
31. 18. Jennet drinks no water.

PART III. (12 leaves.)

32. 84. A Frenche.
33. * Scerdustis. 66.
34. * My Ladie Rothemayes Lilt. 96.
35. 21. Blue breiks.
36. † Aberdeins Currand.
37. * Scullione. 83.
38. 15. My Ladie Laudians Lilt. * 84.
39. 35. Lesleis Lilt.
40. 29. The Keiking Glasse.

41. 3. To dance about the Bailzeis dubb.
42. * I left my love behind me. 28.
43. 12. Alace this night yat we suld sinder.
44. 58. Pitt on your shirt (mail) on Monday. * 65.
45. † Horreis Galziard. * 19 (both omitted).
46. 23. I dowe not qunne (when) cold.
47. 33. My mistres blush is bonie.
48. * I long for her verginitie. 7.
49. † A Saraband.
50. * Trumpeters Currant (anonymous). 13.

PART IV. (12 leaves.)

51. 70. What if a day.
52. 77. Floodis of tears.
53. 66. Nightingale.
54. 74. The willow trie.
55. 55. Marie me marie me quoth the bonie lass.
56. † My Lord Haye's Currand.
57. † Jeane is best of onie.
58. 72. What high offences hes my fair love taken.
59. † Alman Nicholas.
60. 54. Currand Royal (Sir John Hopes Currand).
61. 46. Hunter's Carrier.
62. 6. Blue ribbenn at the bound rod.
63. 49. I serue a worthie ladie.

PART V. (22 leaves.)

64. 80. Canaries.
65. * Pitt on your shirt (mail) on Monday. 44.
66. 71. Scerdustis. * 33.
67. 50. She mowpit it coming owr the lie.
68. 24. Adew Dundie.
69. 31. Thrie sheips skinns.
70. 65. Chrichtons gud nicht.
71. 28. Alace I lie my alon I am lik to die awld.
72. * I love for love again. 98.
73. 73. Sincopas (Cinque-pace).
74. 56. Almane Delorne.
75. 51. Who learned you to dance and a towdle?
76. 19. Remember me at eveninge.
77. † Love is a labour in vaine.
78. 26. I dare not vowe I love thee.
79. † My Lord Dingwalls Currand.
80. 83. Brangill of Poictu.
81. 53. Pantalone.
82. 57. Ane Almane Moreiss.
83. 81. Scullione. * 37.
84. * My Ladie Laudians Lilt. 38.
85. † Queins Currand.

PART VI. (10 leaves.)

86. 61. Then wilt thou goe and leave me her.
87. 48. I will not goe to my bed till I suld die.
88. 13. The Flowres of the Forest.
89. 82. The fourth measur of the Buffins.
90. 39. Shackle of Hay.
91. 62. Com love lett us walk into the Springe.
92. 45. Sa merrie as we have bein.
93. 11. Kilt thy coat Magge, cilt thy coat ti.
94. 75. Shipeherd saw thou not.
95. 2. Peggie is ouer ye sie wi ye souldier.
96. 4. Ladye Rothemayes Lilt. * 34.
97. 52. Omnia vincit amor.
98. 5. I love my love for love again. * 72.
99. 14. Ostend.
100. † Sir John Moresons Currant.
101. † Preludium.

PART VII. (14 leaves.)

102. † Exercises.
103. 44. Gilcreichs Lilt.
104. 43. Blew cappe.
105. 30. Lady Cassilis Lilt.
106. * Blew Breiks. 35.
107. 32. Post Ballangowne.
108. 7. John Andersonne my Jo.
109. 16. Good night and God be with you.
110. † A Sarabande.
111. † Lik as the dum Solsequium.
112. † Come sueat love lett sorrow cease.
113. 79. Veze Setta.
114. † A Sarabande.

J. M. W.

SKETCH (Ital. *Schizzo* ; Germ. *Skizze* ; Fr. *Esquisse*). I. This name is strictly applied to the preliminary jotting down of a musical idea, or to memoranda of special points of development or orchestration, used by composers in the process of bringing their works to perfection. To analyse the various books of extant sketches by great masters would lie outside the scope of this Dictionary ; we may point out that various sketch-books of Beethoven have been published, which are essential to a knowledge of his methods of working.

II. A short movement, usually written for the pianoforte, and deriving its name, in some cases, from its descriptive character, in others.

from the slightness of its construction. Mendelssohn's three little Capriccios, written in Wales for the cousins of Professor Taylor, and now known as op. 16, have also been published under the title of Sketches, and may fairly lay claim to it, though it was not given to them by the composer himself. Schumann's four 'Skizzen' for the pedal-pianoforte (op. 58), are of an altogether different class, and derive their name from the composer's modest appreciation of their calibre; and Sterndale Bennett's three sketches (op. 10), 'The Lake,' 'The Millstream,' and 'The Fountain,' are among his best and most popular works.   W. S. R.

SLIDE. I. (Ger. *Schleifer*; Fr. *Coulé*). An ornament frequently met with in both vocal and instrumental music, although its English name has fallen into disuse. It consists of a rapid diatonic progression of three notes, either ascending or descending, of which the principal note, or note to be ornamented, is the third, and the other two are grace-notes, and are either written of small size (Ex. 1), or, in old music, indicated by an oblique line drawn towards the principal note from the note preceding (Ex. 2).

1. BEETHOVEN, Bagatelle, Op. 119, No. 5.

CHOPIN, Andante Spianato, Op. 22.

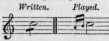

Occasionally, as in the Fitzwilliam Virginal Book, the slide is indicated by a line crossing the stem of the note diagonally :—

Another method of indicating it is by means of a *direct* (∾) placed upon the degree of the stave on which the slide is to commence, and having its right extremity prolonged so as to extend to the position of the principal note (Ex. 3). The short notes of the slide are always executed within the value of the principal note, and not before it, and any note which may accompany it must fall together with the first

note, as in Ex. 3. The accent is on the principal note.

3.   BACH, Suite Française, No. 3.

When a note followed by another, one degree above or below it, is ornamented by a NACHSCHLAG of two notes [vol. iii. p. 346, Ex. 8], the small notes present exactly the appearance of a slide to the second large note, and thus a misapprehension as to the proper rendering might arise. For according to the invariable rule of all grace-notes, the small notes of the Nachschlag would be executed during the latter portion of the value of the first large note (Ex. 4), but those of the slide not until the commencement of the second (Ex. 5). Properly, a slur should be introduced to connect the grace-notes with their own principal note, as in the examples; this prevents the possibility of mistake, but in the absence of the slur—and it is frequently omitted—the performer must be guided by his own judgment.

4. Nachschlag.   5. Slide.

Sometimes the first note of a slide is sustained for the duration of the whole. In old music this was indicated by writing the extreme notes of the slide on a single stem, and drawing an oblique line between them, either upwards or downwards, according to the direction of the slide (Ex. 6). In modern music the same thing is expressed (though not very accurately) by means of a tie (Ex. 7).

6.   Written.   Played.

7. SCHUBERT, 'Momens Musicals,' No. 3.

Slides of greater extent than three notes are not infrequent; groups of three notes leading to a principal note are often met with (Ex. 8), and slides of four and even more notes occasionally (Ex. 9). This extended slide is sometimes called *Tirade* or *Tirata* (from *tirare* to draw, or to shoot). E. W. Wolf, in his *Musikalische Unterricht* (Dresden, 1788), calls such passages 'sky-rockets.'

8.   MEYERBEER, 'Roberto.'

9.   HUMMEL, 'Pianoforte-School.'

Besides the above, a more complicated kind of slide is mentioned by Emanuel Bach and others, called the dotted slide, in which the first grace-note received the addition of a dot. Its execution, however, varies so considerably —as is proved by the two examples by Emanuel Bach, selected from a variety of others (Ex. 10)—that the sign has never met with general acceptance, although the ornament itself, written out in notes of ordinary size, is of constant occurrence in the works of the great masters (Ex. 11).

10.   *Written.*   *Played.*

Written.

Played.

11.   HAYDN, 'Sonata in G.'

BEETHOVEN, 'Sonata Pathétique.'

F. T.

II. (Fr. *Glissade* or *Porte de Voix*; Ital. *Portamento*.) To violinists the 'slide' is one of the principal vehicles of expression, at the same time affording a means of passing from one note to another at a distance. The rules governing the 'slide' are not restricted, as its use and

effect entirely depend upon the judgment of the player, but the following directions are generally observed :—(1) A 'slide' is effected by allowing the finger already upon the string to move up or down to within a fourth or third of the new note. Care should be taken to keep the fingers strictly within the range of each new position. Another kind of 'slide' is made by moving the finger over two or more adjoining semitones, without interruption.

In imitation of the matchless *legato* which the human voice alone can attain, violinists frequently employ a 'slide' limited to adjoining notes. A third 'slide' is entirely of a brilliant type, and belongs to the *virtuoso, par excellence*, having originated with Paganini. It consists in executing chromatic passages, singly or in thirds, octaves, or other combinations, entirely with the same fingers. Paganini's music abounds in this species of 'slide,' as also do the compositions of the masters of the Belgian and French school, who adopted his methods. This 'slide' did not come into general use until the end of the 18th century or beginning of the 19th. Yet its sister acquirements, the tremolo, and shift, were known to violinists a century earlier. Mersenne (*Harm. Universelle*, 1636) speaks with delight of such professional violinists as 'les Sieurs Bocan, Lazarin,' and others, who employed a certain 'tremblement qui ravisient l'esprit,' and the same author mentions the violinists who could mount to the octave on every string. Notwithstanding the lack of any direct mention of the 'slide' previous to the 18th century, the following remark by Jean Rousseau in his *Traité de la Viole* (1687), might indicate that the eminent viola da gamba player, Hottman, was acquainted with it. . . . 'It was he' (Hottman), says Rousseau, 'who in France first composed melodies (*pièces d'harmonie*) regulated for the viol, so as to make the effect of beautiful singing (*beaux chants*) in imitation of the voice.' Corelli in the first half of the 17th century founded the correct position and independence of the left hand, but it is doubtful whether he, or his immediate successors, knew the use of the 'slide.' Even at the beginning of the 18th century the generality of violinists relied mostly upon every species of turn and flourish to give expression to their playing. To the 'Beat,' 'Back Fall,' 'Double Backfall,' 'Springer,' etc., writers of violin methods devoted elaborate attention, and, curiously enough, as though foreshadowing the coming of the 'slide,' these very turns were in France called by the name now employed in that country for its English equivalent, i.e. *Porte de Voix*. Neither Leopold Mozart nor Geminani in the middle of the 18th century mentions the 'slide,' but like their predecessors consider good taste entirely dependent on the judicious employment of turns. But with Viotti's advent, and his establishment of the French School, the old methods began to give way to a truer mode of expression which found its medium in the change of position on the same string. Viotti's most gifted pupil, Rode, was particularly devoted to this method of playing tender phrases, and no violinist cultivated it more carefully than Rode's imitator and admirer Spohr. The compositions of the latter are full of examples of the 'slide' in its most classical form, and his *Violin School* contains some of the best instructions and examples of the art to be found.

Huet, Felix, *Études sur les Differentes Écoles de Violon*; Geminani, F., *The Art of Playing the Violin* ; Bailliot, P., *L'Art du Violon* ; Cartier, J. B., *L'Art du Violon* ; Mersenne, *Harmonie Universelle* ; Rousseau, Jean, *Traité de la Viole, La Chronique Musicale*, August 1873, ' Un Virtuose en 1682 ' ; Scudo, P., *La Musique Ancienne et Moderne* ; Spohr, *Violin School* ; Playford, John, *An Introduction to the Skill of Musick*.   O. R.

III. A contrivance fitted in some form or other to nearly all wind instruments for the purpose of adjusting the pitch by altering the length of the vibrating air-column. It is also applied in a special form to trombones and to some trumpets for the purpose of filling up those notes of the chromatic scale which lie between the various harmonics or ' open ' notes. For this particular use of the slide principle see TROMBONE and TRUMPET.

For the attainment of the first object the slide may be simple, as on the flute, or U-shaped, as is usual on brass instruments. As the slide is used only for the general adjustment of pitch, it should not move too freely, in case the setting should be accidentally altered. In instruments such as the flute and clarinet, the speaking length of which varies with the opening of the different side-holes, any permissible alteration of pitch by means of the tuning-slide, or its equivalent in the form of socketed joints, is necessarily small. The reason for this is that the length added by the extension of the slide cannot bear a uniform proportion to the virtually different lengths of the instrument as determined by the different side-holes ; therefore, no considerable alteration of pitch can be obtained on such an instrument without throwing it out of tune within itself. This apparently trifling matter is practically important, and the want of apprehension of it has led many to underestimate the difficulty and cost of carrying out such a change of pitch as was determined on by the Philharmonic Society of London in 1896, when the present (low) pitch was introduced. The slow progress of the change is largely due to the limitation of the efficiency of the slide, and the consequent need of new instruments constructed to the required pitch.

Attempts have been made to adapt the shifting slide as used on the trombone, to the French horn, but the particular proportions of this instrument and others of the horn type do not admit of a successful application of the slide in this way.   D. J. B.

SLIVINSKI, JOSEPH VON, born at Warsaw, Dec. 15, 1865, studied at Warsaw Conservatorium under Strobl ; at Vienna with Leschetizky for four years; and finally with Rubinstein at St. Petersburg. His first appearance in public was in 1890, and he was not long in finding his way to England, where he first appeared at a recital of his own in St. James's Hall, May 17, 1892. In January 1893 he played at one of Henschel's London Symphony Concerts; at the Crystal Palace, March 4; and at the Philharmonic, March 9 of the same year. In the following November he made his first appearance in New York. His playing is remarkable for poetical feeling, as well as for surprising brilliance of touch. (Baker's *Biog. Dict. of Mus.* etc.)   M.

SLOW MOVEMENT. A generic term for all pieces in slow time, whether separate or forming part of a larger work. It is specially applied to such pieces when they occur in a work in sonata-form. The right of any movement to this title must depend rather on its character than its time indication, for many movements marked Allegretto are strictly slow movements.   M.

SLUR. This word, taken in its original and widest sense, signifies an effect of phrasing which is more commonly expressed by the Italian term *legato*, *i.e.* connected. The sign of the slur is a curved line (Ger. *Schleifbogen* ; Fr. *Liaison*) drawn over or under a group of notes, and the notes included within its limits are said to be *slurred*, and are performed with smoothness, if on a stringed instrument, by a single stroke of the bow, or in singing, on a single syllable. [See LEGATO, vol. ii. p. 665.] But although this was originally the meaning of the word, it is now used in a more restricted sense, to denote a special phrasing effect, in which the last of the notes comprised within the curved line is shortened, and a considerable stress laid on the first. This effect has already been fully described in the article PHRASING [vol. iii. p. 713]. In vocal music the slur is employed to indicate the use of PORTAMENTO, and it is also very generally placed over two or more notes which are sung to a single syllable. In this case, however, the sign is superfluous, since if the passage consists of quavers or shorter notes, the connection can be shown by writing them in groups instead of separate, while even if the notes are crotchets, the fact of there being but a single syllable sufficiently indicates the *legato*. Moreover, an effect analogous to the slur in instrumental music, whereby the second of two notes is curtailed and weakened, is perfectly possible in singing, and may very probably have been intended by the earlier composers where the sign of the slur is employed. This view is insisted upon by Mendelssohn, who in a letter to G. A. Macfarren[1] strongly objects to the engravers of his edition of 'Israel in Egypt' placing the slur over two quavers or semiquavers which are to be sung to one word.

When the slur is used in combination with a series of dots, thus ♪••♪, it indicates the effect called *mezzo staccato*, in which the notes are made of longer duration than if marked with the staccato-sign only, being sustained for nearly their full value, and separated by a very brief interval of silence. [See also STACCATO.]   F. T.

SMALL OCTAVE. See C, vol. i. p. 433.

SMART, GEORGE, a London music-publisher who had some skill as a performer on the double bass. He was one of a musical family, and his son, Sir George Smart, and other relatives attained distinction. Before entering business, he was an assistant to Robert BREMNER, and had been possibly also employed by William NAPIER. He began in the music trade about 1770, his shop being at the corner of Argyll Street, and numbered 331 Oxford Street. He issued many minor publications, such as country dances and sheet music, and remained at 331 Oxford Street until one of the earliest years of the 19th century, the period of his death. George Smart was one of the founders of a benevolent society for musicians.   F. K.

SMART, SIR GEORGE THOMAS, Knight, born May 10, 1776, son of the above George Smart, received his early musical education as a chorister of the Chapel Royal under Dr. Ayrton. He learned organ - playing from Dr. Dupuis and composition from Dr. Arnold. On quitting the choir in 1791 he obtained the appointment of organist of St. James's Chapel, Hampstead Road, and was also engaged as a violinist at Salomon's concerts. At a rehearsal of a symphony of Haydn's for one of those concerts the drummer was absent, and Haydn, who was at the harpsichord, inquired if any one present could play the drums. Young Smart volunteered, but from inexperience was not very successful, whereupon the great composer, ascending the orchestra, gave him a practical lesson in the art of drumming. About the same time he commenced practice as a teacher of the harpsichord and singing. He soon showed an aptitude for conducting musical performances. In 1811, having successfully conducted some concerts in Dublin, he was knighted by the Lord Lieutenant. In 1813 he was chosen one of the original members of the Philharmonic Society, and between that date and 1844 conducted forty-nine of its concerts. From 1813 to 1825 he conducted the Lenten oratorios at one or other of the patent theatres, at one of which in 1814 he introduced Beethoven's 'Mount of Olives' to the English public. In 1818 he directed the City concerts established by Baron Heath. On April 1, 1822, he was appointed

[1] *Goethe and Mendelssohn*, 2nd ed. p. 77.

one of the organists of the Chapel Royal in the room of Charles Knyvett, deceased. In 1825 he accompanied Charles Kemble to Germany to engage Weber to compose an opera for Covent Garden, and when Weber came to England in 1826 to bring out his 'Oberon' he was the guest of Sir George Smart, in whose house he died on June 5. [See *Musical Times*, 1902, p. 533.] It was mainly by the exertions of Sir George Smart and Sir Julius Benedict that the statue of Weber at Dresden was erected, the greater part of the subscriptions having been collected in England. In 1836 Sir George introduced Mendelssohn's 'St. Paul' to England at the Liverpool Festival. [On his duties in connection with the coronation of Queen Victoria, see the *Musical Times*, 1902, p. 18.] On the death of Attwood in 1838 he was appointed one of the composers to the Chapel Royal. To careful musicianship he added an administrative ability which eminently qualified him for the conductorship of musical festivals and other performances on a large scale, and his services were for many years in request on such occasions all over the country. He conducted festivals at Liverpool in 1823, 1827, 1830, 1833, and 1836 ; Norwich, 1824, 1827, 1830, and 1833 ; Bath, 1824 ; Newcastle-upon-Tyne, 1824 and 1842 ; Edinburgh, 1824 ; Bury St. Edmund's, 1828 ; Dublin and Derby, 1831 ; Cambridge, 1833 and 1835 ; Westminster Abbey, 1834 ; Hull, 1834 and 1840 ; and Exeter Hall and Manchester, 1836. He was long resorted to by singers desirous of acquiring the traditional manner of singing Handel's songs, which he had been taught by his father, who had seen Handel conduct his oratorios : among the many he so instructed were Sontag and Jenny Lind. He gave lessons in singing until he was past eighty. He edited Orlando Gibbons's Madrigals for the Musical Antiquarian Society, and the 'Dettingen Te Deum' for the Handel Society. He took an active part in procuring the foundation of the Mendelssohn Scholarship. His compositions consist of anthems, chants, Kyries, psalm tunes, and glees. In 1863 he published a collection of his anthems and another of his glees and canons. Two of his glees, 'The Squirrel' and 'The Butterfly's Ball,' were very popular. He died at his house in Bedford Square, Feb. 23, 1867. [A volume entitled *Leaves from the Journal of Sir George Smart*, by H. B. Cox and C. L. E. Cox, was published in 1907.] A younger son of George Smart, senior, was CHARLES FREDERICK, who was a chorister of the Chapel Royal, and afterwards a double-bass player in the principal orchestras. Older than Charles, but younger than George, was another brother,

HENRY, born in London in 1778 [was for a time in his father's business, and subsequently (about 1803) in that of a brewer. This latter trade being unsuccessful, he returned to the musical profession]. He had begun his musical education at an early age, and studied the violin under Wilhelm Cramer, in which he made such progress that when only fourteen he was engaged at the Opera, the Concert of Antient Music, and the Academy of Ancient Music. He was engaged as leader of the band at the Lyceum on its being opened as an English Opera-House in 1809, and continued so for several seasons. He was leader at the present Drury Lane Theatre from its opening in 1812 until 1821. On June 12, 1819, the band presented him with a silver cup as a token of their regard. He was leader of the Lenten oratorios from the time they came under the management of his brother, Sir George, in 1813, and a member of the Philharmonic Society's orchestra, which he occasionally led. In 1820 he established a manufactory of pianofortes, of a peculiar construction, and on July 22, 1823, obtained a patent for improvements in the construction of pianofortes. He went to Dublin to superintend the début of his pupil, Miss Goward (afterwards Mrs. Keeley), where he was attacked by typhus fever, and died, Nov. 27, 1823. His son,

HENRY THOMAS (known as Henry Smart), a prominent member of the modern English School, was born in London, Oct. 26, 1813, and after declining a commission in the Indian army, was articled to a solicitor, but quitted law for music, for which he had extraordinary natural faculties, and which he studied principally under W. H. Kearns, though he was to a great extent self-taught. In 1831 he became organist of the parish church of Blackburn, Lancashire, which he resigned in 1836. While at Blackburn he composed his first important work, an anthem for the tercentenary of the Reformation, in 1835. In 1836 he settled in London as organist to St. Philip's Church, Regent Street. In March 1844 he was appointed to the organ of St. Luke's, Old Street, where he remained until 1864, when he was chosen organist of St. Pancras. He was an excellent organ-player, specially happy as an accompanist in the service, a splendid extemporiser, and a voluminous and admirable composer for the instrument. But his compositions were by no means confined to the organ. On May 26, 1855, an opera from his pen, 'Berta, or, The Gnome of the Hartzberg,' was successfully produced at the Haymarket. In 1864 he composed his cantata, 'The Bride of Dunkerron' (his best work), expressly for the Birmingham Festival. He produced two cantatas, 'King René's Daughter,' 1871, and 'The Fishermaidens,' both for female voices. An opera on the subject of 'The Surrender of Calais,' the libretto by Planché, originally intended for Mendelssohn, was put into his hands by Messrs. Chappell, about 1852, but though considerable progress was made with it, it was never completed. A sacred cantata, 'Jacob,' was written for the Glasgow Festival, produced Nov. 10, 1873, and

two large anthems for solos, chorus, and organ were written for the Festivals of the London Choral Choirs Association at St. Paul's in 1876 and 1878—'Sing to the Lord,' and 'Lord, thou hast been our refuge.' For many years past his sight had been failing, and soon after 1864 he became too blind to write. All his compositions after that date therefore were committed to paper—like those of another distinguished English composer, Sir G. A. Macfarren—through the truly disheartening process of dictation.

It is as a composer of part-songs and a writer for the organ that Henry Smart will be known in the future. His earlier part-songs, 'The Shepherd's Farewell,' 'The Waves' Reproof,' and 'Ave Maria,' are lovely, and will long be sung; and his organ pieces are full of charming melody and effective combinations. He edited Handel's thirteen Italian duets and two trios for the Handel Society.

His health had for several years been very bad, and cancer on the liver gave him excruciating agony. In June 1879 the Government granted him a pension of £100 a year in acknowledgment of his services in the cause of music, but he did not live to enjoy it, for he died July 6, 1879. He was buried in Hampstead Cemetery. His last composition was a Postlude in E♭ for the organ, finished very shortly before the end. His life was written by his friend Dr. Spark (Reeves, 1881), and the book will always be interesting, though it might perhaps have been more usefully arranged and more accurately printed. [See the *Musical Times* for May 1902.] w. h. h.

SMART, THOMAS, probably brother to the elder George Smart, was an organist at St. Clement's Danes in 1783. He composed many songs and pieces for the pianoforte and harpsichord. He set to music the well-known song on the death of General Wolfe by Tom Paine, beginning 'In a mouldering cave where the wretched retreat.' Dates of birth and death not ascertained.   f. k.

SMEGERGILL, WILLIAM. See CÆSAR, vol. i. p. 443.

SMETANA, FRIEDRICH, born March 2, 1824, at Leitomischl in Bohemia, was a pupil of Proksch at Prague, and subsequently for a short time studied with Liszt. He became a highly skilled pianist, and opened a music school of his own at Prague, where he married the pianist Katharina Kolár. In 1856 he accepted the directorship of the Philharmonic Society of Gothenburg in Sweden, and his wife died there in 1860. In 1861 he made a tour in Sweden, and on the foundation of the National Theatre in Prague, betook himself again to his native country, and eventually became chief conductor of the new institution in 1866, the year of production of his most famous work, 'Die Verkaufte Braut.' He produced three other Bohemian operas, 'Die Brandenburger in Böhmen' (1866), 'Dalibor' (1868), and 'Zwei Witwen'

(1874), before he was compelled, by increasing deafness, to resign his post. Subsequently to his retirement the following were produced: 'Der Kuss' (1876), 'Das Geheimniss' (1878), 'Libussa' (1881), and 'Die Teufelswand' (1882). During his tenure of the conductorship his keen interest in the career of a member of his orchestra, Antonin Dvořák, had a great influence on the younger man's work. Smetana's other works are of great importance though they are not very numerous. The symphonic poem 'Mein Vaterland' is cast in six sections, 'Vysehrad' (Visegrad), 'Vltava' (Moldau), 'Sarka,' 'Aus Böhmens Hain und Flur,' 'Tabor,' and 'Blanik.' It is a work of remarkable power, and very picturesque in treatment. There are besides three other symphonic poems, 'Wallenstein's Lager,' 'Richard III.,' and 'Hakon Jarl'; a 'Triumphsymphonie' dated 1853, and 'Prager Karneval' for orchestra. Two string quartets exist, in E minor and C major ; the first, entitled 'Aus meinem Leben,' is a remarkable piece of chamber music, in which the classical form, somewhat modified, is used to describe the main event of the composer's career, and in which a persistent high note in the finale is understood to be a deliberate statement concerning a note, similarly persistent to his own ear, which was the effect of his deafness. There are also a trio for piano and strings, part-songs, a festival march for the Shakespeare tercentenary, and much piano music. He became insane at the end of his life, and died in an asylum at Prague, May 12, 1884.

Smetana is the first (and, as some think, the greatest) Bohemian composer who deliberately took his stand as an exponent of the art of his native country. But he is a great deal more than this, for, though his music has been long in making its way outside Bohemia, yet it has now obtained so strong a hold that it is most unlikely to be forgotten. If he may not have succeeded in obtaining for his national polka-measure the entry into classical structure that Dvořák won for the *furiant* and *dumka*, yet his attempt to do so marks a point in the history of the development of form. Though his symphonic poems are not realistic, yet there can be no doubt that they carried on the tradition of that form from the hands of Liszt, and increased its power of pictorial expression. The famous opera 'Die Verkaufte Braut' ('Prodana Nevěsta'—'The Bartered Bride'—is the original Bohemian) is one of the most beautiful of modern comic operas, and on a small stage, presented by performers who understand the true comic traditions, it must always impress itself on the audience. Hitherto, though twice brought out in London, it has not achieved a great success with the general public, for Covent Garden and a company accustomed to interpreting the later works of Wagner are not the ideal conditions of its presentment. It was first given by

the Ducal company of Saxe-Coburg and Gotha at Drury Lane on June 26, 1895, and at Covent Garden on Jan. 24, 1907. There is plenty of *vis comica* in it, and lovely music from beginning to end, quite original and characteristic ; but so far nothing has made quite such a success as its overture, which, under the name of 'Lustspiel' or 'Comedy' overture, was widely known and dearly loved long before the opera was produced in England. Monographs on the composer were written by B. Wallek in 1895 and Hostinskh in 1901, the latter being in Czech (Riemann's *Lexikon*, etc.).   M.

SMETHERGELL, WILLIAM, a pianist in London, was author of *A Treatise on Thorough Bass*, 1794, and *Rules for Thorough Bass*, with three sonatas for harpsichord and violin (1795) ; [he composed also six concertos for harpsichord or pianoforte with two violins and violoncello (1785), six duets for two violins, op. 17 (1800), six easy solos for violin (1790), six lessons for harpsichord, six overtures in eight parts, and a second set, op. 8. He also adapted compositions from Jommelli and other composers, and wrote songs. *Brit. Mus. Biog.*]. He was organist of St. Margaret on the Hill, Southwark, and Allhallows Barking.   W. H. H.

SMITH, ALICE MARY (MRS. MEADOWS WHITE), a distinguished English composer, was born May 19, 1839. She was a pupil of Sir W. Sterndale Bennett and Sir G. A. Macfarren ; married Frederick Meadows White, Esq., Q.C. (afterwards a Judge for the County of Middlesex), Jan. 2, 1867, was elected Female Professional Associate of the Philharmonic Society in November 1867, Hon. Member of the Royal Academy of Music in 1884, and died Dec. 4, 1884. She was a prolific composer of works of all dimensions. The list embraces two Symphonies, in C minor (1863), and G ; Overtures to 'Endymion' (1864, rewritten 1871), 'Lalla Rookh' (1865), 'Masque of Pandora,' with two Intermezzi (1878), and 'Jason' (1879) ; a Concerto for clarinet and orchestra (1872) ; an Introduction and Allegro for PF. and orchestra (1865) ; four PF. quartets, in B♭ (1861), D (1864), E, and G minor ; a PF. trio in G (1862) ; three String quartets, in D (1862), A (1870), and G ; also five Cantatas for soli, chorus, and orchestral accompaniment—'Rüdesheim or Gisela' (Cambridge, 1865), Kingsley's 'Ode to the North-East Wind' (Hackney Choral Association, 1880), Collins's 'Ode to the Passions' (Hereford Festival, 1882), Kingsley's 'Song of the Little Baltung' (1883), Kingsley's 'Red King' (1884) ; Part Song, 'The Dream' (1863); Duet (S.T.) ' Maying' ; many solo-songs, duets, etc. 'Her music,' says the *Athenæum* of Dec. 13, 1884, 'is marked by elegance and grace rather than by any great individuality . . . that she was not deficient in power and energy is proved by portions of the "Ode to the North-East Wind," and "The Passions." Her forms were

FRIEDRICH SMETANA

always clear and her ideas free from eccentricity; her sympathies were evidently with the classic rather than with the romantic school.'   G.

SMITH, CHARLES, born in London in 1786, was in 1796 admitted a chorister of the Chapel Royal under Dr. Ayrton, but was withdrawn from the choir in 1798 and became a pupil of John Ashley. In 1800 he sang at the Oratorios, Ranelagh, etc. Upon the breaking of his voice in 1803 he acted as deputy organist for Knyvett and Stafford Smith at the Chapel Royal, and soon afterwards became organist of Croydon Church. In 1807 he was appointed organist of Welbeck Chapel. He composed the music for the following dramatic pieces : 'Yes or No,' 1809 ; 'The Tourist Friend,' and 'Hit or Miss,' 1810 ; 'Anything New,' 1811 ; 'How to die for Love' ; 'Knapschou, or the Forest Fiend,' Lyceum, 1830. In 1815 he appeared, with success, at the Oratorios as a baritone singer. In the next year he settled in Liverpool, where he resided for many years. He composed many songs and ballads, the best of which is 'The Battle of Hohenlinden.' He published in 1844 a work called 'Ancient Psalmody,' consisting of adaptations from music of Ravenscroft, Morley, etc. He ultimately retired to Crediton, Devon, where he died Nov. 22, 1856.   W. H. H.

SMITH, EDWARD SYDNEY, born at Dorchester, July 14, 1839, received his first musical instruction from his parents, and at the age of sixteen went to Leipzig, where he studied the piano under Moscheles and Plaidy ; the violoncello under Grützmacher ; harmony and counterpoint under Hauptmann, Richter, and Papperitz ; and composition under Rietz. He returned to England in 1858, and in the following year he settled in London, where he long enjoyed considerable reputation as a teacher. His compositions, which are confined to PF. pieces, were extremely popular with the numerous class of performers whose tastes are satisfied by a maximum of brilliance combined with a minimum of difficulty. The most successful of his many pieces were 'La Harpe Éolienne,' 'Le Jet d'Eau,' 'The Spinning Wheel,' and a 'Tarantella' in E minor, which (like most of his compositions) have been published, and met with the same popularity on the Continent as in England. He died in London, March 3, 1889, and was buried in Kensal Green Cemetery. W. B. S.

SMITH, FATHER, the usual appellation of BERNARD SCHMIDT, a celebrated organ-builder, born in Germany about 1630, who came to England in 1660 with two nephews, Gerard and Bernard, his assistants. To distinguish him from these and express the reverence due to his abilities, he was called Father Smith. His first organ in this country was that of the Royal Chapel at Whitehall, which Pepys mentions in his Diary as having heard on July 8, 1660. Subsequently he built one for Westminster Abbey, one for St. Giles's-in-the-Fields (1671),

and one for St. Margaret's, Westminster (1675), of which in the following year he was elected organist at a salary of £20 a year. He was now rapidly acquiring fame and was appointed Organ-maker in ordinary to the King, apartments in Whitehall being allotted to him, called in the old plan 'The Organ-builder's Workhouse.'

In 1682 the treasurers of the societies of the Temple had some conversation with Smith respecting the erection of an organ in their church. Subsequently Renatus Harris, who had warm supporters amongst the Benchers of the Inner Temple, was introduced to their notice. It was ultimately agreed that each artist should set up an organ in the church, and in 1684 both instruments were ready for competition. In 1685 the Benchers of the Middle Temple made choice of Smith's organ [which was played by Henry Purcell] ; but those of the Inner Temple dissented, and it was not until 1688 that Smith received payment for his instrument, namely, £1000.

In 1683 he contracted for the organ of Durham Cathedral. In consequence of the reputation he had acquired by these instruments, he was made choice of to build an organ for St. Paul's Cathedral, then in course of erection. This instrument was opened on Dec. 2, 1697. Smith became Court organ-builder to Queen Anne, and died 1708. [His portrait is in the Music School Collection at Oxford.]

According to Hawkins and Burney the two nephews of Schmidt, as above mentioned, were named Bernard and Gerard. But Horace Walpole alters Bernard's name to Christian. These two are very little known, although they built several fine instruments.

In 1755 a Mr. Gerard Smith was organ-repairer to Chelsea Hospital. This was probably a grand-nephew of Father Smith, since from the date he could hardly have been his nephew. V. DE P.

SMITH, GEORGE TOWNSHEND, son of Edward Woodley Smith (born May 23, 1775, chorister of St. Paul's Cathedral, afterwards lay vicar of St. George's Chapel, Windsor, from 1795 until his death, June 17, 1849), was born in the Horseshoe Cloisters, Windsor, Nov. 14, 1813. He received his early musical education as a chorister of St. George's, Windsor. On quitting the choir he became a pupil of Highmore Skeats, the Chapel organist, and afterwards came to London and studied under Samuel Wesley. He next obtained an appointment as organist at Eastbourne, whence he removed to King's Lynn on being chosen organist there. On Jan. 5, 1843, he was appointed organist of Hereford Cathedral. As such he became, ex officio, conductor of the Meeting of the Three Choirs at Hereford, besides discharging the duties of which office he voluntarily undertook the laborious office of honorary secretary to the festival, and by his untiring and energetic exertions, in the

course of the twelve triennial festivals which
he directed, raised it musically, from a low to
a very high condition, and financially, from a
heavy loss to a gain. He composed an 8-voice
anthem and a Jubilate for the festivals, and
other church music, as well as piano pieces of a
popular kind. He died, very suddenly, August
3, 1877, universally beloved and respected.

His brother ALFRED MONTEM, born at
Windsor, May 13, 1828, was also educated in
the choir of St. George's. On quitting it he
became a tenor singer, and after belonging to
the choir of St. Andrew's, Wells Street, succeeded
J. W. Hobbs as lay vicar of Westminster Abbey ;
he was also a gentleman of the Chapel Royal
(1858). He was distinguished as a ballad singer,
and for his skill in recitative. He was a professor of singing at the Royal Academy of Music
and the Guildhall School. He died in London,
May 2, 1891.

Another brother, SAMUEL, was born in Eton,
August 29, 1821. In 1831 he was admitted as
one of the children of the Chapel Royal under
William Hawes. Shortly after leaving the
choir he obtained the appointment of organist
at Hayes Church, Middlesex, and was subsequently organist at Eton and Egham. In 1857
he became organist at Trinity Church, Windsor,
and in 1861 organist of the Parish Church.
He issued some compilations of tunes and
chants.   w. h. h.

SMITH, JOHN, Mus.D., was born at Cambridge
in 1797. On Nov. 23, 1815, he was admitted
to a situation in the choir of Christ Church
Cathedral, Dublin, but failed to secure the
appointment of vicar choral owing to his having
quarrelled and gone to law with the Dean in
1824. On Feb. 5, 1819, he was appointed a
vicar choral of St. Patrick's Cathedral. On
July 7, 1827, the degree of Mus.D. was conferred upon him by the University of Dublin.
He afterwards obtained the appointments of
Chief Composer of the State Music, Master of
the King's Band of State Musicians in Ireland,
and Composer to the Chapel Royal, Dublin ;
and in 1847 was chosen Professor of Music in
Dublin University. He composed 'The Revelation,' an oratorio, some church music, and
several prize glees and other compositions. In
1837 he published a volume of Cathedral Music
containing services and chants, and a 'Veni,
Creator.' He died Nov. 12, 1861.   w. h. h.

SMITH, JOHN (organ-builder). See VOWLES.

SMITH, JOHN CHRISTOPHER, born in 1712,
was son of John Christopher Schmidt, of Anspach,
who, a few years later, came to England and
became Handel's treasurer. [He was agent for
the sale of Handel's music. While John Cluer
engraved the several works published by Handel
on his own behalf, Meares sold them in St. Paul's
Churchyard, and Smith at the sign of 'The
Hand and Musick-Book' in Coventry Street.]
The younger Smith showing a fondness for

music, Handel began teaching him when he
was thirteen years old. He afterwards studied
composition under Dr. Pepusch and Thomas
Roseingrave, and in 1732 produced his English opera, 'Teraminta,' and in 1733 another
opera, 'Ulysses.' In 1738 he composed an
oratorio, 'David's Lamentation over Saul and
Jonathan.' About 1745 he travelled on the
Continent, remaining absent about three years.
In 1754 he was appointed the first organist
of the Foundling Hospital Chapel. (See
Musical Times, 1902, p. 377.) When Handel
became blind Smith was employed as his
amanuensis, and Handel's latest compositions
were dictated to him. He also played the
organ at Handel's oratorio performances. In
1754 he composed the opera of 'The Fairies,'
altered from Shakespeare's 'Midsummer Night's
Dream,' which met with great success, and in
1756 the opera of 'The Tempest,' adapted from
Shakespeare's play, two songs in which, 'Full
fathom five,' and 'The owl is abroad,' long
continued favourites ; and in 1760 'The Enchanter,' a musical entertainment. Handel
bequeathed to him all his original MS. scores,
his harpsichord, his bust by Roubilliac, and his
portrait by Denner. After Handel's death
Smith carried on the oratorios, in conjunction
with Stanley, until 1774, when he retired and
went to reside at Bath. Besides the before-
mentioned works he composed 'Paradise Lost,'
'Rebecca,' 'Judith,' 'Jehoshaphat,' and 'Redemption,' oratorios (besides compiling two
oratorios from Handel's works, 'Nabal,' and
'Gideon') ; 'Dario,' 'Issipile,' and 'Il Ciro
riconosciuto,' Italian operas ; a Burial Service ;
and several miscellaneous vocal and instrumental
pieces. (See Anecdotes of G. F. Handel and
J. C. Smith.) George III. having continued to
Smith a pension which had been granted by his
mother, the Princess Dowager of Wales, Smith
evinced his gratitude by presenting to the King
all Handel's MS. scores—now at Buckingham
Palace—the harpsichord, and the bust by Roubilliac, retaining only the portrait by Denner.
He died Oct. 3, 1795. Three large collections
of Handel's works exist in Smith's MS. : one
belonged to H. B. Lennard, Esq., Hampstead,
and is now in the Fitzwilliam Museum, Cambridge ; another to Dr. Chrysander ; and a third
to the Granville family of Wellesbourne Hall,
Warwickshire.   w. h. h.

SMITH, JOHN STAFFORD, son of Martin
Smith, organist of Gloucester Cathedral from
1743 to 1782, was born at Gloucester in 1750.
He obtained his earliest musical instruction
from his father, and was soon afterwards sent
to London to study under Dr. Boyce, and also
became a chorister of the Chapel Royal under
James Nares. On quitting the choir he sedulously pursued his studies, and became an able
organist, an efficient tenor singer, an excellent
composer, and an accomplished musical anti-

quary. In 1773 he was awarded two prizes by the Catch Club, one for a catch, ' Here flat,' and the other for a canon, ' O remember not the sins.' In the next four years he gained prizes for the following compositions : ' Let happy lovers fly,' glee, 1774 ; ' Since Phillis has bubbled,' catch, and ' Blest pair of syrens,' glee (five voices), 1775 ; ' While fools their time,' glee, 1776 ; and ' Return, blest days,' glee, 1777. He rendered great assistance to Sir John Hawkins in the production of his *History*, not only by reducing ancient compositions into modern notation, but also by the loan of some valuable early MSS. from his extensive and curious library, from which Sir John culled several pieces to enrich his Appendix. In 1779 he published ' A Collection of English Songs, in score, for three and four voices, composed about the year 1500. Taken from MSS. of the same age ' ; among which is the Agincourt song, ' Our king went forth to Normandy.' (See ' English Carols of the Fifteenth Century.') In 1780 he won another prize from the Catch Club by his ode, ' When to the Muses' haunted hill.' He published at various times five collections of glees, containing compositions which place him in the foremost rank of English glee composers. Besides his prize glees they include ' As on a summer's day,' 'What shall he have that killed the deer ? ' ' Hark, the hollow woods resounding,' and the madrigal ' Flora now calleth forth each flower.' Fourteen glees, fourteen catches, four canons, two rounds, an ode, a madrigal, and a motet by him are given in Warren's collections. He also published a collection of songs (1785), and ' Twelve Chants composed for the use of the Choirs of the Church of England.' On Dec. 16, 1784, after having for many years officiated as a deputy, he was appointed a gentleman of the Chapel Royal, and on Feb. 22, 1785, a lay vicar of Westminster Abbey, being installed, after his year of probation, April 18, 1786. In 1790 he was engaged as organist at Gloucester Festival. In 1793 he published a volume of ' Anthems, composed for the Choir Service of the Church of England.' In 1802, upon the death of Dr. Arnold, he was appointed one of the organists of the Chapel Royal, and on May 14, 1805, upon the resignation of Dr. Ayrton, succeeded him as Master of the Children. In 1812 he produced his interesting work ' Musica Antiqua.' [See vol. iii. pp. 328-9.] In June 1817 he resigned the Mastership of the Children of the Chapel Royal. Besides the before-named compositions he produced ' An Ode on the First of April,' for voices and instruments, which was never published. A MS. *Introduction to the Art of composing Music*, by him, is in the library of the Sacred Harmonic Society, which also contains his Musical Commonplace Book. He died in London, Sept. 21, 1836. By his will, dated Jan. 21, 1834, he bequeathed all his property to his only surviving daughter, Gertrude Stafford

Smith, and appointed her sole executrix. A few years afterwards she became insane, and in 1844 the Commissioner in Lunacy ordered that her property should be realised and the proceeds invested for her benefit. Through ignorance or carelessness the contents of her house (which included her father's valuable library, remarkably rich in ancient English musical manuscripts) were entrusted for sale to an incompetent auctioneer. The library was sold April 24, 1844, such books as were described at all being catalogued from the backs and heaped together in lots, each containing a dozen or more works ; 2191 volumes were thrown into lots described as ' Fifty books, various,' etc. The printed music was similarly dealt with ; the MSS. were not even described as such, but were lumped in lots of twenties and fifties, and called so many ' volumes of music.' 578 volumes were so disposed of, and there were besides five lots each containing ' a quantity of music.' The sale took place in Gray's Inn Road ; Smith's name did not appear on the catalogue ; nothing was done to attract the attention of the musical world, and two dealers, who had obtained information of the sale, purchased many of the lots at very low prices. These after a time were brought into the market, but it is feared the greater part of the MSS. is altogether lost.   W. H. H.

SMITH, MONTEM. See under SMITH, GEORGE TOWNSHEND.

SMITH, ROBERT ARCHIBALD, born at Reading, Nov. 16, 1780. His father, a Paisley silkweaver, finding his trade declining in Reading, removed back to Paisley in 1800. Robert soon showed a great aptitude for music, and at ten could play the violin. In 1807 he was appointed precentor at the Abbey Church, Paisley, a situation which he filled for many years. While there he made the acquaintance of Robert Tannahill the poet, many of whose fine lyrics he set to music. One of these, ' Jessie, the Flow'r o' Dunblane,' published in 1808, at once made its mark, and was universally admired.

Smith possessed a fine vein of melody, and in vocal composition had at that time perhaps no equal in Scotland. In 1820 he began to publish [edited by Lady Nairne and other ladies] ' The Scottish Minstrel ' (6 vols. 8vo, 1820-24), containing several hundreds of the best Scottish songs, not a few of them his own, frequently without indication. It is still considered a good compilation. In August 1823 he obtained the leadership of the psalmody at St. George's Church, Edinburgh. Besides anthems and other pieces (published in 1810 and 1819, most of the former written for the boys of George Heriot's Hospital), Smith now found time to publish his ' Irish Minstrel,' [which was suppressed owing to an infringement of Moore's copyright,] followed in 1826 by an ' Introduction to Singing,' and in 1827 by ' Select Melodies of all Nations,' in one volume, one of his best works.

In 1828 he brought out his 'Sacred Harmony
of the Church of Scotland,' by which he is now
best known.   His health was at no time robust,
and he suffered from dyspepsia, under which he
finally sank, Jan. 3, 1829.   He was buried in
St. Cuthbert's churchyard.

'Smith,' says the late George Hogarth, 'was
a musician of sterling talent. . . . His compositions are tender, and tinged with melancholy ;
simple and unpretending, and always graceful
and unaffectedly elegant. . . . He had the admirable good sense to know how far he could
safely penetrate into the depths of counterpoint
and modulation without losing his way ; and
accordingly his music is entirely free from scientific pedantry.'   His most popular pieces are
the songs, 'Jessie, the Flow'r o' Dunblane,' and
'Bonnie Mary Hay' ; the duet, 'Row weel, my
boatie' ; the trio 'Ave Sanctissima' ; and the
anthems, 'Sing unto God,' and 'How beautiful
upon the mountains' ; although many more
might be named which are yet frequently sung.
Owing to the modern alterations in congregational singing, the introduction of German
chorales and ancient ecclesiastical melodies, and
the change from florid to syllabic tunes, Smith's
'Sacred Harmony' is to a great extent superseded.   But it still has its value, even at a
distance of eighty years from its publication.
[An excellent memoir of Smith is attached to an
edition of Tannahill's poems edited by Philip
Ramsay, Edinburgh, 1851.]   D. B.; additions in
square brackets by F. K.

SMITH, SAMUEL.   See under SMITH, GEORGE
TOWNSHEND.

SMOLENSKY, STEPHEN VASSILIEVICH, a
leading authority on Russian church music,
born at Kazan, 1848.   Having had unusual
opportunities of gaining an insight into the
customs and peculiarities of the sect known as
'Old Believers,' who have preserved the church
music in its primitive forms, Smolensky was
led to make a special study of the old manuscripts of the Solovetsky library, preserved in
the Clerical Academy at Kazan.   In 1889 he
became director of the Synodal School and
Choir in Moscow, and in the same year was
appointed successor to the ecclesiastic Razou-
movsky, as professor of the history of church
music at the Moscow Conservatorium.   While
working at the Synodal School, Smolensky has
formed a unique collection of manuscripts from
the 15th to the 19th century, including many
rare chants and other examples of sacred music.
In 1901-3 he directed the Imperial Court
Chapels.   Among his numerous contributions
to the abstruse and complicated subject on
which he is an authority the principal are : *A
Course of Church-Chant Singing* (Moscow, 1900,
5th edition) ; *Old Choral Manuscripts in the
Synodal School, Moscow* (St. Petersburg, 1899) ;
Ancient Notation of the Russian Church-Chants
(1901).   R. N.

SMORZANDO (Ital., 'fading away').   A
term with the same meaning as Morendo, but
used indiscriminately in the course of a piece.
[See MORENDO.]

SMYTH, ETHEL MARY, born in London,
April 23, 1858.   Daughter of General J. H.
Smyth, late of the Royal Artillery.   For a short
time in 1877 she studied at the Leipzig Conservatorium, and under Heinrich von Herzogenberg after leaving that institution.   At Leipzig
a quintet for strings was performed with success in 1884, and a sonata for piano and
violin in 1887.   This latter is numbered
op. 7, opp. 3 and 4 being books of songs.   After
her student days, she does not appear to have
used opus-numbers.   A serenade for orchestra
in four movements, in D, was given at the
Crystal Palace, April 26, 1890 ; and an overture, 'Antony and Cleopatra,' on Oct. 18 of
the same year, the latter being repeated at one
of Henschel's London Symphony Concerts in
1892.   A far more important work, a Solemn
Mass, in D, was performed at the Albert Hall,
under Barnby's direction, Jan. 18, 1893.   This
work definitely placed the composer among the
most eminent composers of her time, and easily
at the head of all those of her own sex.   The
most striking thing about it was the entire
absence of the qualities that are usually associated with feminine productions ; throughout it
was virile, masterly in construction and workmanship, and particularly remarkable for the
excellence and rich colouring of the orchestration.   Miss Smyth did not, however, come
into her own until she was recognised as an
operatic writer.   Her 'Fantasio' (libretto
founded by herself on De Musset) was produced
at Weimar in 1898 in unfortunate conditions,
and it was not until its revival at Carlsruhe
in February 1901 that it could be properly
judged.   The one-act 'Der Wald' was given
at Dresden in September 1901 ; it was produced at Covent Garden, July 18, 1902, with
very great success, given again at the Metropolitan Opera-House, New York, in March
1903, and again at Covent Garden on June 26,
1903.   The distinction of its being revived in
the year after its first production is significant
of its success, to all who know the singular
methods followed by English operatic managers.
It was evident that here was a work of highly
romantic character (the treatment of the spirits
of the wood as the primary agents in the drama
is full of suggestive beauty), by one who had
mastered not only all the secrets of stage effect,
but who understood how to make her climaxes impressive, and how to differentiate her characters.
The German libretto of this, like that of her
former work, was written by the composer
herself.   Her crowning achievement so far, is
the three-act opera, 'Les Naufrageurs' ('The
Wreckers'), produced at Leipzig as 'Strand-
recht' on Nov. 11, 1906.   The libretto, by

H. B. Leforestier, bears some slight traces of being originally intended to suit the conventions of the Paris Opéra-Comique rather than the German stage ; but in any language the wonderful power of the conception, musical and dramatic, must make itself felt. In spite of a performance which was so far from ideal that the composer refused to allow it to be repeated at the same theatre, the work created a profound impression. It was given with far more care and success at Prague on Dec. 22 of the same year, and is accepted for performance at Vienna (1908). While the style is so far modern as that set pieces are dispensed with and Wagner's artistic ideals are fulfilled, there is no attempt to curry favour with the lovers of ugly music, or to write what sounds bizarre for the sake of making a sensation. The fine treatment of the choruses in the first act, the orchestral introduction to the second act, and, in the same section, the great love-duet which rises in intensity of emotion with the rising of the beacon-flame lit by the lovers to warn ships from the dangers of the coast ; and, in the third act, the whole treatment of the final situation, in which the lovers are left by the people to be drowned by the advancing tide, all these points are among the most remarkable things in modern opera, and it is difficult to point to a work of any nationality since Wagner that has a more direct appeal to the emotions, or that is more skilfully planned and carried out. Some charming and delicately written French poems, for mezzo-soprano and very small orchestra, were sung at the Queen's Hall, Nov. 12, 1907.　　　　　　　　　M.

SNARES. A group of four or five pieces of catgut rather loosely stretched across the lower end of the side-drum, which jarring against the parchment when the drum is struck at the other end produces a peculiar rattle characteristic of the instrument.　　　　　　　　　F. K.

SNETZLER, John, was born at Passau in Germany about 1710. This truly eminent organ-builder, after acquiring some fame in his own country, was induced to settle in England [in 1740 ; he built the organ for Chesterfield Church in 1741 and opened a factory in London in 1755. W. H. G. F.]. He built the noble instrument at Lynn Regis (1754) ; a very fine one at St. Martin's, Leicester (1774) ; that of the German Lutheran Chapel in the Savoy, which was the first in this country provided with a pedal clavier ; and many others, including chamber organs of high quality. Two stories are current of his imperfect way of speaking English and his quaint expressions. At the competition for the place of organist to his new organ at Halifax (1766), he was so annoyed by the rapid playing of Dr. Robert Wainwright, that he paced the church, exclaiming, ' He do run over de keys like one cat, and do not give my pipes time to shpeak.' And at Lynn he told the church-wardens, upon their asking him what their old organ would be worth if repaired, ' If they would lay out £100 upon it, perhaps it would be worth fifty.'

Snetzler lived to an advanced age, and died at the end of the 18th or the commencement of the 19th century. Having saved sufficient money, he returned to his native country ; but after being so long accustomed to London porter and English fare, he found in his old age that he could not do without them, so he returned to London, where he died. His successor was Ohrmann. [See HILL, W., & SON.]　V. DE P.

SNODHAM, Thomas. An early London music printer. He was the son-in-law of Thomas ESTE, and succeeded to the latter's business in 1609.

He published a great number of the madrigal books of his period, as Byrd's ' Psalms, Songs, and Sonnets,' 1611 ; Maynard's ' The XII. Wonders of the World set and composed for the Viol de Gamba,' 1611 ; Robert Tailour's ' Sacred Hymns,' 1615 ; a second edition of ' Pammelia,' and other works. By reason of some of his imprints reading ' Thomas Este *alias* Snodham,' it has been considered that Este changed his name. This, however, is a mistake, the fact being that Snodham (who had married into the family and obtained Este's business), merely desired to be associated with the better-known name of Este, Thomas Este having just then died.　　　　　　　F. K.

SNOW, Valentine, was possibly son of Moses Snow, gentleman of the Chapel Royal from 1689 until his death, Dec. 20, 1702, and also lay-vicar of Westminster Abbey (Mus. B. Cambridge, 1606), and a minor composer. Valentine Snow became the finest performer upon the trumpet of his day ; was a member of Handel's oratorio orchestra ; and it was for him that the great composer wrote the difficult obbligato trumpet parts in ' Messiah,' ' Samson,' ' Dettingen Te Deum,' ' Judas Maccabæus,' etc. No better evidence of his ability can be required. In January 1753 he was appointed (in succession to John Shore, deceased) Sergeant Trumpeter to the King, which office he held until his death in December 1770.　　　　　　W. H. H.

SNUFFBOX, Musical. See vol. i. p. 136.

SOCIEDADE DE QUARTETOS DO PORTO (Quartet Society of Oporto). This Society originated in private musical gatherings at the house of a banker of Oporto (Sr. Joaõ Miranda Guimarães). In 1875 the violoncellist J. Casella settled in Oporto, and it was resolved to give public concerts. The first subscription was for twelve concerts, and resulted in a net profit of about £32. Encouraged by these results, the same little body of musicians has continued to give two series of chamber concerts yearly, twelve in the autumn, and six in the spring. They take place on Sunday afternoons in a small concert-room at the S. Joaõ Theatre.

The programmes are entirely instrumental, and consist of movements from the chamber-music of the great masters, as well as from the works of Grieg, Dvořák, Saint-Saëns, Liszt, Grädener, Svendsen, Tchaïkovsky, and Miguel Angelo. Short analytical remarks are written by Sr. B. V. Moreira de Sá, to whose energy and enthusiasm the Society owes much of its success.   w. b. s.

SOCIETA ARMONICA. Founded about 1827 for the purpose of giving subscription concerts in which symphonies, overtures, and occasionally instrumental chamber works were intermingled with vocal numbers usually drawn from the Italian operas. Mr. H. Forbes was the conductor, and Tolbecque and the younger Mori were the leaders of the band. Beethoven's Overture in C major, Berlioz's Overture to 'Les Francs Juges,' Reissiger's Overture in F minor, and the Overture to 'Les Huguenots,' were among the works which gained a first hearing in England at the Society's concerts ; and Weber's Mass in G was also produced. Among the vocalists who assisted in the concerts were Mmes. Grisi, Persiani, Albertazzi, Bishop, Alfred Shaw, Miss Clara Novello, and Miss Birch, Messrs. Phillips, Rubini, Tamburini and Lablache, Mario and Ivanoff. The band included Spagnoletti, A. Griesbach, Willy, Wagstaff, Dando, Patey, Jay, Alsept, Lindley, Hatton, Brookes, Dragonetti, Howell, Card, Ribas, Barrett, Harper, etc. Henri Herz, the pianist and composer, and Hausmann the violinist, made their first appearance in this country at the Societa Armonica. The concerts were successively held at the Crown and Anchor Tavern in the Strand, Freemasons' Tavern, and the Opera Concert room in the Haymarket. They terminated in or about the year 1850. c. m.

SOCIÉTÉ DE MUSIQUE DE CHAMBRE, POUR INSTRUMENTS À VENT. This is a Society for the performance of chamber-music for wind instruments in Paris. It was founded by Mons. Paul Taffanel, the distinguished flute-player, and the first concert took place on Feb. 6, 1879. Six concerts were given in the February, March, and April of each year at 4 P.M. on alternate Thursdays, at the Salle Pleyel ; subscription, 20 francs per season. The executants were all artists from the Conservatoire concerts, or those of Pasdeloup—such as flute, Taffanel ; oboe, Gillet and Boullard ; clarinet, Grisez and Turban ; bassoon, Espaignet and Bourdeau ; horn, Garigue and Brémond ; piano, Louis Diémer. A Society modelled on this, the 'Wind Instrument Chamber Music Society,' did good work in London in the years 1889-93.   g.

SOCIÉTÉ DES CONCERTS DU CONSERVATOIRE. See vol. i. pp. 574, 575.

SOCIETY OF BRITISH AND FOREIGN MUSICIANS. A benevolent society, established in 1822 to provide a fund for the relief of its members during sickness ; to assist in the support of those who, by old age or unavoidable calamity may become unable to follow their profession ; and to allow a certain sum at the death of a member or a member's wife. The office is at 28 Gerrard Street, and the Secretary is Mr. F. Orcherton.   c. m.

SOCIETY OF BRITISH COMPOSERS. This Society was founded in 1905 with the primary object of promoting the publication of works by British composers. As a proof of the need of something of the kind, it may be pointed out that in two years after the Society's formation the number of members (composers) and associates (others interested in the movement) was 254, while there had been published forty-four works of various kinds, principally chamber-music and songs. The Society issues a Year-Book, which is a useful volume, being a complete list of its members' compositions, published or in MS. The publication of music is undertaken by the Society, either by defraying the whole or part of the cost, subject to the approval of an elected council, or at the sole expense of the composer concerned ; the engraving and printing is done at cost price and the terms as to royalties, etc., are of an exceedingly favourable nature. The publications are issued by the publishing company, Charles Avison, Ltd., on behalf of the Society, and the trade agents are Messrs. Breitkopf & Härtel.   n. g.

SOCIETY OF BRITISH MUSICIANS, THE, was founded in 1834 with the object of advancing native talent in composition and performance. In the original prospectus of the Society attention was called to the contrast between the encouragement offered to British painting, sculpture, and the tributary arts at the Royal Academy, and the comparative neglect of English music and English musicians, the overwhelming preponderance of foreign compositions in all musical performances being cited as 'calculated to impress the public with the idea that musical genius is an alien to this country,' and as tending also 'to repress those energies and to extinguish that emulation in the breast of the youthful aspirant, which alone can lead to pre-eminence.' One of the rules adopted was to exclude all foreign music from the programmes of the Society's concerts and to admit none but natives of Great Britain among its members ; but this was set aside in 1841, when the Committee reported in favour of 'introducing a limited proportion of music by composers not members of the Society either British or foreign,' and the suggestion was adopted, though not without strong opposition, in which the editor of the Musical World joined (Musical World of Oct. 14, 1841). In its earlier days the Society achieved a complete success, numbering in 1836 as many as 350 members, while its finances were also in a prosperous state. It not only gave concerts of works of established merit, but adopted a system of trial performances at which many new compositions were heard. The programmes included the names of all the leading English writers of the day, who as a rule conducted their own works, among them Cipriani Potter, G. A. Macfarren, W. H. Holmes, W. L. Phillips, Sterndale Bennett, J. Hullah, J. H. Griesbach, T. German Reed, W. M. Rooke, H. Westrop, Joseph Barnett, H. C. Litolff, C. Lucas, T. M. Mudie, James Calkin, and John Goss. The music included orchestral and chamber compositions, varied by vocal solos and part-music, to which nearly all the above-named composers contributed original works, and the members in turn directed the performances. After 1837 the Society began to decline, and even when the introduction of music by foreign composers was resolved upon, in the hope of creating more general interest in the concerts, it failed to restore the Society to prosperity, and after another period of far from successful management a special appeal for support was put forth at the close of 1854. At that date the members included Messrs. H. C. Banister, W. S. Bennett, H. Blagrove, J. B. Calkin, C. Coote, J. T. Cooper, W. H. Holmes, C. E. Horsley, H. Lazarus, E. J. Loder, Kate Loder (Lady Thompson), C. Neate, W. S. Rockstro, C. Severn, C. Steggall, C. E. Stephens, J. W. Thirlwall, H. J. Trust, F. Westlake, H. Westrop, J. Zerbini, and Sir George Smart. This effort was ridiculed in the *Musical World* of Dec. 16, 1854, on the ground that the Society had no true claim to its title, as many composers and artists of note held aloof from it. The movement served, however, to draw some new friends to the ranks, and as a means of fulfilling its objects prizes were offered for chamber compositions, which were gained in 1861 by Ebenezer Prout and Edward Perry for string quintets ; in 1863 by J. Lea Summers and W. Gibbons, also for string quintets ; and in 1864 by Ebenezer Prout and J. Lea Summers, for quartets for piano and strings. The umpires on these occasions included Joachim, Molique, Piatti, Cipriani Potter, G. A. Macfarren, A. Mellon, T. M. Mudie and H. Leslie. In 1865 the Society was dissolved, its library was sold by Messrs. Puttick & Simpson, and Mr. C. E. Stephens was appointed custodian of the minute-books, etc. The secretaries of the Society were Messrs. J. R. Tutton (its founder), 1834-35 ; G. J. Baker, 1835 until his death in 1851 ; J. Rackham, 1851-54 ; W. W. Grice, 1854-55. The honorary treasurers were the three brothers Erat, in succession to each other, in 1834-58 ; and Cipriani Potter held the post in 1858-65. The Society and its library were housed gratuitously at 23 Berners Street, by Messrs. Erat, from 1834 until 1858, when they gave up the premises ; 1858-59 in Wornum's Music Hall, Store Street ; 1860 in St. Martin's Hall until its destruction by fire on August 26, 1860

(when the Society's property was saved) ; 1860-1862 at 44 Charlotte Street, Fitzroy Square, by permission of Mr. H. Webb ; and 1862-65 at Messrs. Collard's, Grosvenor Street, free of all expense. For the first five years the concerts were given at the Hanover Square Rooms, and the trials of orchestral and chamber works were subsequently held at those rooms or at the above-named buildings. On July 20, 1843, the Society gave a complimentary concert to Spohr at Erat's, and on June 15, 1844, at the same place, a complimentary concert to Mendelssohn. C. M.

SÖDERMAN, AUGUST JOHAN, one of the greatest Swedish composers of modern times, was born in Stockholm, July 17, 1832—his father being director of the orchestra at a minor theatre—and at an early age displayed traces of musical genius. When eighteen years of age he was selected by Stjernström, the director of the orchestra at the Royal theatre in Stockholm, as instructor to a company of musicians, then on a tour to Finland. On his return Söderman wrote his first operetta, with the fantastic title, 'The Devil's first Rudiments of Learning,' which was performed at the Mindre theatre at Stockholm, Sept. 14, 1856. During the following two years he stayed in Leipzig, studying under Richter and Hauptmann ; in the year 1860 he was appointed chorus-master at the Royal Opera in Stockholm ; and from that date until his election as a member of the Swedish Academy of Music, his life was occupied in such minor offices in the musical world as are too often the lot of great composers when cast in a small community. But however poor the offices he held, Söderman filled them with a sincerity and zeal which many a man of inferior talents might have envied. [About 1865 the generosity of Jenny Lind enabled him to continue his studies in Germany.] His works are about sixty in number—operettas, songs, ballads, part-songs, funeral marches, and cantatas ; of which, however, only half have been printed, and these at the expense of the Swedish Government after his death. Of the printed works we can only mention a few, besides the above-mentioned, namely, two operettas, 'The Wedding at Ulfåsa,' and 'Regina von Emmeritz' ; overture and incidental music to 'The Maid of Orleans' ; songs ; Trios for male voices, containing the Finnish national air 'Suomi sång' ; a quartet for female voices, 'Bröllop,' very popular in Germany, a Circassian dance, and a concert-overture, also 'Sacred songs for organ,' containing a number of hymns of great beauty and purity, of which the best known are a Benedictus and an Agnus Dei. Though a Protestant, his *chef-d'œuvre* is a Mass for solos, chorus, and orchestra, which has only been rarely performed in Stockholm, but is considered by his countrymen as equal to any by the great composers, and which is animated by such sincere devotion, and stamped by such a high degree of originality and masterly finish, as to rank among the choicest gems of Swedish music.

Another of his works worth mention is his music to the poetry of Bellman. This poet, whose genius is akin to that of Marlowe, has written a number of rhapsodies, depicting the gay, jovial, and careless nature of the Swede, with a force of animal spirit and genuine originality which few other poets have equalled ; and to these productions, which every Swede knows by heart, Söderman set music.

The foreign composers who seem to have influenced his more elaborate productions are Beethoven, Schubert, and, in particular, Schumann. His compositions, though thoroughly Swedish, are not national ; they bear the impress of the vigorous and energetic nature of the Northerner, which makes Scandinavian compositions so charming. Söderman died Feb. 10, 1876, at the early age of forty-four, and a national subscription was at once raised in Sweden for the benefit of his widow and children. It was a token of the gratitude and respect of a musical nation for a great composer.   c. s⁸.

SOGGETTO (Ital. *Subject* or *Theme*). The true subject of an orthodox Fugue as opposed to the Andamento, which is a subject of abnormal length ; and the Attacco, which is a mere Point of Imitation.

In its most regular form, the Soggetto consists of a single homogeneous section ; as in No. 1 of 'Das Wohltemperirte Clavier.' Occasionally, however, its division into two sections is very clearly marked; as in No. 7 of the same. Subjects of this last-named class frequently make a very near approach to the Andamento, from which they sometimes differ only in their less extended dimensions. [See ANDAMENTO and ATTACCO, and FUGUE, vol. ii. p. 116a.]   w. s. r.

SOKALSKY, PETER PETROVICH, born at Kharkov, Sept. 26, 1832 ; died at Odessa in March 1887. He was educated at the University of Kharkov, and while acting as under-master in one of the public schools in the town began to collect the folk-songs of the district. Later in life (1857-60) he was Secretary to the Russian Consulate in New York, and on his return to Russia became editor of the *Odessa News*. Sokalsky composed several operas : 'Maria' ('Mazeppa'), 'A Night in May,' and 'The Siege of Doubno' (from Gogol's *Tarass Boulba*). His article upon *The Chinese Scale in Russian National Music*, and *Russian National Music* (Kharkov, 1888), are valuable to students of this subject.

VLADIMIR IVANOVICH, his nephew, born at Heidelberg, May 6, 1863, studied law at the university of Kharkov. His unpublished compositions include a symphony in G minor (Kharkov, 1894), a dramatic Fantasia, an

Eastern March, and an Andante Elegiaco for violoncello and orchestra. His pianoforte pieces, 'Impressions Musicales' op. 1, the pianoforte suite 'In the Meadows,' and some songs, have been published.   R. N.

SOKOLOV, NICHOLAS ALEXANDROVICH, composer, born in St. Petersburg, 1859. Here he studied at the Conservatorium from 1877 to 1885 and was a pupil of Rimsky-Korsakov. His chief compositions are : 'Elegy' (op. 4), and incidental music to Shakespeare's 'Winter's Tale,' for orchestra ; three string quartets, opp. 7, 14, and 20 ; eight pieces for violin and pianoforte ; six for violoncello and pianoforte ; seven choruses *a cappella* ; four choruses for female voices ; about eighty songs, and a ballet entitled 'The Wild Swans.'   R. N.

SOL. The fifth note of the natural scale according to the nomenclature of France and Italy ; in English and German G. In the old hymn from which Guido is supposed to have formed the scale it occurs as follows :—

Ut queant laxis *re*sonare fibris,
*Mi*ra gestorum *fa*muli tuorum,
*Sol*ve pollutis *la*bia reatis,
Sancte Johannes.
                                        G.

SOLDAT, MARIE (Madame Soldat-Röger), violinist, was born at Graz on March 25, 1864. In her fifth year she studied the pianoforte under her father, a professional organist. Two years later she began to learn the organ, and was soon able occasionally to act as substitute for her father. Then in her eighth year she took up the violin, under Pleiner, and appeared in public when ten years of age, performing the 'Fantaisie-Caprice' of Vieuxtemps, a type of music with which she has not since been identified. Coming under the influence of Joachim and Brahms she resumed study in the Berlin Hochschule in 1879, remaining there till 1882 and gaining the Mendelssohn prize. She subsequently took private lessons from Joachim, whose répertoire both of solo and chamber music she adopted, making a special study of the Brahms concerto, which she introduced for the first time to a Viennese audience under Richter. In 1889 she was married to Herr Röger, a lawyer by profession, but has since continued her public career. She has travelled a great deal as a soloist, visiting England occasionally (playing for the first time at a concert of the Bach Choir, March 1, 1888), and has a following among those who admire solid before brilliant acquirements.   w. w. c.

SOLESMES. A village near Le Mans, whose Benedictine monastery has become famous through the labours of its monks in the restoration of liturgical music, for which they established a printing press, with special type.

The order of the 'Congregation of France,' better known in England as the 'Benedictines of Solesmes,' was founded in 1833 by Dom Prosper Guéranger, who became the first Abbot.

Under Guéranger and his successors, Solesmes became a centre for the study and execution of plain-song, and was visited by many students from all parts of Europe. In 1901, however, owing to their non-compliance with the new Law of Associations, the monks were expelled from Solesmes, and moved in a body to Appuldur-combe, in the Isle of Wight, where they still are ; but in 1908 they propose to settle at Quarr Abbey, near Ryde. Their printing-press having been confiscated by the French Government, the publication of their works is now carried out by the firm of Desclée et Cie, Tournai, Belgium. Their choir in the Isle of Wight is the practical exponent of their method, and they hold a 'Summer School,' in July and August, for the benefit of those who wish to study and hear plain-song.

The work of reform began under Dom Guéranger, who, wishing to restore Gregorian music to its earliest known form,[1] engaged his colleagues Dom Pothier and Dom Jausions (d. 1870) to examine and compare manuscripts, laying down as a principle that 'where the manuscripts of different periods and different countries agree in their version of a melody, it may be affirmed that the true Gregorian text has been discovered.'

But it was of little use to discover the true text unless the proper method of its performance could also be found. At that time Gregorian music, following the traditions of Zarlino and others, was sung in a slow, heavy, unaccented, and unrhythmical style, and accompanied on the organ by a separate chord to each note. This style was afterwards alluded to by the Solesmes monks as the 'hammered,' ' martelé,' style. Guéranger and Pothier, on studying the theoretical works of the 9th and 10th centuries, found that plain-song had anciently a rhythm peculiar to itself, differing in important particulars from that of measured music. The first result of this discovery was that Dom Guéranger 'was able to give the singing at Solesmes a rhythm that no one had yet dreamed of,'[2] and from henceforth the chief aim of the musicians of Solesmes was to perfect the rhythmical theory as well as the musical readings.

In 1881 the first edition appeared of 'Les Mélodies grégoriennes, d'après la tradition,' by Dom Pothier, treating the whole theory of plain-song from an entirely new point of view. This important work has formed the basis of all subsequent studies.

The investigations now went on more earnestly than ever. Photography was called in to aid, monks were sent to the principal libraries of Europe to photograph codices, and the year 1883 saw the publication by Dom Pothier of the 'Liber Gradualis a Gregorio Magno olim ordinatus, cum notis musicis . . . restitutis in usum Congregationis Benedictinae Galliarum.'

This was followed in 1891 by the 'Liber Antiphonarius pro Vesperis et Completorio,' also by Pothier, and in 1896 by the 'Liber Usualis Missae et Officii,' by Mocquereau.

But others besides the monks of Solesmes were now in the field, endeavouring to reform the liturgical music. Chief among them was Frederic Pustet of Ratisbon, who obtained from Pius IX. a decree under which he was given, by the Congregation of Sacred Rites, the sole right for thirty years of republishing the celebrated 'Medicean' edition, authorised by Paul V. in 1614. The same authority recognised Pustet's publication as the official version of plain-song, and recommended it for use in the whole of the Roman Church. The privileges thus given were confirmed by the next Pope, Leo XIII.

This version (known as the 'Ratisbon' edition), which also claims to be the true music of Gregory, is founded on an entirely different principle from that of Solesmes. It is explained thus in the Magister Choralis of Haberl (Ratisbon, 1893): ' Since the 13th century a principle has existed of improving the melodies by cutting down their enormous length, which arose, partly through a bad method of execution, and partly through the manieren of singers. . . . The revision undertaken by the Congregation of Sacred Rites by order of Pius IX. put the foundation of the Roman Chant on the system followed since the Council of Trent.'

The Solesmes view is that at the time the Medicean edition was authorised, plain-song had reached, not its highest development, but its most decadent stage : that in the time of Palestrina, who is supposed to have had a hand in preparing the edition, the traditions of its proper performance had been forgotten for centuries ; and that its real apogee was immediately after the time of Gregory the Great, when it was collected and written down, and its method of performance described by the theoretical writers.

To support the truth of these views Dom André Mocquereau (now Prior of the Abbey), who brought exceptional musical training to bear on the work, commenced in 1889 a quarterly publication, entitled Paléographie musicale, consisting of photographic facsimiles of Gregorian, Ambrosian, Mozarabic, and Gallican manuscripts, together with exhaustive discussions of the various questions involved. The melodies obtained through the comparative study of many manuscripts on the principle laid down by Guéranger, when sung by the Solesmes choir according to the method explained in the Paléographie, proved to be of greater artistic and æsthetic excellence than any other form of plain-song.

Owing to the support given to the Ratisbon edition, the monks did not at first obtain recognition beyond their monastery and a few similar establishments. Their labours were,

---

[1] For the reason why the earliest form is preferable to that of the time of Palestrina, see PLAIN-SONG, vol. iii. p. 761.
[2] Plain-Chant and Solesmes. Cagin and Mocquereau.

however, rewarded when in 1904 the new Pope, Pius X., who is well versed in music, established a Papal Commission to prepare a new Official Edition, and at the same time wrote to Dom Paul Delatte, the present Abbot, appointing the monks of Solesmes to be the editors. This edition, known as the 'Vatican edition,' has, up to the present date (1907), embraced the Kyriale, or ordinary of the mass, and the Commune Sanctorum. It is primarily based on the 'Liber gradualis'; but in the preparation of that work the learned editor had not the abundant means of research at his disposal which have since been available ; [1] hence certain deficiencies became apparent when the book came into use. These are removed in the Vatican edition, while the monks are issuing for their own use a special Vatican edition containing the marks of expression as performed by them.

The practical application of the laws of Rhythm to the chant is described in the various 'Methods of Plain-Chant' that have issued from the Solesmes and other presses. The theory underlying what is known to modern students of plain-song as 'Free Rhythm' may be briefly described as follows. Free Rhythm arose from the setting of the words of Scripture to music at a time when the idea that melody could have a rhythm of its own, to which the words sung must conform in respect of time-duration, had not yet been thought of. Free Rhythm practically obeys all the laws of modern musical rhythm except that of definitely fixed time-relationship. Writing in the 11th century, when its laws were still understood, and when what we call 'Free' was called by musicians 'Prose Rhythm,' Aribo says : 'Good Prose Rhythm requires that there should be a rough balance in the groups of syllables, and, naturally, also in the groups of accents, and in the members of sentences : but they are not to be subjected to the rigorous laws of metre.'

In 'Syllabic Plain-song,' in which each syllable has a single note (or at most two or three notes very occasionally), the accentuation of the melody is ruled by that of the words. For rhythmical purposes, as well as for the understanding of the ideas to be expressed by them, words are divided into accented and unaccented syllables, and are also grouped into sentences and 'members of sentences.' This is a law of all language, and Syllabic Plain-song is simply prose language uttered in melody instead of being spoken. The technical plain-song names for sentences and members of sentences are *Distinctiones major* and *minor*, and the *distinctiones* are separated by cæsuras. At each cæsura there is a *Mora ultimae vocis* (*ritardando*) which obeys certain rules.

[1] Two monks are now engaged in visiting all the chief libraries of Italy, armed with letters of commendation from the Pope and the Prime Minister. It is said that photographs are arriving at Appuldurcombe at the rate of 1000 a week, and the library possesses some 500 complete codices in facsimile.

In 'Melismatic Plain-song,' of which the short passage quoted below is an example, the same laws of 'distinctions,' cæsuras, and 'morae' are applied, the syllables and words of prose being represented in the melody by the groups of neumes, which may not only occur in connection with the single verbal syllables, but may form long 'Melismata,' apart from the words. The technical name for the melisma is 'Pneuma,' *i.e.* 'Breathing,' which must not be confounded with 'Neuma,' a note, or group of notes. The intimate relation as to rhythm between the neume in melody and the syllable in words is shown by the fact that groups of notes are often called 'Syllabae' by the ancient writers. The chant is now executed more rapidly than in the days of the 'hammered' style ; and the notes have no relative time-value, but take their duration from the syllables in Syllabic, and from certain rules in Melismatic melody.

The opening phrase of the Gradual 'Justus ut palma,' as found in the Ratisbon and Solesmes books respectively, will serve to show the difference between the two versions. The difference in method of performance can only be observed by a visit to one of the many churches in which Solesmes Plain-song is now cultivated. Below it is appended the Solesmes example in modern

RATISBON.

Ju - - stus   ut   pal - ma flo - ré - - bit:

si - cut ce - - - drus Lí - ba - ni   mul-ti-pli-(cabitur)   etc.

SOLESMES.

Ju - stus   ut pal - ma flo - ré - - - - bit:

si - cut   ce - - - drus . . . . Li - ba - - - ni .

mul - ti - pli-(cabitur)   etc.

Ju - stus   ut pal-ma flo-ré - - - - - - - - bit;

rit. e dim.
si-cut ce - - - drus . . . . Li-ba - - - ni .

a tempo   *rit. e dim.*   etc.
mul-ti-pli-(cabitur)

(When using modern notation the Solesmes editors place dots over accented notes: the dots are not to be read as staccato signs.)

notation, as nearly as its rhythm can be expressed, free rhythm not admitting the exact relation implied by crotchets and quavers.

The following is a list of the more important works connected with plain-song published by the monks of Solesmes. The dates are those of the latest editions.

1881. Les Mélodies grégoriennes d'après la Tradition. Pothier.
1883. Liber Gradualis. Pothier.
1889. The Paléographie musicale was commenced by Dom Mocquereau, who has acted as editor and chief contributor. Up to the present it has published :—
Vol. I. Antiphonale missarum Sancti Gregorii. 10th century. St. Gall Library, Codex 339.
Vol. II. and III. The Gradual 'Justus ut palma,' reproduced from over 200 MSS.
Vol. IV. Antiphonale missarum Sancti Gregorii. 10th-11th century. Library of Einsiedeln, Codex 121.
Vol. V. and VI. The earliest known Ambrosian Antiphonary. 12th century. British Museum, Codex Add. MSS. 34, 209.
Vol. VII. and VIII. Antiphonarium Tonale Missarum. 11th century. Library of the School of Medicine, Montpellier, Codex H. 159. This MS. has alphabetical notation above the neumes.
Vol. IX. Monastic Antiphonary. 12th century. Capitular Library of Lucca, Codex 601. (In progress.)
In addition to the above, there is a second series of the Paléographie musicale, not published at definite intervals. The only volume that has appeared as yet contains the Monastic Antiphonary of Hartker. 10th century.
1889. Origine et développement de la Notation neumatique. Mocquereau.
1893. Questions Grégoriennes. Mocquereau.
1897. Liber Antiphonarius pro Vesperis et Completorio. Pothier. Libri Antiphonarii pro diurnis horis. Pothier.
1900. Chants des Offices. Mocquereau.
1902. Manual de la Messe. French and Latin. Mocquereau.
1903. Liber Usualis Missae et Officii. Mocquereau.
1906. Liber Usualis Missae et Officii. Mocquereau.
1907. Kyriale, seu Ordinarium missae cum cantu gregoriano, ad exemplar editionis Vaticanae, concinnatum et rhythmicis signis a Solsmensibus monachis diligenter ornatum.
1907. In the Press. Méthode complète de Chant grégorien. Mocquereau.

C. F. A. W.

SOL-FA. 'To sol-fa' is to sing a passage or a piece of vocal music, giving to the notes, not the words, but the syllables, Do (C), Re (D), Mi (E), Fa (F), Sol (G), La (A), Si (B), Do (C). Why the two syllables Sol and Fa should have been chosen to designate this process in preference to Do Re, or Re Mi, does not appear. For the Tonic Sol-fa system, see Tonic Sol-fa.

In a hymn written by Arrigo Boito and composed by Mancinelli, for the opening of the monument of Guido d'Arezzo at Rome, the seven syllables (see Sol) are thus employed :—

Util di Guido *re*gola superna
*Mi*suratrice *fa*cile de' suoni
*Sol*enne or tu *la*ude a te stessa intuoni,
*Si*llaba eterna.

The roll or stick with which the conductors of church choirs in Italy beat the time is called the Sólfa.   G.

SOLFEGGIO, E GORGHEGGIO. Solfeggio is a musical exercise for the voice upon the syllables Ut (or Do), Re, Mi, Fa, Sol, La, forming the Guidonian Hexachord, to which was added later the syllable Si upon the seventh or leading-note, the whole corresponding to the notes C, D, E, F, G, A, B of the modern Diatonic scale. These names may be considered the result of an accident ingeniously turned to account, the first six being the first syllables of half lines in the first verse of a hymn for the festival of St. John Baptist, occurring upon the successive notes of the rising scale, with a seventh syllable perhaps formed of the initial

letters of Sancte Johannes. [See Sol, Solmisation.]

The first use of these syllables is ascribed to Guido d'Arezzo as an artificial aid to pupils 'of slow comprehension in learning to read music,' and not as possessing any special virtue in the matter of voice-cultivation ; but it is by no means clear that he was the first to use them. At any rate they came into use somewhere about his time. It is probable that even in Guido's day (if voice-cultivation was carried to any grade of perfection—which is hardly likely in an age when nearly all the music was choral, and the capacities of the voice for individual expression were scarcely recognised), as soon as the notes had been learned, the use of syllables was, as it has been later, superseded by vocalisation, or singing upon a vowel. The syllables may be considered, therefore, only in their capacity as names of notes. Dr. Crotch, in his treatise on Harmony, uses them for this purpose in the major key, on the basis of the movable *Do*, underlining them thus, *Do*, etc., for the notes of the relative minor scales, and gives them as alternative with the theoretical names—Tonic, or *Do* ; Mediant, or *Mi* ; Dominant, or *Sol*, etc. The continued use of the syllables, if the *Do* were fixed, would accustom the student to a certain vowel on a certain note only, and would not tend to facilitate pronunciation throughout the scale. If the *Do* were movable, though different vowels would be used on different parts of the voice, there would still be the mechanical succession through the transposed scale ; and true reading—which Hullah aptly calls 'seeing with the ear and hearing with the eye,' that is to say, the mental identification of a certain sound with a certain sign—would not be taught thereby. Those who possess a natural musical disposition do not require the help of the syllables ; and as pronunciation would not be effectually taught by them, especially after one of the most difficult and unsatisfactory vowels had been removed, by the change of Ut to Do, and as they do not contain all the consonants, and as, moreover, voice-cultivation is much more readily carried out by perfecting vowels before using consonants at all,—it was but natural that vocalisation should have been adopted as the best means of removing inequalities in the voice and difficulties in its management. Crescentini, one of the last male soprani, and a singing-master of great celebrity, says, in the preface to his vocal exercises, 'Gli esercizj sono stati da me imaginati per l' uso del vocalizzo, cosa la piu necessaria per perfezionarsi nel canto dopo lo studio fatto de' solfeggi, *o sia, nomenclatura delle note*'—'I have intended these exercises for vocalisation, which is the most necessary exercise for attaining perfection in singing, after going through the study of the sol-fa, or nomenclature of the notes.' Sometimes a kind of compromise has been adopted in exercises of agility, that syllable being used which comes upon the principal or accented note of a group or division, *e.g.*

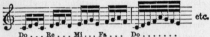

Do ... Re ... Mi ... Fa ... Do ......

The word 'Solfeggio' is a good deal misused, and confounded with 'Vocalizzo' in spite of the etymology of the two words. The preface to the fourth edition of the 'Solfèges d'Italie' says 'La plupart des Solfèges nouveaux exigent qu'ils soient *Solfiés sans nommer les notes.*' Here is an absurd contradiction, and a confusion of the two distinct operations of Solfeggiare and Vocalizzare. We have no precise equivalent in English for Solfeggio and Solfeggiare. The French have Solfège and Solfier. We say, to Sol-fa, and Sol-faing. As a question of voice-production, the wisdom of vocalisation, chiefly upon the vowel *a* (Italian), and certainly before other vowels are practised, and most decidedly before using consonants, has been abundantly proved. The use of the words in question is not therefore a matter of much importance. This appears to be in direct opposition to the advice of a very fine singer and an eminent master, Pier Francesco Tosi, whose book upon singing was published at Bologna in 1723, the English translation by Galliard appearing in 1742. He says, 'Let the master never be tired in making the scholar sol-fa as long as he finds it necessary ; for if he should let him sing upon the vowels too soon, he knows not how to instruct.' 'As long as he finds it necessary,' however, is a considerable qualification. The world lives and learns, and Crescentini's verdict may safely be accepted. The vowel *a*, *rightly pronounced*, gives a position of the resonance-chambers most free from impediment, in which the entire volume of air vibrates without after-neutralisation, and consequently communicates its vibrations in their integrity to the outer air ; this, therefore, is the best preparation, the best starting-point for the formation of other vowels. After this vowel is thoroughly mastered the others are comparatively easy, whereas if *i* or *u* (Italian) are attempted at first, they are usually accompanied by that action of the throat and tongue which prevails to such a disagreeable extent in this country. When the vowels have been conquered, the consonants have a much better chance of proper treatment, and of good behaviour on their own part, than if attacked at the outset of study. Vocalisation upon all the vowels throughout the whole compass of the voice should be practised after the vowel *a* is perfected ; then should come the practice of syllables of all kinds upon all parts of the voice ; and then the critical study and practice (much neglected) of recitative.

The words GORGHEGGIO and GORGHEGGIARE, from *Gorga*, an obsolete word for 'throat,' are applied to the singing of birds, and by analogy to the execution of passages requiring a very quick and distinct movement or change of note, such as trills and the different kinds of turn, also reiterated notes and quick florid passages in general. The English verb 'to warble' is given as the equivalent of *gorgheggiare*, but warbling is usually accepted to mean a gentle wavering or quavering of the voice, whereas agility and brilliancy are associated with the Italian word. A closer translation, 'throat-singing,' would give a rendering both inadequate and pernicious—inadequate, as throat-singing may be either quick or slow, and pernicious as suggesting unnecessary movement of the larynx, and helping to bring about that defective execution so often heard, in which there is more breath and jar than music, closely resembling unnecessary movement of the hand when using the fingers upon an instrument. The fact is, that execution, however rapid, should be perfect vocalisation in its technical sense, and perfect vocalisation has for its foundation the *Portamento*. The Portamento (or carrying of the voice—the gradual gliding from one note to another) removes inequalities in the voice, and facilitates the blending of registers. Increased in speed by degrees, the voice learns to shoot from note to note with lightning-like rapidity, and without the above-named convulsion of the larynx which produces a partial or total cessation of sound, or at any rate a deterioration of sound during the instantaneous passage from note to note. It is this perfect passage from note to note, without lifting off or interrupting the voice, that fills space with a flood of sound, of which Jenny Lind's shake and vocalised passages were a bright example. But this kind of vocalisation is the result of years of conscientious practice and the exercise of a strong will. With such books as those of Garcia, Panseron, Madame Sainton, Randegger, etc. etc., and of course some special passages for individual requirements, to say nothing of those of Rossini, and the numberless vocalizzi of Bordogni, Nava, etc. etc., the 'Solfèges d'Italie,' and the 'Solfèges du Conservatoire,' there is work enough if students will avail themselves of it. Tosi, in speaking of the difficulties in teaching and learning the shake, says, 'The impatience of the master joins with the despair of the learner, so that they decline further trouble about it.'

The first of the two great works just named is entitled 'Solfèges d'Italie, avec la Basse chiffrée, composés par Durante, Scarlatti, Hasse, Porpora, Mazzoni, Caffaro, David Perez, etc. Dédiés à Messeigneurs les premiers Gentilshommes de la chambre du Roi [Louis XV.], et recueillis par les Srs. Levesque et Bêche, ordinaires de la Musique de sa Majesté.' The work is therefore obviously a collection of Italian Solfeggi made in France by Frenchmen. Levesque was a baritone in the King's Chapel from 1759 to 1781, and in 1763 became master of the boys. Bêche was an alto. The first edition of the work appeared in 1768 ; the fourth, published by Cousineau, at Paris in 1786. It forms one large oblong volume, and is in four Divisions : I. The 'indispensable principles' of singing—names of notes, etc., and 62 easy (anonymous) Solfeggi in the G clef with figured bass. II. Solfeggi 63 to 152 for single voices in various clefs—including G clef on second line and F clef on third line—in common, triple, and compound time, all with figured basses. III. Solfeggi 153-241, with changing clefs, and increasing difficulties of modulation and execution—ending with the *Exclamationes* quoted in the text ; all with figured basses. Divisions II. and III. are by the masters named in the title ; each Solfeggio bearing the composer's name. IV. 12 Solfeggi for two voices and figured bass by David Perez, each in three or four movements. The forms of fugue and canon are used throughout the work, and some of the exercises would bear to be sung with words.

A later and very complete collection of exercises and studies is that published in Paris by Heugel under the title of 'Solfèges du Conservatoire, par Cherubini,[1] Catel, Méhul, Gossec, et Langlé,' edited by Edouard Batiste, Professeur de Solfège, etc. It is in eight volumes 8vo, including a hundred preparatory exercises by Batiste himself. The first exercise in the main collection is a short theme with 57 variations. The studies increase in difficulty, and the later ones require great powers of vocalisation. Those by Gossec abound in reiterated notes and in passages of extended compass. There are duets and trios, some of which are very elaborate. A curious one by Cherubini is in free fugal imitation, with the respective entries of the second and third voices taking place at an interval of 24 bars. Canons and fugues are in abundance, amongst them a fugue in 5-4 by Catel. One exercise by Cherubini is without bars, and another by the same composer is headed 'Contrepoint rigoureux à cinq voix sur le Plain Chant.' If these two collections of vocalizzi are *studied* and *conquered*, an amount of theoretical and practical knowledge, as well as control over the voice, will have been gained that will fulfil every possible requirement preparatory to acquaintance with the great operatic and oratorical works. Mention must not be omitted of Concone's useful Exercises, of more modest calibre, which have gained a large popularity throughout musical Europe ; nor of those of Madame Marchesi-Graumann, which give a

[1] Cherubini's Autograph Catalogue [see vol. i. p. 509b] contains an immense number of Solfeggi written between the years 1822 and 1842, in his capacity of Director of the Conservatoire, for the examinations of the pupils of that institution.

great deal of excellent work, and were highly approved by Rossini.   H. C. D.

SOLIÉ, JEAN PIERRE (real name SOULIER), born at Nîmes, 1755, died in Paris, August 6, 1812, was one of the good singers and composers at the Opéra-Comique in its early days. The son of a violoncellist he learnt that instrument, and had a good musical education at the Nîmes *maîtrise*, after which he played in the orchestra and taught singing till his début as a tenor in 1778. His success in the provinces tempted him to go to Paris, but he failed at first, in 1782, and remained away till after three years' success in the largest theatre of Lyons. He was engaged in 1787 for the Opéra-Comique, where he remained, gradually making his way upwards to the first place in the company, especially after relinquishing the part of *tenor de goût* for that of baritone. The baritone was then a novelty, and Méhul wrote for Solié several parts which have since become identified with his name. He next tried his hand at composition, and with equal success, for his opéras-comiques number 33 in all, 'Jean et Geneviève' (1792) being the first, and 'Les Ménestrels,' three acts (1811) the last. 'Le Jockey' (Jan. 6), 'Le Secret' (April 20, 1796), 'Le Chapitre Second' (June 17, 1799) in one act ; and 'Le Diable à quatre' (Nov. 30, 1809), and 'Mademoiselle de Guise' in three (March 17, 1808), were published. Though this music is now entirely out of date, many of its pretty airs became favourites with the vaudeville writers, and were set to a variety of words. Several may be found in the 'Clé du Caveau.'

Solié had several sons ; the eldest drowned himself in 1802 ; but Émile (born in Paris, 1801) published in 1847 two pamphlets on the Opéra-Comique and Opéra, also some short biographies of French musicians. He left a son, Charles, a conductor, who produced at Nice, in 1879, an opéra-comique, 'Scheinn Baba, ou l'intrigue du Harem,' three acts.   G. C.

SOLMISATION (Lat. *Solmisatio*). The art of illustrating the construction of the musical scale by means of certain syllables, so associated with the sounds of which it is composed as to exemplify both their relative proportions, and the functions they discharge as individual members of a system based upon fixed mathematical principles.

The laws of Solmisation are of scarcely less venerable antiquity than those which govern the accepted proportions of the scale itself. They first appear among the Greeks, and after making the necessary allowance for differences of tonality, the guiding principle in those earlier times was precisely the principle by which we are guided now. Its essence consisted in the adaptation to the Tetrachord of such syllables as should ensure the recognition of the Hemitone, wherever it occurred. Now, the Hemitone of the Greeks, though not absolutely identical with our Diatonic Semitone, was its undoubted homologue;[1] and throughout their system this Hemitone occurred between the first and second sounds of every Tetrachord ; just as, in our major scale, the semitones occur between the third and fourth degrees of the two disjunct Tetrachords by which the complete octave is represented. Therefore, they ordained that the four sounds of the Tetrachord should be represented by the four syllables, τα, τε, τη, τω ; and that, in passing from one Tetrachord to another, the position of these syllables should be so modified, as in every case to place the Hemitone between τα and τε, and the two following Tones between τε and τη, and τη and τω, respectively.[2]

When, early in the 11th century, Guido d'Arezzo substituted his Hexachords for the Tetrachords of the Greek system, he was so fully alive to the value of this principle that he adapted it to another set of syllables, sufficiently extended to embrace six sounds instead of four. In the choice of these he was guided by a singular coincidence. Observing that the melody of a hymn, written about the year 770 by Paulus Diaconus, for the festival of St. John the Baptist, was so constructed, that its successive phrases began with the six sounds of the Hexachord, taken in their regular order, he adopted the syllables sung to these notes as the basis of his new system of Solmisation, changing them from Hexachord to Hexachord, on principles to be hereafter described, exactly as the Greeks had formerly changed their four syllables from Tetrachord to Tetrachord.

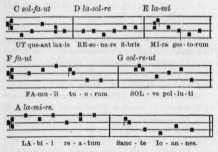

C sol-fa-ut   D la-sol-re   E la-mi

UT que-ant lax-is   RE-so-na-re fi-bris   MI-ra ges-to-rum

F fa-ut   G sol-re-ut

FA-mu-li tu-o-rum   SOL-ve pol-lu-ti

A la-mi-re.

LA-bi-i re-a-tum   Sanc-te Io-an-nes.

It will be seen from this example that the syllables, Ut, Re, Mi, Fa, Sol, La,[3] were originally sung to the notes C, D, E, F, G, A ; that is to say, to the six sounds of the Natural Hexachord ; and that the semitone fell between the third and fourth syllables, Mi and Fa, and these

[1] The Diatonic Semitone is represented by the fraction ¹⁶⁄₁₅; the Greek Hemitone by ²⁵⁶⁄₂₄₃, that is to say, by a Perfect Fourth, minus two Greater Tones.

[2] Though the true pronunciation of the Greek vowels is lost, we are not left without the means of forming an approximate idea of it, since Homer uses the syllable βῆ to imitate the bleating of the sheep.

[3] Gerard Vossius, in his tract De quatuor Artibus popularibus (Amsterdam, 1650), mentions the following Distich as having been written, shortly after the time of Guido, for the purpose of impressing the six syllables upon the learner's memory—
'Cur adhibes tristi numeros cantumque labori ?
UT RElevet (MIserum FAtum SOLitosque LAbores.'

only. [See HEXACHORD.] But, when applied to the Hard Hexachord, these same six syllables represented the notes G, A, B, C, D, E ; while, in the Soft Hexachord, they were sung to F, G, A, B♭, C, D. The note C therefore was sometimes represented by Ut, sometimes by Fa, and sometimes by Sol, according to the Hexachord in which it occurred ; and was consequently called, in general terms, C sol-fa-ut. In like manner A was represented either by La, Mi, or Re ; and was hence called A la-mi-re, as indicated in our example by the syllables printed above the stave. But under no possible circumstances could the semitone occur between any other syllables than Mi and Fa ; and herein, as we shall presently see, lay the true value of the system.

So long as the compass of the melody under treatment did not exceed that of a single Hexachord, the application of this principle was simple enough ; but, for the Solmisation of melodies embracing a more extended range, it was found necessary to introduce certain changes, called Mutations, based upon a system corresponding exactly with the practice of the Greeks. [See MUTATION.] Whenever a given melody extended (or modulated) from one Hexachord into another, the syllables pertaining to the new series were substituted for those belonging to the old one, at some convenient point, and continued in regular succession until it became convenient to change them back again ; by which means the compass of the scale could be enlarged to any required extent.

For instance, in the following example the passage begins at (a), in the Natural Hexachord of C, but extends upwards three notes beyond its compass, and borrows a B♭ from the Soft Hexachord of F. As it is not considered desirable to defer the change until the extreme limits of the first Hexachord have been reached, it may here be most conveniently made at the note G. Now, in the Natural Hexachord, G is represented by the syllable Sol ; in the Soft Hexachord, by Re. In this case, therefore, we have only to substitute Re for Sol at this point ; and to continue the Solmisation proper to the Soft Hexachord to the end of the passage, taking no notice of the syllable printed in italics.

Soft Hexachord.

(a)   Ut Re Mi Fa Sol La

Ut Re Mi Fa Sol La
Natural Hexachord.

At (b), on the other hand, the passage extends

(b)   Hard Hexachord.
La Sol Fa Mi Re Ut

La Sol Fa Mi Re Ut
Natural Hexachord.

downwards, from the Hexachord of G, into that of C. Here, the change may be most conveniently effected by substituting the *La* of the last-named Hexachord for the *Re* of the first, at the note A.

The first of these Mutations is called *Sol-re*, in allusion to its peculiar interchange of syllables ; the second is called *Re-la*. As a general rule, *Re* is found to be the most convenient syllable for ascending Mutations, and *La* for those which extend downwards, in accordance with the recommendation contained in the following Distich.

Vocibus utaris solum mutando duabus
Per *re* quidem sursum mutatur, per *la* deorsum.

This rule, however, does not exclude the occasional use of the forms contained in the subjoined Table, though the direct change from the Hard to the Soft Hexachord, and *vice versa*, is not recommended.

Descending Mutations.

1. *Fa-sol.* From the Hard to the Soft Hexachord, changing on C.
2. *Mi-la.* Nat. to Hard Hex. changing on E.　Soft to Nat. Hex. changing on A.
3. *Re-la.* Hard to Nat. Hex. changing on A.　Nat. to Soft Hex. changing on D.
4. *Re-mi.* Hard to Soft Hex. changing on A.
5. *Re-sol.* Nat. to Hard Hex. changing on D.　Soft to Nat. Hex. changing on G.
6. *Sol-la.* Hard to soft Hex. changing on D.
7. *Ut-fa.* Nat. to Hard Hex. changing on C.　Soft to Nat. Hex. changing on F.
8. *Ut-re.* Hard to Soft Hex. changing on G.

Ascending Mutations.

9. *Fa-ut.* Hard to Nat. Hexachord, changing on C. Nat. to Soft Hex. changing on F.
10. *La-mi.* Hard to Nat. Hex. changing on E.
11. *La-re.* Nat. to Hard Hex. changing on A.　Soft to Nat. Hex. changing on D.
12. *La-sol.* Soft to Hard Hex. changing on D.
13. *Mi-re.*　Do.　　Do.　A.
14. *Re-ut.*　Do.　　Do.　G.
15. *Sol-fa.*　Do.　　Do.　C.
16. *Sol-re.* Hard to Nat. Hex. changing on D.　Nat. to Soft Hex. changing on G.
17. *Sol-ut.* Nat. to Hard Hex. changing on G.　Soft to Nat. Hex. changing on C.

The principle upon which this ancient system was based is that of ' the Movable Ut '—or, as we should now call it, ' the Movable Do ' ; an arrangement which assists the learner very materially, by the recognition of a governing syllable, which, changing with the key, regulates the position of every other syllable in the series, calls attention to the relative proportions existing between the root of the scale and its attendant sounds, and, in pointing out the peculiar characteristics of each subordinate member of the system, lays emphatic stress upon its connection with its fellow degrees, and thus teaches the ear, as well as the understanding. We shall presently have occasion to consider the actual value of these manifold advantages ; but must first trace their historical connection with the Solmisation of a later age.

So long as the ecclesiastical modes continued in use Guido's system answered its purpose so thoroughly, that any attempt to improve upon

it would certainly have ended in failure. But when the functions of the leading-note were brought more prominently into notice, the demand for a change became daily more and more urgent. The completion of the octave rendered it not only desirable, but imperatively necessary that the sounds should no longer be arranged in Hexachords, but in Heptachords or Septenaries, for which purpose an extended syllabic arrangement was needed. We have been unable to trace back the definite use of a seventh syllable to an earlier date than the year 1599, when the subject was broached by Erich van der Putten (Erycius Puteanus) of Dordrecht, who, at pages 54, 55 of his *Pallas modulata*,[1] proposed the use of *BI*, deriving the idea from the second syllable of la*bi*i. No long time, however, elapsed before an overwhelming majority of theorists decided upon the adoption of SI, the two letters of which were suggested by the initials of ' Sancte Ioannes '—the Adonic verse which follows the three Sapphics in the Hymn already quoted.[2] The use of this syllable was strongly advocated by Sethus Calvisius, in his *Exercitatio musicae tertia*, printed in 1611. Since then, various attempts have been made to supplant it, in favour of *Sa, Za, Ci, Be, Te*, and other open syllables ;[3] but the suggested changes have rarely survived their originators, though another one, of little less importance— the substitution of *Do* for *Ut* on account of its greater resonance—has, for more than two hundred years, been almost universally accepted. [See Do.] Lorenzo Penna,[4] writing in 1672, speaks of *Do* as then in general use in Italy ; and Gerolamo Cantone[5] alludes to it, in nearly similar terms, in 1678, since which period the use of *Ut* has been discontinued, not only in Italy, but in every country in Europe except France.

In Germany and the Netherlands far more sweeping changes than these have been proposed from time to time, and even temporarily accepted. Huberto Waelrant (1517-1595) introduced, at Antwerp, a system called ' Bocedisation ' or ' Bobisation,' founded on seven syllables—*Bo, Ce, Di, Ga, Lo, Ma, Ni*—which have since been called the ' Voces Belgicae.' At Stuttgart Daniel Hitzler (1576-1635) based a system of ' Bebisation ' upon *La, Be, Ce, De, Me, Fe, Ge*. A century later Graun (1701-59) invented a method of ' Damenisation,' founded upon the particles, *Da, Me, Ni, Po, Tu, La, Be*. But none of these methods have survived.

In England, the use of the syllables *Ut* and *Re* died out completely before the middle of the 17th century ; and recurring changes of *Mi, Fa, Sol, La*, were used, alone, for the Solmisation of all kinds of Melodies. Butler mentions this

---

[1] *Pallas modulata, sive Septem discrimina vocum* (Milan, 1599), afterwards reprinted, under the title of *Musathena* (Hanover, 1602).
[2] It has been said, that, in certain versions of the Melody, the first syllable of the Adonic verse is actually sung to the note B ; but we have never met with such a version, and do not believe in the possibility of its existence.　　[3] See SI, *ante*, p. 448.
[4] *Albori musicali* (Bologna, 1672).
[5] *Armonia Gregoriana* (Turin, 1678).

method as being in general use, in 1636; [1] and Playford calls attention to the same fact in 1655. [2]

In France the original syllables, with the added *Si*, took firmer root than ever in Italy ; for it had long been the custom, in the Neapolitan schools, to use the series beginning with *Do* for those keys only in which the third is Major. For Minor keys, the Neapolitans begin with *Re* ; using *Fa* for an accidental flat, and *Mi* for a sharp. Durante, however, when his pupils were puzzled with a difficult Mutation, used to cry out, ' Only sing the syllables in tune, and you may name them after devils, if you like.'

The truth is, that, as long as the syllables are open, their selection is a matter of very slight importance. They were never intended to be used for the formation of the voice, which may be much better trained upon the sound of the vowel, A, as pronounced in Italian, than upon any other syllable whatever. Their use is, to familiarise the student with the powers and special peculiarities of the sounds which form the scale ; and here it is that the arguments of those who insist upon the use of a ' fixed,' or a ' movable *Do*,' demand our most careful consideration. The fact that in Italy and France the syllables *Ut* (*Do*), *Re*, *Mi*, *Fa*, *Sol*, *La*, *Si*, are always applied to the same series of notes, C, D, E, F, G, A, B, and used as we ourselves use the letters, exercises no effect whatever upon the question at issue. It is quite possible for an Italian, or a Frenchman, to apply the ' fixed *Do* system ' to his method of nomenclature, and to use the ' movable *Do* ' for purposes of Solmisation. The writer himself, when a child, was taught both systems simultaneously, by his first instructor, John Purkis, who maintained, with perfect truth, that each had its own merits, and each its own faults. In matters relating to absolute pitch, the fixed *Do* is all that can be desired. The ' movable *Do* ' ignores the question of pitch entirely ; but it calls the student's attention to the peculiar functions attached to the several Degrees of the Scale so clearly, that, in a very short time, he learns to distinguish the Dominant, the Sub-Mediant, the Leading-Note, or any other interval of any given key, without the possibility of mistake, and that, by simply sol-faing the passage in the usual manner. It is this quality which is the strongest point in the Tonic Sol-fa system.

One of the strongest objections to the system of the fixed *Do* is that it makes no provision for the indication of flats or sharps. In a tract published at Venice in 1746 [3] an anonymous member of the Roman Academy called ' Arcadia,' proposed to remove the difficulty, by adding to the seven recognised syllables five others, designed to represent the sharps and flats most frequently used ; viz. *Pa* (C♯, D♭), *Bo* (D♯, E♭),

Tu (F♯, G♭), *De* (G♯, A♭), *No* (A♯, B♭). This method was adopted by Hasse, and highly approved by Giambattista Mancini ; but in 1768 a certain Signor Serra endeavoured to supersede it by a still more numerous collection of syllables ; using *Ca*, *Da*, *Ae*, *Fa*, *Ga*, *A*, *Ba*, to represent the seven natural notes, A, B, C, D, E, F, G ; *Ce*, *De*, *E*, *Fe*, *Ge*, *Ao*, *Be*, to represent the same notes, raised by a series of sharps ; and *Ci*, *Di*, *Oe*, *Fi*, *Gi*, *Au*, *Bi*, to represent them, when lowered by flats.

[See the *Sammelbände* of the Int. Mus. Ges. i. 535.]   w. s. r.

SOLO (*Ital.* ' alone '). A piece or passage executed by one voice or performer. Airs are solos ; a pianoforte piece for two hands is a pianoforte solo. A violin solo, strictly speaking, is a piece for the violin alone, like Bach's unaccompanied sonatas ; but the term is often used loosely for a concerto or other piece in which the solo instrument is accompanied by the band, the pianoforte, etc.

In an orchestral piece where one instrument has a passage which is intended to sound out prominently, it is marked ' Solo,' as in the second subject of the Adagio in Beethoven's Symphony No. 4, which is for the 1st clarinet, and marked *Solo* ; in the flute solo near the end of the working-out in the Leonora Overture (where, however, the bassoon, equally solo, is merely marked ' 1 ') ; and in a thousand other instances. In arrangements of pianoforte concertos for two hands, the entry of the solo instrument is marked *Solo*, to distinguish it from the compressed accompaniment.   G.

SOLO ORGAN, a manual or clavier of an organ having stops associated with it which for the most part are intended for use *solo*, that is, in single notes as opposed to chords. The solo organ is generally a fourth manual placed above that of the swell ; but it occasionally supersedes the choir organ, and is then placed below the ' Great ' manual. The stops in a solo organ are most frequently (1) Flutes of 8 ft. and 4 ft. ; (2) A stop of *clarinet*-tone ; (3) a stop of *oboe*-tone (orchestral oboe) ; (4) Reeds of 8 ft. and 4 ft. of *trumpet*-tone (tromba, tuba, etc.). Larger solo organs contain also stops imitative of the violin, horn, piccolo, and other instruments ; perhaps also an open diapason, and, in a few cases, a *carillon* or *glockenspiel*. The solo trumpet-stops are most frequently on a heavy pressure of wind, and in order to obtain special brilliance are sometimes ' harmonic,' as are also the flutes ; that is, they have tubes of twice the ordinary length, pierced with a small hole at their half length. Some of the stops of a solo organ are often used in chords, such for instance as flutes and reeds. This is most commonly done by means of a coupler ' Solo to Great,' by which the diapason or flute tones of the solo organ can be used as a valuable reinforcement of the foundation stops of the Great manual ; and the tone

1 *Principles of Musick*, by C. Butler (London, 1636).
2 *Introduction to the Skill of Musick* (London, 1655).
3 *Riflessioni sopra alla maggior facilità che trovasi nel apprendere il canto*, etc. etc. (Venezia, 1746.)

of the full Great organ can be similarly enriched by coupling the solo reeds. In instruments which contain a *Vox humana*, that stop is perhaps more often found associated with the Swell-manual than with the Solo-manual ; but when placed on the solo its pipes are generally shut up in a separate box with Venetian shutters worked by a second swell-pedal. When composition-pedals are made to act upon the Swell, Great, and Choir organs, it is evidently wise to make the combinations they produce proceed as gradually as possible from *piano* to *fortissimo*. But this simple principle is not applicable to the combinations or rather selections of solo-stops which are made by means of composition-pedals or pistons. The difficulty seems, however, to be overcome by a method suggested some years ago by the writer of this article : namely, to arrange them in the order in which the instruments are found in a modern full-score. Thus, six combination-pedals would act on the solo-stops in the following system :—

(1) Stops of Flute-tone.
(2) Stops of Oboe-tone.
(3) Stops of Clarinet and Bassoon tones.
(4) Stops of Horn-tone.
(5) Stops of Trumpet and Trombone tones.
(6) Stops of Violin and Viola tones.

This method, which is at once simple and exhaustive, might be indefinitely extended ; thus, for example, a carillon, drum, or triangle, would be produced by a composition-pedal or piston lying between the trumpet-stops and violin-stops ; and a vox humana would naturally follow after stops of the violin-tone. Smaller solo organs would probably be easily brought under control by combination-pedals or pistons acting on

(1) Flute.
(2) Oboe.
(3) Clarinet.
(4) Trumpet.

The Solo organ is an introduction of modern times, and followed naturally upon the invention of pipes closely imitating the tones of orchestral instruments.   J. S.

SOLO STOP. (1) A stop or register of a solo organ or fourth manual. (2) Any stop which can be used as a *solo*—that is, in single notes, *e.g.* a clarinet on the choir organ ; a cornopean, hautboy, or other reed on the swell organ ; a clarabella or flute on either of the three manuals great, swell, or choir. The name Solo stop does not necessarily imply that full chords may not be used upon it. [See SOLO ORGAN.]   J. S.

SOLOMON. I. A serenata by William Boyce, to words by Edward Moore, produced 1743. The song 'Softly rise, O southern breeze' was popular for many years.

II. An oratorio of Handel's ; composed between 'Alexander Balus' and 'Theodora.' It was begun on May 5, 1748, and the memorandum at the end of the work is ' G. F. Handel,

Juin 13, 1748, ætatis 63. Völlig geendiget.' The words of the oratorio are supposed to be by Dr. Morell ; but this is not certain. It was produced at Covent Garden Theatre, March 17, 1749, 'with a Concerto,' and was revived by Sir G. Smart at Exeter Hall, April 14, 1836. The Sacred Harmonic Society followed, Dec. 3, 1838 ; and with Costa's additional accompaniments, April 8, 1870.   G.

SOLOVIEV, NICHOLAS THEOPEMPTOVICH, born May 9 (April 27, O.S.), 1846, at Petrozavodsk. He was intended for the medical profession, but entered the St. Petersburg Conservatorium in 1868, eventually passing into Zaremba's class for composition. In 1871, Serov, being then upon his deathbed, entrusted the orchestration of his music-drama, 'The Power of Evil,' to Soloviev. About this time his symphonic picture, 'Russians and Mongols,' was given at one of the concerts of the Russian Musical Society. In 1874, Soloviev became a professor at the St. Petersburg Conservatorium. Of his three operas 'Cordelia' is the best known, having been widely performed in Russia, and also at Prague in 1890. Other compositions comprise a Cantata for the bi-centenary of the birth of Peter the Great ; an Orchestral Fantasia on a folk-song ; and a number of songs and pieces for pianoforte. As a critic, Soloviev has written for the *Novoe Vremya*, *Novosti*, *Rossia*, etc. He is also well known as a collector of folk-songs.   R. N.

SOMBRÉE. *Voix sombrée* is the French term for the veiled voice or *voce velata*, in contradistinction to the *voix claire*. [See VEILED VOICE.]   G.

SOMERVELL, ARTHUR, born at Windermere, June 5, 1863, was educated at Uppingham School from 1877, and Cambridge (King's College), where he took the degree of B.A. in 1883. During his residence at the university he studied with Stanford, and on taking his degree he went to Berlin to study at the Hochschule, where his masters were Kiel and Bargiel. Returning to England in 1885 he entered the Royal College of Music, and after two years there became a private pupil of Parry in 1887. His charmingly graceful songs obtained a wide popularity, but his first ambitious introduction to the world of serious music was in his Mass in C minor, performed by the Bach Choir in 1891. In March 1893 the Philharmonic Society performed his orchestral ballad, 'Helen of Kirkconnell,' and with his first important work for an important festival, 'The Forsaken Merman' (Leeds Festival, 1895), he took a position among the most accomplished composers of the day. In 1901 he was appointed Inspector of Music for England, Wales, and Scotland, in succession to Stainer. He took the degree of Mus.D. at Cambridge in 1903. Besides the works already mentioned, his list of compositions includes choral works, 'A Song of Praise' (Kendal, 1891);

'The Power of Sound' (Do. 1895); 'Elegy' (Robert Bridges, Hovingham, 1896); 'Charge of the Light Brigade' (1896); 'Ode to the Sea' (with soprano solo), Birmingham Festival, 1897; 'Intimations of Immortality' (Wordsworth), Leeds Festival, 1907. 'In Arcady,' a suite for small orchestra, was given at Brighton in 1897; but Somervell's purely orchestral works are very few. Of sacred works the most important is his setting of the Seven Last Words from the Cross. A quintet for clarinet and strings, and a symphony, are still in MS. Two sets of variations for two pianos, and a number of small pianoforte pieces, including some excellent concert-studies, are among his instrumental compositions; and a special success rewarded his song-cycle from Tennyson's 'Maud,' while other songs in series include 'A Shropshire Lad,' and 'James Lee's Wife' (the last with orchestra). His 'Songs of the Four Nations,' and other books of arrangements, are an important addition to the subject of folk-song; and his many songs show remarkable skill in writing for the voice, as well as possessing the charm that makes for popularity while avoiding all that could be thought meretricious.   M.

SOMIS, GIOVANNI BATTISTA, violinist, was born in Piedmont in 1676. He studied first under Corelli at Rome, and afterwards under Vivaldi at Venice. After his return to Turin he was appointed solo violinist to the King, and leader of the royal band, a position he retained until his death, which occurred on August 14, 1763. After having once settled at Turin he appears scarcely ever to have left it; and so few of his compositions were published that there is little opportunity of directly forming an estimate of him as a player; but judging from the style of his numerous and well-known pupils, Somis did not merely hand on the traditions of the great Italian masters, but formed a style of his own, more brilliant and more emotional, marking technically, and also, in a sense, musically, a decided forward step in the art of playing the violin. As the head and founder of the Piedmontese School, and the teacher of Leclair, Giardini, Chiabran, and Pugnani—the latter again the teacher of Viotti —he occupies a prominent place in the history of violin-playing, and forms the connecting link between the classical schools of Italy and France. Fétis names as his only published work 'Opera prima di sonate a violino e violoncello o cembalo. Roma 1722' [but a set of sonatas, op. 4, was published in Paris in 1726, and twelve sonatas, op. 6, in 1734. Besides these, an edition of some of his works appeared at Amsterdam, and a concerto is in MS. in the royal collection at Dresden. *Quellen-Lexikon*.]   P. D.

SOMMER, HANS (actual name, HANS FRIEDRICH AUGUST ZINCKEN, the last name occasionally transformed into 'NECKNIZ'), born at Brunswick, July 20, 1837, was educated at Göttingen, where he became Professor of Physics; subsequently he was appointed Director of the technical High School of his native place, a post he gave up in 1884. In 1885 settled in Berlin, in 1888 in Weimar, and in 1898 returned to Brunswick. He has won success on the operatic stage with his later dramatic works in a fantastic form : 'Der Nachtwächter' and 'Loreley' were both given in Brunswick—the first in 1865, the second in 1891; in 1894, a one-act piece, 'Saint Foix,' was given at Munich; two other one-act operas deserve mention, 'Der Meermann,' at Weimar in 1896, and 'Augustin'; 'Münchhausen,' in three acts, and 'Rübezahl,' were given in Brunswick in 1904; and 'Riquet à la Houppe' at the same theatre on April 14, 1907. It is by his songs that Sommer's name is best known in England : his op. 3, 'Mädchenlieder,' from Julius Wolff's *Wilde Jäger*; his op. 4, three sets of songs from the same poet's *Hunold Singuf*; his op. 5, a set from Wolff's *Tannhäuser*; his op. 6, to words from Carmen Sylva's *Sappho*, and his songs to words of different authors, opp. 8, 9, 10, 11, 12, and 16, contain many things that are effective for the voice, well expressed, original, and full of a sort of ingenuity that delights all cultivated amateurs. In particular, his 'Stelldichein' from op. 4, a vocal obbligato to a brilliant pianoforte waltz, and 'Am Waldteiche,' in which the alternate Latin and German words of the poem are cleverly set to music in different styles, are in their way little triumphs of art. Here and there the composer drifts into rather commonplace ways of expressing himself, but his best songs are things that no educated singer can afford to neglect. He has made several contributions to musical literature, such as his *Ueber die Wertschätzung der Musik* (1898).   M.

SOMMEROPHONE. An instrument of the saxhorn or bombardon class, named after its inventor. It was largely played in the Exhibition of 1851. 'The Euphonic horn of Herr Sommer' is honourably mentioned in the Reports of the Juries (pp. 331, 335) as 'an instrument of great power as well as sweetness of tone.' It possessed no very special peculiarities, and is now seldom, if ever, used.   W. H. S.

SON AND STRANGER. See HEIMKEHR AUS DER FREMDE.

SONATA. The history of the Sonata is the history of an attempt to cope with one of the most singular problems ever presented to the mind of man, and its solution is one of the most successful achievements of his artistic instincts. A sonata is, as its name implies, a sound-piece, and a sound-piece alone; in its purest and most perfect examples, it is unexplained by title or text, and unassisted by voices; it is nothing but an unlimited concatenation of musical notes. Such notes have individually no significance; and even the simplest principles of their relative definition and juxtaposition, such as are necessary to make the most elementary music, had to be drawn from the inner self and the consciousness of things which belong to man's nature only, without the possibility of finding guidance or more than the crudest suggestion from the observation of things external. Yet the structural principles by which such unpromising materials become intelligible have been so ordered and developed by the unaided musical instinct of many successive generations of composers, as to render possible long works which not only penetrate and stir us in detail, but are in their entire mass direct, consistent, and convincing. Such works, in their completest and most severely abstract forms, are sonatas.

The name seems to have been first adopted purely as the antithesis to Cantata, the musical piece that was sung. It begins to come into notice about the same time as that form of composition, soon after the era of the most marked revolution in music, which began at the end of the 16th century; when a band of enthusiasts, led by visionary ideals, unconsciously sowed the seed of true modern music in an attempt to wrest the monopoly of the art in its highest forms from the predominant influence of the Church, and to make it serve for the expression of human feelings of more comprehensive range. At this time the possibilities of polyphony in its ecclesiastical forms may well have seemed almost exhausted, and men turned about to find new fields which should give scope for a greater number of workers. The nature of their speculations and the associations of the old order of things alike conspired to direct their attention first to Opera and Cantata, and here they had something to guide them; but for abstract instrumental music of the Sonata kind they had for a long time no clue. The first suggestion was clearly accidental. It appears probable that the excessive elaboration of the Madrigal led to the practice of accompanying the voice parts with viols; and from this the step is but short to leaving the viols by themselves and making a vague kind of chamber music without the voices. This appears to have been the source of the instrumental Canzonas which were written in tolerable numbers till some way into the 18th century. It does not appear that any distinct rules for their construction were recognised, but the examination of a large number, written at different periods from Frescobaldi to J. S. Bach, proves the uniform object of the composers to have been a lax kind of fugue, such as might have served in its main outlines for the vocal madrigals. Burney says the earliest examples of 'Sonatas' he had been able to discover in his devoted inquiries were by Turini, published at Venice in 1624. His description of those he examined answers perfectly to the character of the canzonas, for, he says, they consist of one movement, in fugue and imitation throughout.

Sonatas did not, however, rest long at this point of simplicity, but were destined very early to absorb material from other sources; and though the canzona kind of movement maintained its distinct position through many changes in its environment, and is still found in the Violin Sonatas of J. S. Bach, Handel, and Porpora, the madrigal, which was its source, soon ceased to have direct influence upon three parts of the more complete structure. The suggestion for these came from the dance, and the newly invented opera or dramatic cantata. The former had existed and made the chief staple of instrumental music for generations, but it requires to be well understood that its direct connection with dancing puts it out of the category of abstract music of the kind which was now obscurely germinating. The dances were understood through their relation with one order of dance motions. There would be the order of rhythmic motions which, taken together, was called a Branle, another that was called a Pavan, another a Gigue; and each dance-tune maintained the distinctive rhythm and style throughout. On the other hand, the radical principle of the Sonata, developed in the course of generations, is the compounding of a limitless variety of rhythms; and though isolated passages may be justly interpreted as representing gestures of an ideal dance kind, like that of the ancients, it is not through this association that the group of movements taken as a whole is understood, but by the disposition of such elements and others in relation to one another. This conception took time to develop, though it is curious how early composers began to perceive the radical difference between the Suite and the Sonata. Occasionally a doubt seems to be implied by confusing the names together or by actually calling a collection of dance-tunes a Sonata; but it can hardly be questioned that from almost the earliest times, as is proved by a strong majority of cases, there was a sort of undefined presentiment that their developments lay along totally different paths. In the first attempts to form an aggregate of distinct movements, the composers had to take their forms where they could find them; and among these were the familiar dance-tunes, which for a long while held a prominent position in the heterogeneous group of movements, and were only in late times transmuted into the Scherzo which supplanted the Minuet and Trio in one case, and the Finale or Rondo, which ultimately took the place of the Gigue, or Chaconne, or other similar dance-forms as the last member of the group.

The third source, as above mentioned, was the drama, and from this two general ideas were derivable: one from the short passages of instrumental prelude or interlude, and the other from the vocal portions. Of these, the first was intelligible in the drama through its relation to some point in the story, but it also

2 k

early attained to a crude condition of form which was equally available apart from the drama. The other produced at first the vaguest and most rhapsodical of all the movements, as the type taken was the irregular declamatory recitative which appears to have abounded in the early operas.

It is hardly likely that it will ever be ascertained who first experimented in sonatas of several distinct movements. Many composers are mentioned in different places as having contributed works of the kind, such as Farina, Cesti, Graziani, among Italians, Rosenmüller among Germans, and John Jenkins among Englishmen. Burney also mentions a Michael Angelo Rossi, whose date is given as from about 1620 to 1660. An Andantino and Allegro by him, given in Pauer's 'Alte Meister,' require notice parenthetically as presenting a curious puzzle, if the dates are correct and the authorship rightly attributed. [These pieces are now known to be spurious (see p. 149a), but genuine specimens of Rossi's works are in Torchi's 'Arte Musicale in Italia,' vol. iii. See also Oskar Bie's *The Pianoforte*, Engl. transl. p. 82.] Though belonging to a period considerably before Corelli, they show a state of form which certainly was not commonly realised till more than a hundred years later. The distribution of subject-matter and key, and the clearness with which they are distinguished, are like the works of the middle of the 18th rather than the 17th century, and they belong absolutely to the Sonata order, and the conscious style of the later period. The actual structure of large numbers of sonatas composed in different parts of Europe soon after this time, proves a tolerably clear consent as to the arrangement and quality of the movements. A fine vigorous example is a Sonata in C minor for violin and figured bass, by H. J. F. Biber, a German, said to have been first published in 1681. This consists of five movements in alternate slow and quick time. The first is an introductory Largo of contrapuntal character, with clear and consistent treatment in the fugally imitative manner; the second is a Passacaglia, which answers roughly to a continuous string of variations on a short well-marked period; the third is a rhapsodical movement consisting of interspersed portions of Poco lento, Presto, and Adagio, leading into a Gavotte; and the last is a further rhapsodical movement alternating Adagio and Allegro. In this group the influence of the madrigal or canzona happens to be absent; the derivation of the movements being—in the first, the contrapuntalism of the music of the Church, in the second and fourth, dances, and in the third and fifth, probably operatic or dramatic declamation. The work is essentially a violin sonata with accompaniment, and the violin-part points to the extraordinarily rapid advance to mastery which was made in the few years after its being accepted as an instrument fit for high-class music. The writing for the instrument is decidedly elaborate and difficult, especially in the double stops and contrapuntal passages which were much in vogue with almost all composers from this time till J. S. Bach. In the structure of the movements the fugal influences are most apparent, and there are very few signs of the systematic repetition of subjects in connection with well-marked distribution of keys, which in later times became indispensable.

Similar features and qualities are shown in the curious set of seven Sonatas for Clavier by Johann Kuhnau, called 'Frische Clavier Früchte,' etc., of a little later date; but there are also in some parts indications of an awakening sense of the relation and balance of keys. The grouping of the movements is similar to those of Biber, though not identical; thus the first three have five movements or divisions, and the remainder four. There are examples of the same kind of rhapsodical slow movements, as may be seen in the Sonata (No. 2 of the set) which is given in Pauer's 'Alte Meister'; there are several fugal movements, some of them clearly and musically written; and there are some good illustrations of dance types, as in the last movement of No. 3, and the Ciaccona of No. 6. But more important for the thread of continuous development are the peculiar attempts to balance tolerably defined and distinct subjects, and to distribute key and subject in large expanses, of which there are at least two clear examples. In a considerable proportion of the movements the most noticeable method of treatment is to alternate two characteristic groups of figures or subjects almost throughout, in different positions of the scale and at irregular intervals of time. This is illustrated in the first movement of the Sonata No. 2, in the first movement of No. 1, and in the third movement of No. 5. The subjects in the last of these are as follows:—

The point most worth notice is that the device lies half-way between fugue and true sonata-form. The alternation is like the recurrence of subject and counter-subject in the former, wandering hazily in and out, and forwards and backwards, between nearly allied keys, as would be the case in a fugue. But the subjects are not presented in single parts or fugally answered. They enter and re-enter for the most part as concrete lumps of harmony, the harmonic accompaniment of the melody being taken as part of the idea ; and this is essentially a quality of sonata-form. So the movements appear to hang midway between the two radically distinct domains of form ; and while deriving most of their disposition from the older manners, they look forward, though obscurely, in the direction of modern practices. How obscure the ideas of the time on the subject must have been, appears from the other point which has been mentioned above ; which is, that in a few cases Kuhnau has hit upon clear outlines of tonal form. In the second Sonata, for instance, there are two Arias, as they are called. They do not correspond in the least with modern notions of an aria any more than do the rare examples in Bach's and Handel's Suites. The first is a little complete piece of sixteen bars, divided exactly into halves by a double bar, with repeats after the familiar manner. The first half begins in F and ends in C, the second half goes as far as D minor and back, to conclude in F again. The subject-matter is irregularly distributed in the parts, and does not make any pretence of coinciding with the tonal divisions. The second Aria is on a different plan, and is óne of the extremely rare examples in this early period of clear coincidence between subject and key. It is in the form which is often perversely misnamed 'lied-form,' which will in this place be called 'primary form' to avoid circumlocution and waste of space. It consists of twenty bars in D minor representing one distinct idea, complete with close : then sixteen bars devoted to a different subject, beginning in B♭ and passing back ultimately to D minor, recapitulating the whole of the first twenty bars in that key, and emphasising the close by repeating the last four bars. Such decisiveness, when compared with the unregulated and unbalanced wandering of longer movements, either points to the conclusion that composers did not realise the desirableness of balance in coincident ranges of subject and key on a large scale ; or that they were only capable of feeling it in short and easily grasped movements. It seems highly probable that their minds, being projected towards the kind of distribution of subject which obtained in fugal movements, were not on the look-out for effects of the sonata order which to moderns appear so obvious. So that, even if they had been capable of realising them more systematically, they would not yet have thought it worth while to apply their knowledge. In following the development of the Sonata, it ought never to be forgotten that composers had no idea whither they were tending, and had to use what they did know as stepping-stones to the unknown. In art, each step that is gained opens a fresh vista ; but often, till the new position is mastered, what lies beyond is completely hidden and undreamed of. In fact, each step is not so much a conquest of new

land, as the creation of a new mental or emotional position in the human organism. The achievements of art are the unravellings of hidden possibilities of abstract law, through the constant and cumulative extension of instincts. They do not actually exist till man has made them ; they are the counterpart of his internal conditions, and change and develop with the changes of his mental powers and sensitive qualities, and apart from him have no validity. There is no such thing as leaping across a chasm on to a new continent, neither is there any gulf fixed anywhere, but continuity and inevitable antecedents to every consequent ; the roots of the greatest masterpieces of modern times lie obscurely hidden in the wild dances and barbarous howlings of the remotest ancestors of the race, who began to take pleasure in rhythm and sound, and every step was into the unknown, or it may be better said not only unknown but non-existent till made by mental effort. The period from about 1600 to about 1725 contains the very difficult steps which led from the style appropriate to a high order of vocal music—of which the manner of speech is polyphonic, and the ideal type of form, the fugue—to the style appropriate to abstract instrumental music, of which the best manner is contrapuntally-expressed harmony, and the ideal type of form, the Sonata. These works of Kuhnau's happen to illustrate very curiously the transition in which a true though crude idea of abstract music seems to have been present in the composer's mind, at the same time that his distribution of subjects and keys was almost invariably governed by fugal habits of thinking, even where the statement of subjects is in a harmonic manner. In some of these respects he is nearer to, and in some further back from, the true solution of the problem than his famous contemporary Corelli ; but his labours do not extend over so much space, nor had they so much direct and widespread influence. In manner and distribution of movements they are nearer to his predecessor and compatriot Biber ; and for that reason, and also to maintain the continuity of the historic development after Corelli, the consideration of his works has been taken a little before their actual place in point of time.

The works of Corelli form one of the most familiar landmarks in the history of music, and as they are exclusively instrumental it is clear that careful consideration ought to elicit a great deal of interesting matter, such as must throw valuable light on the state of thought of his time. He published no less than sixty sonatas of different kinds, which are divisible into distinct groups in accordance with purpose or construction. The first main division is that suggested by their titles. There are twenty-four 'Sonate da Chiesa' for strings, lute, and organ, twenty-four 'Sonate da Camera' for the same instruments, and twelve Solos or Sonatas for violin and violoncello, or cembalo. In these the first and simplest matter for observation is the distribution of the movements. The average, in Church and Chamber Sonatas alike, is strongly in favour of four, beginning with a slow movement, and alternating the rest. There is also an attempt at balance in the alternation of character between the movements. The first is commonly in 4-time, of dignified and solid character, and generally aiming less at musical expression than the later movements. The second movement in the Church Sonata is freely fugal, in fact the exact type above described as a Canzona; the style is commonly rather dry, and the general effect chiefly a complacent kind of easy swing such as is familiar in most of Handel's fugues. In the Chamber Sonatas the character of the second movement is rather more variable; in some it is an Allemande, which, being dignified and solid, is a fair counterpart to the Canzona in the other Sonatas: sometimes it is a Courante, which is of lighter character. The third movement is the only one which is ever in a different key from the first and last. It is generally a characteristic one, in which other early composers of instrumental music, as well as Corelli, clearly endeavoured to infuse a certain amount of vague and tender sentiment. The most common time is 3-2. The extent of the movement is always limited, and the style, though simply contrapuntal in fact, seems to be ordered with a view to obtain smooth harmonious full-chord effects, as a contrast to the brusqueness of the preceding fugal movement. There is generally a certain amount of imitation between the parts, irregularly and fancifully disposed, but almost always avoiding the sounding of a single part alone. In the Chamber Sonatas, as might be anticipated, the third movement is frequently a Sarabande, though by no means always; for the same kind of slow movement as that in the Church Sonatas is sometimes adopted, as in the third Sonata of the Opera Seconda, which is as good an example of that class as could be taken. The last movement is almost invariably of a lively character in Church and Chamber Sonatas alike. In the latter, Gigas and Gavottes predominate, the character of which is so familiar that they need no description. The last movements in the Church Sonatas are of a similar vivacity and sprightliness, and sometimes so alike in character and rhythm as to be hardly distinguishable from dance-tunes, except by the absence of the defining name, the double bar in the middle, and the repeats which are almost inevitable in the dance movements. This general scheme is occasionally varied without material difference of principle by the interpolation of an extra quick movement, as in the first six Sonatas of the Opera Quinta; in which it is a sort of show movement for the violin in a 'Moto continuo'

style, added before or after the central slow movement. In a few cases the number is reduced to three by dropping the slow prelude, and in a few others the order cannot be systematised.

In accordance with the principles of classification above defined, the Church Sonatas appear to be much more strictly abstract than those for Chamber. The latter are, in many cases, not distinguishable from Suites. The Sonatas of Opera Quinta are variable. Thus the attractive Sonata in E minor, No. 8, is quite in the recognised suite-manner. Some are like the Sonate da Chiesa, and some are types of the mixed order more universally accepted later, having several undefined movements, together with one dance. The actual structure of the individual movements is most uncertain. Corelli clearly felt that something outside the domain of the fugal tribe was to be attained, but he had no notion of strict outlines of procedure. One thing which hampered him and other composers of the early times of instrumental music was their unwillingness to accept formal tunes as an element in their order of art. They had existed in popular song and dance music for certainly a century, and probably much more; but the idea of adopting them in high-class music was not yet in favour. Corelli occasionally produces one, but the fact that they generally occur with him in Gigas, which are the freest and least responsible portion of the Sonata, supports the inference that they were not yet regarded as worthy of general acceptance even if realised as an admissible element, but could only be smuggled-in in the least respectable movement with an implied smile to disarm criticism. Whether this was decisively so or not, the fact remains that till long after Corelli's time the conventional tune element was conspicuously absent from instrumental compositions. Hence the structural principles which to a modern seem almost inevitable were very nearly impracticable, or at all events unsuitable to the general principles of the music of that date. A modern expects the opening bars of a movement to present its most important subject, and he anticipates its repetition in the latter portion of the movement as a really vital part of form of any kind. But association and common sense were alike against such a usage being universal in Corelli's time. The associations of ecclesiastical and other serious vocal music, which were then preponderant to a supreme degree, were against strongly salient points, or strongly marked interest in short portions of a movement in contrast to parts of comparative unimportance. Consequently the opening bars of a movement would not be expected to stand out in sufficiently strong relief to be remembered unless they were repeated at once, as they would be in fugue. Human nature is against it. For not only does the mind take time to be wrought up to a fully receptive condition, unless the beginning is most exceptionally striking, but what comes after is likely to obliterate the impression made by it. As a matter of fact, if all things were equal, the portion most likely to remain in the mind of an average listener, is that immediately preceding the strongest cadences or conclusions of the paragraphs of the movement. It is true, composers do not argue in this manner, but they feel such things vaguely or instinctively, and generally with more sureness and justice than the cold-blooded argumentation of a theorist could attain to. Many examples in other early composers besides Corelli, emphasise this point effectively. The earliest attempts at structural form must inevitably present some simply explicable principle of this sort, which is only not trivial because it is a very significant as well as indispensable starting-point. Corelli's commonest devices of form are the most unsophisticated applications of such simple reasoning. In the first place, in many movements which are not fugal, the opening bars are immediately repeated in another position in the scale, simply and without periphrasis, as if to give the listener assurance of an idea of balance at the very outset. That he did this to a certain extent consciously, is obvious from his having employed the device in at least the following Sonatas—2, 3, 8, 9, 10, 11, of Opera 1ma; 2, 4, 7, 8, of Opera 3^{za}; and 2, 4, 5, and 11, of Opera 4ta; and Tartini and other composers of the same school followed his lead. This device is not, however, either so conspicuous or so common as that of repeating the concluding passage of the first half at the end of the whole, or of the concluding passages of one half or both consecutively. This, however, was not restricted to Corelli, but is found in the works of most composers from his time to Scarlatti, J. S. Bach and his sons ; and it is no extravagant hypothesis that its gradual extension was the direct origin of the characteristic second section and second subject of modern sonata section movements. In many cases it is the only element of form, in the modern sense, in Corelli's movements. In a few cases he hit upon more complicated principles. The Corrente in Sonata 5 of Opera 4ta, is nearly a miniature of modern binary form. The well-known Giga in A in the fifth Sonata of Opera 5ta, has balance of key in the first half of the movement, modulation, and something like consistency to subject-matter at the beginning of the second half, and due recapitulation of principal subject-matter at the end. The last movement of the eighth Sonata of the Opera Terza, is within reasonable distance of rondo-form, though this form is generally as conspicuous for its absence in early sonatas as tunes are, and probably the one follows as a natural consequence of the other. Of the simple primary

form, consisting of corresponding beginning and end, and contrast of some sort in the middle, there is singularly little. The clearest example is probably the Tempo di Gavotta, which concludes the ninth Sonata of Opera Quinta. He also supplies suggestions of the earliest types of sonata form, in which both the beginnings and endings of each half of the movement correspond ; as this became an accepted principle of structure with later composers, it will have to be considered more fully in relation to their works. Of devices of form which belong to the great polyphonic tribe, Corelli uses many, but with more musical feeling than learning. His fugues are not remarkable as fugues, and he uses contrapuntal imitation rather as a subordinate means of carrying on the interest, than of expounding any wonderful device of pedantic wisdom, as was too common in those days. He makes good use of the chaconne-form, which was a great favourite with the early composers, and also uses the kindred device of carrying the repetition of a short figure through the greater part of a movement in different phases and positions of the scale. In some cases he merely rambles on without any perceptible aim whatever, only keeping up an equable flow of sound with pleasant interlacings of easy counterpoint, led on from moment to moment by suspensions and occasional imitation, and here and there a helpful sequence. Corelli's position as a composer is inseparably mixed up with his position as one of the earliest masters of his instrument. His style of writing for it does not appear to be so elaborate as that of other contemporaries, both older and younger, but he grasped a just way of expressing things with it, and for the most part the fit things to say. The impression he made upon musical people in all parts of the musical world was strong, and he was long regarded as the most delightful of composers in his particular line ; and though the professors of his day did not always hold him in so high estimation, his influence upon many of his most distinguished successors was unquestionably powerful.

It is possible, however, that appearances are deceptive, and that influences of which he was only the most familiar exponent, are mistaken for his peculiar achievement. Thus knowing his position at the head of a great school of violinists, which continued through several generations down to Haydn's time, it is difficult to disunite him from the honour of having fixed the type of sonata which they almost uniformly adopted. And not only this noble and vigorous school, comprising such men as Tartini, Vivaldi, Locatelli, Nardini, Veracini, and outlying members like Leclair and Rust, but men who were not specially attached to their violins, such as Albinoni and Purcell, and later, Bach, Handel, and Porpora, equally adopted the type. Of Albinoni not much seems to be distinctly known, except that he was Corelli's contemporary and probably junior. He wrote operas and instrumental music. Of the latter, several sonatas are still to be seen, but they are, of course, not familiar, though at one time they enjoyed a wide popularity. The chief point about them is that in many for violin and figured bass he follows not only the same general outlines, but even the style of Corelli. He adopts the four-movement plan, with a decided canzona in the second place, a slow movement first and third, and a quick movement to end with, such as in one case a Corrente. Purcell's having followed Corelli's lead is repudiated by enthusiasts; but at all events the lines of his Golden Sonata in F are wonderfully similar. There are three slow movements, which come first, second, and fourth; the third movement is actually called a Canzona; and the last is a quick movement in 3–8 time, similar in style to corresponding portions of Corelli's Sonatas. The second movement, an Adagio, is the most expressive, being happily devised on the principle above referred to, of repeating a short figure in different positions throughout the movement. In respect of sonata-form the work is about on a par with the average of Corelli or Biber.

The domain of the Sonata was for a long while almost monopolised by violinists and writers for the violin. Some of these, such as Geminiani and Locatelli, were actually Corelli's pupils. They clearly followed him both in style and structural outlines, but they also began to extend and build upon them with remarkable speed. The second movement continued for long the most stationary and conventional, maintaining the Canzona type in a loose fugal manner, by the side of remarkable changes in the other movements. Of these the first began to grow into larger dimensions and clearer proportions even in Corelli's own later works, attaining to the dignity of double bars and repeats, and with his successors to a consistent and self-sufficing form. An example of this is the admirable Larghetto affettuoso with which Tartini's celebrated 'Trillo del Diavolo' commences. No one who has heard it could fail to be struck with the force of the simple device above described of making the ends of each half correspond, as the passage is made to stand out from all the rest more characteristically than usual. A similar and very good example is the introductory Largo to the Sonata in G minor, for violin and figured bass, by Locatelli, which is given in Ferdinand David's 'Hohe Schule des Violinspiels.' The subject-matter in both examples is exceedingly well handled, so that a sense of perfect consistency is maintained without concrete repetition of subjects, except, as already noticed, the closing bars of each half, which in Locatelli's Sonata are rendered less obvious through the addition

of a short coda starting from a happy interrupted cadence. It is out of the question to follow the variety of aspects presented by the introductory slow movement; a fair proportion are on similar lines to the above examples, others are isolated. Their character is almost uniformly solid and large; they are often expressive, but generally in a way distinct from the character of the second slow movement, which from the first was chosen as the fittest to admit a vein of tenderer sentiment. The most important matter in the history of the Sonata at this period is the rapidity with which advance was made towards the realisation of modern harmonic and tonal principles of structure, or, in other words, the perception of the effect and significance of relations between chords and distinct keys, and consequent appearance of regularity of purpose in the distribution of both, and increased freedom of modulation. Even Corelli's own pupils show consistent form of the sonata kind with remarkable clearness. The last movement of a Sonata in C minor, by Geminiani, has a clear and emphatic subject to start with; modulation to the relative major, E♭, and special features to characterise the second section; and conclusion of the first half in that key, with repeat after the supposed orthodox manner. The second half begins with a long section corresponding to the working out or 'free fantasia' portion of a modern sonata movement, and concludes with recapitulation of the first subject and chief features of the second section in C minor; this latter part differing chiefly from modern ways by admitting a certain amount of discursiveness, which is characteristic of most of the early experiments in this form. Similar to this is the last movement of Locatelli's Sonata in G minor, the last movement of Veracini's Sonata in E minor, published at Vienna in 1714, the last movements of Tartini's Sonatas in E minor and D minor, and not a few others. It is rather curious that most of the early examples of what is sometimes called first-movement form are last movements. Most of these movements, however, in the early times, are distinguished by a peculiarity which is of some importance. It has been before referred to, but is so characteristic of the process of growth, that it will not be amiss to describe it in this place. The simple and almost homely means of producing the effect of structural balance by making the beginning and ending of each half of a movement correspond, is not so conspicuously common in its entirety as the correspondence of endings or repetition of cadence bars only; but it nevertheless is found tolerably often, and that in times before the virtue of a balance of keys in the first half of the movement had been decisively realised. When, however, this point was gained, it is clear that such a process would give, on as minute a scale as possible, the very next thing to complete modern binary form. It only needed to expand the opening passage into a first subject, and the figures of the Cadence into a second subject, to attain that type which became almost universal in sonatas till Haydn's time, and with some second-rate composers, like Reichardt, later. The movements which are described as binary must be therefore divided into two distinct classes :— that in which the first subject reappears in the complementary key at the beginning of the second half, which is the almost universal type of earlier times ; and that in which it appears in the latter part of the movement, after the working-out portion, which is the later type. The experiments in Corelli and Tartini, and others who are close to these types, are endless. Sometimes there are tentative strokes near to the later form ; sometimes there is an inverted order reproducing the second portion of the movement first. Sometimes the first subject makes its appearance at both points, but then, may be, there is no balance of keys in the first half, and so forth. The variety is extraordinary, and it is most interesting to watch the manner in which some types by degrees preponderate, sometimes by combining with one another, sometimes by gradual transformation, some nearer and more decisively like the types which are generally adopted in modern times as fittest. The later type was not decisively fixed on at any particular point, for many early composers touched it once or twice at the same period that they were writing movements in more elementary forms. The point of actual achievement of a step in art is not marked by an isolated instance, but by decisive preponderance, and by the systematic adoption which shows at least an instinctive realisation of its value and importance.

These writers of violin sonatas were just touching on the clear realisation of harmonic form as accepted in modern times, and they sometimes adopted the later type, though rarely, and that obscurely ; they mastered the earlier type, and used it freely ; and they also used the intermediate type which combines the two, in which the principal or first subject makes its appearance both at the beginning of the first half and near the end, where a modern would expect it. As a sort of embryonic suggestion of this, the Tempo di Gavotta, in the eighth Sonata of Corelli's Opera Seconda, is significant. Complete examples are—the last movement of Tartini's fourth Sonata of Opus 1, and the last movement of that in D minor above referred to ; the last movement of Geminiani's Sonata in C minor ; the main portion, excluding the Coda, of the Corrente in Vivaldi's Sonata in A major ; the last movement of a Sonata of Nardini's, in D major ; and two Capriccios in B♭ and C, by Franz Benda, quoted in F. David's ' Hohe Schule,' etc.

The four-movement type of violin sonata was not invariably adopted, though it preponderates so conspicuously. There is a set of twelve sonatas by Locatelli, for instance, not so fine as that in F. David's collection, which are nearly all on an original three-movement plan, concluding with an ' Aria ' and variations on a ground-bass. Some of Tartini's are also in three movements, and a set of six by Nardini are also in three, but always beginning with a slow movement, and therefore, though almost of the same date, not really approaching the distribution commonly adopted by Haydn for Clavier Sonatas. In fact the old Violin Sonata is in many respects a distinct genus, which maintained its individuality alongside the gradually stereotyped Clavier Sonata, and only ceased when that type obtained possession of the field, and the violin was reintroduced, at first as it were furtively, as an accompaniment to the pianoforte. The general characteristics of this school of writers for the violin, were nobility of style and richness of feeling, an astonishing mastery of the instrument, and a rapidly-growing facility in dealing with structure in respect of subject, key, modulation, and development ; and what is most vital, though less obvious, a perceptible growth in the art of expression and a progress towards the definition of ideas. As a set-off there are occasional traces of pedantic manners, and occasional crudities both of structure and expression, derived probably from the associations of the old music which they had so lately left behind them. At the crown of the edifice are the Sonatas of J. S. Bach. Of sonatas in general he appears not to have held to any decisive opinion. He wrote many for various instruments, and for various combinations of instruments. For clavier, for violin alone, for flute, violin, and clavier, for viol da gamba and clavier, and so on ; but in most of these the outlines are not decisively distinct from Suites. In some cases the works are described as ' Sonatas or Suites,' and in at least one case the introduction to a church cantata is called a Sonata. Some instrumental works which are called Sonatas only, might quite as well be called Suites, as they consist of a prelude and a set of dance-tunes. Others are heterogeneous. From this it appears that he had not satisfied himself on what lines to attack the Sonata in any sense approaching the modern idea. With the Violin Sonatas it was otherwise ; and in the group of six for violin and clavier he follows almost invariably the main outlines which are characteristic of the Italian school descended from Corelli, and all but one are on the four-movement plan, having slow movements first and third, and quick movements second and fourth. The sixth Sonata only differs from the rest by having an additional quick movement at the beginning. Not only this but the second movements keep decisively the formal lineaments of the ancient type of free fugue, illustrated with more strictness of manner by the Canzonas. Only in calibre and quality of ideas, and in some peculiar idiosyncrasies of structure do they differ materially from the works of the Italian masters. Even the first, third, and fifth Sonatas in the other set of six, for violin alone, conform accurately to the old four-movement plan, including the fugue in the second place ; the remaining three being on the general lines of the Suite. In most of the Sonatas for violin and clavier, the slow movement is a tower of strength, and strikes a point of rich and complex emotional expression which music reached for the first time in Bach's imagination. His favourite way of formulating a movement of this sort, was to develop the whole accompaniment consistently on a concise and strongly-marked figure, which by repetition in different conditions formed a bond of connection throughout the whole ; and on this he built a passionate kind of recitative, a free and unconstrained outpouring of the deepest and noblest instrumental song. This was a sort of apotheosis of that form of rhapsody, which has been noticed in the early Sonatas, such as Biber's and Kuhnau's, and was occasionally attempted by the Italians. The six Sonatas present diversities of types, all of the loftiest order ; some of them combining together with unfailing expressiveness perfect specimens of old forms of contrapuntal ingenuity. Of this, the second movement of the second Sonata is a perfect example. It appears to be a pathetic colloquy between the violin and the treble of the clavier part, to which the bass keeps up the slow constant motion of staccato semiquavers : the colloquy at the same time is in strict canon throughout, and, as a specimen of expressive treatment of that time-honoured form, is almost unrivalled.

In all these movements the kinship is rather with the contrapuntal writers of the past, than with the types of Beethoven's adoption. Even Bach, immense as his genius and power of divination was, could not leap over that period of formation which it seems to have been indispensable for mankind to pass through, before equally noble and deeply-felt things could be expressed in the characteristically modern manner. Though he looked further into the future in matters of expression and harmonic combination than any composer till the 19th century, he still had to use forms of the contrapuntal and fugal order for the expression of his highest thoughts. He did occasionally make use of binary form, though not in these Sonatas. But he more commonly adopted, and combined with more or less fugal treatment, an expansion of simple primary form to attain structural effect. Thus, in the second movements of the first and second Sonatas, in the last of the third and sixth, and the first of the sixth, he marks first a long complete section in his principal key, then takes his way into modulations and development, and discussion of themes and various kinds of contrapuntal enjoyment, and concludes with simple complete recapitulation of the first section in the principal key. Bach thus stands singularly aside from the direct line of the development of the Sonata as far as the structural elements are concerned. His contributions to the art of expression, to the development of resource, and to the definition and treatment of ideas, had great effect, and are of the very highest importance to instrumental music ; but his almost invariable choice of either the suite-form, or the accepted outlines of the violin sonata, in works of this class, caused him to diverge into a course which with him found its final and supreme limit. In order to continue the work in veins which were yet unexhausted, the path had to be turned a little, and joined to courses which were coming up from other directions. The violin sonata continued to make its appearance here and there as has already been mentioned, but in the course of a generation it was entirely supplanted by the distinct type of clavier sonata.

Meanwhile there was another composer of this time, who appears to stand just as singularly apart from the direct high road as Bach, and who, though he does not occupy a pedestal so high in the history of art, still has a niche by no means low or inconspicuous, and one which he shares with no one. Domenico Scarlatti was Bach's senior by a few years, though not enough to place him in an earlier musical generation ; and in fact though his works are so different in quality, they have the stamp that marks them as belonging to the same parallel of time. His most valuable contributions are in the immense number of sonatas and studies which he wrote for the harpsichord. The two names are used as synonyms, for each of the thirty ' Esercizii per Gravicembalo ' is separately entitled ' Sonata.' But whatever they are called they do not correspond in appearance to any form which is commonly supposed to be essential to the Sonata. Neither can they be taken as pure-bred members of the fugal family, nor do they trace their origins to the Suite. They are in fact, in a fair proportion of cases, an attempt to deal with direct ideas in a modern sense, without appealing to the glamour of conscious association, the dignity of science, or the familiarity of established dance rhythms. The connection with what goes before and with what comes after is alike obscure, because of the daring originality with which existing materials are worked upon ; but it is not the less inevitably present, as an outline of his structural principles will show.

His utterance is at its best sharp and incisive ; the form in which he loves to express himself is epigrammatic ; and some of his most effective sonatas are like strings of short propositions bound together by an indefinable sense of consistency and consequence, rather than by actual development. These ideas are commonly brought home to the hearer by the singular practice of repeating them consecutively as they stand, often several times over ; in respect of which it is worth remembering that his position in relation to his audience was not unlike that of an orator addressing an uncultivated mob. The capacity for appreciating grand developments of structure was as undeveloped in them as the power of following widely spread argument and conclusion would be in the mob. And just as the mob-orator makes his most powerful impressions by short direct statements, and by hammering them in while still hot from his lips, so Scarlatti drove his points home by frequent and generally identical reiterations ; and then when the time came round to refer to them again, the force of the connection between distant parts of the same story was more easily grasped. The feeling that he did this with his eyes open is strengthened by the fact that even in the grouping of the reiterations there is commonly a perceptible method. For instance, it can hardly be by accident that at a certain point of the movement, after several simple repetitions, he should fre-quently resort to the complication of repeating several small groups within the repetition of large ones. The following example is a happy illustration of his style, and of his way of elaborating such repetitions :—

etc.

It must not be supposed that he makes a law of this procedure, but the remarkably frequent occurrence of so curious a device is certainly suggestive of conscious purpose in structural treatment. [It is only right to point out the recognised custom of repeating phrases on the harpsichord with a change of registration, which may account in some measure for the habit here referred to.] The result of this mode is that the movements often appear to be crowded with ideas. Commonly the features of the opening bars, which in modern times would be held of almost supreme importance, serve for very little except to determine the character of the movement, and do not make their appear-ance again. On the other hand, he carries the practice before referred to, of making the latter part of each half of the movement corre-spond, to an extraordinary pitch, and with perfect success ; for he almost invariably adopts the key distribution of binary form in its main outlines ; and though it would not be accurate to speak of such a thing as a ' second subject ' in his sonatas, the impression produced by his distribution of repetition and the clearness of his ideas is sufficient, in his best movements, to give a general structural effect very similar to complete binary form on a small scale. In order to realise to what extent the process of recapitula-tion is carried by him, it will be as well to consider the outline of a fairly characteristic sonata. That which stands fifteenth in the easily available edition of Breitkopf & Härtel [1] commences with eight bars only in E minor ; the next forty-six, barring merely a slight and unimportant digression, are in G major. This concludes the first half. The second half begins with reference to the opening figures of the whole and a little key digression, and then a characteristic portion of the second section of the first half is resumed, and the last thirty-four bars of the movement are a recapitulation in E minor of the last thirty-five of the first half, the three concluding bars being condensed into two.

In many respects his principles of structure and treatment are altogether in the direction of modern ways, and alien to fugal principles. That vital principle of the fugue—the per-sistence of one principal idea, and the inter-weaving of it into every part of the structure—appears completely alien to Scarlatti's disposi-tion. He very rarely wrote a fugue ; and when he did, if it was successful that was less because it was a good fugue than because it was Scarlatti's. The fact that he often starts with imitation between two parts is unimportant, and the merest accident of association. He generally treats his ideas as concrete lumps, and disposes them in distinct portions of the movement,

---

[1] It is also the fifteenth in the ' Esercizii ' ; in Pauer's edition it is No. 18 ; in the ' Trésor des Pianistes,' No. 19 ; and occurs on p. 22 of Roseingrave's second volume. It has not yet appeared in Signor Longo's complete edition.

which is essentially an unfugal proceeding; but the most important matter is that he was probably the first to attain to clear conception and treatment of a self-sufficing effective idea, and to use it, if without science, yet with management which is often convincingly successful. He was not a great master of the art of composition, but he was one of the rarest masters of his instrument ; and his divination of the way to treat it, and the perfect adaptation of his ideas to its requirements, more than counterbalance any shortcoming in his science. He was blessed with ideas, and with a style so essentially his own, that even when his music is transported to another instrument the characteristic effects of tone often remain unmistakable. Vivacity, humour, genuine fun, are his most familiar traits. At his best his music sparkles with life and freshness, and its vitality is apparently quite unimpaired by age. He rarely approaches tenderness or sadness, and in the whole mass of his works there are hardly any slow movements. He is not a little 'bohemian,' and seems positively to revel in curious effects of consecutive fifths and consecutive octaves. The characteristic daring of which such things are the most superficial manifestations, joined with the clearness of his foresight, made him of closer kinship to Beethoven and Weber, and even Brahms, than to the typical contra-puntalists of his day. His works are genuine 'sonatas' in the most radical sense of the term—self-dependent and self-sufficing *sound-pieces*, without programme. To this the distribution of movements is at least of secondary importance, and his confining himself to one alone does not vitiate his title to be a foremost contributor to that very important branch of the musical art. No successor was strong enough to wield his bow. His pupil Durante wrote some sonatas, consisting of a Studio and a Divertimento apiece, which have touches of his manner, but without sufficient of the nervous elasticity to make them important.

The contemporary writers for clavier of second rank do not offer much which is of high musical interest, and they certainly do not arrive at anything like the richness of thought and expression which is shown by their fellows of the violin. There appears, however, amongst them a tendency to drop the introductory slow movement characteristic of the violin sonata, and by that means to draw nearer to the type of later clavier or pianoforte sonatas. Thus a sonata of Wagenseil's in F major presents almost exactly the general outlines to be met with in Haydn's works—an Allegro assai in binary form of the old type, a short Andantino grazioso, and a Tempo di Minuetto. A sonata of Hasse's in D minor has a similar arrangement of three movements ending with a Gigue ; but the first movement is utterly vague and indefinite in form. There is also an Allegro of

Hasse's in B♭, quoted in Pauer's 'Alte Meister,' which deserves consideration for the light it throws on a matter which is sometimes said to be a crucial distinction between the early attempts at form and the perfect achievement. In many of the early examples of sonata-form, the second section of the first part is characterised by groups of figures which are quite definite enough for all reasonable purposes, but do not come up to the ideas commonly entertained of the nature of a subject ; and on this ground the settlement of sonata-form was deferred some fifty years. Hasse was not a daring originator, neither was he likely to strike upon a crucial test of perfection, yet in this movement he sets out with a distinct and complete subject in B♭ of a robust Handelian character :—

and after the usual extension proceeds to F, and announces by definite emphasis on the Dominant the well-contrasted second subject, which is suggestive of the polite reaction looming in the future :—

The movement as a whole is in the binary type of the earlier kind.

The period now approaching is characterised by uncertainty in the distribution of the movements, but increasing regularity and definition in their internal structure. Some writers follow the four-movement type of violin sonata in writing for the clavier ; some strike upon the grouping of three movements ; and a good many fall back upon two. A sonata of Galuppi's in D illustrates the first of these, and throws light upon the transitional process. The first movement is a beautiful Adagio of the Arioso type, with the endings of each half corresponding, after the manner traced from Corelli ; the second is an Allegro, not of the fugal or Canzona order, but clear binary of the older kind. A violin sonata of Locatelli's, of probably earlier date, has an Allemande of excellent form in this position, but this is not sufficiently definite in the inference it affords to throw much light on any transition or assimilation of violin sonata-form to clavier sonata-form. Galuppi's adoption of a movement of clear sonata-qualities in this place supplies exactly the link that was needed ; and the fugal or canzona type of movement being so supplanted, nothing further was necessary but expansion, and the omission of the introductory Adagio (which probably was not so well adapted to the earlier keyed instruments as to the violin), to arrive at the principle of distribution adopted in the palmiest days of formalism. Later, with a more powerful instrument, the introductory slow movement was often reintroduced. Galuppi's third movement is in a solid march style, and the last is a Giga. All of them are harmonically constructed, and the whole work is solid and of sterling musical worth.

Dr. Arne was born only four years after Galuppi, and was amenable to the same general influences. The structure of his sonatas emphasises the fact above mentioned, that though the order of movements was passing through a phase of uncertainty their internal structure was growing more and more distinct and uniform. His first sonata, in F, has two movements, Andante and Allegro, both of which follow harmonically the lines of binary form. The second, in E minor, has three movements, Andante, Adagio, Allegrissimo. The first and last are on the binary lines, and the middle one in simple primary form. The third Sonata consists of a long vague introduction of arpeggios, elaborated in a manner characteristic of the time, an Allegro which has only one subject but is on the binary lines, and a Minuet and two Variations. The fourth Sonata is in some respects the most interesting. It consists of an Andante, Siciliano, Fuga, and Allegro. The first is of continuous character but nevertheless in binary form, without the strong emphasis on the points of division between the sections. It deserves notice for its expressiveness and clearness of thought. The second movement is very short, but pretty and expressive, of a character similar to examples of Handel's tenderer moods. The last movement is particularly to be noticed, not only for being decisively in binary form, but for the ingenuity with which that form is manipulated. The first section is represented by the main subject in the treble, the second (which is clearly marked in the dominant key) has the same subject in the bass, a device adopted also more elaborately by W. Friedemann Bach. The second half begins with consistent development and modulation, and the recapitulation is happily managed by making the main subject represent both sections at once in a short passage of canon. Others of Arne's sonatas afford similar though less clear examples, which it is superfluous to consider in detail ; for neither

the matter nor the handling is so good in them as in those above described, most of which, though not rich in thought or treatment, nor impressive in character, have genuine traits of musical expression and clearness of workmanship.

In the same year with Dr. Arne was born Wilhelm Friedemann Bach, the eldest son of John Sebastian. He was probably the most gifted, the most independent, and unfortunately the wildest and most unmanageable of that remarkable family. Few of his compositions are known, and it is said that he would not take the trouble to write unless he was driven to it. Two sonatas exist, which are of different type, and probably represent different periods of his chequered career. One in D major, for its richness, elaborateness, expressiveness, is well worthy of the scion of so great a stock ; the other is rather cheap, and though masterly in handling and disposition of structural elements, has more traces of the elegance which was creeping over the world of music than of the grave and earnest nobleness of his father and similar representatives of the grand period. The first, in D, is probably the most remarkable example, before Beethoven, of original ingenuity manipulating sonata-form under the influence of fugal associations and by means of contrapuntal devices. The whole is worked out with careful and intelligible reasoning, but to such an elaborate extent that it is quite out of the question to give even a complete outline of its contents. The movements are three—Un poco allegro, Adagio, Vivace. The first and last are speculative experiments in binary form. The first half in each represents the balance of expository sections in tonic and complementary keys. The main subject of the first reappears in the bass in the second section, with a new phase of the original accompaniment in the upper parts. The development portion is in its usual place, but the recapitulation is tonally reversed. The first subject and section is given in a relative key to balance the complementary key of the second section, and the second section is given in the original key or tonic of the movement ; so that instead of repeating one section and transposing the other in recapitulation, they are both transposed analogously. In each of the three movements the ends of the halves correspond, and not only this but the graceful little figure appended to the cadence is the same in all the movements, establishing thereby a very delicate but sensible connection between them. This figure is as follows :—

The formal pauses on familiar points of harmony characteristic of later times are conspicuously few, the main divisions being generally marked by more subtle means. The whole sonata is so uncompromisingly full of expressive figures, and would require to be so elaborately phrased and 'sung' to be intelligible, that an adequate performance would be a matter of considerable difficulty. The second Sonata, in C, has quite a different appearance. It is also in three movements—Allegro, Grave, and Vivace. The first is a masterly, clear, and concise example of binary form of the type which is more familiar in the works of Haydn and Mozart. The second is an unimportant intermezzo leading directly into the Finale, which is also in binary form of the composite type. The treatment is the very reverse of the previous sonata. It is not contrapuntal, nor fugal. Little pains are taken to make the details expressive ; and the only result of using a bigger and less careful brush is to reduce the interest to a minimum, and to make the genuineness of the utterances seem doubtful, because the writer appears not to have taken the trouble to express his best thoughts.

Wilhelm Friedemann's brother, Carl Philipp Emanuel, his junior by a few years, was the member of the younger family who attained the highest reputation as a representative composer of instrumental music and a writer on that subject. His celebrity is more particularly based on the development of sonata-form, of which he is often spoken of as the inventor. True, his sonatas and writings obtained considerable celebrity, and familiarity induced people to remark things they had overlooked in the works of other composers. But in fact he is neither the inventor nor the establisher of sonata-form. It was understood before his day, both in details and in general distribution of movements. One type obtained the reputation of supreme fitness later, but it was not nearly always adopted by Haydn, nor invariably by Mozart, and was consistently departed from by Beethoven ; and Emanuel did not restrict himself to it ; yet his predecessors used it often. It is evident therefore that his claims to a foremost place rest upon other grounds. Among these, most prominent is his comprehension and employment of the art of playing and expressing things on the clavier. He understood it, not in a new sense, but in one which was nearer to public comprehension than the treatment of his father. He grasped the phase to which it had arrived, by constant development in all quarters ; he added a little of his own, and having a clear and ready-working brain, he brought it home to the musical public in a way they had not felt before. His influence was paramount to give a decided direction to clavier-playing, and it is possible that the style of which he was the foster-father passed on continuously to the masterly treatment of the pianoforte by Clementi, and through him to the culminating achievements of Beethoven.

In respect of structure, most of his important sonatas are in three movements, of which the first and last are quick, and the middle one slow ; and this is a point by no means insignificant in the history of the sonata, as it represents a definite and characteristic balance between the principal divisions, in respect of style and expression as well as in the external traits of form. Many of these are in clear binary form, like those of his elder brother, and his admirable predecessor, yet to be noted, P. Domenico Paradies. He adopts sometimes the old type, dividing the recapitulation in the second half of the movement ; sometimes the later, and sometimes the composite type. For the most part he is contented with the opportunities for variety which this form supplies, and casts a greater proportion of movements in it than most other composers, even to the extent of having all movements in a work in different phases of the same form, which in later times was rare. On the other hand, he occasionally experiments in structures as original as could well be devised. There is a Sonata in F minor which has three main divisions corresponding to movements. The first, an Allegro, approaches vaguely to binary form ; the second, an Adagio, is in rough outline like simple primary form, concluding with a curious barless cadenza ; the last is a Fantasia of the most elaborate and adventurous description, full of experiments in modulation, enharmonic and otherwise, changes of time, abrupt surprises and long passages entirely divested of bar lines. There is no definite subject, and no method in the distribution of keys. It is more like a rhapsodical improvisation of a most inconsequent and unconstrained description than the product of concentrated purpose, such as is generally expected in a sonata movement. This species of experiment has not survived in high-class modern music, except in the rarest cases. It was however not unfamiliar in those days, and superb examples in the same spirit were provided by John Sebastian, such as the Fantasia

Cromatica, and parts of some of the Toccatas. John Ernst Bach also left something more after the manner of the present instance as the prelude to a fugue. Emanuel Bach's position is particularly emphasised as the most prominent composer of sonatas of his time, who clearly shows the tendency of the new counter-current away from the vigour and honest comprehensiveness of the great school of which his father was the last and greatest representative, towards the elegance, polite ease, and artificiality, which became the almost indispensable conditions of the art in the latter part of the 18th century. Fortunately the process of propping up a tune upon a dummy accompaniment was not yet accepted universally as a desirable phenomenon of high-class instrumental music ; in fact such a stride downward in one generation would have been too cataclystic ; so he was spared the temptation of shirking honest concentration, and padding his works, instead of making them thoroughly complete ; and the result is a curious combination, sometimes savouring strongly of his father's style :—

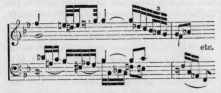

and sometimes coldly predicting the style of the future :—

In general, his building up of movements is full of expressive detail, and he does not spare himself trouble in enriching his work with such things as ingenuity, genuine musical perception, and vivacity of thought can suggest. He occasionally reaches a point of tenderness and poetic sensibility which is not unworthy of his descent, but there is also sometimes an uncomfortable premonition in his slow movements of the posturing and posing which were soon to be almost inevitable in well-bred Adagios. The spirit is indeed not greatly deep and earnest, but in outward things the attainment of a rare degree of point and emphasis, and of clearness and certainty in construction without emptiness, sufficed to give Philipp Emanuel a foremost place among the craftsmen of the art.

P. Domenico Paradies was Emanuel Bach's senior by a few years. Two of his sonatas, at least, are deservedly well known to musicians. The structural qualities shown by the whole set

of twelve, emphasise the opinion that binary form was familiar to composers of this period. They differ from Philipp Emanuel's chiefly in consisting uniformly of two movements only. Of these, the first movements are almost invariably in binary form. That of the first sonata is perfectly complete and of the later type ; many of the others are of the early type. Some details in the distribution of the movements are worth noticing. Thus the last movement of No. 4 is a very graceful and pretty minuet, which had hitherto not been so common an ingredient in sonatas as it afterwards became. The last movement [1] of No. 3 is called an aria ; the arrangement of parts of which, as well as that of the last movement of No. 9, happens to produce a rondo, hitherto an extremely rare feature. His formulation and arrangement of subjects is extremely clear and masterly, and thoroughly in the sonata manner—that is, essentially harmonical. In character he leans towards the style of the latter part of the 18th century, but has a grace and sincerity which are thoroughly his own. In a few cases, as in the last movements of the Sonatas in A and D, Nos. 6 and 10, which are probably best known of all, the character assumed is rather of the bustling and hearty type which is suggestive of the influence of Scarlatti. In detail they are not so rich as the best specimens of Emanuel's, or of Friedemann Bach's workmanship ; but they are thoroughly honest and genuine all through, and thoroughly musical, and show no sign of shuffling or laziness.

The two-movement form of clavier sonata, of which Paradies's are probably the best examples, seems to have been commonly adopted by a number of composers of second and lower rank, from his time till far on in the century. Those of Durante have been already mentioned. All the set of eight, by Domenico Alberti, are also in this form, and so are many by such forgotten contributors as Roeser and Barthélemon, and some by the once popular Schobert. Alberti is credited with the doubtful honour of having invented a formula of accompaniment which became a little too familiar in the course of the century, and is sometimes known as the 'Alberti Bass.' (See vol. i. p. 63a.) He may not have invented it, but he certainly called as much attention to it as he could, since not one of his eight sonatas is without it, and in some movements it continues almost throughout. The movements approach occasionally to binary form, but are not clearly defined ; the matter is for the most part dull in spirit, and poor in sound ; and the strongest characteristic is the unfortunate one of hitting upon a cheap device, which was much in vogue with later composers of mark, without having arrived at that mastery and definition of form and subject

[1] In some modern reprints of this sonata the order of the movements has been reversed.

which alone made it endurable. The times were not quite ripe for such usages, and it is fortunate for Paradies, who was slightly Alberti's junior, that he should have attained to a far better definition of structure without resorting to such cheapening.

There are two other composers of this period who deserve notice for maintaining, even later, some of the dignity and nobility of style which were now falling into neglect, together with clearness of structure and expressiveness of detail. These are Rolle and George Benda. A sonata of the former's in E♭ shows a less certain hand in the treatment of form, but at times extraordinary gleams of musically poetic feeling. Points in the Adagio are not unworthy of kinship with Beethoven. It contains broad and daring effects of modulation, and noble richness of sentiment and expression, which, by the side of the obvious tendencies of music in these days, is really astonishing. The first and last movements are in binary form of the old type, and contain some happy and musical strokes, though not so remarkable as the contents of the slow movement. George Benda was a younger and greater brother of the Franz who has been mentioned in connection with Violin Sonatas. He was one of the last writers who, using the now familiar forms, still retained some of the richness of the earlier manner. There is in his work much in the same tone and style as that of Emanuel Bach, but also an earnestness and evident willingness to get the best out of himself and to deal with things in an original manner, such as was by this time becoming rare. After him, composers of anything short of first rank offer little to arrest attention either for individuality in treatment or earnestness of expression. The serious influences which had raised so many of the earlier composers to a point of memorable musical achievement were replaced by associations of far less genuine character, and the ease with which something could be constructed in the now familiar forms of sonata, seduced men into indolent uniformity of structure and commonplace prettiness in matter. Some attained to evident proficiency in the use of instrumental resource, such as Turini; and some to a touch of genuine though small expressiveness, as Haessler and Grazioli; for the rest the achievements of Sarti, Sacchini, Schobert, Méhul, and the otherwise great Cherubini, in the line of sonata, do not offer much that requires notice. They add nothing to the process of development, and some of them are remarkably behindhand in relation to their time, and both what they say and the manner of it is equally unimportant.

Midway in the crowd comes the conspicuous form of Haydn, who raised upon the increasingly familiar structural basis not only some fresh and notable work of the accepted sonata character, but the great and enduring monument of his symphonies and quartets. The latter do not fall within the limits of the present subject, though they are in reality but the great instrumental expansion of this kind of music for solo instruments. An arbitrary restriction has been put upon the meaning of the word Sonata, and it is necessary here to abide by it. With Haydn it is rather sonata-form which is important, than the works which fall under the conventional acceptation of the name. His sonatas are many, but they are of exceedingly diverse value, and very few of really great importance. As is the case with his quartets, some, which internal evidence would be sufficient to mark as early attempts, are curiously innocent and elementary; and even throughout, with a few exceptions, their proportionate value is not equal to that of other classes of his numerous works. But the great span of his musical activity, reaching from the times of the Bach family till fairly on in Beethoven's mature years, the changes in the nature of keyed instruments, and the development of their resources which took place during his lifetime, make it inevitable that there should be a marked difference in the appearance and limits of different members of the collection. However, he is always himself, and though the later works are wider and more richly expressed, they represent the same mental qualities as the earliest. At all times his natural bent is in favour of simplification, as against the old contrapuntal modes of expression. His easy good-humour speaks best in simple but often ingeniously balanced tunes and subjects, and it is but rare that he has recourse to polyphonic expression or to the kind of idea which calls for it. Partly on this account and partly on account of narrowness of capacity in the instrument to which in solo sonatas he gave most attention, his range of technical resource is not extensive, and he makes but little demand upon his performers. His use of tunes and decisively outlined subjects is one of the most important points in relation to structure at this period. Tunes had existed in connection with words for centuries, and it is to their association with verses balanced by distinct rhythmic grouping of lines, that the sectional tune of instrumental music must ultimately be traced. It appears not to be a genuine instrumental product, but an importation; and the fact that almost all the most distinguished composers were connected with opera establishments, just at the time that the tune-element became most marked in instrumental works, supports the inference that the opera was the means through which a popular element ultimately passed into the great domain of abstract music. In preceding times the definition of subject by hard outlines and systematic conformity to a few normal successions of harmony was not universal; and the adoption of tunes was rare. In Haydn and Mozart the culmination of regularity in the building of subjects is reached.

The virtue of this process is that it simplifies the conditions of structure in the whole movement. When a correct system of centralisation is found by which the subject is restrained within the limits which strictly illustrate but one single tonality, the feelings which this suggests to the hearer are such as will be satisfied with equally simple order in all other parts of the complete structure. If the creative power is not sufficiently concentrated and disciplined to restrain the direction of its activity within comprehensible bounds, the result can only be to make perfect balance and proportion impossible. Thus if the first section of a movement is so decentralised that its connection with any particular key cannot possibly be followed by the hearer, one of the primary conditions of abstract music has been violated, and the balance of parts rendered undistinguishable. Yet the subject or section may range broadly in its course, and touch upon many alien tonalities without violating these conditions ; but then the horizon is broadened so as to necessitate an equal relative extension in every part of the movement. If a poet sets out with a passage expanded to the full with imagery and implication, in which almost every word is suggestive of wide horizons of thought, and carries inference behind it as complicated as those which lie in simple external manifestations of nature, it is useless for him to go back afterwards to a more limited and statuesque mode of expression. Even a person of little cultivation would feel at once the violation of artistic proportion. A relative degree of heat and intensity must be maintained at the risk of the work being as a whole unendurable. But if a more restricted field of imagination be appealed to at the outset, the work may be the more easily and perfectly carried out in simpler and narrower limits. In abstract music, balance, proportion, equality in the range of emotional and structural elements, are some of the most important conditions. Not that there is to be equal intensity all through, but that the salient and subordinate parts shall be fairly proportionate ; and this cannot be tested or stated by formulas of science, but only by cultivated artistic instinct. In music the art of expressing an idea within the limits and after the manner necessary for abstract music had to be discovered. The process of selection from experimental types had brought this to the closest point consistent with completeness in the latter half of the 18th century. At that time the disposition of the musical mind was specially set upon obviously intelligible order and certainty in the structural aspect of works. It was a necessary condition for art to go through ; and though not by any means the sole or supreme condition of excellence, it is not strange that the satisfaction derived from the sense of its achievement should cause people, in social circumstances which were peculiarly favourable, to put disproportionate stress upon it ; and that modern writers who have not been able to keep pace with the inevitable march and change in the conditions of musical utterance should still insist on it as if it were the ultimate aim of art ; whereas in fact its prominence in that epoch was a passing phase having considerable dependence upon unique social conditions, and its existence in art at any time is only one of numberless constituent elements. The condition of art of that time enabled the greatest composers to express the utmost of their ideas, and to satisfy their audiences, within the limits of a very simple group of harmonies. And this simplified the whole process of building their works to the utmost. Haydn manipulates the resources which lie within such limits to admiration. Hardly any composer so successfully made uniformity out of compounded diversity on a small scale. He delights in making the separate limbs of a subject of different lengths, and yet, out of their total sum, attaining a perfect and convincing symmetry. The harmonic progression of the subjects is uniformly obedient to the principles of a form which is on a preconceived plan, and without some such device the monotony of well-balanced phrases must soon have become wearisome. With regard to the actual distribution of the movements, Haydn does not depart from that already familiar in the works of earlier composers. Out of forty sonatas, comprising works for pianoforte alone, for pianoforte with accompaniment, and some adaptations, ten have only two movements, twenty-nine have three, and only one has four, this last comprising the only Scherzando in the whole collection of one hundred and eleven movements. Nearly all the first movements are in binary form with an occasional rondo ; the last is often a rondo, more often in binary form, and occasionally a theme and variations. In the sonatas which have more than two movements, at least twice as many retain the old adagio as those which have the characteristic minuet and trio ; but as a set-off, several of the sonatas either conclude with a dance form, or a rondo, or set of variations in the ' Tempo di Minuetto.'

The actual structure of the movements presents occasional peculiarities. In a few cases the pure old binary type, with repeat of first subject at the beginning of the second half, reappears. A considerable number are in the composite form, in which the first subject makes two distinct reappearances in full in the second half, as before described. The two halves of the movement are generally, but not invariably, repeated—the first half almost invariably ; in fact, the absence of the double bar in the middle of the Sonata in D major (No. 32 in Breitkopf & Härtel's edition) appears to be the only exception. The distribution of subjects in balancing keys appears to be absolutely without exception, as tonic and dominant, or tonic minor and relative major. Each movement has usually two distinct subjects, but occasionally, as is observable in Haydn's predecessors, the second is not strongly marked. In a few cases the same subject serves for both sections. There are a few examples of his anticipating Beethoven's usage of introducing clear accessory subjects to carry on the sections. Haydn illustrates forcibly the usefulness of defining the main division of the movement, not only by emphasising the harmonic formula of the cadence, but by appending to it a characteristic phrase or figure, the position of which, immediately before the full stop, renders it particularly easy to recognise. The purpose and fitness of this has been already discussed. Haydn's cadence-figures are generally peculiarly attractive, and seem to be made so of set purpose.

As a rule the outlines of his binary movements are more persistently regular than those of his rondos. Haydn was the first composer of mark to adopt the rondo with frequency in sonatas. It had existed in isolation and in suites for a long while, and examples there are in plenty by Couperin and other early Frenchmen, who were much given to it ; and also by various members of the Bach family, including the great John Sebastian. But hundreds of sonatas, from the highest to the lowest grade, may be taken at random with a fair probability of not finding a single example. The influence of the opera may probably be here traced again ; in the set tunes and dance types as significantly as in the general structure. However, though Haydn's kind of rondo is peculiarly familiar and characteristic, he does not make use of the form in his sonatas nearly so proportionately often as later composers do. The proportion in comparison with Mozart is almost as one to two. The value and appropriateness of this form is a matter of opinion. The greatest masters have used it frequently, and Beethoven with the profoundest effect. The usage of some other composers may be fairly described as obtrusively obvious, and it lends itself with greater readiness than any other plan of its scope to frivolity and commonplace. Haydn's subjects are often singularly slight, but his development of the form is almost always ingenious. Thus he varies his disposition of the episodes, so that sometimes the main subject and a single episodical subject alternate in different circumstances throughout ; at other times they are disposed so as to resemble the recapitulation in binary form. In the returns of the main theme he always exercises some consideration. In hardly any case does he simply repeat the theme as it stands throughout ; commonly each reappearance is a fresh variation. Occasionally the middle repeats are variations, and the first and last statements simple and identical ; and sometimes variations of theme and episode alternate. In all such points his readiness and energy are apparent, and make his treatment of the form a model in its particular line.

The slow movements of all the composers of sonatas till Beethoven's time are rather artificial and inclined to pose, owing partly to the weakness and want of sustaining power in their instruments. They contain too little of the deep and liberal feeling which is necessary to make the highest impression, and too much decorative finger-play, corresponding no doubt to the roulades and vocal gymnastics for which operatic singers found such admirable opportunities in the slow beats of adagios. Haydn's management of such things is artistic, and he occasionally strikes upon an interesting subject, but hardly any of the movements approach to the qualities expected in the ideal slow movement of modern times.

His distribution of the keys of the movements is simple. In some of the earlier Sonatas all three are in the same, or major and minor of the same key. In more mature examples he adopts the familiar antithesis of subdominant, which in later works, preponderates so strongly. In one case he adopts a very unusual antithesis. This is in the largest and most elaborate of all the sonatas, of which the first and last movements are in E♭, and the middle movement in E♮.

One point requires notice in connection with his violin sonatas, viz. that they are the very reverse of those of the great school of half a century earlier ; for inasmuch as with them the violin was everything, with Haydn it was next to nothing. Except in obviously late sonatas it does little more than timidly accompany the pianoforte. It was in this manner that the violin, having departed grandly by the front door in the old style, crept back again into modern instrumental music by the back. But small as such beginnings were, Haydn's later and fuller examples are the ostensible starting-point of a class of music which in the 19th century has extended the domain of the solo sonata, by enlarging its effective scope, and obtaining a new province for experiment in the combination of other instruments with the pianoforte upon equal terms, and with equal respect to their several idiosyncrasies.

John Christian Bach, the youngest son of John Sebastian, was Haydn's contemporary and junior by three years. In his day he was considered an important composer for the pianoforte, and his style is held to have had some influence upon Mozart. A sonata of his, in B♭, op. 17, is fluent and easily written, but not particularly interesting, and thoroughly in the style of the latter part of the 18th century. It consists of three movements, all in binary form of the older type. Another sonata, in C minor, is, for the date, in very singular form ; beginning with a slow movement, having a fugue in the middle, and ending with a 'Tempo di Gavotta.' Its style is not strikingly massive, but there are many traits in it which show that his parentage was not entirely without influence. The fugue, though ably written, has too much of the hybrid effect common in such works, after the harmonic structural ideas had laid strong hold of men's minds, to be worthy of comparison with the genuine achievements of his father. The style of the work is broad, however, and some ideas and turns of expression may not unreasonably be taken to justify the influence attributed to him.

The difference of age between Haydn and Mozart was twenty-four years, but in this interval there was less change in the form of the sonata than might be expected. It was, in fact, an almost stationary period, when the attainment of satisfactory structural principles by the labours of a century and more of composers left men time to pause and contemplate what appeared to them to be perfection ; the rhythmic wave of progress poised almost balanced for a short time before the rush which brought about an unexpected culmination in Beethoven.

The difference between Haydn and Mozart is plainly neither in structure nor altogether in style of thought and expression, but in advantages of temporal position. Haydn began nearer to the time of struggle and uncertainty. He found much ready to his hand, and he tested it and applied it and improved it ; and when Mozart came there was little to do but adapt his supreme gifts of fluency, clearness, and beauty of melody to glorify the edifice.

The progression of artistic instinct is at present an unexplained phenomenon ; it can only be judged from observation that the children of a later generation are born with a predisposed facility to realise in perfect clearness the forms which preceding generations have been wanderingly and dimly striving after. It is possible that the affinity between genuine music and the mental conditions of the race is so close that the progress of the latter carries the former with it as part of the same organic development. At all events, Mozart was gifted with an extraordinary and hitherto unsurpassed instinct for formal perfection, and his highest achievements lie not more in the tunes which have so captivated the world, than in the perfect symmetry of his best works. Like Haydn's his ideas are naturally restricted within limits which simplify to the utmost the development of the form which follows from them. They move in such perfect obedience to the limits and outlines of the harmonic progressions which most certainly characterise the key, that the structural system becomes architecturally patent and recognisable to all listeners that have any understanding. In his time these formal outlines were fresh enough to bear a great deal of use without losing their sweetness ; and Mozart used them with remarkable regularity. Out of thirty-six of his best-known sonatas, twenty-nine are in the now familiar order of three movements, and no less than thirty-three have the first movement in binary form. That binary form

is moreover so regular, that the same pauses and the same successions of harmony, and the same occurrences of various kinds, may often be safely anticipated at the same point in the progress of the movements. He makes some use, often conspicuously, of the device of repeating short phrases consecutively, which has already been described in connection with Scarlatti's work. Thus in a Sonata in D major for Violin and Pianoforte, the first section of the first movement may be divided into seven distinct passages, each of which is severally repeated in some form or other consecutively. There are some peculiarities, such as the introduction of a new subject in the working-out portion of the work, instead of keeping consistently to development of the principal ideas; and the filling of the episodes of a rondo with a variety of different ideas, severally distinct ; but as these points are not the precursors of further development, they are hardly worth discussing. It only requires to be pointed out that occasionally in pianoforte and other sonatas he makes experiments in novel distribution and entirely original manipulation of the structural elements of binary and other forms ; which is sufficient to prove not only that he recognised the fitness of other outlines besides those that he generally adopted, but that he was capable of adapting himself to novel situations, if there had been any call for effort in that direction. As it happened, the circumstances both of musical and social life were unique, and he was enabled to satisfy the highest critical taste of his day without the effort of finding a new point of departure.

His treatment of rondo-form is different, and less elementary than Haydn's. Haydn most commonly used a very decisively sectional system, in which every characteristic portion, especially the theme, was marked off distinct and complete. This accorded with the primitive idea of rondos as exemplified, often very happily, in the works of early French composers, and in certain forms of vocal music. The root-idea appears in the most elementary stages of musical intelligence as a distinct verse or tune which forms the staple of the whole matter, and is, for the sake of contrast, interspersed with digressions of subordinate interest. It is so obvious a means of arriving at something like structural balance, that it probably existed in times even before the earliest of which evidence remains. In the earliest specimens to be found in sonatas, the traces of their kinship can be clearly followed. Reference has been already made to the two examples in the sonatas by Paradies, which consist of an aria, a contrasting passage, and then the aria pure and simple again, and so forth. Haydn adopted the general outline. He frequently begins with a complete theme systematically set out with double bars and repeats, and a full conclusion. He then begins something entirely different either in a new related key, or in the minor of the principal key, and makes a complete whole of that also, and so on right through, alternating his main tune with one or more others all equally complete. Under such circumstances his principle of giving variations at each return of the theme or repetition of an episode is almost indispensable to avoid monotony. Mozart rarely makes any point of this plan of adopting variations in his sonata-rondos, because it is not required. He does not often cast his theme in such extremely distinct outlines. In structure it is more what an ordinary binary subject would be ; that is, complete and distinct in itself as an idea, without being so carried out as to make its connection with the rest of the movement a matter of secondary rather than intrinsic consequence. Haydn's conception is perfectly just and rational, but Mozart's is more mature. The theme and its episodes are more closely interwoven, and the development of the whole has a more consistent and uniform texture. Mozart does not avoid varying his theme ; on the contrary, he constantly puts in the most delicate strokes of detail and of graceful adornment, and sometimes resorts to delightfully ready development of its resources ; but with him it is not so indispensable, because his conception of the form gives it so much more freedom and elasticity.

The central movement of his three-movement sonatas is almost invariably a slow one, commonly in the key of the subdominant. The style of these is characteristic of the time ; that is, rather artificial and full of graces, which require to be given with a somewhat conscious elegance of manner, not altogether consonant with the spirit of later times. They rarely touch the point of feeling expected in modern movements of the kind, because the conception formed of the proper function of the slow movement in his time was clearly alien to that of the 19th century. As specimens of elegance and taste, however, Mozart's examples probably attain the highest point possible in their particular genus.

The technique of his sonatas, from the point of view of instrumental resource, is richer and fuller than Haydn's, but still thin and rather empty in sound to ears that are accustomed to the wonderful development of the resources of the modern pianoforte ; but the refinement and self-containment of his style make him particularly acceptable to artists who idealise finish and elegance in solo performance, and nicety of *ensemble* in works for combined instruments, as the highest and most indispensable condition of art. His instinct for adapting his thoughts to instrumental idiosyncrasies was of a very high order when the instruments were familiar and properly developed. This with the pianoforte was not yet achieved, and consequently some of his forms of expression are hardly adapted to its nature, and seem in these days to be rather compromises than perfectly suitable utterances.

With regard to the technical matter of the development of the resources of the pianoforte, Mozart's contemporary, Muzio Clementi, occupies a most important position. Clementi, in his early days, according to his own admission, applied himself rather to the development of the resources of playing than to the matter to be played, and attained a degree and a kind of mastery which no one before his time had heard the like of. When he began to apply himself more to the matter, this study served him in good stead ; and his divination of the treatment most appropriate to the instrument, expanded by this means in practical application, marks his sonatas as among the very first in which the genuine qualities of modern pianoforte music on a large scale are shown. They begin to approach to that broad and almost orchestral style which is sometimes said to be characteristic of Beethoven ; and the use of octaves and fuller combinations of sounds, and the occasional irruption of passages which bring into play stronger muscles than those of the fingers, are all in the direction of modern usage. In respect of structure, it is not necessary to consider more than that he commonly accepted the three-movement type of sonata, beginning with a movement in binary form and ending with a rondo, and having a slow movement in the middle. His handling is free and at the same time thoroughly under control. One of his characteristics is the love of importing little touches of learning or scientific ingenuity into the treatment ; as in the Sonata in G (of four movements) in which two canons in direct and contrary motion take the place of the minuet and trio. In another sonata, in F, one figure is woven through the whole substance of the first movement, appearing in the different sections diminished and inverted, and in various phases of expression which quite alter its aspect. His slow movements are sometimes equally simple and expressive, but also frequently of that ornamental order which has been sufficiently commented on.

In one celebrated case he anticipated the modern taste for programme by calling one of his longest and most pretentious sonatas 'Didone abbandonata. Scena tragica.' But appearance of dramatic purpose does not turn him aside from regularity of form any more than in other sonatas. His style is not exempt from the family likeness which is observable in all composers of the latter part of the century. His ideas are large and broad, and not unworthy to have exerted some influence upon both Mozart and Beethoven. A certain dryness and reticence makes him unlikely to be greatly in favour in modern times, but his place as an important figure in the development of the sonata in its relation with the pianoforte is assured.

One further composer who deserves some consideration in connection with the sonata before Beethoven's time is J. L. Dussek, who was born ten years after Clementi, and soon after Mozart. His most noteworthy characteristics are an individual, though not incisive style, and an instinct of a high order for the qualities and requirements of the pianoforte. There is some diversity in point of value between his early and his later sonatas. The former are rather narrow in idea and structure, whereas the latter, such as op. 70 in A♭, are quite remarkable for freedom and elaboration of form and subject. Both in this sonata and in the op. 77 he makes use of the hitherto almost unknown device of extending the effect of the first sections by subordinate transitions as well as by accessory subjects. In the first movement of op. 70 there is the unusual feature of a happy modulation out and back again in the actual substance of the second subject—a characteristic which is common enough in the works of such moderns as Schumann and Brahms, but was exceedingly rare in Dussek's time. Another characteristic which Dussek has in common with more modern writers is the infusion of a certain amount of sense and sentiment even into his passages and flourishes, which with his immediate predecessors had been too commonly barren. He also takes thought to enliven his recapitulations by variation or ingeniously diversified transposition of order in the ideas (as in op. 77). His writing for the instrument is brilliant and sparkling, and has certain premonitions of Weber in it. The ideas are sometimes, even in his best works, trite and vapid, but more often delicate and attractive. The slow movements have a sustained and serious manner, also unusual in his time, and said to be derived from his having studied the organ considerably in his younger days. He stands historically with giants on either hand, and this has contributed to make him appear somewhat of a parenthesis in the direct course of sonata development. Their vastness of artistic proportion did not however suppress his personality, or extinguish his individuality, which is still clear in his own line, and has exerted some influence both upon the modern style of playing and also upon the style of musical thought of a few modern composers for the pianoforte to whom the giants did not strongly appeal.

The direct line of development after Haydn, Mozart, and Clementi is obviously continued in Beethoven. As we have pointed out, the changes which took place after Emanuel Bach's labours were less rapid and remarkable than in times preceding. The finishing touches had been put to the structural system, and men were so delighted with its perfection as structure, that they were content to hear it repeated over and over again without calling for variety or individuality in the treatment, and very often without caring much about the quality of the

thing said. The other side of development was technical. The pianoforte being a new instrument, the manner of musical speech best adapted to it had to be discovered. With the earlier composers forms of expression better suited to other instruments were adopted ; but by degrees experiments in effect and assiduous attention to the capabilities of the hand, such as Clementi gave in his early years, had brought the mechanism of expression to a tolerably consistent and complete state ; so that when Beethoven appeared he was spared the waste of force incident to having to overcome elementary problems of instrumental technique, and the waste of effect incidental to compromises, and was enabled to concentrate all his powers upon the musical material.

Beethoven's works introduce a new element into the problem, and one that complicates matters immeasurably. With his predecessors structural simplicity had been a paramount consideration, and often straitened somewhat the freedom of the idea. The actual subjects seem drilled into a regular shape, admitting of very little variation, in order that the development of the movement might march direct and undeviating in its familiar course. Musicians had arrived at that artificial state of mind which deliberately chose to be conscious of formal elements. Their misconception was a natural one. The existing conditions of art might lead a man to notice that uncultivated people delighted in simple and single tunes, and that cultivated people enjoyed the combination of several, when disposed according to certain laws, and to conclude from this that the disposition was of more importance than the matter. But, in fact, the mind is led from point to point by feelings which follow the ideas, and of these and their interdependence and development it is necessarily conscious ; but of the form it is not actively conscious unless the ideas have not sufficient force to possess it, or the necessities of logical consequence are outrageously violated. It is only under peculiar social and intellectual conditions that structural qualities can be so excessively emphasised. The production of a genuine master must be ultimately reducible to logical analysis, but not on the spot or at once ; and to insist upon art being so immediately verifiable is not only to set the conclusion to be drawn from its historical development upside down, but to refer the enjoyment of its highest achievements to the contemplation of dry bones. The imagination and the reason must both be satisfied, but before all things the imagination.

In the middle years of the 18th century the imaginative side had not a fair chance. Music was too much dependent upon the narrow limits of the taste of polite circles, and the field of appeal to emotion was not free. But when at last the natural man threw off the incubus that had so long oppressed him, the spiritual uprising and the broadening of life brought a new kind of vigour into art and literature. Beethoven was the first great composer to whom the limitless field of unconventionalised human emotion was opened, and his disposition was ready for the opportunity. Even in the ordinary trifles of life he sometimes showed by an apparently superfluous rebellion against polite usages his antipathy to artificiality, and conversely the bent of his sympathy towards unmistakable realities of human feeling. He thus became the prototype of genuine modern music, and the first exponent of its essential qualities ; and the sonata form being ready in its main outlines for his use, and artistic instinct having achieved the most perfect spontaneity in its employment, he took possession of it as an appropriate mode of formulating some of the richest and most impressive of his thoughts. With him the idea asserted its rights. This is not to say that structure is ignored, but that the utmost expansion and liberty is admitted in the expression of the vital parts which can be made consistent with perfect balance in the unfolding of the whole ; and this obviously depends upon the powers of the composer. Under such circumstances he can only be guided by the highest development of instinct, for the process of balance and distribution becomes so complicated that it is almost out of the reach of conscious analysis, much more of the dictation of science. The evolution of this vital ingredient, the idea, is so obscure and difficult that it is out of the question to enter upon it in this place. It is an unhappy fact that the scientists who have endeavoured to elucidate music, with a few great and honourable exceptions, foreseeing that the analysis of ideas was quite beyond their reach, at all events until immense advances are made in the sciences which have direct reference to the human organism, have set their faces to the structural elements, as if music consisted of nothing but lines and surfaces. The existence of idea is so habitually ignored that it necessarily appears to be non-existent in their estimate of art. On the other hand, the philosophers who have said anything about it appear on the surface not to be in accord ; though in reality their views are both compatible and necessary, but require a more detailed experience of the art and of its historical development to explain their interaction. But meanwhile the external method of the scientists gains disproportionate pre-eminence, and conscientious people feel uneasily that there may be no such things as ideas at all, and that they will be doing better to apply themselves to mathematics. And yet the idea is everything, and without it music is absolutely null and void ; and though a great and comprehensive mathematician may make an analysis after the event, a synthesis which is merely the fruit of his calculations will be nothing more than a sham and an imposture. In fact, the formulation of the idea is a most

vital matter in musical history, and its progress can be traced from the earliest times, proceeding simultaneously with the development of the general structure of the sonata. The expressive raw material was drawn from various sources. The style of expression developed under the influences of religion in the ages preceding the beginnings of instrumental music, supplied something ; dance music of all orders, mimetic and merely rhythmic, supplied much ; the pseudo-realism of the drama, in respect of vocal inflexion and imitations of natural circumstances, also something ; and the instincts surviving in the race from countless past ages, the actual cries arising from spontaneous nervous reaction, and many other similar causes, had a share in suggestion, and in actual, though unrealised, motive power. And all these, compounded and inseparably intermingled, supplied the basis of the expressive element in music. Through all the time from Monteverde to Beethoven this expressive element was being more and more clearly drawn into compact and definite proportions ; floating at first vaguely on the surface, springing out in flashes of exceptional brightness here and there, and at times presenting almost perfect maturity by fits of individual good fortune ; but hardly ever so free but that some of the matrix is felt to be clinging to the ore. It obtained complete but restricted symmetry with the composers immediately preceding Beethoven, but arrived only at last with him at that expansion which made it at once perfect and intelligible, and yet boundless in range within the limits of the art-material at the composer's command.

Prior to Beethoven, the development of a long work was based upon antitheses of distinct tunes and concrete lumps of subject representing separate organisms, either merely in juxtaposition, or loosely connected by more or less empty passages. There were ideas indeed, but ideas limited and confined by the supposed necessities of the structure of which they formed a part. But what Beethoven seems to have aimed at was the expansion of the term 'idea' from the isolated subject to the complete whole ; so that instead of the subjects being separate, though compatible items, the whole movement, or even the whole work, should be the complete and uniform organism which represented in its entirety a new meaning of the word 'idea,' of which the subjects, in their close connection and inseparable affinities, were subordinate limbs. This principle is traceable in works before his time, but not on the scale to which he carried it, nor with his conclusive force. In fact, the condition of art had not been sufficiently mature to admit the terms of his procedure, and it was barely mature enough till he made it so.

His early works were in conformity with the style and structural principles of his predecessors ; but he began, at least in pianoforte works, to build at once upon the topmost stone of their edifice. His earliest sonatas (op. 2) are on the scale of their symphonies. He began with the four-movement plan which they had almost entirely reserved for the orchestra. In the second sonata he already produces an example of his own peculiar kind of slow movement, full, rich, decisive in form, unaffected in idea, and completely divested of the elaborate graces which had been before its most conspicuous feature. In the same sonata also he produces a scherzo, short in this instance, and following the lines of the minuet, but of the genuine characteristic quality. Soon, in obedience to the spread of his idea, the capacity of the instrument seems to expand, and to attain an altogether new richness of sound, and a fulness it never showed before, as in many parts of the fourth Sonata (op. 7), especially the Largo, which shows the unmistakable qualities which ultimately expanded into the unsurpassed slow movement of the opus 106. As early as the second Sonata he puts a new aspect upon the limits of the first sections ; he not only makes his second subject in the first movement modulate, but he develops the cadence-figure into a very noticeable subject. It is fortunately unnecessary to follow in detail the various ways in which he expanded the structural elements of the sonata, as it has already been described in the article BEETHOVEN, and other details are given in the article FORM. In respect of the subject and its treatment, a fortunate opportunity is offered by a coincidence between a subordinate subject in a sonata of Haydn's in C, and a similar accessory in Beethoven's Sonata for violoncello and pianoforte in A major (op. 69), which serves to illustrate pregnantly the difference of scope which characterises their respective treatment. Haydn's is as follows :—

and Beethoven's :—

Cello pizz.

etc.

As has been already explained, an expansion of this kind makes inevitable a similar expansion in the whole structure of the movement, and a much wider choice of relative keys than simple tonic and dominant in the expository sections ; or else a much freer movement in every part of the sections, and emphasis upon unexpected relations of harmony. Even without this, the new warmth and intensity of the subject precludes mere reiteration of the accustomed usages, and necessitates a greater proportionate vitality in the subordinate parts of the work. The relative heat must be maintained, and to fall back upon familiar formulas would clearly be a jarring anomaly. In this manner the idea begins to dictate the form. But in order to carry out in equal measure the development of the idea, every resource that the range of music can supply must be admissible to him that can wield it with relevance. Hence Beethoven, as early as op. 31, No. 2, reintroduces instrumental recitative with extraordinary effect. Later, he resumes the rhapsodical movement which Bach and earlier composers had employed in a different sense, as in the Sonata in E♭, op. 81, and in the third division of that in A, op. 101, and in the most romantic of romantic movements, the first in E major of op. 109. And lastly, he brings back the fugue as the closest means of expressing a certain kind of idea. In these cases the fugue is not a retrogression, nor a hybrid, but a new adaptation of an old and invaluable form under the influence of perfectly assimilated harmonic principles. The great fugue in the Sonata in B♭, op. 106, for instance, is not only extraordinary as a fugue, but is distributed in a perfectly ideal balance of long contrasting periods in different states of feeling, culminating duly with a supreme rush of elaborate force, as complex and as inexorable as some mighty action of nature. In these sonatas Beethoven touches all moods, and all in the absolute manner free from formality or crude artifice, which is the essential characteristic of genuine modern music. In a few of the earlier sonatas he reverts to manners and structural effects which are suggestive of the principles of his predecessors. But these occasional incursions of external influence are with rare exceptions inferior to the works in which his own original force of will speaks with genuine and characteristic freedom. The more difficult the problem suggested by the thought which is embodied in the subject, the greater is the result. The full richness of his nature is not called out to the strongest point till there is something preternaturally formidable to be mastered. The very statement of the opening bars of such sonatas as that in D minor, op. 31, No. 2 ; C major, op. 53 ; F minor, op. 57 ; B♭, op. 106 ; C minor, op. 111, is at such a level of daring breadth and comprehensive power, that it becomes obvious in a moment that the work cannot be carried out on equal proportionate terms without almost superhuman concentration, and unlimited command of technical resources, both in respect of the instrument and the art of expression. In such cases, Beethoven rises to a height which has only been attained by two or three composers in the whole history of music, in that sublimity which is almost his peculiar monopoly. But, fortunately for average beings, and average moods of people who have not always a taste for the sublime, he shows elsewhere, on a less exalted scale, the highest ideals of delicate beauty, and all shades of the humours of mankind, even to simple exuberant playfulness. The beauty and the merriment often exist side by side, as in the exquisite little Sonata in G, op. 14, No. 2, and in that in F♯ major, op. 78 ; and in a loftier and stronger spirit in company with more comprehensive ranges of feeling, in the Sonata in A, op. 101. In all these and many more there is an ideal continuity and oneness which is musically felt even where there is no direct external sign of the connection. In a few, however, there are signs of more than this. In the B♭ Sonata, op. 106, for instance, the similar disposition of intervals in the subjects of the various movements has led to the inference that he meant to connect them by transformations of one principal subject or germ. The same occurs with as much prominence in the Sonata in A♭, op. 110, which is in any case a specimen where the oneness and continuity are peculiarly felt. It is possible that the apparent transformations are not so much conscious as the result of the conditions of mind which were necessary to produce the oneness of effect, since concentration upon any subject is liable to exert influence upon closely succeeding action, whether of the mind or body, and to assimilate the fruit unconsciously to the form of the object contemplated. This, however, would not lessen the interest of the fact, but would possibly rather enhance it. It only affects the question whether or no Beethoven consciously reasoned about possible ways of extending and enhancing the opportunities of sonata-form—too large a subject to be entered upon here. As a rule, great masters appear to hit upon such germinal principles in the process of composition, without exactly formulating them in so many equivalent terms ; and those who come after note the facts and apply them as useful resources, or sometimes as invaluable starting-points of fresh lines of development. It is a noticeable fact that Beethoven only seldom indicated a pro-

gramme, and it is extremely rare in him to find even the dimmest suggestions of realism. In fact, as must be true of all the highest music, a work of his is not representative of a story, but of a mental process. Even if it deals with a story it does not represent the circumstances, but the condition of mind which results from its contemplation ; or, in other words, the musical counterpart of the emotion to which it gives rise ; and it is the coherency and consistent sequence of the emotions represented which produce the effect of oneness on the colossal scale of his greatest works, which is Beethoven's crowning achievement. With him the long process of development appears to find its utmost and complete culmination ; and what comes after, and in sight of his work, can be little more than commentary. It may be seen, without much effort, that mankind does not achieve more than one supreme triumph on the same lines of art. When the conditions of development are fulfilled the climax is reached, but there is not more than one climax to each crescendo. The conditions of human life change ceaselessly, and with them the phenomena of art, which are their counterpart. The characteristics of the art of any age are the fruit of the immediate past, as much as are the emotional and intellectual conditions of that age. They are its signs, and it is impossible to produce in a succeeding age a perfect work of art in the same terms as those which are the direct fruit of a different and earlier group of causes ; and it is partly for this reason that attempts to return to earlier conditions of art, which leave out the essential characteristics of contemporary feeling, invariably ring false.

The time produced other real men besides Beethoven, though not of his stamp. Weber and Schubert were both of the genuine modern type, genuinely musical through and through, though neither of them was a born writer of sonatas as Beethoven was. Beethoven possessed, together with the supremest gift of ideas, a power of prolonged concentration, and the certainty of self-mastery. This neither Weber nor Schubert possessed. Beethoven could direct his thought with infallible certainty ; in Weber and Schubert the thought was often too much their master, and they both required, to keep them perfectly certain in the direction of their original musical matter, the guiding principle of a consciously realised dramatic or lyrical conception, which was generally supplied to them from without. As should be obvious from the above survey of the process of sonata development, the absolute mastery of the structural outlines, the sureness of foot of the strong man moving, unaided, but direct in his path, amidst the conflicting suggestions of his inspiration, is indispensable to the achievement of great and genuine sonatas. The more elaborate the art of expression becomes, the more difficult the success. Beethoven probably stood just at the point where the extremest elaboration and the most perfect mastery of combination on a large scale were possible. He himself supplied suggestion for yet further elaboration, and the result is that the works of his successors are neither so concentrated nor so well in hand as his. Weber was nearest in point of time, but his actual mastery of the art of composition was never very certain nor thoroughly regulated, though his musical instincts were almost marvellous. He had one great advantage, which was that he was a great pianist, and had the gift to extend the resources of the instrument by the invention of new and characteristic effects ; and he was tolerably successful in avoiding the common trap of letting effect stand for substance. Another advantage was his supreme gift of melody. His tunes are for the most part of the old order, but infused with new life and heat by a breath from the genius of the people. His two best sonatas, in A♭ and D minor, are rich in thought, forcible, and genuinely full of expression. He always adopts the plan of four movements, and disposes them in the same order as Beethoven did. His treatment of form is also full and free, and he often imports some individuality into it. As simple instances may be taken—the use of the introductory phrase in the first movement of the Sonata in C, in the body of the movement ; the rondo structure of the slow movements, especially in the Sonata in D minor, which has a short introduction, and elaborate variations in the place of exact returns of the subject ; and the interspersion of subjects in the first movement of the Sonata in E minor, op. 70, so as to knit the two sections of the first half doubly together. An essentially modern trait is his love of completing the cycle of the movement by bringing in a last allusion to the opening features of the whole movement at the end, generally with some new element of expression or vivacity. Specially noticeable in this respect are the first and last (the 'Moto perpetuo') of the C major, the last of the A♭, and the first and last in both the D minor and E minor Sonatas. Weber had an exceptional instinct for dance-rhythms, and this comes out very remarkably in some of the minuets and trios, and in the last movement of the E minor.

As a whole the Weber group is a decidedly important item in pianoforte literature, instinct with romantic qualities, and aiming at elaborate expressiveness, as is illustrated by the numerous directions in the A♭ Sonata, such as 'con anima,' 'con duolo,' 'con passione,' 'con molt' affetto,' and so forth. These savour to a certain extent of the opera, and require a good deal of art and musical sense in the variation of time and the phrasing to give them due effect ; and in this they show some kinship to the ornamental adagios of the times previous to Beethoven, though dictated by more genuinely musical feelings.

Schubert's sonatas do not show any operatic traits of the old manner, but there is plenty in them which may be called dramatic in a modern sense. His instincts were of a preeminently modern type, and the fertility of his ideas in their superabundance clearly made the self-restraint necessary for sonata-writing a matter of some difficulty. He was tempted to give liberty to the rush of thought which possessed him, and the result is sometimes delightful, but sometimes also bewildering. There are movements and even groups of them which are of the supremest beauty, but hardly any one sonata which is completely satisfactory throughout. His treatment of form is often daring, even to rashness, and yet from the point of view of principle offers but little to remark, though in detail some perfectly magical feats of harmonic progression and strokes of modulation have had a good deal of influence upon great composers of later times. The point which he serves to illustrate peculiarly in the history of music is the transition from the use of the idea, as shown in Beethoven's Sonatas on a grand and richly developed scale, to the close and intensely emotional treatment of ideas in a lyrical manner, which has as yet found its highest exponent in Schumann. In this process Schubert seems to stand midway—still endeavouring to conform to sonata ways, and yet frequently overborne by the invincible potency of the powers his own imagination has called up. The tendency is further illustrated by the exquisite beauty of some of the smaller and more condensed movements, which lose nothing by being taken out of the sonatas ; being, like many of Schumann's, specimens of intense concentration in short space, the fruit of a single flash of deep emotion. Among the longer movements, the one which is most closely unified is the first of the A minor, op. 143, in which a feature of the first subject is made to preponderate conspicuously all through, manifestly representing the persistence of a special quality of feeling through the varying phases of a long train of thought. Like many other movements, it has a strong dramatic element but more under appropriate control than usual.

As a whole, though illustrating richly many of the tendencies of modern music, the Sonatas cannot be taken as representing Schubert's powers as a composer of instrumental music so satisfactorily as his Quartets, his String Quintet, and some of his finest Symphonies. In these he often rose almost to the highest point of musical possibility. And this serves further to illustrate the fact that since Beethoven the tendency has been to treat the sonata-form with the fresh opportunities afforded by combinations of instruments, rather than on the old lines of the solo sonata.

Two other composers of sonatas of Beethoven's time require notice. These are Woelfl and Hummel. The former chiefly on account of his once celebrated sonata called ' Ne plus ultra,' in which he showed some of the devices of technique which he was considered to have invented—such as passages in thirds and sixths, and ingenious applications of the shake. The matter is poor and vapid, and as throwing light upon anything except his powers as a player, is worthless. Its very title condemns it, for Woelfl had the advantage of being Beethoven's junior ; and it is astonishing how, by the side of the genuine difficulty of Beethoven's masterpieces, such a collection of tricks could ever have been dignified, even by the supposition of being particularly difficult. It seems impossible that such work should have had any influence upon genuinely musical people ; but the sonata has all the signs of a useful piece for second-rate popular occasions ; for which the variations on ' Life let us cherish ' would doubtless be particularly effective.

Hummel in comparison with Woelfl was a giant, and certainly had pre-eminent gifts as a pianoforte-player. Like Weber he had an aptitude for inventing effects and passages, but he applied them in a different manner. He was of that nature which cultivates the whole technical art of speech till able to treat it with a certainty which has all the effect of mastery, and then instead of using it to say something, makes it chiefly serviceable to show off the contents of his finger répertoire. However, his technique is large and broad, full of sound and brilliancy, and when the works were first produced and played by himself they must have been extremely astonishing. His facility of speech is also wonderful, but his ideas were for the most part old-fashioned, even when he produced them—for it must not be forgotten that he was eight years younger than Beethoven and twenty-six younger that Clementi. The spirit which seems to rule him is the consciousness of a pianist before an audience, guided by the chances of display. His modulations are free and bold, but they are often superfluous, because the ideas are not on the level of intensity or broad freedom which necessitates or even justifies them. He probably saw that modulation was a means of effect, but did not realise that there is a ratio between the qualities of subject and the development of the movement that springs from it. From this it will be obvious that his sonatas are not written in the mood to produce works that are musically important. He had the very finest possible opportunities through living in Mozart's house during his most impressionable days, and the fruit is sufficiently noticeable in the clearness with which he distributes his structural elements, and in much of his manner of expressing himself ; but he had not the inventive gift for musical ideas, which contact and even familiar intercourse with great masters seems inadequate to supply. The survival of traits characteristic of earlier times is illustrated by some of his slow movements, in which he brought the most elaborate forces of his finished technique to serve in the old style of artificial adagio, where there is a hyper-elaborated grace at every corner, and a shake upon every note that is long enough ; and if a chord be suitable to rest upon for a little, it is adorned with quite a collection of ingenious finger exercises, artificially manipulated scales and arpeggios, and the like contrivances ; which do not serve to decorate anything worthy of the honour, but stand on their own merits. There are occasional traits of expression and strokes of force in the sonatas, but the technique of the pianist preponderates excessively over the invention of the composer. At the same time the right and masterly use of the resources of an instrument is not by any means a matter of small moment in art, and Hummel's is right and masterly in a very remarkable degree.

After the early years of the 19th century, the sonata, in its conventional sense of instrumental work for a solo or at most for two instruments, occupies a smaller and decreasing space in the domain of music. Great composers have paid it proportionately very little attention, and the few examples they afford have rather an effect of being out of the direct line of their natural mode of expression. In Chopin, for instance, the characteristic qualities of modern music, in the treatment of ideas in short and malleable forms specially adapted to their expression, are found abundantly, and in these his genuine qualities are most clearly displayed. His sonatas are less successful, because, though quite master enough to deal with structure clearly and definitely, it was almost impossible for him to force the ideas within the limits which should make that structure relevant and convincing. They are children of a fervid and impetuous genius, and the classical dress and manners do not sit easily upon them. Moreover the luxuriant fancy, the richness and high colour of expression, the sensuous qualities of the harmony, all tend to emphasise detail in a new and peculiar manner, and to make the sonata-principle of the old order appear irrelevant. The most successful are the Sonatas in B♭ minor for pianoforte, op. 35, and that for pianoforte and violoncello in G minor, op. 65. In both these cases the first movements, which are generally a sure test of a capacity for sonata-writing, are clearly disposed, and free from superfluous wandering and from tautology. There are certain idiosyncrasies in the treatment of the form, as for instance in the recapitulation, which in both cases is almost limited to the materials of the second section, the opening features of the movement being only hinted at in conclusion. The subjects themselves are fairly appropriate to the style of movement, and are kept well in hand, so that on the whole, in these two cases, the impression conveyed is consistent with the sonata-character. In scherzos Chopin was thoroughly at home, and moreover they represent a province in which far more abandonment is admissible. In both sonatas they are successful, but that in the Pianoforte Sonata is especially fascinating and characteristic, and though the modulations are sometimes rather reckless the main divisions are well proportioned, and consequently the general effect of the outlines is sufficiently clear. The slow movements of both are very well known ; that of the Pianoforte Sonata being the Funeral March, and the other being a kind of romance in Chopin's own free manner, which is familiar to players on the violoncello. The last movement of the Pianoforte Sonata is a short but characteristic outbreak of whirling notes, in general character not unlike some of his Preludes, and equally free and original in point of form, but in that respect not without precedent among the last movements of early masters. In the mind of the composer it possibly had a poetical connection with the Funeral March. The other last movement is a free kind of rondo, and therefore more consonant with the ordinary principles of form, and is appropriate, without being so interesting as the other movements. The total effect of these sonatas is naturally of an entirely different order from that of the earlier types, and not so convincing in oneness as the works of great masters of this kind of form ; they are nevertheless plausible as wholes, and in details most effective ; the balance and appropriate treatment of the two instruments in the op. 65 being especially noteworthy. The other sonatas for pianoforte, in C minor and B minor, are more unequal. The first appears to be an early work, and contains some remarkable experiments, one of which at least has value, others probably not. As examples may be mentioned the use of 5–4 time throughout the slow movement, and the experiment of beginning the recapitulation of the first movement in B♭ minor, when the principal key is C minor. In this sonata he seems not to move with sufficient ease, and in the B minor, op. 58, with something too much to have the general aspect of a successful work of the kind. The technical devices in the latter as in the others are extremely elaborate and effective, without being offensively obtrusive, and the ideas are often clear and fascinating ; but as a complete and convincing work it is hardly successful.

Sonatas which followed implicitly the old lines without doing more than formulate subjects according to supposed laws do not require any notice. The mere artificial reproduction of forms that have been consciously realised from observation of great works of the past without importing anything original into the treatment, is often the most hopeless kind of plagiarism, and far more deliberate than the accidents of coincidence in ideas which are obvious to superficial observers.

As examples of independent thought working in a comparatively untried field, Mendelssohn's six sonatas for the organ have some importance. They have very little connection with the Pianoforte Sonata, or the history of its development ; for Mendelssohn seems to have divined that the binary and similar instrumental forms of large scope were unsuitable to the genius of the instrument, and returned to structural principles of a date before those forms had become prominent or definite. Their chief connection with the modern sonata type lies in the distribution of the keys in which the respective movements stand, and the broad contrasts in time and character which subsist between one division or movement and another. Different members of the group represent different methods of dealing with the problem. In the large movements fugal and contrapuntal principles predominate, sometimes alternating with passages of a decidedly harmonic character. In movements which are not absolute fugues the broad outlines of form are commonly similar to those already described as exemplified in Bach's Sonatas, and in the first and last movements of his Italian Concerto. This form in its broadest significance amounts to a correspondence of well-defined sections at the beginning and end, with a long passage of ' free fantasia,' sometimes fugally developed, in the middle. The clearest example in these sonatas is the first movement of the third Sonata, in A major, in which the corresponding divisions at either end are long, and strongly contrasted in the modern quality and more simultaneous motion of the parts, with the elaborate fugal structure of the middle division. In the last movement of the Sonata in B♭ the corresponding sections are very short, but the effect is structurally satisfying and clear. In no case is the structural system of keys used with anything approaching the clearness of a pianoforte sonata. Material is contrasted with material, sometimes simply as subjects or figures, sometimes even in respect of style ; as a chorale with recitative, chorale with fugal passages, or harmonic passages with contrapuntal passages. Sometimes these are kept distinct, and, sometimes, as in the first movement of the Sonata in B♭, they are combined together at the end. The general laying out of the complete works, though based on the same broadest radical principles, is in actual order and manner quite distinct from that of pianoforte sonatas. The longer movements alternate with very short ones, which commonly resemble Romances, Lieder ohne Worte, or such expressive lyrical types ; and occasionally the whole sonata concludes with a little movement of this sort, as No. 3 in A and

No. 6 in D. They are generally in the simplest kind of primary form with a proportionately important coda. In point of actual style and treatment of the instrument there is a great diversity in different sonatas. In some the solid old contrapuntal style predominates, in similar proportion to that in the organ preludes, sonatas, etc. of Bach ; but this rarely occurs without some intermixture of modern traits. The most completely and consistently modern in style is the Sonata in D major, No. 5, which is practically in three divisions. The first is a chorale, the second a kind of 'song without words' in B minor, and the third a species of fantasia, in which the sections are balanced by distinct figures, without more tonal structure than emphasis upon the principal key at the beginning and end, and variety of modulation with some thematic development in the middle. In other sonatas different modes of writing for the instrument are used as a means of enforcing the contrast between one movement and another. Thus in the second Sonata the first division is a kind of prelude in a modern manner, chiefly homophonic and orchestral ; the second corresponds to a distinct romance or 'song without words' with clearly defined melody and graceful and constantly flowing independent accompaniment. In the third movement, which though in 3–4 time has something of a march quality, the modern harmonic character is very prominent, and the last movement is a fugue. Similar distribution of styles and modes of writing are as clearly used in the first and fourth Sonatas ; in the former more elaborately.

Among the few attempts which have been made to add something genuine to the literature of the Pianoforte Sonata, that in F♯ minor, op. 11, by Schumann, first published under the pseudonym of Florestan and Eusebius, is most interesting. This was clearly an attempt to adapt to the sonata-form the so-called romantic ideas of which Schumann was so prominent and successful a representative. The outward aspect of the matter is twofold. First, the absolute subordination of the sectional distribution to the ideas contained, and, secondly, the interchange of the subject-matter so as to connect the movements absolutely as well as intrinsically. The first point is illustrated by the continuity of the Allegro Vivace and the constant shifting and swaying of modulation and changing of tempo ; also by the variety of the subjects and the apparently irregular manner of their introduction, if judged from the point of view of the older sonatas. Thus the part which corresponds to the first section comprises a first subject, containing a figure which may be called the text of the movement, and many subsidiary features and transitions. The second section follows continuously, with new matter and allusions to the first subject, all in a constant sway of transition, till at the end of the first half of the movement

a long continuous subject in A is reached, which in its sustained and earnest calmness seems to supply the point of rest after the long preceding period of activity. This same subject is the only one which is given with complete fulness at the end of the whole movement, the rest of the subject-matter, though all represented in the recapitulation, being considerably condensed and curtailed. The second point is illustrated by the connection between the introduction and the two following movements. The introduction itself is in an elaborate kind of primary form. Its impressive principal subject is reintroduced in the middle of the succeeding allegro ; and the subject of the middle portion serves as the main staple of the beautiful aria which is the central movement of the whole sonata. The success of such things certainly depends on the way in which they are done, and mere description of them gives very little impress of their effectiveness in this case. There can hardly be a doubt that in these devices Schumann hit upon a true means of applying original thought to the development of the structural outlines, following the suggestion which is really contained in Beethoven's work, that the structure is perceptible through the disposition of the ideas, and not only by emphasising the harmonic sections. The actual distribution of the structure which is hidden under the multiplicity of ideas is remarkably careful and systematic. Even in the development portion there is method and balance, and the same is true of large expanses in the last movement. The freedom with which Schumann uses subordinate transitions makes the balance of keys a matter requiring great concentration ; but it is remarkable in his work, as contrasted with similar modern examples by other composers, that he rarely makes random and unrestrained flights, but keeps within the bounds which make proportionate balance possible. It is no doubt a matter of very great difficulty to carry out such principles as this work seems to embody ; but if the sonata form be really capable of any fresh extension it will probably be to a great extent on such lines.

Schumann's second Sonata, in G minor, op. 22, though written during almost the same period, seems to be a retrogression from the position taken up by that in F♯ minor. It is possibly a more effective work, and from the pianist's point of view, more capable of being made to sound convincing. And yet in detail it is not so interesting, nor is it technically so rich, nor so full and noble in sound. He seems to aim at orthodoxy with deliberate purpose, and the result is that though vehement and vigorous in motion, it is not, for Schumann, particularly warm or poetical. The second subjects of the first and last movements are characteristic, and so is a great part of the peculiarly sectional and epigrammatic scherzo. The andantino also has remarkable points about it, but is not so fascinating as the slow movement of the F♯ minor Sonata.

The principles indicated in the sonata opus 11 reappear later with better results, as far as the total impression is concerned, in larger forms of instrumental music, and also in the D minor Sonata for violin and pianoforte. In this there is a close connection between the introduction and the most marked feature of the succeeding quick movement, and similar linking of scherzo and slow movement by means of a reference to the subject of the former in the progress of the latter, with a distinctly poetic purpose. The Sonata in A minor for the same combination of instruments is not on such an elaborate scale, nor has it as many external marks to indicate a decided purpose; but it is none the less poetical in effect, which arises in the first movement from the continuity of structure and the mysterious sadness of spirit which it expresses, and in the slow movement from its characteristic tenderness and sweetness.

Liszt, in his remarkable Sonata in B minor dedicated to Schumann, undoubtedly adopts the same principles of procedure, and works them out with more uncompromising thoroughness. He knits the whole sonata into an unbroken unity, with distinct portions passing into one another, representing the usual separate movements. The interest is concentrated upon one principal idea, to which the usual second subjects and accessories serve as so many commentaries and antitheses, and express the influences which react upon its course. This is further illustrated by the process sometimes defined as 'transformation of themes,' already referred to in connection with Beethoven's Sonatas in B♭ and A♭; which is really no more than a fresh way of applying that art of variation which had been used from almost the earliest times of sonata-writing, in recapitulating subjects in the progress of a movement, as well as in regular set themes and variations; though it had not been adopted before to serve a poetical or ideal conception pervading and unifying the whole work. In the actual treatment of the subject-matter, Liszt adopts, as Beethoven had done, the various opportunities afforded not only by harmonic structural principles, but by the earlier fugal and contrapuntal devices, and by recitative, adapting them with admirable breadth and freedom to a thoroughly modern style of thought. It seems almost superfluous to add that the purpose is carried out with absolute mastery of technical resource, in respect both of the instrument and of the disposition of the parts of the movement.

The pianoforte sonatas of Brahms are as astounding specimens of youthful power and breadth and dignity of style as exist in the whole range of the art; but it must at present be considered doubtful if they represent his maturer convictions. All three appear to have been written before he arrived at the age of twenty; and it is certain that he was then more influenced by the romantic theories which Schumann represented, than he was in his later works. His adoption of shorter and more individual forms, such as cappriccios, intermezzi, rhapsodies, in his mature age, lends at least indirect countenance to the view that the tendency of music is to subordinate form to idea; and that if the classical form of the sonata is not expansible enough, other forms must be accepted which will admit of more freedom of development. This implies a question as to the proper meaning of the word 'sonata,' and a doubt as to its being legitimately assimilable to the tendency to centralise the interest upon the idea, as a contrast to the old practice of making an equal balance between two main subjects as a means of structural effect. If the word is to be so restricted, it will only be another conventional limitation, and, it may be added, must before long put an end to further enrichment of the literature of so-called sonatas.

In the finest of Brahms's three early sonatas, that in F minor, op. 5, the first slow movement is headed by a quotation from a poem of Sternau, and another movement is called Rückblick. These are clearly external marks of a poetical intention. In the actual treatment of the subjects there is no attempt to connect the movements; but the freedom of transition, even in the actual progress of a subject (see the second subject of the first movement), is eminently characteristic of the composer, and of a liberal view of sonata development. In the last movement—a rondo—the most noticeable external mark of continuity is the elaborately ingenious treatment of the subject of the second episode in the latter part of the movement. Brahms added no more to the list of solo pianoforte sonatas, but he illustrated the tendency to look for fresh opportunities in combinations of solo instruments, as in his pianoforte quartets and quintet, which are really just as much sonatas as those usually so designated; in fact, one of the versions of the quintet, which stands as a duet for two pianofortes, is in that form published as a 'sonata.' The three for pianoforte and violin require notice as the work of a great master, but throw very little light on any sort of extension of the possibilities of sonata-form. There seems to be a sort of poetic design in the complicated arrangement of the first half of the first movement in the first Sonata, op. 78, in which the characteristic figures of the first subject reappear, as if to connect each section with the centre of interest; and the half concludes with a complete restatement of the first subject simply and clearly in the original key, as is the case also in the same composer's Serenade in A for small orchestra. It may be observed in passing that this device curiously recalls the early composite form, in which the first subject reappears at the beginning of the second half [see pp. 510, 511]. There is one other slightly suggestive point—namely, the reappearance of the introductory phrase of the slow movement in one of the episodes of the final Rondo. [In the second sonata we may notice the fusion of the Scherzo and slow movement into one.]

Certain traits in his treatment of form, such as the bold digressions of key at the very outset of a movement, and the novel effects of transition in the subjects themselves, have already been described in the article FORM. It is only necessary here to point out that Brahms seems most characteristically to illustrate the tendency in modern music which has been styled 'intellectualism'; which is definable as elaborate development of all the opportunities and suggestions offered by figures, harmonic successions, or other essential features of subjects or accessories, so as to make various portions of the work appear to grow progressively out of one another. This sometimes takes the form of thematic development, and sometimes that of reviving the figures of one subject in the material or accompaniment of another, the object being to obtain new aspects of close and direct logical coherence and consistency. Beethoven is the prototype of this phase of modern music, and the examples of it in his later instrumental works are of the finest description. There are several examples which illustrate this tendency in the F minor Quintet. One of the most obvious is the case in which the cadence concluding a paragraph is formulated, as in the following example at (a), the phrase being immediately taken up by a different instrument and embodied as a most significant feature in the accessory subject which follows, as at (b).

(a) Pianoforte.

(b) Violin.

Under the same head of Intellectualism is sometimes erroneously included that broad and liberal range of harmony which characterises the best composers of the day. This may doubtless call for intellectual effort in those who are unfamiliar with the progress of art, or of inexpansive powers of appreciation, but in the composer it does not imply intellectual purpose, but only the natural step onwards from the progressions of harmony which are familiar to those which are original. With composers of

second rank such freedom is often experimental, and destructive to the general balance and proportion of the structure, but with Brahms it appears to be a special study to bring everything into perfect and sure proportion, so that the classical idea of instrumental music may be still maintained in pure severity, notwithstanding the greater extension and greater variety of range in the harmonic motion of the various portions of the movement. In fact Brahms appears to take his stand on the possibility of producing new instrumental works of real artistic value on the classical principles of abstract music, without either condescending to the popular device of a programme, or accepting the admissibility of a modification of the sonata-form to suit the impulse or apparent requirements of a poetical or dramatic principle.

A sonata which bears more obviously on the direction of modern art in the poetic sense is that of Sterndale Bennett, called 'The Maid of Orleans.' This is an example of programme-music in its purest simplicity. Each of the four movements has a quotation to explain its purpose, and in the slow movement the second section has an additional one. Nevertheless the movements are simple adaptations of the usual forms, the first standing for an introduction, the second representing the usual binary allegro, the third a slow movement in condensed binary form, and the last a rondo. There is but little attempt at using any structural means, such as original distribution of subject-matter, to enforce the poetic idea; so the whole can only be taken as an illustration of a poem in sonata form. But this nevertheless has some importance, as showing the acceptance of the aptitude of sonata-form for such purposes by a composer who was by no means in full sympathy with the lengths to which Schumann was prepared to carry the romantic theories.

Among other recent composers who treat sonata-form in a poetic fashion, we may name Raff and Rubinstein. The works of the former are always admirable in the treatment of the instruments, and both composers frequently present subjects of considerable fascination; but neither have that weight or concentration in structural development which would demand detailed consideration. Poetic treatment is commonly supposed to absolve the composer from the necessity of attending to the structural elements; but this is clearly a misconception. Genuine beauty in subjects may go far to atone for deficiency and irrelevancy in the development, but at best it is only a partial atonement, and those only are genuine masterpieces in which the form, be it ever so original, is just as clear and convincing in the end as the ideas of which it is the outcome.

The whole process of the development of the Sonata as an art-form, from its crudest beginnings to its highest culmination, took nearly two hundred years; and the progress was almost throughout steady, continuous, and uniform in direction. The earlier history is chiefly occupied by its gradual differentiation from the Suite-form, with which for a time it was occasionally confounded. But there always was a perceptible difference in the general tendency of the two. The Suite gravitated towards dance-forms, and movements which similarly had one principal idea or form of motion pervading them, so that the balance of contrasts lay between one movement and another, and not conspicuously between parts of the same movement. The Sonata gravitated towards more complicated conditions and away from pure dance-forms. Diversity of character between subjects and figures was admitted early into single movements, and contrasts of key were much more strongly emphasised; and while in the Suite, except in extremely rare cases, all the movements were in one key, amongst the very earliest Sonatas there are examples of a central movement being cast in a different key from the rest.

In a yet more important manner the capacity of the Sonata was made deeper and broader by the quality and style of its music. In the Suite, as we have said, the contrasts between one movement and another were between forms of the same order and character—that is, between dance-forms and their analogues; but in the Sonata the different movements very soon came to represent different origins and types of music. Thus in the early violin sonatas the slow introductory first movement generally shows traces of ecclesiastical influence; the second, which is the solid kind of allegro corresponding to the first movement of modern sonatas, was clearly derived from the secular vocal madrigals, or part music for voices, through the instrumental canzonas, which were their closest relations. The third, which was the characteristic slow movement, frequently showed traces of its descent from solo vocal music of various kinds, as found in operas, cantatas, or other similar situations; and the last movement earliest and latest showed traces of dance elements pure and simple. A further point of much importance was the early tendency towards systematic and distinct structure, which appears most frequently in the last movement. The reason for the apparent anomaly is not hard to find. The only movement in the group on a scale corresponding to the last was the second, and this was most frequently of a fugal disposition. The fugue was a form which was comparatively well understood when the modern harmonic forms were still in embryo; and not only did it suffice for the construction of movements of almost any length, but it did not in itself suggest advance in the direction of the sonata kinds of form, though it was shown to be capable of amalgamation with them when they in their turn had been definitely brought to

perfection. In the dance movements on the other hand, when the fugal forms were not used, all that was supplied as basis to work upon was the type of motion or rhythm, and the outlines of structure had to be found. As long as the movements were on a small scale the structure which obtained oftenest was the equal balance of repeated halves without contrasting subjects, of which the finest examples are to be found in Bach's Suites. The last movement was in fact so long a pure suite movement. But when it began to take larger dimensions, emphasis began to be laid upon that part of the first half of the movement which was in the dominant key; then the process of characterising it by distinct figures or subjects became prominent; and by degrees it developed into the definite second section. Meanwhile the opening bars of the movement gradually assumed more distinct and salient features, making the passage stand out more clearly from its immediate context; and in this form it was repeated at the beginning of the second half of the movement, the second section being reserved to make a complete balance by concluding the whole in a manner analogous to the conclusion of the first half. So far the change from the suite type of movement rests chiefly on the clearer definition of parts, and more positive exactness in the recapitulation of the subjects; but this is quite sufficient to mark the character as distinct, for in the movements of the Suite (excluding the prelude) balance of subject and key was never systematically recognised. The further development of binary form, in which the recapitulation of the distinct subjects was reserved for the conclusion, took some time to arrive at, but even at this early stage the essential qualities of sonata-form are clearly recognisable. The Violin Sonata was naturally the kind which first attained to perfection, since that instrument had so great an advantage in point of time over the keyed instruments used for similar purposes; and its qualities and requirements so reacted upon the character of the music as to make it appear almost a distinct species from the Clavier Sonata. But in fact the two kinds represent no more than divergence from a similar source, owing to the dissimilar natures of the instruments. Thus the introductory slow movement was most appropriate to the broad and noble character of the violin, and would appeal at once by its means to an audience of any susceptibility; whereas to the weak character of the early keyed instruments, so deficient in sustaining power, it was in general inappropriate, and hence was dropped very early. For the same reason in a considerable proportion of the early clavier sonatas, the third or principal slow movement was also dropped, so that the average type of sonatas for clavier was for a time a group of two movements, both generally in a more or less quick time. In these the canzona movement was early supplanted by one more in accordance with the modern idea, such as is typified in the clavier sonata of Galuppi in four movements [see p. 514], and by occasional allemandes in the earlier sonatas. As keyed instruments improved in volume and sustaining power the central slow movement was resumed ; but it was necessary for some time to make up for deficiencies in the latter respect by filling in the slow beats with elaborate graces and trills, and such ornaments as the example of opera-singers made rather too inviting. The course of the violin solo-sonata was meanwhile distinctly maintained till its climax, and came to an abrupt end in J. S. Bach, just as the clavier sonata was expanding into definite importance. In fact the earliest landmarks of importance are found in the next generation, when a fair proportion of works of this class show the lineaments of clavier sonatas familiar to a modern. Such are the disposition of the three movements with the solid and dignified allegro at the beginning, the expressive slow movement in the middle, and the bright and gay quick movement at the end ; which last continued in many cases to show its dance origin. From this group the fugal element was generally absent, for all the instinct of composers was temporarily enlisted in the work of perfecting the harmonic structure in the modern manner, and the tendency was for a time to direct special attention to this, with the object of attaining clear and distinct symmetry. In the latter part of the 18th century this was achieved ; the several movements were then generally cast on nearly identical lines, with undeviating distribution of subjects, pauses, modulations, cadences, and double bars. The style of thought conformed for a while sufficiently well to this discipline, and the most successful achievements of instrumental music up to that time were accomplished in this manner. Extrinsically the artistic product appeared perfect ; but art could not stand still at this point, and composers soon felt themselves precluded from putting the best and most genuine of their thoughts into trammels produced by such regular procedure. Moreover, the sudden and violent changes in social arrangements which took place at the end of the century, and the transformation in the ways of regarding life and its interests and opportunities which resulted therefrom, opened a new point of public emotion, and introduced a new quality of cosmopolitan human interest in poetry and art. The appeal of music in its higher manifestations became more direct and immediate ; and the progression of the idea became necessarily less amenable to the control of artificialities of structure, and more powerful in its turn of reacting upon the form. This is what lies at the root of much which, for want of a more exact word, is frequently described as the poetic element, which has become so prominent and indispensable a quality

in modern music. By this change of position the necessities of structural balance and proportion are not supplanted, but made legitimate use of in a different manner from what they previously were ; and the sonata-form, while still satisfying the indispensable conditions which make abstract music possible, expanded to a fuller and more co-ordinate pitch of emotional material. Partly under these influences, and partly, no doubt, owing to the improvements in keyed instruments, the Clavier Sonata again attained to the group of four movements, but in a different arrangement from that of the Violin Sonata. The slow introduction was sometimes resumed, but without representing an ingredient in the average scheme. The first movement was usually the massive and dignified Allegro. The two central portions, consisting of a highly expressive slow movement, and the scherzo which was the legitimate descendant of the dance movement, were ruled in their order of succession by the qualities of the first and last movements, and the work ended with a movement which still generally maintained the qualities to be found in a last movement of Corelli or Tartini. The tendency to unify the whole group increased, and in so far as the influence of intrinsic character or of the idea became powerful it modified the order and quality of the movements. For particular purposes which approve themselves to musical feeling the number of movements varied considerably, some exceedingly fine and perfect sonatas having only two, and others extending to five. Again, it is natural that in certain moods composers should almost resent the call to end with the conventional light and gay movement ; and consequently in later works, even where the usual form seems to be accepted, the spirit is rather ironical than gay, and rather vehement or even fierce than light-hearted. The same working of the spirit of the age had powerful effect on the intrinsic qualities of the Scherzo ; in which there came to be found, along with or under the veil of ideal dance motions, sadness and tenderness, bitterness, humour, and many more phases of strong feeling ; for which the ideal dance rhythms, when present, are made to serve as a vehicle : but in some cases also are supplanted by different though kindred forms of expression. In other respects the last movement moved farther away from the conventional type, as by the adoption of the fugal form, or by new use of the Variation-form in a more continuous and consistent sense than in early examples. In many cases the movements are made to pass into one another, just as in the earlier stages the strong lines which marked off the different sections in the movements were gradually toned down ; and by this means they came to have less of the appearance of separate items than limbs or divisions of a complete organism. This is illustrated most clearly by the examples of

slow movements which are so modified as to
be little more than Intermezzi, or introductory
divisions appended to the last movement ; and
more strongly by a few cases where the distinct
lines of separation are quite done away with,
and the entire work becomes a chain of long
divisions representing broadly the old plan of
four distinct movements with kindred subjects
continuing throughout. Since Beethoven the
impetus to concentrate and individualise the
character of musical works has driven many
genuine composers to the adoption of forms
which are less hampered by any suspicion of
conventionality ; and even with sonatas they
seemed to have grasped the object in view with
less steadiness and consistency than in previous
times. Some have accepted the artifice of a
programme, others admit some doubtful traits
of theatrical origin ; others develop poetic and
æsthetic devices as their chief end and object,
and others still follow up the classical lines,
contenting themselves with the opportunities
afforded by new and more elaborately perfect
treatment of details, especially in music for
combinations of solo instruments. In the latter
case it is clear that the field is more open than
in sonatas for single instruments, since the
combination of such instruments as the pianoforte and violin or pianoforte and violoncello
in large works has not been dealt with by the
great masters so thoroughly and exhaustively
as the solo sonata. But in any case it is apparent that fresh works of high value on the
classical lines can hardly be produced without
increasing intellectualism. The origin and
reason of existence of abstract music are, at least
on one side, intellectual ; and though up to a
certain point the process of development tended
to reduce the intellectual effort by making the
structural outlines as clear and certain as possible, when these were decisively settled the
current naturally set in the direction of complication. The inevitable process of accumulating
one device of art upon another is shown in the
free range of modulation and harmony, and in
the increasing variety and richness of detail
both in the subjects and in the subordinate
parts of works. In such cases the formal outlines
may cease to be strictly amenable to a definite
external theory ; but if they accord with broad
general principles, such as may be traced in the
history of abstract music so far, and if the total
effect is extrinsically as well as intrinsically
complete and convincing, it appears inevitable
to admit the works to the rank of ' Sonatas.'
The exact meaning of the term has in fact been
enforced with remarkable uniformity during the
whole period from the beginning to the present
day, and decisively in favour of what is called
abstract music. Fair examples of the successful
disregard of form in favour of programme or a
dramatic conception can hardly be found ; in
fact, in the best examples extant, programme

is no more than the addition of a name or a
story to an otherwise regular formal sonata ;
but on the other hand there is plenty of justification of the finest kind for abstract works in
free and more original forms, and it rests with
composers to justify themselves by their works,
rather than for reasoning to decide finally where
the limit shall be.   C. H. H. P.

SONATINA. This is a work in the same
form and of the same general character as a
sonata, but shorter, simpler, and slenderer. The
average form of the sonata appears to be the
most successful yet discovered for pure instrumental works of large scope. It is admirably
adapted for the expression and development of
broad and noble ideas ; and the distribution of
the various movements, and the clearness with
which the main sections and divisions of each
movement are marked out, give it a dignity and
solidity which seem most appropriate in such
circumstances. But the very clearness of the
outlines and the strength of contrast between
one division and another, make the form less
fit for works of smaller scope. As long as such
a work is laid out on a scale sufficiently large
to admit variety of treatment and freedom of
movement within the limits of these divisions,
there is fair chance of the work having musical
value proportionate to the composer's capacity ;
but if the limits are so narrow as to admit little
more than mere statement of the usual form,
and no more than the conventional order of
modulations, the possibilities of musical sense
and sentiment are reduced to a minimum, and
a want of positive musical interest commonly
results. Consequently sonatinas form one of
the least satisfactory groups of musical products.
The composers who have produced the greatest
impression with short and concise movements
in modern times have uniformly avoided them,
and adopted something of a more free and lyrical
cast, in which there is a more appropriate kind
of unity, and more of freedom and individuality
in the general outlines. It might be quite
possible to group these small pieces so as to
present a very strong analogy to the sonata on
a small scale ; but it has not been attempted,
owing possibly to a feeling that certain limitations of style and character are generally accepted
in the musical world as appropriate for works
of the sonata class, and that it would be superfluous to violate them.

The sonatina form has, however, proved
peculiarly convenient for the making of pieces
intended to be used in teaching. The familiar
outlines and the systematic distribution of the
principal harmonies afford the most favourable
opportunities for simple but useful finger-
passages, for which the great masters have supplied plentiful formulas ; and they furnish at
the same time excellent means of giving the
student a dignified and conscientious style, and
a clear insight into the art of phrasing and into

the simpler rules of classical form. These works may not have any strong interest of a direct kind for the musical world, but they have considerable value in so far as they fulfil the purposes they are meant to serve. The most famous and most classical examples of this kind are Clementi's sonatinas, of opp. 36, 37, and 38. And much of the same character are several by F. Kuhlau, which are excellently constructed and pure in style. Of modern works of a similar kind there are examples by L. Koehler. Those by Carl Reinecke and Hermann Goetz are equally adapted for teaching purposes, and have also in general not a little agreeable musical sentiment, and really attractive qualities. Some of Beethoven's works which are not definitely described as such are sufficiently concise and slight to be called sonatinas : as for instance those in G and G minor, op. 49, which were first announced for publication as ' Sonates faciles ' in 1805. That in G major, op. 79, was published as a ' Sonatine ' in 1810, though it is rather larger in most respects than the other little examples. Prior to Beethoven the average scale of sonatas was so small that it seems difficult to see how a diminutive could be contrived ; and indeed the grand examples which made the degrees of comparison specially conspicuous were not yet in existence. A modern work on such a scale, and made in the conventional manner, would probably be considered as a Sonatina, and apart from teaching purposes it would also be likely to be an anachronism.   C. H. H. P.

SONG. INTRODUCTION. In relation to the study of music, a Song may be defined as a short metrical composition, whose meaning is conveyed by the combined force of words and melody.

The Song, therefore, belongs equally to poetry and music. For the purposes of this Dictionary the subject should properly be treated with exclusive regard to music ; but the musical forms and structure of songs are so much determined by language and metre, and their content by the emotions the words express, that their poetic and literary qualities cannot be put aside. In the strictest sense, lyrical pieces alone are songs ; but adherence to so narrow a definition would exclude many kinds of songs whose importance in the history of music demands that they should be noticed. Attention, however, will be directed chiefly to homophonic forms of secular songs—i.e. songs for one voice or unisonous chorus.

It should, moreover, be mentioned that the history of the Song in this article will be treated in regard to country and not to period. For the study of any other branch of music among the leading nations of Europe,[1] a chronological arrangement would probably be more scientific and instructive ; but the Song is that

branch of music in which national peculiarities and idioms linger longest, and international affinities grow most slowly. Again, without attempting to trace the origin of Song, or to say whether or not Song preceded speech or language, it may safely be asserted that certain successions of sounds or intervals varying with different nationalities, have in all ages possessed some particular significance and conveyed some message of meaning from man to man. So that the music of each nation has qualities and idioms of its own as distinct and definite as those of its language.

Vocal music is probably the oldest branch of the art ; but from the fact that dance-songs preponderate in the music of nations whose musical culture remains in a primitive stage, it is reasonable to conclude that vocal music may have been at first a mere accessory of the dance. (See DANCE - RHYTHM.) Choral singing at religious and other festivals was also a practice of very remote antiquity. Recitations by bards, commemorative of the exploits of heroes, were a further and distinct development of vocal music. Hence the work done by the minstrels, Troubadours and Trouvères, Minnesinger and Meistersinger, will call for notice in their different countries.

Ever since the second quarter of the last century, the Song as a branch of music has assumed great importance. With regard to the Folksong, scientific musicians and composers in most European countries have deemed it worthy of serious study. They have assiduously collected and made use of what remains of the indigenous musical material still left untouched by the hand of civilisation. Governments have given aid to such enterprises, thereby showing the value they attach to the preservation of the songs of their people. Folk-lore has become a scientific study ; societies have been formed to collect and arrange in musical notation the songs orally handed down by uncultured singers, and truly the object is well worthy of the labour. For the folk-song is the origin of all our modern music. From it we have derived not only our scales, but the shape of our melodies, the outlines of our musical form, and indirectly even the art of our harmony and cadences.[2] Hence in treating the history of the Song in each successive country, it is necessary that the folk-song should hold its place.

There is another form of Song which, for want of a better term (where a distinction is necessary), it is convenient to designate by the German phrase Kunstlied, or Art-Song. These songs are more regular and finished compositions, written with conscious art by men who have made music their study. But formerly there was no branch of music so freely handled by inferior and unpractised hands. The lyric song may not need so accurate a knowledge of formal

---

[1] Scotland, Ireland, and Wales are purposely left out of this scheme, as the articles in this Dictionary on the music of those countries give sufficient information on the Songs.

[2] See Parry's Art of Music, p. 52 et seq.

principles as other kinds of music, but it both demands, and at last has received, the care and serious attention necessary for its proper cultivation and appreciation. For the art-song simple 'guitar' accompaniments no longer suffice; the instrumental part must have a beauty, a fulness and elaboration of its own apart from the voice, though primarily its duty is to enhance and support the melody and the meaning of the words. Further, composers have now recognised that no song can be really good without correct accentuation and emphasis; they have turned their attention to the study of accent, and to the proper relations of musical cadence to grammatical punctuation.[1] (See ACCENT, DECLAMATION (iii.).

The importance of the choice of words is happily now manifesting itself in every country, for the necessary dependence of the Song upon poetry is obvious.[2] Until the poet supplies lyrics of adequate power and beauty of form, the skill of the composer alone cannot develop the full capacities of the Song. When, indeed, poets and composers of the first rank have worked together in mutual sympathy and admiration, as did the German poets and composers of Goethe's age, the Song has quickly mounted to the loftiest heights of art. Time alone can produce men of genius and breathe the inspiration of great events, but poets and composers are alike the children of their age, and vividly reflect the dominant emotions of the hour and the scene in which they live. History colours every branch of art, and none more so than the Song, for it is the first and simplest mode of giving expression to strong feeling. Men naturally sing of what fills their heads and hearts; and thus there is a close correspondence between great historic events and the multitudes of songs to which they generally if not invariably gave birth.

Enough has now been said to show the right the Song has to be cultivated as a branch of pure art, and it remains to attempt to trace its history, so far as possible, in each civilised country. In some countries the art of music has not advanced beyond the most primitive stage of national melody, but in others the development of music can be followed from the simplest folk-song to the highest form of artistic composition.

FRANCE

As France was the original home of the Troubadours, France may legitimately occupy

[1] In M. Mathis Lussy's *Traité de l'Expression musicale* clear rules will be found for the correspondence between the musical rhythm and the verse rhythm, with examples which show how the sense of the musical phrase may be destroyed, if it be interrupted by a new line of the verse, and how the verse in turn may be marred by the interruption of rests or pauses in the musical phrase. There the student may learn why the strong and weak accents of the music should coincide respectively with the long and short syllables of the verse, and when the departures from this rule are justifiable. This excellent treatise was translated into English by M. E. von Glehn, and published by Novello & Co.

[2] That the poet's share in the Song is at length recognised, is proved by the poet's name being given nearly as often as that of the composer in the programmes of the present day.

the first place in this scheme. Another valid reason for treating this country first is that it possesses, perhaps, one of the oldest songs in existence. This is a *Complainte* on the death

EX. 1. FACSIMILE OF 'PLANCTUS KAROLI.'[3]

[3] Fétis, *Histoire générale de la Musique,* iv. 474.

of Charlemagne, 813. It may be found in a MS. in *fonds-latin* dated 1154, in the Bibliothèque Nationale in Paris,[1] and has been attributed to S. Columbanus. The music has been reduced to modern notation by both Coussemaker and Fétis, but their versions vary. It must be remembered that there is less certainty on the subject of early music than on early language, for music was handed down solely by oral tradition. And even when about the year 1000 the necessity was felt for some method of musical notation, the plans adopted were so numerous and confused that the question of time or rhythm or actual notes of a mediæval MS. is constantly interpreted differently by musical historians. We therefore give in facsimile a fragment of the MS. (see p. 537), and a few bars of both versions for comparison :—

Ex. 2. COUSSEMAKER'S VERSION.[2]

A so-lis or-tu us-que ad oc-ci-du--a Lit-to-ra ma-ris

Ex. 3. FÉTIS'S VERSION.

A so-lis or-tu us-que ad oc-ci-du-a lit-to-ra ma-ris

The melody has only four notes ; indeed, up to the last phrase only three, showing that the peculiar French fondness for a small compass has survived for 1000 years. Since the 10th century the practice existed of using well-known tunes (which later would be called *timbres*) to different Latin words.[3] And most of the Crusaders' songs which have come down to us from the 11th century are in Latin.[4] But an important exception amongst them is a song commencing 'O Marie, Deu maire,' dated 1096, which is in the vernacular, and this date marks the epoch when the Latin language began to be superseded by the French.

It is necessary to emphasise the close connection which has ever existed—and perhaps in France more than in any other country—between the folk-song and the Church. There is reason to believe that some melodies, or fragments of melodies, of Celtic origin have been preserved from the days before Christianity was introduced into France. The old heathen popular songs were in the early centuries of the Christian era a subject of much trouble to the Church, and Christian people were forbidden to frequent places where they were sung. Even Charlemagne, who ordered a collection of epic songs to be made, condemned the vulgar, reprehensible type of songs which were sung round about the Churches. In speaking of the music of the Church it must be remembered that it had two distinct groups ; first, the liturgical portion, or plain-song, without regular rhythm ; and second, the music to the hymns (prose or sequence, *sequentia*), which was both melodious and rhythmical, and represented the popular part of the service. By degrees, the secular spirit crept into these *proses*[5] and from the 11th century onwards popular songs[6] are to be found in the vulgar tongue side by side with the Latin canticles. These were called *proses farcies* or *epîtres farcies*.[7] Laudable attempts also were made by the Church to adapt secular festivals and customs to Christian purposes. Thus the Christian festival of Easter corresponded with the heathen celebration of the spring. Many of the old Celtic May-day songs[8] still exist, and a great similarity of melody can be traced between them and the Easter music of the Church. The origin of the well-known Easter hymn 'O filii et filiae' is unknown, but it is certainly as old as the 12th century, and has usually been attributed to French sources. It is unlike Gregorian music in character, but its affinity with some of the following examples of old May-day songs, called *Chansons de quête*, still sung in different parts of France, is incontestable.[9]

Ex. 4.

O fi-li-i et fi--li-ae,

Rex coe-les-tis, rex glo--ri-ae

Ex. 5.

En re-ve---nant de--dans les champs, En re-ve--nant de-dans les champs.

Ex. 6.

Mois de mai qu'est ar-ri-vé, c'est au-jour-d'hui qu'il faut chanter.

[1] Another song in the same MS. on the battle of Fontanet, 841, is said to be by one Angelbert, a Frankish warrior, who was present. Fétis, *Histoire générale de la Musique*, iv. 473 *et seq.*

[2] Wekerlin, 'Chansons Pop. du Pays de France,' i. 86.

[3] Fétis speaks of two Latin poems sung to tunes called *Modus libidinis* (l'air de l'amour), and *Modus florum* (l'air des fleurs). *Ibid.* iv. 430.

[4] Such as the beautiful 'Jerusalem Mirabilis,' which is a solemn piece, like a Gregorian hymn, and probably sung by the people in the open air. *Ibid.* iv. 482.

[5] Lavoix, *La Musique Française*, p. 20.

[6] Usually *Complaintes*, recognisable by their rhythm.

[7] For example see Fétis, v. 103.

[8] These contain strange relics of old Celtic words, such as *Trimousette*. See Tiersot, *Histoire*, p. 192.

[9] Tiersot, *Histoire de la Chanson Populaire en France*, p. 361. Other pagan or Celtic festivals, such as midwinter (called *la fête de*

Another example of the resemblance between the Church and folk-songs is afforded by the Tonus Peregrinus, the chant sung to the Psalm 'When Israel came out of Egypt.' Again the origin is obscure, but already in the 9th century it was held to be very old. Like 'O filii et filiae' it differs in many ways from Gregorian music, but several old French songs could be given where the melody is almost note for note that of the Tonus Peregrinus. For instance, the 'Chant des Livrées,' a very old song still sung at country weddings ; or the beautiful 16th-century 'Rossignolet des bois.'[1]

Ex. 7.

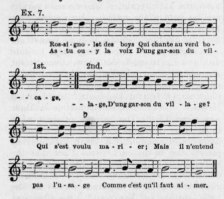

Ros-si-gno - let des boys Qui chante au verd bo -
As - tu ou - y la voix D'ung gar-son du vil -

1st.   2nd.

- - ca - ge,   - - la - ge, D'ung gar-son du vil - la - ge?

Qui s'est voulu ma - ri - er; Mais il n'entend

pas l'u - sa - ge Comme c'est qu'il faut ai - mer.

Though there is no definite evidence in this case that the Church adopted a popular melody for the chant, nor that the people used a chant which they heard in church for their own songs, it proves the popularity of this fine melody, and that it was common property to both. And it will be seen that this practice of intermixing sacred and secular music has continued from those early centuries to the present day.

It was incidentally remarked in the introduction to this article that the folk-songs have given us our scales ; and these scales include not only the modern major and minor but also the ecclesiastical or Gregorian scales and modes. Modal melodies have existed for hundreds of years, and still exist all over France. It must, however, be admitted that the commonest scales for the French folk-songs are the modern major and minor scales.[2] Among the most beautiful modal tunes are those found in Brittany, such as 'Le Clerc du Trémélo,' which is in the ecclesiastical Dorian or first mode ; a singularly pathetic religious song sung in a time of famine, 'Disons le chapelet' in the Phrygian or third mode ; and the well-known 'Ma douce Annette,' or the beautiful 'Le

Paradis' (given below) in the Aeolian or ninth mode.[3]

Ex. 8.

Je crois au pa - ra-dis   J'es - père al - ler un
Jé - sus nous la pro-mis.

1st.   2nd.

jour au glo - ri - eux sé - jour.

The narrative form of song is very popular in France, and the generic terms for this class of song is the *Complainte*. The old Celtic epics and the later collection of epics made by Charlemagne, the *chansons de geste*, the early *romances*, the *légendes* of the Passion and of the Christian saints, and the old pathetic *ballades* of the peasants would all come under that name. The wonderful *légende* called the 'Ballade de Jésus Christ' is still sung in Picardy.[4] The simplicity of the language and the modal melody point to its being of popular origin. The 'Chanson de la Perronelle,' which has lived in the mouths of the people for centuries,[5] resembles the oldest *complaintes* in its poetic form, consisting of couplets of two lines without a refrain.[6]

Ex. 9.
Lentement.

Av' ous point veu— . . . La Per-ron - nel-le Que

les gen-dar - - - mes ont em - me - née?   Ilz

l'ont a - bil - - - - - lée comme ung pai - ge, C'est

pour pas-ser . . . . . le Daul-phi - né.

M. Tiersot calls attention to the strange fact, that although these *chansons narratives* were known to exist, they were far less often included in the collections made from the 13th to the

l'Aguilaneuf or *l'Aguillaneuf*) or midsummer, answering respectively to the Church festivals of Christmas (see CAROL), the Epiphany, or St. John the Baptist, gave rise to masses of songs still sung in France, and common to both kinds of music. Space debars further mention of this subject, but full and interesting information will be found in M. Tiersot's above-quoted volume, p. 186 *et seq.* (In this same chapter the famous 'Maumariée' *Chansons* are alluded to.)
[1] Tiersot, 'Mélodies,' p. 78.
[2] *Ibid., Histoire*, p. 322.

[3] The above are included in M. Bourgault-Ducoudray's 'Trente Mélodies Populaires de la Basse Bretagne' ; and here it would be convenient to state briefly M. Bourgault-Ducoudray's theory. He denies that these modal songs have their origin in the Church. His argument is that the modes found in these and other popular melodies, not only of France, but of Ireland, Scotland, Greece, etc., are actually the survival of music common to the early Indo-European race. He maintains that the Greeks alone cultivated music as an art ; that the Church, taking its scales from Greece and afterwards carrying them to other countries, brought to Brittany, for instance, a kind of music which was already familiar to the Bretons in their popular songs; that the so-called modes may be as old and as common to many nationalities as many of the familiar words common to the different languages of the Indo-European family. On the strength of this, Ducoudray's nomenclature of the modes is the Greek and not the ecclesiastical, and this has been adopted by other continental writers (see MODES). Throughout this article, however, the Church names and Gregorian numbers of the modes are retained, except in the section relating to Song in Greece.
[4] This legend is widely spread in France. It is found in connection with several saints in the *Legenda Aurea* of Jacobus de Voragine. See Champfleury and Wekerlin's 'Chansons pop. des provinces de France.'
[5] The earliest record of the words and music of this song is to be found in a MS. in the Bibliothèque Nationale called 'Chansons du 15ème Siècle,' published by Gaston Paris and Gevaert.
[6] Tiersot, *Histoire*, p. 12.

17th centuries than the *chansons satiriques, chansons d'amour, pastourelles,* etc. Of recent years their extreme beauty has claimed more attention, and many modern collections of them have been published.

To trace the development of song it is now necessary to return to the early Middle Ages. Some strong impulse was evidently given to the human mind in Europe towards the close of the 11th century, and the songs of the Troubadours, like the numerous schools of philosophy which illuminated the 12th century, were fruits of an awakened ardour for intellectual pursuits. With the Troubadours a new type of music was introduced, which may be described as songs written with conscious art. These versifiers, the Troubadours and Trouvères to whom music and literature owe much, derived their names from 'trobar' or 'trouver' (to find or invent). They belonged respectively to the south and north of France, and wrote in the Langue d'Oc and Langue d'Oïl. It was not unnatural that in Provence and Languedoc the new life should especially express itself in music and verse, for the circumstances of those provinces were favourable to the development of sentiment and imagination. The rise of the Troubadours in southern France was quickly followed by the appearance of the Trouvères in northern France. There was less gaiety about these northern versifiers than about the southern, but in other respects the resemblance between them was very close. At first the Troubadours and Trouvères sang their own verses, but the functions of the poet and singer soon became distinct. Hence a class of professional musicians arose, who sang the songs of their own lords and other composers. These wandering singers from Provence and Picardy, known as *Jongleurs* or *Chanteors* in the south, and *Menêtriers* or minstrels in the north,[1] went from court to court, country to country, and joining the Crusaders they returned from the Holy Land filled with enthusiasm and singing songs of love and war. The war-songs or *chansons de geste* were musically uninteresting ; they were merely long chanted tales where the melody only occurs in the short refrain. But the love-songs were poems of exquisite grace, perfect rhythm, and highly expressive. Their very names reveal their origin, such as the *pastourelle, alba* and *serena, tensons* and *sirvente*.[2] To the

Troubadours likewise may be ascribed the *canzo* and *canzone,* the *soula* (soulagement), a merry song, and the *lai,*[3] which is of a melancholy character ; and to the Trouvères more especially the *romance*.[4] The Troubadours and Trouvères were not less fertile in the invention of dance songs, combining solo and chorus. Such were the famous *carol* or *rondet de carol,* the *espringerie* (or jumping dance), and the *ballata.*

The earliest of the Troubadours on record was Guillaume, Duke of Guienne, who joined the first Crusade in 1096. And among the illustrious Troubadours and Trouvères of the 12th and 13th centuries, whose names survive and many of whose melodies have come down to us, there were : Richard Cœur de Lion, Bertran de Born, Pierre Rogier, Bernart de Ventadour, the Châtelain de Coucy, Guirant de Borneil, Blondel de Nesle, Gacé Brulé, Hugues de Lusignan, Thibaut de Champagne (King of Navarre), Jehan Erars, Giraut de Calenson, Perrin d'Angecourt, Adam de la Bassée, Adenet le Roi, and Adam de la Hale. The prime of the Troubadours was past when in the year 1320, the Troubadour Academy of Toulouse was founded for the cultivation and preservation of their art.[5] (See TROUBADOUR.)

The Troubadours and Trouvères owe great debts to the Church and to the Folk-song. Their music was a compound of the folk-song for its melody and form ; and of the Gregorian chant for its declamation and ornament. But inasmuch as the art of literature was then highly developed, and music was still in its infancy, it was impossible to combine the elaborate and highly finished forms of poetry with the music then existing, and a new kind of song, more artistic and more developed, was the result. The Troubadours were eager to invent new, ingenious and graceful phrases, metres, and rhythms,[6] and their work was of real value in handing down the rhyming stanza as the most perfect vehicle for lyrical expression. Also, by the preference the Troubadours gave to the modern major scale they helped to establish it in European music before the close of the 13th century. In this, and in the simple repetitions of their musical phrases, they followed the popular instinct. And though the Troubadour melodies are more developed and finished than those of the *chansons populaires,* it is in many cases impossible to state with certainty which are folk-songs and which are the work of trained musicians. For instance, a pastoral song, 'La reine d'Avril,' belonging to the 12th

<hr />

[1] The Menêtrier seems to have attained a higher standard of culture and taste than the Jongleur, who soon added other modes of popular diversion (such as juggling and acrobatic feats) to his musical accomplishments. It must, however, be remembered that the lower classes in France were untouched by the Troubadour movement, which covered the time from the 11th to the 14th centuries. They had nothing more in common with the *lais, sirventes,* etc. than they had with the old *chansons de geste.* The Jongleurs were the sole connecting link between the people and the courts.

[2] In the *pastourelle* the poet feigned to meet and woo a shepherdess ; the *alba* and *serena* were aubades and serenades. The *tensons* were metrical dialogues of lively repartee on some disputed point of gallantry, and the *sirvente* was an address of a devoted lover to his mistress. To this latter form of composition, which was also much employed in satire, a special celebrity belongs, because its metre—the *terza rima*—was adopted by Dante and Petrarch.

[3] See F. Wolf, *Ueber die Lais.*

[4] The *romance* is the lyrical outcome of the narrative *complaintes* and *chansons de geste* in Northern France. 'Belle Yolans' of the 12th century is an example. See Tiersot, *Histoire,* p. 414.

[5] There were schools in other parts of France where the Gay Science was taught, and whither the Troubadours repaired in Lent (when not allowed to appear in public) to learn new songs and melodies. The minstrels also had rights granted to them to form corporations or guilds in several towns. The earliest charter dates 1338, signed by Robert de Caveran, and lasted until the 18th century.

[6] See P. Aubry, *La rhythmique musicale des Troubadours,* etc., Paris, 1907.

century, is said to be of popular origin; it is melodious and rhythmical, it has a refrain, and the first little phrase is four times repeated. 'L'autrier par la matinée,' by Thibaut, King of Navarre (1201-54), opens with a phrase exactly similar, which is also repeated.[1] There is the same charm of sincerity and pretty sentiment about an older song, the Châtelain de Coucy's (1192) 'Quant le rossignol,'[2] though the form is less concise. It is composed in phrases of seven bars each, like many other mediæval songs.[3] Both are good illustrations of Troubadour songs.[4]

Ex. 10.   *Quant le Rossignol.*

Very few *sirventes*, but many *pastourelles*, have been preserved from the 12th century. This period was specially rich in sacred and secular dramatic representations; and, as before stated, proses and canticles in plain-chant melody are found side by side with light, rhythmical popular tunes. It is thus in 'Daniel Ludus' by one Hilaire, played in 1250. The

'Jeu de S. Nicolas' and 'Le Juif' were of the same type, at once sacred and comic. The character of the mysteries remained faithful to tradition; these were only a continuation of the liturgical dramas of the 11th century.[5] But by the end of the 13th century the Trouvères had broken loose from the Church, and resorted to little village histories or love-stories for their material. 'Aucassin et Nicolete,' the well-known *chant-fable*, belongs to this time. Musically more important was Adam de la Hale's celebrated pastorale 'Le jeu de Robin et de Marion,' which was played at the court of Charles d'Anjou at Naples in 1285. This work has long been attributed solely to Adam de la Hale's own invention, but M. Tiersot has now shown that A. de la Hale probably wrote the play, and then strung together a number of popular tunes (many of them of far older date) to suit his words.[6] Thus this pastoral comedy forms probably the oldest collection of French folk-tunes in existence. Adam de la Hale, together with Guillaume de Machault, should more properly be classed among the *Chansonniers*, or the early musicians, who in the 13th century paved the way for the contrapuntal school, which for two centuries was to be the predominating influence in European music. A. de la Hale, surnamed 'Le bossu d'Arras,' was born in 1240; Machault in 1285, thus forming the link between the Trouvères and the scholar musicians of a little later time. Like the Trouvères they often invented both the words and the melodies of their songs, but they also attempted to write in the polyphonic form of composition; and raw and imperfect as these efforts were, they marked a step in advance. To Adam de la Hale and G. de Machault French music owes much; not only can the form of the future

Ex. 11.

vaudeville be detected in the *pastorale* 'Robin et Marion,' but its chansons are strictly similar

1 Ambros, *Geschichte der Musik*, ii. 227, and Tiersot, *Hist.*, p. 371.
2 Ambros, *Ibid.* ii. 223. Burney and Perne put these into modern notation, and where they differ, Burney's are the lower notes.
3 Another of Thibaut's songs, 'Je me quidoie partir d'amour,' given by Ambros, ii. 228, has an alternating rhythm of two and three bars, but it preserves a perfect symmetry of form.
4 Further examples of Troubadour songs will be found in Wolf's *Ueber die Lais*, Kiesewetter's *Schicksale und Beschaffenheit des weltlichen Gesanges*; J. Stafford Smith's 'Musica Antiqua,' and in the histories of music by Ambros, Fétis, Burney, and others. Also for modernised versions see Wekerlin's 'Echos du Temps passé, vol. i.

5 See Lavoix, *La Musique Française*, p. 41.
6 Space prohibits quoting here at length M. Tiersot's interesting and conclusive arguments. They are given in different places in his *Histoire de la Chanson Pop.* See especially p. 422 *et seq.*, and the article HALE, Adam de la, vol. ii. p. 273.

in structure and character to chansons of modern date. In the old and new alike we find a strongly marked rhythm, easy intervals, and a paucity of notes, repetition of one short melodic phrase, the major mode, the favourite 6–8 time, and an extreme simplicity of general plan.[1] Though hundreds of years have passed since 'Robin et Marion' was written, the song 'Robin m'aime' (ex. 11) is still sung in Hennegau.[2]

In two volumes of old French and Latin poems, the author Guillaume de Machault is styled poet and musician. The forms of the poems are very varied, and among them are a great number of *lais, virelais, ballades, rondeaux,* and *rondelets,* with description of the music to which they are set.[3] Machault seems to have been most renowned for his graceful and rhythmical *ballettes,* which are written, as a rule, in triple or compound time. It should be noted that in the songs of this early period the melody is never protracted and drawn out to the detriment of the words, but closely follows the quick succession of syllables without visible effort. And these old melodies often have the Iambic rhythm, for instance[4]

Ex. 12.　　　　　　　　　ADAM DE LA HALE.

Il n'est　si bon - ne vi - an - de　que ma - tons.

Contemporary with, or a little junior to Machault, was Jehannot Lescurel, who wrote *romances* which are still extant in MS. One of these, 'A vous douce débonnaire,' which has been translated into modern notation by Fétis,[5] exhibits a more developed melody and a more modern tendency than other productions of the same date.

If it be true that during the 14th and 15th centuries, the Church exercised an exclusive dominion over music, she was nevertheless a friend to secular songs. By taking popular tunes for the themes of their masses and motets, such as 'L'omme armé,' 'Tant je me déduis,' 'Se la face ay pale' (used by Dufay); or 'Baisez-moi' (by Roselli), 'Malheur me bat' (by Josquin des Prés), etc.,[6] the musicians of the Church preserved many a melody which would otherwise have perished. 'L'omme armé' is undoubtedly the most famous song of the Middle Ages, and it owes its notoriety not so much to its beauty as to the fact that contrapuntal composers, from Dufay, at the end of the 14th century, to Palestrina, used it more than any other folk-song. (See L'HOMME ARMÉ, vol. ii. p. 687.) From want of such adoption by the Church, some of the airs have been lost to which the curious old Noëls, printed in black letter at the end of the 15th century, were sung, though the names of the airs (such as 'Faulce trahison,' etc.) remain as superscriptions. (See NOËL.)[7]

In that great age of serious polyphonic music a high place was held by the French school, or, to speak more correctly, by the Gallo-Belgian school, for during the 14th and 15th centuries no distinction, as regards music, can be drawn between northern France and Flanders.

The direct use made of secular music for ecclesiastical purposes is remarkably illustrated by the works of Clément Marot. He was a translator of a portion of the Psalms; and the first thirty of them, which he dedicated to his king, François I., were set or 'parodied' to the favourite dance-airs of the Court.[8] Popularity was thus at once secured for the Psalms, which members of the Court could sing to their favourite *courantes, sarabandes,* and *bourrées.* After Marot's death Béza continued his work at Calvin's instance.[9] Much doubt existed for a long while as to whom belonged the credit of having set the Psalms to music. Some ascribed it wholly to Marot, others to Goudimel; but M. Douen has now made it clear that these men, together with Jambe de Fer, Franc, Claudin, and others, adapted the Psalms to old secular songs.[10] In the 'Psautier Flamand Primitif' (1540) all the psalms are for one voice, and with only two exceptions they can all be traced back to their sources in popular French and Flemish songs.[11] (See PSALTER.)

While secular music was thus made to minister to the Church, it had a separate though less conspicuous sphere of its own. This is attested by the *vaux-de-vire* (or drinking-songs),[12] *voix-de-ville* (better known by their modern name of *vaudevilles*) and *airs-de-cour,* collected and published in the 16th

[1] Tiersot, *Histoire,* p. 373.
[2] This example is taken from M. Lussy and E. David's *Histoire de la Notation Musicale,* p. 105.
[3] The volumes were found in 1747 by Count de Caylus in a royal library in France. Burney, *Hist. of Mus.* ii. 303.
[4] Ambros, *Ges. der Musik,* ii. 295.
[5] This song is to be found in the *Revue Musicale,* vol. xii. No. 34.
[6] Ambros, *Ges. der Musik.* iii, 15 et seq.

[7] A list of collections of Noëls is given by Tiersot, *Hist.,* p. 242.
[8] Wekerlin says in his 'Echos du Temps passé,' iii. 136, that when any dance-air became popular, rhymers immediately 'parodied' it, *i.e.* put words to it, so that it could be sung. The term 'parody' thus had no sense of burlesque, but it simply meant adaptation. The Ballards issued a quantity of these songs. 'L'Abeille,' a well-known example, is really a minuet.
[9] Calvin, who detested the arts, recommended music, nevertheless, from the purely utilitarian point of view, 'la parole chantée qui porte beaucoup plus fort.'
[10] See *Clément Marot et le Psautier Huguenot,* i. 606. One of the most noted is the magnificent Huguenot Battle Hymn, 'Que Dieu se montre seulement' (Psalm 68), sometimes called 'La Marseillaise Huguenote.' It is a secular tune of Alsatian origin, and it appeared first in the first edition of the Strasburg Psalter.
[11] For *cantiques,* moreover, as well as masses and psalms, secular airs were openly utilised. And according to Douen (pp. 688 and 703) the Roman Catholics have never ceased to adapt secular airs to ecclesiastical uses from the 16th century down to the present time. He supports this statement by reference to 'La pieuse alouette avec son tire-lire; Chansons Spirituelles, le plupart sur les airs mondains, par Ant. de la Cauchie, 1619'; 'Imitations de Jésus-Christ en Cantiques sur des airs d'Opéras et de Vaudevilles, par Abbé Pelegrin, 1727' (Paris); and 'Concerts Spirituels,' a collection adapted at Avignon in 1835, of masses, hymns, requiems, prayers, etc., on operatic melodies by Gluck, Piccinni, Mozart, Cimarosa, Rossini, Méhul, and others.
[12] Basselin and Jean le Houx, who lived in the little valleys (*vaux*) around Vire in Normandy, in the second half of the 15th century, wrote many favourite drinking-songs, and hence drinking-songs came to be called *vaux-de-vire.* Some writers have confused this term with the *voix-de-ville,* which applied to chansons sung in the streets, and later to any songs with gay airs and light words. Jehan Chardavoine's famous collection of monodic songs of the 16th century is described as containing *vaux-de-ville* and *voix-de-ville,* chansons de ville, pièces littéraires avec leur musique originale, telle que 'Mignonne, allons voir si la rose,' by Ronsard, etc. See Tiersot, *Histoire,* pp. 228 and 433 for other similar collections.

century. Much grace, indeed, and gaiety were evinced in the poetry and music of the songs and *romances* of this period, and it would be wrong to disparage such writers as Guillaume le Heurteur, Noë Faignient, Pierré Vermont, and François I., whose song, 'O triste départir,' with music by A. Muret, is full of feeling. But more important work was undoubtedly being done by their polyphonic contemporaries.[1]

The effects of the great change which came over vocal music at the end of the 16th century were perhaps more marked in France and in the Netherlands than elsewhere. Polyphonic music, whether in masses or in madrigals, had been, as we have seen, the glory of the Gallo-Belgian School; but when once the monodic system had gained universal recognition polyphonic music began to decline, even where it had flourished most; and the French-Flemish School surrendered its individuality by absorption into the Italian School. The French composers were likewise influenced by two other great innovations of this time, namely, the creation of discords by Monteverde, and the application of music to the drama. Henceforward original melodies of their own invention were expected of musicians, and the old practice of choosing themes for their compositions in folk-songs or popular dance-songs died out, though its disappearance was gradual.[2] Songs for one voice, such as the 'Airs de Cour' of the early 17th century, accompanied by lute or harpsichord, began to find favour and to drive airs for several voices from the ground they had occupied for more than 150 years. And that most characteristic type of French song, the *romance*, was soon to commence, or rather resume, a reign of popularity which is not yet ended.

Scudo[3] defines the *romance* as a song divided into several 'couplets,' the air always simple, naïve, and tender, the words to treat of sentiment and love. Unlike the *chanson* it is never political or satirical. It was one of the very earliest fruits of French grace, sensibility, and gallantry; and though its attributes may have varied from time to time, it remained unchanged in its essence from the era of the Troubadours until the 19th century. There

was, it is true, a period after the disappearance of the Troubadours, when the *romance* was threatened with extinction, by its formidable rival, the polyphonic *chanson*, but the 17th century saw it again in possession of all its old supremacy. Louis XIII. wrote several; and his music-master, Pierre Guédron, was perhaps the foremost composer of *romances* of that time. One of the best examples of his work, 'Aux plaisirs, aux délices, bergères,'[4] contains modulations which are remarkable for that date. Guédron's son-in-law, Boësset, was the author of a very famous *romance*, 'Cachez beaux yeux.' And the names of Beaulieu, Deschamps, Colasse, Bernier, Lefêvre, Lambert, and Pierre Ballard may be recorded as composers of this age. The last (whose 'Belle, vous m'avez blessé,' was a favourite) was a member of the famous Ballard family of music-printers and also composers. As printers they preserved a large quantity of *brunettes* (see BRUNETTE), *musettes*[5] and other dance-songs and drinking-songs. Several *brunettes* were included in the great collection of the old French popular songs which A. Philidor copied out with his own hand, and dedicated to Louis XIV. Many were undoubtedly written on old Noël airs, especially those in parts.[6] After the 17th century they became scarcely distinguishable from romances.

For excellent and typical specimens of the romances of the 18th century we may quote J. J. Rousseau's 'Le Rosier' and 'Au fond d'une sombre vallée,' both of which are found in his collection entitled 'Les Consolations des Misères de la vie.' The musicians of this period seem to have been inspired by the grace and delicacy of contemporary poetry to create tender and simple melodies. Insipid as these songs must seem to us now, they are thoroughly representative of the age which produced them. It was the time of that singular phase of thought and feeling which will be for ever associated with the name of J. J. Rousseau; a time of yearnings to return to some imagined state of native innocence, to an ideal pastoral life in some visionary and often artificial Arcadia. All this was faithfully reflected in the works of its poets and musicians. Monsigny instinctively returned to the style of the folk-song, even to the *pastourelle* and *complainte*. His frequent use of the minor seventh of the scale gives a touch of mediævalism to his songs:[7]

---

[1] A celebrated collection, with a dedication to Charles IX., by Ronsard, was published in 1572, under the title of 'Meslanges de chansons,' and it contained songs for four, six, and sometimes eight voices by all the best-known Gallo-Belgian composers, such as Josquin, Mouton, Claudin, etc. These songs, like others of the same date, have strong melodies, and are full of canonic devices. Pierre Ronsard's sonnets were set to music by Philippe de Monte, in five, six, and seven parts, and his songs in four parts, by Bertrand and Reynard. Mention should also be made of Crespel, Raïf, and Clement Jannequin, whose descriptive songs (such as the *Cris de Paris*) formed a new feature in music, also Gombert and Certon. But with the true polyphonic song this article is not concerned.

[2] When public opinion first ceased to approve this practice, composers did not at once abandon it, but they no longer produced vocal pieces which were avowedly parodies or adaptations; it now became their habit to attach their names to all their melodies, whether they were original or borrowed. As a typical case CHARMANTE GABRIELLE may be quoted: neither the words of which were by Henri IV. nor the music by his maître de chapelle, Du Caurroy. The air is really an old Noël of unknown authorship, and probably some court poet, Desportes, perhaps, wrote the words. See also J. B. Wekerlin, 'Chansons Populaires du Pays de France,' ii. 217.

[3] Scudo, *Critique et Littérature musicales*, vol. ii.

[4] Published in Wekerlin's 'Echos du Temps passé,' vol. iii. p. 10. It is taken from a very rare collection entitled 'Airs de Cour de différents auteurs, 5 livres, publiés de 1615 à 1628. Paris, chez Pierre Ballard.' (Guédron's melody is in the first book.)

[5] Here we may mention the drone-bass which occurs so frequently in musettes and other dance-songs. Numerous examples may be found in Wekerlin's 'Echos du Temps passé.'

[6] In Wekerlin's second vol. of his 'Echos du Temps passé' he states that this collection especially characterises the 17th and 18th centuries, and 'though written earlier the songs were only published when their popularity was great enough to justify it.' Wekerlin gives a valuable list of the collections drawn upon for this volume, with full descriptions and dates. The favourite 'Menuet d'Exaudet' (Exaudet was a famous dancing-master), with words by Favart, is included among the *chansons à danser*. All these dance-songs, except the minuet, are in common or 2-4 time and in regular periods.

[7] Tiersot, *Histoire*, p. 525.

Ex. 13.

Son pe-tit   cœur sou - - hai - te.

Grétry, on the other hand, who was a far more advanced musician, consciously set himself the task of reproducing the old melodic form of the folk-song. He confesses to have written the *romance* of Richard Cœur de Lion, ' Une fièvre brûlante,' *dans le vieux style.*[1] And certainly when the little art-songs or *romances* of this period are closely examined, they show externally but little difference from the folk-songs, though in their essence they are wide apart, being artificial rather than natural and spontaneous. As examples it will suffice to mention a few favourites such as : Monsigny's ' O ma tendre musette' (words by La Harpe) ; ' Il pleut, bergère,' by Simon ; ' Les petits oiseaux,' by Rigel ; ' L'amour fait passer le temps,' by Solié ; ' Le point de jour,' by Dalayrac ; ' Annette et Lubin,' by Favart, and ' Que j'aime à voir les hirondelles,' by Devienne.

Although romances were so much in vogue and reached so high a degree of popularity there were songs of other kinds written by the composers of the 18th century of equal importance. Amongst these, political songs are prominent, and in no country have they been more so than in France. The Mazarinade of the 17th century was a vast collection of more than 4000 satirical effusions against Mazarin, adopted to popular airs. Early in the 18th century was heard the famous song, ' Malbrouk s'en va-t-en guerre,'[2] and later on, in the first throes of the Revolution, the Royalists were singing ' Pauvre Jacques' (words by the Marquise de Travenet), and the air resounded with ' Ça-ira,' from the throats of the insurgent rabble of Paris. ' O Richard, ô mon Roi' and ' Où peut-on être mieux' have become historical by their use at the same terrible period. As might have been expected of so profound a movement, the Revolution gave birth to many remarkable songs. To the stormy years at the close of the 18th and the opening of the 19th centuries are due the finest *chants* or patriotic songs of France. Supreme among these stands the ' Marseillaise,' which has won immortality for its author and composer, Rouget de Lisle. Next in fame come three songs of Méhul's, the ' Chant du Départ' (words by Chénier), the ' Chant de Retour,' and the ' Chant de Victoire.' And by the side of these may be set the fine ' Réveil du Peuple' by Gaveaux, and the ' Père de l'Univers' by Gossec. Contemporary with these songs, but on a lower level of political importance and musical value, were ' Cadet Rousselle,' the ' Chanson de Dagobert,' ' Fanfan

la tulipe,'[3] ' Te souviens-tu,' the ' Récit du Caporal,' and many others it would be tedious to enumerate. Of a different kind was the official national anthem of the Restoration, —the beautiful old song ' Vive Henri IV.,'[4] which was much in vogue in 1814 after the Allies entered Paris.

After the accession of Napoleon and the accompanying revival of monarchical traditions, the demand for *romances* was more eager than ever, and there was no lack of composers ready to supply it.[5] The most successful were Plantade, Garat, Pradher, and Lambert. Another popular contemporary, possessing more musical erudition, was Dalvimare, whose ' Chant héroïque du Cid ' is a fine song. Choron was founder of a school whence issued Duprez, Scudo, and others, who were both singers and song composers. The names of several women should also be included among *romance* writers : Mme. Gail, Queen Hortense, Mme. Duchambge, and Loïsa Puget. The first named was the best musician. About Queen Hortense there was more of the amateur composer, and she would trust to Drouet, Carbonnel, or Plantade to put her airs into musical shape. Her best songs were ' Partant pour la Syrie ' and ' Reposez-vous, bon chevalier.' Mme. Duchambge owed her reputation to the skill with which Nourrit sang her songs, and Loïsa Puget was a favourite in schools and convents. Of others who wrote about the same time and in the same manner, it will suffice to mention A. de Beauplan, Panseron, Jadin, Bruguière, Mengal, Dolive, Berton, Lis, and Pollet. As a general reflection on these songs, it may be said that their most common fault is the endeavour to express inflated sentiment with inadequate means. A discrepancy is constantly felt between the commonplace simplicity of the accompaniments and modulations, and the intense sentimentality or turgid pomposity of the words. The disparity could only be concealed by highly dramatic or expressive singing.

Out of the revolutionary era of 1830 there came in France a splendid outburst of lyric poetry. This was the era of Victor Hugo, Lamartine, Delavigne, Alfred de Musset, and Béranger. And it was natural that the song should be responsive to the poetic movement of the time. In 1828 Monpou's setting of Béranger's ' Si j'étais petit oiseau' attracted the notice of the poets of the Romantic School. Many of de Musset's and Victor Hugo's ballades and romances were also composed by him. But Monpou was not a highly trained musician ; though striking and original his music was faulty. He was a slave to the influence of the

[1] Grétry, *Essais sur la Musique,* i. 368.
[2] For further mention of these political and historical songs see separate headings in the Dictionary ; and for the tunes see J. B. Wekerlin's ' Chansons Pop. du Pays de France.'

[3] An old song of irregular metre by Souriquête de St. Marc, set to an old tune, and extremely popular between 1702 and 1802.
[4] Henri IV., 1553-1610. The melody is certainly older than his date, as it first appears as the *timbre* of a Noël in a collection published in 1581.
[5] Specimens of these little songs are to be found in Wekerlin's ' Chansons Populaires du Pays de France.'

Romantic School, and his songs well illustrate the extreme exaggeration to which it was prone. Similar qualities were likewise displayed by an incomparably greater musician, Hector Berlioz. In him there was a depth of poetic insight and a subtle sense of beauty, to which Monpou could make no pretension. Of all Berlioz's works his songs are the least tinged with exaggeration. He wrote twenty-seven in all, of which perhaps the 'Nuits d'été,' op. 7, are the best. 'Sur les lagunes' and 'L'Absence' are especially beautiful. 'La Captive,' op. 12, is a long piece written for contralto voice, with a varied and elaborate accompaniment. 'Fleurs des Landes,' op. 13, consists of five romances for one or more voices, all bearing a distinctively local colouring. No one can study Berlioz's songs without being struck by the fragmentary character of the melodies, and the want of symmetry in the rhythmic phrases. But these defects are atoned for by the exquisite beauty of the melodic fragments, and the rhythmic phrases are never abruptly broken or disjointed without justification. An explanation will always be found in the words, which it was Berlioz's constant study to illustrate with perfect fidelity. Nothing could be more poetical than the opening phrase of his song 'L'Absence.' Berlioz's accompaniments are highly developed, and participate fully in the poetic intention of the words. A proof of his skill in this respect is afforded by the close of the 'Spectre de la Rose,' where, after a full, rich accompaniment throughout, he gives to the last words merely single notes, and thus unmistakably marks the transition from the passionate tale of the rose to its epitaph. Many examples of Berlioz's poetic faculties might be adduced, but enough has already been said to indicate his exalted position as a song-composer. Another musician allied to the Romantic School was Félicien David, who, without being a song-writer, indirectly influenced later composers' songs by introducing the element of orientalism into French music. This, with its strange Eastern rhythms and tonalities, has attracted many subsequent composers.

The French have a manifest preference for dramatic music, and although many of their modern opera-composers, such as A. Thomas, Gounod, Saint-Saëns, Delibes, Bizet, Reyer, Joncières, and Massenet, have written truly lyric songs, they are seldom heard in concert-rooms. The singers and the public prefer the songs extracted from their dramatic works with which they are more familiar. Few composers have regarded song-writing as an important branch of their art, though an exception must be made in the case of Gounod, who had a distinct lyric talent, and who strongly influenced his generation. Much of the present revulsion of feeling against Gounod was engendered by his followers, who imitated his mannerisms

without possessing his gifts. It may be admitted that he set a bad example in the dangerous sentimentality of his sacred songs; but it cannot be denied that many of his other songs are of true and enduring beauty, and always pre-eminently vocal. Among his best may be named 'Le Vallon,' 'Le Soir,' 'The fountain and the river,' 'Ring out, wild bells,' 'Le Printemps,' 'Medjé,' and the collection of twenty songs entitled 'Biondina,' which are full of the Southern spirit. Massenet possesses much the same sensuous vein of melody, but the form of his songs is more concise, and his accompaniments more brilliant. In the songs of Saint-Saëns, Lalo, Bizet, and A. Chabrier there is individuality; but they, as well as Widor, Joncières, Guiraud, Dubois, Paladilhe, Pierné, Boisdeffre, Lefebvre, Augusta Holmès, Thomé, Chaminade, and other lesser composers are greatly indebted to Gounod, and generally speaking may be said to belong to the old school. Delibes and Godard should also be included, but their music has a distinct character of its own. Amongst his other works, Léo Delibes has written many graceful, refined, and typically French songs, full of colour; whilst Benjamin Godard has chiefly distinguished himself in this lyric form by the peculiar charm and melancholy sentiment of his songs.[1]

A totally different school of song from that above described now exists in France. At the present day the old rules of form, cadence, and harmony are discarded; a studied simplification of melody, restless modulation, vague tonalities, and a preference for prose rhythms[2] prevail and indicate a radical change of method. The causes, direct and indirect, are varied. M. Bruneau attributes the new seriousness of French composers to the results of the disastrous war of 1870, and the misery and gloom which overshadowed France. Wagner's influence again penetrated through Opera to Song, realising the importance of the sound of words as well as their meaning, and equalising the importance of the instrumental part and the voice parts. Another incitement to change is based on the revival of the folk-song now used by modern song-writers, not only as a medium of national or local colour but as a source of inspiration.[3] Musicians, no less than painters, have their plein-air school. The love of

[1] Godard has been aptly described as a musician of the autumn or of the twilight (see French Music in the 19th Century, by Arthur Hervey).
[2] A. Bruneau, in La Musique Française, at p. 233, speaks of his efforts to combine prose with music, and adds that Saint-Saëns and he himself agree in thinking that in time prose will supplant poetry in drama and song.
[3] M. Tiersot truly remarks that 'the element of the folk-song vivifies and refreshes art, for it comes direct from the deepest source of inspiration in a nation.' But it is not only the spirit of the peasant's lyric and dramatic songs that modern composers have assimilated; they also make use of the old forms, such as the chansons à danser, ballades, and légendes. These are frequently found in Bruneau's and his contemporaries' works; and Charpentier, in his opera 'Louise,' has used the old cris-de-Paris as Clément Jannequin did centuries ago. Many composers also have thought it worth their while to collect and arrange the folk-songs; see for instance Vincent d'Indy's 'Chansons populaires recueillies dans le Vivarais,' and Bourgault-Ducoudray's beautiful volume of 'Trente mélodies populaires de la Basse-Bretagne.'

nature and its elements, of the earth and of the growths of the soil has asserted its empire in the kingdom of art.[1] But while the influence of the folk-song conduced to simplicity, another influence stamped French song with a new impress. César Franck (a Belgian by birth but a naturalised Frenchman), a profound scholar, an idealist by character and aims alike, raised the level of contemporary art to a greater seriousness, and gave it a more complete emancipation. In his works, depth of feeling, profound humanity and austere beauty combined with a consummate mastery of technique are undeniable qualities. But the special quality assimilated by the younger school of French song-writers is the element of mysticism. In César Franck's song, 'La Procession,' a noble simplicity and fervid mysticism are displayed, which exemplifies what has been said above. In adopting Franck's mysticism, it is stated that some of his followers have forfeited their race qualities of clearness of design and straight-forwardness of expression. But their gains are manifest if we study the songs of Gabriel Fauré, Vincent d'Indy, and Alfred Bruneau, and compare them with the romances and songs of the older school. Among this younger generation song-writing is on a far higher plane. Gabriel Fauré is a song-writer *par excellence*. Both in quality and quantity he ranks highest. His kinship with Schumann and César Franck is apparent, but withal he is original. The exquisite form of his melodies, the fancy displayed in his accompaniments, his whimsical, but always justified harmonies and modulations are all his own. In many of Fauré's songs there is a profound sadness and deep pathos, but without crudeness. Again, over others there is cast a dark veil of mysticism which necessitates an intimate knowledge of the songs before they can be appreciated. In A. Bruneau's songs there is more strength and freedom, humanity and realism, yet great rhythmical beauty. Vincent d'Indy's songs show extreme delicacy and refinement, but a somewhat morbid restlessness. Claude Debussy possesses originality, and a certain aloofness of thought. He seems to wish to express not what he feels and sees, but the passing impressions of his dreams and ideals, and the atmosphere of the poem he sets.

To the above names may be added many others who have treated the form of song with the same serious aims. The following have produced songs of real distinction and interest: G. Charpentier, Reynaldo Hahn, E. Chausson; also L. Wurmser, C. Blanc, E. Moret, P. de Bréville, H. Duparc, H. de Gorsse, E. Trémisot, L. Moreau, P. Vidal, G. Marty, S. Rousseau, Hillemacher frères, G. Ropartz, A. Chapuis, A. Gédalge, De Castillon, G. Hüe, M. Ravel, and many others.

It is necessary to add that modern French poets have had a great influence on these composers, and there exists a close sympathy between them. Obscurity of form, eccentricity, a feverish egoism which tends to over-subjectiveness, a subtlety which to an exaggerated degree substitutes suggestion for expression are the worst features of the school. An aptitude for intensity in the presentment of emotional themes, and an acute perception of the artistic values of personal emotion, a keen appreciation of evasive effects, of the fugitive and illusive beauty of sounds, implied or felt rather than heard,—these are amongst the gifts they have utilised to the full.

To sum up we may quote M. Bruneau's words,[2] that the young French song-writers have all the same aim in view, though they approach it by different roads. Some by the old healthy conventional methods, some through the free paths of life and nature, and others through the labyrinth of unreality and mysticism. But their aim is the same—that of pure art and beauty.

The folk-songs of France vary widely in every part, and each province is worthy of separate study. Fortunately a vast number of these songs have been carefully collected; and all that can be attempted here is to indicate the general characteristics, and refer the student to the various collections.[3] In Paris and the other large cities in France, the popular songs of the hour are only favourite tunes from comic operas, or those which have been heard at a café-chantant.[4] But in the country the real folk-songs still exist, and their distinct attributes are generally determined by the locality to which they belong. The airs of Southern France are distinguished by exuberant gaiety and graceful poetic sentiment. Many of them resemble the old Troubadour Songs, as for instance the well-known 'O Magali.'[5] The songs of Auvergne and Bourbonnais are chiefly *bourrées*, and Burgundy is rich in Noëls[6] and drinking-songs. The Bearnois airs are patriotic and melodious,[7] and their words mostly of love; while, on the other hand, the subjects of the songs of Normandy are generally supplied by the ordinary pursuits and occupations of life. The mill-songs and the begging-songs, called *chansons de part à Dieu*, are especially common in Normandy, and have a character of their own. The couplets of the former consist of two lines with a *refrain*. This *refrain*, in which the audience joins, forms the principal part of the song. The words are usually meaningless syllables of a merry kind, such as *tra la la*, or *ton reloton, ton tontaine, la tontaine*. But the *refrains* occur in the folk-songs of every part of France; each province having its own kind of *refrain* of apparent nonsense-syllables, which can only be explained in *patois*. The May-time songs of Champagne and Lorraine are very numerous and beautiful.[8] The character of the songs of Brittany has been best described by Rousseau: 'Les airs ne sont pas piquants, mais ils ont je ne sais quoi d'antique et de doux qui touche a la longue.' But their grave beauty

---

[1] Bruneau's 'Lieds de France,' and 'Chansons à Danser' form a striking example of the above qualities.

[2] *La Musique Française.*
[3] See especially Champfleury and Wekerlin's 'Chansons Populaires des provinces de France,' where individual examples are given from every part of France with interesting remarks.
[4] A few composers have attempted to supply songs of this kind, such as Pierre Dupont, who wrote for the *peuple*, Darcier for the *ouvrier*, and Nadaud for the *bourgeois* class.
[5] Ambros quotes the modern Provençal air as having a strong resemblance to an old dance-song, anterior in date even to the 12th century. *Geschichte der Musik*, ii. 242.
[6] Philibert le Duc has collected some curious Noëls in his 'Noëls Bressans.'
[7] Champfleury gives a beautiful old example: the 'Cantique Autonnat' by Jeanne d'Albret 'en accouchant Henri IV.'
[8] In nearly every *Chanson de Mai*, from Lorraine, the curious old word *Trimazo* occurs, the meaning of which is as obscure as that of the word *Trimousette* mentioned above.

and pathos can only be fully felt by those who have heard the peasants sing them. Georges Sand and G. de Nerval did much to arouse interest in the songs from Berry and the Île de France by describing the airs and the curious words and customs. But at the present day the folk-song is regarded from a more scientific point of view.

BIBLIOGRAPHY

Burney, Dr. *History of Music* (especially vol. ii.). 1776-89.
Delaborde, J. B., and Roussier, P. J. *Essai sur la Musique.* Paris, 1780.
Grétry, A. E. M. *Mémoires ou Essais sur la Musique.* Paris, 1796.
Toulmon, Bottée de. *De la Chanson Mus. en France.* Paris, 1836.
Wolf, F. *Ueber die Lais.* Heidelberg, 1841.
Scudo, J. P. *Critique et Littérature musicales.* Paris, 1850, 1859.
Chouquet, G. *Les Chants Nationaux de la France* (*L'Art Musical,* October 1867).
Ambros, A. W. *Geschichte der Musik* (especially vols. ii. and iii.).
Fétis, F. J. *Histoire générale de la Musique* (especially vol. iv.). 1869.
Bartsch, C. *Romances et Pastourelles.* Leipzig, 1870.
Hueffer, F. *The Troubadours.* 1878.
Douen, E. O. *Clément Marot et le Psautier Huguenot.* 1878.
David, E., et Lussy, M. *Histoire de la Notation musicale.* Paris, 1882.
Jullien, A. *Musiciens d'aujourd'hui.* Paris, 1882.
Tiersot, J. *Histoire de la Chanson pop. en France.* Paris, 1889.
Lavoix, H. *La Musique française.* 1891.
Imbert, H. *Profils de Musiciens.* Paris, 1888. *Portraits et Etudes.* Paris, 1894.
Bruneau, A. *La Musique française,* 1901.
Hervey, A. *Masters of French Music,* 1894; *French Music in the XIXth Cent.* 1904.
Dietz, F. *Leben und Werke der Troubadours.* Breslau, 1862-82.

COLLECTIONS [1]

Capelle, P. ' La Clé du Caveau,' 2nd ed. 1816.
Rivarez, Fréderic. ' Chansons et airs pop. du Béarn.' Pau, 1844.
Bouillet, J. B. ' Album Auvergnat.' Moulins, 1848.
Wekerlin, J. B. ' Echos du Temps passé.' Paris, 1855.
Kastner, Georges. ' Les Voix de Pris.' Paris, 1857.
Dumersan, and Colet, H. ' Chants et Chansons Populaires de la France.' Paris, 1860.
Champfleury, et Wekerlin, J. B. ' Chansons Populaires des provinces de France.' Paris, 1860.
Arbaud, Damas. ' Chants pop. de la Provence.' Aix, 1862-64.
Gagnon, E. ' Chansons pop. du Canada.' Quebec, 1864, 1880, 1894, and 1900.
Puymaigre, B. de. ' Chants Populaires recueillis dans le pays Messin.' Paris and Metz, 1865.
Nisard, M. E. C. ' Des Chansons populaires.' Paris, 1867.
Villemarqué, Hersat de la. ' Barzas Breiz, Chants populaires de la Bretagne.' Paris, 1867.
Paris, Gaston, et Gevaert, A. ' Chansons du XVe siècle.' Paris, 1875.
Montel et Lambert. ' Chants pop. de Languedoc.' Paris, 1880.
Rolland, E. ' Recueil de Chansons populaires.' Paris, 1885.
Bourgault-Ducoudray, L. A. ' Trente mélodies populaires de la Basse-Bretagne.' 1885.
Tiersot, Julien. ' Mélodies pop. des provinces de France.' 3 vols. Paris, 1887, 1890-91.
d'Indy, V., et Tiersot, J. ' Chansons recueillies dans le Vivarais et le Vercors.' Paris, 1892.
Bugeaud, J. ' Chants et Chansons pop. de l'Ouest.' 1895.
Tiersot, J. ' Chansons pop. des Alpes françaises.' Grenoble, 1903.
Wekerlin, J. B. ' Chansons pop. du Pays de France.' 2 vols. Paris, 1903.
Guillerm, H. ' Recueil de Chants pop. bretons du Pays de Cornouailles.' Rennes, 1905.
Branchet, L., et Plantades, J. ' Chansons pop. du Limousin.' Paris, 1905.
Wekerlin, J. B. ' Chansons pop. de l'Alsace.'
Doncieux, G. ' Le Romancero pop. de la France.'

Numerous old collections of French polyphonic songs are mentioned in Tiersot's *Histoire de la Chanson pop. en France.* Paris, 1889.

(The writer is also indebted to Mr. Walter Ford for permission to quote from his Lectures on French Song, 1905.)

SPAIN AND THE BASQUE COUNTRY

In Spain and Portugal the Song can scarcely be said to have a history. While both countries can boast of numerous celebrated composers of secular and ecclesiastical polyphonic music, in neither has there been any systematic development on the monodic side. The latter remains what it was in the earliest times ; and all the best songs of Spain and Portugal are the compositions of untaught and unlettered musicians. With regard to these folk-songs

---

[1] Most of the collections contain valuable information about the songs given.

---

there is an initial difficulty in determining whether they are more properly songs or dances, because the favourite songs of Spain are, with a few exceptions,[2] sung as accompaniments to dancing.

Spanish literature is rich in remains of antique poetry, and of poetry which from the time of the Troubadours was intended to be sung. The art of these singers, called *La gaya Ciencia* or *Gaya-Saber,* soon crossed over the border from southern France, and flourished especially in the Courts of Aragon and Castile. The words referred chiefly to the adventures of heroes defending their country against the Moors, and dealt with their deeds of chivalry and gallantry ; but the dialect, melodies, and even the notation so forcibly remind one of their Provençal origin, that it is scarcely necessary to dwell on the subject [see FRANCE]. Besides her *Trobadores* Spain had also her *Juglares*[3] (*Jongleurs*) and *Zaharrones,* who were of a lower class than the *Juglares.*[4] Like France, Spain counted kings, princes, and nobles among her *Trobadores* ; for instance, Alfonso II. and X., Pedro III. and IV., the Infante D. Federigo, afterwards King of Sicily, Hugo de Mataplana, Giraldo de Cabrera, Manuel de Esca, Pons de Ortafá, etc. The most prominent names of later *Trobadores* were Pedro Lopez de Ayala, Fernan Perez de Guzman, Sanchez Calavera, and Ausius Marc, called the Spanish Petrarch.[5]

Among the most precious relics Spain possesses are two parchment volumes preserved in the Library of the Escurial. The first contains over 400 *Cantigas* (called the *Cantigas de Santa Maria*), with numerous melodies, some in *gallego* and Portuguese dialect, and some in the Castilian of that time. The second volume consists of 200 *Noventas* in the same languages and in the same musical notation. These were composed in the 13th century by the Troubadour King, Alfonso el Sabio ; but Soriano Fuertes[6] thinks some are of older date, and were only collected by Alfonso. A third MS. (formerly at Toledo) is in the Biblioteca Nacional at Madrid. Nearly all the songs which have their melodies attached to them, are sacred, relating to miracles or various festivals. It is unfortunate that the secular tunes were not preserved ; but the reason probably was that these were improvised by the *Juglares,* and too popular and well known to need writing down.[7] The following example[8] reduced to modern notation by Ambros, is entitled :—

---

[2] Such as the *cañas* and *playeras.*
[3] There were also *Joglaresas, i.e.* women who roamed about with *Joglares* (or Juglares), chiefly as players. *Paleografía Española,* P. Estevan de Terreros, 1758, p. 82.
[4] Marqués de Pidal gives a good account of the *Juglares* in his *Introduccion al Cancionero de Baena sobre la poesia del siglo XIV. y XV.*
[5] *Historia de la Musica Española,* Mariano Soriano Fuertes, i. 93, 123 *et seq.*
[6] Soriano Fuertes, i. 96.
[7] The poems (without the music) were edited by the Marqués de Valmar and published in 1889.
[8] Soriano Fuertes gives numerous examples at the end of vol. i. of his history.

Prologo des milagros y loores de S. Maria.

Ex. 1.

Por - que tro - - bar   e cou - sa en

que iaz   en - ten - di - - - - men-to

po - ren   quen - - - - o   faz, etc.

The 'Cancionero musical de los Siglos XV. y XVI.,' edited in 1890 by Francisco Asenjo Barbieri, is in the library of the Royal Palace at Madrid, and contains nearly 500 sacred and secular songs in parts.[1] Juan del Eucina is one of the principal contributors, and about sixty other native composers are named ; but many of the songs are anonymous.   Close examination will show that the Spaniards of the 15th century stood nearly as high as the French and the Italians in music. Similar and also somewhat later collections exist in Toledo and Seville. Among such literary relics are the celebrated *cancioneros* and *romanceros* of the 15th and 16th centuries, in which a great number of *canciones, invenciones, preguntas, villancicos,* and ballads will be found.[2] The *romanceros* consist chiefly of ballads in 8 - syllabled verse in assonance, the vowels only rhyming. The tunes are stated to have been transmitted by blind ballad-singers who sang them in the streets ; and not one note of music was written down. But these old ballads are still sung by the people in Spain to traditional airs which have passed from mouth to mouth through many generations.

The *villancicos* have always been an important feature in the musical life of Spain.   The term has been variously applied : it may mean the sacred songs sung at great festivals,[3] or it may apply to the peasant's songs in general with their refrains or burdens[4] (*estribillos*), but most probably the *villancicos* of Spain answer to the *noëls* of France.[5] Towards the close of the 15th century secular music was introduced into the churches in order to induce the congregation to join in the singing. Miracle plays and mysteries (especially those relating to the Nativity) were also allowed to be held in the churches, and to the chanted dialogues between

priest and people, the name *villancicos* was given. The greater number refer to the Nativity, such as the following example, which dates about the end of the 15th century :—

Ex. 2.

A-qua do bon   Rey   Da - vid   Da seu li -

- nage de - cen - - - - de, Unbra le cre - - - - da

mi.   De quen   por al - la   mal pren - - de.

There are numerous *villancicos* of later date, and those for six voices by Puebla and the collections of P. de Ruimente,[6] S. Raval, Araniez,[7] and Pardiñas[8] prove that learned musicians turned their attention to them. But in proportion to the quantity of extant words very little of the music has come down to us. Other church festivals, such as the Feast of the Asses (in memory of the Flight into Egypt), the Feast of the Fools, and of the Innocents contain burlesque *villancicos* with long nonsensical verses.[9] (See NOËL, vol. iii. p. 385.) Still, in Spain, the tone of these songs was never so indecorous as in the northern countries of Europe.

For historic reasons there was frequent and close intercourse between Spain and the Netherlands, and many Flemish composers are known to have resided in Spain, and left the deep impress of their learned school. But although many of the Spanish polyphonic composers may have used Flemish folk-songs for their masses and motets, there are scarcely any Spanish folk-songs preserved in this way. A few exceptions may be mentioned, such as, 'Una musque de buscgaya,' used by Josquin des Prés[10] :—

Ex. 3.

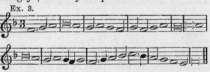

and 'Nunquam fue pena mayor' by P. de la Rue.

On the other hand, there are also many Spanish folk-song survivals in Jewish worship-music.

A most interesting and trustworthy record of the songs of the 16th century is to be found in a book, written in Latin by Franceso de Salinas of Burgos, who died in 1590.[11] In his chapter on rhythm, Salinas quotes as examples numerous popular songs of his period, belonging

[1] See also *Oxford Hist. of Music,* ii. 306 *et seq.,* H. Wooldridge.
[2] The fashion of making such collections, generally called *cancioneros,* was very common in Spain just before and after the introduction of printing ; and many, both printed and in manuscript, have been well preserved. Juan P. Riaño, in his *Notes on Early Spanish Music,* gives descriptions and examples of over seventy medieval MSS. existing chiefly in Toledo and Madrid, and ranging from the 10th to the 16th century. The Bibliothèque Nat., Paris, contains no less than seven collections. See *Cataloga de MSS. Españoles en la Biblioteca Real de Paris,* 378-526, Paris, 1844. See also Ticknor's *History of Spanish Literature,* xxiii. 391.
[3] Riemann.
[4] Soriano Fuertes derives the term from the peasant's songs called *villanas,* i. 92.
[5] Fétis derives *villancicos* from *villano*—peasant, because the shepherds were the first to announce the birth of Our Lord, and most *villancicos* were Nativity Plays or Songs. *Histoire gen. de la Mus.* v. 144.

[6] 'El Parnaso Español de Madrigales y Villancicos' for several voices, published at Antwerp like so much other Spanish music.
[7] 'Villancicos de Natividad,' 1624.
[8] To Pardiñas are also attributed those *Cantares gallegos* which, like the *villancicos,* were sung by troops of pilgrims.
[9] Soriano Fuertes, i. 217, gives a song from the Feast of the Asses. See also Fétis, v. 130 *et seq.* for variants of same.
[10] Printed in Petrucci's 'Canti C. numero Cento Cinquanta,' 1503. This tune was also used by H. Isaak. See Ambros, ii. 293.
[11] Several editions of the book of this learned blind organist were issued at Salamanca between 1577 and 1592.

to various districts. This gives us the authentic age of many tunes still heard in Spain, such as:

Ex. 4.

Ca - sò-me il pa-dre con un ca-ba - lle-ro Ca-da ho - ra mi
lla - ma hi - ja di un pe-chero y yo no lo say.

The national songs of Spain widely differ in the several provinces, and it is the easiest plan to divide them into four geographical groups: (1) those of Biscay and Navarre; (2) Galicia and Old Castile; (3) Southern Spain (Andalusia, etc.); (4) Eastern Spain (Catalonia). In the first of these groups are the songs of the Basques, who are believed to be the oldest inhabitants of the Peninsula.

(1) The exclusiveness with which the Basques have kept themselves a distinct and separate race has made it difficult, if not impossible, to trace their music to any primeval source.[1] Even at first glance we see that the Basque songs and dances have nothing in common with the Greco-Roman or mediæval music.[2] Therefore if the music of the Basques is of great antiquity, it must have sprung up under wholly different conditions from that of other nations. It has a strange affinity with modern music, but this modern effect may be due to the constant use of the leading note and the rapid and incessant changes of key. The Basque melodies are not founded on any particular scale; augmented intervals, whole tones, semitones, and even quarter-tones are freely intermixed, and a curious result is obtained by the constant repetition of a short phrase with alternating major and minor thirds. The time and rhythm of the Basque songs are irregular and complicated. The zorzico, for instance, is in 5–8 or 7–4 time thus:—

Ex. 5.

O id o gui-puz-coa nos en-sen ei-lla-can-cion . . . .
etc.

But generally the bar has two beats, a weak and strong, which alternate in position. The first note of a song is usually surrounded by a grupetto,[3] which gives it an indefinite and uncertain effect. The grupetto, though less elaborate, also sometimes occurs before, or on the last note of a song (see above), but usually the last note has a firm, loud, and long-sustained

sound. The rhythmical grouping of the phrases is absolutely irregular; the periods are unequal in number, and none corresponds with the other. In many cases the last bar of a period is at the same time the beginning of a new melodic phrase. Even the short and comparatively simple 'Sant Basque,' which F. Michel quotes (Le Pays Basque, p. 541) as the most popular tune which the Basques possess, is surprisingly irregular. This imperfect description gives, however, little idea of the originality and peculiar charm of the music of this people; like their language it stands apart.

In Aragon and Navarre the popular dance is the jota, and according to the usage of Spain it is also the popular song. The jota is almost always sung in thirds, and has the peculiarity that in the ascending scale the minor seventh is sung in place of the major. (See JOTA.)

(2) The songs of the second group are less interesting. The rule of the Moors over Galicia and Old Castile was too brief to impart an Eastern colouring to the music of those provinces. It is, however, gay and bright, and of a strongly accented dance-rhythm. The words of the songs are lively, like the music, and in perfect accord with it. To this geographical group belong the boleros, manchegas, and seguidillas, but this last class of songs is also heard in the Moorish provinces. Examples are given in every collection, and as they are also referred to under their own headings in this work, it is not necessary to dwell on them here.

(3) The third group is the most worthy of study. Of all true Spanish songs those of Andalusia are the most beautiful. In them the Eastern element is richest and deepest, and the unmistakable sign of its presence are the following traits: first, a profusion of ornaments around the central melody; secondly, a 'polyrhythmic' cast of music—the simultaneous existence of different rhythms in different parts; and thirdly the peculiarity of the melodies being based on a curious scale, founded apparently on the Phrygian and Mixolydian modes.[4] Another indication of the oriental element is the guttural sound of the voices. Of these characteristics the most obvious is the rhythm. In the Andalusian songs there are often three different rhythms in one bar, none predominating, but each equally important as the different voices are in real polyphonic music. For example:—

Ex. 6.

[1] There has been a good deal of speculation on this point. It is not necessary to put forward the numerous conjectures as to its origin or to its relationship with other European nations, but the writer has noticed a certain likeness between the Basque tunes and those of other nations of Turanian origin, such as the Hungarians and Finns. M. Georges Amé, in an article on Iztueta's collection of Basque dance-tunes, remarks 'that many remind him of Haydn, which is quite possible when we think how many of Haydn's melodies are borrowed from Hungarian themes.'

[2] These remarks are taken from Euskara, an organ in the interest of the Basque Society, and quoted by W. Brambach.

[3] Madame de Villéhélio speaks in her collection of 'Airs Basques' of 'une sorte de grupetto intraduisible, qui est à la phrase musicale ce qu'est une paraphe précurseur d'une majuscule dans certaines exercises calligraphiques.'

[4] Introduction to the Study of National Music, C. Engel.

Or it may be that the accents of the accompaniment do not at all correspond with the accents of the melody ; thus :—

Ex. 7.

The songs of Southern Spain are generally of a dreamy, melancholy, passionate type ; especially the *cañas* and *playeras* which are lyrical. These are mostly for one voice only, as their varied rhythm and uncertain time preclude the possibility of their being sung in parts. In some cases they are, however, sung in unison or in thirds. They always begin with a high note sustained as long as the breath will allow ; and then the phrase descends with innumerable turns, trills, and embellishments into the real melody. The *cañas* are inferior as regards simplicity, both of poetry and music, to the dance-songs—*fandangos, rondeñas*, and *malagueñas*,[1] which have also more symmetry and animation. They usually consist of two divisions : the *copla* (couplet), and the *ritornel*, which is for the accompanying instrument, and is frequently the longer and the more important of the two, the skilful guitar-player liking to have ample scope to exhibit his execution.

(4) In Catalonia and the adjacent provinces, where the Provençal language has predominated since the 9th century, the songs are of a totally different character from those of the rest of Spain. Like the language, the songs both in melody and rhythm have far more in common with those of Southern France. The subjects, too, of the folk-songs are often identical, as for instance, ' La bona viuda ' and the French ' Jean Renaud,' [2] though the tunes vary :—

Ex. 8.

Ma-re mi-a, ma-re, sen-to gran ru - i-do
Ne son las cam - bre-ras, que sal-ten y riu-hen.

Yo no dor-mo no, no es-tich à dormida.

The time is constantly altered during the Catalan songs, and a great quantity possess

---

[1] Songs and dances often derive their name from the provinces or towns in which they are indigenous ; thus *rondeña* from Ronda, *malagueña* from Malaga.

[2] The many varying versions of this famous song, known in Italy as ' Comte Angiolino ' and in Brittany and Scandinavia as ' Sire nan,' and ' Sire Olaf,' are familiar to all students of folk-lore. A. Branchet and Gaston Paris have published articles on this song in the *Revue critique d'histoire et de littérature*. It is remarkable how many Catalan songs have their counterparts among Scandinavian songs, especially as regards the words.

---

tornadas (refrains or burdens), which are an intrinsic part of the song, and may occur in the middle or at the end, as in ' La dama d' Arago.' This is one of the most popular songs in Catalonia :—

Ex. 9.

A - ra - gó n'hi ha una da-ma, qu'es bo - ni - ca com un sol, te la ca - be - lle - ra ros - sa li arri - - - - - ba fins als ta - lons. Ay a - mo - - ro-sa Agua Ma - ri - a rob-a - - - do-ra del a - mor ay del a - mor.

Numbers of old ballads of great length, epic, lyrical, and dance-songs will be found with valuable notes in a collection of ' Cants populars Catalans ' by Francesch Pelay Briz.[3] The religious or legendary songs are especially numerous, and the melodies are very beautiful.[4] The old Provençal troubadour spirit seems to have lingered in many of the lovely little lyrics still sung in Catalonia, and both words and music might belong to that bygone age.

A few words must be said on three essentially national forms of music which have helped to preserve the songs of Spain. The *villancicos* have been already dealt with, and there remain the *tonadillas* and *zarzuelas*. In the early part of the 17th century the *tonadillas* were indiscriminately called *cuatros de empezar, tons, tonadas*, and *tonadillas*, and were pieces sung by women-voices in theatres before the raising of the curtain. The words were chosen from favourite poets and set to popular tunes ; they had nothing to do with the acted piece or opera.[5] Later all kinds of *tonadillas* existed, alternately idyllic or burlesque ; and composers (like for instance Rodriguez de Hita) turned their attention to this form, and cleverly interwove such national dances as the *bolero, jota, tiraña*, or *seguidillas*, and the street-cries of the towns. It may be incidentally remarked that the street-cries, called *los pregones*, are a distinct feature in Spanish town-life. They vary in the different districts and according to the time of year. The following example is centuries old [6] :—

---

[3] See Collections at end.

[4] The Passion songs which are sung from door to door during Lent are among the best. St. Peter and the cock are especially dwelt on in nearly all. ' La Passio ' in vol. iii. of Pelay Briz's collection is a remarkably fine example.

[5] Soriano Fuertes gives many examples in his fourth volume.

[6] From a letter from Antonio Machada y Alvarez to S. D. J. Pitré, 1882.

Ex. 10.

LOS PREGONES.

Cantes del florero.

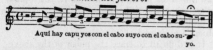

Aqui hay capu yos con el cabo suyo con el cabo su-yo.

The ZARZUELAS form the most truly national part of Spanish art. They are described in their own place.

In the art-songs of Spain there is nothing on which it is profitable to dwell. If publishers' collections may be accepted as evidence, the favourite song-writers would appear to be Tapia, Yradier, Sors, Garcia, Leon, Barbieri, Murgia, Saldoni, Eslava, Arietta, Albeniz, Perez, Cuellar, Tadeo. But although most of these composers have made contributions to song-literature, they have won higher laurels in other branches of music.[1] The limited capabilities of the guitar and mandoline—the invariable accompanying instruments—have naturally dwarfed and stunted the development of accompaniments in Spanish songs.

BIBLIOGRAPHY

Terreros y Pando, Estevan de. *Paleografia Española.* Madrid, 1758.
Ticknor, G. *History of Spanish Literature.* New York, 1849.
Soriano Fuertes, Mariano. *Historia de la Musica Española.* 4 vols. Madrid, 1855-59.
Michel, Francisque. *Le Pays Basque.* Paris, 1857.
Milá y Fontanals. *De los Trovadores en España.* Barcelona, 1861.
Mendel. *Spanische Musik.* (*Mus. Con. Lex.*)
Menendez y Pelayo, M. *Historia de las ideas estéticas en España.* Madrid, 1883.
Riaño, Juan F. *Critical and Bibliographical Notes on Early Spanish Music.* Quaritch, London, 1887.
Brambach, W. *Ueber baskische Musik.* (*Vierteljahrsschrift,* 1887.)
Ridal, Marques de. *Introduccion al Cancionero de Baena, sobre la poesia del siglo XIV. y XV.*
Vinson, J. *Le folk-lore du Pays Basque.* Paris, 1888.
Asenjo Barbieri, Francisco. *Cancionero musical de los siglos XV. y XVI. transcrito y comentado.* Madrid, 1890.
Soubies, A. *Musique Espagnole.* 1899.
Pedrell, Felipe. *Folk-lore musical Castillan du XVI. siècle. Sammelbände* of the I.M.G. 1900, vol. iii.

COLLECTIONS

Kestner, H. 'Auswahl spanischer und portugiesischer Lieder.' Hanover, 1846-59.
Abaud, D. 'Chants pop. de la Provence' (contains many Catalonian songs). Aix, 1862-64.
Caballero, F. 'Cuentos y Poesias populares Andaluces.' Leipzig, 1864.
Berggreen, A. P. 'Spanske Folke-Sange og Melodier.' Copenhagen, 1866.
Pelay Briz, F., Candi, C., and Salto, J. 'Cansons de la Terra' (Cants populars Catalans). Barcelona, 1866-74.
Lacome, P., et Puig y Alsubide, J. ' Echos d'Espagne.' Paris, 1872.
Ocon, Dr. E. y Rivas. 'Cantos Españoles.' Malaga, 1874.
Demofilo. 'Coleccion de Cantos flamencos.' Seville, 1881.[2]
Fouquier, A. 'Chants populaires Espagnols.' Paris, 1882.
Rodriguez Marin, F. 'Cantos populares Españoles.' Seville, 1882-83.
Bertran y Bros, P. 'Cansons y Follies populars.' Barcelona, 1885.
Calleja, R. 'Cantos de la montaña.' Madrid, 1901.
Murphy, Don G. 'Die spanischen Lautenmeister des 16ten Jahrhundert' (contains many songs for one voice). Leipzig, 1902.
Olmeda, F. 'Folklore de Castilla, ó Cancionero popular de Burgos.' Seville, 1903.
Rouenet, J., et Gafil, E. N. 'Répertoire de musique Arabe et Maure.' Alger (en cours de publication), 1905.
Wolff, O. 'Album Spanischer Volkslieder und Gesänge.' Berlin.
Inzenga, J. 'Cantos y Bailes populares de España.' Madrid.
Nunez Robres, L. 'Coleccion de Cantos Españoles.' Madrid.

BASQUE COLLECTIONS

Iztueta's and Moldizteguian's collections of Basque music. 1824 and 1826 (consisting chiefly of dance-tunes).
Santesteban, J. A. 'Coll. de aires Vascongadas.' San Sebastian, 1860.
Salaberry, J. D. J. 'Chants populaires du Pays basques.' Bayonne, 1870.
Santesteban, J. A. 'Chansons basques.' Bayonne, 1870.

[1] See ESLAVA.
[2] The 'Cantos Flamencos' are songs of three or four verses in the Andalusian dialect, composed by the gipsies, and are rarely printed in collections.

Bordes, C. 'Cent chansons populaires basques.' Paris, 1894.
Bordes, C. '12 noëls basques anciens.' Paris, 1897.
Villéhélio, Mme. de. 'Douze airs basques.'
Lamazou's 'Chants Pyrénéens' contains many Basque songs.
De Puymaigre's 'Chants pop. de la vallée d'Ossau' contains many Basque songs.

PORTUGAL

The folk-music of Portugal bears a close affinity to that of Spain, especially in dance-songs. But there are certain clearly-marked differences. The Portuguese is more pensive and tranquil than the fiery excitable Spaniard ; and as all national music is more or less a reflection of racial characteristics, there is a repose and subdued melancholy, and an absence of exaggeration in Portuguese music, qualities seldom found in the more vivacious and stirring music of Spain. From the same cause, and perhaps because the Moorish ascendancy was of briefer duration in Portugal than in Spain, there is less ornament in what music remains to us of an undoubtedly oriental character. The poetry of the two countries has also much in common. Most of the Portuguese epics are of Spanish origin, and even at the present day the Spanish and Portuguese romance forms are almost identical.

In the lyrics of both races the rhyme follows the assonance principle, and is a more important element than the metre. Moreover, the national poets of Portugal used the Castilian language for centuries as much as their own, especially for poetry intended to be sung.

Portugal is less rich than her neighbour in collections of early music. And unfortunately a mass of valuable manuscript and printed music which existed in the splendid library founded by King D. João IV. (1604-56), perished in the Lisbon earthquake in 1755. Much was also destroyed during the demolition of the monasteries and convents which followed the revolution of 1834.

The earliest and most important musical records preserved in Portugal belong to the Troubadour period.[3] D. Diniz, sixth King of Portugal (1279-1325), who founded a university with a chair for music at Coimbra, was a grandson of Alfonso el Sabio, and well versed in the art of the Troubadours. Of D. Diniz's bastard sons D. Pedro, Count of Barcellos, and D. Alfonso Sancho we have nine *trovas*, and a *cancioneiro*[4] consisting of the work of their father and of 127 other Portuguese troubadours. Two copies are extant ; one in the Vatican and one in the Ajuda at Lisbon. The former has the melody indicated for each line, and the other has pictures of the various musical instruments then in use.[5] The *Jogral* (*jongleur*) also

[3] Soriano Fuertes, in his *Historia de la musica Española*, i. 117, gives a hymn of a somewhat earlier date, written by D. Francisco Contiño, Count of Marialva, in the same notation as Alfonso el Sabio used.
[4] A *cancionero* always means a collection of romances. *Trova* has the same meaning as in Provence, only the term continued to be applied in Portugal to all extemporised songs, until the 18th century (*Portugiesische Musik*, Mendel's *Lexikon*) (Platon von Waxel).
[5] *Trovas e Cantares do Conde de Barcellos*, F. A. von Varnhagen, Madrid, 1849.

played an important part in Troubadour life in Portugal ; and the last was Gil Vicente (1470-1536), at once poet, actor, musician, and composer. His works, which give interesting information about the various customs and forms of song of his time,[1] are written partly in Portuguese and partly in Castilian. Interspersed in his pieces are *vilhancetes, cançonetas, cantigas, romances, cançoes pastoris, cantigas de berço, cantigas maritimas,* etc. ; and in his *enselladas* songs with Latin and French words also occur, such as the *chanson,* 'Ay de la noble ville de Paris.'

The *vilhancetes* or *vilhancicos, autos,* and *loãs* were similar to the Spanish in character ; semi-sacred, popular, and yet a form which learned musicians adopted and elaborated, such as Fr. Francisco de Santiago, Gabriel Diaz, and many contrapuntists from Duarte Lobo's celebrated school, as, for instance, Felipe de Magalhães and Lesbio. The earliest *vilhancicos* we hear of were those by Juan del Encina[2] and Gil Vicente[3] in the late 15th century, and the last by the Abbot Luiz Calisto da Costa e Feria in 1723.[4]

The old Pagan festivals and the mediæval Christian festivals blended in Portugal as elsewhere, and heritages from those times are the *Maias* and *Janeiras* songs. These festival songs are still sung on certain days of the year ; the principal ones are 'O São João,' sung on St. John the Baptist's Day (Midsummer) ; 'As Janeiras,' sung at the New Year ; and 'Os Reis,' sung at the Epiphany.[5]

Various forms of songs are given in the works of the poets of the Renaissance, Ribeiro, Juan del Encina, Gil Vicente, Sà de Miranda, and Camoëns, and these were clearly intended to be sung, as the accompanying instruments and the manner of singing them are frequently recorded.[6] Many are identical with the Troubadour forms, for example the *serranhilha* and *solão,* which answer to the *pastoralla* and *soula.* We read also of the *endeixas* or funeral songs ; the *celeumas* sung in chorus by sailors or workmen ;[7] the *descantes* which are always 8-syllabled and

have *estribilhos* (refrains), and the *sonetos.* And among the dance-songs the *xacara* (a gipsy song) and the *chula* which is similar to it, the *captiva* or *mourisca* and the *judenga.* The two latter naturally disappeared with the expulsion of the Moors and Jews.[8]

It is difficult to trace the music of the above-mentioned songs. Still no one can deny the antiquity of many of the *cantigas* and *cançoes* still sung among the peasants in the country districts of Portugal ; and here, unlike Spain, the dance-songs are not more prevalent than other kinds. In some the oriental element is still evident ; there is a careless ease, tinged with melancholy about them, which is the secret of their charm. They are generally sung by one voice without any accompaniment ; and to the ears of foreigners have the sound of recitatives, as the rhythm is often wholly obscured by the singer.[9] The following little song, which the women sing whilst reaping, always inventing new verses, is a fair example :—

Ex. 1.

Foi me acci-fa　ao Por-to San - to As ce - a-ras ama - re-las.

And on the plains the shepherds and labourers may be heard any evening chanting in a minor key, with a pointless, halting measure and vague rhythm *cantigas* which are purely Moorish in character.[10] In the province of Minho it is quite common to hear one peasant in his harsh, guttural Eastern voice challenge another to sing one or more verses against him. The curious custom for the men and women to sing in fourths and fifths still exists in the southern province of Alemtejo. This example, wholly Moorish in character, was heard on a popular feast-day in the little town of S. Thiago do Cacem in 1897[11] :—

Ex. 2.　　　　　*Ribandeira.*

Although the words *cantiga* and *cançao* are used indiscriminately for all kinds of songs, the so-called *Cantiges das ruas* are a special form, and chiefly sung in the towns by blind beggars. Many of the tunes are very old,

1 It is said that Erasmus learnt Portuguese simply to be able to read Gil Vicente's works. Several volumes of various editions are in the British Museum.

2 It is doubtful whether Juan del Encina is Spanish or Portuguese.

3 Gil Vicente was among the first to write *autos,* ' religious pieces resembling in their nature the miracle - plays common all over Europe at the time. . . . Most of these are Christmas pieces, and the dramatists often took advantage of the story of the shepherds to introduce the elements of what may be called pastoral comedy.' *History of Portugal,* by Morse Stephens.

4 Vasconcellos, ii. 191.

5 ' As Janeiras' and ' Os Reis ' are especially sung on the respective eves of the New Year and of the Epiphany. The minstrels go from door to door in the evening, singing the praises of the inmates of the house, and accompanying their songs with metal triangles, bells, etc. They are generally rewarded by the master of the house with money, sausages, or dried figs. But if they get nothing they sing :—

'Esta casa cheira a bren
Aqui mora algum Juden.'

(This house smells of tar ; some Jew lives here) ; or else—

' Esta casa cheira a unto
Aqui mora algum defunto.'

(This house smells of ointment ; there is a dead body in it).

6 Gil Vicente speaks of ' the pleasing way the *sonetos* were sung with guitar accompaniment.' See Th. Braga's *Historia da Litteratura Portugueza,* vol. viii. p. 228.

7 See Camoëns, *Lusiads,* ii. 15.

8 See *Portugiesische Musik,* Mendel's *Mus. Con. Lex.* p. 499 *et seq.* (Platon von Waxel).

9 Nos. 3, 7, and 11 of J. A. Ribas's collection give some idea of this kind of song, but they are spoilt by their accompaniment.

10 It is curious that in the mountainous parts of Portugal no Arab music is heard. The voices also are sweeter.

11 Sent by D. Augustò Machado (Director of the Lisbon Conservatoire) to A. Hammerich. *Studien über isländische Musik, Sammelbände,* I.M.G. 1899, p. 341.

but the words are constantly changed.[1] The *fado* is the most purely national type of dance-song which exists in Portugal, and it has always maintained its integrity.[2] It is seldom heard outside towns, and properly belongs to the lowest classes of the population, though during the last century it acquired popularity among the higher classes.[3] The guitar (which is much less used than in Spain) is always employed for the *fados*, and has a strongly rhythmical and uniform accompaniment :—

Ex. 3.

There are many varieties of *fados* and *fadinhos* in the different towns, but they are all binary in form and have the same rhythm.

Except during the period when the Netherlanders exercised their influence upon the ecclesiastical music of Portugal (that is, during the 16th and 17th centuries) this country can claim no great composers, nor school of its own. For when not avowedly borrowing various forms from other countries, Portugal fell unconsciously under their influence. The *trovas* (Troubadour songs) were merely adopted Provençal forms, the *vilhancicos*, *autos*, and *loãs* were borrowed from Spain and France ; the polyphonic 17th century *tonos* were in reality Italian madrigals written to Spanish words, with *estribilhos* added to them. And late in the 18th century all attempts to form a national opera failed, owing to the invasion of the Italian opera, which has exercised complete hold over Portuguese music for the last two centuries.

It is only in two small and unimportant forms of vocal music, the *fado* and the *modinha*, that Portugal can claim to have created and established a distinct genre of her own. Of the *fados* we have already spoken. The *modinha*, which is the only kind of art-song that Portugal has as yet produced, is, moreover, the direct offspring of the Italian opera. Though written by trained musicians and sung by educated people, neither as regards form nor character can the *modinhas* be assigned high rank as artistic music. Still they have retained their popularity from early in the 18th century down to the present day, and are written as a matter of course by every Portuguese composer.

These *modinhas*, or Portuguese romances, are of a literary as well as a musical form.[4] The first mention of them occurred in the so-called ' Jewish operas,'[5] which rapidly became popular. In the burgher classes *modinhas* remained simple sentimental melodies ; but at the Court and among the more educated classes they developed into highly elaborate brilliant arias, and celebrated composers and poets did not disdain to use this form. In Das Neves' *Cancioneiro de Musicas populares* there are twelve songs (*Modinhas*) from Gonzagas' *Marilia de Dirceu*, which, according to good evidence,[6] were set to music by Marcos Antonio, better known as Portogallo. In 1793 F. D. Milcent published a monthly *Jornal de Modinhas* at Lisbon, from which the following example is taken, to show the brilliant type of *modinha* :—

Ex. 4.
Moda a Solo del S. Ant. da S. Leite M. de Capela no Porte.

Adagio.

Tem - - po que bre - - - ve pas

- - sas - - - - ti que bre - - ve pas - - -

- - sas - - - - - ti tar - de, etc.

Since the 16th century, when Portugal colonised Brazil, there has been continual intercourse between these countries ; and during the first quarter of the 19th century, whilst the Portuguese Court was domiciled in Brazil, the *modinhas* were as fashionable there as in Portugal. But they differed in character ; the *modinhas brasileiras* were always very primitive in form, devoid of workmanship, somewhat vulgar, but expressive and gay. In short, a mixture between the French *romance* of the 18th century and *couplets* from the vaudevilles. And this description applies to the type of Portuguese *modinhas* of the present day, which are written for one or two voices, strophic in form, with easy guitar or pianoforte accompaniments.

A complete list of greater and lesser composers, who have tried their hand at this form of song, is too long to give, but the following are amongst the most celebrated. In the 18th century Portogallo and also Cordeiro da Silva and João de Sousa Carvalho ; a little later, Rego, Bomtempo, Soares, Pereira da Costa, Coelho, Cabral, and João de Mesquita. In Coimbra,[7] José Manricio ; in Oporto, Silva Leite,

---

[1] Numerous examples are given in Das Neves' and other collections.
[2] Platon von Waxel derives this dance-form from the *xacara* of the Portuguese gipsies, and the word from *fatiste* or verse-maker. See also M Roeder's Essay *Dal Taccuino*, p. 145.
[3] A celebrated modern singer of *fados* was José Dias (1824-69), who improvised with wonderful skill. He was a great favourite at the Court, and in the salons at home and abroad. Pinto de Carvalho and Alberto Pimentel have written on the Fados.
[4] The derivation of the word is doubtful. Some say it came from *note* or *moda*, and that it had its origin in Brazil. We certainly read in a folio dated 1729 (*Annals of the Bibl. of Rio de Janeiro*, ii. 129) that on a wedding-feast of the Viceroy ' *um alegre divertimento musico de Cantigas e Modas da terra, de que ha abundancia n'este paiz.*' Also many travellers of that time describe with admiration the *modinhas brasileiras*. For further information see Th. Braga's *Historia da Litteratura Portugueza* (*Filinto Elysio e os dissidentes da Arcadia*), vol. xx. p. 603 *et seq.*
[5] Thus named from Antonio José da Silva, born in 1705, a baptized Jew from Brazil, who wrote Portuguese comedies with these interspersed.
[6] Braga, *Historia da Litteratura Portugueza*, vol. xv. p. 604, note.
[7] The *modinhas* vary somewhat in the different districts.

Nunes, Pires, João Leal, and Edolo;[1] and nearer our own time, Domingos Schiopetta, the two monks J. M. da Silva and José Marquis de Santa Rita, Frondoni (an Italian, long resident in Lisbon), R. Varella, and Vasconcellos de Sà. But the most popular *modinhas*, such as 'A Serandinha,' 'O Salvia,' 'As Peneiras,' 'Mariquinhas meu Amor,'[2] and 'Tem minha amada'[3] are anonymous. An exception is Vasconcellos de Sà's canção, 'Margarida vae à fonte,' which is the favourite *modinha* of the moment.[4]

There are many patriotic and political songs in every collection. The pianist Innocencio wrote a whole series ; Portogallo's 'Hymno da Patria' was the customary national anthem until King Pedro IV.[5] composed his 'Hymno da Carta' in 1826 ; and Frondoni was the author of the popular hymn of the revolution of Maria da Fonte in 1848.

Of late, serious attention has been directed to the national poetry and music of Portugal. One of the first to do so was the poet Almeido Garrett in his *Romanceiro*. He was followed by Vasconcellos and Th. Braga, who in his numerous volumes on the history of Portuguese literature often touches on the musical form.[6] Leading musicians, such as B. Moreira de Sà, A. Machado (Director of the Conservatoire), and J. Vianna da Motta and others have shown their practical interest in the subject.

BIBLIOGRAPHY

Machado, D. B. *Bibliotheca Lusitana.* Lisbon, 1741-59.
Wolf, F. *Proben Portugiesischer und Catalanischer Volkslieder und Romanzen.* Vienna, 1856.
Bellermann, C. F. *Portugiesische Volkslieder und Romanzen.* Leipzig, 1864.
Mendel's *Mus. Cons. Lex.*; *Portugiesische Musik* (Platon von Waxel).
Gazeta da Madeira, 1866-69. *A Musica em Portugal* (Platon von Waxel).
Marques, Joaquim J. *Estudios sobre a historia da musica em Portugal.*
Braga, Th. *Historia da Litteratura Portugueza. Hist. da Poesia Pop. Portugueza.* Oporto, 1867.
Vasconcellos, Joaquim de. *Os Musicos Portuguezes.* Oporto, 1870.
Roeder, Martin. *La musica en Portogallo; Dal Taccuino,* etc. Milan, 1877.
Leite de Vasconcellos, J. *Romances populares portuguezas.* 1880; *Tradições populares.* Oporto, 1882 ; *As Maïs* (May-day songs).
Comte de Puymaigre. *Romanceiro; Choix de vieux Chants Portugais; Traduits et annotés.* Paris, 1881.
Soubies, A. *Histoire de la musique en Portugal.* 1898.
(The writer is also indebted to Senhor Bernardo Moreira de Sà for much information kindly supplied to her by letter.)

COLLECTIONS

Milcent, F. D. 'Jornal de Modinhas, com acompanhamento de Cravo, pelos milhores autores.' Lisbon, 1793.
José do Rego, A. 'Jornal de Modinhas.' 1812.
Edolo, José. 'Jornal de Modinhas.' 1823.
Ferreira, Antonio J. 'Collecção de Modinhas Portuguezas e Brazilieras.' 1825.
Kestner, H. 'Auswahl spanischer und portugiesischer Lieder.' Hanover, 1859.
Garcia, José M., and Machado, R. Coelho. Two large collections of Brazilian Modinhas. 1851.
Berggreen, A. P. 'Portugisiske Folke-sange og Melodier.' 1866.
Ribas, J. A. 'Album de musicas nacionaes portuguezas.'
Neves, A. das e Mello-filho. 'Musicas e canções populares.'
Pires. 'Canções populares do Alemtejo.'
Colaço, A. R. 'Collecção de Fados.'
Thomaz, F. Pedro. 'Canções populares da Beira' (with introduction by Leite de Vasconcellos).

[1] Between 1820 and 1840 José Edolo, a violinist at the opera, was the favourite contributor to the *Jornal de Modinhas.*
[2] These last two are included in Ribas's Collection.
[3] In Berggreen's collection.
[4] The difference between the *canções* and *modinhas* is slight, and the names are constantly interchanged.
[5] Dom Pedro IV., the first constitutional king of Portugal, was a pupil of Sigismund Neukomm, and wrote several choral and operatic works.
[6] Braga also collected the folk-songs of the Azores.

Salvini, G. R. 'Cancioneiro mus. portuguez.' Lisbon, 1884.
Clasing, J. H. 'Zwölf brasilianische Volkslieder.' Hamburg.
Neves, Césardas, and Campos, Gualdino de. 'Cancionero de Musicas Populares.' 3 vols. Porto, 1893-98. (These volumes contain valuable prefaces by Th. Braga, Viterbo and Ramas, and consist of : *canções, serenatas, chulas, danças, descantes, cantigas dos campos e das ruas, fados, romances, hymnos nacionaes, cantos patrioticos, cantigas religiosas de origem popular, canticos liturgicos popularisados, cantilenas, canções do berço,* etc.)

ITALY

Italy was more slowly caught by the poetic flame which the Provençal Troubadours had kindled, than other southern countries. For not until the middle of the 13th century, when Raymond Berenger, Count of Provence, visited the Emperor Frederick II. at Milan, bringing Troubadours and Jongleurs in his train, do we hear of them in this country. A similar patronage was extended to them by Raymond's son-in-law, Charles of Anjou, king of Naples and Sicily. Through which of these two gates the Provençal language entered Italy has ever been a disputed point. But taught by these singers, whom the common people called *Uomini di Corti*,[7] Italy soon produced her own *Trovatori* and *Giocolini*. At first they deemed their native dialect unsuitable to poetry, and used the Provençal language. But it is certain that already, by the time of Dante, the *volgar poesia*, which sprang from it, had reached a stage when it was capable of receiving rules and of being taught in the schools founded for the purpose. After Dante, no Italian could longer doubt the capacities of his own tongue for all forms of poetry. It must not be forgotten that the *terza rima*, used by the Provençal troubadours for the *sirvente*, was adopted by Dante for the 'Divina Commedia' and by Petrarch in his 'Trionfi.' But soon the verse of the Troubadours began to pale before the splendours of the great poet ; and towards the middle of the 14th century, the *Trovatori* declined in numbers and popularity, and after 1450 were heard of no more.[8]

Notwithstanding the subordination of lyric song to other branches of poetry and music in Italy, her long and careful study of *la melica poesia*—poetry wedded to music—has not been surpassed elsewhere. Dante's sonnets and Petrarch's 'Trionfi' were among the earliest poems set to music. Dante's own contemporary and friend Casella[9] (born 1300), who set his sonnet 'Amor che nella mente' to music, is believed to have also composed the music for a *ballata* by Lemmo da Pistoja, still extant in the Vatican.[10] The *ballate* and *intuonate* were perhaps the oldest forms of songs written in the vernacular ; both were love-songs sung to a dance.[11] After them the *maggiolate* or May-day

[7] So called because these singers appeared as retainers from princely courts. Also *Ciarlatani*, because the exploits of Charlemagne were a constant theme of their songs.
[8] For further information about the *Trovatori* see H. von der Hagen's work on the *Minnesingers,* vol. iv.
[9] See the fourth Canto of the 'Purgatorio,' and the second Canzone in the 'Convito,' where Casella's name occurs several times.
[10] Burney tells us that the Vatican MS. No. 3214 is a poem on the margin of which is written : 'Lemmo da Pistoja, e Casella diede il suono.'
[11] Arteaga gives the words of a *ballata* of the 13th century by

songs had their popularity. These also were love-songs, sung in the spring-time by bands of young men. The hunting-songs or *cacci*[1] equally deserve mention. The most celebrated were written by Soldanieri and Sacchetti, and the words are far better than their music by Nicolaus da Perugia, Laurentius, and Ghirardellus. Some are realistic, imitating the sounds of the hunt;[2] others are canonic in form, and others again interesting from the historic side, as they bring in the street-cries of the time.[3] When later the *Canti Carnascialeschi* came into vogue they at first were Carnival songs, but under the skilful hand of Lorenzo di Medici a kind of consecutive drama grew out of them.[4]

During the 14th century there existed a class of dilettante musicians called *cantori a liuto*, whose business it was to set other poets' verses to music and sing them. They differed from the *Trovatori* who were poets, and who sang their own verses to their own music or to that of others, and equally from the *Cantori a libro*, who were the learned professional musicians.[5] Casella (see above) and Minuccio d' Arezzo, mentioned by Boccaccio,[6] would belong to the *cantori a liuto*. It was the habit of these musicians to improvise,[7] for until the 16th century musical notation remained so difficult that only learned musicians were able to avail themselves of it. This is the reason why the melodies of the strophic songs, which contemporary writers[8] show to have been so popular and universal during the 14th and 15th centuries, have not survived.

The compositions of the Netherlands school of music, with their severe contrapuntal style, found their way into Italy in the 15th century, and in time began to exercise a strong influence there. But the prevailing type of Italian secular songs continued to be of a very light order during this and the following century. Petrucci, who issued in 1502 the motets and masses of the Netherland composers, had nothing better to offer of native productions than *frottole* and *villanelle*, tuneful but light part-songs. In form the *villanelle* adhered to the contrapuntal style, though in spirit they

were essentially popular. Gradually the term *frottola* disappeared ; the more serious *frottole* passed into the madrigal, while the gayer, merrier type was merged in the *villanelle*.[9] But although the *frottole* were despised by contrapuntists they showed a sense of form in repeating the first part again, and attention was paid to the words by having different music for each verse, whereas the *villanelle* were strophical—that is, the same melody was repeated for each stanza.[10] Other songs, light in character, were the rustic songs, *Canzone Villanesche*, or *Villotte*, which peasants and soldiers used as drinking-songs. More refined and yet more trifling were the *Villotte alla Napoletana*.[11] The so-called *fa-la-la* was a composition of a somewhat later date and more merit. Those which Gastoldi wrote (about 1590) were good, and so too his *balletti*.

The vocal music to which our attention has been thus far directed, consisted either of songs in parts, or unisonous chorus with little or no accompaniment. Sometimes the principal or upper voice had a sort of *cantilena*, but solo-singing was yet unknown. The first instance of solo-singing is supposed to have occurred in 1539, when Sileno sang in an Intermezzo[12] the upper part of a madrigal by Corteccia, accompanying himself on the violone, while the lower parts which represented the satyrs were taken by wind instruments. But the piece itself shows it was far from being a song for one voice with accompaniment ; the under parts are as much independent voices as the upper one. (See Ex. 1 on next page.)

During the last decades of the 16th century a sweeping change came over music in Italy. Hitherto the highest art-music belonged exclusively to the Church, from which the elements of rhythm, modern tonality, and human expression were rigorously excluded. But the spirit of the Renaissance, which had affected the other arts of poetry, painting, and sculpture many years earlier, gradually asserted an influence over music. With the awakening of the human mind, and its liberation from the bonds of the mediæval Church, which is the real meaning of the Renaissance, it was inevitable that men should seek for a new form in music wherein to express themselves. Each individual now desired to think and speak for himself, and was no longer content to be merged

---

Frederick II., and of another by Dante. See *Le Rivoluzioni del Teatro musicale Italiano*, i. pp. 187, 190.

[1] They may have been written specially for hunting, but Gaspari, in his history of Italian Literature, proves that any quick movement at that time would be called a *Caccia*.

[2] In this they resemble the FROTTOLE.

[3] They are counterparts of the *Cris de Paris*, which Jannequin brought into his motet 'Voulez ouyr les cris de Paris,' the 'Cries of London,' and 'Court Cries' used by Richard Deering. See J. Wolf's article *Florenz in der Musikgeschichte des 14ten Jahrhunderts, Sammelbände*, I.M.G., 1901-2, iii.

[4] Many of these were written by special invitation by Heinrich Isaak (born 1445). Naumann's *Hist. of Mus.* i. 438.

[5] The important part played in Italian music by such a one as Francesco Landini (1325-90) is well described by Fétis, v. 310 *et seq*.

[6] *Decam.* Giorn X. No. 7. See Ambros, *Ges. der Mus.* ii. 497.

[7] The 'improvisatore' has been for centuries a well-known figure in Italian life.

[8] We read in Sacchetti's novels that Dante's *ballate* were everywhere known and sung, and how Dante overheard a blacksmith singing his song and scolded him for having altered it. And Trucchi quotes, in proof of Dante having made the music for his own poems, an anonymous writer of the 13th century, who says Dante was 'dilettossi nel canto e in ogni suono' (*Poesie Italiane inedite*, ii. 140). See also Ambros, *Ges. der Mus.* ii. 489, for further account of the songs in the *Decameron*.

[9] A *frottola*, printed in Junta's Roman collection of 1526, evidently became, ere long, a *villanella*, for it is still sung in Venice with the same words and melody, 'Le son tre Fantinelle, tutti tre da maridar.' Originally, however, it was a part-song with the tune in the tenor. Ambros, iii. 495.

[10] See FROTTOLA, also Ambros, iv. 150 *et seq.*; *Florenz in der Musikgeschichte d. 14ten Jahrhunderts*, J. Wolf; *Sammelbände*, I.M.G., 1901-2, iii. ; *Die Frottole in 15ten Jahrhundert*, R. Schwarz; *Vierteljahrsschrift f. Musikwissenschaft*, 1886.

[11] These were gallant addresses from singing-masters to their feminine pupils. They were as popular in northern Italy as in Naples. For examples, see in Kiesewetter's *Schicksale und Beschaffenheit des weltlichen Gesanges*, app. Nos. 12, and 13 by Cambio (1547) and Donati (1555). Several collections of these songs still exist in the various libraries, and a specially important one at Naples.

[12] The Intermezzi were usually madrigals interspersed in the earlier Italian plays.

Fragment of a Madrigal. Sonato da Sileno con violone, sonando tutte le parti, e cantando il Soprano.

Ex. 1.
1st Tenor.　　　　　　　　　　　CORTECCIA, 1539.

O begl' an-ni de l'o - ro　　O se-col

di - vo　　al-lor　　non rastr'o fal-ce　al -

- - lor non e - ra　　vis-co ne　lac - - cio . .

etc.

in the mass. Thus ecclesiastical music was gradually driven from the field by secular music ; and choral or collective song by pure solo-song, which was the medium best fitted for the expression of the thoughts, emotions, and actions of individuals. Poetry, which had hitherto been smothered in the web of contrapuntal music (where many voices were simultaneously singing different words) once again asserted herself, and claimed attention to her meaning and form.[1] Further, the art of singing, which by the close of the 16th century had reached a highly advanced stage, demanded the prominence of the solo-singer. In short, a different kind of music was now required, and the monodic style supplied the want. Who were the actual inventors of this kind of music it is impossible to decide. Historians have clearly shown that the latent germs must have been present wherever folk-music existed.[2] The predilection for a marked rhythm, the disuse of the old Church scales, the feeling for the dominant, the use of the leading-note which is an essential feature in melody,[3]— all these elements, which form the basis of modern music, were instinctively present in folk-music before being formulated and taught in schools.

According to the historian G. B. Doni, [4] V. Galilei was the first composer who wrote actual melodies for one voice.[5] He further tells us that Galilei set to music the passage of the 'Inferno,' which narrates the tragic fate of Count Ugolino, and that he performed it himself 'very pleasingly,' with viola accompaniment. But be that as it may, an epoch in musical history was undoubtedly marked by Giulio Caccini, when he published in 1601, under the title of 'Le Nuove Musiche,' a collection of *madrigali, canzoni,* and *arie* for one voice. These compositions have a figured bass, and some are embellished with *fioriture.* In the preface [6] to his collection, Caccini gives minute directions as to the proper mode of singing his pieces, and his airs are well supplied with marks of expression, as the following example will show [7] :—

Ex. 2.
(*Scemar di voce. Esclamazione spiritosa.*)　　CACCINI.

Deh! Deh! do-ve son fug-gi - ti, deh! do-ve

(*Escl. più viva.*)　　　　　　　　(*Escl.*)

son spa-ri - ti gl'oc - - chi de quali er - ra - i Io son

(*Trillo.*) (*Senza misura quasi favellando,*

ce - ne-re o - ma - i Au - re au-re di-vi-ne ch'er-

in armonia con la suddetta sprezzatura.)　(*Trillo.*)

ra - te pe - re - gri - ne in　ques-ta par-te e quel - -

(*Escl.*)

- - la, Deh re - - oa-te no-vel - la dell' al-ma lu-ce

[1] Ambros, iv. 178, *et seq.*
[2] See Parry's *Art of Music*, and MONODIA (vol. iii. p. 247).
[3] Zarlino writes in 1558 that the peasants who sing without any art all proceed by the interval of the semitone in forming their closes.

[4] *Op. Omn.* Florence, 1763, tom. ii.
[5] This statement may be doubted, as we hear of Caccini, Viadana, Peri, and Cavalieri all exhibiting the same double talent as Corteccia and Galilei at the same period, *i.e.* in the last decades of the 16th century.
[6] Translated into German in Kiesewetter's *Schicksale und Beschaffenheit,* etc.
[7] For other examples see the beautiful aria 'Fere Selvagge,' reprinted in Gevaert's 'Les Gloires de l'Italie,' and 'Amarilli mia bella' in Parisotti's 'Arie Antiche.'

(*Escl. con misura più larga.*)
1st. (*Trillo.*)

lo - ro, au - re ch'io me-ne mo - - - - ro deh re -

2nd. (*Escl. rinf.*) (*Trillo una mezza battuta.*)

au - re ch'io me-ne mo - - - ro.

Ex. 3.
Lamento. MONTEVERDE.

La - scia - te - mi mo - ri - re! La - scia - te-

- mi mo - ri - re! E che vo - le - te voi,

che mi con - for - te In co - sì du - ra sor-te, in co-sì

gran mar - - ti - re? La - scia - te - mi mo-ri - re!

la - scia - te - mi mo - - ri - re!

Jacopo Peri succeeded Caccini with a work entitled 'Le varie musiche del Sig. J. Peri a una, due, tre voci per cantare nel Clavicembalo o Chitarrone' (Florence, 1609). They are simpler than those by Caccini, and less declamatory.[1] Caccini had numerous followers in the path he had opened, and thus the 'expressive Monodia,' *i.e.* the attempt to render certain thoughts and feelings in music, and to adapt music to the meaning of the words, was virtually established. But these early pioneers of solo-song were amateurs, and it remained for trained musicians to carry on their work systematically. With Monteverde (1567-1643) a turning-point in music was reached. To him we owe that revolution in harmony which showed the use of discords as an effective means of representing the element of expression ; and the development of the recitative which led to the beginning of the Opera—the most important moment in the whole history of music. We also owe to him a debt in the history of Song for having established the so-called ternary form which was soon to become stereotyped for the aria and song. This consisted of an air in three parts ; the last part being a mere repetition of the first, while the middle part contained a passage of contrast. This form was already familiar in the folk-songs of the Middle Ages, but its first appearance in art-music would seem to be in Monteverde's 'Lamento' from 'Arianna' (1608)[2] (Ex. 3). Although in this article the aria proper should be excluded, having already been treated (see ARIA), it is necessary to allude to it here, as the secular monodic song henceforth chiefly showed itself in the aria-form and became, in short, identical with it. Monteverde's successors, Cesti and Cavalli, both showed aptitude for pleasant melodious solo-music of this form, although Cavalli sometimes wrote arias with only two contrasting portions.

Other composers of the transition period which witnessed the growth of the opera and cantata were Radesca da Foggia, who published five books of 'Monodie' in 1616 ; A. Brunelli, who published in the same year and in 1618 two books of 'Scherzi, Arie, Canzonette, and Madrigali' ;[3] G. F. Capello, whose most remarkable work was a set of 'Madrigali a voce sola' ; G. Fornacci, celebrated for his 'Amorosi Respiri Musicali,' which appeared in 1617 ; Sigismondo d' India, Pietro della Valle, Luigi Rossi,[4] and finally Salvator Rosa.[5] A great quantity of these vocal compositions are treated in the strophic form, and the words of all are love-poems of a stilted, artificial character.[6]

If Corteccia's madrigal be compared with the following example from Capello, it will be seen how great an advance had been made in solo-singing in less than a century. And a striking resemblance may be observed between Capello and his successor Stradella.

---

[1] See 'Bellissima Regina' in Parisotti's 'Piccolo album.'
[2] This was afterwards arranged as a madrigal in five parts. See Parry, *Music of the Seventeenth Century* (*Oxford History of Music*), p. 47. Parry further clearly shows how this simple form later dominated one branch of music completely, and indeed 'became the bane of one period of Italian art.'

[3] Brunelli's collection included several pieces by other composers of the Florentine group.
[4] For the numerous existing collections of Rossi's 'Monodie' see ROSSI.
[5] Salvator Rosa certainly was Carissimi's contemporary, but the example Burney gives shows that he wrote much like the aforementioned composers. [6] Ambros, iv. 330.

Ex. 4.
Madrigale a voce sola.   G. F. CAPELLO.

etc.

During the 17th century the influence of Carissimi was great. He had a strong sense for modern tonality and for secular rhythm, and hence his style grew different from that of the older school. The Cantata, which was to become the chief form of chamber-music, reached a high stage of maturity under Carissimi, Legrenzi, Caldara, Stradella, and finally A. Scarlatti. Legrenzi's 'Cantate e Canzonette a voce sola' (published 1676) show his position in the development of the art of his time. (See CANTATA.) With A. Scarlatti's name the *da capo* form of the *aria* is associated, and for the many other debts the classical *aria* owes him, both in the opera and the cantata. (See SCARLATTI.)

We know how fierce the battles were between the monodic and polyphonic systems in Italy. But although the monodic form finally prevailed, it proved to be merely the prelude to the dramatic and not to the lyric form of song. No sooner were the 'expressive monodia' and the recitative started than the opera became firmly established. And in the same way the madrigal and the cantata,[1] which were both important, at least as regards vocal chamber-music during the 16th and 17th centuries, were doomed to insignificance by the use of this great and overshadowing rival. For an account of the origin and marvellous popularity of the OPERA, the reader must turn to that article. It need only be said here that all other kinds of secular vocal music had, and still have to yield precedence in Italy to the opera and its offshoots, the *scena*, *cavatina*, and *aria*.

If we closely examine the vocal works of the great composers of the 17th and 18th centuries, we see how little the *arie*, *ariette*, *canzonette*,

[1] Cantatas, which are really vocal sonatas, became by degrees a mixture of the formal aria and recitative. There was practically no difference in structure and style between the arias from these 'slices out of the opera' and the opera itself. Parry, *Music of the Seventeenth Century* (*Oxford History of Music*).

etc., published separately in collections[2] differ either in form or spirit from the arias extracted from their cantatas and operas. In the latter class some of the most beautiful examples of pure lyrics may be found, like Salvator Rosa's 'Star vicino'; Cesti's 'Intorno all' idol mio'; Stradella's 'Ragion sempre addita'; Leo's 'Ahi, che la pena mia'; A. Scarlatti's 'Voi fuggiste,' 'Le Violette,' and 'Cara Tomba'; and Caldara's 'Come raggio di Sol.' Many of the operas and cantatas from which such lovely airs are taken are dead and forgotten, or their names only remain in history as the shells which contained such treasures.

Turning to another branch of the subject, namely the folk-song, it is clear that in Italy it never held the same place as among other nations. That Italian composers ranked the folk-songs of other countries higher is proved by their choosing French or Gallo-Belgian folk-songs for their masses and motets in preference to their own.[3] In Petrucci's 'Canti Cento Cinquanta,' published in 1503, the best songs belong to France, Germany, and the Netherlands; and the part-songs called *Canzoni alla francese*[4] were among the most popular songs in Italy in the early 16th century. Traces no doubt exist of *canti popolari* of the 15th, 16th, and 17th centuries, but very few have come down to us in their complete or native form. It was in the gay, busy town of Venice that the folk-song first became recognised, and found free development. It was there that Petrucci printed the many *frottole*, *ballate*, *barcajuoli*, etc., which contained folk-songs like 'Le son tre fantinelli' (mentioned above), or the popular 'La Bernardina' used by Josquin des Prés, or 'Lirum bilirum' and 'Quando andarete al monte' used respectively by Rossini di Mantua and J. B. Zesso. It was here, too, that G. Scotto printed the Venetian master A. Willaert's collection which has preserved to us the celebrated 'Canzon di Ruzante.'[5] But though many of the songs used for the polyphonic works bear Italian titles, there is nothing to prove their Italian origin. Only in a few instances have the words been preserved in their integrity, and the melodies have no distinguishing characteristics. They are somewhat dull and formless.[6] Much more akin to the typical *canti popolari* in liveliness and simplicity of style were the

[2] See such collections as—'Arie antiche,' 'Piccolo album di Musica Antica,' Parisotti; 'Echi d' Italia,' Viardot; 'Gloires de l'Italie,' Gevaert; 'Tesori antichi,' M. Roeder; 'Gemme d' antichità,' published by Ashdown; 'Alt-Italienische Canzonetten und Arien,' Lindner.
[3] 'L'homme armé' is a well-known example. It must not be forgotten though, that Italy was for many centuries the meeting-place for musicians from all countries,—hence the cosmopolitan character of the themes chosen for the great contrapuntal works.
[4] 'Canzoni Francesi a due voci, buone da cantare e suonare,' published by Gardano, Venice, 1539. The words are love-songs, and the music chiefly by Sermisy, Peletier, Herteur, and Gardano himself. Gardano had published in the previous year 'Venticinque canzoni francese,' consisting chiefly of four-part songs by Jannequin.
[5] This collection is called 'Canzon Villanesche alla Napolitana di Messer Adriano; a quattro voci con la canzon di Ruzante. Libro i. Venezia, Girolamo Scotto, 1548.'
[6] For an example see 'La Bernardina' in Kiesewetter's *Schicksale*, etc. App. p. 13.

hymn-tunes, known as 'Laudi Spirituali.'
These, in the Middle Ages, were introduced in
the oratorios in order to popularise such per-
formances ; and the connection between these
Laudi with popular dance-songs is obvious.
(See LAUDI SPIRITUALI.)

But although we find within recent years
that the study of the folk-lore of Italy has
received serious attention, materials for a satisfactory treatment of the *canti popolari* do not
exist. Much has been written about the words
of traditional songs, and innumerable collections
of popular poetry have been published,[1] but no
attempt has been made towards a scientific and
systematic work on the melodies, tracing their
origin and development and various forms.
In the many volumes of the *Archivio per lo
Studio delle tradizioni popolari*, edited by
Giuseppe Pitrè and S. Salomone-Marino, and in
G. Pitrè's excellent work, *Bibliografia delle
tradizioni popolari d'Italia* (Clausen, Turin,
1894), mention is made of the various collections
of canti popolari ; and in the former volumes
there are occasional short articles which refer
to the tunes, and give a few musical examples.
During the latter half of the last century
Ricordi and other publishers have issued large
quantities of modern canti popolari in volumes
entitled 'Canzonette Veneziane,' 'Stornelli Toscani,' 'Canti Lombardi,' 'Napolitani,' 'Siciliani,' etc., purporting to be local songs belonging
to the several provinces of Italy. But whether
these songs can be accepted as the genuine
productions which they profess to be, or whether they
are new compositions, or at any rate new
arrangements of old popular tunes, and whether
they are really sung by the peasants in the form
in which they are here given, is very doubtful.[2]
There are exceptions, such as the 'Canti Lombardi,' the melodies at least of which are
genuine ; also the 'Canti Siciliani,' edited by
Frontini, and the 'Canti Abruzzesi,' collected
by P. Tosti and G. Finamore. The latter, in
an interesting article[3] on the harvest-songs of
this district, draws attention to the solemn,
religious character of the melodies, in contrast
to the words, which are merry love-songs. This
peculiarity Finamore attributes to the great
antiquity of the melodies,[4] which have remained
unchanged for centuries, though the words have

altered. The following *Canti della Mietitura*
(harvest) are amongst the commonest ; the tonality of both is curious, the first being pure
Lydian and the second of more or less Phrygian
character.[5]

EX. 5.
Largo.   Given by G. FINAMORE.

Ji' mè-ta mè-ta e la faggij-ja mè-te ca la pa-

- - tron-a m'a da-dà la fij-je.

Aria della notte.[6]
EX. 6.
Largo assai.

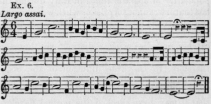

Some of the songs from the Abruzzi collected
by Tosti are of extreme beauty in form, melody,
and words. Many of the Sicilian and Neapolitan songs begin with a long-drawn high
note ; they are sung very fast and strongly
accented.

The wealth of canti popolari is prodigious,
and although (as mentioned above) they vary
greatly in the different districts, their general
characteristics are the same. The harmonic
and formal structure is simple. The accompaniment, which is usually intended for the guitar,
consists merely of the tonic and dominant chords,
and rarely modulates into anything except the
nearest related keys.[7] Few modal canti popolari are extant, although the flattened supertonic
which is characteristic of the Sicilian and
Neapolitan folk-songs recalls the Phrygian
mode.[8] The time is more frequently triple
than duple, and this especially applies to the
dance-songs. The largest proportion of folk-
songs consists of eight-lined verses of eleven
syllables, and are variously called *strambotti,
rispetti,*[9] *dispetti, siciliani,* or *ottavi.* The three-
lined verses are called *ritornelli, stornelli, fiori*
or *fiorette.* But it should be added that the
terms *canti, canzoni, canzonette, stornelli* are

[1] See, for instance, G. Pitrè's *Studii di poesia popolare* (Palermo,
1872) ; Rubieri's *Storia della poesia popolare italiana* (Florence,
1877) ; A. D' Ancona's *La poesia popolare italiana* (Leghorn, 1878).
See also Carducci's *Cantilene e Ballate, Strambotti e Madrigali nei
sec. XIII. e XIV.* (Pisa, 1871) ; and an interesting but unfinished
work entitled *Canzoni antiche del popolo italiano, riprodotte
secondo le vecchie stampe a cura di Mario Menghini,* Rome.

[2] Speaking of Tuscan songs, Miss Busk shows how in these days
of cheap printing and half-educated editing 'the literary songs
(*i.e.* art-songs) have got mixed up with the folk-songs.' As instances,
she quotes 'Stella Confidente,' 'Non mi amara,' 'Ritorna! che t'amo'
which were sung in London drawing-rooms as much as on the way-
sides and in the slums of Italy. Such songs also as Tosti's 'Vorrei
morire' are constantly heard in the streets. *The Folk-songs of Italy,*
p. 261 *et seq.*

[3] *Melodie popolari Abruzzesi ; i canti della Mietitura,* G. Finamore; see vol. 13 of the *Archivio per lo studio delle tradizioni
popolari,* 1894.

[4] 'Chaque acte de la vie de l'agriculture était accompagné de
sacrifice, et on exécutait les travaux en récitant des hymnes sacrés.'
De Coulanges, *La Cité Antique,* p. 184.

[5] From the Vasto district, noted by L. Anelli. It should be
accompanied by the cornemuse.

[6] From the Guardiagrelle district, noted by M. Bruni. Finamore
adds that they are sung in turn by one voice at a time, accompanied
by the *chitarra battente,* a sort of *colascione.* The verses are of
interminable length.

[7] A weak and very modern colouring is imparted to the harmony
of the published folk-songs by an excessive use of the chord of the
seventh.

[8] It has been remarked that the flat supertonic may be found in
the canzonette from the comic operas by Vinci and Leo ; and that
an air from A. Scarlatti's cantata 'Andate o miei sospiri,' marked
alla Siciliana, has the same characteristic, showing that Scarlatti
realised it as essential to the native quality of the melody. (See
E. J. Dent's *A. Scarlatti, His Life and Works,* 1905.)

[9] *Rispetti* are always sung, and as eight lines is the normal
number, the popular mode of speaking either of inventing or singing
them is, *dar l'ottava.* R. Busk, *The Folk-songs of Italy,* p. 20.

very loosely and indiscriminately employed.[1] But speaking generally, *stornelli* are lively songs of love, *canzoni* and *canzonette* narrative songs, and *canto* is a generic term applicable to almost any form. Modern composers generally use the word *melodia* for a lyric song (*Lied*).

A strong claim to the title of ' canti popolari ' may be advanced in favour of the popular melodies taken from operas. Ambros tells us that during the 17th and 18th centuries, favourite ' couplets ' from operas, which at first had nothing in common with the folk-song beyond being melodious and simple, acquired by degrees a place similar to that held by the *Volkslied* in Germany.[2] And the immense popularity of operatic tunes in Italy during the last century cannot surprise us when we remember the theatre is an ubiquitous institution there, and that the quick ear of the Italian instantly catches melodies with a distinct rhythm and an easy progression of intervals.[3] Having regard, therefore, to the wide diffusion of the opera and its influence on all classes during nearly three centuries, it is reasonable to conclude that it may have checked the normal development of songs, and perhaps helped to obliterate the traces of old traditional tunes. It will be seen later that the exactly contrary process took place in some northern countries, where in order to make their operas popular, composers introduced favourite folk-songs or dances, or indeed whole operas were based on national melodies.

The so-called *canti nazionali* belong to a period commencing about the year 1821. They have all been inspired by the political movement of the last century for the regeneration of Italy. Their tone is naturally warlike, but the melodies are ultra-simple and rather weak. The most celebrated of them are : ' Addio, mia bella ' ;[4] 'O dolce piacer, goder libertà' ; ' Daghela avanti un passo';[5] ' Inno di Mameli' ; 'Fratelli d' Italia'; ' La bandiera tricolore ' ; ' Inno di Garibaldi,' and ' All' armi ' by Pieri. The years in which Italy has been most deeply stirred by struggles for independence were 1821, 1848, and 1859, and all the songs whose names have just been cited can be traced to one or other of those revolutionary periods.

For many important forms of both vocal and instrumental music we are primarily and especially indebted to the Italians, but as regards the art-song proper we owe them little. From the latter part of the 17th to the early part of the 19th century, the *canzoni*, and *canzonette da camera* exhibited neither merit nor improvement. Several collections were published at intervals, yet apparently they attracted little attention. Many were of a religious tendency ; not hymns but *canzoni spirituali e morali*, as they were called. Even when the *canzoni madrigaleschi* were reduced to two voices (as, for instance, those by Benedetto Marcello, published at Bologna in 1717) they continued to be essentially polyphonic, one voice imitating the other.

During the 18th century the lyric poet Metastasio exercised a certain effect on vocal music, and many of his *ariette* were set by contemporary musicians ; but his influence was not lasting. A little later, a few inferior composers, such as Asioli, Barni, Federici, Blangini, and Romagnesi[6] (all born in the second half of the 18th century) turned their attention to song-writing, and published quantities of *ariette, canzonette, rondi, notturni,* and *romanze,* but they were too weak to stand the test of time, and such popularity as they may once have known has been brief and fleeting. In fact, few Italian composers of merit ever deemed it worth while to bestow pains on this kind of work ; to write an opera was their natural ambition, and on this they concentrated their powers. ' With all the best talent devoted to the service of the Church or the theatre there was little room left for the more solitary and self-contained expression of lyric feeling.'[7] Nor was there any demand for lyric songs. Just as the ' couplets ' and favourite tunes from the operas supplied the people with many *canti popolari,* the *aria* and *cavatina* provided the vocal pieces which the educated classes preferred. If we look through the work of Paisiello, Cimarosa, Mercadante, Bellini, Donizetti, Verdi, and other celebrated composers of opera, very numerous examples of the above-mentioned miscellaneous kinds of songs may be found, but none evince any serious thought. They were obviously thrown off in leisure moments, and now they are never heard of. An exception, however, must be made in favour of Rossini, some of whose songs have fine melodies and interesting accompaniments.[8] Among song-writers who lived nearer our own time Gordigiani, Mariani, and Giordani are undoubtedly the best for simple melodious songs.[9] They wrote in the true Italian style, with the utmost fluency and sentimentality.

---

[1] *Canzune* is the Sicilian equivalent of *rispetto,* and *ciuri* of *stornello.* The children's songs in Italy are very numerous, and are usually called *Ninne-Nanne* or *Nane* in Venice. Busk, *op. cit.* p. 47.

[2] Orloff recounts how an aria from an opera by P. Cafaro (born 1706), ' Belle luci,' was for half a century the best-known and most widely-sung song all over Italy ; the melody was even painted on china and embroidered on robes (*Essai sur l'Histoire de la musique en Italie,* i. 293). See also the account of the popularity of Piccinni's opera ' La Cecchina ' in the *Oxford History of Music,* vol. 5, *The Viennese Period,* p. 97, W. H. Hadow.

[3] The chorus of an opera is frequently chosen from amongst the workmen and labourers of the place where it is performed ; and thus even difficult choruses may be heard in the streets and suburbs of towns which possess a theatre.

[4] This is an adaptation of Italian words to ' Partant pour la Syrie,' and was probably made during the war of 1820, in which France assisted Italy to liberate herself from the yoke of Austria.

[5] A ballet-song written by P. Giorza in 1858.

[6] These last two composers were better known in Paris than in their own country.

[7] W. H. Hadow, *Oxford Hist. of Music,* v. 325.

[8] See for example ' La Regata Veneziana,' No. 2, where the rhythmical figure in the left hand represents the regular movement of the oars, whilst the right hand has continuous *legato* passages in double notes.

[9] Rossini once aptly summed up the Italian ideal of a song ; ' Il diletto dev' essere la basa e lo scopo di quest' arte—Melodia semplice —Ritmo chiaro.'

With few exceptions Italian songs are marked in a greater or less degree by the same qualities. The voice-part is ever paramount in them, and all else is made to yield to it. The beautiful quality and the wide compass of Italian voices,[1] and the facility with which they execute difficult vocal phrases, tempt the composer to write brilliant and effective passages where a simple melody would be far more appropriate to the words. The words may indeed give the form to the song, and the music may substantially agree with them, but we miss that delicate subtle understanding between the poet and the musician, where the music often interprets the words, or a single word gives importance to a note or passage. Again, the accompaniment holds a very subordinate place. Its sole use is to support the voice ; rarely has it any artistic value of its own,[2] and seldom, if ever, does it assist in expressing the poetic intention of the work.

It would be wrong, however, to apply these criticisms without reserve to all modern Italian composers. P. Tosti, for instance, knows how to rise above the common defects of his countrymen if he chooses ; he possesses a genuine lyric talent, and some of his melodies are charming. Clever accompaniments also are met with in the compositions of Marco Sala, Faccio, Bozzano, Coronaro, and Smareglio. The last two have paid especial attention to the words of their songs. A cycle of songs, entitled ' La Simona,' by Benedetto Junck, would have a high rank assigned to them in any country ; and the same can be said of Sgambati's beautiful songs, with their highly developed accompaniments. E. de Leva's, Enrico Bossi's, P. Tirindelli's, and Rotoli's songs have merit ; and an interesting new composer, Leone Sinigaglia, writes with grace and originality, though his songs are scarcely Italian in character, and he approaches nearer to the German school of song-writers.

Amongst the works of the most celebrated composers of modern Italy, such as Martucci, Boïto, Mancinelli, Catalani, Mascagni, Leoncavallo, Giordano, Franchetti, Puccini, and Cilea, etc., the writer has searched in vain for any mention of songs. It seems as if that branch of music has not yet aroused the interest, nor attained the rank, in Italy which are accorded to it in other countries.

BIBLIOGRAPHY

Arteaga, S. *La Rivoluzione del teatro mus. Ital.* Venice, 1785.
Orloff, G. *Essai sur l'histoire de la mus. en Italie.* Paris, 1822.
Lichtenthal. P. *Dizionario e Bibliog. della Musica.* Milan, 1826.
Von der Hagen, F. *Die Minnesinger.* Leipzig, 1838.
Dietz, F. *Leben und Werke des Troubadours.*
Wolf, F. *Ueber die Lais.* Heidelberg, 1841.
Kiesewetter, R. G. *Schicksale und Beschaffenheit des weltl. Gesanges.* Leipzig, 1841. *Geschichte der Europ.-abendländ. Musik.* Leipzig, 1834.

[1] It is curious to note how limited is the compass of voice for which modern Italian composers write songs intended for circulation in foreign countries, while the songs they write for the home-market often exceed the compass of two octaves.

[2] A point to be taken into consideration as greatly impoverishing and limiting the accompaniments is, that on account of the climate and the outdoor life the Italians lead, the guitar and mandoline are as much used as the pianoforte.

Ambros, W. *Geschichte der Musik.* Breslau, Leipzig, 1862-82.
Florimo, F. *Cenno Storico sulla scuola Mus. di Napoli.* Naples, 1869-71.
Naumann, E. *Italienische Tondichter.* Berlin, 1876.
Pfleiderer, K. *Das ital. Volk im Spiegel seiner Volkslieder.* Leipzig, 1879.
Pitrè, G., e Salomone-Marino, S. *Archivio per lo studio delle tradizioni pop.* Palermo, 1882, etc.
Busk, Rachel. *The Folk-songs of Italy.* London, 1887.
Chilesotti, O. *Sulla melodia pop. del Cinquecento.* Milan, 1889.
Parry, C. H. H. *Music of the Seventeenth Century (Oxford History of Music,* vol. iii.). Oxford, 1902.
The writer also owes her thanks to Signor Domenico Comparetti for information on the folk-songs of Italy.

COLLECTIONS

Florimo, F. ' Eco di Napoli.' Napoli, 1840-60.
Tommaseo, N. ' Canti pop. Toscani.' Venice, 1841-2.
Alverà, Andrea. ' Canti pop. tradizionali.' Vicenza, 1844.
Gordigiani, L. ' Collezione dei Canti pop. toscani' ; 'Stornelli d' Arezzo' ; ' Eco dell' Arno,' etc. Milan, 1850.
Fea, L. A. ' Chants pop. de la Corse.' Paris, 1850.
Ricordi, G. ' Canti pop. lombardi.' 1857-1900.
Giamboni, A. ' I veri Canti pop. di Firenze.' Milano, 1862.
Comparetti, D. ' Saggi dei dialetti greci dell' Italia merid.' Pisa, 1866.
Salomone-Marino, S. ' Canti pop. Siciliani.' Palermo, 1867.
Ferraro, G. ' Canti pop. Monferrini.' Turin, 1870.
Casetti, A. ' Canti pop. delle provincie merid.' Rome, 1871-72.
Bortolini, G. ' Canzoni naz. della Laguna.' Milan, 1873.
Marchetti, F. ' Canti pop. Romaneschi.' Milan, 1874.
Ive, A. ' Canti pop. Istriani.' Rome, 1877.
D' Ancona, A. ' Canti pop. Italiani.' Rome, 1877.
Gialdini, G., e Ricordi, G. ' Eco della Lombardia.' Milan, 1881-84.
De Miglio, V. ' 50 Canzoni pop. Napolitani.' Milan, 1882.
Pinamore, G. ' Canti pop. Abruzzesi.' Milan, 1882-94.
Tosti, F. P. ' Canti pop. Abruzzesi.' Milan, 1882.
Frontini, F. ' Eco della Sicilia.' Milan, 1882.
Sinigaglia, O. ' Stornelli d' Amore.' Palermo, 1884.
Julia, A. ' Baci,' ' Ninne-Nanne.' Naples, 1884.
Ortoli, J. F. B. ' Les voceri de l'île de Corse.' Paris, 1887.
Nigra, Const. ' Canti pop. del Piemonte.' Turin, 1888.
Parisotti, A. ' Le melodie pop. romane.' Rome.
Teschner, G. W. ' Sammlung italienischer Volkslieder.'
Pargolesi, C. ' Eco del Friuli.' Trieste.
Pitrè, G. ' Canti pop. Siciliani.' Palermo, 1891 ; 'Bibliografia delle Tradiz. Pop. d' Italia,' Parte ii. ' Canti e melodie.' Torino, Palermo, 1894.
Giannini, G. ' Canti pop. Lucchesi.' Lucca, 1890-92.
Saviotti, A. ' Canti e Ninne-Nanne Arpinati.' Palermo, 1891.

SWITZERLAND

Although this country is bound together by a strong national feeling, it contains great diversities of idiom. More than half the population speak German ; the rest either French or Italian, and a small fraction Romansch or Ladin. Hence there is little specifically national music, as it generally resembles that of the country to which it lies nearest. For instance, the folk-songs on the southern side are essentially Italian in character, while the French-Swiss and German-Swiss folk-songs are included in the collections of France and Germany. A purely indigenous feature in Swiss music is the cow-call, or *Kuhreihen,* which has been already treated. (See RANZ DES VACHES.) The old watchman-songs should also be mentioned. These date back for centuries, but are probably of German origin ; as in the canton of Tessin, where Italian is the common language spoken, the night watch-call is still sung in Old German. Nearly all the true Alpine songs can be played on the Alphorn, to which in fact they owe their birth. The Swiss peasants have always possessed a remarkable harmonic aptitude. The herdsmen can skilfully improvise songs in many parts, and vary them with *Jodels* as ritornels or refrains. In many of the dance-songs the rhythm, too, is highly developed, necessitating constant changes of time-signature. Otherwise the melodies, like the poetry, are of the simplest character in form and metre.

Looking back on the past history of music in Switzerland we find that the composers of any note in this country have generally identified themselves with other nationalities. Thus in the 16th century the great contrapuntist, Ludwig Senfl's [1] name appears among German composers; in the 18th, J. J. Rousseau is claimed by France, just as Nägeli, Raff, and Schnyder von Wartensee, nearer our own time, are by Germany. But Switzerland has never been without her own musicians, who have striven in all ages to keep up the national feeling, although their names are now scarcely remembered.

The Reformation exerted a great influence in French Switzerland. The Psalms of G. Franc, the two Bourgeois and Davantes are still heard around Geneva. Some of the *coraules* of the Fribourgeois have beautiful refrains, recalling the ecclesiastical sequences; and in many of the old songs used in the peasants' *Festspiele* are traces of Goudimel's fine hymns adapted to secular words. These festival-plays, in which the peasants represent some national legend or historic event by word, dance, and song, are held in different districts, and form a powerful factor in the musical life of Switzerland. In recent years they have incited some of the younger Swiss musicians, such as Baud-Bovy, G. Doret, and F. Niggli, to take down the songs sung on these occasions by the peasants and to write simple popular melodies in the same spirit. Whilst the Church cultivated the taste for hymns and chorales,[2] the frequent wars gave rise to innumerable songs of satire, strife, and politics. Some of the earliest French collections of these songs were printed by P. de Vingle at Neuchâtel in the 16th century.[3] He also printed many books of carols (Noëls Nouveaultx, 1533), usually with very irreverent words set to favourite sacred and secular tunes.

In the 17th and 18th centuries music-schools were formed in the various towns of Zurich, Basle, Berne, and Coire, and their libraries have preserved numerous collections of songs by Dillhern, Simler, Krüger, Briegel, Musculi, the Molitors, Dietbold, Menzingen, and especially L. Steiner (born 1688),—the first Swiss composer to cultivate a love for his country's music. J. Schmidli, who set Lavater's 'Chansons Suisses' to music, and Egli, who published several 'Chansons Suisses avec mélodies,' followed in his steps. After Egli's death in 1810, his pupil Walder carried on his work, together with Ott, Albertin, Bachofen (a special favourite)

Greuter, Felix Huber, Kuhn, and Zwinger, some of whom were national poets as well as musicians and collectors. J. G. Nägeli (as much a German as a Swiss song-composer) did much to promote musical education in the country of his birth. He was joined in this movement by Kunlin, Wachter, Krausskopf, the brothers Fröhlich, and Ferdinand Huber. As song-writers Karl Attenhofer, F. Grast, and Ignaz Heim should be especially mentioned, the latter being perhaps the most popular. Zwyssig composed the 'Cantique Suisse' (the national hymn) and Baumgartner the fine *chant* 'O ma Patrie.' The names of Methfessel, C. and F. Munziger, G. Weber, A. Meyer, and F. Hegar (who is principally famous for his choral songs) may complete the list of that period.

During the latter part of the 19th century, a new impetus has been given to Swiss music by a group of young and enthusiastic musicians, who have strongly felt the necessity of preserving the traditional treasures of their country and developing them with all the resources of modern art. They have hereby endeavoured to prove the essential unity of feeling in the nation. Though composed of such various races, the same patriotism, love of liberty, and independence have animated this little republic in all times of its history. The leaders of this movement are Hans Huber and E. Jaques-Dalcroze; the former bears an honoured name in other branches of music besides songs, and the latter is a refined poet, as well as being a prolific composer. His numerous volumes of 'Chansons romandes,' 'Chansons populaires et enfantines,' 'Chansons des Alpes,' 'Chansons patriotiques,' etc. contain graceful little pictures of national life, in which Jaques-Dalcroze cleverly introduces the types of melody, harmony, and rhythm characteristic of the various cantons.[4]

In the year 1900 the 'Union of Swiss musicians' was formed, which now numbers over 300 members, and holds yearly festivals for the performance of new works of all kinds by these composers. Especial interest is attached to those of the younger generation, all of whom have included song as an important branch of their art. The principal names are as follows: E. Jaques-Dalcroze, V. Andrae, Otto Barblan, E. Bloch, E. Combe, A. Dénéréaz, G. Doret, F. Klose, H. Kling, E. Reymond, Fritz Niggli, J. Ehrhart, R. Ganz, F. Karmin, J. Lauber, W. Pahnke, P. Maurice, W. Rehberg, G. Pantillon, L. Kempter, etc.

The revelation of so much home talent may surprise the world, but it proves that 'a Swiss school of music is rapidly rising, and may in time hold its own.'[5]

---

[1] Senfl contributed largely to the various collections of the 16th century; and in one of these called *Bicinia Gallica*, dated 1545, there occurs the oldest known version of a *Ranz des Vaches*.

[2] Towards the end of the 15th century L. Moser of Basle contributed largely to the popularisation of the Church songs. His book, *Ein vast nothdürftige Materi*, etc. contains a large number of German songs adapted to familiar Church melodies. See Becker, *Hist. de la Musique Suisse*.

[3] The collection of 1509 contains the celebrated *complainte* on the heretics burnt at Berne: 'Die war History von den vier Ketzer Prediger ordens zu Bern in den Eydgenossenschaft verbrannt.'

[4] Jaques-Dalcroze has done much to develop the rhythmical element among his countrymen by his choral, dance, and game-songs, and 'Gymnastiques Rhythmiques.' See also his striking article 'La pedagogia del ritmo' in the *Rivista Musicale Italiana*, Anno xiii.

[5] E. Jaques-Dalcroze, *Die Musik in der Schweiz*.

BIBLIOGRAPHY

Tobler. *Appenzellischer Sprachschatz.* Zurich, 1837.
Schubiger, A. *Die Sängerschule St. Gallens vom 8ten bis 12ten Jahrhundert.* Einsiedeln, New York, 1858.
Becker, G. *La musique en Suisse depuis les temps les plus reculés jusqu'à la fin du 18me siècle,* etc. Geneva, 1874.
Becker, G. *Kulturhistorische Skizzen aus der romanischen Schweiz.* 1878.
Soubies, A. *Suisse (Histoire de la Musique).* Paris, 1899.
Jaques-Dalcroze, E. *Die Musik in der Schweiz (Die Musik,* July, 1905.)

COLLECTIONS

Humbrechtikon, Greuter de. 'Bundtner Lieder.' Coire, 1785.
Egli, J. H. 'Schweizer Lieder.' Zurich, 1798.
Walder, J. J. 'Lieder zum gesellschaftlichen Vergnügen.' Zurich, 1804.
Wagner, S. von. 'Acht Schweizer Kuhreihen.' Berne, 1805.
Kuhn, G. 'Sammlung von Schweizer Kuhreihen und alten Volksliedern.' Berne, 1812-18.
Tarenne, G. 'Recherches sur les Ranz des Vaches ou sur les chansons pastorales des Bergers de la Suisse avec musique.' Paris, 1813.
Wysz, J., and Huber, F., edited the 4th edition of Kuhn's work in 1826.
Huber, Felix. 'Schweizerliederbuch' (532 Lieder). Aarau, 1824. 'Recueil de Ranz de Vaches.' 1830.
Rochholz, E. 'Eidgenössische Lieder-Chronik.' Berne, 1835-42.
Huber, Felix. 'Chants pour la guerre de la Confédération.' Berne, 1840.
Otto, F. 'Schweizer-Sagen in Balladen, Romanzen und Legenden.' Basle, 1842.
Tschudi. 4 vols. of old Swiss songs.
'Chants Valanginois accompagnés de textes historiques.' Neuchatel, 1848.
Forbes, Dr. John. 'A Physician's Holiday, or a month in Switzerland.' (This contains some interesting specimens of the hymns and chants used by the night-watchmen in Switzerland.) London, 1849.
Rochholz, E. 'Alemannisches Kinderlied und Kinderspiel aus der Schweiz' (no music). Leipzig, 1857.
Kurz, H. 'Schlacht- und Volkslieder der Schweizer.' Zurich, 1860.
Buhler, J. A. 'Canzuns en lungatz rhäto-romansch.' Coire, 1865.
Kuella. 'Chansonnier Suisse.' Zurich, 1882.
Wysz, J., and Huber, F. 'Der Schweizer-Sänger.' Lucerne, 1883.
'Chansons et Coraules fribourgeoises.' Fribourg, 1894.
'Chants et Coraules de la Gruyère.' Leipzig, 1894.
'Chansonnier des Zofingiens de la Suisse romande.' Lausanne, 1894.
Dieterich, G. A. 'xxii Alpenlieder.' Stuttgart.

ROUMANIA

Roumania is a Romance country, and embraces both Moldavia and Wallachia. The character of its national music is, therefore, very mixed. Among the educated classes, a preference is shown for French and Italian music, and thus the Latin origin is betrayed. The real folk-music has also much in common with its Slavonic neighbours, and the gipsy element is strongly represented by the *Laoutari*.[1] Without these gipsy lutenists, no christening, wedding,[2] or funeral is held to be complete among the peasants, though at funerals in Roumania, as in Russia, it is the village women who are the professional 'wailers.' Their song of wailing, is a monotonous recitative chanted on a few notes, interspersed by a succession of sharp little cries, whilst the words enumerate all the qualities of the deceased.

The most beautiful of the Roumanian folk-songs are enshrined in their *doinas*.[3] This is a generic term, as it includes songs of various origins. In times past, both pastoral and war-songs were alike called *doinas*, but at the present time they resemble the French *complaintes*, as indeed their name—*doina* = lament—indicates. They are usually in the minor key ; the melody is full of turns, trills, and other embellishments, yet throughout they are of a melancholy cast.

[1] Both Verdi and Liszt have testified their approval of the *Laoutari* in enthusiastic language. See J. Schorr, 'Musik in Roumänien,' in *Die Musik,* 1903, No. 22.
[2] A Roumanian proverb says: 'Mariage sans *Laoutari* c'est-à-dire chose impossible.'
[3] The name *doina,* according to Hâsdeü, is of Dacian origin, and may also be found in Sanscrit, as *d'haina*.

Ex. 1.

Though the folk-songs may be less original and striking than the national dances, they are extremely melodious and full of sentiment. The poetry is rhymed and often in five-lined stanzas. The metre is irregular, and refrains frequently occur either at the end of the line or the stanza, as the following well-known folk-song (*cântec popular*) shows :—

Pentru tine Jano.

Ex. 2.

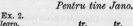

The oldest and most celebrated dance is the *hora,* a slow choral dance written in rondo form usually in this rhythm :—

Ex. 3.

Another dance, equally written in rondo form, but usually in a major key, is the *sărbă* (or *sirba*). Though the prevailing tendency of this country's national music is melancholy, some of the dance-tunes are, nevertheless, gay and light. The occurrence of the augmented second between unusual intervals is frequent, and doubtless due to gipsy influence. Melodies of more recent date consist usually of the first phrase in the major and the second and concluding phrases in the relative minor, as in so many Slavonic tunes.

As mentioned above, the Roumanians seldom sing at all themselves ; the songs are sung to them as solos by the *Laoutari,* and singing in harmony is quite unknown. The melody is also often played by the chief singer on the *cobza,* a sort of flute.

The renaissance of music in this country did not begin until the middle of the 19th century, and its principal promoters were Professor Wachmann (who especially called attention to the national music), Flechtenmacher and

Caudella. The latter was the creator of the Roumanian national opera, and together with Ventura, Scheletti, and Cavadi, composed numerous and favourite songs. These closely resemble the typical French and Italian *romances*, and have little in common with the German or Russian art-song. Mention should also be made of Eduard Hübsch, the composer of the national hymn. Musicescu and Kiriac have reproduced in their compositions the old Roumanian church and folk-songs. Margaritesco, Stephănescu, Spirescu, Ciran, Ercole, and Dumitresco have written numerous songs and ballads, besides other works ; and among the younger generation, Enescu and Lcarlatescu, who have already won for themselves European reputations in more than one branch of music, perhaps stand the highest.

The cultivation of the national poetry and songs is due to the poet Vasili Alexandri,[1] to Asaki, Carmen Sylva, H. Vacaresco, Wachmann, Adamescu, Kogolniceanu, and others. And the establishment of Conservatoires at Bucarest and Jassy, where young musicians can obtain a scientific training in their own country, augurs well for the future of Roumanian song-writers.

There is also a considerable Roumanian colony of Balkan origin in Hungary, who first established themselves here in 1230. They lead a more or less wandering life among the mountains, pasturing flocks. Their language, of a Latin stem, is much intermixed with Albanian, Slavonic, and Hungarian words, but their folk-songs and dances are quite distinct, and essentially their own. Among the dances we find the true Roumanian *hŏra, sirba, tarina*, and *ardeleana* ; and their innumerable songs and ballads are of Balkan rather than Hungarian origin. The oldest are theological or mystical in subject, but in the historical ones the heroes fight against the Turks. Among the *kolindas*, the religious kind are the commonest, treating of the life of our Lord, of the Virgin and saints, and the melodies are in plain-song.[2]

BIBLIOGRAPHY

Sulzer, F. J. *Geschichte des transalpinischen Daciens.* Vienna, 1781-2.
Zustand der Musik in der Moldau, Allg. Musik. Zeitung, xxiii. Leipzig, 1821.
Grenville Murray, E. C. *Doine, or the National Songs and Legends of Roumania.* London, 1854.
Wagner, O. *Das rumänische Volkslied, Sammelbände*, I.M.G. 1902, i.
Schorr, J. *Musik in Rumänien, Die Musik*, 1903, No. 22.
(The principal material for the above sketch was kindly supplied to the writer by M. Margaritesco, Bucarest.)

COLLECTIONS

Pann, A. 'Cântece de stea' (Cantiques de Noël). Bucarest, 1830-48.
Musicescu, G. '12 Melodii nationale armonizate.' Jassy, 1889.
Gebauer, C., and Fedŕr, M. 'Volkslieder und Volkstänze.' Bucarest.
Wachmann, J. A. 'Mélodies Valaques pour le piano.' Müller, Vienna. 'Rumänische Volksmelodien.' Vienna, 1865.
Mikuli, C. 'Airs nationaux roumains.' Léopol.
Ionescu, M. 'Col. de cântece nationale.' Bucarest.
Vacaresco, H. 'Airs pop. roumains.' Bucarest, 1900.

[1] Vasili Alexandri was the first to collect the folk-ballads. His collection was published in 1852. See Otto Wagner's article 'Das rumänische Volkslied,' *Sammelbände*, I.M.G. No. 1, 1902, where the treatment of the literary side of the folk-song is far superior to the musical.
[2] These Roumanians belong to the Greek Church. See G. Moldarau's article 'Die Rumäner' in *Die Oesterreichisch-ungarische Monarchie*, vol. vi.

Paulmann, S. 'Album naţional, colecţiune de arii romanesci.' Bucarest, 1902.
'Chitaristui romān' (Colecţiune de arii si romanţi naţionale). Bucarest, 1903.
Kiriac, D. G. 'Coruri populare romanesti.' Bucarest, 1904-5.

MODERN GREECE

It is difficult if not impossible to avoid the mention of Oriental Songs, when treating those of Greece, because in the islands and on the mainland the songs are intermingled. M. Bourgault-Ducoudray says that in Greece the oriental chromatic scale is often found :—

Ex. 1.

And again in Smyrna and other parts of Asia Minor the Aeolian scale[3] is in constant use. The melodies sung along the coast and in the Ionian islands are very Italian in character, and are easily distinguished from the genuine Greek melodies by being in the European minor scale. But inland, and away from the coast of Asia Minor, the pure Greek songs predominate.[4]

Until within a recent period there existed a number of minstrels or bards who combined the profession of musicians with that of chroniclers, and whose function it was to hand down by word of mouth, and thus keep alive, the great traditions of their country's history. These men were held in high esteem in their time ; but, as in other countries, education and the introduction of printing have brought about their rapid disappearance. Yet we are told that only a few years ago, an old and blind minstrel, by name Barba Sterios,[5] sat, surrounded by a crowd, on the roadside by the gate of Kalamaria in Thessalonica. He played and sang in a melancholy and monotonous tone to his λύρα,[6] without raising his voice to a high pitch, and in pathetic parts drew deep emotion from his audience. In epic recitations of this kind the lyre is only used as an accompaniment in succession to the chanted words, and not with them. For instance, the old man to whom reference has just been made, would start by touching a prelude on his lyre, and then commence intoning a couple of verses, after which the instrument came in again, and so on to the end, alternately playing and singing.[7]

[3] The Greek names of the modes are here retained in preference to the ecclesiastical, and those readers not conversant with the interchange of nomenclature are referred to the article on MODES, ECCLESIASTICAL.
[4] M. Bourgault-Ducoudray says in the preface to his 'Trente Mélodies Populaires de Grèce et d'Orient' (using the Greek names) that the Greek Hypodorian, which only differs from the European A minor scale by the absence of the leading-note, is of frequent occurrence among the popular melodies of Greece. The Greek Dorian, Phrygian, Hypophrygian, and Mixolydian modes are also fairly often met with ; and the Hypolydian with the fourth lowered (which may easily be confused with the Western major scale of F) is at the present time the commonest of all.
[5] *Barba* =uncle, is used as a term of endearment, like *dyadya*=uncle in Russian.
[6] A rough sort of stringed instrument, recalling the classic λύρα with five sheep-guts ; the bow consisting of a stick bent at one end and a bunch of horse-hair strung along it.
[7] G. F. Abbott's *Songs of Modern Greece*.

The τραγούδια τοῦ χοροῦ, or choral songs, are ballads in the original sense of the word, for they are sung as an accompaniment to a complicated set of steps and mimic evolutions. At weddings, Christmas, on May-Day, and similar festivals, men and women may be seen dancing together in a ring, hand in hand, outside their country inns. The leader of the dance as he sweeps on, waves a handkerchief and sings a verse, accompanying it with appropriate gestures, while the rest of the dancers sing alternate verses in chorus. There are also other dance-songs, which are sung antiphonally by distinct sets of voices. This music is of a light and gay kind, consisting of short phrases which often end on the high octave :—

Ex. 2.

with little or no variety in melody or rhythm. The words of the many Greek cradle-songs are of great beauty, but the melodies are monotonous and limited in compass.[1] Greater interest is imparted to the lyric folk-songs belonging to the eastern parts of Greece and the adjacent islands (where the melodies are naturally of an oriental character), by the irregular rhythms and constant change of time, such as alternate 2–4 and 3–4 time.

The Greeks have a gift for improvising or reciting in verse, and the preponderance of open vowels and the facility of rhyming in the Romaic language[2] render their task easy. Also they are keenly sensitive to emotions roused by striking events, and incidents both of past and present history. Many of their songs have reference to the customary periods of absence from home, when the villagers, who follow the professions of merchants or pedlars, descend from their hills to ply their trades in foreign lands.[3] Thus a youth who quits his home for the first time is accompanied a certain distance on the road by his family and friends. Before taking final leave of her son the mother laments his departure in a song either improvised or traditional, and in response the youth bewails the hard fate which drives him from his home.[4] There is proof that among the mass of folk-poetry still extant, much of it dates back to old classical times. For example, the famous swallow-songs, when boys go about the streets greeting in song the reappearance of the swallows, embody a very ancient custom.[5]

[1] The lullabies are called Βαυκαλήματα, Νινυρίσματα, Ναναρίσματα from ναναρίξω, to lull to sleep.
[2] The words of the folk-songs are all in modern Greek, i.e. Romaic, though they vary in dialect. The vernacular language is never taught, but many of the best modern poets have adopted it, and the effort made at the time of the War of Independence for the restoration of the classical language has had but a poor success.
The Romaic language is more easily translated into Italian than any other tongue. Hence the reason that song-collectors such as Bourgault-Ducoudray, Bürchner, and others, make use of it.
[3] Like the Vlachs in the Valley of Zagari who go to Spain.
[4] See Garnett's Greek Folk-Poesy, and Passow's song 'The Exile.'
[5] For the words of the Swallow and May-time songs see Kind and Passow. Many have been translated into English by Miss Lucy Garnett in Greek Folk-Poesy and Greek Folk-songs.

Serenades and aubades are most in vogue in the large towns, and each province has its own special songs ; but there are some ancient songs of great celebrity, such as 'The Fall of Constantinople,' which are the common heritage of all the provinces.

The Fall of Constantinople.[6]

Ex. 3.

In the Greek folk-songs, as among other nations, the last words or lines are often repeated, or the words are broken up into meaningless syllables, recurring three or four times before the word is completed. Or it may be that the words are interrupted by interjections or refrains. It should be noted also that the accents of the words and music do not always agree, which clearly proves that different words were set to already extant melodies. It is difficult to represent these Eastern songs in our present notation, but the following example, of which a few bars are given, is a love-story from the Island of Samos,[7] and shows many of the above-mentioned features, including the peculiar tonality, limited compass, changing time and deep melancholy, inherent to them. Stringed

Ex. 4.

etc.

instruments are used to accompany these songs, and nowadays principally guitars and mandolines.

The literary revival which followed the War of Independence, and the abundance of poetry written in the present day, have, however,

[6] This song was taken down by Bürchner from an old woman of eighty, who again had heard it from her infancy, sung by old people.
[7] Bürchner, 'Griechische Volksweisen,' p. 406.

produced no effect on the music of the country.
The Greek song-writers worthy of mention are
lamentably few; the generality of their published songs are with few exceptions either
trivial or sentimental. Among the Greek
composers who have won European fame, Spiro
Samara may be noted as the best. At an early
period of his career he achieved success in Paris
by his graceful little songs. Other song-
composers scarcely known beyond their own
country are: Zacharopoulos, Sidere, Beloudion,
Lampalete, Karrērē, Rodios, and Leonardos.

The few and best exceptions to the general
average of songs are those in which either the
composer has taken the folk-song as his model,
or the actual folk-songs themselves, such as are
to be found in L. A. Bourgault-Ducoudray's
'Trente Mélodies Populaires de Grèce et
d'Orient'; and more recently in the collection
of M. Pakhtikos, Director of the School of Music
in Constantinople, who personally noted them
down in remote districts of Thrace, Macedonia,
Crete, the Aegean Islands, etc.

BIBLIOGRAPHY AND COLLECTIONS

(The Bibliography and Collections of this country are purposely
classed together.)

Sulzer, F. J. *Geschichte des transalpinischen Daciens.* Vienna,
1781-82, 3 vols. (Contains Greek, Wallachian, and Turkish
tunes.)
Fauriel, C. *Chants populaires de la Grèce moderne* (no music).
Paris, 1824.
Kiesewetter, R. *Ueber die Musik der neueren Griechen.* Leipzig,
1838.
Sanders, D. *Das Volksleben der Neugriechen.* Mannheim, 1844.
Kind, Th. ' Neugriechische Volkslieder.' Leipzig, 1849.
Passow, A. *Liebes- und Klagelieder des Neugriechischen Volkes*
(no music). Magdeburg, 1861; ' Romaic Songs' (Τραγούδια
'Ρωμάϊκα). 1860.
Tantalides, E. ' Collection of songs, including nursery rhymes and
school-songs with music.' Athens, 1876.
Bourgault-Ducoudray. 'Trente Mélodies Populaires de Grèce et
d'Orient.' Paris, 1876.
Rangabé, A. R. *Histoire littéraire de la Grèce moderne.* Paris,
1877.
Sigala, A. ' Recueil de Chants nationaux.' Athens, 1880.
Matza, Pericles. ' 80 mélodies grecques.' Constantinople, 1883.
Garnett, L., and Stuart-Glennie, J. *Greek Folk-Songs* (nothing about
music). London, 1888.
Garnett, L., and Stuart-Glennie, J. *Greek Folk-Poesy.* London,
1896.
Abbott, G. F. *Songs of Modern Greece* (no music). Cambridge, 1900.
Bürchner, L. ' Griechische Volksweisen.' (*Sammelbände of the
I.M.G.* iii. 403.)
Pernot, H., and le Flem, P. 'Mel. pop. de Chio en pays turc.'
Appendix. Paris, 1903.
Pakhtikos, G. D. ' 260 Greek songs (Asia Minor, Macedonia, Cyprus,
Albania, etc.)' Athens, 1905.

RUSSIA

No country is richer in national music than
Russia, and nowhere has it been more carefully
preserved from neglect or oblivion. For many
years the folk-songs and dances of the most
remote districts have been collected by order of
the Government: musicians and savants of the
highest rank [1] have joined in folk-song research
and assisted in the task of compilation. This
was all the more necessary as civilisation is
everywhere gradually killing oral tradition, and
it is only the old people in the villages who
still sing the ancient epic songs. Moreover, the
modern school of Russian music, which holds
so important a place in art, owes, in part, its

[1] Such as Balakirev, Rimsky-Korsakov, Serov, Melgounov, and
others.

strength and magnetic attraction to the ingrain
colour derived from race temperament. Though
Russian music has only lately achieved European
renown, it has always been loved and cultivated
in its own country. Hence from birth onwards
the peculiar harmonies and rhythms of his native
land have so possessed the ear of every Russian
musician, that consciously or unconsciously he
re-echoes them in his works.

The oldest form of national poetry would
seem to be the *builini,* of which there is evidence
that they existed 1000 years ago. They are
national epics akin to the historical romances;
of great length and in unrhymed metre.[2] The
music, which is a kind of monotonous chant,
accompanies one line, or at most two lines of
the song, repeating to the end.

As it befell in the capital Kieff.[3]

Ex. 1.

The *horovodi* or choral songs belong solely to
the Slav races. They celebrate the change of
seasons and the successive festivals of the ecclesiastical or agricultural calendar, while some are
especially appropriate to various peasant occupations.[4] These *horovodi* are sung in a curious
manner: the first voice sings a melody, the
other voices in succession sing variants of the
same melody, and as the voices fall in with one
another a kind of harmony is established, whilst
each voice retains its independence.

Ex. 2.

1st Voice.

2nd Voice.　　　　　　　　　　　　etc.

The historian Melgounov, one of the highest
authorities on Russian folk-music, contends
that from the earliest time it was essentially
polyphonic in structure, and he refutes the
general idea that folk-songs were sung in unison.[5]
In taking down the songs from the peasants he
carefully recorded each voice separately, and
attributed great importance to the preservation
of the popular counterpoint. His examples show
that the secondary parts (*podgoloski*) constitute
really a free imitation of the main melody:

[2] One of the most interesting small collections of *builini* was
made by R. James, an English clergyman, who spent the winter of
1619 in the far north of Russia. His MSS. are now in the Bodleian
Library.
[3] Rimsky-Korsakov,'Chants nationaux Russes,' No. 1. (Communicated by Moussorgsky.)
[4] The singers of the christening, wedding, funeral, or even conscription songs are always elderly women, and no ceremony is
considered properly conducted without them. They are to some
extent 'improvisatrici'—reflecting in their song, past and present,
individual and general conditions. See preface to Dioutsh, Liapounov, and Istomin's ' Songs of the Russian People.'
[5] See preface to J. Melgounov's ' Russian Songs,' and see vol. iii.
p. 105b.

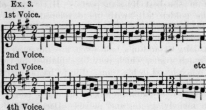

Ex. 3.
1st Voice.
2nd Voice.
3rd Voice.   etc.
4th Voice.

The *piessni* or solo songs are very often sung to the accompaniment of the *balalaïka*, a guitar-like instrument. These are mainly lyrical in character, and reflect the emotions and episodes of peasant life. Some of the love-songs are beautiful, and the wailing songs—*zaplachki*—most pathetic. The melancholy and monotonous cradle-songs have a strange charm of their own ; and the so-called 'laudatory' songs (glorifying some individual indiscriminately, before or after death), which are the peculiar property of the Slav, rank high in importance among the songs of the peasants.[1]

The rhythm of Russian folk-songs is often characterised by extreme irregularity. The tunes usually begin on the first beat of the bar, but the phrases are of unequal length ; they are frequently in 7–4 or 5–4 time, or 2–4 and 3–4 time alternating ; but it must be remembered on the authority of Sokalski and others, that the division of the melodies into bars is arbitrary.[2] The original tunes, handed down by oral tradition, owed their rhythm to no symmetrical repetition of accents, but to the cadences suggested by the flow of the verse itself. Again it frequently happens that the accent of the verse varies, which renders it difficult to arrange under the regular metrical accentuation of the time system. The accent moves from one syllable or one word to another, for instance, *gòry* or *gorỳ* (hills)—as if to avoid monotony ; and the inequality of the number of syllables in each half verse, each of which has one main accent, appears to be one of the characteristics of Russian folk-songs.[3] Naturally the dance-songs have more regular accents and rhythms, especially those of gipsy origin, when the dancers mark the time with their feet. Peasants do not like singing solos ; they prefer to sing in *artel* or companies, in which each member is a performer and composer, owing to the above-mentioned structure of the songs.

Glinka and many other theorists have made the peculiar tonality and harmonisation of Russian songs their life-long study. Melgounov says that they are based on the so-called natural (untempered) scale, which is impossible to represent in our present notation ; and that the foundation of the major and minor scales

is contained in this simple formula : $1 1 \frac{1}{2} 1 1 1 \frac{1}{2}$. That is, if the relative minor of the scale of C is taken descending from dominant to its octave, the result is :—

$$e_1 d_1 c_\frac{1}{2} b_1 a_1 g_1 f_\frac{1}{2} e.$$

This when reversed will be found to be identical with the ecclesiastical Phrygian mode.[4] Certainly there is an indisputable connection between the musical theory of the ancient Greeks and the oldest and actually existing Slavonic melodies founded on these scales, more especially those of the western part of Russia. To modern ears the tonality, therefore, is of an uncertain character, and many melodies commence in the major and bear distinctly the stamp of the major key, until towards the end, where they modulate into the minor key in which they conclude. Further they more often begin and end on the supertonic, or indeed on any degree of the scale rather than the tonic. Another peculiarity we find in the folk and art-songs alike are the florid passages on one syllable ; for instance in 'The Cossack of the Don' and some of Rubinstein's songs. This and many other features in Russian Song could be traced to Asiatic influence, for in Russia the eastern and western temperaments meet and intermingle.[5]

Early in the 19th century national representation was lacking in Russian music. It awaited emancipation from the foreign influences under which it had so long lain. It was Glinka who first began to effect its liberation, and the importance of his work cannot be exaggerated. Though his national opera, 'La vie pour le Czar' (except for a few bars in the opening chorus), incorporates no single folk-song, Glinka so identified himself with the feeling and spirit of the national music, that his melodies became at once familiar to his countrymen. Glinka has truly been named the father of the Russian art-song. Previous to him, other song-composers, such as Alabiev, Varlamov, Kozlovsky, Verstovsky,[6] and Lvov, wrote songs of the simple, popular type, imitating so faithfully the external qualities of the real folk-song, that some, such as Alabiev's 'Nightingale' and Varlamov's 'Red Sarafan' have been accepted as national melodies. Lvov was the composer of the Russian national hymn,[7] the tune of which, though fine and suitable to the words, is not Russian in character.[8] Again, others like

---

[1] The numerous other kinds of songs which the above classifications do not include cannot here be dealt with. They will be found under their different headings in any standard collection. See also Ralston's *Songs of the Russian People*, pp. 34, 39 *et seq.*
[2] Sokalski's *Russian Folk-Songs.*
[3] See preface to Lineff's 'Peasant Songs of Great Russia.'

[4] Tchaikovsky's remarks on the character of the folk-songs are worth quoting. In writing to Tolstoi to acknowledge some songs he had sent him, Tchaikovsky says, 'I must frankly say the songs have not been skilfully treated, and thereby all their original beauty has been lost. The chief fault is, that they have been forced into a regular, formal rhythm. The *builini* have nothing in common with the dances. Besides this, the greater part of these songs are written in the cheerful D major scale, and this does not agree in the least with the tonality of the true Russian Volkslied, which is always of an uncertain tonality, so that one can really only compare them with the old church modes.'
[5] C. Cui remarks that the 'Tartar influence is so strong that there is hardly one Russian folk-song not affected by it.'
[6] Verstovsky, who was hailed for a time as the true Messiah of Russian music, owed his fleeting popularity to his operas more than to his songs.
[7] Composed to order in 1833, the words by Shukovsky.
[8] It has recently been stated that Lvov was not the true composer

Gurilev, Vassilev, and Dübüque arranged a number of national airs, especially the so-called gipsy tunes, to modern words in rhyme and four-line stanzas, with a simple pianoforte accompaniment. Glinka's songs stand on a higher level, though they vary in merit; some of the earlier ones betray the Italian influence, and have elementary accompaniments; some are in dance-rhythm pervaded by a local colouring; others are pure lyrics and very expressive, but his finest effort is the powerful ballad 'The Midnight Review.' Dargomijsky was nearly Glinka's contemporary, and shared the same enthusiasm for his country's music. His songs show more dramatic power; many consist of short declamatory phrases akin to recitative, and all evince a high regard for the meaning and metre of the words. Dargomijsky has, moreover, caught the intense but languorous spirit of the East. His ballads take high rank, especially one called 'Knight Errant.'[1] Rubinstein is a strange paradox. More cosmopolitan and western in feeling than any other Russian composer, it is his eastern songs which are the best. Many of his songs belong to the German *Lied*, the accompaniments being clearly based on Schumann as a model, as for instance, 'Nun die Schatten dunkeln' (Geibel), and 'Nacht' (Eichendorff). But his settings of Mirza Schaffy's words are by far the most beautiful and original of all his songs, and all are essentially vocal.

The following five composers may be said to constitute the new school of Russian music: Borodin, Balakirev, Cui, Moussorgsky, and Rimsky-Korsakov. They are frankly progressive; their aims are high and, generally speaking, they maintain their ideal. They formulated certain principles of their art, one of which directly concerns Song, 'that vocal music should be in perfect accordance with the meaning of the text.' And though each composer with his individual tendencies produced different work, they were unanimous on this point, as may be seen on closer examination of their songs. They were mostly cultivated men, and with regard to the *culte* of their native music they were directly under the influence of Glinka and Dargomijsky. Borodin's songs are of rare beauty and distinction. They are original in form, and remarkable for certain peculiarities of harmony. Borodin had a strong predilection for the rhythms and modes of the East.[2] Balakirev, one of Glinka's true disciples, wrote only twenty-five songs; they are chiefly lyrical in feeling, and all are scrupulously finished and polished. For his words, he chose only

from the best Russian poets. His 'Song of the golden fish,' with its developed and interesting accompaniment, is one of the most perfect specimens of modern Russian songs. Among César Cui's best songs are those set to French words, which may be explained by the French blood in his veins. But he has a special gift for song-writing, and among his numerous songs—over 150 in number—not one is lacking in melody, grace, and polish. Dargomijsky's direct successor may be said to be Moussorgsky, an interesting but unequal composer. Gloom, tragedy, and grim humour are to be found in his songs, but there also exist sincerity and pathos. Rimsky-Korsakov's love for his country's music and his valuable collections have been already alluded to, and throughout his songs this national spirit may be felt. His songs are neither long nor numerous, and their beauty is of a restrained kind. Their chief characteristics are 'beautiful and uncommon harmonies and elaborated accompaniments, by which he gives relief to the melodic phrases.'[3] Rimsky-Korsakov has excelled in the composition of eastern songs, and 'all are characterised by a certain languid monotony, in keeping with the oriental style of the words.'[4] Tchaikovsky cannot be classed in any school; he stands alone. He was more cosmopolitan than the afore-mentioned composers, and more individual than national in his music. The emotional value and the beautiful melodies of his songs compensate for the inadequacy of ill-chosen words and for the defects of a certain diffuseness of treatment. But notwithstanding these artistic demerits, as an expression of passion, tragic or triumphant, his songs make a direct appeal and elicit a direct response. To this quality may be attributed his wide popularity in non-Slavonic countries.

Sacred and spiritual songs are greatly sung in Russia, and in connection with them Lvov, Bortniansky, Bachmetiev, and Dmitriev's names are well known. The eminent antagonistic critics Stassov and Serov also deserve mention, although song-writing was not their forte.

In conclusion it remains to give the names of some other contemporary song-writers; Alpheraky, Antipov, Arensky, Artcibouchev, S. and F. Blumenfeld, Davidov, Glazounov, Gretchaninov, Grodsky, Kopylov, Liadov, Liapounov, Rachmaninov, Rebikov, Scriabin, Sokolov, Stcherbatchev, Wihtol, etc. Some of these musicians are young, and their work varies in merit, but it cannot be denied that in Russia, Song, both the folk- and art-song, is regarded as a serious branch of music, and treated with care and reverence.

BIBLIOGRAPHY

The general histories of Russian music by Youri von Arnold, Famintsine (on old Slavonic music), Sacchetti, Beresovsky, Sokalski (Folk-Song), etc.

---

of this hymn, but merely took the melody of the trio of a *Geschwindmarsch*, composed by F. Bogdanovitch Haas, bandmaster of the St. Petersburg regiment of the Guards, and published in a March Collection in 1822. The notes are identical, the only change being made in the time.

[1] C. Cui says of this ballad: 'It is impossible to put into adequate words all the laconic strength, the picturesque qualities and vivid realism conveyed by this song. It breathes the spirit of the past and appeals to the mind as vividly as a picture.'

[2] See *Borodin and Liszt*, by Alfred Habets, translated by Mrs. Newmarch.

[3] Mrs. Newmarch, *The Art-Songs of Russia*, Sammelbände, I.M.G. iii. 2.   [4] *Ibid.*

Rasoumovsky. *Le chant de l'Eglise en Russie.* Moscow, 1867-69.
Ralston, W. R. S. *Songs of the Russian People.* London, 1872.
Cui, C. *La musique en Russie.* Paris, 1880.
Perepelitzine. *History and Dictionary of Russian Music.* 1884.
Habets, A. *Borodin and Liszt.* London, 1895.
Soubies, A. *Histoire de la musique en Russie.* Paris, 1898.
Mikhuievitch. *L'aperçu de l'histoire de la musique en Russie.*
Lectures and articles by Mrs. Newmarch.
See also the Russian edition of Riemann's *Lexikon* with supplement by J. Engel. Jurgenson, Moscow, 1905.
Extensive work has also been done by the St. Petersburg Song Commission of the Imperial Geographical Society, and the Moscow Musico Ethnographic Committee.

COLLECTIONS

Troutovsky, V. F. 'Russian Songs.' (The first collection.) 1782.
Prach, Ivan. 'Russian Pop. Songs.' St. Petersburg, 1806 and 1815. (Introduction by N. A. Lvov.) 1790.
Doppelmair, G. von. 'Russische Volkslieder.' Leipzig, 1809.
Goetze, P. O. v. 'Stimmen des russ. Volks in Liedern.' Stuttgart, 1828.
Stanovitch, M. 'Recueil de chants pop. russes.' 1834.
Sakarov, J. P. 'Songs of the Russian People.' St. Petersburg, 1838-39.
Kiryeevsky, P. V. 'Russian Folk-Songs.' Moscow, 1860.
Ruibnikov, P. N. 'Songs of the Russian People.' St. Petersburg, 1861-67.
Kashin, D. '115 Russian National Songs.' Moscow, 1833, 1841, 1868.
Bernard, M. 'Chants pop. russes.' St. Petersburg, 1868.
Edlichka. 'Chants Nationaux de la Petite-Russie.' St. Petersburg, 1868.
Philippov and Rimsky-Korsakov. 'Chants nationaux Russes.' 1870.
Hilfering, A. 'Collection of Builini (Bylinas).' 1873.
Prokounin, K., and Tchaikovsky, P. 'Chants pop. russes.' Moscow, 1873.
Melgounov, J. 'Russian Folk-Songs.' Moscow, 1879.
Sokalski, P. P. 'Russian Folk-songs.' Kharkov, 1888.
Dioutsh, Liapounov, and Istomin. 'Songs of the Russian People.' St. Petersburg, 1894.
Paltchinov, N. 'Peasants' Songs.' Moscow, 1896.
Balakirev, M. 'Recueil de Chants pop. russes.' Leipzig, 1898.
Istomine and Nekrasov. '50 Chants du peuple russe.' St. Petersburg, 1901.
Lincff, Eugénie. 'Peasant Songs of Great Russia' (transcribed from phonograms). St. Petersburg and London, 1905.

SOUTH AND OTHER SLAVONIC NATIONS

Much that has been said about the national music of Russia would apply also to other branches of the Slavonic people.[1] There are, nevertheless, important variations in the traits they appear to have in common, and certain characteristics peculiar to each nation which claim notice. The remarks will, however, refer chiefly to the folk-music, as in many of the countries music remains still in its primitive state, or can hardly be said to have developed beyond the stage of national airs ; no musical schools have been formed, and the composers would merely be classed under the generic term, Slavonic.[2] But of the beauty and enormous wealth of the folk-songs in these countries proof has been afforded by the many and valuable collections which already exist and yearly increase.

Indigenous to the Ukraine[3] is a kind of epic song of irregular rhythm recited to a slow chant. These *doumas* were originally improvised by the *Bandurists*, but these wandering minstrels are now nearly extinct, and their function has devolved upon the village women, who invent both the poetry and melodies of the songs which

they sing. Among the peculiarities of these interesting songs, one is, that if the song ends on the dominant or lower octave, the last note of the closing verse is sung very softly, and then without a break the new verse begins loud and accented, the only division between the two being such a shake as described by the German phrase *Bocktriller*. This feature is common also to Cossack songs,[4] and to the songs of that Wendic branch of the Slavonic race which is found in a part of Saxony.

Ex. 1.   *Wendic Folk-song.*

The Wendic songs, except when dance-tunes, are generally sung *tremolando* and very slowly. And the exclamation 'Ha' or 'Hale,' with which they almost invariably commence, may be compared with the 'Hoj' or 'Ha' of the Ruthenians and the 'Ach' of Great Russia. One of the most popular Ruthenian songs is 'Ein Kosakritt,' better known under the name of 'Schöne Minka.'[5] The superior charm of the songs of Little Russia is due, for the most part, to a prevailing cast of melancholy. Inhabited by a people who vie with the Poles in susceptibility to poetic sentiment, Little Russia is naturally rich in songs. The greater part are in the minor, or based on the Church scales, of a slow tempo, and frequently with a halt or drag in the rhythm produced by shortening the first syllable and prolonging the

second, thus :—

Croatian peasants, men or women, never use songs already composed ; they improvise the words as well as the melodies themselves. Hence only those songs which sprang from the people are sung by them.[6] This does not apply to the ritual songs which have been handed down by oral tradition for centuries, and in which the Croatians are very rich. The following song is sung at Midsummer as the men and women leap and dance round the fires lighted on the hill-tops and call to the heathen goddess 'Lado.'[7]

Ex. 3.

La-do! La-do! Bog pomana tomu stanu liepa j' La-do!

[1] Roughly speaking the Slavonic people may be thus divided. East Slavs: Great Russians and Little Russians with Ruthenes, Ukrainians, and the White Russians. West Slavs : Czechs, Slovaks, Moravians, Poles, and Wends. South Slavs : Slovenes, Croats, Serbs, and Bulgarians, including Bosnians, Dalmatians, and Montenegrins.
[2] As for instance Borodin, who is a Georgian composer, is mentioned under Russia.
[3] 'Le dialecte de l'Oukraïne en est tout différent du Russe. Ce n'est pas un patois, c'est un dialecte constitué, qui possède une brillante littérature. C'est surtout la noblesse de Kiev, de la Volhynie, Podolie qui a subi l'influence polonaise ; le *moujik* de l'Oukraine est resté en dehors de son action par la nature de sa vie, et surtout par la différence de religion, car il pratique toujours le rite grec.' Dr. A. Bonmariage, *Notes pour la Russie d'Europe*, p. 430 *et seq.*

[4] The Don Cossacks are Great Russians, and the Zaparogues Cossacks are Little Russians. Dr. A. Bonmariage, *Notes pour la Russie d'Europe*, p. 417.
[5] The music and original words are given in Prach's collection, and the German version in Fink's *Mus. Hausschatz*, No. 157. See also SCHÖNE MINKA.
[6] F. Kuhač in a letter to Mr. Barclay Squire from Agram in 1893.
[7] From F. Z. Kuhač's article in the *Oesterreichisch-ungarische Monarchie*, vol. vii. p. 110 *et seq.*

2 o

The chief dance-song of the Croatians and Serbs is the *kolo*, of which there are many kinds. To the *oro kolo* the peasants sing religious songs; to the *junačko kolo* heroic ballads; to the *zensko kolo* love-songs; and to the *šalgivo kolo* humorous songs. There is a marked difference between the town and village songs. The latter exhibit the truest Croatian feeling; the town songs are more cosmopolitan, and are much influenced by the wandering *Tanburists*, who, like the Hungarian gipsies, sing and play the *tanbura* (the national instrument) in taverns.

Since the Illyrian movement of 1835, a national school of music has arisen in Croatia, and been fostered by educated musicians of the country. Previous to this, a Conservatoire of music had been founded at Agram, but it was not until 1846, when Vatroslav Lisinski's popular opera 'Ljubovi zlova' was given, that Croatian art-music gained notice.[1] Lisinski, Ferdo Livadić, Ferdo Rusan, Ivan Zajc and his pupil G. Eisenhuth, the historian V. Klaić, and the young composer Vilko Novak have contributed to the lyric music of Croatia.[2] F. Z. Kuhač's large collection of South Slavonic folk-songs is of great value. The composer of the Croatian national anthem, 'Liepa naša domovina,' was an officer named Josip Runjanin.

All the Serb songs are of remarkable beauty and expressiveness, and although they resemble the Russian songs as regards their scale and tonality and the same elastic metre prevails, yet the melodies are more sustained and flowing. And

[1] *Musik in Croatien*, by Ferdo Miler, p. 174 *et seq.* in *Oest.-ung. Mon.*
[2] Although Haydn was a Croatian by birth and freely used his native folk-songs in his instrumental works, he is rightly classed among German composers. But the remarkable resemblance between his greatest German song, 'Gott erhalte,' the Austrian National Hymn, and a folk-song from the Bistritz district of Croatia cannot be passed over in silence. It has given rise to much discussion; see for instance, H. Reimann and F. Kuhač in the *Allgemeine deutsche Musikzeitung*, 1893 (Nos. 40-42); also Hugo Conrat's article in *Die Musik*, Jan. 1, 1905; and *Josip Haydn*, by Dr. Kuhač. The tune is as follows:—

Ex. 3.   *Stal se jesem.*

O. Fleischer, whilst admitting the resemblance of Haydn's melody to the folk-song, prefers to trace its origin back to the Church, and quotes many examples of hymns which open with the same phrase as 'Gott erhalte,' thus:—

Ex. 4.

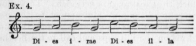

Di - es i - rae   Di - es   il - la

from the Franciscan Requiem; and

Ex. 5.

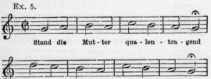

Stand die   Mut-ter   qua - len - tra - gend

An dem   Kreu - ze   und er - kla - gend.

a Stabat Mater from Cantarium S. Galli, 1845 (see *Zur vergleichenden Liedforschung*; *Sammelbände* of the I.M.G. iii. 2). See also Hadow, *A Croatian Composer*.

among these south-eastern nations the affinity with the music of the Arabs and other nations of Western Asia is more often indicated. The Servian drinking-songs are noticeable; grave, solemn, and devotional, they are quite unlike those of any other country; but as among the Serbs the hymns and secular songs are so frequently intermingled, this may be accounted for. Most of the Servian and many of the Bulgarian songs end on the supertonic, as in the Servian national hymn:—

Ex. 6.

The Bulgarian songs are also quite irregular in metre, and far more fragmentary than the Servian:—

Ex. 7.
Lento.

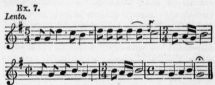

The Bulgarians have a great love for the folk-lore of their country, and the volumes of the Sbornik, which the State publishes yearly, contain legends, ballads, and songs with music.

BIBLIOGRAPHY

The best information on the songs of the above nations is contained in the different volumes of *Die Oesterreichisch-ungarische Monarchie* and the prefaces to the collections.

COLLECTIONS

Lipinski, C. 'Chants du peuple de Gallicie.' Lemberg, 1833.
Kollar, J. 'Národnie Zpiewanky.' Buda Pest, 1834.
Achazel and Korytho. 'Carniolian Songs.' 1839.
Pauli, I. Z. 'Pieśne ludu Ruskiego w Galicyi.' Lemberg, 1839-40.
Haupt and Schmaler. 'Volkslieder der Wenden.' Grimma, 1841
Krasinski, H. 'The Cossacks of the Ukraine.' London, 1848.
Kocipinkim, A. 'Chansons pop. russes en Podolie, l'Oukraine, etc.' 1862.
Roubietz, A. 'Chansons pop. de l'Oukraine.' Moscow, 1872; 'Chansons pop. petit-russiens.' St. Petersburg, 1875.
Kuhač, F. Z. 'Chansons nationales des Slaves du Sud.' Agram, 1878-81. (This contains Servian, Dalmatian, Bosnian, Croatian, etc. songs.)
Chodźko, A. B. 'Les Chants historiques de l'Ukraine.' Paris, 1879.
De Vollau. 'Rutheno-Galician Folk-songs.' 1885. (Publ. by Russian Geog. Soc.)
Stoianov and Ratschow. '24 Chansons notées (bulgares).' 1887.
Kalanz, A. 'Serbische Volksmelodien.' Vienna, 1890.
Vasilev, G. P. '225 Chansons pop. bulgares.' Tirnovo, 1891.
The publications in the *Sbornik* vols. for 1894 and 1897.
Bosiljeva, S. 'Album des Chansons nationales de la Bosnie.' Agram, 1895.
Georgewitch, V. R. 'Mélodies nationales serbes.' Belgrade, 1896.
Gemtchounov, A. and Vl. 'Les Chants des Cosaques de l'Oural.' St. Petersburg, 1899.
Stöhr, A. 'Album Croatien.'
Das musikalische Oesterreich contains Croatian, Carniolian, Dalmatian, and Bosnian Songs. Vienna.
Parlovic. 'Servian Songs.' Agram.
Kocorà. '15 Chants nationaux des Serbes Lusaciens.' Prague.
Manteuffel, Gustav. Freiherr von. 'Deutsche altlivländische Volkslieder.' 1906.

POLAND

The songs of the Poles are mainly presented to us in the form of hymns, or in the form of their national dance-rhythms. One of the earliest and most celebrated examples of the former, dating from the 10th century, is St. Adalbert's hymn to the Virgin ('Boga Rodziça'), which is engraved in plain-chant on his tomb in the cathedral of Gnesen.[1] Here and at Dombrova on the Warka, it is still sung every Sunday. The hymn is, however, well known throughout Poland, as it is used on all solemn occasions, for triumphant or sad ceremonials and on the battlefield[2] :—

Ex. 1.

Another familiar hymn is the 'Hajnaly,' which is heard every morning from the towers of Cracow to awaken the sleeping town. In the old sacred song-books called *Kancyonaly* or *Cancionales*[3] preserved in cathedrals, convents, and in the libraries of the great nobles, many old secular folk-songs are to be found incorporated in masses and motets ;[4] likewise many *kolendas* which are peculiar to the Polish people. These *kolendas* (noëls) are old folk-songs, some dating from the 13th century, and are still sung in every house and street at Christmas time, and it is in one of these *kolendas* that we meet with the rhythm of the polonaise :—

W Zlobie lezy.

Ex. 2.

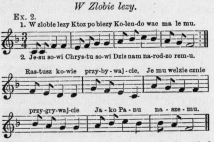

The Poles have ever loved their simple, dignified hymns, and are so familiar with them that they may be truly called their national music.[5]

Unlike the Russian and other Slavonic races the Poles are singularly exempt from Asiatic influences, and are far more European in feeling. At an early date they accepted the Roman Catholic faith ; and while adhering to the Slav language, they adopted the characters of the Latin alphabet. The Poles are excitable and more finely susceptible to romance than the Russians, and their music is full of fire and passion. Their songs are somewhat wanting in melodic invention, though this deficiency is hidden by the wonderful skill with which they are varied and embellished ; and they are marked by a poetic melancholy which makes them attractive. In colouring, they are instrumental rather than vocal, as revealed in their difficult intervals :—

Ex. 3.

It is rather to their characteristic and striking rhythms, free, varied, and elastic and yet contained in dance forms, such as the *polonez*, *krakowiak*, and especially the *mazur* or *mazurek*, that they owe their rare beauty and brilliance. The *mazurek*[6] is usually a melancholy yet quick and strongly accented dance-song in 3–4 time ; the *tempo* is irregular and closely follows the words. These may treat of peasant occupations—hay-making, harvest, vintage, or of love, sorrow, parting, or meeting. Some of the oldest *mazurs*, *polonezes*,[7] and more especially the hymns, take their name from a battle or historic event recounted in the text. The *krakowiak*[8] is described by C. Miaskowski in a book of poems published in 1632, proving that this lively dance-song in duple time has long been popular in the country. And to the same date and genre belong the *gregorianki*—songs which the market-women of Cracow sing on the festival of their patron-saint.

In scientific and ecclesiastical composers Poland excelled for many centuries, but in the 17th century these gave place to Italian musicians who reigned supreme at Court. The first efforts to counteract the Italian influence were made by Kaminsky, J. Stefani, and J. Elsner in the second half of the 18th century. These founders of Polish national opera, by incorporating a large number of their country's songs into their works, won immense popularity. Elsner also wrote many volumes of songs, besides two treatises on the rhythm and prosody of the Polish language and its suitableness for singing. Elsner's melodies are simple and facile ; and though scarcely known beyond the borders of Poland, there, he is still one of the favourite composers.

Rather earlier in the same century the charming poems of François Karpinski were set to music—either to original or adapted tunes, and, sung by rich and poor alike, belonged in their turn to the national song-group, such for instance, as 'Yuz miesionç zeszell' ('Déjà la lune se lève'), which is still heard. In 1816 the poet Niemcewicz published his great work, *Spiewy historyczne z muzyka i rycinami*

---

[1] St. Adalbert was born in 936. Ending life as a member of the Polish hierarchy, St. Adalbert belongs to Poland ; by birth, however, he was Bohemian, and, at one time, Bishop of Prague.

[2] For the hymn (translated into modern notation by F. Lessel) see Sowinski, *Les Musiciens Polonais*, p. 64.

[3] The Bohemian Brothers first printed the *Cancionales* at Prague and at Cracow, in 1558.

[4] This is not the place to speak of the interesting polyphonic school of music which flourished in Poland during the late 15th and 16th centuries, and of the work done by the so-called College of Roratists at Cracow. This school was represented by such composers as Felzstyn, Leopolita, Szamotulski, Szadek, etc., all of whom were clearly under Flemish influence.

[5] Two hymns to the Virgin and a Resurrection hymn are especially celebrated, and these were printed by the Abbé Mioduzewsky in his collections of sacred songs at Cracow in 1838. For further information on these historic hymns, see E. Oloff, *Polnische Lieder-Geschichte*, 1744.

[6] See MAZURKA.   [7] See POLONAISE.   [8] See CRACOVIENNE.

(Historical Songs with Music), and invited the best-known musicians (men and women) of the day to compose or arrange melodies for it. This work, which included some of the oldest hymns (amongst them the celebrated ' Boga Rodziça'), war songs, and legends, stimulated the patriotism of the Polish nation, and is cherished by every class.

In most of the songs belonging to the early part of the last century the national character-istics are to be found ; and especially is this the case with those of Ig. F. Dobrzynski, E. Jenicke, W. Kazynski, Ig. Komorowski, M. Madeyski, J. Nowakowski, A. Sowinski, C. J. Wielhorski, K. Wysoçki, and A. Zarzycki. But while these composers are hardly known beyond their native country, Chopin and Moniuszko have attained a world-wide reputation. Though neither are wholly Poles by birth, they have closely identi-fied themselves with the Polish national spirit. Moniuszko was born in Lithuania, but this country has long been connected with Poland.[1] Both he and Chopin have drawn from the beautiful Lithuanian folk-music, and especially from the *dainos*,[2] which, monotonous as they are, yet possess a peculiar charm.[3] Moniuszko borrowed many traditional tunes from other Slavonic provinces, but all his songs, whether original or borrowed, are delicate, fresh, and varied, and through them all rings a strange but attractive personal note. They are de-servedly loved and sung throughout Poland, Galicia, and Lithuania. Chopin's songs would take higher rank had they not been eclipsed by his instrumental works. Though partly of French extraction, the poetic, chivalrous, and patriotic spirit of the true Pole permeated Chopin's whole being. His seventeen songs, op. 74, were written at different periods of his life, and vary widely in character. The words of most are by his friend S. Witwicki, others are by A. Mickiewicz, Zaleski, and Krasinski. Some of the songs may be traced to traditional sources, so far as the melody goes,[4] but Chopin's exquisitely refined harmony raises them to a high artistic value. Three of the most beauti-ful are the 'Lithuanian Song' (written in 1831), the tender and sad ' Melodya' (1847), and the strange ' Dwojaki koniec' (Two corpses), with the simple chorale-like air. But those in the mazurka form, such as ' Zyczenie' (' Maiden's Desire'), 1829 ; 'Moja Pieszezotka' (' My Joys'), and ' Pieŕscień' (' The Ring'), 1844, are more widely known and sung.

Ig. Paderewski resembles Chopin in one re-spect ; he is national without being a slave to

it, and yet on hearing his songs one feels that no one but a Pole could have written them. In some an undercurrent of sadness prevails, veiled by a proud reserve, as for instance in op. 7. Others are brilliant and effective, and the ac-companiments always developed and interesting.

BIBLIOGRAPHY

Oloff, E. *Polnische Liedergeschichte.* Danzig, 1744. (Chiefly on Sacred Songs.)
Potocki, Tg. *La littérature mus. polonaise.* 1818.
Sikorski, J. *Ruch Musyozny.* 1857-62.
Sowinski, A. *Les musiciens polonais.* Paris, 1857.
Chodzko, J. L. *Histoire populaire de la Pologne.* Paris, 1864.
Gloger, Z. *Singt noch das polnische Volk.*
Jarzemski, A. *Histoire de la Musique en Pologne.*

COLLECTIONS

Fontana, J. ' Polish National Melodies.' Chappell, London, 1830.
Sowinski, J. ' Chants polonais nationaux.' Paris, 1832.
Konopka. J. ' Pieśni ludu Krakowskiego.' Cracow, 1840.
Rhesa, R. S. ' Dainos, oder Litthaunisohe Volksl.' Berlin, 1843.
Mioduszewski (Abbé). ' Pastoralki i Kolendy z Melodyami.' Cracow, 1843.
Nesselmann. '410 Dainos, mit deutscher Uebersetz. und Mus.' Berlin, 1843.
Kolberg, H. O. ' Pieśni ludu polskiego.' Warsaw, 1857-90.
Roger, J. ' Pieśne ludu Polskiego w Gornym Szlasku.' Breslau, 1863.
Berggreen. ' Folke-Sange og Melodier.' Copenhagen, 1866.
Kolberg, H. O. ' Pieśni ludu litewskiego.' Cracow, 1879.
Gloger, Z. ' Ruthenische und lithauische Volksweisen.'
Bartsch, C. ' Dainu Balsai. Melodien lithauischer Volkslieder.' Heidelberg, 1886-89.
Kolberg, H. O. ' La Mazowsze.' Cracow, 1885-90.
Gloger, Z., and Noszlzowski, Z. ' Pieśni ludu.' Cracow, 1892.
Nast, L. ' Die Volkslieder der Lithauer.' Tilsit, 1893.
Juszkiewicz, A. ' Litauische Volksweisen' (new edition). Cracow, 1900.

BOHEMIA

When Christianity was first introduced into Bohemia, the influence of the Church was strenuously exerted to suppress the songs of the people ; but the effort was made in vain, and the nation continued to sing its popular songs. The *Koledy* (*Ansingelieder*), which are still in use, are generally acknowledged to be of pagan origin. As in other countries, the early Christian Church allowed the congregation to join in the Kyrie Eleison, and the oldest Bohemian hymn is merely a translation and development of this ' Krleš.' Tradition ascribes it to St. Adalbert [5] ; it was really a prayer for peace and mercy, and was sung both in churches and on the battlefield as the national song. Another celebrated hymn, which holds the same place, was dedicated in the 13th century to St. Wencelas, the patron saint of Bohemia.[6] These national hymns, and the so-called *Rorate*,[7] are a compound of liturgical melodies and secular folk-songs. They are peculiar to Bohemia, and were allowed to be sung in the vernacular, and thus belonged to the people not less than the Church. Then later, during the Hussite movement, a like popular spirit reasserted itself in the Church. The Hussites and the Bohemian Brothers chose many secular melodies for their hymns, and thus again the hymns passed into genuine folk-songs.[8] One

---

[1] The Lithuanians are said to be of Sanscrit origin, and their language differs widely from that of other Slavonic nations.
[2] A term for secular songs in contradistinction to *ge'sme,* sacred songs.
[3] L. D. Rhesa collected a large quantity of old Lithuanian songs, and published them at Berlin in 1826, with remarks on their metre and rhythm.
[4] Karasowski states that many songs sung by the people in Poland are attributed to Chopin, and chief among them one called 'The third of May,' *Fr. Chopin,* p. 162.

[5] It is given in facsimile in Hostinsky's article on Bohemian Music in *Die Oest.-ung. Monarchie.*
[6] This hymn was composed by Arnest, Archbishop of Prague, and is given in Hostinsky's article referred to above.
[7] The *Rorate* are joyful Advent hymns, and some have been pre served in a beautiful *Cancionale* of the 14th century at Prague.
[8] To John Hus (Huss) only one sacred song can with authority be attributed. ' Stala matka zalostiva,' which contains three strophes of equal length, and a melisma of three notes to a syllable, and is nearly diatonic.

of the earliest and most famous of examples belonging to the first half of the 15th century is the Hussite Battle-Song, of which the first line runs thus :—

Ex. 1.

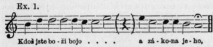

Kdož jste bo - ži bojo . . . .   a zá - ko-na je - ho,

As samples of the secular music of the 15th and 16th centuries the folk-songs preserved in the *Cancionales* are of great value. The Hussite songs are for the most part of a grave and stern character ; while those of the Bohemian or Moravian Brothers have a more tender and sensuous cast. It should be observed that the Bohemians have long been called Czechs, and that name has been adopted for the national language and music. But in their origin the Czechs were only one of the many Slavonic tribes which constitute the nationality of Bohemia and Moravia. There are some differences between the Bohemian and Moravian songs. In the former there is a predominance of songs in the major scale, while those which seem to be in the minor scale more properly belong to the ecclesiastical modes. In Moravia the balance is equal ; the tunes are of a bold decisive character, with a strongly marked rhythm. In this country also, the songs of each district are distinct,[1] and hence flows a greater wealth and variety of song. In Bohemia, on the other hand, which is homogeneous, all parts being alike, a fuller unity exists in the songs. They are more tuneful and tender, their rhythm is simpler, and the form is more regular and developed owing to the influence which German music has exercised in Bohemia.[2] Common to both and characteristic of all Bohemian songs is a vein of natural, unaffected humour, and a close connection between the verbal and musical accents. The tunes rarely begin on the weak beat of the bar, just as in the speaking language the accent is always on the first word, or first syllable. The form is sometimes in three-bar phrases, which in the longer songs develops into four bars in the middle, returning again to the three-bar phrase for the close :—

Ex. 2.

Novinka.

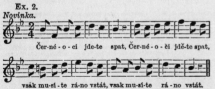

Čer-né - o - ci jde-te spat, Čer-né - o - či jdě-te spat,

vsák mu-sí - te rá-no vstát, vsak mu-sí-te rá - no vstát.

The harmony is always simple, and except in

[1] The Slovaks and Slavonic Czechs are the principal inhabitants of Moravia.
[2] It is interesting to note the difference between the two Slavonic countries. The song may belong to both of them, but with distinct variants, though more perhaps in the words than in the music. The love of nature is a strongly marked characteristic in the Bohemian folk-songs. For instance most of their songs refer to a flower, or a tree, or a bird, or a stream, or a lake, whether it be employed in a literal or metaphorical sense.

the Gipsy songs, the western scales universally prevail. Bohemians have an innate passion for dancing, which imparts marked and exhilarating rhythms to their dance songs. They are generally sung in chorus, and the influence of their national instrument, the 'Dudy,' or bagpipe, is often apparent.

Their many and varied dances (such as the *beseda, dudik, furiant, hulan, kozak, polka, sedlák, trinozka*, etc.) take their names from places or from the occasions on which they have been danced, or even more frequently from the songs with which they are accompanied. There is a close association between the folk-songs and the folk-dances of Bohemia. The greater part of the songs met with in modern collections are of no older date than the 18th century, but there are several exceptions, such as the Hussite Battle-Song, or the tune of 'Proč Kalino,' which was constantly sung in the 15th and 16th centuries, and 'Sedlák z Prahy,' which was composed in 1609.

In the 17th century there was a widespread cultivation of music in Bohemia ; both part-singing and instrumental music were salient features of domestic life. Wenzel Karl Holan (Rovensky) published a large song-book called 'Kaplackrälovski,' which reflected the musical taste of his time, and betrayed deterioration and the secularisation of sacred songs, which was, however, in effect partly due to Italian influence. Nevertheless, the harmony is bold and varied, and the accompaniments for lute and violin or more often wind-instruments, are skilfully composed.

In the 18th century foreign influences were still more marked. German, French, and Italian musicians crowded the principal towns of Bohemia, while the native musicians, such as Benda, Dussek, Reicha, Gyrowetz, etc., on the other hand, sought to win laurels abroad, where their compositions were more likely to attract notice and interest. Meanwhile, the true national music of the country was being kept alive chiefly by the village schoolmasters, who acted as organists, choir and bandmasters. Each parish had its own choir, chorus and band ; and every child was taught the study of music with as much precision as reading, writing, and arithmetic. Naturally, therefore, village music attained to a high level under such conditions.[3]

Then early in the 19th century attempts were made by the Czech composers, F. Dionys Weber, J. Kalliwoda, J. Kittl, and others to restore the lost prestige of their country's music and language. One of the first composers of real Bohemian songs was Ryba, who was followed by Kanka, Dolezalek, and Knīze.[4] But a more

[3] See Burney's *Present State of Music in Germany*, ii. 12, 14, 41.
[4] Knīze's popular ballad 'Bretislava Jitka' is to be found in most collections. For other well-known songs, such as Kroľs 'Husitská,' Škroup's 'Kde domov můj,' Rosenkranz's 'Chaloupka,' Dietrich's 'Moravo,' see Fr. Zahorsky's 'Českých národních písni.'

important factor in music was the national opera. The first and for a long time the favourite opera was written by F. Škroup (or Škraup) and the poet Chmelensky. Škroup's name will, however, be best preserved by his famous song 'Kde domov muj ?'[1] ('Where is my home ?'), which remains to this day the most popular of Bohemian songs. Between 1823 and 1830 Chmelensky and F. Škroup, together with Tomaschek and Th. Krov published many songs. Tomaschek was less successful in his songs than in his other compositions, but he was privileged to win Goethe's approval of his settings of German words. Amongst Krov's many songs with Bohemian words his Hussite song 'Tešme se blahon' has become national.[2] Yet another stimulus to the cultivation of native songs was the collection edited by Chmelensky and Škroup entitled 'Venec' ('The Garland'), which contained songs by thirty-three Czech composers. Among them are the names of Ružička, Drechsler, Vašik (or Vašak) Skřivan, Tomaschek, F. Kittl, J. Vorel, Karas, and Rosenkranz, the author of the popular song 'Vystavim se skromnov chaloupka' ('Let us build a modest hut'). In later editions of the 'Venec' issued by other editors, songs were added by Suchánek, Stasný, Veit, and A. Gyrowetz. Again in 1844 the Moravian composer Ludwig Ritter von Dietrich published a volume of songs which included his fine patriotic song 'Morava, Moravička milá.' Among other song-writers there may be cited the names of Zvonař, Procházka, J. N. Škroup, Kolesovsky, Zelenski, K. Slavik, F. Laub, E. Napravnik, Shukerský, Vojaček, and V. Zavertal. To sum up the general characteristics of their songs, they may be described as a flowing and clear *cantilena*, recalling to mind the traits of Italian song. Their harmony and rhythm are very simple ; and their sentiment and humour have the grace of spontaneity. By their own people these songs are dearly cherished, but in the scale of musical compositions their intrinsic worth is slight.

F. Smetana was the first to reproduce in his own original works the true Bohemian spirit, and mostly so in his national operas and symphonic poems. In the latter he has used many old folk-songs, and one called 'Tabor' is really a splendid polyphonic fantasia on the Hussite battle-song. Nor are the national songs forgotten in A. Dvořák's music. In the overture called 'Husitska' he introduces the St. Wencelas and the Hussite hymns ; and in another called 'Mein Heim' he has made use of 'Kde domov muj' as thematic material. Dvořák, W. Blodek, Rozkošný, Sebor, Hřimaly, Karel Bendl, and Reznicek have tried to carry the merry humorous

[1] This is the blind fiddler's song which Škroup wrote for J. Tyl's musical play *Fidlovačka*, in 1831
[2] This somewhat commonplace song contains a chorale in the middle, and has been used by Liszt, Balfe (in the 'Bohemian Girl') and others. (In Kappey's 'Songs of Eastern Europe' the date 1460 is wrongly given.)

spirit of the Bohemian peasant into their music, and the beauty of Bendl's and Dvořák's tender yet brilliant gipsy-songs is incontestable. Antonin Dvořák is the most Slavonic and the least German of Czech composers. He betrays in his songs both the merits and the defects of his nationality and origin. He has all the Czech wealth of ideas, freshness of invention, and spontaneity of melody, but is somewhat lacking in self-control and intellectual grasp. The simplicity of his themes shows that the folk-songs of his childhood influenced the whole tone of his music ; and his greatest works (such as the Stabat Mater, in which the solo numbers are unmistakably national in origin) are those in which he spoke in the idiom of his own country. Perhaps the most beautiful of his songs, after the already mentioned Zigeunerlieder, op. 55, are the four songs, 'Im Volkston,' op. 73, and the seven Liebeslieder, op. 83. In these we find richness of harmonic colour and bold, unexpected modulations combined with the simplest and most naïve tunes. Thoughout his songs we can trace a close and intimate sympathy with Franz Schubert, of whose works he made a special study. Z. Fibich's few published songs, on the other hand, clearly show the influence of Schumann in their delicate refined workmanship.

The extraordinary development of Bohemian music during the last forty or fifty years is mainly owing to the enthusiasm of modern Czech composers for their country's melodious folk-songs and merry dances. And if a Bohemian school of music can now be said to exist, it is as much due to the peasant as to the conscious efforts of Bendl, Smetana, Fibich, A. Stradal, and Dvořák. For every peasant in Bohemia is a real music-lover, and in this country at least it is not likely that the folk-songs will ever die out.

BIBLIOGRAPHY

Articles in Bohemian newspapers *Dalibor*, and *Literárni příloha*, 1860-65. L. Zvonař.
Meliš, E. *Böhmische Musik.*
Articles in *Die Oesterreich.-ungarische Monarchie : Böhmen* ; (a) *Volkslied und Tanz der Slaven* ; (b) *Musik in Böhmen*, by O. Hostinsky, 1894-96.
Maurice, E. *Bohemia from the earliest times*, etc. London, 1896.
Soubies, A. *Histoire de la Musique. Bohème.* Paris, 1898.
Geschichte der vorhussitischen Gesanges in Böhmen (pub. by the Kgl. böhmische Gesellschaft). Prague, 1904.
Batka, R. *Geschichte der Musik in Böhmen* (still appearing) 1st vol. Prague, 1906.

COLLECTIONS

Kamarýta, J. W. 'Ceski narodní duchovnj Písné.' Prague, 1832.
Ritter von Rittersberg. 'Moravian Songs.' 1835.
Krolmus and Drahorad. Collection, 1845-47.
Erben, K. J. 'Pjsně národnj w čechách.' Prague, 1852-69.
Susil, F. 'Moravské Narodni Pisni.' Brunn, 1853-60.
Berggreen, A. P. 'Folke-Sange og Melodier.' Stockholm, 1866.
Zahn, J. 'Die geistlichen Lieder der Brüder in Böhmen.' Nuremberg, 1875.
Zahorsky, F. 'Českých národnich písni' (no words). Brunswick, 1884.
Malát, Jan. 'Český národni Poklad.' Prague, 1885-95.
Erben, K. J. 'Chansons tchèques populaires.' Prague, 1886.
Bartoš, F. 'Národni pisně moravské.' Brunn, 1889.
Hruschka, A., and Toischer, W. 'Deutsche Volkslieder aus Böhmen.' Prague, 1891.
Swoboda. 'Dítě Vlasti, 100 Českých Národnich Pisni.' Prague, 1895.
Heyduk, F. 'Společensky Zpěvnik český.' Prague, 1901.

HUNGARY

The songs of Hungary comprise both those of the Slovaks and the Magyars, but the music of the Slovaks who inhabit the north-west part of the Hungarian kingdom has such a close affinity with the music of the Slavonic nations that it requires no separate notice. The music of the Magyars,[1] which is generally accepted as the national music, is of Oriental origin. It should be observed that the Hungarian language has nothing in common with the Indo-Germanic. Together with the Finnish, and Turkish (and possibly Basque) languages, it stands isolated in Europe, and belongs to the Turanian or Ural-Altaic family.

Gipsy music also plays an important part in Hungary, but it must be clearly understood that Hungarian music is quite distinct from gipsy music. Indeed the gipsies do not compose ; they simply imitate and perform the music of their adopted countries. It is difficult to discover with any certainty the origin of this wandering race ; but they are supposed to have come from the North-West provinces of India, and to have entered Hungary as well as other parts of Europe in the beginning of the 15th century. It has been pointed out that the gipsies flourish most[2] 'among the Spaniards, Roumanians, and Hungarians, where the national music excels in originality, fantastic rubatos, and a certain rhapsodical spirit.' And it is a recognised fact, that although the same melodic intervals and rhythmic peculiarities occur in Tsigane music all over the world, it was in Hungary, where an affinity of scale existed, that gipsy music reached its highest point. Among the Magyar gipsies—i.e. those gipsies who live among the Magyars and can speak their language, the songs may have gipsy words, but the actual tune and rhythm are Magyar. Moreover, the gipsies rarely sing and nearly always play the songs of other nations, imparting their own fire, impetuosity, and embellishments to the music of their adoption.[3] It is often difficult, when the gipsies play the csárdás, verbunkos, hallgatós, or palatos and other dances, to recognise the original folk-song on which they are based. So full of imagination are they, that the execution of the extremely difficult music always appears to be spontaneous and improvised. It delights Hungarians to hear their own music played and embellished by these wandering musicians, and thus it was in Hungary that gipsy music first became a recognised factor in Art. Many composers, such as Haydn, Hummel, and others, loosely and indiscriminately employed the words all' ongarese and alla zingarese, sometimes with one meaning and sometimes with the other. Likewise Schubert, Liszt, and Brahms, when they coloured their music with the Hungarian character, took the real Magyar folk-songs with their peculiar rhythm and scale, and used also the grace-notes, arabesques, and ornaments which the gipsies had added to the melodies with such skill that they had become an essential feature of the melody. In short, it is clear that although the gipsies have done much to preserve the folk-music of other nations by imitation and adoption, they cannot be regarded as creators of national music in any strict sense.[4]

As in other countries, so in Magyar-land, the introduction of Christianity was followed by a burst of hymn-poetry. But so strong was the national feeling that the hymns were sung even in the churches in the vernacular instead of Latin ; also it seems that the ecclesiastical tonal system never took the same hold of the sacred music as it did elsewhere. A few of these venerable hymns are still sung. Such, for instance, is one sung to the Virgin, by Andreas Vásárheli (printed at Nuremberg, 1484) and another to King Stephen, the patron saint of Hungary. Again, the influence of the Reformation was deeply felt both in music and poetry ; and there arose among the Protestants a literature of hymn-music, such as had already been stirred among the Hungarian Roman Catholics. In 1560 the Roman Catholic Church forbade, under severe penalties, the use in Church of any popular Magyar songs, but the old collections of both churches offer proof that the tunes of the secular songs were always freely used, set either to Latin or Hungarian sacred words.

Further evidence of the cultivation of music in the 16th century is supplied by the Hoffgraff collection[5] and by the songs of Sebastian Tinódi, both published by G. Matray in 1859. Tinódi, commonly called Sebastian the Lutenist, died about 1559, and was the last survivor of Hungary's wandering minstrels. His 'Cronica,' dedicated to King Ferdinand, contains songs of battles lost and won, of the joys and sorrows of the Magyar people, and the vicissitudes of their destiny. Such songs being truly national in their spirit soon passed into folk-songs, and are sung at this day.[6] It should also be noticed that dramatic representations interspersed with songs were introduced by these wandering minstrels, harpists, and lutenists, and secured a great popularity.

Neither in the 17th nor 18th century did the development of music keep pace with that of poetry, except in sacred lyrics. The difference

---

[1] The origin of their language can hardly be traced with certainty. Hungarian philologists are divided ; the 'Orientalists' assert its affinity with the Turco-Tartaric languages, while the 'Finnists' contend that it belongs to the Ugric branch of the Finnish group. That some likeness exists between the Magyar and Finnish language and music has long been recognised.

[2] See Nationality in Music, F. Korbay.

[3] The true gipsy songs are never sung by the 'professional' gipsy in public. Those songs are reserved exclusively for themselves in their tented wanderings, and there they are never played but always sung. See Archduke Joseph's article in vol. vi. (Ungarn) of Die Oesterreich.-ungarische Monarchie, 1902.

[4] For further information about gipsy music, see Archduke Joseph's article ; Die Zigeuner in Ungarn, Die Oesterreich.-ungarische Monarchie, vol. vi. ; L. A. Smith, Through Romany Song-Land, 1889, p. 3 et seq. ; Liszt, Die Zigeuner und ihre Musik in Ungarn, Pressburg, 1861.

[5] The collection contains nineteen songs, chiefly biblical narrative songs, by K. Bajnaj, M. Szártary, M. Tarjai, A. Farkas, and others.

[6] For Tinódi's life see Áron Szilády's Régi Magyar Költök Tára, a recent work on old Magyar poets.

between the melodies of the Roman Catholic churches on the one hand, and of the Protestants on the other is curious and worthy of note. The Roman Catholic melodies were of a florid and ornamented character, with passing notes and chromatic intervals, which may have been due to the instrumental music used in their churches. But the Protestants adhered to severely simple melodies in the style of Goudimel, for a time at least. As the hymns became folksongs, the strong national rhythm prevailed, and changed their character. Thus :—

Ex. 1.

(a) GOUDIMEL. *Psalm xvi.*

(b) FOLK-SONG.

The most remarkable feature, both of the poetry and the music of the Hungarians, is the rhythm. At an early date their lyric poetry shaped itself into sharp and bold strophical sections, and their melodies underwent a corresponding division into distinct phrases and periods. Great diversity of accents, and the unequal length of the lines, impart richness and variety to the musical rhythm. In the music of some nations there is a rhythmical and metrical sameness, but in Hungarian it is far more varied. The prevailing metrical feet are the choriambus : |−◡◡−| and the antispastus : |◡−−◡|. Most tetrapodics are like this : | ♪ ♪.♪ ♪ | ♩ ♩ | ♪♪♪ | ♩ ♪ ♪ |, but constantly three or even five and seven-bar rhythms are met with. The correct accentuation and phrasing of Hungarian music is closely interwoven with the language. Every first syllable has an emphasis of its own, whether short, as in Ex. 2, or long, as in Ex. 3, and

Ex. 2.
Lento.

etc.

Ex. 3.
Far and High the Cranes give Cry.

etc.

hence the reason why no song begins with the up-beat.[1] The constant recurrence of syncopa-

[1] F. Korbay, *Nationality in Music.*

tion and the augmented intervals have already been alluded to under MAGYAR MUSIC, but the Hungarian method of harmonising the airs is peculiar, for where the Germans would employ 'contrary motion' they prefer 'direct.' Again, the scales in which the songs fall are very varied ; numerous instances of the Dorian and Phrygian modes occur, nor are the augmented seconds in the minor scale so prevalent as is generally believed. In many, however, the tonality is most curious, such as

Ex. 4.

The following example begins with the peculiar 'call' found in many Hungarian songs [2] :—

Ex. 5.   *Long pause.*

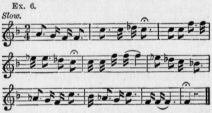

All Hungarian music has a strongly individual character. Its abrupt transition from deep melancholy to wild merriment, its variations of tempo, its richly applied cæsuras, constant ⌒ on different beats of the bar, its unexpected modulations, and its many peculiarities, both melodic and rhythmic, give to it the charm of distinctive originality. A few bars of this beautiful folk-song [3] will suffice to indicate the characteristics here named.

Ex. 6.
Slow.

The time of Hungarian national airs, whether songs or dances, is mostly 2–4. Triple and compound time are rare, excepting 5–4 or 5–8, or 7–4 and 7–8, of which many examples may be found in any collection. The Hungarians are rich in their historic ballads relating to national events. For instance, during the Rakoczy period the celebrated and sturdy Kurutzen songs, or old Crusaders' songs, were revived and widely sung [4] (see RAKOCZY MARCH). The ballads from the Szekler district are very old ; they are mostly sad and simple, as may be seen from this example.[5]

[2] Given by Béla Bartók. An examination of any good collection of these folk-songs would prove the truth of the above remarks.
[3] Called 'Autumn' in J. Kappey's 'Songs of Eastern Europe.'
[4] Julius Káldy published in 1892 about thirty 'Liedweisen aus der Thököly- und Rakoczi-zeit,' under the title of 'Kurutzenlieder.'
[5] This was taken down from the lips of the peasants by the enthusiastic folk-song collector, Béla Bartók.

Ex. 7.
Slow.

Many districts have kept strictly to their own special songs ; and have jealously excluded any outside influence or innovation. Such are the above-named Szekler ballads, the oldest and the most beautiful of the national Hungarian songs ; or the Puszten songs, in which the true Magyar peasant life is reflected, and the Betyar songs. The different classes of songs also fall into clearly distinct sets, such as love and wedding songs, drinking, soldiers', peasants', funeral, and satirical songs, all of which M. Jokai has described in an interesting manner.[1]

The excitable temperament and sensitive organisation of the Hungarian render him keenly susceptible to the refinements of melody and rhythm ; to those qualities he owes also his wealth of poetry and songs, which are of unsurpassed beauty as regards national music. But, on the other hand, the exclusiveness with which he clings to his own music and his neglect of the music of other countries has proved a hindrance to the progress of his musical cultivation. The list of Hungarian composers does not present many celebrated names until we reach the 19th century.

The first national opera ('Béla's Flight') was written in 1823 by Ruzsicska, and though a slight work it contained some songs which immediately became popular. Heinisch and Bartay followed, but the first unmistakably successful opera was Franz Erkel's 'Maria Bathori,' given in 1840, with words by the famous Benjamin Egressy ; and Erkel may with justice be designated as the creator of the Hungarian national opera. Erkel was also a prolific composer of songs, some of which were embodied in his operas ; and he was the author of the Hungarian national hymn. Other successful writers of opera were F. and K. Doppler, Reyer, K. Huber, Szerdahelyi, A. Erkel, G. Császár, and most of these composers freely used their country's folk-songs. Moreover, there is a specifically Hungarian form of drama called the folk-play (Volckschauspiel), the matter for which is taken from the domestic life of the people, and its music consists entirely of folk-songs and folk-dances. E. Szigligetti was the originator of this form, and J. Szerdahelyi, Ig. Bognár, Jul. Káldy, Jul. Erkel, A. Nikolits and others have contributed to establish it. These folk-plays have at least

[1] Die Osterreich.-ungarische Monarchie (Ungarn), vol. i. p. 347.

served to rescue many beautiful melodies from oblivion.

Among the song-writers of the 19th century, who adhered to the national school, the best-known names are Michael Mosonyi[2] and his pupils, the two Erkels and E. Mihalovich. The Magyar songs of this last-mentioned composer are more especially beautiful and poetical. Béla M. Vágvölgyi is also worthy of notice on account of the originality and popularity of his songs entitled ' Szerelmi dalok ' ; and not less worthy of notice is his valuable collection of national airs under the title of ' Népdalgyöngyök.' Other names may be cited, such as E. Székely, Cornel, L. Zimay, K. Huber, Abrányi senior (his ballads are essentially Hungarian), E. Bartay, E. Moór, S. Bartalus, and V. Langer, whose song-cycle ' Ögyek's songs ' is especially noteworthy. Benjamin Egressy likewise maintained a great popularity among the peasants and burghers during the first half of the 19th century. His songs may be found in every national collection, together with those of E. Szentirmay, Limbay, Simonffy, Erkel, Horváth, Füredy, Janko, Bolla, Zagonyi, etc.

F. Korbay's songs, either original or arranged, are well known in England. In the two volumes entitled ' Hungarian Songs,' and the volume of 'Twelve Magyar Songs,' Korbay has taken some of the most beautiful songs of his country,[3] to which he has added skilful and interesting accompaniments, keeping the while true to the national characteristics of harmony and rhythm. Some of the songs included are of Slavonic origin, as for instance[4] ' Azt mondják nem adnak.' Neither Volkmann (Hungarian by adoption) nor Goldmark has added much to song literature, though both have incorporated the spirit of the national songs in their instrumental works.

The greatest Hungarian song-writer is Franz Liszt ; although considering the fact that the larger number of his songs have German texts they would be more accurately classed as belonging to the German school. Moreover, the national elements—the Magyar rhythms and melodies, and the gipsy ornaments which abound in his instrumental music—are, with two exceptions—' Farewell' and the ' Three Gipsies '—absent from his vocal music.[5]

Among Hungarian song-writers of the present day, Emil Abranyi, Pista Dankó, Béla Bartók, and Ernö Lanyi stand on a high level. Many, such as Erdélyi, Bartalus, Káldy, Bognár, Bartók and others, have devoted their time to exploring, collecting, arranging, and publishing

[2] His real name was Michael Brandt.
[3] Amongst them several by Elemér Szentirmay, Benjamin Egressy, Füredy, Kalman de Simonffy, etc.
[4] (Vol. i. No. 13.) Even among the collections of true Magyar songs unmistakable Slavonic melodies are to be found. The external evidence of their origin may lie in the less strongly marked rhythms, the flattened sevenths and the absence of augmented intervals, but also it is clearly shown in the whole character of the song. Compare, for instance, the above-mentioned song, vol. i. No. 13 of Korbay's 'Hungarian Songs,' 'No, they say,' with No. 3 of the same volume—'Far and high the cranes give cry.'
[5] For detailed descriptions see Liszt ; also Vogel's essay published by Kahnt, Leipzig, 1887, and Finck's Songs and Song-Writers.

the old and modern folk-music of their country, greatly assisted by the Kisfaludy Society, which was formed for the express purpose. The Raaber collection, which is still appearing, must also be named.

BIBLIOGRAPHY

Liszt, F. *Die Zigeuner und ihre Musik in Ungarn.* Presburg, 1861.
Die Oesterreichisch-ungarische Monarchie: vol. i. (*Ungarn*) contains, *Die Magyarische Volksdichtung,* by M. Jokai ; *Die ungarische Palastmusik und die Volkslieder,* by S. Bartalus. 1888.
Vol. iii. *Die Kirchliche Musik,* by S. Bartalus, and *Die Weltliche Musik,* by Julius Káldy. 1893.
(Detailed accouuts of numerous collections of songs are given in the above articles.)
Soubies, A. *Hongrie.* (*Hist. de la Musique*), Paris, 1898.
Korbay, F. *Nationality in Music.*
Dr. Pressel's account of Hungarian music in vol. xxxvi. of the *Neue Zeitschrift für Musik,* and the article on Magyar music in this Dictionary.

(The writer also owes her warmest thanks to M. Béla Bartók for information, and for examples from his MS. collection of folk-songs.)

COLLECTIONS

Matray, G. 'Magyar népdalok, etc.' Buda-Pest, 1852-59.
Füredi, M. '100 Magyar Népdal.' Buda-Pest, 1853.
Bartalus, S. 'The Hungarian Orpheus.' 1869. (A collection of 18th and 19th century music, containing many old folk-songs from the Adam Paloczi-Horvath MS.)
Bartalus, S. 'Magyar népdalok.' (7 vols.)
Györffy, J. '50 Magyar népdal, etc.' Buda-Pest, 1871.
Laszlo, Arany. 'Magyar népköltési gyujtémény.' Buda-Pest, 1872-82.
Földes, J., and Demeter, R. 'Emlék.' Buda-Pest, 1876.
Kalmany, L, 'Szeged népe.' Aradon, 1881-82, 1892.
Goll, J. 'Énektan polgári iskolák.' Buda-Pest, 1884-88.
Bornemiszsza, Y. '150 Bordal, etc.' Buda-Pest, 1888.
Berger-Henderson, Mme. 'Album of 16 Hungarian Songs.' London, 1889.
Deák, G. 'Daloskönyv Két és harom szólamu, etc.' Buda-Pest, 1892.
Káldy, G. 'Schätze der alten ungarischen Musik' (1672-1838). Buda-Pest, 1892.
Vágvölgyi, B. M. 'Népdalgyöngyök.' Buda-Pest.
Elemér, Limbay, Bolla G., and Nemesovits, E. 'Magyar dal Album.' Buda-Pest.
Korbay, F. 'Hungarian Songs' and '12 Magyar Songs.'
László, Kún. '1000 Népdalok.' (Still appearing), 1905. 'A Magyar Dal.' Buda-Pest, 3 vols. 1906-7.
Palotasy, G. '101 Legszebb Magyar Nepdal.' Buda-Pest.

FINLAND

Finland (Finnish *Suomi*) is 'the land of a thousand lakes,' vast stretches of moors, deep silent woods, and long dark winters. These elements and scenery are reflected in the gloomy, mystical, fantastic yet monotonous poetry and music of the in-dwellers. No country is more poetic than Finland, as the *Kalevala* proves. This glorious national epic of nearly 23,000 verses has been transmitted from generation to generation from long past ages. The Finns also possess a very large quantity of lyric songs and ballads ; and to Elias Lönnrot (who died in 1884) the credit is due for having given the nation these two treasures in a collected form : the national epics which form the *Kalevala* and the collection of lyrics which are entitled the *Kanteletar.*

The Finnish language, a branch of the Finnish-Ugric stem, is peculiarly melodious and full of open vowels. The verse metre is simple, and consists mostly of trochees, four times repeated—the last foot being lengthened in order to mark the close of the line :

hūwă | kēllŏ | kāuwăs | kŭulŭŭ

This is the usual explanation of the five-beat rhythm in the music, which is the commonest in the old Finnish songs or *runos*,[1]

Ex. 1.

Käwy kasky tai-wa has-ta, Käwy kasky tai-wa has-ta,

Kaiken luondon Hal-di al-da, Kaiken luondon Haldi al-da, [2]

Ex. 2.   RUNO.

Jos mun tut-tu-ni tulisi ja-tu li - - si,

Ar-ma - ha - ni as-te - lei-si, as-te - lei-si

and it is clear that in aiming to make these melodies agree with their poetry the irregular and unsymmetrical 5- or 7-time did not appear to the Finns either forced or unnatural.

As in all other national music, the musical instruments are closely connected with the melodies of the country. In Finland the oldest and most popular instrument is the *kantele*, a kind of lyre or harp with five copper strings tuned *g, a, bb, c, d*, on which five notes a large mass of the old *runo* melodies are formed (see above example). These melancholy and monotonous *runolaulua*, characterised by constant repetition, are usually accompanied by the *kantele*. Mention is made in the *Kalevala* of this instrument being used to accompany the songs ; also of the 'sighing verses' which in the *Runo* songs are a refrain of actual realistic sobbing sighs. Dance tunes also adhere to the *kantele* intervals, and at the same time to the song-rhythms, as :—

Ex. 3.

Some writers,[3] however, deny that this instrument had so great an influence on the old Finnish tunes, and contend that as vocal music is older than instrumental, it is more probable that the melodies were based on the pentatonic scale. A further proof of this theory is that the Finnish-Ugric race is of Asiatic origin.

The *Kanteletar* is a large collection of lyrics and ballads. These songs reflect the restrained melancholy of the national character ; they are full of deep feeling and tenderness, and absolutely natural and spontaneous. A few of these lyric songs are to be found in 5-time, though this time is chiefly confined to the old sacred folk-songs, and more especially to the ancient *runo* melodies. In common with other folk-

---

[1] *Runo* or *runolaulua* means 'air' or 'ballad,' and has nothing to do with the Anglo-Saxon *runes* or runic writing-stones.

[2] Ilmari Krohn, in an article entitled *De la mesure à cinq temps dans la musique populaire Finnoise, Sammelbände* of the Int. Mus. Ges. ii. 1. 1900, considers that the above example (which is a type of the *Kalevala* melodies) is wrongly noted, and suggests two alternative metrical schemes.

[3] See Engel, *Introduction to the Study of National Music,* p. 59 *et seq.*

songs of Western Europe, some of the Finnish melodies have their basis in the ecclesiastical modes ; but there are traces of an older, and as yet unfathomed and unexplained tonal influence which gives a peculiar interest to the music of this country. Those which come from the southern part of Finland, where nature is less severe, possess a certain idyllic cheerfulness, and many which are sung along the coast are undoubtedly of Scandinavian origin. These melodies range over a wider compass, the rhythm is more varied, and they are usually in common or triple time, and more often than not in our modern tonality [1] :—

Ex. 4.

Tuuti las-ta Tuonelahan, Alla nurmen nukkuma - han

Tuonen lasten lau-la-tel-la manan nei-to-jen pi-del-lä.

The herdsmen's songs (*Paimen loilottamus*), as in Scandinavia, are numerous. They are closely akin to the notes of the herdsman's pipe, and of no definite form in tune or words.

Between the 12th and 14th centuries, Sweden took possession of, and christianised Finland, but it was only in towns and at Court that the Swedish language was used. Finland has always been an apple of discord between Sweden and Russia, and the perpetual wars hindered this country's artistic development. Finally, since early in the last century (1809), when it was conquered by Russia, strenuous efforts towards its complete Russification have never ceased. It is, however, highly improbable that Russia will ever succeed in taking away from Finland her own peculiar character and culture. Her national poetry and songs have long stood alone and aloof, independent of foreign bondage and influence.

The modern history of music in Finland begins early in the 19th century, when F. Pacius and B. Crusell, both Germans by birth, settled there. By using Finnish folk-songs in their works, and taking the words of Finnish poets, such as Runeberg, Qvanten, Topelius, etc., for their national songs and hymns, they awoke the spirit of patriotism in Finland, and hence have been justly called the fathers of Finnish music. Pacius, who died at a great age in 1891, wrote many fresh and effective songs, but his name will live for having given Finland her national hymns : ' Our Country ' (' Värt Land ') and ' Finland's Song ' (' Suomen laulu '), which every Finn knows and sings from his childhood. (See Ex. 5.)

His son-in-law, Karl Kollan, wrote also patriotic songs in the peculiar march-like rhythm which is popular in Finland. Crusell was a

[1] For some of the most beautiful, see G. Hägg's collection, 'Soreimmat Soinnut Suomesta.'

Ex. 5.

Hear, the glorious song is ring - ing Thro' the ancient halls of Wai - - no: It is Suomi's song ! It is Suo-mi's song !

prolific and favourite composer, but his melodies are commonplace. K. Greve, L. Bergström, M. Wegelius, Ph. von Schantz, G. Wasenius, F. Ehrstrom, K. Flodin, S. Linsén, H. Borenius, R. Faltin, and a younger generation which includes O. Merikanto (a very popular but somewhat shallow writer), O. Katilainen, P. Hannikainen, and S. Palmgren all belong, more or less, to the same school of song-writers. Whilst introducing many of the old Finnish folk-songs into their works, and choosing the words of Finnish poets for their songs, the music practically belongs to the German Mendelssohn-Spohr period, and cannot in any sense be called racial.

The true national period of Finnish music begins with R. Kajanus. Imbued with the classic-romantic traditions, yet heart and soul a Finn, Kajanus drew his inspirations from the *Kalevala*, and did much to originate and stimulate interest in his country's music. But the actual representative of Finnish music is Jean Sibelius. His art reflects the grave and austere beauty of Finland's scenery and poetry, and expresses the inner life of the people—the despairing and passionate struggles and yearnings, the childlike simplicity and proud melancholy. Hence the worship Sibelius evokes among his countrymen, and his power and influence over his young disciples. His songs, whilst original, dramatic, and powerful, are the true counterpart of the Finnish folk-song. Essentially modern in feeling, yet Sibelius uses frequently the old, simple scale, limited harmony, and the curious uneven rhythm of the folk-songs. One of his most beautiful songs, with a modal melody, is ' Men min Fogel märks dock icke '; ' Svarta Rosar ' (' Black Roses ') is effective ; and ' Atinares Säng,' perhaps the best known, is a fine war-song in march-rhythm. If Sibelius be the lyric and dramatic representative of Finnish music, A. Järnefelt may be called the epic. He has written many songs, but it is the peculiarly national ballad-like feeling in his orchestral works which arrests attention. Mention must also be made of Ilmari Krohn and E. Melartin (born in 1875), whose songs are of distinct merit.

The enthusiasm, patriotism, zeal, and activity of the younger generation of composers, combined with the keen interest and research by students and historians among the national treasures of poetry and song, indicate the prevalence of a new movement in Finland's music.

BIBLIOGRAPHY

Ueber die finnische Musik (*Neue Zeitschrift f. Musik*), vol. xxxiv. p. 205. Leipzig, 1851.
Flodin, K.   *Die Entwickelung der Musik in Finnland* (*Die Musik*, Jahrgang ii.)
Krohn, Ilmari.   *De la mesure à 5 temps dans la musique populaire Finnoise*. *Sammelbände*, I.M.G. i. 1900.
Mendel. *Mus. Lexikon.*
Willibrand, M. von. *Finlande en XIXme Siècle.* Paris, 1900.
Pudor, H.   *Zur Geschichte der Musik in Finnland. Sammelbände*, I.M.G., II. i. 1900.
(The writer is also indebted to Dr. Ilmari Krohn for his kind help.)

COLLECTIONS

Schröter. 'Finnische Runen.' Stuttgart, 1834.
Kollan, K., and Reinholm, A. 'Suomen Kansan Lautaatoja,' Helsingfors, 1849 ; and 'Valituita Suomalaisia Kansan-Lauluja,' Helsingfors, 1854.
Ilberg, F. V. 'Suomalaisia Kansan-Lauluja ja Soetelmia.' Helsingfors, 1867.
Borenius, A., and Linsén, G. 'Suomalaisia Kansan-Lauluja.' Helsingfors, 1880.
Krohn, Ilmari. 'Uusia Suomalaisia Kansanlauluja.' Helsingfors, 1886.
Lagus, E. 'Nyländska Folkvisor' (2 parts). Helsingfors, 1887-1900.
Kajanus, R. 'Suomen Kansan Sävelmiä.' Helsingfors, 1888-92.
'Suomen Kansan Sävelmia' (Melodies of the Finnish People), three series, published by the Finnish Literary Society[1] at Helsingfors ; 1st series, 'Hengellisiä Sävelmiä' (Sacred Melodies), 1898 (still in progress) ; 2nd series, 'Kansanlauluja' (Popular Songs), 1888 ; 3rd series, 'Kansantansseja' (Popular Dances), 1893 (complete with German Introduction). The whole work is edited by I. Krohn.
Hägg, G. 'Soreimmat Soinnut Suomesta.' Stockholm (5th edition), 1904.

SCANDINAVIA

To this group belong Sweden, Norway, Denmark, parts of Finland, Iceland, and the adjacent islands.   There is a great affinity between the Scandinavian languages.   At the present time Danish is the language of the educated class in Norway, although it has a harder pronunciation.[2]   And in an article written early in the last century, entitled *Alte Volksmelodien des Nordens*,[3] it was pointed out that the Swedish songs only differed from the Danish in dialect and not in language. Danish is also as much spoken as Norwegian in the Faroë Islands,[4] where also many Icelandic and Danish songs are heard.

The poetry of Scandinavia is peculiarly rich in ballads, legends, and tales of ancient and mediæval warriors on sea or land—the heroic-epic element being abundant, while the lyric element plays little part except in the refrains to the ballads. The Scandinavians have always been a music-loving nation, but not until comparatively recent times have systematic collections of their folk-music been made.[5] Collectors have found great difficulty in taking down the music of the *Kämpavisor*,[6] owing to the free declamatory way in which they were sung.   The formal melody occurs only in the

refrains, or *Omkväde*, of the *Kämpavisor*. The *Omkväd*[7] (Danish *Omkvœd*), which is undoubtedly of very ancient origin, forms an important part of northern songs.[8]   It may be a line at the end of each verse, used to strengthen the meaning of the poem, or a line interpolated in the middle of the verse corresponding with its contents ; or it may contain satirical or contemptuous remarks sung by a chorus ; or it may only concern the reciter, applauding and encouraging him.[9] Musically the *Omkväd* was the most important part of the song, and remained always intact and unvaried, whereas the actual song was often improvised or changed according to the solo-singer's desire.   In the Faroë Islands, for instance, the old ballads are still sung to the mediæval dances, and collectors often find variants in the songs themselves, whilst the refrains are identical in every part of the islands.   The *Omkväd* naturally influences both the form and harmony of the songs. It necessitates the extension or repetition of a musical phrase, and sometimes a change of time and accent, which impart a great freedom of form to the Scandinavian songs.   Again, if the song be in the minor, the *Omkväd* would be in the major, or *vice versa* ; also if the song be sung as a solo, or in unison, the *Omkväd* is most frequently sung in parts.

Och Jungfrun.

Ex. 1.

Och, jungfrun hon skul-le sig åt   ot-te sån-gen gå;
Oh! the maiden she hurries   to   evensong;

OMKVÄD.

Tiden görs mig lång. Så   gick hon den   vägen åt
Time is   long. So   she went the way by

höga   berget låg ; Men jag vet att sor-gen är tung.
the high   hill ; But I wot that sorrow is heavy.

These refrains are universal in Scandinavian songs, and occur as often in other forms as in the *Kämpavisor*.

It is a well-known fact (and has been briefly alluded to in several sections of this article) that some of the most famous folk-songs of different countries are founded on the same subject, whether it be a legendary or historical event, or an incident of ordinary life.   The accessories of course vary, and impart a local colouring to each version of the song, but the central theme is in all the same.   In like manner the same tunes are the property of

[1] *Suomalaisen Kirjallisuuden Seura.* Dr. Ilmari Krohn says that this publication, which is still in progress, will, when completed, be the fullest and most systematic collection.
[2] Chambers's *Encyclopædia*, 1891 edition.
[3] *Allg. Mus. Zeitung*, No. 35, August 18, 1816.
[4] *Tanz, Dichtung und Gesang auf den Färöern, Sammelbände* of the I.M.G., III. pt. ii. 1902, H. Thuren.
[5] T. Norlind, in his *History of Swedish Music*, speaks of certain isolated collections, such as 'Petri Piae Cantiones,' dated 1582, which contains folk-songs written in parts to sacred words. He calls attention especially to the melodious 'School and Spring Songs.'
[6] That is, the heroic epic folk-poetry or ballads of the Middle Ages. The wandering players called *Leikarar* (or in modern Danish *Legere*) were the professional preservers or 'spreaders' of Scandinavian music at that period, and are mentioned in the old chronicles as honoured guests of the northern kings and nobles.
[7] *Om* (German *um*)=round, about; *Kvœd*=song, singing, 'quoth.'
[8] Jamieson, in his *Popular Ballads and Songs*, Edinburgh, 1806, remarks : 'In our ancient songs equally remarkable and incomprehensible *Omqvads* occur.'
[9] Geijer contends in his *Svenska Folk-visor*, p. 226, that the *Omkväde* had no other significance than that the extemporiser of the song or the listener should use them to gain time—the one to produce his own thoughts, and the other to remember what he had just heard.

different countries.[1] Their identity may not, perhaps, be detected at first, beneath the disguises in which it is enveloped by national varieties of scale and rhythm and harmony ; but it is certain that closer examination would establish many relationships hitherto unsuspected. An especially strong affinity exists between the English, Scotch, Welsh, German, and Scandinavian folk-poetry. This interesting subject, which is well worth separate study, can only be dwelt on shortly, and a few examples given. Geijer in his 'Svenska Folk-visor' quotes three lines of a Norwegian folk-song, also heard in Wermland and Småland—

> Månan skinar (the moon shines),
> Dödman rider (dead men ride),
> Är du inte rädder än, Bolla?
> (Are you not afraid thereof, Bolla ?)

which correspond to the German Lenore ballad [2]—

> Der Mond scheint so helle,
> Die Todten reiten schnelle,
> Feins Liebchen ! graut Dir nicht ?

Geijer also gives the Swedish version of the legend of the Swimmer,[3] the classical story of Hero and Leander, which has a local habitation in Holland, Germany ('Ach Elslein '), Russia, etc. 'The Jolly Beggar' of Scotland is identical with the 'Bettlerlied' still sung in many parts of Germany and Sweden.[4]   The 'Edward' ballad as given in Percy's *Reliques* is the well-known Swedish 'Sven i Rosengård,' the Danish 'Svend i Rosensgaard,' and the Finnish ' Welisurmaäja.' [5]

Ex. 2.

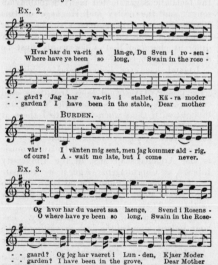

Hvar har du va-rit så lån-ge, Du Sven i ro - sen -
Where have ye been so long, Swain in the rose -

- - gård? Jag har va-rit i stallet, Kä - ra moder
- - garden? I have been in the stable, Dear mother

BURDEN.

vår!   I vänten mig sent, men jag kommer ald - rig.
of ours! A - wait me late, but I come never.

Ex. 3.

Og hvor har du vaeret saa laenge, Svend i Rosens -
O where have ye been so long, Swain in the Rose-

- - gaard?   Og jeg har vaeret i Lun - den, Kjaer Moder
- - garden? I have been in the grove, Dear Mother

[1] See F. Böhme's 'Altdeutsches Liederbuch,' and Oscar Fleischer's *Zur vergleichenden Liedforschung, Sammelbände*, I.M.G. III., ii. 1902.
[2] See also 'Fair Margaret and Sweet William,' and 'Margaret's Ghost' in Percy's *Reliques*.
[3] See 'Svenska Folk-visor,' vol. i. p. 106, and vol. ii. p. 210.
[4] See Crosby's *Caledonian Musical Repository*, 1811, p. 58.
[5] The Swedish and Danish songs are given in Berggreen's collections; the Finnish in Schröter's 'Finnische Runen' and in 'Suomalaisen Kirjallisunden Seuran Toimituksia;' Helsingfors, 1849.

BURDEN.

vor!   I ven - te mig seent eller ald - rig.
of ours! A - wait me late or never.

Ex. 4.   *Welisurmaäja.*

Mis-täs tu-let Kus-tas tu-let, Poi-kan-i i - lo - nen?

Meren ran-nal-ta, meren rannalta äi-ti-ni Kul-ta-nen !

The tunes of the three last-named countries appear to have a common origin, but the tune of the 'Edward' ballad cannot with certainty be traced. Still, as Engel points out, many of our old English tunes bear a strong resemblance to the Scandinavian, both in character and construction ; and the remarkable affinity, especially between the Welsh and Danish songs, has been noticed by Dr. Crotch and others.[6]

But although the Scandinavian nations may have many songs in common, it is evident, on comparing as a whole the collections of the different countries, that there is a great difference in their general character.[7] The Swedish folk-songs are the most beautiful and poetical, and though tinged with melancholy they are not gloomy and tragic like the Norwegian, nor monotonous and regular like the Danish. The latter, however, possess a peculiarly idyllic and pastoral beauty of their own ; they recall the upland meadows, fertile plains, and wooded valleys of the country. The 4- or 8-bar rhythm is usually clearly defined, independently of the refrain [8]:—

Ex. 5.

De va - re syv   og syv-sind sty-ve der de drog

ud fra Hald,   og   der de Komme ti Brat-tings-

OMKVÄD.

- borg, der sloge de der-es tjald. Det don-ner under

ros, de don - ske hofmond der de ud - ri - de.

[6] Engel says, 'One of the most popular of the Welsh tunes, "Ar hyd y nôs," is also current in Denmark, especially among the peasantry in Jutland. It may be worth noticing that Jutland is generally believed to have been inhabited in ancient times by the same Celtic race which we find in Wales. But whether the tune originated in Denmark or in Wales is a question which will probably never be solved' (*Introduction to the Study of National Music*, p. 360). In the introduction to his *Ballad Book*, Allingham calls attention to the similarity between many Scotch ballads, such as the 'Douglas Tragedy,' 'Mary Colvin,' 'Clerk Saunders,' and others, and those contained in the Swedish Folk-song collection by Afzelius and Arvidsson. See also Motherwell's *Minstrelsy, Ancient and Modern*, Glasgow, 1827.
[7] Berggreen, the great Danish collector of folk-songs, draws attention to the close connection between the word-accent and the melodic outline of the three nations' songs.
[8] This is from the old song-cycle, 'King Dietrich Bern,' and is one

The northern melodies usually begin with the up-beat, and by preference with the step of the fourth (as ' Och Jungfrun '). They are very frequently in common or 2–4 time, and adhere to the simplest modulations. The phrases are not repeated on different steps of the scale as in so many other countries, and this gives the melodies great variety. The ' Vermelandsvisa,' one of the most beautiful folk-songs in the world, exemplifies the above qualities ; it begins thus :—

Ex. 6. *Vermelandsvisa.*

It may be safely asserted that nine out of every twelve Scandinavian songs are in the minor, or partly so, for many begin in the minor, and end in the major or *vice versa.* Some of the older melodies recall the Church scales, and especially the Mixolydian and Phrygian modes, but these occur most frequently among the Norwegian and Danish songs.[1] The epic songs which have been collected in Telemarken (in the S.W. of Norway) are evidently of great antiquity, as for instance, the following relating to Sigurd's fight with the dragon, with its curious rhythm and melancholy original melody.[2]

Ex. 7.

Slow.

Important sections of the people's songs are those of the foresters and wood-cutters and the herdsmen. The words of these songs are often mere exclamations, and contain no formal verses. The herdsman or girl calls the cattle home from the mountain-side, either with the cowhorn or *Lur*, or by singing a melody with

the echo formed on that instrument. Another class of songs are those of the sailors and fishermen. Many old ballads relating the brave deeds of the sea-fighting heroes are to be found in the Swedish and Norwegian collections, and many typically nautical songs in the more modern.[3]

The national dances have greatly influenced the melodies, though the *Syvspring, Slängdansar, Halling*, and many others are not usually accompanied by singing.[4] The famous ring or chain-dances, and children's game-songs, and certain festival-songs (such as the old May-Day and Epiphany songs) are relics from mediæval times. In the province of Dalecarlia the 3–4 time dance-songs are especially cultivated ; one called ' Necken's Polska '[5] is widely known. The Norwegian *Springer* is its equivalent. Both dances are sung, whilst the drone fifths in the bass show the old national instrument used. The *Hardangerfele* (*fele*= fiddle) belonging to the Norwegian highlands is the most perfect of their instruments, but it is only used for marches and dances. The peasant marks the time by double tapping of the toe and heel uninterruptedly, playing all the while brilliantly. The richest districts in national songs are Telemarken in the S.W. of Norway, the centre of Jutland,[6] and the southern part of the Faroë Islands. These islands were ever in close connection with Iceland, and many songs show their Icelandic origin. Doubtless the Icelandic Sagas incited many Scandinavian songs, and the poetry and language of this island have much in common with the rest of Scandinavia ; but the music is of such a totally different character that a few words must be devoted to its most salient points.

Iceland has ever been a land of history. With true love and devotion its inhabitants have preserved their old tales, traditions, and customs. Their language, which the Norwegians brought with them when they settled there at the close of the 9th century, remains unchanged, as also their strangely mediæval music.

The chief source for studying Icelandic music is the Arnamagnäan MS. in the University Library at Copenhagen. And if we compare this collection with those of a far later, or even quite recent date, we find the same forms now as then. There has been no development of music in Iceland ; it has been stationary. Iceland, indeed, adopted the form prevailing in the Middle Ages, and has clung to it up to the

---

of the few early northern songs preserved in writing. As here given it was noted down in 1675 by J. Lorentz, an organist at Copenhagen.

[1] There are many examples of modal tunes in Kristensen's ' Gydske Folkeviser.'

[2] Thus given by Lindemann. In Telemarken the refrain is often called *Stev*, but the *Stev* consists really of improvised verses of love or satire, sung on certain festive occasions and gatherings, to traditional tunes. See Landstad and Dr. von Ravn in Mendel's *Lexikon.*

[3] See L. A. Smith's *Music of the Waters*, p. 218.

[4] This does not apply to the Faroë Islands, where musical instruments are practically unknown. Here the inhabitants are passionately fond of dancing, and, as mentioned above, accompany their dances with singing the old epics and ballads.

[5] Lindgren in his *Ur Svenska Musikens Häfder*, p. 137, tells us that the Polska is not of national origin, but was introduced from Poland in the 17th century in the Lute-books under the name of *Polonessa* (polonaise).

[6] This district was called the ' knitting-district,' because until quite recently the peasants used to meet during the winter evenings in different houses knitting woollen goods, and relating or singing tales, songs, ballads, and legends. Their wealth of songs was so great that in many places the same song was not allowed to be sung more than once a year.

present century. The music of her secular songs[1] is of an ecclesiastical character ; instrumental music hardly exists ; the old scales or modes are retained,[2] for the wave of modern tonality which swept over Europe in the 17th century never reached Iceland. An even stronger evidence of mediævalism than the modal tonality is afforded by the peculiar form of part-singing in Iceland, called *Tvisöngur*, which closely resembles Hucbald's *Organum*. Examples are to be found in the Arnamagnäan MS. of the 15th century ; and although earlier traces of it are extant in other countries, Iceland alone has retained it for her secular music down to the present day. This is proved by the following example taken from the 'Icelandic Student's Söngbók,' of 1894[3] :—

Ex. 8.

NATIONAL SONG—*Island.*

Lento. Given by PASTOR THORSTEINSSON.

Island! far-sæl-da frón, og hagsæl-da hrimhvita módir!

Tenor (Melody).

Hvar er pin forn-al-dar frægð frels-ið og mann-dáð-in bezt!

Until the last generation the *Tvisöngur* held its own all over Iceland ; but now in the 20th century it only exists in certain isolated localities. The increasing development of communication with other countries, coupled with the knowledge of musical notation, the spread of choral societies, and the publication of numerous collections of songs and hymns, have all combined to induce the Icelanders to adopt at last the more modern methods of music. 'The *Tvisöngur* is, therefore, fast dying out, and with it the last remains of an interesting episode in musical history.'[4]

The so-called Scandinavian school of music is of very recent birth ; for until the close of the 18th century it was greatly under foreign influence. Thus, during the 16th century, the Court-music of Denmark was chiefly in the hands of Flemish musicians, whilst in the 17th, Dowland and many other Englishmen, besides French, German, Polish, and Italian composers, visited and settled in Copenhagen and Stockholm. The latter part of the 17th and the

first part of the 18th were monopolised by the ballet, and French melodies (especially in Sweden) predominated over all others. A fresh impetus was given to northern music by the operas and Singspiele of German composers, such as B. Keiser, J. A. P. Schulz, and Kunzen. And in the imitations of these by Weyse, Kuhlau, and Hartmann,[5] Scandinavian folk-songs were first introduced on the stage. The compositions in which the vernacular was first used were the sacred and secular cantatas, oratorios and hymns, both by Danish and German composers, such as Iversen, A. Scheibe, and J. E. Hartmann in Denmark, and in Sweden, J. Roman, Per Frigel, and J. B. Struve. But the chief impulse towards a national school of music was given by the literature of the country. Towards the end of the 18th century the didactic school of poetry began to give way to a more natural lyrical style ; and by the beginning of the 19th (influenced by the romanticism of Germany) a strong intellectual national movement arose in Northern poetry. It was greatly promoted in Denmark by the poet Oehlenschläger, in Norway and Sweden by the patriotic 'Norwegian Society,' and by the founding of the so-called 'Götiska förbundet' (Gothic union). About this time the first collections of national songs appeared. Poets and musicians became interested in the old epics and ballads, with their beautiful melodies, and their wealth of new materials both in ideas and form, and hastened to avail themselves of the treasure. Thus within the last hundred years or so a new school of music has arisen, containing in its ranks the distinguished names of Lindblad, Gade, Kjerulf, Grieg, Sjögren, Sinding, etc.

DENMARK. — In Denmark the homely, humorous, or idyllic *Singspiele* especially took root, and it would be legitimate to say that the *Kunstlied* originated in the theatre-songs. Some of these melodies by the elder Hartmann, Schulz, Kunzen, and Zinck—singing of social pleasures, friendship, and wine, or those of a more romantic and sentimental type—are still popular in Denmark, in the Faroë Islands, and far into the north of Norway. It is worthy of notice that the three founders of the Danish school of music, C. E. F. Weyse, F. Kuhlau, and J. Hartmann, were Germans by birth, and that a strong tinge of the German element has prevailed through the works of Danish musicians to the present day. J. Hartmann, the founder of the Hartmann family of composers, is the author of one of Denmark's most national songs, 'King Christian stood by the mast.' Weyse is considered the creator of the Danish romance. Full of romantic feeling, and possessing a fluent gift of melody, the songs from his *Singspiele*, his child-like, pious 'Morning and Evening

---

[1] See especially Olafur Davidsson's 'Islenzkar Skemtanir.'

[2] The Icelanders have an especial love for the Lydian mode with its tritone.

[3] The parallel fifths do not sound so harsh if the melody is taken by loud full voices, and the second (upper) part by a few singers, very subdued, and the whole song sung very slowly and emphatically.

[4] *Studien über isländische Musik,* by A. Hammerich (*Sammelbände* of the I.M.G. I. iii. 1900), to whom the writer is indebted for the above information.

[5] Kuhlau's romantic 'Der Erlenhügel' (1828), and later J. P. Hartmann's 'Liden Kirsten' (1846), (the latter consisting almost wholly of folk-songs) are still popular in Denmark.

Songs,' and more especially his 'Nine Danish Songs' to words by the national lyrists Oehlenschläger, Ewald, Grundtvig, Heiberg, and Winther, are justly popular.   Later in life Weyse devoted himself to collecting and harmonising two volumes of 'Gamle Kæmpewise-Melodier' (Old Hero-songs). He died in 1842. His contemporary, F. Kuhlau, also loved the simple, noble melodies of the *Kämpeviser*, which he had noted down in his youth.   These he used later with success in the romance form, and it is difficult to distinguish them from the genuine folk-songs of this kind.   Still Kuhlau never cared for Danish poetry, and always preferred to use German words.   Contemporary native musicians were less celebrated, and Sörenson, Claus Schall, and Niels Schiorring are names now scarcely remembered.   But the improvement in literature due to the poets Oehlenschläger, Heiberg, Hertz, Hans C. Andersen, and the publications at Copenhagen of the numerous collections of Scandinavian folk-songs, naturally influenced and stimulated the musical feeling and inventive powers of the song-writers.   The consequent development of Danish song we owe to J. P. E. Hartmann, Niels Gade, and P. Heise.   The songs of the latter vary very much in merit, but his fine song-cycles, 'Gudrun's Sorg' and 'Dyvekes Sange' (words by Drachmann), have never received their due appreciation.   J. P. E. Hartmann's songs are gloomy and northern in colouring, and in form less perfect than Heise's and Gade's.   Among the best are the six by Winther's poem 'Hjortens Flugt,' and the nine entitled 'Salomon and Sulamith,' op. 52 ; but at the present day they sound somewhat old-fashioned.   At first, Gade, who was steeped in the atmosphere of Schumann and Mendelssohn, wrote only German songs.   But by degrees— influenced, doubtless, by his old master, Berggreen (the great folk-song collector)—he became more national in feeling, and joined the ranks of the northern romanticists, writing music to Oehlenschläger's and Heiberg's romances. His influence has been great over all subsequent Scandinavian composers, and Gade's cultured musical taste and true cosmopolitan feeling never allowed his art to become bounded by too narrow an horizon. Gade's lyrics are always expressed in the simplest language, and suffer from a certain poverty of rhythm.   He shares with other Danes the preference for the monotonous, swaying 6–8 time, and he rarely modulates beyond the nearest keys.   A group of composers who have treated the song in the same simple and popular way are : H. Rung, Barnekow, A. Winding, J. O. Hornemann, S. Salomon ; and Gade's pupils, K. Attrup and L. Schytte. More individual and more developed in the accompaniment are those by Emil C. Hartmann, C. F. Hornemann, A. Hamerik, O. Malling, A. Enna, and notably R. Hansen and

P. E. Langemüller, whose 'Sulamith' cycle is interesting, and as well known abroad as in Denmark.   A new note in Danish music has been touched by Carl Nielsen (b. 1865).   He has written only a few, but remarkable songs, evincing in his rhythm and modulation a strong originality.

NORWAY.—Although Norway was for a time joined to Sweden, and in the past shared the destinies of Denmark, whose language it still retains, it ever remained the most independent branch of the Scandinavian kingdom.   The people are intelligent and well educated, and intensely jealous of their national rights. Foreign music and literature never had the same influence in Norway as in Sweden and Denmark, and the *Singspiel* and the opera were never popular. The modern period in poetry and music began with the awakening of national life which received its first impulses in 1772, from the 'Norwegian Society';[1] from the national poets, Wergeland (called the Schiller of Norway), Welhaven, Münch, Moë, and Jensen ; from the folk-tale collector Faye, the hymn-writer Landstad, and most of all from the folk-song collectors Bagge and L. M. Lindemann.   The latter did valuable work in familiarising the national melodies of his country. He published them as psalms, hymns, songs, and dances, and his work was carried on by C. Elling.   The first real song-writer of Norway was Halfdan Kjerulf, whose lyrics long suffered from unaccountable neglect.   His two books of 'Sänger och Visor' contain songs of real beauty, as for instance, 'Lokkende Toner,' 'Kärlekspredikan,' 'Saknaden,' 'Eremiten,' 'Mit Hjerte og min Lyre' ('My Heart and Lute'), and 'Natten pas Fjorden.' The voice-part and accompaniments are well written and interesting,[2] and there is no straining for effect or originality.   Among the song-writers born between the years 1837 and 1847, we find the same inclination to represent the national spirit in their art.   But neither Winter-Hjelm, J. Selmer, C. Cappelen, nor even J. S. Svendsen, who wrote two books of highly expressive songs, touched the true note.   This was reserved for R. Nordraak and Eduard Grieg.   Nordraak was a cousin of the poet-novelist Björnson, and modelled his songs, which are of a homely and popular type, after Björnson's peasant-novels. Nordraak died young in 1866, but his patriotism and intimate knowledge and love of his country's songs exercised a strong influence on his friend Grieg, whose taste when young had hitherto been essentially German.   Grieg's talent is curious and delicate.   It is strongly stamped with his own individuality, and not without power,

[1] A band of patriotic Norwegians living in Copenhagen, who combined to found a native university in Christiania in 1811, and to recover their native independence in 1814.

[2] To a certain degree Kjerulf resembles the German song-writer Robert Franz. Both pay the same strict regard to the words and accent, and in both the accompaniments are often treated polyphonically. (See for example Kjerulf's op. 23, No. 2.)

humour, and pathos, but it is limited. His songs, romances, and ballads, especially those set to the northern poets Drachmann, Björnson, Münch, Moë, and Ibsen constitute a characteristic portion of his best work. Owing to the exigencies of the concise song-form, and to Grieg's close study of the folk-music, and his aim, above all, to be simple in form and melody, his songs, though essentially national in colour, never become wearisome or mannered. They may be lacking in intensity of passion, and in the deeper psychological qualities, but they are full of poetry and imagination.

An intimate friend of Grieg's, a celebrated pianist, Agathe Backer-Gröndahl, has written simple and expressive songs, which are very popular in Norway. Other song-writers, born in the second half of the last century, are : J. Holter, Ole Olsen, C. Sinding, Per Winge, and his cousin Per Lasson, C. Elling, J. Halvorsen, Andersen, Alnaes, and Sigurd Lie. The last-named highly gifted composer was born in 1871 and died young. He has left few songs, but they are of rare beauty and poetry. Sinding has an abundance of melodic ideas, and is full of energy, character, and expression, and the strength which works with simple means. He responds to every phase of northern thought ; and such songs as ' Es schrie ein Vogel,' with its harsh colouring, or ' Viel Träume,' with its tender intimacy, or the fine national song ' Vi vil os et Land,' show the intensity with which he realises and reproduces a situation.

SWEDEN.—In the 16th century musical art in Sweden reached a high level. Gustav Vasa was a connoisseur in music, and encouraged composers of the Netherland and Italian Schools to his court. The Thirty Years' War brought Sweden into contact with other European nations, and many Germans flocked thither. Under Charles XII., French music reigned supreme, and long held its sway over all native composers. The Düben family (Germans by origin), who settled in Sweden early in the 17th century, and have been called the ' founders of Swedish music,' hardly deserve this name, for though they did much to further and develop music in Sweden they were entirely under foreign influence. Gustav Düben (died 1690) wrote songs of the type of Heinrich Albert in Germany, whilst his brother Anders Düben, who inclined more to French music, wrote only little arias for the Court of the French chanson kind. In the 18th century the music of German and Italian composers, such as Fux, Graun and Handel, Scarlatti and Lotti, predominated, but simultaneously the Swedish composers J. H. Roman, Agrell, and Zellbell were pursuing the right road towards founding a national school, by using the vernacular in their vocal works. The opera, which has always played an important part in Stockholm, remained chiefly French under Dalayrac and Monsigny, though German dramatic influence was exerted by Gluck, Naumann, Haeffner, etc. The only dramatic composer of Swedish descent was the popular K. Stenborg, who used his native folk-songs in his operas, and led the way through Dupuy and Randel to Hallström, the real creator of the national opera.

The song of the Gustavian period (*i.e.* the close of the 18th century) answers exactly to that of J. A. Hiller, Schulz, Reichardt, and Zelter of Germany, and bore the same homely, popular character, without, however, being in any sense national. The forerunner of the true Swedish Song was Olof Åhlström, who published at the beginning of the 19th century a collection of eighteen volumes called ' Skaldestycken Satte i Musik,' containing songs by himself, by Haeffner, Stenborg, Palm, and others. Many songs in this collection, as well as those by Dupuy, Nordblom, Crusell,[1] etc., still show the same tendency towards the Berlin School, but the words of Swedish poets were used, and attention was thus called at last to Swedish composers. A yet greater service Åhlström did was to edit the songs of that strange original genius C. M. Bellmann, under the title of ' Fredmans Epistlar och Sanger' (1790-95). These are in reality splendidly humorous pictures of Stockholm life, skilfully adapted to favourite foreign (chiefly French) and native airs ; very few tunes are original, but they remain household words in Sweden to the present day.

Literature and music kept pace during the early 19th century, and both drank from the same national source. It is difficult to say whether poetry or music owes most to the so-called Gothic revival, of which Geijer, Afzelius, Tegner, Arwidsson, and Atterbom were the leaders. The first impetus towards the new lyric was given by Afzelius and Geijer in their publication of old Swedish folk-songs in 1814-1816.[2] The melodies in these volumes were revised and harmonised by Haeffner and Groenland. A little later Erik Drake published another series, in which Afzelius joined. Arwidsson (a Dane by birth) devoted himself to the same subject, and published, between 1833 and 1837, three volumes of old war, hunting, and love songs ; Bergström, Hoijer, R. Dybeck, and K. Södling following suit.

The earliest composers who breathed the romantic national atmosphere and sang the characteristic melodies of Sweden, were Geijer, A. Lindblad, J. A. Josephson, Wennerberg, Berwald, Hallström, Rubenson, L. Norman, and A. Södermann. The classic time of the Romanze belongs to the three first named. Geijer's songs are impregnated with the true

1 Crusell would really be considered a Finnish composer, but the interests and destinies of Finland and Sweden have been closely interwoven. This indeed applies to most of the literature and music of the Scandinavian countries, and it is often hard to define to which country the several poets and composers belong.
2 These volumes contain valuable prefaces and notes.

folk-song spirit, and are powerful and expressive, but Lindblad's won wider fame. These also bear the national stamp ; they are pure, natural, unaffected, and withal really poetic and graceful compositions. Among the most interesting are those to Atterbom's words, especially 'Trohet.'[1] And others worthy of mention are 'Saknad,' 'O kom, nij droj,' 'Am Aaren See,' 'Strykningsvisa,' and the nine Heine songs which have more developed and original accompaniments. Lindblad's songs owe their fame and popularity in a great measure to having been sung by Jenny Lind. Josephson surpasses the others in the real lyric ; and the melancholy tenderness which pervades his songs is a racial characteristic. Wennerberg's collection of duets, 'Gluntarne' (Scenes of student-life in Upsala), were once famous, but though his thoughts show independence, his musical treatment is somewhat amateurish. Norman was a truly idyllic composer, and amongst his songs the beautiful 'Skogs Sånger' and 'Månestrålar' should be better known. With the great ballad composer, A. Södermann, Swedish romanticism reached its highest point. Among his solo-ballads and songs, such as 'Tannhäuser,' 'Kvarruinen,' and the 'Black Knight,' we find a great development in the accompaniment. Södermann filled the old forms with new dramatic life, and is therefore considered the great reformer of Swedish Song. Less well-known names are those of J. A. Hägg, A. Körling (whose songs 'Weisse Rosen' and 'Abendstimmung,' of the Mendelssohn type, are favourites), A. Myrberg, V. Svedbom, F. Arlberg (also a fine singer), Henneberg, Kjelander, Byström, Nordquist, A. Bergenson, etc. Among living song-writers, Emil Sjögren holds an important place. Grieg's influence may be traced in his harmonies and Schumann's in his rhythms, but withal he is an independent and interesting composer. The constant repetition of melodic phrases, and the sequences of harsh and ugly discords which occur in his songs, always have their meaning and justification. His settings of Geibel's Spanish Cycle cannot rank with Jensen's, but the beauty of such songs as 'I drommen du är,' 'Så far då väl,' or 'Dröm,' with its lovely vague harmony, and 'Alla mina drömmer,' with its strange impressive tonality, is incontestable.

During the last twenty-five years a change has come over Swedish music. The genius of Berlioz, Liszt, and Wagner has dominated the talents of the living representatives of Swedish romanticism. Of the youngest school of song-writers, Vilhelm Stenhammar, born 1871, stands pre-eminent. His father, P. W. Stenhammar, was a prolific composer of ultra-simple religious, old-fashioned songs. V. Stenhammar is equally successful in any form of song he touches, whether it be the ballad, such as his

[1] Written on the death of the poet's wife.

fine setting of 'Florez and Blanchiflur,' or a little folk-song like 'Irmelin Rose,' or the true lyric, such as the splendid song 'Fylgia.' In freshness, warmth, and wealth of harmony and melody, none of the younger composers have surpassed Stenhammar. In W. Peterson-Berger's Swedish songs, 'Svensk Lyrik' and the cycle entitled 'Ut Fridolin's Lustgård,' the tender, melancholy national tone is reflected ; whereas in his German songs, such as the 'Gesänge nach Nietzsche,' he is more directly under Wagner's spell. Hugo Alfvén, Tor Aulin, and E. Åkerberg belong also, with others, to this group.

In all the modern Scandinavian composers' songs there is the same strong feeling for tone-colour, which may be traced to the innate, deep-rooted love and reverence for the folk-music of their respective homes. And nowhere in Europe has the spirit of romanticism exercised a stronger and higher influence than in these northern countries.

SCANDINAVIAN BIBLIOGRAPHY

Ravn, Dr. von. *Skandinavische Musik* (Mendel).
Hülpher, A. *Histor. Afhandling om Musik och Instrumenter.* Westerås, 1773.
Alte Volksmelodien des Nordens. (*Allg. Musikal. Zeitung*). August 1816.
Lindgren, A. *Ur Svenska Musikens Häfder.*
Cristal, M. *L'Art Scandinave.* Paris, 1874.
Grönvold, Aimar. *Norske Musikere.* Christiania, 1883.
Valentin, Carl. *Studien über die Schwedischen Volksmelodien.* Leipzig, 1885.
Schweitzer. *Geschichte d. Skandinavischen Literatur.* Leipzig, 1886-89.
Spitta, P. *Niels Gade, Zur Musik.* Berlin, 1892.
Norlind, Tobias. *Schwedische Musikgeschichte.* Lund, 1901. *Zur Geschichte der Schwedischen Musik (Die Musik).* August 1904. *Die Musikgeschichte Schwedens in den Jahren 1630-1730.* (*Sammelbände*, I.M.G., I. ii. 1900.)
Thuren, Hjalmar. *Tanz, Dichtung und Gesang auf den Färöern.* (*Sammelbände*, I.M.G., III. ii. 1902.)
Soubies, A. *États Scandinaves.* (*Histoire de la Musique.*) Paris, 1901-3.
Niemann, W. *Die Schwedische Tonkunst.* (*Sammelbände*, I.M.G., V. i. 1903).
Niemann, W. *Die Musik Skandinaviens.* Leipzig, 1906.

COLLECTIONS

Abrahamson, Nyerup, and Rahbek. 'Udvalgte danske Viser fra Middelalderen.' Copenhagen, 1812-14.
Åhlström and Afzelius. 'Traditioner af Svenska Folkviser,' 1814.
Geijer and Afzelius. 'Svenska Folk-visor från Forntiden.' Stockholm, 1814-16.
Rasmussen und Nyerup. 'Udvalg af Danske Viser.' Copenhagen, 1821.
Lyngbye, H. C. 'Foerøske Qvoeder.' Randers, 1822 (no music).
Arwidsson, A. 'Svenska Fornsånger.' Stockholm, 1834-42.
Lindemann, L. 'Aeldre og nyere Norske Fjeldmelodier.' Christiania, 1840.
Dybeck, R. 'Svenska Vallviser och Hornlåtar.' Stockholm, 1846 ; 'Schwedische Weisen,' 1847-48 ; 'Svenske Viser,' 1853-56.
Landstad, M. B. 'Norske Folkeviser.' Christiania, 1853.
Berggreen, A. P. 'Danske, Norske, and Svenske Folkesange og melodier.' Copenhagen, 1861-63.
Lundquist. '100 Svenska Folkviser.' Stockholm, 1866.
Kristensen, E. 'Jydske Folkeviser,' 1871-76-91.
Bohlin, K. T. F. 'Folktöner från Jämtland.' Stockholm, 1883.
Hansen, W. 'Danske Melodier.' (Melodier fra alle Lande, vol. i.) Copenhagen, 1885.
Hammershaimb, V. 'Foerøsk Anthologi.' Copenhagen, 1891. (Chiefly dances and dance-songs.)
Carlheim-Gyllensköld, V. 'Viser och Melodier.' Stockholm, 1892.
Laub, T. 'Danske Folkeviser med gamle Melodier.' Copenhagen, 1899.
Garborg, H. 'Norske Folkeviser.' (In progress) 1903. No. 8 of the 'Norske Folkeskriften.')
'August Bondeson's Visbok.' Stockholm, 1903.
Hansen, W. 'Svenske og Norske Melodier.' (Melodier fra alle Lande, vol. ii.) Copenhagen.
Rocke, L. 'Nordische Volkslieder.'
Åhlström, J. '300 Svenska Folkeviser.' Stockholm. 'Nordiska Folkeviser.' Stockholm.
Bogge, J. '73 Polkskor från Gottland.' Stockholm.
Weyse, C. E. F. '50 gamle Kampevise melodier.' (In progress)
Blumenthal, I. G. 'Delsbostintens Visor' (in progress).

ICELANDIC.—BIBLIOGRAPHY AND COLLECTIONS

De la Borde, J. B. *Essai sur la Musique ancienne et moderne.* (Several Icelandic songs in vol. ii. p. 397 *et seq.*) Paris, 1780.

Berggreen, A. P. 'Folke-Sange og Melodier' (vol. i.). Copenhagen, 1869.
Davidsson, Olafur. 'Islenzkar Skemtanir.' Copenhagen, 1888-92. 'Söngbók hins islenzka Studentafjelags.' Reykjavik, 1894.
Pilet, Raymond. *Nouvelles Archives des Missions scientifiques et littéraires* (vol. vii. pp. 243-271). Paris, 1897.
Panum and Behrend. *Illustrieret Musikhistorie* (vol. i. p. 44, has a reference to the *Tvisöngur*). Copenhagen, 1897-1905.
Hammerich, Angul. *Studien über isländische Musik*. (*Sammelbände*, I.M.G., I. iii. 1900.)
Thuren, Hjalmar. *Tanz, Dichtung und Gesang auf den Färöern.* (This contains many Icelandic songs.) *Sammelbände*, I.M.G., III. ii. 1902.

THE NETHERLANDS

Under this comprehensive term are included the countries which extend from the North Sea to the Somme in France, comprising Holland, Flanders, Belgium, the Walloon country and the chief part of the old province of Artois. The population is partly Teutonic, represented by the Flemings; partly of Romance origin, represented by the Walloons. Two languages are spoken—Dutch and French, for Flemish is nearly akin to Dutch, and the Romance dialect spoken by the Walloons is closely allied to French, which is the official language of Belgium. Still, until the 19th century when Holland and Belgium were formed into independent kingdoms, the Netherlands was practically one country. In dealing with the folk-songs, however, a distinction must be made, as each division of the country possessed its own songs. Yet even so the subject is confusing, for while the official designation of 'Netherlands' is retained by what we now call Holland, the 'Spanish Netherlands,' which in the 16th and early 17th centuries played so important a part in history, and gave birth to the finest songs, comprised rather the districts of Flanders and Belgium. Again, the songs of the North of France and Flanders, and the Low German and Dutch songs, have so much in common, that to write the history of one is to write the history of the other.[1]

The *Trouvères* of the 11th and 12th centuries, with their *langue d'oïl*, belonged equally to Northern France and to Belgium, and as they have already been mentioned under FRANCE it is unnecessary to refer to them again here. Further, the Old French and Flemish schools of music were practically identical, and the Gallo-Belgian School, whose most successful period lies between 1360 and 1460, was considered by other nations as French, and the composers indiscriminately called *Galli* (see *ante*, p. 542). But with the Netherland School proper we are treading on different ground. This school penetrated into every cultured country in Western Europe, formed schools of its own, identified itself with other nationalities, and was held in universal esteem until, in the latter part of the 16th century, the Italians became the leading musical nation in Europe. This great school, however, was essentially polyphonic, and with it and its chief repre-

sentatives (such as Okeghem, Obrecht, Josquin des Prés, Gombert, Orlandus Lassus, and others) this article is only indirectly concerned. These prefatory remarks will explain to some extent the complex character of the history of song in the Netherlands.

Among the earliest traces of the *langue d'oïl* is the 'Cantique de Ste Eulalie' (without music), preserved in the Valenciennes Library, and belonging to the 9th or early 10th century.[2] This language of the *Trouvères* was spoken in Northern France and Belgium for some centuries, and during the 11th, 12th, and 13th numerous songs were composed which, with their melodies, still exist. With regard to the Flemish songs, Fétis says it is more difficult[3] to decide with certainty whether they are as old as they are reputed to be. Of these, one famous song, to judge by the character of the poetry, reaches back to the Norman traditions of the 10th century.[4] It is known by the name of 'Heer Halewijn,' and Willems, who published the song in 1836 with the original text, says it is still heard in Brabant and Flanders.[5] The many versions of the melody make it impossible to date it with accuracy, but the following (in the Hypomixolydian mode) is considered the oldest and purest:—

Ex. 1.   *Heer Halewijn.*

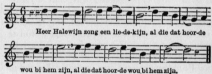

Heer Halewijn zong een lie-de-kijn, al die dat hoor-de

wou bi hem zijn, al die dat hoor-de wou bi hem zijn.

Although it is true that the aim of the representative Netherland School (1425-1625) was polyphonic, it is a mistake to suppose that the work of these learned contrapuntists was the only form of music prevailing in the country at this time. National songs existed contemporaneously with it; and the tunes these great masters used as themes for their glorious masses, motets, and polyphonic chansons were practically their own folk-songs. That such historic French and Flemish tunes as 'L'Homme armé,' 'Cents mille ecus,' 'Forseulement,' 'Je me demande,' 'Myn Hert,'[6] 'Het daghet,'[7] were not merely worthy of local recognition is proved by their constant use throughout Europe.

[1] See Coussemaker's *Chants des Flamands de France*; and Böhme's 'Altdeutsches Liederbuch.'

[2] Fétis, *Histoire Gén. de la Mus.* iv. 485.
[3] *Ibid.* v. 55 *et seq.*
[4] Oscar Fleischer, in *Ein Kapitel vergleichender Musikwissenschaft* (*Sammelbände*, I.M.G., I. i. 1899), shows the resemblance between the Halewijn melody and a Brittany ballad, 'Die drei Monniken' (see Villemarqué, p. 185), and the melody of a hymn, 'Sidus solare,' from a Neapolitan MS. of the 11th and 12th centuries, and discusses which is the older.
[5] F. van Duyse corroborates this by saying that Pol de Mont (poet and folk-lorist) heard the 'Halewijnslied' in 1896 in the environs of Leuwen. (See *Het oude Nederlandsche Lied*, i. 13.) In this standard work Duyse practically includes all the songs found in the Netherlands with the words and tune of each, and their variants. The valuable preface explains the verse metre, rhythm, scales, and general form, and is indispensable to the student.
[6] Used by Pierre de la Rue in a 4-part chanson. See Ambros, iii. 241.
[7] Used by Clemens non Papa in a 3-part chanson. See Duyse, i. 124.

The Netherland masters, however, rarely gave the whole melody even to the leading part, and seldom more than one *couplet* of the words, and hence the fragmentary character of the songs they bequeathed to us. But gradually the spirit of the folk-song began to influence their highest forms of composition, and they realised that in their *chansons, villanelles,* and *canzonettes,* written in four, five, six, seven, or eight parts, 'mechanical invention must be subservient to idea, and euphony and expression should equally be the objects of the composer.'[1] Amongst the works of Dufay, Binchois, Faugues, Busnois, and in Petrucci's 'Canti cento cinquanta,' there are songs which, in regularity of form and simplicity of character, rival the folk-songs. Nor are examples wanting in the minor works of Okeghem, Pierre de la Rue, Josquin des Prés, Gombert, Willaert,[2] Goudimel, Clemens non Papa, Jannequin,[3] Arcadelt, and Orlandus Lassus, of secular melodies conceived in a strain of freshness, naïveté, humour, and brightness, or marked by a power of lyric expression belonging to a much later time.

The picture of an age and its culture is always vividly reflected in its folk-songs; it was therefore the natural result of the intensity of the impulse given to religious life by the 'mystics' that so great a number of sacred songs were created during the 14th century.[4] The ground had already been prepared by the celebrated ascetics Greert Groote and Johann Ruysbrock, and the numerous sacred *Minne-songs*[5] were the especial outcome of the mystic movement. About the middle of the 15th century the early *Rederykers*[6] (who correspond with the German *Meistersinger*) substituted for the harshly realistic secular songs of the day their own carefully prepared sacred songs.[7] For these they either altered the words of the secular songs to give them a sacred meaning, or they adapted totally new religious words, retaining the secular tune unchanged.[8] And this practice prevailed in the Netherlands throughout the 16th and 17th centuries. In 1561 Tylman Susato published his 'Souterliedekens,' consisting of portions of the Psalms according to the rhymed Flemish version, set unaltered to the popular song-tunes.

of the day. This publication was succeeded by Fruytier's 'Ecclesiasticus' (1565) and the various Roman Catholic song-books, such as 'Theodotus,' 'Het Paradijs' (Antwerp, 1621), which similarly contained a mass of secular melodies. Whilst the Church scales were still in use the greater part of the earlier melodies were in the Dorian mode, though the Phrygian and Lydian were also represented.[9]

Very different in character from the sacred songs of the mystics, of the *rederykers,* of the Roman Catholics, or those which the Reformation produced, were the songs of liberty and patriotism sung a generation later during the Spanish oppression. Amongst other collections the famous song-book of the Gueux[10] ('Geusen-Liedenboecxkens,'1588), and Adrianus Valerius' 'Gedenck-Clanck' (1621-26)[11] (see VALERIUS), contain the classics of Dutch musical literature, and are historically of inestimable value. They give us the ballads of 'Egmont and Horn,' the 'Storm of Leyden'; the splendid political songs of satire on the Spanish generals, such as the 'Spotlied op de Bossu,' 'Spotlied op de Alva,' or the patriotic songs such as 'Ein Liedje op den Briel,' or 'De Geuzen bij Antwerpen,' and 'Wilhelmus van Nassouwe'— the Dutch national anthem. (See WILHELMUS VAN NASSOUWE.) These grand old Netherland songs breathe a spirit of protest against tyranny, and of warlike determination tempered with resignation under disaster, which sets them on a distinct plane of their own. In many of the collections only the name of the tune (*stem*) is mentioned to which the song was sung. Such is the case with those in the 'Geusen Lieden-boecxkens,' but Valerius has given the actual melodies as well. Many tunes are derived from foreign sources, and especial interest is attached to those of English origin, of which the following collections contain the most: 'Friesche Lust-thof' (1621);[12] 'Gedenck-Clanck' (1621-26);[13] 'Den singende Zwaen' (1664); 'Stichtelycke Rymen' (1624);[14] 'Bellerophon' (1633);[15] and Thysius's and Vallet's lute-books. At the time of Queen Elizabeth, when the cultivation of music in England was at its height, intercourse between this country and the Netherlands was most frequent. English traders arrived in Dutch harbours, English students studied at Leyden, English actors played in Amsterdam,[16]

---

[1] Naumann's *Hist. of Mus.* i. 368.

[2] In Willaert we clearly see the modern spirit, not only in what he did for harmony but also for his recognition of the value of the solo-voice. In 1536 he arranged some of Verdelot's madrigals for solo-song with accompaniment of lute.

[3] Wooldridge gives a lovely little song, 'Ce Moys de Mai,' by Jannequin, showing the transition between the two styles, where the harmony is in plain chords, but 'the polyphonic element is still present in the melodious flow and independent interest of the separate parts.' *Oxford Hist. of Music,* ii. 277.

[4] See W. Bäumker, *Niederländische geistliche Lieder, Vierteljahrs-schrift,* 1888.

[5] All these songs deal with Christ as the Bridegroom for Whom the loving soul yearns.

[6] For information on the guilds of poets and musicians in the Netherlands, see Motley's *Rise of the Dutch Republic,* i. 75 *et seq.*

[7] For examples from the later *rederyker,* M. van Castelyn's songs (*Diversche Liederkens*), see Duyse, ii. 1530 *et seq.* One of Castelyn's songs, 'Ghepeys, Ghepeys, vol van euvijen,' is included in most collections.

[8] In this manner many secular songs have been preserved intact, instead of only in a fragmentary or mutilated form, such as we have seen the polyphonic writers reduced them to.

[9] Bäumker has given examples of these interchangeable sacred and secular songs from two old MS. collections: one is in the K. K. Fideikommisbibliothek in Vienna, and the other in the Königliche Bibliothek in Berlin. The tunes are nearly all to be found in Böhme's 'Altdeutsches Liederbuch,' and frequently occur again in Dutch collections. See also 'Geistliche und Weltliche Compositionen des XV. Jahrhunderts,' bearbeitet von Guido Adler und Oswald Koller.

[10] Or 'Gentlemen beggars.' For the origin of the word see Motley's *Rise of the Dutch Republic,* i. 432 *et seq.*

[11] Dr. A. Loman has harmonised a selection from the Geusen-liedenboecxkens' and the 'Gedenck-Clanck.' Both, with his interesting prefaces and notes, were published by the Maatschappij tot bevordering der Toonkunst for 1871 and 1872. (See VEREENIGING.)

[12] J. Starter.

[13] See J. P. Land's article on Valerius's 'Gedenck-Clanck' in vol. i. of the *Tijdschrift der vereeniging voor Noord-Nederlands Muziekgeschiedenes.* (Land's references are to the 1st edition of Chappell's *Pop. Music.*) [14] Camphuysen. [15] D. P. Pers.

[16] *Die Singspiele der englischen Komödianten,* Dr. J. Bolte, 1896.

and English soldiers fought side by side with the Dutch against the Spaniards. And it is clear that Dutch musicians were well acquainted with English ballads, for certain songs, such as 'Fortune,' 'What if a day' (identical with 'Wilhelmus van Nassouwe'), 'Barafostus' Dream,' and the 'Cobbler's Jig,'[1] were evidently favourites, as they occur so frequently. The last-named tune is used in the 'Gedenck-Clanck' for the song 'Wie dat sich selfs verheft,' and Valerius calls the *stem* 'Engelslapperken.' On comparing this Dutch song of satire on Alva's standard with the English version, it will be seen that not a note has been altered.

Ex. 2.   *Wie dat.*

Wie dat sich selfs ver-heft te-met, wert wel een ar-me
duc d'Alf u beeld, tot spijt ge-set, waer af-ge-bro-ken

sle-ter,   u boose daed, die ghij begaet bij   al-len toch on-
be-ter,

lij-dig is en strij-dig is met   on-ser Landen staet.

One of the most beautiful songs in this collection, 'Waer datmen sich al keerd of wend' (a fine patriotic poem by Valerius), set to the *stem* 'Pots hondert duijsent'[2] slapperment' (named also by Valerius 'Allemande Pekelharing'), bears a strong resemblance to 'Walking in a country town.'[3]

Ex. 3.   *Waer datmen.*[4]

Waer dat-men sich al keerd of wend, End' waer-men
Waer dat-men reijst of rotst, of rend, End' waer-men

loopt of staet,
he-nen gaet,   Daer vint-men, 'tsij oock op wat ree d'Hol-

lan-der end de   Zeeuw: Sij loopen door de

[1] See Chappell's *Old English Pop. Music* (new edition), i. 75, 100, 148, 279.
[2] *Tausent* in some versions. See Starter's, from whom Valerius possibly took the tune.
[3] Chappell, i. 117.
[4] Thus arranged by Loman. (The opening phrase recalls the Swedish song 'O Wermeland.')

woe-ste   Zee, Als   door het bosch de Leeuw.

Valerius has also included nineteen purely Dutch folk-tunes in the 'Gedenck-Clanck,' and one cannot fail to be struck by the bold sweeping melodic lines, massive structure, and stately dignity of these songs. The Dutch and North Flemish folk-songs have, in fact, much in common with the German Volkslied, which is explicable when we consider the consanguinity of the races, the resemblance of temperament, and the similarity of language and poetical forms.[5] Many of the tunes are modal, and yet have a feeling for harmony which is unusual in such tunes. The melodies most frequently begin on the up-beat, and as the musical rhythm follows the words very closely[6] frequent changes of time are necessitated, although the actual rhythmical figures present little variety :—

Ex. 4.   *Het daghet.*[7]

Het daghet in den Oosten, het   lich-tet o-ver-

-al . . . . .;   hoe luttel weet mijn lief - - -

- ken, och   waer ick he-nen   sal!

The songs are by no means always in regular periods; constantly the first part consists of eight and the second part of five or six bars, or of five and seven bars each as in the 'Spotlied.' (See p. 590, Ex. 5.) Sometimes only one bar is added, as if to give emphasis to the last words. Melodic *melismas* are of frequent occurrence, even in strophical songs, and are probably due to the influence of the Church. And yet, paradoxical as it may seem, the songs never

[5] It may be safely asserted that two-thirds of the songs given in Duyse's famous collection occur also in F. Böhme's 'Altdeutsches Liederbuch' and other German collections, with only slight differences in the words and melodies. As one example, take 'Daer staet een clooster in Oostenrije' (Duyse, i. 472) and 'Es liegt ein Schloss im Oesterreich' (Böhme, 154). Böhme drew attention to this point in his preface, saying: 'The German and old Netherland folk-songs are indistinguishable, for from the last half of the 15th to the end of the 16th century they had a fund of folk-poetry in common. And amongst the songs contained in the Netherland collections (see especially those in the Antwerp Song-book of 1544) many were written both in High and Low German; and in the German collections (see for instance, Rhaw's 'Bicinia') songs occur with Netherland text and sometimes with the mark *Brabantica* annexed. This interchange need cause no surprise when the close intercourse promoted by the Hanseatic League is taken into account.'
[6] Following the verse-metre closely is peculiarly characteristic of Dutch folk-songs.
[7] This 15th-century song is set to Psalm iv. in the 'Souterliedekens' (1540), and was used by Clemens non Papa in a chanson for three voices, and published in Antwerp in 1556. It occurs also in a different form in the Gueux song-book (1575), set to 'Och God wil doch vertroosten,' also in Camphuysen's and many other collections. See Duyse, i. 124.

Ex 5·   *Spotlied op de Bossu.*[1]

Ma-xi-mi-lia-nus de Bos-su ben ick een Graef Ge-hee -

- - - ten,   ick heb ge-weest sijn ad - mi-rael,de Geu-sen te

doo - den   prin - ci-pael, dit had ick mij ver-me-ten.

lose their classical character of regularity of form.

Belgium being a bilingual country the folk-songs are divided into two classes, Flemish and Walloon.[2] The Flemish are more numerous and widespread; indeed they extend north into Holland, where they intermingle with the Dutch. The Walloon songs are more local, though they include all those sung in French or in the curious Walloon dialect.[3] Just as the Flemish people show affinity with the German, the Walloons resemble the French. The grace and liveliness of the French *chanson*, the love the French have for satirical words and strongly marked dance-rhythms,[4] are qualities exhibited by the Walloons. In the district round Liége a particular genre of satirical song exists, called *la pasqueye*, and amongst the numerous Belgian dance-songs, the 'Cråmignons' of the same district should be especially noticed. The following is a favourite :—

Ex. 6.   *Cråmignon.*[5]

Pauv' mohe! quu n'tu sÂ-vér' tu? Wiss' don?

po dri les ca - bus.   Vo - chal vi-now' l'a-

|1st.| |2nd.| *Solo.*

règne, Po v'ni ma-gni l'mohe.   l'mohe, l'a-règne li

Tutti.

mohe, l'a-regne li mohe.   Pauv' mohe! quu n'tu sÂvér'

tu? Wiss'   don?   po dri les ca - bus.

The traditional ballads of the old French

provinces, Lorraine, Picardy, Auvergne, and Provence, survive in the Ardennes. In the Walloon songs the *refrains* follow much the same lines as other countries; rhyme is by no means universal, and is often replaced by mere assonance; the dialogue form is very common, and consists of innumerable strophes.[6] Modal melodies are frequently found amongst the Noëls and other religious songs. The profound sincerity and naïveté of the Noëls must appeal to all, and if a vein of realistic familiarity, attractive to the peasantry, is repellent to the more cultivated taste, none will deny that they possess a touching charm of their own, difficult to convey in words.

It is inevitable that songs handed down century after century should undergo changes, but this is less so in the Netherlands than in most other countries. Conscious of their value, Flemish and Dutch musicians have at all times been assiduous in forming collections of their songs and thus preserving them in their original condition.[7] This has not been the case with the French and Walloon-speaking inhabitants of the country. They have depended on oral tradition, and hence their songs have suffered considerable deterioration in the course of time. Indifference to the folk-song steadily gained ground among this people, and their preference for debased tunes from the *vaudeville* and *opéra-comique* was fostered by inferior composers, who wrote in accordance with the prevailing taste. Fortunately this evil is now being counteracted by earnest musicians,[8] who are devoting themselves to the task of rescuing the folk-songs from neglect, and issuing exhaustive collections from the various districts. The wealth of songs and their beauty have fully justified their labours.

After the 16th century, the glory of the Flemish school[9] waned; the contrapuntal age was over and monody reigned in its place. From henceforth very few musicians of any importance devoted their talents to vocal music. As representative songs of the 18th century we may mention those by the Flemish composer G. de Fesch, who came over to England about 1730 and published there a volume entitled 'Canzonette ed Arie a voce sola.' They are sentimental like the French songs of the period, regular in form, with fairly agreeable harmony. Of greater interest are the songs interspersed in

---

[1] This song does not appear in the first editions of the Gueux song-book, but the melody is given in Luther's hymn-book of 1524 to words by Speratus, 'Es ist das Heil'; afterwards it was used by the Bohemian Brothers, and by the Lutherans in Antwerp in 1573. Winterfeld says in his *Evang. Kirchengesang*, i. 41, that in its original form it was undoubtedly a secular folk-song.

[2] 'Chansons pop. des provinces Belges' (preface), Ernest Closson.

[3] This dialect was dying out, but within the last twenty years efforts have been made by the Liége poet Nicolas Defrecheux and by folk-lorists to preserve it.

[4] 3-4 and 6-8 time are very common among the Walloon songs.

[5] Terry and Chaumont's collection, from which the above is taken, includes over 200.

[6] The (Flemish) lace-makers for instance have their own especial songs with apparently meaningless words, but which represent to them a given number or kind of stitch. Each worker takes up one of these endless verses in turn. See Lootens and Fey's 'Chants pop. Flamands.'

[7] The efforts of the members of the Maatschappij tot bevordering der Toonkunst and their interesting publications have greatly contributed to this end. H. Rogge, J. P. Land, A. D. Loman, J. Röntgen, F. van Duyse, D. F. Scheuleer, and Enschedé also deserve special recognition in this connection.

[8] Among these the names of L. Terry and Chaumont, Lootens and Feys, L. Jouret, E. Closson, O. Colson (the director of the Liége review *Wallonia*, which contains much information about the Walloon folk-songs), and the curé J. Bols hold an honoured place.

[9] Technically, the term Flemish has no longer the same signification as it had earlier; that is to say, it is now more identified with Belgian than with Dutch art.

the short allegorical, mythological, and pastoral plays then much in vogue. Van der Straeten [1] gives as a characteristic example, a pretty little 'Bergère Flamande,' from Lambrecht's 'Vlaemsche Vrede-Vreucht'; but whether it was original or an adopted folk-song is an open question. 'Le Voegge de Chofontaine,' an opéra-bouffe by the Liége composer G. Noël Hamal, contained the favourite couplets and dances in the district in which it was written.[2] By degrees, however, these unimportant local operas died out,[3] and composers sought their laurels in Paris. Both Belgium and France lay claim to Gossec and Grétry as national composers; and similarly Grisar, César Franck, and many others, who, although Belgians by birth, are practically regarded as French composers, having identified themselves with the French school.

BELGIUM.—The year 1834 witnessed the constitution of Belgium as a separate kingdom, and the formation of a Belgian nationality. Up to that date there are no songs worthy of mention, with the possible exception of LA BRABANÇONNE, the national song of Belgium, composed by Van Campenhout in 1830. The generality of composers had hitherto continued to use indiscriminately French and Flemish words for their songs, until within recent years a small group of musicians arose who avowedly are endeavouring to give Flemish art once more a national character. This has been designated the *mouvement flamingant*, and the foremost personalities belonging to it were P. Benoit, whose songs set to Flemish words are full of life and colour, and Edgar Tinel. The latter is an interesting composer with a strong individuality, but his songs are few. Many other excellent musicians, who have all written ballads and songs, joined this movement, such as Lenaerts, Wambach, and Jan Blockx, the most brilliant of them all. Mention must also be made of Blockx's pupil, Vleeshower, and of Van den Eeden, who succeeded Huberti as director of the Mons Conservatoire. Less exclusively Flemish song-writers are Eyken and Tilman, who chiefly confined themselves to sacred songs; Miry, C. Meerens, and A. Goovaerts, who wrote for the most part nursery or school songs; and Van Gheluwe, J. Radoux, A. Samuel, J. Meertens, G. Huberti, and E. Mathieu, who are the best-known names. Mathieu has set many of Goethe's ballads, in which the accompaniments are highly elaborate, and the melodies at times expressive. But they lack proportion and unity, and their great length detracts from their effect. In Mathieu's shorter songs the interest is better sustained. Meertens and Huberti have written songs both graceful and melodious, and of a simple character; whilst those of Jan Blockx, G. Lekeu, Paul Gilson, and the younger school of composers, if somewhat eclectic, manifest originality, novelty, and boldness of invention. The curious phase of thought and the peculiar qualities shown in the literature of Belgium by the writings of Maeterlinck, Rodenbach, and Verhaeren, cannot fail to leave their mark also on the music of the period.

HOLLAND.—After the numerous song-books which appeared in Holland between 1600 and 1700, Dutch composers devoted themselves principally to instrumental music. Even on the title-pages of vocal pieces we find *om te singen of te spelen*; and Sweelinck's skilful organ and clavier variations on the songs were greater favourites than the songs themselves. As lutenists, organists, carillonneurs, or theoreticians, Dutch musicians held a high place in Europe;[4] and although among the works of various members of musical families (and music in Holland was an essentially hereditary gift) we find incidental mention of songs or song-collections, it is evident that this form of art was on the wane. Hooft's anonymous publication, 'Emblemata Amatoria,' is the last collection of any value in the 17th century, though Jacques Vredeman (a member of the Vredeman family of lutenists) is known to have written some *canzoni* and *villanelle* to words in the Frisian dialect.

To the 18th century belong De Koninck and Snep, who were the authors of some 'Nederlandsche liederen met een en twe Stemmen,' with figured bass, but these are of no musical value. The same may be said of the vocal works of the following composers who lived in the early part of the 19th century: A. Ten Cate, J. G. Wilms, G. Hutschenruijter, G. W. Smits, J. Boers, and D. H. Dijkhuijzen. Their names still appear in all popular collections of school and patriotic songs, together with those by composers of a later date and higher rank, such as J. Viotta, J. Antheunis, Van Eyken, Richard Hol, S. de Lange (the elder), Prudens van Duyse, and J. van Riemsdijk. The songs of the last-named composers are best described under the German term *volksthümlich*, though some of them have shown more interesting and original work, as, for example, Riemsdijk in his 'Tranenkruikje' and 'Sant Jans Gheleide.' from the *Loverkens*.[5]

The most typical Dutch composers of the last century, the words of whose songs are in the vernacular, were undoubtedly Richard Hol, J. Verhulst, and W. F. G. Nicolai. The first named is better known for his patriotic songs and choruses. Nicolai, who was a prolific

[1] *La Musique aux Pays-Bas*, E. Vander Straeten, iii. 22.
[2] The opera was revived a short time ago in Paris, edited by L. Terry.
[3] In 1810 Van der Ginste wrote an opera with Flemish words; and later Miry, Van den Acker, and Meertens attempted Flemish vaudevilles, achieving, however, only local success.
[4] D. F. Scheurleer gives an interesting picture of musical life in Holland, *Amsterdam in de 17de eeuwe, Het Muziek leven*, The Hague, 1904.
[5] Hoffmann von Fallersleben's *Loverkens* were favourite words with Dutch composers.

writer and a great favourite, has written melodious and expressive songs, somewhat resembling Mendelssohn. Verhulst was one of the most gifted Dutch musicians, a friend of Schumann's, and also well known abroad. He has set a number of the Flemish poet Heije's words to music, amongst others a volume of children's songs, 'Kinderleeven, 29 Liederen voor eem stem,' which are of great charm. Another very favourite writer of children's songs in Holland is Catarina van Rennes.

Modern Dutch song-writers approach more closely to the German school than to the French; and although at this moment a strong national feeling is asserting itself amidst some of the Dutch composers, the general tendency towards Germany cannot be denied. Space forbids more than the mere enumeration of the following names, many of whom have written songs possessing high qualities: J. Brandts-Buys, J. Wagenaar, Hendrika van Tussenbroek, J. Smulders, S. de Lange, Diepenbrock, Gottfried Mann, Julius Röntgen, B. Zweers, K. Kuiler, A. Spoel, J. H. Loots, H. Viotta, van Brucken-Fock, and Cornelie van Oosterzee.

BIBLIOGRAPHY

Lejeune, J. C. W. *Letterkundig Oversigt en Proevein van de Nederlandsche Volkszangen sedert de 15d eeuw.* Gravesande, 1828.
Coussemaker, C. E. H. de. *Histoire de l'harmonie au moyen âge.* Paris, 1852.
Grégoir, E. G. *Essai historique sur la musique et les musiciens dans les Pays-Bas.* Brussels, 1861.
Dinaux, A. *Les Trouvères de la Flandre; Trouvères, Jongleurs et Ménestrels du Nord de la France et du Midi de la Belgique.* Paris, 1863.
Straeten, E. Vander. *La musique aux Pays-Bas avant le XIXme Siècle.* Brussels, 1867, etc.
Kalff, Dr. G. *Het Lied in de Middeleeuwen.* Leyden, 1884.
Soubies, A. *Belgique, le XIXme Siècle; Hollande, le XIXme Siècle.* Paris, 1901.
Duyse, F. van. *Het eenstemmig, Fransch en Nederlandsche wereldlijk Lied.* Brussels, 1896. *De Melodie van het Nederlandsche Lied en hare rhythmische vormen.* The Hague, 1902.
Various articles in the *Tijdschrift der Vereeniging voor Noord-Nederlands Muziekgeschiedenes,* and general histories by Fétis, Naumann, Ambros, etc.

COLLECTIONS. a. OLD
(This list contains only the most famous of the old collections.)
Susato, Tylman. 'Souterliedekens.' Antwerp, 1561.
Fruytiers, Jan. 'Ecclesiasticus.' Antwerp, 1565.
'Geusen-Lieden Boecxkens.' 1588, etc.
Vallet, Nicolas. 'Le Secret des Muses.' Amsterdam, 1618-19.
Valerius, A. 'Nederlandsche Gedenck-Clanck.' Haarlem, 1626.
Starter, J. 'Friesche Lusthof.' Amsterdam, 1621.
Camphuysen, D. R. 'Nieuwen Jeuchtspiegel' (no music). 1620.
'Stichtelycke Rymen.' 1624.
Theodotus, S. 'Het Paradijs.' 1646.
Swaen, G. de. 'Den Singende Zwaen.' Antwerp, 1664.
'Het Liutboek van Thysius.'
'Cupido's Lusthof' (no music). 1613.
Pers, D. P. 'Bellerophon.' 1633.

COLLECTIONS. b. MODERN AND GENERAL
Fallersleben, Hoffmann von. 'Holländische Volkslieder,' Breslau, 1833; 'Horae Belgicae.' (This contains the 'Antwerpsh Liedebock van 1544.')
Carton, C. 'Oud vlaemsche liederen en andere Gedichten der 14e en 15e eeuwen.' (Vlaem. Biblioph.) 1847.
Willems, J. F. 'Oude Vlaemsche Liederen.' (This contains a valuable list of printed and MS. collections.) Ghent, 1848.
Gevaert, F. A. 'Verzameling van acht oude Vlaemsche Liederen.' Ghent, 1854.
Coussemaker, C. E. H. de. 'Chants pop. des Flamands de France.' Ghent, 1856.
Snellaert, A. 'Oude en nieuwe liedjes.' Ghent, 1864.
Wytsman, Kleens. 'Anciens airs et ch. pop. de Termonde.' 1868.
Brandts-Buys, M. A. 'Liedjes van en voor Nederlands Volk.' Leyden, 1875.
Lummel, H. J. van. 'Nieuw Geuzenliedboek.' Utrecht, 1874 and 1892.
Lootens, A., and Feys, J. 'Chants pop. flamands recueillis à Bruges.' Bruges, 1879.
Scheltema, J. H. 'Nederl. Liederen uit vroegeren tijd.' Leyden, 1885.
Wilder, V. 'Chansons pop. flamandes xv. xvi. et xvii. siècles.' Paris.
Terry, L., et Chaumont, L. 'Recueil d'airs de Crâmignons et d'airs pop. à Liége.' Liége, 1889.

Braekman. 'Oude Nederlandsche Liederen.' (Melodiee uit de Souterliedekens.) Ghent, 1889.
Bamps, C. 'Recherches sur le Mey-Liedje' (hymne pop.). Hasselt, 1889.
Riemsdijk, J. C. van. 'Vier en twintig liederen uit de 15de en 16de eeuw met geestelijken en wereldlijken Tekst.' Amsterdam, 1890.
Vloten, J. van, and Brandts-Buys, M. 'Nederlandsche Baker-en kinderrijmen. Leyden, 1894.
Jouret, L. 'Chansons du pays d'Ath.' Brussels, 1894.
Gilson, P. 'Chansons pop. du pays Borain.' 1894.
Fredericq, P. 'Onze hist. volksl. van vóór de godsdienstige beroerten der 16de eeuw.' Ghent, 1894.
'Nederlandsche Liederboek' (pub. by the Willemsfond). Ghent, 1896.
Lange, D. de, Riemsdijk, C. van, and Kalff, G. 'Nederlandsch Volksliederenboek.' Amsterdam, 1896.
Loon, J. van, and Boer, M. de. 'Frysk Lieteboek.' Leeuwaaden, 1899.
Blyau, A., and Tasseel, M. 'Iepersch (Ypres) oud Liedboek.' Ghent, 1900. (In progress.)
Cock, A. de, and Teirlinck, I. 'Kinderspel 1 Kinderlust en Zuid-Nederland.' Ghent, 1902.
Coers, F. R. 'Liederboek van Groot-Nederland.' Amsterdam, 1898-1902.
Röntgen, Julius. 'Altniederländische Kriegs- und Siegeslieder nach A. Valerius' (1626); '14 Altniederländische Volkslieder nach A. Valerius.' Leipzig, 1903.
Closson, E. 'Chansons pop. des provinces Belges.' Brussels, 1905.
Duyse, F. van. 'Het oude Nederlandsche Lied.' The Hague, 1903-5.
Troelstra, P. J., and Groot, P. de. (New edition by Halbertsma.) 'Nij Frysk Lieteboek. Leeuwaaden, 1905.
See also the publications of the Maatschappij tot bevordering der Toonkunst, and of the Maatschappij der Vlaemsche Bibliophilen.

The writer owes her warm thanks to Professor Julius Röntgen of Amsterdam for his kind help.

ENGLAND

Never within historic times has England been indifferent to the art of music. If John Dunstable who lived early in the 15th century cannot claim to have invented polyphony, at least he was one of the first to bring scientific and artistic order into the chaos of harmony, and raise vocal music to the rank of a structural art. But about the year 1240 [1]—two centuries before the time of Dunstable—the song 'Sumer is icumen in' was written by John of Fornsete, a monk of Reading Abbey. Whether this beautiful canon, still extant, is the sole survivor of many such compositions, or was a solitary inspiration, is hidden from us, but it certainly implied a long previous course of study and practice.

As France gave birth to the Troubadours, and Germany to the Minnesingers, so did England in a remote age produce her own Bards and afterwards her Scalds and Minstrels, her Gleemen and Harpers, all of whom were held in high repute by their countrymen. And there is a record of a company or brotherhood, called 'Le Pui,' formed by some merchants in London, at the end of the 13th century, for the encouragement of musical and poetical compositions. With this purpose they assembled periodically, and competitions were held, though the reluctance of the brotherhood to admit any but members to those meetings prevented their influence being widespread. The name denotes a French origin, which is easily possible considering the close intercourse between France and England after the Norman Conquest and during the time of the Crusades. [2] Of the

[1] Or 1226, according to Dr. Wilibald Nagel's *Geschichte der Musik in England,* i. 76, et seq, where an interesting discussion of that song will be found. (See SUMER IS ICUMEN IN.)
[2] See H. I. Riley's *Liber Custumarum,* p. 589. The languages of Latin, French, and English were for a time intermingled, but by the middle of the 14th century French had become a foreign language, Latin was reserved for ecclesiastics and scholars, and every

abundance of popular tunes in the 14th century evidence is supplied by the number of hymns written to them. For instance, 'Sweetest of all, sing,' 'Good-day, my leman dear,' and many others were secular stage-songs, to which the Bishop of Ossory, who lived about 1350, wrote Latin hymns. While the minstrels flourished, notation was difficult and uncertain, and they naturally trusted to memory and improvisation for the tunes to which their tales should be sung. [See MINSTRELS.] But with the end of the 15th century the Minstrels disappeared, their extinction accelerated by the invention of printing. When the pedlar had begun to traverse the country with his penny books and his songs on broadsheets the Minstrel's day was past.[1] To the time of the Minstrels belongs, however, the famous 'Battle of Agincourt' song,[2] with the date 1415.

Ex. 1.   *The Song of Agincourt.*

To the reigns of Henry VI. and Edward IV. belong also many carols, and amongst them the celebrated 'Nowell, Nowell' and the 'Boar's Head' Carol, sung even now every Christmas

at Queen's College, Oxford.[3] Some of these carols may have been composed by John Dunstable or his contemporaries. Although in England there is little left of this earliest English School of composers, on the Continent recent discoveries have been important. 'O rosa bella,' a three-part love-song, by Dunstable, was found at Rome, and afterwards in a different version at Dijon,[4] and it is evidently counterpoint on a popular song. A number of other MSS. of English composers' works of this period exist at Modena and Trent, and the latter library contains another secular song 'Puisque m'amour' by Dunstable.[5] (See DUNSTABLE.)

In the period between 1485 and 1547,[6] which covers the reigns of Henry VII. and Henry VIII., social and political ballads multiplied fast; and among the best-known productions of these reigns are the following: 'Pastyme with good companye,' composed by Henry VIII. himself; 'The three ravens,' 'John Dory,' 'The hunt is up,'[7] 'We be three poor Mariners,' 'Robin, lend me thy bow,' 'My little pretty one,' 'Sellenger's Round,' 'Westron Wynde,'[8] etc. It should be noticed here that many variations in the copies of old tunes indicate uncertainty in oral traditions. Formerly the general opinion was that the old secular music of European countries was based upon the same scale or mode as the modern major scale, *i.e.* the Ionian mode. But it is now generally acknowledged that the ecclesiastical modes were fully used in England in the composition of all kinds of secular music until early in the 17th century, and many of the popular songs were written throughout this period in the Dorian, Mixolydian, and other modes.[9] Thus, amongst the early songs, 'The King's Ballad,' 'Westron Wynde,' and others agree in some of their many versions with the Dorian mode. And as will be later shown, modal influences exist to the present day in our simplest folk-songs. But in the 16th century the easy Ionian mode was the favourite of strolling singers and ballad-mongers; and in spite of prohibition and censure by the Church and the disdain with which skilled musicians treated what they

Englishman, high or low, spoke his own tongue. *Ges. d. Musik in England*, Dr. W. Nagel, ii. 8 *et seq.*

[1] For further information about the minstrels see *Old English Popular Mus.*, Chappell, i. 1 *et seq.* ; and *Ges. d. Musik in England*, Nagel, i. 96 *et seq.*

[2] *Old English Popular Music*, i. 25. Chappell further says that when Henry V. entered the city of London in triumph after the Battle of Agincourt . . . boys with pleasing voices were placed in artificial turrets singing verses in his praise. But Henry ordered this part of the pageantry to cease, and commanded that for the future no ditties should be made and sung by minstrels or others in praise of the recent victories 'for that he would whollie have the praise and thanks altogether given to God.' Nevertheless among many others, a minstrel piece soon appeared on the *Seyge of Harflett* (Hartfleur), and the *Battagle of Agynkourt*, evidently, says Warton, adapted to the harp, and of which he has printed some portions (*History of English Poetry*, ii. 257). The above song, which was printed in the 18th century by Percy, Burney, and J. Stafford Smith, from a MS. in the Pepysian collection in the Library of Magdalene College, Cambridge, has been shown by Mr. Fuller Maitland to be an incomplete transcript from one in Trinity College, Cambridge, in which the melody stands as above. (See 'English Carols of the 15th Century.')

[3] The words to this carol were printed by Wynkyn de Worde in 1521, but the music appears to be of an earlier date.

[4] See Ambros, *Geschichte der Musik*, Musik Beilage, p. 22, where the Roman version is reprinted.

[5] These were discovered in 1892 by Mr. W. Barclay Squire, and copies are now in the British Museum.

[6] Here the chapter on 'The English School' in Prof. H. Wooldridge's second vol. of the *Oxford Hist. of Mus.* may be studied with advantage.

[7] Any song intended to arouse in the morning, even a love-song, was formerly called a *hunt's up* (Shakespeare so employs it in *Romeo and Juliet*, Act iii. Scene 5). There are many different versions of the tune.

[8] This song is famous for being the only secular song which our Church composers employed; it was the subject of three Masses by Taverner, Tye, and Shepherde in the 16th century. See Chappell, *op. cit.* i. 38 for the melody.

[9] At the time the previous editions of Chappell's work were published this fact had not been freely accepted, and a certain number of the tunes had had sharps and flats added to them, which transformed an ecclesiastical mode into a major or minor key. In the present edition, 1893, these signs have been removed. Moreover, in this edition it is stated that there are 44 Dorian, 19 Mixolydian, and 12 Aeolian tunes out of 118. The other 43 are mostly in the major. The Phrygian, and Lydian modes occur less often, however, in English music than in that of other countries. See Wooldridge's preface to Chappell's *Old Eng. Pop. Music.*

contemptuously termed *il modo lascivo*, this popular scale triumphantly survived the collapse of the Gregorian system, and has formed the basis of our modern system of scales and keys.

Of secular songs antecedent to the middle of the 16th century few have come down to us. The principal relics are the songs in the Fayrfax MS.[1] This manuscript, which once belonged to and was probably written down by Dr. Robert Fayrfax, an eminent composer of the reigns of Henry VII. and Henry VIII., consists of forty-nine songs by the best musicians of that time.[2] They are all written in 2, 3, and 4 parts in the contrapuntal style ; some in the mixed measure —four-time in the one part and three-time in another—which was common at the end of the 15th century. But owing to the want of bars the time is often difficult to discover, and there is also a great confusion of accents. During the latter half of the 16th century musicians of the first rank seldom composed airs of the short rhythmical kind appropriate to ballads, and poets rarely wrote in this metre, for ballad-writing had become a separate employment. It should also be noted that English Church composers did not take popular or folk-songs for the subjects of their masses and motets as was the custom in foreign countries, though they were freely used as themes for variations, or *canti fermi* for polyphonic works by instrumental composers.

In Queen Elizabeth's reign music was generally cultivated, and song was universal : ' tinkers sang catches ; milkmaids sang ballads ; carters whistled ; each trade, even the beggars, had their special songs.'[3] The best-known songs of this period from 1558 to 1603 were ' The Carman's Whistle,' ' All in a Garden Green,' ' Dulcina,' ' The British Grenadiers,' ' Death and the Lady,'[4] ' Near Woodstock Town,' ' Light o' Love,' ' Children in the Wood,'[5] ' The Bailiff's Daughter of Islington,' ' Willow Song,'[6] 'Greensleeves,' ' The Friar of Orders Gray,' ' O Death, rock me asleep,'[7] and ' Frog Galliard.' This last song by John Dowland is almost the only instance to be found in the Elizabethan period of a favourite folk-tune known to have come from the hand of a celebrated composer. Dowland originally wrote it as a part-song to the words, ' Now, O now, I needs must part,' but afterwards adapted it for

one voice with accompaniment for the lute. This practice of writing songs for either one or many voices seems to have been common in England, as in Italy ; and in both countries the lute or theorbo sustained the under parts when sung by one voice. Dowland's contemporary, Thomas Ford, published songs for one or four voices, one of which, ' Since first I saw your face,' not only still retains its popularity, but is remarkable as being one of the earliest melodies written by a trained musician in modern tonality. William Byrd's adoption of the ' Carman's Whistle ' in the Fitzwilliam Virginal Book is well known ; it is a dance-tune, and so also is ' Greensleeves,' and many others. In fact, nearly all the dance-tunes contained in these, and somewhat later collections of lute and virginal music, are the most valuable sources we possess for accurate and trustworthy versions of the music of the folk-songs. They are trustworthy because they were written down at the time by skilled musicians, and therefore escaped the risks of transmission by ear alone. The names or words of many ballads are handed down to posterity in the works of Shakespeare[8] and other Elizabethan dramatists.[9]

A few words may be introduced here on the form of popular English ballads, or, in other words, folk-songs.[10] In dance, or march, or ballad music which has grown from the recitation of words to a chant, or to a short rhythmical tune, the musical design is found to reside chiefly in the rhythm, and not in the balance of keys. The ordinary rhythm of ballads was the even fashion of four-bar phrases, as, for instance, in ' The hunt is up ' :—

Ex. 2.　　　　*The Hunt is up.*

And Harry our King is gone hunting to bring his deer to bay.

The three-bar phrase rhythm is generally met with in the jig and hornpipe tunes of England, such as ' Bartholomew Fair,' but it sometimes occurs in songs of other kinds. Of the rhythm in ' My little pretty one,' which has three phrases of two bars each, and a fourth of three bars, there are several other examples ; and,

---

[1] Mention must also be made of three MSS. in the British Museum. Add. MSS. 5665 contains some ballads. This MS. was discovered by Ritson, and a few pieces were printed in J. S. Smith's ' Musica Antiqua.' Add. MSS. 31,922 is a volume containing no less than thirty-three songs by King Henry VIII. (amongst them ' Green grow the holly,' which is a fine song), the rest by Cornishe, Farthing, John Fluyd, Pygott, and others. Royal MSS. appendix 58 contains tenor-parts of twenty secular songs, perhaps written before 1500. This collection contains many dance-tunes, such as ' My Lady Carew's Dompe,' also printed in ' Musica Antiqua,' with several of the older songs. Davey, *History of English Music*, p. 94 *et seq.*
[2] Burney, ii. 539.   [3] Chappell, i. 59.
[4] A series of ballads from ' The Dance of Death.'
[5] ' Chevy Chace ' was sung to this tune.
[6] ' A poor soul sat sighing.'
[7] This was the first ballad known to have an independent accompaniment ; it was for the lute. Chappell, i. 111.

[8] The following are some of the ballads Shakespeare refers to : 'The hunt is up,' ' Heartsease,' ' Willow, Willow,' ' It was a lover and his lass,' ' Greensleeves,' ' Under the greenwood tree,' ' Bonny Sweet Robin,' etc.
[9] Ben Jonson's poem, ' Drink to me only,' is for ever associated with the equally beautiful 18th-century tune ascribed to Col. Mellish, about 1760.
[10] The word ' ballad ' was applied in a loose sense to every kind of song. The ballad of this period and, indeed, up to the 18th century, usually means ' pieces of narrative verse in stanzas,' the music of the first stanza being repeated for every successive one. It was also used in England for that which in other countries is designated a ' folk-song,' and this term has of recent years been also accepted in England for any form of song which essentially belongs to the people.

Ex. 3. *My Little Pretty One.*

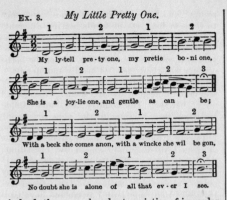

My ly-tell pre-ty one, my pretie bo-ni one,

She is a joy-lie one, and gentle as can be;

With a beck she comes anon, with a wincke she wil be gon,

No doubt she is alone of all that ev-er I see.

indeed, there are abundant varieties of irregular rhythm. But it may be held as a general conclusion that the musical rhythm follows the rhythm and metre of the words, and varies with them. Compound time is very common in English ballads, especially during and after the reign of Charles II., and may be accounted for by the influence of the French dance-music, which Charles II. brought into England. In modulations they exhibit but little variety. The most frequent arrangement is the half-close on the dominant, and the leading note preceding the tonic at the end of the melody, as in 'The hunt is up.' In another arrangement the half-close is on the sub-dominant, and the penultimate note is on the supertonic. In minor-key ballads the relative major-key often takes the place which is held by the dominant in major-key ballads. Another peculiarity of many old ballads are 'burdens.' Sometimes the burden was sung by the bass or basses underneath the melody to support it, as in 'Sumer is icumen in'; or it took the shape of 'ditties,' the end of old ballads, introduced to eke out the words of the story to the length of the musical phrase, as in the 'Willow Song.' In this case the burden was sung continuously by the same voice,

Ex. 4. *Sir Eglamore.*[1]

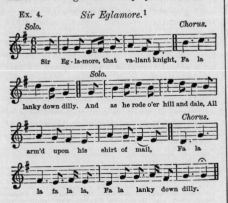

Solo.

Sir Eg-la-more, that va-liant knight, Fa la

Solo.

lanky down dilly. And as he rode o'er hill and dale, All

Chorus.

arm'd upon his shirt of mail, Fa la

la fa la la, Fa la lanky down dilly.

[1] J. Stafford Smith's 'Mus. Ant.' i. 66, taken from the 'Merry Drollery Compleat.'

but in other instances it was taken up by the chorus at the end of a solo song, or solo and chorus combined, as for instance in the burden of 'Sir Eglamore.' The burdens often consist of meaningless syllables, as in 'It was a lover and his lass,' or the last example quoted.[2]

With the advent of the 17th century there commenced a period of transition in the history of music, and more especially in the history of Song. The change was marked by the acceptance of many new principles in musical composition, and by a steady growth of skill in instrumental performances. But its most distinguishing feature was an increase of attention to the conformity of notes with words; that is, to the diligent study of everything that goes to perfect what is called expression in music.[3] And this was the natural development of the monodic revolution whose origin in Italy has already been described.[4] But the success of the new departure was at first as partial and imperfect in England as elsewhere. In Burney's words, 'Harmony and contrivance were relinquished without compensation. Simplicity indeed was obtained, but devoid of accent, grace, or invention. . . . The first attempts at air and recitative were awkward, and the basses thin and unmeaning. Indeed the composers of this kind of music had the single merit to boast of affording the singer an opportunity of letting the words be perfectly well understood, as their melodies in general consisted of no more notes than syllables, while the treble accompaniment, if it subsisted, being in unison with the voice part, could occasion no embarrassment or confusion.'[5]

Nothing was more significant of the change coming over music in England at the beginning of the 17th century than the numerous collections of 'Ayres' or 'Ayres and Dialogues' for solo voices, or for groups of voices accompanied by the lute. These collections also were remarkable for the dainty and delicate poems they contained; in many cases the poet and the composer were one and the same person.[6] Solo songs with instrumental accompaniment had been composed by Byrd,[7] but they were rearranged for several voices when he published them in 1588. The first collections of songs published as solos appeared about the year 1600, contributed by the most eminent composers of this period, Jones, Rosseter, Morley,[8] Coperario, Ford, Ferrabosco, Campion and Johnson.[9] The

[2] For the above remarks on form, see Miss O. Prescott's article entitled *Form or Design in Vocal Music, Musical World,* 1881.
[3] Hullah's *Transition Period of Musical History,* p. 183.
[4] See MONODIA.
[5] Burney's *History,* vol. iii. p. 395.
[6] For instance, Campion and Jones and perhaps Morley.
[7] Twelve in the collection called 'Psalms, Sonets, and Songs of Sadness and Pietie.'
[8] Morley's celebrated 'It was a lover and his lass' appeared in his 'First booke of Aires or Little Short Songes to sing and play to the Lute with the Base-Viol,' in 1600; and Nagel says that previously in 1597 he had arranged a series of canzonets by Italian and English composers as a collection for one voice with lute. Nagel, ii. 136.
[9] Johnson's beautiful air, 'As I walked forth one summer's day,' is given in Hullah's 'English Songs of the 17th and 18th Century.'

style of their solo songs, consisting of a very simple unaffected tune supported by simple harmonies, had a close resemblance to the part-songs, though in some few cases a melodious declamation was attempted. In Rosseter, Jones, Ford, and Campion, the lyric element was more pronounced than in Ferrabosco.[1] Nearly all the above-mentioned composers were among the contributors to the collection published by Sir W. Leighton in 1614. This collection was entitled 'Teares or Lamentacions of a sorrow-full soule,' but its contents were mostly songs in four parts.[2] Ford's song, ' Since first I saw your face,' shows the kind of lute accompaniment employed for these songs.[3]

The popularity of masques at Court offered opportunities to composers for the introduction of lyric songs and dance-tunes. Some scientific musicians may have disdained this kind of work, which only required simple little ditties akin to the folk-songs. Nevertheless Campion, Johnson, and later on Henry Lawes, won great favour in this branch. Henry Lawes merits a special mention as a composer. Known as a professed writer of songs, he was the first Englishman who made it a study to give ex-pression to words by musical sounds,[4] and the care with which he set words to music won him recognition from the chief poets of his day. One of his best-known songs, 'Sweet Echo,' is taken from Milton's 'Comus.' Lawes published also several books of Ayres and Dialogues for one, two, and three voices, with the assistance of his brother, William Lawes, whose fame chiefly rests on his music to Herrick's words ' Gather ye rosebuds.' At this epoch the influence of the Italian recitative style can be plainly traced in all English composers. Henry Lawes was undoubtedly familiar with the works of his Italian contemporaries and recent predecessors, and especially with Monteverde, whose blemishes and beauties were reflected in his own music. A good illustration, both of his skill and of the fragmentary character of his melody, will be found in his music to Waller's ' While I listen to thy voice.'[5]

It was a custom with poets in the 16th and 17th centuries to write new words to favourite old tunes, and this practice has made it almost impossible to assign precise dates to many songs and ballads. Thus in Sir Philip Sidney's poems the heading ' to the air of ' etc. —often a French or Italian tune—constantly

recurs ; and many of the folk-tunes were sung to three or four sets of words bearing different dates, and having little or no relation to each other. Among songs to be found in the principal collections of the first half of the 17th century was the tune of ' Cheerily and Merrily,' afterwards sung to George Herbert's 'Sweet day,' and better known by its later name. ' Stingo, or oil of barley,' 'The country lass,' and ' Cold and raw ' were all sung to the same tune, and many another example might be adduced.

During the Commonwealth secular music flourished in England, and notwithstanding the abolition by the Puritans of cathedral choirs and theatre music, domestic music was much cultivated. A few of the favourite ballads of that time, both Puritan and Loyalist, were, ' Hey then, up we go,' ' Love lies bleeding,' ' I live not where I love,' ' When love was young,' ' When the king enjoys his own again,'[6] and ' I would I were in my own country.' At the end of the Commonwealth the secularisation of music was complete, and with the Restoration of the Stuarts in 1660 a lighter and more melodious kind of music was introduced. In his exile Charles II. had grown fond of French dance music. Ballads, too, came into popular favour again, as the king was partial to lively tunes with strongly marked rhythms. Of the abundant songs of that period, amongst the most celebrated were: 'Here's a health unto his Majesty,' ' Come lasses and lads,' 'Troy Town,' 'Barbara Allen,' 'Under the green-wood tree,' 'Dulce Domum,' ' Lilliburlero,'[7] and 'May Fair,' now better known as 'Golden Slumbers.'[8]

As already mentioned, educated musicians of England were about this time very much under the influence of the Italian and French schools. The style of Pelham Humphrey, whom Charles II. sent to France to study under Lully, was entirely founded on that of his teacher ; and on his return to England Humphrey effected a revolution in English music. Few artists have exercised a more powerful influence on their countrymen and contemporaries than Humphrey ; and his work was all accomplished in the brief space of seven years. He returned from Paris in 1667, and died in 1674, at the early age of twenty-seven. His song, ' I pass all my hours in a shady old grove,'[9] has hardly yet ceased to be sung, and it is a good example of his work, ' which shows a continually varying adaptation of music to changing sentiment of words, and the most fastidious observance of

1 Parry, *Music of the Seventeenth Century (Oxford Hist.* vol. iii.), p. 193 *et seq.*
2 Want of space precludes mention in detail of Playford's, Ravens-croft's, D'Urfey's, Leighton's and the various interesting collections of others, and the reader is referred to the articles under their several names in this Dictionary.
3 Given in Parry's *Music of the Seventeenth Century,* p. 195.
4 See Sonnet addressed to Lawes by Milton in 1645-46.
5 Page 13 of ' Ayres and Dialogues for One, Two and Three Voyces. By Henry Lawes, servant to his late Matie in his publick and private musick. The First Booke, London. Printed by T. H. for John Playford, and are to be sold at his Shop, in the Inner Temple, near the Church door 1653.' Reprinted in Book i. of Playford's ' Treasury of Musick' in 1669. The song will be found with an expanded accompaniment in Hullah's ' 58 English Songs of the Seventeenth and Eighteenth Centuries.'

6 Ritson calls this the most famous and popular air ever heard in this country. See Chappell, i. 214.
7 See LILLIBURLERO.
8 During the 17th century many of our ballad-tunes had found their way into the Netherlands, and were there printed with Dutch words (only preserving the English titles) in most of the miscel-laneous collections of songs. For instance 'The hunt is up' and 'Fortune my foe' appear severally in the Leyden Lute-Book and the 'Nederlandtsche Gedenck-Clanck,'1626. Chappell, *Old English Popular Music,* i. xv. 76, 84. (See *The Netherlands* section of this article.)
9 The words are attributed to Charles II.

their emphasis and quantity.'[1] Many songs of his may be found in the various collections of the time.[2] A fellow-student in the Chapel Royal, to whom Humphrey taught much, was John Blow. In 1700 Blow published a volume of his own songs under the title of 'Amphion Anglicus,' and his setting of Waller's 'Self-Banished' is evidence that he could sometimes compose with tenderness and grace. Then Matthew Lock, the famous masque-composer who wrote 'The delights of the bottle,' a most popular song in its day, is worthy of notice, and he had the honour paid to him of an elegy by Purcell at his death in 1677.

Had Henry Purcell never written anything but songs, he would still have established his claim to be the greatest of English musicians. In dignity and grandeur, in originality and beauty he has no equal among English song-writers. After his death, his songs were collected under the title of 'Orpheus Britannicus,' and 'Full fathom five,' 'Come unto these yellow sands,' 'From rosy bowers,' 'I attempt from love's sickness to fly,' amongst others, have been sung down to our own times. He was a contributor also to Playford's publication 'Choice Ayres and Dialogues,' but his finest songs will be found in the operas and plays for which he composed the incidental music. 'Dido's Lament' should be noted for the skill with which the whole song is constructed on a ground bass of five bars. This is repeated without intermission in the lowest part, but so unconstrained are the upper parts, so free and developed is the rhythm, so pathetic and varied is the melody, that the device would easily escape observation.[3] Between 1683 and 1690 Purcell devoted himself to the study of the great Italian masters, and their teachings are manifest in his music. He did not indeed lose any of his individuality, but the melody of his songs became henceforth smoother and more flowing, and the accompaniments more varied. A common fault of the music of Purcell's time was a too servile adherence to the meaning of the text, and the changing sense of the words was too often blindly followed to the sacrifice of musical construction.[4] Purcell avoided these faults; with his fine instinct for melody and harmony, and his thorough scientific education, no extravagances of any school could lay a strong or permanent hold upon his genius.

From 1700 to 1800 England's previous repute as a land of music sank to a low ebb. Purcell had no successor as a great creative and original musician. There were, however, a number of tunes produced in the 18th century which are still familiar to us. John Eccles

and Richard Leveridge published large selections of songs; and to the latter we owe the famous songs, 'Black-eyed Susan' and 'The Roast Beef of Old England.' A beautiful song called 'Felton's Gavotte,' or 'Farewell, Manchester,' said to have been played by the troops of Charles Stuart in quitting Manchester in December 1745, was originally part of a concerto composed by the Rev. W. Felton. Other popular songs of this period were 'Old King Cole,' 'Down among the dead men,' 'Cease your funning,' 'The Vicar of Bray,' and 'Pretty Polly Oliver.' A marked stimulus was given to song-culture in George II.'s reign by the Ballad-operas, of which the 'Beggar's Opera' (1727) was the first; and it was these operas which brought about the first reaction of the popular taste against Italian music. They were spoken dramas with songs interspersed, the songs being set to old ballad tunes, or imitations of them.[5] Thenceforth most of the popular songs were composed by educated musicians, but the great and enduring popularity of some would entitle them to be classed as national songs. In regard to musical structure they are generally strophical, with an easy accompaniment, a marked rhythm, and a pleasing melody very simply harmonised.

Very popular in his day was Henry Carey, to whom our splendid national anthem was for a time attributed.[6] William Boyce also claims recognition for the spirited 'Come, cheer up, my lads' ('Heart of Oak'), which he wrote to Garrick's words in 1759. A yet greater composer was Thomas Arne, who has been pronounced to be our most national song-writer. 'Rule, Britannia' was written by Arne in 1740 as a finale for the masque of 'Alfred'; and as the song passed from mouth to mouth it soon grew pre-eminent among national airs. It was said by Wagner that the first eight notes of 'Rule, Britannia' express the whole character of the British people. In that same year Arne produced his beautiful songs in *As You Like It*, which he followed with songs in other plays of Shakespeare. In later years Arne's style deteriorated. An imitator of Handel without his genius, Arne overloaded his airs with florid passages, as may be seen in the songs of his opera, 'Artaxerxes.' The obligations of the English people to opera-writers and of the latter to them, have been reciprocal. While some of the best national airs were due to the opera-writers, they in turn won applause by the free introduction of current popular songs into their operas.[7]

Passing on to another generation, we meet with William Jackson of Exeter, who was thirty

---

[1] Hullah's *Transition Period of Musical History*, p. 203.
[2] J. Stafford Smith prints five songs in 'Mus. Ant.' ii. 170 *et seq.*, and also one of John Blow's.
[3] This song is included in Hullah's 'Songs of the Seventeenth and Eighteenth Centuries.'
[4] In fact Lawes's meritorious efforts in this direction were soon exaggerated and overdone by his followers.

[5] See BALLAD OPERA.   [6] See GOD SAVE THE KING.
[7] Most indeed of the best songs of a period extending from Purcell's time down to the early part of the 19th century were once embedded in dramatic pieces; but these pieces have faded into oblivion, while the songs have survived through successive generations. As dramatic forms of song, these compositions lie outside the scope of this article, but as national and popular songs, they come within it. A list of forty operas entirely set to current popular airs is given under ENGLISH OPERA.

years younger than Arne. About Jackson's songs there clings a sense of tameness and insipidity, but in his day no collection was held to be complete without his 'Time has not thinned my flowing hair,' or 'When first this humble roof I knew.' Among his contemporaries, but a little junior to him, were Thomas Carter, Samuel Arnold, Samuel Webbe, and Charles Dibdin, who was a patriotic ballad-writer rather than a musician. The pathos of 'Tom Bowling' has rescued it from neglect, but only by sailors are his other songs remembered now. To Dibdin's generation also belonged John Percy, the composer of 'Wapping Old Stairs,' and James Hook, best known for 'The Lass of Richmond Hill,' and ''Twas within a mile of Edinboro' Town,' a pseudo-Scotch song, like Carter's 'O, Nanny, wilt thou gang with me?' Two better musicians than the foregoing appeared a little later, namely, William Shield and Stephen Storace, both of whom were distinguished by a gift of melody. But their songs are seldom heard now, excepting perhaps 'The death of Tom Moody' by Shield, and Storace's 'With lonely suit.' A well-known song of that period was 'The Bay of Biscay' by John Davy of Exeter.

The special merit of English songs of the late 18th century is their melody, which seems to have then been a common gift ; but the strongest feeling of the nation was patriotism, and the compositions that survive are almost all short songs, expressive of patriotic sentiment, or connected with it by their nautical subjects.[1] John Braham, Charles Horn, and Henry Bishop were all born in the 18th century, but so near its close that their works must be ascribed to the 19th century. Braham himself was a celebrated singer, and his sea-song 'The Death of Nelson'[2] merits the fame which it has won. To Horn we owe 'Cherry Ripe,' and 'The deep, deep sea.' Sir Henry Bishop stood foremost among all his contemporaries and immediate predecessors, alike in science, taste, and facility, and possibly also in invention. His accompaniments are varied and skilful, and though his melodies contain rapid divisions requiring vocal skill, they are graceful and effective. With such care also, did he study correctness of accent, that in his songs the metre of the poetry is seldom disturbed by the rhythm of the music. 'Bid me discourse,' 'Should he upbraid,' and 'Home, Sweet Home' are well-established favourites, which need no eulogy. As other illustrations of the songs of the first part of the 19th century may be mentioned, 'I'd be a butterfly,' by Haynes Bayly ; 'She wore a wreath of roses,' by Knight ; 'The blue bell of Scotland,' by Mrs. Jordan, and others by Rooke, Rodwell, Thomas Cooke, Lee, and

Lover. But speaking generally of these songs and of many others like them, their sole and only merit consisted in the voice-part being pleasant and melodious, and the accompaniments very easy. Weighed in the balance of pure and scientific music they have little value.

It can be easily understood that although this type of song was popular, it had nothing in common with the genuine folk-song. There is indeed an impression that by the end of the 18th century traditional song had died out in England,[3] but this is by no means the case. The many valuable books of traditional songs collected and published during the 19th and present centuries, afford proof that the popularity of song has never been lost in England. Each part of England preserves its special songs as much as its own customs for certain days and seasons. And collectors of songs can bear witness that the habit of inventing songs is not yet extinct among the country people. This circumstance may account for the existence of many quite distinct airs for a set of favourite words.[4] Recent collections also show that the modal influence (already spoken of in this article) is still evident in many of the English folk-songs. Numerous examples of tunes clearly belonging to the ecclesiastical modes could be given, did space permit. Many of the more recently collected folk-songs are mere variants of older versions, and it is often very difficult to trace them back to their original form. The districts where music is largely cultivated among the poorer classes are not those where the old tunes are most carefully preserved and handed down. The reason of this is, that the popular song of the day is ever the enemy of folk-music ; and although the neighbourhood of a town may afford opportunities of musical instruction and cultivation, it likewise offers facilities for acquiring familiarity with this commoner and less desirable class of song. As a general rule the English folk-songs are diatonic in melody and regular in form, and lack any striking characteristics as regards either rhythm or harmony. They hold, however, a high place among the folk-songs of other nations, and they owe it to symmetry of form, simplicity and directness of melody, and the absence of sentimentality.[5]

It would be difficult at this date to write a just appreciation of English songs of the 19th century. Although there have been many composers of real merit, the standard of the general public taste was low, and the demand for high or serious work was limited. A numerous section of song-writers clung to the ever-popular

---

1 Davey's *History of English Music*, p. 425 *et seq.*
2 On the curious similarity of musical idea between this and Méhul's 'Chant du départ' (amounting almost to identity), see Davey, *op. cit.* p. 477.

3 Chappell's 'Old English Popular Music' ends with the close of the 18th century.
4 See preface to 'English County Songs,' by Lucy Broadwood and J. A. Fuller Maitland.
5 Sir Hubert Parry said in his inaugural address to the Folk-song Society : 'The folk-songs are characteristic of our race : of the quiet reticence of our country folk, courageous and content to meet what chance shall bring with a brave heart. All the things that mark the folk-music of the race also betoken the qualities of the race, and as a faithful reflection of ourselves, we needs must cherish it.'

ballad-form, and as they considered the voice-part to be their paramount consideration, they attempted nothing more than the simplest harmonies and accompaniments, and disregarded alike the accent and meaning of the poem for the sake of repeating the same commonplace tune again and again. Yet within these narrow limits there are songs of various degrees of merit ; some composers have raised their songs by force of natural gifts and instinctive taste to a high level.

For a considerable period it seemed as if England knew not how to speak her own language in music. It is an open question whether the effects produced by the Italian opera in Handel's time, and succeeded later by the strong influence of Mendelssohn, were baneful or beneficial to English music. But it is certain that during the first two-thirds of the last century, very few genuine English songs—that is, purely English in idiom and turn of expression, as well as in thought and feeling—could be met with. Of these few exceptions we may name J. L. Hatton's 'To Anthea,' and 'Simon the Cellarer,' J. Hullah's 'Three Fishers,' F. Clay's 'The Sands of Dee,' A. S. Sullivan's 'Orpheus' and his other songs from Shakespeare and Tennyson. In excellence of workmanship many of the above songs cannot compete with those of a perfectly distinct class of writers, among whom W. Sterndale Bennett stands pre-eminent. Of the refinement, delicacy, and perfect symmetry of his songs, such as 'May Dew' and 'Dawn, gentle flower' there could be no question ; and had he not shared in common with Mendelssohn a tiresome mannerism of frequent repetition of the same phrase, his songs would have been more fully recognised and appreciated. To much the same period belong the songs of E. J. Loder, whose graceful 'Brooklet' is one of the best of English songs, W. Davison, G. A. Macfarren, Henry Hugo Pierson, and Edward Bache. The last died very young, but not before he had given promise of high merit in the clearness of his ideas. Pierson's songs displayed strength and originality, but wholly neglected the rules of form. The true English ring of Arthur Sullivan's songs has already been noticed, but there was some other undefined quality, which contributed to secure his great successes. It was not his brilliant humour, for that quality hardly appears in his songs. Possibly the charm lay in some veiled touch of emotion. He wrote various kinds of songs : some nearly descended to the drawing-room ballad, while others rose to a far higher level, such as his Shakespeare songs and the setting of Tennyson's 'The Window, or the Loves of the Wrens.'[1]

[1] These words were written by Tennyson expressly for Sullivan at Sir George Grove's request. The latter had proposed in October 1866 to Tennyson, to write a 'Liederkreis' for Millais to illustrate, and Sullivan to set to music. *Life and Letters of Sir George Grove*, by C. L. Graves, p. 133.

In this last beautiful little cycle there are a tenderness and grace combined with fine workmanship which are enduring qualities. The last word of the ballad-type of song seems to have been said by Sullivan ; since his time, this class of song has not been considered worthy of notice by musicians. Popular taste may not yet have changed, but the aims and work of serious musicians have perceptibly done so.

During the last thirty or forty years Song in England has once more been regarded as one of the most important forms of art, and men have approached it in a different spirit. Once more the importance of the words has been fully recognised, and it is now established that there is no insuperable barrier to the setting of English poetry to music. Some difficulties may no doubt arise from the irregular occurrence of the accents in English poetry ; but accent is a study which has at last received attention, and much is owed to the care and thought which Sir Hubert Parry has bestowed on the due correspondence of the accents of the verse with the rhythm of his music. In his several books of 'English Lyrics' the respect with which he treats the meaning of the words, is also plainly shown, and his influence on this point is evident in the works of the younger generation of English composers. Parry, Stanford, Mackenzie, Elgar, and Goring Thomas have adhered, more or less, to the high standard of song-writing ; but though their names are grouped together as the modern leaders of music in England, each composer has his own individuality. No two composers, indeed, stand farther apart in their songs than Parry and Goring Thomas. The latter's songs, with their long-drawn-out phrases and peculiar romantic atmosphere, are more French in feeling, while Parry's songs, with their elaborate polyphonic accompaniments, incline more to the German school, though throughout, his melodies have a thoroughly English ring. Sir Charles Stanford has written striking and manly ballads, and a vein of true melody traceable to his Irish descent pervades his lyrics. In Elgar's works an exceptionally poetic imagination and great technical skill are manifest, which encourage the hope that he may turn his attention more frequently to song-writing. Feminine song-writers are abundant now, but none have reached the position attained by Maude V. White, whose ever-effective songs are full of expression and refinement ; and a conspicuous merit with her is her choice of good words.

It is interesting to note among the band of earnest young song-writers, the pains and skill bestowed upon the accompaniments of their songs. The accompaniment is now rightly held to be an integral part of the whole composition, and as instrumental skill has reached a very high level, technical difficulties can be ignored. Whether the voice - part is always treated effectively is open to question, but for intrinsic musical value, the modern song has far surpassed the song of former days.

Criticism in detail of the works of living and rising composers is always an invidious task. We stand too near to judge their work without awakening suspicions of prejudice or partiality. Time alone is the true touchstone of merit, and before that high tribunal, the work of the following song-writers must be judged: Granville Bantock, W. H. Bell, Frederick Cowen, H. Walford Davies, Fritz Delius, Edward German, W. H. Hadow, Noel Johnson, C. A. Lidgey, S. Liddle, Hamish McCunn, Albert Mallinson, Roger Quilter, Cyril Scott, Arthur Somervell, S. Coleridge-Taylor, E. Walker, R. Walthew, Amherst Webber, R. Vaughan Williams, and others.

BIBLIOGRAPHY

Burney, Dr. Charles. *History of Music*. London, 1776-89.
Hawkins, Sir John. *History of Music*. Edition of 1853.
Hullah, John. *The Third or Transition Period of Musical History*. London, 2nd edition, 1876.
Rockstro, W. S. *History of Music*. London, 1886.
Naumann, Emil. *History of Music* (edited and added to by Sir F. Gore Ouseley). London, 1882-86.
Parry, Sir C. H. H. *The Evolution of the Art of Music*. London, 1894.
Nagel, Dr. Wilibald. *Geschichte der Musik in England*. Strasburg, 1894-97.
Davey, H. *History of English Music*. London, 1895.
Parry, Sir C. H. H. *Music of the Seventeenth Century (Oxford Hist. of Music*, vol. iii.). Oxford, 1902.
Fuller Maitland, J. A. *The Age of Bach and Handel (Oxford Hist. of Music*, vol. iv.). Oxford, 1902.
Wooldridge, H. *The Polyphonic Period (Oxford Hist. of Music*, vol. ii.). Oxford, 1905.
Sharp, Cecil J. *English Folk-Song, some Conclusions*. 1907.

COLLECTIONS

Smith, J. Stafford. 'Musica Antiqua.' London, 1812.
Sandys, W. 'Christmas Carols, Ancient and Modern.' London, 1833.
Chappell, W. 'Popular Music of the Olden Time.' London, 1855-59.
Wooldridge, H. A new edition of above, called 'Old English Popular Music.' London, 1893.
Hullah, John. '58 English Songs of the 17th and 18th Century.' London, 1871.
Smith, Laura. 'The Music of the Waters.' London, 1888.
Barrett, W. A. 'English Folk-Songs.' London, 1891.
Gould, S. Baring, and Sheppard, H. 'Songs of the West.' London, 1891.
Kidson, F. 'Traditional Tunes.' Oxford, 1891.
Somervell, A. 'Songs of the Four Nations.' London, 1892.
Broadwood, L. E., and Fuller Maitland, J. A. 'English County Songs.' 1893.
Gould, S. Baring, and Sheppard, H. J. 'A Garland of Country Song.' London, 1895-97.
Stokoe, J., and Reay, S. 'Songs and Ballads of Northern England.' Newcastle and London, 1899.
Sharp, Cecil. 'A Book of British Song.' 1902.
Moffat, Alfred, and Kidson, Frank. 'The Minstrelsy of England.' 1902.
Hadow, W. H. 'Songs of the British Islands.' London, 1903.
O'Neill, Norman. 'A Golden Treasury of Song.' London, 1903.
Nicholson, Sydney. 'British Songs for British Boys.' 1903.
Sharp, C. J., and Marson, C. L. 'Folk-Songs from Somerset.' 1905-7.
Duncan, Edmonstoune. 'The Minstrelsy of England.' London, 1905.
Stanford, Sir C. V. 'The National Song-Book.' London and New York, 1906.
Gould, S. Baring, and Sharp, C. 'English Folk-Songs for Schools.' London, 1906.
Kidson, Frank, and Moffat, Alfred. 'English Songs of the Georgian Period.' London, 1907.
See also the Journal of the Folk-Song Society, 1899, etc.

AMERICA

THE UNITED STATES.—Unlike most other countries, America has no distinctive characteristics of her own in music. Her inhabitants are of too mixed a character to constitute a genuine nationality. From all parts of the world representatives of every race have flocked to the United States of America. Dutch, English, Irish, German, Scandinavian, Slavonic, and other races have followed each other in quick succession. And thus it is only natural to find the influence of these different races affecting the music. Deprived as it has been of its natural foundation, *i.e.* the folk-song, her national music must be formed on the individuality of her composers.

Moreover, it should not be overlooked that what may be called America's musical civilisation is of comparatively recent origin. Strangely enough, it was to the Puritan settlers of the 17th century that America owed her first awakening to music. The art remained in a crude and stagnant state at first, developing in the 18th century in the direction only of rough psalmody, under William Billings. Then followed Stephen Foster, who in the first half of the 19th century attempted to interpret the spirit of the Southerners with his so-called 'plantation' or negro-melodies. Excessively sentimental and poorly harmonised as these songs are, no one will deny their melodiousness, nor disparage the hold they have obtained on white and black men alike. (See NEGRO MUSIC.)[1]

It is only within the last fifty years that American song-writers have claimed attention in the musical world. The first composer of musical scholarship was John K. Paine. Although he himself paid little heed to the Song, it is a form much cultivated by Americans, and Paine's numerous pupils have won distinction in this line. Prominent among them is Arthur Foote, whose graceful little 'Irish Folk-Song,' and 'I'm wearing awa',' are favourite songs also in Europe. G. W. Chadwick and his pupil Horatio Parker, are names of greater weight. Parker has done more important work in other branches of music, but the accompaniments of his songs are interesting and varied. Chadwick's songs are very numerous and widely sung. His fine song 'King Death' may be quoted as one of his best compositions. Walter Damrosch's and Mrs. Beach's songs are refined and well-written, and never commonplace or vulgar. The same cannot be said of many other American composers, whose songs, whilst enjoying a great popularity, descend almost to the lowest level of vocal music. These composers have obviously chosen the modern English 'ballad' form as their model. Fortunately others have fallen more under the influence of Schumann, R. Franz and Grieg, and have produced songs of a far higher standard. Edward MacDowell (d. 1908), who justly held the first place among American song-writers, shows traces of his Scottish ancestry and European education. But though no distinct nationality is discernible in his music there is distinct personality. His songs are those of a true and cultivated musician; the voice and instrumental part alike are

---

[1] The patriotic songs such as 'Hail Columbia,' 'Yankee Doodle,' etc., are not alluded to here as they have been dealt with under separate headings in this Dictionary.

moulded and finished with care, whilst the emotional and poetical qualities are seldom lacking. The most popular of his songs are 'Thy beaming eyes,' 'The robin sings in the apple-tree,' and 'Is it the shrewd October wind?'; but the eight songs to words by Howells are among his best and most original. Philip Dalmas's settings of Walt Whitman's words are original and impressive.

The following are the names of a few other song-composers of various kinds and degrees of merit: Ethelbert Nevin, R. de Koven, Van der Stucken, S. Schlesinger, B. O. Klein, Victor Herbert, G. Osgood, C. Hawley, Clayton Johns, E. Stillman Kelley (whose settings of Poe's 'Eldorado,' and his song, 'The lady picking mulberries,' written in the pentatonic scale, have attracted attention); H. Holden Huss, V. Harris, Apthorp, Spalding, Dudley Buck, Whitney Coombs, E. Finck, etc.

BIBLIOGRAPHY

Hood, G. *History of Music in New England.* Boston, 1846.
Gould, N. D. *History of Church Music in America.* Boston, 1853.
Raymond-Ritter, F. *Some Famous Songs.* London, 1878.
Ritter, Dr. F. L. *Music in America.* London, 1884.
Mathews, W. S. B. *Hundred Years of Music in America.* Chicago, 1889.
Dvořák, A. *Music in America. Harper's Magazine,* Feb. 1895.
Elson, Louis C. *The National Music of America.* Boston, 1900.
Hughes, Rupert. *Contemporary American Composers.* 1900.
Finck, H. *Songs and Song-writers.* London, 1901.
'Die Musik, Amerika-Heft.' May 1905.

COLLECTIONS

Wilson, J. 'National Song-Book.' 1813.
Emerick, A. C. 'Songs for the People.' 1848.
'Slave Songs of the United States.' Edited by W. F. Allen, C. P. Ware, and L. M. Garrison. New York, 1867.
Fenner, T. P. 'Cabin and Plantation Songs as sung by the Hampton Students.' New York, 1874.
Trotter, J. M. 'Music and some highly musical People.'
Sousa, J. P. 'National, Patriotic, and Typical Airs, etc., for all Countries.' 1890.
Seward, T. F. 'The Story of the Jubilee Singers with their Songs.' London, 1897.

GERMANY

In no country has the Song held so prominent a place as in Germany, and in no other country has this form of music been carried to greater perfection. Its history has been so thoroughly explored by German writers that its course may be followed from very remote ages, when Song was scarcely distinguishable from speech, and *singen* and *sagen* were convertible terms.[1] But until the time of the Minnesinger the Song had not acquired form either in metre or melody, and this therefore must be our starting-point.

The Minnesinger were the German counterparts of the Troubadours, but they were of rather later date, and the tone of their compositions was somewhat different. While the Troubadours sang generally of love and gallantry, the Minnesinger constantly introduced into their songs praises of the varied beauties of nature. And the expressions of homage to the Virgin, or of other devotional feeling, which burst so frequently from their lips were the outcome of a deeper religious sentiment than any to which the light-hearted Provençals were ever subject. The Minnesinger always sang and accompanied their own compositions, and took no remuneration for the entertainment they gave. They were more numerous in Southern than in Northern Germany; Austria was especially prolific in them. (See MINNESINGER.)

The most representative names in the first period, 1150-1190, were Dietmar von Aiste, Meinloh von Sevelingen, Der von Kürenberc and Spervogel. The second and best period, which was the stage of maturity, was covered by the last years of the 12th century, and at least half of the 13th century. To this period belonged Heinrich von Veldecke, Friedrich von Hausen, Heinrich von Morungen, Reinmar der Alte (the master of Walther von der Vogelweide), Hartmann von der Aue (the author of the celebrated poem 'Der arme Heinrich'), and Walther von der Vogelweide himself, whose fine lyrics won for him a place among national poets. Early in the 13th century the Sängerkrieg, or Minstrel-contest, was held on the Wartburg by the Landgrave Hermann of Thuringia, and among the champions who took part in it, were Heinrich von Ofterdingen, Tannhäuser, and Wolfram von Eschenbach. Wolfram's Minnelieder had some success, but higher renown was gained for him by his Wächterlieder and his 'Parsifal.' The third period was a time of decline, and of transition to the Meistersinger. The art of the Minnesinger then descended to trivial and unpoetic themes, and a growing carelessness as to the forms of poetry plainly revealed its deterioration. Nithart von Reuenthal (whose poems were chiefly descriptive of peasant life), Ulrich von Lichtenstein, Reinmar von Zweter, der Marner, and Konrad von Würzburg were the principal Minnesinger of this period.

Mediæval MSS. contain a great number of the poems of the Minnesinger, and the large Jena and Colmar MSS. the melodies also. These remains attest the especial pains bestowed on the poetic words, the finish of their verses as regards metre and rhythm, and in short the superiority of their poetry to their music. But this perfection was of course only reached by degrees. Beginning with alliterative words they advanced to regular rhymes, and then rules of composition were laid down prescribing the number of lines of which different kinds of song should consist. The structure of the verses was closely followed by the Minnesinger melodies, and as there was necessarily a pause wherever the rhyme fell, a certain form was thus imparted to them. Their mode of notation was similar to that then used in the Church, and their melodies were founded on the ecclesiastical modes. There were three principal kinds of Minnesong: the *Lied* (song), the *Leich* (lay), and the *Spruch* (proverb). The *Lied* was usually

---

[1] Fragments exist of the Hildebrandlied of the 8th century (see list of MSS. and printed collections at end of this section), of which the well-known Volkslied of the 13th century 'Ich will zu Land ausreiten' is an offshoot (Böhme, 'Altdeutsches Liederbuch,' p. 3). Also of the Ludwigslied which was sung in honour of Ludwig III. when he gained the victory over the Normans in 882 at Sancourt. These are the earliest songs in the German language.

divided into three parts ; the first and second
were called *Stollen* (props), and were of the same
metre. These constituted the *Aufgesang*. The
third or concluding section, the length of which
was not prescribed, was called the *Abgesang*.
This, after beginning with a contrasting metre
and melody, usually (but not invariably) repeated
the *Stollen*. A good example is the 'Rügelied'
from the Jena MS., arranged by R. von Kralik
thus [1] :—

Rügelied.

Ex. 1.   HERMANS VON DAMEN.

Aufgesang.

(*Stollen*) Hätt' ich all der   Wel - ten Hul - den,   So wär'
(*Stollen*) Gott verzeih' ihm   sei - ne Schul-den,   der mir

Abgesang.

ich   ein   se - lig Mann.   Ich weiss gar
nur   auf   Missgunst sann.

viel der Schwachen   za - gen,   die den Bie-dern

im - mer nei - den   und das Bös'ste von ihm sa - - gen.

The *Leich*, according to its character, was formed
either from the Church *sequences* or from the
old dance tunes (*Reigen*). If the latter was
the case the *Leich* was composed of differently
constructed strophes and each of these had a
different melody. If taken from the *sequentia*
it exhibited the same monotony and absence of
rhythm as the ecclesiastical melodies of that
time [2] :—

Ex. 2.

Daz   er - ste Syn-gen hie no   tut

Heynrich von Ofterdingen In des e-deln vur - sten dhon.

The *Spruch* was composed of one entire strophe,
or, if other strophes were added they could be
all sung to the same tune. Walther von der
Vogelweide's solitary surviving song (which is
in the Colmar MSS., folio 734) is a *Spruch* [3] ;
it is clearly meant to be sung, and differs from
the ordinary didactic *Sprüche*. It must be
remembered that in speaking of the ' tone ' of
a song, the Minnesinger referred exclusively to
the metrical structure of the strophe, and the

word did not therefore indicate the use of any
especial melody or mode.

The 'fahrenden Sänger' (wandering minstrels),
also called merely *die Fahrenden* or *Gaukler*,
formed a link between nobles and people. Belonging clearly to the ' Jongleur ' class, discouraged by the priests and patronised by courts,
they were at once acrobats, ballad-mongers,
and performers on various instruments. Their
ranks comprised unfrocked monks, disbanded
crusaders, soldiers, serving-men. Essentially
musical, they made known the people's songs
at courts, and transmitted the songs of Church
and Minnesinger to the people. The music was
a fusion of secular and ecclesiastical elements,
their language a mixture of German and Latin.[4]
But they especially loved the Volkslied, and it
is to them that we owe the preservation of these
priceless songs which found their way into the
numerous collections published in the first half
of the 16th century.[5]

In the 14th century feudalism had passed its
prime. With the extinction of the art-loving
Hohenstaufen dynasty, the taste for poetry
and music declined at court, and with it the
patronage extended to the Minnesinger. Power
was slipping from the grasp of princes, prelates,
and nobles into the hands of burghers and
artisans. Out of these middle classes came
the Meistersinger,[6] who supplanted the more
patrician Minnesinger. The name of Heinrich
von Meissen (1260-1318), commonly called
Frauenlob, forms the connecting-link, for by
some he is considered the last of the Minnesinger and by others the founder of the Meistersinger. In 1311 he came to Mainz, and instituted a guild or company of singers, who bound
themselves to observe certain rules. Though
somewhat stiff and pedantic, Frauenlob's poems
evince intelligence and thought ;[7] and the
example set by him was widely imitated. Guilds
of singers soon sprang up in other large towns
in Germany ; and it became the habit of the
burghers, especially in the long winter evenings,
to meet together and read or sing narrative or
other poems, either borrowed from the Minnesinger and adapted to the rules of their own
guild, or original compositions. By the end of
the 14th century there were regular schools of
music at Colmar, Frankfort, Mainz, Prague, and
Strasburg, and a little later they were found also
in Nuremberg, Augsburg, Breslau, Regensburg,

---

[1] *Poesie und Musik der Minnesinger*, R. v. Kralik. (*Die Musik*,
April 1, 1904.)
[2] From the Jena MSS. Fr. Heinrich von der Hagen gives this example in its original notation (iv. 843, No. xxix.). His work on
the Minnesinger is the best authority to consult. In the fourth
volume a very instructive essay on the music of the Minnesinger
will be found, together with many examples of their melodies,
some of which are transcribed in facsimile, whilst others are given
in modern notation. See also the new editions of the Colmar MSS.
by Paul Runge and Hugo Riemann (1896) ; and of the Jena MSS. by
G. Holz, E. Bernouilli, and Fr. Saran (1902).
[3] R. von Kralik gives this song in his above-mentioned work. It
is too long to quote, and the words are certainly of later date.

[4] Schneider, *Das musikalische Lied*, i. 193.
[5] The 'fahrenden Sänger' were also counted as Meistersinger, but
belonged to a different circle. In the 15th century, the greatest
was Michael Beheim (or Behaim), who was a favourite in the courts
of the princes on the Rhine and Danube and at Copenhagen. Reimann in his collection gives an example of his songs, and the
Dresden MSS. of the 15th century contain some mystical hymns
to the Virgin by Behaim. (R. v. Liliencron, *Deutsches Leben im
Volkslied um 1530.*)
[6] The origin of the term Meistersinger is uncertain. Ambros
says that it was applied to every Minnesinger who was not a noble,
and thus became the distinguishing appellation of the burgher
minstrels. Reissmann, however, maintains that the title ' Meister'
indicated excellence in any act or trade ; and that having been at
first conferred only on the best singers, it was afterwards extended
to all members of the guild.
[7] A complete collection of Frauenlob's poems were published in
1843 by Ettmüller, Quedlinburg.

and Ulm. In short, during the 15th and 16th centuries, there was scarcely a town of any magnitude or importance throughout Germany which had not its own Meistersinger. The 17th century was a period of decline, both in numbers and repute. The last of these schools of music lingered at Ulm until 1839, and then ceased to exist; and the last survivor of the Meistersinger is said to have died in 1876.

Famous among Meistersinger were Hans Rosenblüt, Till Eulenspiegel, Muscatblüt, Heinrich von Müglin, Puschman, Fischart, and Seb. Brandt; but the greatest of all by far was Hans Sachs, the cobbler of Nuremberg, who lived from 1494 to 1576. His extant works are 6048 in number, and fill 34 folio volumes. 4275 of them are Meisterlieder or *Bar*, as they were called.[1] To Sachs's pupil, Adam Puschman, we are indebted for accounts of the Meistergesang.[2] The works of the Meistersinger had generally a sacred subject, and their tone was religious. Hymns were their lyrics, and narrative poems founded on Scripture were their epics. Sometimes, however, they wrote didactic or epigrammatic poems. But their productions were all alike wanting in grace and sensibility; and by a too rigid observance of their own minute and complicated rules of composition or *Tablatur* (as they were termed) they constantly displayed a ridiculous pedantry. The Meistersinger clearly adopted (especially in lyric-song) the forms of the Minnesinger, such as the two *Stollen*, and the *Auf-* and *Abgesang*, but without the instrumental preludes, interludes or postludes.[3] Churches were their ordinary place of practice. At Nuremberg, for instance, their singing-school was held in St. Katherine's church, and their public contests took place there. The proceedings commenced with the *Freisingen*, in which any one, whether a member of the school or not, might sing whatever he chose, but no judgments were passed on these preliminary performances. Then followed the contest, in which Meistersinger alone might compete. They were limited to Scriptural subjects, and their relative merits were adjudged by four *Merker* or markers who sat hidden by a curtain at a table near the altar. It was the duty of one of the four to heed that the song faithfully adhered to Holy Writ; of another to pay special attention to its prosody; of a third to its rhyme, and of the fourth to its melody. Should the singer fail in any of the rules of the *Tablatur*, the *Merker* declared him *versungen*

and *verthan*, and the competitor who had the fewest faults obtained the prize, a chain with coins. One of the coins, bearing the image of King David, had been the gift of Hans Sachs, and hence the whole *Gesänge* were called the ' David ' and the prizeman the ' Davidwinner.' Every Davidwinner might have his apprentices, but no charge was made for teaching. The term ' Meister ' (strictly speaking) applied only to those who invented a new metre or melody; the rest were simply ' Sänger.'

The Meistersinger possessed a store of melodies for their own use; and these melodies were labelled with distinctive but apparently meaningless names, such as the blue-tone,[4] the red-tone, the ape-tune, the rosemary-tune, the yellow-lily-tune, etc. A Meistersinger might set his poems to any of these melodies. The four principal were called the *gekrönten Töne*, and their respective authors were Müglin, Frauenlob, Marner, and Regenbogen. So far were the Meistersinger carried by their grotesque pedantry that in setting the words of the twenty-ninth chapter of Genesis to Müglin's *lange Ton*,[5] the very name of the book and the number of the chapter were also included. Thus :—

Ex. 3.

Ge - ne - sis am neun und zwan-zig-sten uns bericht,

wie Ja - cob floh vor sein Bru-der E - sau ent - wicht

Das er in Me - so - po - ta - mi - am kom - men.

To all external appearance the melodies of the Meistersinger (like those of the Minnesinger) had a strong affinity with Church music and kept to the Ecclesiastical modes. But on closer scrutiny many melodies may be found which would sound just like our major and minor scales, were it not for their modal cadences and the many liturgical fragments introduced. Still their songs are for the most part poor and simple, and too devoid of rhythm ever to be really popular, and very few of them found sufficient favour to become *Volkslieder* in the 15th and 16th centuries.[6] On the other hand, the Meistersinger themselves sometimes appropriated Volkslieder. Thus Hans Sachs has

[4] With the Meistersinger the word *Ton* referred to the music only, and not to the poetry, as with the Minnesinger.
[5] Wagner has made us familiar with Müglin's *lange Ton*, in his Meistersinger fanfare:—

and it is evident that Wagner studied and fully understood the Meistersinger melodies, and adopted many genuine ones.
[6] According to Böhme, in the preface to his ' Altd. Liederbuch,' p. xxiii, the writers of the Volkslieder never signed their names, whilst the Meistersinger generally introduced his own name, and very often the date of his composition, into the last rhyme of the poem. A Meistersinger's song can thus be distinguished from a true Volkslied.

[1] The celebrated chorale ' Warum betrübst du dich, mein Herz,' was long believed to be the work of Hans Sachs; but it has been conclusively shown by Böhme (' Altdeutsches Liederbuch,' p. 748) that the words were written by G. A. Oemler, and then set to the old secular tune, ' Dein gsund mein Freud.'
[2] They bear the titles of *Gründlicher Bericht des deutschen Meistergesangs* (Görlitz, 1571); and *Gründlicher Bericht der deutschen Reimen oder Rithmen* (Frankfurt a. O., 1596). Both are partially reprinted in the *Sammlung für altdeutsche Literatur*, edited by F. H. v. der Hagen, J. G. Büsching, and others. Breslau, 1812. See also *Das Singebuch des A. Puschman nebst den Originalmelodien des M. Behaim und H. Sachs*, by G. Münzer (Leipzig, 1906).
[3] *Von den Meistersingern und ihrer Musik.* Curt Mey, 1903.

reproduced the beautiful old Mailied (May-song) in his *Fastnachtsspiel*, ' Der Neydhart mit dem Feyhel,' written Feb. 7, 1562.[1] He calls it a *Reigen* or roundelay, and its original date was evidently anterior to the 14th century. In its 16th-century form it is as follows :—

Ex. 4.

Der Meye, der Meye bringt uns der Blümlein

vil, ... ich trag ein frei Ge - mü - te, Gott

weiss wol, wem ichs wil,   Gott weiss wol, wem ichs wil.

In fine, the Meistersinger cannot be said to have reached a high level of excellence either in poetry or in music, but they undoubtedly exercised an important influence on the formation of the Song by the attention they paid to rhyme, and by their numerous inventions of new metrical arrangements. And they rendered a still greater service to music when they carried it into every German home, and made it a grace and pastime of domestic life.

While more regular and formal varieties of the Song were thus being studied and practised, it had never ceased to issue in its own spontaneous form of Volkslied from the untutored hearts of a music-loving people. From that source it came in native vigour, unforced and untrammelled. And far more was done for melody and harmony by the obscure authors of the Volkslieder than was ever done by Minnesinger or Meistersinger. As Ambros has pointed out,[2] the importance of the part played by the Volkslied in the history of the music of Western Europe was second only to that of the Gregorian modes. Further, the moral struggle against the anti-humanism of the mediæval church found victorious expression in the assertive humanism of the folk-song—anathematised by spiritual authority. A partial reconciliation of the contending forces followed when the great polyphonic masters adopted Volkslied melodies as theme or foundation of their greatest sacred and secular works. Later, a yet closer union was effected in the Chorale of the Reformation period. Whoever were the authors of the Volkslieder, it was not their habit to write them down ; the songs lived on the lips and in the hearts of the people. But happily, even in remote times, there were collectors who made it their business to transcribe these popular songs ; and of collections thus made none are more important than the ' Limburger Chronik ' and the ' Locheimer Liederbuch.' The former work consists of Volkslieder which would seem

to have been in vogue from 1347 to 1380 ;[3] while songs of a little later date are found in the other collection.[4] This book contains forty-four songs, some of great melodic beauty, and showing considerably developed rhythm and structure as well as a delicate sense of poetic feeling. The *Lehrcompendium* of H. de Zeelandia also contains some very fine Volkslieder of the 14th and 15th centuries.[5] Finally, among the many Minnesinger and Meistersinger and other MS. collections named after the various towns (such as the Nuremberg, Prague, Dresden MSS.), numbers of genuine Volkslieder are to be found.[6]

The subjects of the earliest Volkslieder were historical ;[7] they were indeed epic poems of many stanzas set to a short melody. But by the time that the Volkslied had attained to its meridian splendour, about the beginning of the 16th century, almost every sentiment of the human heart and every occupation of life had its own songs. Students, soldiers, huntsmen, pedlars, apprentices, and other classes had their own distinctive songs. The best are undoubtedly the love-songs—those, in fact, where feeling is the strongest. Amongst them the songs of parting (Abschiedslieder) are the most numerous and beautiful, especially the Wächterlieder[8] or Tagelieder, in which the watchman announces the dawn.[9] As a rule, the music of the Volkslied was better than the words. So loose was the structure of the verse that syllables without any sense were inserted to fill up the length of the musical phrase, as :

> Dort oben auf dem Berge
> Dölpel, dölpel, dölpel
> Da steht ein hohes Haus.

or a sentence was broken off in the middle, or meaningless *unds* and *abers* were lavishly interspersed. But notwithstanding these laxities of composition there was a close connection between the words and the melody.

The Volkslied was always strophical in form, and therein differed from the *Sequences* and *Proses* of the Church and the *Leichen* of the Minnesinger. Another marked feature was its rhyme. When the final rhyme had been substituted for mere alliteration and assonance, a definite form was imparted to the verse, and its outline was rendered clearer by the melody of the Volkslied which emphasised the final rhyme, and by covering two lines of the poetry

---

[1] See Böhme's ' Altd. Liederbuch,' p. 366.
[2] Ambros, *Gesch. der Mus.* ii. 276.

[3] In the ' Limburger Chronik ' we are told of a leper monk living by the Rhine, c. 1370. Despite his leprosy, the beauty of his compositions drew men to his cell from all quarters.
[4] Ambros, *Gesch. der Mus.* iii. 375.
[5] From the Prague MS. Ambros (ii. 277) gives one, ' Herr Conrad ging,' both in its original and in modern notation.
[6] For the history of the Meistersinger see J. C. Wagenseil's *Buch von der Meistersinger holdseligen Kunst.* 1697.
[7] For the best authority consult R. von Liliencron's *Die historischen Volkslieder,* etc.
[8] A Wächterlied still sung, ' Der Wächter auf dem Thürmlein sass,' is given in Erk's ' Deutsche Liederhort,' No. 135.
[9] These Abschiedslieder are full of the sounds of nature—described with poetic charm. They were the special property of the Minnesinger (Wolfram von Eschenbach's were the most famous), but equally loved by the people.

with one phrase of the melody constructed a symmetrical arrangement.

Ex. 5. *Meine liebe Frau Mutter.*

Meine lie - be Frau Mut-ter, mit mir ist's aus; jetzt bald

wer-dens mich bald füh-ren beim Schand-thor hin- aus.

It will be noted in the above example that the half-close is on the dominant harmony and the full-close on the tonic, and this principle, which was originally a peculiar attribute of the Volkslied, has been gradually introduced into all other kinds of music, and it is now one of the most important factors of form. (See FORM.) Many of the Volkslieder were composed in different ecclesiastical modes, but by degrees the Ionian mode, in which alone the dominant principle can have full weight, obtained pre-eminence. The form of the Volkslied is generally very concise as in the above example, and this perhaps is the secret of its great charm. But looser forms are sometimes met with, and were probably due to the influence of the Church. To the same influence may be ascribed the melodic *melismata* or vocal flourishes which occur even in strophical songs. In the Gregorian music, where little attention was paid to rhythm, the melody might be indefinitely prolonged upon any syllable; and similarly we sometimes find in the Volkslied many notes given to one word, as in this example:—

Ex. 6. *Abschied.*

Ent - laubet ist der Wal - de gegn die - sem Win -
Be-raubt werd' ich, so bal - de mein Feinalieb macht . .

· · · · · ·ter kalt, Das ich die schönst' muss
· · · · · ·mich alt.

mei · · · · · ·den, die mir ge - fal · · · ·len

thut, bringt mir das heymlich lei - den und

macht mir schwe · · · · · ·ren Mut.

These melodic *melismata* also allow the voice great scope in the so-called *Kehrreim* or refrain. Another noticeable peculiarity of rhythm in the Volkslied is the variety of ways in which the

metre is treated. In many cases the time changes with every bar, and the above example illustrates a different representation of the metre in every line of the stanza.[1] Few of the Volkslieder begin on the first beat of the bar; and therefore the usual metre is Iambic, thus:—

Ich will zu Land aus - rei - ten.

and a preference has always been shown by the Germans for equal or common time; it is a quieter and more formal time than the triple, which is essentially dance-rhythm.[2] Other common, though not invariable attributes of the Volkslied were a diatonic intervallic progression, the reiteration of one note; a limited compass, the key or mode steadily adhered to, and unlike the songs of many other countries, the melody of the Volkslied always maintained a complete independence of the accompanying instrument. In character the old Volkslieder are marked by a certain earnestness and dignified self-restraint. They are cheerful and even gay, but without impetuosity or excitability. There is no attempt at word-painting; the same tune must serve for the numerous verses. Hence the necessity for concise melodies. The tendency of the German spirit is to look inwards, to portray the deeper and more permanent emotions rather than the transient and superficial; to aim less at beauty than expression.

The Volkslied would seem to have been fixed, as it were, instinctively our modern major tonal system; and, moreover, songs even of the 15th century are extant, which correspond to our minor keys. The following example clearly belongs to the old system, but the beginning and close and the intervals on which the principal rhymes fall, make it evident that the key of A minor was intended.[3]

Ex. 7. *Ach Elslein.*

Ach Els - lein,lie-bes Els - lein mein,wie gern wär' ich bei dir!

So sind zwei tief-e Was - - - ser wol zwischen dir und mir!

In Hans Judenkünig's (1523) and Hans Neusiedler's (1536) Lute-books this melody is always in A minor with the G♯ marked. In

1 See Böhme, p. 335, No. 257. The melody and words of this song are taken from the *Gassenhawerlin*, 1535, No. 1. There are many versions of this fine melody; and in collections subsequent to 1540 it is often to be found set to the morning hymn 'Ich dank Dir, lieber Herre,' and with this setting it appears in all chorale books down to the present day.
2 Böhme, however, maintains that until the 14th century no trace of any time except *Tempus perfectum* (which means triple time) can be found. 'Altd. Liederbuch,' Preface, p. 54.
3 Another good example is 'Es warb ein schöner Jüngling' (Georg Forster, *Ein Aufzug guter alter und newer Teutscher Liedlein*, etc., 1539-1556, i. 49). This and 'Ach Elslein, liebes Elslein,' are some of the numerous versions of the legend of the Swimmer. 'Ach Elslein' is found in all the old collections of the 16th century. For instance. in Joh. Ott, 1534, No. 37; Schmeltzel, Quodlibet x. 1544; Rhaw, Bicinia, ii. 1545, No. 19, etc.

the Song-books the sharp was never marked, but undoubtedly always used.

Consideration has thus far been given to the very important contributions of the Volkslied to the determination of permanent form in music; but its influence on contemporary music also requires notice.

It has already been shown that the composers of other countries in the 14th, 15th, and 16th centuries, took secular tunes as themes for their masses, motets, and other sacred works. The German composers did the same to a certain extent, but they more commonly employed the secular tunes in their secular polyphonic works. Nevertheless, as regards Church music the Volkslied occupied a higher place in Germany than elsewhere; for it is not too much to say that more than half the melodies of the chorale-books were originally folk-songs, and these melodies were among the simplest and most beautiful ever created. (See CHORALE.) Heinrich von Lauffenberg (or Loufenberg) in the 15th century systematically set his sacred words to secular tunes,[1] especially using the favourite *Tage* and *Wächterlieder*; but the Reformation made the practice very much more common. The Reformers wished the congregation to join as much as possible in the singing of hymns, and with that object they naturally preferred words in the vernacular, and melodies which were familiar with the people.[2] A well-known example of the combination of sacred words and secular melody is the song 'Isbruck, ich muss dich lassen,' set by Heinrich Isaak in four parts in 1475,[3] with the melody in the upper part—a rare arrangement at that time. After the Reformation this tune was adapted by Dr. Hesse to the sacred words 'O Welt, ich muss dich lassen'; and in 1633 Paul Gerhardt wrote to it the evening hymn 'Nun ruhen alle Wälder,' in which form it still remains a favourite in all Lutheran churches.[4] After many transformations the old love-song 'Mein Gmüth ist mir verwirrt'[5] now lives in one of the most beautiful and solemn chorales of both the Lutheran and Roman Catholic churches, namely 'O Haupt voll Blut und Wunden,' which Bach has introduced so often in his Passion music according to S. Matthew. Again 'Könt ich von hertzen singen' (one of the most famous of the many *Wächterlieder* and *Tageweisen* melodies the Church borrowed) was adapted to the chorale

'Hilf Gott, das mir gelinge'; 'Ich hört ein frewlein klagen' to 'Hilf Gott, wem soll ich klagen'; 'O lieber Hans, versorg dein Gans' to 'O lieber Gott, das dein Gebot'; and 'Venus du und dein Kind' to 'Auf meinen lieben Gott.' Many dance-songs, especially the so-called *Ringel* and *Reigentänze*, were likewise set to sacred words.[6]

It is clear that the chorale gained rather than lost by the adoption of secular melodies; they emancipated it from stiffness and formality; they gave it heart and living warmth. So far removed from irreverence were the secular melodies, and so appropriate to the sacred text, that the music is generally more expressive of the words in the Chorale than in the Volkslied. But perhaps the true explanation of this is, that in the case of the Chorale, the words were either written expressly for a chosen melody, or the melody was selected for its appropriateness to particular words.[7] The melody of that just mentioned, 'O Haupt voll Blut und Wunden,' is obviously secular, but what melody could better express a deep and poignant religious sorrow? In the Roman Catholic Church the use of the Volkslied was chiefly confined to the hymns to the Blessed Virgin (*Marienlieder*) and to the Saints, and to the Christmas Carols, especially the sacred cradle-songs, such as the lovely 'Josef, lieber Josef mein.' But upon the whole, the Roman Catholic hymns are all conceived in the 'traditional fixed cadence of the Gregorian song.'

The progress of polyphonic music in Germany had been checked by the discontinuance of the mass after the Reformation, but a new impetus was given to it by the contrapuntal treatment of the Volkslied by great composers. As examples of such treatment may be mentioned 'Allein dein G'stalt,' 'Ach herzig's herz,' by H. Finck; 'Mir ist ein roth Goldfingerlein,' by L. Senfl; 'Der Gutzgauch auf dem Zaune sass,' by L. Lemlin. This brings us to the *Kunstlied*, which in its primary sense signified only the contrapuntal treatment of the song by learned musicians.[8] With the polyphonic Kunstlied we have here no concern, beyond what just suffices to point out the changes through which it successively passed, and the important part the Volkslied held in it. The composers who used the Volkslied thus were masters of every form of counterpoint; sometimes they worked one melody with another, as Arnold von Bruck, who combined the song 'Es taget vor dem Walde' with 'Kein Adler in der Welt';[9] or if they did not treat the melody as a canon, as Eckel treated 'Ach

---

[1] Ambros, iii. 375.
[2] Naumann (*Hist. of Mus.* p. 454 *et seq.*) points out that Luther being both a practical and theoretical musician saw clearly how powerful a factor the Volkslied had become in tonal practice, and in using it he insisted on the importance of the appropriateness of the melody to the sacred words, and on correctness of accent.
[3] Georg Forster, i. No. 36. The words are supposed to be by the Emperor Maximilian I. in whose court Isaak was living.
[4] See ISAAK. Also Böhme, 'Altd. Liederbuch,' p. 332, where the song is given in its original form with a *melisma*. Böhme also gives an interesting remark on the admiration Bach and Mozart evinced for this song.
[5] This song is to be found in Hans Leo Hassler's *Lustgarten neuer teutscher Gesänge*, etc., Nuremberg, 1601. The melody was also used for a death-song 'Herzlich thut mich verlangen,' and later it was set to the universally sung 'Befiel du deine Wege' (Handel employed it in 1709, previous to Bach).

[6] See Böhme, 'Altd. Liederbuch,' p. 368 *et seq.* Böhme gives a list at p. 810 of secular melodies with sacred words.
[7] The sacred Volkslieder (*geistliche Volkslieder*) differ from the chorale in that the former were printed on broadsheets and sung by the people of every class, whereas the chorales were written for and sung by the cultivated only.
[8] The very much wider signification which the term *Kunstlied* afterwards acquired has been referred to at the outset of this article.   [9] Reissmann, *Gesch. d. deutschen Liedes*, p. 69.

Jungfrau, ihr seid wolgemuth,'[1] they broke it up into fragments for imitation. They were careful always to choose familiar and favourite tunes, so that they might stand out and be easily recognised amidst the web of other parts surrounding them. When composing their own melodies, they always adhered to the ecclesiastical modes, using the new system only when they adopted a Volkslied.[2] The contrapuntal treatment had, however, one great disadvantage—it constantly necessitated the severance of the melody into fragments, and thus the clear, concise form of the song, which the Volkslied had done so much to establish, was in danger of disappearing. But happily at this juncture (about 1600) Hans Leo Hassler came to its rescue. Having studied in Italy, he breathed into his songs the light, secular spirit of the Italian *Villanella* and *Fa-la-la*, and gave more prominence to the melody than to the other voice-parts. His dance-songs also, with their short rhythmical phrases, did much to restore the concise form. Similar characteristics are noticeable in Melchior Franck's, Regnart's, and other contemporary collections of songs.[3]

In the beginning of the 17th century solo songs were first heard in Germany. There, as everywhere else, the introduction of the monodic system was due to the influence of Italy. The revolution begun by that country would seem to have first affected the Church music rather than the secular music of Germany. Innovations of Italian origin are plainly discernible in the sacred works of Praetorius and Heinrich Schütz; but neither of these composers improved the secular monodic song. German poetry had now fallen to a debased condition. It produced nothing better than songs of a vapid and artificial sentiment addressed to a conventional Phyllis or Amaryllis. And the language it employed was a nondescript mixture of French, Latin, and stilted German. Since Luther's death the simple vernacular had ceased to be in repute. But on August 24, 1617, a meeting of German patriots was held, who set themselves to restore their native tongue to

honour, and with that view to study the introduction of method and rule into its grammar and poetry. Other patriotic groups were soon formed with a like purpose, and by the year 1680 these associations numbered 890 members. Their labours quickly bore good fruit. The success of a group of Königsberg poets was specially remarkable, and was doubtless due in a great measure to the skill with which one of the best of them—Heinrich Albert—set his own and his associates' songs to music. His compositions consequently won great popularity, and he has been named 'the father of the volksthümliches Lied.' Schein and Hammerschmidt had preceded Albert in the right path, but their taste and talent had been frustrated by the worthlessness of the words they set to music. The poetry on which Albert worked was not by any means of a high order, although it had sufficient merit to demand a certain measure of attention. And from his uncle, Heinrich Schütz, Albert had learnt the new Italian methods of singing with correct expression and brilliant execution, introducing vocal embellishments.[4] Several of his songs are for one voice with clavicembalo accompaniment, but their harmony is poor. The movement begun by Albert was carried on by J. R. and J. G. Ahle, and Adam and Joh. Krieger. Johann's songs are good, and exhibit a marked improvement in grace and rhythm. The first bars of his song, 'Komm', wir wollen wandeln,' have all the clearness of the best Volkslieder :—

Ex. 8.

Meanwhile the Kunstlied or polyphonic song had ceased to advance. Other branches, especially instrumental and dramatic music, had absorbed composers, songs began to be called 'odes' and 'arias,' and French and Italian influence was strongly felt, both in music and literature. Writing in 1698, Keiser tells us that cantatas had driven away the old German songs, and that their place was being taken by songs consisting of mixed recitatives and arias.[5]

---

[1] Reissmann, *Gesch. d. deutschen Liedes*, p. 72.
[2] Georg Forster's collections contain a large quantity of songs thus treated. See FORSTER.
[3] See, for example, 'Tricinia nova lieblicher amorosischer Gesänge mit schönen poetischen Texten gezieret und etlicher Massen nach Italienischer Art mit Fleiss componirt durch Melchior Francken,' Nürnberg, 1611; and 'Kurzweilige teutsche Lieder zu dreien Stimmen nach Art der Neapolitanen oder Welschen Villanellen durch Jacobus Regnart in Druck verfertigt,' Nürnberg, 1578. The so-called *Gesellschaftslieder* of the 16th and 17th centuries belong to this category of song. They arose when song was cultivated among the burgher and middle classes to a high extent, and ceased with the efforts of the Silesian poets in 1617. At first they resembled the Volkslied in form and spirit, but later they approached more closely to the Kunstlied. Most contemporary musicians took part in this popular development of music, and collected and arranged the favourite songs of the time in parts, either retaining or altering the words. The editors and publishers encouraged the introduction of Italian melodies with translated or imitated words. Between 1540 and 1624, the following musicians (amongst many others) issued collections of such songs : Georg Forster, Orlandus Lassus, Ivo de Vento, Jacob Regnart, Joh. Eccard, C. Demantius, H. L. Hasler, M. Praetorius, M. Franck, E. Widmann, H. Schein, and several Italians. For further information see Hoffmann von Fallersleben, *Die deutschen Gesellschaftslieder*, etc., and R. v. Liliencron, *Deutsches Leben im Volkslied*, etc.

[4] In the preface to the fourth part of his *Arien* Albert says he has borrowed some melodies from other composers, 'Aus Liebe und Wohlgefallen zu denselben Weisen.' He rarely names the composers, but merely calls the songs 'Aria gallica,' 'Aria polonica,' etc. He only used one Italian air, which is the more curious, as in the preface to the sixth part of his *Arien* he says, 'Was für herrliche und geistreiche Compositionen aus Italien . . . sehe ich oftmals mit höchster Verwunderung an.' See L. H. Fischer *Fremde Melodien in H. Albert's Arien, Vierteljahrsschrift*, 1886.
[5] See the preface to his cantata collection. See also Lindner, *Gesch. d. deutschen Liedes*, p. 53.

Among the writers of the 18th century who almost invariably called their songs 'odes' and 'arias' were Graun, Agricola, Sperontes, Telemann, Quantz, Doles, Kirnberger, C. P. E. Bach, Marpurg, Nichelmann, J. G. Krebs, Neefe, and many others. Also large quantities of collections of 'Arien und Oden' were published at this time, either separately or in numbers, of which the most famous was Sperontes' 'Singende Muse an der Pleisse' (Leipzig, 1742-45).[1] J. P. Kirnberger has been called (perhaps not with perfect accuracy) the inventor of the 'durchcomponirtes Lied,' that is, a song with different music for every stanza. C. P. E. Bach used the same form, and his best-known vocal work is his setting of Gellert's 'Geistliche Oden'[2] (1758) ; but he was a musician of a higher and more genial type than the afore-mentioned. Still, this group of composers rendered some services to the song. They set a good example of attention to the words, both as regards metre and expression ;[3] they varied the accompaniments by arpeggios and open chords, and displayed a thorough command of the different forms they employed. But notwithstanding these merits their songs (with few exceptions) must be pronounced to be dry, inanimate, and either deficient in melody, or the melody is overburdened with florid passages and tasteless ornaments, and rarely, if ever, spontaneous.[4]

It might strike the reader as strange if the great names of J. S. Bach and Handel were passed by in silence ; but neither Bach nor Handel ever devoted real study to the Song. Such influence as they exercised upon it was indirect. Bach, it is true, wrote a few secular songs, and a little love-song, 'Bist Du bei mir,' is simple and sincere.[5] His two comic cantatas also contain several of great spirit, and show his use of the Volkslied.[6] And amongst his 'Geistliche Arien' we have the beautiful 'Gieb dich zufrieden' and 'Schlummert ein, ihr matten Augen.' But these are isolated instances, and it was through his choral works that he most powerfully affected the song. Handel's name frequently occurs to songs in 18th-century English song-books, or single sheets, or in collections, but it is difficult to say which are original, and which are adaptations of Italian

songs or minuets set to English words. 'Stand round, my brave boys,'[7] 'From scourging rebellion,'[8] 'The unhappy lovers,'[9] and '"Twas when the seas were roaring'[10] were some of the best-known examples. The Händel-Gesellschaft have published a whole volume of 'German, Italian, and English Songs and Airs,' but Handel's real influence upon the Song was through his operas and oratorios, and there it was immense.[11] Equally indirect, as will be seen presently, were the effects produced on it by the genius of Gluck, Haydn, and even of Mozart.

At the period we have now reached, namely the end of the 18th century, a group of poets, called the 'Göttinger Dichterbund,' or 'Hainbund,' were actively engaged in providing simple lyrics for the people.[12] Simultaneously in music, a new and popular form of the Kunstlied appeared which was the 'volksthümliches Lied.' This term defies exact translation ; but, speaking broadly, it means a simple and popular form of the art-song. The decline of the Volkslied during the 17th century has been sometimes attributed to the distracted state of Germany ; and certainly the gloomy atmosphere of the Thirty Years' War, and the desolation of the Palatinate, cannot have been favourable to it. But no political or social troubles could affect its existence so deeply as an invasion upon its own ground by the Kunstlied. So long as the Kunstlied dwelt apart among learned musicians the Volkslied had little to fear. But when once it had become simple and melodious enough to be caught by the people the Volkslied was supplanted. In churches and schools, at theatres and concerts the public grew habituated to the Kunstlied, and where civilisation existed the old Volkslieder faded from memory.[13] The 'volksthümliches Lied' is, in short, a combination of the Volkslied and the Kunstlied, and its area of capacity is a very wide one. It may rise to a high level of poetic beauty, and may descend to low depths of stupidity or triviality without ceasing to be 'volksthümlich.' Songs there were, undoubtedly, before the time of J. A. Hiller, to which this epithet could be properly applied, but he was the first to secure for them a thorough recognition.[14] He

---

1 Schneider, *Das mus. Lied*, ii. 206, and B. Seyfert, *Das mus. volksthümliche Lied*. Although this collection was popular, it was of a very mixed nature, containing solemn odes, vulgar drinking-songs, parodies, or arrangements of French instrumental pieces, and Italian arias.

2 In his life of C. P. E. Bach, C. Bitter says : 'Mit diesem schönen, edlen Werke ist C. Bach, der Begründer und Schöpfer des deutschen Liedes in seiner jetzigen Bedeutung geworden,' i. 143.

3 Generally speaking, expression and tempo marks were sparingly used until the end of the 18th century. But it is curious to see how the composers of this period indicated the tempo by such words as *fröhlich*, *munter*, *ängstlich*, *traurig*, showing, thereby, their wish to express, above all, the mood or character of the song.

4 Full information and abundant examples of these songs will be found in Lindner's and Schneider's histories of the Song.

5 Another in praise of tobacco, of a different character, is in the same book.

6 P. Spitta, *J. S. Bach*, ii. 561 *et seq.* The English folk-song, 'When Adam was first created' (see Kidson's *Traditional Tunes*, p. 153), was used by Bach in one of these cantatas.

7 A song made for the Gentlemen Volunteers of the city of London, and printed in the *London Magazine*, November 1745.

8 *London Magazine*, July 1746.

9 *Merry Musician*, iv. p. 33, c. 1733.

10 From a *Select Collection of English Songs with their original Airs*, by J. Ritson, London, 1813.

11 See Schneider, *Das mus. Lied*, ii. p. 190.

12 This group consisted of the poets Boie, Hölty, Overbeck, Bürger, Claudius, Voss, and the Stolbergs. They revered Klopstock, and opposed the French tendency.

13 It is, however, well to remember that this new departure of German song which we have been describing may—paradoxical as it sounds—be traced to the zeal displayed by Herder, Goethe, and others in collecting and arousing the enthusiasm for the folk-poetry of Germany and other kindred nations. It was the same desire to return to simple, natural forms, though it led in poetry as in music in different directions.

14 It would have seemed more methodical to trace the rise and decline of particular kinds of songs in separate and clearly defined sections of time, but this is altogether impossible, because their respective periods are situated with one another. Thus the volksthümliches Lied had come into existence, while the Ode and the Aria were at their zenith ; and again composers were using the aria form even after the introduction of the lyric song.

belonged to the second half of the 18th century, and was really an operatic composer. It was indeed the songs in his Singspiele which took so strong a hold of the public, and a favourite tune of his, 'Die Jagd,' will serve as a specimen of his work :—

Ex. 9.

Die Jagd.

J. A. HILLER.

Commodetto.

Als ich auf meine
Da kam aus dem Ge-

Blei - che ein Stückchen garn be - goss Das
sträu - che ein Mädchen a - them - los.

sprach, ach habt er-bar-men, steht meinem Va - ter bei ! Dort

schlag ein Fall dem Armen das linke Bein ent-zwei !

Another, 'Ohne Lieb und ohne Weib,' taken from his Singspiel 'Der Teufel ist los,' and still sung in Germany with much zest, was one of the first Kunstlieder to be received into the ranks of the Volkslieder. J. André, the author of the 'Rheinweinlied,' and J. A. P. Schulz, were contemporaries of Hiller's, and did much for the volksthümliches Lied. Schulz was careful above others of his time to select poetic words for his music, and so long as he kept to the simpler forms, he was always successful; many of his songs are still the delight of German children. Composers were now provided with a store of fresh and natural poems of a popular type by the poets of the Göttingen school, to whom later the names of Körner, Brentano, Arnim, and Uhland [1] may be added; and the love of poetry and song steadily increased in the German nation.

Starting from Hiller and Schulz, the volksthümliches Lied pursued two different roads. Its composers in the Hiller school, such as F. Kauer, Wenzel Müller, and Himmel were shallow and imperfectly cultivated musicians, whose sentimental melodies had for a time a certain superficial and undeserved repute, such as

[1] Körner's patriotic poems and the publication of 'Des Knaben Wunderhorn' acted as powerful incentives to song.

Himmel's 'An Alexis send' ich dich,' or 'Vater, ich rufe dich.' The dramatic composers Winter and Weigl may be reckoned among this school, in so far as they were song-writers; and its tendencies reappeared nearer our own day in Reissiger and Abt. On the other hand, Schulz's followers were real musicians; and if they became too stiff and formal it was the outcome of a strict regard to form and symmetry, and of a praiseworthy contempt for false sentiment. Whenever they chose the volksthümliches Lied they proved their mastery of it; but most of them could write at will in more than one style, and their names must therefore be mentioned in more than one class of song. The first and best of Schulz's school was Mendelssohn's favourite J. F. Reichardt, but his most valuable services to the Song were given on other ground, as will appear later. Next to him came Kunzen, A. Weber, and Nägeli. Zelter, Klein, L. Berger, and F. Schneider are entitled by their songs for male chorus to be counted among the followers of Schulz. The operatic songs of C. Kreutzer and H. Marschner, and the simple melodious songs by C. Krebs, F. Kücken, Silcher, Gersbach, and Gustav Reichardt have proved themselves to be truly *volksthümlich* by their firm hold on the hearts of the people.

In the many collections of so-called Volkslieder, beginning with the South German 'Blumenlese' (1782) and the North German 'Mildheimisches Liederbuch' (1799), down to those which are continually issuing from the musical press of to-day, there will be found numerous volksthümliche Lieder converted into Volkslieder. Some of these are by celebrated authors whose fame was won in other fields,[2] and some by men who wrote nothing but volksthümliche Lieder. Of many songs the authorship is wholly unknown, and of others it is disputed.[3] Worthy

[2] The *Blumenlese*, edited by H. P. Bossler, contains Beethoven's earliest song, 'Schilderung eines Mädchens,' composed when he was eleven. A very good and typical example of the volksthümliches Lied may here be added. It is taken from his Sketch-book of 1815 and 1816 (cited by Nottebohm in the *Mus. Wochenblatt*, Nov. 1878).

Ex. 10.

Die Zufriedenheit.

BEETHOVEN.

Was frag' ich viel nach Geld und Gut, wenn ich zufrie - den

bin? Giebt Gott mir nur ge - sun - des Blut, so

bin ich fro - her Sinn, und sing aus dankbar-

em Gemüth, mein Morgen- und mein Abendlied.

The words of the song are by J. Müller. It has been set also by Mozart and Neefe.

[3] Böhme, in his work entitled *Volksthümliche Lieder der Deutschen im 18. und 19. Jahrhundert*, has done much to rectify current errors

2 R

to be mentioned as representative songs of this class are : ' Es ist bestimmt in Gottes Rath ' ; 'Ach, wie ist's möglich dann' ; 'Prinz Eugenius' ; ' Zu Mantua in Banden ' ; ' Wir hatten gebaut ein stattliches Haus' ; 'Es zogen drei Burschen' ; ' Morgen muss ich fort von hier ' ; ' Aennchen von Tharau ' ; ' Bekränzt mit Laub ' ; ' Gaudeamus' ; 'Es geht bei gedämpftem Trommelklang' ; ' Was blasen die Trompeten ' ; ' Morgenroth ' ; ' Ich weiss nicht, was soll es bedeuten ' ; ' In einem kühlen Grunde ' ; ' Mädele ruck, ruck, ruck ' ; ' So viel Stern am Himmel stehen ' ; ' Es kann ja nicht immer so bleiben ' ; ' Der Mai ist gekommen ' ; ' O Tannenbaum ' ; ' Ich hatt' einen Kameraden ' ; ' Was ist des Deutschen Vaterland' ; 'Die Wacht am Rhein,' etc.[1] None of these songs are vulgar, nor even commonplace. They are familiar in all classes, young and old ; and the heartiness with which they are everywhere sung attests their vitality. Singing in unison is comparatively rare among Germans ; their universal love and knowledge of music naturally predispose them to singing in parts. A regiment on the march, a party of students on a tour, or even labourers returning from work, all alike sing their favourite songs in parts, with remarkable accuracy and precision. And the natural aptitude of the nation for this practice is perpetually fostered by the *Singvereine* which exist in the most secluded corners of Germany.

The mere enumeration of the qualities by which the volksthümliches Lied can be recognised explains its popularity. It is strophical in form, and is easy to sing ; it has an agreeable, usually diatonic melody, a simple and pure harmony, an unpretentious accompaniment, a regular rhythm, and words inspired by natural sentiment. But it lacked the poetic and thoughtful treatment, both of words and music, which subsequently raised the lyric song to the level of true art.

It is now time to inquire in what manner the Song was treated by some of the greatest composers of the 18th and 19th centuries—by Gluck, Haydn, Mozart, Beethoven, Spohr, and Weber. Gluck was the contemporary of Graun, Agricola, and Kirnberger ; and like them he called most of his songs odes. But the standpoint from which he regarded the song was very different from theirs. Applying his theories about the Opera to the Song, he steadfastly aimed at a correct accentuation of the words in the music, and the extinction of the Italian form of the melody, which required the complete subordination, if not the entire sacrifice to itself, of every other element of composition. ' The union,' wrote Gluck to La

Harpe in 1777, ' between the air and the words should be so close that the poem should seem made for the music no less than the music for the poem,' and he conscientiously strove to be true to this ideal in all his work. But though he revolutionised the Opera, he left no deep mark on the Song, for indeed, he never devoted to it the best of his genius. His few songs, chiefly Klopstock's odes, have no freshness about them, they are dry and pedantic ; and with all Gluck's superiority to his contemporaries in aims and principles of composition, his odes are scarcely better than theirs.[2]

With Jos. Haydn the influence of the Volkslied is once more apparent. Hence the vitality of his melodies where this element is strongest. His finest song, the Austrian National Anthem, 'Gott erhalte Franz den Kaiser,' closely resembles a Croatian folk-song [3] (see EMPEROR'S HYMN), and in his instrumental works numerous instances of his use of his native songs could be adduced. Yet, taking the bulk of Haydn's songs it cannot be denied that they are lacking in the freshness displayed in his instrumental works. The melodies are carefully and elaborately written, and the accompaniments often interesting and developed (see for instance ' O süsser Ton,' ' Rückerinnerung,' or ' Der erste Kuss ') ; but his want of interest in the words he chose, and his disregard both for their meaning and proper accentuation, rob them of the first conditions necessary for the true lyric. His songs are conceived too exclusively from the instrumental point of view. As Schneider truly says, Haydn ' treats the vocal melody exactly as a pianoforte or violin motif, under which he places some words which only superficially agree in rhythm with the melody.'[4] Freest from these defects and amongst his best and most popular songs are the twelve canzonets, containing such graceful and melodious numbers as ' My mother bids me,' ' Recollection,' and ' The Mermaid.' These and such simple little German songs as ' Jede meint das holde Kind ' and the pretty serenade ' Liebes Mädchen, hör' mir zu ' will never lose their charm.

The versatility of Mozart's powers is visible in his songs. Some of them might be described as arias, and others as volksthümliche Lieder ; some are lyrical, and others dramatic, and yet Mozart cannot be said to have impressed his own great individuality upon the Song except in a few instances. It was in the Opera that he put forth his whole strength, and his operatic songs often derive from their simple joyous melodies a truly popular character. It is evident that he treated Song, pure and simple, as mere recreation, and bestowed little pains thereon. Many faults of accentuation could be pointed out in his songs, but his exquisite

as regards the authorship of these songs, such as attributing ' Herz, mein Herz, warum so traurig' to Beethoven instead of to F. Glück, and ' Willst du dein Herz mir schenken' to J. S. Bach instead of to Giovannini, etc.
[1] In the various collections mentioned at the end of this article, the reader will find a multitude of other similar songs, including *Studenten-, Soldaten-, Trink-, Fest-, Tanz-, National-, Begräbniss-, Geistliche-, Kinderlieder*, etc.

[2] For a good example see 'Willkommen, o silberne Mond,' given by Schneider, ii. 267.
[3] See the South Slavonic section of this article, p. 570, note 2.
[4] Schneider, *Das mus. Lied*, ii. 269.

melodies and skilful accompaniments almost obliterate such defects. Mozart wrote many volksthümliche Lieder ; some humorous, like ' Die Alte ' (with its amusing expression-mark, ' Ein wenig durch die Nase zu singen '); some fresh and joyous as ' Komm', lieber Mai,' and the favourite ' Ich möchte wohl der Kaiser sein.' [1] But it is in the form of the Aria and *durch-componirtes Lied* that we find his most perfect song-writing. ' Abendempfindung,' with the beautiful opening phrases expressive of the calm moonlight evening, and his masterpiece, ' Das Veilchen,' which he wrote to words by Goethe, are on a level with his best work in other branches.

Some of Beethoven's earlier songs, such as ' An einen Säugling,' 'Das Kriegslied,' 'Molly's Abschied,' and 'Der freie Mann,' are volksthümlich ; the form is small, and the accompaniment nothing more than the melody simply harmonised. The structure is similar in Gellert's sacred songs, op. 48, except in the ' Busslied,' where there is a fuller development, both of voice and accompaniment. ' Adelaide ' is also an early work, but it is written in a larger form, and shows signs of the dramatic treatment which for a while influenced Beethoven's vocal writing. Many other songs cast in the scena and aria form could be instanced, but of far higher interest are those written in the lyrical vein. He set six poems of Goethe's, as op. 75, and three as op. 83, and although there is much in these songs which might have tempted Beethoven to use the scena or the cantata form, he resisted it. He adhered to the strophical divisions, and left it to the instrumental part to satisfy their dramatic requirements. In Mignon's song, ' Kennst du das Land,' each stanza has the same beautiful melody, and the accompaniment alone varies and intensifies. In Jeitteles' Liederkreis, ' An die ferne Geliebte,' op. 98, the unity which makes the cycle is wholly the work of the composer, and not of the poet. It is Beethoven who binds the songs together by short instrumental interludes modulating into the key of the next song, and by weaving the exquisite melody with which the cycle begins into the last song. Most of the songs of this immortal cycle are strophical, but with great variety of accompaniment ; and the just balance of the vocal and instrumental parts, and the warmth and fervour of the expression, equally contribute to the faithful representation of lyric thought and feeling. Enough stress cannot be laid on the importance of Beethoven's work in song-writing, for having effectively shown the power of harmony and modulation as means of expression ; also for having enlarged the part sustained by the pianoforte. He taught his instrument, as it were, to give conscious and intelligent utterance to

the poetic intention of the words. Furthermore, we must recognise that although Beethoven's genius rose to its loftiest heights in other branches of music, it was he who first raised Song from the entirely subordinate position it had hitherto held to an honourable place in the ranks of musical art.

Spohr also wrote lyric songs, and was fitted for the work by his romantic and contemplative nature. But his songs are marred by excessive elaboration of minutiæ, and in the profusion of details clearness of outline is lost. Again, his modulations, or rather chromatic transitions, are so frequent as to be wearisome. Of all his songs, ' Der Bleicherin Nachtlied ' and ' Der Rosenstrauch ' are freest from these faults, and they are his best.

A greater influence was exercised upon the Song by Carl Maria von Weber.[2] He published two books of Volkslieder, op. 54 and op. 64, perfect in their simplicity and of real distinction. Of his other seventy-eight songs the most celebrated are those from Körner's ' Leyer und Schwert '; the cradle-song, 'Schlaf Herzenssöhnchen,' ' Die gefangenen Sänger,' and the finest of all, ' Das Mädchen an das erste Schneeglöckchen.' These songs deserve their celebrity, and there are indeed many others which are not so well known, nor as often heard as they deserve to be. Weber's fame as a song-writer has perhaps suffered somewhat from the circumstance that many of his best songs are in his operas, and it has been partially eclipsed by the supreme excellence of one or two composers who were immediately subsequent to him.

Incidental reference has already been made more than once to Goethe, to whom the obligations of the Song are great. The fine outburst of lyric song which enriched the music of Germany in his lifetime was very largely due to him. The strong but polished rhythm, and the full melody of his verse, were an incentive and inspiration to composers. J. Fr. Reichardt was the first to make it a systematic study to set Goethe's lyrics to music, and between 1780 and 1810 he issued several collections.[3] So long as Reichardt merely declaimed the words in melody, or otherwise made the music subordinate to the verse, he was successful. Goethe's words were, in short, a sure guide for a talent like his. Reichardt was not a great master, but he may claim the honour of having struck the true keynote of lyrical songs, and greater artists than himself immediately followed in his footsteps. Nothing he ever wrote is better than his setting of Tieck's ' Lied der Nacht,' and in this song he clearly shows himself to be the fore-

[1] The little cradle-song, 'Schlafe, mein Prinzchen,' long attributed to Mozart, has recently been proved by Dr. Max Friedländer to have been written by Bernhard Flies.

[2] It is worth while to note that Weber himself says in his literary works, that 'strict truth in declamation is the first and foremost requisite of vocal music. . . . Any vocal music that alters or effaces the poet's meaning and intention is a failure.'

[3] Some of Goethe's words appeared among Reichardt's miscellaneous songs as early as 1780 ; but in 1793 he published a separate collection, entitled ' Goethes lyrische Gedichte,' containing thirty poems. And in 1809 he issued a more complete collection under the title of ' Goethes Lieder, Oden, Balladen, und Romanzen mit Musik, von J. Fr. Reichardt.'

runner of Schubert and Schumann. A younger contemporary, Zelter, also made his reputation by setting Goethe's words to music. Zelter was himself a friend of Goethe's, and so great an admirer was the poet of Zelter's settings that he preferred them to Reichardt's, and, through some strange obliquity of taste or judgment, to those of Beethoven and Schubert. Zelter's early songs were strophical, but in later years he adopted more freely the *durchkomponirte* form. Others of this group of writers were Ludwig Berger and Bernard Klein, albeit they differed somewhat in their treatment, both of the voice and instrumental parts.

If the general results of the period through which we have just passed be now regarded as a whole, it will be seen that the various conditions requisite for the perfection of the Song had matured. The foundations and all the main structure had been built; it required only to crown the edifice. Starting from the *volks-thümliches Lied*, the Berlin composers had demonstrated the necessity of full attention to the words. Mozart and Weber had given it a home in the Opera. Mozart and Beethoven had developed its instrumental and dramatic elements; and had further shown that the interest of the Song is attenuated by extension into the larger scena-form. Nothing, therefore, of precept or example was wanting, by which genius might be taught how to make the compact form of the song a perfect vehicle of lyrical expression. The hour was ripe for the man; and the hour and the man met when Schubert arose.

This wonderful man, the greatest of song-writers, has been so fully and appreciatively treated in other pages of this Dictionary,[1] that it would be superfluous to do more here than examine the development of the Song under him. So fertile was Schubert's genius that we have more than 600 of his songs, and their variety is as remarkable as their number. He was master of the Song in every stage—whether it were the Volkslied, or the Ode, or the *volksthüm-liches Lied*, or the pure lyric song, or the Ballade and Romanze. And the secret of his greatness was largely due to his complete recognition of the principle that the balance between the melodic form and emotional meaning should be perfectly adjusted. The essence of true Song, as Schubert clearly saw, is deep, concentrated emotion, enthralling words and music alike. Full of poetry himself, he could enter into the very heart and mind of the poet; and so wide was his range of sympathetic intuition that he took songs from all the great German poets, and as their styles varied, so did his treatment. His best compositions are lyrical, and it is scarcely possible to conceive higher excellence than is displayed in these masterpieces. Beauty

[1] The reader should also consult Reissmann's *Das deutsche Lied in seiner historischen Entwickelung* and his *Geschichte des deutschen Liedes*. Also Hadow's vol. v. of the *Oxford History of Music*.

and finish are bestowed with so even a hand, both on the voice-part and on the accompaniment, that it would be difficult to say that either takes precedence of the other. In the music which he wrote to the more dramatic, legendary, or ballad-like forms, such as Schiller's 'Der Taucher,' and 'Gruppe aus dem Tartarus,' Collins's 'Der Zwerg,' Mayrhofer's 'Memnon,' or Goethe's 'Ganymed' and 'Schwager Kronos,' the accompaniment is more important than the voice-part. Schubert's treatment of the song-cycle differed from that of Beethoven, inasmuch as Schubert did not weld together the music of the set, but bound them to one another by community of spirit. They can all be sung separately, but the 'Müllerlieder' and 'Winterreise,' which tell a continuous tale, lose much of their dramatic power if they be executed otherwise than as a whole. Some of Schubert's finest songs are strophical in form, and others have a change of melody or accompaniment, or both, for every stanza. But whatever treatment the words might call for, that Schubert gave them with unerring instinct.

Mendelssohn, although he comes after Schubert, belongs to an earlier school of song-writers. His songs exhibit all the best characteristics of the Berlin School; they are perfect in form, melodious, and easy of comprehension. But they lack the marvellous variety we find in Schubert's songs. This is partly owing to the fact that Mendelssohn could not surrender himself completely to the poet whose words he was setting;[2] the words to him were only an aid or incentive to the composition of a song already preconceived in his own mind. He also adhered to certain clearly pronounced types of melody and harmony; so that his songs all bear a strong resemblance to each other. He preferred the strophic form; and ranked the independence of the melody higher than the variations of expression the words demanded. Hence the slight influence Mendelssohn has exercised upon the Song in Germany. Yet granted these limitations, the joyousness of his spring-tide songs, the tranquil beauty of such compositions as 'Scheidend' and the 'Nachtlied,' and the true Volkslied tone of 'Es ist bestimmt,' have rendered his songs popular in the best sense of the word. (See MENDELSSOHN.)

Meyerbeer's songs in general are but little known; but amongst the '40 Mélodies' published in 1840 by Brandus, Paris, many are remarkable and well worth reviving; as, for instance, 'Le moine,' 'Le poëte mourant,' 'Sur le balcon,' 'Du schönes Fischermädchen.' Still, they are open to Mendelssohn's criticism,

[2] It is a strange paradox that Mendelssohn, with all his finished culture and literary tastes, never realised his responsibilities towards the poet, and did not hesitate to change the words if it suited his music better. To give one instance out of many: in Heine's 'Ich wollt' meine Schmerzen ergössen sich,' Mendelssohn substitutes 'Liebe' for 'Schmerzen,' thereby wholly altering the sense. Another strange contradiction is the fact that although Mendelssohn was steeped in Bach and possessed great contrapuntal skill, his accompaniments are never polyphonic.

that they are too pretentious and exaggerated, and are wanting in naïveté and spontaneity. Methods were adopted by Meyerbeer more suitable to the exigencies of opera than to the simple song.

With Robert Schumann we approach a new departure in song-writing ; and no composer since Schubert has exerted so wide and deep an influence upon the subsequent development of this art, both in Germany and in other countries. Schumann was at once poet and musician. His songs are the very soul of romantic poetry. With scrupulous art he reproduces all that runs in the poet's mind, be it ever so subtle and delicate, but he also permeates it with a deeper shade of meaning. This may be seen especially in his settings of the poets Heine, Reinick, Kerner, Geibel, Chamisso,[1] Rückert,[2] and Eichendorff, the last five of whom were essentially romantic poets. Schumann's kindred imagination was stimulated into full activity by the supernatural splendour, mediæval charm, and mystic vagueness of their conceptions. Visions of midnight scenes arise in prompt obedience to the spell of Schumann's music. It conjures up for eye and ear the dark vault of the starry heavens, the solitudes of haunted woods, the firefly's restless lamp, the song of nightingales, the accents of human passion idealised, and all else that makes the half-real and the half-unreal world in which the romantic spirit loves to dwell. It is to Heine that Schumann's nature most deeply responded. Whether the poet be in a mood of subtle irony or bitter mockery, of strong passion or delicate tenderness, of joy or sorrow, with equal fidelity is he portrayed in the composer's music. What Schubert was to Goethe, Schumann was to Heine ; but the requirements of the two poets were not the same. Goethe's thought is ever expressed in clear and chiselled phrase ; while it is a habit of Heine to veil his meaning and leave whatever may be wanting to be supplied by the reader's imagination. The composer who would adequately interpret him must, therefore, have poetic fancy no less than a mastery of his own art. This Schumann had, and none of his songs rank higher than the splendid cycle 'Dichterliebe' from Heine's *Buch der Lieder*. Their melodic treatment is declamatory ; not in recitative, but in perfectly clear-cut strophes, with great attention bestowed on the accentuation of emphatic words. As a general rule the instrumental part of Schumann's songs is too important, too independent to be called an accompaniment ; it is an integral factor in the interpretation of the poem. While the voice-part often seems only to suggest, the pianoforte part unfolds the sentiment of the song, and evolves from the poem a fuller significance than it could ever have owed to the poet's own unaided art.[3] These few remarks will have sufficed to show that together with Schubert in music, and Goethe and Heine in literature, Schumann has lifted Song to a higher pinnacle of excellence than it ever reached before.

We will here allude to another branch of modern German song, which comprises the *Ballade*, the *Romanze*, and the *Rhapsodie*. In the ordinary English sense, the *ballad* is primarily a poem descriptive of an event or chain of incidents, leaving the reader to gather sentiment and reflection from bare narration. But the *Ballade*, as a German form of song, has some other properties. Goethe says it ought always to have a tone of awe-inspiring mystery, which fills the reader's mind with the presence of supernatural powers, and contain strong dramatic elements. The *Romanze* is of the same class as the Ballade, but is generally of more concise form, and by more direct references to the feelings which its story evokes approaches nearer to the lyric song. As distinguished from the Ballade and Romanze, the *Rhapsodie* is deficient in form, and its general structure is loose and irregular. The first poet who wrote poems of the true Ballade type was Bürger ; his example was followed by Goethe, Schiller, Uhland, and others, and then the attention of composers was soon caught. Inspired by Schiller, Zumsteeg composed in this vein, and his work is interesting as being the first of its kind. But Zumsteeg had too little imagination to handle this form successfully, and his best songs belong more correctly to the Romanze. We miss in his Balladen the bold, melodic, principal theme (which should stand out in relief from all secondary themes and ideas, and be repeated wherever the story needs it),[4] although in some of them the details are very well and truthfully painted—for instance, the fine gloomy opening phrase of the 'Pfarrers Tochter.' Neither Reichardt nor Zelter succeeded any better with the Ballade. They treated the 'Erlkönig' as a Romanze, and Schiller's Balladen, 'Ritter Toggenburg,' and 'Der Handschuh,' as Rhapsodies. And even Schubert in his longer pieces was inclined to compose in a rhapsodical form. In some, such as 'Der Taucher,' 'Die Bürgschaft,' 'Der Sänger,' where he is faithful to the Ballade form, and where there are exquisite bits of melody appositely introduced, and the accompaniments are thoroughly dramatic, the general effect of the piece is overlaid and marred by multiplicity of elaborate details, and drawn out to too great length. To the Romanze Schubert gave the pure strophical form, as, for instance, in Goethe's 'Heidenröslein.'

---

[1] Chamisso's cycle 'Frauenliebe und Leben' is described fully under SCHUMANN.
[2] Rückert's verse did not perhaps evoke in Schumann so full a measure of spontaneous melody as Eichendorff and Kerner. The most melodious, and perhaps the best known of the Rückert collection, are Nos. 2, 4, and 11, and these are by Frau Clara Schumann.

[3] Further evidence of the importance of Schumann's innovations in song-writing will be found under SCHUMANN.
[4] Loewe's ballads strikingly illustrate the value of this characteristic.

The founder of the true Ballade in music was J. C. G. Loewe, who caught, as it were instinctively, the exact tone and form it required. His method was to compose a very short, distinct, though fully-rounded melody for one or two lines of a stanza, and then repeat it throughout with only such alterations as were demanded by the narrative. This secures unity for the Ballade, but it necessitates a richly-developed accompaniment to contribute to the dramatic colouring of the incidents. The simpler the metrical form of the Ballade, the better will this treatment suit it. Take, for example, Uhland's ' Der Wirthin Töchterlein.' All Loewe's music to it is developed from the melody of the first line ; though other resources are brought into play as the tragic close draws near, the original idea is never lost to view, and the character with which the accompaniment began is preserved intact to the end. Still more importance is given by Loewe to the pianoforte part in the gloomy Northern Balladen ' Herr Olaf' and ' Der Mutter Geist,' and to his wonderful setting of ' Edward,' ' Archibald Douglas,' and the ' Erlkönig.' But his popular Balladen are ' Heinrich der Vogler,' ' Die Glocken zu Speier,' and ' Goldschmieds Töchterlein.' These have fresh and genial melodies, accompaniments full of characteristic expression, and, stroke upon stroke, they effect a vivid presentment of animated scenes.

Mendelssohn never touched the Ballade form for the solo voice ; and Schumann greatly preferred the Romanze. To his subjective lyric cast of mind the underlying thought was of more concern than external facts. In his beautiful music to Kerner's ' Stirb, Lieb' und Freud' ' he treats the melody as a Romanze, and puts the Ballade form into the accompaniment. On the same plan are his ' Entflieh' mit mir,' ' Loreley,' and ' Der arme Peter,' from Heine. More developed is the powerful ' Löwenbraut,' and the most perfect as regards unity in variety and impressiveness is ' Die beiden Grenadiere.' When Schumann essayed to treat the Ballade melodramatically he failed. Singing, in his opinion, was a veil to the words ; whenever, therefore, he wished them to have emphatic prominence he left them to be spoken or ' declaimed,' and attempted to illustrate the narrative of the song by the musical accompaniment. Still the Ballade form was too small and contracted for this kind of treatment, which is better suited to larger and more dramatic works aided by the orchestra. Subsequent composers have used the Ballade and Romanze form in various ways,[1] but with the exception of Martin Plüddemann none can be said to have devoted themselves exclusively to it. Plüddemann was at first under Wagner's influence : in his musical phrases he attempted to introduce the peculiarly pathetic declamatory

[1] See Brahms's ' Balladen und Romanzen.'

utterances, and the ' leit-motiv' (see, for instance, ' Volkers Nachtgesang' or ' Jung Siegfried '). But, later, he recognised Loewe to be the only true exponent of this form, and on Loewe's methods Plüddemann achieved his greatest success. It is a vexed question whether the repetition of the melody for every verse, or its variation throughout is the better structure for the Ballade ; but the former arrangement would seem to be the best adapted for short and simple pieces, and the latter for lengthier ones. If the melody be repeated for every verse in long Balladen, and unless the varied instrumental part be of paramount importance, an impression of monotony is apt to be created, and the necessarily varying aspects of the poem are imperfectly represented in the music.[2]

The lyric song continued to hold in Germany the high place to which it was raised by Schubert and Schumann, and their traditions have been worthily sustained by their successors, Robert Franz and Johannes Brahms. Franz devoted himself almost exclusively to the Song, which was the form of music best suited to his lyrical temperament. His favourite poets are writers of quiet, pensive verse like Osterwald, Lenau, Geibel, and Eichendorff. There is no lack of melody in his songs, but the chief interest lies in the accompaniments, which are as finely worked out[3] and highly finished as miniatures. Franz's songs are frequently akin to the old Volkslied and Chorale, as the modal harmony and peculiar sequential structure of the melody in his ' Zu Strassburg an der Schanz' (Dorian) or ' Es klingt in der Luft' (Phrygian), among many other examples, will prove. Most are strophical as regards the voice-part, but the richness and fulness of the instrumental part grow with each successive stanza ; or else the harmony is slightly altered to suit the words, as in the subtle change that occurs in the second stanza of ' Des Abends.' Indeed, the perfection of truth with which Franz renders every word is one of his highest merits. There is not, perhaps, enough spontaneity and passion in Franz's compositions to carry us away in a transport of enthusiasm, but the finish of his workmanship compels our deliberate admiration.

All the best tendencies of the 19th century were summed up in the songs of Johannes Brahms. The perfection of formal structure, the high distinction of melody, the beauty and fitness of the accompaniments, the depth of thought, and throughout the ring of truth and sincerity place his songs among the immortal works of the great classical masters. At all times Brahms gave earnest attention to the Volkslied.[4] The simple sentiment and origin-

[2] See Vischer's *Aesthetik*, pt. iii. p. 996 ; Albert Bach's *The Art Ballad* ; Reissmann's *Das deutsche Lied*, p. 236 ; and M. Runze's *Schiller und die Balladenmusik* (*Die Musik*, 4. Jahr. Heft 15).
[3] In his skilful polyphonic accompaniment, such as ' Mutter, sing mich zur Ruh',' Franz shows his close, loving study of Bach's methods.
[4] P. Spitta, *Zur Musik*.

ality of conception in the poetry of the folk-songs of his own and other countries were a strong incitement to him, and were reflected in his music with unsurpassable truth. Even where he uses Hungarian or other idioms, his language is always his own.[1] His use of the old modes and of complex rhythms which had long fallen into disuse,[2] show he had drunk deeply of the past in music, but he ever amalgamated it with his own living musical utterance. Brahms's full, rich accompaniments have also a character of their own. It is clear that he attached the highest importance to the fundamental bass, and there are many songs in which the bass alone is sufficient to support the voice. Again, whilst his consummate skill in the contrapuntal line is shown by the melodic life he has given the inner parts, his complete mastery over every technical resource of his art is visible in the multifarious rhythms and exquisite harmonies he employs.[3] His accompaniments sometimes lead, sometimes follow the voice, or they pursue their own independent course. Many instances of these occur in the magnificent song-cycle from Tieck's *Magelone*. The poetical and intellectual qualities of Brahms's songs, as well as their more serious and spiritual properties, have been fully described elsewhere ; and it suffices to say that the songs of this great artist make it hard to believe that the highest development of the German Lied has not been attained.

Turning to a side-group of composers who have worked more on the lines laid down by Mendelssohn, we find the names of Curschmann, Taubert, F. Lachner, F. Ries, Eckert, Rietz, Reinecke, Raff, and Fanny Hensel. Their best work is unpretending and simple, but they lack the higher qualities of song-writing. Far more interesting, and very different names are those of Cornelius, Jensen, Brückler, Herzogenberg, and Lassen. Jensen was richly responsive to the vein of tender sentiment brought into prominence by the romantic school. The exquisite 'Dolorosa' cycle, the brilliant 'Spanisches Liederbuch' and gay student songs have won success for him. Both he and Hugo Brückler, whose posthumous songs Jensen edited, possessed the true lyric feeling for melody, and both wrote elaborate and interesting accompaniments. But in each of these song-writers we find a want of self-restraint and self-criticism, and an over-feverish imagination. Heinrich von Herzogenberg did not err in this respect ; his refined and thoughtful songs, if lacking in spontaneity, are carefully worked out, and

appeal to those who care for the intellectual side of song-writing. The number of E. Lassen's songs is great, and they vary much in merit. He had a sensitive feeling for the æsthetic side of art ; and the slightness of means and material wherewith he obtains his effects is admirable.[4] But his over-sentimentality and desire for popularity place Lassen on a far lower level than the above-mentioned composers. P. Cornelius stands on a wholly different plane, being as much a poet as a musician, and having too strong an individuality in thought and mode of expression to belong to any school. In Cornelius's personality there is a strange combination of subtle mysticism and transparent simplicity, which imparts a rare charm to his songs. The beautiful 'Weihnachtslieder' cycle, with their childlike sincerity, and the exquisitely poetical 'Brautlieder' cycle represent his best work, but all his songs need to be intimately studied before they can make their full impression.

The history of German song during the last century bears witness to a continuous attempt towards heightening, by means of melody, harmony, and rhythm, the effect of the words. The musical idea, nevertheless, did not subserve the literary, nor were the essentials of pure musical art forgotten. The latest development of German song has carried to the extreme the tendency of giving a place of primary importance to the words, and musical form is sacrificed to literary construction. The composer selects poems with regard to their literary value ; the exigencies of verbal accent are enforced ; repetition or alteration of words and other verbal licences countenanced in past days are prohibited. Musically regarded, the importance and independence of the instrumental part has reached its climax ; declamatory passages have replaced melodic phrases ; all the resources of modern music in modulation, in harmonic and rhythmical combinations have been expended on the song-form with a lavish and often undiscriminating hand.[5] Sounds, musically chaotic, are tolerated by the æsthetic principle which recognises no obligation save the obligation to emphasise the mood or meaning of the verse. Expression, not beauty, is now the composer's ideal. This song-formula was adopted by Hugo Wolf and Richard Strauss, and carried to its apogee by Max Reger and others belonging to the same school of thought — each engrafting thereon his individual qualities and idiosyncrasies. No one can deny the sincerity of these composers' methods of writing. They have realised the æsthetic value of complexity and ugliness, and it needs no defence in their minds. And yet

---

[1] To show the power Brahms had to limit this form to its own compact structure, and without change evolve fresh meaning for every verse, see the pathetic Volkslied 'Schwesterlein.' And that he could equally raise it to the highest development of the art-song is exemplified by his treatment of the Wendic folk-song 'Von ewiger Liebe.'

[2] Compare his use of the *hemiolia* with those which occur in Handel's 'Duetti da Camera.' Spitta, *Zur Musik*.

[3] See, for example, 'Frühlingstrost' and 'O wüsst' ich doch,' from op. 63.

[4] See P. Bachmann's essay on Lassen in *Die Musik*, Feb. 1904.

[5] The application of Wagner's methods to the Song cannot here be discussed, as he practically stood apart from this form, although his indirect influence upon Song has been undeniable, and the few examples he left are of great beauty.

all have shown that if they wished to write anything simple and beautiful they could do so —every resource in musical art being at their command.[1] Strauss and Reger will probably not rank among musicians primarily as song-writers, but with Hugo Wolf his songs are his master-work, and as such he justly holds the highest place. His earliest works show an unerring penetration into the very heart of the poet. His art demanded lyrical objectivity, and he deliberately avoided the subjective poets. This objectivity of theme requires a more vivid imaginative grasp and a wider sympathy than is necessary to a composer who makes the songs only represent his own emotion. There is no diffuseness in Wolf's writing ; the finest thought is compressed into the smallest possible space. He seems to have triumphantly solved the problem of imparting a feeling of unity into the most declamatory and fragmentary phrases of his songs. He produces the effect on the one hand by concentration of imaginative conception, and on the other hand by the more mechanical method of retaining one figure or *motif* throughout the whole song, which adapts itself with wonderful elasticity to each change in the situation. Wolf's accompaniments are usually polyphonic, or consist of kaleidoscopic and unconventional successions of chords and discords, the latter extended also to the voice-part. Songs of extreme beauty are to be found both in the 'Italienisches' and 'Spanisches Liederbuch,' and the 'Geistliche Lieder' of the latter cycle testify to the depth of his nature. In short, what music Wolf wrote was in all sincerity what Wolf felt. Fantastic, realistic, and original he may be, but never wilfully affected or extravagant.

Many interesting and beautiful songs have, moreover, been written by Weingartner, Henschel, Hans Schmidt, Hans Sommer, E. d'Albert, Max Schillings, Th. Streicher, and others.[2] It may also be said that every German composer of modern times, with every diversity of talent, has cultivated the Song as a serious branch of his art. And the reverence of devotion with which the Song is regarded bears full promise for the future.

In connection with essential requisites of the Song, much might be said about the sound of the words in the voice-part, about the incidence of open words on certain notes and careful combination of consonants. Much, too, of the duties and responsibilities of the singer with regard to accentuation and phrasing ; and the varied delivery and interpretation the different kinds of song require. But the discussion of such topics would carry us far beyond the limits of this article. It is hoped, however, that enough has been said in this imperfect sketch to show that the investigation of the history of Song offers a fruitful field for the highest faculties of musical research and exposition.

BIBLIOGRAPHY AND COLLECTIONS

A. MSS. from the 8th to the 17th Century

1. Fragments of the 'Hildebrandlied' (8th century) in the Landesbibliothek, Cassel. (Facsimile published by W. Grimm in 1830. See O. Schade's *Altdeutsches Lesebuch*, 1862-66.)
2. The Wolfenbüttel MSS. (10th century), in the Ducal Library, Wolfenbüttel. (Contains some of the oldest secular songs in Germany.)
3. MSS. of the 'Ludwigslied' (10th century) in the Valenciennes Library. (See Schade's *Altdeutsches Lesebuch*.)
4. The St. Gall Cod. Lat. No. 393 (11th century).
5. Nithart's Song-book'—MSS. (13th century). In the possession of Professor v. der Hagen. (Printed in his work on the Minnesinger.)
6. The Limburg Chronicle (1347-80), in the Limburg Library. (This MS., reprinted in 1617, 1826, and 1860, contains chiefly Knights' and Monks' songs.)
7. The 'Jena Minnesinger Codex' (14th century) in the University Library. (Contains fine specimens of Minnesinger melodies, and amongst them Vogelweide's 'Reiselied.' Latest reprint 1902.)
8. The Colmar Minnesinger MSS. (14th century), at Munich. (Latest reprint, 1896.)
9. H. von. Loufenberg's Song-book (1415-43), at Strasburg. (Destroyed by fire, 1870, but copied previously by Wackernagel.)
10. Spörl's Song-book (end of 14th and beginning of 15th century), in the Imperial Library, Vienna.
11. The Prague MS. (early 15th century), in the University Library, entitled *Ein musikalischer Lehrcompendium d. H. de Zeelandia*.)
12. The Locheim Song-book (1452-60), in the Ducal Library, Wernigerode. (Edited in 19th century by Arnold and Bellermann.)
13. The Dresden Minnesinger MS. (15th century), in the Royal Public Library. (Contains M. Behaim's hymns.)
14. The Vienna Song-book (1533), in the Imperial Library. (Consists of sacred and secular part-books, words and music.)
15. Hager's Meisterliederbuch (1600). (Contains portrait of Hans Sachs, and many Meisterlieder melodies from the Nuremberg School.)
16. Werlin's Song-book (1646), in the Royal State Library, Munich. (Contains many thousand songs ; some are genuine Volkslieder of the 15th and 16th century, and others later and more artificial.)

B. Modern Collections of Volkslieder, Volksthümliche Lieder, and Chorales, and Works relating to the History of German Song, chronologically arranged.[3]

Becker, R. Z. 'Mildheimisches Liederbuch.' Gotha, 1799.
Achim v. Arnim,[4] L., and C. Brentano. 'Des Knaben Wunderhorn.' Berlin, 1806-46.
Herder.[5] 'Stimmen der Völker.' Tübingen, 1807.
Büsching, J. G. G., and F. H. v. d. Hagen. 'Sammlung Deutscher Volkslieder.' Berlin, 1807.
Grimm, J. *Ueber den altdeutschen Meistergesang*. Göttingen, 1811.
Görres, J. von. Altdeutsche Volks- und Meisterlieder (from MSS. in the Heidelberg Library). Frankfurt a/M., 1817.
Erlach, F. K. von. *Die Volkslieder der Deutschen*. Mannheim, 1834-37.
Silcher, F. 'Deutsche Volkslieder,' etc. Tübingen, 1837-40.
Zuccalmaglio and Kretzschmar, A. 'Deutsche Volkslieder.' 1838-44.
Erk, L., and Irmer, W. 'Die Deutschen Volkslieder.' Berlin. 1838-45.
Hagen, F. H. v. d. *Die Minnesinger*. Leipzig, 1838.
Becker, C. F. 'Die Hausmusik in Deutschland in dem 16., 17. und 18. Jahrhunderte,' etc. Leipzig, 1840.
Wolf, F. *Ueber die Lais, Sequenzen und Leiche*. Heidelberg, 1841.
Fallersleben, Hoffmann von, and Richter, E. 'Schlesische Volkslieder,' etc. Leipzig, 1842.
Becker, C. F. 'Lieder und Weisen vergangener Jahrhunderte.' Leipzig, 1843-53.
Lyra, J., and Löwenstein, R. 'Deutsche Lieder.' Leipzig, 1843-58.
Fink, G. W. 'Mus. Hausschatz der Deutschen.' Leipzig, 1843-78.
Schottky, J., and Ziska, F. 'Oesterreichische Volkslieder.' Pesth, 1844.
Fallersleben, Hoffmann v. *Die Deutschen Gesellschafts Lieder des 16. und 17. Jahrhunderts*. Leipzig, 1844-60.
Uhland, L.[6] *Alte Hoch- und Niederdeutsche Volkslieder*. Stuttgart, 1844-46.
Spaun, A. v. 'Die Oesterreichischen Volksweisen.' Vienna, 1845.
Winterfeld, Carl v. *Der Evangelische Kirchengesang*, etc. Leipzig, 1843-47.
Fallersleben, Hoffmann v. 'Deutsches Volksgesangbuch.' Leipzig, 1848.
Meister, C. S. *Das katholische deutsche Kirchenlied*, etc. Freiburg, 1852. (Later edition with Bäumker, 1862-91.)
Stade, W., and Liliencron, R. v. *Lieder und Sprüche aus der letzten Zeit des Minnesanges*. Weimar, 1854.
Becker, C. F. *Die Tonwerke d. 16. und 17. Jahrhunderts*. Leipzig, 1854.

---

[1] Wolf's 'Verborgenheit,' Strauss' 'Traum durch die Dämmerung' and 'Heimliche Aufforderung,' and Reger's 'Mit Rosen bestreut' may be mentioned as isolated examples.

[2] See Dr. Kretzschmar's article, *Das deutsche Lied seit dem Tode R. Wagners*, in the *Jahrbuch der Musikbibliothek Peters*, 1898.

---

[3] It was considered advisable to combine the bibliography and collections together in this section, as the one work frequently embraces both. Take, for instance, Böhme's 'Altdeutsches Liederbuch,' which is at once the best history of the Volkslied and the best collection.

[4] This work contains practically no music, but is necessary to the student of the German Volkslied.

[5] *Ditto.*   [6] *Ditto.*

Silcher, F., and Erk, F. A. 'Allgemeines deutsches Commersbuch.' 1858-88.

Reissmann, A. *Das deutsche Lied in seiner historischen Entwickelung.* Cassel, 1861.

Ambros, A. W. *Geschichte der Musik.* Breslau and Leipzig, 1862-82.

Schneider, C. E. *Das musikalische Lied in geschichtlicher Entwickelung.* Leipzig, 1863-65.

Wackernagel, C. E. P. *Das deutsche Kirchenlied*, etc. Leipzig, 1862-77.

Liliencron, R. v. *Die historischen Volkslieder der Deutschen*, etc. Leipzig, 1865-69.

Härtel, A. 'Deutsches Lieder-lexicon.' Leipzig, 1867.

Vilmar, A. 'Handbüchlein für Freunde d. deutschen Volksliedes.' Marburg, 1867.

Fallersleben, Hoffmann v. *Unsere volksthümlichen Lieder*, Leipzig, 1869.

Lindner, E. O. *Geschichte d. deutschen Liedes im XVIII. Jahrhundert.* Leipzig, 1871.

Von Carolsfeld, Schnorr. *Zur Geschichte d. deutschen Meistergesanges.* Berlin, 1872.

Saran, A. *Robert Franz und d. deutsche Volkslied.* Leipzig, 1872.

Reissmann, A. *Geschichte d. deutschen Liedes.* Berlin, 1874.

Schuré, E. *Histoire du Lied.* Paris, 1876.

Eitner, R. *Das deutsche Lied d. 15. und 16. Jahrhunderts.* Berlin, 1876-80.

Böhme, F. M. *Altdeutsches Liederbuch aus dem 12. bis zum 17. Jahrhundert*, etc. Leipzig, 1877.

Liliencron, R. v. *Deutsches Leben im Volkslied um 1530.* Leipzig, 1884.

Böhme, F. M. *Geschichte des Tanzes in Deutschland.* Leipzig, 1886.

Neckheim, H. 'Kärnthner Lieder.' 1891-1902.

Friedländer, M. 'Commersbuch.' Leipzig, 1892.

Reimann, H. 'Das deutsche Lied.' Berlin, 1892-93.

Wolfram, E. H. 'Nassauische Volkslieder.' Berlin, 1894.

Erk, L., and Böhme, F. M. 'Deutsche Liederhort.' Leipzig, 1894.

Böhme, F. M. *Volksthümliche Lieder der Deutschen im 18. und 19. Jahrhundert.* Leipzig, 1895.

Kufferath, M. *Les Maîtres-Chanteurs de R. Wagner.* Paris, 1898.

Mey, Kurt. *Der Meistergesang in Geschichte und Kunst.* Leipzig, 1901.

Friedländer, M. *Das deutsche Lied im 18. Jahrhundert.* Berlin, 1902.

Riemann, H. *Geschichte des neueren deutschen Liedes.* Leipzig, 1904.

Müller von der Werra, F. C. 'Allgemeine Reichs-Kommersbuch für deutsche Studenten' (edited by Felix Dehn and C. Reinecke). Leipzig, 1904.

Riemann, H. *Geschichte der Musik des 19. Jahrhunderts.* Leipzig, 1905.

Bischoff, H. *Das deutsche Lied.* Leipzig, 1906.

Liliencron, R. v. 'Neue deutsche Volkslieder-Sammlung.' Leipzig, 1906.

Articles in the *Vierteljahrsschrift für Musikwissenschaft, Monatshefte für Musikgeschichte*, and *Sammelbände* of the I.M.G.[1]

For further additions to this list refer to F. M. Böhme's 'Altdeutsches Liederbuch' and 'Volksthümliche Lieder der Deutschen,' where ample catalogues at end, with annotations, will be found.[2]

                    A. H. W.

SONG-SCHOOL. A considerable part in the development of the art of music has been played by Song-Schools. It was the establishment of the *Schola cantorum* at Rome (see SISTINE CHOIR) that led to the development of Gregorian Plainsong in the 5th and 6th centuries, and it was the establishment of other such schools at St. Gall, Reichenau, Metz, etc., which disseminated widely the knowledge of the Roman music. In England such musical centres were set up in the earliest days of the Roman mission, and in the 6th and 7th centuries there was great enthusiasm and much good work done under a succession of teachers who came from the Roman *Schola*. After the Danes had devastated monastic life, and with it the bulk of Saxon culture, musical and other, the recovery took place. Under S. Ethelwold a Benedictine revival took place which recovered music among other things, and English music long preserved some special features which it had learnt in French Benedictine music-schools, particularly at Fleury-sur-Loire.

In the later period before the Reformation two forces were at work in giving practical musical training. In connection with the

monasteries a song-school was almost a necessity. In such song-schools not only foreigners, like Guido of Arezzo or Regino of Prüm, learnt their music, but English musicians too, such as Odington, Tunsted, Hothby, Fairfax, and, finally, Tallis. At Durham, for example, there was in the monastic days a song-school in which six children were taught and kept under a master, who was also bound to play the organ at the chief services. After the dissolution the building was pulled down, but the school continued under its old master in a different position ; and still the song-school flourishes in connection with the present cathedral. Like the monasteries the secular cathedrals had also a song-school, and others were maintained not only by the King for the Chapel Royal, but also by great ecclesiastics and nobles. Secondly, the foundation of chantries tended to multiply song-schools ; for the work stipulated for from the chantry priest after he had said his Mass daily was usually schoolmaster's work, and in many cases either a song-school or a grammar school was annexed to the foundation. Hundreds of these smaller schools were mostly destroyed when Edward VI. confiscated the chantries, and English music has never recovered from the loss. The prevalence of song-schools made it possible for England to be a nation of musicians in the 15th and 16th centuries ; but few survived the Reformation, except in connection with great collegiate or cathedral churches, and England lost its skill.   W. H. F.

In Scotland 'Sang Schools' flourished from the 13th century onwards. A 'scule' for teaching singing existed in almost every one of the cathedral cities in Scotland, and in many of the smaller towns, such as Ayr, Dumbarton, Lanark, Cupar, and Irvine. Even in the far north, in 1544, Bishop Reid founded and endowed a 'Sang School' in Orkney. Prior to the Reformation the teaching in these schools was principally confided to 'musick, meaners, and vertu,' but at a later date it extended to the proverbial 'three R's.' Music, however, seems to have been the chief course of instruction, and the original idea of confining its study to the cathedral singers was so far enlarged, that laymen were admitted to the schools, in which the Gregorian chant had naturally an early and important place. The master of the school was held in high esteem, and was occasionally selected from the clergy, the appointment at times leading to important preferment—thus William Hay, master of the Old Aberdeen School in 1658, was made Bishop of Moray ; and John Leslie, Bishop of Ross, was once a teacher in the Aberdeen School.

Great attention seems to have been paid by the Parliament of the day to the study of music, for a statute was passed in 1574 'instructing the provest, baillies, and counsale, to sett up ane sang scuill, for instruction of the youth in

---

[1] The writer wishes also to express her thanks to Mr. Walter Ford for permission to quote from his Lectures on German Song.

[2] See also Pierre Aubry's *Esquisse d'une Bibliographie de la Chanson populaire en Europe.* Paris, 1905.

the art of musick and singing, quhilk is almaist decayit and sall schortly decay without tymous remeid be providit.' Comparatively little interest seems to have attended either the Edinburgh or Glasgow schools, and from a minute of the Town Council of the latter we gather that the institution collapsed in 1588, 'the scuile sumtyme callit the sang scuile' being sold to defray the expenses incidental to the heavy visitation of a plague. The Aberdeen school appears to have been the one of chief celebrity, attracting teachers of even Continental fame, and the Burgh records contain references of a curious and amusing description. The school existed so early as the year 1370, its class of pupils being the same as those attending the grammar school. Both vocal and instrumental music were taught, as we learn from the title of Forbes's scarce work, 'Cantus, Songs and Fancies both apt for Voices and Viols as is taught in the Music School of Aberdeen' (1662). About this period, Mace, in his *Musick's Monument*, directed the attention of his countrymen to the sang school of Scotland as an institution well worthy of imitation south of the Tweed. A few excerpts from the Burgh records of Aberdeen and other places may not be uninteresting, and we give the following as a fair example of the attention paid by the civic authorities of the day to the subject of music. On Oct. 7, 1496, a contract was entered into between the Town Council of Aberdeen and Robert Huchosone, sangster, 'who obliges himself by the faith of his body all the days of his life to remain with the community of the burgh, upholding matins, psalms, hymns,' etc., the Council also giving him the appointment of master of the Sang School. The four following extracts are also from the Aberdeen Burgh records, as faithfully transcribed by the editors of the Spalding Club publications:—

4th October, 1577.
The said day the counsell grantit the soume of four poundis to the support of James Symsonne, doctour of thair Sang Scuill, to help to buy him cloythis.

23 Nov^r., 1597.
The maister of the sang schoole sall serve bayth the Kirkis in uptacking of the psalmes theirin.

1594.
Item to the Maister of the sang schoile xiiij.

1609.
'The bairnis and scoleris of the sang schoolis' are ordered to find caution for their good behaviour.

From Dundee Records, 1602.
Item to the master of the sang scule lxxx lbs.

From Air Records, 1627.
Item to the M^r of musick scule for teaching of the musick scule and tacking up the psalmes in the kirk x bolls victuall and xiiij of silver.

From Irving Records, 1633.
Our doctour and musicianer jcii.

The stipend of the master of the Edinburgh sang school appears to have been the modest allowance of ten pounds in sterling money.

J. T. F.

SONGE D'UNE NUIT D'ÉTÉ, LE (A Midsummer Night's Dream). An opéra-comique in three acts, an absurd caricature of scenes in the life of Queen Elizabeth and Shakespeare, with no relation to his play. The words are by Rosier and De Leuven, and the music by Ambroise Thomas, and it was produced at the Opéra-Comique, Paris, April 20, 1850.   G.

SONGS WITHOUT WORDS. (See LIED OHNE WORTE, vol. ii. p. 727.)   G.

SONNAMBULA, LA. An Italian opera in two acts; libretto by Romani, music by Bellini (written for Pasta and Rubini). Produced at the Teatro Carcano, Milan, March 6, 1831 ; at the King's Theatre, London, July 28, and at Paris, Oct. 28 of the same year. At Drury Lane (with Malibran) in English, under Italian title, May 1, 1833.   G.

SONNLEITHNER, a noted Viennese family of musical amateurs. The first, CHRISTOPH, born May 28, 1734, at Szegedin, came to Vienna at two years old and learned music from his uncle Leopold Sonnleithner, choir-master of a church in the suburbs. He also studied law, became an advocate of some eminence, was employed by Prince Esterhazy, and thus came into contact with Haydn. He composed several symphonies, which his friend Von Kees (often mentioned in Haydn's life) frequently played with his orchestra ; and also thirty-six quartets, mostly for the Emperor Joseph, who used to call him his favourite composer. His church-compositions, remarkable for purity of form and warmth of feeling, have survived in the great ecclesiastical institutions of Austria, and are still performed at High Mass. Christoph Sonnleithner died Dec. 25, 1786. His daughter, Anna, was the mother of Grillparzer the poet. His son IGNAZ, Doctor of Laws and professor of commercial science (ennobled 1828), was an energetic member of the Gesellschaft der Musikfreunde, and took part in their concerts as principal bass-singer. At the musical evenings held at his house, the so-called 'Gundelhof,' in 1815-24, in which his son, Leopold, took part as chorus-singer, Schubert's 'Prometheus,' though only with piano accompaniment, was first heard (July 24, 1816), as were also part-songs, 'Das Dörfchen' (1819), 'Gesang der Geister über den Wassern' (1821), and the 23rd Psalm for female voices (1822). Ignaz died in 1831. A second son, JOSEPH, born 1766, devoted himself with success to literature and the fine arts, and in 1799 was sent abroad by the Emperor Franz to collect portraits and biographies of *savants* and artists for his private library. During this tour he made the acquaintance of Gerber and Zelter. In 1804 he succeeded Kotzebue as secretary of the Court theatres, and as such had the entire management of both houses till 1814, and also of that 'an der Wien' till 1807. He directed his endeavours principally to German opera, and himself wrote or translated several librettos, including Beethoven's 'Leonore' from the French of du Bouilly (the title of which was changed against the composer's wish to 'Fidelio') ; [1] 'Agnes Sorel' and others for Gyrowetz ; 'Kaiser Hadrian,' and 'Die Weihe der Zukunft'—a *pièce d'occasion* for the visit of the Allies—for Weigl ; 'Faniska' for Cherubini ; an oratorio, 'Die vier letzten Dinge,' for Eybler, and numerous plays from various languages. He edited the Viennese *Theater - Almanach* for 1794, 1795, and 1796, which contains valuable biographies, and articles on the then condition of music in Vienna. For his services as founder (1811) and honorary secretary of the 'Gesellschaft adeliger Frauen zur Beförderung der Guten und Nützlichen' he was made a counsellor. With indefatigable energy he next applied himself to founding (1813) the Gesellschaft der Musikfreunde, and continued to act as its honorary secretary till his death, devoting himself unremittingly to the welfare of the society. Another institution in which he took equal interest was the Conservatorium, founded in 1817.[2] The formation of the archives, and especially of the library, was almost entirely his work, through his acquisition of Gerber's literary remains in 1819, and his legacy of 41 MS. vols. in his own hand, full of valuable materials for the history of music. [His discovery of the S. Gall Antiphoner in 1827 was an important event in the history of old liturgical music. The curious incident of the unique copy of Forkel's collection of 16th century church music, undertaken at Sonnleithner's instance, has been narrated under FORKEL, vol. ii. p. 72*b*.] He lived in close friendship with Schubert and Grillparzer up to his death, which took place Dec. 26, 1835. He received the Danebrog Order and honorary diplomas from several musical societies. His nephew, LEOPOLD EDLER VON SONNLEITHNER, son of Ignaz, advocate and eminent amateur, born Nov. 15, 1797, was a great friend of the sisters Fröhlich, Schubert, Schwind the painter, and Grillparzer. He took great care to preserve Schubert's songs, and to introduce the composer to the musical world, by publishing, with the help of other friends, his 'Erlkönig' and other early songs, for the first time. The 'Erlkönig' was sung by Gymnich [3] at a soirée of the Gesellschaft der Musikfreunde, Jan. 25, 1821, and for the first time in public on the 7th of March following, at the old Kärnthnerthor theatre, by Vogl, with immense success. As member of the Gesellschaft der Musikfreunde (from 1860 an honorary one), Sonnleithner took an unwearied interest in the concerns of the society, to whose archives he left, among other papers, his highly valuable notes on the operas produced, on concerts, and other musical events in Vienna. His

[1] Revised by Treitschke for the revival of the opera in 1814. [See vol. i. p. 191.]
[2] The first scheme of instruction was drawn up by Hofrath von Mosel.
[3] August von Gymnich, an imperial official, and a much esteemed tenor, died Oct. 6, 1821, aged thirty-six.

numerous articles on music are scattered through various periodicals. He was an intimate friend of Otto Jahn's, and furnished him with much valuable material for the life of Mozart, as Jahn acknowledges in his preface. Leopold von Sonnleithner was Ritter of the Order of the Iron Crown, an honorary member of the Gesellschaft der Musikfreunde, and of the Musikvereine of Salzburg, Innsbruck, etc. He died March 3, 1873, and with him disappeared a most persevering investigator and collector of facts connected with the history of music in Vienna, a class which daily becomes rarer, though its labours were never of more value than in the present age of new appearances and general progress. C. F. P.

SONS OF THE CLERGY, THE CORPORATION OF THE. This venerable institution, which was founded in 1655 by sons of clergymen, has for its objects the assisting necessitous clergymen, pensioning and assisting their widows and aged single daughters, and educating, apprenticing, and providing outfits for their children. To aid in procuring funds for these purposes it holds an annual festival (at no fixed date), consisting of a choral service with a sermon, followed by a dinner. The first sermon was preached in the year of foundation at St. Paul's Cathedral by the Rev. George Hall, D.D., minister of St. Botolph's, Aldersgate Street. That similar meetings took place in following years is most probable, but there are no means of proving it, owing to the unfortunate destruction of the early records of the institution by fire, in 1838. We find, however, that in 1674 and 1675 sermons were preached at St. Michael's, Cornhill ; that from 1676 to 1696 they were delivered at Bow Church, Cheapside ; and that from 1697 down to the present year (1907) they have been invariably given at St. Paul's Cathedral. The association was incorporated by charter of Charles II. in 1678. It was in 1698, according to the records, that 'music' (*i.e.* orchestral accompaniment to the service and anthems) was first introduced at the festivals. The compositions then performed were Purcell's Te Deum and Jubilate in D, composed for the celebration on St. Cecilia's Day, 1694, and these were annually repeated until 1713, when Handel's Te Deum and Jubilate, composed on the Peace of Utrecht, were given, from which time the two compositions were alternately performed until 1743, when both were laid aside in favour of the Te Deum composed by Handel to celebrate the victory at Dettingen, which continued to be annually performed (with the exception of one or two years when Purcell's Te Deum was revived) until 1843, after which its performance was discontinued in consequence of the services of the instrumental band being dispensed with in deference to the wishes of the Bishop of London (Blomfield). Handel's overture to the oratorio 'Esther' was almost invariably played as a prelude to the service from near the time of its production in 1720 until 1843. Dr. W. Hayes was at one time conductor of the festivals, and added instrumental parts to the Old Hundredth Psalm tune for their use. Dr. Boyce also was for many years their conductor, and composed for them his two anthems, 'Lord, Thou hast been our refuge,' and 'Blessed is he that considereth the poor and needy,' besides adding accompaniments to Purcell's Te Deum and Jubilate, and expanding several movements in them. After 1843 the services were for some thirty years accompanied by the organ only, the choir being, as before, very largely augmented. Since 1873 orchestral accompaniment has again been called into requisition ; Evensong has taken the place of Matins ; and modern compositions by various living composers, often written expressly for the festival, have been introduced. [A history of the corporation, by Rev. E. H. Pearce, was published in 1904.] 　　　　　　　　　　　　　　　w. h. h.

SONTAG, Henriette, Countess Rossi, was born at Coblenz, Jan. 3, 1806. Her father was a good comedian, her mother an actress of no ordinary merit, to whom the daughter, when at the height of fame, continued to turn for instruction. At six, Henriette made her first public appearance, at the Darmstadt theatre, as Salome, in Kauer's 'Donauweibchen.' Three years later her mother, then a widow, settled at Prague, where Weber was conductor at the theatre. Here Henriette acted in juvenile parts, and in 1815 was admitted, though under the prescribed age, as a pupil to the Conservatorium of the city. She studied singing under Bayer and Frau Czegka, and when only fifteen was suddenly called upon to replace the *prima donna* at the opera in the part of the Princess in Boieldieu's 'Jean de Paris.' Her precocity, appearance, and vocal gifts at once created a great impression, but shortly afterwards her mother removed with her to Vienna, where the next few years were spent, Henriette Sontag singing both in Italian and German opera, and deriving, according to her own statement, incalculable benefit from the counsels and example of Mme. Fodor-Mainvielle. Here Weber, in 1823, after hearing her in the 'Donna del Lago,' went next day to offer her the title-rôle in his 'Euryanthe,' whose production, Oct. 25, was a triumph for Mlle. Sontag. Beethoven could not hear her, but 'How did little Sontag sing ?' was his first question to those who had been at the performance. When, in 1824, his Ninth Symphony and Mass in D were produced, it was she who sustained the difficult and ungrateful soprano part. She was next engaged at Leipzig, and then for Berlin, making her first appearance at the Königstadt theatre, August 3, 1825, as Isabella in the 'Italiana in Algieri.'

Henceforward her career was one unbroken triumph. She made her début in Paris in June 1826, as Rosina in the 'Barbiere,' and became a favourite at once. Her introduction of Rode's air and variations created a furore. She sang also in the 'Donna del Lago' and 'Italiana in Algieri,' and returned to Germany in July with heightened prestige. Everywhere her beauty, charming voice, and exquisite vocalisation combined to excite an admiration amounting to frenzy. At Göttingen her post-chaise was thrown into the river by the ardent crowd, no mortal being counted worthy to make use of it after her. Even Ludwig Börne, after commenting humorously on the extravagance of the public, confesses to have yielded in his turn to the prevailing infatuation. Her figure was slender and *mignonne*, her hair between auburn and blonde, her eyes large, and her features delicate. Her voice, a soprano of clear and pleasing quality, was specially good in the upper register, reaching the E in alt with facility, and in perfection of execution she seems to have been unsurpassed by any singer of her time. But she was deficient in dramatic power, and only appeared to the highest advantage in works of a light and placid style. On her return to Paris, in January 1828, she essayed parts of a different order, such as Donna Anna and Semiramide, with success, but in passion and emotion never rose to the distinction she attained as a songstress.

In England she appeared first on April 19, 1828, at the King's Theatre, as Rosina, and met with a most flattering reception, sharing with Malibran the honours of that and the succeeding season.

At Berlin, Mlle. Sontag had formed the acquaintance of Count Rossi, then in the diplomatic service of Sardinia. An attachment sprang up between them, and was followed by a secret marriage. It was feared that the young diplomat's future might be compromised were he to acknowledge an artist of low birth as his wife. But after a time Count Rossi's efforts to procure Court sanction to his union were successful—the King of Prussia bestowed a patent of nobility on the lady, who henceforth appeared officially as *geb. Frl. von Klarenstein*, and she definitely bade farewell to artistic life. As Countess Rossi she accompanied her husband to the Hague, where he was representative of the Sardinian Court. Occasionally she would sing for public charities, in concerts or oratorio —a style in which she is said to have been unrivalled ; still, for nearly half her lifetime she remained lost to the musical public, following the career of her husband at the Courts of Holland, Germany, and Russia. As to her domestic felicity and the character of her husband, we quote the positive testimony of her brother, Carl Sontag : 'Rossi made my sister happy, in the truest sense of the word. Up to the day of her death they loved each other as on their wedding-day !' But the disorders of 1847-48 had impaired their fortunes, and she

HENRIETTE SONTAG, COUNTESS ROSSI

was tempted to return to the opera. It was notified to Rossi that he might retain his ambassador's post if he would formally separate from his wife—on the tacit understanding that so soon as her operatic career was concluded she should be allowed to return to him. This he, however, at once refused, and resigned his post, though remaining on a friendly footing with the Court. Lumley, then manager of Her Majesty's Theatre, having offered the Countess Rossi £6000 for six months, it was accepted, and in July 1849 her reappearance in London as 'Linda' was announced. The curiosity excited was extreme. Her voice and charms were unimpaired, and the unanimous opinion seems to have been that, in the words of Adolphe Adam, she now united to youth and freshness the qualities of a finished artist. As Amina, though Jenny Lind was fresh in the public memory, she was rapturously received, as also in Desdemona, and Susanna in the 'Nozze,' one of her favourite parts, and pronounced by a German critic the most perfect thing he had seen on any stage. Her extraordinary preservation of her powers was partly due, no doubt, to long exemption from the wear and tear of incessant public singing; but Sontag was always extremely careful of her voice, discarding any rôle that did not lie well within her register. Thus, in an early contract at Berlin, she expressly stipulates that she shall not be bound to sing in the operas of Spontini!

After a tour in the English provinces in the winter of 1849, she went to Paris, where a successful series of concerts, also under Lumley's management, preceded in the spring of 1850 her reappearance at Her Majesty's to win fresh laurels as Norina in 'Don Pasquale,' Elvira in the 'Puritani,' and Miranda in Halévy's new opera 'La Tempesta.' As Zerlina and the 'Figlia del Reggimento,' she appeared for the first time, and with pre-eminent success. In the autumn of 1850 she sang in Italian opera at Paris, Lumley again being director of the company. During this season Alary's 'Tre Nozze' was produced, and the polka-duet between Sontag and Lablache never failed to send the public into ecstasies. It was brought out in London in 1851, with similar results. During this season, Mme. Sontag's last in London, she sang in a round of her favourite parts, and in the production of 'L'Enfant Prodigue.'

In Germany, wherever she went she carried all before her. At a concert at Munich she was expressly requested to stay to hear the last piece. It proved to be a 'Huldigungs Chor' —verses composed expressly in her honour by the Crown Prince, and set to music by Lachner.

In 1852, Mme. Sontag received offers from the United States, which tempted her thither with her husband in the autumn. The results were brilliant. Her voice was strengthened by the climate, and at this time she could sing in

'Lucrezia Borgia' and the 'Figlia del Reggimento' on a single evening without over-fatigue! Her last appearance was made in 'Lucrezia' at Mexico, in 1854. She was attacked by cholera, and on June 17 a brief illness cut short a life of unchequered prosperity.

Berlioz, remarking on the fact that Sontag had less to suffer than other equally famous singers from hostile criticism and party spirit, ascribes it to her having so many favourite qualities—sweetness unsurpassed, fabulous agility, perfect intonation, and expression. In this last her scope was limited, and warranted Catalani's *mot*, 'Elle est la première dans son genre, mais son genre n'est pas le premier.' Her success in certain pathetic rôles must be attributed to the charm of her singing. She used to say, 'A Donna Anna over her father's corpse, a Pamina in the air "Ach ich fühl's," who cannot move the public to tears, has no idea of Mozart.' By her delivery of the short phrase alone, 'Tamino, halt! ich muss ihn sehn,' sung by Pamina behind the scenes, she could rouse the house to the stormiest applause. She was a thorough and conscientious artist, and her style won her the special favour of eminent musicians. Mendelssohn entertained the highest admiration for her, and she obtained a like tribute of praise from connoisseurs in every country. It fell to her lot to achieve an international popularity and fame never before accorded to a German singer.   B. T.

SOPRANO. The human voice of the highest pitch or range. Its peculiar clef is the C-clef upon the lowest line of the stave; but in modern times this has been almost universally superseded by the treble or G-clef on the second line.

The word 'Soprano' is etymologically synonymous with 'Sovrano,' the head, chief, or highest. In the present day the soprano is the highest natural voice of women and boys—the artificial soprani belonging to the past; and in women it is, perhaps, the voice which varies most in compass. That of AGUJARI is the highest and most extended on record, and that of TIETJENS one of the largest in quality and power. But, as with other voices, it is not a question of compass alone, but of timbre. Many mezzosoprani can sing higher notes than many soprani; but there is a middle to every voice, which, as a rule, it is not difficult to find, and about this the *tessitura* (literally texture) of the music and the practice should be woven. Tessitura is the technical term used by the Italians to signify the notes or part of the scale upon which music is framed, and though, as said above, a mezzo-soprano may sing higher notes than a soprano, it would generally be found distressing to the former voice to dwell upon that part of the scale upon which even a limited soprano part is written. [See TESSITURA.] Faustina, Cuzzoni, Mingotti, Anastasia

Robinson, Mara, Banti, Catalani, Mrs. Billington, and Miss Paton are some of the principal soprani of bygone days, possessing exceptionally good voices ; and those of Grisi, Clara Novello, Tietjens, Adelina Patti [and Melba] may perhaps be considered the best natural soprano voices of modern times.   H. C. D.

SORCERER, THE.   Comic opera in two acts ; libretto by W. S. Gilbert, music by Arthur Sullivan.   Produced at the Opéra-Comique Theatre, Nov. 17, 1877.

SORDINO, Mute,[1] or Damper (Fr. Sourdine ; Ger. Dämpfer).   The violin Sordino is described below.

In the pianoforte the contrivance is called in English the damper.   The first pianofortes, as we find Cristofori's and Silbermann's, were made without stops.   In course of time a practice common with the harpsichord was followed in the pianoforte, and led the way to the now indispensable pedals.

The first stops were used to raise the dampers ; and by two brass knobs on the player's left hand the dampers could be taken entirely off the strings in two divisions, bass and treble. C. P. E. Bach, in his Versuch, makes few references to the pianoforte ; but in the edition of 1797 he remarks (p. 268) that the undamped register of the Fortepiano is the most agreeable, and that, with due care, it is the most charming of keyed instruments for improvising ('fantasiren').   The higher treble of the piano is not now damped.   These short strings vibrate in unison with the overtones of deeper notes, and, as a distinguished pianoforte-maker has said, give life to the whole instrument.[2]   The terms 'Senza sordini' and 'Con sordini' applied to the damper stops were used exclusively by Beethoven in his earlier sonatas.   He did not use the now familiar 'Ped.' or 'Pedal,' because the pedal was of recent introduction, and was less commonly employed than the stops, which every little square piano then had.   The 'Genouillière,' or knee-pedal, replaced the damper stops in the German Grands.   For the Italian words signifying Without and With dampers the signs ⊕ and ✳ were substituted by Steibelt, and eventually became fixed as the constant equivalents. The oldest dated square piano existing, one of Zumpe's of 1766, has the damper stops ; as to the Genouillière, Mozart tells us (letter, October 1777) how Stein had one in his improved Grand, and M. Mahillon's Stein of 1780, or thereabouts, accordingly has one.   There is one in Mozart's Walther Grand at Salzburg, and in each of the two Huhn (Berlin) Grands of 1790, or earlier, preserved at Potsdam.   The action of the Genouillière consists of two levers which descend a little below the key-bottom of the piano, and

meet opposite the knees of the player, who, pressing the levers together, by an upward thrust moves a bar which takes the whole of the dampers off the strings. [See Hipkins's History of the Pianoforte, pp. 93, 108, and 110 (footnote).]

Contemporaneous with the employment of the Genouillière was that of the piano stop (German Harfenzug, Fr. Céleste), afterwards transferred, like the dampers, to a pedal.   An interesting anonymous Louis Quinze square piano belonging to the painter M. Gosselin of Brussels had this Céleste as a stop.   Its origin is clearly the harp-stop of the harpsichord, the pieces of leather being turned over so as to be interposed between the hammers and the strings.

A note of directions for the use of the pedals prefixed to Steibelt's three sonatas, op. 35, gives an approximate date. to the use of the pedals becoming recognised, and put under the composer's direction, instead of being left entirely to the fancy of the player.   He says : 'The Author wishing to make more Variety on the Piano Forte finds it necessary to make use of the Pedals, by which alone the tones can be united, but it requires to use them with care, without which, in going from one chord to another, Discord and Confusion would result. Hereafter the Author in all his Compositions will make use of the following signs to denote the Pedals.

⊕ The Pedal which raises the dampers.

✳ The Piano Pedal.

♪ To take the foot off the Pedal that was used before.'

Steibelt's op. 35 was published in 1799, by Longman, Clementi & Co.[3]

The leather was applied in one length to mute the strings more effectually, and was then called in French 'Sourdine.'   John Broadwood was the first to put the 'sordin'—as it is called in his patent of 1783—upon a foot-pedal ; he put the dampers upon a pedal at the same time, and for fifty years the pedal-foot was cloven, to divide the dampers into bass and treble sections, as the stops had previously been divided for the same purpose.   The use of the pianissimo mute was indicated by the Italian word 'Sordino.'   Mr. Franklin Taylor has pointed out to the writer the use of this term in the sense of a mute as late as Thalberg's op. 41 (Ashdown's edition).

The 'Verschiebung,' or shifting pedal, for shifting the hammer first to two strings and then to one (una corda), ultimately gained the day over the muted pedals or stops.   The effect of the 'una corda' was charming, and is expressly indicated by Beethoven in his G major Concerto, in op. 106, etc.   The pp and ppp soft pedal in course of time shared the fate of the divided

---

[1] It will be noticed that the metaphors at the root of the Italian and English terms are deafness in one case and dumbness in the other.

[2] Even in Virdung, A.D. 1511, we find the practice of leaving sympathetic strings in the clavichords ; as he says to strengthen the resonance.

[3] Steibelt gives a description of the pedals, with his signs for them, in his Méthode de Piano, first published by Janet, Paris, 1805.   He names Clementi, Dussek, and Cramer as having adopted his signs. They differ from and are better than Adam's (Méthode de Piano du Conservatoire), also published in Paris, 1802.   Steibelt calls the 'una corda' celeste.

damper pedal ; such refinements were banished as being of small service in large rooms. In the six-pedal Viennese Grand of Nannette Stein at Windsor Castle, the 'Verschiebung' and 'Harfenzug' co-exist.[1] The latter has of late years again come forward, at first in oblique pianos that could not shift, and since more generally ; and has, to a certain extent, gained the favour of amateurs. The material used is cloth or felt. [See also the glossary of terms in Hipkins's *History of the Pianoforte*, p. 123.]   A. J. H.

Most instruments are capable of having their tone dulled for particular effects, and this is accomplished by partially preventing the vibrations by the interposition of a foreign substance. Violins are muted either by placing an ebony, xylonite, or brass instrument upon the bridge,

Violin Mute

or by slipping a coin or strip of horn between the strings above the bridge. These two means produce different results. The brass mute is so heavy as entirely to extinguish the tone, especially of a small or inferior violin, while the strip of horn sometimes produces scarcely any effect at all. A penny squeezed between the bridge and tailpiece produces just the right effect. The brass mute should be reserved as a special effect of itself. On the other hand, the mutes for the violoncello and double-bass are rarely made heavy enough, and this has given rise to the erroneous idea that mutes do not produce much effect on these instruments. The double-bass mutes used by the present writer are of brass, and weigh rather over a pound. They produce a beautiful veiled tone, and it is probable that larger patterned basses would bear even a heavier mute.

Brass instruments can be muted in three ways. The first and most effective is—as in 'stopping' a horn—the introduction of the closed hand or a rolled-up handkerchief into the bell. This raises the pitch of the instrument, but produces a good muffled tone. The second way is by inserting a pear-shaped piece of wood covered with leather into the bell, which it fits, small studs allowing a portion of the wind to pass.

[1] The remaining pedals in Nannette Stein's Grand are the 'Fagotzug,' by which a piece of card or stiff paper is brought into partial contact with the strings, and the 'Janissary' drum and triangle. See STEIN.

The tone thus produced is thin, nasal, and unpleasing. Wagner has frequently used it ('Siegfried,' Acts 1 and 2 ; 'Meistersinger,' last scene) as a comic effect, imitating the sound of a toy-trumpet. The third means produces a very distant-sounding, but still more nasal quality of tone, and is known to orchestral players as the 'coffee-pot effect.' It is obtained by allowing the sound to issue from the small end of a small double cone of metal, styled the 'echo attachment.' A good cornet player can, by these three devices, produce on his instrument exact imitations of the horn, oboe, and bagpipe.

Trombones, Tubas, etc., can also be muted in the same way, and the effect of the former has been tried in Richard Strauss's 'Heldenleben.' For muting by means of the hand in the bell, see HORN, vol. ii. p. 431a.

It has been frequently stated that 'Berlioz muted the Clarinet by enveloping the bell in a bag of chamois leather,' and that 'The Oboes in Handel's time were muted by placing a ball of cotton wool in the bell.' But these devices only affect the bottom note of the instrument, as all others issue from the holes and not from the bell at all.

The laying of any substance, even a handkerchief, on the kettledrums is sufficient to check the vibrations and produce a muffled effect. In the 'Dead March' the big drum is usually beaten enveloped in its cover.

Various means have been used to obtain *sourdine* effects from voices. Berlioz, like Gossec before him [see vol. ii. p. 203], has employed the device of a chorus in a room behind the orchestra ('L'Enfance du Christ'), and the interposition of a veil, or curtain ('Lélio'). He has also suggested that the chorus should hold their music before their mouths, or should sing with their backs to the audience. One important effect, however, deserves more attention than it has received. French composers, especially Gounod, are fond of the device called *à bouche fermée*. The choir *hums* an accompaniment without words, keeping the mouth quite, or nearly, closed. But composers have lost sight of the fact that several totally distinct effects may be thus produced, and they usually confuse the matter still more by writing the sound 'A-a-a' underneath the music—just the very sound which can *not* possibly be produced by a closed mouth. The effect would be better designated by writing the exact sound intended, and consequently the exact position of the mouth. For instance, by closing the lips entirely, the sound of 'n' or 'm' may be hummed *through the nose*. By opening the lips slightly either of the vowel-sounds may be used, each making a distinct effect.   F. C.

SORIANO (or SURIANO, SURIANUS, or SURIANI), FRANCESCO, was born at Rome in 1549, and at the age of fifteen entered the choir at S. John Lateran. After the breaking of his voice he became a pupil of Montanari, then of G. M. Nanini, and lastly of Palestrina. After this his fame went on always increasing. In 1581 we find him Maestro di cappella at S. Ludovico dei Francesi ; in 1583 he was at the Court of Mantua ; in 1587 at S. Maria Maggiore ; in 1599 at S. John Lateran. He returned, however, to S. Maria Maggiore, and in 1603 made his final step to the head of the choir of S. Peter's. He retired in June 1620, died about 1621, and was buried at S. Maria Maggiore. Soriano published his first work in 1581, a book of madrigals, a 5. This was followed by a second in 1592 ; by a book of motets, a 8, 1597 ; by a second book of madrigals, a 4, 1601, 1602 ; by a book of masses for 4, 5, and 6 voices, 1609 ; by a collection of 110 canons on 'Ave Maris Stella,' 1610, and by a second book of psalms and motets, a 8, 12, and 16, 1616. His last work was a Magnificat and Passione, a 4, Rome, 1619, containing his portrait. A complete list of his works is given in the Quellen-Lexikon. He will be remembered longest for having arranged Palestrina's Missa Papae Marcelli for 8 voices. The Passion already mentioned, a Magnificat and five Antiphons, are included in Proske's 'Musica Divina,' vols. iii. and iv., and two Masses in the 'Selectus novus.'   G.

SORIANO-FUERTES, MARIANO, born in Murcia, 1817, a Spanish composer and litté-rateur, according to Riemann was the son of a musician, and so determined in his pursuit of music that though forced into a cavalry regiment he left it for the musical career. His works were many, and in many spheres ; in 1841 he founded a periodical, Iberia musical y literaria ; in 1843 became teacher in the Conservatoire at Madrid ; in 1844 director of the Lyceums at Cordova, Seville, and Cadiz ; conductor of the opera at Seville, Cadiz, and (1852) at Barcelona, where he founded the Gaceta Musical Barcelonesa in 1860. During this period he wrote several 'Zarzuelas' or operettas ; but it is from his literary works that he will derive his chief fame —Musica Arabo-Española (1853) ; History of Spanish Music from the Phœnicians down to 1850 (4 vols., 1855-59) ; Memoir on the Choral Societies of Spain ; and Spain, Artistic and Industrial, in the Exposition of 1867. Soriano died at Madrid, March 26, 1880.   G.

SOSTENUTO, 'sustained' ; a direction which has of late come to be used with a considerable degree of ambiguity. It originally signified that the notes were to be held for their full value, and was thus equivalent to tenuto ; but in music of the modern 'romantic' school it very often has the same meaning as meno mosso, or something between that and ritenuto—i.e. the passage so marked is to be played at a uniform rate of decreased speed until the words a tempo occur. No precise rule can be given for its interpretation, as its use varies with different masters, and even in different works by the same master.   M.

SOSTINENTE PIANOFORTE. The term implies a pianoforte capable of producing a sustained sound, such as that of the organ, harmonium, or violin. It must, however, be borne in mind that by giving the pianoforte this power of sustaining sound, the special character of the instrument is transformed, and in point of fact the 'sostinente' pianoforte is a pianoforte in name only. It is the rapid diminution of the fugitive tone that raises the ordinary pianoforte to that ideal terrain wherein it finds one of its chief excellences, the prerogative of freedom from cloying ; the emotion of the hearer entering actively into the appreciation of its unsubstantial and ethereal tones. Under the head of PIANO-VIOLIN the Hurdy-gurdy is referred to as the germ of sostinente keyed instruments ; and allied to the harpsichord we next meet with it in the Gambenwerk of Hans Haydn of Nuremberg, dating about 1610. The Lyrichord, patented by Roger Plenius in London in 1741, demands notice as being a harpsichord strung with wire and catgut, made on the sostinente principle, and actuated by moving wheels instead of the usual quills, so that the bow of the violin and the organ were imitated. There is no specification to the patent, but a magazine article of 1755, in the possession of the writer, gives a drawing and complete description of the instrument, which was otherwise remarkable for sustaining power by screws, springs, and balanced tension weights for tuning ; for silver covering to the bass strings, like the largest 'Bass-violins' ; for the use of iron to counteract the greater pull of the octave-strings (in the drawing there are apparently four iron bars connecting the wrest-plank and sound-board, thus anticipating the later introduction of steel arches in grand pianofortes for similar service) ; and lastly for the Swell obtained by dividing the lid or cover into two parts, one of which is movable up and down by means of a pedal governed by the foot of the player, a practice followed by Kirkman in his harpsichords, and perhaps by Shudi, until he introduced, about 1766, his important improvement of the Venetian Swell. Another patent of Plenius, in 1745, added the 'Welch harp,' or buff stop (in his patent by a pedal), to the instrument. We have thus dwelt upon the Lyrichord because as an ingenious combination of inventions its importance cannot be gainsaid.[1] Another 'Sostinente' harpsichord was the 'Celestina' of Adam Walker, patented in London in 1772. An important 'Sostinente' instrument was the 'Claviol' or 'Finger-keyed Viol,' the invention of Dr. John Isaac Hawkins of Bordertown, New Jersey, U.S.A., an Englishman by birth, who invented the real upright pianoforte. This upright piano (called 'portable

---

[1] Plenius is said to have been the first to attempt to make a pianoforte in England.

grand ') and the 'Claviol,' which was in form like a cabinet piano, with ringbow mechanism for the sostinente, were introduced to the public in a concert at Philadelphia, by the inventor, June 21, 1802. There is a description of the Claviol in *Rees's Cyclopœdia*, 1819, and also in the *Mechanic's Magazine* for 1845, No. 1150, p. 123. About Hawkins himself there are interesting particulars in *Scribner's Magazine* (1880), in an article on 'Bordertown and the Bonapartes.' Hawkins was in England in 1813 and 1814, exhibiting his Claviol, and in the latter year complained of his idea being appropriated by others through the expiration of his patent. He afterwards lived here and was a prominent member of the Institution of Civil Engineers. Isaac Mott's 'Sostinente Piano Forte,' patented by him in 1817, was a further development of the idea, and is fully described in the patent, No. 4098. Mott claimed the power to increase or diminish the tone at will ; and by rollers acting on silken threads, set in action by a pedal, the 'sostinente' was brought into action or stopped. Mott's instrument had some success, he being at the time a fashionable pianoforte-maker. See PIANO-VIOLIN and MELO-PIANO.[1] [See also p. 95 of Hipkins's *History of the Pianoforte.*]   A. J. H.

SOTO, FRANCISCO, born 1534, at Langa in Spain, entered the college of the Pope's Chapel, June 8, 1562. He was a friend of St. Philip Neri, and in December 1575 took the direction of the music in the Oratory founded by him. He also founded the first Carmelite convent in Rome. He published the 3rd and 4th books of Laudi Spirituali (1588, 1591) in continuation of the two edited by G. Animuccia, and died as Dean of the Pope's Chapel, Sept. 25, 1619.   G.

SOTTO VOCE, 'under the voice,' in an undertone ; a direction of frequent occurrence in instrumental as well as vocal music.   M.

SOUBIES, ALBERT, born in Paris, May 10, 1846, was educated at the Lycée Louis-le-Grand, but, after studying for the legal profession, music was too strong for him, and he entered the Conservatoire, where he studied under Savard, Bazin, and Guilmant. His first essay as a writer on music, a career in which he has had remarkable success, was in the continuation of the *Almanach Duchesne* under the title of *Almanach des Spectacles* (1874 onwards). His principal work has been a history of music in a series of small volumes arranged under different countries : *Allemagne et Russie* occupy two volumes ; *L'Espagne*, three more ; *Le Portugal, La Hongrie, et la Bohême*, three ; *Suisse* and *Hollande*, one each ; *Belgique*, two ; *États Scandinaves*, three ; and *Îles Britanniques*, two. *Les Grands Théâtres Parisiens* is in four volumes, dealing respectively with the Comédie Française,

the Opéra (for sixty-seven years), the Opéra-Comique (for sixty-nine years), and the Théâtre Lyrique, 1851-70. *Une Première par jour* was crowned, with other of Soubies's works, by the Académie, and other non-musical books are in his list. He has collaborated with Ch. Malherbe in the *Histoire de l'Opéra-Comique (1840-1887)*, *Mélanges sur Richard Wagner, L'Œuvre dramatique de Richard Wagner*, and in a *Précis de l'histoire de l'Opéra-Comique*, the last under the name of B. de Lomagne. He has written for the *Soir* since 1876, and for the *Revue de l'Art dramatique* since 1885. He is a frequent contributor to the *Guide Musical*, the *Ménestrel*, etc.   G. F.

SOUND-BOARD or SOUNDING-BOARD. I. In the organ the sound-board is the upper portion of the wind-chest, upon which the pipes stand.

II. In the pianoforte the sound-board is usually called the BELLY. See vol. i. p. 293*b*.

SOUND-HOLES, or *ff* HOLES (Fr. *ouïe* ; Ital. *occhi* ; Ger. *Schalloch*). The two apertures in the form of italic *f*'s which face one another in the bellies of violins—and the instruments of that family—on either side of the bridge. These exercise a powerful influence upon the tone, regulating as they do the entire system of vibrations of the various parts of the instruments, by governing the amount of air which is contained within the body. Scientific investigation has proved that the best tonal results are arrived at when the contained mass of air in the body of a violin answers to 512 vibrations (*i.e.* answering to middle C), and for this reason that standard of vibration has been generally adopted by all good violin-makers since the days of Stradivarius, whose violins are perfect examples of this system. The principle, however, cannot be applied by way of extension to the viola, or violoncello, a fact which was proved by those large violoncellos made by 17th century *luthiers* in accordance with violin measurements by mere augmentation, all of which have had to be reduced in size. According to M. Savart (*Mémoire sur la Construction des Instruments à Cordes et à Archet*) the pitch of the viola being a fifth below that of the violin, and an octave above the violoncello, the instrument should contain a mass of air answering to 341·33 vibrations (*f* : a system, however, not generally followed) ; and the violoncello, being pitched a fifth plus an octave below the violin, should give 170·66 vibrations (F)—neither of which, again, can be said to be arbitrary laws. The form of the *ff* holes and their position are therefore matters of great importance. Savart at first questioned the necessity of curved sound-holes, but his later experiments proved that any deviation from the *f* form, where the belly was arched, had a disastrous effect upon the tone of the instrument. He also tested the effect of dispensing with one sound-hole by covering it

<hr>

[1] Mr. R. B. Prosser of the Patent Office has supplied the references to the Claviol.

with paper, with the result that the tone was immediately diminished, and the note given by the contained mass of air was flattened. A similar effect is produced when the holes are too small ; but when they are too large the vibratory note of the air rises. Practically the proportions of the *ff* holes must depend upon the dimensions, thickness, height, etc., of the instrument, and they must be cut in strict relation to these conditions.

Although an established form and position of the sound-holes did not exist until the latter half of the 16th century, still there are evidences that sound-holes were employed in very early times. The monochord attributed to Ptolemy (*circa* A.D. 139) was apparently provided with a circular sound-hole, like some of the guitars depicted in ancient Egyptian frescoes, which show small sound-holes pierced in the upper table, on either side of the strings. To-day those presumptive descendants of the original inhabitants of Egypt—the Berbers—monopolise a musical instrument called the 'kissar,' considered to be of very ancient origin, which has a circular sound-hole placed in the now generally adopted position. In the 9th century we find a figure from the MS. found by Gerber in the Monastery of St. Blasius in the Black Forest, and copied by him, which shows (Fig. 1) C-shaped sound-holes well placed, but

from that time to the 16th century pictorial and sculptural representations afford evidence that the various small predecessors of the viol properly so called depended entirely upon the whim of their makers for the shape of their sound-holes. Some of the viol's forerunners had as many as six sound-holes pierced in their diminutive bodies, others had four, and others two, but none among them approached the *f* form finally adopted by the violin-makers proper. At the beginning of the 16th century, makers began to show

FIG. 1.

more dexterity in cutting the sound-holes, and even in the previous century some Italian makers had already come very near to realising their correct position. A glance at Fig. 2, reproduced from an early woodcut representation of a seven-stringed viol which ornaments the front page of the 'First Book of Songs' by 'Aurelius Augurellus Ariminensis' (Verona,

1491), a copy of which is in the library of the British Museum, will corroborate this statement. During the first half of the 16th century the woodcut illustrations of bow instruments which appeared in the works of Sebastian Virdung (*Musica getutscht*, 1511), of Martin Agricola (*Musica Instrumentalis*, 1528), and of Hans Gerle (*Musica Teusch*, 1532), show rebecs with the C-shaped sound-holes on either side of the strings—sometimes turned inward and sometimes outward ; also viols with a ' rose ' in the centre and the C-shaped sound-holes set high up in the upper bouts. Far in advance of the German work was that of the contemporary Italians as revealed by Ganassi del Fontego (Venice, 1542), in his *Regola Rubertina*, wherein graceful viols with large *f*-shaped sound-holes appear, and later in the century the still more elegant curves portrayed in

FIG. 2.

FIG. 3.

Domenichino's bass, in his picture of St. Cecilia (Fig. 3). Another form of sound-hole prevalent among viol-makers and extensively employed by them for the viola da gamba is that shown in Fig. 4, known as the 'flaming sword.' Generally speaking, the true era of the *f*-shaped sound-hole began with Andreas Amati (Cremona, about 1520-80) and Gasparo da Salò (Brescia, 1542-1609), and was the outcome of the ceaseless pursuit of perfection which marked the period of the Renaissance. The C-shaped (Fig. 2) sound-holes, it was observed, lacked grace, so makers began to twist them about until they

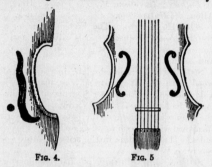

FIG. 4.   FIG. 5

assumed the greater elegance of form. An example of this progression is shown in Fig. 5, which is taken from a tenor viol on one of the carved screens of Cremona Cathedral, dating from the first part of the 16th century. This was a distinct step in the right direction ; but neither Gasparo da Salò nor Andreas Amati could quite throw aside the C-shape, and the first employed that form for some of his grand tenors. Gasparo da Salò's *ff* holes are very long and pointed, stiff in appearance and parallel in position, while Andreas Amati's lack symmetry by reason of their being cut too wide. Gasparo's pupil Paolo Maggini (Brescia, 1590-1640), according to Savart's experiments, committed the same error, the muffled tone of his instruments being due to this cause, the contained volume of air within the body of his violins answering to the vibrations of middle D. The brothers Amati and Jerome's son Nicolas— who added a touch of boldness to his father's *ff*— put grace of design into their sound-holes, but robbed their violins of power by placing them too far apart on the belly. The fallacies inherent to these first attempts were discovered and rectified by Antonius Stradivarius (Cremona, 1644-1737), whose graceful, converging *ff* holes are acknowledged to be perfect in form, position, proportion, and intent. Although Stradivari had an ingenious method for ascertaining the correct place for his *ff* holes on the belly of the violin, and fixed upon the main features of these, yet on no two of his instruments can the *ff* holes be called identical. The spontaneous feeling and charm which characterised the work of his predecessors, who knew neither template nor pattern, or at least did not employ them, were by him preserved with an added touch of necessary exactitude. He realised the efficacy of flatter surfaces and the influence exercised by the contained mass of air, and made his *ff* holes to suit these ruling factors with a resulting balance of parts impossible to surpass. Deviations from the form or position established by Stradivari have never proved satisfactory.

What Joseph Guarnerius gained in power by his more heroic form of sound-hole—magnificent as it is in many cases—was at the sacrifice of the tone of the G string. The E A D of his violins are sonorous and brilliant, but the fourth string suffers from combined effects due to the excessive thickness of the plates, and the size of the sound-holes. In these days the form and position of the sound-holes have reached a point of almost mechanical perfection. With the exception of the attempted innovations made by Savart and Chanot, the present *f* shape has retained its position unchallenged for quite 300 years. Most makers now content themselves with copying the pattern of some one of the great masters, and at the large violin manufactories at MITTENWALD in Saxony and MIRECOURT the imitation is mechanical in the extreme. See the article VIOLIN-MAKING.

Savart, *Mémoire sur la Construction des Instruments à Cordes et à Archet* ; Gallay, *Les Luthiers Italiens* ; Vidal, *Les Instruments à Archet* ; Yussopoff, *Luthomonographie* ; Mordret, *Luthérie Artistique* ; Maugin et Maigne, *Nouveau Manuel complet du Luthier* ; P. Davidson, *The Violin*; Hart, *The Violin*; Hill, *Antonio Stradivari* ; Heron-Allen, *Violin-making* ; *Violin Monthly Magazine*, No. 5 (edited by J. M. Fleming) ; Gallay, *Les Ancêtres du Violon* ; Gerber, *Musical Lexikon* ; von Lutgendorff, *Die Geigen und Lautenmacher* ; Bachmann, *Le Violon*.   E. H-A.

SOUND-POST (Fr. *âme* ; Ital. *anima* ; Ger. *Stimmstock*). A small pillar of pine wood which stands vertically within the body of the violin and the other instruments of that family. Originally it was a mere structural precaution, brought about by the introduction of the higher pitch, and consequent greater pressure upon the belly of the instrument ; but it is in reality the centre round which the vibrations of the body of the instrument focus, and from which they proceed. This important tone-producing factor is made either of fine-grained Swiss pine or spruce wood, and it is placed so that the fibres of its wood run at right angles to those of the belly. Closely fitting against the arching of the back and belly of the instrument, it retains its position under, and slightly behind, the right foot of the bridge, and is kept in position solely by the pressure of the strings upon the belly. Its length depends upon the depth between the back and belly of the instrument for which it is intended, and its diameter is subject to slight alteration, according to the modelling. If the sound-post is too slight, the tone of the instrument in which it is placed will be relatively thin, and the opposite effect is produced where it is too thick. The correct position to be assigned to the sound-post is an important matter, as the smallest variation of position materially alters the tone. The extreme range over which it may be moved is comprised within an area of about a quarter of an inch. As a general rule, when the vibrations of the back of an instrument are sluggish and require to be accelerated before the highest quality of tone of which it is capable can be produced, the sound-post should be brought nearer the bridge ; in a contrary condition of things it should be moved farther away ; and high-built instruments require the sound-post nearer the bridge than do those of flatter model.

The interesting series of experiments made in connection with the sound-post by Mons. Savart, and later by Sir William Huggins, have proved the following axioms :—

(1) That the sound-post conveys the combined vibrations of the belly and sides to the back of the instrument, controlling the action of these parts, and bringing them into unison and equilibrium with the contained mass of air in the body of the instrument.

(2) That the material of which the sound-post is made influences the tone of the instrument, as was evidenced by Sir W. Huggins's introduction of lead, and of sealing-wax, into the centre of the post, whereby the volume of tone was diminished greatly. A sheet of india-rubber firmly wedged in at the upper and lower end of the sound-post, when in position, influenced the tone in a still more disastrous manner.

(3) That the sound-post placed directly under the right foot of the bridge diminished the intensity of tone, rendering it as meagre in quality as it is when the sound-post is dispensed with ; placed under the left foot of the bridge, on the same side as the bass-bar, similarly unsatisfactory results were produced.

The object of the sound-post, therefore, is not so much to convey the vibrations of any of the sections of the violin one to another, as to render the vibrations regular and consonant, and experiment has proved that these results are best obtained by placing the sound-post slightly behind the right foot of the bridge. This conclusion has been borne out by the fact that trial has shown the fallacy and inefficacy of all innovations such (to name but a few) as M. Petizeau's hollow glass sound-post (brought before the Academy of Sciences in Paris a few years ago) ; Haussel's broad, flat, thin sound-post (described in the *Allgemeine Musikalische Zeitung*, 1881 (p. 75) ; and Mr. P. Davidson's sound-post with drilled holes, together with such patents as David Herring's sound-post made elastic, so as to double the amplitude of the vibrations (No. 18,028) ; Simoutre's round-legged or oval sound-post (No. 11,936), and others to be found in the *Abridgements of Specifications relating to Music and Musical Instruments*, published by the Commissioners of Patents.

Huggins, Sir W., LL.D., F.R.S., *On the Function of the Sound-post* (1883) ; Savart, Felix, *Mémoire sur la Construction des Instru-*

ments *à Archet* ; Migge, Otto, *The Secret of the Celebrated Italian Violin-makers* ; Gallay, J., *Les Luthiers Italiens* ; Maugin, J. C., *Manuel de Luthier* ; Davidson, P., *The Violin* ; Heron-Allen, *Violin-making*.   E. H-A.

SOUPIR (a sigh). The French name for a crotchet rest. A quaver rest is called *un demi-soupir* ; a semiquaver ditto, *un quart de soupir*, and so on.   G.

SOURDINE. An obsolete instrument of wood, with a small cylindrical bore, played with a double reed. The larger instruments of this family had two parallel tubes arranged much in the same way as those of the bassoon, and were furnished with several keys, as well as six finger-holes. [For Sourdine in the sense of Mute see SORDINO.]   D. J. B.

SOUSA, JOHN PHILIP, popular bandmaster and composer, especially of marches, was born in Washington, D.C. (U.S.), on Nov. 6, 1856. In 1877 he was a violinist in the orchestra which Offenbach led on his visit to the U.S., and soon after became conductor of travelling troupes. In 1880 he enlisted in the service of the U.S., and was appointed leader of the band of the United States Marine Corps, developing great proficiency among the musicians and laying the foundations for the eminence which he achieved throughout America and in European lands with his own organisation later. He resigned from the service and organised his band in 1892. Facilities which his official post brought him enabled him to compile a useful collection of musical pieces entitled ' National, Patriotic and Typical Airs of All Countries,' which he dedicated to the Secretary of the Navy. He is the composer also of a number of comic operettas, some of which had considerable vogue, though his reputation rests on his marches.   H. E. K.

SPACE. The stave is made up of five lines and four spaces. The spaces in the treble stave, counting upwards, make the word FACE, which is useful as a *memoria technica* for beginners.   G.

SPAGNOLETTI, P. This violinist, who held the post of leader of the King's Theatre orchestra for nearly thirty years, was born at Cremona in 1768 (not, as the *Quellen-Lexikon* says, in 1761), and died in London on Sept. 23, 1834. No complete biographical notice of Spagnoletti has apparently appeared hitherto, but according to some MS. notes sent by the late Mr. George Bently—who was acquainted with some of Spagnoletti's relatives—to Dr. T. Lamb Phipson in 1877, this artist's real name was Paolo Diana. At the age of twelve he was introduced to the Director of the Naples Conservatorio as a very promising pupil, whereupon the director placed an elaborate composition before the young aspirant, who, it is said, astonished his auditors by glancing at the printed sheet for a few moments, and then playing the piece through with the music turned upside down before him. About 1802 he was

brought to London by the celebrated tenor
Vagnoni, who heard him play at Milan, and
shortly after, he was engaged as second violin
in the King's Theatre orchestra.   In 1812 he
was leading the orchestra at the Pantheon, where
Italian Opera was being played, under the
patronage of many of the nobility who had become disgusted with the management of the
King's Theatre.   The following year with the
establishment of the Philharmonic, Spagnoletti
became one of the first thirty-eight Associates
of that Society, and led a Septuor with Vaccari,
Lindley, Hill, Petuder, Cramer, and Holmes,
at one of the first of the season's concerts on
April 19, 1813.   In 1817 he was leader of the
King's Theatre orchestra, and his services were
requisitioned by nearly every important orchestral society in London.   At the Lenten Oratorios
at the King's Theatre, at the Ancient Concerts,
at the Philharmonic, at the Royal Academy of
Music concerts in the Hanover Square Rooms,
at numberless benefit concerts during the season,
Spagnoletti invariably led the orchestra, besides
which he frequently led Quartets at the Philharmonic, and gave a benefit concert in the
Argyll Rooms each year.   Frequent notices of
his performances, 'which were characterised by
an excellent and spirited attack,' appear in
the *Harmonicon* between the years 1823 and
1833.   When Paganini came to London in
1831, the management proposed to engage
another leader for his concerts ; but when the
Genoese virtuoso heard of this, he immediately
demanded that Spagnoletti should be engaged
for all his performances, accompanying his
request with a well-merited compliment on his
abilities.   This occasioned some unpleasant
feeling between the leader and Laporte, especially
when the latter underpaid Spagnoletti for his
services at thirteen Paganini concerts.   A law-
suit ensued, and a letter from Spagnoletti on
the subject appeared in the *Harmonicon* of that
year.   Spagnoletti was of a modest, retiring
disposition, and so ardently devoted to his art
that he invariably put it before all private
interests, the result of which was his acknowledged pre-eminence as an orchestral leader rather
than as a virtuoso.   One of his last appearances—
if not his last—was at Mr. Alsager's 'Queen's
Square Select Society' on March 28, 1834, some
months before his death, when he led the first
performance of Cherubini's 'Requiem' in England.   For several years he had been in a delicate
state of health, owing to two severe strokes of
paralysis, and it was a third seizure which
deprived him of speech and the use of one side
of his body, and to which he eventually
succumbed.   He was buried beside Madame
Spagnoletti in Brompton Cemetery, but all
trace of the grave-stone which marked the
place where he rested has disappeared.   Spagnoletti's favourite violin was a Joseph Guarnerius
of excellent tone but poor preservation.   It

eventually became the property of the late Sir
Howard Elphinstone, V.C., at one time comp-
troller to the household of H.R.H. the Duke
of Edinburgh.   An engraving of Spagnoletti and
Lindley was published by Sharp, after a picture
by Mrs. Wigley of Shrewsbury, in 1836.   He
composed various rather unimportant violin
pieces and some songs.—Parke, *Musical Memoirs*;
Mason Clarke, *Biog. Dict. Fiddlers, Musical
World*, vol. ii. ; James T. Brown, *Biog. Dict.
Mus.*, *Quellen-Lexikon, The Harmonicon* (from
1823 to 1841), *Musical World* (1836) ; W.
Gardiner, *Music and Friends, Musical Recollections of the last Half Century*, chap. iv. vol. i. ; T.
Lamb Phipson, *Celebrated Violinists, The Times*,
and *Morning Post*, Sept. 26, 1834.   E. H-A.

SPARK, WILLIAM, Mus.D., son of a lay-vicar
of Exeter Cathedral, was born at Exeter, Oct. 28,
1823.   He became a chorister there, and in
1840 was articled for five years to Dr. S. Sebastian Wesley.   On Wesley's leaving Exeter for the
Parish Church, Leeds, his pupil went with him,
and soon became deputy-organist of the parish
church, and organist of the churches of Chapel-
town and St. Paul's successively.   He was
next chosen organist to Tiverton, Devon, and
Daventry, Northampton ; and on Wesley's removal to Winchester, in 1850, was appointed to
St. George's Church, Leeds.   His activity in
Leeds, outside his own parish, was remarkable.
Within a year of his appointment he founded
the Leeds Madrigal and Motet Society, and the
People's Concerts, held in the Town Hall, just
then built.   [Municipal business had long required a new Town Hall, the central portion of
which has ever since served the city for its chief
concert-room.]   The organ was built by Gray &
Davison, from the designs of Henry Smart and
Spark.   The hall was opened April 1, 1859, and
after a severe competition Spark was elected the
Borough organist, a post he held until his death,
which took place in Leeds on June 16, 1897.
He took his degree as Doctor of Music at Dublin
in 1861.   In 1869 he started the 'Organists'
Quarterly Journal' (Novello).   It was followed
by the *Practical Choir-master* (Metzler), and in
1881 by a biography of Henry Smart (Reeves,
8vo).   [*Musical Memoirs* (1888), and *Musical
Reminiscences* (1892), contain an amusing
picture of his time, and he did good work
in many Yorkshire towns as a lecturer on
music.]   He also published three cantatas,
various anthems, services, glees, and other
compositions.

[His brother, Frederick Robert Spark, born
Feb. 26, 1831, became editor and publisher of
the *Leeds Express* in the fifties.   He was
officially connected with the Leeds Festival
from its commencement in 1858, being honorary
secretary from 1877.   After the festival of 1907
he retired from active service, and was presented
with a portrait of himself painted by Sir
George Reid.   He is joint author, with Joseph

Bennett, of *A History of the Leeds Musical Festivals 1858-89* (1892). G.; additions by F. K.

SPEAKER-KEYS. On wind instruments of the reed family, certain keys are fitted to facilitate the production of harmonics. These are known as 'speaker-keys.' Two are usually supplied on the oboe, and one on the clarinet, giving octaves on the one instrument and twelfths on the other. These keys open small holes by which the continuity of the air-column is broken, and the setting up of a 'loop,' or point of least variation of pressure, is made easy. The theory of the action of speaker-keys is of much interest in acoustics, but would require more space for exposition than can be allowed in this work.   D. J. B.

SPEAKING-LENGTH. The pitch of the ordinary open flue-pipe on the organ is chiefly determined or controlled by the length of the portion above the mouth of the pipe, which is called the 'speaking-length.' Instances, however, occur in which the speaking-length differs from the true open flue length. See STOPPED PIPE, HARMONIC STOPS, and DIAPASONS. T. E.

SPECIFICATION. The working specification of an organ consists of a detailed description of the stops, materials, pipes, action movements, etc., and the method of procedure requiring to be followed in building the instrument. It is usual to submit the specifications of an organ-builder to an organist or musical expert for his approval.   T. E.

SPECIMENS, DR. CROTCH'S. An interesting collection of musical examples having for its title: *Specimens of various styles of music referred to in a course of lectures read at Oxford and London and adapted to keyed instruments by William Crotch*, 3 vols. folio, London, Robt. Birchall for the author. The lectures themselves were published separately in octavo, and were delivered in 1800-4 and 1820. The first volume of this music was issued by subscription shortly before 1807. The second is dated in the preface 1808, and the third came out a little later. The first volume is probably of the greatest general interest. It consists of 354 melodies of different nations, some published for the first time, and others gathered together from scattered sources. There are a number of Scandinavian, Russian, Chinese, East Indian, Native American airs, and the like. The Old English, Welsh, Scotch, and Irish tunes are mainly from early printed copies. The contents of the other volumes are given below; they are what Crotch states to be 'Scientific music, by which is to be understood such as was composed with a view to harmony.' They are taken from MSS. and scarce printed works, and comprise that early Church music. In the work Dr. Crotch was greatly assisted by a Mr. Malchair, a clever musician and equally gifted water-colour artist, who then resided at Oxford. Dr. Crotch was at that time Professor of Music at the University. The Folk-Song Society has lately become possessed of a very interesting MS. volume of airs noted by Malchair. It was originally one of a series, and shows how deeply Crotch was indebted to Malchair for his 'Specimens.' Malchair seems to have been very learned in national music.

The prefaces to the volumes, besides pointing out from where the specimens were obtained, are otherwise of interest.

VOLUME I.

Symphony to Sommi Dei. Handel.	Italian National Music, 1 example.
Symphony to Jealousy. Handel.	Swiss National Music, 2 examples.
Part of Overture to Ifigénie. Gluck.	German National Music, 8 examples.
Moses and the Children of Israel. Handel.	Spanish National Music, 15 examples.
How excellent (opening). Do.	Polish National Music, 4 examples.
Who is like unto Thee. Do.	Scandinavian National Music, 5 examples.
He rebuked, and He led them. Do.	Norwegian National Music, 21 examples.
Menuet in Berenice. Do.	Danish National Music, 1 example.
Sonata for harpsichord (D). D. Scarlatti.	Russian Music, 16 examples.
Sanctus. O. Gibbons.	Turkish Music, 10 examples.
Allegretto, F (Symphony). Haydn.	Chinese Music, 5 examples.
Jewish Music, 5 examples.	East Indian Tunes, 32 examples.
Irish Music, 60 examples.	Music of North America, 6 examples.
Scotch Music, 76 examples.	
Welsh Music, 42 examples.	
Old English Music, 37 examples.	
French National Music, 20 examples.	

VOLUME II.

VARIOUS STYLES.	
Ambrosian Chant, A.D. 384.	Single Chant. T. Purcell.
Plain Chant. Guido (1022).	Aria, Opri il fato. Anon.
Other Harmonies. Do.	Do. No non amero. Do.
Harmony. Franco.	Do. Due vaghe pupille. Do.
Chant. Josquin des Prés.	Do. Del tuo cor tempri. Do.
1st Psalm O. V. Martin Luther.	Do. Se tu credi. Do.
38th Psalm O. V.	Do. Tanto basti per far. Do.
81st Psalm O. V.	Do. Bella bocca di cinabro. Do.
111th Psalm O. V. French Tune.	Do. Foglio lieve. Do.
I will exalt Thee. Tye.	Do. Tu fuggisti O caro. Do.
Lord, for Thy tender mercies' sake. Farrant.	Do. Crine vezzose. Do.
Gloria Patri. Do.	Do. Dolce Amor mi dice spera. Do.
Deposuit Potentes. Palestrina.	Do. Lusingami speranza. Do.
We have heard with our ears. Do.	Do. Begl' occhi perdonatemi. Do.
Gloria Patri. Tallis.	Do. Col freddo suo velen. Do.
'Dissi a l'amata mia.' Marenzio.	Do. Se il mio labbro. Do.
Bow thine ear. William Byrd.	Do. Gia che amor. Do.
Non nobis Domine. Do.	Do. Se versasti da tuoi lumi. Do.
Double Chant. Morley.	Do. Fantasmi orribili. Do.
Symphony, 3 flutes. Peri.	Cantata, Taci O cruda. Do.
Fate Festa al Signore. E. del Cavalieri.	Aria, Begl' occhi d' amore. Do.
Hosanna. O. Gibbons.	Do. Migravit Juda. Do.
Almighty and everlasting. Do.	Do. Gloria Patri. Dr. Child.
God is gone up. Do.	Do. Dormi dormi ben mio. Cesti.
Gloria Patri. Do.	Part of Cantata, Dite a lei. Stradella.
The Silver Swan. Do.	Cantata, Se gelose, sei Tu. Do.
Awake, Sweet Love. Dowland.	Canzonet, Chi dira. Do.
S' in ch' havro Spirto. Carissimi	Aria, Vado ben spesso. Salv. Rosa.
Movement from Amante che dite. Carissimi.	Gloria Patri. Blow.
Hodie Simon Petrus. Do.	Anthem, I will arise. Creyghton.
Et ululantes—Jephtha. Do.	Duet, Dormino l' aure estive. Durante.
Abiit ergo in montes. Do.	7th Concerto. A. Corelli.
Plorate filiæ Israel. Do.	Part of 2nd Sonata, op. 1. Do.
Deum de Deo. Do.	Fugue from the 4th Sonata, op. 3. Do.
Part of a Cantata, Fortunati miei martire. A. Scarlatti.	Part of the 7th Solo. Do.
Aria, Perche geme O tortorella. Do.	Part of the 11th Solo. Do.
Do. Voglio amar. Do.	Anthem, Out of the deep. Aldrich.
Do. Non da piu peni O cara. Do.	Do. O God, Thou hast cast us out. H. Purcell.
Do. Che piu brami. Do.	Gloria Patri (4 settings).
Do. Il seno de mia vita. Do.	Part of 1st Sonata. 1st set. Do
Cantata, Son ferito. Do.	From 6th Sonata. 1st set. Do.
Aria, Strada penara. Do.	From 9th Sonata. 2nd set. Do.
Do. Il destin. Do.	In guilty night. Do.
Do. Illustre il sangue mio. Do.	Overture to King Arthur. Do.
Do. Con l' arte del mio cor. Do.	Chaconne, before the Play. Do.
Do. Miei fidi a vendetta. Do.	Brave souls to be renowned. Do.
Do. L' innocente diffendete. Do.	Gloria Patri. Dr. Croft.
Duet, Non son piu. Do.	Qui diligit Mariam. Steffani.
Aria, Due bellissime pupille. Do.	Dixit Dominus. Leo.
Do. Il mio figlio. Do.	Part of a Mass. Pergolesi.
Part of Cantata, Che mesta horti sospiro. Do.	Euridice, dove sei (Orfeo). Do.
Motet, Domine quinque talenta. L. Rossi.	Gloria in Excelsis. Do.
Anthem, Teach me, O Lord. Rogers.	4th Psalm. Marcello.

7th Psalm. Marcello.
From Der Tod Jesu. Graun.
Te gloriosus (Te Deum). Do.
Overture to I Pellegrini. Hasse.
Le Porte noi diserra. Do. Do.
Pellegrino è l' uomo. Do. Do.
Overture to Pastor Fido. Handel.

Aria, Son confusa (Poro). Handel.
He is my God (Israel in Egypt).
　Do.
Chorus, The listening crowd. Do.
Do. May no rash intruder. Do.
Double Chorus, He gave them
　hailstones. Do.

VOLUME III.

Fugue (in E). Bach.
No. 2 of the 12 solos for the Violin.
Tartini.
Air, Pupillette vezzosette, from
Ormisda. Vinci.
Air, Infelice abbandonata. Do.
Concerto 6, op. 3. Geminiani.
Concerto 2. Ricciotti.
Part of Sonata 10. Paradies.
Requiem. Jommelli.
Chorus, Santa Speme (Passione).
　Do.
Sonata 3. Crispi.
Part of Sonata 4. Do.
Fantasia. C. P. E. Bach.
Concerto for a full Band. J. C.
Bach.
Overture to Iphigénie en Aulide.
Gluck.
Chorus, Que d'attraits.
Overture, Pierre le Grand.
Grétry.
Do. Don Quichotte. Cham-
pigny.

Overture, Toison D'Or. Vogel.
Part of Sonata 2. Vanhall.
Part of Sonata 2, op. 9. Schobert.
Minuet and trio, Sonata 1, op. 5.
　Do.
Part of Quintet 3, op. 12. Boc-
cherini.
Sonata 3, op. 23. Kozeluch.
Part of Quartet 1. 8th set.
Pleyel.
　Do. 6, op. 8. Do.
Part of Sonata 1, op. 12. Krump-
holtz.
Do. 2, op. 11. Hullmandel.
Do. 2, op. 4. Clementi.
Adagio from op. 11. Do.
Part of Sonata 4, op. 12. Do.
Recordare from Requiem. Mo-
zart.
Benedictus from Do. Do.
Overture, Le Nozze di Figaro. Do.
Part of Quartet 3, op. 76. Haydn.
Sinfonia, in Eb. Do.　F. K.

SPEYER, WILHELM, composer, was born
June 21, 1790, at Frankfort-on-the-Main,
where he died April 5, 1878. He received his
musical education at Offenbach under Thieriot
(the friend of Weber) and André. He was
already a prominent violinist when he went to
Paris in 1812, to become a pupil of Baillot, from
whose instruction and from the acquaintance of
such men as Cherubini, Boieldieu, Méhul, etc.,
he derived much benefit. Returning to Germany
afterwards, he settled down at Frankfort and
exchanged the musical profession for that of a
merchant, but continued to compose—at first
chiefly chamber music. He published string
quartets and quintets, and also violin duets,
which last became widely popular. He afterwards devoted himself chiefly to vocal music,
and it is as a writer of songs that his name is
best known. Amongst his lieder—of which
he published several hundred—many, such as
'The Trumpeter,' 'Rheinsehnsucht,' 'Die drei
Liebchen,' etc., acquired great popularity. He
also wrote vocal quartets and some choral
works.　　　　　　　　　　　　　　　　G.

SPIANATO (Ital.), level, even. A word
used by Chopin in the Andante which precedes
the Polonaise in Eb, op. 22, to denote a smooth
and equal style of performance, with but little
variety.　　　　　　　　　　　　　　F. T.

SPICCATO (Ital.), accurately 'separate,'
'distinct.' A term applied in violin-playing
to a particular vibratory style of bowing.
'Spiccato' and 'Saltato' are both explained
under the head of SPRINGING BOW.　　G.

SPIES, HERMINE, was born Feb. 25, 1857, at
the Löhnberger foundry, near Weilburg, Nassau,
daughter of the resident manager. She was
taught singing by Frau Fichtenberg at the
Conservatorium of Wiesbaden, by Sieber at
Berlin, and by Stockhausen at Frankfort. In
July 1880, while still a student, she sang at
the Mannheim Festival, and in 1882 she made
her début at a concert at Wiesbaden; in 1883

she sang in concerts at Leipzig, Berlin, etc.,
speedily establishing her reputation as an excellent mezzo-soprano or contralto singer. She
also sang in Austria, Hungary, Holland, Denmark, and Russia. On June 3, 1889, she made
her début in England at St. James's Hall at a
Richter Concert, when she sang 'Che farò' and
lieder of Schubert, Schumann, and Brahms.
She attracted immediate attention on account
of her fine voice and her excellent phrasing,
expression, and general intelligence. She confirmed her success at her two recitals in a selection of Schumann's 'Dichterliebe,' etc., also at
the Philharmonic, where she sang in English
Handel's 'Return, O God of hosts,' etc. In
1892 she married Dr. W. A. F. Hardtmuth, of
Wiesbaden, a doctor of jurisprudence, and died
there Feb. 26, of the following year, to the regret of all. She was unrivalled in her singing
the contralto part in Brahms's Rhapsody, op.
53, and in the lieder of the same composer. Her
reading of 'Vergebliches Ständchen' in particular was a perfect work of art. A memoir by
her sister, Minna Spies, appeared in 1894. A. C.

SPINA, CARL ANTON. The successor of the
Diabellis in that famous publishing house at
Vienna, which for so long stood in the Graben,
No. 1133, at the corner of the Bräunerstrasse.
He succeeded them in 1852, and was himself
succeeded by F. Schreiber in July 1872. During
that period Spina's activity showed itself especially in the publication of Schubert's works, a
mass of whose MSS. he acquired from Diabelli.
Chief among these were the Octet, Quintet in C,
Quartets in D minor, G, and Bb; the Overture
in the Italian style, those to 'Alfonso und Estrella,' 'Fierrabras,' 'Rosamunde,' with Entr'actes
in B minor and Bb; the B minor Symphony,
Sonata for PF. and Arpeggione, etc., all in score.
Herr Spina's enthusiasm for Schubert was not
that of a mere publisher, as the writer from personal experience of his kindness can testify. It
was he who allowed the Crystal Palace Company
to have copies of several of the orchestral works
for playing, long before there was sufficient public
demand to allow of their being published.　G.

SPINDLER, FRITZ, pianoforte-player and
composer for that instrument, born Nov. 24,
1817, at Wurzbach, Lobenstein, was a pupil of
F. Schneider of Dessau, and was for many years
resident in Dresden. His published works are
more than 330 in number, the greater part
brilliant drawing-room pieces, but amongst them
much teaching-music, and some works of a
graver character—trios, sonatinas, two symphonies, concerto for PF. and orchestra, etc. His
most favourite pieces are—'Wellenspiel' (op.
6); 'Schneeglöcklein' (op. 19); 'Silberquell'
(op. 74); 'Husarenritt'; six dance themes;
Transcriptions of 'Tannhäuser' and 'Lohengrin.'
He died at Niederlössnitz, near Dresden, Dec.
26, 1905.　　　　　　　　　　　　　　G.

SPINET (Fr. *Épinette, Clavicorde*; Ital.

Spinetta, Clavicordo ; Span. *Clavicordio* ; Eng. *Spinet, Virginal*). A keyed instrument, with plectra or jacks, used in the 16th, 17th, and 18th centuries ; according to Burney (*Rees's Cycl.* 1819, *Harpsichord*) ' a small harpsichord or virginal with one string to each note.' The following definitions are from Florio's *New World of Words*, 1611 :—' *Spinetta*, a kind of little spina . . . also a paire of Virginalles' ; ' *Spinettegiare*, to play upon Virginalles' ; ' *Spinetto*, a thicket of brambles or briars' (see Rimbault's *History of the Pianoforte*, 1860). We first meet with the derivation of spinet from *spina*, ' a thorn,' in Scaliger's *Poetices* (1484-1550; lib. i. cap. lxiii.). Referring to the plectra or jacks of keyed instruments, he says that, in his recollection, points of crowquill had been added to them, so that what was named, when he was a boy, ' clavicymbal' and ' harpsichord' (*sic*), was now, from these little points, named 'spinet.' [See JACK.] He does not say what substance crowquill superseded, but we know that the old cithers and other wire-strung instruments were twanged with ivory, tortoiseshell, or hard wood. (See vol. ii. p. 328.) Another origin for the name has been discovered, to which we believe that Signor Ponsicchi (*Il Pianoforte*, Florence, 1876) was the first to call attention. In a very rare book, *Conclusioni nel suono dell' organo, di D. Adriano Banchieri, Bolognese* (Bologna, 1608), is this passage :—

Spinetta riceve tal nome dall' inventore di tal forma longa quadrata, il quale fù un maestro Giovanni Spinetti, Venetiano, ed uno di tali stromenti hò veduto io alle mani di Francesco Stivori, organista della magnifica comunità di Montagnana, dentrovi questa inscrizione : JOANNES SPINETUS VENETUS FECIT. A.D. 1503.

According to this, the spinet received its name from Spinetti, a Venetian, the inventor of the oblong form, and Banchieri had himself seen one in the possession of Stivori, bearing the above inscription. M. Becker of Geneva (*Revue et Gazette musicale*, in the *Musical World*, June 15, 1878) regards this statement as totally invalidating the passage from Scaliger ; but not necessarily so, since the year 1503 is synchronous with the youth of Scaliger. The invention of the crowquill points is not claimed for Spinetti, but the form of the case—the oblong or table shape of the square piano and older clavichord, to which Spinetti adapted the plectrum instrument ; it having previously been in a trapeze-shaped case, like the psaltery, from which, by the addition of a keyboard, the instrument was derived. [See VIRGINAL ; and also for the different construction and origin of the oblong clavichord.] Putting both statements together, we find the oblong form of the Italian spinet, and the crowquill plectra, in simultaneous use about the year 1500. Before that date no record has been found. The oldest German writers, Virdung and Arnold Schlick, whose essays appeared in 1511, do not mention the spinet, but Virdung describes and gives a woodcut of the Virginal, which in Italy would have been called at that time ' spinetta,' because it was an instrument with plectra in an oblong case. Spinetti's adaptation of the case had therefore travelled to Germany, and, as we shall presently see, to Flanders and Brabant, very early in the 16th century ; whence M. Becker conjectures that 1503 represents a late date for Spinetti, and that we should put his invention back to the second half of the 15th century, on account of the time required for it to travel, and be accepted as a normal form in cities so remote from Venice. Considerable light has been thrown upon the hitherto profoundly obscure invention of the keyboard instrument subsequently known as the spinet, by that erudite searcher and scholar, M. Edmond Vander Straeten, in *La Musique aux Pays-Bas*, vol. vii. (*Les musiciens néerlandais en Espagne*, 1ʳᵉ partie), Brussels, 1885. He quotes, p. 246, from a testamentary inventory of musical instruments which had belonged to Queen Isabella, at the Alcazar of Segovia, dated 1503 : ' Dos Clavicinbanos viejos' that is to say, two old clavecins (spinets). One of her chamberlains, Sancho de Paredes (p. 248), owned in 1500 'Dos Clabiorganos'—two claviorgans or organised clavecins. In a previous inventory, dated 1480 (and earlier), the same chamberlain appears to have possessed a manicorde or clavichord with tangents. But M. Vander Straeten is enabled to give a positive date, 1387 (p. 40, *et seq.*), when John the First, King of Aragon, had heard and desired to possess an instrument called ' exaquir,' which was certainly a keyboard stringed-instrument. He describes it later on as resembling an organ but sounding with strings. The name ' exaquir' may be identified with ' l'eschuaqueil d'Angleterre,' which occurs in a poem entitled ' La Prise d'Alexandrie,' written by Guillaume de Machault in the 14th century. M. Vander Straeten inquires if this appellation can be resolved by ' échiquier' (chequers) from the black and white arrangement of the keys ? The name echiquier occurs in the romance 'Chevalier du cygne' and in the ' Chanson sur la journée de Guinegate,' a 15th-century poem, in which the poet asks to be sounded—

Orgius, harpes, naquaires, challemelles,
Bons echiquiers, guisternes, doucemelles.

The inquirer is referred to the continuance of M. Vander Straeten's notes on this interesting question, in the work above mentioned. It is here sufficient to be enabled to prove that a kind of organ sounding with strings was existing in 1387—and that clavecins were catalogued in 1503, that could be regarded as old ; also that these dates synchronise with Ambros's earliest mention of the clavicymbalum, in a MS. of 1404.

M. Vander Straeten (*La Musique aux Pays-Bas*, vol. i.) has discovered the following references to the spinet in the household accounts of Margaret of Austria :—

A ung organiste de la Ville d'Anvers, la somme de vi livres auquel madicte dame en a fait don en faveur de ce que le xve jour d'Octobre xv. xxii [1522] il a amené deux jeunes enffans, filz et fille, qu'ils ont jouhé sur une espinette et chante à son diner.
A l'organiste de Monsieur de Fiennes, sept livres dont Madame lui a fait don en faveur de ce que le second jour de Décembre xv.xxvi [1526] il est venu jouher d'un instrument dit espinette devant elle à son diner.

The inventory of the Château de Pont d'Ain, 1531, mentions 'una espinetta cum suo etuy,' a spinet with its case ; meaning a case from which the instrument could be withdrawn, as was customary at that time.   M. Becker transcribes also a contemporary reference from the Munich Library :—

Quartorze Gaillardes, neuf Pavannes, sept Bransles et deux Basses-Dances, le tout reduict de musique en la tablature du ieu (jeu) Dorgues, Espinettes, Manicordions et telz semblables instruments musicaux, imprimées à Paris par Pierre Attaignant MDXXIX.

The manichord was a clavichord.   Clement Marot (Lyons, 1551) dedicated his version of the Psalms to his countrywomen :—

Et vos doigts sur les Espinettes,
Pour dire Saintes Chansonettes.

With this written testimony we have fortunately the testimony of the instruments themselves, Italian oblong spinets (Spinetta a Tavola), or those graceful pentangular instruments, without covers attached, which are so much prized for their external beauty.   Miss Marie Decca owns a Rosso spinet dated 1550, and there is another by the same maker (signed Annibalis Mediolanesis) dated 1569, recently in the possession of Herr H. Kohl, Hamburg, who obtained it from the palace of the San Severino family, at Crema, in Lombardy.   These spinets are usually made entirely of one wood, the soundboard as well as the case.   The wood appears to be a kind of cedar, from its odour when planed or cut, at least in some instances that have come under the writer's notice.   The next oldest bearing a date is in the Conservatoire at Paris, by Francesco di Portalupis, Verona, 1523.   The next by Antoni Patavini, 1550, is at Brussels.   In the Bologna Exhibition, 1888, Historical Section, was shown a spinet bearing the inscription 'Alessandro Pasi Modenese,' and a date, 1490.   It was exhibited by Count L. Manzoni.   It is a true Italian spinet in a bad state of repair.   The date, which has been verified, does not invalidate the evidence adduced from Scaliger and Banchieri concerning the introduction of the spinet, but it places it farther back and before Scaliger, who was born in 1484, could have observed it.   This Bologna Loan Collection contained, as well as the earliest dated spinet, the latest dated harpsichord (1802, Clementi) known to the writer.   We have at S. Kensington two by Annibal Rosso of Milan, 1555 and 1577, and one by Marcus Jadra (Marco dai Cembali ; or dalle Spinette), 1568.   [A spinet in

the Dublin Museum of Science and Art, which Mr. Hipkins described in his *History of the Pianoforte*, p. 60, as dated 1590, and the work of Domenico da Pesaro, has since been discovered to be by Francesco da Brescia and to bear the much earlier date 1564.   This inscription, on an inner panel of the instrument, was not discovered till recently.   w. h. g. f.]   Of the date 1568 is also a virginal, or *Spinetta Tavola*, in the collection of M. Terme de Liége ; its compass is A–*f'''*. It has boxwood keys, but the arrangement of the short octave is uncertain, as the lowest note may be G, F, or A.   Signor Kraus has, at Florence, two 16th-century spinets, one of which is signed and dated, Benedictus Florianus, 1571 ; and at the Hôtel Cluny, Paris, there is one by the Venetian Baffo, date 1570, whose harpsichord (clavicembalo) at S. Kensington is dated 1574.

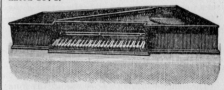

For the pentangular or heptangular model with the recessed keyboard, it is probable that we are indebted to Annibal Rosso, whose instrument of 1555 is engraved in the preceding illustration.   Mr. Carl Engel reprinted in the S. Kensington Catalogue (1874, p. 273) a passage from *La Nobilita di Milano* (1595), which he thus renders :—'Hannibal Rosso was worthy of praise, since he was the first to modernise clavichords into the shape in which we now see them,' etc.   The context clearly shows that by 'clavichord' spinet was meant, *clavicordo* being used in a general sense equivalent to the German *Clavier*.   If the modernising was not the adoption of the beautiful forms shown in the splendid examples at South Kensington—that by Rosso, of 1577, having been bought at the Paris Exhibition of 1867 for £1200 on account of the 1928 precious stones set into the case—it may possibly have been the wing-form, with the wrestpins above the keys in front, which must have come into fashion about that time, and was known in Italy as the Spinetta Traversa ; in England as the Stuart, Jacobean, or Queen Anne spinet, or Couched Harp.   There is a very fine Spinetta Traversa, emblazoned with the arms of the Medici and Compagni families, in the Kraus Museum (1878, No. 193).   Praetorius illustrates the Italian spinet by this special form, speaks (*Organographia*, Wolfenbüttel, 1619) of larger and smaller spinets, and states that in the Netherlands and England the larger was known as the Virginal. The smaller ones he describes as 'the small triangular spinets which were placed for performance upon the larger instruments, and were

2 s

tuned an octave higher.' Of this small instrument there are specimens in nearly all museums ; the Italian name for it being ' Ottavina' (also ' Spinetta di Serenata '). We find them fixed in the bent sides of the long harpsichords, in two remarkable specimens; one of which, by Hans Ruckers,[1] is preserved in the Kunst-und-Gewerbe Museum, Berlin (there is a painting of a similar double instrument inside the lid); the other is in the Maison Plantin, Antwerp, and was made as late as 1734-35, by Joannes Josephus Coenen at Ruremonde in Holland. In rectangular instruments the octave one was removable, as it was in those double instruments mentioned under RUCKERS (p. 183), so that it could be played in another part of the room.

According to Mersenne, who treats of the spinet as the principal keyed instrument (*Harmonie*, 1636, liv. 3, p. 101, etc.), there were three sizes : one of $2\frac{1}{2}$ feet, tuned to the octave of the ' ton de chapelle' (which was about a tone higher than our old ' Philharmonic' or high concert pitch) ; one of $3\frac{1}{2}$ feet, tuned to a fifth above the same pitch ; and the large 5-feet ones, tuned in unison to it. We shall refer to his octave spinet in another paragraph.

The compass of the *Ottavine* was usually from E to C, three octaves and a sixth (*a*) ; of the larger 16th-century Italian *spinette*, four octaves and a semitone, from E to F (*b*). The French *épinettes* of the 17th century were usually deeper, having four octaves and a semitone from B to C (*c*).

The reason for this semitonal beginning of the keyboard is obscure unless the lowest keys were used for ' short octave' measure, an idea which suggested itself simultaneously to the writer and to Professor A. Kraus, whose conviction is very strong as to the extended practice of the short octave arrangement. The Flemish picture of St. Cecilia, in Holyrood Palace, shows unmistakably a short octave *organ* keyboard as early as 1484.[2]

Fortunately, we are not left to such suggestion for the spinet short octave. Mersenne, in a passage which has hitherto escaped notice (*Harmonie*, liv. 3, p. 107), describing his own spinet, which, according to him, was one of the

smallest in use, says : ' The longest string has little more than a foot length between the two bridges. It has only thirty-one steps in the keyboard, and as many strings over the soundboard, so that there are five keys hid on account of the perspective (referring to the drawing)— to wit, three principals and two chromatics ("feintes"), of which the first is cut in two ; but these chromatics serve to go down to the third and fourth below the first step, or C *sol*, in notation , in order to arrive at the third octave, for the eighteen principal steps only make an eighteenth ; that is to say, a fourth over two octaves.' Here is the clearest confirmation of short-octave measure in the spinet, the same as in the organ, both keyboards, according to Mersenne, being conformable. But owing to the fact that the woodcut represents a different spinet from that described (apparently descending to B), the description is not clear. To reach the third octave would require an F, for which one-half the cut chromatic in the spinet described may be reserved. But the B of the drawing would, by known analogy with organ practice, sound G, and A would be found on the C♯, the B also on the D♯ key, though this is generally found retained as E♭ on account of the tuning.[3] It is inferred that F was reached by dividing the lowest natural key ; these diagrams therefore represent what we will call the C short measure, as that note gave the pitch.

A B		A E♭		F A B or E♭
G C D E F		G C D E F		G C D E F

Mersenne's express mention of C as the longest string shows that the still deeper G and A were made so, in his spinet, by weight : an important fact, as we have not seen a spinet in which it could have been otherwise, since in large instruments the bridge is always unbroken in its graceful curve, as it is also in the angles—always preserved—of the bridge of an octave one. The intimate connection of the spinet and organ keyboards must palliate a trespass upon ground that has been authoritatively covered in ORGAN (vol. iii. p. 529). It is this connection that incites inquiry into the origin of the short octaves, of which there are two measures, the French, German or English C one, which we have described, and the Italian F one, which we will now consider. We propose to call this F, from the pitch note, as before. We have reason to believe these pitch notes originally sounded the same, from which arose the original

1 See *ante*, p. 185, No. 5.
2 Hubert, or Jan Van Eyck's St. Cecilia, in the famous 'Mystic Lamb,' may be referred to here although appertaining to the organ and not the spinet, as a valuable note by the way. The original painting, now at Berlin, was probably painted before 1426 and certainly before 1432. The painter's minute accuracy is unquestionable. It contains a chromatic keyboard like the oldest Italian, with boxwood naturals and black sharps. The compass begins in the bass at the half-tone E. There is no indication of a ' short-octave,' but there is one key by itself, convenient to the player's left hand ; above this key there is a latchet acting as a catch, which may be intended to hold it down as a pedal. D is the probable note, and we have in Van Eyck's organ, it seems to us, the same compass, but an octave lower, as is the German Positif of the next century at South Kensington—viz. D, E, then three chromatic octaves from F, and finally F♯, G, A. There is no bottom-rail to the keyboard, nor is there in the painting at Holyrood.

3 It may have been on account of the tuning that A and D were left unfretted in the old 'gebunden' or fretted clavichords ; but the double Irish harp which Galilei (*Dissertation on Ancient and Modern Music*, A.D. 1581) says had been adopted in Italy, had those notes always doubled in the two rows of strings, an importance our tuning hypothesis fails to explain.

divergence of high and low church-pitch ; the C instrument being thus thrown a fourth higher. The Italian short measure having been mis-apprehended we have submitted the question of its construction to the high authority of Professor Kraus, and of Mr. W. T. Best, who made a careful examination of the organs in Italy. Both are in perfect agreement. Professor Kraus describes the Italian short octave as a progression of three dominants and tonics, with the addition of B *molle* (♭) and B *quadro* (♮) for the ecclesiastical tones. The principle, he writes, was also applied to the pedal key-boards, which are called 'Pedaliera in Sesta,' or 'Pedaliera a ottava ripiegata.'[1] Professor Kraus maintains the nearly general use of the short octave in Italian spinets, harpsichords, clavichords, and organs, and to some harpsichords he adds even another dominant.

According to this, the oldest harpsichord known to exist, the Roman one of 1521, at S. Kensington, is a short-octave F instrument. When, in the 18th century, the C short octaves were made long, it was by carrying down the G and A, and giving back the semitonal value to the B and C♯ (sometimes also the D♯) ; but G♯ was not introduced, since it was never required as a drone. The drones had sometimes given way to semitones as early as the 14th and 15th centuries.

What was, then, the original intention of 'short measure'? We find it indicated in Mersenne's Psaltery (G C D E F G A B♭ C d e f g) and in many delineations of Portatives or Regals in pictures of the old masters, whose sincerity, seeing the accurate manner in which they have painted lutes, cannot be questioned. We will confine our references to Orcagna's 'Coronation of the Virgin' (1350), in the National Gallery, London, and Master Stephen's 'Virgin of the Rosary' (1450), at Cologne, with the Holyrood picture of 1484, already referred to as an illustration of a Positive organ with short measure. May not Dr. Hopkins's quotation [ORGAN, vol. iii. p. 525] of two long pipes in an organ of 1418 count as evidence for short measure as much as for pedals? We think so. In fine, we regard short measure as having been intended to supply, in deeper-toned instruments, drones for cadences, and in the shriller regals (which were no more than boxes of pitch-pipes, one, two, or three to a key), to prompt the intonation of the plain-song. The contraction of the

keyboard, whether diatonic or chromatic, to suit the size of the hand, was probably due to these small instruments—

> Orgues avait bien maniables,
> A une seulle main portables,
> Ou il mesmes souffle et touche.
>   *Roman de la Rose.*

The contraction to the short-octave measure might have been intended to get rid of the weight of the heavier pipes not needed for dominants or intonation, and, at the same time, to keep the keyboard narrow. Both contractions —the keyboard and the short measure—were thus ready-made for the spinet, harpsichord and clavichord, when they came into use.

The short-octave group was finally partially doubled, so as to combine with the dominant fourths the ordinary chromatic scheme, by dividing the lowest sharps or chromatics of which there is an example in a spinet by Pleyer or Player, made between 1710 and 1720, exhibited by Messrs. Kirkman at S. Kensington in 1872. This instrument, with black naturals, and apparently $4\frac{1}{4}$ octaves from B to D, has the lowest C♯ and D♯ divided, called in the quotation in the Catalogue (p. 12) 'quarter tones.' But it is difficult to imagine enharmonic intervals provided for the deepest notes. We believe it to have been intended for a 'short octave,' and to be thus explained :—

		D♭ / C♯	E♭ / D♯	
Apparent notes	B	C	D	E
		C♯ / A	E♭ / B	
Real notes	G	C	D	E,

		C♯ / D♭	D♯ / E♭	
or Apparent notes	B	C	D	E
		A / C♯	B / E♭	
Real notes	G	C	D	E

A detailed examination of instruments contributed to the Historic Loan Collection (1885) proves that the natural keys of the Patavini Spinet mentioned on p. 633 are marked with their names. The lowest E key is clearly inscribed Do—C ; on the next, the F, is written F. This writing is not so early as 1550, because Do was not then used for Ut. The probable date is about one hundred years later, when the solmisation was finally giving way before the simple alphabetic notation. There are other instances. As to the cut sharps :[2] the small Maidstone clavichord, said to have been Handel's, has the two nearer or front divisions intended for

---

[1] But not 'Ottava Rubata,' which some inaccurately apply to the lowest octave of the short octave manual. This is a contrivance in small organs with pedals to disguise the want of the lowest diapason octave on the manual, by coupling on to it the contrabasso of the pedals with the register of the octave above.

[2] The oldest spinet with cut sharps in the Historic Loan Collection was, according to the Facies, by Edward Blount ; but on the first key, and less legibly on the jacks, is written 'Thomas Hitchcock his make in 1664.' A similar autographic inscription of this maker, but dated 1703, has been brought forward by [the late] Mr. Taphouse of Oxford. We are thus enabled to find Thomas Hitchcock's working time. We think John Hitchcock came after him, and was probably his son.

fourths below the next higher naturals, the two
further or back divisions being the usual semitones.

A spinet by Keene, dated 1685, in possession
of Mr. H. J. Dale, Cheltenham, and one by the
same maker belonging to Mr. E. R. Hughes, of
Chelsea, have the same apparently enharmonic
arrangement. One by Player (*sic*), sent to South
Kensington about 1882, is to be included with
Messrs. Kirkman's and the Keenes, and also a
Player which belongs to Dr. A. H. Mann of
Cambridge ; but a Keene of Sir George Grove's,
undated, has not the cut sharps, which we are
disposed to regard as for mixed dominants and
chromatics, because the independent keynote
value of the chromatics was, about A.D. 1700,
beginning to be recognised, and the fretted
clavichords were soon to give way to those without frets. It was the dawn of Bach, who set
all notes free as tonics. We see in Keene and
Player's spinets the blending of old and new—
that which was passing away, and our modern
practice.

Returning to the Spinetta Traversa, we find
this model preferred in England in the Stuart
epoch, and indeed in fashion for 150 years. The
favourite makers during the reigns of Charles I.
and II. were Thomas and John Hitchcock and
Charles Haward ; but there is an unaccountable
difference between John Hitchcock's and Charles
Haward's spinets in the fine specimens known
to the writer, both the property of Mr. William
Dale of London, the latter of much older character, though probably made after the former.

Thomas Hitchcock's spinets are better known
than John's. The one in the woodcut belongs
to Messrs. Broadwood, and is numbered 1379.[1]
(The highest number we have met with of
Thomas Hitchcock, is 1547.) Messrs. Broad-

wood's differs from the John Hitchcock of
1630 in having a curved instead of an angular
bent side, and from the naturals being of ivory
instead of ebony. The compass of these instruments—five octaves, from $G_{,}$ to g'''—is so
startling as to be incredible, were it not for the
facts that several instruments are extant with

[1] This is the instrument in Millais's picture of 'The Minuet,'
1962. Thomas dated his spinets ; John numbered them.

this compass, that the keyboard did not admit
of alteration, and that the Sainsbury Correspondence [see RUCKERS, *ante*, p. 184] mentions
that a greater compass obtained in England in
the time of Charles I. than was expected or
required on the Continent. The absence also
of the sound-hole, regarded as essential in all
stringed instruments of that time, where the
sound-board covered the whole internal space,

shows how eminently progressive the Hitchcocks
must have been. Not so Haward, in the instrument here represented. Chas. Haward appears
to have been contemporary with the Hitchcocks,
and yet he is as conservative to old Italian or
French practice as if John Hitchcock had never
made an instrument in England. The Haward
spinet belonging to the Rev. L. K. Hilton, of
Semley, Shaftesbury, is nearly like a Hitchcock,
which proves that Haward did not remain with
the model figured on this page. Mr. Kendrick
Pyne acquired a Haward spinet (now in Mr.
Boddington's collection) dated or numbered
1687, that has sharps like the Hitchcocks, with
a strip of the colour of the naturals let in, in
this instance black.

A John Hitchcock spinet, numbered 1676,
has lately come under our notice. Thomas and
John were probably father and son. The Charles
Haward spinet is small, with short keys and
limited compass, being only of 4 octaves and a
semitone, $B_{,}-c'''$. The naturals are of snake-
wood, nearly black ; the sharps of ivory. There
are wires on each bridge over which the strings
pass, and along the hitchpin block, precisely
the same as in a dulcimer. The decoration of
the sound-board, surrounding an Italian rose, is
signed 'I H,' with 'Carolus Haward Fecit'
above the keys ; and the name of each key is
distinctly written, which we shall again have
occasion to refer to. Pepys patronised Haward
(or Hayward, as he sometimes writes the name).
We read in his Diary :—

April 4, 1668. To White Hall. Took Aldgate Street in my way and there called upon one Hayward that makes Virginalls, and there did like of a little espinette, and will have him finish it for me : for I had a mind to a small harpsichon, but this takes up less room.

July 10, 1668. To Haward's to look upon an Espinette, and I did come near to buying one, but broke off. I have a mind to have one.

July 13, 1668. I to buy my espinette, which I did now agree for, and did at Haward's meet with Mr. Thacker, and heard him play on the harpsichon, so as I never heard man before, I think.

July 15, 1668. At noon is brought home the espinette I bought the other day of Haward ; costs me 5l.

Another reference concerns the purchase of Triangles for the spinet—a three-legged stand, as in our illustration. A curious reference to Charles Haward occurs in *A Vindication of an Essay to the Advancement of Musick*, by Thomas SALMON, M.A., London, 1672. This writer is advocating a new mode of notation, in which the ordinary clefs were replaced by B. (bass), M. (mean), and T. (treble) at the signatures :—

Here, Sir, I must acquaint you in favour of the afore-said B. M. T. that t'other day I met with a curious pair of Phanatical Harpsechords made by that Arch Heretick Charles Haward, which were ready cut out into octaves (as I am told he abusively contrives all his) in so much that by the least hint of B. M. T. all the notes were easily found as lying in the same posture in every one of their octaves. And that, Sir, with this advantage, that so soon as the scholar had learned one hand he understood them, because the position of the notes were for both the same.

The lettering over the keys in Mr. W. Dale's Haward spinet is here shown to be original. It is very curious, however, to observe Haward's simple alphabetical lettering, and to contrast it with the Hexachord names then passing away. There is a virginal (oblong spinet) in York Museum, made in 1651 by Thomas White, on the keys of which are monograms of Gamaut (bass G) and the three clef keys, F *fa ut*, C *sol fa ut*, and G *sol re ut* !

Mace, in *Musick's Monument* (London, 1676), refers to *John* Hayward as a ' harpsichon ' maker, and credits him with the invention of the Pedal for changing the stops. There was a spinet by one of the Haywards or Hawards left by Queen Anne to the Chapel Royal boys. It was used as a practising instrument until the chorister days of the late Sir John Goss, perhaps even later.

Stephen Keene[1] was a well-known spinet-maker in London in the reign of Queen Anne. His spinets, showing mixed Hitchcock and Haward features, accepting Mr. Hughes's instrument as a criterion, reached the highest perfection of spinet tone possible within such limited dimensions. The Baudin spinet, dated 1723 (said to have belonged to Simon Fraser, Lord Lovat), which belonged to the late Dr. Rimbault, and is engraved in his *History of the Pianoforte*, p. 69, was afterwards in the possession of the late Mr. Taphouse of Oxford. Of later 18th-century spinets we can refer to a fine one by

[1] Mr. H. C. Moffatt, J.P., of Goodrich Court, Ross, owns a fine virginal with this inscription on the jack rail :— 'Stephanus Keene, Londini fecit 1668.' The interval between 1668 and 1723 is very long for the work of one man.

Mahoon, dated 1747, belonging to Dr. W. H. Cummings, and there is another by that maker, who was a copyist of the Hitchcocks, at S. Kensington Museum. The late Sir F. G. Ouseley owned one by Haxby of York, 1766 ; and there is one by Baker Harris of London, 1776, in the Music School at Edinburgh. Baker Harris's were often sold by Longman & Broderip, the predecessors in Cheapside of Clementi and Collard. It is not surprising that an attempt should have been made, while the pianoforte was yet a novelty, to construct one in this pleasing wing-shape. Crang Hancock, of Tavistock Street, Covent Garden, made one in 1782 which was long in the possession of the late Mr. Walter Broadwood. It is now at Godalming.   A. J. H.

SPIRITOSO, *i.e.* 'spiritedly,' is, like CON SPIRITO, a designation of style rather than of pace. It is occasionally met with in Haydn, rarely in Mozart, and in not one of Beethoven's original works. In his many arrangements of national airs 'Spirituoso' occurs not unfrequently, as in op. 107, No. 10 ; op. 108, Nos. 13, 22 ; but he probably found it on the copies sent him. Brahms, with a touch of wonted conservatism, uses Con Spirito in the Finale of his Second Symphony.   G.

SPITTA, JULIUS AUGUST PHILIPP, a well-known musical *littérateur*, son of the author of the ' Psalter und Harfe ' ; born at Wechold, Hanover, Dec. 27, 1841 ; studied at Göttingen, and afterwards taught at Reval, Sondershausen, and Leipzig, where he took part in the founding of the Bachverein in 1874. So great was his progress during this time, that in 1875 he was made Professor of Musical History in the Berlin University, and Perpetual Secretary to the Academy of Arts there. At Easter of the same year he became teacher of Musical History in the Hochschule für Musik ; in 1876 entered the direction, and at midsummer 1882 became a permanent director of that establishment. His principal literary work is *J. S. Bach*, in two vols. (B. & H. ; vol. i. 1873, vol. ii. 1880)—an accurate and perfectly exhaustive treatise of all relating to the subject, but sadly wanting a better index. A translation by Clara Bell and J. A. Fuller Maitland was published in three volumes by Novello & Co. in 1884-85. He published a smaller biography of the same master, forming No. 1 of Breitkopf & Härtel's *Musikalische Vorträge*, and another of Schumann, which, though issued as Nos. 37, 38 of the same series, was written for this Dictionary. [See *ante*, pp. 346-383.] His article on SPONTINI, in this work, is the first adequate treatment of that singular individual. An article on Homilius will be found in the *Allg. Deutsche Biographie*, and many other productions of his pen in the *Leipzig Allg. Musikalische Zeitung* for 1875-1878, 1880-82, and in the earlier numbers of Eitner's *Monatshefte für Musikgeschichte*. He was co-editor with Chrysander and Adler of the *Vierteljahrsschrift für Musikwissenschaft*, from 1885 to his death. His critical edition of the organ works of Buxtehude, in two volumes (B. & H. 1875, 1876), is an admirable specimen of editing, and, in addition to the music, contains much valuable information. He also edited the complete edition of Heinrich Schütz, and was a prominent member of the directorate of the 'Denkmäler deutscher Tonkunst.' He died in Berlin, April 13, 1894. A monument by Hildebrandt, the eminent sculptor, was erected to his memory in Berlin.   G.

SPITZFLÖTE, SPITZFLUTE ; *i.e.* Pointed flute. An organ stop, so called because its pipes are slightly conical, that is, taper gradually from the mouth upwards. The diameter of the top is generally one-third of that of the pipe at its mouth. The tone is thin and reedy, but pure and effective. The Spitzflöte may be of 8 ft., 4 ft., or 2 ft. pitch ; in this country, stops of this kind are most commonly of 4 ft. pitch.   J. S.

SPOFFORTH, REGINALD, glee composer, born in 1770 at Southwell, Nottingham, where his uncle, Thomas Spofforth, was organist of the Minster. From him and from Dr. Benjamin Cooke he probably derived all his instruction in music. About 1787 or 1788 he wrote a glee—probably his first—for three male voices, 'Lightly o'er the village green,' and in 1793 obtained two prizes from the 'Glee Club,' for his glees 'See ! smiling from the rosy East,' and 'Where are those hours,' which brought him prominently forward. About 1799 he published a 'Set of Six Glees,' one of which, 'Hail, smiling morn,' at once caught the public ear, and has ever since retained its popularity. Another, 'Fill high the grape's exulting stream,' gained a prize in 1810. Spofforth's masterpieces, however, are not among his prize glees, and 'Come, bounteous May,' 'Mark'd you her eye,' 'Health to my dear,' and 'How calm the evening'—all for male voices—are among the finest specimens of his genius. Few English composers, perhaps, have excelled Spofforth in lively fancy joined to pure, chaste style. For several years before his death his health was bad, and he died at Brompton, Sept. 8, 1827. He was buried at Kensington, where a monument was erected to his memory in St. Mary Abbotts Church. After his death W. Hawes published a number of his MS. glees, but some of these pieces are crude and imperfect, and probably not intended for publication. Reginald's younger brother, SAMUEL, was born in 1780, appointed organist of Peterborough Cathedral when only eighteen, and in 1807 was made organist of Lichfield Cathedral. He died in London, June 6, 1864, and is now best known as the composer of a once popular chant.   D. B.

SPOHR, LOUIS, [1] great violinist and famous composer, was born April 5, 1784, at Bruns-

[1] So, and not Ludwig, he calls himself in his Autobiography.

wick, in the house of his grandfather, a clergyman. Two years after, his father, a young physician, took up his residence at Seesen, and it was there that young Spohr spent his early childhood. Both parents were musical : the father played the flute ; the mother was pianist and singer. The boy showed his musical talent very early, and sang duets with his mother when only four years of age. At five he began to play the violin, and when hardly six was able to take the violin-part in Kalkbrenner's trios. His first teachers were Riemenschneider and Dufour, both amateurs. The latter, a French émigré, was so much impressed with his pupil's exceptional talent, that he persuaded the father to send him for further instruction to Brunswick. Along with his first studies on the violin went his earliest attempts at composition, which consisted chiefly of violin duets.

At Brunswick he attended the grammar-school and continued his musical studies. His teachers were Kunisch, a member of the Duke's band, for the violin, and Hartung, an old organist, for counterpoint. This was the only instruction in the theory of music he ever received. According to his own statement, it was principally through an eager study of the scores of the great masters, especially Mozart, that he acquired mastery over the technicalities of composition. His first public appearance was at a school-concert, when he played a concerto of his own with so much success that he was asked to repeat it at one of the concerts given by the Duke's band. Kunisch then insisted on his taking lessons from Maucourt, the leader of the band, and the best violinist at Brunswick. Spohr was only fourteen when he undertook his first artistic tour. With a few letters of introduction in his pocket he set out for Hamburg. But there he failed even to get a hearing, and after some weeks had to return to Brunswick on foot, greatly disappointed, his slender means thoroughly exhausted. In his despair he conceived the idea of presenting to the Duke a petition asking for means to continue his studies. The Duke was pleased with the lad's open bearing, heard him, was struck with his talent, at once gave him an appointment in his band, and after a short time expressed his willingness to defray the expenses of his further musical education under one of the great recognised masters of the violin. Viotti and Ferdinand Eck both declined to receive a pupil, but the latter recommended his brother, Franz Eck, who was just then travelling in Germany. He was invited to Brunswick, and as the Duke was greatly pleased with his performances, an agreement was made that young Spohr should accompany him on his journeys and receive his instruction, the Duke paying one-half of the travelling expenses and a salary besides. In the spring of 1802 they started, master and pupil, for Russia. They made, however, pro-

LOUIS SPOHR

longed stays at Hamburg and Strelitz, and it was on these occcasions that Spohr profited most from his master's tuition. Latterly this became very irregular. Spohr, however, derived much benefit from constantly hearing Eck, who certainly was a very excellent violinist, though but an indifferent musician. At this pe~od Spohr, who had an herculean frame and very strong constitution, often practised for ten hours a day. At the same time he composed industriously, and among other things wrote the first of his published violin concertos (op. 1) which is entirely in the manner of Rode, and also the violin duets op. 3. In St. Petersburg he met Clementi and Field, of whom he tells some curious traits ; and after having passed the winter there without playing in public, returned to Brunswick in the summer of 1803. There he found Rode, and heard him for the first time. The playing of this great master filled him with the deepest admiration, and for some time it was his chief aim to imitate his style and manner as closely as possible. After having given in a public concert highly satisfactory proof of the progress made during his absence, he again entered on his duties in the Duke's band. An intended journey to Paris in 1804 was cruelly cut short by the loss of his precious Guarnerius violin, the present of a Russian enthusiast. Just before entering the gates of Göttingen the portmanteau containing the violin was stolen from the coach, and all endeavours to recover it proved fruitless. He returned to Brunswick, and after having acquired, with the help of his generous patron, the Duke, another, though not equally good violin, he started on a tour to Berlin, Leipzig, Dresden, and other German towns. His success was everywhere great, and his reputation spread rapidly. At his Berlin concert he was assisted by Meyerbeer, then only a boy of thirteen, but already a brilliant pianist.

In 1805 Spohr accepted the post of leader in the band of the Duke of Gotha. It was there he met and married his first wife, Dorette Scheidler, an excellent harp-player, who for many years appeared with him in all his concerts, and for whom he wrote a number of sonatas for violin and harp, as well as some solo-pieces. Having at his disposal a very fair band, Spohr now began to write orchestral works and vocal compositions of larger dimensions. His first opera, ' Die Prüfung,' which belongs to this period, was performed at a concert. In 1807 he made a very successful tour with his wife through Germany, visiting Leipzig, Dresden, Prague, Munich, Stuttgart (where he met Weber), Heidelberg, and Frankfort. In 1808 he wrote his second opera, ' Alruna '; but this, again, never reached the stage, although accepted for representation at Weimar and apparently gaining the approval of Goethe, at that time manager of the Weimar theatre, who was present at a trial-rehearsal of the work. In the course of this year Napoleon held the famous Congress of Princes at Erfurt. Spohr, naturally anxious to see the assembled princes, went to Erfurt, where a French troupe, comprising Talma and Mars, performed every evening to a pit of monarchs. But on arrival he heard, to his great disappointment, that it was impossible for any but the privileged few to gain admittance to the theatre. In this dilemma he hit on a happy expedient. He persuaded the second horn-player of the band to allow him to take his place ; but as he had never before touched a horn, he had to practise for the whole day in order to produce the natural notes of the instrument. When the evening came, though his lips were black and swollen, he was able to get through the very easy overture and entr'actes. Napoleon and his guests occupied the first row of stalls ; but the musicians had strict orders to turn their backs to the audience, and not to look round. To evade this fatal regulation Spohr took with him a pocket looking-glass, and by placing it on his desk got a good view of the famous personages assembled.

In 1809 he made another tour through the north of Germany, and at Hamburg received a commission for an opera, ' Der Zweikampf mit der Geliebten '— or ' The Lovers' Duel '— which was produced with great success the year after. At this time he had already written six of his violin-concertos, and as a player had hardly a rival in Germany. The year 1809 is memorable for the First Music Festival in Germany, which was celebrated under Spohr's direction at Frankenhausen, a small town in Thuringia. It was followed by another, in 1811, for which Spohr composed his first symphony, in E♭. In 1812 he wrote his first oratorio, ' Das jüngste Gericht ' (not to be confounded with ' Die letzten Dinge,' or ' The Last Judgment '), on the invitation of the French Governor of Erfurt, for the ' Fête Napoléon ' on August 15. He naïvely relates [1] that in the composition of this work he soon felt his want of practice in counterpoint and fugue-writing ; he therefore obtained Marpurg's treatise on the subject, studied it assiduously, wrote half-a-dozen fugues after the models given therein, and then appears to have been quite satisfied with his proficiency ! The oratorio was fairly successful, but after two more performances of it at Vienna in the following year, the composer became dissatisfied, and laid it aside for ever. In autumn 1812 he made his first appearance at Vienna, and achieved as performer a brilliant, as composer an honourable, success. The post of leader of the band at the newly established Theatre ' an-der-Wien ' being offered to him under brilliant conditions, he gave up his appointment at Gotha and settled at Vienna. During the next summer he composed his opera ' Faust,' one of his best works, and

[1] *Selbstbiogr.* i. 169.

soon afterwards, in celebration of the battle of Leipzig, a great patriotic cantata. But neither of these works was performed until after he had left Vienna. During his stay there Spohr naturally came into contact with Beethoven ; but in spite of his admiration for the master's earlier compositions, especially for the quartets, op. 18, which he was one of the first to perform at a time when they were hardly known outside Vienna (indeed, he was the very first to play them at Leipzig and Berlin)—yet he was quite unable to understand and appreciate the great composer's character and works, as they appeared even in his second period. His criticism of the C minor and Choral Symphonies has gained for Spohr, as a critic, an unenviable reputation. He disapproves of the first subject of the C minor as unsuited for the opening movement of a symphony ; considers the slow movement, granting the beauty of the melody, too much spun out and tedious ; and though praising the Scherzo, actually speaks of 'the unmeaning noise of the Finale.' The Choral Symphony fares still worse ; he holds the first three movements, though not without flashes of genius, to be inferior to all the movements of the previous eight symphonies, and the Finale he calls ' so monstrous and tasteless, and in its conception of Schiller's Ode so trivial, that he cannot understand how a genius like Beethoven could ever write it down.' After this we cannot wonder that he finishes up by saying: 'Beethoven was wanting in æsthetic culture and sense of beauty.'[1] But perhaps no great artist was ever so utterly wrapped up in himself as Spohr. What he could not measure by the standard of his own peculiar talent, to him was not measurable. Hence his complete absence of critical power, a quality which in many other cases has proved to be by no means inseparable from creative talent.

Although his stay at Vienna was on the whole very successful, and did much to raise his reputation, he left it in 1815, after having quitted his appointment on account of disagreements with the manager of the theatre. He passed the summer at the country-seat of Prince Carolath in Bohemia, and then went to conduct another festival at Frankenhausen, where he brought out his Cantata ' Das befreite Deutschland,' after which he set out on a tour through the west and south of Germany, Alsace, Switzerland, and Italy. On his road, with the special view of pleasing the Italian public, he wrote the eighth Concerto—the well-known ' Scena Cantante.' He visited all the principal towns of the Peninsula, played the concerto in Rome and Milan, and made acquaintance with Rossini and his music—without approving much of the latter, as will be readily believed.

Returned to Germany, in 1817 he visited Holland, and then accepted the post of conductor

[1] *Selbstbiogr.* i. 202, etc.

of the opera at Frankfort-on-the-Main. Here, in 1818, his opera ' Faust ' was first produced. It was quickly succeeded by ' Zemire and Azor,' which, though hardly equal to ' Faust,' gained at the time even greater popularity. Owing again to differences with the manager he left Frankfort, after a stay of scarcely two years. In 1820 he accepted an invitation from the Philharmonic Society in London, and paid his first visit to England. He appeared at the opening concert of the season (March 6), and played with great success his Concerto No. 8, ' Nello stilo drammatico.' [At a miscellaneous concert on March 22, Spohr was described on the programme as making his first appearance in England.] At the second Philharmonic concert he led his Solo Quartet in E. At the next he would naturally have been at the head of the violins to lead the band, while Ries, according to the then prevailing fashion, presided at the piano. But, after having overcome the opposition of some of the directors, Spohr succeeded in introducing the conductor's stick for the first time into a Philharmonic concert. It was on this occasion (April 10) that he conducted his MS. Symphony in D minor, a fine work, composed during his stay in London. At the last concert of the season another Symphony of his was played for the first time in England, as well as his Nonetto for strings and wind (op. 31). Spohr was delighted with the excellent performance of the Philharmonic Orchestra, especially the stringed instruments. Altogether his sojourn in London was both artistically and financially a great success. At his farewell concert, his wife made her last appearance as a harp-player, and was warmly applauded. Soon after she was obliged, on account of ill-health, to give up the harp for the piano, on which she would occasionally play in concerts with her husband, who wrote a number of pianoforte and violin duets especially for her.

On his journey home, Spohr visited Paris for the first time. Here he made the personal acquaintance of Kreutzer, Viotti, Habeneck, Cherubini, and other eminent musicians, and was received by them with great cordiality and esteem. His success at a concert which he gave at the Opéra was complete, although his quiet unpretentious style was not, and could not be, as much to the taste of the French as it was to that of the German and English public. Cherubini appears to have felt a special interest in Spohr's compositions, and the latter takes special pride in relating how the great Italian made him play a quartet of his three times over. Returned to Germany, Spohr settled at Dresden, where Weber was just then engaged in bringing out his ' Freischütz.' Spohr was no more able to appreciate the genius of Weber than that of Beethoven. It is curious that, without knowing of Weber's opera, he had had the intention of setting a libretto on the same story; but when he heard that Weber had treated the subject, he gave it up. During Spohr's stay at Dresden, Weber received an offer of the post of Hofcapell-meister to the Elector of Hesse-Cassel; but being unwilling to leave Dresden, he declined, at the same time strongly recommending Spohr, who soon after was offered the appointment for life under the most favourable conditions. On New Year's Day, 1822, he entered on his duties at Cassel, where he remained for the rest of his life. He had no difficulty in gaining at once the re-spect and obedience of band and singers, and soon succeeded in procuring a more than local reputation for their performances. Meanwhile he had finished his 'Jessonda,' which soon made the round of all the opera-houses in Germany, with great and well-deserved success. It must be regarded as the culminating point of Spohr's activity as a composer. At Leipzig and Berlin, where he himself conducted the first perform-ances, it was received with an enthusiasm little inferior to that roused a few years before by the 'Freischütz.' In the winter of 1824 he passed some time in Berlin, and renewed and cemented the friendship with Felix Mendelssohn and the members of his family, which had been begun when they visited him at Cassel in 1882. In 1826 he conducted the Rhenish Festival at Düsseldorf, when his oratorio 'The Last Judg-ment' (Die letzten Dinge) was performed (see vol. ii. p. 648b). It pleased so much that it was repeated a few days later in aid of the Greek In-surgents. His next great work was the opera 'Pietro von Abano,' which however, like his next operas, 'Der Berggeist' and 'Der Alchy-mist,' had but a temporary success. In 1831 he finished his great Violin School, which has ever since its publication maintained the place of a standard work, and which contains, both in text and exercises, a vast amount of extremely interesting and useful material. At the same time, it cannot be denied that it reflects some-what exclusively Spohr's peculiar style of playing and is therefore of especial value for the study of his own violin-compositions. It is also true that its elementary part is of less practical value from the fact that the author himself had never taught beginners, and so had no personal ex-perience in that respect.

The political disturbances of 1832 caused a prolonged interruption of the opera performances at Cassel. Spohr, incensed by the petty despot-ism of the Elector, proved himself at this time, and still more during the revolutionary period of 1848 and 1849, a strong Radical, incurring thereby his employer's displeasure, and causing him innumerable annoyances. However he made good use of the interruption to his official duties, by writing his Symphony 'Die Weihe der Töne' (The Consecration of Sound, No. 4, op. 86), which was produced at Cassel in 1832. During the next year, which was saddened by the death

of his wife in 1834, he composed the oratorio 'Des Heiland's letzte Stunden' (Calvary), on a libretto which Rochlitz had offered to Mendels-sohn, but which the latter, being then en-gaged on 'St. Paul,' had declined. Spohr's oratorio was first performed at Cassel on Good Friday, 1835. [In 1836 he married Marianne Pfeiffer, a pianist, who survived him, dying at Cassel, Jan. 4, 1892.] In 1839 he paid his second visit to England, where meanwhile his music had attained great popularity. He had received an invitation to produce his 'Calvary' at the Norwich Festival, and in spite of the opposition offered to the work by some of the clergy on account of its libretto, his reception appears to have surpassed in enthusiasm any-thing he had before experienced. It was a real success, and Spohr for the rest of his life refers to it as the greatest of his triumphs. Soon after his return to Cassel he received from Professor Edward Taylor the libretto of another oratorio, 'The Fall of Babylon,' with a request that he would compose it for the Norwich Festival of 1842. [For the circumstance of the Norwich Festival performances, see *Annals of the Norfolk and Norwich Musical Festivals*, by R. H. Legge and W. E. Hansell, 1896.] In 1840 he conducted the Festival at Aix-la-Chapelle. Two years later he brought out at Cassel Wag-ner's 'Der Fliegende Holländer.' That Spohr, who, in the case of Beethoven and Weber, ex-hibited such inability to appreciate novelty—and who at bottom was a conservative of con-servatives in music—should have been the very first musician of eminence to interest himself in Wagner's talent is a curious fact not easily explained. To some extent his predilection for experiments in music—such as he showed in his 'Weihe der Töne,' his Symphony for two orchestras, the Historic Symphony, the Quartet-Concertante and some other things—may account for it; while his long familiarity with the stage had doubtless sharpened his perception for dra-matic effect, and thus enabled him to recognise Wagner's eminently dramatic genius. But there was in Spohr, both as man and as artist, a curious mixture of the ultra-Conservative, nay almost Philistine element, and of the Radical spirit.

To the great disappointment of himself and his English friends, he was unable to conduct the 'Fall of Babylon' at Norwich, since the Elector refused the necessary leave of absence. Even a monster petition from his English ad-mirers and a special request from Lord Aberdeen, then at the head of the Government, to the Elector, had not the desired result. The oratorio, however, was performed with the greatest success, and Spohr had to be satisfied with the reports of his triumph, which poured in from many quarters. On the first day of his summer vacation, he started for England, and soon after his arrival in London conducted a performance of the new oratorio at the Hanover Square Rooms. On this and other occasions his reception here was of the most enthusiastic kind. The oratorio was repeated on a large scale by the Sacred Harmonic Society in Exeter Hall. The last Philharmonic Concert of the season (July 3) was almost entirely devoted to Spohr, having in its programme a symphony, an overture, a violin-concerto, and a vocal duet of his. By special request of the Queen and Prince Albert an extra concert with his co-operation was given on July 10, in which also he was well represented. A most enjoyable tour through the South and West of England, and Wales, brought this visit of Spohr's to a happy end.

The year 1844 was marked by the composition of his last opera, 'Die Kreuzfahrer' (The Crusaders), for which he had himself arranged the libretto from a play of Kotzebue. It was performed at Cassel and Berlin, but had no lasting success. During his vacations he made a journey to Paris, and witnessed at the Odéon the 32nd performance of the 'Antigone' with Mendelssohn's music. The members of the Conservatoire orchestra arranged in his honour a special performance of his 'Consecration of Sound.' In the same year he conducted the 'Missa Solemnis' and the Choral Symphony at the great Beethoven Festival at Bonn. The year 1847 saw him again in London, where the Sacred Harmonic Society announced a series of three concerts for the production of his principal sacred compositions: 'The Fall of Babylon,' 'Calvary,' 'The Last Judgment,' 'The Lord's Prayer,' and Milton's 84th Psalm. However, on grounds similar to those which had roused so much opposition at Norwich, 'Calvary' was omitted from the scheme, and 'The Fall of Babylon' repeated in its place.

On his return to Cassel, Spohr seems to have been quite absorbed by the great political events then going on in Germany. In the summer of 1848 he spent his vacations at Frankfort, where the newly created German Parliament was sitting, and he was never tired of listening to the debates of that short-lived political assembly. In 1849 he composed a fresh symphony, 'The Seasons'—his ninth. With 1850 a long chain of annoyances began. When his usual summer vacation time arrived, the Elector, probably intending to show displeasure at his political opinions, refused to sign the leave of absence— a mere formality, as his right to claim the vacation was fixed by contract. After several fruitless attempts to obtain the signature, Spohr, having made all his arrangements for a long journey, left Cassel without leave. This step involved him in a law-suit with the administration of the theatre, which lasted for four years, and which he finally lost on technical grounds.

For the London season of 1852 Spohr had received an invitation from the new Opera at Covent Garden to adapt his 'Faust' to the Italian stage. He accordingly composed recitatives in place of the spoken dialogue, and made some further additions and alterations. It was produced with great success under his own direction on July 15, the principal parts being sustained by Castellan, Ronconi, Formes, and Tamberlik. In 1853, after many fruitless attempts which were regularly frustrated by the Elector, he at last succeeded in bringing out Wagner's 'Tannhäuser' at Cassel. In reference to it he says in his Autobiography, 'This opera contains a great deal that is new and beautiful, but also some things which are ugly and excruciating to the ear,' and speaking of the 2nd finale he says: 'In this finale now and then a truly frightful music is produced.' That he considered Wagner by far the greatest of all living dramatic composers he declared as soon as he became acquainted with 'The Flying Dutchman.' From 'Tannhäuser' he would have proceeded to 'Lohengrin,' but owing to the usual opposition of the court, all his endeavours to bring it out were frustrated. In the same year he came for the sixth and last time to England, to fulfil an engagement at the New Philharmonic Concerts. At three of these he conducted not only many of his own works—especially the Symphony for two orchestras—but also the Choral Symphony. At the same time 'Jessonda' was in preparation at Covent Garden. But as it could not be produced before the close of his vacation, Spohr was unable to conduct it himself.

From this time his powers began to decline. He still went on composing, but declared himself dissatisfied with the results. In 1857 he was pensioned off, very much against his wish, and in the winter of the same year had the misfortune to break his arm, which compelled him to give up violin-playing. Once more, in 1858, at the celebration of the fiftieth anniversary of the Prague Conservatorium, he conducted his 'Jessonda' with wonderful energy. It was his last public appearance. He died quietly on Oct. 22, 1859, at Cassel, and thus closed the long life of a man and an artist who had to the full developed the great talents and powers given to him ; who throughout a long career had lived up to the ideal he had conceived in youth ; in whom private character and artistic activity corresponded to a rare degree, even in their foibles and deficiencies. That these last were not small cannot be denied. His utter want of critical power in reference both to himself and to others is fully exposed in his interesting Autobiography,[1] which, however, bears the strongest possible testimony to his rare manly straightforwardness and sincerity in word and deed, and to the childlike purity of mind which he preserved from early youth to latest age. Difficult as it is to understand

[1] *Louis Spohr's Selbstbiographie* ; Cassel und Göttingen, G. H. Wigand, 1860. Two volumes, with portrait and seventeen facsimiles.

his famous criticisms on Beethoven and his interest for Wagner, their sincerity cannot be doubted for a moment. According to his lights he ever stood up for the dignity of his art, with the same unflinching independence of character with which he claimed, not without personal risk, the rights of a free citizen. It is true that he called himself a disciple of Mozart. But the universality of Mozart's talent was the very reverse of Spohr's exclusive individualism ; and except in their great regard for form, and in a certain similarity of melodic structure, the two masters have hardly anything in common. Spohr certainly was a born musician, second only to the very greatest masters in true musical instinct ; in power of concentration and of work hardly inferior to any. But the range of his talent was not wide ; he never seems to have been able to step out of a given circle of ideas and sentiments. He never left the circle of his own individuality, but drew everything within it. At the same time he left much outside of that circle, and his ignorance of the achievements of others was often astounding. This is illustrated by a well-authenticated story. A pupil of his left him, and went for some time to Leipzig to study the piano and other branches of music. On his return to Cassel he called on Spohr, and was asked to play to him. The pupil played Beethoven's sonata in E minor, op. 90. Spohr was much struck, and when the piece was finished made the singular inquiry, ' Have you composed much more in that style, Herr —— ? '

He was fond of experiments in composition— such as new combinations of instruments (to wit the Double Quartets, the Symphony for two orchestras, the Quartet-Concerto, and others), or adoption of programmes ('Consecration of Sound ' ; Concertino, ' Past and Present,' etc.), and thus showed his eagerness to strike out new paths. But after all, what do we find under these new dresses and fresh-invented titles but the same dear old Spohr, incapable of putting on a really new face, even for a few bars ? ' Napoleon,' says Robert Schumann [1] (àpropos of Spohr's Historical Symphony), ' once went to a masked ball, but before he had been in the room a few minutes folded his arms in his well-known attitude. " The Emperor ! the Emperor !" at once ran through the place. Just so, through disguises of the Symphony, one kept hearing " Spohr, Spohr " in every corner of the room.' Hence there is considerable sameness—nay, monotony, in his works. Be it oratorio or concerto, opera or string-quartet—he treats them all very much in the same manner, and it is not so much the distinctive styles peculiar to these several forms of music that we find, as Spohr's peculiar individuality impressed upon all of them. He certainly was not devoid of originality—in fact his style and manner are so entirely his own that no composer is perhaps

[1] Gesammelte Schriften, iv. 89.

so absolutely unmistakable as he is. That an originality so strong and so inalienable, unless supported by creative power of the very first order and controlled by self-criticism, would easily lead to mannerism is obvious ; and a mannerist he must be called. Certain melodious phrases and cadences, chromatic progressions and enharmonic modulations, in themselves beautiful enough, and most effective, occur over and over again, until they appear to partake more of the nature of mechanical contrivances than to be the natural emanations of a living musical organism. The present lack of interest in Spohr's music is probably only the natural reaction from an unbounded and indiscriminating enthusiasm, which, in England at one time, used to place Spohr on the same level with Handel and Beethoven. These temporary fluctuations will, however, sooner or later subside, and then his true position as a great master, second in rank only to the very giants of art, will be again established.

The technical workmanship in his compositions is admirable, the thematic treatment his strong point ; but it would appear that this was the result rather of a happy musical organisation than of deep study. He cannot be reckoned amongst the great masters of counterpoint, and the fugues in his oratorios, though they run smoothly enough and are in a sense effective, can hardly be called highly interesting from a musical point of view.

Symmetry of form is one of the chief characteristics of his works ; but this love of symmetry grew eventually into a somewhat pedantic formalism. A cadenza without its preceding ' passage and shake ' he is reported to have held in abhorrence. His instrumentation shows the master-hand throughout, although his predilection for extreme keys presents much difficulty to the wind instruments, and sometimes, especially in his operas, the orchestra is wanting in perspicuity, and not free from monotony.

To his violin-concertos—and among them especially to the 7th, 8th, and 9th—must be assigned the first place among his works. They are only surpassed by those of Beethoven and Mendelssohn, and are probably destined to live longer than any other of his works. They are distinguished as much by noble and elevated ideas as by masterly thematic treatment ; while the supreme fitness of every note in the solo-part to the nature of the violin, need hardly be mentioned. They are not likely to disappear soon from the repertory of the best violinists. His duets and concertantes for two violins, and for violin and viola, are of their kind unsurpassed. By the frequent employment of double stops great sonority is produced, and, if well played, the effect is charming. The mass of his chamber-music, a great number of quartets, quintets, double quartets, trios, etc., is nowadays most rarely heard in public. Though still favourites with amateurs of the older generation, they are, with few exceptions, all but unknown to the musicians of the present day. The reason for this must be found in the fact that a severer standard of criticism is applied to chamber-music in general, and especially to the stringed quartet, than to any other form of musical composition, not even excepting the symphony. Spohr as a composer of quartets was rarely able to shake off the great violin-virtuoso. Some of the quartets—the so-called Quatuors brillants or Solo Quartets—are avowedly violin-concertos accompanied by violin, viola, and violoncello, and appear to have been written to supply a momentary want. And even those which claim to be quartets in the proper sense of the term, almost invariably give to the first violin an undue prominence, incompatible with the true quartet-style. Allowing all this, it must be maintained that many of the slow movements are of great beauty ; and altogether, in spite of undeniable drawbacks, his quartets contain so much fine and noble music as certainly not to deserve the utter neglect they have fallen into.

His oratorios, still enjoying a certain popularity in England, are but rarely heard in other countries. They contain, no doubt, much beautiful music, and occasionally rise even to grandeur and sublimity. Yet one cannot help feeling a certain incongruity between the character of the words and the musical treatment—between the stern solemnity of such subjects as ' Calvary ' or ' The Last Judgment ' and the quiet charm and sweetness of Spohr's music, which even in its most powerful and passionate moments lacks the all-conquering force here demanded.

Of his many songs a few only have attained great popularity, such as ' The Bird and the Maiden,' and some more.

As an executant Spohr counts amongst the greatest of all times. Through Franz Eck he received the solid principles of the Mannheim School, and Rode's example appears afterwards to have had some influence on his style. He was, however, too original to remain fettered by any school, still less under the influence of a definite model. He very soon formed a style of his own, which again—like his style as a composer—was a complete reflex of his peculiar individuality. It has often been remarked that he treated the violin pre-eminently as a singing instrument, and we can readily believe that the composer of the Scena Cantante and of the slow movements in the 9th and other Concertos, played with a breadth and beauty of tone and a delicacy and refinement of expression almost unequalled. A hand of exceptional size and strength enabled him to execute with great facility the most difficult double-stops and stretches. His manner of . bowing did not materially differ from that of the old French School (Viotti, Rode). Even in quick passages

he preserved a broad full tone. His staccato was most brilliant and effective, moderately quick, every note firmly marked by a movement of the wrist. The lighter and freer style of bowing, that came in with Paganini, and has been adopted more or less by all modern players, was not to his taste. He appears to have had a special dislike to the use of the 'springing bow,' and it is a characteristic fact that, when he first brought out Mendelssohn's Midsummer Night's Dream Overture at Cassel, he insisted on the violins playing the quick passage at the opening with firm strokes.

If Spohr's compositions for the violin do not present abnormal difficulties to the virtuoso of the present day, such was not the case at the time when they were written. They were then considered the *ne plus ultra* of difficulty. We must also remember that he was too great an artist and musician to care for display of executive skill for its own sake, and that in consequence the difficulties contained in his works do not by any means represent the limit of his powers as an executant. He had a large number of pupils, the best known of whom were St. Lubin, Pott, Ferdinand David, Kömpel, Blagrove, Bott, Bargheer. Henry Holmes belonged to his school, but was never his pupil. Spohr was considered one of the best conductors of his time. An unerring ear, imperturbable rhythmical feeling, energy and fire, were combined with an imposing personal appearance and great dignity of bearing.

As a man he was universally respected, although, owing to a certain reserve in his character and a decided aversion to talking, he was not rarely reproached with coldness and brusqueness of manner. At the same time he gained and kept through a long life certain intimate friendships—with Hauptmann [1] and others—and in many instances showed great kindness, and extended not a little courtesy, to brother artists. That this was not incompatible with an extraordinary sense of his own value and importance is evident in every page of his Autobiography, a most amusing work, deserving a better translation than it has yet found. [2]

His works, of which a catalogue is given below, comprise 9 great Symphonies ; a large number of Overtures ; 17 Violin-Concertos and Concertinos ; many other Concert pieces (Potpourris, Variations, etc.) for the violin, for violin and harp ; 15 Violin-Duets ; Duets for violin and PF. ; 4 Concertos and other pieces for clarinet ; 33 String Quartets ; 8 Quintets ; 4 Double Quartets ; 5 PF. Trios ; 2 Sextets ; an Octet ; and a Nonet ; 4 great Oratorios ; a Mass ; several Psalms and Cantatas ; 10 Operas ; a great many Songs, Part-Songs and other vocal pieces—over 200 works in all.

1 Hauptmann's letters to Spohr have been published by Schoene and Hiller. See also *Letters of a Leipzig Cantor*, translated and edited by A. D. Coleridge (1892).
2 *Louis Spohr's Autobiography*, Longmans, 1865.

Catalogue of Spohr's printed Works.

Founded on the Catalogue edited by H. M. Schletterer (B. & H., 1881).[1]

Op.
1. Concerto for Violin (No. 1, A min.).
2. Concerto for V. (No. 2, D min.).
3. 3 Duos Concertants for 2 V.
4. 2 String Quartets (C, G).
5. First Potpourri on Air of Dalayrac for V. with acc. of 2nd V., Viola and Bass.
6. Variations (No. 1, D) for V. solo, 2nd V., Viola, and Bass.
7. Concerto for V. (No. 3, C min.).
8. Variations (No. 2, A min.) for V. solo, 2nd V., Viola, and Bass.
9. 2 Duos Concertants for 2 V. (Nos. 4, 5).
10. Concerto for V. (No. 4, B min.).
11. Quatuor Brillant for 2 V., Viola and Vcello (No. 3, D min.).
12. Overture (No. 1, C min.).
13. Grand Duo for V. and Viola (No. 6).
14. *
15. 2 String Quartets (Nos. 4, 5; C, A).
15a. Overture (No. 2, D), 'Die Prüfung.'
16. Grande Sonate for PF. (or Harp) and V. (B.).
17. Concerto for V. (No. 5, E♭).
18. *
19. *
20. First Symphony (E♭). Peters.
21. Overture (No. 3, E♭), 'Alruna.'
22. Potpourri on themes of Mozart (No. 2, B♭) for V. with acc. of 2nd V., Viola, and Bass.
23. Potpourri on themes of Mozart (No. 3, G) for V. with acc. of Quartet, Flute, Oboe, Clarinet, 2 Bassoons, and 2 Horns.
24. Potpourri on Themes of Mozart (No. 4, B) for V. with acc. of 2nd V., Viola, and Bass.
25. 6 German Songs.
26. Concerto for Clarinet (No. 1, C min.).
27. Quartet for 2 V., Viola, and Violone (No. 6, G min.).
28. Concerto for V. (No. 6, G min.).
29. 3 String Quartets (Nos. 7, 8, 9; E♭, C min., F min.).
30. String Quartet (No. 10, A).
31. Grand Nonetto (F. maj.) for V., Viola, Vcello, Bass, Flute, Oboe, Clarinet, Bassoon, and Horn.
32. Octet (E maj.) for V., 2 Violas, Vcello, Clarinet, 2 Horns, and Bass.
33. 2 Quintets for 2 V., 2 Violas, and Vcello (No. 1, E♭; No. 2, G).
34. Notturno (in C) for wind instruments and Turkish band.
35. Fantasia for Harp (A♭).
36. Variations for Harp (F).
37. 6 German songs (2nd book of Songs).
38. Concerto for V. (No. 7, E min.).
39. 3 Duets for V. (Nos. 7, 8, 9; D min., E♭, E).
40. Grande Polonaise (A min.) for V. with Orch.
41. 6 German Songs (3rd book of Songs).
42. Potpourri. Arrangement for V. and PF. of op. 24.
43. Quatuor Brillant for stringed instr. (No. 11, E).
44. 6 4-part Songs for male voices.
45. 3 String Quartets (Nos. 12, 13, 14; C, E min., F min.).

46. Introduction and Rondo (E) for PF. and V.
47. Concerto for V. No. 8, A min. 'In modo d'una Scena cantante.' ('Gesangsscene ').
48. First Concertante for 2 V. and Orch. (A min.).
49. Second Symphony (D min.) Ded. to Philharmonic Society.
50. Potpourri (F♯ min.) for V. and PF. on Airs from 'Die Zauberflöte.' Peters.
51. Grand Rondo for V. and PF. concertants.
52. Quintet for PF., Flute, Clarinet, Horn, and Bassoon (C min.).
53. Arrangement of op. 52 for PF. and stringed instr.
54. Mass for 5 Solo Voices and 2 5-part Choirs.
55. Concerto for V. (No. 9, D min.).
56. Potpourri for V. and PF. on Airs from 'Das unterbrochene Opferfest.'
57. Concerto for Clarinet (No. 2, E♭).
58. 3 String Quartets (Nos. 16, 17, 18; E♭, A min., G).
59. Potpourri (A min.) on Irish Airs for V. and Orch.
60. 'Faust,' Opera.
61. Quatuor Brillant for stringed instr. (No. 15, B min.).
62. Concerto for V. (No. 10, A min.).
63. 'Jessonda,' Opera.
64. Potpourri (A♭) on Airs from 'Jessonda,' for V. and Vcello with Orch.
65. Double String Quartet (No. 1, D min.).
66. Potpourri (A min.) on Airs from 'Jessonda,' for V. and Orch.
67. 3 Duos Concertants for 2 V. (Nos. 10, 11, 12; A min., D, G min.).
68. Quatuor Brillant (No. 19, A).
69. Quintet for stringed instr. (No. 3, B min.).
70. Concerto for V. (No. 11, G).
71. Scena and Aria for Soprano.
72. 6 German Songs (Book 4 of Songs).
73. 'Der Berggeist,' Opera.
74. 3 String Quartets (Nos. 20, 21, 22; A min., B♭, D min.).
75. Overture, 'Macbeth' (B min.).
76. 'Pietro von Abano,' Opera.
77. Double Quartet for stringed instr. (No. 2, E♭).
78. Third Symphony (C min.).
79. Concerto for V. (No. 12, E maj.).
80. Potpourri for Clarinet (F).
81. Fantasia and Variations for Clarinet (B♭).
82. 3 String Quartets (Nos. 23, 24, 25; E, G, A min.).
83. Quatuor Brillant for stringed instr. (No. 26, E♭).
84. 3 String Quartets (Nos. 27, 28, 29; D min., A♭, B min.).
85. 3 Psalms for Double Choir and Solo Voices.
86. Fourth Symphony, 'The Consecration of Sound.'
87. Double Quartet for stringed instr. (No. 3, E min.).
88. Second Concertante for 2 V. with Orch.
89. 'Erinnerung an Marienbad,' Valses for Orch. (A min.).
90. 6 4-part Songs for Male Voices.
91. Quintet for stringed instr. (No. 4, G min.).
92. Concertino for V. (No. 2, E maj.).

93. Quatuor Brillant for stringed instr. (No. 30, A min.).
94. 6 Songs for Contralto or Baritone (Book 5 of Songs).
95. Duo Concertant for PF. and V. (G min.).
96. Duo Concertant for PF. and V. (F).
97. Hymn, 'St. Caecilia.' Chorus, Soprano Solo.
97a. Psalm 24, for Chorus, Solo Voices, and PF.
98. Hymne, 'Gott, du bist gross' (God, thou art great), for Chorus, Solo Voices, and Orch.
99. Fantasia on Raupach's 'Die Tochter der Luft' in form of a Concert-Overture for Orch. (see op. 102).
100. *
101. 6 German Songs (Book 6 of Songs).
102. Fifth Symphony (C min.). Fantasia op. 99 used as first movement.
103. 6 German Songs with acct. of PF. and Clarinet (Book 7 of Songs).
104. 'Vater unser' (words by Klopstock).
105. 6 Songs (Book 8 of Songs).
106. Quintet for stringed instr. (No. 5, G min.).
107. 3 Duets for Soprano and Tenor with PF.
108. 3 Duets for 2 Sopranos.
109. *
110. Concertino for V., 'Sonst und Jetzt' (No. 3, A min.).
111. Rondo alla Spagnuola (C) for PF. and V.
112. Duo Concertant for PF. and V. (No. 3, E).
113. Sonate Concertante for Harp and V. (B♭).
114. Do. (E♭).
115. Do. (A♭).
116. Historical Symphony (No. 6, G). Dedicated to the Philharmonic Soc., London.
117. Fantasia for PF. and V. on Airs from 'Der Alchymist.'
118. Fantasia for PF. (or Harp) and V. on Airs of Handel and Abt Vogler.
119. Trio Concertant (E min.) for PF., V., and Vcello.
120. 6 4-part Songs for mixed Voices.
121. Double Symphony, 'Irdisches und Göttliches im Menschenleben,' for Double Orch.
122. Psalm 128. Chorus and Solo Voices with Organ or PF.
123. Trio Concertant for PF., V., and Vcello (No. 2, F maj.).
124. Trio Concertant for PF., V., and Vcello (No. 3, A min.).
125. Sonata (A♭) for PF. Dedicated to Mendelssohn.
126. Concert-Overture, 'Im ernsten Styl' (D).
127. 'Elegisch u. humoristisch,' 6 Duettinos for PF. and V.
128. Concerto for V. (No. 15, E min.).

129. Quintet for stringed instr. (No. 5, E min.).
130. Quintet for PF., 2 V., Viola, and Vcello.
131. Quartet Concerto for 2 V. Viola and Vcello, with Orch.
132. String Quartet (No. 31, A).
133. Trio for PF., V., and Vcello (No. 4, B♭).
134. Psalm 84 (Milton). Chorus and Solo Voices with Orch.
135. Sechs Salonstücke for V. and PF.
136. Double Quartet (No. 4, B♭).
137. Symphony (No. 8, G min.). Dedicated to the Philharmonic Soc. of London.
138. Sonatina for PF. and Voice, 'An Sie am Clavier.'
139. 5 Songs (Book 9). Lückhardt.
140. Sextet for 2 V., 2 Violas, and 2 Vcellos (C maj.).
141. Quartet (No. 32, C).
142. Trio for PF., V., and Vcello (No. 5, G min.).
143. Symphony 'The Seasons' (No. 9).
144. Quintet for stringed instr. (No. 7, G min.).
145. Sechs Salonstücke for V. and PF.
146. String Quartet (No. 33, G).
147. Septet for PF., Flute, Clarinet, Horn, Bassoon, V., and Vcello.
148. 3 Duets for 2 V. (No. 1, F)—dedicated to the brothers Holmes. (See opp. 150, 153.)
149. Rondoletto for PF. (G).
150. 3 Duets for 2 V. (No. 2, D). Peters. (See opp. 148, 153.)
151. 6 4-part Songs for mixed Voices.
152. String Quartet, No. 34 (E♭).
153. 3 Duets for 2 V. (No. 3, C).
154. 6 Songs for a Baritone voice with acc. of V. and PF.

WORKS WITHOUT OPUS-NUMBER.
'Der Zweikampf mit der Geliebten.' Opera.
Overture and Bass Air from the Cantata, 'Das befreite Deutschland.'
'Zemire and Azor.' Opera.
'Die letzten Dinge' (The Last Judgment). Oratorio.
'Vater Unser' (words by Mahlman).
'Der Alchymist.' Opera.
'Des Heilands letzte Stunden' (Calvary). Oratorio.
Overture and Song for the play 'Der Matrose.'
'Der Fall Babylons.' Oratorio.
'Die Kreuzfahrer' (The Crusaders). Opera.
36 Violin Studies by Fiorillo, with a 2nd V. part added, fingered and bowed.
A number of Songs, written for and published in various Albums and Collections.
A considerable number of works remain in manuscript.

       P. D.

[1] An earlier catalogue, imperfect but very useful in its time, was that of Jantzen—Verzeichniss, etc., Cassel, Luckhardt.
* Unknown and not to be found in Schletterer's Catalogue. Probably represented by works left in manuscript.

SPONDEE (Lat. *Spondœus*). A metrical foot, consisting of two long syllables (– –), the first of which is enforced by an accent. Its effect is well illustrated in Handel's 'Waft her, Angels.'

Glo - rious there like you to rise.

It is also frequently employed in instrumental movements, as in the third subject of the Rondo of Beethoven's 'Sonate pathétique.'   W. S. R.

SPONTINI, GASPARO LUIGI PACIFICO, born Nov. 14, 1774, at Majolati, near Jesi (the birthplace of Pergolesi), of simple peasants. Three of his brothers took orders, and Gasparo was also destined for the priesthood. An uncle on the father's side took charge of the delicate child of eight, and gave him elementary instruction. It happened that a new organ was to be built for this uncle's church, and the builder, who had been sent for from Recanati, took up his abode for the time at the parsonage. Here he brought his harpsichord, and found an earnest listener in Spontini, who would try to pick out for himself what he had heard, whenever the organ-builder was absent. The latter noticed the boy's talent, and advised his uncle to have him educated as a musician ; but to this the priest would by no means consent, resorting indeed to harsh measures to drive the music out of him. The result was that Spontini ran away to Monte San Vito, where he had another uncle of a milder disposition, who procured him music lessons from a certain Quintiliani. In the course of a year the uncle at Jesi relented, took back his nephew, and had him well grounded by the local musicians.

In 1791 his parents took him to Naples, where he was admitted into the Conservatorio de' Turchini. His masters for counterpoint and composition were Sala and Tritto, for singing, Tarantino.[1] In the Neapolitan Conservatorios a certain number of the more advanced pupils were set to teach the more backward ones. These ' monitors,' as we should say, were called *maestrini* or *maestricelli*.[2] In 1795 Spontini became a candidate for the post of fourth *maestrino*, but the examiners gave the preference to another pupil. This seems to have roused the lad to special industry, and in a short time he was appointed first *maestrino*. His exercise for the competition of 1795 has been preserved, and is now in the archives of the Real Collegio di Musica at Naples. It must be the earliest of his compositions now in existence.[3]

Spontini had already composed some cantatas and church-music performed in Naples and the neighbourhood, and in 1796 had an opportunity of attempting opera. The invitation came from one of the directors of the Teatro Argentina in Rome, who had been pleased with some of Spontini's music which he had heard at Naples. The professors seem to have refused him leave to go, so he left the Conservatorio by stealth, and, reaching Rome, quickly composed 'I puntigli delle donne' with brilliant success. He was readmitted into the Turchini at the intercession of Piccinni, who had lived at Naples since his return in 1791, and gave Spontini valuable advice with regard to composition, particularly for his next opera, ' L'Eroismo ridicolo.'[4] This also

was produced in Rome (1797), as well as a third, ' Il finto Pittore ' (1798). Next followed three operas for Florence, all in 1798. Meantime Naples had begun to fix its attention on Spontini. ' L'Eroismo ridicolo ' (one act) was given at the Teatro Nuovo during the Carnival of 1798, and reproduced in two acts as ' La finta Filosofa ' at the same house in the summer of 1799. In the Carnival of 1800 the same theatre brought out a new work by the industrious composer, ' La fuga in maschera.'[5] It is doubtful if he was present at the performance ; for on Dec. 21, 1798, the Court, alarmed at the advance of the French troops, took flight to Palermo, and Cimarosa, who as maestro di cappella should have gone too, refusing to stir, Spontini was put in his place, and during 1800 composed for the Court in Palermo no less than three operas, in the facile and rapid style of a true disciple of the Neapolitan School. This is specially worth noting, as he afterwards completely changed in this respect, and elaborated most slowly and carefully the very works on which his European fame rests. In Palermo he also began to teach singing, but towards the end of 1800 was forced to leave, as the climate was affecting his health. After supplying more operas for Rome and Venice, he paid a visit to Jesi, and then took ship at Naples for Marseilles. His objective was Paris, and there he arrived in 1803.

From Lulli downwards all Italian composers seem to have been impelled to try their fortunes in the French capital. And, with the solitary exception of Gluck, we may say that each fresh development of French opera has originated with an Italian. Invariably, however, these foreign artists have had to encounter the onslaughts of the national jealousy. The Bouffonists, Gluck, Cherubini, all went through the same experience ; it was now Spontini's turn. The work by which he introduced himself at the Théâtre Italien (as arranged in 1801), ' La finta Filosofa,' was, it is true, well received ; but when he entered on the special domain of the French opéra-comique he was roughly disillusioned. His first work of the kind, ' Julie, ou le pot de fleurs ' (March 1804), failed, and though remodelled by the composer and revived in 1805, could not even then keep the boards.[6] The second, ' La petite Maison ' (June 23, 1804), was hissed off. This fate was not wholly undeserved. Spontini had fancied that the light, pleasing, volatile style, which suited his own countrymen, would equally please the Parisians. The composition of ' La petite Maison ' (three acts) occupied him only two months, and ' Julie ' considerably less. I only know the latter, which was also produced (with-

---

[1] Florimo's *Cenno storico sulla scuola musicale di Napoli* (Naples, 1869), vol. i. p. 50. On p. 673 Florimo speaks of Salieri and not Tarantino as Spontini's master.
[2] Lichtenthal, *Dizionario e Bibliografia della Musica* (Milan, 1826), vol. ii. p. 20. [3] Florimo, pp. 595, 609, and elsewhere.
[4] I can find no quite satisfactory ground for the statement so often

made in print that it was Cimarosa and not Piccinni who gave Spontini instruction in composition.
[5] Fétis speaks of yet another opera, ' L' Amore segreto ' (Naples, 1799), but there is no mention of it in Florimo's 4th volume.
[6] At least so says Fétis, who was living in Paris from the middle of 1804 to 1811, and who not only took great interest in Spontini's works but was personally acquainted with him Ledebur, in his *Berliner Tonkünstler-Lexicon* (Berlin, 1861), p. 501, gives a wholly opposite account, but Fétis seems the more credible witness.

GASPARO LUIGI PACIFICO SPONTINI

out success) in Berlin, Dec. 5, 1808. Here and there some isolated bit of melody recalls the composer of the 'Vestale,' but that is all. Fétis remarks that the forms of this opera are identical with those of the earlier Neapolitans, Guglielmi, Cimarosa, and Paisiello. This is true ; but it must be added that Spontini by no means attains to the sprightliness and charm of his predecessors. The melodies, though very attractive, are often trivial. Stronger work than this was needed to beat the French composers, with Méhul at their head, and Boieldieu, who had already written the 'Calife de Bagdad,' in their ranks. Spontini, however, was not discouraged. During this period Fétis met him occasionally at a pianoforte-maker's, and was struck with his invincible confidence in himself. He was making a livelihood by giving singing-lessons.

Seeing that he had no chance of making an impression with his present style he broke away from it entirely, and tried a new ideal. His very next opera, 'Milton' (Nov. 27, 1804), a little work in one act, is of an entirely different character, the melodies more expressive, the harmony and orchestration richer, the whole more carefully worked out, and the sentiment altogether more earnest. But the most interesting point in the score is the evidence it affords of Mozart's influence. One is driven to the conclusion that Spontini had now for the first time made a solid acquaintance with the works of the German masters. As Cherubini saw in Haydn, so Spontini henceforth saw in Mozart (and shortly afterwards in another German composer) a pattern of unattainable excellence. Even in old age he used to speak of Don Juan as 'that immortal *chef-d'œuvre*,' and it was one of the very few works besides his own which he conducted when director-general at Berlin. The fine hymn to the Sun (No. 4) has something of the mild solemnity which Mozart contrived to impart to the 'Zauberflöte,' and also to his compositions for the Freemasons. The most remarkable number is the quintet (No. 7). Here warmth and nobility of melody, impressive declamation, rich accompaniment, and charm of colour are all united. Such a piece as this is indeed scarcely to be found in his later works. With the Neapolitan school it has nothing in common, but is for the most part drawn from the Mozartean fount of beauty, with traces of that grandeur and nobility so emphatically his own. The change of style which separates his later works from his earlier ones is, at any rate in this quintet, already complete. In other pieces of the opera the Neapolitan is still discernible, as for instance, in the *crescendo*, which became so celebrated in Rossini's works, though known to others besides Spontini before Rossini's day.

'Milton' took at once with the French, and made its way into Germany, being produced in Berlin (translation by Treitschke) March 24, 1806,[1] Weimar, Dresden, and Vienna.

The writer of the libretto, Étienne Jouy, played a considerable part in Spontini's life. He was present at the performance of 'La petite Maison,' but its complete fiasco (the work of a jealous clique) had no effect upon him. He saw in Spontini a man of great dramatic talent, and found in the despised work a host of beauties of the first rank. Meeting the composer the following morning, he offered him a libretto of his own, which Spontini, in no way disheartened by his failure, immediately accepted. This libretto was not 'Milton,' but 'La Vestale.'[2] It was originally intended for Cherubini, but he could not make up his mind to compose it, and after a long delay returned it.[3] To Spontini it afforded the means of ranking himself at once with the first operatic composers of the day.

How 'Milton' and 'Vestale' stand to each other in matter of date it is impossible to ascertain. That the latter was composed before 'Milton' was put on the stage is not probable, since in that case the two must have been written within less than six months. What probably happened was this—an opportunity offered towards the close of 1804 of producing a small opera at the Théâtre Feydeau, and Spontini then broke off the longer work upon which he was already engaged to avail himself of this new chance. He may not have been sorry too to make a preliminary trial of his new style upon the public. On the other hand, we know for certain that the score of the 'Vestale' was finished in 1805. Jouy says that it took three years to overcome the opposition to its production, and the first performance took place Dec. 15, 1807.

He was now fortunately in favour with the Empress Josephine—to whom he dedicated the score of 'Milton'—and was appointed her 'Compositeur particulier.' A cantata, 'L' Eccelsa Gara,' performed Feb. 8, 1806, at the fêtes given in honour of Austerlitz, helped to increase this goodwill, which proved of vital importance to Spontini in maintaining his ground against the opposition of the Conservatoire. To such a length was this opposition carried that at one of the Concerts Spirituels in Holy Week, 1807, an oratorio of his was yelled off the stage by the students. Meantime, however, through the Empress's patronage, 'La Vestale' was in rehearsal at the Opéra. But so prejudiced were the artists against the work that the rehearsals went on amid ridicule and opposition,

---

[1] *Teichmann's Literary Remains*, edited by Dingelstedt (Stuttgart, Cotta, 1863), p. 415.
[2] See Jouy's own account, *Notes anecdotiques sur l'opéra de la Vestale*, in the *Théâtre d'Etienne Jouy* (Paris, 1824), vol. ii. p. 149 *et seq.*
[3] So says Fétis. Others have stated that besides Cherubini it had been offered to Méhul, Boieldieu, Paër, and others, and that the then unknown Spontini was a last resource. That the latter part of the statement is positively untrue we know from Jouy himself, and the rest will not bear examination. The mistakes as to the details of Spontini's life are very numerous. Jouy even did not know the correct date of his birth, for he speaks of him in 1804 as 'à peine âgé de vingt-cinq ans.' For a long time he was universally supposed to have been born in 1778.

both inside and outside the theatre. Some foundation for this no doubt did exist. Even in the 'Finta Filosofa' the orchestra was said to have drowned the voices.[1] Whether this was justified I cannot say, but there is some ground for it in the 'Vestale,' which also fell short in many other points.[2] Fétis attended the rehearsals, and is an unimpeachable witness on this point. Spontini's thoughts were throughout fresh and significant, but, not having before attempted lyric tragedy, he did not in all cases succeed in giving them a satisfactory form. Then began an interminable altering and remodelling on his part; the most trying experiences at rehearsals did not discourage him from again and again re-casting passage after passage, until he had hit on the best possible form. This indefatigable polishing and experimenting became henceforth one of his characteristics, and instead of diminishing, as he acquired command of his means, as might have been expected, each new work seemed to strengthen the habit. He would alter a passage four and five times, each time pasting-on the new version, and not unfrequently, after all this experimenting, he would revert to the original form.

The rehearsals were at length brought to a close after endless trouble, when, at the last moment, the performance was all but postponed, by a command from the Emperor that Lesueur's 'La Mort d'Adam,' which had long been accepted, should be given before it. When, however, the copyist was about to set to work, by some accident Lesueur's score could not be found, and thus Spontini secured precedence for the 'Vestale.' Its success was the most brilliant imaginable, and it long remained a favourite with the Parisians, having been performed 200 times as early as the year 1824. The cast on the first night was as follows: Licinius, Nourrit; Cinna, Laïs; the High-Priest, Dérivis; the Chief-Augur, Bonel; A Consul, Martin; Julia, Mme. Branchu; the Chief Vestal, Mme. Armand. Both composer and poet received permission to dedicate the work to the Empress. A higher distinction than this, however, awaited Spontini. Napoleon had founded a prize to be given every ten years to the new opera which should have made the greatest success within that period. The time of the award drew near. Méhul, Gossec, and Grétry were the judges, and their bestowal of the prize on the 'Vestale,' instead of on Lesueur's 'Bardes,' was a tacit acknowledgment that the organised opposition to the foreigner was at an end. The opera soon became known beyond France. The first per-

formance at San Carlo in Naples (to an Italian translation by Giovanni Schmidt) took place Sept. 8, 1811,[3] with Isabella Colbran as Julia. It made a great sensation, and Spontini might perhaps have found a worthy successor among his own countrymen in Nicola Antonio Manfroce had this talented young man not been carried off by an early death. On the title-page of the 'Vestale' Spontini styles himself Chamber-composer to the Empress, and Maestro di cappella to the Conservatorio of Naples. Whether this title was a new honour, or whether he brought it with him to Paris I know not. Vigano adapted the 'Vestale' as a ballet, and in this form also it was universally popular in Italy. In Berlin the first performance took place Jan. 18, 1811, to a translation by Herklots. It was given at Munich on Jan. 14, and Würzburg, Jan. 10, 1812.

Jouy drew the material of his poem, the action of which takes place in the year of Rome 269, from Winckelmann's 'Monumenti antichi inediti.' It still ranks as one of the best librettos of the 19th century, and justly so. As for the music it is so entirely new, and so utterly unlike the Neapolitan style, that it is not to be wondered at if the malicious story that Spontini was not the composer of it has occasionally been believed. Not that this could have happened if 'Milton' had been better known, for in that little opera the metamorphosis of his style is already complete. His new style Spontini did not evolve entirely from his own resources. Of the influence of Mozart we have already spoken, but that of Gluck, with whose works he became acquainted in Paris, was more important still. 'Iphigénie en Aulide' is said to have been the opera the first hearing of which showed him his future path. Not that Gluck was in his eyes a greater master than Mozart. Some years later, at a banquet given in Spontini's honour at Berlin, some one said in his praise that as a composer he had fulfilled all the requirements of a master of the musico-dramatic art, when he exclaimed hastily, 'No, it is only Mozart who has done that.'[4] But still it is obvious that Gluck was nearer of kin to him than Mozart. With Gluck he shares that touch of grandeur, the refined melancholy of which is often so peculiarly attractive, though as a rule the depth of Gluck's sentiment is beyond the reach of the Italian master. As with Gluck too the dramatic gift preponderates in Spontini over the purely musical. The moment that personal vindictiveness against Spontini ceased it could not but be acknowledged that 'La Vestale' was full of beauties, and that it seized the audience by its grand melodies and fiery outbursts, its depth of passion and truth of expression, its genuinely tragic style, and

[1] *Allg. Musik. Zeitung* for 1804, p. 382.
[2] The 'Vestale' was a marvel of noise for its day, and a good story was current about it in Paris at the time. A well-known physician had advised a friend to go and hear it as a remedy for his deafness, and accompanied him to the theatre. After one of the loudest bursts, 'Doctor,' cried the friend in ecstasy, 'Doctor, I can hear!' but alas, the doctor made no response, the same noise which had cured his friend had deafened him.

[3] See Florimo, *Scuola Musicale di Napoli*, iv. 268. In his earlier work, *Cenno storico sulla Scuola musicale di Napoli* (Naples, 1869), p. 631, he says the first performance took place in 1809.
[4] H. Dorn's *Aus meinem Leben*, pt. 3, p. 9; Berlin, Behr, 1870.

the singularly happy way in which the scenes and characters were individualised. On the other hand there were great shortcomings which could not be ignored. These chiefly lay—outside a certain monotony in the movements—in the harmony. When Berlioz afterwards ventured to maintain that scarcely two real faults in harmony could be pointed out in the score, he only showed how undeveloped was his own sense of logical harmony. It is in what is called unerring instinct for the logic of harmony that Spontini so sensibly falls short in 'La Vestale.'

This, no doubt, arose from the fact that his early training in Naples was insufficient to develop the faculty, and that when he had discovered the direction in which his real strength lay it was too late to remedy the want. Zelter, who in reference to Spontini never conceals his narrow-mindedness, made a just remark when he said that the composer of the 'Vestale' would never rise to anything much higher than he was then, if he were over twenty-five at the time that it was written.[1] He never really mastered a great part of the material necessary for the principal effects in his grand operas. His slow and laborious manner of writing, too, which he retained to the last, though creditable to his conscientiousness as an artist, is undoubtedly to be attributed in part to a sense of uncertainty.

Between the 'Vestale,' which we take to have been finished in 1805, and Spontini's next opera, four years elapsed. To this period apparently belongs a collection of six songs, with accompaniment for PF. or harp, entitled 'Sensations douces, mélancoliques et douloureuses, exprimées en vers par M. de G.—L., et en musique avec accompagnement de Piano ou Harpe par Gaspare Spontini, Maître de Chapelle du Conservatoire de Naples.' Some special series of events seems to have given rise to these pieces, but whether affecting the poet or the composer is not known. The first two are called 'Sentimens d'amour,' the third and fourth 'Regrets d'Absence,' and the last two 'Plaintes sur la tombe.' As might be expected they are all very theatrical, and exhibit many awkwardnesses in the harmony. No. 4 is the best, and its opening phrase deserves quoting as a specimen of refined melancholy :—

Moderato.

Viens, o di - vi - ne me · · · · lo - di - e,
etc.

His next opera was 'Fernand Cortez,' the first performance of which took place Nov. 28, 1809, with Lavigne and Mme. Branchu in the principal parts. The libretto was again by Jouy, and not by Esménard,[2] who merely made some alterations and additions. Napoleon took an interest in the production of 'Cortez,' from an idea

that it might influence public opinion in favour of his plans for the Spanish war, then in progress. As soon as the preparations began Jouy was warned by the Minister of the Interior to introduce into the piece more distinct allusions to the topics of the day. He was specially to strengthen the contrast between the humane views of Cortez and the fanaticism of the Mexicans, and thus suggest a comparison between the liberal-minded French and the bigoted Spaniards of the day. Jouy declining to make these alterations, the Minister proposed Esménard for the work. Napoleon was present at the first performance,[3] but the result did not fully answer his expectations. Spontini had thrown so much life into the character of the Spaniards, and had made them so bold, patriotic, and fearless of death, that the sympathies of the audience were enlisted in behalf of Spaniards in general, and Napoleon ran the risk of witnessing an exactly opposite effect to that which he intended. The success of the opera was very great, equalling if not exceeding that of the 'Vestale.' On the whole we should not be wrong in pronouncing 'Cortez' the more finished work of the two. The faults of harmony are fewer, the tendency (latterly so exaggerated) to pile up means in order to produce imposing effects is still kept within due bounds. Remarkable skill is shown in the treatment of the masses, and the construction of the larger dramatic forms. The martial tone demanded by the subject is well maintained throughout, the savage passions are delineated with an energy often startling, while some pieces are distinguished by grace and dignity. Throughout we are brought in contact with an individual artist, who has created for himself his own means of expression.[4] The certainty of touch, too, in the different characters, especially Cortez, Amazily, and Telasco, is worthy of all praise. The way especially in which the opposite nature of the Spaniards and Mexicans is brought out shows consummate creative power. Here Spontini is seen to be a worthy successor of Gluck, who was the first to attempt this kind of problem in his 'Paris et Hélène.' Gluck had many able successors, such as Winter in Germany and Méhul in France, but Spontini comes still nearer to the great model, and has in his turn served as an example for others. Neither Rossini's 'Guillaume Tell' nor Marschner's 'Templer und Jüdin' would have been quite what they are but for him.

The form in which we know 'Cortez' is not that in which it first appeared. After a long interval it was revived May 26, 1817, in an entirely new shape. Esménard was dead, and for the alterations in the poem Jouy was entirely responsible. The third act now became the first,

[1] Briefwechsel zwischen Goethe und Zelter, vol. i. p. 438.
[2] Riehl (Musikalische Charakterköpfe, 5th ed., Stuttgart, Cotta, 1876, vol. i. p. 192) ; following Raoul Rochette, Notice historique sur la vie et les ouvrages de M. Spontini (Paris, Firmin Didot, 1852).
[3] Théâtre d'Étienne Jouy, vol. ii. p. 199 et seq.
[4] In face of this self-evident fact but little importance will be attached to the discovery made in Paris that the Trio 'Créateur de ce nouveau monde,' was an imitation of an 'O salutaris hostia' of Gossec's. See Journal des Débats for June 1, 1817.

the first act the second, and a part of the second the third ; some passages were suppressed and others added, and the part of Montezuma was entirely new. Jouy had introduced Montezuma into his original sketch, but thinking the part weak and undramatic had omitted it in the first libretto. It now reappeared. The part of Amazily is simplified as regards her appearances, but the character is strengthened. The pianoforte score, arranged by F. Naue, and published by Hofmeister of Leipzig, gives the opera as it stood after a third and final revision made by the poet Théauleon. The full score came out in Paris in the fortieth year after Spontini's retirement from Berlin. The third act in its second form may be found in Jouy's *Œuvres complètes*, vol. ii. p. 187.

In 1810 Spontini became conductor of the Italian opera, which was united with the Comédie Française under the title of ' Théâtre de l'Impératrice,' and located at the Odéon. He formed a distinguished company of singers, improved the orchestra, and threw more variety into the répertoire. One signal service was his production, for the first time in Paris, of ' Don Juan' in its original form. He remodelled Catel's ' Semiramide,' with fresh numbers of his own, and revived it with some success. He also instituted Concerts Spirituels, at which he successfully introduced such works as Mozart's Requiem, Haydn's Symphonies, and extracts from the ' Creation.' But he did not keep the conductorship long. Differences arose between himself and Alexandre Duval, the director of the theatre, and in 1812 Spontini was dismissed from his post by M. de Rémusat, surintendant of the Imperial theatres.

On the restoration of the Bourbons in 1814 Spontini was reinstated, but soon gave up the post to Catalani for a money consideration. His conduct as conductor of the opera does not give a favourable idea of his character. When Count Brühl was in Paris, Spontini was described to him by the managers of the Opéra as ' grasping and indolent ; ill-natured, treacherous, and spiteful.'[1] Catalani, too, always averred that he had treated her badly. Some, however, took a more favourable view, and maintained that he had been both zealous and successful in his efforts for the furtherance of art. Fétis believed that it was not Spontini but Duval who should have been dismissed in 1812. It is curious thus to find the same difference of opinion in Paris with regard to Spontini's character which was afterwards so noticeable in Berlin.

On May 30, 1814, Louis XVIII. became king of France, and in commemoration of the event Jouy and Spontini wrote a festival-opera in two acts called ' Pélage, ou le Roi de la Paix.' The first performance took place August 23, 1814. The work is of no value, and must have been very quickly composed. The subject is idyllic,

breathing only soft emotions, and therefore entirely contrary to the nature of Spontini's talent. The opera was dedicated to the king, who appointed Spontini his ' Dramatic composer in ordinary.' It is often said that Spontini's music displays the spirit of the age of Napoleon. The remark is true so far as the martial splendour, the vehement energy, the overpowering massive effect of his grand operas are concerned. In all this the spirit of the time is recognisable enough. But it resides in the music only ; and it would be very wrong to conclude that Spontini himself was an adherent of Napoleon's politics or person. He was as little of an imperialist as Weber (notwithstanding his songs in the cause of liberty) was a democrat. Art and Politics are two distinct things, and if Spontini did do homage to Louis after enjoying the favour of Napoleon there is no need to blame him.

He next took part with Persuis, Berton, and Kreutzer in an opéra-ballet, ' Les Dieux rivaux,' produced June 21, 1816, in honour of the marriage of the Duc de Berri. Spontini's share was confined to two or three dances, and a song, ' Voici le Roi, Français fidèles,' of little value. Other ballet-music however, composed for Salieri's ' Danaïdes,' rises to the level of ' Cortez ' and the ' Vestale.' The opera, revived with this addition Oct. 22, 1817, was enthusiastically received.

But these *pièces d'occasion* sink into insignificance before the grand opera 'Olympie,' 'imitated' by Briffaut and Dieulafoy from Voltaire's tragedy. Spontini took a most unusual length of time for the composition. He was at work upon the last act in December 1815, and yet the opera was not finished by January 1819.[2] After so much trouble and pains he not unnaturally considered it his best work. ' This score,' he writes Nov. 27, 1819, ' must be ranked higher, for importance and range of subject, than those of " La Vestale " and " Cortez " ' ; and to this opinion he adhered, in spite of many proofs that the public judged otherwise. At the first performance (Paris, Dec. 15, 1819) a bitter disappointment awaited him, for the opera failed in spite of his numerous supporters, and of the generally favourable disposition of the Parisians towards him. Spontini however was not the man to throw up his cause for a first failure. The libretto was chiefly to blame. The writers had adhered too closely to Voltaire, without remembering the requirements of the music, or the established forms of Grand Opera. The tragical conclusion especially was objected to as an innovation. This was remedied first of all, and a happy ending substituted. By February 1820, Spontini was at work on the revision, which he completed in less than a year, and the opera was produced in its new form, May 14, 1821, at Berlin. In 1822 it

---

[1] Letter of Brühl to Frederick William III., Oct. 8, 1819.

[2] Letters from Spontini to Count Brühl, dated Dec. 22, 1815, and Jan. 14, 1819.

was again revised, the changes this time being in the airs for Olympie and Cassandre, the duet for the same in the first act, and a new scene with terzetto in the third. As this last is not included in the printed edition it looks as if the final form of the opera had not even yet been attained. Schlesinger of Berlin published a complete pianoforte-score in 1826.[1] The opera was again put on the stage in Paris, Feb. 28, 1826, and by March 15 it had already been played six times.[2] Each time it pleased more, and at last Spontini was able to count it among his great triumphs. It was, however, only in Berlin, where he settled in 1820, that it kept a permanent place in the repertory. It had a short run at Dresden and Darmstadt in 1822, and was proposed at Vienna, but the performance did not take place. The opera has now completely disappeared from musical life, a fate it shares with Cherubini's 'Médée.' That no attempts have been made to revive it must be attributed partly to the enormous demands which it makes on the dramatic and scenic resources of a theatre, and also to the fact that Spontini's operas are of an individual type and require a peculiar style of representation. The few living musicians who remember the performances of Spontini's operas in Berlin between 1820 and 1830 know the kind of interpretation he used to give of them—one which by no means lay on the surface. Dorn, in his *Recollections*,[3] says that at Leipzig in 1829 the final chorus in the second act of the 'Vestale' was ridiculed as a mere waltz-tune. When Dorn undertook the direction of the opera, and had to conduct the 'Vestale,' he made such good use of his recollections of the way in which it was conducted by the composer, that the chorus in question was scarcely recognised, and all adverse comments were silenced. 'Another fifty years,' continues he, 'and the Spontini traditions will have disappeared, as the Mozart traditions have already done.' It would be more correct to say that *both* have disappeared. The Spontini traditions might possibly have lived longer had his work in Germany been more successful than it was. But there is enough to account for this, and more, in the unsettled condition of all stage matters in Germany for many years past.

'Olympie' and 'Agnes von Hohenstaufen'—written ten years later—stand alone among operas of the 19th century for grandeur of conception. True, in isolated scenes of the 'Huguenots' and the 'Prophète,' Meyerbeer approached his predecessor, but he never succeeded in creating a whole of such magnificent proportions. The unity of design is remarkable, each act seems to be cast in one mould ; and this from the fact that musically the several scenes of each act run into each other in a much more marked manner than in 'Cortez' or the 'Vestale.' There

[1] A full score, in 3 vols. was published by Erard at Paris.
[2] Marx's *Berliner Allgem. Mus. Zeitung* for 1826, p. 104.
[3] *Aus meinem Leben-Erinnerungen* (Berlin, 1870), p. 131 *et seq.*

is also, throughout, the closest connection between the music, the scenes on the stage, and the development of the plot—the *cachet* of the true dramatic artist. The principal characters are well defined, and the tone assigned to each at the start is skilfully maintained. The first entrances, always the most important moment in opera for fixing the character of a part, are always very significant. For instance, it is interesting to observe the entirely different nature of the music at the entrances of Olympia and of Statira. The latter, the principal character in the piece, has no rival, unless it be Cherubini's 'Médée,' or perhaps Gluck's 'Armide.' A sorrrowful woman, burdened with horrible memories and burning for revenge, she is yet a Queen from the crown of her head to the sole of her foot, and a heroine, as all must acknowledge, worthy of Alexander the Great. Bearing in mind the grandeur of the subject, and its background of history, the composer's choice of material does not seem exaggerated.

But these great qualities are accompanied by considerable defects. Apart from the falsified history of the plot, which might easily disturb a cultivated spectator in these days of accuracy, the happy conclusion weakens the interest in the fate of the chief characters. The part of Statira, at any rate, was far more consistent and homogeneous when the ending was tragic. The music, undeniably grandly sketched as a whole, lacks charm in the details. Spontini was not an instrumental composer. His overtures, dances, and marches, are in all cases music without any independent existence, simply intended to introduce or accompany. Instrumental music, from its immense plasticity and variety, is the best possible school for developing all the rich resources of the musical art ; but in this school Spontini had never been properly disciplined, and the neglect makes itself felt in his larger dramatic forms. These are monotonous and wearisome, while his basses are poor, and his accompaniments wanting in variety. It seems strange that with his great reverence for Mozart —the great model in this respect also—he should never have been aware of this want in himself. His melodies lack plasticity, that bold free movement which is absolutely essential if the melody is to remain dominant over all the accumulated masses of sound. He has not sufficient command of language to have always ready to his hand suitable means of expression for the rapid changes of sentiment in the course of a scene. Nor has he the power of assigning the instrumental music its due share in the dramatic development. If all the work is done by the singing and acting, one is tempted to ask what is the object of all this overwhelming apparatus in the orchestra ? The important part played by the instrumental music in an opera, that of preparing and elucidating the sentiments, making them subjectively more credible. and objectively clearer, this problem Spontini either did not grasp, or felt himself unable to solve. In all these respects he was far surpassed by Cherubini and Weber, each in his own line.

Whilst Spontini was busy in Paris composing 'Olympie,' the way was being prepared for the most important event in the second half of his life—his summons to Berlin. As no authentic account of the circumstances of his going there, or of his twenty-two years' sojourn and work in the Prussian capital, has yet been published, we must treat the subject somewhat in detail, from MS. authorities hitherto unused.[1] King Frederick William III., during a visit of two months to Paris (March 31 to the beginning of June 1814), heard Spontini's operas several times, and was deeply impressed by them. Not only was 'Cortez' at once put in rehearsal at Berlin and produced Oct. 15, 1814, but the king, on the return of peace, occupied himself with various plans for improving the state of music in Prussia. An establishment for the promotion of church music was thought of; a Conservatoire for music and declamation was projected, like that at Paris, and, above all, fresh impulse was to be given to the Court Opera by engaging a conductor of acknowledged ability. For this last post Spontini was the man fixed upon. So far back as the autumn of 1814 proposals had been made to him at Vienna, offering him the then immense salary of 5000 thalers (£750) on condition of his furnishing two operas a year for Berlin. Spontini was inclined to accept, but the plan did not meet with the approval of the Intendant of the Royal theatre—Count Brühl, who had succeeded Iffland in Feb. 1815. Brühl's opinion was entitled to the more weight as there had scarcely ever been a theatrical manager in Germany who knew his business so well. He was himself an actor of great experience, had studied several parts at Weimar under Goethe's direction, had sung Sacchini's 'Œdipe' in French, and taken other parts in grand operas at Rheinsberg, Prince Henry's palace. He had even played the horn for months together in the band. He was no inefficient scene-painter; had studied drawing with Genelli, and archæology with Hirt and Bötticher, had devoted some time to architecture, and was personally acquainted with nearly all the important theatres in Germany, Paris, and London. Add to this his refined taste, ideal turn of mind, and high social position, and it will be seen that he possessed qualities rarely found united in the person of a theatrical manager. It is not to be supposed that Brühl ignored the advantage of having so distinguished an artist at the head of the Berlin opera. It was, however, by no means certain that Spontini had had the necessary practice as a conductor, for in Paris no composer conducts his own operas.

His ignorance of German would not only make it difficult for him and his musicians to understand each other, but would also prevent his composing a German opera. As yet he had only composed two operas of acknowledged merit, and it was possible that he would not be able to supply two new ones each year; and if he were able, the price paid for them would be exorbitant, unless it were quite certain that as interpreted under his own direction they would mark a decided step in advance. At this point therefore the negotiations hung fire, until the king returned to Paris in July 1815, when he renewed his offer to Spontini in person, and accepted the dedication of a piece of military music. At his request Spontini sent a collection of his marches to Brühl, following it on Dec. 22, 1815, with a letter, in which he begged him to exert his influence in arranging the matter. This not availing, he got a personal appeal made to him from the Prussian embassy. On March 28, 1816, Brühl returned an evasive answer, and on Nov. 3 wrote decisively that the king had settled the affair adversely to Spontini's wishes, and that he must abandon with regret the pleasure of seeing him settled in Berlin.

The matter now appeared wholly at an end, the king having yielded to the representations of his Intendant. Spontini had at that time no settled appointment in Paris, beyond that of court-composer, and it is easy to understand how tempting so brilliant an offer from Berlin must have seemed. He now entered into a fresh connection with Naples, and received in the following year the title of *maestro di cappella* to the King of the Two Sicilies. The French king also gave him a salary of 2000 francs, and thus all thoughts of Berlin seemed for the time to have vanished.

In 1817 King Frederick William came to Paris for the third time, heard 'Cortez' in its new form, was so delighted that he attended four representations, and directed that the score should be secured at once for Berlin. Spontini received the title of *Premier maître de chapelle honoraire*, and was permitted to dedicate to the king his grand 'Bacchanale,' composed for Salieri's 'Danaïdes.' This he was shrewd enough to arrange for a Prussian military band, introducing an air from the 'Vestale,' 'La paix est en ce jour la fruit de vos conquétes.' To confirm himself in the king's favour he even composed a Prussian national anthem, completed between Nov. 25, 1817, and Oct. 18, 1818. The words, written by the king's private secretary J. F. L. Duncker, begin

Wo ist das Volk das kühn von That
Der Tyrannei den Kopf zertrat?

On the latter date (the anniversary of the battle of Leipzig), Brühl had the work performed for the first time at the Berlin opera-house, and from 1820 to 1840 it was played every year on the king's birthday, August 3. A Volkslied,

[1] The principal sources upon which we have drawn are papers belonging to the royal theatres of Berlin, and to the Prussian Royal Family.

from inherent reasons, it never could become ; but it has a certain chivalrous stateliness and distinction of its own. After the death of Frederick William III. it gradually disappeared from the musical life of Berlin. The king, however, decreed in March 1818 that the 'Vestale' should be performed every year on April 1, in remembrance of the first time he passed in Paris in 1814.

This year also ended without realising the king's project of attaching Spontini to his court. Spontini, aware that Brühl was opposed to his coming, contrived to carry on the negotiations through Major-General von Witzleben, an ardent admirer of his music, and the person who had suggested his composing the Prussian national anthem. The contract was at length drawn up in August 1819, and signed by the king on Sept. 1. It provided that Spontini should receive the titles of chief Capellmeister, and General Director of Music, with an additional one of 'Superintendent-General of the Royal Music' to be borne abroad. He was to take the general superintendence of all musical affairs, and to compose two new grand operas, or three smaller ones, every three years. He was bound to conduct only at the first performances of his own works ; at other times he might conduct or not as he pleased. In addition he was to compose *pièces d'occasion* for the court festivals, and whenever the king pleased. Any other works he chose to compose and produce at the theatre were to be paid for separately. He was also at liberty, with slight restrictions, to produce his operas for his own benefit elsewhere, and to sell them to publishers. His salary was fixed at 4000 thalers, payable half-yearly in advance, besides an annual benefit, guaranteed to yield at least 1050 thalers, and a benefit concert, with the theatre free, and the gratuitous assistance of the members of the Royal opera and orchestra. He was to have four months' leave of absence every year, and an adequate pension after ten years' service. The Prussian ambassador interfered to procure his release from his engagement at Naples, and the king undertook to pay any necessary damages.

Although nominally subordinate to Brühl, Spontini was by this contract virtually made his colleague. Brühl's experienced eye, however, soon detected certain passages in the document admitting of two interpretations, and exposing the management to all the dangers of a divided authority. He could not help feeling mortified at the way he had been superseded in the business ; this would naturally make him mistrust Spontini, and thus the two came together under unfavourable auspices. According to the contract Spontini should have begun work at Berlin on Feb. 15, 1820, but he obtained leave to postpone his coming, first to March 15, and then to May 15, and did not arrive until May 28, 1820. The *corps dramatique*, piqued

at the exorbitant terms of his engagement, did not meet him in the friendliest spirit, but Berlin society was favourably disposed towards him, particularly the court circle. The newspapers were full of the subject, and thus it came to pass that all classes were keenly interested.

The Opera was at this time, thanks to Brühl's exertions, in a high state of efficiency. The company was unusually good—including such singers as Milder-Hauptmann, Seidler-Wranitzky, Schulz-Killitschky, and Eunicke ; Bader, Stümer, Blume, and Eduard Devrient. The band had been well trained by Bernhard Weber. Brühl took immense pains to secure finish in the performances, had added to the répertoire all the great masterpieces, and had introduced 'Fidelio' and 'Armida,' besides establishing other operas of Gluck's permanently in Berlin. He had also mounted the 'Vestal' and 'Cortez' with the utmost care and intelligence, and was entitled to boast that he had made the Berlin opera the first in Germany, as indeed every one allowed. Spontini found neither blemishes to remove nor reforms to introduce. He had at his disposal a company of first-rate artists, his power over them was practically unlimited, and the king's confidence in him unbounded. His obvious duty was to keep matters up to the standard to which Brühl had raised them.

He started with the best intentions. Brühl was informed of various plans for increasing the orchestra, establishing a training-school for the chorus, and introducing new methods into the existing singing-school. He was considering the best means of educating the singers in the dramatic part of their art, and drew up a new set of rules for the band. Little, however, came of all this, partly because several of Spontini's proposals were already in existence in other forms, and partly because of his own want of purpose and temper. In fact, it soon came to a trial of strength between him and Brühl. The latter insisted, a little too firmly, on his rights as supreme manager, and even appealed to the public through the press. Spontini, despotic, and exceedingly sensitive as to publicity, referred to his contract, which had been drawn up without Brühl's concurrence, and which he declined to interpret according to Brühl's views, and stated specifically that he was subject to no one but the King, or possibly the Home-Minister also. Unacquainted with Berlin or the German language, and surrounded by a crowd of parasites, he soon fell into mistakes which it was extremely difficult to rectify with so suspicious a person. A few months of ill-concealed irritation on both sides led to open collision. On Oct. 25, at a meeting to arrange the répertoire for the week, with Brühl in the chair, Spontini spoke of the latter's sketch as 'parfaitement ridicule,' because it did not contain at least two grand operas, the 'Vestale' and 'Armida'; styled the pieces selected 'des misères, des niaiseries,' etc., and talked in the most violent way of the Count's bad management. Brühl tried to give him an idea of what subordination meant in Prussia, but subordination Spontini would not hear of. 'Don't attempt to treat me,' he writes on Nov. 12, 'as a mere subordinate, for I am nothing of the kind, neither by my person, my character, my contract, nor my talent; for although my post happens to be included in your department, it is so in a wholly different sense from what you appear, or pretend, to think.' The whole letter is very angry, and very rude, and it was long before the two were again on terms of even outward civility. Brühl took his grievance straight to the king, and peace was at length re-established. The following extract will show Brühl's opinion of Spontini at this time :—

'He is,' he writes to Witzleben, 'extremely passionate, and once in a passion oversteps all bounds; uses expressions which no man of honour can pardon, and then considers his natural bad temper excuse enough for anything. He is very suspicious, and at the same time very credulous, putting himself at the mercy of any one who will flatter his vanity; and in consequence is surrounded by a host of unsatisfactory characters, who make him their shuttlecock. His pride and vanity have really reached the sublime of the ridiculous; and temper, sometimes assuming the guise of modesty, directs, or rather misdirects, all his actions. . . . And to such a man has been confided the conduct of business of more than ordinary intricacy!'

This description, written under obvious irritation, should in justice be counterbalanced by the consideration of Spontini's great qualities as an artist. But that Brühl's estimate was in the main correct, the sequel will show.

During the preparations for the first performance of 'Olympia,' Spontini had an opportunity of appearing before the court and public with a new composition. In the beginning of 1821 the Grand Duke Nicholas, heir-presumptive to the throne of Russia, and his consort, paid a visit to Berlin, and court festivities on a grand scale were instituted in their honour. Moore's 'Lalla Rookh' was then much talked of, and Brühl conceived the idea of representing the principal scenes in a series of tableaux vivants. Schinkel undertook the scenery and arrangement of the groups, and Spontini composed the songs, introductory march, and dance-music. The performance took place Jan. 27, 1821, at the Royal Palace, and was pronounced to be the most brilliant and quaintly beautiful thing of the kind ever seen. The actors were all members of the court circle. On Feb. 11 the performance was repeated before a select audience comprising the most distinguished artists and scientific men in Berlin. Hensel, Fanny Mendelssohn's husband, was commissioned by the King to paint the tableaux, for presentation to the Grand Duchess.[1] A sort of running commentary on the representation was furnished by a number

of songs written by Spiker, set by Spontini, and executed behind the scenes by the best singers from the opera and a small orchestra.[2] Spontini's work consists of four instrumental and six vocal pieces. One of the latter is a chorus of genii (3 soprani and 1 tenor) sung while Nourmahal is sleeping, and a real work of genius. The singers vocalise on A, while the instruments are playing a light accompaniment. The other vocal pieces are the songs, the second being a free translation of the opening of 'Paradise and the Peri.' Spontini's work now suffers from inevitable comparison with Schumann's music. As an Italian he had neither romantic imagination nor depth of expression enough for the subject. But taking the piece as a whole, it is possibly more in character with Moore's poetry than the oratorio form chosen by Schumann.

The first performance of 'Olympia' was eagerly anticipated. March 5, 1821, was first fixed, but it was postponed till May 14, a delay for which Spontini was entirely to blame. The translator, E. A. Hoffmann, only got the last act from him bit by bit, the chorus-master had not seen a note of it by Feb. 18, nor had the ballet-master been consulted. Spontini insisted on at least three months' rehearsals. The expenditure on the mise-en-scène was so lavish that even the king remonstrated. Statira was played by Milder, Olympia by Schulz, and Cassander and Antigonus by Bader and Blume. The chorus and orchestra were materially strengthened, the scenery was by Schinkel and Gropius, and there were forty-two rehearsals. The result was one of the most brilliant and perfect performances ever seen, and an enormous success. Even Brühl was carried away, and wrote to Milder, 'you have given us a perfect representation, and added another flower to your crown as an artist.' Spontini's triumph was complete. Even his opponents acknowledged that 'Olympia' had no rival among modern operas. Zelter wrote to Goethe that he did not like the work, but could not help going again and again.

Spontini's supremacy in the musical world lasted exactly five weeks, for on June 18, 1821, 'Der Freischütz' was produced at the newly erected theatre in Berlin. Its immediate success may not have been more than equalled that of 'Olympia,' but it soon became evident that the chief effect of the latter was astonishment, while the former set the pulse of the German people beating. 'Olympia' remained almost restricted to the stage of Berlin, while the 'Freischütz' spread with astonishing rapidity throughout Germany and the whole world. Spontini could not conceal that he had, on the morrow of a great triumph, been completely vanquished by an obscure opponent, and that too after consciously doing his very utmost. Even this

---

[1] The importance of this event in Hensel's life may be seen from the *Mendelssohn Family*, vol. i. p. 95.

[2] 'Lalla Rukh. A festival play with songs and dances, performed at the Royal Palace of Berlin, Jan. 27, 1821. Edited by Count Brühl and S. H. Spiker. Berlin, L. W. Wittich, 1822.'

might not have discouraged him, but that in 'Der Freischütz' he was brought face to face with a phase of the German character totally beyond his comprehension. He had no weapons wherewith to encounter this opponent. A man of weaker will would have contented himself with such success as might still be secured in Germany ; but Spontini could brook no rival, and finding that he could not outdo Weber's music, tried to suppress him by means wholly outside the circle of art. As director-general of music many such lay ready to his hand, and that he knew how to use them is shown by the fate of 'Euryanthe' and 'Oberon' in Berlin. The success c˝ ˙Freischütz' did not improve Spontini's relations with Brühl, a personal friend of Weber's, and a great admirer of his music.

From the first night of 'Der Freischütz' the public was divided into two parties. The national party, far the strongest in intellect and cultivation, rallied round Weber. The king and the court persistently supported Spontini, though even their help could not make him master of the situation. The Censorship interfered to check the expression of public opinion against him, and his complaints of supposed slights were always attended to.[1] But his artistic star, which had shone with such lustre after the first night of 'Olympia,' was now slowly setting.

The excellence of that first performance was acknowledged even by Weber himself,[2] and this may be a good opportunity for some remarks on Spontini as a director. Whether he had a specific talent for conducting cannot be determined, for as a rule he conducted only two operas besides his own—'Armida' and 'Don Juan,' and these he knew thoroughly.[3] For the rest of the work there were two conductors, Seidel and Schneider, and two leaders, Möser and Seidler.[4] When Spontini came to Berlin he had had very little practice in conducting, and at first declined to handle the bâton, but made the leader sit by him in the orchestra, and give the tempo according to his directions. Indeed he never completely mastered the technicalities of the art, his manner of conducting recitatives especially being clumsy and undecided. So at least says Dorn,[5] a competent witness, who had often seen him conduct. In reading a score too he was slow and inexpert ;[6] and at the Cologne Festival of 1847 could scarcely find his way in his own score of 'Olympia,' which he had not conducted for some time. He was thus very slow in rehearsing a work, though not for this reason only, for the same laborious accuracy which he showed in composing was carried into every

detail of the performance. He never rested till each part was reproduced exactly as it existed in his own imagination, which itself had to be cleared by repeated experiments. Inconsiderate and despotic towards his subordinates, he wearied his singers and band to death by endless repetitions, his rehearsals not unfrequently lasting from 8 A.M. till 4 P.M., or from 5 P.M. till 11 at night. He only treated others, however, in the same way that he treated himself, for no trouble was too great for him to take in revising his work down to the smallest particulars. When the first night arrived, every member of the orchestra knew his work by heart, and Spontini might beat as he liked, all went like clockwork.[7] If scenery or costumes which had been expressly prepared did not please him he ordered others, regardless of cost. Being a true dramatic artist, his eye was as keen on the stage as his ear in the orchestra, and everything, down to the smallest accessories, must be arranged to express his ideas. Soon after his arrival he fell out with Brühl, because in the 'Vestalin' he wanted Frau Milder to carry the Palladium in public, whereas Brühl maintained, on Hirt's authority, that the Palladium was never shown to the people. He was furious when it was suggested that the burning of the fleet in 'Cortez' should not take place on the stage ; and he once went so far as to send his wife to Brühl to request that a sleeve of Schulz's dress might be altered ! In choosing his actors he not only studied voice, temperament, and dramatic skill, but was most particular about appearance. A distinguished bass singer, recommended to him by Dorn for high-priest parts, was not even allowed to open his mouth because he was 'at least a foot and a half too short.' He insisted on the complete fusion of the vocal and instrumental, the dramatic and the musical elements, and demanded from the chorus, as well as the solo-singers, an entire absorption in their parts, and an intelligent rendering of each situation. His love for the grandiose and the awe-inspiring led him to employ all the resources of decoration, and what then seemed enormous masses of musicians, singers, and dancers ; and also to employ the strongest accents and most startling contrasts. 'His *forte*,' says Dorn, 'was a hurricane, his *piano* a breath, his *crescendo* made every one open their eyes, his *diminuendo* induced a feeling of delicious languor, his *sforzando* was enough to wake the dead.'[8] In this respect he exacted the very utmost from his singers and musicians. He insisted on Milder putting her whole force into Statira's exclamation 'Cassander !' and on one occasion she so overstrained herself as to lose her voice for the rest of the evening. From that moment he considered her useless, and in 1829 had her pensioned off. Seidler-Wranitzky was delicate, and her style

[1] Gubitz, *Erlebnisse*, vol. iii. p. 241. Berlin, 1869.
[2] *Carl Maria von Weber*, by Max von Weber, vol. ii. p. 306, Leipzig, 1864.
[3] He conducted the 99th performance of 'Der Freischütz' (Nov. 6, 1826), for the benefit of Weber's widow and children, which was much to his credit, considering his dislike to the piece.
[4] Bernhard Weber died March 23, 1821.
[5] *Aus meinem Leben*, Part iii. p. 3.
[6] Devrient's *Recollections of Mendelssohn*, p. 28.

[7] Blume on *Alcidor*, in the Theatre archives.
[8] *Aus meinem Leben*, first collection, p. 127.

more suited to Lieder and serious music, so she found little favour with him, in spite of her exquisite singing. 'Il faut braver, Madame,' shouted he, when she showed symptoms of exhaustion at a rehearsal of the 'Vestale'; and he was scarcely moved when she fainted. It was not because he wrote unvocally, or overloaded his voices with accompaniment, that his parts were so trying—for he was too thorough an Italian not to rely upon the voice for his chief effects; but it was his propensity to extreme contrasts, and his want of consideration in rehearsing. It soon became a general complaint among women singers that Spontini ruined the voice. Seidler asked leave to retire on this account in 1826 ; in 1823 Milder begged that 'Olympia' might not be given more than once a fortnight, and Schechner refused an engagement because she was afraid of Spontini's operas. Even Schulz, who was devoted to him, was so angry in March 1824 at the continual strain of her heavy parts, as to lose her temper at rehearsal, and speak so rudely that she would have been punished had he not changed his mind.

Spontini's appearance at the head of his musicians was almost that of a general leading an army to victory. When he glided rapidly through the orchestra to his desk every member of the band was in position, and on the alert to begin. At such moments he looked an aristocrat to the backbone, but also an autocrat who would insist on subjugating all other wills to his own. The pedantic side of his character also came out in many little traits—he could only conduct from a MS. score, and his desk must be of a certain peculiar construction. His bâton was a thick stick of ebony with a solid ivory ball at each end ; this he grasped in the middle with his whole fist, using it like a marshal's staff.[1]

By May 14, 1821, the 'Vestalin,' 'Cortez,' and 'Olympia' had all been produced according to the composer's own ideas at the Berlin opera, where they long remained stock-pieces. But their frequent repetition was more to gratify the king than the public, and indeed the theatre had soon to be filled by a large issue of free admissions. Thus, for 'Olympia,' on Dec. 21, 1821, Spontini obtained from the office fifty free tickets, besides buying twenty-five more. In September 1824 he urged the Intendant not to raise the prices for grand operas (meaning his own), or the public would soon cease to come at all, and begged to have 'ordinary prices' in large letters on the bills for the next performance of the 'Vestalin.' A new opera of his was however still an exciting event, partly because of his own personality and position, partly because the public was sure of a splendid spectacle. He was bound to furnish two grand operas every three years ; 'Olympia'

counted as one, and by the end of 1821 he was thinking of the second. After much consideration he chose the 'Feast of Roses,' from Moore's 'Lalla Rookh,' influenced, no doubt, by the success of his earlier Festspiel, and the prospect, welcome to a slow worker, of using portions of his old material ; but the subject did not seem very congenial. The libretto was written by Herklots, librettist to the Opera. On March 22 Spontini wrote to Brühl that he was working 17 hours a day on the first act, and that there were only two. The first performance of 'Nurmahal' took place May 27, 1822, in honour of the marriage of the Princess Alexandrina of Prussia, to whom the Emperor dedicated the PF. score (Schlesinger). This is not, as has often been said, merely a revised version of 'Lalla Rukh,' comparatively little of that music having been used in it. The introductory march became No. 8 of the opera; Nourmahal's song, No. 26 ; the drum chorus of genii No. 20 ; and the ballet-music was mostly retained. A song was also introduced from his 'Dieux rivaux,' and the ballet from the 'Danaïdes' (Nos. 10 and 14).

The merits of the librettos of the 'Vestalin,' 'Cortez,' and 'Olympia,' outweigh their defects. Not so, however, that of 'Nurmahal'; its plot and characters are alike insipid, and it is in fact a mere *pièce d'occasion*. The oriental colouring, which must have been its attraction for Spontini, still forms its sole interest. But, inferior as it is to 'Oberon,' it gives a high idea of its author's dramatic instinct, when we consider the utter inability of French and Italian composers as a rule to deal with the fantastic and mythical. Its best numbers are the first finale, the duet, No. 17, and the duet with chorus, No. 20. There is a striking passage in the finale—the lovers lying on opposite sides of the stage, and the people dancing about them to a bacchante-like strain, when suddenly the dance ceases, and the voices hold on a chord of the seventh on E, with an indescribable effect of unsatisfied longing. It is a stroke of true genius of which any German composer of the romantic school might be proud. The duet No. 17 contains some conventional thoughts, but the vehemence of its passion is irresistible, and it seems to have been the earliest instance of a kind of sentiment first employed among German composers by Marschner, *e.g.* in No. 17 of his 'Templer und Jüdin.' The spirit chorus No. 20 has a charming sound, produced by means entirely new ; though, compared with Weber's tone-pictures, it strikes the hearer as superficial. It is impossible to help this comparison for many reasons, one being that in No. 21 of 'Nurmahal' one of Spontini's genii sings, 'From Chindara's warbling fount I come.'[2] A glance at the two compositions is enough to

[1] Richard Wagner's *Erinnerung an Spontini; Gesammelte Schriften*, vol. v. p. 116 (Leipzig, Fritzsche, 1872).

[2] Weber's setting of these words was his last composition, dated London, May 25, 1826. F. W. Jähns, *C. M. von Weber in seinen Werken*, p. 409. Berlin, Schlesinger, 1871.

show how far he fell short of the equalities required for this kind of work. The piece contains much that is beautiful, especially some passages in the Andantino malinconico, of startling novelty and expression, the gay introductory chorus, and the melodious Nos. 3, 4, and 5, so entirely in Spontini's Neapolitan manner that they might have been taken from his early operas. Here and there are touches recalling Mozart. The overture and ballets are brilliant and festal, and the overture has an open-airiness of style often found in Italian overtures. Clumsy accentuation of words, however, constantly betrays the fact that the composer is dealing with an unfamiliar language.

On June 9, 1821, Spontini started for a seven months' leave. He went first to Dresden, and there met Weber. Weber was cordial and obliging, while Spontini, though polite in manner, took pains to make his rival feel the newness of his reputation as a composer.[1] By June 29, he was in Vienna trying to arrange a performance of 'Olympia' for the following season ; but this did not take place. Thence he went to Italy, revisiting his birthplace ; and by September was in Paris at work on the revision of 'Olympia.' He also made some experiments on 'Milton,' telling Brühl (Jan. 12, 1823) that he would put it before him in three different forms. By the end of January he was back in Berlin, apparently anxious to keep on good terms with Brühl, though such good resolutions seldom lasted long. One of their many differences was on the subject of star-singers (*Gastspieler*). These Brühl wished to encourage, as a means of testing the artists, and their chance of popularity ; but Spontini disliked the system. An appearance of Carl Devrient and Wilhelmine Schröder in the summer of 1823 evoked another impertinent letter to Brühl, who in reply (July 7) told him to mind his own business.

He had now been in office four years, and the stipulated two grand operas every three years, or smaller one each year, were only represented by a *scena* or two for 'Olympia,' and a couple of pieces for 'Nurmahal.' It was plain that he had undertaken a task wholly beyond his strength, owing to his pedantic manner of working. He thought (August 2, 1823) of turning 'Milton' into a grand opera with recitatives, choruses, and ballets, but soon relinquished the idea, and by Oct. 17 was 'busy, night and day, with "Alcidor."' The libretto was by Théauleon, who had formerly altered 'Cortez.' On coming to Berlin, in Nov. 1823, Théauleon found the first scene already composed, and his business was to fit words to the music. His task was not easy : 'If I wrote lines of ten syllables,' he says, 'Spontini wanted them of five ; scarcely had I hammered out an unfortunate stanza of five, when it had to be

lengthened to twelve or fifteen, and if I expostulated, on the ground that lines of that length were not admissible in French poetry, he would reply in a sort of recitative, accompanying himself on the piano, "The translation will make it all right." Never did so poor a poem cost its author so much trouble.'[2] It is evident from this that Spontini composed to French words, which were afterwards translated by Herklots. Schinkel and Gropius again painted the scenery. The rehearsals began in Sept. 1824, and the first performance took place May 23, 1825. Its reception by Spontini's adherents was unmistakably hearty, and many outsiders were dazzled by its new effects of scenery and music, but the national party were louder than ever in their disapprobation. Among the adverse critiques was a parody in the true Berlin style, in which 'Alcidor eine Zauberoper' was converted into 'Allzudoll eine Zauderoper.'[3] Zelter alone was impartial, but he was no doubt influenced by his prejudice against Weber, and all that he can say is 'The piece was written by Théauleon in French, and set to French music, so we have at last a real Berlin original—that is a new coat turned' ; and again, 'Spontini always reminds me of a Gold-King, flinging his gold at the people, and breaking their heads with it.'[4] Not even a PF. score of 'Alcidor' was published ; nor did it make its way beyond Berlin, any more than 'Nurmahal' had done.

Another grand opera was due for the summer of 1826, and a week after the production of 'Alcidor' Spontini asked Count Brühl whether a revised and lengthened version of 'Milton' would do for the purpose. The Count thought the material too scanty, but the King (June 29) agreed to the proposal. Spontini having obtained eleven months' leave, started for Paris, where he was present at a revival of 'Olympie' on Feb. 28, 1826, returning immediately afterwards to Berlin. Nothing more was heard of 'Milton,' and during this year he furnished no work for the King's theatre. Ernst Raupach was now librettist to the Opera, and Spontini agreed with him on a subject from German mediæval history, which eventually became the opera 'Agnes von Hohenstaufen.' The first act —long enough for a complete opera—was ready by 1827, and performed May 28. The whole three acts were finished in 1829, and produced June 12 for the marriage of Prince Wilhelm, (afterwards the Emperor William I.). Spontini, dissatisfied with his work, had the libretto altered by Baron von Lichtenstein and other friends, and made more vital changes in the music than in almost any other of his grand operas. In this form it was revived Dec. 6, 1837.

German mediæval history at this time occupied much attention, and thus no doubt influenced

[1] *C. M. von Weber*, by Max von Weber, ii. 433.
[2] Ledebur, *Berliner Tonkünstler-Lexicon*, p. 564.
[3] Allzudoll, vulgarism for Allzutoll=quite too mad; Zauderoper =slow opera, because of the time it had taken to write.
[4] *Briefwechsel von Goethe und Zelter*, iv. 39, 40.

Spontini's choice of a subject. He set to work with the seriousness which was his main characteristic as an artist; read, studied, and did everything to imbue himself with the spirit of the epoch, one wholly foreign to anything he had before attempted.[1] The libretto in its final form was a good one on the whole. The scene is laid at Mayence in 1194, during the reign of the Emperor Henry VI. of Hohenstaufen, and the plot turns on the factions of the Guelphs and Ghibellines. The music is thoroughly German, the harmonies richer and more satisfying, the melodies quite national in character; isolated passages recalling Spohr, and even Weber, though without anything like servile imitation. It is throughout the result of an entire absorption in the dramatic situation and characters. A comparison of it with the sentimental ballad-like effusions of even good German composers in similar circumstances will serve to accentuate the difference between them and Spontini. Neither is there any sign of exhaustion of inventive power. The stream of melody flows as freely as ever; indeed there is a breadth, an *élan*, and a fire in some of these melodies, to which he rarely attains in his earlier operas— instance the terzetto in the second act, 'Ja, statt meines Kerkers Grauen,' and Agnes's solo 'Mein König droben.' The criticisms of the day were most unjustly severe; but though the music was never published the MS. score exists, and an examination of it will fully bear out all that we have said. It is not too late to form an impartial judgment, and Germans should recognise that they have a duty to perform to 'Agnes von Hohenstaufen,' as the only opera which deals worthily with a glorious period of German history. When this has been fairly acknowledged it will be time enough to look out for its defects.

It was the last opera which Spontini completed. Various new plans and schemes continued to occupy him, as before, especially during the latter part of his stay in Paris, when 'Louis XI.,' 'La Colère d'Achille,' and 'Artaserse' had in turn been thought of for composition. For a successor to 'Olympia' he thought first of 'Sappho' or of 'Die Horatier,' and then of two of Werner's tragedies, 'Das Kreuz an der Ostsee' and 'Attila,' but none of these projects appear to have advanced far enough even for a preliminary rehearsal. More progress was made with a poem by his old friend Jouy, 'Les Athéniennes,' first offered him in 1819, and accepted in a revised form in 1822. In a review of the poem[2] written in 1830, Goethe implies that the music was complete, but at Spontini's death nothing was found but unimportant fragments.[3] An opera founded on English

history occupied him longer. We have already mentioned the revision of his 'Milton.' His studies for this deepened his interest in the English history of the 17th century. In 1830 Raupach wrote a libretto for a grand opera, 'Milton,' which was bought by the committee of management for 30 Friedrichs d'or, and placed at Spontini's disposal.[4] The only portion of the smaller opera retained was the fine Hymn to the Sun. After completing the revision of 'Agnes von Hohenstaufen,' Spontini wrote to the Intendant (May 9, 1837) that he hoped in the winter of 1838 to produce 'Miltons Tod und Busse für Königsmord' (Milton's death, and repentance for the King's execution). He spent the summer of 1838 in England, studying historical, national, and local colouring for this 'historico-romantic' opera. Raupach's poem, extended and revised by Dr. Sobernheim, had now assumed a political and religious tendency, so distasteful to the King as to make him prohibit the opera. Further alterations ensued, and it became 'Das verlorene Paradies' (Paradise Lost). By May 1840 the score of part of the 1st, and two-thirds of the 2nd act was complete. Up to March 1841 he certainly intended finishing it, but not a note of it has ever been heard. We may add that on June 4, 1838, he mentioned a fairy-opera to the King, and in Dec. 1840 professed himself ready to begin a new comic opera. He was apparently bent on composing fresh dramatic works, and often complained that the management did not offer him sufficient choice of librettos; but he was incapacitated from creation by his increasing pedantry, and by the perpetual state of irritation in which he was kept by his critics.

Spontini's other compositions during his residence in Berlin are unimportant. A hymn for the coronation of the Emperor Nicholas of Russia, to words by Raupach, was performed at Berlin, Dec. 18, 1826, and May 9, 1827.[5] A cantata to Herklots' words, 'Gott segne den König,' had a great success at the Halle Musical Festival in Sept. 1829, which Spontini conducted so much to the general satisfaction as to procure him an honorary Doctor's degree from the University, and a gold medal inscribed *Liricae Tragoediae Principi Germania meritorum cultrix*. A 'Domine salvum fac regem,' *a* 12, with accompaniment of organs, trumpets, violoncelli, and basses, was written on Oct. 15, 1840, for presentation to the King. Besides these he published a number of French, German, and Italian vocal pieces, with PF. accompaniment, the best of which is 'Die Cimbern,' a war-song for three men's voices. As a mere matter of curiosity may be mentioned that he set Goethe's 'Kennst du das Land,' and the Italian canzonet 'Ninfe, se liete,' in which he again clashed unconsciously with Weber's

---

[1] *Spontini in Deutschland*, p. 102 (Leipzig, Steinacker und Hartknoch, 1830).
[2] Goethe's *Works*, Goedecke's edition, vol. xiii. p. 632, Cotta. Also *Spontini in Deutschland*, p. 22. Leipzig, 1830.
[3] Robert's *Spontini*, p. 34. Berlin, 1883.

[4] In *Spontini in Deutschland* this libretto is said to be by Jouy. I have not been able to ascertain whether it was Jouy's work revised by Raupach, or an original production.
[5] Raupach had intended to have *tableaux vivants* to each five stanzas; but this was not carried out.

very graceful composition to the same words (1811).[1]

Considering his great position, Spontini did not accomplish much for music in Berlin. At the opera he made the band play with a fire, an expression, and an *ensemble*, hitherto unknown, forced the singers to throw themselves dramatically into their parts, and used every exertion to fuse the different elements into one coherent whole. He endeavoured to improve the existing school for singers and founded one for the orchestra. But his efforts as a rule were concentrated on the operas which he himself conducted—that is to say, his own, Gluck's 'Armida,' and 'Don Juan.' These works, through his genius, his influence on his subordinates, and his almost absolute power, he brought to a perfection then unequalled. The pieces directed by his vice-conductors went badly, partly because Spontini exhausted the singers, and partly because he took little interest in the general répertoire. He had, too, no power of organisation or administration. As long as the excellent material lasted which Brühl transferred to him in 1820 this defect was not glaring, but when his solo-singers began to wear out and had to be replaced, it was found that he had not the judgment, the penetration, nor the impartiality necessary for such business. Up to the autumn of 1827 he only concluded one engagement himself, and in that instance it was a solo-singer who proved only fit for the chorus. On the other hand he lost Sieber, a good bass, by insisting on reducing his salary to 100 thalers, and had shortly afterwards to re-engage him at 200, as there was no bass in the company capable of taking the parts in his own operas. The art of divining the taste of the public, of at once meeting it, elevating and moulding it—the art, in fact, of keeping the exchequer full without sacrificing artistic position—this was wholly out of his reach. At the King's theatre, the audiences steadily fell off, especially after the opening of the Königstadt theatre in 1823. At times Spontini seems to have felt his incapacity, but unfortunately he was deluded by his own vanity and domineering temper, and the insinuations of so-called friends, into believing that the decline of the opera was owing to Brühl, whereas Brühl might have retorted that everything he proposed was met by a despotic and unreasoning veto. The Count at length, in 1828, wearied out by the unceasing opposition, resigned, and was succeeded by Count Redern, who received from the King a fresh code of instructions, somewhat circumscribing Spontini's powers, and concentrating those of the management. Opportunities for fresh differences still constantly arose, and Count Redern had much to contend with in Spontini's increasing irritability and inconsistency. In time even the admirers of his music felt that his personal influence was bad, and that the opera would never prosper as long as he remained at its head.

Spontini was to have the receipts of the first nights of his own operas for his annual benefit, or in default of such representations a sum of 4000 francs. In the latter case he might give a concert, and in fact he gave a considerable number, both vocal and instrumental. 'My concerts,' in his own words, 'are dedicated to the great masters, whose memory I strive to keep alive with the public, while testifying my own respect by performing their works in the most brilliant and complete manner possible.'[2] His programmes consisted principally of German music, Handel, Haydn, Mozart, and Beethoven. The first performance in Berlin of Beethoven's Symphony in A was at a concert of Spontini's on May 12, 1824, and on April 30, 1828, he gave Beethoven's C minor Symphony, the Kyrie and Gloria from his Mass in D, the overture to 'Coriolan,' and the Credo from Bach's B minor Mass. As Bach's Mass had only just been published by Nägeli of Zurich, Spontini was the first to introduce a portion of it to the public of Berlin, as he had been to acquaint them with Beethoven's Masses. The performance itself seems to have been a poor one, and indeed it could hardly be otherwise, Spontini not having much in common with Bach; but the attempt was praiseworthy.[3] Another point to his credit was that he gave his support to Möser's concerts. The King's band could not play without his permission, so he might have made difficulties if he had chosen.

As we have already mentioned, Spontini's late operas had no success outside Berlin. Except a couple of stray performances of 'Olympia' at Dresden and Darmstadt, they did not even gain a hearing. Occasionally he conducted one of his own works, as for instance the 'Vestalin' at Munich[4] (Oct. 7 and 11, 1827), and Hamburg[5] (Sept. 18, 1834). But such personal contact does not seem to have led to sympathetic relations. Speaking generally, the 'Vestalin' and 'Cortez' were the only operas of his appreciated in Germany.

In Berlin itself, each year added to the number of his opponents. In 1824 Marx entered the lists in his behalf in his *Zeitung*, and was seconded by Dorn ; but Dorn left Berlin in March 1828, and Marx, though sincerely attached to Spontini, occasionally admitted adverse criticisms. Spontini was morbidly sensitive to public opinion, and the loss of his defenders was a serious one. Against the advice of judicious friends he replied in person to anonymous attacks, suffered flatterers to use unpractised pens in his behalf, and even called in the Censorship.

---

[1] Ledebur gives a tolerably complete catalogue of Spontini's smaller works; see p. 570. Also Marx, in the *Berliner Allg. Mus. Zeitung* for 1826, p. 306.

[2] Gubitz's *Erlebnisse*, iii. 242.
[3] Marx, *Berliner Allg. Mus. Zeitung*, 1828, pp. 146 and 152.
[4] Grandaur, *Chronik des königl. Theaters in München*, p. 106. Munich, 1878.
[5] Schmidt's *Denkwürdigkeiten*. Edited by Uhde. Part ii. p. 314. Stuttgart, Cotta, 1878.

Such steps could but damage his cause. The opposition was headed by Rellstab, the editor of the *Vossische Zeitung*, an experienced littérateur with some knowledge of music, a great ally of Weber's, and a blind opponent of everything foreign. In Nos. 23 to 26 of the year 1827 of Marx's *Zeitung* appeared an article utterly demolishing the first act of ' Agnes von Hohenstaufen.' Dorn made a successful reply in Nos. 27 to 29, but far from being silenced Rellstab published a book, *Ueber mein Verhältniss als Kritiker zu Herrn Spontini*,[1] in which he unsparingly attacked Spontini as a composer and director, and exposed the absurd tactics of the Spontini clique.[2] The clique put forth a defence called *Spontini in Germany, an impartial consideration of his productions during his ten years' residence in that country* (Leipzig, 1830). It was, however, anything but impartial, was ignorant and badly done.[3]

Spontini's ten years' contract finished in 1830; it was renewed, on terms more favourable to the Intendant-General, and this, with the fact of his ceasing to compose, gave an opportunity to his enemies, and an unfortunate indiscretion on the part of one of his friends played into their hands. Dorow of Halle, the archæologist, in a collection of autographs (1837) inserted a letter from Spontini (Marienbad, August 12, 1836) lamenting the degeneracy of the dramatic composers of the day. It was done in good faith, Dorow honestly believing that he was serving Spontini by thus publishing his opinions without authority; but his opponents issued the letter in a separate pamphlet with a German translation, and 'explanatory' remarks, in which Spontini was fiercely attacked in terms of ironical respect.[4] In the same year, in Nos. 101 and 102 of the *Komet* appeared a pasquinade by a student named Thomas, stating that Spontini had opposed the production of 'Robert le Diable,' the ' Postillon de Longjumeau,' and ' La Muette de Portici,' till obliged to yield to the express command of the King; that a new code of instructions had altered his position, and made him entirely subordinate to the Intendant; that he had been reprimanded for selling his free admissions, and had had them withdrawn; that the engagements of certain singers contained a clause stipulating that they should not be obliged to sing in Spontini's operas, etc. etc.

Thomas, when called to account, referred to an ' official of high position ' as his authority. And indeed there was a certain amount of truth in the charges. Without directly opposing the production of the operas mentioned, he had not hesitated openly to avow his dislike of them : no new code of instructions had just then been issued, but that of 1831 did materially strengthen the Intendant's position, and to a certain extent make the Director-general his subordinate. Spontini had not himself sold free admissions, but his servant had, and in consequence the allotted number had been diminished, very much to his mortification. It was advisable, however, to prevent such a newspaper scandal from reaching the King's ears, so Count Redern replied, contradicting all the false statements, and passing over in silence all the true ones ; Thomas was induced to make a public apology, and the affair seemed at an end. But Spontini's troubles were not yet over ; and his unpopularity was so great that worse attacks might be expected.

On June 7, 1840, King Frederick William III. died, and Spontini's one mainstay was gone. Though obliged occasionally to express displeasure at his perpetual squabbles with the Intendant, the King had been steadfast in his attachment to Spontini and his music. The new King made no change in his position, but his sympathies were in a different direction, and no place was destined for Spontini in the grand designs he was elaborating. This soon became known. If Spontini could have kept himself quiet the change might have been delayed, but he was injudicious enough to lay before the King a paper complaining of the Management and of Count Redern. The King questioned the Intendant, and was satisfied with his explanations, but to obviate all appearance of partisanship he appointed a commission to inquire into Spontini's grievances. In the meantime the press had taken up the matter. A definite attack was made, to which Spontini was unwise enough to reply (Leipzig *Allgemeine Zeitung* of Jan. 20, 1841) in such a manner as to give Count Redern ground for an indictment for *lèse-majesté*, and (on Feb. 5) to a direct reprimand from the King.

But this disgraceful treatment of the royal house by a foreigner who had enjoyed for years almost unexampled Court favour immensely increased the public feeling against Spontini, and for two months he remained in private. On April 2, however, in spite of repeated warnings, he took his seat to conduct ' Don Juan.' His appearance was the signal for a tremendous uproar, and cries of 'hinaus ! hinaus !'—' off ! off !' He stood firm, began the overture, and would have proceeded with the opera, but a rush was made to get at him on the stage, and he was forced to retire from the theatre. He never entered it again as conductor.

The trial kept Spontini in Berlin all the summer, but he obtained leave from Aug. 31 to Dec. 10, and went to Paris. His connection with the opera was severed by the King on

---

[1] Leipzig, Whistling, 1827.
[2] But see RELLSTAB, *ante*, p. 62*b*. It has been often, and even recently, stated that two articles by Rellstab in *Cäcilia* (*Aus dem Nachlass eines jungen Künstlers*), vol. iv. pp. 1-42, and *Julius. Eine musikalische Novelle*, vol. vi. pp. 1-108) refer to Spontini. This is quite untrue, but it shows how carelessly damaging statements about Spontini are repeated.
[3] Attributed, quite untruly, to Dorn.
[4] *The Lament of Herr Ritter Gasparo Spontini . . . over the decline of dramatic music. Translated from the French, with explanatory remarks by a body of friends and admirers of the great master.* Leipzig, Michelsen, 1837.

Aug. 25, on terms of royal generosity. He was to retain his title and full salary, and live where he pleased, 'in the hope that in repose he might produce new works, which the King would hail with pleasure if he chose to conduct them in person at Berlin.' To these munificent arrangements no conditions whatever were attached. Spontini was convicted of *lèse-majesté*, and condemned to nine months' imprisonment, a sentence confirmed by the higher court to which he appealed, but remitted by the King. In the face of all this he had the effrontery to demand a further sum of 46,850 thalers, on the ground that the Management had not supplied him with a sufficient number of librettos, whereby he had lost the sum guaranteed him for first nights, besides profits from other performances and from publishers—reckoned at 3000 thalers for each opera ! The King referred him to the Law Courts, but Spontini's better nature seems at length to have prevailed, and he withdrew his application Dec. 23, 1841. When he finally left Berlin in the summer of 1842, the King granted him a further sum of 6000 thalers. His friends gave him a farewell concert on July 13, 1842, for which he wrote both words and music of an 'Adieu à mes amis de Berlin.'[1]

He left few friends behind him. His successor at the opera was Meyerbeer, who, with Mendelssohn, received the title of 'Generalmusik-director.' Neither had very friendly feelings towards him, and their paths as artists widely diverged from his. He was, however, long and gratefully remembered by the members of the King's band. The orchestra were proud of their majestic conductor, who so often led them to triumph, and who, moreover, had a tender care for their personal interests. The poorer members found his purse ready of access, and in 1826 he established a fund for them, called by special permission the 'Spontini-Fonds,' to which he devoted the whole proceeds of his annual benefit concerts. The fund speedily attained to considerable proportions, and still exists, though the name has been changed.

That he was badly treated by the Berlin public is indisputable. His ill-natured, unjust, spiteful attacks must have been very irritating, as even those who do not belong to the super-sensitive race of artists can understand, but the last scene at the opera looks like a piece of simple brutality, unless we remember that the real ground of offence was his being a foreigner. The political events of the period beginning with the War of Liberation had roused a strong national feeling in Prussia. The denial of a Constitution had concentrated attention on the stage, which thus became a sort of political arena ; and that a foreigner, and moreover a naturalised Frenchman, should be laying down the law in this stronghold was intolerable.

[1] Robert, p. 52, etc.

In Spontini's character great and mean qualities were almost equally mixed, so that both friends and foes could support their statements by facts, while each shut their eyes to the qualities which they did not wish to see. After his friends had been silenced by the catastrophe of 1841 the verdict of his opponents prevailed, at any rate throughout Germany ; but this verdict, we say emphatically, was unjust. The charge that he despised and neglected German music is simply untrue. That he admired and loved the great German masters from Handel to Beethoven he proved through life in many ways. Robert relates on unquestionable authority that he made great sacrifices for the family of Mozart. When Nissen published his biography Spontini exerted himself immensely to get subscribers, personally transmitted the money to the widow, superintended the translation of the book into French, and rendered all the help in his power.[2] A preference for his own works must be conceded to any artist actively engaged in production, nor is it reasonable to expect from him an absolutely impartial judgment of the works of others. Weber's music was incomprehensible and antipathetic to Spontini, and this did him as much injury in Berlin as anything else. But his delay in performing 'Euryanthe' and 'Oberon' was caused more by inaction than opposition. For Spohr he had a great respect, as he often proved.[3] In Meyerbeer he took a great interest, until the appearance of 'Robert le Diable,' which he could not bear, calling it 'un cadavre' ; but this is no reflection on his taste. For the non-performance of the 'Huguenots' he was not responsible, as the prohibition was the King's. He was certainly not justified in calling Marschner's 'Templer und Jüdin' an 'arrangement after Spontini'—always supposing that the expression was his—but everybody knows that Marschner was deeply influenced by him. He was by no means free from envy and jealousy, but, taking for granted that he allowed himself to be swayed by his passions, foreign composers suffered just as much at his hands as German ones. Of Cherubini he thought very highly (he mounted 'Les Abencérages' and sent the composer a considerable sum from the proceeds), but Auber's 'Muette de Portici,' and Halévy's 'Juive' he thoroughly disliked, took no trouble about their production, and was much annoyed at their pleasing the public. Nor did he like Rossini, his own countryman. His horizon was limited, but if it is possible to reconcile genius with narrow-mindedness, if Spohr may be forgiven for appreciating Beethoven only partially, and Weber not at all, we must not be too hard on Spontini. It is sad to see the incapacity of even cultivated people in Berlin to be just towards

[2] Robert, p. 56, etc.
[3] The statement in the *Mendelssohn Family*, vol. i. p. 124, that he threw obstacles in the way of the performance of 'Jessonda' is quite unfounded. The minutes of the King's Theatre prove the contrary.

him. The Mendelssohn family, at whose house he at one time often visited, and to whom he showed many kindnesses, were never on good terms with him after the appearance of the 'Hochzeit des Camacho.'[1] He may not have done justice to that youthful work, but it is a pity that the noble-minded Mendelssohn should have permitted himself the angry and contemptuous expressions to be found in his letters.[2] The painful close of Spontini's career was enough to atone for all his shortcomings.

Of his last years there is little to relate. On leaving Berlin he went to Italy, and in Jan. 1843 was in Majolati. He had visited his native land several times since 1822. In 1835 he was in Naples, at San Pietro in Majella, and they showed him an exercise he had written forty years before when a pupil at the 'Turchini.' He looked at it with tears in his eyes, and then begged the librarian to tear up 'queste meschine e sconce note' (those wretched misshapen notes) and throw them in the fire.[3] In 1838 he was in Rome, and wrote (June 4) to the King offering his services as mediator between himself and the Pope on the subject of the disturbances in Cologne.[4] In 1843 he left Italy and settled at Paris, where he had many pleasant connections through his wife, an Erard, whom he had married soon after the production of 'Cortez.' He had been a member of the Institute since 1838. In 1844 the Pope made him Count of S. Andrea, and other distinctions followed. But the hope expressed by King Frederick William IV. that he would produce other works was not realised ; Berlin had broken him down physically and mentally. He revisited Germany two or three times. In 1844 he was in Dresden, where Richard Wagner had prepared for him a performance of the 'Vestale,' which he conducted with all his old energy.[5] He was invited to the Cologne Musical Festival of May 1847 to conduct some excerpts from 'Olympia,' and had a warm reception, but was too infirm to conduct, and his place was taken by Dorn, then Capellmeister at Cologne.[6] In August he visited Berlin, and was most graciously received by the King, who gave him an invitation to conduct some of his own operas at Berlin during the ensuing winter. He was much delighted, and thought a great deal about the performances after his return to Paris, and also of the best manner in which he could express his gratitude and devotion to the King ; but the project was never realised, as he was ill all the winter. In 1848 he became deaf, and his habitual gravity deepened into depression. He went back to Italy, and settled at Jesi, where he occupied

himself in founding schools and other works of public utility. In 1850 he removed to Majolati, and there died Jan. 14, 1851. Having no children he left all his property to the poor of Jesi and Majolati. P. S.

SPONTONE, or SPONTONI, BARTOLOMMEO, a madrigal composer, of whom nothing appears to be known beyond the facts that he was a pupil of Nicola Mantovano, and was maestro di cappella in the cathedral of Verona ; that he published a first book of Masses, a 5, 6, and 8, in 1588; a book of four-part madrigals in 1558 ; and three sets of madrigals for five voices at Venice in 1561 (2nd ed. 1583), 1567, and 1583. Others are contained in the collections of Waelrant (1594) and others. Cipriano de Rore prints a Dialogo, a 7, by him in 1568. A Mass, a 6, is in vol. ii of Torchi's 'L'Arte Musicale in Italia.' A fine four-part madrigal of Spontone's, 'The joyous birds,' is given in Hullah's Part Music. G.

SPRING GARDEN. See VAUXHALL.

SPRÜCHE—proverbs or sentences—are sung in the Lutheran service of the Berlin Cathedral after the reading of the Epistle :

1. On New Year's Day, 'Herr Gott, du bist unser Zuflucht.'
2. On Good Friday, 'Um unser Sünden willen.'
3. On Ascension Day, 'Erhaben, o Herr.'
4. On Christmas Day, 'Frohlocket, ihr Völker.'

Mendelssohn set these for eight-part chorus ; and in addition two more :

5. For Passion Week, 'Herr, gedenke nicht unser Übelthaten.'
6. For Advent, 'Lasset uns frohlocken.'

The six form op. 79 of his works. No. 3 ('Erhaben') begins with the same phrase as his 114th Psalm, op. 51, but there the resemblance ceases. No. 2 is dated Feb. 18, 1844, and No. 5 (in minims and for 4-part chorus) Feb. 14, 1844, and each of the two is inscribed 'vor dem Alleluja' —before the Alleluia. They are mostly short, the longest being only fifty bars in length. Schumann entitled one of his little PF. pieces 'Spruch.' [The three 'Fest- und Gedenksprüche' of Brahms, op. 109, are for eight-part chorus a cappella :— (i.) 'Unsere Väter hofften auf dich,' Ps. xxii. 4 ; (ii.) 'Wenn ein starker Gewappneter,' Luke xi. 21, 17 ; (iii.) 'Wo ist ein so herrlich Volk,' Deut. iv. 7, 9.] G.

SQUARCIALUPI, ANTONIO (also called Antonio degl' organi), a famous Florentine organist who lived in the 15th century, and who was living in Siena in 1450, and at the Florentine Court in 1467, as organist of Santa Maria. He died there about 1475. None of his compositions are extant, and he is only known as an esteemed contemporary of Dufay. A letter written by him to Dufay, dated 1467, is given by Otto Kade in the Monatshefte for 1885, No. 2. See also Haberl's 'Dufay' in the Vierteljahrsschrift, i. 436. A volume of music by various

1 Devrient's Recollections, p. 23.
2 Among others see Devrient, p. 74.
3 Florimo, Cenno Storico, p. 595.
4 Whether anything came of this offer is not known, but Gregory XVI. had a high esteem for Spontini, and asked for his views on the restoration of Catholic church-music.
5 For a clever and amusing account of it see Wagner's Gesammelte Schriften, v. 114.
6 Dorn's Aus meinem Leben, vol. iii. p. 21.

early composers, which was in Squarcialupi's possession, is in the Bibl. Laurenziana in Florence, and is described in J. Wolf's *Geschichte der Mensural-Notation*, pp. 228 ff. There is a monument to his memory in the Duomo at Florence.   *Quellen - Lexikon*, Riemann's *Lexikon*.   M.

SQUIRE, WILLIAM HENRY, was born at Ross, August 8, 1871. His father was a clever amateur violinist, and the boy's first teacher. He gained a violoncello scholarship at the Royal College of Music in 1883, which was extended for a further period of three years. He studied under Edward Howell, and made his début at a concert of Señor Albeniz at St. James's Hall, Feb. 12, 1891. At the Crystal Palace he first appeared on April 20, 1895, in Saint-Saëns's Concerto in A. In the same year he held the place of principal violoncello at the Royal Opera, Covent Garden. He was elected an associate of the Royal College in 1889. He has written a concerto for his instrument, very numerous and successful works in a popular style, many songs, two operettas (unpublished), and has had a useful and prosperous career as a concert-player and in orchestras ; he was a prominent member of the original Queen's Hall Orchestra. and for some time after the secession belonged to the London Symphony Orchestra. His sister, Mme. EMILY SQUIRE, is a successful soprano singer, a pupil of the Royal College and the Royal Academy ; she first appeared at Bath in 1888, and at the Crystal Palace in 1891.   M.

STABAT MATER. [This mediæval poem, which has had a greater popularity than any similar composition, is of uncertain authorship. It is generally ascribed to Jacopone or to Pope Innocent III., but on no sufficient evidence. It was not liturgical, and had originally no music of its own ; but it came into popular use as a devotion in the 13th century ; indulgences were granted to those who used it, and finally it crept into liturgical books and was provided with musical settings. It did not obtain its place in the Roman Missal as a Sequence till 1727, nor did a cento from it obtain a place as a Hymn in the Breviary till even later. The musical history of the poem, therefore, is concerned with the polyphonic and later writers.]

The beauty of the poem has rendered it so great a favourite with composers, that the number of fine settings we possess is very great. The earliest example that demands special notice is the 'Stabat Mater' of Josquin des Prés, founded upon the Canto fermo just mentioned, in the Thirteenth Mode transposed.[1] So elaborate is the construction of this work, that not one of the most highly developed of the composer's

Masses surpasses it. The Canto fermo is sustained by the tenor, in Larges, Longs, and Breves throughout, while four other voices accompany it, in florid counterpoint, in constant and ingenious imitation of the most elaborate character.

But not even Josquin's masterpiece will bear comparison with the two grand settings of the 'Stabat Mater' by Palestrina, either of which, as Baini observes, would alone have sufficed to immortalise him. The first and best-known of these, written for a double-choir of eight voices, has long been annually sung, in the Sistine Chapel, on the Thursday in Holy Week, and was first published by Burney in his 'La Musica della Settimana Santa,' on the authority of a copy given to him by Santarelli.[2] It is enough to say that the composition signalises the author of the 'Missa Papae Marcelli' in every page ; and that the opening phrase, containing a progression of three major chords, on a bass descending by major seconds, produces one of the most original and beautiful effects ever heard in polyphonic music.

Palestrina's second 'Stabat Mater' is written for twelve voices, disposed in three choirs ; and is in every way a worthy companion to the preceding work.[3] Ambros, indeed, denies its authenticity, and on the authority of an entry in the catalogue of the Altaemps-Ottoboni Collection in the Library of the Collegio Romano refers it to Felice Anerio, notwithstanding Baini's decisive verdict in its favour : but the internal evidence afforded by the work itself

[1] Pietro Aron quotes this fine composition as an example of the Fifth Mode; and Zarlino, as one of the Eleventh. The work was first printed in Petrucci's 'Motetti della Corona,' Lib. iii. No. 6 (Fossombrone, 1519). About 1840, Choron reprinted it in score, in Paris; and in 1881 it was given in the Notenbeilagen to Ambros's *Geschichte der Musik*, p. 61. The 'Gluck Society' performed it, in London, on May 24, 1881.

[2] It was afterwards published, in Paris, by Choron ; and by Alfieri, in his 'Raccolta di Musica sacra,' vol. vi. (Roma, 1845). For an interesting criticism upon it see Oulibicheff's *Nouvelle Biographie de Mozart*, ii. 72. He was perhaps the first to call attention to it. It was more recently edited, with marks of expression, introduction of solo voice, and other changes, by Wagner.

[3] First printed in Alfieri's 'Raccolta,' vol. vii. (Roma, 1846).

is enough to remove all doubt on the subject. It is not only a genuine work, but one of the finest Palestrina ever wrote. For the effect produced by the union of the three choirs at the words, ' O quam tristis,' as well as the manner of their alternation, in other parts of the Sequence, we must refer our readers to the work itself, in the 7th volume of Breitkopf & Härtel's complete edition.

Few modern settings of the ' Stabat Mater,' with orchestra accompaniments, are finer than (1) that by Pergolesi, for Soprano and Contralto, accompanied by Strings and Organ (to which Paisiello afterwards supplied additional accompaniments for wind).   (2) Haydn's ' Stabat Mater' is a treasury of refined and graceful melody.   (3) Next in importance to this we must rank a very fine one for six voices with accompaniments for two violins, three viole, basso, and organo, composed by Steffani, who presented it to the ' Academy of Antient Musick' in London, on his election as Honorary President for life, in 1724.   (4) Clari wrote another beautiful one, which is among the Fitzwilliam MSS. at Cambridge.   (5) A nearly contemporary work, by Astorga, is one of the best Italian productions of its period.[1]   (6) Winter's Stabat Mater may be taken as a happy example of his refined and graceful style ; and, if not a great work, is at least a remarkably pleasing one.   (7, 8, 9, 10) The Royal College of Music possesses a Stabat Mater, a 3, by Pietro Raimondi, with one composed by Padre Vito, in 1783, and two others, by Gesualdo Lanza, and the Spanish composer, Angelo Inzenga.   (11) The Chevalier Neukomm also wrote one which was very popular among his disciples.   (12) Very different from all these is Rossini's setting of the text, which has made its words familiar to thousands, who would never otherwise have heard of them.   (13) Yet even this does not represent the latest interpretation of these beautiful verses, which have been illustrated, in still more modern, and very different musical phraseology, by Dvořák.[2] [Two important English compositions deserve mention ; (14) by Ernest Walker, still in MS. ; (15) by Sir C. V. Stanford, performed at the Leeds Festival, 1907.]   w. s. r.

STABILINI, GIROLAMO (or HIERONYMO), a violin-player, born at Rome about 1762. Having attained some distinction in Italy he was invited to Edinburgh, to replace Giuseppe Puppo, as leader of the St. Cecilia Hall concerts.

Stabilini arrived at Edinburgh in 1783, and died of dropsy there on July 13, 1815, being buried in the graveyard of St. Cuthbert's or the ' West Kirk.' His tombstone is still to be seen built into an old boundary wall. Stabilini, though he does not appear to have been of very extraordinary talent, was eminently popular in Scotland, a popularity not decreased by his per-

[1] Published in score by Breitkopf & Härtel (1879).
[2] ' Stabat Mater für Soli, Chor, u. Orchester' (Simrock, 1881). Performed by the London Musical Society, March 1883.

formance and arrangement of Scots airs. ' I'll gang na mair to yon toon ' being especially associated with him.

There is a head of him in Kay's *Edinburgh Portraits.*   F. K.

STACCATO (Ital. ; Ger. *abgestossen*), ' detached,' in contradistinction to *legato*, ' connected.' The notes of a staccato passage are made short, and separated from each other by intervals of silence. Staccato effects are obtained on the pianoforte by raising the hand from the keys immediately after striking, usually by a rapid action of the wrist (this is called ' wrist-touch '), though sometimes, especially in *fortissimo*, from the elbow ; and there is also a third kind of staccato-touch called ' finger-staccato,' which is less frequently used, and which, as described by Hummel, consists in ' hurrying the fingers away from the keys, very lightly and in an inward direction.' This kind of touch is of course only applicable to passages of single notes.

On stringed instruments staccato passages are generally bowed with a separate stroke to each note, but an admirable staccato can also be produced, especially in solo music, by means of a series of rapid jerks from the wrist, the bow travelling meanwhile in one direction, from the point to the nut. Staccato on wind instruments is effected by a rapid thrusting forward of the tongue, so as to stop the current of air ; and in singing, a staccato sound is produced by an impulse from the throat upon an open vowel, and instantly checked. A striking example of vocal staccato occurs in Mozart's air, ' Gli angui d' inferno,' from ' Die Zauberflöte.' Upon the harp, or any similar instrument, and likewise upon the drum, a staccato note requires the immediate application of the palm of the hand to the vibrating string or parchment, to stop the sound.

The signs of staccato are pointed dashes ''''', or rounded dots ····, placed over or under the notes, the former indicating a much shorter and sharper sound than the latter. [See DASH, vol. i. p. 664.]   But besides the difference thus shown, the actual duration of staccato notes depends to some extent upon their written length. Thus in the following example the minims must be played longer than the crotchets (though no exact proportion need be observed), in spite of the fact that both are marked staccato alike :—

BEETHOVEN, Sonata Pathétique.

When dots placed over or under notes are covered by a curved line, an effect is intended which is of great value in the rendering of expressive and *cantabile* phrases. This is called *mezzo staccato* (half-detached), and the notes are sustained for nearly their full value, and separated by a scarcely appreciable interval. On stringed and wind instruments indeed they are frequently not separated at all, but are attacked with a certain slight emphasis which is instantly weakened again, so as to produce *almost* the effect of disconnection ; on the pianoforte, however, they must of necessity be separated, though but for an instant, and they are played with a close, firm pressure, and with but little percussion. The following is an example of the use of *mezzo staccato*, with its rendering, as nearly as it is possible to represent it in notes :—

BEETHOVEN, Sonata in C, Op. 53.

When a movement is intended to be staccato throughout, or nearly so, the word is usually written at the commencement, with the tempo-indication. Thus Mendelssohn's Prelude in B minor, op. 35, No. 3, is marked 'Prestissimo Staccato,' and Handel's chorus, 'Let us break their bonds asunder,' is 'Allegro e staccato.' F. T.

STADEN, JOHANN, was born at Nuremberg in 1581 (not 1579, as stated in the *Quellen-Lexikon*). From 1603 to about 1616 he was in the service of the Margrave Christian Ernst of Kulmbach and Bayreuth as Court-Organist. In 1616 he returned to Nuremberg, where he received the appointment of organist, first to the St. Lorenz-Kirche, and shortly afterwards to the more important St. Sebald-Kirche, in which latter post he remained till his death, Nov. 15, 1634. Staden occupies a place of some importance in the transition period of musical history at the beginning of the 17th century, when German musicianship was endeavouring to combine with the older style of pure vocal music the advantages of the newer style of instrumental accompaniment with its greater freedom of harmonic modulation. Staden, however, was on the whole more conservative and less enthusiastically progressive than his contemporaries Michael Praetorius and J. H. Schein, not to mention Heinrich Schütz. His publications were fairly numerous, though all are not preserved complete. There are six of church works proper, partly with Latin, partly with German texts, entitled respectively, 'Harmoniae Sacrae pro festis praecipuis' 4-8 voc., 1616 ; 'Harmoniarum sacrarum continuatio' 1-12 voc., 1621 ; 'Kirchen-musik,' 1 Theil mit 2-14 St., 1625 ; 'Kirchen-musik,' 2 Theil zu 1-7 St., mit violen und anderen Inst., 1626 ; 'Harmoniae novae' 3-12 voc., 1628 ; 'Harmoniae Variatae,'

1-12 voc., 1623. In these works three styles of church music are represented : the pure vocal Motet, in which Basso Continuo is not required ; the Motet with only Basso Continuo ; and the Sacred Concerto with obbligato accompaniment and instrumental preludes and interludes denominated respectively Symphonies and Ritornelli. Another series of Staden's publications consists of sacred music on German texts intended more for private or domestic performance, a kind of music which would seem to have been much in vogue among the Nuremberg citizens of those days. His chief publication of the sort is expressly entitled 'Haus-musik,' which originally appeared in four separate parts in 1623-28, and afterwards in a complete edition in 1646. This work contains 118 mostly short and comparatively simple pieces *a* 3-4 for voices, or instruments *ad libitum*, in a few cases instruments *obbligati*. Another work of the same kind, a little more elaborate, is entitled 'Musicalischer Freuden- u. Andachtswecker oder geistliche Gesänglein' zu 4-6 St., 1630. Other works belonging to the same class entitled 'Hertzentrosts-Musica,' 1630, and 'Geistlicher Music-klang,' 1633, contain mostly Lieder for one voice only with continuo accompaniment for organ, lute, or theorbo. Several of Staden's Lieder found their way into later Chorale-Books. Another department of Staden's activity as a composer consists of secular songs and instrumental dances. Three collections of secular songs *a* 4-5 with an appendix of instrumental dances appeared 1606, 1609, and 1610. Two other collections of dances alone, Pavanes, Galliardas, Courantes, etc., appeared 1618 and 1625. A comprehensive collection of instrumental works by Staden was published posthumously in 1643, containing not only dances, but pieces described as Sonatas, Symphonies, and Canzonas. Staden would appear to have been incited to the composition of these instrumental works by his official connection for a time with the Stadtpfeifer or town musicians of Nuremberg. It only remains to add that a recent volume (Jahrg. viii. Bd. i.) of the Denkmäler der Tonkunst in Bayern contains a selection of Staden's vocal works, including ten Latin Motets *a* 4-8 and twenty-five German pieces *a* 3-8, with a full biographical and critical introduction. A selection from his instrumental works is promised in a succeeding volume.   J. R. M.

STADEN, SIGMUND GOTTLIEB (or THEOPHIL), son of Johann Staden, was born in 1607. At the age of thirteen he was sent by the town authorities of Nuremberg, at the request of his father, to receive further musical instruction from Jacob Baumann, Organist and Stadtpfeifer or town musician of Augsburg. This might seem strange, considering that Johann Staden was himself a more distinguished musician than Baumann, but Baumann appears to have had during his lifetime a greater reputation as

2 u

an instrumentalist. Later on, in 1626, the younger Staden was again sent at the expense of the Nuremberg authorities to Berlin to receive instruction in the playing of the Viola bastarda, a form of the Gamba, from one Walter Rowe or Roy, an English instrumentalist in the service of the Elector of Brandenburg. In 1627 Staden received an appointment as one of the Stadtpfeifer or town musicians of Nuremberg. On the death of his father in 1634, Gottlieb or Theophil Staden, as he is indifferently called, became organist to the St. Lorenz-Kirche in succession to Valentin Dretzel, who took the elder Staden's place as organist to the St. Sebald-Kirche. Whether Staden received any further promotion is unknown. His death took place at Nuremberg, July 30, 1655. This younger Staden is now chiefly known as the composer of the first German operatic work that was ever published, an allegorical Singspiel, the full title of which is 'Das geistliche Waldgedicht oder Freudenspiel genannt Seelewig. Gesangweis auf Italianische Art gesetzet, 1644.' The work is an interesting example of the early monodic style for solo voices with accompaniment of figured Bass, but having also short instrumental preludes and interludes, sometimes for viols or violins only, sometimes for three flutes, at other times for two or three 'schalmeien' or oboes. It has been republished by Robert Eitner in modern form with the harmonies of the figured Bass written out. The text is by G. P. Harsdörffer, one of the founders of the Pegnitz-schäferei Gesellschaft in Nuremberg, who brought from Italy to Nuremberg the peculiar taste for artificial pastoralism in poetry, and for the Florentine monodic style of music in association with allegorical and spiritual dramas. Other poetical texts by Harsdörffer were set by Staden as simple Lieder for one voice with figured Bass. He did not, however, forsake altogether the older style of choral music. In 1637 he put forth a new edition of Hans Leo Hassler's 'Kirchengesänge mit vier stimmen simpliciter gesetzt' (1608), in which he included eleven new chorale-tunes and settings by his father, and five by himself. He also followed in the wake of his father in the encouragement of domestic sacred music, by publishing, in 1644, two collections entitled 'Seelenmusik,' with settings of hymns a 4 with Basso Continuo, and furnishing new melodies to the various Gesang-bücher of the time. The Quellen-Lexikon mentions an Instruction-Book for singing by him, 1648.   J. R. M.

STADLER, MAXIMILIAN, ABBOT, a sound and solid composer, born August 4, 1748, at Melk, in Lower Austria. At ten became a chorister in the monastery of Lilienfeld, where he learnt music, completing his education in the Jesuit College at Vienna. In 1766 he joined the Benedictines at Melk, and after taking priest's orders worked as a parish priest and

professor till 1786, when the Emperor Joseph, who had noticed his organ-playing, made him abbot first of Lilienfeld, and three years later of Kremsmünster. Here his prudence averted the suppression of that then famous astronomical observatory. After this he lived at various country-houses, then privately at Linz, and finally settled in Vienna. [Between 1803 and 1816 he was parish priest at Alt-Lerchenfeld and afterwards in Bohemia.] Haydn and Mozart had been old friends of his, and at the request of the widow he put Mozart's musical remains in order, and copied from the autograph score of the 'Requiem,' the Requiem and Kyrie, and the Dies irae, both copy and original being now in the Hofbibliothek at Vienna. [See vol. iii. p. 308a.] He also came forward in defence of the Requiem against Gottfried Weber, in two pamphlets — Vertheidigung der Echtheit des Mozart'schen Requiem (Vienna, 1825-26), and Nachtrag zur Vertheidigung, etc. (ib. 1827). Stadler was an excellent contrapuntist, and an authority in musical literature and history. His printed compositions include Sonatas and fugues for PF. and organ; part-songs; two requiems; several masses; a Te Deum; 'Die Frühlingsfeier,' cantata, with orchestra, to Klopstock's words; psalms, misereres, responses, offertoriums, etc.; also a response to Haydn's farewell-card for two voices and PF. [See vol. ii. p. 362.] Among his numerous MSS. are fine choruses for Collin's tragedy, 'Polyxena.' Stadler's greatest work, 'Die Befreiung von Jerusalem,' an oratorio in two parts, words by Heinrich and Matthäus von Collin, was given with great success in 1816 at the annual extra concert of the Gesellschaft der Musikfreunde, for the benefit of the proposed Conservatorium, and in 1829 at Zurich. [For list of works see Quellen-Lexikon.]

Stadler died in Vienna, Nov. 8, 1833, highly esteemed both as man and musician.   C. F. P.

STADLMAYR, JOHANN, was born at Freising in Bavaria. Fétis dates his birth 1560, but in the absence of precise documentary evidence Eitner, in the Quellen-Lexikon, considers this far too early, as the works published by the composer himself only begin in 1603 and continue to 1645. On the basis of the indications furnished by the title-pages and dedications of his works, Eitner gives the appointments which he held, as stated below. In 1603 Stadlmayr subscribes himself as a musician in the service of the Archbishop of Salzburg. In 1610 he was Capellmeister to the Archduke Maximilian of Austria probably at Innsbruck. In 1625 he acts in the same capacity to the Archduke Leopold at Innsbruck, and from 1636 he subscribes himself as Music-director to the Archduchess Claudia at Innsbruck. His death took place at Innsbruck on July 12, 1648, and he is then described as having been Hofcapell-meister. Stadlmayr's works are all for the services of the Roman Church, but show the gradual supersession of the earlier pure vocal style of church music by the modern style of instrumental accompaniment. There is, first, the regular employment of Basso Continuo, followed by the substitution *ad libitum* of an instrumental choir, *a* 4 or 8 as the case may be, for one or other of the vocal choirs, and the culminating point is reached in the definite specification of instruments which are now written for in a definitely instrumental style. The dates and titles, somewhat abbreviated, of Stadlmayr's chief publications as given below, will serve to confirm what we have said :—

1603.   Magnificat *a* 5-8. 10 n.   (No mention of Basso Continuo in the title of this or the work following.)
1608.   Magnificat *a* 4-8, 13 n.
1610.   Missae 8 voc., cum duplici Basso ad Organum. 5 n.
1614.   Magnificat. Symphoniae variae secundum varios modos musicos, aliae octonis, una 12 voc., cum Bc.
1616.   Missae 12 voc., cum triplici Bc.
1618.   Cantici Mariani septies variati cum 12 voc. c. triplici Bass. Org.
1625.   Musica super cantum gregorianum.   Pars 1.   Missarum dominicalium Introitus. . . 52 n.   Pars 11.   Festorum introitus. 50 n.   5 voc.   c.   Bc. *ad libitum*.
1628.   Hymni totius anni . . . *a* 4, quibus et alii pro Festis solem-nioribus cum Symphoniis *a* 4-8, accesserunt in quibus pro ratione variant possunt instrumenta Musica cum Basso continuo.
1631.   Missae concertatae *a* 6 adjuncto Choro secundo sive ripieni.
1638.   Odae sacrae. . . *a* 5 v., et totidem instr.
1640.   Salmi *a* 2 et 3 v.   c. 2 V. o Cornetti.
1641.   Psalmi integri *a* 4 voc. concertantibus, quatuor aliis acces-soriis ad lib. accinendis cum 2 Cornet, sive Violin.
1642.   Missae Concertatae *a* 10-12 et instrum., cum 4 partibus pro secundo choro.
1643.   Missae ix voc. primo choro concert. *a* 5 voc.   Secundo pleno cum Symphoniis.
1646.   Apparatus musicus Sacrarum cantorium 6-24 vocib. et instr.

Of all these works, the only one which has as yet appeared in a modern reprint is the Hymni *a* 4, 1628, edited by J. E. Habert for the Denkmäler der Tonkunst in Oesterreich, Band III. Erster Theil. But Habert has only given the simple Hymns *a* 4, without accompaniment. It might have been more interesting, historically, if he had also given the Hymns with instrumental accompaniment and ritornelli.   J. R. M.

STÄNDCHEN (Ger.), 'Serenade.'

STAFFORD, WILLIAM COOKE, born in 1793 at York, published at Edinburgh in 1830 a 12mo volume entitled *A History of Music,* a work chiefly noted for its inaccuracy, but which notwithstanding was translated into French (12mo, Paris, 1832) and German (8vo, Weimar, 1835). [He died at Norwich, Dec. 23, 1876. *Brit. Mus. Biog.*]   W. H. H.

STAGGINS, NICHOLAS, was taught music by his father, a musician of little standing. Although of slender ability he won the favour of Charles II., who, in 1682, appointed him Master of the King's Band of Musick ; and in the same year the University of Cambridge, upon the King's request, conferred upon him the degree of Mus. D.   The performance of the customary exercise being dispensed with, great dissatisfaction was occasioned, to allay which Staggins, in July 1684, performed an exercise, whereupon he was appointed Professor of Music in the University, being the first who held that office. Staggins composed the Odes for William III.'s birthday in 1693 and 1694, and for Queen

Anne's birthday, 1705. [In 1693 he was allowed £200 per annum as Master of the Musick (Calendar of Treasury Papers). W. H. G. F. In 1697 he gave a concert of his own music in York-buildings, London ; in the following year Eccles succeeded him as Master of the King's Musick. *Quellen-Lexikon.*] Songs by him are contained in 'Choice Ayres, Songs and Dialogues,' 1675, and other collections of the time ; and a dialogue, 'How unhappy a lover am I,' composed for Dryden's 'Conquest of Granada,' Part II., is included in J. S. Smith's 'Musica Antiqua.'   He died in 1705.   W. H. H.

STAHLSPIEL (Ger. *stahl,* 'steel,' and *spiel,* 'play'). 1. An instrument consisting of a series of accurately-tuned steel bars loosely fastened to a frame and generally played by means of two small hammers—one in each hand of the performer,—but sometimes constructed so as to be played from a keyboard.   It is used in military music and known by the name Lyra, the steel bars being arranged on a lyre-shaped frame. For orchestral use the bars are arranged in two rows, in the exact relative positions of the white and black keys of the pianoforte.   The compass is from two to two and a half octaves, and the tone incisive and penetrating, but although the instrument is susceptible of very charming effects it should be sparingly used. It is very frequently written for under the names Glockenspiel and Carillon, so much so that in modern use the three names are alternatives for one and the same thing.   Originally the two latter were applied to an instrument consisting of a series of small *bells* ; but steel bars have been found to be more convenient, more easily manipulated, better in tone—being free from the dissonant overtones so particularly prominent in *small* bells,—and capable of the most accurate tuning. Excellent examples of the effective treatment of the instrument will be found in the works of Wagner ('Walküre' and 'Meistersinger'), Tchaikovsky, Strauss, Elgar, Parry, Mackenzie, Cowen, etc.

2. An organ stop consisting of a series of steel bars played from the manuals and generally extending from middle C upwards, but rarely exceeding three octaves in compass.   W. W. S.

STAINER, JACOB, a celebrated German violin-maker, born at Absam, a village near Hall, about one German mile from Innsbruck, July 14, 1621 ; died 1683.   According to one story, the boy had a love of music, which induced the parish priest to send him to an organ-builder at Innsbruck.   This trade, however, he found too laborious. He therefore took to making stringed instruments, serving his apprenticeship to an Innsbruck 'Lautenmacher' ; after which he proceeded to travel, after the usual fashion of German apprentices. In the course of his travels, according to tradition, he visited and worked at Cremona and other places in Italy ; and the common story is that he worked under Antonius or Nicholas Amati, and afterwards spent some time at Venice, where he wrought in the shop of Vimercati. Of all this, however there is not a particle of evidence. It may be said that violins are in existence, signed by Stainer and dated from Cremona ; but these are now believed to be spurious. Probably he found Italian violins in use among the Italian musicians at the court of the Archduke Ferdinand Charles, Count of the Tyrol, at Innsbruck, and after examining their construction and contrasting them with the rude workmanship of the ordinary German Lautenmacher, conceived the idea of making violins on Italian principles. He began at a very early age, if we may trust an apparently genuine label dated 1641. His reputation was very quickly made, for in 1643, according to the *Jahresbericht des Museums in Salzburg* for 1858, he sold a ' Viola bastarda ' to the Archbishop of Salzburg for 30 florins. It is, however, possible that there may be a mistake as to this date. He married in 1645 Margaret Holzhammer, by whom he had eight daughters, and one son, who died in infancy. Henceforward, to his death in 1683, the life of Stainer shows little variety. He made a great number of stringed instruments of all sorts, which he chiefly sold at the markets and fairs of the neighbouring town of Hall. The forests of ' Haselfichte ' [see KLOTZ], which clothe the slopes of the Lafatsch and the Gleirsch, supplied him with the finest material in the world for his purpose ; and tradition says that Stainer would walk through the forest carrying a sledge-hammer, with which he struck the stems of the trees to test their resonance ; and at the falling of timber on the mountain-slopes, Stainer would station himself at some spot where he could hear the note yielded by the tree as it rebounded from the mountain side. In 1648 the Archduke Ferdinand Charles paid a visit to Hall, in the course of which Stainer exhibited and played upon his fiddles, and the Archduke thenceforth to his death in 1662 became his constant patron. Ten years later he received by diploma the title of Hof-geigenmacher to the Archduke, and in 1669 (Jan. 9) the office was renewed to him by a fresh diploma on the lapse of the county of Tyrol to the Emperor Leopold I. Stainer seems to have been always in embarrassed circumstances, owing partly to his dealings with Solomon Hübmer, a Jew of Kirchdorf, with whom he was constantly at law. In 1669, having fallen under a suspicion of Lutheranism, he was imprisoned and forced to recant. In 1672 he sold a viola da gamba and two tenor viols at Salzburg for 72 florins, and in 1675 at the same place a violin for 22 fl. 4 kr. He was still at work in 1677, in which year he made two fine instruments for the monastery of St. Georgenburg. Soon after this date he ceased from his labours. In the same year he presented an ineffectual petition to the Emperor for pecuniary assistance. In his

latter years Stainer became of unsound mind, in which condition he died in 1683, leaving his wife and several daughters surviving him : and in 1684 his house was sold by his creditors, his family having disclaimed his property on account of the debts with which it was burdened. His wife died in great poverty in 1689. There is therefore no truth whatever in the story of his retirement after the death of his wife to a Benedictine monastery, where he is said to have devoted himself to the manufacture of a certain number of violins of surpassing excellence, which he presented to the Electors and the Emperor. Stainer undoubtedly made violins, probably of special excellence, for the orchestras of some of the Electors ; but such instruments were made and sold in the ordinary way of trade. In course of time, when one of his best-finished instruments turned up, the contrast between it and the crowd of common ones which bore his name caused it to be looked on as one of these ' Elector Violins.' These violins, however, cannot have been the work of his last years, during which he was insane, and had to be confined in his house at Absam, where the wooden bench to which he was chained is still to be seen.

Stainer's place in the history of German fiddle-making is strongly marked, and it accounts for his fame and his substantial success. He was the first to introduce into Germany those Italian principles of construction which are the secret of sonority. The degree of originality with which Stainer is to be credited cannot be precisely determined. Some trace his model to the early Tyrolese viol-makers, but in the opinion of other authorities the peculiarities of the Stainer violins are strictly original. As a mere workman Stainer is entitled to the highest rank, and if he had but chosen a better model, his best instruments would have equalled those of Stradivarius himself. Like that celebrated maker he was famous for the great number as well as the excellence of his productions. He made an immense number of instruments, some more, and others less, finely finished, but all substantially of the same model : and the celebrity which he gained caused his pattern to be widely copied, in Germany, in England, and even in Italy, at a time when Stradivarius and Joseph Guarnerius were producing instruments in all respects enormously superior. This endured more or less for a century ; but the fashion passed away, and his imitators took to imitating those Italian makers whose constructive principles he had adopted. All Stainer's works bear his peculiar impress. The main design bears a rough resemblance to that of the Amati, but the model is higher ; the belly, instead of forming a finely-rounded ridge, is flattened at the top, and declines abruptly to the margins ; the middle curves are shallow and ungraceful ; the *f*-holes are shorter, and have a square and somewhat mechanical cut ; the top and bottom volutes of the _f_'s are rounder and more nearly of a size than in the Cremona instruments, but the wood is of the finest quality ; the finish, though varying in the different classes of instruments, invariably indicates a rapid and masterly hand ; and the varnish is always rich and lustrous. It is of all colours, from a deep thick brown to a fine golden amber, equal to that of Cremona ; and in his best works the exterior alone would justify the celebrity of the maker. But to understand the secret of Stainer's success the violin must be opened, and it then appears that the thicknesses of the wood and the disposition of the blocks and linings are identical with those of the Cremona makers. The difference will become more obvious when an old German viol is examined. It will be found that the older German makers, though they finished their instruments with great care and sometimes with laborious ornament, settled their dimensions and thicknesses by guess, and used no linings at all. Stainer's instruments are poor in respect of tone. The combination of height and flatness in the model diminishes the intensity of the tone, though it produces a certain sweetness and flexibility. Popular as the model once was, the verdict of musicians is now unanimous against it, and the Stainer instruments are now valued less for practical use than as curiosities. The violins, which are found of three different sizes, are the best worth having ; the tenors are good for little. The violins are abundant enough, even after allowing for the vast number of spurious instruments which pass under the maker's name ; but they vary greatly in value, according to their class, and the condition in which they are. Their value greatly decreased during the 19th century. A fine specimen that would have brought £100 a century ago will now scarcely produce £20, and the inferior instruments have depreciated in proportion. Small instruments of the common sort, which may be bought very cheap, are useful for children. Stainer's best instruments have written labels : some of the common ones have in very small Roman letterpress in the middle of a large slip of paper, ' Jacobus Stainer in Absom prope Oenipontum Anno (1678).' It is not impossible that some of these may have been made by other hands under his direction. E. J. P.

[On the authority of Herr S. Rüf, whose narrative of Stainer's life the above account follows, Stainer's father—Martin Stainer—married Sabina Gräfinger, by whom he had three sons : (1) Paul, who became a master-joiner and married Ursula Dankler ; (2) Mark, who migrated to Austria where he established himself as a violin-maker but attained no celebrity ; (3) Jacobus, the subject of this biography. This last, by his marriage with Margaret Holzhammer, left eight daughters, two of whom died,

single and in poverty, shortly after their mother in 1689. It must be borne in mind that the generally accepted date of Stainer's death, 1683, is only approximate. This date appears on the tablet attached to his house, and also on the handsome monumental stone erected to his memory in Absam Church in 1842 by the Pastor Herr Lechlatner. The sole evidence that goes to prove that Stainer no longer existed in 1684 is the purchase of his house by his brother-in-law Blasius Kiel, after which Stainer's widow and eight daughters became homeless wanderers. This house is to-day ' a well-to-do picturesque _châlet_, standing in its own garden and courtyard, half overgrown by a flourishing plum-tree that springs from the south-east corner.' It was bought by Stainer from his brother-in-law, Paul Holzhammer, on Nov. 12, 1666, and Blasius Kiel, as already mentioned, bought it for seven hundred florins in 1684. On a tablet affixed to the front of the house is the following inscription—

In diesem Hause lebte seiner Kunst Jakob Stainer, der Vater der deutschen Geige, Geboren zu Absam 14 Juli 1621, hier gestorben 1683.

Although this house was restored, and to some extent reconstructed in 1820, the balcony on which Stainer was known to store his wood still remains and is employed by its present owners for the like purpose. Within, the house is bereft of all relics of the great violin-maker, save the actual bench at which Stainer laboured.

No attempt to gather any record of Stainer's life was made for over one hundred years after his death ; but the deficiency was filled in with numberless romances about ' the father of the German fiddle,' from 1825, when the _Orangenbluter_ published a story entitled ' Jacob Stainer,' to 1878, when a version of Dr. Schuler's novel was published at Innsbruck in the form of a play from the pen of Josef Erler, which adaptation was entitled _Des Kaisers Geigenmacher in Tirol_. Other fanciful versions of Stainer's life have appeared from time to time in various German newspapers and periodicals ; a full list of these, together with the earliest trustworthy account of Stainer, is given by Herr S. Rüf in his biography of the maker.

Rüf, _Der Geigenmacher Jacobus Stainer von Absam in Tirol_, Innsbruck, 1872 ; Oka, F., _J. S. der erste deutsche Meister in Geigenbau_ published in the _Neue Berliner Musikzeitung_ Nos. 22, 23, 31, May 7, June 1854 ; Otto, _A Treatise on the Structure and Preservation of the Violin_ (first edition (German), 1817 ; three English editions translated by John Bishop) ; Stoeving, _Von der Violine_ ; Wasielewski, _Die Violine_ ; Von Lutgendorff, _Die Geigen- und Lautenmacher_ ; Hawkins, _History of Music_ ; Vidal, _Les Instruments à Archet_ ; Grillet, _Les Ancêtres du Violon_ ; Pearce, _Violins and Violin-Making_ ; Reade, _A Lost Art Revived_ ; Racster, _Chats on Violins_ (containing an English translation of Von Gilm's poem); Hill, *Violins and their Makers* (two pictures of Stainer's house); Heron-Allen, *A Pilgrimage to the House of Jacob Stainer* (*Musical Times*, August 1900).   E. H-A.

STAINER, MARCUS, brother of the last mentioned, a celebrated Tyrolese violin-maker. Mark Stainer learned his trade from Jacob, and set up for himself at the village of Laufen. The famous Florentine player Veracini had two violins by this maker, christened 'St. Peter' and 'St. Paul,' and he reckoned them superior to all Italian violins. In sailing from London to Leghorn in 1746 Veracini was shipwrecked and the fiddles were lost. The instruments of this maker are extremely rare. They are made of unusually fine material, of somewhat large size, covered with dark varnish, and are sweet though decidedly feeble in tone. Like those of Jacob Stainer, they usually contain written labels. One of these runs thus: 'Marcus Stainer, Bürger und Geigenmacher in Küfstein, anno 1659.' Occasionally Marcus Stainer yielded to an obvious temptation, and sold his violins under the name of his more famous brother.   E. J. P.

STAINER, SIR JOHN, Mus.D., son of a schoolmaster, was born in London, June 6, 1840, entered the choir of St. Paul's Cathedral in 1847—by which time he was already a remarkable player and an excellent sight-singer—and remained there till 1856, very often taking the organ on occasion. In 1854 he was appointed organist and choirmaster of St. Benedict and St. Peter, Paul's Wharf, of which the Rev. J. H. Coward, classical master to the choristers, was Rector. At the same time he learnt harmony from Bayley, master of the St. Paul's boys, and counterpoint from Dr. Steggall, for whom he sang the soprano part in his Mus.D. exercise at Cambridge in 1852. Through the liberality of Miss Hackett he received a course of lessons on the organ from George Cooper at St. Sepulchre's. In 1856 he was selected by Sir F. Ouseley as organist of his then newly-founded College at Tenbury, where he remained for some time. In 1859 he matriculated at Christ Church, Oxford, and took the degree of Mus.B. Shortly after, he left Tenbury for Magdalen College, Oxford, where after six months' trial he was appointed organist and *informator choristarum*. He then entered St. Edmund Hall as a resident undergraduate, and while discharging his duties at Magdalen, worked for his B.A. degree in Arts, which he took in Trinity Term 1863. Meantime, on the death of Stephen Elvey, he had been appointed organist of the University of Oxford, and was conductor of a flourishing College Musical Society and of another association at Exeter College. But nothing interfered with his duties at Magdalen, where he raised the choir to a very high state of efficiency. In 1865 he proceeded to his Mus.D. degree, and 1866 to his M.A., and became one

of the examiners for musical degrees. In 1872 he left Oxford and succeeded Goss as organist of St. Paul's Cathedral. The services were at that time by no means what they should have been; but Stainer possessed the confidence of the Dean and Chapter, and his hard work, knowledge, and tact, at last brought them to a worthier pitch of excellence.

Dr. Stainer did not confine his activity to his own University. He was a member of the Board of Musical Studies at Cambridge, and for two years was also examiner for the degree of Mus.D. there. He was examiner for musical degrees in the University of London; an Hon. Member of the Royal Academy of Music, and Hon. Fellow of the Tonic Sol-fa College; a Vice-President of the College of Organists, and a Vice-President of the Musical Association, of which he was virtually the founder. He was a juror at the Paris Exhibition of 1880, and at its close was decorated with the Legion of Honour. He was attached to the National Training School, London, as a Professor of Organ and Harmony, from its foundation, and at Easter 1881 succeeded Sullivan as Principal. In 1882 he succeeded Hullah as Inspector of Music in the Elementary Schools of England for the Privy Council. He was also a Member of Council of the Royal College of Music. [In 1888 he was obliged to resign his post at St. Paul's owing to his failing sight. In the same year he received the honour of knighthood. He was appointed Professor of Music in the University of Oxford in 1889, was Master of the Company of Musicians in 1900, died at Verona, March 31, 1901, and was buried at Holywell Cemetery, Oxford, April 6, of the same year. See *Musical Times*, 1901, pp. 297, etc.] His compositions embrace an oratorio, 'Gideon'; a cantata, 'The Daughter of Jairus,' composed by request for the Worcester Festival of September 1878; a cantata, 'St. Mary Magdalen' (Gloucester Festival, 1883); and an oratorio, 'The Crucifixion'—his most popular work—1887. He also wrote many services and anthems, and among his most successful and artistic pieces of church music must be named the well-known 'Sevenfold Amen.' He is the author of the two very popular manuals of *Harmony* and *The Organ* in Novello's series, and of a work on Bible music, and was part editor with W. A. Barrett, of a *Dictionary of Musical Terms* (Novello, 1876 and 1898). He also edited the interesting *Dufay and his Contemporaries*, 1898. Sir J. Stainer was beloved and esteemed by all who knew him, and was an admirable and efficient musician in all branches; but his great excellence was in his organ-playing, and especially his accompaniments, which were unsurpassed. He was a shining example of the excellent foundation of sound musical knowledge which may be got out of the various duties and shifts of the life of a clever chorister in one of our cathedrals.   G.

STAMATY, Camille Marie, son of a Greek father and a very musical French mother, was born at Rome, March 23, 1811. After the death of his father in 1818 his mother returned to France, remained some time at Dijon, and finally went to Paris. There, after long coquetting between music and business as a profession, Stamaty, in 1828, took an employé's post in the Prefecture of the Seine. But music retained its influence on him, and under Fessy and Kalk- brenner he became a remarkable player. An attack of rheumatism forced him from playing to the study of composition. In March 1835 he made his first public appearance in a concert, the programme of which contained a concerto and other pieces of his composition. This led to his being much sought after as a teacher. But he was not satisfied, and in Sept. 1836 went to Leipzig, attracted, doubtless, by the fame of Men- delssohn and Schumann, then both resident there. After a short course of instruction from Mendels- sohn, he returned to Paris early in 1837, and introduced much more classical music—Bach, Mozart, Beethoven, etc.—into his programmes. In 1846 he lost his mother, in 1848 he married, in 1862 was made Chevalier of the Legion of Honour, and on April 19, 1870, closed a long career of usefulness. From a crowd of pupils it is sufficient to name Gottschalk and Saint- Saëns. His most permanent works are educa- tional—' Le Rhythme des doigts,' much praised ; ' Études progressives' (opp. 37-39) ; ' Études concertantes' (opp. 46, 47) ; ' Esquisse' (op. 19) ; ' Études pittoresques' (op. 21) ; ' Six études caractéristiques sur Obéron,' and 12 transcrip- tions entitled ' Souvenir du Conservatoire.'

Besides these, his solo sonatas in F minor and C minor ; a PF. trio, op. 12 ; a concerto in A minor, op. 2 ; sonatas, opp. 8 and 14 ; and other works, were much esteemed at the time. The concerto and some brilliant variations on an original theme (op. 3) were reviewed very favourably by Schumann (Ges. Schriften, ii. 155, 181).   G.

STAMITZ (sometimes called STEINMETZ). A Bohemian musical family of much renown in the 18th century. (1) Johann Wenzl Anton [1] born June 19, 1717, son of the schoolmaster at Deutschbrod ; a man evidently of great origin- ality and force. In 1742 he took part as a solo violinist in the festivities at the coronation of the Emperor Carl VII., and shortly afterwards was taken to Mannheim by the Elector, who in 1745 appointed him his leading violin and director of chamber-music ; he remained there till his death on or before March 27, 1757. He wrote much music for the violin, which shows him to have been a great and brilliant player. Six con- certos, 3 sets of 6 sonatas, and some solo exercises, giving the effect of duets, were published at Paris,

[1] The confusion between Johann and Carl, his son (see below), is made worse by the habit of calling the father ' Johann Carl' as many authorities have done. Eitner says that his son Carl sometimes used the name Johann.

and 21 concertos and 9 solos are still in MS. He also wrote symphonies, of which several sets of 6 were published, as well as concertos and sonatas for the harpsichord. [The thematic catalogue of 45 symphonies and 10 orchestral trios is given in Jhrg. iii. 1 of the ' Denkmäler deutscher Tonkunst in Bayern,' where four of the symphonies and one trio are reprinted. The introduction by Hugo Riemann is the most detailed account of the family that has yet appeared.] The music shows a great advance in effect and expression on anything that pre- ceded them. (2) His brother, Anton Thad- dæus, born 1721, was a violoncello-player ; according to Gerber, he was also in the Mann- heim band. He became a priest, rose to many dignities, and died at Altbunzlau August 23, 1768. Another brother, Joseph, was distin- guished as a painter. Cannabich was one of Johann's pupils ; but a still more memorable one was (3) his eldest son, Carl, born at Mannheim, May 7, 1746, and like his father a remarkable violinist and composer. [He was a second violin in the Mannheim band in 1762-70.] In 1770 he went to Paris, and was known there as a player of the viola and viola d'amore. He played in London in 1778. His opera, ' Der verliebte Vormund,' was given at Frankfort. In 1785 he returned to Germany, and in 1787 we find him at Prague and Nuremberg, in 1790 at Cassel, and then at St. Petersburg, where he remained for some years, and where he brought out a grand opera, ' Dardanus.' He died at Jena in 1801.

His works include 70 symphonies, many published in opp. 1, 2, 3, 4, 6, 9, 13, 15, 16, 18, 19, and 24 ; others are in MS. They are mostly for a larger orchestra than that employed by his father ; some have two 'concertante' violin parts ; there are also many concertos, quartets, trios, etc. (see the summary in Riemann's preface to Denkmäler deutscher Tonkunst, Jhgr. iii. 1). (4) Another son of Johann was Anton, born at Mannheim, 1753. He went to Paris with Carl, and published 13 symphonies, 3 piano concertos, a violin concerto, a violoncello con- certo, and many quartets, trios, and duets. [The family had a great influence on the development of the symphonic form ; the father raised the band to a pitch of superlative excellence, and Carl's experiments in orchestration pointed the way for later men. See Riemann's Lexikon, the Quellen-Lexikon, etc.] He died about 1820.   G.

STANFORD, Sir Charles Villiers, Mus. D., D.C.L., LL.D., was born Sept. 30, 1852, at Dub- lin, where his father, an enthusiastic amateur vocalist, was Examiner in the Court of Chancery. His first teachers were Arthur O'Leary and Sir Robert Stewart, and various efforts in songs, piano pieces, etc., were published while he was yet a child. His first composition is stated to have been a march composed in 1860, and played in the pantomime ' Puss in Boots,' at the Theatre Royal, Dublin, 1863-64 (see Mus. Times, 1898,

p. 785). He matriculated at Queen's College, Cambridge, in 1870, as choral scholar. On his appointment in 1873 to the important post of organist to Trinity College, in succession to Dr. J. L. Hopkins, he 'migrated' as an undergraduate to that college, from which he graduated in 1874 in Classical Honours. He had filled the post of conductor of the Cambridge Amateur Vocal Guild for a year or two before this, and had brought Sir R. Stewart's cantata, 'The Eve of St. John,' to a hearing in 1872. This Society was soon joined to the Cambridge University Musical Society (the choir of which had hitherto consisted of male voices only), and Stanford raised the position of the Society to a remarkably high level, incidentally making Cambridge an important musical centre. He was appointed conductor of the Society in 1873, and his activity was not long in bearing good fruit, in the first performances in England of Schumann's 'Faust' (Part iii.) and many other things, such as Brahms's 'Rhapsodie.' In each year, from 1874 to 1876, he was given leave of absence in order to prosecute his studies first with Reinecke at Leipzig, and then with Kiel at Berlin. In the spring of 1876, on the production of Tennyson's 'Queen Mary' at the Lyceum Theatre, the incidental music was provided by Stanford, having been composed at the poet's suggestion. This work, and a symphony which gained the second prize in a competition held at the Alexandra Palace, in the same year, brought the young composer's name into prominence, and from that time onwards he has been more or less regularly before the public as composer and conductor. In 1877, when he proceeded M.A., he organised and directed a concert at which works by Brahms and Joachim were performed for the first time in England, on the occasion when the Honorary Mus.D. degree was offered to both composers, and accepted by the latter. This was the first of many concerts at which the recipients of honorary musical degrees were similarly honoured. In 1877, too, a Festival Overture was played at the Gloucester Festival, and subsequently given at the Crystal Palace. A setting of Psalm xlvi. was produced at Cambridge, and afterwards at a Richter concert.

The symphony just mentioned, in B flat, was played at the Crystal Palace in March 1879, but like a second 'Elegiac' symphony in D minor, played at Cambridge in 1882, concertos for PF. and for violoncello, etc., is not included in the list of opus-numbers. Stanford's first opera, 'The Veiled Prophet of Khorassan,' to a libretto by W. Barclay Squire, produced at the Court Theatre, Hanover, Feb. 6, 1881, was only given once in England, at Covent Garden, July 26, 1893 ; an orchestral serenade (op. 17) was produced at the Birmingham Festival of 1882. In 1883 he received the hon. degree of Mus.D. at Oxford, and the same

degree at Cambridge in 1888. In 1885 he succeeded Otto Goldschmidt as conductor of the Bach Choir, and in 1887 was elected Professor of Music in the University of Cambridge, on the death of Sir G. A. Macfarren. He devoted his energies to improving the standard of general education required for the musical degrees at Cambridge, and in this and many other ways his influence on the music of the University, and the country at large, has been of great importance. On the opening of the Royal College of Music he became Professor of Composition, conductor of the orchestra and of the annual operatic performances, which have maintained a high standard of excellence, and which have brought many neglected works, old and new, to a hearing. In 1892 he resigned the post of organist to Trinity College, and has since lived in London. In 1901 he was appointed conductor of the Leeds Festival, and received the honour of knighthood ; in 1902 he gave up the conductorship of the Bach Choir. In 1904 he was elected a member of the Royal Academy of Arts at Berlin.

Stanford's Irish descent gives his music a strong individuality, which is not only evident in his arrangements of Irish songs and in his work as a collector (see IRISH MUSIC), but stands revealed in his 'Irish Symphony' (op. 28), in the opera, 'Shamus O'Brien' (op. 61), the two orchestral 'Irish Rhapsodies' (opp. 78 and 84), the 'Irish Fantasies' for violin, and in many other definitely Irish compositions. The easy flow of melody, and the feeling for the poetical and romantic things in legendary lore (illustrated in the early song, 'La Belle Dame sans Merci,' the 'Voyage of Maeldune,' and many other places), are peculiarly Irish traits ; but his rare mastery of every resource of orchestra or voices, the thoroughness of his workmanship, and his remarkable skill as a teacher of composition, are qualities not generally associated even with the more brilliant natives of Ireland. His wonderful versatility allows him to adopt, successfully, styles far removed from one another ; that of the Latin settings of 'Te Deum,' 'Requiem,' 'Stabat Mater,' and of the Mass in G, has an affinity with the Italian composers of the 18th century. Part of his oratorio, 'Eden,' is strictly modal in utterance, a large number of his instrumental compositions are in the classical idioms of Germany, and his use of the fantastic or rhapsodical style of Ireland has been already referred to. In yet another style he has won what is perhaps the greatest success he has yet achieved : the early song, 'In praise of Neptune,' from op. 19, may have been a kind of essay in the nautical style, which reached its full fruition in the splendid 'Revenge' (Leeds Festival, 1886), the choral ballad which is known and loved wherever the best choral music is practised. The five 'Songs of the Sea' (op. 91), for baritone solo, male chorus, and orchestra, have had hardly a less success, and in all these there is a breezy and unmistakably English atmosphere that endears them to all hearers. His use of orchestral colour is full of interest, and his scores are models of effective yet not exaggerated writing ; but in one and all the colouring is properly subordinated to the design, and in the thematic development of his subjects will be found the central interest of these compositions. Although his 'Shamus O'Brien' was a great success, running for many weeks, his more serious operas have not as yet been heard by enough English people to be properly assessed on their real merits. The first, already mentioned, was only given for one extra night after the close of one of Harris's seasons ; his second, 'Savonarola,' brought out at Hamburg April 18, 1884, was only performed for a single night under Richter at Covent Garden, July 9, 1884, owing to difficulties connected with its publication ; the third, 'The Canterbury Pilgrims,' had four performances at Drury Lane Theatre by the Carl Rosa Company, in 1884 ; 'Much Ado about Nothing' (words by Julian Sturgis) was produced with great care and effect at Covent Garden, May 30, 1900, but in spite of the success of its two performances it also disappeared quickly from the repertory. Of course it is necessary to remember the singular methods of operatic management in England before assuming that these works have failed to attract the English public. Neither 'Savonarola' nor 'The Canterbury Pilgrims' has a really good libretto ; the former, which begins with a passionately emotional prologue, loses its dramatic interest before the end is reached, and the frequent allusions to the lovely 'Angelus ad virginem,' though beautiful musically, are of small value on the stage. In the same way, 'Sumer is icumen in' is used as a kind of motto to 'The Canterbury Pilgrims,' and with all the brightness of its first act, and the romantic charm of the second, the impression left by the trial in the third act is not very strong. 'Much Ado about Nothing,' alone of these works, has a remarkably effective close, and the dirge to Hero strikes a note of welcome pathos. 'Shamus O'Brien' was furnished with regular recitatives in place of the original spoken dialogue, for the performance in Germany (Breslau, 1907) ; in its original form, and interpreted by capable actors, it is deliciously bright and characteristic, with a touch of wild and fantastic beauty in the 'caoine' of the banshee.

The list of Stanford's compositions is as follows :—

(Unpublished works are indicated by an asterisk.)

Op.
1. Eight songs from George Eliot's 'Spanish Gypsy.'
2. Suite for pf.
3. Toccata for pf.
4. Six songs by Heine.
5. 'Die Auferstehung,' Resurrection Hymn by Klopstock, for choir and orchestra.
6. Incidental music for Tennyson's 'Queen Mary.' (Lyceum Theatre, 1876.)
7. Six songs by Heine.

Op.
8. Ps. xlvi. for soli, choir, and orchestra.
9. Sonata, pf. and vcello, in A.
10. Morning, Communion, and Evening Service in B flat.
11. Sonata for pf. and vln. in D.
12. Evening Service in A (Festival of the Sons of the Clergy, 1880), for choir, orchestra, and organ.
13. Three Intermezzi, pf. and clarinet.
14. Six songs ('Requiescat,' 'Ode to the Skylark,' 'Sweeter than the violet,' 'There be none of Beauty's daughters,' 'Tragödie,' and 'Le bien vient en dormant').
15. Quartet, pf. and strings in F.
16. 'Awake, my heart,' Hymn by Klopstock.
17. Serenade for full orchestra in G.
18. Three Cavalier Songs (Browning), for baritone and male choir.
19. Six songs ('A Hymn in praise of Neptune,' 'Lullaby,' 'To the Rose,' 'Come to me when the earth is fair,' 'Boat Song,' 'The Rhine Wine ').
20. Pf. Sonata in D flat.*
21. Elegiac Ode (Walt Whitman), for soli and chorus and orch. (Norwich Festival, 1884.)
22. Oratorio, 'The Three Holy Children.' (Birmingham Festival, 1885.)
23. Incidental Music to the 'Eumenides.' (Cambridge, 1885.)
24. 'The Revenge' (Tennyson), choral ballad. (Leeds Festival, 1886.)
25. Quintet for pf. and strings, in D minor.
26. Carmen Saeculare (Tennyson), for soprano solo, and chorus. Composed for Queen Victoria's Jubilee, 1887.
27. Psalm cl. for soprano and chorus. (Opening of Manchester Exhibition, 1887.)
28. 'Irish Symphony' in F minor. Richter, 1887.
29. Incidental music to the 'Oedipus Tyrannus.' (Cambridge, 1887.)
30. A Child's Garland of Songs (Stevenson).
31. Symphony in F. (Berlin, Jan. 14, and Crystal Palace, Feb. 23, 1889.)
32. Suite for vln. and orchestra. (Berlin, Jan., and Philharmonic, March 28, 1889.)
33. Overture, 'Queen of the Seas.' (Armada Tercentary.)
34. 'The Voyage of Maeldune' (Tennyson), soli, choir, and orchestra. (Leeds Festival, 1889.)
35. Trio in E flat for pf. and strings.
36. Morning, Communion, and Evening Service in F.
37. Two Anthems.
38. Anthem, 'The Lord is my Shepherd.'
39. Second Sonata for pf. and vcello in D minor.
40. Oratorio, 'Eden' (Robert Bridges). (Birmingham Festival, 1891.)
41. Choral Ballad, 'The Battle of the Baltic.' (Hereford Festival, 1891.)
42. Six Pf. pieces.*
43. Six Songs, to poems by R. Bridges.
44. String Quartet in G.
45. String Quartet in A minor.
46. Mass in G, for soli, choir, and orchestra.
47. Four part-songs.
48. Incidental Music to Tennyson's 'Becket.' (Lyceum Theatre, 1893.) *
49. Six Elizabethan Pastorals for unaccompanied choir, 1st set.
50. Ode, 'The Bard' (Gray), for baritone, chorus, and orchestra.
51. Three Motets for unaccompanied chorus.
52. Ode 'East to West' (Swinburne) for chorus and orchestra.
53. Six Elizabethan Pastorals, 2nd set.
54. Six Irish Fantasies for vln. and pf.
55. Opera, 'Lorenza.'*
56. Symphony in D, 'L'Allegro ed il Pensieroso.'*
57. Fantasia and Toccata for organ.
58. Ten Dances for pf. (five of them also scored for orchestra as a Suite of Ancient Dances).
59. Concerto, pf. and orchestra, in G.*
60. Moore's Irish Melodies, restored, edited, and arranged.
61. Opera, 'Shamus O'Brien.' (Opera-Comique, London, March 2, 1896.)
62. Choral Ballad, 'Phaudrig Crohoore' (J. S. Le Fanu), for choir and orchestra. (Norwich Festival, 1896.)
63. Requiem for soli, choir, and orchestra in memory of Lord Leighton. (Birmingham Festival, 1897.)
64. String Quartet in D minor.
65. The Clown's Songs from 'Twelfth Night.'
66. Te Deum, for soli, choir, and orchestra. (Leeds Festival, 1898.)
67. Six Elizabethan Pastorals, 3rd set.
68. Cycle of Quartets from Tennyson's 'Princess' with pf. accompaniment.
69. Opera.*
70. Sonata for pf. and vln. in G.*
71. Variations on an English Theme ('Down among the dead men ') for pf. and orchestra.
72. Ballad, 'Die Wallfahrt nach Kevlaar' (Heine), voice and pf.
73. Trio, No. 2, for pf. and strings in G minor.
74. Concerto for vln. and orchestra in D. (Leeds Festival, 1904.)
75. 'The Last Post' (Henley), for choir and orchestra. (Hereford Festival, 1900.)
76. 'Songs of Erin,' a collection of 50 Irish folk-songs.
76a. Opera, 'Much Ado about Nothing.' (Covent Garden, May 30, 1900 ; Leipzig, 1902.)
77. An Irish Idyll (Moira O'Neill), for voice and pf.
78. Irish Rhapsody, No. 1 in D minor.
79. Four Irish Dances for Orchestra.
80. Concerto for clarinet and orchestra.*
81. Morning, Communion, and Evening Service in G.
82. Five sonnets from 'The Triumph of Love' (E. Holmes), for voice and pf.
83. Motet, 'The Lord of Might' for chorus and orchestra. (Festival of the Sons of the Clergy, 1903.)
84. Irish Rhapsody, No. 2, for orchestra.*
85. Quintet for strings, No. 1, in F.*
86. Quintet for strings, No. 2, in C minor.*
87.
88. Six Preludes for Organ.
89. Four Irish Dances for orchestra.
90. Overture in the style of a Tragedy.*

Op.
91. Songs of the Sea for baritone, male choir, and orchestra.
92. Three Rhapsodies from Dante, for pf. solo.
93. Five Characteristic Pieces for vln. and pf. (also for vcello and pf.
94. Symphony in E flat.* (In memoriam G. F. Watts.)
95. Serenade-Nonet in F for strings and wind.*
96. Stabat Mater, Symphonic Cantata for soli, choir, and orchestra. (Leeds Festival, 1907.)
97. Six 'Songs of Faith' (Tennyson and Walt Whitman).
98. Evening Service on Gregorian Tones.
99. String Quartet in G minor.*
100. Wellington (Tennyson) for soli, chorus, and orchestra.
101. Six Short Preludes and Postludes for Organ, 1st set.
102. Overture and Incidental Music to 'Attila' (Binyon). (His Majesty's Theatre, 1907.)*
103. Fantasia and Fugue for organ.
104. String Quartet in B flat. (In memoriam Joseph Joachim.)
105. Six Short Preludes and Postludes for organ, 2nd set.

WITHOUT OPUS-NUMBERS.

Festival Overture. (Gloucester Festival, 1877.)
Symphony in B flat. (Alexandra Palace, 1876.)
Elegiac Symphony, in D minor. (Cambridge, 1882.)
Scherzo in B minor for pf.*
Songs—'Irish Eyes,' 'A Valentine,' 'Three Ditties of the olden Time,' 'La Belle Dame sans Merci,' 'Prospice' (Browning), 'The Tomb,' contr. to an album published by Teague and King (Winchester), 'I liken my love' (contr. to album of Twelve New Songs by British Composers, 1891).
Arrangements of Irish Songs—'Songs of Old Ireland,' 1882 ; 'Irish Songs and Ballads,' 1893.
The 'Petrie Collection of Irish Music' was edited by Stanford for the Irish Literary Society in 1902-5.
The operas, 'The Veiled Prophet,' 'Savonarola,' and the 'Canterbury Pilgrims,' which have no opus-numbers, are referred to above.
Mention should also be made of an Installation Ode for the Chancellor of the University (the Duke of Devonshire), in 1892, which is a 'quodlibet' on well-known tunes. (See for this and many other details of Stanford's career, the *Musical Times* of 1898, pp. 785 ff.)
　　　　　　　　　　　　　　　　　　　　　M.

STANLEY, CHARLES JOHN, Mus.B., born in London, Jan. 17, 1713, at two years old became blind by accident, at seven began to learn music from John Reading, organist of Hackney, and a few months later was placed with Maurice Greene, under whom he made such rapid progress that in 1724 he was appointed organist of All Hallows, Bread Street, and in 1726 organist of St. Andrew's, Holborn. On July 19, 1729, he graduated as Mus.B. at Oxford. In 1734 he was appointed one of the organists of the Temple Church. In 1742 he published 'Six Cantatas, for a Voice and Instruments,' the words by Hawkins, the future historian of music, which proved so successful that a few months later he published a similar set to words by the same author. In 1757 he produced his 'Jephthah,' and in 1760 joined J. C. Smith in carrying on the oratorio performances formerly conducted by Handel, for which he composed 'Zimri,' 1760, and 'The Fall of Egypt,' 1774. In 1761 he set to music Robert Lloyd's dramatic pastoral, 'Arcadia, or The Shepherd's Wedding,' written in honour of the marriage of George III. and Queen Charlotte. [Eight solos for a German flute, violin or harpsichord appeared as op. 1, and Six Concertos in seven parts, for strings, as op. 2 ; another set of flute solos was made from these latter.] He published also 'Three Cantatas and Three Songs for a Voice and Instruments,' and three sets, of ten each, of Organ Voluntaries. In 1774, on the retirement of Smith, he associated Thomas Linley with himself in the conduct of the oratorios. In 1779 he succeeded Boyce as Master of the King's Band of Music. Burney says he was 'a neat, pleasing, and accurate performer, a natural and agreeable composer, and an intelligent instructor.' He died May

19, 1786. His portrait by Gainsborough was finely engraved by Mary Ann Rigg (afterwards Scott), and another portrait, at the organ, was engraved by Mac Ardell. 　　　W. H. H.

STANSBURY, GEORGE FREDERICK, son of Joseph Stansbury, a player upon the flute, bassoon, and viola, residing in Bristol, was born in that city in 1800. When only twelve years old he was proficient on the pianoforte, violin, and flute, and at nineteen was engaged by Mme. Catalani as accompanist during a concert tour through England. He was, in 1820-23, musical director at the Theatre Royal, Dublin. In 1828 he appeared at the Haymarket Theatre as Capt. Macheath in 'The Beggar's Opera,' and on Jan. 15, 1829, at Covent Garden in A. Lee's 'Nymph of the Grotto.' He sang there and at Drury Lane for several years. [He was re-engaged at Dublin from 1833 to 1835 ; his music for 'Life in Dublin' was given there in 1834. W. H. G. F.]

He was engaged as musical director and conductor at the St. James's, the Surrey, and other theatres. He composed music for 'Waverley' (with A. Lee), and 'Puss in Boots,' 1832 ; 'The Elfin Sprite,' and 'Neuha's Cave,' 1833, and other pieces, besides many songs, etc. His voice was of poor quality, but he was an excellent musician, and a ready composer. He died of dropsy, June 3, 1845. 　　　W. H. H.

STANSFIELD, ELY, a Yorkshire musician, settled at or near Halifax in the early part of the 18th century. He issued 'Psalmody Epitomiz'd,' being a brief collection of plain and useful Psalm Tunes, both old and new, in four parts, London, second ed., 1731, 8vo.' The book is of considerable interest as a volume of Yorkshire psalmody, many of the tunes being by Stansfield himself, and named after Lancashire and Yorkshire towns. 　　　F. K.

STAR SPANGLED BANNER, THE. An American national song, the melody being that of an English lyric commencing, 'To Anacreon in Heaven.' The story of the verses is as follows : Francis Scott Key, a young lawyer of Baltimore, during the English and American war in 1814, sought the release of a medical friend who had been captured by the English, and who was detained on one of the English vessels. With a flag of truce and a letter from the President, he rowed out on Sept. 13, 1814, and obtained his request ; but as there had been planned an attack on Fort M'Henry, they were not allowed to leave until the next day. During the bombardment the Baltimore lawyer anxiously watched the stars and stripes floating over the fort until nightfall, and when morning dawned, to his great joy, the flag still held its position. Scott Key wrote the first verse during his detention and completed the song ashore. It was immediately published on a broadside, and in a newspaper, *The Baltimore American* for Sept. 21, 1814. The author had adapted it to the English air which had more than once formed the vehicle for American patriotic songs, 'Adams and Liberty' being one of these effusions. This American popularity for such songs has caused several claims to be set up for the American origin of the air. For one of these see the *Musical Times* for August 1896, p. 516 ff.

The English song associated with the tune, 'To Anacreon in Heaven,' was written for, and sung at all important meetings of the 'Anacreontic Society,' held chiefly at The Crown and Anchor in the Strand. These words were by Ralph Tomlinson, a president of the Society, and the music was by John Stafford Smith, who claimed it as his in his *Fifth Book of Canzonets, Catches, and Glees (circa* 1780), long after its popularity had been established. An early appearance of the words is in *The Vocal Magazine*, 1778. After that date they were reprinted in nearly every subsequent collection.

In America, as before stated, the song was greatly sung, and its fine tune was adapted to numerous songs of a patriotic cast. The Freemasons, too, also used it for one or more songs relating to their Order. It is effectively introduced into Puccini's 'Madama Butterfly.' F. K.

STARCK (von Bronsart), INGEBORG, was born at St. Petersburg, of Swedish parents, 12/24 August 1840. Henselt was one of her first masters. When eighteen she studied for some time under Liszt at Weimar, and then made a long concert tour through the principal towns of Germany, playing at the Gewandhaus Concerts in 1858 and 1859, at Paris and St. Petersburg. In 1862 she married Hans von Bronsart. After staying some time in Leipzig, Dresden, and Berlin, Herr Bronsart and his wife settled in Hanover, where he was Intendant of the theatre. Here she devoted herself entirely to composition. An opera by her, 'Die Göttin von Sais,' had been unsuccessful in Berlin ; but her next dramatic work, a setting of Goethe's 'Jery und Bätely,' was played with great success in Weimar, Cassel, and many other places. In 1870 she wrote a 'Kaiser Wilhelm March,' which was played at Berlin at a state performance, to celebrate the return of the troops. In 1891 her four-act opera, 'König Hiarne,' was produced, the libretto by Hans von Bronsart and Friedrich von Bodenstedt. ['Manfred,' a dramatic tone-poem in five pictures, was given at Weimar in 1901.] After settling in Hanover, Frau von Bronsart, who is a pianist of rare excellence, was seldom heard in public. Her compositions include a concerto and other PF. pieces, many songs, and some music for strings. W. B. S.

STARK, LUDWIG, was born at Munich, June 19, 1831 ; was educated at the University there, and learned music in the good school of the Lachners. In 1856 he went to Paris, and after a short residence there removed to Stutt-

gart, and in conjunction with Faisst, Lebert, Brachmann, and Laiblin, founded the Stuttgart Music School, which has since become so well known. Among the teachers in the School were Speidel, Pischek, Levi, and other well-known names. Dr. Stark's energies were since that time continually concentrated on the school, which has flourished accordingly, and in July 1865 was allowed to assume the title of Conservatorium.

A large number of works have been prepared for the use of the students, among which the 'Grosse Klavierschule' of Lebert and Stark, in 4 vols., is conspicuous. Also by the same— 'Instruktive Klavierstucke' in four grades ; 'Jugendbibliothek' and ' Jugendalbum,' each in twelve parts ; 'Instruktive klassicher Ausgabe,' of various writers, in 21 vols., by Lebert, Faisst, I. Lachner, Liszt, and Bülow ; and many more. The famous Cotta edition of Beethoven's pf. sonatas is the best-known of these publications.

Dr. Stark was made Royal Professor in 1868, and Hon. Dr. Ph. 1873, and had many other distinctions ; he died at Stuttgart, March 22, 1884.

STASSOV, VLADIMIR VASSILIEVICH, a celebrated art critic, and the literary champion of the New Russian School of Music. Born in St. Petersburg, Jan. 14, 1824, he was the son of an architect of great talent. Stassov was educated, like Serov and Tchaikovsky, at the School of Jurisprudence, which he left in 1843. From 1851 to 1854 he resided abroad, chiefly in Rome and Florence, as private secretary to Prince Demidov. In the former city he wrote his first important contribution to musical literature, *L'Abbé Santini et sa collection musicale à Rome.* On his return to St. Petersburg he began by being private assistant to the director of the Imperial Public Library, Baron Korf, and in 1872 was himself appointed director of the department of Fine Arts, a position which he held until his death on Oct. 23, 1906. He wrote indefatigably on a great number of subjects, artistic and literary, and was much preoccupied with the theory—which he shared with Glinka—that the national epics of Russia were mainly of Eastern origin. His earlier musical articles had chiefly an erudite and archæological interest, but with the birth and struggles of the young Russian School they assumed a new and far more vigorous character, and henceforth he stood as the representative champion of nationality in art. His views are clearly and trenchantly defined in such remarkable essays as *Twenty-five Years of Russian Art, The Tracks of Russian Art, Art in the XIXth Century*, etc. His style is intensely individual, his sincerity unquestionable ; while his views invariably incline to the progressive and liberal side. The value of his criticisms is increased by his extensive and accurate learning, which enabled him to use comparative methods most effectually. Apart from polemics, Stassov has collected and published the most valuable materials for the biographies of the chief Russian composers. His monographs upon Glinka, Moussorgsky, Borodin, Cui and Rimsky-Korsakov are indispensable to those who desire to study the development of Russian national music. His influence on contemporary Russian art was immense, and can best be realised in the number of works undertaken at his suggestion, and dedicated to him. His collected works from 1847 to 1886 were published by his admirers in a jubilee edition (3 vols. St. Petersburg, 1894), and a fourth volume, dedicated to Count Tolstoi, was added in 1905.   R. N.

STATUE, LA. Opéra-comique in three acts, text by Carré and Barbier ; music by Ernest Reyer. Produced at the Opéra-Comique, Paris, April 11, 1861. Revived as a grand opera at the Opéra, 1903.

STAUDIGL, JOSEPH, one of the most distinguished and accomplished singers of modern times, born April 14, 1807, at Wöllersdorf, in Lower Austria. His father destined him for his own calling, that of Imperial huntsman (Revierjäger), but for this he was not sufficiently strong, and in 1816 he entered the Gymnasium of Wiener Neustadt, where his beautiful soprano voice soon attracted attention in the church. In 1823 he attended the philosophical college at Krems, and was persuaded, in 1825, to enter upon his noviciate in the Benedictine Monastery at Melk. Here his voice, which had developed into a fine sonorous bass, was invaluable for the church services. A vague impulse drove him in Sept. 1827 to Vienna to study surgery, but money ran short, and he was glad to accept a place in the chorus at the Kärnthnerthor Theatre. Here he took occasional secondary parts, until the sudden illness of one of the solo singers brought him forward as Pietro in the 'Stumme von Portici ' (' Masaniello '), after which all the principal parts fell into his hands. High as was his position on the stage, he was still greater as a singer of oratorio and church music. In 1831 he was admitted to the Court Chapel, and in 1837 sang for the first time at the great musical festival of the Gesellschaft der Musikfreunde in the 'Creation.' In 1833 he sang in the 'Seasons' for the Tonkünstler Societät, a society to which he rendered the greatest services. Though not even a member, he sang at no less than eighty of its concerts, and absolutely declined to accept any fee. Differences with the management of the Court Theatre led him to the Theatre ' an der Wien ' on its reopening in 1845. There he acted as chief manager, and, with Pischek and Jenny Lind, entered on a series of fresh triumphs. He returned to the Court Theatre in 1848, but only to expose himself to fresh annoyance up to February 1854, when an abrupt dismissal embittered the rest of his life. His last appearance in public was in 'St. Paul,' at the Tonkünstler Societät, on Palm Sunday,

1856. A few days after, insanity developed itself, and he was taken to an asylum, which he never quitted alive. His repeated tours abroad spread his fame far and wide, and he had many admirers in England, which he often visited, and where he sang in English. He created the part of ' Elijah ' at the Birmingham Festival of 1846, singing the music at sight at the grand rehearsal. As a singer of Schubert's Lieder he was without a rival. He died March 28, 1861, and half Vienna followed him to the grave.

His youngest son, JOSEPH, born March 18, 1850, possesses a flexible sonorous baritone, which he cultivated with success under Rokitansky at the Vienna Conservatorium till 1874, when he left. He made his mark as an oratorio singer in the principal towns of Germany and Switzerland. In 1875-83 he was frequently engaged at the Court Theatre of Carlsruhe, and was chamber-singer to the Grand Duke. [In 1885 he married Gisele Koppmayer, an Austrian, pupil of Mme. Marchesi, who was a favourite contralto singer in opera at Hamburg, Berlin, Bayreuth, etc. She and her husband sang together in a concert tour in America (*Musik. Wochenblatt*, 1888, p. 349). A. C.]   C. F. P.

STAVE (Lat. *Systema* ; Ital. *Sistema* ; Germ. *Liniensystem, System* ; Fr. *Portée* ; Eng. *Stave, Staff*). A series of horizontal lines, so arranged that the signs used for the representation of musical notes may be written upon or between them.

Though the etymology of the term cannot be proved, its derivation from the familiar Saxon root is too obvious to admit of doubt. Its use, as applied to the verses of a Psalm, Canticle, or ditty of any kind, is very ancient, and, as we shall presently show, the music sung to such verses was originally noted down in such close connection with the verbal text that it may fairly be said to form part of it. When a system of lines and spaces was engrafted on the primitive form of notation, the old term was still retained ; and we now apply it to this, even more familiarly than to the verse itself. The best proof that this is the true derivation of the term lies in the fact that Morley calls the Stave a Verse, and describes the Verse as consisting of Rules[1] and Spaces. [For the early forms of notes see NOTATION.]

About the year 900 a single horizontal line was drawn across the parchment to serve as a guide to the position of the Neumes written upon, above, or below it. This line, the germ of our present Stave, has exercised more direct influence upon the art of notation than any other invention, either of early or modern date. It was originally drawn in red. All Neumes placed upon it were understood to represent the note F. A Neume written immediately above it represented G ; one immediately below it, E. The places of three signs were, therefore,

1 'Rules,' *i.e.* lines. Printers still employ the same term.

definitely fixed ; while those written at greater distances above or below the line, though less certain in their signification, were at least more intelligible than they had been under the previous system.

A yellow line was soon afterwards added, at a little distance above the red one. Neumes written on this line represented the note C, and the position of a whole septenary of signs was thus fixed with tolerable clearness ; for signs placed exactly half-way between the two lines would naturally represent A, while the positions of D and B above and below the yellow line, and G and E above and below the red one were open to very little doubt in carefully-written MSS. When black lines were used instead of coloured ones the letters F and C were written at the beginning of their respective ' rules ' ; and because these afforded a *key* to the Notation they were called *Claves*, or, as we now say, *Clefs*.

Early in the 11th century two more black lines were added to the stave ; one above the yellow line, and the other between the yellow and red ones. The upper black line then represented E, and the lower one A ; and the combined effect of the whole was to produce a four-lined stave ; and when convenience suggested the practice of changing the position of the clefs from one line to another, there remained but little to distinguish the notation of the 12th and 13th century from that now invariably used for plain-song.

[For examples of a stave in which the spaces between the lines were only used, and one in which the lines were used without the spaces, see vol. iii. p. 397.] These collateral inventions soon fell into disuse. The system of alternate lines and spaces was adopted, to the exclusion of all others, in every country in Europe. Henceforth, the only difference lay in the number of lines employed. The natural tendency at first was to multiply them. In early MSS. we constantly find staves of six, eight, twelve, fifteen, and even a still greater number of lines, embracing a compass sufficient for the transcription of an entire vocal score. After a time the difficulty of reading so many lines at once led to the adoption of a more commodious form, consisting of two groups, with four black lines in each, separated by a single red line, on which no notes were written. Staves of this kind are rare ; but an example may be seen at fol. 201*a* of the Chaucer MS. in the British Museum.[1] Finally, these variable forms were relinquished in favour of a fixed standard, which in the 15th and 16th centuries admitted the use of four, five, or six lines only. The stave of four lines was used exclusively for plain-song, and is retained for that purpose to the present day. That of six lines was used for organ Music, and music for the virginals.

[1] Arundel MSS. 248.

[It is not impossible that the six-line stave remained in vogue because paper ruled for lutemusic could be employed.] That of five lines was used for all vocal music except plain-song, and, after the invention of printing, for music of every kind. w. s. r.

STAVENHAGEN, Bernhard, born Nov. 24, 1862, at Greiz (Reuss), studied with Kiel and Rudorff, and became one of the most beloved if not the favourite of Liszt's own pupils. He received the Mendelssohn prize for pianoforteplaying in 1880, and lived till 1885 in Berlin, since when he settled in Weimar, where in 1890 he became Court pianist to the Grand Duke and in 1895 Capellmeister. In 1898 he went to Munich in the latter capacity, and was elected director of the Royal Academy of Music there in 1901, but gave up the post in 1904 and returned to Weimar, where he still lives as teacher, pianist, and conductor. He has composed some piano pieces, of which a minuet is well known. In 1890 Stavenhagen married the singer, Agnes Denis. h. v. h.

STCHERBATCHEV, Nicholas Vladimirovich, pianist and composer, born August 24, 1853. He spent part of his youth in Rome, but on his return to Russia became closely associated with the young Russian School. His compositions, mostly published by Belaiev in Leipzig, are as follows :—

A. *Orchestral.*—' Serenade,' op. 33 ; two Idylls.
B. *Pianoforte.* — ' Féeries et Pantomimes,' op. 8 (two books) ; ' Mosaics,' op. 15 ; ' Scherzo - Caprice,' op. 17 ; ' Echoes,' op. 18 ; ' Allegro Appassionato,' op. 22 ; three Idylls, op. 23 ; two pieces, op. 28 ; ' Expromptu,' op. 29 ; ' Melancholia,' op. 31 ; ' The First Snow,' op. 32 ; ' Barcarolle,' op. 35 ; ' two Expromptus,' op. 36 ; ' Impromptu Vilanelle,' op. 38 ; ' Valses,' op. 21 (3), op. 27 (2), op. 34 (Valse entr'acte) ; Mazurkas, opp. 16, 40, 42 ; Preludes and Interludes, opp. 20, 35, 37 ; Etudes, opp. 19, 26, 30.
C. *Vocal.*—Six songs to words by Count A. Tolstoi, op. 24 ; six songs to words by Heine.

ANDREW VLADIMIROVICH, born Jan. 29, 1869, in the Government of Poltavà. Entered the St. Petersburg Conservatoire in 1887, where he studied under F. Blumenfeld, Liadov, and Rimsky-Korsakov. The composer of a march for orchestra, op. 5, a pianoforte sonata, op. 6, and a considerable number of songs and piano pieces. r. n.

STEFFANI, Agostino. This very remarkable man was born July 25, 1653, at Castelfranco. Of his parentage nothing is known. He appears to have entered one of the Conservatorios early, and become a singing-boy at St. Mark's in Venice, where in 1667 he was heard by a Count von Tattenbach, probably an emissary of the Court of Bavaria. The Count was so delighted with his voice and intelligence, that he carried him off to Munich. He was educated at the expense of the Elector Ferdinand Maria, as appears from a decree[2] of July 26, 1668, ordering a payment of 150 florins to Count Tattenbach for the board and lodging of the ' Welscher Musikus Augustin Steffani ' during the previous year. By another decree of July 9, 1668,

[2] See Rudhardt's *Geschichte der Oper am Hofe zu München. Nach archivalischen Quellen bearbeitet.* Erster Theil, *Die Italiänische Oper, 1654-1787.*

the young ' Churfürstlicher Kammer- und Hofmusikus' had been already apprenticed to
Johann Kaspar Kerl to learn to play (schlagen)
the organ, and to be boarded, for the yearly
sum of 432 florins. A further entry of the pay-
office shows that the yearly cost of the Hof- und
Kammermusikus was, for 1669, 903 fl. 12 kr. ;
for 1670, 997 fl. He remained with Kerl till
Oct. 1, 1671, from which day he was boarded
and lodged by the Churfürstlicher Kammer-
diener Seyler for 156 fl. a year. As Hofmusikus,
Steffani received 300 fl., in addition to a clothing
allowance of 300 fl. a year, by a decree of Jan.
15, 1672. At the commencement of Oct. 1673
he travelled to Rome in order to perfect himself
in his art. Here he began to compose assiduously, for there is a small oblong volume of
motets in the Fitzwilliam Museum at Cambridge,
an original MS., of which there seems no reason
to doubt the authenticity. In it we find the
following compositions, all dated except one.
To speak of them chronologically : the first,
dated Nov. 1678, is a 'Laudate Pueri' a 9.
The next, dated Dec. 30, 1673, is a splendid
'Laudate Dominum' for 8 canti concertati,
divided into two choirs. Again in 1673, with
no month given, we have a 'Tribuamus Domino'
—one short movement for two choirs of S.S.A.T.
In the following year we have a 'Sperate in Deo'
for S.S.A.T.B. in three fine movements, the
last a fugue. The remaining piece, not dated,
is a 'Beatus vir' for S.S.B., with two violins
and a bass.

In Rome he appears to have had a long illness, as he received 50 crowns extra for expenses
incurred while laid up. Bernabei succeeded
Kerl as Capellmeister at Munich in that year.
After his return Steffani again took up his position as Kammermusikus with a pay of 770 fl.
20 kr., and almost immediately published his
first work, 'Psalmodia vespertina volans 8
plenis vocibus concinenda ab Augost. Steffana
in lucem edita aetatis suae anno 19,[1] Monachii,
1674.' This work was a brilliant success for
the young composer, and a portion of it was
thought worthy of being included by Padre
Martini in his Saggio di Contrappunto, published
just a hundred years later. On March 1, 1675,
he was appointed court organist.

But music was not the only study which had
occupied his mind ; he had studied mathematics,
philosophy, and theology with so much success
that in 1680 he was ordained a priest with the
title of Abbate of Lepsing ; and such was the
favour shown to him by the new Elector, his old
friend Ferdinand Maria having died the year
before, that a decree of Nov. 3, 1680, accords
to the 'Honourable priest, Court and Chamber
musician, and Organist Steffani,' a present of
1200 florins for 'certain reasons and favours'
(gewissen Ursachen und Gnaden). Hitherto he

[1] [On this erroneous statement of age see the Quellen-Lexikon.
It is from the same dedications that we know him to have learnt
from Bernabei.]

had confined himself to the composition of
motets and other church music, but now appeared his first work for the stage. The title,
taken from the contemporary MS., evidently
the conducting score, in the Royal Musical
Library at Buckingham Palace, in an Italian
hand, probably that of his secretary and copyist
Gregorio Piva, runs thus :—'Marco Aurelio,
Dramma posto in Musica da D. Agostino Steffani, Direttor della Musica di Camera di S. A. S.
etc. di Baviera, l' anno 1681.' It will be seen
that a further step had been gained—he was
now Director of Chamber-music. In 1683 appeared some Sonate da Camera for two violins,
alto, and bass, and in 1685 a collection of
motets entitled 'Sacer Janus Quadrifrons 3
voc. Monachii,' but no trace of these works is
to be found. For the Carnival of 1685 he composed the opera 'Solone,' which appears to have
been an opera buffa in three acts ; the score,
however, like all the Munich operas by Steffani
with the exception of 'Marco Aurelio,' is
lost. He also composed in this year a musical introduction for a tournament, with the
title : 'Audacia e Rispetto.' The new Elector
Maximilian Emanuel was married at the end
of 1685 to the Archduchess Maria Antonia,
daughter of Leopold I., and the wedding festivities in Munich in the first days of January
1686 began with the opera 'Servio Tullio,'
again by Steffani, with ballets arranged by
Rodier, and music to them by Dardespin, the
Munich Concertmeister, danced by twelve ladies
and gentlemen of the court, with costumes from
Paris. The music made its mark, as we shall
see hereafter. On Jan. 18, 1687, the birthday
of the young Electress, we have an opera—the
text of which was by the new Italian secretary
Luigi Orlandi, whose wife sang on the stage—
called 'Alarico il Balta, cioè l' audace, rè dei
Gothi,' with ballets composed, arranged, and
danced as before. For this opera fresh Italian
singers were brought from Italy. Of the value
of Steffani's music to it no record is given. In
1688 he composed the opera 'Niobe, regina di
Tebe,' probably for the Carnival, the text again
by Orlandi. This was his last work for the
Court of Munich.

Various reasons have been put forward to account for his leaving a court where he had been
so well treated, and where the art of music was
held in such esteem, for Munich had not only at
this time good singers, a good orchestra, and
experienced and intelligent audiences, but had
likewise a splendid musical history. The Elector
had granted him 750 florins on account of his
two operas and for a 'Badekur' in Italy in June
1686. In May 1688 gracious permission was
given to him to go again to Italy, in consideration of his twenty-one years' service ; his salary
was not only paid to the end of June, but from
the beginning of July he was given three years'
salary as a reward ! Not only so, but his debts

were paid by the Court Treasurer out of this, and the balance was sent to him in Venice, where he had gone. The main reason for his deserting Munich was no doubt that on the death of the elder Bernabei at the end of the year 1687 his son, who had come from Italy in 1677 to fill the post of Vice-Capellmeister, was in the early part of 1688 made Capellmeister, thus debarring Steffani from further promotion. Added to this, the Duke of Brunswick, Ernst August, who had been present at the festivities when 'Servio Tullio' was performed, was so delighted with Steffani's music and singing that he had already made him an offer to go to Hanover, and Steffani appears actually to have made use of the leave granted for the Badekur in Italy in 1686 to spend his time in Hanover instead of there. The appointment then of the younger Bernabei to the Munich Capellmeistership must have decided him at once to leave Munich, and from Venice at the end of 1688 or early in 1689 he made his way to Hanover, there to remain and become Capellmeister, and a good deal besides.

If Munich was a pleasant place for a musician of genius, Hanover was not far behind it. It might not have the same glorious musical history ; but Steffani found there congenial society, and singers and players of great excellence. The Court of Hanover was renowned for its magnificence and courtesy, which were, however, combined with a friendly simplicity held to be the best in Germany.[1] One of its principal ornaments was the great philosopher Leibniz, who had resided there since 1676, and who, with the Duchess Sophia, had raised the tone of the Court to a very high intellectual standard. There was also the court poet, Abbate Ortensio Mauro, at once Geheimer Secretär, Hofceremonielmeister, and political agent, who came to Hanover in 1679, and in whom the Duchess placed great confidence. Steffani became the friend of these men. Up to this time the operas at Hanover (chiefly imported from Venice) were given in the small French theatre, but that being deemed too small, a new opera-house was built, which was pronounced to be the most beautiful in all Germany. It created the reputation of its architect Thomas Giusti, and caused him to be called to Berlin and other towns for similar purposes. The new house was opened in 1689 with 'Henrico Leone,' by Mauro and Steffani. The score in Buckingham Palace gives a list of the scenes, machinery, etc., which might astonish even a 20th-century reader. It had a very great success, was given in German in 1696 at Hamburg and in 1697 at Brunswick, and acquired great celebrity. The opera shows marked advance on 'Marco Aurelio.' A remarkable change is found in the instrumentation. There are flutes, hautboys, bassoons, three trumpets and drums, in addition to the

strings, in four parts. There are delightful contrapuntal devices in the scoring, all the wind instruments have obbligato passages, one air a vigorous fagotto obbligato throughout. Chrysander states (Händel) that the opera-company in Hanover was divided into two camps, an instrumental (French) and a vocal (Italian), both, however, working harmoniously. The singers must have been of the best if they could execute these difficult arias ; the band, too, must have been excellent. The leading violin in the orchestra was Farinelli (uncle of the famous singer), who had been much in France and in Spain. Corelli was a great friend of Concertmeister Farinelli, and during his tour in Germany spent some time at Hanover, where he became acquainted with the Electoral family. The hautboys, too, were particularly good, and Chrysander supposes that Handel wrote his first hautboy concerto for this orchestra.

'Henrico Leone' was followed in the summer of this year by 'La lotta d'Alcide con Achelao,' a divertimento drammatico in one act, a charming work, written probably also by Mauro. It seems to have been performed at the Summer Theatre at Herrenhausen. The next opera was 'La superbia d' Alessandro,' in 1690 (the conducting score gives 1691 as the date), the words by Mauro ; a fine work. Many songs have obbligato instrumental parts, especially one in the second act, where two flutes obbligati are sustained by muted violins and alto—a beautiful piece ; also one song with harpsichord solo. This opera also found its way to Hamburg and Brunswick in a German translation. 'Orlando generoso' came out in 1691 —another fine work written in conjunction with Mauro. 'Le Rivali concordi' appeared in 1692, written again by Mauro, and afterwards performed at Hamburg. We now come to 'La libertà contenta' (Mauro) in 1693, in which evidence is given of great further progress, for nothing of such importance had hitherto come from his pen. It is full of beauties of all kinds —a fine overture, fine counterpoint, beautiful melodies, very difficult arias, and powerful recitatives. It had the greatest success, and was most highly thought of at Hamburg. The movements are longer and more developed than in his previous works.

It was in the next year that Steffani issued his celebrated pamphlet, entitled Quanta certezza habbia da suoi Principii la Musica, ed in qual pregio fosse perciò presso gli Antichi. Amsterdam, 1695. Risposta di D. A. Steffani Abbate di Lepsing Protonotario della San Sede Apostolica. Ad una lettera del S[n]. March[e]. A. G. In difesa d' una Proposizione sostenuta da lui in una Assemblea. Hannovera Sett. 1694, 72 pp. in 12. It was translated twice into German : in 1699 by Andreas Werckmeister at Quedlinburg ; in 1760 by Jean Laurent Albrecht at Mühlhausen. Steffani ably discusses the question whether music exists only in the imagination, or is grounded on nature and science. In 1695 we have the opera 'I trionfi del Fato, o le glorie d' Enea,' another charming work. It found its way to Hamburg in 1699. An opera in one act, ' Baccanali,' was also composed this year for the small theatre in Hanover. For the Carnival of 1696 the grand opera of 'Briseide' was composed, the words by Palmieri, Comes Italus. No composer's name is mentioned, and Chrysander thinks it is not by Steffani; but the two scores and collections of Steffani's songs at Buckingham Palace leave little doubt on examination that it is his work, and in his usual manner.

A change was now about to take place in Steffani's circumstances. He was no longer to be the active composer of operas, and capellmeister, but from this time forth was destined to devote his time chiefly to diplomacy, though he never forsook the art of which he was so great an ornament. Ernst August had sent 5000 men to assist the Emperor against the Turks, and some 8000 against the French ; his two eldest sons, George (afterwards King of England) and Frederick Augustus, had served in the field, and three others had been killed in the wars. The Emperor as a reward determined, in 1692, to create a ninth Elector, and raise the younger branch of the house of Brunswick-Lüneburg to the Electorate. This was generally deemed just, but many difficulties stood in the way, and during four years the position of Ernst August as Elector became more and more difficult, so that, in 1696, it was determined to send an Envoy Extraordinary round to the various German Courts to smooth matters over, and Ernst August and Leibniz could find no one among the court *personnel* in Hanover so well fitted for the post as Abbate Steffani. With the title of ' Envoyé Extraordinaire ' he set out on his mission, and so admirably did he succeed, that at the end of the mission he was not only granted a considerably larger salary than he had hitherto had at Court, but Innocent XI. was induced to raise him in 1706 to the dignity of Bishop (*in partibus infidelium*) of Spiga in Anatolia, Asia Minor—the ancient Cyzicus. This was also, perhaps in recognition of Steffani's services, aided by the tolerant Leibniz, in procuring for the Roman Catholics in Hanover the privilege of holding public worship. Steffani was now an accomplished courtier and diplomatist. In the early part of 1698 he was sent to Brussels as Ambassador, and there had his first audience on March 1. In this year the Elector Ernst August died, and Steffani afterwards transferred his services to the Elector Palatine at Düsseldorf, where he became a Privy Councillor as well as the Pope's Protonotarius for North Germany, though at what time this occurred is not known. In 1709 we find Steffani again with two new operas,

one for the Court at Hanover, the other at Düsseldorf. Both are stated in the scores at Buckingham Palace to be by Gregorio Piva— his secretary, whose name he adopted for his compositions after he became a statesman, and this is the earliest date at which it occurs in any of the MSS. of his works, as far as I know. The opera given at Hanover is called ' Enea, or Amor vien dal destino,' in the large copy, but in the conducting score ' Il Turno '—in three acts, and is a very fine work ; again an advance on any previous effort. The Düsseldorf opera, ' Tassilone Tragedia in 5 Atti,' is only repre- sented at Buckingham Palace by a vocal score ; the overture and all instrumental effects are wanting, only the bass being given to the different pieces ; but the singers' names, all Italian, are mentioned. The music is mostly excellent. The movements of both these operas of 1709 are all long, well developed, and broad, and our composer has not failed to march with the times. There remains one more opera to speak of, ' Arminio,' which, according to the full score (one of those brought from Hanover by George I.), was composed for the Court of the Elector Palatine in 1707. Though bearing no com- poser's name, it is without doubt a composition of Steffani, entirely in his manner and one of his very finest ; the instrumental colouring still more full and varied than in any other opera of his. And what further establishes its claim to be considered Steffani's is the fact that the fine air, with fagotto obbligato from ' Henrico Leone,' is introduced with other words, and for a soprano instead of a tenor voice. This opera, and ' Tassilone,' show that the Palatine Court at that time possessed a very fine orchestra, and a splendid company of singers. It is quite possible that Steffani composed more operas than these, and that several may have been written for Düsseldorf which have not come down to us ; but what we have, form a splendid series of masterly works that establish him as a composer of the first rank, equal to Lulli, greatly his superior as a contrapuntist, if possibly, and only possibly, inferior to him in dramatic force. In Hamburg his reputation was so great that no music was thought equal to his. There Bach and Handel as young men must have listened to his operas.

Though, however, his operas were his greatest works, they could not attain the same universal popularity as his well-known duets for various voices, with a bass accompaniment. These are mostly in three long movements, some with recitatives and solos, in the cantata form, following Carissimi and Stradella. Of these celebrated duets there are more than a hundred in the British Museum, and in the splendid copy in 3 vols. in Buckingham Palace. The words were mostly by Ortensio Mauro, Averara, Abbate Conti, Conte Francesco Palmieri, etc. The testimony to the great excellence of these compositions is abundant. Burney says in speaking of these duets, 'Those of the admirable Abbate Steffani were dispersed in MS. throughout Europe.' Mattheson again, ' In these duets Steffani is incomparable to all I know, and deserves to be a model, for such things do not easily become old.' Chrysander also writes, 'These duets are the greatest of their kind.' To the foregoing it is useless to add further commendation. The most renowned singers, Senesino, Strada, and others, delighted in them, and used them constantly for practice in both expressive and florid singing.[1] No copies of these duets are dated, but they were probably all composed after he went to Hanover ; and some of them are known to have been written for the Princess Sophia Dorothea.

The Duke of Brunswick, Anton Ulrich, was converted to Romanism in 1710, and we find Steffani going from Düsseldorf to Brunswick to accept in the name of the Pope a piece of ground as a site for a Catholic church. At the time of the Carnival of this year we find him in Venice in company with Baron Kielmansegge, and he there met Handel, whom he induced to visit Hanover on his way to London. Handel testifies to Steffani's great kindness to him while in Hanover ; he was anxious, too, that he should become Capellmeister at this Court. About the year 1712 the new church in Brunswick was so far ready that the Pope sent Bishop Steffani to consecrate the building and perform the opening service. Two years later the Elector of Hanover became King of England, but Steffani did not accompany him to London ; indeed, we do not meet with his name again till 1724, when the Academy of Ancient Music in London unanimously elected him its Hon. President for life. This Academy, of which Handel was a great supporter, had been instituted by Dr. Pepusch, J. E. Galliard (the only known pupil of Steffani), and other musicians, and had become well known abroad. Many eminent musicians of the Continent were made honorary members, Steffani among the number, who appears to have sent over the following four works for performance—the fine and well-known Madrigal ' Qui diligit Mariam,' for S.S.A.T.B. ; another madrigal, called ' La Spagnuola,' ' Al rigor d' un bel sembiante,' for two altos and tenor, not so remarkable ; and the beautiful madrigal, 'Gettano i Rè dal soglio.' These are generally found in the MS. collections of the time. The fourth piece was the great Stabat Mater, composed for S. S. A. T. T. B., accompanied by strings and organo, and undoubtedly one of the finest works of any composer of the period immediately preceding that of the giants Bach and Handel. His great contemporaries Alessandro Scarlatti and Purcell produced nothing finer. No exact dates can

be assigned to these four works, but they all belong to his later manner. In Steffani is to be found the perfection of counterpoint without stiffness, and with that real sign of genius, exhaustless variety. As in Bach, there is marvellous freedom in the movement of the parts, and no hesitation at a good clashing dissonance produced by this freedom. He was an adept too at writing the charming minuets and gavottes which were then so fashionable, and in which his operas abound. At the British Museum there is likewise a glorious 'Confitebor' for three voices with violins and bass in E minor, said to be of the year 1709, with a splendid bass solo (' Sanctum et terribile ')—a species of accompanied recitative ; the whole work being full of exquisite beauties. No notice of this piece has yet appeared in any life of Steffani. In the library of the Royal College of Music there is a book of ' XII Motteta per celeberrimum Abbatem Stephanum ' for three voices with solos and recitatives, but it is only a vocal score, without the symphonies and accompaniments which all undoubtedly had. In another book in the same library, however, we find two of them complete.

Early in 1727 Steffani was once more and for the last time in Italy ; and Handel met him at Rome in March, where he was living at the Palace of Cardinal Ottoboni. This latter enthusiast still kept up his Monday performances of music, at which Steffani, now seventy-four years old, occasionally sang. Handel tells us (through Hawkins) that ' he was just loud enough to be heard, but that this defect in his voice was amply recompensed by his manner, in the chasteness and elegance of which he had few equals.' From Hawkins we also learn that ' as to his person he was less than the ordinary size of men, of a tender constitution of body, which he had not a little impaired by intense study and application. His deportment is said to have been grave, but tempered with a sweetness and affability that rendered his conversation very engaging ; he was perfectly skilled in all the external forms of polite behaviour, and, which is somewhat unusual, continued to observe and practise them at the age of fourscore.' He was back in Hanover in a short time, and the next year, going to Frankfort on some public business, died there after a short illness, Feb. 12, 1728.

The last word has not yet been said about this remarkable musician, and it is to be hoped that some of his duets, and perhaps his glorious Stabat Mater and Confitebor, may still be heard in the concert-room. His career was certainly one of the most extraordinary in musical history. Born of obscure parents, he raised himself by his talents and industry from the position of a poor choir boy, not only to be one of the foremost musicians of his age, but likewise the trusted confidant of princes and the friend of such a man as Leibniz. The only other instance

[1] [Several movements from these duets are included in 'Duetti da Camera,' edited by J. A. Fuller Maitland.]

2 x

of an artist having become an ambassador is to
be found in the painter Rubens. The materials
for this notice have been chiefly gathered from
Rudhardt, Hawkins, and Chrysander, the latter
having obliged me with some important information hitherto unpublished. [Besides these
authorities the following may be consulted :
A. Neisser's *Dissertation* on ' Servio Tullio,'
1902 ; F. W. Woker's article in the *Verein-
schriften* of the Görresgesellschaft, Bonn, 1885-
1886. For list of extant works, see the *Quellen-
Lexikon*.]   W. G. C.

STEFFKINS, THEODORE, or THEODORUS,
was a foreign professor of the lute and viol,
who lived in London in the latter half of the
17th century. He is commended in Thomas
Salmon's *Essay to the Advancement of Music*,
1672. His brother, DIETRICHT, was one of
the band of Charles I. in 1641, and his two
sons, FREDERICK and CHRISTIAN, were famous
performers on the viol. They were members of
the King's band in 1694, and Christian was
living in 1711.   W. H. H.

STEGGALL, CHARLES, Mus.D., born in
London, June 3, 1826, was educated in the
Royal Academy of Music, from June 1847,
principally by Sterndale Bennett. In 1848 he
became organist of Christ Church Chapel,
Maida Hill ; in 1851 a professor at the Royal
Academy of Music, and in the same year accumulated the degrees of Mus. B. and Mus. D. at
Cambridge. In 1855 he was appointed organist
of Christ Church, Lancaster Gate, and in 1864
organist of Lincoln's Inn Chapel. [In 1884 he
was elected on the Board of Directors of the Academy, and in 1887 was one of those who carried
on the duties of head of the institution between
the death of Macfarren and the appointment of
Mackenzie. In 1903 he resigned his professorship. He was one of the founders of the Royal
College of Organists in 1864, and was examiner
for the Mus. D. degree at Cambridge in 1882
and 1883. He was Hon. Sec. to the Bach
Society, founded by Bennett, from 1849 to its
dissolution in 1870. He died in London,
June 7, 1905.] He composed anthems and
other church music, and lectured upon music
in the metropolis and elsewhere. W. H. H.

His youngest son, REGINALD STEGGALL, was
born in London, April 17, 1867, and was
educated at the Royal Academy of Music, where
he gained the Balfe Scholarship in 1887, afterwards becoming an Associate, in due course
a Fellow, and, in 1895, organ professor. In
1886 he was appointed to the post of organist
of St. Anne's Church, Soho, and some years
afterwards became his father's assistant at
Lincoln's Inn Chapel, being appointed to succeed him in 1905.

He belongs to the more advanced school of
young English composers, and first came
prominently before the public at a concert
organised by Mr. Granville Bantock in 1896 at

the Queen's Hall, when a scena, ' Elaine,' was
performed ; an ' Ave Maria ' was given at
another concert of the same kind, and his
scena ' Alcestis ' was given at the Crystal
Palace earlier in the year. A symphony, and
a mass, together with many anthems, a Festival
Evening Service, and organ pieces, are included
among his compositions.   M.

STEIBELT, DANIEL, a musician now almost
entirely forgotten, but in his own day so celebrated as a pianoforte-player and composer
that many regarded him as the rival of Beethoven, was a native of Berlin, where his father
was a maker of harpsichords and pianofortes of
considerable skill and repute. The date of his
birth is quite uncertain. Most of his biographers state that he was born in 1755 or 1756,
but Fétis declares from personal knowledge that
he was only about thirty-six years of age in 1801,
which would place his birth some eight to ten
years later. The details of his early life are as
much involved in doubt as the time of his birth.
It is, however, certain that his aptitude for music
was early manifest, and that in some way it
attracted the attention of the Crown Prince of
Prussia, afterwards Frederick William II. Kirnberger was then the leading musician of Berlin,
and to him the Crown Prince entrusted the instruction of his protégé in the harpsichord and
composition. How long Steibelt was a pupil of
Kirnberger it is impossible to say, but not a
trace of the learned and somewhat pedantic style
of his master is to be found in his method either
of playing or writing. Indeed the musical
world of Berlin, then under the despotism of
Frederick the Great,[1] does not present any influences to account for the peculiarities which
so strongly marked Steibelt's after-life, though
it may be fairly conjectured that in his father's
workshops he obtained that familiarity with the
mechanism of the pianoforte which he was
always ready to turn to the best account.
Whatever his musical education may have been,
it was interrupted by his joining the army for
a while,[2] and was finally brought to an end, as
far as Berlin was concerned, by his departure
from that city, an event which perhaps took
place as early as 1784.

In what direction he turned his steps seems
wholly unknown, but his career as a composer
and virtuoso commences with his arrival in Paris
at some date between 1787 and 1790. He did
not take up his residence there permanently till
the last-named year, as he was at Munich in
1788, and in 1789 was giving concerts in Saxony
and Hanover, whence he journeyed to Paris by
way of Mannheim ; but his rivalry with Hermann
at Court would appear to suggest that he had
been in Paris before the year that was signalised
by the taking of the Bastile. However this
may be, Steibelt appeared at the French capital

---

[1] For an interesting account of music in Berlin at this period see
Jahn's *Mozart*, ch. 30 (vol. ii. p. 374, etc. in Eng. trans.).
[2] *A. M. Z.* ii. 622.

as a full-fledged performer and composer, and was not long in proving his superiority to his rival. The reasons for his success are obvious. Though Hermann's technique, which was that of the school of C. P. E. Bach, was considered more correct than that of his opponent, he was, nevertheless, emphatically a player of the old style. Steibelt, as emphatically, belonged to the new. Their different characteristics are clearly brought out in the very curious Sonata for the Pianoforte called 'La Coquette,' composed for Marie Antoinette by the two rivals, each of whom contributed one movement to it. Hermann's movement, the first, is good, solid, rather old-fashioned, *harpsichord* music; Steibelt's movement, the Rondo, by its variety of phrasing and the minutiæ of its marks of expression reveals in every line an acquaintance with the resources offered by the pianoforte. The issue of a contest in which the combatants were so unequally matched could not be doubtful, and Steibelt was soon installed as reigning virtuoso. But no musician who aspires to fame in France can neglect the stage, and Steibelt accordingly resolved to essay dramatic composition. One of his patrons, the Vicomte de Ségur, a *littérateur* of some pretensions, who had written for the Opéra a libretto founded on Shakespeare's 'Romeo and Juliet,' entrusted the composition of the music to Steibelt. The score was finished in 1792, but the work was rejected by the Académie. Its authors, nothing daunted, proceeded to alter the piece. The recitatives were suppressed and replaced by prose dialogue, and in this shape the opera was produced at the Théâtre Feydeau on Sept. 10, 1793, with Madame Scio as Juliet. The *Moniteur* of Sept. 23 describes the music as 'learned, but laboured and ugly'—a criticism which, with the music before one, it is impossible to understand. Theatre-goers were of a different opinion, and 'Roméo et Juliette' was a decided success. It was performed with success in Stockholm on Jan. 30, 1815 (and again in 1819), and was revived with great applause in Paris at the Opéra-Comique in 1822. It does not appear that it was ever brought forward on the German stage, but the overture was played in Vienna in 1841. The concert given after Steibelt's death for his son's benefit was closed with the Funeral Chorus from the third act.

The success of this operatic venture completely confirmed Steibelt's position in Paris. His music, though considered difficult, was extremely popular, and as a teacher he counted amongst his pupils the most eminent ladies of the time, including the future Queen of Holland. On his first coming to Paris he had been received with great kindness by Boyer the publisher, who had not only procured for him powerful patronage but even took him into his own house. His services were ill rewarded. Steibelt had already published some Sonatas for the Pianoforte and

Violin (opp. 1 and 2) at Munich. He now added to them a violoncello *ad libitum* part, which merely doubled the bass of the pianoforte part, and sold them to Boyer as new works. The fraud seems to have been discovered about 1796, and though Steibelt made reparation by presenting to the aggrieved publisher his Pianoforte Concertos, Nos. 1 and 2, this transaction, combined with other irregularities, so injured his reputation that he felt it desirable to leave Paris, at any rate for a time. England attracted his attention, and, journeying by way of Holland, he reached London about the close of 1796.[1]

By this proceeding Steibelt challenged comparisons quite as dangerous as those which he had recently risked by bringing out an opera in Paris. Pianoforte music had originated in London a quarter of a century before, and at Steibelt's arrival no fewer than three players and composers of the first magnitude were resident there, Clementi, Dussek, and Cramer. Few particulars of Steibelt's life in London have been recorded. His first public performance seems to have been at Salomon's Benefit Concert on May 1, 1797, and a fortnight later (May 15) he played a pianoforte concerto of his own at an opera concert. Not long after this he wrote the Pianoforte Concerto in E (No. 3), containing the 'Storm Rondo.' Whatever may be thought of the merits of this work now, its popularity at the beginning of the 19th century was enormous, and far exceeded that accorded to any other of Steibelt's compositions. It is not too much to say that it was played in every drawing-room in England; indeed, the notorious 'Battle of Prague' alone could compete with it in popular favour. It was, in all probability, first performed in public at Salomon's concert on March 19, 1798. At the close of the same year (Dec. 11) its author again came forward as a composer for the stage, and again met with a favourable reception. His work on this occasion was an English opera, or, as it was described in the Covent Garden play-bill, 'a new grand Heroic Romance, in three acts, called Albert and Adelaide; or the Victim of Constancy.' It must have been an extraordinary medley. The first two acts were a translation from the German of Schoerer, who had taken them from the French, and the third act was added from another French play. The music was only in part original, and was eked out by the insertion of a Quintet from 'Lodöiska' and the like expedients. Even the 'original' music was not all written by Steibelt, as Attwood contributed some of it.[2] Yet, after all, the most curious part of this curious production must have been

[1] According to Fétis, Steibelt did not leave Paris till 1798; but Messrs. Broadwood & Sons have records in their possession which prove that he was established in London by Jan. 2, 1797. This information is due to the kindness of Mr. A. J. Hipkins.
[2] This information is derived from an advertisement of Longman, Clementi & Co. in the *Morning Chronicle* of Jan. 22, 1799. These pasticcios were common enough then, and until the end of the first quarter of the 19th century.

the Overture, which was 'enlivened by a pantomime'! Such as it was, however, the piece proved sufficiently attractive to keep the boards for some time, and the Overture, arranged for the pianoforte, was published in France, and sold in Germany. As teacher and performer Steibelt appears to have been as fully employed during his stay of three years or so in London as he had been previously in Paris. Whether he was as much liked by his brother artists as by the amateurs seems very problematical; at any rate his music is conspicuous by its absence in the concert programmes of the time. Two other circumstances of interest connected with Steibelt's visit to England have been preserved. The first of these is the fact that he conceived a decided predilection for English pianofortes, always using them in preference to any others: the second is his marriage with a young Englishwoman, described as possessed of considerable personal attractions and as a good player on the pianoforte and tambourine. The last-named accomplishment led her husband to add a tambourine accompaniment to many of his subsequent pieces.

Steibelt now resolved on visiting his native country, from which he had been absent, according to some authorities, as much as fifteen years. He reached Hamburg in September or October 1799, but made no great stay there. His next stopping-place was Dresden, where he met with a very enthusiastic reception. Besides several more or less private performances, he gave a concert of his own on Feb. 4, 1800, with the greatest success. Almost immediately after this he went to Prague. His concert in the Bohemian capital attracted a large audience of the upper classes and brought him no less than 1800 gulden; but his playing made little impression, and he went on forthwith to Berlin.[1] Before the end of April he had given two performances in his native city. It was not very likely that his style would please audiences who still held to the traditions of the school of Bach, and the main result of his visit seems to have been to give great offence to his brother artists. From the capital of Prussia he turned to the capital of Austria, then the metropolis of the musical world, where he arrived about the middle of May. We are told that his reputation was such as to cause some anxiety even to Beethoven's friends. If such was the case they were speedily relieved. At the first meeting a sort of armed truce was observed; but at the second, Steibelt was rash enough to issue a distinct challenge. Beethoven was not the man to decline such a contest, and his victory was so decided that his rival refused to meet him again. [See BEETHOVEN, vol. i. pp. 223a, 234b.] This adventure was not likely to contribute to

Steibelt's success at Vienna, and a concert that he gave at the Augarten-Saal was rather thinly attended. His German tour as a whole was only partially successful, and Steibelt determined to return to the more congenial atmosphere of Paris. He arrived there in August 1800, carrying with him the score of Haydn's 'Creation.' Pleyel, Haydn's favourite pupil, had been despatched to request the veteran composer to come and conduct his own work. Pleyel, however, was unable to reach Vienna [PLEYEL, vol. iii. p. 773b], and the field was thus left open to Steibelt. He made the most of his opportunities. Not content with obtaining 4000 francs from Erard for himself and his assistant, M. de Ségur, as the price of the translation adapted to the music, 3600 francs for himself, and 2400 francs for his fellow-translator from the administration of the Opéra, where the work was to be performed, he transposed the part of Adam to suit the tenor Garat, and in many places even attempted to improve Haydn's music by additions and alterations of his own. In spite of these drawbacks, the performance, which took place on Christmas Eve, 1800, proved a decided success. Public curiosity was much excited; a fortnight before the performance not a box was to be had; an eager crowd surrounded the Opera-House at nine in the morning; at the end of the first part a subscription was started to strike a medal in honour of the composer (nay, so much was the work on every one's lips that one of the vaudeville theatres produced a parody of it three days later called 'La récreation du monde'). Rey directed the performance and Steibelt presided at the pianoforte. The adaptation of the words seems to have been fairly performed; at the alterations made in the score competent judges were, naturally enough, extremely indignant. Moreover, the circumstances of his departure some four or five years before had not been forgotten, and thus, in spite of the éclat of the 'Creation,' Steibelt did not feel very comfortable in Paris. Even the success of his ballet 'Le Retour de Zéphyr' at the Opéra, on March 3, 1802, did not reconcile him to his position, and he embraced the opportunity afforded by the conclusion of the Treaty of Amiens on the 22nd of the same month, and returned to London. [About this time he entered into partnership with Mlle. Erard in a music-publishing business in Paris; in 1805 he gave two concerts in Brussels.]

The next six years of his life, about equally divided between London and Paris, were among the busiest of his busy career. His popularity in London was as great as ever; he lived in the most fashionable part of the town, and was received with applause wherever he went. For the King's Theatre in the Haymarket he wrote two ballets, 'Le Jugement du berger Pâris' in 3 acts (produced May 24, 1804), and 'La belle

Laitière' (produced Jan. 26, 1805). It seems very characteristic of the composer that his work was not ready on either occasion. In the former case several airs had to be written at a very short notice by Winter, who was also responsible for the scoring of the second act ;[1] in the latter case an apology was circulated for the omission of the *dénouement* of the piece, ' Mr. Steibelt not having finished that part of the music.'[2] Both ballets were, nevertheless, received with great favour, the march in the first act of ' Le Juge-ment ' and the pastoral scene in the second act of ' La belle Laitière ' obtaining special applause. He also played his Pianoforte Concerto No. 5 (' à la Chasse,' op. 64) at the Opera concerts, apparently in the summer of 1802, with great success. After his return to Paris Steibelt followed up his dramatic achievements in England with an Intermezzo, ' La Fête de Mars,' composed in celebration of the Austerlitz cam-paign, and performed at the Opéra on March 4, 1806. Encouraged by these successes he again tried his hand on a larger work, ' La Princesse de Babylone,' an opera in three acts. This was accepted by the Académie, and was in active preparation when the importunity of his creditors compelled the composer to leave Paris suddenly in the autumn of 1808. But his energies were by no means confined to writing for the stage. Several of his chief sonatas date from these years. Still more important are the two Concertos in E♭ (Nos. 4 and 5) for the pianoforte, and the ' Méthode ' for that instru-ment published in French, German, and Spanish, in which he claims to have invented the signs for the use of the Pedals adopted by Clementi, Dussek, and Cramer. [See SORDINO, *ante*, p. 622*b*.] Above all, it was on his return to Paris in 1805 that he published his Étude—a collection of fifty studies in two books,—undoubtedly the best of his pianoforte works. In the midst of all this occupation he found time to meditate further travels. Russia, a country that in the previous century had attracted Galuppi, Paisiello, Sarti, Cimarosa, and Clementi, had just furnished an asylum to Boieldieu and a home to Field, was then a sort of Promised Land to French musicians, and it is not strange that Steibelt should have been more than willing to go there, when he received in 1808 the offer of a very advantageous appointment from the Emperor Alexander. Owing to causes already mentioned he left Paris for St. Petersburg in October 1808. His journey was not, however, very speedy when he felt himself out of the reach of his creditors. He stopped at Frankfort to give a great concert on Nov. 2,[3] and at Leipzig made a stay of some weeks and repeated the programme of the Frankfort concert. During his sojourn in Leipzig he put forth (Nov. 24, 1808) a notice in which he complains that some German publishers had

issued very faulty editions of his works, even going so far as to annex his name to composi-tions by other people, and announces his intention of having all his future works published by Breitkopf & Härtel, an intention that was not very consistently carried out. Even after leaving Leipzig he lingered at Breslau and Warsaw to give concerts, so that he could hardly have reached St. Petersburg till the beginning of the spring of 1809.

Here, at last, his wanderings came to an end. He was appointed, it is not very clear when, director of the Opéra Français, and when Boiel-dieu left, at the close of 1810, Steibelt received the title of ' Maître de Chapelle ' to the Emperor in his place. It was, however, a title to which no emolument was attached, and which in no way relieved its possessor from professional duties. In managing and writing for the Opera, and in teaching and composing for the piano-forte, the remaining years of Steibelt's life were spent. About the year 1814 he ceased to play in public, and did not appear again for six years, when the production of his Eighth Pianoforte Concerto induced him to come forward once more as a performer on March 16, 1820. Mean-while his pen was not idle. His early years at St. Petersburg were marked by the ballets ' La Fête de l'Empereur ' in 1809, and ' Der blöde Ritter ' (before the end of 1812) ; and the three Concertos for pianoforte, Nos. 6, 7, and 8, appear to belong to the period of his abstention from playing in public. For the theatre he wrote two operas, each in three acts, 'Cendrillon'[4] and ' Sargines ' ; a third, ' Le Jugement de Midas,' he did not live to finish. He also spent some time in revising ' Roméo et Juliette.' In the midst of these avocations he was seized with a painful disease, of which, after lingering some time, he died on Sept. 20, 1823. A number of his friends combined to honour him with a quasi-public funeral, and the military governor of St. Petersburg, Count Milarodowitsch, organised a subscription-concert for the benefit of his family, who were left in very straitened circumstances.

Comparatively little has been recorded of Steibelt's personal character, but the traits preserved are, to say the least of it, far from prepossessing. Almost the only occurrence that presents him in a pleasing light is his death-bed dedication of the revised score of ' Roméo et Juliette ' to the King of Prussia, in token of gratitude for the kindnesses received from that monarch's father. He appears to have been perfectly eaten up with vanity, which exhibited itself unceasingly in arrogance, in-civility, and affectation. His respect for his art, never too great, was destroyed by the quantity of worthless music that he wrote hastily to meet temporary difficulties, and he

---

[1] *Morning Chronicle*, May 25, 1804.   [2] *Ibid.* Jan. 28, 1805.
[3] The correspondent of the *A.M.Z.* (xi. 170) oddly describes him as ' Steibelt of London.'

[4] It is worth noting that some authorities declare this was written for Paris. This opera has been considered his greatest work.

not unfrequently stooped to expedients still more unworthy. One of these has been already mentioned, but it was not the only one. A device that seems to have been specially common was to add a violin part to a published set of pianoforte sonatas and then bring out the result as an entirely new work.

Most of his numerous pianoforte sonatas have no slow movement at all, consisting merely of an Allegro and a Rondo. When an Adagio or Andante is interpolated, it is either an insignificant trifle of some thirty or forty bars in length, or else a popular melody, such as 'If a body meet a body,' ''Twas within a mile of Edinbro' town,' or the like. He does not seem to have ever realised the powers of the pianoforte for an Adagio, and when a violin part is added, as is often the case in his sonatas, he almost invariably assigns the melody to the latter instrument and accompanies it with a *tremolo* on the pianoforte. His Allegros and Rondos, on the contrary, particularly the former, are often of remarkable merit, and many of his sonatas, such as that dedicated to Madame Bonaparte (in E♭, op. 45), are really fine and original compositions. Yet, even at his best, a want of sustained power makes itself felt. Though the absence of records as to his early life makes it probable that his musical training was not sacrificed to the profitable speculation of exhibiting a youthful prodigy, his constructive skill was never developed. All his music sounds like a clever improvisation that happens to have been committed to paper. Whenever a new idea occurs to the writer it is straightway thrust in, and when no fresh idea presents itself one of the old ones is repeated. Hence it is that his music is now totally forgotten, for, whatever the opinion of contemporaries may be, posterity has invariably consigned to oblivion all music, no matter what other qualities it may possess, that is deficient in design.[1] His contemporaries pronounced the 'Étude' his best work, and time has confirmed their opinion. It has been often republished, and may indeed be said to be the only work of his that still lives. To a modern pianist one of the most striking features of the collection is the fact that several of the pieces (*e.g.* Nos. 3 and 8) anticipate in a very noteworthy manner the style made popular by Mendelssohn in his 'Songs without Words.' The vast mass of Airs with variations, Fantasias, Descriptive Pieces, Potpourris, Divertissements, Bacchanals, and the like, that had a great sale in their day, are now deservedly forgotten. In Germany his reputation was comparatively *nil*. His pianoforte works, however, good and bad, have all the great merit of feasibleness, and invariably lie well under the hand.

For the orchestra and other instruments Steibelt wrote comparatively little—wisely, in

the judgment of one of his biographers.[2] Unfortunately, the scores of many of his operatic works, especially those written for St. Petersburg, are inaccessible and perhaps lost. It cannot, however, be said that an examination of the score of 'Roméo et Juliette' quite bears out the sentence just quoted. We are told that an even division of the interest of the music between the various instruments is one great mark of skilful orchestral writing. If this be so, Steibelt's opera is in one respect skilfully written, for almost every instrument in the orchestra comes to the front in turn. More than this, the composer uses the forces at his command with power and freedom. The trombones are introduced to an extent then unusual, though not excessive. Many of the resources of modern scoring are to be found, especially the employment of wood-wind and strings in responsive groups. The main complaint that can be sustained against the work is that the concerted pieces are unduly protracted and impede the action—this is certainly the case with the Trio in the first act. It should, moreover, be observed that when Steibelt writes for the pianoforte and other instruments, as in his quintets, the pianoforte is not allowed to monopolise the interest. His concertos are formed on the orthodox Mozartean model, and it must be added that they contain, especially in their first movements, some excellent writing. 'The instrumentation of the first movement is quite exceptionally beautiful' was the opinion of one who listened to the performance of his Eighth Concerto in London,[3] and even when the work as a whole is weak, as in the Sixth Concerto, the instrumentation is not deficient in skill and novelty.

Steibelt's originality as a composer was questioned in his own day. It was said that his famous 'Storm Rondo' was a feeble copy of a work for the organ by the Abbé Vogler, a statement on which the thoroughly *pianoforte* character of Steibelt's music throws considerable doubt. His enemies also averred that 'Roméo et Juliette' was a mere plagiarism from Georg Benda's opera of the same name—an allegation that is certainly unfounded. More serious objection may be taken to his Sixth Pianoforte Concerto, 'Le Voyage au Mont St. Bernard,' in which not only the general idea, but even the most striking details — the hymn of the monks, the tolling of the convent bell, and the national music of the Savoyard with accompaniment of triangles—are borrowed from Cherubini's opera of 'Elisa, ou le Voyage au Mont Bernard.' It is, in fact, as it has been aptly described, 'the work, not of an architect, but of a decorator.' On the other hand, Steibelt must be credited with some contributions to musical progress. Modulation he used with a freedom unknown before him. The following passage,

---

[1] Mme. Arabella Goddard, among her numerous revivals, included Steibelt's Sonata in E♭, op. 45, and some Studies.

[2] *A.M.Z.* xxv. p. 725.   [3] *Ibid.* xxiv. No. 25.

for instance, from the Andante of the first Sonata, in op. 37,

was an unheard-of thing in 1799. Of course, nothing is easier than to carry such innovations to excess, and he may be fairly said to have overstepped the line when in the 'working-out' of his Sonata for pianoforte and violin in E minor, op. 32, he introduces the second subject in E♭ major, changing the signature for fifty-six bars. Many other instances of such boldness are to be found.

The list of his works which follows has been compiled with considerable trouble. Not only had Steibelt a careless and, it is to be feared, dishonest habit, of publishing different works under the same opus number, and the same or a slightly altered work under different numbers, but, according to his own protest already mentioned, works were published under his name with which he had nothing to do. In such circumstances the task of drawing up a complete and accurate list is well-nigh hopeless, and this catalogue, though compiled with all the care possible, does not profess to be more than a contribution towards a complete and exact list. An asterisk attached to a work means that it certainly contains *one* sonata (or the number given) and *may* contain more. A date has been added in some cases, where it seemed likely to be of any value.

Op.
1. 3 Sonatas, PF. and Vln. (1788). | Sonata, PF. | 2 Sonatas, PF. | 3 Sonatas, PF. | 3 Sonatas, Harp with Vln. and Vcello. *ad lib.* | 6 Sonatas, PF., with Flute or Vln. and Vcello.
2. * Sonata, PF. and Vln. (1788). | Sonata, PF. | Sonata, PF. and Vln. (1791). | 3 Sonatas, PF., the first with Vln.[1] | 2 Sonatas, PF. | 3 Sonatas, PF., Vln., and Vcello.
3. Sonata, PF., Vln., and Vcello. (1791). | Turkish Overture, PF. Vln. and Vcello.[2]
4. 3 Sonatas, PF. and Vln. | * Sonata, PF., Vln., and Vcello. (1791). | 3 Sonatas, PF., the first with Vln. obbligato.[3]
5. Premier Caprice, PF. (1792). | Preludes and three pieces, PF. (1792).[4] | 3 Preludes, PF.[5]
6. Second Caprice, PF. | Grand Sonata, PF. and Vln.; A (1792). | 3 Sonatas, PF. | 2 Sonatas and 'La Coquette,' PF., the first with Vln. | * Sonata, PF. | Rondo from 3rd PF. Concerto.
7. 3 Grand Sonatas, PF. (1793). | Turkish Overture, PF., Vln., and Vcello.[6] | 3 Sonatas.
8. Grand Sonata, PF. and Vln.; D (1793). | 6 Grand Preludes or Exercises, PF.(1794). | 3 Quartets for Strings (1799).[7] | 'Enfant chéri des Dames,' with var. PF. (1799).[8] | 3 Sonatas, PF., the third with Vln.
9. 6 Divertissements, PF. (1793). | 2 Grand Sonatas, PF. | 'La Coquette,' PF. ; A.[9]
10. Mélange d'airs et chansons en Forme de Scène, PF. (1794).[10]
11. 3 Sonatas, PF. and Flute, or Vln. ; B♭, A, D (1793). | 6 Sonatas, PF. and Vln. | 6 Sonatas, PF. | 6 Sonatas, PF., Nos. 1, 4, 5, and 6, with Vln. obbligato, Nos. 2 and 3 with Flute obbligato. | 3 Sonatas, PF., Vln., and Vcello. | 3 Sonatas, PF. with Vln. acc. (ded. to Mme. Eugenia de Beaumarchois).
12.
13. 6 Airs with var., PF. | Duo, PF. and Harp.
14. 2 Grand Sonatas, PF. (1795). | Duo, Harp and PF.
15. Grand Sonata, PF.
16. Grand Sonata, PF. | Mélange d'airs.[11]
17. 3 Quartets for Strings ; E♭, C, F min. (1797).[12]

[1] See op. 4.   [2] See op. 7.   [3] See op. 2.
[4] This appears to have been also styled Preludes and. Capriccios.
[5] Six Preludes are also published as op. 5. They are probably a combination of the Preludes in the works given.   [6] See op. 3.
[7] Probably part of op. 34, and perhaps the same as op. 17.
[8] See op. 32.   [9] From op. 6.   [10] See op. 16.
[11] See op. 10.   [12] Perhaps the same as op. 8.

Op.
18. 3 Sonatas, PF., Nos. 2 and 3 with Vln. (1797). | 3 Sonatas, PF., with acc. for Flute or Vln. ; G, C, B♭ (1799).
19. 3 Sonatas, PF. (1797).
20. Sonatas, PF.
21.
22.
23. Grand Sonata, PF. ; G min.
24. Preludes, PF. (1797). | 'Ladies' Amusement,' PF.[13] | Trois Caprices en Prélude, PF. | Sonata, PF. ; G.
25. Grand Sonata ('L'Amante disperata '), PF. ; G min. (1797). | Preludes, PF. | 2 Sonatas, PF. and Vln. ; G, B♭.
26. 3 easy Sonatas, PF. and Vln. ; G, F (1799).
27. 6 Sonatas, PF. and Vln. (ded. to Queen of Prussia) ; C, E♭, E, B♭, G, and ? A (1797).[14]
28. 3 Quintets, PF. and Strings ; No. 1, G; No. 2, D; No. 3? (1798).[15] | 3 Sonatas, PF. à 4 mains (1798).[16] | 'A ine tutte le belle,' Rondo, PF., Vln.,and Vcello.; E♭ (1798).[17] | 3 easy Divertissements, PF.
29. 3 Grand Sonatas, PF. | 2 Rondos, PF. ; F, G.
30. 3 Sonatas, PF. and Vln. | Grand Sonata, PF. with acc. for Vln. ; B♭. | 2 Rondos, PF. ; F, A.
31. Grand Trio., PF., Vln., and Bass ; A (1798).[18] | First Quintet, PF. and Strings ; D.[19]
32. Grand Sonata, PF. with acc. for Vln. ; E min. | 'Enfant chéri des Dames,' Air with var., PF., Vln., and Vcello.; E♭.[20] | 2 Sonatas (with Scotch airs), PF.[21]
33. 4 Sonatas of progressive difficulty, PF., with Vln. *ad lib.* ; C, F, G, D (1798). | Concerto No. 3 (' The Storm '), PF. and Orch. ; E (1799).[22] | 2 Sonatas PF., with Vln. and Vcello. *ad lib.* ; B♭, F.[23] | 6 Rondos, PF. ; C, F, G, D, B♭, F.
34. 6 Quatuors concertante for Strings, in two books (1798).[24] | 24 Waltzes, PF. with acc. for Tambourine and Triangle (1800).[25]
35. 3 Sonatas, PF., with Vln. *ad lib.* ; E♭, F, A (1799). | Grand Concerto, No. 3 (' The Storm ') ; E (1799).[26] | 'Amusement pour les Dames' (easy PF. pieces).[27]
36. 3 Sonatas (ded. to Mme. de Boigne), PF. with acc. for Flute, or Vln. ; F, B♭, A (1799).[28] | 3 Divertissements and 5 Rondos, PF. (1799). | 3 easy Divertissements PF. | 3 easy Divertissements and Airs with var., PF. | Sonata for 2 PF. (1800). | 12 Waltzes, PF., with acc. for Tambourine and Triangle.[29] | Combat Naval, PF., with Vln. and Vcello. (and Gr. Tambour *ad lib.*) ; B♭.[30]
37. 3 Sonatas, PF., with Vln. *ad lib.* The first has also a Tambourine obbligato ; C, A, E♭.[31] | 3 Progressive Sonatas, PF. ; C, B♭, F. | 3 Sonatas of progressive difficulty, PF., with Vln. and Vcello. *ad lib.* | Sonata, PF., with Vln. *ad lib.* ; E♭.[32]
38. 3 Sonatas, PF., with acc. for Flute or Vln. ; C, B♭, G.[33] | 3 Sonatas, PF., with acc. for Flute or Vln. ; A, D, B♭. | 12 Divertissements (Marches, Waltzes, and Rondos), PF., with acc. for Tambourine.
39. 3 Sonatas (ded. to Mlle. de Boigne), PF., with acc. for Flute or Vln. (1800).[34] | 6 Bacchanals, PF., with Tambourine *ad lib.*
40. 3 easy Sonatas, PF., with Vln. *ad lib.* ; A min., C, F. | Sonata, PF., with Vln. *ad lib.* ; E♭. | 3 progressive Lessons (also called Sonatas), PF. ; C, B♭, F. | 3 favourite Rondos, PF. ; C, A, E♭.
41. 3 Sonatas, PF. and Flute (1800). | Combat Naval, PF., 1800.[35] | 3 Rondos, PF., with Flute or Vln. ; A, D, B♭. | 3 Sonatas, PF. ; C, B♭, G.[36] | 3 easy, pleasing, and progressive Sonatas. PF.; C, B♭, F. | Easy Sonatas, PF. and Vln. | Easy Sonata, PF.
42. 6 easy and pleasing Sonatinas : Book 1, C, B♭, C ; Book 2, D, E♭, A. | 3 easy Sonatas, PF. and Vln. | 3 Sonatas, PF., with Flute or Vln. ; A, D, B♭.[37] | 'Mamma mia,' arranged as a Rondo, PF. ; E♭. | Naval Fight, a grand national piece, PF.[38]
43. 3 Sonatas, PF. ; D, B♭, E♭. | Rondo, PF. ; D. | 'Amusement pour les Dames,' PF.[39]
44. Grand Sonata, PF., with Flute or Vln. ; A. | Fantasia with var. on ' Der Vogelfänger,' PF.
45. 3 Sonatas, PF., with acc. for Violin ; A, E♭, B♭. | Grand Sonata (ded. to Mme. Bonaparte). PF. ; E♭. | 3 Sonatas, PF., with acc. for Flute or Vln. ; A,D,B♭.[40] | Sonata, PF. and Vln.; A. | Grand Polonaise, PF. and Vln. ; E. | Polonaise, PF.
46. 3 Sonatas (' in which are introduced some admired airs,'), PF., with acc. for Flute or Vln. ; B♭, A, D.[41]

[13] See opp. 35 and 43.
[14] *Selections* from these six appear to have been also published as op. 27.
[15] Six similar Quintets appeared in the following year (see op. 31). These Quintets were especially famous.
[16] These were followed the next year by a fourth, published separately.
[17] Also published for Harp and PF. The air comes from Paisiello's 'La Modista raggiratrice.'
[18] This appears to have been also published for PF., Flute, and Vcello. See op. 28.
[19] This was also published for PF. and Harp. See op. 8.
[20] See opp. 46 and 62.   [21] See op. 35.
[22] These 2 Sonatas are described as ' Liv. 2,' so that another book may have been published.
[23] These Quartets appear to be some sort of arrangement or selection.
[24] In 2 books, each containing 12 Waltzes. The first book was also published (1) for Harp, Tambourine, Flute, and Triangle ; (2) for 2 Violins ; (3) for 2 Flutes. One book was also published as op. 36.
[25] See op. 33.   [26] Also published as op. 43. See op. 24.
[27] These appear to have been also published as op. 39.
[28] Also published for PF., Violin, and Triangle. These Waltzes are part of op. 34.   [29] See opp. 41 and 42.
[30] In 1802, 5 Sonatas with Violin *ad lib.* are announced as forming this work.
[31] It is possible that all the works numbered op. 37 are variants of the first mentioned.   [32] This was also published as op. 41.
[33] These appear to have been also published as op. 36.
[34] See opp. 36 and 42.   [35] See op. 38.
[36] These were also published as op. 45. They may be identical with the preceding.   [37] See opp. 36 and 41.
[38] Also published as op. 35. See op. 24.
[39] Also published as op. 32.
[40] The 'admired airs' are—in No. 1, ' 'Twas within a mile of

Op.
47.
48. 2 Sonatas, PF. ; E♭, A.[1]
49. 6 Sonatas (in 2 books), PF. | Duet for Harp. | 3 Quartets for Strings. | 6 Sonatinas of progressive difficulty, PF.
50. 6 favourite (also called progressive) Sonatas, PF. ; C, B♭, G, D, E♭, A.
51. 3 Sonatas, PF.; C, G, F. | Quartet, PF., Vln., Viola, and Vcello.; A.
52.
53. 6 Bacchanals, PF., with acc. for Flute, Tambourine, and Triangle.
54.
55.
56. 3 Grand Sonatas, PF. and Vln. ; C, D, B♭. | 3 Grand Sonatas. PF. with Vln. ad lib. ; A min., F, C. | 3 Sonatas, PF., Vln., and Vcello. | 2 Sonatas, PF. ; E♭, E.
57. 3 Rondos, PF. ; C, B♭, A.
58. Rondo, PF. ; B♭.
59. Sonata, PF., with Vln. ad lib. ; E♭. | Grand Sonata, PF. | Sonata, PF., Vln., and Vcello.
60. Sonata (ded. to Duchess of Courland), PF. ; E♭. | 6 Sonatas, PF. | 2 Rondos, PF. ; F, A.
61. Grand Sonata, PF. ; E♭. | 3 Sonatas, PF.,with Vln. and Vcello. | 2 Sonatas, PF., with Vln. and Vcello.(ad lib.); G, E♭. | 2 Sonatas, PF., with acc. for Vln. and Vcello. ; F, D. | 2 Sonatas, PF.,Vln., and Vcello. ; B♭, E♭. | Grand Sonata, PF., Vln., and Vcello.[2]
62. 2 Sonatas, PF. ; F, D (1802).[3] | 3 Sonatinas, PF. ; E♭, G, C. | 3 Sonatas, PF., with Vln. or Flute ; C, B♭, G.
63. Sonata, PF. ; D. | 3 Grand Sonatas, PF.; C, F, D (1802). | Sonata, PF.; B♭. | ' Le Rappel à l'armée,' Military Fantasia on an air by Mozart, PF. ; F.[4] | *Rondo, PF.
64. Grand Concerto, No. 5 (' à la Chasse '), PF. and Orch. ; E♭ (1802). | Grand Sonata. PF. ; G. | Second Military Fantasia with a triumphal march by Haydn, PF.
65. 3 Sonatas, PF., Vln., and Vcello. | 3 Sonatas, PF. | ' Le Rappel à l'armée,' Military Fantasia, PF. ; F.[5] | *Rondo, PF.
66. 3 Grand Sonatas, PF., with acc. for Flute or Vln. added by I. Pleyel ; F, G, A (1802). | 3 Sonatas, PF. and Vln. | 2 Sonatas, PF. ; F, A.[6] | Air favori de ' Léonce ' Varié, PF. ; D.[7]
67. 2 Sonatas, PF. | Grand Sonata, PF., with acc. for Vln., Sonata, PF., with Flute or Vln. ; D.
68. 3 Sonatas, PF., with Vln. ad lib. | 2 easy Sonatas, PF. | 6 Bacchanals, PF., with Tambourine ad lib.
69. 3 Sonatas, PF., with Vln., or Vcello., or Bassoon obbligato. | Grand Sonata, PF. and Vln. obbligato ; G min. | ' Les Papillons,' Rondo, PF. ; E♭. | 3 Sonatas, PF., Vln., and Vcello. | Grand Sonata, PF. ; E♭.
70. 3 Sonatinas, PF., with Flute or Vln. ; C, B♭, G. | 3 Sonatas, PF., with Vln. ; G, F, A. | Sonata for Harp.
71. 3 Grand Sonatas, PF., with Vln. obbligato ; G min., G, B♭. | Sonata (with a dance air by Duport), PF. and Flute.
72. 3 Sonatas (or Sonatinas), PF. and Vln., or Flute ; C, B♭, G. | ' La Bohémienne ' (Air by Choron), with var. ; PF. ; G.
73. 3 Sonatas, PF. and Vln. ; G, F, A.[8] | Fantasia with 6 var. on ' Bélisaire,' PF. ; D min.[9]
74. 3 Sonatas, PF. and Vln. ; E♭, A, E min. | 6 Bacchanals, PF., with Tambourine ad lib.
75. 3 Sonatas, PF. | 3 progressive Sonatas, PF., with Vln. ad lib. ; F, G, A. | 2 easy Sonatas, PF. | Fantasia, PF.
76. 3 Grand Sonatas, PF. ; A, G, E♭.[10] | New Turkish Overture, PF., Vln., and Vcello.[11]
77. 6 Sonatinas, PF.[12] | Fantasia with 6 var. on the Romance of Richard Cœur de Lion,' PF. ; C.
78. Étude for PF., containing 50 exercises of different kinds (in 2 books) (1805). | 6 Bacchanals, PF., with Tambourine ad lib.
79. 3 Sonatas, PF. and Flute ; G, F, A.[13] | Grand Sonata, PF. and Vln. obbligato ; E.
80. Grand Sonata, PF. with Vln. obbligato ; B♭. | Military Fantasia on ' La Sentinelle.' PF. ; C.[14]
81. 3 Grand Sonatas, PF.; A, G, E♭.[15] | Grand Sonata, PF. and Vln. obbligato ; B♭.
82. Grand Martial Sonata, PF. ; D.[16] | Grand Fantasia with var. PF. ; D.
83. Grand Sonata, PF., with Vln. ; E min. | 2 Sonatas, PF. ; C, F.
84. Grand Sonata, PF., with acc. for Vln. or Flute ; G. | 3 Sonatas, PF. ; B, G, E♭.
85. Grand Sonata, PF. ; C. | Grand Sonata, PF. ; D.
86. 6 Sonatinas, PF.
87. Grand Sonata, PF., with Vln. ; B♭.
88. Grand Martial Sonata, PF. ; D.[17]
89. Grand Sonata, PF. and Flute ; G.
90. Fantasia en forme de Scène, PF. ; F min. | Fantasia en forme de Scène, PF. ; G.
91. Sonata, PF. ; C.
92.-100.[18]

Edinbro' town' and ' The Caledonian Beauty '; in No. 2, ' The Maid of Selma' and ' Life let us cherish.'
[1] These appear to have been published (1) for PF. and Vln., (2) for PF., Vln., and Vcello.
[2] These last five works are suspiciously like the same thing in different disguises.
[3] The following airs are introduced—in No. 1, ' If a body meet a body,' and Sir David Hunter Blair's Reel ; in No. 2, ' Jesse Macpharlane' (sic), and ' La chantreuse.'
[4] Also published as op. 65.   [5] Also published as op. 63.
[6] The second movement of the first Sonata is on a Scotch song, and the third movement on a Russian theme.
[7] ' Léonce' was an opera by Isouard, 1805.
[8] These appear to have been also published for Flute, both as op. 73 and as op. 79.
[9] ' Bélisaire' was an air by Garat.   [10] Also published as op. 81.
[11] Not, apparently, the same as op. 7.
[12] Selections from these six seem to have been also published as op. 77.
[13] See op. 73.   [14] ' La Sentinelle' was an air by Choron.
[15] Also published as op. 76.   [16] Also published as op. 88.
[17] Also published as op. 82.
[18] At this point, about the date of Steibelt's arrival in Russia, almost all record of his works disappears.

Op.
101. Grand Fantasia (' L'Incendie de Moscou '), PF.
102. Etrennes aux Dames (Favourite Russian Dance with var.), PF. ; G.
103-109.
110. Fantasia (Battle of Neerwinde), PF. (1792).

WORKS WITHOUT OPUS-NUMBERS

1. VOCAL AND ORCHESTRAL.

Six Operas—' Roméo et Juliette,' in 3 acts ; produced at Théâtre Feydeau, Sept. 10, 1793. | ' Albert and Adelaide,' in 3 acts, an English opera, not wholly original, produced at Covent Garden, Dec. 11, 1798. | ' La Princesse de Babylone,' in 3 acts. | ' Cendrillon,' in 3 acts. | ' Sargines,' in three acts. | ' Le Jugement de Midas,' unfinished, but apparently performed.

Five Ballets—' Le Retour de Zéphire ' (Paris Opéra, March 3, 1802). | ' Le Jugement du berger Pâris' (King's Theatre, London, May 24, 1804).[19] | ' La belle Laitière, ou Blanche, Reine de Castile' (King's Theatre, Jan. 26, 1805). | ' La Fête de l'Empereur ' (St. Petersburg, 1809). | ' Der blöde Ritter ' (St. Petersburg, before 1812) ; and an Intermezzo, 'La Fête de Mars' (Paris Opéra, March 4, 1806).

Vocal Music.—The 20 Songs of Estelle, with acc. for PF. or Harp.[20] | 30 Songs with acc. for PF. or Harp, in 5 vols., each of 6 songs.

Music for Orchestra.—Ouverture en Symphonie (1796). | Waltzes for Orch. | Grand Concerto for Harp, with Orch acc. | Potpourri, arranged as Concerto, with acc. for Orch. | 8 Concertos for PF. and Orch., viz.—
No. 1. In C (1796).
   2. In E min. with acc. for Vln. or Full Orch. ad lib. (1796 ?).
   3. In E (' The Storm '). Op. 33 or 35 (1798-99).
   4. In E♭.
   5. In E♭ (' à la Chasse '). Op. 64 (1802)
   6. In G min. (' Le Voyage au Mont St. Bernard ') (about 1816).
   7. In E min. (Grand Military Concerto, 'dans le Genre des Grecs,' with 2 Orchestras) (before 1817).
   8. In E♭ (with Bacchanalian Rondo, acc. by Chorus). (Produced at St. Petersburg, March 16, 1820, and played by Neate at the London Philharmonic Concert of March 25, 1822.)

2. PIANOFORTE.

Fantasias. Of these there are some 30, part with variations, besides those which have opus-numbers. A vast quantity of Rondos, Airs with variations, Potpourris, and specimens of Programme Music exists.

3. MISCELLANEOUS.

I. Amongst the higher class of music that falls under this head may be noticed :—

Méthode de PF. contenant les principes nécessaires pour bien toucher de cet instrument, des gammes dans tous les tons, des exercices pour les doubles cadences, 12 petites leçons, 6 sonates d'une difficulté graduelle, et des grands exercices, le tout doigté, et enfin une instruction sur la manière de se servir des pédales. 1805. | 12 Sonatas, PF. (4 hands)—the first 6 in F, G, G, C, B♭, F. | 6 Sonatas for Harp. | 3 Duets, PF. and Harp. | 6 Duets or Sonatas, 2 PF.s, or PF. and Harp. | 6 Sonatas for Harp, with acc. for Vln. and Vcello. | 6 Sonates périodiques (one with Vln. or Flute ad lib.), PF. | 3 Preludes, PF. | 12 Sonatinas in 2 Books—Bk. 1. C, B♭, G, D, E♭, A : Bk. 2, C, G, F, D, B♭, E♭; PF. | 3 Sonatas (for beginners), PF. | Sonata for Harp with Vln. ad lib. | Elégie (on the death of Marshal Prince Soltykoff), PF. ; D min. (1816). | 2 Airs by Braham (' The beautiful maid' and ' Never think of meeting sorrow ') in Reeve's opera ' The Cabinet' arranged as a Sonata, PF.; B♭. | La Chasse, Sonata, PF., with Vln. ad lib. ; D. | Sonata, PF., with Vln. ; C min. | Overture and Rondo, PF. | Overture and Polonaise, PF.

II. The following are among the chief of his lighter works :—
12 Bacchanals, PF. (with Tambourine ad lib.). | 2 Books of Serenades, PF. | 12 Capriccios, PF. | Turkish March, PF. | Marche de Peterhof, 1811, PF. | Triumphal March on the entry of Alex. I. and Fred. Will. III. into Paris, 1814, PF. | Le Retour de Cavallerie Russe à St. Petersbourg le 14 Oct. 1814, pièce militaire, PF. | Le Départ, Impromptu, PF.; C. | Caprice on ' Non più andrai,' PF. (1816). | 6 Nouvelles Walzes à trois mains (the 6th Waltz is a parody of the finale of the ' Vestale '), PF. | Polonaise, PF.; D. | Turkish Rondo for Harp, with Vln. and Tambourine ad lib. | Air (' Enfant chéri ') with var. PF. and Harp. | Favourite Rondo for Guitar and Flute or Vln. ; D.

In the third book of ' Pandean Music' for the PF., published by N. Corri of Edinburgh, the first number is ' Air from Blaise et Babet by Steibelt'; but no single item of information about ' Blaise et Babet' is forthcoming, except that it does not seem to have been a piece brought out in London.

                              J. H. M.

STEIGLEDER, HANS ULRICH, came of an organist family settled at Stuttgart. The date of his birth is given as 1580. After serving as organist at Lindau on the Bodensee, he was appointed in 1617 Stifts-Organist at Stuttgart, in which capacity he had also to serve as musician generally to the Court of Würtemberg. He died 1635. For the organ he published two works, the first of which is so far remarkable as being the first specimen in Germany of copper-plate engraving for organ or clavier music. As the title informs us, the

[19] The original score of this work came into the possession of Moscheles, and was sold by him on leaving London in 1847.
[20] Some authorities declare that Steibelt only wrote five of this set of 20 songs.

engraving was by his own hands, 'Ricercar Tabulatura, Organis et Organoedis unice inserviens et maxime conducens adornata a J.U.S. . . ejusdemque Autoris sumptibus et manibus propriis Aeri Cupreo insculpta et excusa. Anno 1624.' Although mentioned by Gerber, this work was unknown to modern musicians, until a copy sent from the Royal Library at Stuttgart was shown at the Vienna Musical Exhibition of 1892. The engraving is said to be rather coarsely done. Some account of the music is given in Seiffert, *Geschichte der Klaviermusik*, Bd. I. p. 105. It consists of Ricercari of the earlier Italian fugal type. The other published work of Steigleder is entitled, 'Tabulatur-Buch darinnen dass Vater Unser auf 2, 3 und 4 Stimmen componirt und vierzig mal variirt würdt . . . auf Orgeln und allen andern Instrumenten ordentlich zu appliciren . . . 1627.' This work consists of forty Bearbeitungen or Variations on the melody of the 'Vater Unser im Himmelreich,' which show the influence of the newer technique of the English - Dutch Variation School of Sweelinck, as well as of the South German toccata style of George Muffat. Two specimens are given in Ritter, *Geschichte des Orgelspiels*, Nos. 87 and 88.   J. R. M.

STEIN, a family of pianoforte-makers and players.

1. JOHANN ANDREAS, the founder of German pianoforte-making, was born at Heidesheim in the Palatinate in 1728. Nothing is known of his early life, but he appears to have been in Paris in 1758, and to have remained there for some years. We may conclude that he was engaged in organ-building and harpsichord-making, since he was not only a good musician, but a proficient in both handicrafts, before he turned to pianoforte-making. After Paris we find him at Augsburg, organist of the Barfüsserkirche, the famous organ of which he built, as well as that of the Kreuzkirche. When the article PIANOFORTE was written, special inquiries were made in Vienna and elsewhere, to discover any pianofortes remaining of Stein's make, but without success. [Several examples of Stein's pianoforte, exhibited at Vienna in 1892, are now in the collection of Mr. Steinert of New Haven, Conn., U.S.A.] These inquiries, however, led to the discovery of a grand piano, which was secured by M. Victor Mahillon, of the Museum of the Conservatoire, Brussels. It is inscribed

Jean André Stein
Facteur d'orgues et des Clavecins
Organiste à l'Eglise des Minorites
Augsbourg 1780. [1]

The action of this bichord grand piano is the same as that in vol. iii. p. 725, Fig. 10 of this Dictionary, which was copied from a scarce pamphlet preserved in the Library of the

[1] The last figure is indistinct, and M. Mahillon thinks that it might be 5 or 6 instead of 0.

Gesellschaft der Musikfreunde at Vienna. The wedge damper is Cristofori's ; the escapement and other parts of the action differ entirely from that maker's and from Gottfried Silbermann's as preserved in three instruments at Potsdam, in which the Florentine maker Cristofori is closely followed. This instrument has also the *genouillière* or knee-pedal for raising the dampers, which preceded the foot-pedal. [See SORDINO.] The genouillière and Stein's escapement are described by Mozart with great *gusto* in a letter addressed to his mother, in October 1777, only a very few years before M. Mahillon's piano was made. What action was used by Spaeth of Ratisbon, also referred to by Mozart, we do not know, but M. Mahillon's discovery at Brussels of a square piano, with the rudiments of Stein's action—that is, the same centred percussion without the hopper escapement—leads directly to the conclusion that this simple action, clumsy as Mozart found it without the escapement, was in common use before Stein brought his inventive genius to bear upon its improvement.

Welcker von Gontershausen (*Der Clavierbau*, Frankfort, 1870, p. 173) gives a drawing of this action without hopper escapement, attributing it to Silbermann ; but, as far as we can see, without proof. Many of the early German pianos have neither date nor inscription, which makes the attribution to a maker difficult. We are disposed to think that Silbermann would not have abandoned the good action of Cristofori, which he knew how to finish well, for a crude tentative mechanism ; we therefore conclude that the Seven Years' War having entirely stamped out Saxon pianoforte-making, a new era began with the restoration of peace, and that the merit of founding that German pianoforte-making which was so long identified with the School of Vienna, belongs to Stein, whose inventive talent and artistic devotion were displayed in the good instruments he made, which by 1790 at latest, were adopted as models both in North and South Germany, as the two grand pianos formerly belonging to Queen Louise, made by Huhn, '*Organ-builder*,' of Berlin,[2] and preserved in memory of her at Potsdam, unmistakably show.

Gerber, in his *Lexicon*, has preserved a list of numerous inventions by Stein [of one, the 'Melodica,' the inventor published an account in 1772], of which none are now of value save the escapement and the keyboard shifting by means of a pedal. He introduced the latter in his 'Saitenharmonica' in 1789, carrying the hammers from three strings to one, which he spaced rather away from the other two unisons. This 'una corda' he named 'Spinettchen.'

[2] One of these instruments, and apparently the older one, bears no name outside, but internal examination shows that the maker was the same who made the 1790 one ; both closely resemble Mozart's piano by Walther, at Salzburg, and the original model by Stein of 1780.

A. W. Thayer[1] unearthed a record of Pastor Junker, showing that Beethoven in 1791, when residing at Bonn, always used an instrument of Stein's.

Stein died in 1792, leaving two sons, Matthäus Andreas and Friedrich (see below), and a daughter, Maria Anna, known as NANNETTE, who in 1794 married Streicher, and was really the most prominent of the group.

Though Streicher ultimately succeeded to the business, which had been removed from Augsburg to Vienna, his name does not appear for several years in connection with it. [See footnote to PIANOFORTE, vol. iii. p. 725a, note 2.] The firm as late as 1801 was 'Geschwister Stein'; subsequently 'Nannette Stein' only, which appears as the maker's name on a grand pianoforte with six pedals, existing (1882) in Windsor Castle. For the continuation of the Stein business see STREICHER.   A. J. H.

2. MARIA ANNA, or NANNETTE STEIN, was born Jan. 2, 1769, at Augsburg. When barely eight she played to Mozart on his visit to Augsburg in 1777, and, in spite of the bad habits she had contracted, he said of her 'She may do yet, for she has genius' (Jahn, i. 368). Her talent and capacity were so obvious that her father early initiated her into the details of his business, and on his death, Feb. 29, 1792, she carried it on, in conjunction with her brother Matthäus Andreas, with a decision and energy almost masculine. In 1793 she married Johann Andreas STREICHER, an excellent pianist and teacher from Stuttgart, and then she, her husband, and mother, moved to Vienna. The new firm of 'Nannette and Andreas Stein' (constituted by Imperial decree Jan. 17, 1794) established itself in the 'Red Rose,' No. 301 in the Landstrasse suburb. In 1812 the factory was removed to premises of their own, which had been rebuilt and enlarged some years before, No. 27 in the Ungargasse. In 1802 the brother and sister dissolved partnership, each setting up for themselves, as 'Matthäus Andreas Stein,' and 'Nannette Streicher, geborene Stein.' Streicher, who had hitherto managed only the commercial part of the business, now took his full share of the work. Both firms endeavoured to perfect their instruments in every possible way,[2] while still adhering to the traditions of their father, and Stein of Vienna became as celebrated as Stein of Augsburg had been. In 1823 the Streichers took into partnership their son Johann Baptist (born in Vienna, 1796). Nannette Streicher was at once an energetic and capable woman of business, a pianist of remarkable excellence, a person of great general cultivation, and a model wife and mother. Her name is closely connected with that of Beethoven. It is well known that she

did much to help him in his domestic arrangements, lightened the burden of his housekeeping, and even looked after his bodily health. Thayer, in his Beethoven (iii. 239), gives us a striking picture of their relationship. [See also vol. i. of this Dictionary, pp. 247, 248.] Nannette Streicher died Jan. 10, 1838, and was followed by her husband on May 25 of the same year. The business was carried on successively by their son, J. B. Streicher, and his son, Emil. Her brother,

3. MATTHÄUS ANDREAS STEIN, was born at Augsburg, Dec. 12, 1776, accompanied his sister to Vienna, set up for himself in 1802, married Nov. 12, 1796, and died May 6, 1842. His son,

4. KARL ANDREAS, also a pianoforte-maker and composer, was born in Vienna, Sept. 4, 1797, early showed talent for music, and became an excellent pianist and teacher. He was a pupil of Förster in harmony and composition, and published a considerable number of works principally for his instrument. He also left in MS., among others, two PF. concertos with orchestra, two orchestral overtures, and a comic opera 'Die goldene Gans,' words by Langbein. He appeared several times in public, but latterly devoted himself entirely to the factory, in the working of which his father had early initiated him. In 1829 a patent was granted to him. Karl Andreas travelled much, and his pianos were appreciated abroad, as well as by the first artists of his own country. In 1844 he was appointed Court pianoforte-maker. His book 'on the playing, tuning, and preservation of Stein pianofortes,'[3] contains valuable matter. He died August 28, 1863.   C. F. P.

5. His uncle, FRIEDRICH, was born at Augsburg, May 26, 1784, and at the age of ten went to Vienna, and studied counterpoint and composition with Albrechtsberger. He became one of the first pianoforte-players of the capital, and was considered to be a very promising composer. He appeared rather frequently in the Augarten and Burgtheater concerts as a player of concertos, especially those of Mozart. Reichardt (April 1, 1809) calls him : 'A performer of great power and genius. . . . A rare power, combined with the deepest feeling, characterised his performance. He played some of Beethoven's most difficult pieces, and variations of his own composition, full of invention and deep sentiment, and of monstrous difficulty. Since then I have heard him at home on his magnificent Streicher pianoforte, and am confirmed in my opinion of his assiduous study and great talents.' These eulogies are borne out by other contemporary notices.

Friedrich Stein is the subject of Ries's anecdote (Notizen, p. 115). Beethoven had played his Concerto in G at his own concert, Dec. 22, 1808 (see vol. i. p. 244), with astonishing spirit and

---

1 *Beethoven*, i. 209-215.
2 From this period dates the so-called 'Viennese mechanism,' the principle of which was really the same as that of the Augsburg pianos.

3 *Kurze Bemerkungen ü. d. Spielen, Stimmen, u. Erhalten d. P. P.*, etc., Wien, 1801.

speed, and immediately after called upon Ries to play it in public, with only five days for its study. Ries naturally shirked such a task, preferring to play the C minor one instead. At this his master was offended, and turned to Stein, who accepted the task, but was unable to accomplish it, and played the C minor instead, not satisfactorily.

Stein was an industrious composer, but few of his vocal compositions reached the stage. He left three operettas and a ballet, of which only one —'Die Fée Radiante'—came to public performance. Also a set of Songs, a Violin Concerto, a Grand Sonata for the PF., and a PF. Trio. He also arranged Beethoven's Fourth and Sixth Symphonies for two PF.s.   A. W. T.

STEINBACH, EMIL, born Nov. 14, 1849, at Lengenrieden in Baden, studied at the Leipzig Conservatorium 1867-69, and in 1877 became conductor of the Town Band, and in 1898 Director of the Town Theatre of Mainz. He has composed much chamber and orchestral music and many songs.

FRITZ, born June 17, 1855, at Grünsfeld in Baden, brother of the above, whose pupil he was till he went to the Leipzig Conservatorium in 1873. In 1880 he became second Capellmeister at Mainz till 1886, when he was summoned by the Grand Duke of Meiningen to the post of conductor of his celebrated orchestra, and later on became his general music-director. In 1902 he visited England with the whole of the Meiningen orchestra, and made one of the greatest sensations that has been caused by any musical performances within recent years in this country, his renderings of Bach and Brahms being specially appreciated. All the four symphonies of Brahms were included in his programmes. In 1902 he succeeded Wüllner as Town Capellmeister and Director of the Conservatorium at Cologne. He is also well known as a composer, chiefly through his septet (op. 7) and a violoncello sonata.   H. V. H.

STEINWAY & SONS, an eminent firm of pianoforte-makers in New York, distinguished by the merit of their instruments and by their commercial enterprise, which, in comparatively few years, have placed their firm in equal rank with those famous older makers in Europe whose achievements in the improvement and development of the instrument have become historical.

Henry Engelhard Steinway (originally STEINWEG, see below) was born Feb. 15, 1797, at Wolfshagen, in the Duchy of Brunswick. The youngest of a family of twelve, at the early age of fifteen he was the sole survivor of his family. From the age of seventeen to twenty-one he served in the army, and during that time his natural taste for music led him to learn the zither. On his discharge, which was honourably obtained, from the army, he thought of becoming a cabinet-maker, but was too old to serve the five years' apprenticeship and five years as

journeyman which the guild required prior to his becoming a master. He therefore went for a year to an irregular master, and then turned to organ-building, which was free from the narrow limits of a guild. Circumstances, however, allowed him in 1825 to marry and settle as·a cabinet-maker at Seesen, near the Harz Mountains, where he had been already working ; and in that year (Nov. 25) his eldest son Theodore was born. Steinway in a few years turned his attention to piano-making, and in 1839 exhibited a grand and two square pianos at the State Fair of Brunswick. Seesen being in Hanoverian territory, the foundation of the Prussian 'Zollverein' in 1845 brought Steinway's hitherto flourishing business to a standstill, and the revolution of 1848 destroyed it entirely. The course of events now induced Steinway to leave Germany, and in April 1849 he emigrated to New York, whither his family, with the exception of Theodore, the eldest son, followed him the next year. For three years the father and the three sons, Charles, Henry, and William, worked in different New York piano factories. In March 1853 they agreed to unite and start in business on their own account, and the firm of 'Steinway & Sons' was established. In 1855 they exhibited a square piano in which the American iron frame principle of a single casting was combined with a cross or over-strung scale, forming the foundation of the so-called 'Steinway system,' which, as applied to grand pianos, attracted great attention in the London International Exhibition of 1862. Both Charles and Henry Steinway dying in 1865, Theodore, the eldest son, disposed of his business in Brunswick and became a partner of the New York firm. Their spacious concert-room there was built and opened in 1866. About this time the Steinways began to make upright pianos, and their instruments of all kinds shown at Paris, in the Universal Exhibition of 1867, not only gained them success, but became models for Germany, to the great improvement of the German make and trade. Henry Steinway, the father, died in 1871. In 1875 the firm opened a branch in London, to which a concert-room is attached, and in 1880 another branch establishment at Hamburg.   A. J. H.

[The first grand piano was made by Steinway & Sons in April 1856, the upright in April 1862. In May 1876 the firm was incorporated with a capital of $1,500,000, William Steinway being elected president ; the capital stock was increased to $2,000,000 in 1891. William Steinway, born March 5, 1835, at Seesen, remained its financial head and prime factor in its development until his death on Nov. 30, 1896. C. F. Theodore Steinway, born in Seesen, Nov. 6, 1825, died March 6, 1889, at Brunswick, was the scientific constructor to whom were due many of the inventions which gave the Steinway pianos their high position. The officers of the corporation in 1907 are Charles H. Steinway (son of Henry Steinway, born June 3, 1857), president ; Frederick T. Steinway (son of Henry Steinway, born Feb. 9, 1860), vice-president ; Nahum Stetson, secretary ; Friedrich Reidemeister, treasurer. These gentlemen, together with Henry Ziegler (grandson of the founder of the house, born Oct. 30, 1857), constructor, form the Board of Directors. Among the junior members of the house are two sons of William Steinway, Theodore E. and William R. Steinway. Nahum Stetson entered the service of the corporation as salesman in 1876 ; Mr. Reidemeister has been in the service of the house since 1891.   H. E. K.

STEINWEG, the original of STEINWAY (Grotian, Helfferich, Schulz, TH. STEINWEGS NACHFOLGER). This firm of pianoforte-makers in Brunswick succeeded, as the style implies, to Mr. Theodor Steinweg or Steinway, when he retired, in 1865, from the business founded by his father, to join the New York firm of Steinway & Sons, of which, being the eldest brother, he became the senior partner. Soon after the Steinway system of construction was brought out in America, he introduced it in Germany, and in the season of 1860-61 his concert instruments, made on that principle, were publicly used. His successors in Brunswick have maintained the good reputation he founded for these instruments, which are favoured with the preference of some eminent pianists ; notably of Madame Schumann, who from 1870 used them exclusively in Germany for her public performances. Although the present firm preserve the Steinway model in the main, they claim to have made deviations and alterations, particularly in the action, that give the instruments of 'Th. Steinwegs Nachfolger' their own cachet.   A. J. H.

STENHOUSE, WILLIAM, a writer on Scottish music, was born in Roxburghshire, in 1773, and died Nov. 10, 1827. He was an accountant in Edinburgh, and before 1817 conceived the idea of annotating Johnson's Scots Musical Museum, with historical references regarding both words and music. He contributed specimens of these notes to Blackwood's Magazine for July 1817. For a republication of the Scots Musical Museum, Stenhouse's notes were printed in 1820, but laid aside for a considerable period, being ultimately published in 1839 and again in 1853. Stenhouse's work has been a bone of contention among musical antiquaries since its publication.

There is undoubtedly a vast mass of interesting and trustworthy information in the notes, together with many careless and slipshod references which have caused the whole work to be condemned.

Stenhouse edited the musical portion of James Hogg's Jacobite Relics, 1819-21.   F. K.

STEPHENS, CATHERINE, born in London,

Sept. 18, 1794 [the daughter of Edward Stephens, a carver and gilder in Park Street], having given early indications of aptitude for music, was in 1807 placed under the instruction of Gesualdo Lanza, whose pupil she remained for five years. Early in 1812 she appeared in subordinate parts at the Pantheon as a member of an Italian Opera Company. Soon afterwards her father, dissatisfied with the apparently small progress she made under Lanza, placed her under the tuition of Thomas Welsh. On Sept. 23, 1813, she appeared anonymously at Covent Garden as Mandane in 'Artaxerxes' with decided success. She repeated the part on Sept. 28, as 'Miss Stevens,' and on Sept. 30, under her proper name. On Oct. 22, she sang Polly in 'The Beggar's Opera,' Rosetta in 'Love in a Village,' and afterwards Clara in 'The Duenna,' in each gaining ground in public favour. In March 1814 she was engaged at the Concert of Antient Music, and later in the year she sang at the festivals at Norwich and Birmingham. [She sang in Edinburgh in 1814, and at Dublin in 1816, 1821, and 1825. Dict. of Nat. Biog.] She continued at Covent Garden from 1813 until 1822, when she broke with the managers on a question of terms and transferred her services to Drury Lane. She occupied the principal position on the English operatic stage, at the first concerts, and the festivals, until 1835, when she retired into private life. Her voice was a pure soprano, rich, full, and powerful, and of extensive compass, and her execution neat, although not very remarkable for brilliancy. She somewhat lacked dramatic instinct and power, and her enunciation was very bad, but she excelled in the expression of quiet devotional feeling and simple pathos. In such songs as Handel's 'Angels, ever bright and fair,' and 'If guiltless blood,' and in ballads like 'Auld Robin Gray,' and 'Savourneen Deelish,' she captivated every hearer. On April 19, 1838, she was married to the widowed octogenarian Earl of Essex in his house No. 9 Belgrave Square,[1] and on April 23, 1839, became his widow. She survived him for nearly forty-three years, dying in the house in which she was married, Feb. 22, 1882. [A portrait by John Jackson is in the National Portrait Gallery.]   W. H. H.

STEPHENS, CHARLES EDWARD, nephew of the preceding, was born in Edgware Road, March 18, 1821. Displaying early tokens of musical organisation, he was placed under

[1] In the Parish Register of St. George's, Hanover Square, the marriage was originally entered as having been celebrated in 'the Parish Church.' These last three words were, however, subsequently erased (in two places) with a sharp instrument, and '9 Belgrave Square' written upon the erasures, but without any note, or authentication of the alteration being made in the Register. The original entry is proved by the words 'the Parish Church' remaining unaltered in the certified copy of the Register at Somerset House, until March 1882, when the discrepancy was pointed out by the present writer, and measures taken for its correction. It is to be hoped that this is a solitary instance of so flagrant a violation of the directions of the Act of Parliament as to the mode in which erroneous entries in Registers are to be rectified.

Cipriani Potter for pianoforte, J. A. Hamilton for harmony, counterpoint, and composition, and Henry Blagrove for the violin. In 1843 he was elected organist of St. Mark's, Myddelton Square, and subsequently held the same office at Holy Trinity, Paddington, 1846 ; St. John's, Hampstead, 1856 ; St. Mark's, St. John's Wood, 1862-63 ; St. Clement Danes, 1864-69, and St. Saviour's, Paddington, 1872-75. In 1850 he was elected an associate, and in 1857 a member of the Philharmonic Society, of which he was repeatedly chosen a director. In 1865 he was elected a Fellow of the College of Organists, in 1870 an honorary member of the Royal Academy of Music, and in 1877 a licentiate, *honoris causâ*, of Trinity College, London. His first important composition was a trio for pianoforte, violin, and violoncello, produced at the Society of British Musicians, himself performing the pianoforte part ; his works also include several concert overtures of merit, No. 4 of which, ' A Dream of Happiness,' was played at the Crystal Palace, Nov. 13, 1875. He also composed many works for pianoforte and organ, and much vocal music, comprising anthems and services, songs, ballads, part-songs, etc. His part-song, 'Come, fill ye right merrily,' gained the prize given by Mr. Henry Leslie's Choir in 1858, and in April 1879 he was awarded both the first and second prizes given by Trinity College, London, for the best string quartet. [His symphony in G minor was performed at the Philharmonic Concert in March 1891. He died in London, July 13, 1892, and was buried at Kensal Green.] w. h. h.

STEPHENS, John, Mus.D., educated as a chorister in Gloucester Cathedral, in 1746 succeeded Edward Thomson as organist of Salisbury Cathedral. He graduated as Mus.D. at Cambridge in 1763, conducted the Gloucester Festival in 1766, and died Dec. 15, 1780. A volume of ' Cathedral Music ' by him, edited by Highmore Skeats, was published in 1805. w. h. h.

STERKEL, Johann Franz Xaver (Abbé Sterkel), born at Würzburg, Dec. 3, 1750, was a distinguished amateur. Though music formed a part of his education it was only a part. He went through his college course at Würzburg University, took orders and became vicar and organist of Neumünster. In 1778 he was called to the Court of the Elector of Mainz at Aschaffenburg as chaplain and pianist. Next year the Elector sent him on a journey through Italy ; success attended him everywhere, and at Naples he brought out an opera, ' Farnace,' in 1780, with éclat. In 1781 he returned to Mainz and was promoted to a canonry. All this time he was composing as well as playing in all departments of music. He wrote about this date some German songs which were great favourites, and he formed some excellent pupils—among composers Hofmann and Zulehner, among singers Grünbaum and Kirschbaum. In September

1791 occurred the great musical event of Sterkel's life, though he probably did not know its significance—his meeting with Beethoven, then a youth of twenty. Beethoven came to Aschaffenburg with the band of the Elector of Bonn, and was taken by Ries and Simrock to call on the great player, whose reputation was something like that of Liszt in after years. Sterkel was the first great executant that Beethoven had heard, and the extreme refinement and finish of his style evidently struck him much. He watched him with the closest attention, and not unnaturally declined to play in his turn, till Sterkel induced him to do so by speaking of his twenty-four variations on Righini's ' Venni Amore.' They had been published only a few months previously, and Sterkel declared that they were so hard that he did not believe even the composer could play them. Beethoven played what he could recollect, and improvised others fully equalling the originals in difficulty —but the curious thing was that he adopted Sterkel's delicate style all through. They do not appear to have met again. In 1793 Sterkel succeeded Righini as Capellmeister to the Elector, and this threw him still more into serious composition ; but the French war forced the Elector to leave Mainz, and his Capellmeister returned to Würzburg. In 1805 he became Capellmeister at Ratisbon, where all his old energy revived, and he taught and composed with the greatest vigour and success. The war of 1813 at length drove him back from Ratisbon to Würzburg, and there he died Oct. 21, 1817.

The list of Sterkel's published compositions is immense. [See the *Quellen-Lexikon*.] It embraces 10 symphonies ; 2 overtures ; a string quintet ; a quartet for PF. and strings ; 6 string trios ; 6 do. duos ; 6 PF. concertos ; a very large number of sonatas for PF. both for two and four hands ; variations, and minor pieces ; 10 collections of songs for voice and PF. ; Italian canzonets, duets, etc. The number of editions which some of these went through shows how widely popular Sterkel was in his day. [A Mass, and a Te Deum are in MS.] g.

STERLING, Antoinette, born Jan. 23, 1850 (?), at Sterlingville, in the State of New York. She possessed, even in childhood, a voice of extraordinary range, which afterwards settled into a contralto of great richness and volume, with a compass from $e\flat$ to f''. Her first serious study of singing began in 1867 in New York under Signor Abella, better known as the husband of Mme. d'Angri. She came to England in 1868 and remained a few months, singing chiefly in the provinces, *en route* for Germany. There she was first a pupil of Mme. Marchesi at Cologne, then of Pauline Viardot at Baden-Baden, and lastly of Manuel Garcia in London. She returned to America in 1871, and soon took a high position as a concert-singer. On May

13, 1873, she took leave of her native country in a concert at the Irving Hall, Boston, arrived in England, and made her first appearance on Nov. 5 at the Covent Garden Promenade Concert, under the conductorship of Sir Julius Benedict. At the Crystal Palace she first sang on Dec. 6, and shortly after appeared at the Saturday Popular, Feb. 21, 1874, Sacred Harmonic, Philharmonic, Albert Hall, and London Ballad Concerts. At Gloucester, in the following September, she sang at the Festival. She was married on Easter Sunday 1875, at the Savoy Chapel, to Mr. John MacKinlay; and from that time, excepting a few months in the same year, when she sang in America in a series of forty concerts under Theodore Thomas, resided in London, and was one of the most popular singers there. She was not unknown in classical music. On her first arrival here she sang the Cradle Song from Bach's Christmas Oratorio with much effect, and her repertory contained songs of Mendelssohn and Schumann. But she was essentially a ballad singer. Her voice was one of great beauty and attractiveness; but it was her earnestness and intention, the force which she threw into the story—especially if it was weird or grim, such as 'The three fishers,' 'The sands of Dee,' or 'The three ravens'—and the distinctness with which she declaimed the words, that formed the real secret of her success. [She died at Hampstead, Jan. 9, 1904, and was cremated at the Golder's Green Crematorium. Her son, Mr. Sterling MacKinlay, a baritone singer, published a memoir in 1906.]   G.

STERN, Julius, was born at Breslau, August 8, 1820, but removed at an early age to Berlin, where he learned music under Maurer, Ganz, and Rungenhagen, at the Singakademie and the Royal Academy of Arts and soon began to compose. 'Please enquire about Mr. Julius Stern of Berlin,' says Mendelssohn,[1] 'who has sent me a book of songs with a kind note. From the first glance I think they show talent, but I have not seen or heard anything else about him.' In 1843 he received a travelling scholarship from the King, which led him, first to Dresden for the special study of singing, and then to Paris, where he soon became known as conductor of the German 'Gesangverein.' Here he performed the 'Antigone,' first in the studio of Henry Lehmann the painter,[2] and then at the Odéon Theatre, which drew from Mendelssohn a very characteristic letter (May 27, 1844). In 1846 he returned to Berlin, and in 1847 founded the well-known Singing Society which bore his name. The first performance of 'Elijah' in Oct. 1847 gave a specimen of the powers of the new Association, and the level has since been fully maintained by performances of a very wide range of works both ancient and modern. In 1872 the Society celebrated its

25th anniversary, amid an enthusiasm which conclusively showed how wide and deep was the public feeling. In 1874 ill-health obliged Stern to retire from the conductorship, and he was succeeded by Stockhausen, who was succeeded in 1878 by Max Bruch (till 1880), Emil Rudorff (1880-90), Fr. Gernsheim (1890-1904), and Oskar Fried (1904 to the present time).

Meantime, in 1850, with Kullak and Marx, he had founded his Conservatorium, which, notwithstanding the defection of his two colleagues, still flourishes and has educated many good musicians. From 1869 to 1871 he conducted the Berlin 'Sinfonie-Capelle,' and at Christmas 1873 undertook the Reichshall Concerts, which, however, were not commercially successful, and only lasted for two seasons. He then confined himself to his Conservatorium till his death, Feb. 27, 1883. Stern has published many vocal pieces and arrangements, but his most enduring work will probably be his edition of Exercises by Vaccaj (Bote & Bock), Crescentini (Peters), etc. He was made a 'Königliche Musikdirector' in 1849, and 'Königliche Professor' in 1860.   G.

STERN, Leopold Lawrence, violoncellist, born at Brighton, April 5, 1862. He belonged to a musical family, his father being a German violinist and his mother (née Annie Lawrence) an English pianist. From his early youth he showed strong musical leanings, and as a boy played the drum in the 'Brighton Symphony Society,' of which his father was the conductor. In 1877 he became a student at the South Kensington School of Chemistry, keeping up his music meanwhile, and eventually began the violoncello under Hugo Daubert. In 1880 he accepted a business appointment at Thornliebank near Glasgow; but three years later he finally abandoned chemistry in favour of music and, returning to London, entered the Royal Academy of Music, studying the violoncello first under Signor Pezze and then under Piatti, and subsequently visiting Leipzig in order to take lessons from Julius Klengel and Davidov. Returning to England in 1886, he played both in London and the Provinces, accompanied Patti on one of her tours, and later on played in concerts with Sauret and Paderewski. In Paris he played with Godard and Massenet. In 1895 he visited Prague, where, being favourably impressed by his playing, Dvořák selected him to bring out his Violoncello Concerto, and came himself to London to conduct in person the first public performance of the same, which took place at the Philharmonic Concert in March 1896, when Stern achieved his greatest success. He subsequently played it at Prague, the Leipzig Gewandhaus, and the Berlin Philharmonic.

In 1897 and 1898 Stern toured through the United States and Canada, and henceforth appeared but rarely before an English audience.

Of somewhat delicate health, the strain of public playing slowly undermined his constitution, and finally compelled him in 1893 to abandon an American tour and return to London, where, after a lingering illness, he died at the early age of forty-two on Sept. 10, 1904.

Stern was twice married : firstly, in 1891, to Nettie Carpenter, a violinist of some distinction ; and secondly, in 1898, to Suzanne Adams, the accomplished operatic singer.

In his early years Leo Stern played upon a violoncello by Guidantus, later on the 'General Kyde' Stradivari (an instrument of large proportions), and finally on the 'Baudiot' Stradivari. w. w. c.

STEVENS, RICHARD JOHN SAMUEL, born in London, March 27, 1757, was educated in St. Paul's Cathedral choir under William Savage. He distinguished himself as a glee composer, and obtained prizes from the Catch Club for his glees, 'See, what horrid tempests rise,' 1782, and 'It was a lover and his lass,' 1786. He was appointed organist of the Temple Church, 1786, organist of the Charter House, 1796 (retaining his appointment at the Temple), and on March 17, 1801, was elected Professor of Music in Gresham College. He published three sets of glees, three harpsichord sonatas (op. 1), and songs. Nine glees and a catch by him are included in Warren's collections. Among his best glees may be mentioned 'Ye spotted snakes,' 'Blow, blow, thou winter wind,' 'Crabbed age and youth,' 'Sigh no more, ladies,' 'The cloud-capt towers,' 'From Oberon in fairy land,' all of which still retain their popularity with lovers of that class of composition. He edited 'Sacred Music for one, two, three and four voices, from the works of the most esteemed composers, Italian and English,' an excellent collection in 3 vols. fol. He died Sept. 23, 1837. [He left a valuable collection of music to the Royal Academy of Music.] w. h. h.

STEVENSON, SIR JOHN ANDREW, Knight, Mus.D., son of John Stevenson, a violinist in the State Band in Dublin, was born in Dublin about 1762. In 1771 he was admitted a chorister of Christ Church Cathedral, Dublin, and in 1775-80 was in the choir of St. Patrick's Cathedral. He became a vicar-choral of St. Patrick's in 1783 and of Christ Church in 1800. He composed new music to O'Keeffe's farces, 'The Son-in-Law' (1781), 'The Dead Alive' (1781), and 'The Agreeable Surprise' (1782), to enable them to be performed in Dublin, and also composed for the Irish stage some of the music of 'The Contract,' 1782 ; 'Love in a blaze,' 1799 ; 'The Patriot,' 1810 ; 'The Burning of Moscow,' and 'Bedouins,' 1801. He obtained his honorary Mus.D. degree at Dublin in 1791, and his knighthood from the Lord-Lieutenant (Lord Hardwicke) in 1803. [In 1814 he was appointed the first organist and musical director at the Castle Chapel.] He composed some

Services and Anthems (a collection of which he published, with his portrait prefixed, in 1825), 'Thanksgiving' (Dublin Musical Festival, Sept. 1831), an oratorio, and numerous glees, duets, canzonets, songs, etc. But the work by which he is best known is the symphonies and accompaniments to the collection of Irish Melodies, the words for which were written by Thomas Moore. He died at Headfort House, while on a visit to his daughter, the Marchioness of Headfort, Sept. 14, 1833. [A monument was erected to his memory in St. Patrick's Cathedral. A biographical sketch, by John Bumpus, appeared in 1893.] w. h. h. ; additions and corrections by w. h. g. f.

STEWART, NEIL. One of the early Edinburgh music-publishers. In 1759 he was at the sign of the 'Violin and German Flute' in the Exchange, but before 1761 he had removed to a shop, 'opposite the Head of Blackfriar's Wynd,' which had probably been Bremner's place of business. He again removed to the Exchange, and then to Miln's Square (now demolished), facing the Tron Church. Afterwards the business was in Parliament Square, and finally in South Bridge Street. The stock-in-trade and plates were sold off by auction in 1805. Originally founded by the elder Neil Stewart, the business afterwards developed into a partnership as 'Neil Stewart & Company,' and finally belonged to Neil and Malcolm Stewart, the two sons.

The Stewart publications comprise a great bulk of important works of Scottish music, and include republications of M'Gibbon ; collections of reels and country dances ; marches and minuets ; M'Glashan's works ; Scots Songs ; and great quantities of interesting music sheets. F. K.

STEWART, SIR ROBERT PRESCOTT, Knight, Mus.D., son of Charles Frederick Stewart, librarian of the King's Inns, Dublin, was born in Dublin, Dec. 16, 1825. He was educated as a chorister of Christ Church Cathedral, Dublin, of which he was appointed organist in 1844, in which year he was also appointed organist of Trinity College, Dublin. In 1846 he became conductor of the University of Dublin Choral Society, the members of which defrayed the expenses of the performance of his music for degrees of Mus.B. and Mus.D. which took place in 1851, besides presenting him with his graduate's robes and a jewelled bâton. In 1852 he became a vicar-choral of St. Patrick's Cathedral, and in 1861 was appointed Professor of Music in the University of Dublin. For the great Peace Festival held at Boston in America, in 1872, he composed a fantasia on Irish airs for orchestra, organ, and chorus, but declined the invitation to represent Ireland there. On this occasion he received knighthood from the Lord-Lieutenant (Earl Spencer) [and became Professor of Theory in the Royal Irish Academy of Music]. In 1873 he was

appointed conductor of the Dublin Philharmonic. He died in Dublin, March 24, 1894.
Amongst Sir Robert Stewart's many compositions, his glees deserve particular mention.
In this branch of his art he won numerous prizes
and well-merited renown. His more important
works include an ode for the opening of the
Cork Exhibition of 1852 ; ' Ode on Shakespeare,'
produced at the Birmingham Festival, 1870 ;
and two Cantatas, ' A Winter Night's Wake '
and 'The Eve of S. John.' He edited the
Irish ' Church Hymnal ' (1876).

Sir Robert Stewart enjoyed a high reputation
as an organist and extemporiser ; his playing
at the Great Exhibition of 1851 and at that of
Manchester in 1857 excited general admiration.
As occupant of the Dublin Chair of Music, his
excellent lectures and writings on music bore
evidence to his wide culture and literary skill,
as well as to his high musical attainments.
[He was the first to require candidates for the
musical degrees to pass a literary test, and
the good example was afterwards followed at
Cambridge. A portrait by Sir T. A. Jones is
in the Royal Irish Academy of Music, and his
statue is on Leinster Lawn, Dublin. A biography
by Olinthus John Vignoles appeared in 1898,
and Dr. Culwick's *The Works of Sir R. P.
Stewart*, with a catalogue of his compositions
(Dublin, 1902), may be consulted.] His musical
memory was remarkable.　　　　　　**W. H. H.**

STIASTNÝ, BERNARD WENZEL, violoncellist,
was born at Prague in 1770. Little is known of
him except that he was a member of the Prague
orchestra, studied with Seegr and was probably professor at the Conservatorium, to which
he dedicated his work on the violoncello.
It is remarkable for what may be almost called
a treatise on the accompaniment of recitative
as it was then practised.

STIASTNÝ, JOHANN, brother of the above, was
born at Prague in 1774. We know scarcely
anything of his career except that he was in
the orchestra at Prague in 1800-20. He seems
to have studied harmony and the violoncello at
Prague, under his brother, but he must have
soon left that city, as he is described on the
title of his op. 3 as ' Violoncelle de S. A. R. le
Grand Duc de Frankfort.' According to Fétis
he was musical director at Nuremberg in 1820,
and from thence went to Mannheim. He is
known to have been in London, and he dedicated
two of his finest compositions to Lindley and
Crosdill, as well as his three duets, op. 8, to Sir
W. Curtis. His last and perhaps finest work
was published and probably written in London.
He was also in Paris, where he arranged his op.
11 for violoncello and piano, and he dedicated his
op. 3 to the pupils of the Conservatoire. There
exists a beautiful French edition of his six
grand duets, op. 1, and also of his two sonatas,
op. 2, the latter in score. Though the list of
his works only amounts to thirteen in number,

the originality and purity of them all entitle
him to rank among the very first writers for
the instrument. A list of his works follows :—
op.
1. Six grand duets for two vcellos, dedicated to his brother.
2. Two sonatas for vcello solo with accompaniment for a second
vcello.
3. Divertissement for vcello solo with accompaniments for tenor
and second vcello.
4. Twelve ' Petites pièces pour violoncelle et basse à l'usage de com-
mençants.'
5. Six pièces faciles for vcello and bass.
6. Three grand duets for two vcellos.
7. Concertino for vcello with accompaniments for flute, two tenors,
vcello and contrabass, dedicated to Lindley.
8. Three duets for two vcellos.
9. Six pièces faciles for vcello and bass.
10. Andante with variations for vcello solo with accompaniments
for flute, two violins, tenor, and vcello, dedicated to Crosdill.
11. Six solos for vcello and bass.
12. Theme with variations and rondo with quartet accompaniment.
13. Grand trio for vcello solo with accompaniment for tenor and
vcello, published in London by Welsh & Hawes, but
unknown on the Continent.
　　　　　　　　　　　　　　　　　　G. H.

STICCADO-PASTROLE. An early name
for a kind of wooden dulcimer formed of a
graduated series of rods which being struck give
forth musical sounds. (See XYLOPHONE.) A
trade card, in date about 1770, advertises that
' G. Smart, Sticcado-Pastrole maker, from Mr.
Bremner's music-shop . . . continues to make
the above instruments with improvements.'
The above G. Smart was afterwards a music-
publisher, and was the father of Sir George Smart
the musician.　　　　　　　　　　　**F. K.**

STICH, JOHANN WENZEL, known as PUNTO,
eminent horn-player, born about 1755 in
Bohemia, was taught music and the French-horn
by Matiegka and Hampel of Dresden, at the
expense of Count Thun. On his return to the
Count's household he considered himself ill-
treated, and ran away with some of his comrades. To avoid recognition he Italianised his
name to Punto, and travelled in Germany and
France, settling for a time in Würzburg, Treves,
Coblenz, Paris, etc., and attracting considerable
attention. In Paris he made the acquaintance
of Mozart, who composed for him a Sinfonie
concertante for flute, oboe, horn, and bassoon,
never played and now unfortunately lost.
' Punto plays magnificently' (*bläst magnifique*),
writes Mozart to his father. In 1788 he was
engaged by Mara (with Graff, Fischer, and
Florio) for her concerts at the Pantheon, London.
In Vienna, Beethoven composed his sonata
for PF. and horn (op. 17) for him, and they
played it together without rehearsal, at Punto's
concert, April 18, 1800. It was received
enthusiastically, and at once encored. After
this Punto made another tour with Dussek,
returned to Prague and gave a concert at the
theatre there in 1801. He died after a long
illness, Feb. 16, 1803, and his epitaph runs

Omne tulit punctum Punto, cui Musa Bohema
Ut plausit vivo, sic morienti gemit.

His compositions were published in Paris by
Sieber, Nadermann, Cochet, Imbault, Le Duc,
and Pleyel.　　　　　　　　　　　　**C. F. P.**

STICKER. A light wooden rod used in organ
action for conveying motion by a pushing
movement. (See TRACKER.)　　　　　**T. E.**

STIEHL, HEINRICH, born at Lübeck, August 5, 1829, second son of J. D. Stiehl (1800-73), an esteemed organist there. He studied at Lübeck and Weimar, and at Leipzig under Moscheles, Gade, and Hauptmann. In 1853 he settled in St. Petersburg as organist to the St. Peter's Church, and Director of the Singakademie. In 1867 he moved to Vienna, and after staying there two years went on to Italy. In 1872 and 1873 he was in London, and from Oct. 1874 to 1877 resided in Belfast as conductor of the Philharmonic Society and founder of the Cecilia Society there. He then returned to England, settling as a teacher at Hastings, and in 1880 was called to Reval in Russia, where he held a leading position as professor of music, organist, and conductor of the Musical Society of the town. He gave an excellent performance of Bach's 'Matthew-Passion' (the first in Russia) on March 17, 1883, and repeated it at St. Petersburg, April 6. He died at Reval, May 1, 1886.

Stiehl's compositions are numerous. They include two operas, 'Der Schatzgräber,' and 'Jery und Bätely.' A little orchestral piece called 'The Vision' was produced at the Crystal Palace, April 12, 1873, and was much applauded for its delicate fanciful character. A 'Hexentanz,' 'Ungarisch,' Waltzes, and a Gavotte are also well known in Germany. He published three PF. Trios, a sonata for PF. and Vcello, Sonata quasi Fantasia for PF. solo, and many other works, the latest being a string quartet, op. 172.   G.

STIMME (Germ.), is used both for the human voice and for the individual parts in polyphonic composition or concerted music, whether vocal or instrumental.

STIMMFÜHRUNG (Germ.), PART-WRITING, which see.

STIMPSON, JAMES, a well-known Birmingham musician, born at Lincoln, Feb. 29, 1820, son of a lay vicar of the cathedral, who removed to Durham in 1822, where James became a chorister in 1827. In February 1834 he was articled to Mr. Ingham, organist of Carlisle Cathedral ; in June 1836 was appointed organist of St. Andrew's, Newcastle ; and in June 1841, on Ingham's death, was made organist of Carlisle.

In February 1842 James Stimpson was unanimously chosen organist at the Town Hall and St. Paul's, Birmingham, out of many competitors, and in the following year justified the choice by founding the Festival Choral Society and its Benevolent Fund, in connection with the Triennial Festivals. He continued organist and chorus-master to the Society until 1855. His activity, however, did not stop here. In 1844 he was instrumental in starting the weekly Monday Evening Concerts, of which, in 1859, he took the entire responsibility, to relinquish them only after heavy losses in 1867.

In 1845 Mr. Stimpson had the satisfaction of having the pedals of the Town Hall organ increased from 2 to 2½ octaves, so that he was able to perform the works of J. S. Bach unmutilated. From his weekly recitals in the Town Hall, given throughout the year to audiences varying from 600 to 1000, many a young amateur has derived his first taste for classical music. He was permanent organist of the Birmingham festivals, and Mendelssohn's last visit there was to conduct ' Elijah' for Mr. Stimpson's benefit, April 25, 1847. He introduced Sims Reeves and Charles Hallé to Birmingham, and laboured from 1849 until 1868, in many ways, in the service of good music, gaining thereby the gratitude and respect of his fellow-townsmen. He was for many years Professor of Music at the Blind Institution. He died at Birmingham, Oct. 4, 1886.

D'Almaine published in 1850 'The Organists' Standard Library,' edited by Mr. Stimpson, consisting principally of pieces hitherto unpublished in this country. His other publications consist mostly of arrangements and a manual of theory published by Rudall, Carte & Co. G.

STIRLING, ELIZABETH, an eminent English organist and composer ; born at Greenwich, Feb. 26, 1819 ; learned the organ and piano from W. B. Wilson and Edward Holmes, and harmony from J. A. Hamilton and G. A. Macfarren. She attained a remarkable degree of execution on the organ pedals, as may be inferred from her first public performance, given at St. Katherine's Church, Regent's Park, when, out of fourteen numbers, the programme contained five pedal fugues and preludes, three pedal trios, and other pieces, by J. S. Bach. In Nov. 1839 she was elected organist of All Saints', Poplar, which she retained till Sept. 1858, when she gained the same post at St. Andrew's Undershaft, by competition. This she resigned in 1880. In 1856 she submitted an exercise (Ps. cxxx. for five voices and orchestra) for the degree of Mus. B. Oxon. ; but though accepted it was not performed, owing to the want of power to grant a degree to a lady. She published some original pedal fugues and slow movements, and other pieces for her instrument, as well as arrangements from the works of Handel, Bach, and Mozart. Also songs and duets, and many part-songs for four voices, of which a well-established favourite is 'All among the barley.' In 1863 she married Mr. F. A. Bridge, and died in London, March 25, 1895. G.

STOBAEUS, JOHANN, was born July 6, 1580, at Graudenz, a town in West Prussia on the river Vistula. In 1595 he was sent, for his further education, to Königsberg, where also from 1600 he attended the University. In 1599 he became the pupil in music of Johann Eccard, then Ducal Capellmeister at Königsberg. In 1601 Stobaeus was bass-singer in the Ducal Chapel, and in 1602 was appointed

2 y

Cantor at the Domkirche and the School in connection therewith. In 1626 he received the appointment of Capellmeister to the Elector of Brandenburg at Königsberg, which he retained till his death on Sept. 11, 1646. Stobaeus followed Eccard in the contrapuntal setting of the Chorale-tunes for voices alone, in a style midway between that of the motet proper, and that of mere note-for-note harmony. In 1634 he published 'Geistliche Lieder auf gewöhnliche Preussische Kirchen-Melodeyen durchaus gerichtet und mit fünff Stimmen componirt.' This work contains 102 settings *a* 5 of the Chorale-Tunes, half of them by Eccard, the remainder by Stobaeus. In 1642 and 1644 appeared two parts of ' Preussische Fest-lieder mit 5, 6, 8 Stimmen,' 27 by Eccard, 21 by Stobaeus. In this work the tunes, as well as the settings, are by the composers. It has been reproduced in modern score by Teschner. An earlier publication of Stobaeus is his ' Cantiones Sacrae 5, 6, 7, 8, and 10 vocibus item aliquot Magnificat 5 et 6 vocibus adornatae,' Frankfort, 1624. The Königsberg Library also contains a large number of occasional compositions by Stobaeus, sacred and secular.　　　　J. R. M.

STOCK, FRIEDRICH WILHELM AUGUST, violinist, composer, and conductor of the Theodore Thomas Orchestra in Chicago, U.S.A., was born in Yülich, Germany, on Nov. 11, 1872, the son of a bandmaster in the German army. Under him he began his musical studies, entered the Cologne Conservatory at fourteen years of age, was graduated as a violinist, and then took up seriously the study of theory and composition under Engelbert Humperdinck, Heinrich Zöllner, Gustav Jensen, and Franz Wüllner. In 1895 he went to America to become a member of the Chicago Symphony Orchestra, and in 1899 was appointed assistant to Theodore Thomas (*q.v.*), then conductor of that organisation. In 1903 he conducted the concerts given by the orchestra outside the city of Chicago, and on the death of Mr. Thomas in January 1905, he succeeded him in the conductorship. Mr. Stock has written a considerable number of works in the larger forms,—overtures, symphonic poems, a set of symphonic variations which have been repeatedly played in Chicago, and were brought forward by Franz Kneisel (*q.v.*) at the festival of 1906 in Worcester ; Mr. Kneisel has also taken into his repertory of chamber-music a string quartet of marked originality and strength. In harmonisation and orchestration Mr. Stock belongs to the latter-day German school of vivid colourists.　　　　H. E. K.

STOCK AND HORN, a rude musical instrument mentioned by early writers as being in use among the Scottish peasantry. It appears to have been identical with or similar to the Pibcorn (see vol. iii. p. 739). The instrument is figured in a vignette in Ritson's *Scotish Songs*, 1794, also on the frontispiece to the editions of Ramsay's

Gentle Shepherd, illustrated by David Allan, 1788 and 1808. It was then almost obsolete, for Robert Burns, the poet, had much difficulty in obtaining one. It appears to have been made in divers forms, with either a wooden or a bone stock, the horn being that of a cow. Burns, in a letter to George Thomson, Nov. 19, 1794, thus describes it : ' Tell my friend Allan . . . that I much suspect he has in his plates mistaken the figure of the stock and horn. I have at last gotten one ; but it is a very rude instru-

Stock and Horn.

ment. It is composed of three parts, the stock, which is the hinder thigh bone of a sheep . . . the horn which is a common Highland cow's horn cut off at the smaller end until the aperture be large enough to admit the stock to be pushed up through the horn, until it be held by the thicker end of the thigh bone ; and lastly, an oaten reed exactly cut and notched like that which you see every shepherd-boy have, when the corn stems are green and full grown. The reed is not made fast in the bone, but is held by the lips, and plays loose on the smaller end of the stock ; while the stock with the horn hanging on its larger end, is held by the hand in playing. The stock has six or seven ventages on the upper side, and one back ventage, like the common flute. This of mine was made by a man from the braes of Athole, and is exactly what the shepherds are wont to use in that country. However, either it is not quite properly bored in the holes, or else we have not the art of blowing it rightly, for we can make little of it.'

The illustration given is the Stock and Horn as depicted by David Allan.　　　　F. K.

STOCK EXCHANGE ORCHESTRAL AND CHORAL SOCIETY, THE. The Orchestral Society was founded in Nov. 1883, and gave its first concert on March 5, 1885. On Dec. 18, 1885, the first subscription concert was given at Prince's Hall ; and continuously from that date the Society has given a series of concerts in each season at St. James's and Queen's Hall. The Male Voice Choir was established in Oct. 1886, and gave its first concert in Feb. 1887. The choir made its first appearance with the orchestra in May 1888, and since has always been a regular feature at the concerts. In Oct. 1899 the orchestra and choir amalgamated under the present title. One of the objects of the Society is the production of new works by native composers, and the committee is prepared to consider original choral and orchestral compositions when submitted to them. Mr. George Kitchin, an amateur, was honorary conductor of both orchestra and choir from their foundation until his retirement in 1897. Mr. Arthur W. Payne has conducted the orchestra from Oct. 1897 to the present date, and Mr. Munro Davison the choir from Oct. 1898.

The subscription for members of the orchestra or of the choir and for subscribers is from £1 : 1s. upwards. Membership of the Society is not restricted to the Stock Exchange, though members of that body take precedence in all vacancies occurring in the orchestra and choir. The orchestra numbers 130, and the Male Voice Choir 60 members. Three subscription concerts, at least, are always given in each season. s. J. s.

STOCKFLÖTE. (See Czakan, vol. i. p. 649.)

STOCKHAUSEN, Madame, was born Margarete Schmuck, at Gebweiler in 1803, and trained in Paris as a concert-singer by Cartruffo. She became the wife of the harpist and composer Franz Stockhausen (1792-1868), and the mother of the singer Julius Stockhausen. Husband and wife travelled, giving not very remunerative concerts in Switzerland (1825). Paris was visited later, but Mme. Stockhausen's greatest successes attended her in England, where she was induced to return almost every year from 1828 to 1840, singing at some of the concerts of the Philharmonic and Vocal Societies, and also taking part in the principal private and benefit concerts. She had little or no dramatic feeling, but as she gained in power she grew in public favour, and came to be recognised as a true musician and an accomplished singer. She was frequently engaged at provincial festivals, and her delivery of the music of Mary in Spohr's 'Calvary' evoked special praise among her oratorio parts.

A few years after her farewell appearance in London, a home was made in Colmar, whither the Stockhausens retired to devote themselves to the education of their six children. Up to 1849 Mme. Stockhausen was heard with her son at local concerts ; she left Alsace only occasionally to appear in public, and in her last visit to Paris (1849) her singing showed a great falling off. She died Oct. 6, 1877, nearly ten years after her husband, much regretted by her many friends.   L. M. M.

STOCKHAUSEN, Julius, son of the foregoing, one of the most remarkable singers of his time, was born at Paris, July 22, 1826. His gifts showed themselves early, and his mother was accustomed to say that he could sing before he could speak. He and his younger brother Edward (who died early) accompanied their parents on a concert tour to England, and learnt there to sing Bishop's duet, 'Where are you going, sweet sister Fay ?' In 1833 Julius was placed at a school at Gebweiler in Alsace, where he remained till 1840, with a view to the clerical profession. But such intentions were dispelled by the violent turn for music which asserted itself after a concert at Basle in 1842, at which Mme. Stockhausen made her last appearance. He took a prominent part in the concerts at Gebweiler as singer, accompanist, violin-player, and even drummer. In 1844 he moved to the seminary of Strasburg, and there his performances on the violoncello and organ sealed his fate as a priest. In 1845 and 1846 he visited Paris with his father, took lessons in the piano from Charles Hallé and Stamaty, and in singing from Manuel Garcia, and entered thoroughly into the abundant musical life of the French capital, to the great advantage of his musical education. His devotion to the profession of music was, however, not absolutely decided till 1848, when, at the invitation of Ernst Reiter, the conductor, he suddenly took the part of Elijah in a performance of that oratorio at Basle. His success decided his future course, and he at once threw himself energetically into the art, and for the next few years travelled in all directions, singing at innumerable concerts Schubert's 'Schöne Müllerin' and other songs. In 1849 he came to England, renewed his lessons with Garcia and sang at various concerts. In 1851 he returned, and sang three times at the Philharmonic, April 7, in the Choral Symphony, April 28, in two trios, and June 9 in a scena from Boieldieu's 'Chaperon Rouge.' Taste in England was not then sufficiently advanced to call for the Lieder just mentioned. To these, at the instance, of Schröder-Devrient, he shortly added Schumann's 'Dichterliebe' and others. His first appearance on the stage seems to have been at Mannheim in 1852-53, and he joined the Opéra-Comique at Paris in 1857-59, taking such parts as the Seneschal in 'Jean de Paris.' At this time he became intimate with Ary Scheffer ; and with Mme. Viardot, Berlioz, Duprez, Saint-Saëns, and others, formed one of the circle by whom much German music was performed in the studio of the great painter.

1859 to 1862 were occupied in more concert tours, and it was during this time at Leipzig and Cologne that he first attempted Schumann's 'Faust' music. In 1862 he came to an anchor at Hamburg as Director of the Philharmonic Concerts and of the Singakademie, a position which he retained till 1869, when he was made Kammersinger to the King of Würtemberg at Stuttgart with a salary of 2000 gulden, residing at Canstatt. During all this time he took many concert tours, especially with Mme. Schumann, Joachim, and Brahms. In the latter part of 1870 he brought over his pupil Sophie Löwe to England, sang at the Popular Concerts, and remained till late in 1871. He once more sang at the Philharmonic, and appeared at the Crystal Palace, and the Monday Populars, where he introduced several fine unknown Lieder of Schubert. He and Frl. Löwe reappeared here the next winter, and remained till the end of the summer season of 1872.

In 1874 he moved from Stuttgart to Berlin, and took the direction of the Vocal Society founded by Stern (Sternsches Gesangverein), which under his genial and able direction rose to the highest point of excellence. In the four years that he conducted it there were no less than twenty-eight performances of great works, including Beethoven's Mass in D, Mozart's Requiem, Bach's Matthew-Passion, Schumann's 'Faust' music (complete), and 'Paradise and the Peri,' Brahms's Requiem, etc. In 1878 he again changed his residence, this time to Frankfort, to take the department of singing in the Conservatorium founded by Dr. Hoch, and presided over by Raff. This post, however, he soon gave up, and retired to his house at Frankfort, teaching the many private pupils who resorted to him there. After the death of Raff in 1882 he returned to the Conservatorium. In 1886-87 he published his *Method of Singing* (translated by Mme. Sophie Löwe, new edition, 1907). He died Sept. 22, 1906.

Stockhausen's singing in his best days must have been wonderful. Even to those who, like the writer, only heard him after he had passed his zenith, it is a thing never to be forgotten. Perhaps the maturity of the taste and expression made up for a little falling off in the voice. His delivery of opera and oratorio music—his favourite pieces from 'Euryanthe,' 'Jean de Paris,' 'Le Chaperon rouge,' and 'Le Philtre'; or the part of Elijah, or certain special airs of Bach—was superb in taste, feeling, and execution; but it was the Lieder of Schubert and Schumann that most peculiarly suited him, and these he delivered in a truly remarkable way. The rich beauty of the voice, the nobility of the style, the perfect phrasing, the intimate sympathy, and, not least, the intelligible way in which the words were given—in itself one of his greatest claims to distinction—all combined to make his singing of songs a wonderful event. Those who have heard him sing Schubert's 'Nachtstück,' 'The Wanderer,' 'Memnon,' or the Harper's songs; or Schumann's 'Frühlingsnacht,' or 'Fluthenreicher Ebro,' or the 'Löwenbraut,' will corroborate all that has just been said. But perhaps his highest achievement was the part of Dr. Marianus in the third part of Schumann's 'Faust,' in which his delivery of the scene beginning 'Hier ist die Aussicht frei,' with just as much of acting as the concert-room will admit—and no more—was one of the most touching and remarkable things ever witnessed.   G.

STOCKHORN. A reed instrument on the principle of the bagpipe practice - chanter, but with two parallel cylindrical tubes and independent reeds. These tubes were pierced in a single block of wood, furnished with a horn bell-mouth at one end, and the reeds were sounded by means of a cap or covering-piece placed between the lips, in the same manner as the mouth-piece of the flageolet.

An interesting example in the Museum of Scottish Antiquities, Edinburgh, has fourteen finger-holes, and two thumb-holes at the back, arranged in pairs, so that each finger closes or opens two holes at once. The total length of this instrument is about twenty-two inches, with a bell-mouth expanding to 2¼ inches, and its scale is from f' to g''. The object of the double bore appears to have been the production of a strong beating tone from mistuned consonances as is common in certain native Egyptian instruments at the present day.   D. J. B.

STODART. A family of eminent pianoforte-makers, whose business was founded in Wardour Street, Soho, about the year 1776, by Robert Stodart. It is said he had been in the Royal Horse Guards, to be a private in which corps involved at that time the payment of £100, an amount that must now be estimated by the then higher value of money. Having little duty and much leisure, Stodart became a pupil of John Broadwood to learn pianoforte-making, and in the books of Broadwood's firm appears, during the year 1775, to have taken his share in tuning for customers. It was while he was under Broadwood that he had the privilege, enjoyed by them as friends, of assisting Americus Backers in the invention of the new movement for the grand pianoforte since generally known as the 'English' action. After Backers's death, Stodart, now upon his own account, entered upon grand pianoforte making with energy and ability, and soon made a considerable reputation. The pianoforte was at that time hardly emancipated from the harpsichord, and there were frequent endeavours to combine both principles in one instrument. An endeavour of this nature was patented by Stodart in 1777, which is otherwise remarkable by the first mention of the word 'grand' in connection with a pianoforte. In it he worked his crow-quill registers, and also a swell, by means of pedals.

We find the business in 1795 removed to Golden Square, William Stodart in that year taking out, from that address, a patent for an 'Upright Grand.' This was the horizontal grand turned up vertically in the same way the upright harpsichord had been. The giraffe-like upright grand was then coming into fashion, and the speciality of Stodart's patent was to introduce one in the form of a bookcase. Of the highest importance was the patent of James Thom and William Allen, who were in Stodart's employ, a compensating framing of metal tubes and plates at once secured by Stodart's firm. This meritorious invention, which was really Allen's, was brought out in 1820, and paved the way to the general introduction of iron in pianofortes as a resisting power. [See PIANO-FORTE and the writer's *Pianoforte Primer*, p. 16.] When Malcolm Stodart, who had shown great promise, died, the interest of the survivors ceased, and the business, which had been declining, came, in 1861, to an end.   A. J. H.

STOKES, CHARLES. This excellent musician was born in 1784, and received his first instructions as a chorister in St. Paul's Cathedral. He was afterwards a pupil of Webbe, the glee composer, who was his godfather—and of other masters; but he was most indebted for his musical knowledge to Samuel Wesley, with whom he was long and intimately acquainted. He officiated for several years as assistant-organist to Callcott, at St. Paul's, Covent Garden, and Bartleman at Croydon; but he latterly preferred the quiet pursuit of his own studies, in domestic retirement, to the exertion and fatigue of public engagements. Yet his musical acquirements were of the highest order. Vincent Novello speaks of him as a most able teacher, an excellent organist, a delightful pianoforte-player, a refined and tasteful composer, and one of the most profound musical theorists then living. His name was little known, and his published music was almost confined to the pieces printed in Novello's 'Select Organ Pieces' (from which this notice is derived). That collection contains ten pieces by Stokes, full of quiet feeling, and real, though somewhat antiquated, musicianship. Novello also published an Anthem of his, 'I will lay me down in peace.' He died in London, April 14, 1839.   G.

STOLTZ, ROSINE, celebrated French singer, whose chequered life has afforded materials for more than one romance, was born in Paris, Feb. 13, 1815. According to Fétis her real name was Victorine Noeb, but she entered Ramier's class in Choron's school in 1826 as Rose Niva. She became a chorus-singer at one of the theatres after the Revolution of 1830, and in 1832 made a very modest début at Brussels. In 1833 she sang at Lille under the name of Rosine Stoltz. Her knowledge of music was deficient, and she never became a perfect singer, but nevertheless made a considerable mark in lyric tragedy. The first time she displayed her powers was when acting with A. Nourrit as Rachel in 'La Juive' at Brussels in 1836. She reappeared in the part at the Opéra in Paris, August 25, 1837. Though inferior to Mlle. Falcon, who had created the rôle, the public was interested by a talent so original and full of fire, though so unequal, and Mme. Stoltz became a favourite from the day she appeared in parts written expressly for her. Indeed throughout Léon Pillet's management (1841 to 1847) she reigned without a rival. She created the following mezzo-soprano parts: Lazarillo in Marliani's 'Xacarilla' (1839); Léonore in 'La Favorite' (1840); Agathe in 'Der Frei-schütz' (1841); Catarina in 'La Reine de Chypre' (1841); Odette in 'Charles VI.' (1843); Zayda in Donizetti's 'Dom Sébastien' (1843); Beppo in Halévy's 'Lazzarone,' Desdemona in 'Otello,' and 'Marie Stuart' in Niedermeyer's opera (1844); Estrelle in Balfe's 'Etoile de Séville' (1845); David in Mermet's opera of

that name, and Marie in Rossini's pasticcio 'Robert Bruce' (1846). The last three were failures, and in 1849 she left Paris, but appeared for some time longer in the provinces and abroad. Then no more was heard of her excepting the fact of her successive marriages to a Baron and two foreign princes. Schoen published in her name six melodies for voice and PF. in 1870.

Among the works based on the life of Rosine Stoltz may be mentioned Scudo's *Histoire d'une cantatrice de l'Opéra*; Lamer's *Mme. Rosine Stoltz* (Paris, 1847, 16mo); Cantinjou's *Les Adieux de Mme. Stoltz* (Paris, 1847, 18mo), and Mlle. Eugénie Pérignon's *Rosine Stoltz* (Paris, 1847, 8vo).   G. C.

STOLTZER, THOMAS, a musician of the earlier part of the 16th century, born at Schweidnitz in Silesia, which was then part of the independent kingdom of Bohemia. He became Capellmeister at Ofen or Buda to King Louis, who reigned over both Hungary and Bohemia from 1517 to 1526. Fétis gives the date of Stoltzer's death as August 29, 1526, but although the fact has not been noticed by musical historians, it is somewhat significant that this is merely the date of the Battle of Mohacs, at which King Louis with the flower of the Hungarian nobility fell in fighting against the Turks. But there is no evidence that Stoltzer was with King Louis on this occasion, or that his life came to an end with the taking of Buda shortly afterwards by the Turks. It is very probable that he was still alive between 1536 and 1544, when the greater part of his works appeared in the Collections of the time. A letter of his, addressed to Duke Albert of Prussia, dated Feb. 23, 1526, is extant, which seems to refer to some offer made to him from the Duke to become his Capellmeister at Königsberg. He sent to the Duke an elaborate composition of the 37th Psalm in Luther's German Prose version in seven divisions ('motettisch gesetzt') for three to seven voices. There are four other Psalms of the same kind which, with the one above mentioned, Otto Kade considers to represent the high-water mark of Stoltzer's abilities as a composer. The MSS. of these are now in the Royal Library at Dresden, for which Kade negotiated their purchase in 1858, and one of them, Psalm xii., 'Hilf, Herr, die Heiligen sind abgenommen,' he has since published in score in the *Beilagen* to Ambros's *Geschichte*. Ambros gives considerable praise to the Latin Psalms and Motets of Stoltzer, which appeared in the various collections 1538 to 1545 and 1569. This praise he largely qualifies in the case of the thirty-nine settings *a* 4–5 of Latin Church Hymns, which constitute Stoltzer's contribution to Rhau's 'Hymni Sacri' of 1542. These latter he considers somewhat heavy, though showing solid workmanship. Other German works of Stoltzer are seven settings of Geistliche Gesänge and ten of Weltliche Lieder in the collections of Schöffer, 1536, Forster, 1539, and Ott, 1544. One of the secular songs, 'Entlaubet ist der Walde,' deserves mention, because the tune in Stoltzer's tenor was afterwards adopted as the Chorale-tune for the Hymn 'Ich dank dir, lieber Herre.' The tune itself is said to have been known about 1452, and it also appears in Hans Gerle's Lautenbuch of 1532. Harmonised by Bach, it forms the conclusion of his Cantata, 'Wer da glaubet und getauft wird.' It is given with Stoltzer's own harmony in Schöberlein's *Schatz*, Bd. iii. n. 443. One of the Geistliche Gesänge also deserves mention, 'König, ein Herr ob alle Reich,' because the first words of the three verses form the acrostic 'König Ludwig' (King Louis of Hungary), and the hymn itself first appears in company with the better-known 'Mag ich Unglück nicht widerstehn,' which also forms the acrostic 'Maria,' for Queen Maria, the wife of Louis, and daughter of the Emperor Charles V. A large number of Latin Motets by Stoltzer exist in MS. in the Library at Zwickau.   J. R. M.

STONARD, WILLIAM, Mus. B. Oxon. 1608, was organist of Christ Church Cathedral, Oxford. Some of his compositions are preserved in the Music School, Oxford, and an Evening Service in C in the Tudway Collection (Harl. MS. 7337). The latter is printed in the publications of the Motet Society, vol. ii. p. 78. The words of some of his anthems are in Clifford's Collection. He died in 1630.   W. H. H.

STOPPED PIPE. An organ pipe, the upper end of which is closed by a wooden plug, or cap of metal. The pitch of a stopped pipe is one octave lower (roughly speaking) than that of an open pipe of the same length ; it is usual, therefore, in a specification, to state the pitch of a stopped pipe instead of its length ; thus, ' Open Diapason 16 ft.,' ' Bourdon 16 ft.-tone,' etc. By the former it is understood that the longest pipe is 16 ft. long ; by the latter that the longest pipe (though only 8 ft. in length) gives the same note as an open pipe of 16 ft. For the acoustic law which governs the pitch of closed pipes, see PIPES, VIBRATION OF AIR IN, vol. iii. pp. 752-754.   J. S.

STOPPING is the term used for the action of the fingers of the left hand in playing instruments with strings stretched over a fingerboard, in order to produce the intermediate sounds lying between the notes sounded by the 'open' strings. When a higher note than the fundamental sound of the string is required, the vibrating part of the string must be shortened by stopping the vibration at a certain point between nut and bridge, *i.e.* by using one of the fingers of the left hand as an artificial nut or stopping-point. The nearer this point is to the bridge, the shorter the vibrating part of the strings, and the higher in pitch therefore the sound produced. A correct intonation or playing in perfect tune obviously depends entirely on exactness of

stopping. See also under DOUBLE STOPS and HARMONICS.   P. D.

For stopping as applied to brass instruments, see HORN.

STOPS (HARPSICHORD). Like the organ, the harpsichord had stops, by which, with double keyboard, contrasts as well as changes could be made. The principle, borrowed from the organ, was the simple movement of each rack of jacks forming a register, so that the quills of the jacks might or might not touch the strings. The earliest notice of stops to a keyed stringed instrument appears in the Privy Purse Expenses of Henry VIII., April 1530, published by Sir N. Harris Nicholas in 1827 (Rimbault, *History of the Pianoforte*, 1860, p. 33). The item mentions ' ii payer of Virginalls in one coffer with iiii stoppes.' The term ' Virginals ' in England under the Tudors and up to the Commonwealth, had, like ' Clavier ' in German, the general signification of any keyed stringed instrument. [See VIRGINAL.] We therefore interpret this quotation as a double harpsichord, in one case, with four stops. If this be so, we must perforce limit Hans Ruckers's invention to the ' ottava,' the octave string [see RUCKERS], withdrawing from him the double keyboard and stops. In all unaltered Ruckers harpsichords, we find the registers made as in the old Positive organs,[1] by the prolongation of the racks as rails or slides, so as to pass through and project beyond the right-hand or treble side of the case. Each rail-end has a short loop of cord to pull it by. The late Miss Twining's Andries Ruckers of 1640 (*ante*, p. 188, No. 74), and the Countess of Dudley's Hans Ruckers the younger of 1642 (*ante*, p. 187, No. 41) have only this simple arrangement. But subsequently, to be nearer the hands, the registers were shifted by iron crank levers, and manipulated by brass knobs divided into two groups on either side of the nameboard, and immediately above the keys. The older instruments were often altered and modernised by the addition of this contrivance. The two unison stops were placed to the player's right hand, and as the reversed position of the quills when acting upon the strings required, could be brought into play by squeezing the two brass knobs together, or made silent by pushing them apart. The ottava was placed to the player's left hand, with the Lute and Harp stops, which were of later introduction, and require separate description.

The Lute, a *timbre* or colour stop, doubtless arose from observation of the power which lute-players, like viol- and guitar-players, had of changing the quality of the tone by touching the strings closer to the bridge. Perhaps the earliest reference to an attempt to imitate these instruments on the harpsichord has been found

[1] See the organ depicted in ' Music,' attributed to Melozzo da Forli (1438-94), in the National Gallery, London.

by Count L. F. Valdrighi, of Modena, in a letter in the Este records dated March 3, 1595, by Giacomo Alsise, horn-maker of Padua, who says : ' I have let Messer Alessandro see and hear . . . one of my quill instruments (da penna), of new invention, that with two unisons (due mani di corde) forms three changes of sound.' The passage is obscure, but if, as is probable, two jacks touched one string in Alsise's instrument, one must touch nearer ᴏᴜe bridge than the other, and produce a differᴇnt quality of sound. This might seem far-fetched were not Lady Dudley's Antwerp harpsichord of 1642 actually so made. Here are four certainly original changes, with three strings, two unisons and an octave, and the different quality is sought for upon the octave string. A few years later, and in England, Thomas Mace (*Musick's Monument*, 1676) speaks of the 'Theorboe' stop, which may have been only another name for the Lute stop. Certainly in England in the next century the use of the Lute stop, with its fascinating oboe quality, was universal,[1] and it was frequently added to old harpsichords.

The second fancy stop, the 'Harp,' was contrived to push small pieces of firm leather against the second unison.[2] We have unquestionable authority for this in a double harpsichord of Shudi's, of 1771, that has never been disturbed. From the material being leather, this is often called the 'buff' stop, and a single harpsichord, now at Torquay, inscribed ' Longman & Broderip,' but bearing inside the real maker's name, ' Culliford,' and date 1775, which has all the stops named, has this one marked ' Silent.' The earliest mention of the Harp stop (as ' Welch harp ') is in a patent taken out by Roger Plenius in 1745. The combination of the Lute stop by the first unison on the upper keyboard, and the second unison, which could be muted by the Harp stop on the lower, was effected by a pedal for the left foot. But to allow this pedal to be used, a stop placed inside the case, at the bass end of the keyboards, away from the other stops, had to be pushed back. Culliford's harpsichord gives the name for this pedal stop, the 'Machine,' derived from the ironwork of the pedal movement placed outside the case, and usually concealed by a box covering. The alternation of Lute and Harp with the normal registers of the upper and lower keyboards, is the most pleasing colour effect of the harpsichord. In Kirkman's harpsichord we find the Lute muted, without knowing for certain if this was the original plan. This muting has the high authority of the late Carl Engel, who transferred Messrs. Kirkman's description of the stops from the *Catalogue of the Special*

Exhibition at South Kensington, 1872, to his admirable *General Catalogue of Musical Instruments in the Museum*, 1874, p. 352.

The right-foot pedal is for the Swell. [See SWELL (HARPSICHORD).] Mace attributes the invention of the harpsichord pedal to John Hayward, a ' harpsichon ' maker. Kirkman and Shudi did not place their fancy stops alike. Kirkman's arrangement (and Culliford's), proceeding from the bass, was Harp, Lute, Octave ; Shudi's was Lute, Octave, Harp. In all, the Lute, Octave, and first Unison move to the right ; the Harp and second Unison to the left. Shudi marked this on Frederick the Great's harpsichords, still preserved at Potsdam, with arrows and the English words ' ring ' and ' dumb ' ; the Machine stop, ' open,' ' shut.' The Germans do not appear at that time to have cared for the varieties in the harpsichord given by stops. C. P. E. Bach makes no remarks in his *Versuch* about them. He merely says (1753, p. 131) that on a Flügel with more than one keyboard, the player has the forte and piano ; that is to say, the lower and upper keyboards make those changes.[3] [See *Pianoforte Primer*, p. 86.]　　A. J. H.

STOPS (ORGAN). This word is used in two senses—for the handles or draw-stops which are placed near the organ-player, and by which he can shut off or draw on the various registers ; and for the registers themselves. Thus we speak of a ' stop ' being half-out, meaning the actual handle communicating with the sliders, and at the same time we speak of ' an organ having twenty stops,' meaning twenty registers. The latter use of the word has caused the appearance of a new expression, namely, ' sounding stops ' or stops acting on pipes, as opposed to couplers and other accessory movements governed also by a stop-handle. When the pipes governed by a stop do not go through the whole compass, it is said to be a ' short-stop,' ' incomplete stop,' or ' half-stop.' When a complete row of pipes is acted upon by means of two stops, treble and bass, it is called a ' divided stop.' [See ORGAN, vol. iii. p. 546.]　　J. S.

STORACE, ANN (otherwise ANNA) SELINA, daughter of Stefano Storace (originally Sorace), an eminent Italian contrabassist who had settled in England [and who lived and taught in Dublin in 1750-53], was born in London in 1766. She was first instructed in music by her father, and when only eight years old appeared as a singer at the Haymarket Theatre, in a concert given by Evans, the harper, April 15, 1774. She was afterwards a pupil of Rauzzini, and in 1777 sang in the oratorios at Covent Garden and at Hereford Festival. On April 27, 1778, she had a benefit concert at the Tottenham Street Rooms (subsequently

---

[1] Queen Charlotte's Shudi harpsichord at Windsor Castle has an original Lute stop, and the date is 1740. This instrument, long at Kew Palace, was probably made for Frederick, Prince of Wales, George the Third's father.

[2] Shudi put a spring on the second unison slide, so that it could not be pushed off without moving a rail outside the case, next the Machine.'

[3] In the posthumous second edition, 1797, he recommends Hohlfeld's pedal, which appears to have been a sostenente, for a dynamic change.

the Prince of Wales's Theatre—now the Scala),
'to enable her to pursue her studies, as she
intends to go to Italy in the course of the
ensuing summer.' She accordingly repaired to
Venice, where she became a pupil of the Conservatorio dell' Ospedaletto, under Sacchini.
In 1780 she appeared at La Pergola, Florence,
with great success. [See Michael Kelly's *Reminiscences* and the *Dict. of Nat. Biog.*] In 1781
she sang at Parma, and in 1782 at La Scala,
Milan. In 1784 she was engaged at the
Imperial Theatre, Vienna, at a salary equal to
£500 sterling for the season, a then unprecedented sum. During her stay in the Austrian
capital two important events in her career
happened, (1) her appearance on May 1, 1786,
as the original Susanna in Mozart's 'Nozze di
Figaro,' and (2) her ill-starred marriage with
Fisher the violinist. [See FISHER, JOHN
ABRAHAM.] She returned to England in March
1787, and appeared at the King's Theatre,
March 24, as Gelinda, in Paisiello's 'Gli
Schiavi per amore,' and afterwards in other
comic operas, but she soon abandoned the
Italian for the English stage, on which she
made her first appearance at Drury Lane,
Nov. 24, 1789, in her brother's opera, 'The
Haunted Tower,' and for several years afterwards sustained, with the greatest success, a
variety of characters in comic opera. In 1791
she sang at the Handel Festival in Westminster
Abbey, and in 1792 at Hereford Festival. [She
formed an intimacy with Braham, and toured
with him on the Continent.] In 1801 she was
engaged at Covent Garden, where she continued
to perform till May 30, 1808, when she took
her leave of the public in the opera of 'The
Cabinet.' She lived at Dulwich until her
death, August 24, 1817, and was buried at St.
Mary's, Lambeth. She accumulated a considerable fortune, and by her will, dated August 10,
1797 (twenty years before her death), bequeathed
upwards of £11,000 in pecuniary legacies alone,
including two munificent gifts of £1000 each
to the old Musical Fund (Royal Society of
Musicians) and New Musical Fund. This will
was proved Oct. 11, 1817, the personalty being
sworn under £50,000. It was said in 1820
that after payment of all the legacies, there
remained but little short of £40,000 for her
cousin, Miss Trusler, the residuary legatee.
Her studious concealment, after her return to
England, of her marriage, is evidenced by her
having made her will in her maiden name and
avoided any description in it of her quality
or condition, and also by the fact that her
executor, in proving the will, describes her as a
spinster. [A miniature of her is in the Soane
Museum.]   W. H. H.

STORACE, STEPHEN, brother of the preceding, was born in London, Jan. 4, 1763.
His early taste for music was cultivated by his
father, so that when ten years old he was able

to perform the most difficult violin music of
Tartini and Giardini—the Paganinis of the
day—with correctness and steadiness. When
twelve years old he was placed in the Conservatorio of St. Onofrio at Naples, where he
studied the harpsichord, violin, and composition. On his sister's arrival in Italy, a few
years later, he joined her and visited with her
the principal cities of that country, and eventually went to Vienna, where he produced his
two operas, 'Gli Sposi malcontenti' (June 1,
1785) and 'Gli Equivoci,' the subject taken
from Shakespeare's 'Comedy of Errors,' Dec. 27,
1786. He gained great advantage whilst there
from his association with Mozart. [He wrote,
no doubt, during his Viennese period, two
quintets and a sestet. Many amusing stories
of Storace and his sister are told in Michael
Kelly's *Reminiscences*.] In March 1787 he returned to England and was engaged to superintend
the production of the opera in which his sister
appeared at the King's Theatre, but soon became
disgusted with the prevalent petty jealousies
and intrigues, and retired for a time to Bath,
where he devoted his attention to drawing, for
which he had considerable talent. He returned
to his musical pursuits in the ensuing year,
and on Oct. 25, 1788, produced at Drury Lane
the musical farce of 'The Doctor and the
Apothecary,' adapting some of the well-known
'Doctor und der Apotheker' of Dittersdorf.
On Nov. 24, 1789, he brought out his three-
act opera, 'The Haunted Tower,' the success of which was unbounded; it was performed
fifty nights in the first season and kept its
place upon the stage for nearly half a century.
On April 16, 1790, he produced his charming
little opera, 'No Song no Supper,' in which he
introduced some of the music of 'Gli Equivoci.'
[In the same year he wrote music for 'La
Cameriera Astuta.'] Jan. 1, 1791, witnessed
the production of the opera, 'The Siege of
Belgrade,' in which he introduced much of the
music of Martini's 'La Cosa rara.' This also
long continued an established favourite. On
May 3, in the same year, he produced the 'Cave
of Trophonius,' an adaptation of Salieri's 'La
Grotta di Trofonio,' with some additional music
by himself, but with no success. He fared
better when, on Nov. 20, 1792, he brought
out 'The Pirates,' in which he incorporated
several pieces from 'Gli Equivoci.' The finale
to the first act is regarded as his masterpiece.
In the same year he produced his opera, 'Dido,
Queen of Carthage,' which met with but small
success, notwithstanding that the heroine was
undertaken by Mara. 'The Prize,' musical
entertainment, first performed on his sister's
benefit night, March 11, 1793; 'My Grandmother,' musical farce, produced Dec. 16, 1793;
'Lodoiska,' musical romance, the music partly
adapted from Cherubini and Kreutzer, and
partly composed by himself, performed June 9,

1794 ; 'The Glorious First of June,' occasional piece, produced July 2, 1794 ; the ballet of 'Venus and Adonis' (1794), and the 'Cherokee,' comic opera, Dec. 20, 1794, were all well received, as was also 'The Three and the Deuce,' musical drama, performed Sept. 2, 1795. On March 12, 1796, Colman's 'Iron Chest,' with Storace's music, was performed for the first time, and although the play, owing to accidental circumstances, failed to produce an immediately favourable impression, the music was rapturously received. But few, however, if any, of the gratified and applauding auditors knew or thought that anxiety for the success of that music had impelled its composer to a course which had laid him upon his deathbed. He was then recovering from a severe attack of gout and fever ; yet urged by a sense of duty, he determined, despite the entreaties of his family, to attend the first rehearsal. The consequence was fatal ; he took cold, the gout attacked his stomach, and on March 19,[1] he expired, at the early age of thirty-three years.

At the time of his death he had an opera, 'Mahmoud, or The Prince of Persia,' in preparation for Braham's début in London. This work was left incomplete, but, by the assistance of Kelly, and the selection of some music by the composer's sister, A. S. Storace, it was fitted for performance and produced for the benefit of his widow (a daughter of John Hall the engraver) and his children, April 30, 1796, was well received, and performed many times. Storace's melodies are thoroughly English in character, whilst in his instrumentation the influence of Mozart and the Italian composers is evident. He was almost the first English composer who introduced into his works the modern finale, in which the business of the scene is carried on by concerted music.[2] Some fine examples occur in his works. There is reason for believing that his early death delayed for many years the advance in that direction which might otherwise have been made. W. H. H.

STORNELLO. 'A short poem, in lines of eleven syllables each : it is peculiar to, and liked by the people in Tuscany, who extemporise it with elegant simplicity.' This is the definition of Stornello we find in Mons. Tommaseo's Dictionary, and, in this matter at least, we are not aware of any greater authority. The 'Vocabolario degli Accademici della Crusca,' the stronghold of the purity of the Italian language, does not contain the word ; this fact added to the other, not less significant, that neither Crescimbeni, nor Quadrio, nor Tiraboschi, mention the word in their elaborate works, inclines us to believe that the word Stornello has not the definite meaning that, for instance, Sonnetto has, but is merely a name given in some parts of Italy to very short poems, more with regard

to their purport than their form. Tommaseo again, somewhere else, speaking of Tonio and Beatrice, two peasants who sang and recited popular songs and popular poems to him, says : 'Tonio makes a difference between Rispetti and Ramanzetti ; the latter are composed of only three lines, the former of eight or ten. And those that Tonio called Ramanzetti Beatrice called Strambotti, as Matteo Spinello and King Manfredi did ; and in the territory of Pistoja and in Florence they are distinguished by the name of Stornelli.' Although in the true popular songs of Italy there is a great freedom in the number of lines and rules of rhyming, the two Stornelli we subjoin may be taken as fair examples of this kind of poem.[3]

(1) Tutta la notte in sogno mi venite ;
 Ditemi, bella mia, perchè lo fate ?
 E chi viene da voi quando dormite ?

(2) Fiori di pepe.
 So giro intorno a voi come fa l' ape
 Che gira intorno al fiore della siepe.

The first line may contain either five or eleven syllables ; the other two are of eleven syllables each. The first line rhymes with the third, i.e. the two have the last syllable, and the vowel of the last syllable but one, alike ; the intermediate line, while corresponding in its last syllable with the last syllable of the other two lines, changes the vowel of the accented one. [In the second form given above, the verse begins with the name of a flower. A Stornello is embodied in Browning's 'Fra Lippo Lippi,' and Lola, in 'Cavalleria Rusticana,' sings one.]

The etymology of 'Stornello' is very uncertain ; Tommaseo, however, has some ground for asserting that it is a corruption of 'Ritornello,' or 'refrain.'   G. M.

STRADA DEL PÒ, ANNA. An Italian soprano, brought from Italy by Handel in 1729, with Bernacchi, Merighi, Fabri, and others, for the opera in the Haymarket. She appeared there in 'Lotario,' Dec. 2, 1729 ; in 'Partenope,' Feb. 24, 1730 ; 'Poro,' Feb. 2, 1731 ; 'Ezio,' Jan. 15, 1732 ; 'Sosarme,' Feb. 19, 1732 ; in 'Acis and Galatea,' June 10, 1732 ; and in 'Orlando,' Jan. 23, 1733. She was the only one of Handel's company who did not desert him for the rival new opera in Lincoln's Inn in the end of 1733, and she remained faithful to him till her departure from this country in June 1738, when a quarrel with Heidegger, the manager, put an end to her connection with England. In the interval between 1733 and the last-named date she took part in Handel's 'Ariodante,' 'Alcina,' 'Atalanta,' 'Arminio,' 'Giustino,' 'Berenice' ; also in 'Athaliah' and 'Alexander's Feast.'

Even on her arrival, though, according to Handel,[4] 'a coarse singer with a fine voice,'

---

[1] The day of his death is given on his monument as the 16th.
[2] Dibdin had foreshadowed it in his 'Quaker.'

[3] From Tigri's 'Canto Populare Toscani' (Florence, 1869).
[4] Burney's History, iv. 342. The above information is compiled from the same volume, pp. 339-427.

Strada must have had some brilliant execution, for the first air which she sang on those boards contains no less than thirty opportunities to display her shake. Coming after Cuzzoni and Faustina, and having so little to recommend her to the eye that she was nicknamed the 'pig,' it took her some time to get into favour. But Handel took pains with her, wrote for her, and advised her, and at length rendered her equal to the first singers of the Continent.   G.

STRADELLA, ALESSANDRO, an Italian composer of the 17th century. The earliest and only detailed account of him is given by Bourdelot in his *Histoire de la musique*, written before 1685, published 1715. This is the source of the romantic story of his eloping with the mistress of a Venetian nobleman, of the attempt to murder the composer, of the effect of Stradella's music upon the assassins, and of the ultimate success of the nobleman's plot 'about the year 1670'; there seems no good reason to believe the story, which occurs in a book that is untrustworthy in many particulars. The narrative failed to obtain credence from M. Richard[1] or M. Catelani,[2] whose researches, however, have not led to any positive result.

The place of Stradella's birth is unknown. Wanley[3] thinks he was a Venetian, while Burney[4] states he was a Neapolitan, apparently for no other reason than that he sends Stradella and Ortensia, *en route* for Rome, to Naples, which, he adds, was 'the place of Stradella's nativity.' Fétis,[5] evidently on Burney's statement, but without quoting his authority, describes him as born at Naples about 1645, and the assertion is now an accepted statement.[6] The dates both of his birth and death are in fact unknown. But though we reject the story of his murder at Genoa, it is not impossible that he ended his life there, since the composition, which we may presume to have been his last, is dated from thence.

The date of his death was probably about 1681, since there exists in the Biblioteca Palatina of Modena, a cantata, 'Il Barcheggio,'[7] written for the wedding of Carlo Spinola and Paola Brignole, at Genoa, July 6, 1681. The poem contains numerous allusions to it, and the names of both bride and bridegroom; no mistake is possible as to the real

date of the composition, and thus the dates 1670 and 1678, given by Bourdelot and Burney respectively for his death, are evidently wrong.[8]

The statements that besides being a composer Stradella was a singer,[9] 'an exquisite performer on the harp,'[10] 'a great performer on the violin,'[11] 'excelled in an extraordinary hand, so as to have been accounted the best organist in Italy,'[12] 'was a Latin and perhaps also an Italian poet,'[13] are all more or less gratuitous, and except composing, it cannot be proved that he possessed any of these qualifications. His name is never met with in any of the best treatises of Italian literature, either as a Latin or an Italian poet,[14] and with respect to his skill on the organ, we have been unable to find anything to justify Wanley's assertion, beyond a short Sonata in D for two violins and basso continuo per l'Organo.[15] As to the statements in the *Penny Cyclopædia*, that 'Stradella was not handsome, but remarkable for the symmetry of his form, his wit and polished manners,' and in Wanley's catalogue, that 'he was a comely person and of an amorous nature,' I can do no more than submit them to the reader, as striking instances of the way in which mythical statements gather round a central figure.

Nothing can be positively asserted as to his having been married to Ortensia after the attempted murder at Turin, because the archives of S. Giovanni di Torino, the parish of the court, have been destroyed by fire.

Where or with whom Stradella studied is entirely unknown. In the archives of the Royal Conservatorio di Musica in Naples, where all the documents formerly belonging to the superseded Conservatori are most carefully kept, his name does not occur; nor is it mentioned in Lichtenthal's catalogue.[16] None of his numerous operas are known to have

1 *Le Ménestrel*, 1865, pp. 51, 52; 1866, pp. 1 to 6, and 12 to 18.
2 *Delle opere di A. Stradella esistenti nell' Archivio Musicale della R. Biblioteca Palatina di Modena.* Modena, 1866.
3 *A Catalogue of the Harleian Manuscripts in the British Museum,* vol. i. p. 642, coll. 1272.
4 *A General History of Music,* iv. 100, 101.
5 *Biographie universelle des musiciens.*
6 See *Dictionnaire général de Biographie et d'Histoire* (Paris, 1857); *Dictionnaire de la Conversation et de la Lecture* (Paris, 1858); Mendel, *Mus. Conversations-Lexikon* (1877); Riemann, *Musik-Lexikon.*
7 On the first page of the score is written: 'Il Barcheggio, del Sig. Alessandro Stradella 1681. L' ultima delle sue sinfonie.' After the overture, and before the duet with which the scene opens, at the top of the page is written 'Inuentione per un Barcheggio, 1681. 16 Giugno. L' ultima composizione del Sig. Alessandro Stradella.' This is a cantata for soprano, tenor, and bass, in two parts. Each part is preceded by an overture. The score is for two violins, cornet or trumpet, and bass: a trombone di rinforzo at times with the bass.

8 Burney's mistake is easily explicable, because, when he wrote, ' Il Barcheggio' had not yet been discovered, and he was in possession of a libretto ' La forza dell' amor paterno,' Genoa, 1678, dedicated to Signora Teresa Raggi Soali by Alessandro Stradella, the dedication apparently written by Stradella himself. The facts that the oratorio 'S. Giovanni Battista'—supposed to be that which saved its author's life in Rome—bears the date ' Rome, 1676' and the fact that Bourdelot's account implies a period of two years between Stradella's singing in Rome and his murder in Genoa, induced Burney to believe that Stradella might have met his death in Genoa while attending the rehearsals of his new opera. However, that libretto was seen by Burney only, and has since disappeared.
9 Bourdelot and all biographers.
10 Hawkins's *History*, vol. iv. bk. 2, chap. 10.
11 Burney, *A General History of Music*, iv. 100.
12 *A Catalogue of the Harleian MSS.*
13 Catelani, *Delle opere di A. Stradella esistenti*, etc.
14 *Della Storia e della Ragione di ogni Poesia*, di F. S. Quadrio. Bologna - Milano, 1739-42. Tiraboschi, *Storia della letteratura italiana.* Ginguené, *Histoire littéraire d'Italie.* Giovan Mario Crescimbeni, *Dell' Istoria della volgar Poesia.* In this last work, Stradella is spoken of only where the author, dealing with the *Cantatas*, thus expresses himself: 'They are pretty things and the best and most pleasant diversion that one can enjoy in any honourable and noble conversation; especially when set to music by eminent *maestri*, as, amongst the old ones, are those by the famous Alessandro Stradella, one of which he was sung not long since in the Academy of the Cardinal Ottoboni by Andrea Adami detto il Bolsena.' Vol. i. lib. iv. chap. xii. p. 330. This passage is quoted from the third edition, 1731.
15 'Scielta delle suonate a due violini con il Basso continuo per l' Organo, raccolte da diversi eccellenti autori.' In Bologna per Giacomo Monti, 1680. With the exception of this Sonata, no other of Stradella's compositions was printed in the 17th century.
16 *Dizionario e Bibliografia della Musica del D. Pietro Lichtenthal,* Milano, 1826.

been performed in his lifetime,[1] with the exception of ' Il Trespolo.'[2]

Stradella as a composer is known to modern audiences by the Aria di Chiesa, 'Pietà, Signore!' attributed to him. It is enough to say that no musician, even though but slightly acquainted with the works that are indisputably by Stradella, will attribute it to him. The composer of that beautiful composition is almost certainly Rossini. The words are taken from the second stanza of Arsenio's aria in Alessandro Scarlatti's oratorio 'Santa Teodosia,' two copies of which are in the Biblioteca Palatina of Modena, and bear the signature 'A. S.'

Stradella's name has lately been invested with fresh interest on account of a Serenata attributed to him, in which the subjects of many of the pieces in 'Israel in Egypt' exist in a more or less crude form. [See vol. ii. pp. 286*b*, 514*b*.] A copy of this, formerly belonging to Dr. Gauntlett, is in the Library of the Royal College of Music, London, and another (older) in that of the Conservatoire, Paris ; the original is not known. For a review of the work, by Prof. Prout, see *Monthly Musical Record*, Dec. 1, 1871.

Burney (iv. 105) gives an analysis of his Oratorio di S. Gio. Battista, and mentions a MS. of his opera ' La Forza dell' Amor paterno,' dated Genoa, 1678.

There are 148 of Stradella's compositions at Modena : amongst them six oratorios and six dramas. The library of S. Marco in Venice possesses a collection of 'Canti a voce sola dell' insigne A. Stradella, legate alla Biblioteca S. Marco di Venezia dalla nobile famiglia Contarini.' Some of his compositions are also at the Conservatorio at Naples, and some in that at Paris. Many are in the British Museum. (See the *Quellen-Lexikon*.) The Christ Church Library, Oxford, contains one motet for two voices, and eight cantatas for one and two voices.   G. M.

STRADELLA. 1. French lyric drama, music by Flotow. Produced at the Palais Royal theatre, Paris, Feb. 1837. Then recomposed, as a Grand Opera, and produced at Hamburg, Dec. 30, 1844, as 'Alessandro Stradella.' In English (altered by Bunn) as 'Stradella,' at Drury Lane, June 6, 1846. 2. Opera in five acts, by Niedermeyer ; produced at the Académie, March 3, 1837.   G.

STRADIVARI, ANTONIO, 'brought the violin to the highest perfection and left to Cremona an imperishable name as master of his craft.' Thus the inscription now affixed by the municipality of Cremona to the house in the Piazza Roma where the great violin-maker passed the

most successful years of his life, and where he died on Dec. 18, 1737.

It should be stated at once that the history, that is to say, the whole of the facts available as the reward of untiring effort and affectionate research, concerning the family of the great 'Stradivarius,' as well as his own personality and work, have been amassed in the monumental study which has been, it may be said, the life-work of the sons of William Ebsworth Hill— *Antonio Stradivari, his Life and Work (1644-1737)*, by W. Henry Hill, Arthur F. Hill, F.S.A. and Alfred Hill (London, 1902). Beyond what is collected in this volume there is, probably, nothing more to be discovered or discussed. To this work the writer acknowledges his great indebtedness.

Regarding the etymology of the name Mr. E. J. Payne, in the first edition of the Dictionary, pronounced it to be derived from 'the plural form of "Stradivare," a Lombard variety of "Stradiere," a tollman or douanier, a feudal official who was posted on the Strada (or high road) for the purpose of exacting dues from passengers'; while Signor Mandelli, quoting from the catalogue of ancient rolls of the community of Cremona, compiled by the Piedmontese professor, Astegiano, to the year 1300, and printed at Turin in 1899, states that : ' The form of the name "de Stradaverta" as used in 1298 is derived from "Strada Averta" of the Cremonese dialect ; in Italian "Strada Aperta." A further outcome of Signor Mandelli's researches is the remarkable genealogy of the Stradivari family which he has traced down to 1883. Beginning with Giulio Cesare Stradivari of the parish of S. Michele Vecchio, who married Doralice Milani, a widow of the cathedral parish, on April 10, 1600, we find Antonio Stradivari's father recorded in the register-entry of the son born to them two years later and christened Alessandro, on Jan. 15 in the same church. Later we find this same Alessandro, son of Giulio Cesare Stradivari, entering into the bonds of matrimony with Anna, daughter of Leonardo Moroni, on August 30, 1622, which fact is duly recorded in the marriage register of the parish of S. Prospero. Three children are recorded to have been born of this union : Giuseppe Giulio Cesare, born March 1623 ; Carlo Felice, born Sept. 1626 ; Giovanni Battista, born Oct. 1628. After the birth of the last-mentioned child documentary evidence concerning the family ceases entirely, and no effort has yet dissipated the obscurity which enshrouds the birth of Antonio Stradivari. Every record relating to the subject has, it would seem, been destroyed, or lost, and the only available explanation of this singular deficiency has been furnished by the wars and famine which visited Cremona in 1628, the year Giovanni Battista was born, and again in 1629. Again in 1630 the inhabitants were further harassed by the ravages of

1 The following is the list of books in which the names of Stradella's operas should have been mentioned, if any of them had been performed. Leone Allacci, *Drammaturgia*. Groppo, *Catalogo di tutti i dramme per musica*. Bonlini, *Le glorie della Poesia e della Musica*. C. F. Menestrier, *Des représentations en musique ancienne et moderne*, Paris, 1681. Pietro Napoli Signorelli, *Storia critica de teatri antichi e moderni*. Ditto, *Discorso storico critico da servire di lume alla storia dei teatri*.
2 Performed at Bologna, 1679, and at Modena, 1686.

a plague which caused innumerable deaths, and compelled all those who could do so, to leave the city. It is further recorded that Hieronymus Amati, his wife and his daughters, succumbed to the disease ; but there is no indication that Alessandro Stradivari and his family were still at Cremona at the time, and Mandelli has perhaps rightly interpreted the complete lack of documentary evidence regarding the date and place of Antonio Stradivari's birth, to signify that his parents had fled to some haven of refuge where in the fulness of time Antonio first saw the light. The names of the three children above mentioned are the only entries to be found in the birth registers relating to children born in wedlock to Alessandro Stradivari, and the only direct allusion to the relationship existing between Antonio and Alessandro Stradivari is furnished by the contract for the purchase of his house wherein he signs himself ' Antonio Stradivari, son of the late Alessandro.'

The earliest authentic evidence of Antonio Stradivari's residence in Cremona has been supplied by a violin—dated 1666—recorded by Alfred Hill, in whose hands it has been. The original label in this instrument runs as follows : ' Antonius Stradiuarius Cremonensis Alumnus Nicolai Amati, Faciebat Anno 1666,' followed by the familiar Maltese cross and the initials A. S. enclosed within a double circle. He was then—as will be gathered later—twenty-two years of age and, it may be assumed, had probably served an apprenticeship to Nicolo Amati for the seven or eight preceding years. It is quite possible that he began to insert his own labels some years before 1666, but this date may be said to have marked the later limit of his pupilage ; in any case it proved his competence to claim the authorship of his own instruments, and the labels found in his violins of the following year bear no allusion to Nicolo Amati, nor is there any further reference to his master on the labels of any of his later instruments. Following the same lines of deduction, the year in which Antonio Stradivari was born has been generally accepted as 1644, by reason of his custom of adding his age to his labels during the latter part of his life. It would seem as though the venerable maker, with a pardonable pride, desired to impress his contemporaries, as well as succeeding generations, with his unflagging vigour and skill by recording his age within his instruments. In 1732 he states himself to be ' 89,' in 1736, ' 92 ' and in 1737, ' 93.' Another noticeable feature of these labels is the alteration in the spelling of his name. About the year 1730 he seems to have discarded the first orthography, i.e. ' Antonius Stradiuarius,' and replaced the u with a roman v. The origin of this change may have been a chance misprint which commended itself to him ; but it was certainly not due to any orthographical views on the part of the Stradi-

vari family, for his son, Omobono, still continued to employ the earlier, while Francesco adopted the later spelling.

Accepting the year of Antonio Stradivarius's birth as 1644, we find that he was twenty-three years of age when he married Francesca Feraboschi in 1667. This lady was the widow of Giovanni Giacomo Capra, who had committed suicide in the Piazza S. Agata, Cremona, three years previously, and was Stradivari's senior by a few years. After the union Stradivari and his wife settled in a house known as the Casa del Pescatore, which was situated in his wife's parish of S. Matteo ; and a year after the marriage the Cremona census reports record that a daughter, christened Giulia Maria, had been born to them. Until 1680 Stradivari continued to live at the Casa del Pescatore, where his family was increased by the birth of a second daughter, Catterina, born March 25, 1674 (died June 17, 1748), and four sons : Francesco, born Feb. 6, 1670—who only lived a week ; Francesco, born Feb. 1, 1671 (died May 11, 1743) ; Alessandro, born May 25, 1677 (died June 26, 1732) ; Omobono, born Nov. 14, 1679 (died June 8, 1742). The year following the birth of Omobono Stradivari and his family removed to the house he had purchased in the Piazza San Domenico of a Cremonese family named Picenardi. According to the deed of sale, first brought to light by Signor Lombardini (*Antonio Stradivari e la celebre scuola Cremonese*, 1872), and now preserved in the National Archives of Cremona, Stradivari paid 7000 imperial lires (about £840) for his new home. 2000 lire of this amount he paid in cash, 4990 he agreed to pay within four years, and the balance of ten lire was foregone by the vendors provided he paid the canons of the Cathedral the yearly tithe of six imperial sols. Until his death Stradivari resided in this house, known in his day as No. 2 Piazza San Domenico, but since 1870 as No. 1 Piazza Roma, and for nine years after his demise the remaining members of his family lived there. In 1746 it was let to Stradivari's pupil, Carlo Bergonzi, who occupied the house until 1758. In the following year it was tenanted by Giacomo Caraffe, and until 1777 by Giuseppe Paleari and others ; but in that year Stradivari's grandson, named Antonio after him, sold the house to Signor Giovanni Ancina. During these years the building escaped alteration, but in 1888 the proprietor of the adjoining *caffè* purchased it and carried out such extensive alterations that little of the original form of the structure now remains.

Eighteen years of domestic tranquillity followed the establishment of the Stradivari family —which included Susanna Capra, his wife's only daughter by her first husband—in their new abode, until May 25, 1698, when a break was caused in the home-circle by the death of the violin-maker's wife, Francesca Feraboschi. She was buried with conspicuous honours in a tomb situated in the choir of the church of St. Domenico, and fifteen months after her death Stradivari consoled himself, becoming united in August 1699 to Signora Antonia Maria Zambelli, daughter of Antonia Zambelli, of the parish of S. Donato. This second marriage was blessed with five children: one daughter—named after the first wife—Francesca Maria, born Sept. 19, 1700 (died Feb. 11, 1720); Giovanni Battista Giuseppe, born Nov. 6, 1701 (died July 8, 1702); Giovanni Battista Martino, born Nov. 11, 1703 (died Nov. 1, 1727); Giuseppe, who became a priest, born Oct. 27, 1704 (died Dec. 2, 1781); Paolo Bartolomeo, born Jan. 26, 1708, who was a cloth-merchant (died Oct. 14, 1776). The last named, together with Stradivari's first child, Giulia Maria (by his first wife), were apparently the only members of his family who married.

Immersed in the absorbing interest of his work, it may be safely said that the years passed swiftly over Stradivari's head, so that, notwithstanding the loss of several of his children, the thought of purchasing a family vault did not occur to him until eight years before his own death. It was in 1729 that he is recorded to have purchased, from the heirs of Francesco Villani, the burial-place and tombstone belonging to that noble family. The exact locality of this vault has been entirely lost since the total destruction of the church of S. Domenico and its chapel—named after the Blessed Virgin of the Rosary—which contained the Villani, afterwards the Stradivari tomb. No funds for the restoration of this handsome church were available, and it gradually fell into such a state of decay that the city authorities had the building demolished in 1869, converting the site into the existing public garden. Here a commemorative inscription on one of the decorative vases in the grounds perpetuates the memory of the church of S. Domenico, but the fact that it was the last resting-place of the illustrious violin-maker is not alluded to. The Villani tombstone, however, from which the coat-of-arms and family inscriptions were so imperfectly effaced that they are still visible under Stradivari's name, is now preserved in the Municipal Museum, and the Parish Register of S. Matteo records that Stradivari's second wife was interred in the Villani vault on March 4, 1737. She was the first member of the family to be buried there, and nine months later she was followed by her husband, who was laid to rest on Dec. 19, 1737. The following members of his family were also interred in the same vault: Omobono Stradivari, June 9, 1742; Francesco Stradivari, May 13, 1743; Paolo Bartolomeo Stradivari, Oct. 15, 1776; Giuseppe Antonio Stradivari, Dec. 3, 1781; Catarina Stradivari (spinster), June 18, 1784.

Little or nothing is known concerning the disposition of Stradivari's property after his death. The census returns reveal that his family continued to reside in the Piazza Roma house until 1746. Possibly his sons and daughters divided their father's possessions amicably among themselves, and we may presume that the privilege of using his workshop and tools fell to the share of Francesco and Omobono, who survived their father for five and six years respectively. After the departure of Stradivari's son Paolo Bartolomeo, with his wife Elena Templari and their four children, in 1746, the new tenant, Bergonzi, presumably became the owner of Stradivari's tools and violin-making appurtenances; but during the thirty-nine years or so which elapsed between Stradivari's death and the sale of his designs, moulds, etc., by his descendants to Count Cozio di Salabue, many of these interesting relics necessarily became scattered abroad and passed into different hands. With the exception of his callipers, the great Cremona maker's tools were not included in the Count's collection, which now belongs to the Marchese Dalla Valle in Turin. There are sixteen moulds for violins, and three for violas, in this collection, besides various drawings and designs for the minutest details of his art, which are of great interest. M. Vuillaume, it is said, also preserved some of Stradivari's moulds, and these were presented by him to the Musée of the Paris Conservatoire, whilst the French luthier, M. Chanot-Chardon, owns a set of small planes said to have belonged to Stradivari.

As no genuine portrait of the great Cremona maker exists, we still have to rely on the verbal description of Stradivari handed down to us by Polledro from his master Pugnani, for an idea of his personal appearance. According to M. Fétis (Biog. des Mus.), on whose authority we have the account, Polledro, formerly first violin at the court of Turin (died 1822), records that his master, Pugnani, knew Stradivari during the latter part of his life, and delighted in talking about him. He described him as tall and thin. As a rule his head was covered with a white woollen cap in the winter, and a white cotton cap in the summer; over his clothes he wore an apron of white leather, and, as he rarely ceased from work, his costume varied seldom. M. Fétis also recounts that Stradivari's untiring industry and his frugal habits brought him to an old age of such easy circumstances that his affluence became a standard of comparison to the people of Cremona, who adopted the phrase *Ricco come Stradivari.*

In the opinion of Messrs. Hill, Stradivari was undoubtedly an apprentice in Nicolo Amati's workshop, but they unhesitatingly repudiate the idea that Stradivari assisted Amati in the construction of his later instruments, and this on the grounds that there is no indication of any such help to be found in the latter's work.

The explanation of this is possibly to be found in the fact that Stradivari's superior gifts placed him in a high position of trust, freed him from many of the duties exacted from his comrades, and gave him the privilege of making his own instruments and using his own labels. The question must still be somewhat a matter of surmise, but the above conclusion is certainly strengthened by the excellent violins which issued from Stradivari's hands whilst apparently he still worked in the studio of the great Amati. Again, the termination of Stradivari's apprenticeship can only be approximately stated to have taken place a couple of years before he purchased his house in the Piazza Roma in 1680. Already in 1666—and possibly as early as 1660—Stradivari was making violins in which he affixed his own labels. These early violins are particularly noticeable for their poor material, thick yellow varnish, solid build, and their proportions, which follow those of Amati's smaller pattern, i.e. about 13$\frac{7}{8}$ long ; 7$\frac{1}{8}$ width of lower bouts ; 6$\frac{3}{8}$ width of upper bouts ; 1$\frac{3}{16}$ lower ribs ; 1$\frac{1}{8}$ upper ribs. With one or two exceptions, notably the ornamented violin known as the 'Hellier' Strad (1679), which tends towards the grand Amati in measurement, and is remarkably heavy in style of work, Stradivari adhered to the small model until 1684, after which date he definitely turned his attention to larger-built instruments. There is little doubt that by this time he had gained some *prestige* as a maker, and this, combined with the loss of his master's living influence, gave freedom to and further awakened his inventive faculties. Until 1684 he merely proved himself to be an uncommonly skilled craftsman, but the years which intervened between 1684 and 1700 marked the progress of those experiments which were to culminate in the uttermost perfection of form and balance. It must be observed, however, that notwithstanding the changes which took place in Stradivari's work during this period—generally alluded to as the 'Amatisé period'—the perfect poise and equilibrium, so characteristic of his later work, is to some extent lacking. That Nicolo Amati's precepts still strongly influenced him is proved by his first innovation, which consisted in adopting a standard of length, varying from 14 inches to 14$\frac{1}{16}$ inches, and proportions similar to those of the 'grand' Amati. In some instances he flattened the model, in others arched it almost to a central point, more generally he adhered entirely to the Amati model, though the solidity of his edges always remained the same. The scrolls also, during these years, evidence the master's indecision by the deviating vigour and occasional feebleness. A marked alteration in the detail of his work took place in 1688, when Stradivari first outlined the curves of the scroll in black, and also similarly accentuated the centre-line

or back rib of the scroll. This original idea was one which evidently commended itself to him and to his patrons as, with but few exceptions, he continued to place it on his scrolls until the end of his life. Briefly to summarise this early period, we may say that, between 1684 and 1690, Stradivari principally strove to avoid the defects of others, while seeking new paths for himself ; but in the meantime the beauty, accuracy, and finish of his work was gaining steadily every year. The cutting of his ff holes, the carving of his scrolls, the exquisite precision of the purfling, all prove the complete dexterity with which he handled his knife. Then, as a crowning point to this perfect craftsmanship a new set of proportions suddenly suggested themselves to his maturing brain, and we find him in 1690 creating the 'Long Strad.' The abrupt appearance of this complete innovation is not easy to account for, but the growing demand for strongly toned instruments for use in the churches doubtless influenced Stradivari in the first place, and as the authors of *Gio. Paolo Maggini, his Life and Work* (Hill & Sons) state, the form and proportions were suggested by a Maggini violin which came under his notice. This search for power in Stradivari's work is observable from the moment that he threw off the yoke of the 'small' Amati pattern. He gradually increased his breadths year by year, and even contemporaneously with the 'Long Strad,' he made violins in 1691 and 1692 of still larger proportions, by combining extreme breadth with the utmost length of the long pattern. The dimensions of a typical 'Long Strad' of 1690 will be found recorded in Messrs. Hills' Appendix to their work already mentioned.

During the years following 1684 the varnish upon Stradivari's violins became gradually deeper in colour, and, as on the 'Long Strads,' it is of a rich hue of amber and light red. Until 1698 Stradivari adopted the 'long pattern' almost entirely, then came a return to the proportions which preceded the year 1690, and we get violins of about 14 inches in length, with widths similar to those of the 'Long Strad,' but with outlines more curved, corners longer, body fuller, and a whole of more harmonious appearance. It is interesting to note before leaving this period that the backs of the 'Long Strads' are nearly always cut in one piece ; that the model is rather flat, but sloping gracefully from the centre to the purfling ; that the ff holes, to fall in with the general design, are set rather upright, nearer together, and more open ; the pine is fine grained, the mitres square, and the exquisitely carved scrolls are proportionately long.

With the year 1700 dawned the finest decade of the great Cremona master's greatest period. Slowly but surely he discarded the Amati tradition which had again asserted itself in 1698 and continued to a certain extent until about 1702. We find him still adhering to the 14-inch length, but broadening, developing, and arching the model, until it assumes an unsurpassable grandeur and symmetry. His years of experiment have resulted in a neatly compacted instrument, with light edges, accurate corners, round arching, broadly treated but exquisitely graceful sound-holes and scroll, and a varnish soft in texture, which shades deliciously from orange to red. From 1703 until about 1709, the year of those famous violins 'La Pucelle' and the 'Viotti,' Stradivari seems to have settled upon certain points of construction, from which he rarely departed afterwards. A slight variation of curve is observable, but the main features and general dimensions agree with one another. Then followed years of indecision, in which no consistency of plan is to be traced, and until the end of his career, some minute changes of thickness, width, or length, characterise his work. Yet, in spite of these diversities, the years following 1710 undoubtedly mark the production of some of his finest instruments. In 1711 he made the fine violin known as the 'Parke'; in 1713, the 'Boissier' belonging to Sarasate; in 1714 the 'Dolphin'; in 1715 the 'Gillot' and the 'Alard,' which experts look upon as the master's finest creation; and in 1716 came the 'Messiah.' These years also mark the production of some of his grandest violoncellos, such as the 'Duport,' 1711; the 'Batta,' 1714; and —the most superb of all—the 'Piatti' in 1720. All of these are instruments of smaller proportions (about 29½ inches long) than those he made anterior to the years following 1700, which kept to the dimensions of his contemporaries. That Stradivari did not occupy himself with the proportions of the violoncello, as he did with those of the violin, is hardly to be wondered at, seeing that the capacities of the violoncello were hardly understood in his day. It was not until the latter years of his life that such artists as Franciscello employed it as a solo instrument, and Stradivari—with his usual quick responsiveness to the demands of artistic appreciation—gradually modified the proportions of his instruments from about 31½ inches to about 29½ inches in length, as the progressing technique of the contemporary *virtuosi* exacted a diminution in size.

His violas bear a more distinctive stamp of his creative genius than do his violoncellos. The changes so apparent in his violins are quite as evident in these larger instruments, and the models marked 'TV' and CV' preserved in the Dalla Valle collection evidence that he made these in two sizes, *i.e.* 'Tenor Viola' and 'Contralto Viola.' Before 1690 the influence of the Brescian school, and of the Amatis, still ruled the proportions of his violas, but after that year he adopted a smaller model—about 16₁⁵₆ in length—and to this he mainly adhered. These three members of the string quartet seem to have occupied Stradivari's attention almost exclusively. No authentic double basses or any designs for the same have as yet come to light, and with the exceptions of the remains of a viola-da-gamba, a kit,—now in the Musée of the Paris Conservatoire,—two handsome guitars, dating from the early years of his career, and the head of a third, it may be said with truth that Stradivari's fame rests entirely upon his violins, violas, and violoncellos. His principles of construction are analysed in detail in the work already quoted.

Stradivari's methods have been preserved from century to century, until they have become the fundamental basis of the art of violin-making. No detail of his work was too unimportant for the master's vigilant observation. That he personally designed the pegs, finger-boards, tail-pieces, inlaid patterns, bridges, and even the minutest details of his violin cases, is attested to by the numerous drawings of these in the Dalla Valle collection, while the several sketches for bow-tips and nuts reveal the interesting fact that he also made bows. His material, as already stated, was not always of the finest, owing to the restriction of limited funds during the early part of his career. However, it may be said that in the classification of the relative importance of the various factors required to make a perfect violin, material and dimensions are subservient to varnish, and it was in the application of this that Stradivari surpassed his contemporaries, rather than in the discovery of any new compound for the same. Generally speaking, the so-called 'Lost Cremona Varnish' was, in the writer's opinion, no secret in Stradivari's lifetime, but the common property of the luthiers of the day who compounded it from the materials used by the great painters of the epoch. Space will not admit of our discussing the many theories put forth regarding the component parts which constituted this varnish. Suffice it to state here, that in the opinion of the writer—an opinion which, it must be said, is controverted with some skill by Messrs. Hill—the late Charles Reade's hypothesis of an oil varnish over a spirit varnish is the most fundamentally correct solution of Stradivari's varnishing (vide *Readiana* and the *Pall Mall Gazette*, Letters, 1872). The exigencies of time-limits which have brought a demand for quick-drying varnishes in modern times sounded the death-knell of the brilliant, tender, transparent varnish of the Cremona School, so that the world has been forced to acknowledge that it is now a mere memory. Stradivari's own recipe was inscribed on the fly-leaf of a family Bible, but his descendant Giacomo Stradivari destroyed this, though it is said that he kept a copy of it which he carefully preserved for any future members of the family who might adopt the profession of their illustrious ancestor Antonio Stradivari.

Synopsis of the most Noticeable Violins, etc., made by Antonio Stradivari.—According to Messrs. Hills' careful calculations Stradivari made 1116 instruments between the years 1666 and 1737 ; of these, 540 violins, twelve violas, and fifty violoncellos are actually known to them to-day, whilst they have traces (unconfirmed) of over one hundred more. The earliest dated instruments seen by them are of the years 1666, 1667, and 1669. Count Cozio di Salabue states, however, that Stradivari was working and inserting his own labels in 1659. The following are the names of some of Stradivari's most noticeable violins : The 'Hellier,' 1679 ; the 'Sellière,' made between 1666 and 1680 ; the 'Tuscan,' 1690 (see MOSEL) ; the 'Betts,' 1704 ; the 'Ernst,' 1709 (presented to Lady Hallé by Earl Dudley and others) ; 'La Pucelle,' 1709 ; the 'Viotti,' 1709 ; the 'Vieuxtemps,' 1710 ; the 'Parke,' 1711 ; the 'Boissier,' 1713 ; the 'Dolphin,' 1714 (so named from its iridescent varnish) ; the 'Gillot,' 1715 ; the 'Alard,' 1715 ; the 'Cessol,' 1716 ; the 'Messie,' 1716 (preserved in Count Cozio di Salabue's collection for fifty years without being played on ; hidden by Luigi Tarisio for thirty years in an isolated farm near the village of Fontenato, Italy ; purchased by Vuillaume when Tarisio died in 1854 ; preserved by him in a glass case in his shop ; sold to Mr. E. Crawford, an enthusiastic musical amateur, for £2000, and now the property of Messrs. William Hill). The 'Sasserno,' 1717 ; the 'Maurin,' 1718 ; the 'Lauterbach,' 1719 ; the 'Blunt,' 1721 ; the 'Sarasate,' 1724 ; the 'Rode,' 1722 ; the 'Deurbroucq,' 1727 ; the 'Kiesewetter,' 1731 ; the 'Habeneck,' 1736 ; the 'Muntz,' 1736 (both of these show the shaky hand of the veteran master).

Violas : The 'Tuscan,' 1690, preserved in the Municipal Institute, Florence—it bears Stradivari's monogram stamped on the mortice of the neck, the original finger-board, tail-piece, tail-nut, and bridge ; two violas, 1696, belonging to the quintet of inlaid instruments for some years owned by King Philip IV. of Spain ; the 'Archinto,' 1696 (named after Count Archinto who owned a Quartet of Strads) ; the 'Macdonald,' 1701 ; Paganini's viola, 1731, which inspired Berlioz to write his symphony 'Harold in Italy.'

Violoncellos : The 'Archinto,' 1689 ; the 'Tuscan,' 1690 ; the 'Aylesford,' 1696 ; the 'Cristiani,' 1700 ; the 'Servais,' 1701 ; the 'Gore-Booth,' 1710 ; the 'Duport,' 1711 ; the 'Adam,' 1713 ; the 'Batta,' 1714 ; the 'Piatti,' 1720 ; the 'Baudiot' and 'Gallay,' 1725, comprise some of the finest instruments made by Stradivari (see also QUARTETS OF INSTRUMENTS).

Bibliography.—Alfonso Mandelli, *Nuove In-*

dagini su Antonio Stradivari ; W., A. F., & A. Hill, *Antonio Stradivari* ; Vincenzo Lancetti, *Biografica Cremonese* ; Carl Schulze, *Stradivari's Geheimniss* ; Horace Petherick, *Antonio Stradivari* ; Federico Sacchi, *Gli instrumenti di Stradivari* (*Estratto della Gazzetta Musicale*), Milano, anno 1892 ; Edouard Roche, *Stradivarius* ; Juliet von Lepel Guitz (*née* Buchanan-Austin), *Ein Stradivarius* ; Anonymous (*Enrico Stradivari*), *Cenni sulla celebre scuola Cremonese*, Cremona, 1872 ; F. J. Fétis, *Antonio Stradivari Luthier célèbre*, Paris, 1856 (English translation by John Bishop, London, 1864) ; H. R. Haweis, *My Musical Life*, pp. 314-328, *Stradivarius of Cremona, his House* ; C. Reade, *Cremona Violins* (vide *Readiana*) ; Anon., *A Short Account of a Violin by Stradivari dated 1690* ; W. E. Hill & Sons, *The Tuscan Strad* ; E. J. Payne, *The Violins of Stradivari*, pp. 202-4 ; *Musical Standard*, vol. xxxiv., London, 1888 ; Giovanni di Piccolellis, *Liutai Antichi e Moderni* ; Jules Gallay, *Les Luthiers Italiens aux XVII et XVIII Siècle*, Paris, 1869 (only 500 copies printed) ; Jules Gallay, *Les Instruments des Ecoles Italiennes* ; Richard G. White, *Antonius Stradivarius* (*The Atlantic Monthly*), Boston, vol. xlv. p. 253, 1880 ; *The Stradivarius case at the Violin Loan Exhibition* (*Musical Star*), Edinburgh (secular), No. 167, July 1885 ; J. M. Fleming, *The Stradivarius Violin, the Emperor*, London, 1891 ; Joseph Pearce (jun.), *Violins and Violinmakers* ; A. Vidal, *Les Instruments à Archet* ; G. Hart, *The Violin* ; *The Salabue Strad* (the Messie), W. E. Hill & Sons, London, 1891 ; Louis Perrard, *Le violon, son Histoire* ; Von Lutgendorff, *Die Geigen- und Lautenmacher* ; George Eliot, 'Stradivari' (poem) ; Longfellow, *Tales of a Wayside Inn* ; Robert Fissore, *Les Maîtres Luthiers.*   E. H-A.

STRADIVARI, FRANCESCO and OMOBONO, sons of the above by his first wife, *née* Francesca Feraboschi. Francesco was born at Cremona on Feb. 1, 1671 ; died May 11, 1743 ; and Omobono was also born at Cremona on Nov. 14, 1679 ; died June 8, 1742. Both were interred in the Villani vault. They were the only members of Stradivari's family who embraced their father's profession, and although their work is not without merit, their brilliant and long-lived father entirely eclipsed them. During the latter years of Stradivari's life there is little doubt that they assisted him, probably in conjunction with Carlo Bergonzi, in constructing his violins. This would account for those specimens of the great master's work that frequently give rise to controversy. But for the hand of the vandal these 'doubtful' instruments would bear the label 'sotto la disciplina d'Antonio Stradivari,' by which inscription he distinguished the instruments made in co-operation with his sons. These tickets have, however, in almost every case, been removed, and fresh ones, bearing Antonio Stradivari's name alone, inserted. Of the two brothers, Francesco was the better *luthier*. His work is not without originality, the outline of his *ff* holes in particular differing greatly from that of his father. A picture of one of his violas is included in Mr. George Hart's *The Violin*.　　E. H-A.

STRAIGHT & SKILLERN, a firm of London music-publishers. Thomas Straight and Thomas Skillern were established in Great Russell Street, Covent Garden, and issued a set of Country Dances for 1768. On the death of James Oswald about 1769, they appear to have taken over his business at 17 St. Martin's Lane, and to have reissued some of the Oswald publications, in some instances in conjunction with William Randall. About 1777 or 1778, Thomas Straight either died or gave up business, and Skillern was left alone at 17 St. Martin's Lane, where he remained until about 1799 or 1800, at which time his death occurred, his plates and stock-in-trade being bought by Preston. Skillern's son (presumably) now went into partnership with Challoner (evidently Neville Butler Challoner, the harpist) at 25 Greek Street ; they afterwards, *circa* 1815, were near the corner of Regent Street and Oxford Street.

Thomas Straight, jun., after his father's death, set up a music-business at 138 St. Martin's Lane, removing about 1796, and apparently devoting himself to music-engraving solely, at 7 Lambeth Walk. Another address of the same or another Straight is 4 Green Street, Leicester Square. F.K.

STRAKOSCH, MAURICE and MAX, brothers well known in the United States as *entrepreneurs* of operatic and concert ventures.

Maurice Strakosch, the elder of the two, was born at Lemberg in Moravia in 1825 (Baker's *Dict.*), or 1823 (*Mus. World*). He studied at the Vienna Conservatorium, and from 1845 to 1860 lived in the United States, first as a teacher and then as an impresario. After Rossini's death he gave performances of the ' Messe Solennelle ' at the Salle Ventadour, Paris, where he organised a successful opera season in 1873-74. He was European agent for his sister-in-law, Mme. Patti, from her début in 1859 until her marriage, and also for many other distinguished singers. He joined his brother in management of the Apollo Theatre in Rome in 1884-85. In 1887 he published a volume of memoirs, and died suddenly, Oct. 9, of the same year. His younger brother, MAX, remained in America, when Maurice went to Europe, and managed in his stead. He directed many successful enterprises of Italian opera, managed the Apollo Theatre, in Rome, with his brother in 1884-85, and died in New York, March 17, 1892. A. C.

STRALOCH MS., a famous MS. collection of airs written in lute tablature, for Robert Gordon of Straloch, and dated 1627 and 1629. The MS. was in small oblong octavo of ninety-two leaves, and was entitled, ' An playing Booke

for the Lute. Where in ar contained many cvrrents and other mvsical things. . . . At Aberdein. Notted and Collected by Robert Gordon [Sir Robert Gordon of Straloch]. In the year of our Lord 1627. In Februarie.' On the back of the title was a sketch of a person playing on the lute.

It was given, in 1781, by Dr. George Skene of Aberdeen, to Dr. Burney, who does not appear to have mentioned it or to have made any use of it. It afterwards came into the possession of Mr. James Chalmers of London, at the sale of whose effects it disappeared. In 1839 it was lent to George Farquhar Graham, who made some extracts from it. Graham's original transcript was in the library of the late T. W. Taphouse of Oxford, and was sold in 1905. A fair copy was made by Graham, and deposited in the Advocates' Library, Edinburgh ; other copies, too, have been made from the original transcript, one by the present writer. Though the Straloch appears to be the earliest MS. containing Scottish airs, yet the list of contents (see *Gentleman's Magazine*, February 1823) shows how small a proportion they bear to the English and foreign airs.　　F. K.

STRANIERA, LA (The Stranger). Italian opera in two acts ; libretto by Romani, music by Bellini. Produced at the Scala, Milan, Feb. 14, 1829. In London at the King's Theatre, June 23, 1832, for Tamburini's début.　　G.

STRATHSPEY, a Scottish dance, closely allied to the Reel, derives its name from the strath or valley of the Spey, in the North of Scotland, where it appears to have first been danced. The word does not appear in connection with music till late in the 18th century, but much earlier than that tunes are found suited for the style. Though slower in time than the Reel, the Strathspey calls for more exertion. The former is a gliding dance, while the Strathspey abounds in those jerky motions which call every muscle into play. Thus the music of the Reel is composed of a series of passages of equal quavers, while the Strathspey consists of dotted notes and semiquavers. The latter frequently precede the long note, and this peculiarity has received the name of the ' Scotch snap.' That the two words were formerly almost synonymous, is shown by a volume which is still of the highest authority and of which the title-page runs thus—' A Collection of Strathspeys or Old Highland Reells, with a Bass for the Violincello, Harpsichord, or Pianoforte. By Angus Cumming, at Granton. Strathspey. 1780.' The word Strathspey is here printed in very large letters, while ' Old Highland Reells ' are in the smallest. Moreover, throughout the volume, the word Strathspey is not once used, but always *Reell So-and-so*. No. 5, for example, though clearly a Strathspey, is entitled ' Acharnae Reell.' Reels, and the dance music of Scotland generally, have been

2 z

already noticed.   (See REEL and SCOTTISH
MUSIC.) Something, however, may be said in
regard to Strathspeys specially.   One point of
difference between them and the Reel is in the
tempi of the two ; in the Reel ♩= 126 Maelzel,
in the Strathspey ♩= 94. Another is the smoothness of the notes in the Reel as compared with
the broken notes of the Strathspey.

REEL.   Clydeside Lasses.

It will be seen that in the above all is written
in smooth notes, while the Strathspey consists
almost entirely of broken ones.

STRATHSPEY.   Tullochgorum.

With the Reels and Strathspeys of Scotland
the name of Gow is indissolubly associated.
Niel Gow, the founder of the family, was a man
of strong original genius and admittedly the
greatest player on the fiddle of Scottish dance-
music.   In a short notice of him (published in
the *Scots Magazine*, 1809), Dr. M'Knight, who
had frequently heard him play, and who was
himself a famous fiddler, thus describes his style
of execution : ' His bow-hand as a suitable instrument of his genius was uncommonly powerful ; and when the note produced by the *up-bow*
was often feeble and indistinct in other hands,
it was struck in his playing with a strength and
certainty which never failed to surprise and
delight skilful hearers. . . . We may add the
effect of the *sudden shout* with which he frequently accompanied his playing in the quick
tunes, and which seemed instantly to *electrify*
the dancers, inspiring them with new life
and energy, and rousing the spirits of the most
inanimate.'

Burns wrote some of his finest verses to Strathspeys.   Thus in ' Rothiemurchus' Rant,' the
first part of the tune is almost note for note that
of the Strathspey ; the second part has been
altered so as to make the music more vocal in
its character, the original being strictly instrumental music, with difficulties which the voice
could not well overcome.

Another fine specimen is ' Green grow the
Rashes O' ; an early version of this tune is in the
STRALOCH MS.   It was styled ' a daunce ' then,
as it was later, but has none of the dotted notes
so characteristic of the Strathspey.   In the
' Collection of Original Scotch Tunes,' published
by H. Playford, 1700, there are a few Reel
tunes in addition to the large number of Scotch
measures which it contains.   One called ' Cron-
stoune ' is a very good specimen of the Reel,
whether quick or slow.   Another entitled ' The
Birks of Plunketty ' is a good Strathspey, but

has been written down in 3-4 time by some one
who did not understand the measure.   Another,
' The Cummers (Commères) of Largo,' is styled
a Reel ; being in 9-8 time we should now term
it a Jig.

Many other specimens could be given, but the
above may suffice for our present purpose. T. L. S.

STRAUS, LUDWIG, an excellent violin-
player, was born at Pressburg, March 28,
1835 ; entered the Vienna Conservatorium in
1843, and remained there till the revolution
in 1848 ; was pupil of Böhm for the violin,
and Preyer and Nottebohm for counterpoint ;
made his first appearance (at the same time
with Fräulein Csillag) in a concert at the hall
of the Musikverein, Vienna, in June 1850.
During the next few years he made various
public appearances, besides playing in the
private concerts of several patrons of music,
especially Ober-Finanzrath Baron von Heintl,
at whose réunions he played second fiddle to
Mayseder for three years.   At the Mozart
Centenary Festival in 1856 he met Liszt, and
like many other young artists benefited by his
kindness.   Straus's first concert tour was made
in 1855, and extended as far as Venice and
Florence.   In 1857 he made the acquaintance
of Piatti, with whom he took a second tour
through Germany and Sweden.   In 1860 he
was appointed concertmeister of the theatre
(till 1862) and of the Museum-concerts in
Frankfort (till 1864), giving also quartet concerts, and leading the subscription concerts in
the neighbouring towns.   In 1860 he first visited
England, played at the Musical Union, June 5,
etc., and at the Monday Popular Concert of
June 18.   In 1861 he returned, and appeared
twice at the Philharmonic, April 29 and June
24.

In 1864 he took up his residence in England, settling after a time in Manchester,
where he was leader of Hallé's orchestra.   But
he often visited London, to take either first
fiddle or viola in the Popular Concerts, or to
play solos at the Crystal Palace or the Philharmonic ; during his residence in England he
played at Dresden, Vienna, etc.   Straus was a
member of the Queen's private band, and ' Solo
Violinist ' to Queen Victoria.   [In 1888 he
resigned the leadership of the Hallé orchestra,
and settled altogether in London.   In 1893 he
gave up all active work, being crippled with
arthritis ; he went to live at Cambridge,
where, a short time after his retirement, his
many friends and admirers presented him with
a fine Stradivarius violin.   He died there
Oct. 23 (not 15th as Riemann states), 1899,
retaining to the last his wide interest in the
best music, and endearing himself to a large
circle of friends by his modesty, artistic integrity, and splendid musicianship.]　　G.

STRAUSS, JOHANN, composer of dance-music
of world-wide celebrity, born in Vienna, March

14, 1804. As a child he showed talent for music, and a love for the violin, but his parents, small innkeepers, apprenticed him to a bookbinder, from whom he ran away. A friend met him, took him back, and persuaded the parents to entrust him with the boy's education as a musician. With the son of this benefactor the little Strauss learnt the violin from Polyschansky, afterwards studying harmony and instrumentation with Seyfried. He soon played the viola in string-quartets at private houses, and at fifteen entered Pamer's orchestra at the 'Sperl,' a favourite place of amusement in the Leopoldstadt. At that time the excellent playing of Lanner and the brothers Drahanek was exciting attention ; Strauss offered himself, and was accepted as fourth in the little band. Soon, however, their numbers had to be increased to meet their numerous engagements, and Strauss acted as deputy-conductor till 1825, when he and Lanner parted. In the Carnival of 1826 Strauss and his little orchestra of fourteen performers appeared in the hall of the 'Swan' in the Rossau suburb, and took the hearts of the people by storm. His op. 1, the 'Täuberl-Walzer' (Haslinger), was speedily followed by others, the most successful being the 'Kattenbrücken-Walzer,' called after the Hall of that name. Strauss was next invited to return with his now enlarged orchestra to the 'Sperl,' and with such success as to induce the proprietor, Scherzer, to engage him for six years, which virtually founded the reputation of the 'Sperl' and its orchestral conductor. Meantime Strauss was appointed Capellmeister of the first Bürger-regiment, and entrusted with the music at the court fêtes and balls. As his band was daily in request at several places at once, he increased the number to over 200, from which he formed a select body for playing at concerts, in music of the highest class. He now began to make tours in the provinces and abroad, visiting Pesth in 1833 ; Berlin, Leipzig, and Dresden in 1834 ; West Germany in 1835 ; and North Germany, Holland, Belgium, and the Rhine, in 1836. His next tour began in Oct. 1837, and embraced Strasburg, Paris, Rouen, Havre, Belgium, London, and the larger towns of Great Britain ; he then returned to Belgium, and back to England and Scotland. His success in Paris was unprecedented, notwithstanding the formidable rivalry of Musard and Dufresne, with the former of whom he wisely joined for a series of thirty concerts. A disagreeable intrigue nearly made him throw up the journey to England, but it was only there that his profits at all remunerated him for his enormous expenses. In London he played at seventy-two concerts, and at innumerable balls and fêtes given in honour of the Queen's coronation (June 28, 1838). On his second visit he had great difficulty in keeping his band from dispersing, so weary were they of continual travelling.

He managed, however, to go again to Birmingham, Liverpool, and Dublin, besides visiting Reading, Cheltenham, Worcester, Leicester, Derby, Nottingham, and Sheffield. At Sheffield his receipts were small, and at Halifax still less, but when the amateurs of both places discovered the kind of musician they had been neglecting, a deputation was sent with post-horses to Leeds to bring him back again. He was taken ill at Derby, and only reached Vienna with great difficulty in Dec. 1838. His first reappearance at the 'Sperl' was quite a popular fête. On May 5, 1840, he conducted for the first time in the Imperial Volksgarten, which was crowded whenever his band performed. Strauss now introduced the quadrille, which he had studied in Paris, in place of the galop. His first work of the kind was the 'Wiener Carneval-Quadrille' (op. 124). Henceforward, except waltzes—among which the 'Donaulieder' (op. 127) are still played—he composed only quadrilles, polkas, and marches, including the favourite 'Radetzky-March.' On April 16, 1843, he and the band of his old Bürger-regiment accompanied the body of his old colleague Lanner to the grave. An excursion to Olmütz, Troppau, etc., in the autumn of 1844, was succeeded in the next autumn by one to Dresden, Magdeburg, and Berlin, where he was immensely fêted. The king appeared in person at Kroll's Garden, and invited Strauss to play at the palace. The Prince of Prussia, afterwards the Emperor William I., ordered a performance at Kroll's by more than 200 bandsmen, conducted by the Capellmeister General Wipprecht, before Strauss and his orchestra, when the royal princes, the generals, and the pick of the nobility, attended. On his departure a grand torchlight procession and serenade were given in his honour. On his return to Vienna he was made conductor of the court balls. In the autumn of 1846 he went to Silesia, and the year following again to Berlin and Hamburg, where he revenged himself for some slights caused by professional jealousy by giving a concert for the poor. He returned to Vienna by Hanover, Magdeburg, and Berlin. During the stormy days of March 1848 he did homage to the spirit of the times in the titles of his pieces, but Strauss was at heart a Viennese of the olden time, a fact which caused him much unpleasantness on his next tour, in 1849, by Munich, Stuttgart, Frankfort, and the Rhine, Brussels, and England. He stayed in London and the provinces from April to July. After a brilliant farewell-concert he was accompanied down the Thames by a fleet of boats, one of which contained a band playing the popular air, 'So leb' denn wohl du stilles Haus,' from Raimund's 'Verschwender.' In the midst of this gay scene poor Strauss was oppressed with a presentiment that he should never revisit London. Shortly after his return to Vienna he was taken ill with scarlet fever, to which he succumbed on the fourth day, Sept. 25, 1849. With him departed a feature of Viennese life, and that the people themselves felt this was shown by the vast concourse at his funeral. A Requiem was performed in his honour on Oct. 11 by his own band, and the Männergesangverein of Vienna, the solos being sung by Mesdames Hasselt and Ernst, Aloys Ander and Staudigl, all from the court opera. Strauss married, in 1824, Anna Streim, daughter of an innkeeper, who bore him five children, Johann, Joseph, Eduard, Anna, and Therese. They separated after eighteen years, on the ground of incompatibility of temper. There are numerous portraits from which an idea can be gathered of Strauss's personal appearance. Though small he was well made and distinguished-looking, with a singularly formed head. His dress was always neat and well chosen. Though lively in company he was naturally rather silent. From the moment he took his violin in his hand he became another man, his whole being seeming to expand with the sounds he drew from it.

As an artist he furnished many pleasant hours to thousands, and high and low combined to do him honour, while great masters like Mendelssohn, Meyerbeer, and Cherubini, acknowledged his talent. He raised dance-music to a higher level than it had ever reached before, and invested his copious melodies with all the charm of brilliant instrumentation. Full of fire, life, and boisterous merriment, they contrasted well with Lanner's softer and more sentimental airs, and must be judged by a totally different standard from that of mere dance-music. As a conductor it was his constant endeavour to mingle classical names in his programmes, and thus to exercise an elevating influence on the masses. His works, published almost entirely by Haslinger, number 251, and comprise 152 waltzes, 24 galops, 6 cotillons and contredanses, 32 quadrilles, 13 polkas, and 18 marches, including some without opus-numbers. The bulk of these have made, so to speak, the tour of the world ; each new waltz was in its way an event, not only in Vienna, but wherever the first printed copies penetrated. Innumerable pens, including those of poets, celebrated his works, and the stage itself took part in the general homage, ' Strauss and Lanner ' being the title of a one-act comedy by Töpfer, and a three-act piece by Anton Langer. [His complete works were published in 1889 by Breitkopf & Härtel, in seven volumes.]

Of his three sons, the eldest, JOHANN, scarcely less gifted than his father, was born in Vienna, Oct. 25, 1825. In accordance with the father's wish that none of his sons should adopt his own line of life, Johann, after finishing his education at the Gymnasium and Polytechnic Institute, became a clerk in the savings bank, although he had, with his mother's help, long taken lessons in secret on the violin, and even studied composition with Drechsler. When only six

he composed, at Salmannsdorf near Vienna, where the family used to spend the summer, his first waltz, which was performed on his fiftieth birthday as ' Erster Gedanke.' The constraint put upon him became at length unbearable, and on Oct. 15, 1844, he first appeared as a conductor at Dommayer's, at Hietzing, playing compositions of his own, and his father's 'Loreley Walzer.' His success on that occasion decided his future career. After his father's death he incorporated the two bands, and made a tour to the country towns of Austria, Warsaw, and the more important towns of Germany. He also undertook for ten years the direction of the summer concerts in the Petropaulowski Park at St. Petersburg. On August 28, 1862, he married the popular singer Henriette (' Jetty ') Treffz, and in 1863 became conductor of the court balls. This post he resigned after his brilliant success on the stage, but he had in the meantime composed nearly 400 waltzes, of as high a type as those of his father. His music is penetrated with Viennese gaiety and spirit, and has made its way into all countries. The waltz, 'An der schönen blauen Donau ' (op. 314), became a kind of musical watchword in Vienna, and was played on all festive occasions. ['Tausend und eine Nacht,' ' Man lebt nur einmal,' ' Wiener Blut,' and ' Künstlerleben ' are among the most famous.] Besides Russia, Strauss visited Paris (during the Exhibition of 1867), London, New York, Boston, and the larger towns of Italy. The Theatre 'an der Wien' was the scene of his triumphs as a composer of operettas, which rapidly spread to all the theatres, large and small. ' Indigo und die vierzig Räuber' (his first, 1871), ' Der Karneval in Rom' (1873), ' Die Fledermaus' (1874), 'Cagliostro' (1875), 'Prinz Methusalem' (1877), ' Blindekuh ' (1878), ' Das Spitzentuch der Königin' (1880), ' Der lustige Krieg' (1881), ' Eine Nacht in Venedig' (1883), ' Der Zigeunerbaron' (1885), 'Simplicius' (1887), 'Ritter Pasman' (1892), ' Fürstin Ninetta' (1893), ' Jabuka' (1894), ' Waldmeister' (1895), and ' Die Göttin der Vernunft ' (1897), all published by Spina, were soon known all over the world, and were sung everywhere. Posthumously produced were a ballet ' Aschenbrödel' and an orchestral piece 'Traumbilder.' He died in Vienna, June 3, 1899. A biography by R. von Prochâzka is in Reimann's series of Berühmte Musiker. (See Riemann's Lexikon.) After the death of his wife on April 8, 1878, he married another dramatic singer, Angelica Dittrich.

His next brother, JOSEPH, born August 22, 1827, in Vienna, was also obliged to accommodate himself to his father's wishes, and became an architect. He had, however, studied music in secret, and during an illness of his brother's in 1853 he conducted for him with a bâton, as he did not learn the violin till later. He next collected a band, began to compose,

and published in rapid succession 283 works
(Haslinger and Spina) not less popular than
those of his brother. He had always been
delicate, and the excitement incidental to his
calling increased the mischief year by year. A
visit to Warsaw in 1870, against the wish of
his friends, was very disastrous. Some Russian
officers, having sent for him in the middle of
the night to play for them, so shamefully ill-
treated him for his refusal that he had to take
to his bed. Under the devoted nursing of his
wife (married in 1857) he rallied sufficiently to
return to Vienna, but sank a few days afterwards, July 22, 1870.

The youngest of his brothers, EDUARD, was
born at Vienna, Feb. 14, 1835, and educated
at the Schotten and Akademien Gymnasiums.
His father having died before he grew up he
devoted himself entirely to music, learnt the
harp, and studied composition with Preyer.
In 1862 he made his first appearance as a conductor in the Dianasaal, and was well received
for his father's sake. In 1865 he took his
brother Johann's place at the concerts in St.
Petersburg, and in 1870 became conductor of
the court balls. He and his band have made
repeated tours to Dresden, Leipzig, Breslau,
Berlin, Hamburg, Frankfort, etc. He appeared
regularly in Vienna on fixed days at the Volksgarten, and in the winter in the large hall of
the Musikverein, when his programmes were
always attractive. He composed over 200
pieces of dance-music, published by Haslinger,
and latterly, with few exceptions, by Spina
(Schreiber). Fduard Strauss married in 1863.
[In 1885 his orchestra was engaged at the
Inventions Exhibition in London, when the
daily concerts created a furore. He came also a
few years later and played at the Imperial
Institute.]   c. f. p.

STRAUSS, RICHARD, was born June 11,
1864, at Munich, where his father, Franz Strauss
(born Feb. 26, 1822), was first horn-player in the
Court orchestra. The boy began to play the
piano at four years old, and tried his hand at
composition from the age of six onwards. In
his schooldays he had lessons on piano and
violin, and while at the Gymnasium (1874-
1882) studied composition seriously with the
Court Capellmeister, F. W. Meyer. At school
concerts were performed a couple of choral works,
in 1880 three of his songs were sung in public,
and the Walter Quartet played his string
quartet in A in 1881, in which year Hermann
Levi performed a symphony in D minor in four
movements. Most of these childish and student
efforts are still unpublished. In 1882-83
Strauss was at the University. An unpublished
overture in C minor was played under Radecke
in Berlin, and a serenade for wind instruments at Meiningen under Bülow. Theodore Thomas performed his symphony in F
minor, op. 12, for the first time, in New York,

in Dec. 1884 ; and in 1885, on the occasion
of a visit of the Meiningen orchestra to Munich,
Bülow made him conduct his suite for thirteen
wind instruments (still unpublished), and he
came so successfully through the ordeal that he
was appointed in 1885 to succeed Bülow as sole
conductor. He had gone to Meiningen to profit
by Bülow's hints on conducting, and while there
he appeared as a pianist in the solo part of
Mozart's concerto in C minor. If Bülow fired
him with his own ardent admiration for Brahms,
to Alexander Ritter belongs the responsibility
of having turned the young composer's ideas
into the direction of the more advanced music,
in which he was destined to make such a mark.
In April 1885 he resigned the post of conductor,
and travelled in Italy for a couple of months.
In August he was appointed as third Capellmeister at Munich under Levi. In 1889 he
became assistant to Lassen at Weimar as Court
Capellmeister ; in 1892 he had a dangerous
illness caused by overwork, and went on a
journey to Greece and Egypt on his recovery ;
he returned with the completed opera of ' Guntram,' which was produced at Weimar on May
12, 1894. Later in the year he married Frl.
Pauline de Ahna, a young singer who had
created the principal part in his opera ; in the
same year he became Court Capellmeister at
Munich, and in 1899 a similar position was
conferred upon him at Berlin. In 1896-98 he
undertook extensive tours in different parts of
Europe, with the object of making known his
maturer works ; he visited London in 1897, and
in June 1903 a ' Strauss Festival' was given
in St. James's Hall, with the Amsterdam Orchestra. The composer showed himself a super-
latively fine conductor, one to whom every
detail of orchestral resources was perfectly
clear, and who possessed the power of getting
exactly what he wanted from his band. Such
are, in brief, the main facts of the career of
one who has, more effectually than any man
since Wagner, divided the musical world into
two camps.

The process of his artistic development is
very curious, for he began as a follower of the
classical ideals, and many of his earlier compositions show the influence of Brahms. In a
minute analysis of his work by Gustav Brecher
(Leipzig, 1900) no fewer than six periods are
recognised in his work, and as that division
only goes down to ' Heldenleben' we are probably justified in assuming a new period for
each of the most important subsequent compositions. But only the earlier stages can be taken
as authoritatively analysed. According to this,
opp. 1-11 represent the growth of his technical
skill in absolute music along the classical lines.
It cannot be said that the violoncello sonata or
the horn concerto contains anything that is
very striking in the way of original thought or
beautiful ideas, and even the songs of the same

period have not attained the same popularity as the composer's later lyrics, if we except 'Allerseelen,' the last of op. 10.   In the next period (opp. 12-19) the gradual transition from the classical to the modern ideal seems to be traced in the pictorial mood of the symphonic fantasia 'Aus Italien,' which of course is frankly landscape-painting in music.   The violin sonata is still absolute music, and is a favourable speci-men of the composer's early works.   When 'Aus Italien' was first given in London, at one of Henschel's Symphony Concerts, some dis-appointment was felt at the work not being played in its entirety; it only transpired later that the finale, being based on a tune which Strauss no doubt imagined to be a genuine folk-song, was scarcely suitable to be played before an audience already sated with the air, and fully aware that Signor Denza was its author. The third period embraces little beside 'Macbeth' (op. 23) and 'Don Juan' (op. 20), the latter written after the former, though provided with an earlier opus-number.   This, in the opinion of those best able to judge, represents, with 'Tod und Verklärung,' the composer's highest point so far; both are sincerely felt, and there is a famous theme in 'Don Juan' which has a distinction all too rare in the later works. 'Tod und Verklärung,' op. 24, and the opera, 'Guntram,' op. 25, make up the fourth period, for reasons which may be clear to those who have seen the opera on the stage.   There is much of Liszt's influence in the symphonic poem, and probably a good deal of Wagner's in the opera.   At this point the composer seems to have fully realised the fact that his eccen-tricities of style were a great attraction to the public, and to have considered it his duty to startle his hearers with some new piece of in-dependence (not to say impertinence) with each successive production.   The first work of the fifth period, 'Till Eulenspiegel's lustige Streiche,' op. 28, is a brilliant grotesque; and its real, if rather gruesome, humour more than excuses the realistic details, such as that of the twitching limbs of the knave after he is hung.   As a philosophical treatise, 'Also sprach Zarathustra' may be a valuable addition to the literature of the subject, and it may be a commentary on, or a confutation of, the Nietzschian doctrines that suggested it; but here we reach the vexed question of what is permissible or possible to express in terms of mere music; and the flat contradiction of one key by another at the close is a bold step in the direction of Strauss's new ideal.   In that ideal it would appear that musical beauty has no kind of place; as neither music nor mere noise is competent of itself to inform the hearers of the subject that is being illustrated, there is from hence-forth the absolute necessity for elucidatory pamphlets on the subject of each composition, and the composer's aim is apparently to do

nothing more than to follow the verbal sug-gestions of the programme, mostly by means of his wonderful command of orchestral devices of all kinds.   He is a master of the art of scoring, but though he has gone far beyond Wagner in the quantity of instruments he employs, there is this great difference, that while Wagner puts no single touch into his score that has not its place in the general audible scheme, Strauss allows very many of his effects to be entirely lost even by the most attentive ear. In many places throughout his works elaborate harp-passages are seen in the score, and the listener may watch the persevering exertions of the harpists in the orchestra; but the notes that are played on these instruments might as well be left out for any effect they produce upon the ears of the audience.   The set of orchestral variations, called 'Don Quixote,' op. 35, with which the sixth period begins, is famous for the extremely realistic bleating of sheep that is produced by orchestral means that are almost legitimate, but the introduction of a theatrical 'wind-machine' to give the effect of wind suggests that a real flock of sheep might as well be used for the effect just referred to.   With each successive work, the inevitable discussion on the legitimacy of the means employed and the composer's meaning has given fine opportunity to journa-lists and others, both admirers and detractors, to bring themselves into public notice; but each discussion has been forgotten as soon as the next work has appeared, so that there is some danger of forgetting the successive blows that the composer has administered to the old ideals of beauty, grace, and fitness. 'Ein Heldenleben,' op. 40, for example, has almost passed into the class of the things that are forgotten, since the writers on music have had the 'Sinfonia Domestica' to quarrel about; and in both of these works the use of the explanatory pamphlet has been newly demon-strated.   For as it is never stated in so many words that the pamphlet is written by authority of the composer, one class of his admirers can always say that the explanation is far-fetched and goes beyond the composer's intentions, while the others can quote it as an authori-tative explanation of the meaning of the work.   It was hotly denied, for example, that 'Ein Heldenleben' was a piece of not too modest autobiography, and in the 'Sinfonia Domestica' the usually accepted theory of the baby's toilet was ascribed by European com-mentators to the wicked ingenuity of the American critics (the work having been first performed in the United States).   But in the scores of both works, scores which can hardly lack the composer's sanction, are clear indi-cations that the accepted explanations are right in both cases.   In the former, quotations from Strauss's own earlier works are introduced and

RICHARD STRAUSS

combined with a good deal of skill of a certain kind ; and in the latter printed words occur in the score, which identify the two trumpets with aunts who remark ' Ganz der Papa ! ' and the third trombone with uncles who similarly detect a likeness to the mother. It does not greatly matter, after all, what is the exact topic of any of the symphonic poems, for the ultimate verdict on them must necessarily be based on their merits as music, since they are for choice expressed in terms of music. In this aspect the question is, not ' What poetical or prosaic idea does the music illustrate ? ' but ' Is the frequent harshness and the conspicuous and constant lack of grace in the bulk of the work compensated by any idea of such beauty that the hearer can feel he has not wasted his time ? ' About the middle of the ' Domestic Symphony ' there is a section that is sonorous and more melodious than the rest ; and as many people find it pleasant to listen to, no more need be said ; although it may perhaps be pointed out that the fondness of various distinguished conductors for these extraordinary works is admittedly caused by the interest that must always attach to a task that is especially difficult of accomplishment.

For the present it would seem as if the composer's wish to startle the frequenters of concerts were in abeyance, and he has turned his attention to the possibly harder work of shocking continental opera-goers. As his forthcoming opera, ' Elektra,' has been stated, on good authority, to contain points that will offend, or at least surprise, the most hardened admirers of ' Salomé,' there is no injustice in mentioning this as the primary object of the compositions. In the earlier one-act opera, ' Feuersnot ' (produced in Dresden in Nov. 1901), the dramatic suggestion of the libretto was followed with admirable exactitude, and the central situation lent itself to an instrumental interlude that could be considered as agreeably ' risky,' though it was musically far more conventionally melodious than any of the instrumental compositions of the same period. The author's passion for notoriety is no doubt responsible in great measure for his choice of Oscar Wilde's ' Salomé ' as the subject of an opera, but in the work as produced at Dresden, Dec. 9, 1905, and as performed on all the principal stages of Germany within a short time (six special performances were given in Paris in the following year), the expected shock came from the drama rather than from the music. For music itself cannot be prostituted to base uses, though various qualities incidental to music may be turned to the purposes of pornography. There is plenty of passion in the work, and there is no doubt that on the average hearer it produces a sense of nausea ; but it would be going too far to say that any of the music by itself would have a morally harmful influence on any one. The overture to ' Tannhäuser ' and the second act of ' Tristan ' still remain as the most vivid musical illustrations in existence of the sexual passions. The famous ' Dance of the Seven Veils ' is oddly lacking in musical attraction, but this may arise from the fact that a good chance has been lost, since the oriental dances, of which this is meant as a specimen, gain their power over the hearers' senses by their monotony of rhythm, while this dance-music halts in a kind of compromise with the ballet-music of more conventional opera. The ill-timed realism of the orchestration at the moment when the Baptist's head is cut off is thoroughly characteristic of the composer of ' Till Eulenspiegel ' ; and that he should not see the incongruity of introducing such a touch at such a moment speaks of the same want of the finer perceptions which years before led him to accept ' Funiculì, funiculà ' as a real Italian folk-song.

It is of course too soon to guess what Strauss's position among the musicians of the world may ultimately be ; while he is still young enough to admit that his main object is to shock and startle, he is not too old to change his convictions, as he has already changed them once before. There is a theory that in his later works he is merely laughing at those who profess an unbounded admiration for all he does, but this seems hardly credible, particularly in the face of some of his lyrical work, which, in spite of various rather dull choral works, like the ' Sturmlied,' ' Taillefer,' some male choruses, two anthems, etc., reach a very high level of beauty in the songs of all the various periods. The lovely ' Ständchen ' from op. 17 ; the splendid ' Heimliche Aufforderung ' from op. 27, with its irresistible swing ; ' Morgen ' from the same set, a really expressive song ; the picturesque ' Traum durch die Dämmerung ' from op. 29; ' Ich trage meine Minne ' from op. 32 ; and the characteristic ' Lied des Steinklopfers ' from op. 49, are things that appeal to every one by their musical worth and their fitness for the way in which the feeling of the words is followed. The more ambitious ' Gesang der Apollopriesterin ' and other songs with orchestral accompaniment are less remarkable, and in the incidental music to Tennyson's ' Enoch Arden ' there is not much to divert the hearer's attention from the poem.

A list of Strauss's compositions is appended :—

Op.
1. Festival March for orchestra.
2. String Quartet in A.
3. Five pieces for PF. solo.
5. PF. Sonata in B minor.
6. Sonata for PF. and Vcello.
7. Serenade for wind instruments.
8. Violin Concerto.
9. Stimmungsbilder, five pieces for PF.
10. Eight Songs.
11. Concerto for French Horn.
12. Symphony in F minor.
13. Quartet for PF. and strings.
14. Wanderers Sturmlied for 6-part choir with orchestra.
15. Five Songs.

Op.
16. Aus Italien, Symphonic Fantasia.
17. Six Songs.
18. Sonata, vln. and PF. in E flat.
19. Six Songs (' Lotosblätter ').
20. Don Juan, tone-poem for orchestra.
21. Five Songs (' Schlichte Weisen ').
22. Four Songs (' Mädchenblumen ').
23. Macbeth, tone-poem for orchestra.
24. Tod und Verklärung, tone-poem for orchestra.
25. Guntram, opera in three acts.
26. Two Songs.
27. Four Songs.
28. Till Eulenspiegel's lustige Streiche, tone-poem for orchestra.
29. Three Songs.
30. Also sprach Zarathustra, tone-poem for orchestra.
31. Four Songs.
32. Five Songs.
33 Four Songs, with orchestral accompaniment.
34. Two anthems for 16-part chorus.
35. Don Quixote.   Fantastic variations for orchestra.
36. Four Songs.
37. Six Songs.
38. Enoch Arden, melodrama (music for recitation).
39. Five Songs.
40. Ein Heldenleben, tone-poem for orchestra.
41. Five Songs.
42. Two male choruses.
43. Three Songs.
44. Two ' grössere Gesänge ' for deep voice, with orchestral accompaniment.
45. Three choruses for male voices.
46. Five Songs.
47. Five Songs.
48. Five Songs.
49. Eight Songs.
50. Feuersnot, opera in one act.
51. Das Thal, for bass voice and orchestra.
52. Taillefer, choral ballad with solos, orchestral accompaniment.
53. Symphonia (sic) Domestica, for orchestra.
54. Opera, Salomé, in one act.

WITHOUT OPUS-NUMBERS.

(See also above for early unpublished works.)

Burleske for piano and orchestra.
Soldatenlied for male chorus.
                                M.

STREET, JOSIAH.   A Yorkshire musician,
who issued ' A Book containing great variety
of Anthems in two, three, and four parts.'
London, second edition, 1746.   This was
published by Joseph Lord of Wakefield.   A
previous edition is stated to be circa 1729, but
this is probably too early.   A later one is dated
1785.   F. K.

STREICHER, JOHANN ANDREAS, a professor
of music in Vienna, and, by marriage with
Nannette Stein, the founder of the pianoforte-
making firm in that city, derived from Stein of
Augsburg, that was to become in course of time
the famous house of Streicher und Sohn.   J. A.
Streicher was born at Stuttgart, Dec. 13, 1761 ;
he was a man of education and great intelligence,
and was, moreover, distinguished by his friendship with Schiller.   He brought up his son,
JOHANN BAPTIST, who was born Jan. 3, 1796,
to the business, and long before his death,
which took place May 25, 1833, resigned it to
the son's complete control.   Johann Baptist
maintained the excellent traditions of his worthy
predecessors ; and when he died, March 28,
1871, left his son Emil the proprietor of this
historical business, the services of which in the
improvement of pianoforte construction are duly
recognised in the articles PIANOFORTE and
STEIN.   Ernst Pauer was a grandson of J. A.
Streicher and Nannette Stein, and a great-grand-
son of the object of Mozart's admiration, J. A.
Stein of Augsburg.   [See PAUER.]   A. J. H.

STREICHINSTRUMENTEN (Germ.).
Stringed Instruments, or STRINGS.

STRETTO (Ital.), literally ' close ' or ' narrow ' ;

(Germ. Engführung).   A term used in two
ways. 1. In Fugue it designates the following of response to subject at a closer interval
of time than at first.   This device is usually
employed towards the end of a fugue, so as to
give some impression of climax.   But there are
plenty of exceptions to that custom ; e.g.

BACH 48, No. 1.

which occurs close to the beginning. Some
subjects will bear more than one stretto, in
which case the closer naturally comes last ; e.g.

from the ' Amen ' chorus of Handel's ' Messiah.'
(The inner parts are omitted for the sake of
clearness.)   Still more remarkable instances
will be found in the fugue of Bach's harpsichord Toccata in D minor.   [When several
strettos occur in a fugue, the last is usually
called the Stretto maestrale.]

2. The second use of the word occurs more
especially in Italian opera, when towards the
end of a piece the time is quickened, bringing
the accents closer together.   Thus the title
might be, and sometimes is, applied to the last
prestissimo of the Choral Symphony.   It is
sometimes used, but quite wrongly, as a direction equivalent to accelerando, instead of in its
proper sense of più mosso.   F. C.

STRICT COUNTERPOINT (Lat. Contra-
punctus proprius, vel severus ; Ital. Contrappunto severo ; Contrappunto alla Cappella ; Germ.
Strenger Satz, Kapellstyl ; Fr. Contrepoint sévère).
The art of writing in parts for two or more
voices without the employment of unprepared
discords.

The term is not very well chosen.   The laws
of free part-writing are quite as severe as those
of the so-called strict style.   But the conventional application of the term ' strict ' to the
method which forbids the direct percussion of
a fundamental dissonance, and ' free ' to that
which permits it, has so long been generally
accepted, that it would be impossible now to
introduce a more exact form of terminology.

The laws of Strict Counterpoint are not open,
like those of Harmony, to scientific discussion ;

for Counterpoint is not a science but an art. It is true that its most important rules, when tested by the principles of natural science, are found to coincide with them in all essential particulars ; and to this circumstance alone are they indebted for their unassailable position and promise of future security. Their mathematical accuracy fails, however, to account for their universal acceptance as a code of artistic regulations. Their authority for this rests solely upon the praxis of the great masters of the polyphonic schools ; which praxis was from first to last purely empirical. The refined taste and musical instinct of Josquin des Prés, Willaert, Byrd, Tallis, Palestrina, and their contemporaries, rebelled against the hideous combinations demanded by the rules of Diaphonia and Organum,[1] and substituted for them the purest and most harmonious progressions that art, aided by a cultivated ear, could produce ; but in their search for these they were guided by no acoustic theory. They simply wrote what they felt ; and because the instincts of true genius can never err, that which they felt was uniformly good and true and logical, and based unconsciously upon a foundation firm enough to stand the test of modern mathematical analysis. The leaders of the monodic school rejected the teaching of these great masters ; and in their insane desire for progress, invented new forms of cacophony not a whit less rude than those practised by the Diaphonists of the 13th century. All Italy followed their baneful example, and for a time relapsed into chaos. But German musicians, unwilling to destroy the old landmarks, retained, in their full force, the timehonoured laws relating to the use of Perfect and Imperfect Concords, Syncopations, and Notes of Regular and Irregular Transition, while they extended the system by promulgating new regulations for the government of Fundamental Discords introduced without the customary forms of preparation ; and because such discords had never before been sanctioned this new method of part-writing was called ' free,' though its rules were really more numerous than those of the older one.

It was not until some considerable time after the invention of printing that the laws of Strict Counterpoint were given to the world in the form of a systematic code. Franchinus Gafurius, in his *Practica Musice* published at Milan in 1496, gave a tolerably intelligible epitome of certain rules which at that period were supposed to embody all the information that it was necessary for the student to acquire. The *Musicae activae Micrologus* of Ornithoparcus, printed at Leipzig in 1516, set forth the same laws in clearer language. The *Toscanello in Musica* of Pietro Aron, printed at Venice in 1523, and the *Dodecachordon* of

[1] See DIAPHONIA; ORGANUM; POLYPHONIA.

Glareanus (1547), were illustrated by examples of great value to the tyro, whose labours were still further assisted by the appearance of Zarlino's *Istitutioni harmoniche* in 1558, and Zacconi's *Prattica di Musica* in 1596. In 1597 Thomas Morley published his *Plaine and easie Introduction to Practicall Musicke*—the second treatise of importance in the English language ; and in 1609 John Douland printed an English paraphrase of the *Micrologus* of Ornithoparcus. These works set forth, with gradually increasing clearness, the regulations which in the 15th century had been transmitted from teacher to pupil by tradition only. The compositions of the great polyphonic masters formed a living commentary upon the collective rules ; and with an endless succession of such works within his reach the student of the period ran little risk of being led astray. But when the line of polyphonic composers came to an end, the verbal treatises, no longer illustrated by living examples, lost so much of their value that the rules were in danger of serious misconstruction, and would probably have been to a great extent forgotten, had not Fux, in his *Gradus ad Parnassum*, published at Vienna in 1725, set them forth with a systematic clearness, which, exhausting the subject, left nothing more to be desired. This invaluable treatise, founded entirely on the practice of the great masters, played so important a part in the education of the three greatest composers of the school of Vienna, Haydn, Mozart, and Beethoven, that it is impossible to overestimate its influence upon their method of part-writing. So clear are its examples, and so reasonable its arguments, that it has formed the basis of all the best treatises of later date, of which two only—Albrechtsberger's *Gründliche Anweisung zur Composition* (Leipzig, 1790), and Cherubini's *Cours de Contrepoint et de la Fugue* (Paris, 1835)—are of any real importance. These two, however, are especially valuable ; not, indeed, as substitutes for the ' Gradus,' but as commentaries upon it. For Fux treats only of strict counterpoint, and writes all his examples in the old ecclesiastical modes ; but Albrechtsberger deals both with the strict and the free styles, while Cherubini accommodates the laws of the strict style to the tonality of the modern scale, with such consummate skill, that they bear all the appearance of having been originally enacted in connection with it ; thus solving for the modern student a very difficult problem, which Haydn, Mozart, and Beethoven were left to work out for themselves.

In most important particulars these three great teachers follow the same general plan. All write their examples on Canti fermi, consisting entirely of semibreves ; all make their Canti fermi close by descending one degree upon the tonic or the final of the mode ; and all agree in dividing their exercises into five distinct classes, now known as the Five Orders of Counterpoint, the rules for which may be thus epitomised :—

GENERAL LAWS. The early Contrapuntists insist strongly upon the observance of the four following ' Cardinal Rules ' (*Regulae cardinales*).

I. One Perfect Concord may proceed to another in contrary or oblique motion, but not in similar motion.

II. A Perfect Concord may proceed to an Imperfect Concord in all the three kinds of motion.

III. An Imperfect Concord may proceed to a Perfect Concord in contrary or oblique motion, but not in similar motion.

IV. One Imperfect Concord may proceed to another in all the three kinds of motion.

The intention of these rules is to prevent the possibility of Consecutive or Hidden Fifths, Octaves, and Unisons.

FIRST ORDER (Note against note). One semibreve must be written, in each part, against each semibreve in the Canto fermo. All progressions must be purely diatonic ; the employment of chromatic intervals being utterly prohibited, both in harmony and in melody, in this and all the succeeding Orders. No discords of any kind are admissible. In two parts the only permitted intervals are the three Perfect, and the four Imperfect Concords ; *i.e.* the Unison, Octave, and Perfect Fifth ;[1] and the Major and Minor Thirds and Sixths. In three or more parts the only harmonies permitted are the Major and Minor Common Chords, and the chord of the Sixth. The chord of the 6–4 and the Augmented and Diminished Triads are prohibited ; but the First Inversion of the Diminished Triad is admissible, because none of its intervals are in dissonance with the bass. In three parts each chord should, if possible, consist of a Root, Third, and Fifth ; or a Bass-note, Third, and Sixth. In four parts the Octave should be added. But in cases of necessity any interval may be doubled or omitted. The separate parts may proceed either in conjunct movement, by Major or Minor Seconds ; or disjunctly by leaps of a Major or Minor Third, a Perfect Fourth, a Perfect Fifth, a Minor Sixth, or an Octave. All other leaps, including that of the Major Sixth, are absolutely prohibited. The first semibreve, in two-part counterpoint, must be accompanied by a Perfect Concord ; in three or more parts, one part at least must form a Perfect Concord with the bass. In the remaining semibreves, Imperfect Concords are to be preferred in two parts.

In this, and all other Orders of Counterpoint, the parts may cross each other to any extent.

[1] In Counterpoint the Perfect Fourth, when used alone, or reckoned from the Bass-note, is held to be, and treated as a Discord. When it occurs among the upper notes of a chord, the bass taking no share in its formation, it is treated as a Perfect Concord. The same rule applies to the Augmented Fourth (Tritonus) and the Diminished Fifth (Quinta falsa).

Consecutive Fifths, Octaves, and Unisons, in similar motion, are forbidden in any number of parts. In four or more parts Consecutive Fifths are permitted in contrary motion, but only as a last resource.[2] This licence, however, does not extend to Consecutive Octaves, which were far more carefully avoided by the great masters than Consecutive Fifths, even in contrary motion. But Consecutive Fifths and Octaves are only forbidden when they occur between the same two parts. When produced by different parts, or by making the parts cross each other, they are perfectly lawful. Hidden Fifths and Octaves are as strictly forbidden in two parts as real Consecutives ; but in four or more parts, as at (*d*) in Ex. 3, the great masters never troubled themselves to avoid them.[3]

The False Relation of the Tritonus (Augmented Fourth) is strictly forbidden in two parts ; but permitted in three or more. That of the Octave is forbidden, even in eight parts.

In two parts, the Unison is forbidden, except in the first and last notes. The Octave is permitted in oblique motion, and in contrary motion also, provided it be approached by separation—*i.e.* by the mutual divergence of the parts which produce it ; as at (*c*) in Ex. 2. Its employment by approximation—*i.e.* by the convergence of the parts, as at (*b*) in Ex. 2—is only permitted in the final cadence.[4]

In two-part Counterpoint of this order it is forbidden to take more than three Thirds or Sixths in succession, unless the parts be made to cross each other.

The final Cadence is formed, either by a Major Sixth followed by an Octave, as at (*c*), in Ex. 2 ; or by a Minor Third followed by an Octave, or a Unison, as at (*a*) in Ex. 1. In two parts, these intervals will complete the necessary formula. In more than two parts the same intervals must be given to the Canto fermo and one other part, while the other parts fill up the harmony, in accordance with the laws already laid down, as at (*e*) in Ex. 3. If the last chord be not naturally Major, it must be made so by an accidental Sharp or Natural.[5]

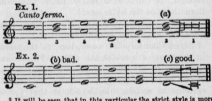

Ex. 1.
Canto fermo.   (*a*)

Ex. 2.   (*b*) bad.   (*c*) good.

[2] It will be seen that in this particular the strict style is more indulgent than the free. Palestrina constantly availed himself of the licence, especially when writing for equal voices.
[3] See HIDDEN FIFTHS AND OCTAVES, vol. ii. pp. 396, 397.
[4] The earlier writers on Counterpoint insist very strongly on the observance of this rule ; and extend its action, with even greater severity, to the unison in the few cases in which the employment of this interval is permitted. Fux (pp. 53, 54) is inclined to treat it with indulgence, provided the converging parts proceed in conjunct movement, but only on this condition. Albrechtsberger forbids the progression in two parts, but sanctions it in three. Cherubini makes no mention of the rule.
[5] For examples of Cadences in all the Ecclesiastical Modes, see MUSICA FICTA, vol. iii. pp. 330-333.

Ex. 3.

Canto fermo.

SECOND ORDER (Two notes against one). In this order two minims must be written in one of the parts against each semibreve in the Canto fermo, except the last, unless the exercise should be in triple time, in which case three minims must be written against each semi-breve.[1] The other parts must all move in semibreves. In the part which contains the minims the same note may not be struck twice in succession. The first bar should begin with a minim rest, followed by a minim in Perfect Concord. In the remaining bars the first minim must always be a Concord, Perfect or Imperfect. The second minim may be either a Concord or a Discord. If a Concord, it may proceed either in conjunct or disjunct movement.—Ex. 4 (g). If a Discord, it must be both approached and quitted in conjunct movement, and lie between two Concords. In other words it must be treated as a Passing Note.—Ex. 4 (f). The part which contains the minims is not permitted to make the leap of a Major Sixth in any circumstances; and not even that of a Minor Sixth, except as a last resource in cases of extreme difficulty.[2] Consecutive Fifths and Octaves between the first Minims of two successive bars are strictly forbidden. Between the second Minims they are tolerated, but only for the purpose of escaping from a great difficulty.

Except in the first and last bars the Unison is forbidden on the Thesis or accented part of the measure; but permitted on the Arsis or unaccented beat. The Octave on the Arsis may be used with discretion; but the Octave on the Thesis (Ital. *Ottava battuta*; Germ. *Streich-Octav*) is only permitted when approached, as in the First Order, either in oblique motion or by separation. Its employment by approximation, as in Ex. 4, bar 5, is permitted only in the final cadence.[3]

In these and all other cases the first minims of the bar are subject to the same laws as the semibreves of the First Order; and the more closely these laws are observed, the better the Counterpoint will be. If the elimination of the second minim in every bar, except the first, and the last but one, should produce good Counterpoint of the First Order, no stronger proof of excellence can be desired.

The Cadence is treated like that of the First

[1] See Fux, p. 63.
[2] See Cherubini, p. 14b of Mrs. Cowden Clarke's translation. (Novello & Co.).
[3] See footnote 4 on previous page.

Order; one of the sounds necessary to form the characteristic intervals being assigned to the Canto fermo, and the other, either to the part which contains the minims—Ex. 4 (h); Ex. 5 (i)—or to some other part written in semi-breves.

Ex. 4.

THIRD ORDER (Four notes against one). In this Order four crotchets must be written, in one of the parts, against each semibreve in the Canto fermo, except the last; the other parts moving in semibreves. The first bar should begin with a crotchet rest, followed by three crotchets, the first of which must form a Perfect Concord with the Canto fermo. The first crotchet in the succeeding bars is subject to the same laws as the first minim in the Second Order. The three remaining crotchets may form either Concords or Discords, provided that, in the latter case, they proceed in conjunct movement, and lie between two Concords; in which respect they must be treated like the unaccented minims in the Second Order.

When the second crotchet forms a Discord with the Canto fermo, in a descending passage, it may, by licence, fall a Third, and then ascend to the necessary Concord, as at (j) in Ex. 6, and (l) in Ex. 7. This very beautiful progression, though forbidden by Cherubini, is sanctioned by the universal practice of the great masters of the 16th century.[4]

The employment of the Tritonus or the False Fifth, as an interval of Melody, is forbidden, not only by leap, but even when the intervening sounds are filled in; thus, the progressions, F, G, A, B, and B, C, D, E, F, are as contrary to rule as F, B, or B, F. This law, however, is only enforced when the dissonant sounds form the limits of the passage; F, G, A, B, C, is therefore perfectly lawful. Consecutive Fifths, Octaves, and Unisons are forbidden between the first and third crotchets in the bar; between the first or third crotchets of two successive bars; and, of course, between the last crotchet of one bar, and the first of the next.

The Cadence will be formed by the Canto fermo either in conjunction with the part containing the crotchets, or with one of the parts written in semibreves, on the same principle as

[4] Fux, p. 65.

that recommended in the Second Order. Ex. 6 (*k*) ; Ex. 7 (*m*).

Ex. 6.

Canto fermo.　(*j*)　(*k*)

Ex. 7.　(*l*)　(*m*)

Canto fermo.

FOURTH ORDER (With Syncopations). In this Order one part must be written in syncopated notes ; while the others accompany the Canto fermo in semibreves.

The first bar must begin with a minim rest, followed by a minim in Perfect Concord with the Canto fermo ; which minim must be tied to the first minim in the following bar, which must always form a Concord with the lowest part Ex. 9 (*r*).

The remaining bars (except the last) will each contain two minims ; the first of which must be tied to the second minim of the preceding bar ; and the second to the first minim of the bar which follows. The tied minims, now known as Syncopations, were formerly called Ligatures.

The second or unaccented minim must always form a Concord with the Canto fermo.

The tied or accented minim may form either a Concord or a Discord with the Canto fermo. In the first case—Ex. 8 (*o*) ; Ex. 9 (*s*)—it may proceed upwards or downwards, either in conjunct or disjunct movement. In the second —Ex. 8 (*n*) ; Ex. 9 (*r*)—it must descend one degree upon a Concord, which forms its natural resolution, and may also serve to prepare a Discord in the succeeding bar, as at (*p*) in Ex. 8. In no case but that of the Ninth is it allowable to let the note into which the Discord is about to resolve be heard simultaneously with the discord itself in any other part than the Bass.

Consecutive Fifths, Octaves, and Unisons are strictly forbidden between the unaccented minims of two successive bars, which must here be guarded as strictly as the accented minims of the Second Order. Indeed, the most severe test that can be applied to this kind of Counterpoint is the excision of the first minim of every bar. If this operation should produce good Counterpoint of the First Order, nothing more can be desired.

All the diatonic discords may be used by Syncopation. But a succession of Ninths, resolving into Octaves, or of Sixths, followed by Fifths, is forbidden ; because in these cases the excision of the accented minims would produce progressions of real Fifths and Octaves.

The Cadence, formed always by the Canto fermo and the part containing the Syncopations,

will consist, either of a suspended Seventh, resolving into a Major Sixth, and followed by an Octave—Ex. 8 (*q*) ; Ex. 9 (*t*) ; or, should the Canto fermo be placed above the Syncopations of a suspended Second, resolving into a Minor Third and followed by a Unison or Octave. This Cadence was called by the old masters the Diminished Cadence, and was used at the close of almost every polyphonic composition.

Ex. 8.　(*n*)　(*o*)　(*p*)　(*q*)

Canto fermo.

Ex. 9.　(*r*)　(*s*)　(*t*)

Canto fermo.

FIFTH ORDER (Florid Counterpoint). In this Order one part will contain a judicious mixture of all the preceding Orders ; while the other parts accompany the Canto fermo in consonant semibreves.

Dotted notes, though forbidden in all other Orders, may here be introduced into the Florid part with excellent effect ; and Quavers also, if used sparingly, and with discretion, as at Ex. 10 (*v*). Tied notes are permitted, on condition that the length of the second note does not exceed that of the first. In modern passages it is sometimes convenient to use a tied note instead of a dotted one.

By a licence analogous to that mentioned with regard to the Third Order, a syncopated Discord, suspended by a tied crotchet, may descend a Third or a Fifth, and afterwards reascend to its resolution,[1] as at (*x*), in Ex. 11 ; or it may ascend a Fourth or a Second, and then redescend to the necessary Concord, as at (*v*) in Ex. 10.

A minim, preceded in the same bar by two crotchets, should always be tied to a minim, or crotchet in the succeeding bar.[2] Ex. 10 (*u*).

The Diminished Cadence—Ex. 10 (*w*)—is used in this Order as well as in the Fourth with many graceful modifications, rendered possible, as in Ex. 11 (*z*), by the employment of dotted and tied notes.[3] These modifications form part of a long list of licences, peculiar to the Fifth Order, and greatly conducing to its beauty, as in Ex. 11 (*y*), though, unfortunately, too numerous for detailed notice in our present article.

Ex. 10.　(*u*)　(*v*)　(*w*)

Canto fermo.

[1] See Fux, p. 76.　[2] *Ibid.* p. 80.　[3] *Ibid.* p. 76.

Ex. 11.

Canto fermo.

Students who have mastered all the difficulties of the Five Orders are recommended by Fux and his successors to employ two or more Orders simultaneously, in place of filling in the free parts with semibreves, and to follow up this exercise by employing the Fifth Order in all the parts except that which contains the Canto fermo.

It will be readily understood that the rules we have here endeavoured to epitomise form but a very small proportion of those laid down by Fux and his successors for the student's guidance ; more especially with regard to the Five Orders of Counterpoint in two parts, the laws of which are excessively severe. We have, in fact, confined ourselves for the most part to the regulations which serve most clearly to distinguish the Strict Style of the 16th century from the Free Part-writing of the 18th and 19th. The true value of these rules lies in the unvarying purity of the harmony produced by their observance. Obedience to their provisions renders harshness of effect impossible. It was for this reason that they were so diligently studied by the great masters of the school of Vienna ; and after them by Mendelssohn and the composers of the later period. It is true that these composers, one and all, have written exclusively in the Free Style. But we have already explained that the laws of the Free Style are not antagonistic to those of Strict Counterpoint. In their treatment of Consonant Harmonies, of Suspensions, and of Passing Notes, the laws of the two styles, as set forth in the works of the great classical writers, are absolutely identical. It is only when dealing with Chromatic Progressions, Appoggiaturas, and Unprepared Discords generally, that the Free Style supplements the older code with new enactments. And since these new enactments concern progressions altogether unknown to the Contrapuntists of the 16th century, they cannot be fairly said to oppose the earlier system. Except when entering upon new ground they neither increase nor diminish the severity of the ancient method. On the contrary, it is a well-known fact that the greatest writers in the Free Style, and the most fearless, are those who have worked hardest at Strict Counterpoint. Hence Beethoven's *bon mot* concerning the necessity for learning rules in order that one might know how to break them, so often misquoted in defence of those who break them through ignor-

[1] Licence. Fifths saved by a tied crotchet, on the authority of Palestrina. At bar 5 the tenor crosses below the bass.

ance. Hence Mendelssohn's microscopic attention to the minutest details in the lessons he gave in Free Part-writing ; and Hauptmann's determined insistence on rules, which, though mentioned by Fux, are unnoticed by Cherubini. All these accomplished musicians used Strict Counterpoint as a stepping-stone to the Free Style ; and if we would know how much the process profited them, we have only to examine Mozart's 'Zauberflöte,' Beethoven's Seventh Symphony, and Mendelssohn's 'St. Paul.' [See also the article COUNTERPOINT, vol. i. pp. 613-623.]   W. S. R.

STRIGGIO, ALESSANDRO, gentleman of Mantua, was born there about 1535. In the judgment of his contemporaries he was a cultivated musician, an organist of renown, a fine lutenist and viola-player. Bartoli (*Ragionamenti accademici*, 1567, p. 37*b*) writes that Striggio was most excellent in playing of the viola 'e far sentir in essa quatro parti a un tratto con tanta leggiadria e con tanta musica, che fa stupire gli ascoltanti,' adding that his compositions were as musical and as good as any to be heard at that time ; and Garzoni (*La piazza universale*, Venetia, 1585, p. 450) mentions among famous players of various instruments ' il Striggio passato nel lauto.' From about 1560 Striggio was at Florence, attached to the Court of Cosmo de Medici, who died 1574 ; on the title-pages of Striggio's works published in 1560, 1565-66, and 1569, he is described as ' gentilhuomo mantovano. Servitore dell' illustrissimo et eccellentissimo Cosmo de Medici, Duca di Firenze e di Siena,' but from 1570 to 1585, he is merely 'gentilhuomo mantovano' and probably was living in Mantua at this later period. He was certainly there in 1574, the bearer of a letter dated Sept. 1, 1574, in which the Emperor Maximilian II. recommends Striggio, 'a man eminent in the art of music,' to the good offices of the Duke Guglielmo of Mantua, with the result that Striggio was released from a dragging lawsuit in which he had been involved. He died in Mantua soon after, Sept. 22, 1587.

Striggio was one of the first to compose music for the Intermedii in representations at Court festivities. An interesting example and one of the earliest is *La Cofanaria, Comedia di Francesco d'Ambra, con gl' intermedii di G. B. Cini.* Firenze, 1566, written on the occasion of the marriage of Francesco de Medici with Johanna of Austria. Striggio set the first, second, and fifth intermedio to music. A copy of this work is in the British Museum ; on p. 16 a description of the music is given with a list of the instruments required, including :—

4 Gravicembali doppl.
4 Viole d' arco.
2 Tromboni.
2 Tenori di Flauti.
1 Cornetto muto.
1 Traversa.
2 Leuti, a Dolzaina, a Stortina, and a Ribechino.

In the *Dialoghi di Massimo Troiano* (Venetia,

1569), recounting the principal events in the festivities celebrated at the wedding of Wilhelm VI. of Bavaria and Renata di Loreno, mention is made (Lib. 3, p. 147) of a motet in 40 parts composed by Striggio, ' il quale fu degno d' ogni honore e laude ' ; it was written for 8 tromboni, 8 viole da arco, 8 flauti grossi, uno instrumento da penna, and un liuto grosso, the rest of the parts being supplied by voices, and was twice performed before large audiences.

In a little book published at Florence in 1579, *Feste nelle nozze del sereniss. Dom Francesco Medici, e della sereniss. Sig. Bianca Cappello, da Raffaello Gualterotti*, p. 20, there is an allusion to the ' diverse musiche, con molte voci ed infiniti strumenti ' composed by Striggio, that most excellent musician. He was also responsible for music to the first, second, and fifth intermedio in the Commedia written for the wedding of Cesare d' Este and Virginia de Medici at Florence (Bastiano de' Rossi, *Descrizione*. Firenze, 1585).

Striggio also composed a great many madrigals ; Morley in his *Plaine and easie Introduction*, 1597, p. 35, gives illustrations of various proportions in ' measured ' music from Striggio's madrigal ' All' acqua sagra ' for six voices, and also includes Striggio's name in the list of ' practitioners the moste parte of whose works we haue diligently perused, for finding the true use of the moods.' Burney scored several of the madrigals : one, ' Invidioso amor' for five voices, from the ' Secondo libro de la muse,' 1559, is in the British Museum, Add. MS. 11,583 ; and another, ' Gravi pene' from ' Madrigali a 4 voci di Cipriano e Annibale,' 1575, is in the Add. MS. 11,588. Another of his madrigals, ' Chi fara fed' al cielo ' for four voices, afterwards used by Peter Philips as a theme for a fantasia (in the Fitzwilliam Virginal Book, i. 312), is to be found rather unexpectedly in a rare book published at Frankfort in 1615, called *Les raisons des forces mouvantes avec diverses machines*, etc., par Salomon De Caus ; in the account of ' La roue musicale (un orgue mécanique)' it is the ' pièce de musique qui est posée sur ladite roue,' and the music, the four parts scored, is reproduced on the back of plate 38.

The following works by Striggio were published, some during his lifetime, others after his death by his son Alessandro :—

Di Alessandro Striggio, gentil'huomo mantovano, servitore dell' illustriss. et eccellentiss. Cosmo de Medici, Duca di Firenze e di Siena. Il primo libro de madrigali a sei voci.
(The earliest edition of this book is not known, it was reprinted in Venice by Antonio Gardano in 1560, 1565, 1569 ; and later editions were published there by Francesco Rampazetto in 1566, by Girolamo Scotto and his successors in 1566, 1578, and 1585, and by Angelo Gardano in 1579 and 1592.)
Il secondo libro de madrigali a sei voci.
(This was also reprinted in Venice, by Girolamo Scotto and his successors in 1571, 1573, 1579, and 1582, and by Angelo Gardano in 1592; the earliest edition is unknown.)
Di Alessandro Striggio, Gentil'huomo mantovano, servitore, etc. Il primo libro de madrigali a cinque voci.
(Of this work again only reprints are known, by Antonio Gardano in 1560 and in 1569, by Scotto in 1560, 1566, and 1585, and by Fr. Rampazetto, *circa* 1566.)
Il secondo libro de madrigali a cinque voci di M. Alessandro Striggio, gentil'huomo mantovano, nouamente posti in luce. In Vinegia appresso Girolamo Scotto, 1570.

(It was reissued by Scotto in 1571, 1573, 1579, and 1583.)
Il terzo libro de madrigali a cinque voci del Sig. Alessandro Striggio, etc., Venetia. Angelo Gardano, 1596.
(Dedicated to the Duke of Mantua by Striggio's son Alessandro, who in alluding to his father, writes of ' this work ' d' uno che nacque suo suddito e visse alcun tempo servitore della felice memoria del sereniss. Sig. suo Padre, che sia in gloria, e mori finalmente servendo l' A.V.')
Il quarto libro de madrigali a cinque voci, etc. Venetia. Angelo Gardano, 1596.
Il quinto libro de madrigali a 5 voci, etc. Venetia. Angelo Gardano, 1597.
(Both books edited by Striggio's son.)
Il cicalamento delle Donne al bucato et la caccia di Alessandro Striggio, Con un lamento di Didone ad Enea per la sua partenza di Cipriano Rore, a 4, 5, 6 e 7 voci. Di nouo posto in luce per Giulio Bonagionta da San Genesi, musico della illus. Signoria di Venezia in S. Marco, Vinegia. Girolamo Scotto, 1567.
(Reprinted in 1569, and again in 1584, with a slightly different title) :—
Il Cicalamento delle donne al bucato e la caccia di Alessandro Striggio a 4, 5, 6 e 7 voci, con il gioco di primiera a cinque voci del medesimo, novamente agionto.
(There is a manuscript copy in five part-books in Ch. Ch. Library. Oxford.)
Other MSS. are to be found in the libraries at
Berlin.—MS. Z, 28, date 1599, a score of ' Faciem tuam ' (' nasce la pena ') for six voices ; the same composition in MS. Z, 32, a 16th-century lute-book. (Eitner.)
Bologna.—A 1613 MS. contains four madrigals for six voices in score. (Gasperini's Cat.)
Brieg.—Imperfect copies of ' Nasce la pena.' (Kuhn's Cat.)
Brussels.—Madrigals in MS. 2289. (Fétis, *Bibl. Royale*.)
Liegnitz.—Eight madrigals for six voices. (Pfudel's Cat.)
Milan.—Conservatoire.—A mass for four voices and a mass for five voices. (Canal.)
Modena.—Bibl. palatina. A canzone with lute accompaniment.
Munich.—MS. 218, dated 1628, ' Ad nitida' (' Chi fara') for five, ' Nascitur cum dolore ' (' Nasce la pena mia') for six, ' Quae mulier' (' All' apparir') for eight voices. (Maier's Cat.)
Proske Library.—In MS. 774 and 75, thirteen madrigals. (Eitner.)
Royal College of Music.—In MS. 1881, four part-books of 17th century, ' Love hath proclaimed ' for six voices. A lute piece in MS. 1964.
Upsala.—MS. J. mus. 108, a piece in organ tablature.
Zwickau.—MS. 732, dated 1587, ' Ecce beatum lucem ' a 40 vocibus in 4 chori, Bassone canato dalle parte più basse del 40 persone. Chorus I. eight voices ; Chorus II. ten voices ; Chorus III. sixteen voices ; Chorus IV. six voices. (Vollhardt's Cat.)
About 41 of Striggio's compositions were also published at Venice in collected works, ranging from the year 1559 to 1626. Five of his madrigals are in Torchi, *Arte musicale in Italia*, vol. i. C. S.

STRIKING REED. A beating reed. One in which the vibrator or tongue strikes the face of the reed. (See REED and REEDSTOP.) T. E.

STRINASACCHI, REGINA, a distinguished violin-player, born at Ostiglia near Mantua in 1764, and educated at the Conservatorio della Pietà in Venice, and in Paris. From 1780 to 1783 she travelled through Italy, and won great admiration by her playing, her good looks, and her attractive manners. She next went to Vienna, and gave two concerts at the National Court Theatre in the Burg on March 29 and April 24, 1784. For the second of these Mozart composed a sonata in B♭ (Köchel 454), of which he wrote out the violin-part complete, but played the accompaniment himself from a few memoranda which he had dashed down on the PF. staves.[1] The Emperor Joseph, noticing from his box above the blank look of the paper on the desk, sent for Mozart and obliged him to confess the true state of the case. ' Strinasacchi plays with much taste and feeling,' writes Mozart to his father, who quite agreed with him after hearing her at Salzburg. ' Even in *symphonies*,' Leopold writes to his daughter, 'she always plays with expression, and nobody could play an Adagio more touchingly or with more feeling than she ; her whole heart and soul is in the

[1] This interesting MS. is now in the possession of Mr. F. G. Kurtz of Liverpool. Mozart filled in the complete accompaniment afterwards in an ink of slightly different colour from that which he first employed, so that the state of the MS. at the first performance can be readily seen.

melody she is executing, and her tone is both delicate and powerful.' In Vienna she learnt to appreciate the gaiety of Haydn's music, so congenial to her own character. She played his quartets before the Court at Ludwigslust, and also at Frau von Ranzow's, with peculiar naiveté and humour, and was much applauded for her delicate and expressive rendering of a solo in one of them. She is also said to have been an excellent guitar-player. She married Johann Conrad Schlick, a distinguished violoncellist in the ducal chapel at Gotha. The two travelled together, playing duets for violin and violoncello. Schlick died at Gotha in 1825, two years after the death of his wife.   C. F. P.

STRING (Fr. *Corde*; Ital. *Corda*; Germ. *Saite*). A slender length of gut, silk, or wire, stretched over raised supports called bridges, between which it is free to vibrate. When weighted to resist the drawing power or tension, the rapidity of its transverse vibrations depends upon the tension, the length, and the specific gravity of the material; and in exact ratio with this rapidity the ear is sensible of the difference of musical pitch. From the 6th century B.C. the monochord or single string, stretched over a sound-board and measured by movable bridges, has been the canon of musical intervals, the relative scale pitch. The string by itself would give but a faint tone in the surrounding air, and a sound-board is necessary to reinforce the tone, and make it sufficiently audible.

Of the materials employed for strings, silk has been much used in the East, but in European instruments gut and wire have had the constant preference. Gut ($\chi o\rho\delta\acute{\eta}$ in Greek, whence the familiar 'chord') was the musical string of the Egyptians, Greeks, and Romans; wire was practically unknown to them, since wire-drawing was invented only about A.D. 1350, synchronising with the probable invention of keyed instruments with strings, such as the clavichord, harpsichord, or virginal. From that epoch gut and wire have held divided rule, as they do in our own day in the violin and the piano. The general name for gut strings is catgut,[1] but it is really made from the intestines of sheep and goats, chiefly the former; the best and strongest being of lamb's gut when the lamb is of a certain age and development, whence it comes that September is the month for fiddle-string making; particularly for first (or E) fiddle-strings, which are the smallest though they have to bear the greatest strain of the four. According to Mr. Hart (*The Violin*, London, 1875) the best catgut strings are the Italian (Roman *par excellence*); next rank the German, then the French; last of all, the English. The author attributes the superior quality of the Italian to climate, an important part of the process of manufacture being, in Italy, carried on in the open air, which is

naturally not always practicable in England. For the deeper-toned strings the gut is overlapped with silver, copper, or mixed metal. According to J. Rousseau (*Traité de la Viole*, 1687) this loading of the string was introduced in France by Sainte Colombe about A.D. 1675. The tension of the four strings of a violin was stated by Tartini, in 1734, to be 63 lb. Mr. Hart, for the English high pitch [happily now discredited] estimates it at about 90 lb.

Wire strings were originally of latten or brass, with which psalteries and dulcimers were strung. As late as the first half of the 18th century, clavichords were generally strung with brass wire only; pianofortes retained a batch of brass strings until about 1830. Steel wire, as the special iron music-wire was called, was, however, very early introduced, for Virdung (*Musica getutscht und ausgezogen*, A.D. 1511) expressly states that the trebles of clavichords were then strung with steel. Early in the 19th century Nuremberg steel was in great request, but about 1820 the Berlin wire gained the preference. The iron of both came from the Harz Mountains. About 1834 Webster of Birmingham brought out cast steel for music wire, and gave piano strings a breaking weight of about one-third more than the German. But in 1850 Miller of Vienna was able to contend for the first place, and in the following year actually gained it at the Great Exhibition, for cast steel wire-drawing. After that, Pöhlmann of Nuremberg came forward and was considered by some experts to have surpassed Miller.[2] Webster's firm has not been idle during a competition to the results of which the present power of the pianoforte to stand in tune owes so much. A trial made under direction of the writer gives for average breaking weight of 24 inches, of No. $17\frac{1}{2}$ wire, Pöhlmann's 297 lb., Miller's 275 lb., Webster and Horsfall 257 lb., all nearly doubling the tension required for use. It is not, therefore, with surprise that we accept the eminent authority of Dr. William Pole, who regarded cast steel music-wire as the strongest elastic material that exists. The earliest covered piano strings, about a hundred years ago, spun in long interstices of brass over steel, have in time become close spun in single, double, and even treble overlayings of copper, or mixed metal composed of spelter and copper, gaining in the largest strings a diameter of 0·21 of an inch, and considerable power of strain. The greatest tension of a string recorded by Messrs. Broadwood in the technical part of their Exhibition book of 1862 is 315 lb. — for the *highest* single string of a Concert Grand. They give the whole tension at that time for Philharmonic pitch (viz. A 454, C 540 double vibrations per second) of two of their

---

[1] The origin of the term catgut has not yet been traced.   e.

[2] Unpublished correspondence of Theobald Böhm, the flautist, shows that Pöhlmann was indebted to him for improving his manufacture.

Concert Grands, as well as the tension of each separate note. The first of the two is 34,670 lb. (15 tons 9 cwt. etc.) ; the other, a longer scale, 37,160 lb. (16 tons 11 cwt. etc.). In later years tension was much increased, but not sufficiently so to account for the much higher totals or for the breaking - weights of wire recorded in Mendel's *Lexikon*. [See the writer's *History of the Pianoforte*, pp. 39, 83, 86.]　　　　　　　　　A. J. H.

STRING. The terms 'Strings,' 'Stringed instruments,' 'String-quartet,' 'String-trio,' have come to be applied in England to instruments of the violin tribe only, the terms answering to the German *Streichquartett, Streichinstrumente*. The term is understood to exclude strings that are not bowed, such as the harp and piano. Thus a quartet for four stringed instruments, usually two violins, viola, and violoncello, is called a String-quartet, to distinguish it from a pianoforte quartet—that is, for piano and three other instruments ; or for any other combination of four, such as a quartet for four horns, four flutes, etc.　　　　　　　　　　G.

STRINGENDO, 'forcing, compelling' ; pressing or hastening the time. This word conveys, besides the idea of simple acceleration of pace, that of growing excitement, working up to some climax.　　　　　　　　　　　　M.

STRING-PLATE (Fr. *Sommier en fer* ; Ital. *Cordiera* ; Germ. *Anhängeplatte, Metallner Saitenhalter*). The iron plate on the hitch-pin block of pianofortes to which the further ends of the strings are now attached. It forms with the tension bars the metal framing of the instrument ; the wooden framing being a bracing more or less complete of wooden beams, in connection with the wrest-plank, which is also of wood, and sometimes covered with metal. [See WREST-PLANK and *History of the Pianoforte*, pp. 13, 15, 16.] The service of the string-plate is one of weight ; it bears an important share in resisting the continual draught of the strings. It was invented, rather with the idea of compensation than resistance, by William Allen, a tuner in Stodart's employ, and was patented by James Thom and Allen in January 1820. A rigid string-plate was introduced by James and Thomas Broadwood in the following year ; it was the invention of one of their workmen, Samuel Herve. The single casting for string-plate and general resistance was the idea of Alpheus Babcock, of Boston, U.S., 1825 ; and was meritoriously improved and rendered practicable by Conrad Meyer of Philadelphia, U.S., in 1833. The important systems of construction that have arisen from the use of iron in string-plates and bars are described under PIANOFORTE.　　　　　　　　A. J. H.

STROGERS, NICHOLAS, an organist in the reign of James I., composer of a Morning and Evening Service printed by Barnard. Two anthems by him, 'Domine non est exaltatum'

and 'O God be merciful,' are in the Library of Peterhouse, Cambridge. An organ part of the latter is in the library of Ely Cathedral. In Christchurch, Oxford, are two entire Services (A minor, D minor), two Motets, and Fancies. [A Fantasia for virginal is in the Fitzwilliam Virginal Book (i. 357), and a piece in Benjamin Cosyn's book is possibly the same. A piece for lute is in Brit. Mus. Eg. MS. 2046.]　W. H. H.

STROHMEYER, CARL, a bass singer, a Kammersänger at Weimar, who sang in a festival at Frankenhausen in June 1810, and is mentioned by Spohr for the extraordinary compass of his voice from D to *g'* (see Spohr's *Selbstbiographie*, i. 142). He was born in the Stollberg district in 1780, and was employed successively at Gotha and at Weimar, at which latter place he died, Nov. 11, 1845.　　G.

STROLLING PLAYERS' AMATEUR ORCHESTRAL SOCIETY, THE, was founded in 1882 by Mr. Norfolk Megone, who gave up his position as conductor of the School of Mines Orchestra to fulfil the duties of honorary conductor. He remained at the head of the Society's operations for a space of twenty years, being succeeded in 1902 by Mr. William Shakespeare, who conducted the concert till 1905, when Mr. Joseph Ivimey was appointed. The first concert was given Dec. 13, 1882, at the School of Dramatic Art, Argyll Street, London. Soon afterwards St. James's Hall was used for the 'Ladies' Concerts,' the smoking concerts being held in St. Andrew's Hall, Newman Street. Now the concerts of both kinds are given in the Queen's Hall. The President is H.R.H. the Duke of Connaught, and the Hon. Secretary is Mr. W. E. Garstin. The annual subscription for members (*i.e.* non-performing members) and for orchestral members alike is two guineas.　M.

STRONG, GEORGE TEMPLETON, an American composer whose career has been made chiefly in Europe, was born in New York City, May 26, 1856. Both of his parents were musical. His mother was a good pianist and sang agreeably, and his father, G. T. Strong, a lawyer associated with the corporation of Trinity Church and a trustee of Columbia College, was an amateur organist, and for four years was president of the Philharmonic Society of New York (see SYMPHONY CONCERTS OF THE U.S.). Naturally the classics were the lad's daily artistic food. He began the study of the pianoforte and violin at an early age, and made essays in composition when he was thirteen years old. A strong predilection for the oboe led him to abandon pianoforte and violin for that instrument, on which he became a professional performer, when a disagreement between himself and his father on the choice of a career cost him the protection of the parental roof. In 1879 he went to Leipzig, where he entered the Conservatorium, abandoned the oboe in favour of the viola, studied harmony with Richard Hofmann, counterpoint and fugue with Jadassohn, and horn with Gumbert of the Gewandhaus orchestra. In Leipzig he belonged to the coterie of Liszt champions of which men like Siloti, Friedheim, Dayas, and Krause were members, and frequently visited that master in Weimar. From 1886 to 1889 he lived in Wiesbaden, associating much with his friend and fellow-countryman Mac-Dowell, and falling under the influence of Raff. He then took up a residence in Vevey, Switzerland, where he still lives, having spent one year (1891-92) in the United States as teacher at the New England Conservatory of Music in Boston. In Vevey he turned his thoughts for a time to water-colour painting, and founded the *Société Vaudoise des Aquarellistes*, having become discouraged by the failure of American composers to find recognition in their native land. Of Mr. Strong's published pieces the most important are two for soli, male chorus, and orchestra : ' Wie ein fahrender Hornist sich ein Land erblies,' op. 26, and 'Die verlassene Mühle,' op. 30, and a symphony entitled 'Sintram,' based on de la Motte Fouqué's romance of that name and Dürer's famous print 'Ritter, Tod und Teufel.' A symphonic poem 'Undine' and a symphony 'In den Bergen' have been successfully played at home and abroad. A considerable number of chamber music-pieces, two 'American Sketches' for violin solo and orchestra, a short dramatic cantata, arrangements for four hands pianoforte of some of Bach's organ works, songs, instrumental solos, etc., remain in manuscript.   H. E. K.

STROUD, CHARLES, born about 1705, was educated as a chorister of the Chapel Royal under Dr. Croft. After quitting the choir he officiated as deputy organist for his instructor and became organist of Whitehall Chapel. He died April 26, 1726, and was buried in the west cloister of Westminster Abbey. He is known as a composer by his beautiful anthem, ' Hear my prayer, O God,' included in Page's ' Harmonia Sacra.'   W. H. H.

STRUNGK, DELPHIN, was born 1601, and died 1694 at Brunswick. He was a capable organist, and held posts successively at the Wolfenbüttel Hauptkirche, 1630-32 ; at Celle, and at the church of St. Martin, Brunswick. In a complimentary dedication to the Burgomaster of Brunswick of his work on music published in 1652, Conrad Matthaei alludes to 'der sehr berühmte Organist, Herr Delphin Strungk' (Vogel, *Handschr. zu Wolfenbüttel*, 1890, p. 182).

Strungk composed music for the organ—an example is printed in Ritter's *Geschichte des Orgelspiels*, 1884, ii. 207, a Choralvorspiel in 4-part writing 'Lass mich dein sein ' ; Dr. Max Seiffert published two more. In a Lüneburg MS. there are six of these organ arrangements (Prof. Junghans, *Bach als Schuler*, 1870) ; other compositions for voices with instruments,

as well as a Choralvorspiel, are in MS. in Berlin. In the Wolfenbüttel Library is an autograph MS. of music for five voice and eight instrumental parts, composed in June 1671, 'Musikalischer Glückwunschender Zuruff (Kommt und sehet die Wercke des Herrn) als . . . Rudolphus Augustus, Herzog zu Braunschweig und Lüneburg in der Erbhuldigungsstadt Braunschweig den Gottesdienst in der Kirchen zum Brüdern erstesmahls beigewohnt.' His son,

NICOLAS ADAM STRUNGK, or STRUNCK, was born at Celle in November 1640. He studied music with his father, Delphin Strungk, and at the age of twelve was acting as organist at the Magnuskirche, Brunswick. Later he entered Helmstadt University, and worked there for some years, taking violin lessons in the vacations from Schnittelbach of Lübeck. In 1660 he was appointed first violin in the Wolfenbüttel Hofkapelle, but changed subsequently to a similar post at Celle, with a yearly salary of 200 thalers. In 1665 he joined the Hofkapelle of the Elector Johann Friedrich of Hanover.

About this time he paid his first visit to Vienna, and played the violin before the Emperor Leopold I. In 1678 he was appointed director of music in Hamburg, where a great effort was being made to foster German musical talent, so long overshadowed by Italian influences. There he wrote and produced many operas : ' Der glückselig-steigende Sejanus,' and ' Der unglücklich-fallende Sejanus ' in 1678, the German libretto by Christ. Richter being adapted from the Italian of Nicola Minato ; ' Esther,' ' Die drei Töchter Cecrops,' ' Doris,' and ' Alceste' in 1680 ; ' Theseus,' ' Semiramis,' and ' Floretto ' in 1683.

Friederich Wilhelm of Brandenburg, when visiting Hamburg, tried to secure Strungk's services as capellmeister, but this was not allowed, Hanover having a prior claim. The Elector Ernst August appointed Strungk chamber organist, and presented him to a canonry at Einbeck, and eventually Strungk accompanied him to Italy and remained there some time. It was at Rome that the meeting between Strungk and Corelli took place, so graphically described by Hawkins (ed. 1875, vol. ii. p. 676). Strungk again visited Vienna, this time playing on the clavier before the Emperor with much success. From 1682 to 1686 he remained a member of the Hanover Hofkapelle, but on Jan. 26, 1688, Johann Georg II. of Saxony appointed him Kammerorganist and Vice-capellmeister to the Dresden Hofkapelle, with a salary of 500 thaler. He was the successor of Carlo Pallavicini, who died on Jan. 29, leaving an unfinished opera which Strungk was asked to complete. The libretto was by Pallavicini's son Stefano. Strungk apparently contributed the music to the third act, and the opera, ' L'Antiope,' was performed four times in Feb. 1689, at Dresden. Strungk seems to have suffered at Dresden from

3 a

the usual friction between the Italian and German musicians, although the Germans were gradually gaining the upper hand, for on March 30, 1688, Elector Johann Georg III. was appealed to because the Italians refused to join in any performance of Strungk's compositions, and would only acknowledge his authority when Bernhard the capellmeister was absent through illness. This resulted in the dismissal of the ringleader Fedeli in the following September. Bernhard died on Nov. 14, 1692, and was succeeded by Strungk, who composed some music in his memory.

On June 13, 1692, Strungk obtained permission from Johann Georg IV. of Saxony to found an opera-house in Leipzig. With the aid of two associates, Glaser and Sartorio, an architect, the work was put in hand in March 1693, and a theatre of wood was erected in the Brühl, at a cost of 10,000 thaler. It was opened on May 8, 1693, with Strungk's opera 'Alceste'; the German libretto by Paul Thiemich was adapted from the original Italian of Aurelio Aureli. A contemporary chronicle narrates that pictured announcements were suspended in the streets of Leipzig, giving a description of the opera, and the time of its performance (*Leipzigisches Geschicht-Buch*, 1714, p. 883). Johann Georg IV. came from Dresden to be present at the opening performance. In 1693 Strungk's opera 'Nero' was also given, and his 'Agrippina' in 1699. Strungk was financially much embarrassed by his Leipzig undertaking, although he retained his Dresden post and salary until 1697, when he retired with a pension. He died Sept. 23, 1700, at Dresden. His daughters Philippine and Elisabeth were two of the principal singers in the Leipzig theatre from 1705 to 1709.

Very little of Strungk's music is known at the present day, and it nearly all remains in MS. He composed a 'Ricercar auf den Tod seiner Mutter, verfertiget zu Venedig am 20. Dec. 1685,' also 'Die Auferstehung Jesu,' first performed on April 21, 1688 ; and he published at Dresden in 1691 'Musikalische Uebung auf der Violin oder Viola da gamba, so wohl zur Ehre Gottes als menschlicher Ergötzlichkeit bestehend, in etlichen Sonaten über die Festgesänge, dann auch etliche Ciaconen mit zwei Violinen.' A selection of his opera airs was published in Hamburg, 1684, 'Ein hundert auserlesene Arien zweyer Hamburgischen Operen, Semiramis und Esther. Mit beigefügten Ritornellen.' A MS. copy is in the Königsberg Library as well as some MS. Choralvorspiele also attributed to Strungk, although they may be the work of his father, Delphin Strungk (see Müller's Cat.). MS. copies of a sonata for two violins and viola da gamba, and a sonata for six strings, are in the Upsala Library. Various MSS. are also in the Berlin and Dresden Libraries, and in the Wolfenbüttel Library, MS. 253 'Les Aires avec les Flauts douces pour son Altesse Seren^{me}

monseigneur le Prince Ludwig Rudolf, Duc de Bruns. et Lüneberg,' containing ten numbers, chiefly dances.   c. s.

STUDIES. See ÉTUDES.

STÜCK (Ger. ' Piece ').

SUB.   The Latin preposition 'under' is used in connection with the organ, and denotes the octave below, as ' Sub Bass,' ' Sub Octave couples,' etc. [See COUPLER.]

SUBDIAPENTE.   A polyglot word, part Latin, part Greek, to signify a fifth below, just as ' Epidiapente' signified a fifth above. A ' Canon in Subdiapente ' was a canon in which the answer was a fifth below the lead. Similarly ' Subdiatessaron ' is a fourth below, and ' Epidiatessaron ' a fourth above.   G.

SUBDOMINANT.   The fourth note of the scale upwards. The note below the dominant, as F in the key of C. The radical bass of the penultimate chord in the Plagal cadence. When groups of movements are balanced together in threes the central one is most frequently in the key of the subdominant, as in sonatas of three movements, the minuet and trio form, marches, valses, etc. In the actual body of a large movement in forms of the sonata order, the key of the subdominant is not antithetically acceptable, and examples of its occurrence in modern music as the key of the second section or second subject are extremely rare, and evidently not well advised. But in dependence on the tonic key it is one of the most important of harmonic centres, and digressions in that direction are very common in modern music.   c. h. h. p.

SUBJECT.   The theme, or leading idea, on which a musical composition is based.   A piece of music can no more be composed without a Subject than a sermon can be preached without a text. Rich harmonies and graceful passages may be strung together in any number ; but if they be not suggested by a leading thought, they will mean nothing. The 'leading thought' is the Subject ; and the merit of the composition based upon that Subject will depend, in the first place, upon the worthiness of the idea, and in the second, upon the skill with which the composer discourses upon it.

Subjects may be divided into as many classes as there are classes of composition ; for every definite art-form is based upon a Subject in harmony with its own peculiar character.

I. The earliest known form of Subject is the ecclesiastical *Cantus firmus*.[1] The most important varieties of this are the plain-song melodies of the antiphon[2] and those of the hymn.[3] The former admits of no rhythmic ictus beyond that demanded by the just delivery of the words to which it is set. The latter fell, even in very early times, into a more symmetrical vein suggested by the symmetry of the verse or prose, cultivated by the great mediæval

[1] See PLAIN-SONG.   [2] See ANTIPHON.
[3] See HYMN.

hymnologists, though it was not until the close of the 15th, or beginning of the 16th century that it developed itself in Germany into the perfectly rhythmic and metrically regular melody of the Chorale.[1]

Upon a phrase of this plain-song the inventors of harmony discoursed at will ; in other words, they treated it as a Subject. Composers of the 11th century discoursed upon it by singing a second part against the given Subject, in plain counterpoint—note against note.[2] They sang this part extempore ; and, because it was sung by a second voice, it was called Discantus—the literal meaning of which is, a song sung by two voices. See DISCANT.

When extempore discant gave place to written counterpoint, the *Cantus firmus* was still retained, and sung by the tenor in long sustained notes, while other voices discoursed upon it, no longer note against note, but, as art progressed, in passages of imitation, sometimes formed from the actual notes of the *Canto fermo*, sometimes so contrived as to contrast with it, in pure harmony, but with unlimited variety of rhythm.[3] And this arrangement brought two classes of theme into simultaneous use—the plain-song basis of the whole, and the point of imitation : the first of which was technically distinguished as the *Canto fermo*, while the last, in process of time, approached very nearly to the true Subject of the modern schools. The two forms are very clearly shown in Palestrina's ' Missa Ecce Sacerdos magnus,'[4] in which the long notes of the *Canto fermo* never fail to present themselves in one or other of the vocal parts, however elaborate may be the imitations carried on in the rest.

II. By a process not uncommon in the development of specific art-forms, the long-drawn notes of the *Canto fermo*, after giving birth to a more vivacious form of Subject, fell gradually into disuse,—appearing, if at all, by diminution, or double diminution, in notes as short as those formerly used for points of imitation. In this manner the ancient *Canto fermo* became a Subject properly so called ; and, as a Subject, was made the groundwork of a regular fugue. This process of development is strikingly exemplified in Palestrina's ' Missa L'Homme armé,' in some of the movements of which the quaint old melody is treated, in Longs and Larges, as a *Canto fermo*, while in others it is written in Semibreves and Minims, as a fugal Subject.[5]

We do not mean to imply that Palestrina invented this mode of treatment ; but only that he availed himself of all the good things that had been used by his predecessors. The laws of fugue were established more than a century before his time. Not the laws of what we now call fugue ; but those of the Real Fugue of the

Middle Ages—a form of composition which differs very materially from that brought to perfection by the great masters of the 18th century. Real Fugue was of two kinds—Limited, and Free.[6] In Limited Real Fugue, the imitation was carried on from the beginning to the end of the composition, forming what we now call Canon. In Free Real Fugue it was not continued beyond the duration of the Subject itself. In the former case the theme of the composition was called a *Guida*—that is, a Subject which serves as a ' guide ' to the other parts, which imitate it, note for note, throughout. In Free Real Fugue the theme was called Subjectum, Propositio, or Dux : Soggetto, Proposta, or, if very short, Attacco ; Führer, Aufgabe, or Hauptsatz. The early English writers called it Point ; but this word is now applied, like the Italian Attacco, to little passages of imitation only, and the leading idea of the fugue is simply called the Subject.

The Subject of the Real Fugue—except in the Limited species—was always very short, frequently consisting of no more than three or four notes, after the statement of which the part was free to move in any direction it pleased. But the treatment of these few notes was very strict. Every interval proposed by the leading part was answered by the same interval in every other part. The Answer, therefore, corresponded exactly with the Subject either in the fifth, or fourth, above, or below ; and it was necessary that its solmisation should also correspond with that of the Subject in another hexachord.[7] But the Subject and the Answer had each a distinguishing name. The Theme and its Reply were called, in various languages, Dux and Comes, Propositio and Responsum, or Antecedens and Consequens ; Proposta and Risposta, or Antecedente and Consequenza ; Führer and Gefährte, or Antwort ; Demande and Réponse. In English, Subject and Answer ; or, more rarely, Antecedent and Consequent.

III. So long as the Ecclesiastical Modes remained in use, Real Fugue was the only species possible ; but, as these were gradually replaced by our modern system of tonality, composers invented a new kind of Fugue, formed upon a Subject the character of which differed entirely from that used by the older masters. This form of composition is now called Tonal Fugue.[8] It is generally described as differing from Real Fugue chiefly in the construction of the answer. Undoubtedly this definition disposes of its most essential characteristic. But there are other differences between the two forms which cannot be thus lightly passed over. So far as the answer is concerned, it is enough to say that its intervals do not furnish an exact reproduction of those of the Subject ; being governed, as to their arrangement, by laws which scarcely fall within the scope of our present article. The

1 See CHORALE.   2 See STRICT COUNTERPOINT.
3 See POLYPHONIA.
4 Published in Breitkopf & Härtel's edition, vol. x.
5 See L'HOMME ARMÉ.

6 See vol. ii. p. 122.   7 See HEXACHORD; SOLMISATION.
8 See vol. ii. pp. 122-3.

Subject, on the other hand, presents so many varieties of form and expression, that it cannot be too carefully considered. In the hands of the great masters it presents an epitome of the entire Fugue, into which nothing is admissible which is not in some way suggested by it ; and, in order that it may serve this comprehensive purpose, it must needs be very carefully constructed. The Subjects employed by the great fuguists are always found to be capable of suggesting a logical Answer, and one or more good Counter-subjects ;[1] of being conveniently and neatly broken into fragments, for purposes of collateral discussion ; of intertwining their various members among the involutions of an ingenious Stretto ; and of lending themselves to a hundred other devices, which are so intimately connected with the conduct of the Fugue itself, that the necessary qualities of the Subject will be better understood by reference to our general article on TONAL FUGUE (vol. ii. p. 122 et seq.), than by separate description here.

IV. We have shown how the fathers of composition treated the Canto fermo ; how their immediate successors enveloped it in a network of ingenious points of imitation ; how, by fusing the points of imitation, and the Canto fermo which suggested them, into a homogeneous theme, the polyphonic composers gave birth to that important factor in composition which we call a Subject ; and how that Subject was treated by the great fuguists of the 18th century. We have now to see how these fuguists revived the Canto fermo, and employed it simultaneously with the newer Subject. Not that there was ever a period when it fell into absolute desuetude ; but it was once so little used, that the term, revived, may be very fairly applied to the treatment it experienced from Handel and Bach, and their great contemporaries.

And now we must be very careful to remember clearly the process by which the Subject grew out of the Canto fermo. The German composer of the 18th century learned the melody of the chorale in his cradle, and used it constantly : treating ' Kommt Menschenkinder, rühmt, und preist,' and 'Nun ruhen alle Wälder,' as Palestrina treated 'Ecce Sacerdos magnus,' and ' L'Homme armé.' Sometimes he converted the traditional melody into a regular Subject, as in the ' Osanna ' of the last-named mass. Sometimes he retained the long notes, enriching them with a florid counterpoint, as in the ' Kyrie.' In the first instance, there was no doubt about the nomenclature ; the term Subject was applied to the choral melody as a matter of course. In the other case there was a choice. When the melody of the chorale was made to pass through the regular process of Fugal Exposition, and a new contrapuntal melody contrasted with it in shorter notes, the former was called the Subject, and the latter

[1] See COUNTER-SUBJECT.

the Counter-subject. When the counterpoint furnished the exposition, and the chorale was occasionally heard against it, in long sustained notes, the first was called the Subject, and the second the Canto fermo. Seb. Bach has left us innumerable examples of both methods of treatment, in his ' Choral-Vorspiele,' ' Kirchen-Cantaten,' and other works. Perhaps the grandest example is the opening movement of the ' Credo ' of the Mass in B minor, in which the plain-song intonation, ' Credo in unum Deum,' is developed into a regular Fugue by the voices, while an uninterrupted counterpoint of crotchets is played by the instrumental bass. In neither of these cases would it be easy to misapply the words Subject, Counter-subject, or Canto fermo ; but the correct terminology is not always so clearly apparent. In the year 1747 Bach was invited to Potsdam by Frederick the Great, who gave him a Subject for the purpose of testing his powers of improvisation. We may be sure that the great fuguist did full justice to this at the moment ; but, not contented with extemporising upon it, he paid the royal amateur the compliment of working it up at home in a series of movements which he afterwards presented to King Frederick, under the title of ' Musikalisches Opfer.' In working this out he calls the theme, in one place, ' Il Soggetto Reale ' ; and, in another, ' Thema regium.' It is quite clear that in these cases he attached the same signification to the terms Thema and Soggetto, and applied both to the principal Subject, treating the violin and flute passages in the sonata, and the florid motivo in the canon, as Counter-subjects. But in another work, founded on a theme by Legrenzi, he applies the term ' Thema ' to the principal motivo, and ' Subjectum ' to the subordinate one.[2] We must suppose, therefore, that the two terms were in Bach's time, to a certain extent, interchangeable.

Handel, though he did occasionally use the Canto fermo as Bach used it, produced his best effects in quite a different way. In the 'Funeral Anthem' he treats the Chorale, 'Herr Jesu Christ,' first as a Canto fermo and then, in shorter notes, as a regularly-worked Subject. ' As from the power of sacred lays ' is founded upon a chorale, sung in plain counterpoint by all the voices ; it therefore stands as the Subject of the movement, while the Counter-subject is entirely confined to the instrumental accompaniment. In ' O God, who from the suckling's mouth,' in the 'Foundling Anthem,' the melody of ' Aus tiefer Noth ' is treated as an orthodox Canto fermo. But this was not Handel's usual practice. His Canti fermi are more frequently confined to a few notes only of Plain-song, sung

[2] 'Thema Legrenzianum pedaliter elaboratum cum subjecto.' The original MS. of this work has disappeared. Messrs. Peters, of Leipzig, have published it in Cahier 4 of their edition of the Organ Works, on the authority of a copy by Andreas Bach ; [and it is given, but without the title quoted, in the B.-G. edition, xxxviii. p. 94].

slowly, to give weight to the regularly-developed Subject, as in 'Sing ye to the Lord,' the 'Hallelujah Chorus,' the last chorus in the 'Utrecht Te Deum,' the second in the 'Jubilate,' the second Chandos Anthem, 'Let God arise,' the last chorus in 'Esther,' and other places too numerous to mention.[1]

The use of the long-drawn *Canto fermo* is fast becoming a lost art ; yet the effect with which Mendelssohn has introduced 'Wir glauben all' an einen Gott,' in combination with the primary Subject of 'But our God abideth in Heaven,' in 'St. Paul,' has not often been surpassed. Mozart also has left us a magnificent instance, in the last finale of 'Die Zauberflöte,' where he has enveloped the Chorale, 'Ach Gott vom Himmel sieh darein,' in an incomparable network of instrumental counterpoint ; and Meyerbeer has introduced two clever and highly effective imitations of the real thing in 'Les Huguenots,' at the 'Litanies' and the 'Conjuration.'

V. The similarity of the *Canti fermi*, and even of the true Subjects, used by great composers, and handed on from generation to generation, has given rise to much ingenious speculation.   1. A remarkable instance of this is a passage of slow notes, rising from the tonic to the subdominant, and then descending towards the note from whence it started.   This passage is constantly found in old ecclesiastical melodies ; among others, in that of the hymn 'Aeterna Christi munera.'   Zarlino used it as a theme for his examples in counterpoint.   In Morley's *Plaine and easie Introduction*, Philomathes gives it to Polymathes, as a Point 'familiar enough, and easie to bee maintained' —*i.e.* developed ; while the 'Master' calls it 'a most common Point,' which 'though it were giuen to all the Musicians of the world, they might compose vpon it, and not one of their Compositions bee like vnto that of another.' Byrd used it in 'NON NOBIS' ; Palestrina, in the first 'Agnus Dei' of his 'Missa brevis' ; Bach, in the 'Gratias agimus' and 'Dona' of his Mass in B minor ; Handel, in 'Sing ye to the Lord,' the 'Hallelujah Chorus,' the last Chorus in the 'Utrecht Te Deum,' the Chamber Duet, 'Tacete, ohimè !' and many other places ; Steffani, in his Duet, 'Tengo per infallibile' ; Perti, in a Fuga *a* 8, 'Ut nos possimus' ; Mendelssohn, in 'Not only unto him,' from 'St. Paul' ; and Beethoven, in the Trio of the Ninth Symphony. The truth is, the passage is simply a fragment of the scale, which is as much the common property of musicians, whether fuguists or composers of the later schools, as the alphabet is the common property of poets.

2. Another Subject, scarcely less universal in its application, embraces a more extended portion of the scale. Bach uses this in the 'Christmas Oratorio' ; Handel, in the 'Hail-

stone Chorus' ; in a remarkable Concerto for two Orchestras, of which the only known copy is the original Autograph at Buckingham Palace ; in 'Worthy is the Lamb' ; in 'When his loud voice,' and in many other places. Mozart used it, in a form all but identical with Handel's, and also in the inverted form, in the Jupiter Symphony. Beethoven used it in his first symphony ; in his pianoforte sonata, op. 31, No. 1 ; and in the inverted form, in his symphony in C minor ; Schumann, in his string quartet, No. 1, and his PF. quartet, op. 47 ; and Brahms, in the finale to his symphony in C minor.

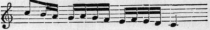

3. These examples deal only with the scale. But there are certain progressions which are as much common property as the scale itself ; just as there are certain combinations of letters which are as much common property as the alphabet. First among these stand the leaps of fifths or fourths, with which countless Subjects begin ; and scarcely less common are the sequences of ascending fourths, and descending fifths, which we so frequently find associated with them ; as in Bach's fugue in E♭—No. 31 of the '48' ; Mozart's overture to 'Die Zauberflöte,' and a hundred other cases.

4. Closely allied to these sequences of fourths and fifths is a form in which a descending third is followed by an ascending fourth. This was used for a Canon by Turini in the 17th century ; in Handel's second hautboy concerto and third organ fugue ; Morley's canzonet, 'Cruel, you pull away too soon' ; Purcell's 'Full fathom five' ; and numerous other cases, including a subject given to Mendelssohn for improvisation at Rome, Nov. 23, 1830.

5. A Subject, characterised by the prominent use of a diminished seventh, and familiar as that of 'And with His stripes,' is also a very common one. Handel himself constantly used it as a theme for improvisation ; and other composers have used it also—notably Mozart, in the Kyrie of the 'Requiem' ; see (*a*).

6. The Intonation and Reciting-Note of the second Gregorian Tone—used either with or without the first note of the Mediation—may also be found in an infinity of Subjects, both ancient and modern, including that of Bach's Fugue in E, No. 33, and the Finale of the Jupiter Symphony ; see (*b*).

The number of Subjects thus traceable from one composer to another is so great that it would be impossible to give even a list of them. The treatment may be original, though the Subject has been used a thousand times ; and these constantly-recurring Subjects are founded upon progressions which, more than any others, suggest new Counter-subjects in infinite variety.

VI. The Subject of Canon differs from that of Fugue, in that it is continuous. The Subject is as long as the Canon itself. Hence it is called the *Guida* or Guide ; each note in the leading part directing those that are to be sung by all the other voices in turn. Subjects of this kind will be found in vol. iii. pp. 77-8, 385*a*, 388-9, and other places ; and many more may be seen in the pages of Burney and Hawkins. Examples of the method of fitting these Subjects together will be found in vol. i. pp. 455*b*, and in vol. iii. pp. 77-8. The number of passages that can be made to fit together in Canon is so limited, that the same notes have been used over and over again by writers of all ages. A remarkable instance of this is afforded by ' Non nobis.' We have seen how many composers have chosen this as a Fugal Subject ; and an account of it, with some solutions in Canon not generally known, will be found at vol. iii. p. 388*b*. It must not, however, be supposed that the older composers alone were able to produce fine Canons. Haydn thoroughly understood the art of writing them [see vol. ii. p. 307*b*] ; and so graceful are Mozart's that their Subjects might very easily be mistaken for those of an ordinary part-song.[1]

VII. Closely allied to the Subject of the Canon is that of the ' Rota' or Round. In this, and in its comic analogue the Catch, the Guida is followed by every voice in turn ; for which reason the composition was formerly written on a single stave. It will be found so written in a *facsimile* of the oldest example we possess, in the article SUMER IS ICUMEN IN ; and it is virtually so written even at the present day ; though, in modern copies, the Guida is *doubled back*, so to speak, each time a new voice enters, so as to give the outward appearance of a score. That it is not really a score is evident, from the fact that there is not a separate part for each voice ; but there is a substantial difference between this and the Canon, though the subject of both is called a Guida. In the Canon, the Subject forms the whole composition. In the Round, it continues only until the entrance of the second voice, the latter sections of the Guida representing Counter-subjects only, and continuing to furnish new Counter-subjects as often as new voices enter.

It is remarkable that this, the oldest form of secular part-writing in existence, should not only have been invented in England, but should still be more highly esteemed in England than in any other country—for it is only in England that the art of singing a round is practised with success, and the success with which we practise it dates from the time of the Plantagenets.[2]

VIII. In turning from the learned complexi-

[1] See a large collection of examples in Merrick's English Translation of Albrechtsberger, vol. ii. pp. 415-432.
[2] See ROUND ; SUMER IS ICUMEN IN.

ties of Fugue and Canon, to the simple Subject of the Dance-tune, we are not, as might be supposed, retracing our steps, but following the line traced out for us by the natural development of art. When instrumental music first began to attract attention, the Fugue was regarded as the embodiment of its highest expression. Lulli ended his overtures with a Fugue ; but as time progressed this form of finale was superseded by that of the Dance-tune. The most common types were those of the Minuet, the Gavotte, the Bourrée, the Courante, the Chaconne, the Sarabande, the Giga, and the closely allied tunes of the Allemande, the Ritornello, the Air, and the March. They originally consisted, for the most part, of two short strains, the first of which stated the Subject, while the second developed it according to its means. It was *de rigueur* that the Minuet should be written in triple time, and that each phrase of its Subject should begin with the down-beat of the bar—though, in later times, most Minuets began with the third beat ; that the Gavotte should be in *Alla breve* time, beginning at the half-bar ; that the Bourrée should be in common time, beginning on the fourth beat ; that the Allemande should be in common, and the Giga in compound common time, each beginning, as a general rule, with a single short note ; and so with the rest. It was indispensable that the first strain, representing the Subject, should be complete in itself, though it did not always end in the key in which it began. The development of the Subject in the second strain usually consisted in the prolongation of the melody by means of phrases, which, in the finer examples, were directly derived from itself : sometimes carrying a characteristic figure through two or more closely-related keys ; sometimes returning, after this process, to the initial strain, and thus completing the symmetry of the movement in accordance with principles of the deepest artistic significance. The most highly-developed forms were those of the Courante and Allemande. In these, the first strain, if in the major mode, almost invariably modulated to the dominant for the purpose of proceeding to a formal close in that key ; if in the minor mode, it proceeded, in like manner, to the relative major. The second strain then started with a tolerably exact reproduction of the initial Subject in the new key, or some other closely related to it ; and the reprise terminated with the transposition to the original key of that portion of the first strain which had first appeared in the dominant or relative major. In these forms the share of interest allotted to the process of development was very small indeed, compared with that absorbed by the Subject itself ; insomuch that, in many very fine examples, the entire movement consisted of little more than a Subject artfully extended by the articulation of two members of not very unequal proportions.

IX. Very different from this was the next manifestation of progressive power. Taking the lines of the Allemande as the limit of the general contour, the first experimenters in 'Sonata-form' (see SONATA) used a primary Subject, of comparatively limited dimensions, as the foundation of a movement of greater length and higher development than any previously attempted. For this form a good Subject was of paramount importance; but its office was that of a text, and nothing more; the real interest of the movement lay in the completeness of its treatment. The essential features of the most beautiful form that the art has yet shown have been treated in the articles FORM, SONATA.

There remains another class of Subjects to which we have as yet made no allusion, but which, nevertheless, plays a very important part in the economy of musical composition. We allude to the Subjects of dramatic movements, both vocal and instrumental. It is obvious that in Subjects of this kind the most important element is the peculiar form of dramatic expression necessary for each individual theme. And because the varieties of dramatic expression are practically innumerable, it is impossible to fix any limit to the varieties of form into which such Subjects may be consistently cast. At certain epochs in the history of the lyric drama consistency has undoubtedly been violated, and legitimate artistic progress seriously hindered by contracted views on this point. In the days of Hasse, for instance, a persistent determination to cast all Melodies, of whatever character, into the same stereotyped form, led to the petrifaction of all natural expression in the most unnatural of all mechanical contrivances—the so-called 'Concert-Opera.' Against this perversion of dramatic truth all true artists conscientiously rebelled. Gluck, with a larger orchestra and stronger chorus at command, returned to the principles set forth by Peri and Caccini in the year 1600. Mozart invented Subjects, faultlessly proportioned, yet always exactly suited to the character of the dramatic situation, and the peculiar form of passion needed for its expression. These Subjects he wrought into movements, the symmetry of which equalled that of his most finished concertos and symphonies, while their freedom of development and elaborate construction not only interposed no hindrance to the most perfect scenic propriety, but, on the contrary, carried on the action of the drama with a power which has long been the despair of his most ambitious imitators. Moreover, in his greatest work, 'Il Don Giovanni,' he used the peculiar form of Subject now known as the 'Leading Theme' with unapproachable effect; entrusting to it the responsibility of bringing out the point of deepest interest in the Drama —a duty which it performs with a success too well known to need even a passing comment.

In 'Der Freischütz,' Weber followed up this idea with great effect; inventing, among other striking Subjects, two constantly-recurring themes, which, applied to the heroine of the piece and the Demon, invest the scenes in which they appear with special interest.

[In the later works of Wagner the use of the Leitmotiv or Leading Subject was developed to the greatest possible extent, and almost all dramatic music since his day illustrates the principle he brought to such perfection. Not merely the characters and the external, tangible objects of the drama were identified with special musical phrases, but the inner dramatic factors, the 'motives' in the non-musical sense, were provided with themes, and in the finest instances, as throughout 'Tristan,' 'Die Meistersinger,' or 'Parsifal,' the themes are not arbitrarily associated with the elements of the play, but are inherently eloquent, so that the hearer who is not acquainted with the labels tacked on to the various themes feels unconsciously how greatly they enhance the appeal of the drama.]

The different forms of Subject thus rapidly touched upon constitute but a very small proportion of those in actual use; but we trust that we have said enough to enable the student to judge for himself as to the characteristics of any others with which he may meet, during the course of his researches, and the more so, since many Subjects of importance are described in the articles on the special forms of composition to which they belong.   W. S. R.

SUBMEDIANT. The sixth note of the scale rising upwards. The note next above the dominant, as A in the key of C. The submediant of any major scale is chiefly brought into prominence as the tonic of its relative minor.   C. H. H. P.

SUBSIDIARY, in a symphonic work, is a theme of inferior importance, not strictly forming part of either first or second subject, but subordinate to one or the other. The spaces between the two subjects, which in the early days before Beethoven were filled up by 'padding' in the shape of formal passages and modulations, are now, in obedience to his admirable practice, occupied by distinct ideas, usually of small scope, but of definite purport. [See vol. i. p. 263.] The 'Eroica' Symphony affords early and striking examples of subsidiary subjects in various positions. Thus, on the usual dominant passage preceding the second subject appears the plaintive melody :—

which becomes of so much importance in the second part. And the same title belongs also to the fresh subject which appears transiently during the 'working-out' with so much effect :—

Equally noticeable is the phrase in a similar situation in the fourth Symphony :—

while the melody which Schubert interpolated as an afterthought in the Scherzo of his great C major Symphony is too well known to require quotation.

These two last, however, are not worked, and can therefore hardly be classed as 'themes,' but are more of the nature of 'episodes.'

In some cases a Subsidiary acquires so much importance in the working out as to rank as a third subject. The Italian Symphony of Mendelssohn supplies a type of this. The subject—

which appears shortly after the double bar in the first movement, though properly speaking merely a Subsidiary, is so insisted upon and elaborated in the working-out and coda as to rival the first subject itself in importance.   F. C.

SUCCENTOR, *i.e.* Sub-cantor. A cathedral officer, deputy to the Precentor. His duty is to supply his principal's place during absence, in the regulation of the service, and other duties of the Precentor.   G.

SUCH, HENRY, violinist, son of Edwin C. Such, Mus.B., was born in London on March 31, 1872. Commenced studying at the age of six, and made his first public appearance when eight years old. Following the advice of Joachim he entered the Hochschule at Berlin in 1885, remaining there till 1892, in which year his first public appearance in Berlin was successfully made. After touring in Germany he studied during 1895-96 with Wilhelmj, and again travelled in Holland and Scandinavia. He then visited Vienna, meeting and playing with Brahms, and in 1896 made two public appearances with Richter conducting. Settled in London in 1898, and was appointed Professor at the Guildhall School of music. He has a large repertory and an excellent technique. His violin is one of the Stradivari instruments formerly possessed by Paganini.   w. w. c.

SUCH, PERCY FREDERICK, brother of the above, was born in London on June 27, 1878. In 1887 went to Berlin and commenced studying the violoncello under Herr Otto Ludemann, pupil of Professor Hausmann, who accepted him as private pupil in 1889, and continued to give him lessons when he joined the Hochschule

in 1892. In the latter institution he remained until 1898, having the advantage of lessons in ensemble-playing from Joachim. His first public appearance in Berlin was with the Philharmonic Orchestra in 1898. Besides playing as soloist, he assisted the Joachim Quartet as second violoncello at many concerts in Germany and Holland, including the Beethoven Festival at Bonn in 1899. Appeared in London first at St. James's Hall with the Joachim Quartet in 1901, and followed with a series of recitals. Held the post of principal violoncello during the two final seasons of the Popular Concerts. His training and purity of style fit him especially for the performance of chamber music. He plays upon an exceptionally fine Gagliano violoncello.   w. w. c.

SUCHER, JOSEF, born at Döbör, Eisenburg, Hungary, Nov. 23, 1844, was brought up in the Löwenburg Convict at Vienna, as a chorister in the Hofkapelle, which he joined on the same day with Hans Richter, the conductor. On completing his course at the Convict he began to study law, but soon threw it aside, worked at counterpoint with Sechter, and adopted music as his profession. Beginning as sub-conductor of a Singing Society in Vienna, he advanced to be 'Repetitor' of the solo singers at the Imperial Court Opera, and conductor at the Comic Opera, and in 1876 went to Leipzig as conductor of the City Theatre. In the following year he married Fräulein Rosa Hasselbeck, the then prima donna of the same house. She was born Feb. 23, 1849, at Velburg in the Upper Palatinate (Brockhaus's *Lexikon* ; but Riemann gives the year of birth as 1845), and is the daughter of one musician and the niece of another. Her first engagement was at Trêves. Thence she went to Königsberg and thence to Berlin and Danzig, where she was engaged by her future husband for Leipzig. From Leipzig in 1879 husband and wife went to Hamburg, where they settled as conductor and prima donna, and where the latter attracted immediate attention by her performance of Chryssa in Rubinstein's 'Nero.' They visited England in 1882, and Mme. Sucher proved her eminent qualities both as a singer and an actress by the extraordinary range of parts in which she appeared at the German opera at Drury Lane. She made her début as Elsa on May 18, and besides singing as Elizabeth and Senta, she sang Eva on May 30, and Isolde on June 20, on the respective productions in England of 'Die Meistersinger' and 'Tristan,' and as Euryanthe on the revival of that opera. Her husband produced a 'Scene' or Cantata entitled 'Waldfräulein' ('The Wood Maiden') for soli, chorus, and orchestra, at the Richter Concert of June 5. Composition is no novelty to Herr Sucher ; even in his chorister days we hear of songs, masses, cantatas, and overtures, one of which, to an opera called 'Ilse,' was brought forward at a concert in Vienna in 1873. One of his best-known published works is a Liedercyclus entitled 'Ruheort.' Frau Sucher gained great renown by her singing of Isolde at Bayreuth in 1886. In 1888 her husband was appointed to the post of conductor at the Hofoper at Berlin; [he retired in 1899, and died April 4, 1908]. G. [Frau Sucher, after successful performances of Kundry and Eva at Bayreuth in 1888, became a prima donna at Berlin, where she remained until 1898, as a noted Wagner singer. On leave of absence, she gave 'Gastspiele' at Bayreuth and other cities of Germany, and in 1892 sang both at Covent Garden and Drury Lane as Brünnhilde in 'Siegfried,' and once as Isolde, and was warmly received. She would have played Isolde again but for a peremptory recall to Berlin, where her services were urgently required. On Nov. 3, 1903, she took a final farewell of the stage at Berlin as Sieglinde.   A. C.]

SÜSSMAYER,[1] Franz Xaver, composer and Capellmeister, born 1766 at Steyer in Upper Austria, and educated at the monastery of Kremsmünster, where he attempted composition in several branches. [Some MS. operas still existing at Kremsmünster are mentioned in the Quellen-Lexikon.] At Vienna he had instruction from Salieri and Mozart. With the latter he formed the closest attachment, becoming, to use Seyfried's expression, 'the inseparable companion of the immortal Amphion.' Jahn details the work he did for the 'Clemenza di Tito' on its production at Prague, whither he accompanied Mozart. Süssmayer was at the composer's bed-side the evening before Mozart's death, while the latter tried to give him the necessary instructions for completing his Requiem, a task for which he was peculiarly fitted by his knack of imitating Mozart's handwriting. Jahn has stated in detail (ii. 172) how much of that work is in all probability Süssmayer's. [See vol. iii. p. 308.]

As a composer Süssmayer's name (as 'pupil of Salieri and Mozart') first appears at Schikaneder's Theatre, where his opera, 'Moses,' was brought out May 4, 1792, revived in 1796, and again in concert-form in 1800. This was followed by 'L' Incanto superato,' a 'musico-romantic fable' (Burgtheater, 1793), and by 'Der Spiegel von Arkadien' (Schikaneder's Theatre, 1794), libretto by Schikaneder, which became a favourite, and was eulogised by the Wiener Zeitung. He became in 1794 composer, and in 1795 Capellmeister, to the Kärnthnerthor Court Theatre, where he produced successively 'Die edle Rache' (1795), 'Die Freiwilligen' (1796), 'Der Wildfang' (1797), 'Der Marktschreier' and 'Soliman der Zweite' (1799), 'Gulnare' (1800), and 'Phasma' (1801). His patriotic cantata, 'Der Retter in Gefahr,' was performed at an entertainment to the Vienna volunteers in the large Redouten-

[1] He signs himself on a symphony SIESSMAYR.

saal at a time of threatened war (1796), and several times repeated in the same building, and by the Tonkünstler Societät. Süssmayer also composed two operas for Prague. Several of the above works were printed, some only in part, while others—masses, and smaller church-works, instrumental pieces, etc.—exist only in MS. Though wanting in depth and originality his works are melodious, and have a certain popular character peculiar to himself. He might perhaps have risen to a higher flight had he not been overtaken by death after a long illness, Sept. 17 (or 16, according to Thayer), 1803. Prince Esterhazy bought his entire MSS. from his widow.   C. F. P.

SUITE. In the period between the latter part of the 16th and the beginning of the 18th century the most conspicuous feature of universal instrumental music is the profusion of dance tunes. All the most civilised nations of that time took equal pleasure in them; and partly owing to the itinerant musicians who traversed divers countries, and partly to the wars which brought representatives of different nationalities into frequent contact, both friendly and hostile, the various characteristic types were spread from one land to another, were adopted universally by composers, irrespective of nationality, and were so acclimatised as to become in many cases as characteristic of and as popular in the countries of their adoption as in that of their origin. This is sufficiently illustrated in Morley's well-known Plaine and easie Introduction, 1597. For when he comes to treat of dance-music, the first things he takes notice of are Pavans and Galliards, Almanes and Branles; of which the first two are of Italian origin, the third probably Suabian, and the last French. The first two were not only in common use for dancing purposes in Queen Elizabeth's time, but were adopted by the great composers of the day and a little later as a favourite basis for instrumental pieces, which were intended as much for private enjoyment as music as for accompaniments to dances; and they are found plentifully scattered in such collections as the Fitzwilliam Virginal Book and 'Parthenia,' among sets of variations, preludes, and fantasias. A large proportion of such dances were naturally taken singly, but composers early perceived the advantage of contrasting one with another. Thus Morley, in the same part of the work just mentioned, speaks of the desirableness of alternating Pavans and Galliards; since the first was 'a kind of staid musick ordained for grave dancing,' and the latter 'a lighter and more stirring kind of dancing'; and he further describes more obscurely the contrast arising from the 4-time and 3-time which subsists between them. Spitta, in his Life of Bach (i. 681, Engl. trans. ii. 73), mentions the same contrast as popular in Germany a little later, and refers to the publication of thirty

Paduans and Gaillards by Johann Ghro of Dresden in 1604. In such a manner originated the idea of joining different dance-tunes together to make an artistic balance and contrast, and in this lies the germ of the Suite ; in which, by selecting dances of various nationalities, and disposing them in the order which displayed their relative bearings on one another to the best advantage, composers established the first secular instrumental cyclic art-form.

It is not possible, for want of materials, to trace fully the process of selection. The Pavans and Galliards dropped out of fashion very early, and Allemandes and Courantes came in, and soon became a sort of established nucleus, to which was sometimes appended a Sarabande, or even several other dance movements, and a Prelude. Indeed, when the principle of grouping movements together was once accepted, the speculations of composers in that line seem to have been only limited by their knowledge of dance-forms. It was in fact by experimenting with various methods of grouping that the most satisfactory succession was arrived at ; and thus many of the earlier suites contain a greater profusion and variety than is found in those of the maturer period. In Purcell's suites, for instance, which date from the last ten or twenty years of the 17th century, besides the Allemande and Courante, which occupy just the very position in which they are found in the Suites of Bach and Handel, in one case the group also comprises a Sarabande, Cebell, Minuet, Riggadoon, Intrade, and March ; while another contains a Trumpet tune and a Chacone, and another a Hornpipe. One of the most curious features in them is the absence of the Jig, which in the mature suite-form was the only one admitted of English origin. The opening with a Prelude is almost invariable ; and this is not astonishing, since this kind of movement (which can hardly be described as a 'form') was as familiar as the dances, from having been so often attempted by the early instrumental composers, such as Byrd, Orlando Gibbons, Bull, and Blow among Englishmen. The order of four movements which served as the nucleus in the large proportion of suites of the mature period is also occasionally, by accident, found very early ; as for instance in one of the Suites of Froberger, which Nottebohm says was written in 1649 ; and another by Lully, which was probably written early in the second half of the same century.

These groups had, however, as yet no uniform distinctive title. In England, in common with other combinations of divisions or movements, they were generally called Lessons, or Suites of Lessons, and continued to be so called till after Handel's time. In Italy similar groups were called Sonate da Camera ; in Germany they were called Parties or Partitas, as in the Clavierübung of Kuhnau published in 1689, and the set of six by Johann Krieger[1] published in 1697 ; and in France they were as yet commonly known as Ordres. Thus the fact evidently existed universally for some time before the name by which it is now known came into general use.

The composers of different countries illustrated in different degrees the tendency towards consolidation which is inevitable in an art-form. The steps taken by the Italians appear to be particularly important as illustrating the distinct tendencies of the Suite and the Sonata. Corelli's earlier Sonate da Camera are scarcely distinguishable from the suite type, as they consist of a string of dance-tunes preceded by a prelude. The later sonatas or solos of his Opera Quinta, however, represent different types. Some still consist of dance-tunes, but many also show a fair proportion of movements of more abstract nature ; and in several the dance element is, in name at least, quite absent. These are indeed a sort of combination of the church and chamber sonata into a secular form, adding a canzona or free fugal movement in the place of the allemande, and transmuting the other dance types into movements with general qualities analogous to the earlier sonatas. Where this abstract character prevailed, the type approached more distinctly to that of the modern sonata ; and where the uniformity of a dance rhythm prevailed throughout, it approached more nearly to the suite type. In these cases the arrangement had already ceased to be a mere crude experiment in antithesis, such as the early balance of galliard and pavan, and attained to the dignity of a complete art-form. With the Italians the remarkable distinction of their[2] violin school led to the greater cultivation of the Violin Sonata, which though retaining a few dance-forms, differed markedly in their distribution, and even in the structure of the movements. In both France and Germany more attention seems to have been paid to the clavier, and with it to the suite form. The former country very early showed many proofs of appreciation of its principles ; as an instance, the suite by Lully in E minor, mentioned above, has the complete series of allemande, sarabande, courante, minuet, and gigue. But a little later, theatrical influences seem to have come into play, and Rameau and Couperin, though in many cases adopting the same nucleus to start with, added to it a profusion of rondeaus and other short movements called by various eccentric names. In one of Couperin's Ordres the number of little pieces amounts to no less than twenty-three ; and in such a case it is clear that a sense of form or complete balance in the whole can hardly have been even aimed at. The movements are strung together in the same key, according to the recognised rule, as a series of agreeable ballet pieces, and the titles point to their belonging to quite a different order of art from that illustrated

[1] See *Musical Times*, 1901, p. 163.   [2] See SONATA.

by the suite in its maturity. In fact their kinship must be attributed mainly to the order of programme music. Thus in the tenth Ordre of Couperin, the first number is called 'La Triomphante' and also 'Bruit de Guerre.' In the eleventh Ordre a series of pieces represents 'Les Fastes de la grande et ancienne Mxnxstrxndxsx,' in five acts, the fourth of which is 'Les Invalides,' etc., in which the right hand is made to represent 'Les Disloqués' and the left 'Les Boiteux,' and the last is 'Désordre et déroute de toute la troupe : causés par les Yvrognes, les Singes, et les Ours.'

In Germany, composers kept their faces more steadfastly set in the direction of purer art-form, and the prevalence of uniformity in their distribution of movements soon became remarkable. Kuhnau's examples have been already referred to, and an example given in Pauer's 'Alte Clavier Musik' illustrates the usual order absolutely. Spitta mentions that the famous organist Buxtehude made a complete suite out of variations on the choral 'Auf meinem lieben Gott' in the form of sarabande, courante, and gigue. Twelve sets of 'Pièces de Clavecin' by Mattheson, which were published in London as early as 1714, two years before Couperin's first set, are remarkably regular. The first, in D minor, has a prelude, allemande and double, courante and double, sarabande, and gigue. The second begins with a toccatina, the fifth with a fantasia, the ninth with a 'Boutade,' and the tenth with a 'Symphonie,' but in other respects most of them follow the same outlines of general distribution. The 'Six Suits of Lessons' of the Dutchman Johann Loeillet, published a little earlier still, are equally precise. From these facts it is quite clear that by the beginning of the 18th century certain definite principles of grouping the movements were generally known and accepted ; and that a nucleus, consisting of allemande, courante, sarabande, and gigue, had become the accepted type of the art-form.

The differences between the structure of suite movements and sonata movements have already been traced in the article SONATA. It remains here only to summarise, with more special reference to the suite. While sonata movements constantly increased in complexity, suite movements remained almost stationary. They were based upon the persistence of the uniform type of a dance rhythm, throughout the whole of each several movement. Hence the ground principles of subject in sonata and suite are altogether different. In the former the subjects are concrete, and stand out in a marked manner both in contrast to one another and to their immediate context ; and it is a vital point in the form that they shall be fully and clearly recapitulated. In the suite, on the other hand, the subject does not stand out at all prominently from its context, but is only a well-marked presentation of the type of motion and rhythm which is to prevail throughout the movement. To this there is no contrasting subject or episode, and definite recapitulation is no part of the scheme at all. In a few cases—which must be regarded as accidents in relation to the logical principles of the form—the opening bars happen to be sufficiently marked to have something of the character of a sonata subject ; and in such cases it may also happen that they are repeated with sufficient simplicity to have the effect of recapitulation. But nevertheless it must be maintained that this is not part of the principle of construction. And with reference to this point it is well to remember that composers did not attain the ultimate distinct outlines of sonata and suite with a definite purpose and plan before them ; but that in working with particular materials they were led almost unconsciously to differentiate the two forms. The plan is found to exist when the work is done ; but it is not theoretically propounded and then worked up to. It is not therefore a matter for surprise that in early times some points in the development of abstract form of the sonata kind were worked out in dance movements of the suite type, and applied and extended afterwards in works which had more distinctly the sonata character. Nevertheless the sonata is not an outgrowth from the suite ; but, inasmuch as both were descended from a kindred stock, before the distinctions had become well defined, it is natural that many works should have continued to exhibit suggestions and traits of both sides promiscuously. On the whole, however, it is remarkable how soon the distinct types came to be generally maintained ; and from the number of instances which conform, the system can be fairly deduced.

The most marked external point is the uniformity of key. In Corelli's earlier Sonate da Camera, which in general are decided suites, the one exception which marks a sonata tendency is that the slow dance is often in a different key from the rest of the movements. In later suites of all sorts the uniformity of key throughout is almost universal. In the whole of Bach's the only exceptions are the second minuet of the fourth English Suite, and the second gavotte in that known as the 'Overture in French Style.'[1] Hence the contrast is purely one of character between the several movements ; and this is emphasised by the absence of any marked contrast of key or subject in the movements themselves. They are almost invariably constructed upon the simple principle of balanced halves, each representing the same material in different phases, and each strengthened by repetition. The first half sets out from the tonic key, and without any marked pause or division modulates so as to settle into the key of the dominant or relative major, and closes in that key. The second half begins afresh from that point, and proceeding in most cases by way of the key of

----

[1] 'Ouverture à la manière Française.'

the subdominant, settles well back again into the original key and concludes. The only break therefore is in the middle ; and the two halves are made purposely to balance one another, as far as may be, without definite recapitulation. In a few movements, such especially as sarabandes and intermezzi, the second half is somewhat extended to admit of a little development and free modulation, but the general principles in the average number of cases are the same, namely, to diffuse the character of the principal figures and features throughout, rather than to concentrate the interest of the subject in definite parts of the movement. In order, however, to strengthen the effect of balance between the two halves, certain devices are common and characteristic, especially with regard to the beginnings and endings of each half. Thus though composers do not seem to have aimed at recapitulation, there is frequently a clear relation between the opening bars of each half. This often amounts to no more than a subtle equivalence in the distribution of the group of rhythms in the bar, or a very loose transcript of its melodic features. But in some cases, most especially in Bach, the opening bars of the latter half present a free inversion of the beginning of the first half, or a sort of free shuffling of the parts approximating to double counterpoint. The first mode is clearly illustrated by the Courante of the third Partita in A minor as follows :—

1st half.

etc.

2nd half.

etc.

The Allemande of the fourth Suite Anglaise supplies a remarkable example of free inversion of figures and parts at the same time :—

1st half.

etc.

2nd half.

etc.

The other point, of even more common occurrence, is the correspondence of the ends of each half, which prevails particularly in allemandes, courantes, and gigues. A very fine and full example is supplied by the Allemande of Bach's first Suite Anglaise ; the Courante of his second Suite Française supplies another of some length ; and among works of other composers the Allemande of Lully's Suite in E minor, the Courante of Mattheson's Suite No. 5 in C minor, the Courante of Handel's fourth Suite, the Gigue of his eighth Suite, and most of his Allemandes, are instances to the point. In the particular manner of the suite movements both these devices are exceedingly effective as emphasising the balance of halves, and in the finest movements the balance of material and modulation is carefully distributed for the same end. Thus much of form applies more or less to all the movements which are based on dance rhythms, or developed on that principle.

Each of the movements has also severally distinct characteristics, upon which the form of the suite as a whole is mainly based. For the better understanding of this it will be best to take the group which forms the average nucleus or so-called canon of the Suite. In the severest simplicity of the form the Allemande comes first, as in all Bach's French Suites, in some of Couperin's, and many by earlier composers. The origin of the movement is obscure, and it is maintained that it is not based upon any dance, since the Allemande of Suabian origin, said to be the only dance-form of that name known, is quite distinct from it. However that may be, its constitution, which is most important, consists mainly of moderately slow 4-time, with regular smooth motion—most frequently of semiquavers—distributed in a figurate manner between the various parts, and its character has been generally regarded as appropriately quiet and sober ; which Mattheson described as the 'Ruhe des Anfangs.' To this the Courante, which almost invariably follows it in the mature suite, is supposed and intended to supply a contrast, but it cannot be maintained that it always does so successfully. The character of this movement varies considerably, owing chiefly to the fact that there are two decidedly distinct forms derived from different sources. The one of Italian origin which is found most frequently in Corelli's Sonatas, in most of Handel's, in some but not all of Purcell's Suites, and in Bach's fifth and sixth French Suites, and fifth Partita, is in 3–4 time, of quick, light, and direct movement, full of rapid passages of simple character, with simple rhythm, and free from complication. This in general supplies in an obvious sense a fair contrast to the Allemande. The other Courante, of French origin, is nominally in 3–2 time, but its characteristic is a peculiar intermixture of 3–2 and 6–4, which is supposed to produce a stronger

antithesis to the smooth motion of the Allemande.
In the original dance it is said that this characteristic was chiefly confined to the last bars
of each half, but in mature suite movements
it was elaborately worked into the body of the
movement with very curious effect.   The
quality is shown as early as Kuhnau, but more
frequently in Couperin's Suites, from whom it is
said Bach adopted it.   The following example
from Couperin's third Suite is characteristic :—

It is possible that Bach adopted this form as
affording opportunities for rhythmic experiments ; he certainly carried it to great lengths,
such as giving the right hand a passage in
3–2 and the left in 6–4 :—

but the result is not on the whole very successful.   In most cases the French Courantes are
the least interesting movement of his Suites,
and as contrasts to the Allemande do not compare favourably with the Italian Courante.   As
an element of contrast the crossing of the time
is rather theoretical than real, and the necessity
of keeping the time moderate in order to make
it intelligible brings the strong beats and the
average quickness of the shortest notes, as well
as the full spread of the bar, too near to those
of the Allemande ; and in the general effect of
the Suite these externals tell more strongly than
the abstract restlessness of crossing rhythms.
It is possible, however, that the French Courante
has one advantage over the Italian : that inasmuch as the latter has more stability in itself,
it calls less for a succeeding movement, and
presents less perfectly the aspect of a link in
the chain than of a movement which might as
well stand alone.   There is a slight touch of
uneasiness about the French Courante which, as
a step towards the Sarabande, is very appropriate.
In this latter movement, which is of Spanish
or possibly Moorish origin, rhythmic principle
is very pronounced, and at the same time simple.

Its external aspect is chiefly the strong emphasis
on the second beat of a bar of three in slow time,
as is clearly illustrated in Handel's Sarabande
in the G minor Suite, in his ' Lascia ch'io pianga,'
and in the Sarabande of Bach's F major Suite
Anglaise.   This is an obvious source of contrast
with both the preceding members of the suite,
since in both Allemande and Courante there is
no pronounced and persistent rhythm, and the
pace, though not necessarily quick, scarcely
ever comes within the range of motion or style
characteristic of definitely slow movements.
There is also a further and equally important
element of contrast.   The first two numbers are
characterised in a considerable proportion of
instances by a similar free motion of parts.
The process of carrying on the figures is sometimes knit by a kind of free imitation, but,
however desirable it may be theoretically to
regard them so, they cannot fairly be described
as movements of imitation.   The process is
rather that of free figuration of two or three
parts, giving in general a contrapuntal effect to
the whole.   In the Sarabande the peculiar
rhythmic character puts both systematic imitation and regular contrapuntal motion equally
out of the question.   Consequently as a rule
a more decidedly harmonic style obtains ; the
chords are fuller, and move more simultaneously
as blocks of harmony.   The character of the
finest examples is necessarily very pliable, and
varies between free melody with simple accompanying harmony, such as those in Bach's Suites
Anglaises in F and D minor, Handel's Suites in
G minor and E minor ; examples in which the
prominent melodic features are distributed successively without regularity between the parts,
as in those in the Suites Anglaises in G minor
and A minor, the Suite Française in B minor, the
Partita in B♭, and several of Couperin's ; and a
few examples in which a figure or characteristic
mode of motion is made to prevail almost
throughout, as in the Suite Française in E♭.
The general effect of the sarabandes is noble and
serious, and the music is more concentrated than
in any other member of the group of movements.
It is thus in various respects the central point
of the suite :—in position ; in musical interest
and unique quality ; and in the fact, as observed
and curiously commented on by Nottebohm,
that the preceding movements generally tend to
the solidity and the succeeding movements to
lightness and gaiety.   The order is in this
respect somewhat similar to that of average
sonatas, and seems to be the art-exposition of
the same ideas of form from the point of view
of the musical sense, though differently carried
out as far as the actual manner and material of
the movements are concerned.
In the most concise examples of the Suite the
Sarabande is followed by the final Gigue ; but
it is so common with all the most notable
writers of suites to interpolate other movements,

that it may be well to notice them first. These appear to have been called by the older writers Galanterien, and more lately Intermezzi ; and seem to have been regarded as a sort of concession to popular taste. But in any way they answer the purposes of form exceedingly well. A very great variety of dances is introduced at this point. The most familiar are the Gavottes, Bourrées, Minuets, and Passepieds. But besides these the most distinguished writers introduced Loures, Polonaises, movements called Arias, and other less familiar forms. Their character on the average is especially light and simple, and in the dance numbers it is remarkable that they always preserve their dance character more decidedly and obviously than any other member of the group. It is not possible to describe them all in detail, as they are too numerous, but their aspect in the group is for the most part similar, and is analogous to that of the Scherzo or Minuet and Trio in the modern sonata. They evidently strengthen the balance on either side of the sarabande both in quality and amount. In many cases there is a considerable group of them, and in these cases it is that the Aria is sometimes introduced. This movement has little connection with the modern piece of the same name, as it is generally a short movement in the same balanced form as the other movements, but free from the dance basis and rule of time. It is generally moderately slow, and sometimes consistently melodious, as in Mattheson's Suite in A ; but often it is little more than a string of figures, without even melody of much importance. The group of Intermezzi is generally contrasted with the Sarabande and the Gigue either by a square time or by the interchange of moderate movement, such as that of the Minuet ; and the conciseness and distinctness of the type is always sufficient to make the relations on both sides perfectly clear.

The Gigue which concludes the series is theoretically, and in most cases actually, of light and rapid style. It is usually based on some rhythmic combination of 3 feet, but even this is not invariable. The balance is in favour of 12–8 time ; but 6–8 is also common, and 12–16 and 3–8 not unfrequent ; while a few are in some form of common time, as the slow Gigue in the first French Suite of Bach, and the remarkable example in his last Partita in E minor. The old fancy for concluding a work with a fugue is illustrated by the common occurrence of fugal treatment in this member alone of the regular group of the true suite series. The treatment is met with in all directions ; in Kuhnau, Mattheson, Handel, Couperin, as well as Bach. The method of application is commonly to begin and carry out a free sort of fugue in the first half, concluding like the other movements in the dominant key ; and to take up the same subject freely 'al rovescio' or by contrary motion in the second half, with regular

answer as in a fresh fughetta, and carry it out on that basis with the usual direction of modulation, concluding in the original key. Thus the fugal treatment is an accessory to the usual form of the suite movement, which is here as regularly and invariably maintained as in the other members of the group.

The most important accessory which is commonly added to this nucleus is the Prelude. It appears in a variety of forms, and under a great variety of names. (It is worth noticing that all six introductory movements of Bach's Partitas have different titles.) The chief point which is most obvious in relation to the other movements is that their characteristic form of nearly equal halves is systematically avoided ; in fact any other form seems to have been taken in preference. In many important examples it is the longest and most elaborate movement of all. In some it is a sort of rhapsody or irregular group of arpeggios and other figures based on simple series of chords. Bach commonly developed it on the same broad outlines as some of his largest sonata movements, and the first and last of the Italian Concerto—that is, the distinct balancing section of clear musical character and full close at the beginning and end of the movement, and the long passage of development and modulation in the middle, sometimes embracing new figures. This is illustrated by the Preludes to the Suites Anglaises in A minor, G minor, F and E minor. In other examples the treatment is fugal, or contains a complete fugue along with other matter of more rhapsodical cast, as in the Toccata of the Partita in E minor ; or yet again it is in the form of a Fantasia, or of the Overture as then understood. The effect is certainly to add breadth and stability to the group in no mean degree, and the contrast with the rest of the movements is in every respect unmistakable. This completes the general outline of the Suite in its finest and most consistently complete form, as illustrated in Bach's Suites Anglaises, which must be regarded as the culminating point of the Suite as an art-form.

In the matter of actual distribution of movements there are plenty of examples of experiments, even in the time when the usual nucleus had come to be generally recognised ; in fact, there is hardly any large collection of suites which does not present some exceptions to the rules. Bach's departures from the usual outlines are chiefly in the earliest examples, such as the Partitas, in one of which he concludes with a rondo and a caprice. The 'Ouverture à la manière Française,' for Clavier, is in appearance a Suite, but it is clear that Bach had not only the Clavier Suite type in his mind in laying out its plan, but also the freer distribution of numbers in the so-called French Overture said to date from Lully. In this there is no Allemande ; the Sarabande has Intermezzi on both sides of it, and it concludes with an ' Echo ' after the Gigue.   The works of his which are now commonly known as Orchestral Suites must be put in the same category.   For the inference suggested by Dehn's trustworthy observations on the MSS. is that Bach regarded them as Overtures, and that the name Suite was added by some one else afterwards.   They depart from the average order of the Clavier Suite even more conspicuously than the above-mentioned work.   In his later compositions for Clavier, as has been already remarked, he was very strict.   Handel's Suites on the other hand are conspicuous departures from the usual order.   They are, in fact, for the most part hybrids, and very few have the genuine suite character as a whole. The introduction of airs with variations, and of fugues, in the body of the work, takes them out of the category of strict interdependent art forms, and makes them appear rather as casual strings of movements, which are often as fit to be taken alone or in different groups as in the group into which he has thrown them.   Moreover they illustrate somewhat, as Nottebohm has also observed, the peculiar position which Handel occupied in art, as not pure German only, but also as representative of some of the finest traits of the Italian branch of the art. The tendency of the Italians after Corelli was towards the Violin Sonata, a distinct branch from the original stem, and to this order some of Handel's Suites tend to approximate.   It was chiefly by thorough Germans that the suite-form was developed in its austerest simplicity ; and in that condition and in relation to their keyed instruments it seems that the usual group is the most satisfactory that has been devised.

It is obvious that the Suite as an art-form is far more elementary and inexpansive than the Sonata.   In fact it attained its maturity long before the complete development of the latter form ; and not a little of the interest which attaches to it is derived from that and collateral facts.   It was the first instrumental form in which several movements were combined into a complete whole.   It was the first in which the ecclesiastical influences which had been so powerful in all high-class music were completely supplanted by a secular type of equally high artistic value.   Lastly, it was the highest representative instrumental form of the contrapuntal period, as the Sonata is the highest of the harmonic period.   It was brought to perfection when the modern sonata was still in its infancy, and before those ideas of key and of the relations of harmonies which lie at the root of sonata-form had become tangible realities to men's minds.   In some respects the complete plan has the aspect of formalism and rigidity. The uniformity of key is sometimes taken

exception to, and the sameness of structural principle in each movement is also undoubtedly somewhat of a drawback ; but it must be remembered that the form is a representative product of a peculiar artistic period, and devised for a particular keyed instrument, and for minds as yet unaccustomed to the varied elaboration of the sonata.   The results are remarkable and valuable in a high degree ; and though this may be chiefly owing to the exceptional powers of the composers who made use of the form, it is possible that as a pattern for the combination of small pieces it may still be worthy of regard. In fact the combination of short lyrical movements such as are characteristic of modern times has strong points of analogy with it. Moreover, since it is obviously possible to introduce modifications of some of the details which were too rigid in the early scheme without destroying the general principles of the form, it seems that genuine and valuable musical results may still be obtained by grafting characteristics of modern treatment and expression upon the old stock.   There already exist several experiments of this kind by modern composers of mark ; and the Suites for orchestra, pianoforte, violoncello, or violin, by Lachner, Raff, Bargiel, Saint-Saëns, Tchaikovsky, Ries, and Cowen, are not by any means among their least successful efforts.   C. H. H. P.

SUK, Josef.   See BOHEMIAN STRING QUARTET.

SULLIVAN, Sir ARTHUR SEYMOUR, was born in London,[1] May 13, 1842.   His father, a native of County Cork, was a bandmaster, and chief professor of the clarinet at Kneller Hall ; he was thus born amongst music.   His first systematic instruction was received from the Rev. Thomas Helmore, Master of the Children of the Chapel Royal, which he entered April 12, 1854, and left on the change of his voice, June 22, 1857.   While at the Chapel Royal he wrote many anthems and small pieces.   One of them, ' O Israel,' a ' sacred song,' was published by Novellos in 1855.   In 1856 the Mendelssohn Scholarship was brought into active existence, and in July of that year Sullivan was elected the first scholar.   Without leaving the Chapel Royal he began to study at the Royal Academy of Music under Goss and Sterndale Bennett, and remained there till his departure for Leipzig in the autumn of 1858. An overture ' of considerable merit ' is mentioned [2] at this time as having been played at one of the private concerts of the Academy. At Leipzig he entered the Conservatorium under Plaidy, Hauptmann, Richter, Julius Rietz, and Moscheles, and remained there in company with Walter Bache, John F. Barnett, Franklin Taylor, and Carl Rosa, till the end of 1861.

[1] A photograph of the house in Lambeth is given in the *Musical Times* for 1901, p. 241.   In the same volume many ancedotes of the composer's youth are related.
[2] *Athenæum*, July 24, 1858.

He then returned to London, bringing with him his music to Shakespeare's 'Tempest' (op. 1 *a*, dedicated to Sir George Smart), which was produced at the Crystal Palace, April 5, 1862, and repeated on the 12th of the same month.

This beautiful composition made a great sensation in musical circles, and launched him into London musical society. Two very graceful pianoforte pieces, entitled 'Thoughts,' were among his earliest publications. The arrival of the Princess of Wales in March 1863, produced a song, 'Bride from the North,' and a Procession March and Trio in E♭ ; and a song entitled 'I heard the Nightingale' was published April 28 of the same year. But his next work of importance was a cantata called 'Kenilworth,' words by the late H. F. Chorley, written for the Birmingham Festival of 1864, and produced there. It contains a fine duet, for soprano and tenor, to Shakespeare's words, 'On such a night as this.' His music to the ballet of 'L'Île enchantée' was produced at Covent Garden, May 16, 1864.

At this date he lost much time over an opera called 'The Sapphire Necklace,' also by Chorley ; the undramatic character of the libretto of which prevented its representation. The music was used up in other works. In March 1866 Sullivan produced a Symphony in E at the Crystal Palace, which has been often played subsequently, there and at the Philharmonic, etc. In the same year he expressed his grief for the loss of his father in an overture entitled 'In Memoriam,' which was produced (Oct. 30) at the Norwich Festival of that year. A concerto for violoncello and orchestra was played by Piatti at the Crystal Palace on Nov. 24. This was followed by an overture, 'Marmion,' commissioned by the Philharmonic Society, and produced by them June 3, 1867. In the autumn of that year he accompanied his friend the Editor of this Dictionary [Sir George Grove] to Vienna, in search of the Schubert MSS., which have since become so well known. At the same time his symphony was played at the Gewandhaus at Leipzig. In 1869 he composed a short oratorio on the story of the 'Prodigal Son,' for the Worcester Festival, where it was produced on Sept. 8. In 1870 he again contributed a work to the Birmingham Festival, the 'Overtura di Ballo' (in E♭), which, while couched throughout in dance-rhythms, is constructed in perfectly classical form. To continue the list of his commissioned works : in 1871, in company with Gounod, Hiller, and Pinsuti, he wrote a piece for the opening of the 'Annual International Exhibition' at the Albert Hall, on May 1—a cantata by Tom Taylor called 'On Shore and Sea,' for solo, chorus, and orchestra. On the recovery of the Prince of Wales from illness, he composed, at the call of the Crystal Palace Company, a Festival Te Deum, for soprano solo, orchestra, and chorus, which was performed there May 1, 1872. At this time he was closely engaged in editing the collection of 'Church Hymns with Tunes' for the Christian Knowledge Society, for which he wrote twenty-one original tunes. In 1873 he made a third appearance at Birmingham, this time with the leading feature of the Festival, an oratorio entitled 'The Light of the World,' the words selected from the Bible by himself. The success of this work at Birmingham was great, and it has often since been performed. Sullivan succeeded Sir Michael Costa as conductor of the Leeds Festival of 1880, and wrote for it 'The Martyr of Antioch,' to words selected from Milman's play of that name. The work lies between an oratorio and a cantata, and was enthusiastically received. He conducted the Leeds Festivals from 1883 to 1898, composing for the latter 'The Golden Legend,' to words selected by Joseph Bennett from Longfellow's poem.

We will now go back to those works which have made Sullivan's name most widely known, not only in Europe but in Australia and America —his comic operettas, and his songs. 'Cox and Box, a new Triumviretta,' was an adaptation by F. C. Burnand of Madison Morton's well-known farce, made still more comic by the interpolations, and set by Sullivan with a brightness and a drollery which at once put him in the highest rank as a comic composer.[1] It was first heard at Moray Lodge (Mr. Arthur J. Lewis's) on April 27, 1867, and produced in public at the Adelphi a fortnight after, on May 11. The vein thus struck was not at first very rapidly worked. 'The Contrabandista' (2 acts, words by Burnand)[2] followed at St. George's Opera House on Dec. 18, 1867 ; but then there was a pause. 'Thespis, or the Gods grown old ; an operatic extravaganza,' by Gilbert (Gaiety, Dec. 26, 1871), and 'The Zoo, an original musical folly,' by B. Rowe (St. James's, June 5, 1875), though full of fun and animation, were neither of them sufficient to take the public. 'Trial by Jury, an extravaganza'—and a very extravagant one too—words by W. S. Gilbert, produced at the Royalty, March 25, 1875, had a great success, and many representations, owing in part to the very humorous conception of the character of the Judge by Sullivan's brother Frederick. But none of these can be said to have taken a real hold on the public. 'The Sorcerer, an original modern comic opera,' by W. S. Gilbert, which first established the popularity of its composer, was a new departure, a piece of larger dimensions and more substance than any of its predecessors. It was produced at the Opéra-Comique, Strand, Nov. 17, 1877, and ran uninterruptedly for 175 nights. The

1 See *Times* of May 13, 1867.
2 This opera was written, composed, and produced in the extraordinarily short space of sixteen days.

company formed for this piece by D'Oyly Carte, including that admirable artist George Grossmith, was maintained in the next, 'H.M.S. Pinafore,' produced at the same house, May 25, 1878. This not only ran in London for 700 consecutive nights (besides an unauthorised series of performances at another theatre), but had an extraordinary vogue in the provinces, and was adopted in the United States to a degree exceeding all previous record. To protect their interests there, Sullivan and Gilbert visited the United States in 1879, and remained for several months. An attempt to bring out the piece at Berlin as 'Amor am Bord'[1] failed, owing to the impossibility of anything like political caricature in Germany. But it was published by Litolff in 1882. The vein of droll satire on current topics adopted in the last two pieces was fully kept up in 'The Pirates of Penzance' (April 3, 1880), and 'Patience, an æsthetic opera' (April 25, 1881), during the run of which the company moved to the Savoy Theatre built especially for these operas, and opened on Oct. 10, 1881. ['Iolanthe' was brought out on Nov. 25, 1882, 'Princess Ida' on Jan. 5, 1884, and the most successful of the whole series, 'The Mikado,' on March 14, 1885. 'Ruddigore' followed it on Jan. 22, 1887, 'The Yeomen of the Guard' on Oct. 3, 1888, and 'The Gondoliers' on Dec. 7, 1889. Up to this time the happy partnership formed between Sullivan, Gilbert, and D'Oyly Carte had remained unbroken, and uniform favour crowned their successive undertakings, the run of each opera only ceasing with the production of its successor. From the time of the rupture, the management relied on revivals of the repertory that had been formed, and upon attempts by others to carry on what were called the 'Savoy traditions.' Sullivan himself contributed 'Haddon Hall' to a libretto by Sydney Grundy, and it was produced on Sept. 24, 1892. The reconcilement of the Savoy differences was a matter of national rejoicing, and on Oct. 7, 1893, the next Gilbert and Sullivan opera was seen, called 'Utopia Limited'; for the next production, a revival of the 'Contrabandista'—to a libretto of Burnand's —with various modifications of the original, was given as 'The Chieftain,' on Dec. 12, 1894. On March 7, 1896, 'The Grand Duke,' a new Gilbert and Sullivan piece, was produced, but after a revival of 'The Gondoliers,' the continuance of the famous collaboration was once more broken, and 'The Beauty Stone,' to a libretto by Messrs. Comyns Carr and A. W. Pinero, was produced on May 28, 1898. With the production of 'The Rose of Persia,' to a libretto by Captain Basil Hood, on Nov. 29, 1899, a new period of success seemed to have been begun, and the reception of the work by the public was almost as great as that given for so many years to the two collaborators. 'The

[1] Arranged for the German stage by Ernst Dohm.

Emerald Isle,' by the same librettist, was brought out on April 27, 1901, some months after the composer's death ; the music was finished by Edward German, who in 'Merrie England' and 'A Princess of Kensington' made an excellent effort to continue the *genre*. For one reason or another it was found impossible to keep the vogue the theatre had so long enjoyed ; but in these latter days, now that the fashion of the rule of the so-called 'musical comedy' seems a little on the wane, the more educated portions of the public have shown a decided inclination to return to the Savoy form of entertainment ; and, while all over the country the popularity of the Gilbert and Sullivan operas has never decreased, the curious prohibition of 'The Mikado,' and the still more curious withdrawal of that prohibition, have placed the work higher in popular favour than it ever was before. It was generally felt that Sullivan was devoting himself too exclusively to the light music in which he was so accomplished a master ; and in the first edition of this Dictionary Sir George Grove expressed the hope that he would 'apply his gifts to the production of a serious opera on some subject of abiding human or national interest.' When a new theatre was built at Cambridge Circus by D'Oyly Carte, for the special purpose of realising this hope, public interest and encouragement reached an extraordinary intensity ; and 'The Royal English Opera House' was opened on Jan. 31, 1891, with the grand opera 'Ivanhoe,' in three acts, to a libretto by Julian Sturgis. Everything was done to ensure the success of the important undertaking, which, had the scheme been a little bolder and more widely based, would no doubt have reached the permanent success at which it aimed. Various circumstances contributed to the ultimate failure of the scheme, and to the establishment of the 'Palace Theatre of Varieties' in its stead. The composer had apparently found it difficult to throw over all the Savoy traditions at once, and accordingly he interspersed, with scenes in which real dramatic interest was displayed, some which were in a flimsy style, quite incongruous with the rest. The impression at the time was that unless a piece ran for at least one hundred nights consecutively, it could not rank as a success, and in order to secure this long run, and in view of the impossibility of any singers repeating trying parts for six or seven performances per week, two casts of principal singers were engaged ; but it was impossible to foresee which representatives would appear on any given night, and as the seats had to be booked long beforehand, the admirers of the composer at last got tired of the uncertainty and withdrew their patronage from the undertaking. Another mistake was made, for although rumours were heard of various new English operas being prepared to take the place of 'Ivanhoe,' none was ready when its popularity was over, and Messager's pretty 'Basoche' was produced; at the close of the run of this piece, the theatre was transformed into a music-hall. Sullivan wrote a good many sets of incidental music to plays, beside 'The Tempest,' with which his first recognition had been obtained. 'The Merchant of Venice,' at the Prince's Theatre, Manchester, 1871; 'The Merry Wives of Windsor,' Gaiety Theatre, 1874; ' Henry VIII.,' Manchester, 1878; 'Macbeth,' Lyceum Theatre, 1888; Tennyson's 'Foresters,' 1892 (first produced in America, and afterwards at Daly's Theatre); and Comyns Carr's 'King Arthur,' Lyceum Theatre, 1894, are the most important of these compositions. The Diamond Jubilee of Queen Victoria was celebrated by Sullivan in two compositions: the ballet, 'Victoria and Merrie England,' produced at the Alhambra, May 25, 1897, in which a danced fugue was the best and most interesting number; and a 'Festival Te Deum,' given at the Chester Festival of 1897. The opening of the Imperial Institute in 1893 suggested a March, and various public events of the same kind were celebrated by compositions, for in some sort Sullivan ranked as a poet laureate of music.] Such unprecedented recognition speaks for itself. But it is higher praise to say, with a leading critic, that 'while Mr. Sullivan's music is as comic and lively as anything by Offenbach, it has the extra advantage of being the work of a cultivated musician, who would scorn to write ungrammatically even if he could.'

Sullivan's songs were in their day as well known as his operettas. They are almost always of a tender or sentimental cast; and some of them, such as 'Sweet day so cool, so calm, so bright'; the 'Arabian Love Song,' by Shelley; 'O fair dove, O fond dove,' by Jean Ingelow; the Shakespeare Songs and the Song-cycle of 'The Window,' written for the purpose by Tennyson, stand in a very high rank. None of these, however, have attained the popularity of others, which, though slighter than those just named, and more in the ballad style, have hit the public taste to a remarkable degree. Such are 'Will he come?' and 'The Lost Chord,' 'O ma charmante' (V. Hugo); 'The Distant Shore' and 'Sweethearts' (both by W. S. Gilbert), etc. [His last composition, in the shape of a single song, was 'The Absent-Minded Beggar' to words by Kipling; this served its purpose of obtaining substantial aid for charities consequent upon the Boer War.]

The same tunefulness and appropriateness that have made his songs such favourites also distinguish his numerous Anthems. Here the excellent training of the Chapel Royal shows itself without disguise, in the easy flow of the voices, the display of excellent, and even learned, counterpoint, when demanded by words or subject, and the frequent examples throughout of that melodious style and independent treatment that marks the anthems of certain periods of the old English school. His part-songs, like his anthems, are flowing and spirited, and always appropriate to the words. There are two sets: one sacred, dedicated to his friend Franklin Taylor, and one secular, of which 'O hush thee, my babie' has long been an established favourite.

His Hymn-tunes are numerous—56 in all—and some of them, such as 'Onward, Christian Soldiers,' have become great favourites. The whole were republished in a volume by Novello in 1902.

If his vocal works have gained Sir Arthur Sullivan the applause of the public, it is in his orchestral music that his name will live among musicians. His music to 'The Tempest' and 'The Merchant of Venice,' his oratorios, his Overture di Ballo, and, still more, his Symphony in E—unfortunately his only work in this department—show what remarkable gifts he had for the orchestra. Form and symmetry he seemed to possess by instinct; rhythm and melody clothe everything he touched; the music shows not only sympathetic genius, but sense, judgment, proportion, and a complete absence of pedantry and pretension; while the orchestration is distinguished by a happy and original beauty hardly surpassed by the greatest masters.

During the early part of his career Sullivan was organist of St. Michael's Church, Chester Square. After this, in 1867, he undertook the direction of the music at St. Peter's, Cranley Gardens, for which many of his anthems were composed, and where he remained till 1871. He was musical adviser to the Royal Aquarium Company from its incorporation in July 1874 down to May 1876, organised the admirable band with which it started, and himself conducted its performances. For the seasons 1878 and 1879 he conducted the Promenade Concerts at Covent Garden for Messrs. Gatti; and for those of 1875-1876, and 1876-77, the Glasgow Festivals. He was Principal of the National Training School at South Kensington from 1876 to 1881, when his engagements compelled him to resign in favour of Dr. Stainer, and he was a member of the Council of the Royal College of Music. He received the Honorary Degree of Doctor of Music from the University of Cambridge in 1876, and Oxford, 1879. In 1878 he acted as British Commissioner for Music at the International Exhibition at Paris, and was decorated with the *Légion d'honneur*. He also bore the Order of Saxe-Coburg and Gotha, and on May 22, 1883, was knighted by Queen Victoria. [At the Leeds Festival of 1898 it was evident that he was in failing health, but he accomplished the difficult task of conducting the performances, although suffering much pain. He died in London, Nov. 22, 1900, and was buried in St. Paul's Cathedral on the 27th. A preliminary funeral service was held in the Chapel Royal.

Besides the compositions already enumerated, Sullivan's list of works includes thirteen anthems, six sacred part-songs, three carols, arrangements, sacred songs, etc. (See *Musical Times*, 1901, p. 24.) In 1868 nine part-songs, an ode for baritone and orchestra, 'I wish to tune,' were composed. The popular 'The long day closes' is among the former. Songs to the number of about seventy were published in his earlier years, most of them before the vogue of the Savoy operas began. Among instrumental works are to be mentioned, beside the symphony, the concerto, and the marches already referred to, a 'Duo concertante' for piano and violoncello, and nine short pieces for piano solo, dating from about 1862 to 1867.

The penalty of excessive contemporary popularity has been paid since Sullivan's death, for although that event came like a national disaster, his more important compositions have been almost entirely neglected from that time. Even the beautiful 'Golden Legend,' which enjoyed enormous popularity for many years, has been only heard comparatively seldom of late years. It is quite probable that the pendulum will swing back some day and a new period of popularity begin.]   G.

SUL PONTICELLO. See vol. iii. p. 790.

SULZER, SALOMON, Precentor of the Jews' synagogue in Vienna, and reformer of their musical service, was born March 30, 1804, at Hohenems in Vorarlberg. The name was derived from Sulz in Würtemberg, the ancient residence of the family. When only thirteen he was made cantor of the synagogue at his native village by the Emperor Franz I., and in 1825 was called to Vienna to conduct the music at the newly built synagogue there. There he took lessons in composition from Seyfried, and set himself earnestly to reform the service by reducing the old melodies to rhythm and harmonising them. His collection of Jewish hymns, under the name of 'Schir Zion' (the Harp of Zion), was used all over Germany, Italy, and even America; but it was not till 1838 that he could succeed in publishing it. It contains a setting of the 92nd Psalm (in Moses Mendelssohn's version) by Schubert, for baritone solo, and four men's voices, made in July 1828, the autograph of which is in possession of the synagogue (Nottebohm's *Catalogue*, p. 229). In 1842 a second edition appeared, and in 1865 a second volume. A collection of home and school songs, entitled 'Dudaim' (Mandrakes), appears to be still in MS. In 1866 a fête was held in his honour and a silver laurel presented to him with the inscription 'The Artists of Vienna to the Artist Sulzer.' From 1844 to 1847 he was Professor of Singing at the Vienna Conservatorium. He was a Ritter of the Order of Franz Joseph (1868), and carried the medals of various societies. His voice, a baritone, is said to have been magnificent, and

he was greatly esteemed and beloved inside and outside of his own community. He died in Vienna, Jan. 18, 1890.   G.

SUMER IS ICUMEN IN (Latin words, *Perspice* X$\tilde{p}$*icola* = *Christicola*). A 'Rota' or Round of great antiquity, the original MS. of which is preserved in vol. 978 of the Harleian collection, in the British Museum.

So important are the questions raised by this document, in connection not only with the history of the English School, but with that of Mediæval Music in all other European countries, that we cannot too earnestly recommend them to the consideration of all who are interested in tracing the development of our present system to its earliest sources. The accompanying facsimile is reduced by photography from $7\frac{7}{16} \times 5\frac{5}{16}$ in., to $6\frac{5}{8} \times 4\frac{1}{2}$, and we add (pp. 750-51) a solution of the Canon, in modern notation, but otherwise scored in exact accordance with the Latin directions appended to the original MS. The only characters employed in the original are, the C clef; the *B rotundum* (= B♭); square black-tailed notes, sometimes perfect by position, and sometimes imperfect; one square black note without a tail; and black lozenge-shaped notes, also without tails; except in one solitary case which we can scarcely conceive to be accidental—the first of the three notes sung to the word 'in.' These are replaced, in the reduction, by the G clef for the four upper parts, and the F clef for the two lower ones, forming the *Pes*; by dotted semibreves for the tailed notes, when perfect, and semibreves without dots for those that are imperfect; by a semibreve without a dot for the single untailed square note; by minims for the untailed lozenge-shaped notes; and by a dotted minim, followed by a crotchet, for the solitary lozenge-shaped note with a tail. For the time-signature, we have used the circle, and the figure 3, indicative of Perfect Time, in combination with the Lesser Prolation—a form closely corresponding with the signature 3-2 in modern music.

We have thought it necessary to print the solution of the Canon *in extenso*, because, to the best of our belief, no correct Score has hitherto [*i.e.* in 1883] been published. Hawkins clearly misunderstood the two Ligatures in the *Pes*, and misprinted the passage, at every repetition. Burney corrected this mistake; but both historians have given an erroneous adaptation of the text to the notes, in bars 41 *et seq.*,[1] at the words 'Wel singes thu cuccu ne swik thu nauer nu'; and both, in bar 40, have systematically misprinted the note sung to the second syllable of 'cuccu,' giving G instead of A every time it occurs. It is true that in certain bars G agrees better than A with Hawkins's misprinted *Pes*, but with Burney's correct *Pes*, it makes a horrible discord.

---

[1] The references are to our own score, the bars in which are numbered for the reader's convenience.

With the facsimile and its solution before them, our readers will be able to criticise the opinions hazarded, from time to time, on the antiquity of the Rota ; which opinions we shall now proceed to consider in detail.

The MS. was first described by Mr. Wanley, the famous antiquary, who, acting in the capacity of Librarian to the Earl of Oxford, wrote an account of it in his *Catalogue of the Harleian MSS.* about the year 1709 ; assigning to it no positive date, but pronouncing it to be by far the oldest example of the kind he had ever met with[1]—an assertion which must be received with all respect, since Mr. Wanley was not only a learned antiquary, but an accomplished musician.

In the year 1770 Sir John Hawkins mentioned the Rota in the first volume of his *History of Music*, illustrating his description by a copy of the *Guida*, in the original square black notes, followed by a not very correct solution of the canon, scored for six voices, including those which sing the Pes. Hawkins imagines the term ' Rota ' to apply to the Latin rather than the English[2] words ; and refers the MS. to ' about the middle of the 15th century, on the ground that the Music is of the kind called *Cantus figuratus*, which appears to have been the invention of John of Dunstable, who wrote on the *Cantus mensurabilis*, and died in 1455.' This statement, however, involves an anachronism which renders Hawkins's opinion as to the date of the MS. absolutely worthless.

Dr. Burney, in the second volume of his *History*, described the composition as not being much later than the 13th or 14th century, printed a copy of the Canon in the original mediæval Notation, and subjoined a complete score, more correct than that supplied by Hawkins, yet not altogether free from errors.

Ritson referred the MS. to the middle of the 13th century ; and fancied—not without reason —that neither Hawkins nor Burney cared to risk their reputation by mentioning a date which could scarcely fail to cause adverse criticism.

In 1819 Dr. Busby reprinted the Rota, following Burney's version of the score, note for note, including its errors, and referring the MS. to the 15th century.[3]

In April 1862 Sir Frederick Madden wrote some memoranda on the fly-leaf of the volume, referring the entire MS., ' except some writing on ff. 15-17 ' (with which we are not concerned), to the 13th century ; and stating his belief that ' the earlier portion of this volume [*i.e.* that which contains the Rota] was written in the Abbey of Reading, about the year 1240. Compare the *Obits* in the Calendars with those in the Calendar of the Cartulary of Reading in the MS. Cott. Vesp. E.V.–F.M. April 1892.'

In 1855 Mr. William Chappell described the MS. minutely in his *Popular Music of the Olden Time*, illustrating his remarks by a facsimile of the MS. printed in the original colours.[4] The author took an intense interest in this most valuable MS. ; and, after much laborious research, collected evidence enough to lead him to the belief that it was written at the Abbey of Reading, by a monk named John of Fornsete, about the year 1226, or quite certainly not more than ten years later. For the grounds on which he bases this conclusion we must refer our readers to his own writings on the subject. One of his discoveries, however, is so important that we cannot pass it over without special notice. The volume which contains the Rota contains also a number of satirical poems, written in rhymed Latin by Gualterus Mahap (Walter Mapes, Archdeacon of Oxford).[5] Among these is a Satire entitled *Apud avaros*,[6] bristling with puns, one of which closely concerns our present subject, and helps, in no small degree, to establish the antiquity of the Rota. The Poet counsels his readers as to the best course to be pursued by those who wish to 'move' the Roman Law-Courts. After numerous directions, each enforced by a pun, he writes as follows :—

Commisso notario munera suffunde,
Statim causae subtrahet, quando, cur, et unde,
Et formae subjiciet canones rotundae.[7]
Apud avaros, 69-71.

Now, the significance of this venerable pun, as a proof of the antiquity of the Rota, is very remarkable. In a poem, transcribed, as Sir Frederick Madden assures us, long before the middle of the 13th century, Walter Mapes, an English ecclesiastic, speaks of 'subjecting Canons to the form of (the) Round,' with a homely *naïveté* which proves that his readers must have been too familiar with both Round and Canon, to stand in any danger of mistaking the drift of the allusion. This form of music, then, must have been *common*, in England, before the middle of the 13th century. Walter Mapes bears witness to the fact that the first English school, as represented by the Rota, is at least a century and a half older than the first Flemish school as represented by the works of Dufay, and we are indebted to Chappell for the discovery of the *jeu d'esprit* in which the circumstance is recorded.

Turning from English to Continental critics, we first find the Rota introduced to the German musical world by Forkel, who, in the year 1788, described it in his *Allgemeine Geschichte der Musik* ; reproducing Burney's copy of the Guida,

[1] See *Catalogue of the Harleian MSS.* (vol. i. No. 978), in the Library of the British Museum.
[2] On this point, he gives the authority of Du Cange, who says that the term 'Rota' was anciently applied to certain hymns.
[3] *A General History of Music*, vol. i. pp. 385-401 (London, 1819).
[4] *Popular Music of the Olden Time*, 2 vols. (London, 1855-59).
[5] See Wanley's remarks, in the *Catalogue of the Harl. MSS.*
[6] Harl. MSS. 978, fol. 85a (formerly numbered 83a, and 106a).
[7] When thou art sent to the Notary pour in thy gifts.
He will then at once extricate thee from the cause, when, why or whencesoever it may have arisen,
And will subject the Canons to the form of the Round.

✠ This sign indicates the bar at which each successive Part is to make its entrance.

† Abbreviated form of *Christicola*.

† Burney and Hawkins have both mistaken this note for G. It is quite certainly A in the original MS. In the four bars which follow, the words and music are incorrectly fitted together in all previous editions.

* Anciently, each voice ceased at the end of the *Guida*, which is here denoted by the sign *. The present custom is for all the voices to continue until they reach a point at which they may all conveniently close together, as indicated by the pause.

in the old black square-headed notation (*Gros-Fa*), and also his modernised score, in semibreves and minims, accompanying these by Wanley's remarks, copied from the Harleian Catalogue. To this he added a corollary of his own to the effect that though the MS. proves this species of Canon to have been well known in the middle of the 15th century, and probably much earlier, the musicians of that period were not sufficiently learned to combine it with good harmony— assertions which lose much of their weight from the self-evident fact that they rest upon information obtained entirely at second-hand, and not even corroborated by examination of the original MS., which it is clear that Forkel never saw.[1]

The next German critic to whom it occurred to touch on the subject was Ambros, who, in volume ii. of his great work, follows Forkel's example, by quoting Wanley's description, and, on the authority of Hawkins, referring the MS. —which he himself clearly never saw—to the middle of the 15th century.[2] It is indeed quite certain that at this period at least Ambros's knowledge of the history of English art was derived entirely from the pages of Hawkins and Burney.

In 1865 the subject was taken up by the Belgian *savant* Coussemaker, who described the MS. as written in the year 1226—or at the latest, 1236—by John of Fornsete, 'a Monk of the Abbey of Reading, in Berkshire.'[3] But the statement rests entirely on information derived from Mr. Chappell, Coussemaker himself never having seen the MS. True, in another work,[4] he speaks more independently ; and in his own name asserts the Rota to have been written by 'the Monk of Reading,' *before* the year 1226. But he nowhere tells us that he examined the MS. for himself.

In 1868 the argument was resumed by Ambros, who, in the fourth volume of his *History*, confessed himself convinced by the arguments of Coussemaker, and undoubtedly refers the Rota to the year 1226. But here again it is clear that the opinion is not his own ; and that he himself never saw the original MS.[5]

And now, having compared the views entertained by the best historians of the past with those set forth by the latest and most competent critics of the present day, it remains only that we should place before our readers the results of our own careful and long-continued study of the original MS.[5]

While receiving with due respect the judgment of the writers already quoted, we cannot but feel that in most cases their authority is weakened, almost to worthlessness, by the certainty that it rests on evidence collected entirely at second-hand. Neither Forkel, Coussemaker,

nor Ambros ever saw the original document ; their statements, therefore, tend rather to confuse than to enlighten the inquirer. Still, great as are the anomalies with which the subject is surrounded, we do not believe them to be irreconcilable. Some critics have trusted to the peculiar counterpoint of the Rota, as the only safe guide to its probable antiquity. Others have laid greater stress upon the freedom of its melody. We believe that the one quality can only be explained by reference to the other, and that the student who considers them separately, and without special reference to the caligraphy of the MS., stands but a slender chance of arriving at the truth. We propose to call attention to each of these three points, beginning with that which seems to us the most important of all—the character and condition of the MS.

1. The style of the handwriting corresponds so closely with that in common use during the earlier half of the 13th century that no one accustomed to the examination of English MSS. of that period can possibly mistake it. So positive are the indications on this point, that Sir Frederick Madden—one of the most learned palæographers of the 19th century—did rot hesitate to express his own conviction, in terms which leave no room for argument. The present librarian, Sir E. Maunde Thompson, unhesitatingly endorses Sir F. Madden's judgment ; and the Palæographical Society has also corroborated it, in connection with an autotype facsimile— Part VIII. Plate 125 (London, 1878)—referred to the year 1240.

Fortunately the MS. is in such perfect preservation that the corrections made during its preparation can be distinctly traced. In a few places the ink used for the Antiphon on the preceding page can be seen through the Vellum ; but apart from the spots traceable to this cause, there are a considerable number of evident erasures, clearly contemporary with the original handwriting, and corrected by the same hand, and in the same ink. The second note on stave 1 was originally an F. The first and second notes on stave 4 were originally two C's ; the fourth note was a D ; and the fifth a C. Between the sixth and seventh notes, in the same Stave, there are traces of a D, and also of an F : the D has certainly been erased to make room for the present notes ; the appearance of the F is produced by a note showing through from the opposite side. The eighth note on this stave was an E. Over the ligature which immediately follows there are traces of a C ; and, towards the end of this stave, a last erasure has been made, for the insertion of the solitary black square note. The marks which show through the vellum are to be found near the beginning of stave 3, and in several other places. Neither these nor the erasures are to be seen in our facsimile, though traces of

[1] *Allg. Geschichte d. Musik*, ii. 490-500. (Leipzig, 1788.)
[2] *Geschichte der Musik*, tom. ii. pp. 473-475. (Breslau, 1862.)
[3] *L'Art harmonique aux xii. et xiii. siècles*, pp. 144, 150. (Paris, 1865.)
[4] *Les Harmonistes des xii. et xiii. siècles*, p. 11.
[5] *Geschichte der Musik*, tom. iv. pp. 440-441. (Breslau, 1863.)

both may be found in the autotype of the Palæographical Society.

2. The mixed character of the Part-Writing has puzzled many an able commentator ; for, side by side with passages of rudest Discant, it exhibits progressions which might well have passed uncensured in the far later days of Palestrina. The 4th, 6th, 7th, 8th, and 24th bars are in Strict Two-Part Counterpoint of the First and Second Order, of irreproachable purity.[1] But, in passing from the 9th to the 10th, and from the 13th to the 14th bars, a flagrant violation of the first cardinal rule[2] results in the formation of Consecutive Fifths between the first and third Cantus parts, in the one case, and between the second and fourth Cantus in the other. The same rule is broken, between Cantus II. and Bassus I., in passing from bar 17 to bar 18 ; and, in bars 37, 38, 39, a similar infraction of the rule produces no less than three Consecutive Fifths between Cantus I. and Bassus II. Between bars 29 and 30, Cantus I. and II. sing Consecutive Unisons ; and the error is repeated, between bars 33, 34, by Cantus II. and Cantus III., simultaneously with Consecutive Fifths between both these Parts and Cantus I. Similar faults are repeated, as the Rota proceeds, with persistent regularity.

Now, the smooth progressions shown in the 4th, 8th, and 24th bars are as stringently forbidden in the Diaphonia of the 11th and 12th centuries as the Consecutive Fifths in bars 37, 38, and 39 are in the Counterpoint of the 15th and 16th, or even in that of the 14th century. To which of these epochs, then, are we to refer the Rota ? The peculiarity of the Part-writing clearly affords us no means whatever of answering the question, but is calculated rather to mislead than to throw new light upon the point at issue.

3. Turning from the Part-Writing to the melody, we find this pervaded by a freedom of rhythm, a merry graceful swing, immeasurably in advance of any kind of polyphonic music of earlier date than the *Fa-las* peculiar to the later decades of the 16th century—to which decades no critic has ever yet had the hardihood to refer the Rota. But this flowing rhythm is not at all in advance of many a Folk-song of quite unfathomable antiquity. The merry grace of a popular melody is no proof of its late origin. The dates of such melodies are so uncertain, that the element of chronology may almost be said to have been eliminated from the history of the earlier forms of national music. In most cases the original poetry and music owed their origin, in all probability, to the same heart and voice. The melodies were not composed, but inspired. If the verses to which they were indebted for their existence were light and tripping, so were they. If the verses were gloomy, the melodies naturally corresponded with them.

And because their authors, however unskilled they might be in the theory of music, were in the constant habit of hearing church melodies sung in the ecclesiastical modes, they naturally conformed, in most cases, to the tonality of those venerable scales. We believe the melody of the Rota to be an inspiration of this kind— a folk-song, pure and simple, in the transposed Ionian Mode, owing its origin to the author either of the English or the Latin verses to which it is wedded.

Now, some folk-songs of great antiquity possess the rare and very curious peculiarity of falling into Canon of their own accord. An old version of ' Drops of brandy ' forms a very fair Canon in the unison for two voices. The melody of the Rota—if we are right in believing it to be a genuine folk-song—possesses this quality in a very remarkable degree. What more probable, then, than that a light-hearted young Postulant should troll it forth, on some bright May-morning, during the hour of recreation ? That a second Novice should chime in a little later ? That the effect of the Canon should be noticed, admired, and experimented upon, until the brethren found that four of them could sing the tune, one after the other, in very pleasant harmony ? There must have been many a learned Discantor at Reading capable of modifying a note or two of the melody, here and there, for the purpose of making its phrases fit the more smoothly together. So learned a musician would have found no difficulty whatever in adding the *pes* as a support to the whole— and the thing was done. The harmony suggested, in the first instance, by a veritable ' Dutch Concert,' became a Round or Canon of the kind proved by Chappell's opportune discovery of the Latin pun [see above], to have been already familiar to English ears ; for which very reason it was all the more likely, in a case like the present, to have been indebted for its confection to a happy accident.

The foregoing suggestion is of course purely hypothetical. We do not, however, make it with the intention of evading a grave chronological difficulty by a mere idle guess. The influence exercised by the point we are considering upon the history of mediæval music in general, and that of the Early English school in particular, is of so great importance, that the element of conjecture would be altogether out of place in any chain of reasoning professing to solve the difficulties of an enigma which has puzzled the best musical antiquaries of the age. We venture, therefore, to propose no conjectural theory, but simply to epitomise the results of a long course of study which has rendered the Reading MS. as familiar to us as our own handwriting ; submitting it to our readers with all possible deliberation, as a means of accounting for certain peculiarities in the Rota which would otherwise remain inexplicable. It

[1] See STRICT COUNTERPOINT, *ante*, pp. 722-23.   [2] *Ibid.* p. 722.

accounts for a freedom of melody immeasurably in advance of that attained by the best polyphonists of the 15th century, whether in the Flemish or Italian school. It accounts for the transcription, in a handwriting of the 13th century, of progressions which were not sanctioned by scholastic authority until the 15th ; and at the same time for the admixture with these of other progressions, which in the 15th century would have been peremptorily forbidden ; in other words, it accounts for simultaneous obedience to two distinct codes of law diametrically opposed to each other ; two systems of part-writing which never were, and never could, by any possibility, be simultaneously enforced—viz. the law of counterpoint, which, in the 14th and 15th centuries, forbade the approach to a Perfect Concord in similar motion ; and that of Diaphonia, which in the 11th and 12th practically enjoined it, by employing no other intervals than doubled Fourths, Fifths, and Octaves. It accounts for the erasures to which we have already called attention ; placing them in the light of improvements, rather than that of necessary corrections. Moreover, it accounts, with still greater significance, for the otherwise inexplicable absence of a whole army of familiar progressions, conventional forms of ornamentation, Cadences true, false, plain, diminished, modal, or medial, and of licences innumerable, which, after the substitution of Counterpoint for Discant, never failed to present themselves at every turn in Polyphonic compositions of every kind, produced in every school in Europe. These anomalies have not been accounted for by any critic who has hitherto treated the subject. Yet surely those who doubt the antiquity of the Rota, on the ground of its advanced construction, owe us some explanation as to the presence of this advanced style in certain passages only. We sorely need some information as to how it came to pass that the piece was written in three distinct styles ; two, of part-writing, separated by an interval of two or three centuries at least ; and one, of melody, which, if not the result of an inspired folk-song, of remotest antiquity, must bring us down to a period subsequent to the invention of Monodia in the 17th century. Our theory, if admissible at all, explains all these things. A learned musician, deliberately intending to write a Canon for six voices would, had he lived in the 12th century, have adopted the style observable in bars 37, 38, and 39, as that of the entire composition. Another, flourishing in the 15th century, would have confined himself to that shown in bars in 4, 6, 8, and 24. But, though the later *savant* would never have passed the Fifths and Octaves, the earlier one, had he possessed sufficient natural genius to enable him to rise above the pedantry of the age, would surely have excused a great deal of what he considered and taught to be licence. Finding that a popular melody of the

day fitted together, in certain places, in a—to his ear—delightful succession of similar Perfect Concords, he would surely have forgiven certain other passages which defied his rules, but, judged by his natural instinct, did not ' sound bad.' Whether John of Fornsete did really construct the Rota on this principle or not we can never know for certain ; but, since the accident we have suggested certainly has happened, and been turned to advantage in other cases, there is nothing improbable in the supposition that it may have happened before, in that which we are now considering.

The fact that no other English Rota of equal antiquity with this has as yet been brought to light proves nothing. The wonder is, not that we can find no similar examples, but that even this one should have escaped the wholesale destruction which devastated our Cathedral and Monastic Libraries, first, during the reign of King Henry VIII., and afterwards, during the course of the Civil Wars. Moreover, we must not forget that the Reading MS., though it contains only one Rota, contains no less than three Latin Antiphons, two for three voices, and one for four ; and that the Chaucer MS.[1] of very little later date, contains several compositions for two voices, all tending to prove the early date at which the art of polyphonic composition was cultivated in England.[2]   w. s. r.

SUNDERLAND, MRS., [whose maiden name was SUSAN SYKES, was born at Brighouse, Yorkshire, April 30, 1819, and was the daughter of a gardener. Her voice first attracted the attention of Luke Settle, a blacksmith at a village near Brighouse, who, hearing her singing in her father's garden, offered to teach her. She afterwards joined the Halifax Choral Society, under the leadership of Dan Sugden, who gave her her first fee, of five shillings, for singing a solo at the quarterly concert of the Society. Her next important appearance as a solo singer was on Feb. 19, 1838, at a concert given in the Exchange Rooms, Bradford. She next had five months' training in London,] and soon became a local celebrity, was styled the ' Yorkshire Queen of Song,' and for more than a quarter of a century was the leading vocalist in the North of England. She was physically robust, and her voice was a high soprano of great force and volume, which she managed with much expression. Her repertory was chiefly composed of the principal songs in the ' Messiah,' ' Judas,' and the ' Creation ' ; but she had also some secular songs, mostly of a popular kind. Her first appearance in London was in the ' Messiah' at Exeter Hall, Nov. 2, 1849, and she continued to sing first soprano for the

---

[1] Arundel MSS. No. 248. See SCORE, *ante*, p. 388. The Montpellier MS. is certainly no older than this, and probably not so old.
[2] Fosbroke, in his *British Monachism* (vol. ii. p. 113), tells us that the song of the Anglo-Saxon monks consisted of a method of figurate Discant, in which the various voices, following one another, were perpetually repeating different words at the same time. Surely this savours strongly of the 'form of the Round.'

Sacred Harmonic Society and other bodies in the 'Messiah,' 'Creation,' 'Elijah,' etc., until 1856. The directors of the Antient Concerts esteemed her voice and expression so much that they offered to send her abroad for further tuition. Indeed, had her early training equalled the quality of her voice and her natural feeling, there can be little doubt that she would have risen to very great general eminence. [She frequently sang at Leeds concerts, notably at the opening of the Town Hall by Queen Victoria in 1858, and at the first of the Leeds Festivals in the same year. Her last appearance in public was in the 'Messiah,' at Huddersfield, June 3, 1864. Mrs. Sunderland married at the age of nineteen, her husband being a butcher. Their golden wedding was celebrated by a concert on June 7, 1888, the proceeds of which helped to found the Sunderland Vocal Prize for natives of the West Riding of Yorkshire. She died on May 7, 1906.] G.; additions in square brackets by F. K.

SUPER. I. The Latin preposition, 'above,' is used in organ terminology to denote the octave above, and is sometimes, but of course erroneously, used for 'octave' (see COUPLER). II. The supernumeraries in a theatre, who appear in crowded scenes, but do not speak, sing, or dance, are technically called 'Supers.'

SUPERTONIC. The second note of the scale upwards, as D in the key of C. It is brought into much prominence in modern music as the dominant note of the dominant key. The strong tendency to find the chief balance and antithesis in that key, and to introduce the second subject of a movement in it, as well as the tendency to make for that point even in the progress of a period, necessarily throws much stress upon the root-note of the harmony which leads most directly to its tonic harmony, and this is the dominant of the new key or supertonic of the original one. It has consequently become so familiar, that its major chord and the chord of the minor seventh built upon it, although chromatic, are freely used as part of the original key, quite irrespective of the inference of modulation which they originally carried. Some theorists recognise these chords as part of the harmonic complement of the key, and consequently derive several of the most characteristic and familiar chromatic combinations from the supertonic root. [For the chord of the sixth on the supertonic see SIXTH, *ante*, p. 478.] C. H. H. P.

SUPPÉ, VON, known as FRANZ VON SUPPÉ, was of Belgian descent, though his family for two generations had lived at Cremona ; he was born at Spalato, or on board ship near it, April 18, 1820, and his full baptismal name was FRANCESCO EZECHIELE ERMENEGILDO CAVALIERE SUPPE DEMELLI. His taste for music developed early. At eleven he learned the flute, at thirteen harmony, and at fifteen produced a mass at the Franciscan church at Zara. [A piece called 'Der Apfel' was produced privately at Zara in 1834.] His father, however, had other views for him, and sent him to the University of Padua. But music asserted itself; he learned from Cigala and Ferrari, and wrote incessantly. At this moment his father died, the mother settled in Vienna, where Francesco joined her ; and after a little hesitation between teaching Italian, practising medicine, and following music, he decided on the last, got lessons from Seyfried, and obtained a gratuitous post as Conductor at the Josephstadt theatre. This was followed by better engagements at Pressburg and Baden, and then (about 1862) at the theatres 'an der Wien,' Quai, and Leopold-stadt in Vienna, with the last-named of which he was connected from 1865 until his death May 21, 1895. His work at these houses, though for long mere patching and adding, was excellent practice, and he gradually rose to more independent things. In 1844 a 'Sommernachts-traum,' founded on Shakespeare, and composed by him, is mentioned in the *A.M.Z.* 'Der Krämer und sein Commis' followed. In 1847 he was at the Theatre 'an der Wien' and (Aug. 7) brought out a piece, 'Das Mädchen vom Lande' (The country girl), which met with wild success. Ten years later (Jan. 8, 1858) a Singspiel, 'Paragraph 3,' spread his fame into North Germany, and from that time a stream of pieces flowed from his pen. His works are said by the careful Wurzbach [1] to reach the astonishing number of 2 grand operas, 165 farces, comedi-ettas, and vaudevilles, etc., as well as a mass ('Missa dalmatica,' Spina, 1877), a Requiem produced at Zara in 1860 under the title of 'L' estremo Giudizio,' etc. etc. A list of 49 of his operatic pieces is given by Wurzbach, but a few only are dated. Another list of 21 is given by Batka in Pougin's supplement to Fétis, but the titles are French, and it is hard to make the dates agree. Some of the pieces are mere parodies, as 'Tannenhäuser,' 'Dinorah, oder die Turnerfahrt nach Hütteldorf.' One, 'Franz Schubert,' is founded on the life of Schubert, and contains five of his songs. In Riemann's *Lexikon* the number of his operettas is given as 31, and 180 'possen' and slighter pieces are mentioned. The only pieces of Suppé's known out of Germany are 'Fatinitza,' produced at Vienna, Jan. 5, 1876 ; at the Alhambra, London, June 20, 1878, and at the Nouveautés, Paris, March 1879 ; and 'Boc-caccio' (originally produced in 1879, and brought out in London, at the Comedy Theatre, April 22, 1882). The overture to 'Dichter und Bauer,' the only one of his overtures known in England, must be his most popular work abroad, since it has been arranged for no less than 59 different combinations of instruments, all published by Aibl of Munich. G.

[1] *Biog. Lexikon des Oesterreich.* Part 40; 1880.

SURIANO. [See SORIANO, *ante*, p. 623.]

SUSANNA. An oratorio in three parts by Handel ; the author of the words is not known. The overture was begun on July 11, 1748, a month after the completion of 'Solomon,' and the work was finished on the 24th of the following month. It was produced during the season of 1749. G.

SUSATO, TYLMAN, printer and composer of music, was born at or near Cologne probably towards the end of the 15th century. His name is regularly written by himself in the full form given above, although the spelling of the first part of it is extremely irregular.[1] A document referred to by Fétis[2] describes Susato as 'son of Tylman.' It is therefore only through an inexplicable forgetfulness of diplomatic usage that Fétis and others[3] have taken Tylman for a surname.[4] These writers have also accepted a conjecture of Dehn[5] that 'Susato' indicated the place of the composer's birth, namely the town of Soest (*Susatum*) ; in one of his books, however, he expressly describes himself as 'Agrippinensis,'[6] which can only refer to Cologne.[7] Consequently we have to consider 'Susato' (or 'de Susato'—as it once occurs, in a document of 1543[8]) as a family name, 'van (or 'von') Soest,' doubtless originally derived from the Westphalian town. By the year 1529 Tylman is found settled at Antwerp, where he maintained himself by transcribing music for the chapel of the Virgin in the cathedral ; in 1531 he is mentioned as taking part, as trumpeter, in the performance of certain masses there. He was also one of the five musicians supported by the city ('stadsspeel-lieden'), and as such possessed, according to a list of 1532, two trumpets, a 'velt-trompet,' and a 'teneur-pipe.' Losing his post on the arrival of Philip II. in 1549, he appears, for some unexplained reason, never to have been again employed by the city. Before this date however, in 1543, he had found another occupation as a printer of music. For a short time[9] he worked in company with some friends ; but from 1543 onwards he published on his own account, bringing out between that year and 1561 more than fifty volumes of music, nearly every one of which contains some compositions of his own. He died before 1564.[10]

Susato's first publication is a first book of four-part 'Chansons' (1543), and his next is entitled 'Premier Livre de Chansons à trois Parties, auquel sont Contenues Trente Et Une Novvelles Chansons conuenables Tant à la Voix comme aux Instrumentz' (1544). Eight of these pieces are by himself. The rest of his publications, so far as they are now extant, include (1) in French, sixteen books of 'Chansons' in 3–8 parts ; (2) 'Madrigali e Canzoni francesi a 5 voci' (1558) ; (3) in Latin three books of 'Carmina,' three of Masses, one of 'Evangelia Dominicarum,' fifteen of 'Ecclesiastical Cantiones' or motets (1553-60), 'Motecta quinis vocibus, auctore Clemente non Papa' (1546), and five books of 'Cantiones sacrae quae vulgo Moteta vocant' [*sic*] (1546). Finally (4) in Dutch there are his three books of songs, etc., (1551), entitled 'Musyck boexken,' and one book (1561), apparently the second of a series of 'Souter-Liedekens' (Psalter-ditties), which are of peculiar interest. The third of the Musyck boexken contains some dances by Susato himself, which are described[11] as 'full of character' and excellently written. The souterliedekens, which Ambros further[12] states to be found in four more Musyck-boexken, are pieces from the Psalms according to the rhymed Flemish version, set without change to the popular song-tunes of the day ('gemeyne bekende liedekens'[13]). The charm, however, of these compositions lies less in the airs adapted in them than in the independence and originality of the part-writing, an art in which Susato was so proficient that some of his three-part songs are composed in such a manner as to be suitable, he states, equally for three and for two voices with omission of the bass. Susato appears also to have co-operated with Clemens non Papa in some of his work, and not to have been merely his publisher.[14] Still it is as a publisher[14] that Susato has hitherto been almost exclusively known, the masters whose works he printed being very numerous, and including such names as Créquillon, Gombert, Goudimel, O. de Lassus, P. de Manchicourt, J. Mouton, C. de Rore, A. Willaert, etc. [See also the *Quellen-Lexikon* for other compositions.] R. L. P.

SUSPENSION is the process of arresting the conjunct motion of one or more parts for a time, while the rest of the components of the chord proceed one step onwards, and thereby come to represent a different root. The part which is stayed in this manner commonly produces dissonance, which is relieved by its then passing on

---

[1] In works with Latin titles Susato writes himself in a great majority of cases *Tilemannus*; *Tielmannus*, *Tilmannus*, *Tylemannus*, and *Tilmannus*, occurring but rarely. In Flemish his favourite form seems to have been *Tielman*. In French *Tylman*, the spelling adapted by Fétis and Mendel is most frequently; *Thielman*, which is preferred by M. Goovaerts is less usual ; while *Tilman*, the spelling which is adopted by M. Vander Straeten and is now practically the accepted one in the Netherlands, is met with only twice.

[2] *Biogr. univ. des Music.* viii. 276; 2nd ed.

[3] Thus Mendel and Reissmann, *Musikal. Convers.-Lex.* x. 355; Berlin, 1881.

[4] Cp. Alphonse Goovaerts, *Histoire et Bibliographie de la Typographie musicale dans les Pays-bas*, pp. 26, 27 ; Antwerp, 1880.

[5] See his letter in Fétis. *l.c.*

[6] Goovaerts, p. 191.

[7] At the same time, M. Goovaerts notes (pp. 26, 27), we are not to confound Susato, as Fétis and Mendel have done, with a contemporary Thielman van Ceulen, who was a brewer, and whose father's name was Adolf.

[8] Edmond Vander Straeten, *La Musique aux Pays-bas avant le xixme Siècle*, v. 258 ; Brussels, 1880.

[9] Goovaerts, pp. 18-26.

[10] *Ibid.* p. 31.

[11] Vander Straeten, v. 261, who says that these dances have been reprinted by Eitner in the *Monatshefte fur Musikgeschichte*, Jahrg. vii. No. 6.

[12] *Geschichte der Musik.* iii. 313 (Breslau, 1868). These, however, are not mentioned by M. Goovaerts, whose general accuracy may lead one to suspect a mistake on Ambros's part.

[13] Ambros, iii. 313.

[14] His publications are rarely found in England, the British Museum only possessing one volume of masses.

to the position it would have naturally occupied sooner had the motion of the parts been simultaneous. Thus in the progression of the chord of the Dominant seventh to Tonic harmony (*a*), the part which takes the upper note (or seventh) can be delayed and made to follow into its position after the rest of the chord has moved, as in (*b*), thereby producing a fourth in place of a third for a time. Similarly the fifth, or the fifth and third, can be suspended, producing a ninth, or a ninth and seventh, against the tonic note ; and the dissonant effect is similarly relieved by their passing on to their normal position in the chord afterwards, as in (*c*). In all such cases the first occurrence of the note in the part whose motion is suspended is called the 'Preparation,' as in the first chord of (*b*)

and of (*c*) : the moment of dissonance resulting from the motion of the other parts, is called the 'Percussion' of the discord, and the release of the dissonance, when the part proceeds to its natural place in the harmony, is called the 'Resolution.'

Suspension was among the very first methods discovered by the early harmonists for introducing dissonance into their music. In the earliest times composers depended chiefly upon the different degrees and qualities of consonances—sixths, thirds, fifths and octaves—to obtain the necessary effects of contrast between one musical moment and another. Then, when, in the natural order of things, something stronger was required, it was found in this process of suspension. But for some time it was used very sparingly, and composers required no more than the least dissonant forms to carry out their purposes. For a long while, moreover, all discords appeared to the early writers as no more than artificial manipulations of the motion of the parts of this kind, and it was only by the use of such means that they even learnt to use some discords, which are at the present day looked upon in a totally different light. About the beginning of the 17th century they began to realise that there was a radical difference in the character and constitution of certain groups of discords, and to use at least one freely as an independent or fundamental combination. From that time discords began to be classified, instinctively, into definite groups. Certain of the less dissonant combinations have in course of time been grouped into a special class, which is freed from the obligation of being prepared, and thereby loses one of the most essential characteristics of suspension. These are the Dominant discords of the minor seventh and major and minor ninths ; certain corresponding chromatic chords on Tonic and Supertonic roots, which have been naturally affiliated upon the key ;

and the chord sometimes known as that of the added sixth. [See SIXTH.] Another class has been created by some theorists, which is much more intimately connected with the class of suspensions ; if indeed they are not actually suspensions slightly disguised. These are the discords which are arrived at by the same process of staying or suspending the motion of a part, but which are distinguished by further motion of the other parts simultaneously with the resolution of the discord, thereby condensing two motions into one ; as in (*d*) and (*e*). When treated in this manner the chords are described by some theorists as 'Prepared discords.' The province of suspensions appears by this process

to have been reduced, but what was lost by the process of classification has been amply made up by the invention of a great variety of new forms.

About the time that composers first began to realise the character of the dominant seventh, they also began to use a greater variety and a harsher description of suspensions. The earliest experiments of note in both directions are commonly ascribed to the same man, namely Monteverde. Since his time the progress has been tolerably constant in one direction ; for the tendency to look for fresh and more vivid points of contrast necessarily leads to the use of suspensions of more complicated and harsher character. At the present time the varieties of possible suspensions are so numerous that it would be almost as absurd to endeavour to make a catalogue of them, as it would be to make a list of possible combinations of sounds. But if the principle be properly understood, it is not necessary to give more than illustrative examples; for the like rules apply to all ; and their kinds are only limited by the degree of harshness considered admissible, and by the possibility of adequate and intelligible resolution. Classical authority not only exists for a great variety of chromatic suspensions, often derived from no stronger basis than a combination of chromatic passing or ornamental notes ; but also for remarkable degrees of dissonance. Beethoven for instance, in the Bb Quartet, op. 130, used the suspended fourth together with the third on which it is to resolve, and put the latter at the top, and the former at the bottom (*f*) ; and Bach supplies many examples of similar character. Certain simple rules are almost invariably observed—such as that the moment of percussion shall fall upon the strong beat of the bar ; and that the progression shall not imply a violation

of rules against consecutive perfect concords, which would occur if the artificial suspension of the part were removed, as in (g).

Composers early discovered a means of varying the character of the process by interpolating notes between the sounding of the discord and its resolution, as in (h). Instances are also to

be found in which some such forms were used as sufficient to constitute resolution without arriving at the normal note,—habit and familiarity with a particular form of motion leading to the acceptance of a conventional formula in place of the actual solution. The following examples from Corelli's 1st Sonata of opera 2da and 5th of opera 4ta are clear illustrations.

This particular device is characteristic rather of the early period of harmonic music up to Corelli's time than of a later period. The following passage from Schumann's andante and variations for two pianofortes (op. 46) is characteristic of modern uses of combined and chromatic suspension, and also of interpolation of notes

(m) 1st Piano.

between percussion and resolution. Some theorists distinguish the combinations which resolve

upwards from those that resolve downwards, styling the former Retardations. [See RETARDATION ; HARMONY.]   C. H. H. P.

SVENDSEN, JOHAN SEVERIN, was born Sept. 30, 1840, at Christiania, where his father was a military bandmaster. At the age of eleven he wrote his first composition for the violin. When fifteen he enlisted in the army, and soon became bandmaster. Even at that age he played, with considerable skill, flute, clarinet, and violin. He soon left the army, and worked during the next few years in the orchestra of the Christiania theatre, and at a dancing academy, for which he arranged some études by Paganini and Kreutzer for dancing. A strong desire to travel drove him, at twenty-one, on a roving tour over a great part of Sweden and North Germany. Two years after, being in Lübeck in extremely reduced circumstances, he fortunately met with the Swedish-Norwegian Consul Herr Leche, whose interest he gained, and who shortly after obtained a stipend for him from Charles XV. to enable him to perfect himself as a violinist ; but being soon afterwards attacked with paralysis in the hand, he was compelled to give up the bow for composition. He went to Leipzig in 1863, and his works being already known there, he was placed in the finishing class of the Conservatorium, receiving, however, instruction in elementary theory of music, which he had never been taught. His instructors were Hauptmann, David, Richter, and Reinecke. He wrote a Quartet in A, an Octet and a Quintet, all for strings ; Quartets for male voices ; and a Symphony in D.

On leaving Leipzig in 1867 he received the great honorary medal of the Academy. After travelling in Denmark, Scotland, and Norway, Svendsen went in 1868 to Paris. The Second Empire was then at its zenith, and his sojourn in the capital of France influenced the composer to a very great extent. Whilst there, he played in Musard's orchestra, and at the Odéon, and became intimately acquainted with Wilhelmine Szarvady, De Bériot, Vieuxtemps, and Léonard. He arranged the incidental music to Coppée's 'Le Passant,' in which both Sarah Bernhardt and Agar performed, but on the whole his Paris productions were few—a Concerto for violin in A, and orchestral arrangements of studies by Liszt and Schubert ; he also began 'Sigurd Slembe,' the overture to a Norwegian drama of that name. He left Paris at the beginning of the war in 1870 for Leipzig, where he had been offered the conductorship of the well-known Euterpe concerts, which however were discontinued, owing to the war. At a great musical festival at Weimar, in the same year, he first met Liszt and Tausig, and his octet was played by a party containing David, Hellmesberger, Grützmacher, and Hechmann, with great approbation. Early in the following year his Symphony in D was performed at the Gewandhaus, and his fame as a composer established. He composed in that year his Concerto for violoncello in D. In the autumn he went to America to be married to an American lady, whom he had met in Paris, and returned the same year to Leipzig, where, after the end of the war, he undertook the leadership of the Euterpe concerts for one year. There he finished the overture to 'Sigurd Slembe,' which was played at the Euterpe then, and in the following year at the musical festival at Cassel, both times with great success. In this year he met Wagner at Bayreuth, and soon became his intimate associate. For the next five years (1872–77) he was conductor of the Christiania Musical Association and teacher of composition, and composed comparatively few works, which may be explained by the unfortunate want of pecuniary independence. The pieces of this period are numbered opp. 10–22 in his list. In 1874 his labours found some appreciation from his countrymen in the shape of an annuity granted by the Storthing, and several decorations conferred on him by the king. After five years of hard work, he was enabled once more to proceed abroad. In 1877 he revisited Leipzig, and conducted a new work at the Gewandhaus; went thence to Munich, and eventually to Rome, where he spent the winter. In 1878 he visited London for the first time, and there met Sarasate, who assisted him in the performance of his quartet, quintet, and octet. From London he went to Paris, where he stayed until 1880, during which time his works were several times performed—as also at Angers, where the post of conductor was offered him by the Musical Association. But Svendsen refused this lucrative appointment, and in the autumn of that year we again find him in his old post as conductor of the Musical Association in Christiania. In 1883 he became court conductor at Copenhagen: in 1888 he visited England again, conducting his Symphony in D at the Philharmonic Concert of May 31. In recent years he has produced only some minor compositions, besides arranging for orchestra several studies by foreign composers.

Svendsen's music is all of very high character, remarkable for strong individuality, conciseness, and the absence of anything national or Scandinavian; as well as for an elaborate finish strictly in harmony with the traditions of the great masters. He is one of the most cosmopolitan composers of the age.

His printed works are as follow :—

Op.		Op.	
1.	String quartet in A minor.	11.	Zorahayde, legend for orch.
2.	Songs for men's voices.	12.	Polonaise for orch.
3.	Octet for strings in A minor.	13.	Coronation march for Oscar
4.	Symphony in D.		II.
5.	String quintet in C.	14.	Marriage Cantata, for chor.
6.	Concerto for violin and orch.		and orch.
	in A.	15.	Symphony No. 2 in Bb.
7.	Do. for violoncello and orch.	16.	Carnaval des artistes Nor-
	in D minor.		végiens.
8.	Overture in C to Björnson's	17.	Rhapsodie Norvégienne No. 1,
	drama of 'Sigurd Slembe.'		for orch.
9.	Carnaval à Paris, for orch.	18.	Overture to Romeo and
10.	Funeral march for Charles		Juliet.
	XV.	19.	Rhapsodie Norvégienne No. 2,

Op.		Op.	
20.	Scandinavian airs arranged for string quartet.	24.	Four songs, French and Norwegian, for voice and PF.
21, 22.	Rhapsodies Norvégiennes Nos. 3, 4.	25.	Romance by Popper, arranged for violoncello and PF.
23.	Five songs, French and German, for voice and PF.	26.	Romance for violin and orch. in G.

C. S^{s.}

SVENDSEN, OLUF, a distinguished flute-player, born in Christiania, April 19, 1832. He learnt the rudiments of playing from his father, a musician; when twelve years old played the flute in small orchestras; and at fourteen was engaged as first flute in the Christiania theatre. In 1851 he went to Copenhagen, and took lessons from Nils Petersen, then a flute-player there. In 1853 he entered the Conservatoire at Brussels, where he studied for two years, after which he was engaged by Jullien for his Concerts in London. In Sept. 1856, he joined the Band of the Crystal Palace, Sydenham, where he remained till the end of 1858. In 1861 Svendsen was appointed first flute in the Queen's private band, and the same year joined the Philharmonic orchestra. He was ten years in the orchestra at Her Majesty's theatre; and from 1867 was professor of his instrument at the Royal Academy of Music. He was well known as a solo-player throughout Belgium, Norway, Sweden, Denmark, and France. He died in London, May 15, 1888. G.

SWEELINCK, or **SWELINCK**,[1] JAN PIETERSZOON, the greatest of Dutch organists, was born of a Deventer family in the summer of 1562. His father, 'Mr. Pieter,' was organist of the Old Church at Amsterdam, which place disputes with Deventer the honour of having given the son birth.[2] Of Sweelinck's boyhood we know nothing, except that he was taught by Jacob Buyck (Buchius), the pastor of the Old Church. There is a tradition that he was sent to Venice to study music under Zarlino and Gabrieli; but with this is connected a mistake of old standing, which places his birth in 1540, twenty-two years too early.[3] Now, as we know that he was in Holland from 1577, at latest, onwards, it becomes barely credible that the lad of fifteen could have followed the instruction of the Venetian masters to any important extent; and it is likely that the whole story is based upon the close study which his works prove him to have devoted to those of 'the apostle of musical science,'[4] whose

---

[1] Of the seven or more ways in which the name is spelled, these two have the warrant of the musician's own signature. The Germans of the time seem to have naturalised him as Schweling; in Amsterdam he was known as plain Jan Pietersz.

[2] Deventer is consistently mentioned by Sweelinck's later biographers; but the Amsterdam claim has the support of the official entry of his marriage there in 1590, in which his birthplace is not stated. The omission was the rule when the person was a native of the city. Else documentary evidence is equally wanting on both sides.

[3] The correction of this and the rest of the mistakes which confuse every single date in Sweelinck's life is due to the essay of F. H. J. Tiedeman, *J. P. Sweelinck, een bio-bibliografische Schets*, published by the Vereeniging voor Nederlandsche Muziekgeschiedenis (Amsterdam, 1876), which supersedes a shorter sketch published by the same writer as an introduction to the 'Regina Coeli,' in 1869. Both are based upon a biography (which remains in MS. in the possession of the Vereeniging) by Robert Eitner, who has done good service by rescuing the works of Sweelinck from the obscurity of the Graue Kloster at Berlin.

[4] So Zarlino is entitled by his modern biographer, F. Caffi, *Della Vita e delle Opere del Prete G. Zarlino* (Venice, 1836). Neither here nor in the chapters on Zarlino and Andrea Gabrieli contained in his *Storia della Musica Sacra*, vol. i, p. 129, etc, (Venice, 1854), does Caffi

'Istitutioni harmoniche' he translated.[1] Some time between 1577 and 1581 Sweelinck was appointed to the organistship previously held by his father (who died in 1573) ; and this post he filled until his death, Oct. 16, 1621. For a generation he was the glory of Amsterdam. When he played the organ there, says a contemporary, 'there was a wonderful concourse every day ; every one was proud to have known, seen, heard the man.'[2] And when he died it was the greatest of Dutch poets, Vondel, who wrote his epitaph, and surnamed him ' Phoenix of Music.' He must also have been a distinguished figure in the society of Amsterdam, then in its greatest brilliancy, not only for his unmatched powers as an organist, but also for his skill, fancy, and charming versatility on the clavicymbel.[3] The town bought him for public service a new ' clavecimpbel ' from Antwerp at a cost of 200 gulden ; and the instrument seems to have travelled with him all over the country.[4]

What was published, however, by Sweelinck in his lifetime was entirely vocal music, and includes—besides occasional canons, marriage-songs, etc.,his 'Chansons françaises' (three parts, Antwerp, 1592-94), ' Rimes françoises et italiennes' (Leyden, 1612), and the great collections of sacred music on which, with his organ works, his fame chiefly rests. These are the ' Pseaumes mis en musique' for 4–8 voices (published in several editions at Leyden, Amsterdam, and Berlin), and the ' Cantiones Sacrae' (Antwerp, 1619. A Regina Coeli from the latter, three Chansons, and eight Psalms in six parts were reprinted, in organ-score, by the Association for the History of Dutch Music (pts. i. v. vi. and vii. ; Utrecht and Amsterdam, 1869-77) ; which has also published for the first time seven of Sweelinck's organ works[5] (pt. iii.) [VEREENIGING. In 1894-1901 Breitkopf & Härtel published Sweelinck's complete works in twelve volumes, edited by Max Seiffert, who added prefaces, etc., see below. The chanson, ' Tu as tout seul' is in vol. i. of ' Arion,' and two of the Italian madrigals are in ' Ausgewählte Madrigale.' The beautiful ' Hodie Christus natus est' is in the Bach Choir Magazine, etc.]

The psalms make an interesting link between the tranquillity of the old polyphonists and the rhythm of modern music. Formally they stand nearest to the earlier style, but the strictness of their counterpoint, the abundance of imitation and fugue in them, does not hinder a general freedom of effect, very pure and full of melody, to a greater degree than is common in works of the time. The organ pieces are also historically of signal importance. Though they may not justify the claim made for Sweelinck as ' the founder of instrumental music,'[6] they at all events present the first known example of an independent use of the pedal (entrusting it with a real part in a fugue), if not with the first example of a completely developed organ-fugue.

It is as an organist and the founder of a school of organists that Sweelinck had most influence, an influence which made itself felt through the whole length of northern Germany.[7] In the next generation nearly all the leading organists there had been his scholars ; his learning and method were carried by them from Hamburg to Danzig. His pupil Scheidemann handed down the tradition to the great Reincke [8] —himself a Dutchman—from whom, if we accept a statement supported alike by unanimous testimony and by exhaustive analysis of their works, it turned to find its consummation in Sebastian Bach.[9]

[The contents of the complete edition are as follows :—

   i. Organ and Clavier works.
      Book I. of Psalms.
   iv. and v. Book II. of Psalms.
   vi. Book III. of Psalms.
   vii. Book IV. of Psalms.
   viii. Cantiones Sacrae.
   ix. Chansons a 5.
   x. Rimes Françoises et Italiennes.
   xi. Miscellaneous and occasional compositions.
   xii. Compositions-Regeln, ed. by Dr. H. Gehrmann.

Two portraits are reproduced, and the prefaces by Dr. Seiffert are given in Dutch and German.]   R. L. P.

SWELL (HARPSICHORD). The desire for a power of increase and decrease on keyboard instruments like the harpsichord and organ, so as to emulate the bow instruments, and even the human voice, in that flow and ebb which are at the foundation of form no less than of expression, has led to the contrivance of mechanical swells as the only possible approach to it. A swell was first attempted on the Organ ; the harpsichord swell was introduced by Robert Plenius in a sostenente variety of the instrument, named by him ' Lyrichord,' and is described (in 1755) as the raising of a portion of the lid or cover of the instrument by means of a pedal. Kirkman adopted this very simple swell, and we find it also in many small square pianos of the 18th century. About 1765 Shudi introduced the Venetian swell, and patented it in 1769. This beautiful piece of joinery is a framing of louvres which open or close gradually by means of the right pedal and thus cause a swell, which may

take any notice of the Dutch scholar. Nor have I been able to discover any trace of his residence at Venice in the MS. collections of S. Marco.
[1] MS. at Hamburg, formerly belonging to the great organist Reincke.
[2] Sweertius, in Tiedeman, p. 16. Sweelinck's portrait at Darmstadt gives his strong irregular features a kindly expression, with a touch of sadness in them. It is reproduced in photograph by Mr. Tiedeman.
[3] On this he was the master of Christina van Erp, the famous lutenist, and wife of the more famous poet, Pieter Corneliszoon Hooft. See the Bouwsteenen of the Vereeniging, vol. i. pp. 13 f.
[4] See an anecdote in Baudartius, Memoryen, xiii. p. 163; cited by Tiedeman, p. 16.
[5] The bibliography of Sweelinck is given at length by Tiedeman, pp. 43-75. To this should be added some supplementary particulars communicated by Dr. J. P. Heije in the Bouwsteenen, vol. i. pp. 39-46.

[6] See Eitner's preface to the edition, and Tiedeman, pp. 54 ff.
[7] The wide distribution of his works is shown by early transcripts existing in the British Museum, and by copies of the extremely rare printed works preserved in the Bibliothèque Nationale. Curiously enough not a single MS. of Sweelinck remains in Holland.
[8] Or Reinken.
[9] Spitta, J. S. Bach, i. 96, 192-213.

be as gradual as the performer pleases. Shudi bequeathed this patent to John Broadwood, who inherited it on the death of Shudi in 1773. When the patent expired, Kirkman and others adopted it, and it was fitted to many old harpsichords, and even to pianos, but was soon proved unnecessary in an instrument where power of *nuance* was the very first principle.

The English organ-builders perceived the great advantage of Shudi's Venetian swell over the rude contrivance they had been using [see ORGAN, vol. iii. p. 536*b*], and it became generally adopted for organs, and has since been constantly retained in them as an important means of effect.   A. J. H.

SWELL-ORGAN. The clavier or manual of an organ which acts upon pipes enclosed in a box, such box having shutters, by the opening of which, by means of a pedal, a crescendo is produced. The shutters are made to fold over each other like the woodwork of a venetian blind, hence the expressions 'Venetian Swell' and 'Venetian Shutters' sometimes found in specifications. To the swell-organ a larger number of reed-stops is assigned than to other manuals.

The first attempt at a 'swelling-organ' was made by Jordan in 1712. The crescendo was obtained by raising one large sliding shutter which formed the front of the box. The early swell-organs were of very limited compass, sometimes only from middle C upwards, but more generally taken a fourth lower, namely, to fiddle G. For many years the compass did not extend below tenor C, and even now attempts are sometimes made to reduce the cost of an organ by limiting the downward compass of some of the stops of the Swell ; but in all instruments with any pretension to completeness the stops run throughout the compass to CC, with the possible exceptions of the Vox Angelica or the Voix Céleste. [See ORGAN, vol. iii. p. 536, etc., and section, p. 545.]   J. S.

SWELL-PEDAL. The pedal in the organ and harpsichord by which the shutters of the swell are opened and closed.   T. E.

SWERT, JULES DE, a representative violoncellist of the Belgian school, was born at Louvain, August 16, 1843. His disposition for music was shown very early. When only eight years of age he began playing in public, though his studies were not completed until 1858, in which year he took first prize in the class of Servais at the Brussels Conservatoire. His subsequent career was that of a travelling virtuoso until 1865, when he became Concertmeister at Düsseldorf. Between 1869 and 1873 he resided at Berlin, where his functions were those of royal Concertmeister and professor at the Hochschule. He also held appointments at Weimar, Wiesbaden, Leipzig, and finally at Ostend. At the latter town he was appointed in 1888 director of the local music school, acting also as professor at the neighbouring Conservatoires of Bruges

and Ghent, until his death, which took place at Ostend, Feb. 24, 1891. As a soloist he visited London first in 1875, and was esteemed as a warm, temperamental player, producing a tone of exceptional volume. As a composer he is less favourably known here. He signed his name to many trashy pieces, probably written to order, for violoncello with pianoforte and with orchestra, but occupied himself also with serious work. Three concertos, one of which was produced with great success at the Berlin Philharmonic in 1886 ; a Symphony, 'Nordseefahrt' ; and two operas, 'Die Albigenser' (Wiesbaden, 1878) and 'Graf Hammerstein,' testify to this ; but it is as soloist that he is best remembered.   W. W. C.

SWIETEN, GOTTFRIED, BARON VAN. A musical amateur of great importance, who resided at Vienna at the end of the 18th century and beginning of the 19th century. The family was Flemish, and Gottfried's father, Gerhard,[1] returned from Leyden to Vienna in 1745, and became Maria Theresa's favourite physician. Gottfried was born in 1734, and was brought up to diplomacy, but his studies were much disturbed by his love of music, and in 1769 he committed himself so far as to compose several of the songs in Favart's 'Rosière de Salency' for its public production at Paris. In 1771 he was made ambassador to the Court of Prussia, where the music was entirely under the influence of Frederick the Great, conservative and classical. This suited Van Swieten. Handel, the Bachs, and Haydn were his favourite masters ; in 1774 he commissioned C. P. E. Bach to write six symphonies for orchestra. He returned to Vienna in 1778 ; succeeded his father as Prefect of the Public Library, and in 1781 was appointed President of the Education Commission. He became a kind of musical autocrat in Vienna, and in some respects his influence was very good. He encouraged the music which he approved ; had regular Sunday-morning meetings for classical music, as well as performances of the great choral works of Bach, Handel, and Hasse, etc.; employed Mozart to add accompaniments to Handel's 'Acis,' 'Messiah,' 'St. Cecilia,' and 'Alexander's Feast,' and Starzer to do the same for 'Judas' ; translated the words of the 'Creation' and the 'Seasons' into German for Haydn ; and himself arranged Handel's 'Athaliah' and 'Choice of Hercules.' He supplied Haydn now and then with a few ducats, and gave him a travelling-carriage for his second journey to England.[2] In his relation to these great artists he seems never to have forgotten the superiority of his rank to theirs ; but this was the manner of the time. Van Swieten patronised Beethoven also [see vol. i. p. 232*a*] ; but such condescension would not be at all to Beethoven's taste, and it is not surprising that we hear very little of it.

1 Evidently not a very wise person. See Carlyle's *Frederick*, Bk. xxi. ch. 5.
2 Griesinger, *Biog. Not.* p. 66.

His first Symphony is, however, dedicated to Van Swieten. He was the founder of the 'Musikalische Gesellschaft,' or Musical Society, consisting of twenty-five members of the highest aristocracy, with the avowed object of creating a taste for good music—a forerunner of the 'Gesellschaft der Musikfreunde,' founded in 1808.

Van Swieten died at Vienna, March 29, 1803. His music has not survived him, but it would be interesting to hear one of the six symphonies which, in Haydn's words,[1] were 'as stiff as himself.'   G.

SWINEY, OWEN, frequently called Mac Swiney, [was born near Enniscorthy, Ireland, in 1680, and was the son of the rector of that place.   w. h. g. f.] In a letter,[2] dated Oct. 5, 1706, and addressed to Colley Cibber, whom he calls in turn 'puppy,' 'his Angel' (twice), 'his Dear,' and finally 'Unbeliever,'—this singular person describes how Rich had sent for him from his 'Quarters in the North,' and how 'he was at a great charge in coming to town, and it cost him a great deal of money last winter,' and 'he served him night and day, nay, all night and all day, for nine months.' He had 'quitted his post in the army' on the faith of promises that, in return for managing 'the playhouse in the Haymarkett' under Rich, he was to have '100 Guineas per annum Salary, a place at Court, and the Devil and all.' This was the somewhat inauspicious beginning of Swiney's theatrical career. Having come up to London, as described, in 1705, he soon found that Rich intended nothing seriously for his advantage; and he announces (in the same letter) that, in consequence of the general discontent of the actors with Rich, and although Rich might have had the house for £3 or £3 : 10s. a day, he (Swiney) had taken a lease for seven years at £5 a day, and meant to begin in a few days.

In 1707 we find him in partnership with Wilks, Dogget, and Cibber in the King's Theatre, having taken the lease from Vanbrugh, and very soon quarrelling with them and petitioning the Lord Chamberlain's interference in his favour. He was mixed up in most of the quarrels and intrigues of the time.

In May 1709 Swiney engaged the famous Nicolini for three years, that great singer having recently made a most successful début in London. Before the completion of this term, however, Swiney appears to have 'absented himself from his creditors' and become bankrupt.

After this he lived for some years in Italy; but on his return to England a place in the Custom-house was found for him, and he was appointed Keeper of the King's Mews. While in Italy with Lord Boyne and Walpole, he wrote to Colman (July 12, 1730) from Bologna,

on the subject of engaging singers for the Opera, then in the hands of Handel. Swiney died Oct. 2, 1754, leaving his fortune to Mrs. Woffington. He was the author of several dramatic pieces, viz. 'The Quacks, or Love's the Physician' (1705); 'Camilla' (1706); 'Pyrrhus and Demetrius' (1709); and an altered version of the first piece.

Two years before his death a fine portrait of Swiney, after Van Loo, was scraped in mezzotint by J. Faber, junr. It represents him, in black velvet, holding in his hand a book, of which the title seems to be Don Quixote.   J. M.

SYLPHIDE, LA. One of the most famous ballets on record ; in two acts ; libretto by A. Nourrit the singer, music by Schneitzhöffer. Produced at the Grand Opéra, Paris, March 12, 1832. The part of La Sylphide was danced by TAGLIONI, and was one of her greatest parts, both in Paris and in London, where the piece was brought out at Covent Garden Theatre, for her benefit, July 26, 1832. Thackeray has embalmed it in Pendennis (chap. xxxviii.)   G.

SYLVANA. See SILVANA.

SYLVIA, OU LA NYMPHE DE DIANE. 'Ballet-pantomime' in two acts and three tableaux; libretto by Barbier, music by Léo Delibes. Produced at the Grand Opéra, Paris, June 14, 1876.   G.

SYMPATHETIC TONE, RESONANCE, or VIBRATION is the term used to describe one of the commonest and most beautiful of accoustical phenomena. Any sound-producing body, such as a stretched string, or any cavity, has one particular note to which it will respond if the same note be sounded in its neighbourhood. The easiest illustration of the fact is given by raising the dampers from the strings of a piano by pressing the right pedal, and then singing a note over the strings ; these will be found to give forth the same notes uttered by the voice, in faint 'sympathy.' The fact has been turned to account in various ways in practical music. The viola d'amore was provided with 'sympathetic' strings below the finger-board, which were usually tuned to the chord of D major, and resounded when notes of that chord were played. The charm of the pianoforte pedal is not so much in prolonging the tone of the notes that are actually struck, as in allowing the sympathetic resonance to be heard from the strings corresponding to the upper partial tones of the lower notes. This power, again, is easy to analyse by placing the fingers successively or simultaneously upon the notes of the chord of C major from middle C upwards (without sounding them), and then striking the bass C firmly ; on releasing this latter key, the upper notes, or overtones, of the chord will be distinctly heard, sounded by sympathetic vibration from the upper strings. The effect of all sympathetic vibration is to enrich the quality of the tone produced ; and the fact that the harp, with its obvious poverty of tone

[1] Griesinger, Biog. Not. p. 67.
[2] In the writer's possession.

as a solo instrument, is one of the most effective members of the full orchestra, is no doubt partly due to the sympathetic vibration reacting on the large surface of strings that are capable of resonance.   M.

SYMPHONIC POEMS (Germ. *Symphonische Dichtungen* ; Fr. *Poèmes Symphoniques*), a term first applied by Liszt to his series of twelve orchestral compositions which, freed from the conventions of actual symphonic form, seemed to him to require some new title. It has been since adopted by Saint-Saëns, and many other followers of the new ideals in music ; it apparently is always held to imply the presence of a ' programme,' in which the function of the music is to illustrate the poetic material, not to be self-subsistent, as in all classical compositions. At present, too, it would seem that the absence of any recognisable design in the composition is considered essential to success, and Liszt's device of transforming his themes and presenting them in new disguises, rather than developing them according to the older principles, seems also to be a rule of the form. As existing specimens from Liszt to Richard Strauss in Germany, and from Saint-Saëns to Debussy in France, have so very little in common with the design of the true symphony, the term ' Tone-Poem ' or ' Tondichtung ' is preferred by some composers, who very likely feel relieved of all responsibility by the adoption of the vaguer title.   M.

SYMPHONY (SINFONIA, SINFONIE, SYMPHONIE). The terms used in connection with any branch of art are commonly very vague and indefinite in the early stages of its history, and are applied without much discrimination to different things. In course of time men consequently find themselves in difficulties, and try, as far as their opportunities go, to limit the definition of the terms, and to confine them at least to things which are not obviously antagonistic. In the end, however, the process of sifting is rather guided by chance and external circumstances than determined by the meaning which theorists see to be the proper one ; and the result is that the final meaning adopted by the world in general is frequently not only distinct from that which the original employers of the word intended, but also in doubtful conformity with its derivation. In the case of the word ' Symphony,' as with ' Sonata,' the meaning now accepted happens to be in very good accordance with its derivation, but it is considerably removed from the meaning which was originally attached to the word. It seems to have been used at first in a very general and comprehensive way, to express any portions of music or passages whatever which were thrown into relief as purely instrumental in works in which the chief interest was centred upon the voice or voices. Thus, in the operas, cantatas, and masses of the early part of the 17th century, the voices had the most important part of the work to do, and the instruments' chief business was to supply simple forms of harmony as accompaniment. If there were any little portions which the instruments played without the voices, these were indiscriminately called Symphonies ; and under the same head were included such more particular forms as Overtures and Ritornelli. The first experimentalists in harmonic music generally dispensed with such independent instrumental passages altogether. For instance, most if not all of the cantatas of Cesti and Rossi[1] are devoid of either instrumental introduction or ritornel ; and the same appears to have been the case with many of the operas of that time. There were, however, a few independent little instrumental movements even in the earliest operas. Peri's ' Euridice,' which stands almost at the head of the list (having been performed at Florence in 1600, as part of the festival in connection with the marriage of Henri IV. of France and Marie de' Medici), contains a ' Sinfonia ' for three flutes, which has a definite form of its own and is very characteristic of the time. The use of short instrumental passages, such as dances and introductions and ritornels, when once fairly begun, increased rapidly. Monteverde, who followed close upon Peri, made some use of them, and as the century grew older, they became a more and more important element in dramatic works, especially operas. The indiscriminate use of the word ' symphony,' to denote the passages of introduction to airs and recitatives, etc., lasted for a very long while, and got so far stereotyped in common usage that it was even applied to the instrumental portions of airs, etc., when played by a single performer. As an example may be quoted the following passage from a letter of Mozart's—' Sie (meaning Strinasacchi) spielt keine Note ohne Empfindung ; sogar bei den Sinfonien spielte sie alles mit Expression,' etc.[2] [The same use of the name for the ritornelli between the verses of a song was common in England down to the middle of the 19th century.] With regard to this use of the term, it is not necessary to do more than point out the natural course by which the meaning began to be restricted. Lully, Alessandro Scarlatti, and other great composers of operas in the 17th century, extended the appendages of airs to proportions relatively considerable, but there was a limit beyond which such dependent passages could not go. The independent instrumental portions, on the other hand, such as overtures or toccatas, or groups of ballet tunes, were in different circumstances, and could be expanded to a very much greater extent ; and as they grew in importance the name ' Symphony ' came by degrees to have a more special significance. The small instrumental appendages to the various airs and so

<hr>

[1] MSS. in the Christ Church Library, Oxford.

[2] ' She does not play a note without feeling, and even in the Symphonies played all with expression.'

forth were still symphonies in a general sense, but the Symphony *par excellence* was the introductory movement ; and the more it grew in importance the more distinctive was this application of the term.

The earliest steps in the development of this portion of the opera are chiefly important as attempts to establish some broad principle of form ; which for some time amounted to little more than the balance of short divisions, of slow and quick movement alternately. Lully is credited with the invention of one form, which came ultimately to be known as the 'Ouverture à la manière Française.' The principles of this form, as generally understood, amounted to no more than the succession of a slow solid movement to begin with, followed by a quicker movement in a lighter style, and another slow movement, not so grave in character as the first, to conclude with. Lully himself was not rigidly consistent in the adoption of this form. In some cases, as in 'Persée,' 'Thesée,' and 'Bellérophon,' there are two divisions only—the characteristic grave opening movement, and a short free fugal quick movement. 'Proserpine,' 'Phaéton,' 'Alceste,' and the Ballet piece, 'Le Triomphe de l'amour,' are characteristic examples of the complete model. These have a grave opening, which is repeated, and then the livelier central movement, which is followed by a division marked 'lentement' ; and the last two divisions are repeated in full together. A few examples are occasionally to be met with by less famous composers than Lully, which show how far the adoption of this form of overture or symphony became general in a short time. An opera called 'Venus and Adonis,' by Desmarets, of which there is a copy in the Library of the Royal College of Music, has the overture in this form. 'Amadis de Grèce,' by Des Touches, has the same, as far as can be judged from the character of the divisions ; 'Albion and Albanius,' by Grabu, which was licensed for publication in England by Roger Lestrange in 1687, has clearly the same, and looks like an imitation direct from Lully ; and the 'Venus and Adonis' by Dr. John Blow, yet again the same. So the model must have been extensively appreciated. The most important composer, however, who followed Lully in this matter, was Alessandro Scarlatti, who certainly varied and improved on the model both as regards the style and the form. In his opera of 'Flavio Cuniberto,'[1] for instance, the 'Sinfonia avanti l'Opera' begins with a division marked *grave*, which is mainly based on simple canonical imitations, but has also broad expanses of contrasting keys. The style, for the time, is noble and rich, and very superior to Lully's. The second division is a lively allegro, and the last a moderately quick minuet in 6–8 time.

[1] MS. in Christ Church Library.

The 'Sinfonia' to his serenata 'Venere, Adone, Amore,' similarly has a Largo to begin with, a Presto in the middle, and a movement, not defined by a *tempo*, but clearly of moderate quickness, to end with. This form of 'Sinfonia' survived for a long while, and was expanded at times by a succession of dance movements, for which also Lully supplied examples, and Handel at a later time more familiar types ; but for the history of the modern symphony, a form which was distinguished from the other as the 'Italian Overture,' ultimately became of much greater importance.

This form appears in principle to be the exact opposite of the French Overture ; it was similarly divided into three movements, but the first and last were quick and the central one slow. Who the originator of this form was it seems now impossible to decide ; it certainly came into vogue very soon after the French Overture, and quickly supplanted it to a great extent. Certain details in its structure were better defined than in the earlier form, and the balance and distribution of characteristic features were alike freer and more comprehensive. The first allegro was generally in a square time and of solid character ; the central movement aimed at expressiveness, and the last was a quick movement of relatively light character, generally in some combination of three feet. The history of its early development seems to be wrapped in obscurity, but from the moment of its appearance it has the traits of the modern orchestral symphony, and composers very soon obtained a remarkable degree of mastery over the form. It must have first come into definite acceptance about the end of the 17th or the beginning of the 18th century ; and by the middle of the latter it had become almost a matter of course. Operas, and similar works, by the most conspicuous composers of this time, in very great numbers, have the same form of overture. For instance, the two distinct versions of 'La Clemenza di Tito' by Hasse, 'Catone in Utica' by Leonardo Vinci (1728), the 'Hypermnestra,' 'Artaserse,' and others of Perez, Piccinni's 'Didone,' Jommelli's 'Betulia liberata,' Sacchini's 'Œdipus,' Galuppi's 'Il mondo alla reversa'—produced the year before Haydn wrote his first symphony—and Adam Hiller's 'Lisuart und Dariolette,' 'Die Liebe auf dem Lande,' 'Der Krieg,' etc. And if a more conclusive proof of the general acceptance of the form were required, it would be found in the fact that Mozart adopted it in his boyish operas, 'La finta semplice' and 'Lucio Silla.' With the general adoption of the form came also a careful development of the internal structure of each separate movement, and also a gradual improvement both in the combination and treatment of the instruments employed. Lully and Alessandro Scarlatti were for the most part satisfied with strings, which the former used crudely enough, but the latter with a good deal of perception of tone and appropriateness of style ; sometimes with the addition of wind instruments. Early in the 18th century several wind instruments, such as oboes, bassoons, horns, trumpets, and flutes were added, though not often all together ; and they served, for the most part, chiefly to strengthen the strings and give contrasting degrees of full sound rather than contrasts of colour and tone. Equally important was the rapid improvement which took place simultaneously in internal structure ; and in this case the development followed that of certain other departments of musical form. In fact the progress of the 'Sinfonia avanti l' Opera' in this respect was chiefly parallel to the development of the Clavier Sonata, which at this time was beginning to attain to clearness of outline and a certain maturity of style. It will not be necessary here to repeat what has elsewhere been discussed from different points of view in the articles on Form, Sonata, and Suite ; but it is important to realise that in point of time the form of this 'Sinfonia avanti l' Opera' did not lag behind in definition of outline and mastery of treatment ; and it might be difficult to decide in which form (whether orchestral or clavier) the important detail first presents itself of defining the first and second principal sections by subjects decisively distinct. A marked improvement in various respects appears about the time when the symphony first began to be generally played apart from the opera ; and the reasons for this are obvious. In the first place, as long as it was merely the appendage to a drama, less stress was laid upon it ; and, what is more to the point, it is recorded that audiences were not by any means particularly attentive to the instrumental portion of the work. The description given of the behaviour of the public at some of the most important theatres in Europe in the middle of the 18th century seems to correspond to the descriptions which are given of the audience at the Italian Operas in England in the latter half of the 19th. Burney, in the account of his tour, refers to this more than once. In the first volume he says, 'The music at the theatres in Italy seems but an excuse for people to assemble together, their attention being chiefly placed on play and conversation, even during the performance of a serious opera.' In another place he describes the card-tables, and the way in which the 'people of quality' reserved their attention for a favourite air or two, or the performance of a favourite singer. The rest, including the overture, they did not regard as of much consequence, and hence the composers had but little inducement to put out the best of their powers. It may have been partly on this account that they took very little pains to connect these overtures or symphonies with the opera, either by character or feature. They allowed it to become almost a settled principle that they should be independent in matter ; and consequently there was very little difficulty in accepting them as independent instrumental pieces. It naturally followed as it did later with another form of overture. The 'Symphonies' which had more attractive qualities were played apart from the operas, in concerts ; and the precedent being thereby established, the step to writing independent works on similar lines was but short ; and it was natural that, as undivided attention would now be given to them, and they were no more in a secondary position in connection with the opera, composers should take more pains both in the structure and in the choice of their musical material. The Symphony had, however, reached a considerable pitch of development before the emancipation took place ; and this development was connected with the progress of certain other musical forms besides the Sonata, already referred to.

It will accordingly be convenient, before proceeding farther with the direct history of the Symphony, to consider some of the more important of these early branches of Musical Art. In the early harmonic times the relationships of nearly all the different branches of composition were close. The Symphony was related even to the early Madrigals, through the 'Sonate da Chiesa,' which adopted the Canzona or instrumental version of the Madrigal as a second movement. It was also closely related to the early Fantasias, as the earliest experiments in instrumental music, in which some of the technical necessities of that department were grappled with. It was directly connected with the vocal portions of the early operas, such as airs and recitatives, and derived from them many of the mechanical forms of cadence and harmony which for a long time were a necessary part of its form. The solo Clavier Suite had also something to do with it, but not so much as might be expected. As has been pointed out elsewhere, the suite-form, being very simple in its principle, attained to definition very early, while the sonata-form, which characterised the richest period of harmonic music, was still struggling in elementary stages. The ultimate basis of the suite-form is a contrast of dance-tunes ; but in the typical early Symphony the dance-tunes are almost invariably avoided. When the Symphony was expanded by the addition of the Minuet and Trio, a bond of connection seemed to be established ; but still this bond was not at all a vital one, for the Minuet is one of the least characteristic elements of the suite-form proper, being clearly of less ancient lineage and type than the Allemande, Courante, Sarabande, or Gigue, or even the Gavotte and Bourrée, which were classed with it, as Intermezzi or Galan-

terien. The form of the Clavier Suite movements was in fact too inelastic to admit of such
expansion and development as was required in
the orchestral works, and the type did not
supply the characteristic technical qualities
which would be of service in their development.
The position of Bach's Orchestral Suites was
somewhat different; and it appears that he
himself called them Overtures. Dehn, in his
preface to the first edition printed, says that
the separate MS. parts in the Bach archives at
Hamburg, from which he took that in C, have
the distinctive characteristics of the handwriting
of John Sebastian, and have for title 'Ouverture
pour 2 Violons,' etc. ; and that another MS.,
probably copied from these, has the title 'Suite
pour Orchestre.' This throws a certain light
upon Bach's position. It is obvious that in
several departments of instrumental music he
took the French for his models rather than the
Italians. In the Suite he followed Couperin,
and in the Overture he also followed French
models. These therefore appear as attempts
to develop an independent orchestral work
analogous to the Symphony, upon the basis of
a form which had the same reason for existence
and the same general purpose as the Italian
Overture, but a distinctly different general
outline. Their chief connection with the actual
development of the modern symphony lies in
the treatment of the instruments ; for all
experiments, even on different lines, if they
have a common quality or principle, must react
upon one another in those respects.

Another branch of art which had close connection with the early symphonies was the
Concerto. Works under this name were not
by any means invariably meant to be show
pieces for solo instruments, as modern concertos
are ; and sometimes the name was used as
almost synonymous with symphony. The
earliest concertos seem to have been works in
which groups of 'solo' and 'ripieno' instruments were used, chiefly to obtain contrasts of
fulness of tone. For instance, a set of six
concertos by Alessandro Scarlatti, for two
violins and violoncello, 'soli,' and two violins,
tenor, and bass, 'ripieni,' present no distinction
of style between one group and the other.
The accompanying instruments for the most
part merely double the solo parts, and leave off
either to lessen the sound here and there, or
because the passages happen to go a little higher
than usual, or to be a little difficult for the
average violin-players of that time. When the
intention is to vary the quality of sound as
well, the element of what is called instrumentation is introduced, and this is one of the earliest
phases of that element which can be traced in
music. The order of movements and the style
of them are generally after the manner of the
Sonate da Chiesa, and therefore do not present
any close analogy with the subject of this
article. But very soon after the time of Corelli
and Alessandro Scarlatti the form of the Italian
overture was adopted for concertos, and about
the same time they began to show traces of
becoming show-pieces for great performers.
Allusions to the performance of concertos by
great violin-players in the churches form a
familiar feature in the musical literature of the
18th century, and the three-movement form
(to all intents exactly like that of the symphonies) seems to have been adopted early.
This evidently points to the fact that this form
appealed to the instincts of composers generally,
as the most promising for free expression of
their musical thoughts. It may seem curious
that J. S. Bach, who followed French models
in some important departments of instrumental
music, should exclusively have followed Italian
models in this. But in reality it appears to
have been a matter of chance with him ; he
always followed the best models which came to
his hand. In this department the Italians
excelled ; and Bach therefore followed them,
and left the most important early specimens of
this kind remaining—almost all in the three-
movement form, which was becoming the set
order for symphonies. Setting aside those
specially imitated from Vivaldi, there are at
least twenty concertos by him for all sorts of
solo instruments and combinations of solo
instruments in this same form. It cannot
therefore be doubted that some of the development of the symphony-form took place in this
department. But Bach never to any noticeable
extent yielded to the tendency to break the
movements up into sections with corresponding
tunes ; and this distinguishes his work in a
very marked manner from that of the generation
of composers who followed him. His art belongs
in reality to a different stratum from that which
produced the greater forms of abstract instrumental music. It is probable that his form
of art could not, without some modification,
have produced the great orchestral symphonies.
In order to get to these, composers had to go
to a different, and for some time a decidedly
lower, level. It was much the same process as
had been gone through before. After Palestrina
a backward move was necessary to make it
possible to arrive at the art of Bach and Handel.
After Bach men had to take up a lower line in
order to get to Beethoven. In the latter case
it was necessary to go through the elementary
stages of defining the various contrasting
sections of a movement, and finding that form
of harmonic treatment which admitted the great
effects of colour or varieties of tone in the mass,
as well as in the separate lines of the counterpoint. Bach's position was so immensely high
that several generations had to pass before men
were able to follow on his lines and adopt his
principles in harmonic music. The generation
that followed him showed scarcely any trace of

his influence. Even before he had passed away the new tendencies of music were strongly apparent, and much of the elementary work of the modern sonata-form of art had been done on different lines from his own.

The 'Sinfonia avanti l' Opera' was clearly by this time sufficiently independent and complete to be appreciated without the opera, and without either name or programme to explain its meaning ; and within a very short period the demand for these sinfonias became very great. Burney's tours in search of materials for his History, in France, Italy, Holland, and Germany, were made in 1770 and 1772, before Haydn had written any of his greater symphonies, and while Mozart was still a boy. His allusions to independent 'symphonies' are very frequent. Among those whose works he mentions with most favour are Stamitz, Emanuel Bach, Christian Bach, and Abel. Works of the kind by these composers and many others of note are to be seen in great numbers in sets of part-books in the British Museum. These furnish most excellent materials for judging of the status of the Symphony in the early stages of its independent existence. The two most important points which they illustrate are the development of instrumentation and the definition of form. They appear to have been generally written in eight parts. Most of them are scored for two violins, viola, and bass ; two hautboys, or two flutes, and two 'cors de chasse.' This is the case in the six symphonies of op. 3 of John Christian Bach ; the six of Abel's op. 10, the six of Stamitz's op. 9, op. 13, and op. 16 ; also in a set of 'Overtures in 8 parts' by Arne, which must have been early in the field, as the licence from George II., printed in full at the beginning of the first violin part, is dated January 174$\frac{4}{9}$. The same orchestration is found in many symphonies by Galuppi, Ditters, Schwindl, and others. Wagenseil, who must have been the oldest of this group of composers (having been born in the 17th century, within six years after Handel, Scarlatti, and Bach), wrote several quite in the characteristic harmonic style, 'à 4 parties obligées avec Cors de Chasse ad libitum.' The treatment of the instruments in these early examples is rather crude and stiff. The violins are almost always playing, and the hautboys or flutes are only used to reinforce them at times as the 'ripieni' instruments did in the early concertos, while the horns serve to hold on the harmonies. The first stages of improvement are noticeable in such details as the independent treatment of the strings. In the 'symphonies before the opera' the violas were cared for so little that in many cases[1] not more than half-a-dozen bars are written in, all the rest being merely

'col basso.' As examples of this in works of more or less illustrious writers may be mentioned the 'Sinfonias' to Jommelli's 'Passione' and 'Betulia Liberata,' Sacchini's 'Œdipus,' and Sarti's 'Giulio Sabino.' One of the many honours attributed to Stamitz by his admiring contemporaries was that he made the violas independent of the basses. This may seem a trivial detail, but it is only by such details, and the way in which they struck contemporary writers, that the character of the gradual progress in instrumental composition can now be understood.

The general outlines of the form were extremely regular. The three movements as above described were almost invariable, the first being a vigorous broad allegro, the second the sentimental slow movement, and the third the lively vivace. The progress of internal structure is at first chiefly noticeable in the first movement. In the early examples this is always condensed as much as possible, the balance of subject is not very clearly realisable, and there is hardly ever a double bar or repeat of the first half of the movement. The divisions of key, the short 'working-out' portion, and the recapitulation, are generally present, but not pointedly defined. Examples of this condition of things are supplied by some MS. symphonies by Paradisi in the Fitzwilliam Museum at Cambridge, which in other respects possess excellent and characteristically modern traits. The first thing attained seems to have been the relative definition and balance of the two subjects. In Stamitz, Abel, J. C. Bach, and Wagenseil, this is already commonly met with. The following examples from the first movement of the fifth symphony of Stamitz's op. 9 illustrate both the style and the degree of contrast between the two principal subjects.

1st subject.

etc.

2nd subject.

etc.

The style is a little heavy, and the motion constrained, but the general character is solid and dignified. The last movements of this period are curiously suggestive of some familiar examples of a maturer time ; very gay and obvious, and very definite in outline. The following is very characteristic of Abel :—

etc.

It is a noticeable fact in connection with the genealogy of these works, that they are almost as frequently entitled 'Overture' as 'Symphony'; sometimes the same work is called by the one name outside and the other in ; and this is the case also with some of the earlier and slighter symphonies of Haydn, which must have made their appearance about this period. One further point which it is of importance to note is that in some of Stamitz's symphonies the complete form of the mature period is found. One in D is most complete in every respect. The first movement is Allegro with double bars and repeats in regular binary form ; the second is an Andante in G, the third a Minuet and Trio, and the fourth a Presto. Another in E♭ (which is called No. 7 in the part-books) and another in F (not definable) have also the Minuet and Trio. A few others by Schwindl and Ditters have the same, but it is impossible to get even approximately to the date of their production, and therefore little inference can be framed upon the circumstance, beyond the fact that composers were beginning to recognise the fourth movement as a desirable ingredient.

Another composer who precedes Haydn in time as well as in style is Emanuel Bach. He was his senior in years, and began writing symphonies in 1741, when Haydn was only nine years old. His most important symphonies

were produced in 1776 ; while Haydn's most important examples were not produced till after 1790. In style Emanuel Bach stands singularly alone, at least in his finest examples. It looks almost as if he purposely avoided the form which by 1776 must have been familiar to the musical world. It has been shown that the binary form was employed by some of his contemporaries in their orchestral works, but he seems determinedly to avoid it in the first movements of the works of that year. His object seems to have been to produce striking and clearly outlined passages, and to balance and contrast them one with another according to his fancy, and with little regard to any systematic distribution of the successions of key. The boldest and most striking subject is the first of the Symphony in D :—

etc.

The opening passages of that in E♭ are hardly less emphatic. They have little connection with the tendencies of his contemporaries, but seem in every respect an experiment on independent lines, in which the interest depends upon the vigour of the thoughts and the unexpected turns of the modulations ; and the result is certainly rather fragmentary and disconnected. The slow movement is commonly connected with the first and last either by a special transitional passage, or by a turn of modulation and a half-close. It is short and dependent in its character, but graceful and melodious. The last is much more systematic in structure than the first ; sometimes in definite binary form, as was the case with the early violin sonatas. In orchestration and general style of expression these works seem immensely superior to the other early symphonies which have been described. They are scored for horns, flutes, oboi, fagotto, strings, with a figured bass for ' cembalo,' which in the symphonies previously noticed does not always appear. There is an abundance of unison and octave passages for the strings, but there is also good free writing, and contrasts between wind and strings ; the wind being occasionally left quite alone. All the instruments come in occasionally for special employment, and considering the proportions of the orchestras of the time Bach's effects must have been generally clear and good. The following is a good specimen of his scoring of an ordinary full passage :—

It has sometimes been said that Haydn was chiefly influenced by Emanuel Bach, and Mozart by John Christian Bach. At the present time, and in relation to symphonies, it is easier to understand the latter case than the former. In both cases the influence is more likely to be traced in clavier works than in those for orchestra. For Haydn's style and treatment of form bear far more resemblance to most of the other com-

posers whose works have been referred to, than to Emanuel Bach. There are certain kinds of forcible expression and ingenious turns of modulation which Haydn may have learnt from him ; but their best orchestral works seem to belong to quite distinct families. Haydn's first symphony was written in 1759 for Count Morzin. Like many other of his early works it does not seem discoverable in print in England. But it is said by Pohl,[1] who must have seen it somewhere in Germany, to be 'a small work in three movements for two violins, viola, bass, two oboes, and two horns' ; from which particulars it would appear to correspond exactly in externals to the examples above described of Abel's and J. C. Bach's, etc. In the course of the next few years he added many more ; most of which appear to have been slight and of no great historical importance, while the few which present peculiarities are so far isolated in those respects that they do not throw much light upon the course of his development, or upon his share in building up the art-form of the Symphony. Of such a kind is the movement (dramatic in character, and including long passages of recitative) in the Symphony in C, which he wrote as early as 1761.[2] For, though this kind of movement is found in instrumental works of an earlier period, its appearance in such a manner in a

symphony is too rare to have any special historical bearings. The course of his development was gradual and regular. He seems to have been content with steadily improving the edifice of his predecessors, and with few exceptions to have followed their lines. A great deal is frequently attributed to his connection with the complete musical establishment which Prince Esterhazy set up at his great palace at Esterház ; where Haydn certainly had opportunities which have been the lot of scarcely any other composer who ever lived. He is described as making experiments in orchestration, and ringing the bell for the band to come and try them ; and, though this may not be absolutely true in fact, there can scarcely be a doubt that the very great improvements which he effected in every department of orchestration may to a great extent be attributed to the facilities for testing his works which he enjoyed. At the same time the really important portion of his compositions were not produced till his patron, Prince Nicolaus Esterhazy, was dead, and the musical establishment broken up ; nor, it must be remembered, till after that strange and important episode in Haydn's life, the rapid flitting of Mozart across the scene. When Haydn wrote his first symphony, Mozart was only three years old ; and Mozart died in the very year in which the famous Salomon concerts in London, for which Haydn wrote nearly all his finest symphonies, began.

[1] *Joseph Haydn*, vol. i. p. 284 (1875).
[2] *Ibid.* pp. 287, 397.

Mozart's work, therefore, comes between Haydn's lighter period and his greatest achievements ; and his symphonies are in some respects prior to Haydn's, and certainly had an effect upon his later works of all kinds.

According to Köchel, Mozart wrote altogether forty-nine symphonies. The first, in E♭, was written in London in 1764, when he was eight years old, and only five years after Haydn wrote his first. It was on the same pattern as those which have been fully described above, being in three movements and scored for the usual set of instruments—namely, two violins, viola, bass, two oboes, and two horns. Three more followed in close succession, in one of which clarinets are introduced instead of oboes, and a bassoon is added to the usual group of eight instruments. In these works striking originality of purpose or style is hardly to be looked for, and it was not for some time that Mozart's powers in instrumental music reached a pitch of development which is historically important ; but it is nevertheless astonishing to see how early he developed a free and even rich style in managing his orchestral resources. With regard to the character of these and all but a few of the rest it is necessary to keep in mind that a symphony at that time was a very much less important matter than it became fifty years later. The manner in which symphonies were poured out, in sets of six and otherwise, by numerous composers during the latter half of the 18th century, puts utterly out of the question the loftiness of aim and purpose which has become a necessity since the early years of the 19th century. They were all rather slight works on familiar lines, with which for the time being composers and public were alike quite content ; and neither Haydn nor Mozart in their early specimens seem to have specially exerted themselves. The general survey of Mozart's symphonies presents a certain number of facts which are worth noting for their bearing upon the history of this form of art. The second symphony he wrote had a minuet and trio ; but it is hardly possible that he can have regarded this as an important point, since he afterwards wrote seventeen others without them ; and these spread over the whole period of his activity, for even in that which he wrote at Prague in 1786, and which is last but three in the whole series, the minuet and trio are absent. Besides this fact, which at once connects them with the examples by other composers previously discussed, there is the yet more noticeable one that more than twenty of the series are written for the same peculiar little group of instruments, viz. the four strings, a pair of oboes or flutes, and a pair of horns. Although he used clarinets so early as his third symphony, he never employed them again till his thirty-ninth, which was written for Paris, and is almost more fully scored than any. In

the whole forty-nine, in fact, he only used clarinets five times, and in one of these cases (viz. the well-known G minor) they were added after he had finished the score. Even bassoons are not common ; the most frequent addition to the little nucleus of oboes or flutes and horns being trumpets and drums. The two which are most fully scored are the Parisian, in D, just alluded to, which was written in 1778, and that in E♭, which was written in Vienna in 1788, and stands first in the famous triad. These facts explain to a certain extent how it was possible to write such an extraordinary number in so short a space of time. Mozart's most continuously prolific period in this branch of art seems to have been when he had returned to Salzburg in 1771 ; for between July in that year and the beginning of 1773, it appears to be proved that he produced no fewer than fourteen. But this feat is fairly surpassed in another sense by the production of the last three in three successive months, June, July, and August 1788 ; since the musical calibre of these is so immensely superior to that of the earlier ones.

One detail of comparison between Mozart's ways and Haydn's is curious. Haydn began to use introductory adagios very early, and used them so often that they became quite a characteristic feature in his plan. Mozart, on the other hand, did not use one until his 44th Symphony, written in 1783. What was the origin of Haydn's employment of them is uncertain. The causes that have been suggested are not altogether satisfactory. In the orthodox form of symphony, as written by the numerous composers of his early days, the opening adagio is not found. He may possibly have observed that it was a useful factor in a certain class of overtures, and then have used it as an experiment in symphonies, and finding it answer, may have adopted the expedient generally in succeeding works of the kind. It seems likely that Mozart adopted it from Haydn, as its first appearance (in the symphony which is believed to have been composed at Linz for Count Thun) coincides with the period in which he is considered to have been first strongly influenced by Haydn.

The influence of these two great composers upon one another is extremely interesting and curious, more especially as it did not take effect till comparatively late in their artistic careers. They both began working in the general direction of their time, under the influences which have been already referred to. In the department of symphony each was considerably influenced after a time by a special circumstance of his life ; Haydn by the appointment to Esterház before alluded to, and the opportunities it afforded him of orchestral experiment ; and Mozart by his stay at Mannheim in 1777. For it appears most likely that the superior abilities

of the Mannheim orchestra for dealing with
purely instrumental music, and the traditions of
Stamitz, who had there effected his share in the
history of the Symphony, opened Mozart's eyes
to the possibilities of orchestral performance,
and encouraged him to a freer style of composition and more elaborate treatment of the
orchestra than he had up to that time attempted.
The Mannheim band had in fact been long considered the finest in Europe ; and in certain
things, such as attention to *nuances* (which in
early orchestral works had been looked upon as
either unnecessary or out of place), they and
their conductors had been important pioneers ;
and thus Mozart must certainly have had his ideas
on such heads a good deal expanded. The qualities of the symphony produced in Paris early in
the next year were probably the first-fruits of
these circumstances ; and it happens that while
this symphony is the first of his which has
maintained a definite position among the important landmarks of art, it is also the first in
which he uses orchestral forces approaching to
those commonly employed for symphonies since
the latter part of the 18th century.

Both Haydn and Mozart, in the course of their
respective careers, made decided progress in
managing the orchestra, both as regards the
treatment of individual instruments, and the
distribution of the details of musical interest
among them. It has been already pointed out
that one of the earliest expedients by which
contrast of effect was attempted by writers for
combinations of instruments, was the careful
distribution of portions for 'solo' and 'ripieno'
instruments, as illustrated by Scarlatti's and
later concertos. In J. S. Bach's treatment of
the orchestra the same characteristic is familiar.
The long duets for oboes, flutes, or bassoons,
and the solos for horn or violin, or viola da
gamba, which continue throughout whole recitatives or arias, all have this same principle at
bottom. Composers had still to learn the free
and yet well-balanced management of their
string forces, and to attain the mean between
the use of wind instruments merely to strengthen
the strings and their use as solo instruments in
long independent passages. In Haydn's early
symphonies the old traditions are most apparent.
The balance between the different forces of the
orchestra is as yet both crude and obvious. In
the symphony called 'Le Matin' for instance,
which appears to have been among the earliest,
the second violins play with the first, and the
violas with the basses to a very marked extent
—in the first movement almost throughout.
This first movement, again, begins with a solo
for flute. The slow movement, which is divided
into adagio and andante, has no wind instruments at all, but there is a violin solo throughout the middle portion. In the minuet a contrast is attained by a long passage for wind band
alone (as in J. S. Bach's second Bourrée to the

'Ouverture' in C major) ; and the trio consists
of a long and elaborate solo for bassoon. Haydn
early began experiments in various uses of his
orchestra, and his ways of grouping his solo instruments for effect are often curious and original.
C. F. Pohl, in his life of him, prints from the
MS. parts a charming slow movement from a
B♭ symphony, which was probably written in
1766 or 1767. It illustrates in a singular way
how Haydn at first endeavoured to obtain a
special effect without ceasing to conform to
familiar methods of treating his strings. The
movement is scored for first and second violins,
violas, *solo violoncello* and bass, all 'con sordini.'
The first and second violins play in unison
throughout, and the violoncello plays the tune
with them an octave lower, while the violas play
in octaves with the bass all but two or three
bars of cadence ; so that in reality there are
scarcely ever more than two parts playing at a
time. The following example will show the
style :—

Violini 1 & 2.

p

Viola.

Violoncello Solo.

Basso.

Towards a really free treatment of his forces he
seems, however, to have been led on insensibly
and by very slow degrees. For over twenty years
of symphony-writing the same limited treatment
of strings and the same kind of solo passages are
commonly to be met with. But there is a growing tendency to make the wind and the lower
and inner strings more and more independent,
and to individualise the style of each within
proportionate bounds. A fine symphony (in E
minor, ' Letter I '), which appears to date from
1772, is a good specimen of Haydn's intermediate stage. The strings play almost incessantly throughout, and the wind either doubles
the string parts to enrich and reinforce them,
or else has long holding notes while the strings
play characteristic figures. The passage from
the last movement, given on the next page, will
serve to illustrate pretty clearly the stage of
orchestral expression to which Haydn had at
that time arrived.

In the course of the following ten years the
progress was slow but steady. No doubt many
other composers were writing symphonies besides
Haydn and Mozart, and were, like them, improving that branch of art. Unfortunately the
difficulty of fixing the dates of their productions

is almost insuperable ; and so their greater re-presentatives come to be regarded, not only as giving an epitome of the history of the epoch, but as comprising it in themselves. Mozart's first specially notable symphony falls in 1778. This was the one which he wrote for Paris after his experiences at Mannheim ; and some of his Mannheim friends who happened to be in Paris with him assisted at the performance. It is in almost every respect a very great advance upon Haydn's E minor Symphony, just quoted. The treatment of the instruments is very much freer, and more individually characteristic. It marks an important step in the transition from the kind of symphony in which the music appears to have been conceived almost entirely for violins, with wind subordinate, except in special solo passages, to the kind in which the original conception in respect of subjects, episodes, and development, embraced all the forces, including the wind instruments. The first eight bars of Mozart's symphony are sufficient to illustrate the nature of the artistic tendency. In the firm and dignified beginning of the principal subject, the strings, with flutes and bassoons, are all in unison for three bars, and a good body of wind instruments gives the full chord. Then the upper strings are left alone for a couple of bars in octaves, and are accompanied in their short closing phrase by an independent full chord of wind instruments, *piano*. This chord is repeated in the same form of rhythm as that which marks the first bars of the principal subject, and has therefore at once musical sense and relevance, besides supplying the necessary full harmony. In the subsidiary subject by which the first section is carried on, the quick lively passages of the strings are accompanied by short figures for flute and horns, with their own independent musical significance. In the second subject proper, which is derived from this subsidiary, an excellent balance of colour is obtained by pairs of wind instruments in octaves, answering with an independent and very characteristic phrase

of their own the group of strings which give out the first part of the subject. The same well-balanced method is observed throughout. In the working out of this movement almost all the instruments have something special and relevant of their own to do, so that it is made to seem as if the conception were exactly apportioned to the forces which were meant to utter it. The same criticisms apply to all the rest of the symphony. The slow movement has beautiful independent figures and phrases for the wind instruments, so interwoven with the body of the movement that they supply necessary elements of colour and fulness of harmony, without appearing either as definite solos or as meaningless holding notes. The fresh and merry last movement has much the same characteristics as the first in the matter of instrumental utterance, and in its working-out section all the forces have, if anything, even more independent work of their own to do, while still supplying their appropriate ingredients to the sum total of sound.

The succeeding ten years saw all the rest of the work Mozart was destined to do in the department of symphony ; much of it showing in turn an advance on the Paris Symphony, inasmuch as the principles there shown were worked out to greater fulness and perfection, while the musical spirit attained a more definite richness, and escaped farther from the formalism which characterises the previous generation. Among these symphonies the most important are the following : a considerable one (in E♭) composed at Salzburg in 1780 ; the 'Haffner' (in D), which was a modification of a serenade, and had originally more than the usual group of movements ; the 'Linz' Symphony (in C ; 'No. 6') ; and the last four, the crown of the whole series. The first of these (in D major) was written for Prague in 1786, and was received there with immense favour in Jan. 1787. It appears to be far in advance of all its predecessors in freedom and clearness of instrumentation, in the breadth and musical significance of the subjects, and in richness and balance of form. It is one of the few of Mozart's which open with an adagio, and that too of unusual proportions ; but it has no minuet and trio. This symphony was in its turn eclipsed by the three great ones in E flat, G minor, and C, which were composed at Vienna in June, July, and August 1788. These symphonies are almost the first in which certain qualities of musical expression and a certain method in their treatment stand prominent in the manner which was destined to become characteristic of the great works of the early part of the 19th century. Mozart having mastered the principle upon which the mature art-form of symphony was to be attacked, had greater freedom for the expression of his intrinsically musical ideas, and could emphasise more freely and consistently the typical characteristics which his inspiration led him to adopt in developing his ideas. It must not, however, be supposed that this principle is to be found for the first time in these works. They find their counterparts in works of Haydn's of a much earlier date; only, inasmuch as the art-form was then less mature, the element of formalism is too strong to admit of the musical or poetical intention being so clearly realised. It is of course impossible to put into words with certainty the inherent characteristics of these or any other later works on the same lines; but that they are felt to have such characteristics is indisputable, and their perfection as works of art, which is so commonly insisted on, could not exist if it were not so. Among the many writers who have tried in some way to describe them, probably the best and most responsible is Otto Jahn. Of the first of the group (that in E♭), he says, 'We find the expression of perfect happiness in the charm of euphony' which is one of the marked external characteristics of the whole work. 'The feeling of pride in the consciousness of power shines through the magnificent introduction, while the Allegro expresses the purest pleasure, now in frolicsome joy, now in active excitement, and now in noble and dignified composure. Some shadows appear, it is true, in the Andante, but they only serve to throw into stronger relief the mild serenity of a mind communing with itself and rejoicing in the peace which fills it. This is the true source of the cheerful transport which rules the last movement, rejoicing in its own strength and in the joy of being.' Whether this is all perfectly true or not is of less consequence than the fact that a consistent and uniform style and object can be discerned through the whole work, and that it admits of an approximate description in words, without either straining or violating familiar impressions.

The second of the great symphonic trilogy—that in G minor—has a still clearer meaning. The contrast with the E♭ is strong, for in no symphony of Mozart's is there so much sadness and regretfulness. This element also accounts for the fact that it is the most modern of his symphonies, and shows most human nature. E. T. A. Hoffmann (writing in a spirit very different from that of Jahn) says of it, 'Love and melancholy breathe forth in purest spirit tones; we feel ourselves drawn with inexpressible longing towards the forms which beckon us to join them in their flight through the clouds to another sphere.' Jahn agrees in attributing to it a character of sorrow and complaining; and there can hardly be a doubt that the tonality as well as the style, and such characteristic features as occur incidentally, would all favour the idea that Mozart's inspiration took a sad cast, and maintained it so far throughout; so that, notwithstanding the formal

passages which occasionally make their appearance at the closes, the whole work may without violation of probability receive a consistent psychological explanation. Even the orchestration seems appropriate from this point of view, since the prevailing effect is far less soft and smooth than that of the previous symphony. A detail of historical interest in connection with this work is the fact that Mozart originally wrote it without clarinets, and added them afterwards for a performance at which it may be presumed they happened to be specially available. He did this by taking a separate piece of paper and rearranging the oboe parts, sometimes combining the instruments and sometimes distributing the parts between the two, with due regard to their characteristic styles of utterance.

The last of Mozart's symphonies has so obvious and distinctive a character throughout, that popular estimation has accepted the definite name 'Jupiter' as conveying the prevalent feeling about it. In this there is far less human sentiment than in the G minor. In fact, Mozart appears to have aimed at something lofty and self-contained, and therefore precluding the shade of sadness which is an element almost indispensable to strong human sympathy. When he descends from this distant height, he assumes a cheerful and sometimes playful vein, as in the second principal subject of the first movement, and in the subsidiary or cadence subject that follows it. This may not be altogether in accordance with what is popularly meant by the name 'Jupiter,' though that deity appears to have been capable of a good deal of levity in his time; but it has the virtue of supplying admirable contrast to the main subjects of the section; and it is so far in consonance with them that there is no actual reversal of feeling in passing from one to the other. The slow movement has an appropriate dignity which keeps it in character, and reaches, in parts, a considerable degree of passion, which brings it nearer to human sympathy than the other movements. The Minuet and the Trio again show cheerful serenity, and the last movement, with its elaborate fugal treatment, has a vigorous austerity, which is an excellent balance to the character of the first movement. The scoring, especially in the first and last movements, is fuller than is usual with Mozart, and produces effects of strong and clear sound; and it is also admirably in character with the spirit of dignity and loftiness which seems to be aimed at in the greater portion of the musical subjects and figures. In these later symphonies Mozart certainly reached a far higher pitch of art in the department of instrumental music than any hitherto arrived at. The characteristics of his attainments may be described as a freedom of style in the ideas, freedom in the treatment of the various parts of the score, and independence and appropriateness of expression in the management of the various groups of instruments employed. In comparison with the works of his predecessors, and with his own and Haydn's earlier compositions, there is throughout a most remarkable advance in vitality. The distribution of certain cadences and passages of *tutti* still appear to modern ears formal; but compared with the immature formalism of expression, even in principal ideas, which was prevalent twenty or even ten years earlier, the improvement is immense. In such structural elements as the development of the ideas, the concise and energetic flow of the music, the distribution and contrast of instrumental tone, and the balance and proportion of sound, these works are generally held to reach a pitch almost unsurpassable from the point of view of technical criticism. Mozart's intelligence and taste, dealing with thoughts as yet undisturbed by strong or passionate emotion, attained a degree of perfection in the sense of pure and directly intelligible art which later times can scarcely hope to see approached.

Haydn's symphonies up to this time cannot be said to equal Mozart's in any respect; though they show a considerable improvement on the style of treatment and expression in the 'Trauer' or the 'Farewell' Symphonies. Of those which are better known of about this date are 'La Poule' and 'Letter V,' which were written (both for Paris) in 1786 and 1787. 'Letter Q,' or the 'Oxford' Symphony, which was performed when Haydn received the degree of Doctor of Music from that university, dates from 1788, the same year as Mozart's great triad. 'Letter V' and 'Letter Q' are in his mature style, and thoroughly characteristic in every respect. The orchestration is clear and fresh, though not so sympathetic nor so elastic in its variety as Mozart's; and the ideas, with all their geniality and directness, are not up to his own highest standard. It is the last twelve, which were written for Salomon after 1790, which have really fixed Haydn's high position as a composer of symphonies; these became so popular as practically to supersede the numerous works of all his predecessors and contemporaries except Mozart, to the extent of causing them to be almost completely forgotten. This is owing partly to the high pitch of technical skill which he attained, partly to the freshness and geniality of his ideas, and partly to the vigour and daring of harmonic progression which he manifested. He and Mozart together enriched this branch of art to an extraordinary degree, and towards the end of their lives began to introduce far deeper feeling and earnestness into the style than had been customary in early works of the class. The average orchestra had increased in size, and at the same time had gained a better balance of its component elements. Instead of the customary little group of strings and four wind instruments, it had

come to comprise, besides the strings, two flutes, two oboes, two bassoons, two horns, two trumpets, and drums. To these were occasionally added two clarinets, as in Haydn's last three (the two in D minor and one in E♭), and in one movement of the Military Symphony. Neither Mozart nor Haydn ever used trombones in symphonies; but uncommon instruments were sometimes employed, as in the 'Military,' in which Haydn used a big drum, a triangle and cymbals. In his latest symphonies Haydn's treatment of his orchestra agrees in general with the description already given of Mozart's. The bass has attained a free motion of its own; the violas rarely cling in a dependent manner to it, but have their own individual work to do, and the same applies to the second violins, which no longer so often appear merely 'col 1mo.' The wind instruments fill up and sustain the harmonies as completely as in former days; but they cease merely to hold long notes without characteristic features, or slavishly to follow the string parts whenever something livelier is required. They may still play a great deal that is mere doubling, but there is generally method in it; and the musical ideas they express are in a great measure proportioned to their characters and style of utterance. Haydn was rather fond of long passages for wind alone, as in the slow movement of the Oxford Symphony, the opening passage of the first allegro of the Military Symphony, and the 'working out' of the Symphony in C, No. 1 of the Salomon set. Solos in a tune-form for wind instruments are also rather more common than in Mozart's works, and in many respects the various elements which go to make up the whole are less assimilated than they are by Mozart. The tunes are generally more definite in their outlines, and stand in less close relation with their context. It appears as if Haydn always retained to the last a strong sympathy with simple people's-tunes; the character of his minuets and trios, and especially of his finales, is sometimes strongly defined in this respect; but his way of expressing them within the limits he chose is extraordinarily finished and acute. It is possible that, as before suggested, he got his taste for surprises in harmonic progression from C. P. E. Bach. His instinct for such things, considering the age he lived in, was very remarkable. The passage on the next page, from his Symphony in C, just referred to, illustrates several of the above points at once.

The period of Haydn and Mozart is in every respect the principal crisis in the history of the Symphony. When they came upon the scene, it was not regarded as a very important form of art. In the good musical centres of those times—and there were many—there was a great demand for symphonies; but the bands for which they were written were small, and appear from the most natural inferences not to have been very efficient or well organised. The standard of performance was evidently rough, and composers could neither expect much attention to *pianos* and *fortes*, nor any ability to grapple with technical difficulties among the players of bass instruments or violas. The audiences were critical in the one sense of requiring good healthy workmanship in the writing of the pieces—in fact much better than they would demand in the present day ; but with regard to deep meaning, refinement, poetical intention, or originality, they appear to have cared very little. They wanted to be healthily pleased and entertained, not stirred with deep emotion ; and the purposes of composers in those days were consequently not exalted to any high pitch, but were limited to a simple and unpretentious supply, in accordance with demand and opportunity. Haydn was influenced by these considerations till the last. There is always more fun and gaiety in his music than pensiveness or serious reflection. But in developing

the technical part of expression, in proportioning the means to the end, and in organising the forces of the orchestra, what he did was of the utmost importance. It is, however, impossible to apportion the value of the work of the two masters. Haydn did a great deal of important and substantial work before Mozart came into prominence in the same field. But after the first great mark had been made by the Paris Symphony, Mozart seemed to rush to his culmination ; and in the last four of his works reached a style which appears richer, more sympathetic, and more complete than anything Haydn could attain to. Then, again, when he had passed away, Haydn produced his greatest works. Each composer had his distinctive characteristics, and each is delightful in his own way ; but Haydn would probably not have reached his highest development without the influence of his more richly gifted contemporary ; and Mozart for his part was undoubtedly very much under the influence of Haydn at an important part of his career. The best that can be said by way of distinguishing their respective shares in the result is that Mozart's last symphonies introduced an intrinsically musical element which had before been wanting, and showed a supreme perfection of actual art in their structure ; while

Haydn in the long series of his works cultivated and refined his own powers to such an extent that when his last symphonies had made their appearance, the status of the symphony was raised beyond the possibility of a return to the old level. In fact he gave this branch of art a stability and breadth which served as the basis upon which the art of succeeding generations appears to rest ; and the simplicity and clearness of his style and structural principles supplied an intelligible model for his successors to follow.

One of the most important of the contemporaries of Haydn and Mozart in this department of art was F. J. Gossec. He was born in 1733, one year after Haydn, and lived like him to a good old age. His chief claim to remembrance is the good work which he did in improving the standard of taste for instrumental music in France. According to Fétis such things as instrumental symphonies were absolutely unknown in Paris before 1754, in which year Gossec published his first, five years before Haydn's first attempt. Gossec's work was carried on most effectually by his founding, in 1770, the 'Concert des Amateurs,' for whom he wrote his most important works. He also took the management of the famous Concerts Spirituels, with Gaviniés and Leduc, in 1773, and furthered the cause of good instrumental music there as well. The few symphonies of his to be found in this country are of the same calibre, and for the same groups of instruments, as those of J. C. Bach, Abel, etc., already described ; but Fétis attributes importance to him chiefly because of the way in which he extended the dimensions and resources of the orchestra. His Symphony in D, No. 21, written soon after the founding of the Concert des Amateurs, was for a full set of strings, flutes, oboes, clarinets, bassoons, horns, trumpets, and drums ; and this was doubtless an astonishing force to the Parisians, accustomed as they had been to regard the compositions of Lully and Rameau as the best specimens of instrumental music. But it is clear from other indications that Gossec had considerable ideas about the ways in which instrumental music might be improved, analogous on a much smaller scale to the aspirations and attempts of Berlioz at a later date. Not only are his works carefully marked with *pianos* and *fortes*, but in some (as the Symphonies of op. xii.) there are elaborate directions as to how the movements are to be played. Some of these are curious. For instance, over the first violin part of the slow movement of the second symphony is printed the following : ' La différence du Fort au Doux dans ce morceau doit être excessive, et le mouvement modéré, à l'aise, qu'il semble se jouer avec la plus grande facilité.' Nearly all the separate movements of this set have some such directions, either longer or shorter ; the inference from which is that

Gossec had a strong idea of expression and style in performance, and did not find his bands very easily led in these respects. The movements themselves are on the same small scale as those of J. C. Bach, Abel, and Stamitz ; and very rarely have the double bar and repeat in the first movements, though these often make their appearance in the finales. The style is to a certain extent individual ; not so robust or so full as that of Bach or Stamitz, but not without attractiveness. As his works are very difficult to get sight of, the following quotation from the last movement of a symphony in B♭ will serve to give some idea of his style and manner of scoring :—

Another composer of symphonies, who is often heard of in juxtaposition with Haydn and Mozart, and sometimes as being preferred to them by the audiences of the time, is Gyrowetz. His symphonies appear to be on a larger scale than those of the prior generation of composers of second rank like himself. A few of them are occasionally to be met with in collections of 'Periodical overtures,' 'symphonies,' etc., published in separate orchestral parts. One in C, scored for small orchestra, has an introductory

Adagio, an Allegro of about the dimensions of Haydn's earlier first movements, with double bar in the middle ; then an Andante *con sordini* (the latter a favourite device in central slow movements) ; then a Minuet and Trio, and, to end with, a Rondo in 2–4 time, Allegro non troppo. Others, in E♭ and B♭, have much the same distribution of movements, but without the introductory Adagio. The style of them is rather mild and complacent, and not approaching in any way the interest or breadth of the works of his great contemporaries ; but the subjects are clear and vivacious, and the movements seem fairly developed. Other symphony writers, who had vogue and even celebrity about this time and a little later, such as Krommer (beloved by Schubert), the Rombergs, and Eberl (at one time preferred to Beethoven), require no more than passing mention. They certainly furthered the branch of art very little, and were so completely extinguished by the exceptionally great writers who came close upon one another at that time, that it is even difficult to find traces of them.

The greatest of all masters of the Symphony followed so close upon Haydn, that there is less of a gap between the last of Haydn's Symphonies and his first than there was later between some of his own. Haydn's last was probably written in 1795. When Beethoven wrote his first cannot be ascertained ; sketches for the Finale are found as early as the year last mentioned ; but it was not actually produced in public till April 2, 1800. Like Schumann and Brahms in later days, he did not turn his attention to this branch of composition till comparatively late. The opus-number of his first symphony is 21. It is preceded by eleven pianoforte sonatas, several works for pianoforte combined with other instruments, the well-known Septuor in E♭, and several chamber compositions for strings. So that by the time he came to attacking Symphony he had had considerable practice in dealing with structural matters. The only works in which he had tried his strength with the orchestra were the two piano concertos—the B♭, op. 19, which was written in or about 1795, and the C major, op. 15, which was written about 1796. He showed himself at once a master of the orchestra ; but it is evident that at first he stepped cautiously in expressing himself with such resources. The first Symphony is less free and rich in expression, and has more elements of formality, than several works on a smaller scale which preceded it. This is explicable on the general ground that the orchestra, especially in those days, was not a fit exponent of the same kind of things which could be expressed by solo violins, or the pianoforte. The scale must necessarily be larger and broader ; the intricate development and delicate or subtle sentiment which is quite appropriate and intelligible in the intimacy of a domestic circle, is

out of place in the more public conditions of orchestral performance. This Beethoven must have instinctively felt, and he appears not to have found the style for full expression of his personality in either of the first symphonies. The second is even more curious in that respect than the first, as it comes after one of the richest and most interesting, and another of the most perfectly charming and original of the works of his early period, namely the Sonatas in D minor and E♭ of op. 31. However, even in these two symphonies there is a massiveness and breadth and seriousness of purpose, which mark them as products of a different and more powerfully constituted nature than anything of the kind produced before. At the time when the first Symphony appeared, the opening with the chord of the minor 7th of C, when the key of the piece was C major, was looked upon as extremely daring ; and the narrow-minded pedants of the day felt their sensitive delicacy so outraged that some of them are said never to have forgiven it. The case is very similar to the famous introduction to Mozart's C major String Quartet, about which the pedants were little less than insulting. Beethoven had to fight for his right to express what he felt to be true ; and he did it without flinching ; sometimes with an apparent relish. But at the same time, in these early orchestral works he seems to have experimented with caution, and was content to follow his predecessors in a great deal that he put down. There are characteristic things in both symphonies ; for instance, in the first the transitional passage which begins at the 65th bar of the Allegro, passing from G to G minor and then to B♭ and back again, and the corresponding passage in the second half of the movement. The working out of the Andante cantabile and the persistent drum rhythm are also striking points. In the second Symphony the dimensions of the Introduction are unusual, and the character of all the latter part and the freedom of the transitions in it are decisive marks of his tendencies. The Slow Movement has also a warmth and sense of genuine sympathy which is new ; the Scherzo, though as yet short, has a totally new character about it, and the abrupt sforzandos, and short striking figures and still more the coda, of the Finale, are quite his own. In the orchestra it is worth noting that he adopted clarinets from the first, apparently as a matter of course ; in the first two symphonies he continued to use only the one pair of horns, as his predecessors had done; in the third he expanded the group to three. In the fourth he went back to two, and did not use four till the ninth. The disposition of his forces even in the first two is more independent and varied than his predecessors. The treatment of the several groups of instruments tends to be more distinct and appropriate, and at the same time more perfectly assimilated in the total effect of the music. The step to the third Symphony is however immense, and at last shows this branch of composition on a level with his other works of the same period. It is surrounded on both sides by some of his noblest achievements. Op. 47 was the Sonata in A for violin and pianoforte, known as the 'Kreutzer.' Op. 53 is the Sonata in C major, dedicated to Count Waldstein. Op. 54 is the admirable little Sonata in F major. Op. 55 is the Symphony, and op. 57 the Sonata known as the 'Appassionata.' It appears that Beethoven had the idea of writing this symphony as early as 1798, but the actual work was probably done in the summer and autumn of 1803. There seems to be no doubt that it was written under the influence of his admiration for Napoleon. His own title-page had on it 'Sinfonia grande. Napoleon Bonaparte,' and, as is well known, the name ' Eroica ' was not added till Napoleon became Emperor ; after which event Beethoven's feelings about him naturally underwent a change. To call a great work by the name of a great man was quite a different thing from calling it by the name of a crowned ruler. However, the point remains the same, that the work was written with a definite purpose and under the inspiration of a special subject, and one upon which Beethoven himself assuredly had a very decided opinion. The result was the richest and noblest and by far the biggest symphony that had ever yet appeared in the world. It is very possible that Beethoven meant it to be so ; but the fact does not make the step from the previous symphonies any the less remarkable. The scoring throughout is most freely distributed. In the first movement especially there is hardly any one of the numerous subjects and characteristic figures which has not properties demanding different departments of the orchestra to express them. They are obviously conceived with reference to the whole forces at command, not to a predominant central force and appendages. The strings must necessarily have the greater part of the work to do, but the symphony is not written for them with wind as a species of afterthought. But it is still to be noticed that the balance is obtained chiefly by definite propositions and answers between one group and another, and though the effect is delightful, the principle is rendered a little obvious from the regularity of its occurrence. The second movement is specially noticeable as reaching the strongest pitch of sentiment as yet shown in an orchestral slow movement. In the earliest symphonies these movements were nearly always remarkably short, and scored for fewer instruments than the first and last. Frequently they were little better than 'intermezzi,' attached on both sides to the more important allegros. Even Mozart's and Haydn's latest examples had more grace and sweetness than deep feeling, and frequently showed a tendency to formalism in the expression of the ideas and in the ways in which

the ornamental *fioriture* were introduced. In the Eroica the name ' Marcia funebre ' at once defines the object ; and though the form of a march is to a certain extent maintained, it is obvious that it is of secondary importance, since the attention is more drawn to the rich and noble expression of the finest feelings of humanity over the poetically imagined death of one of the world's heroes, than to the traditional march form. The music seems in fact to take almost the definiteness of speech of the highest order ; or rather, to express the emotions which belong to the imagined situation with more fulness and comprehensiveness, but with scarcely less definiteness, than speech could achieve. In the third movement appears the first of Beethoven's large orchestral scherzos. Any connection between it and the typical Minuet and Trio it is hard to see. The time is quicker and more bustling ; and the character utterly distinct from the suave grace and somewhat measured paces of most of the previous third movements. The main points of connection with them are firstly the general outlines of form (that is, the principal portion of the Scherzo corresponding to the Minuet comes first and last, and the Trio in the middle) and secondly the humorous element. In this latter particular there is very great difference between the *naïf* and spontaneous fun of Haydn and the grim humour of Beethoven, sometimes verging upon irony, and sometimes, with evident purpose, upon the grotesque. The scherzo of the Eroica is not alloyed with so much grimness as some later ones, but it has traits of melancholy and seriousness here and there. The effect in its place is chiefly that of portraying the fickle crowd who soon forget their hero, and chatter and bustle cheerfully about their business or pleasure as before ; which has its humorous or at least laughter-making ironical side to any one large-minded enough to avoid thinking of all such traits of humanity with reprobation and disgust. The last movement is on a scale more than equal to that of all the others, and, like them, strikes an almost entirely new note in symphonic finales. The light and simple character of Haydn's final rondos is familiar to every one ; and he was consistent in aiming at gaiety for conclusion. Mozart in most cases did the same ; but in the G minor Symphony there is a touch of rather vehement regretfulness, and in the C major of strength and seriousness. But the Finale of the Eroica first introduces qualities of massiveness and broad earnest dignity to that position in the symphony. The object is evidently to crown the work in a totally different sense from the light cheerful endings of most previous symphonies, and to appeal to fine feelings in the audience instead of aiming at putting them in a cheerful humour. It is all the difference between an audience before the revolutionary epoch and after. The starting-point of the movement is the same theme from the Pro-

metheus music as that of the pianoforte variations in E♭ (op. 35). The basis of the whole
movement is mainly the variation-form, interspersed with fugal episodes ; and a remarkable
feature is the long Andante variation immediately
before the finale Presto—a somewhat unusual
feature in such a position, though Haydn introduced a long passage of Adagio in the middle of
the last movement of a symphony in F written
about 1777, but of course in a very different
spirit. The Finale of the Eroica as a whole is
so unusual in form, that it is not wonderful that
opinions have varied much concerning it. As
a piece of art it is neither so perfect nor so convincing as the other movements ; but it has
very noble and wonderful traits, and, as a grand
experiment in an almost totally new direction,
has a decided historical importance.

It is not necessary to go through the whole
series of Beethoven's Symphonies in detail, for
one reason because they are so generally familiar
to musicians and are likely to become more and
more so ; and for another because they have been
so fully discussed from different points of view in
this Dictionary. Some short simple particulars
about each may, however, be useful and interesting. The order of composition of the works
which succeeded the Eroica Symphony is almost
impossible to unravel. By opus-number the 4th
Symphony in B♭, comes very soon, being op. 60;
but the sketches for the last movement are in
the same sketch-book as parts of 'Fidelio,' which
is op. 72, and the Concerto in G, which is
op. 58, was begun after ' Fidelio ' was finished.
It can only be seen clearly that his works were
crowded close together in this part of his life,
and interest attaches to the fact that they represent the warmest and most popular group of
all. Close to the B♭ Symphony come the Overture to ' Coriolan,' the three String Quartets,
op. 59, the Violin Concerto, the PF. ditto in
G major, the Symphony in C minor, and the
' Sinfonia Pastorale.' The B♭ is on a smaller
scale than its predecessor, and of lighter and
gayer cast. The opening bars of the Introduction are almost the only part which has a trace
of sadness in it ; and this is probably meant to
throw the brightness of the rest of the work into
stronger relief. Even the Slow Movement contains more serenity than deep emotion. The
Scherzo is peculiar for having the Trio repeated
—altogether a new point in symphony-writing,
and one which was not left unrepeated or un-
imitated. What the symphony was meant to
express cannot be known, but it certainly is as
complete and consistent as any.

The C minor which followed has been said to
be the first in which Beethoven expressed himself freely and absolutely, and threw away all
traces of formalism in expression or development
to give vent to the perfect utterance of his
musical feeling. It certainly is so far the most
forcible, and most remote from conventionalism
of every kind. It was probably written very
nearly about the same time as the B♭. Nottebohm says the first two movements were written
in 1805 ; and, if this is the fact, his work on
the B♭ and on the C minor must have overlapped.
Nothing, however, could be much stronger than
the contrast between the two. The C minor
is, in the first and most striking movement,
rugged, terrible in force ; a sort of struggle
with fate, one of the most thoroughly characteristic of Beethoven's productions. The second
is a contrast : peaceful, though strong and
earnest. The Scherzo again is one of his most
original movements ; in its musical spirit as
utterly unlike anything that had been produced
before as possible. Full of fancy, fun, and
humour, and, notwithstanding the pauses and
changes of time, wonderful in swing ; and containing some devices of orchestration quite
magical in their clearness, and their fitness to
the ideas. The last movement, which follows
without break after the Scherzo, is triumphant ;
seeming to express the mastery in the wrestling
and striving of the first movement. It is
historically interesting as the first appearance
of trombones and contrafagotto in modern
symphony ; and the most powerful in sound
up to that time. The next symphony, which
is also the next opus-number, is the popular
' Pastoral,' probably written in 1808, the second
of Beethoven's which has a definitely stated
idea as the basis of its inspiration, and the
first in which a programme is suggested for
each individual movement ; though Beethoven
is careful to explain that it is ' mehr Empfindung
als Malerei.' Any account of this happy inspiration is clearly superfluous. The situations
and scenes which it brings to the mind are
familiar, and not likely to be less beloved as
the world grows older. The style is again in
great contrast to that of the C minor, being
characterised rather by serenity and contentment ; which, as Beethoven had not heard of
all the troubles of the land question, might
naturally be his feelings about country life.
He used two trombones in the last two movements, but otherwise contented himself with
the same group of instruments as in his earliest
symphonies.

After this there was a pause for some years,
during which time appeared many noble and
delightful works on other lines, including the
pianoforte trios in D and E♭, the Mass in C
minor, op. 86, the music to ' Egmont,' op. 84,
and several sonatas. Then in one year, 1812,
two symphonies appeared. The first of the
two, in A major, numbered op. 92, is looked
upon by many as the most romantic of all of
them ; and certainly has qualities which increase
in attractiveness the better it is known and
understood. Among specially noticeable points
are the unusual proportions and great interest
of the Introduction (*poco sostenuto*) ; the singular

and fascinating wilfulness of the first movement, which is enhanced by some very characteristic orchestration ; the noble calm of the slow movement ; the merry humour of the Scherzo, which has again the same peculiarity as the fourth Symphony, that the trio is repeated (for which the world has every reason to be thankful, as it is one of the most completely enjoyable things in all symphonic literature) ; and finally the wild headlong abandonment of the last movement, which might be an idealised national or rather barbaric dance-movement, and which sets the crown fitly upon one of the most characteristic of Beethoven's works. The Symphony in F, which follows immediately as op. 93, is again of a totally different character. It is of specially small proportions, and has rather the character of a return to the old conditions of the Symphony, with all the advantages of Beethoven's mature powers both in the development and choice of ideas, and in the treatment of the orchestra. Beethoven himself, in a letter to Salomon, described it as 'eine kleine Symphonie in F,' as distinguished from the previous one, which he called 'Grosse Symphonie in A, eine meiner vorzüglichsten.' It has more fun and light-heartedness in it than any of the others, but no other specially distinctive external characteristics, except the substitution of the graceful and humorous 'Allegretto scherzando' in the place of the slow movement, and a return to the Tempo di Menuetto for the scherzo. After this came again a long pause, as the greatest of all symphonies did not make its appearance till 1824. During that time, however, it is probable that symphonic work was not out of his mind, for it is certain that the preparations for putting this symphony down on paper spread over several years. Of the introduction of voices into this form of composition, which is its strongest external characteristic, Beethoven had made a previous experiment in the Choral Fantasia ; and he himself spoke of the symphony as 'in the style of the Choral Fantasia, but on a far larger scale.' The scale is indeed immensely larger, not only in length but in style, and the increase in this respect applies to it equally in comparison with all the symphonies that went before. The first movement is throughout the most concentrated example of the qualities which distinguish Beethoven, and the new phase upon which music entered with him, from all the composers of the previous half-century. The other movements are not less characteristic of him in their particular ways. The second is the largest example of the typical scherzo which first made its appearance for the orchestra in the Eroica ; and the supreme slow movement (the Theme with variations) is the finest orchestral example of that special type of slow movement ; though in other departments of art he had previously illustrated it in a manner little less noble and

deeply expressive in the slow movements of the B♭ Trio and the B♭ Sonata (op. 106). These movements all have reference, more or less intelligible according to the organisation and sympathies of the hearer, to the Finale of the Symphony, which consists of a setting of Schiller's ode 'An die Freude.' Its development into such enormous proportions is of a piece with the tendency shown in Beethoven's previous symphonies, and in some of his sonatas also, to supplant the conventional type of gay last movement by something which shall be a logical or poetical outcome of the preceding movements, and shall in some way clench them, or crown them with its weight and power. The introduction of words, moreover, gives a new force to the definite interpretation of the whole as a single organism, developed as a poem might be in relation to definite and coherent ideas. The dramatic and human elements which Beethoven introduced into his instrumental music to a degree before undreamed of, find here their fullest expression ; and most of the forms of music are called in to convey his ideas. The first movement of the symphony is in binary form ; the second in scherzo, or idealised minuet and trio form ; the third in the form of theme and variations. Then follows the curious passage of instrumental recitative, of which so many people guessed the meaning even before it was defined by the publication of the extracts from the MS. sketch-books in the Berlin Library ; then the entry of the noble tune, the theme of the entire Finale, introduced contrapuntally in a manner which has a clear analogy to fugal treatment ; and followed by the choral part, which treats the theme in the form of variations apportioned to the several verses of the poem, and carries the sentiment to the extremest pitch of exultation expressible by the human voice. The instrumental forces employed are the fullest; including, with the usual complement, four horns, three trombones in the scherzo and finale, and contrafagotto, triangle, cymbals, and big drum in the finale. The choral forces include four solo voices and full chorus, and the sentiment expressed is proportionate to the forces employed.

In Beethoven's hands the Symphony has again undergone a change of status. Haydn and Mozart, as above pointed out, ennobled and enriched the form in the structural sense. They took up the work when there was little more expected of the orchestra than would have been expected of a harpsichord, and when the object of the piece was slight and almost momentary entertainment. They left it one of the most important branches of instrumental music, though still to a great extent dependent on formal perfection and somewhat obvious artistic management for its interest. Their office was in fact to perfect the form, and Beethoven's to use it. But the very use of it brought about a new ratio between its various elements. In his work first clearly appears a proportion between the forces employed and the nobility and depth and general importance of the musical ideas. In his hands the greatest and most pliable means available for the composer could be no longer fit for lightness and triviality, but only for ideal emotions of an adequate standard. It is true that earlier composers saw the advantage of adopting a breadth of style and largeness of sentiment when writing for the orchestra ; but this mostly resulted in positive dulness. It seems as if it could only be when the circumstances of history had undergone a violent change that human sentiment could reach that pitch of comprehensiveness which in Beethoven's work raised the Symphony to the highest pitch of earnest poetic feeling : and the history of his development is chiefly the co-ordination of all the component elements ; the proportioning of the expression and style to the means ; the expansion of the form to the requirements of the expression ; the making of the orchestration perfectly free, but perfectly just in every detail of expression, and perfectly balanced in itself ; and the eradication of all traces of conventionalism both in the details and in the principal outlines, and also to a great extent in the treatment of the instruments. It is chiefly through Beethoven's work that the symphony now stands at the head of all musical forms whatever ; and though other composers may hereafter misuse and degrade it as they have degraded the opera, the cantata, the oratorio, the mass, and such other forms as have equal possibilities with the symphony, his works of this kind stand at such an elevation of human sympathy and emotion, and at such a pitch of individuality and power, in expression and technical mastery, that it is scarcely likely that any branch of musical art will ever show anything to surpass them.

It might seem almost superfluous to trace the history of Symphony further after Beethoven. Nothing since his time has shown, nor in the changing conditions of the history of the race is it likely anything should show, any approach to the vitality and depth of his work. But it is just these changing conditions that leave a little opening for composers to tread the same path with him. In the millions of the human species there are endless varieties of mental and emotional qualities grouped in different individuals, and different bands or sets of men ; and the many-sided qualities of artistic work, even far below the highest standard, find their excuse and explanation in the various groups and types of mind whose artistic desires they satisfy. Those who are most highly organised in such respects find their most perfect and most sustained gratification in Beethoven's works ; but others who feel less deeply, or are less wide in their sympathies, or have fewer or

different opportunities of cultivating their tastes in such a musical direction, need musical food more in accordance with their mental and emotional organisation. Moreover, there is always room to treat an accepted form in the mode characteristic of the period. Beethoven's period was much more like ours than that of Haydn and Mozart, but yet it is not so like that a work expressed entirely in his manner would not be an anachronism. Each successive generation takes some colour from the combination of work and changes in all previous generations ; in unequal quantities proportioned to its amount of sympathy with particular periods. By the side of Beethoven there were other composers, working either on parallel lines or in a different manner on the same lines. The succeeding generations were influenced by them as well as by him ; and they have introduced some elements into symphony which are at least not prominent in his. One of the contemporary composers who had most influence on the later generation was Weber ; but his influence is derived from other departments, and in that of Symphony his contribution is next to nothing—two only, so slight and unimportant, as probably to have had no influence at all.

Another composer's symphonies did not have much immediate influence, chiefly because they were not performed ; what they will have in the future remains to be seen. In delightfulness, Schubert's two best works in this department stand almost alone ; and their qualities are unique. In his earlier works of the kind there is an analogy to Beethoven's early works. Writing for the orchestra seemed to paralyse his particular individuality ; and for some time after he had written some of his finest and most original songs, he continued to write symphonies which were chiefly a mild reflex of Haydn and Mozart, or at most of the early style of Beethoven. His first attempt was made in 1813, the last page being dated October 28 of that year, when he was yet only sixteen years old— one year after Beethoven's Symphonies in A and F, and more than ten years before the great D minor. In the five following years he wrote five more, the best of which is No. 4, the Tragic, in C minor ; the Andante especially being very fine and interesting, and containing many characteristic traits of the master. But none of the early works approach in interest or original beauty to the unfinished one in B minor, and the very long and vigorous one in C major ; the first composed in 1822, before Beethoven's No. 9, and the second in 1828, after it. In these two he seems to have struck out a real independent symphony-style for himself, thoroughly individual in every respect, both of idea, form, and orchestration. They show singularly little of the influence of Beethoven, or Mozart, or Haydn, or any of the composers he must have been familiar with in his early days at the Convict; but the same spirit as is met with in his songs and pianoforte pieces, and the best specimens of his chamber music. The first movement of the B minor is entirely unlike any other symphonic first movement that ever was composed before. It seems to come direct from the heart, and to have the personality of the composer in it to a most unusual degree. The orchestral forces used are the usual ones, [excepting only that he uses three trombones, an unusual thing in first movements at the date,] but in the management of them there are numbers of effects which are perfectly new in this department of art, indicating the tendency of the time towards direct consideration of what is called 'colour' in orchestral combinations, and its employment with the view of enhancing the degree of actual sensuous enjoyment of a refined kind, to some extent independent of the subjects and figures. Schubert's mature orchestral works are, however, too few to give any strong indication of this in his own person; and what is commonly felt is the supreme attractiveness of the ideas and general style. As classical models of form none of Schubert's instrumental works take the highest rank; and it follows that no compositions by any writer which have taken such hold upon the musicians of the present time, depend so much upon their intrinsic musical qualities as his do. They are therefore in a sense the extremest examples that can be given of the degree in which the status of such music altered in about thirty years. In the epoch of Mozart and Haydn, the formal elements absolutely predominated in importance. This was the case in 1795. The balance was so completely altered in the course of Beethoven's lifetime, that by 1824 the phenomenon is presented of works in the highest line of musical composition depending on the predominating element of the actual musical sentiment. It must be confessed that Schubert's position in art is unique; but at the same time no man of mark can be quite unrepresentative of his time, and Schubert in this way represents the extraordinary degree in which the attention of musical people and the intention of composers in the early years of the 19th century were directed to the actual material of music in its expressive sense as distinguished from the external or structural aspect.

The relation of the dates at which more or less well-known symphonies made their appearance about this time is curious and not uninstructive. Mendelssohn's Reformation Symphony was produced only two years after Schubert's great Symphony in C, namely in 1830. His Italian Symphony followed in the next year; and Sterndale Bennett's, in G minor, in 1834.

The dates and history of Spohr's productions are even more striking, as he was actually a contemporary of Beethoven's and senior to

Schubert, while in all respects in which his style is characteristic it represents quite a later generation. His first Symphony (in E♭) was composed in 1811, before Beethoven's 7th, 8th, and 9th, and when he himself was twenty-seven years old. This was followed by several others, which are not without merit, though not of sufficient historical importance to require special consideration. The symphony of his which is best known at the present day is that called the 'Weihe der Töne,' which at one time enjoyed great celebrity. The history of this work is as follows. He intended first to set a poem of the same name by his friend Pfeiffer. He began the setting in 1832, but finding it unsatisfactory he abandoned the idea of using the words except as a programme; in which form they are appended to the score. The full description and purpose of the work as expressed on the title is 'Characteristisches Tongemälde in Form einer Sinfonie, nach einen Gedicht von Carl Pfeiffer'; and a printed notice from the composer is appended to the score directing that the poem is to be either printed or recited aloud whenever the symphony is to be performed. Each movement also has its title, like the Pastoral of Beethoven; but it differs from that work not only in its less substantial interest, but also in a much more marked departure from the ordinary principles of form, and the style of the successive movements.

The earlier part of the work corresponds fairly well with the usual principles of structure. It opens with a short Largo of vague character, passing into the Allegro, which is a continuous movement of the usual description, in a sweet but rather tame style. The next movement might be taken to stand for the usual slow movement, as it begins Andantino; but the development is original, as it is broken up by several changes of tempo and time-signatures, and is evidently based upon a programme, for which its title supplies an explanation. The next movement again might be taken as an alternative to the Minuet and Trio, being marked 'Tempo di Marcia,' which would suggest the same general outline of form. But the development is again independent, and must be supposed to follow its title. From this point all connection with the usual outlines ceases. There is an Andante maestoso, based upon the plain-song of the Te Deum, a Larghetto containing a second hymn-tune, and a short Allegretto in simple primary form to conclude with. From this description it will be obvious that the work is an example of thoroughgoing 'programme music.' It is clearly based rather on the musical portrayal of a succession of ideas in themselves independent of music, than upon the treatment of principles of abstract form, and ideas intrinsically musical. It derives from this fact a historical importance which its musical qualities taken alone would not warrant, as it is one of the very first German examples of its kind possessing any high artistic excellences of treatment, expression, and orchestration. It contains a plentiful supply of Spohr's characteristic faults, and is for the most part superficial, and deficient in warmth of feeling and nobility of thought ; but it has also a fair share of his good traits—delicacy and clearness of orchestration, and a certain amount of poetical sentiment. Its success was considerable, and this, rather than any abstract theorising upon the tendencies of modern music, led him to several further experiments in the same line. The symphony (in C minor) which followed the 'Weihe der Töne' was on the old lines, and does not require much notice. It contains experiments in unifying the work by unusual references to subjects, as in the first movement, where conspicuous reference is made in the middle part of the Allegro to the characteristic feature of the slow introduction ; and in the last, where the same subject is somewhat transformed, and reappears in a different time as a prominent feature of the second section. In the next symphony, and in the 7th and 9th, Spohr again tried experiments in programme. Two of these are such curiosities as to deserve description. The 6th, op. 116, in G is called 'Historische Symphonie,' and the four movements are supposed to be illustrations of four distinct musical periods. The first is called the Period of Handel and Bach, and dated 1720 ; the second, the Period of Haydn and Mozart, and dated 1780 (i.e. before any of the greatest instrumental works of either Haydn or Mozart were produced) ; the third is the Period of Beethoven, and dated 1810 ; and the fourth, 'Allerneueste Periode,' and dated 1840. This last title seems to imply that Spohr regarded himself as belonging to a different generation from Beethoven. The first period is represented by an introductory Largo in contrapuntal style, and an Allegro movement, part after the manner of the old Canzonas, and part a Pastorale, introduced for contrast. The style has scarcely the least affinity to Bach, but the Handelian character is extremely easy to imitate, and hence in some respects it justifies its title fairly well. The slow movement which follows has good qualities and graceful points. It has more the flavour of Mozart than Haydn, and this is enhanced by the Mozartian turns and figures which are introduced. One which is very conspicuous is the short figure—

which is found in several places in Mozart's works. The second subject, moreover, is only an ingenious alteration of the second subject in the slow movement of Mozart's Prague Symphony in D :—

Nevertheless, the whole effect of the movement is not what its title implies. The scoring is fuller, and the inner parts richer and freer in their motion than in the prototypes, and the harmonisation is more chromatic, after Spohr's manner. The Scherzo professes to be in Beethoven's style, and some of his characteristic devices of harmony and rhythm and treatment of instruments are fairly well imitated (e.g. the drums in G, D, and E♭), though in a manner which shows they were but half understood.

The last movement, representing the then 'latest period,' has of course no names appended. Spohr probably did not intend to imitate any one, but was satisfied to write in his own manner, of which the movement is not a highly satisfactory example. It is perhaps rather to the composer's credit that his own characteristics should peep out at all corners in all the movements, but the result can hardly be called an artistic success. However, the experiment deserves to be recorded and described, as unique among works by composers of such standing and ability as Spohr ; and the more so as it is not likely to be often heard in future. His next Symphony (No. 7, in C major, op. 121) is in many respects as great a curiosity of a totally different description. It is called 'Irdisches und Göttliches in Menschenleben,' and is a double symphony in three movements for two orchestras. The first movement is called 'Kinderwelt,' the second 'Zeit der Leidenschaften,' and the last (Presto) 'Endlicher Sieg des Göttlichen.' In the first two the second orchestra, which is the fuller of the two, is little more than an accompaniment to the first. In the last it has a good deal of work to do, uttering chiefly vehement and bustling passages in contrast with quiet and sober passages by the first orchestra ; until near the end, when it appears to be subdued into consonance with the first orchestra. The idea seems to be to depict the divine and the worldly qualities more or less by the two orchestras ; the divine being given to the smaller orchestra of solo instruments, and the worldly to the fuller orchestra. The treatment of the instrumental forces is on the whole very simple ; and no very extraordinary effects seem to be aimed at.

Spohr wrote yet another programme symphony after this (No. 9, in B, op. 143) called 'Die Jahreszeiten,' in which Winter and Spring are joined to make Part I., and Summer and Autumn to make Part II.

The work approaches more nearly to the ordinary outlines of the Symphony than his previous experiments in programme, and does not seem to demand so much detailed description. In fact, but for his having been so early in the field as a writer of thoroughgoing programme-music, Spohr's position in the history of the Symphony would not be an important one ; and it is worthy of remark that his being so at all appears to have been an accident. The ' Weihe der Töne ' would not have been a programme symphony but for the fact that Pfeiffer's poem did not turn out to be very suitable for a musical setting. It is not likely that the work would have attained such popularity as it did but for its programme ; but after so good a result in relation to the public, it was natural that Spohr should try further experiments on the same lines ; and hence he became one of the earliest representatives of artistic speculation in a direction which has become one of the most conspicuous subjects of discussion among modern musical philosophers. As far as intrinsic qualities are concerned it is remarkable how very little influence he has had upon the subsequent history of the Symphony, considering the reputation he enjoyed in his lifetime. His greatest excellence was his treatment of his orchestra, which was delicate, refined, and extremely clear ; but it must be confessed that he erred on the side natural to the virtuoso violinist, and was too fond of bringing his first violins into prominence. His ideas and style generally were not robust or noble enough to stand the test of time. His melodies are not broad or strong ; his harmonisation, though very chromatic to look at, is not radically free and vigorous ; and his rhythm, though sometimes complicated and ingenious, is neither forcible nor rich in variety. None of his works, however, can be said to be without their good points, and the singularity of his attempts at programme-music give them an interest which the unlikelihood of many performances in the future does not by any means diminish.

An interesting fact in connection with Spohr and the history of the Symphony is that he was the first to conduct an orchestra in England with a baton ; the practice having previously been to conduct ' at the pianoforte.' The occasion was one of the Philharmonic Concerts in 1820. [See BATON, CONDUCTING, SPOHR.] The habit of conducting at the pianoforte was evidently a tradition continued from the days when the Symphony was an appendage of the Opera, when the principal authority, often the composer in person, sat at the principal clavier in the middle of the orchestra giving the time at his instrument, and filling in the harmonies under the guidance of a figured bass. Almost all the earlier independent symphonies,

including those of Philip Emanuel Bach of 1776, and some of Haydn's earlier ones, have such a figured bass for the clavier-player, and an extra bass part is commonly found in the sets of parts which may be reasonably surmised to be for his use.[1] The practice was at last abrogated in England by Spohr, possibly because he was not a clavier but a violin player. In Germany it was evidently discontinued some time earlier.

The most distinguished composers of symphonies who wrote at the same time as Spohr, were entirely independent of him. The first of these is Mendelssohn, whose earliest symphonies even overlap Beethoven, and whose better-known works of the kind, as before mentioned, begin about the same time as Spohr's best examples, and extend over nearly the same period as his later ones. The earliest which survives in print is that in C minor dedicated to the London Philharmonic Society. This work was really his thirteenth symphony, and was finished on March 31, 1824, when he was only fifteen years old, in the very year that Beethoven's Choral Symphony was first performed. The work is more historically than musically interesting. It shows, as might be expected, how much stronger the mechanical side of Mendelssohn's artistic nature was, even as a boy, than his poetical side. Technically the work is extraordinarily mature. It evinces not only a perfect and complete facility in laying the outline and carrying out the details of form, but also the acutest sense of the balance and proportion of tone of the orchestra. The limits of the attempt are not extensive, and the absence of strong feeling or aspiration in the boy facilitated the execution. The predominant influence is clearly that of Mozart. Not only the treatment of the lower and subordinate parts of the harmony, but the distribution and management of the different sections and even the ideas are like. There is scarcely a trace of the influence of Beethoven, and not much of the features afterwards characteristic of the composer himself. The most individual movements are the slow movement and the trio. The former is tolerably free from the influence of the artificial and mannered slow movements of the Haydn and Mozart style, and at the same time does not derive its inspiration from Beethoven : it contains some very free experiments in modulation, enharmonic and otherwise, a few characteristic figures similar to some which he made use of later in his career and passages of melody clearly predicting the composer of the Lieder ohne Worte and the short slow movements of the organ sonatas. The Trio is long and very original in intention, the chief feature being ingenious treatment of arpeggios for the strings in many parts. The other movements are for the most part formal.

---

[1] Mendelssohn's early Symphonies are marked ' Klavier mit dem Basse.' [See vol. iii. p. 114a, note 1.]

The Minuet is extraordinarily like that of Mozart's G minor Symphony, not only in accent and style, but in the manner in which the strings and the wind are grouped and balanced, especially in the short passage for wind alone which occurs towards the end of each half of the movement. It was possibly owing to this circumstance that Mendelssohn substituted for it the orchestral arrangement of the Scherzo of his Octet when the work was performed later in his life. In the last movement the most characteristic passage is the second subject, with the short chords of pizzicato strings, and the tune for the clarinet which comes after the completion of the first period by strings alone. He used the same device more than once later, and managed it more satisfactorily. But it is just such suggestions of the working of the musical spirit in the man which make an early work interesting.

His next symphony happened to illustrate the supposed tendency of the age towards programme. It was intended for the tercentenary festival of the Augsburg Protestant Confession in 1830, though owing to political circumstances its performance was deferred till later. He evidently had not made up his mind what to call it till some time after it was finished, as he wrote to his sister and suggested Confession Symphony, or Symphony for a Church Festival, as alternative names. But it is quite evident nevertheless that he must have had some sort of programme in his mind, and a purpose to illustrate the conflict between the old and new forms of the faith, and the circumstances and attributes which belonged to them. The actual form of the work is as nearly as possible what is called perfectly orthodox. The slow introduction, the regular legitimate allegro, the simple pretty scherzo and trio, the short but completely balanced slow movement, and the regular last movement preceded by a second slow introduction, present very little that is out of the way in point of structure; and hence the work is less dependent upon its programme than some of the examples by Spohr above described. But nevertheless the programme can be clearly seen to have suggested much of the detail of treatment and development in a perfectly consistent and natural manner. The external traits which obviously strike attention are two; first, the now well-known passage which is used in the Catholic Church at Dresden for the Amen, and which Wagner has since adopted as one of the most conspicuous religious motives of 'Parsifal'; and secondly, the use of Luther's famous hymn, 'Ein' feste Burg,' in the latter part of the work. The Amen makes its appearance in the latter part of the opening Andante, and is clearly meant to typify the old church; and its recurrence at the end of the working out in the first movement, before the recapitulation, is possibly meant to imply that the old church still holds its own: while in the latter portion of the work the typical hymn-tune, introduced softly by the flute and by degrees taking possession of the whole orchestra, may be taken to represent the successful spread of the Protestant ideas, just as its final utterance fortissimo at the end of all, does the establishment of men's right to work out their own salvation in their own way. There are various other details which clearly have purpose in relation to the programme, and show clearly that the composer was keeping the possible succession of events and circumstances in his mind throughout. The actual treatment is a very considerable advance upon the Symphony in C minor. The whole work is thoroughly Mendelssohnian. There is no obvious trace either in the ideas themselves, or in the manner of expression of the Mozartian influence which is so noticeable in the symphony of six years earlier. And considering that the composer was still but twenty-one, the maturity of style and judgment is relatively quite as remarkable as the facility and mastery shown in the work of his fifteenth year. The orchestration is quite characteristic and free; and in some cases, as in part of the second movement, singularly happy. The principle of programme here assumed seems to have been maintained by him thenceforward; for his other symphonies, though it is not so stated in the published scores, are known to have been recognised by him as the results of his impressions of Italy and Scotland. The first of them followed very soon after the Reformation Symphony. In the next year after the completion of that work he mentioned the new symphony in a letter to his sister as far advanced; and said it was 'the gayest thing he had ever done.' He was in Rome at the time, and it appears most probable that the first and last movements were written there. Of the slow movement he wrote that he had not found anything exactly right, 'and would put it off till he went to Naples, hoping to find something to inspire him there.' But in the result it is difficult to imagine that Naples can have had much share. Of the third movement there is a tradition that it was imported from an earlier work; and it certainly has a considerable flavour of Mozart, though coupled with traits characteristic of Mendelssohn in perfect maturity, and is at least well worthy of its position; and even if parts of it, as is possible, appeared in an earlier work, the excellences of the Trio, and the admirable effect of the final Coda which is based on it, point to considerable rewriting and reconstruction at a mature period. The actual structure of the movements is based upon familiar principles, though not without certain idiosyncrasies; as for instance the appearance of a new prominent feature in the working-out portion, and the freedom of the recapitulation in the first movement. In the last movement, called Saltarello, he seems to have given a more free rein to his fancy in portraying some scene of unconstrained Italian gaiety of which he was a witness; and though there is an underlying consistency in the usual distribution of keys, the external balance of subjects is not so obvious. The last movement is hence the only one which seems to depend to any extent upon the programme idea; in all other respects the symphony belongs to the 'classical' order. Indeed such a programme as the purpose to reproduce impressions of particular countries is far too vague to lend itself to exact and definite musical portrayal of external ideas, such as might take the place of the usual outlines of structure. In fact it could lead to little more than consistency of style, which would be equally helpful to the composer and the audience; and it may well have served as an excuse for a certain laxity and profusion in the succession of the ideas, instead of that difficult process of concentrating and making relevant the whole of each movement upon the basis of a few definite and typical subjects. The characteristics of the work are for the most part fresh and genial spontaneity. The scoring is of course admirable and clear, without presenting any very marked features; and it is at the same time independent and well proportioned in distribution of the various qualities of sound, and in fitness to the subject-matter.

In orchestral effects the later symphony—the Scotch, in A minor—is more remarkable. The impressions which Mendelssohn received in Scotland may naturally have suggested more striking points of local colour; and the manner in which it is distributed from first page to last serves to very good purpose in unifying the impression of the whole. The effects are almost invariably obtained either by using close harmonies low in the scale of the respective instruments, or by extensively doubling tunes and figures in a similar manner, and in a sombre part of the scale of the instruments; giving an effect of heaviness and darkness which were possibly Mendelssohn's principal feelings about the grandeur and uncertain climate of Scotland. Thus in the opening phrase for wind instruments they are crowded in the harmonies almost as thick as they will endure. In the statement of the first principal subject again the clarinet in its darkest region doubles the tune of the violins an octave lower. The use of the whole mass of the strings in three octaves, with the wind filling the harmonies in rhythmic chords, which has so fine and striking an effect at the beginning of the 'working out' and in the coda, has the same basis; and the same effect is obtained by similar means here and there in the Scherzo; as for instance where the slightly transformed version of the principal subject is introduced by the wind in the Coda. The same qualities are frequently noticeable in the slow movement and again in the coda of the last movement. As in the previous symphony, the structure is quite in accordance with familiar principles. If anything, the work errs rather on the side of squareness and obviousness in the outlines both of ideas and structure; as may be readily perceived by comparing the construction of the opening tune of the introduction with any of Beethoven's introductions (either that of the D or B♭ or A Symphonies, or his overtures): or even the introduction to Mozart's Prague Symphony. And the impression is not lessened by the obviousness of the manner in which the succeeding recitative passages for violins are introduced; nor by the squareness and tune-like qualities of the first subject of the first movement, nor by the way in which the square tune pattern of the Scherzo is reiterated. In the manipulation of the familiar distribution of periods and phrases, however, he used a certain amount of consideration. For example, the persistence of the rhythmic figure of the first subject of the first allegro, in the inner parts of the second section of that movement, serves very good purpose; and the concluding of the movement with the melancholy tune of the introduction helps both the sentiment and the structural effect. The scherzo is far the best and most characteristic movement of the whole. In no department of his work was Mendelssohn so thoroughly at home; and the obviousness of the formal outlines is less objectionable in a movement where levity and abandonment to gaiety are quite the order of the day. The present Scherzo has also certain very definite individualities of its own. It is a departure from the 'Minuet and Trio' form, as it has no break or strong contrasting portion in the middle, and is continuous bustle and gaiety from beginning to end. In technical details it is also exceptionally admirable. The orchestral means are perfectly suited to the end, and the utterances are as neat and effective as they could well be; while the perfect way in which the movement finishes off is delightful to almost every one who has any sense for art. The slow movement takes up the sentimental side of the matter, and is in its way a good example of his orchestral style in that respect. The last movement, Allegro vivacissimo, is restless and impetuous, and the tempo-mark given for it in the Preface to the work, 'Allegro guerriero,' affords a clue to its meaning. But it evidently does not vitally depend upon any ideal programme in the least; neither does it directly suggest much, except in the curious independent passage with which it concludes, which has more of the savour of programme about it than any other portion of the work, and is scarcely explicable on any other ground. It is to be noticed that directions are given at the beginning of the work to have the movements played as quickly as possible after one another, so that it may have more or less the effect of being one piece. Mendelssohn's only other symphonic work was the Lobgesang, a sort of ecclesiastical counterpart of Beethoven's ninth Symphony. In this of course the programme element is important, and is illustrated by the calls of the brass instruments and their reiteration with much effect in the choral part of the work. The external form, as in Beethoven's ninth Symphony, is that of the three usual earlier movements (1) Introduction and Allegro, (2) Scherzo, or Minuet and Trio, and (3) Slow Movement (which in the present case have purposely a pietistic flavour), with the Finale or last movement supplanted by the long vocal part.

The consideration of these works shows that though Mendelssohn often adopted the appearance of programme, and gained some advantages by it, he never, in order to express his external ideas with more poetical consistency, relaxed any of the familiar principles of structure which are regarded as orthodox. He was in fact a thoroughgoing classicist. He accepted formulas with perfect equanimity, and aimed at resting the value of his works upon the vivacity of his ideas and the great mastery which he had attained in technical expression, and clearness and certainty of orchestration. It was not in his disposition to strike out a new path for himself. The perfection of his art in many respects necessarily appeals to all who have an appreciation for first-rate craftsmanship; but the standard of his ideas is rather fitted for average musical intelligences, and it seems natural enough that these two circumstances should have combined successfully to obtain for him an extraordinary popularity. He may fairly be said to present that which appeals to high and pure sentiments in men, and calls upon the average of them to feel at their best. But he leads them neither into the depths nor the heights which are beyond them; and is hence more fitted in the end to please than to elevate. His work in the department of Symphony is historically slight. In comparison with his great predecessors he established positively nothing new; and if he had been the only successor to Beethoven and Schubert it would certainly have to be confessed that the department of art represented by the Symphony was at a standstill. The excellence of his orchestration, the clearness of his form, and the accuracy and cleverness with which he balanced and disposed his subjects and his modulations, are all certain and unmistakable; but all these things had been attained by great masters before him, and he himself attained them only by the sacrifice of the genuine vital force and power of harmonic motion and freedom of form in the ideas themselves, of which his predecessors had made a richer manifestation. It is of course obvious that different orders of minds require different kinds of artistic food,

and the world would not be well served without many grades and standards of work. Mendelssohn did good service in supplying a form of symphony of such a degree of freshness and lightness as to appeal at once to a class of people for whom the sternness and power of Beethoven in the same branch of art would often be too severe a test. He spoke also in the spirit of his time, and in harmony with it; and as illustrations of the work of the period in one aspect his symphonies will be among the safest to refer to.

Among his contemporaries the one most natural to bracket with him is Sterndale Bennett, whose views of art were extraordinarily similar, and who was actuated in many respects by similar impulses. His published contribution to the department we are considering is extremely slight. The symphony which he produced in 1834 was practically withdrawn by him, and the only other work of the kind which he allowed to be published was the one which was written for the Philharmonic Society, and first played in 1864. The work is slight, and it is recorded that he did not at first put it forward as a symphony. It had originally but three movements, one of which, the charming minuet and trio, was imported from the Cambridge Installation Ode of 1862. A slow movement called Romanze was added afterwards. Sterndale Bennett was a severe classicist in his views about form in music, and the present symphony does not show anything sufficiently marked to call for record in that respect. It is singularly quiet and unpretentious, and characteristic of the composer, showing his taste and delicacy of sentiment together with his admirable sense of symmetry and his feeling for tone and refined orchestral effect.

The contemporary of Mendelssohn and Sterndale Bennett who shows in most marked contrast with them is Robert Schumann. He seems to represent the opposite pole of music; for as they depended upon art and made clear technical workmanship their highest aim, Schumann was in many respects positively dependent upon his emotion. Not only was his natural disposition utterly different from theirs, but so was his education. Mendelssohn and Sterndale Bennett went through severe technical drilling in their early days. Schumann seems to have developed his technique by the force of his feelings, and was always more dependent upon them in the making of his works than upon general principles and external stock rules, such as his two contemporaries were satisfied with. The case affords an excellent musical parallel to the common circumstances of life: Mendelssohn and Sterndale Bennett were satisfied to accept certain rules because they knew that they were generally accepted; whereas Schumann was of the nature that had to prove all things, and find for himself that which was good. The result was, as often happens, that Schumann affords examples of technical deficiencies, and not a few things which his contemporaries had reason to compare unfavourably with the works of Mendelssohn and Sterndale Bennett ; but in the end his best work is far more interesting, far more deeply felt, and far more really earnest through and through than theirs. It is worth observing also that his feelings towards them were disinterested admiration and enthusiasm, while they thought very slightly of him. They were also the successful composers of their time, and at the head of their profession, while he was looked upon as a sort of half amateur, part mystic and part incompetent. Such circumstances as these have no little effect upon a man's artistic development, and drive him in upon his own resources. Up to a certain point the result for the world in this instance was advantageous. Schumann developed altogether his own method of education. He began with songs and more or less small pianoforte pieces. By working hard in these departments he developed his own emotional language, and in course of time, but relatively late in life as compared with most other composers, he seemed to arrive at the point when experiment on the scale of the Symphony was possible. In a letter to a friend he expressed his feeling that the pianoforte was becoming too narrow for his thoughts, and that he must try orchestral composition. The fruit of this resolve was the B♭ Symphony (op. 38), which was produced at Leipzig in 1841, and was probably his first important orchestral work. It is quite extraordinary how successfully he grappled with the difficulties of the greatest style of composition at the first attempt. The manner is thoroughly symphonic, impressive and broad, and the ideas are more genuinely instrumental both in form and expression than Mendelssohn's, and far more incisive in detail, which in instrumental music is a most vital matter. Mendelssohn had great readiness for making a tune, and it is as clear as possible that when he went about to make a large instrumental work his first thought was to find a good tune to begin upon. Schumann seems to have aimed rather at a definite and strongly marked idea, and to have allowed it to govern the form of period or phrase in which it was presented. In this he was radically in accord with both Mozart and Beethoven. The former in his instrumental works very commonly made what is called the principal subject out of two distinct items, which seem contrasted externally in certain characteristics and yet are inevitable to one another. Beethoven frequently satisfied himself with one principal one, as in the first movements of the Eroica and the C minor ; and even where there are two more or less distinct figures, they are joined very closely into one phrase, as in the Pastoral, the No. 8, and the first movement of the Choral. The first movement of Schumann's B♭ Symphony shows the same characteristic. The movement seems

almost to depend upon the simple but very definite first figure quoted on p. 375a which is given out in slow time in the Introduction, and worked up as by a mind pondering over its possibilities, finally breaking away with vigorous freshness and confidence in the ' Allegro molto Vivace.' The whole first section depends upon the development of this figure ; and even the horns, which have the last utterances before the second subject appears, continue to repeat its rhythm with diminishing force. The second subject necessarily presents a different aspect altogether, and is in marked contrast to the first, but it similarly depends upon the clear character of the short figures of which it is composed, and its gradual work up from the quiet beginning to the loud climax, ends in the reappearance of the rhythmic form belonging to the principal figure of the movement. The whole of the working-out portion depends upon the same figure, which is presented in various aspects and with the addition of new features and ends in a climax which introduces the same figure in a slow form, very emphatically, corresponding to the statement in the Introduction. To this climax the recapitulation is duly welded on. The coda again makes the most of the same figure, in yet fresh aspects. The latter part is to all intents independent, apparently a sort of reflection on what has gone before, and is so far in definite contrast as to explain itself. The whole movement is direct and simple in style, and, for Schumann, singularly bright and cheerful. The principles upon which he constructed and used his principal subjects in this movement are followed in the first movements of the other symphonies ; most of all in the D minor ; clearly in the C major ; and least in the E♭, which belongs to the later period of his life. But even in this last he aims at gaining the same result, though by different means ; and the subject is as free as any from the tune-qualities which destroy the complete individuality of an instrumental subject in its most perfect and positive sense. In the first movement of the D minor he even went so far as to make some important departures from the usual outlines of form, which are rendered possible chiefly by the manner in which he used the characteristic figure of his principal subject. It is first introduced softly in the latter part of the Introduction, and gains force quickly, so that in a few bars it breaks away in the vigorous and passionate allegro in the following form—

which varies in the course of the movement to

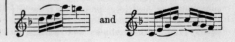

In one or other of these forms it continues almost ceaselessly throughout the whole movement, either as actual subject or accompaniment ; in the second section it serves in the latter capacity.   In the latter part of the working-out section a fresh subject of gentler character is introduced, seeming to stem and mitigate the vehemence expressed by the principal figures of the first subject ; from the time this new subject makes its appearance there continues a sort of conflict between the two ; the vehement subject constantly breaking in with apparently undiminished fire, and seeming at times to have the upper hand, till just at the end the major of the original key (D minor) is taken, and the more genial subject appears in a firm and more determined form, as if asserting its rights over the wild first subject ; and thereupon, when the latter reappears, it is in a much more genial character, and its reiteration at the end of the movement gives the impression of the triumph of hope and trust in good, over the seeds of passion and despair. The result of the method upon which the movement is developed is to give the impression of both external and spiritual form.   The requirements of key, modulation, and subject are fulfilled, though, from the point of view of classical orthodoxy, with unusual freedom. The spiritual form,—the expression in musical terms of a type of mental conflict, so depicted that thinking beings can perceive the sequence to be true of themselves—is also very prominent, and is the most important element in the work, as is the case in all Schumann's best works ; moreover in this movement everything is strongly individual, and warm with real musical life in his own style ; which was not altogether the case with the first movement of the B♭.   In the C major Symphony (op. 61) the first allegro is ushered in by a slow introduction of important and striking character, containing, like those of the two just mentioned, anticipations of its principal figures.   In the allegro the two principal subjects are extremely strong in character, and the consistent way in which the whole movement is developed upon the basis of their constituent figures, with allusions to those of the introduction, is most remarkable. Here again there is a sort of conflict between the principal ideas.   The first subject is just stated twice (the second time with certain appropriate changes), and then a start is instantly made in the Dominant key, with new figures characteristic of the second section ; transition is made to flat keys and back, and an allusion to the first subject ends the first half ; but all is closely consistent, vigorous, and concise.   The development portion is also most closely worked upon the principal subjects, which are treated, as it seems, exhaustively, presenting especially the figures of the second subject in all sorts of lights, and with freshness and warmth of

imagination, and variety of tone and character. The recapitulation is preceded by allusions to the characteristic features of the introduction, considerably transformed, but still sufficiently recognisable to tell their tale.   The coda is made by fresh treatment of the figures of the principal subjects in vigorous and brilliant development.

The Symphony in E♭ has no introduction, and Schumann seems to have aimed at getting his strong effects of subject in this case by means other than the vigorous and clear rhythmic forms which characterise the first movements of the earlier symphonies.   The effect is obtained by syncopations and cross rhythms, which alternately obscure and strengthen the principal beats of the bar, and produce an effect of wild and passionate effort, which is certainly striking, though not so immediately intelligible as the rhythmic forms of the previous symphonies.   The second subject is in strong contrast, having a more gentle and appealing character ; but it is almost overwhelmed by the recurrence of the syncopations of the principal subject, which make their appearance with persistency in the second as in the first section, having in that respect a very clear poetical or spiritual meaning.   The whole development of the movement is again consistent and impressive, though not so fresh as in the other symphonies. As a point characteristic of Schumann, the extreme conciseness of the first section of the first movement in the B♭, D minor, and C major Symphonies is to be noticed, as it bears strongly upon the cultivated judgment and intelligence which mark his treatment of this great instrumental form.   The first half is treated almost as pure exposition ; the working-out having logically the greater part of interesting development of the ideas.   The recapitulation is generally free, and in the D minor Symphony is practically supplanted by novel methods of balancing the structure of the movement.   The coda either presents new features, or takes fresh aspects of the principal ones, enhanced by new turns of modulation, and ending with the insistence on the primary harmonies of the principal key, which is necessary to the stability of the movement.   In all these respects Schumann is a most worthy successor to Beethoven.   He represents his intellectual side in the consistency with which he develops the whole movement from a few principal features, and the freshness and individuality with which he treats the form ; and he shows plenty of the emotional and spiritual side in the passionate or tender qualities of his subjects, and the way in which they are distributed relatively to one another. Schumann's symphonic slow movements have also a distinctive character of their own. Though extremely concise, they are all at the same time rich and full of feeling.   They are somewhat in the fashion of a 'Romanze,' that in the D minor

Symphony being definitely so called ; and their development depends rather upon an emotional than an intellectual basis ; as it seems most just that a slow movement should.   His object appears to have been to find some noble and aspiring strain of melody, and to contrast it with episodes of similar character, which carry on and bear upon the principal idea without diverting the chain of thought into a different channel.   Hence the basis of the movements is radically lyrical ; and this affords an important element of contrast to the first movement, in which there is always an antithetical element in the contrast of the two principal subjects. The romanze of the D minor is constructed on a different principle ; the sections and musical material being strongly contrasted ; this may be partly owing to the closeness of its connection with other parts of the symphony, as will be noticed farther on.   The scherzos, including that in the 'Overture, Scherzo, and Finale' (op. 52), have a family likeness to one another, though their outlines are different ; they all illustrate a phase of musical and poetical development in their earnest character and the vein of sadness which pervades them.   The light and graceful gaiety of most of the minuets of Haydn and Mozart is scarcely to be traced in them ; but its place is taken by a certain wild rush of animal spirits, mixed up in a strange and picturesque way with expressions of tenderness and regret.   These scherzos are in a sense unique ; for though following in the same direction as Beethoven's in some respects, they have but little of his sense of fun and grotesque, while the vein of genuine melancholy which pervades them certainly finds no counterpart either in Spohr or Mendelssohn ; and, if it may be traced in Schubert, it is still in comparison far less prominent.   In fact Schumann's scherzos are specially curious and interesting, even apart from the ordinary standpoint of a musician, as illustrating a phase of the intellectual progress of the race.   Schumann belonged to the order of men with large and at the same time delicate sympathies, whose disposition becomes so deeply impressed with the misfortunes and unsolvable difficulties which beset his own lot and that of his fellow-men, that pure unmixed lightheartedness becomes almost impossible.   The poetical and thoughtful side of his disposition, which supplied most vital ingredients to his music, was deeply tinged with sadness ; and from this he was hardly ever entirely free.   He could wear an aspect of cheerfulness, but the sadness was sure to peep out, and in this, among thoughtful and poetically disposed beings, he cannot be looked upon as singular.   Hence the position of the scherzo in modern instrumental music presents certain inevitable difficulties. The lively, almost childish, merriment of early examples cannot be attained without jarring upon the feelings of earnest men ; at least in

works on such a scale as the symphony, where the dignity and importance of the form inevitably produce a certain sense of responsibility to loftiness of purpose in the carrying out of the ideas.   A movement corresponding to the old scherzo in its relation to the other movements had to be formed upon far more complicated conditions.   The essential point in which Schumann followed his predecessors was the definition of the balancing and contrasting sections.   The outlines of certain groups of bars are nearly always very strongly marked, and the movement as a whole is based rather upon effects attainable by the juxtaposition of such contrasting sections than upon the continuous logical or emotional development which is found in the other movements.   The structural outline of the old dance-forms is still recognisable in this respect, but the style and rhythm bear little trace of the dance origin ; or at least the dance quality has been so far idealised as to apply rather to thought and feeling than to expressive rhythmic play of limbs.   In Schumann's first Symphony the scherzo has some qualities of style which connect it with the minuets of earlier times, even of Mozart ; but with these there are genuine characteristic traits of expression.   In the later scherzos the poetical meaning seems more apparent.   In fact the scherzo and the slow movement are linked together as the two sections of the work most closely representative of human emotion and circumstance ; the first and last movements having more evident dependence upon what are called abstract qualities of form.   In its structural outlines Schumann's scherzo presents certain features.   In the Symphonies in B♭ and C he adopts the device of two trios.   Beethoven had repeated the trio in two symphonies (4th and 7th), and Schumann advanced in the same direction by writing a second trio instead of repeating the first, and by making the two trios contrast not only with the scherzo, but also with each other ; and as a further result the trios stand centrally in relation to the first and last statement of the scherzo, while it in its turn stands centrally between them, and thus the whole structure of the movement gains in interest.   It is worthy of note that the codas to all Schumann's scherzos are specially interesting and full ; and some of them are singular in the fact that they form an independent little section conveying its own ideas apart from those of the principal subjects. His finales are less remarkable on general grounds, and on the whole less interesting than his other movements.   The difficulty of conforming to the old type of light movements was even more severe for him than it was for Beethoven, and hence he was the more constrained to follow the example set by Beethoven of concluding with something weighty and forcible, which should make a fitting crown to the work in those respects, rather than on the principle of sending the audience away in a good humour. In the B♭ Symphony only does the last movement aim at gaiety and lightness ; in the other three symphonies and the Overture, Scherzo, and Finale the finales are all of the same type, with broad and simple subjects and strongly emphasised rhythms. The rondo form is only obscurely hinted at in one ; in the others the development is very free, but based on binary form ; and the style of expression and development is purposely devoid of elaboration.

Besides the points which have been already mentioned in the development of the individual movements, Schumann's work is conspicuous for his attempts to bind the whole together in various ways. Not only did he make the movements run into each other, but in several places he connects them by reproducing the ideas of one movement in others, and even by using the same important features in different guises as the essential basis of different movements. In the Symphony in C there are some interesting examples of this ; but the Symphony in D minor is the most remarkable experiment of the kind yet produced, and may be taken as a fit type of the highest order. In the first place all the movements run into each other except the first and second ; and even there the first movement is purposely so ended as to give a sense of incompleteness unless the next movement is proceeded with at once. The first subject of the first movement and the first of the last are connected by a strong characteristic figure, which is common to both of them. The persistent way in which this figure is used in the first movement has already been described. It is not maintained to the same extent in the last movement ; but it makes a strong impression in its place there, partly by its appearing conspicuously in the accompaniment, and partly by the way it is led up to in the sort of intermezzo which connects the scherzo and the last movement, where it seems to be introduced at first as a sort of reminder of the beginning of the work, and as if suggesting the clue to its meaning and purpose ; and is made to increase in force with each repetition till the start is made with the finale. In the same manner the introduction is connected with the slow movement or romanze, by the use of its musical material for the second division of that movement ; and the figure which is most conspicuous in the middle of the romanze runs all through the trio of the succeeding movement. So that the series of movements are as it were interlaced by their subject-matter ; and the result is that the whole gives the impression of a single and consistent musical poem. The way in which the subjects recur may suggest different explanations to different people, and hence it is dangerous to try and fix one in definite terms

describing particular circumstances. But the important fact is that the work can be felt to represent in its entirety the history of a series of mental or emotional conditions such as may be grouped round one centre ; in other words, the group of impressions which go to make the innermost core of a given story seems to be faithfully expressed in musical terms and in accordance with the laws which are indispensable to a work of art. The conflict of impulses and desires, the different phases of thought and emotion, and the triumph or failure of the different forces which seem to be represented, all give the impression of belonging to one personality, and of being perfectly consistent in their relation to one another ; and by this means a very high example of all that most rightly belongs to programme music is presented. Schumann, however, wisely gave no definite clue to fix the story in terms. The original autograph has the title 'Symphonische Fantaisie fur grosses Orchester, skizzirt im Jahre 1841 ; neu instrumentirt 1851.' In the published score it is called 'Symphony,' and numbered as the fourth, though it really came second. Schumann left several similar examples in other departments of instrumental music, but none so fully and carefully carried out. In the department of Symphony he never again made so elaborate an experiment. In his last, however, that in E♭, he avowedly worked on impressions which supplied him with something of a poetical basis, though he does not make use of characteristic figures and subjects to connect the movements with one another. The impressive fourth movement is one of the most singular in the range of symphonic music, and is meant to express the feelings produced in him by the ceremonial at the enthronement of a Cardinal in Cologne Cathedral. The last movement has been said to embody 'the bustle and flow of Rhenish holiday life, on coming out into the town after the conclusion of the ceremony in the Cathedral.' [1] Of the intention of the scherzo nothing special is recorded, but the principal subject has much of the 'local colour' of the German national dances.

As a whole, Schumann's contributions to the department of Symphony are by far the most important since Beethoven. As a master of orchestration he is less certain than his fellows of equal standing. There are passages which rise to the highest points of beauty and effectiveness, as in the slow movement of the C major Symphony ; and his aim to balance his end and his means was of the highest, and the way in which he works it out is original ; but both the bent of his mind and his education inclined him to be occasionally less pellucid than his predecessors, and to give his instruments things to do which are not perfectly adapted to their

[1] For Schumann's intention see Wasielewski, 3rd ed., pp. 269, 272.

idiosyncrasies. On the other hand, in vigour, richness, poetry, and earnestness, as well as in the balance which he was able to maintain between originality and justness of art, his works stand at the highest point among the moderns whose work is done ; and have had great and lasting effect upon his successors.

The advanced point to which the history of the Symphony has arrived is shown by the way in which composers have become divided into two camps, whose characteristics are most easily understood in their extremest representatives. The growing tendency to attach positive meaning to music, as music, has in course of time brought about a new position of affairs in the instrumental branch of art. We have already pointed out how the strict outlines of form in instrumental works came to be modified by the growing individuality of the subject. As long as subjects were produced upon very simple lines, which in most cases resembled one another in all but very trifling external particulars, there was no reason why the structure of the whole movement should grow either complex or individual. But as the subject (which stands in many cases as a sort of text) came to expand its harmonic outlines and to gain force and meaning, it reacted more and more upon the form of the whole movement ; and at the same time the musical spirit of the whole, as distinguished from the technical aspects of structure, was concentrated and unified, and became more prominent as an important constituent of the artistic *ensemble*. In many cases, such as small movements of a lyrical character for single instruments, the so-called classical principles of form were almost lost sight of, and the movement was left to depend altogether upon the consistency of the musical expression throughout. Sometimes these movements had names suggesting more or less of a programme ; but this was not by any means invariable or necessary. For in such cases as Chopin's Preludes, and some of Schumann's little movements, there is no programme given, and none required by the listener. The movement depends successfully upon the meaning which the music has sufficient character of its own to convey. In such cases the art form is still thoroughly pure, and depends upon the development of music as music. But in process of time a new position beyond this has been assumed. Supposing the subjects and figures of music to be capable of expressing something which is definite enough to be put into words, it is argued that the classical principles of structure may be altogether abandoned, even in their broadest outlines, and a new starting-point for instrumental music attained, on the principle of following the circumstances of a story, or the succession of emotions connected with a given idea, or the flow of thought suggested by the memory of a place or person or event of history, or some such means ; and that this would serve as a basis of consistency and a means of unifying the whole, without the common resources of tonal or harmonic distribution. The story or event must be supposed to have impressed the composer deeply, and the reaction to be an outflow of music expressing the poetical imaginings of the author better than words would do. In some senses this may still be pure art ; where the musical idea has really sufficient vigour and vitality in itself to be appreciated without the help of the external excitement of the imagination which is attained by giving it a local habitation and a name. For then the musical idea may still have its full share in the development of the work, and may pervade it intrinsically as music, and not solely as representing a story or series of emotions which are, primarily, external to the music. But when the element of realism creeps in, or the ideas depend for their interest upon their connection with a given programme, the case is different. The test seems to lie in the attitude of mind of the composer. If the story or programme of any sort is merely a secondary matter which exerts a general influence upon the music, while the attention is concentrated upon the musical material itself and its legitimate artistic development, the advantages gained can hardly be questioned. The principle not only conforms to what is known of the practice of the greatest masters, but is on abstract grounds perfectly unassailable ; on the other hand, if the programme is the primary element, upon which the mind of the composer is principally fixed, and by means of which the work attains a specious excuse for abnormal development, independent of the actual musical sequence of ideas, then the principle is open to question, and may lead to most unsatisfactory results. The greatest of modern programme composers came to a certain extent into this position. The development of pure abstract instrumental music seems to have been almost the monopoly of the German race ; French and Italians have had a readier disposition for theatrical and at best dramatic music. Berlioz had an extraordinary perception of the possibilities of instrumental music, and appreciated the greatest works of the kind by other composers as fully as the best of his contemporaries ; but it was not his own natural way of expressing himself. His natural bent was always towards the dramatic elements of effect and dramatic principles of treatment. It seems to have been necessary to him to find some moving circumstance to guide and intensify his inspiration. When his mind was excited in such a manner he produced the most extraordinary and original effects ; and the fluency and clearness with which he expressed himself was of the highest order. His genius for orchestration, his vigorous rhythms, and the enormous volumes of sound of which he was as much master as of the most delicate subtleties of small combinations of instruments, have the most powerful effect upon the hearer ; while his vivid dramatic perception goes very far to supply the place of the intrinsically musical development which characterises the works of the greatest masters of abstract music. But on the other hand, as is inevitable from the position he adopted, he was forced at times to assume a theatrical manner, and a style which savours rather of the stage than of the true dramatic essence of the situations he deals with. In the 'Symphonie Fantastique,' for instance, which he also called 'Episode de la Vie d'un Artiste,' his management of the programme principle is thorough and well-devised. The notion of the ideal object of the artist's affections being represented by a definite musical figure, called the 'idée fixe,' unifying the work throughout by its constant reappearance in various aspects and surroundings, is very happy ; and the way in which he treats it in several parts of the first movement has some of the characteristic qualities of the best kind of development of ideas and figures, in the purely musical sense ; while at the same time he has obtained most successfully the expression of the implied sequence of emotions, and the absorption consequent upon the contemplation of the beloved object. In the general laying out of the work he maintains certain vague resemblances to the usual symphonic type. The slow introduction, and the succeeding Allegro agitato—representing his passion, and therefore based to a very great extent on the 'idée fixe'—are equivalent to the familiar opening movements of the classical symphonies ; and moreover there is even a vague resemblance in the inner structure of the Allegro to the binary form. The second movement, called 'Un bal,' corresponds in position to the time-honoured minuet and trio ; and though the broad outlines are very free there is a certain suggestion of the old inner form in the relative disposition of the valse section and that devoted to the 'idée fixe.' In the same way the 'Scène aux Champs' corresponds to the usual slow movement. In the remaining movements the programme element is more conspicuous. A 'Marche au supplice' and a 'Songe d'une nuit de Sabbat' are both of them as fit as possible to excite the composer's love of picturesque and terrible effects, and to lead him to attempt realistic presentation, or even a sort of musical scene-painting, in which some of the characteristics of instrumental music are present, though they are submerged in the general impression by characteristics of the opera. The effect produced is of much the same nature as of that of passages selected from operas played without action in the concert-room. In fact, in his little preface, Berlioz seems to imply that this would be a just way to consider the work, and the condensed statement of his view of programme music there given is worth quoting :

'Le compositeur a eu pour but de développer, dans ce qu'elles ont de musical, différentes situations de la vie d'un artiste. Le plan du drame instrumental, privé du secours de la parole, a besoin d'être exposé d'avance. Le programme (qui est indispensable à l'intelligence complète du plan dramatique de l'ouvrage) doit donc être considéré comme le texte parlé d'un Opéra, servant à amener des morceaux de musique, dont il motive le caractère et l'expression.'[1] This is a very important and clear statement of the position, and marks sufficiently the essential difference between the principles of the most advanced writers of programme music and those adopted by Beethoven. The results are in fact different forms of art. An instrumental drama is a fascinating idea, and might be carried out perfectly within the limits used even by Mozart and Haydn ; but if the programme is indispensable to its comprehension those limits have been passed. This does not necessarily make the form of art an illegitimate one ; but it is most important to realise that it is on quite a different basis from the type of the instrumental symphony ; and this will be better understood by comparing Berlioz's statement with those Symphonies of Beethoven and Mendelssohn, or even of Raff and Rubinstein, where the adoption of a general and vague title gives the semblance of a similar use of programme. Beethoven liked to have a picture or scene or circumstance in his mind ;[2] but it makes all the difference to the form of art whether the picture or story is the guiding principle in the development of the piece, or whether the development follows the natural implication of the positively musical idea. The mere occurrence, in one of these forms, of a feature which is characteristic of the other, is not sufficient to bridge over the distance between them ; and hence the 'instrumental drama' or poem, of which Berlioz has given the world its finest examples, must be regarded as distinct from the regular type of the pure instrumental symphony. It might perhaps be fairly regarded as the Celtic counterpart of the essentially Teutonic form of art, and as an expression of the Italo-Gallic ideas of instrumental music on lines parallel to the German symphony ; but in reality it is scarcely even an offshoot of the old symphonic stem ; and it will be far better for the understanding of the subject if the two forms of art are kept as distinct in name as they are in principle.

The earliest and most eminent follower of Berlioz, working on similar lines to his in modern

[1] 'The composer has aimed at developing various situations in the life of an artist, so far as seemed musically possible. The plan of an instrumental drama, being without words, requires to be explained beforehand. The programme (which is indispensable to the perfect comprehension of the dramatic plan of the work) ought therefore to be considered in the light of the spoken text of an Opera, serving to lead up to the pieces of music, and indicate the character and expression.'

[2] This important admission was made by Beethoven to Neate: 'I have always a picture in my thoughts when I am composing, and work to it.' (Thayer, iii. 343.)

times, is Liszt; and his adoption of the name 'Symphonic poem' for such compositions sufficiently defines their nature without bringing them exactly under the head of symphonies. Of these there are many, constructed on absolutely independent lines, so as to appear as musical poems or counterparts of actual existing poems, on such subjects as Mazeppa, Prometheus, Orpheus, the battle of the Huns, the 'Préludes' of Lamartine, Hamlet, and so forth. A work which, in name at least, trenches upon the old lines is the 'Faust Symphony,' in which the connection with the programme-principle of Berlioz is emphasised by the dedication of the piece to him. In this work the connection with the old form of symphony is perhaps even less than in the examples of Berlioz. Subjects and figures are used not for the purposes of defining the artistic form, but to describe individuals, ideas, or circumstances. The main divisions of the work are ostensibly three, which are called 'character-pictures' of Faust, Margaret, and Mephistopheles severally; and the whole concludes with a setting of the 'Chorus mysticus.' Figures are used after the manner of Wagner's 'Leit-motiven' to portray graphically such things as bewildered inquiry, anxious agitation, love, and mockery, besides the special figure or melody given for each individual as a whole. These are so interwoven and developed by modifications and transformations suited to express the circumstances, as to present the speculations of the composer on the character and the philosophy of the poem in various interesting lights; and his great mastery of orchestral expression and fluency of style contribute to its artistic importance on its own basis; while in general the treatment of the subject is more psychological and less pictorially realistic than the prominent portions of Berlioz's work, and therefore slightly nearer in spirit to the classical models. But with all its striking characteristics and successful points the music does not approach Berlioz in vitality or breadth of musical idea.

The few remaining modern composers of symphonies belong essentially to the German school, even when adopting the general advantage of a vague title. Prominent among these are Raff and Rubinstein, whose methods of dealing with instrumental music are at bottom closely related. Raff almost invariably adopted a title for his instrumental works; but those which he selected admit of the same kind of general interpretation as those of Mendelssohn, and serve rather as a means of unifying the general tone and style of the work than of pointing out the lines of actual development. The several Seasons, for instance, serve as the general idea for a symphony each. Another is called 'Im Walde.' In another several conditions in the progress of the life of a man serve as a vague basis for giving a certain consistency of character to the style of expression, in a way quite consonant with the pure type. In

one case Raff comes nearer to the Berlioz ideal, namely in the Lenore Symphony, in some parts of which he clearly attempts to depict a succession of events. But even when this is most pronounced, as in the latter part of the work, there is very little that is not perfectly intelligible and appreciable as music without reference to the poem. As a matter of fact Raff is always rather free and relaxed in his form; but that is not owing to his adoption of programme, since the same characteristic is observable in works that have no name as in those that have. The ease and speed with which he wrote, and the readiness with which he could call up a certain kind of genial, and often very attractive ideas, both interfered with the concentration necessary for developing a closely-knit and compact work of art. His ideas are clearly defined and very intelligible, and have much poetical sentiment; and these facts, together with a very notable mastery of orchestral resource and feeling for colour, have ensured his works great success; but there is too little self-restraint and concentration both in the general outline and in the statement of details, and too little self-criticism in the choice of subject-matter, to admit the works to the highest rank among symphonies. In the broadest outlines he generally conformed to the principles of the earlier masters, distributing his allegros, slow movements, scherzos, and finales, according to precedent. And, allowing for the laxity above referred to, the models which he followed in the internal structure of the movements are the familiar types of Haydn, Mozart, and Beethoven. His finales are usually the most irregular, at times amounting almost to fantasias; but even this, as already described, is in conformity with tendencies which are noticeable even in the golden age of symphonic art. Taken as a whole, Raff's work in the department of symphony is the best representative of a characteristic class of composition of modern times—the class in which the actual ideas and general colour and sentiment are nearly everything, while their development and the value of the artistic side of structure are reduced to a minimum.

Rubinstein's works are conspicuous examples of the same class; but the absence of concentration, self-criticism in the choice of subjects, and care in statement of details, is even more conspicuous in him than in Raff. His most important symphonic work is called 'The Ocean'—the general title serving, as in Raff's symphonies, to give unity to the sentiment and tone of the whole, rather than as a definite programme to work to. In this, as in Raff, there is much spontaneity in the invention of subjects, and in some cases a higher point of real beauty and force is reached than in that composer's works; and there is also a good deal of striking interest in the details. The most noticeable external feature is the fact that the symphony is in six movements. There was originally the familiar group of four, and to these were added, some years later, an additional slow movement, which stands second, and a further genuine scherzo, which stands fifth, both movements being devised in contrast to the previously written adagio and scherzo. Another symphony of Rubinstein's, showing much vigour and originality, and some careful and intelligent treatment of subject, is the 'Dramatic.' This is in the usual four movements, with well-devised introductions to the first and last. The work as a whole is hampered by excessive and unnecessary length, which is not the result of the possibilities of the subjects or the necessities of their development ; and might be reduced with nothing but absolute advantage.

The greatest representative of the highest art in the department of Symphony is Johannes Brahms. His four examples [1] have that mark of intensity, loftiness of purpose, and artistic mastery which sets them above all other contemporary work of the kind. Like Beethoven and Schumann he did not produce a symphony till a late period in his career, when his judgment was matured by much practice in other kindred forms of instrumental composition, such as pianoforte quartets, string sextets and quartets, sonatas, and such forms of orchestral composition as variations and two serenades. He seems to have set himself to prove that the old principles of form are still capable of serving as the basis of works which should be thoroughly original both in general character and in detail and development, without either falling back on the device of programme, or abrogating or making any positive change in the principles, or abandoning the loftiness of style which befits the highest form of art ; but by legitimate expansion, and application of careful thought and musical contrivance to the development. In all these respects he is a thorough descendant of Beethoven, and illustrates the highest and best way in which the tendencies of the age in instrumental music may yet be expressed. He differs most markedly from the class of composers represented by Raff, in the fact that his treatment of form is an essential and important element in the artistic effect. The care with which he develops it is not more remarkable than the insight shown in all the possible ways of enriching it without weakening its consistency. In appearance it is extremely free, and at available points all possible use is made of novel effects of transition and ingenious harmonic subtleties ; but these are used in such a way as not to disturb the balance of the whole, or to lead either to discursiveness or tautology. In the laying out of the principal sections as much freedom is used as is consistent with the possibility of being readily followed and understood. Thus in the recapitulatory portion of a movement

the subjects which characterise the sections are not only subjected to considerable and interesting variation, but are often much condensed and transformed. In the first movement of the second symphony, for instance, the recapitulation of the first part of the movement is so welded on to the working-out portion that the hearer is only happily conscious that this point has been arrived at without the usual insistence to call his attention to it. Again, the subjects are so ingeniously varied and transformed in restatement that they seem almost new, though the broad melodic outlines give sufficient assurance of their representing the recapitulation. The same effect is obtained in parts of the allegrettos which occupy the place of scherzos in both symphonies. The old type of minuet and trio form is felt to underlie the well-woven texture of the whole, but the way in which the joints and seams are made often escapes observation. Thus in the final return to the principal section in the Allegretto of the second Symphony, which is in G major, the subject seems to make its appearance in F♯ major, which serves as dominant to B minor, and going that way round the subject glides into the principal key almost insensibly. [2] In the Allegretto of the Symphony in C minor the outline of a characteristic feature is all that is retained in the final return of the principal subject near the end, and new effect is gained by giving a fresh turn to the harmony. Similar closeness of texture is found in the slow movement of the same symphony, at the point where the principal subject returns, and the richness of the variation to which it is subjected enhances the musical impression. The effect of these devices is to give additional unity and consistency to the movements. Enough is given to enable the intelligent hearer to understand the form without its appearing in aspects with which he is already too familiar. Similar thoroughness is to be found on the other sides of the matter. In the development of the sections, for instance, all signs of 'padding' are done away with as much as possible, and the interest is sustained by developing at once such figures of the principal subjects as will serve most suitably. Even such points as necessary equivalents to cadences, or pauses on the dominant, are by this means infused with positive musical interest in just proportion to their subordinate relations to the actual subjects. Similarly, in the treatment of the orchestra, such a thing as filling up is avoided to the utmost possible ; and in order to escape the over-complexity of detail so unsuitable to the symphonic form of art, the forces of the orchestra are grouped in masses in the principal characteristic figures, in such a way that the whole texture is endowed with vitality. The impression so conveyed to some is that the orchestration is not at such a high level of

---

[1] [See below as to the third and fourth.]

[2] For a counterpart to this see the first movement of Beethoven's pianoforte Sonata in F, op. 10, No. 2.

perfection as the other elements of art ; and certainly the composer does not aim at subtle combinations of tone and captivating effects of a sensual kind so much as many other great composers of modern times ; and if too much attention is concentrated upon the special element of his orchestration it may doubtless seem at times rough and coarse. But this element must only be considered in its relation to all the others, since the composer may reasonably dispense with some orchestral fascinations in order to get broad masses of harmony and strong outlines ; and if he seeks to express his musical ideas by means of sound, rather than to disguise the absence of them by seductive misuse of it, the world is a gainer. In the putting forward and management of actual subjects, he is guided by what appears to be inherent fitness to the occasion. In the first movement of the Symphony in C minor, attention is mainly concentrated upon one strong subject figure, which appears in both the principal sections and acts as a centre upon which the rest of the musical materials are grouped ; and the result is to unify the impression of the whole movement, and to give it a special sentiment in an unusual degree. In the first movement of the Symphony in D there are even several subjects in each section, but they are so interwoven with one another, and seem so to fit and illustrate one another, that for the most part there appears to be but little loss of direct continuity. In several cases we meet with the devices of transforming and transfiguring an idea. The most obvious instance is in the Allegretto of the symphony in D, in which the first Trio in 2-4 time (a) is radically the same subject as that of the principal section in 3-4 time (b), but very differently stated. Then a very important item in the second Trio is a version in 3-8 time (c) of a figure of the first Trio in 2-4 time (d).

Of similar nature, in the Symphony in C minor, are the suggestions of important features of subjects and figures of the first Allegro in the opening introduction, and the connection of the last movement with its own introduction by the same means. In all these respects Brahms

illustrates the highest manifestations of actual art as art ; attaining his end by extraordinary mastery of both development and expression. And it is most notable that the great impression which his larger works produce is gained more by the effect of the entire movements than by the attractiveness of the subjects. He does not seem to aim at making his subjects the test of success. They are hardly seen to have their full meaning till they are developed and expatiated upon in the course of the movement, and the musical impression does not depend upon them to anything like the proportionate degree that it did in the works of the earlier masters. This is in conformity with the principles of progress which have been indicated above. The various elements of which the art-form consists seem to have been brought more and more to a fair balance of functions, and this has necessitated a certain amount of 'give and take' between them. If too much stress is laid upon one element at the expense of others, the perfection of the art-form as a whole is diminished thereby. If the effects of orchestration are emphasised at the expense of the ideas and vitality of the figures, the work may gain in immediate attractiveness, but must lose in substantial worth. The same may be said of over-predominance of subject-matter. The subjects need to be noble and well marked, but if the movement is to be perfectly complete, and to express something in its entirety and not as a string of tunes, it will be a drawback if the mere faculty for inventing a striking figure or passage of melody preponderates excessively over the power of development ; and the proportion in which they are both carried upwards together to the highest limit of musical effect is a great test of the artistic perfection of the work. In these respects Brahms's Symphonies are extraordinarily successful. They represent the austerest and noblest form of art in the strongest and healthiest way ; and his manner and methods have already had some influence upon the younger and more serious composers of the day. [The third and fourth symphonies of Brahms more than fulfil the expectations raised by the first two, here reviewed. The third, in F, op. 90, is given remarkable unity by the use, before the first subject of the opening movement, of a kind of motto-theme which reappears in the finale unaltered, and plays no insignificant part in the slow movement. The first subject of the opening section, too, recurs at the very end in the form of a subtle allusion in the violins as their *tremolando* passages descend to the last chords. The *poco allegretto* of this symphony is one of Brahms's most individual inspirations, one which for plaintive grace and delicate expression has not its fellow in music. The fourth symphony in E minor, op. 98, is a masterpiece of thematic development, and is remarkable for the adoption of the Passacaglia form for the finale.]

It would be invidious, however, to endeavour to point out as yet those in whose works his influence is most strongly shown. It must suffice to record that there are still many younger composers who are able to pass the symphonic ordeal with some success. Among the most successful are the Bohemian composer Dvořák, and the Italians Sgambati and Martucci ; and among English works may be mentioned with much satisfaction the Scandinavian Symphony of Cowen, which was original and picturesque in thought and treatment ; the Elegiac Symphony of Stanford, in which excellent workmanship, vivacity of ideas, and fluency of development combine to establish it as an admirable example of its class ; and an early symphony by Sullivan, which had such marks of excellence as to show how much art might have gained if circumstances had not drawn him to more lucrative branches of composition. It is obvious that composers have not given up hopes of developing something individual and complete in this form of art. It is not likely that many will be able to follow Brahms in his severe and uncompromising methods ; but he himself has shown more than any one how elastic the old principles may yet be made without departing from the genuine type of abstract instrumental music ; and that when there is room for individual expression there is still good work to be done, though we can hardly hope that even the greatest composers of the future will surpass the symphonic triumphs of the past, whatever they may do in other fields of composition. [Among modern writers there are very few whose fame rests mainly on their symphonies, apart from the composers of 'symphonic poems.' Anton Bruckner's eight complete symphonies, Gustav Mahler's six, and Weingartner's two, have achieved great success in Germany at different dates ; but among those that have attained universal acceptance all over the cultivated world, none are more remarkable than the three later works of Tchaikovsky, and the seven of Glazounov. The last composition of the former reached an astounding degree of popularity in London owing to the circumstances of the composer's death just at the time of its introduction into England ; in the matter of form it differs from his other symphonies, which are on strict classical lines, in certain particulars, such as ending with the slow movement, and giving to the second subject of the first movement a rate of speed as well as a character in sharp contrast with those of the first subject.]   C. H. H. P.

SYMPHONY CONCERTS. Under this title are grouped the descriptions of some of the most famous organisations in Great Britain and America, at which the performance of symphonic works is the main object in view. The occasional performance of a symphony at a miscellaneous or choral concert is not enough to justify the title of 'Symphony Concert,' and

the attempt here made must be understood to deal only with more or less permanent institutions. There is little hope that it can be complete, even for the countries already named ; in Germany, where every small town has its orchestral concerts as a matter of course, and in France, where there is much less centralisation than among ourselves, the task of cataloguing even the names of the various bodies which are founded for the performance of symphonic works would be impracticable.

LONDON

The first English organisation of the kind is the PHILHARMONIC SOCIETY, founded 1813, for which see vol. iii. pp. 698-703. The NEW PHILHARMONIC SOCIETY (see vol. iii. p. 366) was the next, founded in 1852. In 1855 the famous Crystal Palace Saturday Concerts began their long and useful career, which was carried on until 1901, being for all that time under the able direction of August Manns. (See vol. iii. p. 42, for their early history.) The concerts began with the first Saturday in October, and lasted, with an interval at Christmas, till the end of April. The orchestra consisted of 16 first and 14 second violins, 11 violas, 10 violoncellos, and 10 double basses, with single wind, etc. The programmes usually contained two overtures, a symphony, a concerto, or some minor piece of orchestral music, and four songs. The distinguishing feature of the concerts was their choice and performance of orchestral music. Not to mention the great works of Haydn, Mozart, Beethoven, Mendelssohn, Spohr, Weber, and other time-honoured classics, the audience were familiar with Schumann's symphonies and overtures, and with Schubert's symphonies and ' Rosamunde ' music, at a time when those works were all but unknown in the concert-rooms of the metropolis. Mendelssohn's Reformation Symphony was first played here ; so was his overture to ' Camacho ' ; Brahms's Symphonies, Pianoforte Concertos, Variations on a theme of Haydn and ' Song of Destiny ' ; Raff's various Symphonies ; Liszt's ' Ideale ' ; Rubinstein's Symphonies ; Goetz's Symphony, Concerto, and Overtures ; Smetana's ' Vltava ' ; Schubert's Symphonies in chronological order ; Wagner's ' Faust ' Overture ; Sullivan's ' Tempest ' Music and Symphony in E ; Benedict's Symphony in G minor, and many other works were obtained (often in MS.) and performed before they were heard in any other place in the metropolis. Bennett's ' Parisina ' was first played there after an interval of a quarter of a century. A very great influence was exercised in the renaissance of English music by the frequent performance of new works of importance by Mackenzie, Parry, Stanford, Cowen, and others.

A disposition was apparent in the managers of the concerts to present the audience with pieces of special interest; such as the MS. works of Schubert, and of Mendelssohn; Beethoven's arrangement of his Violin Concerto for the piano, and his Overture, 'Leonora No. 2'; an alternative Andante written by Mozart for his Parisian Symphony; the first version of Mendelssohn's 'Hebrides' Overture, and other rare treasures of the same nature.

The performances were of that exceptional quality which might be inferred from the ability, energy, and devotion of the conductor, and from the fact that owing to the wind and a portion of the strings of the orchestra being the permanent band of the Crystal Palace, Manns had opportunities for rehearsal which were at that time enjoyed by no other conductor in London.   G.

The establishment of the RICHTER CONCERTS in 1879 was the next event in the history of symphony concerts in London. For these see *ante*, pp. 93-94.

The history of the first series called LONDON SYMPHONY CONCERTS has been related under the heading HENSCHEL, vol. ii. p. 381. The concerts were founded in 1886, and brought to an end with a notable performance of the 'Matthew-Passion' on April 1, 1897.

The opening of the Queen's Hall in 1893 was followed by the formation of the Queen's Hall Choral Society, and in 1895 the experiment was tried of reviving public interest in Promenade Concerts, which had for some seasons languished in London. Mr. Henry J. Wood tried the bold experiment of giving the public at large an opportunity of hearing the great masterpieces of music, and the result showed that the attempt was surprisingly successful. Although symphonies were given regularly at these concerts, not at first on every occasion, the regular series of SATURDAY SYMPHONY CONCERTS began on Jan. 30, 1897, and have been carried on ever since. They were at first given weekly (subsequently fortnightly) up to the end of May, and their influence was less important on British music than on that of the contemporary Russian school, the chief representatives of which obtained frequent hearings for their works. The 'Pathetic' symphony of Tchaikovsky, though introduced at a Philharmonic Concert, acquired its great popularity under Mr. Wood, and for some years its continual performances stood in the way of more interesting work being done; but in due time the views of the authorities have become broader, and the programmes have shown a more catholic taste, as well as giving opportunities, more or less frequent, to the younger English composers. It must not be forgotten that the question of Sunday concerts was importantly affected by the series of Sunday Afternoon Orchestral Concerts founded in Oct. 1895, with Mr. Randegger as conductor. Mr. Wood became the regular conductor in the third season, 1897-98; in Nov. 1898 a dispute as to the legality of Sunday concerts, and licensing questions, made it imperative to close the hall on Sunday, Nov. 27, 1898, and led to the formation of a Sunday Concert Society, by means of which it was found possible to continue the concerts without transgressing the existing laws. The Sunday, as well as the Promenade Concerts, and the Saturday Afternoon Symphony Concerts, are still flourishing.

In 1902 a large number of the orchestra, who had acquired under Mr. Wood a very remarkable degree of excellence, particularly in accompaniment, refused to re-engage themselves to the Queen's Hall managers, owing to differences of opinion as to the right to employ deputies, and other points into which it is not necessary to enter. In course of time a new body of players was formed by Mr. Wood, and the malcontents organised themselves into the LONDON SYMPHONY ORCHESTRA, an institution whose internal economy differs from that of other English bodies of the kind. It is run at the joint risk of the members, who share in the profits and have a voice in the direction of the affairs. No permanent conductor is engaged, but various distinguished English conductors have appeared from time to time, and certain illustrious foreign conductors have also directed them. The Richter Concerts have been virtually transferred to this orchestra, a great part of whose concerts are now directed by that great conductor. Excellent work has been done in regard to performances and programmes by this body, so that the breach with the older institution has brought about nothing but artistic good.

Of Mr. Thomas Beecham's NEW SYMPHONY ORCHESTRA it is perhaps rather early to speak, as its organisation is scarcely as yet finally settled. In several seasons very interesting programmes have been given, the conductor being a man of wide musical reading, who has adopted the wise plan of reviving the older works written for a small orchestra under the original conditions. For the Symphony Concerts given in London by the various amateur bodies of players' societies, see ROYAL AMATEUR ORCHESTRAL SOCIETY (*ante*, p. 172); STOCK EXCHANGE ORCHESTRAL AND CHORAL SOCIETY (*ante*, p. 698); and STROLLING PLAYERS' ORCHESTRAL SOCIETY (*ante*, p. 728).   M.

BOURNEMOUTH.

In 1893 Mr. Dan Godfrey was engaged to provide a military band of thirty performers for the summer season; gradually, as in the case of the Crystal Palace Concerts, the authorities ventured upon classical concerts, and in 1895 a series of Symphony Concerts was organised and given in the Winter Gardens with full orchestra. These were so successful that the Municipality decided to make the undertaking a permanent one, and the annual series of concerts have attained great importance, being given on Monday and Thursday afternoons during the season. Many centenaries and other anniversaries in musical history have been observed more carefully than has usually been the case in London, and very frequently composers have conducted their own works at the concerts, Mr. Godfrey filling the post of regular conductor with great distinction.   M.

BRADFORD.

The Bradford Permanent Orchestra was founded in 1892, and is partly professional, partly amateur. The band is about eighty strong, and the post of conductor has been held successively by Mr. W. B. Sewell, Mr. A. E. Bartle, Dr. Cowen, and Mr. Allen Gill, the last of whom has been in office five years. The season 1907-8 included five concerts, at which works by most of the classical composers, and of modern musicians like Sibelius, Humperdinck, German, and York Bowen, were performed. The orchestra is a private and self-supporting institution. It is now usually engaged for the concerts of the Bradford Festival Choral Society. Among the conductors who have directed their own works have been Sir Arthur Sullivan, Sir Hubert Parry, Sir C. V. Stanford, Sir Edward Elgar, and Mr. E. German.   H. T.

HARROGATE.

Here also a permanent Municipal Orchestra has lately been formed and is now under the direction of Mr. Julian Clifford. On Wednesday afternoons, during a great part of the year, symphony concerts are given, and 'composers' afternoons' take place frequently.   M.

HULL.

The Hull Symphony Orchestra consists of local players who are engaged at theatres and music-halls, so that the concerts are given always in the afternoon. They were established in 1906, and under the conductorship of Arthur Wallerstein have done good work.

LEEDS.

The Leeds Municipal Orchestra was organised in the autumn of 1903 by Mr. A. H. Fricker, organist of the Town Hall; the first concert was given on Oct. 17 of that year. The orchestra at first consisted of fifty of the best professional musicians in the immediate neighbourhood, and the number has since been increased to over sixty. It has no direct subsidy from public money, but as the conductor receives no further remuneration than his stipend as organist, and as the concerts take the place of the customary Saturday evening organ recitals, there is no expense for hall, lighting, etc., and

the small charges made for admission (2d., 6d., and 1s.) have hitherto just sufficed to maintain the institution. The scheme for the season of 1907-8 consisted of ten concerts, at which symphonies by Haydn, Beethoven, Schubert, Tchaikovsky, and Dvořák, together with orchestral pieces by Mozart, Weber, Mendelssohn, Liszt, Saint-Saëns, Brahms, Svendsen, Smetana, Sibelius, Debussy, Elgar, German, were given. Among the composers who have conducted their own works are Sir C. V. Stanford, Mr. E. German, Dr. Vaughan Williams, Mr. York Bowen, Mr. J. W. Nicholl, Mr. F. Cliffe, Mr. Havergal Brian, Dr. Bairstow, Mr. William Wallace, Mr. Joseph Holbrooke, Mr. Percy Godfrey, and Mr. F. K. Hattersley.   H. T.

LIVERPOOL.

For the Liverpool Philharmonic Society, see vol. ii. p. 754.

MANCHESTER.

For the Gentleman's Concerts and Hallé Concerts, see vol. iii. pp. 36-37.

NEW BRIGHTON.

For the excellent series of concerts organised at the Tower, New Brighton, by Mr. Granville Bantock, in 1897-1901, see vol. i. p. 181.

SCOTLAND.

See SCOTTISH ORCHESTRA, *ante*, p. 402.

SYMPHONY CONCERTS IN THE UNITED STATES. Throughout the 18th century the concert life of America, so far as it existed in the principal cities of the Atlantic coast (such as New York, Philadelphia, Boston, Baltimore, and Charleston), was in every particular a reflex of the concert life of London. Practically all the influences were English, and English they remained for a full century; the colonists, as soon as they were in a position to enjoy the embellishments of civilisation, sought them in their English manifestations. As an illustration it may be pointed out that 'Ranelagh Gardens' were opened in 1765, at which 'a complete band of music' was engaged, and 'Vaux Hall Gardens' in Charleston in 1767, and New York in 1769. As to the vigour with which instrumental music, still subordinate to vocal the world over, was cultivated in America under the auspices of organisations of amateurs and professionals corresponding to the *Collegia musica* of Germany, it may suffice here to say that concerts in which solos on the harpsichord, violin, oboe, bassoon, flute, and horn were played date back to the fourth decade of the 18th century; and that the symphonies of Haydn, Pleyel, Stamitz, Gyrowetz, and their fellows, the overtures of Handel, Gretry, Gossec, and others, as well as the *concerti grossi* of Corelli, figured largely on the programmes of the concerts given in New York and Philadelphia in the latter half of the same century. Charleston, S.C., still maintains a Caecilia Society, organised in 1762, which gave fortnightly concerts from the beginning of its career with a band of amateurs, helped out by professionals, and in 1771 advertised in the newspapers of New York, Philadelphia, and Boston for a first and second violin, 2 hautboys, and a bassoon with whom the Society was willing to enter into a contract for one, two, or three years. There is little evidence to be found concerning the size and constitution of the bands of this period, though the intimations of the programmes are suggestive. In 1786, at a 'Grand Concert of Sacred Music' in Philadelphia, which had been inspired by the Handel Commemoration in Westminster Abbey, the chorus numbered 230 and the band 50. It is worthy of note in this connection that a number of musicians who sat in the band at the Commemoration were large factors in the development of instrumental music in America afterwards; among them were Gillingham, Reinagle, Gehot, Pick, Phillips, Mallet, and R. Shaw. (Readers desirous of pursuing this branch of the subject further are recommended to read Mr. O. G. Sonneck's *Early Concert-Life in America* (*1731-1800*), published by Breitkopf & Härtel, 1907.)

German influences began to make themselves felt in the second quarter of the 19th century, and to them is largely due the present status of symphonic culture in the United States, with one phase of which this article is particularly concerned. The intermediate stage between the instrumental elements of the concerts of the 18th century and the symphony concerts maintained in the musical centres of the country is still disclosed in a large number of cities where the theatre has a sufficient patronage to justify the employment of a considerable number of orchestral musicians. In these cities—Cleveland, Detroit, Indianapolis, St. Louis, Denver, New Orleans, New Haven, St. Paul, Minneapolis, and San Francisco may be taken as examples —the local orchestral musicians are brought together a few times in each season, and concerts given at the instance of either an enthusiastic or ambitious local leader or of a body of citizens who are prompted to make the inevitable financial sacrifice by a mixture of musical love and civic pride. Each of the larger and more firmly grounded institutions, whose stories are to be told presently, moreover carries on a propagandism within a large radius of its home; and there is, therefore, wide familiarity with orchestral music of the highest class, at least in the larger towns and cities of the northern tier of states. It is the custom to speak of all the orchestras (except one) which come in for discussion below as 'permanent.' The purpose of this is to distinguish them as organisations whose members play only at symphony concerts during the regular season and under a single conductor,

from the bands which are assembled for occasions, and whose members otherwise play as they list. It may be well to remember that the term is loosely applied; for no orchestra in the country is so firmly grounded as the Philharmonic Society of New York which, through sixty-five years of good and evil fortune, has never failed to give a series of symphony concerts every season, and has maintained the loftiest standard in programme and performance; yet its members are variously employed in theatre and other concert bands, when not called on for duty by their own corporation. Permanency would seem to call for an endowment in perpetuity, since no orchestra in the country has yet succeeded in making receipts and expenses cover each other except the New York Philharmonic, which lives on the co-operative plan. The Chicago Orchestra has an endowment in its hall built by popular subscription; the Boston Orchestra is the philanthropic enterprise of an individual; the others depend, year after year, on the generosity and public spirit of their guarantors, and may, therefore, be said to be just as permanent or impermanent as the moods and motives of the patrons.   H. E. K.

BOSTON.

THE BOSTON SYMPHONY ORCHESTRA owes its existence and its large perpetual endowment to the generosity and taste of Mr. Henry Lee Higginson, a well-known citizen of Boston, and affords a good instance of the munificent way in which the Americans apply their great riches for the public benefit in the service of education and art. Mr. Higginson had for long cherished the idea of having 'an orchestra which should play the best music in the best way, and give concerts to all who could pay a small price.' At length, on March 30, 1881, he made his intention public in the Boston newspapers as follows :—The orchestra to number sixty, and their remuneration to include the concerts and 'careful training.' Concerts to be twenty in number, on Saturday evenings, in the Music Hall, from middle of October to middle of March. Single tickets from 75 to 25 cents (3s. to 1s.); season tickets (concerts only) 10 to 5 dollars; one public rehearsal, 1s. entrance.

Mr. Georg Henschel was appointed conductor, and Mr. B. Listemann leader and solo violin. A full musical library was purchased, and the first concert took place on Oct. 22, 1881. There were twenty concerts in all, and the last ended with the Choral Symphony.   G.

Mr. Henschel remained as conductor of the orchestra for three years. He was succeeded at the beginning of the season of 1884-85 by Wilhelm Gericke of Vienna. Mr. Gericke's advent led to important improvements in the orchestra, many changes in the *personnel* by the importation of young and ambitious musicians from Europe, especially from Vienna, and the establishment of a higher standard of efficiency in performance. One of his most important steps was the engagement, as leader, of Franz Kneisel, beginning with the season of 1885-86, who occupied that highly important post until the end of the season 1902-3. After five years, during which Mr. Gericke had raised the standard of the orchestra to a plane approximating the founder's ideal, he was succeeded by Arthur Nikisch, who remained conductor for four years. After him came Emil Paur for five years, when, in the autumn of 1898, Gericke was recalled. He continued as conductor until the end of the season of 1905-6, when Dr. Karl Muck, of Berlin, was engaged for two years.

The orchestra has been considerably enlarged since its establishment. It now (1908) numbers an effective force of about ninety-seven men. The support given to the orchestra in Boston is loyal and enthusiastic; the concerts are crowded, and a system of premiums for choice of seats at the regular subscription sale each season greatly increases the normal receipts. Only in one season, however, have the receipts equalled the expenditures. In the other seasons the deficits met by Mr. Higginson have ranged from $2000 to $40,000. The annual series of concerts now numbers twenty-four, given on Saturday evenings, with public rehearsals (which are to all intents and purposes the same as the concerts) on the preceding Friday afternoons. For twenty years the concerts were given in the old Music Hall. In the autumn of 1901, however, the orchestra took possession of a fine new Symphony Hall, built especially for its accommodation. A series of nightly popular concerts, extending over a period of two months, is given every summer.

An important element of its work which has reached a firmly established basis in recent years is that accomplished outside of Boston. Besides appearing frequently in New England cities near Boston the orchestra makes five trips a year, in season, to Baltimore, Philadelphia, and New York, giving one concert on each visit to the first two cities and three in New York (two in the Borough of Manhattan and one in the Borough of Brooklyn). The concerts in New York have been given uninterruptedly since 1887. In 1903 the orchestra took an important step in establishing a pension fund, formed by the self-assessment of the members, the proceeds of two special concerts given annually, and contributions of friends of the organisation. R. A.

BROOKLYN.

THE PHILHARMONIC SOCIETY, incorporated 1857, has for its declared object 'the advancement of music in the city of Brooklyn, by procuring the public performance of the best works in this department of art.' Its affairs are controlled by a directorate of twenty-five

members, chosen annually from which a government is appointed. Membership is secured by payment of the subscription annually designated by the directors, who also prescribe the number of these subscriptions, limited, for several years, to 1200. Beginning in the autumn of 1857, five or more concerts have been given in each season, that at the close of the twenty-first season, May 10, 1879, being the 108th—each preceded by three public rehearsals. During the first five seasons the concerts were given at the Brooklyn Athenæum. Since 1862 the Brooklyn Academy of Music, a large theatre holding nearly 3000 people, has been made use of. The orchestral conductors have been—Theodore Eisfeld, 1857-62; Theodore Thomas, part of 1862; Mr. Eisfeld again, until the election of Carl Bergmann, Sept. 5, 1865; Mr. Thomas, re-elected Sept. 4, 1866; Mr. Bergmann again, 1870-73; succeeded May 26, 1873, by Mr. Thomas, who retained the position until his departure for Chicago (see below), assisted by William G. Dietrich, who had charge of the orchestra at the first two rehearsals of each concert. The concerts have always been of a high order; the orchestra large and composed of the best musicians procurable; the programmes of a catholic nature, no especial school of music having undue prominence. Important works have been produced for the first time in America, including several by native composers. Large choral works have occasionally figured on the Society's programmes, as well as solos and instrumental concertos. The Society's Library contains the scores and parts of over 100 orchestral works.　　　　F. H. J.

What was formerly the city of Brooklyn, N.Y., is now a borough of the American metropolis. Nevertheless the Philharmonic Society retains the corporate name by which it has been known since 1857. Theodore Thomas, with his orchestra, gave its concerts from 1873 till 1891. On his departure for Chicago an arrangement was made by which the concerts (five annually, by the Boston Symphony Orchestra) were continued under the joint auspices of the Philharmonic Society and the Institute of Arts and Sciences. After the destruction of the Academy of Music, Nov. 29, 1903, the concerts were transferred to the Baptist Temple.　　　　H. E. K.

CHICAGO.

THE THEODORE THOMAS ORCHESTRA of Chicago is in several things unique amongst the concert institutions of the United States, but in none so much as its history, which illustrates achievement through the persistence of a man of dominant ambition and iron will, the courage and steadfastness of a coterie of friends and music-lovers, and the public spirit of a young city of amazing resource and indomitable energy. The orchestra is the only one in the United States which bears officially the name of its creator ; it is also the only one of its kind which occupies its own hall. This hall is its endowment, an endowment which may fairly be said to be more enduring than that of any other concert institution in the country, inasmuch as it does not depend upon the wealth and inclination of an individual, a body of guarantors or the interests of the players themselves as is the case of one or the other of the Societies discussed in this article. The management of the Theodore Thomas Orchestra is in the hands of the Orchestral Association of Chicago, and for fifteen years it was known as the Chicago Orchestra, though popularly spoken of by the name by which it is now officially known. It had its origin primarily in the admiration excited by Mr. Thomas (*q.v.*) in the metropolis of the Middle West in the course of a long series of concerts given by him when he was still the leader of an itinerant orchestra which went out from New York, and a series which he gave every summer for a number of years in a building erected for exposition purposes on the Lake Front. The first Thomas concert was given in Chicago in 1869, when the city was only thirty-four years old as a municipal corporation, and when it was surpassed in population by Cincinnati and St. Louis. But the love of good music which Mr. Thomas implanted in the city would not have yielded its present fruit had it not been for the disasters which overwhelmed Mr. Thomas's private enterprises during the last few years of his sojourn in New York City. The chief causes, which operated against his efforts to maintain his own orchestra in the American metropolis may be looked for in the variety and number of interests developed by the growth of musical culture in New York. In 1890, when he ended his labours in the city which had been his home since childhood, orchestral concerts were regularly given by the Philharmonic and Symphony Societies, the Boston Symphony Orchestra, and the band conducted by Anton Seidl. Mr. Thomas had himself helped to raise the Philharmonic Society to a proud position, and many circumstances conspired to prevent him from commanding the large allegiance which his ambition and ideals exacted. Moreover, Grand Opera, which hitherto had been an exotic, had taken firm root in the Metropolitan Opera-House (see OPERA IN THE UNITED STATES, vol. iii. pp. 466-472) and gathered unto itself a munificent public patronage. In a sense, Mr. Thomas's missionary labours were done in New York, and it was for the good of music that he transferred his work to Chicago.

It was in the summer of 1890, when Mr. Thomas had abandoned all of his individual enterprises in New York, that he was met by C. Norman Fay, his brother-in-law, of Chicago, and from him received the suggestion that he

come to that city and organise an orchestra there. He agreed, provided that a guarantee fund of $50,000 a year for three years should be raised. Fifty-two citizens of Chicago were found who subscribed $1000 a year for three years, an official invitation was extended and accepted, and Mr. Thomas took a habitation in the city in 1891, spending the intermediate time in organising his new band. Meanwhile the Orchestral Association, which was conceived as a self-perpetuating body, was organised by N. K. Fairbank, C. Norman Fay, E. B. M'Cagg, A. C. Bartlett, and C. D. Hamill. This association entered into an agreement with Mr. Thomas and the guarantors to give two concerts a week, on Friday afternoons and Saturday evenings, for twenty weeks each season for three years. The musicians were engaged for twenty-eight weeks, eight of which were devoted to concerts outside Chicago. The Chicago concerts were given in the Auditorium, a new theatre with a seating capacity of between 4000 and 5000. At the end of the contract period the losses entailed by the concerts amounted to $153,000, which fact, together with certain unpleasant experiences in which Mr. Thomas had become involved as Musical Director of the World's Fair held in 1893, had a discouraging effect upon the guarantors. Originally there were fifty-two ; two of them failed to pay their assessments, and twenty declined to renew their subscriptions. The Orchestral Association was now reorganised, and new subscriptions were asked on a basis of a unit of $50, each unit to entitle the subscriber to a vote for the trustees who were to take over the financial administration. An effort to create another three years' term failed, and the guarantee fund for the fourth season amounted to only $30,000, which proved to be $4000 less than the cost of the concerts. The fifth, sixth, and seventh seasons created deficits of $27,000 and $39,000 respectively, the last largely due to injudicious travelling. The guarantee for these seasons being only $22,000 for each year a debt of $30,000 accumulated, for which a special subscription was raised. This was done, the debts paid, and a contingent fund of $30,000 was created, which soon disappeared under the flood of losses. On guarantees raised from year to year the orchestra continued the concerts until the final phase of the enterprise was reached. On Feb. 13, 1903, the patrons of the concerts were asked by the trustees of the Association to subscribe to a fund for the purpose of building a hall which should be a permanent home of the organisation, the theory of the trustees being that a hall with a seating capacity of 2500 would secure better support than one with so many seats that there was little if any inducement to subscribe for the season. It was argued, besides, that the saving in rentals and an income from the same source would put the orchestra on a self-supporting basis. A system was adopted which appealed for subscriptions to all classes of the population, and 8000 subscriptions were secured, ranging in amount from 10 cents to $25,000, and amounting to $650,000. Building operations were begun in May 1904, and the hall which cost $750,000 was dedicated on Dec. 14 of the same year. Up to this time the losses on each season had been as follows; 1st season $53,000; 2nd, $51,000; 3rd, $49,000; 4th, $34,000; 5th, $27,000; 6th, $27,000; 7th, $39,000; 8th, $16,000; 9th, $16,000; 10th, $26,000; 11th, $30,000; 12th, $20,000; 13th, $21,000; 14th, $19,000; 15th, $15,000. In March 1907 the treasurer, Frederick J. Wessels, wrote touching the result of the new policy of the Orchestral Association: 'The theory of the Trustees has proved correct. The ticket sales have increased every year, the demand for seats being sufficient to induce the Trustees to lengthen the season of 24 weeks (48 concerts) to 28 weeks (56 concerts). The present patronage, together with the building rentals and hiring of the hall for outside attractions is sufficient to keep the orchestra on a no-loss basis, notwithstanding the large interest and tax expenditures to be met.' Mr. Thomas lived to conduct only five concerts in the new hall, the last on Dec. 24, 1904. He died on Jan. 4, 1905, and was succeeded by Frederick A. Stock (*q.v.*), who had been his assistant.   H. E. K.

CINCINNATI.

THE CINCINNATI SYMPHONY ORCHESTRA. Concerts of symphonic music were given by this organisation from Jan. 1895 to April 1907, under the auspices of the Cincinnati Orchestra Association, whose affairs are administered by a Board of Directors composed of women, and supported financially by bodies of shareholders, stockholders, and subscribers to a guarantee fund. The Association was organised in 1895 for the purpose of promoting the culture of high-class orchestral music, which for fifteen years had been dependent upon the somewhat desultory and sporadic efforts of the College of Music of Cincinnati. The concerts of the first season, given between January and April of 1895, were divided into three series of three concerts each, preceded by afternoon public rehearsals, and were conducted by Frank Van der Stucken, Anton Seidl, and Henry Schradieck. Mr. Van der Stucken was then engaged as sole conductor, and remained such for twelve years, during which period ten afternoon and ten evening concerts were given annually. At the close of the thirteenth season (1906-7), the Orchestra Association, rather than submit to the dictation of the American Federation of Musicians, disbanded the orchestra and resolved to invite the orchestras of the eastern cities and Chicago to give concerts under its auspices.   H. E. K.

NEW YORK.

THE PHILHARMONIC SOCIETY OF NEW YORK is the oldest orchestral body in continuous service in the United States devoted to the performance of instrumental music. Incidentally it also extends help to its superannuated members, and to that end maintains a pension fund created by gifts from its friends, one half of the initiation fees paid by new members on their election, fines assessed against members and a share of the earnings of the concerts. It is a communistic body of professional musicians, with three classes of members, viz. Actual, Honorary, and Honorary Associate. In the first class there are none but professional players upon orchestral instruments. The title of Honorary Member is bestowed by vote of the Society upon musicians whose eminence entitles them to that distinction in the eyes of the members; that of Honorary Associate upon laymen for the same reason. Election to membership in the three classes requires a unanimous vote. Active devotion to the Society's interests is enforced on the part of the Actual Members by a system of fines. At the concerts of the Society, which take place only in the regular musical season the actual members constitute a little less than two-thirds of the performers, generally numbering from 90 to 110. The additional players are engaged by the Directors in the ordinary way, and paid the ruling rate of wage. At the end of each season the money in the hands of the Treasurer, save a small sum withheld for contingent expenses, is divided equally among the members who have participated in the concerts. All the officers of the Society are musicians except the President, who as a rule, is a citizen of New York distinguished by love of music and devotion to its interests. The conductor need not be a member of the Society, but must be elected like the other officers. His salary is fixed by agreement between him and the Board of Directors. The regular subscription concerts of the Philharmonic Society now (in 1908) number sixteen in each season, and are given in pairs on Friday afternoons and Saturday evenings from November to April, the programmes of each pair of concerts being identical. Until 1906 it was a rule of the Society that its name should not be used for any concerts except those given under its own auspices; but the advent of 'star conductors' led to a modification of the rule in the hope that the Society might participate in other concerts than its own, thus adding to its income and recouping it for the large salaries demanded by the 'stars.' The results of the first season did not justify the change. Among the Honorary Members of the Society since its foundation have been Vieuxtemps (the first one, elected in 1843), Spohr, Mendelssohn, Jenny Lind, Sontag,

Alboni, William Vincent Wallace, Thalberg, Mme. Parepa-Rosa, Franz Liszt, Richard Wagner, Joachim Raff, Anton Rubinstein, and Dvořák.

The history of the Philharmonic Society of New York had its beginning at a meeting of professional musicians called by Ureli Corelli Hill (an American musician, violinist, and conductor, pupil of Spohr in Cassel) held on April 2, 1842. The impulse to organise such a Society seems to have come from the artistic success achieved at a 'Musical Solemnity' given in June 1839, in honour of the memory of Daniel Schlesinger, one of the first thoroughly trained musicians to make his home in New York. The most prominent musicians in the city were present at this meeting and the meetings which followed, at which the organisation of the Society was perfected. Among them were Mr. Hill ; A. P. Heinrich, an eccentric Bohemian composer who presided at the first meeting, but took no further interest in the affair ; Charles E. Horn (q.v.) ; William Vincent Wallace, who was a member during the first two years ; Alfred Boucher, a connection of Alexandre Jean Boucher (q.v.) ; Dr. Edward Hodges, an English Cathedral musician, afterwards organist of Trinity Church ; H. C. Timm and William Scharfenberg, pianists of German birth and training ; George Loder, a member of the English family of musicians of that name ; and D. G. Etienne, a French pianist who could play the horn when required. To Loder, who was connected with the Society throughout the first decade, fell the honour of conducting the first performance in the United States of Beethoven's Choral Symphony at a concert of the Society on May 20, 1846. Three concerts were given in the first season (1842-43), and the first programme is such excellent testimony to the seriousness of the founders' aims that it deserves publication here.

First Concert, Dec. 7. 1842—Symphony No. 5, in C minor, Beethoven (conducted by U. C. Hill); Scena from 'Oberon,' Weber (Madame Otto) ; Quintet in D minor, for pianoforte, violin, viola, violoncello, and double-bass, Hummel (Messrs. Scharfenberg, Hill, Derwort, Boucher, and Rosier) ; Overture 'Oberon,' Weber, (conducted by Mr. Etienne) ; Duet from ' Armida,' Rossini (Madame Otto and Mr. C. E. Horn) ; Scena from 'Fidelio,' Beethoven (Mr. C. E. Horn) ; Aria Bravura, from 'The Seraglio,' Mozart (Madame Otto) ; New Overture in D, Kalliwoda, (conducted by Mr. Timm). The orchestra during the vocal music was directed by H. C. Timm.

For the next sixteen years four regular concerts were given each season, then for ten years five. In the twenty-seventh season the number was increased to six, and this remained the rule until the fifty-sixth season, when the number was increased to eight. Out of a custom of admitting amateurs to the rehearsals of the Society which was inaugurated in the second season there grew the so-called public rehearsals which for several decades differed in nothing but name and the time of performance from the regular concerts. In 1906 the title 'public rehearsals' was abandoned for 'Afternoon Concerts.' This explains the statement, heretofore made, that now the Society gives sixteen subscription concerts annually. It was the custom during the early years of the Society, when the president was a professional musician and necessarily a member of the Society, to leave the conducting of the concerts in his hands, though for a number of years that official found it expedient to share the duty with the leading members of the Society, especially such as were at the head of singing and other musical societies. Thus in the first season, though only three concerts were given, five members officiated at the conductor's desk, viz : U. C. Hill, H. C. Timm, W. Alpers, Alfred Boucher, and George Loder. D. G. Etienne aided Hill, Loder, and Alpers in the second season. Two new men, one of whom was destined to play an important rôle in the history of the Society, appeared in the seventh season. They were Theodore Eisfeld, who came from Europe with experience gained in conducting concerts in Paris and elsewhere ; and Max Martezek, whose real activities belonged in the field of opera. In Eisfeld's second season the directors changed their policy and elected Eisfeld sole director for the season. In 1854 Carl BERGMANN was associated with him and H. C. Timm, who was then president, and thereafter for ten years, save the fifteenth and sixteenth seasons conducted solely by Eisfeld and the fourteenth and seventeenth conducted by Bergmann, these two men conducted alternately. Bergmann was sole conductor from 1865 to 1876. Then came an interregnum of three years with Dr. Leopold DAMROSCH, Theodore THOMAS, and Adolph Neuendorff as conductors. Mr. Thomas was conductor for the next twelve years, Anton SEIDL for the next seven (holding the position at the time of his death on March 28, 1898) ; and Emil PAUR for four. Under the artistic administration of Messrs. Thomas and Seidl, the Society grew steadily in prosperity and reached its zenith. A falling off in popular interest during the Paur regime and the one season, the sixty-first, in which Walter DAMROSCH was conductor, led to the adoption of the custom, which had gained a foothold in some of the European capitals, of engaging a different conductor for each concert, instead of one for the entire season. These 'guests' in the sixty-second season were Edouard Colonne of Paris, Gustav F. Kogel of Frankfort, Henry J. Wood of London, Victor Herbert of Pittsburgh, Felix Weingartner of Munich, and Richard Strauss of Berlin. In the sixty-third season the conductors were Gustav F. Kogel, Edouard Colonne, Wassili Safonoff of Moscow, Felix Weingartner, and Karl Panzner of Bremen ; Theodore Thomas, who had also accepted the invitation of the directors, died before the concert which he was to conduct, and Herr Kogel was called back from Frankfort to take his place. In the sixty-fourth season the

Society's invitation was accepted by Willem Mengelberg of Amsterdam, Victor Herbert, Max Fiedler of Hamburg, M. Safonoff, Dr. Ernst Kunwald of Frankfort, and Fritz Steinbach of Cologne. At the end of this season an engagement was made with M. Safonoff as sole conductor for three years. To carry out these new policies a number of public-spirited citizens placed a considerable fund at the service of the Society.

(For a history of the Society see *The Philharmonic Society of New York*, a memorial by Henry Edward Krehbiel published on the occasion of the Fiftieth Anniversary of the founding of the Society, April 1892, London, Novello, Ewer & Co.)   H. E. K.

THE NEW YORK SYMPHONY SOCIETY. This organisation is a successor, *de jure* if not *de facto*, of a Society of like name, which was founded in 1878 by Dr. Leopold DAMROSCH. During the early years of its existence the New York Symphony Society maintained an exceedingly active competition with the orchestra of Theodore THOMAS, and the rivalry of the organisations had much to do with familiarising the New York public with the works of the German, French, and Russian composers as fast as they were published, and even before, since Dr. Damrosch and Mr. Thomas were both in the habit of securing manuscript copies of their compositions from the leading authors of Europe. After the death of Dr. Damrosch in 1885 his son Walter succeeded to the conductorship of the Society, and has remained its administrative as well as artistic head ever since. The Society has passed through many vicissitudes, and has several times appeared to be moribund, only to be awakened to renewed life by its energetic and indefatigable conductor. The concerts were permitted to lapse in 1899, when Mr. Damrosch devoted a year to composition ; again when he travelled with his own opera company, and still again when he became conductor for a season (1902-3) of the Philharmonic Society of New York (*q.v.*). Retiring from that post Mr. Damrosch organised what for four years was called the New York Symphony Orchestra, on a co-operative basis, profit and loss being shared by the members of the organisation and a committee of guarantors. The plan proved to be unsatisfactory, and in the spring of 1907 the guarantors called the old Symphony Society back to life, and resolved to proceed under the old style and in the old manner, paying the players weekly wages throughout the season, and assuming all financial responsibilities. At the same time it was determined to increase the number of concerts in New York City to twenty-eight, half of them to be given on Sunday afternoons. In the season 1905-6 Felix Weingartner alternated with Mr. Damrosch in conducting concerts in New York and other cities ; for, unlike the Philharmonic Society, this band makes tours to many cities and towns in the United States. It also remains intact during the summer months, and provides music for large and fashionable resorts near Philadelphia and Chicago. H. E. K.

PEOPLE'S SYMPHONY CONCERTS OF NEW YORK. Under this title a series of concerts are annually given in the chief American city by an orchestra of excellent proportions and artistic character, and with programmes of a high class, for which there is little more than a nominal charge for admission, the prices varying from ten cents to fifty. The concerts are also given in pairs, first in the large hall of Cooper Union, situated in the densely populated district known as the East Side ; then in Carnegie Hall, the home of all the fashionable concerts, the purpose being to reach all classes of the people whose tastes the concerts are designed to educate. Under the title 'The People's Symphony Concerts' auxiliary chamber concerts are also given by local combinations of players. All the concerts, which were called into being by Franz Xavier Arens in 1902 and have been directed by him ever since, are given under the auspices of an organisation incorporated under the laws of the State of New York, and are maintained largely by the contributions of philanthropic persons interested in musical culture. These contributions range from $2500, which sum entitles the donor to be a founder, to a dollar a year. Receipts and expenses are about $12,000 a year, and at the end of 1905 the organisation had a permanently invested fund of the same amount.   H. E. K.

YOUNG PEOPLE'S SYMPHONY CONCERTS OF NEW YORK. For the purpose of giving children and young people an opportunity not only to hear standard symphonic works but also to become familiar with their structure and contents Frank DAMROSCH organised an annual series of concerts under the above title in 1898. Appreciation of the compositions is helped by explanatory remarks made by the conductor, in which the forms are briefly analysed and the poetic contents suggested, themes and phrases being played in illustration by the orchestra. The concerts are given at popular prices, and teachers and pupils of the public schools of the city receive tickets at half price. Inasmuch as the orchestral has full symphonic dimensions, that of the New York Symphony Society being employed and solo artists are frequently engaged, the expenses are not always covered, though for years all the seats in Carnegie Hall have been subscribed for, and the resulting deficit is usually met by private subscription of public-spirited music-lovers. The management of the concerts is in the hands of a small committee of ladies ; there is no official organisation. H. E. K.

PHILADELPHIA.

THE PHILADELPHIA ORCHESTRA, whose affairs are administered by the Philadelphia Orchestra

Association, aided by committees of ladies from towns and cities contiguous to Philadelphia, was organised in 1900. The Orchestra Association is composed of about 300 men and women, prominent in social and artistic affairs, who annually guarantee the cost of the enterprise. Until now (1908) the yearly losses have ranged from $50,000 to $70,000, but Philadelphia has repeated the story of Chicago in its self-sacrificing devotion to the ideal which it has set for itself in respect of orchestral music. The history of the Philadelphia Orchestra does not differ essentially from that of a number of the other institutions discussed in this article; though the desire of the city's society element to have adequate performances of opera as a feature of the social season was largely instrumental in its formation. Readers of the article in this Dictionary on OPERA IN THE U.S. (vol. iii. pp. 466-472) will have observed that for a long time in the latter part of the 18th and the first decades of the 19th centuries Philadelphia was a vigorous rival of New York in operatic activity, but that in the course of time supremacy went to the latter city. So long as Theodore Thomas was a factor in the orchestral music of the eastern cities, his orchestra gave concerts with greater or less regularity in Philadelphia; but the abandonment of his individual enterprises in 1891 left the music-lovers of the old Federal capital without regular concerts of high-class orchestral music. The Boston Orchestra, on its travels, supplied the want for several years, but could not satisfy the ambitions of a city properly proud of the part which it had played in the political, commercial, social, and artistic history of the country. In the season of 1894-95 there was something like an awakening of the dormant musical interests of the city. In 1895-96 a committee was formed to promote an opera season, and a season of opera in English of forty performances was given under a guarantee with Mr. Gustav Hinrichs as director. In the next season Mr. Walter Damrosch supplied local operatic needs; in 1897-98 Messrs. Damrosch and Ellis, and in 1898-99 Mr. Charles Ellis alone with Mr. Damrosch as conductor and director. Thereafter, the local committee of opera guarantors made annual arrangements for opera from year to year with Maurice Grau and Heinrich Conried.

During this period of operatic interest orchestral matters were also in a ferment. While Mr. Hinrichs was director of the opera he gave orchestral concerts, and tried to develop a symphonic band out of the material which he found at hand. In the same season the Musical Fund Society, an old foundation, created conditions which made it possible for a local concert orchestra, the Germania, to increase the number of its members and to give a series of Friday afternoon concerts under the direction of William

Stoll, Jr., a well-known violinist. The concerts of the Germania continued for two years, whereupon Henry Gordon Thunder, director of the Philadelphia Choral Society, took up the work and out of the same material organised a Philadelphia Orchestra; his concerts, like those of Mr. Stoll, however, were tentative in character, and served chiefly to disclose the inadequacy of the players. After five years of these praiseworthy but futile efforts a number of the most prominent men and women in social and musical circles formed the Orchestral Association. Some of the foremost workers in the new enterprise were the cultivated amateurs who had formed a 'Symphony Society of Philadelphia' in 1893, with Dr. W. W. Gilchrist as conductor; this Society gave concerts from time to time until the new orchestra, a brief forerunner of the present organisation, appeared on the field. This new orchestra gave two concerts in the spring of 1900 with Fritz Scheel as conductor. Mr. Scheel had been an assistant to Dr. von Bülow in Hamburg, and was a man of fine musical parts and splendid energy. The success of the two concerts was such as to induce the Association to send him abroad to recruit the orchestra, and make of it a first-class symphonic organisation. The first regular season of the newly recruited orchestra was given in 1900-1, and from that time till his death in February 1907, Mr. Scheel remained conductor of the band; he was succeeded in the season of 1907-8 by Karl Pohlig. The Philadelphia Orchestra does not confine its ministrations to Philadelphia, but besides twenty afternoon and twenty evening concerts there, gives concerts each year in other neighbouring towns and cities, such as Wilmington, Del., Harrisburg, Pa., Trenton, N.J., Easton, Pa., Reading, Pa., Baltimore and Washington.   H. E. K.

PITTSBURGH.

PITTSBURGH SYMPHONY ORCHESTRA. The incentive to organise a permanent concert orchestra in Pittsburgh, Pennsylvania, came with Andrew Carnegie's gift to the city of a building that should contain a library, art gallery, museum, and music hall. The building was dedicated in 1895, and the Art Society undertook to raise funds to support an orchestra for three years. The first season of the Orchestra was begun on Feb. 27, 1896. Frederic ARCHER was conductor. Twenty concerts were given that year in Pittsburgh, and in the two years following, twenty in Pittsburgh and in other towns, seven in the season 1896-97, and five in 1897-98. Mr. Archer was chiefly known as an organist, but he had had some experience in the English provinces as a conductor. He was succeeded as conductor by Victor HERBERT in 1898. In the season of 1898-99 the concerts given numbered twenty in Pittsburgh and nine in other places. The next season the number in the regular series was increased to thirty-six, and so it remained for the next five years. At the same time the Orchestra entered upon a much greater activity in giving concerts outside of Pittsburgh. Tours were undertaken, and the concerts varied in number from twenty-seven to forty-five. In 1904 Mr. Herbert was succeeded by Emil PAUR, who for five years, from 1893 to 1898, had been conductor of the Boston Symphony Orchestra. The number of concerts in the Pittsburgh season was reduced to thirty ; but in that season forty-three concerts were given in other cities and towns and eighty-five in the season of 1905-6.

From the beginning the Art Society of Pittsburgh has been responsible for the Orchestra ; but it has asked of the public guarantees of a fixed sum in periods of three years, each representing the term for which the conductor is engaged. The first year the total guarantee was $25,000. Each year the sum has been increased, until for the three-year term beginning with the season of 1904-5 the amount was $40,000 a year. At no time in the history of the organisation has it been necessary to ask the guarantors to pay the maximum of their subscriptions, but the deficit in the first eleven years was over $250,000. It is not expected that the Orchestra shall pay expenses ; in fact, the Committee of the Art Society has declared that its maintenance ought to be regarded as an obligation upon the public-spirited and well-to-do citizens of Pittsburgh. The out-of-town concerts have formed an increasingly important part of the activities of the Orchestra, and through them its influence has been great in Cleveland, Buffalo, Toledo, and Detroit, and particularly in Toronto and other Canadian cities and towns. As at present (1908) constituted, the Orchestra numbers sixty-five players.   R. A.

SYMPSON, CHRISTOPHER. See SIMPSON, ante, pp. 455-456.

SYNCOPATION. [An alteration of regular rhythm, produced by placing the strongest emphasis on part of the bar not usually accented. In a bar of common time, the simplest form of syncopation is produced by giving three notes of the value of a crotchet, a minim, and a crotchet respectively. This last crotchet is often tied on to the first crotchet of the next bar, so that for several bars the displaced accentuation obtains the mastery. The fourth species of STRICT COUNTERPOINT (see ante, p. 724) is in in syncopation.] In the Coda of the great Overture 'Leonora No. 3' Beethoven has a passage given out syncopated on the wind and naturally on the strings, then vice versa. It was not, however, always sufficient for Beethoven's requirements, as may be seen from a well-known place in the Scherzo of the Eroica, where he first gives a passage in syncopation—

and then repeats it in common time, which in this instance may be taken as an extreme form of syncopation.

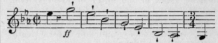

Schumann was fonder of syncopation than any other composer. His works supply many instances of whole short movements so syncopated throughout that the ear loses its reckoning, and the impression of contra-tempo is lost : e.g. Kinderscenen, No. 10 ; Faschingsschwank, No. 1, and, most noticeable of all, the opening bar of the 'Manfred' Overture.

Wagner has one or two examples of exceedingly complex syncopation : an accompaniment figure in Act 2 of 'Tristan und Isolde,' which runs thus throughout

and a somewhat similar figure in Act 1 of 'Götterdämmerung' (the scene known as 'Hagen's watch'), where the quavers of a 12-8 bar are so tied as to convey the impression of 6-4. The prelude to Act 2 of the same work presents a still more curious specimen, no two bars having at all the same accent.

[The figure at the beginning of Tchaikovsky's string quartet in D, op. 11, is an interesting instance of syncopation carried out for many bars at a time.

Brahms's favourite device of crossing rhythms in triple time is not usually called syncopation, though it belongs to the same class of devices.]   F. C.

SYNTAGMA MUSICUM. See PRAETORIUS, vol. iii. pp. 805-808.

SYREN. [See SIREN, ante, p. 471.]

SYRINX. [See PANDEAN PIPE, vol. iii. pp. 611, 612.]

SYSTEM. The collection of staves necessary for the complete score of a piece—in a string quartet, or an ordinary vocal score, four ; a PF. trio, four ; a PF. quartet, five ; and so on. Two or more of these will go on a page, and then we speak of the upper or lower system, etc.   G.

SZARVADY, MADAME. See CLAUSS-SZAR-VADY, vol. i. p. 548, and add date of death, in Paris, Sept. 1, 1907.

SZYMANOWSKA, MARIE, a distinguished pianist of her day, who would, however, hardly have been remembered but for Goethe's infatuation for her. She was born about 1790, of Polish parents named Wolowski, and was a pupil of John Field's at Moscow. She travelled much in Germany, France, and England, and died at St. Petersburg of cholera in August 1831. One of her daughters married the famous Polish poet Mickiewicz, whom she had introduced to Goethe in July 1829. Goethe knew her as early as 1821, and even then overpraised her, setting her above Hummel ; 'but those who do so,' says Felix Mendelssohn, who was then at Weimar,[1] 'think more of her pretty face than her not pretty playing.' Goethe renewed the acquaintance in August 1823, at Eger, where she and Anna Milder were both staying, calls her 'an incredible player,' and expresses his excitement at hearing music after an interval of over two years in a remarkable letter to Zelter of August 24, 1823, again comparing her with Hummel, to the latter's disadvantage. Mme. Szymanowska appears to have helped to inspire the 'Trilogie der Leidenschaft,' and the third of its three poems, called 'Aussöhnung,' is a direct allusion to her. In 1824 she was in Berlin. 'She is furiously in love (rasend verliebt) with you,' says Zelter to the poet, 'and has given me a hundred kisses on my mouth for you.'

Her compositions were chiefly for the PF., with a few songs.   G.

[1] *Goethe and Mendelssohn*, p. 25.

ADDENDA ET CORRIGENDA FOR VOL. IV

RANZ DES VACHES. Line 9, after 'rant' add 'and the Irish *raun*—a song.'

REGGIO, PIETRO. Add that Evelyn heard him sing in Sept. 1680 and July 1684, and says that Reggio had set some of Abraham Cowley's poems to music.

RIMSKY-KORSAKOV. In list of works, under 'Choral with Orchestra,' *for* 'The Legend of St. Olga' *read* 'The Ballad of the Doom of Oleg,' for tenor and bass soli, male choir and orchestra (performed at the Newcastle Festival, 1909).

ROUSSEAU, SAMUEL. Add that his lyrical drama, in four acts, 'Leone,' to a libretto by George Montorgueil, was produced at the Opéra-Comique, Paris, March 7, 1910.

SAINT PATRICK'S DAY. P. 207, add that the air has been long known, traditionally, in northern England as 'Barbary Bell.' In the south it is sometimes called 'Bacon and Greens,' and is used as a Morris dance-tune.

SAINT-SAËNS, CAMILE. P. 208a, line 36, add that he was in the United States from October to December 1906.

SAN MARTINI. Add that he died about 1750.

SANTLEY. P. 222b, line 24 from bottom, *for* '1876' *read* '1875,' next line *for* 'Lyceum' *read* 'Princess's,' and add that he appeared as Figaro on the opening night of the season, continuing with the company in 1876, when he sang the Flying Dutchman at the Lyceum.

SCARLATTI, FRANCESCO. Line 5 from end of article, add that the concert took place in May 1720 at Hickford's Room, and consisted mainly of his own compositions.

SCHUMANN-HEINK, ERNESTINE. Add that she created the part of Clytemnestra in Strauss's 'Elektra' at Dresden, Jan. 25, 1909. Her third marriage, with Mr. William Rapp, son of a publisher in Chicago, her business-manager, took place on May 27, 1905.

SICILIAN MARINER'S HYMN. Line 5 of article, after '1794' add 'but to have been previously issued in America in 1793.'

SMYTH, ETHEL. P. 490b, bottom line, add that 'The Wreckers' was produced in English at the Afternoon Theatre (His Majesty's Theatre), June 22, 1909, and at Covent Garden, March 1, 1910.

SONG. P. 601, to list of books on American music, add *History of American Music*, by L. C. Elson, 1904. Revised edition, 1915.

STANFORD, SIR CHARLES VILLIERS. Add to list of compositions:—
Op.
106. Four Part-songs for male voices.
107. A Welcome Song for the opening of the Franco-British Exhibition, 1908 (to words by the Duke of Argyll), for chorus and orchestra.
108. Installation March for the Chancellor of the University of Cambridge, for wind band, published in an arrangement for organ.
109. Three Military Marches.
110. Four Part-songs for mixed choir.
111. Three Part-songs for mixed choir.
112. Four Songs.
113. Four Bible Songs, for voice and organ.
114. Ave atque Vale, overture with choral portions, written for the Haydn Centenary in 1909.
115. Morning, Evening, and Communion Service in C.
116. Two organ pieces, 'Te Deum Laudamus,' and 'Canzona.'
117. Five 'Songs of the Fleet,' for baritone solo and chorus.
118. Cushendall, an Irish song cycle.

STODART. Line 22 from end, add that William Southwell of Dublin had patented an upright piano in 1794.

STRAUSS, RICHARD. To list of compositions add 'Elektra,' opera in one act, founded on von Hoffmansthal's tragedy, produced at Dresden, Jan. 25, 1909, at New York, Feb. 1, 1910, and at Covent Garden, Feb. 19, 1910.

SYMPHONY CONCERTS IN THE UNITED STATES. P. 803b, last line, add that the Cincinnati Symphony Orchestra was reorganised in 1909, and Leopold Stokowski was appointed conductor.

END OF VOL. IV